ENCYCLOPAEDIA JUDAICA

ENCYCLOPAEDIA JUDAICA

SECOND EDITION

VOLUME 19
Som–Tn

Fred Skolnik, *Editor in Chief*
Michael Berenbaum, *Executive Editor*

MACMILLAN REFERENCE USA
An imprint of Thomson Gale, a part of The Thomson Corporation

IN ASSOCIATION WITH
KETER PUBLISHING HOUSE LTD., JERUSALEM

THOMSON
GALE

Detroit • New York • San Francisco • New Haven, Conn. • Waterville, Maine • London

THOMSON GALE

ENCYCLOPAEDIA JUDAICA, Second Edition

Fred Skolnik, *Editor in Chief*
Michael Berenbaum, *Executive Editor*
Shlomo S. (Yosh) Gafni, *Editorial Project Manager*
Rachel Gilon, *Editorial Project Planning and Control*

Thomson Gale
Gordon Macomber, *President*
Frank Menchaca, *Senior Vice President and Publisher*
Jay Flynn, *Publisher*
Hélène Potter, *Publishing Director*

Keter Publishing House
Yiphtach Dekel, *Chief Executive Officer*
Peter Tomkins, *Executive Project Director*

Complete staff listings appear in Volume 1

For more information, contact
Macmillan Reference USA
An imprint of Thomson Gale
27500 Drake Rd.
Farmington Hills, MI 48331-3535
Or you can visit our internet site at
http://www.gale.com

LIBRARY OF CONGRESS CATALOGING-IN-PUBLICATION DATA

Encyclopaedia Judaica / Fred Skolnik, editor-in-chief ; Michael Berenbaum, executive editor. -- 2nd ed.
v. cm.
Includes bibliographical references and index.
Contents: v.1. Aa-Alp.
ISBN 0-02-865928-7 (set hardcover : alk. paper) -- ISBN 0-02-865929-5 (vol. 1 hardcover : alk. paper) -- ISBN 0-02-865930-9 (vol. 2 hardcover : alk. paper) -- ISBN 0-02-865931-7 (vol. 3 hardcover : alk. paper) -- ISBN 0-02-865932-5 (vol. 4 hardcover : alk. paper) -- ISBN 0-02-865933-3 (vol. 5 hardcover : alk. paper) -- ISBN 0-02-865934-1 (vol. 6 hardcover : alk. paper) -- ISBN 0-02-865935-X (vol. 7 hardcover : alk. paper) -- ISBN 0-02-865936-8 (vol. 8 hardcover : alk. paper) -- ISBN 0-02-865937-6 (vol. 9 hardcover : alk. paper) -- ISBN 0-02-865938-4 (vol. 10 hardcover : alk. paper) -- ISBN 0-02-865939-2 (vol. 11 hardcover : alk. paper) -- ISBN 0-02-865940-6 (vol. 12 hardcover : alk. paper) -- ISBN 0-02-865941-4 (vol. 13 hardcover : alk. paper) -- ISBN 0-02-865942-2 (vol. 14 hardcover : alk. paper) -- ISBN 0-02-865943-0 (vol. 15: alk. paper) -- ISBN 0-02-865944-9 (vol. 16: alk. paper) -- ISBN 0-02-865945-7 (vol. 17: alk. paper) -- ISBN 0-02-865946-5 (vol. 18: alk. paper) -- ISBN 0-02-865947-3 (vol. 19: alk. paper) -- ISBN 0-02-865948-1 (vol. 20: alk. paper) -- ISBN 0-02-865949-X (vol. 21: alk. paper) -- ISBN 0-02-865950-3 (vol. 22: alk. paper)
1. Jews -- Encyclopedias. I. Skolnik, Fred. II. Berenbaum, Michael, 1945-
DS102.8.E496 2007
909'.04924 -- dc22

2006020426

ISBN-13:

978-0-02-865928-2 (set)
978-0-02-865929-9 (vol. 1)
978-0-02-865930-5 (vol. 2)
978-0-02-865931-2 (vol. 3)
978-0-02-865932-9 (vol. 4)
978-0-02-865933-6 (vol. 5)
978-0-02-865934-3 (vol. 6)
978-0-02-865935-0 (vol. 7)
978-0-02-865936-7 (vol. 8)
978-0-02-865937-4 (vol. 9)
978-0-02-865938-1 (vol. 10)
978-0-02-865939-8 (vol. 11)
978-0-02-865940-4 (vol. 12)
978-0-02-865941-1 (vol. 13)
978-0-02-865942-8 (vol. 14)
978-0-02-865943-5 (vol. 15)
978-0-02-865944-2 (vol. 16)
978-0-02-865945-9 (vol. 17)
978-0-02-865946-6 (vol. 18)
978-0-02-865947-3 (vol. 19)
978-0-02-865948-0 (vol. 20)
978-0-02-865949-7 (vol. 21)
978-0-02-865950-3 (vol. 22)

This title is also available as an e-book
ISBN-10: 0-02-866097-8
ISBN-13: 978-0-02-866097-4
Contact your Thomson Gale representative for ordering information.
Printed in the United States of America

10 9 8 7 6 5 4 3 2

TABLE OF CONTENTS

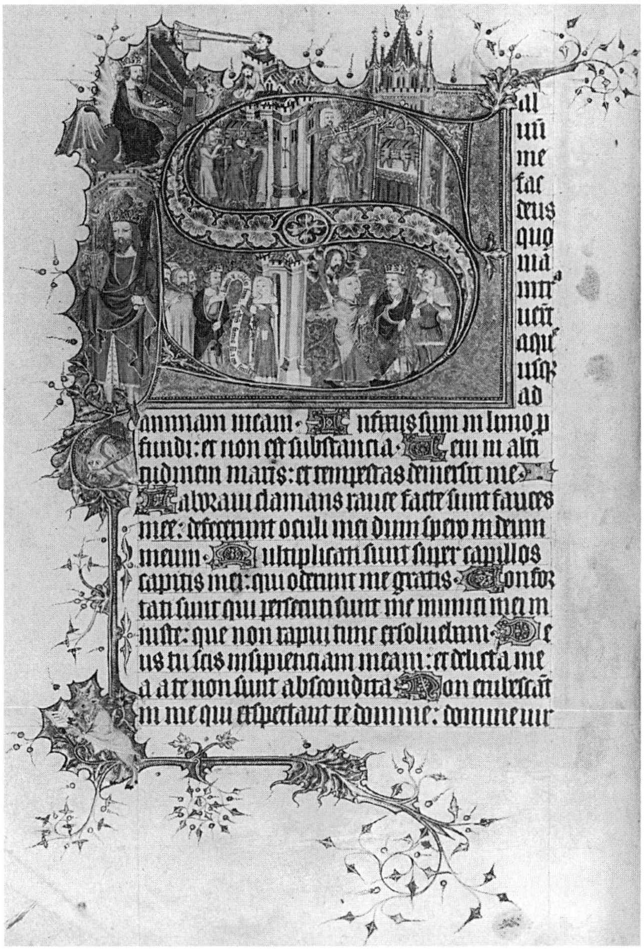

Illuminated initial letter "S" of the word Salvus *at the opening of Psalm 68 (Vulgate; 69 according to the Masoretic text) in the* Bohun Psalter, *14th century. The four scenes from the story of David are, top left, the Ark being carried up to Jerusalem (II Sam. 6:1–15); right, Michal watches David dancing before the Ark (*ibid., *16); bottom left, David reproves Michal for her criticism of him (*ibid., *20–23); right, the prophet Nathan assures David of the endurance of his kingdom (II Sam. 16). London, British Museum, EG 3277, fol. 46v.*

SOM-SZ

SOMARY, FELIX (1881–1956), Austrian banker and economist. Born in Vienna, Somary began his career with the Anglo-Austrian Bank under Charles *Morawitz. During World War I he took part in the financial administration of the German-occupied part of Western Europe. From 1919 he was active as a banker in Zurich and later assisted in drafting the Young Plan designed to regulate German reparations to the Allied Powers. During World War II he was in the United States on behalf of the Swiss government and private interests.

He published his autobiography *Erinnerungen aus meinem Leben* (1955, 1959[3]). His many publications on international economics and finance include *Bankpolitik* (1915, 1934[3]); *Wandlungen der Weltwirtschaft seit dem Kriege* (1929; *Changes in the Structure of World Economics Since the War,* 1931); *Krisenwende!* (1933; *End the Crisis!* 1933).

[Joachim O. Ronall]

°**SOMBART, WERNER** (1863–1941), German political economist and sociologist. Born in Ermsleben, Sombart acquired a reputation through his work *Der Moderne Kapitalismus* (2 vols., 1902, 1916[2]) in which he traced the development of capitalism from the late Middle Ages. In 1917 he was appointed professor of political economy at the University of Berlin. He wrote two works on capitalism and the Jews: *Die Juden und das Wirtschaftsleben* (1911; *The Jews and Modern Capitalism,* 1913, 1951), and *Die Zukunft der Juden* (1912) which aroused considerable controversy. In Sombart's view, the Jews were the principal cause of the disruption of the medieval economic system and its replacement by capitalism. The Jews, he held, were foreigners and came up against the hostility of the guilds which controlled the commerce of the medieval cities. Consequently they sought to break away from the restrictive economic framework of city life and, by doing so, became the pioneers of international trade. In this way they helped to lay the foundation of the capitalist system. Sombart maintained that the Jewish intellect, "concrete, stubborn, and systematic," was ideally suited to fostering a capitalist economy: "When Israel appears upon the face of Europe, the place where it appears comes to life; and when it departs, everything which had previously flourished withers away." Such statements made for the ambivalent reception of Sombart's work among Jews at the time. Thus, while liberal Jews strongly criticized Sombart as an antisemite, others, particularly in the Zionist camp, praised him as a nonpartisan researcher and held up his theses as evidence of Jewish perseverance and as acknowledgement of the special contribution of the Jews.

Although it has been generally accepted that Jews played an important part in the early development of capitalism, Sombart's theories were generally considered to be wildly exaggerated. They provided Nazi Germany with considerable material for antisemitic propaganda, since he stressed the incompatibility of Jewish commercialism with the spirit of the "nordic farmer," and in *Deutscher Sozialismus* (1934) favored the Nazi policy of excluding Jews from German economic and cultural life.

In 1911, David Ben-Gurion translated Sombart's *Sozialismus und Soziale Bewegung im XIX Jahrhundert* into Hebrew. A Hebrew translation of Sombart's *Die Juden und das Wirtschaftsleben* was published in 1912 in Kiev by a group of young Zionists.

BIBLIOGRAPHY: Ziegler, in: AZDJ, 75 (1911), 271–2; I. Taglicht, *Juden und Judentum in der Darstellung Werner Sombarts* (1911); J. Henningsen, *Professor Sombarts Forschungsergebnisse zur Judenfrage* (1913^3); H. Wätjen, *Das Judentum und die Anfaenge der modernen Kolonisation; Kritische Bemerkungen zu Werner Sombarts "Die Juden und das Wirtschaftsleben"* (1914); A. Philipp, *Die Juden und das Wirtschaftsleben; Eine antikritisch-bibliographische Studie* (1929). **ADD. BIBLIOGRAPHY:** A. Mitzman, *Sociology and Estrangement…* (1973); F. Raphael, *Judaisme et capitalisme …* (1982); M. Appel, *Werner Sombart …* (1992); F. Lenger, *Werner Sombart 1863–1941…* (1995); J. Backhaus, *Werner Sombart (1863–1941)* (2000).

SOMBOR (Hung. **Zombor**), city in N.W. Yugoslavia, in the district of Bačka, province of Vojvodina; part of the Austro-Hungarian Empire until 1918. The first (registered) Jewish families came to settle in the mid-18th century. By the middle of the 19th century, a Jewish school existed where teaching was done in Hebrew and Yiddish, the use of the latter language eventually being objected to by the authorities and prohibited. The first synagogue in Sombor was erected in 1825 and the second in 1865. Among the founders of the *kehillah* was Jacob Stein. Conservative in doctrine, its first rabbi was David Kohn (d. 1884). By the end of the 19th century there were 200 Jewish taxpayers, and 650 Jews out of a total population of 25,000. The community had a *bikkur ḥolim* society and during the century the town and its *kehillah* grew considerably. In 1910 there were 1,000 Jews out of a population of 35,000, and by 1940 there were 1,200 out of 45,000 inhabitants in the city. A *talmud torah* was founded in 1925. In the 1920s and 1930s various youth and Zionist organizations opened chapters in Sombor. The last rabbi before the Holocaust was Michael Fischer. Like other places in Vojvodina, the Hungaro-German occupation resulted in the extermination of this once active Jewish community. The last Jews were sent to Auschwitz via Backa Topola on April 5, 1944. In 1953 a monument to the victims of the Holocaust was erected. The synagogue was used by a local commercial enterprise.

BIBLIOGRAPHY: S. Guttman, *A szombori zsidók története* (1928); *Magyar Zsido Lexikon* (1929), s.v. *Zombor*; L. Fischer, in: *Jevrejski Almanah…*, 4 (1928/29), 76. **ADD. BIBLIOGRAPHY:** Z. Loker (ed.), *Yehudei Vojvodina be-Et he-Ḥadashah* (1994), with Eng. summary.

[Zvi Loker]

SOMECK, RONNY (1951–), Hebrew poet. Someck was born in Baghdad, Iraq, and came to Israel as a child. He studied Hebrew literature and philosophy at Tel Aviv University and sketching at the Avni Art Institute. He worked as a counselor with street gangs, taught literature, and led writing workshops. Someck began publishing poetry in 1968 and published his first collection, *Goleh* ("Exile"), in 1976. Other collections include *Solo* (1978), *Asphalt* (1984), *Sheva Shurot al Pele ha-Yarkon* ("Seven Lines on the Wonder of the Yarkon River"), *Panter* (1989), *Bloody Mary* (1994), *Gan Eden le-Orez* ("Rice Paradise," 1996). The bustling life and alienating effect of the modern city, primarily Tel Aviv, figures prominently in his poetry, which addresses collective Israeli concerns, the ethnic issue as well as private experience. In 1997 Someck recorded with the musician Elliot Sharp the CD *Revenge of the Stuttering Child*. In 1998, together with artist Benny Efrat, Someck presented the exhibition "Nature's Factory" at the Israel Museum. With Shirley Someck he wrote a book for children, *Kaftor ha-Ẓeḥok* ("The Laughter Button," 1998). Someck's ninth poetry collection, *Maḥteret ha-Ḥalav* ("The Milk Underground"), appeared in 2005. He received the ACUM special Jubilee Prize, and in 2004 was awarded the Yehuda Amichai Prize. A collection of *Selected Poems* appeared in English translation (1999) as well as *The Fire Stays in Red* (2002).

BIBLIOGRAPHY: G. Moked, *"Al Sheloshah Meshorerim Ẓe'irim (Someck, Bachar, Perez Banai),"* in: *Yedioth Aharonoth* (November 16, 1979); O. Bartana, *Teritoriyyiah Ḥadashah ve-Efsharuyotehah*, in: *Yedioth Aharonoth* (December 26, 1980); A. Barkai, in: *Al ha-Mishmar* (February 27, 1981); A. Balaban, *Ereẓ Tel Aviv*, in: *Yedioth Aharonoth* (January 30, 1981); T. Avgar, *Bein Gimgum le-Mahapekhanut Kevuyah*, in: *Moznayim*, 52:1 (1981), 61–62; Y. Mazor, *Al Tomru Lanu Shalom*, in: *Iton 77*, 183 (1995), 18–23; Y. Ben David, *"Shirah – Be-Millim shel Sedot Te'ufah,"* in: *Ahavah mi-Mabat Sheni* (1997), 206–9; Y. Mazor, "The Silky Vigor of the Boxing Glove: R. Someck in the Arena of Contemporary Hebrew Poetry," in: *World Literature Today*, 72:3 (1998), 501–6; M. Forcano, *R. Someck, música d'Um Kultzum à Tel Aviv*, in: *Tamid*, 2 (1998–99), 205–8; S. Dayyan and R. Yagil, in: *Ma'ariv* (April 29, 2005).

[Anat Feinberg (2nd ed.)]

SOMEKH, ABDALLAH BEN ABRAHAM (1813–1889), rabbi and *posek* of Baghdad. Abdallah was born in *Baghdad and was a pupil of Jacob b. Joseph ha-Rofe. At first he engaged in business, acquiring considerable wealth. When he perceived that the study of Torah was being neglected, however, he abandoned his business and devoted himself to the dissemination of learning. He founded the *bet midrash* Abu Menashe which was established with funds provided by the philanthropist Ezekiel b. Reuben Manasseh, after whom it was named. In 1840 he founded, with the help of the same philanthropist, the renowned Midrash Bet Zilkhah. He died in a plague that swept through Baghdad, and was buried there, against the orders of the government, in the court of the traditional tomb of the high priest Joshua. This caused an outbreak of riots, in consequence of which rabbis and communal leaders were imprisoned. After three months, Somekh's body had to be exhumed and buried in another cemetery.

Somekh was regarded as the supreme halakhic authority by communities of Baghdadi origin throughout the Far East. He was the author of *Zivḥei Ẓedek* (2 pts., 1899), halakhic decisions on the *Yoreh De'ah* with appended responsa. In manuscript are two more parts of the same work; *Eẓ ha-Sadeh* on the tractate *Beẓah*; novellae on most tractates of the Talmud; a commentary on the Passover *Haggadah*; *Ḥazon la-Mo'ed*, on the calendar; and responsa.

BIBLIOGRAPHY: A. Ben-Yaacob, *Toledot ha-Rav Abdallah Somekh* (1949); idem, *Yehudei Bavel* (1965), index.

[Abraham Ben-Yaacob]

SOMEKH, SASSON (1933–), professor emeritus of Arabic literature at Tel Aviv University. Born in Baghdad, he immigrated to Israel and specialized in modern Arabic literature and Semitic philology. Research, editing, and translating characterized his academic career, along with lecturing in Israeli, Swedish, and U.S. universities. Among his books are *The Changing Rhythm* (1973), a monograph on the Egyptian novelist Naguib Maḥfūẓ; *Genre and Language in Modern Arabic Literature* (1991); three books (in Arabic) on the novelist Yūsuf Idrīs; four anthologies of modern Arabic poetry, translated into Hebrew; and an autobiography (in Hebrew), *Baghdad Yesterday* (2004). He was awarded the Israel Prize in Oriental Studies in 2005.

SOMEN, ISRAEL (1903–1984), public figure in Kenya. Born in London, Somen was taken to South Africa when he was a child, and in 1923 went to Kenya where he joined the colonial service. Somen was mayor of Nairobi from 1955 to 1957 and honorary consul for Israel before Kenya's independence. He was also president of the Nairobi Hebrew congregation.

SOMLYÓ, ZOLTÁN (1882–1937), Hungarian poet. Tried to earn his livelihood by writing and had a lifelong struggle against poverty. His lyric poetry is founded on the feeling of love and the Jewish feeling of loneliness. He wrote *Az àtkozott költö* ("The accursed poet," 1911).

SOMMER, EMIL (1869–1947), Austrian soldier. Born in Dorna Watra / Vatra Dornei, Bukovina, Sommer was one of the top graduates from the cadets' school and served on the general staff. During World War I he commanded a regiment and was highly respected. In 1923 he retired as a full colonel and later received the brevet rank of major general. Sommer was head of the Austrian Jewish War Veterans (Bund juedischer Frontsoldaten Oesterreichs) until the organization split over his strong monarchist views in March 1934. He and his supporters founded a monarchist-oriented War Veterans Organization (Legitimistische Juedische Frontkaempfer). Following the *Anschluss* newspapers reported that he was forced to sweep the streets in his general's uniform with all his decorations. This false report was a pure invention; he was, however, arrested. In 1942 he and his wife, Anna, née Mittler, were deported to Theresienstadt. He managed to survive and after the liberation returned to Vienna. Sommer immigrated to the United States, where he died.

ADD. BIBLIOGRAPHY: E.A. Schmidl, *Juden in der K. (u.) K. Armee* 1788–1918 (1989), 148; *The National Jewish Monthly* (Nov. 1946), 90–91.

[Mordechai Kaplan / Albert Lichtblau (2nd ed.)]

SOMMERSTEIN, EMIL (1883–1957), Zionist leader in Galicia and Polish Jewish leader. Born in the village of Hleszczawa in the district of Tarnopol, Galicia, Sommerstein practiced law in Lvov. His Zionist activities began during his student years, when he founded the Zionist Students' League in Galicia (1906). He later played a leading role in the Galician Zionist Federation, of which he became chairman. He was a member of the Polish Sejm from 1922 until 1939 (with a break from 1927–29). He was active in several Jewish institutions and organizations, especially economic ones. Due to him, the Jewish Academic House, the first of its kind in Europe, was established in Lvov in 1910. He specialized in economic and financial law and published several books on these subjects in Polish (1924–28). Sommerstein took part in the establishment of the *World Jewish Congress. At the end of September 1939, with the entry of the Soviet army into Lvov, he was arrested and taken to Kiev. He was transferred from prison to prison until he was liberated at the beginning of 1944 in a general amnesty.

In spring 1944 Sommerstein was invited by the Soviet authorities to represent Polish Jewry in Moscow and was even received by Stalin. Together with the Soviet-sponsored Association of Polish Patriots, he followed in the wake of the Soviet army's advance into Polish territory. He was co-opted onto the Polish Committee for National Liberation, which was established in Chelm in July 1944 and became the provisional government of liberated Poland. He moved to Lublin with the government and then to Warsaw (February 1945). Sommerstein was among the founding members of the Central Committee of Polish Jewry and also served as its president. He played an important role in arranging for the repatriation of 140,000 Polish Jewish refugees from the Soviet Union. He was a member of the editorial board of the central Jewish organ, *Dos Naye Lebn*, which commenced publication in liberated Poland. In April 1946 he headed a delegation of Polish Jews to the U.S., where he suffered from a paralytic disease from which he never recovered. He died in New York and his remains were taken to Israel and buried in Tel Aviv (See also *Poland, Contemporary).

BIBLIOGRAPHY: N.M. Gelber, *Toledot ha-Tenu'ah ha-Ẓiyyonit be-Galizyah*, 2 vols. (1958), index; AJYB, 59 (1958), 477.

[Nathan Eck]

SOMMO, JUDAH LEONE BEN ISAAC (also known as **Leone De Sommi Portaleone, Leone di Somi, Leone Ebreo de Somi, Leone de' Sommo Portaleone, Yehuda Sommo**; 1527–1592), dramatist, theater director, and poet in Hebrew and Italian. An outstanding contributor to the development of the theater during the Renaissance, Sommo, born in Mantua, was a descendant of the aristocratic *Portaleone family. He was educated in the spirit of the Renaissance in general and in Jewish subjects by Rabbi David b. Abraham *Provençal who planned to found a Jewish academy of sciences at Mantua. Provençal, however, opposed Jewish participation in the theater. In his youth Sommo served as tutor and copier and invented a method for manufacturing ink, which is mentioned in *Shiltei ha-Gibborim* (Mantua, 1612), authored by his relative Abraham Portaleone. At the age of 23 he wrote a five-act prose play, *Ẓaḥut Bediḥuta de-Kiddushin* ("An Eloquent Marriage Farce"), which is the oldest Hebrew *drama extant. In 1557 he participated in a satirical literary competition on the subject of women, in their praise or censure. He submitted a long macaronic poem, *Magen Nashin* ("In Defense of Women"), with alternate stanzas in Hebrew and Italian, which he dedicated to Anna *Rieti.

Sommo seems to have been active from an early age in writing and staging plays for the Gonzaga court theater where European dignitaries were often in attendance. Each year the Jewish community of Mantua was obliged to present a play before the duke; Sommo was placed in charge of these performances. In 1565 he submitted to Cesare Gonzaga, patron of the literary school Accademia degl' Invaghiti ("Academy of the Lovesick"), *Dialoghi in materia di rappresentazioni sceniche* ("*Dialogues on the Art of the Stage*," ed. F. Marotti, Milan, 1969). In recognition of this work Sommo was admitted a year later as the only Jewish *scrittore* ("writer") in the academy. He ultimately became renowned throughout Europe as a dramatist and director, as well as an expert in stage design, make-up, and lighting effects. Sommo pioneered in the use of lighting by placing torches around the hall or on the stage. The torches were brightened or dimmed at appropriate times to heighten the emotional atmosphere of the play. The famous playwright Manfredi insisted that Sommo was the only director capable of staging his *Semiramis*. He befriended many famous actors and actresses who came to Mantua.

Although Sommo reached the height of fame in European theater, he did not neglect his activities in the Jewish community. In 1574 he aided Azariah dei *Rossi in publishing his controversial book *Me'or Einayim*. Like other famous Jewish artists and performers granted similar privileges, Sommo was exempted in 1580 from wearing the yellow *badge required of the Jews. In 1585 he was allowed to buy property in Mantua upon which he built a synagogue. In the same year Sommo was involved in an unsuccessful attempt to have the duke of Mantua crowned king of Poland after the former king died leaving no male heir. In 1588 he submitted to the first duke of Vincenzo a prose comedy, *Le tre sorelle* ("The Three Sisters," ed. F. Marotti, Milan, 1970).

Sommo's literary output, which remained in manuscript until the 20th century, comprised 16 volumes. Those works composed in Italian included 13 plays (comedies in prose and rhyme, pastorales, intermezzos), the *Dialoghi in materia di rappresentazioni Sceniche, 45 Salmi Davidici* ("Psalms of David"), poems, canzones, and satires. However, 11 of the Italian volumes, stored in the National Library of Turin, were destroyed by a fire in 1904. Only *Le tre sorelle*, the rhymed pastorale *L'Hirifile*, and a few Italian poems survived. Numbered among his Hebrew works are the first Hebrew play (four copies), two short dialogues (one of which, *Shetei Siḥot Tinok Omenet ve-Horim*, is the earliest piece of *children's literature in Hebrew), and several poems. J. *Schirmann discovered *Ẓaḥut Bediḥuta de-Kiddushin* in 1930 and it was subsequently printed for the first time in 1946, some 400 years after it was written. In 1937, *Dialogues on the Art of the Stage* first appeared in print in A. Nicoll's English translation and in 1969 it was first printed, together with *Le tre sorelle*, in Italian.

Sommo's greatest works are the *Dialoghi* and his Hebrew comedy of betrothal. The *Dialoghi*, among the most valuable discussions on Renaissance theater, are written in a lively and humorous style. Four in number, the *Dialoghi* are conducted by Veridico, a Jewish embroiderer of Mantua who directs performances at the ducal court, like Sommo himself, and two Italian devotees of the theater. Veridico tells his friends how he selects, rehearses, and readies a play for performance. Sommo's writings, although echoing the style of Aristotle and Horace who were very popular in Italy at that time, ventures the original opinion that it was the Jews who contributed drama to world literature. He maintains that the Book of Job, whose authorship Jewish tradition ascribes to Moses, was the first drama in history and influenced Plato to write in dialogue form, which, in turn, inspired the Greek dramatists. In the second dialogue Sommo asserts that dramatists divide their plays into five acts and limit the number of actors appearing on the stage at any time to five in order to correspond to the number of books in the Pentateuch. To prove the antiquity of Jewish drama he cites the Aramaic dramatic allegory "The Current of Life" ("*Corso della Vita*"), and traces the origin of the Italian word *scena* ("scene") to the Hebrew *shekhunah* ("street" or "neighborhood"). Much of interest is to be found in his detailed discussion of various aspects of theatrical production (acting, costuming, makeup, and lighting); his advice on the method of acting resembles Hamlet's monologue on the same theme.

Written mainly in biblical Hebrew, *Ẓaḥut Bediḥuta de-Kiddushin* is cast into the characteristic style of Renaissance comedy. The heroes are based on the stock figures of *commedia dell'arte* and the plot is taken from an *aggadah* of Midrash Tanḥuma: a father on his deathbed bequeaths all his property to his slave, leaving to his only son, who is abroad, the right to choose only one article from the estate as his own. The plan is based on the assumption that the son, upon his return, will choose the slave and thus, since a master automatically acquires all that belongs to his slave, he will obtain the whole estate. Until the son's return the inheritance will be safely guarded by the slave. However, the parents of the son's fiancée, believing that their intended son-in-law has been disinherited, cancel the engagement. The youth then plans to seduce his beloved in a vineyard and marry her by *nissu'ei bi'ah* ("marriage by intercourse"). In the finale, Rabbi Amittai ("speaker of truth," the counterpart of Veridico in the *Dialoghi*) solves the predicament and the youth regains both his fiancée and his inheritance. The comedy was designed not only to amuse the audience but also to criticize contemporary Jewish behavior in matters of betrothal and marriage and to demonstrate the literary potential of Hebrew. The play was apparently staged in Sommo's lifetime and later during the 17th century in Italy. It was produced for the first time in Israel in 1963 by a Hebrew University troupe and in 1968 by the Haifa Theater, which performed it two years later at the Venice Festival.

BIBLIOGRAPHY: J. Schirmann (ed.), *Ẓaḥut Bediḥuta de-Kiddushin* (1965²), 173–6 (bibliography); A. Nicoll, *The Development of the Theatre* (1966⁵), 253 (bibl.); A. Holtz, in: *Tarbiz*, 36 (1967); I. Gour, in: *Bamah*, 31 (1967), 14–25; Judah Leone ben Isaac Sommo, *Dialoghi in materia di rappresentazioni sceniche* (1969); idem, *Le tre sorelle* (1970). **ADD. BIBLIOGRAPHY:** D. Namery, in: HUSL, 9:2 (1981), 147–74; *Tre sorelle: comedia*, ed. G. Romeo (1982); *A Comedy of Betrothal = Tsahoth B'dihutha D'Kiddushin*, transl. A.S. Golding (1988); *The Three Sisters: Le tre sorelle*, transl. D. Beecher and M. Ciavolella (1988); W.S. Botuck, *Leone de' Sommi: Jewish Participation in Italian Renaissance Theatre* (1991); Y. David, in: RMI, 61:1–2 (1995), 119–128; J. Guinsburg, in: *Iberia Judaica* (1996), 307–15; A. Belkin (ed.), *Leone de' Sommi and the Performing Arts* (1997); K. Werchowsky, in: REEH, 5 (2001), 171–81; A.L. Benharrosh, in: *Cahiers du Judaïsme*, 14 (2003), 25–43.

[Dan Almagor]

SOMOGYI, BÉLA (1868–1920), Hungarian political journalist. Born in Halastó, he taught in secondary schools and edited the social-democrat organ *Népszava*, as well as the German language organ *Volksstimme*. After the October Revolution (1918), he became director-general of the Ministry of Education. Under the brief Communist regime, he resigned. Nevertheless, when Somogyi protested against the murders of the White Terror (see *Hungary), he was kidnapped and with his companion, a non-Jewish author, B. Bacsó, murdered and his body thrown into the Danube. Somogyi wrote *A francia népoktatás* (1905) and *Az ipari szövetkezetek* (1905).

BIBLIOGRAPHY: Magyar *Zsidó Lexikon* (1929), 796; *Magyar Irodalmi Lexikon*, 3 (1965), 77.

[Baruch Yaron]

ŞOMREI SABAT, Christian sect in *Transylvania; though chronologically the latest, it was the most extreme faction in the Reformation in Hungary. Founded in the 1580s in central Transylvania, the sect had distinct anti-Trinitarian trends. During its long history the sect passed from denial of the Trinity to rejection of the New Testament until it approached very close to Judaism. The inhabitants of the Transylvanian village *Bezidul Nou, the majority of whom were adherents of the sect, converted to Judaism in 1868–69, and their descendants were completely absorbed in Judaism.

Ideologically, the history of the sect, which in 1971 still had a small number of followers in Transylvania, may be divided into two periods. In the first period, on the instructions of the sect's founder, the Transylvanian nobleman András Eössi (d. c. 1602), the Şomrei Sabat almost completely abandoned the principles of Christianity, though they still recognized Jesus as the messiah to reappear. But by that time, in religious as well as everyday life, they behaved according to the biblical precepts, observing "the Jewish Sabbath" as the day of rest instead of Sunday, and celebrating Jewish festivals according to the Jewish calendar: Passover, the New Moon, etc. In that early period the prayer rite of the sect was already influenced by Jewish liturgy. The Şomrei Sabat also refrained from eating ritually unclean food.

The second period, beginning in 1630, was marked by the outstanding personality of Simon *Péchi (c. 1575–1642), the adopted son of Eössi. A scholar with a command of the classical languages as well as Hebrew, Péchi performed important functions in the political administration of independent Transylvania and was chancellor at the princely courts. In 1621 Péchi was dismissed from all his posts, probably in connection with his religious views. Thereafter he devoted himself to the organization and development of the Şomrei Sabat sect and also became involved in clandestine activities. In this period the sect deviated even more from Christianity and came conspicuously close to Judaism. The leader of the sect as well as his disciples translated into Hungarian many Hebrew prayers of the Sephardi rite. At that time the Şomrei Sabat based themselves only on the Old Testament, observing the Jewish precepts and completely rejecting the principles of Christianity. It is estimated that the membership of the sect was then about 20,000.

In 1638, on instructions from the prince, the Transylvanian authorities started to persecute the members of the sect and its leaders. Some emigrated to *Turkey where several of them converted to Judaism. Those who had remained in Transylvania were put on trial, their property was confiscated, and some were sentenced to death. The leader of the sect also became impoverished as a result of the confiscations and spent the last years of his life in his rural home under house arrest. As a result of the persecutions the membership of the sect greatly diminished.

The spiritual leaders of the sect created a varied literature, including prayers, religious poems, etc., partly independent original literary creations but most of them showing Jewish influence. The outstanding Hungarian author, Zsigmond Kemény (1814–1875), gives a vivid description of the life of the sect, the persecutions, and the life of its leader, Péchi, in his historical novel *A rajongók* ("The Devoted"; first published in 1858).

BIBLIOGRAPHY: *S. Kohn, A szombatosok* (1889) = *Die Sabbatharier in Siebenbuergen* (1894); M. Guttmann and S. Harmos, *Péchi Simon szombatos imádságos könyve* (1914); A. Pirnat, *Die Ideologie der Siebenbuerger Antitrinitarier* (Budapest, 1961); B. Varjas, *Szombatos énekek* (1970).

[Yehouda Marton]

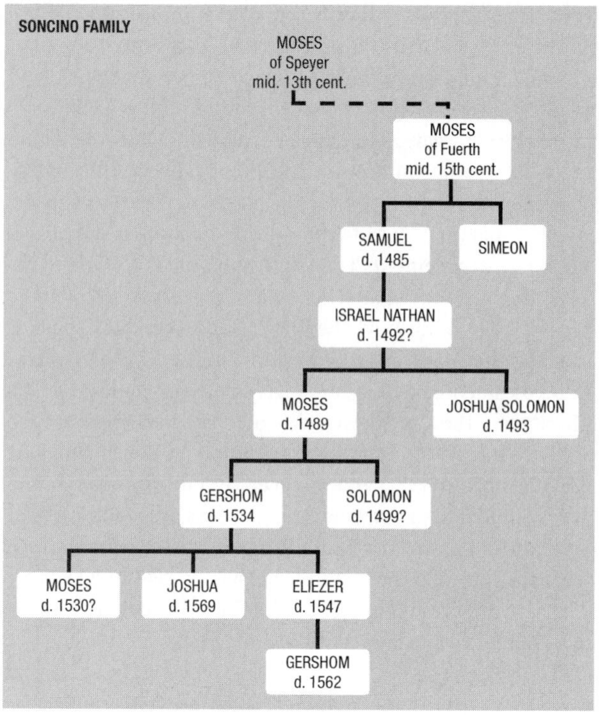

SONCINO, family of Hebrew printers active in Italy, Turkey, and Egypt in the 15th and 16th centuries. The Soncino family originated in Germany and claimed among their ancestors Moses of Speyer, mentioned in the *tosafot* by *Eliezer of Touques (13th century). Five generations later another MOSES, resident at Fuerth, succeeded in driving the wandering Franciscan monk and rabble-rouser John of Capistrano (1386–1456) out of the town (see title page of David Kimḥi's *Mikhlol*, Constantinople, 1532–34). His sons SAMUEL and SIMON left Fuerth for Italy, where in 1454 they obtained permission from Francesco Sforza, duke of Milan, to settle in Soncino near Cremona, from which they took their surname. Samuel's son ISRAEL NATHAN (d. 1492?), a physician, was renowned for his talmudic scholarship and piety; he died in Brescia. Printing had taken place in Italy from 1465, and it was, no doubt, under the influence of Israel Nathan and in partnership with him and his other sons (Benei Soncino) that his son JOSHUA SOLOMON (d. 1493) set up a Hebrew printing press which in 1484 produced its first book, the Talmud tractate *Berakhot*, with commentaries in the arrangement which became standard. This was followed by a complete, voweled Hebrew Bible (1488), the *Maḥzor Minhag Roma* (Soncino and Casalmaggiore, 1486), and 15 other works (to 1489). His were the first printed editions of the Hebrew Bible and Talmud tractates. From 1490 to 1492 Joshua Solomon printed at least nine works in Naples, and altogether more than 40 works are ascribed to his press.

His nephew GERSHOM BEN MOSES (d. 1534), also called Menzlein – perhaps for having learned the art of printing in Mainz – became one of the most successful and prolific printers of his time – and one of the finest of all times – printing from 1489 to 1534, not only in Hebrew (and Judeo-German?), but also in Latin, Greek, and Italian and using for non-Hebrew literature the names Hieronymus, Geronimo, or Girolamo. During his extensive travels, to France in particular, he obtained valuable manuscripts for publication, e.g., the *tosafot* of Eliezer of Touques which he was the first to publish. He was also the first to use woodcut illustrations in a Hebrew work (Isaac ibn Sahula's *Meshal ha-Kadmoni*, Brescia, c. 1491), and to produce secular Hebrew literature (Immanuel of Rome's *Maḥberot*, Brescia, 1492). Soncino also printed in small, pocket-size format, assembling an expert staff of literary advisers, typesetters, and proofreaders. His letters were cut by Francesco Griffo da Bologna, who also worked for the well-known Aldus Manutius.

Apart from Soncino and Casalmaggiore, Soncino also printed in Brescia, Barco, Fano, Pesaro, Ortona, Rimini, Ancona, and Cesena; both his Hebrew and non-Hebrew productions exceeded 100 volumes each, of which about 20 were Hebrew *incunabula (before 1500). His constant wanderings were due as much to the chicaneries of the local overlords as to fierce and perhaps unfair competition, though in the decade 1494–1504 (with an interval from 1499 to 1502) he was the world's only Hebrew printer. Eventually Soncino had to leave Italy for Turkey, where he continued to print in *Salonika (1527) and *Istanbul (from 1530), assisted by his son ELIEZER (d. 1547). Gershom Soncino exerted himself in bringing relief to the victims of the Spanish and Portuguese expulsions of 1492 and 1497.

His brother SOLOMON is mentioned as printer in only one work: Jacob b. Asher's *Arba'ah Turim* (1490?), though he belonged no doubt to the collective Benei Soncino. His son MOSES printed a number of books in Salonika from 1521 to 1527. Eliezer b. Gershom Soncino continued printing after his father's death, and after he died the press was taken over by his partner Moses b. Eliezer Parnas. His son GERSHOM printed in Cairo, Egypt, in 1557, being the last of the known Soncino printers. JOSHUA *SONCINO (d. 1569) of Istanbul was the author of a volume of responsa and novellae (*Naḥalah li-Yhoshu'a*, 1531). It is believed that the Hebrew press in Prague, where printing began in 1512, was founded by the Soncino family.

BIBLIOGRAPHY: A.M. Habermann, *Ha-Madpisim Benei Soncino* (1933); A. Yaari, in: KS, 13 (1936/37), 121–30; idem, *Ha-Defus ha-Ivri be-Kushta* (1967), 21–22; D.W. Amram, *Makers of Hebrew Books in Italy* (1909), index; M. Marx (Hieronymus) in: HUCA, 7 (1930), 427–50; C. Roth, *Jews in the Renaissance* (1959) index.

[Abraham Meir Habermann]

SONCINO, JOSHUA (d. 1569), rabbi and halakhic authority; a scion of the famous *Soncino family from Italy, some of whose descendants settled in Turkey. Soncino was the rabbi of the Sephardi Great Synagogue (Sinagoga Mayor) in Constantinople. In one of his responsa he intimates that his Ashkenazi friends disapproved of his holding that post. He maintained contact with R. Isaac *Luria and R. Bezalel *Ashkenazi, and was a close friend of R. Moses *Almosnino. His responsa and his commentaries on the tractates *Eruvin* and *Shevu'ot* were published by his grandson R. Joshua b. Menahem Soncino, under the title *Naḥalah li-Yhoshua* (Constantinople, 1731). One of his responsa can be found in *Divrei Rivot* by R. Isaac *Adarbi (Salonika, 1582, no. 60). He was asked by Dona Gracia *Nasi to render halakhic decisions on business matters (responsa 12, 20). At the time of the proposed *Ancona boycott in 1556–57, which caused a great stir among Turkish Jews, Soncino originally favored the proposals, but later took up an attitude of vehement opposition. As the representative of Italian Jews who had settled in Turkey, he was of the opinion that pressure on the city by Turkish Jewry would further imperil the situation of Ancona's Jews (responsa 39–40). He thought that the solution to the difficulties facing Italian Jewry lay in their migration to the East.

BIBLIOGRAPHY: Rosanes, Togarmah, 2 (1937/38), 79ff.; C. Roth, *The House of Nasi* (1947), 134–74; I. Sonne, *Mi-Paulus ha-Revi'i ad Pius ha-Ḥamishi* (1954), 146–59; A. Yaari, *Meḥkerei Sefer* (1958), 309–11.

[Abraham David]

SONCINO GESELLSCHAFT DER FREUNDE DES JUEDISCHEN BUCHES, Jewish bibliophile society, founded in Berlin in 1924, and liquidated by order of the Nazi government of Prussia in 1937.

The Society aimed at the typographic improvement of the Jewish and Hebrew book; 15 regular publications were primarily intended to introduce to the Jewish book-world suitable models to be imitated by the commercial producers. The Society, therefore, commissioned all the different types of literary products likely to appear in print, such as scholarly works and periodicals, novels, short stories, plays, texts illustrated by modern artists, and reprints of interesting rare books. The texts were chosen from Jewish literature of all periods and languages. Leading master-printers selected the printing type, size, and paper of each individual publication in order to design an external appearance in accordance with its contents.

The most ambitious enterprise of the Society was the creation of a new Hebrew printing type, a task not attempted for many generations. The letters were designed by Markus Behmer, who based his work on the script used by Gershom *Kohen in his *Haggadah*, printed in 1527 in Prague. The "Behmer type" appeared for the first, and last, time in the Pentateuch printed for the Society in 1930–33 by E.W. Tieffenbach at his "Officina Serpentis" printing press in Berlin.

The Society published *Soncino Blaetter; Beitraege zur Kunde des juedischen Buches*, edited between 1925 and 1937 by Herrmann Meyer, the founder and honorary secretary of the Society. In addition, *Mitteilungen der Soncino Gesellschaft* appeared between 1928 and 1932 with A. Horodisch as editor.

BIBLIOGRAPHY: J. Rodenberg, *Deutsche Bibliophilie in drei Jahrzehnten* (1931), 199–210; F. Homeyer, *Deutsche Juden als Bibliophilen und Antiquare* (1963), 67–69; 128–34. **ADD. BIBLIOGRAPHY:** A. Horodisch, in: *Bibliotheca docet: Festgabe fuer Carl Wehmer* (1963), 181–208; idem, in: *Imprimatur* Neue Folge 8 (1976), 243–54; M. Brenner, *The Renaissance of Jewish Culture*… (1996) 173–77.

[Herrmann M.Z. Meyer]

SONDERKOMMANDO, JEWISH. In May 1942, in the framework of the clandestine plan known as the "Final Solution of the Jewish Question," the mass-annihilation of the European Jewry began in the biggest extermination camp – Auschwitz-Birkenau. The killing process, which was characterized by its technical and industrial methods, was executed in the form of a production line run by SS personnel. Staff members were rewarded for their murderous activities with special rations, additional vacation, and a personal promotion.

To operate the crematoria and remove all traces of their crimes, the SS selected prisoners for a special squad shortly after their arrival without knowing the real aim of the work. For practical and ideological reasons the SS selected for this purpose mostly Jews, who from the middle of 1942 were the majority of the new prisoners coming to the camp. Ideologically, this was one the Germans' cruelest ways to humiliate the Jews and stamp them as sub-humans ("*Untermenschen*"). The inevitable death of these prisoners was a continuation of their spiritual death, which occurred during their horrible work in the death installations. The squad of prisoners thus symbolized the double death of the Jews: the mental and the physical. Another reason for choosing Jews for this squad could have been the desire to blur the distinction between the criminals and their victims, and to forcibly involve Jewish slave laborers in the process of mass killing and impose on them the onus of crimes committed solely by the Germans.

The SS euphemistically called these Jewish prisoners "*Sonderkommando*," "special squad." The members of the squad were given several privileges, which helped those who remained the professional core of the Sonderkommando survive. These prisoners got better food, improved living conditions, medical treatment from their own doctors, and from 1944 exemption from bodily punishment. They were always kept in isolated barracks, guarded day and night, and were not allowed to contact other prisoners. By giving them privileges, the administration of the camp achieved an additional moral separation of the *Sonderkommando* members from the other prisoners, who tended to accuse them of being collaborators. As a matter of fact these miserable and abused *Sonderkommando* prisoners had no choice at all. Anyone who refused to obey the orders or claimed that he was incapable of working was immediately shot by the SS.

The members of the *Sonderkommando* were organized in a hierarchic structure. At the base were the majority of ordinary workers. A few were "functionaries," e.g., the "*Vorarbeiter*" (foreman) and "*Kapo*" (head of work unit). The "*Oberkapo*" (head Kapo) and the "*Blockaelteste*" (head of the barrack) stood at the top of the *Sonderkommando* hierarchy. Orders, however, always came from the SS men, and through the functionaries were delivered to all members of the unit. The first *Sonderkommando* started to work in May 1942, in the old crematorium in the main camp (Stammlager-Auschwitz), as well as in the provisional gas chambers on the outskirts of the Birkenau camp. Parallel to this there operated from August 1942 the so-called "*Krematorium-Kommando*" in the main camp.

Between March and July 1943 four multifunctional crematoria were put into action in Birkenau. The work in the old crematorium at the main camp was stopped completely in July 1943. From May 1942 to January 1945 about 2,200 prisoners were recruited into the *Sonderkommando*. The number of members depended on the killing potential and the policy of extermination, as decided by the camp administration. The number at any one time ranged from 100 to 874 men.

As so-called "secret bearers," these direct witnesses to the genocide of the Jewish people were doomed to death by the SS and were usually murdered after the completion of the bigger killing actions, on December 9, 1942; February 24, 1944; December 23, 1944; October 7, 1944; and November 26, 1944. As it was desired that the skilled and experienced workers in the commando should stay alive until the end, there was only one complete liquidation of the whole squad, on December 9, 1942.

The members of the commando were forced by their tormentors to welcome the Jews who were entering the dressing room, to calm them, to carry those who were not able to go to the gas chambers by themselves, to ensure a quick undressing process and fast movement into the gas chambers. After the killing by gas the prisoners were obliged to evacuate and clean the gas chambers, to inspect the bodies of the victims for valuables, to cut their hair (mainly women's hair), to clean hair earmarked for industrial uses, to pull out gold teeth, and to remove prostheses. Subsequently, the prisoners were forced to burn the bodies of those murdered in the crematoria ovens or in the burning pits, to crush the remaining bones, and to spread the ashes. In the dressing room they were forced to collect all the belongings of the victims and to prepare these for dispatch by train. In the case of killing by shooting, they were obliged to distract the victims and hold them by force.

The total hopelessness and overwhelming helplessness in this extreme situation paralyzed almost every form of resistance and created an atmosphere of apathy and a loss of moral values among some of the members. Nevertheless, and amazingly, the will to survive remained in the hearts of many prisoners in the squads, who even developed an optimistic attitude.

Not only the contact with death was traumatic but also meeting the victims shortly before their deaths, including friends and relatives, not to mention the accusations by other prisoners. All this exacerbated the moral dilemma of *Sonderkommando* prisoners and their mental suffering. The prisoners found themselves in an extreme psychological situation, full of self-contempt and self-reproach. As the sole eyewitnesses to the killing process, these prisoners were the last to have contact with the victims before they were murdered. For this reason, the Germans preferred to choose prisoners for the Sonderkommando who spoke the same language as the victims, especially before big killing actions. The members of the unit, in the age range from 16 to 54, came from 18 countries altogether, mostly from Poland, Slovakia, France, Holland, Greece, Romania, and Hungary, and communicated in 11 languages. Despite the common fate that awaited them, the society of the *Sonderkommando* members could not achieve complete solidarity, mainly because of differences in social and cultural backgrounds.

Motivated by a historical conscience, several members of the *Sonderkommando* clandestinely wrote the history of the mass murder of the Jews and their own histories of the *Sonderkommando*. These manuscripts were buried in the grounds of Birkenau, discovered in part between February 1945 and October 1980, and later published.

Wishing to warn the still living Hungarian Jews before their deportation to Auschwitz, the *Sonderkommando* men supplied the four Jewish prisoners Vrba, Wetzler, Rosin, and Mordowicz who escaped from Auschwitz successfully in spring 1944 with important information and evidence of the crimes committed in the camp. Unfortunately this information could not prevent the mass murder of the Hungarian Jews.

With the completion of four new crematoria in Birkenau between March and July 1943, the living and working conditions of the *Sonderkommando* improved significantly. This enabled the creation of an underground movement of prisoners within the *Sonderkommando*, which initially was part of the general underground movement in the camp. This movement planned a general armed uprising of prisoners. Because of basic misunderstandings and incompatible interests, the general plan for an uprising was canceled, and only the *Sonderkommando* continued to plan an uprising of its own. The preparations for such an action took place in the months of spring and summer 1944. During the preparation period, young Jewish female prisoners smuggled explosives from the Union Metallwerke for the use of the Sonderkommando fighters. Four of these women were publicly hanged on January 6, 1945.

The uprising, an act of despair, was launched on October 7, 1944, in an attempt to destroy the killing installations, to avenge the crimes against the Jews committed in the camp, and to ensure that at least someone remained alive from the commando to bear witness to what had occurred in the camp.

The uprising was crushed after few hours, ending in a bloodbath of 451 *Sonderkommando* prisoners who fell in the battle or were shot in retaliation. The fighters of the *Sonderkommando* succeeded in burning one of the crematorium buildings (No. IV), killing three SS members, and wounding probably 12 others. After the uprising was crushed, the remaining prisoners of the commando were obliged to burn the bodies of their fallen comrades and destroy the remaining crematorium buildings.

By the end of October 1944, after the gas chambers in Auschwitz-Birkenau were used for the last time, more than 1,100,000 Jews had already been murdered in the death factory of Auschwitz. The last surviving members of the commando left the camp on January 18, 1945. On the long death marches they were first deported to Mauthausen.

Altogether, about 110 men of the *Sonderkommando* survived the Shoah. Sixty years after the evacuation of Auschwitz 18 former *Sonderkommando* prisoners were still alive, most of them in Israel and the United States.

[Gideon Greif and Andreas Kilian (2nd ed.)]

SONDERLING, JACOB (1878–1964), rabbi. Sonderling was born in Lipine, Silesia. His mother was a descendant of the Yismaḥ Moshe, the founder of Hungarian Ḥasidism. An ardent Zionist from youth, Sonderling was referred to as "my fighting rabbi" by Theodor Herzl.

After studying at the University of Vienna and Breslau as well as at seminaries in Vienna, Breslau, and Berlin, Sonderling received his Ph.D. from the University of Tuebingen in 1904. In 1908, he became rabbi of Hamburg's celebrated Israelitischer Temple Verein, the birthplace of Reform Judaism but in his congregation, the bastion of Reform Judaism, men and women sat separately. He was such an eloquent orator and prominent rabbi that the Hamburg synagogue offered him the position despite its well known anti-Zionism and his advocacy of Zionism. His tenure there was interrupted when, during World War I, he served as a German Army chaplain on the staff of Field Marshal Paul von Hindenburg, who was later the president of Germany. He was the chief Jewish chaplain on the German Eastern front and spent the war years in Russia, Poland, and Lithuania, where he ministered not only to German soldiers but to Eastern European Jews he encountered. He looked like the embodiment of a rabbi, with a long beard and distinguished face that as he aged became ever more impressive. His picture appeared on postcards of the Kaiser's Army. He was called "God's word on a horse." At the war's conclusion, he returned to his pulpit and remained until 1923, when he immigrated to the United States. Within weeks of his arrival in the United States he was lecturing on Zionism and drawing large audiences to hear his passionate advocacy. He then held pulpits in Chicago, New York, and Providence, where he developed what his Los Angeles colleague called new approaches to an old tradition. Religion must appeal to the senses – all five senses – not only to the ear and to the mind.

Upon moving to Los Angeles in 1935, he founded the Center for Jewish Culture (Fairfax Temple). Where else but in Hollywood could one combine art and religion? While living and working in Los Angeles, he collaborated with many well-known musicians. He inspired Eric Zeisl to compose his requiem and Maria Jeritza to perform it. During World War II, he discovered that Arnold Schoenberg, then a refugee from Nazi Germany, needed some money, so he commissioned him to write the *Kol Nidre* service. He also worked with Ernst Toch in writing the text for "Cantata of the Bitter Herbs." In 1941, he commissioned Erich W. Korngold to write the "Passover Psalm," Opus 30.

Earlier in his career he inspired Freidrich *Adler (1878–1942), who died in Auschwitz and had been a member of his congregation, to make Jewish ceremonial objects. Adler was a master of applied art who worked with furniture, architecture, and functional ware. For the Cologne Werkbund of 1914, Adler designed a synagogue interior and Torah ornaments as well as an entire group of ceremonial objects for Sabbath and holiday home observances. The remaining part of that collection is the eternal light, which is in the collection of the Spertus Museum. The first piece of ceremonial art that Adler created was a *seder* plate of pewter and embossed and cut-out glass. Incorporated onto the *seder* plate is a lid that lifts up to hold the *matzot*, and when the lid is closed the cup of Elijah fits on top in the center of the plate. It is on loan to the Skirball Cultural Center from the family of Jacob Sonderling 363 days a year and returned each year just in time for the *seder*.

His colleague, Hollywood Rabbi Max Nussbaum, commented that in Los Angeles Sonderling "initiated the Seder in drama and music and the dramatization of the Bible at Friday evening services. Basically, Sonderling himself was a fusion of religion and art."

His colleagues considered him more a teacher of teachers, a rabbi of rabbis, and he held his own with some of the most dominant personalities in the Los Angeles rabbinate. He considered himself an Orthodox rabbi among the Reform and a Reform rabbi among the Orthodox. Nussbaum said, "He represented the totality of our Jewish heritage at its best."

BIBLIOGRAPHY: M. Nussbaum, "Jacob Sonderling," in: *Proceedings of the Central Conference of American Rabbis* (1965.); J. Sonderling, "Five Gates: Casual Notes for an Autobiography," in: *American Jewish Archives* (1964).

[Michael Berenbaum (2nd ed.)]

SONDHEIM, STEPHEN (Joshua) (1930–), U.S. composer and lyricist born in New York. His meeting with his neighbor Oscar *Hammerstein II in Pennsylvania (where he moved with his mother) led him to write lyrics for stage shows. Winning the Hutchinson Prize for music at Williams College enabled him to study privately with Milton *Babbitt. Sondheim leapt to the forefront of Broadway lyricists while still in his twenties when he coauthored the songs (with Leonard *Bernstein) for *West Side Story* (1957). He followed this hugely successful musical with another lyrical triumph, Jule Styne's *Gypsy* (1959), and then wrote both the music and lyrics for *A Funny Thing Happened on the Way to the Forum* (1962). *Company*

(1970) revolutionized the art form, and *Follies* (1971) marked the start of Sondheim's collaboration with Hal Prince. *A Little Night Music* (1973) contained his most popular song "Send in the Clowns," while *Pacific Overtures* (1976) broke new ground with its use of Japanese *kabuki* theater techniques. *Sweeney Todd* (1979) is his biggest work. In *Sunday in the Park with George* (1984), Sondheim, inspired by a painting by Seurat, conveyed his images of the pointillist style through use of musical minimalism. His later works include *Into the Woods* (1987), *Assassins* (1991), and *Passion* (1994), his most symphonic score. He also wrote film scores. Sondheim's musical language, in which melody and harmony are closely argued, retains strong affinities with Ravel and *Copland, while making sophisticated use of jazz and dance idioms; it is intensely personal. His use of counterpoint is the anchor which separates him from most of today's theatrical composers. Sondheim is on the Council of the Dramatist Guild, having served as its president from 1973 to 1981. In 1983 he was elected to the American Academy of Arts and Letters. He was appointed the first Visiting Professor of Contemporary Theatre at Oxford University (1990) and was a recipient of the Kennedy Center Honors (1993), a National Medal of Arts Award (1997), and the Praemium Imperiale, Japan's highest honor, for a lifetime of artistic achievement (2000). In 2002 he received the ASCAP Richard Rodgers Award. Most of his scores have won Tony and New York Drama Critics' Circle Awards. "Sooner or Later" from *Dick Tracy* won an Academy Award, and *Sunday in the Park with George* was awarded the 1985 Pulitzer Prize for Drama. *The Sondheim Review* is a quarterly magazine dedicated to his works. Sondheim productions in translation have also spread to Spain, Germany, the Netherlands, and elsewhere.

BIBLIOGRAPHY: Grove Music Online; J. Gordon (ed.), *Stephen Sondheim: A Casebook* (1997); M. Secrest, *Stephen Sondheim: A Life* (1998); M. Gottfried, *Sondheim* (2000).

[Jonathan Licht / Naama Ramot (2nd ed.)]

SONDHEIMER, FRANZ (1926–1981) organic chemist. Born in Stuttgart, Germany, he was educated at Highgate School, London (1940–43) before gaining his Ph.D. from Imperial College, London. He was a research fellow at Harvard University (1949–52) and associate director of research at Syntex S.A. in Mexico City (1952–56) before becoming head of the organic chemistry department of the Weizmann Institute (1956–64) and also Rebecca and Israel Sieff Professor of Organic Chemistry (1960–64). During this period he retained his association with Syntex as vice president of research (1961–63). He returned to England as Royal Society Research Professor of Organic Chemistry, first at Cambridge University (1964–67), where he was also a Fellow of Churchill College, and from 1967 at University College, London. Sondheimer's research concerned the total synthesis of many natural products and in particular steroid hormones and their analogues and novel macrocyclic compounds. His many awards included the Israel Prize in exact sciences (1960), election to the Royal Society of London (1967), and the American Chemical Society's Sigma Award for creative work in synthetic organic chemistry (1976). His other main interest was classical music.

[Michael Denman (2nd ed.)]

SONG, ANGELIC. The song of praise which the angels sing to God is a common theme in the Jewish and Christian apocalyptic and mystic literature. In his vision Isaiah heard the *seraphim* uttering (Isa. 6:3) what later became known as the **Kedushah* (in Greek *Trishagion*). The idea of the angels singing in the heavenly spheres is very likely an old one; it is the counterpart of the song which the levites sing in the Temple (e.g., I Chron. 6:16–17). In the apocalyptic literature the seer translated to heaven sees, among other things, the throne of God surrounded by angels singing their perpetual song to God (II En. 39–40). This part of the vision may be called the mystical core of the apocalyptic experience. The angelic song in the apocalyptic literature is generally a development of Isaiah 6:3 and Ezekiel 3:12. The song of the angels is mentioned often in II Enoch, where it is revealed to the seer (Version II 23:2; cf. also Test. Patr., Levi 3:8). Particularly rich in its angelic doxologies, or songs of praise, is the Jewish-Christian Book of Revelation. The Qumran sect had a highly developed angelic liturgy (see Strugnell, in: VT, Supplement, 7 (1959), 318–45).

The *heikhalot* literature of the Jewish mystics of the talmudic period is replete with angelic songs. Even the throne of God sings a special song to God (*Heikhalot Rabbati*, 24–26). The angelic songs which the mystic hears are not short doxologies as in the apocalyptic writings, but long lyrical expressions of the divine holiness, appropriately called "numinous hymns" (R. Otto, *The Idea of the Holy* (1923), 34). There are several references to the angelic song in talmudic and midrashic literature. The two main ideas expressed there are:

(a) the angels do not repeat their song (which is always that of Isa. 6:3 and Ezek. 3:12); when they have finished singing it, they disappear;

(b) there is a special order according to which the angels divide the song among themselves.

There are also differences of opinion as to when the angels sing their song: during the day only (Lam. R. 3:23; Hul. 91b); during the night, when Israel does not pray (Ḥag. 12b; Av. Zar. 3b); or during both day and night (SER 7:34).

BIBLIOGRAPHY: H. Bietenhard, *Die himmlische Welt im Urchristentum Spaetjudentum* (1951), 137ff. (incl. bibl.); G. Scholem, *Jewish Gnosticism…* (1965), 20–30; Van Unnik, in: *Vigiliae Christianae*, 5 (1951), 204–48 (Eng.); Flusser, in: *Abraham, Unser Vater… Festschrift Otto Michel* (1963), 129–52.

[Ithamar Gruenwald]

SONG OF SONGS (Heb. שִׁיר הַשִּׁירִים), the book of the Hebrew Bible which normally follows Job in the Hagiographa and precedes the Book of Ruth. It thus stands first among the Five Scrolls. In Protestant and Roman Catholic Bibles, the book follows Proverbs and Ecclesiastes, in accord with Jewish (then later Christian) tradition that Solomon was the author of all three, for the arrangement of the books in the Septuagint has continued to exert its influence on the Christian canon into modern times (see *Bible, Canon). The title is derived from the superscription, *shir ha-shirim asher li-shelomo*, usually understood as "the best of Solomon's songs," although Hebrew normally does not form superlatives this way. (Comparisons with "king of kings," or "slave of slaves," are irrelevant because these are superlative by function: a king who rules other kings (= emperor); a slave owned by another slave; see Tur-Sinai, 354–55.) The book is also called the Song of Solomon or Canticles, the latter name being derived from the Latin translation of the Hebrew title. Fragments of the Song were found at Qumran.

The Character of the Song of Songs

The Song of Songs is composed entirely of a series of lyric (Septuagint: *asma*) love songs which vary in length, often consisting of brief stanzas, in which two lovers express to one another, and occasionally to others, the delights and anguish of their mutual love. Bold imagery and striking hyperbole characterize the songs, producing extravagant expressions and incongruous comparisons:

I have compared thee, O my love,
To a mare in Pharaoh's chariots.
Thy cheeks are comely with circlets,
Thy neck with beads (1:9–10; on the mare see M.H. Pope, in BASOR, 200 (1970), 56–61).
My beloved is unto me as a cluster of henna
In the vineyards of En-Gedi (1:14).
I am a rose of Sharon,
A lily of the valleys (2:1).

Several songs in chapters 4–7 exhibit qualities that distinguish them somewhat from the other poems in the book, for they lavishly praise the physical features of the two young lovers:

The roundings of thy thighs are like the links of a chain,
The work of the hands of a skilled workman.
Thy navel is like a round goblet,
Wherein no mingled wine is wanting;
Thy belly is like a heap of wheat
Set about with lilies.
Thy two breasts are like two fawns
That are twins of a gazelle (7:2b–4).

Because such poems belong to the same literary genre as a similar type of Arabic love poetry, they are called *waṣfs*, after the Arabic technical term meaning "description." Such lyrical imagery and forthright expression are admittedly sensual and suggestive, but the poems are never coarse or vulgar. (Similar seductive language is employed by the married seductress of Prov. 7:16–17, but there it leads to a bitter end.) The composer has employed vivid imagery to set a mood and create an aura of emotion, which invites the hearers to participate and share his joy and delight. Such poetic finesse in part accounts for the timeless appeal and lasting popularity of these songs. The flickering flames of love that rise and fall throughout the book leap to a final crescendo in 8:6–7:

Set me as the seal upon thy heart,
As the seal upon thine arm;
For love is strong as death,
Jealousy is cruel as the grave;
The flashes thereof are flashes of fire;
A very flame of the Lord [or "mighty flame"],
Many waters cannot quench love,
Neither can the floods drown it.

The Bible, because of its primary concern with religious themes, contains poetry which deals principally with sacred topics in hymns, laments, songs of praise and thanksgiving, etc. There are also a number of songs with a secular flavor and dealing with the more mundane affairs of life scattered through its pages, but the Song of Songs is unique in the Bible, for nowhere else within it can be found such a sustained paean to the warmth of love between man and woman. It is completely occupied with that one theme. No morals are drawn; no prophetic preachments are made. Perhaps more than any other biblical book, the Song presents a picture of "gender mutuality" (Meyers).The female lover is given more lines to speak than the male, and the presence of the "daughters of Jerusalem" is most prominent. It is likely that several of the poems originated among women bards.

A remarkable feature of the book is that God receives no mention, and theological concerns are never discussed. While the Book of Esther also fails to mention God, an unmistakable spirit of nationalism permeates its pages; but the Song lacks even this theme. Another unique feature of the book is the extended description of the woman's dreams (3:1–5; 5:1–6:3). These are the only biblical examples of dreams not followed by interpretation.

While the Song of Songs appears unique in the Bible, it is quite at home in the literature of the Ancient Near East. Numerous texts recovered from both Egypt and Mesopotamia have brought to light the long history of love poetry in the ancient world. Even the earliest civilization of ancient Mesopotamia, that of Sumer, produced passionate love songs that reflect a remarkable similarity of expressions, implications, situations, and allusions to parts of the Song of Songs, even though the latter are "far superior to their stilted, repetitive, and relatively unemotional Sumerian forerunners" (S.N. Kramer, in *Expedition*, 5 (1962), 31; Cooper, 1970). Fox has demonstrated close parallels in Egyptian love songs, and Held has called attention to a dialogue between lovers in an Akkadian work of the Old Babylonian period. Still others have compared Greek love lyrics. Upon reflection it is only natural to expect that such songs existed in the culture of ancient Israel. Song, music, and dance, both sacred and secular, have been vehicles for expressing the deepest human emotions from time immemorial, and it is doubtful that the line dividing the one from the other was as clear to the ancients as it appears to moderns.

The Song of Songs consists of only eight chapters numbering 117 verses, yet in it occur 49 words peculiar to itself and an additional number of unusual words. The syntax of the Song is also marked by oddities. The *vav* consecutive of biblical Hebrew is completely lacking; frequent incongruities exist, with masculine forms of verbs, pronouns and suffixes often appearing rather than the expected feminine forms; the personal pronoun is used pleonastically with finite verbs with no apparent emphatic connotations; the infinite absolute is never used and the infinitive construct only rarely; and what appears to be an Aramaic construction occurs at 3:7 (*miṭṭato she-li-Shelomo*, literally, "his bed, Solomon's").

The Song exhibits characteristic features of Hebrew *poetry – parallelism, meter based on stress, repetitive patterns of structure, the use of chiasmus and ballast variants, assonance, and occasionally paranomasia. A variety of repetitive patterns may be found including a number with archaic features.

The diverse features of the Song, which support the view that the work is a collection, are somewhat muted by the uniformity of language, representing a late stage of biblical Hebrew along with features that are regular in Aramaic and in later Mishnaic Hebrew. This uniformity is apparently the result of linguistic leveling which was arrested by the final redaction of the book, leaving it essentially as it now exists in the Masoretic Text.

The Interpretation of the Song of Songs

Despite its brevity, the Song of Songs has been the inspiration for more literature about itself than any other book of its size in the Bible. It holds a magnetic attraction for those who feel compelled to explain its inclusion in the Bible, its meaning, and the linguistic peculiarities in it. Near the close of the first century C.E., when the book had long been a part of the Jewish national literature, arguments against its inclusion among the books that were to be considered canonical were suppressed by no less an eminent and vociferous advocate than R. Akiva. The rabbis and the early Church Fathers quoted, paraphrased, and sermonized from it. In medieval Europe, Bernard of Clairvaux produced 86 sermons extracted from its imagery. Still, despite the voluminous writings of Jewish and Christian exegetes, in the 17th century the Westminster Assembly's annotations on the Song of Songs state, "It is not unknown to the learned, what the obscurity and darknesse of this Book hath ever been accounted, and what great variety of Interpreters, and Interpretations have indeavoured to clear it, but with so ill successe many times, that they have rather increased, then removed the cloud" (*Annotations upon all the Books of the Old and New Testament* (1951^2)). Advances in biblical scholarship have been made since then, but scholars are still divided on such important matters as the unity of the book, its origin, its divisions, its purpose, the number and identity of its characters, and its date.

The Song as an Allegory

The history of the interpretation of the Song of Songs necessarily begins with its interpretation as an allegory in which the love of God for His people was expressed. By this means a mystical message of comfort and hope could be derived from the text. The lover in the songs, operating under the guise of Solomon and the shepherd youth, was now recognized as the Lord God of Israel, and His beloved was the people Israel. Thus a literary product which seemed devoid of any apparent religious connotations was transformed into a vehicle for expressing the very deepest kind of spiritual relationship existing between God and His people. (The development of Jewish allegorization is generally traced to Greek influence. Though the term allegory is Greek in origin, the assumption of borrowing the method is gratuitous, however, for the germinal concepts and interpretative tendencies possessing the potential for allegorization existed in Jewish schools of thought and in the Bible. Noteworthy in this respect are for example the marital images found in Hos. 2; Jer. 2:2; and Isa. 50:4–7.) The allegorical view of the book had gained widespread currency among the rabbis by the first century C.E., and it was doubtless the predominant view of the populace as well; there is evidence in the Mishnah, however, that the allegorical interpretation was not universally accepted. The Tosefta (Sanh. 12:10) records the famous admonition of R. Akiva: "He who trills his voice in the chanting of the Song of Songs in the banquet-halls and makes it a secular song has no share in the world to come."

It is difficult to determine with any degree of accuracy when the allegorization of the Song of Songs began, but the disturbing conditions imposed by Rome upon Jewish life in the first century C.E. were advantageous to its expansion. In light of this and of the unusual features of the work, there can be little wonder that arguments arose among the rabbis over the retention of the Song among the books that "defile the hands," that is, that were considered canonical. At the Council of Jabneh, c. 90 C.E., the matter was discussed, but we know little of the details. In any event, current scholarly opinion does not attribute authoritative canonization of biblical books to the Jabneh council. It is clear that the songs had an innate popular appeal, and they had been ascribed to King Solomon because of the several occurrences of his name in the text and the association of the references to a king with him. A generation after Jabneh, R. Akiva denied that there had ever been any controversy about the sacred character of the Song: "God forbid that it should be otherwise! No one in Israel ever disputed that the Song of Songs defiles the hands. For all the world is not worthy as the day on which the Song of Songs was given to Israel, for all the Writings are holy, but the Song of Songs is the Holy of Holies" (Yad 3:5; cf. Eduy. 5:3; Tosef., Yad 2:14). R. Akiva's defense of the work was most certainly based on the mystical allegorical interpretation, and it is significant that he had attained a certain fame as a mystic (Tosef., Hag. (ed. Lieberman), 2:3–4). According to another tradition the Song along with Proverbs and Ecclesiastes, the other "Solomonic" works, though holy, had at first been kept out of the public curriculum (*genuzim*) but were made accessible to the public thanks to the exegesis of the men of the Great Assembly (ADRN (ed. Schechter), 2; Zakovitch, 31).

The mystical emphasis was in time displaced by historical and eschatological allegories. The Targum interpreted the Song as an allegory of the history of Israel from the Exodus to the age of the Messiah and the building of the Third Temple. Allegory was an extension of a general interpretative tendency which sought to discover the supposed deeper meaning of the sacred texts with a consequent de-emphasis of the literal meaning. This permitted every generation to find consolation, solace, and hope appropriate to its own time and circumstances. Later Jewish exegetes such as Saadiah Gaon, Rashi, Samuel b. Meir, and Abraham ibn Ezra found in the symbolism of the Song words of consolation and strength for their contemporaries. A particularly interesting interpretation advocated by a few medieval and later commentators was the view that the bride represented wisdom.

When the Christian Church included the Hebrew Bible as a part of its canon, the allegorical interpretation of the Song of Songs was taken over with it, but the allegory was modified so that it conformed to the doctrinal needs of the Church. The Song was now understood as a portrayal of the love of Christ for his church and as speaking of his dealings with it. Modern scholarship has largely abandoned the allegorical interpretation.

The Song as a Drama

The popularity in scholarly circles of the allegorical interpretation began to decline during the late 18th century, thereby giving rise to other interpretative views. An early contender was the view that the Song of Songs was best explained as a drama, complete with characters, a plot, and a moral to be drawn. The two-character version identified Solomon and the Shulammite of 7:1 as the leading dramatis personae. The king is attracted to the beautiful country girl, and he takes her from her rustic surroundings to his capital for his bride. Through a series of romantic interludes, however, she enables him to rise above mere sensual infatuation and attain a higher and nobler form of love. This version lacked drama and any convincing moral purpose; the three-character version, however, finds Solomon vying with a youthful shepherd for the love of the maiden. Despite the concerted efforts of the king to win her affections (which included carrying her off to his harem in Jerusalem), she adamantly rejects his amorous endeavors. Her constant longing for her shepherd lover ultimately dampens the king's ardor. In the end he graciously allows her to return to her home and a happy reunion with her true love. The obvious moral of virtue triumphant, unfortunately, demeans Solomon.

The conception of the Song as a drama was not a new invention of 18th-century scholars. As early as the third century C.E. the Christian scholar, Origen, had described the book as a nuptial poem in dramatic form, and two important manuscripts of the fourth and fifth centuries, Codex Sinaiticus and Codex Alexandrinus, indicate in their margins the identity and order of speakers. The popularity of the theory could not be sustained, because of its inherent weaknesses. When approached without bias, the Song of Songs obviously lacks the elements of a drama. The identification of the speakers, stage directions, appropriate divisions into acts or scenes, a plot – all these must be imposed upon the text to sustain the dramatic theory. A further drawback to the theory is the figure of Solomon, for while he is made central in the drama he does not appear so in the text itself, and he is actually absent in the supposed climax (8:11ff.).

The Song as a Cultic Liturgy

Early in the 20th century a new theory was suggested in which the Song of Songs was understood as a Jewish liturgy which was derived ultimately from the pagan rituals of the Tammuz (Adonis) cult. This cult, mentioned specifically in the Bible only in Ezekiel 8:14 and alluded to elsewhere (some compare Isa. 17:10–11), reenacted annually the myth of Tammuz, the god of fertility. The lover of the Song is seen as the dying-rising god, and the maiden is the goddess who laments him until his return, whereupon a sacred marriage (see Klein) ensues. It is suggested that much of the poetic material in the Bible came from cultic backgrounds, and that the liturgy that underlies the Song of Songs came into Israelite traditions through the celebration of a ritual marriage at the annual New Year's festival. The old Tammuz liturgy was revised in order to make it acceptable to the monotheistic ideas of Israel, or the liturgy may simply have been reduced to folk poetry. Proponents of the theory call attention to the reading of the Song of Songs during Passover to bolster their case, but the practice was not regularly followed until the medieval period.

As intriguing as the theory appears at first glance, it cannot explain the wholly secular character of the existing Song. The Song may very well contain mythological allusions, but it is unlikely that these would have been known outside of a small circle of bookish savants.

The Literal Interpretations

Two interpretations of the Song of Songs existed in the first century C.E. – the allegorical and the literal. The rabbis suppressed the latter while the allegorical view in its manifold variations dominated the interpretation of the Song for centuries. The literal view was never completely suppressed, however, for the discussions on canonization were retained and transmitted through the Mishnah, and the natural view of the Song subtly surfaced in a later rabbinic discussion on the order in which Solomon wrote Proverbs, Ecclesiastes, and the Song of Songs. R. Jonathan argued on the basis of human behavior: "When a man is young, he sings songs. When he becomes an adult, he utters practical proverbs. When he becomes old, he speaks of the vanity of things" (Song R. 1:1, no. 10). The literal interpretation, however, was advocated only rarely until the late 18th century when J.G. Herder interpreted the book on the basis of the plain meaning of the words, understanding it as a collection of love songs.

A variation of the literal view was initiated when in 1873 J.G. Wetzstein drew attention to the wedding customs of the peasants of Syria. The bride and groom are treated as king and queen during a seven-day round of festivities which include songs sung by the guests, praising the physical beauty of both bride and groom, and a "sword dance" performed by the bride before the groom. In 1893 the proposal was advanced by K. Budde that the book is actually a collection of Palestinian wedding songs. This fascinating theory held the attention of scholars for a generation thereafter, but it left disturbing problems unresolved. Not all the songs could so easily be identified with nuptial ceremonies, nor even with marital love. The division of the Song into seven sections for the seven feast days proved unconvincing. It was also illusory to assume that marriage customs of modern Syrian peasants who are composed of mixed ethnic origins could be realistically projected back over two millennia and imposed on a Jewish milieu, particularly when it was uncertain that the Syrian wedding customs described in the theory actually obtained even in modern Palestine.

The predominant trend of modern scholarship is to take the Song of Songs literally, as a collection of lyric love songs. The anthology includes songs appropriate for use at wedding feasts and others that simply celebrate the joys of youthful love. The redeeming value of this view, if one is needed, is that love in all its manifestations is the work of the Creator who made all things and pronounced them good.

Authorship, Date, and Origin

Tradition ascribed the Song of Songs to Solomon, but Solomonic authorship has been rejected for the most part by modern scholars. The diverse poems and variety of poetic elements preclude, too, the unity which the traditional view assumes. The language of the book indicates a relatively late date. The shape of the verb, *naṭar* (Song 1:6, 8:11, 12) replacing earlier *nāẓar*, "guard," for example, shows that it was borrowed from Aramaic after the internal Aramaic sound shift from the phoneme preserved in Arabic as [ظ], to [ṭ] sometime in the seventh century B.C.E. The Persian loanword *pardes*, "orchard" (4:13) is well post-Solomonic as is the hapaxlegomenon *egoz*, "walnut" (6:11). The *aperion*, "palanquin," in 3:9 may be of Greek origin. There are sufficient archaic elements in the book (Albright), however, to suggest that some of the songs are pre-Exilic.

The mention of Tirzah in 6:4 has been used to support a date for 6:4–7 before Omri moved the capital of the Northern Kingdom to Samaria (c. 800 B.C.E.). The geographical horizons of the Song include North Israel, Syria, Transjordan, and Judah, with northern places predominant so that several of the songs may have originated in that area. The destruction of the Kingdom of Israel in 722 B.C.E. did not necessarily mean the loss of that literary heritage. Ample opportunity existed for the preservation in Judah of the literary and oral traditions of the north when the Kingdom of Judah stood alone. It may be assumed that older songs, carried into Exile with the people, were brought together with later compositions and were edited, probably during the fifth century B.C.E. Older parts of the Song may have undergone minor changes in vocabulary through the replacement of older words with those more familiar before a final editing.

The discovery since 1929 of the Ugaritic texts has provided an important new research tool for biblical scholars. Through comparative linguistic studies several grammatical and syntactical problems in the Song of Songs have been partially clarified, and a number of archaic features have been identified in its text (Avishur). The direct value of the Ugaritic texts for the study of the Song of Songs is limited, however, because no work of a comparable theme has yet been discovered at Ugarit.

[Keith N. Schoville / S. David Sperling (2nd ed.)]

In the Liturgy

The Song of Songs is included in the liturgy of Passover. It is read on the Intermediate Sabbath where there is one; when the first day of Passover falls on Sabbath it is read in Israel on the first day and in the Diaspora on the eighth. Under kabbalistic influence it was instituted as a voluntary reading before the Friday evening service, being observed by Sephardi Jews, particularly during the Sabbaths between Passover and Shavuot.

In the Arts

Like the Book of Psalms, the Song of Songs has been a major influence in literature, art, and music – largely as a result of its mystical interpretation in Jewish and, even more, in Christian tradition. In early medieval times there were notable translations by Notker Labeo and Williram in Old High German; others appeared during the Renaissance era in various languages, including one in Spanish (c. 1561) by the New Christian humanist Luis de *León which may have been based on the original Hebrew; and, in more recent times, there were translations by Moses *Mendelssohn, *Goethe, and *Herder (in German), and by *Bossuet and *Renan (in French). In poetry, drama, and fiction the Song of Songs figures mainly in works of the 19th and 20th centuries. The French poet Victor Hugo, who first skirted the theme in his "Salomon" (*La légende des siècles*, 1877), developed it more fully in his "Cantique de Bethphagé," a poem contained in his posthumous collection, *La Fin de Satan* (1886). Treatments of the theme by Jewish writers include Heinrich *Heine's poem "Salomo" (in *Romanzero*, 1851), inspired by Song 3:7ff.; Abraham *Goldfaden's Yiddish operetta, *Shulamit* (1880); Julius *Zeyer's Czech drama, *Sulamit* (1883); and *Die Weisheit Salomos*, a German drama by Paul *Heyse, which S.L. *Gordon published in Hebrew as *Shulamit; o Ḥokhmat Shelomo* (1896).

The Song of Songs has continued to appeal to many writers of the 20th century, as well. In Russia, for example, Alexander Ivanovich Kuprin published the romance, *Sulamif* (1908; Eng. trans. 1923); in Argentina, Arturo Capdevila was the author of *La Sulamita* (1916), a play about the Song of Songs; and the French dramatist Jean Giraudoux wrote *Cantique des cantiques* (1938). A number of modern Jewish authors have also turned to the subject, including the Russian Samuel *Marshak, whose poem on the theme dates from his early, pre-Soviet, "Jewish" period, and the Romanian poet Marcel Breslaşu (*Cîntarea Cîntarilor*, 1938).

In art the subject was chiefly popular in the Middle Ages, when it was given a symbolic interpretation. Thus, in Byzantine miniatures, illustrations to "Behold, it is the litter of Solomon; Threescore mighty men are about it, Of the Mighty men of Israel" (3:7) sometimes show Jesus in place of Solomon, the "mighty men" being depicted as angels with lances. The subject appears in 12th-century Byzantine miniatures such as the *Homilies of the Monk James* (Vatican Library, Bibliothèque Nationale, Paris) and in the 12th-century *Hortus Deliciarum*. The Shulamite or Beloved symbolized the Church (i.e., the bride of Jesus), and hence the virgin Mary (the Church is representative). In the *Hortus Deliciarum* the Beloved is shown as the virgin flanked by monks and laity with the daughters of Zion at her feet, and the Beloved is also shown as Mary in the 16th century *Story of the Virgin* tapestry in Rheims Cathedral. Figures of the madonna from medieval France and Spain sometimes have blackened heads. These "black madonnas" have been thought to derive from the description of the Beloved who is "black, but comely" (1:5). The metaphors for the Beloved, such as the "rose of Sharon" (2:1), the "garden shut up" (4:12) and the "fountain of gardens" (4:15) became attributes of the virgin.

Two representations of the 19th century are "The Shulamite," by the English painter Albert Joseph Moore (1841–1893; Walker Art Gallery, Liverpool), and "The Song of Solomon" (1868), a drawing by the English pre-Raphaelite artist Simeon *Solomon (1840–1905; Municipal Gallery of Modern Art, Dublin). Modern Jewish works include a series of paintings by Marc *Chagall, illuminations (1923) by Ze'ev Rabban (1890–1970), illustrations by the Israel artist Shraga Weill (1918), and engravings by the Canadian David Silverberg (1961).

In the music of the 15th, and more frequently of the 16th, century settings of the (Vulgate text of the) Song of Songs were generally composed for liturgical purposes, since the verses and sections form part of many Marian celebrations. Early examples are *Quam pulchra es* by John Dunstable and by King Henry VIII of England. Sixteenth-century composers of motets and motet-cycles on the text include most of the great "Netherlanders" and their Italian successors. In the 17th century, the functions and forms of the settings became more diverse. Monteverdi's choral *Nigra sum* and *Pulchra es* were still in use as Marian praises, while his *Ego flos campi* and *Ego dormio* had already been composed as songs for alto voice and continuo. Among Schuetz's many settings in both Latin and German, *Ich beschwoere euch* (1641) is a *dialogo* approaching the dramatic form. The German Protestant settings were mostly intended as wedding songs; with the rise of Pietism they once more assumed a religio-allegorical function. *Meine Freundin du bist schoen* by Johann Christoph Bach, another wedding piece, practically concludes a period in the musical history of the Song of Songs. The 18th century did not favor the text, although one rare exception was William Boyce's *Solomon, a Sereneta... taken from the Canticles* (1743), with dialogues between "He" and "She," and choirs. In the 19th and 20th centuries the dramatic, or at least dialogic potential of the text again appealed to composers. The 19th-century works include *Tota pulchra es* by Bruckner; Chabrier's cantata, *La Sulamite*; Leopold *Damrosch's oratorio, *Sulamith*; and the oratorios titled *Canticum canticorum* by Enrico Bossi and Italo Montemezzi. Twentieth-century composers include Ralph Vaughan Williams (*Flos campi*, for viola solo, wordless voices, and small orchestra); Virgil Thompson (*Five phrases from the Song of Solomon*, for soprano and percussion); Jacobo Ficher (*Sulamita*, symphonic poem); Rudolf Wagner-Régeny (*Schir haschirim*, for choir; German text by Manfred Sturmann); Lukas *Foss (*Song of Songs*, for soprano and orchestra); Jean Martinon (*Le Lis de Saron*, oratorio); Stanislaw Skrowaczewski (*Cantique des cantiques*, for soprano and 23 instruments); Arthur Honegger (*Le Cantique des Cantiques*, ballet); Natanaël Berg (*Das Hohelied*, for choir); and Mario *Castelnuovo-Tedesco (*The Songs of Songs*, scenic oratorio; also settings of "Set me as a seal upon thine heart," etc., for Reform Jewish wedding ceremonies).

Among settings by Israel composers the best known are the oratorio *Shir ha-Shirim* by Marc *Lavry, and the solo song *Hinakh Yafah* by Alexander Uriah *Boscovich (the latter based on the traditional Ashkenazi intonation of the text). Several choral settings have also been composed for the introductory parts of the Kibbutz **seder* ceremonies, which traditionally open with the celebration of Spring. The folk-style settings of single verses and combinations of verses (often out of their original sequence) are especially numerous. Their role was particularly important in the formative years of the Israel folk-dance movement (during the late 1940s). The need for lyrical couple-dances – as against prevailing communal dances such as the *Horah and those derived from it and the "jolly" couple-dances taken over from Europe – led to an ideological conflict which was resolved by basing the new, more tender dances on the "historical" precedent of the Song of Songs.

The Song scarcely appears in traditional Jewish folk music outside its liturgical function – no doubt because of the rabbinic prohibition against singing it "like a folksong" (Sanh. 101a; see The Five *Scrolls, musical rendition).

[Bathja Bayer]

BIBLIOGRAPHY: R. Gordis, *The Song of Songs* (1954); M.H. Segal, in: VT, 9 (1959), 470–90; W.F. Albright, in: *Festschrift... G.R. Driver* (1963), 1–7; H.H. Rowley, in: *The Servant of the Lord and Other Essays on the Old Testament* (1965), 197–245; E.M. Yamauchi, in: JBL, 84 (1965), 283–90; G.D. Cohen, in: *The Samuel Friedland Lectures 1960–66* (1966), 1–21; R. Soulen, in: JBL, 86 (1967), 183–90; G. Fohrer, *Introduction to the Old Testament* (1968); K.N. Schoville, *The Impact of the Ras Shamra Texts on the Study of the Song of Songs* (Ph.D. dissertation, University Microfilms, 1970); C.D. Ginsburg, *The Song of Songs* (1857; 1970[2] with introd. by S.H. Blank). **ADD. BIBLIOGRAPHY:** N.H. Tur-Sinai, in: *Ha-Lashon ve-ha-Sefer*, vol. 2 (1959), 351–88; M. Held, in: JCS, 15 (1961), 1–26; J. Cooper, in: JBL, 90 (1970), 157–62; idem, in: I. Finkel and M.Geller (eds.), *Sumerian Gods and their Representations* (1997), 85–97; Y. Avishur, in: *Beth Mikra*, 19 (1974), 508–25; M. Pope, *Song of Songs* (AB; 1977); P. Trible, *God and the Rhetoric of Sexuality* (1978); W. Hallo, in: L. Gorelick and E. Williams-Forte (1983), 7–17; idem, in: *Bible Review*, 1 (1985), 20–27; idem, in, JANES, 22 (1993), 45–50; M.V. Fox, *The Song of Songs and the Ancient Egyptian Love Songs* (1985); D. Pardee, in: J. Marks and M. Good (eds.), *Love and*

Death in the Ancient Near East Essays…Pope (1987), 65–69; C. Meyers, *Discovering Eve* (1991); Y. Zakovitch, *Song of Songs* (1992); J. Snaith, *Song of Songs* (1993); R. Weems, in: NIB 5 (1997), 361–434; J. Klein, in: ABD, 5:866–70; R. Murphy, in: ABD, 6:15–55 (with bibliography); E. Matter, in: DBI, 2:492–96; D. Carr, in: JBL, 119 (2000), 233–48; T. Longman, *Song of Songs* (NICOT; 2001); P. Dirksen, in: *Biblia Hebraica Quinta*, vol. 18 (critical edition; 2004).

SONG OF SONGS RABBAH, aggadic Midrash on the Song of *Songs, the product of Palestinian *amoraim*. In geonic and medieval rabbinic literature *Song of Songs Rabbah* is also referred to as *Midrash Ḥazita* or *Aggadat Ḥazita*, the name deriving from its opening passage: "This is what Scripture states in the words of Solomon (Prov. 22:29): 'Seest thou (*ḥazita*) a man diligent in his business? He shall stand before kings.'" In the *editio princeps* of the work, it is called *Shir ha-Shirim Rabbati and Midrash Shir ha-Shirim*. (For the name *Song of Songs Rabbah*, see **Ruth Rabbah*.)

It is an exegetical Midrash which expounds the *Song of Songs consecutively, chapter by chapter, verse by verse, and sometimes even word by word. In the *editio princeps* the work is divided into two sections, the first an exposition of Song of Songs 1:1–2:7; the second of 2:8 to the end. Later editions, however, are further subdivided into eight chapters corresponding to those of the biblical book. The Midrash begins with five proems characteristic of amoraic Midrashim, starting with an extraneous introductory verse which is subsequently connected with the opening verse of the biblical book expounded by the Midrash. Here the proems, most of which are anonymous, are introduced by verses from the Hagiographa (three from Proverbs and one from Ecclesiastes, both ascribed, as is the Song of Songs, to Solomon).

The language of the Midrash is mishnaic Hebrew with an admixture of Galilean Aramaic and with a liberal representation of Greek words.

Song of Songs Rabbah drew from tannaitic literature, the Jerusalem Talmud, *Genesis Rabbah*, and *Leviticus Rabbah*, as well as **Pesikta de-Rav Kahana* in a recension somewhat different from its present form. There is no evidence, however, to support the suggestion that it also made use of *Lamentations Rabbah*, the greater likelihood being that both of these drew upon a common source. Conversely, *Song of Songs Rabbah*, even though in a recension other than that extant, served as a source for **Pesikta Rabbati*. It is employed in the *piyyutim* of Meshullam b. Kalonymus and is referred to in *Teshuvot ha-Ge'onim* (ed. A. Harkavy (1887) 36). This Midrash contains much original tannaitic and amoraic material. It interprets Song of Songs as an allegory of the relationship between God and Israel. It also contains many *aggadot* dealing with the messianic redemption, as well as polemical expositions against Christianity. The work was apparently redacted in Ereẓ Israel about the middle of the sixth century C.E.

There are several later additions in the Midrash, some of them the work of copyists. On Song of Songs 1:2, for example, a copyist added an entreaty that his nephew might acquire a knowledge of the Torah.

Editions

Songs of Songs Rabbah was first published in Pesaro in 1519 together with the *midrashim* on the four other scrolls (although entirely unrelated to them) and has often been reprinted on the basis of this edition. There are several extant manuscripts of the Midrash, the earliest being the Parma manuscript, dated 1270, in which *Song of Songs Rabbah* occurs in the middle of *Pesikta Rabbati* between sections 18 and 19, associated with the festival of Passover, when the Song of Songs is customarily read. An English translation by Maurice Simon appeared in the Soncino Midrash (1939).

BIBLIOGRAPHY: Zunz-Albeck, Derashot, 128; Theodor, in: MGWJ, 28 (1879), 97ff., 164ff., 271ff., 337ff., 408ff., 455ff.; 29 (1880), 19ff.; Urbach, in: *Tarbiz*, 30 (1960/61), 148–70; Sachs, in: JQR, 56 (1965/66), 225–39.

[Moshe David Herr]

SONG OF THE THREE CHILDREN AND THE PRAYER OF AZARIAH, an apocryphal addition to the ancient versions (Greek, Latin, Syriac, Coptic, Ethiopic, Armenian, Arabic) of the canonical text of the Book of Daniel, inserted between 3:23 and 3:24. The interpolation, which may have been composed in Hebrew in the second or first century B.C.E., is in three sections: (a) the Prayer of Azariah (1–22), praising God, confessing Israel's sins, and imploring divine deliverance; (b) details concerning the heating of the fiery furnace (23–27); and (c) the Song of the Three Children (28–68). The last is in two parts: the opening liturgy addressed to God (29–34) and a series of exhortations addressed to all creatures, animate and inanimate, to praise the Lord (35–68). The unknown author of the addition derived much of his inspiration from the antiphonal liturgies in Psalms 136 and 148.

BIBLIOGRAPHY: See Bibliography in *Susanna and the Elders.

[Bruce M. Metzger]

SONNABEND, YOLANDA (1934–), stage designer and painter. Yolanda Sonnabend was born in Rhodesia, but studied at the Académie des Beaux-Arts, Geneva, at Rome University, and at the Slade School of Fine Art, London. She was a resident of London from 1964. A well-known stage designer and painter, she collaborated on productions at Sadler's Wells and the Royal Opera House, London, at the Old Vic, the Stuttgart Staatsoper, and the Aldeburgh Festival. These productions included the *Oresteia* trilogy by Aeschylus, Monteverdi's *Orfeo*, *The Maids* by Genet, Shakespeare's *The Tempest*, *Othello*, *Henry IV*. and Benjamin Britten's opera, *The Turn of the Screw*. Her work was noted for intensity of vision and an extremely personal use of color and decoration. Among her finest efforts have been the plays of Genet, which require fantastic settings. She held exhibitions of stage designs in London, New York, and Italy, and her paintings appeared in numerous mixed exhibitions. She is represented in the collections of the Victoria and Albert Museum, London, and the Arts Council of Great Britain.

[Charles Samuel Spencer]

SONNE, ISAIAH (1887–1960), scholar, historian, and bibliographer. Born in Galicia, Sonne studied at Swiss and Italian universities and at the Collegio Rabbinico in Florence, where he later became a lecturer in Talmud, philosophy, and Jewish history after having taught at the Hebrew high school in Lodz. In Florence he also taught German in a state high school and worked in the libraries and archives of the Jewish communities in Italy. From 1936 to 1939 he headed the rabbinical seminary in Rhodes, and in 1940 became lecturer and librarian at Hebrew Union College, Cincinnati.

Sonne's scholarly interests extended to history, particularly that of Italian Jewry; biography (Judah Abrabanel, Uriel d'Acosta, Leone Modena); philosophy (Spinoza, Pascal); Hebrew literature (Immanuel of Rome); bibliography; and Jewish art. He was a scholar of penetrating insights, able to extract underlying historical theories from seemingly trivial details, e.g., his article in the *Alexander Marx Jubilee Volume* (1950, Hebrew section, 209–32). Sonne discovered a number of hitherto unknown works and documents, his main work consisting of articles that he published in learned periodicals and Festschriften. His books include *Avnei Binyan le-Toledot ha-Yehudim be-Italyah* ("Documents in the History of the Jews in Italy," 1938–40) and *Mi-Paulus ha-Revi'i ad Pius ha-Ḥamishi* "From Paul IV to Pius V," 1954); among his bibliographical studies is his "Expurgation of Hebrew Books; the work of Jewish Scholars" (in: *Bulletin of the New York Public Library*, 46 (1942), 975–1013). Of a polemical bent, Sonne was involved in a number of scholarly controversies. He bequeathed his collection of books and manuscripts to the Ben-Zvi Institute, Jerusalem, which published a memorial volume in his name in 1961.

BIBLIOGRAPHY: E.E. Urbach, in: *Sefunot*, 5 (1961), 11–16; N. Ben-Menahem, *ibid.*, 17–25 (bibl.); A.M. Habermann, in: *Haaretz* (Dec. 30, 1960); A.S. Halkin, *ibid.* (July 28, 1960).

[Jerucham Tolkes]

SONNEBORN, RUDOLF GOLDSCHMIDT (1898–1986), U.S. businessman and Zionist leader. Sonneborn was born in Baltimore, Maryland. He served as a navy pilot during World War I. In 1920 he joined his family's oil and chemical firm, L. Sonneborn and Sons of New York City, with which he remained associated. He was a director of the Commercial State Bank and Trust Company of New York, and president of the American Financial and Development Corporation for Israel and the Israel American Petroleum Corporation. Sonneborn was first attracted to Zionism during his student years. In 1919, when he was 21, he served on the *Zionist Commission to Palestine and journeyed alone to Damascus to confer with Emir Feisal. His wide connections in the American-Jewish community well equipped him as leader of a small group of prominent American Jews, called the Sonneborn Institute, who worked secretly with the Haganah in the years after World War II to provide the Palestine *yishuv* with desperately needed arms, ships (including the famous *Exodus*), and supplies. After the establishment of the State of Israel, the group continued its activities as Materials for Israel, of which Sonneborn was president until 1955. In addition to his business activities on behalf of the Jewish State, Sonneborn served in executive capacities with the United Jewish Appeal, the United Israel Appeal, and the Zionist Organization of America. He married Dorothy *Schiff, owner and publisher of the *New York Post*.

ADD. BIBLIOGRAPHY: L. Goldstein, *The Pledge* (2001).

[Hillel Halkin]

SONNEMANN, LEOPOLD (1831–1909), German banker, newspaper publisher, politician; founder and owner of the *Frankfurter Zeitung*. He was born in the town of Hochberg, Bavaria, to a traditional Jewish family. Following the death of his father in 1853, Sonnemann successfully turned the family's cloth-trade business into an international banking house. In 1856, at the age of 25, he joined forces with another Frankfurt banker, H.B. Rosenthal, in establishing a liberal financial paper, *Frankfurter Geschäftsbericht*, later renamed *Frankfurter Handelsblatt*. In 1859, the paper was transformed into the *Neue Frankfurter Zeitung* and, in 1866, into the *Frankfurter Zeitung* (FZ), by then published in Sonnemann's Frankfurter Societaets-Druckerei. In 1867, he became sole proprietor and editor. Under his direction, the FZ soon developed into one of the leading liberal dailies in Germany. Deeply impressed as a boy by the revolutionary events in 1848/49, Sonnemann was one of the founders of the *Volkswirtschaftlicher Kongress* (German Economic Congress), to which he reported on banking and stock exchange systems until 1885. From 1871 to 1876 and from 1878 to 1884, he was a member of the Reichstag, representing the *Deutsche Volkspartei* (Southern German Democratic Party). He was also a member of the Frankfurt city council. In his will, he asked that the *Frankfurter Zeitung* remain a liberal voice, and so it continued until it was closed on the personal instructions of Hitler in 1943.

BIBLIOGRAPHY: H. Simon, *Leopold Sonnemann* (Ger., 1931). **ADD. BIBLIOGRAPHY:** A. Giesen (ed.), *Zwölf Jahre im Reichstage. Reichstagsreden von Leopold Sonnemann* (1901); Wininger 5 (1930), 571–2; E. Kahn, in: LBIYB, 2 (1957), 228–35; K. Gerteis, *Leopold Sonnemann* (1970); W.E. Mosse, in: LBIYB, 15 (1970), 125–39; B.B. Frye, in: LBIYB, 22 (1976), 143–72; A. Estermann, *Dokumente zu Leopold Sonnemann* (1995).

[Lawrence H. Feigenbaum / Johannes Valentin Schwarz (2nd ed.)]

SONNENFELD, BARRY (1953–), U.S. director-producer. Born in New York City, Sonnenfeld grew up in Washington Heights and attended the High School of Music and Art in Manhattan. He majored in political science at New York University, but completed his senior year at Hampshire College in Amherst, Massachusetts. Following a cross-country trip, Sonnenfeld decided to enroll in NYU's Graduate Institute of Film and Television. He earned money making industrial films, directing commercials, music videos, and X-rated movies. In 1982, Sonnenfeld worked as a cinematographer on the documentary *In Our Water*, which earned an Academy Award nomination. After he met fellow NYU film student Joel *Coen at a party, the two became friends. Sonnenfeld helped Coen raise money for the noir thriller *Blood Simple* (1984), for which he was the cinematographer. In 1985, he won an Emmy Award for his work on an ABC television special, *Out of Step*. He was the cinematographer for several feature films, including the Coen brothers' *Raising Arizona* (1987) and *Miller's Crossing* (1990) and Rob *Reiner's *When Harry Met Sally…* (1989) and *Misery* (1990). Sonnenfeld directed *The Addams Family* (1991), a big-screen adaptation of the 1960s sitcom inspired by Charles Addams' cartoons, which earned more than $110 million, and the sequel, *Addams Family Values* (1993). He turned down the opportunity to direct *Forrest Gump* (1994), preferring instead to adapt the Elmore Leonard novel *Get Shorty* (1995), which earned actor John Travolta a Golden Globe. After directing the quirky sci-fi comedy hit *Men in Black* (1997), Sonnenfeld began moving into production with two Elmore Leonard projects, television's *Maximum Bob* (1998) and the Steven *Soderbergh-directed feature *Out of Sight* (1998). After directing *Wild Wild West* (1999), a big-budget flop, Sonnenfeld returned to his crime roots directing the Dave Barry comedy *Big Trouble* (2002) and the sequel to his 1997 hit *Men in Black II* (2002). He delved further into Leonard's lead character from *Out of Sight* with the short-lived television show *Karen Sisco* (2003). In 2004, he produced the Coen brothers' remake of *The Ladykillers* and Lemony Snicket's *A Series of Unfortunate Events*.

[Adam Wills (2nd ed.)]

SONNENFELD, JOSEPH ḤAYYIM BEN ABRAHAM SOLOMON (1849–1932), first rabbi of the separatist Orthodox community in Jerusalem. Born in Verbó (Slovakia), Sonnenfeld was orphaned at the age of four. As a child he studied both in a *talmud torah* and in a general school, but in his youth he decided to devote himself entirely to rabbinic study. After pursuing his studies in the yeshivah of his native town, in 1865 he went to Pressburg, where he lived in great poverty while studying in the yeshivah of Abraham Samuel Benjamin Sofer. In 1870 he received the title of honor *Morenu* from his teacher in a letter full of laudatory references to his great learning. The same year he went to Kobersdorf (Burgenland), where he became a pupil of A. Shag, who thought highly of him. In 1873 Sonnenfeld accompanied his teacher to Ereẓ Israel and settled in the Old City of Jerusalem, and until the end of his life meticulously refrained from remaining outside the walls of the Old City for more than 30 days. He formed a close association with M.J.L. *Diskin and was his right hand in his communal activities, such as the founding of the large orphanage and schools and the struggle against the secular schools. Sonnenfeld was one of the most active and influential personalities in the community centered in the Old City. He headed the Hungarian *kolel* Shomerei ha-Ḥomot ("the guardians of the walls"), founded the Battei Ungarn quarter, and helped in the establishment of other quarters in Jerusalem. In 1919 he was one of a group of rabbis headed by A.I. Kook which visited the newly established settlements in order to influence them with regard to the observance of Judaism.

Sonnenfeld stood for complete separation between the Orthodox and the non-Orthodox; he strongly opposed the bringing of the institutions of the old *yishuv* under the control of the Zionist bodies and the participation of the Orthodox in the official community, Keneset Yisrael, and fought for the statutory right of every individual to opt out of it. When the Jewish Battalions were founded in World War I he opposed enlistment of Orthodox Jews in the battalions. He was one of the founders of the Va'ad ha-Ir le-Kehillat ha-Ashkenazim ("City Council for the Ashkenazi Community"), as well as of its *bet din*, in opposition to the official Jerusalem rabbinate. He was also a founder of *Agudat Israel in Ereẓ Israel.

As a result of his adherence to the doctrine of separation, Sonnenfeld was one of the chief opponents of A.I. Kook, and led the opposition to his appointment as rabbi of Jerusalem, and later as chief rabbi of Ereẓ Israel, even though on the personal level their relationship was one of friendship and esteem. In 1920 Sonnenfeld was elected rabbi of a separate Orthodox community. In his struggle for the emergence of the separatist community he was especially aided by the Dutch publicist Jacob Israel de *Haan, who took care that eminent non-Jewish visitors would meet Sonnenfeld, and they were duly impressed by his personality. He was a member of the separatist Orthodox delegation that appeared, on de Haan's initiative, before Hussein, king of the Hedjaz, when the latter visited Transjordan. He appeared before the U.S. King-Crane Commission (see: *Palestine, Inquiry Commissions); he also instructed his followers to meet Lord Northcliffe on his visit to Ereẓ Israel. On all these occasions Sonnenfeld expressed a positive attitude to the Jewish resettlement of Ereẓ Israel and the return to Zion, and in the census declared Hebrew as his language. He generally preached loyalty toward the government. He also inclined to moderation toward the Arabs of Ereẓ Israel and strove to establish peace between them and the Jewish population.

His published works include glosses to the *Aguddah* on *Bava Kamma* (Jerusalem, 1874) and on all of *Nezikin* (1899), a pamphlet, *Seder ha-Purim ha-Meshullash* (1898ff.); *Salmat Ḥayyim*, responsa to Shulḥan Arukh *Oraḥ Ḥayyim* and *Yoreh De'ah* (193842).

BIBLIOGRAPHY: M. Blau, *Ammuda di-Nehora* (1932, 1968²); idem, *Al Ḥomotayikh Yerushalayim* (1946), 114–9; I. Breuer, in: *Nach'lath Z'wi*, 2 (1932), 193–201; S. Daniel, in: *La-Mo'ed*, 1 (1959), 281–5; A.B. Schurin, *Keshet Gibborim* (1964), 93–97; Tidhar, 1 (1947), 61f.

[Zvi Kaplan]

SONNENFELD, SIGISMUND (1847–1929), journalist, philanthropist, and communal leader, born in Vagujhely (then in Hungary). After graduating in philosophy, Sonnenfeld joined the staff of *Pester Lloyd* in Budapest. In 1890 he settled in Paris where he became director of the philanthropic institutions of Baron de *Hirsch; as such he took part in planning relief for East European Jewry. From 1891 to 1911 he was a director of ICA (*Jewish Colonization Association), undertaking several study tours in Russia, Romania, and Argentina. He also was a member of the central committee of the *Alliance Israélite Universelle.

BIBLIOGRAPHY: Wininger, Biog, 5 (1930), s.v.

SONNENFELDT, HELMUT (1926–), political adviser and scholar. Born in Berlin, Sonnenfeldt fled Nazi Germany with his family, settling in the United States in 1944. He was educated at Johns Hopkins University, earning his bachelor's degree in 1950 and his master's degree in 1951.

Sonnenfeldt joined the U.S. Department of State in 1952, becoming director of the Office of Research on the Soviet Union and Eastern Europe, a position he held until 1969. That year he was appointed as a National Security Council aide on Soviet affairs, working under Henry Kissinger, who was President Richard Nixon's national security adviser. Sonnenfeldt's close relationship with Kissinger, as well as their agreement in foreign policy matters, led to his inclusion in Kissinger's wide-ranging diplomatic ventures, including the early initiatives toward normalization of relations with China and the extensive negotiations leading to the Strategic Arms Limitation Talks.

Following Kissinger's appointment as secretary of state in 1973, Sonnenfeldt returned to the State Department, holding the position of counselor from 1974 to 1977. An expert political analyst, Sonnenfeldt also had a reputation as an anti-Communist. His departure from the department in 1977 was purportedly driven by a misunderstanding over remarks about the Soviet Union.

Sonnenfeldt continued his career as a consultant and political analyst, writing and lecturing on international issues. He became a visiting scholar at the School of Advanced International Studies at Johns Hopkins University. In 1978 he was named a guest scholar at the Brookings Institution, a position he still held in 2006. In 1988 and 1989 he served as a member of the executive committee of the International Institute of Strategic Studies. He wrote and lectured extensively on Asian-Pacific affairs, national security, U.S.-European relations, and executive and congressional relations. His works include *Soviet Politics in the 1980s* (1985), *Soviet Perspectives on Security* (with William Hyland, 1979), and *Soviet Style in International Politics* (1985). He contributed numerous articles to academic journals.

Sonnenfeldt serves as a trustee of Johns Hopkins University and was a member of the Executive Panel of the Chief of Naval Operations. He was director of the Atlantic Council of the United States and was a member of the advisory council of numerous organizations, including the Balkan Action Committee, the Defense Policy Board Advisory Committee, and the World Affairs Council.

[Dorothy Bauhoff (2nd ed.)]

SONNENFELS, ALOYS VON (**Ḥayyim Lipmann Perlin; Aloys Wiener**; d. c. 1775–80), apostate Hebrew interpreter in Vienna. Son of a Brandenburg rabbi, Sonnenfels went to *Mikulov (Nikolsburg), Moravia, as an agent of the local noblemen. He adopted the Roman Catholic faith between 1735 and 1741 and had his two sons baptized. His wife, however, remained in the Jewish faith. Moving to Vienna, he became teacher of Oriental languages at the university there and court interpreter to *Maria Theresa. He was knighted in 1746. A year earlier he had published *Or Nogah, Splendor lucis*, a "physico-kabbalistic" exposition in Hebrew and German of the problem of the philosopher's stone. In 1753 he translated the *Shai Takkanot* (see *Moravia) for the compilation of the *Polizey-ordnung* of 1754. That same year he wrote to R. Isaac Landau of Cracow offering to go to Poland to assist in the struggle against the Frankist blood libel (see Jacob *Frank and the Frankists), publishing *Juedischer Blut-Eckel* in Latin and German against the blood libel (1753). In it he argued that such false, superstitious accusations prevented Jews from recognizing the truth of Christianity. When Jacob Selekh, the representative of Polish Jewry, went to ask for the renewal of the papal *bulls in refutation of the blood libel, Sonnenfels submitted an Italian translation of his book. He published a christological apology, *Controversiae cum Judaeis* ("Controversies with the Jews"), in Latin in 1758. When proposing, in 1760, that he should write a book in defense of the Talmud, which was then under attack at the court of Pope Clement XIII, he requested financial support for this project from the Italian communities. The book, which was also to include proof that the Gospels could be explained by the Talmud, did not materialize.

His son JOSEPH (1732–1817) became the chief representative of the ideology of enlightened despotism, and as adviser to Maria Theresa, *Joseph II, and Leopold II, one of the most influential men in the Hapsburg Empire in the second half of the 18th century. Born in Mikulov and baptized at the age of three, he never mentioned his Jewish origin. After graduating from the philosophy faculty of Vienna University, he joined the army in 1749. On his discharge (1754) he studied law, becoming a professor of political science in 1763. As he was proficient in nine languages, Hebrew among them, he succeeded his father as court interpreter.

Joseph von Sonnenfels published more than 150 books and pamphlets and his textbooks on national economy, particularly mercantilism, were influential for decades (*Grundsaetze der Polizey-Handlung und Finanzwissenschaft*, 3 vols., 1765–67, 1819–22). Sonnenfels opposed excessive urbanization and held that it was the responsibility of the state to guarantee all who were willing to work the minimum means of subsistence. In his *Ueber die Liebe des Vaterlandes* (1771) he introduced the concept of the "fatherland" into Hapsburg lands. He favored indirect taxation and opposed revenue farming. Sonnenfels had literary ambitions, aspiring to be the first Austrian author to attain international fame. He founded the periodical *Der Mann ohne Vorurteil* (1765–75). He eliminated the *Hanswurst* ("buffoon") from the popular Viennese stage and was involved in a controversy with Gotthold Ephraim *Lessing. In Austria he was remembered mainly for the part he played in the abolition of torture in judicial procedure (*Ueber die Abschaffung der Tortur*, 1775, 1782²). He also fostered educational reform.

Sonnenfels drafted the *Toleranzpatent of Joseph II, which shows the imprint of his theories. In 1782 he published in Berlin a pamphlet titled *Das Forschen nach Licht und Recht* in which he requested Moses *Mendelssohn to become a Christian. Mendelssohn's reaction to this was published in his *Jerusalem* (1783). In 1784 Sonnenfels made Mendelssohn a member of his Deutsche Gesellschaft (German scientific society) and of the Vienna Academy of Sciences. Although highly honored during his lifetime (becoming *Wirklicher Geheimrat*, Real Aulic councillor in 1779, twice rector of Vienna University, head of the Academy of Sciences in 1810), Sonnenfels was known in Vienna as "the Nikolsburg Jew." A statue of him was erected in front of Vienna city hall when the antisemite Karl *Lueger was mayor; it was removed under Nazi rule (1938) and restored in 1945.

BIBLIOGRAPHY: R.A. Kann, *A Study in Austrian Intellectual History* (1960), 146–244; bibl., 310–35; Holzmann and Portheim, in: *Zeitschrift fuer die Geschichte der Juden in der Tschechoslowakei*, 1 (1930/31), 198–207; 2 (1931/32), 60–66; Nirtl, *ibid.*, 3 (1932/33), 224; W. Mueller, *Urkundliche Beitraege… maehrischen Judenschaft* (1903), 83–84; F. Kobler, *Juden und Judentum in deutschen Briefen* (1938), 50–51; 103–14; L. Loew, *Gesammelte Schriften*, 2 (1891), 363–6; 405–6; idem, *Aron Chorin* (Ger., 1863), 137–40; G. Wolf, *Das Unterrichtswesen in Oesterreich unter Kaiser Josef II nach… Joseph von Sonnenfels* (1880); Zielenziger, in: ESS, 14 (1954), 258–9; S. Simonsohn, *Toledot ha-Yehudim be-Dukkasut Mantova* (1963), index; Katz, in: *Zion*, 29 (1964), 112–32; R. Kestenberg-Gladstein, *Neuere Geschichte der Juden in den boehmischen Laendern*, 1 (1969), index.

[Meir Lamed]

SONNENSCHEIN (née **Jassol**), **ROSA** (1847–1932), early American Zionist and editor. Sonnenschein was born in Hungary but immigrated to America where she soon became prominent in literary circles, serving as special correspondent for several St. Louis and Chicago newspapers while attending the Paris Exposition.

At the Columbian Exposition held in Chicago in 1893 she read a paper on the need for a literary journal for women, which was followed by her founding the first independent English-language Jewish women's journal in the United States, *The American Jewess*, which appeared from 1895 to 1899, when it was discontinued for financial reasons, despite the fact that it was supported by the National Council of Women and had many well-known contributors, including Israel *Zangwill, Max *Nordau and Isaac Meyer *Wise.

During her numerous trips abroad, she met Theodor *Herzl and became an ardent Zionist and was a delegate to the First Zionist Congress held in Basle in 1897.

In 1864, she married Rabbi Solomon Hirsch Sonnenschein who was a rabbi in Prague and subsequently in New York, St. Louis, and Des Moines, Iowa. They were divorced however in the 1890s.

BIBLIOGRAPHY: J.N. Porter, in: *American Jewish History* (1978), 78; J. Zausmer, *Be-Ikve ha-Dor* (1957); A. Lebeson, *Recall to Life: The Jewish Women in America* (1970), 228–33.

[Jack Nusan Porter]

SONNENTHAL, ADOLF RITTER VON (**Neckwadel**; 1834–1909), Austrian actor and theatrical director. Apprenticed to a tailor, Sonnenthal decided to become an actor on seeing a performance by Bogumil *Dawison. For several years he acted in theaters in Temesvar, Hermannstadt, and Graz, until he was invited by Heinrich Laube to join the Burgtheater in Vienna in 1856. After an indifferent debut, he triumphed in Don Carlos and was given a contract that kept him at the Burgtheater for life. Though not handsome, he nevertheless excelled in drawing-room comedy, but he gained his great reputation in Shakespeare, Goethe, Schiller, Ibsen. Among his most impressive roles were Romeo, Hamlet, Macbeth, Wallenstein, Faust, King Lear, Nathan the Wise, and Uriel Acosta. He became Oberregisseur of the Burgtheater in 1884 and its provisional general manager in 1887–88 and 1889–90. Sonnenthal was a practicing Jew and resisted attempts to convert him. More than once he was a target of antisemitic attacks. The emperor made him a nobleman in 1881. He made guest appearances in Russia and the U.S.

BIBLIOGRAPHY: L. Eisenberg, *Adolf Sonnenthal* (Ger., 1900). **ADD. BIBLIOGRAPHY:** J. Bab and W. Handl, *Deutsche Schauspieler …* (1908); J. Minor, *Aus dem alten und neuen Burgtheater* (1920); J. Handl, *Schauspieler des Burgtheaters* (1955).

[Gershon K. Gershony / Jens Malte Fischer (2nd ed.)]

SONNINO, (Giorgio) SIDNEY (1847–1922), Italian statesman and economist who twice became prime minister of Italy. The son of a wealthy Jewish merchant from Pisa and a Protestant mother whose faith he adopted, Sonnino graduated from the University of Pisa and was variously occupied as a journalist, lawyer, and diplomat. In 1880 he entered parliament where he rapidly established himself as an authority on financial policy. In 1893 he became undersecretary of the treasury and was made minister of finance in 1896 when, together with Luigi *Luzzatti, he helped reduce the Italian budget deficit.

Sonnino served two short periods as prime minister (in 1906 and 1909–10) and was foreign minister during World War I, signing the Treaty of London in 1915 by which Italy sided with the Allies. He remained foreign minister after the war and headed the Italian delegation at the Versailles Peace Conference in 1919. Sonnino retired in 1920 and was made a senator for life. He left two books dealing with his political life: *Discorsi per la Guerra* (1922) and *Discorsi parlamentari* (3 vol., 1925).

BIBLIOGRAPHY: M. Viterbo, *Sidney Sonnino* (It., 1923); A. Savelli, *S. Sonnino* (It., 1923); C. Montalcini, *Sidney Sonnino* (It., 1926). **ADD. BIBLIOGRAPHY:** G Haywood, *Failure of a Dream:*

Sidney Sonnino and the Rise and the Fall of the Liberal Italy (1999); E. Minuto, *Il partito dei parlamentari: Sidney Sonnino e le istituzioni rappresentative(1900–1906)* (2004).

[Giorgio Romano]

SONNTAG, JACOB (1905–1984), Ukrainian-born editor and author. The son of a bookbinder, Sonntag was educated in Vienna and elsewhere in Central Europe, fleeing to England in 1938. He devoted himself to Anglo-Jewish cultural affairs and made repeated attempts to found a periodical for Jewish writers and artists. Sonntag finally succeeded with *The Jewish Quarterly,* which he founded in 1953. Edited almost single-handedly, it provided the main periodical venue in England for intelligent discussion of Jewish issues and published the early works of a range of distinguished Anglo-Jewish writers, including Dannie *Abse, Jon *Silkin, and Arnold *Wesker. It continued to be published after Sonntag's death. He also edited the anthology *Caravan* (1962).

BIBLIOGRAPHY: ODNB online; R. Sonntag, "Jacob Sonntag: A Personal Memoir," in: S.W. Massil (ed.), *The Jewish Year Book 2003*, xiii–xviii.

[William D. Rubinstein (2nd ed.)]

SON OF MAN (Heb. בֶּן אָדָם; pl. בְּנֵי אָדָם, Aram. בַּר אֱנָשׁ).

In the Bible

In the Bible the phrase "son of man," or "sons of man" (*adam*), is used as a synonym for a member of the human race, i.e., descendants of Adam. It occurs frequently in Psalms in the plural, and the most cogent examples of its meaning are Psalms 90:3, "Thou turnest man to contrition, and sayest, return, ye sons of man"; 115:16, "the heavens are the heavens of the Lord, but the earth hath He given to the sons of man"; and repeatedly in Psalm 107. In Psalm 49:3 a distinction is made between "the sons of *Adam* and the sons of *Ish*, rich and poor together," and it would appear that insofar as the two are distinct, the former refers to the common man, while *Ish* refers to the upper strata (cf. Isa. 2:9 and 11). The phrase "son of man" is merely the singular of *benei adam*, and in the Bible has no theological or mystical connotation. It is most frequently used by Ezekiel, mostly as the form of address to him by God, where it occurs 79 times, and it seems, as is clear from chapter 33, that he wishes thereby to emphasize that he is possessed of no special qualities or powers different from those of any other person, except that he has been selected as the "watchman" of his people.

[Louis Isaac Rabinowitz]

Post-Biblical Concept

The eschatological figure commonly identified with the Messiah occurs in chapter 7 of the Book of Daniel in a vision which is explained by the angel in a collective way as the holy ones of the most high, i.e., Israel or the pious among them. The author of Daniel based himself upon a more ancient tradition according to which the title son of man was a designation of a special eschatological figure. This idea existed possibly by the third century B.C.E.; the designation "man" for messiah already occurs in the Greek translation of the Pentateuch (see *Messiah) of this period.

The son of man is named "man" also in IV Ezra, and in Hebrew "son of man" and "man" is identical. In the whole literature in which it is mentioned, the son of man is always portrayed with the same economy of line. The son of man has a superhuman, heavenly sublimity. He is the cosmic judge at the end of time; seated upon the throne of God, he will judge the whole human race with the aid of the heavenly hosts, consigning the just to blessedness and sinners to the pit of hell; and he will execute the sentence he passes. Frequently he is identified with the Messiah, as in the Book of Enoch, chapters 37–71, and in IV Ezra. According to a later part of the Book of Enoch (ch. 71) the son of man is identified with Enoch himself as the heavenly scribe. According to the apocryphal Testament of Abraham the son of man is literally Adam's son Abel who was killed by the wicked Cain, for God desired that every man be judged by a man (the identification is based upon a verbal understanding that son of man in Hebrew is *ben-Adam*). Though in the Dead Sea Scrolls there were also other messianic concepts, the concept of son of man is also reflected in them. The eschatological figure occurring in the Thanksgiving Scroll (3, 5–18) resembles or is identical with the son of man of other Jewish literature. In one of the fragments from the Dead Sea Scrolls Melchizedek figures as the judge at the end of time. In company with angels from on High he will judge man and the wicked spirits of Belia'al. Thus the son of man could be even identified with the biblical Melchizedek according to a mythical understanding.

The idea of son of man originated possibly from a midrashic interpretation of Ezekiel 1:26, "… and the likeness as the appearance of a man above upon it." In the Book of Enoch (46: 1, 2) the son of man is presented with similar words "with Him was another being whose countenance had the appearance of a man… And I asked the angel who went with me and showed me all the hidden things, concerning that son of man, who he was…."

Thus it seems that the concept preceded the final identification of the son of man with the Messiah, which became common at the end of the Second Temple period. It was so applied in the time of Jesus, who used to speak of the son of man as the heavenly judge, and it seems that finally he identified himself with this sublime figure.

[David Flusser]

BIBLIOGRAPHY: POST-BIBLICAL CONCEPT: D. Flusser, in: *Christian News from Israel* (1966), 23–29; S. Mowinckel, *He That Cometh* (1956); E. Sjöberg, *Der Menschensohn in dem aethiopischen Henochbuch* (1946).

SONS OF LIGHT (Heb. בְּנֵי אוֹר, *benei or*), phrase used specially in the *Dead Sea Scrolls denoting the godly, by contrast with the phrase "sons of darkness" (Heb. בְּנֵי חֹשֶׁךְ, *benei ḥoshekh*) denoting the ungodly. It is so used, notably in the **War Scroll*, where "the sons of light put forth their hands to make a beginning against the lot of the sons of darkness" (1QM 1:1). The "sons of light" are here particularized as "the sons of Levi, the sons of Judah, the sons of Benjamin, the dispersion of the wilderness"; the "sons of darkness" as the hosts of Edom, Moab, the Ammonites, Philistia, and the Kittim, aided by those who transgress the covenant. In the event described, the sons of light annihilate the sons of darkness. From the viewpoint of the Qumran community, the sons of light are members of the community and their sympathizers. On entry into membership the candidate swears "to love all the sons of light, each according to his lot in the council of God, and to hate the sons of darkness, each according to his guilt in the vengeance of God" (1QS 1:9–11). The apostate is to be "cut off from the midst of the sons of light" (1QS 2:16). The sons of light are so chosen through God's predestinating decree. When God created man, He appointed two spirits to govern him: "dominion over all the sons of righteousness is in the hand of the Prince of Lights, and they walk in the ways of light; all dominion over the sons of perversity is in the hand of the Angel of Darkness, and they walk in the ways of darkness" (1QS 3:20ff.). The Angel of Darkness, indeed, makes even the sons of light go astray, but they can count on the aid of "the God of Israel and the angel of His truth" (1QS 3:24ff.). The designation "sons of light" is one of the links between the Qumran texts and the New Testament; in the latter it is found on the lips of Jesus (Luke 16:8, where it is opposed to the "sons of this age", John 12:36) and in the Pauline writings (Eph. 5:8; I Thess. 5:5). In both bodies of literature the ultimate background is the separation made by God in the beginning when He called light into being as the first of His creative works and separated it from the darkness (Gen. 1:3ff).

BIBLIOGRAPHY: A.R.C. Leaney, *Rule of Qumran and Its Meaning* (1966), 79ff., passim.

[Frederick Fyvie Bruce]

SONTAG, SUSAN (1933–2004), U.S. critic and author. Born in New York City, Susan Sontag taught philosophy and aesthetics at the City College of New York, Sarah Lawrence College, and from 1961 to 1965 at Columbia University.

Her first novel, *The Benefactor*, was published in 1963, but her reputation grew largely from her literary criticism, which appeared throughout the 1960s in a number of journals and was collected in *Against Interpretation* (1966) and *Styles of Radical Will* (1969). Consciously avant-gardist, it argued for a purely formalistic approach to literary values, while at the same time seeking to reconcile this position with her left-wing political views. A second novel, *Death Kit* (1967), was concerned, like her first, with the relation between illusion and reality. She also wrote and directed a movie, *Duet for Cannibals* (1969). Later works include plays, among them *Alice in Bed: A Play in Eight Scenes* (1993). In addition to stories and essays, Sontag has written books that include the 1992 novel *The Volcano Lover: A Romance.* A selection of her writings was collected in the 1982 *A Susan Sontag Reader.* In her capacity as literary critic she has edited *Antonin Artaud: Selected Writings* (1988) and *A Barthes Reader* (1982). Her reflection on the relationships amongst photography, history, and perception, *On Photography*, appeared in 1977. Her own battle with cancer led her to write *Illness as Metaphor* (1978), followed in 1989 with a complementary study, *Aids and Its Metaphors.* In 2000, her sweeping novel of late 19th century America, and the fortunes of Maryna Zalezowska, was published with the title *In America: A Novel.* It received the National Book Award. *Conversations with Susan Sontag*, edited by Leland Pogue, appeared in 1995.

A member of the American Academy of Arts and Sciences and the American Academy of Arts and Letters, Sontag has been the recipient of many awards including the 1978 American National Book Critics prize. She was created Officier de l'Ordre des Artes et des Lettres in France in 1984.

ADD. BIBLIOGRAPHY: L. Kennedy, *Susan Sontag: Mind as Passion* (1995); C. Rollyson, *Reading Susan Sontag: A Critical Introduction to Her Work* (2001); S. Sayres, *Susan Sontag: the Elegiac Modernist* (1990).

[Rohan Saxena and Lewis Fried (2nd ed.)]

SOPRON (Ger. **Oedenburg**), city in W. Hungary on the Austrian border, within proximity of the "Seven Communities" of *Burgenland. Jews were living there during the 14th century, according to the prevailing custom in a "Jewish street." Their residence in Sopron was guaranteed by King Charles Robert in 1324. The land registry records of 1379 show that 27 houses were owned by Jews. After King Louis the Great expelled the Jews in 1360, those who lived in the town left for nearby *Wiener Neustadt in Austria, where some of them made their fortune and became well-known financiers. When Louis authorized their return in 1365, their houses were transferred to Christian ownership. During their absence the debts owed to them were canceled by Rudolf, prince of Austria, upon the request of the citizens of Sopron. Upon their return the Jews demanded that the validity of their promissory notes be recognized, but the townsmen succeeded in revoking them.

Their situation did not improve until the reign of Matthias Corvinus, when the office of *Praefectus Judaeorum was established. From 1495 a special tax was imposed on the Jews by the governor of the town until in 1523 the king took them under his protection. The Jews then numbered 400. Rabbis of Sopron at the close of the 14th century were R. Meir (mentioned in *Sefer ha-Minhagim*) and R. Judah (mentioned in the *Shalshelet ha-Kabbalah* as a distinguished scholar in the Germanic countries). Fifteen codices recently discovered attest the erudition of the Jewish scholars of Sopron.

When the whole of Hungary was conquered by the Turks in 1526, the Jews were expelled from the town "forever." They infiltrated back into Sopron in the 18th century but its gates remained closed to them until freedom of residence was authorized by law in 1840. In 1855, 180 Jews were living there. New settlers came mainly from the "Seven Communities" of Burgenland where they had lived under the protection of the Eszterházy family from the 16th century. The municipal council of Sopron again attempted to oppose them, and in 1858 anti-Jewish riots broke out in the town; these were suppressed by the central authorities. In 1857 the Jews were authorized to organize themselves as a community but they did not possess a cemetery or synagogue. In 1862 the municipal council prevented the community from purchasing land for a cemetery and the Jews were compelled to acquire an estate for this purpose (1869). A synagogue was erected in 1876, and in 1884 a school was built. The community remained *status quo ante after the schism in Hungarian Jewry of 1868–69 (see *Hungary). In 1868 L. Alt was appointed rabbi of Sopron but he was dismissed in 1872. It was only 20 years later that M. *Pollak was appointed as the first, and also the last, rabbi of the status quo ante community (1894–1944). An Orthodox community was organized in 1872; its rabbi was Menahem Gruenwald (1872–1930). A *talmud torah* was established in 1874, and a yeshivah was founded in 1917 by S. Posen, the rabbi of the town (1930–44), who later settled in the United States.

The Jewish population numbered 1,152 in 1881; 1,632 in 1891; 2,255 in 1910; 2,483 in 1920; and 1,885 in 1930. They were mainly occupied as merchants, and included industrialists and contractors, as well as a number of craftsmen and members of the liberal professions. The anti-Jewish tradition in the town continued and its German inhabitants rapidly adopted the theory of racism.

Holocaust and Contemporary Periods

During World War II, after the German occupation (March 19, 1944), the Jews, numbering 1,861 in 1941, were confined in a ghetto. On July 5, around 3,000, including Jews from the surrounding area, were deported to the death camp at Auschwitz. Only a few returned. Even after the deportation, the inhabitants of Sopron did not help to alleviate the suffering of the thousands of Jews from the forced labor camps who passed through the town on their last halt before being sent to the death camps in Germany.

After World War II, only 274 Jews remained in Sopron (1946), and only 47 in 1970.

BIBLIOGRAPHY: M. Pollák, *A zsidók története Sopronban* (1896) = *Geschichte der Juden in Oedenburg* (1929); S. Scheiber, *Héber kódexmaradványok magyarországi kötéstáblákban* (1969); idem, *Magyaroszági zsidó feliratok* (1960); *Magyar Zsidó Lexikon* (1929), 798–801; MHJ, 6 (1961), index; 11 (1968), index; F. Grünvald, in: MIOK évkönyv (1970), 52–64.

[Baruch Yaron]

SORAUER, PAUL KARL MORITZ (1839–1916), German plant pathologist. Sorauer was born in Breslau, the son of a cabinet maker, and after studying horticulture went to Berlin for further training in plant physiology. In 1872 he was appointed director of an experimental station for plant physiology at Proskau. He was given the rank of professor in 1892, but was obliged to relinquish his post the following year because of a long-standing eye ailment. He moved to Berlin and lectured for a time at the Humboldt Academy. At the age of 63 he was made a *Privatdozent* at the University of Berlin.

Sorauer was the author of many publications on plant diseases, which bear the stamp of his unique amalgam of practical knowledge and physiological science. He was the founder of the *Zeitschrift fuer Pflanzenkrankheiten*, established in 1891. A major work was his *Handbuch der Pflanzenkrankheiten*, first published in 1874, which went through three editions. Sorauer was an influential teacher, and trained a large number of European plant pathologists.

BIBLIOGRAPHY: *Zeitschrift fuer Pflanzenkrankheiten*, 26 (1916), 6–17.

[Mordecai L. Gabriel]

SORCERY. First and foremost among the "abhorrent practices of the nations" mentioned in the Bible are the various forms of sorcery: "let no one be found among you who… is an augur, a soothsayer, a diviner, a sorcerer, one who casts spells, one who consults ghosts or familiar spirits, or one who inquires of the dead. For anyone who does such things is abhorrent to the Lord" (Deut. 18:9–14). *Divination and soothsaying (Lev. 19:26) and the turning to ghosts and spirits (Lev. 19:31 and 20:27) had been proscribed separately before, and witchcraft in general is outlawed with the lapidary "Thou shalt not suffer a witch to live" (Ex. 22:17). It was to be the characteristic of Judaism that nothing would be achieved by *magic, but everything by the will and spirit of God: hence the confrontations of Joseph and the magicians of Egypt (Gen. 41), of Moses and Aaron and Egyptian sorcerers (Ex. 7), of Daniel and the Babylonian astrologers (Dan. 2), etc., and hence also the classification of crimes of sorcery as tantamount to idolatrous crimes of human sacrifices (Deut. 18:10) and to idolatrous sacrifices in general (Ex. 22: 19) and its visitation, just as idolatry itself, with death by stoning (Lev. 20:27; see *Capital Punishment). In a God-fearing Israel, there is no room for augury and sorcery (Num. 23:23; Isa. 8:19), and the presence of astrologers (Isa. 47:13) and fortune-tellers is an indication of godlessness (Naḥ. 3:4; Ezek. 13:20–23; et al.). Nonetheless, magic practices remained widespread throughout, and not only with idolaters (see, e.g., I Sam. 28:4–20; II Kings 18:4; Chron. 33:6).

Talmudic law differentiated between capital and noncapital sorcery, retaining the death penalty only for those species for which the Bible expressly enjoined it, namely witchcraft (*kishuf*; Ex. 22:17) and conjuring a death (*ov* and *yidoni*; Lev. 20:27; Sanh. 7:4). *Kishuf* is nowhere exactly defined, but a distinction is drawn between actual witchcraft, committed by some overt and consummate act which resulted in mischief, and then punishable, and the mere pretense at witchcraft which, however unlawful and prohibited, is not punishable (Sanh. 7:11 and 67b). Witchcraft appears to have been widespread among women (cf. Avot 2:7), and Simeon b. Shetaḥ is reported to have ordered the execution of 80 witches in Ashkelon on a single day as an emergency measure (Sanh. 6:4 and Maimonides in his commentary thereto). It is witchcraft that makes for the devastation of the world (Sot. 9:13). All other species of sorcery are painstakingly defined in talmudic sources, apparently upon patterns of contemporary pagan usage. Thus, *ov* conjures the dead to speak through his armpit, while *yidoni* makes them speak through his mouth (Sanh. 7:7), both using bones of the dead in the process (Sanh. 65b). The aggravating circumstance, deserving of capital punishment, obviously is the use of human remains for purposes of sorcery, for he who simply communicates with the dead (in cemeteries or elsewhere) and serves as their mouthpiece (*doresh el ha-metim*) is punishable with flogging only (Yad, Avodat Kokhavim 11:13) – and this would, presumably, apply also to modern spiritualism (*Da'at Kohen*, no. 69). Other offenses punishable with flogging (both for committing and soliciting them) are *niḥush*, defined as superstitions based on certain happenings or circumstances (Sanh. 65b; Yad, Avodat Kokhavim 11:4); *kesem*, being fortune-telling from sands, stones, and the like (Maim., loc. cit. 11:6); *onanut* (done by the *me'onen*), being astrological forecasts of fortunes (R. Akiva in Sanh. 65b; Maim. loc. cit. 11:8); and *ḥever*, the incantation of magic and unintelligible formulae for purposes of healing or of casting spells (Maim. loc. cit. 11:10). It is presumably because these practices were so widespread that it was postulated that judges must have a thorough knowledge of magic and astrology (Sanh. 17a; Maim. Yad, Sanhedrin 2:1; and see *bet din*).

While there is no information about the measure of law enforcement in this field in talmudic and pre-talmudic times, it seems certain that this branch of the law fell into disuse in the Middle Ages. Superstitions of all kinds not only flourished and were tolerated, but found their way even into the positive law (see YD 179, passim, for at least eight instances). What became known as "practical Kabbalah" is, legally speaking, sorcery at its worst. The penal provisions relating to sorcery are a living illustration of the unenforceability of criminal law (whether divine or human) which is out of tune with the practices and concepts of the people. In modern Israeli law, witchcraft and related practices are instances of unlawful false pretenses for obtaining money or credit (Penal Law Amendment (Deceit, Blackmail, and Extortion), Law, 5723 – 1963).

See also *Divination; *Magic.

BIBLIOGRAPHY: A. *Lods, La croyance à la vie future et le culte des morts dans l'antiquité Israélite* (Thesis, Paris, 1906); L. Blau, *Das altjuedische Zauberwesen* (1914²); I.S. Zuri, *Mishpat ha-Talmud*, 6 (1921), 91; M. Gaster, *Studies and Texts in Folklore, Magic, Medieval Romance, Hebrew Apocrypha and Samaritan Archaeology*, 3 vols. (1925–28); A. Berliner, *Aus dem Leben der Juden Deutschlands im Mittelalter* (1937), 72–83; EM, 1 (1950), 135–37; 2 (1954), 710f.; 4 (1962), 348–65; ET, 1 (1951³), 113–16; 7 (1956), 245–48. **ADD. BIBLIOGRAPHY:** M. Elon, *Ha-Mishpat ha-Ivri* (1988), 1:424; 2:987; idem, *Jewish Law* (1994), 2:519–20; 3:1193; M. Elon and B. Lifshitz, *Mafte'aḥ ha-She'elot ve-ha-Teshuvot shel Ḥakhmei Sefarad u-Ẓefon Afrikah* (legal digest) (1986), 2:340; *Enẓiklopedyah Talmudit*, vol.1, s.v. "*Ov*," 244–49; vol.1, s.v. "*aḥizat einayim*," 460–63; vol. 5, s.v. "*doresh el ha-metim*," 245–48; vol.7, s.v. "*darkhei ha-Emori*," 706–12; vol.13, s.v. "*ḥover ḥaver*," 1–4; index.

[Haim Hermann Cohn]

SOREK, VALLEY OF (Heb. נַחַל שׂוֹרֵק, Naḥal Sorek; from the root שרק, "red grapes"), valley on the border of Philistia and the territory of the tribe of Dan. The only biblical reference to it places the meeting of Samson and Delilah there (Judg. 16:4). It is generally identified with Wadi al-Ṣarār, present-day Naḥal Sorek, near which are the ruins of Byzantine Chaparsorech (Eusebius, Onom. 160:2), now Khirbat Surayk. The Sorek Valley was one of the main approaches into the mountains of Judah and several important cities, such as Ekron (Khirbat Mukanna') and Beth-Shemesh, were situated along it. At present, the Jerusalem–Tel Aviv railway runs in the valley.

BIBLIOGRAPHY: Abel, Geog, 1 (1933), 405; 2 (1938), 96.

[Michael Avi-Yonah]

SORGHUM, the summer plant *Sorghum cernicum*, called in Arabic *durra* or *doḥ'n*. The Arabs of Israel sow it extensively, both for fodder and for flour, from which they make *pittah* ("flat bread"). It is thought to have been introduced into Ereẓ Israel only during the time of the Second Temple. According to Pliny (*Natural History* 18:55), a plant resembling *Millium* ("*millet"), which has large kernels, was brought to Rome from India during his time, and the reference seems to be to sorghum. It is possible that the plant reached Babylon at an earlier date, for it would appear to be identical with the *doḥan* from which Ezekiel made the mixed bread he ate for a period of 390 days (Ezek. 4:9). Some think that *Panicum* ("millet") is meant here, but millet is the *peragim* of the Mishnah. In rabbinic literature *doḥan* is mentioned with *rice and *peragim* as a summer crop (Shev. 2:7, et al.) from which bread was sometimes made, but since these are not included in the *five species of grain they are not treated as bread with respect to the laws of **ḥallah*, blessings, and leaven on Passover (Ḥal. 1:4; Ber. 37a). Bread made of sorghum was regarded as less tasty than that made from rice (Er. 81a). Today the red-seeded sorghum brought from California is cultivated by Jews in Israel. Some species of sorghum grow wild there.

BIBLIOGRAPHY: Loew, Flora, 1 (1926), 738–46; H.N. and A.L. Moldenke, *Plants of the Bible* (1952), index; J. Feliks, *Olam ha-Ẓome'aḥ ha-Mikra'i* (1968²), 154–5.

[Jehuda Feliks]

SORIA, city in Old Castile, N. central *Spain. The Jewish community of Soria was a major cultural and religious center in Castile. Nothing is known about the beginnings of the Jewish settlement in Soria. During the 12th century the Jews there benefited from a number of rights which were mentioned in several articles of the town *fuero* ("charter"). This also included regulations concerning jurisdiction over, and protection of, the merchants who came to trade in Soria. At first, the Jewish quarter was situated in a fortress, where about 50 families lived during the middle of the 13th century and throughout the 14th. (At that time there were 700 families in the town.) In the 13th century the community was very well organized. Jews continued to live there until the expulsion. During the second half of the 13th century, Soria was renowned for its kabbalists. According to tradition, *Jacob ha-Kohen was born there. Toward the close of the 13th and early 14th century, Shem Tov b. Abraham *Ibn Gaon lived in Soria; there was also a school of

Jewish illuminators who were members of this family and illuminated the famous Kennicott II and Sassoon 82 bibles, both in the Bodleian Library in Oxford. It was in Soria that Moses Narboni completed his commentary on the *Guide of the Perplexed*. Joseph *Albo, originally from Daroca in Aragon, lived there for many years and died there.

The 39,895 maravedis levy imposed on the Soria community in 1290 is an indication of its economic strength. According to an estimate of F. Cantera, there were over 1,000 Jews living in the town at the close of the 13th century. Their occupations included trade, the cultivation of vineyards, and crafts. During the civil war (c. 1366–69) between the brothers Pedro the Cruel and Henry of Trastamara, one of the tax farmers of Soria, Samuel ibn Shoshan, joined Pedro's camp and was compelled to flee from the kingdom after Henry's victory.

Although devastated by the persecutions of 1391 (see *Spain), the community appears to have recovered gradually, and in 1397 they were granted certain rights in respect of their quarter in the fortress by Henry III. A leader in the rehabilitation of the community was Don Abraham *Benveniste, who organized a convention of the delegates of the communities of Castile in Valladolid in 1432. In the 15th century, Soria was among the most important communities in Castile. Around 300 Jewish families lived in the city, constituting around 20% of the population. They were merchants, moneylenders, and artisans. Several of the inhabitants of Soria were important tax farmers. In 1465, Henry IV exempted the Jews of Soria from some taxes in appreciation of their services to the crown. Since the tax imposition in 1474 was 5,000 maravedis, it would appear that the community no longer ranked among the largest and wealthiest. In 1490, however, it paid 80,915 maravedis. The anti-Jewish policy adopted by the crown from the 1470s was felt in Soria by the restriction of the Jews to a special quarter and by the actions and attitude of the municipal council vis-à-vis the local Jews. In 1485, a levy of 308,000 maravedis was imposed on ten Jews of Soria to cover the expenses of the war against Granada. During the same year Ferdinand and Isabella authorized the Jews to maintain workshops and shops in various quarters of the town on the condition that they did not work on the Christian festivals and did not eat or sleep in these quarters. At the time of the expulsion of the Jews from Castile (1492) some Jews of Soria left for the kingdom of Navarre and most of them for Portugal. The crown ordered that debts still owed to Don Isaac *Abrabanel and other Jews in Soria be collected for them.

From the very beginning, and until the expulsion, the Jews of Soria lived in the fortress. The fortress has disappeared and on its grounds there is a park.

BIBLIOGRAPHY: Baer, Spain, index; Baer, Urkunden, index; J. Weill, in: REJ, 74 (1922), 98–103; F. Cantera Burgos, in: *Sefarad*, 16 (1956), 125–9; Suárez Fernández, Documentos, index. **ADD. BIBLIOGRAPHY:** F. Cantera Burgos, in: *Revista de dialetogía y tradiciones populares*, 32 (1976), 87–102; idem, in: *Homenaje a Fray Justo Pérez de Urbel*, OSB, vol. 1 (1976–7), 445–82; D. Gonzalo Maeso, in: *Celtiberia*, 56 (1978), 153–68; E. Cantera Montenegro, in: *Anuario de estudios medievales*, 13 (1983), 583–99; M. Diago Hernando, in: *Sefarad*, 51 (1991), 259–97; J. Edwards, in: *Past & Present*, 120 (1988/o, 3–25; idem, in: *Pe'amim*, 48 (1991), 42–53 (Heb.)).

[Haim Beinart / Yom Tov Assis (2nd ed.)]

SORKIN, AARON (1961–), U.S. writer-producer. Born in Manhattan and raised in Scarsdale, New York, Sorkin began acting in the eighth grade and in high school he joined the school drama club. He studied theater at Syracuse University, graduating with a bachelor's degree in 1983. While trying to break into acting in New York, Sorkin began writing plays. His first, *Removing Doubt*, was unsuccessful, but *Hidden in This Picture* (1988) was staged at the West Bank Cafe Downstairs Theater Bar in New York. His next play, *A Few Good Men* (1992), was inspired by his sister, who had gone to the U.S. Marine base at Guantanamo Bay in Cuba to arbitrate a murder case. The play appeared on Broadway, and Sorkin was hired to write the screenplay for the motion picture starring Jack Nicholson and Tom Cruise. In 1993, he helped write the screenplay for *Malice*, and was invited by Stephen *Spielberg to help polish the script for *Schindler's List*. He took two years to write the screenplay for *The American President* (1995), which earned him a Golden Globe nomination. During this time Sorkin admitted to a cocaine problem, for which he sought treatment at the Hazelden Institute in Minnesota. Sorkin took inspiration from ESPN's *Sportscenter* for his first foray into television, ABC's *Sports Night* (1998–2000), which was favorably reviewed by critics but never found its audience. In 1999, he debuted his Emmy Award-winning show about the White House, NBC's *The West Wing*, which featured Sorkin's trademark rapid-fire dialogue. Tensions over budgets and production delays grew between Sorkin and Warner Brothers, which produced *West Wing*, leading to Sorkin's departure from the show after the season finale in 2003.

[Adam Wills (2nd ed.)]

SORKIN, MICHAEL (1948–), U.S. urbanist and architectural critic. Sorkin received his training at Harvard and MIT. For seven years he wrote for the *Village Voice*, a New York newspaper, and later became director of the Graduate Urban Design Program at the City College of New York. From 1993 to 2000 he was professor of urbanism and director of the Institute of Urbanism at the Academy of Fine Arts in Vienna. He taught at numerous schools, including Cooper Union, Columbia, Yale (holding both the Davenport and Bishop Chairs), Harvard, Cornell (Gensler Chair), Nebraska (Hyde Chair), Illinois, Pennsylvania, Texas, and Minnesota. Sorkin is the principal of the Michael Sorkin Studio in New York City. This small firm specializes in urban designs both practical and theoretical and does not wait for clients to come with their requests but takes the lead in tackling projects that are sometimes visionary, such as planning for a Palestinian capital in East Jerusalem. This project was an outgrowth of a conference he organized "to bring Palestinian, Israeli, and other architects and urbanists together to discus the future of the city in physical terms, via the medium of a design proposal. The assumption was that there were certain issues – the environment, neighborhood development, transportation, sprawl – that could be discussed outside the discourse of politics." Quickly, after the World Trade disaster in New York City, Sorkin, together with Sharon Zukin and 17 of New York's best urbanists studied the attack and its aftermath. They dealt with the history of neighborhood conflicts in New York and predicted many of the struggles between various interests that have rendered the rebuilding of the site problematic. In 2002 he edited *Variations on a Theme Park, The Next Jerusalem: Sharing the Divided City*, and *After The World Trade Center: Rethinking New York City*.

[Betty R. Rubenstein (2nd ed.)]

SOROKI (Rom. Soroca), city in N. Moldova, in the region of Bessarabia. The first mention of Jewish settlement in Soroki is in 1657. However, information concerning an organized community there only dates from the beginning of the 18th century. In 1817 there were 157 Jewish families. In the early 19th century, R. David Solomon Eibenschutz served as rabbi and encouraged the study of Torah in the city. The community grew in the 19th century with the Jewish immigration to Bessarabia, and at the end of the century, also with the frequent expulsions of Jews from the neighboring border area and from the villages. In 1864, 4,135 Jews were registered in Soroki and in 1897 there were 8,783 Jews (57.2% of the total population). In 1863 a government Jewish school was opened. At the end of the century among the teachers in Soroki were the writers Noah Rosenblum, and Kadish-Isaac Abramowich-Ginzburg, who laid the foundations of a new system of Jewish education and culture among the Jews of the town on a secular and national basis. Many of the Jews of Soroki engaged in agriculture, primarily in the growing of tobacco, grapes, and other fruit. In 1900 the Jewish Colonization *Association established a training farm near Soroki. From the 1880s the economic situation of the Jews deteriorated and a wave of immigration to the United States began. In 1930 there were 5,462 Jews (36.3% of the entire population). Before World War II several educational and social institutions existed in Soroki, including Hebrew elementary and secondary schools, a hospital (founded in 1885), and an old-age home. The community was destroyed with the entry of the Germans and Romanians into Bessarabia in July 1941. The Jewish life of Soroki is described by Shelomo Hillels in the novel, *Har ha-Keramim* (1930). In the late 1960s the Jewish population was estimated at about 1,000. The only synagogue was closed down by the authorities in 1961. In April 1966 the matzah bakery was closed down by the authorities, the bakers were arrested, and the baking of matzah was discontinued. Use of the cemetery and ritual poultry slaughtering were still permitted in 1970.

BIBLIOGRAPHY: S. Hillels, in: *Pirkei Bessarabyah*, 1 (1952), 94–120; E. Feldman, *Toledot ha-Yehudim be-Bessarabyah* (1963), includes summary in English.

[Eliyahu Feldman]

SOROS, GEORGE (1931–), financier and philanthropist. Born in Hungary, Soros spent a year as a child in hiding during the Holocaust. In 1947 after the communist takeover, he moved with his family to Britain. He studied at the London School of Economics, subsequently moving to New York. There he worked as a Wall Street trader but in 1969 established the Quantum Fund, that eventually would invest billions of dollars in various parts of the world. The Soros Foundation, described as the world's largest philanthropy, distributes more than $300 million annually in over 60 countries.

On September 16, 1992 (subsequently referred to as "Black Wednesday"), Soros, as a currency speculator, "broke the Bank of England" by placing a hedge bet that the UK would devalue the pound sterling. This audacious act earned him one billion dollars in a single day.

Much of Soros' activities are directed to Eastern Europe, where in 1992 he founded and funded the Central European University, with branches in Budapest and Prague. In 1993 and 1994 he provided one-third of Russia's scientific research budget. In 1993 he set up the Quantum Emerging Growth Fund to invest in Third World countries. In 1993 he also created the Open Society Institute (OSI), of which he was chairman. A private operating and grant-making foundation, the OSI works to support the Soros foundations worldwide and strives to shape public policy to promote democratic governance, human rights, and economic, legal, and social reform.

Soros is the author of *Alchemy of Finance* (1987); *Opening the Soviet System* (1990); *Underwriting Democracy* (1991); *Soros on Soros: Staying Ahead of the Curve* (1995); *The Crisis of Global Capitalism* (1998); *Open Society* (2000); *George Soros on Globalization* (2002); and *The Bubble of American Supremacy: The Cost of Bush's War in Iraq* (2004).

BIBLIOGRAPHY: *Time* (July 10, 1995), 32–38; R. Slater, *Soros: The Life, Times, and Trading Secrets of the World's Greatest Investor* (1996); M. Kaufman *Soros: The Life and Times of a Messianic Billionaire* (2003).

[Ruth Beloff (2nd ed.)]

SOROTZKIN, ZALMAN BEN BEN-ZION (1881–1966), Lithuanian rabbi and communal leader. Sorotzkin was born in Zakhrina, Russia, where his father was rabbi. After studying under his father, he proceeded to the yeshivot of *Slobodka and *Volozhin. His renown as a brilliant student came to the attention of Eliezer *Gordon, the head of the yeshivah of Telz, whose daughter he married. After his marriage he studied for several years in Volozhin. On returning to Telz he undertook the administration of the yeshivah, displaying great organizational ability. The yeshivah building was destroyed by a conflagration, and he succeeded in rebuilding it within a short time. In 1911, after the death of his father-in-law, he was invited to serve as rabbi in the small town of Voronovo (Werenow), near Vilna, where he founded a yeshivah for young students. After some years he was appointed rabbi of Zittel in Lithuania, where he also developed extensive communal activities, particularly in founding an educational network. After the outbreak of World War I, he was forced to wander with his family into Russia and arrived in Minsk. There he devoted himself to public activity and vigorously opposed the false charges and discriminatory decrees against the Jews, which were constantly being issued by the czarist government. After the war he returned to Zittel, but shortly afterward was appointed rabbi of Lutsk, capital of Volhynia (then in Poland), which had a Jewish community of 30,000, and he remained there until the outbreak of World War II. During his rabbinate in Lutsk he became renowned as one of the outstanding Polish rabbis and was one of the leaders of Agudat Israel and of Orthodox Jewry generally. When Lutsk was occupied by the Russians after the outbreak of World War II, they threatened to imprison him if he continued his activities. He was compelled to flee with his family to Vilna, where Ḥayyim Ozer Grodzinski, rabbi of Vilna, charged him with reorganizing the many yeshivot, most of whose students had escaped to Lithuania. He remained in Vilna until the entry of the Russian army, when he left, and after many vicissitudes finally arrived in Ereẓ Israel.

There he threw himself into communal work. He established the Va'ad ha-Yeshivot charged with the care of the yeshivot in Israel on the model of the Vilna Va'ad ha-Yeshivot (of which he had been one of the founders), and he headed it until his death. He was elected vice chairman of the Mo'eẓet Gedolei ha-Torah of Agudat Israel, and after the death of Isser Zalman *Meltzer served as its chairman, a position he held until his death. He also headed the independent educational network (Ḥinnukh Aẓma'i) set up by Agudat Israel. Sorotzkin was an outstanding preacher, and many of his homilies appear in his work *Ha-De'ah ve-ha-Dibbur* (1937), on the Pentateuch. Toward the close of his life he published *Oznayim la-Torah* (1951–60), a commentary on the Pentateuch, and *Moznayim la-Mishpat* (1955), a collection of responsa in two parts. Some of his responsa are still in manuscript. His commentary *Ha-Shir ve-ha-Shevaḥ* on the Passover *Haggadah* (1971) was published posthumously.

BIBLIOGRAPHY: *Rabbi Zalman Sorotzkin...* (Heb., 1967).

[Itzhak Goldshlag]

SOSIS, ISRAEL (1878–after 1936), Russian historian. Sosis, born in Balta, southern Russia, joined the *Bund, and took part in the Russian Revolution of 1905. He contributed to the party's publications and was imprisoned several times for revolutionary activities. During World War I Sosis was active in *YEKOPO. He published articles on the history of social classes in Russian Jewry in *Yevreyskaya Starina* (1914–16). With the left wing of the Bund, he joined the Communist Party after the 1917 Revolution. From 1924 he lectured on Jewish history at the Institute for White-Russian Culture in Minsk, and published articles on the history of Lithuanian and White-Russian Jews in Russian-Jewish periodicals. Sosis' main work, "The History of Jewish Social Trends in Russia in the 19th Century" (1919), though Marxist in outlook and method, did not slavishly follow the official Soviet historiographical line, and showed some objectivity and national Jewish feeling. The "deviations" led to his transfer, in 1930, to the Institute for Jewish-Proletarian Culture in Kiev. When the institute was closed in 1936, Sosis was arrested and his fate remains unknown.

BIBLIOGRAPHY: Rejzen, Leksikon, 2 (1927), 602–4; B. Shohetman, in: KS, 8 (1931/32), 343–6; Greenbaum, *Jewish Scholarship in Soviet Russia* (1959); LNYL, 6 (1965), 303–5.

[Yehuda Slutsky]

°**SOSIUS, GAIUS**, Roman general, governor of Syria, and conqueror of Jerusalem in 37 B.C.E. After the Parthian conquest of Judea and the consequent appointment of *Antigonus the Hasmonean to the throne in Jerusalem (40 B.C.E.), Herod made his way to Rome and was recognized by Antony and the senate as king of Judea. He returned to Palestine at the head of a considerable force but was eventually forced to turn to Antony for assistance in subduing the country. After his conquest of Samosata, Antony appointed Sosius governor of Syria, with orders to support Herod. Sosius immediately sent two legions and himself followed with the remainder of his army. He joined forces with Herod. The two laid siege to Jerusalem in the spring of 37 (although certain discrepancies exist regarding the precise date of the siege and fall of Jerusalem; cf. Jos., Ant., 14:475 n. a, p. 694; A. Schalit, *Hordos ha-Melekh* (1964), 509–11). The ensuing battle appears to have been fierce, and Josephus stresses that Jerusalem fell – as in the conquest by Pompey – "on the day of the fast." Scholars have interpreted this to mean either the Day of Atonement or the Sabbath (according to Dio Cassius, 49:22), but it is also possible that the reference is to a special fast declared at the time of the siege to arouse divine intercession (cf. Schalit, op. cit., 510). On the fall of the city Antigonus came before Sosius and begged for mercy, only to be jeered at for his tragic change of fortune by the Roman general who, after calling the Jewish leader "Antigone," had him put in chains and eventually put to death. Sosius furthermore explicitly instructed his soldiers to plunder the city, and after perpetrating a terrible massacre they were finally restrained only by Herod, who promised to distribute to them rewards from his own funds.

BIBLIOGRAPHY: Jos., Wars, 1:327, 345–57; 5:398, 408–9; idem, Ant., 14:447, 468–9, 481–8; Schuerer, Gesch, 1 (1901^3), 357–9.

[Isaiah Gafni]

SOSKICE, SIR FRANK, BARON STOW HILL (1902–1979), British politician. Soskice was born in Geneva, the son of DAVID VLADIMIROVICH SOSKICE (1866–1941), a Jewish lawyer and journalist from the Ukraine who was an important liberal activist against the czarist regime and was briefly an official of the Kerensky government. He lived in England for most of the period after 1898. Frank Soskice's mother was a gentile, the niece of the Pre-Raphaelite painter Ford Maddox Brown. Soskice was educated at St. Paul's School and Oxford. He became a barrister in 1926, the same year he became a naturalized British subject. In 1945 he was appointed a KC and was also elected to Parliament as a Labour member, serving until 1966, although briefly losing his seat in 1950 and 1955–56. Upon entering Parliament he was immediately appointed solicitor-general, with a knighthood, and was regarded as an able holder of this post. When Labour returned to power in 1965, Harold *Wilson appointed him to the senior post of home secretary. Soskice, in poor health, was not successful in this position and was moved to the office of Lord Privy Seal, but still with a seat in the cabinet, in 1965. He retired in 1966 and was given a life peerage.

BIBLIOGRAPHY: ODNB online.

[William D. Rubinstein (2nd ed.)]

SOSKIN, SELIG EUGEN (1873–1959), pioneer agronomist and politician. Soskin was born in Churubash in the Crimea, Russia, but settled in Palestine (1896) where he served as plantation expert for Ḥovevei Zion. Together with Aaron *Aaronsohn, he explored the country and conducted agricultural experiments. He was a member of the Zionist Inquiry Commission on the * El-Arish project (1903) and he served as agricultural adviser in German South West Africa (1906–15). He was director of the settlement department in the central office of the Jewish National Fund, then in The Hague (1918–23). Soskin advocated intensive farming on small irrigated plots, as opposed to the "mixed" farming on larger units practiced by the Zionist Organization. In 1934 he founded Nahariyyah, where he established an experimental intensive farm. Soskin advocated growing plants in water (hydroponics) or in saturated soil, and in 1945 he founded an experimental station in hydroponics in Ramat Gan.

In 1926 Soskin joined the Revisionist movement and became its spokesman on agricultural settlement. From 1927 he acted as political representative of the Union of Zionist Revisionists to the League of Nations in Geneva. After the split in the Revisionist movement (1933), he joined the Jewish State party. He held controversial views on the importance of land exchange to enable the Jewish state to build up its holding of national land under the proposals of the Peel Commission. He published many studies on his work in Africa and Palestine including *Small Holding and Irrigation* (1920), *Intensive Cultivation and Close Settlement* (1926), *The Escape from the Impasse* (1927), and *Land settlement in Palestine* (1929).

[Joseph Ben-Shlomo / Michael Denman (2nd ed.)]

SOSNOWIEC (Rus. **Sosnovets**), city in Katowice province, S. Poland. There were 2,600 Jews living in Sosnowiec around 1890 (29.8% of the total population), who earned their livelihood mainly in the clothing, food, building, and machine industries, and bookkeeping. A Jewish cemetery was opened in 1896, a *linat ẓedek* ("paupers' hostel") was founded in 1907, a *talmud torah* in 1908, and a *mikveh* in 1913. The city's growth in the 20th century, especially after the Russian retreat in World War I, was accompanied by an increase in the Jewish population which reached 13,646 (16% of the total) in 1921. Approximately one-third engaged in light and medium industry, crafts and trade, including clothing and shoe manufacture, coal mining, and manufacture of coke. About 2,000 Jews were employed as laborers or clerks in industry or business; a considerable number engaged in the professions. In the early 20th century a Jewish labor movement was organized through the *Bund and *Po'alei Zion. The Jewish workers of Sosnowiec took part in revolutionary activities in 1905–06, and 30 were imprisoned and exiled to the Russian interior. Through the efficient workers' organization the Jewish mine owners were able to compete with large industrial concerns. The mine owned by H. Priwer produced 25,000 tons of coal in 1920, and that of B. Meyer 32,000 in 1922.

The Jewish population continued to grow in the interwar period, from 20,805 in 1931 to 28,000 in 1939 (22% of the total). New arrivals came mainly from Kielce province attracted to Sosnowiec by more favorable work opportunities. The communal organization expanded; in addition to a Jewish hospital, secondary schools for girls and boys were established, and associations of artisans, merchants, and industrialists were formed.

[Arthur Cygielman]

Holocaust Period

The German army entered Sosnowiec on Sept. 4, 1939. On the same day it organized an attack on the Jewish population, and 13 Jews were killed. On September 9 the Great Synagogue on Dekert Street was set on fire. In 1942, Jews were deported to *Auschwitz death camp in three groups: 1,500 on May 10–12; 2,000 in June; and over 8,000 on August 12–18. After the last deportation the Germans established a ghetto in the suburb of Srodula. On March 10, 1943, the ghetto was sealed off. On August 16, 1943, all the inhabitants, with the exception of about 1,000 people, were deported to Auschwitz where they perished. The last 1,000 Jews in Sosnowiec were murdered in December 1943 and January 1944. Previously there had been considerable underground activity among the Jews, mostly organized by the youth organizations Ha-No'ar ha-Ẓiyyoni, Gordonia, and Ha-Shomer ha-Ẓa'ir, whose main leader was Ẓevi Dunski.

After the war about 700 Jews resettled in Sosnowiec, but almost all of them emigrated shortly afterward.

[Stefan Krakowski]

BIBLIOGRAPHY: W.A.P. Lodz, Piotrkowski Rząd Gubernski, *Kanc. Prez.*, 500, 623; *Wydział administratywny*, 2446, 8118; *Wydział* Pr. 211d; *Zarzad żand.* 119/1906 (= CAHJP, ḤM 6421, 6432, 3489, 6329, 6920, 7193f.); B. Wasiutyński, *Ludność żydowska w Polsce w wiekach XIX i XX* (1930), 29; S. Bronsztejn, *Ludność żydowska w Polsce w okresie międzywojennym* (1963), 278; N.E. Szternfinkiel, *Zagłada Żydów Sosnowca* (1946); J. Jaras, in: BŻIH, 35 (1960), 91–97; M.S. Gashur (Grukner), *Le-Korot ha-Ir Sosnowiec ve-ha-Sevivah* (Heb. and Yid., 1969).

SOTAH (Heb. סוֹטָה; "Errant Wife"), the fifth tractate in the current edition of the Mishnah order of *Nashim*, with Tosefta and *Gemara* in the Babylonian and Jerusalem Talmuds. Dealing mainly with the laws concerning a woman suspected of adultery (Num. 5:11–31), the tractate also discusses incidentally extraneous matters like the rite of the *eglah *arufah* and the rules of exemption from military service (Deut. 20:1–9;

24:5). In some manuscripts it is put sixth in the sequence of tractates in *Nashim*.

The contents of the nine chapters of this tractate are as follows: Chapter 1 discusses the form in which the husband has to manifest his jealousy and how the Sanhedrin urges the woman to admit her guilt rather than undergo the ordeal; the first stages of the ordeal are also discussed. The last passages of this chapter are of aggadic nature, debating the principle of measure for measure in divine justice. Chapters 2–3 deal with the "meal-offering of jealousy" and the writing of the "scroll of curses." Incidentally, the question of whether daughters should be taught Torah is considered, and information is given on the differences between men and women in respect of various *halakhot*. The "bitter water" is discussed in chapter 4, mainly those cases exempted from this ordeal. Chapter 5 is dedicated to the *halakhot* which were taught *bo va-yom* ("on the very same day"), i.e., when Rabban Gamaliel was deposed and R. Eleazar b. Azariah was made *nasi*. Only the first Mishnah in this chapter deals with *sotah*.

Chapter 6 is concerned with the question of the "minimum evidence" necessary to decide the woman's guilt without her having to undergo the ordeal. Since it is laid down that the declarations with regard to the *sotah* may be made in any language, chapter 7 lists other biblical passages to which this applies and then enumerates passages which must be read in Hebrew. In connection with this it is related how King Agrippa, who was partly of Edomite descent, wept when he read the sentence "thou mayest not put a foreigner over thee," but the people encouraged him, exclaiming: "Thou art our brother!" Chapter 8 speaks first of the priest anointed for war, since his address to the army (Deut. 20:3–4) has to be in Hebrew, and then deals in detail with the whole passage, including the grounds for exemption from military service. Of particular interest is the concluding paragraph, stating that the exemption applied only to optional wars of conquest like those of King David but not to obligatory wars, like those of Joshua's conquest of the Holy Land, or to defensive wars at any time. The second half of chapter 9, which deals with *eglah arufah*, is of a general aggadic nature, which is introduced by the observation that with the great increase in murders (the reference is to a time of civil disorder preceding the destruction of the Temple) the rite of breaking the heifer's neck was discontinued, and with the increase of immorality the ordeal of bitter water was abolished. The chapter goes on to describe how at various times, especially at the time of the destruction of the Temple, other laws and customs were abolished or fell into disuse and how scholarship and piety declined after the death of the great sages, such as Ben Azzai and Ben Zoma. Many other profound aggadic passages are also found in the Babylonian and Jerusalem *Gemara* and in the Tosefta. The Babylonian Talmud (22b) lists seven types of hypocrites and in connection with this cites Alexander Yannai's well-known observation that neither sincere Pharisees nor sincere Sadducees should be feared, only the hypocrites. In 49b there is a description of the struggle between Aristobulus and Hyrcanus; an interesting distinction is made in this context between the Greek language and Greek wisdom.

The Mishnah of *Sotah* was taught at the end of the Temple era. The main early portions of the Mishnah belonging to this period are 1:2 and 4–6; 2:2; 3:1–4; and 7:1–9:15. The account of Agrippa and the reading of "the chapter of the king" described in 7:8 almost certainly refers to Agrippa *II and the incident which took place in 62 C.E., since the Tosefta says of this Mishnah: "On that same day R. *Tarfon saw a lame man standing and sounding the *shofar*." Mishnah 9:9 is by Johanan b. Zakkai, who testifies about something which occurred in his time, as is also clear from a comparison with Tosefta 14:1. Basing himself on this, Epstein believes that the main part of chapters 8 and 9 is from the Mishnah of Johanan b. Zakkai. The order of procedure in dealing with the *sotah* differs in several details from those given in the Bible, and this is already discussed in the sources themselves (Sot. 3a; TJ 1:5, 17a). Since the Mishnah was taught in Temple times, it obviously gives the procedure customary during this period. Other differences are reflected in various books of Philo, and some of them are alluded to in early *beraitot* and fragments of them (see Epstein in bibliography). The Babylonian Talmud to *Sotah* has a distinctive style: it contains passages in Hebrew (39b); it does not use the phrase "there is a lacuna" (*ḥassurei meḥassera*); and it usually gives the final decision (*mistavra keman de-amar*). This tractate was translated into English and published by the Soncino Press (1936).

BIBLIOGRAPHY: Epstein, Tanna'im, 394–413; Epstein, Amora'im, 84–93; Ḥ. Albeck, *Shishah Sidrei Mishnah, Seder Nashim* (1954), 227–31.

[Arnost Zvi Ehrman]

SOUL.

In the Bible

The personality was considered as a whole in the biblical period. Thus the soul was not sharply distinguished from the body. In biblical Hebrew the words *neshamah* and *ru'aḥ* both mean "breath" and *nefesh* refers to the person or even the body (cf. Num. 6:6). For ways of expressing mind see *Heart.

Rabbinic Doctrine

For the rabbinic view of the soul see *Body and Soul.

In Medieval Jewish Philosophy

The soul in medieval Jewish philosophy is often depicted as the king and ruler of the body, its principle of life, organization, and perception. It is likened, in similes which go back to antiquity, to the rider of a steed, the captain of a ship, and the governor of a state. Yet, paradoxically, the soul is also often considered as a stranger on earth, an alien yearning for its supernal home. Philosophers view this latter characteristic, indicative of the soul's ability to survive the death of the body, as a function of its intellectual as well as moral perfection. Intellectual perfection was understood to comprise a true understanding of the nature of all being, both physical and metaphysical, including the nature of the soul. Descriptions of the soul followed Platonic and Aristotelian views, with later Greek thought supplying the models by which man's soul was related to heavenly substances. *Saadiah Gaon had a partial familiarity, derived from Pseudo-Plutarch's *De placitis philosophorum*, with these and many other systems of thought, none of which consistently appealed to his primarily theological perspective. He delared that each soul is created from nothing by God – the sole eternal being – at the moment of the completion of the formation of the body, and that body and soul form a unit bound together in this life and, eventually, in the hereafter. The soul requires the good acts of the body to perfect its peculiarly immaterial, celestial-like substance, even as the body needs the faculties of sensation and reason which the soul provides. Saadiah believed, with Plato (see *Republic* 4:435b; *Timaeus* 69c), that the soul has intellectual, spiritual, and passionate expressions; however, following Aristotle, he maintained that these were faculties of a single soul, located in the heart (*Book of Beliefs and Opinions*, Treatise 6).

Man's soul was believed by most of the philosophers to have affinities with the souls of plants and animals, on the one hand, and with either the World Soul of the Neoplatonists or, in the Aristotelian system, the souls of the celestial bodies – the soul of a celestial body being a kind of rational principle separate from and responsible for the movement, if not life, of the sphere – on the other. In the Neoplatonic cosmology accepted by Isaac *Israeli, Solomon ibn *Gabirol, Joseph ibn *Ẓaddik, and Pseudo-*Baḥya, the World Soul emanates from the Universal Intellect and therefore has intellectual powers, which it transmits, together with the subsequently emanated physical qualities of Nature, to the individual soul. Man's soul, a substance or form independent of the body, thus contains "natural" or vegetative, animal, and rational aspects, and as such reflects the World Soul. These faculties are usually treated as separate, distinct souls, located respectively in the liver, heart, and brain.

From Israeli on, the vegetative soul is generally held responsible for nourishment, growth, and generation; the animal soul, for a type of instinctive intelligence known as estimation, as well as for locomotion and sensory perception; and the rational soul, for discursive knowledge, both practical and theoretical. Israeli, following the Arab philosopher al-*Kindī, also introduced into Jewish philosophy the Proclean stages of purification and illumination of the soul, substituting an ultimate stage of "spiritualization," i.e., a union with the First Form, the Supernal Wisdom or Intellect, for Proclus' divine union. The ascent of the soul, the upward way, is facilitated by withdrawal from the soul's passions and appetites, an ascetic direction particularly emphasized by Baḥya ibn Paquda (*Duties of the Heart*, ch. 10). Paradise is, for Israeli, union with the supernal light of wisdom, and hell the failure to attain this stage, the soul being weighed down by its corporeal aspects (see A. Altmann and S.M. Stern, *Isaac Israeli* (1958), 165–70, 185–94).

Aristotle's *De anima*, seen through the eyes of such Greek commentators as *Alexander of Aphrodisias and *Themistius, and such Arab scholars as al-*Fārābī and *Avicenna, serves as the main inspiration for Abraham *Ibn Daud, Moses *Maimonides, and most subsequent philosophers. They view the soul as the form of the body, a single substance comprised (in addition to the earlier tripartite division) of nutritive, sensitive, imaginative, appetitive, and rational faculties. Descriptions of the functional anatomy of these faculties mostly follow Galen as well as Aristotle, with the emotions of the appetitive faculty particularly responsible for ethical behavior, and the imagination and intellect considered as the organs of prophecy. The Aristotelians, like the Neoplatonists, teach that the good is the mean between psychic extremes (see Maimonides, *Shemonah Perakim*, 1 and 4). The ideal of most philosophers is an extremely intellectual as well as virtuous person, whose intellect has reached a stage of completely immaterial, actual perfection. In this state the individual "acquired" intellect, which is comprised of universal intelligibles, may conjoin with the Active Intellect. It is this conjunction with the Active Intellect that constitutes immortality (Maimonides, *Guide*, 1:70, 72; 3:27; 54).

This impersonal and incorporeal approach to immortality was heightened by the view of Averroes as propounded, for example, by *Moses of Narbonne, in which the individual intellect is understood to be essentially related to the Active Intellect from its very beginning as a potential intellect. Against such denials of personal immortality, *Levi b. *Gershom contended that the "acquired" intellect became an independent eternal substance (*Milḥamot Adonai*, 1:12); while Ḥasdai *Crescas, in a general critique of his predecessors' views, claimed the same status for the soul itself, using the term "soul" as more than a euphemism for the intellect. Crescas believed that the perfection of the soul was achieved more through love than through knowledge of God (*Or Adonai*, 2:6, 1). His attack upon Aristotelianism calls to mind that of *Judah Halevi, who mentions in passing the Aristotelian view of the soul (*Kuzari*, 5:12, 14, 21). Judah Halevi's own contribution to the subject was to posit a divine yet "natural" endowment *(ha-inyan ha-Elohi)* which, apparently related to the Jewish soul, made the Jew a superior being (*Kuzari*, 1:95; 2:14). A somewhat similar view was advanced by Judah Halevi's 12th-century contemporary, *Abraham bar Ḥiyya, who believed that the rational soul in all its purity was to be found among the elect of Israel alone. Such national feelings have little place in Crescas' more rigorously argued philosophy, and even less in the 16th-century *Dialoghi di Amore* of Judah *Abrabanel. Judah Abrabanel believed that love was a universal expression of both the animated structure of the universe, and of its yearning for unity with God. Through intellection and conjunction with the Active Intellect – which, following Alexander of Aphrodisias, Abrabanel identified with God – man could enter into a direct relationship with the Divine (*Dialoghi*, 3). This mixture of love and intellect is pronounced in the synthesis of Aristotelian and Cartesian ideas effected by *Spinoza, in which the influence of medieval Jewish philosophy is marked. Spinoza advocated the impersonal approach to immortality, consistent with his denial of independent substantial existents of any kind. He believed that all things are ensouled, or endowed with a psychic dimension of intelligibility that is ultimately part of God. The emotions, he felt, could be controlled through an analysis of their causes, allowing for an intellectual love of God which follows the mind's knowledge of its inherent oneness with God/Nature. The man who reaches this degree of knowledge is blessed with the thought that his mind, as part of God, is eternal (*Ethics*, 5).

See also *Imagination; *Intellect.

BIBLIOGRAPHY: Husik, Philosophy, index; Guttmann, Philosophies, index; H. Davidson, in: A. Altmann (ed.), *Jewish Medieval and Renaissance Studies* (1967), 75–94; H. Malter, in: JQR, 2 (1911–12), 453–79; S. Horovitz, *Die Psychologie bei den juedischen Religionsphilosophen des Mittelalters von Saadia bis Maimuni*, 4 vols. (1898–1912).

[Alfred L. Ivry]

SOUL, IMMORTALITY OF.

In the Bible

Unlike the gods of Mesopotamia and Canaan, e.g., Apsu, Tiamat, Baal, and Mot, who, while they could not die a natural death, could incur a violent one, the God of Israel is the living God (Hos. 2:1; Ps. 18:47). His lordship extends from heaven to Sheol (Ps. 139:8; Job 26:6); He puts to death and brings to life (I Sam. 2:6; I Kings 17:17–22; II Kings 4:18–37); and He can preserve His faithful from Sheol (Ps. 16:10).

Among the peoples of the Ancient Near East, the Egyptians were very optimistic about the afterlife. They believed that the dead lived a life almost identical with that in this world (cf. *The Book of the Dead*, 110). The Babylonians, on the other hand, were pessimistic about life after death. The average human being had no means of escaping his fate: one day he would die and descend to the netherworld, which was governed by a god and goddess of death. There were, however, special cases in which man could attain immortality. Theoretically, man could become immortal, or at least rejuvenated, by means of a mysterious food or drink (cf. *Adapa*, frag. B; Pritchard, Texts, 101–2; *Gilgamesh*, Tablet 11, lines 265–90, Pritchard, Texts, 96). Immortality could be acquired by a special favor of the gods in their assembly (see *Gilgamesh*, Tablet 11, lines 190–8). A god could also resurrect the dead: Ishtar threatens the gatekeeper of the netherworld, saying: "I will raise up the dead … so that the dead will outnumber the living" (*Descent of Ishtar*, line 20; Pritchard, Texts, 107).

In the Bible two persons are said to have left this world in a special way: Enoch "was taken by God" (Gen. 5:24) and Elijah "was taken up to heaven in a whirlwind" (II Kings 2; cf. Ps. 49:16). The exact implication of these traditions is not clear.

The crucial passage of Proverbs 12:28 has been translated differently through the centuries. Saadiah Gaon already understood it as immortality, as did F. Delitzsch many centuries later. M. Dahood (in: *Biblica*, 41 (1960), 176–81) related the Hebrew אַל מָוֶת *ʿal mawet*) in this verse to the Ugaritic *blmt*, "not dying."

It is also possible that the Masoretic Text of Proverbs 14:3 contains the hope of a better life than that in Sheol (cf. Ps. 16:9–11; 73:24; A.W. van der Weiden, in: VT, 20 (1970), 339–50). However in Daniel 12:2 the resurrection to eternal life for some is unequivocally predicted. Only in the post-biblical period did a clear and firm belief in the immortality of the soul take hold (e.g., Wisd. 3) and become one of the cornerstones of the Jewish and Christian faiths. See *Death; *Resurrection.

In the Talmud

The rabbis of the Talmud believed in the continued existence of the soul after death, but differed with regard to the nature of this existence. On the one hand, the view was widespread that the righteous person immediately after his death enters the Garden of Eden, where he is vouchsafed to be in a special section of the garden (Shab. 152b; BM 83b), while the wicked go to *Gehinnom (Ḥag. 15a; Ber. 28b; Er. 19a; whether in corporeal form or not is not mentioned). On the other hand, the view is expressed that the soul of man – at death – is severed from any connection with the body and its pleasures, ascends upward, and is gathered into "the treasury" beneath "the throne of glory" (Shab. 152b), where it had its pre-existential origin in the upper heaven called "*Aravot*"; "where are right and judgment and righteousness, the treasures of life, the treasures of peace, the treasures of blessings, the souls of the righteous, the spirits and souls yet to be born, and the dew wherewith the Holy One will eventually revive the dead" (Ḥag. 12b); while the souls of the wicked "continue to be imprisoned" (Shab. 152b), are "cast about on the earth" (Eccles. R. 3:21; ARN[1] 12:50), and are cast from the slings of destructive angels (Shab. 152b).

Alongside the belief in the heavenly "treasury" to which the soul returns after death, the ancient belief was widespread in the talmudic era (and later) that the soul of man after death continues with the body in the netherworld, either for a brief or for an extended period. In one passage (TJ, MK 3:5, 82b; TJ, Yev. 16:1, 15c) R. Levi says that the soul hovers over the body for three days, hoping that it will return to it, and departing only when the hope is belied (a belief found also in Zoroastrianism). Elsewhere it states that "a man's soul mourns for him all the seven days of mourning" (Shab. 152a), and also that "for full 12 months the body continues to exist and the soul ascends and descends" and only after this period, when the body is decomposed, "the soul ascends nevermore to descend" (Shab. 152b). Similarly, there is neither uniformity nor consistency concerning the extent of the consciousness retained by the dead. In one passage it is stated that the dead hear everything spoken in their presence until the grave is sealed (*ibid.*), while elsewhere it is stated that the dead are aware (apparently eternally) of their own pain ("worms are as painful to the dead as a needle in the flesh of the living," Shab. 13b) and shame. For this reason it was forbidden to walk in a cemetery wearing *tefillin or reading from a *Sefer Torah*, since it seemed like a mockery of the dead (Ber. 18a). It is related that R. Ḥiyya and R. Jonathan were walking in a cemetery, and Ḥiyya told Jonathan to gather up his *ẓiẓit so that the dead should not say: "Tomorrow they are coming to join us and now they insult us" (*ibid.*).

The dead even have contact with the living and direct them in worldly affairs: the father of Samuel appeared to him, on returning from "the heavenly yeshivah," and revealed to him where the money of orphans, which had been deposited with him, was to be found (Ber. 18b); and similarly a woman innkeeper informed Zeiri after her death where the money he deposited with her was lying (*ibid.*). The dead also hold conversations with the living: Some men digging in the field of R. Naḥman heard the sound of the deep breathing of a corpse, and when Naḥman came he conversed with him (Shab. 152b). Deceased women adorn themselves in their clothes and ornaments. The innkeeper who came into contact with Zeiri requested that her mother send her a comb and cosmetics through a woman about to die. Another complained to her neighbor that she was unable to rise and wander about the upper worlds because she was buried in a matting of reeds (Ber. 18b). The dead wander about and hear "from behind the curtain" what was decreed upon the living (*ibid.*). The sages spoke especially highly of the power of the righteous after their death. According to Simeon b. Lakish, the sole difference between the living righteous and the dead is the faculty of speech (TJ, Av. Zar. 3:1). Likewise they said that "if a statement is said in a person's name in this world, after his death his lips move in the grave" (Sanh. 90b). It is also related of Judah ha-Nasi that after his death he used to visit his house every eve of the Sabbath, and only ceased to do so out of respect for the scholars (Ket. 103a). All these views, however, did not prevent others from saying that "if one makes remarks about the dead, it is like making remarks about a stone" (Ber. 19a) and that at the most the dead know their own pain (Ber. 18b) but not what transpires in the world.

[Yehoshua M. Grintz]

In Medieval Jewish Philosophy

The doctrine of the immortality of the soul, as it appears in the writings of *Philo as well as in the works of some later Jewish philosophers, shows strong influences of Platonism (see Plato and *Platonism), which saw a complete separation between body and *soul.

PHILO. Philo's statements that the human soul is mortal are usually ambiguous, but he often refers to the various ranks which the souls achieve after death. According to Philo, Abraham achieved the rank of the angels, which are incorporeal, Isaac ranks higher, and Moses achieved a yet higher rank, since he is close to God.

SAADIAH. Saadiah Gaon held the opinion – apparently according to views of the Muslim *Kalām, which reflected a non-Platonic Greek philosophical tradition – that the soul is "a more pure, transparent and simple substance than are the spheres," i.e., that the soul is a fine body. At the time of death, the soul separates from the body of man, and "during the first period after its separation from the body, however, the soul exists for a while without a fixed abode until the body has decomposed; that is to say, until its parts have disintegrated. It consequently experiences during this period much misery, occasioned by the knowledge of the worms and the vermin and the like that pass through the body, just as a person would be pained by the knowledge that a house in which he used to live is in ruins and that thorns and thistles grow in it" (*Book of Beliefs and Opinions*, 6:7). Saadiah had no clear conception of the condition of the soul during the transition period from the time of death until the resurrection of the dead, which was characteristic of many medieval Jewish thinkers, and illustrates their difficulties in reconciling the notion of the immortality of the soul with a belief in resurrection. According to Saadiah, the soul is reunited with its body at the time of resurrection and this combined state continues thereafter.

ISAAC ISRAELI. Unlike Saadiah, his older contemporary, Isaac *Israeli, was deep within the Platonic tradition. According to him, the soul is an incorporeal substance. Man's soul does not die with the death of his body: "he becomes spiritual, and will be joined in union to the light which is created, without mediator, by the power of God, and will become one that exalts and praises the Creator for ever and in all eternity. This then will be his paradise and the goodness of his reward, and the bliss of his rest, his perfect rank and unsullied beauty" (*Book of Definitions*, see A. Altmann and S.M. Stern, *Isaac Israeli* (1958), 25–26). While the upper souls are above the heavens, the lower ones are beneath them and are tortured by fire, according to a belief which was also held in Greco-Roman paganism.

SOLOMON IBN GABIROL. A similar Platonic spirit pervades the writings of Solomon ibn *Gabirol in his book *Mekor Ḥayyim*. He does not express a clear opinion in this book with regard to the immortality of the soul, but he does mention the idea of Platonic recollection (see S. Pines, in: *Tarbiz*, 27 (1958), 231). One section of *Mekor Ḥayyim*, which is cited by Moses ibn *Ezra, attests more clearly than does the Latin translation to the central role played by Platonic recollection in the thought of Ibn Gabirol.

This idea, if accepted simply, presupposes a belief in the existence of the soul prior to its conjunction with the body, since it assumes that it is this conjunction which caused the soul to forget its previous knowledge, which it may again recollect. In contrast to this view, in his poem *Keter Malkhut* Ibn Gabirol expresses a traditional Jewish outlook when he states that the souls of the righteous rest beneath the throne of glory.

JOSEPH IBN ẒADDIK. Joseph ibn *Ẓaddik was influenced by both Ibn Gabirol and Israeli. According to him, the soul is incorporeal, existed before its conjunction with the body, and continues to exist after the passing of the body. If the soul attained the necessary level of knowledge, it returns after death to its place of origin, i.e., to the world of the intelligibles; but if it remained ignorant, it is pulled by the motion of the celestial sphere and tortured by fire. It is then likened to a traveler who cannot find the way back to his homeland.

ABRAHAM BAR HIYYA. Abraham bar Ḥiyya describes the intelligible soul by the term "form" (*Meditation of the Sad Soul* (1969), 46ff.) which continues to exist even after its separation from the body. Abraham b. Ḥiyya has a multiple account of what happens to the soul after death. If the man was wise and righteous, his soul ascends to the upper world "and attaches itself to the pure high form, enters into it and never separates from it." If he was wise and wicked, his soul arrives after death at the world of the spheres "and it revolves under the circles of the sun, whose heat appears to it as an image of a perpetually scorching fire, and it has neither the right nor the power to remove itself from the heavenly sphere in order to attach itself to the supernal light." If the man was ignorant and righteous, his soul returns "a second and third time" to bodies until it acquires wisdom and is able "to separate from the air of the lower world and to ascend above it; and its righteousness or wickedness at that particular time will determine the order of its ascent and its ultimate rank." If the man was ignorant and wicked, his soul too will die "a death of a beast and an animal."

JUDAH HALEVI. According to Judah *Halevi (*Kuzari*, 1:103), Judaism is "the religion which insures the immortality of the soul after the demise of the body." It is nonetheless clear that the character of the Jewish scholar in the work (who expresses Judah Halevi's thought) wants to broaden and crystallize this idea. Thus, his interlocutor, the king of the Khazars, is able to point out, with certain justification: "The anticipations of other religions are grosser and more sensuous than yours" (*ibid.*, 1:104).

It appears that Judah Halevi realized the difficulty with which his successors were to contend, namely, that Scripture does not express clearly the notion of the immortality of the soul. In answer, Judah Halevi was able to state that the nature of the Jewish prophets and godly men approaches, even in their lifetime, the condition of souls in their immortality (*ibid.*, 1:109).

ABRAHAM IBN DAUD. Abraham ibn *Daud is considered – with certain justification – as the first Spanish Jewish Aristotelian. It appears, however, that because of *Avicenna's influence on him, he was not an orthodox Aristotelian. Like Avicenna, Ibn Daud maintains that the individual human soul continues to exist after the death of the body (*Emunah Ramah*, ed. by S. Weil (1852, ch. 7, 34–39). Contrary to Avicenna, however, he speaks at great length about the condition of the souls after death.

MAIMONIDES. The great majority of the Spanish Aristotelians, both Jewish and Muslim, did not follow Avicenna and did not believe in the immortality of the individual soul. Nothing remains of man after death, they held, except his intellect, which bears no trace of individuality and the exact nature of which was a source of controversy among them (see *Intellect). Judah Halevi had already established – possibly on the basis of the views of his Muslim contemporary, *Avempace, which were known to him – that the philosophers do not affirm the immortality of the individual soul. It may be thought that even *Maimonides, to the extent that he was a philosopher, believed in the immortality of the intellect rather than of the soul. It is possible to find traces, and even clear statements, of this idea in his *Guide of the Perplexed*.

In his *Mishneh Torah*, which essentially deals not with philosophic ideas but rather with *halakhah* and principles of faith, Maimonides states that in the **olam ha-ba* there are no bodies, but only the souls of the righteous, without body, serving as the angels of God. Since there are no bodies in the world to come, there are in it neither eating, nor drinking, nor any of the things which human bodies need in this world. Neither do the souls perform any of the actions of the body, such as sitting and standing, sleeping and dying, weeping and laughing. It is obvious that there is no body since there is no eating and drinking (Yad, Teshuvah, 8:2). It becomes manifest, however, that these things refer not to the soul, as it was conceived by the Aristotelians, but to the intellect, which can be deduced from Maimonides' statements that the soul referred to in this connection is not the soul which is needed for the body, but is rather the form of the soul which is the knowledge it derives from God according to its ability. This is the form which is called "soul" in this reference (*ibid.*, 8:3). This rejection of individual immortality, which is in accordance with the teachings of Averroes, caused a furor among Jews as well as among the 13th-century Christian scholastics and gave rise to bitter dispute. Echoes of the Christian notions, which reject the opinion of Averroes, can be seen in the *Tagmulei ha-Nefesh* of Hillel of *Verona, who argued for individual immortality.

ISAAC ALBALAG AND HASDAI CRESCAS. Isaac *Albalag also affirms the immortality of the individual soul, but it is doubtful that this was his true opinion (see G. Vajda, *Isaac Albalag* (1960), 239–49). On the other hand, the position of Ḥasdai *Crescas on this matter is entirely clear. He directs harsh criticism against the views of the Aristotelians regarding the intellect and states that, since man is a spiritual being, his soul remains immortal after its separation from the body (*Or Adonai*, 2:6). According to his view, which rejected Aristotelian intellectualism and saw love and not knowledge as the highest good, the love between man and God is what determines the immortality of the soul. The souls of the righteous after death enjoy the splendor of the *Shekhinah, i.e., they attach themselves to God to an extent which was denied them while they were in the body, and their union with God is constantly being strengthened. When the soul is unable to reach this union (because of its sins), it suffers great sorrow, which is so complete in some souls that it leads to their total destruction (*ibid.*, 3:3).

JOSEPH ALBO. Joseph *Albo devoted a large section of his *Sefer ha-Ikkarim* (fourth treatise) to the question of the immortality of the soul. Unlike the Aristotelians, he maintains that the soul is a spiritual being, which has an independent existence, is not intellectual in nature, but is capable of attaining knowledge (4:29).

[Shlomo Pines]

In Modern Philosophy

MOSES MENDELSSOHN. Outstanding among 18th-century works on the immortality of the soul is Moses *Mendelssohn's *Phaedon oder ueber die Unsterblichkeit der Seele* ("Phaedon or On the Immortality of the Soul," 1767). In its methodology, this work follows Plato's *Phaedo*, but its content is based on modern philosophy. In it, Mendelssohn attempts to answer the question: How would Socrates prove to himself and his friends the idea of the soul's immortality if he lived in modern times?

Mendelssohn rejects the theory that the soul, after its separation from the body, enters a state similar to sleep or fainting. All rational beings, he states, are destined to increase their perfection. The whole world was created for the sake of the existence of rational beings who progressively increase their perfection, and herein lies their bliss. It is not possible that these beings, who struggle for their perfection in this world, should be frustrated in these efforts in the world to come. This would be a contradiction of the order of the universe. It was not in vain that the Creator instilled in man a desire for eternal bliss. It is both possible and necessary that this desire should be fulfilled, despite all the setbacks and obstacles. In the same way that certain disorders in the physical world, such as storms, earthquakes, diseases, etc. are negated within the infinite totality of the cosmos, so in the realm of morality all the temporary disorders lead toward the eternal perfection. Even suffering reinforces a person's powers, without which he cannot attain moral bliss. It is impossible to know God's design. In order to understand the life of even one man, it would be necessary to view all life in its totality, and then we would not complain but would rather revere the creator's mercy and wisdom, which are revealed in the life of each intelligible being, when viewed in its totality.

MORITZ LAZARUS. In the 19th century, with a general change in the intellectual climate, the question of the immortality of the soul lessened in importance. Several Jewish thinkers attempted to show that Judaism is not concerned with the immortality of the individual after death.

Moritz *Lazarus deals with this question in his *Ethik des Judentums* (1898, para. 137ff.). In his opinion, the attitude of Judaism was summarized in two sayings of R. Jacob in *Pirkei Avot* (4:16, 17). One states: "This world is like a vestibule before the world to come: prepare thyself in the vestibule that thou mayest enter into the banqueting hall." Lazarus sees this saying's "weak side" in that it speaks only of the individual, while in the realm of ethics it is the society which plays the major role. This saying is based only on the philosophy of the "I," while true knowledge of man's fate can only be attained by a philosophy of "we." Thus Lazarus rejects completely the notion of individual immortality or, at least, he is not concerned with this notion. This attitude emerges even more clearly in Lazarus' treatment of R. Jacob's second saying, which is inverted by Lazarus to read as follows: "Better is one hour of bliss in the world to come than the whole life of this world; [but] better is one hour of repentance and good works in this world than the whole life of the world to come." Lazarus does not hesitate to change the saying in order to make it conform to his own emphasis on this world rather than the next.

HERMANN COHEN. Hermann *Cohen also holds that Judaism views the soul's immortality as applying to the people as a whole rather than to the individual (*Religion der Vernunft* (1918), ch. 15). The people never dies, he states, but rather has an eternal continuing history. The individual soul is perpetuated by means of this history and is real only within the context of the continuity of the people. This concept of immortality is taught by the Bible, while the place of individual immortality is in the realm of mythology. Individual immortality only means that the individual is constantly required to strive for his moral perfection. True immortality of the soul is its spirit, i.e., the possibility and the obligation to effect the principles of truth and morality in this world. The soul is spirit – beyond this there is no need to think about man's fate after death.

AḤAD HA-AM. *Aḥad Ha-Am regards belief in immortality of the soul solely as a sign of weakness. Many people, he says, lack the courage to face death and, in old age, fall back on a belief in immortality to give the "I" back its "future," a future in which they will compensate for what was lacking in the past. Thus Aḥad Ha-Am ridicules a belief in the world to come and in the immortality of the soul (see his article *Avar ve-Atid*). In his article *Ḥeshbon ha-Nefesh*, Aḥad Ha-Am characterizes the belief in an afterlife as a "sickness of the spirit." He attributes the manifestation of this belief to the desire to escape from life during times of depression. This belief, he states, does nothing to encourage positive activity in life, since it teaches that man's fate on earth depends on his continued fate after death.

RABBI KOOK. In dealing with the question of death and immortality, A.I. *Kook holds that death is a defect in creation. The Jewish people is called upon to remove this taint from the world and to save nature from death. Death is wholly imaginary, but it is difficult for man to free himself from this image. Original sin, which led man to a distorted world view, brought about death and fear of death, but repentance will overcome both. R. Kook saw indications of the retreat of death in modern times in the increase of life expectancy. The modern Hebrew poet Aaron Zeitlin gave a striking expression to this idea of the delusionary nature of death by coining the word LHA-MA-M, formed from the initial letters of the Hebrew sentence, *Lo hayah mavet me-olam* ("death has never existed").

[Samuel Hugo Bergman]

In Kabbalah

In contrast with speculations in medieval Jewish philosophy, in Kabbalah immortality of the soul is not a matter requiring justification and defense in the face of doubts and arguments. To the kabbalists, immortality of the soul was an incontrovertible fact based on the primary doctrine of the soul common to all, that the soul and all its parts are a spiritual entity (or spiritual entities), whose origin (or origins) is in the supernal worlds and from the divine emanation, and that it evolved downward and entered the body only in order to fulfill a specific task or purpose. Its special spiritual essence guarantees its immortality after death. The forms visualized for this immortality differ widely and are connected with the respective views of the kabbalists regarding reward and punishment. The reward is included in the many-staged ascent to the primal dwelling place of the soul. This ascent begins with the entrance of the soul into the earthly Paradise. From there it ascends to the heavenly Paradise, and from there into even higher spiritual worlds, until it reaches its original anchorage both in the world of creation and in the world of emanation – two of the four worlds acknowledged by most kabbalists after the *Zohar. The absorption of the soul or of its upper parts, such as the spirit (and in the Lurianic Kabbalah, also the life, *ḥayyah*, and the entity, *yeḥidah*) into the world of the *Sefirot* apparently does not cancel its personal individuality – in any case, not in the period preceding the universal resurrection of the dead. Afterward a more basic absorption is possible, to the extent of the abolition of the separate existence of the soul and its complete adherence to its divine source.

The punishment awaiting sinners, which is also connected with the immortality of the soul, takes on two forms: hell and reincarnation. In these two, the quality of justice which befits the soul exists according to the particular circumstances of its deeds. There is no general agreement in the kabbalistic systems on the details of reward and punishment, and there are many variations in the details, but these do not affect the principle of immortality of the soul, its designation for eternal life, and the rectification of its defects by different means. Only the question of the punishment of *karet*, which the Torah designates for several sins, presented the kabbalists with the problem that in special cases the existence of the soul may be completely abolished, and it would have no chance of immortality. For the most part the kabbalists gave the punishment of *karet* the interpretation which sees in it a special type of the punishment of reincarnation. The soul was indeed cut off from its supernal roots and lost its predetermined group. Despite this, its existence was not completely abolished; it only passed to other fields of existence of lower value than its source of origin. In the Lurianic Kabbalah the problem of immortality of the soul became complex, because, according to this doctrine, there are five different sources for the five principal elements of which the soul is composed – *nefesh*, *ru'aḥ*, *neshamah*, *ḥayyah*, *yeḥidah*. Life, spirit, and soul are the three lower souls; the two higher elements can be attained only by elects. In addition, the soul also has sparks (*niẓoẓot*) of other souls close to it, in accord with its essence. There is no one vision of what will happen to the different parts of the soul after their separation from the body, because each one undergoes individual refinements and purifications and ascends to a different place in the supernal worlds. Only with the resurrection of the dead do all the parts return and become unified, and from that time they remain connected to the total spiritual unity.

[Gershom Scholem]

BIBLIOGRAPHY: IN THE BIBLE: F. Delitzsch, *Das Salomonische Spruchbuch* (1873), 207ff.; J. Derenbourg, *Oeuvres complètes de R. Saadia*, 6 (1894), 70; J. Touzard, in: RB, 7 (1898), 207ff.; L.F. Burney, *Israel's Hope of Immortality* (1909); A. Heidel, *The Gilgamesh Epic and Old Testament Parallels* (1949²), 137ff.; W.F. Albright, in: VTS, 4 (1957), 257. IN MEDIEVAL JEWISH PHILOSOPHY: Guttmann, Philosophies, index; Husik, Philosophy, index, s.v. *Immortality*; H.A. Wolfson, *Philo*, 1 (1947), 260ff.; H. Davidson, in: *Jewish Medieval and Renaissance Studies* (1967), 75–94; S. Horovitz, *Die Psychologie bei den juedischen Religionsphilosophen des Mittelalters von Saadia bis Maimuni*, 4 vols. (1898–1912); G. Vajda, in: *Archives d'historie doctrinale et littéraire du Moyen Age*, 15 (1946).

SOULTZ (Ger. **Sulz**), town in the department of Haut-Rhin, E. France (not to be confused with the place of the same name in lower Alsace, where the settlement of the Jews was of a later date). The presence of Jews in Soultz is confirmed from 1308. In 1338 some fell victim to the *Armleder excesses; in the *Black Death persecutions of 1349 the community was destroyed. From 1371 onward a number of Jews returned to Soultz. During the 17th century Jews were engaged as moneylenders, physicians, wine merchants, and livestock merchants. After reunion with France the number of Jews increased, rising from 102 in 1784 to 231 in 1808. After 1918 the community declined and by the outbreak of World War II had ceased to exist. E. *Carmoly, the chief rabbi of Belgium (1802–1875), was a native of Soultz.

BIBLIOGRAPHY: M. Ginsburger, *Histoire de la Communauté israélite de Soultz* (1939); idem, in: *Revue d'Alsace*, 70 (1923), 405–16, 508–14; I. Bloch, in: REJ, 14 (1887), 116f.; Germ Jud, 2 (1968), 811f.

[Bernhard Blumenkranz]

SOURASKY, Mexican family of industrialists, bankers, philanthropists, community leaders, and active Zionists, originally from Bialystok, Poland, from where the family emigrated in 1909. In 1917 the brothers LEÓN (1889–1966), JAIME (1894–1962), and ELÍAS (1899–1986) settled in Mexico. Each of them acted independently in many areas of general and Jewish community life in Mexico: assistance to the needy, institutional organization, Zionist activity, promotion of excellence in scientific research and education, promotion of Jewish and Hebrew education, defense against antisemitic attacks. They were also very active in the political and material support of the Zionist idea, and the establishment of the national Jewish homeland in Ereẓ Israel, the establishment of the State of Israel during the War of Independence and its strengthening afterwards. Many general and Jewish institutions in Mexico and Israel were supported by them and subsequently named after them. They also instituted many prestigious prizes in Israel and Mexico. In 1968 Elías Sourasky received from the

Mexican government the "Águila Azteca," the highest decoration Mexico awards foreigners.

[Efraim Zadoff (2nd ed.)]

SOUS, largest province in *Morocco, including the southern slopes of the Grand Atlas, the valley of the Oued Sous, the Anti-Atlas, the Noun (to the Atlantic Ocean), and the southern Darʿa. Early legends mention the existence of two pre-Islamic Jewish kingdoms in the Sous: one in *Ofran (Ifrane) and the other in the Darʿa. The Jews always lived dispersed in the Sous; in some of its regions they found secure, if remote, shelter. The larger urban centers did not attract great numbers of Jews, not even the ancient capital, Taroudant; however, the small community of this town, although relegated to quarters outside the city walls, for many centuries imposed its own *takkanot* and *minhagim* upon the numerous Jewish centers and communities of the Sous.

There were many wars and political upheavals over the centuries, and towns such as Tiyout and Tidsi, seats of prosperous Jewish communities, passed out of existence; in many localities ancient cemeteries remain as the only sign of Jewish life. The Marabout movement of the 15th and 16th centuries severely damaged the Jewish community. Forced conversions eliminated all aspects of Jewish life from territories where the Jews had formerly been numerous, with traces remaining only in names such as Aït-Mzal and Aït-Baha, and in the land of the Ammeln, where some of the present-day tribes are still called by names such as Aït-Aouday ("Tribe of the Jews"). In the Aït-Jerrar, Ida-ou-Milk, Chtouka, Aït-Ba Amran, and other places there are parts of *Berber tribes which may well have once been Judaized, or even Jews. In about 1510 the survivors of the persecutions joined together in Tahala, where they remained until 1957 when they left en masse for Israel, as well as in other centers of the Anti-Atlas where they met with different fates. By the 17th century the Jews of the important center of Illigh had become an influential community; 100 years later the Jewish populations suffered during a series of rebellions and upheavals, and their synagogues, like those of *Agadir, were destroyed around 1740. About 1792 Bou-Hallais gave the Jews of Ofran the choice of conversion or death. In the 19th century the occupation of the Sous by the central government offered the opportunity to pillage and massacre the Jewish population. In 1840 the Jewish village of Tatelt was destroyed, and 40 years later Tillin suffered the same fate; in 1882 the Jewish quarter of Goulimine was pillaged, and in 1900 the soldiers of the Makhzen razed the quarter of Ouijjane. In some instances the Jews resisted fiercely and succeeded in saving many of their settlements and in some cases they even went on the offensive.

In the high mountains, in often inaccessible localities, far from the troubled life of the plains, the Jews of regions such as Ounein, Tifnout, and Azilal – considered by modern ethnologists and ethnographers as the remnants of very ancient migrations – were probably Berber tribes that had become Jewish in pre-Islamic times. In these forbidding regions the Jews lived as autochthonous populations, detached from all outside influences. As in the case of many of their brethren in the Marrakesh Atlas, their common language was Berber, not Arabic. At the southwestern end of the Sous, the region of Noun, whose ancient center of Tagaost was destroyed and replaced by Goulimine, was the foremost supplier of ostrich feathers; from ancient times it was also one of the market outlets for numerous Sahara caravans, which until the end of the 19th century carried the continent's basic raw materials, such as slaves, ivory, ebony, pelts, and gold, from the heart of Africa. Some of the richest Jews controlled a vast part of this trade. In the 15th and 16th centuries their trade with the neighboring Canary Islands was of great importance. Moreover, from 1505 to 1540 a number of Marranos who had found shelter in those islands came to the Sous region and returned to Judaism. After 1880 almost every Jew became a retailer or a small artisan. Only after 1936 did the economic situation change somewhat for the better.

The surplus Jewish population of the Sous was regularly sent to the urban centers of Morocco, especially to Marrakesh and *Mogador where they contributed to the overcrowding of the local mellahs. It is estimated that up to the 18th century the Jewish communities of the Sous formed 20% of the total Jewish population of Morocco. Droughts and epidemics of plague and cholera in 1799, 1805, 1818, and 1878 decimated the local population, and in 1884 Charles de Foucault estimated that there were about 7,000 persons. Adding some Jewish communities not included in his studies to his figure, the number of about 8,500 is arrived at. In 1951 A. de la Porte des Vaux – whose calculations are the most detailed and reliable among available statistics – estimated that there were 6,420. After 1955 the Jewish population literally evacuated the Sous en masse, the great majority immigrating to Israel.

BIBLIOGRAPHY: V. Monteil, in: *Hesperis*, 33 (1946), 385–405; 35 (1948), 151–62; J. Chaumeil, *ibid.*, 40 (1953), 227–40; A. de la Porte des Vaux, in: *Bulletin Economique et Social du Maroc* (1952), 448–59, 625–32; P. Flamand, *Diaspora en Terre d'Islam* (1960); D. Corcos, in: *Sefunot*, 10 (1966), 58–60, 72–75, 77–83. **ADD. BIBLIOGRAPHY:** D.J. Schroeter, *Merchants of Essaouria: Urban Society and Imperialism in Southwestern Morocco, 1844–1886* (1988).

[David Corcos]

SOUTH AFRICA, republic comprising nine provinces – Western Cape, Eastern Cape, Northern Cape, North West, Gauteng, Limpopo, Mpumalanga, Free State, and KwaZulu-Natal. Prior to 1994, when multiracial democracy was introduced, there were four provinces, viz. Cape, Natal, Orange Free State, and Transvaal.

The first European settlement in southern Africa was founded in *Cape Town, today capital of the Western Cape, in 1652 by the Dutch. It became a British colony in 1806; Natal was a British colony from 1843; the Free State and the Transvaal, founded by Dutch (Afrikaner or Boer) emigrants from the Cape, were republics until annexed by Britain in 1902 after the Boer War. In 1910 the colonies were merged

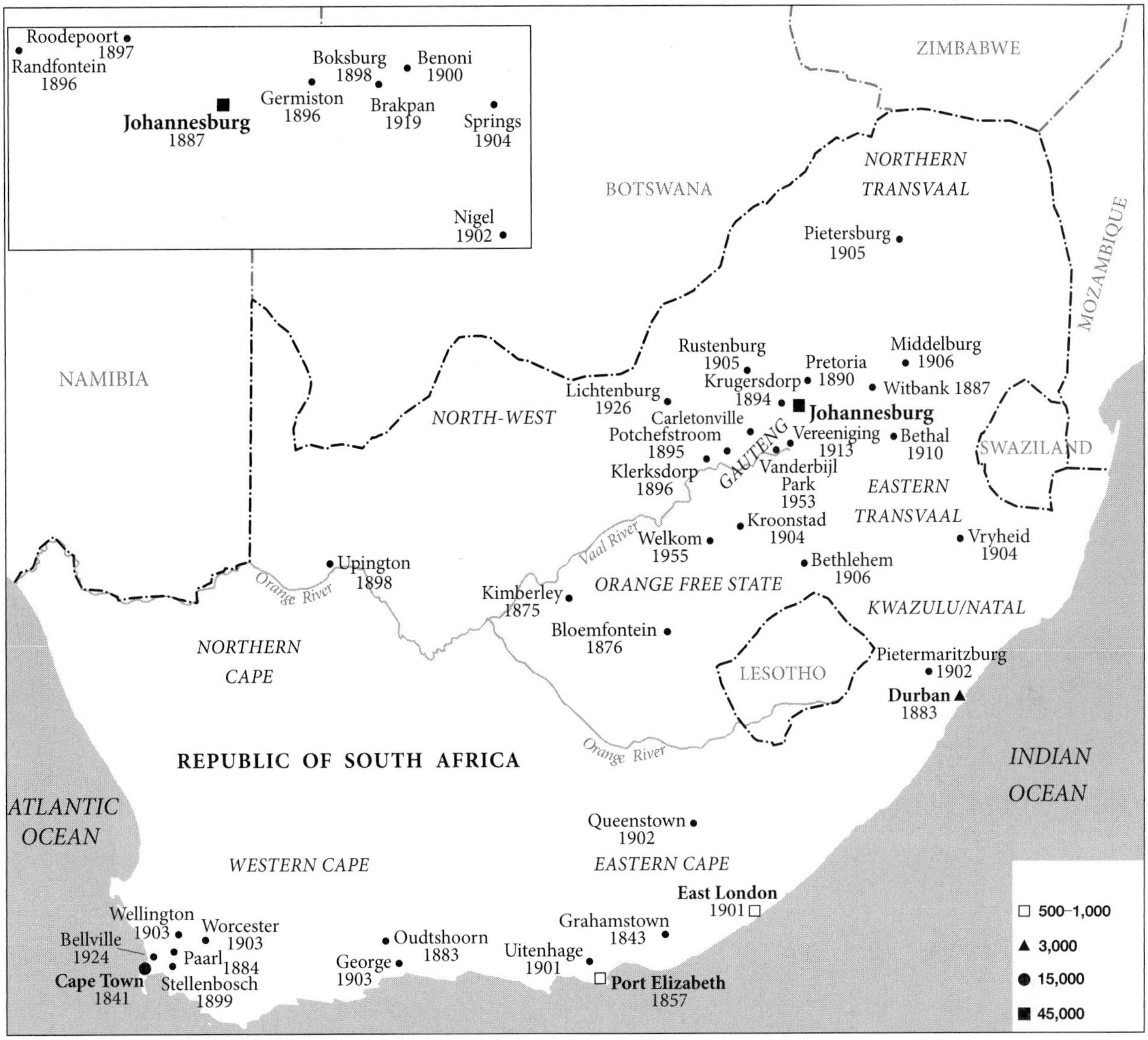

Historical Jewish communities of South Africa with dates of establishment. Main 21st century communities in bold face with population figures based on 2004 census. (Discrepancies in dates in the records may be partially due to varied definitions of what constitutes the establishment of a congregation.)

as the Union of South Africa under the British flag. In 1961 the Union became a republic outside the British Commonwealth. Until 1994, South Africa was ruled by the white minority. Black majority rule was ushered in by the country's first democratic, non-racial elections, held on April 27 of that year.

Settlement

Jewish associations with South Africa date back a long way. Jewish scientists and cartographers in Portugal contributed to the success of Vasco da Gama's voyage which led to the discovery of the Cape of Good Hope in 1497. Jewish merchants in Holland were associated with the Dutch East India Company, which established the white settlement at the Cape in 1652, and Jewish names appear in the early records of the settlement. These were probably converts to Christianity who had come to Holland from Central and Eastern Europe. The company required all its servants and settlers to be professing Protestants. Identifiably Jewish settlement began only after the introduction of complete religious tolerance under the Batavian Republic in 1804 and its confirmation by the British who took over the Cape in 1806. Enterprising Jewish individuals then began to arrive, mainly from Germany and the British Isles. Some made their way from Cape Town (where the first congregation was founded in 1841) deep into the interior and played pioneering roles in the development of what was then a backward country with a thinly scattered white population. Prominent individuals were Nathaniel *Isaacs, Benjamin *Norden, Jonas *Bergtheil, the *Mosenthal brothers, the *Solomon family, and Joel *Rabinowitz.

By the end of the 1860s, when the Jews in the Cape numbered a few hundred families in a white population of something over two hundred thousand, there were two main centers of Jewish settlement in the colony, the older in Cape Town and environs, and the other in the eastern region, mainly in Grahamstown, *Port Elizabeth and district, and Graaff Reinet. Individuals – itinerant traders and storekeepers, with a few professional men – had also penetrated into the more remote inland areas. Though small in number, they made a significant contribution to the economic advancement of the country and to its social and civic life.

The opening up of the diamond fields in Griqualand West (*Kimberley) in 1869 and of the gold mines of the Witwatersrand in 1886, marked a turning point in the economic and political history of South Africa. From being predominantly pastoral, it developed rapidly into a modern industrial society. The new economic opportunities attracted Jews among the emigrants from Britain, Germany, and elsewhere on the continent of Europe, as well as from America and Australia, and other countries. They were the forerunners of the mainstream of Jewish immigrants who began to arrive from Eastern Europe in the 1880s, a tributary of the vast outflow escaping czarist oppression and economic deprivation and seeking freedom and new opportunity, of whom the majority found their way to North America. Many of these immigrants settled in Cape Town and nearby towns, but later spread to more distant rural areas, and also found their way to the goldfields in the Witwatersrand. Few villages in the Cape, the Orange Free State, and later in the Transvaal, were without their Jewish peddlers or storekeepers, who were usually joined in time by their families and kinsmen from overseas. They formed small communities, and in some cases (as in the ostrich feather center *Oudtshoorn) larger Jewish settlements. The mainstream of Jewish migration, however, flowed to *Johannesburg and other towns on the Witwatersrand, which soon after the Boer War (1899–1902) – during which there was an exodus of war "refugees" – became the nucleus of the largest concentration of Jews in South Africa. There was also a smaller movement into Natal, particularly to *Durban.

The steady extension of Jewish settlement to the new areas was reflected in the dates when the first congregations were established: Kimberley – 1875; Oudtshoorn – 1883; Durban – 1883; Johannesburg – 1887; *Pretoria – 1890; *Bloemfontein – 1876.

Immigration

Official statistics on immigration became available only after the Boer War (1899–1902), but it can be conjectured that the Jewish population in 1880 was about 4,000. Ten years later it had grown to about 10,000. Around 1900 it was in the vicinity of 25,000, and in the 1904 official census it had reached a total of some 38,000. These figures reflect clearly how the Jewish population was growing through the addition of newcomers from abroad. Between 1880 and 1910, some 40,000 Jewish immigrants entered the country. Thereafter, for various reasons, the numbers decreased, with the exception of the years 1924 to 1930. In all, in the half-century from 1910 to 1960, it is estimated that there were perhaps 30,000 Jewish immigrants.

Until about 1890, the majority of Jewish immigrants came from Britain, and in lesser numbers from Germany. Thereafter, the influx of "Russian" Jews (as the East European Jews were officially designated) increased and within a couple of decades the "greeners" outnumbered the older elements. They came predominantly (approximately 70%) from Lithuania and the other territories on the eastern shores of the Baltic (South African Jewry came to be described as "a colony of Lithuania") and also from Latvia, Poland, Belorussia, and further afield. In their escape from oppression and poverty in Eastern Europe the Jews who went to South Africa were encouraged by success stories of individuals, reports of the sympathetic attitude of the Boers (Afrikaners) to Jews as the "Chosen People," the helping hand stretched out by older settlers, and inflated stories of the fortunes made from the gold mines. Most of the East Europeans at first encountered great hardships and difficulties economically before achieving prosperity. South Africa's attitude to Jewish immigration was influenced by various factors, among them conservative official policies in regard to immigration generally, partly due to the internal struggle between the rival English-speaking and Afrikaner sections of the population. The changing political and economic situation in the country, and at times, the relatively high proportion of Jews among immigrants from alien (non-British) countries, also played their part.

Although, in an overall historical perspective, and by comparison with other countries, South Africa's attitude was not an unfavorable one, Jewish leaders frequently felt the need for vigilance against discrimination, and at certain periods Jewish immigration became a subject of intensive political agitation (see below, legal and social status). In 1902, Jewish immigrants faced a crisis because a new literacy test at the Cape (designed to exclude Asiatics) called for the ability to read and write "in the characters of a European language." There were moves to deny this status to Yiddish because it was written in Hebrew characters, but the language was officially accorded recognition in the Cape Immigration Law of 1906. This provision was also incorporated after Union in the basic Immigration Act of 1913. In the early 1920s Jewish communal leaders were engaged in a lengthy dispute with the government on the interpretation of the immigration laws, which had resulted in severe restrictions on economic grounds. These restrictions were removed in 1924, but the increased Jewish immigration which followed led in 1930 to the enactment of a law generally referred to as the "Quota Act." This did not restrict Jewish immigration per se but by imposing numerical limitation upon all immigration from specified countries of Eastern and southern Europe, it substantially reduced the admission of Jewish immigrants. Soon afterward the influx of Jewish refugees, from Nazi Germany – and especially the dramatic arrival in 1936 of a chartered boat, the *Stuttgart*, with 537 German Jewish refugees on board – resulted in a major

Jews in South Africa

Year	Total
1904	38,101
1911	46,919
1918	58,741
1921	62,103
1926	71,816
1936	90,645
1946	104,156
1951	108,498
1960	114,762
1970	118,200
1980	117,963
1991	91, 925
2001	71,800

agitation and precipitated the enactment of the "Aliens Act" of 1937. This law gave plenary powers to an Immigrants Selection Board, which was required, among other considerations, to apply the criterion of "assimilability." The number of Jewish refugees from Germany then dropped considerably, the total between 1933 and 1940 being approximately 5,500.

During World War II, Jewish immigration virtually ceased and in the immediate postwar period was largely limited to aged parents and children of persons already living in South Africa and to other specified categories. Following the virtual destruction, in the Holocaust, of the communities from which South Africa had drawn its Jewish immigrants, as well as the movement toward the State of Israel, the overall figure of Jewish immigration to South Africa dropped to a few hundred annually.

DEMOGRAPHIC ASPECTS. The growth of the South African Jewish population through both immigration and natural increase is shown in the Table; figures are based on official census returns:

Until 1936, when the proportion of Jews in the population reached its peak of 4.52%, the annual Jewish increase was proportionately higher than that of the white population generally. In the succeeding 25 years (1936–1960), however, it was only 1.77% compared with 2.26% for the white population as a whole, and in the decade 1950 to 1960, it was only one-half of the general figure. The relative decline of the Jewish percentage was due to the restrictive immigration laws; the lower birth rate of Jews compared with that of the general white population; a certain amount of emigration; and the higher number of Jews in the older age groups.

In the early years, the high masculinity in sex distribution was similar to that of all typical immigrant communities, but later it dropped sharply. In 1904, there were 25,864 males and 12,237 females, while by 1960, males numbered 57,198 and females 57,563. The proportion of foreign-born to local-born Jews had also radically changed. Whereas in 1936, 46.69% were South African-born (for females the figure was 50%), the large majority are now South African-born.

In 1970, according to the official census of that year, the Jewish population reached an all-time high of 118,200. This figure remained static during the next decade, with losses to emigration being partially offset by immigration from Rhodesia (today *Zimbabwe), other African countries, and Israel. The Jewish population declined precipitously during the 1980s as a result of social, economic, and political unrest. The adjusted 1991 census, when adjusted upwards based on the national percentage of those who omitted the "religion" question on the census form, gave the Jewish population as 91,925, comprising 1.8% of the white population and 0.3% of the total population.

According to the 2001 census, this figure had declined still further. A total of 61,670 whites gave their religion as Jewish, suggesting a total of between 72,000 and 75,000 when the proportion of those who omitted the religion question was taken into account. These were overwhelmingly concentrated in the three provinces of Gauteng (47,700, more than 90% of whom lived in Johannesburg), Western Cape (18,360, mainly in Cape Town), KwaZulu-Natal (3,470, mainly in Durban) and Eastern Cape (1,390, mainly Port Elizabeth and East London), while the combined total of the remaining five provinces was estimated at about 1,500. Once a substantial proportion of the total, the number of Jews still living in rural districts had declined to a few hundred, mainly elderly people. Despite the steep decline in the Jewish population, there were signs early in the new century that Jewish emigration was leveling off and that a modest influx of new immigrants, as well as some returning emigrants, was beginning to swell its ranks once more.

Legal and Social Status

As an integral part of the white population, Jews have full equality and participate in all aspects of South Africa's national, political, civic, economic, and cultural life. During the white minority rule years, although the usual forms of anti-Jewish prejudice in gentile societies were occasionally encountered, both of the main white population groups – the English-speaking and the Afrikaans-speaking – remained faithful, generally speaking, to the traditions of religious tolerance which characterized the homelands – England and the Netherlands – from which their forefathers came. In the post-1994 era, there has been little evidence of anti-Jewish sentiment in the majority black population, with antisemitism being primarily confined to elements within the Muslim community.

There have nevertheless been periods in South Africa's history when Jews faced special problems which arose, in particular, from the complex racial and political tensions of the country. There were exceptional periods when the status of Jews was challenged. While the Cape was under the control of the Dutch East India Company prior to 1795 (see above), and all in the Company's service had to profess the Christian Reformed religion, there could be no professing Jews in the country until a liberal religious policy was introduced. Thereafter, however, whether in the British or the Afrikaner territories,

Jews enjoyed religious tolerance and freedom of conscience. Indeed, a notably sympathetic attitude was shown by the Boers toward the early Jewish immigrants from Eastern Europe.

The situation in the Afrikaner Transvaal Republic, however, differed from that in the Orange Free State, where full equality was enjoyed by the Jews. The Grondwet (constitution) of the Transvaal Republic (1864; reaffirmed in 1896) stipulated that membership in the Volksraad (parliament) and also the holding of official positions in the state service, were to be restricted to Christian Protestants. Catholics, and also Jews, were consequently debarred from military posts and from the offices of the presidency, state secretary, and Landdrost, nor could they become members of the first or second Volksraad or superintendents of the natives or of mines. These disabilities applied even to individuals who had become burghers of the republic. There were also educational disabilities: as education had to be based on a strictly Christian Protestant religious foundation, Catholic and Jewish children were debarred from attending government schools and their parochial schools were denied state aid. These disabilities did not arise from expressly anti-Jewish motives, but flowed from the rather harsh Calvinist constitution of the republic. In the last years of the republic, Jewish deputations to the government sought to have them removed, but without success. Eventually in 1899, President Kruger tried unsuccessfully to persuade the Volksraad to replace the requirement of the Grondwet that all members of the Raad must be Protestant by a provision that they must "believe in the revelation of God through His Word in the Bible." The Jews in the Transvaal reacted variously to these disabilities which were also somewhat obscured by the fact that the Jews were in most cases foreigners (*uitlanders*) with their own far-reaching grievances. Such limitations also did not weigh much upon the relatively recent arrivals from Eastern Europe, who appreciated their situation in the Boer republic, so markedly in contrast to the oppressive conditions of czarist Russia. All the disabilities disappeared when the Transvaal republic came under British rule in 1902. Thereafter, whether under the colonial regimes in the Transvaal and in the rest of the country prior to Union in 1910 or subsequently, Jewish citizens living in South Africa enjoyed legal equality in all respects.

However, further immigration of Jews, more particularly from Eastern Europe, did periodically become a public issue. In the 1930s the influx of refugees from Nazi Germany led to active agitation for the complete prohibition of Jewish immigration. In the result, while no specific anti-Jewish provisions were written into the immigration laws, restrictions were introduced which were expressly designed to cut down the flow of Jewish immigrants. The supporters of these restrictive policies were not confined to one political party only, and many disclaimed an anti-Jewish prejudice, asserting that the measures were necessary to prevent the growth of antisemitism by maintaining the existing balance between the various elements of the white population. (South Africa never favored an open-door immigration policy, the Afrikaans-speaking section, in particular, often contending that the aliens were a threat to the economic and political status of the established population).

South Africa became the scene of open antisemitic agitation among certain sections of the population – not shared by the majority of the citizens – from the time of the accession of the Nazis in Germany in 1933 until the end of World War II. Organized antisemitic movements arose, among them the "shirt" movements like the Greyshirts, Blackshirts, and South African Fascists, and semi-political bodies like the Ossewa Brandwag and the New Order, with fully-fledged National Socialist programs. These developments eventually had their impact upon the official opposition party, the National Party, which in 1937 included a plank on the "Jewish question" in its official program. Its demands included the total prohibition of further Jewish immigration, stronger control over naturalization, and the introduction of a "quota" system for Jews in various branches of economic life. In Transvaal province, too (but not in the other provinces), Jews were banned from membership in the National Party. When the United Party government, headed by Jan Christiaan *Smuts, declared war against Germany in 1939, the National Party formally proclaimed its neutrality.

The anti-Jewish agitation grew more subdued as World War II moved to its climax and sharp ideological differences emerged within the National Party. The moderate elements finally gained the upper hand, and in his political manifesto prior to the general election in May 1948, the Nationalist Party leader, Daniel François Malan, later prime minister, announced a new policy. Denying that the party's attitude on immigration was motivated by anti-Jewish feelings, he affirmed positively that his party did not support discriminatory measures between Jew and non-Jew who were already resident in the country. Consistently with that declaration, when the National Party won the election and became the government, Malan announced his goal to be the removal of the "Jewish question" from the life and politics of South Africa. The reestablishment of confidence was not effected without difficulty. Jews generally tended to hold aloof from the National Party. However it fulfilled its pledge not to countenance antisemitism in public life. Successive National Party prime ministers reaffirmed government policy to be one of equality and non-discrimination between all sections of the white population.

Apart from the 1930s and early 1940s, antisemitism has never manifested as a serious problem in South Africa and Jews continue to participate fully in all aspects of national life on the basis of equality. Levels of recorded antisemitic incidents have been dramatically lower than those of other major Diaspora communities, consistently averaging around 30 annually. During the apartheid years, most antisemitic activity emanated from the white extreme right. During the 1980s and 1990s, the community became increasingly perturbed by the growing prevalence of organized neo-Nazi movements and other antisemitic organizations. Among these were the Afrikaanse Weerstands Beweging (Afrikaner Resistance Movement), Boerenasie, and the Blanke Bevrydingsbeweging (White Liberation Movement). These organizations largely ceased to operate following the transition to majority rule in 1994.

In recent years, most antisemitism has emanated from radical elements within South Africa's large Muslim minority, numbering around 800,000 in 2001 (about 2% of the population). The post-1994 ethos in the country, however, is strongly anti-racist, with numerous laws – including a comprehensive Bill of Rights in the Constitution – proscribing any form of abuse, discrimination, or hate speech based on race, color, creed, or ethnicity.

Communal Organization and Structure

HISTORICAL SURVEY. The earliest pattern of communal organization was established by Jews of German, English, and Dutch extraction. Their congregations provided elementary facilities for worship, classes for Hebrew and religious instruction of the young, and philanthropic aid, and also attended to the rites for the dead. The authority of the chief rabbi of England was accepted in ecclesiastical matters. Joel Rabinowitz (officiated 1859–82), Abraham Frederick *Ornstein, and Alfred P. *Bender (1895–1937), all of whom administered to the Cape Town Congregation, and Samuel I. Rapaport (1872–95), the minister in Port Elizabeth, all emigrated from England.

By the end of the 19th century or soon after, the "greener" East Europeans had broken away from the "English" synagogues in most communities to form their own congregations. Their parochial loyalties were reflected in the many separate associations for religious worship and talmudic study and the numerous *Landsmannschaften (fraternal associations) of persons who had come from the same town or village in Lithuania or Poland. Leading rabbinical personalities in this formative period were: in Johannesburg, Judah Loeb *Landau (officiated 1903–42), from Galicia; the more "Westernized" Joseph Herman *Hertz (1898–1911) who arrived via the United States (he later became chief rabbi of the British Empire); Moshal Friedman (beginning in 1891), from Lithuania; Chief Rabbis L.I. *Rabinowitz (1945–61); B.M. Caspar (1963–1988) and C.K. Harris (1988–2004) and in the Cape, M.Ch. Mirvish (d. 1947), also from Lithuania and I. *Abrahams (1937–68). In lay matters, Jews of English and German origin usually took the lead, but East Europeans also began to assert their influence.

The communal structure gradually underwent change in response to the new social forces – the slowing down of immigration, increasing acculturation and growing homogeneity. Splinter congregations rejoined the older synagogues or new amalgamations took place. By the 1940s most of the Landsmannschaften had disappeared or continued to survive on nostalgic memories. Emerging social and cultural needs called forth a variety of new institutions, such as the lodges of the Hebrew Order of David, the Zionist and Young Israel Societies, the branches of the Union of Jewish Women, the *B'nai B'rith Lodges, the Ex-Servicemen's organizations, the *Reform movement in religious life, Jewish social and sports clubs and, since the early 1990s, communal security organizations. Important work in social outreach and upliftment in the non-Jewish community is carried out by such organizations as MaAfrika Tikkun, the Union of Jewish Women, the United Sisterhood and ORT-South Africa, amongst others. Increased communal cohesion began to be reflected in the organizational structure of education, congregational affairs and philanthropy, and overall communal representation. However, older forms of organization, inherited or adapted from the East European tradition, yielded slowly to change. The most striking exceptions were in the Hebrew educational sphere and in the proliferation of Jewish sports clubs.

The main concentration of Jewish communities is now in two areas: the Johannesburg-Pretoria complex in the north, and the Cape Peninsula in the south, where 66% and 25% respectively of the Jewish population now live. Because of the geographic distance and differences of outlook, the regional bodies in the south until fairly recently maintained virtually autonomous religious and educational organizations parallel to the national bodies up north. However, since the mid-1980s the trend has been toward greater coordination and unity, as shown, inter alia, by the establishment of a national Union of Orthodox Synagogues and Bet Din in 1987. All the major national Jewish bodies have their headquarters in Johannesburg, which has now become the focal point of Jewish life.

RELIGIOUS INSTITUTIONS. The great majority of Hebrew congregations in South Africa, about 85% of the total, are Orthodox, with most of the remainder being Reform (Progressive). The Conservative movement as known in America virtually does not exist in South Africa, apart from the small Shalom Masorti Independent Congregation in Johannesburg, formed after one of the Reform congregations broke away from the Progressive movement in 1992.

In 1966, there were 29 Orthodox congregations and four Reform temples in Johannesburg and 12 Orthodox congregations and two Reform temples in Cape Town. In 2004, the number of Orthodox congregations in Johannesburg had grown to 51 while the Reform temples had declined to three. In Cape Town, the number of Orthodox congregations had increased to 18 and Reform Temples to three. There is at least one Orthodox and one Reform congregation each in Durban, Port Elizabeth, and East London. Outside of the main urban centers, virtually all of the smaller country synagogues had closed, with those remaining functioning only with great difficulty.

The Union of Orthodox Synagogues of South Africa (UOS) is the umbrella body for Orthodox congregations throughout South Africa and has affiliated to it most Orthodox congregations countrywide. It consists of just under 100 synagogues (including many *shtiebels*) and claims a membership enrollment of approximately 20,000 families. The UOS appoints and maintains the office of the chief rabbi and the Bet Din (ecclesiastical court). At the end of 2004, Scottish-born Rabbi Cyril Harris, who had served as a rabbi in London before coming to South Africa, retired after seventeen years as chief rabbi and was replaced by Rabbi Dr. Warren Goldstein, the first locally born rabbi to have been appointed to the position.

There is a single national Bet Din, based in Johannesburg with an office in Cape Town. This deals with conversions to the Jewish faith, the issuance of divorces, supervision of *kashrut*, and similar matters. Although the UOS established and maintains the Bet Din, and also appoints the *dayyanim*, the Bet Din is an independent body, exercising supreme plenary authority in Orthodox religious matters. The UOS publishes a quarterly magazine, *Jewish Tradition*. There is an Orthodox Rabbinical Association of South Africa, its members being drawn from the clergy of all parts of the country.

The period after 1970 saw young people becoming progressively more involved in religious life, in part because of more religion-focused Jewish day schools such as Yeshiva College and also because of the advent of dynamic outreach movements such as the Kollel Yad Shaul, Chabad (Lubavitch), Ohr Somayach, and Aish HaTorah. Johannesburg in particular is today widely regarded as a model *ba'al teshuvah* (return to Orthodoxy) community, while Cape Town and Pretoria were also experiencing an upsurge in religiosity by the turn of the century. The impressive growth of the *ba'al teshuvah* movement was shown by the proliferation of *shtiebls* (small synagogues, characterized by a high level of observance amongst its members) in Johannesburg, which numbered over 30 in 2004.

The Progressive movement was started in South Africa in 1933 by Rabbi Moses Cyrus Weiler (1907–2000) and was later led by Rabbi Arthur Saul Super (1908–1979) in the teeth of strong Orthodox opposition. The Reform movement became established in all the larger communities, at its height claiming support from about 20% of the whole Jewish population. This had declined to between 10 and 15% by the end of the century. In South Africa Reform has been relatively conservative in its religious approach, avoiding some of the radical manifestations of the American movement, and it has always been strongly pro-Zionist. In contrast to the Orthodox synagogues, which confined their activities largely within the Jewish community, Reform congregations broke new ground by adopting programs for Christian-Jewish goodwill and by fostering social welfare projects among non-whites, particularly for children. Several Orthodox congregations, notably the prestigious Oxford shul in Johannesburg, subsequently also became involved in social outreach and upliftment projects in the general community.

The Progressive congregations are associated together in the South African Union for Progressive Judaism, religious issues being handled by a central ecclesiastical board. The latter consists of rabbis and a few laymen, with a rabbi elected annually as its chairman. The ladies guilds in Orthodox synagogues are affiliated to the Federation of Synagogues' Ladies Guilds, and the Reform sisterhoods to the National Union of Temple Sisterhoods.

Both Orthodox and Reform congregations for many years had difficulties in finding rabbis and ministers. The sources in Europe which provided them with trained and experienced ministers no longer existed. By the closing years of the 20th century, however, an increasing number of the community's Orthodox rabbis were emerging from locally established rabbinical training institutions, most notably the Yeshiva Gedolah. Many products of the religious day schools, moreover, were returning to South Africa after gaining *semikhah* overseas, and serving the community both from the pulpit and as teachers within the burgeoning Jewish day school system.

SOUTH AFRICAN JEWISH BOARD OF DEPUTIES. A single representative organization, the South African Jewish Board of Deputies, is recognized by Jews and non-Jews alike as the authorized spokesman for the community. It is charged with safeguarding the equal rights and status of Jews as citizens and generally protecting Jewish interests. A Board for the Transvaal was formed in 1903, on the initiative of Max *Langerman and Rabbi Joseph Hertz, with the encouragement of the High Commissioner, Lord *Milner, and was named after its prototype in England. At first it encountered opposition from the Zionists. Among its early leaders were Bernard *Alexander, Manfred *Nathan, and Siegfried Raphaely. An independent Board for the Cape was formed in 1904 through the efforts of Morris *Alexander and David Goldblatt, despite opposition from the Rev. Alfred P. Bender and his congregation.

Following the unification of the four provinces in 1910, the two bodies were unified in the South African Board of Deputies (1912). Its main concern was to prevent discrimination against Jews in respect of immigration and naturalization and to rebut defamatory attacks on Jews. It led the community's efforts in rendering relief to Jews in Europe after World War I, and later was active also on behalf of German Jewry and the displaced persons of World War II through the instrumentality of the South African Jewish Appeal (1942). A relatively small and weak body, the Board underwent reorganization in the early 1930s to meet the challenge of Nazism and antisemitism. While Johannesburg remained the headquarters, provincial committees were set up in Cape Town – the seat of Parliament – Durban, Port Elizabeth, East London, Pretoria, and Bloemfontein. The position of chairman of the executive council was held by Cecil Lyons (1935–40); Gerald N. Lazarus (1940–45); Simon M. Kuper (1945–49); Israel A. *Maisels (1949–51); Edel J. Horwitz (1951–55); Namie Philips (1955–60); Teddy Schneider (1960–65); Maurice Porter (1965–70); David Mann (1970–74), Julius Rosettenstein (1974–78), Israel Abramowitz (1979–83), Michael Katz (1983–87), Gerald Leissner (1987–91), Mervyn Smith (1991–95), Marlene Bethlehem (1995–99), Russell Gaddin (1999–2003), and Michael Bagraim (from 2003). Its secretary and later general secretary for many years was Gustav Saron. Aleck Goldberg held this position for most of the 1980s while Seymour Kopelowitz did so for most of the next decade. As new needs had to be met, the Board became a functional agency in various fields. Today, it publishes a quarterly journal, *Jewish Affairs*, runs a Country Communities Department to cater to the needs of Jews still living in isolated country areas, maintains in Johannesburg an important library of Jewish information and archives relating to South African Jewry, and publishes information on the community through its website and communal directories. In 1993 it also took the lead in founding, and subsequently in running, the *African Jewish Congress, a representative and coordinating body for the Jewish communities in Sub-Saharan Africa. There is frequent consultation and cooperation between the Board and the Zionist Federation. In 1949 the Board launched the United Communal Fund (UCF) for South African Jewry, which provides the budgets – in whole or in part – of the Board itself, and of a number of other important communal organizations, including the Office of the Chief Rabbi, Community Security Organisation, Union of Jewish Women (UJW) and S.A. Board of Jewish Education. The UCF combined with the Israel United Appeal in 1984 to form the IUA-UCF. In line with important rationalization initiatives introduced during the late 1990s, the Board, Zionist Federation, IUA-UCF, UJW, S.A. Union of Jewish Students, and a number of other, smaller, Zionist and Jewish communal organizations today share single premises in all the major Jewish centers country-wide.

PHILANTHROPY. Institutions to assist the poor and needy early became an established feature of communal organization. In the wake more particularly of the East European immigration, there was a proliferation of many kinds of philanthropic institutions or fraternal bodies having philanthropic objects, such as Landsmannschaften, free-loan societies, societies to visit the sick, and especially for the provision of financial and material help to those in need. Many of these institutions bore the hallmark and followed the methods of East European traditions of *ẓedakah*. Today, for instance, the largest welfare body in Johannesburg, the *Chevra Kaddisha* combines extensive philanthropic work with the activities of a burial society. The organizational structure and also the underlying principles of Jewish social welfare subsequently underwent changes under the impact of changing social conditions. In recent years, the *Chevra Kaddisha* has incorporated a number of other important welfare institutions under its umbrella, amongst them the two Jewish aged homes Sandringham Gardens and Our Parents Home, Jewish Community Services, the Jewish Women's Benevolent Society, and the Arcadia Jewish Orphanage. Other important welfare institutions include the free-loan societies, the Witwatersrand Hebrew Benevolent Association (founded 1893) and the more recent Rambam Trust, the Selwyn Segal Home for Jewish Handicapped (1959), Yad Aharon, Hatzollah (medical rescue), Kadimah Occupational Centre, B'nai B'rith, and Nechama (bereavement counseling).

Leading bodies in the Cape include the Astra Centre (incorporating Jewish Sheltered Employment), B'nai B'rith, Cape Jewish Welfare Council, Glendale Home for the Intellectually Disabled, Hebrew Helping Hand Association, Highlands House (Jewish Aged Home), and Jewish Community Services (incorporating Jewish Board of Guardians, founded 1859, and the Jewish Sick Relief Society). The Jewish community has assumed financial responsibility for all its welfare needs, the large budgets being met by fees, membership dues, contributions, and bequests. Some advantage has been taken of government grants for specific welfare projects.

FRATERNAL ORGANIZATIONS. In the first decades of the 20th century many of the communal organizations provided some form of philanthropic and fraternal services to assist the integration of the immigrant generation. As late as 1929, of the 68 Jewish institutions in Johannesburg then affiliated to the Board of Deputies, 38 were either wholly or partly philanthropic. An indigenous South African institution of this type, the Hebrew Order of David, founded successive lodges after 1904 and, as members began to be recruited among the South African-born generation, added social, cultural, and communal objectives. The Grand Lodge has its headquarters in Johannesburg.

UNION OF JEWISH WOMEN. In the women's sphere the Union of Jewish Women of South Africa plays a major role. The first branch was formed in Johannesburg in 1931 and a national body in 1936. In 1969 the Union had 64 branches throughout the republic with a total membership of between 9,000 and 10,000 women, its national headquarters being in Johannesburg. The subsequent concentration of most Jews in the main urban centers, with the resultant closure of most rural and small town branches, saw the number of branches shrinking to 10 by 2004, with a total membership of about 7,500 women. The Union maintains a wide range of activities and acts as a coordinating body for Jewish women's organizations. A distinctive aspect of its program is its nondenominational work, educational and philanthropic, serving all sections of the population. Some branches run creches and feeding depots for indigent colored and African children and adults. Branches of the Union have established Hebrew nursery schools, friendship clubs, services for the aged, youth projects, and a wide program of adult education. In recent years, the UJW has become extensively involved in HIV/AIDS relief work.

EDUCATION. There are a plethora of Jewish day schools in Johannesburg and Cape Town, all of which provide a complete secular education, with Jewish studies integrated into the general curriculum, up to matriculation standard. The mainstream schools in Johannesburg are the three King David schools, located in Linksfield, Victory Park, and Sandton. The first two provide Jewish education from pre-school to matriculation level while the third goes up to primary school level. King David's counterparts in Cape Town are the Herzlia schools, while there is also a small Jewish day school in Port Elizabeth, Theodor Herzl.

The ideological basis of the King David, Herzlia, and Theodor Herzl schools is officially described as "broadly national traditional," a formula intended to indicate both the religious and the Zionist character of the education. Pupils receive a full education following a state syllabus and a Jewish studies program, including religion, history, literature, and Hebrew language. The mainstream Jewish day schools accept children of mixed marriages and Reform converts. However, many demanded more intensive religious instruction and greater religious observance. Protagonists of this type of education, together with Bnei Akiva religious youth movement, created in 1958 Yeshiva College, originally established as the Bnei Akiva Yeshiva seven years previously. This developed into a full-time day school from nursery school up to matriculation and steadily grew from an initial few dozen pupils to well over 800 by the turn of the century. In 1995, the school received the Jerusalem Prize for Jewish Education in the Diaspora. Yeshiva College could be regarded as centrist Orthodox in its approach. More right-wing Orthodox schools that subsequently were established include Torah Academy and Cape Town's Hebrew Academy (both under Chabad's auspices), Yeshivas Toras Emes, Shaarei Torah, Bais Yaakov, Hirsch Lyons, and Yeshiva Maharsha.

The Progressive movement also maintains a network of supplementary Hebrew and religious classes at its temples. These schools are affiliated with the Union for Progressive Jewish Education.

Overall supervision of the King David schools is undertaken by the South African Board of Jewish Education (SABJE), established in 1928, which operates from headquarters in Johannesburg. Affiliates include Yeshiva College and Torah Academy in Johannesburg, Theodor Herzl in Port Elizabeth, and the Herzlia schools in Cape Town. The SABJE has direct responsibility, both financial and administrative, for the Jewish day schools in Johannesburg. It also involves itself with Jewish children who attend state schools and whose main access to Jewish education is through the *Cheder* program and by means of religious instruction booklets sent into the schools. It administers a network of Hebrew nursery schools according to the standards laid down by the Nursery School Association of South Africa. The Cape Council of the South African Jewish Board of Education has its own religious instruction program for Jewish pupils who attend the state schools in the Western Cape Province.

In 2003, over 80% of school-going Jewish children in Johannesburg, Cape Town, and Port Elizabeth (whose Theodor Herzl School by then had a mainly non-Jewish enrollment) were attending one of the Jewish day schools. Those still in government schools had their Jewish educational requirements catered to by the United Hebrew Schools (under the SABJE) in Johannesburg and the Religious Instruction Department of the SAJBE in Cape Town. Jewish pupils in Pretoria and Durban received Jewish education through a special department at the Crawford College branches. This arrangement came about following the take-over of the Carmel College Jewish day schools in those cities by Crawford during the 1990s. The total pupil enrollment in the day schools in 2004 was about 8,000, substantially more than the 1969 figure of 6,000 even though the overall Jewish community had by then declined by more than a third. Government policy precludes financial support to new private schools, of whatever denomination, and financing of Jewish education remains a problem.

At the tertiary level, university students are able to take Jewish studies through the Semitics Department of the University of South Africa (UNISA); the Department of Hebrew and Jewish Studies of Natal University; and the Department of Hebrew and Jewish Studies (including the Isaac and Jessie Kaplan Centre for Jewish Studies and Research) at the University of Cape Town.

Programs of adult education continue to be provided by the SABJE, the South African Zionist Federation and the various affiliates, including most particularly the Union of Jewish Women, the Women's Zionist Council and the South African Zionist Youth Council. Other bodies, which have significantly contributed to the general cultural life of South African Jewry, include the Histadrut Ivrit, Yiddish Cultural Federation and the South African National Yad Vashem Foundation. Courses of Jewish study are offered at the University of Natal in Durban, and the University of South Africa.

Social Life

INFLUENCE OF IMMIGRATION STREAMS. Following the congregational beginnings in Cape Town in 1841, loss of identity through assimilation was gradually arrested, although the immigrants became quickly integrated into the general economic and cultural life. In secular matters, as also in religious, they maintained ties with Anglo-Jewry, and this tradition was followed also by the immigrants from Germany. The latter, socially influential, often assumed the leadership, but do not appear to have made a specifically German-Jewish cultural contribution.

The growing numbers of East Europeans led in time to social, religious, and cultural ferment. Social distance, and even open friction and conflict, developed between the "greeners" and the older sections, due to differences in ritual tradition, in intensity of religious observance, or in attitudes to Jewish education and Zionism. Nonetheless, many aspects of the Anglo-Jewish pattern persisted, although it underwent changes in spirit and content.

Elements of the legacy of Lithuanian Jewry may be identified in certain characteristics of South African Jewry: generous support for all philanthropic endeavors, respect for Jewish scholarship and learning, exemplified in the status accorded to the rabbinate and concern for Jewish education; and a conservative outlook toward religious observance (at least in externals). However, as the community became largely South African-born and homogeneous, the barriers that formerly separated the various immigrant groups all but disappeared. The Yiddish language, the only vernacular used by the East European immigrants, became confined to a small minority. (In the 1936 census, 17,861 persons declared Yiddish as their home language; by 1946 the figure was 14,044, and in 1951, it had fallen to 9,970. In 1960, of the large Jewish population in Johannesburg, only 2,786 declared Yiddish to be their home language). By 2004, only a handful remained.

FORCES STRENGTHENING GROUP IDENTITY. The normal trends of acculturation and integration – linguistic, cultural, and economic – were accelerated by the rapid rise in the material condition of many Jews. South African Jewry has thus far escaped large-scale manifestations of assimilation and maintains a vigorous group life. A major community survey jointly conducted in 1998 by the Institute for Jewish Policy Research (U.K.) and Kaplan Centre for Jewish Studies and Research (Cape Town) showed remarkably high levels of Jewish identification, both in the religious and Zionist sphere, and an intermarriage rate of less than 10%. Various factors have contributed to this. During the apartheid years, the country's cultural and political climate, which emphasizes the distinctiveness of the various linguistic, cultural, and ethnic groups of the population, and especially the coexistence of the English and Afrikaans language and culture, was favorable to the preservation of a separate Jewish group life. There was no pressure upon the Jew to drop his identity or to become an "unhyphenated" South African. This has continued into the post-1994 era, where the right of ethnic and religious communities to express their identity within the greater multicultural society is constitutionally protected, and indeed encouraged. The advent of democracy has therefore scarcely impinged, if at all, on Jewish identity, which has in fact been considerably strengthened by the strong upsurge in religiosity, particularly in Johannesburg.

THE ZIONIST MOVEMENT. The greatest influence, however – itself part of the Lithuanian heritage – has been exerted by the Zionist movement in the evolution of South African Jewry. Lithuanian Jewry's support of *Ḥibbat Zion was continued by the emigrants to South Africa. There was at first lukewarmness, and even active opposition, from some of the older anglicized groups, some right-wing Orthodox ministers, and also a small group of *Bund members and socialists. In time, however, the Zionist outlook achieved an unchallenged position.

Even before the first Basle Congress in 1897, there were a few Ḥovevei Zion societies in the country. An association of Zionist societies in the Transvaal, formed in 1898, convened a countrywide conference which led to the creation of the South African Zionist Federation, the first all-national Jewish body. The first all-South African Zionist conference was held in 1905. Although the fortunes of the Zionist movement fluctuated in the post-Herzl era, its strength was revealed during World War I, when the first South African Jewish Congress was held in Johannesburg, in April 1916, convened jointly by the Zionist Federation and the Board of Deputies in order to mobilize public opinion for the Jewish claim to Palestine. Zionist activity expanded greatly in the post-*Balfour Declaration period, owing much to its effective leaders, among them, Samuel Goldreich, Jacob *Gitlin, Idel Schwartz, A.M. Abrahams, Rabbi J.H. Hertz, Rabbi J.L. Landau, Benzion Hersch, Isaac Goldberg, Joseph Janower, Lazar Braudo, Katie Gluckman, Nicolai Kirschner, Bernard Gerling, Simon M. *Kuper, Joseph *Herbstein, Leopold *Greenberg, Edel J. Horwitz, and Israel A. Maisels. Its most influential officials included Jack Alexander, Zvi Infeld, and Sidney Berg. The Zionist Movement acted as a counterforce to weakening religious observance, and also unified the widely scattered communities. During the 1960s and 1970s, contributions per capita to Zionist funds were believed to have been higher in South Africa than elsewhere, even though the country's laws did not allow tax reductions for such donations. These contributions have been significantly reduced in the modern era, partly due to the decline of the South African currency relative to other currencies and because of government restrictions.

The South African Zionist Federation has been held up as a model of an all-embracing territorial Zionist organization. It takes the lead in, and coordinates, a many-faceted program. Its activities range from fundraising, the promotion of *aliyah*, tourism, and other forms of assistance to Israel, to youth work, adult education, and the fostering of Jewish culture generally. With its national headquarters situated in Johannesburg, it has officials in the main provincial centers and also an office in Tel Aviv, which carries out many varied functions in Israel itself. The strength of the Zionist movement lies particularly in its women's and youth sections. Organizations affiliated to the Zionist Federation include the Women's Zionist Organization of South Africa, whose fundraising projects are directed mainly toward the needs in Israel of women and children and land reclamation. The South African Maccabi Association, which promotes sport with Israel and is responsible for South Africa's participation in the *Maccabi Games. In 2004, there were four Zionist youth movements nationally, the largest being Bnei Akiva, followed by Habonim-Dror, Betar, and Netzer (representing the Reform movement). These conduct cultural programs, organize youth activities, and run summer camps. University youth have their representative organization – the South African Union of Jewish Students (SAUJS) affiliated to both the SAJBD and SAZF. In addition, many Zionist Societies and numerous synagogues are affiliated to the Federation. Fundraising is conducted through various channels, mainly through the Israel United Appeal campaign. Additional funds are raised for the Jewish National Fund, the Magen David Adom, South African Friends of various Israeli universities and educational institutions including the Hebrew, Bar-Ilan, Ben-Gurion and Haifa universities and the Technion, amongst other causes. The executive council of the Zionist Federation, elected by a biennial conference, includes representatives of the Women Zionists, Youth, Maccabi, and Medical Councils, and of other bodies within the Zionist movement.

South African Zionism has been noteworthy for its practical character, and the many projects which it has sponsored in Israel, among them the South African Palestine Enterprise (Binyan Corporation Ltd.) 1922, which granted mortgage loans at low interest rates; the African Palestine Investments, which participated in the Palestine Cold Storage and Supply Co.; and the Palestine Shippers Ltd. The South African Jewish Appeal promoted an important housing project and the building of the garden village in *Ashkelon. The Women's Zionist Council erected and maintains the WIZO Mothercraft Center. The Union of Jewish Women endowed the first dormitory for women students at the Hebrew University and is responsible for the maintenance of the Parasitology Laboratory. Significant endowments made by individuals to the Hebrew University include the Bialik Chair of Hebrew, the Ruth Ochberg Chair of Agriculture, the Cootcher Museum of Antiquities, the Joffee Marks wing of the Jewish National and University Library, the Silas S. Perry Endowment for Biblical Research, and the Percy A. Leon building in the geology complex.

Comparatively large numbers of South African Jews settled in Israel. By 1948 they numbered about 200, and by the beginning of 2004 the figure was estimated at around 18,000. Former South Africans who achieved high distinction in the state are Abba Eban, Michael Comay, Louis (Aryeh) Pincus, Arthur Lourie, and Jack Geri (who for a time was minister of commerce). In periods of crisis many volunteers from South Africa spontaneously left for Israel. In the 1948 War of Liberation, men and women who had served in the South African forces during World War II went to the defense of the Jewish state. A few thousand volunteered, but only 800 were sent and of these, approximately one-quarter remained permanently in the country. A stream of volunteers again left for Israel in the 1956 Sinai crisis, at the time of the Six-Day War in June 1967, and in the 1973 Yom Kippur War. An increasing number of students continued their studies at various seats of higher learning in Israel. The Jewish day schools send large groups of pupils to Israel for extended courses, and great numbers of tourists visit Israel regularly. Increasing contacts between South African Jewry and Israel have enriched the content of Jewish life and strengthened Jewish consciousness in South Africa.

Political Attitudes and Involvement

Apart from a few exceptional situations, opportunities to participate in all aspects of civic and political life have been open to Jews at all levels – national, provincial and local. An impressive number of Jews regularly participated in local government as elected councilors, both in the large cities and in the rural villages (until the exodus to the cities). Many were elected to the position of mayor (including 22 in Johannesburg and 13 in Cape Town). The provincial councils and Parliament also have always included Jewish representatives, with these after 1948 largely belonging to opposition parties. Four Jews, Henry *Gluckman, Louis Shill, Joe *Slovo, and Ronnie Kasrils have to date attained cabinet rank, while Gill Marcus, as well as Kasrils, have served terms as deputy ministers. In 1999, Tony Leon became the country's first Jewish Leader of the Opposition when his party, the Democratic Alliance, became the second largest party in Parliament following the general election of that year.

Throughout the 20th century, relations between the white and non-white sections of the population formed the warp and woof of party politics in South Africa, and there was likewise no collective Jewish attitude in regard to these. Because of the great diversity of opinions among individuals, and the complexity of the racial and political tensions within the country, the Jewish community found it impossible to advocate any specific group policy. The majority espoused moderate policies. Some Jews were among the foremost protagonists of the non-white sections of the population. One of the best-known was Helen *Suzman, the sole representative of the Progressive Party in the South African Parliament from 1961 to 1974. Within the ranks of the anti-apartheid liberation movements, Jews were likewise disproportionately involved, whether as academics, trade unionists, political organizers, or within the armed wings of the liberation groups. Many of these were jailed, including Denis Goldberg, who was convicted alongside Nelson Mandela and other leading black opposition figures at the famous Rivonia Trial in 1964. Many more were compelled to go into exile, where they continued to be active in anti-apartheid activities in places like London and Lusaka in Zambia. Some returned after the unbanning of the various liberation movements in 1990 and several of these, amongst them Joe Slovo, Ronnie Kasrils, Ben Turok, and Gill Marcus, played an important role in the subsequent process of transition to multiracial democracy.

During the apartheid years of white minority rule, the activities of individual Jews or of the Jewish community as such led to occasional controversy, often revealing the impact of the political, ideological, and racial tensions in South Africa upon attitudes toward Jews. The fact that so high a proportion of Jews were engaged in anti-apartheid activities, often as members of the banned Communist Party, led to the loyalties of the Jewish community as a whole being called into question. The mainstream Jewish leadership, represented by the SAJBD, found it necessary from time to time to emphasize that there was no collective Jewish viewpoint in regard to the racial policies advocated by the respective political parties, and that Jewish citizens act in such matters not as members of a group, but as individuals. As opposition to apartheid intensified, both locally and internationally, the mainstream communal leadership became increasingly torn between its traditional mission of safeguarding the Jewish community and the need to condemn the injustices of the apartheid policy in accordance with Jewish moral values and historical experience.

By the mid-1980s, the SAJBD was speaking out more forthrightly against the apartheid policy. At its national conference of 1985, and again in 1987, the Board explicitly rejected apartheid. It also released statements condemning evictions of black leaders and pass-law arrests, detention without trial, a university quota system for blacks, and the treatment of black squatters near Cape Town. The ruling National Party's move away from pure apartheid attracted some Jewish support although the majority of Jews continued to support the liberal opposition Progressive Federal Party, later transformed into the Democratic Party and thereafter the Democratic Alliance. A substantial number of Jews were engaged in social action and welfare activities. Jews were prominent in various activist organizations including Lawyers for Human Rights, the Legal Resources Centre, and the End Conscription Campaign (which sought changes to laws regarding compulsory military service for whites). Two specifically Jewish activist organizations were founded in the mid-1980s: Jews for Social Justice in Johannesburg and Jews for Justice in Cape Town. In 1987 Jews for Social Justice participated in the founding of the Five Freedoms Forum, a broad grouping of 25 white organizations opposed to apartheid. The SAJBD fully endorsed the moves away from apartheid by President De Klerk after 1989, and devoted much of its efforts during the following decade to preparing the Jewish community for the transition to black majority rule. In 1992, it threw its weight behind a "yes" vote during an all-white referendum on whether or not the reform process should be continued.

The majority of Jews tended to vote for opposition parties during the 1948–94 period, and in the elections of 1999 and 2004 overwhelmingly supported the Democratic Alliance. Nevertheless the Jewish community collectively – as distinct from individual Jewish citizens – has played no part in politics (except in exceptional situations, such as during the 1930s, where Jews felt that their status as full and equal citizens was being threatened).

Economic Life and Social Structure

That Jews have played a significant role in the economic development of the country is generally acknowledged. They were able to make a distinctive contribution because of the specific economic situation prevailing in the country at various periods, which required and gave scope for their particular talents and enterprise.

In the early part of the 19th century, before the discovery of the diamond fields, the economy was largely pastoral and agricultural. Economic prospects of the Cape were revived, however, by the increased trade and shipping around the southern route between Europe and the East. Furthermore, the aftermath of the English industrial revolution had encouraged some emigration to South Africa; and included the group known as the 1820 Settlers from Britain, which settled along the eastern frontier of the Cape (see *Norden family). During the 1830s, the interior was further opened up by the Boer voortrekkers. The relatively small number of Jewish immigrants from England and Germany brought with them an aptitude for and experience in trade and finance, and filled a special niche in the economically undeveloped society. They were merchants and small traders, with a sprinkling of professional men and craftsmen. Through their knowledge of foreign markets they helped to develop the export of such products as wool, hides, skins, and wine. They also contributed to the improvement of the Cape wool and mohair industries, the foundation of South Africa's future development as one of the world's producers. The Mosenthals from Germany, in particular, left a permanent mark on the economy through their initiative and diversity of interests. From bases in Cape Town and Port Elizabeth they set up a chain of trading stations in the interior of the Cape, usually manned by Jewish immigrants whom they had brought out from Germany. They helped to stabilize the rural economy by providing long-term credits to storekeepers and, through them, to farmers, particularly in bad seasons. Before the advent of commercial banking, the firm's banknotes were widely accepted in the development of banking, the financing of diamond and gold mining, and the establishment of secondary industries in the Cape and Transvaal. The *De Pass brothers, who came from Britain in the 1840s, developed shipping, fishing, and coastal trading enterprises in the southwestern Cape. They had interests in the newly discovered diamond fields in South-West Africa, then a German possession. Daniel De Pass was one of the pioneers of the sugar industry in Natal. The itinerant Jewish traders and peddlers (locally known as "smouses") traveled on foot or used animal-drawn transport to penetrate long distances, often amidst great hazards and hardships, to scattered hamlets and the extensive farms. They sold their wares and also provided a channel through which the products of the land could reach the ports and world markets. Many settled in the villages and at wayside stations as shopkeepers, so that eventually there was hardly a small town without one or more Jewish stores. These Jewish middlemen had a recognized place in the economy of the Cape and subsequently in the northerly territories.

Then came the revolution which transformed South Africa's economic structure: the discovery of diamonds at Kimberley (1870) and the opening of the Transvaal gold mines (1886; see *Johannesburg). The exploitation of mineral wealth called for enterprise, technical and managerial initiative, ability and great capital resources. There was a demand for commercial techniques, and the way was opened for the later development of secondary industries to supply the new communities which sprung up. The majority of Afrikaners, still largely a rural community, were not ready for the challenges of this new economic era, and the lead was taken by the English-speaking elements and foreigners of various nationalities, who flocked to the country. Among them Jews, mainly from Western Europe, became leaders of the mining industry (see B.I. *Barnato, the *Joels, Lionel *Phillips, George *Albu and David *Harris). With Cecil John Rhodes, Barnato founded De Beers Consolidated Mines which controlled the production and marketing of diamonds (see also *Diamond Industry and Trade). On the discovery of gold the same men, using the wealth and skill they had acquired in the diamond fields, took the lead in developing the gold mines. In later years, Ernest *Oppenheimer and his son Harry were at the head of De Beers and established widespread interests in the goldfields of the Transvaal and the newer goldfields of the Orange Free State, in the production of base minerals and uranium, and in the development of manufacturing industries. Many of the early

Jewish magnates had only flimsy associations with the Jewish community, and some actually abandoned Judaism. Later, other Jewish mining magnates, financiers, and executives also became leading figures in the mining industry, though in relatively small numbers.

The next major movement forward – a latecomer in South Africa – was the development of secondary industry, which occurred after World War I and was greatly intensified during and after World War II. Jews, many of them from Eastern Europe, contributed greatly to this development through their pioneering spirit and readiness to take risks. Often starting from humble beginnings as peddlers, storekeepers, and handicraftsmen (tailors, shoemakers, cabinetmakers, bricklayers, and so on), they produced some of the most enterprising industrialists. Among the pioneers were Samuel *Marks, who immigrated to South Africa in the 1860s, and his partner Isaac Lewis, who, with the help of state concessions established a number of industries in the Pretoria area, from the production of dynamite for the mines to a distillery and glass works. The steel plant which they established in Vereeniging was the forerunner of the South African state-controlled iron and steel industry. Assisted by protective tariffs and by wartime conditions, industries for manufacturing food, clothing, textiles, furniture, leather articles, and others were established by Jewish enterprise. Clothing and textile factories, in particular, were developed into one of the most important sectors of South African industry, and Jews remained leaders in that field. In the 1930s, the refugees who arrived from Germany also introduced many new industries. The younger generation of South African-born Jews later diversified into other spheres like electronics, engineering, the chemical industries, and large-scale building construction. Jewish town planners, property developers, and builders were largely responsible for the modernization of Johannesburg and other cities to meet the needs of an increasingly urbanized population. Entrepreneurs, notably I.W. *Schlesinger, were among the leading figures in the tertiary industries (insurance, mass entertainment, hotel keeping, catering, and advertising). Jews were among the first in South Africa to introduce modern distribution techniques in the retail trade, such as the department store, the supermarket and the discount house. The largest chain stores were founded by Jews, most of whom started from small beginnings. Although few Jews took up agriculture, Jewish farmers, especially in the maize industry, fruit growing, dairy farming and viticulture, set examples of successful scientific farming. Schlesinger's citrus undertaking in the Transvaal became one of the largest of its kind in the world. Ostrich farming and marketing, until the decline of the industry after 1914, was developed by Jews in the Oudtshoorn area of the Cape, notable among them being the Rose brothers, Max and Albert.

The South African-born generation of Jews turned in increasing numbers to the professions, to medicine, law, pharmacy, and later to accountancy, engineering, architecture, and pure and applied science, often achieving positions of eminence. A high proportion of young people regularly study at the universities. There have been distinguished Jewish lawyers in the past, Simeon Jacobs, Manfred *Nathan, Leopold Greenberg, Philip *Millin, J. Herbstein, H.M. Bloch, Percy Yutar, Simon Kuper, Cecil Margo, Isie Maisels, Richard Goldstone, Sydney Kentridge, Albie Sachs, and Arthur Chaskalson, many of these going on to serve with distinction on the bench. In 2001, Arthur Chaskalson was appointed chief justice. Many Jews have distinguished themselves in medicine, medical research, and the development of health and hospital services.

Jews in the Armed Forces

Jewish service as volunteers in the armed forces of the nation dates back to the Anglo-Boer War of 1899–1902, when Jews fought on both sides. Jewish participation in army service has been in greater numbers, proportionally, than the rest of the white population. Thus in World War I, there were some 3,000 Jewish volunteers representing about 6% of the entire Jewish population of that time. In World War II over 10,000, above 10% of the Jewish population, were listed in the records kept by the South African Jewish Board of Deputies of Jews serving in the Union Defense Forces and with other Allied forces. Of these 357 were killed, 327 were wounded or injured, 143 were mentioned in dispatches, and 94 received various awards for distinguished service. Compulsory military conscription for white males was introduced in the early 1970s, which began at six months and eventually was extended to two years plus two further years of military camps. Shortly thereafter, in 1976, South Africa became embroiled in a war against South West African liberation fighters and Cuban forces on the Angola-South West Africa border. The war continued until 1989, when South West Africa, now called Namibia, gained its independence from South Africa. A number of Jewish conscripts, perhaps a dozen in all, were amongst those who lost their lives in the conflict.

During the years of compulsory military conscription, chaplaincy services to Jewish men in the armed forces were provided by a Chaplaincy Committee, composed of representatives of the Board of Deputies, the Federation of Synagogues (later the UOS), the Union of Progressive Judaism, the Jewish Ex-Servicemen's organization, the Union of Jewish Women, and the Rabbinical Association. The chaplains were usually ministers or rabbis serving communities in the areas where military camps were located. Most of the administrative work of the Chaplaincy Committee was carried out by the Board of Deputies. There were 30 Jewish chaplains serving in the field in World War II. Chaplaincy services were discontinued in 1994.

Cultural Life

Jews have participated actively in all aspects of the cultural and artistic life of the country. Their work is recognized as part of South African culture. That they are Jews may not be irrelevant to their work, but does not determine the nature of their contributions. In the literary field, they have produced an imposing list of writers and artists, some of the first rank, including South Africa's foremost novelist, Sarah Gertrude *Millin. Also from South Africa are the Jewish novelists Dan *Jacobson and Nadine *Gordimer. Since for the most part Jews have been living in the cities where English is the dominant language, it is not surprising that they have had a greater share in English culture than in Afrikaans, although several have made worthy contributions to Afrikaans literature and more and more Jews are becoming fluent in both Afrikaans and English (see *South African Literature). One of the founders of the *Rand Daily Mail* and both founders of the *Mail & Guardian* were Jews, and Jews figure prominently in journalism. As patrons of art, music, and literature, they have provided stimulus in many aspects of the cultural life of the country, notably, perhaps, in musical and dramatic enterprise. Jewish painters include Irma *Stern and John Henry *Amshewitz, and among sculptors of notable standing is Moses *Kottler. South African playwrights, composers, musicians, producers, and actors have contributed largely to the cultural scene. While Yiddish was still in vogue among substantial numbers of the community, several South African writers made worthy literary contributions in that medium. There has also been literary creativity in Hebrew.

Relations with Israel

South Africa's official relations with Israel were founded, significantly, in a month decisive for the destinies of both people, May 1948. Chaim Weizmann, describing May 15, the day after the establishment of the State of Israel, wrote: "I bethought myself of one surviving author of the Balfour Declaration and addressed a cable to General Smuts. This was closely followed by South African recognition (of Israel)" (*Trial and Error*, p. 585). In the same month, however, Smuts and his United Party were defeated in the South African elections and succeeded by Malan's Nationalist Party. Smuts had had a longstanding familiarity with Zionism, whereas the new government was less involved with the story of Zionism and the cause of Jewish statehood. The Smuts administration had steadfastly supported the Zionist cause in international forums and was among the governments which had voted in the United Nations for the partition of Palestine on Nov. 29, 1947. Under the Nationalists, South Africa continued to support Israel, voted for its admission to the United Nations in 1949, and backed it on a number of subsequent issues in that forum. South Africa's recognition of Israel was followed by the establishment of an Israel consulate-general in Johannesburg and an Israel legation in Pretoria. Out of consideration for its economic interests and ties with the Arab States, however, South Africa was for long reluctant to establish any diplomatic mission in Israel. Nevertheless, Prime Minister Malan made a personal visit to Israel in 1952.

During the 1960s, attitudes to Israel underwent a change, because of the statements and votes by Israel representatives at the United Nations, which were critical of South Africa's racial policies. The reactions at times caused considerable tension between the South African government and the Jewish community. When the Israel-Arab war broke out in 1967, however, public sympathy was strongly on Israel's side. Following the 1973 Yom Kippur War, ties between Israel and South Africa, particularly in the military sphere, were steadily strengthened, a factor that contributed significantly to anti-Israel sentiment within the majority black population.

The establishment of these links between Israel and South Africa brought increasing and severe international criticism. Chaim Herzog, then Israel ambassador at the UN, revealed the hypocrisy of these allegations by his disclosure of details concerning large-scale secret trade between Arab, Asian and African nations and South Africa. On numerous occasions it was made plain by Israel that it had reservations about South African internal policies, but that it believed that it was essential to continue to foster cooperation between the countries despite differences of opinion on internal policies.

South Africa consolidated warm relations with Israel through the 1980s. However, as Western pressure against South Africa intensified, Israel was forced into reassessing this relationship. The United States threatened to cut military assistance to countries engaged in military trade with South Africa. In 1987 Israel agreed "to refrain from new undertakings between Israel and South Africa in the realm of defense." In line with its general opposition to sanctions as a policy, the South African Jewish leadership urged Israel not to take that step. Notwithstanding Israeli policy, the South African government continued to accept "approved enterprise to certain categories of investment" in Israel, among them residential housing, subject to certain conditions.

During the 1980s, left-wing and Islamist groups, such as the PAC, the Azanian Peoples' Organization (AZAPO), Call of Islam, and Qibla (a Muslim fundamentalist movement) pursued a vigorous anti-Zionist line. Their support was built upon black disappointment at close ties between South Africa and Israel and suspected military cooperation. Anti-Zionist sentiment was already evident at the time of the Lebanon War (1982) and consolidated during the first *intifada*. In particular the Muslim population of over 500,000 pursued a vigorous stance against Israel. This was very evident during the First Gulf War, intensifying during the years of the Oslo peace process and reaching unprecedented heights following the outbreak of the second *intifada* in September 2000. Notwithstanding sympathy for the Palestinian people, black leaders made a clear distinction between anti-Zionism and antisemitism. Nonetheless, there were indications of substantial "social distance" between blacks and Jews, including anti-Jewish attitudes among blacks.

The advent of black majority rule in 1994, which resulted in an overwhelming victory for the strongly pro-Palestinian African National Congress (ANC), saw a radical change in the government's attitude towards Israel. The relationship remained reasonably cordial during the years of the Oslo peace process but deteriorated sharply with the outbreak of the second *intifada*. While often critical of Israeli policy, however, the ANC (which was returned to office with increased majorities in the elections of 1999 and 2004) remains committed to dialogue and strengthening already strong trade ties between the two countries.

BIBLIOGRAPHY: L. Feldman, *Yidn in Johannesburg* (1956); *Jewish Affairs*, 15 (1960); *Zionist Record* (March 21, 1961); idem, *Jewish Affairs*, vol. 15 no. 5 (May, 1960), M. Shain, *The Roots of Anti-Semitism in South Africa* (1994); S.E. Aschheim, in: JJS 12, 2 (Dec. 1970), 201–31. **ADD. BIBLIOGRAPHY:** I. Suttner (ed.), *Cutting Through the Mountain – Interviews With South African Jewish Activists* (1997); G. Shimoni, *Jews and Zionism: The South African Experience, 1910–1967* (1980); G. Shimoni, *Community and Conscience: The Jews in Apartheid South Africa* (2003); M. Shain and R. Mendelsohn (eds.), *Memories, Realities and Dreams – Aspects of the South African Jewish Experience* (2002); *Jewish Affairs*, Vol. 58, No. 3 (Rosh Hashana 2003) (South African Jewish Board of Deputies centenary issue); M. Kaplan and M. Robertson (eds.), *Founders and Followers – Johannesburg Jewry, 1887–1915* (1991); M. Arkin (ed.), *South African Jewry – A Contemporary Survey* (1984); M. Kaplan, *Jewish Roots in the South African Economy* (1986); *Jewish Affairs* 60th anniversary issue, Vol. 57, No. 3 (Rosh Hashana 2002).

[Gustav Saron and Milton Shain / David Saks (2nd ed.)]

SOUTH AFRICAN LITERATURE.

Biblical Influences

The Afrikaans-speaking people of South Africa are mainly descended from Dutch Calvinist and French Huguenot immigrants of the 17th century. The Bible has been an important factor in their life and thinking. The Afrikaans language (a variant of Dutch) took shape in the late 19th century, and biblical influences were reflected in it and in the early literature. Scriptural themes were common in the Afrikaans novel, and some Afrikaans verse was influenced in its subject matter and style, notably by Psalms and Ecclesiastes.

In South African English literature, with its natural affinities to the literature of England, biblical influences were less pronounced. They were to be seen chiefly in style and language in the works of the non-Jewish Olive Schreiner (1855–1920), Pauline Smith (1884–1959), and Alan Paton (1903–1988), and the Jewish writer Sarah Gertrude *Millin (1889–1968). Dan *Jacobson (b. 1929) wrote *The Rape of Tamar* (1970), which is an imaginative reworking of a biblical subject.

The Figure of the Jew

While the Hebrews of the Bible were esteemed by the Afrikaners, the Jews of modern times were generally less favorably dealt with by Afrikaans writers, who tended to portray a traditional stereotype of the "bad Jew," shrewd, grasping, and ruthless in his dealings with the simple Afrikaner. However, there were some instances of the "good Jew" as well. Jewish characters were frequently represented as speaking a heavily accented Afrikaans. D.F. Malherbe, Jochem van Bruggen, C.M. Van den Heever, and Abraham Jonker, who focus on the changeover that took place in the 1920s and 1930s from an agricultural to a capitalist mode of production, create Jewish characters with a mixture of grudging admiration and condemnation. J. van Melle and C.J. Langenhoven's characterizations are more sympathetic. Abraham Jonker's non-fictional *Israel die Sondebok* (1940) (translated as *The Scapegoat of History*, 1941), vigorously condemned antisemitism. Etienne Leroux (1922–1989) wrote several novels. In *Sewe Dae by die Silbersteins* (*Seven Days at the Silbersteins*, 1962) Jewish characters are more fully developed. *Een vir Azazel* (1964) contains biblical motifs. *Onse Hymie* (1982) deals sympathetically with a *smous* (itinerant peddler). Generally, in later Afrikaans literature, Jews seldom appear.

After the advent of the State of Israel, a number of descriptive and historical accounts of the Holy Land by Afrikaans writers usually exhibited a sympathetic approach. B. Gemser, who in 1937 had published a collection of Afrikaans translations of Hebrew short stories, issued a Hebrew-Afrikaans grammar in 1953.

In South Africa's English-language literature, in the work of non-Jewish writers, both white and black, Jewish characters invariably appear in three distinct stereotypes, of which the unscrupulous Jewish shopkeeper or businessman is the most common. The wandering Jew appears as the itinerant peddler, a typical occupation for newly arrived Jews from the end of the 19th century. A philo-semitic approach is rarer. Alan Paton's *Too Late the Phalarope* (1953) and the work of the colored (mixed-race) Peter Abrahams, are examples of portrayals of sympathetic Jews. Some writers were viciously antisemitic. A.A. Murray's *Anybody's Spring*, (1959) is a striking example. In later English fiction Jews often appear as leftists, involved in the struggle of the black people for freedom, a perception which reflects the prominent presence of Jews in the struggle for a democracy.

The Jewish Contribution

Jews did not reach South Africa in significant numbers until the second half of the 19th century. Most settled in towns, and Jewish writers mainly used Yiddish and, increasingly, English. The Jewish contribution to the emergent Afrikaans literature came later and was smaller, though not negligible.

Writers in English

FICTION. Among the major figures in South African English fiction a number are Jewish. However, not all identify as being Jewish, nor does their writing always reflect Jewish themes. Except for some specifically Jewish social, political, and communal concerns, Jewish writers, following the general trend, concern themselves with general South African topics, not least with the issue of race and color, understandably so for a people with a history of persecution. The family saga, particularly immigration from eastern Europe and, more latterly, emigration from South Africa, is another recurrent theme. However, there is no "Jewish" school, and it is noteworthy that some Jewish writers display evidence of Jewish self-rejection. Overall, the Jewish contribution to South African literature has been contemporary in setting, realistic in mode, and liberal in political outlook. Jewish characters occur more frequently in the fiction of Jewish writers than in that of gentiles, where the Jew more often than not appears in a minor, and stereotyped, role. Perhaps because of concern with the overshadowing white-black racism, antisemitism is a theme that seldom becomes a central issue.

Louis Cohen, a half-Jewish immigrant from England, was a journalist in Kimberley during the 1870s and wrote scurrilous sketches concerning Jews. Sarah Gertrude Millin, one of the most prolific of South African writers, published 18 novels. For many years she was the outstanding personality in South African creative writing and her works were translated into many languages. Her novel *God's Stepchildren* (1924) was the first major South African work of fiction to deal with miscegenation and the plight of the colored people. *The Coming of the Lord* (1928) deals with the problems of minority groups, including the Jews. In later years her writings tended to reflect more conventional South African views on color.

Nadine *Gordimer's work and Dan Jacobson's early writing revealed an intense awareness of the currents of social and race conflict in South Africa. Gordimer's international standing culminated in the award of the Nobel Prize for literature in 1991. Her 13 novels and many books of short stories are among the finest of South African writing. Apart from in her early work, references to Jews are few, and some, such as in *A Sport of Nature* (1987), are depicted in stereotypical fashion. Dan Jacobson, who immigrated to London, wrote an important novel, *The Beginners* (1966), portraying on a broad canvas the fortunes of a Jewish immigrant family, their adjustment to South African conditions, and emigration. *The Price of Diamonds* (1957) and several masterly short stories, including "The Zulu and the Zeide" (1958), satirize Jewish assumptions about race and morality and interrogate the Jewish stereotypes. His non-fictional writing includes *Heshel's Kingdom* (1999), which deals with a retrieval of Lithuanian roots.

The works of Arthur Markowitz (*Facing North*, 1949; *Market Street*, 1959) and Arthur Segal (*Johannesburg Friday*, 1954) also treat Jewish South African life, as do the sketches in *Millionaires and Tatterdemalions* (1952) by Victor Barwin.

Lewis Sowden in *The Crooked Bluegum* (1955) and Gerald Gordon (1909–1998) in *Let the Day Perish* (1952) deal with social and racial themes. Harry Bloom's *Episode* (1956) is considered a classic on the subject. A pioneer in a related field was Herzl J. Schlosberg who, under the pen name Henry John May, was co-author with J. Grenfell Williams of *I Am Black* (1936), the first South African novel to view life from the black African's standpoint. Wolfe Miller published *Man in the Background* (1958).

Lionel Abrahams (1928–2004), who wrote *The Celibacy of Felix Greenspan* (1977) and *The White Life of Felix Greenspan* (2002), was one of South Africa's most eminent writers, editors, teachers, and critics, having worked with distinction in almost all genres. His great contribution to South African letters was recognized by the award of two honorary doctorates. Among lesser-known figures the following authors are those who have published at least one novel or novella. Only one reference is given in each case. Ronald Segal (*The Tokolosh*), Rhona Stern (*Cactus Land*), Phyllis Altman (*The Law of the Vultures*), Bertha Goudvis (*Little Eden*), Maurice Flior (*Heralds of the East Wind*), Myrna Blumberg (*White Madam*), Sylvester Stein (*Second Class Taxi*), Olga Levinson (*Call Me Master*), Rose Moss (*The Family Reunion*), Rose Zwi (*Another Year in Africa*), Shirley Eskapa (*The Secret Keeper*), Dennis Hirson (*The House Next Door to Africa*), Lynne Freed (*Home Ground*), Eddie Lurie (*The Beginning Is Endless*), Gillian Slovo (*Ties of Blood*), Maja Kriel (*Rings in a Tree*), David Cohen (*People Who Have Stolen from Me*), Tony Eprile (*The Persistence of Memory*), Patricia Schonstein (*The Alchemist*), Mona Berman (*Email from a Jewish Mother*), Johnny Steinberg (*Midlands*), Diane Awerbuck (*Gardening at Night*), and Ken Barris (*Summer Grammar*). The renowned actor Antony Sher, who moved to England, imaginatively and even grotesquely dealt with the subject of immigration in *Middlepost* (1988).

Collections of short stories have come from Bertha Goudvis, Barney Simon (*Jo'burg Sis!*), David Medalie (*The Killing of the Christmas Cows*), Maureen Isaacson, Shirley Eskapa, Maja Kriel, Sandra Braude, Marc Glaser, and Ken Barris. Lilian Simon, Pnina Fenster, and Marcia Leveson are among the numerous others whose stories have appeared in South African literary journals. Humorous fiction was written by, among others, D. Dainow, M. Davidson, S. Levin, and Barbara Ludman.

POETRY. Jews have made substantial contributions to South African poetry. Phillip Stein published *Awakening* (1946) and Victor Barwin's *Europa and Other Poems* appeared in 1947. Lewis Sowden published three volumes of verse, notably *Poems from the Bible* (1960), and Florence Louie Friedman produced original verse and translations from the French and Zulu.

Among the most important voices in South African English poetry were those of Sydney Clouts (1926–1982) (*One Life*) and Ruth Miller (1919–1969) (*The Floating Island*). Jewish aspects were not reflected in their poetry. These do appear, however, in the work of many of South Africa's other Jewish poets. Jacob Stern's *Proverbs* is one such volume. Lionel Abrahams published several volumes of poetry on philosophical and political issues, love, and his home city, Johannesburg. Helen Segal (*Footprint of a Fish*) wrestles with moral, aesthetic, and religious issues. Bernard Levinson in *From Breakfast to Madness* and elsewhere draws on his experience as a psychiatrist. Sinclair Beiles (*Ashes of Experience*) and Roy Joseph Cotton (*Ag Man*) employ surrealism. Riva Rubin (*The Poet-Killers*) writes among other things on biblical themes, and her experiences of Israel where she settled in 1963. Chaim Lewis, an Anglo-Jewish author, wrote poetry on South African and Jewish themes during his long stay in the country. Experience of Israel is also apparent in the work of Jeremy Gordin (*With My Tongue in My Hand*). Among the many others whose work has appeared in their own anthologies or in journals are Robert Berold (*The Door to the River*), David Friedland (*After Image*), Lola Watter (*Images from Africa*), Edgar Bernstein, Elias Pater (Jacob Friedman), Jean Lipkin, Elaine Unterhalter, Mannie Hirsch, Dennis Diamond, Dennis Hirson, Allan Kolski

Horwitz, Rose Friedman, Sheila Basden, Sandra Braude, Roy Blumenthal, Debra Aarons, Marc Glaser, Peter and Mike Kantey, Karen Press, Keith Gottshalk, Steve Shapiro, Terry Sussman, Adam Schwartzman, Barry Feinberg, Ken Barris, Gail Dendy, Cyril Edelstein, Jessie Prisman, and Freda Freeman. Gloria Sandak-Lewin's poetry contains many Jewish themes. Israel Ben Yosef, in collaboration with Douglas Reid Skinner, published *Approximations* (1989), translations into English of contemporary Hebrew poetry.

DRAMA. The Jewish contribution to the performing arts has been highly significant in South Africa. *The Verdict* (1911), written by T.J. Holzberg in collaboration with I.K. Sampson (a non-Jew), was probably the first South African play by a Jew. One of Lewis Sowden's plays, *The Kimberley Train* (1958), brought the color question onto the South African stage, and ran for more than 100 performances. Bertha Goudvis wrote several plays on Jewish themes, *A Husband for Rachel* (1926) being the best known. Sarah Gertrude Millin's novel *Mary Glenn* (1925) was dramatized and staged abroad, as were two adaptations of works by Dan Jacobson, notably his short story "The Zulu and the Zeide," which was staged as a musical on Broadway. The first internationally successful South African musical, *King Kong*, which premièred in Johannesburg in 1959, was, except for the music, a largely Jewish production with African actors, with the book by Harry Bloom, orchestration by Stanley Glasser, set design by Arthur Goldreich, and direction by Leon Gluckman (all of whom subsequently emigrated).

Internationally acclaimed Leonard *Schach was involved in every stage of the development of theater in South Africa between 1925 and 1994. He was the inspiration behind Cape Town's Cockpit Theater, and until his death, divided his time as a director between South Africa and Israel. He published his memoirs in 1996. Other influential directors in the post-war years were Celia Sonnenberg and Rene Ahrenson, who founded "Shakespeare in the Park" at Maynardville in Cape Town and, later, the "Company of Four." Leon Gluckman, one of the country's most creative directors, was particularly interested in fostering black theater. Moira Fine, a major supporter of the Space Theater in Cape Town, also ran Volute Productions. For a lengthy period the doyenne of South African theater actor-directors and managers was Taubie Kushlick. The Johannesburg Children's Theater was the work of Joyce Levinsohn. A co-founder and artistic director of the famous Market Theater, the home of political protest theater in South Africa, was Barney Simon, who was a leading director and facilitator-playwright, stimulating his actors into creative improvisations. One of the most successful of these was the internationally acclaimed *Woza, Albert!* A significant book, tracing the first decade of the existence of this theater, was written by the Johannesburg journalist Pat Schwartz in 1988. The Junction Avenue Theater Company, under the leadership of Malcolm Purkey, applied workshop methods to create *The Fantastical History of a Useless Man* and other important plays, including *Sophiatown*, a recreation of a black township destroyed by government edict. Purkey became artistic director of the Market Theater. Among other Jewish playwrights whose work has been staged in South Africa are Bernard Sachs, Geraldine Aron, Sinclair Beiles, Michael Picardie, David Peemer, Gary Friedman, and Henry Rootenberg. Shawn Slovo produced a film, *A World Apart*, based on the experiences in political detention of her mother, Ruth First. William Kentridge, renowned artist, collaborated with the Handspring Theater Company to produce such innovative works as *Faustus in Africa!* which had worldwide success. In the field of satire and social commentary, Adam Leslie was for many years a household name, as are the half-Jewish and half-Afrikaans Pieter-Dirk Uys and David Kramer.

For over 50 years, one of South Africa's most influential theater and film critics was Percy Baneshik. Percy Tucker wrote his memoirs as the creator of a theater-booking agency. Among promoters of the arts in general in South Africa is Phillip Stein, who was director of the Vita Awards made annually for distinguished work in the performing, literary and visual arts.

AUTOBIOGRAPHY, BIOGRAPHY AND MEMOIRS. Jewish writers have been greatly concerned with the recreation of the past – the general South African past, their own life-stories, and the history of immigrant families. In this field Sarah Gertrude Millin was prominent. She wrote the lives of *Rhodes* (1933), *General Smuts* (1936), and two autobiographical volumes, *The Night is Long* (1941) and *The Measure of My Days* (1955). Nathan Levi, a Dutch-Jewish journalist in Pretoria, produced the first biography of General Smuts in English (1917). The memoirs of Lionel Phillips, *Randlord*, first appeared in 1924. Henry Raymond, Richard Lewinsohn and S. Joel each chose Barney *Barnato as a subject (1897, 1937 and 1958), and Felix Gross wrote *Rhodes of Africa* (1956). Manfred *Nathan wrote a standard biography of the Boer leader, Paul Kruger (1941). The memoirs of Sir David *Harris, South African pioneer, soldier, and politician, appeared in 1930. The explorer Nathaniel *Isaacs was also a literary pioneer with his *Travels and Adventures in Eastern Africa...* with a Sketch of Natal (1836; reissued 1935–36). Sir Harry Graumann published a review of the gold industry in 1936. Enid Alexander wrote the life of her husband, Morris *Alexander (1953), and Morris Kentridge's published reminiscences of his public career. The historian, Phyllis Lewsen, produced an authoritative edition of the letters of the South African statesman John Xavier Merriman (4 vols. 1960–69). Her own memoir is titled *Reverberations* (1996). Bernard Friedman wrote a biography of J.C. Smuts. Bertha *Solomon's memoirs, *Time Remembered,* appeared in 1968. Martin Rubin wrote on Sarah Gertrude Millin. The mercantile Mosenthal family was researched by D. Fleischer and A. Caccia. Isie Maisels, a leading advocate in human rights cases, wrote his memoirs. Eric Rosenthal recaptures the spirit of South Africa in the 20th century. Lola Watter evokes the literary and artistic life, particularly of Johannesburg. In *Strange Odyssey* (1952) Betty Misheiker wrote of an immigrant group, and Geoff Sifrin's *To Gershn* (1995) is a recreation of his widely spread family from their days in eastern Europe. Richard Mendelsohn wrote on *Sammy Marks: The Uncrowned King of the Transvaal* (1991). Phyllis Jowell documented the life of her father-in-law, a key figure in Namaqualand, in *Joe Jowell of Namaqualand* (1994) and, with Adrienne Folb a pictorial history of the Jews of Namaqualand. In 2000 Chief Rabbi Cyril Harris recorded highlights of his ministry. Others in the autobiographical field include Lyndall Gordon, eminent scholar and biographer who immigrated to England and wrote a memoir of life in Cape Town during the 1950s titled *Shared Lives* (1992). Helen *Suzman, long-time sole representative in parliament of the Progressive Party under the Apartheid government, wrote memoirs, as did Jack Penn, Ali Bacher, David Susman, Pauline Podbrey, Hilda Bernstein, Harold and AnnMarie Wolpe, Ben Turok, Benjamin Pogrund, Norma Kitson, Ronald Segal, Lionel (Rusty) Bernstein, Baruch Hirson, Joel Joffe, Rudy Frankel, Ronnie Kasrils, and Alfred Honikman, former mayor of Cape Town. Benjamin Pogrund also wrote on activist Robert Sobukwe and Paul Clingman on the Hon. A.E. Abrahamson. Ruth First and Albie Sachs wrote of their experiences in an apartheid prison. Joe *Slovo, the renowned South African communist, recorded his life; and Mendel Kaplan, industrialist, former chairperson of the Board of Governors of the Jewish Agency, and later chairman of the World Jewish Congress produced several books chronicling Jewish immigration and the Jewish contribution to the economic development of the country. Julian Roup, in *Boerejood* (2004), contributed a different slant with the point of view of the sometimes intermarried community of Afrikaner-Jews.

Included in the memoirs of survivors of the Holocaust are those of Levi Shalit, *Beyond Dachau* (1980), Henia Brazg, *Passport to Life* (1981), Maja Abramowitch's *To Forgive... But Not Forget* (2002), and Madeleine Heitner's *Breaking through Buttonholes* (2004). Gwynne Schrire edited a selection of the memories of Cape Town Holocaust survivors, *In Sacred Memory* (1995).

OTHER FIELDS. In belles lettres, Jewish writers included Joseph Sachs (*Beauty and the Jews*, 1937; *The Jewish Genius*, 1939); Wulf Sachs (*Black Hamlet*, 1937; later published as *Black Anger*); George Sacks (*The Intelligent Man's Guide to Jew-baiting*, 1935); and Adèle Lezard (*Gold Blast*, 1936). Bernard Sachs wrote a miscellaneous collection of essays on *Personalities and Places* (2 vols., 1959–65). Contributions to literary criticism were also made by Edward Davis, Phillip Segal, and many others not collected in volume form.

NON-FICTION. Non-fictional literary prose of a very high order, in the form of scholarly, journalistic, historiographical, biographical, and polemical works, has been produced by many distinguished Jewish South Africans. Not only have books and studies appeared, but there have been innumerable contributions to newspapers and journals and important editorships, not only in the Jewish field but also in the general world of scholarship and letters. For Jewish scholarship and historiography, the influential *Jewish Affairs* (started in 1941 under the editorship of Edgar Bernstein, and for 16 years under the editorship of Amelia Levy, once secretary of the Society of Jews and Christians) is crucial. The Isaac and Jessie Kaplan Center for Jewish Studies and Research at the University of Cape Town currently produces outstanding work in this field.

Sidney Mendelssohn compiled a monumental *South African Bibliography* (1910) and wrote *Jewish Pioneers of South Africa* (1912). Bernard Sachs published several volumes of autobiographical, political, and other essays, as well as a study of H.C. Bosman, writer of Afrikaans extraction connected with the South African Jewish community in the 1930s and 1940s. He has been the subject of a biography by Valerie Rosenberg, *Sunflower to the Sun*. Rosenberg and Lionel Abrahams edited several volumes of his writing, which, until recent scholarly updating, have been authoritative. Edgar Bernstein published a collection of essays titled *My Judaism, My Jews*, while Neil Hirschson has published some polemical work on Jew-hatred and Shakespeare. Michael Wade and Steven Clingman published major studies of the novels of Nadine Gordimer. *The Cape Town Intellectuals – Ruth Schechter and her Circle, 1907–1934* (2001) was written by Baruch Hirson, a political activist who immigrated to England. Reuben Musiker has published six books and 150 articles in the field of South African bibliography. Among the many Jewish scholars directly engaged in academic work on South African Jewish historiography and writing are Louis Herrman, who wrote *A History of the Jews in South Africa from the Earliest Times to 1895* (1935), and Gustav Saron and Louis Hotz, who were the editors of the influential *The Jews in South Africa: A History* (1955). Marcus Arkin edited *South African Jewry: A Contemporary Survey* in 1984. Among several other surveys of the South African Jewish community are those of L. Feldberg, N. Berger, N.D. Hoffman, D.L. Sowden, M. Konvisser, T. Hoffman, and A. Fischer. Marcia Gitlin's *The Vision Amazing* (1950) and the work of the prominent scholar now living in Israel, Gideon Shimoni (*Jews and Zionism*, 1980), analyze the strong bonds between the South African community and Israel. R. Musiker and J. Sherman edited *Waters out of the Well*, a collection of articles and essays on Jewish themes. *Memories, Realities and Dreams*, with international as well as local contributions, edited by Milton Shain and Richard Mendelsohn, is an important documentation of more recent thinking responses to and construction of a new identity in the light of political change in South Africa. In recent years a team of volunteers working for the South African Friends of Beth Hatefutsoth has been producing handsome illustrated books as part of its ongoing record of the dwindling Jewish country communities. Joseph Sherman made available in translation much of the neglected Yiddish writing from South African authors in *From a Land Far Off* (1987). Milton Shain produced a great deal of ongoing research on the South African Jewish community and a seminal work, *The Roots of Anti-semitism in South Africa* (1994). Jocelyn Hellig, who wrote *The Holocaust and AntiSemitism* (2003), lectured and published on issues such as antisemitism and comparative religion. Marcia Leveson published on the image of the Jew, including *People of the Book: The Image of the Jew in South African Fiction 1880–1992* (1996). Immanuel Suttner's collection of interviews with South African Jewish activists, *Cutting through the Mountain* (1997), is an important repository of research material. A.A. Dubb, Shirley Kossick, John Simon, Gwynne Schrire, David Saks, Franz Auerbach, Rose Norwich, and a host of other scholars published original research into the many facets of the wide Jewish contribution to the development of South Africa. Claudia Braude published a collection of contemporary Jewish writing in 2001. Veronica Belling compiled a *Bibliography of South African Jewry* (1997).

In other fields, Martin Orkin published *Shakespeare against Apartheid* (1987) and Clive Chipkin *Johannesburg Style* (1993). Esme Berman, Steven Sack, Neville Dubow, and Mona Berman made significant contributions in the field of art and art history. Mona de Beer wrote on an aspect of Cape urban history, Joel Mervis on South African newspapers, Ellison Kahn on law, Rod Suskin and Alexandra Levin on esoteric matters, and Raymond Ackerman on his life and business. Arnold Benjamin was a long-serving journalist on *The Star* and produced a book on graffiti. Elaine Katz wrote on trade unions and disease in the South African gold mines. Adam Levin wrote on travel in Africa, and Matthew Krouse, assisted by Kim Berman, co-edited a book on gay and lesbian writing. Shirli Gilbert wrote on South African music and music in the Holocaust. Numerous handsome cookbooks have been published by Jewish writers, and Geraldine Mitton and Linda Friedland publish on health issues. *The Jewish Report* has since 1998 been a popular national Jewish weekly newspaper, and several well-known Jewish journalists are active in the media world.

Writers in Afrikaans

A significant contribution to Afrikaans literature was made in the early 19th century by a Dutch Jewish convert to Christianity, Joseph Suasso de Lima (1791–1858). In 1844 he wrote the first booklet of its kind on the subject, in which he championed the developing Afrikaans language. He also wrote (in Dutch) the first history of the Cape of Good Hope (1823) and a number of other works. Another convert to Christianity, Jan Lion Cachet (d. 1912), who came from Holland in 1861, published *Sewe Duiwels en wat hulle gedoen het* ("Seven Devils and What They Did"). Written in serial form, it appeared in one volume in 1907. There are several Jewish characters, chiefly unsympathetically drawn. Cachet ranks as one of the founders of literary Afrikaans. Sarah Goldblatt (d. 1975), a writer of Afrikaans children's books and short stories, was the literary executrix of C.J. Langenhoven (1873–1932), a foremost Afrikaans writer. Another Jewish pioneer of Afrikaans literature, best known for his stories and sketches of animal life, was J.M. Friedenthal (1886–1959).

In later years, South African-born Olga Kirsch, who settled in Israel in 1948, published highly acclaimed collections of Afrikaans verse, including *Die Soeklig* ("The Searchlight," 1944), dealing with racial issues, *Geil Gebied* (Fertile Territory 1976) and four other collections which dealt with general Jewish and Israeli themes. Peter Blum, an immigrant, won an Afrikaans literary prize for his first collection of poems (1955).

In Judaic studies, links between Hebrew and Afrikaans were established by Rabbi Moses Romm, in his translations of the Jewish prayer book and the *Ethics of the Fathers*; and by Roman B. Egert, who published an Afrikaans version of the *Haggadah* (1943). Israel ben Yosef wrote *Nofim Reḥokim.* ("Verre Landskappe"), translations of Afrikaans poems into Hebrew, in collaboration with S.J. Pretorius (1985), and *Olyfwoestyn. Poësie uit Verre Lande.* ("Poems from Far-off Lands," 1987), Hebrew poems translated into Afrikaans in collaboration with Johan Steyn. The Yiddish writer Jacob Mordecai Sherman was extremely interested in Afrikaans, publishing several essays on its literature.

Writers in Yiddish

From 1881 onward, the influx of Yiddish-speaking Jewish immigrants enormously increased the size of the existing South African Jewish population. And of these many laid the foundations for the development of an indigenous South African Yiddish literature.

YIDDISH NEWSPAPERS AND JOURNALS. The pioneer of Yiddish journalism in South Africa was the professional belletrist, Nehemiah Dov Ber Hoffmann (1860–1928), who in 1889 brought the first Hebrew-Yiddish typeface to the land. Moving from the Cape to the Transvaal in 1890, he founded South Africa's first Yiddish weekly, *Der Afrikaner Israelit*, which lasted six months. Returning to the Cape, Hoffmann started a second weekly – Cape Town's first – titled *Ha-Or*, which lasted from April 1895 to July 1897. David Goldblatt's weekly, *Der Yiddisher Advokat*, which appeared regularly from 1904 until 1924, was recognized by the government as an official newspaper. Hoffmann's volume of memoirs, *Sefer Ha-zikhroynes* (1916) was the first full-length Yiddish book to be printed in South Africa. It describes the author's experiences in Europe, America (in Hebrew), and Africa. He was the first writer to record the eastern European immigrant response to life in South Africa. His account of the hardships experienced by the traveling Jewish *smous* was the first appearance in South African Yiddish literature of what was to become one of its major themes. His *Yearbook* of 1920 contains important information about country communities.

Yiddish weekly newspapers before World War II were short-lived. In Johannesburg between 1920 and 1948, six books of short stories and essays and four volumes of poetry were published. Solomon Fogelson founded a Yiddish weekly, *Der Afrikaner*, in Johannesburg in 1911, and at least three Yiddish periodicals were being published at the same time. Fogelson's newspaper survived for over 20 years until it was amalgamated with the *Afrikaner Idishe Tsaytung* in 1933, directed by Boris Gershman. After his death in 1953, the newspaper was bought by Levi Shalit in partnership with Shmarya Levin; it closed in 1983. At its peak, it had a weekly readership of 3,000 and carried regular contributions from distinguished overseas writers. Shalit exerted a powerful influence on local Yiddish writing through his finely wrought prose.

There were many short-lived journals, the most robust of which came from socialist groups. Between 1912 and 1939 organizations such as the *Gezerd* [*Gezelshaft far Erdarbet*], *Po'alei Zion*, and the *Yiddisher Arbeter Klub* produced several periodicals. The literary journal that did most to stimulate local creative writing at this time was *Dorem Afrike*, the organ of the *Yiddisher Literarisher Farayn*, which appeared first in nine issues between 1922 and 1923 and reappeared as a monthly from July 1928 to January 1931.

At a national conference called in Johannesburg in May 1947, Di Dorem Afrikaner Yiddishe Kultur Federatzie was established, and its monthly organ, a new *Dorem Afrike*, the first issue of which appeared in September 1948, was edited by Melekh Bakalczuk-Felin. In 1954 the editorship passed to David Wolpe, who ran the journal until 1970 and was succeeded by a committee chaired by Zalman Levy. It closed in 1991.

In 1949, Pacific Press and its ancillary, Kayor Publishers, were founded by Nathan Berger and Joseph Borwein. Between them, Kayor and the *Kultur Federatzie* inaugurated the most productive era in local Yiddish publishing. South Africa became an important center of Yiddish creativity. From 1949 to 1962, Kayor, in association with the *Kultur Federatzie*, published six collections of essays and short stories, six volumes of poetry and one novel, together with all the journalism and most of the Yiddish and Hebrew occasional publications in South Africa.

The horrors of the Holocaust were movingly chronicled by two survivors, Levi Shalit (b. 1916) and A. Peretz, who lived in South Africa before they emigrated to Israel.

THEMES AND AUTHORS IN SOUTH AFRICAN YIDDISH PROSE. A normative figure in early South African Jewish life was the old bachelor, who stayed single because he could not afford to bring over a bride from the Old Home. For some, brides were sent out from Lithuania. Married men often could not afford to bring their families to join them. There was also considerable intermarriage with Afrikaans, black, and colored women in country districts. Sensitively treated, all these matrimonial complexities, common in the immigrant experience, became recurring subject matter. Many immigrant Jews went to work in the exploitative stores-cum-eating-houses which the mining companies granted by concession to entrepreneurs, mostly Jewish themselves. There they lived solitary lives, working long hours in unhygienic conditions. To describe these places and those who worked in them, Yiddish speakers created two neologisms which entered the language as unique South Africanisms: *kaffireater*, the place, from the pejorative English title "kaffir eating-house"; and *kaffireatnik*, which became one of the stock figures of South African Yiddish literature. The problem of adaptation and the ensuing conflict between traditional ways of Jewish life and the demands of accommodation are understandably another chief focus of the writing. The love-hate relationship between Afrikaners and Jews recurs in different forms, but the alienating and bitter gulf between black and white most profoundly touches sensitive observers.

The earliest, most important figures in South African Yiddish literature were Hyman Polsky (1871–1944), Morris Hoffman (1885–1940), and Jacob Mordecai Sherman (1885–1958). Polsky, a journalist on Fogelson's Yiddish weekly, assumed its editorship in 1933 and remained its chief contributor. A selection of his best stories was published in Warsaw under the title *In Afrike* in 1939, republished in 1952. Morris Hoffman spent most of his life as a shopkeeper in the Little Karoo and published a major anthology of poetry, *Woglungsklangen* ("Songs of a Wanderer"), in Warsaw in 1935. After his death, his widow published a selection of his stories titled *Unter Afrikaner Zun* ("Under the African Sun") in 1951. Apart from contributing extensively to all the country's Yiddish publications and editing several periodicals himself, Sherman worked in almost all literary genres and produced South Africa's first Yiddish novel, *Land fun Gold un Zunshayn* ("Land of Gold and Sunshine"). His fiction, which was often autobiographical, depicted the relationships in farming communities between Afrikaner and Jew and between black and white. He also concentrated on the problem of marriages outside the faith.

Black-white relations, and the hardships of black people, were powerfully drawn by Richard Feldman (1917–1968), prominent in Transvaal labor movements. His volume of short stories, *Shvarts un Vays*, was published in South Africa in 1934, and republished in America 20 years later.

Der Regn hot Farshpetigt ("The Rains Came Late"), short stories by Nehemiah Levinsky (1901–1957), showed insight and compassion concerning the interrelationships between Jews, blacks and coloreds, and a deep understanding of African tribal customs. The most prolific Yiddish humorist was Hersh Shisler (1903–1978). Hyman Ehrlich published a book of satirical sketches in 1950, titled *Ot Azoy* ("That's the Way"), and a book of childhood reminiscences, *Dankere*, in 1956. A gifted short-story writer was Samuel Leibowitz (1912–1976), a regular contributor to all the local Yiddish periodicals. Other talented writers were Leibl Yudaken (1904–1989); Wolf Rybko (1896–1955), who wrote in Hebrew and Yiddish; and Chaim Sacks, who published in 1969 a series of vignettes of life in his father's rabbinical household in Poland titled *S'Iz Geven a Mol* ("Once Upon a Time").

Mendel Tabatznik (1894–1976) produced South Africa's second Yiddish novel, *Kalman Bulan*, a family saga which shows a realistic appreciation of the inexorable processes of assimilation. His stories, one-act plays, two volumes of memoirs and two volumes of poems sensitively examine all aspects of Jewish life in South Africa. Memoirs have always been a chief feature of all Yiddish literature, and 15 volumes have appeared in South Africa. Some writers never really adjusted to life in the African environment and looked back with sadness to the world left behind in eastern Europe, forever obliterated by the Holocaust.

Foremost among the writers of non-fiction was the polemicist and researcher, Leibl Feldman (1896–1975), a passionately committed Yiddishist with strong historicist leanings, who became the earliest chronicler of South African Jewish life. He published five books of history, providing indispensable documentation of early Jewish settlement in South Africa, particularly in Oudtshoorn and Johannesburg. He was also interested in the history of the Indians in South Africa and wrote a controversial essay of impressions after visits to Israel. David Wolpe (b. 1908) produced two volumes of literary criticism and a substantial book of short stories, and in 1997 and 2002 two volumes of his autobiography. Published in Argentina under the series title *Musterwerk fun der Yidisher Literatur* ("An Outline of Yiddish Literature"), volume 50 was dedicated to South African Yiddish Literature: *Dorem-afrikanish – fragmentn fun forsharbrtn tzu der kharakteristik un zikhrones* ("South African – Fragments of Research Works, Literature and Memoirs," 1971).

SOUTH AFRICAN YIDDISH POETRY. Yiddish in South Africa found its most profound expression in poetry. Here women made an impressive contribution. Anthologies came from Chaya Fedler (d. 1953), Rachiel Levin-Brainin (d. 1980), and Leah Benson-Rink. Sarah Eisen (d. 1981) wrote poetry in both Yiddish and Hebrew. Her subjects ranged from memories of eastern Europe to impressions of Israel and pictures of African life. Hyman Ehrlich (1908–1981) wrote children's verses before moving to more somber lyrics of two later volumes.

Outstanding among the introspective lyricists were Michael Ben Moshe (1911–1983) and David Fram (1903–1988). While Ben Moshe explored the anguish of personal pain in anthologies like *Opris*, Fram changed his style from the lyrics that had established his reputation in Lithuania to incorporate some of the vibrancy of tribal Africa. Fram's epics, published in 1947–1948, were *Efsher* ("Perhaps") and *Dos Letste Kapittel* ("The Last Chapter"). His last anthology, *A Shwalb Oifn Dakh* ("A Swallow on the Roof"), appeared in 1983. South African Yiddish verse continued to achieve international distinction in the work of David Wolpe, whose substantial modernist anthology, *A Wolkn un a Weg* ("A Cloud and a Way," 1978), was awarded the Itzik Manger Prize for Yiddish Literature in Jerusalem in 1983. Among other volumes *Krikveg, lider – poemes* ("The Way Back – Poems") appeared in 1991 and *Iber meine vegn, lider, poemes, dertzaylungen* ("Above My Ways, Poems and Stories") in 2002.

YIDDISH DRAMA IN SOUTH AFRICA. Yiddish plays, mainly written by overseas playwrights, were staged in South Africa from 1895. Most of the local work produced between 1916 and 1954 was light entertainment, performed from typescript, sometimes appearing in ephemeral local journals. Only Hirsch Brill (1891–1925) attempted to deal with serious dramatic themes and published two collections. Steadily declining communal interest and commercial competition slowly forced all Yiddish theater from South Africa's boards.

There is growing interest in Yiddish literature and in keeping Yiddish alive as a spoken language in South Africa. In 1983 the University of the Witwatersrand established a Yiddish library.

Hebrew

The most remarkable South African achievement in Hebrew came from Judah Leib *Landau, who arrived to assume a rabbinical position in South Africa in 1903. Between 1884 and 1923, he published overseas eight five-act epic dramas on mainly historical themes. Two were staged in Johannesburg. Only one dealt with African issues, the rest were concerned with the problems of westernization and assimilation, which he treated in the many essays he contributed on South African Jews during the period when he was chief rabbi of Johannesburg. A volume of his poetry was published in Warsaw. N. Levinsky and Z.A. Lison published in Israel fiction concerning South African life.

S. Aisen, M. Hoffman, and I. Idelson also published poetry in Israel. B. Beikenstadt published an anthology of translations from the Hebrew and Yiddish in 1930. I. Ben Yosef's *Links of Silence* was translated by Rachelle Mann and appeared in Tel Aviv in 1983. Azila Talit Reisenberger published poetry in both English and Hebrew. Her volume *Maḥazor Ahavah* ("Cycles of Love," 2002) appeared in Israel, as did her volume of short stories, *Mi-Po ad Kaf ha-Tikvah ha-Tovah* ("From Here until the Cape of Good Hope," 2004). As well she wrote plays and published on Jewish identity in South Africa.

In the 1930s Jack Rubik founded a monthly Hebrew newspaper, *Barkai*, and produced it regularly until his death in 1978. The newspaper died with him. A monthly Hebrew supplement, the *Musaf Ivrit,* to the weekly *Zionist Record* ran from the 1960s and closed in 1987.

BIBLIOGRAPHY: D. Sowden, *The Jew in South Africa* (1945); idem, *South African Jewry* (1965), 119–39; South African Jewish Board of Deputies, *Books and Writers* (1948); E. Bernstein, in: *South African Jewish Yearbook* (1959/60), 21–26; idem, in: JBA, 18 (1960/61), 54–61; idem, in: *Jewish Affairs*, 15, no. 5 (1960), 27–32; A. Coetzee, ibid., 38–41 (Afrikaans); H.D.A. du Toit, ibid., 21, no. 4 (1966), 16–20; S. Liptzin, ibid., 23 no. 9 (1968), 28–32; S.I. Mocke, ibid., 6, no. 6 (1951), 7–10 (Afrikaans); R. Pheiffer, in: *Die Burger* (March 11 and 12, 1970). **ADD. BIBLIOGRAPHY:** C.N. Van der Merwe, *Breaking Barriers: Stereotypes and Changing of Values in Afrikaans Writing 1875–1990* (1994); M. Leveson, *People of the Book: Images of the Jew in South African English Fiction 1880–1992* (1996); V. Belling, *Bibliography of South African Jewry* (1997).

[Louis Hotz, Dora Leah Sowden, and Joseph Sherman / Marcia Leveson (2nd ed.)]

SOUTHAMPTON, major port in S. England. Its small medieval community was expelled in 1236 (Runceval, a house owned by the Jewish financier, Benedict of Winchester, was excavated in the 1960s). During the 16th century, Marrano agents boarded ships docking at Southampton to inform Marrano refugees from Portugal whether it was safe for them to proceed to their destination in Flanders. The modern community dates from 1833, though individual Jews lived in Southampton in the late 18th century and some were navy agents during the Napoleonic Wars. A split in the early congregation was settled soon after the appointment of Nathan Marcus *Adler as chief rabbi of Anglo-Jewry in 1844. Later Southampton was the port largely used by Jews traveling to and from South Africa. In 1969 the Jewish population numbered 150, out of a general population of 210,000. In the mid-1990s the Jewish population numbered approximately 105. According to the 2001 British census, there were 293 declared Jews in Southampton. It had an Orthodox synagogue. The University of Southampton has emerged as one of the major academic centers of Jewish history in Britain and contains the Parkes Library, which holds a number of important collections of Anglo-Jewish material.

BIBLIOGRAPHY: C. Roth, *The Rise of Provincial Jewry* (1950), 100; JYB; Roth, England, index.

[Vivian David Lipman / William D. Rubinstein (2nd ed.)]

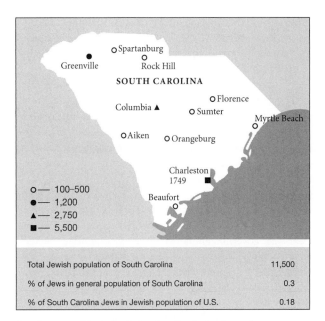

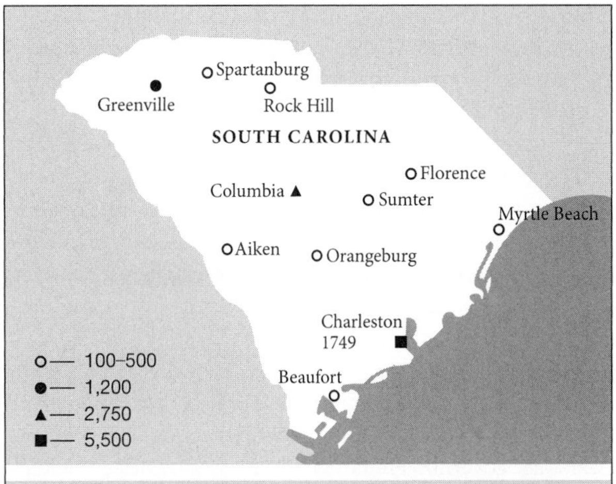

Total Jewish population of South Carolina	11,500
% of Jews in general population of South Carolina	0.3
% of South Carolina Jews in Jewish population of U.S.	0.18

Jewish communities in South Carolina. Population figures for 2001.

SOUTH CAROLINA, southeastern state of the United States, bordering the Atlantic Ocean and the states of North Carolina and Georgia. Jews arrived in the British colony of Carolina in the early days of European settlement. A new outpost in the mercantile traffic of the Atlantic basin, Carolina offered economic opportunities and a degree of religious tolerance remarkable for the time. The colony's Fundamental Constitutions of 1669, drafted by philosopher and physician John Locke, who was secretary to one of the eight Lords Proprietors, granted freedom of worship to "Jews, Heathens, and other Dissenters from the purity of the Christian Religion." Although the colonial assembly never endorsed the provision, British *Charleston became known as a place where people of all faiths – except Catholics – could do business and practice their religion without interference. In 1696, Jews in Charleston allied with French Protestants to safeguard their rights to trade, and the next year to secure citizenship.

Most of Carolina's first Jewish settlers traced their roots to Spain or Portugal. Expelled during the Inquisition at the end of the 15th century, the Sephardim dispersed around the globe and established themselves in capitals and port cities in northern Europe, the Mediterranean, and the West Indies. In 1749, Charleston's Jewish community chartered Kahal Kadosh Beth Elohim – one of the first five Jewish congregations in America. Like her sister synagogues in New York, Newport, Savannah, and Philadelphia, Beth Elohim was Sephardi in ritual and practice. Charleston's congregation remained so for two generations after the Revolutionary War, though by then the majority of South Carolina Jews were Ashkenazi, hailing from central or eastern Europe.

Following the Revolutionary War, South Carolina's Jewish population surged. When Columbia became the state capital in 1786, seven Jewish men from Charleston were among the first to buy town lots. Jews in Georgetown, Beaufort, and Camden belonged to the business and civic elites. By 1800, Charleston was home to the largest, wealthiest, and most cultured Jewish community in North America – upwards of five hundred individuals, or one-fifth of all Jews in the nation.

Carolina's Jews pursued the same goals as their white neighbors. Those who could afford it owned slaves. The affluent lived in finely furnished houses and traveled abroad. Many Ashkenazim adopted traditional Sephardi practices and assumed an aristocratic view of themselves as "earliest to arrive."

Charleston's highly acculturated Jewish community produced the first movement to reform Judaism in America. In 1824, a group of young Jewish men, mostly American-born, petitioned the governing body of Kahal Kadosh Beth Elohim for shorter services, a sermon preached on the Sabbath, and prayers in English. Rebuffed in their efforts, the dissidents drafted a constitution and established the Reformed Society of Israelites. For eight years the reformers worshiped separately, then returned to the traditional congregation. But in 1840 the reform faction prevailed. With the blessing of Beth Elohim's popular minister, Gustavus Poznanski, a proposal to install an organ in the new synagogue – a Greek revival temple that replaced the original structure, which had burned in the great fire of 1838 – was adopted by a narrow margin. The traditionalists seceded and formed Shearit Israel (Remnant of Israel), with its own burying ground adjacent to Beth Elohim's Coming Street cemetery. A brick wall separated the dead of the two congregations.

While schism in Beth Elohim divided traditionalists and reformers, a new group of immigrants introduced another brand of orthodoxy to Charleston. People of modest means – peddlers, artisans, metalworkers, bakers – the newcomers gave the city's Jewish population a more foreign appearance than before. As early as 1852, these eastern European Jews began meeting under the leadership of Rabbi Hirsch Zvi Levine, recently arrived from Poland. In 1855, they formally organized as Berith Shalome (now Brith Sholom) or "Covenant of Peace," the first Ashkenazi congregation in South Carolina and one of the first in the South.

As the southern states began seceding from the Union in 1860 and 1861, Jews rallied to the Confederate cause. Thousands of Jewish men served in the southern armies, while Jewish women, in accord with their gentile sisters, threw themselves into the war effort, sewing uniforms, knitting socks, rolling bandages, preparing boxes of clothes and provisions, and working in hospitals to care for the sick and wounded.

After the war, during the period of Reconstruction, some South Carolinians of Jewish descent, including the notorious "scalawag" governor, Franklin J. Moses, Jr., supported the Radical Republicans' drive to build a new society. However, most backed the Redeemers' crusade to restore white rule. Jewish women such as Octavia Harby Moses and Phoebe Yates Levy Pember were prominent in memorializing the "Lost Cause." In the shared experience of defeat, Jewish Confederates demonstrated their fierce sense of belonging.

Beginning in the 1880s, East European migration to America brought about a dramatic increase in the nation's Jewish population. Charleston's Jewish population, which had remained flat for decades at around 700, doubled between 1905 and 1912. The neighborhood where the "greenhorns" settled was called "Little Jerusalem." Immigrant men commonly started out as peddlers, then established small businesses. At one time some 40 stores on upper King Street were closed on Saturday, in observance of the Jewish Sabbath. The men held prayer services above stores. The women kept kosher homes. They trained their African American help to make potato *kugel* and *gefilte* fish, and they learned, in turn, to fix fried chicken and okra gumbo.

By World War I, Jewish communities in the midlands and upcountry had grown large enough to support synagogues. Meanwhile, some country clubs, fraternities, and sororities barred Jews, who responded by forming their own social groups and athletic teams modeled on the ones that kept them out. These organizations helped unify Jews around an ethnic identity without regard to place of birth, date of arrival in America, and degree of observance.

The revival of the Ku Klux Klan disturbed southern Jews' sense of well-being. In the heyday of Jim Crow, however, the primary targets of discrimination were blacks. Jews generally found themselves on the safe side of the racial divide. They demonstrated their loyalty to country and region in patriotic parades and party politics. When the United States entered World War II, Jewish southerners joined in the mobilization to fight the Japanese and Nazi foes.

As a result of the Holocaust in Europe, America's place in world Jewry changed radically. Now more than half of all Jewish people were living in the United States. In many ways, South Carolina was a microcosm of the nation. The class of Jewish merchants had begat a generation of lawyers, doctors, accountants, and college teachers, who shifted the Jewish economic niche away from retail business. With the rest of the white American mainstream, urban Jews abandoned the old neighborhoods and moved to the suburbs – a migration that coincided with the first stirrings of the civil rights movement and the rise of Conservative Judaism.

By the end of 20th century, Jewish populations in most small towns across the South had dwindled, while suburban and resort congregations were continuing to grow. South Carolina's Jews remained prominent in political life. Solomon Blatt, of Barnwell, served for 30 years in the state legislature, ending his final term as Speaker of the House in 1970. Numerous other Jewish lawmakers have filled seats in both houses, and, since World War II, more than a dozen Jews have been elected as mayors of South Carolina towns and cities.

South Carolina mirrors the nation in the drift toward more traditional observance – a trend in all divisions of Judaism. The Addlestone Hebrew Academy in Charleston and Lubavitcher Chabads in Myrtle Beach and Columbia teach Hebrew and religious studies in day schools to an increasingly diverse student population that includes newcomers from other parts of America, and from Russia and the Middle East as well.

BIBLIOGRAPHY: S. Breibart, *Explorations in Charleston's Jewish History* (2005); B.A. Elzas, *The Jews of South Carolina, From the Earliest Times to the Present Day* (1905, reprint, 1972); "The Diary of Joseph Lyons (1833–35)," a new and unabridged transcript edited, annotated, and introduced by M. Ferrara, H. Greene, D. Rosengarten, and S. Wyssen, in: *American Jewish History*, 91:3 (Sept. 2003); B. Gergel and R. Gergel, *In Pursuit of the Tree of Life: A History of the Early Jews of Columbia and the Tree of Life Congregation* (1996); J.S. Gurock, *Orthodoxy in Charleston: Brith Sholom Beth Israel & American Jewish History* (2004); J.W. Hagy, *This Happy Land: The Jews of Colonial and Antebellum Charleston* (1993); Jewish Heritage Collection. Special Collections, College of Charleston Library, Charleston, South Carolina. For excerpts from the JHC oral history archives, see www.cofc.edu/~jhc; C. Reznikoff and U.Z. Engelman, *The Jews of Charleston: A History of an American Jewish Community* (1950); R.N. Rosen, *The Jewish Confederates* (2000); T. Rosengarten and D. Rosengarten (eds.), *A Portion of the People: Three Hundred Years of Southern Jewish Life* (2002). See on-line version of the exhibition "A Portion of the People" at www.lib.unc.edu/apop.

[Dale Rosengarten (2nd ed.)]

SOUTH DAKOTA, state in the upper Midwest sector of the United States; general population 756,000 (2001) with approximately 300 Jews. As a result of the gold rush, Jews settled in the Dakota territory as early as 1876. Two utopian agricultural communities, Cremieux and Bethlehem Yehudah, were founded in 1882 by the *Am Olam. They were defunct by 1885. Other Jewish homesteaders, particularly in the western part of the state stayed on the land longer. Movement to towns and to commercial activity was common.

There were once congregations in Deadwood, Lead, Sioux Falls, Aberdeen, and at Ellsworth Air Force Base in Rapid City. Today there are two: Mt. Zion in Sioux Falls and the newer Synagogue of the Hills in Rapid City, both

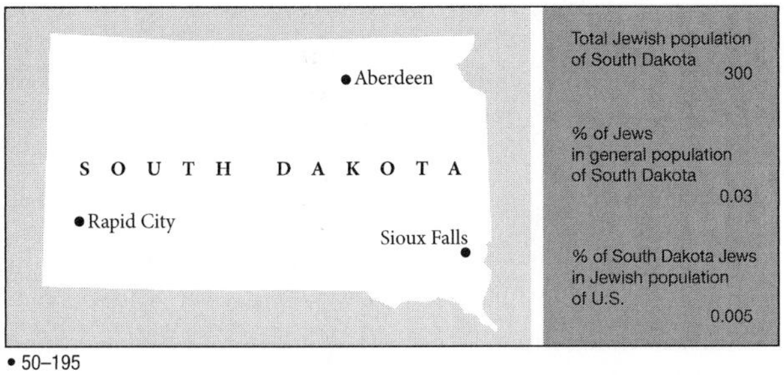

Jewish communities in South Dakota. Population figures for 2001.

served by student rabbis. Blanche Colman, a native of Deadwood, became the first woman to practice law in the state and worked as legal counsel for the Homestake Mining Company. She is buried, along with her family and other Jewish gold seekers, in the "Hebrew Hill" section of the communal Mt. Moriah Cemetery, where Wild Bill Hickock and Calamity Jane are also interred. Other noteworthy South Dakota Jews include agronomist Sam Bober, who in the 1920s and 1930s developed rust resistant strains of wheat and the Adelstein family of Rapid City whose Northwestern Engineering Company is one of the largest private civil engineering firms in America.

[Linda M. Schloff (2nd ed.)]

SOUTH WEST AFRICA (Namibia). Jewish connections with the territory were established even before its conquest by the Germans when it became a German colony. During the middle of the 19th century the *De Pass brothers, Jewish merchants from Cape Town, established trading posts on the Namaqualand coast, and in 1861 started the Pomona Copper Company. German Jews were allowed much more scope in the territory after its establishment as a colony. Carl *Fuerstenberg, a German Jewish banker, was responsible, as head of the Berliner Handellgesellschaft, for the development of the diamond industry, and he also organized the construction of the railway line from Luderitz Bay to Kubub. Emil *Rathenau created the German South West African Mining Syndicate and established a research company in 1907 for the study of irrigation problems. Walther *Rathenau was one of the two experts sent by Kaiser Wilhelm II to report on administrative reforms. The number of Jews in South West Africa under German rule was no more than about 100, most of them in Swakopmund. During the campaign of 1915, which ended in the conquest of the territory by South African forces, the men were interned and their families sent to Windhoek. After South Africa was granted a mandate over it by the League of Nations after World War I, however, the Jewish population increased, and in 1965 there were 400–500 Jews in a total white population of about 68,000, of whom the overwhelming majority lived in Windhoek, which has a Hebrew congregation (dating from 1917), a synagogue (completed in 1925), a *talmud torah*, a communal hall, named after Simon (Sam) *Cohen, the most prominent Jew and benefactor of the community, an active Zionist movement supported by generous contributions, and the only Jewish minister in the territory. The only other community, at Keetmanshoop, which had about 12 families, a congregation (founded in 1910), and a synagogue, ceased to exist when the number of Jewish families was reduced to five and their *sifrei torah* were sent to Windhoek. In addition, there are a few families in Swakopmund and Walvis Bay. L. Kerby served as town clerk of Windhoek for many years, and was responsible for the layout and upkeep of the beautiful cemetery which is one of the showpieces of Windhoek.

Jack Louis Levinson, the husband of Olga *Levinson, who has been a member of the municipal council for 25 years was mayor from 1963 to 1965 and was succeeded by Sam Davis. Mr. George May was another Jewish councilor.

In November 1980 Windhoek became a twin city with Kiryat Telshe Stone, a settlement outside Jerusalem.

The political developments including the cancellation of the League of Nations mandate by the United Nations and the proclamation of the establishment of an independent republic, called Namibia, has brought about a considerable dwindling of the Jewish population.

[Lewis Sowden]

SOUTHWOOD, JULIUS SALTER ELIAS, FIRST VISCOUNT (1873–1946), British newspaper owner. The son of Polish immigrants who settled in Birmingham, England, and then moved to London, Southwood started his career in London as an office boy and became one of the leaders of the newspaper industry. At the age of 21 he joined the jobbing printers firm of Odhams Brothers. Four years later he was appointed a director and became managing director in 1920. From 1906 Odhams published Horatio Bottomley's populist and scurrilous weekly, *John Bull*, which at its peak sold two million copies. After Bottomley was jailed for fraud, Southwood rebuilt the firm, adding more newspapers and magazines with vast circulations. Among them were the Labor paper *Daily Herald*, which reached a circulation of 2,000,000, and the weekly, *The People*, with 3,000,000. Other papers Odhams controlled were *John Bull, Illustrated, Sporting Life, Woman*, and *News Review.* Southwood was the only one of Britain's leading "presslords" to support the Labour Party, serving as deputy leader of the Labour Party in the House of Lords. Southwood associated himself with many charities and was chairman of funds in aid of hospitals, boys' clubs, children, and the blind. He was made a baron in 1937, taking the title of Lord Southwood, and a viscount in 1946. He was buried as an Anglican; his biography, *Viscount Southwood*, published in 1954 by R.J. Minney, makes no mention of the fact that he was Jewish.

BIBLIOGRAPHY: H. Herd, *March of Journalism* (1952), 262; *The Times* (April 11, 1946). **ADD. BIBLIOGRAPHY:** ODNB online.

[Irving Rosenthal]

SOUTINE, CHAIM (1893–1943), Russian-French painter. Soutine was born at Smilovitchi in Lithuania, the tenth of eleven children of a poor tailor. Chaim was interested in nothing but drawing, and at the age of fourteen he ran away, first to Minsk, then to Vilna, where he enrolled at the School of Fine Arts. Attending school during the day, Soutine worked at night. In 1913, a physician who appreciated his talent provided him with money to go to Paris. There he met Amedeo *Modigliani, nine years his senior, who tried to help him. At one time, he and Modigliani shared a garret in Montmartre that contained only one cot, on which they took turns sleeping. To make a living, Soutine copied old masters at the Louvre, worked as a porter at a railroad station, or as a ditch digger. Overcome by despair, he once tried to commit suicide. His situation improved after the dying Modigliani recommended him to his art dealer. Thanks to the dealer's efforts, the American art collector, Albert C. Barnes, visited Soutine's studio and bought more than fifty of his paintings (they are now all at the Barnes Foundation at Merion, near Philadelphia, Pa.). After this meeting in 1922, Soutine produced many oils, and his reputation spread to England and the United States. When World War II broke out, he refused opportunities to go to the United States. After the Nazi invasion of France he was forced to hide in a small village in Touraine. The constant threat of being discovered made him ill with ulcers. In August 1943 a friend rushed him to a hospital in Paris where, after an operation, he died at the age of 50. Soutine never drew subject matters from memories of his early life in the ghetto. Instead, he portrayed the people, places, and scenes around him. He was an expressionist who rendered in violent color all the agony that he felt in his subject matter. He used paint in heavy impasto, and his colors, even more than his technique, betrayed his troubled mind. His canvases often remind one of bleeding, tortured flesh. Everything is broken, twisted, distorted. Even in his landscapes, there is a continuous cataclysmic movement. The body of his work consists of about six hundred oil paintings, many of which were acquired by museums all over the world.

BIBLIOGRAPHY: A. Forge, *Soutine* (Eng., 1965); M. Tuchman, *Chaim Soutine* (Eng., 1968), catalog of exhibition (Los Angeles); R. Cogniat, *Soutine* (Fr., 1945); E. Szittya, *Soutine et son temps* (1955).

[Alfred Werner]

SOVERN, MICHAEL IRA (1931–), U.S. legal scholar and arbitrator. Sovern, who was born in New York City, received his law degree from Columbia Law School in 1955. He taught at the University of Minnesota Law School in 1955–58, then at Columbia Law School, becoming a full professor in 1960, the youngest modern Columbia faculty member to achieve this rank. As a legal scholar Sovern's main interest was labor relations and employment discrimination. He published *Legal Restraints on Racial Discrimination in Employment* (1966) and was co-author of the text *Cases and Materials on Law and Poverty* (1969). He served as special counsel on the New York State Joint Legislative Committee on Industrial and Labor Conditions. Working for effective legal services for the poor, Sovern helped found the Legal Services Unit of Mobilization for Youth. He supervised legal education for civil rights lawyers and chaired the committee on labor and industry of the American Civil Liberties Union. Sovern devoted effort to advancing public understanding of the U.S. legal system through his television series *Due Process for the Accused.*

As a labor arbitrator in public and private disputes, he arbitrated disputes in the New York City public schools, Pan American World Airways, and the New York Telephone Company, among others. Active in mediation during the 1968 disorders at Columbia, he presided over the faculty executive committee, which examined the causes of the disruption and made recommendations for their alleviation, which were adopted. In 1970 he was appointed dean of Columbia Law School, the first Jew to hold this post. He emphasized that skill in conciliation, as well as in adversary proceedings, should be a task of law school education. In 1979 he was named executive vice president for academic affairs and provost of the university. He assumed the role of university president in 1980, serving in that capacity until 1993. During his tenure as president he effected such achievements as creating the university's intellectual property policy, which began to bring in an annual revenue of $100 million; opening Columbia College to co-education without compromising Columbia's affiliate, Barnard College for women; increasing student scholarships and expanding the enrollment of minority students; and negotiating the sale of Columbia's land under Rockefeller Center to the Rockefeller family for $400 million, which enabled the university to improve its facilities and increase salaries. In 1993 he was named president emeritus and returned to teaching at the university's law school.

Sovern wrote *Legal Restraints on Racial Discrimination in Employment* (1966) and *Of Boundless Domains* (1994).

[Ruth Beloff (2nd ed.)]

SOVETISH HEYMLAND ("Soviet Homeland"), the only Yiddish literary journal in the post-Stalinist Soviet Union, published as an organ of the Soviet Writers' Union. *Sovetish Heymland* made its appearance in July–August 1961, originally as a bi-monthly and, from January 1965, as a monthly. Apart from a few books in Yiddish that began to be published in Moscow in 1959, this magazine was a partial response of the Soviet authorities to the continued and forceful demands, mostly external, made upon them to reverse the process inaugurated at the end of 1948 of completely obliterating all manifestations of Jewish cultural life. This process had led to the execution of important Yiddish writers in the Soviet Union on August 12, 1952.

The editorial board, headed by Aaron *Vergelis, was composed of the few surviving Yiddish writers and changed significantly in the 1970s and 1980s, when some members died, immigrated to Israel, or quarreled with Vergelis. Like other periodicals of its kind appearing in the USSR, *Sovetish Heymland* devoted about two-thirds of its space to belles lettres and the remainder to literary criticism, research papers, ideological articles, memoirs, an account of Jewish cultural events in the Soviet Union and abroad, regular columns (such as the one on old Jewish books), polemical sections, etc. Most of the contributors were Yiddish authors living in the Soviet Union. The magazine also frequently presented translations of Soviet authors and, from time to time, contributions by Yiddish and Hebrew writers living outside the Soviet Union, provided, as a rule, that they were sympathizers of the communist movement. The magazine was illustrated and well edited and earned the reputation of being one of the most attractive Yiddish journals published at the time.

The material published by *Sovetish Heymland* fully reflected the ideology of Soviet patriotism prevailing in the publications in other languages in the USSR. Thus, compared to Soviet magazines that followed a "liberal" line in literature, such as *Novy Mir, Sovetish Heymland* displayed much greater circumspection. The literary standard was often lower than that of Soviet Yiddish literature before the liquidation of 1948, although every issue contained interesting and appealing items. Most of the contributors were the disciples of the liquidated writers. Their Jewish aspect was expressed primarily by works dealing with the Holocaust and World War II and by attempts to portray Soviet Jewish life; initially the liquidation of Yiddish literature was only hinted at, but from 1988 it became one of the main topics. Until 1970 the journal exercised great restraint over any topic related to Israel and did not contain the vicious attacks on the state found in other Soviet publications, especially after the Six-Day *War (1967). On the other hand it sharply refuted reports on the situation of Soviet Jewry published in the West. *Sovetish Heymland* fulfilled a positive role in domestic Jewish life by providing Yiddish material to a considerable readership and serving as a symbol of Jewish identity in a country that had so few opportunities for Jewish expression.

From 1970, when the journal became a forum for virulent anti-Zionist propaganda, it lost many readers and friends in the country and, especially, abroad. In the 1980s the editorial office trained a group of younger writers, such as Boris *Sandler (1950–) and Velvl Chenin (1958–). Following the collapse of the Soviet state-sponsored publishing system, the journal was saved by foreign sponsors and appeared sporadically in 1993–97 under the name of *Di Yidishe Gas* ("Jewish Street").

BIBLIOGRAPHY: M. Abramowicz, in: *Molad*, 163 (1962), 11–17; H. Sloves, in: *Yidishe Kultur* (N.Y., Oct. 1966), 4–17; J. and A. Brumberg, *Sovetish Heymland, An Analysis* (1966); *Midstream*, 12 (1966), 49; E. Schulman, in: *Judaism*, 14, no. 1 (Winter, 1965), 6071; idem, in: *Reconstructionist*, 37, no. 4 (June 11, 1970), 13–17. **ADD. BIBLIOGRAPHY:** G. Estraikh, in: *East European Jewish Affairs*, 25:1 (1995), 1–12; idem, *Soviet Yiddish* (1999), index; idem, in: T. Parfitt and Y. Egorova (eds.), *Jews, Muslims and Mass Media* (2004), 133–43.

[Chone Shmeruk / Gennady Estraikh (2nd ed.)]

SOYER, MOSES (1899–1974), U.S. painter. Born into a cultured family, Moses Soyer, his twin brother Raphael *Soyer, and younger brother Isaac Soyer all became well-known artists associated with the Social Realist style of painting. The family was forced out of czarist Russia in 1912, at which time they immigrated to the United States, ultimately settling in the Bronx. Soyer took free art classes at the Cooper Union and the National Academy of Design in the late 1910s; met the Ashcan artist Robert Henri at the Ferrar Art School, whose uncompromising representations of city life greatly influenced him; and studied at the Educational Alliance, where he formed friendships with Peter *Blume and Chaim *Gross. In 1923 Soyer began teaching at the Educational Alliance, where he continued to work intermittently throughout his life.

Soyer spent a year in Europe after winning a travel scholarship from the Educational Alliance (1926). After enjoying his first one-person exhibition at J.B. Neumann's Art Circle Gallery in 1929, Soyer showed his work regularly.

As a Works Progress Administration artist, Soyer painted ten portable murals addressing the life of the child, which were installed at children's hospitals and libraries throughout New York, and jointly designed a mural for the Kingsessing Station post office in Philadelphia with Raphael. During the Great Depression he also painted images of the unemployed and homeless in a representational fashion.

Inspired by the work of Edgar Degas, one of his favorite artists, and his dancer-wife, beginning in the 1940s Soyer made canvases of dancers rehearsing and at rest with a gestural, loose brushstroke. Throughout his life Soyer remained a figurative painter, frequently imaging studio nudes naturalistically. Indeed, Soyer's models are often shown at introspective, even troubled moments, and those who sat for portraits with the painter, notably many of the artist's friends, were never unnecessarily flattered. As Soyer accurately observed: "Most of my paintings reflect an interest in the casual moments in the life of plain people, the gestures and natural attitudes they fall into when they perform habitual tasks, when they are in thought, and when they are not observed by other people." Soyer's work was shown at a posthumous retrospective at the Whitney Museum of American Art in 1985.

BIBLIOGRAPHY: C. Willard, *Moses Soyer* (1962); A. Werner, *Moses Soyer* (1970); M. Soyer, *Moses Soyer: A Human Approach* (1972).

[Samantha Baskind (2nd ed.)]

SOYER, RAPHAEL (1899–1987), U.S. painter and printmaker. Born in Borisoglebsk, Russia, Raphael Soyer was one of three of the six Soyer children – along with his twin brother Moses *Soyer and younger brother Isaac Soyer – who became artists. In 1912, when the family was forced to leave Russia because their "Right to Live" permit was revoked, they immigrated to the United States, settling in the Bronx.

After taking drawing classes at the Cooper Union (1914–17), Soyer studied at the National Academy of Design (1918–22) and the Art Students League, where he attended classes intermittently from 1920 until 1926. Soyer enjoyed his first one-man show at New York's Daniel Gallery in 1929. It was there that his painting *Dancing Lesson* (1926, Collection Renee and Chaim Gross, New York), often understood as the exemplar of Jewish American art, was first exhibited publicly.

Throughout his career, Soyer was interested in Social Realist themes, which he both painted and showed in prints. During the Great Depression he often created dark-hued, compassionate renderings of the down-and-out in works such as *In the City Park* (1934, private collection, New York).

Soyer retreated into his studio in the 1940s and 1950s. Indeed, self-portraits at his easel and studio scenes of female nudes comprise Soyer's artistic interests at this time, as did portraits of his artist-friends and artists he admired. At a 1941 one-man show at the Associated American Artists Gallery, 23 of Soyer's artist-portraits were exhibited in a section entitled "My Contemporaries and Elders." Among the paintings displayed were portraits of Phillip Evergood and Abraham *Walkowitz. In the late 1950s Soyer started to paint outdoor scenes again, most of which were figurative canvases, such as *Farewell to Lincoln Square* (1959, Hirshhorn Museum and Sculpture Garden, Washington, D.C.). Inspired by Soyer's eviction from the Lincoln Arcade Building, where he kept a studio for 14 years, the large, colorful painting includes a self-portrait of the artist.

Remaining a representational artist in an abstract art scene, Soyer founded the periodical *Reality: A Journal of Artists' Opinions*, published annually from 1953 to 1955 to declare the importance of imaging "man and his world."

After meeting Isaac *Bashevis Singer in the elevator of his New York apartment building, Soyer worked on several projects with the Yiddish writer. Soyer illustrated a Limited Editions Club publication of two Singer stories, "The Gentleman from Cracow" and "The Mirror" (1979), and the second and third volumes of Singer's memoirs, *A Young Man in Search of Love* (1978) and *Lost in America* (1981). Soyer chronicled aspects of his life in four autobiographies.

BIBLIOGRAPHY: L. Goodrich, *Raphael Soyer* (1972); S. Cole, *Raphael Soyer: Fifty Years of Printmaking, 1917–1967* (1978); M. Heyd and E. Mendelsohn. *"Jewish' Art? The Case of the Soyer Brothers,"* in: *Jewish Art* (1993–94), 194–211; S. Baskind, *Raphael Soyer and the Search for Modern Jewish Art* (2004).

[Samantha Baskind (2nd ed.)]

SPACE AND PLACE (in Jewish Philosophy).

Philo

The term "place" has three meanings for *Philo, one physical and two theological: (1) the space taken up by a body, (2) the divine *logos, and (3) God Himself (Som. 1:11, 62–64). The first definition is probably derived from Stoic philosophy and is, in fact, similar to Aristotle's definition. In contrast to the latter, however, Philo's conception is based on the existence of three-dimensional space, which is itself independent of the bodies which fill it. The second definition does not relate to physical space; the place identified with the divine logos is said to be wholly filled by God Himself. On the other hand, it is characteristic of Philo's thought to ascribe a spatial relationship to the place of the third definition: "God Himself is called a place, by reason of His containing things, and being contained by nothing whatever… for He is that which He Himself has occupied, and naught encloses Him but Himself. I, mark you, am not a place, but in a place; and each thing likewise that exists… and the Deity, being contained by nothing, is of necessity Itself Its own place."

Philo's third definition relates to Jewish tradition. Jewish sources often refer to God as "Place" (*Makom*); a usage which was prevalent before Philo's time. Several Greek writers who preceded Philo, in referring to the God of the Jews, used the term *makkif* ("containing"), which appears in Philo's third definition. Later midrashic texts (e.g., Gen. R. 8:10) state explicitly that God is "the place of the world and His world is not His place."

In the Muslim world the first Karaite thinkers accepted the atomistic theories of the Mu'tazilites (see *Kalām), according to which not only bodies composed of atoms are inseparable, but there also exist equal and indivisible units of space, of time, of motion, and of the different qualities. Within a unit of motion, the atom passes from one unit of space to an adjoining unit. The existence of void space may be assumed, because (according to the notion also held by Greek atomists) the atoms could not move from place to place in a world which has no void.

Saadiah Gaon

Saadiah's definition of space is "the meeting of two contiguous bodies… each one of them becomes the place of the other. Thus one part of the earth, as it revolves, serves as the locale for the other" (*Beliefs and Opinions*, 1:4). This definition is probably based on an incorrect reading of Aristotle's conception, and the conclusions which Saadiah derives appear contradictory: at times he uses Aristotle's view as a proof that God, being incorporeal, cannot be in a particular place; at other times he seems to be saying that God is everywhere. In his commentary to *Sefer Yeẓirah*, Saadiah speaks of two kinds of air which are found everywhere:

(1) tangible air, and

(2) the fine air, which he identifies with the biblical "glory of God" (see *Shekhinah).

Jewish Aristotelianism

Ibn Abī Sa'īd, the first Jewish Aristotelian, appears to have accepted, in general, Aristotle's definition of place as "the limit of the encompassing body." This conception, which was commonplace in Muslim and Jewish philosophy, was totally rejected by Abu al-Barakat Ḥibat Allah (Nethanel) *al-Baghdadi, a Jewish philosopher who converted to Islam in his old age. He held the notion that space is a three-dimensional extension, which can be seen as both void and filled with bodies. The human intellect, according to him, has an image of void space before having an image of filled space. Contrary to Aristotle, whose views he criticizes at length, he believes that space is infinite.

Solomon ibn Gabirol

According to Solomon ibn Gabirol (in his *Mekor Ḥayyim*), there is a hierarchy of different kinds of place, some of which are spiritual (when the spiritual being is the place of spiritual form, and "will" is the place of both matter and form), and others physical. He refers to the existence of various other types of bodies as the "known place." God (the first agent) is the infinite place (or space).

Abraham ibn Daud

Abraham ibn *Daud attempts (in his *Emunah Ramah*) to establish the derivation of the three dimensions from prime matter, "which God created in the beginning," and which in itself is apparently non-spatial. The first form which it takes on, the corporeal form, is identified with continuity. This form affords something a certain measure of solidity and allows the three dimensions to come into existence.

Maimonides

*Maimonides accepts the Aristotelian view of physical place. He distinguishes between "particular" and "general" place (*Guide of the Perplexed*, 1:8): the particular place is the place of every individual body, which is the body referred to in Aristotle's definition; the general place, which contains all bodies, encompasses within its area the upper sphere, and the two are identical since, like Aristotle, Maimonides sees the world as finite. The term "place," when used to refer to God, designates His greatness.

Naḥmanides

*Naḥmanides recounts the midrashic notion that God is "the place of the world." The sages, in his opinion, meant by this dictum that God is the form of the world, since form is the realization (the entelechy) of the perfection of what is contained in the world, and is also its limit since it prevents the spreading out of the world's dimensions beyond its form.

Ḥasdai Crescas

A basic criticism of the Aristotelian conception of space and place is found in Ḥasdai *Crescas' *Or Adonai*, whose point of view and opinions are sometimes similar to those of Ḥibat Allah. It appears that Crescas was influenced in this critical attitude by the anti-Aristotelian physical theories of 14th- and 15th-century Christian scholastics. Crescas substitutes for the Aristotelian conception of two-dimensional place the conception of three-dimensional space (using the term *makom* ("place") to designate both place and space). This three-dimensional space is found within the limits of the world which is full of bodies. Crescas' notion that the world is infinite, however, leads him to reject the assumption that the existence of a void is impossible. It is his opinion that infinite void can exist outside the limits of the world, and even within the world itself. Crescas also assumes the possibility of the existence of more than one world. He maintains, however, that the human intellect is incapable of arriving at well-founded conclusions in regard to this matter. Like Naḥmanides, Crescas holds that referring to God as "the place of the world" means that God is the form of the world.

Apparently under Crescas' influence his disciple, Joseph *Albo, substituted the three-dimensional conception of space for the Aristotelian conception (*Sefer ha-Ikkarim*, 2:17).

BIBLIOGRAPHY: I.I. Efros, *The Problems of Space in Jewish Medieval Philosophy* (1917); H.A. Wolfson, *Crescas' Critique of Aristotle* (1929), index, s.v. *Place*; idem, *Philo* (1948²), index s.v. *Place, Space*; S. Pines, in: REJ, 103 (1938), 3–64; idem, in: PAAJR, 24 (1955), 103–36; Ch. Touati, in: *Archives d'histoire Doctrinale et Littéraire du Moyen Âge*, 21 (1954), 203–4.

[Shlomo Pines]

SPAIN (in Hebrew at first אספמיא then ספרד), country in S.W. Europe. The use of the word "Spain" to denote "Sepharad" has caused some confusion in research. Spain came into being long after the Jews had been expelled from the Crowns of Castile and Aragon, which were jointly ruled by the Catholic Monarchs, Isabella of Castile and Ferdinand of Aragon, at the time of the expulsion. When Spain emerged, incorporating also the Kingdom of Navarre, there were no Jews officially living in the Iberian Peninsula. Sepharad was used in the Middle Ages to indicate the entire peninsula and the Jews who lived there whose culture emerged as result of the encounter of Judaism with Greco-Arabic culture that developed in Al-Andalus. Many major works devoted to Jewish history and culture treated as one unit the Jews of all the Hispanic kingdoms that subsequently constituted Spain, leaving out Portugal. Baer's monumental history does exactly that and he is followed by many scholars.

According to various legends, there were Jews living in Spain in biblical times, but no proof exists in support of such stories. Most probably, the first group of Jews settled there under the Roman Empire and the communities grew rapidly. A tombstone inscription attests the presence of Jews in Adra (the ancient Abdera) in the third century C.E. They thus witnessed the conversion of the inhabitants of the Peninsula to Christianity, which is probably why the Council of *Elvira (305) attempted to effect or maintain a separation between the members of the two faiths by forbidding Christians to live in the houses of Jews, or to eat in their company, or to bless the produce of their fields.

Under Visigothic Rule

The weakening of the empire and the arrival of the Visigoths changed the face of Spain. From their court in Toledo they attempted to restore the shattered Hispanic unity, initially on the religious plane, through the conversion of their king Reccared, originally an Arian, to Catholicism (587). Subsequently, in the political sphere, King Sisebut (612–21) broke down the last Byzantine stronghold in Spain. It is therefore hardly surprising that the Church councils of *Toledo, which were as much political as religious assemblies, should have played so important a role in the Visigothic state, and thus in the determination of its policy toward the Jews. As in the case of all other subjects, the policy was to have them adopt Catholicism, which had by then become the state religion. Reccared approved the decision of the third Council of Toledo (589) laying down that the children of a mixed Jewish-Christian marriage should be baptized by force. Going even further, Sisebut inaugurated a policy of forcible conversion of all the Jews in the kingdom. From 613 they were ordered to be baptized or leave the kingdom. Thousands of Jews then left Spain, while others were converted. Most of the latter, however, took the opportunity of returning to Judaism under the rule of his more tolerant successor Swintila (621–31). They were joined at this time by a number of exiles returning to Spain. At that period the official Church doctrine on conversion was formulated: Jews must not be baptized by force, and the fourth Council of Toledo (633) accepted this. King Sisenand (631–36) supported this attitude but, like the council, insisted that those Jews who had been converted by Sisebut and reverted to Judaism under Swintila must return to Christianity.

However, this relatively moderate attitude was revoked again under King Chintila (636–39) who compelled the sixth Council of Toledo (638) to adopt a resolution proclaiming that only Catholics might reside in the kingdom of Spain; he even anathematized those of his successors who did not hold to his decrees against the Jews. Numerous Jews accepted baptism and signed a declaration that they would respect Christian rites; others chose exile. Under Chintila's successor, Chindaswinth (641–49), the application of these laws had been neglected to such an extent that his successor, Recceswinth (649–72) complained to the eighth Council of Toledo (653) about the presence of Jews in the kingdom. Probably some of the exiles had come back and some of the converts had returned to Judaism. The king commanded that they be brought back within the fold of Christianity, by force if necessary. Those who had relapsed had to sign a new declaration, promising to be good Catholics, to reject all Jewish rites, and to execute themselves those of their erring brethren who backslid into Judaism. However, they were permitted to abstain from eating pork, which they abhorred. The king decided not to drive the unconverted Jews to the font but to make it impossible for them to practice Judaism by prohibiting circumcision and forbidding them to celebrate the Sabbath and the festivals. However, these ordinances were honored more in the breach than in the observance and, thanks to various allies, even among the clergy, the Jews were able to survive in Spain; so much so that the tenth Council of Toledo had to remind Christians that they were obliged to observe the laws relating to the Jews.

The next king, Wamba (672–80), expelled the Jews from Narbonne and probably also from Septimania (then part of Spain), but they did not all leave the Visigothic kingdom. They were there when Erwig (680–87) convoked the 12th Council of Toledo to obtain in spite of the traditional ruling of the Church, the forced baptism of the Jews. Within a year every Jew had to foreswear Judaism, accept baptism for himself and his family, and pledge his fidelity to the Christian faith. Those who refused were to be penalized by having their belongings seized, by corporal punishment, and finally by exile. Similar penalties were to be imposed on those who, baptized or not, observed Jewish rites. The priests were to gather all the Jews in the churches to read out to them the text of the law so that none could claim he was unaware of it. Any noble who helped the Jews to evade these laws was to lose his rights over the Jews and pay a heavy fine. The execution of the laws was the task of the clergy, the king reserving several penalties for them if they were lax in carrying out his orders. Yet the Jews continued to Judaize and even to attack Christianity on some occasions for the king could not count on the assistance of his people in carrying out the whole of his anti-Jewish policy. His successor, Egica (687–702), reversed his attitude, restating once more the prescription on forced baptism and suppressing those disqualifications which oppressed converted Jews, while at the same time increasing the benefits to be gained from becoming Christian. He passed several measures tending to impoverish the Jews and make it impossible for them to buy protection from powerful nobles. They were forced to sell, at a price fixed by the king, all slaves, buildings, lands, and vineyards which they had acquired from Christians. On pain of perpetual servitude and confiscation of their goods, they were forbidden to conduct commercial transactions with Christians or overseas. At the same time their taxes were considerably increased. In spite of its ratification by the 16th Council of Toledo (693), this policy was unsuccessful. Soon it was rumored that the persecuted Jews were thinking of appealing to the Muslim invaders, who had shown themselves to be decidedly more tolerant than the Visigoths. Alarmed, Egica convened a 17th council on Nov. 9, 694, accusing the Jews of treason and demanding that the severest measures be taken against them. Declared as slaves and their possessions confiscated, all the Jews of Spain were given into the hands of Christian masters in various provinces. Their masters were charged to see that they did not practice Jewish rites and to take their children to be brought up from the age of seven by Christian tutors and later married to Christians. Those Jews who were able to, escaped; the rest were taken into servitude.

[Simon R. Schwarzfuchs]

Muslim Spain

When Tarik b. Ziyad in 711 crossed the Straits of Gibraltar, and overran the Visigothic Kingdom, there were no communities of openly professing Jews in Spain. But there remained in the country many secret Jews who welcomed the Muslims as their saviors from long oppression and flocked to join them. According to reliable Arabic sources the Muslim invaders made it their custom to call together the Jews wherever they found them and to hand towns which they had conquered over to them to garrison. They mention that this happened at Córdoba, Granada, Toledo, and Seville. Since the number of Muslim soldiers was relatively small, there can be no doubt that they appreciated the military help of the Jews who enabled them to continue their campaigns without having to leave behind them sizable units. So the situation of the Crypto-Jews changed abruptly and they occupied the enviable position of a group allied with the new rulers of the peninsula. Probably their economic situation changed too, since most of the Visigothic nobles had fled and they could appropriate abandoned estates. The immediate sequel of the conquest of Spain by the Arabs was apparently that many Jews who had left Spain at the time of the religious persecutions by the Visigothic kings or their descendants returned from North Africa where they had found shelter. But soon the Jews began to suffer from the exactions of the new rulers who imposed on them (as on the Christians) heavy taxes. Even the party strife and civil wars which flared up among the Arabs brought down many calamities upon them.

UMAYYAD RULE. The *Umayyad kingdom in Spain was established by ʿAbd al-Raḥmān I in 755 with its capital at Córdoba in Andalusia. There was relative economic prosperity throughout Umayyad rule and Jews were represented in many occupations, including medicine, agriculture, commerce, and crafts. Jews continued to work in these fields after the fall of the Umayyad regime. The tolerance of the Umayyad regime rendered Muslim Spain a refuge for the Jews and their numbers increased within the country. In 839 the Frank bishop *Bodo converted to Judaism in *Saragossa, married a Spanish Jewess, and wrote a tract against Christianity to which Alvaros of Córdoba replied.

Jewish scholarship and culture flourished alongside its Arab counterpart and was influenced by it. The Babylonian *geonim* corresponded with rabbis and scholars in the centers of *Lucena and *Barcelona. R. *Amram Gaon sent his prayer book to Spanish scholars. The academy at Lucena flourished into the 12th century and is mentioned in responsa as early as the ninth. Later Arab geographers cited Lucena, Granada, and *Tarragona as "Jewish cities." The real Jewish cultural revival began in the tenth century under ʿAbd al-Raḥmān III (912–961), who assumed the title of caliph in 929 in Córdoba. At that time Córdoba was a center of both Arab and Jewish culture. This was the time of the political rise of the court physician *Ḥisdai ibn Shaprut, who attained the position of chief of customs and foreign trade. Ḥisdai was also a diplomat who negotiated with Christian rulers on behalf of the caliphate. In addition, he was a patron of the two leading Hebrew philologists, *Dunash b. Labrat and *Menahem b. Saruk. The Jewish literati acquired a sense of aesthetics and an appreciation of physical beauty from the artistic accomplishment of the Arabs in Spain. This sensitivity took root in the mid-tenth century and found expression in the Hebrew poetry of medieval Spain almost right up to the general expulsion in 1492.

As head of Spanish Jewry, Ḥisdai appointed *Moses b. Ḥanokh, who came from Italy, chief rabbi and head of a yeshivah at Córdoba. Thus, Spanish Jewry's reliance on the Babylonian *geonim* in halakhic matters decreased. Ḥisdai is the first example of the many-faceted Jewish statesman, communal leader, and intellectual who was characteristic of the community in Muslim Spain. After his death the post of rabbi of the Córdoba community was disputed by Joseph b. Isaac *Ibn Abitur, supported by the wealthy silk merchant *Ibn Jau, and R. *Ḥanokh b. Moses. The latter emerged victorious and his appointment was sanctioned by Caliph al-Ḥakam II, the patron of the Jewish geographer Ibrahim b. Yaʿqūb. During the reign of al-*Manṣūr (d. 1002) the great Hebrew philologist *Ḥayyuj (Abu Zakariyyā Yaḥyā b. Daʾud), who established the principle of the trilitteral root, lived in Córdoba.

THE PETTY PRINCIPALITIES. With the decline of Umayyad rule after al-Manṣūr's death, the *Berber conquest of Córdoba (1013), and the demise of the dynasty in the 1030s, Córdoba lost its former prominence and the capitals of the various Berber and Arab principalities became cultural and commercial centers. Jewish taxfarmers, advisers, and physicians served at the different courts. The relatively tolerant rulers welcomed and esteemed Jewish financiers, advisers in matters economic and political gifted writers, scholars, and scientists. The ethos of this Jewish upper class was distinguished by several features: the desire for and attainment of political power, the harmony of religion and secular culture, the study of the Talmud along with poetry and philosophy, equal proficiency in Arabic and Hebrew. The epitome of the fulfillment of this ideal was the poet and halakhist *Samuel ha-Nagid, a refugee from Córdoba who served as vizier and commander of the army of Granada from about 1030 to his death in 1056; he was also head of the Jewish community. His remarkable career and military exploits are recorded in both Hebrew and Arabic sources, including his own poetry. Samuel was succeeded by his son *Joseph ha-Nagid, whose pride and ambition aroused the enmity of certain Muslims, who assassinated him in 1066. Inspired by fanatics, Muslims then attacked Granada Jewry and many survivors moved to other towns, particularly Lucena. The Granada massacre marked the first persecution of Jews in Muslim Spain.

Prominent communities in the middle to late 11th century also included Seville, then ruled by the *Abbasid dynasty. (See Map: Muslim Spain.) Jewish courtiers included Abraham b. Meir ibn *Muhajir, to whom Moses *Ibn Ezra dedicated his *Sefer ha-Tarshish* (*Sefer ha-Anka*). Under al-Muʿtamid, Isaac ibn *Albalia served as court astrologer and as chief rabbi of Seville, and the scholar Joseph *Ibn Migash was sent on diplomatic missions. Lucena remained an important center of learning. Its academy was led by the great talmudist Isaac *Alfasi. His successors were Isaac *Ibn Ghayyat and Joseph ibn Migash. During Samuel ha-Nagid's term of office, the Jew *Jekuthiel, who was later murdered by political rivals, served as vizier in Saragossa. A dynamic cultural center, Saragossa was the home of the philologist and grammarian *Ibn Janāḥ, the controversial Bible commentator Moses ha-Kohen ibn *Gikatilla, the important neoplatonic philosopher and poet Solomon ibn *Gabirol, and the ethical writer *Baḥya ibn Pakuda. The latter's major work, *Farāʾiḍ al-Qulūb* (Heb. *Ḥovot ha-Levavot*, "The Duties of the Hearts"), shows the influence of Muslim ascetic ideals. Other important communities were *Denia, a major port in eastern Spain and the residence of the talmudist R. *Isaac b. Reuben al-Bargeloni, *Tudela, *Almeria, and *Huesca. Eleventh-century Toledo, capital of a Berber king-

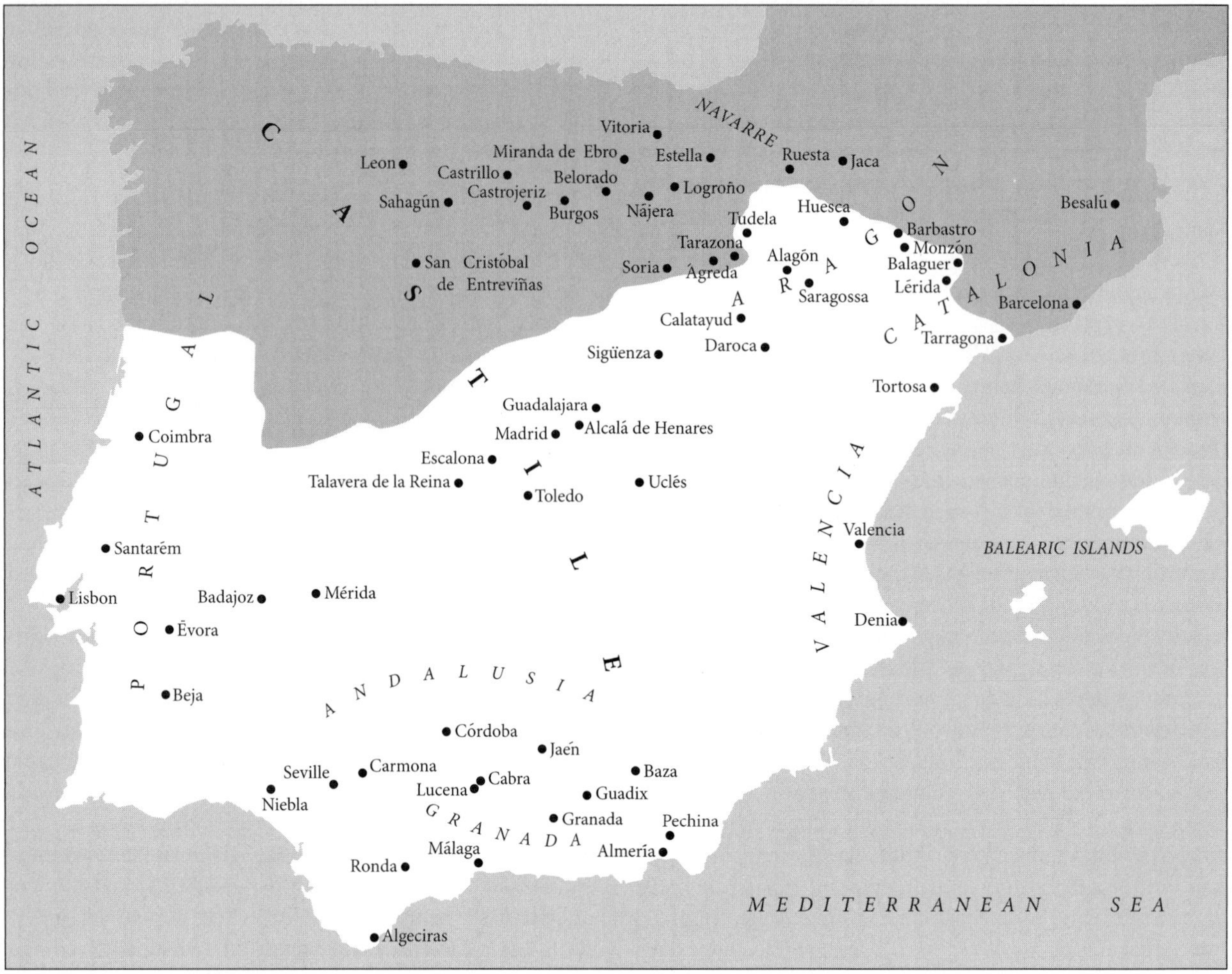

Map 1. Jewish communities in Muslim Spain in the 11th century. Shaded area indicates the extent of Christian expansion by 1030.

dom, had a Jewish population of 4,000 and a *Karaite community as well. It was taken by the Christians in 1085.

THE ALMORAVIDS. The advance of the reconquest prompted al-Mutʿamid of Seville to request the aid of Yūsuf ibn Tāshfīn of North Africa, the leader of the fanatic *Almoravid sect. In 1086 the latter led the Muslim armies to victory at Zallaka against the Castilians commanded by Alfonso VI. Yūsuf attempted to force Lucena Jewry to convert to *Islam, but payment of a large sum of money caused him to rescind his decree. Under his son, Ali (1106–43), Abu Ayyūb Sulaymān ibn Muʿallim served as court physician and Abu al-Ḥasan Abraham b. Meir ibn Kamaniel was sent on diplomatic missions. During Ali's reign the poets Abu Sulaymān ibn Muhājir and Abu al-Fath Eleazar ibn Azhar lived in Seville. Córdoba continued to prosper and was a cultural center and the residence of the gifted poet Joseph b. Jacob *Ibn Sahl (d. 1123) and the philosopher Joseph ibn *Ẓaddik.

THE ALMOHADS. In 1146 the *Almohads, an even more fanatic Berber dynasty of *Morocco, led by ʿAbd al-Muʾmin, began their conquest of Muslim Spain, which put an end to the flourishing Jewish communities of Andalusia. The practice of the Jewish religion was forbidden by the authorities. Synagogues and yeshivot were closed and Jews were compelled to embrace Islam. Many emigrated to Christian Spain; others outwardly professed Islam but secretly observed Judaism, an ominous portent of the Conversos in Christian Spain a century later. R. Abraham *Ibn Ezra composed a moving elegy on the demise of the Andalusian communities. In 1162 these secret Jews were active in a revolt against the Almohads, particularly in deposing them in Granada. Almohad rule in Spain lasted longer than a century.

In the mid-13th century the Castilians conquered a great part of Andalusia. The Muslims retained only the kingdom of Granada in southeastern Spain. This kingdom, which was ruled by the Arab dynasty of Banū al-Aḥmar and existed for nearly 250 years, contained the important communities of Granada, *Málaga, and Almeria. Although there were periods when the rulers of Granada inclined toward religious fanaticism, they employed Jewish counselors and court physicians. Jews from Christian Spain immigrated to Granada as their situation deteriorated. The poet, historian, and talmudist Saadiah b. Maimon *Ibn Danan was rabbi of Granada in the late 15th century. At that time Isaac *Hamon was court physician and very influential in government circles. When Granada surrendered to Ferdinand and Isabella in 1492, the last Muslim king stipulated that Jews enjoy the same rights as other subjects, i.e., judicial autonomy, freedom to practice their religion, and permission to emigrate. According to this treaty, Conversos who had come from Christian Spain could leave within a month. The Catholic monarchs, however, did not keep their word and proclaimed the edict of the expulsion of the Jews in Granada.

[Eliyahu Ashtor]

The Reconquest Period

For many years the history of the Jews in Christian Spain became an element in the struggle for the reconquest. In the early stages of this the Jews suffered alongside the Muslims from the violence of the newly-founded Christian state in Oviedo, which regarded itself as the successor of the Visigoths and felt bound to punish the so-called treason of the Jews. However, in many Christian principalities the influence of the Carolingian Empire was paramount and the Jews were treated more moderately.

Little is known about the Catalonian Jewish communities during this period; their presence is attested by a few tombstones. More records are available on the communities in the county of León. In this province a problem arose which perplexed the Christian kings of the reconquest for many years: how to settle, colonize, and develop regions won back from the Muslim invaders. It is fairly clear that this preoccupation prompted a change in their attitude toward the Jews so that gradually they began to consider them a useful and even essential section of the population. Relations with the Christian population changed, and this period saw the emergence of organized communities, influential in trade and industry, in northwest Spain. In the new capital, León, from the tenth century the Jews controlled the commerce in textiles and precious stones. They also owned many estates in the kingdom. In the young state of Castile the judicial status of the Jews was almost equal to that of the Christians. In the meantime the Jewish population in the small Christian states was insignificant.

At the beginning of the 11th century, assisted by the decline of the caliphate, the Christian hold in Spain increased through the initiative of Alfonso v of León (999–1027), who set himself out to attract settlers to his lands by granting them privileges and freedom. Among these new settlers were numerous Jews, who shared the same advantages as the Christians. It is difficult to establish their origins: did they come from France or from Muslim Spain, where their situation was now less secure than before? At any rate it is highly likely that at the beginning of the 11th century, especially with the onset of the Berber invasions, many Jews from the Muslim region made their way to the Christian kingdom, attracted by the advantages offered to new settlers, to join earlier Jewish arrivals. The face of Spanish Jewry was transformed; for the first time the influence of Oriental Jewry penetrated a Christian land, dislodging the influence of Franco-German Jewry from its monopolistic position.

In spite of the internal reverses and setbacks disturbing the countries of Christian Spain, which also had an effect on the Jews, Jewish communities were organized and securely established. Their status was clearly defined: whether they lived on territory belonging to nobles, monastic orders, or elsewhere, the Jews belonged to the king, who protected them and to whom they owed fealty. For some time this principle was interpreted literally – as the blood money due on the killing of a Jew had to be paid directly to the king. The abortive Crusade of 1063 did not affect the development of the Jewish communities. According to legend, the great national hero El Cid employed Jews as treasurers, financial agents, lawyers, and administrators. Alfonso vi certainly employed as his physician and financier the Jew Joseph ha-Nasi *Ferrizuel, called Cidellus or little Cid, who did a great deal to help his coreligionists. It appears that Alfonso was the Spanish king who inaugurated a tradition that lasted as long as Spanish Jewry itself: that of the Jewish courtiers who, while still remaining faithful to their religion, exercised considerable authority over the inhabitants of the kingdom. During Alfonso's reign the reconquest suffered a setback with the defeat of Zallaker in 1086; no doubt there were some who cast aspersions on the Jews of the king who had refused to fight.

In the meantime in *Barcelona the Jews continued to be important landowners. According to some estimates, in the 11th and 12th centuries they owned around one-third of the estates in the county, which explains why the second Council of Gerona demanded that they continue to pay the tithes due to the Church on land that they had purchased from Christians. In 1079 there were at least 60 Jewish heads of families in Barcelona. This was the milieu which produced the first great figures of Spanish Jewish culture: the rabbi Isaac b. Reuben al-Bargeloni ("from Barcelona") the many-faceted *Abraham b. Ḥiyya ha-Nasi, and the rabbi *Judah b. Barzillai al-Bargeloni. Writing in a Christian land, these three authors belonged to a totally different cultural environment from their contemporary, Rashi, and attest the originality of Spanish Jewish thought which, from the end of the 11th century, gained in importance and impact.

The Golden Age in Spain

When Toledo fell to Alfonso i of Castile in 1085 the Jewish inhabitants, unlike the Muslims, did not flee the town, and it seems that they continued to live in their old quarter, joined there by newcomers from old Castile and León and refugees from Muslim lands. On the death of the king in 1109, the security of the Jews was revealed as illusory since it was based solely on royal favor, which more tardily was again extended by Alfonso's successor. In the meantime Christianity gained ground in Spain. *Tudela fell to King Alfonso i of Aragon in 1115. Jews and Muslims alike were granted full religious freedom, but while the Muslims were ordered to leave the town itself the Jews were granted permission to remain in their own quarter, which lay within the city walls. Thus, preferred to the Muslims, they were no longer an object of fear to the Christians. The Jews of *Saragossa, conquered in 1118, enjoyed the same privileges and this precedent was followed in almost all towns on the way of the triumphant Christian advance.

The county of Barcelona, united with the kingdom of Aragon in the time of Count Ramón Berenguer IV (1131–62), had also taken part in the reconquest. In 1148 *Tortosa fell to the count who, having given important possessions to the Jews there, promised supplementary freedoms to any of their coreligionists who wished to settle in the town. When *Lérida was conquered in 1149, the Jews were once more asked to stay and preferred to the Muslims. Nevertheless they were not always protected from the maneuverings of the Christian lords, who cared more for immediate gain than for future settlement. At this time the focal point of Spanish Jewry had shifted from the Muslim south to the Christian north, where the Jewish population had increased considerably. However, the internal structure of the communities changed little and the rule of the notables remained firmly established. The court Jews still occupied all important positions, which scarcely troubled newcomers, who were above all concerned with establishing themselves and finding a means of livelihood. They tended to settle in the towns more than in the countryside. Occasionally the Christian kings gave them the citadel of a conquered town and there they established themselves, assuring at the same time their internal communal autonomy and external security. Engaged largely in commerce and industry and in the administration of the possessions of the nobles, the Jews were barely concerned with moneylending.

The Jews were serfs of the king, property of the royal treasury alone, but in times of stability this meant no more than an obligation to pay taxes; the king took no interest in the internal structure of the communities, which remained autonomous organizations. Known as **aljama* (the Arabic name being retained), the Jewish communities were each independent political entities paying taxes directly to the royal treasury, with full administrative and judicial autonomy, under the very general supervision of a royal functionary. In the case of suits with Christians, the Jews had to take a special *oath *more judaico* and were forbidden to engage in judicial duels. From the end of the 12th century, however, municipal legislation weighed more heavily on the Jews: the municipalities were desirous of curbing the power of rich Jewish businessmen. But in spite of their efforts they did not succeed in supplanting the king as the supreme authority over the Jews. Meanwhile in Barcelona, Toledo, and Saragossa the Jewish courtiers, an aristocracy in their own right, acquired even greater importance. They were tax farmers and undertook diplomatic missions and were frequently looked upon askance by the communities too, whose authority they sometimes tried to avoid. It is therefore hardly surprising that from the early 13th century the first signs of a democratic reaction were apparent, the poorer demanding a voice in the communal councils alongside the rich. In this period the *Maimonidean controversy split Spanish Jewry. Beginning in Provence, it spread through the Midi, developing into a dispute on the very validity of philosophy within Judaism. It was the first sign of self-examination by the communities and of the renunciation of ideas absorbed from the Muslim and then from the Christian background. This tendency was expressed in the condemnation of the writings of Maimonides, several of them being suppressed. The controversy simmered down, only to break out with renewed ferocity some time later.

In the meantime the reconquest proceeded apace. James I of Aragon (1213–76) took the Balearic Islands (1229–35) and Valencia (1238). Ferdinand III of Castile (1217–52) captured *Córdoba (1236), *Murcia (1243), and *Seville (1248). Alfonso X (1252–84) extended the conquest so far that only the kingdom of Granada remained in Muslim hands. All these kings had employed Jews in their armies and all had requested them to settle in towns evacuated by Muslims. Everywhere the Jews who had lived under Muslim rule were permitted to remain in their old quarter, were preferred to Muslims, and their previous privileges were confirmed. Their ownership of land expanded, for the kings frequently granted them lands and other possessions in order to attract them to settle. More Jewish shops opened in the towns, arousing the opposition of the municipalities, who wished to limit their commerce. Around the middle of the 13th century King *Alfonso X prepared a code of laws covering all the inhabitants of his kingdom. This code, known as *Las Siete Partidas*, was formulated around 1263, but was only very gradually applied, especially from 1348. It defined with great precision the principles of royal policy toward the Jews and in this respect was extremely influential. The Jews were accorded complete religious liberty, on condition that they did not attack the Christian faith; measures were taken to prevent the possibility of *blood libels; and they were forbidden to leave their homes during Easter. They were also prohibited from holding positions of authority over Christians. The number and size of synagogues were strictly limited, but it was forbidden to disturb the Jews on the Sabbath, even for legal reasons. No force was to be used to induce them to adopt Christianity, while those who had converted were not to be taunted with insults about their origins, nor to lose their rights of succession to the property of their former coreligionists. By contrast, any Christian who converted to Judaism was to be put to death and his property declared forfeit. Jews and Christians were not to occupy the same house, and Jews could not own Christian slaves. They were also to carry a special badge which identified them as Jews. Thus the policy of the Church triumphed. The *aljamas*, turned more in on themselves, reinforced their autonomy. Under the direction of their **muqaddamin* (or **adelantados*) they established their own courts of law, but maintained the right of appeal before the royal court. At this period the king appointed a functionary, known as the *rab de la corte*, to supervise the affairs of the Jewish communities. It appears that his nomination by the king did not give rise to any special problems, for he generally did not interfere with the internal organization of the communities.

Jewish courtiers, largely in Castile, rose to the highest positions. Therefore their fall was usually attended by the most brutal consequences for the communities to which they belonged, and thus the latter could not consider them as *shtadlanim*, but rather as high functionaries and financiers whose influence depended more on their talents than on any representative status. The Castilian monarchs seem to have been well satisfied by their services. As Jews they could not aim for political power nor could they ally themselves with the nobility or the clergy. Thus there developed in the Christian lands the custom, long widespread in the Orient, of employing Jews in the highest administrative and financial positions. The nobles imitated the kings in employing Jewish experts. Some of these Jewish courtiers, while still holding to the Jewish faith, were influenced by the Christian environment; wishing to live as nobles, they competed for royal favor. Veritable dynasties of courtiers emerged: the powerful families wielded considerable importance in their communities. Don Solomon *Ibn Ẓadok of Toledo, known as Don Çulema, was ambassador and *almoxarife major.* His son and successor, Don Isaac ibn Ẓadok, known as Don Çag de la Maleha, played an important role in reestablishing the finances of Alfonso x, who granted him and his associates authority to farm taxes owing on the previous 20 years in return for payment of the enormous sum of 80,000 gold maravedis for the years 1276 and 1277. This kind of contract could be very remunerative although the king frequently went back on his word. It sometimes happened that, as in the case of Don Çag, a Jewish courtier fell from royal favor and, as a result, lost his life. The very financial success of the courtiers tempted the kings to impose enormous taxes on the Jewish communities, which were impoverished by their efforts to pay them. The Church, the Cortes, and the nobility frequently cast a jaundiced eye on the rise of the Jewish courtiers, who competed with them for royal favor and gave too powerful a hand to the strengthening of the monarchy. Thus they frequently put pressure on the king to dislodge his Jewish courtiers. In spite of all efforts, however, the institution of the Jewish courtier increased in influence in Castile, rather than the contrary.

In Aragon Jewish courtiers were to be found at the court of James i, who used them as interpreters in his survey of the Arab lands he had reconquered. The king also invited the Jews to settle in his newly acquired lands; they were to receive their share of the conquered territory on the sole condition that they settled on it. There too they were preferred to Muslims, for the problem of resettling the former Arab lands was ever present. Thus Jews from the north of Aragon spread gradually southward, establishing new communities. By the edict of Valencia, March 6, 1239, the king confirmed the authority of the *bet din* in suits between Jews, except in cases of murder. He also recognized the need for witnesses of each religion in cases involving Christians and Jews. The validity of the *oath more judaico* was reaffirmed. Any Jew who was arrested had to be freed between midday on Friday and Monday morning. The king took the Jews and their property under his protection and forbade anyone to harass them except for a debt or crime which could be firmly established. This charter often served as the model for similar charters in towns throughout Aragon. James i also undertook to protect the Jews of newly conquered Majorca. As these measures proved insufficient to populate the new communities, on June 11, 1247, James promised safe conduct and citizenship to any Jew coming by land or sea to settle in Majorca, Catalonia, or Valencia. As far as the internal life of the communities was concerned, he confirmed and extended their autonomy. By the privilege granted to the community of *Calatayud on April 22, 1229, he authorized the community to appoint a rabbi and four directors (*adenanti*) to control their affairs, and to dismiss these officials if they deemed it necessary. They were also authorized to arrest and even sentence to death any malefactors in their midst. The community did not have to account for any death sentences it passed but had to pay the king 1,000 solidos for every one of these. The four *adenanti* directing the community could, with the agreement of the *aljama*, pronounce excommunication. Thus the elected heads of the community exercised considerable power, especially the authority to impose the death sentence, which in fact was only pronounced against informers. The king rarely attempted to interfere with this autonomy, leaving the communities to direct their own affairs.

Beginning of the Christian Reaction

However, early in the 13th century, a Christian reaction made itself felt, under the influence of *Raymond de Peñaforte, Dominican confessor to the king. From Barcelona he attempted to limit the influence of the Jews by fixing the interest rate on moneylending at 20%, by limiting the effectiveness of the Jewish oath, and restating the prohibition on Jews holding public office or employing Christian servants (Dec. 22, 1228). The Council of Tarragona (1235) restated these clauses and forbade Muslims to convert to Judaism or vice versa. The Cortes increased their attempts to suppress Jewish moneylending.

Thus the climate had changed. Following the example of France, the kingdom of Aragon initiated a large-scale campaign to convert the Jews through exposing the "Jewish error." From 1250 the first blood libel was launched in Saragossa. Soon the example of Louis ix found Spanish imitators: James i found himself obliged to cancel debts to Jews (1259). Soon after, an apostate Jew carried over to Spain the work of Nicholas *Donin of France, provoking a disputation between Pablo *Christiani and the most famous rabbi of the day, *Naḥmanides. Held before the king, the bishops, and Raymond de Peñaforte, the disputation took place in Barcelona on July 20, 27, 30, and 31, 1263 (see *Barcelona, Disputation of). Central to the disputation were the problem of the advent of the Messiah and the truth of Christianity; probably for the last time in the Middle Ages, the Jewish representative secured permission to speak with complete freedom. After a somewhat brusque disputation, each side claimed the victory. This constituted no check to Christian missionary efforts; forced conversion remained prohibited but the Jews were compelled to attend conversionist sermons and to censor all references to Jesus or Mary in their literature. Naḥmanides, brought to trial because of his frankness, was acquitted (1265), but he had to leave Spain and in 1267 settled in Jerusalem. By his bull *Turbato corde*, proclaimed at this time, Pope Clement IV gave the Inquisition virtual freedom to interfere in Jewish affairs by allowing the inquisitors to pursue converted Jews who had reverted to their old religion, Christians who converted to Judaism, and Jews accused of exercising undue influence over Christians and their converted brethren. It was becoming apparent that the Jews had outlived their usefulness as colonizers, except in southern Aragon. The old hostility toward Judaism reappeared, but for the time being was content with efforts to convince the Jews of the truth of Christianity. At this period Raymond *Martini, one of the opponents of Naḥmanides, published his *Pugio Fidei*, a work which served as the basis for anti-Jewish campaigns for many years. But the economic usefulness of the Jews was still considerable: in 1294 revenue from the Jews amounted to 22% of the total revenue in Castile. In spite of mounting hostility on the part of the burghers, the state was very reluctant to part with such a valuable source of income.

The very existence of the Jewish communities posed problems for the burgher class. The *aljama* was a neighbor of the Christian municipality but was free from its authority because of its special relationship with the king. The *judería* thus often seemed to be a town within a town. The *aljama* itself in this period reinforced its authority and closed its ranks, limiting the influence of the courtiers, who were increasingly becoming a dominant class with no real share in the spiritual life of the people. The different communities in Aragon had developed on parallel lines without any centralized organization. At times their leaders met to discuss the apportionment of taxes, but this had never led to the development of a national organization. Within the communities the struggle continued between the strong families who wielded power and the masses. In general the oligarchy succeeded in dominating the communal council with the assistance of the *dayyanim* who, since they were not always scholars, had to consult the rabbinical authorities before passing judgment according to Jewish law. Around the end of the 13th century the *dayyanim* began to be elected annually, the first step toward greater control by the masses. Soon after, these masses managed to secure a rotation of the members of the council, but nevertheless these were nearly always chosen from among the powerful families.

Such a climate of social tension, aggravated by the anxiety caused by the insecure state of the Jews, proved fruitful for the reception of kabbalistic teachings, transplanted at the beginning of the 13th century from Provence to Gerona. Mainly due to the works of Naḥmanides, the kabbalistic movement developed widely (see *Kabbalah). Between 1280 and 1290 the Zohar appeared and was enthusiastically received. Philosophy appeared to be in retreat before this new trend. At this very moment the Maimonidean controversy broke out once more, beginning in Provence where the study of philosophy had received a new impetus through the translations of works from Arabic by the Ibn *Tibbon and *Kimḥi families. The quarrel reached such dimensions that the most celebrated rabbi of the day, Solomon b. Abraham *Adret, rabbi of Barcelona, was obliged to intervene. A double *ḥerem* was proclaimed on those who studied Greek philosophy before the age of 25 and on those who were too prone to explain the biblical stories allegorically. Exceptions were made on works of medicine, astronomy, and the works of Maimonides. This ban was probably another sign of the decline of the Jewish community of Aragon and its increasing tendency to withdraw into itself. During the same period Jewish courtiers lost their influence and left the political arena.

In Castile, on the other hand, Jewish courtiers continued to play an important role in spite of the efforts of other courtiers to be rid of them and of the Church to condemn them as usurers. Apostates were at the fore in this struggle, especially *Abner of Burgos who, becoming a Christian in 1321 and, taking the name Alfonso of Valladolid, tried to remain in close contact with the Jewish community, the better to influence it. Around the same period, Gonzalo *Martínez de Oviedo, majordomo to the king, obtained the temporary dismissal of Jewish courtiers and planned the eventual expulsion of all the Jews of the kingdom. Soon himself accused of treason, he was put to death (1340) and his plan fell into abeyance. At the beginning of the 14th century *Asher b. Jehiel became rabbi of Toledo, the principal community in the kingdom, holding this office from 1305 to 1327. After the imprisonment of his master, *Meir b. Baruch of Rothenburg, he had been the leading rabbinic authority in Germany, a country he fled from in 1303. Practically as soon as he arrived in Spain he was involved in the philosophic controversy and signed the ban proclaimed by Solomon b. Abraham Adret. On the latter's death he became the leading rabbinic scholar in Spain, where he disseminated the methods of the tosafists and the ideals of the *Ḥasidei Ashkenaz. The attitude of the Catholic monarchy toward the Jews continued to vacillate. Alfonso XI resolved to root out Jewish usury but to permit the Jews to remain (1348). The *Black Death, which reached Spain at this period, did not give rise to persecutions like those which swept central Europe. Alfonso's successor, Pedro the Cruel (1350–69) brought Jewish courtiers back into his employment and allowed Don Samuel b. Meir ha-Levi *Abulafia, his chief treasurer, to build a magnificent synagogue in Toledo in 1357 (it was later turned into a church and subsequently into a museum). Despite the fall of Don Samuel, who died in prison, other Jewish courtiers retained their positions and influence. During the civil war between Pedro and his bastard half-brother, Henry of Trastamara, the Jews sided with the king, who, therefore, was even called the king of the Jews. When Burgos was taken by the pretender (1366), the Jewish community was reduced to selling the synagogue appurtenances to pay its ransom. Some of its members were even sold into slavery. Henry's victory, augmented by the capture of Toledo (in which many Jews fell victim), reduced the local community to destitution: the king had seized at least 1,000,000 gold maravedis. However, this did not prevent the king from appointing Don Joseph *Picho as tax farmer and other Jews from filling important positions. Incited by the Cortes, he imposed the Jewish badge and forbade Jews to take Christian names, but he did not dismiss his Jewish courtiers. Meanwhile the condition of the Jews in the kingdom deteriorated. In 1380 the Cortes, as a result of the secret execution of Don Joseph Picho as an informer on the orders of the rabbinical tribunal, forbade the Jewish communities to exercise criminal jurisdiction and to impose the death penalty or banishment. In Castile the first part of the 14th century was dominated by the personality of *Jacob b. Asher, third son of Asher b. Jehiel, who was *dayyan* in Toledo. Around 1340 he published his *Arba'ah Turim*, a codification of the law combining the Spanish and the Ashkenazi traditions, which was widely distributed. His brother *Judah b. Asher succeeded his father in Toledo and became in effect the chief rabbi of Castile.

The situation in Aragon was generally both less brilliant and less disquieting. There the influence of the Jews at court had practically disappeared with the dismissal of the Jewish courtiers. The Jews were tolerated and had the right to royal protection within the limits of Church doctrine on the matter. The taxes raised from the Jews were an important source of revenue and so they were allowed to pursue their commercial ventures and direct their own internal affairs. Under the reign of James II (1291–1327) the Inquisition had begun to show an interest in the Jews but the king declared that their presence was an affair of state and not a religious concern, an attitude characteristic of the monarchy for many years. James gave no assistance to the efforts to convert the Jews. When the *Pastoureaux arrived in Aragon, the king resisted them vigorously in his efforts to spare the Jews from this menace. During his rule (1306) Jews expelled from France were permitted to settle in Spain. Unlike in Castile, in Aragon the Black Death gave rise to anti-Jewish excesses. In Saragossa only 50 Jews survived and in Barcelona and other Catalonian cities the Jews were massacred. So shattered were the communities by these riots that their leaders convened in Barcelona in 1354 to decide on common measures to reestablish themselves. They resolved to establish a central body to appeal to the papal curia to defend them against allegations of spreading the plague and to secure for them some alleviation in their situation. A delegation sent to Pope Clement VI in Avignon succeeded in having a bull promulgated which condemned such accusations.

It would seem that the attempt to create a central organization did not succeed, but the Aragon communities had nevertheless to reorganize. From 1327 the Barcelona community succeeded in abolishing all communal offices which were acquired by royal favor. Authority and power within the community were henceforth vested in the Council of 30, elected by the community notables. The 30 were trustworthy men, judges or administrators of charities, who were empowered to issue *takkanot* and apportion taxes. They were elected for three-year terms and could serve more than one term; however, close relatives could not sit on the same council. Although in effect the aristocracy remained in power, they were no longer all-powerful. The presence in Barcelona of eminent masters of the law counterbalanced the ambition of the powerful families. Nissim b. Reuben *Gerondi (d. c. 1375), *av bet din* in Barcelona, exercised great influence over all Spanish Jewry, as attested by his many responsa (the majority of which are unfortunately no longer extant). Ḥasdai *Crescas, born in Barcelona around 1340, who seems to have been close to court circles, became the most venerated authority in Spanish Jewry. *Isaac b. Sheshet Perfet, also born in Barcelona (1326), rapidly became known as a leading rabbinic authority. A merchant by trade, he later served as rabbi in various communities. On April 2, 1386, Pedro IV approved a new constitution for the Barcelona community which constituted slight progress toward democratization. The community was divided into three classes, almost certainly according to their tax contribution. Each class was empowered to nominate a secretary and elect ten members of the council. With the secretaries, the 30 elected members made up the grand council of the community. Five representatives of each class and the secretaries constituted the smaller council. The secretaries served for one year only and could only be renominated after two years had expired. One-third of the 30 members had to be renewed each year. The council had limited powers only, being unable to establish tax allocations without the approval of the 30. Tax assessors had to be chosen from among the three classes. The influence of the powerful families was thus curbed, extending only over the class of the community of which they were members.

The smaller communities, of course, established a less complex system of administration. Councils were not appointed there until the second half of the 14th century. In many places the local oligarchy seems to have maintained its power. In Majorca, essentially a mercantile community, this oligarchy was composed of merchants who prevented any democratization of the administration. The royal administration recognized the existence of *judíos francos*, descendants of courtly Jewish families who paid no taxes to the community and took no part in communal life. They married among themselves and generally remained true to their faith. The communities were also concerned with the moral life of their members. An institution almost unique to Spain in the Middle Ages was the **berurei averah*, notables who watched over the religious life of their communities. The latter also exercised authority over *informers, punishing them with loss of a limb or death, with the approval of the king. The death sentence was generally carried out immediately, which to some seemed dangerous or arbitrary. To avoid the possibility of abuse, in 1388 Ḥasdai Crecas was appointed judge over all informers in the kingdom.

The Persecutions of 1391

Soon the face of Spanish Jewry was brutally altered. In 1378 the archdeacon of Ecija, Ferrant *Martinez, launched a campaign of violent sermons against the Jews, demanding the destruction of 23 local synagogues. On the death of the archbishop in 1390, he became virtual ruler of the diocese, using this situation to intensify his anti-Jewish campaign and declaring that even the monarchy would not oppose attacks on the Jews. After unsuccessful interventions by the communities, the death of King John I of Castile (1390) left the crown in the hands of a minor who did not attempt to check the redoubtable preacher. On the first of Tammuz 5151 (June 4, 1391) riots broke out in Seville. The gates of the *judería* were set on fire and many died. Apostasy was common and Jewish women and children were even sold into slavery with the Muslims. Synagogues were converted into churches and the Jewish quarters filled with Christian settlers. Disorder spread to Andalusia, where Old and New Castile Jewish communities were decimated by murder and apostasy. In Toledo, on June 20, Judah, grandson of Asher b. Jehiel, refused to submit and was martyred. Attacks were made in *Madrid, *Cuenca, Burgos, and Córdoba, the monarchy making no efforts to protect the Jews. So many people had been involved in the riot that it proved impossible to arrest the leaders. In July violence broke out in Aragon; the Valencia community was destroyed on July 9 and more than 250 Jews were massacred. Others, including Isaac b. Sheshet Perfet, managed to escape. The tardy measures taken by the royal authorities were useless. Many small communities were converted en masse. In the Balearic Islands the protection of the governor was to no avail: on July 10 more than 300 Jews were massacred. Others took refuge in the fortress, where pressure was put on them to compel them to convert. A few finally escaped to North Africa. In Barcelona more than 400 Jews were killed on August 5. During the attack on the Jewish quarter of Gerona on August 10 the victims were numerous. The Jews of *Tortosa were forcibly converted. Practically all the Aragon communities were destroyed in bloody outbreaks when the poorer classes, trying to relieve their misery by burning their debts to the Jews, seized Jewish goods. Yet the motive behind the attacks was primarily religious, for, once conversion was affected, they were brought to an end.

Although he did not encourage the outbreaks, John I of Aragon did nothing to prevent or stop them, contenting himself with intervening once the worst was over. Above all he was concerned to conserve royal resources and on Sept. 22, 1391 ordered an enquiry into the whereabouts of the assets of the ruined communities and dead Jews, especially those who had left no heirs. All that could be found he impounded. At this point Ḥasdai Crescas became in effect the savior of the remnants of Aragonese Jewry, gathering together the funds necessary to persuade the king to come to their defense, appealing to the pope, and offering assistance to his brethren. The assassins were barely punished, but when a fresh outbreak seemed imminent early in 1392 the king swiftly suppressed it. Subsequently he took various measures to assist Ḥasdai Crescas in his efforts to reorganize the communities and reunite the dispersed members. Meanwhile, in Barcelona and Valencia, the burghers, freed from their rivals, seemed opposed to the reconstitution of the shattered Jewish communities. A small community was reestablished in Majorca. In the countryside the communities could reorganize more easily; there the Jews were indispensable and less a target of the jealousy of the Christian burghers.

The Conversos

In this period the problem of Jews who had converted by force became acute. Illegal though forced conversion was, in the eyes of the Church a Converso was a true Christian and thus forbidden to return to Judaism. There were indeed a number of Jews who took their conversion to heart and, filled with the zeal of neophytes, reproached their former coreligionists for their "errors" and launched a campaign to bring them to the font. Chief among these was Solomon ha-Levi of Burgos who became *Pablo de Santa Maria in 1391 and later bishop of Burgos. In their desperate state, the Jews could hardly respond energetically. The Christian missionary spirit did not rest content with the successes achieved. The notorious friar Vicente *Ferrer preached in the towns of Castile in 1411–12. Although opposed to forced conversion, he was ready to compel Jews to listen to him and was unconcerned by the anti-Jewish violence which was consequent on his sermons. Following on his activity the government of Castile proclaimed on Jan. 2, 1412, new regulations concerning Jews. Henceforth, in towns and in villages, they were to inhabit separate quarters and, to distinguish them from Christians, had to grow their hair and beards, and could no longer be addressed by the honorific, "Don." They were forbidden to take employment as tax farmers or fill any other public office, nor could their physicians treat Christians; lending on interest was also prohibited. All professions were closed to them and all commerce by which they might ameliorate their miserable existence forbidden. For a time even their internal autonomy and freedom of movement were in question.

In Aragon the situation was more favorable. The community of Saragossa, spared because of the presence of the king in the town, was able to play an important role in the reconstitution of the Aragonese communities. The action of the king gave a semblance of stability to the new Jewish groups. In 1399 the *aljama* of Saragossa, where Ḥasdai Crescas was rabbi, obtained a new statute from Queen Violante defining its power and organization. In June 1412 Ferdinand I became new king of Aragon, thanks to the assistance and support of Vicente Ferrer, who seized the opportunity to extend his activities against the Jews of Aragon. At that moment Joshua *Lorki, who had previously disputed with Pablo de Santa Maria, decided to accept baptism under the name of Geronimo de Santa Fé. In August of the same year he sent a pamphlet to the antipope Benedict XIII which served as the basis for the public disputation soon to be held in Tortosa. The pope invited the Aragonese communities to send representatives to a public disputation to be held in Tortosa on Jan. 15, 1413; it actually took place the following February (see *Tortosa, Disputation of). Probably the antipope wished to achieve a

Map 2. Major Jewish and Converso communities in Christian Spain, 1474. From map by H. Beinart in Y.Baer, A History of the Jews in Christian Spain, *Philadelphia, 1961.*

great religious success at the moment the split Church was attempting to reunite at the Council of Constance. The Jewish delegates presented themselves without great enthusiasm for the issue of the disputation was in no doubt and freedom of expression had been virtually refused. The leading Jewish delegates were *Zerahiah b. Isaac ha-Levi from Saragossa and the philosopher Joseph Albo; as was to be expected Christianity triumphed and the defeat of the Jews resulted in a wave of conversion. The rabbis were given no real opportunity to defend themselves. The major topics of the disputation were the messianic problem and the veracity of the Talmud, and the Jewish delegates, despairing of being truly heard, wished to end the disputation. Only Zerahiah b. Isaac ha-Levi and Joseph Albo defended Judaism against all attack but they failed to convince their colleagues that there was any point in replying. The disputation finally ended in December 1414 and the Jewish delegates returned home.

Acting on a bull promulgated by Benedict XIII on May 11, Ferdinand I ordered on July 23, 1415 the Jews to submit their copies of the Talmud so that all passages deemed anti-Christian might be censored. The Jews were also forbidden to read the **Toledot Yeshu*. Any attack on the Church was prohibited. Jewish judges lost their authority over criminal cases, even those involving informers. They were also forbidden to extend their synagogues. Christians could no longer employ Jewish agents and the Jews were confined to a special quarter. Apostates could inherit from their Jewish parents. With this even heavier burden to bear, many Aragonese communities were destroyed and conversions were numerous, especially among the higher classes. Aragon Judaism was close to the abyss when Benedict XIII was dismissed from the papacy (1416). On the death of Ferdinand in the same year they acquired a temporary respite.

John II, the new king of Castile (1406–54), and his contemporary, Alfonso V of Aragon (1416–58), had little taste for the religious fervor of their predecessors. The new pope was similarly disinclined to reopen this particular battle. Almost all anti-Jewish measures were therefore abrogated (1419–22). Copies of the Talmud and synagogue buildings were restored to the Jews. In the meantime the Aragonese communities were greatly reduced; those of Valencia and Barcelona had disappeared altogether. In Majorca, the Jews who remained were dispersed by a blood libel in 1432. Only the rural settlements in the province of Aragon had escaped persecution. At the moment of the expulsion there was an estimated 6,000 Jewish families in Aragon, a meager percentage indeed of the country's total population.

In Castile there were around 30,000 Jewish families, aside from innumerable Conversos, many of whom were in fact Jews. The large communities, Seville, Toledo, and Burgos, had lost their former influence as a result of the apostasy of many members of the ruling class. Henceforward the decisive weight in the Jewish life of the kingdom was maintained by the small rural communities whose numbers rarely exceeded 50 families. The Jews were merchants, shopkeepers, or artisans, with a number of physicians. Some Jewish courtiers managed to retrieve their positions at court; Abraham *Benveniste de Soria was the treasurer of John II, who also appointed him *rab de la corte*, chief rabbi of the kingdom. Abraham Benveniste used his position to undertake the reorganization of Castilian Jewry, convoking in 1432 a convention of representatives of Spanish communities in Valladolid to formulate and adopt new regulations. Their primary concern was to reorganize systems of instruction, to be effected through a tax imposed on slaughter, on wine, on marriages, and on circumcisions. Any community of 15 families or more was to support one primary school teacher, and a community of 40 families must employ a rabbi. It was also laid down that a community consisting of ten families must maintain a place of prayer. Various measures were formulated to regulate the election of judges, who had to act in accord with the rabbi and notables. It was also possible to appeal to the *rab de la corte*. The former laws covering informers and slanderers were abrogated; in future the *rab de la corte* could, under certain conditions, sentence informers to death. Forced betrothals and marriages were strictly forbidden. The *rab de la corte* also had to approve the appointment of any Jew to royal commissions. No Jew was allowed to obtain from the king exemption from payment of the communal taxes. Other decisions of the convention concerned sumptuary laws. Through this strict centralization the Castilian communities found a solution to their problems. It is difficult to ascertain if the regulations of *Valladolid were strictly applied, but they were an answer to the plight of communities greatly reduced in numbers and wealth.

Yet the most pressing problem of Spanish Jewry no longer concerned the communities, for the question of the Conversos became progressively more acute. Showing their awareness and suspicion of the true nature of the mass conversions, Spanish Christians were in the habit of referring to "New" and "Old" Christians and effecting a veritable racial distinction between them. It is undoubtedly true that many Conversos were Christians in name only, acquiring their new status through force alone, and many others had accepted baptism as a means of breaking down social, economic, and political barriers. In pursuit of these aims they had begun to marry into the great Toledan families. Yet they too became concerned when in 1449 the rebels of Toledo issued a statute proclaiming that all New Christians – regardless of the fervor of their faith – were infamous and unfit for all offices and benefices, public and private, in Toledo and all its dependencies. They could be neither witnesses nor public notaries. The king and pope condemned this proclamation, more through the desire to hasten the conversion of the Jews, which it rendered henceforth impossible, than through any sense of justice. Great harm was done by this proclamation, giving rise to a widespread policy of eradication of real or suspected Jewish influence. Subsequently all religious and political agitation tended to this end.

Steps Toward the Expulsion

The marriage of Isabella, heiress to the throne of Castile, and Ferdinand, heir to the throne of Aragon, in 1469 had disastrous consequences for Spanish Jewry. The two kingdoms were united in 1479. At first they took no heed of the Jewish communities as such, but they considered the Conversos a danger to national unity. The Catholic monarchs continued to employ Jewish functionaries – such as Don Abraham *Seneor, chief rabbi of Castile and tax controller for the whole kingdom, and Isaac *Abrabanel, tax farmer for part of Castile – and a number of Conversos as well. However, in 1476 the right of criminal jurisdiction was taken from the Jewish communities. Soon the Catholic monarchs launched a direct attack on the Conversos, inviting the *Inquisition to extend its activities to the kingdom, which their predecessors had always refused to countenance, fearing the great power of this institution. On Sept. 27, 1480, two Dominicans were named inquisitors of the kingdom of Castile, and they began their activities in Seville in January 1481. Soon after, the first Conversos condemned as Judaizers were sent to their deaths. According to the chronicler Andres Bernaldez, more than 700 Conversos were burned at the stake between 1481 and 1488 and more than 5,000 reconciled to the Church after enduring various punishments. Inquisitors were appointed in 1481 for Aragon, where the papal Inquisition, which had been in existence for some time, was considered insufficiently effective. From 1483 the Jews were expelled from Andalusia, no doubt because it appeared to the inquisitors to be impossible to root out Jewish heresies from among the Conversos while practicing Jews still lived in their midst.

Tomás de *Torquemada, confessor to the queen, was appointed inquisitor-general in the autumn of 1483, providing the Inquisition with a new impetus and stricter organization. His activities stretched from town to town throughout the whole kingdom, bringing terror to Jewish communities everywhere since they were inevitably linked with the Conversos. In less than 12 years the Inquisition condemned no less than 13,000 Conversos, men and women, who had continued to practice Judaism in secret. Yet these were no more than a fraction of the mass of Conversos. When the last bastion of Muslim power in Spain fell with the triumphant entry of the Catholic monarchs into Granada on Jan. 2, 1492, the urge toward complete religious unity of the kingdom was reinforced. The scandal of the Conversos who had remained true to Judaism had shown that segregation of the Jews and limitation of their rights did not suffice to suppress their influence. They must be totally removed from the face of Spain. Thus on March 31, 1492 the edict of expulsion was signed in Granada, although it was not promulgated until between April 29 and May 1. All Jews who were willing to accept Christianity were, of course, to be permitted to stay.

In May the exodus began, the majority of the exiles – around 100,000 people – finding temporary refuge in Portugal (from where the Jews were expelled in 1496–97), the rest making for North Africa and Turkey, the only major country which opened its doors to them. A few found provisional homes in the little kingdom of Navarre, where there was still an ancient Jewish community in existence, but there too their stay was brief, for the Jews were expelled in 1498. Considerable numbers of Spanish Jews, including the chief rabbi Abraham Seneor and most of the members of the influential families, preferred baptism to exile, adding their number to the thousands of Conversos who had chosen this road at an earlier date. On July 31 (the 7th of Av), 1492, the last Jew left Spain. Yet Spanish (or Sephardi) Jewry had by no means disappeared, for almost everywhere the refugees reconstituted their communities, clinging to their former language and culture. In most areas, especially in North Africa, they met with descendants of refugees from the 1391 persecutions. In Ereẓ Israel they had been preceded by several groups of Spanish Jews who had gone there as a result of the various messianic movements which had shaken Spanish Jewry. Officially, no Jews were left in Spain. All that were left were the Conversos, a great number of whom remained true to their original faith. Some later fell victim to the Inquisition; others managed to flee from Spain and return openly to Judaism in the Sephardi communities of the Orient and Europe.

See also *Anusim; *Conversos; *Marranos; *New Christians; *Portugal; *Sephardim.

Cultural Life

From the beginning, the cultural life of Spanish Jewry under the Christian reconquest followed on the style set under Muslim rule. Eastern influence lost none of its force even though a frontier henceforward separated the communities of the north from those of the south. In fact, the contrary was the case, since the Jews of Christian Spain often appeared to be indispensable agents in the diffusion of the Eastern cultural tradition. Consequently, many of them were translators of Arabic; some, like the *Kimḥis and the Ibn *Tibbons, even carried their work as translators to the north, to Provence. In Christian Spain the Jews continued to study the sciences, medicine in particular, and the Christian kings employed numbers of Jewish physicians. They were also well versed in astronomy and shortly before the expulsion Abraham *Zacuto prepared the astronomical tables that Christopher Columbus used on his voyage. The Jewish "nobility" had frequently received the same education as their Christian counterparts, reaching a cultural integration rarely equaled in Jewish history. Of course this process only affected the families of Jewish courtiers, but this type of assimilation goes a long way toward explaining both the phenomena of Marranism – entailing the need to lead a double life – and the ability to abandon the Jewish heritage without regret and join the Christian fold. Yet the majority of people still looked to their traditional Jewish cultural heritage, which remained central to their lives. The relation of the journey of *Benjamin of Tudela to the communities of Europe and Asia, and the work of the historian Abraham *Ibn Daud in his account of the continuity of Jewish tradition are well worthy of mention. The main stress, however, lay on the study of the Hebrew language and of the Bible and Talmud, and on the development of a style of Hebrew poetry which took the profane as well as the sacred for its subject matter. In all fields there was no real break with the Judeo-Arab milieu. For many years the Babylonian academies continued to be a major influence, but rabbinical scholarship in Spanish Jewry came to maturity in the 11th century with the work of Isaac b. Jacob ha-Kohen *Alfasi. The latter, assisted by his pupils, especially Joseph b. Meir ha-Levi *Ibn Migash, created a Spanish Jewish talmudic academy which proceeded to develop its own methods. The theories of the grammarians in Muslim Spain were already known in the north and were accepted there. Poets flourished in the retinue of Jews who were wealthy or well placed at court. Poetry often remained a profession. Along with many of his contemporaries, *Judah Halevi left Muslim Spain for the Christian part of the country without finding success there. His poems were torn between the two worlds and Judah Halevi finally left for the Holy Land. Along with Judah Halevi and Moses *Ibn Ezra, Solomon ibn *Gabirol brought Hebrew poetry to a peak of perfection. Their religious poems, the main body of their work, permanently enriched the liturgy. At the same time they gave a new dimension to Hebrew poetry by extending it beyond its liturgical framework to cover every variety of a benevolent patron. The interest in poetry also gave rise to liturgical and biblical studies; biblical Hebrew once more predominated over rabbinical Hebrew. Following in the path of Menahem b. Saruk and *Dunash b. Labrat were such grammarians as Judah b. David *Ḥayyuj, Jonah *Ibn Janaḥ, Moses ha-Kohen ibn *Gikatilla, and above all Abraham *Ibn Ezra, who produced their grammatical treatises in Hebrew and so enabled the Jewish grammarians of France and Germany to become aware of and adopt the theories of their Spanish counterparts. The same writers often produced biblical commentaries: Joseph b. Isaac *Ibn Abitur on Psalms, Moses ha-Kohen ibn Gikatilla on Isaiah, the Latter Prophets, Psalms, and Job, and Abraham ibn Ezra on the entire Bible (although some portions of his commentary are no longer extant). In this period the **maqāma* – an Arabic verse form – made its debut in Jewish literature with the *Taḥkemoni* of Judah *Al-Ḥarizi. Yet the golden age of Hebrew poetry in Spain was already drawing to a close.

During the 11th century talmudic studies took root in Spain with the arrival of Isaac b. Jacob *Alfasi and continued to be greatly influenced by his work. With the aim of summing up the discussions of the sages and pointing out the correct *halakhah*, he prepared a resumé of the Talmud. In this work, he stressed practical observance, an attitude which was characteristic of the great Spanish talmudists. His main pupil, Joseph b. Meir ha-Levi ibn Migash, followed in his footsteps and, like his teacher, wrote a number of responsa clarifying points of the law. The greatest stimulus to talmudic studies was the work of Maimonides, who spent his formative years in Spain and can be considered a Spanish scholar. He, too, produced works of *codification of the law, the *Mishneh Torah* and *Sefer ha-Mitzvot*, and wrote numerous responsa. Like other Spanish rabbis, he did not hesitate to bring out his works in Arabic so that they could be understood by all. This bilinguality in Hebrew and Arabic was a mark of the first era of Spanish Jewry. Another equally important characteristic was its enthusiasm for philosophical debates. Spanish Jewry's integration into the contemporary Arab culture obliged it to face the same problems, though generally with an avowedly polemic intent. Writers were largely concerned with demonstrating that revelation and philosophy were not necessarily contradictory and that in any case Judaism represented the superior truth. Although Ibn Gabirol's philosophical work *Fons Vitae* has no specifically Jewish character, Judah Halevi devoted himself to a vigorous apology for Judaism. *Baḥya ibn Paquda, a moralist, attempted to show the superiority of ethical conduct over the ceremonial law, which becomes falsified if the "duties of the heart" are neglected. However, the greatest representative of the philosophic trend was Maimonides, who followed it to formulate his classic definition of the dogmas of Judaism. Nevertheless, from the beginning of the 13th century the supremacy of philosophy was challenged in the controversy over Maimonides' works (see *Maimonidean Controversy), especially in the north of Spain, which had then reverted to Christian rule. The change in attitude was influenced by disillusionment arising from the changed conditions of Jewish life, by the renewed interest in talmudic studies due to the work of the Franco-German tosafists, and by the new trends in Jewish mysticism which first appeared in Provence before reaching Spain. At the beginning of the 14th century the Franco-German talmudic tradition came face to face with the Spanish through the arrival of *Asher b. Jehiel, resulting in the preservation of unity in the field of Jewish law. Warmly received by the greatest Spanish scholar of the day, Solomon b. Abraham *Adret, Asher b. Jehiel cooperated with him in restoring peace: the study of philosophy was permitted, but under clearly defined conditions. Time, too, had done its work and the controversy was soon stilled. In the meantime the Kabbalah became increasingly important, especially in the group at Gerona. The celebrated talmudist Naḥmanides became one of its leading advocates. The appearance of the *Zohar, the largest part of which was produced by *Moses b. Shem Tov de León between 1280 and 1286, gave a powerful impulse to the development of the kabbalistic trend which became predominant in Spain. Talmudic studies too gained a new impetus through the commentaries, novellae, and responsa of Naḥmanides, Solomon b. Abraham Adret, Asher b. Jehiel, and Nissim b. Reuben *Gerondi. *Jacob b. Asher, son of Asher b. Jehiel, produced his codification of the law, the *Arbaʿah Turim*, which remains to this day the archetype of the rabbinic code and was one of the bases of the Shulḥan Arukh. Another code, *Sefer Abudarham*, was compiled by David b. Joseph *Abudarham of Seville. Following in the same path, *Menahem b. Aaron ibn Zerah of Navarre composed his *Ẓeidah la-Derekh*. *Yom Tov b. Abraham Ishbili was especially noted for his many novellae; Isaac b. Sheshet Perfet, who had to leave Spain in 1391, wrote many responsa. Biblical commentaries (frequently showing kabbalistic influences) also came to the fore once more with the works of Naḥmanides, Baḥya b. Asher, and Jacob b. Asher, although the latter resolutely avoided kabbalistic speculation. Nevertheless the persecutions had grave consequences for scholarship too. The Judeo-Arab heritage began to disappear. Those conditions which had drawn Spanish Jews toward the study of science, medicine, and astrology in particular ceased to exist. This decay became more marked in the 15th century. Apart from the philosophic works of Ḥasdai Crescas and Joseph Albo, whose *Sefer ha-Ikkarim* was a new attempt to define the dogmas of Judaism, the creative period had passed. The messianic upheaval, exacerbated by persecution, only prolonged it slightly; the spirit of this period is best expressed in the works of Isaac b. Judah Abrabanel, who in 1492 preferred exile to apostasy. Probably stimulated by fear for the future, interest in kabbalistic speculation continued unabated. The expulsion itself did not mark a final end of the development of this specific type of culture. Abraham Zacuto finished his rabbinical history on the way to exile. The intellectual activity of Spanish Jewry was transferred to Eastern and European centers. Even the use of the Spanish language continued unchanged (see *Ladino; *Sephardim). Such was the vitality of this outlook that it remained seminal in Jewish life for many centuries

[Simon R. Schwarzfuchs]

Modern Period

Though the edict of expulsion of 1492 was not formally repealed until December 1968 and was consequently, on the Spanish statute book until that date, Jews had been allowed to live in Spain as individuals, though not as an organized community, from the late 19th century. The Republican Constitution of 1868 introduced for the first time in modern Spain the principle of religious tolerance. This was maintained in subsequent legislation and transformed into the more enlightened formula of religious freedom by the amendment to the *Fuero de los Españoles*, adopted by the referendum of December 1966. The new statute guaranteed the right of non-Catholics to maintain their organized institutions, public worship, and religious education. Jews, as such, were not specifically mentioned in any legal enactment but, as non-Catholics, they enjoyed equal rights with their Catholic fellow citizens. The only instance of "Jewish legislation" is a decree of December 1924 which granted to Sephardi Jews living abroad the right to claim Spanish nationality and settle in Spain, if they wished.

This decree, although initially referring only to the Sephardi groups of *Salonika and *Alexandria, afforded the legal basis for extending the protection of the Spanish authorities to many Jews in Nazi-occupied countries during World War II.

[Jeonathan Prato]

Holocaust Period

From 1933 until the Civil War, Spain became a haven for about 3,000 Jewish refugees. The Civil War caused most of them to leave, and after the nationalist victory, when all non-Catholic communities had to close their institutions, Jewish public and religious life was destroyed. After the fall of France, Spain served for tens of thousands of refugees as a landbridge to the high seas, which were dominated by the Allies. By the summer of 1942, over 20,000 Jewish refugees had passed through Spain, 10,500 of whom were assisted by the *HICEM office in Lisbon. Less than 1,000 were unable to continue the journey, however, and were imprisoned with other refugees in jails or in the *Miranda de Ebro concentration camp. Some refugees who crossed the border illegally were sent back to France. In the summer of 1942, when the "Final Solution" was initiated by Germany, a new wave of Jewish refugees reached Spain, and their numbers grew after the occupation of southern France. Initially there was no change in Spain's policy: refugees were accepted and arrested, and some were deported. In December 1942, however, when the Allies wanted French deserters to cross the Spanish border, Spain had to agree to stop deporting refugees and allow them to leave for North Africa and Portugal. In April 1943, Spain permitted the establishment in Madrid of the Representation of American Relief Organizations, most of whose budget came from the American Jewish *Joint Distribution Committee (AJDC). About 5,600 Jews survived by fleeing to Spain during the second half of the war. In 1943, Spain was faced with an additional rescue problem. Four thousand Jews – of whom 3,000 were in France and the rest in the Balkans as well as a number of Jews from Spanish Morocco who were living in French Morocco, possessed partial or full Spanish citizenship. Most of the Spanish consuls protected these Jews, even when they were instructed to act only when Spanish sovereignty was affected. On Jan. 28, 1943, *Eichmann and his associates presented Spain with the alternative of either recalling these Jewish subjects within a specified time or abandoning them to slaughter. On March 18, 1943 Spain decided that only those who could prove their Spanish citizenship would be permitted to enter the country. They would have to live in specified towns and would remain in Spain until they could be removed elsewhere. As long as there was one group of these "repatriates" in Spain, the next group could not enter the country. This policy was strictly adhered to. Since the Allies delayed for a year and a quarter the establishment of a refugee center in North Africa, which they had agreed upon at the *Bermuda Conference, the AJDC could not remove the "expatriation" by Spanish consuls without having recourse to repatriation; the rest died or saved themselves. In the last stages of the Holocaust, Spain joined the rescue operation in Hungary by giving protection certificates to 2,750 Jews who were not Spanish citizens.

[Haim Avni]

After World War II

The improving economic, social, and general conditions prevailing in Spain after World War II attracted an increasing number of Jews. According to an unofficial estimate some 8,000 Jews lived in Spain in 1968, distributed as follows: 3,000 in Barcelona, 2,500 in Madrid, 1,400 in Melilla, 600 in Ceuta, 300 in Malaga, and 50 in Seville. Individual Jews were scattered in many other cities. Until 1945 the bulk of the community was constituted of families originating from East Mediterranean, Balkan, and East and Central European countries. Since then a considerable number of Jews from former Spanish and French Morocco settled in the Peninsula: about 85% were of Sephardi origin. Until 1967 a Jewish community could not obtain legal recognition as a religious body (the community of Madrid was registered as a corporation under the law of private associations). Nevertheless they maintained an almost complete range of religious activities and services. In Barcelona a community center housed the synagogue, a rabbinical office, and a cultural center. In Madrid a new synagogue was officially inaugurated in December 1968 in the presence of government and ecclesiastical authorities. To mark the importance of the event, the Spanish government issued a formal repeal of the edict of expulsion. An increasing effort was made to provide Jewish education to the new generation. In Madrid a primary school had some 80 children in 1968. Hebrew lessons were given to pupils attending private schools. Two summer camps in Madrid and Barcelona were attended by 200 youngsters. A Maccabi movement, functioning in Madrid and Barcelona, afforded a framework for an increasing number of young people. The Council of Jewish Communities of Spain, established in 1963 for the coordination and study of common activities and problems, issued a monthly bulletin in Spanish, *Ha-Kesher* (1963–), dealing with local and general Jewish affairs.

In the 1960s, Spain saw a revival of studies of general and Hispanic Jewish culture. The universities of Madrid, Barcelona, and Granada had chairs of Hebrew language, Jewish history, and Jewish literature. In 1940 the Arias Montano Institute of Jewish and Near Eastern Studies was established in Madrid under the guidance of distinguished Hebrew scholars; its quarterly publication *Sefarad* acquired a reputation in the field of Sephardi culture. The Spanish Council of Scientific Research, in conjunction with the World Sephardi Federation, organized an Institute of Sephardi Studies in Madrid for the study of all aspects of Sephardi culture since the expulsion, throughout the world. In 1964 a Sephardi Center was created in Toledo by a decree of the head of state: its board included the president of the Jewish Community of Madrid and a professor of Jewish history of The Hebrew University of Jerusalem, both *ex officio*, a representative of the World Sephardi Federation, and three outstanding personalities of the Sephardi world. The new climate created in the Catholic world as a result of Vatican Council II made possible the organization of the Amistad Judeo-Christiana with the approval of the Church hierarchy in Madrid and Barcelona. This organization revised school textbooks, eliminating from them passages offensive to the Jewish people and religion.

In the post-Franco era (from 1975) the position of the Jews in Spain improved to a considerable extent, mostly as a result of the radical social changes which took place in the country. During the 1970s the number of Jews in Spain grew to about 12,000, the majority (90%) of Moroccan, Algerian and Tunisian origin, and the remainder from Eastern Europe, France, Turkey and the Balkan countries.

At the end of 1978 a major change in the constitution of Spain took place when, following a national referendum, the Catholic Church was disestablished as the state religion, as a result of which Jews were given equality with all the other religious denominations, such as the Protestant Church. Organized communities existed in Madrid, Barcelona, and Malaga. Madrid's impressive new synagogue, built in 1968, served as a center for social activities. Both Madrid and Barcelona had rabbis. Educational and social activities in Barcelona took place in the spacious communal hall attached to the synagogue and courses for youth were conducted by emissaries from Israel. There was no rabbi in Malaga, with communal affairs in the hands of a lay committee. Kosher meat was imported from Morocco.

In 1992, in a symbolic gesture, King Juan Carlos repealed the 1492 expulsion order. The two major Jewish centers remained Madrid (with about 3,000 Jews in the early 21st century) and Barcelona (also with about 3,000), followed by Malaga and with smaller communities in Alicante, Benidorm, Cadiz, Granada, Marbella, Majorca, Torremolinos, and Valencia. The total Jewish population in the early 21st century was around 12,000. The majority of Jews were Sephardi. In Spanish North Africa there were communities in Ceuta and Melila. The 1970s and 1980s saw immigration from Latin America. The Latin Americans took the initiative in forming groups that brought Jews together for cultural and intellectual events. The communities were united in the Federacion de Comunidades Israelitas de Espana. Jewish day schools operated in Barcelona, Madrid, and Malaga.

In the absence of laws restricting hate propagation or Holocaust denial, Spain served as a publishing and distribution center for neo-Nazis and other extreme rightists.

RELATIONS WITH ISRAEL. Though no diplomatic relations existed between Spain and Israel until 1986, Spain nevertheless maintained a Consulate General in Jerusalem, which had existed prior to the establishment of the State of Israel. There was no parallel Israel representation, however, in Spain. In the Israel-Arab conflict, Spain adopted a markedly pro-Arab line, seeing itself as a bridge between Western Europe and the Arab world. However, sympathy for Israel was not negligible. Trade, tourist, and shipping relations between Israel and Spain developed substantially. Exports from Israel to Spain increased from $500,000 in 1960 to $616 million in 2004, imports from $100,000 to $652 million. In 2004, 21,400 Spanish tourists arrived in Israel, up from 7,800 in 1980.

[Jeonathan Prato]

BIBLIOGRAPHY: GENERAL: **ADD. BIBLIOGRAPHY:** C. Sáncez-Albornoz, *Spain, a Historical Enigma*, 2 vols. (1975), 2:757–873; L. Suárez Fernández, *Judíos españoles en la edad media* (1980) (French trans. *Les Juifs espagnols au Moyen Âge* (1983)); idem, *Los Reyes Católicos: la expansión de la fe* (1990), 75–120; J. Stampfer (ed.), *The Sephardim: A Cultural Journey from Spain to the Pacific Coast* (1987); Y. Assis, in: *Encuentros and Desencuentros, Spanish Jewish Cultural Interaction* (2000), 29–37; idem, in: A. Rapoport-Albert and S.J. Zipperstein (eds.), *Jewish History, Essays in Honour of Chimen Abramsky* (1988), 25–59; A. Mirsky, A. Grossman, and Y. Kaplan (eds.), *Exile and Diaspora; Studies in the History of the Jewish People Presented to Professor Haim Beinart* (1991) (2 vols. one in Hebrew, the second in other languages); J.L. Lacave, *Sefarad: La España judía* (1987); idem, *Juderías y sinagogas españolas* (1992); D. Romano, in: *Proceedings of the 10th World Congress of Jewish Studies* (1900), Division B, vol. 2, 135–42; H. Beinart, ed., *The Sephardi Legacy* (1992), 2 vols.; idem, *The Expulsion of the Jews from Spain* (2002) (trans. from Hebrew); E. Kedourie (ed.), *Spain and the Jews; The Sephardi Experience, 1492 and After* (1992); V.B. Mann, J.D. Dodds, and T.F. Glick (ed.), *Convivencia: Jews, Muslims, and Christians in Medieval Spain* (1992); H. Méchoulan (ed.), *Les Juifs d'Espagne; histoire d'une diaspora* (1992). MUSLIM PERIOD: Ashtor, Korot; E. Ashtor, in: *Zion*, 28 (1963), 34–56; Ibn Daud, Tradition; R. Dozy, *Spanish Islam* (1913); E. Lévi-Provençal, *Histoire de l'Espagne Musulmane*, 2 vols. (1950); H.J. Schirmann, in: YMḤSI, 2 (1936), 117–212; 4 (1938), 247–96; 6 (1945), 249–347; idem, in: *Zion*, 1 (1936), 261–83, 357–76; idem, in: JSOS, 13 (1951), 99–126; Schirmann, Sefarad, 1–2 (1960–61²), passim; L. Torrés-Balbas, in: *Al-Andalus*, 19 (1954), 189–97; A.S. Halkin, in: L. Finkelstein (ed.), *The Jews*, 2 (1960³), 1116–49; M. Margaliot, *Hilkhot ha-Nagid* (1962), 1–11; S.D. Goitein, *A Mediterranean Society* (1967), index. **ADD. BIBLIOGRAPHY:** S.D. Gotein, in: *Orientalia Hispanica*, 1:1 (1974), 331–50; N. Allony, in: *Sefunot*, n.s., 1 (1980), 63–82; A. Pinero Saenz, in: J. Peláez del Rosal (ed.), *The Jews in Cordoba (X–XII) Centuries* (1987), 9–27. CHRISTIAN PERIOD: Baer, Spain; Baer, Urkunden; Neuman, Spain; H. Beinart, *Anusim be-Din ha-Inkvizizyah* (1965); J. Juster, in: *Etudes d'histoire juridique offertes à Paul Frédéric Girard* (1912), 275–335; F. Cantera Burgos, in: C. Roth (ed.), *World History of the Jewish People*, 2 (1966), 357–81; J. Regné, *Catalogue des actes de Jaime Ier, Pedro III et Alfonso III, rois d'Aragon, concernant les Juifs* (1911–14); I. Epstein, *Responsa of R. Solomon ben Adreth of Barcelona (1235–1310) as a Source of History of Spain* (1925); I.S. Revah, in: REJ, 118 (1959), 29–77; *Sefarad*, 1 (1941–71); R. Cansinos-Asséns, *España y los judíos españoles. El retorno del éxodo* (1917); idem, *Los judíos en Sefarad: episodios y símbolos* (1950). **ADD. BIBLIOGRAPHY:** Y.H. Yerushalmi, in: *Salo Wittmayer Baron Jubilee Volume on the Occasion of His Eightieth Birthday* (1974), 1023–58; M. Kriegel, *Les Juifs à la fin du Moyen Âge dans l'Europe méditerranéene* (1979); D. Romano, in: *Sefarad*, 39 (1979), 347–54; idem, in: *ibid.*, 51 (1991), 353–67; idem, in: *Hispania sacra*, 40 (1988), 955–78; H. Beinart, in: *Zion*, 51 (1986), 61–85; Y. Assis, in: *Zion*, 46 (1981), 251–77 (Heb.); idem, *ibid.*, 50 (1985), 221–40 (Heb.); idem, in: REJ, 142 (1983), 209–27; idem, in: *Sefunot*, 3:18 (1985), 11–34; idem, in: J. Dan (ed.), *Tarbut ve-Historiyah (Culture and History)* (Heb., 1987), 121–45; idem, in: *Jewish Art*, 18 (1992), 7–29; idem, in: D. Frank (ed.), *The Jews of Medieval Islam* (1995) 111–24; idem, in: S. Kottek (ed.), *Medical Ethics in Medieval Spain (13th–14th Centuries)* (1996), 33–49; idem, *The Golden Age of Aragonese Jewry* (1997); idem, *Jewish Economy in the Medieval Crown of Aragon* (1997); E. Gutwirth, in: *Misceláneo de Estudios Áreabes y Hebraicos*, 30:2 (1981), 83–98; idem, in: *ibid.*, 34:2 (1985), 85–91; idem, in: *Sefarad*, 49 (1989), 237–62; M. de Menaca, in: *Les pays de la Méditerranée occidentale au Moyen Âge; études et recherches* (1983), 235–53; J. Hacker, in: R.I. Cohen, *Vision and Conflict in the Holy Land* (1985), 111–39; idem, in: *Sefunot*, n.s. 2 (1983), 21–95; B. Leroy, *L'aventure séfarade* (1986); J.R. Magdalena Nom de Déu, in: *Calls*, 2 (1987), 7–16; J. Riera i Sans, in: *Calls*, 3 (1988–89), 9–28; P. León Tello, in: *Anuario de estudios medievales*, 19 (1989), 451–67; D. Schwatz, in: *Pe'amim*, 46–47 (1991), 92–114 (Heb.); HOLOCAUST PERIOD: N. Robinson, *Spain of Franco and its Policies Towards the Jews* (1953). **ADD. BIBLIOGRAPHY:** H. Avni, *Spain, the Jews and Franco* (1982). CONTEMPORARY PERIOD: J. Goodman, in: AJYB, 68 (1967), 332–41; H. Beinart, *Ha-Yishuv ha-Yehudi he-Ḥadash bi-Sefarad, Reka, Meẓi'ut ve-Ha'arakhah* (1969).

SPANDAU, city in Germany; since 1920 part of the metropolitan area of *Berlin. Jews settled in Spandau as early as the 13th century. Although a source dated 1307 gave Jews permission to maintain a communal slaughterhouse, meat selling was limited to those who maintained a house in the city. Jews were engaged mostly in moneylending, having been given permission to do so providing they charged a reasonable rate of interest and refrained from debasing the coinage. In part, the granting of the privilege was intended to help provide the funds for the building of the city walls. As an additional stimulus to Jewish settlement, Duke Rudolph submitted to the city council (1324) a plan for exempting Jews from all taxes for a period of two years. A cemetery was noted in 1324 and a synagogue in 1342. (In 1955–56, 19 Jewish gravestones which dated from 1284 to 1947 were unearthed in Spandau.) The Jews of Berlin buried their dead in Spandau until the 15th century. While some Jews reached high levels of governmental administration in the financial service of Duke Louis, the Jewish community itself went through a period of considerable unrest at the time of the *Black Death persecutions. In 1496 there were 50 Jews in the city. In 1510, however, Jews were accused of desecrating the *Host and were driven from the city. Their cemetery and synagogue were confiscated. No Jews lived in Spandau until the 18th century. In 1782 there were eight Jews in the city, and in 1812 there were 52. Religious services were held in a private home, and a religious school was established in 1854. The Jews of Spandau joined with those of Nauen and Kremmen as a single community until 1894. After that time the Jews of Spandau again maintained a separate community, building a synagogue in 1895. Expanded commercial activity brought additional Jews to the city. By 1880 there were 165 Jews in Spandau; 316 in 1910; 514 in 1925; 725 in 1933. In 1937 there were 381. On the eve of the Nazi accession to power, the community maintained a religious school and three philanthropic organizations. Its fate during the Holocaust was part of that of the Jews of all Berlin. In 1989 a memorial was consecrated to the former synagogue that was destroyed in 1938.

BIBLIOGRAPHY: *Germania Judaica*, 2 (1968), 772–4; vol. 3 (1987), 1382–84; F. Kohstall, *Aus der Chronik der Spandauer Juedischen Gemeinde* (1929); FJW, 62. **ADD. BIBLIOGRAPHY:** A. Kaulen and J. Pohl, *Juden in Spandau. Vom Mittelalter bis 1945* (1988) (Reihe Deutsche Vergangenheit, vol. 33; Staetten der Geschichte Berlins); *Juedische Buerger Spandaus nach 1933: Informationen zur Ausstellung einer Arbeitsgruppe der Carl-Diem-Oberschule Spandau* (1991).

[Alexander Shapiro]

SPANEL, ABRAM NATHANIEL (1901–1985), U.S. industrialist, inventor, philanthropist. Spanel was the founder of one of the biggest corset and brassiere companies in the U.S. and an inventor who held more than 2,000 patents. He was probably best known, however, for the editorials he wrote as paid advertisements in scores of newspapers all over the country for more than 40 years. In them, he offered his opinions on world affairs, with particular emphasis on matters affecting the State of Israel, whose cause he championed.

Born in Odessa, Russia, the son of a tailor and a laundress, he was taken to Paris by his family at an early age, and then to Rochester, N.Y., when he was 10. He was a student at the University of Rochester for three years, then invented a garment bag that could be aired and moth-proofed with a vacuum cleaner. He made his first million dollars with his first business, the Vacuumizer Manufacturing Company. In 1932 he founded the International Latex Corporation, which later became the International Playtex Corporation. Playtex was the first company to make a bra with elastic, the first to package intimate apparel and sell it as a brand, and the first to advertise it on television. It was also the first to use live women modeling bras in TV commercials. Spanel retired as chairman of International Playtex in 1975, but remained active as head of the Spanel Foundation and Spanel International Ltd., a business he started in 1976 to manufacture some of his inventions. Spanel was awarded patents on an eclectic range of products, including a hair-cutting device to be used in the home and a pneumatic stretcher for transporting military personnel wounded in combat. His philanthropic interests focused on medical research, especially child care. He established the Spanel Foundation for Cancer Research in New York City and the Playtex Park Research Institute at his company's headquarters in Dover, Delaware. His employees were provided with free Vitamin C tablets and were among the first workers to have air-conditioning, paid health and life insurance, and a profit-sharing plan. During World War II, Spanel contributed more than $1.5 million to the war effort, the profits he had made on war contracts. A staunch advocate of Franco-American relations, he was made a Commander of the Legion of Honor by France.

BIBLIOGRAPHY: W.H. Waggoner, *New York Times* (April 2, 1985).

[Mort Sheinman (2nd ed.)]

SPANIER, ARTHUR (1889–1944), German scholar and librarian. Spanier, who was born in Magdeburg, studied classical languages at the University of Berlin and Hebrew at the Lehranstalt fuer die Wissenschaft des Judentums (1908–13). In 1914–15 he worked as a school teacher in Berlin, and then served in the German army. After the war he resumed teaching, first in Berlin, and then in Koenigsberg. He was appointed a research fellow at the newly founded *Akademie fuer die Wissenschaft des Judentums in 1919–20. He received his Ph.D. in Freiburg/Breisgau in 1920. In 1921 he entered the service of the Prussian State Library, becoming head of the Hebraica and Judaica division in 1926, specializing also in the Armenian language. As a "non-Aryan" he was pensioned off in 1935. From 1937 he lectured at the *Hochschule fuer die Wissenschaft des Judentums. In 1938 he was taken to the Sachsenhausen concentration camp, but was released, whereupon he immigrated to the Netherlands in 1939. He perished at *Bergen-Belsen.

Spanier's main scholarly interests and works were in Talmudics. He wrote *Die Toseftaperiode in der Tannaitischen Literatur* (1922), in which he suggested that Tosefta had its origin in marginal notes to the Mishnah; *Die Massoretischen Akzente* (1927); *Das Berliner Baraita Fragment* (1931); *Zur Frage des Literarischen Verhaeltnisses zwischen Mischnah und Tosefta* (1931).

BIBLIOGRAPHY: E. Taeubler, in: HJ, 7 (1945), 96; E.G. Lowenthal (ed.), *Bewaehrung im Untergang* (1965), 162ff. **ADD. BIBLIOGRAPHY:** W. Schochow, in: *Mitteilungen der Staatsbibliothek Preussischer Kulturbesitz* 1 (1990), 36–38.

[Archive Bibliographia Judaica]

SPANISH AND PORTUGUESE LITERATURE.

Biblical and Hebraic Influences

One result of the Christian struggle against Muslim invaders of the Iberian peninsula from the eighth century onward was the blending of national and religious aspirations, which revealed itself in Spanish literature. Jews and Christians cooperated in translating the Bible into the vernacular, and the Old Testament version was taken direct from the Hebrew in renderings that antedate 1250. Thus, although Juan I of Aragon prohibited such activities in 1233, *Alfonso the Wise (Alfonso X of Castile, 1221–1284) enthusiastically encouraged the translation of the Bible into Spanish. Indeed, Alfonso himself, in his *General e grande Estoria*, linked the history of the world as known in his time with the Hebraic history of the Bible. In the 15th century further biblical projects were promoted by Jews or Conversos. The version by Moses *Arragel (1422) was followed by that published by Abraham *Usque, whose Ferrara Bible (1553) appeared in two slightly differing editions. Usque's Bible inspired Jewish translations into Judeo-Spanish or *Ladino, the dialect of Spanish which Jewish exiles took with them after the Expulsion of 1492. With the official Catholic ban on Spanish versions of the Bible a century later, these became a Jewish monopoly, and after 1600 Spain ceased to be a Bible-reading country until the Spanish hierarchy changed its policy at the end of the 18th century.

During the Renaissance, however, the Bible was a significant influence in Spanish and Portuguese literature, though more especially among writers of Jewish or *Marrano origin, whether in the Iberian peninsula or abroad. Luis de *León (1527–1591), a humanist scholar and poet whose New Christian descent was responsible for his spending five years in the cells of the Inquisition, is said to have translated the Song of Songs from the Hebrew, and biblical themes and metaphors greatly influenced his original verse. Much the same may be said of the mystical poets of the Spanish Renaissance, notably Saint John of the Cross (1542–1591). Biblical echoes can even be found in the works of a completely secular writer such as Garcilaso de la Vega (1503–1536). Diego Sánchez (c. 1530) composed a *Farsa de Salomón* and other plays on Abraham, Moses, and David; Micael de Carvajal (c. 1575) wrote a drama about Joseph; and the 96 biblical *autos* of the Madrid Codex (1550–75) include 26 on Old Testament subjects. Solomón *Usque (c. 1530–c. 1596), a professing Jew of Marrano origin, wrote a Spanish Purim play, *Ester*, first staged in the Venice ghetto in 1558.

BIBLICAL DRAMA. Biblical drama and poetry really became prominent, however, from the 17th century. In Spain the prolific Tirso de Molina (Gabriel Téllez, c. 1584–1648) composed *La mejor espigadera* (1634), based on the story of Ruth; and *La venganza de Tamar* (1634), a drama about Absalom. The Old Testament played an even more important part in the writings of Pedro Calderón de la Barca (1600–1681), who made use of the biblical themes of the Babylonian captivity (in *La cena de Baltasar*), the Ark of the Covenant, David, Solomon, and Job for his *autos sacramentales* (religious plays). The *auto* of Spain's Golden Age had been anticipated to a great extent by the religious plays and moralities of Gil Vicente (c. 1465–c. 1536), a Portuguese court dramatist, many of whose works were written in Spanish. Writers of Jewish origin inspired by the Bible include Felipe *Godínez (c. 1588–c. 1639), a Seville dramatist and preacher, who wrote plays about Isaac, David, Haman and Mordecai, Job, and Judith. Others who left the peninsula to take refuge abroad were Francisco (Joseph) de *Caceres, whose *Los siete Días de la Semana* (1612) was an adaptation of a Creation epic, *La Semaine*, by the French Protestant *Du Bartas; David *Abenatar Melo, a Marrano revert to Judaism, who published a Spanish verse rendering of the Psalms (1626); and Antonio Enríquez *Gómez, an immensely popular writer, whose works include the biblical epic, *El Sansón Nazareno* (1656) and *La Torre de Babilonia* (1647). Two Portuguese Marrano poets who found inspiration in the Bible were João (Mose) *Pinto Delgado (d. 1653), a leader of the Crypto-Jewish community in Rouen, who dedicated to Cardinal Richelieu his *Poema de la Reyna Ester, Lamentaciones del Profeta Jeremías*, and *Historia de Rut* (Rouen, 1687); and Miguel de *Silveyra, whose baroque masterpiece, *El Macabeo* (Naples, 1638), was written in Spanish. The early 18th-century author Isaac Cohen de *Lara wrote a graceful *Comedia famosa de Amán y Mordochay* (Amsterdam, 1699), based on the Book of Esther and the related midrashic traditions, and a ballad about Jacob which was printed in the same volume. The works of Abraham de *Bargas, a refugee Marrano author and physician, included ethical discourses on the Bible, *Pensamientos sagrados y educaciones morales* (Leghorn, 1749).

During the 18th and 19th centuries biblical and other Hebraic themes became less common in Spanish and Portuguese literature, perhaps as a result of political and social conservatism and the disappearance of the Jews. Even in the 20th century, interest in these subjects has been largely restricted. A remarkable exception was the eminent Spanish novelist and critic Rafael Cansinos-Assens (1883–1964) of Marrano descent. Reverting to Judaism, he studied Hebrew and wrote a series of works on Jewish themes. These include *Psalmos. El candelabro de los siete brazos* (1914), love poems in "biblical" style; *Las bellezas del Talmud* (1919), translated selections; *Salomé en la literatura* (1919); *Cuentos judios* (1922); *Las luminarias de Hanukah; Un episodio de la historia de Israel en España* (1924), a novel; and *El amor en el Cantar de los Cantares* (1930), with texts in Hebrew and Spanish.

The Image of the Jew in Spanish Literature

Jews have generally been portrayed in Spanish literature in an unfavorable guise. Their earliest appearance is in the epic *Poems del Cid* (or *Cantar de Mío Cod* (c. 1140)) in which two moneylenders, Raquel and Vidas, are cheated by El Cid, the national hero, giving him 600 marks on the security of a richly decorated chest filled with sand. The episode has been variously interpreted, but it must have appealed to the antisemitism of the audiences listening to a troubadour telling the story. In his *Milagros de Nuestra Señora*, the poet Gonzalo de Berceo (c. 1195–c. 1265) repeats several miracles involving Jews, tales which enjoyed a European vogue: the Jews who are converted are saved, the others are portrayed as diabolical figures deserving the punishments of Hell. The 13th-century *Disputa entre un cristiano y un judío*, typical of the disputation literature written by Christians, Muslims, and Jews in Spain, is remarkable only for its coarseness and for the Christian's prurient interest in the Jewish rite of circumcision. Perhaps the most favorable medieval Spanish treatment of the Jew is found in the works of the infante Don Juan Manuel (1282–1348). In his *Libro de los castigos* Juan Manuel wrote with great sympathy of his doctor, Don Salamón, and recommended him in glowing terms to his son. In the 14th century, the poet and historian Pedro Lopez de Ayala (1332–1407) castigated the powerful court Jews in his *Rimado de Palacio*, a work satirizing all the contemporary ills of the nation as he saw them, and not specifically antisemitic. In the same century, the archpriest of Hita (Juan Ruiz, c. 1283–c. 1350) composed songs for Moorish and Jewish dancing girls, as well as for Christians. The late 14th- or early 15th-century *Danza de la muerte* (Dance of Death) hispanicizes a widespread European type of satire in that it includes a Moorish *alfaquí* and a rabbi among those whom Death invites to dance, treating them no better and no worse than the other victims.

Conversos and Marranos

Not surprisingly, the literature of the 15th century, reflecting the mounting tensions and hatreds of the period, is full of antisemitic references. Both Jews and Conversos (especially the latter) are objects of scorn, and are depicted as cowardly, sly, and mercenary. Juan Alfonso de *Baena's *Cancionero* (1445), an anthology of the 14th- and 15th-century verse, contains several attacks on Jews and Conversos, as well as one or two contributions by Jews. The somewhat later *Coplas del Provincial*, a vicious libel on the highest nobility of the country, accuses the *hidalgos* mainly of sexual deviation and Judaizing. The Converso poet Rodrigo de *Cota de Maguaque (c. 1460), who alluded to Jewish customs of his time, was outspokenly hostile to both Jews and Marranos. For this he was vigorously attacked by another Converso poet, Antón de *Montoro, who also engaged in a poetic feud with a third New Christian writer, Juan (Poeta) de *Valladolid.

The post-expulsion literature of the 16th and, even more, of the 17th centuries – Spain's Golden Age of letters – had its share of anti-Jewish attacks and plays on words and concepts. Ecclesiastical censorship limited the range of satire, but the Conversos were one of the acceptable targets. To call a man a "Jew" was a serious insult, and even the slightest reflection on his **limpieza de sangre* ("purity of blood") was considered grossly offensive. Satirical references were made to the supposed physical imperfections of the Jew, to his desire for social position, and to his beliefs and practices. Names suggestive of Jewish identity were ridiculed, and the allegation that a person had an aversion to pork was a stock-in-trade insult. Even the verb *esperar* (to wait) became a cliché, referring to the patience of the Jews awaiting the Messiah. The satirist Quevedo (Francisco Gómez de Quevedo y Villegas, 1580–1645) attacked his literary rival, Luis de Góngora (1561–1627), with allusions to his nose – it was commonly believed that the nose revealed a man's Jewish origin – and threatened to anoint his own poems with bacon so that Góngora would be deterred from stealing them. Quevedo's writings were probably the most insistently anti-Jewish of the period, except for specifically anti-Jewish literature, such as sermons at *autos-da-fé, which were printed and widely read. By contrast, the Navarrese physician and writer Juan *Huarte de San Juan displayed marked sympathy for the Jews in his *Examen de ingenios para las ciencias* (1575), where he even suggested that Jews were especially suited to the practice of medicine. The great novelist Miguel de *Cervantes Saavedra who (like Huarte de San Juan) has been claimed as a Marrano, occasionally indulged in anti-Jewish poems, but derided the doctrine of *limpieza*. Two of his plays barely disguise his admiration for the Jew's religious tenacity and national vitality.

Other writers who used conventional attacks and jokes at Jewish expense were Tirso de Molina, Lope de Vega, Alonso Castillo Solórzano (1854–c. 1648), and Calderón. A more vicious accusation (found in Tirso's *La Prudencia en la mujer*, 1634) was that Converso doctors murdered their Christian patients. Lope de Vega's play, *El niño inocente de la Guardia* (1617), repeated the charge that the Marranos committed ritual murder (see *Blood Libel). Such an accusation was rare after 1492, when New Christians often occupied positions of power and could be formidable enemies. The story of the *Jewess of Toledo, the mistress of Alfonso VIII, provided the theme for *comedias* by Lope de Vega (*Las paces de los reyes y judía de Toledo*, 1617), Antonio Mira de Amescua (c. 1574–1644), and Juan Bautista Diamante (1625–1687) whose *La judía de Toledo* (1673) endows the Jews with noble characters. The best work of the 18th-century neoclassical theater in Spain is *La Raquel* (1778), a tragedy on the same theme by Vicente García de la Huerta (1734–87).

Modern Spanish Writers

Jewish characters are relatively unimportant in modern Spanish literature. The 19th-century romantics, Bécquer, Larra, and Zorrilla, occasionally wrote of exotic Jewish types, but displayed little sympathy for them. Among novelists, Benito Perez Galdós (1843–1920) in *Misericordia* (1897) created the delightful character of Almudena, who is described as a Moor but whose patois is based on some linguistic elements of *Ladino speech. In *Fortunata y Jacinta* (1886–87) Galdós shows that in the late 19th century Marranos were still thought to dominate Madrid business circles. Pío Baroja y Nessi (1872–1956), who was opposed to almost everything, also displayed literary antisemitism. In the 20th century, Vicente Blasco Ibáñez (1867–1928), a revolutionary writer who claimed Jewish descent, dealt with the problem of Majorca's *Chuetas in his novel, *Los Muertos mandan* (1909; "The Dead Command," 1919). Another liberal writer, Salvador de Madariaga (1886–1978), recreated in his novel *El corazón de piedra verde* (1943; "The Heart of Jade," 1944) the violent and romantic world of the 16th-century half-Jewish *conquistador* Sebastiano Garcilaso (d. 1559), father of the Peruvian historian, Garcilaso de la Vega ("El Inca," c. 1540–1616). A monumental work is the three-volume *Judíos en la España moderna y contemporánea* (1962) of Julio Caro Baroja. Among works by R. Cansinos Asséns in the same field are *España y los judios espanoles…* (1917) and *Los judíos en la literatura Española en Sefard; episodios y símbolos* (1950).

The Image of the Jew in Portuguese Literature

In general, the attitude toward Jews in Portuguese literature parallels that of Spanish writers. Portuguese literature is of somewhat later origin than Castilian, and medieval references are rare. There are occasional anti-Jewish remarks in the *Cantigas d'escarnho e maldizer* (13th–14th century), and it is worth recording that Alfonso x of Castile wrote his *Cantigas de Santa María* in Galician, a dialect of Portuguese. Fifteen of the miracles described here deal with Jews, who are portrayed as child-murderers, cheats, and agents of the devil. The *Cancioneiro Geral* (1516) of García de Resende (1470–1536) contains many satirical references to Jews, and Anrique da Mota pokes fun at the misfortunes of a Jewish tailor in his *Farsa do Alfaiate*. Jewish characters appear in several works by the versatile dramatist Gil Vicente who wrote in both Portuguese and Spanish and who witnessed the expulsion and forced conversion of the Jews in Portugal. In his religious *Autos de Moralidade das Barcas* and the *Diálogo sôbre a Ressurreiçào*, he presented the stereotyped arguments about the Jews as deicides, identified with the devil, but elsewhere he portrayed Jews more realistically. In the farces *Inês Pereira* (1523) and *Juiz da Beira* (1525), Vicente's Jewish characters and customs are based on personal observation, and if there is in them an element of caricature, this is also true of his other characters. In the first part of the *Auto da Lusitânia* (1532) the main characters are a Jewish tailor, D. Juda, and his wife and daughter, who are treated with remarkable delicacy and respect. In other works Vicente discreetly protested against the forced conversion of Jews and brutal attacks on New Christians.

After the expulsion of 1497, Portuguese Conversos and their descendants were subjected to literary attacks. In his *Apólogos Dialogaes* (1721) Francisco Manuel de Melo (1608–1666) wrote satirically of the converts in business, as did Manoel Monteiro, in *Academia nos montes* (1642). During the 16th and 17th centuries there were also many anti-Jewish doctrinal works, some by baptized Jews such as João Baptista de Este, but these were not of a literary nature.

In the 19th century the theme of love between a Christian youth and a beautiful Jewess was used by the Visconde de Almeida Garrett (1799–1854) in his *Romanceiro e Cancioneiro Geral* (3 vols., 1843–51) and by the Brazilian romantic poet Antônio de Castro Alves (1847–71). The same theme is the basis of the much-recited romantic poem "A Judía" of Tomás Ribeiro (1831–1901). A defense of the Jews was put forward by Alexandre Herculano de Carvalho e Araújo (1810–1877) in his classical *História da origem e estabelecimento da Inquisção em Portugal* (3 vols., 1854–59). Other writers who championed the Jews were the novelists Camilo Castelo Branco (1825–1890), himself of Jewish descent, and José Maria de Eça de Queirós (1846–1900), who wrote a scathing denunciation of German antisemitism and Bismarck's anti-Jewish policy in the sixth of his *Cartas de Inglaterra* (1903) and gave a remarkably vivid picture of life in Jerusalem at the time of Jesus in his novel *A Relíquia*. The martyred 18th-century playwright Antônio José da *Silva, was the central character of several works, including Castelo Branco's novel, *O Judeu* (2 vols., 1866), and the romantic drama, *Antônio José – o Poeta e a Inquisição*, by the Brazilian Domingos José Gonçalves de Magalhães (1811–1882).

The Jewish Contribution to Spanish Literature

The contribution of the Sephardim to Spanish literature was from the 12th to the 17th centuries, but a distinction must be made between the literary role of professing Jews and that of Conversos or New Christians, who were merely of Jewish origin. Spanish literature's earliest monuments, whose importance was discovered only in the 20th century, are intimately related to the two Semitic peoples living in Andalusia. These are the *jarchas* – short poetic endings, in colloquial Arabic or Mozarabic transcribed into Arabic or Hebrew characters, to longer compositions in classical Arabic or Hebrew, known as *muwashashat*. Of the more than 50 *jarchas* that are known, at least 20 form the endings to Hebrew *muwashshat*. The earliest was part of a *muwashshat* ("girdle poem") written by Joseph the Scribe and dedicated to Ismail ibn Nagrela (i.e., *Samuel ha-Nagid) and his brother Isaac. Believed to have been written before 1042, it constitutes the oldest known lyric poetry in any language of western Europe, antedating even the earliest Provençal poems. *Jarchas* are to be found in *muwashshat* of the great Hebrew poets of Spain, Moses *Ibn Ezra, *Judah Halevi, and Meir ben Todros ha-Levi *Abulafia.

TRANSLATORS AND POETS. The Jews of medieval Spain also distinguished themselves as translators, forming an important bridge between Oriental, scientific, and ethical knowledge and the nascent European culture (see *Translations). Possessing a knowledge of Arabic, Hebrew, and one or another of the Romance languages, they were invaluable collaborators. The task of imparting Arabic learning to the western world was not limited to any one center, but of them all the most important was Toledo. In the 12th century Archbishop Raimundo (d. 1152) gathered Jews, Christians, and Moors there to translate Arabic scientific and philosophical texts. The prologue to the Latin version of *Avicenna's *De Anima* tells how the work was done. Juan Hispano, a Converso, translated orally from Arabic into Romance, which Dominicus Gundisalvi in turn translated into Latin. The Latin was written down by a scribe. In the 13th century Toledo was again a center of cultural activity, but now works were translated from Arabic into Castilian, reflecting the wish of Alfonso X to make the spoken language of his country that of government and culture. Alfonso's Jewish translators were Isaac ibn Cid, Don Abraham, and R. Judah ben Moses ha-Kohen (Judah Mosca). Judah (Jafuda) *Bonsenyor of Barcelona (d. 1331) compiled for James II of Aragon a volume of maxims in Catalan, mainly derived from Arabic and Jewish sources, titled *Libre de Paraules e dits de Savis e Filosofs* (c. 1300). Another Jewish savant was Isaac al-Carsoni, whose Hebrew astronomical tables, compiled for Pedro IV (1336–1387), were later translated into Latin and Catalan.

An early and famous Jewish composer of Spanish verse was Shem Tov b. Isaac Ardutiel, known to Spaniards as *Santob de Carrión and Don Santo. His *Proverbios morales*, written probably between 1355 and 1360, are the first examples of aphoristic verse in Spanish. Moses de Zaragua *Acan (c. 1300) rivals Santob as a Jewish literary pioneer in Spain. His Catalan verse treatise on chess was translated into Spanish in 1350. Jews also contributed to medieval Spanish culture through the *literatura aljamiada*, the name given to works in Spanish written in Arabic or Hebrew characters. An example of the latter is to be found in one of the four manuscripts in the Cambridge University Library of Santob's *Proverbios* (ed. by Ig. Gonzalez Wubera, 1947). This also contains a poetic treatment of the biblical story of Joseph, called *Coplas de Yoçef*, which was influenced by *Josephus and the Midrash, and later became important in Ladino literature.

JEWISH AND CONVERSO WRITERS. The writers active in Spain from the 15th century onward were invariably Marranos or Conversos, rather than professing Jews. The massacres that began in 1391, mass conversions, and the expulsion of 1492 combined to bring to an end Spanish Jewry's Golden Age and the open practice of Judaism in Spain. There were, of course, Converso writers before 1492, such as the moralist *Petrus Alfonsi in the 12th century (*Disciplina clericalis*, 1120), or the Christian apologist Alfonso de Valladolid (*Abner of Burgos) in the 14th. But the 15th century saw a completely new internal situation in Spain: a whole class of "New Christians" came into being, and at the same time popular antisemitism made a sharp cleavage between peoples and religions that had previously at least coexisted. The intellectual élite was composed largely of Conversos, and many of the writers and humanists who set the tone of the century were New Christians. They also rose to fame in the Church and at court. Ferdinand and Isabella, who signed the decree of expulsion, were not averse to having their deeds recorded by Conversos. Diego de Valera (c. 1412–88), who wrote the *Crónica de los Reyes Católicos*, was the son of Alonso *Chirino (d. 1430?), the baptized physician of Juan II of Castile and author of some curious works on medicine. The official chronicler of the Catholic monarchs and secretary to the queen was Hernando del Pulgar (1436–1493), also thought to have been a Converso.

New Christians were among the poets active in the reign of Juan II (1458–79), and later in the century several writers of minor stature testified to the psychological state of the converts. As members of a minority group scorned and upbraided by the majority, they often took refuge in satire directed against each other – or even against themselves. In literary polemics of the era, the accusation of being a Marrano (Crypto-Jew) was frequently leveled, whether or not with justification. Among Spanish writers of real or imagined New Christian extraction were Juan *Ávarez Gato, Rodrigo de Cota de Maguaque, Juan (Poeta) de Valladolid, Juan de España, el Viejo, Juan de Mena (1411–1456), Antón de Montoro, and Alfonso de la *Torre. Beneath the badinage and cynical laughter, however, one feels the bitterness of the outcast. Two famous prose works written in the reign of Isabella of Castile were by New Christians: the *Cárcel de Amor* (1492) of Diego de San Pedro and *La Celestina* (1499), written either entirely or in large part by Fernando de *Rojas. Both works are the products of the sadness and suffering of the Conversos.

The Later Conversos

While New Christians undoubtedly played an important part in Spanish cultural life throughout the 16th and 17th centuries, it is not easy to determine their contribution with any precision, since they found it advisable to conceal their origin. As a result of the statutes on purity of blood (see *limpieza de sangre*), known Conversos found their opportunities for ecclesiastical, social, and political advancement severely limited, and even the most orthodox Catholics were affected. The grandfather of Spain's greatest saint and mystic, Santa Teresa of Avila, had been penanced by the Inquisition for Judaizing, and there is evidence that the father of the great 16th-century humanist, Juan Luis *Vives, was burned as a Judaizer, and that he himself attended a secret synagogue as a child.

Conversos also distinguished themselves as innovators in Spanish prose. The first pastoral novel written in Spanish was *Diana* (1559?) by Jorge de Montemayor (c. 1520–1561), a writer of Portuguese origin who was taunted with Jewish ancestry by one of his contemporaries. The picaresque novel, considered a peculiarly Spanish invention, owes much to Converso writers. The anonymous author of the first such work, *La vida de Lazarillo de Tormes* (1554), may have been a New Christian, as a brief passage at the beginning of the work is a veiled satire on racial prejudice. No picaresque novels appeared during the reign of Philip II (1556–98), but the year following his death saw the publication of the first part of *Guzmán de Alfarache* (1599) by Mateo *Alemán. Luis Vélez de Guevara (1579–1644) contributed to the genre with *El diablo Cojuelo* (1641), as did Antonio Enriquez Gómez (see above), with *El siglo pitagórico y Vida de don Gregorio Guadaña* (1644). No Converso appeared in the first rank of dramatists during Spain's Golden Age, but several had their works produced on the Madrid stage. Apart from Enríquez Gómez, they include the prolific Juan Pérez de Montalván (1602–1638), the son of a New Christian bookseller and publisher, who nevertheless was appointed a notary of the Holy Office and who became a friend and follower of Lope de Vega; and Felipe Godinez (see above). From the 18th century onward, there were undoubtedly many Spanish writers of Jewish descent, but by then the question had become less important. In the 19th century, José *Taronji y Cortés, a Spanish priest and Catalan poet of Marrano origin, testified to the prejudice besetting the *Chuetas* of Majorca. So far as Spanish literature is concerned, however, *marranismo* was unimportant after the 17th century.

REFUGEE WRITERS. In the Marrano diaspora, on the other hand, professing Jews – refugees or their descendants – made an important contribution to Spanish letters throughout the 17th and 18th centuries. Refugees active in Amsterdam in the latter half of the 17th century were Joseph Semah (Ẓemaḥ) *Arias, a former Spanish army captain; Francisco (Joseph) de Caceres; two poetesses, Isabel (Rebecca) de *Correa and Isabel *Enríquez; Isaac *Gómez de Sossa, whose father had been physician to the infante Fernando of Spain; Isaac Cohen de Lara; and Nicolás (Daniel Judah) de *Oliver y Fullana, a former Spanish colonel. Miguel (Daniel Levi) de *Barrios was one of the most eminent of these exiles. His travels took him to the West Indies and to the Low Countries, where he led a double life as a Spanish army captain in Brussels and as a Jew in Amsterdam.

The Jewish Contribution to Portuguese Literature

In medieval Portugal there were Jewish, as well as Moorish, troubadours, one of whom was called "O Judeu de Elvas" (the Jew of Elvas). Most Portuguese writers of Jewish descent were Marranos, and many fled their native land in the 16th and 17th centuries. Samuel *Usque's *Consolaçam ás Tribulaçoens de Israel*, though published abroad (Ferrara, 1553), is considered a classic of Portuguese literature. The novelist and poet Bernardim *Ribeiro, known as the father of Portuguese bucolic literature (*Hystoria de Menina y Moça*, Ferrara, 1554), was probably a Marrano. Manoel *Fernandes Villereal was one of the many 17th-century Portuguese authors who wrote mainly in Spanish. Perhaps the most famous victim of the Portuguese Inquisition was Antônio José da Silva ("O Judeu," 1705–1739), who was born in Rio de Janeiro, Brazil. Da Silva was one of the few important Portuguese dramatists of the 18th century, and although his career was cut short at the age of 34, his works continued to be performed and published, albeit anonymously, long after his death. Although many Portuguese writers from the 19th century onward proudly claimed Jewish ancestry, specifically Jewish contributions to the literature of Portugal effectively came to an end by 1700.

[Kenneth R. Scholberg]

The Jewish Contribution to Latin-American Literature

During the 16th and 17th centuries many writers of Marrano origin left Spain and Portugal for the New World, in the hope of finding greater freedom there. Marranos were among the most cultivated members of the new American society. In Mexico, the martyred Luis de Carvajal El Mozo (1566–1596; see *Carvajal family), nephew of the governor of New Leon, was a competent poet; in Peru, Antonio de León Pinelo (1591–1658) was one of the first American bibliographers. Two eminent Marrano writers denounced to the Brazilian Inquisition were Ambrósio Fernandes *Brandão, author of the *Diálogos das Grandezas do Brasil* (c. 1618), and Bento *Teixeira Pinto, author of the epic *Prosopopéia* (1601^2), the first literary work written in Brazil.

By the 19th century, Marrano culture had disappeared, and only a few Latin Americans were still conscious of their Jewish descent. In Venezuela, Abigail Lozano (1821–1866) and Salomón López Fonseca (1853–1935) were noted poets. Two other writers were Abraham López-Penha, a Dominican writer, and Efraim Cardozo, a Paraguayan historian. The Colombian novelist, Jorge *Isaacs, author of the classic, *María* (1867), was not of Sephardi origin, being the son of a converted English Jew. In time more liberal ideas promoted a somewhat romantic reassessment of the Crypto-Jews of Latin America, exemplified by *La hija del judío*, a story by Justo Sierra (1814–1861), and the novel *Moisén* (1924) by Julio Jiménez Rueda, both Mexican non-Jews. *Moisén* is notable for its bizarre presentation of the Marranos and their secret religion. Exotic Jewish characters frequently appear in the short stories of Jorge Luis Borges (1899–1986), one of the outstanding Argentine writers of the 20th century. Borges, who was partly of Marrano descent, used kabbalistic and other Jewish elements to heighten the suspense in his tales of mystery, some of which were collected in *El Aleph* (1949; *The Aleph and Other Stories 1933–1969*, 1970). His admiration for the Jewish State prompted two poems about Israel written in June 1967 at the time of the Six-Day War. Four years later, in April 1971, Borges was awarded the Jerusalem Prize for his contribution to the freedom of the individual at the Fifth International Book Fair held in Israel's capital.

Contemporary Jewish Writers

Toward the end of the 19th century, Ashkenazi Jewish communities grew steadily, especially in Argentina, where the *Jewish Colonization Association (ICA) resettled thousands of Jews from Russia. Two of Argentina's foremost Jewish writers, Alberto *Gerchunoff, author of *Los Gauchos Judíos* (1908–10), and Samuel *Eichelbaum were raised in the Argentine Jewish colonies. Carlos Moises Gruenberg (1903–1968), a prominent lawyer and poet, was known for his *Mester de Judería* (1940); a keen Zionist, he translated Hebrew poetry into Spanish, and he was considered a masterly stylist. Salomón Resnick (1895–1946), an essayist and translator, who edited the weekly *Mundo Israelita* and the literary periodical *Judaica*, made Yiddish literature known to the Spanish-speaking reader. Lázaro *Liacho (1897–1969), a journalist and poet, and his father, Jacob Simon Liachovitzky (1874–1937), a journalist and a leading Zionist, both wrote on Jewish themes. Enrique Espinoza (Samuel Glusberg, 1898–1987) wrote tales of Jewish life in Buenos Aires and edited *Babel*, a literary magazine, first in Buenos Aires and later in Santiago, Chile. César *Tiempo (Israel Zeitlin, 1905–1980), a leading poet and playwright, played a prominent part in the fight against Argentine antisemitism. Bernardo Verbitzky (1902–1979), a journalist and novelist, portrayed Jewish life and the fate of the poor. Some other Argentine writers were the novelist Max Dickmann (1897–1991), Máximo José Kahn (1897–1953), and Marcelo Menasché (1913–). Literary essayists and historians included Albert Palcos (1894–1965), León *Dujovne, and Antonio Portnoy (1903–1958).

Max *Aub (1903–1972), who settled in Mexico, was a staunchly anti-Fascist poet, playwright, and novelist. His tragedy, *San Juan* (1943), dealt with the fate of Jewish refugees on a doomed ship in the Mediterranean. Jewish writers in Brazil included Fernando Levisky (1910–1982), author of *Israel no Brasil* (1936); the poet Idel Becker; the playwright Pedro Bloch; the novelist Clarice Lispector; Kurt Loewenstamm; and Henrique Iussim (who wrote under the name Ẓvi Yotam after emigrating to Israel).

Despite their strong Zionist sympathies, Latin America's Jewish writers rarely dealt with Ereẓ Israel in their works. One exception was Samuel Eichelbaum, whose short story, *Una buena Cosecha*, is set in Rosh Pinnah. A non-Jewish Venezuelan poet, Vicente Gerbasi (1913–1992), who was his country's ambassador to Israel (1960–68), included poems on Jerusalem and its Jewish inhabitants in his verse collection, *Poesía de viajes* (1968).

[Paul Link]

Younger Judeo-Argentinian writers continued to explore the process and problems of acculturation and assimilation which appear in the works of earlier writers like Gerchunoff. Germán Rozenmacher (1936–1971) presented an intergenerational conflict between an immigrant cantor and his Argentinian-born son in his play *Requiem para unviernes a la noche* (1964). Mario Szichman (b. 1945) in his novels, *Crónica falsa* (1969) and *A las 20:35 la señora entró a la inmortalidad* (1981), depicted the odyssey of a Jewish family against the background of the Peronist era. David Vinas (b. 1929), Marcos Aguinis (b. 1935), Gerardo Mario Goloboff (b. 1939), Alicia Steimberg (b. 1933), and Marion Satz (b. 1944) were other writers of this new generation of Jewish intellectuals.

Although Argentina, because of the size of the community and the vigor of the cultural milieu, contained the largest nucleus of Jewish authors, there were a number of writers in other Latin American countries, such as the Peruvian novelist Isaac Goldemberg (b. 1945), who told the story of an eastern European Jewish immigrant in *The Fragmented Life of Don Jacobo Lerner* (1976). In Venezuela Isaac Chocrón (b. 1932), one of the country's most prominent playwrights, examined his Sephardi background in a novel, *Rómpase en caso de incendio* (1975).

Despite maintaining strong Zionist sympathies, Latin America's writers only occasionally set their works in Israel. In *El caramelo descompuesto* (1980), a novel by Ricardo Feierstein, a young Argentinian narrator looks critically at life on a kibbutz.

A non-Jewish Venezuelan poet, Vicente Gerbasi (1913–1992), who was his country's ambassador to Israel (1960–68), included poems on Jerusalem and its Jewish inhabitants in his verse collection *Poesiás de viaje* (1968).

The Palestinian-Israeli conflict from a pro-Arab point of view was dealt with by the well known Mexican novelist, Carlos Fuentes, in his *La cabeza de la hidra* (1978; "The Hydra Head," 1978).

[Edna Aizenberg]

Latin American Jewish literature developed specifically in the 1970s and 1980s, and can be defined as the treatment of Jewish values in two languages – Spanish and Portuguese, as conceived and spoken in Latin America; and more particularly, as the way in which these languages have left their mark on Latin American Jewry, through those authors who use them as their vehicle.

In other words, the Jewish literature of Latin America exploits the possibilities of expression offered by the Portuguese and Spanish languages to translate, both at the personal and the collective level, the way in which basic Jewish values are experienced and interpreted in the framework of living conditions in this part of the world. In the words of literary critic Saul Sonowski, "Jewish literature in Latin America is not built exclusively on the basis of motifs which can easily be identified as Jewish, but as a function of the relationship of these motifs to concrete realities which are in a process of development and transformation: the realities of the Latin American societies in which they must evolve." What he means basically is that the Latin American Jewish writers are an inseparable part of their respective national literatures. Their acknowledgment of their Jewishness resides in their perception of themselves as Uruguayan, Brazilian, Mexican, Venezuelan, Chilean, or Argentine writers whose works and thought integrally include a Jewish thematic variation, which may be more or less frequent, more or less intense, and can be formulated and reelaborated in an infinite variety of ways. The Jewish variation cannot be isolated from the totality which gives it meaning, nor placed in a hierarchy to the detriment of the totality. Nevertheless, Latin American Jewish writers, in order to consolidate their respective identities as Latin American writers, also have to take their positions as Jews. In their work, Jewish and Latin American themes, far from constituting an irreconcilable antithesis, as is often alleged by explicitly antisemitic and implicitly discriminatory theses, have become strongly complementary and inseparable.

For many years, in the Latin American cultural arena, the need for an alternative was solicited equally zealously by both the nationalist right and the Marxist-Leninist left: strictly specific characteristics, such as those implicit to the Jewish condition, were to be merged into the national identity (right) or the international proletariat identity (left). Considered "foreign" by the former and "reactionary" by the latter until well into the 1970s, Judaism seemed to have no future as a variation in the composite profile of the Latin American writer. However, the situation began to change in the 1970s. Government terrorism, which raged in every corner of the continent, but with an especially bloody genocide in the southern tip of Latin America, gave rise to a new phenomenon in the region – a diaspora. This bitter experience strongly paralleled Jewish memories.

Discrimination, censorship, persecution, torture, imprisonment, and death were practiced with systematic tenacity by the successive dictatorships, especially against anyone daring to challenge the regime in force; fearing for their lives, many fled their country or even the continent. Jewish writers naturally drew parallels between past and present. At the same time, the seeds of today's Communist crisis were already present. Against this background, the meaning of Judaism, as a constituent element of the personal and historic identity of so many writers, underwent an intense process of redefinition, inspired not only by the suffering but also by its dialectic complement – the spirit of struggle, the capacity to confront adversity. Judaism was beginning to be seen as a determined demand for pluralism, for democratic ideals, for a thirst for dialogue, in open opposition to dogmatism and contempt for differentness. Beyond its possible adherence to theological arguments and religious options of one kind or another, Judaism was conceived, by contemporary Latin American writers, as a moving metaphor of their own experience, and was thus ultimately acknowledged as an inalienable part of an individual identity.

"In the countries of Latin America, which have experienced a repression unprecedented in their history, survival – perhaps the basic motif of all Jewish literature – has obviously played a major role" (Saul Sosnowski). And "it is under identical circumstances that some Jewish motifs have become precision instruments in interpreting a reality that centuries of persecution and exile have imprinted in the cultural tradition of the historic Jew" (Saul Sosnowski).

In addition to the decisive theme of survival, other fundamental themes began to appear in poetry, fiction, and drama. Man's dialogue with God, with its innumerable variations, the sufferings imposed by prejudice and intolerance, the intensity of nostalgia, exile and its indelible shadow, the meaning of death, the value of memory, mysticism, the warmth of family life, the immigrant origin, the Jewish holidays and history, the unexpected recording of one's own life as an "immigrant," and the presence and ethical and even esthetic weight of tradition, all to a great extent shape the repertory of themes which, in numerous forms, run through Latin American Jewish literature. And just as European or North American Jewish literature, for instance, have distinctive traits, specific only to a country or a continent, so Latin American Jewish literature has its own, unique characteristics. Its treatment of proverbially Jewish questions has an unmistakably Latin American emphasis, in that the Jewish models are presented through the subjective, social, and historic experience of the countries of Latin America, with their specific conflicts, resources, and conditions. The Jewish statement is made through the Spanish and Portuguese languages, with their own cultural imprint, and thereby receives a specific bias – accorded by the distinctive intonation of the language in every country and region where it is spoken. This intonation is not only that of the language's rhythm, its euphony, but also that of its semantic weave, which, in each locality, and in each consciousness, links the repertoire of resources offered by the language to its users, giving birth to that fertile "hybrid" condition noted by writer Ricardo Feierstein; and to the theme which, among so many other nationalities, both incorporates the Jewish element in, and separates it from, the Bolivian, Peruvian, Colombian, or Cuban element and elegantly frames a Jewish individuality which, while obviously related to others, is not one of them. This "hybridism" is simply the permanent interweaving of two originally separate traditions – the Jewish and Latin American, which, through the meeting of circumstances, ultimately shaped a new expression. The value and quality of this possibility of expression characterizes Latin American Jewish literature.

In other words, Spanish and Portuguese are not the languages into which the universal nature of Judaism is translated, but the means through which it is constituted and conceived in Latin America. Based in these languages, Jewish poetry, fiction, and drama, as well as essays and critical reviews, are seen as the highest grade of conceptual elaboration which Jewish experience has attained in Latin America. While Latin American Jews do not have to be aware of this in order to be what they are, it is no less true that this knowledge constitutes for them a privileged resource for a greater and better understanding of their identity.

Since the reestablishment of democratic institutions in the 1980s, in particular, Latin American Jewry has encountered a fertile terrain in which to shape itself, demonstrating that a complete manifestation of the universality of Jewish values is possible only when inspired by a concrete historic circumstance. It is in the light of their experience as Latin

Americans that the validity of the meaning of Jewishness can be projected in the contemporary world. Every literary work, beyond its value as a comparative model, expresses that moment of luminous encounter between past and present which imbues the experience it describes, the statement it makes, with both an individual, specific, and even regional nuance, and an archetypal, metaphoric, and revealing dimension whose symbolic stature is universal. In this way the yesterday of previous generations who sustained, enjoyed, and suffered the Jewish condition, becomes the today shaped by our circumstances, which are no less worrying or fascinating than those of the past. Through looking at the past one learns to see those who observe from the present; observations of the present bring to the acknowledgment of the validity of this millennia-old message. Latin American Jewish literature proves this eloquently. It is one of the basic indications of Latin American Jewry's intense desire to attain self-understanding. Indeed, to a very great extent literary activity in the 1980s evidenced the resolute initiative and great persistency of this community in examining its condition. Among the events demonstrating this orientation should be noted: two encounters of Latin American Jewish writers held in Buenos Aires in 1986 and in 1988; the proliferation of poetry, fiction, and essays, which join together with remarkable elegance the double source of personal identity – Jewish and Latin American; the appearance of *Noaj*, the first Jewish literary review in Spanish and Portuguese edited in Israel; the creation, also in Israel, of a Jewish writers' association in both languages. All these proved decisive acts and showed the extent of Latin American Jewry's eagerness for self-exploration and self-expression. Certainly it is not by chance that all these developments were taking place at a time when the values of political democracy were being progressively restored. Democracy is the most propitious condition for the institution of pluralism; and Judaism, freed from the oppressive yoke placed upon it by totalitarian thinking, finds itself with an auspicious opportunity to say and affirm what it is, and to begin once again to question its own meaning.

[Santiago Ezequiel Kovadloff]

BIBLIOGRAPHY: L. Magnus, in: E.R. Bevan and C. Singer (eds.), *Legacy of Israel* (1927), 483–505; R. Cansinos Assens, *Los judíos en la literatura española* (1937); J.P.W. Crawford, *Spanish Drama Before Lope de Vega* (1937); A. Portnoy, *Los judíos en la literatura española medieval* (1942); S. Resnick, *Cinco ensayos sobre temas judíos* (1943); R.A. Arrieta, *Historia de la literatura argentina*, 6 vols. (1958–60), incl. bibl.; A. Wiznitzer, *Jews in Colonial Brazil* (1960), incl. bibl.; J. Caro Baroja, *Los judíos en la españa moderna y contemporánea*, 3 vols. (1962), incl. bibl.; C. Láfer, *O Judeu em Gil Vicente* (1963); Baer, Spain; E. Weinfeld, in: *Judaica* (Buenos Aires, Jan. 1944), 1–13; S. Resnick, in: *Hispania*, 34, no. 1 (1951), 54–58; E. Glaser, in: *Nueva revista de Filología Hispánica*, 8 (1954), 39–62; F. Lehner, in: L. Finkelstein (ed.), *The Jews, Their History, Culture and Religion*, 2 (1960), 1472–86; *Echad: An Anthology of Latin American Jewish Writings*, ed. by R. and R. Kalechofsky (1980); D. McGrady, *Jorge Isaacs* (1972); K. Schwartz, in: *The American Hispanist* (Sept. 1977), 9–12; E. Aizenberg, in: *Anuario de letras* (Mexico), 15 (1977), 197–215; idem, in: *Revista Iberoamericana*, 46 (1980), 533–44.

SPARROW (Heb. צִפּוֹר דְּרוֹר, *zippor deror* or דְּרוֹר, *deror*, but sometimes the word *zippor* "bird" refers to the sparrow), the *Passer domesticus biblicus*, the house sparrow, which is the most common bird in Israel during all seasons of the years. It "dwells in the house as in the field" and its name *zippor deror* ("free bird") is explained by the fact that "it does not submit to authority" (Beẓah 24a); and, despite the fact that it lives in populated areas, it cannot be domesticated. It nests in the interstices of rooftops and stone walls. It is referred to as nesting between the stones of the Temple (Ps. 84:4), and to this day some make their nests between the stones of the *Western Wall. It possesses the characteristics of a *kasher* bird (see *Dietary Laws) and there are Jewish communities which permit it for food. "Two *zipporim*" were used for the purification ceremony of the leper (Lev. 14:4) and for the house cleansed from leprosy (*ibid.*, 14:49); according to the Mishnah (Neg. 14:1) *zipporei deror*, i.e., house sparrows, are meant. Some would identify the *deror* with the swallow, but the descriptions of the *deror* in rabbinical literature leave no doubt that it refers to the sparrow.

BIBLIOGRAPHY: Lewysohn, Zool, 187 (no. 237), 206–9 (nos. 256 and 257); F.S. Bodenheimer, *Animal and Man in Bible Lands* (1960), 56, 119, 120 (no. 20); J. Feliks, *Animal World of the Bible* (1962), 61. **ADD. BIBLIOGRAPHY:** J. Feliks, *Ha-Ẓome'aḥ*, 222.

[Jehuda Feliks]

SPARTA, city in Greece; ancient city-state in the Peloponnesus, called Mistra in Crusader times. The earliest information on the relations between Sparta and the Jews is the letter said to have been sent by Areus, king of Sparta (309–265 B.C.E.), to the high priest *Onias I (I Macc. 12:20–23). In this letter Areus sends his greetings to the Jews and proposes a full alliance in the words, "your cattle and goods are ours, and ours yours." It also refers to a written tradition that the two peoples are of the stock of Abraham (cf. Jos., Ant., 14:255; see *Pergamum). This was apparently included in one of those books dealing with the genealogy of the various nations, which were widespread in the Hellenistic era, or it may have been based on the well-known work of *Hecateus of Abdera. It is possible that the contemporary political situation, the relations between the *Ptolemies and Sparta on the one hand and the Jews on the other (idem, 109) forms the background to this alliance, as well as perhaps some sympathy of ideas (cf. Y. Baer, in: *Zion* 17 (1952), 35). Josephus, who quotes the text of the letter (Ant. 12:22–26), adds some details which do not appear in I Maccabees. I Maccabees (12:6–18) also quotes a letter of Jonathan the Hasmonean to the Spartans and (14:20–23) a letter of the Spartans to Simeon the Hasmonean. Some scholars regard these letters as either wholly or in part fictitious (see F.M. Abel, *Les Livres des Maccabées* (1949), 231–3). Corroborating evidence for these relations is to be found in II Maccabees (5:9) which describes the flight of the high priest Jason to Sparta because its people were close to his. The inhabitants of Sparta are also mentioned in I Maccabees (15:23), but it is doubtful whether the existence of a Jewish settlement can be inferred from there, as some scholars have attempted to do. There is no explicit mention of a Jewish settlement in Sparta, though Jews were living in the Peloponnesus during the first century C.E. (Philo, *Legatio and Gaium*, 281).

[Uriel Rappaport]

During the tenth century there were Jews in Sparta; they were engaged in commerce. When a plague broke out in Sparta, the monk Nikon (10th century) refused to come to the village's aid as long as the Jews, who were an obstacle in the spreading of Christianity, were not expelled. His incitement was without effect. The presence of Jews is mentioned during the reigns of the Palaeologi emperors (1261–1453). When Sigismondo Malatesta conquered Mistra in 1465, he burnt down the Jewish quarter. There is evidence of the presence of Jews again during the 16th and 17th centuries. They were engaged in the silk industry and in commerce. The French author Chateaubriand, who visited Greece in 1806, mentions the Jewish quarter of Sparta. During the Greek Revolution (1821–1829), the Albanians, who invaded Peloponnesus, destroyed the Jewish community.

[Simon Marcus]

BIBLIOGRAPHY: F.R. de Chateaubriand, *Itinéraire de Paris à Jérusalem*, 1 (1859), 161, 166; M. Schwab, *Rapport sur une Mission de Philologie en Grèce* (1913), 117f.; A. Andréades, in: *Economic History*, 3 (1934–37), 1–23; Rosanes, Togarmah, 3 (1938), 129–200.

SPÄTH, JOHANN PETER (**Moses Germanus**; 1642/45–1701), German Christian Hebraist who converted to Judaism. Späth was born either in Augsburg or in Vienna between 1642 and 1645 to a Roman Catholic family. He became a teacher in a Protestant family and this contact made him question his own faith. Influenced by the Protestant theologian Philipp Jacob Spener (1635–1705), Späth converted to the Lutheran church and he became a follower of Spener. His religious doubts, however, did not weaken. On the contrary, he became disappointed because of the controversy among the Lutherans, and this made him decide in 1681 to return to the Roman Catholic Church. However, he continued to have doubts. Several years later Späth appeared to be living in Amsterdam, where he met people from various religious movements such as the Mennonites, the Collegiants, and the Socians. During that period, he converted once again to become a Quaker. Thus he came into contact with the Christian Hebraist and Kabbalah scholar Francis Mercury of Helmont (1614–1699). At that time, Späth moved to Sulzbach to help with a Latin translation and the publication of a large corpus of Kabbalistic texts.

The chronological records of the subsequent years are not very clear, but in 1696 we find Späth in Amsterdam once again, where he officially converted to Judaism. From then on he was known as Moses Germanus. A year later he was circumcised and was accepted into the Portuguese-Jewish community in Amsterdam. He had previously married a Jewish woman, and was appointed as a teacher. Späth died in Amsterdam on April 27, 1701.

His conversion to Judaism caused the customary scandal in those days. Many of his contemporary Christian scholars expressed their disapproval of the facts. The most complete record of his life and his conversion written at that time is to be found in the work of Johann Jacob Schudt (1664–1722) entitled *Jüdische Merckwürdigkeiten* (= Jewish curiosities) in which he also talks about the dismay of the Christian scholars. Späth defended his conversion in a number of letters addressed to scholars in his area.

A great deal of that correspondence has been preserved, such as several letters to Johannes Leusden (1624–1699) dating from the period in which Späth converted, addressed by Leusden to Moses Germanus Judäus.

BIBLIOGRAPHY: J.J. Schudt, *Jüdische Merckwürdigkeiten, vorstellende was sich Curieuses und Denckwürdiges in den neuern Zeiten bey einigen Jahrhunderten mit Denen in alle IV Theilen der Welt, sonderlich durch Teutschland zerstreuten Jüden zugetragen, sammt einer vollständigen Franckfurter Juden-Chronik, darinnen der zu Franckfurt am Mayn wohnenden Jüden von einigen Jahrhunderten, biss auff unseren Zeiten*, 4 vols. (1714–1718); H.J. Schoeps, *Philosemitismus im Barock. Religions- und Geistesgeschichtliche Untersuchungen* (1952), 81–87; idem, *Barocke Juden – Christen – Judenchristen* (1965), 83–92; A.P. Coudert and J.S. Shoulson, *Hebraica Veritas? Christian Hebraists and the Study of Judaism in Early Modern Europe* (2004); A.P. Coudert, in: M. Mulshow and R.H. Popkin (eds.), *Secret Conversions to Judaism in Early Modern Europe* (2004).

[Monika Saelemaekers (2nd ed.)]

SPECTER, ARLEN (1930–), U.S. senator, chairman of the Judiciary Committee. Spector was born in Kansas, the son of Russian immigrants. His family moved to Russell, Kansas, the home town of another United States senator, Robert Dole. Specter was educated at the University of Oklahoma, and transferred to the University of Pennsylvania, where he received his B.A. (1951). He was in the Air Force from 1951 to 1953 during the Korean War. He returned to attend Yale Law School, where he edited the law journal and graduated in 1956.

He served as assistant district attorney in Philadelphia as a Democrat from 1959 to 1963 and then went to Washington, where he was assistant counsel to the Warren Commission investigating the assassination of President John F. *Kennedy. He devised the single bullet theory, contending that one bullet hit the president and Texas Governor John Connally, who was riding in the limousine and was also wounded. He sought the Democratic nomination for district attorney but was rebuffed by the Democratic machine so he ran as a Republican reform candidate and won an upset victory. He narrowly lost the race for mayor of Philadelphia the next year. He served for eight years as district attorney and then suffered a series of political losses that ordinarily doom a political candidate. Specter lost a race for district attorney in 1973; he lost for the U.S. Senate in 1976 and lost for governor in 1978. He won the 1980 race in the Reagan landslide and then proceeded to vote against the Reagan Administration more often than any other Republican senator.

He played a major role during the Iran-Contra hearing, where his talent as a cross examiner came into play again. He concluded that the intelligence system was in need of an overhaul and proposed the creation of an inspector general of the CIA. His role on the Senate Judiciary Committee was controversial vis-à-vis his Republican colleagues. He voted against Robert Bork for the Supreme Court. He was an ardent defender of Judge Clarence Thomas' nomination to the Supreme Court and an intense interrogator of Anita Hill, whom he accused of perjury. His performance did not endear him to women. In 1996 he was a candidate for president, but withdrew before the first primary as it was clear that the Republican Party was not going to nominate a pro-choice Republican moderate. After Orrin Hatch completed his six years as chairman, Specter was in line to become chairman of the Judiciary Committee, a move opposed by some Republican colleagues, who were fearful of his moderation and his support of abortion. He further enraged his colleagues by warning the administration not to appoint someone who was going to overturn Roe v. Wade. He was forced to clarify – some say disavow – his statement. Surrounded by his Republican Judiciary Committee colleagues, he said: "I have no reason to believe that I will be unable to support any individual President Bush finds worthy." In addition to tackling the major legislative business before the Senate in 2005, Specter also engaged in a personal battle with Stage IVB Hodgkin's lymphoma cancer. He underwent nearly five months of chemotherapy but still maintained all of his senatorial duties, including chairing hearings, voting, and brokering important legislative initiatives. On July 22, 2005, Specter received his last chemotherapy treatment and subsequently received a clean bill of health.

In 2005 and early 2006 his leadership was tested in the nomination of John Roberts to be chief justice of the Supreme Court, the nomination and withdrawal of nomination of Harriet Miers, and finally the nomination of Samuel Alito as associate justice. His wife, Joan, is a former City Council member in Philadelphia.

BIBLIOGRAPHY: K.F. Stone, *The Congressional Minyan: The Jews of Capitol Hill* (2000); L.S. Maisels and I. Forman (eds.), *Jews in American Politics* (2001).

[Michael Berenbaum (2nd ed.)]

SPECTOR, JOHANNA (1920–), U.S. ethno-musicologist, filmmaker, and educator. Johanna Spector was born and grew up in Latvia where her husband, Robert Spector, was killed by the Nazis in 1941. She spent the war years in concentration camps. She immigrated to the U.S. in 1947. She received her doctorate in Hebrew Letters from the Hebrew Union College (Cincinnati, 1950) and obtained a master's degree in anthropology from Columbia University in 1960. She was a research fellow at the Hebrew University, Jerusalem (1951–53) and until 1957 she spent half the year in Israel, undertaking fieldwork on the Yemenite, Kurdish, and Samaritan communities. In 1954 she joined the Jewish Theological Seminary, New York, and founded its department of ethno-musicology in 1962, becoming associate professor in 1966 and full professor in 1970. In the course of her research in Jewish music, she made an extensive collection of recordings. Her personal archive of 11,000 tape recordings includes Arabic, Persian, Turkish, Samaritan, Yemenite, and Indian (Cochin and Bombay) music of Jewish communities. They are accompanied by thousands of photographs, and later films from which she made documentaries, particularly on the Yemenites and Samaritans; she published several studies on them. A large part of her collection is at the National Archives of the Hebrew University. She helped to found the Society for the Preservation of Samaritan Culture and the Friends of the Samaritan Museum in 1968, with the object of establishing a museum at Shechem (Nablus).

[Amnon Shiloah (2nd ed.)]

SPECTOR, MORDECAI (1858–1925), Yiddish novelist and editor. Born in Uman, Ukraine, of a hasidic family, he came under the influence of Haskalah literature and began to write realistic sketches based on his personal experiences and observations of ordinary people in workshops and marketplaces. A. *Zederbaum, editor of the St. Petersburg *Yidishes Folksblat*, published Spector's first novel in weekly installments under the title *Roman On a Nomen* ("Novel without a Title," 1883). Spector later became assistant editor of this paper. His second novel, *Der Yidisher Muzhik* ("The Jewish Farmer," 1884), aroused great interest since it advocated the return of Jews to productive labor on their ancestral soil, a doctrine then propagated by the Ḥovevei Zion. Spector also influenced *Shalom Aleichem to set his literary sights on the provinces and on *shtetl* life, then a neglected area in Yiddish literature. In 1887, he settled in Warsaw, where, during the following decade, he reached the height of his fame, writing feuilletons, travel sketches, short stories, and novels, and editing a series of anthologies, *Der Hoyzfraynd* ("The Family Friend"), a landmark in the development of modern Yiddish literature. In 1894, together with I.L. *Peretz and D. *Pinski, he launched the *Yontev Bletlekh* ("Holiday Leaflets"), another literary landmark. Other literary ventures followed during the ensuing two decades. After the Communist Revolution, he experienced hardships in Odessa. He escaped in 1920, and arrived in the U.S. in 1921. Living in New York, he completed a volume of memoirs, *Mayn Lebn* ("My Life," 1927), which has great literary, historical, and cultural value. Spector was a writer for the masses, whom he tried to entertain, educate, and uplift. Though neither an original thinker nor a subtle psychologist, he was an excellent observer of reality, faithfully reproducing the colloquial speech of Jewish men and women in their homes, shops, and alleys. He was a pioneer of Yiddish folklore and of Yiddish writing for children, and was one of the first Yiddish writers to take a positive attitude toward Ḥasidism. His collected works appeared in 10 volumes (1927–29). His stories have been translated into eight languages, including English (cf. I. Howe and E. Greenberg, ed. *A Treasury of Yiddish Stories* (1953), 250–5).

BIBLIOGRAPHY: *Spektor-Bukh* (1929), incl. bibl.; Rejzen, Leksikon, 2 (1927), 691–708; LNYL, 6 (1965), 518–27; *Dertseylers un Romanistn* (1946), 11–129; S. Niger, *Bleter Geshikhte fun der Yidisher Literatur* (1959), 382–403; Y. Yeshurin, in: M. Spektor, *Der Yidisher Muzhik* (1963), 264–8. **ADD. BIBLIOGRAPHY:** D. Roskies, *A Bridge of Longing* (1995), 170–2.

[Moshe Starkman]

SPECTOR, NORMAN (1949–), Canadian diplomat, public servant, and media commentator. Spector was born and raised in Montreal, where he attended Talmud Torah and Herzliah day schools, worked part time as a packer for Steinberg's grocery chain, and graduated from McGill University. After obtaining his doctorate in political science from Columbia and a master's degree in communications from Syracuse, he taught for a year at the University of Ottawa in 1974–75 before taking a position in the Ontario Ministry of Communications.

Spector moved to British Columbia, where he served as deputy minister to Social Credit Premier Bill Bennett from 1982 to 1986. He was heavily involved in the government's battle with labor unions. His talents and fluency in French drew him to employment in the federal government, and he became secretary to the cabinet for federal-provincial relations in 1986, then chief of staff to Prime Minister Brian Mulroney in 1990. Spector became one in a series of Jews who held very senior positions with Canadian prime ministers of different political stripe. These include Mel Cappe, Eddie Goldenberg, Stanley Hartt, Chaviva Hosek, Hugh Segal, and David Zussman. In Ottawa Spector played a major role in negotiating the unsuccessful 1987 Meech Lake Accord, which would have had Quebec accept the Canadian Constitution passed by the Trudeau Liberals in 1982. In 1992 Spector became Canadian ambassador to Israel and the Palestinian Authority. As Canada's first Jewish ambassador to Israel, and as someone not from the ranks of the diplomatic corps, his appointment caused some opposition within the established foreign service community. Spector proved evenhanded and studied Arabic to go along with his fluency in Hebrew.

Returning to Canada in 1995, Spector became president of the Atlantic Canada Opportunity Agency and an executive with Imperial Tobacco. He returned to Israel briefly in 1997 as publisher of *The Jerusalem Post*. Following his tenure at *The Jerusalem Post* he settled in Victoria, British Columbia. He remains a frequent columnist for *The Globe and Mail* and commentator on Canadian television news, often on Middle East affairs. In 2003 he published *Chronicle of a War Foretold: How Mideast Peace Became America's Fight*, based on his articles in the Middle East.

[Morton Weinfeld (2nd ed.)]

SPECTOR, PHIL (**Harvey Philip**; 1940–), vastly influential rock music producer, who produced, arranged, and co-wrote some of rock & roll's earliest classic tunes in the late 1950s and early 1960s; member of the Rock and Roll Hall of Fame. Spector was born in the Bronx to Bertha and Benjamin, a Russian Jewish immigrant who committed suicide in 1949. Spector, his mother, and sister, Shirley, moved to Los Angeles in 1953, where Spector quickly proved proficient on numerous instruments and became acquainted with L.A. rhythm and blues musicians, including songwriters Jerry *Leiber and Mike *Stoller, with whom he would later collaborate on the No. 1 hit "Spanish Harlem." By 1958, having secured a small recording contract, Spector wrote and performed what became his first No. 1 hit, "To Know Him Is To Love Him," inspired by words written on his father's gravestone. In 1960, having apprenticed himself to Los Angeles music veterans, including Lee Hazlewood, Spector began producing numerous pop singles for journeyman singers. Two years later, having become a millionaire from "Spanish Harlem" and other early hits, Spector developed his own, innovative production method. Later known as the "Wall of Sound," Spector massed Los Angeles musicians and instruments into elaborate arrangements that produced pop classics of undisputed emotional and sonic impact. The lyrics for Spector's songs were often produced by the mainly Jewish songwriting teams Carole *King and Gerry Goffin, Ellie Greenwich and Jeff Barry, and Barry Mann and Cynthia Weil. His hits included "Be My Baby," by the Ronettes, and "Da Doo Ron Ron," by the Crystals, both "girl groups," a genre Spector is credited with having defined. The Ronettes were led by Veronica "Ronnie" Bennett, later one of Spector's three wives. In 1965, "You've Lost That Loving Feeling" by the Righteous Brothers reached No. 1, despite being nearly four minutes long – one-third longer than the accepted standard. Spector got around that rule by deliberately misprinting the song's time on the record's label. Spector's rule of the charts faded after that, and he went into self-imposed exile. He repeated his success in the early 1970s with individual members of the Beatles, producing memorable albums for George Harrison (*All Things Must Pass*) and John Lennon (*Plastic Ono Band*), but Spector earned the longstanding enmity of Beatle Paul McCartney for adding strings, horns, and chorus to the uncompleted tapes of the Beatles' *Let It Be* album. He was named to the Rock and Roll Hall of Fame in 1989. Spector's litigious and eccentric behavior tarnished his reputation, and he was accused of pulling weapons on several of his artists, including Leonard *Cohen, with whom he worked in the 1970s. In 2003, an actress was found shot dead in Spector's Los Angeles home, and he was slated to stand trial for murder in 2006.

[Alan D. Abbey (2nd ed.)]

SPEISER, EPHRAIM AVIGDOR (1902–1965), U.S. Orientalist and archaeologist. Born in Skalat, Galicia, Speiser emigrated to the United States (1920). In 1926–27 he surveyed northern Iraq, discovering Tepe Gawra, whose excavation, along with that of the adjacent Tell Billa, he directed during 1930–32 and 1936–37. In 1927 Speiser taught comparative Semitics at the Hebrew University of Jerusalem. From 1928 to the end of his life he lectured in Semitic languages and literatures at the University of Pennsylvania. During World War II,

Speiser served as the chief of the Near East section of the Research and Analysis Branch of the Office of Strategic Services. From 1955 he was a key member of the translation committee of the Jewish Publication Society of America that produced a new English version of the Torah (1962).

Speiser was one of the pioneers in the discovery of the *Hurrians and their culture. He clarified the scope and significance of the Hurrian component in Western Asia during the second millennium B.C.E. and investigated the structure of their language in the still standard *Introduction to Hurrian* (1941). In *The United States and the Near East* (1947, 1950^2) he illuminated the modern problems of the region by his expert knowledge of its long history. Speiser's philological and synthetic studies in Mesopotamian civilization displayed its values, with emphasis upon the centrality of law and the influence of Mesopotamian legal conceptions on peripheral peoples, including Israel. During the last decade of his life he devoted much time to the origin of Israel's history and faith. He regarded these as both a reflex of, and a critical reaction to, the Egyptian and Mesopotamian cultures from which Israel emerged. His biblical research culminated in the volume on Genesis in the *Anchor Bible* (1964).

Speiser's scholarly, humanistic, and professional distinction was nationally recognized. He was a president of the American Oriental Society, a member of the American Philosophical Society, and a fellow of the American Academy for Jewish Research.

BIBLIOGRAPHY: D.D. Finkelstein and M. Greenberg (eds.), *Oriental and Biblical Studies: Collected Writings of E.A. Speiser* (1967), 587–616; J.B. Pritchard et al. in: BASOR, 79 (1965), 2–7; M. Greenberg, in: JAOS, 88 (1968), 1–2.

[Moshe Greenberg]

SPEKTOR, ISAAC ELḤANAN (1817–1896), Lithuanian rabbi. Spektor was born in the province of Grodno, Russia, and one of his teachers was Benjamin Diskin. After serving as rabbi in various towns, Spektor went to Kovno, where he officiated until his death. In Kovno he attained eminence as a rabbinic authority and established a yeshivah (*kolel avrekhim)* for the training of outstanding rabbis. He was unsuccessful in his struggle to obtain official recognition for rabbis who were not government appointees. On the other hand he struggled successfully against a law requiring an official examination in Russian from Jewish teachers and also secured the withdrawal of a government decree prohibiting Jewish instruction in the *ḥeder.* At Spektor's instigation Samson Raphael *Hirsch wrote his book on the relationship of the Talmud to Judaism, which was submitted to the Russian government. He supported Isaac *Dembo of Petersburg in his successful campaign against the ban on *sheḥitah* in Russia. He frequently organized aid for stricken communities in Russia, Lithuania, and other countries. Individuals and communities in distress, from all areas of Jewish settlement, turned to him. He sought government permission for the provision of *kasher* food to Jewish soldiers, and maintained a soup kitchen in Kovno until his death. He was the only rabbi invited to the conference of Jewish leaders held in St. Petersburg (Leningrad) in 1881–82 to discuss the deteriorating position of the Jews. He later dispatched a manifesto to David *Asher, secretary of the chief rabbi of London, which resulted in protest meetings being held in England, France, Italy, and the U.S. These meetings, whose resolutions were submitted to the Russian government, attracted much publicity and led to the establishment of welfare funds. In later years he made similar pleas and participated in subsequent conferences of Jewish leaders, maintaining confidential contact with influential Jewish circles.

With the increasing Jewish emigration from Russia, he supported the efforts of the Ḥovevei Zion movement, thereby adding greatly to the movement's prestige. The preparatory meetings for the appointment of representatives to the *Kattowitz conference were held in his home, two delegates being appointed, though he refused to accept nomination as honorary trustee at the Ḥovevei Zion conference held in Druskininkai in 1887. After the movement was given official recognition, he publicly proclaimed the religious duty of settling in Ereẓ Israel, signing an appeal for the collection of funds for this purpose in synagogues on the eve of the Day of Atonement. On the question of agricultural labor in Ereẓ Israel in a *shemittah* ("sabbatical") year, he favored its permission by the nominal sale of land to a non-Jew, a measure which is employed to the present day. His ban on Corfu *etrogim* enabled the Palestinian variety to enter the market. He also concerned himself with the amelioration of the spiritual and religious needs of Jewish settlers in Argentina and the U.S. Spektor won universal admiration for his broad-mindedness and peace-loving disposition. In 1889 he was elected an honorary member of the *Society for the Promotion of Culture among the Jews of Russia. He was frequently requested to serve as arbitrator. In a dispute over *sheḥitah*, referred to him from London in 1891, he supported the chief rabbi against the ultra-Orthodox element.

His works are *Be'er Yiẓḥak* (1858; 1948^2); *Naḥal Yiẓḥak* (2 pts., 1872–84); *Ein Yiẓḥak* (2 pts., 1889–95); *Eẓ Peri* (1881; 1903); *Devar ha-Shemittah* (1889). His letters have been printed in various collections. His works contain commentaries and novellae to the Shulḥan Arukh, particularly responsa to questions submitted to him from the various Jewish communities in which he was regarded as the leading authority of his generation. Spektor exercised leniency, particularly in relieving the burden of many *agunot. His 158 responsa on this subject reveal only three cases where he could not find a basis for permitting the woman to remarry. Many Torah institutions, including the Rabbi Isaac Elchanan Theological Seminary in New York, were named after him.

BIBLIOGRAPHY: E. Shimoff, *Rabbi Isaac Elchanan Spektor* (Eng. and Heb., 1961); J. Lipschitz, *Toledot Yiẓḥak* (1896); L.P. Gartner, *Jewish Immigrant in England, 1870–1914* (1960), index; Mirsky, in: *Guardians of our Heritage*, ed. by L. Jung (1958), 301–15; A. Druyanov, *Katavim le-Toledot Ḥibbat Ẓiyyon…*, 1 (1919), xiii (index); 2 (1925), 28 (index); 3 (1932), 400–1; J. Nissenbaum, *Ha-Dat ve-ha-*

Teḥiyyah ha-Le'ummit (1920), 130; J. Mark, *Gedoylim fun Undzer Tsayt* (1927), 105–24; J. Lipschitz, *Zikhron Ya'akov* (1924–30), passim; Mirsky, in: *Talpioth*, 3 (1947/48), 121–5; Hill, *ibid.*, 7 (1960), 558–81; J.L. Maimon, *Lema'an Ẓiyyon Lo Eḥesheh*, 1 (1954), 34; S.B. Hoenig, in: JBA, 28 (1970/71).

[Geulah Bat Yehuda (Raphael)]

SPELLING, AARON (1923–2006). U.S. television producer, writer, and actor. Born in Dallas, Texas, Spelling enlisted in the U.S. Army Air Force in 1942 and served in Europe during World War II. He briefly worked as a reporter for the Army's newspaper, *Stars and Stripes*, and produced theatrical events for the Army's special services branch. After attending the University of Paris for one year, Spelling returned to Texas in 1946 to study drama at Southern Methodist University under the GI Bill. There he wrote several plays, two of which took Eugene O'Neill Awards. After graduating in 1950, he directed local theater and then moved to Los Angeles, where he began acting in television programs. He returned to writing and in 1956 sold a script, *Unrelenting Sky*, to *Zane Grey Theater*. Spelling continued writing for the program and in 1960 was named producer of the series. He continued creating and producing shows, including *The Lloyd Bridges Show* (1962–63) and *Burke's Law* (1963–66). In 1968, Spelling hit it big with the action series *The Mod Squad* (1968–73), kicking off similar shows, such as *The Rookies* (1972–76), *S.W.A.T.* (1975–77), *Starsky and Hutch* (1975–79), and *Charlie's Angels* (1976–81). In 1976, Spelling and Mike Nichols took a chance with *Family* (1976–80), but the Emmy-nominated series about a middle-class family that was a win with critics failed to find its audience. Spelling also sought to balance his lighter fare with socially responsible television movies, such as *The Boy in the Plastic Bubble* (1976) and *The Best Little Girl in the World* (1981). Riding high from his success with *Charlie's Angels*, Spelling introduced shows that blended action with glitz, such as *Love Boat* (1977–84), *Fantasy Island* (1978–84), *Vega$* (1978–81), and *Hart to Hart* (1979–84). In 1981, Spelling further refined his formula for commercial success by focusing on the trials and tribulations of the wealthy with *Hotel* (1983–88), *Dynasty* (1981–89), and its spin-off *The Colbys* (1985–87). His first feature film was the hit family comedy, *Mr. Mom* (1983). Just as the late 1980s saw a decline in Spelling's appeal, the launch of the Fox network helped reinvigorate his empire with more youth-oriented shows, such as *Beverly Hills, 90210* (1990–2000) and *Melrose Place* (1992–9). In 1993, Spelling produced HBO's *And the Band Played On*, an expose of the social, political, and personal realities of AIDS. After producing more than 200 television shows, Spelling said he had found personal satisfaction in the success of *7th Heaven* (1996–2006), a television series about a functional religious family.

BIBLIOGRAPHY: A. Spelling, in: *St. James Encyclopedia of Popular Culture*, 5 vols. (2000); A. Spelling, in: Contemporary Authors Online (Thomson Gale, 2004).

[Adam Wills (2nd ed.)]

SPELLMAN, FRANK (1922–), weightlifter, Olympic and Maccabiah medalist, member of the U.S. Weightlifting Hall of Fame and the Helms Hall of Fame. Born in Malvern, Pennsylvania, Spellman was orphaned at the age of seven and raised in a Jewish orphanage in Philadelphia. Originally trained in track and gymnastics, in his late teens Spellman came under the tutelage of weightlifter Dan Leone, and in 1942 he won the U.S. junior middleweight title. In December of that year he was drafted into the Army Air Corps, where he served until his honorable discharge in December 1945. Spellman, who had maintained his training, returned to Pennsylvania and was accepted to the well-known York Barbell team. At the 1946 U.S. Amateur Athletic Union (AAU) competition, he took first place in the middleweight division, and later that year finished 3rd at the World Championships in Paris, while helping the American weightlifters win the world team title. In 1947, Spellman moved down a notch to second place at the AAU Nationals, but moved up to second place at the World Championships in Philadelphia. Now at the peak of his form, in 1948 for the second time in his young career he won the AAU middleweight national title. Then, as the No. 1 middleweight lifter for the U.S. Olympic team, Spellman won the gold medal at the 1948 London games. After 1948, Spellman remained a force in weightlifting, finishing in second place in the AAU Nationals four times between 1949 and 1954. In addition, he won a gold medal at the 1950 Maccabiah games. Spellman did not compete in the national or world championships after 1954, though he did compete in the California State Championships, taking first place in 1954, 1957, and 1958. At the age of 38 and after a two-year hiatus from participation in any competitions, Spellman decided to close out his career by making one final appearance at the 1961 AAU National Championships, in Santa Monica, California. To the surprise of many weightlifting enthusiasts, Spellman overcame the odds to win the middleweight division for his third U.S. title. Besides his championship titles and two gold medals over the course of his 16-year career, Spellman set four American records and two Olympic world records. From 1957 to 1961, Spellman was the coach and mentor of Carl Miller, who became a highly-acclaimed weightlifting and strength trainer. Spellman eventually settled in Florida, and was still lifting into his eighties and acting as an unofficial coach of aspiring weightlifters.

[Robert B. Klein (2nd ed.)]

°**SPENCER, JOHN** (1630–1693), English theologian and Hebraist. Spencer was master of Corpus Christi College, Cambridge, from 1667 onward and in 1677 became dean of Ely. He published a *Dissertatio de Urim et Thummim* (1669), a kind of prologue to his more famous work, *De legibus Hebraeorum Ritualibus et earum Rationibus* (1685), which laid the foundations of the science of comparative religion. In this work Spencer maintained that many Jewish laws and customs could be linked with those of other Semitic peoples, producing examples from sacrificial rites, the Temple and its appurtenances, and the institution of the scapegoat.

In the second work (2 vols., 1727), which only appeared years after his death, he expanded his thesis to include rabbinic institutions (e.g., *tefillin*), basing much of his speculation on *Maimonides' *Guide of the Perplexed*. A third edition of the work, also in two volumes, was published at Tuebingen in 1732. Some of Spencer's writings appeared in Blasio Ugolino's *Thesaurus Antiquitatum Sacrarum* (Venice, 1744–69).

BIBLIOGRAPHY: C.M. Pfaff, in: J. Spencer, *De Legibus*... (Tuebingen, 1732); W.R. Smith, *Religion of the Semites* (1956), v–xi; J. Guttmann, in: *Festschrift ... D. Simonsen* (1923), 258–76. **ADD. BIBLIOGRAPHY:** ODNB online.

SPERBER, DAN (1942–), French social and cognitive scientist. His father was the Galician-born novelist and essayist Manès Sperber. Born in France, Dan Sperber was educated at the Sorbonne, where he earned a Licence ès Lettres in 1962, and at Oxford, where he received a B.Litt. in 1968. The director of research at the Centre National de Recherches Scientifiques (CNRS) in Paris, Sperber was well known for his work in developing what he terms an "epidemiology of representations" in his naturalistic theory of culture.

Sperber's early research focused on the anthropology of religion from the perspective of innate mental structures; he argues that these structures have played an important role in the development of religious beliefs and in the way that beliefs "fixate" in the human mind and are "extraordinarily catching." His studies of linguistics, experimental psychology, the philosophy of science, and evolutionary biology led to his further exploration of cultural theory, using a naturalistic approach linked to evolution. His works include *Rethinking Symbolism* (1975); *On Anthropological Knowledge* (1985); and *Explaining Culture: A Naturalistic Approach* (1996). His "epidemiology of representations," which may be conceived as a "contagion" of ideas, concerns the processes of replication and transformation of cultural beliefs, which Sperber likens to models of the transmission of disease.

Sperber also developed, with British linguist Deirdre Wilson, a cognitive approach to communication that has become known as "relevance theory." Their 1986 work, *Relevance: Communication and Cognition*, has received much attention; their theory, though influential, has also generated controversy, as has Sperber's "epidemiology of representations." In *Relevance*, the authors argue that human cognition relies on perceived relevance: that humans pay attention only to information that seems relevant. The work also approaches the study of reasoning by considering the role of contextual information, and questions contemporary views on the nature of verbal comprehension.

Sperber was a visiting lecturer at several institutions, including Cambridge University, the British Academy, the London School of Economics, the Van Leer Institute in Jerusalem, the University of Michigan, the University of Bologna, the University of Hong Kong, and the Institute for Advanced Study at Princeton University.

[Dorothy Bauhoff (2nd ed.)]

SPERBER, DANIEL (1940–), historian and Talmud scholar. Born in Wales in 1940, he moved to Israel after high school and studied at the Kol Torah and Hebron yeshivot. In the 1960s he studied the history of art at England's Courtauld Institute. In 1978 he became a full professor of Talmud at Bar-Ilan University. He has written on economic history, as in *Roman Palestine, 200–400: Money and Prices* and in *Roman Palestine. 200–400: The Land* and on Jewish art and history, *Minhagei Israel* (1998), *Why Jews Do What They Do* (1999), and the *City in Roman Palestine* (2001), among other topics. From 1985 he was a member of the Academy of the Hebrew Language. In 1992 he received the Israel Prize for Jewish Studies.

SPERBER, MANÈS (1905–1984), French author and editor. Born in Zablotov, Eastern Galicia, Sperber spent much of his youth in Vienna, where he was prominent in the *Ha-Shomer ha-Ẓa'ir Zionist youth movement. He was assistant to the psychologist Alfred *Adler, whose life and work Sperber discussed in a study published in 1926. From 1927 to 1933 he taught psychology in Berlin and founded a psychological review. For some years he was an active communist, but finally left the party in 1937. After the Nazis came to power in Germany, he escaped to France. Later he became a director of the important French publishing house of Calmann-Lévy and turned to literature, first writing in German and later in French.

His main works were *Et le Buisson Devint Cendre* (1944; *The Burned Bramble*, 1951); *Plus Profond que l'abîme* (1949; *The Abyss*, 1952); *La Baie Perdue* (1952; *Journey Without End*, 1954), an epic of the underground; the essay *Le Talon d'Achille* (1957; *The Achilles Heel*, 1959); and *Man and His Deeds* (1970), an alternative to the politics of the present. Like Arthur *Koestler, he depicts the moral collapse of the revolutionary edifice and the disillusionment of its architects. He parts company with Koestler when he propounds a positive attitude to Jewishness and is deeply immersed in Jewish culture. This is particularly noticeable in the story "*Qu'une larme dans l'oçean*," which forms part of *La Baie Perdue*. Here the novelist sets forth the eternal spiritual resistance of the Jews. In his preface to the book, André Malraux (d. 1976) eulogized it as "one of the Jewish people's greatest stories."

BIBLIOGRAPHY: C. Lehrmann, *L'Elément Juif dans la Littérature Française*, 2 (1961), 178–83; G.L. Mosse, in: *New York Times* (Nov. 11, 1970).

[Arnold Mandel]

SPERO, NANCY (1926–), U.S. painter. Cleveland-born, feminist artist Nancy Spero studied at the Art Institute of Chicago (1945–49) and at the Atelier André l'Hote and the Ecole des Beaux-Arts (1949–50) in Paris. While at the Art Institute, she met the artist Leon *Golub, whom she married in 1951.

Conceived while Spero and Golub were living in Paris from 1959 until 1964, her early *Black Paintings* show figures materializing from a dark background. Several of these canvases portray women segregated into stereotypical roles, such as a mother or a prostitute. In Paris, Spero had her first solo exhibition at the Galerie Breteau (1962). Following the couple's move to New York in 1964, Spero initiated *The War Series*

(1966–70), a group of gouache drawings on paper that often show the effects of bombing by utilizing iconography that equates the male phallus with annihilation. From 1969–72, Spero worked on the *Codex Artaud*, her first scroll and a format she would explore for many years. Based on the writings of Antonin Artaud, Spero juxtaposes typed excerpts from Artaud's poems with painted imagery arranged in a collage-like fashion on strips of paper. For Spero, Artaud's prose, which describes his alienation and anguish, metaphorically articulated the position of women in a patriarchal world.

Spero began designing museum installations in the late 1980s. After reading Bertolt Brecht's poem about Marie Sanders, a woman who slept with a Jew and was subsequently murdered for her perceived transgression, Spero made several installations about her, including *Ballad of Marie Sanders, The Jew's Whore* at Smith College Museum of Art, Northhampton, Massachusetts (1990) and *The Ballad of Marie Sanders/Voices: Jewish Women in Time* at the Jewish Museum (1993). The latter installation reproduced photographs showing victimized women in the Warsaw Ghetto, concentration camps, and other Nazi-related brutalities, as well as women in a more powerful position, such as female Israeli soldiers and female Israeli and Palestinian peace activists. Spero also depicted Sanders in a paper print and a scroll.

From 1969 Spero was a member of Women Artists in Revolution (WAR), a group dedicated to female equality in the arts. She co-founded the Artists in Residence Gallery, an art gallery for women based in New York City, in 1972.

BIBLIOGRAPHY: D. Nahas, *Nancy Spero: Works Since 1950* (1987); N. Spero, *Nancy Spero: Woman Breathing* (1992); K. Kline and H. Posner, *Leon Golub and Nancy Spero: War and Memory* (1994); J. Bird, J. Isaak, and S. Lotringer, *Nancy Spero* (1996).

[Samantha Baskind (2nd ed.)]

SPERO, SHUBERT (1923–), U.S. rabbi. Born in New York City, Spero received his rabbinic ordination at Yeshiva and Mesifta Torah VaDaath in 1947. After serving as rabbi at the Young Israel of Brookline, Mass. (1947–50) he assumed the same position at Young Israel of Cleveland (1950–83). He holds a B.S.S. from the CCNY, an M.A. from Case Western Reserve University, and a Ph.D. from Case Western Reserve University (1971). His thesis was on the subject, "The Justification and Significance of Religious Belief." He also served as the secretary of the Orthodox Rabbinical Council of Cleveland and lecturer in philosophy at the Cleveland Institute of Art. After making *aliyah* to Israel in 1983, he has served as Irving Stone Professor of Basic Jewish Thought at Bar-Ilan University.

For over 40 years Spero made contributions to Jewish thought in areas of moral philosophy, aesthetics, religious Zionism, and the accommodation between traditional Judaism and modern life. His published works include *Faith in the Night (A Bedside Companion for the Sick)* (1957); a compilation of Maimonides' writings, *The Faith of a Jew* (1949); and *Story of Chasam Sofer* (1946). His book *God in All Seasons* (1967) discusses Jewish festivals as an integral force in the life of the observant Jew. His major philosophical work *Morality, Halakha and the Jewish Tradition* (1982) is an attempt to present a comprehensive study of the morality of Judaism. In this work he argues that the ultimate creative task of man is to create himself as a moral personality.

After many years of research he published his second major work, *Holocaust and Return to Zion* (2000). In this book he analyzes the idea of history from both a Jewish and a philosophical perspective. He presents a novel interpretation of exile in Jewish history, in which it has the special function of bringing about the slow, progressive development of certain key factors in Jewish and world history that make a renewed Jewish sovereign polity possible.

These key factors are from the Jewish side: the presence of a sizable number of Jews, identifiable as Biblical Israel, in Europe by the middle of the 19th century, in possession of a Torah which had been elaborated into a viable philosophic worldview and a comprehensive way of life, and from the side of the larger society, the spread of liberal democracy, the doctrine of human rights, the growth of science and technology, and the serious efforts to establish institutions working toward an international order. As he understands it, the improbable conjunction of these key factors made possible the reestablishment of the Jewish state within the historic boundaries in 1948 – a return that had been promised by the Hebrew prophets.

Spero suffered a great personal tragedy in the 2003 suicide bombing at Café Hillel in Jerusalem. Both his son-in-law, physician Dr. David Appelbaum, and his granddaughter, Nava, who was to be married the next day, were killed in the blast. Spero and his family in the following years dedicated themselves to establishing humanitarian and religious projects in memory of his son-in-law and granddaughter.

[Shalom Freedman (2nd ed.)]

SPERTUS INSTITUTE OF JEWISH STUDIES (formerly the College of Jewish Studies), Chicago educational institute organized in 1924 by the Board of Jewish Education of Chicago to provide opportunities for systematic Jewish studies and for training teachers. The College opened under the leadership of Alexander Dushkin, the executive director of the Board of Jewish Education, with five students, who met in rented quarters in different parts of the city. Dushkin later established the Department of Education at The Hebrew University. In 1935 Leo Honor, the college's administrator, succeeded Dushkin as director of the Board of Jewish Education with Samuel M. Blumenfield serving as registrar and, later, dean of the college. Under the leadership of Dr. Leo Honor and Rabbi Samuel Blumenfield, the identity of the college as a distinct institution began to emerge. In 1942, it was authorized to grant degrees by the Illinois Department of Education. As a result of the steady growth of the college, the Board of Jewish Education recommended that it become a separate corporation with its own board of governors. In 1945 the college was incorporated as a Not-for-Profit Illinois Corporation. In its charter, issued that year, the institutional mission was defined as "Maintaining and operating a College in which youths and adults may receive an education on a college and post graduate level in… any subject relating to Jews and Judaism." This represented an expansion of the college's original mission of being primarily a teachers' training institution. In 1946 it moved into its own building and expanded its program to include studies leading to the Bachelor of Hebrew Literature degree and teachers' diplomas. With the addition to the faculty of distinguished scholars from Europe and Israel, the college initiated graduate studies. Spertus College now offers eight post-graduate degrees, and through distance learning options serves students in 36 U.S. states and six foreign countries. The Spertus Center for Nonprofit Management provides working professionals with tools to succeed in the nonprofit and public service sectors, through its master's program and continuing education opportunities.

From the 1940s until the 1960s, the college served as the central institution in Chicago and in the American Midwest for the training of Jewish educators and as the central institution in Chicago for Hebrew culture, thereby expressing the ideology of Cultural Zionism that characterized its early history, programs, and curricula. By 1948, a department of graduate studies offering bachelor's, master's, and doctoral degrees had been initiated. During the late 1950s and early 1960s, cantors and choir directors were trained for synagogues through its Institute for Jewish Music. From 1965 the college has served other colleges and universities as a department of Judaic studies, in which students may pursue a major or minor curriculum as well as elective courses. From the 1940s until the mid-1960s, the college operated a summer camp, Camp Sharon, and initiated and substantially expanded continuing education programs in Chicago and surrounding suburbs. Many renowned refugee scholars who migrated to America to escape Hitler served on the Spertus faculty during these years.

In 1968, Maurice Spertus donated his impressive collection of Jewish ceremonial objects to the college, thus beginning the Spertus Museum. In 1970, the College of Jewish Studies honored the outstanding and ongoing support of the families of Maurice and his brother Herman Spertus by changing its name to the Spertus College of Judaica. In 1974, Spertus moved to its present Michigan Avenue location. That same year, Norman and Helen Asher, recognizing the importance of a first class library, endowed what is now the Norman and Helen Asher Library, which contains more than 100,000 books. The Asher Library also includes the Targ Center for Jewish Music and the Chicago Jewish Archives.

In 1968, the College of Jewish Studies was officially separated from the Board of Jewish Education. Among the distinguished scholars who served on the faculty were Simon Halkin, Simon Rawidowicz, Meyer Waxman, Samuel Feigen, Moses Shulvass, Judah Rosenthal, and Byron Sherwin. Samuel B. Blumenfield was its first president, followed in 1954 by Abraham Duker, and in 1962, by David Weinstein. In 1984, Dr. Howard A. Sulkin became the organization's seventh president.

In 1971, Spertus College started the first college level course in the Midwest in Holocaust Studies, and in 1975 Spertus Museum created the Bernard and Rochelle Zell Holocaust Memorial, the first permanent Holocaust exhibition in North America, the centerpiece of the Bernard and Rochelle Zell Center for Holocaust Studies.

In 1987, Spertus College established The Joseph Cardinal Bernardin Center for the Study of Eastern European Jewry. Jointly sponsored with the Archdiocese of Chicago, the center is dedicated to promoting interfaith dialogue and increased understanding between eastern European and Jewish communities.

In 1993, the Spertus College of Judaica officially became the Spertus Institute of Jewish Studies, reflecting its multidisciplinary identity. Along with the name change, reflecting its multifaceted approach to the study of Jewish culture, came a renewed declaration of institutional goals and new long term strategies on how to implement them.

[Samuel M. Blumenfield]

SPEWACK, BELLA (1899?–1990), U.S. journalist, screenwriter, and playwright. Born in Transylvania, Bella Cohen emigrated with her mother to the Lower East Side of New York in 1903. After graduating from Washington Irving High School, she began writing for the socialist newspaper *The Call* and also worked as a press agent for various organizations. Among them was the Girl Scouts, where she is reputed to have invented the idea for the Girl Scout cookie. In 1922, Bella Cohen married Samuel Spewack, a newspaperman for the New York *World*, and they traveled together to Berlin and Moscow as foreign correspondents. While in Berlin in 1922, Spewack penned her posthumously-published memoir, *Streets: A Memoir of the Lower East Side* (1995) and also began writing short stories. "The Laugh," published in *Best Short Stories of 1925*, was one of more than 40 short stories she wrote in her twenties. Developing their talent in association, Bella and Sam Spewack wrote a number of successful comedies for stage and screen, including the plays *Boy Meets Girl* (1935), a satire on Hollywood which ran on Broadway for 669 performances; *Clear All Wires* (1932), a farcical newspaper melodrama; *My Three Angels* (1953); and *The Festival* (1955); and films such as *My Favorite Wife* (1940), starring Cary Grant; and *Weekend at the Waldorf* (1945), starring Ginger Rogers. Perhaps their best known works are the books they wrote for two highly successful Cole Porter musicals, *Leave It To Me!* (1938), and *Kiss Me Kate* (1948), which won the Tony Award that year. Spewack was deeply involved in the theatrical and intellectual world of mid-twentieth century New York City. Her papers, in the Samuel and Bella Spewack Collection in the Rare Book and Manuscript Library of Columbia University, include correspondence with George and Ira Gershwin, George S. Kaufman, Thornton Wilder, Mary Martin, Lillian Hellman, Eleanor Roosevelt, and many others. In 1953 the Spewacks founded a sports club in Ramat Gan, Israel, for child victims of poliomyelitis.

BIBLIOGRAPHY: J. Mersand, *Traditions in American Literature, a Study of Jewish Characters and Authors* (1939), 73–77; S.J. Kunitz (ed.), *Twentieth Century Authors*, first supplement (1955).

[Andrea Most (2nd ed.)]

SPEYER (Fr. **Spire**; Eng. sometimes **Spires**), city in the Rhenish Palatinate, Germany. Although local traditions, largely legendary, speak of Jewish settlement in Speyer in Roman times, Jews probably first came to the city in the early 11th century. Documentary evidence for a Jewish settlement in the city dates only from 1084, when Bishop Ruediger settled Jews in the village of Altspeyer, which he incorporated into Speyer "to increase the honor of the town a thousand fold." At that time Jews fled from *Mainz for fear of persecution because of a fire they were accused of having caused. The bishop allotted them a special residential quarter and gave them a plot from Church lands to be used as a cemetery. They were also allowed to build a protective wall around their quarter. In a privilege, dated Sept. 13, 1084, Bishop Ruediger granted them unrestricted freedom of trade and considerable autonomy. The **archisynagogos*, later also called "bishop of the Jews" (*Judaeorum episcopi*), was the spiritual head of the community; in lawsuits between Jews he was permitted to give rulings in accordance with Jewish law. The Jews were also expressly allowed to sell to Christians meat which was ritually unclean for Jews, and they did not have to pay any duties or tolls when entering or leaving the city. They also had the right to engage Christian servants. The privilege granted by Bishop Ruediger was confirmed by Emperor Henry IV on Feb. 19, 1090, to *Judah b. Kalonymus, David b. Meshullam, and Moses b. Jekuthiel of Speyer; in addition to renewing the privileges granted by Bishop Ruediger, the emperor guaranteed the Jews freedom of trade in his empire as well as his protection. Henry's privilege document is of more than passing interest to the historian, since city privileges were at the time a new category of constitutional documents in Germany. By 1096 a synagogue had been built. The *mikveh*, first mentioned in 1125, was in the vicinity.

The Jewish community of Speyer was one of the first Rhine communities to suffer during the First *Crusade. On a Sabbath, the eighth of Iyyar (May 3, 1096), a mob of crusaders surrounded the synagogue intent upon attacking the community while all were gathered in one spot. Forewarned, the Jews had concluded their service early and fled to their homes. Nevertheless, 10 Jews were caught outside their homes and killed. One woman committed suicide rather than submit to baptism, an act that was to be repeated frequently during the period. When Bishop John heard of what occurred, he came to the defense of the Jews with his militia, prevented further bloodshed, and punished some of the murderers. As an added precaution, he hid some of the Jews in villages surrounding Speyer, where they stayed until the danger had passed. The Jews returned to their homes, still fearful of attacks against them. Jews living in Altspeyer (the upper part of the city) did not attend the synagogue located in the lower portion of the city because of such fears. Instead, they held services at the *bet midrash* of R. Judah b. Kalonymus until a new synagogue was erected in Altspeyer in 1104.

The community grew and prospered during the 12th century; its economic position was excellent and it established itself as a center of Torah. Among the scholars of Speyer in this period were Eliakim b. Meshullam ha-Levi, a student of *Isaac b. Judah of Mainz; Kalonymus b. Isaac, known as a mystic as well as a talmudist; *Isaac b. Asher ha-Levi; Jacob b. Isaac ha-Levi, a German tosafist and author of a dirge on the Crusade period; *Samuel b. Kalonymus he-Ḥasid; Shemariah b. Mordecai, a correspondent of R. Jacob *Tam and a great talmudic authority; Meir b. Kalonymus, the author of a commentary to the *Sifra, Sifrei*, and *Mekhilta*; and Judah b. Kalonymus b. Meir, the author of a talmudic lexicon, *Yiḥusei Tanna'im ve-Amora'im*. In 1195, after severe persecutions following a *blood libel, Emperor Henry VI demanded that the Jews be compensated for damages and that the burned synagogue and ruined houses be rebuilt. Under the guidance of R. Ḥezekiah ha-Nagid, the Jews rebuilt their community. Early in its history the community developed a close relationship with the other Rhine communities and particularly with the closely allied cities of Mainz and Worms (see *Shum). In a series of synods beginning in 1196 they promulgated a series of communal decrees known as *takkanot Shum*, later to be of decisive influence on all Ashkenazi communities. The synod of 1223 took place in Speyer; among the most important scholars participating in the synods was R. *Simḥah b. Samuel of Speyer, although Speyer had then lost the dominant position it had held as a Torah center.

A flourishing community continued to exist in Speyer until the middle of the 14th century, although the Jews were drawn into a conflict between the bishop and the burghers in 1265, and in 1282 a blood libel brought suffering upon the community. In 1286 many Jews of Speyer and the neighboring communities of Worms, Mainz, and *Oppenheim were involved in the ill-fated attempt at immigration to Ereẓ Israel led by *Meir b. Baruch of Rothenburg. In December 1339 both the bishop and the municipality promised their protection to the Jewish community for a period of ten years. The city possessed a *Judengasse* but Christians lived on it as well, and Jews owned houses elsewhere in the city. The community had a high degree of autonomy, administered by a "*Judenbischof*" together with a Jewish municipal council. In this period the community maintained not only a synagogue and a cemetery but also a communal wedding hall, a hospital for the indigent poor (**hekdesh*), and a *matzah* bakery. The community suffered somewhat during a blood libel in 1342; it was, however, to meet its destruction during the *Black Death persecutions. In January 1349 a mob gathered and stormed the Jewish quarter. Some Jews locked themselves into their houses and set fire to them; others were killed by the mob, while a small number allowed themselves to be baptized in order to save their lives. Among the martyrs was the scholarly R. Eliakim, treasurer of the community's hospital. The loss of life was very great; out of fear of contamination, the burghers packed Jewish corpses in wine barrels and threw them into the Rhine. A small number were able to flee to neighboring communities such as *Heidelberg and Sinzheim. All Jewish property was confiscated or destroyed by the mob in an attempt to find hidden gold in Jewish homes. Tombstones were dragged away and utilized in the building of towers and walls, while the graveyard was plowed and sown with corn. All debts owed to the Jews were annulled. Emperor Charles IV absolved the city's inhabitants of any wrongdoing and allowed the city to retain confiscated Jewish properties. Although their houses in Altspeyer remained in Christian hands, Jewish autonomy was restored in 1354 and part of the cemetery returned, together with the right to rebuild communal institutions.

With much difficulty the community was rebuilt, but without any of its prior standing as a center of learning. Emperor *Wenceslaus issued a new letter of protection (see **Schutzjuden*) to the Jews of Speyer in 1394. Nevertheless, in 1405 they were expelled from the city and allowed to return only in 1421. In 1430 they were again expelled, returning again in 1434, only to be driven out once more a year later. After an interval of 30 years they were again domiciled in Speyer. In 1467 the city granted the Jews their protection for a period of ten years. Yet in 1468 and 1472 Bishop Matthias von Rammung issued anti-Jewish decrees, including a ban on charging interest and practicing usury; forbidding Jews to appear publicly on Christian feast days; forcing Jews to wear distinctive clothing; forbidding the building of a school or synagogue without the bishop's permission; and an edict confining Speyer Jews to a ghetto. By that time, however, the number of Jews in Speyer was very small. In fact, from the 16th to the 18th centuries, only individual Jews lived in the city. Those who fled from Speyer settled in neighboring places such as *Bruchsal, Berghausen, Harthausen, Dudenhofen, Otterstadt, and *Landau.

In the 19th century the community was renewed; by 1828 it was flourishing once more. A new *talmud torah* was opened, employing a permanent teacher. In 1829 the statutes of the community, which determined the synagogue regulations in particular, were published. In 1831 a Jewish elementary school was dedicated and in 1837 a synagogue, with an adjoining *mikveh*; the synagogue was enlarged in 1866. A new Jewish cemetery was consecrated in 1888. There were several societies for social self-help, which united in 1910 to aid the needy. The board of the community consisted of five members in 1920. At the beginning of the 20th century Dr. Adolf Wolf *Salvendi and Dr. Steckelmacher were rabbis of Speyer.

Holocaust Period

In 1933 there were 269 Jews in Speyer, since many had previously moved to other German cities. That same year all the community's cultural associations as well as the Jewish youth societies were banned. The Speyer municipal government investigated the proprietors of firms and placed orders only with "Aryan" firms. In May 1934 the community initiated courses for the study of Hebrew; in 1935 a conference of Jewish youth took place in Speyer. In subsequent years, up to the outbreak of the war, many emigrated because of increasing antisemitic excesses. Almost all young Jews left the city. In 1939 there were still 77 Jews there; in 1940 there were 60. Of these, 51 were deported on Oct. 22, 1940, to the *Gurs concentration camp in France and almost all the rest to camps in Eastern Europe, where they perished. No new community was established in Speyer after the war. The synagogue that had been built in 1836 was destroyed in 1938, but the cemetery still existed in 1971. Remains of the old Jews' court and Jewish public baths were preserved in the Palatinate Historical Museum in Speyer, along with a number of Jewish tombstones from the 12th and 15th centuries and Jewish ritual objects from the former community.

The medieval synagogue in Speyer, dating back to 1104, is the oldest Jewish religious structure preserved in Germany. Archaeological excavations in 2001 brought new findings about the history of the building, the interior, and the early history of the Jews in the episcopal city. In 2004–2005 the Palatinate Historical Museum in Speyer held the exhibition "The Jews of Europe in the Middle Ages," which included a computer-based reconstruction of the synagogue. Near the site of the synagogue, a plaque (inaugurated in 1978) commemorates the building that was destroyed in 1938. Another memorial to the former Jewish community was consecrated in 1992, bearing the names of all the Speyer Jews who perished during the Nazi era.

After 1990 Jews from the former Soviet Union settled in Speyer. They are partially affiliated with the Jewish community of Rhine Palatinate in Neustadt. In 2005 there were about 50 members. The Neustadt community planned to open a new community center with a synagogue in 2006. Besides Jewish immigrants from the former Soviet Union, a Jewish community was founded in Speyer in 1996. There were 100 members in 2005.

BIBLIOGRAPHY: *Germania Judaica*, 1 (1963), 326–66; 2 (1968), 775–82; vol. 3 (1987), 1384–1401; FJW; E. Carlebach, *Die Rechtlichen und sozialen Verhaeltnisse der Juedischen Gemeinden Speyer, Worms und Mainz…* (1901); A. Epstein, *Juedische Alterthuemer in Worms und Speyer* (1896); L. Rothschild, *Die Judengemeinden zu Mainz, Speyer und Worms von 1349–1438* (1904); R. Herz, *Gedenkschrift zum 100-jaehrigen Bestehen der Synagoge in Speyer* (1937); F.J. Hildebrand, *Das Romanische Judenbad im alten Synagogenhofe zu Speyer* (1900); A. Neubauer and M. Stern, *Hebraeische Berichte ueber die Judenverfolgungen waehrend der Kreuzzuege* (1892), passim; M. Wiener, in: MGWJ, 12 (1863), 161–77, 255–68, 297–310, 417–31; 454–66; D. Kaufmann, *ibid.*, 35 (1886), 517–20; O. Stobbe, in: ZGJD, 1 (1887), 205–15; M. Stern, *ibid.*, 3 (1889), 245–8; R. Strauss, *ibid.*, 7 (1937), 234–9; R. Krautheimer, *Mittelalterliche Synagogen* (1927), 145–50; G. Stein, *Judenhof und Judenbad in Speyer am Rhein* (1969); idem, *Zur Datierung des Speyerer Judenbades* (1964); Finkelstein, Middle Ages; A. Kober, in: PAAJR, 14 (1944), 187–220; Aronius, Regesten, no. 168; Kisch, Germany, index; *Monumenta Judaica* (1963), index; A.M. Habermann, *Gezerot Ashkenaz ve-Ẓarefat* (1946); K. Duewell, *Die Rheingebiete in der Judenpolitik des Nationalsozialismus vor 1942* (1968), index. **ADD BIBLIOGRAPHY:** *Geschichte der Juden* *in Speyer* (Beitraege zur Speyerer Stadtgeschichte, vol. 6) (1981); G. Stein, Speyer, *Judenhof und Judenbad* (Grosse Baudenkmaeler, vol. 238) (1989^7); S. Wipfler-Pohl, "Vom Leben Juedischer Frauen," in: F. Ebli (ed.), *Frauen in Speyer. Leben und Wirken in zwei Jahrtausenden* (1990); J. Bruno and L. Moeller, *Der Speyerer Judenhof und die mittelalterliche Gemeinde* (2001); J. Bruno and E. Dittus, *Juedisches Leben in Speyer* (2004). **WEBSITES:** www.alemannia-judaica.de; www.jgs-online.de; http://museum.speyer.de/de/histmus; www.speyer.de/de/tourist/sehenswert/judenhof.

[B. Mordechai Ansbacher / Larissa Daemmig (2nd ed.)]

SPEYER, German and American family of international bankers and philanthropists. Progenitor of the family was MICHAEL ISAAC SPEYER (d. 1692) who, on his marriage in 1644, established residence in the Frankfurt ghetto and became community head. His great-grandson ISAAC MICHAEL SPEYER (d. 1807) was an Imperial Court Jew. The latter's nephew JOSEPH LAZARUS SPEYER (1783–1846) married into the Frankfurt banking family Ellissen, and his son LAZARUS JOSEPH SPEYER (1810–1876) carried on business from 1836 under the hyphenated name Lazard Speyer-Ellissen. The latter's partner, PHILIPP SPEYER (1815–1876), moved to New York in 1837. Together with his brother GUSTAV (1825–1883) he established the bank Philipp Speyer & Co. in 1845, later Speyer & Co. Together with its Frankfurt affiliate, it placed the first North American Civil War loan in Germany. Gustav's American-born sons, JAMES (1861–1941) and EDGAR (1862–1932) piloted the family concern to its height. While remaining partners of the Frankfurt house, whose last head was their brother-in-law EDUARD BEIT VON SPEYER (1860–1933), James conducted the American business and Edgar took charge of Speyer Brothers, London. Edgar was made a baronet, but, suffering defamation during World War I, returned to New York. Speyer & Co. alone, and sometimes jointly with *Kuhn, Loeb & Co. and National City Bank, led syndicates which raised European capital for investment in American industry. This movement was reversed after World War I, when a subsidiary, New York & Foreign Investing Corporation, mobilized American capital for investment, mainly through the Frankfurt branch, in German and other Central European issues. Absorbing a Berlin private bank in 1927, the Frankfurt branch became temporarily prominent in the international expansion of the German rayon industry. However, the worldwide crisis after 1929 stopped the trans-atlantic flow of capital, and the German and American houses were liquidated in the 1930s. Institutions benefiting from the family's philanthropic interests included Frankfurt University; Museum of the City of New York; and Mount Sinai Hospital, New York.

BIBLIOGRAPHY: B. Baer, *Stammtafeln der Familie Speyer* (1896); K. Grunwald, in: LBYB, 12 (1967), 176; S. Birmingham, *Our Crowd* (1968).

[Hanns G. Reissner]

SPEYER, BENJAMIN (18th century), communal leader and *shtadlan*, merchant in Mogilev-Podolski, and purveyor to the Russian government. In 1768 Speyer acted with Baruch Yovon (Yavan) to foil Jacob *Frank's appeal to the Russian government for protection. In 1770 Speyer successfully obtained the suspension of a decree expelling Jews from Courland and Riga. When the Frankists sent the "red letters" to the Jews of Russia in 1800, Speyer translated them for Governor-General Gudovich of Kamenets-Podolski, signing himself with the title "court councillor." In 1804 he proposed to the government council in charge of legislation for Jews that they eliminate unfair taxation.

BIBLIOGRAPHY: Yu. Hessen, in: YE, 16 (c. 1912), 82.

[Yehuda Slutsky]

SPEYER, SIR EDGAR (1862–1932), British railway financier. Edgar Speyer, a member of the famous German banking family, was born in Frankfurt and came to England in 1887 as a director of Speyer Brothers, the family bank, engaged in currency exchange and railway finance. He was naturalized in 1892. From the mid-1890s he was one of the most important figures in procuring the finance and development of London's "tubes," its electric-powered subways, usually in conjunction with the American railway builder C.T. Yerkes. London's Underground system owes much to Speyer. He was made a baronet (a hereditary knight) in 1906 and was made a member of the Privy Council in 1909. During World War I, Speyer was the victim of a concerted, highly unpleasant campaign against him as an alleged pro-German. In 1915 he offered to resign as a privy councilor, but the offer was declined by the prime minister; at nearly the same time, a lawsuit was brought against him and Sir Ernest *Cassel, another German-born member, requiring them to justify their continued membership. As a result of these pressures, Speyer moved permanently to New York. According to historians, however, there seems no doubt that Speyer was, in some sense, pro-German and was in regular touch with his Frankfurt business. In 1921 he was struck off the list of privy councilors and was accused, in a government white paper, of "trading with the enemy" in wartime. He continued to live in New York but died after an operation in Germany, ironically less than a year before Hitler came to power.

BIBLIOGRAPHY: ODNB online; D. Kynaston, *The City of London, 1* (1994).

[William D. Rubinstein (2nd ed.)]

SPICES. The Bible has no special word for spice. In the talmudic and midrashic literature the term *tavlin* is used, from the verb *tavel* (תבל), which is apparently connected with the root *balol* ("to mix"). This term was employed metaphorically by R. Joshua b. Ḥananiah in his reply to questions by "the emperor" (probably Hadrian): "Why has the Sabbath dish such a fragrant odor?" To this R. Joshua replied: "We have a certain spice (*tavlin*) called the Sabbath, which we put into it [the Sabbath dish] and which gives it a fragrant odor" (Shab. 119a). Spiced foods were very popular among the Jews of Ereẓ Israel and Babylonia, even as they are today among Jews from Oriental countries who know several dozen varieties of spices, special favorites being the pungent-tasting ones, principally pepper, that stimulate the appetite. Such spices apparently also have some disinfectant action under the inferior conditions of food hygiene prevalent in the East. The general name for spices is משביחי אוכלין (*mashbiḥei okhelin*, "food improvers"; Sif. Deut. 107, where seven kinds of spices are mentioned). Another term used is צִיקֵי קְדֵרָה (*ẓikei kederah*; Yoma 75a; Ḥul. 77b; et al.).

Among the "food-improving" spices may also be included pungent-tasting vegetables, such as *garlic, the *leek, the *onion, etc. Some aromatic plants (*incenses and perfumes), such as *cinnamon and *saffron, were also used as spices. In addition to these aromatic plants and vegetables, the Bible mentions four kinds of spices, *hyssop, *caper, *cumin, and *fennel-flower, while talmudic literature refers to dozens of varieties, the most important of which are the following.

AMOMUM. The word *ḥamam* mentioned in the Mishnah (Uk. 3:5; et al.) refers, according to Asaph ha-Rofe, to the seed of the pungent-tasting, aromatic plants of the genus *Amomum* of the Zingiberaceae – ginger family – such as *Amomum cardamomum*. Called *hel* in Arabic, it is popular among Oriental communities as an additive to coffee. Some hold that the "principal spices" (Ex. 30:23) refer to these plants.

ASAFETIDA. The *ḥiltit* of the Mishnah is the plant *Ferula asafetida*, the congener of *galbanum*, and, like it, has an unpleasant aroma but flavors a dish, and is still used in Iran. Mentioned together with asafetida is a spice named *ti'ah* (Uk. 3:5), held by some to be the root of the same plant.

CAPER. The fruit, *aviyyonah*, and the flower buds, *ẓalat*, of the caper plant were eaten pickled either in salt or in vinegar.

CARAWAY. The *karbos* of the Mishnah (Kil. 2:5 – this is the correct reading), which is identified in the Jerusalem Talmud (MS Rome, *ibid.* 2:5, 27d) refers to *Carum carvi*, the seed of which was used as a spice and the thick root as a vegetable.

COSTUS. The *kosht*, which is mentioned among the "food improvers" (Sif. Deut. 107; cf. Uk. 3:5) and among the ingredients of the incense used in the Temple (Ker. 6a), has been identified with the aromatic spice *Costus*, which was extracted from species of plants belonging to the ginger family. According to another view, the *Costus* of the ancients is to be identified with *Aucklandia costus* (= *Aplotaxixhappa*), a fragrant plant which is a member of the Compositae family.

CUMIN. The seed of the *kammon* of the Bible and the literature of the sages was used as a spice on bread during baking.

DILL. Called *shevet* in the Mishnah, dill is the plant *Anethum graveolens* used today mainly as a spice in pickled cucumbers. In mishnaic times its foliage, stems, and seed were used as a spice (Ma'as. 4:5), and it was sown for this purpose (Pe'ah 3:2). It is an umbelliferous plant with yellow flowers, which grows wild in the Negev (it is popularly but erroneously called *shamir*).

DODDER. This plant is identified with plants of the genus *Cuscuta* of which there are many species that are parasitic on cultivated and wild plants in Israel. Dodder is called in the Mishnah *keshut*, the meaning of which is "hair," since these plants are leafless and have the appearance of entwined hair. The seed sprouts on the ground, and the plant winds itself around the stem of another plant, extracting its sap by putting forth suckers into it. The fruit of the dodder was used as a spice, mainly in wine (Pliny, *Historia naturalis* 13:46). In the Talmud it is mentioned that the dodder is a parasitic plant, its life depending on the plant to which it is attached (Er. 28b).

FENNEL. The umbelliferous plant *Foeniculum vulgare*, leaves of which are used as a spice similar to dill, fennel is called *gufnan* in the Mishnah (Dem. 1:1) and *shumar* in the Talmud. The Jerusalem Talmud (Dem. 1:1, 21d) states that the Galileans did not consider it a spice, but it was regarded as such in Judah.

FENNEL-FLOWER. Known as *keẓah* in the Bible and the literature of the sages, the seed of the fennel-flower was used as a spice on bread.

GINGER. The Indian plant *Zingibar officinale*, from the rootstock of which an aromatic spice was made, ginger is called *zangevila* in the Talmud and was sold both dried and fresh (Ber. 36b; Yoma 81b). In the Talmud (*ibid.*) it is also called "the *himalta* which comes from India."

HYSSOP. The plant *Majorana syriaca* is called *ezov* in the Bible and in the literature of the sages; its leaves were used as a spice. Of the allied genera, reference is made to the spice plants (*ezov koḥeli*), which is *Hyssopus officinalis* (Neg: 14, 6, where *ezov romi* is also mentioned), *evreta*, *maru-ḥiyyura*, and *shumshuk* (Shab. 109b), species that belong to the genera *Majorana* or *Origanum*.

LAVENDER. The plant *Lavandula officinalis* (*spica*) is known as *ezovyon*, and its leaves are used as a perfume and as a medicine (Shab. 14:3).

MINT. The plant *Menta piperita*, the leaves of which are used as a spice and yield an ethereal oil, is called *minta* in the Mishnah (Uk. 1:2) and *na'ana* (which is also its Arabic name) in the Jerusalem Talmud (Shab. 7, 10a). Four species of mint grow wild in Israel.

MUSTARD. Known as *ḥardal* in the literature of the sages, *mustard is extracted from the seed of species of *Sinapis* and *Brassica*.

PEPPER. The most important and popular spice, black *pepper is know as *pilpel*, and *Piper longum* as *pilpela arikhta*.

RUE. The small shrub *Ruta graveolens*, whose leaves have a pungent aroma (regarded by some as unpleasant), is popular among Oriental communities. In the Mishnah (Uk. 1:2; et al.), it is called *pigam*, and in Arabic *fijn or rudah* (= *Ruta*). The Mishnah (Shev. 9:1) also mentions a rue that grows wild, the reference being to *Ruta bracteosa*, which grows in the woods in Israel. To the family of rue – *Rutaceae* – belong species of the *Citrus*.

SAFFLOWER. The prickly plant *Carthamus tinctorius* has reddish-yellow leaves, *ḥallot ḥari'a* (Uk. 3:5), which were used as a spice, and its seed, *benot ḥari'a* (Tosef. Ma'as. Sh. 1:13), as food as well as a spice. In the Talmud *koẓah, kurtama*, and *morika* are used as synonyms for safflower. Today the safflower is grown largely for the oil extracted from its seed. The petals of the flower's corolla were formerly used as a dye (see *Dye Plants).

SAFFRON. Known as *karkom* in the Bible and the literature of the sages, the stigmas of its flower were used as a spice and a dye.

SAVORY. Called *si'ah* in the Mishnah, savory is mentioned there, together with hyssop and thyme, among plants which were grown as spices; it also grew wild (Shev. 8:1; Ma'as. 3, 9). According to the Jerusalem Talmud (Shev. 7:2, 37b), *si'ah* is identified with *ẓatrah*, which is *Satureia tymbra Savory*, an aromatic dwarf shrub of the family *Labiatae*, that grows wild on mountains. The Arabs call these three species *za'ar*.

SESAME. The summer plant *Sesamum orientalis* (*indicum*), sesame was used in the preparation of delicacies and as a spice in various kinds of pastry (Shev. 2:7; TY 1:5). Its seed consists of 50% oil, which was used as a food and in lamps (Ned. 6:9; Shab. 2:2).

SUMAC. The *og* of the Mishnah, the fruit of the sumac tree was used as a spice.

THYME. Called *koranit* in the Mishnah, thyme is a diminutive dwarf shrub which grows extensively in Israel on the kurkar hills near the coast and on mountains. Its tiny, pungently aromatic leaves were used as a spice, like hyssop and savory, together with which it is mentioned (Ma'as. 3:9).

The above are the most probable identifications, others having been suggested by commentators for these plants, as well as for kinds of spices common in their day. Among these, mention should be made of the poppy, the plant *Papaver somniferum*. Its seed is used as a spice and also in various kinds of pastry. In modern Hebrew the poppy is called *parag* or *pereg*, on the basis of the identification given in the *Arukh* and by other commentators for פרגים in the Mishnah, which are, however, none other than *millet. Although several species of *Papaver* grow wild in Israel, it is impossible to determine whether the cultivated poppy was grown. The only reference to *ofyon* (opium is extracted, as is known, from poppy) occurs in the Jerusalem Talmud (Av. Zar. 2:2, 40d). It was considered dangerous to buy *ofyon* from heathens (see *Havdalah).

BIBLIOGRAPHY: Loew, Flora, respective articles and 4 (1934), 93f.; S. Krauss, *Kadmoniyyot ha-Talmud*, 2 (1929), 243–9; J. Feliks, *Olam ha-Ẓome'aḥ ha-Mikra'i* (1968), 176–85; idem, *Kilei Zera'im ve-Harkavah* (1937), index. **ADD. BIBLIOGRAPHY:** Feliks, *Ha-Tzome'aḥ*, 19, 22, 24, 41, 65, 66, 69, 73, 85, 89, 100, 104, 123, 125, 132, 137, 147, 148, 154, 157, 197.

[Jehuda Feliks]

SPICE TRADE. In their original settlements in the East Mediterranean and Near East, Jewish merchants traded in luxury goods, including *spices. This latter trade became more evident in the Diaspora era, when Jews, along with Greeks and Syrians, appeared as traders in Western Europe. Because of their relationship with the Orient, they were able to supply these products, which were grown mainly in the countries from southern Arabia to the Moluccas and were used for medicinal purposes, in the preparation of food and beverages, and in perfumes. At first the Syrians led this trade, losing their position to the Jews only after the conquest of the Syrian coast by the Arabs. Writing on the trade routes in the years between 854 and 874, Ibn Kordabheh, postmaster of the caliph of Baghdad, mentioned that Radhanites traded in musk, aloes, camphor, cinnamon, and other commodities between France and China. From the tenth century the northern route through the Slav countries became increasingly important to Jewish traders as they were displaced in the Mediterranean by Italian merchants. When visiting Mainz around 978, Ibrahim Tartuschi, an Arab from the Iberian Peninsula, was astonished to find the markets filled with large quantities of spices which could only be found in the Far East; it was generally believed that these were brought by Jewish merchants from the Orient by way of Kiev. The activities of Jewish traders on the Mediterranean and Indian Ocean trade routes and ports are revealed in 11th- to 13th-century *genizah* documents and responsa. The disuse of the Eastern routes with the expansion of Tatar and Turkish conquest added to the increased Christian participation in overseas trade and the restriction of Jewish commercial activities, and caused the Jews to lose their position as intermediaries with the Orient, being replaced by the Italians and especially the Venetians.

Jewish merchants once more played a part in the spice trade with the opening of the direct route to East India by the Portuguese. Prominent among these merchants was the New Christian *Mendes family, probably descendants of the Spanish *Benveniste family. Rui Mendes (de Brito) sent a ship to East India with Vasco da Gama's second voyage in 1502, and in 1505, in association with the German Lucas Rem, armed three ships for East India. He was probably a close relative of the brothers Francisco and Diogo *Mendes who, the former in Lisbon and the latter in Antwerp, controlled a major part of the commerce in pepper and other spices in northern Europe, the largest market at that time. After the death of Diogo Mendes (1542 or 1543), Francisco's widow, Beatrice de Luna, carried on the Antwerp branch of the enterprise. As J.A. Goris has shown (see bibl.), about 12 other New Christians in Antwerp were engaged in the spice trade, on the basis of annual contracts made with the king of Portugal. For some time the Perez family and other Spanish merchants, who were probably also New Christians, were the representatives of these *contractadores*. When Philip II succeeded to the throne of Portugal, he tried to renew the system of contracts, which had been in the hands of the German Konrad Rott during the last years of Portuguese independence. After Rott's bankruptcy, the Lisbon and Antwerp branches of the Ximenes and D'Évora families participated in the European contract. From 1592 to 1596 the Indian contract was in the hands of a consortium of New Christians: Tomáz and André Ximenes, Duarte Furtado de Mendoza, Luis Gomes d'Elvas, Heitor Mendes, and Jorge Rodriguez Solis. Attacks on Portuguese ships by English pirates, the revival of the Levantine spice trade from Alexandria and Syria to the Mediterranean ports, and the opening of East Indian navigation by the Dutch and English, all contributed to the decline of the Portuguese monopoly and thus of the activities of the New Christian groups. However, their participation in the spice trade in Hamburg and Amsterdam remained prominent. Among the 16 spice importers in Amsterdam in 1612, 11 were "Portuguese," i.e., Sephardim. According to Bloom (see bibl.), in the first part of the 18th century the spice trade still represented a considerable proportion of the commercial activities of the Sephardi community in Amsterdam.

BIBLIOGRAPHY: W. Heyd, *Geschichte des Levantehandels im Mittelalter* (1879); P. Lambrechts, in: *Antiquité Classique*, 6 (1937), 357ff.; J. Brutzkus, in: ZGJD, 3 (1931), 97f.; L. Rabinowitz, *Jewish Merchant Adventures, a Study of the Radanites* (1948); S.D. Goitein, *A Mediterranean Society*, 1 (1967), index; Roth, Marranos, index; C. Roth, *House of Nasi, Doña Gracia* (1947); J.A. Goris, *Etude sur les Colonies Marchandes Méridionales à Anvers de 1488 à 1567* (1925); Brugmans-Frank, 1 (1940); D. Gomes, *Discursos sobre los Comercios de las dos Indias*, ed. by M.B. Amzalak (1943); J.G. da Silva, in: *XIII Congresso Luso-Espanhol para o Progresso das Ciências*, Lisbon, 1950; J.L. de Azevedo, *Epocas de Portugal Economico* (1947[2]); H.I. Bloom, *Economic Activity of the Jews of Amsterdam in the Seventeenth and Eighteenth Centuries* (1937); C. von Rohr, *Neue Quellen zur zweiten Indienfahrt Vasco da Gamas* (1939); J. Polišenský and P. Ratkoš, in: *Historica*, 9 (1964), 53–67; H. Kellenbenz, in: *Monumenta Judaica* (1963), 199f.; idem, *Sephardim an der unteren Elbe* (1958); idem, *La Participation des Capitaux de l'Allemagne Méridionale aux Entreprises Portugaises d'Outre-Mer au Tournant du XVe siècle et XVIe siècle* (1966).

[Hermann Kellenbenz]

SPIDER (Heb. עַכָּבִישׁ, *akkavish*). Isaiah (59:5–6) compares the evil designs of those who plot against the righteous to the webs which the spider spins to trap insects, while Job (8:14–15) compares the house of the wicked to the spider's fragile web. There are hundreds of species of spider in Israel, all having poisonous glands in their maxillaries. The poison in most spiders is a mild one, but there are species capable of killing a bird or a mouse. It would appear that the *akhshuv* (Ps. 140:4) which is mentioned together with the snake as a poisonous animal is merely the *akkavish* with the letters transposed. The Tosefta (Par. 9:6) enumerates it among the species of spiders. Some erroneously identify the spider with the *semamit* (Prov. 30:28) which is the *gecko.

BIBLIOGRAPHY: Lewysohn, Zool, 299–301, nos. 400 and 401; F.S. Bodenheimer, *Animal and Man in Bible Lands* (1960), 116, nos. 336–40; J. Feliks, *Animal World of the Bible* (1962), 135.

[Jehuda Feliks]

SPIEGEL, DORA (1879–1948), third president of the National *Women's League of the United Synagogue of America. Spiegel led the organization through the difficult years of the Depression and World War II. Born in Ungvar, Hungary, to Pepi Josephine (Fullman) and Rabbi Daniel Rosenberg, Dora Rosenberg arrived in the United States with her parents in 1882. Although Dora and Dr. Samuel Spiegel (a New York physician, whom she married in 1900) had no children of their own, she dedicated her energy to serving Jewish children and their mothers. Spiegel attended Teachers College of Columbia University, receiving a B.S. degree in 1916 and an M.A. in 1920, with a special diploma as Advisor to Women. In New York she taught at the Educational Alliance, training immigrants in "Americanization."

A close friend and supporter of Mathilde *Schechter, Spiegel was a founder and president (1918–28) of the New York Metropolitan branch of the Women's League of the United Synagogue of America, and served as national president from 1928 to 1944, when poor health forced her to step down before the conclusion of her term. During World War II, Spiegel's "President's Chats" columns in the League's magazine *Outlook* encouraged members to help with war-relief efforts. Women responded by giving blood, selling bonds, serving in canteens, and taking and teaching first-aid classes. During her presidency, Spiegel also led the League to begin the Torah Fund Campaign to establish a Seminary dormitory and a scholarship fund, which would allow rabbinical students to study full-time. She also encouraged the creation of two additional scholarship funds (the Mathilde Schechter Scholarship Fund and the Cyrus Adler Scholarship Fund). In addition, the plan for building a dormitory for female students developed during her tenure as president. She also helped found the Women's Institute of Jewish Studies at the Jewish Theological Seminary of America.

BIBLIOGRAPHY: *They Dared to Dream: A History of National Women's League, 1918–1968* (1967); S. Weintraub, "Spiegel, Dora," in: P.E. Hyman and D. Dash Moore *Jewish Women in America: An Historical Encyclopedia* (1997).

[Aleisa Fishman (2nd ed.)]

SPIEGEL, ISAIAH (**Yeshayohu Spiegel**; 1906–1990), Yiddish poet, fiction writer and essayist. Born in Balut, a poor suburb of Lodz, Poland, Spiegel was encouraged by I. *Katzenelson and M. *Broderzon, and was one of the group of young Yiddish poets active in Lodz in the 1920s. From 1926 to 1933 he taught in Yiddish schools and wrote for Yiddish journals in Poland and abroad. Spiegel was one of the few Yiddish writers of distinction to survive the Holocaust. For almost five years he lived in the Lodz ghetto; upon its destruction he was sent to Auschwitz and later to a labor camp in Saxony. He returned to Lodz after the liberation (1945) and from 1946 to 1948 taught in its Jewish school; there, he dug up a manuscript he had buried. From 1951 he lived in Israel. He published two volumes of verse and an autobiographical novel, but his most important work is his Holocaust fiction, especially his short stories: *Malkhes Geto* ("Ghetto Kingdom," 1947), *Shtern Ibern Geto* ("Stars Over the Ghetto," 1948), *Mentshn in Thom* ("People in an Abyss," 1949), *Likht Funem Opgrunt* ("Light from the Precipice," 1952), and *Vint un Vortslen* ("Wind and Roots," 1955). With restraint and perception, Spiegel records the fate of multitudes of ordinary men and women in his stories. Most of his stories originally written during the Holocaust were considerably revised, the documenting witness giving way to the memorializing artist.

BIBLIOGRAPHY: J. Glatstein, *In Tokh Genumen, Eseyen 1948–1956* (1956), 453–65; idem, *In Tokh Genumen, Eseyen 1949–1959*, 1 (1960), 279–86. **ADD. BIBLIOGRAPHY:** N. Gris, *Fun Finsternish tsu Likht: Yeshayohu Shpigl un Zayn Verk* (1974); LNYL, 8 (1981), 782–4; Y. Szeintuch (ed.), *Yeshayohu Shpigl: Proza Sifrutit Migeto Lodzh* (1995); L. Prager, in: S. Kerbel (ed.), *Jewish Writers of the Twentieth Century* (2003), 533–4.

[Leonard Prager]

SPIEGEL, LUDWIG (1864–1926), Czech educator and politician. Spiegel, who was professor of constitutional law at the German University of Prague, was one of the leaders of the German Democratic Party and a member of the Senate (upper chamber of deputies; 1920–25). In 1926 he was elected rector of the university in spite of his being a Jew (see also Samuel *Steinherz), but died before assuming office. His works include *Die Geschichtliche Entwicklung des Oesterreichischen Staatsrechts* (1905), *Die Verwaltungsrechtswissenschaft* (1909), *Gesetz und Recht* (1913), and *Die Entstehung des Tschechoslowakischen Staats* (1921).

[Chaim Yahil]

SPIEGEL, NATHAN (1905–1995), scholar of Jewish studies. Born in New York, Spiegel grew up in Galicia, Moravia, and the Ukraine. He received his doctorate in 1931 from the University of Lvov in classical studies and ancient philosophy. After World War II he was a high school teacher in Poland and from 1952 the rector of a Warsaw institute of education. He immigrated to Israel in 1957 where he was director of a special library at the Hebrew University of Jerusalem. In 1965 he began to teach at Ben-Gurion University and served as head of the department of general studies. Among his works are books on leading figures of the Greek and Hellenic world, such as Socrates, Aristotle, Homer, and Seneca, as well as on trends and schools of thought in the Greek world. Spiegel received the 1990 Israel Prize for Jewish Studies.

[Fern Lee Seckbach]

SPIEGEL, PAUL (1937–2006), German-Jewish journalist and politician. Born in Warendorf (Westphalia), Spiegel fled with his family to Holland after the outbreak of World War II. He wrote as a journalist for German-Jewish newspapers, and between 1965 and 1972 was editor of the Juedische Pressedienst and assistant to the general secretary of the Zentralrat der Juden in Deutschland. Between 1974 and 1986 he directed the office of public affairs at the Rheinische Sparkassen und Giroverband. In 1986 he founded an international Kuenstleragentur. In 1984 Spiegel was elected president of the Duesseldorf Jewish community, in 1989 president of the Zentralwohlfahrtsstelle der Juden in Deutschland. After the death of Ignatz *Bubis, Spiegel was elected president of the Zentralrat der Juden in Deutschland in January, 2000. He was an active promoter of German-Jewish understanding, an author on Jewish matters, and a prominent figure in German public life.

SPIEGEL, SAMUEL P. (1901–1985), U.S. motion picture producer. Born in Jaroslau, Austria, Spiegel came to the United States in 1939. Ultimately becoming one of the top producers of his time, Spiegel's films include *Tales of Manhattan* (1942), *The Stranger* (1945), *We Were Strangers* (1949), *The African Queen* (1951), *On the Waterfront* (Academy Award for Best Picture, 1954), *The Bridge on the River Kwai* (Academy Award for Best Picture, 1957), *Suddenly Last Summer* (1950), *Lawrence of Arabia* (Academy Award for Best Picture, 1962), *The Night of the Generals* (1966), *The Happening* (1967), *Nicholas and Alexandra* (Oscar nomination for Best Picture, 1971), *The Last Tycoon* (1976), and *Betrayal* (1983). Spiegel, who was also known for a time as S.P. Eagle, was the only person to win the Best Picture Oscar three times as a sole producer within eight years. He was the brother of Shalom *Spiegel.

In 1964 he received the Irving G. Thalberg Memorial Award, given to a creative producer who has been responsible for a consistently high quality of motion picture production.

ADD. BIBLIOGRAPHY: A. Sinclair, *Spiegel: The Man behind the Pictures* (1987); A. Sinclair, *S.P. Eagle: A Biography of Sam Spiegel* (1988); N. Fraser-Cavassoni, *Sam Spiegel: The Incredible Life and Times* (2003).

[Jonathan Licht / Ruth Beloff (2nd ed.)]

SPIEGEL, SHALOM (1899–1984), scholar, writer, and educator. Born in Romania and educated in Vienna, Spiegel was for a number of years a leader of Jewish youth who were preparing to live in collectives in Israel as members of Ha-Shomer ha-Ẓa'ir. He taught in Ereẓ Israel 1923–29, then went to New York, and was professor of medieval Hebrew literature at the Jewish Theological Seminary (1944–84). Trained in art and aesthetics, among other areas, he brought the appreciation of the sensitive critic to what he taught, studied, or wrote. His *Hebrew Reborn* (1930, repr. 1962), a series of chapters on Jewish men of letters in modern times, is a lucid, cultural analysis of the works of the authors it surveys. He also gave attention to the biblical and the medieval periods of Jewish cultural history. He published studies on Hosea, Amos, Jeremiah, Ezekiel, and Job. These exhibit both his erudition and thoroughness and also his style and finesse. Spiegel prepared a definitive edition of the liturgical compositions of Eleazar *Kallir. He also prepared a volume of what remains of the religious poetry by Kallir's predecessors and contemporaries. His discussion of the sacrifice of Isaac (**Akedah*) in the Hebrew liturgy of the 12th and 13th centuries is a notable example of his penetrating approach (*The Last Trial*, translated from the Hebrew by J. Goldin, 1967).

In 1996 the Jewish Theological Seminary established the Shalom Spiegel Institute for Medieval Hebrew Literature. The

Institute provides fellowships to graduate students in the field, fosters international research projects, and provides access to Spiegel's copious collection of research materials.

He was the brother of film producer Samuel P. *Spiegel.

[Abraham Solomon Halkin / Ruth Beloff (2nd ed.)]

SPIEGEL-ADOLF, MONA (Anna Simona; 1893–1983), colloid chemist. Spiegel-Adolf studied medicine in her native Vienna and worked there on medical colloid chemistry until 1931, when she became professor of colloid chemistry at the medical school of Temple University, Philadelphia. Her research covered physical chemistry of proteins and lipids, cancer, amaurotic family idiocy, etc. She wrote *Die Globuline* (1930) and co-authored *X-ray Diffraction Studies in Biology and Medicine* (1947).

SPIEGELBERG, HERBERT (1904–1990), philosopher. Of Jewish origin, Spiegelberg was raised as a Christian. Born in Strasbourg, he received his Ph.D. from the University of Munich. He went to the U.S. in 1938 and taught at Swarthmore College in Pennsylvania (1938–41) and Lawrence College in Wisconsin (1941–63). In 1963 he was appointed to the philosophy department of Washington University in St. Louis, Missouri, where he stood out as a phenomenologist and historian of phenomenology. He retired as professor emeritus in 1971.

Spiegelberg belonged more to the "Older Phenomenological Movement" than to the Freiburg School, influenced by Alexander Pfaender's approach. He was very influential in developing interest in phenomenological thought in the Anglo-American world through his lectures and writings. His *Phenomenological Movement* has provided a historical study and interpretation to this philosophy from Brentano to the present.

His major writings include *Anti-relativismus* (1935), *Gesetz und Sittengesetz* (1935), *The Phenomenological Movement* (2 vols., 1960, 1965^2), *Alexander Pfaender's Phaenomenologie* (1963), the translation of Pfaender's *Phenomenology of Willing and Motivation* (1967), *Phenomenology in Psychology and Psychiatry* (1972), *Doing Phenomenology* (1975), *The Content of the Phenomenological Movement* (1981), and *Steppingstones toward an Ethics for Fellow Existers* (1986).

BIBLIOGRAPHY: *H. Spiegelberg, Phenomenological Perspectives: Historical and Systematic Essays in Honor of Herbert Spiegelberg* (1975).

[Richard H. Popkin / Ruth Beloff (2nd ed.)]

SPIEGELMAN, ART (1948–), U.S. cartoonist. Born in Stockholm, Sweden, to parents who survived the Holocaust, Spiegelman grew up in Queens, N.Y. In 1968, while attending Harpur College in Binghamton, N.Y., he had a nervous breakdown, but he recovered. Shortly after, his mother, a survivor of Auschwitz, committed suicide. Spiegelman later included the tragic and traumatic event in his groundbreaking comic books, *Maus I* and *Maus II*, which tell the story of his parents' wartime ordeal and paint an indelible portrait of the widowed father in old age, an insufferable, maddening survivor, noble despite himself. The first book, *Maus: A Survivor's Tale*, also known as *Maus: My Father Bleeds History*, won a special Pulitzer Prize in 1992. It had the distinction of appearing on *The New York Times* bestseller list as a work of fiction, but after Spiegelman's dignified objection, as nonfiction. The second volume, *Maus: And Here My Troubles Began*, followed in 1991. *Maus*, depicting Jews as mice, Nazis as cats and Poles as pigs, attracted an unprecedented amount of critical attention for a work in the form of comics, including an exhibition at the Museum of Modern Art. Before gaining widespread attention with *Maus*, Spiegelman had illustrated many of the Wacky Packages and Garbage Pail Kids stickers and cards. He founded two significant comics anthology publications, *Arcade* and RAW, the latter with his wife, Francoise Mouly, who later became art editor of *The New Yorker.* Spiegelman worked for *The New Yorker* for ten years, producing memorable work, but resigned a few months after the terrorist attacks of September 11, 2001. Spiegelman's post-September 11 cover for the magazine, inspired by Ad Reinhardt's black-on-black paintings, at first appears to be totally black, but upon close examination reveals the silhouettes of the World Trade Center towers in a slightly darker shade of black. The attack had a profound effect on Spiegelman, who witnessed the victims' frantic last minutes as he left his apartment not far from the site. Spiegelman said his resignation from the magazine was a protest against "the widespread conformism of the mass media in the Bush era." In 2004 he published *In the Shadow of No Towers*, an attempt to capture the essence of the morning when the terrorists struck. It features a series of ten large-format comic strips that ran in the course of a year in eight weekly publications around the world. It was printed on thick cardboard and had to be held sideways to read each two-page spread. In the back, Spiegelman added reprints of some early comic strips, from Krazy Kat to Little Nemo in Slumberland, that he said gave him comfort after the attacks. Spiegelman was a tireless advocate for the medium of comics. He was quoted as saying that "comic books are to art what Yiddish is to language – a vulgar tongue that incorporates other languages into its mix, a vital and expressive language that talks with its hands. It's a form that's even laid out like a Talmudic text, a form that avoids the injunction against graven images by turning pictures into words, or at least into word-pictures."

[Stewart Kampel (2nd ed.)]

SPIEGELMAN, SOL (1914–1983) U.S. research microbiologist. He was born in New York City, where his interest in biology began in childhood. He gained his B.S. in mathematics and physics at the College of the City of New York (1933–39), a course lengthened by switching from biology and a research period at Crown Heights Hospital, Brooklyn (1936–37). He earned his Ph.D. in cellular physiology and mathematics from Washington University, St Louis (1944), after an initial period at Columbia University (1940–42). He worked successively in the bacteriology department of Washington University School of Medicine (1945–48), as a U.S. Public Health Service Fellow at the University of Minnesota, Minneapolis (1948), and at the University of Illinois, Urbana (1948–69), where he became professor of microbiology. He returned to New York (1969) as director of Columbia University's Institute of Cancer Research and professor of human genetics and development in the University's College of Physicians and Surgeons (1975). Spiegelman's research profoundly influenced our understanding of the control of normal cell growth and its disruption in cancer cells. His work has also had important implications for understanding the origins of life in self-replicating nucleic acid sequences. His experiments were based on the novel hypothesis that unregulated activation or deactivation of genes controlling enzyme production is followed by uncontrolled cell growth. Progress in his studies and in molecular biology in general was revolutionized by his technical innovation, RNA/DNA hybridization, which made it possible to detect and characterize specific RNA sequences. Spiegelman and his colleagues first showed that only one strand of DNA's double helix transmits the genetic information for protein synthesis. They also identified and purified the first viral nucleic acid polymerase that could detect specific viral RNA in the RNA of infected cells. In his later work his laboratory concentrated on methods for screening human cancer tissue and the blood of cancer patients for specific viral RNA or DNA sequences or the RNA viral enzyme, "reverse transcriptase," and for antigens found in cancer cells but not normal cells. This, however, has proved to be a difficult and complex field. His many honors include the Lasker Award for Basic Medical Research (1974) and the Feltrinelli Prize, awarded by the Italian National Academy of Sciences (1981). Spiegelman was also greatly respected for his early recognition of scientists' social responsibilities and for his self-deprecation over the fame brought by scientific discovery.

[Michael Denman (2nd ed.)]

SPIELBERG, STEVEN (1946–), film director, writer, producer. Born in Cincinnati, Ohio, Spielberg began his career early in his youth, directing home movies. At age 13 he entered and won his first contest with a 40-minute war film. While attending California State College, he directed five films and made his professional debut with a 24-minute short, *Amblin*, which was shown at the 1969 Atlanta Film Festival. Its success led to a contract with Universal Studios that soon found Spielberg directing movies for television such as *Duel* (1971) and *Something Evil* (1972). His debut as a feature film director was *Sugarland Express* (1974). Spielberg followed this with a series of some of the most successful motion pictures in cinema history, including *Jaws* (1975), *Close Encounters of the Third Kind* (Oscar nomination for Best Director, 1977), *Raiders of the Lost Ark* (Oscar nomination for Best Director, 1981), *E.T.* (Oscar nominations for Best Director and Best Picture, 1982), *Indiana Jones and the Temple of Doom* (1984), *Indiana Jones and the Last Crusade* (1989), *Always* (1989), and *Jurassic Park* (1993). Spielberg also attempted more serious cinematic fare with *The Color Purple* (Oscar nomination for Best Picture, 1985) and *Empire of the Sun* (1987), but neither of these films prepared the movie-going public for *Schindler's List* (1993), a brilliant and devastating portrait of Oskar *Schindler, an Austrian industrialist who saved more than 1,000 Polish Jews during the Holocaust. *Schindler's List* won the 1993 Academy Award for Best Picture as well as delivered an Oscar to Spielberg for Best Director. In 1990 the Academy of the Motion Pictures, Arts and Sciences presented Spielberg with the Irving Thalberg Memorial Award for his ongoing contribution to the Excellence of Cinema. Spielberg's subsequent directorial efforts include *Amistad* (1997), *Saving Private Ryan* (Oscar winner for Best Director and nomination for Best Picture, 1998), *The Unfinished Journey* (1999), *Artificial Intelligence: AI* (2001), *Minority Report* (2002), *Catch Me If You Can* (2002), *The Terminal* (2004), and *War of the Worlds* (2005).

Spielberg, who also wears a producer's hat, has released more than 100 films and television features since 1978. In 1995 he co-founded the production company DreamWorks SKG with Jeffrey Katzenberg and David Geffen. In addition to producing many of the films he directed, Spielberg was the producer of such films as *I Wanna Hold Your Hand* (1978), *Continental Divide* (1981), *Poltergeist* (1982), *Twilight Zone: The Movie* (1983), *Gremlins* (1984), *Back to the Future* (1985), *The Money Pit* (1986), *Who Framed Roger Rabbit?* (1988), *The Flintstones* (1994), *Men in Black* (1997), *The Mask of Zorro* (1998), the TV series *Band of Brothers* (Emmy Award for Outstanding Mini-series 2001) and *Taken* (Emmy for Outstanding Mini-series, 2002), and *Memoirs of a Geisha* (2005).

Spielberg was married to actress Amy *Irving from 1985 to 1989. Since 1991 he has been married to actress Kate Capshaw.

BIBLIOGRAPHY: F. Sanello, *Spielberg: The Man, the Movies, the Mythology* (1996); J. McBride, *Steven Spielberg: A Biography* (1997); S. Rubin, *Steven Spielberg: Crazy for Movies* (2001); I. Freer et al., *The Complete Spielberg* (2001).

[Jonathan Licht / Ruth Beloff (2nd ed.)]

SPIELMAN(N), English family that contributed extensively to Jewish and English communal and cultural literature. The family was descended from ADAM SPIELMAN (1812–1869), a banker, who married the sister of Samuel *Montagu. Adam's three best-known sons were SIR ISIDOR SPIELMAN (1854–1925), who was the founder and director of the art exhibitions branch of the Board of Trade and represented Britain at numerous international exhibitions from 1897 onward. He organized the Anglo-Jewish Historical Exhibition of 1887 and was president of the Jewish Historical Society, 1902–04. When Russian anti-Jewish excesses were at their height, he edited *Darkest Russia*, a supplement to the *Jewish Chronicle* (1890–92). He was knighted in 1905. MARION HARRY ALEXANDER SPIELMAN (1858–1948), art critic, was editor of the *Magazine of Art*, for 17 years. He wrote on art for the *Pall Mall Gazette* and the *Westminster Gazette*, and wrote a history of the first 50 years of the London satirical weekly, *Punch* (1895).

An authority on portraiture, he wrote *The Portraits of Geoffrey Chaucer* for the Chaucer Society (1901), *The Portraits of Shakespeare* for the Stratford Town Edition of Shakespeare's works (1907), and *British Portrait Painting*, 2 vols., 1910. His *Iconography of Andreas Vesalius*, commissioned by the Belgian government, was published in 1925. SIR MEYER ADAM SPIELMAN (1856–1936), the third son, was an educator and an inspector of Home Office Schools. He engaged in child welfare work, and was knighted in 1928 for his work on the prevention of juvenile delinquency. He was a founder and chairman of managers of a reformatory school established in 1921 for Jewish boys (converted to general use in the 1960s because Jewish child delinquency had almost disappeared). Sir Meyer held office in several Jewish charitable societies. His wife, LADY (GERTRUDE) EMILY SPIELMAN, the daughter of the banker George Raphael, was also prominent in social welfare and in 1919 was the first woman to be elected to the Board of Deputies of British Jews. Their daughter EVA MARIAN HUBBACK (1886–1949), educated at Cambridge, was a well-known social reformer and educator. She was the principal of Morley College in south London, which was noted for employing leading musicians, and was the author of *The Population of Britain* (1947). PERCY EDWIN SPIELMANN (1881–1964), a son of Marion Spielman, was a chemist who became a leading expert on coal tar, petroleum, and road making.

ADD. BIBLIOGRAPHY: ODNB online for Eva Hubback; R. Sebag-Montefiore, "From Poland to Paddington: The Early History of the Spielman Family, 1828–1948," in: JHSET, 32 (1990–92), 237–58; D. Hopkinson, *Family Inheritance: A Life of Eva Hubback* (1954); W.R. [Winifred Jessie Spielman], *Gertrude Emily Spielman, 1864–1949: A Memoir* (1950).

[John M. Shaftesley / William D. Rubinstein (2nd ed.)]

SPIELMANN, RUDOLF (1883–1942), Austrian chess master. Spielmann was regarded as the most successful of attacking chess players. He defeated *Nimzovich, *Tartakover (twice), *Réti, Stahlberg, Lundin, Eliskases, Bogoljubow, and Stolz in match play and won first prizes in 18 master tournaments between 1910 and 1935.

[Ed.]

SPIELVOGEL, CARL (1928–), U.S. businessman, diplomat. Born in Brooklyn, N.Y., Spielvogel graduated from the City College of New York and joined *The New York Times* as a copyboy while an undergraduate. He became a reporter for the business section in 1955, and three years later he was named the newspaper's first advertising columnist. He left the paper in 1960 to join the advertising firm McCann-Erickson, where he rose to executive vice president and general manager before joining McCann's parent, the Interpublic Group of Companies, in 1972. There he eventually became chairman of the executive committee. He left Interpublic in 1979 to form Backer & Spielvogel, one of the leading advertising agencies of the early 1980s. Mergers created Backer Spielvogel Bates Worldwide, where he was chairman until 1994. At his departure, Bates Worldwide was one of the world's leading marketing and advertising communications companies, with 185 offices in 65 countries. As an entrepreneur, Spielvogel was chairman and chief executive officer of United Auto Group, the nation's largest publicly owned automobile dealership group, from 1994 to 1997. In 1995 Spielvogel was appointed by President Bill Clinton to the U.S. Broadcasting Board of Governors, which was responsible for the Voice of America, Radio Free Europe, and other governmental broadcasting ventures. In 1997 he was named chairman of the international board of advisors of *The Financial Times* of London. In 2000, Clinton named him ambassador to the Slovak Republic, where he sought to promote trade. He served until 2001. Spielvogel was on the board of a number of cultural organizations in New York City, including the Metropolitan Museum of Art, Lincoln Center for the Performing Arts, and the Asia Society. He served for more than 20 years as a trustee of Mount Sinai Medical Center and aided Eureka Communities, which works to rebuild inner cities. His wife, Barbara Diamonstein-Spielvogel, is the author of 18 books on art, architecture, and public policy.

[Stewart Kampel (2nd ed.)]

SPIELVOGEL, NATHAN (1874–1956), Australian author. The son of a Galician immigrant who became a goldminer and storekeeper, Spielvogel was born in the gold-rush town of Ballarat, Victoria. He was raised in a warm, religious atmosphere and, despite the remoteness and isolation of his environment, always remained closely attached to Jewish tradition. Spielvogel gained distinction as one of the only Australian Jewish writers of the era. His first published work, a short story entitled "Mike Hardy's Folly," appeared in the *Ballarat Courier* (Dec. 22, 1894) and for the next sixty years he contributed to practically every Australian literary periodical and to the Jewish press. As a country schoolteacher, he traveled widely in the eastern Australian outback and also made a journey to London.

His recorded experiences were first serialized and then published in book form. Spielvogel's *A Gumsucker on the Tramp* (1906) was an early Australian best seller, some 20,000 copies appearing in several editions. Much of what he wrote about early Australian bush life is of historical interest and importance and in some instances is the only source of information. This is also the case with his descriptions of Jewish immigrant types arriving from England and Europe. Spielvogel portrayed their manner of work and trade and their synagogue, communal, and youth activities at the turn of the century. A limited edition of his prose and verse, *Selected Short Stories of Nathan Spielvogel*, was published in 1956. He was a close friend of many noted Melbourne artists and writers of his time, including Norman Lindsay. Spielvogel lived in Ballarat from 1924, serving as a school principal. He was a major influence in fostering a Jewish cultural presence in Australia at a time when the community was very small.

BIBLIOGRAPHY: N. Spielvogel, in: *Journal of the Australian Jewish Historical Society*, 6 pt. 1 (Dec. 1964), 1–27 (autobiog., ed. by

L.E. Fredman). **ADD. BIBLIOGRAPHY:** ADB, 12, 36–37; H.L. Rubinstein, Australia 1, 279–80, 440–41.

[Shmuel Gorr]

SPIER, LESLIE (1893–1961), U.S. anthropologist. Born in New York City, he became a student of Franz *Boas, later serving as assistant anthropologist at the American Museum of Natural History. From 1939 he taught at the University of New Mexico where he established a department of anthropology. Influenced also by R.H. *Lowie and C. Wissler, he did his field work on various North American Indian tribes, principally among the Zuñi and Yumans.

In North American ethnology Spier studied cultural traits over a continuous geographical area to achieve a historical reconstruction of human history. Such a paper as "Sun Dance of the Plains Indians" represents a significant contribution to cultural historical analysis by mapping the distribution of different elements in a cultural complex. He also studied the ghost dance and nativistic movement in the Northern Plains in 1890. Spier worked among the Indians of the Northern plains to salvage the vestiges of dying cultures.

All of Spier's work is characterized by methodological restraint and sobriety. He founded and edited anthropological journals and helped to establish American anthropology as an academic discipline.

BIBLIOGRAPHY: H.W. Basehart and W.W. Hill, in: *American Anthropologist*, 67 (1965), 1258–77, incl. bibl.; IESS, 15 (1968), 130–1, incl. bibl.

[Ephraim Fischoff]

SPIKENARD (**Nard**; Heb. נֵרְדְּ, *nerd*), spice mentioned three times in the Song of Songs. It grew in the imaginary spice garden to which the loved one is compared (Song 4:12–14) and she perfumed herself with it while waiting for her beloved (1:12). According to an ancient *baraita*, spikenard was one of the 11 spices from which the Temple incense was prepared (Ker. 6a; see *Incense and Perfumes and *Pittum ha-Ketoret*). It is called spikenard (*Nardostachys*) because of its appearance, which is similar to that of an ear of corn. It was extracted from the plants *Nardostachys jatamansi* and *N. grandiflora* that grow in the Himalayas. The name *nard* is derived from the Sanskrit *nalada* which means "spreading fragrance." This highly valued perfume was extracted both from the stalk (Lat. *spicatum*) which is the spikenard and from the leaves (Lat. *foliatum*). The Tosefta mentions *polyaton* oil among the luxuries whose use according to one view was forbidden after the destruction of the Temple as a sign of mourning (Tosef., Sot. 15:9).

BIBLIOGRAPHY: Loew, Flora, 1 (1926), 309; 2 (1924), 15; 3 (1924), 483; J. Feliks, *Olam ha-Ẓome'aḥ ha-Mikra'i* (1968²), 244–5; H.N. and A.L. Moldenke, *Plants of the Bible* (1952), index.

[Jehuda Feliks]

SPINA, GERI (Schreiber; 1896–1944), Romanian journalist. Born in *Jassy, Spina contributed to Romanian papers and magazines, including the Jewish periodicals *Hatikva* and *Adam*. With Isac *Ludo he edited the magazine *Absolutio* from 1913, and in 1914 published poems, *Senzaţii inutile* ("Vain Sensations"). In 1934 he published *Evreii în Literatura lui Ionel Teodoreanu*, a study of Jews in the writings of the Romanian author Teodoreanu. In 1944 he fought for the exposure of Nazi war criminals in Romania, was arrested, and died in prison.

SPINGARN, two U.S. brothers of wide intellectual interests, both devoted to the development of the National Association for the Advancement of Colored People. JOEL ELIAS SPINGARN (1875–1939) was a literary scholar and champion of African-American integration. The son of an immigrant Austrian merchant, Spingarn was born in New York. His doctoral thesis, *A History of Literary Criticism in the Renaissance* (1899), was widely acclaimed by scholars, and he thereafter had a successful academic career at Columbia University, becoming professor of comparative literature at the age of 24. With *Critical Essays of the Seventeenth Century*, a three-volume work which he edited in 1908, he established himself as a recognized exponent of the "New Criticism," which judged art on its own terms. However, a clash with Columbia's president, N.M. Butler, led to his dismissal in 1910. The correspondence between the two men was published a year later as *A Question of Academic Freedom*. Although he continued to publish literary criticism, Spingarn never returned to academic work. He wrote *The New Criticism* (1911) and *Creative Criticism* (1917). In 1919, on his return from war service in France, he helped to found the publishing firm of Harcourt, Brace and Howe, whose editorial consultant he remained until 1932. He edited *Scholarship and Criticism in the United States* (1922), wrote *Poems* (1924), and then retired to his home in Amenia, New York, where he became an authority on flower cultivation and issued the *Troutbeck Leaflets* (1924–31), occasional literary papers. One of the founders of the NAACP and its chairman from 1913 through to 1919, Spingarn was president of the association at the time of his death. In the association, he served as a bridge between the integrationists and the Black nationalists, led by W.E.B. Du Bois, editor of the NAACP's magazine *Crisis*. Although ideologically Spingarn was an integrationist, his friendship with and admiration for Du Bois allowed him to work with the editor until Du Bois resigned in 1934.

ARTHUR BARNETT SPINGARN (1878–1971) was a prominent lawyer active in the New York City Bar Association. His interest in questions of the black man led him to begin an extensive collection of Black literature, which he gave to Howard University. Resigning his position in the Bar Association in 1966, Spingarn, as honorary president of the NAACP, continued to support the organization and the cause for which he and his brother had worked.

BIBLIOGRAPHY: Howard University, Libraries, *Dictionary Catalog of the Arthur B. Spingarn Collection of Negro Authors* (1970); E. Rudwick, *W.E.B. Du-Bois* (1960); *Crisis*, passim; *New York Times* (July 27, 1939, July 14, 1958, Jan. 3, 1966). **ADD. BIBLIOGRAPHY:** M. Van Deusen, *J.E. Spingarn* (1971).

[Richard Cohen]

SPINKA, JOSEPH MEIR WEISS OF (1838–1909), *ẓaddik*, founder of a ḥasidic dynasty. The son of Samuel Ẓevi of Mukachevo (Munkacs), Joseph Meir was the disciple of Shalom of *Belz, Mendel of *Vizhnitsa, Isaac Eizik of *Zhidachov, and Ḥayyim *Halberstam of Zanz. On many occasions he visited Isaac of Zhidachov and regarded himself as his successor. Renowned for his ecstatic prayers, he also practiced extreme self-mortification. From 1876 he was revered as a *ẓaddik* by thousands of followers.

His works are *Imrei Yosef* (1910–27), a commentary on the Pentateuch in four volumes; *Imrei Yosef* (1931), sermons on the festivals and their customs; *Hakdamat Likkutei Torah ve-ha-Shas* (1911), sermons and an anthology of ḥasidic teachings; *Perush la-Haggadah shel Pesaḥ* (1964); and *Tefillot u-Minhagim* (1912).

His son, ISAAC EIZIK (1875–1944), was murdered by the Nazis. He was an outstanding authority on *halakhah* and famous as a cantor. From 1909 he too was a *ẓaddik* in Spinka. After the outbreak of World War I, he took his family and his retinue to Mukachevo, where he established his *bet midrash* and yeshivah. There he remained for a few years and, as in Spinka, his *bet midrash* became a center of learning and Ḥasidism. After the war he moved to Selishche, where he also established a large *bet midrash* that continued for 14 years. Isaac is the author of *Ḥakal Yizḥak*. His grandson JACOB JOSEPH WEISS, who was regarded as the most prominent leader of Spinka Ḥasidism after the Holocaust, maintained a yeshivah in Jerusalem. There were two additional *ẓaddikim* of Spinka Ḥasidism in Israel, grandsons of Joseph Meir of Spinka.

BIBLIOGRAPHY: Weiss, *Imrei Yosef*, 1 (1910), introd.; A. Feuer, *Zikhron Avraham* (1924); A.S. Weiss, *Pe'er Yosef* (1934); *Ḥasidut Spinka ve-Admoreha* (1958); J.L. Levin, *Beit Spinka* (1958); A. Stern, *Meliẓei Esh*, 1 (1962), 206, no. 120; S. Rozman, *Zikhron Kedoshim* (1968), 118–27.

[Esther (Zweig) Liebes]

SPINOZA, BARUCH (Bento, Benedictus) DE (1632–1677), philosopher born in Amsterdam of Portuguese background, who became one of the most important representatives of the rationalist movement in the early modern period.

Introduction

In the Jewish and National Library in Jerusalem, Spinoza's writings, unlike those of Jewish philosophers such as Philo of Alexandria or Maimonides, are not in the Judaica reading room, but in the general reading room, between the writings of Descartes and Leibniz. The decision of the library reflects a broad consensus in the way his work is perceived: Spinoza is not considered a Jewish thinker but one who belongs to the general history of philosophy. To be sure, Spinoza was excommunicated from Amsterdam's Jewish community for things he apparently said and did as a young man, and he went on to become the most radical and arguably the most interesting thinker of the early modern period. From the end of the 17th century onward his work played a central role in a variety of intellectual contexts: from the Enlightenment and German Idealism to the "higher criticism" of the Bible. Today Spinoza's ideas are debated not only in philosophical circles of both analytical and continental orientation, but also among scientists such as the neurologist Antonio Damasio, who claims that his research confirms how Spinoza conceived the relationship between body, mind, and affects of human beings. And yet, Spinoza's relationship to Judaism, and in particular to Jewish philosophy, is complicated: it is marked by continuity and criticism that sometimes remain in unresolved tension. Much of his philosophical project is, in fact, best understood in light of the Jewish background. In Spinoza's thought ideas from many sources come together, ranging from Plato to the Kabbalah. But of particular importance are, on the one hand, various traditions of Jewish thought and, on the other, the writings of Descartes and Hobbes which were at the center of philosophical discussions in the Netherlands of Spinoza's time. His first commitment, of course, was not to this or that intellectual current, but to the truth: "I do not claim to have found the best philosophy, but I know that I understand the true one [*sed veram me intelligere scio*]" (*Letter* 76).

Life and Works

Spinoza's father, Michael (d. 1654), fled from Portugal to the relatively tolerant Dutch republic where, he became a member of Amsterdam's Sephardi community and a successful merchant. Spinoza studied Hebrew, the Bible, and rabbinic literature at the local *talmud torah* school. The community's most renowned scholars, Isaac Aboab, Menasseh ben Israel, and Saul Levi Morteira, were presumably among his teachers and influenced him directly or indirectly. Aboab translated Abraham Cohen Herrera's kabbalistic treatise *Puerta del Cielo* (The Gate of Heaven), with which Spinoza seems to have been familiar, from Spanish into Hebrew. Morteira, who inclined to a rationalist interpretation of religion, could have introduced him to medieval Jewish philosophy. Menasseh ben Israel edited in 1628 the *Sefer Elim* by the Galilei student Joseph Delmedigo, of which Spinoza had a copy, and that may have introduced him into post-Copernican cosmology. Through Menasseh, Spinoza may also have made his first acquaintance with Christian thought, as well as with the ideas of Isaac La Peyrère, against whose treatise, *Prae-Adamitae*, Menasseh wrote a refutation. Spinoza later used the book for his critique of Scripture; among others, La Peyrère claims that Moses was not the only author of the Pentateuch and that human beings existed before Adam and Eve. When his half-brother, Isaac, died in 1649 Spinoza's help was required in the family's importing business. Although an outstanding student, he could thus not complete the higher level of the educational curriculum which would have prepared him for a career as a rabbi. The process that led to Spinoza's alienation from traditional Judaism, culminating in his excommunication (*ḥerem*) in 1656, cannot be precisely reconstructed from the available sources. A significant role must presumably be assigned to heterodox Jewish thinkers in Amsterdam such as Uriel da Costa, who had been excommunicated twice a generation earlier and whose writings Spinoza certainly knew, and Juan de Prado, who was excommunicated at the same time as Spinoza. Despite the unusual harshness of the *ḥerem*, it does not make explicit the content of the accusations, mentioning only "abominable heresies" and "monstrous deeds." But from various indirect sources Spinoza's views that were perceived as heretical can be established with reasonable certainty: they seem to have included the denial that the Torah is of divine origin, the denial that the immortality of the soul is a biblical doctrine, and a "philosophical" concept of God incompatible with that of popular tradition. All three issues show a certain affinity to doctrines of Da Costa and appear to have been endorsed in one way or another by De Prado as well. Spinoza probably explained and defended his views in a treatise now lost, but whose Spanish title is preserved in later sources: *Apologia para justificarse de su abdicacion de la sinagoga* ("Defense to justify his departure from the synagogue"). There are good reasons for assuming that some of the material contained in the *Apologia* was later incorporated into the first part of the *Tractatus Theologico-Politicus* (TTP; "Theological-Political Treatise").

The encounter with the former Jesuit and freethinker, Franciscus van den Enden, played an important role in Spinoza's intellectual development. In van den Enden's school, which he already started to frequent before his excommunication, Spinoza learned not only Latin, but was also introduced into ancient literature and philosophy, as well as into contemporary debates, in particular those provoked by the writings of Descartes and Hobbes. Descartes presumably also occupied an important place in his studies at the University of Leiden, at the time a center of Dutch Cartesianism. That Spinoza had mastered Descartes' philosophy is clear from his *Principia Philosophiae Cartesianae* ("Principles of Cartesian Philosophy"), an exposition of Descartes' *Principia Philosopiae* in the "the geometric manner," published in 1663 together with an appendix, *Cogitata Metaphysica* ("Metaphysical Thoughts"), that reflects both medieval Jewish and Scholastic sources. Neither presents Spinoza's own views, as he instructed his friend and doctor, Lodewijk Meyer, to emphasize in a preface introducing the two works. On the contrary: the treatises originate in notes that Spinoza used for teaching his student Caesarius, concerning whom he urges his friends "not to communicate my views to him until he has reached greater maturity" (*Letter* 9). Indeed, even earlier Spinoza had made no secret of his disagreement with Descartes on fundamental issues such as "the first cause and origin of all things" (*Letter* 2).

But whereas the scope of Descartes' influence on Spinoza and its relation to the influence of Jewish philosophers remain an object of controversy among scholars, it is uncontroversial that already in his earliest writings devoted to the exposition of his own philosophy Spinoza appears as a highly original thinker. Between the end of the 1650s and the beginning of the 1660s he was working on two treatises: the *Tractatus de Intellectus Emendatione* ("Treatise on the Emendation of the Intellect"), which remained incomplete and was published only in the *Opera Posthuma*, and a first outline of his metaphysics, anthropology, epistemology, and ethics which was intended for circulation only among his friends, apparently because he feared that "the theologians of our time" would attack him with "their usual hatred" (*Letter* 6). Already the work's title, *Korte Verhandeling van God, de Mensch en des zelfs Welstand* ("Short Treatise on God, Man, and His Wellbeing"), names the constitutive themes of Spinoza's philosophical project. From 1661 to 1675, he systematically reworked the ideas sketched in the *Korte Verhandeling* into his main philosophical work, the *Ethica Ordine Geometrico Demonstrata* ("Ethics Demonstrated According to the Geometrical Method"). In 1665 Spinoza interrupted his work on the *Ethica* for several years to set forth his critique of religion and his political philosophy in the *Tractatus Theologico-Politicus* ("Theological-Political Treatise"), published anonymously in 1670. His goal was to contribute to defending the freedom of thought and religious tolerance, which had been secured in the Dutch republic governed by Jan de Witt, but now seemed threatened by the alliance of monarchists and Calvinist orthodoxy. Since the critique of religion is grounded on a critique of Scripture, and the correct understanding of Scripture requires a thorough understanding of Hebrew (TTP 7), Spinoza's *Compendium Grammatices Linguae Hebraeae* ("Compendium of the Grammar of the Hebrew Language") can be seen as a tool for carrying out the critical theological-political project. But the striking parallel between the account of nouns, adjectives, and participles in the Hebrew Grammar and the account of substance, attributes, and modes in the *Ethica* also suggests an interesting (if unclear) connection to Spinoza's metaphysics. The scandal triggered by the critique of religion in the TTP led to the book's prohibition in 1674. Under these circumstances Spinoza did not even attempt to publish the *Ethica*. Like the *Tractatus Politicus* ("Political Treatise") that he was not able to complete and the equally unfinished Hebrew Grammar, it appeared only in 1677 in the *Opera Posthuma*. Finally, Spinoza's extant correspondence must be mentioned which contributes significantly to clarifying specific issues in his work.

Philosophy

OUTLINE OF THE PHILOSOPHICAL PROJECT. The *Tractatus de Intellectus Emendatione* (TIE) begins with a description, stylized as autobiographical, of the author's conversion to the philosophical life. An examination in the Socratic sense leads to the decision to turn away from "what men consider to be the highest good [*summum bonum*]," i.e., "wealth, honor, and sensual pleasure," in order to seek the "true good" that provides the "highest joy [*summa laetitia*] eternally." The passage, whose immediate source is a treatise by the Jewish Renaissance Platonist Leone Ebreo, takes up the foundational concern of ancient ethics: the quest for the good life. Since the TIE was originally conceived as a methodological introduction to Spinoza's philosophical system, this opening passage in a sense provides the point of departure for his philosophical project as a whole. Indeed, choosing a life devoted to the pursuit of knowledge would surely be a mistake if it were not the best life. The *Ethica*, as before the *Korte Verhandeling*, can be seen as the guide to that goal which Spinoza describes as "happiness [*beatitudo*]" and as "salvation [*salus*]" (*Ethica* v, Prop. 36, Schol.). The true good for Spinoza is God. What leads to this good is "understanding" culminating in "knowledge of God [*Dei cognitio*]" (*Ethica* iv, Prop. 27 and 28). Since knowledge of God and of things "insofar as we conceive them to be contained in God and to follow from the necessity of the divine nature" (*Ethica* v, Prop. 29, Schol.) is accompanied by "joy [*laetitia*]," it gives rise to the "intellectual love of God [*Amor Dei intellectualis*]" (*Ethica* v, Prop. 32, Cor.). Spinoza speaks in this context of knowledge "under the aspect of eternity [*sub specie aeternitatis*]" (*Ethica* v, Prop. 29) because both God and things conceived as necessarily following from God are eternal and immutable. From knowledge of eternal things Spinoza draws a conclusion that continues to puzzle scholars: that the part of the mind which loves God intellectually becomes itself eternal, i.e., is in some way preserved after the destruction of the body (*Ethica* v, Prop. 22 and Prop. 23). It seems, therefore, that "salvation" for Spinoza is a form of intellectual immortality. But the *Ethica* not only intends to instruct the reader how to reach happiness and salvation; in a way it also puts these instructions into practice. The geometric form of the argument, which deduces philosophical propositions from definitions and axioms, entails a claim to definitive validity. From the first part, that demonstrates God's existence and characteristics, to the fifth part, that shows how human freedom consists in the activity of intellectually loving God, the *Ethica* can be seen as part of the knowledge *sub specie aeternitatis*. In this sense it contributes to bringing the quest for the "true good" to conclusion that was the point of departure of the TIE. At the end of the "road [*via*]" set out in the *Ethica* the seeker is prepared to turn into a "wise man [*sapiens*]" who "suffers scarcely any disturbance of spirit, but being conscious, by virtue of a certain eternal necessity, of himself, of God and of things, never ceases to be, but always possesses true spiritual contentment [*animi acquiescentia*]" (*Ethica* v, Prop. 42, Schol.). Many of the arguments on which Spinoza's project of the good life relies – from those for the intellectual love of God to those for the immortality of the mind – were articulated in similar ways by Jewish rationalists such as Abraham Ibn Ezra, Maimonides, Gersonides, and Leone Ebreo. It is presumably in their writings that Spinoza encountered them for the first time.

METAPHYSICS. In order to show of what the good life consists, it is necessary to understand the nature of human beings and their place in the order of existents. This in turn requires understanding the nature and order of existents themselves. The first part of the *Ethica* is thus devoted to ontology. Since for Spinoza ontology and philosophical theology coincide, it is titled *De Deo* (About God). By identifying God with reality as a whole, Spinoza radically breaks with the concept of divine transcendence. God neither is located outside the natural order, nor does he lack what Spinoza takes to be the essential attribute of the physical world: extension. In light of this it is not surprising that he can speak of "God or Nature [*Deus sive Natura*]" (*Ethica* iv, Praef.). God is defined as "an absolutely infinite being [*ens absolute infinitum*], i.e., a substance consisting of infinite attributes, each of which expresses eternal and infinite essence" (*Ethica* i, Def. 6). According to this definition, God encompasses all logically possible kinds of being, each of which is infinite in its kind. But only two kinds can be apprehended by human beings: "thought [*cogitatio*]" and "extension [*extensio*]," i.e., the essential attributes of the two realms of reality accessible to us. God, therefore, is both "thinking thing" and "extended thing," but also an infinite number of other things that lie beyond human cognition (*Ethica* ii, Prop. 1 and 2 and *Letter* 64). That God exists follows from the fact that the concept of a substance with infinite attributes is not contradictory (*Ethica* i, Prop. 10, Schol.) and that the essence of a substance entails its existence (*Ethica* i, Prop. 11). Since the existence of two substances with the same attribute is impossible (*Ethica* i, Prop. 5), and since God has all attributes, Spinoza's substance monism follows: "Except for God no substance can be or be conceived" (*Ethica* i, Prop. 14). This God is not static, but has an "active essence [*essentia actuosa*]" (*Ethica* ii, Prop. 3, Schol.) and produces as "immanent cause [*causa immanens*]" (*Ethica* i, Prop. 18) "infinite many things in infinite many ways" (*Ethica* i, Prop. 16) in himself "with the same necessity by which he apprehends himself [*seipsum intelligat*]" (*Ethica* ii, Prop. 3, Schol.). Spinoza here takes up and modifies the doctrine of God found in the writings of medieval Jewish Aristotelians who conceived God as the activity of a pure intellect apprehending itself (*Ethica* ii, Prop. 7, Schol.). The difference is that Spinoza's God is not only intellectual activity but also extending activity and an infinite number of other activities. Spinoza holds, moreover, that increasing God's ontological scope does not conflict with God's unity, for "the thinking substance and the extended substance are one and the same substance, comprehended now under this now under that attribute" (ibid.). Since Jewish rationalists before Spinoza took God to be incorporeal, the attribution of extension to God appears to be a fundamental departure from their premises. But also this step had been prepared by the Jewish critic of Aristotelianism, Hasdai Crescas, who argued for the existence of an infinitely extended empty space which he describes as a "metaphor [*dimayon*]" for God. Moreover, Spinoza uses arguments drawn from Crescas in *Ethica* i, Prop. 15, Schol. for defending God's extension. It would thus be inaccurate to say that Spinoza substitutes a philosophical God for a religious God. His move beyond medieval philosophy is better characterized as an attempt to solve specific ontological problems arising from the causal relation, which his predecessors had to posit between an incorporeal God and a corporeal world. As absolutely infinite activity that produces all logically possible kinds of being, Spinoza's God is all-powerful (*Ethica* i, Prop. 35). Although he is not free to choose what he does, he is free in the sense that his activity is determined only by the necessity of his own nature (*Ethica* i, Prop. 17, Cor. 2). Since the same necessity governs the order of things that God creates in himself, this order is completely determined (*Ethica* I, Prop. 29). In this context the distinction between creator and creation is replaced through that between *natura naturans* and *natura naturata* (ibid., Schol.) of which the former refers to substance insofar as it is an active cause and the latter to the infinite number of modifications produced under each of its attributes. Like substance, the series of modes is one; it consists in ideas when considered under the attribute of thought, in extended things when considered under the attribute of extension, and in an infinite number of other things when considered under the attributes unknown to us (*Ethica* II, Prop. 7, Schol.). There are two kinds of modes: those of the first kind are eternal and infinite and subdivided into modes following immediately from one of God's attributes and modes that are mediated through a mode following immediately from one of God's attributes. Modes of the second kind, by contrast, are transitory and finite. Since an eternal and infinite thing cannot be the cause of a transitory and finite thing, it is unclear how the modes of the second kind are supposed to be caused by God. Although Spinoza does not address the problem, a possible solution is to take finite modes to be dependent on God not individually, but as an eternal and infinite chain of causes and effects. Spinoza also makes little effort to explain the first kind of modes. The "infinite intellect" is the mode immediately following from the attribute of thought, "motion and rest" the mode immediately following from the attribute of extension, and the "face of the whole universe [*facies totius universi*]" a mediate eternal and infinite mode of extension (*Letter* 64). The notion of "motion and rest" suggests that Spinoza has the fundamental laws of nature in mind. The "face of the whole universe" appears to refer to the stable order of nature, since Spinoza links the notion to *Ethica* II, Lemma 7, Schol., where "the whole of nature" is described as an infinite individual that remains unchanged, while its constituents vary in infinite ways.

In an appendix to the first part of the *Ethica*, Spinoza explains the devastating consequences of his philosophical theology for popular views of God. A providential God, who interferes in the course of nature according to his free will, rewards and punishes, and performs miracles, is nothing but the "refuge of ignorance [*asylum ignorantiae*]" of the superstitious.

EPISTEMOLOGY, PSYCHOLOGY, AND ETHICS. From the subsequent parts of the *Ethica* it is clear that Spinoza is not interested in a general account of the order of modes, but in the structure of one particular mode: the human being, consisting of "mind and body [*mens et corpus*]" (*Ethica* II, Prop. 13, Cor.) which – as in the case of substance and all other modes – are one and the same thing considered under the attribute of thought and under the attribute of extension. While Spinoza thus avoids the problems involved in dualistic accounts of mind and body, the unity he assumes is not without obscurities of its own. He describes the mind as the idea of the body (*Ethica* II, Prop. 13) and its cognitive power as corresponding to the body's complexity and hence ability to interact with its environment (ibid., Schol. and Prop. 14). Of particular importance for Spinoza's epistemology are the three kinds of knowledge that he distinguishes in Prop. 40, Schol. 2: "imagination [*imaginatio*]" which draws on random sense-perceptions and their arbitrary association; "reason [*ratio*]" which draws on common notions and adequate ideas of the properties of things; finally "intuitive knowledge [*scientia intuitiva*]" which infers the essence of things from the essence of God's attributes. Whereas the first kind of knowledge is fallible, the other two kinds are necessarily true (*Ethica* II, Prop. 41). Although a true idea must correspond to its object (*Ethica* I, Ax. 6), this is not the criterion of truth for Spinoza. What is decisive is if the idea is "adequate" or not, whereby an "adequate" idea is one that has the "intrinsic characteristics of a true idea" (*Ethica* II, Def. 4). As a consequence, "he who has a true idea knows at the same time that he has a true idea, and cannot doubt its truth" (*Ethica* II, Prop. 43). Truth thus becomes "the standard both of itself and of falsehood [*norma sui et falsi*]" (ibid., Schol.).

The third part of the *Ethica* contains Spinoza's psychology in form of a theory of human affects. Crucial for understanding the affects is the striving "to persist in one's being" (*Ethica* III, Prop. 6) which Spinoza calls *conatus* and takes to be the essence of all things. Only God has absolutely unlimited power in himself to attain the goal of the *conatus*. The power of the modes, on the other hand, depends on God and is limited to varying degrees within the order of nature, which necessarily follows from God's essence, and in which the modes are determined by God to act on one another. In human beings the *conatus* takes on the form of "desire [*appetitus* or *cupiditas*]" which gives rise to two further basic affects: "joy [*laetitia*]" and "sadness [*tristitia*]." The former is caused by an object that increases a person's power and whose possession is, therefore, desired. The latter is caused by an object that decreases a person's power and which he or she will thus attempt to avoid (*Ethica* III, *Definition of the Affects* 1–3). Fundamental, moreover, is the distinction between active affects, of which human beings are the "adequate cause," and passive affects that are caused by external objects. With this, Spinoza has set up the conceptual framework for a detailed account and explanation of human affects "in the geometric manner" (*Ethica* III, Praef.), as well as for the ethical discussion of the fourth and fifth part of the *Ethica*.

Spinoza's ethics is clearly egoistic: to act virtuously means "to preserve one's own being [...] under the guidance of reason," which in turn means to act with a view to "one's own advantage [*proprium utile*]" (*Ethica* IV, Prop. 24). As a consequence, goodness or badness are not inherent properties of things or actions but depend on their utility or lack of utility for attaining the objects of desire (*Ethica* IV, Def. 1 and 2). Since intellectual perfection is the highest level of power accessible to human beings, they – insofar as they are rational – desire nothing but "understanding [*intelligere*]" (*Ethica*

IV, Prop. 26) which, as already indicated, has the "knowledge of God" as its ultimate goal. This, therefore, is "the highest good" and the "highest virtue" of the mind (*Ethica* IV, Prop. 27 and 28). The power derived from understanding is manifold: it liberates human beings at least to some extent from the "bondage [*servitus*]" to passive affects, since next to the highest good, external things that are good or bad, but beyond their control, become less important. Moreover, their affective reaction to what happens to them will diminish and their tranquility increase through the knowledge that all things are predetermined and that human beings are "part of the whole of nature" (Appendix). By means of the better rational control over their affects, human beings become less vulnerable to external causes that toss them back and forth "like the waves of the sea when driven by contrary winds" (*Ethica* III, Prop. 59, Schol.). At the same time, intellectual activity is an active affect and entirely under our control. It thus represents the highest form of freedom in the sense of self-determination accessible to human beings. Since knowledge *sub specie aeternitatis*, according to Spinoza, allows the mind to participate in God's eternity, it constitutes the goal of the striving to "persist in one's being." Finally, the increase in power gained through understanding is a source of constant joy, leading to the "intellectual love of God."

It is important to note that Spinoza takes his ethical egoism to be perfectly compatible with the wish to give to one's fellow human beings every possible assistance to attain the same degree of perfection that one desires for oneself. For "no individual thing in nature is more advantageous to man than a man who lives by the guidance of reason" (*Ethica* IV, Prop. 35, Cor. 1). Moreover, in contrast to material goods, "the greatest good," i.e., knowledge of God, "can be enjoyed by all equally" (*Ethica* IV, Prop. 36). Solidarity and mutual help are thus good for purely utilitarian reasons.

CRITIQUE OF RELIGION. The *Tractatus Theologico-Politicus* also fits into Spinoza's project of the good life. Its goal may be described as creating the conditions for the project's implementation. After all, a philosophical life cannot be led by someone who does not have the "freedom to philosophize [*libertas philosophandi*]," or whom the "prejudices of theologians" prevent from "devoting [*applicare*]" his life to philosophy. These, according to Spinoza, were the main reasons for working out his critique of religion in the TTP (*Letter* 30). The chief purpose of this critique is to show that Scripture can make no legitimate claim to truth. This will take away both the fear felt by the potential philosopher when a demonstrated proposition conflicts with a theological doctrine and the authority of the theologian to persecute a person for holding views that disagree with the teachings of Scripture. Of crucial importance for attaining this purpose are the first two chapters of the TTP, which deal with "prophecy or revelation [*prophetia sive revelation*]" and with the biblical prophets. Spinoza recurs to a distinction between intellect and imagination that was common in the Aristotelian tradition and that Maimonides had already used for explaining prophecy. According to Maimonides, the prophet has both a highly developed intellect and a highly developed imagination, whereby the latter allows him to translate his intellectual insights into a simple and vivid language that can be understood by his uneducated audience. According to Spinoza, on the other hand, the prophet does not excel through his "more perfect intellect," but only through his "more lively imagination [*potentia vividius imaginandi*]" (TTP 2). Prophetic discourse, therefore, has no true cognitive content; it is only persuasive through images and symbols which are adjusted to the audience's limited capacity for understanding and help securing obedience to the law. Moreover, Spinoza intends to show through a detailed examination of the meaning of biblical terms that when the Bible describes the prophets as being filled with "the spirit of God or the holy spirit," it only intends to highlight their "exceptional virtue." This is an implicit attempt to refute the doctrine of the Calvinist Church which grounds the authority of Scripture on its super-rational inspiration by the holy spirit (TTP 1). Prophecy thus understood is neither specifically Jewish, nor can a claim to "election [*vocatio*]" be derived from it. For Spinoza Israel's election refers only to the political success of the ancient Hebrew state based on Moses' legislation. The election ended with the state's disintegration. That the Jewish people nonetheless continues to exist he explains through its insistence to keep up "external rituals" such as the "sign of circumcision [*signum circumcisionis*]" through which it sets itself apart from other nations and provokes their hatred (TTP 3). Moses' legislation, in particular the "ceremonial law [*ceremoniae*]" (TTP 5), is exclusively political in nature. As a "human law [*lex humana*]" (TTP 4) it aims only at "preserving life and the commonwealth," promising no more than "worldly happiness [*temporanea foelicitas*]" to those who observe it (TTP 5). By contrast, the "divine law [*lex divina*]" aims at the "highest good, i.e., the true knowledge and love of God," thus leading to "man's highest happiness [*summa hominis foelicitas*]" (TTP 4). Also the distinction between human and divine law Spinoza took over from Maimonides, at the same time turning it against its original intention. Whereas Maimonides identified the Torah with the divine law and presented Moses as a philosopher and lawgiver in the Platonic sense, Spinoza demotes Moses to a simple lawgiver whose legislation became obsolete after the downfall of the Hebrew state. This reversal of the Maimonidean model is a good example for the influence of Uriel da Costa and other Jewish heterodox thinkers on Spinoza. Their denial that the immortality of the soul is a biblical doctrine presumably underlies his claim that the Mosaic Law only promises "worldly happiness," and not eternal happiness which is the reward of "the true knowledge and love of God."

Also the miracles related in Scripture cannot be used as testimony for the authority of revelation, since miracles in the sense of God suspending the laws of nature are impossible in the order of nature, which is eternally and necessarily determined through God's essence. The reason for the belief in miracles, according to Spinoza, is the ignorance of causal connections (*TTP* 6).

The demolition of the traditional notion of revelation allows Spinoza to refute the premises of the exegesis promoted by Maimonides which attempts to harmonize philosophy and Scripture. In Spinoza's view this amounts to the "distorting and explaining away of Scripture" (*TTP* 7) with the goal to "extract" from it "Aristotelian nonsense [*nugas Aristotelicas*]" (*TTP* 1). It allows him likewise to refute the central claim underlying the hermeneutics of the Calvinist Church: that the understanding of Scripture requires the super-rational illumination by the holy spirit. Against these approaches Spinoza calls for the unconditional acceptance of Scripture's literal sense based on the methodological principle that "the knowledge of all the contents of Scripture must be sought from Scripture alone." The focus is no longer the "truth [*veritas*]" of a proposition in Scripture but its "meaning [*sensus*]" (*TTP* 7). In order to determine the meaning, the Bible scholar proceeds in an analogous way to the scientist whose aim is to explain nature. Both work out a "history [*historia*]," i.e., a methodological account, of the object of their study (ibid.). For the Bible scholar this means collecting and ordering the data contained in Scripture and then interpreting them in light of the relevant historical and socio-cultural contexts, as well as the psychological peculiarities of the prophets, insofar as these can be reconstructed from the available sources. In much of his discussion in the preceding chapters Spinoza follows the methodological rules laid out in *TTP* 7 and shows that from a philosophical point of view almost every statement in Scripture is false.

In *TTP* 8–10 he goes on to examine the composition and transmission of the biblical books. Taking a number of cryptic remarks in Abraham Ibn Ezra's commentary on the Bible as his point of departure, Spinoza arrives at the conclusion that much of the Pentateuch cannot have been written by Moses. He likewise questions the traditional attribution of several other books of the Bible. The comprehensive rejection of the claim to truth of revelation leads to the goal of the theological part of the *TTP*: the strict separation of philosophy and religion. The authority to determine truth and falsehood belongs only to philosophers who rely on rational insight. The task of theologians, relying on revelation, is to assure "obedience [*obedientia*]" to the law by teaching – like the prophets led by their imagination – "pious dogmas" whose truth is not important. Philosophy and theology thus become two independent disciplines: "the goal of philosophy is nothing but the truth, the goal of faith is nothing but obedience" (*TTP* 14). Consequently "reason" cannot be "the handmaid of theology [*ancilla theologiae*] nor theology the handmaid of reason [*ancilla rationis*]." Spinoza calls the former position "skepticism," for it "denies the certainty of reason," and exemplifies it through Judah Alfakhar, one of the leaders of the opposition to philosophy in medieval Judaism. Alfakhar is a stand-in for the position of the Calvinist Church, which Spinoza refrained from attacking openly. The latter position he calls "dogmatism" and illustrates it by means of Maimonides' philosophical exegesis which reinterprets every biblical passage that contradicts a doctrine established by reason (*TTP* 15). From this point of view the *TTP* marks the end of classical Jewish philosophy, whose fundamental premise was the agreement of revelation with all propositions demonstrated by reason. More importantly: it destroys the traditional notion of religion as a whole insofar as it is grounded on the truth of revelation. In this lies one of Spinoza's most momentous contributions to modernity.

RELIGION AS A REPLACEMENT OF PHILOSOPHY. Nevertheless, Spinoza's attitude to religion is considerably more complicated. For despite the radical critique of religion, there are a significant number of passages throughout his work – from the *Cogitata Metaphysica* to the *Tractatus Politicus* and the late correspondence with Henry Oldenburg – in which he attributes a true core to Scripture, often presented as its allegorical content. This striking inconsistency seems to stem from a twofold commitment that Spinoza was ultimately unable to reconcile: he not only wants to criticize religion in order to defend the freedom to philosophize; he also wants to use religion as a replacement of philosophy for non-philosophers. The concept of religion as a replacement of philosophy which guides non-philosophers to virtue is precisely the "dogmatic" view of Maimonides (and, in fact, the standard view of medieval Islamic and Jewish philosophers) that Spinoza rejects in the *TTP*. The main idea is that the positive content of religion – biblical narratives, laws, rituals and so forth – is a pedagogical-political program designed by philosophers to guide non-philosophers. The allegorical content of religion, on the other hand, corresponds to the doctrines demonstrated in philosophy. Religion's authority thus depends on the assumption that the teachings of religion are true on the allegorical level. Before Spinoza started working on the *TTP* in 1665, he consistently endorsed the dogmatic position whenever he discussed the character of Scripture (*Cogitata Metaphysica* II, 8 and the correspondence with W. van Blyenbergh between 1664 and 1665). But different versions of it reappear also in his later writings. They include the attribution of true moral convictions to the biblical prophets (*TTP* 1 and 2), the attribution of true metaphysical doctrines such as God being *causa immanens* to "all ancient Hebrews" (*Letter* 73), the presentation of Christ as an accomplished philosopher instructing non-philosophers by means of allegories (*TTP* 4; cf. E IV, Prop. 68, Schol.), and the claim that the "uncorrupted" core of Scripture corresponds to the "universal religion" described in the *TTP* (12–14). None of these can be justified through the exegetical method that Spinoza claims to have adopted in the *TTP*: "to neither affirm anything of [Scripture] nor to admit anything as its teaching which I did not most clearly derive from it" (*TTP* Preface). The textual evidence gives rise to a number of questions: why did Spinoza adopt the medieval position in his early writings, why did he refute it in the *TTP*, and why did he continue to make use of it even after having refuted it? For one thing, Spinoza clearly shares the view of Maimonides and many other medieval philosophers that the good life based on knowledge (i.e., the life he himself chose according to the opening passage of the *TEI* and for which the *Ethica* serves as a guide) is accessible only to a small group of philosophers: "only a few in proportion to the whole of humanity acquire a virtuous disposition under the guidance of reason alone" (*TTP* 15; cf. *Ethica* v, Prop. 42, Schol.). This leads to the question how guidance can be provided to non-philosophers. The evidence of Spinoza's early writings shows that he in principle agrees with the medieval solution which takes the positive content of religion to be a pedagogical-political program designed to lead non-philosophers to virtue. A second reason for adopting the medieval position is that the perception of philosophy as coinciding with the allegorical content of religion facilitates its acceptance in a religious society. Finally, the medieval position, which has philosophy determine the true core of religion, neither seems to interfere with Spinoza's philosophical project in the *Ethica* nor with the freedom to philosophize that he sets out to defend in the *TTP*. But if this is the case, why did he refute it at all? It is clear that Spinoza's main opponent in the *TTP* is not the "dogmatic" position represented by Maimonides, but the "skeptical" position of the Calvinist Church, in particular the view that the authority of Scripture overrides the authority of reason. This he takes to be the chief threat to the freedom to philosophize (*TTP* Preface). The only efficient way to refute this position, in Spinoza's view, is to show that Scripture contains no truth. But although the medieval position and the position of the Reformed Church are in a sense opposed to each other, both depend in different ways on the premise that Scripture is true. Thus the refutation of the one entails the refutation of the other. While his target is the Reformed Church, Spinoza has no choice but to give up the medieval position as well. At the same time he has no new solution for the problem of non-philosophers. This explains why, despite its refutation, he continues to use the dogmatic position in various contexts in his later writings.

POLITICAL PHILOSOPHY. In the *Ethica* Spinoza argues that the essence of human beings is the *conatus*, i.e., the striving "to persist in one's being." In the political part of the *TTP* and in the *Tractatus Politicus*, following Thomas Hobbes, he equates the power to do so with a person's natural right in the state of nature, and explains the social contract as the decision to submit to a sovereign power in exchange for peace and safety (*TTP* 16). But, against Hobbes, Spinoza maintains that the natural right is not given up under the social contract: "the supreme power in a state has no more right over a subject than is proportionate to the power by which it is superior to the subject" (*Letter* 50).

Besides Hobbes, Spinoza was also influenced by ancient political thought, in part mediated through medieval Jewish sources. Indeed, the fear of being harmed through the power of others is not the only motive for forming a political community. Since, on their own, human beings are not self-sufficient, they must collaborate with one another. Hence the Aristotelian definition "which makes man a social animal, has been quite pleasing to most." Spinoza in any case is certain that "we derive from the society of our fellow men many more advantages than disadvantages" (*Ethica* IV, Prop. 35, Schol.). Moreover, according to Spinoza, social harmony is weakened when the actions of the citizens are guided by the idiosyncratic goals of their passions, whereas it is strengthened when their actions are guided by reason which prescribes the same goal to all (idem, Dem.). It follows that the "end [*finis*]," for which the state is established, is not simply peace in the sense of "the absence of war [*privatio belli*];" its positive aim is to enhance the rationality of the citizens, i.e., their virtue, for "reason" is the "true virtue and life of the mind" (*Tractatus Politicus* 5, IV – VI). Since Spinoza equates virtue and knowledge, culminating in the intellectual love of God, and since he takes the "uncorrupted" true core of Scripture to be the call "to love God above all and one's neighbor as oneself" (*TTP* 12), the fundamental convergence of the purpose of his philosophical, religious, and political project becomes apparent: to foster a community based on solidarity and on freedom of thought, whose members assist one another in attaining the best life, i.e., a life devoted to the love of God.

INFLUENCE. Although during the first century after his death Spinoza was less famous than infamous, reviled as a notorious atheist, his influence was nonetheless considerable: not only on philosophers such as Leibniz, but, most importantly, on the different currents of the unfolding Enlightenment. Indeed, some scholars argue that the Enlightenment of the 18th century was no more than a *post-scriptum* to the dynamic of the radical Enlightenment set off by Spinoza's writings. He determined the intellectual agenda not only of those who agreed with him, but also of those who attempted to refute him and of those who adopted intermediate positions (cf. J. Israel). The most fruitful reception of his philosophy took place in Germany in the second half of the 18th century. The event which put Spinoza's work at the very center of the thriving German intellectual culture of the time was the so-called "*Pantheismusstreit*." This quarrel broke out when F.H. Jacobi accused Lessing after his death of being a crypto-Spinozist, in a public exchange of letters with Moses Mendelssohn that was widely debated in Germany's literary and philosophical circles and stirred up renewed interest in Spinoza's thought. A typical response to Jacobi's identification of Spinozism with atheism was that of the great Romantic poet Novalis, who described Spinoza as a "God-intoxicated man." Spinoza also significantly contributed to shaping Goethe's worldview, as well as that of many other central figures of Germany's literary scene. In a dedication that J.G. Herder wrote into a copy of Spinoza's *Opera Posthuma*, given to Goethe as a Christmas gift in 1784, he expresses his wish that the "holy Spinoza" may always remain their "holy Christ." In philosophy, Spinoza's ontological monism influenced the systems of German idealists probably as much as Kant's criticism. According to Hegel, Spinoza's thought is the "essential beginning of all philosophizing [*wesentliche Anfang alles Philosophierens*]." Nietzsche arrived at the conclusion that his own philosophical project agreed with Spinoza's on most fundamental issues. As mentioned in the introduction, Spinoza today continues to be debated by philosophers of a wide range of intellectual affiliations. Turning to his critique of religion, Spinoza may be said to have laid the foundation for the scientific study of the Bible. He also had a considerable impact on Jewish thinkers, beginning with David Nieto in the 17th century. In Jewish Haskalah circles of the 18th century, Mendelssohn's cautious Spinoza-reception stands next to Salomon Maimon's enthusiastic encounter with Spinoza's system that he relates in his *Autobiography*. Maimon's metaphysics, which takes up and combines ideas derived from Maimonides and Spinoza, was the first to make the transition from Kant to an idealist position. Spinoza also left his imprint on 19th-century *maskilim*. Moreover, he became an important source of the secular worldview of prominent Zionists, among them David Ben-Gurion who proposed to revoke the *ḥerem* against him. Albert Einstein wrote a poem "On Spinoza's Ethics." His "God who does not throw dice" clearly has Spinozistic features, as does his notion of a "cosmic religion."

[Carlos Fraenkel (2nd ed.)]

As a Bible Scholar

Spinoza's biblical criticism in part follows earlier attempts, but integrates them for the first time into a rational system, laying the groundwork for all later critical works on the Bible up to the present. His biblical criticism is closely connected to his philosophical system and political project. Based on the knowledge of the Bible that he acquired in his childhood, and after long years of reflection, his critical views of the Bible were expressed in the *Tractatus Theologico-Politicus*, as well as in a few letters and conversations. In opposition to the many misuses of the Bible that he observed in Judaism and Christianity, Spinoza developed what he took to be the true method of biblical exegesis. Every person has the right to engage in biblical interpretation; it does not require supernatural illumination or special authority. Spinoza's supreme principle is that the Bible must be interpreted on its own terms. The method of the interpretation of the Bible is the same as the method of the interpretation of nature. "For, as the method of interpreting nature consists essentially in putting together a history [i.e., a methodical account] of nature, from which, as from sure data, we deduce the definitions of natural phenomena, so it is necessary for the interpretation of Scripture to work out a true history of Scripture, and from it, as from sure data and principles, to deduce through legitimate inference, the intention of the authors of Scripture" (*TTP* 7). The history of Scripture should comprise three components: (1) an analysis of the Hebrew language; (2) the compilation and classification of the expressions [*sententiae*] of each of the books of the Bible; (3) research into the original contexts of the biblical writings, as far as they still can be ascertained, i.e., into "the life, the conduct, and the pursuits of the author of each book, who he was, what was the occasion and the epoch of his writing, whom did he write for, and in what language. Further it should inquire into the fate of each book: how it was first received, into whose hands it fell, how many different versions there were of it, by whose advice was it received into the Canon, and lastly, how all the books now universally accepted as sacred were united into a single whole" (ibid.). In accordance with this program, Spinoza analyzed the biblical writings in an attempt to determine their authors (*TTP* 8–10). He spelled out, and substantially expanded on, the considerations that led the medieval commentator Abraham Ibn Ezra to allude to the possibility that the Pentateuch did not derive in its entirety from Moses. Although some of the Pentateuch did originate with Moses (The Book of the Wars of God, the Book of the Covenant, the Book of the Law of God), it was only many centuries after Moses that the Pentateuch as a whole appeared. The Pentateuch, together with the books of Joshua, Judges, Samuel, and Kings, forms a single larger historical work, whose author, Spinoza conjectures, was Ezra. Ezra was prevented by his premature death, or perhaps some other reason, from revising these books. They contain numerous repetitions and contradictions, e.g., of a chronological nature, that lead to the conclusion that the wealth of material was compiled from works of different authors, without being arranged and harmonized. I and II Chronicles were written long after Ezra, perhaps even after the restoration of the Temple by Judah Maccabee. The Psalms were collected and divided into five books in the Second Temple period; Proverbs is from the same period or, at the earliest, from the time of Josiah. The Prophetic books contain only fragments assembled from other books, but not in an order established by the prophets. Spinoza adopts Ibn Ezra's hypothesis concerning Job, according to which Job was translated from a gentile language; if this were the case it would entail that the gentiles also had holy books. Daniel is authentic only from chapter 8 on; the previous chapters, presumably taken from Chaldean chronicles, are in any case an indication that books can be holy even though they are not written in Hebrew. The Book of Daniel forms with the books of Ezra, Esther, and Nehemiah a work by a historian who wrote long after the restoration of the Temple by Judah Maccabee, using the official annals of the Second Temple in his work. These theories lead to the conclusion that the canon could have originated only in the time of the Hasmoneans. It is a work of the Pharisees, not Ezra, in whose time the Great Assembly did not yet exist. Spinoza criticizes various decisions of the Pharisees, such as the inclusion of Chronicles in the canon and the rejection of the Wisdom of Solomon and Tobit, and he regrets "that holy and highest things should depend upon the choice of those people." Spinoza discovers in the Prophets numerous contradictions in their conceptions of natural and spiritual phenomena. He concludes that God adapted his revelation in these matters to the limited intellectual power of the prophets, and that philosophical knowledge is not to be found in their works. The purpose of the revelation to the prophets is rather to teach the right way of life to an uneducated audience (*TTP* 1–2). The example of Balaam indicates that there were prophets not only among the Hebrews.

The election of the Hebrews should not be understood as an indication that they excelled over other nations with respect to intellect and virtue; their election refers only to their political kingdom and ended with the latter's downfall (*TTP* 3). The ceremonies prescribed in the Bible, in fact the entire Mosaic law, were applicable only as long as the kingdom lasted; after it ended they no longer contributed to happiness and blessedness (*TTP* 4–5). According to Spinoza, stories in the Bible are not to be believed literally; they are intended to instruct the members of the community, who could not comprehend philosophical arguments in which propositions are deduced from definitions and axioms (*TTP* 5). Spinoza is aware of the difficulties that stand in the way of a conclusive understanding of the Bible on the basis of his method, for example our incomplete knowledge of Hebrew and of the circumstances of the composition of the biblical books, some of which (in particular those of the New Testament) are not extant in the language in which they were composed (*TTP* 7).

[Rudolf Smend / Carlos Fraenkel (2nd ed.)]

BIBLIOGRAPHY: SOURCES: Spinoza, *Opera*, ed. C. Gebhardt, 4 vol., (1925); *The Collected Works of Spinoza*, vol. 1, ed. and Eng. trans. E. Curley (1985); *Complete Works*, Eng. trans. S. Shirley, ed. M.L. Morgan (2002); SCHOLARLY LITERATURE: M. Joel, *Spinozas theologisch-politischer Traktat auf seine Quellen geprüft* (1870); idem, *Zur Genesis der Lehre Spinozas* (1871); J. Freudenthal, "Spinoza und die Scholastik," in: *Philosophische Aufsätze – Eduard Zeller zu seinem fünfzijährigen Doctor-Jubiläum gewidmet* (1887), 85–138; idem, *Die Lebensgeschichte Spinoza's* (1899); idem, *Spinoza, Leben und Lehre* (1927); K.O. Meinsma, *Spinoza en zijn kring* (1896; French trans. 1983); H.H. Joachim, *A Study of Spinoza's Ethics* (1901); C. Gebhardt, "Spinoza und der Platonismus," in: *Chronicon Spinozanum*, 1 (1921), 178–234; L. Roth, *Spinoza, Descartes and Maimonides* (1924); L. Strauss, *Die Religionskritik Spinozas als Grundlage seiner Bibelwissenschaft* (1930; Eng. trans. 1965); idem, "How to Study Spinoza's *Theological-Political Treatise*," in: *Proceedings of the American Academy of Jewish Research*, 17 (1948), 69–131; H.A. Wolfson, *The Philosophy of Spinoza: Unfolding the Latent Process of His Reasoning*, 2 vol. (1934); I.S. Révah, *Spinoza et Juan de Prado* (1959); S. Zac, *Spinoza et l'interpretation de l'écriture* (1965); M. Gueroult, *Spinoza I, Dieu* (1968); idem, *Spinoza II, L'Ame* (1974); S. Pines, "Spinoza's Tractatus, Maimonides and Kant," in: *Scripta Hierosolymitana*, 20 (1968), 3–54; A. Matheron, *Le Christ et le salut des ignorants chez Spinoza* (1971); W.Z. Harvey, "Maimonides and Spinoza on the Knowledge of Good and Evil," in: *Iyyun*, 28:4 (1978), 167–185 (Heb.); idem, "A Portrait of Spinoza as a Maimonidean," in: *Journal of the History of Philosophy*, 19:2 (1981), 151–72; C. Cramer, W.G. Jacobs, W. Schmidt-Biggemann (eds.), *Spinozas Ethik und ihre frühe Wirkung* (1981); J.P. Osier, *D'Uriel da Costa à Spinoza* (1983); J. Bennett, *A Study of Spinoza's Ethics* (1984); K. Gründer and W. Schmidt-Biggemann (eds.), *Spinoza in der Frühzeit seiner religiösen Wirkung* (1984); J. Dienstag, "The Relation of Spinoza to the Philosophy of Maimonides," in: *Studia Spinozana*, 2 (1986), 375–416; H.E. Allison, *Benedict de Spinoza – An Introduction* (1987); R.H. Popkin, and M.A. Singer, *Spinoza's Earliest Publication?* (1987); E. Curley, *Behind the Geometrical Method – A Reading of Spinoza's Ethics* (1988); Z. Levy, *Baruch or Benedict – On Some Jewish Aspects of Spinoza's Philosophy* (1989); Y. Yovel, *Spinoza and Other Heretics*, 2 vols. (1989); M. Dorman, *The Spinoza Dispute in Jewish Thought – From David Nieto to David Ben-Gurion* (Heb. 1990); M. Della Rocca, *Representation and the Mind-Body Problem in Spinoza* (1996); S.B. Smith, *Spinoza, Liberalism, and the Question of Jewish Identity* (1997); S. Nadler, *Spinoza: A Life* (1999); J. Israel, *Radical Enlightenment* (2001); J.S. Preus, *Spinoza and the Irrelevance of Biblical Authority* (2001); H. Ravven and L. Goodman (eds.), *Jewish Themes in Spinoza's Philosophy* (2002); C. Jaquet (ed.), *Les Pensées métaphysiques de Spinoza* (2004); J. Lagrée, *Spinoza et le débat religieux: lectures du traité théologico-politique* (2004); Y. Melamed, "Salomon Maimon and the Rise of Spinozism," in: *Journal of the History of Philosophy*, 42:1 (2004), 67–96; C. Fraenkel, "From Maimonides' God to Spinoza's *Deus sive Natura*," in: *Journal of the History of Philosophy*, 44:2 (2006).

SPIRA (Spiro), NATHAN NATA BEN SOLOMON (c. 1585–1633), Polish kabbalist. Spira, who was born in Cracow, maintained a well-known yeshivah. During the last years of his life he apparently served as head of the rabbinic court. One of the first protagonists in Poland of pseudo-Lurianic Kabbalah, particularly in the version disseminated by Israel *Sarug, he was interested mainly in the mysticism of numbers rather than in systematic speculation. His *Megalleh Amukkot*, published by his son after his early death (Cracow, 1637), became one of the classics of Ashkenazi Kabbalah and was reprinted several times. It offered 252 interpretations of one single passage, Moses' prayer in Deuteronomy 3:23ff. The author was "intoxicated" with numbers; he was concerned less with using the qualities of numbers in order to elucidate matters of Kabbalah and *halakhah* than in employing the Kabbalah as material for showing his great power with different numerical combinations, and there is no doubt that he had an extraordinary mathematical mind. Where other people think in words, he thought in numbers. His way of thinking and interpreting was frequently imitated by kindred spirits in the next 200 years. Spira mentions a similar book of his in which he had interpreted the letter *alef* in the word *Va-Yikra* in Leviticus 1:1 (which is written in a particularly small form) in 1,000 different ways. His commentary on the whole Pentateuch was not published until much later (Lvov, 1785), under the same title. The rabbinical approbations of an elaborate commentary on Spira's classic by David b. Moses from Zuelz were published in Dyhernfurth in 1707, but the work itself never appeared.

BIBLIOGRAPHY: S.A. Horodezky, in: *Iyyim*, 1, section 4 (1928), 54–61; J. Ginzburg, in: *Ha-Tekufah*, 25 (1929), 488–97; S.A. Horodezky, *Shelosh Me'ot Shanah shel Yahadut Polin* (1946), 127–32; G. Scholem, in: RHR, 143 (1953), 34–36.

[Gershom Scholem]

SPIRE, ANDRÉ (1868–1966), French poet and Zionist leader. Born in Nancy, Spire was descended from an old established family of Lorraine and the son of a rich industrialist. After studying law, he became a member of the Conseil d' État in 1894, specialized in employment problems at the French Ministry of Labor (1898–1902), and was inspector general in the Ministry of Agriculture from 1902 to 1926 when he retired. Spire was roused from his assimilationist lethargy by the *Dreyfus Affair, in which he played an active role. He fought a duel with the antisemite *Drumont, and struggled to gain a revision of the trial. Much to the dismay of assimilated French

Jewry, Spire speedily became a militant advocate of Jewish national revival, first supporting the Russo-Jewish self-defense organizations during the pogroms, then organizing the Association des Jeunes Juifs in order to organize the recent Jewish immigrants to France. Writing from Basle where he was attending a Zionist Congress in 1911, Spire declared: "The most despicable Jews are those who deny their own identity.… They were cursed by the Prophets and will be banished from the New Jerusalem.… Assimilation is death. Zionism is life." After the Balfour Declaration, Spire founded in 1918 the Ligue des Amis du Sionisme, and a year later represented the French Zionists at the Paris Peace Conference; in 1920 he joined a delegation to Ereẓ Israel. Following a rift with *Weizmann, Spire withdrew from active participation in official Zionism. During World War II he took refuge in the U.S., where he taught and lectured on French culture and poetry. He worked for refugees during the Nazi period, and supported Hillel Kook's activist "Hebrew National Liberation Movement" on the eve of the birth of the State of Israel.

Spire is best remembered as the leader of the Jewish revival movement in 20th-century French literature, and also as a literary theorist and innovator. His verse, which overflows with passion and humor, defends freedom and justice, and chastises the cowardly and the rich. Spire's main verse collection, *Poèmes Juifs* (1919, 1959^3), lashes the assimilated and calls for a Jewish revolt. In *Samaël* (1921) Spire develops a dramatic vision of good and evil, man's destiny and happiness. His inexhaustible verve also expressed itself in tales such as the fanciful "Le Rabbin et la Sirène" (in *Mercure de France*, Aug. 15, 1931; "The Rabbi and the Siren," in J. Leftwich, *Yisröel*, 1933, rev. 1963); his critical judgment and insight appears in the essays *Quelques Juifs* (1913), enlarged in a second edition as *Quelques Juifs et demi-Juifs* (2 vols., 1928). He was a rare combination of a Frenchman attached to his country and steeped in its culture, and of a Jew, fully identified with the spiritual and national aspirations of his people.

BIBLIOGRAPHY: S. Burnshaw *André Spire and his Poetry* (1933), essays and translations; *Hommage à André Spire* (1939); C. Lehrmann, in: *Revue des Cours et Conférences* (June 15, 1938), 465–79; idem, in: *L'élément Juif dans la Littérature Française*, 2 (1961), 145–54; P.M. Schuhl, in: *Cahiers de l'Alliance Israélite Universelle* (Sept.–Oct. 1959), 51–64; P. Jamati, *André Spire* (Fr., 1962), incl. bibl.; P. Moldaver, *La Technique Poétique d'André Spire* (1966); *L'Amitié Charles Péguy. Feuillets Mensuels*, 132 (1967).

[Moshe Catane]

SPIRO, EUGEN (1874–1972), U.S. painter, illustrator, printmaker. Son of Abraham Beer Spiro, chief cantor of the Storch Synagogue, Breslau, Spiro studied in Breslau, Munich, and France. He studied with Franz van Stuck at the Munich Academy of Art. After visiting Paris from 1906 to 1914, he traveled to Berlin, where he taught at the Staatlichen Kunstschule and chaired the Berlin Secession. He immigrated to Paris in 1935 after the Nazis stripped him of his position and qualifications and denounced his portraits as "degenerate." He was imprisoned at the French concentration camp of Gurs; however, in 1941 Spiro and his family successfully escaped Nazi-occupied France, fleeing to New York via Marseilles and Portugal, in part through the support of Alfred H. Barr, the director of the Museum of Modern Art. Spiro was active as a painter of landscapes, which reflected his study of Cezanne, van Gogh, and the Impressionists. He also made still lifes, self-portraits, and interiors, and was well known for his portraits, including those of Leni Riefenstahl (1924), Albert Einstein, Thomas Mann, and the artist Balthus in 1947. The latter artist was his nephew, and Spiro also painted a portrait of his sister Elisabeth Dorothea Spiro, Balthus' mother, as a strict schoolteacher in 1902. Spiro made numerous simple but descriptive drypoint etchings of North African subjects, including soldiers, snake charmers, and the Alhambra, all of which seek to invoke the images with exoticism. He taught at the Wayman Adam School in Elizabethtown, New Jersey. His work is in the collections of the Fine Arts Museum, San Francisco. He exhibited at the Museum of Modern Art and the St. Etienne Galerie, New York. The Galerie von Abercorn in Cologne mounted a retrospective of his work in 1978. A catalogue raisonné of his art, edited by Wilko von Abercron, was published in 1990.

BIBLIOGRAPHY: S. Barron, *Exiles and Emigrés: The Flight of European Artists from Hitler* (1997); S. Rewald, "Balthus Lessons: Five Controversial Works by the French Artist," in: *Art in America* (Sept. 1977); W. Schwab and J. Weiner, *Jewish Artists: the Ben Uri Collection: Paintings, Drawings, Prints, and Sculpture* (1987).

[Nancy Buchwald (2nd ed.)]

SPIRO, GYÖRGY (1946–), Hungarian novelist, poet, and literary historian. His volume of essays *A közep-kelet-europai dráma* ("The Drama in Central-East-Europe," 1986) analyzes the political era. He dealt mainly with historical and Slavonic subjects.

[Eva Kondor]

SPIRO, KARL (1867–1932), German physiological chemist. Born in Berlin, he worked at the University of Strasbourg from 1894 until 1918, when it became difficult there for Germans, and he went to Switzerland. From 1921 he was professor of physiological chemistry at the University of Basle. He was one of the first to apply concepts of physical chemistry to biology, such as pH buffering, and chemical kinetics to enzyme actions. He discovered some of the building blocks of proteins, such as pyrrolidinecarboxylic acid and phenylethylamine.

SPIRO, MELFORD ELLIOT (1920–), U.S. anthropologist. Born in Cleveland, Ohio, Spiro received his Ph.D. from Northwestern University in 1950. He taught at Connecticut University from 1952 to 1957; from 1957 to 1964 he was professor at Washington University, and from 1965 to 1967 at the University of Chicago. In 1968 he became a founding member of the Department of Anthropology at the University of California, San Diego. After retiring from teaching, he was named professor emeritus of anthropology at UCSD.

Spiro's primary research interest is the comparative analysis of social systems, especially problems of cultural motivation and control, and the interrelation of personality, culture, and society. In a theoretical chapter in *Studying Personality Cross-Culturally* (ed. B. Kaplan, 1961), he discussed culture and personality study in relation to the central issue in the social sciences – the explanation of social cohesion and functioning. He saw personality and culture as systems of motivational tendencies. Among his studies were *Kibbutz: Venture in Utopia* (1956) and *Children of the Kibbutz: A Study in Child Training and Personality* (1958), based on his research in the kibbutz as a participant observer. He analyzed the child-rearing methods on the collective settlements and the outcome in the personality of the kibbutz child. He also conducted fieldwork in Micronesia and Burma. In 1991 he received the Distinguished Contribution Award from the Society for Psychological Anthropology.

Spiro's publications include *Burmese Supernaturalism* (1967), *Buddhism and Society* (1970), *Gender and Culture: Kibbutz Women Revisited* (1979), *Oedipus in the Trobriands* (1982), *Culture and Human Nature* (1987), and *Gender Ideology and Psychological Reality* (1997). He also edited *Context and Meaning in Cultural Anthropology* (1965).

[Ephraim Fischoff / Ruth Beloff (2nd ed.)]

SPITZ, MARK ANDREW (1950–), U.S. swimmer, holder of the record for most gold medals won in a single Olympics with seven, and tied for most gold medals overall with nine; member of the International Swimming Hall of Fame and U.S. Olympic Hall of Fame. Born in Modesto, California, the eldest of three children to Lenore and Arnold, a steel executive, Spitz began swimming at age two, when his family moved to Honolulu and Spitz would swim at Waikiki Beach every day. The family returned to California four years later, and Spitz received his first competitive training at six at the Sacramento YMCA. By the time he was 10, he held 17 national age-group records and one world record, the 50-yard butterfly, which he completed in 31 seconds, and was named "the world's best 10-and-under swimmer." The family moved to Santa Clara when Spitz was 14, so he could train at the famed Santa Clara Swim Club. In 1965 at age 15, he swam at the Maccabiah games in his first international competition, winning four gold medals. At age 16 he won the 100-meter butterfly at the 1966 National AAU Championships, the first of his 24 AAU titles. The next year he won five gold medals at the Pan-American Games in Winnipeg, and laid claim to ten world records. By the time Spitz was 18, he had won 26 national and international titles, and broken 10 world and 28 U.S. records. At the 1968 Olympic Games in Mexico City, where much was expected of him, Spitz came away disappointed after predicting he would win six gold medals. He won two gold medals, in the 4 × 100 m and 4 × 200 m freestyle relays, a silver medal in the 100m butterfly, and bronze in the 100m freestyle. Spitz spent the next four years at Indiana University, winning almost every conceivable award and setting almost every world record in existence, as he prepared for the 1972 Olympics in Munich. He returned to Israel for the 1969 Maccabiah Games, winning another six gold medals. By the spring of 1972, Spitz had set 23 world records and 35 U.S. records. Driven by ambition and sheer single-mindedness, Spitz won seven Olympic gold medals in 1972 at the Munich Games – a feat unequaled by any Olympic athlete – with a world record in each of the seven events (the 100 m freestyle, 200 m freestyle, 100 m butterfly, 200 m butterfly, 4 × 100 m and 4 × 200 m freestyle, and the 4 × 100 m medley). The next week he was on the September 11, 1972, cover of *Time* magazine. Spitz's 11 total medals in the two Olympics are tied for the most medals ever won by a U.S. Olympian. Hours after he won his last medal, Palestinian terrorism claimed the lives of 11 Israeli sportsmen, and security personnel whisked Spitz out of Munich. Over his career, Spitz set 26 individual world records in the freestyle and butterfly, contributing to another seven relay world records; 38 American records; 24 National AAU championships; and eight NCAA titles. He was named "World Swimmer of the Year" in 1967, 1971, and 1972 and became the first Jewish recipient of the James E. Sullivan Award in 1971, given annually to the Amateur Athlete of the Year. Spitz attempted a comeback at age 41 in an attempt to qualify for the 1992 Barcelona Olympics, after filmmaker Bud *Greenspan offered to pay him a million dollars if he succeeded in qualifying. Filmed by Greenspan's cameras, Spitz failed to beat the qualifying limit – his best time was 58:03, but he needed 55:59. Spitz was named a member of the International Swimming Hall of Fame in 1977 and the U.S. Olympic Hall of Fame in 1983. He wrote *The Mark Spitz Complete Book of Swimming* (1976) and his autobiography, *Seven Golds: Mark Spitz Own Story* (1981).

[Elli Wohlgelernter (2nd ed.)]

SPITZ, RENE A. (1887–1974), child psychiatrist and psychoanalyst. Born in Vienna, Spitz worked in Hungary, Austria, and France before he immigrated to the United States at the end of the 1930s. From 1940 to 1957 he was on the faculty of the New York Psychoanalytic Institute, where he became a research consultant in pediatrics and psychiatry. During part of this time he was an adjunct psychiatrist at the Mount Sinai Hospital, New York City (1940–43). As visiting clinical professor of psychiatry at the University of Colorado's school of medicine from 1957, he was active in the fields of psychoanalysis, psychiatry, and normal and disturbed infant development. He was vice president of the New York Psychoanalytic Society (1950–52). In 1959 he published *Genetic Field Theory of Ego Formation*. After his retirement, he went to live in Geneva, Switzerland, where he continued to teach and write.

Spitz earned international fame for his pioneering research in infant development. In order to clarify psychoanalytic theories that had previously been based in the retrospective analysis of adults, he carried out direct observation and photographic documentation of infant behavior. His observation of children in hospitals led to one of his most important contributions to psychoanalytic theory – the concept of anaclitic depression, a severe disturbance of infant development resulting from separation from a maternal object and leading to malnutrition and sometimes death. This condition was regarded by subsequent analysts as an attachment disorder. The books Spitz wrote in his later years, *No and Yes* (1957) and *The First Year of Life* (1965) provide rich documentary evidence on the early development of infant communication, perceptual development, relation to objects, and development of the mother-child relationship. In them, Spitz tried to conceptualize early development and to correlate the psychological theory of Jean Piaget (1896–1980) with psychoanalytic theory.

ADD. BIBLIOGRAPHY: H. Gaskill, *Counterpoint: Libidinal Object and Subject: A Tribute to Rene A. Spitz* (1963); R. Emde (ed.), *Rene A. Spitz: Dialogues from Infancy* (1984).

[Joseph Marcus]

SPITZER, ELIOT (1959–), New York State attorney general. Born in the Bronx in New York City, Spitzer graduated from Princeton University in 1981 and received his J.D. degree from Harvard Law School, where he was an editor of the *Harvard Law Review* in 1984. He clerked for U.S. District Court Judge Robert W. Sweet in New York, then entered private practice at the firm of Paul, Weiss, Rifkind, Wharton, and Garrison.

From 1986 Spitzer worked as an assistant district attorney in Manhattan, under District Attorney Robert Morgenthau. He pursued investigations into organized crime, eventually becoming chief of the Labor Racketeering Unit. In 1992, in perhaps his most famous case, Spitzer led the investigation into the Gambino family's control of trucking in Manhattan's garment industry. That same year he left the District Attorney's office and joined the firm of Skadden, Arps, Slate, Meagher, and Flom, and he was later a partner at Constantine and Partners.

In 1994 Spitzer made his first bid for the office of New York State Attorney General. He failed to win the Democratic nomination, and Democratic candidate Karen Burstein lost the general election to Dennis Vacco. Spitzer again sought the nomination in 1998, this time successfully, and defeated Vacco in the general elections. In 2002 he was reelected with a large margin.

As attorney general, Spitzer was credited with redefining the role of the office, taking on cases that formerly had been deferred to federal prosecution. His office investigated securities fraud, insurance practices, occupational safety, marketing fraud, and violations of environmental protection. *Time* magazine named him "Crusader of the Year" in 2002. That year Spitzer sued several investment banks for inflating stock prices by, among other practices, using affiliated firms to offer biased advice. He negotiated a settlement of these lawsuits for $1.4 billion in compensation and fines, and new rules were imposed for analysis of the market. Also in 2002, he filed suits to address violations of the Clean Air Act.

In 2004 Spitzer's office investigated the music industry, uncovering $50 million in unpaid royalties to musicians. Numerous other cases addressed commissions in the insurance industry, disclosure policies regarding clinical trials in the pharmaceutical industry, and fraud in the marketplace.

Spitzer announced in 2004 that he would seek the Democratic nomination for governor of New York in 2006. Senator Charles Schumer, who had been favored in the polls, had announced that he would not run but would remain in his Senate seat. Governor George Pataki announced in 2005 that he would not seek reelection, and Spitzer was considered a strong candidate for not only the Democratic nomination but in a run against possible Republican contenders.

[Dorothy Bauhoff (2nd ed.)]

SPITZER, FREDERIC (**Samuel**; 1814–1890), Hungarian-born collector and dealer in paintings, armor, and objets d'art. Spitzer, son of a cemetery guard, began by selling a Duerer painting he bought cheaply in Italy while serving with the Austrian army in 1848. He later dealt in old weapons and armor. He settled in Paris and built up a magnificent collection which the French state offered to buy. Spitzer rejected this offer and the collection was sold after his death for ten million francs. The armor was purchased by King Edward VII.

SPITZER, HUGO (1854–1937), Austrian philosopher and scientist. Spitzer, who was born in Einoede, Carinthia, was professor of philosophy and natural science at Graz from 1903 to 1924. He was an ardent supporter of Darwin and wrote *Beitraege zur Deszendenztheorie und zur Methodologie der Naturwissenschaft* (1886). In common with Haeckel, Spitzer claimed that consciousness could be derived from matter (in his *Ueber Ursprung und Bedeutung des Hylozoismus* (1881)). Spitzer also wrote *Kritische Studien zur Aesthetik der Gegenwart* (1897), and *Untersuchungen zur Theorie und Geschichte der Aesthetik* (1923^2), in which he tried to clarify the relationship between aesthetics and the philosophy of art.

BIBLIOGRAPHY: *Zeitschrift fuer Aesthetik und allgemeine Kunstwissenschaft*, 18 (1924), Festschrift H. Spitzer; E. Binder, in: *Archiv fuer Philosophie und Soziologie*, 30 (1926), 181–90.

[Richard H. Popkin]

ŠPITZER, JURAJ (1919–1995), Slovak writer, literary critic, scriptwriter. Špitzer was born in Krupina, Slovakia. In 1944 he participated in the Slovak National Uprising against the Germans. From 1951 to 1970 he worked at the Institute of Slovak Literature of the Slovak Academy of Sciences. In 1970 he lost his job (punishment for his activities in 1968). Špitzer wrote several movie scripts and a number of stories, such as *Patrím k vám* ("I Belong to You," 1964) about the political trials of the 1950s and *Letná nedeľa* ("The Summer Sunday," 1991). The narrative *Nechcel som byť Žid* ("I Did Not Want to Be a Jew," 1995) is based on a factual "Report on Nováky," which describes the Jewish concentration camp in central Slovakia between 1942 and 1944. After Špitzer's death, a collection of essays and memoirs appeared entitled *Svítá, až keď je celkom tma* ("It Is Getting

Light, until the Darkness Is Coming," 1996). The main topic was the so-called "Jewish question" and the Holocaust.

BIBLIOGRAPHY: V. Mikula, *Slovník slovenských spisovatelů* (1999)

[Milos Pojar (2nd ed.)]

SPITZER, KARL HEINRICH (1830–1848), first Jewish victim of the March 1848 revolution in Vienna. He was born in Bzenec (Bisenz), Moravia, where the family had settled after the expulsion of the Jews from Vienna in 1670. From the age of 10 he lived in Vienna, where he was educated, and was influenced by the French Enlightenment, and the writings of Ludwig *Boerne. Dissatisfied with political conditions under the Hapsburgs and tending to radicalism, he intended to emigrate to the United States. In the 1848 revolution in Vienna, Spitzer was among the first five fighters at the barricades to be shot outside the building of the Lower Austrian Estates *(Landhaus)* on March 13. Spitzer was glorified as a martyr of the revolution by the Jews of the Hapsburg Empire. His father, Leopold, is reported to have said that he praised God because his son had helped to free the fatherland and gave new life to millions by his death. On the initiative of the Roman Catholic chaplain of the students organization the Jewish victims, Spitzer and Bernard Herschmann, were buried in a common grave with Christians who also lost their lives at this time. I.N. *Mannheimer eulogized them in a celebrated sermon. This unique procedure was not repeated for the Jews shot in Vienna in October 1848.

BIBLIOGRAPHY: *Oesterreichisches Central-Organ…*, 1 (1848), 6–11; *Juedisches Archiv*, 1 no. 6 (1928), 16–18. **ADD. BIBLIOGRAPHY:** C. Von Wurzbach, *Biographisches Lexikon des Kaiserthums Oesterreich*, s.v.; K. Streng, *Ausfuehrliche Biographie des am 13. Maerz in Wien Gefallenen Freiheitshelden Karl Heinrich Spitzer* (1848).

[Meir Lamed / Albert Lichtblau (2nd ed.)]

SPITZER, LEO (1939–), scholar and author. Born in Bolivia to Austrian Jewish parents fleeing Nazi persecution, Spitzer moved to the United States with his family in 1950. He was educated at Brandeis University, where he received a B.A. in Spanish literature (1961), and at the University of Wisconsin, where he earned a master's degree in Latin American history (1963) and a Ph.D. in African history (1969). He joined the faculty of Dartmouth College in 1967 as an instructor, becoming an assistant professor in 1969 and an associate professor in 1974. He became the Kathe Tappe Vernon Professor of History at Dartmouth.

A multilingual scholar who speaks Spanish, German, Portuguese, and Krio, and reads French and Xhosa, Spitzer published widely on African culture and responses to colonialism and racism. From 1963 to 1965 he was the recipient of a Ford Foundation Foreign Area Training Fellowship for research in England and Sierra Leone, and in 1972 he received a Social Science Research Council fellowship for a comparative study of the intellectual reactions to Western culture of Afro-Brazilian freedmen and the Sierra Leone Creoles. In 1974 and 1975 he was awarded grants from the comparative world history program of the University of Wisconsin. His works include *The Creoles of Sierra Leone: Responses to Colonialism* (1974); *Lives in Between: Assimilation and Marginality in Austria, Brazil, West Africa, 1780–1945* (1989); and *Acts of Memory: Cultural Recall in the Present* (as editor, with Mieke Bal and Jonathan Crewe, 1999).

Spitzer perhaps received the most attention for his 1998 work, *Hotel Bolivia: The Culture of Memory in a Refuge from Nazism*, which was widely and favorably reviewed as a significant contribution to Holocaust studies. The work is part memoir, part ethnographic study of the Jews who fled to "Hotel Bolivia," as they called the country that most regarded as a temporary haven. It includes letters, family photographs, and interviews with surviving refugees, and the work explores the issues of displacement, grief, and nostalgia for an obliterated past.

Spitzer has been the recipient of several honors. He was the Lucius Littauer Fellow at the National Humanities Center in 1992 and 1993. From 1996 to 1998 he was a National Humanities Center Distinguished Lecturer. His latest work is a collaboration with Marianne Hirsch on a study of Jewish families from Czernowitz before, during, and after the Holocaust.

[Dorothy Bauhoff (2nd ed.)]

SPITZER, MOSHE (1900–1982), Israeli publisher and typographer. Moshe Spitzer was born in Boskovice, Moravia, studied at the University of Vienna, and then earned his Ph.D. at the University of Kiel in Indian Studies. In the late 1920s he served as Martin Buber's secretary, assisting the philosopher in his German translation of the Bible, and from 1933 he worked for the Schocken Publishing Company in Berlin. In 1939, Spitzer went to Palestine, where in 1940 he established Tarshish Books. Over the years he published over 100 editions of Hebrew literature (Samuel Beckett, Nelly Sachs) and the classics (Dante, Shakespeare). In 1942 he opened a composing (typesetting) shop for his own books and for other publishers. As a partner in the Jerusalem Type Foundry (1950–1960), he revived neglected Hebrew typefaces and initiated the casting on new ones: *Romema, Rahat*, and *Hatzvi.* Because of his unceasing demands on compositors and printers, his innate good taste, and his familiarity with European fine printing, he succeeded in raising the level of book production in Israel from the mediocre to the best possible with the materials then available in the country. He commissioned leading Israeli artists to illustrate many of his editions. His publications included *The Birds' Head Haggadah* (1965–67), the facsimile of a manuscript in the Israel Museum. Spitzer designed books for Schocken, established and managed the Jewish Agency's publishing department from 1945, and directed publishing at the Bialik Institute. He wrote articles on the history of the Hebrew letter. In 1981 he was elected to the Double Crown Club of England for his contribution to fine printing, and he was honorary chairman of Yedidei ha-Sefer, the Israel Bibliophiles. His own publications were exhibited in the Israel Museum (1970) and at the Jewish National and University Library (1981).

BIBLIOGRAPHY: H. Goldberg, "The Work of Dr. Moshe Spitzer: Leader in Modern Hebrew Printing and Publishing," Master's thesis, Hebrew University of Jerusalem, School of Library and Archive Studies (1982); Israel Museum, *From the Collection of Dr. Moshe Spitzer, Jerusalem*, (1982; Cat. No. 172); idem, *The Typographical Work of Moshe Spitzer* (1970; Cat. No. 73); H.J. Katzenstein, *Dr. Moshe Spitzer: Books, Typography, Design* (1980); I. Soifer, "The Pioneer Work of Dr. Moshe Spitzer, in: *Penrose Annual*, 63 (1970), 127–47."

[Leila Avrin]

SPITZER, SAMUEL (1839–1896), Hungarian rabbi and scholar. Spitzer, who was born in Keszthely, Hungary, studied with S.J. *Rapoport in Prague. In 1856 he became rabbi in Eszek (now Osijek, Croatia), where he engaged in the study of the history of Jewish and general culture.

His published works include *Das Heer und Wehrgesetz der alten Israeliten, Griechen und Roemer* (1869); *Das Mahl bet den alten Voelkern* (1878); *Urheimisch in Slavischen Laendern* (1880); *Das Jubilaeum in Woertlicher und Historischer Beleuchtung* (1882); and *Ueber Sitte und Sitten der alten Voelker* (1886).

[Baruch Yaron]

SPITZER, SOLOMON (**Benjamin Solomon Zalman**; 1826–1893), known as Reb Zalman Spitzer; rabbi and leader of Austrian Orthodox Jewry. Born in Ofen (Budapest), he studied under R. Moses Schick, in St. Jur, R. Meir Ash *Eisenstaedter in Ungvar, and R. Abraham Samuel Benjamin *Sofer in Pressburg. In 1849 he married the daughter of R. Moses *Sofer (Schreiber). On the suggestion of Ignaz *Deutsch, in 1853 he was appointed rabbi of Vienna's Pressburger *Shool*, a small community of Orthodox Jews mainly from Pressburg and from Hungarian provincial communities. Under Spitzer's leadership the community soon outgrew the small premises they occupied and by 1864 a new synagogue, Adass Yisroel, was built in Grosse Schiffgasse and known as the Schiff *Shool*. In conjunction with the synagogue he founded the Schiff *Shool bet ha-midrash*. In 1858 he was appointed assistant rabbi to Eliezer Horowitz. On the latter's death in 1868 Spitzer was offered the post of chief rabbi, on condition that he modify his strictly traditional standards, but he refused. In 1871 Adolf Jellinek, aided by Simon *Szanto, the influential editor of the *Neuzeit*, and Ignaz *Kuranda, the new president of the Kultusgemeinde, wished to introduce some radical reforms into the order of the service, including the elimination of all mention of an ultimate return to Zion and Jerusalem, and the exclusion from the prayer books of all references to the reinstitution of sacrifices and to a belief in the Messiah. Although the government openly sympathized with the reformers, the Orthodox community opposed the proposals. Spitzer called a protest meeting attended by some 500 people – approximately one quarter of the whole of Vienna's synagogue membership. A compromise was found: the reforms were called modifications, the organ was not introduced into any Vienna synagogue, and the controversial prayers were to be recited in silence by the congregation.

Spitzer resigned from the rabbinate of the Kultusgemeinde and devoted his energies entirely to the affairs of the Schiff *Shool* and to its flourishing subsidiary institutions. It was his lifelong desire to settle in Jerusalem and in preparation he sent his library on ahead with a son-in-law who migrated there. However, Spitzer's teacher, Moses Schick, prevailed upon him not to leave Vienna, saying "a conscientious general does not leave his soldiers to fight on by themselves." He died in Vienna and, in accordance with his last wish, was buried in Pressburg.

A large number of responsa in his teacher's work, the "Responsa of Maharam Schick," are addressed to Spitzer, as are a number of responsa in the *Ketav Sofer* by Abraham Samuel Benjamin Sofer, the *Shevet Sofer* of Simḥah Bunim Sofer, and the Responsa of Akiva *Eger. The only original work published by Spitzer is the *Tikkun Shelomo* (1892), consisting of 100 sermons and eight funeral orations, together with *Simlat Binyamin*, talmudic discourses. He also published the speech he made at the protest meeting in Vienna (1871).

BIBLIOGRAPHY: I. Gastfreund, *Wiener Rabbinen* (1879), 115–7; J.J. Greenwald, *Le-Toledot ha-Reformazyon ha-Datit be-Germanya u-ve-Ungarya* (1948), 14 n. 25; *Ha-Maggid*, 15 (1871), 50, 58; *Der Israelit*, 34 (1893), 1835f., 1879f.

[Alexander Scheiber]

SPIVACKE, HAROLD (1904–1977), U.S. music librarian and musicologist. Born in New York, Spivacke studied at New York University and the University of Berlin, where he received his Ph.D. in 1933. He also studied privately with d'Albert and Hugo *Leichtentritt. He was assistant chief of the music division of the Library of Congress from 1934 to 1937 and chief from 1937 until his retirement. The music division was greatly developed under his administration. Spivacke was also a member of various directive and advisory bodies in American and international musicological organizations and president of the Music Library Association from 1951 to 1953; he held offices in the National Music Council and the American Musicological Society. He published *Paganiniana* (1945) and various articles.

BIBLIOGRAPHY: Grove Music Online.

[Amnon Shiloah (2nd ed.)]

SPIVAK, ELYE (1890–1950), Yiddish linguist and pedagogue. Born in the Ukraine, Spivak was renowned as a Yiddish teacher before the Revolution. The author of scores of Yiddish primers and literary anthologies for schoolchildren, he trained Yiddish teachers at several institutes. After Nahum Shtif's death in 1933, Spivak was appointed director of the linguistic section of the Institute for Jewish Proletarian Culture at the Ukrainian Academy of Sciences in Kiev and editor of its journal, *Afn Shprakhfront*. In 1937, after the dissolution of the Institute, which had supported more than a hundred workers, a small Office for the Study of Yiddish Literature, Language, and Folklore was established, with Spivak continuing as director. The office was evacuated to the East during World War II and closed in 1949, when Spivak, a member of the *Jewish Anti-Fascist Committee, was arrested under charges of Jewish nationalism. He died in prison in 1950. The main administrator of Soviet Yiddish research in the 1930s and 1940s, Spivak was the authority on the lexicon and terminology. His crowning work was *Naye Vortshafung* ("Creating Neologisms," 1939), which demonstrated impressive expertise in Yiddish morphology, etymology, and language history and structure. The short-lived policy of dehebraization of Yiddish suggested by Shtif and I. Zaretski was, from 1931–1939, consistently opposed by Spivak, who argued for the componential integrity of the language.

BIBLIOGRAPHY: LNYL, 6 (1965), 509–13; B. Kagan, *Leksikon fun Yidish Shraybers* (1986), 410–11; R. Peltz, in: J. Fishman (ed.), *Readings in the Sociology of Jewish Languages* (1985), 125–50; S. Redlich, *War, Holocaust and Stalinism* (1995), 153, 454; E. Rozental-Shnayderman, *Oyf Vegn un Umvegn*, 3 (1982), 163–79; J. Rubinstein and V. Naumov (eds.), *Stalin's Secret Pogrom* (2003), 127.

[Rakhmiel Peltz (2nd ed.)]

SPIVAK, NISSAN (known as "**Nissi Belzer**"; 1824–1906). Lithuanian cantor and composer. Spivak sang in the choir of Yeruḥam *Blindman, whose cousin he married, and became cantor in Belz, where he acquired his additional name. Later he was cantor in Kishinev and, from 1877 until his death, in Berdichev. He was largely self-taught, and although his voice was impaired by an accident in childhood, he became widely known because of his talents as a composer and choral conductor. His vocal limitation actually led him to develop a new style of synagogue music. Instead of using the choir merely for accompaniment and responses, he assigned to them long ensembles with solos and duets and reduced the role of the cantor to a minimum. He also took his choir on visits to other towns and the courts of ḥasidic rabbis. Successful as a teacher, he attracted many young cantors to study with him at Berdichev. His own compositions were preserved by his pupils. Two of them were published in Idelsohn's *Hebraeisch-orientalischer Melodienschatz* (bibl.).

BIBLIOGRAPHY: Prachtenberg, in: Jewish Ministers-Cantors Association of America, *History of Hazanuth* (1924), 163; Idelsohn, Melodien, 8 (1932), XXII–XXIII, nos. 250, 251; Friedmann, Lebensbilder, 3 (1927), 129; Sendrey, Music, indexes.

[Joshua Leib Ne'eman]

SPIVAKOVSKY, TOSSY (1906/7–1998), Russian-American violinist. Spivakovsky was born in Odessa. He studied with the Italian violinist Arrigo Serato and with Willy Hess in Berlin, where he made his concert debut at the age of ten. Spivakovsky became leader of the Berlin Philharmonic Orchestra in 1926. He then toured Europe (1920–33) and Australia (1933–39), where he taught at the Melbourne Conservatorium (1934–39).

In 1940 he settled in the United States and made his debut at New York's Town Hall. Playing with the Cleveland Orchestra in 1943, Spivakovsky introduced Bartok's *Violin Concerto* to the United States. He subsequently appeared with the most important American orchestras. In addition to an active performing career, Spivakovsky taught violin and chamber music at the Juilliard School from 1974 to 1989. His repertory ranged from the classics to contemporary works. A brilliant virtuoso, he had an exceptionally fast vibrato and advocated new bowing techniques which proved controversial. He was capable of frequently expressive playing with a highly volatile temperament. He published violin transcriptions and "Polyphony in Bach's Works for Solo Violin," in *The Music Review*, 28:4 (Nov. 1967), 277–88.

ADD. BIBLIOGRAPHY: *Baker's Biographical Dictionary of Musicians* (1997); "Tossy Spivakovsky Dies" (obituary), in: *The Strad*, 109 (Oct. 1998), 1041; J. Gottlieb, "The Juilliard School Library and Its Special Collections," in: *Notes*, 56 (Sept. 1999), 11–26.

[Max Loppert / Naama Ramot (2nd ed.)]

SPLIT (also **Spliet;** It. **Spalato;** in Jewish sources **אישפלטרא**), Adriatic port in Croatia. A Jewish community with a cemetery existed in nearby Salona (now Solin) in the third century C.E. When Salona was destroyed by the Avars in 641, the Jews seem to have fled to Diocletian's fortified palace which later became the town of Split. The register of the Church's properties in 1397 mentions a building that served as a synagogue. The first Jewish tombstones on the Marjan hill date, however, from 1573.

In the 16th century there were two groups of Sephardi Jews in Split; the Ponentine ("western") and the Levantine ("eastern") Jews. The first group came from Italy or from Spain via Italy, Split being a Venetian possession, and the second from the Ottoman territories in the Balkans. Both groups later merged into one Sephardi congregation whose notable families were Pardo, Macchiero, Misrai (Mizraḥi), Penso (Finzi), Jesurun (Yeshurun). There were also some Ashkenazi Jews, e.g., the Morpurgo family from Maribor.

The Jews of Split were mainly merchants, physicians, and tailors. The Venetian authorities protected them from the Inquisition and favored them in the interest of the trade with the Ottoman Empire. In 1592 the Jew Daniel Rodriguez succeeded, with the authorization of the Senate of Venice, in establishing a free port in Split. Jewish merchants from the Ottoman Empire wanting to settle in Split were exempted from paying the residence tax; and immunity of person and capital was guaranteed to Jewish merchants traveling to Venice via Split. The free port prospered. Some Jews became wealthy from traveling to the Ottoman territories in the Balkans and exporting the wares brought to Venice; later they had agents in major cities. In the 17th century Joseph Penso, consul of the Jews, became instrumental in expanding the free port's activities. The increasing wealth of Split's Jews brought a prohibition on real estate ownership except by special license, to prevent gentiles from pledging houses and land to Jews.

During the Turkish attack in 1657 the Jews were assigned the defense of a tower which later became known as the Jewish position [*posto degl' Ebrei*].

In the beginning of the 18th century there were several abortive attempts to exclude Jews from the food trade (1719, 1748), and from tailoring (1724, 1758). The law of 1738, regulating Jewish rights and duties in Venetian possessions, was applied in Split. It included the wearing of a yellow hat cover by Levantine, and of a red one by other Jews; confinement to the ghetto between midnight and sunrise; not leaving it at all Thursday and Friday of holy week; closing the shops in the ghetto on Christian holidays; and an interdiction to employ Christians.

The general decadence of Venice in the late 18th century and the anti-Jewish measures of 1779 caused many Jewish families to leave. In 1796 there were 173 Jews left in Split. The ghetto was abolished by the Napoleonic regime. When Split passed to Austria in 1814, the Jewish laws valid in Austria were applied there, and full emancipation was granted only in 1873. Many families left for Italy during the 19th century, and with the influx of Jews from Croatia and Bosnia, the community became increasingly Croatian-speaking.

Holocaust Period

When on April 6, 1941, the Italian Army occupied the town, there were 400 Jews living there, some being refugees from Austria, Czechoslovakia etc. Although Dalmatia nominally belonged to *Pavelić's quisling Croatian state, the Italian army prevented his regime from persecuting the Jews, and some 3,000 refugees from Poland, Austria, and Czechoslovakia had passed through Split by 1943.

In June 1942 a mob devastated the synagogue, community offices, shops, and private houses. Under German pressure refugees were interned in Italian camps on the Dalmatian islands. When Italy capitulated in September 1943, and before the Germans entered the town, several hundred Jews crossed the Adriatic in small boats to Italy and to partisan-held islands, while others joined the partisan forces on the mainland. All remaining male Jews were made to register with the German authorities, and on October 13 were arrested and sent to the Sajmište camp near *Belgrade where most of them perished. Around 150 Jews from Split died in the Holocaust.

Contemporary Period

In 1947 there were 163 Jews in Split, and in 1970 some 120; there was no rabbi and very little communal activity. The new military hospital inaugurated in 1965 bears the name of Dr. Isidore Perera-Molić, the founder of the Yugoslav Army Medical Corps. During reconstruction work in the Diocletian Palace engravings of *menorot* were discovered, confirming earlier allusions regarding a Jewish presence there in the 2nd or 3rd centuries. The nearby camp at Pirovac, which was formerly a summer resort for Jewish youth from all parts of the country, served as an absorption center during the 1992 evacuation of the Jews of Bosnia and Herzegovina (mainly from *Sarajevo and Mosta). The successful rescue operation was a joint venture of the Federation of Jewish Communities in Belgrade, the Jewish community of Sarajevo, the Jewish Agency, and the respective civil and military authorities of the Bosnian Moslems, Croats, and Serbs. A number of Jews were evacuated by air to *Belgrade; others through Herzegovina to Dalmatia (Split) by land across several zones held by the three warring parties. About 100 Jews lived in Split in 2004.

BIBLIOGRAPHY: G. Novak, *Židovi u Splitu* (1920); C. Roth, *Venice*, (1930), 67, 186, 305–10, 343; Frey, Corpus, 1 (1936), no. 680; *Jevrejski Almanah* (1959/60), 7–14, 29–53; Hananel-Eškenazi, 2 (1960), 199. HOLOCAUST PERIOD: *Jevrejski Almanah* (1957/58), 125–8; Savez jevrejskih opština, *Zločini fašističkih okupatora…* (1952).

[Daniel Furman / Zvi Loker (2nd ed.)]

SPOEHR, ALEXANDER (1913–1992), U.S. anthropologist. Born in Tucson, Arizona, Spoehr specialized in American Indian and Pacific ethnology and archaeology. In 1940 he worked as assistant curator of American ethnology and archaeology at the Field Museum in Chicago. During World War II, he was commissioned as a lieutenant in the Naval Reserve, where he served in air combat intelligence and air-sea rescue operations in the western sea frontier and central Pacific area, which included the Marshall (Majuro), Gilbert, and Caroline islands. When he returned to the Field Museum in 1946, he worked for eight years as curator of Oceanic ethnology, supervising the reorganization of the museum's massive collection of artifacts from Oceania. In 1953 he was appointed professor of anthropology at Yale University. He moved to Hawaii later that year to assume the directorship of the Bernice Pauhi Bishop Museum in Honolulu. In 1961 he became chancellor of the East-West Center at the University of Hawaii. In 1964 he was appointed professor of anthropology at the University of Pittsburgh, where he remained until his retirement. He served as chairman of the Pacific Science Board of the National Academy of Sciences (1958–61) and was president of the American Anthropological Association (1965). In 1972 he was elected to the National Academy of Sciences.

When Spoehr retired from teaching in 1978 he returned to Honolulu, where he did a study of the tool-using techniques of Japanese-American carpenters. He also did research on the history of the Hudson's Bay Company in 19th-century Hawaii.

Spoehr wrote several books on his fieldwork, which was mainly among the American Indians and the peoples of the Pacific islands. He is best remembered for defining the prehistoric ceramic culture known as Lapita, a community of hunter-gatherers that lived in Oceania from 1500 B.C.E. to 500 B.C.E. and whose handiwork included elaborately decorated pottery and a wide variety of tools made from shells.

His major works include *Camp, Clan and Kin among the Cow Creek Seminole of Florida* (1941), *Majuro, a Village in the Marshall Islands* (1949), *Acculturation and Material Culture* (with G. Quimby, 1951), *Saipan, the Ethnology of a War-Devastated Island* (1954), *Zamboanga and Sulu: An Archaeological Approach to Ethnic Diversity* (1973), *Protein from the Sea* (1980), and *Maritime Adaptations* (1980).

[Ephraim Fischoff / Ruth Beloff (2nd ed.)]

SPOLETO, town in central Italy. A Jewish community possibly existed in Spoleto before 1298 when the distinguished Roman family De *Pomis settled there after the head of the family, Elijah, was condemned to death by the Holy Office. In the 15th century the principal activity of the Jewish community in Spoleto was moneylending. The notable Spoleto Jews included the physicians David De' Pomis (1525–88) and Moses *Alatino (1529–1605). The Jews were expelled from Spoleto and the rest of the Papal States by Pius V in 1569. Some returned for a brief period under Sixtus V (1587). There is still in Spoleto the Church of S. Gregorio della Sinagoga.

BIBLIOGRAPHY: Roth, Italy, index; Milano, Italia, index; Ravà, in: *Annali di Statistica*, 9 (1884), 201–8.

[Ariel Toaff]

SPORKIN, STANLEY (1932–), U.S. federal judge. Born in Philadelphia, Sporkin received his bachelor's degree from Pennsylvania State University in 1953 and graduated from Yale Law School in 1957. After a clerkship with a presiding justice in the U.S. District Court, Sporkin entered private practice in 1960. In 1961 he began a 20-year career with the Securities and Exchange Commission, first as a staff attorney; he became chief attorney for the SEC Enforcement Bureau in 1963. In 1968 he became an associate director and from 1973 to 1981 served as the director of the SEC Division of Enforcement. He taught as an adjunct professor at Antioch Law School from 1974 to 1981 and at Howard University in 1981.

Sporkin became general counsel for the Central Intelligence Agency in 1981, serving under Director William Casey during the Iran Contra era. In 1985 President Ronald Reagan appointed him as a federal judge in the U.S. District Court for the District of Columbia. Judge Sporkin ruled in several notable cases, including an early settlement between the Justice Department's Antitrust Division and Microsoft Corporation. In 1995 he rejected a proposed settlement between the parties as too narrow and potentially ineffective in reducing Microsoft's monopolistic practices. His ruling was overturned by a panel of three federal appeals judges. Sporkin served on the bench until his retirement in 2000, when he joined the firm of Weil, Gotshal, and Genges as partner and counseled parties in corporate governance and litigation matters, acted as an arbitrator, and provided mediation services. He contributed numerous articles to professional journals.

In his long career of public service, Sporkin received numerous awards and honors. In 1976 he received the National Civil Service League's Special Achievement Award and in 1978 the Rockefeller Award for Public Service from the Woodrow Wilson School of Public and International Affairs at Princeton University. In 1979 he was the recipient of the President's Award for Distinguished Federal Civilian Service, the highest honor that can be granted to a member of the federal service.

In 1994 Sporkin received the William O. Douglas Award for Lifetime Achievement from the Association of Securities and Exchange Commission Alumni, and in 1996 he was presented the H. Carl Moultrie Award for Judicial Excellence by the Trial Lawyers of Washington, D.C. In 2000 he received the Federal Bar Association's Tom C. Clark Award. That same year he received the Judicial Excellence Award from Judicial Watch.

[Dorothy Bauhoff (2nd ed.)]

SPORN, PHILIP (1896–1978), U.S. electrical engineer. Sporn was born in Galicia, and taken to the United States in 1907. He joined the staff of the American Electric Power Company in 1920 and held many positions in this company, including chief engineer, executive vice president, and chairman of development. He was also president of the Electric Power Service Corporation, the Indiana-Kentucky and Ohio Valley Electric Corporations, and the Nuclear Power Group.

Sporn served in various consultative capacities with numerous studies and projects on nuclear power production under the aegis of the U.S. government, the Atomic Energy Commission, the National Research Council, and large companies. He was vice president of the American Nuclear Society. Sporn was chairman of the Seawater Conversion Commission of the government of Israel. As well as papers on the generation and distribution of electric power, he wrote (with Ambrose and Baumeister) *Heat Pumps* (1947) and *Integrated Power System as the Basic Mechanism for Power Supply* (1950). He received many awards.

[Samuel Aaron Miller]

SPORTS. There is no evidence of sports among the Jews during the obscure period between the close of the Bible and the Maccabean periods. At the beginning of this latter period, in the second century B.C.E., circumstances conspired to make sporting activities as such, i.e., sport not as associated with the need for physical exercise or as an aspect of military training but competitive sport "for the sake of the game," repugnant to the Jews as the very antithesis of Jewish ideals, and this approach remained characteristic of Judaism until the dawn of the modern period.

A number of circumstances contributed to the negative and antipathetic attitude toward sport. The first was that, with the conquest of Alexander the Great in the fourth century B.C.E., hellenistic culture began to infiltrate into Ereẓ Israel, and the attempt of Antiochus *Epiphanes to forcibly hellenize Judea led to the outbreak of the Maccabean War. One of the overt signs of this process was the establishment of a gymnasium in Jerusalem by *Jason in 174 B.C.E., where the participants engaged in their sporting activities in the nude. The antithesis between the gymnasium as an expression of *Hellenism and Judaism was dramatically and almost symbolically highlighted by the fact that some of the Jewish participants, according to the Book of I Maccabees (1:15), actually underwent operations for the purpose of concealing the fact that they were circumcised. Sport thus became associated with the alien and dangerous hellenistic culture. An additional factor was that the Olympic games were connected with an idolatrous cult, particularly of the Greek deity of Hercules, and it is significant that during the period of hellenization, when a Jewish contingent went to the games held at Tyre concurrently with the 152nd Olympic games in Greece, they refused to bring the customary gifts, which were dedicated to Hercules, unless they were devoted to a non-idolatrous cause.

Nevertheless, there is some evidence that in countries under Greek influence, sports were indulged in by Jews. Claudius warned the Jews of Alexandria that they "should not strive in gymnasiarchic and cosmetic games" (Philo, *Legatio ad Gaium*), and one interpretation of a second- or third-century inscription in Hypaepa, Asia Minor, has it refer to a sports association of young Jews.

This opposition to sport became even more intensified when, following the intervening period of independence, Roman overlordship was substituted for Greek, and theaters and *circuses were linked together as the very antithesis of "synagogue and school." To the considerations which applied to the gymnasia were the added factors of cruelty associated with Roman sport, which was not confined to the characteristic aspect of gladiatorial contests, and also the fact that at the theaters the Jews were made the butt of satire, parody, and mockery (cf. Lam. R. intro. 17). The first sentence of the Book of Psalms, "Happy is the man… who sat not in the seat of the scorners" was made to apply to those who refrained from attending "theaters and circuses and did not attend gladiatorial combats" (Pes. 148b), and the humane aspect of the opposition finds expression in the ruling that "one is permitted to go to stadiums if by his shouting he may save the victim" (Av. Zar. 18b). At one period of his life the famous *amora* Simeon b. Lakish (Resh Lakish) was a professional gladiator (Git. 47a), but he justified this on the grounds of grim necessity. The very vehemence of the denunciation of the rabbis would seem to point to the fact that participation in, or at least attendance at, those sports by Jews was widespread.

The first Jewish ruler to encourage sports was Herod. Between 37 and 4 B.C.E. he erected sports stadia in Caesarea, Sebaste, Tiberias, Jericho, and other cities, and also introduced a Palestinian Olympiad with sports competition every five years. He brought athletes from all parts of the world to compete in gladiatorial games and contests of boxing, racing, archery, and other sports, and also contributed large sums to the Olympic games in Greece. His extensive activities in this sphere were, however, part of his program of the "romanization" of the realm.

Middle Ages

There are a few references to organized sport during the Middle Ages. According to *Shevet Yehudah* (ch. 8), Jews in Spain distinguished themselves in the art of fencing. An examination of all the data given in I. Abrahams' *Jewish Life in the Middle Ages* (1932², repr. 1960, 397–411) reveals that, almost without exception, the instances which purport to prove that the Jews indulged in sport belong either to recreations like strolling, self-defense, dancing, and intellectual pastimes, such as chess and riddles, or to children's games. There is a reference by Jerome in the fourth century to Jewish boys in Syria lifting heavy stones "to train their muscular strength" (to Zech. 12:4) and in the 13th century it was the custom to hold tournaments and jousts as part of marriage celebrations. Isaac Or Zaru'a refers to "young men who go out on horseback to greet the bridegroom, and indulge in combats with one another, and tear one another's garments or cause injury to the horse" (Hil. Sukkot ve-Lulav no. 315). He ruled that the injured party had no claim for damages since he had been partaking in a joyous occasion. In Provence the Jews trained falcons and engaged in hawking on horseback. On the other hand, in the 15th century Israel *Bruna, in answer to a question whether it was permitted to even attend non-Jewish horse-racing competitions, gave guarded permission only because one could thereby judge the quality of the horses and learn to ride "in order to escape from one's enemies." "Nevertheless," he added, "I doubt whether it is permitted to go and see such races as are intended merely as jousting tournaments for pleasure" (Resp. 71).

The most popular sports in the Middle Ages appear to have been ball games. Although the Midrash (Lam. R. 2:4) gives as one of the reasons for the destruction of the Temple that "in Tur Malka they played ball games on the Sabbath." Moses Isserles, disagreeing with Joseph Caro, permitted ball playing on the Sabbath and festivals and stated that in his time (16th century) it was customary to do so (Sh. Ar., OḤ 308:45), and on festivals (when there is no prohibition against carrying) it is permitted "even in a public domain and even for pure sport" (*ibid.* 518:2). He based himself upon Tosafot (to Beẓah 12a), which states explicitly that "we find that they play with the ball called *pelota*" (cf. the modern Basque game called by the same name). No details are given; according to one authority, however, "it was very like handball but, instead of being struck by the hand, the ball was caught in a long narrow scoop-like basket attached firmly to the wrist and thrown against the wall" (JQR, 26 (1935/36), 4).

In 1386 there were Jewish tourneys in Wiesenfeld, Germany. In the 15th century, competitions were held in Augsburg, Germany, in running, jumping, throwing, and bowling, in which Jews also participated. *Immanuel of Rome mentions "boys who trained in stone throwing" (in his *Maḥbarot* 22, no. 42). In this same century, at the popular festivals initiated in Rome, sports competitions were also included: Monday was for youth, Tuesday for Jews (under 20 years of age), Wednesday for older boys, and so on. The Jews were obliged to provide precious carpets as prizes. It is known that Jews distinguished themselves in these games in 1487, 1502, and 1595. There is even a song about Jewish runners, composed in 1513. These games and festivals continued for some 200 years despite the fact that during these years the mob interfered with the Jewish runners, who participated half naked. In 1443 there was a registration of a Jew who knew "wrestling without shedding blood."

In the 16th century there was a famous Austrian converted Jew by the name of Ott who was outstanding at the Augsburg games and was even invited to the court of the Austrian prince in order to train the courtiers. He wrote a book in which wrestling was separated from fencing for the first time and was known as "Ottish Wrestling." There was also a book on fencing published by Andres Jud, who, together with his brother Jacob Lignitzer, took special care of fencing. The decrees of Rudolph II show how important fencing was for the Jews in Germany. Among these decrees was one which forbade Christian fencing teachers to train Jews and, later on, also forbade competitions between Jews and Christians. There is little information about sport in the 17th and 18th centuries.

Despite the examples given, there is no doubt that S.W. Baron is correct in stating that during the Middle Ages sporadic voices in favor of recreational pauses were as ineffective as those which advocated physical exercises. Northern Jewry especially had little use for physical education and paid little heed even to the injunction of a talmudic sage that a father give his son instruction in swimming as a "life-saving precaution." It is only in the modern period that sports became popular and widespread among Jews.

Modern Era

Though most Jews in the 19th century lived in conditions unfavorable to athletic pursuits, a number of them in England, Germany, Hungary, Canada, France, Austria, and the United States did well in a variety of sports. In 1896, six Jewish athletes won 13 medals at the first modern Olympic games in Athens.

In a speech before the Second Zionist Congress in 1898, Max *Nordau asked the Jewish people to renew their interest in sports and physical fitness. Nordau's call for "muscular Judaism" was answered by the *Maccabi movement, which spread first to the countries of Europe and Palestine and then around the world. Over 100 Maccabi clubs were in existence in Europe by the beginning of World War I. The largest of these clubs – Ha-Koah of Vienna, Bar Kochba of Berlin, and Ha-Gibor of Prague – became famous for their outstanding teams. It was Hungary, however, that produced the most successful Jewish athletes in Europe. Hungarian Jews won numerous Olympic medals in various sports.

Early in the 20th century immigrant Jewish children in Great Britain and the United States learned to play the games of their new countries in youth clubs, settlement houses, and YM-YWHAs. Living in crowded urban areas, they became proficient in sports which required little space and equipment, such as boxing, handball, table tennis, basketball, gymnastics, and wrestling. Professional sports, particularly boxing and basketball, attracted many Jews, who used athletic scholarships to gain admission to some U.S. colleges.

The sports picture changed radically for Jews following World War II. In the affluent communities of North and South America and in Western Europe, the emphasis shifted to social sports, such as tennis, golf, polo, yachting, and squash. Most Jews attending colleges in the United States could afford to pay tuition fees and participate in university sports for recreation. When Jews were excluded from established yacht and country clubs they organized their own.

Jews were active in formulating sports programs in the Soviet Union during the 1920s, and after World War II they contributed to that nation's successful entry into international competition. Many Soviet Jews have been accorded the title "Honored Master of Sport."

[Jesse Harold Silver]

In Israel before 1948

Physical education was first introduced into Jewish schools in Ereẓ Israel toward the end of the 19th century by Yeshayahu *Press and Heinrich Eliakum *Loewe. The first Jewish sports clubs in the country, the Rishon le-Zion Club in Jaffa and the Bar Giora Club in Jerusalem, were established in 1906 by Leo Cohen and Aviezer *Yellin, respectively, and shortly afterward the first qualified club leaders were appointed. In 1908, the first national sports competition – the Reḥovot Festival – was organized under the leadership of Ẓevi Nishri (d. 1973) and was held annually until the outbreak of World War I. Sports outside the framework of the schools were organized by voluntary organizations associated in varying degrees with social or political movements.

MACCABI. Maccabi started as an apolitical sports organization, but was favored by the General Zionists. The first Maccabi club was established in Jerusalem in 1911 and soon had 300 members. A second club was formed in Petaḥ Tikvah, and the two clubs, together with the Rishon le-Zion Club in Jaffa, formed the countrywide Maccabi Organization in 1912. Maccabi did not confine its activities to sports. It was active in cultural affairs and fought for the recognition and dissemination of the Hebrew language, the employment of Jewish labor, and Jewish self-defense. On the eve of World War I, it had about 1,000 members in 15 clubs. With the participation of Maccabi and the *Ha-Shomer movement in the Reḥovot Festival in 1913, a genuine national Jewish sports movement seemed to have emerged.

Even before the outbreak of World War I, however, the first signs of the dissolution of this movement were visible. Maccabi boycotted the Reḥovot Festival of 1914 because Arab guards and Arab workers were employed in the village. On the other hand, the Jewish workers alleged that the Maccabi clubs had fallen under the control of the landowners and employers. It therefore came as no surprise when the Reḥovot Festival was not revived after the war and Maccabi organized its own festival, the first Maccabi games, in 1920.

DEVELOPMENT OF PHYSICAL EDUCATION. Physical education in Palestine was given a new lease by the arrival of several experienced Jewish athletes as part of the wave of Jewish immigration that followed the end of World War I. The newcomers included David Almagor, gymnast and wrestler from Cairo, Yehoshua Alouf, one of the best gymnasts in Maccabi-Warsaw, and Dr. Emanuel Simon, one of the best track and field men in the Bar-Kochba Club in Berlin, who all contributed to the expansion and improvement of physical education in the schools and the Maccabi clubs.

ESTABLISHMENT OF HA-POEL. The workers, for their part, began to organize their sports clubs in 1924, and in 1926 they founded a countrywide workers' sports organization under the name of '*Ha-Poel as an affiliate of the *Histadrut. A year later Ha-Poel joined the International Workers' Sports Federation. Initially, the main objective of Ha-Poel was to cater to the masses, rather than to breed champion athletes. In 1935 there were 10,000 participants in its fourth festival. These festivals are still held once every five years. Maccabi, by contrast, laid greater emphasis on competitive sports and devoted its energies to organizing them on a national basis, as well as introducing Palestine to the international sports arena.

SOCCER INTRODUCED. The establishment of the British Mandatory regime in Palestine after World War I had a marked effect on local sports. Whereas prior to the war, gymnastics had been the dominant sport, under Eastern and Central European influence, it was now supplanted by soccer due to the influence of the British army teams which competed with the Maccabi teams. In 1925 the Organization of Jewish Soccer Clubs was founded. In 1928 the Palestine Football Association – the first national sports federation – was established. It comprised British, Jewish, and Arab teams and was the only body in which Maccabi and Ha-Poel cooperated until after the establishment of the State of Israel. Through the association, Palestine – and later Israel – has been represented in the World Cup Championships regularly since 1936.

THE MACCABIAH: ENTRY INTO INTERNATIONAL SPORTS. Maccabi initiated the establishment of the Palestine Amateur Sports Federation in 1931 in order to take part in international competitions, and was accepted by most federations. Two years later, the Palestine Olympic Committee was set up. Maccabi's greatest achievement prior to World War II was the organization of the international *Maccabiah Games in 1932, in which 500 Jewish athletes from 23 countries participated and 1,500 in a gymnastic display. At the second Maccabiah, in 1935, there were 1,700 participants from 27 countries. As many of the athletes, accompanying personnel, and tourists remained in the country after the contest was over, the Maccabiah became not only a means of stimulating sports, but also an important lever for the promotion of *aliyah*. The Second Maccabiah was even more of an "Aliyah Maccabiah," since most of the participants and their escorts remained in Palestine, in view of the wave of antisemitism sweeping Europe after the Nazi accession to power in Germany. Y. Alouf was the chief organizer of the first five Maccabiah Games.

Maccabi was also the first body to send a delegation to an official event in Asia (the West Asian Games in New Delhi in 1934) and to an international event for women (the London Games in 1934). In the same period, Ha-Poel athletes twice represented Palestine in Workers' Olympics, in Vienna (1931) and Antwerp (1937). An invitation to participate in the Berlin Olympics in 1936 under the Nazi regime was rejected for obvious reasons and, as a result, the appearance of Palestinian or Israel athletes in the Olympics was delayed for 16 years. (The Games were not held in 1940 and 1944. In 1948 the Palestine Olympic Committee no longer existed, the Israel Olympic Committee had not yet been recognized, and Israel was fighting for survival.)

Between 1924 and 1939 young Jews from Palestine studied physical education in Denmark, and the number of qualified physical education teachers in the schools increased. In 1938, Yehoshua Alouf was appointed the first supervisor of physical education. One of his achievements was the organization of the first countrywide inter-school competitions. In 1939 the Va'ad Le'ummi set up a department of physical education, which was to become the government body responsible for sports on the establishment of the State of Israel (since 1961 it has been known as the Sports Authority). The department, as it was then, introduced a course for physical education teachers that was later expanded into a permanent college for physical education teachers. The department also published books on physical education.

In the State of Israel

PHYSICAL EDUCATION. With the establishment of the State of Israel, the number of schools increased enormously, and sports facilities improved. Physical education is taught twice weekly in schools throughout Israel. Some 70,000 pupils participate in annual sports competitions, which include track and field, basketball, volleyball, handball, swimming, and soccer. About 70,000 pupils participate annually in the "Sports Badge" trials, and outstanding pupils are invited for advanced training lasting from three to twelve days.

In addition to supervising sports and physical education in the schools, the authority encourages sports throughout the country and gives financial assistance to the Wingate Institute for Physical Education, which comprises a three-year college for physical education teachers run by the Ministry of Education and Culture, a three-year school for physiotherapists, a one-year course for coaches, and a school for physical training instructors of the Israel Defense Forces.

The Sports Authority lays special emphasis on popular sports, such as marching, running, swimming, etc. It provides financial assistance for the provision of sports facilities and the publication of sports literature. In addition to the one at the Wingate Institute, there are three other colleges of physical education in the country: one in Tel Aviv, at a seminar run by the kibbutz movements; one in Beersheba; and a third, a religious college, at Givat Washington.

ORGANIZATION OF SPORT IN ISRAEL. World War II took a heavy toll of Jewish athletes, and it was only with great reservations that the Third Maccabiah was organized in 1950. On this occasion, Israel's team for the first time included athletes from Maccabi and Ha-Poel, and this made a major contribution to the unification of Israeli sports one year later. The Maccabiah was held again in 1953 and then 1957 and was a quadrennial event thereafter. In 1951, Maccabi and Ha-Poel agreed to cooperate on the Israel Olympic Committee and the Israel Sports

Federation. The two associations were already represented on the Israel Football Association.

In 1970, over 40,000 athletes participated in organized competitive athletics in Israel. Fifteen thousand came under the jurisdiction of the Israel Sports Federation, which controls 14 sports; 13,000 belonged to the Israel Football Association; 9,000 to the Israel Basketball Association; and the rest to smaller associations controlling tennis, judo, and other sports. All sports are amateur, and a much greater number of people are active in noncompetitive sports. The major sports organizations are: Ha-Poel, with 300 branches and 85,000 members; Maccabi, with 75 branches and 18,000 members; Elitzur (founded 1939) for religious youth, with 80 branches and 10,000 members; Betar (founded in 1924), affiliated to Ḥerut, with 74 branches and 5,000 members; Academic Sports Association (1953) with nine branches in the institutes of higher education and 5,000 members.

IN INTERNATIONAL SPORTS. Israel participated in the Olympic Games for the first time in Helsinki in 1952 and thereafter at all subsequent games. Since 1954 it has also competed at the Asian Games (with the exception of the Jakarta Games in 1962, which were canceled due to a boycott of Israel by Indonesia). Israel has made endeavors to integrate into Asian sport, except in basketball and volleyball, where it belongs to the zone covering Europe and the Mediterranean countries. The efforts of Arab countries to boycott Israel have generally been frustrated by international sports bodies. Israel's achievements in international sports have been modest. The Israel national soccer team reached the World Cup Championships in Mexico in 1970, after defeating Australia in the eliminating round, and acquitted itself creditably. The small Israel team at the 1970 Asian games at Bangkok won six gold medals, six silver, and five bronze, finishing in sixth place. Israel tennis players have competed at Wimbledon and in Davis Cup matches, and since 1962 a youth team has competed at Miami Beach. Gliding has been practiced in Israel for over 30 years, and free-fall parachuting has recently been introduced. Israel won the Asian Football Championships once, the Asian Youth Championships four times, and the Asian Champions' Cup twice. Up to June 1969, Israel's basketball team had won 62 out of 126 official international games.

In recent years, dinghy sailing has become popular, and in 1969 Ẓefania Carmel and Lydia Lazarov won the world championships in the 420 class in Sweden. In the following year the championships were held in Israel off Tel Aviv.

NONCOMPETITIVE SPORTS. The most popular noncompetitive sports event in Israel are the annual Three-Day March to Jerusalem, organized by the Israel Defense Forces, the swim across Lake Kinneret (Sea of Galilee, started by Ha-Poel), and the cross-country race around Mount Tabor. The Three-Day (originally Four-Day) March is in a category of its own. It is not the same as hiking, which may be motivated by the wish to "get away from it all"; nor is it comparable with the walking race, for it is not a race at all. It has been most aptly described as Israel's folk "happening," although the idea was taken from a similar Dutch event. Thousands of people of all ages – organized in clubs or in family groups, coming from offices, factories, banks, or hospitals, and some individuals – go out tramping over the hills around Jerusalem together with contingents of soldiers in training. Visitors from overseas also participate. The army builds camps and lays on entertainment facilities for the participants, and the event culminates in a march through the streets of Jerusalem. One-day marches are also held in other parts of the country organized by Maccabi and Ha-Poel, and an Israel Defense Forces contingent participates every year at the annual Four-Day March in Holland. Ha-Poel has organized sports activities in factories and offices. Cross-country running also has a special Israel character: the route, and sometimes the date of the event, is usually related to some event in the Bible or Jewish history. On *Ḥanukkah, for instance, relays of runners from Maccabi carry torches from Modi'in, birthplace of the Maccabees, to the presidential residence in Jerusalem, as well as to various other parts of the country. There is also the annual run around Mount Tabor. The annual swim across Lake Kinneret, from Ein Gev to Tiberias; the Haifa Bay swim; and the "crossing of the Red Sea" at Eilat, are mass events with a competitive element. As in the annual marches, all participants who complete the course are awarded certificates and, for some events, medallions.

[Yehoshua Alouf and Uriel Simri]

1968–2005. The third decade of the existence of the State of Israel was marked by a significant improvement of its representative sports and by the intervention of politics into the activities of Israel sports on the international scene. At the beginning of the decade the improvement was modest. Thus at the Olympic Games of Mexico (1968), Israel had only a fifth place in soccer to show. Two years later, however, the soccer team of Israel was to return to Mexico as one of the 16 teams participating in the World Cup (for professionals and amateurs).

The year 1969 saw Israeli athletes gain their first world championship, when Zefanya Carmel and Lydia Lazarov became world champions in sailing in the (non-Olympic) 420 class. Since then Israel has gained six more world championships in this event, the recipients being Joel Sela, Yoram Kedar, Mordechai Amberam, Eitan Friedlander, Shimshon Brockman, and Amnon Samgura.

In 1970 Israel was represented by 27 athletes in the Asian Games at Bangkok, and they returned with 6 gold, 6 silver and 5 bronze medals. Four years later the Israeli delegation (61 athletes) was to return with 7 gold, 4 silver and 8 bronze medals from the Asian Games in Teheran. The appearance at the games in Teheran may have been Israel's last major appearance on the scene of Asian sports which, under Arab influence, has increasingly brought politics into the sphere of sports, with the result that Israel was excluded from the Asian Games of 1978, under the pretext of "security reasons" and it was prevented from participating in many other Asian events.

Arab terrorism played havoc on Israeli sports, and 11 Israeli coaches and athletes paid with their lives during an Arab attack on the Olympic Village at Munich on September 5, 1972. This attack, however, did not prevent Israel from appearing on the international sport scene. In fact, it returned with a bigger and stronger delegation to the Olympic Games in Montreal (1976), gaining a fifth (Edouard Weitz in weightlifting), a sixth (Esther Rot in hurdling), a seventh (Rami Meron in wrestling), and a twelfth place (Micha Kaufmann in shooting) in individual events, while the national soccer team reached the last eight in the Olympic tournament. Esther Rot can definitely be considered Israel's top athlete of this decade, having been elected five times (1970, 1971, 1974, 1975, 1976) athlete of the year in Israel.

Tennis has come to the fore as a popular sport, with 14 centers having opened in various parts of Israel. The most outstanding Israeli tennis player is Shlomo Glickstein (b. 1958), who first entered the national Israeli youth championship competition at the age of 10 and won the title for his age group. He went on to compete in international events, and by the end of 1981 was seeded 30 in the rankings of the Association of Tennis Professionals.

Basketball continued to be Israel's best representative sport during this period. Major achievements were: Asian Games championships (1970, 1974), the European Cup for nations (1976) and the victory of Maccabi Tel Aviv in the European Cup for champions in 1977 and 1981. Furthermore, basketball became the first sport in which an Israel national team defeated a national team of the U.S.S.R. when Israel won its game in the European junior championship in 1972. Israel also placed sixth in the Intercontinental Cup of 1977 and fifth in the European championship of that year. A striking victory in this sphere of sport was the defeat of the Washington Bullets, the champions of the U.S. National Basketball Association by Maccabi Tel Aviv in September 1978 by the narrow margin of 98–97. The major sport events in Israel during this period were again the Maccabiah Games (the eighth in 1969, the ninth in 1973, the tenth in 1977, the eleventh in 1981), and the International Hapoel Games (the ninth in 1971 and the tenth in 1975). Other major events held in Israel include: The Olympic Games for the Disabled (1968); the International Spring Cup in volleyball (1970, 1976); the world championship in sailing in the 420 class (1970); the Eight Nations' Cup in swimming (1971, 1978); and the European junior championship in judo (1974).

At the end of the 1970s Israel was attempting to enter the European sport scene, as a result of its rejection by Asian sport organizations. Up to date Israel has been accepted into the European region of seven sports and is continuing its efforts to be accepted in more European federations.

In January 1979, the praesidium of the Israel Olympic committee issued a statement breaking off all sporting relations with South Africa, apparently in order to remove any objection to Israel's participation in the Olympic Games scheduled to be held in Moscow the following year. At a plenary meeting of the IOC held a few days later, however, it rejected the statement. Ultimately Israel did not participate in the 1980 Moscow Olympics.

[Uriel Simri]

The following years were noted in Israel's sports for two major breakthroughs – one in the political domain, the other in the athletic arena.

The political breakthrough began in 1989, when the Soviet Union, under President Gorbachev, relented in its opposition to the acceptance of Israel into the European zone of the various international sport federations. Thus Israel, which had been without a continental affiliation since its expulsion from Asian sports in the mid-1970s, was able to enter the European federations and their regular activities. By 1992 this procedure had been completed for all practical purposes, the European Soccer Federation (UEFA) being one of the last federations that had not granted Israel full membership status. At the same time, from 1987 UEFA invited Israel's youth teams to participate in its championships and in 1992 invited the national champion as well as the cup-holder to participate in the annual competitions organized by it.

The major breakthrough in athletics occurred during the Olympic Games in Barcelona in the summer of 1992, when two Judokas succeeded in bringing to Israel for the first time Olympic medals – Yael Arad returning with the silver medal in women's 61 kg. class and Oren Smadja with the bronze medal in the men's 71 kg. class.

Israel had, in fact, been very close to gaining its first Olympic medals already at Seoul in 1988. However, Joel Sela and Eldad Amir had to be satisfied with a fourth place in the Flying Dutchman class of the Olympic yachting competitions, after forfeiting one race because it was held on Yom Kippur. The same couple was placed eighth in the 1984 Olympics at Los Angeles. Similar placings, which were the best during those Olympics, were achieved by the yachtsmen Shimshon Brockman and Eitan Friedlander in the 470 class, as well as by the marksman Yitzchak Yonassi.

In Israel's representation at the Barcelona Olympics, 11 out of the 31 representatives were newcomers to the State of Israel, primarily from the former Soviet Union. The top achievements of those newcomers were the sixth place of weightlifter Andre Danisov in the 100 kg. class and the eighth place of Yevgeni Krasnov in the pole vault.

The significant improvement of the standard of the top athletes can further be seen from a list of achievements in recent years in other sports. In July 1992 Johar Abu-Lashin, a Christian Arab from Nazareth, became the first Israeli professional athlete to gain a world champion's title, when he became lightweight champion of the World Boxing Federation. The same year windsurfer Amit Inbar was placed second in the world championship (and a disappointing eighth in the Olympics), after having ranked first in the previous year. Another newcomer from the Soviet Union, the wrestler Max Geller, succeeded in winning the silver medal at the European championships in freestyle wrestling in 1991.

On the other hand basketball, which had been the outstanding sport in Israel for its quality for a long time, had its ups and downs. Whereas the men's national team was placed second in the European championship in 1979, sixth in 1981, and fifth in 1983, it receded to ninth place in 1985, to eleventh in 1987, and thereafter did not qualify for the final stages of the championship (until 1993). However, in 1986 the team succeeded for the second time in history (after 1954) to qualify for the final stages of the world championship, where it came seventh.

The Maccabi Tel Aviv basketball team also did not succeed in repeating its earlier successes (wins in 1977 and 1981) in the European Champions' Cup games. Although the team reached the finals three years in a row (1987–1989), it was beaten at that stage by teams from Italy and Yugoslavia. The women's national team in basketball succeeded in 1990 to reach the "final eight" in the continental championship, but this turned out to be a one-time achievement.

Israel's tennis managed to be in the limelight from 1986 until 1989, when the men's team held its place among the top 16 nations in the world within the framework of the Davis Cup games. As of 1990 attempts to return to the top have not been successful. The above achievement was mainly due to Israel's no. 1 player, Amos Mansdorf, who at the peak of his career (in 1987) ranked no. 18 in the world. In the following years Mansdorf had a ranking around no. 30.

While soccer remained Israel's most popular sport, the Football Association had very little to show as far as achievements on the international scene were concerned. In 1989, Israel came closest to repeating its appearance in the final stages of the World Cup (the first and only time was in 1970), but drew with Colombia in Ramat Gan, after losing by a single goal in the away game. Israel reached this stage after winning the zone of Oceania, to which it was removed by FIFA as a result of the Asian boycott and UEFA's refusal, up to that time, to let Israel participate in the European zone.

In 1988 the Knesset passed the "Sports Law," after tabling it for 13 years. Its major provisions called for mandatory certification of coaches and instructors; mandatory health and loss of income insurance of athletes participating in competitive sports; mandatory periodical medical examinations for participants in competitive sports; and prohibition of the use of any doping materials. The Minister of Education and Culture was given a number of regulatory powers within the framework of the law.

The Knesset also approved, early in 1991, the appointment of a deputy minister in the Ministry of Education and Culture to be in charge of sports. When the Labor Party returned to power in 1992, it too appointed a deputy minister.

The quadrennial Maccabiah and the Hapoel Games continued to be the major sports events in the country. While the participation in the Maccabiah Games expanded – in 1989 athletes from the former Communist bloc participated for the first time – the athletic standard of the Games left much to be desired. The Hapoel Games, on the other hand, developed in scope and in standard up to 1987, but were greatly reduced in 1991 as a result of a serious financial deficit.

Israeli team sports in the 1990s and early 2000s were dominated by the Maccabi Tel Aviv basketball team, which continued to sweep local league play and won three European championships under Coach Pini *Gershon (2001, 2003, 2004) after a long drought in international competition. Local basketball also developed a number of superstars, most playing for Maccabi but some also for European teams. Among them were Doron Jamche, Doron Shefer, Gur Shelef, Tal Burstein, and Oded Katash, who led Greece's Panathinaikos to a championship win over Maccabi, his former team, in 2000. In women's basketball, Elitzur Holon built a parallel dynasty, taking 18 Israeli cups and 20 Israeli league championships between 1977 and 1996. Israeli Shay Doron was an All-American guard at Maryland and led the Terrapins to an NCAA Championship in 2006.

Women's tennis also made great strides, with two standouts on the WTA tour. Anna Smashnova finished the 2002 and 2003 seasons with a No. 16 world ranking and through 2005 had taken 11 titles (in 11 finals), chalking up over $2 million in winnings. Nineteen-year-old Shahar Peer climbed to No. 23 in June 2006. In 2002 Alex Averbach took the gold medal in the pole vault at the European championships, a first for an Israeli athlete, and in 2004 Gal Fridman won Israel's first Olympic gold medal, taking it in windsurfing.

[Uriel Simri / Elli Wohlgelernter (2nd ed.)]

JEWISH ATHLETES

Association Football (Soccer)

Shortly after 1900, the Bohr brothers, Neils Henrik David (1885–1962) and Harald August (1887–1951), of Denmark, became famous soccer players in Scandinavia. In 1908 Harald won a silver medal in the first Olympic soccer competition. Other *Olympic medalists included Sandor Geller (Hungary) in 1952 (gold); Boris Razinsky (1933–) (U.S.S.R.) in 1956 (gold), and Arpad Orban (1938–) (Hungary) in 1964 (gold). In the 1920s, Austria's Hakoah-Vienna All-Stars, an outstanding all-Jewish team, played a series of matches in Palestine and the United States. In New York City in 1926 Hakoah-Vienna set a U.S. single-game attendance record (46,000) that was not broken for over 40 years. Many of the teammates of Hakoah-Vienna left Austria in the 1930s and continued their soccer careers in Palestine and the United States. Bela Guttmann (1900–1981), a Hungarian who also played for Budapest's MTK Club, became one of the world's top soccer coaches in the 1950s and 1960s.

The Meisel brothers, Hugo (1895–1968) and Willy (1897–1967), were Austrian soccer personalities. Willy, who became one of Europe's most respected sportswriters, was a goalkeeper for the Austrian national team; Hugo founded the International or World Cup competition in 1927 and was head of the Austrian Football Association in the 1930s. Hungary produced many outstanding Jewish players, coaches, and administrators, beginning with a member of the first national team, Olympic swimmer and medalist Alfred Hajos (Arnold Guttmann)

(1878–1955), the first modern Olympic swimming champion, and his brother, Henrik. Mark Lazarus (1938–) was a British soccer player. In the Soviet Union, Mikhail Romm was one of the organizers of soccer in the 1920s, and Mikhail Loshinsky played on the national team before World War II.

The Israel Football Federation was founded in Palestine in 1928 and its first international match was played in 1934. The first side representing the State of Israel played in New York City in 1948. Israel reached the quarterfinal round in the 1968 Olympic Games and the final round of 16 in the World Cup competition in 1970. The star of the team was the captain, Mordechai ("Mottele") Spiegler.

American soccer pioneer Nathan Agar (1887–1978) introduced soccer in the New York City area in 1904 and helped found the United States Football Association in 1913. In 1929 the all-Jewish Hakoah All-Stars of New York City won the National Challenge Cup.

Johan Neeskens (1951–) played for Ajax of Amsterdam, which won the European Cup in 1971–73, and for World Cup finalist Netherlands in 1974 and 1978. As a player for the New York Cosmos, he was named to the North American Soccer League All-Star team in 1979.

Goalie Shep *Messing (1949–) was a member of the 1972 United States Olympic team and the 1977 North American League champion New York Cosmos. Goalkeeper Arnold Mausser (1954–) of the Tampa Bay Rowdies was named American Player of the Year in the North American Soccer League in 1976, and goalie Alan Mayer was accorded the same honor in 1978. Mayer played for the San Diego Sockers.

The Maccabee Club of Los Angeles, which included a number of Israeli students, won the United States National Challenge Cup in 1973, 1975, and 1977–78.

Alan Rothenberg, a lawyer, was elected president of the U.S. Soccer Federation in 1990. Rothenberg served as commissioner of soccer in the 1984 Olympic Games. In 1990 Henry Kissinger, former U.S. secretary of state, was named vice chairman of the U.S. World Cup '94 organizing committee.

Yair Allnut was a member of the 1992 U.S. Olympic Games team and a gold medalist in the 1991 Pan American Games. Jeff Agoos (1968–) had 134 international appearances with the national team, played with the U.S. Under-15, Under-17, Under-20, World University and Indoor National Teams, and was a member of five championship teams during his MLS career. Debbi Belkin played with the U.S. gold medal team in the inaugural Women's World Championships in China in 1991. Arcady Gaydamak (Ari Barlev, 1952–), a Russian-Israeli billionaire, bought the Betar Jerusalem soccer team in August 2005. He is also owner of the Hapoel Jerusalem basketball team. His son, Alexandre "Sasha" Gaydamak, bought a 50 percent share of the Portsmouth FC soccer team in January 2006.

Automobile Racing

Britain's Woolf Barnato (1895–1948), a director of Bentley Motors and son of Barney *Barnato of South African diamond fame, won three consecutive Le Mans 24-hour Grand Prix of Endurance races in 1928–30. In a 14-year career, Rene Dreyfus (1905–1993) of France triumphed in 36 races and gained the Grand Prix of Monaco (1930) and the Grand Prix of Belgium (1934). After winning the national driving championship in 1936, Mauri *Rose (1906–1981) of the United States drove to three victories (1941, 1947, and 1948) in the Indianapolis 500-mile classic. Sheila Van Damm (1922–1987) of Great Britain was the European women's driving champion in 1954–55. Robert Grossman (1923–) of the United States placed among the top ten finishers in six consecutive Le Mans races (1959–64). Peter Revson (1939–1974) of the United States won the World Challenge Cup in 1968, the 1973 British and Canadian Grand Prix events and was runner-up at the 1971 Indianapolis 500, but was killed during a practice run in 1974. American Steve Krisiloff placed fourth in the 1978 Indianapolis 500. Jody *Scheckter (1950–) of South Africa placed third in the world driving championships in 1974 and was runner-up in 1977. His Grand Prix victories included Swedish (1974 and 1976); British (1974); South African (1975) and Argentinean, Monegasque and Canadian in 1977. In 1979 Scheckter won the Belgian, Monegasque and Italian Grand Prix events and became South Africa's first world driving champion. He retired from international racing competition after the 1980 season. Kenny Bernstein (1944–) won a record-tying four consecutive U.S. National Hot Rod Association Funny Car Championships in 1985–88. He switched to the Top Fuel class in 1990 and the following year had a record six victories in a season. In 1992 Bernstein recorded four wins and became the first drag racer to cover a quarter mile at more than 300 miles per hour.

Baseball

Jews early developed an interest in baseball, which had its origins in the 1840s. Lipman E. (Lip) *Pike became baseball's first professional in 1866 when he played third base for the Philadelphia Athletics at a salary of $20 per week. In 1882 Louis Kramer (1849–1922) helped organize the major league American Association, and was its president in 1891. Aaron S. Stern (1853–1920), a clothing merchant, was a co-founder of the American Association and owner of the Cincinnati Reds in 1882–90. The Reds won the first American Association championship in 1882. Other officials of the Cincinnati club included Edgar Mayer Johnson (1836–?), secretary, 1877–80, and Nathan Menderson (1820–1904), president, 1880. Jacob C. (Jake) Morse (1860–1937), who became a noted sportswriter, was manager of the Boston team in the Union League in 1884. Barney *Dreyfuss, president of the Louisville Colonels in 1899 and owner of the Pittsburgh Pirates from 1900 to 1932, founded the World Series in 1903. One of the game's most controversial owners, Andrew Freedman (1860–1915), a lawyer and a power behind New York City's Tammany Hall, was president of the New York Giants in 1894–1902. Louis W. Heilbroner (1861–1933) managed the St. Louis Cardinals in 1900, and nine years later founded baseball's first statistical bureau. Harry (Judge) Goldman (1857–1941) was an organizer of the American League in 1900, and with the Frank brothers, Moses and Sydney, served as an official of the Baltimore club in the new league in 1901–2. Besides Pike, the outstanding players prior to 1900 were William M. (Billy) Nash (1865–1929), a third baseman who played in the major leagues for 15 years, a member of pennant-winning teams in 1890 (Boston, Players League) and 1891–93 (Boston, National League), and manager of Philadelphia in 1896; James John (Chief) Roseman (1856–1938), an outfielder with the New York team that won the American Association pennant in 1884, and player/manager of the St. Louis club in the same league in 1890; and Daniel E. Stearns (1861–1944), first baseman on the Cincinnati team that won the first American Association championship in 1882.

Players who gained success in the major leagues after 1900 included Hank *Greenberg (1911–1986), the first Jewish member of the Baseball Hall of Fame; pitching great Sandy *Koufax (1935–), first Jewish pitcher and youngest player ever elected to the Baseball Hall of Fame; and Lou *Boudreau (1917–2001), a member of the Hall of Fame whose mother was from an Orthodox Jewish family. Al *Rosen (1924–), third baseman, American League home run champion in 1950 and 1953, voted the league's Most Valuable Player in 1953; Erskine Mayer (1891–1957), a pitcher who won 21 games for the Philadelphia Phillies in 1914 and 1915; Charles Solomon (Buddy) Myer (1904–1974), an infielder with Washington and Boston for 17 years who played in the 1925 and 1933 World Series, won the League batting title of 1935, and compiled the lifetime batting mark of .303; Larry *Sherry (1935–), pitching hero of the Los Angeles Dodgers in the 1959 World Series; Art *Shamsky (1941–), an outfielder who hit four home runs in four consecutive at bats and batted.300 for the 1969 World Champion New York Mets; and Kenny Holtzman (1945–), who had the most number of wins for a Jewish pitcher and who pitched no-hitters in 1969 and 1972.

Also George R. Stone (1876–1945), an outfielder for the St. Louis Browns who won the American League batting title in 1906; Barney Pelty (1880–1939), pitcher, compiled a 2.62 earned run average in a ten-year (1903–12) American League career with the St. Louis Browns and Washington Senators; Benjamin M. (Benny) Kauff (1890–1961), outfielder, was the batting champion of the Federal League in 1914 and 1915, and a member of the National League champion New York Giants in 1917; Sid *Gordon (1917–1975), 1941–43, 1946–55; Harry Danning (1911–2004), 1933–42; Saul Rogovin (1922–1995), 1949–53, 1955–57; Samuel A. (Sammy) Bohne (Cohen) (1896–1977); Andrew (Andy) Cohen (1904–1988), 1926, 1928–29; Calvin (Cal) *Abrams (1924–1997), 1949–56; Morris (Morrie) Arnovich (1910–1959), 1936–41, 1946; Harry Eisenstat (1915–2003), 1935–42; Harry Feldman (1919–1962), 1941–46; Myron (Joe) Ginsberg (1926–), 1948, 1950–54, 1956–62; Moe *Berg (1902–1974), an outstanding linguist as well as baseball player and a member of the U.S. Intelligence who undertook espionage in Japan and Germany, and worked for the Office of Strategic Services (OSS) during World War II, 1923, 1926–39; Barry Latman (1936–), 1957–67; James (Jim) Levey (1906–1970), 1930–33; Jimmy *Reese (1904–1994), 1930–32; Jacob (Jake) Atz (1879–1945), 1902, 1907–09; Goodwin (Goody) Rosen (1912–1994), a Canadian, 1937–39, 1944–45; Philip (Mickey) Weintraub (1907–1986), 1933–35, 37–38, 1944–45; Norman (Norm) Miller (1946–), 1965– ; Michael P. (Mike) Epstein (1943–), 1966– ; Steve *Stone (1947–), 1971–81, won the Cy Young Award in 1980; Ross Baumgarten (1955–), 1978–82; Ron Blomberg (1948–), 1969, 1971–76; Jeff Newman (1948–), 1976–84; Steve Yeager (1948–), 1972–86; Larry Rothschild (1954–), 1981–82; Scott Radinsky (1968–), 1990–93, 1995–2001; Jesse Levis (1968–), 1992–99; Alan Levine, (1968–), 1996, 1998– ; Brad Ausmus (1969–), 1993– ; Shawn *Green, (1972–), 1993– ; Mike Lieberthal, (1972–), 1994– ; Scott Schoeneweis (1973–) 1999– ; Gabe Kapler, (1975–), 1998– ; Jason Marquis, (1978–), 2000– ; Kevin Youkilis (1979–), 2004– ; Justin Wayne (1979–), 2002–2004, Adam Stern (1980–), 2005– ; and Adam Greenberg (1981–), who was hit in the head by the first pitch he saw in the Major Leagues on July 9, 2005, and was out for the remainder of the season.

Jacob A. (Jake) Pitler (1894–1968) was an infielder for the Pittsburgh Pirates (1917–18) and a popular coach for the Brooklyn Dodgers (1948–57), and Al *Schacht (1892–1984) pitched for the Washington Senators (1919–21), was a coach for the Senators and Boston Red Sox and became known as the "Clown Prince of Baseball." He was followed by Max *Patkin (1920–1999), who was also known as the "Clown Prince of Baseball" for his goofy antics as a rubber-necked, double-jointed comic genius. Dolly *Stark (1897–1968) and Al Forman (1928–) were National League umpires.

Baseball executives of the modern era included Judge Emil E. Fuchs (1879–1961), owner and manager (1929) of the National League Boston club in 1923–35; Leo J. Bondy (1883–1944), vice president of the New York Giants, 1934–44; Sidney Weil (1891–1966), owner of the Cincinnati Reds, 1930–33; William Benswanger (1892–1972), son-in-law of Barney Dreyfuss, president of the Pittsburgh Pirates, 1932–46; Harry M. Grabiner (1890–1948), vice president of the Chicago White Sox, 1939–45, and part-owner and vice president of the Cleveland Indians, 1946–48; Hank Greenberg, vice president and general manager, Cleveland Indians, Chicago White Sox, 1948 to 1963; Gabe *Paul (1910–1998), was vice president and general manager of the Cincinnati Reds (1951–1960), president and general manager of the Cleveland Indians (1961–1973), president of the New York Yankees (1974–1977), and president of the Indians (1978–1984). Jerold C. Hoffberger (1919–1999) helped return major league baseball to Baltimore in 1953, became principal owner of the Orioles in 1965, and sold the team in 1979; Marvin Milkes, general manager of the Seattle (1969) and Milwaukee (1970) teams of the American League; Charles R. Bronfman was chairman and principal owner of the Montreal Expos from 1968 to 1990. Fred Wilpon (1936–) is owner of the New York Mets; Walter Haas Jr. (1916–1995) was owner of the Oakland Athletics from 1980–1995; Lewis

Wolff, U.S., owner of the Oakland Athletics; Jerry *Reinsdorf (1936–) has been owner of the Chicago White Sox since 1981 (and the Chicago Bulls since 1985). Jeffrey Loria bought the Florida Marlins in 2002; the president is David Samson, the vice chairman is Joel Mael, and the general manager is Larry Beinfest. Stuart Sternberg became principal owner of the Tampa Bay Devil Rays in October 2005.

Al Rosen served as president of the New York Yankees (1978–79), Houston Astros (1980–1985) and San Francisco Giants (1985–1992). Bob Lurie was owner of the San Francisco Giants (1976–1992). Theo N. Epstein (1973–), son of novelist Leslie *Epstein (1938–) and grandson of Oscar-winning screenwriter Philip G. *Epstein (1909–1952), is general manager of the Boston Red Sox (2002–). Andrew Friedman is executive vice president of the Tampa Bay Devil Rays.

Harold (Lefty) Phillips (1969–71) and Norman *Sherry (1976–77) managed the American League California Angels; Larry Rothschild managed the Tampa Bay Devil Rays from 1998–2001, and was pitching coach for the Cincinnati Reds (1992–1993), Florida Marlins (1995–1997) and Chicago Cubs (2001–present).

Hank Greenberg's son, Steve, served as the deputy commissioner of baseball from 1989–93. Bud *Selig (1934–), former owner of the Milwaukee Brewers, was named chairman of baseball's executive council in 1992 and given the authority to act as commissioner.

Marvin *Miller (1917–) served as the executive director of the Major League Baseball Players Association from 1966 to 1984.

Basketball

Invented in 1891 in the United States, the game was ideally suited to the crowded urban areas where most of the nation's Jewish population lived. Jewish settlement houses on New York's East Side and Chicago's West Side gave Jewish youth their first opportunity to play the game and set many players on their way to stardom. Jews played basketball in the 1890s, and in 1900 the first Jewish professional player, Paul ("Twister") Steinberg (1880–1964), began his career at Little Falls, New York. Later he coached at Cornell University (1910–12), and for many years acted as referee at college games. Frank Basloe (1887–1966), professional player and coach of the Herkimer, New York, team, organized a squad that toured the country in 1903–23. Basloe was president of the New York State League in 1937–48. Harry Baum (1882–1959), a New York City settlement worker and professor of electrical engineering at the City College of New York, developed a style of play that made outstanding professional players of Barney *Sedran, Louis Sugarman (1890–1951), Jake Fuller (Furstman), and Max (Marty) Friedman (1889–1986). Friedman captained the World War I American Expeditionary Force team that won the Inter-Allied Games basketball tournament and introduced the sport to Europe. Other outstanding professionals of the 1910–25 era were William Cone and Emanuel (Doc) Newman (1890–?). Henry Hart Elias (1882–1941) was the first Jewish college player. He played on the initial Columbia University team in 1901; was the team's captain in 1903, and the school's first basketball coach in 1904–05. The first Jewish player to win collegiate honors, Samuel Melitzer (1888–1970), an All-East selection in 1907, and an All-American in 1909, was also from Columbia. William Laub, 1926; Louis Bender (1910–?), 1930, 1932, and David Newmark (1946–), 1966, also received All-America recognition at Columbia. From 1909 to 1950 the City College of New York produced teams that were among the best in the nation and were nearly all-Jewish. With the exception of Ira Streusand (1890–1964), 1908, professional star Nat *Holman trained all the other Jewish players from CCNY who were selected as All-Americans, namely Louis Farer, 1922; Pincus (Pinky) Match (1904–1944), 1925; Moe Spahn, 1932; Mo Goldman (1913–?), 1934; Bernard Fliegel, 1938; William (Red) *Holzman (1920–1998), 1942, and Irwin Dambrot (1950). All-America selections from other New York City schools (New York University, Long Island University, and St. John's) were Maclyn (Mac) Baker (1898–1985), 1920–21; Milton Schulman, 1936; Robert Lewis, 1939; Jerome (Jerry) Fleishman (1922–), 1943; Sid *Tannenbaum (1925–1988), 1946–47; Dolph *Schayes (1928–), 1948; Donald Forman (1926–), 1948; Barry Kramer (1942–), 1963–64; Ben Kramer (1913–1999), 1936; Jules Bender (1914–1982), 1937; John Bromberg, 1939; Daniel Kaplowitz, 1939; Irving Torgoff, 1938–39; Oscar (Ossie) Schectman, (1919–), 1941; Jackie Goldsmith (1921–1968), 1946; Max (Mac) Kinsbrunner (1909–1972), 1930; Max (Mac) Posnack, 1931; Nathan Lazar, 1933; Jack (Dutch) Garfinkel (1920–), 1939; Harry Boykoff (1922–1978), 1943, 1946; Hyman (Hy) Gotkin, 1944–45; and Allan Seiden, 1958–59. In 1928–31 Kinsbrunner, Posnack, Albert (Allie) Schuckman and Jack (Rip) Gerson were members of the "Wonder Five," one of college basketball's most famous teams.

Other All-America players included Cyril Haas, Princeton, 1916–17; Leon (Bob) Marcus, 1918–19; Samuel Pite, Yale, 1923; Emanuel (Menchy) Goldblatt (1904–1994), Pennsylvania, 1925–26; Carl M. Loeb Jr., Princeton, 1926; Edward Wineapple, Providence, 1929; Louis Hayman, Syracuse, 1931; Jerry Nemer (1912–1980), Southern California, 1933; Herbert Bonn, Duquesne, 1936; William Fleishman, Western Reserve, 1936; Marvin Colen, Loyola of Chicago, 1937; Meyer (Mike) Bloom, Temple, 1938; Bernard Opper (1915–2000), Kentucky, 1939; Louis Possner, DePaul, 1940; Morris (Moe) Becker (1917–1996), Duquesne, 1941; Irving Bemoras (1930–), Illinois, 1953; Len Rosenbluth (1933–), North Carolina, 1955–57, college player of the year in 1957; Lawrence Friend (1935–1998), California, 1957; Donald Goldstein, Louisville, 1959; Jeff Cohen, William and Mary, 1960–61; Arthur Heyman (1941–), Duke, 1961–63, college player of the year in 1963; Howard Carl, DePaul, 1961; Robert I. (Rick) Kaminsky (1942–), Yale, 1964; Talbot (Tal) *Brody (1943–), Illinois, 1965, and subsequently a star in Israel; Neal Walk (1948–), Florida, 1968–69; and Dave Kufeld, Yeshiva U. 1977–1980, and a 10th-round draft pick of the NBA's Portland Trailblazers.

College coaches included Leonard Palmer (1882–?), first CCNY coach, 1909–16; Edard Siskind (1886–1955), Fordham, 1910; Samuel Melitzer, NYU, 1911; Michael Saxe, Villanova, 1921–26; Louis Sugarman, Princeton, 1921; David Tobey (1898–1988), Savage School of Physical Education, 1924–42 and Cooper Union, 1947–60, an outstanding referee from 1918 to 1945 and the author of the first book on basketball officiating (1943), and a member of the Basketball Hall of Fame; Leonard D. Sachs (1897–1942), Loyola or Chicago, 1924–42, had a 224–129 record; Emil S. Gollubier (1890–1969), Chicago Hebrew Institute, 1918–62; Dolly Stark (1897–1968), Dartmouth, 1929–36, 1945–46; Bernard (Red) *Sarachek (1912–2005), Yeshiva, 1943, 1946–69; Harry Stein (1916–1959), Brandeis, 1949–58; Samuel Cozen, Drexel Tech, 1952–68, had a 213–94 record; David Polansky, CCNY, 1953–54, 1957–58, 1960–68, 1970–71; Roy Rubin, Long Island University, 1961– , in 1968 LIU was the small college national champion; Harold (Hal) Blitman, Cheyney State, 1962–69; Jules Rivlin, Marshall, 1956–62; Irving Olin (1917–1970), Brandeis, 1964; and Harry *Litwack (1907–1999), Temple, at the Philadelphia school beginning in 1925 as a player and coach. He became head coach in 1953 and his teams won over 300 games, including the 1969 National Invitational Tournament in New York City.

The majority of the players who made All-America in college went on to play professional basketball. Other Jewish players who excelled as professionals were David (Pretzel) Banks (1901–1952), the Original Celtics; George (Red) Wolfe (1905–1970), Shikey Gotthoffer and Inky Lautman of the Philadelphia Sphas; Louis Spindell and Phil Rabin (Rabinowitz) of the American League; National Basketball Association players Leo Gottlieb, Sidney (Sonny) Hertzberg, Max *Zaslofsky (1925–1985), all-NBA guard in 1947–50, who led the league in scoring in 1948, and Danny Schayes, son of Dolph.

Coaches, managers, and owners of professional teams included Jack (Nibs) Neiman, manager of the Rochester, New York, Centrals, 1902; Eddie *Gottlieb (1900–1979), organized, played for, and coached the South Philadelphia Hebrew Association (Sphas) team in 1918–45. In 1946 he helped found the Basketball Association of America (which became the National Basketball Association) and from 1947 to 1968 was a coach and owner of the Philadelphia Warriors; Abe *Saperstein (1902–1966), founder, owner, and coach of the Harlem Globetrotters; Barney *Sedran (1891–1964), a coach and promoter in 1932–46; Les *Harrison (1904–1997), coach and owner of the Rochester Royals of the NBA, 1949–1958; Benjamin (Ben) Kerner (1917–), owner of the Tri-Cities/Milwaukee/St. Louis Hawks in the National Basketball League and the National Basketball Association, 1946–68; Max Winter, owner of the Minneapolis Lakers in the 1950s; Mark *Cuban (1958–), owner of the Dallas Mavericks; Jerry Reinsdorf (1936–), owner of the Chicago Bulls; Leslie Alexander, Houston Rockets; Micky Arison, Miami Heat; William Davidson, Detroit Pistons; Abe *Pollin (1923–) Washington Wizards; Donald Sterling, Los Angeles Clippers; Herb Kohl, Milwaukee Bucks; and Howard Schultz, Seattle Supersonics.

Arnold (Red) *Auerbach (1917–), was Boston Celtics coach and general manager; Red Holzman played for the Rochester Royals in 1946–54, and led the New York Knicks to the NBA championship in 1970 and 1973. Maurice *Podoloff (1890–1985) was elected president of the Basketball Association of America in 1946 and served as the first commissioner of the National Basketball Association until 1963. Marty *Glickman (1917–2001) was a radio broadcaster and founding father of basketball on radio, and is a member of the Basketball Hall of Fame. Leo Fischer (1897–1970), an outstanding sportswriter, was president of the National Basketball League in 1940–44, and Harry Rudolph (1907–1973), president of the Eastern League. Larry *Fleisher (1930–1989) was head of the NBA players union from 1962–1988, and a member of the NBA Hall of Fame as contributor.

Referees who gained prominence were Sam Schoenfeld (1907–1956), who starred at Columbia University in 1928–30 and later founded and was first president of the Collegiate Basketball Officials Association; Mendy *Rudolph (1928–1979), who became an NBA official in 1953 and in 1969 became the league's chief of referees; and Norman Drucker, who after 15 years with the NBA became supervisor of ABA officials in 1969. Jews coached and won medals at the Olympic *Games. Julius Goldman, an American, coached Canada to an Olympic medal in 1936, and Alexander Gomelsky did the same for the Soviet Union in 1964 and 1968. Canadian Olympic coaches include Men Abromowitz (1948) and Ruben Richman (1934–). Harry D. *Henshel served as chairman of the United States Olympic Basketball Committee in 1956, and Harold Fischer coached United States gold medal teams at the 1951 and 1967 Pan-American Games. Tanhum (Tanny) Cohen-Mintz of Israel was named to the European All-Star team in 1964 and 1965. Members of the Basketball Hall of Fame are Leonard D. Sachs, David Tobey, Barney Sedran, Nat Holman, Red Auerbach, and Abe Saperstein.

Ernie *Grunfeld won gold medals as a member of the American men's teams at the 1975 Pan-American Games and the 1976 Olympic Games, and Nancy *Lieberman (1958–) was a member of the American women's teams which gained Pan-American Games gold and Olympic Games silver medals. Lieberman was named outstanding college player twice, winning the Wade Trophy following the 1978–79 and 1979–80 seasons, when her school Old Dominion won the women's championship. In 1979 she helped the United States win the FIBA World Championship and a silver medal in the Pan-American Games.

Larry *Brown (1940–) was named Coach of the Year in the American Basketball Association in 1973 and 1975. In 1979 Brown moved to the college ranks to coach at UCLA. His team reached the finals of the national collegiate (NCAA) championship in his first season. Brown, basketball's traveling man, then went to the NBA New Jersey Nets (1981–1983), and then to the University of Kansas, which won the NCAA championship in 1988. He returned to the NBA in 1988 with the Antonio Spurs, which went from a 21–61 record in Brown's first year to 56–26 the following year – the 35-game swing from one season to the next an NBA record. In 1992 he moved from San Antonio to the Los Angeles Clippers, then to the Indianapolis Pacers (1993–1997), Philadelphia 76ers (1997–2002), Detroit Pistons (2003–2004), and New York Knicks (2005–2006). His brother Herb (1936–) is also a veteran coach.

Alexander Gomelsky (1928–2005) returned to coach the U.S.S.R. national team in 1977. His team won an Olympic bronze medal in Moscow.

Players Dolph Schayes (1972) and Max (Marty) Friedman (1971); coach Harry Litwack (1976); and contributors Edward Gottlieb (1971) and Maurice Podoloff (1973) were elected to the Basketball Hall of Fame.

David Stern became the commissioner of the National Basketball Association in 1983 and in 1992 was named the most powerful person in sports by a national sports publication. *The Sporting News* said of him, "As a direct result of David Stern's progressive leadership, the NBA now has the greatest universal appeal of any professional sport."

Mickey *Berkowitz (1954–) is considered the greatest basketball player in Israel's history.

Senda Abbott *Berenson was the "Mother of Women's Basketball" and was inducted into the International Basketball Hall of Fame in 1985.

Billiards

John M. Brunswick (1819–1886), who was born in Bengarten, Switzerland, and settled in Cincinnati, Ohio, was one of the earliest manufacturers of billiard equipment in the United States. He built the country's first perfect billiard table in 1845. Moses Bensinger (1839–1904), Brunswick's son-in-law, invented the balkline game in billiards in 1883, and in 1890 became president of his father-in-law's firm, which had been moved to Chicago. Outstanding American professional billiard players were Leon Magnus, winner of the first world three-cushion championship in 1878; Harry P. Cline, world three-cushion (1907) and 18.2 balkline (1910) champion, and Arthur Rubin (1905–?), world professional three-cushion champion (1961 and 1964); Sydney Lee (1903–?), the British amateur champion in 1931–34 and winner of the world amateur billiard championship in 1933, American amateurs Max Shimon, winner of the national three-cushion championship in 1929 and 1930, and Simon ("Cy") Yellin, national pocket billiard champion in 1929.

Bowling (Tenpin)

The Brunswick Company entered the bowling business in 1888 and helped establish the tenpin game around the world. Bowling pioneers Samuel Karpf (1866–1923) and Dutch-born Louis B. Stein (1858–1949) helped organize the American Bowling Congress in 1895. One of the first to write about bowling in the United States, Karpf served in 1896–1907 as the first secretary of the American Bowling Congress. Stein, an outstanding bowler, established 300 as the score in tenpin bowling and determined that the weight of the ball should be 16 pounds. The Bowling Hall of Fame includes charter member Mortimer ("Mort") Lindsey (1888–1959); Phil Wolf, American Bowling Congress champion (1928); and Sylvia Wene Martin (1928–), women bowler of the year in 1955 and 1960.

Mark *Roth (1951–), Bowler of the Year in 1977, 1978, 1979, and 1984, is a member of Pro Bowlers Association (PBA) Hall of Fame. Roth, Barry Asher (1972–73), and Marshall Holman (1977–78) gained All-America selections. Holman was player of the year in 1987. Roth and Holman were voted into the U.S. Professional Bowlers Association's Hall of Fame in 1987 and 1990, respectively. Veteran Barry Asher joined the PBA Hall of Fame in 1988, and the American Bowling Congress' Hall of Fame added Norman Meyers in 1983 and Al Cohn in 1985.

Boxing

The most active years of Jewish participation in professional boxing were in the latter part of the 18th and the first quarter of the 19th centuries in England, and in the first half of the 20th century in the United States. The best boxers of the early era were Daniel *Mendoza (1764–1836), champion of England in 1792–95, and Samuel ("Dutch Sam") Elias (1776–1816), credited with the invention of the uppercut. Other English Jews who fought in the ring during this period were Barney Aaron ("the Star of the East"; 1800–1850); Henry Abrahams; the Belasco brothers – Abraham ("Aby") (1797–?), Israel (1800–?), Samuel, and John; Isaac Bittoon (1778–1838); Elisha Crabbe (d. 1809); Abraham da Costa; Barnard Levy; Keely Lyons; Daniel Martin; Isaac Mousha; Abraham Robes; Solomon Sodicky; and the cousins of Daniel Mendoza, Angel Hyams and Aaron Mendoza.

A number of English fighters bridged the gap between the early and modern eras. Barney ("Young Barney") Aaron (1836–1907), son of Barney Aaron, Asher Moss, nephew of Daniel Mendoza and Israel ("Izzy") Lazarus (1812–1867); and his sons Harry (1839–1865) and Johnny, who emigrated to the United States in the 1850s and 1860s and helped build interest in boxing by giving lessons and putting on exhibitions around the country. "Young Barney" Aaron won the lightweight championship of the United States in 1857.

The first Jewish boxer to win a world championship under Marquis of Queensberry rules was Harry ("The Human Hairpin") Harris (1880–1959), bantamweight, 1901–02.

Other American world professional champions were light heavyweight Battling *Levinsky (Barney Lebrowitz; 1891–1949) in 1916–20; Maxie ("Slapsie") *Rosenbloom (1904–1976) in 1930–1934; and Bob Olin (1908–1956) in 1934–35; middleweights Al McCoy (Albert Rudolph; 1894–1966) in 1914–17; Ben Jeby (Morris Jebaltowsky; 1907–1985), 1932–33; and Solly Krieger (1909–1964), 1938–39; welterweights Jackie *Fields (Jacob Finkelstein; 1907–1987) in 1929–30, 1932–33; and Barney *Ross; lightweights Benny *Leonard; Al ("The Bronx Beauty") Singer (1907–1961) in 1930; and Barney *Ross; featherweights Abe *Attell (1884–1970) in 1901–12; Louis ("Kid") Kaplan (1902–1970) in 1925–27; and Benny Bass (1904–1975) in 1927–28; bantamweights Abe Goldstein (1898–1907) in 1924;

Charley ("Phil") Rosenberg (Green; 1902–1976) in 1925–27; and flyweight Izzy ("Corporal") Schwartz (1900–1988) in 1927–29. Other world champions were Ted ("Kid") *Lewis, Great Britain; Victor ("Young") Perez (1911–1942), France (Tunisia), flyweight 1931–32; Robert Cohen (1930–), France (Algeria), bantamweight 1954–56; and Alphonse Halimi (1932–), France (Algeria), bantamweight 1957–59. World junior champions were Mushy Callahan (Vincent Morris Sheer; 1905–1986), welterweight 1926–30; Jack Bernstein (John Dodick; 1899–1945), lightweight 1923; and Jackie ("Kid") *Berg (Judah Bergman; 1909–1991), Great Britain, welterweight 1930–31. Other noted American boxers were Monte Attell (1885–1960), Abe's brother; Jacob ("Soldier") Bartfield (1892–1970); Joe Bernstein (1877–1931); Harry Blitman (1908–1972); Phil ("Ring Gorilla") Bloom (1894–?); "Newsboy" Brown (Dave Montrose; 1904–1977); Joe Choynski (1869–1943); Leach Cross (Louis Wallach; 1886–1957); Charley Goldman (1887–1968), who was also a successful trainer; Ruby ("The Jewel of the Ghetto") *Goldstein (1907–1984), both a boxer and referee; Willie Jackson (Oscar Tobler; 1897–1961); Danny Kramer (1900–1971); Harry Lewis (Besterman; 1886–1956); Ray Miller (1908–1987); Young Montreal (Morris Billingkoff; 1897–1978); Young Otto (Arthur Susskind; 1886–1967); Dave Rosenberg (1901–1979); Johnny ("Young") Rosner (1895–1974); Lew Tendler (1898–1970); Sid ("Ghost of the Ghetto") Terris (1904–1974); Al "Bummy" *Davis (Albert (Avraham) Davidoff; 1920–1945), welterweight boxer; Abe ("The Newsboy") *Hollandersky (1887–1966, who engaged in more professional bouts (1,309) than any other fighter in boxing history; and Mike Rossman, who won the World Boxing Association light heavyweight championship in 1978 at age 21, the youngest claimant of the light heavyweight title. He lost the championship in 1979.

Champions of Europe included British boxers Anshel ("Young") Joseph, welterweight, in 1910; Matt Wells (1886–1953), lightweight in 1911–12; Harry Mason, lightweight, in 1923; Johnny Brown (d. 1975), bantamweight, in 1923 and Al Phillips, featherweight, in 1947; and also Albert Yvel, France, light heavyweight, in 1950–51. Winners of national professional titles were Jack Bloomfield in 1922, Joe Fox (1892–1965), in 1921; and Harry Mizler (d. 1990) in 1934 of Great Britain; Al Foreman, Curly Wilshur (Barney Eisenberg), Sammy Luftspring and Maxie Berger of Canada; Tiger Burns (Dan Levine), Al James, and David Katzen of South Africa; and Waldemar Holberg of Denmark. In 1971, Henry Nissen of Australia (1948–) won the British Commonwealth flyweight title.

Jews have been involved in all other activities connected with the boxing business as managers, trainers, and promoters. Promoters included Mike *Jacobs (1880–1953), Joe *Jacobs ("Yussel the Muscle"; 1896–1940), Harry Markson, Herman Taylor, Lew Raymond, Johnny Attell, Sam Becker, Larry Atkins, Goldie Ahearn, Archie Litman, Irving Schoenwald, Willie Gilzenberg, Bonnie Geigerman, and Jack Begun of the United States; Bella Burge, Jack *Solomons, Nathan Shaw, Mickey Duff, Esther Goldstein, and Harry Levene of Great Britain; Ludwig Japhet of South Africa; Gilbert Benaim of France; and Paul Damski of Germany. Ray *Arcel (1899–1994) is considered the greatest trainer in the sport. Whitey (Morris) *Bimstein (1897–1969) was another outstanding boxing trainer. Teddy *Brenner (1917–2000), considered the greatest matchmaker in boxing history, is a member of the International Boxing Hall of Fame. Lou *Stillman (Louis Ingber; 1887–1969) was owner of Stillman's Gym.

The Boxing Hall of Fame, founded by ring historian Nat *Fleischer, has enshrined charter members Daniel Mendoza, Benny Leonard, Abe Attell, Barney Ross, Joe Choynski, Lew Tendler, Ted ("Kid") Lewis, Battling Levinsky, Barney ("Young") Aaron, and Max *Baer.

Gilbert Cohen of France won the light middleweight championship of Europe in 1978.

Australian Henry Nissen was the Commonwealth flyweight champion in 1971–74. Victor Zilberman of Romania won a bronze medal in welterweight division, and Rollie Schwartz served as manager of the very successful American team at the 1976 Olympic Games.

American Saoul Mamby won the World Boxing Council's version of the world junior welterweight championship in 1980. Shamil Sabyrov of the USSR won a 1980 Olympic gold medal in the light-flyweight division. Dmitry *Salita, a religious Jew who does not box on Shabbat, won the NABA junior welterweight championship in August 2005.

French boxers Gilles Elbilia and Fabrice Benichou enjoyed ring successes in the 1980s and 1990s. Elbilia won the French and European welterweight titles in 1982 and 1983 while Benichou won the World and European featherweight championships in 1989 and 1991.

Scotland's Gary (Kid) Jacobs defeated an Australian opponent and won the British Commonwealth welterweight championship in 1988. He lost the title the following year. In 1992 he became the British welterweight champion.

Bullfighting

Jewish bullfighters include Sidney *Franklin of the United States and Randy Sasson (*El Andaluz*) of Colombia.

Canoeing

The sport began in 1865 and four years later Montagu Mayer competed in canoe races in England. In 1880 Arthur *Brentano and Adolph Lowenthal were among the 25 canoeists who founded the American Canoe Association. Leo Friede (1887–1959) of the United States won canoe sailing's oldest trophy, the International Sailing Challenge Cup, in 1913 and 1914. Olympic medalists include Leon Rottman (Romania) two gold (1956) and one bronze (1960); Imre Farkas (Hungary), two bronze (1956, 1960); Laszlo Fabian (Hungary), gold (1956); Klara Fried (Hungary), bronze (1960), and Naum Prokupets (U.S.S.R.), bronze (1968).

The two-man whitewater team of Joe Jacobi and his partner won a Olympic Games gold medal in 1992. It was only the fifth canoeing or kayaking gold medal won by the U.S. in Olympic Games history.

Cricket
The first Jewish cricket players of note played at Oxford and Cambridge. D.L.A. Jephson represented Cambridge University in 1891 and 1892 and John E. Raphael played for Oxford from 1903 to 1905. Both later represented Surrey County. International cricket players included the South Africans Manfred J. Susskind, Norman ("Mobil") Gordon, Dennis Gamsy and Aron ("Ali") Bacher. The last, a physician who devoted his early years of medical practice to nonwhites, achieved widespread distinction as a cricketer in the South African victory over Australia in 1966. He was appointed captain of the South African team for the 1970 test matches against England, the first Jew to reach such a position. Though an outspoken advocate of multiracial cricket, he was to have led his all-white team in the Commonwealth Matches at Edinburgh in 1970, but violent opposition in England to South African apartheid in sport caused cancellation of his team's participation.

Prue Hyman of Great Britain was captain of the women's team at Oxford and represented her country in international competition. Patrons of the game were Sir Julian Cahn of Great Britain, Wilfred Isaacs of South Africa, and John I. Marder (d. 1975), president of the United States Cricket Association. Cricket has been played in Israel since the Mandate period and later gained popularity with tours of Israel by Maccabi teams and still later by teams from England. Dr. Aron (Ali) Bacher of South Africa served as the first Jewish captain of a national cricket side in 1970–74. In 1979 Julian Wiener became the first Jewish cricketer to play for Australia's full international Test side.

Cycling
Louis Gompertz of Great Britain perfected the gear rope, or bicycle chain, in 1821. Felix Schmal of Austria won one gold and two bronze medals at the first Olympic Games in 1896.

Equestrian
American Neal Shapiro won an Olympic silver and bronze medal in 1972 in show jumping, and his countrywoman Edith Master gained a 1976 Olympic bronze medal in dressage. Mark Laskin, Canada's top rider in 1978 and 1979, helped his country win the gold medal at the "alternate Olympics" in Rotterdam, the Netherlands, in 1980. Margie Goldstein was named the 1989 and 1991 American Grand Prix Rider of the Year. In 1991 she became the first show jumper to win eight Grand Prix events in one season. Serious injuries cost her an Olympic Games opportunity in 1992.

Fencing
Between 1896 and 1976, 38 Jewish fencers won 76 medals (39 gold, 22 silver, and 15 bronze) in Olympic competition. Over the years they won numerous world, national, European, British Empire, Commonwealth, and Pan-American games (see *Olympic Games). Olympic medalists include Eduard Vinokurov (silver, 1972 and gold, 1976), Mark Rakita (silver, 1972) and Grigori *Kriss (bronze, 1972), all of U.S.S.R., and Ildiko Uslaky-Rejtoe (silver, 1972), Hungary. Kriss won the world epee title in 1971. Albert (Albie) *Axelrod (1921–2004) was one of the greatest American fencers in history, competing in five consecutive Olympics from 1952 to 1968 and winning a bronze in 1960. Allan *Jay (1931–) was a British fencer and a silver medalist in Individual and Team Epee at the 1960 Olympic. In 1975 Martin Lang of the United States won a Pan-American Games gold medal. Americans Yuri Rabinovich of Wayne State and Paul Friedberg of Pennsylvania won the sabre event in the national collegiate championships in 1979 and 1980. Leonid Dervbinsky was national epee champion in 1980 and Peter Schifrin (gold) and Edgar House (silver) won Pan-American Games medals in 1979. American medalists in the Pan American Games were Elaine Cheris, Paul Friedberg, and Jeff Bukantz in 1987 and Nick Bravin, John Friedberg, Chris O'Loughlin, and Joseph Socolof in 1991. Israel's Udi Carmi placed fourth in the foil competition in the 1987 World Championships.

Field Hockey
A women's Olympic Games gold medalist in 1984, and a bronze medal winner in 1988, Carina Benninga carried the Netherlands flag at the Olympic Games opening ceremony in 1992.

Football (American and Canadian)
In 1870, a year after college football began in the United States, Moses Henry Epstein represented Columbia University against Rutgers in the third game ever played. The following year, Emil G. *Hirsch, a future Reform rabbi, appeared in the initial football game at Pennsylvania University. In 1874, Henry Joseph, a Canadian, played for McGill University against Harvard in an important series of contests. Lucius Littauer, future "Glove King of America" and congressman from New York State, played for Harvard in 1875 and 1877. Littauer returned to his alma mater in 1881 and became college football's first coach. Phil King of Princeton University, one of early football's greatest players, was an All-American selection in 1890–93 and a member of the College Football Hall of Fame. He later coached at his alma mater and at Wisconsin University. Sam Jacobson, a member of the Syracuse Athletic Association, helped organize the first football team at Syracuse University in 1889.

Those who followed King as All-American selections were Sigmund ("Sig") Harris (1883–1969), Minnesota, 1903–04; Israel ("Izzy") Levene (1885–1930), Pennsylvania, 1905–06; Joseph Magidsohn (1888–1969), Michigan, 1909–10; Arthur ("Bluey") Bluethenthal (1891–1918), Princeton, 1911–12; Leonard Frank (1889–1967), Minnesota, 1911; A. Harry Kallet (1887–1965), Syracuse, 1911; Victor H. Frank (1900–), Pennsylvania, 1918; Joseph Alexander (1898–1975), Syracuse, 1918–20; Ralph Horween (1896–1997), Harvard, 1916; his brother Arnold Horween, (1898–1985), Harvard 1920; Max Kadesky (1901–1970), Iowa, 1922; George Abramson (1903–1985), Minnesota, 1924; Milton ("Irish") Levy, 1925; Benny *Friedman (1905–1982), Michigan, 1925, and a member of the College and Professional Football Hall of Fame; Ray

Baer (1905–1968), Michigan, 1927; Benny Lom, California, 1927–29; Lou Gordon (1908–1976), Illinois, 1927; Fred Sington (1910–1998), Alabama, 1929–30; and Mike Alexander, a member of the College Football H all of Fame; Gabriel Bromberg, Dartmouth, 1930; Aaron Rosenberg (1912–1979), Southern California, 1932–33, and a member of the College Football Hall of Fame; Harry "Doc" Newman (1909–2000), Michigan, 1932; Franklin Meadow (1912–1989), Brown, 1932; David Smukler (1914–1971), Temple, 1934; Isadore ("Izzy") Weinstock (1913–1997), Pittsburgh, 1934; Marshall *Goldberg (1917–), Pittsburgh 1937–39, and a member of the College Football Hall of Fame; Sid *Luckman (1916–1998), Columbia, 1937–38, and a member of the College Football Hall of Fame; Leroy Monsky (1916–1981), Alabama, 1937; A. Sidney Roth (1916–2001), Cornell, 1938; Mervin Pregulman (1922–), Michigan, 1943; Dan Dworsky (1927–), Michigan, 1947; Bernard Lemonick, Pennsylvania, 1950; Al Goldstein (1936–1991), North Carolina, 1958; Ron *Mix (1938–), Southern California, 1959; Rich Stotter (1945–), Houston, 1967; Bob Stein (1948–), Minnesota, 1967–68; Michael Andrew Seidman (1981–), Carolina Panthers; and Igor Olshansky (1982–), San Diego Chargers.

Among other leading football coaches were Israel Levene (1885–1930), an All-American selection, who played for Pennsylvania and later coached at the University of Tennessee and at his alma mater; Fred Lowenthal (1879–1931), who starred at the University of Illinois and later coached its team; Edward Siskind (1886–1955), who played and coached at Fordham University; Frank Glick (1893–1979) of Princeton University, who coached at his university and at Lehigh; Arnold Horween, All-American at Harvard and coach of the team in 1926–30. Others were Benny *Friedman, Joe Alexander, Louis Oshins (1902–1975), Marv *Levy (1926–), and Maurice ("Mush") Dubofsky (1910–1970), captain of the Georgetown University team.

Although professional football began officially in 1895, the Syracuse, N.Y., Athletic Association played the game for money before that date. Jewish members of the team included the manager and coach, Samuel Jacobson; the Freeman brothers, David and Chuck (1882–?), and an outstanding running back, Paul (Twister) Steinberg (1880–1964). Steinberg was also a member of the champion Philadelphia Athletics in 1902, and the famous Canton Bulldogs in 1905–06. In 1898, Barney *Dreyfuss of baseball fame was co-owner and manager of the Pittsburgh Athletic Club, the champions of professional football. Other professional players included John Barsha (Abraham Barshofsky) (1898–1976), 1919–20; Leonard Sachs (1897–1942), 1920–26; the Horween brothers, Arnold, 1921–24, head coach of the Chicago Cardinals in 1923–24, and Ralph (1896–1997), 1921–23; Joseph Alexander, 1921–22, 1925–27, head coach of the NY Giants in 1926; Jack Sack (Jacob Bernard Sacklowsky) (1902–1980), 1923, 1925–26; Samuel Stein (1906–1966), 1926, 1929–32; Saul Mielziner (1905–1985), 1929–34; Ollie (Bernard Oliver) Satenstein (1906–1959), 1929–33; Benny *Friedman, 1927–34, head coach of the Brooklyn Dodgers in 1932; Philip (Motsy) Handler (1908–1968), 1930–36, head coach of the Chicago Cardinals in 1943–45, 1949; Louis Gordon, 1930–38; Harry "Doc" Newman (1909–2000), 1933–37, in 1933 he led the National Football League in passing for the N.Y. Giants; Charles (Buckets) *Goldenberg (1911–1986), 1933–45; Edwin Kahn (1911–1945), 1935–37; David Smukler, 1936–39, 1944; Marshall "Biggie" Goldberg (1917–), 1939–43, 1946–48; Sidney *Luckman (1916–1998) 1939–50, a member of the Professional Football Hall of Fame; Alexander (Allie) *Sherman (1923–), 1943–47, head coach of the N.Y. Giants, 1961–68; Herbert Rich, 1950–56, an all-league selection in 1952; Sidney Youngelman, 1955–63; Michael Sommer, 1958–63; and Ron Mix, 1960–69, a member of the all-time American Football League team. Sid *Gillman (1911–2003) served as head coach of the Los Angeles Rams in 1955–59 and Los Angeles and San Diego Chargers in 1960–69. Al *Davis (1929–) was head coach and is now owner of the Oakland Raiders, and was commissioner of the American Football League in 1966. Benjamin F. Lindheimer (1896–1960) was commissioner of the All-America Conference in 1946–47; and Art *Modell (1925–), owner of the Cleveland Browns which became the Baltimore Ravens, and president of the National Football League in 1967–70. Referees of note were Norman ("Bobie") Cahn (1892–1965), Joseph J. Lipp (1889–1958), Joseph Magidsohn (1888–1969), and Samuel A. *Weiss (1902–1977).

Canadian professional football executives included Louis Hayman, Harry Sonshine, Neville Winograd, David Loeb, Samuel Berger, and G. Sydney Halter, the first commissioner of the Canadian Football League. Halter and Abe Eliowitz (1910–1981), a U.S. player, are members of the Canadian Football Hall of Fame.

Gary Wichard, quarterback, C.W. Post (1971), Randy Grossman (1952–), end, Temple (1973) and David Jacobs (1957–), kicker, Syracuse (1978) won All-America honors. Grossman played professionally with the Pittsburgh Steelers.

Ron Mix (1938–), offensive tackle with the San Diego Chargers, retired in 1973 after a 13-year career. He was named to the Professional Football Hall of Fame in 1979. Harry Newman, an All-America quarterback at Michigan in 1932, was named to the College Football Hall of Fame in 1975.

In 1972 Carroll *Rosenbloom (1907–1979) exchanged ownership of the Baltimore Colts for the same position with the Los Angeles Rams of the NFL. Zygmunt Wilf, a child of Holocaust survivors, became owner of the Minnesota Vikings in 2005. Other owners include Al Lerner (1933–2002), Cleveland Browns; Arthur Blank (1942–), Atlanta Falcons; Robert *Kraft (1942–), New England Patriots; Daniel Snyder, Washington Redskins; Malcom Glazer (1928–), Tampa Bay Buccaneers (and majority owner of Manchester United), Jeffrey Lurie (1951–), Philadelphia Eagles; and Robert *Tisch (1926–2005), co-owner of the New York Giants.

Players who performed on Super Bowl teams were Lyle Alzado (1949–1992), Los Angeles Raiders, 1984; Ed Newman (1951–), Miami Dolphins, 1985 and John Frank (1962–) and Harris Barton (1964–), San Francisco 49ers, 1989 and 1990.

Alzado, Newman, Barton, and Brad Edelman of the New Orleans Saints were named to All-Pro teams during this period. Barton, an offensive tackle, was an All-Pro in 1990 and 1992.

Coach Marv Levy, the Phi Beta Kappa scholar who was hired by the Buffalo Bills in 1986, led the Bills to four consecutive Super Bowl appearances (1991–1994). Coach Sid Gillman and Al Davis were voted into the Professional Football Hall of Fame in 1983 and 1992. In 1989 Gillman was also named to the College Football Hall of Fame. Beginning in 1960, Davis served as a personnel assistant and scout, head coach, general manager, league commissioner, principal team owner, and chief executive officer. Davis was a Gillman assistant in 1960.

Golf

The development of outstanding Jewish golfers was slow as most established golf clubs barred Jews from membership. Elaine V. Rosenthal (1896–?) of the United States was one of the first successful golfers. She won a number of tournaments after placing second in the national amateur championship in 1914. Herman Barron (1909–1978) was a leading player on the United States professional tour in the late 1940s, a member of the United States Ryder Cup team in 1947, and world professional senior champion in 1963. Sidney Brews (1899–1972) of South Africa had a long career as a professional golfer. Beginning in 1925, he won 30 Open championships in six countries. South African national amateur champions and international players included Brews' brother-in-law, Mickey Janks, South African national champion of 1948; Betty Bental Peltz; Florrie Josselsohn; Rita Levitan; Isabel Blumberg; and Judy Angel. Martin (Marty) Fleckman of the United States won the national collegiate title in 1965 and two years later became the first golfer in history to win the first tournament he entered as a professional. In 1968, Bruce Fleisher (1948–) won the United States amateur championship, and, with Richard Siderowf, was a member of the winning U.S. team at the world amateur championships in Australia. Fleckman, Fleisher, Siderowf, and Arnold Blum were all members of winning U.S. teams in Walker Cup competition. Douglas Silverberg of Canada and Roberto Halpern of Mexico were also international golfers. Jane Weiller Selz, an American, won the women's national amateur championship of Mexico in 1960. In 1960–61, Lord (Lionel) Cohen of Great Britain served as captain of the famous Royal and Ancient Golf Club of St. Andrews, Scotland. Israel opened its first golf course at Caesarea in 1961.

American Amy *Alcott (1956–) had 29 career wins, including five majors, and was inducted into World Golf Hall of Fame in 1999. Richard Siderowf, an American, won the Canadian Amateur in 1971 and the British Amateur in 1973 and 1976.

After 13 years as a club professional, Bruce Fleischer returned to the tour and won his first Professional Golf Association tournament in 1991. In 1992, Monte Scheinblum won the National Long Drive championship. Entertainer Dinah Shore was the 1985 recipient of the Patty Berg Award for outstanding contributions to women's golf.

Gymnastics

Germany's Flatow cousins, Alfred (1869–1942) and Gustav Felix (1875–1945), won six medals (five gold) in gymnastic competition at the first modern Olympic Games in 1896. Other Olympic medalists included Imre Gellert (Hungary), silver, in 1912; George Gulack (1905–1986; United States), gold, in 1932; Philip Erenberg (1909–1992); United States), silver, in 1932; Agnes *Keleti (1921– ; Hungary), 11 medals, including five gold, in 1948–52, and 1956; Alice Kertesz (Hungary) gold and silver, in 1956; Mikhail Perelman (U.S.S.R.), gold, in 1952; and Vladimir Portnoi (U.S.S.R.), silver and bronze, in 1960. Abie *Grossfeld (1934–) and Mark Cohn (1943–) of the United States won gold medals in the Pan-American Games, and Daniel Millman (1946–) of the United States became the first world trampoline champion in 1964. Joseph Salzman was co-coach of the United States Women's Olympic team in 1948. Harvey Berkman, who was physical education director of Chicago's Jewish People's Institute from 1908 to 1922, was responsible for the training of some of America's best gymnasts.

Abie *Grossfeld coached the United States men's team at the 1972 Olympic Games. Marshall Avener was a 1972 Olympian and a 1975 Pan-American Games gold medalist. Sharon Shapiro of UCLA won all four individual events and the all-around title at the United States women's college championships in 1980.

Olympic medalists included Mitch *Gaylord (1961–) of the U.S., who won a gold, silver, and two bronze medals in 1984; Valeri Belenki of Azerbaijan, a gold and bronze winner in 1992; and Kerri *Strug (1977–) of the U.S., who won a gold medal at the 1996 Games.

Soviet gymnast Maria *Gorokhovskaya (1921–) won seven medals at the 1952 Olympics. Americans Lucy Wener and Brian Ginsberg won Pan American Games gold medals in 1983 and 1987.

Handball

This is a very popular sport with American Jews. During the 1960s, the membership of the United States Handball Association was 35 percent Jewish. The game has had numerous Jewish national champions including Vic *Hershkowitz (1918–), handball's greatest all-round player, and Jimmy *Jacobs (1931–1988), the best player of the 1960s. Hershkowitz won a record 40 national titles in one-wall, three-wall, and four-wall play between 1942 and 1968. Jacobs' victories were gained in three-wall and four-wall competitions.

Handball held its first national championship in 1919, and the following year Max Gold won the title. Other players who gained national singles titles were George Nelson, Ken Schneider, Paul Haber, Simon ("Stuffy") Singer, Martin Decatur, Ken Davidoff, Steve Sandler, Michael Schmookler, Irving Jacobs, Harry Goldstein, Jack Londin, David Margolis, Joseph Garber, Arthur Wolfe, the Alexander brothers Seymour and Morton, and Sheila Maroschick. Members of the Helms Handball Hall of Fame include players Hershkowitz and Schneider and Hyman Goldstein and Judge Joseph Shane, both national commissioners of the United States Handball Association.

Paul Haber (1970–71) and Fred Lewis (1972, 1974–76, 1978) won United States Handball Association singles titles.

Horse Racing

An English Jew named Lamego was engaged in this sport as early as the 18th century. Active in English racing during this period were Baron Maurice de *Hirsch, who gave all his racing winnings to charity, and Sir Ernest *Cassel. Philip Levi (1821–1898) was an early patron of the sport in Australia. In the United States, Ben Cohen was an officer of the Maryland Jockey Club in 1830, and six years later a horse owned by Aaron Philip Hart won the first running of the King's Plate in Canada.

America's leading jockey before the Civil War was Jacob Pincus (1838–1918) who began to ride in 1852. Pincus became a trainer and in 1881 he saddled the first American-bred horse to win England's Epsom Derby. One of those who employed Pincus as a trainer was August *Belmont, who had entered the sport in 1866 as a founder of Jerome Park and was the first president of the American Jockey Club. This club included many Jewish horse owners. Other prominent American owners and trainers in the 19th century were David Gideon (1846–1929), Charles Fleischmann (1834–1897), Moses Goldblatt (1869–1941), and Julius (Jake) Cahn (1864–1941), owner and trainer of the 1897 Kentucky Derby winner, Typhoon II.

Georges Stern (1882–1928) of France earned the title "King of the Jockeys" during a career that ran from 1899 to 1926. During that time Stern won almost every major European event, including the 1911 Epsom Derby. America's Walter Miller (1890–1959), another successful jockey of the same era, is a member of the national Jockeys Hall of Fame. He had ridden in the United States (1904–09) and Europe before weight problems forced his retirement. Miller was the American riding champion in 1906–07 and had ridden 388 winners in 1906, a record that lasted until 1952. Other outstanding American jockeys were Lewis Morris; the Renick brothers, Joseph (1910–?) and Sam (1912–1999); Robert Merritt (1912–); Willie *Harmatz (1931–); and Walter ("Mousy") *Blum (1934–), who rode over 3,000 winners from 1953 and was national riding champion in 1963–64. Harry ("Cocky") Feldman (1915–1950) was the national riding champion of South Africa seven times during an 18-year career. He was killed in a riding accident, as was Britain's Reginald Sassoon (1893–1933), an amateur steeplechase rider. Nikolai Nasibov was the Soviet Union's leading jockey in the 1960s.

The most noted American trainers, who were also owners and breeders, were Hirsch *Jacobs (1904–1970) who saddled more winners (3,596) than any other trainer in history; his brothers Eugene and Sidney; the Byer brothers, Nathaniel, Frank, and Jacob; Mose Shapoff; the Lowenstein brothers, Jake (1889–1971) and Mose; Philip Bieber, founder and first president of the Horsemen's Benevolent and Protective Association; Kentucky Derby winners Sol Rutchick and Jacob ("Jack") Price; Arnold Winick; Howard ("Buddy") Jacobson (1931–1989), the national training champion in 1963–65; and Yevgeni Gottlieb of the U.S.S.R.

Prominent owners and breeders included Sir Ellice V. Sassoon (1881–1961), who had four Epsom Derby winners; the Joel brothers, Jack (1862–1940) and Solomon ("Solly"; 1866–1931); Nat Cohen (d. 1988), winner of the 1962 Grand National Steeplechase at Aintree; Stuart Levy (1908–1966); Heinrich Loebstein; Michael Sobell; Sir Henry *d'Avigdor-Goldsmid; and Evelyn *Rothschild, Great Britain; Jean Stern (1874–1962), who won the Grand Steeplechase of Paris four times; Georges *Wildenstein (1893–1964) and his son Daniel; Alec Weisweiller; Barons Edouard (1868–1949), James (1878–1957), Maurice (1891–1957) and Guy de Rothschild, France; Sir Adolph Basser (1887–1964), Australia, winner of the Melbourne Cup in 1951; Abe Bloomberg and G.M. Jaffee, South Africa; and the Americans Benjamin Block (1873–1950) and John D. Hertz (1879–1961; Hertz and his wife Frances (1881–1963) won the Triple Crown in the United States in 1943 with Count Fleet; Herbert M. Woolf (1880–1964), J.J. (Jack) Amiel, Harry F. *Guggenheim, and Isaac Blumberg were all Kentucky Derby winners; Bernard M. *Baruch, William Littauer (1865–1953); Harry M. *Warner (1881–1958); Alvin Untermeyer (1882–1963); Louis B. *Mayer; Albert Sabbath (1889–1969) whose horse Alsab cost him $700, earned $350,000 from him and sired winners who earned $4,000,000. There were also Nelson I. Asiel (1886–1965); Robert Lehman, Arlene Erlanger (1895–1969); Louis K. Shapiro (1897–1970); Irving Gushen (1899–1963), president of the Horsemen's Benevolent and Protective Association in 1953–63; Stanley Sagner (1908–1964); John M. *Schiff; Jacob Sher (1889–1972); Louis E. Wolfson; Isador (Colonel) Bieber (1887–1974); Maxwell H. Gluck (1896–1984); Jack Dreyfus Jr. (1914–?), chairman of the Board of Trustees of the New York Racing Association in 1969–70; and David J. Davis, whose Australian thoroughbred, Phar Lap, was considered by many to have been the greatest racehorse of all time.

American racing executives included Louis Smith (1888–1968), Benjamin F. Lindheimer (1890–1960), Leonard Florsheim (1880–1964), Joseph Schenck (1878–1961), Morris Shapiro (1883–1969) and his son John D., the originator of the Washington, D.C., International Classic and president of the Thoroughbred Racing Association; Mervyn *Leroy (1900–1987); J.J. ("Jake") Isaacson (1896–?); David Haber; Nat Herzfeld; Joseph Cohen; Joseph Gottstein (1891–1971); the Cohen brothers, Herman and Ben, who controlled Maryland's famous racetrack, Pimlico; Dr. Leon Levy (1895–?) and his son Robert; Hyman N. Glickstein, Saul Silberman (1896–1971), Philip H. Iselin, and J. Samuel Perlman (1900–), a Canadian, who was publisher and editor of the *Daily Racing Form* and *Morning Telegraph*.

Harness racing became a major sport in the United States in 1940 when George Morton Levy (1889–1977) introduced night racing at Roosevelt Raceway in New York. Levy also encouraged and backed the invention of the mobile starting gate. He is a member of the Hall of Fame of the Trotter. Even before 1940, track-owner Louis Smith modernized the sport by eliminating the use of heats to determine winners; he built and owned New England's first modern racetrack, Rockingham. Sacher ("Satch") Werner (1898–?), was the outstanding American trainer and driver; before turning professional he was an amateur champion of Vienna, Austria. Amateur drivers included Nathan S. *Straus (1848–1931), who gave up racing and yachting to devote himself to philanthropies which helped lay the foundations of the State of Israel; and Neal Shapiro, won an Olympic silver and bronze medal in 1972 in show jumping.

American jockey Walter Blum (1934–) retired after the 1975 season, after a 22-year riding career with 4,383 winners. Maxwell Gluck (1977) and Louis Wolfson (1978) were named the outstanding American thoroughbred owner-breeders of the year. Wolfson's horse Affirmed won the 1978 Triple Crown (Kentucky Derby, Preakness, and Belmont Stakes) and was named Horse of the Year in 1978 and 1979. Sir Michael Sobel and Sir Arnold Weinstock's Troy won the 200th running of the English Derby and Harry Meyerhoff's Spectacular Bid won the Kentucky Derby.

Jockeys Walter Blum and Jacob Pincus were enshrined in the U.S. Thoroughbred Racing Hall of Fame in 1987 and 1988. Blum rode 4,382 winners in a 22-year career (1953–1975), and Pincus, a leading 19th-century jockey, was also an outstanding trainer. Another Hall of Fame entry in 1990 was owner Sam Rubin's John Henry, a two-time American Horse of the Year.

In 1983, with 2,500 victories to his credit, South African jockey Stanley Amos retired, the same year another South African jockey, Basil Barcus, recorded his 1,000th win.

Ice Hockey

Defense man Yuri Lyapkin of the U.S.S.R. won an Olympic gold medal in 1976.

Mathieu *Schneider (1969–) is a two-time NHL All-Star and was a member of the U.S. Olympic team and Team U.S.A.

Gary *Bettman (1952–) has been commissioner of the National Hockey League since 1993. Edward and Peter Bronfman, owners of the Montreal Canadiens since 1971, sold the team in 1978. Steve Ellman is owner of the Phoenix Coyotes, and Ed Snider owns the Philadelphia Flyers. Stan *Fischler (1932–) is an author, broadcaster, and leading authority on ice hockey.

Ice Skating (Figure and Speed)

American Scott Cramer won the men's professional figure skating gold medal at the world championships in 1980. Dr. Alain Calmat, an Olympic silver medalist in figure skating in 1964, became France's Minister of Youth and Sports in 1984. American Judy Blumberg and her partner won bronze medals in ice dancing in the World Figure Skating Championships in 1983–85. They placed fourth in the 1984 Olympic Games.

In speed skating, American Andrew Gabel (1964–) is a four-time Olympian (1988, 1992, 1994, 1998) and holds a silver medal as a member of the 1994 5,000 m Short Track relay team. In figure skating, Sasha *Cohen (1984–), Sarah *Hughes (1985–), and Irina *Slutskaya (1979–) all skated in the Olympics and have won numerous medals.

Jai Alai

Richard I. Berenson (1893–1967) was responsible for the success of jai alai in the United States. He was president and general manager of the Miami Fronton from 1929 until his death. He was succeeded by his son, L. Stanley ("Buddy") Berenson. Among Americans who played professional jai alai were Martin Perfit and Howard Wechsler.

American Joey Cornblit, a professional for 20 years, won the Tournament of Champions (a meeting of the sport's top players) in 1992, when he also won his ninth Florida singles championship.

Judo

In 1964, when this sport was added to the Olympic program for the first time, James Bregman (1941–) of the United States won a bronze medal in the middleweight division. Other internationalists included Gabriel Goldschmied, Mexico, a bronze medalist in the 1967 Pan-American Games; Ronald Hoffman (1944–), Bernard Lepkofer (1933–), and Irwin Cohen of the United States; Ivan Silver of Great Britain; Salvadore Goldschmied of Mexico, and Jorge Gleser (1947–) of Argentina and the United States.

Irwin Cohen (1971–72, 1974, 1976–78), Steve Cohen (1974–75, 1977) and David Pruzansky (1973) won United States national titles. Jesse Goldstein won a 1979 Pan-American Games silver medal for the United States in the heavyweight division. Amy Kublin won American women's titles in 1976–78, 1980.

After 40 years, Israel won its first Olympic medals in 1992. Yael *Arad gained a silver medal in women's competition and Shay Oren Smadga took a bronze in the men's events. Other Olympic medalists were American Robert Berland, silver, and Canadian Mark Berger, bronze, in 1984.

Pan American Games medalists in 1983 and 1987 included Berland, Berger and also American Damon Keeve.

Karate

Between 1986 and 1988, Kathy Jones won two silver and four bronze medals in World Cup and World Championship competition. Danny Hakim of Australia won a silver medal in the 1988 World Championships.

Lacrosse

Early internationalists were Henry Joseph of Canada, who in 1876 played in a game before Queen Victoria in London, and Lionel Moses of the United States, the first known Jewish captain of an intercollegiate sports team. Like Joseph, Moses was a member of teams that toured Great Britain before 1900. Bernard M. Baruch played the game at the City College of New York in the late 1880s. Another early American player was Clarence M. Guggenheimer, who played for Johns Hopkins and later for Harvard. Milton Erlanger (1888–1969), also of

Johns Hopkins, served as president of the Intercollegiate Lacrosse Association and was later elected to the Lacrosse Hall of Fame. Other members of the Lacrosse Hall of Fame include Henry S. Frank, captain of the 1909 Johns Hopkins team, and Victor K. Ross, who starred at Syracuse University and led his team to victory over Oxford-Cambridge in 1922.

Lawn Bowling

This is a very popular game with the Jews of South Africa. In the 1960s, when Jews represented 1% of the total population, 25% of all lawn bowlers in the country were Jewish. South African bowlers and administrators included Alfred ("Alf") Blumberg, who in 1950 became his country's first Jewish lawn bowling internationalist and winner of an Empire Games' gold medal in Auckland, New Zealand, that year; Abraham (Pinky) Danilowitz, 1958 Empire Games gold medalist in singles, and Leon Kessel who represented South Africa in the first world lawn bowling championship in 1966. Harry Hart of Rhodesia was awarded the MBE for his services as player and administrator in 1964. David Magnus was one of Australia's star players.

Luge (Toboggan)

American Gordy Sheer won gold medals in the North American Championships doubles in 1990 and 1991. Sheer also participated in the 1992 Olympic Games.

Motorboat Racing

In 1905, two years after the sport began, America's Jacob Siegel won the inboard hydroplane National Championship Trophy. The following year, Britain's Lionel de *Rothschild was co-owner of the winning boat at the Harmsworth Trophy event in Ireland. Bernard M. Baruch and his brother Hartwig won the National Championship Trophy in 1906–09. Herbert Mendelsohn was victorious in the 1937 Gold Cup race, and S. Mortimer Auerbach (1901–) won the National Sweepstakes in 1939. Donald Aronow of the United States, a boatbuilder, designer, and driver, won the world title in ocean racing in 1967 and 1969. In the latter year, the Union of International Motorboating awarded him its Gold Medal of Honor. Other American ocean drivers were Jerry Langer (1966 national outboard champion), Peter Rothschild (1966 national inboard champion), and William Wishnick (1924– ; 1970 national inboard champion). In 1967, Milton Horwitz of the United States won the national title in predicted-log competition. Horwitz, Aronow, Langer, and Rothschild are members of the Gulf Marine Hall of Fame. Other international drivers included Arnie Levy and his son Derrick, South Africa; and Alan Bernstein, Rhodesia.

American William Wishnick won the 1971 world ocean racing title and Dr. Robert Magoon (1971–73) and Joel Halpern (1976–77) United States national ocean racing championships.

Don Aronow, American boat designer and two-time world offshore powerboat champion (1967 and 1969), died in 1987.

Motorcycling

In 1936 Australia's Lionel Maurice Van Praag (1908–?) won the world's first speedway championship in Wembley, England, and Benjamin Kaufman (1911–), of the United States, gained national speedway titles in 1936–37.

Olympic Games

Israel joined the United States and a number of other nations in the 1980 boycott of the Moscow Olympic Games as a protest against the U.S.S.R. invasion of Afghanistan. See *Olympic Games for list of Jewish medal winners.

Polo

A favorite sport of the Rothschild banking family since the 1890s, they helped popularize polo in Austria and France. Leading Rothschild players were Baron Louis (1882–1954), Austria; Barons Edouard Alphonse James (1869–1949), Robert (1880–1946), and Elie (1917–), France and Evelyn (1931–), Great Britain. American players included William Littauer (1865–1953); the *Fleischmann brothers, Julius (1872–1925) and Max (1877–1951); Robert Lehman (1891–1969); Adam Gimbel (1893–1969); Samuel Cohen (1896–1965); and John M. Schiff (1904–1987).

Roller Skating

American Scott Cohen, who won the world free skating championships in 1985, 1986, 1989, and 1990, became the first singles skater to win the title four times. Cohen also won a Pan American Games silver medal in 1987.

Rowing

In 1858, Britain's Sir Archibald Levin Smith (1836–1901) rowed in the Cambridge University crew that defeated Oxford and triumphed in the Henley Royal Regatta. During the 1870s Henry Altman (1854–1911), Isaac N. *Seligman (1856–1917), and Lucius *Littauer were engaged in collegiate rowing in the United States. Seligman rowed at Columbia, Littauer at Harvard, and Altman helped to establish the sport at Cornell University. The Lone Star Boat Club of New York City, America's first Jewish rowing group, was organized in 1887. Samuel G. Sterne was its president.

In Olympic competition, Allen P. Rosenberg (1931–) coached the 1964 American rowing team to a pair of victories. As a coxswain, Rosenberg won a gold medal in the 1955 Pan-American Games. Between 1963 and 1966 Donald Spero (1939–) of the United States won seven national, two Canadian, and the 1966 world championship, in single-sculls. He was an Olympic finalist in 1964 and winner of the Diamond Sculls in Britain's Henley Royal Regatta in 1965. Spero and Rosenberg are members of the Helms Rowing Hall of Fame. Frederic Lane stroked the University of Pennsylvania to victory in the Grand Challenge Cup of England's Royal Henley Regatta in 1955, to defeat a Soviet crew. George Hermann, Herbert Senoff James Kreis, Jerry Winkelstein, James Fuhrman (1943–), and Lawrence Gluckman (1946–) were Pan-American Games gold medalists.

Allen Rosenberg coached and David Weinberg was coxswain of the American crew that won the 1974 eight-oared heavyweight race at the World Championships.

Seth Bauer won an Olympic Games bronze medal in 1988. Other American participants in the 1988 Olympic Games were Sherri Cassuto and Jon Fish. Bauer, Fish, and Cassuto won Pan American Games and World Championships medals between 1985 and 1991.

Pablo Bulgach of Argentina and Betsy Kimmel, U.S., won Pan American Games gold medals in 1987 and 1991.

Rugby

John E. Raphael (1882–1917) represented England nine times in international rugby competitions in 1902–06, and Bethel Solomons (1885–1965), later a leading gynecologist, played for Ireland ten times in 1908–10. Aaron ("Okey") Geffin of S. Africa was the hero of the 1949 test series victory over New Zealand. Samuel Goodman was the manager of the United States Olympic gold medal teams in 1920 and 1924. Australia's Albert A. Rosenfeld (1885–) and Britain's Lewis Harris were outstanding Rugby League players. Rosenfeld appeared in the first test series between England and Australia in 1909, and during the 1913–14 season he scored a record 80 tries for Huddersfield in the Northern Rugby Football League. Harris was a member of the Hull Kingston Rovers when they won the Challenge Cup in 1925 and were Northern Rugby Football League champions in 1921 and 1923.

Shooting

In 1868, Philo Jacoby (1837–1922) won the Berlin shooting championship as the representative of the American Sharpshooters Association of New York. During the next 30 years Jacoby made many trips to Europe, where he triumphed in numerous shooting tournaments. In 1876 he captained the California team that won the world shooting championship at the Centennial Exposition in Philadelphia. For many years he was editor and publisher of *The Hebrew*, one of the first Jewish newspapers in San Francisco. Among outstanding U.S.S.R. modern shooters were Olympic medalists Lev Vainshtein, 1952; Allan Erdman, 1956; world champion Mikhail Itkis, 1958; and Larissa Gurvich, 1967. Gurvich won the European and World skeet championships in 1975. Joelle Fefer of Canada won three Pan American Games medals in 1983 and 1987. Thomas Bernstein, a member of the Norwegian national team, won the U.S. national collegiate (NCAA) rifle championship in 1988.

Squash Racquets & Racquetball

Victor Niederhoffer won United States squash racquets championships in 1972–75, and the Canadian and North American Open titles in 1975. In 1977 Selwyn Machet won the South African amateur championship. American Stuart Goldstein won the World professional title in 1978.

In racquetball Martin Hogen won the United States championship in 1978, and his second and third national professional racquetball titles in 1979 and 1980. Kathy May Teacher won the United States women's national paddle tennis championship in 1980.

Surfing

South African Shaun Tomson won the 1975 American Championship Cup and the World professional title in 1977; he remained among the world's best surfers in 1985. After a decade of competition Tomson had recorded the most victories in the Association of Surfing Professionals world tour.

Swimming and Water Polo

Jews were active in competitive swimming from the time the sport began in the 19th century. Marquis Bibbero of England participated in swimming races in the 1860s and G. Cohen set an American record for the 440-yards in 1878. In 1896, Jews triumphed in all three swimming events at the first modern Olympic Games. They were Alfred Hajos (Guttmann; 1878–1955), of Hungary and Paul Neumann (1875–), of Austria (see *Olympic Games). Hajos, an architect, built Budapest's main swimming pool and in 1924 won a silver medal in the Olympic Art competition. Otto Wahle (1880–1963), an Austrian Olympian, immigrated to the United States, where he became a coach and helped influence the course of American swimming and coached the American Olympic teams in 1912 and 1920. His Olympic successor was William (Bach) Bachrach (1879–1959), who coached the Illinois Athletic Club swimming team in 1912–54. Bachrach trained many national and Olympic champions, including the great Johnny Weissmuller, and headed the Olympic swimming teams in 1924 and 1928. During the same period, Charlotte Epstein (1885–1938) established swimming as a sport for women in the United States. She founded the Women's Swimming Association in 1917 and was responsible for women's swimming being included in the 1920 Olympic Games. Miss Epstein was manager of the women's Olympic swimming teams in 1920, 1924, and 1932, and served as chair of the United States Olympic Women's Swimming Committee. She was also chair of the United States Maccabiah Games Swimming Committee in 1935. Leo Donath of Hungary headed the International Swimming Federation in the 1930s. Mark *Spitz (1950–), who won four medals in the 1968 Olympic Games, set records in the butterfly stroke. In 1967, when he was named "world swimmer of the year," Spitz won five gold medals in the Pan-American Games. In 1972, the year after he became the first Jewish sportsman to win the Sullivan Award as the outstanding American amateur athlete, Spitz won an unprecedented seven gold medals and set seven world records at the Olympic Games. In 1983, Spitz was one of the first 20 Olympians named to the U.S. Olympic Hall of Fame and Museum. Chosen by the National Association of Sportscasters and Sportswriters, Spitz received the second highest number of votes cast; only Track and Field great Jesse Owens received more. Other swimming Olympic medalists were Eva *Szekely (1927–) Hungarian-born swimmer who set ten world records, five Olympic records, and over 100 Hungarian national records while winning two Olympic medals, ten

World University Championships and 68 Hungarian National Championships over her 19-year career. She is a member of the International Swimming Hall of Fame. Other winners are Andrea Gyarmati, Hungary (silver and bronze), 1972, Wendy Weinberg, United States (bronze), 1976; and Lenny *Krayzelburg (1975–), who won four Olympic gold medals.

Israel's star swimmers and divers in the 1960s were Yoav Raanan, Yvonna Toviss, Abraham Melamed, Gershon Sheffa, Moshe Gartel, and Yoram Schneider.

Jews were prominent too in water polo at the Olympics (see *Olympics). Bela Komjadi (1892–1933), coach of the Hungarian national team in the late 1920s and early 1930s, established Hungary as an Olympic power in water polo. American Peter Asch won a 1972 Olympic bronze medal in water polo. Australia's Russell Basser and American Charles Harris represented their countries in the 1984 and 1992 Olympic Games. Harris was a silver medalist in the 1991 Pan American Games.

In 1980, Helen Plaschinski of Mexico won the Latin Cup 100 meter freestyle gold medal in Madrid, Spain. Barbara Weinstein won the United States indoor platform diving title in 1979 and the outdoor event the following year. She also won the 1979 Pan-American Games gold medal in platform competition.

Dara Torres won her second gold and third Olympic medal in 1992. She gained her first gold in 1984 and received a Olympic bronze medal in 1988. Other American medalists in major international competition were John Witchel, 1987, Pan American Games, two golds, and Cheryl Kriegsman, Dan Kutler, and Dan Kanner in the World University Games in 1987 and 1991.

Olympic finalists in 1988 and 1992 were Vadim Alekseev, U.S.S.R., and Tomas Deutsch, Hungary. Alekseev, who is now an Israeli, won a Goodwill Games silver medal in 1990.

In Synchronized Swimming, Americans Tracy Long and Ann Miller won Pan American Games gold medals in 1987 and 1991.

Al Schoenfield, publisher and editor of swimming publications, and Dr. Paul Neumann, Austria, 1896 Olympic gold medalist, were named to the International Swimming Hall of Fame in 1985 and 1986.

In water polo, American Peter Asch won a 1972 Olympic bronze medal. Australia's Russell Basser and American Charles Harris represented their countries in the 1984 and 1992 Olympic Games. Harris was a silver medalist in the 1991 Pan American Games.

Table Tennis

Table tennis was organized as a modern sport in the 1920s. It proved a very popular game with Jews and several became world champions. The Honorable Ivor Montagu (1904–1984) served as president of the English or International Table Tennis Federation from 1922 to 1967. His mother, Lady Swaythling (1879–1965), was also president of the English Table Tennis Federation and in 1926 donated the men's world team cup which bears her name. M. Cohen of Great Britain won the second English open championship in 1922, and Marcus Schussheim of the United States was the first American champion in 1931. Dr. Roland Jacobi of Hungary triumphed in men's singles at the initial world championship in 1927. Other world champions in singles, doubles, and mixed doubles were Hungary's Zoltan Mechlovitz; Gyozo Viktor *Barna (1911–1972), who won 22 world titles including five singles championships; Richard *Bergmann (1919–1970), an Austrian who won four singles titles; Alfred Liebster, Austria, and Angelica *Adelstein-Rozeanu (1921–), Romania; the sisters Thelma Thall and Leah Thall Neuberger, United States; and Svetlana Grinberg, U.S.S.R.

Ivor Montagu of Great Britain, who became the first chairman of the Table Tennis International Federation and held the post for over 40 years, died in 1984.

Tennis and Squash

As most tennis facilities were located in private clubs that barred Jewish membership, progress in this sport was slow. Conditions improved after World War II, as did the rankings of Jewish players. The first Jewish player officially ranked in the United States was Dr. William Rosenbaum (1882–1951) in 1908, and the first to gain the top-ten was Julius Seligson (1909–1987) in 1929. In Europe, Mikhail Stern represented Romania in the 1922 Davis Cup competition, and in 1928–30 Baron Hubert de Morpurgo (1897–?) of Italy received world ranking. Other players who achieved world ranking included Daniel Prenn (1905–), 1929 Germany, and 1932 Great Britain, 1934 (doubles); Ladislav Hecht (1910–), Czechoslovakia, 1934 (doubles), who defeated Britain's Davis Cup player Bunny Austin; Angela *Buxton (1934–) Great Britain, who was a Wimbledon doubles title winner in 1956. Outstanding tennis players also included Abraham Segal (1931–), South Africa, winner of South African singles championship in 1967; Pierre *Darmon (1934–) France, 1958, 1963–64; Tom ("the Flying Dutchman") Okker (1944–), Netherlands, Dutch national champion who won the Italian national singles title in 1968; Dick *Savitt (1927–) an American who was Wimbledon champion in 1951 and came out of retirement to win both the singles and doubles championships at the 1961 Maccabiah Games; Herbert *Flam (1928–), who won more top world rankings than any other Jewish tennis player and represented the U.S. Davis Cup team in 1951 and 1952; Americans Barbara Breit, 1955, 1957; Anita Kanter, 1952; and Julie M. Heldman (1945–), who as a girl of 12 won her first national title, the Canadian Junior Championship, and later won the Italian National Women's singles title in 1968; and Pete *Sampras (1971–), whose father is Jewish and who is considered by many tennis analysts to be the greatest tennis player of all time. Among Israel players of note was Eleazar Davidman.

Americans Julie Heldman (1974), Harold *Solomon (1975–77, 1979), Brian Gottfried (1977–79), and Eliot Telscher (1980) were ranked among the world's top ten players. Heldman played in Federation and Wrightman Cup competition and Solomon and Gottfried in Davis Cup play. Solomon was South African Open champion in 1975 and 1976, and Gottfried won the French (1975 and 1977), World (1975) and Wimbledon (1976) doubles championships. Brian Gottfried and Harold Solomon, retired from the professional tour in 1984.

In 1976 Ilana Kloss of South Africa won the French mixed doubles and the United States women's doubles titles. American Bruce Manson won a 1975 Pan-American Games gold medal, and Dana Gilbert the 1978 United States women's Clay Court championship.

American Dick Savitt, 1951 Wimbledon winner, was included in the International Tennis Hall of Fame in 1976.

Other Americans Eliot Telscher, Brad *Gilbert (1961–), Aaron Krickstein, and Jay Berger and Israel's Amos Mansdorf and Argentina's Martin Jaite joined the world's tennis elite in the 1980s. These players and Shlomo Glickstein, Shahar Perkiss, and Gilad Bloom of Israel and Andrew Sznajder of Canada played in Davis Cup competition. Elise Burgin represented the U.S. in Federation Cup play.

American Jim Grabb was a member of the men's doubles combination that won the U.S. Open championship in 1992, and Brad Gilbert won a men's singles bronze medal in the 1988 Olympic Games.

Joseph Cullman III, who helped launch the women's pro tour, was inducted into the International Tennis Hall of Fame in 1992. Anna Smashnova was ranked No. 16 on the woman's tour in 2002 and 2003.

National champions in American squash racquets and squash tennis were Victor Niederhoffer, Victor Elmaleh, Abraham M. Sonnabend (1897–1964), Milton Baron, and James Prigoff. Prigoff served as president of the National Squash Tennis Association, and Roger Sonnabend held the same position with the National Squash Racquets Association. Cecil Kaplan, David Duchen, and Jeffery Maisels were South African national champions and internationalists.

Track and Field

Modern track and field had its beginnings in England in the 1850s and 1860s. An early American runner was Lipman *Pike, a professional baseball player. Pike ran 100-yards against a Canadian Indian on the Capitoline Grounds in Brooklyn, New York, in 1869 and four years later became the Maryland State 100-yard champion. Daniel Stern (1849–1923) began to race-walk in 1873 and three years later won the one-and three-mile events at the first American track-and-field championships. He was an early member and officer of the New York Athletic Club and served on the committee charged with building the first cinder track in the United States. In 1875, Philo Jacoby (1837–1922) participated in the San Francisco Olympic Club's first outdoor athletic games. Victor E. Schifferstein (1863–?) represented the same California club when he won the national long-jump championship in 1888. Earlier that year, Schifferstein ran 100 yards in ten seconds to equal the world record of the time. The greatest American runner of the 19th century was Lawrence ("Lon") *Myers. He set world records in the 440- and 880-yard runs, and won American, Canadian, and British national championships in 1879–85. In 1900, Myer Prinstein (1880–1925) of the United States became the first Jewish medalist in Olympic track-and-field competition. He won the triple jump and placed second in the long jump. Earlier that year Prinstein had established a new world mark of 24 feet, 7.25 inches in the long jump. He repeated his Olympic triple-jump victory in 1904 and added a gold medal in the long jump. In 1906, Prinstein won another gold medal in Athens in the long jump, in what was then considered the Olympic Games, but some 50 years later the 1906 competition was ruled not to have been an Olympiad. Michael Spring (d. 1970) won the Boston marathon race in 1904. Abel Kiviat (1892–1991) won a silver medal at the 1912 Olympics, and set a world 1,500 m record that year. England's most famous track star was Harold *Abrahams who won the 100 meters race at the 1924 Olympic games; and his brother Sir Sydney *Abrahams also represented Britain at the Olympic Games. Harold Abrahams in 1969 became chairman of the British Amateur Athletic Board. Fanny ("Bobbie") Rosenfeld (1905–1969) in addition to starring in ice hockey, basketball, and softball, tied the women's world record for the 100-yard dash in 1925, excelled at the Olympics in 1928, and was hailed by the Canadian press as her country's "outstanding woman athlete of the half-century." Lillian *Copeland (1904–1964) was an Olympic gold and silver medallist, and member of U.S. Track & Field Hall of Fame. Deena Kastor (1973–) won a bronze medal in the women's marathon at the 2004 Olympics. Marty *Glickman (1917–2001) was a U.S. sprinter and a track star who was pulled from the 1936 Berlin Olympics because he was Jewish.

Jews were also medalists in European, British Commonwealth and Empire, Pan-American, and Asian Games.

Irena *Kirszenstein-Szewinska (1946–) of Poland won seven Olympic medals and ten European Championship medals, and is a member of the International Women's Sports Hall of Fame. Faina Melnik-Velva of the U.S.S.R. won an Olympic gold medal in the discus throw in 1972.

Abigail (Abby) Hoffman of Canada won a Pan-American Games gold medal in the 800-meter run in 1971 and silver and bronze medals in the 1975 Pan-American Games. In 1974 Y.C. Yohanna of India won the long jump event and set an Asian record in the Asian Games.

Israeli-born Boris (Dov) Djerassi won the United States national hammer throw in 1975 and 1978, and Ron Wayne won the U.S. national marathon championship in 1974.

Svyetlana Krachevskya of the U.S.S.R. won a 1979 bronze medal in the World Cup and a silver medal in the 1980 Olympic Games in the shot-put.

American Pincus (Pinky) Sober (1905–1980), was chairman of the International Amateur Federation's technical committee and longtime Madison Square Garden track announcer.

In 1992 Mel Rosen served as the U.S. men's Olympic coach, and Yevgeniy Krasnov of Israel placed eighth in the Olympic pole vault competition.

American Ken Flax won medals in the World University Games in 1989 and 1991 (gold) and was named the ninth ranked hammer thrower in the world in 1991.

In 2002, Russian-born Israeli Alex Averbach took the gold medal in the pole vault at the European championships.

Fred Lebow (Ephraim Fishl Lebowitz, 1932–1994) was president of the New York Road Runners Club and founder and director of the New York Marathon and the Fifth Avenue Mile.

Volleyball

Jews have also had a prominent part in volleyball. Sid Nachlas' (1920–) achievements brought him election to the Helms Volleyball Hall of Fame. Harlan Cohen (1934–) coached the American women's Olympic team in 1968. Eugene Selznick (1930–) is a member of the Volleyball Hall of Fame. Doug Beal and Israel's Arie Selinger coached the U.S. Olympic men's and women's teams to gold and silver medals in 1984. These were the first medals ever won by American teams in Olympic competition.

In 1992, Selinger coached the Netherlands men to an Olympic silver medal. Selinger's son Arbital was a member of the Dutch team. Other Olympic Games medalists were Bernard Rajzman, Brazil, silver, 1984; and Dan Greenbaum, U.S, bronze, 1992.

Water Skiing

David Nations pioneered this sport in Great Britain. He founded the British Water Ski Federation in 1951 and was the national overall champion in 1955–56.

Weightlifting

Britain's Edward Lawrence Levy (1851–1932) was among the first to engage in amateur weightlifting in the 19th century. He won the first English and international competitions in 1891, and five years later served as a weightlifting judge at the first modern Olympic Games. There have been many Olympic weightlifting medalists (see *Olympics). Jews also engaged in the European, Commonwealth, Empire, and Pan-American Games. Oscar State (1911–1984), OBE, of Great Britain organized the weightlifting competitions at the Olympic Games in 1948 and 1956, and officiated at nine Olympic Games, 21 Regional meets such as the Pan-Am, Maccabiah, Asian and Commonwealth Games, two World Games, 24 World Weightlifting Championships, 27 World Bodybuilding Championships, nine Mr. Olympias, 51 international bodybuilding contests and 101 international weightlifting contests, served as secretary of the International Weightlifting Federation, and is a member of the International Federation of Bodybuilding & Fitness Hall of Fame. David A. Matlin, a weightlifting official, served as the 33rd president of the Amateur Athletic Union of the United States in 1967–68. Isaac ("Ike") Berger (1936–), U.S. Olympic weightlifter, winner of gold and two silver Olympic medals, and a member of U.S. Weightlifters Hall of Fame.

David Rigert of the U.S.S.R. won a 1976 Olympic gold medal in the 198-pound division. Commonwealth Games medalists were Terrance (Terry) Perdue, England (bronze), 1974, and Ivan Katz, Australia (silver), 1978.

Grigory Novak, U.S.S.R. world champion in 1946 and 1952 Olympic silver medalist, died in 1980.

David Lowenstein of Australia won a Commonwealth Games silver medal in 1986, and Giselle Shepatin and Rachel Silverman won silver medals for the U.S. in the Women's International Weightlifting Tournaments in 1985 and 1987. Allon Kirschner of Israel won a gold medal in the World Powerlifting Championships in 1989.

Windsurfing

Gal *Fridman (1975–) was the first Israeli ever to win an Olympic Gold medal (2004), and the first Israeli to win two Olympic medals.

Winter Sports

In 1900–20, Cecil *Hart (1883–1940) pioneered amateur ice hockey in Canada. He entered the professional game in 1921 and became a successful coach with the Montreal Canadians. Samuel E. Lichtenhein (1871–1936) owned the Montreal Wanders hockey team (National Hockey Association) in 1911–18. Americans who owned teams in the National Hockey League included Sidney Solomon Jr. and Sidney Solomon III of the St. Louis Blues and Edward M. Snider of the Philadelphia Flyers. In 1964 the all-Jewish Ha-Koah-Melbourne team won the Australian ice hockey championship.

Louis Rubenstein of Canada introduced figure skating into North America in the late 1870s. He won many titles, including the 1890 world championship in Russia. One of the organizers of the 1890 world competition was Baron Wolff of the St. Petersburg Skating Club. Rubenstein's brothers and sisters, Moses, Abraham, and Rachel, were all champion skaters. Lily Kronberger of Hungary was world figure skating champion in 1908–11. Joel Liberman (1883–1955) of the United States was founder of the New York Skating Club and an Olympic judge in 1928 and 1932. Benjamin Bagdade (1902–) served as president of the American Skating Union in 1947–51 and was manager of the U.S. team at the 1948 Olympic Games. Irving *Jaffee (1906–1981) is a member of the Speed Skating Hall of Fame. France's Alain Calmat, world figure skating champion (1965), was awarded the Legion d'Honneur by President de Gaulle.

Alice Damrosch Wolf Kiaer (1893–1967), a daughter of conductor Walter *Damrosch, organized the first United States women's ski team in 1935 and the following year served as manager of the Olympic team. Richard Rubitscek of Austria won a gold medal in skiing in the 1933 European Maccabiah games and was a founder of the Arlberg ski method. American Hayley Wolff won a grand prix mogul gold medal in 1983 and a silver medal in the first world freestyle championship in 1986. Baron Robert de Rothschild (1880–1946) was the 1936 bobsledding champion of France, and in 1888 E. Cohen of the United States won the Grand National of Tobogganing at St. Moritz, Switzerland. The Montreal Curling Club numbered Canadian Jews among its members in the early 1800s. In 1965, Terry Braunstein skipped the Manitoba rink to the Canadian curling title.

Wrestling

There were a large number of medalists in wrestling at the Olympics. Jews also won medals for wrestling in European, Commonwealth, Empire, and Pan-American Games. Alfred Brull (1876–1944) of Hungary was president of the World Wrestling League.

David Pruzansky of the United States (1971) and Howard Stupp of Canada (1975, 1979) won Pan-American Games gold medals. Keith Peache of England won a Commonwealth Games gold medal in 1974, and Victor Zilberman of the U.S.S.R. was a silver medalist at the European championship. Zilberman later competed for Canada.

Pan American Games medalists included Canada's Gary Kallos, sambo wrestling, gold, 1983; Andrew Borodow, free and Greco-Roman wrestling, two silvers, 1991; and also American Andrew Seras, Greco-Roman wrestling, gold, 1991. Seras and Borodow competed in the Olympic Games in 1988 and 1992.

Ralph (Ruffy) Silverstein (1914–1980) was United States national collegiate champion in 1935 and Maccabiah Games coach in 1965.

Yachting

In 1969, Israel won its first world title in any sport when Ẓefania Carmel and Lydia Lazarov sailed to victory in the 420 class championship. In the United States, Emil ("Bus") Mosbacher, *Jr. (1922–1997), triumphed in American Cup races in 1962 and 1967, and his brother Robert Mosbacher (1927–) won the world title in the Dragon Class in 1969. Olympic medalists in yachting were Robert ("Buck") Halperin (1908–?), United States, in 1960; and Valentin Mankin, U.S.S.R. in 1968 (gold). The Levinson brothers, Alan and Harry, won a silver medal for the United States in the 1967 Pan-American Games. Other yachtsmen included Baron Phillipe de Rothschild (1902–1988) and Baron Edmund de Rothschild (1845–1934), France; and August *Belmont (1816–1890), Mortimer L. Schiff, and Walter N. *Rothschild (1892–1960), United States.

In Olympic Games competition, Valentin Mankin of the U.S.S.R. won gold (1972, 1980) and silver (1976) medals, and Daniel Cohan of the United States was a bronze medal winner in 1972.

American helmsman Larry Klein won four world's championships between 1983 and 1991. He was named U.S. Yachtsman of the Year in 1989.

[Jesse H. Silver /Elli Wohlgelernter (2nd ed.)]

BIBLIOGRAPHY: I. Abrahams, *Jewish Life in the Middle Ages* (1932², repr. 1960), 381–90; L. Rabinowitz, *Social Life of the Jews of Northern France in the 12th–14th Centuries* (1938), 225–29; Baron, Community, 1 (1942), 16, 197–98. B. Postal et. al. (eds.), *Encyclopaedia of Jews in Sports* (1965). **ADD. BIBLIOGRAPHY:** J.M. Siegman, *Jewish Sports Legends* (2000³); R. Slater, *Great Jews in Sports* (rev. 2000).

SPRACHMAN, ABRAHAM (1896–1971) and **MANDEL** (1925–2002), Canadian theatrical and institutional architects. Abraham Sprachman was born in Honczarow, near the Carpathian mountains between Lvov and Chernovitz. His family settled in Toronto when Abe was a youngster. While he was studying bookkeeping in secondary school, a school inspector noticed his artistic talents and transferred him to a program in architecture. In about 1919 he opened his first architectural office in his bedroom. When a degree in architecture became required in 1935, he was retroactively made a member of the Ontario Association of Architects and the Royal Architectural Institute of Canada. Sprachman lived and worked in an almost exclusively Yiddish world, and most of his clients were Jews. With architectural opportunities for Jews limited in Canada, he first designed homes for Jewish clients referred to him by a friend building an accounting firm. Just as the Depression began, one of these clients gave him his first theatrical commission, the Circle Theatre. Theater architecture was something of an architectural extension of the largely Jewish movie business in which Jewish producers in Hollywood created the films that Jewish entrepreneurs exhibited in small neighborhood theaters, affectionately known as the "Nabes." Sprachman and a partner, Harold Kaplan, built many substantial neighborhood movie houses in Canada for the Famous Players, Loew's, 20th Century, and Premier Operating chains. Their most significant theaters were in the Art Deco style: the Vogue in Vancouver (1941) and the Eglinton in Toronto (1936), which was honored with the Governor General's medal. As his list of theater designs grew, American architects came to Toronto to study Sprachman's work.

Although theaters were their most prominent contribution to the Canadian streetscape, Kaplan and Sprachman also designed a number of Jewish community buildings including Jewish community centers in Toronto and Hamilton, the Toronto Mt. Sinai Hospital, the Baycrest Home for the Aged in Toronto, and several synagogues in Toronto and across western Canada.

Abe's son, Mandel, also became an architect known for his theater designs, albeit in a much changed Canada. Mandel was a child of the movies. He had spent his childhood in his father's movie theaters and at building sites doodling at the drawing board. In 1951 he translated his love of theater and screenwriting into a degree in architecture from the University of Toronto. After graduating, Mandel worked in Sweden, then in his father's office before opening his own firm in 1958. Like his father, Mandel designed movie houses that reflected the tastes of his times. Among his innovations were the first multiplexes, incorporating several screening rooms in one building and using televisions in the lobbies to promote the films.

Mandel was a striking man, known for his bowties and lapel pansies. Like his father, Mandel designed a number of striking synagogues in Ontario. His crowning achievement was his successful struggle to restore the 1913 Elgin Wintergarden Theatre in Toronto. One of the few remaining "doubledecker" or stacked Edwardian theaters in the world, the Elgin

Wintergarden had been the flagship of the Loew's chain of vaudeville theaters. Under Mandel's direction, it was painstakingly restored with added backstage and lobby areas. It reopened in 1989 and was soon a Toronto landmark.

[Paula Draper (2nd ed.)]

°**SPRINGER, AXEL CAESAR** (1912–1985), German publisher. Born in Altona/Hamburg. As he was unfit for war services, he did not fight as a soldier in the German Wehrmacht during World War II. Until 1941 Springer was editor in his father's newspaper *Altonaer Nachrichten*, whose publication was stopped due to a Nazi order. After the war he first started as a book publisher, but soon after that he founded many popular German magazines and newspapers. With the daily newspaper *Bild* Springer reached his greatest success, though critics complained about the one-sided conservative political opinions spread by this tabloid and a lack of serious journalism. In 1967, Springer postulated as the four main goals to which every editor of the Springer Press had to subscribe: The engagement for the German re-unification in freedom and in a united Europe, the reconciliation between Germans and Jews as well as the defense of the rights of the Israeli people, the rejection of political totalitarianism, and the defense of the free social market economy. In addition, the Springer Press always demonstrated sympathy and solidarity for American politics, particularly during the Vietnam War. As a non-Jew, Springer was a known friend of the Jewish People and Israel. This fact irritated many left-wing critics, who viewed in the the conservative Springer Press their main enemy. During the student protests in the 1960s, *Bild* condemned the protesters and many critics accused *Bild* of "heating-up" the atmosphere. In 1972 the Springer Publishing House in Berlin was the target of a bomb attack carried out by leftist extremists.

Springer gave substantial donations to Israel and Jewish organizations, e.g., for the library of the Israel Museum in Jerusalem (1966) and the Leo Baeck Institute in New York (1963). In 1968, Springer endowed $250,000 for the establishment of the Ottilie Springer Chair at Brandeis University. As a result of his social and political engagement Springer was honored with numerous awards, such as the Leo Baeck Medal (1978), and honorary doctorates from Temple University in Philadelphia (1971), Bar-Ilan University in Ramat Gan (1974), and the Hebrew University of Jerusalem (1976). In 1983, Springer was awarded the title "*ne'eman Yerushalayim*" (preserver of Jerusalem). In 1984, he received the gold medal of the Israeli Association of Daily Paper Publishers and in 1985 the gold medal of the B'nai B'rith League. Moreover, Springer was an honorary member of the Weizmann Institute of Sciences in Reḥovot, Israel.

In 1972, Springer published a collection of his speeches and essays: *Von Berlin aus gesehen. Zeugnisse eines engagierten Deutschen.*

BIBLIOGRAPHY: Axel-Springer-Verlag (ed.), *The Axel Springer-Group's Commitment to Israel* (2001); E. Cramer, A. Springer, "Israel und die Juden," in: A. Nachama et al (eds.), *Aufbau nach dem Untergang. Deutsch-jüdische Geschichte nach 1945* (1992), 347–56; G. Kruip, *Das "Welt"-"Bild" des Axel Springer-Verlags. Journalismus zwischen westlichen Werten und Deutschen Denktraditionen* (1999).

[Monika Halbinger (2nd ed.)]

SPRINGFIELD, city in Massachusetts. As of 2005, Springfield and its suburbs had a total population of 251,000, including an estimated 10,000 Jews, a figure largely unchanged in the past quarter-century. Jews did not begin to settle in Springfield in large numbers until the East European immigration of the 1880s, though individual Jews were recorded in the city previously, among them Leopold Karpeles (1838–1909), a Congressional Medal of Honor winner in the Civil War who lived in Springfield before the war. The first synagogues – B'nai Jacob and Beth Israel – were organized in 1891–92, and within a decade five other Orthodox congregations were established to serve the rapidly growing community, whose numbers increased from about 300 to 3,000 between 1901 and 1907 alone. YMHA was organized in 1905 and a Jewish Home for the Aged in 1912. One of the first local Jews to attain prominence in these years was the Lithuanian-born Henry Lasker (1878–1953), the first local Jew to be admitted to the bar and who between 1908 and 1916 was first elected alderman and then president of the city council. Lasker was a leader of B'nai B'rith and many other Jewish and civic organizations. Two other prominent Jews were the Russian immigrants Moses Ehrlich, who had a successful scrap-iron business and Raphael Sagalyn (1881–1949), a successful wholesale dry goods and real estate businessman. Ehrlich was a prime initiator and first president of Congregation Kodimoh; Sagalyn was founder of the United Hebrew Schools and president of its board of directors.

Following the restrictive immigration laws of the 1920s, the Jewish population of Springfield ceased its rapid growth but institutional life continued to develop. In 1921, the first Conservative synagogue, Congregation Beth El, was founded, and in 1932 a Reform congregation, Sinai Temple. The Jewish Community Council (predecessor to the Jewish Federation of Greater Springfield) was established in 1925, and the Jewish Social Service Bureau was established in 1927. In 1966, eight synagogues and temples were in existence in Greater Springfield, five Orthodox, two Conservative, and one Reform. The initial settlement took place in the city's older residential areas, primarily the North End area. After World War II, both the newer urban areas and the suburb of Longmeadow became increasingly popular. By 1966, only 5% of Greater Springfield's Jews still lived in the older area of settlement, while 60% lived in the newer urban areas. Of the 35% who resided in the suburbs, all but 3% were in Longmeadow, which adjoins the largest of the newer urban areas within Springfield proper, Forest Park. Accordingly, three of the largest Jewish institutions in the city, Temple Sinai, Congregation Beth El, and the Jewish Community Center, are all located near each other on the Longmeadow – Forest Park line, with two other synagogues remaining in Forest Park.

High educational achievement and occupational affiliation characterized the Jewish community in the late 1960s. Among adults, 40% had had at least some college education. One-fourth were engaged in professional work and 40% were managers or proprietors. An additional 27% were employed as clerical or sales workers; only 8% of the Jews were blue collar workers. Almost 80% of the Jews of Springfield were affiliated with a congregation; slightly more persons were members of Orthodox synagogues (41%) than of Conservative congregations (39%), and 20% belonged to the Reform Temple. Part-time religious schools were affiliated with the various synagogues, and there were the community-wide United Hebrew School and two day schools, the Heritage Academy and the Lubavitcher Yeshiva Academy. Two-thirds of all children between 5 and 14 years of age were enrolled in some program of Jewish education.

At the turn of the twenty-first century, a different picture has emerged, consistent with demographic trends throughout the country. Springfield's Jewish affiliation rate is now approximately the same as the national average of just above 40%. Although Springfield's Jewish community remains highly educated, much of the population is engaged in the professions (medicine, law, etc.), with very few proprietors and entrepreneurs. The Jewish population is increasingly older, with a small number of young families continuing to move to the area. In 2005, Springfield/Longmeadow had two day schools (Heritage Academy, Lubavitcher Yeshiva Academy) and six synagogues: three Orthodox (Congregation Kodimoh, Kesser Israel, and Beth Israel), two Conservative (Beth El and B'nai Jacob), and one Reform (Sinai Temple).

The Jewish community has grown significantly in the area just north of Springfield to the Vermont border. The communities of Northampton and Amherst, in particular, have witnessed significant Jewish growth, with approximately 5,000 Jews in these communities. Home to the University of Massachusetts, Amherst College, Smith College and others, the area attracts many academics, artists, and young professionals from larger cities. In 2005, the Upper Pioneer Valley boasted four synagogues, two of them with several hundred families. There are two Conservative synagogues (B'nai Israel, Northampton; Temple Israel, Greenfield), one Reform (Beit Ahavah, Northampton), and one Reconstructionist (Jewish Community of Amherst). Founded in the 1990s, the Solomon Schechter School of the Pioneer Valley has opened its doors to 100 students.

A variety of organizations and services continue to cater to the needs of the community. The Springfield Jewish Community Center traces its origins to the YMHA. The Jewish community supports a wide range of Zionist and fraternal organizations, with a strong Federation and an active Hadassah chapter, as well as many groups under temple auspices. The community is also the home of the Harold Grinspoon Foundation. Among notable members of the Springfield Jewish community are Frank Freedman, mayor, elected in 1967; Alan Sisitsky, state representative, elected in 1968; Paul Akerman, city councilman; Joel Levitt, president of the Springfield Jewish Federation (founded in 1938) and president of the Springfield Sugar Company; Irving Geisser, executive director of the federation and a member of the executive committee of the National Jewish Community Relations Advisory Council; Charles Nirenberg, Founder of Dairy Mart; and Harold Grinspoon, nationally recognized philanthropist and founder of Aspen Square Management.

[Sidney Goldstein / Harold Berman (2nd ed.)]

SPRINZAK, JOSEPH (1885–1959), Israeli labor leader and first speaker of the Knesset, member of the First to Third Knessets. Sprinzak was born in Moscow. His father, a manufacturer, was a member of Ḥovevei Zion and was active in Jewish community affairs. In 1891, when the Jews were expelled from Moscow, Sprinzak's family moved to Kishinev and then to Warsaw. Their home was a center for young Hebrew writers and active Zionists. In 1903, Sprinzak took part in organizing the Zionist group Ha-Teḥiyyah, led by Yitzhak *Gruenbaum. In Warsaw he worked for a while in the Hebrew publishing house Ahi'asaf, and wrote for Hebrew and Yiddish newspapers. In 1905 he returned to Kishinev, where he was a cofounder of the *Ẓe'irei Zion movement in Southern Russia, and in 1906 he participated as its delegate at the *Helsingfors Conference of Russian Zionists, after having formulated the Ẓe'irei Zion program together with Haim *Greenberg.

In 1908, after spending several months in Constantinople, where he was in touch with various Zionist leaders, including David *Wolffsohn, Menahem *Ussishkin, Nahum *Sokolow, and Vladimir *Jabotinsky, in an attempt to influence the new regime of the Young Turks, Sprinzak went to study medicine at the American University in Beirut. However, in 1910 he was asked by Ha-Po'el ha-Ẓa'ir to discontinue his studies, and become the party's secretary in Palestine. Inter alia, he was active in the absorption of the immigrants from Yemen. At the 11th Zionist Congress in Vienna in 1913, Sprinzak organized a faction of 41 delegates, consisting of members of Ha-Po'el ha-Ẓa'ir and Ẓe'irei Zion. During World War I he remained in Palestine and was instrumental in organizing help for the *yishuv* in general and the Jewish workers in particular. After the war he took part in creating the framework of the world movement *Hitaḥadut, which encompassed Ha-Po'el ha-Ẓa'ir and Ẓe'irei Zion. At its founding conference in Prague in 1920, together with Aharon David *Gordon, Hugo Bergmann, and Eli'ezer *Kaplan, he was the moving spirit of the Ha-Po'el ha-Ẓa'ir delegation from Palestine. Chairing the conference's meetings, he summed up its deliberations. At the 11th Zionist Congress in Carlsbad in 1921, he was the first representative of the labor movement in Ereẓ Israel to be elected to the Zionist Executive. For seven years he served on the Executive as head of the Labor Department and later of the Aliyah Department as well. In the 1920s, Sprinzak was a co-founder and leading member of the *Histadrut, a member of the Tel Aviv municipality, and played an active role in the establishment of Asefat ha-Nivḥarim and the Va'ad Le'ummi, and in the formation of

*Mapai through the merger of *Aḥdut ha-Avodah and Ha-Po'el ha-Ẓa'ir. In 1942–59, he served as chairman of the presidium of the Zionist Executive, and in 1944–49 served as the secretary general of the Histadrut.

After the establishment of the State of Israel in 1948, he was elected to chair the Provisional State Council. He was elected to the three first Knessets on behalf of Mapai, and served as Knesset speaker from 1949 until his death in 1959. As the Knesset's first speaker, he played a major role in molding the written and unwritten rules of Israel's parliamentary life. Sprinzak oversaw the competition for the planning of the new Knesset building at Givat Ram, but its construction began only after his death. His friendly, warm, and moderate character endeared him to both Israeli citizens and Jews abroad. His sense of humor and sensitivity enabled him to overcome conflicts. He favored a form of humanist, social-democratic Zionism, which regarded the process of national regeneration as an evolutionary one in which the workers were to play a major role in both urban and rural settlements.

Sprinzak's son Ya'ir was a scientist who worked at the Weizmann Institute, and was a member of the 12th Knesset on behalf of Moledet.

Among his writings are *Bein ha-Teimanim* ("Among the Yemenites," 1918); *Bi-Khetav u-be-al Peh*, a collection of articles and speeches (1952); and Yosef Shapira (ed.), *Iggerot Yosef Sprinzak*, a collection of letters (1965–69).

[Susan Hattis Rolef (2nd ed.)]

SQUADRON, HOWARD MAURICE (1926–2002), American Jewish communal leader. Squadron was born in New York City and graduated in law from Columbia University, where he was an editor of the *Columbia Law Review*. After teaching at the University of Chicago, he practiced law in New York, and after spending two years as staff counsel for the American Jewish Congress, he reentered private practice in 1954. He ultimately became the senior partner at Squadron, Ellenoff, Plesen & Sheinfeld.

Active in the American Jewish Congress for 25 years, and serving as its senior vice president, chairman of the National Governing Council, chairman of the national Commission on Law and Social Action, and chairman of the Congress's New York Metropolitan Council, he was elected president in 1978, retaining the position until 1984. In that capacity, he helped spearhead an assembly of mayors from around the world held annually in Jerusalem. At the 1999 conclave, Squadron was awarded the Guardian of the City of Jerusalem Medal. Squadron was an active participant in the America-Israel "Dialogue," an annual symposium conducted by the American Jewish Congress in Jerusalem. From 1980 to 1982 he served as chairman of the Conference of Presidents of Major American Jewish Organizations.

Active in the cultural life of New York City, Squadron was chairman of the executive committee of the Foundation for Joffrey Ballet, Inc., as well as of the Fifty-fifth Street Dance Theater Foundation.

SQUILL (Heb. חָצָב, *ḥaẓav* (mish.) or חָצוּב, *ḥaẓuv*), the *Urginea maritima*, a plant with a very large bulb that grows wild in almost every district of Israel. It lies dormant in the summer, its leaves withering, but later a stalk with a large inflorescence bearing hundreds of flowers bursts out of the bulb. The roots are very long and descend vertically into the earth as if digging into it, and some connect its name (*ḥaẓav*; "to dig") with this characteristic. Because of this the squill was sometimes used for demarcating fields (cf. BB 55a). According to tradition Joshua marked out with it the boundaries of Israel and of the tribes (TJ, Pe'ah 2:1, 16d). It was said that "the squill cripples the wicked" (Beẓah 25b), because it prevents them from removing the boundaries. The rind of its bulb is juicy and was used by some for implanting fig shoots (Kil. 1:8; so too Theophrastus, *Historia Plantarum*, 2:5, 5). Its leaves and bulb contain poisonous matter and few animals eat it. According to the *baraita* (Shab. 128a) it was eaten by gazelles and Noah prepared "squills for the gazelles" (Gen. R. 31:14) in the ark.

BIBLIOGRAPHY: Loew, Flora, 2 (1924), 188–94; E. and H. Ha-Reubeni, *He-Ḥaẓav* (1938); J. Feliks, *Kilei Zera'im ve-Harkavah* (1967), 161–2; H.L. Ginsberg, *Kohelet* (1961), 131–2; idem, *Five Megilloth and Jonah* (1969), 77. **ADD. BIBLIOGRAPHY:** Feliks, Ha-Ẓome'aḥ, 68.

[Jehuda Feliks]

SRAFFA, PIERO (1898–1983), British economist. Sraffa was born in Turin, Italy, the son of a professor of law. He became a professor of economics at the University of Caligari, Sardinia, at the age of 28 but was forced to flee to Britain the following year after his writings offended Mussolini. Sraffa spent the rest of his life at Cambridge University, where he served as Marshall Librarian, fellow of Trinity College, and reader in economics. Sraffa developed a legendary reputation as one of the great theoretical innovators in 20th-century economics, originating the theory of imperfect competition and making significant and influential contributions to the orthodox theory of value. He wrote little, but some of his ideas appeared in his *Production of Commodities by Means of Commodities* (1960). He is equally well known for his co-editing of 11 volumes of the correspondence of David *Ricardo, published in 1951–73, regarded as one of the great works in the history of economics. Sraffa also exerted a strong influence on many of the leading intellectual figures of his time and is credited with helping Ludwig *Wittgenstein move away from his earlier logical positivism to his later orientation towards linguistic analysis.

BIBLIOGRAPHY: ODNB online.

[William D. Rubinstein (2nd ed.)]

SREM (Ger. **Schrimm**; Pol. **Szrem**; Yid. **Strim**), town in Poznan province, W. Poland. Jews settled in Srem in the late 16th century and engaged in commerce, weaving, and goldsmithery. In 1656, during the war between Poland and Sweden, the Polish general S. Czarniecki persecuted the Jews of Srem, and those who survived left the town. In the 1670s Jews resettled in Srem and a community was organized. In 1683 a meeting of the council of the *galil* (province) of Poznan (see

*Council of the Lands) took place there. In the 18th century Srem Jews engaged in the trade of agricultural products, tailoring, shoemaking, and liquor production. In 1765 the Jewish community numbered 327. In the mid-18th century Samuel b. Azriel of Landsburg was the rabbi of Srem. From 1815, under Prussian rule, the Jewish population increased, numbering 924 (27% of the total) in 1840 and 1,127 (19%) in 1871. The Jews were engaged mostly in the building trade, tailoring, transportation, and shopkeeping. In the late 1870s many Jews left for Poznan and other cities in central Germany. In 1895 only 607 Jews were left (11%), and this number decreased to 318 (4.5%) by 1910. In the early 20th century the Srem community maintained charitable institutions and an association for Jewish historical and literary research. In 1921, in independent Poland, there were 103 Jews (1.5%) there.

[Arthur Cygielman]

Holocaust Period

Before World War II there were 26 Jews in Srem. Under German occupation, it belonged to the Regierungsbezirk Posen of the Warthegau. In October 1939 the Jews were deported to a transit camp in Poznan, from where they were probably sent to the General Government or to a larger town in Warthegau.

[Danuta Dombrowska]

BIBLIOGRAPHY: Halpern, Pinkas, index; B. Wasiutyński, *Ludność żydowska w Polsce w wiekach xix i xx* (1930), 167; A. Heppner and J. Herzberg, *Aus Vergangenheit und Gegenwart der Juden und der Juedischen Gemeinden in den Posener Landen* (1909–29), index; D. Lewin, *Judenverfolgungen im zweiten Schwedisch-polnischen Kriege* (1901), 28, 31.

SS AND SD (SS – **Schutzstaffeln**, "Protection Squad"; SD – **Sicherheitsdienst des Reichsfuehrers SS**, "Security Service of the Reichsfuehrer SS"), Nazi order that executed the "*Final Solution" (see also *Holocaust: General Survey) and other acts of mass and individual terror committed by the Nazis in Europe. The organization from its inception was connected with the idea of the "security" of the leader, and grew up as a racial elite formation around the myth of *Hitler the Fuehrer and his "mission."

The SS was originally a select group of bodyguards charged with protecting Hitler and the Nazi elite. It was set apart from other Nazi organizations by its distinctive black shirts, and eventually adopted the insignia of the death's-head. Its first leader was Jules Schreck, a personal body guard and chauffeur to Hitler. Other local party groups established similar means of protection, which were used not only defensively but offensively. The SS participated in the 1923 Munich Putsch and was outlawed together with the Nazi Party for a short time afterward.

In 1929, Heinrich *Himmler was appointed Reichsfuehrer-SS (RFSS), and as the party expanded he transformed the SS into a racial elite formation. From several hundred members in 1929, it expanded to some 50,000 by 1932 before Hitler came to power. In 1931, two years before the Nazis came to power, Himmler set up an intelligence service exclusively for the SS, headed by Reinhard *Heydrich: the Sicherheitsdienst (SD). The SD assisted in keeping an eye on deviators in the party, but at the time the Nazis rose to power it was still only a skeleton organization. He also established the Race and Settlement Office (RhSHA) to protect the racial purity of the SS. Special emphasis was placed on loyalty and disciplined appearance in uniforms, and racial criteria were established for membership, including an Aryan appearance and a registry of ancestors, including those of wives. The SS attracted and recruited people of a higher social class than the SA (storm troops). The SS was divided along military lines model into platoons, companies, and regiments. Its distinctive black uniform was first used in 1932.

When Hitler took power, Himmler began to attain control over all the internal security organs of Germany. Within a year the SS increased fourfold and Himmler consolidated his power. Beginning as the commander of the Bavarian political police, he soon took over the political police of other German states, and in 1934 the *Gestapo, the secret political police of Prussia. In 1934, the SS led the assault against Ernst Rohm and the SA and destroyed it decisively. In July 1934 after the assault, the SS became independent of the SD within the party. Afterwards there were no potential rivals to its power and its status rose.

The SS, the political police, and the concentration camps acted as a three-fold system devised to shadow the enemies of the regime and intern or destroy them politically or physically. Of particular importance was the vesting of the authority over concentration camps in the SS system and not subordinated to government authority, thus constituting what became known as the SS-state. In the process of differentiation of special tasks of the SS, special units were established, such as SS Totenkopfverbaende (Death's Head Units) to guard the concentration camps and SS Verfuegungstruppe, which served as a nucleus of the armed (Waffen) SS.

In 1936, Himmler became head of the entire German police, as the Reichsfuhrer SS and Chef der Deutschen Polizei im Ministerium des Innern. Himmler created a series of homes for wives of the SS men and single mothers to breed the master race – Lebensborn, the Well of Life. The Ancestral Heritage Society tried to document the superiority of the master race. The SS was envisioned by Himmler as the paradigm of the master race, the core of its future development.

Until World War II

By the time World War II broke out (1939), the SS numbered hundreds of thousands of members and millions of helpers. The duplication and competitiveness of the departments in the complicated, vast SS administration were intentional. To control the administration of both state and party functions, Himmler set up a field organization of SS and higher police leaders (Hoehere SS – und Polizeifuehrer – HSSPF). A nucleus of SS men engaged in work abroad, including intelligence work against future victims of Germany, and, last but not least, the "mobile killing units" (the Einsatzgruppen), which followed along with the Wehrmacht to the occupied countries to deal with "internal security matters."

Some ambitious younger men, including Adolf *Eichmann, Dieter Wisliceny, and Herbert Hagen, became experts in the Jewish question. Section II/112 of the SD began dealing with classifying world Jewry and its institutions according to the German organizational tables, studied Jewish literature and newspapers, and spied on Jewish leaders and organizations, in the full belief that the Jews had a worldwide intelligence service. The SD also began pressing to speed up Jewish emigration by all means and sought to work out practical ways to do so. One suggestion was to incite and organize riots such as the *Kristallnacht*, carried out two years later. The annexation of Austria in March 1938 permitted the SD executive initiative to establish (through Eichmann) the *Zentralstelle fuer juedische Auswanderung in Vienna, the first compulsory Jewish emigration center. Eichmann personally supervised the registration of Jews and expropriation of their property prior to their emigration. This first initiative led to the establishment of similar offices in the Protectorate of Bohemia–Moravia and in Germany itself. Eichmann headed the centers, and the director of the Gestapo, Heinrich *Mueller, acted as the chief supervisor. Thus the SD became an executive arm alongside the Gestapo, and finally the two authorities, the SD and the Gestapo, were united under the SS reorganization scheme in November 1939.

The SS organization now split up into main offices (Hauptaemter), among which the most important were the *RSHA – Reich Security Main Office (Reichssicherheitshauptamt); WVHA – Main Office for Economy and Administration (Wirtschafts-und Verwaltungshauptamt); and RuSHA – Main Office for Race and Settlement (Rasseund Siedlungshauptamt). The RSHA, which was essentially a combination of the security police and the SD, was given charge over internal security, the liquidation of enemies in the first stages of conquest by the Germans, and the dispatch of prisoners to camps. The prisoners were subordinate to the WVHA, on a combined ideological and "economic" base. The WVHA exploited the prisoners in the giant SS enterprises and in private German enterprises, while life in the camps and the work itself were functionally organized to bring about the physical "neutralization" or decimation of many of them. The WVHA also carried out pseudomedical experiments on human beings on orders given by "scientific and research" institutes of the SS and by Himmler, who wished to establish proofs for his racial concepts.

With the German invasion of Poland in September 1939, the SS attained almost sole responsibility for the Jews of Poland. The security police and SD, together with the regular police, interned the Jews in ghettos, deprived them of all their means, and starved them. To reduce all the Jews to the same level in the uniform repression scheme, *Judenraete were set up to assume direct and personal collective responsibility for the Jews, with the German authorities in charge. In the RSHA, several suggestions for a radical "Solution of the Jewish Question" were made during 1940, including the concentration of Jews in a "reservation" in Poland or their dispatch to Madagascar (see *Madagascar Plan). Historians have come to view local initiatives to deal with the local problem of Jews as an essential component of what later developed into the "Final Solution." Many emphasize the functionalist approach, with the destruction of Jews being a priority in solving a local problem, the apparatus of destruction evolving locally before being centralized and implemented throughout the German-controlled areas. Meanwhile, the invasion of Soviet Russia was in the offing. It commenced on June 22, 1941. Hitler decided that in the final stage of the "struggle for the vast Lebensraum in the East," the Jews of Russia and the Baltic states along with gypsies and Soviet commissars should be murdered by SS Einsatzgruppen with the cooperation of the army and the civil occupying administration. The Einsatzgruppen were divided into Einsatzkommandos (assault commando units) and Sonderkommandos (special commando units).

The "Final Solution."

The killing of Jews evolved in stages. First the mobile killing units, the Einsatzgruppen, went into towns and villages captured by the Wehrmacht and alone or together with local gendarmeries, and native antisemites assembled the Jews, confiscated their possessions, and murdered them one by one, town by town, village by village. After the murder of several hundred thousand Jews in the East by execution, gas vans were developed by the SS personnel on the ground, using retrofitted trucks. Many of these initiatives were taken locally, but this process proved to be too public, disquieting for inhabitants of conquered territories, and psychologically difficult for the killers. Thus a new mode of achieving the "Final Solution" (a camouflage term – see *Nazi-Deutsch) of the "Jewish Question" in all of Europe was initiated. The RSHA, with Eichmann as its Jewish expert and Mueller as the chief executor, was in charge of the dispatch of Jews to the death camps. The extermination centers differed from the older concentration camps as the former were constructed to deal with the immediate mass murder of the arrivals under the direction of the WVHA. A gigantic network was organized for the mass-scale plundering of property and possessions of the murdered, and for exploiting the victims' clothing, hair, and gold teeth. Not infrequently, concentration camps were set up alongside the death camps for exploiting the condemned for slave labor until the inmates, suffering from starvation and maltreatment, were "selected" for the gas chambers for automatized murder run by the SS technicians. Through its various agents, of which the SS was chief, the German occupiers compelled the various Judenraete in the ghettos to supply them with batches of victims for the death chambers and, until the ghettos' liquidation, with slave laborers for German industry. Throughout, the goal of utilizing Jewish labor by economic arms of the SS was at odds with the overriding goal of the "Final Solution" – the killing of the Jews. Dead Jews could not work. The ghettos were steadily reduced, until the final liquidation of all their inhabitants at the end of 1943 (with Lodz, the most notable exception). The use of camouflaged language and the dispatch of Jews in varying stages and by different bodies – sometimes by the RSHA and sometimes by the security police commanders (all of which were part of the SS and served one aim) – helped to keep in check any possible revolt or resistance by the Jews. In the Western countries and satellite states of the Reich, the SS maintained experts whose task was to dispatch the Jews.

The organizational principles that aided Himmler in his first steps turned the SS finally into a monster organization with millions of officials and soldiers with thousands of multiple and duplicate functions. In 1943 Himmler, the Reichsfuehrer SS, also became minister of the interior of the Reich, and in 1944 he drafted many foreigners to the legions of the Waffen-SS, including members of those considered by Nazi ideology to be of "inferior races." The attempts in 1939–41 of the SS to solve by mass extermination such problems as the existence of mentally ill and retarded children in German society, or its war against the churches, failed largely due to protests among the German public. But the murder of Jews, gypsies, Soviet prisoners of war, and members of "inferior peoples" was carried out without inhibition and virtually without protest. At the end of 1944, Himmler, as commander of the reserves and battlefront, retreated from the "Final Solution." He apparently still believed that the Jews under his control could be used as a bargaining chip to divide the Allies and forge a separate peace with the United States and Great Britain against the Soviet Union. He presumed that the Allies would accept his SS organization as an instrument of order and security in Germany. However, the Allies condemned the SS at the Nuremburg trials as a criminal organization and sentenced some of its heads to death. Many others were sentenced to severe punishments, but received amnesty. From the 1960s, the German judiciary dealt with the subsidiary organizations of the SS in a series of trials.

BIBLIOGRAPHY: G. Reitlinger, *SS, Alibi of a Nation* (1956); H. Hoehne, *The Order of Death's Head: The Story of Hitler's SS* (1969); H. Krausnick, et al., *Anatomy of the SS State* (1968); S. Aronson, *Reinhard Heydrich und die Fruehgeschichte von Gestapo und SD* (1970); E. Neusuess-Hunkel, *Die SS* (1956); L. Stein, *Die Waffen-SS* (1965); E. Kogon, *The Theory and Practice of Hell* (1960²); A. Bullock, *Hitler, a Study in Tyranny* (1962²), index. **ADD. BIBLIOGRAPHY:** R. Hilberg, *Destruction of the European Jews* (1961, 1985, 2003).

[Shlomo Aronson / Michael Berenbaum (2nd ed.)]

STACHEL, JACOB (Jack; 1900–1966), U.S. Communist leader. Stachel, born in Galicia, was taken by his family to New York City in 1911. He became active in the Socialist Party Youth and in 1924 joined the Communist Party. By 1927 Stachel headed the party's national organizational secretariat, and in 1933 he became director of its Trade Union Educational League. His main geographical area of responsibility in the 1930s was Michigan, where he staged a demonstration of 100,000 unemployed workers in Detroit in 1930 and pressed for Communist Party support of the Congress of Industrial Organizations (CIO) when it was founded in 1936. In 1939 Stachel was made executive secretary of the party's central executive committee, giving him much power behind the scenes until his indictment under the Smith Act in 1950, along with ten other party leaders, for advocating the violent overthrow of the United States government. After serving a five-year term in a federal penitentiary Stachel remained active in the party until his death.

BIBLIOGRAPHY: *New York Times* (Jan. 2, 1966), 73; M. Epstein, *Jew and Communism* (1959), 405–7.

STADTHAGEN, JOSEPH (d. 1715), German rabbi. One of a venerable line of rabbis, he was born in Metz and was *Landesrabbiner* of Schaumburg-Lippe for many years, taking his name from his home in Stadthagen. An acknowledged rabbinical authority (author of *Divrei Zikkaron*, Amsterdam, 1705), with a thorough knowledge of the New Testament and apologetic works, he participated in several religious disputations. In July 1704 he was called upon by Leffman *Behrend, the powerful Hanoverian *Court Jew, to accept the challenge of an apostate, who had been making the rounds of Jewish communities, challenging the scholars to disputations and blackmailing them into paying him to desist. The disputation was held in the presence of the elector of Hanover, the future George I of England, and his court. Stadthagen deftly refuted the stock charges of the apostate, gained the sympathy of the tolerant court, and established his intellectual and moral superiority. He made a vivid impression on the electress Sophie who parted from him with the words, "We all have but one God." The debate was transcribed by Stadthagen in Hebrew and Yiddish in his *Minḥat Zikkaron*, which was edited, translated, and published by A. Berliner, *Religionsgespraech* (1914).

BIBLIOGRAPHY: D. Kaufmann, in: REJ, 22 (1891), 98f.; J. Rosenthal, in: *Aresheth*, 2 (1960), 159.

STAHL, FRIEDRICH JULIUS (1802–1861), German conservative politician and political thinker. Born Julius Jolson in Wuerzburg, Bavaria, he grew up in an Orthodox Jewish family, but converted to Lutheranism in 1819, seemingly more out of inner conviction than in order to obtain a government post in a Catholic country. Stahl studied law at various Bavarian universities and was prominent in the Burschenschaften movement (see *Student Fraternities, German). After his doctorate and a first position in Munich, he became a professor of law in Erlangen and Wuerzburg. During this time, he completed his two main works *Die Philosophie des Rechts nach Geschichtlicher Ansicht* (2 vols., 1830–37), a historical view of the philosophy of law based on Christian theology, and *Die Kirchenverfassung nach Lehre und Recht der Protestanten* (1840), an important contribution to the debate about the structure of the Protestant church.

In 1840 Stahl succeeded Edward *Gans as professor of law at the University of Berlin where his lectures attracted widespread attention. He expounded his conservative opinions on contemporary politics in his lectures and published a series of pamphlets calling for the mobilization of the Christian state against liberalism and republicanism. Following the suppression of the 1848 revolution, he was made a member of the Prussian Upper House and gained considerable political influence at the court of Friedrich Wilhelm IV. While his political ideas have frequently been described as extreme and reactionary, it is now evident how important Stahl's contribution was for the modernization of German conservative thought, including the acceptance of constitutionalism.

Stahl rejected the full emancipation of the Jews and especially defended the exclusion of non-Christians from state functions. As a zealous and rhetorically gifted defender of traditional rights, justice and order, his views were approved of by *Bismarck and *Treitschke who were, nevertheless, troubled, as were his contemporaries, by the figure of a former Jew from Catholic Bavaria, forging the ideology of Prussian Lutheran conservatism. Stahl's philosophy was later repudiated by the Nazis as an expression of Jewish theocracy.

BIBLIOGRAPHY: R.A. Kann, in: YLBI, 12 (1967), 55–74; E. Hamburger, *Juden im oeffentlichen Leben Deutschlands* (1968), 197–209 and index. **ADD. BIBLIOGRAPHY:** W. Bussmann, in: M. Greschat (ed.), *Gestalten der Kirchengeschichte* (1985), 325–43; W. Fuessl, *Professor in der Politik: Friedrich Julius Stahl (1802–1861)* (1988); C. Link, in: H. Heinrichs (ed.), *Deutsche Juristen Jüdischer Herkunft* (1993), 59–83; J.B. Mueller, in: H.C. Kraus (ed.), *Konservative Politiker in Deutschland* (1995), 69–88.

[Uffa Jensen (2nd ed.)]

STAHL, HEINRICH (1868–1942), president of the Jewish community of *Berlin under the Nazi regime. A prominent insurance executive, Stahl was a liberal Jew who attached great value to Jewish tradition. He became president of the Berlin community in May 1933, when its executive consisted of seven liberals (Reform), three Zionists, and one Orthodox representative. He was influential in the establishment of the Reichsvertretung der Deutschen Juden, and signed its first proclamation. In November 1935, the Nazi authorities demanded the reduction of the executive to seven members, and the Zionists put in their claim for 50% of the seats. Stahl saved the situation by reducing the number of his own liberal faction from seven to three. He attempted to retain a special status for the Berlin community vis-à-vis the *Reichsvertretung. He did not succeed, though it was agreed that its headquarters would remain in Berlin. Stahl, the patrician businessman, did not see eye to eye with the scholarly rabbi, Leo *Baeck. Deported to *Theresienstadt in 1942, in the month preceding his death he became deputy chairman of the camp's *Judenrat under Jacob *Edelstein.

[Kurt Jakob Ball-Kaduri]

°STALIN (Dzhugashvili), JOSEPH VISSARIONOVICH (1879–1953), Bolshevik revolutionary, ruler of the Soviet Union, and leader of world *Communism. Through his entire career, Stalin had to deal with the "Jewish question," and as the autocratic ruler of the Soviet Union his policy had a profound influence on the fate of the Jewish people. At the early stages of the factional strife in the Russian Social Democratic Party, during which Stalin unreservedly joined *Lenin and the Bolsheviks, he became involved in the Jewish problem through their bitter dispute with the *Bund. In 1913, with Lenin's approval, he published an essay titled "Social Democracy and the National Question" (later renamed "Marxism and the National Question"), in which the Jews figured prominently as the subject of a theoretical analysis of ethnicity and nationhood. In this essay Stalin denied the existence of one national Jewish entity throughout the world, stressing the differences between the Jewish communities in East and West. He conceded that certain ethnic characteristics exist in each Jewish community separately, but denied the Jews any national status and adhered to Lenin's concept of the unavoidable progressive assimilation and disappearance of the Jews under advanced capitalism (e.g., in Western Europe and in America) and certainly under Socialism.

In contrast to this view, Stalin, as commissar of nationalities in the first Soviet government (1917–23), was responsible for the policy of fostering Yiddish cultural and educational activity, Jewish administrative institutions, and agricultural settlement, and it was he who gave the formal permit to the young Hebrew theater *Habimah in Moscow. In his controversy and blood feud with L. *Trotsky, G. Zinovyev, L. *Kamenev, K. *Radek, and other members of Lenin's old guard, hardly any anti-Jewish allusions were discernible. He did not refrain, however, from accusing his prominent Jewish victims of being agents of the Nazis and the *Gestapo. Although there were Jews among the executors of the bloody purges, the upheaval of the party and government structure caused by these purges resulted in a reduction of Jewish personnel in many branches of the bureaucracy.

At the same time a marked change occurred in Stalin's policy toward Jewish cultural activity and to the evolution of Jewish settlement and territorial autonomy, which had culminated in the *Birobidzhan project. Stalin's trend, concurrent with the great purges, was to liquidate the Yiddish school system, Yiddish publications, research institutes, theaters, etc., so that at the end of the 1930s only token vestiges of them remained (as, e.g., the State Jewish Theater in Moscow). During his rapprochement with Nazi Germany (1939–41) he suppressed in the Soviet press and radio all mention of Nazi antisemitism and anti-Jewish atrocities, but himself refrained from using anti-Jewish allusions while attacking the Western "imperialist" powers. He extradited to the Nazi regime German communists who had fled to the Soviet Union, many of them Jews. The German attack on the Soviet Union (June 22, 1941) and his adherence to the anti-Nazi alliance induced Stalin to establish the Jewish *Anti-Fascist Committee, which, for the enlistment of Western Jewish support for the Soviet war effort, was allowed to exploit the sentiments of world Jewish solidarity and "brotherhood" and even use Jewish historical and nationalist rhetoric, in full contradiction to his original ideological concept of Jewish identity. Immediately after the war, when he was presented with a plan to allow returning Jewish evacuees to settle in the Crimea, Stalin opposed it on the grounds that in the event of war a "Jewish Crimea" would constitute a security risk for the Soviet Union.

An exceptional episode in Stalin's attitude to Jewish nationhood was his resolute and energetic support in 1947–48 for the establishment of a Jewish state in Palestine, a policy clearly directed against Britain's position in the Middle East and largely reversed during the explicitly antisemitic (and "anti-Zionist") stance of his last years (1948–53), which coincided with the Cold War. An ominous prelude to these "black years" was the camouflaged assassination of the de facto head of Soviet Jewry Solomon *Mikhoels, the chairman of the Jewish Anti-Fascist Committee, on Jan. 13, 1948, a crime to which Stalin was at least a passive accomplice.

From the end of 1948 until his death, Stalin displayed an extremely hostile attitude toward everything Jewish (mostly labeled "Zionist"). He embarked on a course of complete liquidation of the last Jewish institutions and personalities who engaged in Yiddish literature and culture. The Jewish Anti-Fascist Committee and the publishing house Der Emes were closed down. Mass arrests of leading Jewish writers and artists followed. Jewish intellectuals and professionals active in various fields were also arrested. Among the arrested was Molotov's Jewish wife, whom Stalin believed to be sent by Zionists to spy on her husband. These purges were accompanied by a vituperous campaign of the Soviet press against Western-oriented *"Cosmopolitans" in which Jews were the obvious target. In mid-1952 a closed trial was held against members of the Anti-Fascist Committee and other leading personalities in Jewish cultural life, 26 of whom were secretly executed on August 12 of that year. They were accused of Jewish nationalism, of having maintained contact with Western espionage, and of having planned to detach the Crimea from the Soviet Union. Jews were assigned a prominent role in the Slánský *Trials, staged in Czechoslovakia on Stalin's orders, and based mainly on an alleged link between Jews, Zionism, and U.S. espionage. This trial indicated Stalin's intentions to use antisemitism not only in the Soviet Union, but also in the satellite countries of Eastern Europe. The *"Doctors' Plot," staged under Stalin's supervision in 1952 and published on January 13, 1953, represented his fears and suspicions of the Jews. It is generally believed that Stalin's death on March 5 of that year prevented a major disaster to Soviet Jews.

Personal Anti-Jewish Bias

Stalin's ruthlessness and secretive nature make it impossible to prove conclusively when and to what extent a personal anti-Jewish bias played its role in his policy toward individual Jews and the Jewish people. Jews were known to him from his childhood and adolescence, since both Georgian towns – Gori, his birthplace, and the capital Tbilisi, where he received his Greek-Orthodox education – had a sizable Jewish population. A jest to which he referred in an article in 1907, in which the Bolsheviks' rivals, the Mensheviks, were portrayed as a "Jewish" faction of the Social-Democratic Party, and the humorous allusion made to the fact that it would not have been a bad idea if the Bolsheviks staged an intraparty "pogrom" seemed to indicate a certain train of thought. On the other hand, on Jan. 12, 1931, in an interview with a representative of the Jewish Telegraphic Agency, Stalin made one of the sharpest statements ever made against antisemitism, describing it as "the most dangerous vestige of cannibalism," and in 1936 he allowed this statement to be published in the Soviet Union (*Pravda*, Nov. 30). However, there is a series of indications of a personal anti-Jewish bias, as, e. g., a remark made to General Sikorski, the head of the Polish government in exile, in 1941 ("the Jews are rotten soldiers"), and various hints and remarks he uttered in 1948 to the Yugoslav Communist Milovan Djilas, or, in his family life, his disapproval of his son Yakov's marriage to a Jewess, his highly emotional irritation over his daughter's romance with the Jewish film director Kapler (having him arrested and sent to a labor camp) and avoiding meeting his Jewish son-in-law. The enthusiastic response of Soviet Jews to the establishment of the State of Israel in 1948 seemed to have reinforced his antagonism. He said to his daughter, Svetlana, that the entire older generation of Soviet Jews was contaminated with Zionism and that they were teaching it to their young people. Thus it seems evident that, while consciously exploiting deep-rooted anti-Jewish suspicions of the populace for his political ends – through the anti-"Cosmopolitan" campaign, the Slánský Trials, and the Doctors' Plot, which highlighted his nationalist, anti-Western Cold War policy – Stalin himself became more and more paranoid and disturbed in his attitude to Jews and the Jewish people.

See also *Antisemitism: In the Soviet Bloc.

BIBLIOGRAPHY: I. Deutscher, *Stalin: A Political Biography* (1949, 1963[3]); S.M. Schwarz, *The Jews in the Soviet Union* (1951); idem, *Yevrei v Sovetskom Soyuze*, 2 (1966[4]); M. Djilas, *Talks with Stalin* (1962); S. Allilueva, *Twenty Letters to a Friend* (1967); idem, *Only One Year* (1969).

[Shimon Redlich]

STAMFORD, town in Lincolnshire in northeastern England. In 1190 the local Jews were attacked by the crusaders assembled there at the Lent fair and those unable to find shelter in the royal castle were massacred. The community later reestablished itself and in the 13th century there was an **archa*. In 1222 members of the community were arrested on a charge of mocking Christianity, possibly the result of a misunderstanding of a Purim masquerade. No Jewish community has been established in modern times.

BIBLIOGRAPHY: Roth, England, index; Rigg-Jenkinson, Exchequer, index.

[Cecil Roth]

STAMFORD, corporate and finance center in Connecticut; population (2004) 111,000; Jewish population (2004) est. 14,000. The earliest Jewish merchants were Nehemiah Marks (1720), and Jacob Hart (1728), who by 1738 was the fifth highest taxpayer in town. He owned property also in Greenwich and Darien but as a Jew was not eligible to vote or serve on the grand jury. Hart's children were the first of the Jewish faith born in Stamford. Jewish families came from New York during the American Revolution, among them were Isaac Pinto who translated the first English High Holy Day prayer book in America (1761) and the daily English prayer book in 1766 but did not remain afterwards. Sporadic Jewish settlers continued to come until 1856 when Wolff Cohen advertised his clothing store in *The Advocate*. In 1868 there were five Jewish-owned businesses but no community or congregation. Through the 1870s Jewish owned saloons as well as clothing and fancy and dry goods establishments. The first Jewish marriage with a full *minyan* was held in 1805, but it was not until 1871, when Rabbi Henry Vidaver of New York married Henry Bernhard and Rachel Cohen, that a description of the ceremony and reception were printed in full detail in *The Advocate*. Samuel H. Cohen, Stamford's first Jewish attorney, was appointed probate judge in 1876. In 1881 Jacob Rosenblum arrived in Stamford; he is considered the first Eastern-European Jew from Lithuania to reach there, coming via Sharon, Pennsylvania. Young, single peddlers, Isadore Alexander and Solomon Osmansky, followed. The first worship services were held in an attic on Cedar St. In 1887 David Cohen, a new arrival, reports that the first High Holy Day services were held in Stamford in Jacob Rosenblum's tenement flat on Stillwater Ave. The same year Pacific St. began to develop as the retail hub for the new arrivals who opened a variety of retail stores and small manufacturing. By World War I, this street had become Stamford's version of New York's Lower East Side. Mainstream Jewish stores were also on Main St. and Atlantic Street. In 1889 a congregation was chartered as Agudath Sholom with 22 signers. In 1891 a cemetery association was chartered with the name of Agoodat Solima and purchased land on West Hill Rd. The congregation during this decade was dormant and by 1901, it was simply reported as "The Hebrew Society" with no building of its own. In 1904 a second charter for a Cong. Agudath Sholom was issued and ground was broken for the first synagogue, completed 1908. There were secular Jewish organizational chapters, such as L'Maan Zion that began in 1902, and the Independent Lodge started in 1903, which also established its own cemetery on Hoyt St. in Darien in 1904. B'nai B'rith was chartered in 1910, and the National Council for Jewish Women in 1911; a Stamford Hebrew Political & Social Club was chartered in 1907. Of all the aforementioned groups, only the Independent Lodge survives. In 1911 attorney Alfred Phillips was elected to the state legislature, and in 1913 he became the first Jewish secretary of state in Connecticut. In 1916 The Hebrew Institute was founded as the meeting place for social and later also some worship activities of the community. It dissolved in 1927 and was succeeded by The Stamford Jewish Community Center which dedicated its building on Prospect St. in 1930. Roosevelt Lodge of the Masonic Order was founded 1922, because Jews were refused membership in Stamford's Union Lodge F.&A.M. The JCC moved to its present location on Newfield Avenue in 1982. Temple Beth El, a Conservative congregation, was founded in 1920 and met in the Hebrew Institute until 1927, when its first synagogue was dedicated on Prospect St. The congregation moved to its newer structure on Roxbury Rd. in 1974. Temple Sinai, a Reform congregation founded in 1954, has a synagogue complex on Lakeside Drive. The Orthodox Congregation Agudath Sholom has worshiped since 1965 in its current building, which also has a *mikveh*, on Colonial Road. Young Israel is an Orthodox congregation with a synagogue on Oaklawn Avenue. Chabad is constructing a school complex on High Ridge Rd., and The Fellowship of Jewish Learning, founded 1973, is a liberal congregation sharing a meeting house on Roxbury Rd. All congregations have religious schools. The Bi-Cultural Day School founded in 1956 is renowned for its full curriculum from kindergarten through grade eight. Jewish Family Services has offices to serve all in need of assistance. Offices of The United Jewish Federation, and The Jewish Endowment are located in the JCC. The Jewish Historical Society of Lower Fairfield County was founded in 1983 in Stamford. Julius Wilensky was elected and served as the first and only mayor of the Jewish faith of The City of Stamford, 1969–73. Stamford is the birthplace and boyhood home of United States Senator Joseph Lieberman who was the first candidate of the Jewish faith to be nominated and run for vice president of the United States.

[Irwin Miller (2nd ed.)]

STAMPFER, JEHOSHUA (1852–1908), a founder of *Petaḥ Tikvah. Born in Szombathely, western Hungary, Stampfer attended Azriel *Hildesheimer's yeshivah at Eisenstadt. The obtainment of national independence by Hungary in 1867 aroused in Stampfer a desire to go to Ereẓ Israel to ensure the survival of the Jewish people and the Torah. Leaving home in 1869 and completing his journey to Jerusalem on foot, he joined a group of young people who were trying to establish an agricultural settlement in the country. In 1878 he and his companions settled on land that belonged to the village of Mulabbis, near the Yarkon River, and founded the first Jewish agricultural settlement, *Petaḥ Tikvah. For many years Stampfer was chairman of the Petaḥ Tikvah local council, which sent him abroad to collect funds from philanthropists and also encourage settlement in Ereẓ Israel. In 1903 he attended the *Zikhron Ya'akov assembly, which was convened to form the organizational framework of the *yishuv*; he was the representative of the conservative faction, which had as one of its aims the abolition of women's right to vote. He administered the affairs of Petaḥ Tikvah in an ultra-Orthodox spirit and accepted the first pioneers of the Second Aliyah with mixed feelings: he was pleased by the influx of new blood to the country and tried to help the newcomers integrate and learn farming, but, on the other hand, he bitterly opposed their detached attitude toward religion and feared their influence on the settlers and their children. Stampfer's son, SOLOMON ISAAC STAMPFER (1877–1961), became the first mayor of Petaḥ Tikvah in 1934.

BIBLIOGRAPHY: Y. Yaari-Poleskin, *Ḥolemim ve-Loḥamim* (1946^2), 38–46; idem (ed.), *Sefer ha-Yovel le-Petaḥ Tikvah* (1929), 107–22; M. Smilansky, *Mishpaḥat ha-Adamah*, 1 (1944), 65–68.

[Yehuda Slutsky]

STAMPFER, JOSHUA (1921–), U.S. Conservative rabbi, historian. Stampfer was born in the Jewish Quarter in the Old City of Jerusalem and was brought at the age of two to the United States, where he grew up in Akron, Ohio. He earned his B.S. from the University of Chicago in 1943 and his M.S. from the University of Akron in 1945. He returned to Jerusalem to study at the Hebrew University and volunteered to fight with the *Haganah in Israel's War of Independence. He was ordained at the *Jewish Theological Seminary in 1949 and received a D.H.L. from the *University of Judaism in 1972. In 1987, he was awarded an honorary Ph.D. from Pacific University. He served as rabbi of Congregation Tifereth Israel in Lincoln, Nebraska (1949–53) before becoming rabbi of Congregation Neveh Shalom in Portland, Oregon (emeritus since 1993). Under his leadership, Neveh Shalom grew to more than 1,000 families, to become one of the leading Conservative synagogues in the Pacific Northwest. Influenced by his teacher Mordecai *Kaplan, Stampfer initiated egalitarian changes, encouraging women to read the Torah and counting them in the *minyan* long before it became more commonplace within the movement.

A past president of both the Oregon Board of Rabbis and the Pacific Northwest Region of the *Rabbinical Assembly, Stampfer brought dynamism to the greater Oregon Jewish community as well. In addition to developing innovative educational programs at his own synagogue, Stampfer was instrumental in founding the first Jewish day school in the city, Hillel Academy (now the Portland Jewish Academy). He established and chaired the Oregon Jewish Historical Society, the Oregon Holocaust Resource Center, the Oregon Jewish Museum, and the Oregon Israel Jubilee Committee. In 1983, he founded the Institute for Judaic Studies, sponsoring symposia and conferences (in conjunction with the University of Oregon and Portland State University, where he serves on the faculty) that bring Jewish scholars to an area of the country considered remote. Remembering the influence of Shlomo *Bardin's Brandeis Camp on his own life, Stampfer founded and directed Camp Solomon *Schechter, the only Conservative Jewish summer camp in the Pacific Northwest.

Stampfer created and nurtured organizations beyond the boundaries of Oregon as well. His travels and contacts with the remnants of the ancient Jewish community of Kaifeng, China, and the Converso families of Belmonte, Portugal, led him to become the founding president of the Society for Crypto-Judaic Studies, to support research on the vanishing traces of the *Diaspora. He was also an organizer and the first vice president of the Sino-Judaic Institute.

Stampfer has maintained close personal and professional ties with Israel. He spent his sabbaticals working for and teaching at the fledgling Center for Conservative Judaism in Jerusalem. He encouraged support for Israel at home and led more than a dozen community and clergy tours to Israel. He was a co-founder of Oregonians for Peace Now and a member of the national board of Americans for Peace Now.

Stampfer was a long-standing appointee to the Oregon Government Ethics Commission and was actively involved in interfaith dialogue with Muslim and Christian leaders. He was the author of *Pioneer Rabbi of the West: The Life and Times of Julius Eckman* (1984), and a volume on ancient history, *Cradle of Civilization in the Middle East* (n.d.). In addition, Stampfer edited six books: *Prayer and Politics: The Twin Poles of A.J. Heschel* (1985); *Dialogue, the Essence of Buber* (1986); *The Sephardim*: A *Cultural Journey from Spain to the Pacific Coast* (1987); *All Its Paths Are Peace* (1987); *Islam and Judaism, 1400 Years of Shared Values* (1988); and *The Last Crypto Jews of Portugal* (1990). A biography of Stampfer's life, *To Learn and to Teach* (by David Michael Smith) appeared in 2003.

[Bezalel Gordon (2nd ed.)]

STAMPS. The first post offices in the Holy Land were established by the European great powers, by arrangement with the Sublime Porte, in the mid-19th century (see *Israel: Postal Services for further details).

The following post offices were established by the European powers:

(a) French Post Offices. There were three French post offices in Ereẓ Israel. The office in Jaffa was opened in June 1852, while those in Jerusalem and Haifa were opened in 1900 and 1906, respectively. The postage stamps of France were in use until 1885, when they were replaced by stamps specially issued for the French post offices in the Levant.

(b) Austrian Post Offices. The post offices in Jaffa and Haifa were opened in 1854 and that in Jerusalem in 1859. Postage stamps were introduced in 1863 with the issues of Lombardo-Venetia, followed in 1867 by the first stamps for the Austrian post offices in the Levant.

(c) Russian Post Offices. The Russian post offices in Ereẓ Israel were in Jaffa, Jerusalem, Acre, and Haifa.

(d) The Italian Post Office. This was the only postal service to issue stamps specially overprinted with the name of the city "Gerusalemme."

The period of the Turkish post offices ended with the conquest of Ereẓ Israel by General Allenby (1917–18). The British then opened post offices, staffed by army personnel, in the principal towns and cities. At that time there were no postal facilities for the civilian population, and the inhabitants of Ereẓ Israel were unable to communicate with their relatives and friends abroad. Cut off from the outside world for a long time, the people of Ereẓ Israel eagerly awaited the resumption of postal services. On Dec. 9, 1917, approval was given by the military authorities for printing the first stamp under the British occupation. This stamp, first issued on Feb. 10, 1918, bears the initials EEF ("Egyptian Expeditionary Forces") and cost one piaster. A total of 338,881 of these stamps were printed on ungummed paper, and they remained in use until July 1, 1920. In addition, 20 separate stamps of various monetary denominations, all appearing with the same basic design, were issued. The Civil Administration replaced the Military Administration on July 1, 1920, when the letters OET (or OETAEEF), the abbreviation for "Occupied Enemy Territory Administration, Egyptian Expeditionary Force," were removed from the obliterators used in all post offices. It was decided by the government to issue stamps bearing inscriptions in the then official languages of the country: English, Hebrew, and Arabic. The inscription on these stamps, issued in September 1920 in the official languages, read "Palestine"; the Hebrew inscription having the additional letters א״י (the abbreviation for Ereẓ Israel) added after the word "Palestine" (פלשתינה א״י). These stamps were used in various overprints, until the appearance in 1927 of the only pictorial set to be issued by the British government, and which continued in use until the State of Israel was established in 1948. This pictorial issue had four basic designs: Rachel's Tomb near Bethlehem for the 2, 3, and 10 mil values; the Dome of the Rock in the Old City of Jerusalem for the 4, 6, 8, 13, and 15 mil values; the Tower of David near Jerusalem's Jaffa Gate for the 5, 7, and 20 mil values; and Tiberias and the Sea of Galilee for the 50, 90, 100, 200, 250, 500 mil, and £ P1 values. Three sets of postage due stamps were also issued; these stamps were normally used to collect charges on taxed letters or letters with insufficient postage.

On the departure of the British in April–May 1948, many of the post offices were taken over by the Minhelet ha-Am, and, from May 15, 1948, by the Government of Israel. During the War of Independence communications were extremely difficult, and from time to time the supply of postage stamps ran out. In order to overcome this shortage and to continue a regular postal service until the Government of Israel could supply the new stamps, many issues of a local and provisional nature appeared. Noteworthy among these, and eagerly sought by philatelists, are the Jewish National Fund labels overprinted with the word *Do'ar* ("Post") and the local issues of Safed, Rishon le-Zion, and Petaḥ Tikvah. On May 9, 1948, while Jerusalem was under siege, the first set of local Jerusalem stamps were issued. These were JNF stamps showing the map of Ereẓ Israel with the frontiers of the Jewish State and the "International" city of Jerusalem as proposed by the United Nations in its decision of Nov. 29, 1947. Overprinted with the word *Do'ar* and their value in mils in Hebrew lettering, the stamps were in use until June 20, 1948, when the stamps of the State of Israel became available.

The first stamps issued by the State of Israel were printed on a small letter-press machine under strict secrecy. On May 16, 1948, the *Do'ar Ivri* ("Hebrew Post") stamps bearing pictures of ancient Jewish coins were put on sale throughout Israel. Since the name of the new state was not known until the Proclamation of Independence on May 15, the designation *Do'ar Ivri* was used. The nine values of this first set are today a highly prized collector's item. From 1948 to the end of 2005 Israel produced a total of 1,827 stamps, including souvenir sheets and special issues. Their attractive and colorful designs have won them international recognition. The definitive series of ancient coins, the twelve tribes, the signs of the zodiac, and emblems of the towns and cities of Israel; airmail issues of birds, landscapes, and exports of Israel; annual Jewish New Year and Independence Day commemoratives; and many other fascinating subjects have introduced Israel to philatelists throughout the world. Many philatelic clubs, both in Israel and abroad, are devoted to the study of the postal history of Ereẓ Israel. Collections of Ereẓ Israel stamps are regularly displayed at philatelic shows such as at the Philympia exhibition in London, where a number of exhibitors of Ereẓ Israel stamps were awarded medals. Israel stamps are much in demand, and the early issues, for example, sell for high prices. They have also been a considerable source of revenue to the state.

[Moshe Hesky / Alan Karpas]

Jews and Judaica on Stamps

Over the years philatelists the world over have increasingly devoted their collections to a single theme, subject, or country. One such thematic category is "Judaica" and "Jews on Stamps." These stamps, issued by Israel and many other countries, depict religious symbols and objects, synagogues, portraits of famous Jews in all walks of life, sites of significance in Jewish history, Bibles, statues of and by Jews, and almost every aspect of life connected with Judaism and Jews. There are a number of enthusiasts all over the world who devote themselves to this aspect of stamp collecting, and who have united themselves into societies. One of these publishes the *Judaica Historical Philatelic Journal* in the U.S.

Among the subjects in the Judaica collection are the following:

Nobel Prize Winners: Niels Bohr, Paul Ehrlich, Fritz Haber, and Albert Einstein.

Statesmen: Benjamin Disraeli, Walther Rathenau, Paul Hymans, and President Zalman Shazar (on a Brazilian stamp issued in honor of his visit to that country in 1966).

Scientists and Scholars: Heinrich Hertz, Armin Vámbéry, David Schwarz, Robert von Lieben, Ferdinand Widal, Walemar Haffkine, Otto Lilienthal.

Philosophers: Henri Bergson, Maimonides.

Musicians: Anton Rubinstein, Henri Wieniawski, Karl Goldmark, Felix Mendelssohn-Bartholdy, Gustav Mahler, Paul Dukas.

Artists: Isaac Levitan, Amadeo Modigliani, Marc Chagall, Mark Antokolsky.

Actors: Rachel, Sarah Bernhardt.

Poets and Writers: Heinrich Heine, Shalom Aleichem, Ḥ.N. Bialik.

Revolutionaries and Resistance Fighters: Rosa Luxemburg, Karl Marx, Jacob Sverdlov, Mátyás Rákosi.

Other subjects include the Bible; Hebrew letters (on the stamps of the UN, Russia, Denmark, and Jordan); and synagogues of Prague, Surinam, Cochin, Panama, and the Netherlands Antilles. A field of special interest to collectors of Judaica is the period of the Holocaust, including antisemitic issues, and the Ghetto stamps.

[Alan Karpas and Shaul Dagoni]

BIBLIOGRAPHY: M.J. Wurmbrand (comp.), in: *Philatelic Literature Review*, 5, no. 3 (1955); H.F. Kahn, in: *Postal History Journal* (Jan. 1966), incl. bibl.; I. Livni, *Livni's Encyclopedia of Israel Stamps.*

Catalogue 1969 (Heb. and Eng. 1968); London. Mosden Stamp Company. *Catalogue of the Postage Stamps of the State of Israel* (1959); idem, *Holy Land and Middle East Philatelic Magazine; Holy Land Philatelist: Israel's Stamp Monthly* (Tel Aviv); *Israel Philatelist: Official Organ of the Israel Philatelic Exchange Club* (Tel Aviv); *Simon's Catalogue of Israel Stamps* (Heb.). **ADD. BIBLIOGRAPHY:** *Stamps of Israel Encyclopedia and Catalogue*, CDD-ROM (1998); M. Arbell, *The Spanish and Portuguese Jews in Postage Stamps* (1988).

STAND, ADOLF (1870–1919), Zionist leader in Galicia and one of the leaders of world Zionism. Born in Lemberg, Stand became a Zionist in the 1880s. He was very active in the organization of Zionist societies and was the editor of the fortnightly Polish-language paper *Przyszłość* ("Future") and later of the important Zionist annual in Polish *Rocznik Żydowski* ("Jewish Yearbook"). He joined Theodor *Herzl and always regarded himself as his disciple. A period of great activity ensued for Stand as, traveling through Galicia, he won over audiences with his Zionist speeches and established various Zionist groups. He was considered one of the finest speakers of his generation. In addition to his Jewish education, he had mastered German and Polish cultures, and put them to good use in his speeches.

He largely built up the Zionist movement in Galicia. In 1907 he was elected to the Austrian parliament for the district of Brody-Zloczow in eastern Galicia, and was among the founders of the Club of Jewish Members of Parliament, the first of its kind in Jewish parliamentary history. Despite his great admiration for Herzl, he opposed the *Uganda Scheme. In opposition to Herzl, Stand favored practical settlement activity in Ereẓ Israel. On the outbreak of World War I, Stand fled to Vienna together with other Jewish refugees from the areas of Galicia conquered by the Russian army but was unable to adapt himself to his new circumstances, although he joined the Austrian Zionist leadership, and with the end of hostilities was appointed chairman of the East Galician National Council Mission in Vienna. In fact, his position as the leader of Galician Jewry had come to an end in 1914. After World War II, letters from Herzl to Stand were discovered and transferred to the Zionist Archives in Jerusalem. A Hebrew selection of his writings, *Kitvei Stand*, was published in Tel Aviv in 1942.

BIBLIOGRAPHY: N.M. Gelber, *Toledot ha-Tenu'ah ha-Ẓiyyonit be-Galiẓyah*, 2 vols. (1958), index; Z.F. Finkelstein, *Stuermer des Ghetto* (1924).

[Aryeh Tartakower]

STANDE, STANISLAW RYSZARD (1897–1939), Polish poet and translator. Stande's numerous verse collections were political salvoes for communism and range from *Młoty* ("Hammers," 1921) to *Nasz krok* ("Our Step," 1937). From 1931 he was an exile in the USSR, where he joined the editorial board of the monthly *Internatsionalnaya Literatura*. During the Stalinist purges of the late 1930s Stande died in prison.

STANISLAV (Pol. **Stanislawow**; now called **Ivanov Frankovsk**), city in Ukraine; under Poland-Lithuania until 1793; under Austria until 1918; and in Poland until 1939. A few months after the town was founded on his estates by Hetman Jedrzej Potocki (1662), he granted the Jews the right to settle there, extending to them other rights as well. The Jewish population consisted of leaseholders, innkeepers, craftsmen, and merchants, the last in competition with the Armenians living in the town. As a result of a succession of epidemics in the first 20 years of the 18th century, the number of Jews declined considerably, but within a dozen years or so this situation changed for the town's squires tried to attract Jews to the town. Around 1720 Józef Potocki confirmed the rights granted to the Jews in 1662. In 1745 the bishop of Lvov gave Stanislav Jews permission to erect a new synagogue but it was never built. Permission was obtained once more, with certain limitations, in 1761. In the fire of 1868 a large part of the town, including the synagogue and many Jewish houses, was burnt down.

The Jewish population grew from 404 families (about 45% of the total population) in 1793 to 2,237 persons (41.5%) in 1801; 6,000 (55%) in 1849; 10,023 (53%) in 1880; 15,860 (30.7%) in 1921; and 24,823 (41.3%) in 1931. From 1784 until the Holocaust, members of the *Horowitz family were rabbis in Stanislav. In the first half of the 19th century, influenced by the center in *Tysmenitsa, the Haskalah movement spread there. By the mid-19th century the rich merchants and the intelligentsia, who had assimilationist tendencies, dominated the community, but in 1880 Zionist influence became predominant in these groups. A regional Zionist committee was founded in Stanislav in 1898, and the Bar Kochba Students' Association at the beginning of the 20th century. Markus (Mordecai Ze'ev) *Braude played an important role in the development of Zionism and in the social and cultural life of the Jews of Stanislav. The Yiddish weekly, *Stanislaver Nakhrikhten*, edited by B. Hausmann, was published from 1902 to 1912. Other Yiddish weeklies were *Der Yidisher Veker* (1905–07) and *Stanislaver Gloke* (1909–14). A Hebrew literary monthly, *Ha-Yarden* (1906–09), was edited by Eleazar *Rokach.

During World War I Stanislav was twice occupied and destroyed by the Russian army; the synagogue was burnt down, and a large number of Jews escaped to Bohemia and Vienna. In 1918 the town was the temporary seat of the authorities of the West Ukrainian Republic; the Jewish National Council for East Galicia also had its seat there. During this period, in spite of the Ukrainian nationalist repressions, the social and cultural life of the Jews flourished; they organized a Jewish militia for *self-defense which included demobilized soldiers. In May 1919 the units of Jeff Haller (see Haller's *Army) entered the town, instigating pogroms and looting Jewish property.

[Jacob Goldberg]

In Independent Poland

In June 1919 the Polish authorities, influenced by the *Endecja party, dismissed the heads of the Jewish community of Stanislav, as well as all Jewish officials in the municipality, the post office, and railroad. Jewish teachers were not allowed to teach at public or private schools. By the end of August 1919 the situation improved somewhat after the visit of Henry Morgenthau (see Morgenthau *Commission). At the end of the year the Zionist leader Karl Halpern was appointed head of the community. At the 1922 elections to the Polish *Sejm, three Jewish delegates were elected from Stanislav and the province. In 1923, 13 Jews were elected to the 36-member municipal council. In order to minimize the importance of the Jewish community in the municipality, the Polish authorities incorporated several surrounding villages into Stanislav, thereby decreasing the percentage of Jews in the total population. At the 1927 municipal elections the Zionist leader Alexander Rittermann was elected deputy mayor, and out of eight town councilors three were Jews. The Jewish hospital was reopened in 1922. From 1922 the economic situation of Stanislav Jews considerably improved. In addition to wholesale and retail trade, they were occupied in the developing tanning industry, wood processing, and the production of alcoholic beverages and industrial alcohol. In 1924 the local yeshivah reopened. A Jewish secondary school was opened in 1924/25 and had 300 pupils a year later. There was also a Hebrew school, Safah Berurah. Vocational training institutes for boys, girls, and adults were established in the 1920s. A Yiddish weekly, *Dos Yidishe Vort*, close to Po'alei *Zion, appeared in 1918–19, and *Shtegen*, a Yiddish literary monthly edited by Max Tabak, was published from 1932 to 1935. Between the two world wars there were 55 synagogues and prayerhouses in Stanislav (including one of the Sadagura Ḥasidim).

[Arthur Cygielman]

Holocaust Period

The number of Jews in Stanislav had increased to approximately 30,000 in 1939. The Soviets occupied Stanislav on Sept. 18, 1939, and immediately prohibited the activities of the various Jewish organizations. However, for a while, Zionist youth organizations continued to function underground. Public trials against Jewish merchants were staged, and Zionist and other leaders were imprisoned.

When the German-Soviet War broke out in June 1941, the town was occupied by the Hungarian army, and soon the Ukrainians carried out acts of murder, robbery, and degradation against the local Jews. At the same time over 1,000 Hungarian Jews were brought into the city. When the town came under direct German administration (July 26, 1941), a Judenrat was appointed, headed by Israel Zeiwald. The first victims of the German extermination policy were 1,000 Jews of the local intelligentsia who were massacred in a nearby forest. In the largest and most ruthless *Aktion*, on Oct. 12, 1941, over 10,000 Jews were put to death at the local Jewish cemetery. Two months later the ghetto was established. Starvation and epidemics claimed further victims. On March 31, 1942, all the refugees from Hungary as well as 5,000 local Jews were dispatched to *Belzec extermination camp. On the basis of a rumor spread in August 1942 that a young Jew had struck a Ukrainian policeman, the Germans asked Mordecai Goldstein, then chairman of the Judenrat, to deliver 1,000 Jews to the Nazis. When he refused, he was hanged together with all the other members of the Judenrat; and over 1,000 Jews were murdered. On the first day of Rosh Ha-Shanah 1942, German soldiers broke into the ghetto, rounded up some 5,000 Jews, and sent them to Belzec. Many others were killed on the spot. There were further round-ups and in one of them the Germans shot about 1,000 Jews caught without labor permits (Jan. 26, 1943). The murder of the remainder of the community took place on Feb. 22, 1943, at the local Jewish cemetery. During the last stages of the liquidation of the Jewish community of Stanislav, several groups of young Jews organized themselves into partisan units. One group was headed by Oskar Friedlender of Buchach, and in another, a young woman engineer, Anda Luft, was known for outstanding partisan activities.

Some 1,500 Jews from Stanislav, some of whom had escaped prior to the Nazi occupation, survived in various parts of the world. In the city itself the Jewish community was not reestablished after the war. Organizations of Jews from Stanislav function in Israel and in the United States.

In later years, the renewed Jewish community in Ivanov-Frankovsk established a synagogue, a Jewish day school, and a community center. In 2003 the Jewish community opened an exhibition entitled "Jewish Stanislav." Dedicated to the history and development of the Jewish community in Stanislav, the exhibition depicts the history of the local community and synagogue. A new Holocaust memorial was erected near the city.

[Aharon Weiss / Ruth Beloff (2nd ed.)]

BIBLIOGRAPHY: D. Sadan and M. Gelehrter (eds.), *Sefer Stanislav (Arim ve-Immahot be-Yisrael*, vol. 5, 1952); E. Weitz, *Al Ḥorvotayikh Stanislavov* (1947); L. Streit, *Dzieje Wielkiej Miejskiej Synagogi w Stanislawowie* (1936); A. Szartowski, *Stanisławł i powiat Stanisławowski pod wzglłem historycznym* (1887); S. Barcaz, *Pamitki miasta Stanislawowa* (1858); Leibesmann, in: *Yad Vashem Bulletin*, 14 (1964), 64–66; H. Jonas, in: *Chwila* (Sept. 17, 1933).

STANISLAVSKY, SIMON JUDAH (1849–1921), author and scholar. Born in Nikopol, S. Russia, Stanislavsky received a traditional education, and influenced by I. *Orshanski, entered a Russian gymnasium at the age of 23.

His first contribution to the Hebrew press dealt with problems of education, especially for girls. Later he wrote studies on the history of Russian Jewry as well as monographs on Isaac Erter, Abraham Abba Glusk, the Maggid of Dubno (Jacob *Kranz), Mendel *Lefin, Israel *Zamosc, and others. Most of his works were published in the Russian-Jewish press, mainly in *Yevreyskaya Biblioteka* and *Voskhod*. He also contributed to Hebrew periodicals, such as *Ha-Shilo'aḥ* and *Reshummot*. Stanislavsky was one of the first *maskilim* in Yekaterinoslav (*Dnepropetrovsk) where he resided, contributing many reports on the activities of his community to the Hebrew and Russian-Jewish press.

BIBLIOGRAPHY: *S.J. Stanislavsky; Autobiografiya*, in: N. Sokolow (ed.), *Sefer Zikkaron* (1889); *Haaretz* (Sept. 9, 1921); S. Levin, *Mi-Zikhronot Ḥayyai*, 3 (1939), 215; Y.L. Baruch, in: *Hed Lita* (1924), no. 23, 13–14.

[Yehuda Slutsky]

STAR, DARREN (1961–), U.S. television writer and producer. Star was born in the Washington, D.C., suburb of Potomac, Md., the eldest son of an orthodontist father and freelance-writer mother. As a child, he was obsessed with Hollywood. By age 15, he had a subscription to the trade publication *Variety*, and, while in high school, he took screenwriting classes at American University. After graduating college from UCLA, Star worked odd jobs to support his writing career, and at age 24 sold his first screenplay, *Doin' Time on Planet Earth*, a sci-fi movie for teens (starring Adam West of TV's *Batman*). In 1990, Fox paired Star with famed TV producer Aaron *Spelling (*Charlie's Angels, Dynasty*) to write the pilot for a dramatic series set in high school, and *Beverly Hills, 90201* (1990–2000) was born. It was an enormous hit, which spawned another Fox series, *Melrose Place* (1992–99), based on an apartment complex in Los Angeles where Star once lived. Star's first solo venture, *Central Park West* (1995), lasted only 17 episodes. However he followed this with the HBO cable hit, *Sex & the City* (1998–2004), a racy comedy about a New York sex columnist (Sarah Jessica *Parker) and her three best friends (Cynthia Nixon, Kim Cattrell, and Kristen Davis), which was groundbreaking in its depiction of stylish contemporary women and their relationships. It was a critical hit with many nominations and awards, including winning Golden Globes for Best Comedy Series (2000, 2001, 2002) and the Emmy for Outstanding Comedy Series (2001). Star continued to create new shows, including *Miss Match* (2003) starring Alicia Silverstone, and *Kitchen Confidential* (2005).

[Amy Handelsman (2nd ed.)]

STARA ZAGORA, city in central Bulgaria. It seems that refugees from Spain established a community in Stara (Old) Zagora. In 1858 there is a mention of the Jewish quarter. The Russians, who conquered the town in 1877, looted the houses of the Jews and the synagogues; some of the Jews lost their lives. In 1884 an Alliance Israélite Universelle school was opened. In 1885 there were 332 Jews in the town and in 1893, 480. The Jews engaged in the export of grain. In 1943 there were 560 Jews in the city. After the establishment of the State of Israel, most of the Jews of Stara Zagora immigrated there together with other Bulgarian Jews. In 2004 there were 110 Jews in the city, affiliated to the local branch of the nationwide Shalom organization. For further information on the Holocaust Period, see *Bulgaria.

BIBLIOGRAPHY: S. Mézan, *Les Juifs Espagnols en Bulgarie* (1925), 53, 77; Rosanes, Togarmah, 6 (1945), 125–8.

[Simon Marcus / Emil Kalo (2nd ed.)]

STARER, ROBERT (1924–2001), U.S. composer of Austrian birth. Starer was born in Vienna, where he studied from the age of 13 at the State Academy of Music. After the *Anschluss* he settled in Jerusalem and continued his studies at the conservatory with Josef *Tal, Solomon *Rosowsky, and Oedeon *Partos. After serving with the British Royal Air Force from 1943 to 1946, he went in 1947 to the U.S. on a Juilliard School of Music postgraduate scholarship, studied with Aaron *Copland in Tanglewood in 1948, and joined Juilliard's faculty in 1949, teaching there until 1974. In 1957 he received American citizenship. In 1966 he was appointed professor of music at Brooklyn College and at the Graduate Center of the City University of New York, where he taught until 1991 and was named a Distinguished Professor (1986). Starer was elected a member of the American Academy of Arts and Letters (1994) and awarded the Medal of Honor for Science and Art by the president of Austria (1995). He received an honorary doctorate from the State University of New York in 1996.

Starer is the author of *Rhythmic Training* (1969), *Basic Rhythmic Training* (1986), and an autobiography, *Continuo: A Life in Music* (1987).

Starer wrote a great deal of ballet music, including *The Story of Esther* for Anna *Sokolow (first performed 1960), *The Dybbuk* for Herbert *Ross (Berlin Festival, 1960), *Samson Agonistes* (1961) and *Phaedra* (1962) for Martha Graham. His operas include *The Intruder* (1956) and *Pantagleize* (1973). He also wrote *Kohelet* (1952); *Sabbath Eve Service* (1967) *Psalms of Woe and Joy* (1975); *Anna Margarita's Will*, (1979); *Letter to a Composer*, (1994), two symphonies (1950, 1951); three piano concertos (1947, 1953, 1972); violin concerto, 1979/80; viola concerto, 1986; cello concerto, 1988; *Nishmat Adam* for narrator, choir and orchestra (1990); concerto for two pianos (1996).

Starer was a composer of eloquent style in a post-Bergian atonal idiom. His works reflect his encounter in Palestine with Arabic scales and rhythms, and his affinity to jazz he learned in the U.S. He absorbed some influences of the 1960s avant-garde and turned them into vehicles of his penchant for dramatic processes.

BIBLIOGRAPHY: Grove Music Online.

[Yuval Shaked (2nd ed.)]

STARK, ALBERT ("**Dolly**"; 1897–1968), U.S. baseball umpire, radio announcer, and college basketball and baseball coach. Stark was born on the Lower East Side. His father died when he was a youngster, and his mother became blind, leading to a poverty-stricken childhood and forcing Stark to earn money as a pushcart peddler. Stark played for Jersey City and Newark in the International League, before failing in his tryout with the Washington Nationals for his lack of hitting. Stark umpired college baseball for a few years and then began officiating in the Eastern League in 1927. On February 3, 1928, he was appointed an umpire in the National League. He became one of the most celebrated and popular umpires in baseball from 1927 until 1940, so much so that on August 24, 1935, Stark was given a "day" at the Polo Grounds and presented with an automobile before the scheduled game, an event virtually unheard of for umpires. In 1934 and 1935 he was voted the most popular umpire in a player's poll. In 1936 Stark became the first umpire in history to hold out for more money, sitting out the season and working as a radio announcer in Philadelphia. He returned the following year, retired in 1939, came back in 1942, and then retired for good. In the off-seasons Stark coached basketball at Dartmouth College, as head coach of the freshman team from 1925 to 1928 and coach of the varsity from 1929 to 1936 and 1945–46, finishing with a 102–59 record. After his career, Stark became a successful designer of women's clothes, known for the originality of his "Dolly Stark" dress.

[Elli Wohlgelernter (2nd ed.)]

STARK, EDWARD (1863–1918), U.S. *ḥazzan* and composer. Stark was the son of a *ḥazzan* and became *ḥazzan* of Temple Emanu-El in San Francisco in 1893 and remained there for 20 years. He was one of the most influential musicians in the service of the American Reform Synagogue. His compositions evince the influence of *Sulzer and *Lewandowski and the style of the classical oratorio, but are based for the most part on traditional Jewish thematic material. He insisted on the use of the *ḥazzan* as soloist, thus reversing previous trends in the Reform synagogue. Under the title *Anim Zemiroth*, he published compositions for the Sabbath and the High Holidays (1909–13). In *Day of God* (1898) he arranged the **Kol Nidrei* melody for soprano solo, choir, and small orchestra.

STARK, LOUIS (1888–1954), U.S. journalist. Stark, a leading labor reporter for almost 20 years, worked on *The New York Times* from 1917 until his death. He wrote firsthand accounts of fights in the Kentucky coalfields, sit-down strikes, and lockouts, and among the awards he won for his reporting was the Pulitzer Prize (1942). From 1931 to 1951 Stark was in Washington covering the White House. He then returned to New York to join the *Times* editorial board.

STARKENSTEIN, EMIL (1884–1942), pharmacologist. Born in *Poběžovice, Bohemia, Starkenstein was professor of pharmacology at the Prague German University from 1920 until 1938. Initially he studied purines, inosite, and metabolism of purines. Later he investigated the metabolism of inorganic substances and the effect of compound drugs in the treatment of pain. His study of seasickness led him to develop an effective counteracting drug. Starkenstein endeavored to further collaboration between the Czech and the German universities of Prague. He resigned at the time of the Sudeten crisis (1938) and moved to the Netherlands in 1939, where he concentrated on research into quinine. He was arrested after the Nazi occupation and killed in the concentration camp of Mauthausen. Starkenstein had a keen interest in the history of pharmacology and of Bohemian Jewry, and published articles on the history of his family (he was a descendant of Eleazar *Loew) and on his native community (see bibliography there). Starkenstein took a leading part in the activities of the territorial lodge of *B'nai B'rith in Czechoslovakia.

He published more than 300 articles. His books include *Der Einfluss experimentell-pharmakologischer Forschung auf Erkennung und Verhuetung pharmakotherapeutischer Irrtuemer* (1923); *Pharmakologie der Entzuendung* (1929); and in collaboration with J. Pohl and E.E. Rost: *Lehrbuch der Toxikologie* (1929).

BIBLIOGRAPHY: M. Matoušek and J. Kok, in: *Arzneimittelforschung – Drug Research*, 14 (1964), 1367–68 (bibl. of articles published in 1939–42 on p. 1368); S.R. Kagan, *Jewish Medicine* (1952), 219–20; *Biographisches Lexikon der hervorragenden Aerzte*, 2 (1993); S. Hermann, in: HJ, 8 (1946), 104.

[Suessmann Muntner]

°**STARKEY, JOHN LLEWELYN** (1895–1938), British archaeologist. After World War I, he excavated with *Petrie at Qau and Badari. From 1924 to 1926 he was field director of the University of Michigan expedition to Kom Washim. In 1926 he joined Petrie's expedition to Palestine, working at Tell Jamma (1926), Tell Sharuhen (1927), and Tell al-ʿAjjūl (1929–31). He directed the Wellcome-Marston expedition to Tell *Lachish from 1932 to 1938. Starkey was a successful field director with efficient methods. During the 1936–39 riots he was assassinated by Arabs while on his way to Jerusalem for the opening of the Palestine Archaeological Museum.

[Michael Avi-Yonah]

STAROBINSKI, JEAN (1920–), Swiss literary critic and author. The son of a physician, Starobinski was born and educated in Geneva, where he obtained doctorates in both literature and medicine. He lectured on French literature at Johns Hopkins University from 1953 to 1956 and then returned to Geneva University, where he became professor of French literature in 1964. He published articles and books on a vast range of subjects – medicine (*Histoire de la Médecine*, 1963; *A History of Medicine*, 1964); psychoanalysis, psychiatry (*L'Invention de la Mélancolie*, 1960); architecture and art (*L'Invention de la Liberté*, 1964; *The Invention of Liberty*, 1964); sociology, linguistics, and above all literature, especially that of the 18th century. Two works in this last field were *Montesquieu par lui-même* (1953) and *Jean-Jacques Rousseau: la Transparence et l'Obstacle* (1957). In *L'Invention de la Liberté* Starobinski traced the birth of the concept of freedom in the plastic arts, and in *L'Oeil Vivant* (1961) dealt with phenomena such as literary creation and a comprehensive vision of the world. Starobinski was also a leading exponent of the "structuralist" school of criticism, which considered a work of art in terms of a "significant structure" (i.e., the psyche of the creator, or the creative psyche of a social class), and the written word as a sign embodying the precarious balance between the *signifié* and the *signifiant* (i.e., content and expression). Raised in a staunchly Jewish and Zionist home, Starobinski was greatly interested in the Jewish aspects of modern literature, particularly the works of *Kafka, to whom he devoted several analytical studies, the first in 1943. His continued preoccupation with Jewish and Israel cultural affairs found expression in his preface to Claude *Vigée's French translaton of David *Rokeaḥ's verse collection, *Les Yeux dans le rocher*, 1968. He is married to Prof. Esther Starobinski, née Safran, the daughter of the chief rabbi of Geneva. She taught Jewish philosophy at its university.

BIBLIOGRAPHY: L. Le Sage, *The French New Criticism* (1967), 141–8; G. Poulet, in: *Critique*, 19 (1963), 387–410.

[Claude Gandelman]

STARODUB, city in Bryansk oblast, Russian SFSR. Jewish settlement in Starodub is first mentioned in connection with the *Chmielnicki massacres of 1648–49, when the Cossacks conquered the town and murdered its Jewish inhabitants. Later, Jews once more inhabited Starodub, but during the Northern War, when the town was occupied by the Swedish army (1708), soldiers again killed about 50 Jews. In 1847 the number of Jews registered in the community was 2,558, and in 1897 there were 5,109 Jews (42.5% of the total population). The community was largely influenced by *Ḥabad Ḥasidism, which during the middle of the 19th century established a large yeshivah. This was closed down by the authorities, however, in 1881 as a result of a denunciation by one of the town's *maskilim* who accused the Ḥasidim of evading military service and of being involved in forgery and fraud. In October 1905 pogroms took the lives of several Jews in Starodub. Under the Soviet regime the community and its institutions were dissolved. In 1926 there were 3,317 Jews (26.6% of the total population). Under the German occupation (1941) all Jews who did not manage to escape were killed.

BIBLIOGRAPHY: Y.F. Schneersohn, in: *He-Avar*, 3 (1955), 125–30; 4 (1956), 104–11; *Die Judenpogrome in Russland*, 2 (1909), 324–8.

[Yehuda Slutsky]

STARO-KONSTANTINOV (referred to by the Jews as Old Konstantin), city in Kamenets-Podolski oblast, Ukraine. Under Polish rule Staro-Konstantinov was an important commercial center renowned for its fairs. Jews lived there from the end of the 16th century; in 1629 there were 130 Jewish families (about 25% of the total population) and the community was the second largest in Volhynia. During the *Chmielnicki massacres (1648–49), Jews from the whole of the surrounding region sought refuge within the fortified city. The Cossacks broke into the city on the Ninth of Av, however, and massacred all the Jews. Staro-Konstantinov was also destroyed several times during the *Haidamack persecutions of the early 18th century. Jews continued to settle in the city, however, and by 1765, 1,801 Jews were counted as paying the poll tax in Staro-Konstantinov and its vicinity. Under Russian rule Staro-Konstantinov became a district city of the region of Volhynia. In 1802 Jews numbered 2,053. Riots broke out in Staro-Konstantinov in 1827 when the order of Czar Nicholas I on the mobilization of Jews into the Russian army was published. By 1847, there were 6,611 Jews in the community, and in 1897 the number had increased to 9,212 (60.7% of the total population). Most of the local Jews were Ḥasidim and followers of the *ẓaddikim* of the Chernobyl and Sadagora dynasties. With the establishment of the Soviet regime in Volhynia in 1920 Jewish community life was dissolved. This period also marked the economic collapse of the city proper and the departure of many of its inhabitants. By 1926 there were again 6,934 Jews (41.3% of the population) in Staro-Konstantinov supporting a large Yiddish secondary school. At the end of 1931 there were 4,837 Jews (about 33% of the population) in the city, of whom over a quarter were deprived of voting rights ("Lishentsy"). During World War II when the Nazis invaded the city those Jews who did not succeed in escaping were exterminated. In 1959 there remained only 800 Jews among the city's 20,000 inhabitants. Staro-Konstantinov was the birthplace of A.B. *Gottlobor and A. *Goldfaden.

BIBLIOGRAPHY: S. Ettinger, in: *Zion*, 21 (1956), 107–42; Nathan Hannover, *Yeven Meẓulah* (1966 ed.), passim, esp. 53ff.; A. Margolis, *Geshikhte fun Yidn in Rusland* (1930), 402–4; S. Lipshitz, *Vegn Shtetl* (1932), 34–68; A.B. Gottlober, *Zikhronot mi-Ymei Ne'urai* (1880).

[Yehuda Slutsky]

STARR, JOSHUA (1907–1949), U.S. Jewish historian and communal worker. Starr, born in New York, studied at the Teachers' Seminary of the Jewish Theological Seminary, at the Universities of New York and Chicago, and at Columbia University. During 1933–35 he was a research student at the American School of Oriental Research in Jerusalem. Starr served on the staff of the American Jewish Congress and the American Jewish Joint Distribution Committee. During 1947–49 he was secretary of the Commission for European Jewish Cultural Reconstruction, on whose behalf he was instrumental in recovering part of the religious and cultural treasures looted by the Nazis. Starr's main scholarly interest was in Byzantine and post-Byzantine Jewish history, on which he published: *The Jews in the Byzantine Empire, 641–1204* (1939); *Life in Crete Under the Rule of Venice* (PAAJR, 12 (1942), 59–114); and *Romania; the Jewries of the Levant after the Fourth Crusade* (1949). He also wrote on the New Testament and on Christian sects. In the field of contemporary Jewish history he took part in the publication of the *Jewish Population Studies* (1943) on behalf of the Conference on Jewish Relations, and edited *Jewish Social Studies*. Starr contributed numerous articles to learned publications, as well as pamphlets and articles for the World and American Jewish Congresses. A *Joshua Starr Memorial Volume* was published in 1953, containing a biography (by Abraham G. Duker) and a bibliography (9–15).

[David Jacoby]

STASZOW (Pol. **Staszów**; Rus. **Stashev**), town in Kielce province, central Poland. The Jewish settlement there developed from the beginning of the 18th century. In 1765 there were 609 Jews paying the poll tax in Staszow and 169 in the surrounding villages. Jews in this period were occupied in tailoring, hatmaking, goldsmithery, glaziery, and soap manufacture. Between 1823 and 1862 Jewish settlement in the town was restricted by the authorities of Congress Poland. The Jewish population numbered 2,062 (52% of the total) in 1827; 3,246 (64%) in 1857; and 4,885 (62%) in 1897. In the second half of the 19th century Jews in Staszow established tanneries and factories for shoes and clothing, and engaged in small-scale trading. Owing to the residence there of the *ẓaddik* R. Israel (1763–1831), son of R. Meir ha-Levi Hurwitz of Apta, the influence of Ḥasidism within the community was strong. There were 4,704 Jews living in Staszow (56% of the population) in

1921. In 1932 antisemites perpetrated a pogrom against the Jews of the town. The community's institutions included *battei midrash*, two yeshivot, schools, two hospitals, and libraries. The celebrated *ḥazzan* Joseph (Yossele) *Rosenblatt was born in Staszow.

[Shimshon Leib Kirshenboim]

Holocaust Period

On the outbreak of World War II there were about 5,000 Jews in Staszow. The Germans entered the town at the end of June 1941. A ghetto was established in June 1942, in which 5,000 Jews from Staszow and 2,000 from its vicinity were concentrated. The Jewish community was liquidated on Nov. 8, 1942, when hundreds of Jews were murdered and the remainder deported to *Belzec death camp. During these deportations many Jews fled to the nearby forests and succeeded in hiding there. After the war the Jewish community of Staszow was not reconstituted. Organizations of former residents of Staszow are active in Israel, the United States, Argentina, Brazil, and Uruguay.

BIBLIOGRAPHY: *Słownik geograficzny Królestwa Polskiego*, 11 (1890), 286; R. Mahler, *Yidn in Amolikn Poyln in Likht fun Tsifern* (1958), index; B. Wasiutyński, *Ludnosć żydowska w Polsce w wiekach XIX i XX* (1930), 31; *Sefer Staszow* (1962, Heb., Yid., and Eng.).

STATISTICS.

Official Statistics

Prior to the 19th century, statistical data on Jews were obtained irregularly, either from mere estimates, or as a by-product from administrative records specifically relating to Jews. As modern official statistics developed in Europe and American countries during the 19th century, they began to provide some statistical information on Jewish inhabitants. But enumeration of the number of Jews in some European countries, before the latter part of the 19th century, is considered to be incomplete. The growth of official statistics in general, and statistics on Jews in particular, was a gradual process. During the 20th century, official statistics on the number of Jews in the general population have been compiled in some Asian and African countries. The most favorable conditions for statistical information on Jews from official sources prevailed in the first decades of the 20th century until World War II. The majority of Jews were then living in countries – especially in Eastern and Central Europe – that rather regularly collected and published vital and migratory statistics, in addition to census data on Jews as a distinct group within the general population. These data not only supplied the overall numbers of the Jewish populations but also reflected their composition and demographic patterns. The Jews were distinguished in three ways: by religion, by ethnic group (termed "nationality" in Eastern Europe), and by language, i.e., according to the use of Yiddish or Ladino. Sometimes all three criteria were used concurrently by the same country. During the Nazi ascendancy, some countries made counts of persons of "Jewish descent." The wide-ranging changes in the period after World War II also affected the quantity and quality of statistics on Jews. On the one hand, the State of Israel has provided competent and detailed statistics on both its Jewish and non-Jewish inhabitants, and on the other hand, there has been a great reduction in the volume of official statistics on Diaspora Jewries. The Holocaust and subsequent migrations diminished the numerical importance of the Jews in Eastern and Central Europe. In addition, the policy of the new Communist regimes in that part of the world was to discontinue religious and, in some countries, ethnic, classification in official statistics. In the West, when religious information is not collected, this is attributed to "separation of church and state." Nevertheless, some liberal and democratic Western countries have developed a tradition of either distinguishing or not distinguishing religious groups in their official statistics (e.g., Canada, the Netherlands, Switzerland differentiate; the U.S., Belgium, and France do not). A new circumstance which, in recent decades, has complicated the collection of data on Jews, is the increased number of "marginal" Jews who are apt to conceal their Jewish identity and indicate on statistical returns that they are "without religion." At present about 70% of Diaspora Jewry, i.e., more than 50% of world Jewry, live in countries without regular official statistics on Jews. Even where such inquiries are made in Diaspora countries, the information published on the composition of the Jewish population is usually meager, often no more than a geographical breakdown cross-classified by sex. The situation in the major countries of Jewish residence in the Diaspora is as follows: the U.S., which has the largest Jewish population of any country, does not distinguish Jews in its decennial population census. Some figures on the number and residential distribution of the Jews were obtained by a "census of religious bodies," but this was last taken in 1936. The separate classification of Jews in U.S. immigration statistics was discontinued in 1943. There are no official vital statistics on religious groups in the U.S. (except for marriage and divorce data collected in two states).

After World War II the U.S.S.R., another major center of Jewish population, had two population censuses, in 1959 and 1970. The published results distinguished Jews as well as the many other ethnic groups in the Soviet Union. The number of Jews in the U.S.S.R. recorded by the censuses was contested by Jewish circles as being too low. However, it should be remembered that there were conceptual and practical problems of identification of Jews in the U.S.S.R. In any case, no reliable means exist for making alternative estimates because there is no statistical information on the manifold changes in the Jewish population which took place during and since the Holocaust on the territory of the U.S.S.R. (which was enlarged after World War II). In France and Great Britain there are virtually no official statistics on Jews, and those in Argentina are scanty.

Of the Diaspora countries with several hundred thousand Jews after World War II, Canada has had the most detailed official statistics on Jews. But even in this case, conceptual difficulties affected the results of the 1951 and 1961 censuses, relevant vital statistics on Jews no longer extend to all provinces, and the separate designation of Jews was recently omitted from the immigration statistics.

Jewish institutions in several countries made successful efforts to use, as they became available, the electronically processed material of official statistics for preparing special tabulations on Jews in response to Jewish initiatives.

Jewish-Sponsored Data Collection

In countries where there are no official statistics on the Jewish population, the only practical way to obtain any numerical information about it is through Jewish-sponsored data collection. The customary method, local community surveys, has been used sporadically over the last few decades, especially in the U.S. In the case of large Jewish groups, these surveys are necessarily sample studies. Many improvements have been incorporated in the technique of some Jewish surveys to make them more sophisticated. However, isolated community surveys have essential shortcomings, e.g., the local focus, the differences in content and method between the various studies, and the fact that they are conducted at different times even within the same country. Hence their usefulness for countrywide or larger statistical syntheses is very limited. "Marginal" Jews who have little desire to identify themselves as Jews and who have few or no organizational ties with the Jewish community are now not few in number in many Diaspora countries. While official statistics may not adequately identify individuals in the general population as Jews, Jewish-sponsored surveys have difficulty in reaching the total number of Jews in a community. In the collection of demographic data the concept "Jewish" should be construed in the widest sense. But in the tabulations various categories within the Jewish population should be distinguished according to attachment to Jewish practices, mixed marriages, etc. At any rate, the customary "master list," i.e., the combined information on Jews from various institutional and organizational records, is often insufficient as the sole source for surveying a Jewish population.

Another field of Jewish-sponsored statistical activity is the collection of vital statistics. These, however, often reflect only those activities which take place under the auspices of Jewish religious institutions, e.g., synagogue marriages, circumcisions, and burials with religious ceremonies. But the marriages, births, and deaths of Jews which are not accompanied by religious ceremonies are unrecorded in the statistics of Jewish institutions. The increasing assimilation and secularization of Diaspora Jews, and the consequent absence of "marginal" Jews from the data collected by Jewish institutions, are apt to vitiate the data's demographic value. In some Diaspora countries, interested organizations make counts of Jewish immigrants who have received assistance as well as estimates of the total number of Jewish immigrants. Sociological and socio-psychological investigations which supply data on Jews have only limited demographic value because their subjects are often unrepresentative of the entire Jewish population or their figures are too small. In a few European countries where the Jewish communities are recognized by public law, permanent population registers are kept by the community.

From the 1960s, the Institute of Contemporary Jewry of The Hebrew University, Jerusalem, designed a new and more efficient type of Jewish-sponsored population survey. These surveys inquired into demographic, economic, and social characteristics as well as aspects of Jewish identity, and permitted many cross-tabulations of population characteristics. They were preferably on a countrywide basis, with improvements in sampling technique and especially designed to include "marginal" Jews. The first survey of this type was taken in Italy in 1965. Better information on Jewish vital statistics is also partially obtainable from population surveys. Jewish-sponsored surveys are not only substitutes for nonexistent governmental statistics on Jews but are, in fact, the only means of investigating aspects of Jewish identity. Jewish-sponsored data collection on topics other than population statistics usually relates to the working of Jewish institutions and organizations, international, national, and local. In general, the data are collected within the framework of the respective agencies themselves.

Research Activities

The copious statistical material on Jews which accumulated before World War II encouraged scholars and others to compile comparative statistics of various countries, and to analyze the available data in detail. Among the major contributors to the field of Jewish demographic research have been A. *Nossig and J. *Jacobs, toward the end of the 19th century; and in the 20th century, A. *Ruppin, J. *Thon, B. *Blau, J. Segall, F. Theilhaber, I. Koralnik, L. *Hersch, J. *Lestschinsky, H.S. Linfield, A. *Tartakower, and R. *Bachi. Important centers for demographic and statistical research on the Jews were the Bureau fuer Statistik der Juden (Berlin) and *YIVO. Periodicals of importance in this field were *Zeitschrift fuer Demographie und Statistik der Juden; Bleter far Yidishe Demografye, Statistik un Ekonomik*; and *Shriftn far Ekonomik un Statistik*.

The period after World War II has seen not only the diminution of official data on Jews, but also the passing of the previous generation of scholars in Jewish statistics. The present scholarly emphasis in Jewish population statistics has partially shifted, of necessity, from the analysis and comparison of available data to the methodology and promotion of data collection. Several Jewish research institutions have been engaged primarily in statistical and demographic work on a local and national level: the Bureau of Social and Economic Research of the Canadian Jewish Congress, Montreal; the Statistical and Demographic Research Unit of the Board of Deputies of British Jews, London; and Instituto de Investigaciones Sociales of the Asociacion Mutual Israelita Argentina (AMIA), Buenos Aires. Some permanent institutions for social and historical research on the Jews which have given part of their attention to statistical and demographic matters are: Centre National des Hautes Etudes Juives, Brussels; Communauté, Paris; Oficina Latinoamericana of the American Jewish

Committee and Centro de Estudios Sociales of the Delegación de Asociaciones Israelitas Argentinas (DAIA), Buenos Aires; and the Jewish Museum of the Czech State, Prague.

In some cases, scholars have carried out ad hoc demographic and social surveys of local Jewish populations at the invitation of the community leadership. There are many such instances in the U.S., the most notable through to the mid-1960s being the surveys taken in Washington (1956), Los Angeles (1959 and 1965), Providence (1963), Camden Area (1964), Boston (1965), and Springfield (1966). Elsewhere, local surveys were taken in recent years in São Paulo (Brazil); Melbourne (Australia); Leeds and Edgware (England); Brussels (Belgium); and Wroclaw (Poland). For Dutch Jewry, a survey based on records only, without home visits, was made in 1954; a similar survey of Dutch Jewry took place in 1966. Counts based on community population registers are available for the Jews in Vienna, Austria, in the German Federal Republic, and to some extent in Italy and the Netherlands. Additional countrywide sample surveys of Jewish populations were planned for the U.S., France, and other countries (in the U.S. under the auspices of the Council of Jewish Federations and Welfare Funds).

Israel has a very active Central Bureau of Statistics (headed by R. Bachi until 1972), whose work also illuminates important aspects of Jewish demography in the Diaspora. On the international level, the Division of Jewish Demography and Statistics in the Institute of Contemporary Jewry of The Hebrew University, Jerusalem, also headed by R. Bachi, has advanced the study of Jewish demography throughout the world by encouraging and coordinating data collection and research, refining methodology, developing technical services (world bibliography, documentation center), and training specialists. It is also the seat of the Association for Jewish Demography and Statistics, which serves as the international organization for interested scholars and laymen. Other international Jewish research bodies whose activities include some statistical work are: The Institute of Jewish Affairs (in London since 1966), YIVO, and *Yad Vashem.

[Usiel Oscar Schmelz]

Sources

The amount and quality of documentation on Jewish population size and characteristics is far from satisfactory. Reviewing the sources since 1990, however, one finds that important new data and estimates have become available for several countries through official population censuses and Jewish-sponsored sociodemographic surveys. National censuses yielded results on Jewish populations in Ireland, the Czech Republic, and India (1991); Romania and Bulgaria (1992); the Russian Republic and Macedonia (1994), Israel (1995), Canada, South Africa, Australia, and New Zealand (1996 and 2001); Belarus, Azerbaijan, Kazakhstan, and Kyrgyzstan (1999); Brazil, Mexico, Switzerland, Estonia, Latvia, and Tajikistan (2000); the United Kingdom, Hungary, Croatia, Lithuania, and Ukraine (2001); the Russian Republic, and Georgia (2002). Permanent national population registers, including information on the Jewish religious, ethnic or national group, exist in several European countries (Switzerland, Norway, Finland, Estonia, Latvia, and Lithuania), and in Israel.

In addition, independent sociodemographic studies have provided most valuable information on Jewish demography and socioeconomic stratification as well as on Jewish identification. Surveys were conducted over the last several years in South Africa (1991 and 1998); Mexico (1991 and 2000); Lithuania (1993); the United Kingdom and Chile (1995); Venezuela (1998–99); Israel, Hungary, the Netherlands, and Guatemala (1999); Moldova and Sweden (2000); France and Turkey (2002); Argentina (2003 and 2004). In the United States, important new insights were provided by two large surveys, the National Jewish Population Survey (NJPS, 2000–01) and the American Jewish Identity Survey (AJIS, 2001). Several further Jewish population studies were separately conducted in major cities in the United States (notably in New York City in 2002) and in other countries. Additional evidence on Jewish population trends can be obtained from the systematic monitoring of membership registers, vital statistics, and migration records available from Jewish communities and other Jewish organizations in many countries or cities, notably in the United Kingdom, Germany, Italy, Buenos Aires, and São Paulo. Detailed data on Jewish immigration routinely collected in Israel helps in the assessment of changing Jewish population sizes in other countries. Some of this ongoing research is part of a coordinated effort aimed at updating the profile of world Jewry.

Following an International Conference on Jewish Population Problems held in Jerusalem in 1987, initiated by the late Roberto Bachi of the Hebrew University and sponsored by major Jewish organizations worldwide, an International Scientific Advisory Committee (ISAC) was established, chaired by Sidney Goldstein of Brown University. An Initiative on Jewish Demography, sponsored by the Jewish Agency under the chairmanship of Sallai Meridor, led to an international conference held in Jerusalem in 2002 and to an effort of data collection and analysis implemented over the years 2003–2005. The Jewish People Policy Planning Institute (JPPPI), chaired by Ambassador Dennis Ross, provides a framework for policy analyses and suggestions, including Jewish population issues.

Definitions

A major problem with Jewish population estimates periodically circulated by individual scholars or Jewish organizations is a lack of coherence and uniformity in the definitional criteria followed – when the issue of defining the Jewish population is addressed at all. Simply put, the quantitative study of Jewish populations can rely only on operational, not normative, definitional criteria. Three major concepts must be considered in order to put the study of Jewish demography on serious comparative ground.

In most countries outside of Israel, the *core Jewish population* includes all those who, when asked, identify themselves as Jews; or, if the respondent is a different person in the same household, are identified by him/her as Jews. This is an intentionally comprehensive and pragmatic approach reflecting the nature of most available sources of data on Jewish population. In countries other than Israel, such data often derive from population censuses or social surveys, where interviewees have the option to decide how to answer relevant questions on religious or ethnic preferences. Such a definition of a person as a Jew, reflecting *subjective* feelings, broadly overlaps but does not necessarily coincide with *halakhah* (rabbinic law) or other normatively binding definitions. Inclusion does *not* depend on any measure of that person's Jewish commitment or behavior in terms of religiosity, beliefs, knowledge, communal affiliation, or otherwise. The *core* Jewish population includes all converts to Judaism by any procedure as well as other people who declare they are Jewish. Also included are persons of Jewish parentage who claim no current religious or ethnic identity. Persons of Jewish parentage who adopted another religion are excluded, as are other individuals who in censuses or surveys explicitly identify with a non-Jewish group without having converted out. In the State of Israel, personal status is subject to the rulings of the Ministry of the Interior, which relies on criteria established by rabbinical authorities. In Israel, therefore, the *core* Jewish population does not simply express subjective identification but reflects definite legal rules, those of *halakhah*. Documentation to prove a person's Jewish status may include non-Jewish sources.

The question whether Jewish identification according to this *core* definition can or should be mutually exclusive with other religious corporate identities emerged on a major scale in the course of the 2000–01 NJPS. The solution chosen – admittedly after much debate – was to allow for Jews with multiple religious identities to be included under certain circumstances in the standard definition of Jewish population. In the latter survey, at least in the version initially processed and circulated by UJC, "a Jew is defined as a person whose religion is Judaism, OR whose religion is Jewish and something else, OR who has no religion and has at least one Jewish parent or a Jewish upbringing, OR who has a non-monotheistic religion and has at least one Jewish parent or a Jewish upbringing." A category of Persons of Jewish Background (PJBS) was introduced: some of these were included in the Jewish population count and others were not. By the same token, Jews with multiple ethnic identities were included in the standard Jewish population count in Canada. The adoption of such extended criteria by the research community tends to stretch Jewish population definitions further than had usually been done in the past and beyond the above-mentioned typical *core* definition. These procedures tend to limit actual comparability of the same Jewish population over time and of different Jewish populations at the same time.

The *enlarged Jewish population* includes the sum of (a) the *core* Jewish population; (b) all other persons of Jewish parentage who – by *core* Jewish population criteria – are *not* Jewish currently (or at the time of investigation); and (c) all of the respective further non-Jewish household members (spouses, children, etc.). Non-Jews with Jewish background, as far as they can be ascertained, include: (a) persons who have themselves adopted another religion, even though they may also claim to be Jewish by ethnicity or religion – with the caveat just mentioned for recent U.S. and Canadian data; and (b) other persons with Jewish parentage who disclaim being Jews. As noted, some PJBS who do not pertain to the *core* Jewish population naturally belong under the *enlarged* definition. It is customary in sociodemographic surveys to consider the religio-ethnic identification of parents. Some censuses, however, do ask about more distant ancestry. For both conceptual and practical reasons, the *enlarged* definition does not include other non-Jewish relatives who lack a Jewish background and live in exclusively non-Jewish households.

The *Law of Return, Israel's distinctive legal framework for the acceptance and absorption of new immigrants, awards Jewish new immigrants immediate citizenship and other civil rights. According to the current, amended version of the Law of Return, a Jew is any person born to a Jewish mother or converted to Judaism (regardless of denomination – Orthodox, Conservative, or Reform), who does not have another religious identity. By ruling of Israel's Supreme Court, conversion from Judaism, as in the case of some ethnic Jews who currently identify with another religion, entails loss of eligibility for Law of Return purposes. The law as such does not affect a person's Jewish status – which, as noted, is adjudicated by Israel's Ministry of the Interior and rabbinical authorities – but only the specific benefits available under the Law of Return. The law extends its provisions to all current Jews, their children, and grandchildren, as well as to the respective Jewish or non-Jewish spouses. As a result of its three-generation and lateral extension, the Law of Return applies to a large population, one of significantly wider scope than the *core* and *enlarged* Jewish populations defined above. It is actually quite difficult to estimate what the total size of the Law of Return population could be. These higher estimates in some of the major countries reach values double or three times as high as those for the *core* Jewish population.

The significant involvement of major Jewish organizations in Israel and in the U.S. – such as the Jewish Agency, the American Joint Distribution Committee, HIAS or UJC – in sponsoring data collection tends to complicate research issues. Organizations are motivated by the needs of their constituencies more than by neutral analytic criteria. In turn, the understandable interest of organizations to continue functioning and securing budgetary resources tends to bring them to take care of Jewish populations increasingly closer to the *enlarged* than to the *core* definition.

For further developments see *Population; Vital Statistics.

[Sergio DellaPergola (2nd ed.)]

BIBLIOGRAPHY: A. Nossig (ed.), *Juedische Statistik* (1903); Bureau fuer Statistik der Juden, *Statistik der Juden* (1918); Israel, Central Bureau of Statistics, *Official Statistics in Israel* (1963; Heb., 1966²);

R. Bachi, in: *La vie juive dans l'Europe contemporaine* (1965); idem, in: JJSO, 8 no. 2 (1966), 142–9; U.O. Schmelz, *ibid.*, 8 no. 1 (1966), 49–63; idem, *Jewish Demography and Statistics* (1961), bibliography for 1920–60; U.O. Schmelz and P. Glikson, *Jewish Population Studies 1961–1968* (1970). **ADD. BIBLIOGRAPHY:** U.O. Schmelz, P. Glikson, and S.J. Gould (eds.), *Studies in Jewish Demography: Survey for 1969–1971* (1975), 60–97; M. Corinaldi, "Jewish Identity," chap. 2, in: M. Corinaldi, *Jewish Identity: The Case of Ethiopian Jewry* (1998); S. DellaPergola and L. Cohen (eds.), *World Jewish Population: Trends and Policies* (1992); B.A. Kosmin, S. Goldstein, J. Waksberg, N. Lerer, A. Keysar, and J. Scheckner, *Highlights of the CJF 1990 National Jewish Population Survey* (1991); L. Kotler-Berkowitz, S.M. Cohen, J. Ament, V. Klaff, F. Mott, and D. Peckerman-Neuman, with L. Blass, D. Bursztyn, and D. Marker, *The National Jewish Population Survey 2000–01: Strength, Challenge, and Diversity in the American Jewish Population* (2003); S. DellaPergola, *Jewish Demography: Facts, Outlook, Challenges*, JPPPI Alert Paper 2 (2003); *The Jewish People Policy Planning Institute Assessment 2005*, Executive Report 2 (2005); S. DellaPergola, World Jewish Population, *American Jewish Year Book*, 100 (New York, 2005), 87–122.

°STATIUS, PUBLIUS PAPINIUS (c. 45–96), Roman poet. He referred to the fall of Jerusalem and of Judea (which he calls Idyme, i.e., Idumea) at the hands of Titus and Vespasian (*Silvae* 5:2, 138) and the triumphs celebrated by them in 71 C.E. (*Silvae* 3:3, 138–42). He also praised the date groves of the country and the balsam which he described as "Hebrew juices."

BIBLIOGRAPHY: M. Stern, *Greek and Latin Authors on Jews and Judaism*, vol. 1 (1974), 515–20.

[Jacob Petroff / Shimon Gibson (2nd ed.)]

STATUS QUO ANTE, term applied to those communities in Hungary which after the schism that occurred at the Hungarian General Jewish Congress of 1868–69 (see *Hungary) did not join the *Neologist organization or the Orthodox communities (1871) but retained their former pre-Congress status. As they did not have a central representation, they conducted their affairs on a separate basis, while their relations with the government were maintained through the local authorities. It was only in 1927 that they organized themselves into a national organization – the Status Quo Ante Communities of Hungary – recognized by the government in 1928.

During the time of the schism in 1868–69, a number of communities, including some of the larger and more important ones, sought to maintain their traditional character. Thus for example, Abraham S. Sofer (Schreiber), rabbi of Pressburg (Bratislava), asked M. Perls to continue his rabbinical position at the head of the united community. Only a small number of them, however, succeeded in their objectives because the separate organization of the Orthodox claimed that the united communities were no longer faithful. The status quo ante communities were ostracized by the Orthodox, with their rabbis and *shoḥatim*. The communities which did not join the Neologists or Orthodox were thus completely isolated. According to the census of 1930, the membership of the status quo ante communities was 17,440, compared with 292,159 for the Neologists, and 134,972 for the Orthodox.

The most important status quo ante communities were those of *Debrecen, *Eger, Gyöngyös, and *Nyiregyhaza, and outside Hungary, between the two world wars, Nagyszombat (Trnava) in Czechoslovakia, and Nagykároly (*Carei Mare) in Romania. When the Jewish communities were united by a governmental order of 1950, the status quo ante organization was also closed down.

BIBLIOGRAPHY: S. Ha-Kohen Weingarten, in: *Areshet, Sefer Shanah shel Iggud Soferim Datiyyim* (1943), 431–8.

[Baruch Yaron]

STAUB, HERMANN (1856–1904), German jurist. Born in Nicolai, Upper Silesia, Staub practiced as a lawyer in Berlin and achieved considerable fame through his work *Kommentar zum Deutschen Handelsgezetzbuch* (1891–93; 1921–32[12]), a commentary on the new German commercial code. Here he explained the commercial code section by section and it became the leading work on the subject running into a number of editions. Many of Staub's interpretations were specifically approved by the German Supreme Court and his book was also considered an authoritative work in Austria. He wrote works on the law of contracts, company law, and the stock exchange and was a founder and editor of the legal magazine *Deutsche Juristenzeitung*. A proud Jew, Staub refused to convert to Christianity and used his influence to prevent a numerus clausus in the legal profession in Germany

BIBLIOGRAPHY: S. Kaznelson, *Juden im deutschen Kulturbereich* (1959), 650–1, 671; Wininger, Biog, 5 (1928), bibliography; AZDJ, 37 (1904), 438–9.

STAVI (Stawsky), MOSES (1884–1964), Yiddish and Hebrew writer. He was born in Antopol, Belorussia. Stavi for many years wrote in Yiddish; it was only in Ereẓ Israel, where he settled in 1911, that he gradually began to write in Hebrew. His early stories were translated into Hebrew, among them his best-known work, *Lavan ha-Arami* (1910), which in its Hebrew version went through many editions and remained popular for a long period. His first stories deal with the world of nature; in Ereẓ Israel his subjects also came to include the Arab village and the life of the working man.

Comprehensive collections of his stories appeared under the titles of *Ha-Boker Or* (1930), *Sefer ha-Behemot* (2 vols., 1930), *Ba-Derekh le-Ereẓ ha-Osher* (1954, stories and legends for old and young), and *Ha-Zore'im be-Dimah* (1960, village stories). In his latter years, Stavi's interest in rural life and in labor led him to research of the language of terminology used in Hebrew literature in these two fields, which resulted in two books: *Pirkei Teva ve-Lashon* (1958), and *Geluyyot u-Setumot ba-Lashon* (1961). In *Ha-Kefar ha-Arvi* (1946) he describes life and work in Arab villages. A list of his works translated into English appears in Goell, Bibliography, 2524–29.

BIBLIOGRAPHY: Kressel, Leksikon, 2 (1967), 538. **ADD. BIBLIOGRAPHY:** G. Shaked, *Ha-Sipporet ha-Ivrit*, 2 (1983), 65–67.

[Getzel Kressel]

STEEL, DANIELLE (1947–), U.S. author. Danielle Fernande Schuelein-Steel, one of the bestselling authors in American history, was born in New York to a German-Jewish father and a Portuguese mother. Steel, who studied at the Parsons School of Design in New York, New York University, and in Europe, had sold more than 500 million copies of the romance novels for which she is best known by 2005. From her first published book, *Going Home* (1973), to *The House*, one or more of her 67 novels were on *The New York Times* bestseller list for almost 400 consecutive weeks, and 21 of them were adapted for television. Her books, which explore subjects like kidnapping, incest, illness, death, divorce, adoption, marriage, loss, cancer, war, and suicide, appear in 47 countries and in 28 languages. Her historical themes sometimes shed new light on familiar events.

After she completed her education, Steel worked in public relations in New York and then in advertising in San Francisco. In addition to her novels for adults, Steel wrote the "Max and Martha" series of books for young readers. They comprise 10 illustrated storybooks written to comfort youngsters as they face such problems as a new stepfather, new baby, new school, loss of a grandparent, or other crucial problems. She also wrote four "Freddie" books about real-life situations in children's lives, like a visit to the doctor and the first night away from home. She published a book of poetry and two nonfiction books, *Having a Baby* and *His Bright Light*, about the life and death by suicide of her son Nicholas Traina. As a result of her own dysfunctional family – she was married five times, twice to convicts – Steel was said to have maintained a strong interest in children's well-being. She raised nine children, seven of them her own. In 2002 she was decorated by the French government as a chevalier of the Order of Arts and Letters for her lifetime contribution to world culture. She founded and ran two foundations, one named for her late son, which finances organizations involved in mental illness and child abuse. The second was established to assist the homeless. In 2003 she opened an art gallery in San Francisco to show emerging artists.

[Stewart Kampel (2nd ed.)]

°**STEFAN, METROPOLITAN** (**Stoyan Popgueorguiev**; 1878–1957), head of the Bulgarian Orthodox Church in World War II and Righteous Among the Nations. Starting from January 1940, the government of Bulgaria was headed by a Fascist regime which favored a pro-German alignment, with the consent of King Boris III and most members of the Parliament (Subranie). There were somewhat over 50,000 Jews in the country. To please the Germans, Bulgaria promulgated the Law for the Protection of the Nation at the end of 1940 (ratified in early 1941), with the intent to seriously limit the rights of Jews in the life of the country. The Bulgarian Orthodox Church, headed by Metropolitan Stefan, took a strong stand against the Law. In a statement on November 15, 1940, the Holy Synod of the Bulgarian Orthodox Church denounced the Law, the intent of which was to repress the rights of the Jewish population without regard whether Jews had committed any offense against the State. On the eve of the Law's promulgation, in January 1941, Stefan convened the Holy Synod and reiterated its denunciation, since "the principle of racism which encourages persecution, in this case of the Jewish race, has no justification.... One cannot turn the Law for the Protection of the Nation into a means of oppression and persecution of the Jewish minority in the land." The Law was nevertheless ratified by Parliament, on January 23, 1941. In the following years, the Law served as the basis for further restricting the rights of Jews. In September 1942, in a sermon, Metropolitan Stefan emphasized that no one has the right to treat the Jews cruelly and persecute them. He asked that the rights of Jews as well as converts to Christianity be respected. According to Abraham Alfasi, a leader of the Jewish community in Sofia, when, in March 1943, it became known that the Bulgarian government was about to acquiesce to German demands to deport Bulgarian Jews, Metropolitan Stefan told the king that in that event he would give instructions to open the gates of the churches and monasteries to shelter the Jews. Stefan then called a plenary session of the Holy Synod, which protested the increased persecution of Jews, underlining that "God's law, which transcends all human laws, unequivocally obliges us not to be indifferent in the face of the sufferings of innocent people, of whatever race.... The Bulgarian Orthodox Church is of the opinion that she cannot deny help and protection to the persecuted and oppressed. If she were to refuse such help, she would be unfaithful to herself." When the government decided to expel the Jewish population in Sofia to small outlying locales, a step which many interpreted as a prelude to their delivery to the Germans, Metropolitan Stefan again decided to intervene. In a telephone conversation between Stefan and King Boris, on May 25, 1943, Stefan spoke out boldly: "Boris, my son, I am not at all satisfied about you. One hears lately of many things done to our Israelite brethren. Think very hard; it is unworthy of you and of the Bulgarian people.... Things have come to my knowledge which I would rather not believe. They are a disgrace and shame to you and to the Bulgarian people. I cannot explain them to you by telephone. If you wish, come to me, or I shall come to you at once." The king declined. The following day, Stefan was again on the phone with the king and pontificated to him on the anti-Jewish measures: "Boris, you forgot yourself. You elude me and hide.... You know that one time I saved your father's head and your throne. But it is doubtful whether I, after these acts of yours, shall be able to save your head. Give the matter serious thought and uproot this demonic influence from your heart." He then sent the king a telegram reading: "Do not persecute, so that you may not be persecuted. With what measure ye mete, it shall be measured to you again. I know, Boris, that from heaven God will keep watch over your actions." Stefan was then subjected to police searches which impounded documents of hasty conversions of Jews, carried out in order to exempt them from the government's anti-Jewish measures. Metropolitan Stefan's constant intervention on behalf of Bulgarian Jews, with the backing of the Bulgarian Orthodox Church, as well as the outcry by other public figures, caused the government to postpone the delivery of the Jews to the Germans, and eventually led to the cancellation of this plan, and the more than 50,000 Jews of Bulgaria proper (with the exception of Jews in the annexed territories of Macedonia and Thrace) were saved.

BIBLIOGRAPHY: Yad Vashem Archives M31-9375; F.B. Chary, *The Bulgarian Jews and the Final Solution 1940–1944* (1972).

[Mordecai Paldiel (2nd ed.)]

STEFANESTI (**Ştefăneşti**), town in Botoşani province, Moldavia, N.E. Romania. The first Jews settled in Stefanesti at the beginning of the 17th century. After the neighboring province of Bessarabia passed to Russia in 1812, Stefanesti became a border town and consequently began to develop. In 1814 the ruler of Moldavia authorized the settlement of additional Jews. In 1883, however, when the municipality bought land to sell to the inhabitants, the Romanian parliament prohibited the Jews from acquiring any property. The Jewish population numbered 628 in 1838, and 3,886 (76.5% of the total population) in 1886. The first synagogue was erected at the beginning of the 18th century; it was rebuilt in 1854. There were eight organized congregations, two formed by tailors; a *mikveh* built in 1854; and a primary school. Stefanesti was well known among Romanian Jewry for the ḥasidic "court" established there by the Friedman family, descended from the *Ruzhin dynasty. Abraham Mattathias Friedman acted as ḥasidic *ẓaddik* in the town for 70 years (1863–1933). After World War I, when Romania regained Bessarabia and the town was no longer on the border, its commercial importance diminished. The number of Jews decreased in 1930 to 2,361 (26.5% of the total).

In World War II the Jews of Stefanesti were deported to Botosani. From there they were sent to forced labor camps. A few returned after the war, numbering 870 in 1947 and 600 in 1950. In 1969 about 12 Jewish families remained in Stefanesti.

BIBLIOGRAPHY: M. Schwarzfeld, *Excursiuni critice asupra istoriei evreilor în România* (1888), 31; V. Tufescu, *Târguşoarele din Moldova şi importanţa lor economică* (1942), 105, 140; PK Romanyah, 255–7.

[Theodor Lavi]

STEG, ADOLPHE (**Ady**) (1925–), French surgeon and Jewish community leader. Steg was born in Verecky, Czechoslovakia, and taken to France in 1932. After completing his medical studies, Steg became a surgeon in Paris and professor of urological surgery at the faculty of medicine in Paris (1976). From World War II, Steg has been prominent in many Jewish organizations. Initially he was active in student circles and was president of the Union of Jewish Students in Paris (1948) and vice president of the World Union of Jewish Students (1949). He was a leading member of the Fonds Social Juif Unifie, the Consistoire, and the Alliance Israélite Universelle. He took part in the creation of the Coordinating Committee of Jewish Institutions in May 1967 on the eve of the Six-Day War. Steg was the founder of the French Association of the Friends of the Hebrew University which he headed from 1965 to 1986. He served as the president of the Conseil Representatif des Juifs de France (CRIF) from 1969 to 1974 and from 1985 as president of the Alliance Israélite Universelle, and he was a member of the Fondation pour la Mémoire de la Shoah. Steg was a member of the Académie de Chirurgie and of the Académie Nationale de Médecine. From 1984 he was secretary general of the European Urological Association and from 1986 president of the French Urology Association. He was a Grand Officier of the Legion of Honor, a Commandeur of the Ouissam Alaoui, and a Grand Croix dans l'Ordre National du Mérite. He received an honorary doctorate from the Hebrew University of Jerusalem. He was a member of the Economic and Social Council of France from 1979.

[Michael Denman (2nd ed.)]

STEIG, WILLIAM (1907–2003), U.S. cartoonist and author. Born in Brooklyn, N.Y., to immigrant parents, Steig was reared in the Bronx. He graduated from high school at 15, studied for two years at the City College of New York, three years at the National Academy of Design, and five days at the Yale School of Fine Arts. When his father could not find a job during the Depression, Steig began selling his drawings. In his first year, he earned $4,500, which was enough to support the entire family. For more than six decades Steig created many of the *New Yorker* magazine's best covers and cartoons and also wrote some of the most beloved of children's books, including *Shrek!* and the award-winning *Sylvester and the Magic Pebble*. In all, Steig created more than 100 *New Yorker* covers, starting with the one that appeared on May 7, 1932, depicting a father glaring at his son's report card as the child timidly glances up at him. Steig had a cartoon gallery of street-tough kids, satyrs, damsels, dogs, and drunks; and he wrote more than 25 children's books about brave pigs, donkeys, and other creatures. *Shrek!* was made into a movie in 2001 and won an Academy Award as the best animated feature film. A sequel followed in 2004. From his first *New Yorker* cartoon in 1930, a picture of a prison inmate telling another, "My son's incorrigible, I can't do a thing with him," Steig produced more than 1,600 drawings for the magazine and 117 covers, many of which were later published in books of collected drawings. In 1936 Steig ended his career as a traditional gag cartoonist, and he married Elizabeth Mead, the sister of the anthropologist Margaret Mead. Soon after he began whittling figures out of stacking wood. Three years later he had his first one-man show, an exhibition of his carvings. Also in 1936 Steig started making his "symbolic drawings" of people enduring shame, embarrassment, and other emotional problems. He published these in *About People* (1939), *The Lonely Ones* (1942), and *All Embarrassed* (1944). In the 1940s Steig discovered Wilhelm

Reich, who became a psychological mentor. Steig saw Reich for therapy 40 times and credited him with saving his life as well as his mother's. He also bought an orgone box, a booth made of cardboard, steel wire, and metal that is supposed to collect the world's orgone, or orgasmic energy. Steig sat in his energy accumulator every day. What Steig got from Reich was a confirmation of his belief that people should be emancipated from the inhibitions that society and government impose on children and adults. It was in 1968 that Stein began writing for children, and his *CDB!*, a book that uses letters to stand for words, became a minor classic. CDB, in other words, is See the Bee! Steig also helped changed the nature of the greeting-card industry. His symbolic drawings were licensed to appear on cocktail napkins, glasses, and cards. In addition to the classic *Shrek!*, the story of an ogre who marries a princess, Steig's books in the 1990s included *Grown-Ups Get to Do All the Driving, The Toy Brother, Zeke Pippin, Doctor De Soto Goes to Africa,* and *Spinky Sulks.*

[Stewart Kampel (2nd ed.)]

STEIGER TRIAL, trial held in 1924–25 in Lvov against the Jew Stanislaw Steiger on the trumped-up charge that he had conspired to assassinate the Polish president. As a result of the tension among the Ukrainians in Galicia in the wake of international recognition of Polish rule over this region, an unsuccessful attempt was made to assassinate President S. Wojciechowski when he officially opened the "Fair of the East" in the town. It was clear to all that this was an act perpetrated by a clandestine Ukrainian organization which sought to undermine the Polish rule. The real conspirator, Teofil Olszański, succeeded in escaping across the border and found refuge in Berlin, while the police arrested a Jewish student on the spot as a suspect. In order to substantiate the accusations against Steiger, the prosecution produced a lengthy series of dubious testimonies serving Polish political interests, which attempted to minimize Ukrainian agitation in the region and divert public attention to the alleged crime of the Jew.

The manifestations of hysteria which accompanied the giving of evidence set off storms of mass antisemitism in the streets. Distinguished Jewish advocates, such as Nathan *Loewenstein (von Opoka) and Leib Landau, took part in the defense. As a result of the tension, Jewish public leaders were imprisoned and the life of Steiger was endangered. Israel *Waldman, who maintained friendly relations with Ukrainian statesmen in Vienna, endeavored to convince the responsible leaders publicly to admit their role in the act. Once his efforts had failed, he revealed all the details of his negotiations in Vienna and Berlin on this subject when he testified before the tribunal in Lvov. Nathan Rand, who had previously been in the service of the Ukrainian government-in-exile, followed his example. The impact of these revelations brought about Steiger's acquittal on Dec. 20, 1925.

BIBLIOGRAPHY: N. Loewenstein, *O sprawie Steigera* (1926).

[Moshe Landau]

STEIMAN, BEYNUSH (1897–1919), Yiddish poet and playwright. Born in Kreslavka, Latgale, Latvia, Steiman began writing poetry when he was 13. After being trained as a chemist's assistant, he spent two years in Vilna working in a pharmacy. Then he established a Yiddish elementary school in his home town, as well as a dramatic club to finance the school. During that period, in addition to writing poetry, he wrote dramas and dramatical poems. At the end of August 1919 he enrolled at the Kultur-Lige's teachers' seminary in Kiev, but was recruited for defense work in which he was killed. Steiman's works were not published during his lifetime. His first drama *Baym Toyer* ("Near the Gate") appeared posthumously in the Kiev literary periodical *Oyfgang* (1919). The dramatic poem *Meshiekh ben Yoysef* ("Messiah, Son of Joseph") was published in *Eygns* (vol. 2, Kiev 1920) and was also printed in book form. In 1926 it was produced in New York and in 1927 a Hebrew translation appeared in Jerusalem. *Dos Royte Kind* ("The Red Child"), his third and last extant work, is included in the volume *Dramen* ("Dramas," Warsaw, 1921) and was also printed in the first issue of *Shtrom* (1922). He also completed a translation of Oscar Wilde's *Salome* (published in 1924). Steiman's plays, which deal primarily with social reform, have religious intensity and motifs. The fundamental and persistent prophetic quality of his writing is manifested in his repeated use of the theme of redemption (the figure of the Messiah appears in all three plays), which is here, however, not drawn from traditional Jewish sources, but rather is a collective character representing the spirit of the people which is given the leading role.

BIBLIOGRAPHY: Rejzen, Leksikon, 4 (1929), 578–82. **ADD. BIBLIOGRAPHY:** LNYL, 8 (1981), 613–14; Y. Dobrushin, in: B. Steiman, *Dramen* (1921), 3–9; N. Meisel, *Noente un Vayte*, 2 (1926), 214–22.

[Yechiel Szeintuch]

STEIMBERG, ALICIA (1933–), Argentinean author. Born in Buenos Aires, Steimberg was trained as an English teacher and translator. Her works earned her some of the most prestigious awards in Argentinean letters, including the Premio Planeta in 1992.

Steimberg's first novel, *Músicos y relojeros* (1971), is a somewhat autobiographical narrative of Jewish life in Buenos Aires as seen through the eyes of the young narrator growing up in a family of immigrants. It has been translated into English as *Musicians and Watchmakers* (1998). The author's characteristic use of humor is evident in the novel and remains a constant in most of her subsequent works. To a certain extent her next novel, *Su espíritu inocente* (1981), continues where the first left off. Again the narrator is a young girl struggling to find her own identity and come to terms with the difficulties of being Jewish in a mostly Catholic country.

Her other novels also use humor to examine Argentinean social reality. This is the case of *La loca 101* (1973), a rather chaotic tale that casts a critical eye on social mores and politics, and *El árbol del placer* (1986), a satirical portrayal of the world of psychoanalysis that is so prevalent in Buenos Aires. Her erotic novel *Amatista* (1989) was a finalist for the celebrated La Sonrisa Vertical literary prize. In *Cuando digo Magdalena* (1992), Steimberg returned, at least in part, to a more specifically Jewish context. This novel was also translated into English as *Call Me Magdalena* (1992). Finally, the novel *La selva* (2000) narrates the story of an older Jewish woman who unexpectedly falls in love with a man while on vacation in Brazil. Simultaneously, it tells the story of her struggle with a drug-addicted son. Steimberg is also the author of the short-story collections *Como todas las mañanas* (1983) and *Vidas y vueltas* (1999). Steimberg earned a well-deserved reputation as one of Argentina's best contemporary writers.

[Darrell B. Lockhart (2nd ed.)]

STEIMER, MOLLY (1897–1980), anarchist and advocate on behalf of political prisoners; the only person ever to have been deported from both the United States and the Soviet Union. Born in Dunaevtsy, Russia, Steimer immigrated to New York with her parents and siblings at the age of 15. She soon became involved with *Frayheyt* (Liberty), a Jewish anarchist group that secretly published and distributed materials in both Yiddish and English supporting the Russian Revolution and opposing World War I.

These activities led to the arrests of Steimer and six other *Frayheyt* members in August 1918 for conspiring to violate the Sedition Act, an emergency war measure that made it a crime to criticize either the United States government or the Constitution. Their two-week trial, which took place in October 1918, became a *cause célèbre*. The mistreatment of the defendants, one of whom died from injuries sustained upon arrest, as well as the harsh sentences handed down, 15 years for Steimer and 20 for three of the other co-defendants, led to outrage in liberal circles. When the Supreme Court upheld the convictions, attorney Harry Weinberg, a well-known defender of political radicals, rallied leading lawyers and intellectuals on the anarchists' behalf. Despite Steimer's objections, Weinberg negotiated a solution through which Steimer and her colleagues were deported to the Soviet Union and granted full pardons, with the stipulation that they never return to the United States. Soon after her arrival in the Soviet Union in 1921, Steimer met and fell in love with fellow anarchist Senya Fleshin, a Russian Jew who had immigrated to the United States and returned after the Revolution. The two remained life-long companions.

Steimer did not fare well in the hands of the Soviet authorities, who, like the American government, felt threatened by the anarchist movement. Steimer and Fleshin were expelled from the Soviet Union in 1923 and spent the next 15 years helping political prisoners and anarchist exiles, taking part in radical political debates of the day, and running a photographic studio in Berlin. They were living in Paris at the outbreak of World War II, and after a brief period in a French internment camp, both were able to flee to Mexico City. There, they joined a growing group of political exiles and opened another photographic studio. Steimer maintained strong connections with fellow radicals throughout her years in Mexico and had become a much admired veteran of the international anarchist movement when she died in 1980 in Cuernavaca, Mexico.

BIBLIOGRAPHY: E.L. Goldstein, "Steimer, Molly," in: P.E. Hyman and D. Dash Moore (eds.), *Jewish Women in America: An Historical Encyclopedia*, vol. 2 (1997), 1313–14; G.R. Stone, *Perilous Times and Free Speech in Wartime from the Sedition Act of 1798 to the War on Terrorism* (2004).

[Nadia Malinovich (2nd ed.)]

STEIN, ARTHUR (1871–1950), Austrian historian. Stein was born in Vienna. His first book, *Untersuchungen zur Geschichte und Verwaltung Aegyptens unter Roemischer Herrschaft* (1915), earned him the post of lecturer at the German University of Prague, where he became a full professor in 1923. Under the German occupation of Czechoslovakia he was deprived of his professorship, and confined to the Theresienstadt concentration camp until 1945.

Stein was interested primarily in the history of the Roman Empire, which he elucidated through the study of its administration and prosopography. He and Edmund Groag were entrusted by the Berlin Academy with the preparation of a new edition of the *Prosopographia Imperii Romani saeculorum I. II. III.* (1933–). He was primarily responsible for the biographies in the *Prosopographia* of members of the equestrian class. His other studies include *Roemische Reichsbeamte der Provinz Thracia* (1920); *Der roemische Ritterstand, ein Beitrag zur Social-un Personengeschichte des roemischen Reiches* (1927); *Die Legaten von Moesien* (1940); *Die Reichsbeamten von Dazien (1944); and Die Praefekten von Aegypten in der roemischen Kaiserzeit* (1950).

[Irwin L. Merker]

STEIN, AUGUST (1854–1937), Czech-Jewish communal leader. Son of a rabbi in a small town in southern Bohemia, Czechoslovakia, Stein studied law at Prague University. As a student he joined the Czech national movement as represented by the "Old Czech Party" and became influenced by Siegfried *Kapper, the spiritual father of the Czecho-Jewish assimilationist movement (see Svaz *Čechů-Židů). In 1881 he became the first editor of the Czecho-Jewish almanac. He joined the municipal administration of Prague and headed the "sanitation" program for the old Jewish quarter. In 1922 he was elected president of the Prague Jewish community. During the first years of his administration there were many conflicts between his assimilationist movement and the Zionists, but in later years some reconciliation was achieved. In 1930 the Czecho-Jews were defeated in the elections to the community council and the presidency passed to Stein's Zionist opponent Ludvik *Singer. When the Supreme Council of the Federations of Jewish Religious Congregations of Bohemia, Moravia, and Silesia was constituted in 1926, Stein became its first chairman and served in that capacity until 1931, when he was replaced by Joseph *Popper. He devoted much energy to the translation of the Pentateuch and of the *siddur* into Czech.

His widow and four children perished in concentration camps during the Holocaust.

BIBLIOGRAPHY: O. Guth, in: *Česko-židovský kalendář* (1929/30), 5–6; M. Poper, in: *Věstnik*, 11 no. 23 (1949), 265.

[Chaim Yahil]

STEIN, SIR AUREL (Mark; 1862–1943), British archaeologist. Stein was born in Budapest, the son of a prosperous merchant. His family, although Jewish on both sides, were advocates of assimilation and Stein was baptized as a Lutheran and educated at Christian schools. He attended three universities in Central Europe, and went to India in 1888 to take up the positions of principal of Oriental College in Lahore and registrar of Punjab University. From 1889, when he entered the Indian Education Service, he was constantly engaged in journeys of archaeological exploration. He traveled in Central Asia, West China, Persia, Iraq, and Transjordan. His work can be classified as follows: expeditions to Central Asia (1900–01; 1906–08; 1913–16, and 1930); expeditions to Baluchistan and Iran between 1927 and 1936 (to examine the traces of the Mesopotamian and Indus Valley civilizations); journeys to establish the marching routes and battlefields of Alexander the Great; a reexamination of the Roman-Parthian frontier to fix the western terminus of the silk trade. As a result of the Hungarian Geological Survey of Tun-huang in 1897, Stein made his greatest discoveries there of ancient Chinese art of the fourth century: *Cave Shrines of the Thousand Buddhas* (1907). There he brought to light beautiful Chinese murals and paintings and some Chinese manuscripts from the fifth to tenth centuries as well as the oldest specimen of a printed book (dated 868 C.E.). Stein also explored the Graeco-Buddhist monuments of Northwest India and intended to explore Afghanistan, but died a few days after his arrival. From 1884, Stein spent much of his time in London and became a naturalized British subject in 1904.

Stein was knighted in 1912 and given honorary degrees by Oxford and Cambridge universities. His work threw much light on the history of ancient civilizations.

Among his books are *Rins of Khotan* (1903), *Ancient Khotan* (1907), *Serindia* (1921), *Innermost Asia* (1928), *The Thousand Buddhas* (1921), *An Archaeological Tour in Gedrosia* (1931), *Archaeological Reconnaissances in Northwestern India and Southeastern Iran* (1937), *On Old Routes of Western Iran* (1940), and *On Ancient Central-Asian Tracks* (1964) with a biography by J. Mirsky. Stein was one of the most famous explorers and archaeologists of his time.

BIBLIOGRAPHY: Oldham, in: *Proceedings of the British Academy*, 29 (1943), 329–48; Smith, in: JJRAS (1919), 49–61; JRAS (1946), 86–89. **ADD. BIBLIOGRAPHY:** ODNB online; J. Mirsky, *Sir Aurel Stein: Archeological Explorer* (1977); A. Walker, *Aurel Stein: Pioneer of the Silk Road* (1995).

STEIN, EDITH (1891–1942), German philosopher. Born in Breslau, of an Orthodox Jewish family, Edith Stein studied philosophy under Edmund *Husserl at Goettingen and then became his first assistant at Freiburg University. Her dissertation, *Zum Problem der Einfuehlung* (1917; *On the Problem of Empathy*, 1964), played an important role in the phenomenological movement. She also prepared some of Husserl's works for publication. In 1922, after reading the autobiography of St. Theresa of Avila, she converted to Catholicism, gave up her university post, and went to teach at a Dominican girls' school in Speyer. Here she studied Catholic philosophy, especially that of Thomas Aquinas, and translated his treatise *Quaestiones disputatae de Veritate* (*Untersuchungen ueber die Wahrheit*, 1931). Her study in the *Husserl-Festschrift*, "*Husserls Phaenomenologie und die Philosophie des heiligen Thomas von Aquino*" (1929) attempted to show the points of contrast between phenomenology and Thomism. In 1932, Edith Stein was appointed lecturer at the Institute for Pedagogy at Muenster, but in 1933, with the advent of the Nazi regime, she had to give up this position, and entered a Carmelite convent in Cologne as Sister Teresa Benedicta of the Cross. Here she completed her large work *Endliches und ewiges Sein* (*Werke*, vol. 2, 1950), relating Thomism and contemporary phenomenological and existentialist thought. In 1938, to escape Nazi persecution, she was taken to a monastery at Echt in Holland, where she wrote *Kreuzeswissenschaft* (*Werke*, vol. 1, 1950; *The Science of the Cross*, 1960), on the life and teaching of St. John of the Cross. Shortly after finishing the work she, along with other priests and nuns of Jewish origin, was arrested by the Gestapo as a reprisal for the condemnation by the Dutch bishops of Nazi antisemitism. She died in the Auschwitz gas chambers. In 1998 she was canonized by the Catholic Church.

BIBLIOGRAPHY: H.C. Graef, *The Scholar and the Cross* (1955); H.C. Bordeaux, *Edith Stein: Thoughts on Her Life and Times* (1959), includes bibliography; A.A. Devaux et al., in: *Les Etudes Philosophiques*, 11 (1956), 427–72, incl. bibl.; H. Spiegelberg, *The Phenomenological Movement* (1960), index; *The Writings of Edith Stein*, selected, translated, and introduced by H. Graef (1956), 7–18, biographical introd.; C. Alexander, *Der Fall Edith Stein. Flucht in die Chimaere* (1970).

[Richard H. Popkin]

STEIN, EDMUND MENAHEM (1895–1943), Polish scholar and writer. Born in Dobromil, Galicia, from 1929 he was a professor at the Institute of Judaistic Sciences (Instytut Nauk Judaistycznych) in Warsaw, teaching the history of the Jews during the Hellenistic period, Jewish philosophy in the Middle Ages, and Midrash. In 1935 he was elected rector.

Among his numerous works in Polish, Hebrew, German, and Latin was his famous polemical work *Judaizm i Hellenizm* (1929) in which he subjected Tadeusz Zieliński's *Hellenizm i Judaizm* (2 vols., 1927) to devastating criticism. Zieliński belittled the influence of Judaism on Christian civilization and condemned what influence there was as negative and even destructive. Among Stein's other major works are *Pilon Alexandroni* ("Philo of Alexandria," 1937); *Dat ve-Da'at* ("Faith and Wisdom," 1939); and Hebrew translations from the Latin of Josephus' autobiography, with an introduction (1933); of the works of Philo (1937), and of the popular philosophical works of Cicero (1937).

Stein was elected chairman of the Union of Hebrew Writers in Warsaw. An ardent Zionist, he visited Palestine in 1935. During the German occupation of Poland he was in Warsaw, where he suffered together with all the Jews in his community. In spite of this he managed to be active in cultural endeavors like the society Tekumah, where he lectured on Philo and the great Greek philosophers. In 1940 he organized courses on Judaica, where he taught the subject of his specialty. At the same time he translated into Hebrew the works of Anacreon, Plato, and other Greek thinkers and writers. In 1943 his wife and son Gabriel were deported to Treblinka, where they were killed by the Germans. The same year he was deported to Trawniki, near Lublin, where he was killed.

BIBLIOGRAPHY: H. Seidman, *Yoman Getto Varshah* (1946); idem, in: *Jewish Morning Journal* (July 13, 1947); Y. Rosenthal, in: *Personalities in Judaic Scholarship* (1959), 361. **ADD. BIBLIOGRAPHY:** M. Neustadt (ed.) *Ḥurban u-Mered shel Yehudei Varshah* (1946), index.

[Hillel Seidman]

STEIN, ELIEZER LIPMAN (c. 1778–1851), Hungarian talmudist and preacher. Stein corresponded on *halakhah* with Moses *Sofer (Responsa *Ḥatam Sofer*, pt. 6, no. 48), with Meir *Eisenstadt and with his teacher Judah Aszo, author of the responsa *Mahari Aszo*. Stein served as *av bet din* of the community of Gyöngyös. During his period of office there, a quarrel arose between him and the community because he disqualified a *shoḥet*. The community referred the dispute to a non-Jewish judge who ruled that the *shoḥet* was capable of carrying out his duties. As a result of this ruling, the community deducted from the rabbi's salary the payment that they were accustomed to receive from the slaughter of animals, because this had decreased as a result of the ban. He resolved to resign his office and was accepted as rabbi in the community of Mór, but in the end the community yielded and became reconciled with him, and he remained there until 1837 when he went as rabbi and *av bet din* to Nagyszöllös (Vinogradov). Shortly thereafter, at the age of 60, he decided to immigrate to Ereẓ Israel. With this in mind he went to Pressburg and obtained from Moses Sofer a letter of recommendation to the philanthropists of Hungary. In the letter Sofer describes Stein's greatness as a talmudist and asks the Jewish philanthropists to appoint him to offices that would enable him to support himself in Ereẓ Israel and also that they pay the expenses of the journey. During Stein's visits from town to town to make the necessary arrangements he went to Dunaszerdahely and was appointed to the then vacant office of rabbi and *av bet din*. He abandoned his previous plan and remained there until his death.

He was the author of several works on contemporary problems, including *Hishanot ha-Bimah* (1943), against siting the **bimah* in the synagogue in front of the ark. He also wrote *Evel Moshe* (1840), a eulogy on Moses Sofer, and *Ir Shushan* (1849), homilies and responsa.

BIBLIOGRAPHY: J.J. (L.) Greenwald (Grunwald), *Zikkaron la-Rishonim* (1909), 22 no. 5; idem, *Mekorot le-Korot Yisrael* (1934), 91; idem, *Toyzend Yor Idish Lebn in Ungarn* (1945), 249f.; idem, *Maẓẓevat Kodesh* (1952) 33; M. Stein, *Even ha-Me'ir* (1909), 19 no. 113; P.Z. Schwartz, *Shem ha-Gedolim me-Ereẓ Hagar*, 1 (1913), 63b. no. 69; S. Buechler, in: *Magyar Zsidkó Szemle*, 7 (1890), 470, 472, 474.

[Samuel Weingarten-Hakohen]

STEIN, ERWIN (1885–1958), conductor, music critic, and editor. Born in Vienna, Stein studied composition with Arnold *Schoenberg. For a time he was engaged as an opera conductor in Germany and from 1924 until 1934 was an editor at the music-publishing firm of Universal Edition in Vienna. At the time of the *Anschluss* he left Vienna for London, where he settled, joining the firm of Boosey and Hawkes. He wrote for many music magazines, edited numerous modern music scores, and published a collection of essays, *Orpheus in New Guises* (London, 1953). He was a particular champion of Schoenberg's music at the time of its greatest rejection by critics and the public. He also gave much support, in print and as a publisher, to the music of Benjamin Britten.

[Max Loppert (2nd ed.)]

STEIN, GERTRUDE (1874–1946), U.S. author, critic, and patron of modern art and literature. Born in Allegheny, Pennsylvania, into a wealthy German Jewish family, Gertrude Stein spent her childhood in Vienna and Paris and was fluent as a child in various languages including German and French. In 1879, the family moved to Oakland, California. Stein studied psychology at Radcliffe College under William James and started but never completed a medical course at Johns Hopkins University, Baltimore. In 1902, she joined her brother Leo in Europe. Eventually she and Leo settled in Paris, where Stein immersed herself in the bohemian life of the literary and artistic avant-garde. Stein studied the art of the new painters and collected the as yet unknown works of Picasso, Braque, and Matisse. Picasso's portrait of her is one of his best-known early works. Her apartment, at 27 rue de Fleurus, which she first shared with Leo and later with her lifetime companion, Alice B. Toklas, was covered from floor to ceiling with paintings by the "new moderns." Stein also began to write, attempting to accomplish a linguistic and stylistic revolution akin to the visual revolution attempted by her artist friends. By the 1920s her apartment had become a center of artistic life and a place of pilgrimage for the aspiring expatriate American writers she dubbed "the Lost Generation," including F. Scott Fitzgerald and Ernest Hemingway.

Stein's first original work, *Three Lives* (1909), the story of three working-class women, included "Melanctha," a study of the consciousness of an American mulatto girl involved in an unhappy affair with a black doctor. "Melanctha" made a great impression on the practitioners of the "new writing," with its use of vernacular black English and stylistic experimentation, attracting many to her salon. Her later works moved toward ever greater experimentation, with Stein rejecting realistic, linear narratives for linguistic free play, playing with words both for their sound and rhythm and for their subconscious associations. At first she had to pay for the publication of her work, yet she could also write lucidly and engagingly, and her reputation grew. Even at its height, attitudes toward her swung between adulation and scorn; nonetheless, her own circle regarded her as a great writer, and she had a powerful impact on later modernist and postmodern writers. In *Tender Buttons* (1914), a series of "portraits" of inanimate objects, she tried to establish a type of abstract writing which some critics called "cubist," others "primitivistic." It was terse, sometimes childlike, and often repetitive. Her most quoted line, "A rose is a rose is a rose is a rose" (*Geography and Plays*, 1922), is indicative of the absurd linguistic play at the heart of much of her work. While many of her most experimental books were not appreciated in her lifetime, including her 1,000 page semi-autobiographical *The Making of Americans* (1925), a plot-less exploration of the assimilation of American immigrants, her most conventional work, *The Autobiography of Alice B. Toklas* (1933), was widely read. This autobiographical work, ostensibly written by her secretary and companion, told the history of her salon and of her relationship with the new literature and art.

Her later work included experimental plays, poems, novels, and criticism. She made sweeping generalizations about the character of nations and peoples, and the relationship of American and European cultures (*The Geographical History of America: the Relation of Human Nature to the Human Mind*, 1936). She used orthodox prose effectively and even nostalgically in *Paris, France* (1940); but *Four Saints in Three Acts*, produced as an "opera" with music by Virgil Thomson in 1934, proved amusing but largely unintelligible. Her World War II experiences in Belignin, in the south of France, where she remained in safety and comparative seclusion, were described in two entertaining books, *Wars I Have Seen* (1945) and *Brewsie and Willie* (1946). On the liberation of Paris, she returned there and continued her sponsorship of new writing.

Many of Gertrude Stein's unpublished manuscripts were deposited in the Yale Library. Among those published after her death are *Four in America* (1947), *Two: Gertrude Stein and Her Brother, and Other Early Portraits, 1908–12* (1951), and *Mrs. Reynolds* (1952), an experimental novel. Gertrude Stein's brother LEO STEIN (1872–1947) was a painter and art critic, who made Cézanne his chief interest in life. He wrote *Appreciation: Painting, Poetry and Prose* (1947) and his letters and papers, edited by Edmund Fuller, appeared as *Journey into the Self* in 1950.

BIBLIOGRAPHY: A. Stewart, *Gertrude Stein and the Present* (1967); F.J. Hoffman, *Gertrude Stein* (1961); Dupee, in *Commentary*, 33 (1962), 519–23; R. Bridgemen, *Gertrude Stein in Pieces* (1941). **ADD. BIBLIOGRAPHY:** J. Mellow, *Charmed Circle: Gertrude Stein and Company* (1974).

[Frederick J. Hoffman / Craig Svonkin (2nd ed.)]

STEIN, HENRI (1862–1940), French bibliographer and historian. Stein, who was born in Pierry, Marne, became archivist at the Archives Nationales in 1885. Here his access to the rich documentary sources enabled him to produce an enormous number of works in many different areas. After his retirement in 1923 from the chief curatorship of the ancient section, he taught the history, use, and conservation of documents at the Ecole des Chartres until 1933. Stein was not a specialist in one area or period, but was, rather, a universal scholar: bibliographer, archivist, archaeologist, general historian, local historian, art historian, and topographer. His work in French history was particularly important.

He founded and directed the periodical *La Bibliographie Moderne*, and created the Société Française de Bibliographie. Among his many books are *Les Archives de l'Histoire de France* (with C.V. Langlois, 3 vols., 1891), *Manuel de Bibliographie Générale* (1897), *Répertoire Numérique des Archives du Châtelet de Paris* (1898), *Bibliographie Générale des Cartulaires Français ou Relatifs à l'Histoire de France* (1907), *Les Architectes des Cathédrales Gothiques* (1911), *Charles de France* (1919), and *Répertoire Bibliographique de l'Histoire de France, 1920–1931* (with P. Caron, 1931).

[Irwin L. Merker]

STEIN, HERBERT (1916–1999), U.S. economist. Stein was born in Detroit, Michigan. After graduating from Williams College in 1935, he obtained his doctorate from the University of Chicago. For 22 years he was on the staff of the Committee for Economic Development (known as CED), an influential, privately sponsored research and policy-formulating organization. Subsequently, he joined the Brookings Institution and was appointed to the President's Council of Economic Advisers by President Nixon soon after his election (1969–71). In 1972, Stein became the Council's chairman, serving until 1974, after which he taught at the University of Virginia. He was appointed a member of the Advisory Committee of National Growth Policy Processes in 1976 and adjutant scholar of the American Enterprise Institute, and scholar in 1977. Stein, who had long opposed government intervention in private price and wage decisions, played a major role in the first attempt by a peacetime administration to enforce price and wage controls, although he was not optimistic about the program's success. Stein is credited with developing the concept of the "full employment budget" during the 1940s. This concept establishes government expenditures on the basis not of actually expected government income, but of income that would be received in a fully prosperous economy. Along the same lines is the view, represented in the early post-World War II years by the CED, that budgetary deficits are not always bad.

Stein was a senior fellow at the American Enterprise Institute and the A. Willis Robertson Professor of Economics Emeritus at the University of Virginia.

In 2000 the National Association for Business Economics created the Herbert Stein Public Service Award, which is presented to a policy adviser or policymaker in the U.S. or abroad with an outstanding record of public service. The first award was presented to Stein posthumously in September 2000.

Stein's publications include *The Fiscal Revolution in America* (1969), the novel *On the Brink* (with B. Stein, 1977), *Moneypower* (with B. Stein, 1979), *Presidential Economics* (1984), *Washington Bedtime Stories* (1986), *The New Illustrated Guide to the American Economy* (with M. Foss, 1995), *On the Other Hand* (1995), and *What I Think* (1998).

His son Ben Stein is a noted writer, scholar, and humorist.

[Joachim O. Ronall / Ruth Beloff (2nd ed.)]

STEIN, HERMAN D. (1917–), U.S. social work educator. Born in New York, Stein taught social work research at the New York School of Social Work, Columbia University, from 1945 to 1947. He then worked for three years with the *American Jewish Joint Distribution Committee (director of welfare department, 1948–50), and returned to the New York School of Social Work, where from 1958 to 1964 he was a professor. From 1959 to 1964 he also directed its research center. In 1964 he became professor and dean of the School of Applied Social Services, Case Western Reserve University, Cleveland, and in 1967 provost for Social and Behavioral Sciences, Case Western Reserve University. The many national and international committees on which Stein served include the National Institute of Mental Health (chairman, social work committee, 1958–62); the Council of Social Work Education (president, 1966–69); and the International Association of Schools of Social Work (president, elected 1968). He was an expert adviser for UNESCO and UNICEF.

In 1998 the CWRU's Mandel School of Applied Social Sciences initiated the annual Herman D. Stein Lectureship in International Social Welfare to honor Stein's "extraordinary lifework and accomplishments in building international social services."

A book of Stein's selected papers, *Challenge and Change in Social Work Education*, was published in 2003. Among the books Stein edited are *Social Perspectives on Behavior* (with R.A. Cloward, 1958) and *Social Theory and Social Invention* (1968), a collection of essays; and *The Crisis in Welfare in Cleveland* (1969). His many articles included studies of Jewish social work in the United States.

[Joseph Neipris / Ruth Beloff (2nd ed.)]

STEIN, ISAAC (d. 1495), rabbi, *rosh yeshivah*, and halakhic authority. Stein probably came from the village of that name near Nuremberg, a district in Bavaria (i.e., Stein bei Nuernberg). He studied under Israel *Isserlein, to whom he invariably refers as "the *Gaon*," basing himself upon the halakhic rulings he heard from him, as well as upon the customs he saw practiced in his home in Wiener Neustadt. He resided in Regensburg and often refers to rulings he gave in that city. Stein was regarded in his day as one of the greatest halakhic authorities, Joseph *Colon referring to him and his brother, Aaron Pappenheim, during their lifetime, as "two distinguished scholars" (lit. "golden pipes") and numbering them among "the four leaders" who were the outstanding scholars of the time. While in Nuremberg he debated with "the *lomedim*" (the local scholars) on the question of the date of the compilation of the Talmud and when it was committed to writing, and at their request wrote a comprehensive essay on the subject, revealing an original approach and a power of critical analysis.

Stein's main reputation, however, rests upon his commentary and novellae to the *Sefer Mitzvot Gadol* ("*Semag*") of *Moses b. Jacob of Coucy. He mentions many *halakhot* and emendations of the "*Semag*" which he received from Tevele of Nuremberg and suggestions given him by a certain Rabbi Samuel. The "*Semag*" was highly regarded both as a popular, practical, and readily accessible reference work of *halakhah* and as an authoritative source. As a result, many copies of the work were in circulation. Two editions published in Rome (1480) and Soncino (1488) are included in the list of Hebrew *incunabula. Many manuscripts of the work came into Stein's possession, but he found in them "obscure matters and passages that seemed labored." As a result he came to the conclusion that it was necessary to compose a new edition, including his own explanations as well as giving emendations, noting sources, and adding complementary material. To ensure that the work would be of practical use in his time, he added some of the customs and traditions of the Jews of Germany. While in Regensburg he assembled a considerable amount of material, noting variant readings. According to his son, he collected the material for his book over a period of many years, noting down customs of which he had heard or had actually seen, copying glosses from the margins of the books of early scholars, collecting anonymous responsa, and investigating and comparing different versions, both from the Talmud and the works of the *posekim*, to determine the correct reading.

He adopted a method original for his time. He wrote down his notes on hundreds of separate pieces of paper, like index cards, and then placed each piece in its relevant place between the pages of the "*Semag*." Since he "did not hide his copy of the *Semag* from the eyes of men," some people secretly copied these pieces of paper before the author had examined and emended any mistakes which crept into them. When the author became aware of this, "he was displeased and in order to prevent any harm arising," assembled a number of authoritative scholars in *halakhah* in the city of Gunzenhausen, and together with them, worked on the "*Semag*" for a number of years until the expulsion of the Jews from the city in 1495. Each note was subjected to a thorough discussion until the final version was decided upon by majority vote. He put his pen through the pieces of paper that were rejected, but preserved them inside the "*Semag*" "like the broken tablets which were preserved in the Ark." He began to write his book from the corrected notes shortly before his death, but only reached the middle of precept 65 (on the laws of the Sabbath).

He died in Regensburg. He bequeathed the copy of the "*Semag*" upon which he was working, together with the portion arranged in his own handwriting, and the corrected and rejected pieces of paper, to his son, Aviezri. At first the son hesitated to undertake the completion of the work and only ten years later (in 1506), began sorting the material and methodically arranging it. In his introduction, the son warns against "those who possess unamended copies." Fifty-two years after the author's death, the work, sometimes called "the *Nimmukim* ["reasons"] of Isaac Stein" appeared as an appendix of the *Sefer Mitzvot Gadol* (Venice, 1547), without mentioning that it was only an uncorrected part of the whole work. *Nimmukim* contains valuable material for the study of the folklore of German Jewry and the linguistic usages of those days. Interesting too are the author's observations on Jewish social life, such as the attitude to Hebrew as a spoken language, neighborly relations with gentiles, divination, the flogging of transgressors, and public confession. It serves as a source of great value because of its halakhic summaries and because of its fund of quotations from the works of early scholars. Many incomplete copies of Stein's work are extant. One in Oxford is said to be in the handwriting of the author's son, but this claim has still to be confirmed.

BIBLIOGRAPHY: *Resp Maharik*, nos. 169–70; Mirsky, in: *Talpioth*, 7 (1957), 33–71, 317–59; 8 (1961), 3–37, 420–50; Y.L. Bialer, *Min ha-Genazim* (1967), 9–29.

[Yehuda Leib Bialer]

STEIN, JANICE GROSS (1943–), Canadian scholar, Middle East expert. Stein was born in Montreal and received an M.A. from Yale and a Ph.D. from McGill, becoming Belzberg Professor of Conflict Management and Negotiation and Director of the Munk Centre for International Studies at the University of Toronto. She wrote widely on negotiation theory, foreign policy decision-making, and international conflict and conflict management. She authored over 80 books, book chapters, and articles.

As a Middle East specialist, Stein addressed a range of important theoretical problems in political science and psychology. Her first book, *Rational Decision Making: Israel's Security Choices, 1967* (1980), used the 1967 war as a case study to test three contrasting models of decision-making. It won the Edgar Furniss Award of the Mershon Centre for outstanding contribution to the study of national security and civilian military education. Other works on Jewish or Middle East subjects include *Powder Keg in the Middle East: The Struggle for Gulf Security* (1995), *Peacemaking in the Middle East* (1985), and *Contemporary Antisemitism* (2005).

Stein was a member of international advisory panels, including the Committee on International Conflict Resolution of the National Academy of Sciences in Washington, the American Association for the Advancement of Science, and the United States Institute for Peace. In Canada, Stein was chair of the Research Advisory Board to the Minister of Foreign Affairs and chair of the Advisory Board to the Canadian Centre for Foreign Policy Development as well as member of the Middle East Advisory Group in the Ministry of Foreign Affairs. She is a fellow of the Royal Society of Canada and a Trudeau Fellow. She provided regular commentary on Middle East and other international issues for Canadian television.

[Judith E. Szapor (2nd ed.)]

STEIN, JOSEPH (1912–), U.S. dramatist. Born in New York City, Stein grew up in the Bronx. His father, a Polish immigrant, read him the stories of *Shalom Aleichem, and Stein would later remember them when he developed the musical *Fiddler on the Roof.* Earlier, Stein graduated from the City College of New York and earned a master of social work degree from Columbia University. He spent the next six years as a psychiatric social worker. In 1946 Stein began writing for radio, and two years later he and a writing partner, Will Glickman, began contributing sketches to Broadway revues. Stein was also a writer for the comedian Sid *Caesar's television shows. One of his first works for Broadway was the musical *Plain and Fancy* (1955), about the adventures of a pair of sophisticated New Yorkers living among the Amish in Pennsylvania. Then came *Mr. Wonderful* (1956), a vehicle for Sammy *Davis Jr., and, with Sheldon Harnick, the musical *Body Beautiful* (1958). In 1959 it was *Take Me Along*, an original musical, and in 1963, *Enter Laughing*, a comedy. Stein then produced the book (and Harnick and *Jerry Bock the music) for *Fiddler* (1964), the story of Tevye the milkman and his five daughters that played on Broadway, first with Zero *Mostel in the starring role, until 1972. It was revived on Broadway four times in the next 32 years, was made into a movie starring Chaim *Topol, the Israeli star, and spawned productions all over the world, including such unlikely venues as Japan. Audiences devoured the music ("If I Were a Rich Man," "Sunrise, Sunset") and related to the universal truths espoused by a poor Jew in the fictional shtetl of Anatevka, where the Jews' lives were as shaky as that of a fiddler on a roof. Stein won the Tony Award and Drama Critics Circle Award for *Fiddler.* His other musicals included *Zorba* (1968), for which he received a Tony nomination; *Rags* (1986), another Tony nomination; and *The Baker's Wife*, which won the Laurence Olivier award in London. He also wrote the screenplays for *Enter Laughing* and for *Fiddler on the Roof.*

[Stewart Kampel (2nd ed.)]

STEIN, JULES CEASAR (1896–1981), U.S. entertainment executive; ophthalmologist. Stein was born in South Bend, Indiana, to Orthodox retailer M. Louis and Rose (nee Cohen) Stein. Stein's mother was an invalid, and the resulting financial drain for her medical care forced Stein to work at age 12, playing the violin and saxophone. He had established his own band and was booking musical acts by 1910 and graduated high school early two years later at age 16. Stein went on to attend the University of West Virginia (1912–13), the University of Chicago (1915), University of Chicago's Rush Medical College (1921) and the University of Vienna (1921). Following a residency in ophthalmology at Cook County Hospital in Chicago, Stein set up a private practice in 1923. He continued to book bands on the side, and, with William Goodheart, in

1924 Stein co-founded the Music Corporation of America, an agency that excelled at setting up exclusive contracts and perfected packaging, which would provide venues for an entire season of bookings and net the agency a separate fee. In 1938, he sent employee Lew Wasserman to Hollywood to open an MCA film division. As the agency gained momentum in southern California, Stein moved his family to Beverly Hills. In 1946, he turned the presidency of MCA over to Wasserman, but remained chairman. MCA was active in breaking the standard seven-year studio contract, and in 1952 Screen Actors Guild President Ronald Reagan helped secure a deal that would allow MCA to represent and hire actors for the agency's television production company Revue Productions. In 1959 the agency's name was officially changed to MCA and went public. MCA also purchased Decca Records in 1959 and started acquiring other businesses, including a consolidated Universal Pictures, Spencer Gifts, and book publisher G.P. Putnam's Sons. In 1962, the Justice Department forced MCA to give up its agency, leaving the company to focus on television and film production. Stein began promoting vision research in 1960, founding Research to Prevent Blindness, Inc., which helped pave the way for corrective surgical procedures. The University of California at Los Angeles dedicated the Jules Stein Eye Institute in 1966, and two years later Stein pushed for Congress to establish the National Eye Institute under the umbrella of the National Institutes of Health. In 1973, after undergoing surgery a few years earlier for an intestinal disorder, Stein turned over chairmanship of MCA to Wasserman, but remained primary shareholder of the company. Upon his death from a heart attack, Stein left behind an estate worth $150 million.

BIBLIOGRAPHY: "Stein, Jules," in: *The Scribner Encyclopedia of American Lives*, vol. 1: 1981–1985 (1998); Jules Stein – American Society of Cataract and Refractive Surgery, http://www.ascrs.org/Awards/Jules-Stein-MD.cfm; T. Schatz, "The Last Mogul," *The Nation* (June 30, 2003), http://www.thenation.com/docprint.mhtml?i=20030630&s=schatz.

°STEIN, BARON KARL VOM UND ZUM (1757–1831), German statesman and patriot. Stein opposed the political emancipation granted to Jews during and after the French Revolution, even though his own ordinance of Prussian municipal government of 1808 had granted them municipal citizenship. Numerous antisemitic statements of his have been recorded, especially those he made against the patrician banking families of Berlin. When Frankfurt on the Main was freed from French rule in 1813, Stein, plenipotentiary for all conquered territories, refused to intervene on behalf of the Jewish community which was in danger of losing its rights. Under his sponsorship the Westphalian estates of 1827 proposed a series of restrictive measures against the "harmful" Jewish population.

BIBLIOGRAPHY: I. Freund, *Die Emanzipation der Juden in Preussen*, 1 (1912), 104ff.; M.J. Kohler, *Jewish Rights at the Congresses of Vienna and Aix-La-Chapelle* (1918), 6, 36–38; S. Baron, *Die Judenfrage auf dem Wiener Kongress* (1920), 33f., 185.

STEIN, LEONARD (**Jacques**; 1887–1973), barrister, author, and Zionist historian. Born in London, the son of a merchant, Stein was educated at St. Pauls and Oxford, where he was the first Jewish president of the Oxford Union, and was called to the bar in 1912. He was a captain in the British Army in World War I, after which he served as a political officer in the military administration in Palestine and as military governor of Safed. In 1920 Chaim *Weizmann appointed him political secretary and legal adviser of the Zionist Organization, a position which he held from 1920 until 1929, when he left over a disagreement on the official policy of the Zionist leadership. In 1932 he returned to practicing law and achieved a reputation as a foremost expert on taxation. He continued to advise the Jewish Agency and drafted the Zionist case before the Palestine Royal Commission (1936) and the Woodhead Commission (1938; see *Palestine, Inquiry Commissions). Stein's testimony before the Shaw Commission, which investigated the causes of the 1929 riots, was described by Weizmann as "the crowning glory of Stein's outstanding services to Zionism." He was president of the Anglo-Jewish Association (1939–49) and exerted considerable influence on this body which had not been favorably disposed toward political Zionism, although Zionist circles felt that in the 1945–48 period his representations to the British government on behalf of the Anglo-Jewish associations were not always helpful to Zionist policy.

Stein wrote extensively on Zionist history and compiled an anthology of official documents pertaining to Zionism and Israel, *Promises and Afterthoughts*, and, together with Leon Simon, edited *Awakening Palestine* (1923). His most outstanding book is the *Balfour Declaration* (1961), the most authoritative, documented, and detailed work on the subject, which revealed many facts previously unpublished. He also edited and published (together with Gedalia Yogew) *The Letters and Papers of Chaim Weizmann* (vol. 1, 1889–1902). Stein wrote a number of standard works on revenue law. He was a director of the *Jewish Chronicle* newspaper for 36 years; it established a lectureship in Medieval Hebrew at Oxford to mark his 80th birthday in 1967.

ADD. BIBLIOGRAPHY: ODNB online.

[Getzel Kressel]

STEIN, LUDWIG (1859–1930), philosopher. Born in Erdöbenye, Hungary, he studied philosophy at Berlin under Zeller, at Halle, and at the Jewish Theological Seminary of Berlin, where he became a rabbi and functioned in that capacity for a couple of years. He taught at Zurich (1886–91) and then was professor at Berne. Stein edited the *Archiv fuer Geschichte der Philosophie, Archiv fuer Systematische Philosophie und Soziologie, Berner Studien zu Philosophie und ihrer Geschichte, Bibliothek fuer Philosophie*, and *Nord und Sued*. During World War I he was involved politically with the moderate Gustav Stresemann. Stein wrote extensively on philosophy and sociology. He was a cultural and political optimist of religious tendencies, opposing the pessimism of Nietzsche and Spengler, a Humean in epistemology, and interested in biology. Stein's writings deal with the history of philosophy, Jewish thought, social questions, sociology, and optimistic philosophy.

His chief works include *Die Willensfreiheit und ihr Verhaeltnis zur Goettlichen Praescienz und Providenz bei den Juedischen Philosophen des Mittelalters* (1882); *Freidrich Neitzsches Weltanschauung und ihre Gefahren* (1893); *Die soziale Frage im Lichte der Philosophie* (1897, 1923[4]); *Wesen und Aufgabe der Soziologie* (1898); *Der Sinn des Daseins* (1904); *Der soziale Optimismus* (1905); *Philosophische Stroemungen der Gegenwart* (1908), on neo-Kantiansim; *Gegen Spengler* (1925); and *Evolution and Optimism* (lectures in America; 1926).

BIBLIOGRAPHY: Koigen, in: *Archiv fuer Systematische Philosophie und Soziologie*, 33 (1929), 1–12; Dyroff, *ibid.*, 34 (1931), 153–76.

[Richard H. Popkin]

STEIN, RICHARD (1898–), Israeli ophthalmologist. Stein was born in Bohemia, the son of a farmer. After serving as an officer in the Austrian army during World War I, in which he was taken prisoner by the Italians, he studied medicine at the University of Prague and worked at the eye clinic of the university until the Nazi invasion of Czechoslovakia in 1938. During World War II, he was incarcerated in the Theresienstadt concentration camp and was put in charge of health services there. After the war he founded an ophthalmological department in a hospital in Prague but in 1949 immigrated to Israel, having been invited to treat soldiers who had suffered eye injuries in the War of Independence. He established the ophthalmological department of Tel ha-Shomer (now Chaim Sheba) Hospital and was the first to perform retinal transplants in Israel. He was appointed professor of ophthalmology at Tel Aviv University in 1966. Stein was president of the Israel Ophthalmological Association for six years and a member of the International Ophthalmological Association. He was awarded the Israel Prize in 1973.

STEIN, WILLIAM HOWARD (1911–1980), U.S. biochemist. Born in New York City, Stein studied at Harvard and Columbia, receiving his doctorate in 1938 and joining the staff of Rockefeller University, where he was appointed professor in 1952. In 1960 he was elected to the National Academy of Sciences and made a fellow of the American Academy of Arts and Sciences. He served as chairman of the editorial committee of the American Society of Biological Chemists (1958–61) and chairman of the *Journal of Biological Chemistry* (1968–71). He was a member of the medical advisory board of the Hebrew University-Hadassah Medical School in Israel and a trustee of the Montefiore Hospital. Stein was stricken with polyneuritis in 1969 and was confined to a wheelchair until his death in 1980. In 1972 he was awarded the Nobel Prize for chemistry jointly with Dr. Stanford Moore, also of Rockefeller University, for research in proteins, peptides, and amino acids, in which he had been engaged for over 30 years.

STEIN, YEHEZKIEL (1926–), Israeli physician and medical research scientist. Born in Cracow, Poland, he graduated as an M.D. from the Hebrew University of Jerusalem-Hadassah Medical School (1953) and after graduation joined the department of medicine at Hadassah where he received postgraduate training in biochemistry (1955–56). He was a visiting research scientist at Yale University and the Rockefeller University, New York (1959–61) on a Magnes Fellowship. After returning to Hadassah, he was appointed director of the Lipid Research Laboratory (1965–94), professor of medicine since 1969, and chairman of the department of medicine (1969–94). Stein's research centers on the contribution of high levels of lipoproteins rich in cholesterol (LDL) to atherosclerosis, a common disease of blood vessels including coronary artery disease. He also studied the lipoprotein HDL which removes cholesterol from the circulation. He used experimental tissue culture systems, human biochemical investigations, epidemiological surveys especially in the Jerusalem region, and clinical trials in broad and imaginative combination to elucidate the mechanisms underlying the development of atherosclerotic disease. His findings have helped to identify risk factors for developing atherosclerosis such as genetic predisposition, obesity, diet, and smoking. He has also investigated the intriguing observation that religious orthodoxy reduces the risk of myocardial infarction ("heart attacks"). Most of his more than 350 research publications were co-authored by his wife, Olga Stein, professor of experimental medicine, who also obtained her M.D. from Hadassah (1953). He participated in many international epidemiological surveys and was visiting professor at many leading U.S. university departments with shared research interests. He played a leading part in national and international committees concerned with atherosclerosis research and with education and research in medical science in general. Stein's achievements and international reputation in this field have been recognized by many honors and awards. These include the Heinrich Wieland Prize with O. Stein (1978), election to the Israel Academy of Sciences and Humanities (1980), honorary membership in the American Association of Physicians (1987), the Humboldt Research Award with O. Stein (1993), and the Israel Prize for medicine (1996).

[Michael Denman (2nd ed.)]

STEINACH, EUGEN (1861–1944), physiologist and biologist. He was born in Hohenems (in the Tyrol) and became professor of physiology at the German University of Prague, where he established a laboratory for general and comparative physiology, particularly of the sexual organs. In 1912 he was appointed director of the department of experimental biology at the Vienna Academy of Science. Steinach also contributed to the study of the physiology of elastic tissue, of the sense organs and nervous system. He coined the name "puberty gland." Steinach devised an operation for rejuvenation which consisted in the ligation of the vas deferens to produce atrophy of the spermatogenic apparatus of the testes and consequently, as he supposed, proliferation of the interstitial tissue and increased production of the hormone testosterone. In 1920 he published a book on the subject entitled *Verjuengung* *durch experimentelle Neubelebung der alternden Pubertaetsdruese.* He died in Montreux.

BIBLIOGRAPHY: S.R. Kagan, *Jewish Medicine* (1952), 169; *Biographisches Lexikon der hervorragenden Aerzte.*

[Suessmann Muntner]

STEINBACH, ALEXANDER ALAN (1894–1978), U.S. rabbi and author. Steinbach, born in Baltimore, Maryland, was ordained a rabbi by Hebrew Union College. From 1921 to 1934 he filled several pulpits before becoming rabbi of Temple Ahavath Sholom in Brooklyn, New York. Rabbi Steinbach served as president of the New York Board of Rabbis, the Brooklyn Board of Rabbis, and the Jewish Book Council of America, and was active on the boards of charitable, cultural, and civic agencies both in the Jewish and the general community.

As an author, Rabbi Steinbach wrote volumes ranging from notes to the tractate Bava Meẓia (1927), sermons, and textbooks to volumes of original essays *Musings and Meditations* (1941), *Faith and Love* (1959), and prize-winning poetry, *When Dreamers Build* (1939). He was editor of the *Jewish Book Annual* from 1954 and of *In Jewish Bookland* (*Nat'l* JWB) from 1960.

[Gladys Rosen]

STEINBACH, EMIL (1846–1907), Austrian lawyer and politician who became minister of finance. Born in Vienna, Steinbach practiced and taught law until 1874 when he was appointed an official in the Ministry of Justice under Julius *Glaser. Following his baptism in 1886 he was made a department head in the Ministry of Justice and pioneered legislation in social reform and workers' insurance. On becoming minister of finance in 1891 Steinbach introduced tax reforms and a new currency, the crown in place of the florin, basing it on the gold standard. After the fall of the government following the defeat of his electoral reform bill, Steinbach became a supreme court judge. He was president of the Supreme Court from 1904 until his death. His publications include *Die Moral als Schranke des Rechtserwerbs und der Rechtsausuebung* (1898); *Zur Friedensbewegung* (1899), *Der Staat und die modernen Privatmonopole* (1903).

BIBLIOGRAPHY: A. Spitzmueller, in: *Neue Oesterreichische Biographie 1815–1918*, 2 (1925), 48–62, incl. bibl.; L. Wittmayer, in: *Jahrbuch fuer Gesetzgebung, Verwaltung und Volkswirtschaft* (1907), 553–75.

[Josef J. Lador-Lederer]

STEINBARG, ELIEZER (Shtaynbarg; 1880–1932), Yiddish educator, cultural activist, and author. Born in Lipkany, Moldava (former Bessarabia), Steinbarg received extensive Jewish instruction from kabbalist Yosele Dayen, and was self-taught in Russian and German literature. Like his older cousin, Hebrew writer Judah *Steinberg, he was a teacher, and, for many years, director of a Hebrew-Yiddish school in Lipkany. In 1911, Steinbarg met with Ḥ.N. *Bialik and Y.Ḥ.*Rawnitzki in Odessa; their plan to publish Steinbarg's fables was abandoned with the outbreak of World War I. From 1919 until his death, Steinbarg lived with his wife, Rivke, in Czernowitz, where Jewish national consciousness was finding increasing expression. A keen Hebraist, Steinbarg was also a proponent of Yiddish phonetic orthography. He published an illustrated Yiddish primer (*Alef-Beys*, 1921) and a Yiddish-language method for learning Hebrew (*Alfon*, 1921), intertwining the pedagogy of *taytsh* with the aesthetic pleasure of whimsy. From 1920 to 1928, he was the animating force behind Yiddish-language children's theater and summer camps. He was director of a Sholem Aleichem school in Rio de Janeiro (1928–30), before returning to Czernowitz, where he resumed the leadership of Yiddishist cultural activities. The 20th anniversary of the Czernowitz Language Conference saw the publication of *Durkh di Briln* ("Through My Eyeglasses"), a limited edition of 12 of Steinbarg's rhymed fables, and was the occasion for the "discovery" of literary Yiddish Romania, then at its apogee, whose towering figures were two "neo-folk poets," Steinbarg and Itsik *Manger. While public performances of Steinbarg's fables had long been popular locally, it was through Herz Grossbart's artistic recitals that these Yiddish tales gained international renown. When Steinbarg died in March 1932, his collection *Mesholim*, was in galley proofs. Published a few months later, the book became a bestseller; the texts have been widely translated and anthologized. *Mayselekh* ("Short Stories) was published in Czernowitz (1936), and a supplementary volume of fables, *Mesholim II*, in Tel Aviv (1956). The revised, standard edition of *Mesholim* (with 150 fables) was issued in 1969. Rivke Steinbarg died in Israel in 1968. In 1972, Eliezer Steinbarg's archives were donated to the National and University Library (Jerusalem) by her brother, Yehudah Heilprin, and Eliezer Steinbarg's siblings, Shemuel and Rivke. Steinbarg is the outstanding master of the Yiddish fable both in content and form. An admixture of mordant wit, trenchant analysis, and deep humanism, the fables are largely indeterminate and rarely offer a clear moral. Each protagonist is depicted through characteristic syntax and discourse; the speaking subjects include lyric figures, animals, and inanimate objects, notably exploring power relations. Fables of alphabetic characters (*oysyes*) are particularly innovative. Steinbarg combines motifs from traditional Hebrew study with modern literary language informed by conversational folk sources. He also enriched Yiddish culture with new idioms and reshaped proverbs.

BIBLIOGRAPHY: Rejzen, Leksikon, 4 (1929), 588–93; S. Bickel, *Rumenye* (1961), 205–34; G. Kressel, Leksikon, 2 (1967), 909–10. **ADD. BIBLIOGRAPHY:** Sh. Niger, *Yidishe Shrayber fun Tsvantsikstn Yorhundert* (1973), 211–28; D. Leibel, in E. Steinbarg, *Mesholim* (1969), 323–34; *Afn Shvel*, 306 (April-June 1997) (special Steinbarg issue).

[Nikki Halpern (2nd ed.)]

STEINBERG, Canadian family. Montreal's Steinberg family history exemplifies the classic model of poor immigrants from humble origins who succeeded in business and amassed a large fortune. The family immigrated to Montreal from Hungary in 1911. They eked out a living largely through the efforts of IDA ROTH STEINBERG, who opened in 1917 a small grocery store on St. Lawrence Boulevard in the heart of the immigrant area. IDA and WILLIAM STEINBERG (Sternberg in Hungary) had six children, of whom SAM STEINBERG (1905–1978) was the second eldest and ultimately the most prominent. All six children worked in the family store but Sam proved to be especially bright, talented, and innovative. He was also highly motivated and had a remarkable entrepreneurial sense. As a young man, he became the dominant figure in the family enterprise and guided the firm as it became a main grocery chain serving the Quebec consumer and an integral part of the Quebec scene. Under Sam's leadership the Steinberg's supermarket chain also expanded beyond Quebec into Ontario and had major interests in the United States. Known for quality products, innovation, top customer service, and high ethical business standards, through the second half of the 20th century the Steinberg's chain was recognized as one of the most successful Jewish-owned companies closely associated with the growth of the Montreal Jewish community.

Sam Steinberg controlled the company until his death in 1978. While he was alive, the company also remained very much a family business, employing many family members, though this ultimately proved to be a weakness. Of the other Steinberg siblings, NATHAN played a key role as a senior vice president and Sam's right-hand man. In the next generation, Sam's son-in-law, MEL DOBRIN, became president of the firm and Nathan's son ARNOLD STEINBERG was executive vice president. By the 1970s, however, the family enterprise encountered difficulties adapting to the changing business conditions. The situation became more acute after Sam died with no clear succession plan in place. Deteriorating relationships between the family and the firm's professional management and among several family members led to discord, much of which became public, and ultimately resulted in the sale of the company in 1989.

Sam Steinberg's two obsessions were the business and his family. He had little time for community activities and was often at odds with Sam *Bronfman, the titular leader of the Montreal Jewish community during Sam Steinberg's active years. Nevertheless Steinberg did head the organizing committee for the Pavilion of Judaism at Expo '67, Montreal's world fair. He also served as president of the Montreal Jewish General Hospital and was active in the Canadian Council of Christians and Jews.

Most of the Steinberg clan, nearly 100 descendants of Sam Steinberg and his five siblings, remain in Montreal, where several have played significant roles in and provided financial support to Jewish and large community activities. Despite the healing of some of the family rifts that developed before the sale of the family business, the family no longer acts as a coherent unit.

[Harold M. Waller (2nd ed.)]

STEINBERG, AARON (1891–1975), author and philosopher. Steinberg, a brother of Isaac Nahman *Steinberg, was born in Dvinsk, and studied in Russia and Germany. During World War I he was interned in a German village. After the war Steinberg helped to found an institute of learning in Leningrad where the intellectual leaders of Russian Jewry came together to sponsor and create new cultural values. Here and at the university, Steinberg lectured on the history of Jewish philosophy. He was a close friend of Simon Dubnow, with whom he collaborated. The climate, however, soon became unfriendly for Jewish scholars and in 1922 he moved to Berlin, where he helped to establish the Gesellschaft für Juedische Wissenschaft, as well as the Yiddish Scientific Institute, *YIVO. He published a book on Dostoevsky's *Philosophy of Freedom* and was co-editor of the Yiddish *Algemeyne Entsiklopedye*, which after many years was continued in London under the title *Jewish People, Past and Present.* It was Steinberg's translation of Dubnow's ten-volume *World History of the Jewish People* that made Dubnow well known in German-speaking countries. Together with Dubnow, he wrote a three-volume *History of the Jewish People* published shortly before World War II. He also edited a memorial volume to mark Dubnow's centenary in 1960, *Simon Dubnow: The Man and His Work (1860–1960)* (1963). Steinberg wrote fluently in Hebrew, English, Yiddish, French and German and his scholarly articles were published in various journals. He settled in England in 1934 and headed the Cultural Department of the World Jewish Congress until 1971. He was Honorary President of the Association of Jewish Journalists and Authors.

[Josef Fraenkel]

STEINBERG, AVRAHAM (1947–), Israeli physician and ethicist. Born in Germany, Steinberg immigrated with his parents as an infant to Israel (1949). After graduating high school Steinberg studied at Yeshivat Merkaz ha-Rav Kook in Jerusalem (1965–66). He then studied medicine at the Medical School of Hebrew University-Hadassah in Jerusalem and graduated in 1972. After serving in the army as a medical officer in the Air Force (1973–76), Steinberg trained in pediatrics at the Shaare Zedek Medical Center in Jerusalem, and in pediatric neurology at the Albert Einstein College of Medicine and at Montefiore Hospital Medical Center in the Bronx, New York (1976–82). Steinberg has worked as a senior pediatric neurologist at Shaare Zedek and Bikkur Cholim Hospitals in Jerusalem, as well as in the various health maintenance organizations in Jerusalem. Between 1986 and 1999 Steinberg served as secretary and treasurer of the Israel Society of Pediatric Neurology. From 1969 Steinberg researched and published extensively in the fields of general and Jewish medical ethics, history of medicine and medicine and law. He wrote many papers in Israeli and international journals, and he lectured in medical ethics at the Hebrew University Medical School as well as in many national and international forums. Steinberg chaired several national committees on medical-ethical issues, including the National Israeli Committee for Evaluation of Living Organ Donors, the National Advisory Committee to the Minister of Health for Enacting a Law Concerning the Terminally Ill, the National Advisory Committee for Amendments of the Anatomy and Pathology Law, and the National Forum Concerning Organ Donations in Israel. In 1999 Steinberg received the Israel Prize for his monumental work *Encyclopedia of Jewish Medical Ethics* (1988–98, 2,740 pp.). Steinberg was the director of the Medical Ethics Unit and senior pediatric neurologist, Shaare Zedek Medical Center, Jerusalem, Israel.

[Bracha Rager (2nd ed.)]

STEINBERG, ISAAC NAHMAN (1888–1957), Russian revolutionary, jurist, writer, and leader of the *Territorialist movement. He was born in Dvinsk (Daugavpils, Latvia) into a family in which Jewish tradition and Haskalah coexisted. His father was a well-established merchant and his mother was the sister of the Yiddish literary critic *Baal-Makhshoves. Steinberg received a traditional Jewish education, which had a marked influence on him until the end of his life. He studied law at Moscow University, from which he was expelled because of revolutionary activities. In 1910 he completed his legal studies at Heidelberg University, receiving the title of Doctor of Laws for his dissertation *Die Lehre vom Verbrechen im Talmud* (1910; "Penal Law in the Talmud"), published as a book. For a few years before the outbreak of World War I he practiced as a lawyer in Moscow.

Steinberg had begun his revolutionary activity in 1906, when as a student he joined the Social Revolutionary Party. He was arrested, imprisoned, and exiled abroad. In 1910 he returned to Russia. After the February 1917 Revolution, when the Social Revolutionary Party split up, Steinberg joined its left-wing faction. When the faction joined the first Soviet government headed by Lenin, Steinberg represented his party in it serving as commissar for law (minister of justice) from December 1917 to March 1918. After the split between the left-wing Social Revolutionaries and the Bolsheviks Steinberg was arrested several times. He left Russia, and from 1923 lived in Berlin. There he acted as representative abroad for his party, and went on lecture tours on its behalf. From 1933 to 1939 Steinberg lived in London, and in 1943 settled in New York. There, among other activities, he was a member of the board of directors of *YIVO, on whose behalf he made several journeys to South Africa and South America.

Steinberg began his literary activity by contributing to legal and general periodicals in Russia. Subsequently he continued as one of the editors of party organs in Moscow and Berlin. He also contributed to the general socialist press, and to the Yiddish *Zukunft* in New York. From 1926 to 1937 Steinberg published and edited the series in Yiddish *Fraye Shriftn farn Yidishen Sotsialistishn Gedank* in which he attempted to formulate his ideas in the spirit of ethical socialism, which combined Jewish ethics with the ideal of universal justice and human solidarity. From 1943 to 1956 he edited the monthly *Oyfn Shvel* of the Freeland League, founded by Ben *Adir. Apart from numerous articles of literary and political interest, Steinberg published a series of books in Russian, Yiddish, and German on the Russian Revolution, which were translated into English and other languages. He also wrote a social drama in German, *Der Dornenweg* ("The Thorny Path," 1927; Yid. trans. 1928), which was produced in Germany. His best-known book is his comprehensive work on the Russian revolutionary Maria Spiridonova (Eng., 1935; Yid., 1936; Heb., 1936). His socialist credo is expressed in his *Der Moralisher Ponim fun der Revolutsiye* ("The Moral Aspect of the Revolution," Yid., 1925; Rus., 1925); *Gewalt und Terror in der Revolution* (Ger., 1931); *In the Workshop of the Revolution* (1953; 1955). He wrote on his brief experience as minister of justice in Russia in *Als ich Volkskommissar war* (Ger., 1929; *Memoirs of a People's Commissar*, Eng., 1931; Yid., 1931).

His activity in the Territorialist movement forms a special chapter in Steinberg's life. Hitler's rise to power in Germany, and subsequently the outbreak of World War II, led him to advocate the idea of Territorialism. He argued that the safety of European Jews could not await a change in the British policy in Palestine, and accordingly founded the territorialistic Freeland League which advocated Jewish colonization in other countries. In pursuit of this aim Steinberg went to Australia and proposed the creation of an autonomous Jewish colony in the northwestern Kimberley. His efforts failed, however, the Australian government being prepared to accept Jewish refugees but not to tolerate a separate national unit on its territory. After the failure of the Australian project, Steinberg promoted a similar plan, though on a more limited scale, in Surinam, which also ended in failure. He wrote on his ideas on Territorialism and attempts to put them into practice in *Gelebt un Gekholemt in Australie* (Yid., 1945; *Australia – The Unpromised Land*, Eng., 1948), and to some extent also in *Mit Eyn Fus in Amerike* (1951), on personalities, events, and ideas.

Steinberg's was an unusual personality, in which varying and seemingly conflicting elements combined. While an extreme left-wing revolutionary, and among the leaders of the party which relied on the Russian peasant, Steinberg was an observant Orthodox Jew, with Jewish national ideas, and active in Jewish politics. He was a prolific writer, with a lucid style, as well as an accomplished speaker and controversialist.

BIBLIOGRAPHY: Rejzen, Leksikon, 4 (1930), 604–8; *Yiẓhak Naḥman Steinberg Gedenk-Bukh* (1961); M. Enav, *Be-Sa'arat ha-Ḥayyim* (1967).

[Simha Katz]

STEINBERG, JACOB (1887–1947), Hebrew poet, short story writer, and essayist; born in Belaya Tserkov in the Ukraine. Little is known of his early life, except what may be gathered from his short stories and novelettes. These, with their portrayal of poverty, family squabbles, the vagaries of self-education, revolt against tradition, and flight to the city suggest the usual background of a Hebrew writer in Eastern Europe prior to World War I. At 14 Steinberg ran away to Odessa where he met Ḥ.N. Bialik, who encouraged him, and Z. Shneour, who became his close friend. In 1903 he moved to Warsaw where he published his first Hebrew poem and contributed to Hebrew and Yiddish periodicals, winning literary acclaim in both languages. At the outbreak of World War I he immigrated to Palestine and, except for the years 1923 to 1925 spent in Berlin, lived out his life there. In Palestine he ceased writing Yiddish and contributed regularly in Hebrew to *Ha-Po'el ha-Za'ir*, *Moledet*, and *Davar*. From 1942 he was one of the editors of *Moznayim*, the literary periodical of the Hebrew Writers' Association. His Hebrew writings were republished in 1957 as part of the Dvir Classical Library. The collected works appeared in 1964.

Poetry and Poetics

Steinberg's work is highly original, notwithstanding that he was not an innovator. Though he never acknowledged any influence, that of Bialik is clearly discernible in his earlier poems and short stories. But his insight into the work of Baudelaire and Verlaine and the lesson derived from the Russian realists are equally evident in what may be described as his "spiritual realism."

In his quest for flawless form, in his pained introspection, and in his objection to the excesses of didacticism, he is thus reminiscent of Baudelaire. The recurrent mood of ennui with its accompanying motifs of decay, poison, tombs, and riddles also recalls the French poet and the later symbolists. From Baudelaire and his disciples he apparently derived the doctrine of enigmatic affinities, also sharing their predilection for analogy and oxymorons.

Like the symbolists, Steinberg distrusts descriptive verse; the poet, he maintains, should neither initiate nor analyze but uncover the essential correspondences between things. Analogy alone reveals that things are not haphazard, opaque, or fragmentary. It alone can ensure the conception of a unified world which is the sum total of all its analogies brought together by poetic imagination. The poet is thus capable of reconciling opposites without diminishing their polar tension, the latter being the key to and the manifestation of the mystery of life.

Steinberg's style, essentially biblical, deliberately archaic, with a manifest contempt for "the lightsome present," is nevertheless exact and specific. He is perhaps the only modern Hebrew poet who succeeded in forging a biblical style into an adequate tool for the expression of a basically modern sensibility, without recourse to pastiche or a technique of fragmentation. Despite its insistence on the discovery of new relationships, his poetry is not given to modernistic analogies that "make it new" by their sheer incongruity. On the contrary, he often resorts to a conventional imagery which comes alive by dint of a single word or expression. The main strength of his idiom lies in the endowment of abstract spiritual entities with almost sculptural concreteness. His phrases and word formations, ostensibly biblical but intrinsically his own, cannot be paraphrased and would greatly lose in translation. They epitomize fully realized moments drawn from intense personal experience yet emanating, as it were, from the wisdom of the ages. These "moments," enigmatic "documents of life," as he calls them, are not susceptible to logical reduction but they are equally hostile to the spirit of generalizing abstractions and are not satisfied with mere "musical" vagueness – qualities Steinberg disliked in poetry as in life. Hence his predilection for the powerful realism in the narrative books of the Bible.

Steinberg's emphasis on such pregnant moments is reinforced by a theoretical preoccupation with the smallest structural and semantic unit – the verse line and the single word, provided it contains what he calls "an epic of life." He saw the history of Hebrew literature as a gradual estrangement from the life-engendering verse line and as an immersion in rhetorical garrulity, inattentive to life or inimical to it. The very indifference of the Jew to aesthetic perception is symptomatic of the malaise of an uprooted people. Whoever envisages a future for Jewish poetry, he argues, envisages a future for the Jewish nation. The return of Hebrew poetry to the "line" implies the return of the Jew to normal life.

More than any of his contemporaries, Steinberg thus pointed out the major weakness of contemporary Hebrew literature of his day, though his own poetry was not always untainted by the very things he abhorred. His condemnation of a cliché-ridden rhetoric constituted a reaction against a tradition which had exhausted itself, and, in the eyes of its modern opponents, had adulterated the language of poetry. Like the imagists, Steinberg sought to return to the hard core of poetry, which he too calls image. His assertion that at the dawn of a new epoch the image-analogy is first to awaken to a new life, is the essence of the imagist credo. As prototype of his image, Steinberg points to the ambiguous word-entity fashioned by biblical realism. The ancient Hebrews, he argues, were unskilled in the arts of building and sculpture but excelled in sculpting abstract notions into word monuments. In this resides the strength of the Hebrew language itself whose words are "chiseled, solid stones, not formless sand as in Slavic and Germanic tongues." This insistence on hardness and meaningful directness is evinced in Steinberg's late lyrics and in his accomplished love poems in which he evokes the experience with unsparing truthfulness and almost scientific detachment. On the whole his poetry marks one of the most impressive achievements of modern Hebrew literature.

Stories

Steinberg wrote some 20 stories whose themes and landscapes are taken mainly from the life of the Jewish communities in the small towns of the Ukraine. These depict a lowly world of frustration, unhappy love affairs, the squalor of an existence under constant persecution – a world stirred by the echoes of far-off change and revolution. Most of them resolve in death, defeat, suicide, the waste of strong passions doomed to slow extinction and transformed into forces of destruction.

Out of this gallery of uprooted, washed-out, withered souls – portrayed with restraint, with close attention to the pregnant minor detail, and without a trace of melodrama – rises a specter of the writer's own early incurable afflictions.

But beyond autobiography, the stories are a psychological study of the rootless Jew in the midst of a hostile world. Here

Steinberg allies himself with J.H. Brenner, S.Y. Abramovitsh (Mendele Mokher Seforim), and a long succession of Jewish writers in a blunt scrutiny of what he considers the only race of man forced out of the orbit of nature and living for the sake of death in the absence of any earthly purpose to devote itself to. The condemnation of the *galut* is absolute, but even when describing the Diaspora Jew as "a freakish specter," Steinberg remains the observer rather than the preacher. The sense of a common lot and the echoes of pogroms turn this predicament, too, into an occasion of self-revelation. This is where the stories and the poems touch.

Essays

His essays, ostensibly written about "occasional" subjects, are set in the realities of Ereẓ Israel. Whether he writes about the *ḥamsin*, the atmosphere of the café, or the plethora of languages in the city of his day, he constantly reverts to the subject that haunts him: the impoverished spiritual life of a small and arid community of immigrants, as opposed to the glory that was Judah. These essays, halfway between the conventional essay form and the prose poem, do not register fleeting moods or impressionistic intimacies, but adhere to the lesson Steinberg learned from the Bible (one of the few masterpieces, he maintains, in which a whole nation revealed its soul) and from the nature of the Hebrew language as he interpreted it.

Despite their affinity to Zionist ideology, his ideas, couched like his poems in biblical language, are concerned with and addressed to the select few. Indeed, the strengthening of the individual is seen by Steinberg as the main task of Hebrew renascence.

The essays won a wider acclaim than the poems. Only after the War of Independence, with the advent of a new generation of Hebrew writers inveighing against the rhetorical excesses of their predecessors, were his works more closely read and revalued.

BIBLIOGRAPHY: G. Shaked, in: J. Steinberg, *Yalkut Sippurim* (1966), 7–27; A. Epstein, in: *Sefer ha-Shanah li-Yhudei Amerikah*, 4 (1939), 228–35; J.M. Ben-Eliezer, in: *Ha-Tekufah*, 21 (1924), 501–3; J. Silbershlag, in: *Bitzaron*, 1 (1940), 333–44; M. Rabinson, in: *Haolam*, 26 (1937/38), 138f.; 617f.; I. Cohen, *Ya'acov Steinberg Vi-Yẓirato* (1972). **ADD. BIBLIOGRAPHY:** M. Ungerfeld, "*Y. Steinberg*," in: *Hadoar*, 51 (1972), 528–29; A. Komem, *Darkhei ha-Sippur shel Ya'akov Steinberg* (1976); A. Brakai, *Mishka'im Bialikiyyim be-Shirat Meshorerim* (1976); G. Shaked, *Ha-Sipporet ha-Ivrit*, 1 (1977), 250–1; Y. Cohen, "*Y. Steinberg*," in: *Moznayim*, 47:5 (1979), 283–88; Z. Sivan, *Ha-Yesod ha-Dramati be-Shirat Y. Steinberg* (1979); H. Herzig, *Ha-Sippur ha-Ivri be-Reshit Shenot ha-Esrim* (1992); Z. Luz, *Y. Steinberg, Monografyah* (2000); A. Komem, *Shenei Ekronot Yesod be-Shirat Ya'akov Steinberg* (2004).

[Natan Zach]

STEINBERG, JOSHUA (1825–1908), Hebrew writer, linguist, and teacher, son-in-law of A.B. Lebensohn (Adam ha-Kohen). A graduate of the Vilna Government Rabbinical Seminary, Steinberg served as a government-appointed rabbi in Bialystok and Vilna (1860–66), and was active in the establishment of governmental Russian-Jewish schools. In 1867 he was appointed lecturer in Hebrew and Aramaic at the Vilna Rabbinical Seminary and was censor of Hebrew books from 1883 to 1905. From time to time Steinberg wrote articles in which he preached the ideas of the Haskalah. The body of his work was connected with the study of Hebrew and its grammar. He wrote textbooks in Russian for the study of Hebrew and Aramaic; translated the Pentateuch and several books of the Prophets into Russian with Hebrew and Russian commentary; compiled a Russian-Hebrew dictionary (1880), and a frequently reprinted Russian-Hebrew pocket dictionary. In his book of grammar, *Ma'arekhei Leshon Ever* (1884), he employed his own method, whose main principle was the acceptance of the Ashkenazi pronunciation of vowels and the use of two- and three-letter roots. His biblical dictionary, *Mishpat ha-Urim* (1891; revised edition, *Millon ha-Tanakh*, 1940), has retained its value. Steinberg was a scrupulous purist who wrote only in the biblical idiom. Aḥad Ha-Am, who printed his article "*Toledot ha-Safah ve-Torat Darwin*" ("History of Language and Darwin's Theory," in: *Ha-Shilo'aḥ* (2 (1897), 24–37)), referred to his writings as examples of the inability of biblical style to express modern scientific thought. Steinberg greatly influenced the methods of teaching Hebrew language and grammar.

His works also include: translation of M.J. Lebensohn's poems into German, *Gesaenge Zions* (Vilna, 1859); epigrams and proverbs, *Or la-Yesharim* (1865); and three chapters of *Sybilline Oracles* translated into Hebrew in *Ha-Me'assef* (Warsaw, 1886).

BIBLIOGRAPHY: H.Y. Katznelson, in: *Hadoar*, 11, nos. 11, 12 (1932), 173–4.

[Yehuda Slutsky]

STEINBERG, JUDAH (1863–1908), writer and Hebrew educator. Born into a ḥasidic family in Lipkany (Bessarabia), Steinberg became attracted to Haskalah and taught himself Russian, science, and mathematics. His first book, *Niv Sefatayim* (1893), a writing manual, was unsuccessful, and Steinberg himself burned many copies of the book. His book of proverbs, *Ba-Ir u-va-Ya'ar* (1923^2), was warmly received as was *Siḥot Yeladim* (1899), a children's story book. In 1897 Steinberg became a teacher in Leovo. His failing health forced him to give up teaching and in 1905 he went to Odessa and there served briefly as the correspondent of the New York Yiddish daily *Di Warheit*.

Steinberg wrote many stories, which he published in Hebrew and Yiddish journals, and several textbooks. His children's stories were drawn from contemporary society and written in a simple style which combined biblical, mishnaic, and midrashic Hebrew. His heroes are Jews of all types depicted in romantic fashion with all their faults and virtues. Many of his stories deal with the Hebrew teachers of his time and their attitude toward their students. His attempts to write longer stories, "*Av u-Veno*" and "*Dr. Orlov*," were unsuccessful.

Steinberg's ḥasidic stories reflect the positive romantic attitude of Hebrew writers to Ḥasidism which in his day began to replace the critical view held by earlier modern Hebrew authors. He does not write about the great figures of Ḥasidism or about the movement's central problems, but concentrates on the simple, humble ḥasid, in all his innocence and optimism (*Gedalyahu ha-Tam*). Perhaps his most popular work is *Ba-Yamim ha-Hem* (1906), a moving, long short story depicting the suffering of a young *cantonist. After his death, his works were published by the Odessa literary circle, in six volumes (two of them, stories for young readers); several collections of his Yiddish stories were also published. A list of English translations of his works appears in Goell, Bibliography, 79, 96, 97.

BIBLIOGRAPHY: Steinberg, in: *Genazim*, 1 (1961), 139–42; Klausner, in: *Ha-Shilo'aḥ*, 18 (1908), 278–82; Fichmann, in: *Kol Kitvei Yehudah Steinberg* (1959), v–x; P. Lachower, *Meḥkarim ve-Nisyonot*, 1 (1925), 159–62; Ofek, in: *Moznayim*, 16 (1963), 140–1; Orlan, *ibid*, 18 (1964), 303–5; Kressel, Leksikon, 2 (1967), 910–1; Waxman, Literature, 4 (1960²), 62–70.

[Yehuda Slutsky]

STEINBERG, MARTIN R. (1904–1983), U.S. medical administrator. Born in Russia and educated in the U.S., he was appointed assistant professor of otolaryngology at the graduate school of the University of Pennsylvania in 1935. In 1948 he became director of New York City's Mount Sinai Hospital and in 1964 he was also appointed professor and chairman of the department of administrative medicine of the Mount Sinai School of Medicine. He was president of the Greater New York Hospital Association and of the Hospital Association of New York State.

STEINBERG, MAXIMILIAN OSSEJEVICH (1883–1946), composer and teacher. Born in Vilna, Steinberg graduated from St. Petersburg University (1907, natural sciences faculty) and St. Petersburg Conservatory (1908, composition). Being the student and son-in-law of Rimsky-Korsakov, Steinberg followed his tradition and edited many of his scores and books (including *Foundations of Orchestration* (2 vols., 1913). His career developed from teaching composition and orchestration at the St. Petersburg Conservatory from 1908 until the end of his life. There he was dean of the faculty from 1917 to 1931 and vice rector from 1934 to 1939. Steinberg's compositions were influenced by his master, and by his interest in Asiatic music. He wrote five symphonies and other orchestral works, ballets, and chamber and piano music. Many prominent Soviet composers were Steinberg's pupils, including Dmitri Shostakovich, Vladimir Shcherbachev, and Yuri Shaporin.

BIBLIOGRAPHY: A. Rimsky-Korsakov: *Maximilian Shteinberg* (1928); M. Gnesin, *"Maximilian Shteinberg,"* in: *Sovetskaya muzyka*, 12 (1946), 29–36; V. Bogdanov-Berezovsky, *Maximilian Shteinberg* (1947); L. Nikol'skaya, *"Simfonicheskoe tvorchestvo M.O. Shteinberga"* and O. Dansker, *"Shostakovich v dnevnikakh M.O. Shteinberga,"* in: L. Kovnatskaya (ed.), *Shostakovich: mezhdu mgnoveniem i vechnostiu* (2000), 83–148

[Marina Rizarev (2nd ed.)]

STEINBERG, MILTON (1903–1950), U.S. Conservative rabbi. Steinberg was born in Rochester, New York, and ordained a rabbi by the Jewish Theological Seminary (1928). His first congregation was in Indianapolis, Indiana, and in 1933 he moved to the Park Avenue Synagogue in New York, an institution that was still part of the Reform movement and lived in the shadow of the larger and more prestigious institutions that were nearby, Kehillath Jeshurun with Rabbi Joseph *Lookstein as its leader and Temple Emmau-El and Central Synagogue. Steinberg brought the synagogue into the Conservative movement. He attracted new members and built up the congregation. He was a fine preacher. An ardent Zionist, he worked with the Zionist Organization of America and also with Hadassah. Park Avenue Synagogue is now among the most prestigious in the Conservative Movement. A student of Morris Raphael *Cohen, Steinberg was concerned with a philosophical approach to Judaism. He dealt with issues such as the nature of God, His relation to humanity and history, the problem of evil, the confrontation of faith and reason, and so forth. While at the seminary, the most profound influence on Steinberg was Mordecai M. *Kaplan. Steinberg was early identified with Kaplan's Reconstructionist movement and was one of the founders of its publication. For a year he was managing editor of *The Reconstructionist* (1937), and in the 1940s helped edit the *Reconstructionist Sabbath Prayer Book* (1945) that was widely criticized in traditional circles for its abandonment of the chosen people concept and the sacrificial order. Steinberg later expressed criticism of the movement. His main points were that while Reconstructionism was a sound ideology, it lacked a philosophic concern and was deficient in poetry. Steinberg's novel, *As a Driven Leaf* (1939), was considered one of the best novels written with the talmudic period as a background. The work deals with the heretic *Elisha ben Avuyah and the conflict of religion and philosophy which his life represents. Elisha eventually realizes that one is not superior to the other but both are based upon the acceptance on faith of undemonstrated basic premises. This realization prevents Elisha from denouncing religion as inferior. The work is still read more than 65 years after its writing and is still a fine orientation to the time of Rabbinic Judaism. *The Making of the Modern Jew* (1934) was Steinberg's attempt to sort out the history of the Jew and the meaning of that history for a Jew in the 20th century. The book did not actually deal with the 20th century, and Steinberg published *A Partisan Guide to the Jewish Problem* (1945) which, although not a sequel, gave indication of the type of modern Jew that he believed would emerge from this interplay of past and present. His work *Basic Judaism* (1947) enjoyed wide popularity as an attempt to set down the basics of the Jewish religion. It, too, is still widely read, especially by those who are becoming Jews by choice. In addition, Steinberg was active in Zionist circles and devoted much time to furthering the Zionist cause in the U.S. A number of volumes of essays were published posthumously: *A Believing Jew* (1951); *From the Sermons of Milton Steinberg* (1954); and *Anatomy of Faith* (1960).

BIBLIOGRAPHY: A. Cohen, in: M. Steinberg, *Anatomy of Faith* (1960), 11–60; J. Goldin, in: *Jewish Frontier*, 27 (May 1950), 5–8; P.S. Nadell, *Conservative Judaism in America: A Biographical Dictionary and Sourcebook* (1988).

[Michael Berenbaum (2nd ed.)]

STEINBERG, PAUL (1926–2005), U.S. Reform rabbi, psychologist, academician. Steinberg was born in New York City and attended the College of the City of New York, where he earned a B.S. (1946) and M.S. (1948) and served as a fellow in the Department of Education (1946–48). During those years leading up to the creation of the State of Israel, he worked for Americans for *Haganah, an organization that smuggled arms to Jewish fighters in mandatory Palestine. A disciple of Stephen S. *Wise, he was ordained at the *Jewish Institute of Religion in 1949 and received an Ed.D. from Teachers College, Columbia University in 1961. In 1985, he was awarded an honorary D.H.L. by Baltimore Hebrew University. The recipient of a Guggenheim Fellowship for Research and Travel in Israel, he served as a visiting lecturer in the School of Social Welfare and the Department of Education at the *Hebrew University in Jerusalem (1949–50). Returning to the United States, he became director of the *B'nai B'rith Hillel Foundation at the University of California in Berkeley (1950–52) before entering the pulpit rabbinate at Temple Israel of Northern Westchester, Croton-on Hudson, N.Y. (1952–57). He also served as chaplain of the Franklin D. Roosevelt Veterans Administration Hospital in Montrose, N.Y. (1952–57) and lectured at the New York University School of Education (1956).

In 1958, Steinberg accepted a full-time appointment as associate professor at the New York campus of the Hebrew Union College-Jewish Institute of Religion, where he had been a part-time instructor for the two preceding years. In 1961, he was elevated to professor of human relations and education and dean, a position he retained until 1985. In addition to being responsible for all the departments at the school that train rabbis, cantors and educators, he served as executive dean of the HUC Biblical and Archaeological School in Jerusalem (1963–70), as well as director of the American Office of the HUC-JIR Jerusalem School and director of the Summer Programs in Israel, including archaeological excavations. Steinberg is credited with inaugurating the New York institution's Year-in-Israel Program for its students (1971) and establishing an Israel Rabbinical Program in the 1980s to strengthen Progressive Judaism in Israel. He also helped develop a music degree program and set up satellite schools in the suburbs offering certification in Jewish education.

A New York State Department of Education Research Fellow in Israel (1967) and Eleanor Sinsheimer Distinguished Service Professor in Jewish Religious Education and Human Relations (1970), Steinberg was a member of the board of directors of the Council of Higher Educational Institutions of the City of New York (1957–1973). In 1985, he was named HUC-JIR's vice president for communal affairs and dean of faculty, serving in that post for 20 years. He was HUC-JIR's longest serving dean when he succumbed to illness at the age of 79.

A certified psychologist, Steinberg combined his academic career with a professional one outside the halls of academe: he was a consultant to industry and management at Richardson, Bellows & Henry (1958–60) and a professional associate at BFS Psychological Associates of New York. He was also an expert examiner for the New York State Civil Service Commission and a speaker at executive development seminars conducted by the Department of Defense and the American Management Association. In addition, he was a member of the Boards of Trustees of the Albright Institute of Archaeological Research – American Schools of Oriental Research (Jerusalem, Israel) and of the Jewish Braille Institute of America as well as a Fellow of the American Association for the Advancement of Science.

BIBLIOGRAPHY: The Nearprint Files of the American Jewish Archives, Cincinnati.

[Bezalel Gordon (2nd ed.)]

STEINBERG, SAUL (1914–1999), U.S. artist and cartoonist. Born near Bucharest, Romania, Steinberg studied sociology and psychology at the University of Bucharest but moved to Italy and received a doctoral degree in architecture from the Reggio Politecnico in Milan in 1940. There, he began his career as an artist, founding a magazine with Giovanni Guareschi, an Italian novelist, and began publishing his drawings. His visual language was a thin sharp line that was always remarking on its own existence. Often his drawings poked fun at the art of drawing, the artist growing out of his own pen and winding up as a square, or becoming entangled in his own fancies, or unable to break out of a never-ending spiral. His art also played on the theme of emigration and the bureaucratic guises of identity: fingerprints, passports, signatures. As a foreign Jew living in Milan under a Fascist regime that was growing more antisemitic, he was awarded his diploma by Victor Emmanuel III, King of Italy, King of Albania, and Emperor of Ethiopia, identified as "of the Jewish race." In 1941, he fled to the United States using what he described as a "slightly fake" passport, one he stamped with his own rubber stamp. It got him to neutral Portugal and then to Ellis Island, from where he was deported to Santo Domingo, Dominican Republic, because the tiny quota of Romanians was already filled. He sent some cartoons to *The New Yorker*, hoping the magazine would support his entry into the United States. His first *New Yorker* drawing appeared on October 25, 1941, an artist's playful rendition of a reverse centaur, one with a man's rear end and a horse's head. Steinberg arrived in the United States the following year. In 1943 Steinberg had his first American one-man show. On the same day that he became a United States citizen, he was given an ensign's commission in the Navy. He was assigned to teach Chinese guerillas how to blow up bridges, and for a year flew the mountainous route known as the Hump from China to India, making sure the explosives reached their destinations. He was then sent to North Africa to draw cartoons that would inspire anti-Nazi resistance inside Germany. *The New Yorker* published Steinberg's visual reports from Asia, North Africa, and Europe, and satiric drawings of Nazis. In one, "Benito and Adolf – Aryan Dancers," Mussolini and Hitler are wrestling half naked. His wartime work was published in *All in Line* (1945), the first of many collections of his drawings. In 1946, the year Steinberg was discharged from the Navy, he won his first recognition as a serious artist, when his work was included in "Fourteen Americans" at the Museum of Modern Art in New York. After the war his style changed, becoming more abstract, philosophic, and symbolic. In the 1950s he devised a roster of characters: cats, sphinxes, and empty-looking men and women, then crocodiles, his emblem for primitive political society, horses, and knights. By the 1960s his work was filled with geometrical forms, baroque comic-strip balloons, letters of the alphabet, numbers, and punctuation marks. In the late 1960s and 1970s he did architectural fantasies, watercolor landscapes, and savage pictures of New York street life that indicated a pessimism about urban life. His art was shown at several important venues: Galerie Maeght in Paris (1953) and the Sidney Janis Gallery (1973) in New York, and he had a retrospective at the Whitney Museum of American Art (1978). For *The New Yorker*, he produced 85 covers and 642 drawings. But none was more famous than the New Yorker's conception of the world, which appeared on March 29, 1976, and shows a shortsighted view of the rest of the world, in which everything in the landscape recedes according to its cultural distance from Manhattan. The idea was copied in knockoffs made for London, Paris, Rome, Venice, and just about every other city. Steinberg, as he lamented late in life, was known as "the man who did that poster." More than once Steinberg was photographed with one of his paper-bag masks over his face. That, he once said, is what people do in America, "manufacture a mask of happiness for themselves."

[Stewart Kampel (2nd ed.)]

STEINBERG, WILLIAM (1899–1978), conductor. Born in Cologne, Steinberg became assistant to Otto *Klemperer and later first conductor at the Cologne opera. He was director at the Frankfurt opera (1929–33), and made it into one of the centers of progressive music. From 1933 to 1936 Steinberg was active as conductor in the *Juedischer Kulturbund, and in 1936 went to Palestine upon the invitation of Bronislaw *Huberman to organize the Palestine (later Israel Philharmonic) Orchestra for its premiere under Toscanini. In 1937 he became assistant conductor of the NBC Symphony Orchestra in New York, and subsequently conductor of the Buffalo Philharmonic, the Pittsburgh Symphony, and part-time conductor of the London Philharmonic orchestras. Steinberg was chief conductor of the Boston Symphony Orchestra from 1969 to 1972, when he resigned on account of ill health, but continued as musical director of the Pittsburgh Symphony Orchestra.

STEINBERGER, JACK (1921–), physicist, Nobel laureate. Steinberger was born in Bad Kissingen, Germany, and immigrated to the United States in 1935. He studied at the University of Chicago, from which he received his B.Sc. in chemistry in 1942 and his Ph.D. in physics in 1948. He was a professor at Columbia University from 1950 to 1971, with the title of Higgins Professor from 1967 to 1971.

He was affiliated with the European Center for Nuclear Research (CERN) from 1968, serving as its director from 1969 to 1972. In the early 1960s Steinberger and two colleagues, Melvin *Schwartz and Leon M. *Lederman, using the proton accelerator at Brookhaven National Laboratory near New York, developed a method to detect neutrinos, subatomic particles, with spin of one-half, no electric charge, very small mass, and therefore velocities very close to the speed of light, and very weak interactions, which make them elusive, difficult to detect, but also very useful in the study of the structure of the nucleon. In an experiment performed in 1962 they found a second variety of neutrinos in addition to the neutrino which was known to be emitted by some radioactive nuclei. This was an important step towards the present understanding that elementary particles are grouped in families. For this discovery they were awarded the Nobel Prize in physics in 1988.

STEINBRUCH, AARÃO (1915–1992), Brazilian journalist, lawyer, and politician. The son of a *shoḥet*, Steinbruch was born in Porto Alegre. He was elected as a labor deputy to the Federal Chamber of Deputies in 1950 (serving until 1962) and initiated the law known as "The Thirteenth Salary," which was designed to discourage absenteeism in factories. In 1963 he became the first Jewish federal senator in Brazil representing the Movimento Democratico Brasileiro party (Laborist; serving until 1969), and in 1964 he was elected president of his party. Steinbruch presided over the Federação Israelita do Estado de Rio de Janeiro (Federation of Jewish Societies of the state of Rio de Janeiro) from 1958 to 1962 and visited Israel on several occasions. He was also editor of three journals, *Revista de Justiça*, *Revista do Trabalho*, and *Tres Poderes*. His wife, JULIA VAENA (1933–), was also a member of the Federal Chamber of Deputies.

[Paul Link]

STEINEM, GLORIA (1934–), U.S. feminist, writer, speaker, co-founder and contributor to *Ms. Magazine*, which became the most prominent mass-circulation feminist journal published and edited by women, from its inception in 1972 until it was sold in the 1980s. Born in Toledo, Ohio, of a Jewish father and a non-Jewish mother, Steinem was baptized in a Congregational church. Educated at home by her mother, she did not attend school regularly until she was 10, when her mostly absent father left the family permanently. Steinem came to link her mother's depression and other psychological ailments to the fact that she had given up her career for marriage, a realization that reinforced Steinem's dedication to the women's movement.

Steinem graduated with highest honors from Smith College in 1956, where she had majored in government. Her 1956 engagement to a Jewish fiancé ended in 1958 after Stein spent two years in India, following an abortion in England. Her abortion experience fueled her later "conversion" to feminism, which she attributed to an abortion rights rally in New York City in 1969. Steinem began her career as a magazine and television writer and became a founding editor of *New York Magazine* in 1968.

A widely sought public speaker and campaigner for women's rights in employment, politics, and social life, Steinem was often characterized as a Jewish feminist. She became a participant in the first feminist women's *seders* which started in 1976 and supported women's and minority rights in other walks of life. Her six books include *Outrageous Acts and Everyday Rebellions* (1983), a bestseller that was translated into 11 languages; *Moving Beyond Words* (1986); *Revolution from Within: A Book of Self-Esteem* (1992); and *Feminist Family Values* (1996). Her numerous essays made a deep impact on the feminist movement and beyond.

Steinem helped found the National Women's Political Caucus in 1971, to encourage women to seek political office and to work for women's rights legislation; co-founded the Women's Action Alliance, to fight discrimination against women; helped found Ms. Foundation for Women in 1972, to assist underprivileged girls and women; and was a founding member of the Coalition of Labor Union Women in 1974. She planned and attended the first of its kind National Women's Conference in Houston, Texas, 1977. Steinem was honored as *McCall's Magazine*'s Woman of the Year, 1972, and was inducted into the National Women's Hall of Fame in Seneca Falls, New York, 1993.

BIBLIOGRAPHY: C. Fuchs Epstein, "Steinem, Gloria," in: *World Book Online Reference Center,* at: www.aolsvc.worldbook (2005); C.G. Heilbrun, *The Education of a Woman: The Life of Gloria Steinem* (1996); P. Cronin Marcello, *Gloria Steinem: A Biography* (2004); S.L. Stern, *Gloria Steinem: Her Passions, Politics, and Mystique* (1997).

[Harriet Hartman (2nd ed.)]

STEINER, GEORGE (1929–), literary critic. Born in Paris, Steiner moved to the United States with his family in 1940 and was educated at American and French universities and at Oxford and Cambridge. From 1961 Steiner lived in England, where he was a fellow of Churchill College, Cambridge, and, later, Weidenfeld Professor of Comparative Literature at Oxford. He also held a wide range of visiting positions at universities in America and Europe. His early works include *The Death of Tragedy* (1961); *Anno Domini*, three short novels (1964); and *Language and Silence*, a volume of essays (1964). Steiner was appointed president of the English Association in 1975 and was a fellow of the Institute for Advanced Study, Princeton. His distinguished career was recognized by the universities of East Anglia and Louvain, which both awarded him honorary doctorates.

Steiner's later publications include *Extraterritorial: Papers on Literature and the Language Revolution* (1971) and *In Bluebeard's Castle: Some Notes Towards the Re-definition of Culture* (1971), which contains his most comprehensive theory of modern antisemitism. *After Babel* was published in 1975 and he also published *Martin Heidegger* (1980) and a collection of essays, *On Difficulty and Other Essays* (1978). His reputation as one of the world's leading literary critics was confirmed with the publication in 1984 of the anthology *George Steiner: A Reader.*

Steiner's literary criticism, in later years, was complemented by two works of fiction, *The Portage to San Cristobal of A.H.* (1979) and *Antigones* (1984). Both works won critical acclaim and the 1982 stage version of *The Portage to San Cristobal of A.H.* excited a prolonged exchange of letters and articles on the meaning of the Holocaust and modern antisemitism. Steiner exhibited both an astonishing range as a literary critic and incomparable understanding of Central European Jewish culture. His autobiography, *Errata: An Examined Life*, was published in 1997. He is one of the best-known public intellectuals in contemporary Britain. His wife, Zara Steiner, is also a well-known historian.

[Bryan Cheyette]

STEINER, HANNAH (1894–1944), Czech leader of women Zionists and social worker. She was born in Ceska Lipa. While studying in London before World War I, Hannah Steiner (née Dub), joined the Zionist movement. After her marriage in 1920 to Ludwig Steiner, a secondary school teacher, she settled in Prague. She was one of the founders of the WIZO in Czechoslovakia and its president from its foundation, as well as a member of the executive of world WIZO. From 1927 she edited, with Miriam Scheuer, the *Blaetter Fuer die Juedische Frau*, a women's supplement in **Selbstwehr,* the central Zionist weekly which appeared in Prague. As a result of her influence and leadership, the Czechoslovak WIZO played a central role in the pioneer training of young women, Hebrew education, and in caring for the impoverished Jews of *Sub-Carpathian Ruthenia, the eastern part of Czechoslovakia. Hannah Steiner also was active in general Zionist work, at first within the Radical Party and later within the General Zionists, and in fundraising. When thousands of Jewish refugees fled from Germany to Czechoslovakia in 1933, she and Marie *Schmolka became leaders of the relief committee for refugees (Juedisches Hilfkomité), which later became the Czechoslovak branch of HICEM.

On March 16, 1939, the day after the Nazi occupation of Prague, Hannah Steiner was arrested, but was released a few weeks later. While arranging the *aliyah* of their son and daughter she and her husband chose to remain with their oppressed coreligionists. They were interned in the ghetto of *Theresienstadt, where she was in charge of the relief service for women (*Frauenhilfsdienst*). In 1944 she and her husband were deported to *Auschwitz, where she died in the gas chambers.

BIBLIOGRAPHY: F. Grove and D. Pollak (eds.), *Saga of a Movement; Wizo: 1920–1970* (1971), 234–9; C. Yahil, *Devarim al ha-Ẓiyyonut ha-Czechoslovakit* (1967).

[Chaim Yahil]

STEINER-PRAG, HUGO (1880–1945), Czech painter, etcher, and designer. Steiner-Prag hyphenated his name with that of his native city, Prague, where he was educated. In 1907 he was appointed professor at the State Academy in Leipzig. Dismissed by the Nazis in 1933, he founded a school for applied art in Prague. After 1939, he fled to New York. Steiner-Prag contributed notably to the improvement of book production-typography, binding, jacket, and was known for his illustrations to the classics. In 1936 he designed a *Maḥzor* (a prayer book for the holidays). This proved to be his crowning achievement.

STEINFELD, J.J. (1946–), Canadian playwright, novelist, and short story writer. An only child, Steinfeld was born of Jewish survivors of the Holocaust, Esther (Biezunska) and Leon Steinfeld, in a displaced persons' camp in Munich, Germany. The family migrated to the U.S. in 1947. Steinfeld earned a B.A. from Case Western Reserve University in 1968, moved to Canada in 1972, and earned an M.A. from Trent University (Peterborough, Ontario) in 1978. After being enrolled for a Ph.D. at the University of Ottawa, Steinfeld left after completing his comprehensive exams and moved to Charlottetown, Prince Edward Island, to be a full-time writer. He continued to reside there.

Steinfeld published a novel, *Our Hero in the Cradle of Confederation* (1987) and nine short story collections: *The Apostate's Tattoo* (1983), *Forms of Captivity and Escape* (1988), *Unmapped Dreams: The Charlottetown Stories of J.J. Steinfeld* (1989), *The Miraculous Hand and Other Stories* (1991), *Dancing at the Club Holocaust: Stories New and Selected* (1993), *Disturbing Identities* (1997), *Should the Word Hell Be Capitalized?* (1999), *Anton Chekhov Was Never in Charlottetown* (2000), and *Would You Hide Me?* (2003).

Although his work does not always feature Jewish themes, many of the harrowed protagonists of Steinfeld's Kafkaesque fiction are members of the Second Generation (the children of Jewish survivors of the Holocaust), often artist figures. For these characters, Jewish identity, as refracted through their parents' experience and consciousness as Shoah survivors, threatens both sanity and life. Exploring the nuances of Jewish survival, displacement, memory, and meaning in a post-Shoah world, Steinfeld juxtaposes the horrors of his protagonists' inherited memories and knowledge of genocide with the more mundane reality of a mostly complacent and apathetic Canadian society – often to jarringly powerful effect. "Courtroom Dramas," a story in his latest collection (*Would You Hide Me?*), extends the legacy of the Shoah to the Third Generation. The unnamed protagonist has so fully identified himself with his beloved grandmother and her survival of the death camps that he, in an act of revenge, pushes a man he perceives to be a Nazi (he is wearing a swastika-armband) down an escalator at a Toronto shopping mall, killing him. The story is the poignant account of the protagonist's trial for murder.

Steinfeld won numerous literary awards for his plays (most unpublished) and his fiction, including the Norma Epstein Award for Creative Writing in 1979, the Okanagan Short Story Award in 1984, and the Creative Writing Award from the Toronto Jewish Book Committee in 1990.

[Alexander Hart (2nd ed.)]

STEINGUT, family of U.S. politicians who were leaders of the Brooklyn (New York) Democratic Party. IRWIN (1893–1952), born in New York, combined his law career and real estate and insurance business with diligent work for the Brooklyn Democratic Party, led by John H. McCooey, whom Steingut succeeded in 1934. Entering the state assembly in 1922, he became minority leader in 1930 and speaker in 1935. He was a sponsor of the Unemployment Act of 1935 and the State Social Security Bill (enacted in 1937). Both governors F.D. *Roosevelt and H.H. *Lehman found Steingut valuable in putting through reform legislation they sponsored, including greater state aid for municipalities, rent control measures and more state aid for education, and the establishment of a state university with a medical college. He was also true to his party in opposing many of the *La Guardia reforms of New York City's government. Steingut served as director of the Brooklyn Federation of Jewish Charities and as a trustee of the Hebrew Orphan Asylum. After his death, his son STANLEY (1920–1990) assumed the legislative position and political power of his father in Brooklyn politics, where he maintained the conservative structure and policies of the traditional Democratic machine (from 1953). In 1969 he was made minority leader of the state assembly. At that time he retired from the Democratic leadership of Brooklyn. Subsequently he instituted a statewide campaign against the legislature's cuts in support of education, health, and welfare, favoring tax reforms (specifically, the closing of loopholes) to supply the necessary funds. He served as speaker of the New York State Assembly from 1975 to 1978.

BIBLIOGRAPHY: IRWIN STEINGUT: *New York Times* (Sept. 27, 1952) 1:5; A. Nevins, *Herbert H. Lehman and His Era* (1963), passim; W. Moscow, *Politics in the Empire State* (1948), passim. STANLEY STEINGUT: *New York Red Book*, 78 (1969–70), 145.

[Judith S. Stein]

STEINHARDT, JAKOB (1887–1968), painter and printmaker. Born in Zerkow, Germany, he left home in 1906 to study in Berlin, first at the Museum of Arts and Crafts. Thanks to stipends he received from the Jewish community of Posen, he learned engraving under Hermann Struck. From 1909 he studied in Paris under Laurens and Matisse. He returned to Berlin in 1912 and, together with Ludwig Meidner and Richard Janthur, founded the *Pathetiker* Group, with whom he exhibited. Steinhardt was an early disciple of German expressionism, and his early subject matter was almost exclusively religious and social. He served as a soldier in Lithuania and Macedonia during World War I, and his on-the-spot drawings were exhibited in Berlin in 1917. During the war he had been exposed to the misery of Jewish life in the traditional little towns of Lithuania. This traumatic confrontation with the difficulties encountered by Jews was later significant to the content of his art. In 1933 Steinhardt immigrated to Ereẓ-Israel, choosing to live in Jerusalem. In 1949 he was appointed head of the graphics department of the Bezalel School of Art, of which he was director between 1954 and 1957. Awarded many international prizes for his outstanding woodcuts, in 1955 he received the first international prize in graphic arts at the SCO Paulo Biennale, and in 1960 the Arta Liturgica Prize at the Venice Biennale.

Steinhardt's art was recognized by his unique woodcut technique. This technique was adapted and developed in a very "primitive" way by the German Expressionists who influenced his art. Direct carving with sharp edges and forms, as well as strong contrasts of black and white, were part of his method (*Haggadah*, 1921). The romantic themes of death and suffering that appeared in Steinhardt's art were also a reflection of his Expressionist attitude. In 1925 colors were added to the woodcuts. Steinhardt chose a dark tonality instead of the bright sunlight colors he used in his oil paintings. In Jerusalem, during the 1930s and the early 1940s, the woodcuts expressed his depressed mood caused by the horrible information about the Jews in Europe, while they also were concerned with the shtetl atmosphere of the Old City of Jerusalem. Later he articulated his anger against God for allowing the Holocaust to happen, mostly by dealing with biblical themes.

The political situation in Israel became part of Steinhardt's content. A perusal of his art over the years reveals a complicated attitude toward the Arab figures. Hagar, Rachel, Jacob, and Esau expressed the suffering on both sides and the desire for peace. Studies by Prof. Ziva Amishai-Maisels have confirmed this complex process. His later work concentrated on rhythm and color was often introduced, as exemplified in his Ḥasidic scenes.

BIBLIOGRAPHY: E. Bar-On (ed.), *The Late Woodcuts of Jacob Steinhardt*, 1987; Berlin, Juedisches Museum, *Jakob Steinhardt – Der Prophet*, 1995; Tefen, The Open Museum, *Jacob and Israel, Homeland and Identity in the Work of Jacob Steinhardt*, 1998.

[Yona Fischer / Ronit Steinberg (2nd ed.)]

STEINHARDT, JOSEPH BEN MENAHEM (1720–1776), German rabbi and *posek*, Steinhardt studied at the yeshivah of Jacob b. Benjamin ha-Kohen *Poppers, in Frankfurt. In 1746 he lived in Schwabach, Bavaria. He later served as rabbi of Alsace, with his seat at Rixheim. In 1755 he was appointed chief rabbi of Niederenheim in Lower Alsace, and from 1763 until his death served as rabbi of Fuerth. Among his pupils were Mordecai *Banet of Mikulov, Moses Tobiah Sondheimer of Hanau, and Benjamin Ze'ev Wolf *Heidenheim. His fame as a halakhic authority was such that problems were addressed to him from Hungary (his: *Zikhron Yosef* 4c, et al.), Italy (5c, 48a, 87b), Amsterdam (84c), and Switzerland (58b). He maintained a regular correspondence with his brother-in-law, Isaiah b. Judah Leib *Berlin, with whom he communicated on various problems. In his work Steinhardt quotes comments and novellae by his learned wife, Kreindel, Isaiah Berlin's sister; Kreindel also urged her husband to publish his work. He was the author of: *Zikhron Yosef* (Fuerth, 1773), responsa and rulings on the four divisions of the Shulḥan Arukh, with an appendix of his novellae and sermons: *Mashbir Bar* (1828), commentaries on the Pentateuch; and *Ko'aḥ Shor*, novellae to *Bava Batra*. The last two works were published by his grandson, Akiva Steinhardt, the rabbi of Kubin, Hungary. He declined to give a ruling on his own authority in difficult problems, emphasizing that he was one of "those apprehensive of giving rulings," and suggested that the concurrence of authoritative rabbis be sought (*Zikhron Yosef* 39a–b, 65b, 77b, et al.). He took a firm stand on fundamental issues that were likely to undermine morality and religion. He was especially opposed to mixed dancing, and stressed in his responsum that "any rabbi and instructor is obligated to protest and to abolish any type of mixed dancing that is planned for his city during a festival." In the course of his responsa, he describes how he canceled a dance arranged in Niederenheim, even after the Jewish community had obtained permission from the secular authorities (22d no. 17). In the introduction to his responsa he inveighs against the Shabbateans, and particularly against the *Ḥasidim. Because of his inimical attitude toward them, the Ḥasidim took steps to have those sections of his introduction directed at them removed, and in many editions the whole of the introduction is indeed missing.

Steinhardt mentions that he was "greatly punished by the death of children and grandchildren … and few of many remained to him." His son MOSES (d. 1799) was the author of a Judeo-German commentary to the *Sha'ar ha-Yiḥud* of Baḥya's *Ḥovot ha-Levavot* (Fuerth, 1765).

BIBLIOGRAPHY: Loewenstein, in: JJLG, 6 (1908), 190–9, 218, 222f.; Y.A. Kamelhar, *Dor De'ah* (1935), 90f.; R.N.N. Rabinovicz, *Ma'amar al Hadpasat ha-Talmud* (1952²), 123f.

[Yehoshua Horowitz]

STEINHARDT, LAURENCE ADOLF (1892–1950), U.S. attorney and diplomat. Steinhardt was born in New York City. After his admission to the bar in 1916 he entered the U.S. Army in 1917, moving up from private to a commission and service on the provost marshal general's staff. He was active for a time in the Federation of American Zionists and the American Zion Commonwealth. From 1920 to 1933 he practiced law in his uncle Samuel *Untermyer's firm, Guggenheimer, Untermyer, and Marshall, and wrote articles on medical jurisprudence, labor unions, and economics. One piece attacking President Herbert Hoover's budgetary and financial policies brought him to Franklin D. Roosevelt's attention, and Steinhardt worked for Roosevelt's election in 1932. Roosevelt appointed him minister to Sweden in 1933, the beginning of Steinhardt's 17 years in six diplomatic posts, all but the last of them requiring great resources of judgment in a series of delicate situations. He served in Sweden (1933–37), when the economic effects of the Depression and the political and military problems posed by the rise of Hitler were predominant; as ambassador in Peru (1937–39), when Roosevelt was seeking to solidify a policy of collective security for Latin America; and in the USSR (1939–41), from the time of the nonaggression pact to the German invasion of the Soviet Union. Steinhardt served in Turkey (1942–45), when that country's neutrality was pivotal to the Allied war effort. During his service in Russia Steinhardt lent his influence to the stringent U.S. immigration laws, which from 1940 operated virtually to exclude Jewish refugees. However, as U.S. ambassador in Turkey he vigorously cooperated with the U.S. War Refugee Board, the Jewish Agency, and Ira Hirschmann by persuading that government to permit the entry and passage of European Jews in ever-increasing numbers. The lives of tens of thousands were thus saved through his efforts. He also served in Czechoslovakia (1945–48), when communist pressure built up to the 1948 coup. Steinhardt's last ambassadorial post was in Canada, where he served from 1948 until his death in an airplane crash.

BIBLIOGRAPHY: *New York Times* (March 29–31, April 1, 1950); H.L. Feingold, *The Politics of Rescue* (1970), 285–9.

STEINHARDT, MENAHEM MENDEL BEN SIMEON (1768–1825), rabbi and author. Steinhardt, a nephew of Joseph *Steinhardt, was born in Fuerth. He published his responsa, *Divrei Menaḥem* (Offenbach, 1804), while he served as rabbi in Minden, and in the same year he was appointed rabbi of Hildesheim. When the consistory of the kingdom of Westphalia was set up in 1808 in Cassel by Israel *Jacobson, Steinhardt was appointed one of its members, together with Leib Meir Berlin and Simeon Isaac Kalkar. They were requested by the government to adopt and formulate the constitution and theology of Judaism on the pattern of the French *Sanhedrin established on the initiative of Napoleon. Steinhardt, like the other members of the consistory, aspired to a moderate form of Judaism, an aspiration well reflected in *Divrei Menaḥem* and in *Divrei Iggeret* (Roedelheim, 1812). The latter work was published by his friend Binyamin Ze'ev *Heidenheim, who added notes and glosses to the book. Steinhardt was the first German rabbi to omit portions from the liturgy. One of his well-known lenient rulings – permitting the use of legumes on Passover – aroused the vehement opposition of the Orthodox rabbis. He was one of the first rabbis to deliver sermons in German. In 1810 he taught Talmud at the Teachers' Training Seminary in Cassel. In 1813 he was appointed rabbi of Warburg, and in 1815 became rabbi of Paderborn, where he spent the rest of his life.

BIBLIOGRAPHY: Graetz, Gesch, 11 (1900^2), 280f., 375; Zunz, Ritus (1919^2), 171; Lewin, in: MGWJ, 53 (1909), 363; Lazarus, *ibid.*, 58 (1914), 185f., 459–82, 542–61.

[Abraham David]

STEINHARDT, MICHAEL H. (1940–), U.S. financier. Steinhardt, who was born in Brooklyn, N.Y., became interested in the stock market when his father gave him 200 shares of Penn Dixie Cement and Columbia Gas System stock as a bar mitzvah present. At 13 he began studying brokers' reports. At 16 he enrolled in college, graduating from the University of Pennsylvania's Wharton School of Finance in three years. He began his Wall Street career as a research associate, staff writer, and securities analyst before starting his own company, Steinhardt Partners, where he made a fortune in the risky field of hedge-fund management. In 1995 Steinhardt dissolved four hedge funds managed by the Steinhardt Management Company. From 1967 to 1995, as the manager of nearly $5 billion, the average annual return of his investors was 31 percent, before fees. But in his final years he and his partners paid more than $70 million in fines to settle charges of collusion in a Treasury note-trading scandal. In the early years of the 21st century, his liquid assets of more than $300 million were managed by more than 30 other money managers spread among an array of investments.

A professed atheist, Steinhardt, who grew up in a Jewish household, is especially interested in finding a way to perpetuate what he calls the philosophy of Jewish culture for the next generation of American Jews without relying on theology. He spent millions of dollars financing Jewish day schools, Hillel activities at colleges, trips to Israel for young people, and a drop-in center for young adults in Manhattan. He also became involved with an assortment of higher education institutions. He joined the board of Brandeis University, was chairman of the board of Tel Aviv University, and gave $10 million to the School of Education at New York University, where he was a trustee. The gift, the largest in the school's history, was used to create an endowment to support faculty development, doctoral fellowships, and research. A portion was allocated to support fellowships in a newly established doctoral program in education and Jewish studies offered by the school in collaboration with the Skirball Department of Hebrew and Judaic Studies. The school was renamed the Steinhardt School of Education in 2001.

One of his passions was art. He collected in five areas: ancient art, Judaica, 20th-century works on paper, Peruvian feathered textiles, and Chinese art. A gallery of sixth-century Greek art at the Metropolitan Museum of Art was named after him and his wife, Judy. Horticulture and wildlife were also deep interests, flowing from his love of his estate in Bedford, New York, which he filled with 120 varieties of fruit trees and a large array of wildlife creatures.

[Stewart Kampel (2nd ed.)]

STEINHAUS, HUGO DYONIZY (1887–1972), Polish mathematician. Steinhaus was one of the founders of the so-called Lvov school in mathematics; with S. Banach he founded its organ, *Studia Mathematica*, which he continued to edit. From 1920 to 1941 he was professor at the University of Lvov, and in 1945 became professor at Wroclaw. In 1961–62 he taught at the University of Sussex, England. Apart from serious mathematical works such as *Theorie der Orthogonalreihen*

("Theory of Orthogonal Rows," with S. Kaczmarz, 1935), *Sur la localisation d'objets au moyen des rayons* (1938), and *Sur les fonctions indépendantes* (1948), Steinhaus popularized his subject in books such as *Kalejdoskop matematyczny* (1938; *Mathematical Snapshots*, 1960^2) and *Orzel czy rzeszka* ("Heads or Tails," 1961), and also wrote on the subject of establishing paternity, as in *Dochodzenie ojcowstwa i alimentów* (1958; *Remarks ... on the Establishment of Paternity and Maintenance Rights*, 1958).

STEINHEIM, SALOMON LUDWIG (1789–1866), physician, poet, and theologian. Born near Hamburg-Altona, he studied at the University of Berlin and received his medical degree at the University of Kiel. He practiced medicine in Altona from 1813 to 1845 and was active in the struggle for Jewish emancipation in Germany, collaborating in political activity with Gabriel *Riesser (1806–63), and publishing essays in Riesser's literary journal *Der Jude*.

He spent the last 20 years of his life in Rome as a Jewish scholar. There he completed his magnum opus on revelation in Judaism, *Die Offenbarung nach dem Lehrbegriffe der Synagoge*, ("Revelation According to the Doctrine of Judaism"; 4 vols., 1835–65). Steinheim undertook this work to stem the tide of assimilation and conversion to Christianity by Jews emerging from the ghettoes in the post-Napoleonic era to become integrated in a more open society. He aimed to demonstrate the truths of Judaism's revealed religion as superior to the metaphysics of contemporary philosophies and Christian theology. He rejected the attempts of Jewish thinkers to reformulate the revealed doctrines of Judaism in terms or concepts of the philosophic systems of Schelling, Hegel, and other contemporary German philosophers.

The key to Steinheim's work is his contention that reason is deficient in its comprehension of reality. Reason's view of reality is bound by the law of causality. God is "necessarily" existent as the first cause initiating the chain of cause and effect which produced the world, life, and human beings. Reason is bound by another "necessary" principle, *ex nihilo nihil fit*, out of nothing comes nothing. The physical world could not have emerged out of nothing.

Reason is, therefore, compelled to assume the eternity of physical matter, an assumption that clashes with the law of causality, which demands some initiating cause, a beginning in time, contrary to the eternity of physical matter. There is no escape from this contradiction in which reason stumbles over itself except through the revealed doctrine of God as Creator who made the world out of nothing. The idea of God acting in absolute freedom, creating something out of nothing, and, derivatively, the idea of man's freedom of will, independent of the law of causality, cannot be rationally conceived. Such knowledge can come to us only through revelation.

Steinheim recognized as revelation only doctrines, ideas, principles. Formulations of civil and cultic laws (*Halakhah*) are in Steinheim's view derivative, conditioned by time and place and secondary in importance.

Among his most original thoughts are his criteria for the validation of revelation. One of these is that revelation must have the character of novelty; it must be new truth not previously known, better yet, it must contradict previously held knowledge; it should not coincide with rational awareness since the supreme spirit would not solemnly announce to us truths which we already know or can determine for ourselves.

Another criterion of revelation is its historical appearance in time and place. Natural religion develops out of human consciousness in the course of generations. Divine revelation suddenly bursts upon the scene. It is an unprecedented illumination. Yeḥezkel *Kaufmann and Leo *Baeck also stressed the mystery of monotheism's sudden appearance as a radical departure from a pagan environment of polytheism.

Also cited as validation of revelation is the historical uniqueness of the Jewish people. The unparalleled survival of the Jews testifies to a supernatural element received through revelation.

Steinheim was not an anti-rationalist as charged by his critics, but a supra-rationalist. He used rational arguments with rigorous logic to demonstrate the superiority of revelation over *speculative* reason as a source of ultimate truths. At the same time, he recognized *critical* reason as an indispensable tool with which to detect misunderstandings of revelation and validate its truths. Nevertheless, the charge of anti-rationalism stuck and doomed his work to a century of neglect and obscurity.

Steinheim's isolation was further accentuated by his rejection of both Reform and neo-Orthodoxy. Reform, in his view, had embraced a shallow rationalism and degenerated into a "blind reforming mania." Neo-Orthodoxy was vainly trying to puff up Jewish tradition with zeal for ceremonial observance. Neither side addressed itself to the core of beliefs which is the essence of Judaism.

The revival of Jewish theological thought in the 20th and 21st centuries, initiated by Franz *Rosenzweig, and, in the wake of the Holocaust, disenchantment with the power of reason which had been so tragically overestimated, may make Steinheim's supra-rationalism more acceptable, and he may at last receive the recognition due him as a major Jewish thinker in keeping with Heinrich Graetz's judgment that "no one of his time or earlier, understood the foundations of Judaism as profoundly as did he."

BIBLIOGRAPHY: J.O. Haberman, *Philosopher of Revelation: The Life and Thought of S.L. Steinheim* (1989); idem, "S.L. Steinheim's Critique of Messianism," in: *Jerusalem Studies in Jewish Thought*, 11 (1993), XXV–XXXVI; A. Shear-Yashuv, *The Theology of Salomon Ludwig Steinheim* (1986); idem (ed.), *Shelomoh Levi Steinheim, Iyyunim be-Mishnato* (1994); J.H. Schoeps (ed.) *"Philo des 19. Jahrhunderts": Studien zu Salomon Ludwig Steinheim* (1993).

[Joshua O. Haberman (2nd ed.)]

STEINHERZ, SAMUEL (1859–1944), Prague medievalist. Born in Grassing (Burgenland), Steinherz taught history at the

Prague German University from 1901, and specialized in papal diplomacy, on which he published four volumes (between 1898 and 1914). When Steinherz was elected rector in 1922 he did not follow the custom of Jewish professors of declining the honor but declared that he felt and acted as a German. Antisemitic students' organizations asked for his resignation, organized a strike, occupied the buildings, and prevented Jewish students from entering them demanding the imposition of the *numerus clausus. The riots spread to German universities all over Europe, mainly in Austria. In February 1923, becoming aware of obstruction by his colleagues, Steinherz submitted his resignation, which the Czechoslovak minister of education, Rudolf *Bechyne, a Czech Social Democrat, refused to accept. Finally Steinherz went on leave. The "Steinherz affair" caused a crisis in Jewish circles in Czechoslovakia advocating assimilation into German culture, and influenced Steinherz himself. He turned to research in Jewish history, mainly the epoch of the Crusades. He edited *Die Juden in Prag* (1927) and was among the founders of the Society for History of the Jews in the Czechoslovak Republic in 1928. That year he retired from the university and became head of the society and editor of its yearbook (JGGJČ) throughout its existence, from 1929 until 1938. In 1942, nearly blind, Steinherz was deported to *Theresienstadt. In the camp he lectured on the history of the Jews in Bohemia. He died in Theresienstadt on his 85th birthday.

BIBLIOGRAPHY: H. Gold, in: *Zeitschrift fuer Geschichte der Juden in der Tschechoslowakei*, 5 (1938), 51–56; V. Stein, *ibid.*, 57–58; *Selbstwehr*, 16 no. 47 (1922), 1–3; no. 48 (1922), 1; no. 50 (1922), 3; 17 no. 8 (1923), 1; *Židovské zprávy*, 4 no. 32 (1922), 3; no. 33 (1922); no. 34 (1922), 5; 5 no. 7 (1923), 8; R. Kestenberg-Gladstein, in: *Zion*, 5 (1940), 281–93; *Věstník židovské obce náboženské v Praze*, 17 (1955), 569; B'nai B'rith, *Mitteilungen* CSR (1937), 297–302.

[Meir Lamed]

STEINITZ, WILHELM (1836–1900), chess master. Born and educated in Prague, he went to London in the early 1860s and took an active part in the chess life of the city. Soon after his arrival he defeated Blackburne in a match and in 1866 challenged Anderssen for the unofficial championship of the world. Steinitz won, and is often regarded as having been world chess champion for 28 years, until he was defeated by Emanuel *Lasker in 1894. Formally, however, Steinitz became world champion only in 1886, when he defeated *Zukertort in the first official championship match. From 1866 until 1894 Steinitz won all the matches he played (some for title, some informally) against the greatest players including Blackburne, Zukertort (twice), Tchigorin (twice), Gunsberg, and Schiffers. In 1894 he lost the title to Emanuel *Lasker and failed to regain it. He was the first to be aware of the strategic elements in the great tactical performances of players such as Morphy, Anderssen, Blackburne, and Zukertort. On the basis of this analysis he developed the Steinitzian technique which is now a basic principle accepted by all chess players. Steinitz stressed in his teaching the importance (in the opening moves) of the center, the desirability of accumulating small advantages, and above all, the value of a well-integrated defense system, the main components of the so-called classical school of chess strategy. These teachings appear in his book *The Modern Chess Instructor* (2 vols., 1889–95), in the columns of the London *Field*, a journal in which he was the chess editor, and in *The Chess Monthly* which he edited. The latter years of his life were spent in New York, where he died in poverty.

BIBLIOGRAPHY: C. Devide, *A Memorial to William Steinitz* (1901); H.F. Chesire, *Hastings Tournament 1895* (1896); *The Living Age* (Dec. 22, 1900), 759–67; L. Bachmann, *Schachmeister Steinitz* (1910). **ADD. BIBLIOGRAPHY:** D. Hooper and K. Whyld, *The Oxford Companion to Chess* (1996), 395–97; C. Devide, *William Steinitz: Selected Games* (1974); K. Landsberger, *William Steinitz, Chess Champion: A Biography of the Bohemian Caesar* (1993); idem, *The Steinitz Papers* (2002).

[Gerald Abrahams / William D. Rubinstein (2nd ed.)]

STEINMAN, ELIEZER (1892–1970), Hebrew writer. Born in Obodovka, Steinman was ordained a rabbi, and began to write at an early age, but it took some time before his first stories appeared in print. Steinman pursued literary work (provided by D. *Frischmann) and was also a part-time Hebrew teacher in Odessa. He contributed regularly to *Ha-Ẓefirah* and worked on translations, which were not published until a later date. During this period, he began to publish long stories ("*Bi-Ymei ha-Besht*," in: *Ha-Ẓefirah*), as well as essays and articles. In 1920 he left Russia. During those unsettled times, having been mistaken for the Yiddish writer Baynush Steinman, a rumor was spread of his death, and he was eulogized in the Hebrew daily press and in literary periodicals, as well as in foreign-language publications. Steinman published "*Teshuvah le-Maspidai* ("Reply to my Eulogists"), in *Ha-Ẓefirah*.

Settling in Warsaw, he continued his regular contributions of stories, essays, and articles to *Ha-Ẓefirah* and wrote for *Der Moment*. Steinman founded the monthly, *Kolot*, which provided a forum for young writers. It was also the first attempt (later expanded in *Ketuvim*) to compare the thought of R. *Naḥman of Bratslav and Aaron Samuel *Tamares (*Aḥad ha-Rabbanim ha-Margishim*; "one of the sensitive rabbis") with those of St. Francis of Assisi, Ibsen, and others. (Eleven numbers of *Kolot* were published in the period 1923–24.) During his Warsaw period he published a collection of stories (*Sippurim*, 1923), a novel (*Ester Ḥayyot*, 1922), a collection of articles (*Sefer ha-Ma'amarim*, 1924), and two Yiddish books of essays and stories on the pogroms against Ukrainian Jews.

In 1924, Steinman settled in Tel Aviv. He wrote for *Haaretz* and *Ha-Olam* and, together with other young writers, became active in the Writers' Union. On behalf of the Union he edited its literary collection *Mesibbah* (1926) and, afterward, its organ *Ketuvim* (1926–33). Here he continued his attempts to find a synthesis between ancient and modern Jewish literature and culture, and world literature. He published stories and novels, including *Zugot* (1930) and *Duda'im* (1931), and collections of essays: *Ha-Yesod ba-Ḥinnukh* (1930), *Meshiḥiyyut* (1930), *Be-Mizreh ha-Zeman* (1931), and *Sha'ar ha-Vikku'aḥ* (1933). When

Ketuvim closed, he became a columnist for *Davar*, also contributing regularly to literary periodicals and collections in Israel and abroad.

Steinman claims that the primary function of a critical essay is to improve man's view on life and art, and that therefore it is permissible and desirable to apply present-day views in studying works of the past. His memoirs contain a great deal of literary gossip. In his reconstruction of the "conversations," Steinman aims at giving a very subjective account of the conversants' views rather than a stenographic recording of their actual remarks.

Steinman was the most prolific Hebrew writer of his generation. While the essays published (in *Davar* and in the book form, *Perudot* (1965)), comprise a large part of his total output, works still in manuscript would fill dozens of volumes of fiction, memoirs, and autobiography. His books included *Sodot* (2 vols., 1938); *Sefer Me'ah Shanah* (with J.J. Trivaks and Y. Yaari-Poliskin, from 1938 onward), on the heroes and pioneers of Ereẓ Israel for the past 100 years and more; *Bi-Netivot ha-Emunah* (1943); *Be-Ma'agal ha-Dorot* (1944); *Koh Amar Frischmann* (1950), conversations and memoirs of Frischmann; *Kitvei Eliezer Steinman*: vol. 1, *Gan-Eden shel Anshei Shelomenu Sippur ha-Sippurim* (1956); vol. 2, *Ha-Beḥirah be-Ereẓ ha-Beḥirah* (1956); vol. 3, *Zeman Hayyeinu* (1956); vol. 4, *Alim me-Eẓ ha-Ḥayyim* (1958); *Perudot* (1965); *Ha-Har ha-Yarok* (1965), stories; *Barekhi Nafshi* (1965), essays; *Sippurim Keẓarim* (1966); *Ha-Yaḥid ve-ha-Olam* (1966), short essays; *Ayin Lo Ra'atah* (1967), stories; *Ha-Melech Ayef* (1968), a story on Saul and David, and *Le-Kol he-Ḥalil* (1968), essays.

In later years he also undertook a massive project designed to make the resources of Jewish culture more readily available by rendering the texts in his own version and adding his own introductory notes and essays. The first book, *Be'er ha-Ḥasidut* (1951), was followed by a series of nine books on Ḥasidism (1958–62) and a collection of ḥasidic stories, *Kankan ha-Kesef* (4 vols., 1969). He also wrote *Be'er ha-Talmud* (4 vols., 1963–65), on the Talmud.

BIBLIOGRAPHY: I. Norman, *Ḥalil ha-Ro'im* (1931); Y. Zmora et al., in: *Moznayim*, 14 (1961/62), 185–203, 291–5; M. Ravitch, *Mayn Leksikon* (1958), 418f.; Waxman, Literature, 4 (1960), 196f.; 5 (1960), 62–64, 183–5. **ADD. BIBLIOGRAPHY:** B.Y. Michali, "*E. Steinman be-Masotav u-ve-Prudotav*," in: *Moznayim*, 22 (1966), 382–92; A. Cohen, "*E. Steinman*," in: *Hadoar*, 49 (1970), 642–43; A.B. Jaffe, "*Mardut she-Hishlimah*," in: *Moznayim*, 31 (1970), 190–96; M. Yanai, *Koh Amar Steinman: Yoman ha-Sikhot shel Meir Yanai* (1976); G. Shaked, *Ha-Sipporet ha-Ivrit*, 3 (1988), 26–32; N. Shaḥam, *Sefer Ḥatum* (1989).

[Getzel Kressel]

STEINSALTZ (Even Yisrael), ADIN (1937–), Israeli rabbi and author. Born in Jerusalem, Steinsaltz acquired a background in Jewish studies, as well as chemistry, mathematics, and physics, at The Hebrew University of Jerusalem. He was also ordained as a rabbi. After working in education for 13 years in the Negev, he returned to Jerusalem where he taught, did research, and wrote for various periodicals. In 1988 he received the Israel Prize in Jewish Studies.

In 1965 he founded the Israel Institute for Talmudic Publications which undertook the production of a vocalized Babylonian Talmud, accompanied by Hebrew translation and commentary; over 30 volumes of a projected 42 had appeared by the early 2000s. An English translation of the series was begun by Random House, and volumes have appeared in French, Russian, and Spanish. Rabbi Steinsaltz founded the "Mekor Ḥayyim" yeshivah in 1984, an institute which has as one of its aims the bridging of the gap between religious and non-religious Jews. In February 1989 he initiated the founding of a yeshivah in Moscow, called the Center for the Study of Judaism.

Each year Rabbi Steinsaltz lectures widely outside of Israel, and his books, a number of which have been translated into English, such as *The Essential Talmud* (1976), *The Thirteen-Petalled Rose* (1980), and *Guide to Jewish Prayer* (2000), reach readers the world over. He has published works on Talmud, biblical figures, repentance, stories of Rabbi Naḥman of Bratslav, and other topics. He has also published over 600 papers on Jewish and scientific subjects.

STEINSCHNEIDER, MORITZ (1816–1907), father of modern Jewish *bibliography, among the founders of the "Science of Judaism" (*Wissenschaft des Judentums). Born the son of the Talmud scholar Jacob Steinschneider (1781–1856) and Hani Zadek-Weizenkorn (1792–1859) in Prossnitz, Moravia, Steinschneider received his early education in his native town, where he was influenced by his uncle Gideon *Brecher. He also attended a Christian school and studied music, an interest he maintained throughout his life. At age 13, he entered the yeshivah of R. Nehemiah *Trebitsch and in 1833 he left for Prague to take up secular studies. By that time, Steinschneider had already acquired a thorough knowledge of French and Italian from private tutors. He became a tutor in these languages, and in 1836 received a teacher's diploma for Hebrew in the Hebraeische Lehranstalt in Prague. That same year he left for Vienna, where he began to study Semitic languages; there he made the acquaintance of Leopold *Dukes, who aroused his interest in the study of medieval literature, Hebrew manuscripts, and Jewish bibliography.

In 1839 Steinschneider went to Leipzig. Though he stayed only half a year, this short stay proved crucial for his career as he both studied and formed close relationships with Heinrich L. *Fleischer and Franz *Delitzsch. After six months Steinschneider went on to the university in Berlin, where he also made the acquaintance of Leopold *Zunz and Abraham *Geiger; Zunz especially encouraged the young scholar and provided other forms of assistance. Returning to Prague in 1841, Steinschneider earned a living for three years as a private tutor and teacher in a Jewish girls' school. In 1843 he received a formal rabbinical diploma from the rabbi of his native town, Hirsch B. Fassel, and also a very warm recommendation from Salomon L. *Rapoport. While in Prague, Steinschneider unsuccessfully applied for a number of positions, including censor of Jewish books. After his friend Michael *Sachs left Prague upon accepting an invitation to Berlin, Steinschneider soon followed in 1845. Later, the friendship with Sachs cooled due to his disapproval of Sachs' Orthodox religious tendencies. In Berlin Steinschneider gave private lessons, preached sermons, officiated at weddings, and engaged in occasional work as a translator and author of textbooks for the elementary study of Hebrew. In 1848 he received Prussian citizenship.

In 1859, he received his first regular appointment as lecturer at the Veitel-Heine-Ephraimsche Lehranstalt, where he taught for 48 years. Many of his students later became prominent Jewish scholars, including I. *Goldziher, Solomon *Schechter, Ḥayyim *Brody, Judah L. *Magnes, H. *Malter, A. *Marx, George A. *Kohut. From 1860 to 1869, he was in charge of administering the **oath more judaico*, the Jewish oath. Another regular appointment came in 1869, when Steinschneider became assistant at the Berlin Royal Library, a position he held until his death. In the same year, he also became the head of the girls' school of the Jewish community, a position from which he retired in 1890. In appreciation of his scholarly contributions, the Prussian government made him an honorary professor in 1894. Steinschneider also received several other honors from various universities and academies, including Columbia University in New York (1887). On the occasion of his 80th birthday, a *Festschrift* was published in his honor. Steinschneider was buried as an honorary member of the Berlin Jewish community at the Weissensee cemetery.

Steinschneider's literary output was tremendous; his bibliography contains more than 1,400 items. His main lifelong interest was the study of the relationship between Jewish and general cultures, especially during medieval times. Upon his early realization that the preliminary requirement for carrying out such studies was a thorough and scientific bibliographical record of all available printed and manuscript materials, Steinschneider devoted himself to the preparation of library catalogs and subject bibliographies. In addition to catalogs and bibliographies, he also provided general introductions to Jewish literary history and Jewish booklore. In collecting and organizing the materials for his studies on the role of the Jews in medieval culture, his research led him also to the study of the history of medieval philosophy, especially medieval medicine, the sciences, and mathematics. His works are not only a contribution to Jewish learning, but also to Arabic literature and to general medieval cultural history. Steinschneider regarded his bibliographical, philological, and Oriental studies in Jewish literature as a contribution to general cultural history, which in his opinion was the original object of world history and of all intellectual effort. With this scholarly program, he stood in the tradition of his fatherly friend Zunz.

The following works are of particular note: *Die hebraeischen Uebersetzungen des Mittelalters und die Juden als Dolmetscher* (1893), his magnum opus containing a wealth of information based on manuscripts and printed sources in many languages about the transmission of philosophy and the sciences throughout the Middle Ages. It also shows how classical Greek knowledge reached Europe and Western culture through the intervention of Arabic and Hebrew writers. *Die arabischen Uebersetzungen aus dem Griechischen* (1897) and *Die europaeischen Uebersetzungen aus dem Arabischen* (1904–05) supplemented this work and carried its subject far beyond purely Jewish interests. These three works together provided a pioneering contribution to the understanding of Western civilization's dependence on classical sources and the contribution of Muslim and Jewish civilizations to them.

Another of Steinschneider's major works, *Die Arabische Literatur der Juden* (1902), lists all of the Jewish authors who wrote in Arabic and includes detailed biographies and bibliographies. His lectures on the same subject appeared in English in the *Jewish Quarterly Review* (1897–1901). A further work dealing with the relationships between Jews, Arabs, and Christians is his *Polemische und apologetische Literatur in arabischer Sprache zwischen Muslimen, Christen und Juden* (1877). Not only is the typical full bibliographical and biographical apparatus provided in this work, but it also classifies and enumerates the main areas of religious controversy. Steinschneider's unbelievable industry and erudition also manifested itself in a series of catalogs and bibliographies, among which the most important is his *Catalogus Librorum Hebraeorum in Bibliotheca Bodleiana* (1852–60). Upon the request of the chief librarian of the Bodleian Library at Oxford University, Steinschneider prepared a catalog of all the printed books up to 1732 in that great library over a period of many years, during which time the library was also dynamically enriching its Hebrew collections through the acquisition of important private libraries. Over the course of five summers in Oxford, Steinschneider described all the Hebrew items there, at which time he also made generous use of all the Hebrew manuscript materials. The catalog is arranged according to the name of the authors (with the exception of anonymous works), gives all the available information on their lives, and is followed by a list of their works and all the references to them in the secondary literature available at that time. At the end follows a list of all printers, patrons, etc., who were associated with the publication of the works, as well as a geographical index providing the Hebrew forms of many geographical names. With this book, Steinschneider raised Hebrew bibliography to a scholarly level and corrected misinformation. Steinschneider also published classic catalogs of the Hebrew manuscript collections of the following libraries: Leiden (1858), Munich (1875; 2nd ed. enlarged, 1896), Hamburg (1878, reprint with new introduction, Hellmut Braun, 1969), and Berlin (1878–97). In all of these he identified many hitherto unknown writings and historical research.

Some aspects of his detailed, painstaking research were organized into more general presentations. For the *Ersch und Gruber Allgemeine Encyclopaedie*, he wrote a systematic survey of Jewish literature (1850) which was translated into English (*Jewish Literature from the 8th to the 18th Century*, 1857) and later into Hebrew by Henry *Malter, one of his pupils (*Sifrut Yisrael*, 1897–99). For the same encyclopedia, he co-wrote, together with David *Cassel, *Juedische Typographie und Juedischer Buchhandel* (1851), a still-valuable general survey of

Jewish printing and book trade. But both scholars failed to publish a planned *Real-Encyclopaedie des Judentums* (1843) for unknown reasons despite several years of intensive preparation. Another work of Steinschneider's which still remains the most systematic and broadest treatment of the subject, is *Vorlesungen ueber die Kunde Hebraeischer Handschriften* (1897; Hebrew translations, with additions by A.M. Habermann *Harẓa'ot al Kitvei Yad Ivriyyim*, 1965; also printed in *Aresheth*, 84 (1966)). Also significant are his contributions to the history of the study of the Hebrew language and his work on Jewish writers of history and historiography (*Die Geschichtsliteratur der Juden*, 1905). Finally, he published the journal *Ha-Mazkir* (*Hebraeische Bibliographie. Blaetter fuer neuere und aeltere Literatur des Judentums*, 1858–65, 1869–81) to which he contributed more than 500 articles concerning bibliography, library history, booklore, philology and cultural history.

Steinschneider's major works were reprinted several times in their original form in the 1930s, 1960s, 1970s, and 1980s; the last reprinting of his Bodleian Catalog dates from 1998. Unfortunately, the author's own numerous additions and corrections to his works, as preserved in the copies of his works at the Jewish Theological Seminary in New York, as well as other new materials, were not incorporated into these reprints. In the early 2000s, a web-based translation and revision of the *Hebraeische Uebersetzungen des Mittelalters* was in preparation by Charles H. Manekin (University of Maryland) in collaboration with Y. Tzvi Langermann (Bar-Ilan University), and Hans Heinrich Biesterfeld (Bochum University).

Steinschneider spent most of his life in the pursuit of his great scholarly projects, but he also wrote some lighter belletristic and journalistic works. He also commented – though rarely – on the major contemporary events of his day and for a while was actively involved in a society founded by his friend Abraham *Benisch, the aim of which was the promotion of Jewish resettlement in Ereẓ Israel. He withdrew from the group in the early 1840s and later assumed a very negative attitude toward political Zionism. However, he welcomed the 1848 Revolution in Germany, and even helped to build barricades in Berlin, but shied away from radicals. Steinschneider published some letters by Hirsch B. Fassel, dealing with Samson R. *Hirsch's religious views (*Hereb Zion*, 1839); for this edition he wrote under the pen name of M.S. Charbona, adding some of his own remarks that revealed his position toward the Reform movement, about which he maintained a rather conservative view, particularly in his advocacy of the Hebrew language in the synagogue and in Jewish scholarly literature. In this publication, he formulated his views on the tasks and methods of Jewish scholarship, aiming for objective truth and impartial research as well as the creation of the scholarly foundations of Jewish learning. He vehemently rejected superficial attempts at popularization and the replacement of original research by empty phrases. He also opposed, like Zunz, *rabbinical seminaries as centers of scholarly research, fearing the introduction of theological considerations into what he considered to be pure, objective scholarship.

BIBLIOGRAPHY: G.A. Kohut, in: *Festschrift… M. Steinschneider* (1896), v–xxxix; idem, *A Tribute to his Eighty-Fourth Birthday* (1900); idem, *A Tribute Written on the Occasion of his 90th Birthday* (1906); idem, in: *Studies in Jewish Bibliography and Related Subjects* (1929), 65–127; idem, in: MGWJ, 78 (1934), 211–32; A. Golderg, in: ZHB, 5 (1901), 189–91; 9 (1905), 90–92; 13 (1909), 94–95; F.H. Garrison, in: *Sudhoffs Archiv fuer Geschichte der Medizin*, 25 (1932), 249–78; A. Marx, *Essays in Jewish Biography* (1947), 112–84, incl. extensive bibl. up to 1947, 294–6; idem, in: *Studies in Jewish History and Booklore* (1944), 346–68; idem, in PAAJR, 5 (1934), 95–153; idem, in: *Jewish Studies in the Memory of Georg A. Kohut* (1935), 492–527; S. Baron, in: *Alexander Marx Jubilee Volume* (1950), 83–148 (English section) (reprint in: idem, *History and Jewish Historians* (1964), 276–312); P.O. Kristeller, in: PAAJR, 27 (1958), 59–66; F. Rosenthal, *ibid.*, 67–81; J. Dienstag, in: *Sinai*, 66 (1970), 347–66; A. Paucker, in: YLBI, 11 (1966), 242–61; K. Wilhelm, in: BLBI, 1 (1957), 35–42. **ADD. BIBLIOGRAPHY:** Wurzbach, *Biographisches Lexikon des Kaisertums Oesterreich*, 38 (1878), 160–67; S. Schechter, in: *Seminary Addresses and Other Papers* (1915), 119–24; S. Almoni, in: *Ost und West* (1907), 181–86; I. Elbogen/A. Goldberg, in: AZJ, 13 (1916), 149–54; I. Elbogen, in: *Soncino-Blaetter*, 1 (1925–1926), 155–58; I. Schorsch, in: HUCA, 53 (1982), 241–64; J. Ziegler, in: *Medieval Encounters*, 3/1 (1997) 94–102; L. Fuks, in: *Studia Rosenthaliana*, 13/1 (1979), 45–100; M. Steinschneider; *Briefwechsel mit seiner Verlobten Auguste Auerbach* (1995); M.L. Steinschneider, in: *Archiv Bibliographia Judaica*, 2–3 (1990), 195–210; H.I. Schmelzer, in: *Occident and Orient* (1988), 319–29; Ch. H. Manekin, in: JSQ, 7/2 (2000), 141–59.

[Menahem Schmelzer / Gregor Pelger (2nd ed.)]

STEINTHAL, HERMANN HEYMANN (1823–1899), German philologist and philosopher. He studied in Berlin and Paris (where he spent three years in the study of Chinese language and literature), was appointed lecturer in philology and mythology at Berlin University in 1850 and in 1855 associate professor of general philology. In 1872 he was appointed to the chair of biblical studies and philosophy of religion at the Hochschule fuer die Wissenschaft des Judentums. Steinthal and his brother-in-law, Moritz *Lazarus, founded the science of racial psychology (*Voelkerpsychologie*) and the *Zeitschrift fuer Voelkerpsychologie und Sprachwissenschaft* (from 1860). Having studied under Wilhelm von Humboldt, he edited the latter's *Sprachwissenschaftliche Werke* (1884) and wrote extensively in this field, e.g., *Die Sprachwissenschaft Wilhelm von Humboldts und die Hegelsche Philosophie* (1848), *Die Klassifikation der Sprachen* (1850), *Der Ursprung der Sprache im Zusammenhang mit den letzten Fragen alles Wissens* (1851), *Die Entwicklung der Schrift* (1852), *Geschichte der Sprachwissenschaft bei den Griechen und Roemern* (1863), *Abriss der Sprachwissenschaft* (1871–78), *Gesammelte kleine Schriften* (1880), and *Allgemeine Ethik* (1885). Steinthal also retained a lifelong interest in, and devotion to, Judaism and Jewish life. Serving as a director of the *Deutsch-Israelitischer Gemeindebund he frequently lectured and wrote newspaper articles in his capacity as a Jewish spokesman. His essays *Zu Bibel und Religionsphilosophie* (1890, 1895) reflect his ethical and aesthetic (rather than higher critical) approach to the Bible. In his collection of essays and addresses, *Ueber Juden und Judentum* (1906), he showed his pride in his Jewish roots. Steinthal polemicized against Bruno *Bauer and others who showed Christian prejudice in their treatment of Judaism and he defended both Jews and Judaism against antisemitic attacks. He saw in prophetism the distinguishing mark of ancient Israel, setting it apart from other peoples, even as for him both Germanism and Judaism were inspirations for moral action.

BIBLIOGRAPHY: T. Achelis, *Heymann Steinthal* (Ger., 1898); Baumgardt, in: YLBI, 2 (1957), 205ff.; W. Bumann, *Die Sprachtheorie Heymann Steinthals* (1965).

[Jakob J. Petuchowski]

STEKEL, WILHELM (1868–1940), Austrian psychoanalyst. Born in Vienna, Stekel was one of the small group of physicians who gathered around Freud from 1902 onward to learn the practice of analysis. In 1895, before having heard of Freud, Stekel had already written a paper on sexual activity in childhood. In about 1901 he was treated successfully by Freud for a neurotic complaint. He wrote a defense of Freud's theory of dreams and in 1903 began the practice of psychoanalysis. It was on Stekel's suggestion that the first psychoanalytic group met at Freud's home. In 1909 Stekel published *Dichtung und Neurose* and in 1911 his extensive *Sprache des Traumes*. E. Jones says it contained many "bright ideas but also many confused ones." Freud found it "mortifying." Stekel wrote prolifically in many fields, publishing papers on a wide range of subjects extending from the psychology of everyday errors to the psychological treatment of epilepsy. His books include *Der Wille zum Schlaf* (1915), *Der Wille zum Leben* (1920), and *Stoerungen des Trieb-und Affektlebens* (9 vols., 1924–27).

E. Jones wrote that Stekel had very little interest in theory, was very practical, and had a ready access to the unconscious. He was a naturally gifted psychologist, contributing greatly to our knowledge of symbolism, a field in which he had greater intuitive genius than Freud. Unfortunately, according to Jones, these talents went with an unusual incapacity for judgment, and his intuition and speculations were not to be depended on. When Freud founded the monthly *Zentralblatt fuer Psychoanalyse und Psychotherapie*, Stekel became its joint editor, but he resigned his membership from the Vienna society in 1912, and, Freud's group having withdrawn their subscriptions from the periodical, it ceased publication a year later. In 1933 Stekel wrote *Der Seelenarzt* and in 1938 moved to London where he wrote his last book, *Technik der analytischen Psychotherapie* (1938). In his preface to the latter book Stekel criticized the cult of orthodoxy in psychoanalysis, and the length and expense of its treatment, and foresaw the collapse of orthodox analysis if its practitioners could not adapt themselves. He considered medical training indispensable to the psychoanalyst, "since the boundaries between psychic and somatic determination can never be easy to establish."

BIBLIOGRAPHY: E. Jones, *Life and Work of Sigmund Freud…*, 2 (1955), index. **ADD. BIBLIOGRAPHY:** W. Stekel, *Autobiography* (1950); M. Stanton, in: E. Timms and N. Segal (eds.), *Freud in Exile* (1988), 163–74; E. Timms, in: C. Brinson et al. (eds.), *"England? Aber wo liegt es?"…* (1996), 47–58.

[Louis Miller]

STEKELIS, MOSHE (1898–1967), Israel archaeologist, born in Kamenets-Podolski in the Ukraine. He studied at Odessa, also serving as the deputy director of the Archaeological Museum and the director of the Archaeological Library there (1921–24). As a result of his Zionist activities, he was exiled to Siberia. In 1928 he settled in Palestine and was appointed lecturer (later professor) in prehistoric archaeology at the Hebrew University in 1948. He directed various archaeological expeditions to prehistoric sites: Bethlehem; Jebel al-Qafza (with R. Neuville); Abu ʿUṣba (Mt. Carmel); the megaliths in Transjordan; the Yarmukian site of Sha'ar ha-Golan; the Kabbāra cave and Naḥal Oren on Mt. Carmel; and al-ʿUbaydiyya in the Jordan Valley. Stekelis was the founder of a prehistory library in Jerusalem and a museum in Haifa.

[Michael Avi-Yonah]

STEMATSKY, AVIGDOR (1908–1989), Israel painter. He was born in Odessa, Russia, and was brought in 1920 to Palestine. He studied at the Bezalel Academy of Art and Design, Jerusalem, and in Paris. In 1947/48, he was one of the founders of the "New Horizons" group. He taught painting at the Avni Institute of Painting and Sculpture in Tel Aviv for several years. He was for many years a landscapist, but about 1948 began to work in an abstract style, using color contrasts, and constantly suggesting a link with nature. His watercolors are subtle, whereas his oils are violent and dramatic.

BIBLIOGRAPHY: B.Tammuz, *Art in Israel* (1966), 33; Ḥ. Gamzu, *Painting and Sculpture in Israel* (1951), 41.

[Yona Fischer]

STENCL, ABRAHAM NAHUM (Avrom-Nokhem Shtentsl; 1897–1983), Yiddish poet and editor. Born in Czeladź, Poland, his father was ḥasidic *dayyan* of Czestochowa and his brother head of the local yeshivah. To avoid military conscription, he fled to Holland in 1919, later living in Germany. Wrestling with secular culture, he came early to the vocation of poet and chose to write in Yiddish. Arriving in London in 1936, he lived the rest of his life in a council flat in Whitechapel, organizing the Friends of Yiddish and editing its journal, *Loshn un Lebn*. His poems and essays printed in Germany include *Un Du Bist Got* ("And You Are God," 1924) and *Fisherdorf* ("Fishing Village," 1933). His London writings appeared in his *Heftlekh* and *Loshn un Lebn* and in such collections as *Vaytshepl Lebt* ("Whitechapel Lives," 1951) and *Vaytshepl Shtetl Debritn* ("Whitechapel, A *Shtetl* of Britain," 1961). His papers are at the School of Oriental and African Studies, London.

BIBLIOGRAPHY: Rejzen, Leksikon, 4 (1929) 624–6; S.S. Prawer, *A.N. Stencl, Poet of Whitechapel* (1984); L. Prager, *Yiddish Culture in Britain* (1990), 597–9.

[Leonard Prager (2nd ed.)]

STENDAL, city in Brandenburg, Germany. A Jewish community existed around the middle of the 13th century. The Jews of Stendal held a key position among those of Brandenburg and adjacent territories, and the tax problems and customs of the community had crystallized by the latter part of the century. In 1297 its members were granted the privilege of acquiring property, for which they had to pay a low rent; only Jews owning ten silver marks were to be admitted as burghers. The community's total tax of ten marks was to be divided between the margraves and the city. On its part the city had to protect the Jews against any interference by ducal officers. Jewish law was to be respected, but the Jewish *oath in front of the synagogue had to be taken in German. This privilege was upheld by the Magdeburg court in 1331. The community continued to develop, the Jews' Street being first mentioned in 1327. About 1350 the Jews suffered persecution, either in consequence of the civil war or in connection with the *Black Death. The burghers, however, were granted amnesty for the misdeeds committed against the Jews, as well as permission to readmit Jews under the previous conditions. In 1446 all the local Jews were imprisoned and subsequently expelled from Stendal (presumably on papal and royal orders), but in 1453–54 they were readmitted. In 1490, too, a few new Jewish settlers were admitted; but in 1520 all Jews were banished from Brandenburg, including Stendal.

However, Elector Joachim II (1535–71) favored settlement of Jews in Stendal. Therefore, by 1564 nine Jewish families had settled in the city, but they were expelled after his death. Only after 1847 did Jews resettle there. By 1849, there were 38 Jews living in Stendal; 49 in 1871; 104 in 1892; 85 in 1903; and 93 in 1905. They formed a small community that had a cantor-teacher. Their number declined to 60 by 1913 (0.22% of the total population) and to 34 in 1925 (0.11%). In 1933 there were 61 Jews; 23 in 1939; and three in 1942. No Jews lived in Stendal after 1945. In 1995 a commemorative plaque was consecrated to the former synagogue, which is now privately owned. The Jewish cemetery is preserved.

BIBLIOGRAPHY: *Germania Judaica*, 2 (1968), 791–4; 3 (1987), 1410–13; I.A. Agus, *Rabbi Meir of Rothenburg* (1947), 502–5; *Handbuch der Juedischen Gemeindeverwaltung* (1913), 60; (1932–33), 115; Kisch, Germany, index; idem, *Jewry Law in Medieval Germany* (1949), 140–2; Baron, Social 2, 9 (1965), 211; 11 (1967), 14; W. Heise, *Die Juden in der Mark Brandenburg bis zum Jahre 1571* (1932). **ADD BIBLIOGRAPHY:** M. Brocke, E. Ruthenberg, and K. Schulenburg, *Stein und Name* (Veroeffentlichungen aus dem Institut Kirche und Judentum, vol. 22) (1994), 618–19; B. Bugaiski, I. Leubauer, and G. Waesche, *Geschichte der Juedischen Gemeinden in Sachsen-Anhalt* (1997), 250–4.

[Toni Oelsner]

STENGEL, ERWIN (1902–1973), psychiatrist. Stengel was born in Vienna, of East European parentage and was educated at Vienna University, where he received his M.D. in 1926. He studied with Sigmund *Freud and, before 1929, had worked together with Paul *Schilder and Heinz *Hartmann. In 1937, he became senior lecturer in psychiatry and neurology at Vienna University, where he worked with Wagner, V. Jauregy, and Poetzel and did research into the relation of frontal brain pathology to obsessional problems. In 1938, he left Austria for Britain as a refugee from Nazism, and after working with Mayer-Gross in Creighton (1942) he was appointed a research fellow in psychiatry at Edinburgh and, in 1949, became reader in psychiatry at London University, also serving as consultant to the Bethlehem Royal and Maudsley hospitals. In 1957, he was appointed to the newly established chair of psychiatry at the University of Sheffield, and on his retirement in 1967 was granted the title of emeritus professor. He served as president of the Royal Medico-Psychological Association in 1966, and was president of the International Association for Suicide Prevention.

In his earliest publications (with Hartmann), *Studien zur Psychologie des Induzierten Irreseins* (Arch. Psychia. Nervenkrank. (95), 1931) he maintained that certain paranoiacs have a specific motivation to establish a following, and his subsequent works were concerned with the examination of anxiety and compulsive wandering. In 1950, however, he began his researches on suicide, on which he became a world authority.

In 1958, he published a monograph (with N.G. Cook) on attempted suicide. His definitive work in the field, published in the Pelican series, appeared in 1964 as *Suicide and Attempted Suicide.* In 1969, Stengel addressed the opening session of the 11th Congress of the Israel Neuro-Psychiatric Society in Haifa, his subject being "recent progress in suicide research and prevention." He was active in the promotion of suicide prevention centers and techniques.

BIBLIOGRAPHY: O. Fenichel, *The Psychoanalytic Theory of Neurosis* (1945), 656. **ADD. BIBLIOGRAPHY:** ODNB online.

[Louis Miller]

STENN, REBECCA, U.S. modern dancer and choreographer. She was born in Ohio and spent her childhood in Canada studying with Deanne Shorten; she later studied at the Juilliard School. As a member of Momix Dance Theater from 1989 to 1995, she toured extensively throughout Europe, the Far East, and the Americas and appeared as a feature performer in films for Italian, Spanish, and French television. She assisted in the choreography and performed in the Emmy award winning film *Pictures at an Exhibition.* In 1996 Stenn formed The Perks Dance Music Theater, a company performing with a live band on stage, integrating the musicians and their instruments. The Perks' repertoire includes over 30 works using original music ranging from funk/rock to ethnic and to the classically inspired; its *Left of Fall* (2003) is a contemporary choreographic and musical interpretation of the 1913 ballet *The Rite of Spring.* Improvisation has always been a strong force in her work. In 1990 she established the first improvisational group for Lincoln Center Institute. She collaborated with Moses Pendelton in the making of *Passion* to the music of Peter Gabriel, and assisted him in the choreography of Lina Wertmuller's *Carmen* at the Munich State Opera, also performing as a principal dancer. She also collaborated on a multimedia piece for the Copenhagen Festival 96, with Japanese and Danish musicians and dancers. Stenn was a contributing editor of *Dance* magazine and wrote for the *International Journal of Dance.*

[Amnon Shiloah (2nd ed.)]

STENT, GUNTHER SIEGMUND (1924–), U.S. molecular biologist. He was born Guenter Stensch in Berlin. He immigrated to the U.S. where he was educated at Hyde Park School, Chicago, and gained his Ph.D. in physical chemistry at the University of Illinois (1948). He worked on the synthetic rubber research program of the U.S. War Production Board (1944–48), apart from a period as a document analyst for the Field Intelligence Agency in Occupied Germany (1946–47). After post-doctoral fellowships at the California Institute of Technology, Pasadena (1948–50), the University of Copenhagen and the Pasteur Institute, Paris (1950–52), he returned to the faculty of the University of California at Berkeley (1952–94). He became professor of molecular biology from 1959, director of the virus laboratory (1980–86), and founding chairman of the department of molecular and cell biology (1987–92). From 1994 he was professor emeritus of neurobiology at Berkeley. Stent was an extraordinary polymath who achieved universal recognition in three fields of endeavor. His initial research in phage genetics (bacteria infecting viruses) made early contributions to the rapidly developing field of molecular biology. The significance of this research is summarized in the highly influential book *Phage and the Origins of Molecular Biology* (1966) he wrote with James D. Watson and John Cairns. His research on developmental neurobiology is based on the leech and dates from a sabbatical visit to Harvard University (1972). He is also distinguished for his writings on the history and philosophy of science. His many highly regarded books in this field include *Morality as a Biological Phenomenon* (1978) and his autobiography, *Nazis, Women and Molecular Biology* (1998). Stent made major contributions to the organization of biological research at the University of California at Berkeley. He was a visiting professor at many leading universities in the U.S., Europe, and Japan. He was a member of the U.S. National Academy of Sciences and the American Philosophical Society.

[Michael Denman (2nd ed.)]

STERLING, SIR JEFFREY, BARON STERLING OF PLAISTOW (1934–), British businessman. Sterling was educated at Reigate Grammar School and the Guildhall School of Music but became a stockbroker and established an investment house, the Sterling Guarantee Trust Company. He became a director of P. & O., one of Britain's oldest and most famous shipping lines, in 1980, and its chairman from 1983. He was instrumental in developing its cruise ship business and spearheaded the revival of sea cruises from the last few decades of the 20th century through P. & O. Cruises, which he headed. Sterling was chairman of the Queen Elizabeth Golden Jubilee Weekend Trust, responsible for the celebrations marking the British monarch's 50th year on the throne in 2002. He has been active in Jewish affairs and was chairman of World ORT in 1969–73. He was knighted in 1985 and received a life peerage in 1991.

[William D. Rubinstein (2nd ed.)]

STERN, family of English merchant bankers and philanthropists. Originally, several brothers born in Frankfurt established banks in different European countries. DAVID DE STERN (1807–1877) and his brother HERMANN DE STERN (1815–1887) founded the firm of Stern Brothers in London, a bank which was highly successful in handling loans for various governments. In 1869 the king of Portugal made David Stern a hereditary viscount (as "Viscount De Stern") and Hermann Stern a baron (as "Baron De Stern") in gratitude for such services and they added the prefix "de" to their names. David de Stern became a director of the Imperial Bank and the family bought Strawberry Hill, Horace Walpole's famous Gothic mansion near London. Although they were related by marriage to such "Cousinhood" families as the Rothschilds and Goldsmids, they were never fully accepted as part of the financial aristocracy and were certainly not household names. Nevertheless, they were among the most successful English merchant bankers of their day. Hermann de Stern left an estate of £3.5 million, one of the very largest Victorian fortunes. SYDNEY JAMES STERN, FIRST BARON WANDSWORTH (1845–1912), elder son of David de Stern, joined the family firm, but retired early. After several unsuccessful attempts he was elected a member of Parliament for Stowmarket in 1891 and was elevated to the peerage in 1895. Stern Brothers lost its previous prominence in later years. Hermann's son HERBERT STERN, FIRST BARON MICHELHAM (1851–1919) also became a partner in the family bank and was also made a peer, in 1905, but without having served in the House of Commons. SIR EDWARD STERN (1854–1933), younger son of David, held a number of Jewish communal offices, including the presidency of the Jewish Deaf and Dumb Home. He was knighted in 1904 and received a baronetcy in 1924. By the 1920s, Stern Brothers had sadly declined as a major City merchant bank and, indeed, became something of a byword for generational decline. HERMANN DE STERN, brother of David de Stern, was a generous benefactor of Jewish charities and also held several communal offices. He was a director of the Imperial Bank, the London and San Francisco Bank, the Bank of Roumania, and the East London Waterworks Co. LAURA JULIA DE STERN (d. 1935), a daughter of Hermann, took part in communal work and married the inventor Sir David Lionel *Salomons. Her cousin, SIR ALBERT GERALD STERN (1878–1966), who was educated at Eton and Oxford, was a pioneer of tank warfare in World War I.

ADD. BIBLIOGRAPHY: ODNB online; DBB.

[John M. Shaftesley / William D. Rubinstein (2nd ed.)]

STERN, ABRAHAM JACOB (1762–1842), Polish *maskil* and mathematician. Stern was born in Hrubieszów (Lublin province) and then moved to Warsaw, where he was able to widen the scope of his education. While developing his interest in mathematics, he also acquired profound talmudic erudition. He revealed his technical talents in his improvements in the mechanism of the watch and his invention of a threshing machine and a calculating machine (1812). The senator N.

Norosiltsev introduced him to Czar Alexander I in 1815 and obtained an annual pension for him from the state treasury. Stern also wrote ethical and occasional poems of some linguistic originality. When the Committee for Jewish Affairs was established in 1825, Stern was a member of its consultative council. Submitting the project of the proposed rabbinical seminary to be established in Warsaw, he stressed its role in the campaign against Ḥasidism. In 1826, however, when he was offered the position of principal of this institution, he politely refused since he felt that it would produce rabbis who were not truly devoted to their religion and would be more active in Polonization than in propagating culture among the Jewish masses.

Remaining strictly Orthodox, Stern was opposed to assimilation, maintaining that rather than breaking with the past it was important to enrich general culture with the values of Judaism. He was one of the few *maskilim* who did not cut himself off from Jewish nationalism and because of his individuality was a popular figure in Warsaw. During his travels he visited various countries, especially Germany, and acquired a knowledge of foreign languages. The Poles and Russians respected his great erudition. He was the only Jew to be honored with membership in the Royal Society of the Friends of Science, where he demonstrated the operation of his calculating machine. Together with Jacob *Tugendhold he also acted as censor of Hebrew. Stern was the father-in-law of Ḥayyim Zelig *Slonimski, whom he influenced in the spheres of his interests and work.

BIBLIOGRAPHY: S. Lastik, *Z dziejów Oświęcenia żydowskiego* (1961), 180–4; A. Levinson, *Toledot Yehudei Varshah* (1953), 116–7; J. Shatzky, *Geshikhte fun Yidn in Varshe*, 1–3 (1947–53), indexes; idem, in: *The Joshua Starr Memorial Volume* (1953), 203–18; R. Mahler, *Ha-Ḥasidut ve-ha-Haskalah* (1961), index; idem, *Divrei Yemei Yisrael*, 5 (1970), index.

[Moshe Landau]

STERN, ADOLPHE (1848–1931), Romanian lawyer and political leader. Born in Bucharest, Stern studied law, and in 1891 became the secretary of Benjamin *Peixotto, the first consul of the United States in *Romania. In 1873 he was elected secretary of the Zion Brotherhood in Bucharest. In 1886 Stern became president of the B'nai B'rith lodge in Romania and in 1889 he headed the central board of all the lodges in Romania.

Stern took the initiative in creating the first political representation for Romanian Jews, the Union of Native Jews, in 1909, and served as its president until 1923. During World War I he made contact with G. Clemenceau and other political personalities informing them of the situation of Romanian Jews and asking for intervention in recognizing their rights of Romanian citizenship. From 1922 to 1926 he was a member of the Romanian parliament and chairman of the Jewish Club where he urged the inclusion in the constitution of provisions in the Paris peace treaty concerning naturalization for Jews in Romania. He published a series of judicial works, and translated into Romanian several plays of Shakespeare. The three volumes of his memoirs, *Insemnări din viața mea* (vol. 1, 1915; vol. 2, 1921; and vol. 3 fragmentarily in the paper *Renașterea Noastră* ("Our Revival"), are an important source for the political history of Romanian Jews of his time.

BIBLIOGRAPHY: *Sinai*, 2 (Bucharest, 1929).

[Theodor Lavi]

STERN, ALFRED (1846–1936), historian. Born in Goettingen, Stern immigrated to Switzerland where he was professor of history first at the University of Bern (1874–87) and thereafter (until 1928) at the Polytechnikum, renamed in 1911 Eidgenoessische Technische Hochschule of Zurich. His books involved the origins and development of European liberalism. Among them were a study of the Peasants' Revolt of 1525 (1869); a work on Milton (*Milton und seine Zeit*, 2 vols., 1877–79), which was followed by a history of England's mid-17th century revolution (*Geschichte der Revolution in England*, 1881). His major work was a ten-volume history of 19th-century Europe, *Geschichte Europas seit den Vertraegen von 1815 bis zum Frankfurter Frieden von 1871* (1894–1924), a politically oriented, fully documented, and dispassionate account in the tradition of Leopold von Ranke. Other works included a biography of Mirabeau (*Das Leben Mirabeaus*, 2 vols., 1889; *Viede Mirabeau*, 2 vols., 1895) and books on Swiss and Prussian history. Stern aided the Jewish community of Bern in a lawsuit involving the *Protocols of the *Elders of Zion*, and financially assisted numerous young Jewish scholars. He also treated Jewish historical topics such as the state of the Jews in Prussia. He contributed to the German *Encyclopaedia Judaica*.

BIBLIOGRAPHY: A. Stern, *Wissenschaftliche Selbstbiographie* (1936), obituary in: *Juedische Preßzentrale*, No. 887 (April 3, 1936), 3.

[Walter L. Arnstein]

STERN, ANATOL (1899–1968), Polish poet, author, and translator. Born in Warsaw, Stern was a political radical and a leading member of the futurist school, playing an important part in Polish literary life between the world wars. He was especially well known as a representative of Poland's new writing with strongly defined social tendencies. Stern's works include the verse collections *Futuryzje* (1919); *Anielski cham* ("Angelic Lout," 1924); *Ziemia na lewo* ("Earth to the Left," 1924), written in collaboration with Bruno *Jasienski; *Bieg do bieguna* ("Race to the Pole," 1927); *Europa* (1929); and *Rozmowa z Apollinem* ("Conversation with Apollo," 1938). He also published the novel *Namiętny pielgrzym* ("The Passionate Pilgrim," 1933) and the play *Szkoła genjuszów* ("School for Geniuses," 1933), which was staged in Warsaw. After the outbreak of World War II, Stern fled to the USSR, where he was promptly arrested and sentenced to a year's imprisonment. In 1942 he was transferred to the Middle East as a soldier in the Free Polish army and remained in Palestine until 1948, when he returned to Poland.

His later works include the novel *Ludzie i syrena* ("People and the Siren," 1955) and two volumes of verse: *Wiersze i poematy* (1956) and *Poezje* (1918–1968) (1969). Stern also published translations from French and Russian literature. A volume of his recollections and essays, *Poezja zbuntowana* ("Poetry of Revolt"), appeared in 1964; and *Legendy naszych dni* ("Legends of Our Time"), a collection of sketches, in 1969.

BIBLIOGRAPHY: *Słownik współczesnych pisarzy polskich*, 3 (1964), 214–20.

[Stanislaw Wygodzki]

STERN, ARTHUR C. (1909–1992), U.S. public health engineer. Born in Petersburg, Virginia, Stern became director of New York City air pollution survey (1935–38); chief industrial hygiene engineer, New York State (1942–54); and chief of the engineering laboratory of the U.S. Public Health Service Sanitary Engineering Center (1955–1962). From 1962 he was assistant director of the National Center for Air Pollution Control in Washington. He edited *Air Pollution*, 3 vols. (1962, second edition 1968–69). In 1968 Stern accepted an appointment as professor of air hygiene in the Department of Environmental Sciences and Engineering at the University of North Carolina in Chapel Hill. Although he retired from the position in 1978, he remained active until the day of his death.

Stern received many honors. These included chairmanship of the Electric Power Research Institute Advisory Committee and of the U.S. Environmental Protection Agency's National Air Quality Criteria Advisory Committee, and presidency of the International Unions of Air Pollution Prevention Associations. In 1976 he was elected to the National Academy of Engineering Societies.

STERN, AVRAHAM (underground name, **Ya'ir**; 1907–1942), leading underground fighter in Palestine, founder of the organization later called *Loḥamei Ḥerut Israel (Leḥi). Born in Suvalki (then Russian Poland), Stern studied at the Hebrew high school there. In 1925 he went to Palestine and continued his studies at the Hebrew University in Jerusalem. Active in the *Irgun Ẓeva'i Le'ummi (IẒL) from its formation in 1931, he collaborated with David *Raziel in compiling a Hebrew manual on the use of the revolver and wrote underground poetry, including *Ḥayyalim Almonim* ("Anonymous Soldiers," 1933), which became the anthem of IẒL and later of Leḥi. When IẒL split in 1937, he did not join the *Haganah, but became a member of the IẒL command. He went to Europe to acquire arms and to establish contact with the Polish authorities for the organization of courses for IẒL instructors in Poland. In August 1939 he was arrested together with the other members of the IẒL command and was imprisoned until June 1940. While in prison, his opposition to a suspension of the anti-British attacks for the duration of World War II caused a new split in IẒL and the formation of a separate group, which, after his death, called itself Loḥamei Ḥerut Israel (and which was also known as the Stern Group). He composed a manifesto for the new organization entitled *Ikkarei ha-Teḥiyyah* ("The Principles of Revival"). Early in 1942, the authorities offered a reward for his capture, and on February 12 the Palestine Police traced him, forced an entry into the house in Tel Aviv in which he was hiding, and killed him outright. The house now contains an archive in his memory established by ex-Leḥi members.

Stern was notable for his fanaticism in the armed struggle for Jewish independence, which, he contended, could succeed only if conducted by an underground force independent of all "legal" bodies (even that of *Jabotinsky and his movement). Because of his doubts that the Allies would win World War II, he tried to establish contact with the Italians and the Germans and to persuade the Axis to adopt a pro-Jewish policy in Palestine.

The final work by Moshe *Shamir was *Ya'ir* (2001), a biographical novel.

See also Irgun Ẓeva'i *Le'ummi; Loḥamei Ḥerut *Israel.

BIBLIOGRAPHY: Jabotinsky Institute in Israel, *Avraham Stern (Ya'ir)* (Heb., 1956); D. Niv, *Ma'arekhot ha-Irgun ha-Ẓeva'i ha-Le'ummi*, 3 (1967), index; *Loḥamei Ḥerut Yisrael*, 1 (1959), passim; I. Eldad, *Ma'aser Rishon* (1950), passim; J. Banay, *Ḥayyalim Almonim, Sefer Mivẓa'ei Leḥi* (1958), passim; Yellin-Mor, in: *Etgar*, no. 23 (1962), 4–5; W.O. von Hentig, *Mein Leben – eine Dienstreise* (1962), 338–9.

[David Niv]

STERN, BERNHARD JOSEPH (1894–1956), U.S. sociologist. Born in Chicago, Stern was educated at universities in the U.S. and England and was also ordained as a rabbi at Hebrew Union College in Cincinnati. He taught at the City College in New York, the University of Washington, the New School for Social Research, and Columbia University, but failed to receive a permanent appointment because of his membership in the Communist Party. He was, however, secretary for many years of the Eastern Sociological Society and received research assignments. Stern was editor of *Science and Society*, a Marxist-oriented social science journal. Contrary to other Marxist social scientists in the United States, he was always outspoken about his adherence to the principles of historical materialism and his abhorrence of exploitation in any shape or form. Bearing in mind this background, his contribution to medical sociology and to the sociology of minorities is remarkable.

His major books were *Social Factors in Medical Progress* (1927), *The Family, Past and Present* (1938), and *Society and Medical Progress* (1941). He co-edited *When Peoples Meet* (1942, 1946^2) and *Outline of Anthropology* (1948). His selected papers, *Historical Sociology*, were published posthumously in 1959.

BIBLIOGRAPHY: *Science and Society*, 21 (1957), 1–9, 28–29, includes bibliography of his writings.

[Werner J. Cahnman]

STERN, BERTHA GLADYS (1890–1973), English novelist who wrote under the name "G.B. Stern" and also used the name "Bronwen Gladys Stern." Born in London, G.B. Stern became a writer and journalist after abandoning hopes of a stage career. A prolific author, she published over 50 books, beginning with *Pantomime* (1914). Her own home background and her travels in Germany and Italy provided color for many of her works, not least those on Jewish themes. Her *Matriarch Chronicles* (1936) was really the culmination of a series of novels about the Rakonitz family and the pre-Hitler world of assimilated, middle-class European Jewry, and on these works G.B. Stern's once-considerable reputation was based. They include *Children of No Man's Land* (1923), *Tents of Israel* (1924), *Mosaic* (1930), and *Shining and Free* (1935). The Jewish element is superficial, however, since the novelist's characters – whether they live in Vienna, London, or New York – jealously retain their family loyalties, but not their Judaism. *Tents of Israel* was published in the U.S. as *The Matriarch* (1925), and this was the title given to the book's successful stage adaptation (1929), a sequel being *The Young Matriarch* (1942).

G.B. Stern's other works, which range from novels to autobiography, include *Debonair* (1928), *Little Red Horses* (1932), *Ten Days of Christmas* (1950), and *Promise Not to Tell* (1964). Like several of her fictional heroines, G.B. Stern married a non-Jew and abandoned Judaism. *All in Good Time* (1954) dealt with her conversion to Catholicism.

BIBLIOGRAPHY: S.J. Kunitz, *Twentieth Century Authors*, first supplement (1955), incl. bibl. **ADD. BIBLIOGRAPHY:** ODNB online.

STERN, BEZALEL (1798–1853), educator and pioneer of the *Haskalah in southern Russia. Stern, who was born in Tarnopol, Galicia, was educated in the school of Josef *Perl, where he later taught for ten years. During the late 1820s he was invited by the community of Odessa, which was headed by natives of Galicia (the "Brodyists"), to become director of the Jewish school which had been founded in 1826 by a group of moderate *maskilim* led by Simḥah *Pinsker and Isaac Hurwitz. Under Stern's direction, the institution expanded, the number of its classes was increased from four to six, sections for boys and girls were opened, and the number of pupils rose to 400. Stern instituted changes in the curriculum by expanding instruction in the sciences and languages (German and Russian) at the expense of Jewish studies. He rapidly won the approval of the Russian *maskilim*, who corresponded with him on the subject of changes and reforms in the life of the Jews of the country. The Orthodox elements of the community were opposed to these changes, but Stern relied on the support which he received from the municipal authorities, particularly from Governor-General Vorontsov.

In 1837 Nicholas I visited the school and expressed his satisfaction with the institution's course of studies. In spite of this, when the government decided to establish a network of governmental schools for the Jews, Max *Lilienthal, a newcomer to Russia, was appointed to supervise the project. This aroused the anger of Stern, who refused to collaborate with Lilienthal. In 1843 Stern was appointed member of the commission which was to ratify the curriculum of the Jewish governmental schools. The other members of the commission were R. Isaac b. Ḥayyim*Volozhiner, head of the yeshivah of Volozhin, R. Menahem Mendel *Schneersohn, the leader of Ḥabad Ḥasidism, and Israel Heilperin, an Orthodox banker of Berdichev. Stern represented the *maskilim* but his influence was equivalent to that of all his colleagues because he enjoyed the support of the government. In 1852 Stern was dismissed from his position as director of the Jewish school and its administration was assumed by Christian inspectors.

In addition to his educational activities, Stern also took an interest in Jewish history and archaeology. He maintained relations with Abraham *Firkovich. He also occupied himself with the problems of the Jewish community, as shown by his memorandum on the collection of the meat tax (**korobka*) in Odessa.

BIBLIOGRAPHY: S.M. Stanislavski, in: *Voskhod*, 4 (1884); O.M. Lerner, *Yevrei v malorossiyskoy kraye* (1901); A. Druyanow, *Pinsker u-Zemanno* (1953), 9–10, 20; P. Friedman, in: *Fun Noentn Over*, 2 (1938), 99.

[Yehuda Slutsky]

STERN, BILL (1907–1971), U.S. sports broadcaster, member of the Radio Hall of Fame, National Sportscasters and Sportswriters Hall of Fame, and American Sportscasters Hall of Fame. Stern began broadcasting in 1925, when he was hired to cover football games for WHAM in his hometown of Rochester, New York. His dramatic flair as an announcer was bolstered by his experience in theater and vaudeville, most notably his appointment as Radio City Music Hall's first stage director when it opened its doors in 1932. In 1937, Stern was hired by NBC and was given his own nationally syndicated, 15-minute radio show, *Bill Stern Review*. The show, which featured Stern rifling off sports scores, telling stories of amazing coincidences and heroism (some true, some concocted), and interviewing famous entertainers, became a fixture of the radio. From 1939 to 1951, he hosted *The Colgate Sports Newsreel*, and until 1956, *Bill Stern Sports*. Stern's voice was also made famous by his calling Friday night fights for NBC, as well as narrating MGM's *News of the Day* newsreels shown in movie theaters from 1938 to 1952. Stern also played himself in the 1942 movie classic *Pride of the Yankees*. At the height of his popularity, Stern was selected for 13 consecutive years (1940–52) as the top sports commentator by a poll of American radio editors. Stern broadcast the first-ever televised sports event – Princeton vs. Columbia in baseball – on May 17, 1939, as well as the first televised football game between Waynesburg and Fordham on September 30, 1939. After a health-related hiatus in the late 1950s, Stern returned to finish his broadcasting career as sports director for the Mutual Broadcasting System throughout the 1960s. He wrote *Bill Stern's Favorite Sports Stories* (1946), *Bill Stern's Favorite Football Stories* (1948), *Bill Stern's Favorite Boxing Stories* (1948), *Bill Stern's Favorite Baseball Stories* (1949), *Bill Stern's Sports Quiz Book* (1950), and an autobiography, *The Taste of Ashes: A Famous Broadcaster's Comeback from Addiction and Disaster* (1959).

[Robert B. Klein (2nd ed.)]

STERN, CHAIM (1930–2001) U.S., Reform rabbi, liturgist. Stern, acknowledged as the foremost liturgist of Reform Judaism, was born in Brooklyn, New York. He studied in Orthodox yeshivot as a child, but the Holocaust caused him to become far more secular than his family. He received a B.A. from City College (1952) and attended Harvard Law School, but left Harvard after a year to enroll in *Hebrew Union College, where he was ordained in 1958. In 1983, HUC-JIR awarded him an honorary D.D. While serving as rabbi of Temple Sholom in River Edge, New Jersey (1958–62), he taught at the HUC-JIR School of Sacred Music. An outspoken political activist, he traveled to Mississippi to fight for civil rights as a Freedom Rider in 1961. In 1962, he became rabbi of the Liberal Jewish Synagogue in London, England, returning in 1965 to assume the pulpit at Congregation Emanu-El B'ne Jeshurun in Milwaukee, Wisconsin. He spent the year 1967–8 back in London, lecturing at Leo Baeck College and serving as rabbi of Westminster Synagogue. From 1968 to 2000, he was the senior rabbi at Temple Beth El of Northern Westchester in Chappaqua, New York, where he also served as president of the Northern Westchester and Putman Rabbinic Council and the Chappaqua Interfaith Council as well as on the regional board of the Anti-Defamation League. He was serving as senior rabbi of Temple Israel in Miami, Florida, at the time of his death.

In 1971, as a result of Stern's having co-edited two new prayer books for the Liberal Movement of England – *On the Doorposts of Your House* and *Gates of Joy* – he was appointed by the *Central Conference of American Rabbis to edit the new liturgy of the Reform movement. Over the course of three decades, he compiled the entire *Gates* series of prayer books: *Gates of Prayer*, published in 1975, became the official year-round **siddur* of Reform Judaism's 800 congregations, while his **mahzor Gates of Repentance*, which appeared three years later, played the same role for the High Holy Days. (U.S. President Bill Clinton publicly quoted a passage on contrition from *Gates of Repentance* when he discussed atoning for the Lewinsky sex scandal.) The series also comprises *Gates of the House* (1977), containing prayers related to ritual observances in the home; *Gates of Heaven: Services for Children and Their Parents on the Days of Awe* (1979); *Gates of Forgiveness* (1980), a companion volume to *Gates of Repentance* focusing on the **selihot* service recited in the weeks preceding Rosh Ha-Shanah and the Day of Atonement; and *Gates of Freedom*, a popular *Passover **Haggadah*.

Stern translated many of the prayers from the original Hebrew, wrote passages himself and incorporated words of wisdom ranging from ancient Jewish texts to such eclectic modern voices as Martin *Buber, e.e. cummings, and Norman *Mailer. The old-fashioned "thee" and "thou" were rendered as "you," while references to "our fathers" in traditional prayers, considered sexist, became "our ancestors." All references to God as King were changed to Sovereign.

Stern also wrote *Pirke Avot: Wisdom of the Jewish Sages* (1992) and **Isaac: The Link in the Chain* (1977). In addition, he co-authored (with Gunther *Plaut) *The Book of Genesis*, a translation and commentary of the first book of the Bible (1974), and *The Haftarah Commentary* (1996). He co-edited (with Lisa Pemstein) *Day by Day: Reflections on the Themes of the Torah From Literature, Philosophy, and Religious Thought*, a collection of meditations to accompany the cycle of the Jewish year, and (with Rossel and Chanover) *When a Jew Seeks Wisdom: The Sayings of the Fathers* (1975). He adapted several of his works for special occasions, including *Gates of Prayer for Weekdays and a House of Mourning* (1992). His final work, *Paths of Faith: The New Jewish Prayer Book for Synagogue and Home* – containing devotions for weekdays, *the Sabbath and festivals – appeared in 2003.

BIBLIOGRAPHY: The Nearprint Files of the American Jewish Archives, Cincinnati.

[Bezalel Gordon (2nd ed.)]

STERN, DAVID (1942–), U.S. basketball executive, fourth commissioner of the NBA. Born and raised in the Chelsea section of Manhattan, Stern worked his way through school at his father's deli, near Madison Square Garden, which was open six days a week and closed only on the Jewish High Holidays. Stern was a passionate sports fan and developed his love for basketball and the skills and ease of dealing with the public while serving the diverse deli customers. After studying at Rutgers University and Columbia Law School, Stern noted: "Others talk about working as clerks for Supreme Court justices or federal judges, but I enjoy saying that my first clerkship was at Stern's Delicatessen." From the time he joined the legal firm of Proskauer and Associates in 1966 to his appointment as NBA legal counsel in 1978, Stern dedicated almost all his professional activities to NBA work. As an NBA executive, Stern was determined to radically renovate the league's image tainted by public perceptions of drug abuse, lazy work ethics, and astronomic salaries. Stern played a major role in changing popular perceptions in the early 1980s via two milestone agreements with the NBA Player's Association: drug testing, and instituting team salary caps. His tenure as commissioner, starting in 1984, reflects the unprecedented success of the NBA. In particular, the league's appeal to a young audience increased not only in the U.S. but also worldwide. The pinnacle achievement of this international enthusiasm was the unprecedented decision to include NBA players on the U.S. basketball "Dream Team" at the Barcelona Olympics in 1992. Highlighting the skills of stars such as Larry Bird, Magic Johnson, and Michael Jordan helped the NBA achieve not only equality with other American professional sports, but even seemingly to surpass them. NBA players were now the most famous athletes in the world, appealing to an international audience and starring in commercials all over the globe. Additional achievements by Stern include the expansion of the NBA to 30 teams (2005); the opening of international offices; the creation of the Women's National Basketball Association in 1997; and the 1999 launch of NBA.com TV, a 24-hour digital network. Stern also serves on the boards of numerous public institutions including Columbia University, Beth Israel Medical Center, and the NAACP, and is a contributor to various charities, including the United Jewish Appeal.

BIBLIOGRAPHY: D. Halberstam, *Playing For Keeps; Michael Jordan and the World He Made* (1999).

[Yitzchak Mais (2nd ed.)]

STERN, ELIZABETH GERTRUDE LEVIN (1889–1954), social worker and author of 13 books that received much popular and critical attention. Details of Stern's birth remain uncertain. Although she consistently maintained that she was born in Königsberg, Prussia, and came to the United States in 1892 with her parents, Sarah Leah (Rubenstein) and Aaron Kleine Levin, a cantor and rabbinical assistant, her oldest son later revealed that while raised by the Levins, his mother actually had been born out of wedlock in Pittsburgh to Lillian Morgan and Christian Limburg, a store owner and merchant.

After graduating from the University of Pittsburgh in 1910, Stern moved to New York City and enrolled in the New York School of Philanthropy (later renamed the New York School of Social Work) where she met, and in 1911 married, fellow student Leon Stern. From 1912 to 1913, they lived in Galveston, Texas, assisting Jacob Schiff's efforts to reroute American Jewish immigration from New York to the Southwest. A decade later, they co-authored *My Friend at Court* (1923), a "casebook" of a female probation officer based on cases with which they were familiar. The mother of two sons, Stern was an active professional and a writer. Her social work achievements were recognized with an honorary master's degree from the University of Pittsburgh in 1918.

Stern, who began writing for local newspapers as early as 1908, began to publish feature articles in *The New York Times* in 1914. By 1926, she was writing for the *New York Evening World* and the *Philadelphia Public Ledger*, for which she assumed the pen name Eleanor Morton. In 1926, she adopted the pseudonym Leah Morton for the popular and critically acclaimed *I am a Woman – and a Jew* (rep. 1986, with a new introduction by E.M. Umansky). This book purports to be the autobiography of an Eastern European Jewish immigrant who comes to America as a child and spends her youth in the Jewish section of a small city along the Ohio River. The focus is on the author's struggle to meet familial and professional demands while she struggles to come to terms with her Jewish identity. Contemporary reviewers assumed the book was Morton/Stern's personal story. However, Leah's struggle to establish a career despite her husband's objections and the conflicts created by marrying a non-Jew were fictional. Still, like Stern's earlier autobiographical novel, *My Mother and I* (1917), this book illuminated the spiritual journey and generational tensions experienced by many modern Jews, especially women.

Stern's religious attachment to Judaism remains unclear. By 1928 she had joined the Philadelphia Ethical Society, a branch of Ethical Culture, and she later became a member of the Religious Society of Friends, devoting much of her time and energy to Quaker organizations.

BIBLIOGRAPHY: T. Noel Stern, *Secret Family* (1988); E.M. Umansky. "Representations of Jewish Women in the Works and Life of Elizabeth Stern," in: *Modern Judaism*, 13 (1993), 165–76.

[Ellen M. Umansky (2nd ed.)]

STERN, EPHRAIM (1934–), Israeli archaeologist, expert on the Land of Israel during the Iron and Persian periods. Born in Haifa in 1934, he studied at the Reali High School and was a member of the local branch of scouts known as "the Carmel Wanderers." His military service was undertaken from 1952 and eventually he reached the rank of officer. In 1955 he began his studies at the Hebrew University in Jerusalem, taking courses in archaeology and the history of Israel, and finally receiving his Ph.D. in 1968 for "The Material Culture of the Land of the Bible in the Persian Period," supervised by Prof. Benjamin Mazar. His ground-breaking research on the Persian period is regarded as a milestone in the archaeology of Israel. He began teaching archaeology at Tel Aviv University in 1964, but in 1971 he returned to the Hebrew University and began teaching at the newly founded Institute of Archaeology at the request of his mentor, Yigael Yadin. He was appointed full professor there in 1984, eventually holding the Bernard M. Lauterman Chair in Biblical Archaeology, and continued teaching until his retirement in 2002. Stern was director of the Yad Ben-Zvi Institute in Jerusalem between 1993 and 1996. As a student Stern participated in numerous excavations in Israel, notably at Masada, Hazor, Beersheba, and En Gedi. He subsequently conducted his own excavations at a number of sites, including Gil'am, Tel Kadesh, and Tel Mevorakh, but most of his scientific energy was directed towards 20 years of digging at Tel Dor (Tanturah). Stern served as editor of the Hebrew archaeological journal *Qadmoniot* (published by the Israel Exploration Society), as well as editor of the distinguished *New Encyclopedia of Archaeological Excavations in the Holy Land* (1988–93). Stern published numerous research papers, excavations reports, and books, including *Dor – Ruler of the Seas: Ten Years of Excavating a Phoenician Israelite Harbour Town on the Carmel Coast* (1994); *Archaeology of the Land of the Bible*, vol. II. *The Assyrian, Babylonian, and Persian Periods* (732–332 B.C.E.) (2001). He was the recipient of many awards and prizes, including the Ben-Zvi Prize (1979), the Biblical Archaeology Society Publication Award (1984), the P. Schimmel Prize (1994), two Irene Levi-Sala Book Prizes (1995, 2002), and the Emet Prize on behalf of the Prime Minister of Israel for Distinguished Scholarly Achievements (2005).

[Shimon Gibson (2nd ed.)]

STERN, ERICH (1889–1959), psychologist, physician, and educator. Born in Berlin, Stern was an associate professor at the University of Giessen from 1924 to 1928, when he went to Mainz to lecture at the Institute of Pedagogy and direct the Mainz Institute of Psychology. In 1933 he migrated to Paris, where he was active in the children's neuropsychiatry clinic of the University of Paris medical school. During the Nazi occupation of France he worked with the underground, and after the war, engaged in the rehabilitation of Jewish children. From 1950, he was in charge of research in the National Center of Scientific Research in Paris.

Stern was active with *OSE, and wrote some studies on the psychology of immigrants. His books include *Ein-*

leitung in die Paedagogik (1922), *Jugendpsychologie* (1923, 1951[5]), and *Gesundheitliche Erziehung* (1928). He also published the *Jahrbuch der Erziehungswissenschaft und Jugendkunde.*

[William W. Brickman]

STERN, ERNEST (1876–1954), stage designer. Stern was born in Bucharest, going to Munich at the age of 19 to study under Franz van Stuck. He worked as a caricaturist for *Jugend* and *Simplizissimus* and began to contribute to political cabarets. He moved to Berlin in 1905 as illustrator on the *Lustigen Blatter* and in the same year began his historic collaboration with Max Reinhardt, with the famous production of Shakespeare's *Midsummer Night's Dream.* The following year he was taken on by Reinhardt as artistic director, a position he held for 16 years. There followed a series of remarkable productions which made both men world famous: works by Shakespeare, the pantomime *Samurun* (1910), *Faust* (1911), the remarkable *Miracle* (1914), *Danton's Death* (1916), *John Gabriel Borkman* (1917). Between 1919 and 1929 Stern also worked for the German cinema, including films by Ernst *Lubitsch. Before the advent of Nazism Stern was already famous on the London stage, designing Noel Coward's *Bitter Sweet* in 1929, followed by a series of spectacular musicals including Offenbach's *La Belle Héléne* and *White Horse Inn.* In 1934 he settled in London where he lived for the rest of his life. He continued to design the plays of Shakespeare, especially for the actor Donald Wolfit, and popular musical plays. An artist of deep historical knowledge and remarkable imagination, Ernest Stern had a profound effect on 20th-century stage design. He was regarded as one of the outstanding stage designers of the century.

[Charles Samuel Spencer]

STERN, SIR FREDERICK CLAUDE (1884–1967), British banker. Stern was a partner in the London banking house of *Stern Brothers. His father, James Stern, and his older brother, Sir Albert Stern, devoted their energies during World War I to the construction of the newly invented tank, while Frederick had a distinguished career on active service, mainly on the Turkish front. During World War I he came into contact with Lloyd George and served temporarily as his secretary during the Versailles Peace Conference. He was knighted in 1956. Outside his professional life he was widely known as a skillful and enthusiastic gardener, particularly as a breeder of lilies and daffodils. At his country mansion, Highdown House, near Worthing, West Sussex, Stern created a famous garden which has been the subject of several books. After his death, his widow left the house and grounds to the Worthing Council. He wrote extensively on botanic subjects and was prominent in the Linnean Society and the Royal Horticultural Society and was master of the Drapers' Co., one of London's ancient guilds. Among his writings are *Study of Genus Paeonia* (1946) and *Snowdrops and Snowflakes* (1956), a study of the general *Galanthus* and *Leucojum.*

BIBLIOGRAPHY: *Royal Horticultural Society Journal*, 92 (Sept. 1967), 379–81.

[Joachim O. Ronall]

STERN, FRITZ RICHARD (1926–), U.S. historian of German-Jewish background. Stern grew up in then German Breslau (Wroclaw) as the son of parents of Jewish background. He was brought up as a Protestant, his godfather being the Nobel Prize-winning chemist Fritz *Haber. His family had to leave Germany, and he settled in the United States in 1938. He received his Ph.D. in history at Columbia University, having studied with another German emigrant, Hajo Holborn. Stern spent most of his teaching career at Columbia University, first as Seth Low Professor, later as University Professor. He retired in 1997. He was a permanent visiting professor at the University of Konstanz and taught at numerous European universities. The main focus in his publications is the prehistory of the rise of National Socialism in Germany, which he analyzed mainly through illiberal tendencies in central European thought. His celebrated book *Gold and Iron* (1977) centered on the relationship between German Chancellor Bismarck and his Jewish banker Gerson von Bleichroeder. Stern was active in political debates and his voice was heard far beyond the scholarly realm. In Germany, he gave a public speech in the parliament, the Bundestag, in 1987 as the first non-German citizen at the anniversary of the failed East German revolt of 1953. He received numerous prizes, such as the Lionel Trilling Award and the Peace Prize of the German Book Trade (1999), Germany's most renowned literary award. He also served as assistant to Ambassador Richard Holbrooke during the latter's tenure in Germany in 1993/94. Stern always tried to understand the causes of the German catastrophe in the 20th century and draw lessons for a peaceful future for Europe. He was eager to build bridges between Germans and Jews, Europe and the United States.

BIBLIOGRAPHY: *Who's Who in America 2002*, 5092; *International Biographical Dictionary of Central European Émigrés 1933–1944* (1999), 1123–24.

[Michael Brenner (2nd ed.)]

STERN, GERSHON (1861–1936), Transylvanian rabbi and author. Stern was a pupil of Moses Schick and Abraham Judah ha-Kohen Schwartz. He served as rabbi of Marosludas from 1885. In 1881 he published in the *Ha-Tor* of Abraham Guenzler (fourth year, no. 6) an attractive article on the need to revive the Hebrew language and the joy that filled him on the appearance of Hebrew papers. He visited Ereẓ Israel and then wrote his small work, *Masei Benei Yisrael* (1910), in German with Hebrew script. In "*Ḥatimat ha-Sefer*" ("conclusion") of the *Yalkut ha-Gershuni, Hilkhot Terefot* (1907), he wrote in ornate language of his love and yearnings for Ereẓ Israel.

He also wrote of his ties with Ereẓ Israel in his testament (*Yalkut ha-Gershuni, al Aggadot ha-Shas*, pt. 1 (1922), 41a). He was very concerned about the yeshivot in his province and wished to raise their standards both economically and spiritually. To this end he published many articles in the *Allgemeine Juedische Zeitung*, and then issued them in a special pamphlet *Marbeh Yeshivah* (1902). His *Yalkut ha-Gershuni* is in 13 parts: three parts contain novellae and expositions of themes in the Talmud and *posekim*, arranged in alphabetical order (1894–96); two parts are on the Bible (1899–1900); four parts are on the Shulḥan Arukh (1901–08); three parts are on talmudic *aggadot* (1922–27); and one part is on *Avot* (1906). He also frequently published talmudic novellae in the *Tel Talpiyyot*. His *Masei Benei Yisrael* was translated into Hebrew by N. Ben-Menahem (*Mi-Sifrut Yisrael be-Ungaryah* (1958), 9–49), which gives a detailed bibliography of his writings (317–26).

[Naphtali Ben-Menahem]

STERN, GRIGORI (d. 1940), Soviet army officer. Stern was chief adviser to the Republican army in Spain from 1936 to 1937 when he was sent to the Far East as chief of staff of the Soviet Far Eastern forces. He defeated the Japanese at the battle of Lake Khasan and was promoted to colonel general and given command of the Soviet forces. In the following year he defeated the Japanese at the battle of Khalkhin-Gol and drove them out of Soviet Mongolia. Stern died during the Finnish campaign.

STERN, HANS (1922–), Brazilian jeweler. Born in Essen, Germany, Stern immigrated to Brazil in 1939 with his family and settled in Rio de Janeiro. In 1940 he found work with a firm that exported Brazilian semiprecious stones such as tourmaline, topaz, and aquamarine, and he soon rose to the position of manager. In 1945 he sold his accordion for $200 and used the money to start his own jewelry business, H. Stern Comercio e Industria, to buy, polish, set, and sell such stones in original designs. Aided by his flair for aggressive and imaginative promotion, the company developed within a few years into Brazil's largest undertaking in the field. It had an annual volume of many millions of dollars and more than 200 stores in principal cities all over the world, earning Stern the title of "the king of colored gems." The company is owned today in equal shares by his sons: Roberto, Ronaldo, Ricardo, and Rafael.

BIBLIOGRAPHY: S. and K. Seegers, in: *Reader's Digest* (Jan. 1968), 203–8.

STERN, HARRY JOSHUA (1897–1984), Canadian Reform rabbi. Stern was born in Eragoly, just outside Kovno, Lithuania. One of eight children, Stern describes in his memoir growing up in a traditional family and studying at his local *ḥeder*. After his mother died, Stern's father remarried and had four more children. Between 1906 and 1908 the family moved, in stages, to Steubenville, Ohio, from where Stern applied to study at Hebrew Union College. Unlike most of his fellow students, Stern was fluent in Yiddish and, like his role model, Stephen *Wise, became a Zionist, even though Zionism was treated with disdain by most HUC faculty. Stern earned a bachelor of Hebrew literature from HUC in 1919, a B.A. from the University of Cincinnati in 1920, and was ordained in 1922.

Stern assumed his first pulpit in 1922, in Uniontown, Pennsylvania. He developed a reputation for oratory, interfaith work, Zionist activism, and social welfare. In 1927 he moved to Montreal's Temple Emanu-el, where he remained until his retirement in 1972. Stern preached the principles of Reform Judaism with an emphasis on the social responsibility. During the Depression he chastised factory owners, including some of his own congregants, for firing employees in order to hire cheaper labor in the rural areas. Stern also supported adult education, establishing the College for Jewish Studies the year after his arrival. Stern hired Jews of various stripes, including avowed socialist David *Lewis, to teach both adults and children. Stern also exchanged pulpits with Protestant ministers. Even more remarkably, Stern had regular contact with French Catholics. His first meeting did not occur in Quebec but rather on a ship where Stern, traveling with some students to Palestine in 1929, met the Quebec Jesuit Joseph Paré, who was also traveling with students to Rome. The two continued their contact and on several occasions in the 1930s tried to turn the Quebec Church hierarchy against antisemitism. Because of these contacts, the Canadian Jewish Congress assigned Stern a prominent role in its Joint Public Relations Committee. If little headway was made during the 1930s, it was hardly for lack of effort. Stern also championed the end of discrimination at McGill University and in housing.

In the postwar years, Stern continued to work for better Jewish-Christian relations, calling on Jews to recognize the prophetic quality of some of the teachings of Jesus the Jew, and on Christians to abandon their negative attitudes to the Jewish faith. A number of volumes of Stern's sermons have appeared in print. Biographical details are contained in K.I. Cleator and H.J. Stern, *Harry Joshua Stern: A Rabbi's Journey* (1981). Stern received numerous awards for his work in Jewish-Christian relations.

BIBLIOGRAPHY: *Who's Who in Canadian Jewry* (1965), 93; G. Tulchinsky, in: M. Van Die (ed.), *Religion and Public Life in Canada* (2001), 313–28; P. Anctil, *Le Rendez-vous manqué* (1988).

[Richard Menkis (2nd ed.)]

STERN, HORACE (1879–1969), U.S. jurist. Born in Philadelphia, Stern graduated from the University of Pennsylvania Law School, where he went on to lecture in real estate law for ten years. In 1903 he formed a law partnership with Morris Wolf. He served in the U.S. army during World War I, rising to the rank of major. In 1930 he was appointed a judge of the Common Pleas Court of Philadelphia. The following year he was elected to a full ten-year term. In 1935 he was elected to the Pennsylvania Supreme Court, on which he served as chief justice from 1952 until his retirement in 1957. Generally liberal in outlook, his judicial opinions were characterized by their independence of mind and careful adherence to sound legal principles.

Besides acting as a trustee of the University of Pennsylvania, Stern belonged to numerous civic organizations and was highly active in Jewish affairs. He was director for many years of the Philadelphia Federation of Jewish Charities, served briefly as president of Dropsie College, and was vice president of the Jewish Publication Society of America from 1914 to 1965, when he was declared honorary president. A collection of his articles and addresses was published in 1953 as *The Spiritual Values of Life*.

STERN, HOWARD (1954–), U.S. broadcasting personality. Born in Jackson Heights, Queens, Stern was raised in nearby Long Island. He graduated from Boston University, where he produced bawdy comedy like the *King Schmaltz Bagel Hour* on the campus radio station. (Stern was first introduced to radio by his father, Ben Stern, a radio engineer.) Stern started at a tiny radio station in Briarcliff Manor, a New York City suburb, for $4 an hour and moved to stations in Hartford, Conn., and Detroit, Michigan, before landing a choice spot on a Washington, D.C., station, where his unadulterated, scrappy on-air personality was honed. Stern was fired but landed in New York City in 1982 in the coveted afternoon drive home slot on WNBC-AM. His outrageous humor on WNBC was terminated after two years, and he joined WXRK on the FM band in New York in 1985. There he produced one more outrageous program after another. Stern's audience grew as his show went into syndication, beginning in Philadelphia in 1985. Stern's conduct cost his employer Infinity Broadcasting $600,000 in fines for indecency. He was forced to apologize when he said that he prayed for the death of the chairman of the Federal Communications Commission. In 1990 Stern started a television version of his show, essentially a visual version of his radio show, although nudity was obscured. Nevertheless his popularity grew and the radio and television shows got high ratings in such cities as Los Angeles, New Orleans, Cleveland, Las Vegas, and Baltimore. In 1994 Stern ran for governor of New York on the Libertarian Party ticket on a platform that included bringing back the death penalty and eliminating daytime traffic construction. Stern abandoned the race but the newly elected governor signed the Howard Stern Bill, which restricted construction to nighttime on state roads on Long Island and in New York City. Stern wrote an autobiography, *Private Parts*, which became the basis for a movie of the same name in 1997. Another book, *Miss America*, was published, concentrating on the inner workings of the show. Both books reached the top of the bestseller list. After the World Trade Center attacks of September 11, 2001, Stern continued live broadcasts in a subdued tone and won praise from many listeners. In February 2004, Stern was indefinitely suspended by Clear Channel Communications, his syndicator, in six markets, supposedly because of his sex-charged conversation with an on-air guest. Fed up with constantly butting heads with the FCC and feeling unsupported by his corporate parent, Stern signed a five-year, $500-million deal with Sirius Satellite Radio, with broadcasts beginning in January 2006. The arrangement, in which Stern can be as uninhibited as he wants because he is not using public airways, relied on the potential for Stern to increase the Sirius subscribers from 1 million to 8 million. Sirius devoted two round-the-clock channels for Stern's show and other material he developed.

[Stewart Kampel (2nd ed.)]

STERN, IRMA (1894–1966), South African painter. Irma Stern was born of a German family in Schweizer-Renecke, Transvaal, but was taken to Europe as a girl. She studied in Vienna and Berlin. Back in South Africa after World War I, she shocked the public with her bold palette and expressionist method, which were regarded as aggressively modern. Within a few years, however, she came to be recognized for the vital qualities of her work and her paintings were bought for many public and private collections. She used exuberant harmonies and heavy draftsmanship. Sometimes her still lifes and flower pieces tended to grossness, but more often her compositions were relieved by a vein of tenderness and, especially in her watercolors, by poetry and simplicity of approach. She portrayed colored, Malay, and Indian types, and traveled to the Congo and Zanzibar, bringing back many African and Arab studies. She exhibited in Johannesburg and Cape Town and in Europe. In 1971 the University of Cape Town established an Irma Stern Museum to exhibit her work.

BIBLIOGRAPHY: Sachs, in: *Jewish Affairs*, no. 1 (1967), 38–43; Eglington, *ibid.*, 21, no. 9 (1966), 20–21; Martienssen, in: *Lantern* (Dec. 1968). **ADD. BIBLIOGRAPHY:** I. Below, *Hidden Treasures, Irma Stern: Her Books…* (2000); N. Dubow, *Irma Stern* (1974); K. Schoeman, *Irma Stern: The Early Years, 1894–1933* (1994).

[Lewis Sowden]

STERN, ISAAC (1920–2001), U.S. violinist. Born in Kremenets, Ukraine, the following year he was taken to San Francisco, where his mother worked as pianist and teacher. He took up the violin at the age of eight. Following his recital début (1935) Stern was soloist with the San Francisco Orchestra under Pierre *Monteux (1936). During the years 1943–4 he played for Allied troops. In America he acquired a reputation, which became worldwide after World War II. Stern made his European début in 1948 under Munch and thereafter he toured Europe regularly (except Germany, where he consistently refused to appear). His work with the cellist Pablo Casals at the Prades Festivals was important in his development. During the Cold War he toured the USSR. Stern had very strong ties with the State of Israel. He appeared frequently with the Israel Philharmonic Orchestra, most memorably in the concerts on Mount Scopus with Bernstein after the Six-Day War in 1967, and in the 1991 Gulf War, during which he continued his performance while sirens wailed to signal an Iraqi Scud missile attack. Stern founded the Jerusalem Music Center and became president of the America-Israel Cultural Foundation and a sponsor of Israeli artists, such as *Perlman, *Zukerman, *Fried, and *Mintz. In keeping with his long-standing commitment to working with young musicians, Stern held a number of chamber music workshops in Israel and at Carnegie Hall over the years. He was always active in chamber music with his piano partner Alexander Zakin and in a trio with *Istomin and *Rose (1961–1984); he performed regularly with Emanuel *Ax, Jaime Laredo and Yo Yo Ma and Yefim *Bronfman. For more than 60 years Stern appeared on the world's most prestigious concert stages. Recognized as one of the great violinists of his generation, he was particularly noted for his warm, rich tone in a repertoire that ranged from the Baroque to the modern. He premiered violin works by Bernstein, Penderecki, *Rochberg, Schuman, and Dutilleux and gave first American performances of works by Bartok and Hindemith. Stern is one of the most recorded musical artists of our time; he recorded all the great concertos, numerous chamber music recitals, and soundtracks for films (such as *Fiddler on the Roof*, 1971). He appeared frequently on television and documentaries. The film of his trip to China, *From Mao to Mozart*, received an Academy Award in 1981. Active in wider fields, he took part in the movement which saved Carnegie Hall in New York from demolition and became president of the Carnegie Hall Corporation. He was also a co-founder of the National Endowment for the Arts in 1964. Stern received many of the nation's and the world's highest honors, among them honors from the U.S., Japanese, Danish and French governments; the Albert Schweitzer Music Award for a life dedicated to music and devoted to humanity; a Fellow of Jerusalem (1986); Israel's Wolf Prize (1987); and the Presidential Medal of Freedom (1992). He received honorary degrees from many institutions, such as Columbia, Harvard, New York University, Oxford, the Hebrew University of Jerusalem, the Juilliard School, and Tel Aviv University. His biography, with Chaim Potok, entitled *My First 79 Years*, was published in 1999.

BIBLIOGRAPHY: Grove Music Online; *Baker's Biographical Dictionary of Musicians* (1997); H. Roth, *Violin Virtuosos: From Paganini to the 21st Century* (1997); A. Mischakoff Heiles, "Isaac Stern Remembered," in: *The Instrumentalist*, 56 (Nov. 2001), 72–77.

[Uri (Erich) Toeplitz / Rohan Saxena and Naama Ramot (2nd ed.)]

STERN, JACK (1926–), U.S. Reform rabbi. Stern was born in Cincinnati, Ohio, and received a B.A. at the University of Cincinnati in 1948. In 1952, he was ordained at *Hebrew Union College, which awarded him an honorary D.D. in 1977. After ordination, he became assistant rabbi at Temple Beth El in Great Neck, N.Y. (1952–55), where his then soon-to-be father in law, Jacob *Rudin, was senior rabbi. Next he served as rabbi of Temple Emanu-El in Westfield, N.J. (1955–62), until he was appointed rabbi of Westchester Reform Temple in Scarsdale, N.Y. (1962–91, when he became emeritus). He also lectured in Modern Jewish Thought at the College of New Rochelle, New York, as part of the Jewish Chatauqua Society Lectureship program.

Stern was a social activist in both the Jewish and general communities, as a trustee of the Federation of Jewish Philanthropies of Greater New York, president of the Westchester Board of Rabbis, co-chairman of the Scarsdale Committee for Senior Housing, and a member of the Human Relations Advisory Council in Scarsdale. As a member of the board of the Scarsdale Family Counseling Service, he had a special interest in mental health and participated in a National Institute of Mental Health pilot project on "Religion and Mental Health." He extended his charitable efforts beyond Scarsdale by establishing an ongoing relationship with the poor Jewish elderly in the Bronx, finding clothing and jobs for refugee Vietnamese families, and participating in countrywide interfaith efforts to feed the hungry and shelter the homeless. He ventured forth from the suburbs in the service of his own congregants as well, as one of the pioneering rabbis to bring religious study to them at their places of business (on Wall Street, for example).

In the Reform movement, Stern was chairman of the Task Force on Jewish Ethics of the *Union of American Hebrew Congregations and chaired the *Central Conference of American Rabbis' Committee on Ethics. He also chaired the CCAR Committee on Youth and served on both the Joint CCAR-UAHC Commission on Social Action and the CCAR's executive board. In 1982, he was elected vice president of the CCAR; in 1984, he succeeded Gunther *Plaut as CCAR president. During his tenure in office, Stern worked at what he called "setting up dialogues" – with the goal of bringing together Christians and Jews in order to share Jewish values in interfaith settings, but primarily with his Conservative and Orthodox counterparts at the *Rabbinical Assembly and *Rabbinical Council of America, respectively. While defending Reform Judaism's position on patrilineal descent against vehement opposition from both the Conservative and Orthodox camps, Stern managed to hammer out with his colleagues a historic "Statement of Unity" that was read aloud in congregations affiliated with all three denominations on *Shabbat ha-Gadol. This step forward for the benefit of *Kelal Yisrael* was made possible by drawing a distinction between the "Covenant of Fate" – that all Jews share – and the "Covenant of Faith," about which the movements agreed to disagree.

Also during his presidency, Stern tackled the issue of intermarriage from two new perspectives: he called on the institutions of Reform Judaism to create an environment in which young Jews would consider dating outside the faith unacceptable *a priori*, thus adopting a proactive rather than reactive stance against serious interfaith relationships. Secondly, he prevailed on the *Union of American Hebrew Congregations to issue a statement asking its synagogues not to discriminate against rabbinic candidates who refused to officiate at interfaith weddings as a matter of principle.

Following his term of office, Stern served on the board of governors of HUC-JIR and was alumnus-in-residence at HUC-JIR in Cincinnati. In 1996, he was asked by the CCAR to chair the Committee on Sexual Abuse by Clergy, which recommended procedures and sanctions that were adopted by all the institutions of the Reform movement. He also served as a trustee of Mazon, a Jewish response to hunger.

BIBLIOGRAPHY: The Nearprint Files of the American Jewish Archives, Cincinnati.

[Bezalel Gordon (2nd ed.)]

STERN, JACQUES (1881–1949), French politician. Born in Paris, Stern became private secretary to Leon Bourgeois when the latter was minister of foreign affairs and was elected to the National Assembly in 1914. He established himself as an authority on financial affairs and devised a plan for a supranational organization to solve the problem of reparations and inter-allied debts after World War I. His scheme was frustrated largely because of the frequent change of government in France. Stern held office in several French governments as minister for the merchant marine (1930 and 1933) and minister for the colonies (1935–39). He immigrated to the United States in 1942 where he published *Les Colonies françaises, passé et avenir* (1943). He later committed suicide.

[Shulamith Catane]

STERN, JOSEPH (1803–1858), Hungarian rabbi. Stern was the son-in-law of Menahem *Stern. He studied with Ḥayyim of Kosov in the home of his father Menahem Mendel of Kosov. Stern claimed that he had studied the Shulḥan Arukh, *Yoreh De'ah*, 140 times and the other sections of the Shulḥan Arukh 111 times. He was ordained rabbi by the scholars Abraham David Wahrmann, rabbi of Buchach, and Nathan Nata Mueler, rabbi of Podgaytsy, and was first appointed *rosh bet din* ("head of the *bet din*") and then *av bet din* of Sighet. A bitter quarrel broke out in Sighet, as some of the community wanted to appoint in his stead Eleazar Nissin Teitelbaum, son of Moses Teitelbaum. Stern, who hated contention and strife, wanted to divide the rabbinic post, with Teitelbaum as rabbi and himself as head of the *bet din*. Nevertheless, this did not stop the dispute. Troublemakers accused Stern of attacking the government in his sermons, and he was imprisoned. Nearly all the inhabitants of the town condemned this step, and the government authorities were also convinced of his complete innocence. On the third day of his imprisonment the district officer, together with high government officials, entered the prison and asked forgiveness of the rabbi for the unpleasantness caused him and assured him that the transgressors would be severely punished. After six years of dissension and quarreling Teitelbaum left the town. The only one who supported Stern during difficult times was Jekuthiel Asher Zalman Ansel Zusmir, rabbi of Styria. Of Stern's writings only his introduction to his father-in-law's *Derekh Emunah* (vol. 1, 1856) and one responsum (no. 50) in the *She'elot u-Teshuvot* (1882, 48a–49a) of Zusmir are known.

BIBLIOGRAPHY: J.J.(L.) Greenwald (Grunwald), *Zikkaron la-Rishonim* (1909), 26–28; idem, *Maẓẓevat Kodesh* (1952), 28–38; N. Ben-Menahem, *Mi-Sifrut Yisrael be-Ungaryah* (1958), 94–99.

[Naphtali Ben-Menahem]

STERN, JOSEPH ZECHARIAH (1831–1903), Lithuanian rabbi and talmudist. Stern was born in Neustadt-Shirwint (Woldislovava) in the Suwalki district of Russia to a family which had produced many generations of rabbis. He married the daughter of Mordecai Gimpel *Jaffe and at the age of 20 was appointed rabbi of Jasenovko, Grodno district, where he remained for ten years. He was subsequently appointed rabbi of Shavli, Lithuania, which post he retained until his death. With his phenomenal memory, he mastered ancient and modern Hebrew literature and also interested himself in various branches of Jewish and general knowledge. He published articles on *halakhah* and topical matters (mainly in *Ha-Levanon*), some of them polemics against Moses Leib *Lilienblum who advocated religious reform (1869–70). The poet Judah Leib *Gordon, during his stay in Shavli as a teacher, came to know Stern and regarded him as a symbol of religious fanaticism and inflexibility, portraying him in his poem *Koẓo shel Yod* (in the character Vafsi Hakuzari – a name made by a transposition of the letters of Joseph Zechariah) as a fanatical rabbi with "the soul of a Tatar." This assessment of Stern was severely criticized by those who knew him. Many claimed that he was indeed one of the lenient rabbis, even though he was of a resolute mind and a nonconformist. He displayed a positive attitude toward the Ḥibbat Zion movement and settlement in Ereẓ Israel, but it was expressed only in his letters and writings, and not in actual activity. He wrote responsa and corresponded on halakhic topics with rabbis in many countries.

He was the author of *Zekher Yehosef* (1860), novellae on the Talmud; *Zekher Yehosef* (1899–1902), responsa on the Shulḥan Arukh in four parts; commentaries on the five scrolls (Song of Songs, 1875; Ruth, Lamentations, Ecclesiastes, and Esther, 1876); the Passover *Haggadah* (1898); and *Tahalukhot ha-Aggadot* (1902), on the *aggadah* (appended to *Zekher Yehosef*, pt. 4).

BIBLIOGRAPHY: Sefer ha-Yaḥas, in J.Z. Stern, *Zekher Yehosef* (Responsa), 1 (1899); Z.A. Rabiner, *Ha-Rav Yosef Zekharyah Stern* (1943); B. Jaffe, in: *Yavneh*, 3 (1942), 153–60; G. Katzenelson, *Ha-Milḥamah ha-Sifrutit bein ha-Ḥasidim ve-ha-Maskilim* (1954), 103ff.; *Yahadut Lita*, 3 (1967), 97.

[Benjamin Jaffe]

STERN, JULIUS (1820–1883), conductor and teacher. Born in Breslau, Stern founded the Stern'scher Gesangverein in 1847, and conducted it until 1874. The choir's performance of Mendelssohn's *Elijah* in 1847 established his reputation as a conductor. In 1850 he founded with Adolf Bernhard *Marx and Theodor Kullak the Berlin Conservatory, and was its sole director from 1856. It became one of the main centers of musical education in Germany. In 1869, he conducted the Berlin Symphony Orchestra and in 1873–75 he led the Reichshalle concerts. Stern composed an opera and works for voice, piano, and strings.

STERN, JULIUS DAVID (1886–1971), U.S. newspaper publisher. Stern, who was born in Philadelphia, worked as a reporter on several newspapers during 1908–10, and in 1911–12 was general manager of the Providence *News*. Stern purchased the New Brunswick, New Jersey, *Times* in 1912 and acted as its president until 1914; he then bought the Springfield, Illinois, *News* and *Record* and served as publisher of both from 1915 to 1919, when he bought the Camden, New Jersey, *Evening Courier.* His fast-paced, honest *Memoirs of a Maverick Publisher* (1962) begins with his purchase of the Camden *Morning Post* in 1926, to which he added the Philadelphia *Record* in 1928. Purchasing the New York *Post* in 1933, when it was losing $4,000 a day, Stern determined to make it the most liberal New York newspaper. He installed Ernest *Gruening as its editor, and then Henry Sayler, a long-time associate. Using puzzle competitions and low-priced book offers as well as more conventional features, he restored the paper's circulation before selling it in 1939. An advocate of crusading liberal journalism throughout his newspaper career, Stern supported Franklin D. Roosevelt before Roosevelt's first Democratic presidential nomination in 1932, and in 1940 and 1944 he produced a newspaper for the Democratic National Committee. Stern served as general chairman of the Publishers and Advertisers Division of the United Palestine Appeal in 1936, which raised $1,500,000. In his novel *Eidolon: A Philosophical Phantasy Built on a Syllogism* (1952), Stern pursued the theme of the compatibility of science and religion as paths to truth.

STERN, KURT GUNTER (1904–1956), U.S. biochemist. Born in Tilsit, Germany, Stern worked at the Rockefeller Institute, New York, at the Virchow Hospital, Berlin, and at the Courtauld Institute of Biochemistry, London, finally immigrating to the U.S. in 1935. He was at Yale University School of Medicine (1935–42), and from 1944 professor of biochemistry at the Brooklyn Polytechnic Institute. He also served with the Marine Biological Laboratory of Woods Hole from 1938. His research fields included the structure of genes, techniques of ultracentrifugation, and electrophoresis. He co-authored *Allgemeine Chemie der Enzyme* (1932) and *Biological Oxidation* (1939). He was chairman of the chemists' division of the United Jewish Appeal.

BIBLIOGRAPHY: J.C. Poggendorff, *Biographisch-Literarisches Handwoerterbuch,* 7A (1961), s.v.; H. Mark, in: *Nature,* 177 (1956), 556.

[Samuel Aaron Miller]

STERN, LEONARD (1938–), U.S. entrepreneur. Born in New York City, Stern graduated from New York University. His initial wealth was inherited from his father, Max *Stern, vice chairman of the board of trustees of Yeshiva University, for whom its Stern College for Women was named. Max had emigrated from Weimar Germany to the United States in the 1920s, where he developed the family business, Hartz Mountain, the pet food supplier. After Leonard graduated from college in 1957, he bought out his brother's and sister's share of the family business. By the early 1960s he exercised absolute control of Hartz Mountain. Using questionable techniques that were later the subject of antitrust lawsuits, Hartz captured the pet supply market that catered to dog, cat, and bird owners. Stern broadened Hartz's distribution channels from variety stores into more than 30,000 supermarkets and mass merchandisers. Under his leadership, the Hartz trademark became the most widely known pet supply brand in the United States. By 1984 Hartz controlled 75 to 90 percent of the U.S. market for most U.S. pet supply goods. Its pet supply business was estimated to be worth $400 million and was earning $40 million in annual profits. But there were image problems. Over 20 years Hartz Mountain was the subject of more than a dozen antitrust suits and of investigation by the Federal Trade Commission and the Justice Department. Officials of the company pleaded guilty in March 1984 to a variety of white-collar crimes. In 1979 Hartz Mountain agreed to pay $42 million to A.H. Robins Company, which had accused Hartz Mountain of bribery, perjury, and antitrust violations such as strong-arming distributors and offering stores special deals to sell only Hartz Mountain products.

In 1966 Stern began a major diversification of his business interests by going into active real estate development. By the early years of the 21st century it had become one of the largest privately held real estate companies in the United States. Stern started the real estate operations by purchasing land in New Jersey's Meadowlands near New York City for $20,000 an acre. By 1987 Meadowlands real estate was selling for $500,000 an acre. The value of Stern's property there jumped from $10 million to over $1 billion by the late 1980s. Among the companies that moved their corporate offices from Manhattan to his Meadowlands commercial properties were Equitable Life Assurance Society, Paine Webber, Panasonic, and ITT. He completed a 24-story luxury office tower in Manhattan in 1987 and located the corporate offices there.

From 1986 through 1999, Stern successfully built Stern Publishing into the leading publisher of alternative weekly newspapers, with a total circulation of more than 900,000. Stern published *The Village Voice* in New York, *L.A. Weekly,* the *Seattle Weekly,* the *Cleveland Free Press,* and *City Pages* in Minneapolis. He sold his publishing interests in March 2000.

Over the years Stern built and sold numerous other businesses, including SM/Cork, the largest nonfoods service distributor in the United Kingdom, Harmon Homes, which published 180 free circulation local *Homes* magazines, and the Carpet Magic Company, which manufactured and serviced carpet cleaning machine rental centers in 20,000 retail stores.

In December 2000, in order to concentrate on the management of his growing real estate and financial interests, Stern sold the Hartz Mountain Pet Company, thus ending the family's 76 years of ownership. In recognition of a $30 million donation and his many years as a university trustee, NYU renamed its graduate and undergraduate schools of business the Leonard N. Stern School of Business.

[Stewart Kampel (2nd ed.)]

STERN, LINA SOLOMONOVNA (1878–1968), Russian physiologist and biologist. Born in Lithuania, Lina Stern qualified in Geneva and was later appointed professor of biochemistry at that university. In 1925 she was appointed professor of physiology at the Second Medical Institute of Moscow University and later chief professor and director at the Physiological Scientific Research Institute. In 1932 she was elected a member of the German Academy of Natural Sciences and in 1939 became the first woman to be admitted to the USSR Academy of Sciences. She was the recipient of the Stalin Prize and several Orders of Merit. During the 1948–49 purges in the Soviet Union she was accused of "rootless cosmopolitanism" and removed from her positions, but after the death of Stalin in 1953 was rehabilitated, with all her previous honors restored. Lina Stern made significant contributions to the study of the physiology of the central nervous system, the problems of sleep, the endocrine system, catalase, oxidation ferments, and related subjects. She investigated the hematoencephalic barrier, described the role of the carotid plexus in the brain, the exchange of blood in the plexus and the liquid of the rachis. She published papers in German and Russian, among them "*Die Katalase*" (with F. Battelli, 1910); "*Ueber den Mechanismus der Oxydationsvorgaenge im Tierorganismus*" (1944); and others.

BIBLIOGRAPHY: S.R. Kagan, *Jewish Medicine* (1952), 175–6.

[Suessmann Muntner]

STERN, LOUIS (1904–1972), U.S. businessman and communal leader. Stern, born in Newark, New Jersey, was a partner in the New York stock brokerage firm of Stern and Byck. He was active in the Jewish community of South Orange, New Jersey. On a national level he was president of the *Council of Jewish Federations and Welfare Funds (CJFWF, 1962–64) and the Jewish Community Council of Essex County (1952–55), becoming president of the *National Jewish Welfare Board (JWB) in 1965 and chairman of the CJFWF Overseas Services Committee in 1971. Vice president of the Bureau for Careers in Jewish Service, he was a member of the Board of Governors of the American Jewish Committee and chairman of its Task Force on the Future of the Jewish Community. He was also a member of the Rockefeller Foundation Commission to Study Voluntary Health and Welfare Agencies.

STERN, MALCOLM HENRY (1915–1984), U.S. Reform rabbi, historian, genealogist. Stern, who has been called "the father of Jewish genealogy in America," was born in Philadelphia, Pennsylvania. He received his B.A. from the University of Pennsylvania in 1935, and was ordained at *Hebrew Union College in 1941. In 1957, he earned his D.H.L. from HUC-JIR, which also awarded him an honorary D.D. in 1966. He began his rabbinic career as assistant rabbi at Reform Congregation Keneseth Israel in Philadelphia (1941–47), interrupted by three years of service as a chaplain in the U.S. Army Air Corps during World War II (1943–46), including more than a year in hospital recovering from a near fatal plane crash in North Africa. In 1947, Stern was appointed rabbi of Congregation Ohev Sholom in Norfolk, Virginia, where he remained for 17 years. His activity on behalf of civil rights and the Jewish community earned him the 1964 *B'nai B'rith Man of the Year Award in Norfolk. In 1964, he became the unanimous choice of his colleagues in the *Central Conference of American Rabbis to create their placement office and served as the first director of rabbinic placement for Reform Judaism, a position he held until his retirement in 1980. He also chaired CCAR committees that published three hymnals for Reform Judaism: *Union Songster* (1960); *Songs and Hymns for Gates of Prayer* (1977) and *Shaarei Shirah: Gates of Song* (1987).

In 1981, Stern joined the faculty of the New York campus of Hebrew Union College-Jewish Institute of Religion, initially as counselor for student field work and subsequently as adjunct professor of American Jewish History. There he continued his research, begun in 1950, as genealogist for the American Jewish Archives and the American Historical Society. He was a founding member and president emeritus of the Jewish Genealogist Society, the first organization of its kind. He was also the first and only Jewish member elected a Fellow of the American Society of Genealogists, eventually rising to become that organization's president as well. In addition, he was a Fellow of the National Genealogical Society, and a board member and vice president of the Federation of Genealogical Societies. In 1978, he was appointed Genealogical Representative on the U.S. National Archives Advisory Council, where he served until the year of his death. In 1980, he organized the Genealogical Coordinating Committee, comprising the nation's major genealogical organizations; under their auspices, he established the National Archives Gift Fund, seeking $1.00 per year per genealogist to create finding aids for genealogical research at the National Archives and its regional branches. He was also president of the Jewish Historical Society of New York, and served on the Board of Trustees of the American Jewish Historical Society.

Stern compiled the pioneering volume *American Families of Jewish Descent* (1960), an eight-pound tome containing 26,000 names researched over the course of 10 years of labor. It was the first genealogical survey of Jewish families who settled in the United States between 1654 and 1840, and was lauded as an invaluable research tool in the fields of American and Jewish history. Many American Protestants and Catholics first learned of Jewish roots and branches in their family trees from Stern's data, which served as an important source for Stephen Birmingham's best-selling novel, *The Grandee*. For the United States Bicentennial, the American Archives and American Jewish Historical Society published a revised and enlarged edition, entitled *First American Jewish Families: 600 Genealogies, 1654–1977*. The latest updated third edition, *First American Jewish Families* (1991), contains 50,000 family trees of every Jewish family established in North America by 1840, traced to the present. Stern became such a popular lecturer at genealogical conferences that his speaking engagements were booked as far as 12 years in advance.

In addition to the three celebrated editions of his magnum opus, Stern contributed numerous articles to academic journals and co-authored two books: *American Airlines' Guide to Jewish History in the Caribbean* (with Bernard Postal) and *Life Begins at 40* (1980).

BIBLIOGRAPHY: The Nearprint Files of the American Jewish Archives, Cincinnati.

[Bezalel Gordon (2nd ed.)]

STERN, MAX (1898–1982), U.S. businessman and philanthropist. Stern, who was born in Fulda, Germany, went to the U.S. in 1926. In 1932 he became president of the Hartz Mountain Products Corporation, which subsequently became one of the largest pet food suppliers in the U.S. Extremely active in Jewish affairs and a major supporter of Orthodox institutions, Stern endowed the Stern College for Women of Yeshiva University (1954), was vice chairman of Yeshiva University, and was a founder and member of the board of governors of the University's Albert Einstein College of Medicine. He was president of the Jewish Center in New York and chairman of the International Committee of Shaarei Zedek Hospital. He was also a member of the board of directors of the American Fund for Israel Institutions, and chairman of the board of directors of the Union of Orthodox Congregations of America.

STERN, MAX EMANUEL (Mendel; 1811–1873), Hebrew publisher and writer. Born in Pressburg, he studied in a yeshivah and began teaching at the age of 14. In 1833 he went to Vienna and worked as a proofreader at a printing press; from 1838 he was director of its Hebrew division. He was editor and publisher of *Kokhevei Yiẓḥak* (36 vols., 1845–69), a Hebrew periodical which included poetry, prose, scholarly articles, and translations. He also issued old Hebrew texts with German translations.

BIBLIOGRAPHY: Kressel, Leksikon, 2 (1967), 919.

[Getzel Kressel]

STERN, MENAHEM (d. 1834), Hungarian rabbi. Stern was born in a small village near Sziget (Sighet). Among his teachers were Moses Leib of Sasov, the *Maggid* of Kuzhnitz (Kozienice), and Menahem Mendel of Kosov, and he was ordained rabbi by Meshullam Igra of Tismanitz. Stern served as rabbi of Kalush, Galicia, and then, from 1802, as rabbi and *rosh bet din* ("head of the *bet din*") of Sziget. On the death of Judah ha-Kohen *Heller, author of the *Kunteres ha-Sefekot*, he was appointed *av bet din* of Sziget in 1819, a post in which he served until his death. He was most concerned at the lack of religious knowledge and observance in the Maramures region, and he traveled about the outlying villages and saw simple Jews, farm workers who had forgotten the Torah and were becoming indistinguishable from their Walachian and Ruthenian neighbors. He visited the villages once or twice a month, gathering the inhabitants together and giving them instruction. He established synagogues and ritual baths and arranged **eruvin* in every village of Maramures. He used to say: "Maramures is my garden; I planted it." Stern was the author of *Derekh Emunah* (1856–60), on the Torah and the festivals. He also wrote a book on the four parts of the Shulḥan Arukh, as well as one on the Psalms, but these were apparently lost in the Holocaust.

BIBLIOGRAPHY: J.J.(L.) Greenwald (Grunwald), *Zikkaron la-Rishonim* (1909), 16–20; idem, *Maẓẓevat Kodesh* (1952), 23–28; N. Ben-Menahem, *Mi-Sifrut Yisrael be-Ungaryah* (1958), 87–94.

[Naphtali Ben-Menahem]

STERN, MENAHEM (1925–1989), historian. Born in Poland, Stern immigrated to Israel in 1938. Stern's specialization was the period of the Second Commonwealth, and Greek and Roman texts dealing with Jews and Judaism. His main publications are *Greek and Latin Authors on Judaism and Jews from Herodotus to Plutarch*, (3 vols. 1974–1984); *Studies in Jewish History. The Second Temple Period* (Hebrew), ed. by M. Amit, I. Gafni, and M.D. Herr (1991); *Hasmonean Judaea in the Hellenistic World: Chapters in Political History* (Hebrew), ed. by D.R. Schwartz (1995) (published posthumously). Stern was awarded the Israel Prize in 1977 for the history of Ereẓ Israel and the Jewish people. While walking on his way to the National Library in Jerusalem, he was murdered by a terrorist on June 22, 1989.

[Emmanuelle Main (2nd ed.)]

STERN, MORITZ (1864–1939), German rabbi and historian. Stern, who was born in Steinbach, Germany, was rabbi at Kiel (1891–98), head of the Jewish secondary school in Fuerth (Bavaria) until 1899, and of a religious school in Berlin until 1905, when he was appointed librarian of the *Berlin Jewish Community Library. Under him, this library developed into one of the most important institutions of its kind in Europe with over 70,000 volumes. Stern also acted as curator of the art collection of the Berlin community from its inception in 1917 until 1930, and organized in 1929 the Moses Mendelssohn bicentenary exhibition.

Stern's main interests in scholarship were his researches into the history of German Jews in the Middle Ages, the blood libel, and communal, family, and individual histories. He compiled the "Bibliographie der Schriften A. Geigers," in Ludwig Geiger's *Abraham Geiger* (1910).

BIBLIOGRAPHY: Shunami, Bibl., nos. 2271–72, 3549.

STERN, MOSHE (1935–). Born in Budapest, the son of Israel Stern, who was chief cantor, Stern immigrated to Israel in 1950. In 1955 he was appointed *ḥazzan* to the chief synagogue in Reḥovot, and in 1958 to the *Hechal Shlomo Synagogue in Jerusalem. From 1963 to 1968 he was chief cantor of the Great Synagogue in Johannesburg, and from 1968 to 1977 of Beth-El Synagogue in Boro Park, New York. In 1977 he returned to Israel. Subsequently the High Holidays saw Stern *daven* for more than a decade at Club Hebraica in Sao Paulo, Brazil, while the rest of the holidays would often find him presiding at the pulpit of the Great Synagogue on Allenby Street in Tel Aviv. Stern was regarded as one of the greatest cantors and extemporizers of our time and was constantly touring the Jewish world giving concerts of Jewish liturgical music.

He made many recordings, often of his own compositions, which though traditional in nature are always memorable and showstoppers.

[Akiva Zimmerman / Raymond Goldstein (2nd ed.)]

STERN, NOAH (1912–1960), Hebrew poet. Born in Jonava, Lithuania, he moved to the U.S. when he was 17. In 1935 he settled in Palestine where he worked as a news translator for **Davar* and as a teacher in a Tel Aviv high school. During World War II he served for four years in the Jewish Brigade. A growing mental depression, which was aggravated by the Holocaust, appears to have prevented him from striking roots in postwar Israel. His few poems, published in various periodicals, aroused little attention, though his translation of T.S. Eliot's *The Waste Land* (*Ereẓ ha-Shemamah*, 1940), was lauded by many critics. He served a prison term for attempted manslaughter, and in 1960 he committed suicide. His poems, *Bein Arfillim* ("In the Haze," Tel Aviv, 1966), a sheaf of prose sketches, and literary reviews were published posthumously. In his early verse, along with his attempts at more immediate and more intense expression, much is awkward, obsolescent, and graceless. In the poems written under the impact of his war experiences, sensitivity gives way to solemn rhetoric verging on the banal. The more personal imagery – recurring metaphors of decay and disease – sometimes appears as conventional trappings rather than a genuine expression of an immediate experience. But it would be unfair to measure Stern's poetry solely by the poem as a whole. The single phrase, the concise cluster of images that flare suddenly from the half-extinguished ashes are his most effective skills. It is here that the strange, unexpected epithet – at times, undoubtedly, a corollary of his unwieldy language – evokes a vital, highly suggestive presence. Perhaps his most impressive poems are those which, like *Mikhtav Beinayim* ("An Interim Letter," 1942), take to task the realities of Ereẓ Israel as they existed for the immigrant of the 1930s, with a keener awareness of conflict and contradiction and in a manner more outspoken and unadorned than that of many of his confreres who enjoyed wider popularity at the time. Here his poetic shortcomings are more than offset by the balance between the pungent statement and the resonant image. With the publication in 1966 of his collected work, interest in Stern greatly revived. A collection of poems, *Egrof ha-Goral*, appeared in 2002.

BIBLIOGRAPHY: A. Broides, in: N. Stern, *Bein Arfillim* (1966), 5–16. **ADD. BIBLIOGRAPHY:** H. Schimmel, *"Demut ha-Sofer ha-Ivri N. Stern,"* in: *Moznayim* 31 (1971), 358–62; B. Link, *"Shirato shel N. Stern ve-Zikkatah le-Merkazei ha-Sifrut ha-Ivrit bi-Shenot ha-Sheloshim,"* in: *Ha-Kongres ha-Olami le-Mada'ei ha-Yahadut, Yerushalayim* 10, 2–3 (1990), 289–294.

[Natan Zach]

STERN, OTTO (1888–1969), physicist and Nobel prizewinner. Born in Sorau, Stern worked with *Einstein in Prague and Zurich. From 1915 to 1921 he lectured in theoretical physics at the universities of Frankfurt and Rostock, and in 1923 was appointed professor of physical chemistry at Hamburg. This was his most fruitful period. Stern succeeded in making the molecular beam method a sufficiently sensitive tool for measuring nuclear magnetic moments. He provided proof that the movements of atoms and molecules could be represented by the propagation of de Broglie waves. His work confirmed Planck's quantum theory and the dual nature of matter. In 1933, at the first sign of Nazi interference in the affairs of his department, Stern left Germany for the U.S., and the Buhl Foundation built him a laboratory at the Carnegie Institute of Technology in Pittsburgh, Pennsylvania. There, with I. Estermann, a former colleague expelled by the Nazis, he carried on research in molecular physics. In 1943 Stern was awarded the Nobel Prize for his research in the development of the molecular beam method of detecting the magnetic moment of protons. From 1945 he lived in Berkeley, California.

BIBLIOGRAPHY: *Mc-Graw-Hill Modern Men of Science* (1966), 446–8.

STERN, PHILIP COHEN (1847–1933), Jamaican lawyer and politician. Stern was born in Kingston and educated at University College, London, becoming a barrister in London in 1869 and in Jamaica in 1870. He was also admitted as a solicitor in Jamaica, where he lived until 1878 and after 1893. In 1883 he founded and edited *Pump Court*, the Temple newspaper and review. Ill health forced him to leave England soon afterward and he returned to Jamaica where he rapidly established a reputation as an outstanding lawyer and was involved in most of the famous legal cases in Jamaica during the next few decades. Stern sat in the Legislative Council from 1895 to 1908. On his retirement from the council he was appointed its clerk (1908–24) and served as registrar of the Supreme Court (1909–10). He was three times mayor of Kingston.

[Bernard Hooker]

STERN, ROBERT A.M. (1939–), U.S. architect. Stern was born in New York City and received his bachelor's degree from Columbia University. He was appointed dean of Yale School of Architecture in 1999. In achieving this position, he returned to the school where he graduated in 1965 with a master's degree. He worked first with architects Richard Meier and John S. Hagmenn. From the time of his graduation, Stern emerged as a world-class architect as well as a prolific author of analytical books on earlier forms of architecture, especially the architectural development of New York City, and a fellow of the American Institute of Architects. His commentaries on New York's architecture also include extensive analysis of architectural designs of Manhattan synagogues. Stern suggested, for example, that the classical design of Congregation Shearith Israel on West 19th Street in New York marked a sign of assimilation and dissociation of the local Jewish community from the Moorish style in synagogue design. Stern suggests that Congregation Emanu-El on Fifth Avenue, which uses more of an Italian style, was designed to compete with major cathedrals in the city. In addition to analytical writing, Stern also hosted, in 1986, a multi-part public television series on architecture entitled "Pride of Place: Building the American Dream."

As with many architects who were schooled in this period, Stern was influenced strongly by Frank Lloyd Wright and the Bauhaus, particularly Le Corbusier. Wright's influence is most striking in the Jewish Center at Princeton University (1993), which echoes aspects of Wright's style as well as the Prairie School of architecture. In 1975, Stern wrote a biography of Philadelphia architect George Howe, famous for his design of the Philadelphia Savings Fund Society Building (1929–32), heralded as the first American skyscraper in the International Style, as well as his association with Louis Kahn and Oscar Stonorov.

Stern has suggested the need for architects to create what he calls "a compelling sense of place." His architectural achievements include the Center for Jewish Life at Princeton University, public libraries in Nashville, Bangor, Miami Beach, Jacksonville, and Columbus, Ga.; he has designed many country houses in his "Shingle-style" which harkened back to early 20th-century houses, American homes with a rambling character. In the mid-1980s, Stern developed an association with the Walt Disney Company, embarking on many projects including the planned community of Celebration in Orlando, Fla. Other educationally oriented buildings include the Brooklyn Law School Building, Darden School of Business at the University of Virginia, the Ohrstrom Library at St. Paul's School in Concord, N.H., and the American Revolution Center at Valley Forge, Penn. In 2004, Stern won the Palladio Award for the John L. Vogelstein '52 Dormitory at the Taft School in Watertown, Conn.

Stern's work has been exhibited extensively in American museums and he was also selected on three occasions (1976, 1980 and 1996) to be included in the Venice Biennale.

BIBLIOGRAPHY: P.M. Dixon, *Robert A.M. Stern: Buildings and Projects 1999–2003* (2003); V. Scully, *Robert A.M. Stern: Buildings and Projects 1987–1992* (1992).

[Stephen Feinstein (2nd ed.)]

STERN, SAMUEL MIKLÓS (1920–1969), Orientalist. Stern belonged to the great tradition of Hungarian Jewish Orientalist scholarship. After studies at the Hebrew University and in Oxford, he was employed on the new edition of the *Encyclopaedia of Islam* and in the coin room in the Ashmolean Museum in Oxford before becoming, in 1957, a fellow of All Souls College, Oxford, where he remained for the rest of his life.

Stern's large scholarly output encompassed many areas of Jewish and Islamic scholarship. He wrote on Islamic numismatics and history, on *Fatimid documents, on the so-called *Epistles of the Brethren of Purity*, and on early Islamic philosophy, as well as editing an English translation of Ignaz *Goldziher's *Muhammedanische Studien*, one of the foundation stones of modern Orientalist scholarship. But his prime achievement, accomplished at a very early stage in his career, was the recognition that the mysterious *kharjas*, or endings, to the *muwashshahāt*, a genre of strophic poetry in Arabic (or in Hebrew) produced in medieval al-Andalus, Islamic *Spain, were occasionally not in Arabic (or Hebrew), but in a form of early Spanish transliterated into Arabic letters. These were in fact among the very earliest witnesses to the character of early Spanish. His interpretation of the very difficult material aroused much controversy (some of it colored by antisemitism), and discussion of details in it continues, but its overall correctness is undisputed. The material contributes greatly to our understanding of medieval Iberian social relations, linguistic behavior, and much else.

Among Stern's other contributions to Jewish scholarship was a study (with A. Altmann) of *Isaac Israeli, a Neoplatonic Philosopher of the Early Tenth Century* (1958).

BIBLIOGRAPHY: S. Sela, "The Interaction of Judaic and Islamic Studies in the Scholarship of S.M. Stern," in: M. Kramer (ed.), *The Jewish Discovery of Islam* (1999), 261–71; Bibliography of Stern's writings by J.D. Latham and H.W. Mitchell, in: L.P. Harvey (ed.), S.M. Stern, *Hispano-Arabic Strophic Poetry* (1974), 231–45.

[David J. Wasserstein (2nd ed.)]

STERN, SIGISMUND (1812–1867), German teacher and leader of the Berlin Reform movement. After studying philology in Berlin, in 1835 Stern succeeded I.M. *Jost as headmaster of the Berlin Jewish boys' school. In 1845 he gave a series of lectures on the tasks of Judaism which aroused wide interest and controversy. He wished to bring about a revival of religious life, waking it from its then current lethargy, which he felt was caused by the contradictions and frustrations faced by Jews in the modern world. Following his proposal calling for the erection of a "German-Jewish church," leading classes of Berlin Jewry responded by forming an "Association for Reform in Judaism," in which Stern played a central role. Contending that Judaism must free itself from its national heritage, he initiated radical reforms and the separate organization of the reformers in Berlin. In 1848, after standing unsuccessfully as candidate for that year's National Assembly, Stern accepted the directorship of the Frankfurt on the Main Philanthropin Jewish school. He enlarged the institution, raised its academic standards, and introduced pedagogic (but not religious) innovations, which made him an acknowledged leader of the German methods.

BIBLIOGRAPHY: A. Galliner, *Sigismund Stern* (1930); idem, in: YLBI, 3 (1958), 177–81; W.G. Plaut, *Rise of Reform Judaism* (1963), 288. **ADD. BIBLIOGRAPHY:** M.A. Meyer, *Response to Modernity: A History of the Reform Movement in Judaism* (1988), 125–29.

STERN, STEVE (1947–), U.S. novelist and short-story writer. Stern was born in Memphis and educated at Rhodes College, where he received his B.A., and at the University of Arkansas at Fayetteville, where he received an M.F.A. in creative writing. Among the most gifted writers of his generation, Stern brought an unusual locale to American-Jewish writing: the "Pinch," the once-vibrant East European Jewish community of Memphis. He had become acquainted with the Pinch while working at the Center for Southern Folklore, making transcriptions of oral histories. He became the director of the "Lox and Grits" project, one that involved preserving the recollections of those who lived in the Pinch.

It was only when he began to write in his mid-twenties that he discerned the echoes of the literature that became important to him. Among the influences on his work are Kafka and Peretz: he calls them "palate-cleansers." Babel and Malamud are what he terms "compasses" that he refers to when his work "goes awry."

His work keeps alive the grand traditions of mythographic narrative. In his fiction, Jewish characters find themselves confronting angels, the figure of death, and tales within tales that ensnare the teller and the listener. His writing can be placed in the long tradition of Yiddish folktales and *aggadah* that see our daily life as carried out within a culture's embroidered rendition of the sacred. His works can also be placed alongside Jewish writers who separated a strict realism from the poetics of the imagination: a choice between how the world empirically appears, as opposed to the possibilities we imagine the world to contain. Among his works are *Isaac and the Undertaker's Daughter* (1983); *The Moon and Ruben Shein: A Novel* (1984); *Lazar Malkin Enters Heaven: Stories* (1986); *Harry Kaplan's Adventures Underground* (1991); *A Plague of Dreamers: Three Novellas* (1994), *The Wedding Jester* (1999; National Jewish Book Award Winner), and *The Angel of Forgetfulness* (2005).

[Lewis Fried (2nd ed.)]

STERN, WILLIAM (Louis; 1871–1938), German philosopher and psychologist; grandson of Sigismund *Stern. Stern, who was born and educated in Berlin, was the founder of personalistic psychology and a pioneer in many other fields of psychology. He taught philosophy and psychology at Breslau (1897–1915), before becoming professor of psychology and philosophy at the University of Hamburg and head of the Institute of Psychology (1916). Stern co-edited *Zeitschrift fuer angewandte Psychologie* (1907–33). Expelled by the Nazis, he fled to Holland (1933) and from there went to the U.S. In 1934 he became professor of psychology at Duke University (North Carolina), where he remained until his death. At Breslau, Stern invented an instrument, the Tonvariator, to effect changes in pitch, and studied the perception of change in many sense modalities. His approach foreshadowed the methods of Gestalt psychology. Its importance lay in its opposition to the "constancy hypothesis," the notion that there has to be a simple one-to-one relationship between stimulus and response. Stern was also interested in the psychology of the courtroom and of the witness stand. Child psychology engaged his attention throughout his life, and formed a basis for his studies in IQ and personalistic psychology. He and his wife, Clara, studied their own and other children by making use of questionnaires and the direct observation technique. This work led to a study of intelligence, and it was in this connection that he improved the method of Binet by introducing the ratio of mental age to chronological age (IQ), as an age-independent index of intelligence (1912). Stern found that a wealth of influences arrayed themselves in a unified pattern in the developing individual. He called it a *unitas multiplex* ("a whole of many parts"). His convergence theory stressed the convergence of character traits with the totality of environmental influences. His studies of Helen Keller (1910) were an attempt to validate his theories.

Stern divided his energies between the applied work of his institute, famous for its early identification of gifted children, and his studies of the individual as a living, unique whole, capable of goal-directed behavior and experience, a concept intended to weld the multiplicity of psychological functions into a complex unity. It was in connection with this personalistic theory that he rejected his early formulation of the IQ as too narrow, although he defended its heuristic value. Although his ideas were not readily accepted in American psychology and he gained few disciples, his point of view foreshadowed many of the trends which later gained prominence in formulations of psychological theory.

His works include *Die Analogie im volkstuemlichen Denken* (1893); *Psychologie der Veraenderungsauffassung* (1898); *Psychologie der individuellen Differenzen* (1900); *Zur Psychologie der Aussage* (1902); *"Helen Kellers Persoenliche Eindruecke"* in *Zeitschrift fuer angewandte Psychologie*, 3 (1910), 321–33; *Die psychologischen Methoden der Intelligenzpruefung und deren Anwendung an Schulkindern* (1912); *Person und Sache* (3 vols., 1906, 1918, 1924); *Psychologie der fruehen Kindheit bis zum sechsten Lebensjahre* (1914) transl. as *Psychology of Early Childhood up to the Sixth Year* (1930); *Allgemeine Psychologie auf personalistitscher Grundlage* (1935), transl. by H.D. Spoerl as *General Psychology, from the Personalistic Standpoint* (1938). In collaboration with Clara Stern he wrote *Die Kindersprache* (1907) and *Erinnerung, Aussage und Luege in der ersten Kindheit* (1908).

[Helmut E. Adler]

Stern's wife, CLARA JOSEEPHY (1878–1945), was a child psychologist. She collaborated with her husband on research projects involving the growth and development of their three children. This joint effort resulted in two monographs on the mental and spiritual development of the child from birth through the primary school years. The first, *Die Kindersprache* (1907, 1922³), an investigation from the psychological and linguistic standpoints, traced the development in children from the ability to articulate the first word to that of composing sentences. As source materials, Clara Stern used the diaries recording observations of her own children as well as available scientific literature. The second monograph, *Erinnerung, Aussage und Luege in der ersten Kindheit* (1908, 1931⁴), interpreted children's statements in psychological and personal terms. Her diaries were the basis of her husband's *Psychology of Early Childhood up to the Sixth Year* (1928).

[William W. Brickman]

BIBLIOGRAPHY: *A History of Psychology in Autobiography*, 1 (1930, repr. 1961), 335–88; G.W. Allport, in: *Character and Personality*, 5 (1936/37), 231–46; H. Werner, *ibid.*, 7 (1938/39), 109–25; G.W.

Allport, in: *American Journal of Psychology*, 51 (1938), 770–4; idem, in: B.B. Wolman (ed.), *Historical Roots of Contemporary* (1940), 1–15 (Ger.); *William Stern bibliography*, compiled by Eva Michaelis-Stern (1971).

STERNBERG, ERICH-WALTER (1898–1974), composer. Sternberg was born in Berlin, where he studied law and also music (with Hugo Leichtentritt and Adolf Aber). His first compositions already incorporated material from East European Jewish folklore (the finale of the First String Quartet was based on Eliakum *Zunser's *Der Parom*, "The Ferry"). After a visit to Ereẓ Israel in 1924, he settled there permanently in 1932 with the first wave of composers trained in Western Europe.

Many of his works had biblical themes: *Joseph and his Brethren*, a suite for string orchestra (1938); *The Twelve Tribes of Israel*, variations for orchestra (1942); *David and Goliath*, a cantata for bass-baritone and chamber orchestra (text by Mathias Claudius, transl. by J. Aḥai); and *Noah's Ark*, a symphony. Others are connected by their themes or texts with liturgical traditions: *Yishtabbaḥ*, for choir, baritone solo, and speaker, to words by Judah Halevi (1945), and *Shema Yisrael*, a symphonic poem. Settings of texts from European literature are more frequent in Sternberg's work than in that of other Jewish composers: a major work is *The Raven* (based on Edgar Allan Poe's poem in the translation by Vladimir Jabotinsky), for baritone and orchestra. Other works of note are a children's opera *Dr. Dolittle* (1932); a suite for his stage music to the Habimah production of Shalom Aleichem's *Amkha* (1935); *The Resurrection of Israel*, for baritone and orchestra; and various vocal, choral, chamber, and orchestral works.

BIBLIOGRAPHY: *Who Is Who in ACUM* (1965); P.E. Gradenwitz, *Music and Musicians in Israel* (1959), 36–39, 159–60; I. Shalita, *Enziklopedyah le-Musikah. Ishei ha-Musikah ha-Yisra'elit ve-ha-Kelalit* (1959), 770–3.

[Bathja Bayer]

STERNBERG, JACOB (1890–1973), Yiddish editor, poet, and dramatist. Born in Lipkany, Moldova (former Bessarabia), Sternberg attended a Russian secondary school in Kamenets-Podolski. In 1908 he began publishing poetry and short stories in the Yiddish press, and in 1911 the Odessa daily *Gut Morgn* printed his translation of Ḥ.N. *Bialik's popular poem "*Hakhnisini Taḥat Kenafekh*" ("Take Me under Your Wings"). In 1914 he settled in Romania and wrote and produced nine short plays and satiric dramatic revues for the Yiddish theater in Bucharest in collaboration with Jacob *Botoshansky (1917–18). He directed the Vilna Troupe during its extended stay there (1924–26), staging plays by I.L. *Peretz, *Sholem Aleichem, Osip *Dymov, and Gogol. Between 1920 and 1930 he also edited several short-lived Yiddish periodicals. In 1935 he collected his lyrics and grotesques in the volume *Shtot in Profil* ("City in Outline"). In 1940 Sternberg moved to Bessarabia but soon fled from the Nazis to Uzbekistan. In 1945 he returned to direct the Yiddish theater of Kishinev, capital of the Soviet Moldavian Republic. Sternberg was a member of the *Jewish Anti-Fascist Committee in Moscow, and was thus arrested in 1948 and spent five years in a Siberian labor camp. His reputation was rehabilitated after the death of Stalin, and a collection of his poems was published in 1959 in Russian translation. After 1961 his Yiddish essays and critical articles were frequently printed in *Sovetish Heymland*, of whose editorial board he was a member. A volume of his collected poetry *In Krayz fun Yorn* ("In the Circle of the Years") appeared in Bucharest (1970), and his collected essays in Tel Aviv (1987); a selection of his lyrics in Hebrew translation appeared in 1967.

BIBLIOGRAPHY: Rejzen, Leksikon, 4 (1929), 628–31; S. Bickel, *Rumenye* (1961), 235–53. **ADD. BIBLIOGRAPHY:** LNYL, 8 (1981), 649–52; A. Spiegelblatt, in: *Di Goldene Keyt*, 73 (1971), 200–11; W. Tambur, in: *Bukareshter Shriftn*, 8 (1985), 5–15.

[Sol Liptzin]

STERNBERG, JOSEF VON (1894–1969), film director. Von Sternberg, born in Vienna (though the "von" was a Hollywood addition), was one of the best-known film directors of the 1920s and 1930s. He used the camera as it had not been used before, capturing the play of light and the symbolism of shadow. Out of his struggle against the commercialism of the major studios came films of distinction and influence. He first drew attention with *The Salvation Hunters* (1925), a realistic presentation of the lower depths of American life. For Paramount studios he made the first gangster film, *Underworld*, in 1927. In 1930 he went to Germany to direct the Ufa company's first talking picture, *The Blue Angel*. He cast the unknown Marlene Dietrich in the leading role and the film became a part of cinema history. There followed six more films with Dietrich in Hollywood. During World War II, he made films for the Office of War Information. Von Sternberg amassed a noteworthy collection of 20th-century art. He published his autobiography, *Fun in a Chinese Laundry*, in 1965.

BIBLIOGRAPHY: H.G. Weinberg, *Josef von Sternberg* (Eng., 1967); G. Castello, in: *Encyclopedia Dello Spettacolo*, 9 (1962), 356–60, incl. bibl.

[Stewart Kampel]

STERNBERG, KURT (1885–1942), German philosopher. He was born in Berlin and taught there at the Lessing Hochschule. A rigorous neo-Kantian advocating a faithful return to Kant, he was involved in the neo-Kantian discussions over the relationship between *Naturwissenschaften* and *Kulturwissenschaften* and wrote on the nature of historical studies, *Zur Logik der Geschichtswissenschaft* (1914). He criticized Spengler's pessimism in his *Idealismus und Kultur* (1923). Other writings deal with Hauptmann, Heine, and Rathenau. His last books treat philosophical problems in the Bible. Among his main works are *Beitraege zur Interpretation der kritischen Ethik* (1912), *Neukantische Aufgaben* (1931), and *Die Geburt des Etwas aus dem Nichts* (1932). He was murdered in Auschwitz.

[Richard H. Popkin]

STERNBERG, LEV YAKOVLEVICH (1861–1927), Russian anthropologist, born in Zhitomir. He was sentenced in 1886 to ten years' exile in Sakhalin as a member of the Narodnaya Volya (Populist Party). Like his friends V.G. *Bogoraz and V. *Jochelson, Sternberg studied ethnography and resolved to devote himself to this subject. He became an authority on the culture of the Gilyaks of northeast Siberia, and later he and his two friends participated in the great Jessup North Pacific Expedition headed by Franz *Boas, in which he was responsible for investigation of the Gilyak culture. After his return from exile (1897), Sternberg was appointed ethnographer at the St. Petersburg Museum of Anthropology and Ethnography and wrote a number of papers on the customs and languages of the east Siberian peoples. After the Russian Revolution Sternberg was appointed professor of ethnography at the University of Leningrad and of anthropology at the Geographical Institute, and with Bogoraz helped to develop these academic disciplines in the USSR. An energetic Marxist, he carried forward certain doctrines in that tradition, for example, primitive communism, and its familial correlate, group marriage, according to the theory of Engels; he polemicized on behalf of these views against the doctrines of Schmidt, *Freud, and *Lévy-Bruhl. Yet his ethnological theory was eclectic and "idealistic," stressing the creativity of the human spirit. As a result, his Marxist orthodoxy was impugned but he was permitted to continue his teaching. He was a member of the Academy of Science in St. Petersburg (later Leningrad), and with Bogoraz assisted in the cultural development of the Siberian peoples, utilizing his ethnological knowledge to foster the political modernization of indigenous peoples in transition. Sternberg took an active part in Jewish social and cultural life. He was one of the founders of the "Popular Jewish Group" (the *Vinawer-*Sliosberg group) and edited its periodicals, participated in the Jewish Historical Ethnological Society, and contributed to Jewish periodicals, such as *Yevreyskaya Starina*, which he edited and where he published papers on the anthropology and social psychology of Jews. Sternberg was one of the group of Jewish scholars in Leningrad who endeavored to continue research on Jewish subjects under the Soviet regime.

BIBLIOGRAPHY: L. Krader, in: IESS, 2 (1968), 116–9 s.v. *Bogoraz* (incl. bibl.); E. Kagaroff, in: *American Anthropologist*, 31 (1929), 568–71; B. Brutskus, in: *National Jewish Monthly*, 43 (1928/29), 234ff., 241; M.A. Krol, *Stranitsy moyey zhizni*, 1 (1944); Z. Rudi, in: *He-Avar*, 16 (1969), 182–91.

[Ephraim Fischoff]

STERNBERG, SARAH FRANKEL (1838–1937), daughter of ḥasidic rabbi Joshua Heschel Teomim Frankel and wife of the *ẓaddik* Hayyim Samuel Sternberg of Chenciny, a disciple of the famed Seer of Lublin. Sternberg was one of the few women who attained any stature in the ḥasidic courts of the 19th century. After her husband's death, Sarah Sternberg functioned successfully as a *rebbe* in Chenciny and was highly regarded for her piety and asceticism. She fasted regularly and avoided meat, except on the Sabbath. She also became well-known for her wise parables, and other famous rabbis consulted her and requested her blessing. As a charismatic leader, Sternberg was most famous for her apparently miraculous powers. Many women made pilgrimages to see her and left *kvittlach* (written petitionary prayers), a common practice among ḥasidim, who believed that the intervention of a *rebbe* would assure that their request to God was granted. One of Sarah's original letters of blessing has been preserved in a late 20th-century authorized history of the Chencin-Ozherov ḥasidic dynasty; it is affirmed with her personal seal, evidence that suggests she was considered a legitimate *rebbe*. Sarah had many children and a number of her sons and grandsons were well-known *rebbes* and respected scholars. At least one of her daughters, Hannah Brakhah, also participated in the ḥasidic court, along with her husband Elimelekh of Grodzinsk. Hannah remains one of the few ḥasidic women who were active while married. Sarah Frankel Sternberg lived to the age of 99 and was survived by more than 250 grandchildren and great-grandchildren. According to contemporary reports 10,000 people attended her funeral.

BIBLIOGRAPHY: N. Loewenthal, "Women and the Dialectic of Spirituality in Hasidism," in: E. Etkes et al., *Be-Maglei Ḥasidim: Kovez Mehkarim shel Professor Mordecai Wilensky* (1999); N. Polen, "Miriam's Dance: Radical Egalitarianism in Hasidic Thought," in: *Modern Judaism* 12 (1992), 1–21; E. Taitz, S. Henry, and C. Tallan, *The JPS Guide to Jewish Women: 600 B.C.E.–1900 C.E.* (2003).

[Emily Taitz (2nd ed.)]

STERNBERG, SIR SIGMUND (1921–), British businessman, interfaith activist, and patron of Reform Judaism. Born in Budapest, Hungary, Sternberg came to England in 1939 when antisemitic laws made it difficult to receive a higher education in Hungary. After the war he became a leading metal recycler and smelter and was later president of the Metal Trades Industry Association. He also served as chairman, for 15 years, of ISYS Ltd., the computer firm. Sternberg is best known, however, for his remarkable activities on behalf of interfaith work in Britain. He was chairman of the executive of the International Council of Christians and Jews and was one of the founders of the Three Faiths Forum, which includes representatives of Islam. In 1988 Sternberg was awarded the Templeton Prize in Religion for having "advanced the public understanding of God and spirituality." He received numerous international honors and in 1985 became one of the few Jews to be made a papal knight. He was also one of the most important leaders of Reform Jewry in Britain, in 1981 endowing the Sternberg Centre for Judaism, the headquarters of Reform Judaism in the country, and he was president of the Reform Synagogues of Great Britain. He was knighted in 1976.

[William D. Rubinstein (2nd ed.)]

STERNE, HEDDA (1916–), U.S. painter, printmaker, educator. Born Hedda Lindenberg in Bucharest, Romania. Between 1932 and 1934 she studied art history and philosophy at Bucharest University, and then in Vienna and Paris. She affiliated herself with the Surrealists, especially Victor Brauner, and exhibited in the Paris Salon of Surrealist Independents in 1938. Sterne arrived in the U.S. in 1941. She exhibited at Peggy Guggenheim's Art of This Century Gallery that same year. The artist had her first solo exhibition at the Betty Parsons Gallery in 1943, a show consisting of assemblages recalling totems. Also in 1943, Sterne married cartoonist Saul Steinberg. She is probably most familiar to students of art history as the only woman featured in the famous photograph of the Abstract Expressionists, "The Irascibles" by Nina Leen, published in the January 15, 1951, issue of *Life* magazine. She often signed her work "H. Sterne" to mask her identity as a woman, a strategy necessary when the work of female artists in 1950s New York encountered the risk of being dismissed as "delicate." Sterne adopted many different styles throughout her career, often at the same time: While a painting like *Birds* (1944–45) recalled the simple, evocative shapes of Adolph Gottlieb, a composition titled *Fixtures* of the same year depicts a stylized, but definitively representational interior, complete with radiator. As late as 1997, Sterne returned to a motif she had established in the 1940s, that of a cruciform in *U.S.A.* Sterne also painted portraits throughout her career. She received a Fulbright Fellowship to study in Venice in 1973. Her work has been exhibited at the Art Institute of Chicago, the Corcoran Gallery, the Museum of Modern Art, and the Whitney Museum. A retrospective at the Krannert Art Museum, University of Illinois is scheduled for 2006. Her art is in the collections of the Art Institute, the Carnegie Museum, the National Museum of Women in the Art, and the Whitney Museum, among other institutions. She lives in New York.

BIBLIOGRAPHY: A.E. Gibson, *Abstract Expressionism: Other Politics* (1997); C. Greenberg, "Review of Exhibitions of Hedda Sterne and Adolph Gottlieb," in: *Arrogant Purpose, 1945–49*, vol. 2. *Clement Greenberg: The Collected Essays and Criticism.* ed. by John O'Brian (1986).

[Nancy Buchwald (2nd ed.)]

STERNE, MAURICE (1877–1957), U.S. painter, educator, printmaker, and sculptor. Born in Libau, Latvia, his family moved to Moscow; at the age of 10, the artist immigrated to the United States. In America, he first studied map engraving, then painting and drawing at the National Academy of Design (1894–99) under the tutelage of Thomas Eakins. He also studied at Cooper Union in New York City. After receiving a Mooney Traveling Scholarship from the National Academy, he traveled widely in Europe and Asia from 1904 to 1915, although maintaining a base in New York City. In fact, Sterne became an American citizen in 1904. He first traveled to Paris, absorbing the lessons of Degas, Renoir, and Cezanne, then to Italy, where he studied Mantegna and Piero della Francesca. Sterne next lived in Greece, studying 4th- and 5th-century statuary. In 1916, he traveled to Taos, New Mexico, where he and his wife Mabel Dodge devoted themselves to the study and preservation of American Indian culture. Sterne's images from this time include sensitive portraits of Indians, with great attention to details of dress. Two years later, he returned to Italy. By 1910, he was in Germany, where he executed many commissioned paintings. From 1910 to 1914, he visited Bali, Java, Burma, and India. Work from this time, characterized by a movement away from the lessons of academic painting to a more decorative and spontaneous use of line and form, and brighter palette, reflected Sterne's enchantment with the people and places he encountered here. He was elected president of the Society of American Painters in 1929. In this same year, Sterne won a competition to create a public sculpture in Worcester, Massachusetts. Made of limestone, the Rogers-Kennedy memorial depicts a couple pulling a plow atop a base featuring an array of bas-reliefs which illustrate events in the life of an agricultural community. In 1933 he had a retrospective show at the Museum of Modern Art, the first for an American artist. The critic Lewis Mumford praised Sterne's Balinese paintings as the highlight of the exhibition. Sterne worked in a variety of media: paint, charcoal, etching, and marble, among others. Sterne's subjects included portraits, still-lifes, genre-scenes, seascapes, as well as themes borrowed from the Impressionists. The latter include dancehall scenes such as *Entrance of the Ballet*, which appropriates the subject matter, and the economy of light and form characteristic of Degas and Toulouse-Lautrec. Sterne's talents as an artist emerge most forcefully in his depictions of women, whether the quietly luminous marble *Sitting Figure* (1932) or the water, crayon, and charcoal *Study of My Wife*, which captures a figure in a few emotive and economical strokes. Sterne's style underwent a radical change after an illness suffered in 1945, becoming looser, freer, and more colorful. Sterne taught at the California School of Fine Arts (1935–36) and the Art Students League in New York. He divided his time between New York and Provincetown. His work is in the collections of the Metropolitan Museum of Art, the Museum of Fine Arts, Boston, the National Gallery of Art, the Pennsylvania Academy of Fine Art, the San Francisco Museum of Modern Art, the Smithsonian American Art Museum, and the Whitney Museum.

BIBLIOGRAPHY: C.L. Mayerson (ed.), *Shadow and Light: The Life, Friends and Opinions of Maurice Sterne* (1965); C. Roth, *Jewish Art. An Illustrated History*, revised ed., Bezalel Narkiss (1971).

[Nancy Buchwald (2nd ed.)]

STERNE, SIMON (1839–1901), U.S. lawyer and reformer. Sterne, who was born in Philadelphia, was admitted to the bar in Pennsylvania (1859) and New York (1860). He practiced law in New York and concurrently pursued the study and teaching of political economy, which he called the "science of liberty," and helped to introduce a number of practical reforms. On a visit to England in 1865, he encountered some of the leading personalities in social reforms, including John Stuart Mill, John Bright, and Thomas Hare, who were proponents of proportional representation. They encouraged Sterne's energetic espousal of a number of causes, including free trade, proportional representation, improvement in the drafting of legislation, democratizing political party methods and standards, and improving the accountability of railroads to the public, all of which he supported in his speeches, articles, and organizational activities.

Sterne was most widely known for the achievement of two successful reforms: demolition of the Tweed ring's hold on New York City politics and the regulation of railroads in the public interest through the creation of the Interstate Commerce Commission (ICC), the first U.S. regulatory commission. As the secretary of the Committee of Seventy, which for several years pursued New York City's boss Tweed and the "corrupt judges, venal legislators, and complacent lawyers" who had cooperated to put and retain him in power, Sterne was instrumental in obtaining Tweed's conviction in 1873 for forgery and larceny. Sterne's role in the creation of the ICC began with his drafting a state railroad regulation bill in 1874. He conducted the investigations of the New York State Hepburn Commission into railroad administrative abuses (1879–80), and in 1882 the legislature passed a railroad commission act along the lines of Sterne's draft.

The legislative commission's report became a model for local and national government investigation and regulation of railroads. When the U.S. Senate began preparing legislation for national regulation, Sterne was consulted. He drafted some of the provisions of what was to be the law establishing the Interstate Commerce Commission, and was retained as counsel in some of the commission's most important lawsuits. In his private law practice Sterne was counsel for a number of corporations, railroad companies, and businesses.

BIBLIOGRAPHY: J. Foord, *Life and Public Services of Simon Sterne* (1903).

STERNHARZ, NATHAN (1780–1845), disciple and companion of Naḥman of *Bratslav, organizer of Bratslav Ḥasidism, and its leader after Naḥman's death. Nathan was born in Neirov and was known as a scholar and talented writer even in his youth. In 1793 he married the daughter of David Ẓevi, rabbi of Shargorod and a *Mitnagged*. Nathan was drawn to Ḥasidism and visited some of the great Ḥasidim. The decisive event of his life was a meeting with Naḥman of Bratslav in 1802, when the two formed a deep and unique friendship that lasted until Naḥman's death. Nathan soon became Naḥman's most devoted disciple. He spread knowledge about his teacher and expounded his teaching. In fact, Naḥman's personal charisma became integral to the thought and habits of his followers through Nathan's devotion and efforts. Although Nathan became the actual leader of Bratslav Ḥasidim on Naḥman's death in 1810, he refused to assume the official title of ḥasidic rabbi, a gesture which established the special character of Bratslav Ḥasidim who acknowledged Naḥman as their only rabbi. Nathan worked arduously to spread Naḥman's teachings. He guided and extended the movement of Naḥman's followers. He often visited the Bratslav Ḥasidim and sent them numerous letters, thus spreading the rabbi's teaching and encouraging the Ḥasidim who suffered persecutions that culminated in their excommunication in 1835 by Moses Ẓevi of *Savran. With charm and moderation he refuted the calumnies against the movement and, at the same time, encouraged the Ḥasidim in their firm belief in the greatness of Naḥman and in the truth of his teachings. Despite violent personal persecution (including denunciation to the authorities and arrest), Nathan not only succeeded in establishing the basic patterns and direction of the movement (e.g., visiting Naḥman's tomb in Uman) but also succeeded in maintaining and even increasing the number of its followers. Nathan transcribed and edited Naḥman's teachings, everyday talks, and stories.

He published, on his own initiative, Naḥman's principal books, *Likkutei Moharan* (Ostrog, 1808), *Sefer ha-Middot* (Mogilev, 1811), and *Sippurei Ma'asiyyot* (Berdichev, 1895). His own literary activity was prolific and varied. He wrote, for example, *Ḥayyei Moharan* (1875), *Siḥot ha-Ran* (1864), and *Shivḥei ha-Ran* (1864), depicting his teacher's life and greatness. Fulfilling Naḥman's request "to turn his teaching into prayers," he wrote also *Likkutei Tefillah* (Bratslav, 1824–27), a poetic work based on *Likkutei Moharan*. He continued to expound and develop Naḥman's teaching in his great work, *Likkutei Halakhot* (1847–48). Nathan died in Bratslav and was buried in Uman beside his teacher.

BIBLIOGRAPHY: H. Zetlin, *R. Nakhman Braslaver* (Yid., 1952).

[Adin Steinzalts]

STERNHEIM, CARL (1878–1942), German playwright. The son of a banker, Sternheim was born in Leipzig and, after university studies, lived in several German cities. His early writing showed little originality, bearing the imprint of Hauptmann, Wedekind, Wagner, Nietzsche, and George. His creative breakthrough occurred in *Die Hose* (1911), the first in a series of witty and abusively anti-bourgeois comedies, later grouped together in the cycle *Aus dem buergerlichen Heldenleben* with plays such as *Buerger Schippel* (1913) and *Der Snob* (1914). Sternheim admired the feudal aristocracy but showed a distaste for the upper middle class. In attacking the bourgeoisie he was attacking the bourgeois in himself, just as his often vitriolic antisemitic outbursts were a form of self-abuse, as in his essays *Berlin oder Juste Milieu* (1920) and *Tasso oder Die Kunst des Juste Milieu* (1921). Sternheim thus unwittingly played into the hands of Hitler. His comedies are nevertheless remarkable for their immaculate construction and for the terseness of their diction. In his short stories, mostly collected in *Chronik des zwanzigsten Jahrhunderts* (2 vols., 1918), Sternheim allowed linguistic experimentation to get out of hand; this has made his only novel, *Europa* (1920), unreadable. A document of strange interest is Sternheim's autobiography, *Vorkriegseuropa im Gleichnis meines Lebens* (1936). He suffered from a nervous disorder and died in Brussels.

BIBLIOGRAPHY: H. Karasek, *Carl Sternheim* (Ger., 1965); W. Wendler, *Carl Sternheim, Weltvorstellung und Kunstprinzipien* (1966), 307–22 (bibl.); S. Kaznelson (ed.), *Juden im deutschen Kulturbereich* (1962³), 52–53; W. Stauch and V. Quitzow, *Carl Sternheim, Bewusstsein und Form* (1969).

[Wolfgang Paulsen]

STERNSCHUSS, MOSHE (1903–1992), Israeli sculptor and winner of the Dizengoff and Jerusalem prizes for sculpture. Born in Poland, Sternschuss immigrated to Palestine in 1926. He studied at the Bezalel Academy of Art and Design in Jerusalem, and developed as a sculptor. He began as a realist but later evolved towards a semi-abstract stylization of the human form.

STERNSTEIN, JOSEPH PHILIP (1925–), Conservative rabbi and Zionist leader. Sternstein graduated Brooklyn College (1944) and received his law degree from St. John's University and his rabbinic ordination from the Jewish Theological Seminary (1948) and a D.H.L. in 1961.

After serving as a rabbi in Glen Cove, Long Island (1948–50), Dayton, Ohio (1950–61), and New York City (Temple Ansche Chesed, 1964–69), he was appointed rabbi of Temple Beth Sholom of Roslyn Heights, New York. A prominent Zionist, he became a member of the executive of the World Union of General Zionists, and was president of the Zionist Organization of America (ZOA) (1974–78). He was president of the American Zionist Federation and served on the presidium of the World Zionist Council. He was also a national president of the Jewish National Fund. Sternstein wrote extensively on modern Jewish and Zionist affairs and is the author of *Diagnosis and Prognosis* (1956), a study of American Zionism. He also wrote on *The Theology of the Sfat Emet of Rabbi Yehudah Aryeh Leib of Ger (1847–1905)* (1961).

[Mordecai S. Chertoff / Michael Berenbaum (2nd ed.)]

STERN-TAEUBLER, SELMA (1890–1981), German historian. Selma Stern-Taeubler, born in Kippenheim (Baden), was the first girl to attend the Gymnasium in Baden-Baden. She then studied history and languages at the universities of Heidelberg and Munich, graduating in 1913. She specialized at first in general German history, but became interested in the history of German Jewry. In 1919 she was appointed a research fellow at the Akademie fuer die Wissenschaft des Judentums in Berlin at the invitation of its founder and director, the historian Eugen *Taeubler, whom she married in 1927. Her special field was compiling source material on the relationship between the Prussian state and its Jews from 1648 to 1812. Her scholarly publications were based on the premise that Judaism had to be studied in the context of the political and cultural environment.

The first two volumes of her chief work, *Der preussische Staat und die Juden*, were published in 1925, and a third volume followed in 1938, but almost the entire edition was destroyed by the Nazis. *Jud Suess. Ein Beitrag zur deutschen und zur juedischen Geschichte* was published in 1929 (repr. 1973), and many scholarly articles appeared in magazines. In 1934 the Akademie was closed by the Nazis, and in 1941 Selma Stern-Taeubler and her husband immigrated to the United States, settling in Cincinnati. In 1947 she became the first archivist of the American Jewish Archives (at the Hebrew Union College, Cincinnati), a post she held until her retirement in 1957. In 1960 Selma Stern-Taeubler moved to Basle, Switzerland, where, between 1970 and 1975, she completed the following four volumes of *Der preussische Staat und die Juden*.

During and after her stay in the United States she continued to write important scholarly works, including *The Court Jew; A Contribution to the History of the Period of Absolutism in Central Europe* (1950; repr. 1985) and *Josel von Rosheim, Befehlshaber der Judenschaft im Heiligen Roemischen Reich Deutscher Nation* (1959; Eng. 1965). Her historical novel, *The Spirit Returneth…* (1946; Ger. 1972: *Ihr seid meine Zeugen*), deals with the persecution of the Jews during the time of the Black Death and helped the author to understand the persecutions of her own time.

ADD. BIBLIOGRAPHY: Fritz Bamberger, in: *Aufbau*, vol. 26 (July 29, 1960); M. Sassenberg (ed.), *Apropos Selma Stern* (1998); idem, *Selma Stern…* (2004; with bibl.); idem, *Selma Stern, erste Frau in der Wissenschaft des Judentums* (2005).

[Frederick R. Lachman / Archiv Bibliographia Judaica (2nd ed.)]

STETTIN (Szczecin), city in Pomerania, N.W. Poland. Jews are first mentioned there in 1261 in a charter granted by Duke Barnim I which extended *Magdeburg law to the city. In all probability, however, they had been living there for some time. The charter was renewed in 1371 by dukes Casimir IV and Swantibor III. All Jews were expelled from *Pomerania in 1492/93 and they did not return until the 17th century. Jews were occasionally employed at the Prussian mint in Stettin; in 1753 the medalist Jacob Abraham of Strelitz worked there as a die cutter, while at the same time Moses Isaak and Daniel *Itzig supplied the mint with silver. Permanent residence was denied to the Jews throughout the 18th century. The modern community grew up from 1812. In 1818 it numbered 18, including the Hebrew grammarian Ḥayyim b. Naphtali Coeslin (J.H. Borchard), and by 1840 had increased to 381. The first synagogue was built in 1834/35. The community grew through emigration from Posen (Poznan) and West Prussia, reaching 1,823 in 1871; in 1875 a new synagogue was dedicated; an organ was introduced in 1910. From 1867 the community also had an Orthodox prayer room. During the course of the 19th century, Jewish books were printed in the city. The community maintained a religious school from 1850; the cemetery was opened in 1821. The Jewish population increased to 2,757 in 1910, then declined to 2,703 in 1930 and 2,365 in 1933. The following rabbis officiated in Stettin: W.A. Meisel (1843–59); Abraham Treuenfels (1860–79); Heinemann *Vogelstein (1880–1911); Max *Wiener (1912–26); Max Elk (1926–35); K. Richter (1936–38); and H. Finkelscherer, who served from 1938 until the deportation in 1940; he perished with the other deportees. On the eve of the Nazi accession to power, the community maintained an orphanage and an old-age home, as well as numerous charitable organizations.

During the night of Feb. 11/12, 1940, the Jews of Stettin were deported together with other Pomeranian Jews to Belzyce, Glusk, and Piaski. After the so-called population transfers of a few Jews, the remainder were murdered in Belzyce on Oct. 28, 1942. Only a very few survived. Following the departure of the last "non-Aryans" (partners of mixed marriages) after World War II, Jews from Poland settled in Stettin, which had become part of Poland. A new community was organized, numbering 1,050 in 1959. In 1962 two Jewish producers' cooperatives were active, and the community maintained a school and a synagogue. The majority of Jews left after the Six-Day War.

BIBLIOGRAPHY: U. Grotefend, *Geschichte und rechtliche Stellung der Juden in Pommern* (1930); FJW, 73–75; I. Bialostocki, in: BŻIH, no. 71/72 (1969), 83–105; J. Peiser, *Die Geschichte der Synagogen-Gemeinde zu Stettin* (19652); *Lebenszeichen aus Piaski. Briefe Deportierter aus dem Distrikt Lublin 1940–43* (1968); Germ Jud, 2 (1968), 795–6; E. Taeubler, *Mitteilungen des Gesamtarchivs der deutschen Juden*, 1 (1909), 37–41.

[Bernhard Brilling]

STEUERMAN, ADOLF RODION (1872–1918), Romanian poet and journalist. Born in *Jassy, Steuerman became a physician there, but devoted himself mainly to literature and journalism. He became chief editor of the local newspaper, *Opinia*, and for three years also of *Răsăritul*, a Zionist weekly published in the city. He contributed to many Romanian journals and reviews as well as to almost all the Romanian Jewish periodicals of his day. He became known as one of the wittiest and most ironical social critics in his attacks on the tyrannical regime and his struggle for democracy. As a poet, Steuerman was noted especially for his collections: *Sărăcie* ("Poverty") and *O toamnă la Paris* ("An Autumn in Paris"), both published in 1897, and *Lirice* ("Lyrics"). Many of these poems deal with the theme of Jewish homelessness in an antisemitic society. In 1915 he collected all his poems on Jewish themes into a volume entitled *Spini* ("Thorns"). As a translator, he was often drawn to Jewish themes, publishing Romanian versions of poems by writers such as *Heine and Judah *Halevi. In World War I, Steuerman served as a medical officer. His experiences and reflections in those years are expressed in the sonnets published posthumously by his friend, the writer Eugen *Relgis, under the title *Frontul roșu* ("The Red Front", 1920). *Cartea băiatului meu* ("My Son's Book", 1924), another product of Steuerman's war experiences, contains autobiographical notes meant for his son; it contains much interesting material on Jewish life in Jassy during his early years. After his return from the front, Steuerman became increasingly depressed and committed suicide.

BIBLIOGRAPHY: Ibrăileanu, in: *Lumea Nouă* (Feb., 1898); N. Iorga, *Istoria Literaturii Române Contemporane* (1934); M. Schwarzfeld, pref. to *In depărtări* (1936), Botez, in: *Insemnări Literare* (1918), no. 85; *Poeții "Contemporanului"* (1956).

[Abraham Feller]

STEUERMANN, EDWARD (1892–1964), pianist and teacher. Born in Lemberg, Poland, Steuermann studied piano with Busoni and theory with Arnold *Schoenberg in Berlin. Later he taught at the Jewish Conservatory in Cracow, Poland. In 1936 he settled in the United States where he taught at the Philadelphia Conservatory and at the Juilliard School of Music. Steuermann devoted himself to the dissemination of modern music, particularly that of Schoenberg. He gave the first performances of all of Schoenberg's piano works and chamber works with piano accompaniment, and transcribed his orchestral works for piano.

°**STEUERNAGEL, CARL** (1869–1958), Protestant German Bible critic. Born in Hardegsen, Steuernagel taught Bible at the University of Halle. In 1914 he was appointed professor at Breslau. A prolific writer, he wrote the commentaries on Deuteronomy (1899; 1923^2) and Joshua (1899; 1923^2) for the *Handkommentar zum Alten Testament* in addition to a general introduction to the Hexateuch (1900), and the volumes of Job (1923), Proverbs (1923), and Esther (1923) for *Die Heilige Schrift des Alten Testaments*. His *Der Rahmen des Deuteronomiums* (1894) and *Die Enstehung des deuteronomischen Gesetzes* (1895, 1901^2) are attempts to explain the composition of Deuteronomy as a composite redaction of a number of Deuteronomic strands which are characterized by forms of address and the usages of singular and plural elements of speech. He maintained that Isaiah 40–55 was written at the same time by the same hand, immediately before the Return (538 B.C.E.); that "the Servant of the *Lord" is a personification of the people Israel, a view which later influenced R. Kittel, L. Gautier, T.H. Robinson, O. Eissfeldt, and others; and that Hosea 3 is an account by the prophet of the incident reported in chapter 1 by people from his environment. In the *K. Marti Festschrift* (in: BZAW, 41 (1925), 266–73), he pleaded for the importance of biblical theology as a historical discipline in its own right which complements the historical study of the Hebrew religion.

From 1903 he edited the *Zeitschrift des deutschen Palaestina-Vereins*, and he wrote an introduction to the study of the Bible, Apocrypha, and Pseudepigrapha (*Lehrbuch der Einleitung in das Alter Testament, mit einem Anhang ueber die Apokryphen und Pseudepigraphen*, 1912) which stressed archaeological and textual insight. Besides numerous articles, he produced the following works: *Die Einwanderung der israelitischen Staemme in Kanaan* (1901); *Hebraeische Grammatik* (1903; 1948^{11}); *Methodische Einleitung zum hebraeischen Sprachunterricht* (1905); and *Neue Beitrage zu Colonia Agrippinensis* (1916, with R. Schultze).

BIBLIOGRAPHY: M. Noth, in: ZDPV, 74 (1958), 1–3; W. Schmauch, in: *Theologische Literaturzeitung*, 83 (1958), 547–50.

[Zev Garber]

STEUSS, DAVID (d. 1387 or 1388), head of a family of bankers in Austria. The Steuss were the most important financiers of their time, serving Austrian and foreign rulers, ecclesiastical lords, and noblemen. The grandfather of David, banker of the first Hapsburgs in Austria, moved from Klosterneuburg to Vienna in 1241. David, son of Hendlin, was the banker of Duke Albert II and archdukes Rudolf IV and Albert III, financing their campaigns and the construction of St. Stephen's in Vienna. Among other business ventures he lent a considerable sum to the city of Bruenn. Steuss had business relationships with the city of Vienna, heads of the Church, and government officials far from the borders of Austria. He was exempt from all jurisdiction excepting that of the archduke himself. He collected and allocated the contributions levied on the Jews and was able to amass great wealth, but was finally imprisoned in 1382 by Albert III in order to extort an exorbitant sum of money. The business records of the Steuss family with Hebrew marginals have been preserved, and the names of David, his sons Jonah, Jacob, and Hendlin, and other relatives appear frequently in debt registers. David's son-in-law was the celebrated Vienna rabbi *Meir b. Baruch ha-Levi. The archduke's treasurer Bishop John of Brixen characterized David as an honest and wise man. At one time in 1364 he lent money to Bishop John who designated his cathedral as collateral. David's son Jonah died a victim of the Vienna persecutions of 1420 (*Wiener Gesera*) when the Steuss properties were confiscated by the archduke.

BIBLIOGRAPHY: J.E. Scherer, *Rechtsverhaeltnisse der Juden in deutsch-oesterreichischen Laendern* (1921), 398–9; S. Krauss, *Wiener Geserah von dem Jahre 1421* (1920), index; *Juedisches Jahrbuch fuer Oesterreich* (1932/33), 132–5; REJ, 96 (1933), 199–209; M. Grunwald, *Vienna* (1936), index; B. Bretholz, *Bruenn* (1938), 66; Baron, Social^2, 9 (1965).

[Hugo Knoepfmacher]

STIEGLITZ (18th century), Russian bankers from Waldeck, Germany, where BERNHARD (HIRSCH) became court agent to the Prince of Waldeck in 1767. His sons NICOLAI (1772–1821) and LUDWIG (1778–1843) were baptized and immigrated to St. Petersburg, Russia. There they formed a successful banking house which acquired a virtual monopoly in Russian banking and the *Rothschilds transacted their Russian business through Stieglitz. In 1826 Ludwig Stieglitz, the head of the house, was made a baron. His son, ALEXANDER (d. 1884), was instrumental in establishing the Russian State Bank and served as its first president (1860–66). In 1863 he liquidated his father's bank. A great philanthropist, he founded the School of Arts in St. Petersburg. Members of the Stieglitz family married into the Baltic and Russian nobility, and their St. Petersburg house was a famous social and artistic center.

BIBLIOGRAPHY: H. Schnee, *Die Hoffinanz und der moderne Staat*, 3 (1955), 90–94; S. Ginzburg, *Meshumodim in Tsaristishn Rusland* (1946), 199.

[Joachim O. Ronall]

STIEGLILTZ, ALFRED (1864–1946), U.S. photographer. Stieglitz, who was born in Hoboken, New Jersey, led the way to the emergence of photography as an art form. His contributions to photography were closely matched with his efforts on behalf of modernist painters in their struggle for recognition. In the dual role of craftsman and prophet, Stieglitz took pictures thought to be impossible and gave a rising generation of modernist painters a place to show their work. His photography was hung in nearly every major museum, the first photographer to be so honored. After Stieglitz's family moved to New York in 1871, he enrolled at the City College of New York at 17 to study engineering. In 1881 he went to Berlin, but soon terminated his engineering studies after he bought his first camera there. He became the first amateur photographer in Germany, and he soon defied tradition. Instead of pictures by daylight, Stieglitz took them at night. He was the first to use a camera in snow or rain, the first to photograph skyscrapers, clouds, and airplanes and was a pioneer in the use of color. He left Europe in 1890 and returned to the United States with a large camera, a tripod, and a small box with a ground glass and bellows and a shutter that cost 50 cents. He made some of his greatest images with this unpretentious equipment. His first major collection traced the development of New York. Two of his most popular pictures were taken in 1892: a horsecar lumbering up Fifth Avenue in a raging blizzard and a driver watering his steaming horses at an old rail terminal. "Winter – Fifth Avenue" and "The Terminal – Street Car Horses" became internationally known. Stieglitz then turned to nature studies of clouds, trees, grass, and woods and branched out to things made by man: houses, barns, autos, planes. He allowed no retouching and no eccentric angle shots. Also, he took no money for his photographs, and later found himself living in poverty. His best photographic work ended in the 1920s.

Stieglitz also ran an art gallery, known as 291, where he showed the works of Cezanne, Matisse, Picasso, Braque, Brancusi, John Marin, and Marsden Hartley. He also launched the careers of Charles Demuth, Arthur Dove, Max Weber, and Georgia O'Keeffe, whom he married in 1924. Under Stieglitz, O'Keeffe's paintings of flowers and simple landscapes, many done at his retreat in Lake George, N.Y., found their way into American collections. A simple photograph of O'Keeffe's hands became a classic. Inside the gallery, Stieglitz took a number of portraits that rhymed the faces of his sitters with the shapes on the walls. His portrait of his daughter, Kitty, with a fuzzy hat on, rhymes with Picasso's "Head of a Woman" just behind her. The gallery was closed in 1917, but in 1929 Stieglitz opened An American Place, which also became an influential gallery. In 1934 *Equivalents* allowed celebrated poets, writers, artists, and leading photographers to contribute their interpretation of Stieglitz both as artist and personality. His brother was the chemist Julius Oscar *Stieglitz.

BIBLIOGRAPHY: D. Norman, *Alfred Stieglitz: Introduction to an American Seer* (1960); H.J. Seligmann, *Alfred Stieglitz Talking* (1966); D. Norman (ed.), (1947).

[Stewart Kampel (2nd ed.)]

STIEGLITZ, JULIUS OSCAR (1867–1937), U.S. organic chemist. Born in Hoboken, New Jersey, Stieglitz was from 1892 professor at the University of Chicago, and from 1915 chairman of its chemistry department. He was attached to the U.S. Public Health Service 1918–31. He published papers on molecular rearrangements, catalysis, the theory of color production, and the application of the electronic theory of valency and wrote *The Elements of Qualitative Chemical Analysis* (2 vols.,

1911) and *Chemistry and Recent Progress in Medicine* (1926), and edited *Chemistry in Medicine* (1928). He was president of the American Chemical Society and of the Institute of Medicine of Chicago.

STIGLITZ, JOSEPH E. (1943–), U.S. economist, professor; joint winner of the 2001 Nobel Prize for economics. Born in Gary, Indiana, to parents Nathaniel and Charlotte, he received a B.A. from Amherst College, and a Ph.D. from Massachusetts Institute of Technology (MIT). Stiglitz began his academic career teaching at such prestigious institutions as Yale, Stanford, Oxford, and Princeton. Stiglitz was an economic adviser to President Clinton from 1992 to 1997, and then spent three years (from 1997 to 2000) as a chief economist and senior vice president at the World Bank. He then taught economics and international and public affairs at Columbia University in New York in the Columbia Business School, the Graduate School of Arts and Sciences department of economics, and the School of International and Public Affairs. In 2000, Stiglitz founded the Initiative for Policy Dialog (IPG), based out of Columbia University. Along with teaching and work with the IPG, Stiglitz was a prolific writer, with a number of books and articles on world and national economics.

Growing up in a middle-class family in industrial Gary, Stiglitz took note of the struggling steel town where plants were laying off hundreds of employees, or closing outright. He writes in his autobiography for the Nobel Prize that "the poverty, the discrimination, the episodic unemployment could not but strike an inquiring youngster: why did these exist, and what could we do about them." As to the Gary of Stiglitz's youth, he goes on to describe that he had "the good fortune of having dedicated teachers, who in spite of relatively large classes, provided a high level of individual attention." First physics, and then economics, were his interests at Amherst, where he felt he could marry his passion for history, writing, and applying mathematics to social issues. At MIT, Stiglitz had at least four Nobel Prize winners as professors, no doubt catalysts for his later becoming a Nobel Prize winner as well.

As chief economist at the World Bank, Stiglitz's outspoken criticism of policies undertaken by the World Bank's sister organization, the International Monetary Fund (IMF), caused a stir that led to his resignation in 2000. His issues with the IMF are discussed in some of his writings, including *Globalization and Its Discontents*.

Stiglitz founded the Initiative for Policy Dialogue (IPD) in July 2000 at Columbia University. A global network of economists, political scientists, policymakers and others, the IPD was created as a think tank for solutions to global economic policy-making. The IPD analyzes economic policies and alternatives, and helps countries solve growth and globalization problems through task forces, dialogues, workshops, and research.

The Royal Swedish Academy of Sciences awarded the Bank of Sweden Prize in Economic Sciences in Memory of Alfred Nobel (known as the Nobel Prize) to Stiglitz and two others (George A. Akerlof and A. Michael Spence) in 2001, based on their individual contributions to the field of research in markets known as "asymmetric information." Stiglitz's contributions were in the form of clarifying the opposite type of market adjustment, showing that asymmetric information offers keys to understanding market phenomena such as unemployment and credit rationing. Stiglitz's other recognitions include the American Economic Association's John Bates Clark Award (1979). He was also a fellow to the National Academy of Sciences, the American Academy of Arts and Sciences, the Econometric Society, the American Philosophical Society, and the British Academy.

Among Stiglitz's body of written work is *The Roaring Nineties* (2004); *Globalization and Its Discontents* (2002); *Whither Socialism?* (1994); and others, including titles edited by Stiglitz, and a variety of articles published in journals and magazines.

[Lisa DeShantz Cook (2nd ed.)]

°**STILES, EZRA** (1727–1795), U.S. scholar and theologian, and president of Yale. Stiles, born in North Haven, Connecticut, was ordained in 1749, and, after teaching at Yale College (1749–55), served as a minister in Newport, Rhode Island, until the Revolution of 1776. His early missionary urge led him to seek descendants of the *Ten Lost Tribes of Israel in the American Indians and clouded his attitude toward the Jews, but he soon entered into a close and friendly relationship with the Newport Jewish community, attending the dedication of the Touro Synagogue in 1763. From 1769 Stiles kept a *Literary Diary* (published in 3 vols., 1901) which contained a detailed account of Newport Jewry, its leading members (such as the merchant Aaron *Lopez, whom he greatly admired), and its synagogue, where he often attended services. One of the outstanding American scholars of his age, Stiles made his lifelong aim the pursuit of knowledge, studying Hebrew from 1767 and mastering the Bible commentators, some Talmud, the Zohar, Syriac, and Arabic within the next five years. When the Ereẓ Israel emissary Raphael Ḥayyim Isaac *Carigal visited Newport in 1773 and preached in the synagogue, Stiles, greatly impressed by the former's scholarship and personality, sought his company and maintained a correspondence with him for several years. From 1778 until his death Stiles was president of Yale – a post in which he had been preceded by an earlier American Hebraist, Timothy Cutler (1694–1765) – and was also professor of ecclesiastical history and divinity. He made the study of Hebrew compulsory for all freshmen at Yale, and at the commencement exercises of 1781 delivered an oration in Hebrew. To the end of his life Yale's president was devoted to the Hebrew language and culture, which he thought essential to a liberal education and sound grasp of the Bible.

BIBLIOGRAPHY: A. Holmes, *Life of Ezra Stiles* (1798); G.A. Kohut, *Ezra Stiles and the Jews* (1902); W. Willner, in: AJHSP, 8 (1900), 119–26; M. Jastrow, *ibid.*, 10 (1902), 5–36; F. Parsons, *Six Men of Yale* (1939).

STILLER, BEN (1965–), U.S. writer, director, actor. Born in New York, N.Y., to comedy duo Jerry Stiller and Ann Meara, Stiller attended college at UCLA for just nine months, but made his acting debut in New York in John Guare's *The House of Blue Leaves* (1984). He followed this with his film debut in *Fresh Horses* (1986). In 1989, he went to work for *Saturday Night Live*, but lasted only five weeks, describing the backstage atmosphere as "very negative." Stiller returned to Los Angeles, creating a half-hour sketch comedy show, *The Ben Stiller Show*, which aired on MTV before being picked up by Fox. Although the show was canceled after 12 episodes, it won great critical acclaim, winning a 1993 Emmy for Outstanding Writing in a Variety or Music Program. Stiller next directed and acted in *Reality Bites* (1994) (also starring Winona *Ryder, Ethan Hawke, and Janeane Garofalo). He then played a young father searching for his birth parents in the comedy *Flirting with Disaster*, directed by David O. Russell. The film was both a commercial and critical hit. Two comedies followed: *The Cable Guy* (starring Jim Carrey and Matthew Broderick), which Stiller directed; and *There's Something about Mary*, a mega-hit, gross-out comedy in which Stiller starred with Cameron Diaz. Since 2000, Stiller has been incredibly prolific, starring in cult comedies such as *Zoolander* (2001), flops such as *Duplex* (2003) and *Envy* (2004), giant commercial successes such as *Meet the Parents* (2000) and its sequel *Meet the Fockers* (2004), as well as being the animated voice of Alex in *Madagascar* (2005).

[Amy Handelsman (2nd ed.)]

STILLING, BENEDICT (1810–1879), German pioneer in surgery and anatomy. Stilling, who was born in Kirchlain, Hesse, studied at Marburg, and in 1833 was appointed district surgeon in Cassel, where from 1840 he concentrated on his private practice. He was the first German surgeon to perform ovariotomy by the extraperitoneal method. However, this method did not immediately attract the attention of his colleagues and was "rediscovered" ten years later by the British surgeon Doffin. Stilling was the first to transplant a section of the cornea from the eye of one rabbit to that of another, and preserve the transparency. He coined the term "vasomotoric nerves" and was the first to prove the vasomotor function of the sympathetic nervous system. Stilling also studied the anatomy and physiology of the central nervous system and wrote numerous books on various aspects of the structure of the spinal cord. He introduced the sliding microtome and serial section into microscopic technique. His son JACOB BENEDICT STILLING (1842–1915) was born in Cassel. In 1884 he was appointed professor of ophthalmology at the University of Strasbourg. He first described pseudo-isochromatic tables and made significant contributions to the study of color sense, color blindness, and perimetry. His numerous publications deal mainly with the subjects of color sense and myopia.

BIBLIOGRAPHY: S.R. Kagan, *Jewish Medicine* (1952), 148–9, 516; *Biographisches Lexikon der hervorragenden Aerzte*, 5 (1934).

[Suessmann Muntner]

STILLMAN, LOUIS (**"Lou" Ingber**; 1887–1969), U.S. boxing gym manager and owner. In 1921, Stillman was hired by businessman Alpheus Geer to manage his Marshall Stillman Movement gym, despite Stillman's knowing nothing about the sport of boxing. Shortly after his appointment, an antisemitic incident at a nearby gym led to a mass transfer of the disaffected Jewish clientele, amongst them a number of quality fighters. Now calling himself Lou Stillman to simplify things, he started charging admission not only to those who trained, but also to those who wanted to watch. The scheme led to a cycle of increasing numbers of attention-hungry fighters and trainers, followed by more spectators willing to pay the famous 15-cent entrance fee. In 1931, Stillman purchased the gym outright from Geer and moved it to 919 8th Avenue in Manhattan, where it became a magnet for America's greatest boxers. Located two blocks from the old Madison Square Garden, "the University of 8th Avenue" boasted the likes of Joe Louis, Jack Dempsey, Gene Tunney, Sugar Ray Robinson, and Rocky Graziano. The attraction of Stillman's Gym was magnified by the regular presence of entertainment stars such as Frank Sinatra, Dean Martin, Jerry Lewis, Buddy Hackett, and Tony Bennett, who were all boxing enthusiasts. When asked to portray Rocky Graziano, Paul Newman spent many hours studying Stillman's Gym, and in the resulting film, *Somebody Up There Likes Me*, Matt Crowley played the role of Lou Stillman. Those who remember the gym in its heyday were struck not only by the quality of the fighters and constant stream of VIPs, but equally by the physical dilapidation and filth of the gym that Stillman relished as the perfect environment for grooming the next generation of toughened prize fighters. Stillman himself was remembered as a colorful if irascible character who always wore a .38 pistol at his side and who treated everyone with equal contempt, but who also enjoyed hosting unskilled boxers if their banter was particularly humorous. When Stillman finally sold his gym in 1959, over 35,000 boxers had trained in its legendary confines.

[Robert B. Klein (2nd ed.)]

STILLMAN, NORMAN ARTHUR (1945–), U.S. historian. Born in New York, Stillman was educated at the University of Pennsylvania (B.A. 1967, Ph.D. 1970), with postgraduate work at the Jewish Theological Seminary (1970–71). Stillman taught at New York University, 1970–73, the State University of New York at Binghamton, 1973–95, and from 1995 at the University of Oklahoma, where he was the Schusterman/Josey Professor of Judaic History. He was a visiting professor at Haifa University, 1979–80, and lectured at many universities. He was a fellow of the National Endowment for the Humanities, a Bronfman Fellow, and a Littauer Fellow. He was a member of the Middle East Studies Association of North America, the American Oriental Society, the Association for Jewish Studies, the Conference on Jewish Social Studies, the Society for Judeo-Arabic Studies, the Israel Historical Society, and the Societe de l'histoire du Maroc.

Stillman was a student of S.D. *Goitein, whom he considered his mentor, and his work carried on in the field of studies established by Goitein's work on Jewish life and culture in Islamic societies. He is a recognized authority on the history of the Islamic world and of Sephardi and Middle Eastern Jewish culture as well as an advocate of Israel and Zionism. While his account of Sephardi and Middle Eastern Jewish history is sympathetic, it has attracted some criticism from non-Ashkenazi Israeli Jews, who feel that he sees their history through a European Zionist framework that distorts it and minimizes the hardships and disabilities they experience in Israeli society.

Stillman has been quoted as having said that he affiliated himself with academic Jewish studies rather than Middle East studies because of "barely veiled antisemitism" in Middle East studies departments. His principal published works are *The Jews of Arab Lands: A History and Source Book* (1979), *Studies in Judaism and Islam* (edited with Shelomo Morag and Issachar Ben-Ami, 1981), *The Language and Culture of the Jews of Sefrou* (1985), *The Jews of Arab Lands in Modern Times* (1991), *Sephardi Religious Responses to Modernity* (1995), and *From Iberia to Diaspora: Studies in Sephardic History and Culture* (edited with Yedida K. Stillman, 1999). With his late wife Yedida Kalfon Stillman, a Moroccan-Israeli scholar, he published a translation of *Travail in an Arab Land* by Samuel Romanelli (1989), and he edited her posthumous work *Arab Dress: A Short History* (2000). He has also published numerous scholarly articles and reviews. For his publications in Hebrew, he writes under the name Noam Stillman.

[Drew Silver (2nd ed.)]

STINE, R.L. (1943–), U.S. author. Born in Columbus, Ohio, Robert Lawrence Stine graduated from Ohio State University, where he was renowned locally by the name Stine, the editor of the campus humor magazine, *The Sundial.* Upon graduation he moved to New York City, where he became head writer of the Nickelodeon series *Eureka's Castle,* and for 10 years was editor in chief of *Bananas,* a humor magazine for children. During that time, Stine wrote dozens of joke books and humor books for children under the name Jovial Bob Stine. Under the name Hammering Hank, Stine wrote a number of humor books for young readers, some of which are "instructional manuals" like *How to Be Funny: An Extremely Silly Guide* (1978) and *Don't Stand in the Soup* (1982). In the 1990s Stine was catapulted to fame with the bestselling *Goosebumps* series, which sold more than 220 million copies. The *Goosebumps* books feature spooky tales for ages 8–11 and became a popular live-action children's television show on the Fox network. They were translated into 16 languages in 31 countries. The plots of his books usually involve naïve teenagers or preteens who fall into situations having to do with the supernatural or the occult. His other major series, *Fear Street,* for ages 9–14, got more gory. The *Fear Street* books sold more than 80 million copies. This was considered the first horror series for teenagers. Stine's first hardcover collection of terrifying tales for children, *Nightmare Hour,* was published in 1999, and featured illustrations by well-known artists like Bernie Wrightson and Ed Koren. Stine published an autobiography, *It Came From Ohio! My Life as a Writer* (1997).

[Stewart Kampel (2nd ed.)]

ST. LOUIS, VOYAGE OF THE. In 1938 and 1939, the Nazi regime intensified its efforts to force Germany's Jews to emigrate by using terror, discriminatory legislation, and the expropriation of property. Tens of thousands of Jews lined up at foreign consulates to obtain visas and immigration papers, and in the space of some ten months, more than 115,000 Jews had left Germany.

In April 1939, Germany's Hamburg-America Line announced the upcoming departure of the passenger liner, the MS *St. Louis,* for Cuba. Within weeks all the tickets were purchased, mostly by Jews anxious to flee Germany. The shipping line calculated that more than 95 percent of the passengers were Jewish. On May 13, the *St. Louis* set sail from Hamburg, carrying 937 passengers, for a two-week trip to Cuba. The vast majority of the Jewish passengers had applied for U.S. visas, and had planned only to remain temporarily in Cuba until their quota numbers for the United States were called.

Unbeknown to those on board the ship, the political situation in Cuba was ominous. Some eight days before the *St. Louis* departed Hamburg, the Cuban president, Laredo Bru, had invalidated the landing permits which most of the passengers carried and required that henceforth only visas authorized by the Cuban Secretaries of State and Labor and the posting of a $500 bond were acceptable. Although the German government and the Hamburg–America Line had been informed of the new decree, the ship left port with the understanding that permits purchased prior to the decree would be accepted.

By May 1939, the political climate in economically depressed Cuba had turned against the increased influx of refugees. On May 8, the single largest antisemitic demonstration took place in Havana, attended by some 40,000 persons. News of the *St. Louis*'s pending arrival further fanned the flames of hatred and focused more public and official attention on the sale of landing permits by the Director-General of Cuba's immigration office, Manuel Benitez Gonzalez. Such certificates were to be given out *gratis* to tourists who were awaiting visas for the United States or other countries, but they were routinely sold for $150 or more to desperate refugees seeking haven from Nazi persecution. American officials in Havana estimated that Benitez Gonzalez had accrued a personal fortune of $500,000 to $1,000,000 through the sale of landing permits.

When the *St. Louis* docked in Havana harbor on May 27, 1939, Cuban officials allowed only 28 passengers holding proper visas to enter the country. The remaining passengers, all carrying landing permits signed by Benitez Gonzalez, were denied admittance. The following day, the American Jewish *Joint Distribution Committee dispatched Lawrence Berenson, an attorney with extensive business and political connections, to Cuba, to negotiate on behalf of the passengers.

Newspapers from around the world soon began printing stories about the plight of the passengers on board the ill-fated ship. Without breaking off the talks, Bru ordered the ship to leave Cuban waters. Several days later, after failing to reach agreement on the appropriate bond for each passenger, the Cuban president ended the negotiations.

In the hopes of gaining admission to the United States, the ship's captain, Gustav Schroeder, sailed close to the Florida coast, where the passengers could see the lights of Miami. The United States Coast Guard thereupon signaled the *St. Louis* to remain outside the country's territorial waters. Urgent appeals by the ship's passengers to the State Department and President Franklin Delano Roosevelt went unanswered. Concerned Americans, including Hollywood celebrities, such as Edward G. Robinson, Carl Laemmle, Melvyn Douglas, Sylvia Sidney, Luise Rainer, and writer Dashiell Hammett, also requested aid for the refugees. The State Department, however, was ordered by the White House not to officially intervene with Cuban authorities, only to stress the humanitarian aspects of the situation, and not to permit the ship to land in the United States. Its standard response to requests to grant the passengers haven was that they "must await their turns on the waiting list and then qualify for and obtain immigration visas before they may be admissible into the United States." American public opinion, though sympathetic to the plight of the refugees and increasingly antagonistic toward Nazi Germany, still supported immigration restrictions, and few politicians, including the president, were willing to challenge the prevailing mood of the nation.

With little hope of refuge in the New World, and supplies running short, the *St. Louis* was forced to head back to Europe on June 6. The passengers, fearing a return to Nazi Germany, continued their international appeals. Working with Jewish and other organizations in Europe, the American Jewish Joint Distribution Committee negotiated with the governments of Great Britain, France, the Netherlands, and Belgium to arrange for temporary haven for the passengers in those countries. By June 14, agreement had been reached on the number of refugees for each country: Great Britain would accept 287, France, 224, Belgium, 214, and the Netherlands 181. (During the voyage to Cuba, one passenger died and another attempted suicide in the Havana harbor but was later transported to England.) The *St. Louis* docked in Antwerp on June 17, after being at sea for over a month, and the refugees were dispersed to their new homes.

At the time, European and American newspapers, Jewish organizations, and the passengers themselves viewed the ship's landing in Belgium as a major success story. A few months later, the plight of the passengers once again turned tragic. With the German attack on Poland in September 1939, and particularly after the May 1940 invasion of Western Europe, many of the former passengers found themselves declared "enemy aliens" because most still carried German passports. Dozens of them, even perhaps a few hundred, were interned by Belgian, British, and French authorities. Those detained in French camps often remained there after the country's surrender to Germany, awaiting permission to leave for the United States or elsewhere.

Like other Jews in German-controlled Europe, they were subjected to discriminatory legislation and deportation. Of the 908 passengers who returned to Europe, only those who were admitted to Great Britain were relatively safe. Although the outbreak of war severely restricted trans-Atlantic passages, a number of these refugees reached the United States when their numbers on the immigration quota came up.

The chances for survival on the European mainland were slim after the mass deportations from Western Europe to the Nazi extermination camps began in 1942. Some of the *St. Louis* passengers were hidden by non-Jews in France, Belgium, and the Netherlands, while a few managed to emigrate abroad. Those who could not find refuge were deported to the Theresienstadt ghetto and the Auschwitz and Sobibór killing centers. More than 250 of the former passengers died during the Holocaust.

[Steven Luckert (2nd ed.)]

°STOBBE, OTTO (1831–1887), German legal historian. Stobbe was a professor at the universities of Koenigsberg, Breslau, and Leipzig. His book on the legal, social, and economic conditions of medieval German Jewry, *Die Juden in Deutschland waehrend des Mittelalters in politischer, sozialer und rechtlicher Beziehung* (1886, repr. 1902, 1923), republished in 1969, prefaced by Guido *Kisch, is considered both a pioneer work and a classic. It received unanimous acclaim among Jewish scholars, who accepted its authority unquestioningly, as did nearly all contemporary legal and economic historians and latter-day sociologists. His influence can be discerned particularly in Max Weber. Stobbe influenced the historiography of medieval German Jewry to a very large extent. The importance of his work is in its definition of the status of Jewish serfdom as comparable to that of *ministerialis* and vassals and in his utilization of the records of medieval civic court proceedings and other archival material concerning Jews. In many respects Stobbe, nevertheless, transmitted the bias inherent in semi-scholarly general and historical works on the Jews of the 18th and early 19th centuries and gave it new currency. Many earlier errors were reintroduced. In depicting the Jews as the only merchants before the Crusades, Stobbe strengthened the image of the Jews as a commercial people. Proceeding from a misunderstanding of the canonic usury prohibition as prohibiting all credit dealings and ignoring the history of credit dealings among Christians, he vastly exaggerated the role of the Jews as moneylenders, while ignoring or minimizing evidence on landed properties held by them.

After Stobbe's work, many collections of medieval sources published by German regional commissions and individual cities, as well as improved texts of lawbooks, along with progress in solid Jewish scholarship on the history of medieval German Jewry, have helped to correct and supersede Stobbe's views. While a professor at Breslau University (1859–71), Stobbe was in close contact with H. *Graetz. In 1886 he joined the Commission on Research on the History of German Jewry and contributed an article on the privileges granted the Jews of Speyer and Worms (1084 and 1090) by the Holy Roman Emperor Henry IV, for the first volume of the commission's journal, *Zeitschrift fuer die Geschichte der Juden in Deutschland* (1887). His other works were in the field of general legal history.

BIBLIOGRAPHY: K. Maurer, in: *Kritische Vierteljahrschrift fuer Gesetzgebung und Rechtswissenchaft*, 9 (1867), 564–81; H. Bresslau, in: ZGJD, 2 (1888), 105–8; E. Landsberg, in: *ADB*, 36 (1893), 262–6; G. Kisch, in: *Forschungen zur Rechts-und Sozialgeschichte der Juden in Deutschland waehrend des Mittelalters* (1955), 199–210, with bibl.; T. Oelsner, in: YLBI, 7 (1962), 188ff.; idem, in: YIVOA, 12 (1958/59), esp. 176–95; Baron, Social, 11 (1967), 8; idem, in: *Essays and Studies... Abraham A. Neuman* (1969), 46.

[Toni Oelsner]

STOCKADE AND WATCHTOWER (Heb. חוֹמָה וּמִגְדָּל, *Ḥomah u-Migdal*), type of settlement established in Palestine between 1936 and 1947 in planned surprise operations to provide immediate security against Arab attacks. The *Jewish National Fund had acquired large tracts of land in areas distant from Jewish population centers, where de facto possession was in jeopardy unless the land was settled and ordinary methods could not be used because of Arab antagonism. Convoys carrying hundreds of helpers, prefabricated huts, and fortifications set out at daybreak, protected by Jewish Settlement Police. By nightfall they completed the erection of the settlement, surrounded by a double wall of planks with a filling of earth and stones, dominated by a central tower equipped with a searchlight and electric generator to enable the countryside to be scanned for signs of hostility. The 118 settlements established in this way included Tirat Ẓevi, Nir David, and Sedeh Naḥum in the Beth-Shean Valley, Massadah and Sha'ar ha-Golan in the Jordan Valley, and Ḥanitah in Upper Galilee.

BIBLIOGRAPHY: A. Bein, *Return to the Soil* (1952), 481–95; J. Weitz, *Hitnaḥalutenu bi-Tekufat ha-Sa'ar* (1947), index; Dinur, Haganah, 2, pt 3 (1965), index.

[Misha Louvish]

STOCK EXCHANGES. Jews came to the stock exchange by way of their medieval occupation of *moneylending and their activity in the modern period as *Court Jews and in *banking. Soon after the founding of the first European international exchange at Antwerp (1536), **anusim* arrived there and for a short time played a prominent role in it until their expulsion by *Charles V. Many of them then moved to Amsterdam, the economic capital of Europe in the 17th and early 18th centuries. By 1674, 13% of the total number of investments on the stock exchange was in "Portuguese" Jewish hands, though the size of their individual investments was not great. A contemporary noted that many brokers refrained from visiting the stock exchange on Saturday, when the Jews were absent. The first book to describe the practices of the Amsterdam stock exchange was published in Spanish by Joseph *Penso de la Vega in 1688. Jews were excluded from most of the commodity exchanges in Germany. Benjamin and Abraham *Goldsmid were prominent on the Royal Exchange in London at the end of the 18th and the beginning of the 19th centuries, and after the Napoleonic Wars they were eclipsed by N.M. Rothschild who was the dominant figure on the London Exchange.

In the United States Ephraim *Hart was among the 22 founders of the first board of stockbrockers in New York in 1792. August *Belmont was the representative of the Rothschilds in the 19th century. In the mid- and late 19th century a number of German-Jewish underwriting firms were prominent on the board: J. and W. Seligman and Co., run by the eight *Seligman brothers and led by Joseph Seligman, and Kuhn, Loeb, and Co., which was raised to international repute by Jacob *Schiff, Otto *Kahn, and Paul M. *Warburg. The battle between Hill-Morgan and Harriman-Schiff for control of the Northern Pacific railway stocks resulted in the stock exchange crash known as "Black Thursday."

Even at the height of their activity, Jews were never the largest nor the most prominent group on the exchanges in England and the United States; by the mid-20th century their number and proportion had declined considerably. In Continental Europe Jews were more prominent on the stock exchange (see Isaac *Pinto). Jews attended the exchanges of Lyons and Paris as early as the 18th century but it was only with the rise of the house of Rothschild in the post-Napoleonic era that they became prominent there; the initiative of this house in floating railroad stocks was followed by the *Fould house and others. The *Pereire brothers founded the Crédit Mobilier, the first joint-stock bank. In the aftermath of the Panama Canal stock scandal (1892–93), in which Baron Jacques Reinach was incriminated, antisemitic attacks were made on Jewish activity on the exchanges.

Jews were not allowed into the Frankfurt stock exchange, the most important in Germany at the time, until 1811, but from then until the Nazi regime they played a dominant and later a leading role, partly attributable to the activity of the house of Rothschild and other Jewish financial magnates. The stock exchange of Berlin was a relative latecomer. The patrician Jewish families of Berlin – *Gomperz, *Veit, *Ephraim, Riess, and Wulff, who had amassed wealth as court jewelers, army contractors, and mint purveyors – played a predominant part from its foundation. The statutes of the bourse corporation of 1805 found it necessary to lay down that two of the four chairmen must be Christians. In 1807, 159 of the 174 member firms were Jewish. Such marked preponderance of Jewish firms continued for a short period only. As in banking, the role of the Jews on the stock exchanges declined rapidly with the founding of public banks. In 1882 there were 2,908 Jews in Prussia engaged in stocks and banking, 22% of the total; by 1925 the absolute number of Jews in these fields had increased to 5,620 but their percentage of the total was only 3.84%, although many of this small ratio were in key positions. The economic recession of 1873–76 was blamed on stock speculators, some of whom were Jews, and this was one of the factors behind the antisemitic movement led by A. *Stoecker. In Vienna H. *Todesco and other leading Jewish financiers were prominent from the foundation of the exchange, on which a Rothschild soon came to play a leading role. The number of Jewish stockbrokers was also high. In the stock exchanges of Budapest, Prague, and Bucharest, Jews filled important positions in the 19th and early 20th centuries. The Jewish role decreased as a result of antisemitic economic nationalism.

It was not only in times of economic crisis and financial speculation that the activity of Jews on the stock exchange was seized on as a pretext for antisemitic outbursts; anti-Jewish agitators magnified their influence out of all proportion, creating an anti-Jewish stereotype out of "Jewish mastery" over the stock exchange. In this they were aided by the theories of men like Werner *Sombart, who ascribed the creation and workings of the stock exchange to the "capitalist Jewish spirit."

For stock exchange in modern Israel, see Israel, State of: Economic *Affairs.

BIBLIOGRAPHY: G.N. Hart, in: AJHSP, 4 (1896), 215–8; S. Mayer, *Die Wiener Juden* (1917); R. Lewinsohn, *Juedische Weltfinanz?* (1925); H. Goslar, in: *Gemeindeblatt der juedischen Gemeinde zu Berlin*, 21 (1931), 14–18; J. Lestschinsky, *Das wirtschaftliche Schicksal des deutschen Judentums* (1932); H.I. Bloom, *Economic Activities of the Jews of Amsterdam* (1937); P.H. Emden, *Money Powers of Europe* (1938); H. Rachel, *Berliner Grosskaufleute und Kapitalisten*, 2 (1938), 541ff.; R. Strauss, in: JSOS, 3 (1941), 15–40; D. Bernstein, in: S. Kaznelson (ed.), *Juden im deutschen Kulturbereich* (1959²), 720–59; E.V. Morgan and W.A. Thomas, *The Stock Exchange* (1962); R. Glanz, *The Jew in the Old American Folklore* (1961), 166ff.; R. Sobel, *The Big Board* (1965); A. Hertzberg, *French Enlightenment and the Jews* (1968), 74ff., 143–4, 146–7; S. Birmingham, *Our Crowd* (1968).

[Henry Wasserman]

STOCKHOLM, capital of *Sweden. The first Jew to settle in Stockholm was the gem-carver and seal-engraver, Aaron Isaac, who arrived in 1774. A year later the Jewish community was founded when the right of residence in the Swedish capital was granted to him, his brother, his business partner, and their families. By 1778–79 there was already a community of 40 families. Land for a cemetery, which was named Aronsberg after Aaron Isaac, had been acquired in 1776. In 1780 the first rabbi, Levin Hirsch Levi, arrived in Stockholm from Strelitz, *Mecklenburg. Three years later, at his request, he was awarded the title of chief rabbi of Sweden, which was subsequently held by all the rabbis of the Stockholm community. Until 1838 the community was organized on the usual pattern of German communities of the time. It was at first headed by a committee of three laymen, which in 1807 was enlarged to five. In 1838, the year which marked the beginning of emancipation in Sweden, the authorities laid down new rules for the organization of the community, which were drafted in consultation with Aaron Levi Lamm, then president of the community. As in many other European places, equal rights were granted at the price of abrogation of autonomy. From then on communal records were kept in Swedish instead of in Yiddish, and sermons in the synagogue had to be delivered in Swedish, Danish, German, or French. The independent activity of the community was restricted to charity and Jewish education; the latter was steadily declining.

In 1832 a rabbi with an academic degree (Loeb Seligman) was appointed in Stockholm for the first time. He introduced innovations from the *Reform movement into the prayers and customs, but the movement did not gain strength in the community until the 1860s. A powerful trend toward assimilation, however, was evident even before then, and in 1843 between 80 and 90 men and women out of the 400 members of the community converted to Christianity. It was only toward the close of the century, after the achievement of complete emancipation in 1870, that the patriarchal structure of the Mosaic Congregation of Stockholm was replaced by a more democratic system of electing members to the communal board. From 1882 membership of the community was conditional on Swedish nationality. The rabbis of Sweden were always invited from abroad. The liberal Gottlieb *Klein (1882–1914), a scholar born in Hungary, was succeeded by the Zionist Marcus *Ehrenpreis (1914–48), formerly chief rabbi of Bulgaria. His successor, Kurt *Wilhelm (1948–65), was born in Germany and took up his post in Stockholm after living in Jerusalem. In addition to the Great Synagogue in Stockholm, which was inaugurated in 1870, there are two smaller Orthodox synagogues which are supported by the community.

The character of the Stockholm Jewish community changed between the late 19th century and the post-World War II period, due to the influx of immigrants and refugees fleeing the effects of persecution and war. In 1900 there were 1,631 members in the community (41% of all the Jews in Sweden), and in 1920 that number had risen to 2,747. Of these 1,353 were born in Sweden and 1,394 abroad. Until the rise of Hitler the situation remained unchanged. The principal activities on behalf of the refugees and negotiations with the authorities were necessarily concentrated in Stockholm. The community played a role in organizational activity and fundraising. In the most critical period, however – before 1939 and the first phase of the war – its success was very limited. Thousands of requests for entry permits remained unanswered and the community itself was compelled to give negative replies. This situation changed with the arrival of refugees from Norway in 1942, and in particular with the escape of Jews from Denmark in October 1943. At the end of the war, a significant stream of refugees arrived from the concentration camps. Between 1933 and 1950 Stockholm spent a total of 17,500,000 Swedish kronor (7 kronor = 1 U.S. dollar) in relief, the community providing slightly over 5,000,000 kronor from taxes and appeals, while the remainder was paid by international Jewish organizations (about 8,000,000 kronor) and the Swedish Ministry of Social Affairs. After the war the Jewish community of Stockholm numbered 7,000 (including children). With the assistance of the *Claims Conference a community center was erected, and on the initiative of Zionist circles, whose influence increased after the establishment of the State of Israel, a Jewish elementary school was established and recognized by the Ministry of Education. The importance of the Jews of Stockholm was apparent in commerce, science, the arts, the press, and in publishing (the famous publishing company of Bonniers was founded in 1831, and by the close of the century it had attained the important position which it continued to hold in the literary life of Sweden). A quarterly review, *Församlingsblad*, founded by the Stockholm community in 1940 and edited by David Köpniwsky, contained news of communal life and from time to time published articles on the history of Swedish Jewry.

In 2005 the Jewish community of Stockholm numbered just over 5,000 members, with estimates of at least another 3,000–5,000 Jews living in Stockholm who are not affiliated.

Paideia

One recent addition to the Stockholm Jewish community scene is the Paideia Institute, a pan-European initiative to revitalize Jewish knowledge and interest in Jewish culture. It came about through cooperation between European governments, Jewish organizations, and the business community towards the end of the 1990s, with the aim of examining and counterbalancing the consequences of the Holocaust and of reviving Jewish knowledge, culture, and traditions that were largely wiped out by the ravages of the Holocaust.

The Paideia Institute is a pan-European Jewish educational institution that has the recognition of the Swedish parliament and generous support from the World Jewish Congress and the Jewish Central Committee of Sweden, among others. In the first three years of its existence, it attracted 57 students from 17 countries – including Israel – who have returned to their home countries and helped nurture a flourishing revival of Jewish studies and Jewish-interest programs.

BIBLIOGRAPHY: E. Olan, *Judarna på svensk mark: historien om israeliternas invandring till Sverige* (1924); *Gamla judiska gravplaster i Stockholm* (1927); M. Ivarsson and A. Brody, *Svenskjudiska pionjärer och stamfäder* (1956); H. Valentin, *Judarna i Sverige* (1964), incl. bibl. **Add Bibliography:** L. Dencik, *Jewishness in Postmodernity: The Case of Sweden* (April 2003).

[Leni Yahil / Ilya Meyer (2nd ed.)]

°**STOECKER, ADOLF** (1835–1909), German antisemitic preacher politician. Stoecker became a renowned figure in the 1870s as an influential and popular Protestant theologian and as an advocate for a conservative social reform movement. He founded the Christian Social Workers' Party in 1878 (renamed Christian Social Party in 1881), originally intended as an instrument against the Social Democratic Party, whose following he failed to attract. During the first year of its existence, the powerful, modern-style demagogue increasingly used the party to promote anti-liberal and antisemitic ideas. He was thereby able to create a right-wing mass movement of discontented artisans and small shop owners, who were later joined by members of the conservative educated classes, civil servants, officers, and students. In mass rallies Stoecker used stereotype slogans in attacking the Jews as the moneyed power in Germany and as a group which dominated German cultural life, and castigated the liberal press, in which he believed Jews to be prominent. Blending the religious issue with an extreme nationalism that stigmatized Jews as aliens, he advocated the limitation of Jewish civil rights, their exclusion from public office and from the staffs of public schools, and a *numerus clausus in high schools and universities, as well as the limiting of Jewish immigration. His inflammatory demagogy paved the way for the rampant antisemitic movement in Berlin in the early 1880s which spread to provincial cities and the countryside.

Imperial court chaplain from 1874, Stoecker was a member of the Prussian Diet from 1879 to 1898. In 1881 he was elected to the Reichstag for a Westphalian district which he represented (except for the years 1893–98) until 1908. After Stoecker had been invited to the Luther Festival in London in 1883, the lord mayor revoked his permission to speak at Mansion House; he thus suffered his first public defeat. Two libel suits in the following years brought him further adverse publicity. Public opinion began turning against anti-Jewish attacks and his influence declined from 1885. In 1889 he had to curtail his political activities, and in 1891 was forced to resign from his position as court chaplain. However, he continued to stir up antisemitic issues in the Reichstag. Stoecker's mass movement provided fertile soil for the more radical antisemitic parties which followed in the mid-1880s.

BIBLIOGRAPHY: P.G.J. Pulzer, *Rise of Political Anti-Semitism in Germany and Austria* (1964); M.A. Meyer, in: YLBI, 11 (1966), 139–45. **ADD. BIBLIOGRAPHY:** G. Brakelmann, M. Greschat, and W. Jochmann, *Protestantismus und Politik. Werk und Wirkung Adolf Stoeckers* (1982); D.A.J. Telman, in: *Jewish History*, 9 (1995), 93–112; G. Brakelmann, *Adolf Stoecker als Antisemit* (2004).

[Toni Oelsner / Uffa Jensen (2nd ed.)]

STOICISM, one of the influential post-Socratic philosophies of antiquity, founded by the Hellenized Phoenician Zeno (335–263 B.C.E.). It was popular with Roman jurists and became a major ingredient in Greco-Roman rhetorical culture. As such it met Judaism, probably even before the Hasmonean revolt. The extent and nature of this meeting are still under debate. Stoicism lent itself to an explanation of how the bridging of the chasm between God and man, actualized in creation, revelation, and history, was accomplished in detail (mediation). The Stoic theory of the Logos ("Word," "Reason") became therefore central in Philo and after him in the Gospel according to St. John, and traces of it are found in the Midrash. The metabolism of elements, the World Soul, and Providence appear in the Wisdom of Solomon, shades of the quasi-material Spirit and of ecpyrosis (successive conflagrations of the world) in the Midrash. Less obvious is the possibility that the large-scale midrashic attempt to see latent "ethical" situations everywhere in cosmos and history may have been furthered by the panlogistic mood of Stoicism and its doctrine of cosmic "sympathy." Rabbinism, however, insisted on *hashgaḥah peratit* ("individual providence") and rejected the impersonal Stoic concept (Greek *pronoia*). Stoicism in all these adaptations has sometimes been regarded as an aid to the clarification of earlier Jewish beliefs. Occasionally, Jewish sources such as Josephus and the talmudic dialogues about *Antoninus Pius try to outdo the Stoicism of the Stoics (IV Macc.) or to portray Pharisaic Judaism as an up-to-date Stoicism. The Jewish and Hellenistic bureaucrat-scholar classes, i.e., the rhetorician-philosophers, Philo, and the rabbis, were compelled to reinterpret sacred writ in an age of change. Stoic allegory came to their aid. Both were involved in legal exegesis, and Stoic techniques of expounding and expanding law were useful. Some rabbinic hermeneutical rules have thus been regarded as having a Stoic-rhetorical coloring, at least in their terminology. Stoic casuistry was known to the rabbis, and the prevailing sense of "etiquette" is reflected in rules for table and toilet in Cicero and the Talmud alike.

Perhaps the Stoic mood is most strongly in evidence in rabbinic ethics, part of which could thus be considered as an intercultural ideology of a bureaucrat-scholar class elevating the ideal Sage. Here values and problems emerge that were not found (or not stressed) in the Bible: health, the simple life, self-improvement, fortitude, the ethos of work, *imitatio dei*, generosity, theory versus practice, the good versus the merely valuable, new interpretations of suffering etc. The biblical roots *amal* ("to labor") and *zaʿar* ("to take pains") acquire positive connotations. Beyond these, however, the native ethos prevailed: empathy, repentance, hope, and rule over the emotions, not their extirpation. Strong, too, is the acceptance of Stoic-rhetorical literary forms in rabbinism, such as catalogs of virtues and vices, sorites, consolation formulae (life as a deposit), eristic dialogues, diatribic sequences, and certain similes (athletics, household, civic life). The *Letter of Aristeas* is an example of Stoic instructions for kings. The immediate source for rabbinism (and early Christianity) must have been Greco-Roman rhetoric rather than the ubiquitous Posidonius of earlier research. Yet, "what is received is received according to the way of the receiver," i.e., selectively, and is synthesized with the unaffected transcendental and humanitarian tradition of Judaism.

[Henry Albert Fischel]

Medieval Jewish Philosophy

Stoic influence on Jewish religious philosophy in the medieval period was mainly indirect, that is, through the Neoplatonic philosophers (see *Neoplatonism) and commentators on Aristotle who had undergone Stoic influence. The Stoic ideal of the cosmopolis, a state covering the whole of mankind, may have had some influence on the political ideas of al-Fārābī and through him on *Maimonides in his conception of the Law of Moses as the constitution of the ideal state and in his vision of the Messianic age (Yad, Melakhim, end). It is possible that Isaac *Abrabanel was influenced by Stoic views in his criticisms of luxurious living and its consequences for human life. In *Spinoza, one finds a material conception of God which is analogous to the Stoic conception, and Spinoza's ideal of the free man corresponds to that of the Stoic sage.

[Lawrence V. Berman]

BIBLIOGRAPHY: Kaminka, in: REJ, 82 (1926), 233–52; L. Wallach, in: JQR, 31 (1940/41), 259–86; Daube, in: HUCA, 22 (1949), 239–64; S. Lieberman, in: A. Altmann (ed.), *Biblical and Other Studies* (1963), 123–41; Urbach, in: Israel Academy of Sciences and Humanities, *Proceedings*, 2 (1966), no. 4. MEDIEVAL JEWISH PHILOSOPHY: Guttmann, Philosophies, index; H.A. Wolfson, *Philosophy of Spinoza*, 2 vols. (1934), index; idem, *Philo, Foundations of Religious Philosophy*, 2 vols. (1947), index.

STOKES (Wieslander), ROSE PASTOR (1879–1933), U.S. socialist writer and lecturer. Born in Augustow, Poland, her impoverished family emigrated to London in 1882 and then settled in Cleveland, Ohio, when she was 12 years old. She educated herself while working as a cigar maker, and in 1903 moved to New York to work at the *Jewish Daily News*, which had earlier published some of her poems. Through an assignment to interview the prominent railway president, J.G. Phelps Stokes, she became active in the latter's social projects in the University Settlement on the Lower East Side, and she married Stokes in 1905. Both became socialists, but while her husband left the Socialist Party in 1917, Rose joined the left wing and was later one of the founders of the Communist Party. Rose Stokes toured the U.S., lecturing and writing articles expounding her radical views. She was a prominent figure in the hotel and restaurant workers' strike and in the shirtwaist workers' strike and was one of the leaders of the birth control movement. She divorced Stokes in 1925 and shortly afterward married Isaac Romaine, a language instructor with similar political views. She died in Frankfurt. Her works include a three-act play, *The Woman Who Wouldn't* (1916), and a translation of Morris Rosenfeld's *Arbeter-Lider as Songs of Labor* (1914).

BIBLIOGRAPHY: *New York Times* (June 21, 1933), 17.

[Edward L. Greenstein]

STOLBTSY (Pol. **Stolpce**; Yid. **Stoybts, Shtoptsi**), town in Minsk district, Belorus; until 1793 and between the two world wars within Poland. Jews settled there from the end of the 16th century. In 1632 the Minsk community, among others, assisted the Jews in Stolbtsy in combating a blood *libel. Jewish merchants of Stolbtsy are referred to in legal archives of Minsk (1678) and of the supreme tribunal of Lithuania (1704), as traders in salt and salted fish. During the 18th century Jews there engaged in the export of agricultural products, flax, and lumber (floated down the Niemen River) to Koenigsberg in East Prussia, and the import of salt, spices, and cloths. The Jewish population numbered 259 in 1811; 1,315 in 1847; and 2,409 (64% of the total) in 1897. In the second half of the 19th century Jews developed the timber trade – from tree felling to sawing and other by-products – and in the 20th century founded sawmills which employed some Jewish workers. A Ḥovevei Zion society was established as early as 1885 and Zionist activity began from the beginning of the 20th century. A *Bund group was organized in Stolbtsy in 1905–06, and a branch of the Po'alei *Zion in which Zalman Rubashov (*Shazar) was active. In the same period Jewish youth and workers in Stolbtsy organized *self-defense against pogroms by the population of the neighboring villages.

During World War I about half of the Jews of Stolbtsy left the city. Those remaining suffered severely during the civil war in 1919–20 from the struggle for control of the area between the Red Army and those who opposed it. In 1921 Stolbtsy was incorporated within Poland as a border town. There were then 1,428 Jewish inhabitants (48% of the total). The Jewish economy was severely affected as a result of the city being cut off from its previous markets, and particularly as a result of the hostile attitude of the antisemitic government, as well as by the organized Polish competition. In the interwar period all Jewish parties were active in Stolbtsy and a *hakhsharah* farm of *He-Ḥalutz was organized. Jewish educational institutions were developed, and included a *Tarbut school and two Orthodox schools, "Ḥorev" for boys, and a Beth Jacob for girls.

[Dov Rubin]

Holocaust Period

After the outbreak of World War II, during the period of Soviet rule in Stolbtsy (1939–41), the Jewish community institutions were disbanded and all Jewish political activities were prohibited. In the spring of 1941 Jewish youth were mobilized in the Soviet army, and later fought against Germany. After the outbreak of war between Germany and the Soviet Union (June 22, 1941), groups of Jewish youth attempted to reach the Soviet interior, but were prevented by the Soviets. At the beginning of the German occupation there were more than 3,000 Jews in the town. As early as July 1941 about 80 of them were executed. A ghetto was established at the end of 1941. In February 1942 hundreds of Jews were murdered at the local Jewish cemetery. In the spring of 1942 an underground resistance group was organized in the ghetto, and attempts were made to acquire arms. On May 15, 1942, the first group left the ghetto for the forests to make contact with the partisans. In September 1942 most of the Jewish population was killed, about 500 skilled workers remaining in the ghetto. Some were sent to the camps at Baranovichi and Minsk. A few Jewish groups escaped to the forests, joined the partisans, and carried out important combat operations against the Germans and their collaborators.

[Aharon Weiss]

BIBLIOGRAPHY: *Akty izdavayemye Wilenskoy Kommissiyei dlyarazbora drevnikh aktov*, 29 (1902), 48, 312; S. Dubnow (ed.), *Pinkas ha-Medinah* (1925), 55; Kh. G. Korobkov, in: *Yevreyskaya Starina*, 4 (1910), 23–24; Vaysrusishe Visnshaft-Akademye, *Tsaytshrift*, 4 (1930), 72; *Sefer Stoybts* (1965); Z. Shazar, *Kokhevei Boker* (1950^3), 117ff.; E. Tcherikower, *Anti-semitizm un Pogromen in Ukraine 1918–19* (1928), 146–7; *Haynt* (July 25–27, 1939); *Sefer ha-Partizanim ha-Yehudiyyum*, 1 (1959), 568–72.

STOLIN, city in Pinsk district, W. Belarus. Jews are assumed to have settled in Stolin in the 17th century. They acquired land from the owner of the estate, Stachowski, who had divided the area into building plots. They built houses and contributed toward the development of Stolin. At the end of World War I, the Jews suffered at the hands of armies passing through the town, such as the gangs of *Petlyura, the Germans, the Russians, and finally the Poles who took the town. The Jews earned their livelihood from minor trade and crafts. The economic occupations of Jews, however, hardly provided for their needs, and many were compelled to emigrate. During Poland's independence the hardships of Jews increased because of the government's Polonization policy which aimed to support and strengthen merchants and craftsmen. Social and cultural activity among the Jews was highly developed. During the 19th century Ḥasidism wielded much influence and a court of the Stolin-*Karlin dynasty was active. At the beginning of the 20th century Zionist influence was intensified. The last rabbis of the town were Israel Perlow (d. 1922) and his son Moses Perlow. In 1921 there were 2,966 Jews (62.4% of the population).

[Shimon Leib Kirshenboim]

Holocaust Period

Soviet authorities took over in Stolin in September 1939. When Germany attacked the USSR on June 22, 1941, the Soviet army retreated and Ukrainian nationalists took over the local government and began organizing pogroms against the Jews. The Jewish community, to ensure its safety, set up a committee (including Rabbis Moses Perlow, Aaron Dorczin, and Solomon Polak) which prevented the impending attacks. On August 22 the district German authorities arrived from Rovno, and imposed a fine of 1,000,000 rubles on the Jewish community. The Judenrat, headed by Nathan Bergner (a refugee from Lodz), used every means at its disposal, including personal contacts and bribes, in an attempt to aid the Jewish population. In the fall of 1941 all the Jews from the towns and villages in the vicinity were sent to Stolin but the Ukrainian authorities prevented their admission into the city. The Judenrat intervened with the authorities to allow the entrance of 1,500 refugees. Public kitchens were set up for them. The ghetto, containing 7,000 persons, was established on the eve of Shavuot 1942. On September 10 the Judenrat members were executed and the following day the Germans and their Ukrainian collaborators rounded up all the inmates in the market square. The sick and elderly were shot in their beds. All the Jews of Stolin and the vicinity were led off in groups of 500 and killed in the forest near Dolin. Some Jewish groups tried to reach the forests. Moses Glazer and Asher Shapira, who sought contact with the partisans, were turned over by Ukrainian peasants to the Germans and hanged. The few survivors made their way to partisan units in the vicinity. After the war the Jewish community of Stolin was not rebuilt. A society of former residents of Stolin functions in Israel.

By 2005, a Jewish community center had been established in Stolin.

[Aharon Weiss]

BIBLIOGRAPHY: *Sefer Zikkaron li-Kehillat Stolin ve-ha-Sevivah* (1952).

STOLLER, SAMUEL (1898–1977), agronomist. Stoller was born in Moscow and after studying philology and history at the local university studied agriculture and science at the University of Simferopol. He immigrated to Ereẓ Israel in 1920, joining kibbutz Kinneret. He was one of the first agricultural settlers to do research on progressive farming methods. When banana planting was begun in Ereẓ Israel in 1922 he devoted his research to it, visiting the Canary Islands for this purpose; he also did pioneering research in conjunction with the first plantation of table grapes in Kinneret in 1925 and the date palm in 1933, and was largely responsible for the development of all three. From 1934 he applied himself to agricultural problems in the Jordan Valley and from 1947 headed the Ruppin Agricultural High School in Bet Yeraḥ in the Jordan Valley. A collection of his research papers appeared in 1960. He was awarded the Israel Prize for agriculture in 1965.

STOLYARSKI, PETER SOLOMONOVICH (1871–1944), violin pedagogue. Born in Lipovtsy, Ukraine, Stolyarski came from a family of *klezmorim* (see *Music). As a child he played with a band at Jewish wedding ceremonies and attracted the attention of the Polish violinist Barcewicz, upon whose advice he went to study at the music school in Odessa. After his graduation in 1900 he devoted himself to teaching talented children, often as young as four years old; he developed special teaching methods which gained recognition. In 1920 he became professor at the Odessa Conservatory. In 1933 he founded a music school for youths, which consisted of a ten-year course combining music studies with general instruction. His system was widely adopted in the USSR, and similar institutions, mainly at high school level, now exist in many countries. His most celebrated pupils, David *Oistrakh and Nathan *Milstein, exemplified and continued Stolyarski's tradition of purity and flawless technique in violin playing.

BIBLIOGRAPHY: M. Goldstein, *Shkola imeni Stolyarskogo* (1947).

[Michael Goldstein]

STOLZ, JOSEPH (1861–1941), U.S. rabbi. Born in Syracuse, he went to public schools and then to the University of Cincinnati, where he received his B.L. in 1883. A year later he was ordained in the second class of Hebrew Union College. In 1880 he received a D.D., writing on the "Funeral Agenda," and a half century later an honorary D.H.L. Upon ordination he was appointed rabbi in Little Rock, Arkansas, at B'nai Israel Temple and then in 1887 he moved to Chicago as assistant to Bernard Felsenthal at Zion Temple. After eight years, he moved to the South Side of Chicago, at a time when Jews were moving to that part of Chicago from the West Side, and formed a new congregation with his migrating members. Under his leadership they formed Temple Isaiah, meeting in the Oakland Club Hall in 1896. Two years later, they had built and dedicated a building. He remained there for the rest of his career. He was active in the affairs of his community, serving as a member of the Chicago Board of Education for six years (1899–1905), appointed by the mayor, Carter Harrison, and as a member of the Chicago Criminal Commission. He was president of the Chicago Rabbinical Association from 1920 to 1925 and of the Chicago Federation of Synagogues. On a national level, he was also active in the CCAR and was its president from 1905 to 1907. In 1921 he led the merger efforts of Temple Israel and Isaiah Temple.

His wife, BLANCHE A. STOLZ (née Rauth), brought the Union to Reform Judaism. A young man came to her husband in preparation for his marriage to a young woman coming from Germany. In the ensuing months he had to make all the wedding arrangements as well as assure his future in-laws that he could provide a simple home for their daughter. Rabbi and Mrs. Stolz took an interest in the young man and took him under their wing. Mrs. Stolz found it interesting that many messages of good wishes came for the bride and groom from Germany in identical envelopes. Later on, Rabbi and Mrs. Stolz learned from the bride that the Jewish girls' club she belonged to in Germany used a special message blank to raise funds for their charities. Some years later, after she became a delegate to the founding convention of the National Federation of Temple Sisterhoods (now Women of Reform Judaism), Mrs. Stolz recalled the messages sent to this couple and became convinced that identical message blanks could be used by sisterhoods and their members.

BIBLIOGRAPHY: T. Schanfarber, "Joseph Stolz," in: *American Jewish Year Book*, vol. 43 (1941–42); *Universal Jewish Encyclopedia* (110:69); K.M. Olitzky, L.J. Sussman, and M.H. Stern (eds.), *Reform Judaism in America: A Biographical Dictionary and Sourcebook* (1993).

STONE, DEWEY D. (1900–1977), U.S. business executive and communal leader. Stone was born in Brockton, Massachusetts. He went into business in his native state and rose to become president of the Harodite Finishing Company as well as a board member of various corporations. A personal friend of Chaim Weizmann, he was long active in Zionism. From 1955 to 1963 he served as national chairman of the United Jewish Appeal. He was also chairman of the United Israel Appeal and the Jewish Agency, and active in numerous cultural and economic enterprises for Israel. His main interest was the Weizmann Institute of Science in Reḥovot, of which he was chairman of the board of governors from the institution's establishment in 1944, as well as chairman of the board of directors of its American Committee.

ADD. BIBLIOGRAPHY: N. Kaganoff, *Solidarity and Kinship: Essays on American Zionism in Memory of Dewey Stone* (1980).

[Hillel Halkin]

STONE, I.F. (Isidore Feinstein; 1907–1989), U.S. journalist, born in Philadelphia. Stone edited the liberal weekly *The Nation*, 1940–46. From 1952 until 1971 he published *I.F. Stone's Weekly* written by himself and noted for its criticism of American society and policy. Regarded as one of the most influential liberal journalists of the postwar period, Stone has been quoted as saying, "If you want to know about governments, all you have to know is two words: governments lie." Originally pro-Israel, he reported the 1948–49 War of Liberation but became hostile after the Six-Day War.

Stone was the author of *Business as Usual* (1941); *Underground to Palestine* (1946); *This Is Israel* (with R. Capa, 1948); *The Hidden History of the Korean War* (1952); *The Truman Era* (1953); *The Haunted Fifties* (1963); *In a Time of Torment, 1961–67* (1967), a collection of pieces from his weekly; *Polemics and Prophecies, 1967–1970* (1970); *The Killings at Kent State* (1971); *The I.F. Stone's Weekly Reader* (1973); *The War Years 1939–1945* (1988); and *The Trial of Socrates* (1988).

[Ruth Beloff (2nd ed.)]

STONE, IRVING (1903–1989), biographer and novelist. After he had written a number of plays, Stone interested himself in biography and produced a number of very successful works, including *Lust for Life* (1934), on Vincent Van Gogh; *The Agony and the Ecstasy* (1961) as well as other books about Michelangelo; *Lincoln, A Contemporary Portrait* (1962); and *The Passions of the Mind* (1971), about Freud. His other well-known works include *They Also Ran* (1943), *Clarence Darrow for the Defense* (1941), *Earl Warren* (1948), and *Those Who Love* (1965). He also edited *Dear Theo: The Autobiography of Vincent Van Gogh* (1937).

STONE, JULIUS (1907–1985), jurist and international lawyer. Born in Leeds, England, Stone studied in England and at Harvard, where he was assistant professor of law 1933–36. From 1938 to 1942 he was dean of the Faculty of Law at the University of New Zealand and in 1942 was appointed professor of international law and jurisprudence at the University of Sydney. His appointment to the Sydney chair was marked by controversy. Stone was attacked as a judicial radical by conservatives; these attacks often had antisemitic overtones. Stone was awarded the O.B.E. in the New Year's Honors of 1973. Stone's many books include *International Guarantees of Minority Rights* (1932), *International Court and World Crisis* (1962), *The Province and Function of Law* (1961⁴), *Legal Controls of International Conflict* (1954), and *Aggression and World Order* (1958). His greatest contribution to the study of law is his trilogy, *Human Law and Human Justice* (1965), *Legal Systems and Lawyers Reasoning* (1966); and *Social Dimensions of Law and Justice* (1967), regarded as a milestone in the history of jurisprudence, which attempts to assess law in terms of logic, justice, and society, corresponding to analytical, ethical, and sociological jurisprudence.

An active figure in Jewish affairs in Australia, Stone published in 1944 a booklet, *Stand Up and be Counted*, in which he challenged the anti-Zionist views of Sir Isaac *Isaacs and called upon Australian Jewry to rally behind the Zionist cause. From 1968 to 1970 he was academic director and head of the Truman Center for the Advancement of Peace at the Hebrew University of Jerusalem. He remained a staunch supporter of Israel in the Australian public sphere until his death. A *Festschrift*, *Legal Change: Essays in Honour of Julius Stone*, edited by A.R. Blackshield, appeared in 1983. Leonie Star's *Julius Stone: An Intellectual Life* (1992) is a comprehensive biography.

[Isidor Solomon]

STONE, OLIVER (1946–), U.S. film director. Born in New York, Stone spent two years in Vietnam (1967–68) as a U.S. Infantry Specialist 4th class and received both the Purple Heart and a Bronze Star with Oak Leaf Cluster honors. Stone began his feature film career at the highest level, writing the screenplay of Alan Parker's *Midnight Express* (1978), for which he received an Oscar. Stone then wrote the script for *Scarface* (1983) and then directed his first feature, *Salvador* (1986), which he also co-scripted and co-produced. Stone's next writing and directorial effort was the hugely successful *Platoon* (1986), which received the Academy Award for Best Picture of the year and an Oscar for Stone for Best Director. Stone then directed *Wall Street* (1987) and *Talk Radio* (1988), both of which he also co-scripted. His next film, *Born on the Fourth of July* (1989), won him his second Academy Award for Best Director. Stone then directed *The Doors* (1990); the highly controversial *J.F.K.* (Oscar nominations for Stone as writer, director, and producer, 1991); *Heaven & Earth* (1993); the even more controversial *Natural Born Killers* (1994); *Nixon* (Oscar nomination, 1995); *U Turn* (1997); *Any Given Sunday* (1999); *Comandante* (2003); *Persona Non Grata* (2003); the TV movie *Looking for Fidel* (2004); and *Alexander* (2004). In addition to writing the screenplays for many of his films that he directed, Stone also wrote the screenplay for *Conan the Barbarian* (1982); *Year of the Dragon* (1985); *8 Million Ways to Die* (1986); and *Evita* (1996).

Stone's published works include *A Child's Night Dream* (1997) and *Oliver Stone's U.S.A.* (2000).

ADD. BIBLIOGRAPHY: F. Beaver, *Oliver Stone: Wakeup Cinema* (1994); J. Riordan, *Stone: The Controversies, Excesses and Exploits of a Radical Filmmaker* (1996); C. Salewicz, *Oliver Stone: Close Up* (1998); N. Kagan, *The Cinema of Oliver Stone* (2000); C. Silet (ed), *Oliver Stone: Interviews* (2001); E. Hamburg, *JFK, Nixon, Oliver Stone and Me* (2002).

[Jonathan Licht / Ruth Beloff (2nd ed.)]

STONE, PETER (1930–2003), U.S. movie and theater writer. Born in Los Angeles, Stone went to Bard College in New York State and earned a master's degree from the Yale School of Drama. After a stint in journalism, he turned to writing for television. In 1956 he wrote an episode for the highly regarded *Studio One* series. He earned an Emmy award for a 1962 episode of *The Defenders*, a series about a father-son team of lawyers who often delved into social issues. In the early 1960s he wrote a movie script that was rejected all over Hollywood until he turned it into a novel. Hollywood beckoned, so he turned it back into a screenplay that became the 1963 movie *Charade*, starring Cary Grant and Audrey Hepburn. He won an Oscar the following year for his reprise with Grant, *Father Goose*. Subsequent film thrillers, *Mirage* (1965) and *Arabesque* (1966), were not so successful. Stone became known for his adaptations. In 1969 he adapted for the screen the Broadway musical *Sweet Charity.* For NBC television he adapted George Bernard Shaw's *Androcles and the Lion* (1967), and Billy Wilder's *Some Like It Hot* for Broadway as the musical *Sugar* (1972), as well as the novel *The Taking of Pelham One, Two, Three* for the screen (1974). Stone had been asked years earlier to write a Broadway musical about the Founding Fathers. By the late 1960s, he decided Americans could use a history lesson wrapped in a different package. The result was *1776*, an unlikely hit that told of the days leading up to the signing of the Declaration of Independence, which won him one of his three Tony awards. He was nominated six times for Tonys and won three, scoring on Broadway with the Lauren *Bacall musical *Woman of the Year* (1981) and *Titanic* (1997). He later worked sporadically in film, with his credits including *Who Is Killing the Great Chefs of Europe?* (1978), adapted from a novel. A much-respected craftsman, show doctor, and wit, Stone had legions of friends in Hollywood and New York and was the uncredited collaborator on dozens of major film and theatrical productions.

[Stewart Kampel (2nd ed.)]

STONE, RICHARD BERNARD (1928–), U.S. politician. Born in New York, Stone graduated from Harvard in 1949 and from Columbia University Law School in 1954. He was admitted to the Florida bar in 1955. He was city attorney of Miami 1966–67 and was elected to the Florida State Senate in his first try for office, serving 1967–70. He was then elected Florida secretary of state, serving from 1971 until he resigned to run for the U.S. Senate on the Democratic ticket in 1974. He was elected the first Jewish senator to serve Florida since 1845 but was defeated in the 1980 elections. Stone was active in Jewish and Zionist affairs.

In July 1975, he was named to the Presidential Committee on U.S. Participation in the Olympics by President Gerald R. Ford. Stone served as ambassador at large and special envoy to Central America (1983–84) and as U.S. ambassador to Denmark (1992–93).

STONE, STEVEN MICHAEL (Steve; 1947–), U.S. baseball player and sportscaster, 1980 Cy Young Award winner. Born in Euclid, Ohio, Stone was an all-around athlete as a child, shooting a hole in one at golf at age 11 and winning the Cleveland junior tennis title at age 13. In 1965, Stone graduated Bush High School in Cleveland, where he won All-State honors in baseball as a junior and captained the team as a senior, and was the winning pitcher in a state high school All-Star game. Stone attended Kent State University, and signed with the San Francisco Giants on February 15, 1969, before graduating. After three years in the minor leagues, Stone made his Major League debut on April 8, 1971. He played for the San Francisco Giants (1971–72), Chicago White Sox (1973), Chicago Cubs (1974–76), Chicago White Sox (1977–78), and Baltimore Orioles (1979–81). Stone had never won more than 15 games until he dazzled the baseball world in 1980 with a 25–7, 3.23 ERA season to win the Cy Young Award, and was named American League Pitcher of the Year by *The Sporting News.* He also started and pitched three perfect innings in the All-Star game, and in one stretch won 14 games in a row, two shy of the AL record. Tendonitis curtailed his season in 1981, and in June 1982 Stone announced that he was retiring from baseball. Stone finished with a 107–93 record, and an ERA of 3.96 in 1,789 innings, and 1,065 strikeouts. He is 3rd on the all-time list of wins and strikeouts by a Jewish pitcher, behind Ken *Holtzman and Sandy *Koufax, and fourth in games. Stone was the rare pitcher who called his own pitches from the mound, giving signs to the catcher on what he would throw. After retiring, Stone worked for the Cubs as a broadcaster from 1983 to 2000 and in 2003–4, when he left amid a controversy involving Cubs players who felt he was being overly critical of their performance. Stone was hired the next year by Chicago radio station WSCR to host a weekly talk show, and by ESPN to work some of the network's baseball telecasts.

[Elli Wohlgelernter (2nd ed.)]

STOPNICA, small town near Busko, in Kielce province, central Poland. Jews settled there in the 17th century. They owned 12 houses in the town in 1663. The Jews of Stopnica had certain trading rights in this period and were exempt from services to the governor (*starosta*). They were granted a royal privilege in 1752 authorizing their communal autonomy and rights to engage in trade and crafts, the latter being regulated by an agreement concluded in 1773 between the leaders of the community and the municipal authorities. The representatives of the province (*galil*) of *Sandomierz, within the framework of the *Councils of Lands, convened in Stopnica in 1754 and 1759. There were 375 Jews paying the poll tax in Stopnica and 188 in the surrounding villages in 1765. Between 1823 and 1862 the authorities of Congress Poland placed difficulties in the way of Jewish settlement in Stopnica because of its proximity to the Austrian border. In 1869 Stopnica lost its status as a city. During the 19th century *Ḥasidism gained influence within the community.

The Jewish population numbered 1,014 (49% of the total) in 1827; 1,461 (69%) in 1857; 3,134 (71%) in 1897; and 3,328 (76%) in 1921. They were mainly occupied in small-scale trade and crafts, including tailoring, shoemaking, and carpentry, and in carting.

[Shimshon Leib Kirshenboim]

Holocaust Period

During the German occupation Stopnica belonged to the General Government, *Radom District, in Busko County. At the outbreak of World War II there were about 2,600 Jews in Stopnica. In the course of the fighting the town center – mainly inhabited by Jews – was burnt down. After the Germans entered, shooting Jews on the streets became a common phenomenon. The Jews were compelled to pay a high "contribution" (fine) and in order to ensure payment the Germans took as hostage leading Jewish personalities, some of whom were killed. On the eve of Passover 1940, 13 Jews were dragged from their homes and shot. An "open" ghetto was set up but the Jews were forbidden under penalty of death to leave it. Tailoring workshops were established, providing the craftsmen with some employment and small wages. The number of Jews grew gradually with the influx of deportees and refugees from *Plock, *Gabin, Radom, *Lodz, and *Cracow, and in 1942 from the surrounding villages. By November 1940 there were 3,200 Jews in Stopnica; in May 1941, 4,600; in April 1942, 5,300; and in June 1942, 4,990. On the eve of Passover 1942, the police shot the president of the Judenrat and his son.

On Nov. 5–6, 1942, the liquidation of the ghetto took place. The German police and Ukrainian formations, with the help of the Polish police and the fire-brigade, shot 400 elderly and children at the Jewish cemetery, sent 1,500 young men to labor camps in *Skarzysko-Kamienna, and drove the remainder, about 3,000, on foot to the train station in Szczuczyn (Shchuchin). On the way many were killed. Jews caught in hiding in the ghetto were shot or included in the transport. The victims were sent by train to *Treblinka. In Stopnica itself about 200 young Jewish men and women remained alive, employed in workshops and on road building. This group was sent in January 1943 to labor camps in Sandomierz and Poniatow.

[Danuta Dombrowska]

BIBLIOGRAPHY: Halpern, Pinkas, 389, 394, 399, 528; *Słownik geograficzny Królestwa Polskiego*, 11 (1890), 374; R. Mahler, *Yidn in Amolikn Poyln in Likht fun Tsifern* (1958), index; B. Wasiutyński, *Ludność żydowska w Polsce w wiekach XIX i XX* (1930), 54, 71, 76, 78; A. Rutkowski, in: BŻIH, no. 15–16 (1955), 148, 174; no. 17–18 (1956), 106–28, passim.

STORA (Satorra), Algerian family. ABRAHAM (15th century) spent time in several Algerian cities and eventually settled in Bougie, where he was a merchant and community leader. REUBEN (16th century) served as an interpreter for the Spanish forces during their conquest of *Oran in 1509. In 1512, he was given a house by the Spanish in the old Jewish quarter. His grandson succeeded him but was put to death in the mid-16th century for unknown reasons. The post was then given to Jacob Cansino. The Storas remained loyal to the Spanish during the Moorish invasions of Oran in the 17th century, despite Spanish injustices to the Jews. PAUL (20th century) was president of the consistoire of Algiers. During World War II, when offered the position of president-general of the Union of Algerian Jewry, which was organized by the Vichy government for collaborationist purposes, he courageously refused.

BIBLIOGRAPHY: Hirschberg, Afrikah, 2 (1966), 99–100, 114.

STORAX (Gr. στύραξ), a sap with medicinal properties. According to Pliny (*Natural History* 12:81) and Dioscorides (*De materia medica* 1:79) it was extracted from trees growing wild in Syria and the vicinity. Some identify it with the "balm" enumerated among the "choice fruits of the land" that Jacob sent to Egypt (Gen. 43:11), and among the wares brought "from Judah and the land of Israel" (Ezek. 27:17) to Tyre. Balm of Gilead is mentioned (Gen. 37:25; Jer. 8:22, 46:11), and is praised by Jeremiah as a remedy for wounds (46:11; 51:8). Linnaeus, who determined the scientific names of plants, thought that storax was extracted from the tree called in modern Hebrew *livneh refu'i* which he termed *Styrax officinalis*. However in the light of tests made in Israel it is very doubtful if a sap with medicinal or aromatic qualities can be extracted from this tree. The storax of the ancients was probably extracted from a different tree, seemingly from the *Liquidambar orientalis* which grows wild in northern Syria and may even have been grown in Israel; from it is extracted an aromatic sap with healing qualities called *storax liquidis*. This may possibly be the biblical balm, though other sources led to the conclusion that *ẓori* ("balm"), *nataf*, and *ketaf* are synonyms for *balsam.

The *Styrax officinalis* is widespread in the forests of Israel, and Hosea (4:13) mentions "*alon, livneh,* and *elah*" (*oaks, *livneh*, and *terebinths) among the shady trees used as sites for idol worship. The reference seems to be to the tree called in Arabic *avḥar* and also *livnah* or *luvnah*, a name connected with the silvery white color of the underside of its leaves (for the *livneh* of Gen. 30:37 see *Poplar). The flowers of this tree are sweet smelling and similar in shape to citrus blossom. The poisonous fruit is used for trapping fish. Arabs do not fell this tree because of the legend that "demons recline beneath it."

BIBLIOGRAPHY: Loew, Flora, 3 (1924), 388–95; G.M. Crowfoot and L. Baldensperger, *From Cedar to Hyssop* (1932), 108; H.N. and A.L. Moldenke, *Plants of the Bible* (1952), index; J. Feliks, *Olam ha-Ẓome'aḥ ha-Mikra'i* (1968²), 118; idem, in: *Teva va-Areẓ*, 10 (1968), 168–78.

[Jehuda Feliks]

STORK (Heb. חֲסִידָה, *ḥasidah*). The stork, the *Ciconia ciconia*, has been identified with the *ḥasidah*, enumerated among birds forbidden as food (Deut. 14:18). According to the Talmud it derives its name ("the kindly") from the fact that it shows kindness to its fellows (Ḥul. 63a), a reference to the harmony of a flight of storks. These flights pass over Israel in the autumn and spring during their migrations to and from northern and southern countries. Jeremiah (8:7) notes that the bird has fixed times of migration. Small flights of the young birds remain in Israel during the summer, but the stork does not hatch its eggs in Israel and the verse "as for the stork the juniper trees [Heb. *beroshim*] are its house" (Ps. 104:17) refers to the stork's hatching its eggs on the *juniper trees in Lebanon. Although this identification of the *ḥasidah* can be taken as certain, it should be noted that some commentators took it to refer to a different bird, with the result that in certain localities in Spain the stork was mistakenly permitted by Jews as food. Generally however, the stork is regarded as an unclean bird (*Beit Yosef* to Tur, YD 92).

BIBLIOGRAPHY: R. Meinertzhagen, *Nicoll's Birds of Egypt*, 2 (1930), 430–2; F.S. Bodenheimer, *Ha-Ḥai be-Arẓot ha-Mikra*, 2 vols. (1949–56), index, s.v. *ḥasidah*; J. Feliks, *Animal World of the Bible* (1962), 83.

[Jehuda Feliks]

STOROZHINETS (Rom. **Storojineț**; Ger. **Storozynetz**), city in Chernovtsy district, Ukraine, in the historic region of Bukovina; until World War I, within Austria, and between the two world wars within Romania. Jews settled there at the close of the 18th century, but severe restrictions imposed by the Austrian authorities hindered the expansion of the Jewish settlement. The number of Jews nevertheless increased, mainly as a result of immigration from Galicia and Russia. In 1865, a Jew of Galician origin, who had established himself in the town in 1828, received a royal authorization, the first of this category to be granted there, to acquire real estate and trade without restriction. The Jewish population numbered 1,601 (32.9% of the total) in 1880, and 4,832 (48.3%) in 1910. The local Jews mainly engaged in commerce and industry connected with the products of the forest in the vicinity, and in timber processing, as well as in crafts and the liberal professions. At the beginning of the 20th century, 99% of the tailors, shoemakers, and carpenters of the town were Jews. Communal institutions were organized as the Jews became established. From 1890, the community was reorganized in accordance with the Austrian law concerning the communities which then came into force. A large main synagogue was erected at the beginning of the 20th century. There were also many ḥasidic and other houses of prayer. The members of the community, most of whom were Ḥasidim, belonged to various trends of Ḥasidisim, principally *Vizhnitsa and Sadagora. The community also had *ḥadarim* and yeshivot, but from 1871 many Jewish children also attended the general schools. In 1909 the community established a private Jewish secondary school for boys and girls that functioned, with a few interruptions, until 1938. In World War I, many Jews left the town during the fighting in the area. After the war, under Romanian rule, community life again flourished despite the antisemitic and oppressive regime. Zionist organizations were active there between the two world wars. Jews took part in municipal life.

Holocaust and Contemporary Periods

In 1940, Storozhinets was occupied by the Red Army. Many Jews lost their property as a result of nationalization, and relations between the local Jewish Communists and the other members of the community became strained. In 1941, the town was restored to the Romanian authorities, then collaborating with the Germans, During that year, most of the 2,482 Jews in the town were deported to the death camps in *Transnistria.

After World War II, at the commencement of the Soviet regime, a small number of Jews still remained in the town but this number subsequently declined.

BIBLIOGRAPHY: H. Gold, *Geschichte der Juden in der Bukowina*, 2 (1962), 108–13.

[Yehouda Marton]

°**STORRS, SIR RONALD** (1881–1955), British military governor (1917–20) and district commissioner (1920–26) of *Jerusalem. Storrs, who came from a distinguished English family, was a brilliant classics student at Cambridge University. In 1904 he joined the Egyptian service, became Oriental secretary, and during World War I was a member of the Arab Bureau at British military headquarters in *Cairo. After political service in Mesopotamia, he was appointed military governor of Jerusalem. There Storrs, who had a great sense of the historical occasion, was in his element. More of a diplomat than an administrator, he did a great deal for the city, founding the Pro-Jerusalem Society, with financial support from influential friends in Britain and elsewhere, to preserve and restore the Old City and revive its indigenous crafts. In 1926 he became governor of Cyprus and later of Northern Rhodesia.

His memoirs, *Orientations* (1937), and his work *Lawrence of Arabia: Zionism and Palestine* (1940) contain reservations about Zionism and the activities of the Zionist Commission, headed by Chaim *Weizmann. During the Arab riots of 1920 and 1921 the leaders of the *yishuv* and the Hebrew press accused Storrs of deliberate leniency toward the Arab rioters. Jewish leaders' demands for his resignation in 1921 were rejected by the high commissioner, Sir Herbert *Samuel.

ADD. BIBLIOGRAPHY: ODNB online.

[Edwin Samuel, Second Viscount Samuel]

°**STRABO** (first century C.E.), Greek historian and geographer. Born in Pontus, he traveled widely, and received the conventional education of his day. He wrote a comprehensive history in 47 books. Of this work only a few extracts have been preserved, most of them in *Josephus' *Antiquities*. It is not surprising that the bulk of these extracts deal with matters relating to the history of the Jews, Josephus having used Strabo as a source for his history of the Hasmonean state. To what extent Josephus was further indebted to Strabo it is impossible to gauge. In any event, the history of Strabo, who was free from the pro-Herodian tendencies and the Syrian-Greek viewpoint of *Nicholas of Damascus, provided to some extent a counterbalance to the latter's writings. In his history Strabo frequently quoted the literary sources to which he had recourse; thanks to this the few extracts from him in *Antiquities* have preserved the evidence of other historians who wrote about the Jews (Timagenes, *Hypsicrates of Amisus).

The earliest event in Jewish history known to have been mentioned by Strabo was *Antiochus Epiphanes' attack on the Temple in Jerusalem (Jos., Apion, 2:84). His comments on the penetration of Jews throughout the entire inhabited world, on their status in Cyrene, and on the organization of the Jewish settlement in Egypt (Jos., Ant., 14: 115ff.) are particularly interesting. On the authority of Timagenes, Strabo depicts *Aristobulus I in a favorable light (*ibid.* 13:319), contrary to Josephus' previous assessment of him, which was based on Nicholas. The final quotation from Strabo's history deals with the execution of *Antigonus, and from it the affection of the Jewish people for Herod's rival can be gauged.

Strabo's other great work, his *Geographica* in 17 books, has survived in its entirety. It is a comprehensive geography in which Ereẓ Israel is described in the 16th book. Here, Strabo states that the most acceptable view about the origin of the Jews is that which regards them as descended from the Egyptians. According to him, the Jewish religion and nation originated with an Egyptian priest called Moses, who came to realize that the Egyptians were misguided in depicting their gods in the form of animals. The same applied to the Greeks, with their anthropomorphic conception of the gods. Moses held that God embraces all things, the earth and the sea, that He is in reality "what we call heaven, the universe, and the nature of things." Having succeeded in persuading intelligent men of this, Moses led them to the place now known as Jerusalem, where he established a just regime which his direct heirs maintained for a certain time. Later, however, they had priests who were superstitious and subsequently even tyrannical. These changes led to acts of brigandage, as a result of which Judea and the neighboring countries suffered. Strabo briefly mentions the kingdom of *Alexander Yannai and the conquest of *Pompey (Jos., Ant., 14:34–6). Generally he displays great respect for Moses and the ancient Jewish regime but rejects its later development. The last event in the political history of Judea quoted in Strabo's geography is the banishment of *Archelaus in 6 C.E. In his geographical survey, Strabo describes at some length the region of Jericho and the Dead Sea, which he confuses with the Sirbonian Lake. His knowledge of the geography of Ereẓ Israel is poor, and he apparently did not really know the country.

BIBLIOGRAPHY: Schuerer, Hist, 97, 179, 329 n. 11; Reinach, Textes, 89–113; K. Albert, *Strabo als Quelle des Josephus* (1902); Heinemann, in: MGWJ, 63 (1919), 113–21; Norden, in: *Festgabe Harnack* (1921), 292–301; F. Jacoby, *Fragmente der griechischen Historiker*, 2A (Texts) (1926), 92f., 430–6; 2A (Commentary) (1926), 83, 291–5; Roos, in: *Mnemosyne*, 2 (Ger., 1935), 236–8; W. Aly, *Strabonis Geographica*, 4 (Ger., 1957), 191ff.

[Menahem Stern]

°STRACK, HERMANN LEBERECHT (1848–1922), German Orientalist and theologian. Strack was born in *Berlin, where he became professor of Oriental languages and director-founder of the university's Institutum Judaicum. He was recognized as a leading non-Jewish scholar in the field of Bible and Talmud, Hebrew and Aramaic linguistics, Masorah, etc. Serving as an expert in German courts on a number of cases with antisemitic overtones, Strack took a firm line in defense of Judaism, and at the same time was active in the Protestant missionary movement (he edited *Jahrbuch der evangelischen Judenmission* and *Zeitschrift fuer die Arbeit der evangelischen Kirche in Israel*).

In the field of linguistics his main publications were *Grammatik des Biblisch-Aramaeischen* (1921^6); *Hebraeische Grammatik* (1952^{12}; also in English (1886)); *Juedisches Woerterbuch* (1916), a Yiddish dictionary; and *Lehrbuch der neuhebraeischen Sprache und Litteratur* (1884). Of importance for the study of Masorah was his *Dikduke ha-Te'amim des Ahron ben Moscheh ben Ascher* (1879), edited in cooperation with S. *Baer; *Catalog der hebraeischen Bibelhandschriften der... Bibliothek in St. Petersburg* (with A.E. Harkavy, 1875); and *Prophetarum posteriorum Codex babylonicus Petropolitanus* (1876). He also took part in the controversy surrounding the *Firkovich forgeries (*A. Firkowitsch und seine Entdeckungen*; 1876). Strack wrote *Einleitung in das Alte Testament* (1906^6) and edited, together with O. Zoeckler, a short Bible commentary ($1891–1905^2$), to which he contributed several biblical books; he also published a translation of and commentary on Ben Sira (1903). He wrote, with P. Billerbeck, a commentary to the New Testament which was based on Talmud and Midrash (4 vols., 1922–28) and demonstrated the Jewish rabbinic origin of most of Jesus' sayings. He also issued annotated translations of several Mishnah tractates with Billerbeck, including *Avot* (1915^4), together with a vocalized text. Strack's *Einleitung in Talmud und Midrash* (1921^5) became a standard reference work, the English edition, *Introduction to the Talmud and Midrash* (1931), which is based on the last but revised German one, being sponsored by the Central Conference of American Rabbis.

In fighting the malicious accusations against Judaism, Strack wrote *Das Blut im Glauben und Aberglauben der Menschheit* (1911^8), which was translated into English by H. Blanchamp as *The Jew and Human Sacrifice...* (1909). Works in the same vein include: *Sind die Juden Verbrecher von Religionswegen?* (1900); *Juedische Geheimgesetze?* (1925^9); *Herr Adolf Stoecker christliche Liebe und Wahrhaftigkeit* (1886^2); and *Die Aufhebung der Juden-Emanzipation und ihre rechtliche Begruendung* (1895; cf. also his *Das Wesen des Judentums*; 1906). Strack's courageous stand against growing German antisemitism brought him bitter denunciation by antisemitic writers such as K. Erbsreich and Th. *Fritsch; on the other hand his missionary activities came under attack from Jewish writers (P. Meyer, *Woelfe im Schafsfell*, 1893).

STRAKOSCH, MAURICE (1825–1887), pianist and impresario. Born in Gross-Seelowitz, Moravia, Strakosch toured Europe as a pianist and immigrated to the U.S. in 1848. From 1856 he worked chiefly as an operatic impresario, managed the concerts of his sister-in-law, the celebrated soprano Adelina Patti, and toured with his company in the U.S. and Europe. Strakosch composed one opera *Giovanni di Napoli*, and pieces for piano, and wrote *Ten Commandments of Music for the Perfection of the Voice* (posthumous, 1896), and *Souvenirs d'un Impresario* (1887).

STRAND, PAUL (1890–1976), U.S. photographer. The son of immigrants from Bohemia, Strand was born in New York City and given his first camera at the age of 12 by his well-to-do father. He was sent to the Ethical Culture School in 1904 for an education that gave equal weight to individual creativity and social engagement. There his teacher was Lewis Hine, who at the time was photographing immigrants arriving at Ellis Island. Hine introduced him to Alfred *Stieglitz, and in 1916 Strand had his first one-man exhibition at Stieglitz's famed "291" gallery. The last two issues of Stieglitz's *Camera Work* in 1917 were devoted to Strand's photography, whose principal early subjects were Manhattan life and 20th-century machinery. Several of his images from that period, including "Wall Street" (1915), "The White Fence" (1916) and "Blind" (1916), are considered revolutionary in their starkness and use of light and shadow. Strand's street photos of 1916, taken with a special camera designed to capture his subjects unawares, emulated Hines' engaged stance. He focused on the city's rich cultural mix (two Orthodox Jewish men deep in conversation; an elderly woman with a time-creased face in Washington Square Park), but he also portrayed the city's dispossessed, including a picture of a disheveled woman yawning and a man with dazed eyes in an Irish slum.

After service in the Army Medical Corps, where he was introduced to X-ray and other medical camera procedures, Strand collaborated with Charles Sheeler on the film *Manhattan*, released as *New York the Magnificent* in 1921. Strand made his exquisitely composed landscape and nature photographs in the 1920s. With the onset of the Depression, Strand became active in politics. A socialist, he worked with the Group Theater, which had been formed in New York by Harold *Clurman, Cheryl Crawford, and Lee *Strasberg in 1931. The Group was an attempt to create a theater collective with a company of trained players dedicated to presenting works by contemporary writers. Members of the group tended to hold left-wing political views and wanted to produce plays that dealt with important social issues. In 1935 Strand visited the Soviet Union and met the radical film director Sergei *Eisenstein. When Strand returned to the United States, he began to produce socially significant documentary films, including *The Plow That Broke the Plains* in 1936, his film on trade unions in the Deep South, *People of the Cumberlands* the following year, and *Native Land* in 1942. The latter evolved from a Congressional hearing on anti-labor activities. When it was released on the eve of World War II, its message was considered politically divisive.

In 1936 Strand joined with Berenice Abbott to establish the Photo League in New York, whose initial purpose was to provide the radical press with photographs of trade-union activities and political protests. The Museum of Modern Art in New York held a full-scale retrospective of Strand's work in 1945. Later in that decade, the Photo League was investigated by the House Un-American Activites Committee. Several members were blacklisted and Strand decided to leave the United States and live in France. There he produced *A Profile of France* with Claude Roy in 1952, *A Village* with Cesare Zavattini in 1955, and *Tir a'Mhurain*, about the Hebrides, with Basil Davidson in 1968.

[Stewart Kampel (2nd ed.)]

STRANGERS AND GENTILES. Ancient Israel was acquainted with two classes of strangers, resident aliens and foreigners who considered their sojourn in the land more or less temporary. The latter were referred to as *zarim* (זָרִים) or *nokhrim* (נָכְרִים), terms generally applied to anyone outside the circle the writer had in view (e.g., Ex. 21:8; 29:33). They retained their ties to their original home and sought to maintain their former political or social status. On occasion they came as invaders (II Sam. 22:45–46; Obad. 11). More often they entered the land in the pursuit of trade and other commercial ventures. The usual laws were not applicable to them, and they were protected by folk traditions concerning the proper treatment of strangers (cf. Job 31:32) and by special conventions resulting from contractual arrangements between the Israelites and their neighbors (cf. I Kings 20:34). In the legislation of Deuteronomy, an Israelite may charge a foreigner usury though he may not do so to a fellow Israelite (Deut. 23:21), and the septennial remission of debts does not apply to the debts of foreigners (Deut. 15:3). On the other hand, barred from the cult (Ex. 12:43), the foreigner was also not bound by the ritual laws, and it was permissible to sell him animals that had died a natural death (Deut. 14:21). The fact that Deuteronomy includes a special prohibition against foreigners' ascending the throne (Deut. 17:15) and that Solomon specifically requested that God listen to their prayers (I Kings 8:41) may indicate the important position some foreigners occupied during the age of the monarchy.

In contrast with the foreigner, the *ger* (גֵּר), the resident alien, lived more or less permanently in his adopted community. Like the Arabic *jār*, he was "the protected stranger," who was totally dependent on his patrons for his well-being. As W.R. Smith noted, his status was an extension of that of the guest, whose person was inviolable, though he could not enjoy all the privileges of the native. He, in turn, was expected to be loyal to his protectors (Gen. 21:23) and to be bound by their laws (Num. 15:15–16).

Prior to the Exodus, resident aliens as a class were unknown in Israel. On the contrary, the Israelites themselves were *gerim* (Ex. 22:20) as were their ancestors (Gen. 15:13; cf. 23:4; Ex. 2:22). Aliens were apparently attracted to their ranks when they left Egypt (Ex. 12:38, 48), and their numbers were further augmented during the time of the conquest of Canaan (Josh. 9:3ff.). By far the greatest number of *gerim* consisted of the earlier inhabitants of Canaan, many of whom were neither slain as Deuteronomy commands (cf. e.g., 7:2) nor reduced to total slavery (cf. I Kings 5:29; II Chron. 2:16–17). Immigrants also were numbered among them – foreigners who sought refuge in times of drought and famine (cf. Ruth 1:1) and refugees who fled before invading armies.

Since all of the landed property belonged to Israelites (cf. Lev. 25:23–24), the *gerim* were largely day laborers and artisans (Deut. 24: 14–15; cf. 29:10). Both the Book of the Covenant which classed them among those who were dependent (Ex. 23:12) and the Decalogue which referred to them as "your stranger" (*gerkha*; Ex. 20:10; cf. Deut. 5:14) attest their inferior position in Israelite society. While a few acquired wealth (cf. Lev. 25:47), most of them were poor and were treated as the impoverished natives. Thus, they were permitted to share in the fallen fruit in the vineyard (Lev. 19:10), the edges of the field, and the gleanings of the harvest (Lev. 23:22; see also Poor, Provisions *for). Like the other poor folk they were also granted a share in the tithe of the third year (Deut. 14:29) and the produce of the Sabbatical Year (Lev. 25:6).

Since the foreigners' defenselessness made them vulnerable, the Israelites were frequently reminded of God's special concern for the weak (Ex. 22:21–22; cf. Deut. 10:17–19) and were enjoined not to molest them (Ex. 22:20; cf. Jer. 7:6). They were not to be abused (Deut. 24:14) and were to receive equal treatment before the law (Deut. 1:16; cf. 24:17; 27:19). In case of accidental homicide, the cities of refuge were open to them as well (Num. 35:15), for there was to be "one standard for stranger and citizen alike" (Lev. 24:22). Moreover, the Israelites were enjoined to be especially solicitous of the welfare of the *ger* and to befriend him as one of their own, since they could recall the sufferings of their own people in the land of Egypt (Lev. 19:34; cf. Deut. 10:19).

With the passage of time, the *gerim* were assimilated culturally and religiously. Doeg the Edomite, for instance, was a worshiper of YHWH by the time of Saul (I Sam. 21:8), as was Uriah the Hittite in the reign of David (II Sam. 11:11). Hence, the *ger*, in contrast to the *nokhri*, was required in many cases to conform to the ritual practices of the native Israelite. Thus, *gerim* were subject to laws dealing with ritual purification (Num. 19:2–10), incest (Lev. 18:26) and some of the food taboos (Lev. 17:10–16; but cf. Deut. 14:21). They were expected to observe the Sabbath (Ex. 20:10; Deut. 5:14), participate in the religious festivals (Deut. 16:11, 14), and fast on the Day of Atonement (Lev. 16:29). They were permitted to offer up burnt offerings (Lev. 17:8; 22:18; Num. 15:14ff.) and, if circumcised, even to sacrifice the paschal lamb (Ex. 12:48–49; Num. 9:14). Indeed, they, no less than the Israelites, were expected to be loyal to YHWH (Lev. 20:2; cf. Ezek. 14:5–8).

However, social differences did remain, and some *gerim* were better received than others. While third generation offspring of Edomites and Egyptians might "be admitted into the congregation of the Lord" (Deut. 23:8–9), Ammonites and Moabites were not to be admitted "even in the tenth generation" (23:4). Furthermore, even while the Holiness Code admonished Israelites not to subject their fellows to slavery (Lev. 25:39), they were specifically permitted to do so to the children of resident aliens (25:45–46). A Hebrew slave belonging to a *ger* could be redeemed immediately, and if not redeemed served until the Jubilee Year (25:47ff.), but one belonging to an Israelite served until the *Jubilee (25:39ff.). Correspondingly, a Hebrew could serve as a hired or bound laborer (25:40) of an Israelite, but only as a hired laborer of an alien (25:50). Indeed, the humble position of the *ger* generally was emphasized by the usage of the term in the Holiness Code: e.g., "The land is Mine; you are but strangers resident with Me" (25:23; cf. 25:35, but see *Proselyte).

In practice, of course, there were Israelites who became propertyless and destitute and had to support themselves as day laborers (Deut. 24:14; cf. Lev. 19:13), and no doubt there were also *gerim* who became prosperous and acquired land. This narrowed the gap between the two classes and resulted in frequent intermingling. Marriages between the two groups did take place, only marriages between Israelites and the aboriginal inhabitants of Palestine being prohibited in Deuteronomy 7:3–4. On close examination it appears that even in the theory (and it was hardly more) of the author of Ezra-Nehemiah only marital alliances with the non-Israelites of Palestine were illegitimate, because the laws of Deuteronomy 7:3–4 and 23:3–9 applied to them. The absorption of converts from other nations is reported with equanimity – Ezra 2:59–60 (= Neh. 7:61–62); Ezra 6:21; Nehemiah 10:29 ("and everyone who withdrew from the uncleanness of the peoples of the lands [note the plural] to the teaching of God"). The phenomenon of such conversions is alluded to in Isaiah 56:3 and Zechariah 2:15; 8:20ff., and the predictions of the conversion of the gentiles in Isaiah and Jeremiah are well known. In late Second Temple times, the term *ger* had become virtually synonymous with "proselyte," and strangers were admitted to the religious fellowship of Israel (Jos., Apion, 2:28).

[David L. Lieber]

Whereas, as stated, the word *ger* in the Bible was taken to refer to the proselyte, the *ger toshav*, the "resident stranger," was regarded as belonging to a different and special character. He was a non-Jew who accepted some, but not all of the commandments of the Torah, as a result of which he was permitted to reside in the land of Israel and enjoy many of the privileges of citizenship. Various views are expressed by the rabbis as to the qualifications which entitle the resident gentile to be accepted as a *ger toshav*, ranging from the renunciation of idolatry to one who accepts the whole of the discipline of the Torah with the exception of the dietary laws (Av. Zar. 64b). The *halakhah* was decided that it applies to the person accepting the seven "Noachide Laws" (Maim. Yad, Issurei Bi'ah 14:7; Sh. Ar., YD 124:1). The laws, privileges, and restrictions of the *ger toshav* are exhaustively dealt with in the Talmud. As, however, it was laid down that the acceptance of a *ger toshav* was permitted only during the period that the Jubilee was in force, and that law was no longer in power in talmudic times, the discussion was purely academic.

For a full discussion of the post-biblical period see *Gentile.

BIBLIOGRAPHY: W.R. Smith, *Lectures on the Religion of the Semites* (1889, 1956), 75–79; M. Guttmann, in: HUCA, 3 (1926), 1–20; T.J. Meek, in: JBL, 49 (1930), 172–80; Pedersen, Israel, 1–2 (1926), 40ff., 505; 3–4 (1940), 397, 583–4; Kaufmann Y., Toledot, 2 (1947), 191–2, 459; idem, *Golah ve-Nekhar*, 1 (1954²), 226ff.; L.A. Snijders, in: OTS, 10 (1954), 1–154; de Vaux, Anc Isr, 74ff.; ET, 6 (1965), 296–304.

STRÁNSKÝ, JAROSLAV (1884–1973), Czech politician. Stránský was born in Brno, the son of Adolf Stránský (1855–1931), one of the leading Jews in the National Democratic Party, who was a member of the Austro-Hungarian Parliament before World War I and became the first minister of commerce in Czechoslovakia when it became an independent state in 1918. He had abandoned Judaism, however, and his son was raised as a Christian. Jaroslav Stránský played a leading role in the Czech National Socialist Party (founded before, and having no connection with, the National Socialist Party of Hitler) and, on the outbreak of World War II, went into exile in England with the president of Czechoslovakia, Edvard Beneš. He served in the cabinet of the Czechoslovak government-in-exile in London and was deputy prime minister, minister of education, and minister of justice in the postwar government of the country. In 1948, he returned to Great Britain, and later settled in the United States, but again returned to England, where he died. Stránský was conscious of his Jewish origin. In 1922, he took over the ownership of the Czech-language daily *Lidové Noviny* in Brno, which had been founded by his father, and transformed it into a liberal daily of international standard. It was one of the few Czech newspapers to support Jewish aims in Ereẓ Israel under the Mandate and to defend Jews against antisemitism both in the pre-Hitler era and the period preceding the Nazi occupation of Czechoslovakia after the Munich agreement.

BIBLIOGRAPHY: J.W. Bruegel, in: *The Jews of Czechoslovakia*, 2 (1971); K. Baum, in: *Jewish Chronicle* (Aug. 24, 1973).

STRANSKY, JOSEF (1872–1936), conductor and composer. Born in Humpolec, Bohemia, Stransky studied medicine (receiving his M.D. in Prague, 1896), and music in Leipzig and then in Vienna with Dvořák and Bruckner. Stransky conducted a student orchestra in Prague, and in 1898 had his first professional engagement at the Neues Deutsches Theater there. In 1903 he moved to the Hamburg Opera as principal conductor and in 1910 worked with the Bluethner Orchestra in Berlin. In 1911 he succeeded *Mahler as conductor of the New York Philharmonic Society (to the distress of Strauss, who thought Stransky would give German conducting a bad name abroad). A large bequest (by Joseph Pulitzer) enabled him to carry out successfully the sweeping reforms instituted by Mahler. He pleased his New York audience with his uncontroversial but not altogether unspiced programs. He conducted the première (1922) at the Philharmonic of *Schoenberg's Bach chorale-prelude transcriptions, despite having received a sulphurous letter from Schoenberg. In 1923, he became conductor of the newly formed New York State Symphony Orchestra, but gave up conducting in 1925 to work as an art dealer. Stransky published the book *Modern Paintings by German and Austrian Masters* (1916); composed an operetta, *Der General*; songs; orchestral and other instrumental music. His editions include an adaptation of Berlioz's *Béatrice et Bénédict*, which he felt needed reorchestration for modern taste.

BIBLIOGRAPHY: Grove Music Online; *Baker's Biographical Dictionary of Musicians* (1997); O.G. Villard, "Joseph Stransky Resigns," in: *The Nation*, 116, no. 3008 (February 28, 1923).

[Naama Ramot (2nd ed.)]

STRASBERG, LEE (1901–1982), U.S. theatrical director and teacher. Born in Budanov (then Austria-Hungary), his family moved in 1909 to New York, where Strasberg became entranced with the theater, largely through the influence of the Chrystie Street Settlement House. In 1923, after seeing a performance of the Moscow Art Theater then touring under the direction of Stanislavsky, he enrolled in the American Laboratory Theater, which followed Stanislavsky's realistic principles. He began his professional career in 1924 with the Theater Guild, first as assistant stage manager and then as an actor. In 1931 Strasberg, Cheryl Crawford, and Harold Clurman founded the Group Theater, which came to exercise a profound influence on the American stage. He directed several plays, of which *Men in White* (1933) won a Pulitzer Prize, but resigned in 1937 after a policy dispute. In 1947, he joined the Actors Studio and became its artistic director in 1948. The Studio was largely shaped by him and became famous for its "Method" approach to acting. Its pupils won acclaim for an intense personal style. Strasberg has said, "Acting is to live on a stage. This means an actor must be able to react to an imaginary stimulus just as hard as he would to a real stimulus." Strasberg maintained close ties with Jewish theater and directed several productions for *Habimah, the National Theater of Israel.

He made his film debut at age 73, portraying a Jewish mobster in *The Godfather, Part II* (1974), which garnered him an Oscar nomination for Best Supporting Actor. Subsequent films include *The Cassandra Crossing* (1976); the TV movie *The Last Tenant* (1976); *And Justice for All* (1979); *Boardwalk* (1979); *Going in Style* (1979); and the TV movie *Skokie* (1981).

His book *A Dream of Passion: The Development of the Method* was published in 1987.

His daughter, SUSAN (1938–1999), a film and stage actress, was best known for her performance on Broadway in the title role of *The Diary of Anne Frank* (1955), which earned her a Tony nomination for Best Actress. A close friend of Marilyn Monroe's, she wrote *Marilyn and Me* (1992), as well as *Bittersweet* (1990).

BIBLIOGRAPHY: *Current Biography Yearbook, 1960* (1961), 406–8; *Enciclopedia dello Spettacolo* (1962), s.v., incl. bibl. **ADD. BIBLIOGRAPHY:** C. Adams, *Lee Strasberg: The Imperfect Genius of the Actors Studio* (1980); L. Hull, *Strasberg's Method as Taught by Lorrie Hull* (1985); J. Strasberg, *Accidentally on Purpose* (2000).

[Raphael Rothstein / Ruth Beloff (2nd ed.)]

STRASBOURG (Ger. **Strassburg**), capital of the department of Bas-Rhin, Alsace, E. France. The earliest conclusive evidence on the presence of Jews in Strasbourg dates from 1188. During the anti-Jewish persecutions connected with the Third Crusade, the Jews fled from the town and a number of other towns, but they appear to have returned after a short while. The statutes of the town (from about 1200) mention the Jews, who were by then living in a special quarter. At the beginning of the 13th century at the latest, they already owned a cemetery; the oldest remaining epitaph belongs to the year 1213. The synagogue is not mentioned until 1292. The size of the Jewish community, as well as its economic power, is reflected in the fact that in 1242 it paid the highest tax of all the Jewish communities of the empire. Until about 1260, the Jews of Strasbourg were subjected to the authority of the bishop. From the first half of the 13th century, some Christians bore the surname of "Jew" (*Jude*), which probably attests to their Jewish origin. In spite of demographic losses due to conversions, the number of Jews in Strasbourg was constantly on the rise as a result of immigration from other Alsatian localities, as well as other Germanic localities, so that in 1306, with additional arrivals from France, the Jewish population numbered about 300. *Moneylending appears to have been their sole economic activity, their customers including Christian religious institutions and noblemen. Loans ran as high as 6,000 livres.

In his account of the massacre of the Jews of Strasbourg after they had been accused of propagating the *Black Death, a local chronicler points out that the real poison by which the Jews of Strasbourg had perished was usury. In addition, the Jews also suffered as a result of the battle for municipal power between the patricians and the master craftsmen. The patrician municipality sought to protect the Jews, and at the end of 1348, when rumors spread that the Jews were poisoning the wells in order to spread the plague, it preferred to refrain from any action until an inquiry had been conducted in the localities where similar accusations had been voiced (including *Lausanne, *Chillon, *Berne, *Colmar, *Cologne, and *Freiburg in Breisgau). Although the guilt of the Jews was taken for granted almost universally, the council of Strasbourg remained convinced of their innocence and even took up their defense. On Feb. 9, 1349, however, Mayor Peter Swarber and two counselors were compelled by the craftsmen to resign. On February 13, the new council decided to burn the Jews. According to tradition, the decision was enforced on Saturday, February 14, when 2,000 Jews perished. The only ones spared were those who accepted baptism; however, a number of those converts were the victims of a new persecution in the summer of 1349, when the plague actually reached the town and took a heavy toll of lives. On Sept. 12, 1349, Emperor Charles IV officially pardoned the town for the massacre of the Jews and the plunder of their possessions. Until the French Revolution, two calls upon a horn, played nightly, perpetuated the memory of the supposed treason of the Jews.

In spite of the town's decision to prohibit the settlement of Jews for a period of 100 years, a number of Jews were authorized to reside there from 1369 onward, though against the payment of extremely high fees. They numbered at least 25 families when they were again expelled from Strasbourg at the end of 1388, on this occasion "forever." Those banished established themselves in surrounding villages, from where they continued to maintain commercial relations with the inhabitants of Strasbourg. Magistrates frequently intervened (e.g., in 1570) to prohibit these relations completely or reduce them to a minimum. From at least 1512, and probably much earlier, the Jews who wished to enter the town were required to pay an expensive toll. In time, this admission fee was increased by an additional payment to the municipal servant who accompanied each Jew in all his movements and supervised the lawfulness of his activities. When the exceptional Jew was authorized to spend the night in Strasbourg – normally at the Corbeau Inn or at the Ours-Noir Hotel – he had to pay a double toll, that is, the fee which he would have paid had he returned the next day. On certain occasions, such as in 1639, this supervision was accompanied by an interrogation and a search at the gates of the town to determine the goods which the Jews brought and the persons with whom they intended to establish contact. The Jews endeavored to circumvent both the payment of toll rates and humiliating treatment by concluding their transactions outside the town. The municipality, in order to protect its handsome income, would then intervene against such practices. In 1648, for example, it prohibited the sale of horses at any site other than the horse market of the town.

Relations between the Jews and the Council of Strasbourg were not always hostile. Joseph Joselmann b. Gershom of Rosheim, in particular, succeeded through his diplomatic talents in obtaining the council's support. In 1537 he obtained a letter of recommendation to the prince-elector of Saxony, and in 1541 called the attention of the council to the anti-Jewish pamphlet of the Strasbourg preacher M. *Bucer, and in 1543 to the writings of M. *Luther, "Concerning the Jews and Their Lies" and "Concerning the Shem ha-Meforash" (Tetragrammaton). He thereby succeeded in obtaining an order against new publications of these writings.

Once the town came under French sovereignty (1681), the severity of the anti-Jewish measures was eased or they were even temporarily suspended, such as in time of war to enable the Jews of the surrounding area to take refuge in the town. The minister R.L. de Voyer Marquis d'Argenson, however, was compelled to intercede in favor of Moses Blim, a purveyor of the army, and his Jewish partners to enable them to reside in Strasbourg until 1748. Again, the intervention of the royal authorities was required in 1767 to permit *Cerfbeer, also an army purveyor, to reside in Strasbourg during the winter and, from 1771, during the entire year. The numerous members of Cerfbeer's family and the persons engaged in his service also benefited from this personal authorization, so that in 1785 he occupied three or four houses with 60–70 people. In the letters patent of 1785, which abolished the "corporal toll," a special mention was made of Strasbourg, where "the Jews are subjected to a corporal tax which reduces them to the level of animals… a levy which appears to debase humanity." In spite of the king's commitment to indemnify the town for the loss of income, Strasbourg was reluctant to apply this edict.

A few years later there was almost unanimous opposition to granting the rights of citizenship to the Jews. Immediately after the National Assembly had done so, however, many Jews established themselves in Strasbourg. In the revolutionary year II, it was especially the Jews who became the target of the antireligious campaign. A contradictory situation resulted: it was the Republic which revived medieval practices by seizing, together with religious objects, all the Jewish books, particularly those of the Talmud, to be burned in an immense auto-da-fé. In 1806 seven delegates represented the 1,500 Jews of Strasbourg at the *Assembly of Notables. Immediately after the constitution of the Consistories, Joseph David *Sinzheim, until then chief rabbi of Strasbourg, became chief rabbi of the Central Consistory. The community, which was constantly growing, soon developed exemplary institutions. In addition to the synagogues, it supported a vocational school from 1825, an old age home called "Elisa" from 1853, and a rabbinical seminary for a short while from 1885. The German annexation of 1871 was responsible for the departure of a number of Jews for France. There was a particularly rapid numerical growth between the two world wars. Immigration from abroad was much lower than in other towns. In 1931, of almost 8,500 Jews living in Strasbourg, over 60% were born in France.

[Bernhard Blumenkranz]

Hebrew printing

In 1504 Johann Grueninger published in Strasbourg G. Reysch's *Margarita Philosophica*, which included a Hebrew grammar by Pelican, a Hebrew alphabet, and other Hebrew texts, all printed by woodblocks. In 1541 Paul *Fagius was appointed professor of Hebrew at Strasbourg University, and this led to the production of Hebrew textbooks for his students by the press of Johann Knobloch (or his successors). Fagius' own edition of parts of *Targum Onkelos* appeared in these texts in 1546, probably together with reprints of other texts, which he and Elijah Levita had published at Isny and Konstanz in the preceding years. In 1589 Elias Schadaeus set up a Hebrew press for which he himself prepared the Hebrew type, and in 1591 printed an edition of Proverbs, Ecclesiastes, and Song of Songs.

It was only toward the end of the 18th century that Hebrew printing resumed in Strasbourg, with the publication of Bezalel Ashkenazi's *Shitah Mekubeẓẓet* on *Ketubbot* and Solomon Algazi's *Leḥem Setarim*, by Jonah Lorenz in 1777. This printing venture was inspired and financed by Cerfbeer and his brother-in-law, David Sinzheim. The auxiliary personnel were experienced typesetters, correctors, etc. from other printing centers, such as Hanau.

Holocaust Period

With the outbreak of World War II in September 1939, the entire population of Strasbourg was evacuated to the southwest of France. After the French capitulation (June 1940), the Jewish community succeeded in making basic provisional arrangements in southwestern France – setting up a synagogue and a welfare bureau in Périgueux and a synagogue in Limoges. As a result, a large number of Jews from Strasbourg were able to survive the war. Chief Rabbi René *Hirschler, mobilized in 1939, continued in his post as an itinerant rabbi after the defeat and Nazi occupation, and visited the Strasbourg Jewish community dispersed in more than 50 localities south of the Loire. In Strasbourg proper, the Nazis set fire to the Quai Kléber synagogue erected in 1898 and systematically destroyed all traces of the structure. Strasbourg Jews played a major role in educational work, welfare, sanitation, and in armed resistance. They set up agricultural schools and helped to direct them in the framework of the Jewish French scouting movement (Eclaireurs Israélites de France). Under the auspices of *OSE, they helped open clinics and children's homes. They also organized flight to Switzerland or to Palestine (via Spain) for infants and older children and joined in the armed resistance. As a result of their participation in these activities, Rabbis Hirschler, Robert Brunschwig and Elie Cyper, along with youth leader Léo Cohn, were arrested and deported to death camps. Rabbis Samy Klein and Aron Wolf were also killed in the course of their resistance work.

Contemporary Period

About 10,000 Jews lived in Strasbourg on the eve of World War II. Eight thousand came back after the liberation, 1,000 died in concentration camps, and another 1,000 decided to settle elsewhere. In 1965 there were 12,000 Jews in Strasbourg (4.5% of the total population). This increase was the result of natural growth (300), immigration from smaller Alsatian centers (1,200), immigration from Central Europe (500), and settling of refugees from North Africa (2,000). The Jewish population had been diminishing since 1955; however, in the late 1960s the birthrate was 7.5% and the mortality rate 12%; the number of mixed marriages increased by 40% between 1960 and 1965. Nevertheless, the community was strengthened by the absorption of an independent Polish-rite group in 1948 and North African Jews, for whom oratories were built or arranged in several neighborhoods. By the turn of the century the Jewish population had increased to around 15,000. Strasbourg Jewry was one of the most active communities on the continent of Europe after World War II. Institutions created since 1945 stress Jewish education, contrary to the trend prevalent before. They included a kindergarten, a full-time school, two boarding houses for high school and university students, two yeshivot, a monthly bulletin, and a weekly radio program. The University of Strasbourg had a chair of Jewish studies held by André *Neher. The Synagogue of Peace was inaugurated in 1958. It includes a large community center, which has often been the site of national and international Jewish congresses. The latent antisemitism of the Alsatian population was expressed by the establishment of organizations to prevent the return of Jewish property (confiscated in 1940) to the owners, and later to prevent the erection of a synagogue on city land.

[Lucien Lazare]

BIBLIOGRAPHY: Germ Jud, 1 (1963²), 367–72, 552; 2 (1968), 798–805; A. Glaser, *Geschichte der Juden in Strassburg* (1924 Strasbourg²); I. Loeb, in: *Annuaire de la Société des études juives*, 2 (1883), 137–98; H. Bresslau, in: ZGJD, 5 (1892), 115–25, 307–34; *La Révolution Française*, 52 (1907), 553–4; E. Schnurmann, *La statistique de la population juive de Strasbourg* (1935); P. Hildenfinger, in: REJ, 58 (1909), 112–28; M. Ginsburger, *ibid.*, 79 (1924), 61–78, 170–86; 80 (1925), 88–94; A. Hermann and L. Weil, *Les oeuvres sociales israélites privées à Strasbourg* (1922); *La synagogue de la Paix* (1958); *A nos martyrs* (1951). Printing: A. Marx, *Studies in Jewish History and Booklore* (1944), 318ff.; L. Rostenberg, in: *Journal of Jewish Bibliography*, 2 (1940), 47ff.; B. Friedenberg, *Toledot ha-Defus ha-Ivri… Eiropah…* (1937), 93–94; A. Hertzberg, *French Enlightenment and the Jews* (1968), 171 n.82.

STRASBURGER, EDUARD (1844–1912), German botanist and one of the founders of modern plant cytology. Strasburger, born in Warsaw, was made director of the Botanical Institute at Jena in 1869, and two years later, when only 27 years of age, was appointed full professor there. In 1880 he became professor at Bonn, where he worked until his death. Under his direction, the botanical institute became a world center for research in botany and especially in the newly emerging science of cell biology.

Strasburger's early research dealt with the embryology of liverworts, ferns, and conifers. He recognized the homology of the archegonium of the fern with the embryo sac of conifers. This discovery helped lay the basis for one of the fundamental generalizations of plant evolution: the essential correspondence of the life cycles of higher and lower plants. Among Strasburger's pioneer contributions to cell biology were his description of mitotic cell division in plants and his observation of the longitudinal splitting of the chromosomes in the process. Strasburger arrived at the conclusion that the cell division process was the same in plants and animals and set forth the generalization that nuclei arise only from preexisting nuclei. His observation of the union of male and female nuclei in the reproduction of plants was of the utmost significance in establishing the universal character of the phenomenon of fertilization and the role of the nucleus as the vehicle of heredity. Strasburger was the author of the important book *Ueber Zellbildung und Zelltheilung* (1875), and an influential *Lehrbuch der Botanik fuer Hochschulen* (1894, 1967^{29}; *Textbook of Botany,* 1898, 1965^{7}).

BIBLIOGRAPHY: G. Karsten, in: *Berichte der Deutschen botanischen Gesellschaft*, 30 (1912), (61)–(86) (second pagin.), incl. bibl. of his writings.

[Mordecai L. Gabriel]

STRASHUN, MATHIAS (Mattityahu; 1819–1885), talmudic scholar, founder of the Strashun Library. Mathias, the son of Samuel *Strashun, was born in Vilna. His family was well-to-do and at the age of 13 he married the eldest daughter of the wealthy Joseph Elijah Eliasberg and was financially independent during his whole life. According to his own testimony (*Ha-Maggid*, 3 (1859), 158), in his youth he already began to make marginal notes on every book he read and acquired a profound mastery of every branch of Jewish scholarship. He knew Greek and Latin, as well as Russian, Polish, and German, and had an extensive knowledge of philosophy, history, and astronomy. When H.M. *Pineles and H.S. *Slonimski had a difference of opinion on an astronomical-calendrical point, they agreed to submit the dispute to Strashun for his final decision (*ibid.*, 12 (1868), 149). He was approached to accept the position of rabbi of Berlin but refused. Besides his scholarly activities, he was a prominent communal leader, the head of the Ẓedakah Gedolah (which in effect was the official organization of the community of Vilna) of the *ḥevra kaddisha*, and was responsible for the collection of funds for Ereẓ Israel. He was one of the heads of the *Mekiẓe Nirdamim society. Independent, he adopted a firm attitude and showed considerable initiative. Strashun was held in esteem by the government authorities; he was appointed to the city council of Vilna and was a member of the Vilna branch of the Russian Imperial Bank in 1869, and was decorated by the government.

Only one work by Strashun has been published, the *Mattat Yah* (1892), a commentary on, and annotation to, the *Midrash Rabbah*, edited by his friend Shalom Pludermacher, who included it in a bibliographical list of Strashun's 316 periodical publications. It was in those publications, including *Pirḥei Ẓafon, Kerem Ḥemed, Ha-Maggid*, and *Ha-Levanon*, that, generally under the title *Minḥah Belulah ba-Shemen*, Strashun published his researches, but mostly not under his own name, using a wide variety of noms de plume, either initials, or such names as Ani Ve-Hu, Ve-Hu Ve-Hu, etc. They also appeared in the *Israelitische Literaturblatt* (1883) and his annotations to the Midrash were published in A. *Wuensche's German translation of the *Midrash Rabbah.* His selected writings appeared in Hebrew in 1969.

[Shillem Warhaftig]

Strashun was a devoted bibliophile and book collector and his extensive library, bequeathed to the Vilna community, contained over 5,700 volumes, many personally annotated by him. The library was opened to the public in 1892, and in 1901 it was transferred to a house specially erected for the purpose in the courtyard of the synagogue. The first director of the library, Samuel Strashun, edited and published a catalog of the library in his *Likkutei Shoshannim* (1889). After his death, the library was headed by his son Isaac Strashun. The librarian Khaykel Lunski, who supervised the reading room, became one of the most popular figures in Vilna. Over the years, many books were added to the library, mainly from the contributions and estates of authors and rabbis of Vilna. From 1928 the University of Vilna sent a copy of every book published in Poland in Hebrew or Yiddish to the library. By the late 1930s, there were over 35,000 books in the library, the overwhelming majority of them dealing with Hebraica and Judaica. There were also 150 manuscripts and five incunabula. The library served the vast number of students, teachers, journalists, and authors of Vilna. Various scientific circles convened in the library building. Zalman *Shneour described it in his poem "Vilna." When the Nazis occupied the town in the summer of 1941, they destroyed some of the books and transferred others to Frankfurt. Several thousand books were found after World War II and distributed among the YIVO Library in New York and the National Library and other libraries in Ereẓ Israel.

[Yehuda Slutsky]

BIBLIOGRAPHY: D. Radner, in: *Keneset ha-Gedolah*, 1 (1890), 3rd pagination, 25f.; *Ha-Asif*, 2 (1886), 45–47; 3 (1887), 122; S. Pludermacher, "*Zikkaron la-Ḥakham*," in: M. Strashun, *Mattat Yah* (1892); K. Lunski, in: Y. Yeshurin (ed.), *Vilne; A Zamlbukh…* (1935), 273–87; J.L. Maimon, *Middei Ḥodesh be-Ḥodsho*, 6 (1960), 111ff.; Z. Haravy, *Le-Ḥeker Mishpeḥot* (1953), 47f.; idem, in: *Aresheth*, 3 (1961), 426–9; idem, in: S. Federbush (ed.), *Ḥokhmat Yisrael be-Ma'arav Eiropah*, 3 (1965), 345–55; S. Federbush, *Ḥikrei Yahadut* (1965), 319–24; M. Berger, in: Z. Scharfstein (ed.), *Ha-Ḥinnukh ve-ha-Tarbut ha-Ivrit be-Eiropah Bein Shetei Milḥamot ha-Olam* (1957), 511–9; Ḥ. Lunski,

Me-ha-Getto ha-Vilna'i (1921), 54ff.; Ḥ.N. Maggid-Steinschneider, *Ir Vilna*, 1 (1900), 283–7.

STRASHUN (Zaskovitzer), SAMUEL BEN JOSEPH (1794–1872), Lithuanian merchant and talmudic scholar. Originally called Zaskovitzer, after the place of his birth, Zaskovitz, Strashun adopted the surname of his father-in-law, David Strashun. David Strashun acquired a business in Vilna, and also opened a *Klaus* named after him. Samuel, relieved by his father-in-law of all material cares, devoted himself to study there. His teacher was R. Abraham *Danzig, who refers to him in his *Binat Adam* and *Ḥokhmat Adam* under his original name. Even after his father-in-law's death in 1843, he was able to continue his studies while his wife and brothers ran a department store in Vilna. Strashun was also one of the leaders of the Vilna community. He refused to accept an appointment as rabbi of Suwalki, devoting himself entirely to study and teaching.

Strashun's fame rests upon his extensive annotations and glosses on almost every tractate of the Talmud and of the Mishnah. He followed the example of Elijah Gaon of Vilna, eschewing, as he himself testifies (in a letter to R. Heshel Levin), the method of *pilpul*, confining himself to giving sources, establishing the correct text, commenting, and giving original interpretations. He dealt with individual words and even letters, often pointing out how a mistake in explaining initials had distorted the text. He did not hesitate to suggest new halakhic rulings, not all of which were accepted. His annotations on the Talmud take up about 100 folio pages. In addition he annotated the *Midrash Rabbah*, adopting the same method. Strashun's commentary reveals his wide knowledge of Hebrew grammar and his acquaintance with history, geography, and foreign languages. In addition to the above commentaries, which are included in the Romm (Vilna) editions of the Talmud and Midrash, he wrote novellae to Maimonides' *Mishneh Torah*, to the Shulḥan Arukh *Oraḥ Ḥayyim*, and to the *Sifrei*. He also composed glosses to the *Ma'aseh Rav*, on the customs of Elijah Gaon of Vilna (1887).

Of his children the best known was Mathias *Strashun.

BIBLIOGRAPHY: D. Radner, in: *Keneset ha-Gedolah*, 1 (1890), 3rd pagination 22–24; Ḥ.N. Maggid-Steinschneider, *Ir Vilna* (1900), 250; Z. Harkavy and R. Katzenellenbogen, in: S. Strashun, *Mekorei ha-Rambam la-Rashash* (1956), 53ff.; idem, *Le-Ḥeker Mishpaḥot* (1953), 44ff.; J.L. Maimon, *Middei Ḥodesh be-Ḥodsho*, 6 (1960), 109ff.

[Shillem Warhaftig]

STRASSFELD, MICHAEL (1950–), U.S. rabbi and educator. Born to a rabbinic family, his father Meyer Strassfeld was an Orthodox rabbi in Dorchester, Massachusetts, who moved to a Conservative synagogue in Marblehead. A graduate of Brandeis University (B.A. 1971, M.A. 1972), Strassfeld was influenced by American anti-establishment "counterculture" in the late 1960s. He was active in the *havurah* (Jewish religious fellowship) movement as part of a Jewish counterculture, cultivating personal involvement and knowledge as alternatives to the passivity and superficiality of Judaism as practiced in the conventional American middle-class synagogue. Between 1973 and 1980, while a member of havurot in Boston and New York, he co-edited the three volumes of the highly popular *The Jewish Catalog*, a do-it-yourself guide to Jewish living designed to make Jewish knowledge and *havurah*-style practice accessible to Jews disaffected with the conventional synagogue. Between 1979 and 1982 he served as chairperson of the National Havurah Committee, the coordinating body of independent havurot in North America.

In 1982 Strassfeld assumed the first of a series of positions in Congregation Ansche Chesed in New York City, a run-down synagogue amenable to experimenting with innovative practices in order to survive. He opened the synagogue as a venue for several havurah-inspired *minyanin* (prayer quorums) accommodating different prayer styles, and applied insights derived from the Jewish counterculture to the congregational setting.

His realization that the synagogue as the central institution of American Jewry could be a venue for innovation in Jewish life led him to pursue rabbinical studies. In 1991 he was ordained by the Reconstructionist movement, which had cultivated havurot and a participatory spirit of innovation since its inception as a distinct denomination in the early 1960s. From 1991 to 2001 Strassfeld served as rabbi of Congregation Ansche Chesed. In 2001 he became rabbi of the Society for the Advancement of Judaism in New York, a congregation known for its creative approach to Judaism since its establishment by Mordecai M. Kaplan in 1922.

Strassfeld has been active in infusing elements of the ecstatic worship and intimate community associated with Ḥasidism into American Jewish life. The resulting synthesis, known as "neo-Ḥasidism," draws from the egalitarianism of the *havurah* while recognizing a role for the "rebbe," or charismatic spiritual leader. Neo-Ḥasidism originated in the late 1960s as a motif differentiating the Jewish counterculture from "establishment" Judaism of that time. In his books and teaching, and especially by assuming the rabbinate of an urban congregation, Strassfeld has embodied the principle of introducing neo-Ḥasidism into the mainstream of contemporary American Judaism.

His major publications include *A Book of Life* (2002); *A Night of Questions: A Passover Haggadah*, co-editor J. Levitt. (2000); *The Jewish Holidays* (1985); *A Shabbat Haggadah*, editor (1981); *The Third Jewish Catalog*, co-editor S. Strassfeld (1980); *A Passover Haggadah*, editor (1979); *The Second Jewish Catalog*, co-editor S. Strassfeld (1975); *The Jewish Catalog*, co-editors R. Siegel and S. Strassfeld (1973). He has also contributed articles to Jewish periodicals, notably *Response*, *Shma*, and *Tikkun*.

[Peter Margolis (2nd ed.)]

STRASSFELD, SHARON (1950–), U.S. Jewish educator, feminist, and community organizer. Educated at the Providence Hebrew Day School in Rhode Island and the University of Massachusetts (B.A. 1971), Strassfeld participated in the Jewish "counterculture" through the *havurah* movement as a member of "Havurat Shalom" in suburban Boston from 1971 to 1975. Drawing from this experience, she co-edited the three volumes of *The Jewish Catalog*, (1973, 1975, and 1980), inspired by the countercultural *Whole Earth Catalog* which had appeared several years earlier. Strassfeld was instrumental in establishing the annual Havurah Summer Institute, a week-long educational and cultural retreat first held in 1979, and an innovative Jewish day school, the Abraham Joshua Heschel School in New York, which opened in 1983.

Strassfeld is also noted for introducing women's sensitivities into the Jewish counterculture, which despite its purported egalitarianism had initially been male-dominated. Following the birth of her daughter, she (with then-husband Michael Strassfeld) pioneered the *simḥat bat* ceremony in the 1970s as the girls' equivalent of the male *brit milah*. Through her writing and educational activities she has become a proponent in the Jewish mainstream for the equality of women in Judaism that she originally voiced in the Jewish counterculture.

Strassfeld applied her business acumen to effect a synthesis between conventional financial activities and Jewish countercultural values of *tikkun olam* (repairing the world). As a businesswoman, her real estate and construction activities have generated resources that enabled her to support creative programs such as Ohel Ayalah (free High Holiday services for non-affiliated Jews in New York) and the Jewish Appleseed Foundation (outreach to isolated Jewish communities). She has headed Strassfeld Consulting, providing real estate services for non-profit organizations, and is a principal of the Soul Support Foundation, a philanthropic fund.

Her major publications include *Everything I Know: Life Lessons from a Jewish Mother* (1998); *The Jewish Family Book*, co-edited with K. Green (1983); *The Third Jewish Catalog*, co-edited with M. Strassfeld (1980); *Behold a Great Image*, co-edited with B. Aron (1980); *The Second Jewish Catalog*, co-edited with M. Strassfeld (1975); *The Jewish Catalog*, co-edited with R. Siegel and M. Strassfeld (1973). She also contributed articles to Jewish periodicals, notably *Response* and *Shma*, and wrote a weekly column syndicated in the Jewish press titled "Dear Molly."

[Peter Margolis (2nd ed.)]

STRAUBING, city in Bavaria, Germany. A Jewish community existed there by the 13th century. A tosafist, Solomon of Straubing, lived in the town. The tombstone of R. Azariah b. Hosea, with a Hebrew inscription of 1328, was located beside a house in the former Jews' street. In the privilege granted the town by Duke Stephen I of Bavaria in 1307, the Jews along with the Christians were designated as "free inhabitants." They were called upon to build or repair fortifications. In 1338, following a rumor of *Host desecration, the Jews in Straubing were massacred. The duke pardoned the burghers and awarded them the property of the victims. A new community came into being before 1400. In 1439 the Jews were expelled from the newly created duchy of Straubing-Bavaria. The *oath *more Judaico* is contained in the Straubing Town Book, or Red Book, compiled between 1472 and 1482 from older sources dating back to the 14th century. Straubing Jews are mentioned in Regensburg in 1466. After the emancipation in Bavaria (1872), Jews again moved to Straubing and the adjoining region. By 1890, 253 of them lived in the town and neighboring localities. In 1897 they formed the Lower Bavarian Jewish community. A synagogue and community center was consecrated in Straubing in 1907, and a cemetery was acquired in 1923. The community numbered 141 in 1913 (0.64% of the total population) and 115 in 1925–33 (0.5%), with approximately 110 in the affiliated localities. More than half subsequently emigrated. The synagogue was burned down in 1938. Fifty Jews from Straubing and 41 from the affiliated localities perished in the Nazi deportations. After the end of World War II approximately 700 Jews who had arrived in Straubing on their forced march from concentration camps stayed there; 100 of them remained until 1948. The community was reestablished and in 1968 numbered 112 persons and 119 in 1970. In 1964 a memorial plaque for the Holocaust victims was dedicated in the rebuilt synagogue. In 1988 a commemorative plaque was consecrated by the city of Straubing in memory of the Jewish victims of the Nazi era. The synagogue was restored in 1988–89. The Jewish community numbered 141 in 1989 and 1,729 in 2004. The increase is explained by the immigration of Jews from the former Soviet Union.

BIBLIOGRAPHY: E. Rosenthal, *Zur Rechtsgeschichte der Staedte Landshut und Straubing* (1883), 207, 251–4, 318; H. Maor, *Ueber den Wiederaufbau der juedischen Gemeinden in Deutschland seit 1945* (1961) 30, 61; R. Straus, *Urkunden und Akten zur Geschichte der Juden in Regensburg* (1960), no. 168 (22); *Germania Judaica*, 2 (1968), 680, 685–6, 806–8; 3 (1987), 1433–38; S. Schwarz, in: K. Bosl (ed.), *Festschrift Straubing* (1968), 295–304; I.A. Agus, *Rabbi Meir of Rothenburg* (1947), 584 no. 632; *Deutsche Reichstagsakten*, 13 (1908), no. 24; 14 (1935), no. 142; *Handbuch der juedischen Gemeindeverwaltung* (1913), 135; FJW, 139. **ADD BIBLIOGRAPHY:** B. Ophir and F. Wiesemann (eds.), *Die juedischen Gemeinden in Bayern 1918–1945* (1979), 71–73; I. Schwierz, *Steinerne Zeugnisse juedischen Lebens in Bayern* (1992^2), 333–34; A. Unterholzner, *Straubinger Juden – juedische Straubinger* (1995).

[Toni Oelsner / Larissa Daemmig (2nd ed.)]

STRAUS, U.S. family of department store merchants, industrialists, public servants and philanthropists. Its founder, LAZARUS STRAUS (1809–1898), went to the U.S. in 1852 and settled in Talbotton, Georgia. Straus's three sons, all of whom were born in Otterberg, Rhenish Palatinate, and his wife joined him in 1854. Moving his family to New York City in 1865, Straus became a crockery importer there.

His eldest son, ISIDOR (1845–1912), was a merchant, congressman, and philanthropist. During the Civil War he worked as (aide to) a London-based Confederate agent and as a Confederate bond salesman there and in Amsterdam. After returning to the U.S. in 1865, Isidor entered the family business in New York. He and his brother Nathan became partners in the R.H. Macy Department Store in 1874, and the store's sole owners in 1887. Isidor subsequently became a partner in Abraham and Straus (1893). He was elected to Congress to fill an unexpired term (1894–95), served as a member of the New York and New Jersey Bridge Commission, and was a founder of the Reform Club of New York. Active in Jewish affairs, he was president of the Educational Alliance, a member of the American Jewish Committee, and a founder of an endowment fund for the Jewish Theological Seminary. He died in the sinking of the *Titanic*.

Lazarus's second son, NATHAN (1848–1931), was a merchant and philanthropist. He served as New York park commissioner (1889–93), health commissioner, and as a member of the New York Forest Preserve Board. Nathan's lifelong interest in public health manifested itself in his establishment in New York City of a milk pasteurization laboratory and milk distribution stations (1892, 1894, 1897); an emergency relief system for the distribution of coal and food to the poor (winter of 1892–93); and a chain of boarding houses which supplied a bed and breakfast to the poor for five cents (winter of 1893–94). During the severe winter of 1914–15 Straus served one-cent meals in the milk stations he had established earlier. He also established the Pasteur Institute in Palestine, and endowed Hadassah's Nathan Straus child health welfare stations and the Nathan and Lina Straus health centers in Jerusalem and Tel Aviv. It was estimated that Straus gave two-thirds of his fortune to various projects in Palestine; in recognition, *Netanyah was named for him.

The youngest brother, OSCAR SOLOMON (1850–1926), was a diplomat, author, public servant, and jurist. Oscar was educated at Columbia University (L.B. 1873). While his father and brothers were expanding their crockery store into a far-flung mercantile firm, he was drawn through his law practice into the circles of political reformers. A "mugwump" who worked for the election of Grover Cleveland in 1884, Straus was rewarded by the Democrats with the post of minister to Turkey. On that mission (1887–89) and during two subsequent missions (minister, 1898–1900; ambassador, 1909–10) he dealt with the problems of missionary rights, the protection of naturalized U.S. citizens, and the course of "dollar diplomacy."

In matters of foreign policy Oscar was usually the anti-imperialist and pacifist. Active in the organized peace movement, he labored continuously for the establishment of legal machinery for the amicable settlement of international disputes. During World War I and its aftermath he championed the idea of a league of nations. Theodore Roosevelt appointed Straus to the International Court of Arbitration at The Hague, an appointment which was renewed four times. In domestic affairs Straus stressed political reforms (e.g., direct primaries) as the best means to preserve the democratic system. A Cleveland Democrat who broke with the party when it backed free silver, he stood for sound money, low tariffs, liberal immigration policies, and civil service reform. He emphasized the interest of the public in the clashes between capital and labor, and, like Theodore Roosevelt, he advocated cooperation with business and regulation of trusts when he served as Roosevelt's secretary of commerce and labor (1906–09). In 1912 he followed Roosevelt into the Progressive Party, and he ran as that party's candidate for governor of New York.

The first Jew to hold a cabinet post, Straus displayed a strong sense of responsibility toward the Jewish community. On numerous occasions he interceded with U.S. and foreign statesmen on behalf of the suffering Jews of Russia and Romania. In 1906 he helped found the *American Jewish Committee. Opposed to political Zionism, he nonetheless contributed to various projects for the physical rehabilitation of Palestine and he supported territorialist schemes for the settlement of persecuted Jews. As a founder and officer of the Baron de Hirsch Fund he also worked to ease the plight of the newly arrived immigrants to the United States. Straus, a Reform Jew, found ideological similarities between the missions of Judaism and Americanism. As first president of the American Jewish Historical Society, and in numerous writings, particularly *The Origin of the Republican Form of Government in the United States of America* (1887, 1925), he stressed the impact of Hebraic concepts upon U.S. culture. His other writings include: *Roger Williams, the Pioneer of Religious Liberty in the United States* (1896) and *Under Four Administrations* (1922), an autobiography.

JESSE ISIDOR (1872–1936), the son of Isidor Straus, graduated from Harvard in 1893. He went to work for Macy's in 1896, was subsequently elected firm president in 1919, and supervised its growth into the world's largest department store. Governor Franklin D. Roosevelt appointed Straus to serve first on the New York State Commission for the Revision of Tax Laws and then as head of the New York State Temporary Emergency Relief Administration (1931). In his latter position he was responsible for supervising the disbursement of $20 million in unemployment funds. Straus, who organized the Roosevelt Business and Professional League to work for Roosevelt's election as president, was appointed ambassador to France by Roosevelt in 1933. As ambassador he urged the removal of trade barriers between the U.S. and France. He resigned in 1936 because of ill health. His son JACK ISIDOR (1900–1985) inherited the management of Macy's, of which he became director in 1928, vice president in 1939, president in 1940, and chairman of the board in 1956. A second son, ROBERT KENNETH (1905–1997), was active in New Deal politics in Washington, where he served as deputy administrator of the National Recovery Act before going into business.

NATHAN JR. (1889–1961), the son of Nathan Straus, was born in New York City and worked as a reporter for the New York *Globe* (1909–10). He resigned to devote himself to the family interests at R.H. Macy (1910–13), but soon resumed his editorial career. From 1913 to 1917 he was editor and publisher of the humorous magazine *Puck*. After World War I service as a navy ensign, Straus was assistant editor of the New York *Globe*. He resigned in 1920 in opposition to the paper's support for Harding and its anti-League of Nations stand. From 1920 to 1926 Straus served in the New York State Senate as a Democrat, where he became interested in public housing legislation. He subsequently served as state administrator for the National Recovery Administration (1934), was a member of the New York City Housing Authority (1936), and head of the U.S. Housing Authority (1937–42). He resigned from the latter position as a result of dissatisfaction among conservative congressmen over his leadership of the authority. As president of radio station WMCA, he steered the station into an increasingly liberal stance on public issues. Straus wrote *Seven Myths of Housing* (1944), and *Two-Thirds of a Nation – A Housing Program* (1952).

His son, R. PETER (1917–), took over the management of WMCA while purchasing additional radio stations to form the Straus Broadcasting Group. He also served as executive assistant to the director of the International Labor Organization in Geneva from 1950 to 1955 and director of the U.S. office from 1955 to 1958. In 1967 he was appointed by President Lyndon B. Johnson to be assistant director of the U.S. foreign aid program to Africa until 1969. Under President Jimmy Carter he served as director of the Voice of America (1977–79). After WMCA was sold in 1986, the company broadened into Straus Communications, a private chain that owns 11 radio stations and eight newspapers, of which Straus served as chairman. He was married to Ellen Sulzberger Straus for 45 years until her death in 1995. In 1998 he married writer Marcia Lewis, the mother of Monica Lewinsky. He wrote several books, including *Is the State Department Color Blind?* (1971); *The Buddy System in Foreign Affairs*; (1973); and *The Father of Anne Frank* (1975).

ROGER WILLIAMS (1893–1957), the son of Oscar Solomon Straus, graduated from Princeton in 1913. He married the daughter of Daniel *Guggenheim, and joined the American Smelting and Refining Company, owned by the Guggenheim family, becoming company president in 1941 and board chairman in 1947. Active in Republican Party politics, Straus was New York City manager for Thomas E. Dewey's 1948 presidential campaign and vice chairman of the Republican National Campaign Committee (1944). In 1954 he served as a member of the U.S. delegation to the UN General Assembly. Appointed in 1947 to the New York State Board of Regents, the supreme educational body in the state, Straus was named its chancellor in 1956. He was a founder of the National Conference of Christians and Jews (1928) and of the World Council of Christians and Jews (1947), and a member of the executive boards of the Union of American Hebrew Congregations, the American Jewish Committee, and the American Financial and Development Corporation for Israel. His son OSCAR II (1914–) served with the State Department in Washington from 1940 to 1945 before going into his father's business. In 1963 he became president of the Guggenheim Exploration Company. He was the first chairman of the Board of Trustees of the Rensselaerville Institute think tank and served for many years, after which he became honorary chairman. His younger brother, ROGER WILLIAMS JR. (1917–2004), went into publishing and in 1945 founded the prominent New York publishing house of Farrar, Straus, and Company in partnership with John C. Farrar.

BIBLIOGRAPHY: G.S. Hellman (ed.), *The Oscar Straus Memorial Volume* (1949); S. Birmingham, *Our Crowd* (1967), index; N.W. Cohen, *Dual Heritage. The Public Career of Oscar S. Straus* (1969), includes bibl. **ADD. BIBLIOGRAPHY:** M. Harriman, *And the Price Is Right: The R.H. Macy Story* (1958); I. Marmash, *Macy's for Sale* (1989).

[Naomi W. Cohen and Hanns G. Reissner / Ruth Beloff (2nd ed.)]

STRAUS, OSCAR (1870–1954), composer. Born and educated in Vienna, Straus also studied in Berlin with Max Bruch. In 1901, after conducting various theater orchestras in Austria and Germany, he became conductor at the satirical cabaret "Ueberbrettl" in Berlin. There he began writing musical sketches and chansons, including *Die Musik kommt*, and quickly proceeded to full-scale operettas, joining the mainstream of the "silver age" of the operetta which had just begun to establish a vigorous school at Berlin that paralleled the Viennese productions. His first works, such as *Die lustigen Nibelungen* (1904), were Offenbach-like parodies of Wagnerian operas. In 1907 he composed the first of his international successes, *Ein Walzertraum* ("A Waltz Dream"), and in 1908 the second one, *Der tapfere Soldat*, based on G.B. Shaw's *Arms and the Man*; it was known in English as the *The Chocolate Soldier* (New York premiere in 1909). Further successes followed almost yearly. In 1927 Straus settled in Vienna. After his works were banned by the Nazi regime he lived in Switzerland and France, and stayed in the United States from 1940 to 1948, when he returned to Europe. His last work, *Božena* (premiere Munich, 1952), is a work in the style of a folk opera based on Slavic material; it emphasizes the use of ensembles and choral scenes. He also wrote some orchestral, chamber, and piano works, as well as music for films, of which the music to Max Ophuls' *La Ronde* (1950) yielded a perennial waltz favorite.

The original form of his name was Strauss, but the spelling was changed because of pressure from German nationalistic elements who resented the possibility of linking the composer's name with the presumably Aryan Viennese Strauss family of composers. Ironically, the Viennese Strauss family were also discovered to have been of Jewish descent – a fact which the Nazi authorities hushed up by a manipulation of the documentary evidence after their takeover of Austria. Genealogical research has not, however, established any direct relationship between Oscar Straus and the Viennese Strausses.

BIBLIOGRAPHY: Riemann-Gurlitt; MGG, incl. bibl.; Grove, Dict; Baker, Biog Dict; B. Grun, *Prince of Vienna; the Life, the Times and the Melodies of Oscar Straus* (1955); H. Jaeger-Sunstenau, *Johann Strauss; der Walzerkoenig und seine Dynastie. Familiengeschichte, Urkunden* (1965), 84–87, 91.

[Bathja Bayer]

STRAUS, RAHEL GOITEIN (1880–1963), pioneering woman physician trained in Germany. Born and raised in an Orthodox family in Karlsruhe, Rahel Goitein was selected as valedictorian of the first graduating class of the first Girls' Gymnasium in Germany in 1899; she went on to become the first matriculated woman student at the University of Heidelberg. In order to complete her medical education, Rahel Goitein had to overcome many obstacles and much discrimination against her as a woman. Some faculty members, including the dean, tried to discourage her; she needed special permission to take courses and even to sit for her final exams. Nevertheless, she persevered; a month before her marriage to Eli Straus, a lawyer, in 1905, she passed her state medical boards and in 1908, she received her doctorate in medicine. For 25 years, Rahel Straus maintained a private medical practice in Munich, while at the same time running a model Jewish household and raising five children.

An ardent Zionist since her youth, Straus organized and led various women's Zionist groups in Munich, including the Association of Jewish Women to Support Cultural Work in Palestine before World War I and WIZO, the Women's International Zionist Organization, thereafter. She also served as vice president of the Jüdischer Frauenbund. She belonged to several radical feminist organizations, joining the German Association for Woman Suffrage in 1905 and the Women's International League for Peace and Freedom after the war.

Soon after the death of her husband in 1932, Straus emigrated to Palestine with her children. She set up a medical practice in Jerusalem, but, encountering difficulties adapting to a new language and environment, she retired in 1940, at the age of 60. Once again, she became involved in volunteer activities on behalf of women, establishing a homemaking school to train young immigrant girls, a service to collect, repair and distribute used clothing and furniture among the needy, and an occupational therapy workshop for handicapped women. She also established AKIM, a training institute for the rehabilitation of disabled children, which is still known as Beit Rahel Straus. In 1952, she helped found the Israeli branch of the Women's International League for Peace and Freedom and remained its honorary president until her death.

After retiring from medical practice, Rahel Straus wrote her memoirs, *Wir lebten in Deutschland: Erinnerungen einer deutschen Jüdin* (1961), discussing life in Germany before the Nazi era. She began to paint and to write poetry; she also became the author of a popular children's book of fairy tales in Hebrew. Her papers are found in the Leo Baeck Institute Archives at the Center for Jewish History in New York City.

BIBLIOGRAPHY: H. Pass Freidenreich, *Female, Jewish, and Educated* (2002); M. Krauss, "'Ein voll erfülltes Frauenleben': Die Ärztin, Mutter und Zionistin Rahel Straus (1880–1963)," in: H. Häntzschel & H. Bussmann (eds), *Bedrohlich gescheit: Ein Jahrbunder Frauen und Wissenschaft in Bayern* (1997), 236–41.

[Harriet Pass Freidenreich (2nd ed.)]

STRAUS, RALPH (1882–1950), English novelist and biographer. Born in Manchester and educated at Harrow and Cambridge, Straus is best known as the author of *Dickens, a Portrait in Pencil* (1928) and *Dickens, the Man and Book* (1936). He also wrote a mystical fantasy, *The Dust Which Is God* (1907); *The Unseemly Adventures* (1924); *Married Alive* (1925); and *Five Men Go to Prison* (1935).

STRAUS, ROGER, JR. (1917–2004), U.S. publisher. Roger Williams Straus, Jr., was born in New York City, the son of two prominent German Jewish families. His father was a member of the R.H. *Straus family that owned Macy's department store, and his mother was Gladys Guggenheim of the mining company. His father was the president of the American Mining and Smelting Company and worked for his father-in-law, David Guggenheim, a copper mine owner and a philanthropist. Straus's paternal grandfather was Oscar S. Straus, U.S. ambassador to Turkey and secretary of commerce in President Theodore Roosevelt's administration. An indifferent student, young Straus left the boarding school St. George's because he felt uncomfortable there as a Jew, went to Hamilton College and left, and later graduated from the school of journalism at the University of Missouri. The next year he married a childhood friend, Dorothea Liebmann, granddaughter of the founder of the Rheingold brewery. With the security of two trust funds, Straus became a reporter for the *White Plains Daily Reporter.* During World War II he served in the U.S. Navy, doing public relations work and writing speeches. He rose to the rank of lieutenant.

Following the war, Straus and John Farrar founded a publishing company with additional funds from James Van Alen (who later invented the tiebreak in tennis). Van Alen's parents, though, did not want their son's name to appear as a partner because Straus was a Jew. Although the company achieved success with Gayelord Hauser's *Look Younger, Live Longer,* a nutritional manual, in 1950, Straus realized he did not have the capital to compete with more commercial publishers, so he decided to become a literary house, stressing quality writers. Straus went abroad and signed Carlo *Levi and Alberto *Moravia, which attracted Edmund Wilson, Shirley Jackson, and Marguerite Yourcenar. It acquired other companies and their well-known writers, including Marguerite Duras and Francois Mauriac. In 1964 the firm became Farrar, Straus & Giroux, and Robert Giroux brought more distinguished authors, including T.S. Eliot, Robert Lowell, Flannery O'Connor, and Bernard *Malamud. New editors brought in Tom Wolfe, Joan Didion, Philip *Roth, Arthur *Miller, Maurice Sendak, and William *Steig. Over the years his authors received the most important literary prizes. The Nobel Prize, Pulitzer Prize, and National Book Awards were won by Joseph Brodsky, Robert Lowell, John McPhee, Czeslaw Milosz, Isaac Bashevis *Singer, Aleksandr I. Solzhenitsyn, Scott *Turow, and Susan *Sontag.

In 1994 when he recognized that his house could no longer compete financially as an independent in a world of conglomerates, he sold Farrar, Straus to one of the foreign media companies he so scorned, Georg von Holtzbrinck Publishing Group, in Stuttgart, Germany, although, as he insisted in the wake of the deal, which reportedly brought him more than $30 million, the arrangement was such that for all practical purposes he remained in charge and the house remained virtually independent.

[Stewart Kampel (2nd ed.)]

STRAUSS, ARYEH LUDWIG (1892–1953), Hebrew and German poet, short story writer, and literary critic. Born in Aachen, Strauss first distinguished himself as the author of poems and stories in German, writing a volume of tales, *Der Mittler* (1916), and the verse collection *Wandlung und Verkuendigung* (1918). He became a Zionist and, after World War I, associated himself with the *Ha-Po'el ha-Ẓa'ir movement, serving as editor of *Ha-Avodah*, its German language periodical. Following his first visit to Ereẓ Israel in 1924, Strauss published the drama *Tiberius* (1924) and a story, "*Der Reiter*" (1929). During the years 1929 and 1933 he taught German literature at the University of Aachen and specialized in literary history. He paid a second visit to Palestine in 1934 and his impressions were recorded in a volume of German poems, *Land Israel* (1934), a Hebrew version of which appeared as *Sha'ot ve-Dor* (1951). Two other works of this period were the poem "*Nachtwache*" (1933) and *Die Zauberdrachenschnur* (1936), a collection of fairy tales. When the Nazis came to power, Strauss left Germany, settling in Ereẓ Israel in 1935. He first joined kibbutz Ha-Zore'a and taught at Ben Shemen. Later he moved to Jerusalem, where he taught at the Hebrew University. He was one of the first German-Jewish immigrants to write poetry in Hebrew.

Strauss specialized in textual analysis, applying modern critical methods to the whole of Hebrew literature. His critical essays profoundly influenced contemporary literary criticism in Israel. His work also afforded new insights into the poetry of Ḥ.N. *Bialik, which he translated into German. His last works include the poem *Heimliche Gegenwart* (1952) and *Wintersaat* (1953), a book of aphorisms. His collected German works were published posthumously by Werner Kraft (1962). T. Ruebner published his essays and lectures on aesthetics and on Hebrew and general literature in *Be-Darkhei Sifrut* (1959). Tuvia Ruebner and Yedidya Peles translated Strauss's *Ha-Adam ve-ha-Shirah* (1985). Dan Pagis translated *Ha-Kad ha-Atik: Aggadot* (1961; 1986). There has been a growing interest in the writings of Strauss in Germany, with a number of publications of his own German works as well as books on his life and writing. Among these are B. Witte, *Ludwig Strauss, Dichter und Germanist* (1982) and Hans Otto Horch (ed.), *Ludwig Strauss: Beitraege zu seinem Leben und Werk* (1995).

BIBLIOGRAPHY: Kressel, Leksikon, 2 (1967), 917–8. **ADD. BIBLIOGRAPHY:** T. Ruebner, "*Hedei Shir*," in: *Dappim le-Meḥkar ba-Sifrut, Haifa* (1984), 241–58.

[Getzel Kressel]

STRAUSS, BENNO (1873–1944), German inventor. Born in Fuerth, Bavaria, Strauss worked with the Krupp company at Essen, and from 1921 to 1934 was director of Friedrich Krupp A.G. In 1912 he was made a professor by the Prussian Ministry of Education. Strauss discovered the greater corrosion resistance of nickel-chromium steels, thus inventing stainless steel.

STRAUSS, EDUARD (1876–1950), German chemist, born in Kreuznach. Strauss worked as a nutritional chemist in Munich and in 1907 went to Frankfurt to the Biological Institute and the Georg Speyer Haus, working mainly on albumen and other nutritional factors. A communal leader and Zionist, Strauss did much to foster Jewish education in Frankfurt. He went to New York in 1939 and joined the Crown Heights Hospital in Brooklyn.

STRAUSS, GEORGE RUSSELL, BARON (1901–1993), British politician. The son of Arthur Strauss (1847–1920), who was a Conservative member of Parliament from 1910 to 1918, George Strauss was educated at Rugby and entered the family firm of tin merchants. He served as a Labour member of Parliament in 1929–31 and 1934–79. He was also a prominent figure in the London County Council, on which he served in 1926–31 and 1932–46. In 1945 he was made parliamentary secretary to the Ministry of Transport. Strauss became minister of supply in 1947, and was responsible for executing the nationalization of the steel industry in 1949. During the 1930s Strauss was on the left of the party, helping to fund the left-wing weekly *Tribune*. Later he moved to the party's center. In 1968 he helped secure the abolition of theater censorship. From 1974 to 1979 he was the "Father of the House," the longest-serving Member of Parliament. He was made a life peer in 1979.

ADD. BIBLIOGRAPHY: ODNB online.

[Vivian David Lipman / William D. Rubinstein (2nd ed.)]

STRAUSS, GUSTAVE LOUIS MAURICE (c. 1807–1887), English author. Born in Trois Rivières, Canada, Strauss settled in England after serving as a surgeon with the French Foreign Legion and being expelled from France for alleged revolutionary activities. His works include *Moslem and Frank* (1854), *Reminiscences of an Old Bohemian* (2 vols. 1882), *The Emperor William* (1887), and various translations. The *Athenaeum's* attacks on his novel, *The Old Ledger* (1865), led to two famous libel actions. Strauss was well known in bohemian circles in London and was one of the founders of the Savage Club. He claimed to be of "Italian, French, German, and Sarmatian [sic] blood," and had no obvious connection with the Jewish community. He has an entry in *The Jewish Encyclopedia* of 1904, but did not receive an obituary in *The Jewish Chronicle*.

ADD. BIBLIOGRAPHY: ODNB online.

STRAUSS, JOHANN, JR. (**Baptist**; 1825–1899), composer, conductor, and violinist. He was the eldest son of the celebrated composer and violinist Johann Strauss (1804–49), known as the "Waltz King." Strauss, Jr., who began composing when he was six, became an accomplished pianist. He wished to become a professional musician but his father intended him for a business career. His mother arranged for him to study secretly with the leader of his father's orchestra. He also studied harmony, counterpoint, and violin. In 1844 Strauss made his first public appearance as conductor of his own ensemble at Hietzing. In 1845 he was offered the honorary position of Bandmaster of the 2nd Vienna Citizens' Regiment and in 1847 begun his long and fruitful association with the influential Wiener Maennergesang-Verein for which he wrote the waltz *An der schoenen blauen Donau* (1867). During the 1848 Vienna Revolution he supported revolutionary elements and then switched his allegiance and tried to ingratiate himself with Emperor Franz Joseph. He consolidated his initial success after his father's death (1849), when he united his father's band with his own. With his brother Josef, Johann held sway over Vienna's dance-music scene from the late 1850s. He also performed in Russia and the United States and won numerous medals and honors. He brought the waltz to a height of musical artistry, endowing it with new melodic, rhythmic, and orchestral richness. He wrote more than 400 waltzes and numerous quadrilles, polkas, polka-mazurkas, marches, and gallops. Strauss composed a number of operettas, including *Die Fledermaus* (1874) and *Der Zigeunerbaron* (1885), and cemented his position as the leading figure of "Silver Age" Viennese operetta. Strauss also championed the music of Liszt and Wagner. When the Nazis realized the Jewish ancestry of the family, they falsified the parish register at St. Stephen's Cathedral in 1939 to make the family racially pure.

BIBLIOGRAPHY: Grove Music Online; P. Kemp, *The Strauss Family: Portrait of a Musical Dynasty* (1985, 1989^2); F. Mailer, *Johann Strauss, 1825–1899* (1999); C. Crittenden, *Johann Strauss and Vienna: Operetta and the Politics of Popular Culture* (2000).

[Naama Ramot (2nd ed.)]

STRAUSS, LEO (1899–1973), philosopher and political scientist. Born in Germany, Strauss began his association with the Academy of Jewish Research in Berlin in 1925, and ended it with Hitler's rise to power. On arriving in the U.S. he taught at the New School for Social Research, New York, from 1938 to 1949, and then joined the University of Chicago, where he was professor of political science until 1968.

Strauss's scholarship encompasses the tradition of Western political philosophy. Of particular interest is his work on the reception and adaptation of Greek philosophy by medieval Jewish and Muslim writers. He sees the most profound and intransigent confrontation as that between Athens and Jerusalem, between philosophic doubt and faith. In examining that conflict he studies ancient and modern texts with a presumption of their vitality, seriousness, and thoughtful composition. His wish to understand past authors as they understood themselves – explicit even in his earliest books, *Die Religionskritik Spinozas* (1930; *Spinoza's Critique of Religion*, 1965), and *Philosophie und Gesetz* (1935) – led him to investigate carefully those philosophers' manner of writing. Strauss revived the distinction (familiar from antiquity until the 19th century) between exoteric and esoteric speech – public orthodoxy, be it political or religious, and private heterodoxy. Through studies of Maimonides, Halevi, and Spinoza in *Persecution and the Art of Writing* (1952), he explicates the art of "writing between the lines" by illustrating the art of reading between the lines. In teaching and writing, Strauss has used these arts to restate for contemporaries the insights and relevance of classical political philosophy against prevailing modes of thought, and has attempted to state a systematic political philosophy in defense of classical natural law. In doing so he has rendered problematic much that was noncontroversial, because unexamined, in modern political science.

The range of Strauss's general and Jewish scholarship is shown in his *On Tyranny* (1948, 1963); *Natural Right and History* (1953); *Thoughts on Machiavelli* (1958); *What Is Political Philosophy?* (1959); his introduction to Pines' translation of Maimonides' *Guide* (1963); *Liberalism: Ancient and Modern* (1968). His writings are listed in J. Cropsey, *Ancients and Moderns* (1964), 317–22.

BIBLIOGRAPHY: Momigliano, in: *Rivista Storica Italiana*, 79 (1967), 1164–72.

[Ralph Lerner]

STRAUSS, LEVI (1829–1902), U.S. garment manufacturer and philanthropist. A native of Bavaria, Germany, Strauss followed his two brothers to New York in 1848. In 1850, during the gold rush, he started a dry goods business in Sacramento, California, and three years later in San Francisco. He began to manufacture pants from blue denim, reinforced with copper rivets, which under the trademark "Levis" became popular with gold miners. They were taken up by Western farmers and, as the years went by, were sold to an ever-widening public. By the mid-20th century they were being marketed all over the world. Strauss, a bachelor, took first his brothers, then his brother-in-law, David Stern, and finally the latter's four sons into partnership in Levi Strauss & Co. A multimillionaire, he assumed directorship of a bank, an insurance company, wool mills, and the San Francisco Board of Trade. His charities included scholarships at the University of California, and he left large sums to Jewish, Protestant, and Catholic orphanages. He was a member of Congregation Emanu-El, San Francisco. In 1968, with WALTER A. HAAS, SR. (1889–1979), a grandnephew of Strauss's, as chairman of the board, and his sons WALTER A., JR. (1916–1995), president, and PETER E. (1918–), executive vice president, Levi Strauss & Co.'s sales topped $200 million. The owners have participated in local and national public and charitable activities, both general and Jewish. In 1953 Walter and his wife established the Evelyn and Walter Haas Jr. Fund, dedicated to helping disadvantaged youths, families, and the elderly, reducing hunger and homelessness, and encouraging volunteerism and philanthropy. Peter was the director of the Levi Strauss Foundation and vice president of the Miriam and Peter Haas Fund. The Levi Strauss firm has been a leader in "equal opportunity" employment and actively encourages minority group enterprises in the ghettos. By 1995 the company had become the largest brand-name clothing manufacturer in the world, with 36,000 employees and an annual revenue of $6.1 billion.

BIBLIOGRAPHY: I. Dunwoody, in: *National Jewish Monthly*, 82 (Nov. 1967). **ADD. BIBLIOGRAPHY:** R. Dru, *The First Blue Jeans* (1978); E. Cray, *Levi's* (1978); M. Goldish, *Levi Strauss: Blue Jean Tycoon* (1993); K. McDonough and L. Downey, *This Is a Pair of Levi's Jeans* (1995); C. Ford, *Levi Strauss: The Man behind Blue Jeans* (2004).

[Hanns G. Reissner / Ruth Beloff (2nd ed.)]

STRAUSS, LEWIS LICHTENSTEIN (1896–1974), U.S. governmental official, navy rear admiral, and banker. Strauss was born in Charleston, West Virginia, and grew up in Richmond. He became a traveling salesman for his family's wholesale shoe business. In 1917 he presented himself to Herbert Hoover, who was then organizing volunteers in the cause of Belgian relief. Strauss remained with the volunteers, and when Hoover became head of the Food Administration, Strauss became his secretary, later accompanying him on several European missions. Strauss caught the attention of Kuhn, Loeb & Co., which hired him in 1919. In 1923 he married Alice Hanauer, daughter of a partner in the firm, and in 1929 he himself became a partner. Avidly keeping abreast of technological developments, Strauss was an initial investor in Kodachrome. His interest in the atom was spurred by the deaths of his parents from cancer, and he funded the construction of a surge generator to produce isotopes for cancer treatment. From 1926 Strauss was in the Navy Reserve and was called to duty in 1941, becoming adviser to Navy Undersecretary Forrestal. He directed the development of the radar proximity fuse, conceived the Big "E" war production incentive program, and in 1945 was promoted to rear admiral by President Truman. In 1946 Truman appointed him to the Atomic Energy Commission (AEC) where he served through 1950. He was reappointed by President Eisenhower in 1953, this time as chairman. Strauss, who was then president of Temple Emanu-El, New York City, opened the first meeting under his chairmanship with a prayer, "that the fruits of our labor be peace and not war."

Strauss was thrust into public controversy twice during his tenure. In 1953 the White House suspended the security clearance of commissioner J. Robert *Oppenheimer. Strauss eventually voted against Oppenheimer's reinstatement but sought to have him retained in the Princeton Institute for Advanced Study and other nuclear undertakings. The second controversy flared a year later, when the AEC engaged the Dixon-Yates combine to erect a power plant in West Memphis, Arkansas. Strauss, a deeply conservative Republican, was eager then to admit private industry into the atomic field. But liberals saw in the Dixon-Yates contract a threat to the Tennessee Valley Authority and public power. They attacked the contract so vigorously that in 1955 President Eisenhower canceled it. In 1959 Eisenhower nominated Strauss secretary of commerce, but the Senate refused to confirm him. Soon thereafter he returned to private life.

BIBLIOGRAPHY: *Fortune* (Jan. 1955); *New York Times* (Feb. 25, 1959); L. Strauss, *Men and Decisions* (1962).

STRAUSS, ROBERT SCHWARZ (1919–), U.S. lawyer, businessman, Democratic political leader, member of the Cabinet, ambassador, statesman. Strauss was born in Lockhart, Texas, and raised in Stamford, a small town in West Texas where his immigrant father owned a small general store. His maternal great grandfather, Heinrich Schwarz, was the first ordained rabbi in the state of Texas (1873). The Strausses were the only Jewish family in Stamford, a town without a synagogue or rabbi, and although the Strauss home was deeply culturally Jewish, Bob Strauss received no formal Jewish education.

Robert Strauss received his undergraduate and law degrees from the University of Texas in Austin. During law school, Strauss began a life-long friendship with John Connally, who later was elected governor of Texas. After law school, he served as a special agent in the FBI until the end of World War II. He then moved to Dallas where he established his own law firm. Akin, Gump, Strauss, Hauer and Feld has become one of the great law firms in the United States, and has branches in 15 cities around the world. It is considered one of the premier law-lobbying firms in the nation's capital.

Strauss has become an icon of American politics. After serving as Democratic National Committeeman from Texas and Treasurer of the DNC, Bob Strauss was elected Chairman of the Democratic Party in 1972 following the electoral debacle of the McGovern presidential campaign, the first Jew to serve as chairman of a national political party. In that role Strauss worked tirelessly and brilliantly to reunite a badly splintered party, patiently coaxing disparate and hostile factions to work together around common programmatic goals. His almost mystical powers of persuasion and leadership were manifest at the hugely successful Democratic National Convention in New York City in 1976 which nominated a moderate southern governor, Jimmy Carter, who went on to win the presidency of the United States in a campaign that Strauss managed.

President Carter appointed Strauss to the cabinet level post of US Special Trade Representative, where he masterfully completed the Tokyo Round of Multilateral Trade Negotiations. Impressed by Strauss' negotiating skills, Carter then appointed him as his Personal Representative to the Mideast Peace Negotiations.

Although an unparalleled Democratic Party political leader, Bob Strauss was no stranger to Republican presidents. Indeed he served as a friend and advisor not only to Lyndon Johnson, Jimmy Carter, and Bill Clinton, but also to Ronald Reagan, George Herbert Walker Bush, and George W. Bush. President George H.W. Bush appointed Strauss to serve as the United States ambassador to the Soviet Union, and after the breakup of the Soviet Union in 1990, Strauss was appointed by President Bush to serve as the first United States ambassador to Russia. For Strauss' quietly effective work on the Wallenberg Holocaust case while serving as ambassador to the Soviet Union and Russia, he was awarded the prestigious Raoul Wallenberg Award

Strauss occupied the Lloyd Bentsen Chair at the Lyndon Baines Johnson School of Public Affairs at the University of Texas, and served on the Boards of major U.S. corporations, including Xerox and Archer Daniels Midland. He was the chairman of the U.S.-Russia Business Council, a member of the Council on Foreign Relations, and a Trustee of the Center for Strategic and International Studies.

Strauss is and will always be considered one of the true giants of American politics. Strauss – national party chairman, member of the Cabinet, ambassador, and statesman – who served as mentor to a new generation of American politics and advised six American presidents, has written that, at the end of the day he owes whatever he has accomplished in life to the experience of growing up in the only Jewish family in a small town in West Texas.

[Mark Siegel (2nd ed.)]

STRAUSS-KAHN, DOMINIQUE (1949–), French economist. Strauss-Kahn graduated in law and then specialized in economics. From 1980 to 1990 he was professor at Paris' Nanterre University. From 1986 he was a deputy in the National Assembly, where he was president of the finance committee before being appointed minister of industry and foreign trade (1991–93), being regarded as one of the leading experts in the Socialist party on economic affairs. Among his many activities as minister were special efforts to strengthen trade relations between France and Israel. In 1995 Strauss-Kahn was elected mayor of Sarcelles and in 1997 was appointed minister of the economy, finance, and industry, leading France to a period of prosperity. Accused of receiving a bogus fee from an insurance company, he resigned in 1999, denying any guilt. He became a deputy again in 2001.

[Gideon Kouts]

°STRECKFUSS, ADOLF FRIEDRICH KARL (1779–1844), Prussian official and writer. In 1833 Streckfuss published a pamphlet, *Ueber das Verhaeltniss der Juden zu den christlichen Staaten*, in which he stated that the 1812 edict emancipating the Jews had been premature, as had been demonstrated by the unanimous opposition of the provincial estates to full emancipation. He claimed that the Jews had remained an unassimilable foreign body or "nation" within the state because of their special ritual and belief in the forthcoming Messiah. Nevertheless Streckfuss was prepared to grant conditional political rights to individuals of the thin upper layer of Jewish society. But, according to Streckfuss, the remaining mass of ignorant and superstitious peddlers and innkeepers had to remain without rights until they proved themselves worthy of citizenship. Because of Streckfuss's official position as *Geheimrat* (government counselor), the leading young intellectuals of German Jewry, such as G. *Riesser, felt obliged to refute him at length. Ten years later, after his retirement, Streckfuss published a work under the title *Zweite Schrift ueber das Verhaeltniss der Juden…*, this time proclaiming his sincere conversion to the cause of complete and immediate emancipation of the Jews.

BIBLIOGRAPHY: F. Friedlaender, in: MGW 78 (1934), 291 305; V. Eichstaedt, *Bibliographie zur Judenfrage* (1938), index; H. Fischer, *Judentum, Staat und Heer in Preussen* (1968), index. **ADD. BIBLIOGRAPHY:** G. Riesser, in: *Gesammelte Schriften*, vol. 3 (1867), 507–64; S. Dubnow, *Weltgeschichte des jüd. Volkes* (1929), 9:46, 52; H. Berding, *Moderner Antisemitismus in Deutschland* (1988), 45–50; J. Katz, *Vom Vorurteil bis zur Vernichtung…* (1989), 194f.; R. Erb, W. Bergmann, *Die Nachtseite der Judenemanzipation…* (1989), 121.

[Uri Kaufmann (2nd ed.)]

°STREICHER, JULIUS (1885–1946), Nazi propagandist and antisemitic agitator, publisher of a crude antisemitic newspaper which characterized the Jews in quasi-pornographic fashion. Born in Fleinhausen, Swabia, Streicher was a teacher by profession. He was a founder of the German Socialist Party, which soon merged with the Nazi Party. Limited in his education, ambitious, and emotionally disturbed, he was enabled by the antisemitism of the Third Reich to give vent to his abnormal tendencies. In 1921 he founded the Nuremberg branch of the Nazi Party and participated in the attempt to remove Hitler from the party leadership. But he won Hitler's confidence by his participation in the Beer Hall Putsch (1923), which led to his arrest. In the same year Streicher founded *Der *Stuermer*, a weekly which achieved a circulation of 500,000 copies. He became its editor only in 1935 and was its owner. Hitler appointed him Gauleiter of Franconia (1928–40). He was elected to the Reichstag, made a general in the SA (storm troops) in 1932, and was charged with organizing the annual party convention, the Nuremberg Rally. Despite all his titles, Streicher had no real influence on policy making. Many of the party's leaders loathed him and plotted against him and his newspaper. In 1939 he was forbidden to make speeches and from 1940 was confined to his estate, Pleikershof. However, Streicher was esteemed by academic circles engaged in the "scientific" development of antisemitism. He achieved his fame and influence as a result of his fanatical incitement against the Jews. In hundreds of articles in *Der Stuermer* and in his speeches, in which he portrayed the Jews as the devil, the enemies of humanity, inferior beings, and dangerous germs, Streicher demanded their total extermination. He organized the economic boycott of the Jews (April 1, 1933), and his sadistic depictions of Jews in *Der Stuermer* as "defilers of the race" prepared the ground for the *Nuremberg Laws (1935). Even before **Kristallnacht* (1938), Streicher presided over the destruction of the Nuremberg synagogue, and on the morrow of the riots (Nov. 10, 1938) publicly justified it. Captured in 1945, after a period of hiding in disguise, he was brought before the Nazi war criminal court at Nuremberg and sentenced to death under the Crimes Against Humanity clause for his part in the preparation of German public opinion to accept the "*Final Solution." He was hanged in October 1946.

BIBLIOGRAPHY: L.W. Bondy, *Racketeers of Hatred* (1946); E. Davidson, *Trial of the Germans* (1966), 39–58; G.M. Gilbert, *Nuremberg Diary* (1947), 301–6; R. Hilberg, *Destruction of the European Jews* (1961), index. **ADD. BIBLIOGRAPHY:** R.L. Bytwerk, *Julius Streicher* (1983).

[Nathan Feinberg / Michael Berenbaum (2nd ed.)]

STREICHMAN, YEḤEZKEL (1906–1993), painter. Born in Kovno, Lithuania, the son of Isaac, a wealthy timber merchant, and Hasia Streichman, Yeḥezkel Streichman already received personal training in art at the Hebrew Gymnasium. In 1924 he immigrated to Ereẓ Israel and studied at Bezalel in Jerusalem. From 1927 to 1931 Streichman continued his art training at the Brerra Academy in Florence, Italy. From Italy he returned to Kovno, where he lived and worked until 1936, when he returned to Ereẓ Israel. He lived most of his life in Tel Aviv with his wife, Tzilla, and was an art teacher in schools as well as at the Avni College. In 1945 he established The Studio atelier in Tel Aviv, together with *Stematzky, where many young artists received their art education. Together with other painters and sculptors, he founded the New Horizons group and participated in all its 11 exhibitions until 1964.

Streichman's art was sent to the Venice and the Sao Paulo Biennales more then once. In 1990 he was awarded the Israel Prize.

In his art Streichman enlarged the portrait genre. Most of his portraits described members of his family as well as friends. His wife, Tzilla, became a recurring subject for more than 30 years. Landscape was another theme appearing in Streichman's art.

While the paintings of his early years employed dark colors, using expressive brush movements, during the 1940s Streichman discovered the French painting style, which became one of the factors that led to the brightening of the tonal language and to the dominance of the contour line.

From the 1940s on, Streichman believed that modern art drew the artist's path toward the abstract, though he reached abstract style only around the 1960s. The starting point for his abstract work was the landscape, with the paintings' names being those of the painted places. Later he repeated the motif of the tree and the fenced windows (*Soaring Bird*, 1970, Israel Museum, Jerusalem). The reflections of local places expressed Streichman's belief in the existence of a unique Israeli painting. He described himself as an Israeli artist in that his style was open, bright, and happy. Zionist ideology had a powerful influence on his life, and he strongly believed that his painting style with its free vibrating and vital atmosphere was a part of the Zionist vision. All those tendencies found expression through the modernist language, the abstract.

Streichman's participation in the New Horizons group located him in the center of the Israeli art world. Streichman's power as an influential figure, however, was also forged thanks to his being an impressive, didactic figure. As a teacher, and later as an interlocutor, he influenced the young Israeli artists who were the next generation of the Israeli art world.

BIBLIOGRAPHY: Israel Museum, *Yehezkel Streichman* (1987); Y. Fischer, *Streichman, The Israeli Phoenix* (1997).

[Ronit Steinberg (2nd ed.)]

STREISAND, BARBRA (1942–), U.S. singer and actress. Born in Brooklyn, New York, Streisand worked as a switchboard operator and theater usher until she won a singing contest at a Greenwich Village bar. After some appearances on television, she made her first Broadway success in the musical *I Can Get It for You Wholesale* (1962). Streisand made a great hit in the Broadway show *Funny Girl* in 1964, playing the part of Fanny Brice, and won an Academy Award for her role in the film version in 1968. Her television show, *My Name Is Barbra*, received a Peabody Award and five Emmy Awards in 1965.

Her subsequent film roles include *Hello, Dolly!* (1969); *On a Clear Day You Can See Forever* (1970); *The Owl and the Pussycat* (1970); *Up the Sandbox* (1972); *What's Up, Doc?* (1972); *The Way We Were* (Oscar nomination for Best Actress, 1973); *For Pete's Sake* (1974); *Funny Lady* (a sequel to *Funny Girl*, 1975); *A Star Is Born* (produced, 1976. Oscar for Best Song, "Evergreen," making her the first female composer to win an Academy Award); *The Main Event* (produced, 1979); *All Night Long* (1981); *Yentl* (wrote, produced, and directed, 1983), based on a story by Isaac Bashevis Singer in which she played a yeshivah student in pre-War Poland; *Nuts* (produced, 1987); *The Prince of Tides* (produced and directed; Oscar nomination for Best Picture, 1991); *The Mirror Has Two Faces* (produced and directed; Oscar nomination for Best Song, "I Finally Found Someone," 1996); and *Meet the Fockers* (2004). She was the first woman to produce, direct, write, and star in a major motion picture (*Yentl*).

In 1979 Streisand established her own film production company, called Barwood Productions. In addition to serving as the vehicle for the films in which she starred, Barwood produced other films as well, such as the 1995 TV movie *Serving in Silence*, a film about the attitude toward homosexuality in the military; *Rescuers: Stories of Courage*, (1997–98), a series of six two-part dramas about non-Jews who heroically saved Jews in the Holocaust; and *The Long Island Incident* (1998) on the issue of gun control.

As a singer, Streisand's record albums achieved wide popularity. She went on to achieve legendary status in the American entertainment world, commanding huge sums for her rare live performances and earning several Grammy Awards. Through 2005 she recorded 60 albums, of which 49 were gold and 30 platinum; 18 of her albums achieved multi-platinum status in record sales, surpassing any other female singer. Streisand rates an all-time second in topping the charts, exceeded only by Elvis Presley. For her single recordings, she had nine gold and five platinum records.

Among her many awards and accolades, Streisand won two Academy Awards, ten Grammys, six Emmys, a Tony, two Peabody Awards, eleven Golden Globes, and a Lifetime Achievement Award from the American Film Institute.

Beyond the realm of arts and entertainment, Streisand established the Streisand Foundation in 1986. Contributing to a wide variety of causes and charitable organizations, the foundation's scope includes gaining women's equality; the protection of human rights and civil rights and liberties; the needs of children at risk in society; and the preservation of the environment.

Streisand was married to actor Elliot Gould from 1963 to 1971. She was married to actor James Brolin from 1998.

BIBLIOGRAPHY: *Time Magazine* (April 10, 1964); *Newsweek* (Jan. 5, 1970). **ADD. BIBLIOGRAPHY:** R. Riese, *Her Name Is Barbra* (1994); N. Bly, *Barbra Streisand: The Untold Story* (1994); J. Spada. *Streisand: Her Life* (1995); B. Dennen, *My Life with Barbra* (1997); A. Edwards, *Streisand: A Biography* (1998); C. Nickens and K. Swenson, *The Films of Barbra Streisand* (2001).

[Lee Healey / Jonathan Licht / Rohan Saxena and Ruth Beloff (2nd ed.)]

STREIT, SHALOM (1888–1946), Hebrew writer. Born in Tlumach (Galicia), Streit settled in Ereẓ Israel in 1908 and was one of the founders of the village Ein-Ḥai (Kefar Malal), serving as its secretary for many years. Later he taught, mainly at the Aḥad Ha-Am High School in Petaḥ Tikvah, which he founded in 1926. His house was a meeting place for Hebrew writers.

He began writing while still in Galicia, publishing articles on literature and feuilletons in *Ha-Miẓpeh*. In Ereẓ Israel, encouraged by *Brenner, he continued writing, especially literary reviews, although he also tried his hand at fiction. Streit's criticism is a blend of impressionistic comments and pedagogical remarks. A collection of his essays was published under the title *Ba-Alot ha-Shaḥar* (1927) and *Penei ha-Safrut* (2 vols., 1939).

BIBLIOGRAPHY: Waxman, Literature, 4 (1960²), 429.

[Getzel Kressel]

STRELISK, URI BEN PHINEHAS OF (d. 1826), disciple of R. Solomon of *Karlin. Opposed to wonder-workers, Uri b. Phinehas required ethical perfection from his Ḥasidim. His ecstatic manner of praying brought him the name *Ha-Saraf* (the seraph). It was said of him that every day before saying his prayers he bade farewell to his wife and family for fear that he might die of ecstasy in the middle of his devotions. Once he said, "In the Torah there are 600,000 letters; and there are 600,000 souls among the People of Israel; and just as the Torah scroll is unfit for use if one letter is missing, so the *Shekhinah* [Divine Presence] does not rest upon the people if one soul is missing from Israel." His book is entitled *Imrei Kadosh* (1871). His son, R. Solomon, died several months after his father's death and Uri b. Phinehas's outstanding student, R. Judah Ẓevi *Stretyn, inherited Uri's post.

BIBLIOGRAPHY: Dubnow, Ḥasidut, index; L.I. Newman, *Ḥasidic Anthology* (1963), index; M. Buber, *Tales of the Hasidim*, 2 (1966³), 145–9.

[Zvi Meir Rabinowitz]

STRELISKER, MARCUS (1806–1857), Hebrew scholar and poet. Born in Brody, in his youth he was close to N. *Krochmal and I. *Erter and was greatly influenced by them. In the early 1850s he moved to Mihaileni, Romania, where he officiated as cantor and also engaged in commerce.

He contributed poems and research on the Bible and Talmud to many Hebrew periodicals, especially Galician publications. He published several collections of poetry; included among them were a number of occasional poems: *Ta'aniyyat Yeshurun* (1835), on the death of Franz I; *Zekher Olam* (1848), a dirge on his father, together with his biography; *Shirah le-Kohen* (1860); *Todah u-Verakhah* (1868); *Shenei ha-Me'orot ha-Gedolim* (1873).

BIBLIOGRAPHY: Shunami, Bibl, no. 4364; Zeitlin, Bibliotheca, 389.

[Getzel Kressel]

STRETYN, JUDAH ẒEVI HIRSCH (Brandwein) OF (d. 1854), founder of a ḥasidic dynasty in eastern Galicia. Judah Ẓevi Hirsch was a scion of a prominent family of rabbis and *ẓaddikim* and the outstanding disciple of Uri (*Ha-Saraf*) b. Phinehas of *Strelisk. After the death of his teacher, he left his work as a *shoḥet* and succeeded Uri as leader of the Strelisk Ḥasidim. Like his teacher, he emphasized the importance of ecstatic prayer. Judah Ẓevi Hirsch did not deliver many ḥasidic teachings, and only a few were collected later in *Degel Maḥaneh Yehudah*.

His name is included in a list of 12 leading *ẓaddikim* in Galicia appended to a detailed memorandum on the ḥasidic movement which the chief of police in Lemberg sent to the provincial authorities. As an example of the negative elements in the ḥasidic "cult of the *ẓaddik*" the chief of police forwarded a remedy formula (*segullah*) which had been found during a search in the house of a Ḥasid, which Judah Ẓevi had written for a follower whose wife was having difficulties in childbirth. His son ABRAHAM OF STRETYN (d. 1865) succeeded him. His other sons, ELIEZER OF OZOPOL and SAMUEL ZANVIL (d. 1887), also continued as *ẓaddikim*, and their descendants established a small ḥasidic community in Ereẓ Israel. One of them was Yehudah Ẓevi *Brandwein, kabbalistic author and the "rabbi of the Histadrut." Their teachings and stories about them are found in Eliezer Brandwein's *Degel Maḥaneh Yehudah* (1912) and Israel Berger's *Eser Ẓaḥẓaḥot* (1909).

BIBLIOGRAPHY: R. Mahler, *Ha-Ḥasidut ve-ha-Haskalah* (1961), index.

STRICH, FRITZ (1882–1963), German literary historian. Born in Koenigsberg, East Prussia, Strich studied at the University of Munich, where he became a professor in 1915. He was elected to the chair of modern German literature at the University of Berne in 1929. Not until his encounter with the art historian Heinrich Woelfflin did Strich find the teacher he sought. In 1916 Strich published a pioneering essay, applying Woelfflin's method and insight to German literature of the 17th century, defining the style of literary baroque.

Strich broke new ground with *Deutsche Klassik und Romantik, oder Vollendung und Unendlichkeit: Ein Vergleich* (1922, 1928³). Whereas the history of literature had hitherto largely been a chronicle of works and writers, origins and influences, Strich clearly regarded it as an art with basic forms and possibilities of artistic expression, such as the "classical" search for perfection and permanence, or the "romantic" effort to capture the ever changing variety, impermanence, and infinitude of the world. For Strich these fundamental literary styles and categories always represent expressions of the human mind and soul; and the individual work of literature always exists in the larger context of historical time and of national and social culture. In an essay on *Kafka, Strich called on the Jewish writer to speak in the authentic voice of Jewish commitment. There could be no dissociation of art from life, a conviction clearly expressed in the titles of Strich's collected essays – *Dichtung und Zivilisation* (1928); *Der Dichter und die Zeit* (1947); and *Kunst und Leben* (1960). He also edited the works of *Heine, Schiller, and Wedekind.

BIBLIOGRAPHY: *Weltliteratur: Festgabe... Fritz Strich zum 70. Geburtstag* (1952); S. Kaznelson (ed.), *Juden im deutschen Kulturbereich* (1962³), 346ff.

[Ludwig W. Kahn]

STRICK, JOSEPH (1923–), U.S. film director and producer. Born in Pittsburgh, Pennsylvania, Strick started his career with documentaries and later applied documentary realism to feature films. He gained a reputation with such films as *Muscle Beach* (1948), *The Big Break* (produced, 1950), *The Savage Eye* (wrote and produced, 1960), and *The Balcony* (produced, 1963). The outstanding example of his method was *Ulysses* (wrote and produced, 1967), a version of the novel by James Joyce. He directed *Tropic of Cancer* (1970), *Interview with My Lai Veterans* (1971), *Road Movie* (1974), *A Portrait of the Artist as a Young Man* (1977), and *Criminals* (1996).

Strick also produced *The Legend of the Boy and the Eagle* (1967); *Ring of Bright Water* (1969), a film based on Gavin Maxwell's book on porpoises; *The Darwin Adventure* (1972); and *Never Cry Wolf* (1983). He co-produced the TV movie *Survive the Savage Sea* (1992).

[Ruth Beloff (2nd ed.)]

STRICKER, ROBERT (1879–1944), Zionist leader and journalist. Born in Bruenn (Brno), Stricker worked as an engineer for the state railways, rising to the position of chief surveyor. He was a member of the students' Zionist association, Veritas, and a contributor to the *Juedische Volksstimme* (Bruenn), founded by Max *Hickl. Stricker was a co-founder of Emunah, an association of Jewish shop assistants and clerks. Before World War I he edited the Vienna *Juedische Zeitung*, the official organ of Austrian Zionists, and in 1915 he founded the Jewish War Archives, of which Nathan *Birnbaum was secretary. After the collapse of the Austrian monarchy, Stricker became president of the Jewish People's Party (Juedische Volkspartei), and in 1919 was elected to the Constituent National Assembly of the Federal Austrian Republic, to which he belonged until 1920.

Stricker founded and edited the only German-language Jewish daily, the *Wiener Morgenzeitung* (1919–28), and from 1928 edited the lively Zionist weekly *Die Neue Welt*. In 1912 he was elected to the board of the Viennese Jewish community (Israelitische Kultusgemeinde) and in 1932 he became its vice president. He was a member of the Executive of the *World Jewish Congress and president of its Austrian section. At the 12th and 13th Zionist Congresses in Carlsbad (1921, 1923), he proposed that Chaim *Weizmann be elected president of the Zionist Organization, but in 1924 he opposed Weizmann's policy and resigned as vice president of the Zionist General Council. He was a co-founder of the Radical Zionist Faction. In 1931 he joined the *Union of Zionist Revisionists, and after it split in 1933 became one of the founders of the *Jewish State Party. After Austria was annexed to Nazi Germany (1938), he had the opportunity to leave the country, but refused, saying: "I cannot. I must stay with my constituents." He was arrested by the Nazis, and sent to Dachau, Buchenwald, and then to Theresienstadt. Even in the concentration camp he preached hope, maintaining his belief in the defeat of Hitler and in the establishment of a Jewish state. In the autumn of 1944 he and his wife Paula were transported from Theresienstadt to the gas chambers of Auschwitz. A selection of his speeches and essays, *Wege der juedischen Politik*, was published in 1929.

BIBLIOGRAPHY: J. Fraenkel (ed.), *Robert Stricker* (Eng., 1950); L. Lipsky, *A Gallery of Zionist Profiles* (1956), 116–20.

[Josef Fraenkel]

STRIGLER, MORDECAI (**Motl**; 1918–1998). Yiddish and Hebrew writer and journalist. Born near Zamość, Poland, he attended a Musar yeshivah in that city and then studied in other yeshivot (e.g., Lutsk, and Kletsk under Rabbi Aaron *Kotler). In 1937 he settled in Warsaw and became a journalist, writer, and preacher in the Great Synagogue. Interned in 12 concentration camps, Strigler survived the Holocaust. In Buchenwald he worked in the Jewish cultural underground, which organized the education of 800 children. He edited the first periodical of Holocaust survivors (*Tkhiyas ha-Meysim*, May 4, 1945). He then settled in Paris (1945–52), where he was contributor to and editor of *Unzer Vort*. From 1953 he lived in New York, where he edited the Labor-Zionist *Yidisher Kemfer* (at first with Baruch Zukerman, later as sole editor until 1995, published in collaboration with Jacob *Glatstein). From 1987 until his death he edited the Yiddish *Forverts*. Strigler was one of the most learned and prolific Jewish writers of the second half of the 20th century. His works dealt with Jewish life in Poland before World War II and reported on and interpreted his experiences in the slave labor and death camps as well as the lives of Holocaust survivors in postwar Paris. His published books include *Tsu Aykh Shvester un Brider Bafrayte* ("To You Liberated Sisters and Brothers," 1945); *In a Fremdn Dor: Lider un Poemen* ("In an Alien Generation: Poems," 1947); *Maydanek* (1947); *In di Fabrikn Fun Toyt* ("In the Factories of Death," 1948); *Di Ershte Libe fun Kopl Matsh: Roman* ("The First Love of Kopl Matsh: A Novel," 1948); *Verk Tse* ("Factory 'C,'" 2 vols., 1950); *Goyroles* ("Destinies," 2 vols., 1952); *Georemt Mitn Vint: Historisher Roman fun Yidishn Lebn in Poyln* ("Arm in Arm With the Wind: A Historical Novel of Jewish Life in Poland," 1955); *Inzlen Oyf der Erd: Noveln* ("Islands on the Earth: Novellas," 1957); *Shmuesn Mit der Tsayt* ("Conversations With Time," 2 vols. 1959–61). Several of his Yiddish and Hebrew novels, as well as over a thousand short stories and essays, and thousands of articles in scores of Yiddish and Hebrew periodicals (under his name and more than 20 pseudonyms), have not yet been published in book form.

BIBLIOGRAPHY: J. Glatstein, *In Tokh Genumen* (1947), 283–7; 2 (1960), 221–8; idem, *Mit Mayne Fartogbikher* (1963), 555–69; H. Leivick, *Eseyen un Redes* (1963), 287–91. **ADD. BIBLIOGRAPHY:** Y. Szeintuch, in: *Chulyot*, 9 (2005), 223–7.

[Yechiel Szeintuch (2nd ed.)]

STRISOWER, LEO (1857–1931), Austrian jurist. Born in Brody, Galicia, Strisower was appointed lecturer in international law at the University of Vienna in 1908. He rose to become full professor in 1924 and was made president of the Institut de Droit International. He represented Austria in a number of international arbitrations. Strisower was an active supporter of Jewish student organizations in Vienna. At the time of his death he was engaged in preparing a critical analysis of the legality of the British White Paper on Palestine of 1931.

The author of several books and articles on international law, Strisower's publications include *Der Krieg und die Voelkerrechtsordnung* (1919), and *"L'Exterritorialité et ses principales applications,"* in: Académie de Droit International de La Haye, *Receuil des Cours*, 1 (1923).

BIBLIOGRAPHY: J.L. Kunz, in: *Revue de Droit International*, 7 (1931), 419–28.

[Josef J. Lador-Lederer]

STRNAD, OSKAR (1879–1935), Austrian architect and interior decorator. Born in Vienna, Strnad was head of the department of architecture at the Wiener Kunstgewerbeschule, from 1914 until his death. He had received a classical training, and aspired to purity of form. One of his chief architectural works was the middle building in the Winarsky Hof, Vienna (1924–25). He was equally active designing interiors, furniture, and stage and cinema sets.

STROCHLITZ, SIGMUND (1916–), Holocaust survivor, businessman, and major figure in institutionalizing Holocaust commemoration. The eldest of three children, Strochlitz was raised in a Zionist home in Bendzin, Poland, and in 1936 graduated from the Furstenberg School, a Hebrew high school. He enrolled at the Jagiellonian University in Cracow, but his studies were interrupted by the war in 1939. During the partition of Poland, Strochlitz escaped into the Soviet zone but then secretly crossed back into the German zone to be with his family in Bendzin. In August 1943, he and his family were sent to Auschwitz-Birkenau. Strochlitz's parents, sisters, and wife were killed upon arrival. Strochlitz spent 15 months in Birkenau. He was then deported to the concentration camps at Stuthoff, Hailfingen, Dautmergen, and ultimately Bergen-Belsen, where he was liberated by the British army in April 1945.

After liberation, Strochlitz married Rose Grinberg (1913–2001), a Polish-born Holocaust survivor from the Radziner ḥasidic family. They emigrated to New York in 1951. In 1957, Strochlitz bought a Ford dealership in New London, Connecticut, naming it Whaling City Ford. He moved to New London, and the dealership became his principal business.

Strochlitz and the writer Elie *Wiesel formed a close working relationship after the war, undertaking many Holocaust commemoration projects as well as other Jewish and humanitarian ventures. In 1978, when President Jimmy Carter created the President's Commission on the Holocaust, he appointed Wiesel as chairman and Strochlitz as a Commission member. The two continued in those roles on the United States Holocaust Memorial Council, which established and oversees the United States Holocaust Memorial Museum. Strochlitz was the first chairman of the Commission's and later the Council's Days of Remembrance committee. He organized the first National Commemoration of the Holocaust, held in the Capitol Rotunda on Yom ha-Shoah. President Jimmy Carter, Vice President Walter Mondale, the speaker of the House, and the Senate majority leader participated in the first commemoration. It became the model of the annual ceremony held in Washington. Strochlitz persuaded state and federal officials to hold annual Holocaust commemorations in all 50 state capitals and in Washington, D.C. Strochlitz also led the international campaign in support of Wiesel's candidacy for the Nobel Peace Prize.

Among other distinctions, Strochlitz served as the president of the American Friends of Haifa University, a governor of Bar-Ilan University, a founding member of the American Society for Yad Vashem, a trustee of the American Jewish Congress, a member of the board of Lawrence & Memorial Hospital in New London, and, at the appointment of President George H.W. Bush, a member of the United States Commission on the Preservation of American Heritage Abroad. He endowed the Strochlitz Institute of Holocaust Studies at Haifa University and the Strochlitz Judaic Teaching Fellowship at Bar-Ilan.

[Richard Primus (2nd ed.)]

STROHEIM, ERICH VON (1885–1957), film actor and director. Born in Vienna, Austria, Von Stroheim, with his bullet-shaped head and his monocle, became famous for his Teutonic roles and was dubbed "the man you love to hate." He directed and acted in Hollywood, and his film *Greed* (1923) is still considered a masterpiece. Regarded as an indulgent, extravagant director, Von Stroheim directed such films as *Blind Husbands* (1919); *The Devil's Passkey* (1920); *Foolish Wives* (1922); *The Merry Widow* (1925); *The Honeymoon* (1928); *The Wedding March* (1928); *Queen Kelly* (1929); and *Hello Sister* (1933).

In 1937 he went to France to play in Jean Renoir's film *La Grande Illusion*. The son of a lower middle-class Jewish hat manufacturer, Von Stroheim had created his own "grand illusion" about himself in the film industry, fabricating the persona of a Prussian aristocrat and a decorated military officer. As his Jewish identity was not known, he was able to work in France after the Nazi occupation and appeared in some 30 films before going back to Hollywood to act in *Five Graves to Cairo* (1943); *The North Star* (1943); *The Lady and the Monster* (1944); *Storm over Lisbon* (1944); *The Great Flamarion* (1945); *Scotland Yard Investigator* (1945); *The Mask of Dijon* (1946); *Sunset Boulevard* (1950); and *Orient Express* (1954).

He was nominated for an Academy Award as Best Supporting Actor for his performance in *Sunset Boulevard*. In 1957 he was awarded the Legion of Honor in France.

BIBLIOGRAPHY: R. Koszarski, *The Man You Loved to Hate: Erich Von Stroheim and Hollywood* (1983); N. Henry, *Ethics and Social Criticism in the Hollywood Films of Erich Von Stroheim, Ernst Lubitsch, and Billy Wilder* (2000); R. Koszarski, *Von: The Life and Films of Erich Von Stroheim* (2004).

[Ruth Beloff (2nd ed.)]

STROMINGER, JACK (1925–), U.S. biochemist. Born in New York, he graduated in psychology from Harvard University and received his M.D. from Yale University. After clinical training at Barnes Hospital (1948–49) and an American College of Physicians research fellowship in the department of pharmacology at Washington University School of Medicine, St. Louis (1949–51), he worked at the National Institutes of Health (NIH), Bethesda (1951–54). Next he visited the Carlsberg Laboratory, Copenhagen, and the Molteno Laboratory at Cambridge University, England, as a Commonwealth Fund Fellow (1954–55). He returned to Washington University School of Medicine (1958–64) where he was professor of pharmacology and microbiology from 1961. He moved to the University of Wisconsin Medical School, Madison, as professor of pharmacology and chemical microbiology and chairman of the department of pharmacology (1964–68). In 1968 he joined the staff of Harvard University as professor of biochemistry in the department of biochemistry and molecular biology (1968–83), where he was department chairman (1970–73), director of basic sciences in the Sidney Farber Cancer Center (1974–77), and head of the division of tumor virology from 1977. He became the Higgins Professor of Biochemistry. Strominger's early research clarified the mechanism by which penicillin kills bacteria by blocking the production of bacterial cell walls. His research interests then centered on immunology. With his colleague, the late Don Wiley, he investigated the structures on cell surfaces, called histocompatibility or "MHC" antigens, that largely distinguish one individual's tissues from another. Some of these antigens capture protein fragments derived from invading microorganisms. The immune system identifies and destroys these cells as a major defense mechanism against infection. MHC antigens are also central to the problems of organ transplant rejection and autoimmune diseases resulting from an immune attack against "self" antigens. Strominger and Wiley worked out the precise structure of the most important MHC antigens and the manner in which these combine with protein fragments to stimulate an immune response. Subsequently Strominger, who continued to work in his laboratory, and his colleagues investigated autoimmune diseases, especially multiple sclerosis, with the aim of using protein fragments to block harmful immune responses. He founded Peptimmune, a company that produces small proteins for therapeutic purposes. His administrative skills helped to establish Harvard's renowned department of molecular and cellular biology whose alumni have also had a major influence on teaching and research in other institutions. He has also contributed to the activities of WHO and other international organizations. His many honors include membership of the U.S. National Academy of Sciences, the Pasteur Medal (1990), the Lasker Award for Basic Medical Science (1995), and the Japan Prize (the last two prizes with Don Wiley).

[Michael Denman (2nd ed.)]

STROOCK, U.S. family of lawyers, philanthropists, and businessmen. MARCUS STROOCK immigrated to the U.S. from Germany in the mid-19th century and founded a large woolen mill in Newburgh, New York. His eldest son, LOUIS S. (1855–1925), was active in S. Stroock & Co. for 50 years, and eventually became its president. He was president of the Board of Trustees of Congregation Bnai Jeshurun and a treasurer and trustee of Beth Israel Hospital. Stroock was a generous philanthropist, and a year before his death he gave 20 scholarships to graduates of preparatory schools who would not otherwise have been able to afford college. His brother MARK (1863–1926) was a director and officer of S. Stroock & Co. MOSES J. (1866–1931), another brother, was a lawyer. Stroock was admitted to the bar in 1888 and practiced law at first with Platzek and Stroock and later with his brother, Solomon Marcuse (see below), in Stroock & Stroock. He was especially involved in the area of higher education, as a trustee of City College in 1911 and chairman of the board of trustees in 1925, and as chairman of New York City's board of higher education from its establishment in 1926. Stroock was active in Jewish organizations, especially the Federation for the Support of Jewish Philanthropic Societies.

Another brother, JOSEPH (1869–1946), was president and chief executive officer of S. Stroock & Co. He was a close friend of Stephen S. *Wise and helped him financially in setting up the Free Synagogue and the institution which ultimately became the Jewish Institute of Religion, later a part of Hebrew Union College. His second wife, REGINA (1875–1948), was chairman of the women's division of the United New York Appeal for the Joint Distribution Committee. She was on the board of the Hebrew Orphan Asylum and of the Jewish Child Care Association. Mayor La Guardia appointed her to the board of the Children's Center of New York. Regina Stroock founded the Girls Home Club, a residence organization for working girls.

SOLOMON MARCUSE (1874–1945), another brother, was a lawyer. By 1907 he and his brother Moses were practicing law together. He specialized in constitutional law and appeared before the New York State Supreme Court. He was chairman of a number of legal committees, including the legal education committee (from 1933) of the Bar Association of the City of New York. Stroock served as president (1924–26) of the YMHA of New York and from 1925 to 1930 headed the Metropolitan League of Jewish Community Centers while acting as president of the Federation for the Jewish Philanthropic Societies in New York City. In 1934 he was made chairman of the executive committee of the American Jewish Committee and in the year of his death became president of that organization. He was among the founders of the Jewish Agency for Palestine and a member of the non-Zionist section of that organization. His wife, HILDA (1876–1945), born in New York City, sponsored a cardiac clinic for children at Montefiore Hospital, of which she was a trustee, and was vice chairman of the City Work and Relief Administration and a member of the board of directors of the State Conference on Social Work. Actively involved in the Federation for the Support of Jewish Philanthropic Societies, she sponsored the first women's conference on Jewish affairs in 1938.

Solomon and Hilda Stroock's son ALLAN (1907–1985) became a lawyer. From 1934 to 1936 he was a law clerk for Supreme Court Justice Benjamin *Cardozo. Following that he joined Stroock & Stroock, first as an associate (1936) and later as a partner (1939), until 1942, when be became a member of Stroock & Stroock & Lavan. While remaining active in legal organizations, Stroock, like his father, supported the Jewish Theological Seminary of America – becoming chairman of the board in 1947 and president of the corporation of the Seminary in 1963; the Federation of Jewish Philanthropies; and the American Jewish Committee. In 1960 he was made trustee at large of the Federation. He served as vice president of the American Jewish Committee from 1948 to 1951 and from 1955 to 1958; in 1958 he became chairman of its administrative committee. He was also a trustee of New York University.

The Alan and Katherine Stroock Fund supports many projects in education and the arts.

°**STROOP, JUERGEN** (originally **Josef**; 1895–1951), SS general; the Nazi commander who destroyed the *Warsaw ghetto. Born in Detmold into a family of lower middle class Roman Catholic policemen, Stroop was educated in a nationalist and militarist spirit. He served in World War I, where he was wounded twice and reached the rank of captain. By profession a surveyor, he joined the SS in 1932, and embarked upon a meteoric career after Hitler's advent to power. At the outbreak of World War II he was appointed chief of the Selbstschutz ("self-protection") of the Germans in the Posen area, where he organized the terror against the Polish population. In June 1941, Stroop served first in the Waffen-SS. During 1942 and the beginning of 1943 he was SS and police chief for several towns of southern Russia. He hunted partisans and persecuted the local population. On Feb. 6, 1943, he was attached to the office of the police and SS in Galicia but not long afterward was dispatched to Warsaw to crush the ghetto revolt. Apparently, the commanders had little faith in Ferdinand Sammern-Frankenegg, the local commander. Stroop suppressed the revolt by physically destroying the ghetto, setting it on fire, house by house, street by street, and killing the inhabitants. He wrote a meticulous report detailing the revolt and conducted the action as a military campaign, employing some 2,000 troops. He concluded his report with the words: "The Jewish Quarter of Warsaw is no longer." He marked his victory by blowing up a synagogue. Appointed SS and police chief in *Greece in September 1943, Stroop ordered the registration of Jews and limited their freedom within the German zone (Oct. 3, 1943). In November 1943 *Himmler made him SS and police leader of Rheinland-Westmark, in which post he remained until the collapse of the Third Reich. In 1947 Stroop was condemned to death by a U.S. military court for his atrocities in Greece and the murder of U.S. prisoners of war, but Poland requested his extradition. He was then extradited to Poland, where he was sentenced and hanged for his crimes in the Warsaw ghetto.

His illustrated report on the suppression of the Warsaw ghetto uprising was published as *The Stroop Report: The Jewish Quarter of Warsaw Is No More* (1979), and in Hebrew as *Mered Getto Varsha be-Einei ha-Oyev*, with introduction and notes by J. Kermish (1966).

BIBLIOGRAPHY: *Nazi Conspiracy and Aggression*, 3 (1946), 719–75; J. Wulf, *Das dritte Reich und seine Vollstrecker* (1961), index.

[Yehuda Reshef / Michael Berenbaum (2nd ed.)]

STROUSBERG, BETHEL HENRY (**Baruch Hirsch Strausberg**; 1823–1884), German financier. Born in Neidenburg, East Prussia, he left Germany after his father's death, embraced Christianity, and went to England and the United States, where he worked as a journalist. He returned to Germany in 1855 and began his business career by forming railway companies on behalf of a group of English investors. The tracks eventually covered more than 1,500 miles (2,600 km.) through Prussia and Hungary. Strousberg undertook the construction of locomotive works, rolling mills, mines and collieries, sometimes using questionable business methods. At one time his concerns employed over 100,000 people and his speculations involved hundreds of millions of dollars, but when, in 1872, his public loan for railway construction in Romania was not granted, his empire collapsed overnight. Bankruptcy proceedings were begun against him in Germany, Austria, and Russia; his assets were sold at a fraction of their value, and he died impoverished in London, where he was earning a meager living as a journalist. The collapse had serious political and economic consequences. Public inquiries into the case showed that corruption connected with railway construction and financing had penetrated the highest and most respected circles in Germany; this contributed largely to the change in public opinion in favor of public control and ownership of railways.

BIBLIOGRAPHY: K. Grunwald, in: YLBI, 12 (1967), 192–8; E. Achterberg, *Berliner Hochfinanz*, 2 vols. (1965). **ADD. BIBLIOGRAPHY:** M. Ohlsen, *Der Eisenbahnkoenig Bethel Henry Strousberg* (1987); J. Borchart, *Der europäische Eisenbahnkönig Bethel Henry Strousberg* (1991); R. Roth, in: *Jahrbuch fuer Antisemitismusforschung* 10 (2001) 86–111.

[Joachim O. Ronall]

STROUSE, MYER (**Meyer Strauss**; 1825–1878), U.S. congressman and lawyer. Born in Oberstrau, Bavaria, Strouse was taken by his father to Pottsville, Pennsylvania, in 1832. In 1848 he founded the *North American Farmer*, a Philadelphia newspaper, which he edited until 1852. After studying law, he was admitted to the bar in 1855. In 1862 and in 1864 Strouse was elected to the U.S. Congress as a Democrat from the 10th Pennsylvania Congressional district, serving on different committees: Roads and Canals; Territories; Expenses; and Mines and Mining. He returned to his law practice in 1867, and in 1876–77 defended the notorious miners' organization, the Molly Maguires.

[Max Vorspan]

STRUCK, HERMANN (1876–1944), graphic artist. Struck, born into an Orthodox Berlin family, studied at the Berlin Academy under Max Koner, where Hans Meyer introduced him to the art of etching. Struck joined the Zionist movement at an early age. in 1903, after several study trips throughout Europe, he visited Palestine and, on his way back to Germany, stopped in Vienna and met Herzl. This meeting inspired the famous portrait etching of the Zionist leader. During World War I Struck served with the German army in Lithuania. There he came in contact with East European Jews and was deeply impressed by their way of life. *Skizzen aus Litauen, Weissrussland und Kurland* (1916) and *Das ostjuedische Antlitz* (1920) reflect this experience. In 1923 he moved to Palestine and settled in Haifa. Struck's favorite technique was copper etching and its related processes although he did lithographs as well. His early work, done in pure etching, was usually signed with his Hebrew name, Ḥayyim Aharon ben David. From 1902 he mixed etching with *vernis mou* and aquatint. A master of his craft and an excellent teacher, Struck taught graphic techniques to such fellow artists as Chagall, Liebermann, Israels, and Corinth. His book *Die Kunst des Radierens* (1923[5]), a popular guidebook for artists and connoisseurs, provides technical explanations and practical instruction. Struck excelled as a portraitist. Among his sitters were Ibsen, Nietzsche, Freud, and Einstein. He also did landscapes, Jewish types and scenes from Jewish life as well as many ex libris. Struck, who remained an Orthodox Jew, participated in Jewish public life and attended several Zionist congresses as one of the leaders of the Mizrachi Party. He was a member of the London Society of Painters, Etchers and Engravers.

BIBLIOGRAPHY: A. Donath, *Hermann Struck* (Ger., 1920); H. Hirschberg (ed.), *Der Humor bei Struck* (1916); Y. Wolfsberg, *Professor Ḥayyim Aharon "Hermann" Struck* (Heb., 1946); Y. Mann (ed.), *Hermann Struck, ha-Adam ve-ha-Amman* (1954); A. Fortlage and K. Schwarz, *Das graphische Werk yon Hermann Struck* (1911).

[Elisheva Cohen]

STRUG, KERRI (1977–), U.S. gymnast, Olympic medal winner, member of the U.S. Gymnastics Hall of Fame, and 1996 U.S. Olympic Spirit Award recipient. Strug was a gifted child in gymnastics, and at the age of 13 her parents allowed her to leave her home in Tucson, Arizona, to study in Houston, Texas, with the world-renowned coach Bela Karolyi. Over the next five years, Strug helped lead the U.S. women's gymnastics team to a series of high finishes, including a silver medal at the 1991 World Gymnastics Championships, a bronze medal at the 1992 Olympics, a silver medal at the 1994 World Team Championships, and a bronze medal at the 1995 World Championships. Strug also showed great ability in individual all-around competitions, winning several American championships, and finishing in the top 15 in a number of international contests, including the 1992 Olympics. On March 2, 1996, she won her first major international competition, the American Cup. But Strug's defining moment came at the 1996 Summer Olympics in Atlanta. In the finals of the vault competition, Strug fell on her first attempt, severely twisting her left ankle. Karolyi calculated that Strug needed a score of at least 9.6 and encouraged her with his now-famous, "You can do it, Kerri, you can do it." Having heard a popping noise, Strug knew that she was risking her chance to make a recovery in time for the all-around competition, but decided nevertheless to give her team a chance of ensuring the win. She limped back to the runway and then managed a near-perfect run, vault, and landing. Strug immediately lifted the injured leg and grimaced before collapsing to the canvas. She had torn two ligaments and now had a third-degree sprain. But Strug's score on the vault was 9.712, the U.S. had its gold, and Strug had won a place in Olympic lore. Reacting to people expressing surprise at her Jewishness, Strug wrote, "I think about the attributes that helped me reach that [medal] podium: perseverance when faced with pain, years of patience and hope in an uncertain future, and a belief and devotion to something greater than myself. It makes it hard for me to believe that I did not look Jewish up there on the podium. In my mind, those are attributes that have defined Jews throughout history." After retiring, Strug attended Stanford University. She is the author of *Heart of Gold* (1996) and *Landing on My Feet: A Diary of Dreams* (1997).

[Robert B. Klein (2nd ed.)]

STRUNSKY, SIMEON (1879–1948), U.S. journalist and author. Strunsky, Russian by birth, was an editorial writer for the *New York Evening Post* from 1906 to 1920 and editor until 1924. He then joined *The New York Times* and for 15 years wrote anonymously his urbane daily commentary on the news, *Topics of the Times*. His books include *The Patient Observer* (1911), *Belshazzar Court* (1914), *Professor Latimer's Progress* (1918), *The Living Tradition* (1939), *No Mean City* (1944), and *Two Came to Town* (1947).

STRY (Pol. **Stryj**), city in Lvov district, Ukraine. With the development of trade between eastern Poland and Hungary at the beginning of the 16th century, Jews were invited to settle in Stry by the governor, Jan Tarlowski, who wanted to counterbalance the number of Ruthenians (i.e., Ukrainians) in the city. In 1576 King Stephen Báthory (1575–86) issued the first legal confirmation of permanent Jewish settlement, granting the Jews the same terms as the other townsmen. The leaders of the city fought for almost 100 years against this privilege. In 1589 King Sigismund III Vasa confirmed the rights of the Jews, warning the townsmen not to harm them. Stry's Jews engaged in wholesale and retail trade, leasing of customs, brewing beer, and making and selling wine. At the end of the 17th and during the 18th century Jews imported wine and horses from Hungary, exported bulls, grain, and salt, leased estates and flour mills, bred cattle, and traded in cloth. A few of them were goldsmiths and tailors. The extent of their trade is reflected in the enterprise of Samuel Haymovich, who sold 18,000 barrels of salt annually between 1701 and 1704. The volume of their trade in Hungarian wines and horses is recorded in Ber of Bolechow's *The Memoirs of Ber of Bolechow 1723–1805* ((1922), index).

An organized Jewish community, subordinate to the district of *Przemysl, existed from the end of the 16th century.

In 1634 Stry's Jews were allowed to buy land for a synagogue (built in 1660) and a cemetery. There were 70 Jews (5% of the total population) living in the city in 1662. Between 1652 and 1670 Jews acquired 11 houses. The ruler of the city, John Sobieski (later king of Poland, 1674–96), ordered in 1663 that the municipal authorities include two representatives of the *kahal* in every consultation on the city's taxes. As king he ordered in 1676 that a second market day be held every Tuesday since the regular market day was on Saturday. Finally, in 1696, the city authorities reached a compromise with the Jews and transferred the market day from Saturday to Friday. The community was permitted to build a new wooden synagogue in 1689. Accusing them of stealing sacred objects from a church, Stry's Catholic priests brought certain Jews to trial in 1697; the case dragged on until 1708, when the charge was dropped. In 1714 the Jewish community paid a poll tax of 2,000 zlotys, and in 1756 there were 1,727 Jews in Stry and its district who paid this tax. The city became part of the Austrian Empire in 1772, remaining as such until 1918. In 1795 the community was composed of 444 Jewish families living in the city and nine in its suburbs. At the end of the 18th century Ḥasidism began to exert an influence in Stry. Notable rabbis of Stry were Aryeh Leib b. Joseph ha-Kohen *Heller (1788–1813) and Jacob *Lorberbaum (1830–32).

Since limitations were imposed on wine selling and leasing of estates in the 1820s, the number of Jewish families earning their living from tailoring, the fur trade, bakery, carpentry, and tinsmithing increased. In the 1870s Jewish entrepreneurs established a foundry, wood mills, a soap factory, and a match factory. In 1873 a Jewish hospital was built. In the mid-1880s the Hebrew author Isaac Aaron Bernfeld was a teacher of religion in the governmental secondary schools, which were attended by more than 400 Jewish students in 1910. In the same year a boarding school for 30 Jewish students from the area was opened. The nationalistic awakening among young educated Jews led to the foundation of the Admat Yisrael society (1891) to support Jewish settlement in Ereẓ Israel. In 1893 the first Jewish workers' association in Stry (Briderlekhkeyt) was organized.

At the beginning of World War I the Jewish community suffered during the Russian invasion of Galicia. With the disintegration of the Hapsburg Empire in 1918, a Jewish *self-defense group with approximately 40 members was organized. In 1918–19, during the period of the Ukrainian independence, a Jewish National Assembly, headed by E. *Byk and M. Binenstock (1881–1923), and a Jewish militia were established, and a weekly newspaper, *Yidishe Folksshtime*, was published in Stry. Between the two world wars, when Stry was part of Poland, all the Zionist parties and Agudat *Israel had branches there. A vocational school set up by the American Jewish Joint Distribution *Committee (Joint), a *Tarbut school, and a Safah Berurah school were founded during the 1920s. The historian and geographer Abraham Jacob *Brawer and the educator and poet Eisig *Silberschlag were born in Stry which was also the home of the Polish-Jewish author J. *Stryjkowski who describes Jewish life there prior to World War II in many of his works. The Jewish population of the city was 10,988 (40% of the total) in 1921, 10,869 in 1931, and approximately 12,000 in 1939.

[Arthur Cygieman]

Holocaust Period

When the city was occupied by the Soviet Union after the outbreak of World War II, organized Jewish life came to a standstill. All charitable, religious, and cultural institutions were closed, and some of the leaders of the community were arrested and deported. In 1941, before the Germans entered Stry, even official Soviet Jewish leaders were arrested, including Beni Garfunkel and Benjamin Klein, and some others were executed. When the Germans occupied Stry, on July 2, 1941, hundreds of Jews were immediately killed by the Ukrainians aided by the Nazis. Oskar Hutrer was appointed head of the *Judenrat. At the first mass execution, in November 1941, 1,200 Jews were shot in the Holobotow Forest. The winter of 1941–42 was marked by frequent manhunts for young Jews, who were sent to labor camps, where many of them died. The second mass *Aktion* took place in May 1942. On Sept. 1, 1942 thousands of Jews were sent to the *Belzec extermination camp. This was followed by the deportation of 2,000 Jews to the same camp on Oct. 17–18, 1942. Before the local ghetto was established, on Dec. 1, 1942, small numbers of Jews managed to escape to Hungary via the Carpathian Mountains. Further *Aktionen* took place in February 1943, when 2,000 Jews were killed in the city itself, and on May 22, 1943, when 1,000 Jews were murdered in the local cemetery. The ghetto was finally liquidated at the beginning of June 1943, Jewish houses were systematically burned down, and any Jews hiding in the ruins were killed. In July the labor camps were also liquidated, so that by August 1943 Stry became **judenrein*. In the following months Jews in hiding were caught and executed. When the Soviet army occupied Stry on Aug. 8, 1944, there were only a few Jewish survivors. No Jewish community was reestablished. Societies of Stry Jews were established in Israel and the United States.

[Aharon Weiss]

BIBLIOGRAPHY: Halpern, Pinkas, index; B. Wasiutyński, *Ludność żydowska w Polsce w wiekach XIX i XX* (1930), 123, 131, 148, 154; S. Borensztejn, *Ludność żydowska w Polsce w okresie międzywojennym* (1963), 279; M. Bersohn, *Dyplomataryusz, dotyczący Żydowska w Polsce* (1910), no. 294; A. Prohaska, *Historja miasta Stryja* (1926); I. Schiper, *Dzieje handlu żydowskiego na ziemach polskich* (1937), index; *Sefer Stry* (1962).

STRYJKOWSKI, JULJAN (originally **Pesach Stark**; 1905–), Polish novelist. Born in Stryj, Galicia, Stryjkowski joined a Zionist youth movement as a boy, but later became a Communist. In 1939 he fled to the USSR, where he remained during World War II, returning to Poland in 1946. He was active in postwar Polish literary life and was a co-editor of the literary monthly *Twórczość*.

Stryjkowski's first major work was *Bieg do Fragala* ("Run to Fragala," 1951), which depicted the life of a poverty-stricken village in Calabria, Italy. A stage version was performed in

Wrocław (Breslau) by the Polish National Theater in 1953. This was followed by *Pożegnanie z Italji* ("Farewell to Italy," 1954); *Głosy w ciemności* ("Voices in the Dark," 1955), a novel about Jewish life in his native Stry before World War I; *Czarna Róża* ("The Black Rose" 1962); and the story *Imię własne* ("First Name," 1961). A later novel, *Austeria* (1966), portrayed the Jews of a town in eastern Galicia at the outbreak of World War I. Stryjkowski's works were translated into many languages and the writer himself translated works by the French author Louis-Ferdinand Céline and the Russian writer Leonid Maximovich Leonov.

BIBLIOGRAPHY: D. Desantis, in: *Peuples amis*, 101 (1957); *Słownik współcrzesnych pissarzy polskich*, 3 (1964), 241–3.

[Stanislaw Wygodzki]

STRYKOW (Pol. **Stryków**), town in the province of Lodz, central Poland. An organized Jewish community existed there from the early 18th century under the jurisdiction of the *Leczyca community. In 1765 there were 488 Jewish poll-tax payers in Strykow, and 137 (including nine persons in *Zgierz) in 21 surrounding villages. The Jews then owned 41 houses, including a synagogue and a hostel for the poor. In 1789 a Jewish merchant established a tannery. The Jewish population numbered 868 (70% of the total) in 1808, 1,394 (62%) in 1827, and 1,713 (65%) in 1857. They engaged in trade, and particularly in crafts, benefiting from the development of the town until the middle of the 19th century, when it declined as a result of the development of the industrial towns of *Lodz and Zgierz. In 1897 the community numbered 1,799 (58%). They were mainly engaged in tailoring, shoemaking, small trade, and transportation. During the 19th century Strykow became a center of Ḥasidism. At the beginning of the century the kabbalist Ephraim b. Isaac Fishel (d. 1825) lived in the town. The *ẓaddikim* Elimelech Menahem Mendel Landau (d. 1877) and Ze'ev Wolf Landau (d. 1891) had their "courts" in Strykow. In 1921 there were 1,998 Jews living in the town (48%). Between the two world wars there was a Jewish elementary school and a library.

[Shimshon Leib Kirshenboim]

Holocaust Period

On the outbreak of World War II, Strykow underwent heavy bombardment. Many of the nearly 2,000 Jews there fled to the outlying villages and some became the first victims of the advancing German troops. In December 1939 nearly 1,600 Jews were deported to Glowno, situated in the General Government territory. The deportees were turned away by the mayor of Glowno and obliged to look for shelter on the periphery of the town. They stayed until the spring of 1940, when the Glowno authorities drove them back to Strykow. The mayor of Strykow refused them entry and the deportees had to return once more to Glowno, where they probably remained and shared the fate of the Jews there.

After the first deportation of Jews in December 1939, only 378 Jews remained behind in Strykow. In time a number of refugees also arrived. In the years 1940–42 the Jews in Strykow were concentrated within a tiny ghetto. In April or May 1942 all the Jews were deported to Brzeziny (Loewenstadt) – the only other Jewish settlement still existing, besides Lodz, in the whole province. In the course of the liquidation of the Brzeziny ghetto and soon afterward, the 300 Jewish laborers from Strykow were sent with 3,000 "selected" Jews from Brzeziny to the Lodz ghetto.

[Danuta Dombrowska]

BIBLIOGRAPHY: Halpern, Pinkas, index; R. Mahler, *Yidn in Amolikn Poyln in Likht fun Tsifern* (1958), index; B. Wasiutyński, *Ludność żydowska w Polsce w wiekach XIX i XX* (1930), 28; E. Ringelblum, in: *Miesięcznik żydowski*, no. 11–12 (1933), 233; D. Dąbrowska, in: BŻIH. 13–14 (1955), 122–84, passim.

STUDENTS' FRATERNITIES, GERMAN (Ger. **Burschenschaften**). Different types of German students' associations have existed since the establishment of universities. As part and forerunners of the German national movement the specific German students' fraternities called Burschenschaften were founded in Jena in June 1815. Fanned by the reaction against Napoleon, the Burschenschaften rapidly expanded to include almost all German universities. The movement's outlook was essentially romantic, imbued with Christian, patriotic, and radical sentiments. However, at the beginning the organization was not overtly anti-Jewish in tone and Jews even took part in the foundation of some local Burschenschaften, as in Freiburg in 1816, and as so-called Alte Herren (Old Boys) were active members of the alumni organizations. Later, though, antisemitic agitation – particularly of the *Stoecker brand – found eager supporters among the student generation. The Verein Deutscher Studenten (VDST) (Union of German Students) aligned itself with the antisemitic petition demanding from the government the suspension of the legal emancipation of the Jews. It was also distributed by and among German students and handed over to Bismarck in April 1881. As early as 1878 the Viennese fraternity, Libertas, had passed a motion excluding Jews on racial grounds. By 1890 fraternities declared themselves *judenrein*, both in Germany and in Austria. In 1896 the member-fraternities Waidhofener Verband "dishonored" Jewish students by refusing to give them satisfaction in duels. By 1908 alumni associations also joined in ostracizing Jews. In Austria *Schoenerer emulated Stoecker by setting himself up as an anti-Jewish mentor to the students. Jewish students reacted to the increasingly antisemitic climate from the late 1880s by forming separate organizations. The first to be established was the Viadrina in 1886 at Breslau University, later part of the *Kartell-Convent der Verbindugnen Detuscher Studenten juedischen Glaubens (KC). From the start Jewish fraternities were socially excluded and repeatedly dissolved by university administrations.

From 1900 to 1914 there was a recess in general antisemitic agitation, but the war and its aftermath reactivated *Volk* and racist fanaticism. In 1920, at their general convention in Eisenach, German fraternities extended their racial ostracism to all members who married Jewish or colored partners. Throughout the Weimar Republic German fraternities were predominantly right-wing, *voelkisch*, and antisemitic, as was the student corpus as a whole. After Hitler assumed power they widely embraced the new development, although they had to join in the National Socialist students' organization (Nationalsozialistischer Deutscher Studentenbund) and hence give up their own organizational framework. After World War II the student fraternities reestablished their pre-war organizations, the umbrella organization of the German fraternities, the Deutsche Burschenschaft (DB), became active again in 1950. They are still predominantly politically conservative but are no longer openly antisemitic. There are still different kinds of student associations in the sense of fraternities to be found on German campuses.

BIBLIOGRAPHY: O.F. Scheuer, *Burschenschaft und Judenfrage…* (1927); E. Siecke, *Die Judenfrage und der Gymnasiallehrer…* (1880). **ADD. BIBLIOGRAPHY:** H.H. Brandt, *Der Burschen Herrlichkeit. Geschichte und Gegenwart des studentischen Korporationswesens* (1998); M. Gruettner, *Studenten im Dritten Reich* (1995); D. Heither, *Blut und Paukboden. Eine Geschichte der Burschenschaften* (1997); K.H. Jarausch, *Students, Society and Politics in Imperial Germany. The Rise of Academic Illiberalism* (1982); M.H. Kater, *Studentenschaft und Rechtsradikalismus in Deutschland 1918–1933. Eine sozialgeschichtliche Studie zur Bildungskrise in der Weimarer Republik* (1975); A. Kurth, *Maenner-Buende-Rituale. Studentenverbindungen seit 1800* (2004).

[Emmanuel Beeri / Miriam Ruerup (2nd ed.)]

STUDENTS' MOVEMENTS, JEWISH. In Central Europe in the 19th and 20th centuries most gentile students' societies did not accept Jews (see *Students' Associations, German). This experience, which continued also after World War I, except in the less numerous left-wing student associations, was one of the powerful motivations which led Jewish students to adhere to prevalent ideologies, whether revolutionary-internationalist or Zionist.

In eastern Europe, and particularly in the Russian Empire with its **numerus clausus*, very few Jews could enter universities or even high schools. Many of them went to Swiss, German, or Austrian universities, and their associations and debating societies became nuclei of revolutionary and Zionist movements. In Poland between the two world wars Jewish students were often physically assailed by their antisemitic colleagues and sometimes even allotted segregated "ghetto" benches in the classrooms. As a result, many became either extreme revolutionaries (in practice, mostly members of illegal Communist cells), or Jewish nationalists, i.e., Zionists. Thus, Jewish students and students' societies played an important role at the inception of the Zionist movement, e.g., in Vienna (*Kadimah) and Prague (*Bar Kochba). Subsequently a number of other students' organizations and associations with cultural and literary aims played a significant part: in Berlin (e.g., the Russian Jewish Scientific Society), and in Russia and among Russian émigré students (e.g., *He-Ḥaver). In Germany the overall Jewish students' federation, *Kartell Juedischer Verbindungen (KJV), became Zionist, partly under the impact of the hostile "Aryan" ideology of their gentile colleagues. In the Baltic countries of the 1920s and 1930s *Revisionist students organized themselves in German-style "corporations" (such as "Hasmonaea" in Riga), including wearing "colors," collective beer drinking, fencing, etc., whereas Zionist and Labor Zionist students formed groups without these trappings (as He-Ḥaver and Ha-Shaḥar). Religious Zionist students formed the Yavneh society. After World War II no Jewish student groups were allowed to exist in Communist eastern Europe, except, for a short time, a semi-legal group in Poland in 1967–68, named after the Russian Jewish writer Isaac *Babel.

In Great Britain

Although Jews were admitted to British universities from the mid-19th century, their numbers did not at first encourage the establishment of Jewish student societies, and these were mainly inaugurated from the second decade of the 20th century. Immediately after World War I, in 1919, the Inter-University Jewish Federation (IUJF) was set up to coordinate the activities of Jewish student societies that had begun to spring up independently in London, Oxford, Cambridge, and the major provincial cities, such as Birmingham, Glasgow, Leeds, Liverpool, and Manchester. The Federation's aim was to foster an interest among Jewish students in Judaism and Jewish history and culture, members being encouraged to involve themselves after graduation in the social and religious life of the Anglo-Jewish community. The University of London Jewish Union Society (ULJUS), an "umbrella" organization for the various student societies in the metropolitan area, was founded in 1922.

Student Zionist activity, which dates in Britain from the years immediately following the First Zionist Congress, met sufficient resistance in some Jewish students' societies to encourage the formation of separate Zionist associations and, from about 1924, the Universities' Zionist Federation (UZF) functioned alongside, and to some extent in competition with, the IUJF. During the 1930s the UZF amalgamated with the Association of Young Zionist Societies (mainly a non-student body), but organizational and other difficulties led to the old UZF's revival as the Universities' Zionist Council (UZC) shortly before the outbreak of World War II. Student Zionist activity intensified during the war years and the late 1940s. Both IUJF and UZC helped to organize cultural activities for their members. IUJF also published various periodicals, while UZC issued publications of its own. The two student organizations began to work in harmony after 1948, later operating together as IUJF-UZC, and finally merging in the 1960s when Zionism became part of the IUJF platform.

With the rapid increase in the number of Britain's "redbrick" universities after World War II, many more Jewish student societies were founded, in new areas. Major support was given to the Jewish students' organizations by the B'nai B'rith Hillel Foundation in London, which eventually set up Hillel

Houses in London, Birmingham, Leeds, Liverpool, Manchester, Sheffield, and other university towns. From the early 1960s a chaplaincy commission operated with varying degrees of success, mainly in Oxford, Cambridge, and the smaller university towns, where Jewish students felt themselves to be isolated from the main community.

A high proportion of Jews studying at British universities took no part in the activities of the organized Jewish student body. Semi-independent religious groups existed within the general Jewish student framework, such as Liberal and Reform associations and the Orthodox Yavneh movement. There were in 1971 over 10,000 Jewish students in the British Isles, some two-thirds of whom had no connection with IUJF or any other Jewish student group. About 80 Jewish student societies and Israel societies were affiliated to IUJF. Jewish students were prominent in protest movements such as CND (the Campaign for Nuclear Disarmament) in the 1960s and, later, in demonstrations on behalf of Soviet Jewry. They were active in the World Union of Jewish Students (see below). In recent decades the Union of Jewish Students has had to deal with venomous anti-Zionism at some British campuses, especially during the period in the 1980s when the militant left controlled much of student life. Since about 1990, British campuses have been more quiescent, although demands to boycott Israeli universities and goods surfaced again during the 2002–05 period. Many Jews have found the anti-Zionism of extreme left-wing groups on British campuses little different from right-wing antisemitism. The British Union of Jewish Students was affiliated with the European Union of Jewish Students.

[Godfrey Edmond Silverman / William D. Rubinstein (2nd ed.)]

In France

The Union of French Jewish Students (Union des Etudiants Juifs de France; UEJF) was founded in Paris in 1945 and is affiliated to the World Union of Jewish Students (WUJS). Before World War II there was no Jewish student movement in France. Organized Jewish life in France had mainly centered on religious or philanthropic activity, and entry to a university was thought of as a further step toward integration into French society. Only one institution provided a meeting place for Jewish students: this was the *kasher* canteen opened in Paris in 1921, intended for poor and Orthodox students. Pierre *Mendès-France, then a law student, was active in the establishment of this canteen, the Foyer israélite. The UEJF was formed by young Jewish resistance fighters, militants of the Eclaireurs israélites (see *Scouts), the Communist youth, and youth of Zionist organizations. It aimed to help needy students by offering scholarships, opening university canteens, and setting up a centralized employment bureau; to contribute to the revitalizing of Jewish life through the universities; and to develop an awareness of Jewish cultural values and Israel society through courses, publications, and trips to Israel. Branches were set up in various university cities: Paris, Lille, Nancy, Strasbourg, Lyons, Grenoble, Toulouse, Montpellier, Marseilles, etc. During the following ten years the Communists and Zionists struggled for the leadership in the administration of the UEJF. A measure of reawakening occurred between 1958 and 1962 due to political events associated with the war in Algeria. From 1967 the UEJF took an openly pro-Israel stand. The general student agitations in May 1968 stimulated its developments and confirmed it in its support for Israel.

The number of Jewish students attracted by the Jewish student movement never exceeded 10% of the total. The upheavals experienced in many French universities in 1969 and 1970 sometimes became confrontations between Jewish groups divided on the question of the Middle East conflict. Relations between the UEJF and communal institutions were often strained: the students complained that they were not allowed to participate in the direction of Jewish life and that they were not granted the funds necessary for the realization of their program. The communal leaders, on the other hand, suspected the Jewish youth movement of compromising with the Communist party and left-wing organizations. The achievements of the UEJF were modest. Private and communal initiative resulted in the establishment of residential buildings and university restaurants in Paris and Strasbourg, as well as a Jewish study center in the capital and clubs in a number of university cities. Although active in these institutions, the UEJF was not always associated with their foundation and direction. A periodical, *Kadimah*, was published sporadically by the UEJF and, in association with private publishers, it organized the printing and distribution of various works on Judaica. The UEJF continues to be active in such matters as Holocaust memorialization, antisemitism, and Israel.

[Lucien Lazare]

In the U.S.

The oldest Jewish student organization on a North American campus, Zeta Beta Tau (ZBT) fraternity, was founded in New York City in 1898 to encourage the study of Jewish life and culture among Jewish students. Soon afterward, however, it was converted into a Greek-letter fraternity. Additional Jewish student clubs emerged at the City College of New York (1902), Minnesota (1903), Harvard and Columbia (1905), Illinois and Texas (1907), Yale (1909), and California (1910). Most of these groups were gradually absorbed by the Intercollegiate Menorah Association, which was founded by Henry *Hurwitz at Harvard in 1906, and grew to 50 chapters by 1930. Designed to promote the academic study of Jewish culture in the university and to serve as a platform for the nonpartisan discussion of Jewish problems, the association sponsored a speakers' bureau, provided Judaica for several university libraries, tried unsuccessfully to stimulate university study of Jewish history and culture, and published the *Menorah Journal* (1915–62). No Menorah chapter remained in existence after World War II; the Menorah Association was dissolved in 1963.

Zionist societies sprang up at several major universities, independent of the Menorah Association. They formed the Collegiate Zionist League in 1905, which merged in 1915 with other Zionist student groups to become the Intercollegiate

Zionist Association. At its peak in 1919 it had a membership of 2,500 in 33 chapters, but it disbanded shortly after the Zionist Organization of America withdrew support in 1920. Five years later a successor organization, Avukah, was founded. It grew to 56 chapters in the United States and Canada by 1939 but was dissolved in 1942, largely as a result of the rapid turnover of student leadership and a persistent lack of funds.

Professional direction combined with organized program services and community support for Jewish collegiate activities were provided for the first time with the coming of the B'nai B'rith Hillel foundations to the American campus. Founded at the University of Illinois in 1923, and funded, since 1925, primarily by B'nai B'rith, with supplements from Jewish federations and welfare funds, Hillel maintained, in 1969, a network of 274 foundations (chapters with full-time professional staff) and counselorships (part-time staff). Of the total, 252 were in the United States and Canada and 22 were in Australia, Brazil, Great Britain, the Netherlands, Israel, South Africa, Switzerland, and Venezuela. Hillel also supported chairs of Judaic studies (Iowa, Missouri, Vanderbilt), and Hillel staff members taught accredited courses in Judaic studies at 40 additional institutions. Hillel's campus activities included lectures and classes in Jewish thought and life, the holding of religious services and holiday observances, the running and support of international, national, and regional student institutes, social service and social action projects, counseling services, student publications, and social programs. Hillel was governed by the B'nai B'rith Hillel Commission, and the international Hillel office in Washington, DC, provided resources and administrative guidance for the individual Hillel chapters.

In the 1970s and 1980s Hillel's effectiveness declined after a cutback in funding, but it revived in the late 1980s under the direction of Richard Joel. In the early 2000s it had approximately 250 affiliates in the U.S. and Canada serving college and university students on more than 500 campuses, an additional three dozen campus and community-based affiliates in other countries, and a global budget in excess of $60 million. Hillel was viewed widely as one of the early 21st century's major success stories in Jewish organizational life. Thirty-four percent of Jewish undergraduate students in the U.S. participate in Hillel activities, according to a market research study conducted in 2005.

Similar student programs, with full-time professional staff but independent of Hillel, existed at Rutgers-Newark, Columbia (Counselorship for Jewish Students, established in 1929), New York University (Jewish Culture Foundation, established in 1937), and Long Island University in Brooklyn. Unaffiliated Jewish student groups without professional guidance existed at more than 120 colleges and universities in 1969.

As the number of Jewish students increased, additional student groups were organized, mainly along denominational or ideological lines, among them Atid, the college-age organization of the Conservative movement (founded in 1960); Yavneh, an organization of Orthodox Jewish students (founded in 1960); and T'hiyah, a Reconstructionist university fellowship. The Reform movement maintained a college service department but no separate collegiate organization. In addition, the United Synagogue of America subsidized, and the National Council of Young Israel (Orthodox) sponsored or subsidized, student houses and kosher dining clubs.

Attempts were also made to reestablish an effective Zionist campus program. After Avukah's dissolution, the Intercollegiate Zionist Federation of America (IZFA) was founded in 1946 with the partial support of the American Zionist Youth Commission. During the period immediately preceding the founding of the State of Israel, IZFA's membership rose to 10,000, but it dropped after the state was established, and the organization was dissolved in 1953. A year later, it was succeeded by the Student Zionist Organization (SZO), which was sponsored and supported by the American Zionist Youth Foundation. SZO had about 2,500 members in 70 college chapters in the United States and Canada in 1963 but lost membership rapidly in the second half of the '60s and was replaced by American Students for Israel and similar, often radical, groups supported mainly by the American Zionist Youth Foundation.

Jewish participation in student activism became prominent from the middle 1960s on. Accurate statistics are not available, but several studies estimate that one-third to one-half of the committed identifiable radicals on the most activist campuses were Jewish. They were found to come largely from families which were urban, well-educated, professional, and affluent, with a high degree of permissiveness, a stress on democratic interpersonal relations and on values other than achievement – dominant characteristics of the urban middle-class Jewish group. Initially, Jewish students participated primarily in general activist or radical organizations. Many of them, unidentified with organized Jewish life, were motivated less by Jewish commitments than by their general social and political concerns. However, in the late 1960s Jewish students also began to form specific Jewish activist campus groups as a result of their rejection by the black movement, their disappointment with the growing anti-Israel stance of the New Left, and a growing self-awareness which turned them to the needs of the Jewish community as the arena for acting out their moral and social convictions. Their objectives included the establishment of accredited Jewish studies programs at universities, the development of "Free Jewish Universities" involving students and faculty in the study of Jewish thought and life, political action on behalf of Israel and Soviet Jewry, the stimulation of supportive action for peace and social justice by the Jewish community, and action countering the anti-Israel activities of the New Left and Arab students. In 1969–70 such groups were operating on about 80 campuses under various names – Jewish Student Bund, Concerned Jewish Students, Jewish Student Union, Jewish Activist League, Na'asseh. Many published campus newspapers; membership generally ranged from 10 to 50 in each branch.

Social and professional fraternities constituted still another facet of Jewish group life on the campus. ZBT, the first

Jewish fraternity, was followed by Sigma Epsilon Delta (1901) for dental students, Phi Delta Epsilon (1904) for medical students, and Iota Alpha Pi (1903), the first sorority. The number of social groups grew steadily with the increase in Jewish enrollment and the exclusion of Jews from the general fraternities and sororities. In 1941, 12 national social Jewish fraternities, five national sororities, and 17 professional fraternities had 540 local chapters and a membership of 85,000, in addition to several local organizations without national affiliation. Several national groups were nondenominational, but their membership was almost exclusively Jewish, and although most of them occasionally supported Jewish projects or programs, their chief purpose was social.

After World War II, in response to changing university policies and the growing public demand for the elimination of discriminatory restrictions, most Greek-letter societies began to accept members regardless of social, racial, or religious background. Deprived of one of their major reasons for existence, most Jewish groups experienced a significant drop in membership, leading to mergers of several national groups and the closing of local chapters by the late 1960s.

[Alfred Jospe]

In Israel

During the school year 1970–71 about 44,000 students (including Arabs, Druze, and Jews from abroad) were studying at ten universities and colleges. In 2004–5, 245,000 students were registered in eight universities, 23 colleges, and 26 teacher colleges. The Israel students' average age is higher than that of students in other countries because most of them serve in the army for three years prior to their university attendance. During their studies the students are frequently called to the army reserves. Many are married and most of them work to support themselves. All these are factors limiting political, social, and cultural activity. Social and political activity among students is often outside the framework of the students' organizations. About 15% of the students are active in student "cells" of the political parties, in local student unions, and in the National Union. A National Union of Students, to represent all the students, was first set up in the 1930s (local unions had begun to function in the 1920s). It is the roof organization of the local unions and is headed by a presidium composed of the chairmen of the local unions. Elections to the local unions and the National Union are held yearly. The National Union is the Israel branch of the World Union of Jewish Students and the chairman of the union is the vice chairman of WUJS.

WORLD UNION OF JEWISH STUDENTS. The World Union of Jewish Students (WUJS, or UMEJ in French and Spanish) was founded in 1924 by a number of European Jewish student unions and had among its early presidents and officers such personalities as Albert *Einstein, Chaim *Weizmann, Simon *Dubnow, Sigmund *Freud, Stephen S. *Wise, Ḥayyim Naḥman *Bialik, and Sir Hersch *Lauterpacht. Most of the archives of the organization were destroyed during the Holocaust, and afterward the officers themselves discarded old records. During its initial stages WUJS concerned itself with such problems as the numerus clausus in eastern European universities, the building of a student house at The Hebrew University campus on Mount Scopus in Jerusalem, etc. During World War II the center was transferred from Paris to Switzerland, and the most important activity of WUJS was to provide refuge for Jewish students, victims of Nazi persecution. After World War II, until 1948, WUJS had member organizations in Czechoslovakia, Bulgaria, Egypt, Iraq, Lebanon, Poland, and Romania, as well as official connections with the youth of the Jewish Anti-Fascist Committee of the U.S.S.R. In 1948, back in Paris, WUJS involved itself in the work of the World Student Relief, the International Student Service, and UNESCO. In the late 1950s, after some years of lethargy, the organization recovered and remained centered in Paris until 1968, when the secretariat was moved to London.

The core of WUJS's activities until 1967 was the furthering of Jewish identity, but following the *Six-Day War (1967) WUJS became openly pro-Zionist, supporting *aliyah* and other activities centered on Israel, and it affiliated to the World Zionist Organization in 1968. A process of political radicalization characterized the Union during 1967–70. However, the decrease of the impact of the New Left in the early 1970s led to a renewed interest in furthering Jewish education. In 1971 WUJS comprised 30 national union members and correspondent student organizations, as well as individual Jewish student affiliates from countries where the functioning of Jewish institutions is not permitted. The total membership was estimated at 100,000 to 110,000, of which approximately 50,000 were represented through the North American Jewish Students' network and 35,000 are members of the National Union of Israel Students. The supreme authority of the union is the WUJS Congress, where national Jewish student unions are represented proportionately to their membership (with a maximum of eight delegates). The Congress generally convenes in Israel every three years.

The main activities of WUJS fall into three categories: educational, political, and Israel-oriented or Zionist. WUJS published numerous pamphlets and journals on basic Judaism. Political activity is centered mainly on action to combat antisemitism and neo-Nazism with the cooperation of non-Jewish student organizations, and action in connection with the Israel-Arab conflict. There were also protests, demonstrations, picketing, and the coordination of activities all over the world on behalf of Jews in Arab countries (especially after the Baghdad executions) and in defense of Soviet Jewry. Contacts were maintained with general international organizations, particularly with the International Students' Organization. Many WUJS activities are oriented around and centered in Israel. In addition to various summer schemes in Israel, in 1967 WUJS established an International Graduate Institute at Arad, its program allowing participants to learn Hebrew, basic Judaism, and Israel studies.

WUJS provides an umbrella framework for nearly all different trends existing in the Jewish world. The weight of each of its trends varies continuously, and it is therefore difficult to define the composition of its leadership. Student unions in Germany, France, Italy, and Belgium have usually provided an extreme-left Zionist approach. Unions in Switzerland, U.K., Ireland, South Africa, and Australia were strongly Zionist with a religious predominance. North America is mostly represented through the Radical Zionists. Latin America, constantly in a very isolated position, represents the "middle-way" Zionist.

[Edy Kaufman]

STUDENT STRUGGLE FOR SOVIET JEWRY (SSSJ), 1964–1991, the first American national movement to free Russian Jews. Its combination of imaginative demonstrations, Congressional lobbying, and information dissemination helped generate the wave of international public pressure which ultimately forced open the gates of the Kremlin to mass emigration and the release of refuseniks and Prisoners of Conscience. A grassroots effort, SSSJ became a unifying factor among the diverse streams of American Jewry, and continually challenged the Jewish Establishment to act with greater vigor on behalf of its Russian brethren.

SSSJ was founded at a meeting at Columbia University on April 27, 1964, initiated by Jacob Birnbaum, Glenn Richter, Arthur Green, and James Torczyner, all involved in the American civil rights movement, just months after the famed March on Washington and but two months before Mississippi Summer. Four days later, it staged a public demonstration of over 1,000 students at the Soviet Union's Mission to the United Nations, which garnered a page 2 story in the *New York Times* the next morning. Within months, SSSJ drew political figures to its rallies. In 1965, noted Jewish singer Rabbi Shlomo Carlebach penned SSSJ's marching tune "Am Yisrael Chai!" (the people of Israel live!) It became the signature song of the Soviet Jewry freedom movement, both without and within the U.S.S.R.

SSSJ saw four main pressure points: the Kremlin, the US government, public opinion, and the American Jewish community. From 1964 to 1971, much effort was spent sparking a slowly growing interest in the issue and pressuring Establishment Jewish organizations to allocate a budget and staff to deal with the crisis. After the notorious Leningrad Trials which began in December 1970 of Jews who sought to escape from the U.S.S.R., SSSJ initiated, along with its adult activist counterpart of the Union of Councils for Soviet Jews (UCSJ), widespread Congressional lobbying to first pass, then maintain, the Jackson-Vanik Amendment. The bill linked trade credits to the U.S.S.R. with freedom of emigration. Intense pressure was kept on Establishment Jewish bodies not to abandon the Amendment despite pressures from the Nixon Administration, which had been so supportive of Israel to do so.

SSSJ differed from many other Jewish groups in that its leadership consisted of activist young rabbis, such as Rabbis Shlomo Riskin, Yitz Greenberg, Charles Sheer, and Avi Weiss. They inspired many students, who were soon further motivated by books revealing American public political and Jewish inaction during the Holocaust. This generation, raised in less self-conscious times, swore to be different. Israel's spectacular victory during the Six-Day War spurred more visible young American Jewish identification, and SSSJ provided a suitable vehicle. SSSJ continually utilized overt Jewish symbols, such as the *shofar*, and biblical phrases, such as "Let my people go."

By the early 1970s, SSSJ had developed methods to bring out from the USSR. an increasing stream of information about and appeals by refuseniks (Jews denied exit) and Prisoners of Conscience (Prisoners for Zion), which were widely disseminated. These efforts bypassed the control of the Israeli government, which attempted to keep a lid on this documentation. SSSJ's method was to focus on individual stories to understand the plight of millions of Russian Jews. To that end, SSSJ encouraged both popular and legislative mail and phone communication with refusenik and prisoner families, despite widespread KGB interference, as well as missions into the USSR to visit these Jews.

The enthusiasm of SSSJ's many volunteers far exceeded the movement's meager budget, raised in part by sale of protest buttons, bumper stickers, stamps, Prisoner of Conscience and refusenik bracelets. The successful effort to rescue a fifth of world Jewry, so soon after the Shoah, became a transformative experience for many young American Jews. They learned advocacy skills that were soon put to use for Israel and other causes, and understood that in their hands could lie the seeds of Jewish redemption.

[Avi Weiss (2nd ed.)]

STUDY. The study of the Torah (*talmud Torah*) as a supreme religious duty is one of the most typical and far-reaching ideas of rabbinic Judaism. Talmudic literature is full of references to the *mitzvah* of Torah study, especially of the difficult halakhic portions which require the fullest application. C.G. Montefiore (*A Rabbinic Anthology* (1938), introd., 17), though more than a little unsympathetic to this side of rabbinism, observes: "For all these legal discussions, all this 'study of the Law,' all these elaborations and minutiae, were to the Rabbis the breath of their nostrils, their greatest joy and the finest portion of their lives."

An early Mishnah (Peah 1:1), after describing such duties as honoring parents and performing acts of benevolence among the *mitzvot* for which there is reward both in this world and the next, concluded that the study of the Torah is "equal to them all." A tannaitic treatise, *Baraita Kinyan Torah* (Avot 6), devoted to the ideal of Torah study, contains the advice (6:4): "This is the way of the Torah: a morsel of bread with salt to eat, water by measure to drink; thou shalt sleep on the ground, and live a life of hardship, whilst thou toilest in the Torah. If thou doest thus, happy shalt thou be, and it shall be well with thee; happy shalt thou be – in this world, and it shall be well with thee – in the world to come." Quoting the verse, "This is the Law (Torah): when a man dieth in a tent" (Num. 19:14), the third-century teacher Resh Lakish taught: "The words of the Torah become firmly established only for one who kills himself (in study) for it" (Ber. 63b). Dedicated students, "toiling in the Torah," were found to number in the thousands in the great Palestinian and Babylonian academies during the first five centuries of the present era. Only against such a background of unqualified devotion does the saying of the second-century R. Jacob become intelligible: "If a man was walking by the way and studying and he ceased his study to declare, 'How fine is this tree!' or 'How fine is this plowed field' Scripture reckons it to him as though he were guilty against his own soul" (Avot 3:7). Of Rava it was said (Shab. 88a) that he was once so engrossed in his studies that he was unaware that his fingers were spurting blood. It was taken for granted that a scholar would be incapable of diverting his mind from Torah study; hence it was ruled that a scholar is forbidden to remain in unclean alleyways where Torah should not be studied (Ber. 24b).

The ideal of Torah study had a twofold aim. First it was believed to lead to the practical observances, since without knowledge of what it is that the Torah enjoins full observance is impossible. "An empty-headed man cannot be a sin-fearing man, nor can an ignorant person be pious" (Avot 2:5). Secondly, Torah study was itself a religious duty of the highest order. This dual function of study is presumably given expression in the discussion said to have taken place in the early part of the second century: "R. Tarfon and the Elders were once reclining in the upper story of Nithza's house in Lydda, when this question was put to them: 'Which is greater, study or practice?' R. Tarfon replied: 'Practice is greater.' R. Akiva replied: 'Study is greater for it leads to practice.' Then they all answered and said: Study is greater, for it leads to practice" (Kid. 40b). Yet study without any intention of carrying out the precepts was seen as having no value. "Whoever says that he has only [an interest] in the study of the Torah, he does not even have [the study of] the Torah" (Yev. 109b). There is evidence of tension between the scholarly ideal and that of extraordinary piety without learning. The famous scholars were committed to Torah study as the highest pursuit, yet they were compelled to recognize the achievements of men of outstanding piety who were in no way renowned for their learning. The scholars yielded only grudgingly, as in the tale (Ber. 34b) of the miracle-working saint, R. Ḥanina b. Dosa, who prayed successfully for the recovery of R. Johanan b. Zakkai's son, whereas the prayers of R. Johanan would have accomplished nothing. When R. Johanan's wife asked him, "Is Ḥanina greater than you are?" he replied, "No; but he is like a servant of the king who can enter his presence at any time whereas I am like a nobleman who is allowed only to appear at fixed times."

The qualifications for study were carefully mapped out, 48 "excellences" by which the Torah is acquired being listed (perhaps for rehearsal by the prospective student):

> By study, by the hearing of the ear, by the ordering of the lips, by the understanding of the heart, by the discernment of the heart, by awe, by reverence, by humility, by cheerfulness; by attendance on the Sages, by consorting with fellow-students, by close argument with disciples; by assiduity, by knowledge of Scripture and Mishnah; by moderation in business, in worldly occupation, pleasure, sleep, conversation, and jesting; by long-suffering, by a good heart, by faith in the Sages, by submission to sorrows; by being one that recognizes his place and that rejoices in his lot and that makes a fence around his words and claims no merit for himself; by being one that is beloved, that loves God, that loves mankind, that loves well-doing, that loves rectitude, that loves reproof, that shuns honor and boasts not of his learning, and delights not in rendering decisions; that helps his fellow to bear his yoke, and that judges him favorably, and that establishes him in the truth and establishes him in peace; and that occupies himself assiduously in his study; by being one that asks and makes answer, that hearkens and adds thereto; that learns in order to teach and that learns in order to practice; that makes his teacher wiser; that retells exactly what he has heard, and reports a thing in the name of him that said it (Avot. 6:6).

The demands made on the student were thus both of intellect and of character. The successful student acquired in addition to factual knowledge the capacity for skill in debate. Of particularly brilliant scholars it was said that they were able to provide 24 answers to every problem (Shab. 33b; BM 84a). It was not unusual for teachers to encourage their disciples to cultivate alertness of mind by appearing on occasion to act contrary to the Law, to see whether the error would be spotted (Ber. 33b; Ḥul. 43b; Nid. 4b). The debators were compared to mighty warriors taking part in the "battles of the Torah" (Sanh. 111b). Another comparison was that to competent craftsmen. The "craftsmen and the smiths" (II Kings 24:14) were identified with the scholars and said to possess acute reasoning powers (Sif. Deut. 321). Of a text presenting severe problems of interpretation it was said that neither a carpenter nor his apprentice could provide the correct solution (AZ 50b). In similar vein keen scholars were compared to builders (Ber. 64a), to pearl divers capable of reaching great depths in pursuit of treasure (BK 91a), and to weavers (Ber. 24a). The purveyor of the difficult halakhic teachings was compared to a dealer in precious stones for the connoisseur, whereas the more popular but less profound aggadic teacher was compared to the retailer of cheap tinsel goods which all can afford to buy (Sot. 40a).

While the saying of R. Judah in the name of Rav, that a man should study the Torah even if his motives were not of the purest (*she-lo li-Shemah*), was generally accepted because the right motive would eventually emerge (Pes. 50b), the rabbinic ideal was that of Torah "for its own sake" (*li-Shemah*). R. Meir said: "Whoever labors in the Torah for its own sake merits many things; and not only that, but the whole world is indebted to him: he is called a friend, beloved, a lover of the All-present, a lover of mankind; it clothes him in meekness and reverence; it fits him to become just, pious, upright and faithful; it keeps him far from sin, and brings him near to virtue; through him the world enjoys counsel and sound knowledge, understanding and strength" (Avot 6:1). The *Sifrei* (Deut. 41 and 48) remarks: "Suppose you say, I am learning Torah that I may get rich, or that I may be called Rabbi, or that

I may gain reward (from God) – the teaching of Scripture is: 'To love the Lord your God' (Deut. 11:13)." "Suppose you say, I will learn Torah in order to be called learned, to have a seat in the academy, to have endless life in the world to come – the teaching is: 'To love the Lord your God.'"

From the rabbinic period and onward great centers of Jewish learning were established. In Palestine there was the academy at the sea-coast village of Jabneh, which came into especial prominence after the destruction of the Temple; at Lydda under the guidance of R. Eliezer b. Hyrcanus and R. Tarfon; at Bene-Berak under R. Akiva; at Usha in Galilee; and there were also centers in Sepphoris, Tiberias, and Caesarea. R. Yose b. Kisma said: "I was once walking by the way, when a man met me and greeted me and I returned his greeting. He said to me, 'Rabbi, from where are you?' I said to him, 'I come from a great city of sages and scribes.' He said to me, 'If you are willing to dwell with us in our place, I will give you a thousand golden dinars and precious stones and pearls.' I said, 'If you were to give me all the silver and gold and precious stones in the world, I would not dwell anywhere but in a home of the Torah'" (Avot 6:9). "Homes of the Torah" rose to a position of importance in third-century C.E. Babylonia. At the beginning of this century two Palestinian-trained scholars, Rav and Samuel, returned to their native Babylonia, the former to found the academy at Sura, the latter to revive the long-established academy at Nehardea. When Nehardea was destroyed during the Roman-Persian wars in the year 259 C.E., Samuel's disciple, R. Judah b. Ezekiel, founded an academy at Pumbedita which existed as a sister and rival institution of Sura for over eight centuries. After the decline of Sura and Pumbedita in the 11th century, new schools sprang up in North Africa and Europe to take their place. The schools of Paris, Troyes, Narbonne, Metz, Worms, Speyer, Altona, Cordoba, Barcelona, and Toledo were renowned in the Middle Ages. From the 16th century, Poland, with its own academies, emerged as the Jewish intellectual center.

Yet it should not be imagined that the rabbinic ideal of Torah study was for the scholar alone. It was binding on every Jew as a *mitzvah*. R. Johanan said in the name of R. Simeon b. Yoḥai, "Even though a man reads no more than the *Shema* morning and evening he has thereby fulfilled the precept of 'This book of the law shall not depart'" (Josh. 1:8). It is, however, forbidden to say this in the presence of the ignorant (who would draw the consequence that detailed Torah study is not important). But Rava said it is meritorious to say it in the presence of the ignorant (so that they should not despair of having no part in Torah study; Men. 99b). There is no doubt that the rabbinic ideal was devotion to Torah study on the part of every Jew. Maimonides follows his rabbinic mentors in ruling (Yad, Talmud Torah 1:8): "Every man in Israel is obliged to study the Torah, whether he is firm of body or a sufferer from ill-health, whether a young man or of advanced age with his strength abated. Even a poor man who is supported by charity and obliged to beg at doors, and even one with wife and children to support, is obliged to set aside a period for Torah study by day and by night, as it is said: Thou shalt meditate therein day and night."

The Laws of Study

Three benedictions are to be recited before studying the Torah (Singer, Prayer 5). Since the whole of the Jew's waking life is a time for study these benedictions are recited at the beginning of each day and suffice for the whole day's study. It is considered meritorious to set aside a fixed time each day for Torah study, preferably in the company of others. Each community is expected to have a special "house of study" (*bet ha-midrash*), the sanctity of which is greater than that of a synagogue. As evidence of this it is ruled that while it is not permitted to run from a *bet ha-midrash* to a synagogue it is proper to run from a synagogue to a *bet ha-midrash*. A person unable to study himself should assist in supporting students of the Torah, in whose learning he will then have a share (Sh. Ar., YD 246:1). The Psalmist (Ps. 19:19) speaks of the precepts as "rejoicing the heart." Consequently, it is forbidden to study the Torah during the week of mourning for a close relative or on the Ninth of Av. The rabbis believed in the psychological value of verbal expression and therefore advised that Torah study should not be a purely mental exercise but the words of the text should be uttered aloud, customarily with a chant. Since the study of the Torah is equal to all the other precepts, a man should not interrupt his studies to do a good deed unless there is no one else to carry it out. At the completion of the study of a whole tractate of the Talmud it is customary to celebrate the occasion with a festive meal.

Scope of Study

"At five years the age is reached for the study of Scripture, at ten for the study of Mishnah, at thirteen for the fulfillment of the commandments, at fifteen for the study of Talmud" (Avot 5:21). This may reflect the actual ages when the young students were gradually introduced to the more complex subjects of study. Elsewhere (Kid. 30a) it is said that a man should divide his study time so that a third is devoted to Scripture, a third to Mishnah, and a third to Talmud. In the Middle Ages, especially in France and Germany, most of the students' efforts were directed to the study of the Babylonian Talmud, in particular to its halakhic portion, with a certain neglect of other topics. Typical is the admission of Rabbenu Tam (Tos. Kid. 30a s.v. *lo*) that the rabbinic schools relied on the fact that the Babylonian Talmud is full of all matters, containing Scripture and Mishnah. This tendency toward a certain narrowing of studies to the virtual exclusion of all except *halakhah* became more and more the norm in Russia and Poland. The medieval thinkers, however, not only urged the study of their discipline but tended to identify philosophical investigation with the highest type of Torah study. Maimonides (Yad, Yesodei ha-Torah 4:13) identified the esoteric disciplines known as the "Work of Creation" and "Work of the Chariot" with Aristotelian physics and metaphysics, respectively, and ranked them higher in the Jewish scale of studies than talmudic debates. Similarly, the kabbalists zealously regarded their subject – the "soul of the Torah" (Zohar III 152a) – as the highest pursuit. The kabbalist Ḥayyim Vital (*Sha'ar ha-Hakdamot*, introd.) recommended that a man should spend an hour or two each day on halakhic casuistry in order to remove the coarse "shell" which surrounds the "fruit," but should devote the rest of his study time to the true science of the kabbalistic mysteries. In the 16th century R. Moses Isserles (YD 246:4) summed up the rabbinic attitude as follows: "A man should only study Scripture, Mishnah, and Gemara, and the Codes based on them. In this way he will acquire this world and the next. But he should not study other sciences. However, it is permitted to study other sciences occasionally, provided that this does not involve in the reading of heretical works. This is called by the Sages 'strolling in Paradise.' A man must not 'stroll in Paradise' until he has filled his stomach with meat and wine, namely, the knowledge of that which is forbidden and that which is permitted and the laws of the precepts."

The rise of the ḥasidic movement in the 18th century presented a serious challenge to the ideal of Torah study as the supreme religious duty. The early ḥasidic masters accused the conventional scholars of engaging in Torah study for motives of fame, wealth, and prestige. Prayer, in the traditional scheme inferior to study, was frequently elevated by the Ḥasidim above study. In addition, the rabbinic ideal of *Torah li-Shemah* ("for its own sake") was interpreted in early Ḥasidism to mean attachment to God (*devekut*), while studying, especially in the sense of intense concentration on the letters of the text, was believed to reveal on earth the divine forces by means of which God governs the world (see J.G. Weiss in: *Essays Presented to... I. Brodie* (1966), Heb. sec. 151–69). The comparatively large number of classical talmudic scholars among the second and third generations of ḥasidic masters prevented, however, any radical departure from the older ideal. In a statement which combines the older ideal with the new ḥasidic emphasis on attachment to God while studying, R. Shneour Zalman of Lyady describes (*Tanya*, ch. 5, *Likkutei Amarim* (1912), 17–19) the religious significance of even the legalistic debates:

> Behold, with regard to every kind of intellectual perception, when one understands and grasps an idea in one's mind, the mind seizes the idea and encompasses it in thought so that the idea is held, surrounded, and enclosed in the mind in which it is comprehended. Conversely, the mind is clothed by an idea it has grasped. For instance, when one understands fully a rule in the Mishnah or the Gemara, his mind seizes the rule and encompasses it and, at the same time, his mind is encompassed by the rule. Now, behold, this rule is the wisdom and will of the Holy One, blessed be He, for it rose in His will that, for instance, when A pleads thus and B thus the rule will be thus. And even if, in fact, a case of this kind will never come before the courts, nonetheless, seeing that it rose in the will and wisdom of the Holy One, blessed be He, that this is the rule, it follows that when a man knows and grasps this rule in his mind in accordance with the decision laid down in the Mishnah or the Gemara or the Codes he grasps, seizes hold of, and encompasses in his mind the will and wisdom of the Holy One, blessed be He, of whom no thought can conceive.

A less mystical approach is advocated in the famous broadside fired against the Ḥasidim by the disciple of the Gaon of Vilna, R. Ḥayyim of Volozhin (*Nefesh ha-Ḥayyim*). R. Ḥayyim reiterates the conventional view that Torah study even out of ulterior motives is not to be despised and that, moreover, Torah for its own sake does not mean that the student should have God in mind when he studies the texts (such an attempt, R. Ḥayyim argues, would interfere with the intense concentration required for the mastery of the difficult halakhic studies he favored above all else). The student should have a few moments of prayer and devout thoughts before his actual studies and then he should immerse himself in the texts. For R. Ḥayyim (*Nefesh ha-Ḥayyim* (1874), 4:9, 40a) the Torah student has little need for the moralistic and devotional literature (*Musar*) in order to become God-fearing. The Torah itself possesses the property of inducing the fear of God in the hearts of its diligent students. A work in similar vein, from the same school, singing the praises of traditional Torah study, is *Ma'alot ha-Torah* by Abraham, brother of the Gaon of Vilna. The book expresses the ideal taught in the yeshivah of Volozhin and in the Lithuanian yeshivot influenced by it in the 19th and 20th centuries, in which, however, *Musar* did eventually come to occupy a considerable place.

In Western Europe, from the beginning of the 19th century, more and more time had to be found for secular studies, frequently to the detriment of Torah study. Samson Raphael Hirsch adapted the rabbinic ideal of "Torah and *Derekh Ereẓ*" ("worldly occupation") so that the latter came to embrace Western learning and culture. Moreover, the critical investigation of the classical sources known as *Juedische Wissenschaft* posed problems of its own for the traditional ideal of Torah study. In a sense the objective, "scientific" scholarship that is the ideal of this school is opposed to that of study as a devotional exercise, if only because it is far more difficult to treat as sacred texts those that are critically examined, and, conversely, acknowledging the sanctity of a text tends to prejudge critical questions regarding its background and authorship. The achievements of *Juedische Wissenschaft* have shed new light on many obscure corners of Jewish thought and history, but critics such as G. Scholem (*Perakim be-Yahadut*, ed. by E. Spicehandler and J. Petuchowsky (n.d.), 312–327) have questioned whether the movement has ever had any real religious significance. There have undoubtedly emerged two vastly different worlds of Jewish studies: the world of the yeshivot indifferent or even hostile to critical scholarship, and the world of modern learning with no formal interest in study as an act of religious worship. To date there has been little meeting between these two worlds.

[Louis Jacobs]

Historical Aspects

The ideal of Torah study as a lifelong pursuit incumbent upon all Jews found ample concretization in the course of Jewish history. Indeed, *ḥevrot* (voluntary study groups) devoted to the regular study of one or another traditional text constitute a significant feature of Jewish social history. Although early medieval sources do not specifically mention the existence of such associations, it is clear from the responsa literature of the period that householders were in the habit of engaging tutors – where required – to give them regular instruction in the sacred texts (see Neuman, Spain, 2 (1942), 293 n. 31, for references to the relevant responsa). The first such study circles, which date back to talmudic and geonic times, appear to have been devoted to the perusal of mystical texts. There is some evidence that the initial impulse toward the formation of organized study groups for laymen originated with the 16th-century Safed school of mystics, who regarded daily study of the Torah in groups as an essential part of their program of mystical exercise; and this hypothesis is confirmed by the fact that the first references to such study circles come from early 16th-century Palestine (see B. Dinur, *Be-Mifneh ha-Dorot* (1955), 162–63). A visiting Italian rabbi, Obadiah of *Bertinoro, found the sight of such groups in Jerusalem sufficiently novel to warrant noting it in his travel diary. A letter from Palestine dating from the same period describes the local practice in these terms: "Even a hired laborer would not go out to his work or affairs in the morning after services, before studying Torah" (A. Yaari, *Iggerot Ereẓ Yisrael* (1943), 208).

From Palestine the practice spread to Italy. Thus, the *ketav rabbanut* (rabbinic contract) of a Veronese rabbi of the first half of the 16th century specified that he conduct classes in Jewish studies for laymen. In the last quarter of the century *Judah Loew b. Bezalel (the Maharal of Prague), inspired by the mystic significance which the Lurianic Kabbalah ascribed to the study of the Mishnah, organized groups for laymen to study Mishnah regularly. With the rapid spread of such circles, an early 17th-century author, Joseph Yuspa *Hahn (*Yosef Omeẓ*, Frankfurt, 1823, pt. 2, *Perek ha-Torah* (1928 ed.), 265ff.), prescribes the regulations by which they should be governed. Shabbetai Sheftel *Horowitz, the early 17th-century rabbi of Frankfurt, urged every householder to join one of the local circles so that he might devote at least one hour daily to study. At that time such groups included the entire adult male population of the community. In some communities – Prague for example – participation in a study group was an obligation imposed by communal regulation (1611). A similar ordinance adopted in Worms in 1667 made it mandatory for every adult male to devote at least one hour a day to study.

By the end of the 17th century study groups, usually meeting daily, were to be found in virtually every community of any size. Similar groups were established in Poznan (Poland) under the influence of Shabbetai Horowitz, who had moved there from Frankfurt, and their example was soon followed throughout Poland. The community there developed a novel feature in its zeal for learning. In the *bet ha-midrash*, professional students, supported by the local community, were organized in relays so they might study in turn around the clock. This practice of marathon study, recorded by Jacob *Emden in connection with the Great Bet ha-Midrash of Vilna, was widespread in Poland; and in 1741 it was introduced into the Amsterdam community. The extent to which universal adult study was a matter of communal concern is seen in the minute book of the Lithuanian Council (see *Councils of the Lands) which prescribed that every layman had a duty to study at least one chapter of the Mishnah every day (*Pinkas ha-Medinah*, ed. by S. Dubnow (1925), pars. 590, 959). Study was not only carried on in societies specifically constituted for this purpose, but also in most voluntary associations, whatever their primary function. Thus, for example, the Ḥevrat Bikkur Ḥolim in 17th-century Mantua required its members to gather for study on Sabbaths and festivals (see S. Simonsohn, *Toledot ha-Yehudim be-Dukkasut Mantovah*, 2 (1964) 405–7). A similar practice prevailed among the guilds of Jewish artisans in Poland (see M. Hendel, *Melakhah u-Va'alei Melakhah be-Am Yisrael* (1965), 7ff.)

A curious sidelight on the universal preoccupation with study is afforded by the opposition to it evinced by leading rabbinic authorities of the 18th century. Jacob Emden based his opposition on the grounds that the study of the Talmud was intended for scholars and not for mere laymen who were certain to become skeptics when they read some of the more fantastic aggadic tales found there. He argued, moreover, that these laymen used their own study of the Talmud as a pretext for exempting themselves from the support of those who devoted their full time to it (see J. Emden, *Siddur Yaveẓ Ammudei Shamayim Hilkhot Talmud Torah*). In a similar vein, Jonathan *Eybeschuetz, a contemporary of Emden, exhorted laymen to study *Oraḥ Ḥayyim* (the laws of daily religious life) and moralistic texts rather than the Talmud; and still others urged that Baḥya ibn Paquda's pietistic-philosophic text *Ḥovot ha-Levavot* ("Duties of the Heart") be read in place of the Talmud.

[Theodore Friedman]

Women and Torah Study

Most rabbinic texts presume that Jewish women are not obligated to engage in Torah study, just as they are exempt from other communal obligations such as public prayer at mandated times (Tosefta Sotah 7:6; Lieberman 7:9; similarly Ḥag. 3a), commenting on the commandment that the entire community must gather to hear divine teachings and so learn to observe them (Deut. 31:12), quotes R. Eleazar b. Azariah to the effect that the men come to learn Torah but women come only to hear. A frequently cited tannaitic Midrash claims that "And you shall teach them to your children (*binekhem*)" (Deut. 11:19) should be understood to mean, "Your sons, but not your daughters" (*Sifre Devarim* 46; similarly TJ, Eruv. 10:1, b. Ber. 20b; TB, Kid. 29b).

A central debate between the sages Ben Azzai and R. Eliezer over whether women should study Torah appears in Sotah 3:4, in reference to the ordeal of a woman accused of adultery. While the content of the debate has several ambiguities, the positions of the protagonists are clear. Ben Azzai says that a man is obligated to teach his daughter Torah while R. Eliezer disagrees, opining that "whoever teaches his daughter Torah teaches her *tiflut*" (obscenity or lasciviousness; sometimes translated as foolishness). And while it is possible to read this passage narrowly, as limited to its particular context, later rabbinic tradition read it broadly, as a wholesale exclusion of women from Torah study. The Palestinian Talmud (Sot. 3:4, Ḥag. 1:1) contrasts Ben Azzai's positive view with the negative opinion of R. Eleazar b. Azariah, cited above. This passage goes on to relate a story about the depths of R. Eliezer's antipathy to women studying Torah, in which he refuses to answer a question posed by a wealthy matron, telling her, "A woman's wisdom is only in her spindle." When his son expresses concern that R. Eliezer may jeopardize the financial support this woman provides to him, he replies, "Better the words of Torah be burned than be given to a woman."

The Babylonian Talmud on *Sotah* 3:4 (Sot. 21a) takes it for granted that women are exempt from Torah study: a woman who studies voluntarily is said to be meritorious but she does not merit the larger reward of fulfilling a commandment. Ideally, women should garner merit in this area by arranging for their sons to learn Torah and by waiting patiently for their husbands to return from studying with the rabbis (similarly Ber. 17a).

The medieval legal tradition also exempted women from study. *Maimonides (Laws of Torah Study, 1:13) writes that women are not obligated to learn Torah and goes on to say that "the sages have commanded that a man not teach his daughter Torah, since most women's minds are not properly directed to being taught, but rather they turn the words of Torah into words of triviality (*tiflut*) …" While distinguishing between different levels of Torah study, since it is the "Oral Torah" that a woman will especially fail to understand, Maimonides rules that a man should not even teach his daughter written Scripture. However, if he does so, he has not taught her *tiflut*. Maimonides goes on to say that a woman who studies Torah voluntarily receives merit, albeit less than a man who studies in order to fulfill the commandment. Joseph *Caro repeats Maimonides' rulings in the Shulḥan Arukh (YD 246:6); in his commentary for Ashkenazi Jewry, Moses *Isserles adds that a woman is, nevertheless, obligated to learn the laws that pertain to women's lives.

Some women did receive Torah education in both the rabbinic and medieval periods. For example, M. Nedarim 4:3 rules that if person A has vowed to receive no benefit from person B, person B may nonetheless "teach his (A's) sons and *daughters* Bible." Similarly, Kiddushin 4:13 discusses whether women may teach Bible to young children, which suggests that at least some women must have been sufficiently educated to do so. References to female Bible teachers also appear in the Cairo **Genizah* and in the responsa of Maimonides (Goitein, 64–65, 69–71). Tosefta *Berakhot* 2:12 includes menstruants and women who have recently given birth among those who may "read from the Torah, and study mishnah, midrash, and *halakhot*," despite being in a state of ritual impurity. The Babylonian Talmud includes several stories about the scholarly *Beruriah, whose accomplishments included learning "300 teachings in a day from 300 teachers" over three years (Pes. 62b).

Several medieval Ashkenazi sources rule that if a woman wishes to study Torah, she may do so and should say the appropriate blessing (*Maḥzor Vitry* 359; *Siddur Rashi* 267; Rashi, responsa 68). A Jewish school for girls is recorded in Rome in the 15th century. By the late Middle Ages, a literature of vernacular Bible translations, commentaries, and collections of ethical and aggadic materials, directed at a non-scholarly readership that included women, became popular in European communities, particularly following the invention of printing. There were also a few women throughout the medieval period who were noted for their advanced Jewish learning. The 12th-century Spanish traveler Petahiah of Regensburg (Ratisbon) reported that the daughter of Baghdad *gaon* Samuel ben Ali (d. 1194) taught Scripture and Talmud to men through a window (Goitein, 64). As in this case, such women were usually daughters, wives, and mothers of noted rabbinic scholars. It may be that it was precisely under such conditions that a woman could have access to advanced Jewish learning, or perhaps it is because of their connections to noted men that some such women were remembered to history.

It is in the modern period that most radical changes in women's relationship to Torah study have taken place. In the 19th and 20th centuries, particularly in Eastern Europe, opinions against teaching women any form of Torah knowledge were dominant. While boys and men could dedicate themselves to intense study of Jewish texts, girls received no formal Jewish education and sometimes attended secular schools. Concerned for the social effects this was having on girls' commitment to Jewish life and practice as they matured, Sarah *Schnirer founded a girls' school, *Beth Jacob, in Cracow in 1917. By 1924, there were 53 Beth Jacob schools in Poland; on the eve of World War II, nearly 40,000 girls across Europe and elsewhere were being educated in Beth Jacob schools.

Schnirer faced initial resistance from the religious establishment, but received support from a leading authority of the day, Rabbi *Israel Meir ha-Kohen (known as the Ḥafeẓ Ḥayyim). He wrote that Maimonides' ban on teaching women Torah could no longer hold in changing times: "It seems that this applies only in times before us, when everyone lived in the place of his ancestors and the tradition of the ancestors was very strong among all, to behave as their ancestors had behaved… and in such case one could say not to teach Torah [to a woman] and her behavior will rely on [the model of] her ancestors. But now, when our ancestors' tradition has become very weak… those women who are accustomed to learning foreign language and writing, certainly it is a great commandment to teach them Pentateuch, and the Prophetic books, and the Writings, and the ethical writings of the sages…" (*Sefer Likkutei Hilkhot Sotah* 21a).

The mandate to teach women advocated by the Ḥafeẓ Ḥayyim was limited in scope and excluded advanced subjects such as Talmud or other rabbinic writings; it remains the case that Talmud is not taught in schools affiliated with the Beth Jacob system. A few strict ḥasidic and Orthodox communities continue to refuse to teach girls any Torah subject beyond the necessary rules and customs of Jewish practice. In many other early 21st century Jewish communities, however, opportunities for Jewish girls and women to study Torah have continued to expand. In the Reform, Conservative, and Reconstructionist movements, it is generally expected that Jewish education will be egalitarian, up to and including rabbinic ordination. Similarly, a number of Orthodox Jewish day schools in the United States, Israel, and elsewhere teach Talmud and related subjects to girls as well as boys, either in separate or co-educational classes. A variety of women's yeshivot, notably in Jerusalem and New York City, teach college age and adult students at a variety of levels, including some offering advanced study in rabbinic literature.

[Gail Labovitz (2nd ed.)]

BIBLIOGRAPHY: Sh. Ar., YD 246; G.F. Moore, *Judaism*, 2 (1927), 239–47; S. Zevin, *Le-Or ha-Halakhah* (1946), 159–64; E.E. Urbach, *Ḥazal, Pirkei Emunot ve-De'ot* (1969), index s.v. *Torah*; Assaf, Mekorot; A. Shoḥat, in: *Ha-Ḥinnukh*, 28 (1957), 404–18; Baron, Community, index s.v. *Education*. **ADD. BIBLIOGRAPHY:** J.R. Baskin, *Midrashic Women* (2002); idem, "The Education of Jewish Girls in the Middle Ages in Muslim and Christian Milieus," in: *Pe'amim*, 82 (2000), 1–17 (Heb.); S.D. Goitein, *Jewish Education in Muslim Countries* (Heb., 1962); A. Grossman. *Pious and Rebellious* (2004); T. Ilan, *Integrating Women into Second Temple History* (1999); S.P. Zolty. *"And All Your Children Shall Be Learned"* (1993).

STUERMER, DER, antisemitic German weekly, founded and edited by Julius *Streicher. It appeared in Nuremberg between 1923 and 1945, at first a local paper with a small circulation, but after 1935 with a circulation of 500,000. Its slogan, *"Die Juden sind unser Unglueck"* ("The Jews are our misfortune"), was pasted on walls in the streets and schools, thereby popularizing racial antisemitism among the masses. *Der Stuermer* encouraged the economic boycott and social isolation of Jews, further demanding that they be exterminated "root and branch." It contained sensational gossip tinged with sadism. It defined the Jews as "defilers" of the "pure and superior Nordic race," using crude lies, repetition of catchphrases, and caricatures depicting the stereotyped hideous *Rassenjude* ("Jew by race"), a devil in human form that destroyed everything good and healthy. In its "Ritual Murder" issue (May 1939), *Der Stuermer* revived the *blood libel accusation, with presumed proofs from the Talmud and frequent quotations from the Protocols of the *Elders of Zion. World War II was portrayed as the ritual murder of the whole of humanity by "World Jewry." Because of its vulgarity, *Der Stuermer* aroused distaste even among Nazi leaders, who occasionally tried to silence it. Though *Der Stuermer* was crude and vulgar, it was not ineffective in shaping the concept of the Jew in the minds of certain segments of the German Public.

BIBLIOGRAPHY: L.W. Bondy, *Racketeers of Hatred* (1946), ch. 3 and index; W. Hagemann, *Publizistik im Dritten Reich* (1948); Y. Wulf, *Presse und Funk im Dritten Reich* (1966).

[Nathan Feinberg / Michael Berenbaum (2nd ed.)]

STULBERG, LOUIS (1901–1977), U.S. labor leader. Stulberg, a lifelong unionist, began as a teenage garment cutter and rose to become president of the International Ladies Garment Workers Union (ILGWU), leading that organization for 10 years. In contrast with his predecessor, the fiery, high-decibel David *Dubinsky, Stulberg was regarded as a quiet but efficient leader and an astute financial manager. He was born in Poland but his family immigrated to Toronto, Canada, when he was three. His first job was as a cutter, but he was blacklisted in Toronto because of union activities and the family moved to Chicago, where he joined the ILGWU. He attended the University of Chicago for one year, played semi-pro baseball, and briefly considered a career as a shortstop. Devoting himself instead to union activities, he moved around the Midwestern U.S., working as a cutter and organizer in Toledo, Ohio, and Chicago before settling in New York City in 1927 and joining Cutters Local 10. Within two years, he was a business agent for Local 10 and in 1933 was named its business manager. As head of the cutters' dress department, he helped bring thousands of new members to the union during an East Coast organizing drive just before the start of World War II. In 1945, Stulberg joined the union's general staff as assistant executive secretary. Two years later he became manager of Local 62, which made women's undergarments, and was elected a vice president and member of the general executive board. In 1956 he was appointed by Dubinsky as executive vice president of the ILGWU, a non-elective position. He was elected general secretary-treasurer in 1959, making him Dubinsky's heir apparent. Stulberg became president of the ILGWU in 1966 and was reelected three times. He resigned as president in 1975, citing health problems. Stulberg's decade as president was marked by a major shift in ILGWU membership, from largely Jewish and Italian workers to Hispanics and African-Americans. Although membership had reached an all-time high of well over 400,000 in 1968, it began to fall as more apparel makers moved their operations to low-wage countries. It was during Stulberg's administration that the ILGWU broke away from the Liberal Party, which it had helped found. The union's leaders, including Stulberg, said the party had weakened the liberal-labor political coalition, contributing to Republican victories in New York State. Stulberg was also a vice president of the AFL-CIO and was a U.S. representative at the United Nations. He was also a fellow at Brandeis University in Waltham, Mass., where in 1969 the Louis Stulberg Chair of Law and Politics was established. In 1973, on the 25th anniversary of the State of Israel, he was awarded the Prime Minister's Medal.

[Mort Sheinman (2nd ed.)]

STURMAN, ḤAYYIM (1891–1938), *Haganah leader in Ereẓ Israel. Born in the Kiev district, Ukraine, Sturman settled in Ereẓ Israel with his parents in 1906. He then became an agricultural worker at Sejara. He joined the founders of *Ha-Shomer and participated in the establishment of *Merḥavyah and afterward of the Ha-Shomer settlement of *Tel Adashim. During World War I Sturman participated in the secret activities to provide the *yishuv* with arms. He was discovered and arrested by the Ottoman authorities, and he returned to

Tel Adashim after his release. Following the war he moved to Kevuẓat *Kinneret and was one of the organizers of the *Gedud ha-Avodah (Labor Legion) settlement activities in the Harod area. In 1921 he participated in the founding of *En-Harod, of which he was a member until his death.

Sturman was among those primarily responsible for the defense of the Harod bloc and an active member of the national center of the Haganah. He traveled as a political and agricultural emissary to neighboring countries, aided by his fundamental knowledge of Arabic and the Arab way of thinking. During the Arab riots of 1936–38 he was constantly in responsible positions for the defense of his area. At the same period he was one of Orde *Wingate's advisers and friends. When he was returning from a visit to the *stockade and tower settlement of *Tirat Ẓevi together with two friends, all three were killed when their car went over a road mine near the Arab village of Samaria. The school shared by En-Harod and Tel Yosef, and the nearby Bet Sturman, which serves as a museum institute for research of the eastern Jezreel Valley, were established in his memory and kibbutz Ma'oz Ḥayyim was named after him.

His son, MOSHE, fell in the Israel War of Independence and Moshe's son, ḤAYYIM, was killed in 1969 in the Israel Defense Forces' commando action on Green Island at the mouth of the Suez Canal.

BIBLIOGRAPHY: Bet Ḥayyim Sturman, *Ḥayyim Sturman, Aharon Etkin, D. Mossinsohn…* (1968); *Moshe Sturman, le-Zikhro* (1965).

STURMANN, MANFRED (1903–1989), Israeli author writing in German. Born in Koenigsberg (East Prussia), his first book, *Althebraeische Lyrik* – a rendering of biblical poetry into German – appeared in 1923 with an introduction by Arnold Zweig. This was followed by several books of his own lyrical poems, the first of which, *Die Erben* (1929), was awarded the Lyrics Prize of the City of Munich. After his immigration to Ereẓ Israel in 1938, he continued writing poetry as well as short stories in German. He dealt with the involved problem of an "Israel poet in the German language" in an essay published in *Meilensteine – Vom Wege des Kartells Juedischer Verbindungen KJV in der Zionistischen Bewegung* (Tel Aviv, 1972). He stated that both the serene landscape of the years of his youth and "the discovery of the Zionist dream" had a decisive influence on his outlook, his thinking, and his writing.

Some of the short stories Sturmann wrote in Israel were inspired by his experience in the war of 1948, his social work in Jerusalem, and his deep love of this city and the country: *Die Kreatur* (1952) and *Abschied von Europa* (1963) contain a representative selection of his short stories. He was the literary administrator of Else *Lasker-Schueler.

[Erich Gottgetreu]

STUTSCHEWSKY, JOACHIM (1891–1982), composer, cello player, and folklorist. Stutschewsky was born in Romny (Ukraine) to a family of musicians who had been *klezmerim* (entertainment players) for several generations. After studying at the Leipzig Conservatory (1909–11) he joined the Jena string quartet and played with the local orchestra. From 1918 to 1924 he stayed in Zurich, where he was active as soloist, chamber-music player, and cello teacher, and began to write his treatise on the art of cello playing which became recognized as one of the major modern manuals and has also been published as an official method in Russia. In Zurich, Stutschewsky began to promote lectures on and concerts of Jewish music, in cooperation with the movement begun by the Society for Jewish Folk Music. From 1924 to 1938 he stayed in Vienna and undertook concert tours dedicated to Jewish music in several countries. Going to Ereẓ Israel in 1938, he established himself as one of the most influential musical personalities in the country, continuing as a cello pedagogue, composer, lecturer, and writer.

Stutschewsky's style as a composer began in the East European vein and also absorbed in Israel the local influences of the Near Eastern Jewish communities and the emergent new folk-song styles. His earlier writings, as well as his many arrangements of folk and traditional melodies, were a part of the efforts made during the 1920s and 1930s to propagate the cause of Jewish music as such. In the later ones, such as the book *Ha-Klezmerim* (1959) and the collections *Zemer Am* (1940) and *120 Niggunei Ḥasidim* (1950), he turned to specific tasks of collection and preservation including, in *Ha-Klezmerim*, invaluable reminiscences and materials from his own family and regional traditions of the *klezmer*'s life and activities. In the field of general music Stutschewsky published a considerable number of arrangements and transcriptions for cello, which also became repertoire standards, and augmented his cello manual by several books of etudes. His other compositions include a symphonic poem *Safed* (1960) and other orchestral work; incidental music for the *Ohel Theater's *Fishke ha-Ḥigger*, based on *Mendele Mokher Seforim's novel (1939); cantatas to texts by S. Shenhod; chamber music for various combinations; piano pieces (including *Ze'eiriyyot*, Miniatures for Children, 1946); cello pieces; numerous original and arranged songs to Hebrew texts; and arrangements of East European Jewish songs. He also wrote *Mein Weg zur juedischen Musik* (1936), and autobiographical notes in *Tazlil*, 8 (1968), 65–67.

[Bathja Bayer]

STUTTGART, city in Wuerttemberg, Germany. A small Jewish community with a synagogue was in existence by 1330–40. In November 1348 during the *Black Death persecutions, most of the Jews were burned to death, but some survivors were recorded in *Esslingen in 1385. In 1393 one Jew was recorded as living in Stuttgart. A new community had come into being by 1434, comprising eight families by 1470. Both a synagogue and a *mikveh* date from that period. Some time after 1492 Jews were banished in consequence of the will (enacted as a state law in 1498) of Count Eberhard Ill of Wuerttemberg. At the beginning of the 16th century Count Ulrich attempted to employ Jews in the economic development of the territory. However, the banishment was reaffirmed by Emperor Charles v in 1521. In 1597 Duke Frederick i invited the Italian-Jewish inventor Abraham Colorni to experiment with saltpeter potassium but imprisoned him after a few unproductive months; Colorni later escaped. The duke's attempt in 1559 to attract a Portuguese-Jewish manufacturer met with ecclesiastical opposition. By 1710 a few Jews doing business with the ducal court were allowed to reside in Stuttgart, and by 1721 there were seven families in residence there. In 1734 Joseph Suess *Oppenheimer was appointed financial adviser by Duke Alexander; he fell into disfavor after the duke's death in 1737 and was executed in 1738. Newly admitted Jews were expelled in 1739. By 1770, four Jewish families lived in Stuttgart, among them Nathaniel Seidel, director of the mint, and the two brothers Seligmann (see *Eichthal-Seligmann family), lessees of the salt-mine concession from 1758.

After the admission of the merchant-banking *Kaulla family in 1779, a new community came into being. In 1831 the Central Wuerttemberg Jewish Council was organized in Stuttgart under state and church supervision. In 1834 a cemetery was acquired (a new one in 1876); in 1835 Joseph Maier, the first Wuerttemberg rabbi with the required Ph.D. degree (from Tuebingen University), was appointed; a prayer hall was consecrated in 1837. The growth of the community followed the two emancipation laws of 1828 and 1864. In 1808, 109 Jews lived in Stuttgart; the numbers rose to 211 in 1844; 847 in 1861; 1,169 in 1864; 1,801 in 1871; 3,015 in 1910; and 3,818 (1.4% of the total population) in 1913. In nearby Cannstatt, incorporated with Stuttgart in 1905, there were 469 Jews in that year. In 1925 the Jewish population of Stuttgart and Cannstatt was 4,870 (1.4% of the total population) and 4,490 in June 1933.

A synagogue was consecrated in 1861, and a separate Orthodox group maintained a prayer hall from 1880. The rabbis Maier (1794–1873) and Moses Wassermann (1811–1892) were raised to the nobility by the Wuerttemberg kings. From the 1890s the community had youth and cultural associations and branches of political organizations. From 1924 to 1938 it published a monthly for the Wuerttemberg Jewish communities, and a *Lehrhaus* (adult education center) was open from 1925 to 1938. In 1933 Jews in public office (among them eight jurists) and in cultural institutions were dismissed. Karl Adler, director of the conservatory for 11 years, founded the Jewish Arts Council for lay choirs. A Jewish school was founded in 1933, and a school for teachers of physical education in 1935. The B'nai B'rith Stuttgart Lodge was dissolved in 1937, and Polish Jews were deported on Oct. 26, 1938. Following the November 1938 pogrom, Adler organized an Emigration Aid and Self-Help Agency, which was led, after his emigration in May 1941, by the jurist Alfred Marx. The Wuerttemberg Jewish Central Council was dissolved in 1943. By 1941, 2,690 Jews had emigrated. The remainder were concentrated in a Jewish quarter, the older members of the community being evacuated to small towns and villages. From late 1941 through early 1945 Stuttgart was the collection point for the deportation of all Wuerttemberg Jews, beginning on July 1, 1941, to Riga (where the deportees were subsequently massacred), in 1942 first to *Izbica, *Auschwitz (four transports 1942–43), and then to *Theresienstadt (Aug. 5, 1942 to Feb. 1945). About 1,000 Stuttgart Jews died in deportation or in concentration camps.

[Toni Oelsner]

Post-World War ii

About 20 Jews survived in Stuttgart, some by going into hiding; 45 returned from Theresienstadt (among them Alfred Marx) and a few from other concentration camps. In two Displaced Persons' camps in the city in 1945 there were more than 2,000 Jews. By the end of 1946, 1,276 Jews remained in Stuttgart, decreasing to 569 in 1950; in 1968 the community had 480 members. A synagogue (built by the surviving architect Ernst Guggenheim), the only one in Wuerttemberg, was consecrated in 1952; the enlarged community center was completed in 1964. Among the survivors, Dr. Richard Perlen (d. 1961) was appointed president of the Wuerttemberg supreme court. The house of Albert *Einstein's mother's family in Cannstatt-Stuttgart has been preserved. Stuttgart is the seat of the Jewish community of Wuerttemberg, which numbered 677 in 1989. There were 2,881 in 2004, among them about 1,500 members living in Stuttgart. The increase is explained by the immigration of Jews from the former Soviet Union. In 1989 the majority were living in Stuttgart; in 2004 about 45% were living outside Stuttgart. In 1999 the community opened an old age home.

[Toni Oelsner /Larissa Daemmig (2nd ed.)]

BIBLIOGRAPHY: M. Zelzer, *Weg und Schicksal der Stuttgarter Juden* (1964); P. Sauer, *Die juedische Gemeinde in Wuerttemberg* (1966); *Germania Judaica*, 2 (1968), 809–11; 3 (1987), 1441–43; A. Freimann, *Gazetteer of Hebrew Printing* (1946), 69; L. Adler, in: YLBI, 5 (1960), 279–98; K.J. Ball-Kaduri, in: *Zeitschrift fuer die Geschichte der Juden*, 2 (1965), 73–98; T. Kroner (ed.), *Festschrift zum 50 jaehrigen Bestehen der Synagoge zu Stuttgart* (1911); A. Taenzer, *Die Geschichte der Juden in Wuerttemberg* (1937), 5–9, 120–6, 136–43, 162–73; A. Marx, *Schicksal der juedischen Juristen in Wuerttemberg und Hohenzollern 1933–1945* (1965). **ADD BIBLIOGRAPHY:** W. Braunn, *Quellen zur Geschichte der Juden bis zum Jahr 1600 im Hauptstaatsarchiv Stuttgart und im Staatsarchiv Ludwigsburg* (Thematische Repertorien, vol. 1) (1982); *Spurensuche: Juden und Judentum in Stuttgart* (1991); J. Hahn, *Friedhoefe in Stuttgart*, vol. 3 (Veroeffentlichungen des Archivs der Stadt Stuttgart, vol. 57) (1992); S. Dietrich, W. Schulze, and J. Wessel, *Zwischen Selbstorganisation und Stigmatisierung* (Veroeffentlichtungen des Archivs der Stadt Stuttgart, vol. 75) (1998); P. Sauer and S. Hosseinzadeh, *Juedisches Leben im Wandel der Zeit* (2002). **WEBSITES:** www.alemannia-judaica.de; www.irgw.de.

STUTTHOF (Pol. **Sztutowo**), German concentration camp established in a secluded area 22½ mi. (36 km.) E. of Danzig, which existed from Sept. 2, 1939, until May 9, 1945. Surrounded by water on three sides, the land was wet and almost at sea level. It was situated along the Danzig-Elbing highway. Initially a civilian camp, it became a concentration camp in January 1942. Jewish prisoners (several hundred men, mostly residents of Danzig) were brought there as early as Sept. 17, 1939. Among them were the writer and journalist Jacob Lange and the cantor of the Danzig synagogue, Leopold Schufftan. Almost all of these prisoners died within a few weeks. The initial population of prisoners were Poles; it also housed Soviet prisoners of war as well as Norwegians and Danes. Jews were a distinct minority. As it appeared that the war would last longer than planned and labor shortages would be prolonged, the work of these slaves became more valuable and thus conditions were slightly improved for the non-Jewish prisoner population precisely as the conditions of Jews became more lethal throughout German-occupied territory. The camp was expanded in 1943 and wooden barracks were replaced by concrete ones. Stutthof was a site of forced labor. Inmates worked at private industrial enterprises, foremost among them was the airplane factory of Focke-Wulff. They also worked in farming and in camp workshops. The camp staff were SS men and Ukrainian auxiliary police.

Until 1943 only small numbers of Jews from Warsaw, Bialystok, and some other places were deported to Stutthof. In the autumn of 1943, several hundred Jews found in hiding in Bialystok after the Bialystok ghetto uprising were brought there. Early in 1944 all the surviving Jewish prisoners were deported to the *Auschwitz concentration camp.

Besides the central camp 105 subcamps were built, notably in Stolp, Heiligenbeil, Gerdauen, Jesau, Schippenbeil, Seerappen, Praust, Burggraben, Thorn, and Elbing. About 20,000 Jewish prisoners, mostly women, were imprisoned there. In spring 1944 several thousand Jews from concentration camps in Ostland (in Latvia and Lithuania) were deported to Stutthof, and in the early summer thousands of Jewish women arrived from Hungary. The greatest increase of Jewish prisoners occurred in June–October 1944, when over 20,000 Jews were shipped to Stutthof from Auschwitz. These were mostly women from Hungary and the Lodz ghetto. Most of these people died in the first weeks from hunger and lack of water, or were gassed in the gas chamber, where, as in Auschwitz, Zyklon B rather than carbon monoxide was used. In the last months of 1944 about 12,000 Jewish prisoners (including almost 4,000 women) were deported from Stutthof to concentration camps in Germany: *Dachau, *Buchenwald, Neuengamme, and Flossenbuerg. In January 1945 forced evacuation – death marches – from Stutthof and its satellite camps began. At that time about 29,000 Jewish prisoners (including almost 26,000 women) were still alive in these camps. Five thousand marched to the Baltic sea coast and were executed by machine gun fire. The remaining prisoners were marched toward Lauenberg but were stopped by Soviet advances and returned to Stuthoff. In April 1945, with the front collapsing, the prisoners were again moved. Some were shot in the sea; others were transported by boat to Neuengamme. En route many died. When the camp was liberated on May 9 there were some 100 prisoners still alive at Stutthof.

About 26,000 Jews were killed or drowned during the evacuation. It is estimated that altogether over 52,000 Jewish prisoners passed through Stutthof and its satellite camps. Only about 3,000 of them survived.

BIBLIOGRAPHY: K. Dumin-Wasowicz, *Obóz koncentracyjnyStutthof* (Pol. with Eng. summary, 1966); O.M. Picholz-Barnitsch, in: *Yad Vashem Bulletin*, no. 17 (1965) 34–41; K. Dunin-Wasowics in: BZIH, no. 63 (1967) 3–37. **ADD. BIBLIOGRAPHY:** Y. Gutman and A. Saf (eds.), *The Nazi Concentration Camps: Structure and Aims; the Image of the Prisoner: The Jews in the Camps.* Proceedings of the Fourth Yad Vashem International Historical Conference (1984).

[Stefan Krakowski / Michael Berenbaum (2nd ed.)]

STYBEL, ABRAHAM JOSEPH (1884–1946), publisher and literary patron. Born in Zharki, Poland, Stybel engaged in the leather business. From his youth he was deeply interested in Hebrew literature. During World War I he moved from Warsaw to Moscow and became wealthy from his business dealings. He then decided to devote himself to fostering the advancement of Hebrew literature. In 1917 he founded the Stybel publishing house and invited David *Frischmann to be his chief editor. They began the systematic translation of some of the world's best literature by leading Hebrew writers, and also published a literary quarterly, **Ha-Tekufah*. After the October 1917 Revolution, when publishing of Hebrew literature was forbidden, Stybel moved to Warsaw and then to Berlin, and opened branches in New York (where he published the literary monthly *Miklat* under the editorship of Y.D. *Berkowitz) and in Ereẓ Israel. He published hundreds of books, both translations and original works (such as the complete works of M.J. *Berdyczewski and J.Ḥ. *Brenner). When his economic situation deteriorated, Stybel transferred his publishing and manuscripts to N. Twersky in Tel Aviv. In 1938 he renewed his publishing activities in Warsaw, and at the outbreak of World War II moved to the United States. There he reestablished his publishing house in 1945 under the name of The Institute of Goslava and A.J. Stybel, and printed an additional volume of *Ha-Tekufah* (vol. 36). He also published his notes and memoirs. His publishing house greatly advanced Hebrew book publication.

BIBLIOGRAPHY: J. Twersky, in: *Ha-Tekufah*, 32–33 (1948), 11–25; N. Touroff, *ibid.*, 26–32; J. Pogrebinski, in: *Ha-Sefer ha-Ivri*, 10 (1952), 37; I. Rabinowitz, in: *Gilyonot*, 20 (1946), 26–29; Z. Voyeslavsky, in: *Moznayim*, 23 (1946), 118–20; M. Ribalow, in: *Hadoar*, 25 (1946), 907–8; A. Litai, in: *He-Avar*, 3 (1956), 51–59.

[Yehuda Slutsky]

STYNE, JULE (1905–1994), U.S. songwriter and theatrical composer. Born in London as Julius Stein, he went to the U.S. as a young boy, settling in Chicago with his family. At eight he began studying at the Chicago College of Music and won a medal in a Chicago Symphony competition for children. He moved to New York and became a vocal coach and then joined 20th Century Fox in Hollywood coaching such stars as Shirley Temple. He wrote songs including "I Don't Want to Walk Without You," with Frank *Loesser. He met Sammy *Cahn and they turned out a stream of popular hits, including "It's Been a Long, Long Time" and "I've Heard That Song Before." Many of their songs were written for Frank Sinatra, including the Oscar-winning "Three Coins in the Fountain."

In 1987, Styne estimated that he had written 2,000 songs, had published 1,500, and had had 200 hits.

His tunes became standards for three generations and he composed such classic Broadway musicals as *Gypsy, Gentlemen Prefer Blondes, Bells Are Ringing*, and *Funny Girl*. The songs from the shows bore the stamp of the singers who introduced them: Ethel Merman, Carol Channing, Judy *Holliday, and Barbra *Streisand. His collaborators included Stephen *Sondheim and Betty *Comden and Adolph *Green. Styne was honored in 1990 by the John F. Kennedy Center for the Performing Arts for his cultural contributions to the nation.

[Stewart Kampel (2nd ed.)]

STYRIA (Ger. **Steiermark**), province in S.E. and central Austria, originally a duchy connected with the *Hapsburgs from 1186. The presence of Jews in Styria from the 11th century may be learned from place names such as *Judenburg (first mentioned c. 1080), Judendorf near *Graz (mentioned 1147), and Leoben (mentioned 1230). The existence of Jewish communities is attested only from the second half of the 14th century (in Graz, e.g., from 1389). The legal position of the Jews was based on the adaptation by Premysl *Otakar and Rudolph of Hapsburg of the Fridericianum of 1244 (see *Frederick II of Babenberg). In the early Middle Ages, Jews were occupied as traders, and later primarily moneylenders, and were instrumental in effecting Styria's shift to a money economy. Their moneylending activities often involved the formation of a consortium to lend money on a large scale to municipalities; even monasteries were frequently involved in such transactions. In 1310 or 1312 Jews were massacred in Fuerstenfeld (because of an alleged desecration of the *Host and blood *libel) and in Judenburg. After repeated requests by the Estates, *Maximilian I expelled the Jews from the region in 1496, the Estates undertaking to reimburse him for the consequent loss of taxes. The exiles settled primarily in *Burgenland and the north Italian Hapsburg provinces from which they traded intensively with Styria. Individual Jews settled in Styria in 1753 and 1775; a decree permitted the attendance by Jews at the Graz markets in 1781, but the expulsion edict of 1496 was renewed repeatedly, for the last time in 1828. Even after the 1848 Revolution their economic activities were restricted; only from 1861 could they acquire real estate.

In 1903 Jews lived in 47 localities. They took an active part in the development of heavy industry and the railway to Hungary; some engaged in farming. At the resort of Gleichenberg-Trautmannsdorf a Jewish hospital was founded in 1884. Antisemitism was strong in Styria, though not violent in its manifestation until 1938. Many holiday resorts would not admit Jews. After the *Anschluss* (March 1938), Polish citizens among the Styrian Jews were compelled to leave for Poland while others, mainly from Graz, were deported to the *Dachau concentration camp; Jewish businesses were "aryanized." From Aug. 1, 1939, no Jew was permitted to live on Styrian territory.

After the end of World War II a community was reestablished in Graz in 1949. Styria has been depicted in Hebrew literature in the writings of Gershon *Shofman, who lived in a village there between the two world wars.

BIBLIOGRAPHY: E. Baumgarten, *Die Juden in Steiermark* (1903); A. Rosenberg, *Beitraege zur Geschichte der Juden in Steiermark* (1914); J.E. Scherer, *Die Rechtsverhaeltnisse der Juden* (1901), 455–517; M.K. Schwarz, in: J. Fraenkel (ed.), *The Jews of Austria* (1967), 391–4; *Germania Judaica*, 2 (1968), 785–7; D. Herzog, in: MGWJ, 75 (1931), 30–47; 79 (1935), 31–49; 80 (1936), 58–79, 118–21; 81 (1937); 44f.; idem, in: *Zeitschrift fuer die Geschichte der Judea in der Tschechoslowakei*, 3, no. 2 (1932), 95–106; 5, no. 1 (1938), 1–12.

[Meir Lamed]

SUARÈS, ANDRÉ (**Félix André Yves Scantrel**; 1868–1948), French essayist, poet, and critic. Born near Marseilles, Suarès was of Portuguese-Jewish descent. At the Ecole Normale Supérieure in Paris he was a lifelong friend of the great writer Romain Rolland, to whom he apologetically revealed his Jewish origin. Except for scattered remarks, the fragmentary manuscript *L'Antisémitisme*, and letters written under a pseudonym in all of which he defends *Dreyfus and attacks injustice, his writings have no Jewish interest. A disciple of *Nietzsche, he adopted a negative attitude toward Judaism.

Possessed of an encyclopedic mind, Suarès was equally at home in literature, art, music, politics, and philosophy. He published poetry and several plays, including *La Tragédie d'Elektre et d'Oreste* (1905), *Cresida* (1913), and *Orphée* (1935), which were never performed. A solitary and secluded life enabled him to devote himself to writing prolifically on the historical, artistic, and literary figures who for him incarnated genius or the heroic soul, and reflected his ideal of grandeur and beauty. His portraits and studies include *Images de la grandeur* (1901), *Troits Hommes: Pascal, Ibsen, Dostoievski* (1913), *Debussy* (1922), *Goethe, le grand Européen* (1932), and *Trois grands vivants: Cervantès. Tolstoï, Baudelaire* (1937). Among his meditative writings are *Voici l'Homme* (1906), *Sur la Vie* (3 vols., 1909–12), and *Valeurs* (1936).

BIBLIOGRAPHY: G. Savet, *André Suarés, Critique* (1959); M. Maurin, in: *Preuves*, 2 (1952), 21–32; S.D. Braun, in: *Publications of the Modern Language Association of America*, 7 (1955), 285–91; idem, in: *Romanic Review*, 58 (1967), 254–70.

[Sidney D. Braun]

SUAREZ, family of Egyptian bankers of Spanish descent, settled in *Egypt during the 19th century. About 1875 EDOUARD SUAREZ together with his brothers FELIX and RAPHAEL formed the Maison Suarez & Cie. which, after various reorganizations, carried on until its nationalization in 1956. During the 1880s, in cooperation with others of the family, he established the Crédit Foncier Egyptien, the leading mortgage lending institution, the Helwan and other railway constructions, the Cairo Omnibus Company, and the Tanta Water Supply. The Suarez family together with the *Cattaui family established Egypt's first successful sugar refineries and contributed to the country's agricultural development. They also took part in, and supplied managers to, important projects such as the Wadi Kom-Ombo Scheme and other industrial undertakings. LEON SUAREZ, son of Felix Suarez, entered his father's business in 1895. In 1903 he became administrator of two other Suarez business interests, the Société Cheikh Fadl and Société Wadi Kom-Ombo. He left the firm of Maison Suarez & Cie. on his father's death in 1906 to take the latter's place as administrator of the National Bank of Egypt and of the Crédit Foncier Egyptien. EDOUARD (EDGAR) SUAREZ, grandson of the firm's founder, served during 1914–17 as president of the *Alexandria Jewish community. Edgar had a great estate and was one of Egypt's great industrialists; he was president of the Eliyahu ha-Navi Lodge of B'nai B'rith in the years 1899–1903. EDMOND was the president of the Alexandria community; EMILE was the president of the *Tanta community in 1938; JOSEPH was a member of the school committee of Alexandria in 1854; CARLO was an author. His wife, NADIN TILCHE, was in 1913 the first woman to pass the matriculation exams and in 1921 the first woman physician in Egypt. MENACHEM was one of the wealthy Jews of 19th-century in Egypt.

ADD. BIBLIOGRAPHY: J.M. Landau, *The Jews in Nineteenth-Century Egypt* (1969), index; S. Raafat, in: *Egyptian Mail* (Nov. 16, 1996), 1–4; M. Fargeon, *Les Juifs en Egypte depuis l'origine jusqu'à ce jour*, (1938); Z. Zohar, *Masoret u-Temurah*, 12, 252; S. Stambouli, in: J.M. Landau (ed.), *Toledot ha-Yehudim be-Mizraim ba-Tekufah ha-Otmanit* (1988), 117–23; J. Hassoun, in: ibid., 564–70; L. Bornstein-Makovetsky, in: ibid., 208.

[Joachim O. Ronall / Leah Bornstein-Makovetsky (2nd ed.)]

SUASSO, family of bankers originally from Spain with branches in Holland and England in the 17th and 18th centuries. One of its most distinguished members was ANTONIO (ISAAC) LOPEZ SUASSO (second half of the 17th century), who lived in The Hague and was considered one of the wealthiest merchants in Holland. He was also one of the leading shareholders of the West India Company, his investments in 1674 amounting to 107,677 gulden. In recognition of his diplomatic services, King Charles II of Spain granted him an estate in Brabant, together with the title of baron, despite the fact that he was a Jew. An ardent supporter of the House of Orange, Isaac Lopez placed 2,000,000 gulden unconditionally at the disposal of William III when he set out for England in 1688. His son, FRANCISCO (ABRAHAM ISRAEL) LOPEZ, second baron of Avernas de Gras, acted as the trustee for the affairs of Queen Christina of Sweden (1632–54) in Hamburg during the years following her abdication. He married Judith, the daughter of Manuel de Teixeira de Sampaio, and his daughter married Isaac Teixera d'Andrade. His sons were ANTONIO (ISAAC) LOPEZ, who in 1714 married the daughter of Moses Mendes da Costa, the governor of the Bank of England, and ALVARO (JACOB ISRAEL) LOPEZ, who in 1735 became a member of the Royal Society. ANTONIO LOPEZ (1776–1857), great-grandson of the first baron of Avernas de Gras, was born in Amsterdam, and, in accordance with the will of his maternal grandmother, assumed his mother's name, Diaz de Fonseca, and was converted to Christianity. He joined the British army, fought against the French, and in 1829 retired with the rank of captain. His last years were devoted to writing about political and military matters, his most important work being *La Politique Dégagée des Illusions Libérales* (2 vols., 1838).

BIBLIOGRAPHY: J.S. da Silva Rosa, *Geschiedenis der Portugeesche Joden te Amsterdam* (1925), index; Baron, Social, 2 (1937), 180, 230; 3 (1937), 133; H.I. Bloom, *The Economic Activities of the Jews of Amsterdam* (1937), index; Brugmans-Frank, 400, 416, 585, 597; A.M. Hyamson, *The Sephardim of England* (1951), index; H. Kellenbenz, *Sephardim an der unteren Elbe* (1958), index, s.v. Lopes Suasso; Landa, in: JHSET, 13 (1932–35), 273, 276, 287; C. Roth, *ibid.*, 15 (1939–45), 16f.; Sutherland, *ibid.*, 17 (1951–52), 87; Rubens, *ibid.*, 18 (1953–55), 103, 110.

SUBBOTIN, ANDREY PAVLOVICH (1852–1906), Russian economist and writer. In 1887 Subbotin made a journey to the *Pale of Settlement in order to determine the economic condition of the Jews. His findings first appeared in the *Ekonomicheskiy Zhurnal* in 1887, and in 1888 and 1890 were published separately as *V cherte yevreyskoy osedlosti*. In this work Subbotin described the life of the Jewish working people, giving statistical information on their commerce, handicraft, and industry. His study was considered one of the first serious efforts to describe the economic situation of the Jews of the area.

Subbotin also participated in the plans of the *Jewish Colonization Association (ICA) for a study of the Jews in Russia. In his work, *Yevreyskiy vopros v yego pravilnom osveshchenii* ("The Jewish Problem in its True Light," 1910; also in *Yevreyskaya Biblioteka*, 10 (1903), 63–123), he presented the main features of Ivan S. *Bliokh's writings on the situation of the Jews in Russia. Thus the important results of Bliokh's work were preserved when the bulk of Bliokh's writings were destroyed by fire during printing.

BIBLIOGRAPHY: S. Ginzburg, *Historishe Verk*, 2 (1946), 213.

SUBCARPATHIAN RUTHENIA (also known as **Ruthenia**, **Carpathian Ruthenia**, **Carpatho-Russia**, **Carpatho-Ukraine**, **Carpathia**, and **Transcarpathian oblast**; Rus. **Zakarpatskaya oblast**), historic region, part of (western) Ukraine. Its territory adjoined Romania, Hungary, Czechoslovakia, and Poland. Formerly part of Hungary, at the end of World War I the bulk of this territory passed to Czechoslovakia, becoming a province; a section of the county of Máramures was incorporated into Romania; in 1938, 1939, and 1940 most of the territory was gradually annexed by Hungary; after the reconstruction of Czechoslovakia, it was ceded in 1945 to the Soviet Union. The capital of the oblast is *Uzhgorod; its important towns are *Mukacevo, *Beregovo, *Vinogradov, and *Khust.

Documents confirm the presence of Jews in Subcarpathian Ruthenia from the first half of the 17th century. Some survivors from the *Chmielnicki massacres of 1648 who escaped from Poland to Hungary settled in this region and on the estates of noblemen there in this period. According to the government census of Jews in the region, there were about 100 families, or 450 persons, between 1725 and 1728. This number is, however, unreliable since, because of the numerous changes in sovereignty over sections of the region, it is difficult to determine the accuracy of the census lists; they were occasionally of a very general nature and referred to places and districts which became excluded from the present area of Zakarpatskaya oblast.

The almost exclusive occupations of the Jews during this period were the manufacture and sale of liquor and beer (see Wine and Liquor *Trade) on the estates of the noblemen, a limited amount of agricultural activity, and the maintenance of flour mills. The Jews were compelled to pay various taxes to both the owners of the estates and the government authorities. The taxes were a heavy burden, while the livelihood earned by the local population was meager. The number of Jews nevertheless steadily increased. In 1745 the government took the initiative of expelling the Jews from the Máramures district and sought to reduce their numbers in general. Despite this, further waves of Jewish immigration arrived from beyond the Carpathians – from Galicia and Poland, where the situation of the Jews had deteriorated. The new settlers scattered in many localities and there were some villages with only one or two Jewish families. This resulted in a degree of dissociation from the sources of traditional Jewish life. In most localities there was no *minyan* for the first few years, and there were few rabbis and Jewish teachers in the area. This cultural and spiritual desolation enabled the movement of Jacob *Frank to win many adherents in Subcarpathian Ruthenia. After the Frankist crisis, rabbis from beyond the Carpathians arrived and taught among the Jews of the towns and villages. Later the various trends of Ḥasidism also reached the Jews of the region. Its influence increased and remained strong until the liquidation of the Jews during the Holocaust.

Economic life also began to develop. The Jews of Galician origin were naturally inclined to establish commercial relations with their country of origin. During the early 19th century closer relations were also established with the center of the state, Hungary. During this period the influence began to be felt of the Orthodox disciples of the Ḥatam Sofer, Moses *Sofer, many of whom took up rabbinical office in communities of the region. In consequence, after the schism in Hungarian Jewry in 1868–69 (see *Hungary), most of the Jews in Subcarpathian Ruthenia and their community organizations remained Orthodox. The numerous Ḥasidim adhered to *ẓaddikim* of Galicia and Bukovina, predominantly to the ḥasidic "court" of *Kosov, as well as to those of *Vizhnitsa, *Zhidachov, and *Belz. Between 1825 and 1848 the Jewish population also increased in the smaller localities; a considerable number of villages had a Jewish population of over 100. In the public and political debates which then took place in Hungary, the question of the *emancipation of the Jews was also raised; many Christian leaders in the region supported the granting of equal rights to the Jews on condition that they would endeavor to assimilate from the external and cultural aspects into the Christian population. During the same period antisemitic criticisms were voiced against the Jews in Subcarpathian Ruthenia, their rapid natural growth, and their economic role within the general population.

In the four districts which in time formed the territory of the oblast (including Máramures, of which only a part belongs to this region from 1918 and at present) the Jewish population numbered about 93,000 in 1891, and about 120,000 in 1910.

In 1897 the Hungarian government investigated the impoverished social condition of the region's inhabitants. The investigator, E. Egán (1851–1901), an expert on agriculture, submitted antisemitic conclusions and sought discrimination against the Jews in the economic sphere. His conclusions became the basis of widespread violent anti-Jewish agitation, which was expressed in a series of articles by the publicist Miklós Bartha (1848–1905), later collected in *Kazár földön* ("In the Land of the Kazhars"). This work, published for the first time in 1901, was republished during the Nazi antisemitic period in 1939 and served as a manual for the renewed persecutions of the Jews of Subcarpathian Ruthenia. Despite the accumulation of obstacles against the Jewish population, there were large communities with numerous institutions, including yeshivot and charitable institutions, toward the close of the period of Hungarian rule at the end of World War I. Though the general cultural standard of the Jews was slightly inferior to that of the Jews in the other parts of Hungary, internal Jewish life flourished, and there were also frequent disputes between **Mitnaggedim* and Ḥasidim. The spoken language of most of the Jews in the region was Yiddish. The overwhelming majority of them, however, also knew Hungarian. Many Jewish professionals were to be found in the towns, mainly lawyers and physicians.

After the end of World War I almost the whole of the territory was incorporated into Czechoslovakia and the remainder into Romania. During this period the Jews rapidly adapted themselves to the democratic way of life of the new Czechoslovak state. According to the constitution of the Czechoslovak Republic, Jews were recognized as a national minority. They took part in municipal life and the political struggles. In many towns Jews were well represented on the municipal councils, and they also succeeded in sending a deputy to parliament in Prague. The Jews in the region numbered 93,341 (15.39% of its total population) in 1921, and 102,542 (14.14%) in 1930, when they formed 28.73% of Czechoslovakian Jewry.

Economically and socially, this period was characterized by extensive activity and development. A particular phenomenon of Subcarpathian Ruthenia was the considerable Jewish agricultural population. Two-thirds of the Jews lived in villages, and many of them engaged in agriculture. Their economic situation differed little from that of the Christian farmers. The region, in general, was poor and there were many unemployed among the Jews of the towns and villages. The American Jewish Joint Distribution *Committee established important institutions for the relief and assistance of the Jews of the region. The traditional yearning for the Land of Israel had already before this period prompted Jews to immigrate to the Holy Land where they joined the old *yishuv*, mainly in Jerusalem. From its inception, political Zionism found adherents in Subcarpathian Ruthenia. Between the two world wars the movement developed to considerable dimensions among both the adults and youth. There was a considerable *aliyah*, mainly of working-class people and farmers. Zionist initiative was also evident in internal political life, in both the municipal and national spheres, the framework for this activity being the Jewish Party (see Zidovská *Strana). To a smaller but noticeable extent, Jews were also active within the Hungarian minority movement. Exceptional in this part of Central Europe was the network of Hebrew schools established in Subcarpathian Ruthenia. The first Hebrew elementary school was opened in Mukacevo in 1920, to be followed by the Hebrew secondary school in the same town in 1925, and another secondary school in Uzhgorod, in 1934.

Hebrew printing presses also functioned. Jewish newspapers published in Hebrew, Yiddish, and Hungarian became the platforms for lively polemics between the representatives of the various trends among the Jews in the region. Zionist publicists were active and also fought Ḥasidism through this medium. It may be estimated that about 10,000 Jews from Subcarpathian Ruthenia emigrated between 1918 and 1938, and at least an equal number moved to the western parts of Czechoslovakia.

Holocaust Period

As various parts of Subcarpathian Ruthenia were annexed by Hungary (1938; 1939; 1940), anti-Jewish persecutions were immediately initiated. At first these took the form of administrative measures by the new Hungarian government; they subsequently reached the stage of physical annihilation. Jews of military age were conscripted into labor battalions and sent to the eastern front, where most of them perished. From the spring of 1944 the Hungarian Fascist regime and the German Nazis collaborated in concentrating the Jews in ghettos and deporting them to the death camps. After March 19, 1944, when the extermination of Hungarian Jewry was set in motion, the authorities began their activities in Subcarpathian Ruthenia. A special operational garrison was organized within the framework of the eighth zone of the Hungarian gendarmerie within which territory the region was situated. The pretext for the speeding up of these activities was that the Jewish population would most likely collaborate with the approaching Red Army. Ghettos were set up in Mukacevo, Uzhgorod, Khust, Vinogradov, Beregovo, and other places. After the deportations to the camps had been accomplished, one of the most flourishing and variegated Jewish populations was effectively liquidated.

Contemporary Period

Only 10,000 to 15,000 Ruthenian Jews, out of over 100,000, survived the Holocaust. Several thousands of these did not return to their former residence and joined the movement of Displaced *Persons (see also *Beriḥah); up to 8,000 moved upon the cession of Ruthenia to the Soviet Union westward to Czechoslovakia, most of them to towns in the Sudeten area depleted of their former German population. Some groups resettled in their former places of residence in Ruthenian towns and smaller localities. Later, other Jews arrived there from distant parts of the Soviet Union, mainly office workers and technical administrators employed in industry. Differences developed between the two Jewish groups, and they did not amalgamate. Culturally also, the character of the Jewish population changed. The Western Hungarian-Czech-German cultural influence was gradually replaced by Eastern Soviet culture. According to Soviet estimates, there were 13,000 Jews in the district in 1971, but there is reason to believe that their actual number was greater. They formed an amorphous group and Jewish life was in a process of disintegration, the remnant of the Jewish heritage being maintained mainly by the few survivors of the original population.

BIBLIOGRAPHY: EG, 7 (1959); MHJ, 7 (1963), 19–23, also Index Locorum s.v. *Bereg, Máramaros, Ugocsa*; P. Meyer et al., *Jews in the Soviet Satellites* (1953), 49ff.; R.L. Braham (ed.), *Hungarian Jewish Studies*, 1 (1966), 223–35; A. Sole et al., in: *Jews of Czechoslovakia*, 1 (1968), 125–54; S. Goldelman, in: *Juedischer Almanach* (1933), 78–86; H. Hoffmann, in: *Juedische Wohlfahrtspflege und Sozialpolitik*, 6 (1936), 123–35.

[Yehouda Marton]

SUBOTICA (Hung. **Szabadka**), city in the district of Bačka, Vojvodina province, in Serbia, part of the federation of Serbia and Montenegro; formerly known as Maria-Theresiopol. Modern Subotica, with *Novi-Sad – the most important urban center of Vojvodina – was founded in 1775. At that time some Jews probably lived there as the treaty between the city and the royal authorities at Pressburg, concluded in 1743, already stipulated that "Greeks, Armenians, Jews, and gypsies may be admitted by the [city] senate" (*Judaeorum et Ziganorum admissio a solo oppidani huius magistratus arbitrio dependebit*). In fact, the senate granted such a permission in 1775 to Jacob Heschel, known as "Hirsch from Paksch [Hungary]." Barely ten years later Jews asked and obtained authorization to found their own religious community, and a "Jew's judge" was elected and subsequently confirmed in office. Before the end of the 18th century there was a synagogue, and 13 families had official status in the city.

At the beginning of the 19th century 43 Jewish families lived there, and the first rabbi, Lew Hirschmann, was installed, inaugurating an era of growth and prosperity. Jews were accepted as importers, middlemen, custom officials, etc. As they were not prevented from engaging in new fields, they became initiators of the food and spirits industries and gradually entered the liberal professions as well. Many Subotica Jews participated in the Austro-Hungarian war of 1848 on the Hungarian side, a large number losing their lives or becoming war invalids.

Under the leadership of the novelist Isidor Milko the community inaugurated a new synagogue in 1901, which is still standing (1971). A *talmud torah* was built soon after, and religious and communal life was intensified during the office of Rabbi Benat (Bernard) Singer. An exclusive achievement of Subotica's Jews was the opening of the Jewish Bernat Singer Hospital, named for the rabbi, in 1923. It operated until the Holocaust, when the Hungarian occupiers took it over. It served not only local needs but also those of other Yugoslav Jewry. In 1925 a short-lived Zionist weekly, *Szombat* (Sabbath), was published in Hungarian by Dr. Imre Vidor. Zionism became active under the leadership of the lawyer Moses (Moshe) Schweiger, son of Rabbi Hermann Schweiger of Zenta. In 1940 there were 6,000 Jews in Subotica out of a total population of about 100,000, and in addition to the numerous national and local communal organizations in the city there was a small Orthodox (ḥasidic) religious group.

Holocaust Period

When the Hungarian Fascist troops entered the city on April 11, 1941, the only resistance was made by several Jewish youths who threw bombs. Most of them were secretly tried and executed. During the occupation the fate of Subotica Jews was little different from that of Novi Sad and Vojvodina Jewry. They were arrested en masse, placed in an improvised ghetto nearby, transferred to Bacsalmas in old Hungary, and then deported to and murdered at *Auschwitz. The remaining Jews of Novi Sad and smaller places in the Bačka were first gathered in a four-story mill in Subotica – 3,500 people – before being herded into cattle wagons and sent to Poland. After the war the survivors tried to continue communal life. In 1948 about 800 of the remaining Jews left for Israel. The Jewish population of Subotica was approximately 400 in 1970 and 220 in 2004. The synagogue was partially restored and returned to use.

BIBLIOGRAPHY: M. Vidor, in: *Jevrejski Almanah* 4, Belgrade (1928/29), 1–4; L. Fišer, *ibid.* (1955/56), 86–96; *Magyar Zsidó Lexikon* (1929), s.v. *Szabadka*. **ADD. BIBLIOGRAPHY:** D. Jelić et al., in: *Zbornik*, 5 (1989), Subotica Jewry issue.

[Zvi Loker]

SUBSTANCE AND ACCIDENT (Heb. עֶצֶם and מִקְרֶה respectively). According to Aristotle (*Categories*, ch. 5, *Metaphysics*, 5:8), substance is that which is neither predicable of a subject nor present in a subject, e.g., the individual man or horse; accident, something which may possibly either belong or not belong to any one and the selfsame thing (*Topics*, 1:5), e.g., the "sitting position," which may belong or not belong to one and the selfsame thing (the man may be sitting at one time, not sitting at another). Aristotle further distinguishes (*Categories*, ch. 5) between primary substances, such as the individual man or horse, and secondary substances, such as the species "man" and the genus "animal." Accidents occur in nine categories: quantity, quality, relation, place, time, position, possession, action, and affection. This account of substance and accident was generally accepted by medieval Jewish philosophers, as, for example, Abraham ibn Daud (*Emunah Ramah*, 1:1), Joseph ibn Ẓaddik (*Olam Katan*, 1:2), and Joseph Albo (*Sefer ha-Ikkarim*, 2:2).

Maimonides followed Aristotle in his definition of substance as the highest, most inclusive, genus, and of accident as the universal which can be either more general or more limited than the species. Thus, for example, movement in relation to man is more general than the species; blackness is both more limited than the human species, which is not all black, and also more general, since it is found also outside of man. There are two kinds of accidents: one inheres permanently and inseparably in its subject, like the blackness of pitch and the heat of fire; the other is a separable accident, like the standing or sitting of a person (*Millot ha-Higgayon*, 10, tr. by I. Efros, in: PAAJR, 8 (1937–38), 34–65; see also, Samuel ibn Tibbon's glossary to his translation of the *Guide of the Perplexed, Perush me-ha-Millot ha-Zarot*, s.v. *mikreh, sikhut*).

Whether substance and accident are relative or absolute terms forms a significant controversy between Solomon ibn Gabirol and Ibn Daud. Ibn Gabirol holds that some things are substance in one respect and accident in another respect, while Ibn Daud maintains that the same thing cannot be both. For Ibn Daud, since the substance of a thing determines what it is, the selfsame thing cannot both be and not be a substance without being and not being itself simultaneously, which is impossible. In Ibn Gabirol's system, however, the terms substance and accident do not refer to the internal constitution of individual things but to their external relation to each other. It is the relation of things to one another in the hierarchy of emanated substances which determines their relative self-sufficiency, and hence the sense in which they are either substances or accidents.

The distinction between substance and accident also had a bearing on the medieval discussion concerning God and His attributes, for medieval philosophers inquired whether these two notions, derived from an analysis of the created world, were equally applicable to God. In addition, medieval philosophers also distinguished between essential attributes, attributes closely related to the essence, such as existence and unity, and accidental attributes, independent of the essence, such as mercy and anger, and they inquired in what way these attributes may be applied to God.

Saadiah, a representative of Kalām philosophy, investigated in great detail whether substance and each of the accidents can be predicated of God and came to the conclusion that they cannot be (*Book of Belief and Opinions*, 2:8–12). God who created all substances and accidents must be unlike them and, hence, he cannot be described directly by any of them. If terms referring to substances and accidents are applied to both God and creatures, they must be applied to God figuratively. He also held that such terms as living, omnipotent, and omniscient do not introduce any multiplicity into the essence of God: while men use a multiplicity of terms, the properties to which these terms refer are identical with the essence of God (*Book of Beliefs and Opinions*, 2:4). In passing, Saadiah refers to the distinction between essential and active (accidental) attributes (2:12; cf. 2:4), seemingly holding that essential attributes are to be understood as negations, while accidental attributes are to be understood as referring to God's actions. The same position is also held by Baḥya ibn Paquda (*Ḥovot ha-Levavot*, 1:10). Judah Halevi, though differing from the Kalām in his overall position, follows this school of thought in his account of attributes. According to him, attributes applied to God must be understood as negations, relations, or actions (*Kuzari*, 2:2).

The question of divine attributes took a new turn with the beginning of the Aristotelian period in Jewish philosophy. The discussion now rested on a distinction between the views of the Islamic philosophers Avicenna and Averroes concerning attributes. Discussing essential attributes, Avicenna held that such attributes are "accidents" superadded to the essence to which they belong, while Averroes maintained that they are contained within that essence. It followed for Avicenna that essential attributes had to be understood as negations, while, for Averroes, they could have a positive meaning. Among Jewish philosophers Maimonides followed Avicenna and Levi b. Gershom, Averroes.

Maimonides inquired (*Guide*, 1:53) whether attributes applied to God can be understood as definitions, parts of definitions, qualities, or relations and came to the conclusion that the attributes can be none of these. Only attributes of action can be applied to God: all accidental attributes must be understood as attributes of action. In another discussion (*Guide*, 1:57–58) he maintained that all essential attributes must be understood as negations. Levi b. Gershom (*Milḥamot Adonai*, 5:3, 12) opposed Maimonides (Avicenna), holding that there exists a similarity between attributes applied to God and creatures, though such attributes (e.g., substance, one, existing, gracious, strong, mighty) are applied to God in a primary and more perfect sense than they are applied to creatures. Ḥasdai Crescas (*Or Adonai*, 1:3, 1–4) agreed with Levi b. Gershom that attributes applied to God can have a positive meaning though he differed from him in his understanding of God and the exact nature of the attributes.

With the decline of Aristotelian philosophy, the distinction between substance and accidents and the relation of these two notions to God and His attributes lost their importance in Jewish philosophy.

See also *Categories; Attributes of *God.

[Jacob Haberman]

SUCCESSION, devolution of the deceased person's property on his legal heirs.

Order of Succession

The Pentateuchal source of the order of succession is "If a man die and have no son, then ye shall cause his inheritance to pass unto his daughter. And if he have no daughter, then ye shall give his inheritance unto his brethren. And if he have no brethren, then ye shall give his inheritance unto his father's brethren. And if his father have no brethren, then ye shall give his inheritance unto his kinsman that is next to him of his family and he shall possess it. And it shall be unto the children of Israel a statute of judgment, as the Lord commanded Moses" (Num. 27:8–11).

Scripture makes no mention of the father inheriting from his son but this is laid down in the Mishnah: "The father has precedence over all his offspring" (BB 8:2). An interpretation that son and daughter inherit like shares in their father's estate – and that Scripture merely indicates that daughters inherit all of the estate in the absence of sons – was raised and rejected in the Talmud (BB 110a–b) and it was confirmed that the daughter only inherits if there is no son (see below). A daughter succeeding to her father's estate was enjoined to marry "only into the family of the tribe of their father… So shall no inheritance of the children of Israel remove from tribe to tribe; for the children of Israel shall cleave everyone to the inheritance of the tribe of his fathers" (Num. 36:6–7; cf. also Philo, Spec. 2:126). In the Book of Tobit (6:10–11) two additional elements were attached to the above law: firstly, the enjoinder that the daughter marry "someone from a clan of her father's tribe" was interpreted as a duty imposed not only on a daughter upon her father's death, but also on the father – if he had no sons – to marry his daughter to one of his kinsmen; secondly, the father's violation of the enjoinder was treated as punishable by death, "according to the law of the Book of Moses" (*ibid.*, 6:13). The sages of the Talmud laid down that the duty of the daughter to marry as above mentioned was applicable only to the particular generation to whom the enjoinder was directed (BB 120a and *Rashbam* ad loc.).

Jewish law has the parentelic system of succession, conferring the right of inheritance on all the kin of the deceased in the agnate (paternal) line of descendancy and ascendancy. Precedence among the heirs is determined, firstly, according to the degree of kinship with the deceased: the first parentela includes the deceased's children and their descendants, to the end of the line; the second includes the deceased's father and his descendants; the third, the father's father and his descendants; and so on in an ascending order – "that the estate may ultimately find its way to Reuben (the eldest son of the Patriarch Jacob)" (BB 8:2; TB, BB 115a–b). The nearer parentela takes precedence over and excludes more distant ones from the inheritance: "the lineal descendants of any one with a priority to succession take precedence" (BB 8:2).

The mother's family is not regarded as kin for the purposes of inheritance and therefore she does not inherit from her sons nor do her brothers or other relatives. Sons do, however, succeed to their mother's estate (BB 8:1). In post-talmudic times the mother too was recognized as a legal heir in a number of *takkanot* (see Gulak, Yesodei, 3 (1922), 94).

Relatives of the deceased, even if born out of wedlock or of an invalid marriage, are his kin and legal heirs for all purposes as if born of a valid marriage, except for the offspring of a bondswoman or a non-Jewess, who take the status of their mother and are not numbered among the father's family (Yev. 2:5; Sh. Ar., ḤM 276:6).

"Inheritance in the Grave" (Yerushah ba-Kever)

According to this principle, the place of a son who predeceases his father is taken by his children in inheriting the portion which he, but for his death, would have inherited (BB 115a; Yad, Naḥalot, 1:3, 5). If the deceased's sole survivors should be a daughter and a son's daughter, the latter will inherit the whole estate since she takes the place of her father to the exclusion of his sister; the Sadducees, however, held the opinion that in such event the inheritance is shared between the deceased's daughter and his granddaughter (BB 115–116a). A son who predeceases his mother "does not inherit from his mother to transmit the [inheritance] to [his] brothers on his father's side" (BB 114b).

Primogeniture

The firstborn son of the father takes a double portion in his estate: "… he shall acknowledge the firstborn,… by giving him a double portion of all that he hath; for he is the firstfruits of his strength; the right of the firstborn is his" (Deut. 21:16–17). The firstborn is entitled to the double portion even if he is a *mamzer*. On the other hand, the law of the firstborn does not apply to daughters who inherit in the absence of sons (Sif. Deut. 215). The firstborn only takes a double portion from the estate of his father and not from that of his mother or any other relative (Yad, Naḥalot, 2:8). If the firstborn predeceases his father, the double share which he would otherwise have inherited from his father's estate is taken by his heirs (Sh. Ar., ḤM 277:15). If the firstborn is born after his father's death (or in the case of twins) he does not receive a double portion (BB 142b).

The inheritance due to the firstborn equals the portions of two ordinary heirs. Thus if the deceased is survived by five sons including the firstborn, the latter takes a third, i.e., two-sixths of the estate, and the other four heirs take one-sixth each; if there are nine sons, the firstborn takes a fifth and each of the others takes one-tenth (Yad, Naḥalot, 2:1).

The portion of the birthright is fixed according to the state of the inheritance at the time of its devolution. Hence it is neither diminished by the birth of another son after the father's death, nor is it increased by the subsequent death of a son (BB 142b). The firstborn only receives a double portion out of the *muḥzakim*, i.e., estate assets already held by the deceased in his possession at the time of his death. With regard to *re'uyim*, i.e., assets contingent to come to the deceased but not held by him at the time of his death, the firstborn takes only the share of an ordinary heir. Hence the firstborn does not take a double portion of an inheritance that accrues to his father after the latter's death, nor of the unrecovered debts owing by others to the latter – whether verbal or witnessed by deed. The firstborn does, however, take a double portion of all such outstanding debts owing to his father as were secured by pledges held by the latter in his possession at the time of his death (Bek. 8:9; Sh. Ar., ḤM 278:7). Just as he takes a double portion, so the firstborn is obliged to defray a double portion of the outstanding debts owed by his deceased father (BB 124a).

The Husband as Heir to His Wife

The husband is heir to his wife and takes precedence over all her other heirs. Opinions are divided in the codes as to whether the husband's right to succeed to his wife's estate stems from the Pentateuchal or the rabbinical law (Yad, Naḥalot 1:8; Sh. Ar., EH 90:1 and *Beit Shemu'el* thereto, n. 1). The husband is heir to his wife even if their marriage was a prohibited one – as for example between a priest and a divorcee (Yad, Naḥalot 1:8) – provided only that they were still married to each other at the time of her death (Tur, EH 90). It does not matter that the husband was planning to divorce his wife, but if he had claimed that his marriage was based on a mistake, for example if he had raised a plea of blemish or defect on the part of his wife, he forfeits his right of inheritance (*Teshuvot Maimoniyyot*, Ishut, no. 35). In explaining this *halakhah* the *aḥaronim* expressed the opinion that although mere admission by the husband concerning his wife's defect does not suffice to dissolve their marriage, yet for the purposes of inheritance the husband's admission is like the testimony of 100 witnesses and therefore upon the death of the wife her husband will not be regarded as one who is heir to his wife's estate (*Ḥelkat Meḥokek*, EH 90, n. 15). According to some scholars, even a *mored* (see *Husband and Wife) or a husband who has refused to cohabit with his wife due to his vow, forfeits his right to inherit her estate (*Rema*, EH 90:5). The husband only inherits the part of his wife's estate in her possession at the time of her death and he does not take her place in inheriting her contingent inheritance (Sh. Ar., EH 90:1). If she became entitled to an inheritance during her lifetime but she died before gaining possession thereof, the inheritance will nevertheless be deemed to have been held by her and it will pass to her husband (Maharashdam, resp. EH no. 98).

The husband's right to inherit his wife's estate proved to be to the detriment of the wife's relatives and heirs since they received nothing at all from her estate. Various *takkanot* accordingly came to be made, aimed at defining the inheritance rights of the wife's heirs and limiting those of her husband. The first of these, dating from the mishnaic period, is known as the *ketubbat benin dikhrin* (i.e., *ketubbah* of male children). In terms thereof the husband inherited his wife's estate, but if the wife predeceased her husband leaving sons from the latter, these sons would upon their father's death inherit her *ketubbah* and dowry in addition to their portions in the estate of their father shared with his other sons. The object of the *takkanah* was "in order that all men might thereby be encouraged to give to a daughter as much as to a son" (Ket. 52b; Sh. Ar., EH 111), i.e., so that the father should not hesitate to give his daughter a large dowry since it would remain in the hands of his descendants and not with his daughter's husband. In geonic times the need for this *takkanah* fell away and it was abolished, since it had anyhow become customary for fathers to give more to their daughters (Tur, EH 111). Later many of the *posekim* sought to revive the validity of this *takkanah* but its abrogation was confirmed by Isserles (*Rema*, EH 111: 16).

In the period of the *rishonim* various *takkanot* were made to limit the husband's right to inherit his wife's estate. In some communities, if the wife died without issue, it became customary for the whole of the dowry given to her upon marriage to be inherited by her father or his heirs, and in other communities for the dowry to be divided between the husband and the wife's heirs on the paternal side (Sh. Ar., EH 118:19; *Teshuvot Maimoniyyot*, Ishut no. 35).

In France and Germany one of the ordinances known as the *takkanat* **Shum* (שו"ם – Speyer, Worms, Mainz) came to be widely accepted. The effect thereof was to oblige the husband to return whatever remained of his wife's dowry – save for deduction of burial expenses – to the donor thereof or to her heirs, if she died childless within a year of her marriage; the second part of the ordinance laid down that upon the death of either husband or wife within the second year of their marriage, half of the dowry was to be returned to the heirs of the deceased if there were no surviving children (*Rema*, EH 52:4). In Spain similar *takkanot* were made. The most important of these, the *takkanah* of Toledo, laid down that if the wife was survived by her husband and any children of their marriage, her estate was to be shared equally between them; if there were no surviving children, her estate was to be divided between her husband and those who would have succeeded to her estate had she survived her husband. The object of the *takkanah* was to prevent the entire inheritance of the wife's family from going to her husband, and in this manner the scholars restricted the husband's rights as legal heir to his wife – in the opinion of some of the *posekim* even in accordance with the Pentateuchal law (see above) – and afforded him only one-half of her estate (Rosh, resp. 55:1,6; *Rema*, EH 118:8).

The Wife's Rights to Her Husband's Estate

The wife is not a legal heir to her husband's estate (BB 8:1) but has a number of rights which afford her a share therein and ensure provision for her sustenance and essential needs until her death or remarriage. The *widow receives from the estate her husband's *ketubbah* obligations, the *dowry increment, and her own property brought into the marriage and she is further entitled to maintenance from the husband's estate until her death or remarriage.

Important changes were introduced by the *takkanot* of Toledo and Molina with regard to the widow's rights to the estate of her deceased husband. These had the object of strengthening the hand of the husband's heirs against the widow's claims upon the estate, and laid down that if the husband was survived by any children the wife might claim no more than one-half of the total value of the estate toward payment of her dowry, *ketubbah*, and its increment. Thus the husband's heirs were afforded the option of settling the widow's claims in full – as was usually done when the total amount thereof did not exceed one-half of the estate – or settling her claims by paying her one-half of the value of the estate, even if less than due to her. If there were no children and the widow's claims were directed against the other heirs to her husband's estate, the latter would first return to her whatever remained – in specie, at the time of her husband's death – of the dowry she had brought him, and from the remainder of the estate she would recover her *ketubbah* and its increment in an amount not exceeding one-half of the value of the estate, the option as above mentioned again residing with the heirs (Rosh, resp. 50:9; Sh. Ar., EH 118:1; *Beit Shemu'el* ad loc. no. 1). In a *takkanah* of Castile it was laid down that a wife surviving her husband, without any children of their marriage, might take from the estate everything proved to have been brought by her as a dowry and remaining in specie at the time of her husband's death, and from the rest of the estate one-quarter, with three-quarters going to the husband's heirs (Rashba, resp., vol. 3, no. 432).

Inheritance Rights of Daughters

Since by law sons exclude daughters as heirs (see above), it became necessary to make provision for the support of daughters after the father's death. This was achieved by the scholars through an obligation imposed on the heirs of the deceased to maintain his daughters and by way of giving daughters part of the estate as a dowry.

MAINTENANCE OF DAUGHTERS. The rule is: "If a man died and left sons and daughters, and the property was great, the sons inherit and the daughters receive maintenance; but if the property was small, the daughters receive maintenance and the sons go a-begging" (Ket. 4:6; 13:3; 9:1). By mishnaic times this obligation had become part of the generally accepted law as a *tenai bet din* (i.e., a *takkanah* of the early scholars). Daughters are entitled to maintenance out of the estate of their deceased father until they reach the age of majority, or become betrothed (Ket. 4:11; 53b). Since the daughter's right to maintenance, as distinct from her right to a dowry, stems from the *ketubbah* deed (of her parents), any testamentary instruction of the deceased in deprivation of this right will have no legal validity (Ket. 68b; Sh. Ar., EH 112:10). Daughters only receive maintenance out of the estate of their deceased father if he is survived by sons as well; if the father is survived by daughters only, the latter share his estate – even though any of them be minors – and the question of their maintenance is no longer relevant (Sh. Ar., EH 112:18).

DOWRY. Sons are obliged to give their deceased father's daughters part of his estate as a dowry, as if the father were alive. This obligation is known as *issur nekhasim* (i.e., giving the daughter one-tenth of the estate), in terms whereof an assessment is made of what the father would have given his daughter as a dowry – according to his disposition, gathered from his friends and acquaintances, his transactions and standing – and if this cannot be established by the court, she is given one-tenth of the estate as the *parnasat ha-bat* (i.e., dowry; Sh. Ar., EH 113:1, based on Ket. 68a). According to some scholars, a daughter is also entitled to receive a dowry out of her deceased mother's estate (EH 113:1), but this is disputed by other scholars (*Rema*, EH 113:1). The father may deprive his daughter of a dowry by testamentary instruction since the *parnasat ha-bat* is merely an assessment of the father's disposition (Ket. 68b). Although the daughter's dowry is recoverable at the time of her marriage, the court may earlier decide on what she should be given upon her marriage (*Beit Yosef* and *Darkhei Moshe*, EH 113).

The dowry is regarded as a charge in favor of the daughter on the estate of her father, as at the time of his death, and she may seize from third parties any of the estate assets sold or mortgaged by her brothers. However, debts incurred by the deceased himself, as well as the obligations for the *ketubbah* of his widow and maintenance for the latter and her daughters, take preference over the daughters' dowry (Ket. 69a; Sh. Ar., EH 113: 5, 6).

See also *Parent and Child.

Shetar Ḥaẓi Zakhar

In post-talmudic times it became customary in the Ashkenazi communities for a father to allot to his daughter one-half of a son's share in his estate, for which purpose there was evolved a special deed known as the *shetar ḥaẓi zakhar* ("deed for half of the male child's share"). The deed was written by the father – and sometimes by the mother too (*Naḥalot Shivah*, no. 21, n. 1) – in favor of the daughter or her husband. It was generally written at the time of the daughter's marriage, the father undertaking to pay his daughter a specified sum of money, generally a very high amount, to fall due for payment one hour before his death, with a condition exempting his sons from liability for such debt after his death if they should give the daughter one-half of a son's share in his estate (*Rema*, ḤM 281:7). This development was an important step toward the regulation of the daughters' right of inheritance in Jewish law (for further details see Assaf, bibl.).

Proselytes as Heirs

A proselyte is regarded as a newborn person whose ties of kinship with his family have been severed for inheritance purposes. The scholars ruled, however, that a proselyte may accept an inheritance from his gentile father, lest the loss thereof tempt him to return to his former ways. A proselyte's estate is inherited by sons born after his conversion to the exclusion of his other sons, whether or not proselytized along with himself (Kid. 17b; BB 142a). The estate of a proselyte who dies without any legal heirs may be acquired in the same way as abandoned property, by the firstcomer, who is regarded as an heir for the purposes of estate liabilities in favor of third parties (*Rema*, ḤM 275:28).

Devolution of Inheritance and Renunciation

Upon death the estate passes automatically and immediately into the ownership of the heirs. Hence an heir cannot renounce his share by waiver thereof, since in Jewish law a person cannot waive something that already belongs to him but only that which is yet to come to him, and the heir can only transfer his share in the same way as any other property is transferred through one of the recognized modes for its assignment or alienation (see *Acquisition, Modes of). An exception to this rule is the birthright portion of the firstborn (see above), as distinguished from his ordinary share (Tur, ḤM 278; Sh. Ar.; ḤM 278:10). An heir may, however, abandon his share in the same way as he abandons any of his own property (*Sma*, ḤM 278, no. 27) and a husband's renunciation of his right to his wife's estate is valid if made prior to their marriage, but not thereafter (Ket. 9:1, 83a).

Debts of the Deceased

It is a *mitzvah* for the heirs of the deceased to pay his debts. They will be compelled to do so if they inherit land and, according to a *takkanah* of the *geonim*, the creditor may recover from the heirs even when they inherit movable property. If they inherit both, the heirs prevail if they want payment to be made out of the land rather than the movable property as desired by the creditor (Sh. Ar., ḤM 107:1). For the purposes of her dowry (see above) a daughter takes only from the land left by the deceased, a rule that survived the above-mentioned *takkanah* of the *geonim* (Sh. Ar., EH 113:2).

Payment is always recovered from the poorest quality land (i.e., *ẓibburit*, Sh. Ar., ḤM 108:18). A stipulation by the creditor to recover payment out of the debtor's best (*iddit*) or medium (*beinonit*) land is not binding on the latter's heirs unless this was expressly provided for in the stipulation (*ibid.*; see also *Execution). If the heirs of the deceased inherit nothing from him, they will not be obliged – not even morally – to defray his debts, since they do not have to do so out of their own property (Sh. Ar., ḤM 107:17). An heir is not heard if he should plead, "I do not take nor will I pay" (*Rema*, ḤM 107:1; and Sh. Ar., ḤM 278:10). The heirs are liable for debts of the deceased to the extent that these do not exceed the value of the assets held by the deceased at the time of devolution of the inheritance, his contingent assets (*re'uyim*) being excluded for this purpose (*Rema*, ḤM 104:16). However, a debt due to the deceased is considered part of the assets held by him at the time of his death. Some scholars have explained this special rule on the basis of the extensive development that took place with regard to credit transactions, with creditors coming to rely upon such as upon movable property rather than as contingent assets (Rosh, resp. 36:3), and other scholars have regarded loans due to the deceased as property held by him upon death since the money of the loan had previously been in his possession (*Beit Shemu'el*, EH 100, no. 3).

The creditor recovers his debt from each of the heirs on a pro-rata basis (Tos. to BB 107a s.v. *u-va ba'al ḥov*). A field hypothecated (see *Lien) by the deceased is recovered by the mortgagee from the heir who receives it as part of his share, and he may recoup from the remaining heirs (Sh. Ar., ḤM 175:4). Similarly, if a creditor should experience difficulty when seeking to recover a proportionate share of the debt from each of the heirs, he may recover the whole debt out of the share of any one of them, and that one may recoup from the others (Rosh, resp. 79:7).

A verbal debt (see *Obligations, Law of) is not recoverable from the heirs of the debtor except in the following cases: the debtor had before his death and from his sickbed admitted such indebtedness; the loan was for a fixed period and not yet due for payment; or the debtor had refused to make payment notwithstanding a judgment of the court, maintaining his refusal until death. In each of these three cases the creditor recovers without swearing an oath (Sh. Ar., ḤM 108:11). A debt witnessed by deed is only recoverable after the creditor has sworn that the debt is still outstanding (Sh. At., ḤM 108:17). If the heir should plead that he was left no property by the deceased and the creditor plead with certainty that the deceased did leave property, the heir will be exempted from liability upon taking the equitable *oath (*shevu'at hesset*; Sh. Ar., ḤM 107:2). A creditor holding a bond of indebtedness with a credency (*ne'emanut*) clause in his favor (see **Shetar*) will not be exempted from delivering an oath when seeking to recover from the debtor's heirs unless he was so exempted expressly with reference to the debtor and his heirs (Sh. Ar., ḤM 71:14–17). In case of a similar clause in favor of the debtor with regard to a plea of payment of the bond, the creditor will not be entitled to recover from the former's heirs on such bond (Sh. Ar., ḤM 71:21).

Debts of the deceased are not recoverable from his heirs as long as they are minors regardless of any clause whatever stipulated in the bond of indebtedness, lest contradictory evidence come to light (*ibid.*, 108:3). However, in the three events mentioned above in which a verbal debt of the deceased is recoverable from his heirs, his debts will be recoverable from the minor orphans too (*ibid.*). The court has the discretion to allow debts to be recovered from the minor orphans if this be to their advantage, e.g., because the creditor is prepared to waive part of the debt in return for recovering the balance forthwith (*Rema*, ḤM 110:1), and the minor heirs may also be recovered from when they are liable to a penalty for nonpayment on due date (*Siftei Kohen*, ḤM 110, no. 3). If some of the heirs are majors the creditor recovers from them pro-rata to their share in the estate. For the purpose of division of the estate the court will appoint a guardian for the minor (Sh. Ar., ḤM 110:1).

Commorientes

Where two persons die at or about the same time and it is unknown who died first, the rights of their heirs are determined in accordance with the following order of priority: If one of the claimants is a "certain" heir – i.e., whatever the sequence of the deaths – and the other a "doubtful" heir – i.e., only upon a particular sequence of death – the former claimant excludes the latter and takes all (*Rashbam*, BB 158b); if both claimants are doubtful heirs they take equal shares of the inheritance (Yev. 38a; Yad, Naḥalot 5:5); if one of the claimants is kin to the deceased himself and the other has become entitled through the death of a relative who is kin to the deceased, the former claimant takes all in both cases (Yad, Naḥalot 5:6), for the reason that the inheritance is not to be diverted from the kin of the deceased unless this is warranted by proof of a particular sequence of deaths (see M. Silberg, *Ha-Ma'amad ha-Ishi be-Yisrael* (1965), 314–22).

On the inheritance of public offices, see **Mishpat Ivri*; *Public Authority; on the inheritance rights of apostates, see *Apostasy (Family Law).

In the State of Israel

Matters of inheritance are governed by the Succession Law, 5725 – 1965, the provisions whereof accord with Jewish law in a number of respects and digress therefrom in others. Thus, as in Jewish law, the law lays down, inter alia, that children born out of wedlock and even *mamzerim* are included among the heirs (sec. 3 (c)). The Jewish law principles with reference to commorientes (see above) were adopted virtually without change. On the other hand the law differs from the traditional approach in laying down that the line of succession ends with the grandparents and their descendants, whereafter the state succeeds, and that both husband and wife are in the line of succession to each other. So too the law recognizes no distinction between sons and daughters, between the paternal and maternal lines (sec. 10), nor does it mention the double portion of the firstborn. (On the question of the absorption of Jewish law in these matters, see Elon, bibl.). An important principle incorporated in the law is that of the widow's right to maintenance out of the estate; unlike Jewish law, this right is extended to other relatives of the deceased besides the widow and daughter, and is also wider in scope (secs. 57, 58).

See also *Apotropos; *Wills.

[Shmuel Shilo]

In the Regulations of the Chief Rabbinate of Israel

In 1943 the first steps were taken to promulgate regulations by the Chief Rabbinate to provide for equal distribution of a decedent's estate between sons and daughters, and between husband and wife. The Mandatory Succession Ordinance of 1923 provided that, where a person died intestate, and owned land classified as *miri* at the time of his death, the provisions of the Ordinance – mandating an equal distribution to sons and daughters, to the man and the woman – were binding upon the religious courts as well. The Israeli rabbinical courts complied with this Ordinance, but it was difficult to anchor this custom in the rule of *dina de'malkhuta dina* (see **Dina de-Malkhuta Dina*), insofar the majority of halakhic decisors ruled that *dina de-malkhuta dina* does not apply to matters of inheritance. Thus, the rabbinical courts adopted an approach whereby the equal distribution was carried out on the basis of the agreement of both parties, entered into with a *kinyan*, to distribute the estate in a manner differing from the manner prescribed by Torah. (The rabbinical courts act in this fashion today as well, unless the parties have agreed that the rabbinical court adjudicate according to the rules set forth in Torah, pursuant to Section 155 of the Succession Law.)

In 1943, regulations were enacted setting forth the procedural rules in the rabbinic courts. Sections 182 and 183 of the regulations provide that, regarding *miri* land – the rabbinic court is to rule pursuant to the Succession Ordinance. Thus, the rabbinical courts accepted the regulations set forth in the Succession ordinance regarding certain portions of the inheritance as binding upon the parties by force of the Chief Rabbinate's regulations, and not only by force of rabbinical acquiescence de facto to an arrangement based on an authority external to the rabbinical court. However, the incorporation provisions of the Succession ordinance should not be understood as a halakhic-normative provision that henceforth, Jewish Law mandates equal rights in the distribution of an estate between the sons and the daughters, and husbands and wives – i.e. as a substantive change in the laws of succession in Jewish law.

An attempt to make that substantive change in Jewish Law was made by Chief Rabbi Isaac Herzog in the years preceding the establishment of the State of Israel, and in the first years thereafter. Rabbi Herzog proposed that the Chief Rabbinate, together with the other prominent rabbis of that generation, should enact regulations regarding inheritance to provide for equal distribution of the inheritance between sons and daughters. His suggestion was that, at the time of the parents' marriage, a condition should be written in the *ketubbah* stating that the distribution of the "*estate*" (and not "the inheritance") be carried out in such a manner that the daughter would "receive" (and not "inherit") an equal share with the son, so long as she is unmarried, rather than only a tenth of the assets. Rabbi Herzog assumed that, if such regulations were enacted, the rabbinic courts would be conferred jurisdiction to adjudicate matters of inheritance, whereas without such regulations – and insofar as the rabbinic courts would rule according to the Shulḥan Arukh – the Knesset would revoke the jurisdiction of the rabbinical courts over this issue and possibly over other issues relating to personal status. Rabbi Herzog hoped that, after promulgating these enactments, it would be possible to introduce a legislative proposal before the Knesset for the enactment of a Succession Law based on Jewish law. Beyond these considerations, Rabbi Herzog believed that such enactments were necessary as a substantive matter as well, just as he believed that enactments (*takkanot*) should be promulgated in many other areas. In view of the changes that had occurred in society over the course of time, as a result of which women were insisting upon their rights and demanding equality, it was the duty of the rabbinate to make efforts to find a solution that would address the feelings of women that they were discriminated against by Jewish Law. Rabbi Herzog proposed the promulgation of similar enactments regarding the inheritance of the eldest son and the inheritance by the husband of his wife's holdings. It should be emphasized that his proposals were based on halakhically acceptable measures and earlier regulations that had been promulgated in these matters.

Like Rabbi Herzog, Rabbi Ben Zion Meir Ḥai Ouziel, his Sephardi counterpart in the Chief Rabbinate, believed that equal distribution of the parents' property among sons and daughters could be provided for at the time of the marriage of the parents, through a will. Rabbi Herzog's proposals for rabbinical enactments were not accepted by the other members of the Chief Rabbinate Council, and the proposed enactments never proceeded beyond the "proposal" stage.

Regulations Promulgated by the Moroccan Sages in the Mid-Twentieth Century

In the 1950s, proposals were raised before the Rabbinical Council of Morocco, regarding the promulgation of regulations to equate the status of daughters and sons. The reasons invoked by the Moroccan sages to justify such regulations were the changes that had occurred over time in the general outlook and in the situation, status and role of women, which was equal to that of men in the workplace and in terms of earning a livelihood. The regulatory proposal included a grant of equality to married women as well as unmarried women, representing a novel approach in comparison to the regulations that had been promulgated throughout the ages in this regard. These proposals were never promulgated as regulations, because shortly after this proposal was raised, Morocco gained political independence and the rabbinic courts' jurisdiction over questions of personal status was revoked. Nevertheless, these proposals of the Moroccan Rabbinical Council are instructive regarding the approach of the North African sages to the promulgation of regulations in our time, as opposed to the stricter approach, limiting halakhic creativity, adopted by the Ashkenazi sages since the time of the Emancipation in Europe (see **Takkanot*).

[Menachem Elon (2nd ed.)]

BIBLIOGRAPHY: I.M. Hazan, *Successione per Israele* (1851); H.B. Fassel, *Das mosaisch-rabbinische Civilrecht*, 1 (1852), 274–320; A. Wolff, *Das juedische Erbrecht* (1888); M. Bloch, *Das mosaisch-talmudische Erbrecht* (1890); I.S. Zuri, *Mishpat ha-Talmud*, 3 (1921), 1–24; Gulak, Yesodei, 3 (1922), 71–112; Ch. Tchernowitz, in: *Jewish Studies… I. Abrahams* (1927), 402–15; S. Assaf, in: *Emet le-Ya'akov, Sefer Yovel… J. Freimann* (1937), 8–13 (Heb. section); Ch. Cohen, in: *Yavneh*, 3 (1948/49), 80–83; J.D. Cohen, in: *Ha-Torah ve-ha-Medinah*, 2 (1949/50), 18–24; B.M.H. Ouziel, *ibid.*, 9–17; ET, 2 (1949), 16–20; 5 (1953), 152–6; 6 (1954), 279–82; 9 (1959), 536–42; A. Karlin, in: *Ha-Peraklit*, 9 (1952/53), 22–26; J. Hakohen, in: *Ha-Torah ve-ha-Medinah*, 5–6 (1952/54), 177–90; B.M.H. Ouziel, in: *Talpioth*, 5 (1952), 451–74; 6 (1953), 51–64; J. Herzog, *ibid.*, 6 (1953), 36–50; A. Karlin, *Divrei Mishpat*, 1 (1954) (*Dinei Yerushot ve-Ẓavva'ot*); S.D. Revital, in: *Sugyot Nivharot be-Mishpat* (1958), 442–69; E.J. Waldenburg, in: *Sefer Yovel le-Shimon Federbusch* (1960), 221–6; Elon, Mafte'ah, 92–104; E.E. Urbach, in: *Divrei ha-Congress ha-Olami ha-Revi'i le-Madda'ei ha-Yahadut*, 1 (1967), 133–41; Engl. summary: *ibid.*, 263 (Eng. section); B. Schereschewsky, *Dinei Mishpahah* (19672), 224–70; M. Elon, in: ILR, 4 (1969), 126–40. **ADD. BIBLIOGRAPHY:** M. Elon, *Ha-Mishpat ha-Ivri* (1988), 1:135, 474f, 670ff., 679ff.; 3:1337f., 1362, 1389, 1413ff. and index; idem, *Jewish Law* (1994), 1:152; 2:578, 828f., 837ff.; 3:1596f., 1625, 1656, 1683ff.; idem, *Ma'amad ha-Ishah* (2005), 255–96; idem, *Ḥakikah Datit* (1968), 42–43; idem, "*Yiḥuda shel Halakhah ve-Ḥevrah be-Yahadut Ẓefon Afrikah mi-le-aḥar Gerush Sefarad ve-ad Yameinu*," in: M. Bar Yuda (ed.), *Halakhah u-Petiḥut Ḥakhmei Moroko ke-Posekim le-Doreinu* (1985), 29ff.; M. Elon and B. Lifshitz, *Mafte'aḥ ha-She'elot ve-ha-Teshuvot shel Ḥakhmei Sefarad u-Ẓefon Afrikah* (legal digest) (1986), 169–73; B. Lifshitz and E. Shochetman, *Mafte'aḥ ha-She'elot ve-ha-Teshuvot shel Ḥakhmei Ashkenaz, Ẓarefat ve-Italyah* (legal digest) (1997), 110–15; Y. Cohen, "The Inheritance of a Wife of her Husband in the Communal Enactments," in: *Shenaton ha-Mishpat ha-Ivri*, 6–7 (1979–1980), 133–75 (Heb.); I. Gruenfeld, *The Jewish Law of Inheritance* (1987); Y. Herzog, in: I. Warhaftig (ed.), *Teḥukah le-Yisrael al-pi ha-Torah*, 2 (1989); Y. Rivlin, *Ha-Yerushah ve-ha-Ẓavva'ah ba-Mishpat ha-Ivri* (1999); E. Shochetman, "The *Halakhah*'s Recognition of the Laws of the State of Israel," in: *Shenaton ha-Misphat ha-Ivri*, 16–17

(1991), 417 (Heb.); Z. Weinman, "Law of Inheritance in the Rabbinical Courts – Applied *Halakhah*," in: *Shenaton ha-Mishpat ha-Ivri*, 8 (1981), 490ff. (Heb.).

SUCCOTH (Heb. סֻכּוֹת; "booths"), name of two places mentioned in the Bible.

(1) A locality in the Jordan Valley; according to the etiological explanation in Genesis 33:17, it was named after the booths for cattle erected there by Jacob. It belonged to the kingdom of Sihon, from whom it passed to the tribe of Gad (Josh. 13:27). The city refused to aid Gideon in his pursuit of the Midianites and was consequently punished when he returned victorious; in this narrative it is also related that the city had 77 elders and there was apparently a high standard of literacy among its inhabitants (Judg. 8). It is mentioned with Zarethan as the metallurgic center where the brass vessels of the Temple were cast (I Kings 7:46; II Chron. 4:17, as Zeredah). According to Yadin, Succoth should be read in place of "booths" in II Samuel 1:11 and I Kings 20:12, 16. In his view, it served as David's secondary strategic center during his assault on Rabbath-Ammon and on the *Arameans; hence the reference to it in the Victory Psalm (Ps. 60:8; 108:8). Also according to Yadin's reading, it served as a base for *Ben-Hadad during his unsuccessful assault on Samaria. Succoth is identified in the Talmud (TJ, Shev. 9:2, 38d) with Ter'ela, the present-day Tell Deir ʿAllā to the north of the junction of the Jabbok and the Jordan. Excavations carried out at the site by a Dutch expedition under H.J. Franken revealed a settlement dating from about the 15th century B.C.E. to the period of the monarchy. A Late Bronze Age sanctuary discovered there was destroyed in the early 12th century, as dated by an Egyptian cartouche of the late 19th Dynasty. Unique and still undeciphered clay tablets were found in this level. In the levels of the Israelite period, traces of metallurgic industries were found, in accordance with biblical tradition.

(2) The second station of the Israelites, located between Rameses and Etham, on the route of the Exodus (Ex. 12:37; 13:20; Num. 33:5, 6). In Egyptian texts the name occurs as *t-k-w*. The favored identification is with Tell Maskhūṭa, a border fortress in the eastern part of Wadi Ṭumaylāt (the biblical land of Goshen, west of the Bitter Lakes).

BIBLIOGRAPHY: N. Glueck, in: AASOR, 25–28 (1951), 308–10, 347ff.; Y. Yadin, *The Art of Warfare in Biblical Lands*, 2 (1963), 271–2, 305–8; Aharoni, Land, index; E.G. Kraeling, *Bible Atlas* (1956), 104, 106; Abel, Geog, 2 (1938), 469–70.

[Michael Avi-Yonah]

SUCCOTH-BENOTH (Heb. סֻכּוֹת־בְּנוֹת; LXX, *Socchôth/bainith/benithei/banitha, Rochchôthbaineithei*), unidentified deity worshiped by the Babylonians who were settled in Samaria after the fall of the Northern Kingdom (c. 722 B.C.E.; II Kings 17:30). Succoth-Benoth is a corrupted form of the name of a popular Babylonian god or goddess. A theory based on the Septuagint rendering proposes to identify Succoth-Benoth as *Sarpanītu*, Marduk's consort, popularly known as *Zêr-banitu*, "creative seed." Another theory sees in Succoth-Benoth the Babylonian *SAG. KU* (Ninurta?), as in Amos 5:26.

See also Sikkuth and *Chiun.

BIBLIOGRAPHY: M. Jastrow, *The Religion of Babylonia and Assyria* (1898), 121–3; J.A. Montgomery, *Commentary on Kings* (ICC, 1951), 473–4; S. Yeivin, in: *Eretz Israel*, 3 (1953), 27; G.R. Driver, *ibid*, 5 (1959), 18, 20.

SUCEAVA (Ger. **Suczawa**), town in Suceava province, Bukovina, N. Romania; formerly capital of Moldavia, from 1774 to the end of World War I under Austria. Jews lived there from the beginning of the 18th century. In 1774 there were 50 Jewish families (209 persons) living in the town. Although the Jews were oppressed by the Austrian authorities, their number increased as a result of immigration from Galicia and Russia. In 1782, 92 Jews were expelled from Suceava, the authorities claiming that they were unable to pay the taxes. Representatives of Suceava Jewry took an active part in the struggle of the Jews of Bukovina against the oppressions of the Austrian authorities. There were 160 Jewish families in Suceava in 1791, and 272, with the Jews in the vicinity, according to data of 1817. After 1848 their numbers increased rapidly, and the Jewish population numbered 3,750 (37.1%) in 1880; 6,787 in 1901; and 8,000 on the outbreak of World War I. With the advent of Romanian rule, many Jews moved to *Chernovtsy and other places; 3,496 Jews remained in 1930.

The communal institutions included a Jewish school, opened in 1790. A large synagogue was erected at the beginning of the 19th century. Jews also prayed in many *battei midrash* and a number of houses of prayer (*kloysen*). Ḥasidic influence in the community was strong. Zionist activity had been initiated during the Ḥibbat Zion period and an organization of Zionist students existed in Suceava before the First Zionist Congress. A number of smaller Jewish communities were affiliated to the Suceava community until they became independent. Jews engaged in the trade of liquor, wine, and beer. The cultural orientation was German. Jews played important roles in both municipal and national political life.

Holocaust and Contemporary Periods

The local Jews were persecuted by the Nazi German and Romanian authorities between 1940 and 1941. When deported to *Transnistria in 1941, they numbered 3,253. Only 27 remained in the town.

After World War II, when northern Bukovina was annexed by the Soviet Union, many Jews from Chernovtsy and other places in northern Bukovina who arrived in Suceava chose to remain there. Their numbers rose to 4,000 and community life was active during that period. The number of Jews subsequently declined as a result of emigration to Israel and other places. In 1971, there were still about 290 Jewish families in the town and Jewish life was maintained to a limited degree. Prayers were held in the central synagogue and a number of other places.

BIBLIOGRAPHY: H. Gold, *Geschichte der Juden in der Bukowina* 2 (1962), 113–8.

[Yehouda Marton]

SUEDFELD, GABRIEL (1799–1872), private scholar, tutor, Hebrew writer; father of Max *Nordau. Born in Krotoszyn, he studied at the Lissa Yeshivah; although ordained, he never practiced as a rabbi. He became a follower of the Haskalah and published in the journal **Bikkurei ha-Ittim*, yet he remained strictly religious. After studying at the universities of Berlin and Breslau, he was a tutor in the households of *S.J. Rapoport in Prague, Rabbi M. *Schreiber (Sofer) in Pressburg, and the Fischhof family in Buda. Suedfeld eventually settled in Pest, where he earned a meager living teaching Hebrew and German. A master of the three classical languages, Hebrew, Greek, and Latin, Suedfeld also knew German, French, and Italian. He wrote philosophical and linguistic studies in Hebrew, as well as poetry, both original and translations, and miscellaneous prose in German. His Hebrew writings include *Aḥuzzat Mere'im* (1825), and *Reḥovot ha-Be'ur* (1850), a German translation of Ecclesiastes, with Hebrew commentary.

BIBLIOGRAPHY: M. Nordau, in: *Kol Kitvei Re'uven Brainin*, 2 (1936), 57–58. **ADD. BIBLIOGRAPHY:** M. Nordau, in: *Eine Gartenstadt fuer Palaestina. Zum 70. Geburtstag v. M. Nordau* (1920), 21–22; idem, *Erinnerungen* (1928), 10; S. Bettelheim, *Zurueck zur Bibel!* (1922), 145–49.

[Gedalyah Elkoshi / Archiv Bibliographia Judaica (2nd ed.)]

SUESS, EDUARD (1831–1914), Austrian geologist and politician. Suess was born in London, the son of a Christian father and a Jewish mother, but spent most of his life in Austria. He became an assistant at the Hofmuseum in Vienna in 1852, and five years later joined the staff of the University of Vienna, where he held the chair of geology from 1867 to 1901. While his early specialty was invertebrate paleontology, once he began teaching at the university, he devoted himself mainly to geology. His study of the formation of the Alps, *Die Entstehung der Alpen*, appeared in 1875, but his great work was *Das Antlitz der Erde* (4 vols., 1885–1907; *Face of the Earth*, 1904–09), which had a major influence on modern geotectonics. Investigating geological, geographical, and historical sources from all countries, Suess was – and remains – the only researcher ever to master singlehandedly the regional geological literature of the entire world.

A liberal in politics, Suess was elected to the provincial diet of Lower Austria in 1869, and for over 30 years from 1873 was a deputy for Vienna in the lower house of the Austrian parliament. He was president of the Austrian Academy of Sciences from 1898 to 1911. Although he always declared that he was not a Jew, he was a member of the Austrian association for defense against antisemitism.

[Leo Picard]

SUESSKIND VON TRIMBERG (c. 1200–1250), German minstrel (*Minnesaenger*), identified as "Suesskind the Jew of Trimberg" and portrayed wearing a beard and a Jew's hat in the 14th-century Manesse Codex, which preserves six Middle High German lyrics ascribed to this otherwise unknown poet. In one of these lyrics, the *Minnesaenger* claims that since he has fallen out of grace with the lords, he will take up life in the manner of old Jews. These few lines, a variation of the conventional *Armutsklage* or minstrel's lament of his poverty, have given rise to much speculation about Suesskind's Jewishness and even about an alleged influence of biblical and rabbinical literature on his lyrics.

BIBLIOGRAPHY: J. Kastein, *Suesskind von Trimberg, oder die Tragoedie der Heimatlosigkeit* (1934); Spanier, in: ZGJD, 7 (1937), 138–55; Straus, in: JSOS, 10 (1948), 19–30; C. von Kraus, *Deutsche Liederdichter des 13. Jahrhunderts* (1953); Prawer, in: YLBI, 8 (1963), 150–2; Germ Jud, 1 (1963), 384–7. **ADD. BIBLIOGRAPHY:** D. Gerhardt, *Suesskind von Trimberg* (1997); R.K. Weigand, in: M. Stone and G. Sharman (eds.), *Jenseits der Grenzen* (2000), 13–30; R. Bauschke, in: *Juden in der deutschen Literatur des Mittelalters* (2002), 61–86.

°**SUETONIUS (Caius Suetonius Tranquillus**; c. 69–140 C.E.), Roman biographer. Suetonius' *"Lives of the Caesars"* (*De Vita Caesarum*) yields a good deal of information on the Jews under the Julio-Claudian and Flavian emperors. Details which do not occur elsewhere are his observations on the mourning by the Jews after the murder of *Julius Caesar (*Divus Iulius*, 84), the negative attitude of *Augustus to Judaism (*Divus Augustus*, 93), the anecdote about *Tiberius and the Jewish grammarian Diogenes on the island of Rhodes (*Tiberius*, 32), and the account of the interrogation of a Jewish nonagenarian in connection with the Jewish tax under *Domitian (*Domitianus*, 12). He mentions (contradicted by Dio) Claudius' expulsion of the Jews from Rome because of a riot caused by a certain Chrestus: this seems to constitute a reference to the early diffusion of Christianity. He also refers to Josephus' prediction that Vespasian would become emperor. While Suetonius' attitude toward Christianity is clearly derogatory (*Nero*, 16), he refrains from expressing an opinion on Judaism, and similarly does not explicitly censure the spread of Oriental cults in Rome. Suetonius, however, was closely attached to his ancestral Roman religion, and he stresses the negative attitude of Augustus, his ideal ruler, toward the Jewish and Egyptian cults equally. The general impression one gains of his attitude is that foreign cults are associated with unworthy emperors.

BIBLIOGRAPHY: Reinach, Textes, 327–33; H.J. Leon, *The Jews of Ancient Rome* (1960), 23–27.

[Menahem Stern]

SUFFERING. The presence of suffering in the world poses a problem for religion insofar as it seems to contradict the notion of an all powerful benevolent God. It would seem that if God were good, He would not want His creatures to suffer, and if, all powerful, He would be able to prevent their suffering. Judaism has attempted to cope with the problem of suffering in various ways. The Bible is from the very beginning aware of suffering as a characteristic of human existence (Gen. 3:19; Job 5:7), as is rabbinic Judaism (PR 189b). In kabbalistic doctrine the existence of the world and man as distinct from God by definition entails the pain of separation from God. A similar position is taken by Leibnitz when he defines suffering in the "best of all possible worlds" as a necessary feature of finiteness, and Paul *Weiss when he says "No matter how good and concerned God might be, there is always metaphysical evil to mark the fact that the universe is not God and God not the universe" (N. Glatzer (ed.), *The Dimensions of Job* (1969), 193).

Philosophical Explanations

Some religious philosophies overcome suffering by denying either its importance (Stoicism) or its reality (Spinoza), or by seeking release from existence in the world (Buddhism). A certain other-worldly emphasis is also characteristic of certain types of Christian thought. Augustine formulated the classic philosophical view of evil which states that since everything that exists must have been created by God and must be good, evil is not an existent but is merely privation, i.e., the absence of good. This essentially neoplatonic doctrine also has a long tradition in Jewish philosophy, Maimonides being among those who adopted this view (*Guide of the Perplexed*, 3:8–25). While he does not deny that suffering does exist, he believes that the particular evils which befall one are for the good of the universe as a whole. He opposes the doctrine that the innocent sometimes suffer in order to be rewarded in the **olam ha-ba*, holding that all suffering is punishment for priorly committed sins (*Guide*, 24). Among modern Jewish philosophers, Buber holds that evil is really only a "turning away" from the good toward "nothingness." He adhered to this view even after the Holocaust, explaining that there is a turning away that is so far gone that it can never be turned back (M. Buber, *Good and Evil*, 1952). Judaism in its nonphilosophic form acknowledges the utter reality of evil and suffering. Indeed, God Himself is often described as suffering with man. Man is challenged to remedy suffering wherever it can be remedied, and to endure it without complaining wherever it is irremediable. M. Bred in *Heidentum, Christentum, Judentum* (2 vols., 1921) considers the attitude toward suffering the major distinguishing factor between Judaism and Christianity.

Compassion for the Suffering of Others

Judaism demands that man extend active sympathy toward the suffering of others. So that it may be remediable, the essence of suffering must be perceived not in death or natural catastrophes but in illness and poverty. "The poor are God's people," and they exist so that others may help others out of their poverty (BB 10a). Man is admonished to share in the suffering of the community and not enjoy himself while others are suffering (Ta'an. 11a). The historic Jewish penchant for medicine and social reform may have its source in the biblical and rabbinic attitude toward suffering. It is forbidden, according to Jewish law, to inflict suffering on animals (*ẓa'ar ba'alei ḥayyim*; BM 32a; Ex. 20:10). With the coming of the Messiah, illness, poverty, and even death will be abolished (Ex. R. 46:4).

Punishment and Purification

The primary traditional explanation of suffering is that it constitutes punishment for sin: "When a man sees that he is being chastised let him examine his ways" (Ber. 5a; Sanh. 27b). There is a didactic element in this explanation insofar as it encourages man to refrain from sin in order to avoid suffering. However, it is difficult to uphold this explanation in the face of the suffering of the innocent and the prosperity of the wicked (Jer. 19:1, Eccles. 7:15, Job). One way of coping with the moral imbalance in the world is to formulate a doctrine of *reward and punishment in the *afterlife. Another explanation of the existence of suffering is that it is a process of purification. The Talmud terms such suffering "afflictions of love" (*yissurin shel ahavah*). Suffering was thought to be the ultimate form of divine purification leading to *unio mystica* (A. Rote, *Shomer Emunim*, 1 (1959), 111a, ch. 8). Nevertheless there is room within Judaism for protest to be leveled at God when suffering is thought to be undeserved. Among those who reproached God for inflicting suffering unjustly were *Abraham, *Job, and *Ḥoni ha-Me'aggel, and *Levi Isaac of Berdichev. The *Holocaust has in the 20th century aroused much concern with the problem of suffering.

See also *Good and Evil; *Reward and Punishment.

[Steven S. Schwarzschild]

SUFISM (Ar. **Taṣawwuf**). The Arabic form *Taṣawwuf* is the name by which Islamic mysticism has been known since the early 9th century C.E. and to which many paths (*ṭarīqa*, pl. *ṭuruq*) and individuals still adhere today. The name derives, most probably, from *ṣūf*, wool, and refers to the rough woolen garment (*jubbat ṣūf*) with which ascetics, mystics, and prophets have been associated since biblical times. Sufis themselves prefer to point to another derivation: the root *ṣ-f-w*, which, in various verbal forms, denotes "purity" (*ṣafā*) and "[divine] choice" (*ṣafwa, iṣṭifā*). In their self-appraisal Sufis see these latter principles as more crucial than ascetic practices such as wearing wool. Primarily, Sufis see themselves as seekers (*murīdūn*) and wayfarers (*sālikūn*) on the path to God. The search for God (*irāda, ṭalab*) and the wayfaring (*sulūk*) on the path (*ṭarīq*) involve a gradual inner and ethical transformation through a number of stages or stations (*maqāmāt*). These include repentance (*tawba*), scrupulous performance of the divine commandments (*wara'*), abstention (*zuhd*), poverty (*faqr*), perseverance (*ṣabr*), trust in God (*tawakkul*) and surrender (*riḍā*). Although some of these stations are ascetical in nature, their primary functions are ethical, psychological and educational: they are designed as a means for combating the lower-self (*mujāhadat al-nafs*) and as a tool for its training and education (*riyāḍat al-nafs*). The lower-self (*nafs*), being the seat of personal will and desire, is seen as the main obstacle for attaining God. In order to combat and train the lower-self, Sufis practice fasting (*ṣawm*), food and drink deprivation (*jū'*), wakefulness at night for the recitation of koranic passages (*qiyām al-layl*), periods of seclusion (*khalawāt*), roaming uninhabited places in states of poverty and deprivation, and lengthy meditations (*murāqaba, jam' al-hamm*). The effortful path of self-denial and transformation through gradual stages (*maqāmāt*) is interwoven with effortless mystical experiences (*aḥwāl*). These are seen as spontaneous and intense inner occurrences in which divine truths are revealed to the heart (*qalb, sirr*). They portray the dynamic and ecstatic aspect of the mystical life and are richly depicted in Sufi literature, poetry and vocabulary. The culmination of the mystical states is the self-absorption, or annihilation (*fanāʾ*) in God. Mystical experiences often produce states of ecstasy (*wajd*) and drunkenness (*sukr*), which may result in the exclamation of poetic verses, uncontrollable utterances, involuntary bodily movements, fainting and even death. The ecstatic exclamations (*shaṭaḥāt*) are at times shocking and seemingly blasphemous. The most notorious among the latter are attributed to Abū Yazīd al-Bisṭāmī (d. ca. 875) and to Manṣūr al-Ḥallāj. One of the most traumatic events in the history of Sufism is associated with the ecstatic utterances of al-Ḥallāj, in particular his "I am the Truth" (*anā al-ḥaqq*), for which, among other accusations, he was publicly executed in *Baghdad in the year 922.

For their proper training Sufi seekers are urged to put themselves under the guidance of a master (*murshid, shaykh*). Spiritual masters are revered men, and occasionally women, who constitute a "sacred hierarchy" and are known as "the Friends of God (*awliyāʾ allāh*). These are the protagonists of many edifying stories, recorded in Sufi compilations, which narrate of their miraculous acts (*karāmāt al-awliyāʾ*). The master directs the disciples in religious, ethical, psychological, and spiritual matters, including the interpretation of their dreams, perplexities and mystical experiences. Under the guidance of the master, or his deputy, the disciples perform the ritual known as "Remembrance of God" (*dhikr allāh*), in which God's names, as well as certain sacred formulae, are invoked repeatedly. Another practice that is often associated with Sufism is the spiritual concert, or "listening," *samāʿ*, in which poetic recitations, music and dances are performed by the participants, sometimes in states of ecstasy and elation.

The early Sufi circles of the 9th–11th centuries became the *nuclei* for the large Sufi Paths, or Brotherhoods (*ṭarīqa, ṭuruq*), which emerged from the 12th century on. The Brotherhoods are named after their believed founders, who had passed the teaching down to their disciples; they, in turn, pass it on to their own disciples in an uninterrupted "chain of transmission" (*silsila*). Currently, in spite of the general decline of Sufism due to disapproval from both modernists and fundamentalists, Sufi Brotherhoods and their local branches are still active throughout the Muslim world, as well as in the West. At present, as in the past, Sufism is an important factor in the spread of Islam, especially among Western seekers.

In the Middle Ages, especially in Muslim *Spain and later on in *Egypt, Sufism left its mark on some Jewish pietistic writers and circles. The most popular Sufi-inspired Jewish work, written in *Judeo-Arabic in 11th-century Saragossa, is *Baḥya ibn Paquda's "The Duties of the Heart" (*Ḥovot ha-Levavot*). In Egypt, Sufism was highly regarded by the Pietist Circle of the Egyptian ḥasidim and their masters, in particular R. Abraham *Maimonides and his descendants, who saw in Sufi practices the continuation of biblical prophetic traditions.

BIBLIOGRAPHY: S.D. Goitein, *Jews and Arabs* (1964), 148–54; A. Schimmel, *Mystical Dimension of Islam* (1975); G. Böwering, *The Mystical Vision of Existence in Early Islam* (1980); P. Fenton, *The Treatise of the Pool* (1981); C. Ernst, *Words of Ecstasy in Sufism* (1984); J.S. Trimingham, *The Sufi Orders in Islam* (1998^2); R.E. Cornell, *Early Sufi Women* (1999); L. Lewisohn (ed.), *The Heritage of Sufism*, 3 vols. (1999); A. Knysh, *Islamic Mysticism. A Short History* (2000). A new periodical, researching Sufism, *The Journal of the History of Sufism*, has started publication in English and French.

[Sara Sviri (2nd ed.)]

SUGAR, SIR ALAN (1947–), British businessman. Born in north London, the son of an East End tailor, Sugar left school at 16 and founded the Armstrad Home Electronics group in 1968. It became nationally known in 1983 when it sold the first inexpensive home computer, retailing at the time at £300. In the 1980s Armtrad was regarded as a serious competitor for other major international computer firms like Apple, but in the 1990s the firm ran into difficulties, and in 1997 it was divided into two separate concerns, Betacom and Viglen. In the early 1990s Sugar became the chief owner of the Tottenham Hotspur football club. Known for his aggressive style, Sugar was given a knighthood in 1999. In 2005 he became host of a popular BBC television series, U.K. Apprentice. In 2005 he was estimated to have been the 55th richest man in Britain, worth £760 million.

[William D. Rubinstein (2nd ed.)]

SUGAR INDUSTRY AND TRADE. In the Middle Ages sugar was a luxury article, and sugar for European consumption was produced in Syria, Palestine, Crete, Egypt, Sicily, and southern Spain. The Cairo **Genizah* records reveal that making and selling sugar from sugarcane was one of the most common occupations of Jews in the Middle Ages; Sukkari was a common family appellation from the beginning of the 11th until the end of the 13th centuries in Egypt and in North Africa. Sugar refineries were often in Jewish hands. Jews are mentioned as exporters of sugar from Crete in the 15th century. When sugar began to be used for everyday consumption (15th century), *Marranos played a leading role in introducing sugarcane cultivation to the Atlantic islands of Madeira, the Azores, the Cape Verde Islands, and São Tomé and Príncipe in the Gulf of Guinea, and in the 16th century to the Caribbean Islands. They also brought the cultivation of sugarcane from Madeira to America, and the first great proprietor of plantations and sugar mills, Duarte Coelho Pereira, allowed numerous Jewish experts on sugar processing to come to Brazil. Among them was one of the first important Jewish proprietors of sugar mills, Diego Fernandes.

In Europe Marranos who were active in international commerce, such as the merchant family of Ximenes, played an important role in the import of sugar to Lisbon and thence to northwestern Europe, especially *Antwerp. During the 16th and the beginning of the 17th centuries there were many Jews among the merchants of Antwerp, the Portuguese colony, which was central to the sugar trade in the port and played a vital part in the development of Antwerp as the central European sugar market, where many refineries were established. They made Brazil, where several Portuguese Jews had established sugar plantations and mills, the most important area of sugar production in the world. From around the 1620s *Amsterdam took the place of Antwerp in the sugar trade, and many Marranos left Brazil and Portugal to settle in Amsterdam. Some Jews (e.g., Abraham and Isaac *Pereire and David de Aguilar) owned refineries in Amsterdam. In 1639 ten of the 166 *"engenhos"* in Dutch Brazil belonged to declared Jews, while others belonged to Marranos who kept their Jewishness secret. The Jews of Brazil were not important as proprietors of mills but rather as financial agents, brokers, and export merchants. When Brazil came again under Portuguese rule in the second half of the 17th century, many Jews emigrated to Surinam, Barbados, Curaçao, and Jamaica, where they acquired large sugarcane plantations and became the leading entrepreneurs in the sugar trade. Benjamin d'Acosta introduced sugarcane to Martinique in 1655, bringing with him 900 Jews (who were expelled in 1683). Sugar production was introduced into South Africa in the 1840s by Aaron de Pass of Natal. From the beginning of the 17th century Hamburg played a growing role in the European sugar trade – to a considerable extent thanks to the activities of the Marranos who had settled there. Early in the 18th century Portuguese Jews lost their leading position in the sugar trade, in Hamburg because of the growth of competition, and in Brazil because of persecutions of the Marranos and the general decline of the trade in that country. In the first half of the 18th century, London gradually ousted Amsterdam as the center of the sugar trade; at the same time the role of the Jews became less important.

Jews also played a leading role in the development of the sugar-beet industry in Poland, Russia, the Ukraine, Hungary, and Bohemia. In eastern Europe Jews were the traditional buyers of agricultural produce from the estates and often leased the local refinery and mill from the landowners. Requests by Polish Jews to erect sugar refineries were turned down by the authorities in 1816, 1827, 1834, and 1837. Finally, Hermann Epstein built his first refinery in 1838 and by 1852 his was the largest and most modern in Poland. He was joined by L. *Kronenberg and other leading Polish Jewish industrialists and financiers. In the Ukraine Israel *Brodsky first helped finance Count Bobrinski, pioneer of Russian sugar-beet, and later he and his sons established numerous refineries. Other Jews entered this field (such as M. Halperin and M. Sachs) until, by 1872, one-quarter of the total sugar production in Russia was in Jewish hands. In 1914, 86 refineries in Russia (32% of the total) were owned by Jews; 42.7% of the administrators of the joint-stock sugar companies were Jewish, and two-thirds of the sugar trade was in Jewish hands. The percentage of Jewish workers, managers, technicians, and scientists employed in the field was correspondingly high. Between the two world wars, Jews in Poland were squeezed out of the sugar trade through the antisemitic economic policy. In Hungary a pioneering role in the development of the sugar-beet industry was played by Ignac Deutsch; his grandson Sándor de Hatvany Deutsch (1852–1913; see *Hatvany-Deutsch family) enlarged the firm and represented Hungary at international sugar conferences.

[Hans Pohl / Henry Wasserman]

In Israel

In the early 1950s two sugar-beet refineries were established in Afula and Kiryat Gat, both for economic reasons and for social considerations, such as providing employment in development areas. Sugar-beet production grew from 21,000 tons in 1955 to a peak of 295,000 in 1965 (when 37,000 tons of sugar were produced). In 1969 only 22,500 tons of sugar were produced (18% of consumption) because low international prices led to decreased profits for growers and benefits for the economy. Since that time Israel's sugar industry has continued to decline, though in 2006 Tate & Lyle formed a joint venture with Gadot Biochemicals to build and operate a sugar plant in Israel.

[Zeev Barkai]

BIBLIOGRAPHY: S.D. Goitein, *Mediterranean Society*, 1 (1967), index; H. Landau, in: *Shriften far Ekonomik un Statistik*, 1 (1928), 98–104 (Yid.), 16–17 (Ger.); E.O. von Lippmann, *Geschichte des Zuckers* (1929²); B.D. Weinryb, *Neueste Wirtschaftsgeschichte der Juden in Russland und Polen* (1934), index s.v. *Zucker*; P. Friedman, in: *Jewish Studies in Memory of G.A. Kohut* (1935), 231–2, 241 (Ger.); H.J. Bloom, *Economic Activities of the Jews of Amsterdam* (1937), index: N. Deerr, *History of Sugar*, 2 vols. (1949–50); H. Kellenbenz, *Sephardim an der unteren Elbe* (1958); N. Shapira, in: *Gesher*, 4 (1958), no. 3, 101–12; Roth, Marranos, 284, 290, 292; A. Wiznitzer, *Jews in Colonial Brazil* (1960), index; idem, in: JSOS, 18 (1956), 189–98; H. Pohl, in: *Jahrbuch fuer Geschichte von Staat, Wirtschaft und Gesellschaft Lateinamerikas* (1967), 348–73; J.C. Pick, in: *Jews of Czechoslovakia*, 1 (1968), 382–6.

SUGERMAN, SIR BERNARD (1904–1976), Australian judge. Born in Sydney, the son of a salesman, Sugerman was educated at Sydney University and was a lecturer there on property law before becoming the first editor of the *Australian Law Journal* from 1927 to 1946. After a career at the bar (Sugerman became a KC in 1943), he was appointed to the Commonwealth Court of Conciliation in 1946–47 and then served as head of the New South Wales Land and Valuation Court from 1947 to 1961. He served as a member of the Supreme Court of New South Wales from 1961 to 1970 and was then president of the New South Wales Court of Appeal from 1970 until his death. He was knighted in 1970. Sugerman was active in many Jewish causes in Sydney.

BIBLIOGRAPHY: ADB, 16, 342–43.

[William D. Rubinstein (2nd ed.)]

°**SUGIHARA, CHIUNE-SEMPO** (1900–1985), Japanese diplomat in World War II and Righteous Among the Nations. Sugihara served as consul-general of Japan in Kaunas (Kovno), Lithuania, from the fall of 1939 until August 31, 1940, when, after Lithuania's annexation to the Soviet Union, the Soviet authorities ordered all foreign legations closed. Before that, in early August, Sugihara was approached by a delegation of Jewish refugees from Poland, headed by Dr. Zeraḥ *Warhaftig, with a request for Japanese transit visas. These, Warhaftig explained, were needed in order for his group of people to acquire Soviet transit visas on their way, via Japan, to the distant Carribean island of Curacao – in the mistaken belief that no end visa was required for this island, under control of the Dutch government-in-exile. Staying in Lithuania meant for the refugees the prospect of having the Soviet authorities force them back to Poland, presently under German occupation. Sugihara asked for a few days to consider the request in the light of instructions from his superiors not to issue visas on a mass scale as well as to make sure that refugees would not prolong their stay in Japan on their way to a final destination. Recalling that momentous event years after the war, Sugihara related the struggle in his mind as he tried to come to a decision. "I really had a difficult time, and for two whole nights was unable to sleep. I eventually decided to issue transit visas.... I could not allow these people to die, people who had come to me for help with death staring them in the eyes. Whatever punishment might be imposed upon me, I knew I had to follow my conscience." Having decided positively, on August 10, 1940, Sugihara began issuing Japanese transit visas to anyone requesting them, the numbers reaching several thousand in an operation that continued to the day of Sugihara's departure from Kaunas at the end August for a different assignment. The visa recipients, which included hundreds of yeshivah students (notably those of the Mir Yeshivah), left the area in time, before the German attack on the Soviet Union on June 21, 1941, and were thus saved – passing through Russia and Japan enroute to various destinations (Shanghai, the Philippines, Canada, and Palestine). Ironically, none of them headed for Curacao. In 1985, Yad Vashem awarded the aged Sugihara Chiune-Sempo the title of Righteous Among the Nations.

BIBLIOGRAPHY: Yad Vashem Archives M31–2861; H. Levin, *In Search of Sugihara* (1996); M. Paldiel, *The Path of the Righteous* (1993), 252–55.

[Mordecai Paldiel (2nd ed.)]

SUICIDE. The duty of preserving life, including one's own, is one of the paramount injunctions of Judaism (see **pikku'aḥ nefesh*). The prohibition of suicide is a natural corollary to this, and yet it is nowhere explicitly forbidden in the Talmud. However, post-talmudic authorities considered suicide a most heinous sin, even worse than murder. It was thought to be a denial of the doctrines of reward and punishment, the world to come, and the sovereignty of God, and the opinion was expressed that the suicide forfeits his portion in the world to come. Suicide is sharply to be differentiated from martyrdom, which, under certain circumstances, is the greatest *mitzvah* of Judaism; a difference must also be made between letting oneself be killed and active suicide (see **Kiddush ha-Shem* and *Ḥillul ha-Shem*).

Four definite suicides are recorded in the Bible. Samson (Judg. 16:30), Saul and his armor-bearer (I Sam. 31:4–5), and Ahithophel (II Sam. 17:23). The first three are regarded as "suicide under mitigating circumstances," so to speak. The Midrash, which regards suicide as rare (Gen. R. 82:8), includes the prohibition of suicide ("self-strangulation") in the injunction "and surely your blood of your lives will I require" (Gen. 9:5), but specifically excludes Saul as well as *Hananiah, Mishael, and Azariah (Gen. R. 34:13). The Shulḥan Arukh (YD 345:3) takes Saul as an example of permitted suicide "because he knew that the Philistines would do with him as they wished, and put him to death" (*Siftei Kohen*, ad loc.). Samson's suicide, which brought in its train the death of the Philistines, is extolled as *kiddush ha-Shem*. The most famous act of suicide in Jewish history is the mass self-immolation of the garrison of *Masada in 73 C.E. as reported by Josephus (Wars, 7:320ff.). It has been suggested that they acted in accordance with their interpretation of the *halakhah* which included slavery and subjection to a foreign power as one of those principles concerning which one was enjoined "to be killed rather than transgress" (Rabinowitz, see bibl.). Other cases of suicide – such as the mass suicide in York in 1190 – which were motivated by either a desire to avoid forced conversion or fear, are considered to be acts of martyrdom.

It was only in the late post-talmudic tractate *Semaḥot* (Evel Rabbati 2:1–5) that the laws regarding suicide are formulated. It is laid down that no rites are to be performed in honor of the dead (e.g., **keri'ah* and **hesped*), but everything which appertains to respect for the mourners is permitted (YD 345:1; Maim. Yad, Evel 1:11). Solomon b. Abraham *Adret states that the "nothing to be done" does not include burial and shrouds (Rashba, Resp., vol. 2, no. 763). R. Ishmael states that an announcement was made concerning the suicide, "Woe, he has taken his life," but R. Akiva disagreed, saying to him, "Leave him in silence. Neither honor him nor curse him." Two cases are mentioned in the context of children (not necessarily minors) who committed suicide out of fear of punishment. The suicides were granted the full respects due to the dead. The moral which the rabbis derived from it was that it is better to punish than threaten punishment (Sem. 2:4–5).

A distinction is made between suicide while of sound mind (*la-da'at*) – to which alone these restrictions apply and suicide while of unsound mind (*she-lo la-da'at*), to which they did not apply; thus the suicide of a minor is not regarded as culpable. Only when there is the clearest evidence of felo-de-se, deliberate intent, is a suicide to be considered as being of sound mind. "Who is a suicide of sound mind? It is not so regarded if a man climbed a tree or a roof and fell to his death, but only where he states, 'I am climbing the roof or the tree and I am going to throw myself to my death,' and one sees him acting accordingly... a man found strangled or hanging from a tree or cast upon a sword is regarded as a suicide while of unsound mind" (Sem. 2:2–3). It was, and in some places still is, the custom to bury suicides in a special section of the cemetery, but in recent years the tendency has grown to remove this stigma from the suicide, since the verdict is usually suicide while of unsound mind. The slightest indication is enough to establish a state of "unsound mind" (J.M. Tukacinsky, *Gesher ha-Ḥayyim*, 1 (1960^2), ch. 25, which also contains a full list of the laws regarding a suicide).

Apart from exceptional circumstances, such as during the Nazi persecutions, the incidence of suicides among Jews has been small. The mass suicides which took place during the Middle Ages to avoid forcible baptism, which are generally regarded as belonging to the category of *kiddush ha-Shem*, were not without their critics (see the incident recounted in *Da'at Zekenim*, to Gen. 9:5). The self-immolation of Meir Feinstein and Moshe Barazani who blew themselves to death in prison in Jerusalem in 1947 on the eve of their execution in order to cheat the hangman, was justified on the analogy of Saul. Their original intention, to commit the act on the way to the scaffold, causing the simultaneous death of their potential executioners, was based on the example of Samson. Rabbi S. *Goren (see bibl.), the chief rabbi of the Israel Defense Army, expressed the view that a soldier taken prisoner was entitled, and even obliged, to commit suicide if he feared that he might not be able to withstand torture, or that under it he might reveal military secrets. He was, however, subjected to considerable criticism for this view. However, with the growth of acculturation in the Western world, there is evidence that the rate among Jews is rising and approximating to that of the general population. See *Mental Illness.

[Louis Isaac Rabinowitz]

In Jewish Law

"But for your own life-blood I will require a reckoning" (Gen. 9:5) – these are the suicides whose blood is claimed by God (Gen. R. 34:13; Yad, Roẓe'aḥ 2:3). The "reckoning" is, of course, God's only, but on earth the suicide is denied certain honors due to the dead, provided the surviving mourners are not aggrieved by such denials (Sem. 2:1; YD 345:1). The suggestion that words of scorn be exclaimed at this grave was met by R. Akiva with the rejoinder, "do not abase him and do not praise him" (Sem. 2:1). In order to be reprehensible, the suicide must be voluntary and premeditated (*me'abbed aẓmo la-da'at*, that is, he must knowingly destroy himself). A person destroying himself is presumed to do so without the necessary premeditation (*she-lo la-da'at*) – whether from pathological depression and not being in possession of his mental faculties (cf. Yad, Sanhedrin 18:6), or from "duress" (see *Penal Law). Duress includes not only compulsion, such as the necessity to kill oneself rather than surrender to the enemy or violate God's laws (see below), but also the (subjectively) reasonable despair of life or the identification with a person who just died. Most of the suicides reported in Bible, Talmud, and Midrash fall into either of these categories, which may explain the fact that they are not adversely or deprecatingly commented upon. (For those in the Bible, to which the (possible) suicide of Zimri (I Kings 6:18) may be added, see above.) Examples in the Talmud are that of the servant of Judah ha-Nasi who killed himself when learning of his master's death (Ket. 103b), and of the pagan executioner who joined Hananiah (Ḥanina) b. Teradyon in the flames (Av. Zar. 18a).

Duress is also present where the suicide amounts to self-inflicted punishment for real or imagined sinfulness: the apostate Yakum of Ẓerorot is said to have entered paradise after having taken his own life in a manner devised to combine all four modes of judicial execution (Mid. Ps. to 11:7); and Ḥiyya b. Ashi is said to have caused his own death in despair over an offense he intended to commit and thought he had committed, though in fact he had not committed it at all (Kid. 81b). Where a man chooses to die rather than surrender to the heathen, no question of duress arises, because his conduct is highly praiseworthy (Git. 57b); the most notable instances are those related in the Books of the Maccabees (e.g., II Macc. 14:37–46) and the reported mass suicide at Masada (which has recently given rise to some halakhic discussion). As for the violation of Divine law, while every man has to decide for himself whether he will kill himself rather than commit any such violation (Git. 57b), the law was settled to the effect that where he is required to commit idolatry, adultery (*gillui arayot*), or murder, he must kill himself or let himself be killed rather than commit any of those crimes (Sanh. 74a; Sh. Ar., YD 157).

The scope of duress being as wide as it is, the law will presume that a man found dead from his own hand took his life involuntarily and without premeditation (Sem. 2:3), until the contrary is proved from what the man himself had been heard to say before his death (Sem. 2:2). As far as minors are concerned, the presumption of duress appears to be irrebuttable (Sem: 2:4–5; YD 345:3). So long as the presumption is not rebutted, a suicide may not in any way be discriminated against (Yad, Evel 1:11). The law, however, has to take cognizance of attempted suicide: a person who does any act by which he endangers his own life is liable to disciplinary *flogging (*makkat mardut*; Yad, Roẓe'aḥ 11:5). Opinions are divided whether a man may inflict nonfatal wounds on himself (BK 91b); and the law is that while he is not allowed to do so, he is not punishable if he does so (BK 8:6; ḤM 420:31); yet not only might he be punished at the hands of heaven (Tosef., BK 9:31), but the disciplinary flogging may always be imposed in lieu of punishment (Yad, Roẓe'aḥ 11:5; ḤM 427:10). If suicide attempts are epidemic or otherwise constitute a threat to national security, the court may exercise its emergency powers and impose not only floggings but also *imprisonment (cf. Yad, Roze'ah 2:4–5).

[Haim Hermann Cohn]

Suicide to Avoid Severe Torture

Throughout the generations halakhic authorities have confronted questions concerning the permissibility of suicide in situations other than when it becomes necessary to avoid committing one of the three cardinal prohibitions previously discussed. These questions arose during periods of anti-Jewish violence and pogroms and attempts to coerce Jews into to apostasy.

Rabbenu Tam (Tos. Avodah Zarah, 18a) ruled that it is a *mitzvah* to commit suicide in order to escape extreme pain and torture, especially when used against a person to coerce apostasy. According to other halakhic authorities, suicide under such circumstances, is not required but permitted (Maim., Torat ha-Adam), while according to other authorities, such suicide is prohibited (Maharshal, *Yam shel Shelomo*, BK 8:59).

During the *Holocaust, this question again arose in a practical context. In Resp. *Mi-Ma'amakim* (1.6), Rabbi Ephaim Oshry relates to a question submitted by a Jew from the Kovno ghetto who asked whether he was allowed to commit suicide to avoid a horrible death accompanied by severe suffering as well as to avoid witnessing the deaths of his family.

The responsum discusses the opinions of earlier authorities, and cites the incident of the suicide of King Saul (I Samuel 31:4), The answer given was that, under the circumstances, suicide was permitted, but the author requested that the responsum not be publicized to prevent it from providing assistance to Nazi murderers by sowing despair among the Jews.

The responsum concludes with the following comment: "Nonetheless we may take pride in the fact that there were no suicides in the Kovno ghetto with the exception of three people whose morale was completely shattered. The remaining Ghetto residents continued to believe and were fully confident that God would not abandon His people and would halt the murderers."

[Menachem Elon (2nd ed.)]

BIBLIOGRAPHY: S. Goren, in: *Maḥanayim*, 87 (1964), 7–12; L.I. Rabinowitz, in: *Sinai*, 55 (1964), 329–32; Ch. W. Reines, in: *Juda*, 10 (1961), 160–70. IN JEWISH LAW: A. Roth, *Eine Studie ueber den Selbstmord, vom juedischen Standpunkte* (1878); J. Ginzburg, *Mishpatim le-Yisra'el* (1956), 247–57, 307f.; J. Nedava, in: *Mishpat ve-Kalkalah*, 3 (1956/57), 87–99; Z. Rabinowicz, in: *Harofe Haivri*, 34 (1961), 153–6; ET, 12 (1967), 681f. **ADD. BIBLIOGRAPHY:** M. Elon, *Ha-Mishpat ha-Ivri* (1988), 2:1156; idem, *Jewish Law* (1994), 3:1389; A. Ben Zimra, *"Kedushat ha-Ḥayyim u-Messirut Nefesh bi-Ymei ha-Shoah al-pi ha-Halakhah,"* in: *Sinai*, 80 (1977), 151–85; J.D. Bleich, *Judaism and Healing* (1981), 158–61; S. Goldstein, *Suicide in Rabbinic Literature* (1989); S. Goren, *"She'elah u-Teshuvah be-Niddon Gibborei Meẓadah,"* in: *Or ha-Mizraḥ*, 7:3 (1960), 22–27; M.Z. Neriah, *"Hitabdut le-Da'at – Giborei Meẓada le-Or ha-Halakhah,"* in: *Or ha-Mizraḥ*, 8 (1961) 8–12; A. Steinberg, *Enẓiklopedyah Hilkhatit Refu'it*, 1: 7–17; idem, *"Hitabdut le-Or ha-Halakhah,"* in: *Halakhah ve-Refu'ah* (1988) 281–95.

SUKENIK, ELIEZER LIPA (1889–1953), Israel archaeologist. Born in Bialystok, Poland, he settled in Ereẓ Israel in 1912. In 1914, he began his teaching career, and eventually was appointed field archaeologist at the Hebrew University. He directed the excavations of the synagogues of *Beth-Alpha (1928) and *Hammath-Gader (1932) and participated with L.A. *Mayer in the clearance of the remains of the Third Wall in *Jerusalem (1925–27). From 1931 to 1933 he was a member of the expedition to *Samaria. In 1935 he was promoted to lecturer in archaeology and in 1938 he was appointed professor; in the same year he also became director of the University Museum of Jewish Antiquities. He excavated a number of synagogues and Jewish tombs in the vicinity of Jerusalem, the latter containing remains which he claimed were evidence of early Christianity, as well as Chalcolithic remains in Ḥaderah, including a tomb, and a Bronze Age site at Tell Jarisha. In 1947 Sukenik was instrumental in acquiring part of the *Dead Sea Scrolls – whose importance he immediately recognized – and he devoted the rest of his life to their study.

His many publications include excavation reports on Beth-Alpha, Hammath-Gader, Japhia and Salbīt Sha'alvim synagogues (published in the *L.M. Rabinowitz Bulletin*) and a study of the Dura-Europos synagogue, as well as the *Dead Sea Scrolls* (1958).

[Michael Avi-Yonah]

His wife, HASYA SUKENIK-FEINSOD (1889–1968), was a pioneer kindergarten teacher. Also born in Bialystok, she settled in Ereẓ Israel in 1912, where she was among the founders of the kindergarten system and served as supervisor of kindergartens and director of kindergarten teachers' seminaries. She was a member of the *Asefat ha-Nivḥarim and the leader of the Women's Equal Rights Association. Their sons were: Yigael *Yadin, soldier and archaeologist; Yoseph Yadin, actor; and Matityahu Sukenik, a pioneer Israel Air Force pilot who fell in the War of Independence.

[Abraham Aharoni]

BIBLIOGRAPHY: *Eretz Israel*, 8 (Sukenik volume, 1967).

SUKKAH (Heb. סֻכָּה), booth erected for the festival of *Sukkot, in accordance with the biblical commandment "Ye shall dwell in booths seven days" (Lev. 23:42). The reason for the commandment given in the Bible is "that your generations may know that I made the children of Israel to dwell in booths, when I brought them out of the land of Egypt" (Lev. 23:43). Since the Israelites in the desert dwelt in tents and not in booths, the Talmud records a dispute between R. Eliezer and R. Akiva on whether the *sukkot* in Leviticus 23:43 were actual or metaphorical booths, the latter referring to the protective "clouds of glory" (Suk. 11b) which accompanied the Israelites throughout their 40-year sojourn. Details of the *sukkah's* construction are discussed in the talmudic tractate *Sukkah. According to *Bet Shammai (whose ruling is here accepted, Maim. Yad, Shofar, Sukkah ve-Lulav, 6:8), the *sukkah* must be large enough to contain a man's head, most of his body, and his table (Suk. 2:7), an area defined as seven handbreadths square (Sh. Ar., OḤ 634:1; Yad, loc. cit. 4:1; for a conical or circular shaped *sukkah*, see Suk. 8a). The height of the structure must not be less than ten handbreadths, nor more than 20 cubits (Suk. 1:1; see also *Weights and Measures). The most important section in the construction of the *sukkah* is the roof made of covering known as *sekhakh*. The *sekhakh* must be cut from that which grew in the soil and which is not susceptible to ritual impurity (Suk. 1:4; 9b; Rashi, ad loc.; Yad, loc. cit. 5:1). An overhanging tree, for example, is invalid as *sekhakh* (Suk. 1:2). The *sekhakh* must be so arranged that the shaded area within the *sukkah* will exceed the unshaded (Suk. 9b–10a; Sh. Ar., OḤ 626:1). Any material may be used in the construction of the walls (Suk. 1:5), at least two of which must be complete, while the third may be partial (Suk. 6b; Yad, loc. cit. 4:2; Sh. Ar., OḤ 630:2). It is particularly meritorious to begin construction of the *sukkah* at the conclusion of the *Day of Atonement (Isserles to Sh. Ar., OḤ 625:1). Despite the opinions quoted in the Jerusalem Talmud (Ber. 9:4, 14a, and see also Rashi to Mak. 8a), no benediction is said on the construction of the *sukkah* because the biblical commandment is fulfilled by "dwelling" in it and not in its construction (Sh. Ar., OḤ 641:1).

"Throughout the seven days ('and nights,' Suk. 43a) of the festival, the *sukkah* must be regarded as one's principal abode, and the house merely a temporary residence" (Suk. 2:9). Thus, it is forbidden to eat any major repast or to sleep outside the *sukkah* (Suk. 26a; Yad, loc. cit. 6:6; Sh. Ar., OḤ 639:2), and it is obligatory to eat in the *sukkah* on the first night of the festival (Suk. 2:6; Yad, loc. cit. 6:7; Sh. Ar., OḤ 639:3). These laws do not apply to women, slaves, and infants (Suk. 2:8; Yad, loc. cit. 6:1; Sh. Ar., OḤ 640:1); and if rain is likely to spoil one's food, it is permitted to transfer the meal to the house (Suk. 2:9; Yad, loc. cit. 6:10; Sh. Ar., OḤ 639:5). Each time one eats in the *sukkah* the blessing "to dwell in the *sukkah*" (Suk. 46a) is recited, usually after the blessing over bread (Sh. Ar., OḤ 643:3). On the first night of the festival these blessings are made before the *She-Heḥeyanu* *benediction, since the latter can thereby be made to apply both to the observance of the festival and to the first performance of the duty to dwell in the *sukkah* (Suk. 56a; Yad, loc. cit. 6: 12, Sh. Ar., OḤ 643:1). However, in the Diaspora, the order of the benedictions is reversed on the second day of the festival (*ibid.* 661). It is customary to decorate the *sukkah* with fruit (which may not be eaten during the festival, Suk. 10a–b), and with the symbols of Sukkot, and to recite special welcomes to the seven "guests of the festival" (the *Ushpizin*), Abraham, Isaac, Jacob, Moses, Aaron, and David, on each day of Sukkot (see Zohar, Lev. 103b). According to the Midrash (Gen. R. 48:10), the Children of Israel were divinely protected in the wilderness by the shelter of the Tabernacles solely because the Patriarch Abraham had given shelter to three strangers beneath the tree on his property (Gen. 18:2–5). It is also customary to construct a *sukkah* at the synagogue (see *Oẓar ha-Ge'onim*, (1934), 33 nos. 51–53), where a token meal (usually a *Kiddush*), is held after the holiday services. In present-day Israel the Samaritans erect the *sukkah* inside their houses, while Jews construct *sukkot* on the sidewalks, roofs, and balconies of their houses reminiscent of what is described in Nehemiah: "So the people went forth… and made themselves booths, every one upon the roof of his house, and in their courts, and in the courts of the house of God…" (8:16–18).

*Philo suggested that the *sukkah* was built to show misfortune at a time of good fortune and to remind the rich of the poor (Spec. Leg. 2:208–9) and Maimonides similarly interprets the lesson of the Tabernacle (Guide 3, 43). There are modern scholars who see the origin of the custom in a reinterpretation of some ancient agricultural rite but the nature of this is disputed.

BIBLIOGRAPHY: S.J. Zevin, *Ha-Mo'adim ba-Halakhah* (1963[10]), 90–103; E. Munk, *The World of Prayer*, 2 (1963), 272–4; H. Schauss, *Guide to Jewish Holy Days* (1966[4]), 200–3.

SUKKAH (Heb. סֻכָּה; "booth"), sixth tractate of the order *Mo'ed* in the Mishnah, Tosefta, and Babylonian and Jerusalem Talmuds. It deals, in five chapters, with laws relating to the festival of *Sukkot (Tabernacles). The festival is sometimes referred to simply as the *ḥag* ("the holiday"; Num. 29:12; Neh. 8:14, etc.), and in fact, this name is employed throughout this tractate, indicating that it was considered the most outstanding festival. The observances with which this tractate is primarily concerned are the "dwelling in booths" and the taking of the four *species. Two other ceremonies dealt with are the ceremony of the willow branches and the rite of water libation.

Chapter one covers the making of the *sukkah*; chapter two continues the subject, and goes on to define the term "dwelling" in the *sukkah*. The question of exemptions is also touched upon. Chapter three deals with the four species. Chapter four gives further information on the various ceremonies, including the above-mentioned ceremony of the willow branches and the rite of the water libation, and chapter five describes vividly the festivities surrounding the festival of the water drawing. Information is also given about other occasions when the trumpets were sounded, as well as on how the various sacrificial duties were distributed among the priestly divisions and how they shared the sacrificial portions.

The Mishnah of *Sukkah* can be divided into two main sections: chapters 1–3 and chapters 4–5. Both the language and the contents as well as the places mentioned therein show that the latter belong to the period of the Second Temple. Nevertheless these two chapters are not of the same source, and differences in language are recognizable in them. The reason is that though in the main they belong to the time of the Temple, they were adapted and worded by later *tannaim*, some of whose names have remained there, such as R. Judah (5:4) and Johanan b. Beroka (4:6). The Babylonian *Gemara* to tractate *Sukkah* is unique compared with most other tractates. Especially numerous in this tractate are the "transposed themes," i.e., the themes which contradict the same themes found in parallel passages in other tractates, both in the circumstances attributed to them (*ukimta*) and the discussions themselves. On the other hand the *Gemara* displays a remarkable similarity to that of the Jerusalem Talmud, to which there is no parallel with regard to the other tractates of the Babylonian Talmud. On this basis, J.N. Epstein has come to the conclusion that despite the fact that it shows many similarities to other tractates, *Sukkah* is to be regarded as belonging to a class of its own. In addition *Sukkah* contains a considerable number of the disputes between Abbaye and Rava and a comparatively large number of additions of the *savoraim*. *Sukkah* was translated into English in the Soncino Talmud by I.W. Slotki (1938).

The tractate ends with an obscure reference to the priestly watch of Bilgah (see I Chron. 24:14), which was in various ways discriminated against. The alternate reasons for this are given in the Tosefta (4:28; variations in TJ 5:8 and TB 56b), namely that they were disgraced by a female member, Miriam, who became an apostate and traitor and married a Greek captain during the Hasmonean struggle against the Syrio-Greeks. The other reason given is that they were negligent in their Temple service. Other aggadic points to be noted are the description of the splendor of the Great Synagogue in Alexandria, which is referred to as a Great Basilica (Tosef. 4:6), and the story of Trajan's persecution of the Jews and its reasons (TJ 5:1, 55b). Of interest also are the discussions of the relative merits of charity and sacrifices (TB 49b) and observations on the problem of freedom of will (TB 52b).

BIBLIOGRAPHY: Epstein, Tanna'im, 37–40, 346–53; Epstein, Amoraim, 45–53; Ḥ. Albeck, *Shishah Sidrei Mishnah*, 2 (*Seder Mo'ed*; 1958), 253–8.

[Arnost Zvi Ehrman.]

SUKKOT (Heb. סֻכּוֹת; "booths" or "tabernacles"), the festival, beginning on the 15th day of Tishre, which commemorates the *sukkot* in which the Children of Israel dwelt in the wilderness after the Exodus. The festival lasts for seven days, of which the first (and the second in the Diaspora) is a *yom tov* (a festival on which work is prohibited) and the other days *ḥol ha-mo'ed* (intermediate days on which work is permitted). Immediately after Sukkot, on the eighth day (and the ninth in the Diaspora), is the festival of Shemini Aẓeret ("the eighth day of solemn assembly") which is a *yom tov*.

In the Bible

Tabernacles, the "feast of ingathering" (Ex. 23:16ba; 34:22ba), was celebrated by the Israelites at the time of the ingathering from the threshing floor and wine press (Deut. 16:13; cf. Ex. 23:16b; Lev. 23:39a) "at the end of the year" (Ex. 23:16b; cf. "at the turn of the year," 34:22b). The last of the three Israelite feasts connected with the agricultural year (Ex. 23:16; 34:22; Lev. 23:34–36, 39–43; Num. 29:12–38; Deut. 16:13–15), Tabernacles was from ancient times one of the most important feasts of the Israelites and is therefore called "the feast of the Lord" (Lev. 23:39; Judg. 21:19) or simply "the feast" (I Kings 8:2, 65; 12:32; Ezek. 45:25; Neh. 8:14; II Chron. 5:3; 7:8). The seven-day feast (Deut. 16:13a; cf. I Kings 8:65 [= II Chron. 7:8]) was originally – like *Passover – congruent with the period of a week; the date (in the month of Etanim, i.e., the seventh month (Sept./Oct.), I Kings 8:2) was determined by the end of the harvest. After the Exile (Ezek. 45:25) it was dated to the 15th to the 21st of the seventh month (Lev. 23:34–36a, 39–41; Num. 29:12–38) and prolonged by one day, the *aẓeret*, on the 22nd day of the month (Lev. 23:36b; Num. 29:35; Neh. 8:18; II Chron. 7:9). The note that Jeroboam I celebrated this feast one month later, on the 15th of the eighth month (I Kings 12:32–33), did not have any climatic or calendaric reasons. It may be a Deuteronomistic reproach for the king's incorrect cultic behavior (cf. 12:33a). The third agricultural festival, like the other two, was taken over from the Canaanites. According to Judges 9:27, the Shekhemites celebrated a feast of joy at the end of the grape harvest; a similar Israelite feast in the vineyards, at which the girls danced, was celebrated every year in Shiloh according to Judges 21:19–21. Festival joy is shown in other places to be a main feature of the feast (Lev. 23:40; Deut. 16:14; Neh. 8:17). It is not yet mentioned in Judges 21:19–21, but later in the Bible the seven-day dwelling in booths became the central custom of the feast (cf. Lev. 23:42; in Jerusalem this was carried out at the Temple square according to Neh. 8:14ff.); hence the name "Feast of Booths" or "Tabernacles" (Lev. 23:34; Deut. 16:13, 16; 31:10; Zech. 14:16, 18–19; Ezra 3:4; II Chron. 8:13). As the main feast of the year, Tabernacles was the occasion for the consecration of Solomon's Temple (I Kings 8). According to the Deuteronomistic construction, in every seventh year the law was to be read before the gathered people on the same occasion (Deut. 31: 10–11). At the end of days all the peoples would assemble for the feast in Jerusalem to worship the Lord (Zech. 14:16ff.). Unlike Passover and Pentecost the Feast of Booths was rather late, its connection with the Exodus was, therefore, forced. According to Leviticus 23:42–43, the Israelites were to dwell in booths as they did during the Exodus from Egypt; but in the wilderness at the time they did not have booths, but tents.

Critical Theories Concerning Origin

According to the Bible, the Feast of Booths was a thanksgiving festival. Recent information concerning cult and feasts in Mesopotamia has led biblical sholars to use new methods of research to gain further knowledge about this feast. P. Volz and – independently – S. Mowinckel tried to understand the Feast of Booths as an old Israelite New Year's festival. Through the cultic-mythic explanation of the so-called "Psalms of Enthronement" (Ps. 47; 93; 96–99) and a number of other psalms, Mowinckel reconstructed a feast of YHWH's enthronement which was celebrated every year at the time of the Feast of Booths (1922); from the structure of the Sinai pericope he derived the ritual of this celebration which centered around the reading of the law as the expression of the divine will and covenant between God and people (1927). British and Swedish scholars have interpreted the Israelite Feast of Booths as a New Year's festival by connecting it with a so-called "cultic pattern" which they suppose to have existed in the Ancient Near East. The object of the ritual in which the sacral king had a central part was the securing of life (Johnson, Widengren, and others). On the other hand, G. von Rad, going beyond Mowinckel, found the structure of the "feast of the renewal of the covenant" ("*Bundeserneuerungsfest*") in the Book of Deuteronomy and in Joshua 24 (in connection with Deut. 27). Because according to Deuteronomy 31:10–11 and Nehemiah 8 the law was read during the Feast of Booths, it has been concluded that this feast is identical with the Feast of Booths. As Mowinckel supposed the feast of enthronement, including the procession of the ark, to be the highlight of cultic life in Israel and the "*Sitz im Leben*" of most of the psalms and their literary forms, so A. Weiser maintained that the "feast of the covenant," including a cultic theophany of YHWH, was the highlight. H.J. Kraus assumed that a "feast of tents" had been celebrated as a nomadic forerunner of the Feast of Booths in a cultic camp around the tent sanctuary (possibly in Beer-Sheba), as a reminder of the march through the wilderness from Egypt to Palestine. For the pre-Exilic period, Kraus, referring to II Samuel 6, 7 and Psalms 132, reconstructed a "royal Zion Feast" to be held on the first day of the Feast of Booths. This feast, held on the first day of the festival, which included a procession of the ark (cf. II Sam. 6 and I Kings 8), celebrated the election of Jerusalem and of the Davidic dynasty. Under the influence of Deutero-Isaiah, this feast became a celebration of the beginning of the kingship of God over his people, and, thus, the Feast of Booths secondarily became a feast of YHWH's enthronement.

These theses have – to varying extents – influenced research, but all of them also called forth important objections. Nowhere in the Bible is it said that one of these subjects is always connected with the Feast of Booths. The feast of ingathering was celebrated, according to Exodus 23:16, "at the end [not at the beginning] of the year" (E. Kutsch, in: ZAW, 83 (1971)). It was thought to be at the "beginning" of the year because it was dated on the 15th to the 21st of the seventh month, and the first day of this month – in the post-biblical period (RH 1:1, 2; but cf. already Lev. 23:24b, 25; Num. 29:1–6; Neh, 8:2) – became New Year's Day. The feast itself never was a New Year's feast; therefore it lacks any important equivalent in relation to Mesopotamian parallels. Further, the formula "*YHWH malakh*" (Ps. 93:1; 96:10; 97:1; cf. 47:9) does not mean "YHWH has become king" but "YHWH rules as king" (D. Michel, in: VT, 6 (1956), 40–68); it emphasizes God's kingship, but not an enthronement acted out in the cult. II Samuel 6 and I Kings 8 report two different transfers of the ark (to the City of David, to the Temple), each of which took place only once, and therefore do not reflect a regularly held procession of the ark. A "feast of the covenant," or "feast of the renewal of the covenant," cannot have existed because *berit* in the Bible does not mean "covenant" (E. Kutsch, in: ZAW, 79 (1967), 18–35), and because Israel did not interpret her relationship to YHWH as a "covenant" (E. Kutsch, in: *Tuebinger Theologische Quartalschrift*, 150 (1970), 299–320). Deuteronomy 31:10–11 prescribes a proclamation of the law before the people, which constitutes a statement of their commitment to YHWH (not a covenant), to take place – if at all – every seventh year on the Feast of Booths. After the Exile such an act could be dated to the first or second of the seventh month (Neh. 8:1ff.), to Pentecost (II Chron. 15:10ff.; cf. Ex. 19:1), to the 24th of the seventh month (Neh. 10:1ff. in connection with 9:1), or the beginning of the first month (II Chron. 29:10; cf. 29:3). Joshua 24:25 and II Kings 11:17a; 23:3 do not give any fixed date. Such an act of commitment was at no time bound to a certain feast, therefore it was not bound to the Feast of Booths. Furthermore, it is impossible to derive (cf. Weiser) from Joshua 24 or the Psalms a connection between the commitment of the people and the proclamation of the divine salvatory acting ("*Heilshandeln*") as the contents of the Feast of Booths. Kraus wrongly presupposes that the "Tent of Meeting" and the Ark were jointly used in an early Israelite cult (according to PC) and that the "Tent of Meeting" stood at some time in Shiloh (I Sam. 1:7, 9, 24; 3:3, 15 against Joshua 18:1; 19:51 (both belonging to PC); I Sam. 2:22). On the other hand the basis of the "royal feast of Zion" (the parallelism between II Sam. 6 and I Kings 8 (see above) and the traditional historical connection between II Sam. 6 and 7) cannot be proved.

In the New Testament the Feast of Booths in John 7 is the background of Jesus' appearance in Jerusalem. The fact that according to 7:37, Jesus "on the last [i.e., on the seventh] day of the feast" calls the ones who thirst to come to him is connected with the custom of pouring water from the first to the seventh day of the feast that was common in the time of Jesus. On the other hand, no motives of the Feast of Booths are presupposed in Mark 9:2ff.

[Ernst Kutch]

Sukkot in Rabbinic Literature

Two special observances are mentioned in the Book of Leviticus (Lev. 23:39–43): that the people should dwell in booths for seven days, so "that your generations may know that I made the Children of Israel to dwell in booths, when I brought them out of the land of Egypt," and that the people were to take on the first day "the fruit of goodly trees, branches of palm trees, and boughs of thick trees, and willows of the brook" to "rejoice before the Lord." Rabbinic authorities named these the *arba'ah minim*, "the *four species" (of plant); the "fruit of goodly trees" is the citron (*etrog*); the "boughs of thick trees" are myrtle twigs (*hadasim*); the palm branch is the *lulav*; and the willows are *aravot*. In the Book of Nehemiah, it is said that from the days of Joshua to Nehemiah, the people had not dwelt in booths (Neh. 8:17), but in the same chapter it is stated: "Go forth unto the mount, and fetch olive branches, and branches of wild olive, and myrtle branches, and palm branches, and branches of thick trees, to make booths as it is written" (Neh. 8:15). There is no mention of olive branches in Leviticus and none of willows in Nehemiah. Moreover, from Nehemiah it would appear that the various plants were used to cover the booths (and this was, in fact, the interpretation of the *Sadducees) whereas in the rabbinic tradition, the command to dwell in booths and the command to "take" the four species are treated as two separate precepts. In Zechariah's vision all the nations of the world will come to Jerusalem in the new age to celebrate the festival of Sukkot (Zech. 14:16).

According to the rabbis, biblical law obliges every male Jew to take *arba'ah minim* in the hand on the first day of Sukkot (based on Lev. 23:40). The rabbis, however, understood the reference in the verse to "rejoice before the Lord your God seven days" to apply to the Temple, where the *arba'ah minim* had to be taken each day. After the destruction of the Temple, Johanan b. Zakkai ordained that wherever Jews celebrate Sukkot, the *arba'ah minim* should be taken in the hand for seven days in commemoration of the Temple (Suk. 3:12). The four species were to be held in the hand while *Hallel* (Ps. 113–8) is chanted and they were to be waved at the beginning of Psalm 118 and while reciting verse 25 of the Psalm (Suk. 3:9). The *lulav* was to be held in the right hand together with three *hadasim* and two *aravot* and the *etrog* in the left hand (Suk. 3:4). The *lulav*, the largest of the four species, gives its name to the four so that the benediction is: "Blessed art Thou… Who has sanctified us with His commandments and commanded us to take the *lulav*." (Suk. 46a; for laws concerning the *sukkah*, see **Sukkah*.)

Rabbinic authorities mention a special ceremony of "water-libation" during the seven days of Sukkot (Suk. 4:9). The Sadducees rejected the ceremony because they could find no support for it in Scripture (Suk. 4:9 and 48b; Jos., Ant. 13:372). The special rites of "water-libation," accompanied by the playing of the flute, took place only on *ḥol ha-mo'ed* (except on the Sabbath), not on *yom tov*. The ceremony was known as Simḥat Bet ha-Sho'evah ("the rejoicing of the place of water-drawing"), based evidently on Isaiah 12:3 "Therefore with joy shall ye draw water out of the wells of salvation" (Suk. 5:1). There were said to be three huge golden candlesticks in the Temple court which were lit on these occasions "and there was not a courtyard in Jerusalem that did not reflect the light of the Bet ha-Sho'evah" (Suk. 5:2–3). "Men of piety and good works used to dance before them with burning torches in their hands, singing songs and praises" (Suk. 5:4). It was further said that whoever had not seen the Simḥat Bet ha-Sho'evah, had never witnessed real joy in his life (Suk. 5:1).

Laws and Customs of Sukkot

It is customary to use leaves or straw as the roof covering of the *sukkah*; the walls, however, may be of any material. The *sukkah* must be so well covered that there is more shade (i.e., covered space) than open space but the covering should not be so thick that even strong rain cannot penetrate. It must have at least three walls (the third need only be one handbreadth in width), and be beneath the open sky, not under a tree or inside a house. It should be decorated in accordance with the general rule that precepts be "adorned." On the first night of the festival, a person is obliged to eat at least the equivalent of an olive's bulk of bread in the *sukkah* but not during the remainder of the festival. If meals are eaten, they must be partaken of in the *sukkah*. In modern times, in colder regions, many do not sleep in the *sukkah* since the rules of *sukkah* do not apply where there is severe discomfort. The pious have heated *sukkot* so that they can fulfill the obligation of sleeping there. Not only is a person not obliged to sleep or eat in the *sukkah* when rain penetrates, but he is forbidden to do so, on the grounds that it is indelicate and presumptuous to insist on carrying out a religious duty from which there is exemption. It is customary to build a *sukkah* adjacent to the synagogue for the benefit of congregants who have no *sukkah* of their own. In some Reform congregations, a symbolic *sukkah* is erected in the synagogue itself, even though it has no validity as a *sukkah* in Jewish law. A custom, originating with the school of Lurianic Kabbalah in the 16th century, is to "invite" each day one of the biblical heroes to the *sukkah*. These **Ushpizin* ("guests") are: Abraham, Isaac, Jacob, Moses, Aaron, Joseph, and David; they correspond to the seven *Sefirot* of lovingkindness, power, beauty, victory, splendor, foundation, and sovereignty.

The *lulav* is held with the spine facing the holder. On the first day it is necessary for each person to take his own *arba'ah minim*, but on the other days of the festival they may be borrowed. *Arba'ah minim* purchased by the congregation can, however, be taken even on the first day, since each congregant has had a share in them. The *arba'ah minim* are waved while the *Hallel* is recited. They are waved first toward the east, then the south, the west, the north, above and below. Toward the end of the service in the synagogue, a scroll is taken from the Ark and the congregation walks in procession around the *bimah* holding the four species as a reminder of the processions around the altar in Temple times. In liturgy, Sukkot is referred to as *zeman simḥatenu* ("the season of our rejoicing").

Hoshana Rabba

The seventh day of Sukkot is known as Hoshana Rabba ("the Great *Hoshana*"); the name is taken from the word *hoshana* ("Save, I Pray") which is frequently used in the prayers of the day. The *hoshana* prayers for a good harvest in the year to come are recited during a procession seven times around the *bimah* after which five *aravot* bound together are beaten. In Temple times, *aravot* were carried around the altar seven times on this day (Suk. 4:5). In post-talmudic times, the day became a supplement to the *Day of Atonement, a special day of judgment on which God's decrees for the coming year are finalized. Consequently, it is the custom to spend the night of Hoshana Rabba in prayer and study, particularly of the Book of Deuteronomy.

Shemini Azeret

"On the eighth day ye shall have a solemn assembly (*aẓeret*): ye shall do no manner of servile work" (Num. 29:35). The eighth day of Sukkot is treated by the rabbis as a separate festival, *regel bifenei aẓmo*. The *Yizkor* (Memorial service) and a special prayer for rain (*Tefillat Geshem*) are recited during **Musaf* (in Israel before it), in the synagogue. The Book of Ecclesiastes is read in the synagogue on the intermediate Sabbath of Sukkot or, when there is no intermediate Sabbath, on this day. Among the reasons given for the reading are: Its melancholy nature which makes it appropriate reading for the autumn festival; and the verse: "Divide a portion into seven, yea, even into eight" (Eccles. 11:2) applied by the rabbis to the seven days of Sukkot and to this eighth day (see The Five *Scrolls).

Simḥat Torah

The last day of the festival is *Simḥat Torah ("rejoicing in the Torah) which in Israel coincides with Shemini Aẓeret. On this day, the annual reading of the Torah from the scroll in the synagogue is concluded. Simḥat Torah is a post-talmudic festival, but was known in the geonic period. Over the years, a number of ceremonies have grown up around the day. The person called to the reading of the last portion of the Torah is known as *Ḥatan Torah* ("the bridegroom of Torah"). A new cycle of Torah reading is begun as soon as the old cycle is concluded. The person called to begin the new cycle is known as

Ḥatan Bereshit ("the bridegroom of Genesis"). The "bridegrooms" invite their fellow-congregants to a party in honor of the day (see *Bridegroom of the Law). On Simḥat Torah eve, and again during the day, all the scrolls are taken from the Ark and carried in procession around the synagogue while songs of praise are chanted. In many communities it is the custom to dance with the scrolls.

See *Simḥat Torah; **Hakkafot*; Festivals; **Hoshanot*.

[Louis Jacobs]

In Art

Elongated receptacles for the *lulav* are traditionally made of knotted palm leaves; silver receptacles are also found, sometimes similar to the short-lived palm leaf holder, but they are comparatively late. The use of containers for the *etrog* is also late. These most frequently take the form of a rectangular box ranging in style from the simple to the baroque; there are others, more unusual, shaped like the fruit and usually featuring a stem, the reason being that the stem of the *etrog* must remain intact throughout the duration of the festival. In Eastern Europe the *etrog* was very often kept in a silver box originally intended to be used for some secular object such as sugar.

Despite its austere associations, the *sukkah* has in traditional practice always been richly decorated. Different fruits hang from its roof of foliage, and very often there are pictures and tapestries on the wall. Some of these pictures are called *ushpizin*.

Some *sukkot* are collapsible. One of the best known originates from Fischbach in southern Germany and dates from the early 19th century. It is now in the Israel Museum. The structure is complete with numbered boards and beams, and its walls are elaborately decorated with paintings depicting the city of Jerusalem, the Temple, the Western Wall, the Levites, Moses on Mt. Sinai, Elijah in the valley of Kerith, and a secular scene of a man going hunting while his wife waits for him outside their house.

On the last day of Sukkot, which is also Simḥat Torah, the Scrolls of the Law are carried around the *bimah* and the members of the congregation wave gaily decorated flags, which have constituted a very attractive form of folk art.

[Abram Kanof]

BIBLIOGRAPHY: IN THE BIBLE: P. Voltz, *Das Neujahrfest Jahwes* (1912); S. Mowinckel, *Psalmenstudien*, 2 (1922); idem, *Le décalogue* (1927); D.J. Bornstein, in: EJ, 10 (1934), 681–6; G. von Rad, *Das formgeschichtliche Problem des Hexateuch* (1938); H. Riesenfeld, *Jésus transfiguré* (1947); A. Weiser, *Die Psalmen* (19503), 19636); H.-J. Kraus, *Die Koenigsherrschaft Gottes im Alten Testament…* (1961); idem, *Gottesdienst in Israel…* (19622); A.R. Johnson, *Sacral Kingship in Ancient Israel* (1955); G. Widengren, *Sakrales Koenigtum im Alten Testament und im Judentum* (1955); E. Kutsch, *Das Herbstfest in Israel* (1955); idem, in: *Tuebinger Theologische Quartalschrift*, 150 (1970), 299–320; E. Auerbach, in: VT, 8 (1958), 1–18; G.W. Mac-Rae, in: CBQ, 22 (1960), 251–76; K.-H. Bernhardt, in: VTS, 8 (1961); W. Michaelis, in: *Theologisches Woerterbuch zum Neuen Testament*, 7 (1964), 369–96; H. Cazelles, *La Fête des tentes en Israel* (1965), 32–44; H. Schauss, *The Jewish Festivals* (1938), s.v.; Y.T. Lewinsky (ed.), *Sefer ha-Mo'adim – Sukkot*, 4 (1952). GENERAL: J. Fabricant, *A Guide to Succoth* (1958); L. Finkelstein, *The Pharisees*, 1 (19623), 102–15; 2 (1962[3]), 700–8; A. Yaari, *Toledot Hag Simḥat Torah* (1964); S.J. Zevin, *Ha-Mo'adim ba-Halakhah* (1967), 90–141.

SULAMITH, first German-language periodical for Jews. Founded in 1806 by David Fraenkel (1779–1856), the Dessau educator, and Joseph Wolf (1762–1826), and edited by the former, it carried the masthead, "A periodical for the advancement of culture and humanism among the Jewish nation"; by 1810, however, the word "Israelites" had replaced the words "Jewish nation." Fraenkel viewed his creation as a continuation of the Koenigsberg **Me'assef* and fully supported *Mendelssohn and his program as interpreted by his radical followers. Through poems and edifying discourses, the paper advocated a return to a purified and tolerant Judaism. It endorsed the modern education of rabbis, emphasized preaching and sermons in the service, and supported the modern educational efforts made in *Seesen, *Frankfurt, and *Dessau, and the religious innovations introduced there. The list of subscribers (not confined to Germany alone) was relatively small, but it included financiers, manufacturers, and court advisers who were generally also leaders of their respective communities and advocates of the reforms proposed by *Sulamith*.

BIBLIOGRAPHY: S. Stein, in: ZGJD, 7 (1937), 193–226; W. Grossert, in: *Judentum – Wege zur geistigen Befreiung* (2002), 158–69.

[Andreas Kennecke (2nd ed.)]

SULEIMAN I (the Magnificent), Ottoman sultan 1520–1566, called al-Qānūnī, "the Legislator," "the Lawgiver," as the Turks referred to him for his extensive legislative achievements in fiscal and feudal law. The epithet "the Magnificent" was given to him by the Europeans as a tribute to the fact that his rule coincided with the golden period of the *Ottoman Empire. The Jews called him "King Solomon," not only because of his name, but also because of his wisdom and legislative activities. Suleiman conquered *Hungary and laid siege to Vienna in 1529. He annexed *Iraq and *Yemen and extended Ottoman control of North Africa from *Egypt to the borders of *Morocco. Generally he followed the positive system of his father and grandfather toward the Jews, but there were also some problems, caused especially by his tax policy and the pressure to get money from the Jewish population. The long years of his reign represented the pinnacle of Ottoman Jewry, and under his reign the Jewish communities achieved their highest political and economic status, and also benefited from the involvement of Jews in Suleiman's court. In these years thousands of Jews, many of them *anusim* from Portugal, immigrated into the Ottoman Empire. The Jewish population in his days achieved records in communal, social, economic, and intellectual life. Under Suleiman's rule the Jewish settlement in Ereẓ Israel, especially in *Safed, had a strong presence. Like his father and grandfather, Suleiman used the sürgün system, and transferred Jewish residents from their native cities to other cities. In 1523 he transferred 150 Jewish families from *Salonika to *Rhodes just after its conquest in 1522. According to one testimony, 150 of the richest and most respected Jewish landlords in Salonika (men, women, and children) were transferred at the command of Sultan Suleiman. He wanted to develop Rhodes and to establish it economically. The Jews were forced to remain on the island, but there were people who did succeed in escaping from there. Suleiman had followed this system after he captured Buda in 1526. Despite the fact that the Jews were among the few who had remained in Buda and had delivered the keys to the city into his hands, he still took the Jews with him, leading them off in boats as sürgün. The Jews were dispatched as sürgün, in the category of craftsmen and tradesmen. The Jews of Buda were settled in Sofia, Kavalla, and according to one source, in Salonika as well. Other Jews from Buda settled during Sultan Suleiman's reign in *Edirne (Adrianople), *Istanbul, and perhaps even in Safed. Joseph b. Solomon Ashkenazi, who handed Suleiman the keys to the city of Buda, was awarded, together with his descendants, tax exemption and special grants. The firman written by Suleiman to Ashkenazi was renewed during the Ottoman era by other sultans.

Generally Suleiman was strict, in accordance with the laws of *Islam and state legislation. Suleiman codified the regulations regarding the attire of his subjects, and during his reign the obligation of the Jews to preserve all *Omar regulations was discussed. The Jews had to obtain firmans from the sultan, permitting them to restore several synagogues in some cities. On the other hand, Suleiman did not enforce all of Omar's regulations. For example, Moses *Hamon, his physician and adviser, acquired the right to build a four-story house, and there are sources about Jews in Istanbul who felt free to dress in expensive wool and muslin, silky atlas and cotton cloaks and expensive shoes. Preserved in the Ottoman archives are dozens of firmans written by Suleiman dealing with the status of the Jews of Ereẓ Israel and other communities. Suleiman ordered local Ottoman officials to change their attitude toward the Jewish population and to prevent pressure and extortion. Many of these orders were written in response to letters of complaint sent to Suleiman by the Jews.

A number of Jews held important posts during Suleiman's rule, some acting as diplomatic agents of the Ottoman Empire in European capitals. As one of his Jewish advisers, the aforementioned Moses Hamon accompanied the sultan on his travels and campaigns. Hamon also interceded on behalf of the Jews with the sultan. Following the Amasya blood libel in 1553, Hamon persuaded the sultan to issue a special decree prohibiting provincial judges from trying cases of blood libel and requiring them to refer such cases to the Imperial divan for trial. Hamon was in close contact with the party in the court led by Hurrem Sultan (Roxelana), Suleiman's favorite wife, and Grand Vizir Rustem Pasha. Hamon is also believed to have interceded with Suleiman to exert pressure on Venice to facilitate the departure of the Mendes-Nasi family for the Ottoman Empire. Moses Hamon was the man who influenced Suleiman to bring Gracia Mendes to Istanbul in 1552 and to protect her on the way from Italy to the Ottoman capital. Hamon strived to assist Jews in the Ottoman Empire who requested his political help. But there is no proof that he took up the request of the impoverished clothiers of Salonika to intervene on their behalf at the court of the kadi of Istanbul. On the other hand, he did intervene in the quarrel in the community of Salonika about the activity of the wealthy Barukh.

Another Jew who had an important role in the state, especially in foreign affairs, was Don Joseph *Nasi. Deeply impressed by Nasi's erudition and financial and diplomatic talent, the sultan made him one of his confidants, and gave him his protection and several economic monopolies. In 1555 Suleiman, at Nasi's request, urged Pope Paul IV, who had burned a group of Portuguese *anusim* in Ancona, to release the Ottoman Jewish subjects who had been arrested. When the Nasi family declared that their agents, who were Ottoman subjects, were among the prisoners, Suleiman urged the pope to free them. Since some of the Ancona prisoners were Nasi's agents, they could be considered Ottoman subjects. The effort failed and the Jews were burned. Suleiman also made efforts in 1555 to release confiscated possessions of Jewish merchants in the papal territory. Suleiman protested, claiming that this act had caused many Jews of Salonika and Istanbul to go bankrupt, so they were unable to pay their taxes to the Ottoman treasury. In the last days of his reign, in 1666, Suleiman, under Jewish influence at his court, interceded concerning money interests of some Levantine Jewish merchants who owed debts to Venetian merchants. In the course of this crisis, Grand Vizier Mehmed Sokollu intervened, and a sultanic messenger was sent to Venice, with a special firman issued by Suleiman. This intervention was in favor of the Segura family, whose members were close to Joseph Nasi and possessed important businesses in the empire.

Finally the sultan gave Gracia Mendes, as a *multazima* during the years 1560–1566, the ruined city of *Tiberias and its environs, and permitted her to build the walls of the city. Details about this agreement are written in the orders of Suleiman to the governor of *Damascus and to other Ottoman officials. The chronicler Joseph ha-Kohen writes about the important role of Joseph Nasi in developing the city of Tiberias.

During Suleiman's rule the Jews of the Ottoman Empire made great cultural and economic progress. They developed the empire's commerce and succeeded in renting from the sultan the right to collect taxes, especially customs duties. Despite this, at the same time there were the first indications of financial pressure on the Jews by the authorities, and it required great efforts on the part of the Jews close to the court to keep such pressure to a minimum.

Suleiman had connections with two Jewish women called **Kiera* (kira) who had good relations with the wives in the harem. When he ascended to the throne, in 1520/1521, he gave the Jewish kira, Stronillah, who served his mother Hafsa Sultan, an exemption from taxes for her and her descendants. This woman adopted Islam at the end of her life and received the name Fatma. We do not know if her conversion was under pressure by the sultan. Another kira, Esther *Handali, was certainly active in the harem before the death of Suleiman, and served Nur-Banu, the favorite concubine of Selim II, continuing her services to that woman during the reign of Selim II. Under Suleiman's reign the two kiras did not gain political influence but did have opportunities to become wealthy.

The Ottoman censuses organized by Sultan Suleiman have considerable importance for the history of the Jews in the 16th century. In Ereẓ Israel four censuses were carried out in his time. Suleiman built the wall around the Old City of Jerusalem which still stands (see *Jerusalem, Under Ottoman Rule). This deed made a great impression throughout the Jewish Diaspora.

The attitude of Suleiman to the Jews of Salonika was described by many writers and historians. In 1537 Suleiman visited Salonika and granted the Jewish residents a decree exempting them from the obligation of being "celep" (that is, rich men chosen by the Ottoman officials to use their own money to buy thousands of sheep and to drive them to Istanbul, where they would sell the sheep to the butchers of the city at a fixed price, which often resulted in a financial loss) and from the obligation to be the operators of the silver mines in Siderokapisi, near Salonika. But in 1545 this document was burned in the Great Fire which broke out in Salonika, and the Jews lost these rights. For 20 years the Jews of Salonika sent emissaries to Istanbul to attempt to renew the old order, but their efforts failed. R. Moses *Almosnino did succeed in obtaining the reissue of the order.

The death of Suleiman in Transylvania (September 6, 1566) and his funeral (November 22, 1566) are described by the same Moses Almosnino, who was present in Istanbul at that time, in his book *History of the Ottoman Kings*. In a second work he described Sultan Suleiman's reign. The entire book is full of admiration for Suleiman's wisdom and statesmanship as well as his attitude toward his subjects, Muslim and non-Muslim. He calls Sultan Suleiman "Our great master Sultan Suleiman, may his memory live forever." The feelings of admiration toward Suleiman are noted also in the colophon of the response by R. Isaac Bar Sheshet published in Istanbul in 1556. The publisher, Shemuel ha-Levi, wrote at the time of the publication, "In Istanbul, the fine city, the city of a great king, a faithful shepherd, our master the Sultan Suleiman, may his splendor be exalted, and his honor grow, and in his times and ours Judea and Israel be redeemed, and may the redeemer come to Zion." Sultan Suleiman was the first Ottoman sultan in whose honor a special poem was written in Hebrew. This poem was written by the Istanbuli poet Shelomo ben Mazal Tov (d. 1545).The last book published in Istanbul during Suleiman's reign was *Sefer Yuḥasin* by R. Abraham *Zacuto. It was printed in 1566, a few months before Suleiman's death during his campaign in Hungary, and the publisher expressed his wishes for the sultan: "...May the Lord bring him back here in peace without obstacles, and may the Lord cause all his enemies to be defeated by him ..."

BIBLIOGRAPHY: Rosanes, Togarmah, 2 (1937²), 1–94; S.N. Fisher, *The Middle East, a History* (1959), 218–29; U. Heyd, in: *Sefunot*, 5 (1961), 139, 144–8. **ADD. BIBLIOGRAPHY:** A.H. Lybyer, *The Government of Suleiman* (1966); S.W. Baron, in: *Joshua Finkel Festschrift* (1974), 29–36; A. Cohen and B. Lewis, *Population and Revenue in the Towns of Palestine in the Sixteenth Century* (1978); A. Bridge, *Suleiman the Magnificent* (1983); M.A. Epstein, The *Ottoman Jewish Communities and their Role in the Fifteenth and Sixteenth Centuries* (1980); A. Shmuelevitz, *The Jews of the Ottoman Empire in the Late Fifteenth and Sixteenth Centuries* (1984); *Yehudim be-Darkhei ha-Shayyarot u-be-Mikhrot ha-Kesef shel Makedonia* (1984); R. Lamdan, in: Z. Ankori (ed.), *Mi-Lisbon le-Saloniki ve-Kushta* (1988), 135–54; L. Bornstein-Makovetsky, ibid., 69–94; A. Cohen, in: *Journal of Turkish Studies*, 10 (1986), 73–78; H. Inalcik, in: *Essays in Honor of Bernard Lewis:* (1989), 525, 529 n. 22; A. Cohen, ibid., 467–77; Y.H. Hacker, in: *Zion*, 55 (1990), 27–82; A. Cohen, in: *Cathedra*, 57 (1990), 31–51; Hacker, in: A. Rodrigue (ed.), *Ottoman and Turkish Jewry: Community and Leadership* (1992), 27–31, 58–62; M. Rozen, *ibid.* (1992), 141–44, 162; M. Rozen, *Bi-Netivei ha-Yam ha-Tikhon* (1993), 47–50, 69–70, 147, 157–58, 164; A. Cohen and E. Simon-Pikali, *Yehudim be-Veit ha-Mishpat ha-Muslemi* (1993), index; L. Bornstein-Makovetsky, in: Sh. Trigano (ed.), *Société juive à travers les âges*, 3 (1993), 433–62; A. Levy, *The Jews of the Ottoman Empire* (1994); T. Be'eri, in: *Pe'amim*, 59 (1994), 68–69; B. Arbel, *Trading Nations, Jews and Venetians in the Early Modern Period* (1995); K. Metin and C. Woodhead, *Suleiman the Magnificent and his Age* (1995); M. Rozen, in: M. Rozen (ed.), *Yemei ha-Sahar* (1996), 13–37; M.Z. Benaya, *Moshe Almosnino Ish Saloniki* (1996); M.M. Weinstein, in: *Studies in Bibliography and Booklore*, 20 (1998), 145–76; N. Shor, *Bonim Ḥomah bi-Yrushalayim* (2000), 96–108; M. Rozen, *A History of the Jewish Community in Istanbul, The Formative Years, 1453–1566* (2002); Y. Hacker, in: *Kehal Israel*, 2 (2004), 287–309.

[Abraham Haim / Leah Bornstein-Makovetsky (2nd ed.)]

SULEIMANIYA (al-), Kurd province in N.E. *Iraq in which there were about ten Jewish communities and village settlements. The most important communities were in Suleimaniya, Ghūlambar, Zardiāwa, Halabja, Halībrūy, Mazūrān, Mīrwa, Sūrdash, Fishdal, and Franjawīn. In 1827 the traveler David d'Beth Hillel found about 100 Jewish families in the provincial town of Suleimaniya. They owned a beautiful synagogue, most of them were merchants, others were craftsmen, and the community was led by a *nasi* who was the banker (*ṣarrāf bāshī*) of the pasha. During the 1890s there were 180 Jewish families in the town and the number of Jews who spoke Jebel (mountain) Aramaic increased at the beginning of the 20th century. In 1906 the number of Jews was about 1,500. According to official statistics of 1930, however, there were 47,510 inhabitants in the whole of the al-Suleimaniya region, of whom 900 were Aramaic-speaking Jews. In 1948 they all immigrated to Israel.

BIBLIOGRAPHY: A. Ben-Yaacob, *Kehillot Yehudei Kurdistan* (1961), 111–6.

[Abraham Ben-Yaacob]

SULITA (Rom. **Suliţa**), village in Botosani district, Moldavia, Romania. Founded in 1817, the town passed in 1840 to the ownership of the Moldavian ruler Prince Michael Sturza who was interested in developing the locality. In 1843 when a conflagration destroyed the town, the Jews there wished to leave but the ruler helped them to reestablish their dwellings and exempted them from taxes for 25 years. Their community increased from 496 in 1831 to 1,831 (63% of the total population) in 1899; 80% of the Jews were occupied as craftsmen, and others were merchants. Some were occupied in sheep raising and marketing. The community had five prayer rooms, a *ḥeder* and a primary school (founded in 1890 with the aid of the *Jewish Colonization Association), a ritual bath, and a hostel for poor travelers.

During the Peasants' Rebellion in 1907 nearly all the houses belonging to the Jews were pillaged and destroyed. By 1930 the Jewish population had decreased to 1,062, but their proportion in the population had increased to 76.1%. In 1932 the landlord of the estate on which the town was built brought a lawsuit to have the Jews expelled, but lost the case. In World War II the Jews in Sulița were deported to Botosani. A few returned after the war, numbering 380 in 1947, and 250 in 1950. In 1969 there were fewer than ten Jewish families in Sulița.

BIBLIOGRAPHY: E. Schwarzfeld, *Împopularea, reimpopularea si întemeierea târgurilor și a târgușoarelor în Moldova* (1914), 44, 84–85; PK Romanyah, 185–6.

[Theodor Lavi]

SULIȚEANU, GHISELA (1920–2006), Romanian ethnomusicologist. She played a very special role within the discipline of Romanian ethnomusicology. She joined the Institute of Folklore immediately after its founding in 1949 and was one of its most assiduous workers until her retirement in 1979. However, she continued to work on her incredibly large musical collections from the field as well as on her theoretical ideas. She earned her Ph.D. at the University of Bucharest in 1974; her thesis was on the psychology of folk music, a quarter of which was published in 1980. She collected a great deal of Sephardi and Ashkenazi folk music as well as religious (synagogal) music. The only anthology of Jewish folk music in Romania was published by Emil Săculeț in the late 1950s, but Sulițeanu also worked on this anthology, even writing the foreword for the book's first edition (1956), which was destroyed – withdrawn from the market immediately after it was printed, then recycled as scrap paper. Despite fears and lack of institutional support, Sulițeanu was the only one among the remaining Jewish colleagues who continued to collect, transcribe, write, and publish on Jewish music. In later years she very much wanted to see the publication of her long commentary and huge transcription of the *Purimspiel Joseph and His Brothers* that she identified and recorded in Romania in the early 1970s. She also worked hard on a book devoted to her studies from 1960 to 1980 on the folk music of the Turkish and Tartar communities in southeastern Romania. Sulițeanu embraced many modern subjects and approaches, familiarizing local academic research with ideas and books coming from the West (she was the first, and actually the only one to plead for the introduction into Romania of the ideas of the famous international ethnomusicologists Lomax, Ellis, Merriam, and Blacking). Although she was allowed to travel abroad and contribute papers read at various international congresses and conferences, she was never invited to teach in Romania at the university level. Thus, she shined individually and modestly without transforming or turning specifically Romanian scholarship toward the paradigms and perspectives she was capable of opening up. Among her numerous works are volumes devoted to the folk dance music in Muscel (1976), ballads in southeastern Romania – Brăila County (1980) – a huge lullaby anthology (1986), her *Psihologia folclorului muzical* ("Psychology of Folk Music"), and numerous academic essays found in various ethnomusicological journals, proceedings, and collective books.

[Marin Marian (2nd ed.)]

SULLAM, SARA COPPIO (1592?–1641), Italian poet. Born into a wealthy Venetian family – her father and uncle were benefactors of Leone *Modena and financed the printing of several of his works – Sara Sullam spent her life in Venice. She became known through the sonnets and letters she exchanged with Ansaldo Cebà, a Genoese nobleman and monk. This correspondence, which was conducted at a remarkably high literary level (somewhat resembling the platonic "game of love" then in vogue), arose from Cebà's publication of a verse epic on Queen Esther (1615–16). When this work came to Sara's attention it aroused her enthusiasm, and from 1618 to 1622 the two writers exchanged sonnets, letters, and gifts. Sara lavished praise on Cebà for choosing the tragic figure of Esther as a literary theme, thus departing from the conventional use of motifs drawn from classical Greek and Roman sources, and even declared her spiritual love for him. In reply, Cebà praised Sara who, "though a Jewess," revealed in her writings her thorough humanistic education and the purity of her soul. Cebà's replies were, however, primarily aimed at inducing her to convert. Shortly before his death, having despaired of these endeavors and in the hope of gaining merit for himself as a faithful Christian, he published the letters and poems which he had written to Sara (*53 Lettere di Ansaldo Cebà, scritte a Sara Copia Sullam e dedicate a Mare Antonio Doria*, Genoa, 1623). The letters written by Sara were, however, omitted from this publication.

In 1614 Sarah had married Jacob Sullam, a prominent member of the Venetian Jewish community, and she took an active part in the city's cultural life, her house serving as a meeting place for Jewish and Christian scholars. In 1621 Baldassar Bonifaccio (later Cardinal of Cape d'Istria) attacked her in a pamphlet, claiming that the poetess had denied the immortality of the soul, a belief shared by Jews and Christians alike. The religious liberty which Venetian Jewry then enjoyed enabled Sara to make public her reply in a witty and mordant manifesto refuting Bonifaccio's allegations. She also answered his charge with two caustic sonnets in which she declared her pride in her faith. In 1619 Leone Modena dedicated to Sara Coppio Sullam his Italian version of Salomon *Usque's tragedy *Esther*, and also composed her epitaph. A volume of her collected sonnets (ed. L. Modena) appeared in 1887.

BIBLIOGRAPHY: M.A. Levy, *Sara Copia Sullam…* (Ger., 1862); M. Soave, *Sara Copia Sullam…* (It., 1864); E. David, *Sara Copia Sullam* (Fr., 1877); F. Kobler, *A Treasury of Jewish Letters*, 2 (1952), 430–48; C. Roth, *Venice* (1938).

[Joseph Baruch Sermoneta]

°**SULPICIUS SEVERUS** (fourth century), Christian writer. Severus used the Bible and classical authors in his history of the world. He sees the siege of Jerusalem in 70 C.E. as divine retribution for the Jews' part in the crucifixion of Jesus. He disagrees with Josephus (perhaps following a lost passage from Tacitus) and blames Titus for the destruction of the Temple (*Chronica* 2:30).

[Jacob Petroff]

SULTANSKY, MORDECAI BEN JOSEPH (c. 1772–1862), Karaite scholar and writer. He was born in Lutsk, Volhynia. His father was a *ḥazzan* and a head of the *bet din* in Lutsk. Sultansky served as a teacher in his native town. At the age about 40, apparently after a large fire that broke out in 1813/4 in Lutsk, Sultansky moved to the Crimea where he functioned as *melammed* in *Chufut-Qaleh, and later as *ḥazzan* in *Yevpatoriya. At the end of his life he went to his son Isaac, who lived in Kherson, Ukraine. In Chufut-Qaleh Sultansky, together with A. Firkovich, was engaged in publishing Karaite books in the printing house of Eupatoria. Sultansky was widely read in both Karaite literature and such rabbinic authors as Maimonides, Abraham ibn Ezra, Judah Halevi, Bahya ibn Paquda, and Levi b. Gershom, and he also studied Talmud. The most important of his printed works is his *Zekher Ẓaddikim* (also entitled *Kiẓẓur Aggadah*; ed. by S. Poznanski, 1920), a detailed account of Karaite history from its beginnings to the author's time. This book demonstrates anti-rabbinic tendencies and contains numerous incorrect historical data and other errors. Since it lacks a critical approach it is of little scientific value. This book is an example of modern Karaite historiography, which demonstrates at the same time an interest in modern research and manipulation of the facts for the ideological and political purposes of the community. His main concepts concerning Karaite history, presented in this book, were adopted by Sultansky's disciple A. *Firkovich before the latter started his public and research activity.

Sultansky also published a Hebrew grammar entitled *Petaḥ Tikvah* (pt. 1, Yevpatoriya, 1857); *Tetiv Da'at* (ibid., 1858), a philosophical defense of Karaism, containing many quotations from old rabbinic and modern Hebrew authors, and polemics against Rabbanism and Ḥasidism; *Sefer ha-Ta'am* (IOS SPb A 132) – answers to questions posed by a counselor of Czar Alexander I about the origins of Karaites; *Palgei Mayyim*, a commentary on the Lamentations of Jeremiah (IOS SPb B 429). Most of his works remained unpublished, among them *Or ha-Ganuz* (philosophical composition); *Hod Malkhut* – the treatise about Karaism and against Rabbanism which he planned to present to Czar Nicholas I, but for some unknown reason did not; *Yalkut Yosef* (commentaries on the Torah); *Mikhtam Sur me-Ra* (ethical composition). Sultansky also studied new Hebrew written works belonging to the Haskalah. He was on a friendly terms with Peretz Smolenskin and Efraim Deinard.

BIBLIOGRAPHY: E. Deinard, *Massa Krim* (1878), 18, 71; R. Fahn, *Sefer ha-Kara'aim* (1929), 99–100; Mann, Texts, 2 (1935), index, 1570; L. Nemoy, *Karaite Anthology* (1952), 6; M. Polliack (ed.), *Karaite Judaism: A Guide to Its History and Literary Sources*, (2003), index.

[Golda Akhiezer (2nd ed.)]

SULZBACH, town in Bavaria, Germany (united with the village of Rosenberg in 1934). A Jewish settlement is first mentioned in 1305. It suffered during persecutions in 1337, and during the Black *Death persecutions of 1349 it was probably annihilated. A community was reestablished only 300 years later, in 1666, under the rule of Duke Christian-August of Pfalz-Sulzbach. During the early history of the new community its settlers were mainly *Schutz juden* with limited residence permits. After the first three families had arrived, a cemetery was consecrated. In the wake of the expulsion of Jews from Vienna in 1670 additional settlers came to the town, and in that year the community's first rabbi, Joseph Moses Hause, took office. By 1682 the community had an organized school under the direction of David Brot. In 1685 a liberal charter of privileges was granted, and was renewed in 1712. According to the charter the recognized head of the community acted as its representative in all negotiations with the authorities. At first, public prayers were held in a private house, but in 1687 a house was converted into a synagogue, and in 1737 a new synagogue was built. By 1699 there were 15 Jewish families in Sulzbach. Among the important personages of the community was Joseph b. Eliezer Oettingen, author of *Edut be-Yosef* (Sulzbach, 1741), a Bible commentary. The Schwabacher family, its members noted for their work as court factors and merchants, also lived in Sulzbach in the 18th century. In 1745 there were 22 families in the community, in 1829, 65. The community possessed a *Memorbuch*, of importance in tracing its history and development. The synagogue was destroyed by fire in 1822 and another was built in 1824. An elementary school for Jewish children was founded in 1825, and functioned until 1923. In accordance with the *Toleranzpatent of 1813 there were to be no more than 65 families in the town, and that number was roughly maintained until the middle of the 19th century when the Jewish population was gradually reduced by emigration. By 1933 there were only eight Jews living in Sulzbach.

Hebrew Printing

The inclination of Duke Christian-August toward mysticism and Kabbalah aroused his interest in the Hebrew language and led him to grant an authorization in 1669 for the founding of a Hebrew press in his town. As a result Sulzbach became renowned in the Jewish world. The first of the Jewish printers was Isaac bar Judah Yudeh Katz of Prague. In 1684 the ownership of his press passed to the Bloch family, and from 1699 until 1851, the year the press shut down, it was held by the Frankel-Arnstein family. The Sulzbach press printed 702 works, which consisted mostly of *siddurim*, *mahzorim*, Bibles, three editions of the Talmud, and popular *musar* (ethical) literature in Judeo-German. The press first achieved fame as a result of its excellent edition of the Zohar, printed in 1684. The half-folio edition of the *maḥzor enjoyed a wide circulation ever since 1699 when it first appeared; there was hardly a community in southern Germany ("Ashkenazi ritual") where it was not employed as *maḥzor-kahal* (community *maḥzor*) by the *ḥazzan*. The publication of the Talmud in Sulzbach was the cause of a serious dispute with the Proops *brothers of Amsterdam. The demise of the press was due partly to the prohibition on importing Hebrew books into the Austrian Empire as well as to the excellent quality of work produced by Wolf *Heidenheim's press in *Roedelheim, with which the Sulzbach press could not compete.

BIBLIOGRAPHY: M. Weinberg, *Geschichte der Juden in der Oberpfalz*, 5 (1927); idem, *Die hebraeischen Druckereien in Sulzbach* (1904); idem, in: JJLG, 15 (1923), 125–55; 17 (1925), 89–94; 21 (1930), 319–70; FJW, 269; Germ Jud, 2 (1968), 812; Salfeld, Martyrol, 264.

[Jacob Rothschild]

SULZBACH, ABRAHAM (1838–1925), educator and scholar. Sulzbach, born in Hamburg, studied rabbinics with the local chief rabbi (A. Stern), S.B. *Bamberger in Wuerzburg, and M. Landsberg in Berlin; in Wuerzburg and Berlin he also attended university, studying history and philology. From 1862 to 1912 he taught German, history, geography and talmudic subjects at the high school (*Realschule der Israelitischen Religionsgesellschaft*) that S.R. *Hirsch had established in Frankfurt.

Among his published works are *Renan und der Judaismus* (1867); *Dichterklaenge aus Spaniens besseren Tagen* (1873, 1903[2]); *Die religioese und weltliche Poesie der Juden vom 7. bis zum 16. Jahrhundert* (1893; later in J. Winter and A. Wuensche, *Die juedische Literatur seit Abschluss des Kanons*, vol. 3); *Bilder aus der juedischen Vergangenheit* (1914, 1923[2]); *Die Ethik des Judentums* (1923; extracts from R. Judah he-Ḥasid, *Sefer Ḥasidim*); and he edited an anonymous commentary on Job (1911). Sulzbach also translated the book of Esther (*Das Buch Esther*, 1904[3]; 1906[4]; incl. the evening prayer for Purim) and the *Targum Sheni* of Esther (1920) into German and edited some prayer books with translation, such as *Sefer ha-Ḥayyim* (1905[8], 1930[10]; repr. 1983) and *Koheleth Schelomo* (1908).

BIBLIOGRAPHY: *Der Israelit* (July 9, 1925); H. Schwab, *Chachme Ashkenaz* (Eng., 1964), 120; P. Arnsberg, *Die Geschichte der Frankfurter Juden*, vol 3, 454–55.

[Archiv Bibliographia Judaica]

SULZBACH, WALTER (1889–1969), sociologist. Sulzbach was born in Frankfurt and was a professor at the university there until the Hitler regime. In 1937 he immigrated to the United States, where he assumed various teaching and research positions. Sulzbach's writings are chiefly concerned with the sociology of nations, social classes, and political parties. He conceived of a nation entirely as a political unit, disregarding other criteria such as language and ethnicity. His position regarding imperialism and social classes was Marxist with the addition of socio-psychological components. It was from this point of departure that he wrote *Vorurteile und Instinkte; Eine Untersuchung ueber die Rassenabstossung und den Anti-semitismus* (1923). His most important contribution was an article on the concept of the nation, "*Begriff und Wesen der Nation*," in *Dioskuren*, 2 (1923). He also wrote *Nationales Gemeinschaftsgefuehl und wirtschaftliches Interesse* (1929) and *National Consciousness* (1943).

BIBLIOGRAPHY: W. Bernsdorf (ed.), *Internationales Soziologenlexikon* (1959), incl. bibl.

[Werner J. Cahnman]

SULZBERGER, ARTHUR HAYS (1891–1968), U.S. publisher of *The New York Times*. Sulzberger, who was born in New York, married Iphigene B. Ochs, the only child of Adolph S. *Ochs, publisher of *The New York Times*, in 1917. He joined the staff of the paper in 1919, after his release from service in World War I as a lieutenant in the field artillery. Given wide-ranging training and responsibilities in all areas of the paper's operation, he was named publisher of the paper and president of The New York Times Co. when Ochs died in 1935. Under his direction, the paper was successful not only in perpetuating Ochs's high traditions of comprehensive, responsible, and impersonal journalism, but also in extending the scope and influence of its coverage through increased attention to interpretative reporting, news of consequence in political and economic affairs, and the world of culture and the arts. As the newspaper's top executive, he also played a dominant role in its affiliated operations, including: the Chattanooga *Times*, the paper published by Ochs at the time he went to New York; the Spruce Falls Power and Paper Co. Ltd., of Canada, the largest newsprint producer in the world; and Interstate Broadcasting Co.

As his father-in-law had done, he too trained a son-in-law to succeed him, Orvil Eugene Dryfoos (1912–1963), who had married his daughter Marian. When Sulzberger went into semi-retirement in 1961, he continued as chairman of the board but turned over day-to-day direction of the paper to Dryfoos as publisher. When Dryfoos died suddenly (in 1963), he was succeeded by ARTHUR OCHS SULZBERGER (1926–), son of Arthur Hays Sulzberger. Sulzberger had joined *The New York Times* staff after service with the U.S. Marines. He devoted several years to gaining extensive experience in both its editorial and business operations. After serving as a cub reporter on *The New York Times*, he worked for a year as a reporter for *The Milwaukee Journal*, and then returned to *The New York Times* for assignments on the foreign news desk, as a correspondent in London, Paris, and Rome. He returned to New York in 1955 as assistant to the publisher. He was named assistant treasurer in 1958, and was president and publisher from 1963 until 1992 and served as chairman until 1997. In 1972 he won the Pulitzer Prize for publishing *The Pentagon Papers*. In 2005 he received the Katharine Graham Lifetime Achievement Award from the Newspaper Association of America. His son ARTHUR OCHS SULZBERGER JR. (1951–) became the publisher of *The New York Times* in 1992 and chairman in 1997. Sulzberger's first cousin CYRUS LEO SULZBERGER (1912–1993) was a prominent *New York Times* foreign affairs columnist. He wrote a large number of books, among them *Seven Continents and Forty Years: A Concentration of Memoirs* (with A. Malraux, 1977).

BIBLIOGRAPHY: Mandell, in: J. Fraenkel (ed.), *The Jews of Austria*. **ADD. BIBLIOGRAPHY:** S. Tifft and A. Jones, *The Trust: The Private and Powerful Family behind The New York Times* (1999).

[Irving Rosenthal / Ruth Beloff (2nd ed.)]

SULZBERGER, MAYER (1843–1923), U.S. jurist and communal leader. He was born at Heidelsheim, Germany, and was to remember the cries of the mobs that were part of the anti-Jewish movement that followed the Revolution of 1848. His father, a *ḥazzan* and teacher, immigrated to the United States in 1849 and settled in Philadelphia. Sulzberger studied law in the office of Moses A. *Dropsie, was admitted to the bar in 1865, and became one of the leading lawyers of Philadelphia. He was elected a judge of the Court of Common Pleas in 1895. In 1909 President William Howard Taft wished to appoint him U.S. ambassador to Turkey but Sulzberger preferred to remain a judge. He served until 1915 when, by this time president judge of the Court of Common Pleas, he refused to run for reelection so that he might devote himself to his Hebrew studies. However, he was a member of a commission to revise the constitution of Pennsylvania in 1920. As a judge he impressed the lawyers practicing before him not only by his legal learning but by his impatience with words that lacked substance. He regarded judicial precedents as "more or less tentative hypotheses," to be followed only when they were socially serviceable and to be ignored or set aside when they led to conclusions at war with new social needs.

In 1906 he helped organize, and was the first president of, the *American Jewish Committee. As its president, he helped bring about the abrogation of the commercial treaty between the United States and Russia because of Russia's refusal to recognize U.S. passports when issued to Jewish citizens. He was also a founder and the first president of the Young Men's Hebrew Association of Philadelphia, a vice president of the Philadelphia Jewish Hospital, which his father had helped found, and a trustee of the Baron de Hirsch Fund. Although he believed in making Ereẓ Israel a place of refuge and a home for Jews, he was not a Zionist and did not believe in a Jewish state.

While still in his early twenties, Sulzberger had helped Isaac *Leeser in the publication of *The Occident* and *American Jewish Advocate* and, after Leeser's death in 1868, he continued its publication for a year. He was one of the founders of the *Jewish Publication Society of America and, for many years, chairman of its Publication Committee. He helped reorganize, in 1901, the *Jewish Theological Seminary of America in New York and was a governor of *Dropsie College in Philadelphia. He had been secretary of the board of trustees of Maimonides College, the first Jewish seminary in the United States (1867–73), and was a trustee of *Gratz College from its foundation. He was also one of the original members of the *American Jewish Historical Society. Among his other communal activities was that of trustee of the Jefferson Medical College. He collected an important library of Hebrew books and manuscripts and in 1902 presented this to the Jewish Theological Seminary as the nucleus of its library. Sulzberger lectured on Hebrew jurisprudence and government at Dropsie College and at the Jewish Theological Seminary.

The lectures, based principally on a study of the text of the Bible, were published as *The Am Ha-Aretz – the Ancient Hebrew Parliament, a Chapter in the Constitutional History of Ancient Israel* (1909); *The Policy of the Ancient Hebrews* (1912); *The Ancient Hebrew Law of Homicide* (1915); and *The Status of Labor in Ancient Israel* (1923). His conclusions in the lectures (so he wrote in the preface to the last of these publications) may at first sight seem "bizarre" and "will scarcely meet with ready acceptance since they depart from notions very generally entertained," but their object was to stimulate the students to follow them "without preconceived opinions," and also to stimulate research. It was in this last volume that he pointed out that "a great movement for the protection and improvement of the laboring mass was initiated in Israel more than three thousand years ago, and continued to promote its life and literature, becoming indeed a part of the mental condition of the people."

BIBLIOGRAPHY: M. Ben-Horin, in: JSOS, 25 (1963), 249–86; 27 (1965), 75–102; 30 (1968), 262–71; *Addresses Delivered in Memory of Mayer Sulzberger* (1924); L.E. Levinthal, *Mayer Sulzberger, P.J.* (1927); M. Davis, *The Emergence of Conservative Judaism* (1963), 362–5; A. Marx, *Essays in Jewish Bibliography* (1947), 223–38; S. Solis Cohen, in: AJYB, 26 (1924–25), 382–403; L.E. Levinthal, in: *University of Pennsylvania Law Review*, 75 (1926–27), 99–121, 227–46; A. Friesel, *Ha-Tenu'ah ha-Ẓiyyonit be-Arẓot ha-Berit ba-Shanim 1897–1914* (1970), index.

[Charles Reznikoff]

SULZER, SOLOMON (1804–1890), Austrian cantor and reformer of liturgical music. He was cantor in his native town of Hohenems, Tyrol, at the age of 16, and from 1826 officiated at the New Synagogue in Vienna. His singing won the admiration of Schubert and Liszt. Sulzer adopted a path of moderate reform, for which he won the support of the head of the community, Isaac Noah *Mannheimer. He sought to "renovate" traditional *ḥazzanut* by taking into consideration the musical trends of the time. Sulzer applied his principles in his great work *Shir Ẓiyyon* (Song of Zion), in the first part of which, published in 1840, he purified many melodies of their unbecoming additions and trimmings. He allowed his choral music, however, to be dominated by the style of Christian church music of his time, even using Christian compositions. The second part, published in 1866, included recitatives in the ancient Polish style, taken from Polish or Russian cantors, with improvements.

Though his innovations aroused little sympathy among the cantors of Eastern Europe, they were not considered as foreign or "un-Jewish," like those of the Reform movement, and they were widely adopted in modern synagogues between 1835 and 1876. Actually, as was later to become evident, Sulzer offered his community only a compromise between his own musical compositions and prevailing practice. He himself would have preferred complete reform. In a memorandum written in 1876, he suggested the introduction of an organ, curtailment of the liturgy, the use of German hymns, and even abolition of the traditional cantillation of the Torah. His approach to *ḥazzanut* was that of a professional musician seeking a complete break with the old style. This brought him criticism from Eastern European Jewry or only partial acceptance. Nevertheless, Sulzer restored splendor to the prayer service and enjoyed wide respect in Central Europe.

A new scientific edition of Sulzer's *Shir Ẓiyyon* appeared in Vienna in the series *Denkmaeler der Tonkunst in Oesterreich.*

[Ernst Daniel Goldschmidt / Akiva Zimmerman]

BIBLIOGRAPHY: Mandell, in: J. Fraenkel (ed.), *The Jews of Austria* (1967), 221–9; Idelsohn, Music, 246–60; A. Friedmann, *Der synagogale Gesang* (1908), 121ff.; Sendrey, Music, indexes; A.L. Ringer, in: *Studie Musicologia*, 11 (1969), 355–70; M. Wohlberg, in: *Journal of Synagogue Music* (April 1970), 19–24.

SUMAC (mishnaic Heb. אוֹג), the Arabic name for the *Rhus coriaria.* This shrub or low tree, belonging to the family Anacardiadeae, which includes the *terebinth and the *pistachio, grows wild in the groves of Israel. The tree is dioecious, with pinnate leaves containing a high proportion of tannin which is used in the manufacture of leather, whence its Hebrew name *og ha-bursaka'im* ("tanner's sumac"). The female trees bear reddish fruits (in Ar. *sumac* means "red") arranged in dense clusters. The fruits are shaped like lentils, and are hairy with an acrid taste. It is used as a spice by some Oriental communities. It was cultivated in mishnaic times and is therefore reckoned with those fruits to which the law of *pe'ah* applied (Pe'ah 1:5), but in Judea where it grew wild abundantly it was not very highly valued and a lenient attitude was adopted about *pe'ah* (Dem. 1:1).

BIBLIOGRAPHY: Loew, Flora, 1 (1925), 200–2. **ADD. BIBLIOGRAPHY:** Feliks, Ha-Ẓome'aḥ, 19.

[Jehuda Feliks]

SUMBAL (Sunbal), SAMUEL (d. 1782), Moroccan diplomat. After a prosperous career in trade, Sumbal entered the service of the sultan of *Morocco as an interpreter and confidential adviser. Ultimately, he was responsible for the conduct of the sultan's foreign policy and was the Moroccan representative in all negotiations with the envoys of the European states. In recognition of his potential utility, the Spanish government granted him a yearly allowance. In 1751 he was sent on a special mission to *Denmark as ambassador.

Sumbal occupied an important position in the life of the Moroccan Jewish communities and was recognized as their **nagid.* In 1780 he fell into disgrace on the charge of smuggling currency abroad, but escaped from prison and made his way to Gibraltar. There he helped to provision the fortress during the siege which was in progress. He subsequently returned to Morocco, and died in *Tangier.

Sumbal's son JOSEPH ḤAYYIM SUMBAL (d. 1804) then went to Denmark, where he successfully asserted his father's financial claims. In 1787 he created a great stir by proclaiming a new syncretistic religion. Later he settled in *London where by his eccentricity he attracted great attention. In 1794 he was appointed Moroccan ambassador to the English court. In 1797 he married a well-known actress and journalist, Mary Wells, who converted to Judaism. Subsequently, they quarreled and separated, as she recorded in lurid detail in her autobiography. He ultimately settled in Altona (Hamburg), where he died.

BIBLIOGRAPHY: M. Sumbel (Wells), *Memoirs of the Life of Mrs. Sumbel, late Wells*, 3 vols. (London, 1811); C. Roth, in: *Commentary*, 10 (1950), 569–76 (= *Jewish Monthly*, 4 (1940), 339–53); idem, in: *Studies and Reports of the Bev-Zvi Institute*, 3 (1960), 13–17 (Heb. sect.).

[Cecil Roth]

SUMER, SUMERIANS.

Prehistory

Sumer (Akk. *Šumer* ī Sumerian *Kengir*) is the earliest known name of the land corresponding roughly to the southern half of Iraq. It was first settled about 5000 B.C.E. by agriculturists from the hilly regions to the north and/or east, known as Ubaidians because their remains were first uncovered in al-Ubaid, a tell near Ur. Nothing is known about their language except for traces left in a number of geographical names and words, relating to agriculture and technology, borrowed by the Sumerians. Following the settlement of the land by the Ubaidians, nomadic Semites from the north and west infiltrated the land as settlers and conquerors. The Sumerians themselves did not arrive until about 3500 B.C.E. from their original home, which may have been in the region of the Caspian Sea. Sumerian civilization, therefore, is a product of the ethnic and cultural fusion of Ubaidians, Semites, and Sumerians; it is designated as Sumerian because at the beginning of recorded history it was the Sumerian language and ethos that prevailed throughout the land.

History

History of a legendary character begins in Sumer in the first half of the third millennium with the three partly contemporaneous dynasties of Kish, Erech (Uruk), and Ur. Some of the outstanding rulers of this era were: Etana of Kish, a figure of legendary fame; Enmerkar, Lugalbanda, and Gilgamesh of Erech, three heroic figures celebrated in a cycle of epic tales; and Mes-anne-padda of Ur, the first ruler from whom we have contemporary inscriptions. The three-cornered struggle among these cities so weakened Sumer that for a century or so it came under the domination of the Elamite people to the east. It recovered during the reign of Lugal-anne-mundu of Adab (c. 2500), who is reported to have controlled not only Sumer but some of the neighboring lands as well.

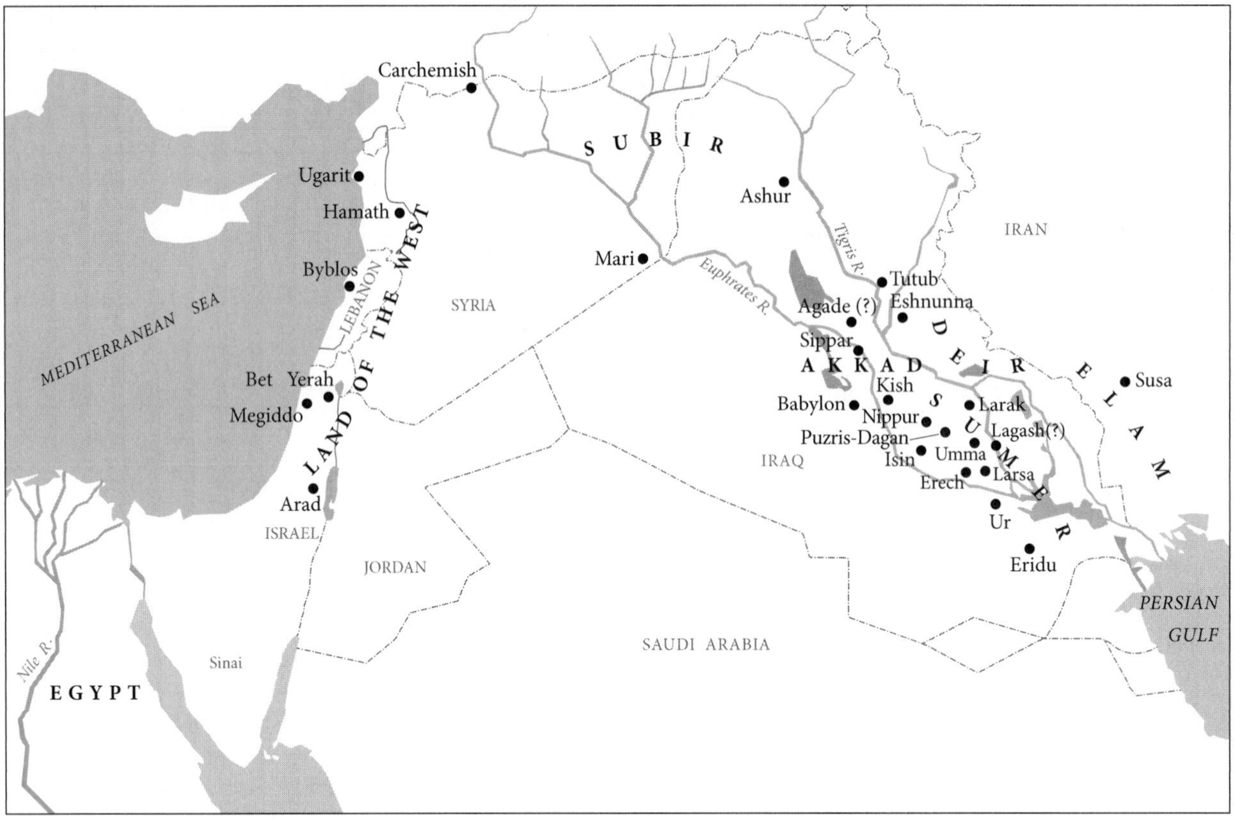

The Near East in the third millennium B.C.E., *showing Sumer lying between the Tigris and Euphrates rivers. Boundaries of modern states are outlined in gray. After Y. Aharoni,* Carta's Atlas of the Bible, *Jerusalem, 1964.*

Authentic history, recorded on significant contemporary documents, begins with the second half of the third millennium. The earliest-known ruler from this period is Mesilim (c. 2475), noted for arbitrating a dispute between the two rival city states, Lagash and Umma. In the century that followed, Lagash played a dominant political role in Sumer; under one of its rulers, Eannatum (c. 2425), it became for a brief period the capital of Sumer. Its last ruler, Urukagina (c. 2360), was history's first-known social reformer; the documents from his reign record a sweeping reform of a whole series of bureaucratic abuses and the restoration of "freedom" to the citizens. Urukagina was defeated by Lugal-zagge-si (c. 2350) of Umma, an ambitious king who moved his capital to Erech and succeeded in making himself ruler of all Sumer. By this time, however, Semites from the north and west had infiltrated northern Sumer, and one of their leaders, Sargon (c. 2325), defeated Lugal-zagge-si and conquered all Sumer, and indeed much of ancient western Asia. Later generations claimed that his power extended even to Egypt and India. Sargon built a new capital, Agade (biblical, Akkad), and following his reign the land came to be known as "Sumer and Akkad."

The Dynasty of Akkad endured for over a century. Toward the end of its rule, Sumer suffered a humiliating invasion by the Gutians from the Zagros hills, and thus came under Gutian domination for close to a century (c. 2200–2100). Throughout much of this period, however, the city of Lagash seemed to flourish, and one of its rulers, Gudea (c. 2140), whose statues and inscriptions have made him one of the figures best known to the modern world, exercised considerable power in spite of the Gutian overlordship.

Sumer was finally liberated from its Gutian yoke and, under the Third Dynasty of Ur, founded by Ur-Nammu (c. 2100), a king noted as the promulgator of the first-known law code, it experienced a remarkable renaissance. Ur-Nammu's son, Shulgi (c. 2080), was one of the great monarchs of the ancient world. A rare combination of statesman, soldier, administrator, and patron of music and literature, he founded Sumer's two leading academies at Nippur and Ur. The last of the dynasty, the pious, pathetic Ibbi-Sin (c. 2015), was a victim of infiltration by the nomadic Amurru from the west, of unrelenting military attacks by the Elamites from the east, and of traitorous intrigues by his own governors and generals. Ur was finally destroyed and Ibbi-Sin carried off to Elam, a calamity long mourned by the poets of Sumer in dolorous laments. Following the destruction of Ur, Ishbi-Irra, one of Ibbi-Sin's traitorous generals, established a dynasty in Isin (c. 2000) that lasted for some 200 years. Isin was destroyed by Rim-Sin (c. 1800), a king of neighboring Larsa, who, in turn, was subjugated by Hammurapi (c. 1750) of Babylon. With the reign of

Hammurapi, the history of Sumer comes to an end, and that of Babylonia begins.

Society

Sumerian society was predominantly urban in character; large and small cities dotted the landscape and shaped its social, political, and economic life. Physically the city was rather drab and unattractive. Streets were narrow, crooked, and winding; they were unpaved, uncleaned, and unsanitary. Houses were thick-walled mudbrick compounds of several rooms, with here and there a more elegant two-story home. But the city had its broad boulevards, busy bazaar, and tempting public square. Above all, there was the sacred precinct with its monumental temple and sky-reaching ziggurat. The citizen took great pride in his city and loved it dearly, as is manifest from the heart-breaking laments in which the poets bewailed its destruction.

The population of the city, which may have varied from 10,000 to 50,000, consisted of free citizens, serf-like clients, and foreign and native slaves. Some of the free citizens were high temple functionaries, important palace officials, and rich landowners; together these formed a kind of noble class. The majority of free citizens were farmers and fishermen, artisans and craftsmen, merchants and scribes. The serf-like clients were dependents of the temple, palace, and rich estates; they were usually given small plots of land for temporary possession, as well as rations of food and wool. Slaves were the property of their owners, but had certain legal rights: they could borrow money, engage in business, and buy their freedom.

The basic unit of society was the family. Marriage was arranged by the parents, and the betrothal, often accompanied by a written contract, was legally recognized as soon as the groom presented a bridal gift to the bride's father. Women had high legal standing: they could hold property, engage in business, and qualify as witnesses. But the husband could divorce his wife on relatively slight grounds and could marry a second wife if the first was childless. Children were under the absolute authority of the parents and could be disinherited or even sold into slavery.

Politically, the cities were governed by a viceroy who was subject to the king. Kingship was hereditary, but usurpers were frequent, and capitals changed from time to time. The king's word and authority were supreme, but he was not an arbitrary despot; as intermediary between the people and their gods, it was his responsibility to insure the prosperity and well-being of the land by leadership in war, the upkeep of the irrigation system, the building and restoration of the temples and their ziggurats, and the preservation and promotion of law and justice. There were also city assemblies of free citizens which originally wielded considerable power, but later became consultative bodies.

Religion

The Sumerians believed that the universe and everything in it were created by four deities: the heaven-god An, the air-god Enlil, the water-god Enki, and the mother-goddess Ninhursag. To help them operate the universe effectively, these four deities, with Enlil as their leader, gave birth to, or "fashioned," a large number of lesser gods and goddesses, and placed them in charge of its various components and elements. All the gods were anthropomorphic and functioned in accordance with duly prescribed laws and regulations; though originally immortal, they suffered death if they over-stepped their bounds. Man was created for the sole purpose of serving the gods and supplying them with food and shelter, hence the building of temples and the offering of sacrifices were man's prime duties. Sumerian religion, therefore, was dominated by priest-conducted rites and rituals; the most important of these was the New Year sacred marriage rite celebrating the mating of the king with the goddess of love and procreation. Ethically, the Sumerians cherished all the generally accepted virtues. But sin and evil, suffering, and misfortune were, they believed, also divinely planned and inevitable; hence each family had its personal god to intercede for them in time of misfortune and need. Worst of all, death and descent to the dark, dreary netherworld were man's ultimate lot, and life on earth was therefore man's most treasured possession.

The Written Word

Sumer's most significant contribution to civilization was the development of the cuneiform system of writing into an effective tool of communication. It began about 3000 B.C.E. as a crude pictographic script used for simple administrative memoranda, in which the signs represented ideograms or logograms; it ended up a thousand years later as a flexible phonetic syllabary adaptable to every kind of writing: legal, historical, epistolary, and literary. To teach and disseminate it, schools were established throughout the land, and thus formal education came into being. For purposes of instruction, the schoolmen developed a curriculum consisting of copying and memorizing especially prepared "textbooks" inscribed with long lists of words and phrases that covered every field of knowledge available to them: linguistic, botanical, zoological, geographical, mineralogical, and artifactual. An important part of the curriculum was mathematics, since no scribe could function as a competent secretary, accountant, or administrator without a thorough knowledge of the sexagesimal system of notation current throughout the land; the students had to copy, study, and memorize scores of tablets involving all sorts of mathematical operations, as well as numerous problem texts involving their practical application.

See also *Mesopotamia.

Biblical Echoes

There are a number of biblical words that go back in all probability to Sumerian origin: *ʿanak* (Sumerian *naga*), "tin"; *ʿeden* (*edin*), "Eden"; *gan* (*gan*), "garden"; *hekhal* (*egal*), "palace"; *ḥiddeqel* (*idiglat*), "Tigris"; *ʾikkar* (*engar*), "farmer"; *kisse* (*guza*), "chair"; *malaḥ* (*malaḥ*), "sailor"; *perat* (*buranum*), "Euphrates"; *shir* (*sir*), "song"; *tammuz* (*dumuzi*), "Tammuz"; *tel* (*dul*), "mound"; *tifsar* (*dubsar*), "scribe"; *tomer* (*nimbar*), "palm-tree." Far more significant are the literary motifs, themes, patterns, and ideas that go back to Sumerian prototypes: the existence of a primeval sea; the separation of heaven and earth; the creation of man from clay imbued with the breath of life; the creative power of the divine word; several "paradise" motifs; the Flood story; the Cain-Abel rivalry; the Tower of Babel and confusion of tongues; the notion of a personal, family god; divine retribution and national catastrophe; plagues as divine punishment; the "Job" motif of suffering and submission; the nature of death and the netherworld dreams as foretokens of the building of temples. Not a few of the biblical laws go back to Sumerian origins, and in such books as Psalms, Proverbs, Lamentations, and the Song of Songs there are echoes of the corresponding Sumerian literary genres. Sumerian influence on the Hebrews came indirectly through the Canaanites, Assyrians, and Babylonians, although to judge from the Abraham story and the often suggested Ḥabiru-Hebrew equation, the distant forefathers of the biblical Hebrews may have had some direct contact with the Sumerians. The Biblical word for Sumer is generally assumed to be Shinar (Heb. שִׁנְעָר; Gen. 10:10). It has also been suggested that Shinar represents the cuneiform *šum(er)-ur(i)*, i.e., Sumer and Akkad, and that the biblical equivalent of Sumer is Shem (from cuneiform *šum(er)*); hence the *anshe ha-shem* of the days of yore in Genesis 6:4.

BIBLIOGRAPHY: SELECTED BIBLIOGRAPHY: S.N. Kramer, *The Sumerians* (1963), 343–6. SPECIALIZED AND DETAILED BIBLIOGRAPHY: C.J. Gadd, *The Cities of Babylonia* (CAH², 1962), 54–60; idem, *The Dynasty of Agade and the Gutian Invasion* (CAH², 1963), 49–54; idem, *Babylonia c. 2120–1800* B.C.E. (CAH², 1965), 50–56; idem, *Hammurabi and the End of His Dynasty* (CAH², 1965), 55–62.

[Samuel Noah Kramer]

SUMMERS, LAWRENCE H. (1954–) U.S. economist, secretary of the Treasury, 27th president of Harvard University. Born in New Haven, Connecticut, Summers is the son of two noted economists, Robert and Anita Summers, and nephew of two Nobel laureates. His father's brother, Paul *Samuelson, won the Nobel prize in economics in 1970, and his mother's brother, Kenneth *Arrow, won the same prize two years later.

Larry Summers grew up in Penn Valley, Pennsylvania, in the Philadelphia suburbs, and attended the Lower Merion public schools. At 16 he was accepted for admission to Massachusetts Institute of Technology, where he majored in economics and was an active member of the debate team before graduating in 1975. For graduate school, Summers moved down the Charles River to Harvard University and studied under renowned economist Martin Feldstein. After completing his dissertation, "An Asset-Price Approach to Capital Income Taxation," Summers received his Ph.D. in economics in 1982. He had already been a member of the economics faculty at MIT for three years, where he had been named an assistant professor in 1979 and an associate professor in 1982.

Upon receipt of his Ph.D., Summers went to Washington to serve as a domestic policy economist for the President's Council of Economic Advisors. One year later, Summers, then 28, returned to Harvard as the youngest member of the economics faculty to be granted tenure.

Summers' research at Harvard was broad ranging, with many of his most important contributions coming in the fields of public finance, labor economics, financial economics, and macroeconomics. He also produced research on topics in international economics, developmental economics, economic demography, and economic history.

In 1987, Summers was named Nathaniel Ropes Professor of Political Economy at Harvard and was the first social scientist to win the Congressionally established Alan T. Waterman Award from the National Science Foundation. In 1993, Summers received the prestigious John Bates Clark Medal from the American Economic Association, an award given every two years to the outstanding American economist under the age of 40.

Summers returned to Washington in 1991, serving this time as vice president of development economics and chief economist at the World Bank. Summers guided the Bank's research, statistics, and training programs, and created strategies for assisting developing nations and the Bank's global loans. Among his highest profile efforts was a publication that demonstrated the tremendous return on investing in educating girls in developing countries.

Two years later, President Clinton appointed Summers undersecretary of the Treasury for International Affairs, under then-Secretary Lloyd Bentsen, giving Summers authority over building and executing U.S. international economic policy. In 1995, incoming Secretary Robert Rubin promoted Summers to the Treasury Department's number two post, deputy secretary of the Treasury, where he played a high-profile role handling many of the United States' economic, financial, and tax matters on the domestic and global stages. At this time, Summers worked closely with Alan Greenspan, chairman of the Federal Reserve, formulating governmental responses to several financial crises in developing nations around the world.

When Rubin announced his resignation in 1999, President Clinton chose Summers to be the next secretary of the Treasury, and the Senate confirmed him on July 2. Summers remained Treasury secretary until President Clinton's second term ended in January 2001. As secretary, Summers served as the president's chief financial advisor. He managed a diverse department with a workforce of almost 150,000 employees spread across over a dozen bureaus and offices in such areas as trade policy, law enforcement, and currency production.

Summers's efforts as secretary of the Treasury include helping build an enormous pay down of U.S. national debt, managing the enactment of the most sweeping financial deregulation in 60 years, reforming the International Monetary Fund and international financial architecture as a whole, and securing debt relief for the world's poorest nations. At the conclusion of his term, Summers received the department's highest honor, the Alexander Hamilton Medal, named after the first secretary of the Treasury.

After leaving Treasury, Summers served as the Arthur Okun Distinguished Fellow in Economics, Globalization, and Governance at the Washington-based think-tank, the Brookings Institution. His work there continued to focus on international financial crises.

In the spring of 2001, after a nine-month search to replace outgoing President Neil Rudenstine, the President and Fellows of Harvard College announced their election of Summers, then 47, as the 27th president of Harvard University. Summers officially assumed the office on July 1, 2001. His tenure as president was marked by such university priorities as enhancing financial aid for students from families of modest means, expanding opportunities for students to study and work outside the United States, encouraging a comprehensive review and renewal of the undergraduate academic experience, spurring a range of interdisciplinary initiatives in the sciences as well as other academic domains, and planning for a major physical expansion of the Harvard campus. His address focusing attention on antisemitism in the world from the Chapel of Harvard University generated international attention. Summers began these well-publicized remarks by expressing astonishment that the world situation had so changed that he would have to speak forthrightly of this problem. Summers resigned the Harvard presidency in March 2006.

[Sheryl Sandberg (2nd ed.)]

SUMPTUARY LAWS, enactments issued by communities against luxury and ostentation; frequently combined with a distinctly class aim – that each should dress according to his standing in the community – allied to the wish to help people withstand the temptation of conspicuous consumption beyond their means. The sumptuary laws were also designed to put an end to anti-Jewish agitations stemming from accusations of ostentatious living. **Takkanot* of a sumptuary nature referred either to dress and jewelry or to the size of banquets held at weddings and circumcision ceremonies and the number of guests permitted to attend them: e.g., the Rhenish *synods of 1202–23 limited banquets to those who participated in the religious ceremony. A conference held in 1418 at Forlí, Italy, limited the number of guests who could be invited to a wedding to 20 men, ten women, five girls, and all the relatives up to second cousins. They also permitted the wearing of fur-lined jackets, in any color other than black, provided that the sleeves and the garments themselves were not fringed with silk. The Castilian synod convened at Valladolid in 1432 forbade Jews aged 15 and over to "wear any cloak of gold thread, olive-colored material, or silk, or any cloak trimmed" with these materials on occasions other than "a time of festivity or at a reception of a lord or a lady, or at balls or similar social occasions." In the 16th and 17th centuries the communities of Salonika, Mantua, and Rome issued periodic anti-luxury regulations. The Cracow community ordinances of 1595 contained paragraphs on sumptuary laws. The Lithuanian Council (see *Councils of the Lands) in 1637, referring to its previous regulations which had been wholly disregarded, empowered local rabbis to decide how many guests might be invited to festive meals. The Polish Council of Four Lands in 1607 enjoined Jews from wearing gentile apparel "in order that the Jews be distinguished by their dress." In 1659 the number of invited guests at a circumcision was scaled according to the host's means: "a person who pays two zlotys in taxes may invite 15 persons, four zlotys 20 persons, six zlotys 25 persons, including the rabbi, the preacher, the cantor, and the beadle." In Moravia the cost of wedding clothes was determined by the amount of the dowry. In Carpentras, the papal possession in southeastern France, sumptuary regulations were adopted in three stages (1712–40). In many places these statutes were honored more in the breach than in the observance.

BIBLIOGRAPHY: Baron, Community, 2 (1942), 301–7; Halpern, Pinkas, 17, 91, 460; J.R. Marcus, *Jew in Medieval World* (1960), 193–7.

[Isaac Levitats]

SUN (Heb., שֶׁמֶשׁ; poetical form חַמָּה; Isa. 24:23; 30:26; Song 6:10, et al.). A deity for Israel's neighbors, the sun is for Israel "the greater light to rule the day", created on the fourth day of creation (Gen. 1:16). In Joseph's dream, the sun and the moon personify his parents (Gen. 37:9–10). In Joshua 10:12–14, the sun is said to have stood still to give the Israelites time to defeat the Amorites.

Cult

In the Bible, the sun is either feminine or masculine in gender. As a deity it is masculine in Mesopotamia, and feminine in Ugarit, South Arabia, and other places. The Hittites worshiped a god and a goddess of the sun. Under the Sumerian name Uta or the Semitic Shamash, the sun, as the god of justice, was worshiped especially at the temple of Ebabbar in Sippar, in northern Babylonia. In the stele of Hammurapi's code from Susa, Hammurapi is depicted standing before Shamash who is seated on a throne (see Pritchard, Pictures, 175, no. 515).

The rare word for sun חֶרֶס (Job 9:7; cf. *har ḥeres* in Judg. 1:35, identical with *ir shemesh* in Josh. 19:41) has no known cognate in the Semitic languages.

The cult of the sun, very popular in Palestine – as is attested by place-names such as Beth-Shemesh, En-Shemesh, Ir-Shemesh – was forbidden in Deuteronomy 4:19 and 17:3. It was, nevertheless, introduced into Judah by Manasseh (II Kings 21:3, 5). King Josiah abolished the cult (II Kings 23:5) and destroyed the horses and chariots of the sun placed "by the kings of Judah at the entrance of the Temple" (23:11).

See Host of *Heaven; *Moon; *Sundial.

In the *Aggadah*

The usual word for "sun" in rabbinic literature is *ḥammah*, although *shemesh* also occurs. The sun and the moon were created on the 28th of Elul (PD-RE 8). Although they were originally equal in size, jealousy induced dissensions between them, each claiming to be greater than the other. This necessitated the reduction in size of one of them, and the moon was chosen to be degraded because it had unlawfully intruded into the sun's domain. This is based on the phenomenon that the moon is sometimes visible while the sun is still above the horizon (PD-RE 6; Gen. R. 6:3). Originally, the sun was designated as Jacob's tutelary luminary but later God assigned it to Esau, the moon being designated for Jacob. For this reason the Jewish people reckon by the lunar calendar (Gen. R. 6:3). It was God's original intention that the sun alone should furnish light to the earth. However, when He foresaw the future idolatrous worship of the heavenly objects, He decided that it would be better to have two large celestial bodies so that the danger of one becoming a central deity would be minimized (Gen. R. 6:1). For this reason, the sun and moon stand in judgment daily before God, ashamed to go forth, pleading "People worship us and anger the Holy One, blessed be He!" (Mid. Ps. to 19:11). When Joshua bade the sun stand still it first refused, but complied when Joshua said, "Faithless servant! Did not my ancestor [Joseph] see you in his dream, bowing down to him?" (Gen. R. 84:11).

God placed the sun in the second firmament because placing it in the one nearest the earth would have consumed all beings by its heat (Mid. Ps. to 19:13). Indeed, the sun is kept in a sheath. In the future, God will draw forth the sun from its sheath and the wicked will be consumed by its intense heat. Hence during that period there will be no Gehinnom (Ned. 8b). Simultaneously, the sun will heal the righteous of all ills, and will be a glorious ornament for them (Ned. 8b). The sun ascends by means of 366 steps, and descends by 183 in the east and 183 in the west. There are 366 windows in the firmament through which the sun successively emerges and retires. These windows are arranged so as to regulate the sun's movements in accordance with the *tekufot* ("seasons") of the year. The sun bows down before God and declares its obedience to His commands. Three letters of God's name are written on the sun's heart, and it rides in a chariot. One set of angels leads it by day and another set leads it by night (PD-RE 6).

The rotation of the sun causes the emission of beams and rays just as dust is produced by sawing wood. The sound which the sun makes during its rotations would be heard were it not for the din of the city of Rome (Yoma 20b). The rabbis differ as to the color of the sun. One holds that its natural color is truly red as it appears at sunrise and sunset, yet it appears white during the day because its powerful rays dim the sight of man. Another says the sun is actually white, but it appears red in the morning when it passes through and reflects the red roses of the Garden of Eden, and also toward evening when it passes through and reflects the fires of Gehinnom (BB 84a). The Talmud deduces the healing efficacy of sunlight from the verse "But unto you... shall the sun of righteousness arise with healing in its wings" (Mal. 3:20; Ned. 8b). Abraham possessed a precious stone which healed the sick. When he died God set it in the sphere of the sun (BB 16b). Sunshine on the Sabbath is considered a blessing for the poor because they have the leisure time to enjoy its rays (Ta'an. 8b).

An eclipse of the sun is an evil sign for the gentiles while an eclipse of the moon augurs evil for the Jews. When the solar eclipse occurs in the eastern horizon it forecasts bad tidings for the inhabitants of the East; if in the western horizon it betokens ill to those of the West; while if it occurs in the zenith it threatens the entire world. When the color of the eclipse is red it symbolizes war; when gray, famine; when changing from red to gray, both war and famine. When the eclipse occurs in the beginning of the day or of the night it signifies that evil will come soon; if late in the day or night, then it will arrive tardily. Jews who are true to their faith need not worry about these premonitions since the prophet already said: "....be not dismayed at the signs of heaven, for the nations are dismayed at them" (Jer. 10:2; Suk. 29a).

See also *Sun, Blessing of.

BIBLIOGRAPHY: Ginzberg, Legends, index.

[Alfred Rubens]

SUN, BLESSING OF THE (Heb. בִּרְכַּת הַחַמָּה), a prayer service in which the sun is blessed in thanksgiving for its creation and its being set into motion in the firmament on the fourth day of the world (Gen. 1:16–19). The ceremony is held once every 28 years. It takes place after the morning prayer, when the sun is about 90° above the eastern horizon, on the first Wednesday of the month of Nisan. The date is based on calculations by the *amora* *Abbaye, according to whom the vernal equinox cycle (called *maḥzor gadol*) always begins then (Ber. 59b). Although Abbaye's method became obsolete after the adoption of R. *Adda's calendar, the ceremony has not fallen into desuetude. The order of the recital is as follows: Psalms 84:12, 72:5; 75:2, Malachi 3:20, Psalms 97:6 and 148, the benediction: "Praised be the Maker of creation," which is followed by Psalms 19 and 121, the hymn *El Adon* (of the *Shaḥarit* prayer of the Sabbath), the *baraita* of Abbaye (Ber. 59b), and the quotation of an *aggadah* by R. Hananiah b. Akashya (Mak. 3:16). The rite ends with a short thanksgiving prayer in which the congregation expresses gratitude for having been sustained until this day, and the hope to live and reach the days of the Messiah and of the fulfillment of the prophesy of Isaiah "and the light of the sun shall be sevenfold, as the light of the seven days" (Isa. 30:26). The dates for the ceremony in the second half of the 20th century were April 8, 1953 and March 18, 1981. For the first half of the 21st century the dates are April 1, 2009 and March 18, 2037

See also *Calendar.

BIBLIOGRAPHY: Sh. Ar., OḤ 229:2; Maim. Yad, Berakhot, 10:18; S. Segner, *Or ha-Ḥammah* (1897); J.M. Tukaczinsky, *Kunteres Birkat ha-Ḥammah* (1897); Eisenstein, Yisrael, s.v. *Birkat ha-Ḥammah*; I. Epstein (ed.), *The Babylonian Talmud*, Zera'im, 1 (1948), 369–71n.; ET, 4 (1952), 453–55.

SUNBAT (**Sambutia**), town of Lower *Egypt. The Jewish community seems to have been very old because one of *Abraham b. Sahlan's ancestors is mentioned in his family tree as having lived there in the ninth century. The community is also mentioned in the list of contributions for the redemption of prisoners in the middle of the 12th century. *Maimonides appealed to the Jews of Sunbat, in a circular letter addressed to the communities of the eastern region of the Delta, and Anatoli b. Joseph, the *dayyan* of *Alexandria at that time, wrote a poem dedicated to Shabbetai, a teacher in Sunbat. It seems that the community existed until the 17th century because Joseph b. Isaac *Sambari reports that in 1623 a *Sefer Torah* was transferred from Sunbat to a synagogue in *Cairo.

BIBLIOGRAPHY: Mann, Egypt, 1 (1920), 96, 244; 2 (1922), 290; Mann, Texts, 1 (1931), 412–3; Neustadt (Ayalon), in: *Zion*, 2 (1936/37), 253; Ashtor, in: JJS, 18 (1967), 34–36.

[Eliyahu Ashtor]

SUNDERLAND, industrial city in N.E. England. The first Jewish settler in Sunderland was Abraham Samuel, a jeweler and silversmith. A community probably existed in the 1750s; a rabbi, Jacob Joseph, came from Holland in 1790, while the first cemetery dates from slightly earlier. Since in the 18th century Sunderland was a coal port of some importance, trading with Holland, Scandinavia, and Danzig, it attracted Jewish settlers from Holland, Bohemia (after foreign Jews were expelled in 1763), and Poland (between 1760 and 1780). The two congregations, Polish and Israelite (Dutch and Bohemian settlers), combined in 1857 to form the Sunderland Hebrew Congregation. Around the 1870s immigration began from Krottingen (Lithuania), again by way of the cheap sea route from Danzig. A larger influx followed the great fire in Krottingen in 1889. This element and other Orthodox Eastern European Jews in the 1890s formed the *bet ha-midrash* which has contributed to Sunderland's reputation for Jewish observance and learning. It has a yeshivah and a *kolel* (institute for higher talmudical studies). In 1968 there was an estimated Jewish population of 1,350. In the mid-1990s the estimated Jewish population dropped to approximately 210. The 2001 British census found 45 declared Jews in Sunderland. One reason for this apparent sharp decline in population probably lies in the fact that *Gateshead, with its famous yeshivah, is situated in the same conurbation in northeast England. Sunderland has an Orthodox synagogue.

BIBLIOGRAPHY: A. Levy, *History of the Sunderland Jewish Community* (1956); JYB.

[Vivian David Lipman]

SUNDIAL. Although sundials can be traced back to earlier periods in Egypt and Mesopotamia, the earliest textual reference to a sundial appears to be II Kings 20:8–11 (cf. Isa. 38:7–8). There a shadow-tracking device, ascribed to Ahaz, is used for a sign that Hezekiah would be healed. The Masoretic Text speaks of *ma'alot ahaz*, literally "the steps of Ahaz." Various ancient versions and commentators disagree over whether the device is an actual sundial or a set of stairs attached to Ahaz's palace. Unfortunately, 1QIsa[a], which contains the variant *ma'alot 'lyt*, does not resolve this question.

A fragment of a portable, disk-shaped sundial excavated at Tel Gezer has been dated to the reign of Merneptah (1225–1215 B.C.E.) whose cartouches were inscribed on its back. Earlier representations of this type were found on the ceilings of the early 15th century tombs of Amenhotep I and Serenmuth. These appear as a circle subdivided by radiating lines into 24 equiangular sections.

A later development, the sundial found at Qumran, was shaped like a shallow bowl with three circular dials and a small vertical *gnomon* in its center. The upper dial was divided into approximately 90 sections. The middle dial resembled those known from I Enoch 72, with 18 equiangular 20° "parts." This appears to be a shallow form of the *hemisphaericum of Aristarchus* described by Vitruvius (end first cent. B.C.E.).

For the preceding two dials, since the increments were represented by equally spaced "steps" on each dial, and since the movement of the shadow of the gnomon travels faster at midday and slower at the day's beginning or end, the actual time that the shadow spent within each step varied accordingly. Also, the number of steps through which the shadow passed each day either increased or decreased depending on the season. The solstices, equinoxes, and months (or "gates") were tracked by noting where the first shadow of the gnomon became visible on the dial or by the rising of certain constellations at night.

The latest and most common sundials were the typical Greco-Roman, quarter-spherical *hemicyclium*, and the "conical" *conicum*. Twelve equiangular sections on these dials measured hours which in real time varied both according to the time of the day and season. Three concentric circles, running perpendicular to the hour lines, marked the full extent of the shadow at the four cardinal points of the year.

BIBLIOGRAPHY: S. Adam, "Ancient Sundials of Israel," in: *BSS Bulletin* 14 (2002), 52–57, 109–114; Y. Yadin, "*Ma'alot Ahaz*," in: *Eretz Israel* 5 (1959), 91–96; pl. 10 (Heb.).

[Stephen Pfann (2nd ed.)]

SUPERCOMMENTARIES ON THE PENTATEUCH, commentaries mostly on the chief commentators of the Pentateuch – *Rashi, Abraham *Ibn Ezra, and *Naḥmanides. Supercommentaries began to be composed soon after the appearance of the original commentaries. By far the largest number of such supercommentaries are on Rashi, the most popular commentator on the Pentateuch. An early supercommentary was *Minḥat Yehudah* (Leghorn, 1783). It was compiled by *Judah b. Eliezer, probably in Troyes, in the year 1313. The author quotes comments on Rashi by his teacher and earlier authorities. The most extensive supercommentary is by Elijah *Mizraḥi. It was printed for the first time in Venice in 1527, some time after the author's death, and in itself is largely quoted and discussed by later supercommentators. Prominent rabbis who wrote supercommentaries on Rashi included: Israel *Isserlein (*Be'urim al Perush Rashi…*, Venice, 1519); Obadiah di *Bertinoro (*Amar Neke*, Pisa, 1810); Samuel *Almosnino, whose supercommentary was printed in c. 1525 in Constantinople with three other supercommentaries; Solomon *Luria (*Yeri'ot Shelomo*, Prague, 1608); Moses *Mat (*Ho'il Moshe, ibid.*, 1611); Mordecai *Jaffe (*Levush ha-Orah*, Prague, 1604); *Ḥayyim b. Bezalel (*Be'er Mayim Ḥayyim*, 1694–99); *Judah Loew b. Bezalel (*Gur Aryeh*, Prague, 1578–79); Issachar Baer Eilenburg (*Ẓeidah la-Derekh*, Prague, 1623–24); *David

b. Samuel ha-Levi, author of *Turei Zahav* (*Divrei David*, Dyhernfurth, 1689); David *Pardo (*Maskil le-David*, Venice, 1760); and Ḥayyim *Palache (Palaggi) (*U-Vaḥarta baḤayyim*, Smyrna, 1874). *Siftei Ḥakhamim* (Frankfurt on the Main, 1712) by Shabbetai *Bass is primarily a selection from other supercommentaries. A critical edition of the text of Rashi's commentary with a supercommentary, called *Zekhor le-Avraham*, was prepared by Abraham *Berliner (1866).

The concise, abrupt, and enigmatic style of Abraham ibn Ezra gave rise to numerous supercommentaries, not only on his commentary on the Pentateuch, but also on those to other books of the Bible. However, most of these have remained in manuscript. Small selections from some of them have been published in modern times. Early supercommentaries on Ibn Ezra's Pentateuch commentary which appeared in print were *Ẓafenat Pa'ne'aḥ* (complete edition 1911–30) by Joseph b. Eliezer Bonfils, *Mekor Ḥayyim* (Mantova, 1559) by Samuel *Zarza, and *Megillat Setarim* (Venice, 1554) by Samuel ibn *Motot – all three from the 14th century. Another 14th century product, *Perush ha-Sodot shel ha-RABE al ha-Torah* deals only with Ibn Ezra's enigmatic statements. An abridged version of it was published in 1903 (in I. Last, *Asarah Kelei Kesef*, pt. 2). The work has been doubtfully ascribed to Joseph ibn *Kaspi. Other supercommentaries on Ibn Ezra were written by Moses *Almosnino, Yom Tov Lipmann *Heller, and Solomon *Maimon. Modern supercommentaries includes those by Moses Cremieux, Judah Leib Krinski, Isaac Meijler, and Leopold Fleischer. The supercommentary of Solomon Zalman Netter, which was first published in 1859, is to a large extent based on early supercommentaries.

One of the chief commentators on the Pentateuch, Naḥmanides, was widely quoted and discussed by subsequent commentators. His critical observations on Rashi were dealt with by Rashi's supercommentators, while kabbalists elucidated his kabbalistic allusions. Special treatises dealing with these kabbalistic references were written by the 14th-century kabbalists Shem Tov b. Abraham *Ibn Gaon, Joshua *Ibn Shu'ayb, Meir ibn *Sahula, and *Isaac b. Samuel of Acre. Isaac *Aboab ("the last *Gaon* of Castille") wrote a supercommentary on Naḥmanides (Constantinople, 1525). Joseph *Caro was said to have written explanations on parts of Rashi's and Naḥmanides' commentaries. Among rabbis and scholars of modern times who wrote supercommentaries or explanatory notes on Naḥmanides may be mentioned Mordecai Gimpel *Jaffe, Abraham Lieblein, Jacob Aryeh Frankel, Isaac *Maarsen, Aryeh L. Steinhart, and Joseph Patsanovski. New critical editions of Naḥmanides' commentary accompanied by a supercommentary were prepared by Ẓevi Menahem Eisenstadt (1958–61; on Genesis only) and by C.D. Chavel (1959–60; on the whole Pentateuch).

BIBLIOGRAPHY: I. Schapiro, *Parshanei Rashi al ha-Torah* (1940) (repr. from *Bitzaron*, 2 (1940), 26–37); M. Friedlaender, *Essays on the Writings of Abraham ibn Ezra* (1877), 213–52; N. Ben-Menahem, in: *Aresheth*, 3 (1961), 71–92; Benjacob, Oẓar, 475, 479 (no. 729); I. Rivkind, in: KS, 4 (1927/28), 276; M. Kasher and J.B. Mandelbaum, *Sarei ha-Elef* (1959), 59–60.

[Tovia Preschel]

SUPRASKY, YEHOSHUA (1879–1948), General Zionist leader in Ereẓ Israel. Born in Goniadz, Bialystok district, Suprasky engaged in trade and industry. He was a delegate to the Zionist Conference in Minsk (1902), was a member of the Zionist central committee in Russia, and worked for investment in Ereẓ Israel. He visited Ereẓ Israel in 1912 and in 1914 and settled there in 1920. He founded the Ha-Manḥil Company to build houses in Tel Aviv as well as the Tiberias Hot Springs Co. Ltd., and the Kinneret Company in Tiberias. He was a member of the Tel Aviv municipal council (1925–32), vice chairman of the community board, and a member of the Va'ad Le'ummi. A leader of the *General Zionists in Palestine and of the world movement, he advocated the encouragement of private initiative in the settlement and upbuilding of Ereẓ Israel. Suprasky was also a member of the Zionist General Council (1921–48), a delegate to 14 Zionist Congresses (from the fifth to the 19th), and a founder of the Mifdeh Ezraḥi (a building and loan fund). Neveh Yehoshu'a in Ramat Gan is named in his honor.

[Abraham Aharoni]

SURA, site of one of the leading Babylonian academies. In fact, two different settlements by the name of Sura are mentioned in the Babylonian Talmud. One was located in Syria at the northern extremity of the Euphrates, a 15-days' journey from *Pumbedita. It was an important station on the caravan route from Pumbedita to Ereẓ Israel (Av. Zar. 16b, which describes the journey and the encampment of R. Zeira during his *aliyah* to Ereẓ Israel from Babylonia). This settlement, however, was not a center of Torah study and therefore little is related about it.

The famous Sura, the important center of Torah studies for several centuries, was located in southern Babylonia, where the Euphrates divided into two rivers. The soil of Sura and its environs was noted for its great fertility. Agricultural activity was centered around vineyards, orchards, wheat, and barley, and the farmers of Sura, among them scholars, were intensively involved in these pursuits. They irrigated their fields with the waters of the Euphrates, planted vineyards, engaged in wine growing and its trade, and reared livestock.

The Persian Period

The growth of Sura was due to the Torah center which was established there by *Rav after going to Babylonia from Ereẓ Israel in 219. There is no knowledge of an earlier *bet midrash* in Sura, and it seems that Sura's earlier inhabitants were unfamiliar with Jewish laws. In the course of time, Rav succeeded in surrounding himself with hundreds of students from the Diaspora; his *bet midrash* and *bet din* became the basis of one of the two most important religious centers in Babylonia. Rav's *takkanot* and legal decisions, his halakhic and aggadic statements and the discussions which opened in their wake, and his actions in public and private life provided the foundation for the Babylonian Talmud. After Rav's death in 247 Sura lost its central role for seven years, during which time the decisive authority in matters of *halakhah* was wielded by Samuel in *Nehardea.

After Samuel's death in 254, Sura regained its prominence under the leadership of Rav *Huna, the disciple of Rav. It maintained this status until the end of the third century. At the end of the 290s the academy of Pumbedita rose in importance, and under the leadership of *Judah b. Ezekiel became the center of *halakhah* in Babylonia. A *bet midrash* for the study of the Torah and teaching continued to exist in Sura, but its importance and decisive authority were not regained until the days of Rav *Ashi (367–427), who even managed to broaden the scope of the academy. In addition to the masses of students who streamed there, especially during two months of the year, he also instituted the *Shabbeta de-Rigla* in Sura, which was attended by the eminent *ḥakhamim* of Babylonia, headed by the *exilarch and his retinue. Rav Ashi also built a new synagogue. During his time the academy was transferred to *Mata Meḥasya, which was very near Sura. After the death of Rav Ashi, who was one of the most important editors of the Babylonian Talmud, the central religious role of Sura diminished. In the period of the **savoraim* the number of *ḥakhamim* and students decreased as a result of the upheavals which followed the persecutions of Firūz and Yazdagird.

BIBLIOGRAPHY: Neusner, Babylonia, indexes; B.M. Lewin (ed.), *Iggeret R. Sherira Ga'on* (1921), 100–2, 105–8, 114–8; Assaf, Ge'onim, 42–70, 261–78; S. Assaf, in: *Ha-Shilo'aḥ*, 39 (1921), 218–20; idem, in: *Tarbiz*, 11 (1939/40), 146–52, 156–9; J. Mann, ibid., 5 (1933/34), 148–79, 280–1; Mann, Texts, 1 (1931), 63–75, 145–79; Abramson, Merkazim, 14, 35–37, 59, 73–76, 113, 159; Neubauer, *Chronicles*, 2 (1887), 78, 83–84; A. Scheiber, in: *Zion*, 18 (1953), 6–13; R.S. Weinberg, in: *Sinai*, 65 (1969), 69–99; Shapira, in: B.M. Lewin (ed.), *Ginzei Kedem*, 3 (1925), 3–13; Dinur, Golah, 1 pt. 2 (1961^2), 102–5; S. Schechter, *Saadyana* (1903), 63–74; L. Ginzberg, *Geonica*, 1 (1909), 37–52; G. Margoliouth, in: JQR, 14 (1902), 307–11; A. Cowley, ibid., 18 (1906), 399–405; S. Poznański, in: REJ, 62 (1911), 120–3; J. Mann, in: JQR, 7 (1916/17), 463–4; 8 (1917/18), 362–6; 9 (1918/19), 153–60; 11 (1920/21), 409–22; B. Eshel, *Jewish Settlements in Babylonia during Talmudic Times* (1979), 194–197.

[Eliezer Bashan (Sternberg)]

SURAT, port N. of Bombay. In the 17th century, Portuguese, Dutch, and English trading companies arrived in Surat, for centuries the main trading center between Europe and Asia. A few Jews were among them, often diamond merchants; Anglo-Portuguese Jews in London developed a flourishing trade with Surat though they were not allowed to settle there. A permanent Jewish settlement came into existence in the last decades of the 17th century. First to settle were Dutch-Portuguese merchants from Amsterdam, headed by Pedro Pereira who conducted widespread commercial transactions associated with both the Dutch and the English East India companies. Around 1740, they were followed by Anglo-Ashkenazi Jews, such as Abraham Elias and then, toward the end of the 18th century, by Arabic-speaking Jews from *Aleppo, *Baghdad, and *Basra. One of Surat's leading merchants was Moses *Tobias, who played a prominent role in the affairs of the city. When *Bombay became the British administrative center and *Calcutta rose to prominence, the Jewish settlement in Surat declined and most of its inhabitants moved to one of these two cities. In the 19th century a few individual Jews in government service settled in Surat. Some Jewish tombstones of the 17th and 18th centuries are still preserved.

BIBLIOGRAPHY: Fischel, in: PAAJR, 33 (1965), 1–20.

[Walter Joseph Fischel]

SURE, BARNETT (1891–1960), U.S. biochemist, born in Vilkomir (Ukmerge), Lithuania. Sure went to the U.S. in 1908. He became professor and head of agricultural chemistry department, University of Arkansas in 1927. Sure was an independent discoverer of vitamin E and of a new member of the vitamin B complex. He wrote *The Vitamins in Health and Disease* (1933) and *Little Things in Life: The Vitamins, Hormones and Other Minute Essentials for Health* (1937).

°**SURENHUIS, WILHELM (Surenhuysen, Gulielmus Surenhusius**; (1666–1729), Dutch Hebraist. Surenhuis was professor of Greek and Hebrew at the Amsterdam Athenaeum Illustre and was in close touch with the German Orientalist Johann Christof *Wolff of Hamburg. He published *Dissertatio de natura Pandectarum Hebraicarum* (1704), the exegetical "New Testament catalogue" *Sefer ha-Mashweh* (1713), and *De oratione Dominica Hebraica* (1715), a Hebrew version of the Christian "Lord's Prayer" (with various translations into other languages). However, he is best remembered for his monumental *Versio Latina Mischnae et Commentationes Maimonidis et Obadjae Bertinoro…* (6 vols., 1698–1703) in Hebrew and Latin. Although Surenhuis used a manuscript Spanish version by Jacob *Abendana in preparing his edition, much of the work was original and 40 tractates of the Mishnah were translated by the editor himself. An earlier Latin version by Isaac Abendana, Jacob's brother, remains in manuscript (University of Cambridge, 1663–75). A catalogue of Surenhuis' library appeared in 1730.

BIBLIOGRAPHY: Steinschneider, Cat Bod, 2663; J.W. Wesselius and P.T. van Rooden, in: *StRos*, 26 (1992), 136–48. P.T. van Rooden, in: *Hebrew Study from Ezra to Ben-Yehuda* (1999), 257–67.

[Irene E. Zwiep (2nd ed.)]

SURETYSHIP (Heb. עֲרֵבוּת), one person's undertaking to fulfill the obligation of another toward a third person (called the *arev*, *ḥayyav*, and *nosheh*, respectively). In Jewish law fulfillment of an obligation is secured primarily through the assets of the debtor – "a man's possessions are his surety" (BB 174a; see *Lien) – and it is in addition to this that a person may serve as a surety for the fulfillment of the debtor's obligation toward his creditor.

Suretyship in the Bible and the Talmud

The biblical term *'eravon* ("pledge"), although philologically related to the term *'arev* or *'arevut*, occurs in the sense of an obligation secured by property and not personally (Gen. 38:17ff.; and see Targ. Onk. and Rashi thereto; cf. Neh. 5:3). The form of personal pledge mentioned in the matter of Judah's undertaking to Jacob to be surety for Benjamin's safe return (Gen. 43:9) has no bearing on the present discussion, since Judah was at one and the same time surety and principal debtor (ibid., 8; and see *She'iltot* 32). Detailed discussion of suretyship is to be found in Proverbs, where the surety's undertaking is described as given verbally and accompanied by a handshake (*teki'at kaf*; Prov. 6:1–5; 11:15; 17:18; 22:26; see also Job 17:3). It is likely that a handshake also served as the mode of establishing other kinds of obligations (see Ezra 10:19). In the Book of Proverbs there is a strong exhortation against undertaking a suretyship obligation because, if it is unfulfilled, the creditor might levy payment even on the surety's garments and bedding (20:16; 22:27; 27:13). Since this is the extreme consequence with which the surety is threatened, it may be deduced that the creditor is forbidden to subject the surety to personal bondage, just as he is forbidden from so subjecting the debtor (see *Obligations, Law of). Suretyship involving the bodily subjection of an individual is to be found only in the field of military law, with reference to the taking of hostages in time of war (II Kings 14:14; II Chron. 25:24).

A guarantee to present the debtor before his creditor and the court (on due date) is described in the Talmud as "the law of the Persians" (BB 173b). The existence of this phenomenon in Jewish law was hinted at in geonic times (*She'elot u-Teshuvot ha-Ge'onim*, no. 213), but Maimonides denied the validity of this form of suretyship (Yad, Malveh, 25:14; also see *Hassagot Rabad* and *Maggid Mishneh* thereto). The unfavorable attitude expressed in Proverbs toward the very act of undertaking a suretyship obligation is reflected also, although to a lesser degree, in the apocryphal books (Ecclus. 8:13; 29:17–20). Even in talmudic times suretyship is mentioned as one of the things a man is advised to avoid (Yev. 109a).

Formation of Suretyship

At first Jewish law recognized suretyship only insofar as it was undertaken before or at the time of the creation of the debtor's principal obligation (BB 10:7; "If a man loaned his fellow money on a surety's security..."), because in such an event "he had lent him the money through his trust in the surety" (ibid., 8). R. Ishmael decided that a written suretyship was valid even if it was given after creation of the principal obligation (ibid.; and cf. Ket. 101b–102b). Some of the early *amoraim* held that such a suretyship was valid even if it was undertaken verbally, but the *halakhah* was decided in accordance with the opinion of R. Naḥman, to the effect that a verbal suretyship is valid if given at the time of creation of the principal obligation ("at the time the money is handed over"); otherwise (i.e., "after the money has been handed over") it will only be valid if accompanied by a *kinyan sudar* (see *Acquisition, Modes of; BB 176a–b and Codes). The distinction stems from the general principle in Jewish law that the promissor's "final making up of the mind" (*gemirat ha-da'at*, see *Contract) is an essential precondition of a valid undertaking. Hence it may be presumed that this requirement is satisfied on the part of the surety whenever the loan is given "on his security" – even if undertaken verbally – since he is aware that the very loan is given on the strength of his suretyship; the position is different, however, if the suretyship is given after the execution of the loan transaction, since then the surety's final decision is not manifest unless his verbal undertaking is accompanied by the formality of a *kinyan sudar*. According to the view of the Babylonian *amoraim*, which was accepted as the *halakhah*, the possible absence of a *gemirat ha-da'at* was to be feared more with a suretyship undertaking than with any other kind of undertaking, since the very essence of the suretyship undertaking is tainted with the defect of **asmakhta* – i.e., the surety's confident assumption that the borrower will pay the debt and the claim against him will never materialize. The invalidating effect of *asmakhta* on suretyship was overcome by the scholars through reasoning that the surety derives pleasure from being regarded as trustworthy and a man of means.

In the following cases a verbal suretyship without a *kinyan* is valid even if it is undertaken after establishment of the principal obligation: if it is given on the instructions of the court (BB 176b and codes); if on the strength of the suretyship the lender has returned to the borrower the bond of indebtedness or pledge (Sh. Ar., ḤM 129:3); and if the surety is not an individual but the community or its representative (Resp. Maharam of Rothenburg, ed. Prague, no. 38; see also *Public Authority). Alternatives to a *kinyan sudar* also came in to being. Thus, according to some of the *posekim*, a written suretyship obviates any need for a *kinyan* (Nov. Ramban, and *Beit ha-Beḥirah*, BB 176; Sh. Ar., ḤM 129:4). Suretyship may also be established by handshake whenever custom decrees that an obligation may be established in this way (*Darkhei Moshe*, ḤM 129:5; *Rema*, ḤM 129:5). It is interesting to note the historical changes concerning the use of a handshake as a means of establishing a suretyship obligation. In biblical times it had this function; it fell into complete disuse during the talmudic period, and it appeared again in post-talmudic times under the influence of its use in other contemporary legal systems. According to some of the *posekim*, even a verbal suretyship undertaken after the establishment of the principal obligation is valid if it is the custom to dispense with the need for a formal *kinyan* (see **Minhag*).

Arev and Arev Kabbelan

The *tannaim* and the *amoraim* of Ereẓ Israel knew the regular form of surety (*arev*) in which the creditor must first sue and seek to recover payment from the debtor; only when the debt cannot be satisfied out of the debtor's property may the creditor turn to the surety for payment, because it is presumed that it was the surety's intention to become liable for the debt only in such an event. A creditor who wished to ensure effective recovery of the debt could stipulate with the surety that "I shall recover from whomever I choose," whereupon he could claim directly from the surety whether or not the debtor had sufficient property to satisfy the debt. R. Simeon b. Gamaliel's opinion, that as long as the debtor has property, payment must always be demanded from him first, was not accepted as *halakhah* (BB 10:7; TJ, BB 10:14, 17d, and see statements of R. Johanan, loc. cit.). The Babylonian *amoraim*, however, interpreted these mishnaic statements (in the light of R. Johanan's variant version) to mean that even when the creditor has stipulated with the surety as mentioned above, he may not, in the opinion of all, demand payment from the surety as long as the debtor's known assets, such as land, have not been exhausted. In their opinion, the only case in which the creditor may claim directly from the surety without first excusing the debtor (even if he has known assets) is when the surety is an *arev kabbelan*, that is, when he has carefully formulated his undertaking in a particular manner so as to avoid the use of terms such as "loan" or "suretyship," saying instead, e.g., "Give to him and I shall give to you." Thus, once more, R. Simeon b. Gamaliel's contrary opinion, that the debtor must first be excused if he has any property even if the surety is an *arev kabbelan*, was not accepted as *halakhah* (BB 173b and Tos. ad loc. s.v. *Ḥasurei Meḥasrei*).

An explanation for the restraint on the freedom of contract in suretyship, contrary to the general principle of Jewish law that "contracting out of the Torah" is permissible in matters of civil law, lies in the apprehension expressed by the Babylonian *amoraim* about the surety's lack of final resolve when making a suretyship undertaking, and the resulting inference that the surety does not seriously intend to be bound by his undertaking as long as the debt may be recovered from the principal debtor – even if he has expressly agreed to it (Rashba, Nov. BB 173b). In post-talmudic times the scholars sought ways in which to overcome the restriction on the freedom of stipulation in suretyship because of its limiting effect on the scope of credit transactions. Some scholars interpreted the statements of the Babylonian *amoraim* to mean that they, like the *amoraim* of Ereẓ Israel, held the opinion that the creditor might claim directly from the surety once he has stipulated with the latter to recover "from whomever I choose" (Ibn Miggash, quoted in *Sefer ha-Terumot*, 35:2; Yad, Malveh 25:4; and see Elon, bibl., 203ff.). Other scholars considered the version "I shall recover from whomever I choose" to be ineffective and distinguished it from one worded "I shall recover first from whomever I choose," holding that this entitles the creditor to claim directly from the surety whether or not the debtor has any property (Ramban, Nov. BB 173b; Tur, ḤM 129:17, et al.). The *halakhah* was decided according to the former opinion (Sh. Ar., ḤM 129:14).

The post-talmudic socioeconomic realities spurred a number of further developments designed to enable the creditor to claim directly from the surety, including a regular surety, even without prior stipulation to this effect. Thus it was laid down that if the debtor is violent and does not comply with the judgment of the court, or if he is abroad and the suit against him involves many difficulties, or if he has died, the creditor may claim directly from the surety (Yad, Malveh 25:3; 26:3 and *Maggid Mishneh* thereto; Sh. Ar., ḤM 129:8–12). The creditor always retains the right to claim first from the debtor, even when he is entitled to claim directly from the surety, and the debtor is not entitled to refer him to the surety; however, if the surety is a *kabbelan* who has personally received the money of the loan from the lender and passed it on to the borrower, no legal tie will have been created between lender and borrower, and the lender will be entitled to recover the debt from the surety alone (Yad, Malveh 26:3; Sh. Ar., ḤM 129:15, 19).

Substance and Scope of Suretyship

The surety's obligation is secondary to that of the principal debtor; hence the validity of the suretyship obligation is coextensive with that of the principal obligation, and extinction of the latter automatically terminates the suretyship: "if there is no debt, there is no suretyship" (Resp. Maharashdam, ḤM no. 218). Thus, e.g., if the principal obligation is void because the debtor was acting under duress (see *Ones), the suretyship will be equally ineffective – even though it was undertaken according to the law (ibid. and Resp. Reshakh, pt. 1, no. 44). Moreover, the same result follows even when the underlying principal obligation is essentially valid but cannot be realized against the debtor on account of a procedural defect, as may happen if the name of the debtor and other details mentioned in a bond of indebtedness fit two persons and do not allow for his proper identification, thus barring proceedings against him. In such an event the surety, too, cannot be called upon for payment, not even in the case where he is surety to two debtors who have identical names (Bek. 48a; Tur and Sh. Ar., ḤM 49: 10; cf. also the contrary opinion of *Rema*, ḤM 129:8 and *Baḥ* thereon).

On the other hand, suretyship may be undertaken in respect of only a part of the principal obligation, and the surety may also stipulate that his obligation shall only be in effect for a specified period after the debt has fallen due (Resp. Rashba, vol. 1, no. 1148; *Rema* and standard commentaries to Sh. Ar., ḤM 129:1 and Tur, ibid.; *Arukh ha-Shulḥan*, ḤM 129:7). Suretyship may be undertaken in respect of either an already existing principal obligation or one about to be established, the sole distinction between them being their two different modes of establishment (see above). The validity of suretyship in respect of a debt of an unfixed amount is a matter on which there is a division of opinion in the codes. It was held by some scholars that if the surety has said, "I am surety for whatever amount you shall give," he is liable for the whole amount, "even if one hundred thousand" (Yad, Malveh, 25:13; see Samuel b. Hophni, bibl., ch. 3). According to other *posekim*, the surety is not liable at all in such an event: "since he does not know what it is that he has bound himself for, neither can he have made a final resolve nor has he bound himself" (Yad, loc. cit.). A third opinion is that the suretyship is binding to the extent of the amount for which the surety may reasonably be presumed to have bound himself, with attention given to his financial means (*Hassagot Rabad* and *Maggid Mishneh* loc. cit.). The *halakhah* was decided to the effect that a suretyship for an unspecified amount is valid (Sh. Ar., ḤM 131:13).

Scope of the Surety's Liability

The suretyship obligation includes liability for the expenses incurred by the creditor in claiming payment, such as the costs of a legal suit (Sh. Ar., ḤM 129:10 and *Sma* n. 29), and for any other reasonable loss suffered by the creditor (Tur, ḤM 131:7–10 and Maharik, quoted in *Beit Yosef*, ibid., Sh. Ar., ḤM 131:7–8). According to the majority of the *posekim*, a regular surety is discharged from liability if the creditor, after due date of payment, neglects to recover the debt from the debtor when he has the possibility of doing so (Tur and Sh. Ar., ḤM 131:4; *Beit Yosef* and *Baḥ* thereto). Similarly, "if the debtor was present in the town when the debt fell due for payment and the creditor allowed him to depart the town, he cannot claim from the surety" (*Keneset ha-Gedolah*, ḤM 129; Tur no. 58). The surety is likewise discharged from liability if the creditor releases any of the debtor's property which he holds as a pledge (Resp. Rashba, vol. 1, no. 892; Sh. Ar., ḤM 129:8 and *Rema* thereto; *Sma* ḤM 129–26; *Arukh ha-Shulḥan* ḤM 129:26).

Suretyship in Respect of Different Kinds of Obligations

In general, suretyship may validly be undertaken with reference to all kinds of obligations, regardless of the manner in which they arise (for instance from loan, the most common case, tort (Git. 49b), and so on). In certain cases, however, this has been a matter of halakhic dispute, particularly with reference to the husband's **ketubbah* obligation. Among the *tannaim* and *amoraim* of Ereẓ Israel, and for most of the period of the Babylonian *amoraim*, there was never any doubt that a person could be surety for the husband's obligations toward his wife in respect of her *ketubbah* (BB 9:8; BB 174b, in the matter of Moses bar Azri). However, in the sixth generation of the Babylonian *amoraim*, following on their raising the problem of the invalidating effect of *asmakhta* on suretyship (see above), they likewise called into question the measure of final resolve and seriousness with which the surety might undertake his obligation in respect of a *ketubbah* liability. There were two reasons for this: firstly, because it was considered that in such a case the surety intends no more than to perform a *mitzvah* and to bring about a matrimonial tie between the couple concerned; secondly, because in this case the husband undertakes to give his wife an amount which comes out of his own pocket and not one which the wife has initially expended – unlike the case of a loan, for instance, in which the creditor is made to incur an actual expenditure. Special requirements were accordingly laid down for the validity of suretyship as regards the *ketubbah*. Some scholars held regular suretyship to be entirely ineffective here, except if the surety is the groom's father (because of the kinship the existence of *gemirat ha-da'at* may be presumed), in which case it is valid if executed by *kinyan sudar*; other scholars held that regular suretyship is effective when executed by *kinyan sudar*, and that this formality is unnecessary when the surety is the groom's father. If the suretyship is of the *kabbelan* type, the scholars agree that it is valid in all cases and there is no need for a *kinyan* (BB 174b; Yad, Malveh 25:6; Ishut 17:9 and *Hassagot Rabad* thereto).

With regard to a gift, the scholars are further divided on the question of whether the suretyship undertaking in respect of this is to be treated like suretyship for the *ketubbah* (because in gift also the donee will suffer no actual loss if the transaction is not carried out), or whether it should be regarded otherwise since in the case of a gift it cannot be said that the surety's intention is the performance of a *mitzvah*; (Tur, ḤM 129 and *Beit Yosef* thereto, no. 5; Sh. Ar., EH 102:6 and *Rema* thereto).

A Surety's Right of Recourse Against Debtor

A surety has the right to recoup from the debtor whatever he has paid to the creditor in discharge of the principal obligation. In order for him to succeed in his claim against the debtor, it will not suffice for the surety to present the bond of indebtedness as holder thereof; he must prove – by way of the creditor's certification or in some other equally persuasive manner – that he has actually discharged the debt (Tosef. BB 11:15; Yad, Malveh, 26:7–8; Sh. Ar., ḤM 130:1, 3). The surety's right of reimbursement is to be explained either on the basis of an implied agreement between the debtor and the surety that the latter will be entitled to reimburse himself from the former if he discharges the principal obligation, or that upon receiving payment from the surety the creditor assigns to him (by way of subrogation) his right of recovery against the debtor (BB 32b and *Rashbam* thereto; *Maggid Mishneh*, Malveh 26:8; and see below).

The right of recourse against the debtor is available to the surety only when his suretyship has been solicited by the former and, in the case of a regular surety, only after the creditor has already proceeded against the debtor (Yad, loc. cit. 6; Sh. Ar., ḤM 131:2). For if he is a surety on his own initiative, "any person who wishes to avenge himself of his neighbor might do so by becoming surety for him in order to turn to the latter after discharging his debt" (Resp. Radbaz no. 2084); an unsolicited surety is in the position of a volunteer who pays another's debt without the latter's knowledge or approval and as such also has no right of action against the debtor (Ket. 107b–108a; Yad, loc. cit.; Sh. Ar., ḤM 128:1; see also *Unjust Enrichment). Suretyship established in the debtor's presence will be presumed to have been undertaken with his approval (Resp. Radbaz, no. 2084; *Leḥem Mishneh* to Yad, Malveh 26:6). There is also an opinion that the surety has a right of recourse against the debtor even if he has not been solicited by him (Maggid Mishneh, relying on the opinion of Rabad to Yad, Malveh, 26:6; cf., however, Tur, ḤM 129 and Resp. Radbaz no. 2084, where this view is contested and Rabad's opinion interpreted differently). The surety's right of recourse extends not only to the amount of the principal obligation but also to the expenses he has incurred in the matter, because it is presumed that the debtor "takes upon himself… to compensate for and make good all loss… even without expressly stipulating to this effect" (Resp. Rosh 18:7; Tur and Sh. Ar., ḤM 131:7ff.), except for unreasonable expenses such as "interest much above the customary" (*Beit Yosef*, ḤM 131, n. 7; and see above with regard to the scope of the surety's liability).

Plurality of Sureties and Debtors

If there are several sureties, the creditor may not claim more from each than his proportional share of the debt, unless he has expressly contracted for the right to recover the whole amount of the debt from any of them (Tosef. BB 11:15). Maimonides, contrary to this *halakhah*, held that the creditor may recover the whole of the debt from any one of several sureties, and Abraham b. David of Posquières was of the opinion that the matter is determined by local custom, but other *posekim* confirmed that a proportional share only may be recovered from each (Yad, Malveh 25:10 and *Hassagot Rabad* thereto; Sh. Ar., ḤM 132:3 and standard commentaries). Where several debtors are jointly involved in a single legal transaction – such as "two who borrow on the same bond… or a partner who borrows on behalf of the partnership" – some of the *posekim* hold that each is a principal debtor in respect of the whole debt, but the majority opinion is that each is liable as principal debtor in respect of his proportional share only and must be considered a regular surety as regards the rest of the debt; i.e., the creditor must first claim from each his proportional share, and only if one of them is unable to pay will the other be liable as surety for him (TJ, Shevu. 5:1, 36a; Yad, 5:9 and standard commentaries; Tur and Sh. At., ḤM 77:1–2; for further particulars see *Obligations, Law of).

In the State of Israel

In 1967 the Knesset enacted the Surety Law, which replaces the provisions of the *Mejelle* (Ottoman law) on this subject. Although largely based on Jewish law, it nevertheless deviates from it on one central matter. The law provides that "the surety and debtor are jointly and severally liable to the creditor, but the creditor may not require of the surety fulfillment of his suretyship without first requiring the debtor to discharge his debt" (sec. 8). The creditor is not required to make prior demand of the debtor if this need is waived by the surety, or if it is clear that the debtor has no property, or if service of the demand against him involves special difficulties. The law accordingly allows the creditor to turn directly to the surety, even a regular one, since a demand from the debtor is a mere formality and it is not necessary that legal proceedings be instituted against him. This accords with the attitude of both the *Mejelle* (arts. 643, 644) and English law, both of which dispense even with the need for a prior demand from the debtor, a requirement which is indeed of little practical value (E. Jenks, *Digest of English Civil Law*, 1 (1938^3), 277, no. 682). On the other hand, Swiss law (*Code des obligations*, para. 495–6) and the Nordic Draft Code of 1963 (see V. Kruse, *A Nordic Draft Code* (1963), para. 1301) accord with Jewish law in this respect and require the creditor, in the absence of an express agreement to the contrary, to claim first from the principal debtor and to exhaust execution proceedings against him before turning to the surety, except if there are special difficulties involved in suing the debtor. Swiss law furthermore recognizes the institution of *Solidarbuergschaft* (ibid. para. 496), which is akin to the *arev kabbelan* in Jewish law.

[Menachem Elon]

Arevut and Asmakhta

According to Professor Berachyahu Lifshitz, a regular surety (hereinafter – guarantee) signifies a promise to pay a creditor if the debtor defaults, and is the prototype for all forms of promises. This is the case in Roman law as well as in Jewish law. Indeed, various sources indicate that the word *'arevut* did not originally connote a specific kind of undertaking, being rather a generic term for undertaking. This is also indicated by the verses from the Book of Proverbs cited in the relevant passage in Bava Batra 173b: According to their literal meaning, they deal with a commitment given by one person to another, and not necessarily in the context of a third party, the debtor.

In Jewish law there is a dispute whether a promise (= **Asmakhta*) is binding or not. This is the import of the Talmudic statement (ibid.) that the validity of a guarantee depends on the aforementioned debate. It is also the reason for Rabbi Ashi's statement (ibid.), which became the accepted explanation for the validity of the guarantee obligation – that the guarantor "assumes the responsibility." In other words: from that moment onward the guarantor becomes indebted, thereby removing the guarantee transaction from the category of a general promise, the fulfillment of which is contingent upon a future occurrence. The pleasure imputed to the guarantor by reason of the creditor's trust in him (upon the transfer of the money) causes him to agree to this type of undertaking. If the guarantee is given after the transfer of money, there is a requirement for a *kinyan sudar*, a symbolic act of transfer whose mode of operation, legally, creates a bond "as of now," due to some benefit purportedly derived by the person giving the undertaking. A conditional guarantee is invalid, just like any other conditional undertaking, unless given according to the halakhic rules governing conditions.

According to this approach, the *arev kablan* is also considered the recipient of the funds just like the "real" debtor, and therefore it is possible to collect payment directly from him without first attempting to collect from the principal debtor, for he too is considered a "debtor."

In the Decisions of the Israeli Supreme Court

Reliance on the laws of guarantee in Jewish law is found in the case of *Maor* (CA 8034/95 *Maor v. John*, 52 (4) PD 97; Justice Y. Englard). In that case, at the request of his creditor, a restraining order was issued against the debtor to prevent him from leaving the country. In order to obtain the creditor's consent to the debtor's leaving the country for a short period in order to raise funds, a third party signed a *shetar arevut* (deed of guarantee), in which he gave a commitment that the debtor would return to Israel by a specific date, and if not – the guarantor would be responsible for all his debts. The debtor delayed his return to Israel, and two weeks after the date he was supposed to return he was killed in a traffic accident abroad. His body was brought to Israel for burial. The guarantor argued that the guarantee had never taken effect, because the debtor had intended to return to Israel, even though he was late, and it was only because of his death that he had not returned; and if, on the other hand, the guarantee had gone into effect, then the return of his body to the country annulled it. The exceptional circumstances of this case made it difficult to find a solution in accordance with the Israeli Guarantee Law, and the Court drew inspiration from the provisions of Jewish law in this matter. The Court begins its argument by mentioning the distinction in Jewish law between *guarantee* involving the guarantor's personal liability (*shi'bud ha-guf*), as distinct from liability of his assets (*shi'bud mammon*), and refers to various sources that discuss this distinction (see bibliography). The Court interprets the significance of a guarantor's obligation to bring the debtor to court, in light of the statements of Rabbi Naḥshon Gaon quoted in the *Tur* (ḤM 129), in which he states that "upon his bringing him to Court the surety shall be exempted (from his obligation)... if he brought him on the Shabbat eve at dusk and he escaped after the Shabbat, then the guarantor is not exempted." The author of *Be'er Heitev* explains that the guarantor is not absolved from his obligation because the presentation of the principal debtor before the Court must be done in such a manner as to enable the conduct of a judicial hearing and to compel the principal debtor to pay, and in the case mentioned his presentation before the Court was only for the duration of the Shabbat, during which it was impossible to conduct a hearing, for "if it was impossible to adjudicate the case in his presence and to have him take an oath, then it was as if he had never been brought before the Court, and the guarantor is obliged to bring him again" (*Be'er Heitev*, ḤM 129:10,29). From this the Court infers that no significance attaches to the fact that the debtor's body was brought back to Israel after his death, and that in order for the surety to be released from the obligation of his guarantorship the debtor's presentation must be in a manner which enables the law to be enforced upon him.

In his minority opinion in the *Maor* case, Justice (Ret.) Yaakov Türkel opined that "the appellant in our case has taken a strictly legal approach, attempting to base it on the dry, lifeless wording of the deed of guarantee... it is incumbent upon us to 'release the shackles' imposed by the written words, and to plumb their true import, reflecting the intentions of the contracting parties. We must restore the 'spirit of life' to the words of the guarantee, and interpret it according to its real intention, in view of the duty of good faith mandated by section 39 of the Contracts Law. Consequently, the appellant's action to enforce the guarantee deed should be dismissed (ibid. 113, 114). Regarding the duty of good faith in Jewish Law, Justice Tirkel refers to the judgment of Justice Menachem Elon in CA 391/80 *Lasserman et al. v. Shikun Ovedim Ltd.* 38 (2) PD 197, 263–264 (see *Contract (the principle of Good Faith).

In another case the Supreme Court deliberated on principles of the laws of guarantee in Israeli law with respect to a third party's surety to indemnify the father for payment of maintenance for children, in case the father is sued for additional amounts beyond the maintenance determined in the divorce agreement, see CA 255/81 *Kott v. Kott*, 36(1) PD 236; FH 4/82 *Kott v. Kott*, 38(3) PD 197. That case concerned an indemnification agreement between the mother and the father which provided that the implementation of the agreement would be deferred until the child grew up. The judgment discussed the question of whether this deferral also affected the guarantor's undertaking – "Does the fact that the performance of the undertaking of the principal debtor (the mother) is deferred affect the guarantor's performance of his obligation, under the provisions of the Guarantee Law? Can the guarantor rely on the defense plea provided in section 7 (a) of the Guarantee Law, whereby "Any plea that the debtor may have against the creditor in relation to the obligation shall also be available to the creditor?" (*Kott*, p. 240). Deputy President Menachem Elon addressed this question basing himself on the Guarantee Law, 5732 – 1967 and the sources of Jewish Law (Yad, Creditor and Debtor, 26:2; Sh. Ar., ḤM, 129:9, *Siftei Cohen*, ḤM 129 (23). Justice Elon wrote that "in the case before us, the guarantor cannot invoke this claim. The wife's obligation to indemnify is deferred because her financial position does not enable her to discharge that obligation without impinging on the satisfaction of the child's maintenance needs, whereas the essence of the guarantee is to ensure the obligation of indemnification in the event that the woman – who is obliged to indemnify – is unable to do so. From that perspective, it is irrelevant if the temporary deferral of the wife's discharge of her obligation to indemnify was legally mandated, for reasons of the child's best interest" (*Kott*, p. 241).

On guarantee for the person in *geonic* literature and its connection to corresponding Muslim literature, see *Law, Jewish and Islamic, a Comparative Review, as well as the bibliography.

[Menachem Elon (2nd ed.)]

BIBLIOGRAPHY: *Samuel b. Hophni, Sefer ha-Arevut ve-ha-Kabbelanut, ed.* by S. Assaf, in: *Zikhronot... shel ha-Rav Kook (1945)*, 139–59; I.S. Zuri, *Mishpat ha-Talmud*, 5 (1921), 139–41; A. Abeles, in: *MGWJ*, 66 (1922), 279–94; 67 (1923), 35–53, 122–30, 170–86, 254–7; Gulak, *Yesodei*, 2 (1922), 88–95; idem, *Oẓar*, 59–65, 107–9, 152, 259–66; idem, *Toledot ha-Mishpat be-Yisrael bi-Tekufat ha-Talmud*, 1 (*Ha-Ḥiyyuv ve-Shi'budav, 1939*), 81–88; Herzog, Instit, 2 (1939), 197–208; *ET*, 7 (1956), 61–63; 12 (1967), 717–21; S.M. Stern, in: *JJS*, 15 (1964), 141–7; Elon, *Mafte'aḥ*, 222–5; idem, in: *Divrei ha-Congress ha-Olami ha-Revi'i le-Madda'ei ha-Yahadut*, 1 (1967), 197–208; Engl. abstract: ibid., Engl. section, 268f.; idem, in: *ILR*, 4 (1969), 4–96; A. Greenbaum, in: *KS*, 46 (1970/71), 154–69. **ADD. BIBLIOGRAPHY:** M. Elon, *Ha-Mishpat ha-Ivri* (1988), 1:64, 113, 128f., 137, 485, 572, 576, 743, 775f.; 2:838f., 900f., 950f., 960f., 990, 1000, 1259; 3:1345f., 1448f., 1628; idem, *Jewish Law* (1994), 1:72, 127, 144f, 155; 2:590, 705, 710, 916, 942f.; 3:1026f., 1095f., 1151f., 1161f., 1197, 1210, 1505; 4:1606f., 1721f., 1939; M. Elon and B. Lifshitz, *Mafte'aḥ ha-She'elot ve-ha-Teshuvot shel Ḥakhmei Sefarad u-Ẓefon Afrikah* (legal digest) (1986), 2:346–49; B. Lifshitz and E. Shochetman, *Mafte'aḥ ha-She'elot ve-ha-Teshuvot shel Ḥakhmei Ashkenaz, Ẓarefat ve-Italyah* (legal digest) (1997), 237–40; B. Daube, "Sponsor and the History of Contract," in: *LQR*, 62 (1946), 266; B. Kahana, *Guarantee* (1991); G. Libson, "Recourse of Surety to Debtor in Maimonides and Muslim Writings," in: *Shenaton ha-Mishpat ha-Ivri*, 14–15 (1998–99), 153; idem, "A Guarantee to Present the Debtor," in: *Shenaton ha-Mishpat ha-Ivri*, 13 (1987), 121; idem, "Two Sureties: A Comparative Study," in: *Shenaton ha-Mishpat ha-Ivri*, 11–12

(1984–86), 337; idem, "Guarantee for Responsibility," in: *Meḥkarei Talmud*, 1 (1980), 305; B. Lifshitz, *Promise, Obligation and Acquisition in Jewish Law* (1988), 187ff.; idem, "Payment from the Surety when it is Impossible to Collect from the Debtor," in: *Shenaton ha-Mishpat ha-Ivri*, 16–17 (1990–1991), 243; idem, "On Surety and the Terminology of Undertaking," in: *Shenaton ha-Mishpat ha-Ivri*, 13 (1987), 185; idem, "A Guarantee for the Body – Halakha and Aggada," in: *Studies in Talmudic and Midrashic Literature in Memory of Tirzah Lifshitz* (2005), 231; idem, "A Guarantee Which is a Guarantee for the Body," in: *Alei Mishpat*, 1 (2000), 353–68; idem, "A Promissory Note and Suretyship – Acquisition and Obligation," in: *Essays in Memory of Prof. G. Tedeschi* (1995), 401; H. Soloveitchik, "Surety in Jewish-Gentile Money-Lending Contracts," in: Zion, 37 (1972), 1.

SURGUN, ISAAC (1701–1791), merchant in the service of the Dutch East India Company. Originally from Constantinople, Surgun settled on the Malabar Coast in Calicut and *Cochin early in the 18th century. Dealing in a variety of commodities, he owned warehouses, factories, and ships. His commercial transactions brought him into contact with many native Indian and Muslim potentates and European merchants; Dutch, English, and Hebrew sources stress his linguistic abilities, including Arabic and Portuguese. When in 1759 the Dutch East India Company needed a spokesman to represent its interests before the new Mysore rulers, Haidar Ali Khan and his son Tipu Sahib, Surgun's ability and prestige made him a natural choice. In 1779 he secured the freedom of a group of English visitors who had been imprisoned in Calicut. With his death, the family fortunes declined.

BIBLIOGRAPHY: E. Fay, *Original Letters from India*, ed. by E.M. Forster (1925); W.J. Fischel, *Ha-Yehudim be-Hodu* (1960), 112–9; idem, in: REJ, 126 (1967), 27–53.

[Walter Joseph Fischel]

SURINAME, republic on the northeastern coast of South America, between Guiana (formerly British Guiana), Brazil, and French Guyana and bordered on the north by the Atlantic Ocean. The first permanent settlement was founded in 1652 by the English governor of Barbados, Francis Lord Willoughby, and three vessels with English and Jewish settlers were sent to Suriname. Jews leaving Remire in *French Guyana joined them in 1663. A second group from Remire was brought to Suriname by English ships in 1667. Maps from that same year show Jewish plantations in the colony. On August 17, 1665, the English authorities published an official grant of privileges to the Hebrew Nation in Suriname, to be considered English-born, to practice and perform all ceremonies and customs of their religion, including marriages and wills, the observance of Sabbath and holidays, to maintain a tribunal of their own, and a grant of a plot of land in the capital, Thorarica, for a place of worship, a school, and a cemetery.

In 1667, the Dutch occupied Suriname and confirmed the privileges given to the Jews; in 1669 additions were made to them giving permission to work on Sundays, with free passage on that day and also noting that Spanish-Portuguese Jews "having been plagued by debts on property seized by the Inquisition, should not be seized for non-payment." A special military unit was composed of Jews.

With these privileges the Dutch prevented the evacuation of the Jews as English citizens to *Jamaica, and only a small group left.

On a hill on the banks of the Cassipoera creek, where the majority of the Cayenne Jews had settled, a wooden synagogue was consecrated; downhill a Jewish cemetery was located, its oldest grave dating from 1667.

Gradually Jews moved to a healthier area on the banks of the Suriname River, where they were joined by the Jews in Thorarica. The region, still called the "Jewish Savanna," began to flourish. Jewish knowledge of planting and processing sugar and other tropical produce attained a high level. A township known geographically as "Jews Town" (Joods Dorp) was called by the Jews "Jerusalem on the Riverside." In 1685 a brick synagogue was built called Berakha ve-Shalom, which also housed communal authorities and the Jewish Court of Law. The plantations around it that became small settlements had biblical names, such as Mahanaim, Succoth, Gilgal, Beersheba, Carmel, Goshen. By 1694 the population of the Savanna was composed of 570 Jews employing 9,000 laborers in 40 plantations; in the mid-eighteenth century the Jewish population reached 2,000, the majority of the white population of Suriname, in 115 plantations, employing tens of thousands of workers. Portuguese Jews from Amsterdam and Ashkenazi Jews from Rotterdam joined their brothers in Suriname.

In 1759 a "siva" (brotherhood) of liberated slaves and mulattoes descended from Jewish planters was established, called "Darkhe Yesharim" (The Way of the Righteous), whose members gradually became assimilated into the Jewish community after following the Jewish faith and intermarrying with Jews.

A series of disastrous attacks by the French navy, slave rebellions, and the production of sugar from beets in Europe led to the decline of the Jewish Savanna at the end of the eighteenth century. The planters began moving to the capital Paramaribo; in the nineteenth century about one hundred impoverished Jews still lived in the Savanna, with Jewish residence continuing until the synagogue was destroyed by fire in 1932.

In Paramaribo the community became one of small shopkeepers, anti-Jewish feelings became more prominent, and in 1925 the special privileges of the Jews were discontinued. The Portuguese Jewish synagogue Zedek ve-Shalom was erected in Paramaribo in 1716, followed by the High German (Ashkenazi) synagogue Neve Shalom in 1735. The floors of the two synagogues are covered with sand and the Sephardi rite is followed in them. By the close of the 20th century the two communities were praying together. The Jewish population dropped to 1,500 at the beginning of the 20th century; in 1923, there were 1,818 Jews. By the time of the independence of Suriname (1975), it had declined to 500 and by the end of the 20th century it was about 200 among a general population of 400,000.

The Neve Shalom synagogue was restored at the end of the 20th century. The furnishings of Zedek ve-Shalom were transferred to the Israel Museum, and the building abandoned. Community life, however, still functions.

BIBLIOGRAPHY: D. d. I. Cohen Nassy, *Essai Historique sur la Colonie de Surinam: sa foundation, ses revolutions, ses progres, depuis son origine jusqu'a nos jours* (1788; Eng. trans., in Papers of the AJA, No. 8 [1974]); F. Oudshans Dentz, *De Kolonisatie van de Portugeesch Joodsche natie in Suriname en geschiedene van de Joden Savanne* (1925); M. Arbell, *The Jewish Nation of the Caribbean – The Spanish-Portuguese Jewish Settlements in the Caribbean and the Guianas* (2003); Ph. A. Samson, *Historische Proeve over de Kolonie Suriname* (1948).

[Mordechai Arbell (2nd ed.)]

°SUROWIECKI, WAWRZYNIEC (1769–1827), Polish aristocrat; the most celebrated Polish economist of the late 18th–early 19th century. In his book *On the Decline of Industry and Towns in Poland* (1810) he discussed the theory that the Jews had played a negative role in Poland, stating that certain characteristics criticized in them were caused by their bad living conditions and the influence of religious orthodoxy, and maintaining that these characteristics also appear in all groups engaged in commerce. The Jews, he considered, played a basic role in the historical development of the Polish economy and he concluded that they were bound to raise the level of Polish commerce, agriculture, and industry. In his view they had the necessary qualities to perform this task: industry, thrift, and the ability to learn new ways. The fact that they were able to survive difficult times was thanks to the close relationship between their personal and general interests which, Surowiecki averred, was a basic Jewish quality.

[Itzhak Goldshlag]

SURVIVORS OF THE SHOAH VISUAL HISTORY FOUNDATION, THE. The foundation was established in 1994 by filmmaker Steven *Spielberg, with the goal of recording the visual testimony of Holocaust survivors and eyewitnesses so that future generations will have direct unmediated access to their experiences. Spielberg was moved by the power of oral history during his experience creating *Schindler's List*. The oral histories provided him with specific details that made his movie only more vivid. He was beseeched by survivors coming forward to tell their stories, and he undertook a public commitment to record 50,000 testimonies and to disseminate such testimonies in five initial repositories: Yad Vashem in Jerusalem, the Simon Wiesenthal Center in Los Angeles, the Museum of Jewish Heritage in New York, the United States Holocaust Memorial Museum in Washington, and the Fortunoff Archives of Holocaust Testimonies at Yale University in New Haven, Connecticut. Since its inception, the task of dissemination has become both more modest and more extensive. Until the technology enables the entire archive to be available off site at a reasonable cost, segments of the archive, often site specific, are being made available at multiple sites.

This project was not the first oral history project. The Fortunoff archive was begun in 1978 and has been recording testimonies ever since. And during the 1980s and 1990s, as video technology evolved, regional and local projects were developed in many communities throughout the United States and Canada. The United States Holocaust Memorial Museum began its oral history project in the late 1980s, and the Hebrew University and Yad Vashem began their projects, which were audio and not video recording projects, as early as the 1950s. Still, no project of this size and scope had ever been developed regarding the Holocaust, and none was as global in reach, especially once the project fully developed.

It was a race against time. Survivors were rapidly aging. Within a few years, the last witnesses would be gone. Just after the war, many survivors had been anxious to tell the world about their experiences, their tragedies, but were silenced by disbelief or incredulity. In midlife, many wanted to share with their children, but they were afraid of upsetting them.

As they were approaching old age, these survivors were invited to give testimony to ensure that their stories would be preserved. They understood that it was time to relate their experiences. These memories would have to be shared if they were to go forth to the future. *Schindler's List* and Holocaust museums had heightened interest in the Event. The more distant we become from the Event, the more the significance of the Holocaust intensifies. In classrooms throughout the world the encounter between survivors and students – the transmission of memories, a discussion of values, and a warning against prejudice, antisemitism, racism, and indifference – has become intense.

Between 1994 and 2000, 51,700 Holocaust survivors and other victim groups and/or witnesses were interviewed. The testimonies were taken in 56 countries and in 32 languages. The Foundation interviewed Jewish survivors, homosexual survivors, Jehovah's Witness survivors, liberators and liberation witnesses, political prisoners, rescuers and aid providers, Roma and Sinti survivors, survivors of eugenics policies, and war crimes trials participants. Almost half of the archive's testimonies were collected in English – most of them in the United States. Among the 31 other languages, more than 7,000 are in Russian and more than 6,300 are in Hebrew. There are approximately 1,000 Dutch interviews, 1,800 French, 1,300 Hungarian, 1,400 Polish, and 1,300 Spanish interviews. The following languages are represented with approximately 500 to 1,000 testimonies: Bulgarian (600), Czech (500), German (900), Portuguese (500), Slovak (500), Yiddish (500).

Testimonies collected usually include discussions about one's prewar (20%), wartime (60%), and postwar (20%) experience. The Shoah Foundation had amassed 232,906 videotapes, more than 31,978 miles of tape – more than the circumference of the earth. It has collected more than 116,453 hours, which would take a viewer 13 years, 3 months and 12 days, working night and day, to see in their entirety. The longest interview is 17 hours and 10 minutes, and the average interview is two hours and fifteen minutes. The archive is diverse. It centers on the experiences of Jews but includes testimonies from each of the Nazis' victim groups, as well as rescuers, liberators, and other important eyewitnesses. It does not, however, include perpetrators, as perhaps a complete video record of the Holocaust should.

Why Oral History?

Without oral histories, we would know almost nothing of the death marches, the forced marches of the winter of 1944–45, in which beleaguered concentration camp victims walked hundreds of miles without food or shelter. They were stretched beyond the limits of human endurance. Oral testimony fills in the gaps, it gives us a more complete picture of the *gestalt*, it individualizes and personalizes the event. Without oral histories, how could we learn of the life of a hidden child, too young to write and to record, but later still able to remember? To many the victims were nameless and faceless. The survivors are not.

Oral history is an effective educational tool. Professional movie makers recognize its power and respect the effectiveness of oral history. In the decade between 1995 and 2005, seven documentaries based almost exclusively on oral history won Academy Awards. Some historians are uncomfortable with oral history. They contend the information is unreliable, or at best far less reliable than documentary evidence or evidence created at the time, such as diaries and notes. They are correct, yet they miss the point. No oral history should be viewed uncritically as historical evidence. It must be evaluated within the context of everything else people know. If some oral histories are self serving, so too are some documents, speeches, memos, and other accounts of the time. Oral histories should be considered alongside other forms of documentation, and they should at least be considered by historians, subject to verification and classification. However, even historians who most vociferously object to oral history do rely upon it to provide context and texture. They do interview people who were participants in historical events. They read their memoirs and review court testimony. And the material assembled by these oral histories will provide the possibility of a people's history of the Holocaust.

To date the Survivors of the Shoah Foundation has produced several movies from this material, including its Academy Award-winning film *The Last Days*, produced and directed by founding co-executive director James Moll, and several films in European languages. In early 2006 the Shoah Foundation became part of the University of Southern California, which will be responsible for the preservation and dissemination of this material, as well as of creative educational products from the archival holdings.

Since achieving its goal of more than 50,000 testimonies, the Foundation has struggled for a mission whose clarity resembles the original goal. It has spoken of not only teaching the Holocaust and teaching tolerance, but of transforming the attitude of students toward a more tolerant world. With the incorporation to USC, it has spoken of expanding the archival collection to include other genocidal events, such as Darfur and Rwanda.

[Michael Berenbaum (2nd ed.)]

SUSAN, ISSACHAR BEN MORDECAI (c. 1510–after 1580). Issachar Susan was a member of the Ben Susan family, which claimed descent from the tribe of Benjamin. He was born in Fez and about 1527 he and his father moved to Jerusalem where he studied under *Levi ibn Ḥabib. Some years later he went to Safed where he continued to study in very straitened circumstances. He was active in the Maghreb (North Africa) congregation and as a result became friendly with the leaders of the Mostarabian community (the original Jewish community which existed before the influx following the expulsion from Spain). During that period he occupied himself with research into the synagogue customs of the various Jewish communities, both in Ereẓ Israel and the Diaspora, particularly those connected with the scriptural readings, as well as with the calendar. In the hope of overcoming his poverty, he left Ereẓ Israel in 1538 and traveled to Egypt, Turkey, Italy, and other countries. It was during this period that he wrote his book, which contains a full and detailed summary of all the sources for the customs he gave. He wrote the first text in 1538, but was able to revise it from time to time before its publication, under the titles *Tikkun Yissakhar* (Constaninople, 1564) and *Ibbur Shanim* (Venice, 1579). The book was well received by the various Jewish communities and became a kind of code of synagogue customs. It circulated mainly among the communities of Yemen, India, and other countries of the east. Joseph Caro, who was at that time already compiling the Shulḥan Arukh, was able to include Susan's conclusions and deal with them extensively in his works. The book throws light on everything connected with Mostarabian custom in Ereẓ Israel and the adjoining countries, and contains much information on liturgical usage not given in any other sources, as well as customs first mentioned by him (e.g., the eating of fruit on *Tu bi-Shevat). It also contains vivid portraits of the unique way of life of the scholars of Safed of the time (among them Joseph Caro), and their discussions on subjects mentioned in his work.

In the period between the publication of the two editions of his work, Susan returned to Safed where he administered a yeshivah for youth, among whom were many from the Yemen and other countries. During this period he translated the whole Bible and the *Megillat Antiochus* into the Arabic spoken at that time in the east. This book, written between 1571 and 1574, was never published; manuscripts exist in the D. Sassoon collection and in the British Museum.

BIBLIOGRAPHY: Fuenn, Keneset, 704; J.M. Toledano, *Ner ha-Ma'arav* (1911), 109; J. Ben-Naim, *Malkhei Rabbanan* (1931), 79b; Ben-Zvi, in: *Sinai*, 5 (1939), 383–5; Freed, *ibid.*, 60 (1966/67), 130f.; Hakohen, in: *Sinai, Sefer Yovel* (1958), 421f.

[Nathan Fried]

SUSANN, JACQUELINE (1918–1974), U.S. novelist. Born in Philadelphia, Susann went to New York in 1936, a beauty contest winner anxious to break into show business. She got bit parts in movies and commercials and in 1939 married Irving Mansfield, a press agent, and got better jobs. In 1955 she acquired a pet poodle, Josephine, and a contract to be the fashion commentator of an overnight television show. In 1963 she published *Every Night, Josephine*, about her experiences with her poodle, whom she sometimes dressed up in outfits to match her own. The book was widely viewed as a novelty but sold well enough for her to get a contract for a novel, *Valley of the Dolls* (1966). The book channeled her inside show business savvy into a bestselling combination of romance, lurid sex, and sensationalism. The main characters were loosely based on the lives of the singers Judy Garland and Ethel Merman. Susann and her husband launched an all-out drive to publicize the book, effectively promoting it on television talk shows, and Susann became as famous as her books. *Valley of the Dolls*, a lurid saga of three young women coping none too well with the challenges of show business, was made into a film of the same name (1967). Susann also wrote *The Love Machine* (1969) and *Once Is Not Enough* (1973). Her books were hugely successful, despite savaging by critics, with *Valley of the Dolls* becoming one of the 10 most widely distributed books of all time.

[Stewart Kampel (2nd ed.)]

SUSANNA AND THE ELDERS, apocryphal work added to the canonical Book of Daniel in ancient versions. In several uncial Greek manuscripts (B A Q), the Old Latin, and the Bohairic, Susanna precedes chapter 1; its traditional position, however, in accord with the Septuagint and the Latin Vulgate (and versions based on it), is after chapter 12. The story of Susanna (whose name means "lily") concerns the virtuous and beautiful wife of a prosperous Jew of Babylon, named Joakim. Unjustly accused by two Jewish elders of having committed adultery, and condemned to death, she is proved innocent when the elders, interrogated by Daniel, disagree about the tree under which the adultery allegedly took place. In accord with Deuteronomy 19:18–19 the elders were executed, and God and Daniel are praised for Susanna's vindication. Scholars have debated the question whether the original language of the addition was in Hebrew or Greek. Already in the third century (C.E.) Julius Africanus, rebutting Origen's defense of the genuineness and canonicity of the account, pointed out that the play on words in verses 54f. and 58f. are possible only in Greek. During the Middle Ages the story attained great popularity.

[Bruce M. Metzger]

In the Arts

Susanna is one of the outstanding heroines of the Apocrypha, and her story has inspired many writers and artists. In literature, two of the earliest treatments are the mid-14th century English *Epistill of Swete Susane* and a 15th-century French play, *Une vie de Saincte Susanne*, staged at Chambéry in 1470. The subject particularly attracted Renaissance dramatists because of the religio-didactic significance of the central theme – the vindication of innocence and virtue. A work of high quality was Sixtus Birck's German drama, *Susanna* (1532), a neo-Latin version of which was published by the playwright in 1537. One of its novel effects was the insertion of appropriate Old Testament passages at certain points in the action which were sung by the chorus. Some other works of the period were *Susana čista*, a play by the Montenegrin religious poet Mavro Vetranović of Ragusa (1482–1576); a neo-Latin *Susanna* by the Dutch humanist Georgius Macropedius (c. 1475–1558) and Jan Kochanowski's early Polish epic, *Zusanna* (1562). It was in England that the theme attracted the greatest attention, beginning with Ralph Radcliffe's *The Delivery of Susanna*, performed at Hitchin in 1540. Outstanding among the English plays was Thomas Garter's *The Commody of the moste vertuous and Godlye Susanna* (London, 1578) which, though clearly influenced by Ovid's erotic works, righteously maintained the biblical notion of divine justice in its highly moral conclusion. The subject continued to attract writers throughout the 17th and 18th centuries. In France, Antoine de Montchrétien wrote the verse play, *Susane ou la Chasteté* (1601), and in Greece, M. Dephrana was the author of the poem, *Istoria tēs Sōsannēs* (1667, 1671[2]). Fresh attention was paid to the story by a number of 20th-century writers, some of whom have displayed a satirical or frankly iconoclastic approach. Modern works include *Susanna im Bade* (1901), a German verse play by Hugo *Salus; and the Scottish playwright James Bridie's *Susannah and the Elders* (1937). Bridie made Susanna an incorrigible flirt, and, as Daniel himself is forced to admit, deserves less sympathy than the sorely provoked elders, who stoically accept their unjust condemnation. An original treatment of the post-World War II era was *Het boek van Joachim van Babylon…* (1947, 1948[4]; *The Book of Joachim of Babylon*, 1951), a Flemish novel by Jan Albert Goris, to which a sequel was added in 1950.

Susanna and the elders is a theme that frequently occurs in early Christian art. In the second-century prayers of the *Commendatio Animae*, Susanna delivered from false accusation symbolizes the soul of the elect protected from various perils. Other symbols of this type are Daniel in the lions' den and the three Hebrews in the fiery furnace. All were common in the funerary art of the catacombs and sarcophagi. Susanna is generally shown flanked by the two elders; in a fresco from the fourth-century cemetery of Pretextat she is symbolized as a lamb between wolves. Two episodes from the history of Susanna especially caught the imagination of artists. The judgment of Daniel (Susanna 44–62), like the judgment of Solomon, appealed to the Middle Ages as an example of justice, and was often represented in law courts. It appears in early Christian as well as medieval art, and there is a painting of the subject attributed to Giorgione (Glasgow Art Gallery). The sequel – the stoning of the elders – figures in a painting by Albrecht Altdorfer (Munich Pinakothek). The other episode, Susanna bathing (Susanna 15), was popular from the 16th to the late 18th centuries, when subjects were chosen for human interest rather than for moral or iconographic significance. Accordingly, this apocryphal story was treated as an opportunity for painting a beautiful woman in the nude. There is a study by Altdorfer, and a number of paintings by the great Venetians of the 16th century, notably by Paolo Veronese (Dresden, the Prado, and the Louvre) and by Tintoretto (the

Louvre, Vienna Museum). Paintings by Rubens are in the art galleries of Munich and Turin, the Stockholm National Museum, and the Academia San Fernando, Madrid. The two versions of the subject by *Rembrandt are in The Hague and Berlin museums. Later paintings included the ribald, satirical interpretations by the German artist Lovis Corinth and that by Oskar Kokoschka.

IN MUSIC. Paul Rebhun's school play with music, *Ein geistlich Spiel von der gotfurchtigen und keuschen Frawen Susannen* (1536), has an important place in the history of so-called school drama and as one of the precursors of the oratorio movement (see *Musikbibliothek Werner Wolffheim*, 2 (1928–29), 310–1,340; MGG s.v. Schuldrama). At the same time the subject was taken up by many composers of motets and chansons. The Latin (Vulgate) text, beginning *Ingemuit Susanna*, was set by Thomas Crecquillon and Jacobus Gallus (Handl); for *Susanna se videns rapi* there are settings by Adriaen Willaert, Philippe de Monte, Orlando di Lasso, and Palestrina; the latter also wrote a motet, *Susanna ab improbis*. A French poem, *Susanne un jour*, which appeared in a collection of chansons by an unknown composer, published in 1548, was the most influential: the melody was reset by Orlando di Lasso, and also used by him in a mass and for a German adaptation, *Susannen frumb* (see G. Reese, *Music in the Renaissance* (1954), 393–4, 696f., 709, and index: s.v. *Susanne un jour*). The text, and very often also parts of Lasso's setting, were used by Nicolas Gombert, Cipriano de Rore, Claude le Jeune, and others, and the melodic material was reworked by several composers as a lute or keyboard piece. The popularity of the song in England is attested by William Byrd's *Susanna fayre sometime assaulted was* and other settings. Another English text began with the words "There dwelt a man in Babylon"; this appears in the central "song scene" of *Shakespeare's *Twelfth Night* (Act II, scene 3ff.), and the tune was probably that of the Lasso setting. In the 17th century the subject entered the field of oratorio, in works such as Virgilio Mazocchis' "intermedio," *L'historia di Susanna* (Rome, 1643), and Alessandro Scarlatti's *Il martirio di Santa Susanna* (Florence, 1706); it also appeared in Germany (Johann Franck, *Die in deutsche Tracht verkleidete Susanna*, 1658). The emphasis on the pious moral did not always prevail: Alessandro Stradella's *Susanna* (Modena, 1681) is called by Schering "one of the most lubricious pieces of the entire literature, frivolous to the end" (cf. A. Schering, *Geschichte des Oratorios* (1911), 109, and *ibid.* on the "oratorio erotico"). In the 18th century only Handel's oratorio *Susanna* deserves mention (première at Covent Garden, London, 1749; librettist unknown); and 19th-century works are also few and negligible. The 20th century has seen the appearance of several operas on literary variations and even parodies of the subject, in which the biblical story is seldom adhered to strictly, such as Jean Gilbert's operetta, *Die keusche Susanne* (1910; later turned into an Argentinian film); Paul Hindemith's *Sancta Susanna* (text by August Stramm, 1922); Paul Kurzbach's *Die Historia der Susanna* (1948); Knudage Riisager's *Susanne* (1948/49); and Carlisle Floyd's *Susannah* (1955), which was first performed in New York in 1956.

See also Daniel in the Arts.

[Bathja Bayer]

BIBLIOGRAPHY: Schuerer, Gesch, 3 (1909⁴), 452–8; Kay, in: Charles, Apocrypha, 1 (1913), 638–54; R.H. Pfeiffer, *History of New Testament Times* (1949), 434–54; B.M. Metzger, *Introduction to the Apocrypha* (1957), 107–13. IN THE ARTS: G. Antonucci and G. Di Lentaglio, in: *Emporium*, 70 (1929), 3–19; M.T. Herrick, in: *Studies... T.W. Baldwin*, ed. by D.C. Allen (1958); M. Roston, *Biblical Drama in England* (1968), index; Pilger, in: *Zeitschrift fuer deutsche Philologie*, vol. 11, pp. 129ff.

SUSITA OR HIPPOS, Greek city established above the E. bank of the Sea of Galilee (Pliny, *Natural History* 5:15). The Greek name Hippos is a translation of the Semitic name Susita. The coins of the ancient city usually show a horse (Heb. *sus*, Gk. *hippos*). Officially, the city was known as "Antiochia by Hippos," because it was probably founded by the Seleucids. It was captured by Alexander Yannai (Jannaeus) and was later reestablished as a city of the Decapolis by Pompey (Jos., Ant., 14:75). Augustus gave the city to Herod, but the citizens bore Herodian rule unwillingly, and after his death, it reverted to Syria (Jos., Ant., 15:217; 17:320; Wars, 1:396; 2:97). The city was attacked by the Jews in the Jewish War against Rome (Jos., Wars, 2:459) and the Jews in the city were interned (*ibid.*, 2:478). Some of them were found among the defenders of Taricheae (*ibid.*, 3:542). The territory of Susita bordered on the Sea of Galilee (Jos., Life, 153). It was located 30 stadia (4 mi.; c. 6½ km.) from Tiberias, with which Susita lived in constant rivalry, despite the commercial relations between the two cities (Lam. R. 1: 17, no. 52; TJ, Shev. 8:3, 38a).

In Byzantine times, Susita was the seat of a bishop. The city was part of *Palaestina Secunda*. Jewish villages in its territory were freed from such obligations as tithes and the Sabbatical Year (Tosef., Shev. 4:10). It has been identified with Qalʿat Ḥuṣn, a ruin on a mountain above *En-Gev. Remains on the site include fortification walls, a gate, a colonnaded street, a forum, a sanctuary (temenos) with the remains of Hellenistic and Roman temples, four churches, and an aqueduct. A new survey of the city was made in 1999, and from 2000 excavations were conducted there by A. Segal on behalf of Haifa University.

BIBLIOGRAPHY: Schuemacher, in: ZDPV, 9 (1886), 327ff.; Schuerer, Gesch, 2 (1906⁴), 155f.; Avi-Yonah, Geog, 158–9; Schulman, in: BDASI, 6 (1957), 30–31; Anati, *ibid.*, 31–33; Avi-Yonah, *ibid.*, 33; Press, Ereẓ, s.v. **ADD. BIBLIOGRAPHY:** A. Segal, *Hippos-Sussita: Fifth Season of Excavations 2004. And Summary of All Five Seasons (2000–2004).*

[Michael Avi-Yonah / Arthur Segal (2nd ed.)]

SUSMAN, MARGARETE (1874–1966), German essayist and poet. She lived in Hamburg (where she was born), Frankfurt, and – from the Nazi period – in Zurich. Margarete Susman combined scholarship and existentialist philosophy with considerable poetic talent.

Her verse collections include *Mein Land* (1901) and *Lieder von Tod und Erloesung* (1922) and a selection of her poetry is contained in *Aus sich wandelnder Zeit* (1953). Her essays on Jewish problems include *Das Buch Hiob und das Schicksal des juedischen Volkes* (1946), *Gestalten und Kreise* (1945), and *Deutung biblishcher Gestalten* (1955). Her major works include: *Vom Sinn der Liebe* (1912), a philosophical analysis of the tragic nature of love; *Frauen der Romantik* (1929), a collection of essays on Caroline and Dorothea von *Schlegel, Rahel (Levin) *Varnhagen von Ense, and Bettina Brentano; and *Deutung einer grossen Liebe* (1951), on the friendship between Goethe and Charlotte von Stein. In her 90th year she published her autobiography, *Ich habe viele Leben gelebt* (1964).

BIBLIOGRAPHY: *Auf gespaltenem Pfad. Festschrift fuer Margarete Susman* (1964; incl. bibl.).

[Sol Liptzin]

SUSSKIND, DAVID (1920–1987), U.S. producer. Born in New York, Susskind was press agent for Warner Brothers after World War II but later went into television, specializing in serious drama. By 1969 he had produced 26 plays, including Euripides' *Medea; Rashomon*; and *Othello*. He conducted his own discussion shows on television, notably *Open End* (1958–66) in which he talked with leading personalities about contemporary issues.

Susskind's TV series productions include *Armstrong Circle Theatre* (1950–63), *Goodyear Television Playhouse* (1951–57), *The Dupont Show of the Month* (1957–61), *Play of the Week* (1959–61), the sci-fi drama series *Way Out* (1961), the police drama series *East Side/West Side* (1963–64), the sitcom *Alice* (1976–85), and the Watergate miniseries *Blind Ambition* (Emmy nomination, 1979).

Among his many TV feature productions are *Pinocchio* (1957), *Ten Little Indians* (1959), *Meet Me in St. Louis* (1959), *The Power and the Glory* (1959), *A Month in the Country* (1959), *Our Town* (1959), *The Waltz of the Toreadors* (1959), *Miracle on 34th Street* (1959), *Death of a Salesman* (1966), *The Glass Menagerie* (1966), *Mark Twain Tonight!* (Emmy nomination, 1967), *The Crucible* (1967), *Johnny Belinda* (1967), *Laura* (1968), *A Hatful of Rain* (1968), *The Price* (Emmy nomination, 1971), *The Country Girl* (1973), *A Moon for the Misbegotten* (Emmy nomination, 1975), *Eleanor and Franklin* (Emmy Award for Outstanding Special, 1976), *Harry S. Truman: Plain Speaking* (Emmy nomination, 1976), *Eleanor and Franklin: The White House Years* (Emmy Award for Outstanding Special, 1977), *Johnny, We Hardly Knew Ye* (1977), *Who'll Save Our Children?* (1978), *Sex and the Single Parent* (1979), *The Bunker* (1981), *Mister Lincoln* (1981), *Ian McKellen* (1982), and *Rita Hayworth: The Love Goddess* (1983).

In 1960, Susskind won the Peabody Award for his production of *The Moon and Sixpence* (1959), which featured Laurence Olivier in his American television debut. The stellar cast included Judith Anderson, Hume Cronyn, Jessica Tandy, Cyril Cusack, Denholm Elliot, Geraldine Fitzgerald, and Jean Marsh.

Susskind also produced a number of feature films for the movies. Among these are *Edge of the City* (1957), *A Raisin in the Sun* (1961), *Requiem for a Heavyweight* (1962), *All the Way Home* (1963), *Lovers and Other Strangers* (1970), *Alice Doesn't Live Here Anymore* (1974), *Buffalo Bill and the Indians* (1976), and *Goldenrod* (1976).

BIBLIOGRAPHY: T. Morgan, *Self-Creations: 13 Impersonalities* (1965); E. Asinof, *Bleeding between the Lines* (1979).

[Ruth Beloff (2nd ed.)]

SUSSKIND, (Jan) WALTER (1913–1980), conductor, pianist, and composer of Czech birth. He studied composition with Suk and Karel Hába, piano with Hoffmeister at the Prague Conservatory, and conducting with *Szell at the Academy of Music in Prague. Susskind became Szell's assistant at the German Opera, Prague, and played piano with the Czech Trio (1933–38). After the German occupation he went to London where he served as pianist with the exiled Czech Trio until 1942. He resumed his conducting career (1941) and became a naturalized British subject (1946). He assumed directorships with the Carl Rosa Opera Company in London (1943–45), the Scottish National Orchestra (1946–52), the Victoria Symphony Orchestra (SO), Melbourne (1953–55), the Toronto SO (1956–65), the Aspen (Colorado) Music Festival (1962–68), and the St Louis SO (1968–75). His last position was with the Cincinnati Orchestra (1978–80). Susskind also appeared regularly as guest conductor with the major orchestras of Europe, the United Kingdom, and North America and taught at the University of Southern Illinois (1968–75). He was a highly accomplished conductor, being a technically secure and polished musician. During his time in Toronto he expanded the orchestral repertory widely, introducing new works such as Bruckner's and Mahler's symphonies. He continued this policy of exploratory program building with the St. Louis SO, which under his direction became a leading American orchestra. Together they made over 200 recordings. He founded the National Youth Orchestra of Canada (1960) and was known as a great mentor of young conductors. Susskind wrote several compositions among them *4 Songs for Voice and String Quartet* (1935), *9 Slovak Sketches for Orchestra*, *Passacaglia for Timpani and Chamber Orchestra* (1977), and scores for films and the theater.

BIBLIOGRAPHY: J. Hunt, Grove Music Online; *Baker's Biographical Dictionary of Musicians* (1997); *Makers of the Philharmonia* (1996).

[Naama Ramot (2nd ed.)]

SUSSMAN, ABRAHAM (1861–1943), Israel agronomist. Born in Odessa, Sussman joined the *Bilu movement, but was not among the original settlers in Ereẓ Israel. In 1885 he established and ran a model farm near Odessa on which he trained Jewish youth for about seven years. He accompanied *Aḥad Ha-Am on his visit to Ereẓ Israel in 1900 as an emissary of the Odessa Committee of Ḥovevei Zion. In this capacity Sussman toured the Jewish settlements and later published a detailed report of the journey together with his traveling companion. After the Russian Revolution (1917), Sussman was the director of a farm near Odessa that trained groups of pioneers, including the founders of Kibbutz *Kiryat Anavim in the Jerusalem Hills. He settled in Palestine in 1924 and, among other activities, engaged in agricultural research and training.

BIBLIOGRAPHY: D.B., in: *Ha-Po'el ha-Ẓa'ir*, no. 35 (1943); Tidhar, 10 (1959), 3589.

[Yehuda Slutsky]

SUSSMAN, EZRA (1900–1973), Hebrew poet and translator. Born in Odessa, Sussman emigrated to Ereẓ Israel in 1922. He began writing poetry and prose in Russian, in a monthly that his father edited in Odessa. In Palestine, he was a regular contributor to *Davar* from its founding, and there published poems, both in original and translation, as well as drama criticism, and became a member of the editorial board. He translated Voltaire's *Candide* (1946), the selected poetry of Boris Pasternak, *Mivḥar Shirim* (1961), and poems by Anna Akhmatova. With S. Grodzensky he edited the periodical *Akhsanyah* (1956). Among his books are *Shirim* (1968), *Yalkut Shirim* (with a bibliography, 1984), and the posthumously published collection *Ḥaẓot ve-Neẓaḥ* (1998). A volume of translations appeared in 1985, preceded by a collection of theater reviews, *Aḥarei Bekhorah* (1981).

ADD. BIBLIOGRAPHY: A. Hagorni-Grin, *Be-Or Panehah shel Shirat Ezra Sussman* (1969); U. Shavit, *"Ha-He'alem ve-ha-Hester,"* in: *Haaretz* (1973), 20; Y. Zemorah and E. Sussman, in: *Al ha-Mishmar* (Sivan 3, 1974); G. Leshem, *"Umdanim ve-Ovdanim,"* in: *Moznayim*, 57:1–2 (1983), 69–71; B. Link, *Iyyunim be-Shirat E. Sussman* (1983); Y. Sukari, *Shirat Ezra Sussman* (1997).

[Getzel Kressel]

SUSSMAN, YOEL (1910–1982), president of the Israel Supreme Court. Born in Cracow, Poland, Sussman moved to Germany with his parents and completed his secondary education there and studied law. He settled in Palestine in 1934 and remained in private practice until the War of Independence, when he served as deputy judge advocate-general in the Israel Defense Forces with the rank of captain. In 1949 he became a district court judge in Tel Aviv and in 1953 was nominated to the Supreme Court. He lectured at Tel Aviv University and at the Hebrew University Law School in Jerusalem. His major studies are the following: *Das Wechselrecht Palestinas* (1937), *Bills of Exchange* (1945), *Dinei Shetarot* (1951), *Dinei Borerut* ("On Arbitration," 1953), *Sidrei Din ha-Ezraḥi* (1959). In 1970 he was appointed permanent deputy president of the Supreme Court and in 1976 its president. In 1975 he received an Israel Prize.

BIBLIOGRAPHY: *Jerusalem Post* Archives

[Alexander Zvielli]

SUTRO, ABRAHAM (1784–1869), German rabbi. He was appointed by the *Kassel consistory as a teacher in Reichenbach in 1811, and became one of the first rabbis to preach in German. In 1815 he became rabbi of *Muenster, and in 1828 of *Paderborn as well. An opponent of *Reform, Sutro objected to the introduction of the organ into the synagogue. However, he supported vocational training for Jews and persuaded A. *Haindorf to found a pedagogical institution bearing his name in Muenster. In 1853 he began to organize petitions to the Prussian authorities against discrimination in the appointment of Jews to governmental, particularly juridical, offices. Sutro wrote an anti-Reform work, *Milḥamot Adonai* (4 vols., 1836–65).

BIBLIOGRAPHY: *Der Israelit*, 10 (1869), 829–31; F. Lazarus, in: MGWJ, 58 (1914), 550ff.

SUTRO, ADOLPH HEINRICH JOSEPH (1830–1898), U.S. engineer and civic leader. Sutro, who was born in Aachen, Prussia, left school at 16, when his father died, to manage the family's woolen cloth mill. At the request of a Memel businessman who bought the factory, Adolph went to Memel to set up and run the mill for the new owner. In 1848 he immigrated with his family to the United States, traveling to California in 1850 and selling goods in Stockton and San Francisco. In 1860 he visited Nevada's silver mines and conceived of a tunnel through the Comstock Lode for drainage, ventilation, and more efficient silver mining. His Sutro Tunnel Company began construction in 1869 and completed the tunnel, which ran four miles from Sutro City, a "planned city," to Virginia City, in 1878. The great mining period of the Comstock Lode was over, however, and though Sutro was rumored to have made as much as $5 million through the sale of his tunnel stock in 1880, his profit was probably no more than $900,000. Sutro planned to run for a Senate seat from Nevada in 1880, but his scheme to embarrass his opponent was betrayed to the opposition by one of his advisers, and his campaign collapsed. Sutro then moved to San Francisco and invested his money in San Francisco land, eventually purchasing one-twelfth of the city's land and building up a fortune of several million dollars. He bought a home and grounds, known as Sutro Heights, which he landscaped, furnished with a seal pool, and decorated with statuary he believed to be edifying, and opened the grounds to the public. He built and ran a street railway from the city to the Heights so that San Franciscans could make the trip on a single fare rather than the double fare that the existing railway charged. He also built Sutro Baths, a public indoor pool opened in 1896 which would admit about 10,000 persons at a time. An obsessive book buyer, he amassed a library of about 125,000 bound books, including something under 3,000 of the existing 20,000 incunabula (largely destroyed in the 1906 fire), sometimes buying up whole bookstores in person or through his European agents. Only the Sutro Library, built after his death to house his collection and now a branch of the California State Library on the campus of the University of San Francisco, and the Medical Center at the University of California Medical School at San Francisco, for which he left a bequest, remain. In 1894 Sutro was elected mayor of San Francisco as a People's Party (Populist) candidate on a platform of maintaining the five-cent street railway fare and defeating a bill benefiting the Southern Pacific Railway, which Sutro consistently referred to as the Octopus. He served as mayor from 1895 to 1897. The inadequacies of the city's charter and Sutro's inability to work with others led the San Francisco *Examiner* to the judgment that "The Mayor's power is barely more than that given by his tact… He passed his term in a state of exasperation." A believer in charity rather than in any religion, Sutro gave land to the Home for Aged Israelites, as well as to other charitable causes, and left a personal bequest to the founder of *Ethical Culture to avoid supporting that organization.

BIBLIOGRAPHY: R.E. and M.F. Stewart, *Adolph Sutro* (1962).

[Robert E. Levinson]

SUTRO, ALFRED (1863–1933), English playwright. The son of a German physician and grandson of a rabbi, Sutro was educated at the City of London School and in Brussels, and became a successful wholesale merchant. After his marriage – his wife was a sister of the first Marquess of *Reading – he devoted himself exclusively to writing. He made his reputation in 1904 with a social comedy, *The Walls of Jericho*, which was followed during the next quarter century by many other West End stage successes, generally on stock themes but always written with wit and polish.

His plays include *The Fascinating Mr. Vanderveldt* (1906), *The Perplexed Husband* (1913), *The Desperate Lovers* (1927), and *Living Together* (1929). Sutro showed a deeper vein in his essays and sketches – *About Women* (1931) – where satire is sometimes edged with bitterness. He was also a talented translator, mainly of the works of his lifelong friend, the Belgian dramatist Maurice Maeterlinck. Sutro was a friend of many noted writers of his day, including George Bernard Shaw and D.H. Lawrence. He wrote an autobiography, *Celebrities and Simple Souls* (1933).

ADD. BIBLIOGRAPHY: ODNB online; L. Sawin, *Alfred Sutro: A Man With a Heart* (1989).

SUTTON, PHILIP (1928–), painter. Sutton was born in London, and studied at the Slade School of Fine Art where he subsequently taught. As a young man he was awarded scholarships for travel in France and Italy, and also spent some time in Israel. Between 1963 and 1965 he lived for two years on Fiji with his wife and four children. Sutton was influenced chiefly by Matisse and the German Expressionists. He was foremost a colorist and, apart from an early period of landscape painting, his chief subjects, like those of many Jewish artists, were firstly members of his family, and secondly the female nude. He was a bold draughtsman, particularly effective in his woodcuts, and a lover of hot, sensuous color, and was regarded as one of the most gifted English painters of his generation. He is represented in the Tate Gallery and leading museums throughout the world. He was elected a member of the Royal Academy in 1988. *Model with Yellow Hair* is one of his largest and most striking woodcuts. It was published in 1969 in a small, limited edition of 30 impressions. *Woodcuts by Philip Sutton: 1950s–1970s* appeared in 1998.

[Charles Samuel Spencer]

SUTZKEVER, ABRAHAM (1913–), Yiddish poet. Born in Smargon (Belorussia), Sutzkever fled with his family to Siberia to escape the German occupation of his hometown during World War I, returning to Vilna after the war. He was not educated in the city's secular Yiddish schools, but rather at a Polish-Hebrew secondary school. He taught himself about Yiddish literature as a teenager through disciplined self-study, later auditing classes on Polish Romanticism at University of Vilna and studying early Yiddish literature under Max *Weinreich at YIVO. He first discovered his poetic calling when, in 1930, he joined the Jewish scouts and befriended Leyzer *Wolf, a leader of the literary group *Yung-Vilne. His membership in that group was initially rejected because his poetry lacked political engagement, but in 1934, the year of his literary debut, he was accepted. He emerged as a defiant aesthetic voice that resisted the highly politicized nature of Yiddish writing in Poland in favor of a joyous, affirmative poetic. In 1935 he appealed to Yiddish modernist Aaron *Glanz-Leyeles in New York, who, impressed by Sutzkever's talent, invited him to contribute regularly to his prestigious monthly, *In Zikh*. Sutzkever's first book, *Lider* ("Songs," 1937), secured his reputation as a rising international literary star at age 24. The volume includes a sonnet sequence about Siberia that transforms the setting into a landscape of sound, color, and childhood wonder. His second volume, *Valdiks* ("Of the Forest," 1940), is an ecstatic hymn to nature and celebration of existence. During the initial weeks of the Nazi occupation of Vilna, he composed a cycle of poems while in hiding. He divided his energies in the ghetto between creative work (he received first prize in a ghetto literary competition in 1942) and his underground association with the United Partisans Organization. He also played a critical role in the rescue of treasures from YIVO's archive as part of the secret "Paper Brigade." His wartime writings range from private confessions of sorrow and rage to the crafting of collective myth. He and his wife, Freydke, escaped the liquidation of the ghetto in September 1943, joining Jewish partisan units in the Lithuanian forest. The *Jewish Anti-Fascist Committee in Moscow, with Ilya *Ehrenberg's assistance, arranged for his rescue. In the Soviet Union he was greeted as a symbol of Jewish sacrifice in the fight against fascism. After Vilna's liberation, he returned with Yung-Vilne colleague Shmerke *Kaczerginski to dig up treasures hidden by the Paper Brigade, which were sent to YIVO in New York to keep them out of Communist hands. In Moscow, he completed his memoir, *Fun Vilner Geto* ("From the Vilna Ghetto," 1946), and gathered his wartime poetry for the volumes *Di Festung* ("The Fortress," 1945) and *Lider fun Geto* ("Poems of the Ghetto," 1946). Additional writings from and about the Holocaust period include *Yidishe Gas* ("Jewish Street," 1948) and *Di Ershte Nakht in Geto* ("The First Night in the Ghetto," 1979). *Geheymshtot* ("Secret City," 1948), one of only two book-length epics in his career, crafts a mythopoeic universe of Jews hiding from Nazis in the sewers of Vilna, including the figure of the poet, who lives to bear witness to pain which must be transformed into beauty. The prose symbolism of "Green Aquarium," published in *Ode tsu der Toyb* ("Ode to the Dove," 1955), explores his faith in poetry as a regenerative force. *Lider fun Yam-Hamoves* ("Poems from the Sea of Death," 1968) is the official canon of his wartime writings. Sutzkever testified at the Nuremberg trials (1946), and represented Yiddish literature at the International PEN Congress in 1947, the same year he immigrated to Palestine, settling in Tel Aviv with his wife and young daughter. There he established and edited the world's most important postwar Yiddish quarterly, *Di Goldene Keyt* ("The Golden Chain," 1949–95). His life in Israel produced the most sustained engagement with Zionism in all of Yiddish poetry. *In Fayer Vogn* ("In the Chariot of Fire," 1952) communicates his ecstasy over his encounter with Jewish life reborn in Israel and his anxieties about the way European Jewry will be remembered. The volume *In Midber Sinay* (1957; *In the Sinai Desert*, 1987), about the 1956 Sinai Campaign, imagines direct links between the generation of ghetto fighters and Israel's fighting spirit. *Gaystike Erd* ("Spiritual Soil," 1961; with original woodcuts by Arthur Kolnik) tells of the birth of Israel and the War of Independence. A two-volume edition of his collected writings, *Poetishe Verk* (1963), appeared in honor of his 50th birthday. His mature period, best represented by *Lider fun Togbukh* ("Poems from a Diary," 1977), offers meta-poetic and philosophical musings that stake the highest claim for poetry. Additional volumes include *Sibir* (1953; with illustrations by Marc Chagall; *Siberia*, 1961), *Oazis* ("Oasis," 1960), *Firkantike Oysyes un Mofsim* ("Square Letters and Miraculous Signs," 1968), *Tsaytike Penemer* ("Ripe Faces," 1970), *Di Fidlroyz* (1974; *The Fiddle Rose*, 1990), *Dortn vu es Nekhtikn di Shtern* ("There Where the Stars Spend the Night, 1979), *Fun Alte un Yunge Ksav-Yadn* (1982; *Laughter Beneath the Forest*, 1996), *Tsviling-Bruder* ("Twin Brother," 1976), *Di Nevue fun Shvartsaplen* ("The Prophecy of the Inner Eye," 1989), *Der Yoyresh fun Regn* ("Heir of the Rain," 1992), *Baym Leyenen Penimer* ("Face Reading," 1993), and *Tsevaltike Vent* ("Shaky Walls," 1996). Other English translations include *Burnt Pearls* (1981), and the comprehensive *A. Sutzkever: Selected Poetry and Prose* (1991). Sutzkever's poetry distinguishes itself by inventive word-play, experimentation with sound and rhythm, mastery of form, and the poet's romantic sense of his artistic calling. For these and many other reasons, he was called the "Ariel" of Yiddish poetry at an early stage in his career, only to be proclaimed "the uncrowned Jewish poet laureate" by one recent critic. Honors include the Itsik Manger Prize (1969), an exhibition in recognition of his life at the Jewish National and University Library, Jerusalem (1983), and the Israel Prize (1985).

BIBLIOGRAPHY: S. Bickel, *Di Brokhe fun Sheynkayt* (1969); I. Biletzky, *Essays on Yiddish Poetry and Prose Writers* (1969), 207–31; J. Leftwich, *Abraham Sutzkever: Partisan Poet* (1971); Z. Shazar, et al. (eds.), *Yoyvel-Bukh tsum Fuftsikstn Geboyrntog fun A. Sutzkever* (1963). **ADD. BIBLIOGRAPHY:** J. Cammy, in: *Yiddish After the Holocaust*, (2004), 240–65; *Di Goldene Keyt*, 136 (1993) (Sutzkever issue); B. Harshav, in: *A. Sutzkever: Selected Poetry and Prose* (1991), 3–23; Y. Mark, *Avrom Sutzkevers Poetisher Veg* (1974); Sh. Niger, in: *Yidisher Shrayber fun Tsvantsikstn Yorhundert* (1973), 55–98; A. Novershtern, *Avrom Sutzkever Bibliografye* (1976); idem, *Avrom Sutzkever: Tsum Vern a Benshivim* (1983); D. Roskies, *Against the Apocalypse* (1984), 225–57; D. Sadan, et al. (eds), *Yikhes fun Lid* (1983); Ruth Wisse, in: *Commentary*, 76 (1983), 41–8; idem, *Abraham Sutzkever: The Uncrowned Jewish Poet Laureate* (National Yiddish Book Center recording, 1994); Y. Yanasovitsh, *Avrom Sutzkever: Zayn Lid un Zayn Proze* (1981)

[Justin D. Cammy (2nd ed.)]

SUWALKI (Pol. **Suwálki**; Yid. **Suvalk**), town in Bialystok province, N.E. Poland. The town began to develop toward the end of the 18th century under Prussian rule; Jews then settled there, numbering 44 (3.5% of the total population) in 1808. In 1815 Suwalki was incorporated within Congress Poland and between 1823 and 1862 restrictions of residence in some of the sections of the city were imposed upon a number of Jews. An organized community was formed at the beginning of the 1820s, and in 1827 numbered 1,209 (32% of the total population). A synagogue was built in 1821. During the 19th century Jews in Suwalki developed trade relations with Germany, in particular for *agricultural produce, timber, and horses. They also engaged in retail trade and crafts including tailoring, shoemaking, building, and transportation. In the second half of the 19th century, Jews in Suwalki engaged in the manufacture of prayer shawls, fulling, and tanning. During the Polish uprising in 1863 many Jews in Suwalki and the surrounding area took an active part in the struggle against the Russian army. Two of them, Leib Lipman and Leib Lejbman, were executed by the czarist authorities. Following persecutions and disasters of nature Jews emigrated from Suwalki, among them, in the early 1880s, a number of followers of the "*Am Olam" movement. In 1866 a "benevolent society for natives of Suwalki" was founded in New York. The Jewish population numbered 6,587 (62% of the total) in 1857, and 7,165 (40%) in 1897. From the latter year until 1914 Jewish traders and craftsmen supplied the garrison stationed in the locality.

Jewish national activity in the community began as early as the movement for settlement in Ereẓ Israel in 1881. In 1891 the Safah Berurah Society for the propagation of Hebrew in Suwalki had 70 members. A Jewish workers' association was formed in 1901. Members of the *Bund and *Po'alei Ẓion in Suwalki took an active part in the revolutionary period of 1905–06, and organized *self-defense against *pogroms.

In World War I the Jews in Suwalki suffered severely during the retreat of the Russian army in the beginning of the summer of 1915. In the interwar period, under Polish rule, Jews opened factories for woolen textiles, and timber and food products. The Jewish population numbered 5,747 (34% of the total) in 1921, and 5,811 in 1931. Jewish institutions in Suwalki included schools of the *Tarbut and CYSHO (see *Education), a *talmud torah* (founded in 1861), and a yeshivah (1936). A Jewish self-defense organization in 1936 prevented a pogrom by the Polish population.

Among distinguished rabbis who served in Suwalki in the second half of the 19th century were Isaac Eisik *Wildmann (Ḥaver) (1850–53); Jehiel b. Aaron *Heller (1853–57); Samuel b. Judah Leib *Mohilewer (1860–68); and David Tevel *Katzenellenbogen (in the 1890s). Personalities born in Suwalki or active there include the educator Alexander M. *Dushkin; Pinhas *Sapir (Israeli cabinet minister); and Avraham *Stern (leader of Leḥi).

[Dov Rabin]

Holocaust Period

Before the outbreak of World War II there were about 6,000 Jews in Suwalki. The Jewish community was liquidated at the end of November 1939 when the Jews were deported to *Biala Podlaska, *Lukow, *Miedzyrzec-Podlaski, and *Kock and shared the fate of these communities. After the war the Jewish community of Suwalki was not reconstituted.

BIBLIOGRAPHY: *Yisker Bukh Suvalk* (1961); B. Wasiutyński, *Ludność żydowska w Polsce w wiekach XIX i XX* (1930), 37, 41, 67, 72, 74, 79, 188; S. Bronsztejn, *Ludność żydowska w Polsce w okręsie międzywojennym* (1963), 278; A. Wein (ed.), *Żydzi a powstanie Styczniowe* (1963), index; *Caret i klasy posiadające w walcz z rewolucją. 1905–07 w krolestwie Polskim* (1956), index; I. Schiper, *Dziejehandłu żydowskiego na ziemach polskich* (1963), index.

SUWALSKI, ISAAK (1863–1913), Hebrew writer and editor. He was born in Kolno, Lomza province, and from 1881 contributed articles to the Hebrew press (*Ha-Levanon, Ha-Ẓefirah, Ha-Meliẓ*), written in the spirit of religious orthodoxy. In 1890–91 he published in Warsaw a literary collection, *Keneset ha-Gedolah*. His book *Ḥayyei ha-Yehudi al pi ha-Talmud* (1889) gathered talmudic sayings, arranged by subject matter, that reflect the sages' views of man and society. This collection went through several editions and was translated into German and Danish. In 1895 he migrated to London where he single-handedly established the Hebrew weekly *Ha-Yehudi* (1897–1913), of which he was publisher, editor, compositor, and staff writer. He also dealt in Hebrew books and organized charitable institutions in the Jewish quarter in the East End of London.

BIBLIOGRAPHY: *Ha-Ẓefirah*, no. 102 (1913); JC (May 23, 30, 1913); Kressel, Leksikon, 2 (1967), 476–7; Waxman, Literature, 4 (1960^2), 446.

[Yehuda Slutsky]

SUZIN, SOLOMON MOSES (d. 1835), rabbi of Jerusalem. Suzin was appointed *rishon le-Zion* in 1824 as the successor of Yom Tov Danon. He did a great deal for the Jewish population of Jerusalem, and held the position until his death. He was responsible for a considerable number of *takkanot* and his approbations are included in many contemporary works. From them it would appear that at first he lived in Hebron. In 1826 he proceeded to the countries of North Africa as an emissary of Jerusalem.

He was the author of *Pinkas le-Inyenei Halakhah* (Jerusalem, National Library, Heb. 8° 378), halakhic novellae on various subjects. The work contains much material on the comtemporary history of Ereẓ Israel in general and of Jerusalem in particular. A number of his responsa are published in the works of the scholars of his day.

BIBLIOGRAPHY: Frumkin-Rivlin, 3 (1929), 194f.; M.D. Gaon, *Yehudei ha-Mizraḥ be-Ereẓ Yisrael*, 2 (1937), 478; Yaari, Sheluḥei, 567f., and index.

SUZMAN (née **Gavronsky**), **HELEN** (1917–), South African politician and parliamentarian of liberal views. Born in Germiston, Transvaal, she lectured on economic history at the University of the Witwatersrand. She was first elected to Parliament as a member of the United Party, the official opposition (1953), but, with 12 other members, broke away in 1959, because of differences on race policies. They formed the Progressive Party and continued to sit in Parliament as a separate opposition group. Helen Suzman was reelected for the same constituency (Houghton) as a candidate of the Progressives in 1961, the only Progressive candidate to be successful. She was the sole representative of her party in Parliament for a total of 13 years until the election of 1974, when a further six Progressive candidates were elected to the house. A formidable debater, she was a determined opponent of discrimination based on race or color, and a champion of the rights of the African people. At the time of her resignation from Parliament in 1989, Suzman was the longest-serving South African MP. Her struggle for equal rights for South Africa's people of color resulted in her receiving two nominations for the Nobel Peace Prize as well as over 28 honorary degrees, including honorary doctorates from Oxford (1973), Harvard (1976), and Witwatersrand (1976) universities. She wrote two autobiographies, *Time Remembered* (1968) and *In No Uncertain Terms* (1993).

[David Saks (2nd ed.)]

SUZMAN, JANET (1939–), actress. Born in Johannesburg, Suzman was educated at the University of Witwatersrand. She first appeared on stage in 1962 in *Billy Liar*, but her modulated voice and diction, elegance and authority led quickly to classical theater, where she specialized in Shakespeare and Classical and 19th-century theater. Her roles with the Royal Shakespeare included Portia, Rosalind, Ophelia, and Cleopatra. In 1976 she received the *Evening Standard* Award for her portrayal of Masha in Chekhov's *The Three Sisters*. Her many television appearances included participation in the BBC Shakespeare series along with such varying roles as Charlotte Bronte, Florence Nightingale, Edwina Mountbatten, and Clytemnestra. In films she portrayed Alexandra in *Nicholas and Alexandra* (1971), receiving an Academy Award nomination for best actress for her portrayal of the imperious czarina. In Peter Greenaway s film *The Draughtman's Contract*, her portrayal of the sensual, decadent aristocrat brought great critical acclaim. She turned increasingly to character roles and has directed for television (*Othello*) and the theater. She was a civil rights activist following in the footsteps of her aunt, Helen *Suzman.

[Sally Whyte]

SVERDLIK, ODED (**Enrique**; 1938–1996), Argentinean-Israeli poet, author, literary critic, and journalist. His grandparents immigrated at the turn of the century to the Argentinean Jewish colonies established by Baron Hirsch. Born in Buenos Aires, Sverdlik was very active in leftist Zionism, one of the founders of the Ha-Shomer ha-Ẓa'ir "Mordehai Anilevich" youth group and editor of the newspaper *Nueva Sión*. His first book of poems, *Las hambres consumadas* ("The Accomplished Hungers," 1961) won him an award from the Argentine Writers Association. He published in Argentina *Las tremendas decisiones* ("The Tremendous Decisions," short stories, 1964) and *Memorias del transeúnte* ("Memories of the Passerby," poems, 1970), before he established himself in Israel in 1965. He lived in a kibbutz for five years. From 1970 to 1988 he was editor of information and study materials in Spanish at the World Zionist Organization Youth Department. His first book in Hebrew was *Ereẓ Lo Noda'at* ("Unknown Territory," short stories, 1972), followed by *Parashei ha-Ishon* ("The Riders of the Pupil of the Eye," poems, 1980) and *Ḥalonot ba-Saḥaf* ("Windows in Erosion," poems, 1986). From 1987 to 1991 Sverdlik was a member of the Hebrew Writers Association's Executive Board. In 1988 he was awarded the Levi Eshkol Prize for literary creation. In 1990 he published a Spanish anthology of self-translated poems, *Brindis* ("Toast"), and in 1992 a new book of poems in Hebrew, *Ad Kelot ha-Devash* (To the End of the Honey). At his death, he was working on another book of poems, *Ma'agal Kama'i* ("Primordial Circle"). In his last years, he became a member of the Mexican Academy of Literature and was general secretary of the Israeli PEN Club. Sverdlik also devoted himself to poetry translation from Hebrew to Spanish and vice versa, and was literary advisor and reviewer for newspapers, journals, and publishing houses in Spanish and Hebrew. His poems have been translated into English, French, German, Italian, Romanian, Hungarian, Serbian, Russian, and Lithuanian.

BIBLIOGRAPHY: A.N. Rosero (ed.), *Poesía hebrea contemporánea 1950–1983* (1986); E. Toker (ed.), *Panorama de la poesía judía contemporánea* (1989); F. Goldberg and I. Rozen (eds.), *Los latinoamericanos en Israel* (1988); M. Braver and J. Braver (eds.), *Cien años de narrativa judeo-argentina* (1990); I. Beser (ed.), *Mivḥar Shirim she-Ra'u Or bi-Meruẓat 20 Shanah be-Iton 77* (1996).

[Florinda F. Goldberg (2nd ed.)]

SVERDLOV, YAKOV MIKHAILOVICH (1885–1919), Russian revolutionary and Communist leader. Born in Nizhni-Novgorod (now Gorki), Sverdlov founded the revolutionary movement in his youth. He established the Nizhni-Novgorod Revolutionary Committee on an organized basis. He was imprisoned on two occasions and in 1910 was exiled to Siberia. Sverdlov returned to Petrograd in April 1917 and was a member of the Central Committee of the Communist Party. Shortly after the October Revolution he was elected chairman of the All-Russian Central Executive Committee and thereby titular head of state. He died suddenly on his way to a congress of the Soviets in Kharkov. Sverdlov was considered one of the outstanding figures of the Bolshevik Revolution. Lenin paid a warm tribute to him as a brilliant organizer. In 1924 the name of the city Yekaterinburg was changed to Sverdlovsk in his memory.

BIBLIOGRAPHY: K.T. Sverdlova. *Yakov M. Sverdlov* (Rus., 1960²); T.S. Bobrovskaya, *Der erste Praesident der Republik der Arbeit* (1933); L. Shapiro, *The Communist Party of the Soviet Union* (1960, 1962²), index: E.H. Carr, *The Bolshevik Revolution, 1917–1923*, 3 (1950), index.

SVETLOV, MIKHAIL (1903–1967), Soviet-Russian poet and playwright. Svetlov edited various periodicals of the Young Communist League before studying at the University of Moscow. His early volumes of lyrics, *Relsy* ("Rails," 1925) and *Korni* ("Roots," 1925), depict the heroism of the Revolution, and his famous poem *Grenada* (1926) glorifies the internationalism of the working classes. Two plays, *Skazka* ("Fairy Tale," 1939) and *Dvadtsat let spustya* ("Twenty Years Hence," 1940), portray the devotion of Russian youth to the building of the Socialist homeland.

Other poems and plays by Svetlov laud the heroism of those who fought in the Communist Revolution, the Russian civil war, and World War II. Svetlov's works reflect the conflict between his political identification and his feelings for Judaism. He frequently emphasized his Jewishness and praised the Revolution for having freed the Jews from oppression. In a series of eight poems in *Korni* called "Stikhi o rebe" ("Verses about the Rabbi"), he expressed Jewish melancholy and a yearning for the Jewish way of life which was being destroyed by the waves of revolution. He nevertheless argued that the Revolution was more important and declared that he would himself be prepared to burn the synagogue, if the Revolution required him to do so.

BIBLIOGRAPHY: A.O. Boguslavski and L.I. Timofeyev (eds.), *Russkaya sovetskaya literatura* (1936); B.Y. Braynina and E.F. Nikitina, *Sovetskiye pisateli*, 2 (1959), 304–10; E.J. Simmons, *Through the Glass of Soviet Literature* (1953), 188–9.

[Irving Malin]

SVEVO, ITALO (pen name of **Ettore Schmitz**; 1861–1928), Italian novelist. Svevo's mother was an Italian, his father an Austrian. He was educated in Germany, and on returning to his native Trieste worked as a bank clerk. From 1889 he was a partner in an industrial concern which he managed until his death, carefully separating his business from his literary life. After publishing two unsuccessful novels, *Una vita* (1892; *A Life*, 1963) and *Senilità* (1898; *As a Man Grows Older*, 1932), Svevo immersed himself in commerce for over 20 years. His talent was first discovered by the Irish writer James Joyce, who spent some time in Trieste from 1903 onward. Their friendship was mutually fruitful, and the correspondence between the two novelists, *Carteggio inedito Italo Svevo-James Joyce*, was published in 1949. It was as a result of the favorable attention it attracted in England and France that Svevo's masterpiece,

La Coscienza di Zeno (1923; *The Confessions of Zeno*, 1930), came to be recognized in Italy itself as a classic of modern Italian literature. Partly autobiographical, the book is in effect an extended monologue, self-analytical and deeply introspective, telling the story of a man's life as he observes it from the outside. A member of a middle-class mercantile family, the hero regards his life as empty of meaning, a succession of failures. Caught up in dreams and visions and beset by psychological complexes, he becomes a melancholic and ironical spokesman of the absurdity of the human condition. Like the people in similar condition with whom he comes in contact, he finds life full of irremediable disappointments. Svevo's own rejection of the unremitting flow of life is thus projected onto his hero. In spite of the fact that Svevo never explicitly related to Jews or to a Jewish milieu in his literary works, some scholars have considered them crypto-Jewish. This thesis appeared in the late 1920s in an article by Giacomo Debenedetti, one of the outstanding Italian literary critics of the last century (a Jew himself), and since then it has been proposed many times in several different versions. According to Debenedetti, Svevo symbolically describes in his works the uneasiness of the emancipated Jew not completely belonging to European Christian society, and his approach to Judaism is in some way close to the negative attitude of the Jewish-born philosopher Otto Weininger.

Svevo's colloquial style was something of an innovation in Italian writing. His cosmopolitan background and education undoubtedly contributed to his unique position in his country's literature. Immediately before and after his death in an automobile accident some of his short novellas were published. They include *Una burla riuscita* (1928; *The Hoax*, 1929) and *La novella del buon vecchio e della bella fanciulla* (1929; *The Nice Old Man and the Pretty Girl*, 1930), both successfully combining pessimism with humor and gentle irony. Two other posthumous publications are his *Corto viaggio sentimentale* (1949; *Short Sentimental Journey and Other Stories*, 1967), a collection of novellas; and a volume of essays, *Saggi e pagine sparse* (1954). His collected works, edited by B. Maier, appeared in 1954 (in English, 1962ff.).

BIBLIOGRAPHY: M. Penter, *Italo Svevo* (It., 1936); G. Spagnoletti, *La Giovinezza e la formazione letteraria di Italo Stevo* (1953); B. Maier, *Profilo della critica su Italo Svevo* (1954); E. Levi, in: *Scritti... Sally Mayer* (1956), 122–38; idem, *Opere di Italo Svevo* (1958), preface; L. Veneziani Svevo, *Vita di mio marito* (1958²); A.L. de Castris, *Italo Svevo* (It., 1959); R. Ellman, *James Joyce* (Eng., 1959), index; G. Luti, *Italo Svevo* (It., 1961); Roditi, in: Svevo, *Confessions of Zeno* (1962), 7–25; M. Forti, *Svevo romanziere* (1966); P.N. Furbank, *Italo Svevo* (Eng., 1966). **ADD. BIBLIOGRAPHY:** G. Voghera, *Gli anni della psicanalisi* (1980), 45–51 and passim; H. Stuart Hughes, *Prisoners of Hope* (1983), 33–42; P. Puppa, "Italo Svevo. La scrittura in scena," in: M. Carlà and L. De Angelis, *L'ebraismo nella letteratura italiana del Novecento* (1995), 33–42; L. De Angelis, "La reticenza di Aron. Letteratura e antisemitismo in Italo Svevo," in: *ibid.*, 43–85.

[Joseph Baruch Sermoneta / Ariel Rathaus (2nd ed.)]

SVIRSKI, ALEXEY IVANOVICH (1865–1942), author. After a nomadic youth, Svirski turned to literature, one of his early works being *Rostovskiye trushchoby* ("Slums of Rostov," 1893). Two of his best-known books were *Ryzhik, priklyucheniya brodyago* ("Ryzhik, the Adventures of a Vagrant," 1912), a popular children's story, and the autobiographical *Istoriya moyey zhizni* ("Story of My Life," 1930, 1947³). *V Cherte* ("In the Pale") and Yevrei ("Jews," 1934) were collected short stories about Jews.

SVISLOCH (Pol. **Swisłocz**), town in Grodno district, Belarus; within Poland before 1795 and between the two world wars. A number of Jews settled there at the beginning of the 18th century on the invitation of the owners of the locality, the princes of Tyszkiewicz. In 1752 the Council of Lithuania (see Councils of *Lands) imposed a poll tax of 215 zlotys on the Svisloch community, which numbered 220 in 1766. Until the middle of the 19th century the Jews of Svisloch earned their livelihood mainly from trade in timber and grain, shopkeeping, and crafts; they later also engaged in innkeeping and the lease of public houses. After a great fire, in which most of the Jewish shops were destroyed, the fairs were no longer held in Svisloch and the Jews were deprived of their principal sources of livelihood. Around 1870 Jews began to pioneer in the tanning industry and improved methods of manufacture with the assistance of German experts whom they invited. By the end of the 19th century a number of tanneries had been established in Svisloch, which employed hundreds of workers. Many Jews from the surrounding areas went there in search of employment. As early as the middle of the 19th century Jewish craftsmen in Svisloch attempted to organize themselves into guilds. At the beginning of the 20th century the *Bund Movement developed in Svisloch and it embraced the whole of the Jewish working populace (tanners, tailors, shoemakers, carpenters. smiths, and bakers), who organized strikes for the amelioration of working conditions in tanneries and factories. In 1905 the workers' organization was established for Jewish self-defense against pogroms. After World War I Zionist Socialism gained ground within the community. A *hakhsharah* farm was established by the He-Ḥalutz movement. A *Tarbut school and a school of the CYSHO (see *Education) were established. The Jewish population numbered 977 in 1847; 2,086 (67.3% of the total) in 1897; and 1,959 (66.7%) in 1921. The community came to an end in the Holocaust. Its last rabbi, Ḥayyim Jacob b. Moses Judah Mishkinski, perished together with the members of his community.

Ẓevi Hirsch *Edelman (Ḥen-Tov) and Samuel *Belkin were born in Svisloch.

BIBLIOGRAPHY: *Yizkor li-Kehillat Svisloch* (1961); A. Ain, in: *Volkovisker Yisker-Bukh*, 2 (1949); idem, in: YIVO *Bleter*, 24 (1945), 47–66; 25 (1945), 382–401; idem, in: YIVOA, 4 (1949), 86ff.; I. Halpern, *Tosafot u-Millu'im le-"Pinkas Medinat Lita"* (1935), 56ff.

[Dov Rubin]

SWABIAN LEAGUE, league of free cities in S. Germany. First formed in 1331, the league continued to exist in various forms for two centuries. Under the leadership of *Ulm, 14 cities were the basis of the revitalized league of 1376. When Charles IV put a ban on Jud *Jaecklin, a Jewish moneylender who had lent large sums to Ulm and to other member cities, Ulm refused to turn him over to the authorities, since Jaecklin had helped the city to increase its territory by forcing indebted nobles to sell their estates to it. Charles IV waged war against Ulm but was forced to acknowledge defeat, recognize the league, and repeal the ban. In 1384 the Jewish community of *Noerdlingen, a member city, was massacred and persecutions also took place in Windsheim and Weissenburg. The league forced the latter cities to indemnify the victims and ordered Noerdlingen to return the confiscated books of deceased Jews. The council of Noerdlingen procrastinated and finally paid a sum to the emperor *Wenceslaus in order to obtain a pardon; as a result, Noerdlingen was ejected from the league. Emperor Wenceslaus, who was deeply in debt and interested in enriching his treasury, opened negotiations with the league. The result of these negotiations (in which the Rhenish league also took part) was the decision to liquidate a portion of all debts owed to Jews (*Judenschuldentilgung*). On June 10, 1385 the cities agreed not to harbor any nonlocal refugee Jews. All Jews were arrested on June 16, 1385, and their books confiscated. The emperor received 40,000 gulden from the cities, but the total financial benefit was actually greater. The debts of the nobility were transferred to the cities for payment. Five years later. however, Wenceslaus declared a total moratorium on debts owed to Jews. This act in favor of the nobles was in effect a blow against the cities of the league, which lost much potential revenue as a result. In the process of Wenceslaus' financial manipulations, many Jews were ruined.

BIBLIOGRAPHY: A Suessmann, *Judenschuldentilgungen unter Koenig Wenzel* (1907), index s.v. *Schwaebischer Bund*; H. Dicker, *Geschichte der Juden in Ulm* (1937), 25–40; L. Wallach in: HJ, 8 (1946), 184–6; Baron, Social2, 12 (1967), 194–6; I. Stein, *Juden der schwaebischen Reichsstaedte im Zeitalter Koenig Sigmunds: 1410–37* (1902).

SWADESH, MORRIS (1909–1967), U.S. anthropological linguist. Born in Holyoke, Massachusetts, Swadesh served as research associate at Yale from 1933 to 1937. He taught anthropology at various universities and was appointed research professor of prehistoric linguistics at Universidad Nacional Autónoma de México, Mexico City.

His particular interest was in the recording and description of various languages, notably the American Indian dialects. He also studied the reconstruction of prehistory through comparative linguistics as well as methods of teaching languages, culture history, and general theories of culture. One of his major contributions was to glottochronology or lexicostatistics, which is a linguistic method for determining the relative time depth when related languages become separated from their common source. Swadesh was also an important contributor to the study of numerous American Indian languages.

[Ephraim Fischoff]

SWANSEA, second largest industrial city and seaport in Wales. Swansea's Jewish community (the first in Wales) was established in the mid-18th century; the first settler known by name was David Michael, who came from Germany in 1741. Religious services were held soon afterward and a cemetery acquired in 1768. The first synagogue was opened in 1780, being replaced by one erected in 1818. As in most British provincial centers, the community consisted of silversmiths, watchmakers, jewelers, and other shopkeepers and craftsmen; by 1850 it numbered around 100–150, increasing to 1,000 in 1914 as a result of immigration from Russia. In 1969 the Jewish population numbered 418 (0.3% of the total). In the mid-1990s the Jewish population was estimated at approximately 245. The 2001 British census found 170 declared Jews in Swansea. Its old synagogue was destroyed in an air raid in 1941 and a new one, which still functions, was erected after World War II.

BIBLIOGRAPHY: C. Roth, *Rise of Provincial Jewry* (1950), index; V.D. Lipman, *Social History of the Jews of England: 1850–1950* (1954), index; R.P. Lehmann, *Nova Bibliotheca Anglo-Judaica* (1961), 156, 192.

[Vivian David Lipman]

SWARSENSKY, HARDI (**Bernhard**; 1908–1968), journalist and publisher. Born in Berlin, Swarsensky graduated as a lawyer and practiced law briefly until he was debarred by the Nazis in 1933. During the next few years he devoted himself to Jewish communal life in Germany and was active in the leadership of the Reichsverband der Juden in Deutschland. In 1939 he immigrated to Buenos Aires, where in 1940 he founded the German-Jewish weekly *Juedische Wochenschau*, which he edited until his death. A passionate Zionist and supporter of Israel, he was president of the Theodor Herzl Gesellschaft from 1942 and of the large German-Jewish communal organization Nueva Comunidad Israelita from 1942 until 1953. He was also a leading figure in the World Jewish Congress and one of the founders of Centra, the umbrella organization of Central-European Jewish organizations in Latin America. In 1942 he founded the publishing house Estrellas, which issued works by German-Jewish and Argentine-Jewish authors, including many of his own writings: *Von Basel nach Jerusalem* (1945), *Eroberung durch Aufbau* (1949), *Walter Rathenau* (Sp., 1967), *Noche de Cristal* (1968), and *Pogrom ueber Deutschland* (1969).

SWEATSHOP POETRY, movement in American Yiddish literature whose main representatives are Joseph *Bovshover, David *Edelstadt, Morris *Rosenfeld, and Morris *Vinchevsky. The mass immigration of East European Jews to the United States beginning in the 1880s confronted many of the immigrants for the first time with a metropolis, where a large portion of them found employment in the garment industry, many in the sweatshops of New York City. The American Yiddish press, which developed during the same period, generally espoused radical political tendencies and sought to win over working-class readers to the causes of socialism, communism, and anarchism. Throughout the 1880s and 1890s, newspapers such as *Arbeter Tsaytung, Forverts, Di Varheyt, Der Folksadvokat*, and *Fraye Arbeter Shtime* published poems of social protest, describing the oppressive working and living conditions of their readers, which aimed at stirring their mass audiences to social revolution. The poetry produced within this context represents the first phase of Yiddish literature in America.

BIBLIOGRAPHY: I. Howe, *World of Our Fathers* (1976), 420–24; C. Madison, *Yiddish Literature* (1968), 138–40; S. Liptzin, *Flowering of Yiddish Literature* (1963), 131–48; idem, *A History of Yiddish Literature* (1972), 89–7.

[Marc Miller (2nd ed.)]

SWEDEN, kingdom in N. Europe, part of the Scandinavian peninsula. It is unlikely that there were Jews in Sweden in pagan times or in the Catholic Middle Ages, nor was their presence favored in Lutheran Sweden. Several regulations issued in 1685, directed against the presence of Jews in the country, seem to indicate that Jews had resided there illegally for certain periods. In the first ordinance, which referred to the Jews as "revilers of Christ and his communion" and justified their removal from the country in order to protect the pure Lutheran faith, permission to stay was granted in exceptional cases only. Some Jewish creditors of Charles XII, who had followed the king from Turkey, were allowed to stay in Sweden with their families for about ten years.

The position changed under the rule of the enlightened monarch Gustav III (1771–92). In 1774 Aaron Isaac, a seal engraver from Buetzow, Mecklenburg, arrived in Stockholm; in the following year he received the king's permission to settle there, along with his brother, his partners, and their families. A cemetery was consecrated with royal permission in 1776; subsequently it was named Aronsberg in honor of Aaron Isaac. In 1779 Parliament, with the king's support, granted Jews the right to settle in Stockholm, Göteborg, and Norrköping, under certain conditions and with a measure of religious freedom. Accordingly, in 1782 the royal office of trade and commerce issued "regulations governing those members of the Jewish people who wish to enter the country." The Swedish regulations were modeled on those of other European countries, especially *Prussia, but in certain respects they were more liberal, so as to attract potentially useful Jewish immigrants. Jews were allowed to settle only in the three cities mentioned above, where they could hold religious services, acquire real estate, and engage in industry and in those trades that were not subject to the guilds. According to the country's constitution, non-Christians were excluded from all government positions and were not entitled to vote. On the other hand, following the practice of other European countries, Jews were allowed autonomy in their own affairs, including religious worship and welfare activities, inheritances, guardianships, and marriages. Intermarriage was prohibited, with the exemption of a few wealthy Jews. While these laws were in force, Jews in the cities were regarded as rivals and intruders, while the predominantly liberal-minded officialdom came to their defense. The accusations against the Jews, as well as the arguments in their defense, were basically the same as those found on the European mainland. The financial crises which afflicted Europe after the Napoleonic wars led to antisemitic agitations in Sweden as elsewhere.

To those influenced by economic liberalism, including King Charles XIV John and his minister of finance, the 1782 regulation governing Jewish immigration appeared increasingly obsolete. It was repealed on June 30, 1838, and replaced by a royal decree by which the Swedish Jews, hitherto a colony of foreigners enjoying defined rights, were incorporated into the Swedish state. From then on they were to be called "adherents of the Mosaic faith," an appellation which remained officially valid. The former *kehillot* were termed Mosaic communities and Jewish autonomy was abolished. The restrictions on Jews contained in the constitution and the civil code could not be lifted without the approval of Parliament, but virtually all administrative practices detrimental to them were wiped out. However, the new decree aroused such strong and widespread opposition that in September of the same year the government was obliged to abrogate the regulation entitling the Jews to settle anywhere in the country. Henceforth, foreign Jews were permitted to reside only in Stockholm, Göteborg, and Norrköping as before, with the addition of Karlskrona. Despite these concessions to anti-Jewish feelings, no reform in the history of Swedish Jewry can compare in significance with the decree of June 1838, which marked the beginning of a development that led to complete political emancipation and basic acceptance as citizens and members of the community. This decree, albeit modified in a few points, governed the civil rights of Swedish Jews until 1951. Due to the conservative immigration policy of the government, the number of Jews in 1838 was still small, amounting to about 900 persons, more than 800 of whom lived in Stockholm and Göteborg.

During the 1840s, free trade principles prevailed in Sweden; this led to the lifting of almost all existing restrictions on Jewish occupations and, in turn, to the elimination of the conflict of interest between the Jews and the rest of the population. On the initiative of the government and liberal-minded members of Parliament, the emancipation of the Jews was completed during the ensuing decades. They were entitled to reside in any part of the country, to acquire real estate, to intermarry, and to participate in municipal elections. The last barrier fell in 1870. After long debates the Jews (and the Catholics) were given the franchise and entitled to hold political office. Nevertheless, until 1951 membership of the Swedish state church was a requirement for ministerial office. Paralleling emancipation, assimilation made rapid gains. Religious services were modeled on those of German Reform Jewry. The psalms were chanted in Swedish and sermons delivered in that language. The liturgy, although shortened, continued to be in Hebrew, but Swedish prayers were interpolated. The community of Göteborg led the way toward Reform and was the first to introduce the use of the organ in the synagogue (1855). Members of the Henriques and Warburg families were

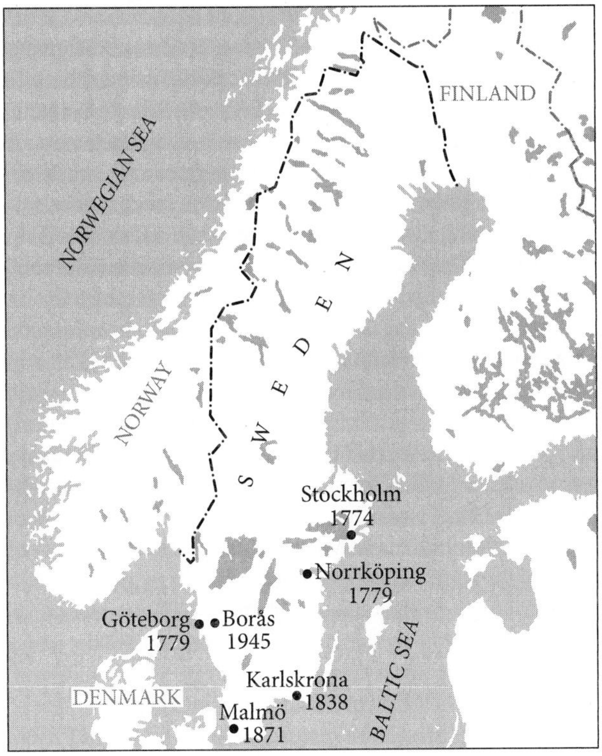

Jewish communities in Sweden, with dates of establishment.

especially active in favor of Reform, backed by the chief rabbi of Göteborg, Carl Heinemann (1837–68).

The rise of political antisemitism in Central Europe was of little significance for the Jews of Sweden. Their relationship with the non-Jewish population remained harmonious, although there was a perceptible increase in antisemitic manifestations. The Jews played a major role in the cultural life of Sweden, out of proportion to their numbers, especially in the fields of music, painting, and literary criticism. However, Jewish activities declined. During that period, the chief rabbi of Stockholm, Hungarian-born Gottlieb Klein (1882–1944), was the outstanding representative of liberal theology. Immigration from eastern Europe proved to be one of the most significant events of the period between the 1860s and 1933. The new immigrants were more pronouncedly Jewish than the old Swedish-Jewish families that dominated the congregations founded during the 18th century. They supported the existing congregations and founded new ones in the provinces, for example in Malmö. According to official statistics, in 1880 about 3,000 Jews lived in Sweden. The 1930 census recorded 7,044 Jews in the country, 1,391 of whom were non-citizens. About 4,000 resided in Stockholm, and the majority of the others in Malmö and Göteborg.

Holocaust Period

The victory of National Socialism in Germany (1933) created in Sweden a Jewish and a refugee problem. Efforts by Swedish Jewish refugee organizations to save German Jews by transferring them to Sweden were impeded by the country's restrained refugee policy. The authorities feared that the refugees would increase unemployment, from which Sweden suffered badly as a result of the 1929 world crisis, and that antisemitism would grow because of an increasing Jewish population. The upper echelon of Swedish society had been pro-German from earlier days, and although the Nazis were never powerful in Sweden, antisemitism increased as Hitler's power expanded. In 1938, when it became publicly known that the Jews in Germany were in imminent physical danger, the Swedish Jewish and other refugee organizations increased their pressure on the Swedish government to develop a more liberal immigration policy. The consequence was sensational counter-measures in business circles, polemics in the press, and even denouncements, by various student organizations and other bodies, of the so-called "Jewish invasion." The motivations behind these measures were usually not directly antisemitic, but stressed in particular the dangers connected with unemployment. The consideration of the so-called "racial question" was undeniable, however. The government yielded to public pressure, and the fact that Sweden abolished the regulation allowing every alien to remain in the country for three months without a visa was of far-reaching importance. The obligation to have a visa was from then on dealt with very strictly, especially for Jews, and thousands of requests were denied, even when the required material guarantees were provided by Swedish Jews. Up to the beginning of the war, about 3,000 refugees were able to leave Germany, Austria, and Czechoslovakia for Sweden, in addition to 1,000 so-called transmigrants who traveled on from Sweden to other countries. After *Kristallnacht* (Nov. 1938), 150 adults and 500 children (without their parents) were granted entry permits. A Jewish immigration committee was charged with the painful task of choosing out of the many applications, so that the quota would not be surpassed. Among those who were unable to continue their trip because of the outbreak of the war were a few hundred *ḥalutzim* (members of Zionist youth movements intending to settle in Palestine) who – following the Danish example – were admitted temporarily to agricultural and other training centers (*hakhsharah*). During World War II public opinion changed in favor of the refugees, for several reasons. The crimes of the Nazis, which many circles had previously refused to admit, became publicly known. Instead of unemployment there now was a shortage of workers. Moreover, it was realized that, with some good will, it would be possible to receive many more refugees than was previously thought. The turning point in the history of Swedish refugee policy and antisemitism came in November 1942, when Jewish persecutions in German-occupied Norway began. These provoked a general feeling of disgust and angry protests throughout Sweden. About 900 Norwegian Jews who were able to escape to Sweden were readily admitted.

How decisive the change of mind was became obvious in October 1943, when Danish Jewry took flight in order to escape deportation. After a fruitless démarche to the German Foreign Office, the Swedish government officially offered asylum to the fleeing Jews, setting an example of humane policy.

Encouraged by the turning tide of the war, the unanimous public opinion in Sweden, and the acclaim of the free world, the Swedish government not only received about 8,000 Jews and some of their relatives from Denmark, but also an almost equal number of Danes fleeing from the German occupation. Moreover, it tolerated the establishment of a clandestine organization on its soil, providing the Danish resistance movement with steadfast communication with the Allies. The communication lines were initiated and maintained with the organizational and financial aid of the Swedish and Danish Jews, among whom Ivar Philipson, a Stockholm lawyer, took a prominent part. Some leaders of the Jewish community in Stockholm were also instrumental in bringing about the mission of Raoul *Wallenberg to Hungary (1944), where he became one of the main benefactors and rescuers of the Budapest Jewish community. Under the guidance of the *World Jewish Congress (WJC), toward the end of the war, Sweden became an important center for the dispatch of food parcels to concentration camp inmates, mainly in Germany. Finally the ties formed by the representative of the WJC, Hillel Storch, with Himmler's masseur, Kersten, led to the historic meeting of Norbert Mazur with Himmler on the eve of Germany's final defeat (April 20–21, 1945). Following their negotiations, many more thousands of concentration camp inmates were included in the rescue operation of Count Folke *Bernadotte. Among the almost 21,000 thus rescued were 3,500 Jews, mostly women. After the war some 10,000 more were brought to Sweden by the Red Cross and UNRRA. Altogether, more than 200,000 refugees – Finns, Norwegians, Danes, Jews and others – reached Sweden during and after the war.

[Hugo Mauritz Valentin]

Post-War Period

Almost all the Jews of Norway and Denmark who escaped to Sweden returned to their native countries at the end of the war. About half the refugees liberated from concentration camps who went to Sweden toward the end of the war or immediately afterward emigrated overseas, mostly to the United States and Canada or to Israel, while half remained and became citizens of Sweden. As a result, the 1970 Jewish population in Sweden was double that of 1933 and was estimated at 13,000–14,000. According to a 1961 estimate, approximately 1,500 lived in Göteborg, 1,500 in Malmö, 7,000 in Stockholm, 350 in Borås (almost all survivors of the Holocaust), 150 in Norrköping, and the rest were dispersed in smaller centers. Of the total number, over 5,000 were considered veteran citizens and their descendants, i.e. Jews who had come to Sweden before 1933; over 2,000 were refugees from Central Europe from 1933–39; about 5,500 were survivors of the concentration camps; and approximately 500 were refugees who fled from Hungary in the wake of the 1956 revolution. To these should be added about 1,500 refugees from Poland who went to Sweden after 1968.

The absorption of the many refugees presented Swedish Jewry with new and difficult problems. At the end of World War II the Jewish communities levied an additional income tax on their members. Half of the revenue from this tax was designated for aid to refugees. Fifteen special schools were opened for refugee children and over 700 students were enrolled in 1946. The aid granted by the Swedish government and the Jewish community was augmented by international Jewish funds, mostly from the American Jewish *Joint Distribution Committee, and later from the *Conference on Jewish Material Claims. Gradually a considerable degree of amalgamation of the refugees and the veteran Jewish community was achieved. In the late 1950s it was possible to state that the majority of the refugees were absorbed in Sweden, from an economic and professional standpoint, and some even socially and culturally.

The shock of the Holocaust, which nearly reached the gates of Sweden, and the experience of encounter with the refugees left a deep impression on Swedish Jewry, in contrast to the isolationist trend that had predominated until the war. The consciousness that they were part of world Jewry and responsible for their brethren found expression in increased participation in world and European Jewish organizations, such as the *World Jewish Congress, ORT, and later the Conference on Jewish Material Claims Against Germany, as well as the Standing Conference of European Jewish Communities. Increased activity on behalf of the establishment of a Jewish state and support of the State of Israel after its establishment were also expressions of the new attitude of the Swedish community. The Zionist movement, which was supported only by a small minority before the war, expanded, and many refugees and veterans joined it. Even most professed non-Zionists participated in activity on behalf of the *yishuv*. A special appeal for the *Haganah in the winter of 1947–48 collected $300,000, the greatest amount ever reached by an Israel appeal in Sweden (with the exception of the emergency campaign during the *Six-Day War in 1967). A group of young Jews participated as volunteers in the *War of Independence in 1948. The movement on behalf of Israel was further strengthened by the attitude of the Swedish public, which supported the Jewish people's struggle for a state not only through moral and political support but also by providing material aid.

The law of freedom of religion in 1951 abolished the regulation of 1838 requiring that citizens affiliate with a religious organization, on the grounds that a citizen has the right to free decision. The new law aroused great concern among the Jewish communities, which feared that their economic position would be undermined. Apparently these fears were unjustified, for only 350 Jewish adults broke away from their communities. In the postwar period Jewish life was characterized by considerable activity in comparison with the prewar period. Particularly noteworthy were the women's organizations (*WIZO and the General Organization of Jewish Women), in addition to increased activity on the part of the Zionists. Other organizations included that of the Nazi victims, the Scandinavian Organization of Jewish Students (SJUF), and the *Bnei Akiva youth movement. Chapters of *B'nai B'rith were founded in the three major cities, Stockholm, Göteborg, and Malmö. The struggle within the communities between Zionists and non-Zionists continued, but the crux of the dispute was not support for Israel, but rather the question of separate Jewish education. On the initiative of the Zionists and the Orthodox, the Hinnukh association established the Hillel Day School in Stockholm. In addition, the communities provided religious instruction in the public schools and ran day camps and summer camps. Cultural activities expanded due to the establishment of a cultural institute on the initiative of newspaper editor Daniel Brick; the cultural club attached to the Israeli embassy; and a large community center established in Stockholm in 1963 with the aid of the Conference on Jewish Material Claims against Germany. Brick published the bi-weekly *Judisk Kronika* (1932–). A learned monthly, *Judisk Tidskrift*, was founded by Marcus *Ehrenpreis in 1928 and later edited by Hugo *Valentin, the veteran of the Zionist movement, a historian of Swedish Jewry, and perhaps the most admired figure among Sweden's Jews in his generation. Some time after his death in 1963, the monthly ceased publication.

The economic situation of Swedish Jewry is generally healthy. Jews are active in business, industry, and the liberal professions; they do not hold key positions in the economy, however, with the exception of department stores, which developed mainly through their initiative. Jews occupy a respectable position in cultural and literary life, in the theater, and in the graphic arts. Ragnar *Josephson was a member of the Swedish Academy, which numbers only 18 members and awards the Nobel Prize for Literature. There were no Jews outstanding in Swedish political life, with the exception of Hjalmar Mehr, who served as mayor of Stockholm in the early 1960s. Antisemitism was not widespread; indeed, the extremist antisemitic group led by Einar Åberg had merely a marginal influence on society. Most of the Swedish people rejected antisemitism and were sometimes active on behalf of persecuted Jews. From the 1960s there were conspicuous Swedish efforts on behalf of Jews in the Soviet Union and Arab countries. Swedish Jewry not only enjoys equality, but finds few cultural barriers as well, which has resulted in an increase in the number of intermarriages. While the Holocaust experience and the absorption of the refugees strengthened Jewish identity, the small number of Jews and the openness of Swedish society have worked in the opposite direction.

[Chaim Yahil]

By the mid-1990s, there were 18,000 Jews living in Sweden, a figure that remained stable. The main communities are Stockholm, Göteborg, and Malmö. There are also communities in Borås, Varberg, and Uppsala, and a number of Jews live in Helsingborg, Lund, Norrköping, and Växjö. A number of emigrants from the former Soviet Union have also settled in Sweden. The communities are linked by the Official Council of Jewish Communities in Sweden. Swedish Jewry is very active in international Jewish welfare and in supporting development projects in Israel. Stockholm has three synagogues (two Orthodox, one Conservative) and two rabbis. Göteborg has two (one Orthodox, one Conservative) and Malmö one. A Jewish primary school and a kindergarten operate in Stockholm. The community still publishes the bimonthly *Judisk Kronka*, and there is a weekly Jewish radio program. Göteborg has long had a Jewish kindergarten, Noah's Ark, which was relocated to new multi-purpose premises at a community center that also houses the Jewish retirement home and a kosher food store. In 2002 a Jewish primary school was opened in Göteborg, already doubling in size the following year. The Göteborg community also broadcasts a weekly hour-long Jewish radio program with music, interviews, cultural reviews, and news, repeated on the weekend.

The *Chabad movement established a small presence in Göteborg in 1991, and in 1992 opened a kindergarten, Gan Chaya Mushka, followed five years later by a primary school.

The Swedish legal system permits the expression of antisemitic, racist, and xenophobic ideas, including Holocaust denial, under liberal freedom of speech legislation. Right-wing extremist groups, often with neo-Nazi sympathies, number a few thousand members. The Palestinian Intifada in Israel in the early 2000s was accompanied by a sharp rise in antisemitic attacks in Sweden and a far harsher, less nuanced tone in both the Swedish media and among many of the country's politicians.

See also *Scandinavian Literature.

[Chaim Yahil / Ilya Meyer (2nd ed.)]

Relations with Israel

The supportive attitude of most of the Swedish people toward the Jews also found expression in Swedish-Israel relations. Because of Sweden's neutrality, her representatives more than once filled important positions in connection with the Palestine question. In 1947, Emil Sandström served as chairman of the special United Nations Committee on Palestine (UNSCOP), which recommended the partition of the country. Count Folke *Bernadotte was the first mediator on behalf of the United Nations on the Israel-Arab conflict in 1948. Dag Hammarskjöld, the secretary-general of the United Nations, was occupied with the problem of Palestine; General von Horn was chief of staff of the United Nations truce observers; and Gunnar Jarring was a special envoy of the UN after the Six-Day War. The assassination of Bernadotte in Jerusalem (1948) overshadowed Swedish-Israel relations for some time and contributed to a delay in the establishment of diplomatic relations between the two countries until 1950 (ambassadorial level, 1957). But this tragic affair did not alter the basic sympathy of most of the Swedish people toward Israel, and in the course of time regular, friendly relations were established. Swedish policy – traditionally framed by long-dominant Labor governments – has generally supported several principles which were the foundation of Israeli policy: the aspiration for peace, the principle of direct negotiations to solve the Israel-Arab conflict, condemnation of the Arab economic boycott, freedom of passage through the Suez Canal and the Straits of Tiran. On the other hand, Sweden has had – and often voiced – reservations about retaliatory raids and preventive acts on the part of Israel. Her sympathy toward Israel is traditionally echoed in all mainstream political parties – the liberal movement; the evangelical religious movements; the conservative movement. In the late 1960s a "New Left" movement developed with a critical or even hostile attitude toward Israel. Swedish sympathy with Israel has in the past been expressed by financial support from Rädda Barnen, the Swedish branch of Save the Children Fund, and special committees, the most important of which was founded by Selma Arnheim and has supported Youth Aliyah for many years. Swedish funds have established a village in the south of Israel and a children's institution in Jerusalem; women's organizations have participated in the establishment of a training center in Haifa, for communal work in developing countries; and professional unions at one time aided border settlements. Since the 1980s, much of this support has been eroded by increasing sympathy for the Palestinian cause, aided by widespread media and political activity. This general sympathy for the Palestinian cause has resulted in a sizable downturn in Swedish tourism in Israel, in stark contrast to the seven-fold increase in tourism between 1960 and the Six-Day War, for example. There are strong trade links between Sweden and Israel, although the traditional Israeli exports of fruit, vegetables, flowers, and chemicals have been replaced by high-tech products, mainly in the fields of advanced electronics, communications, and medical equipment. Mutual chambers of commerce have been established in both countries. A wide network of cultural connections between the two countries has been systematically expanded. Cultural relations were cemented with the granting of the Nobel Prize for Literature to S.Y. Agnon in 1966, and there is now a vibrant cultural exchange between the two countries, despite frequent calls for boycotts of all Israeli products as well as of sports and cultural exchanges by an increasingly polarized Left and the highly political pro-Palestinian, anti-Israel stance taken by the head of the Swedish Church, Archbishop K.G. Hammar. Leagues for Swedish-Israel friendship exist in both countries

[Chaim Yahil / Ilya Meyer (2nd ed.)]

BIBLIOGRAPHY: GENERAL: H. Valentin, *Judarnas historia i Sverige* (1924); idem, in: YIVOA, 8 (1953); V. Jacobowsky, *Göteborgs mosaiska församling* (1955); W. Siegel, *Mosaiska församlingen i Malmö 75 a'r* (1946). 17th TO 19th CENTURIES: M. Ivarsson and A. Brody, *Svensk-judiska pionjärer och stamfäder...* (1956); B. Tarschys, *Chevra Kaddischa 150 år* (1944). HOLOCAUST AND CONTEMPORARY PERIOD: L. Yahil, *Rescue of Danish Jewry* (1969); idem, in: *Yad Vashem Studies*, 6 (1967), 181–220; Adler-Rudel in: YLBI, 11 (1966), 220–41; H. Valentin, *Judarna i Sverige* (1964). **ADD. BIBLIOGRAPHY:** *Mosaiska församlingen i Göteborg 200 år* (1980); I. Lomfors, in: S. Scharfstein, *Judisk historia från renässansen till 2000-talet* (2002); F. Bedoire, *Ett judiskt Europa – kring uppkomsten av en modern arkitektur 1830–1930* (1998); B. Moback, *Livet är ingen banalitet – judiska röster* (2001).

SWET, GERSHON (1893–1968), journalist. Born in the Ukraine, Swet went in 1921 to Berlin as a correspondent for the Warsaw Yiddish newspaper *Moment*. While increasingly active in the Zionist movement, he became an expert in two fields: international politics, especially Jewish, and music. After two years in Paris (1933–35) he went to Palestine and was a member of the editorial staff of *Haaretz*. He also served as chairman of the Association of Journalists in Jerusalem; in addition, in 1938, he edited the musical journal *Musica Hebraica*. In 1948 *Haaretz* sent him as a correspondent to the United Nations in New York. There he wrote regular columns for the German-Jewish *Aufbau* and the Russian *Novoye Russkoye Slovo*. He also conducted his own weekly news programs on the radio in Russian and Yiddish, and served as press officer of the Jewish Agency and foreign correspondent for *La Pensée Russe* in Paris.

SWIDNICA (Ger. **Schweidnitz**), town in Silesia, Poland. A synagogue existed in Swidnica in 1285 and a cemetery also served neighboring communities, its oldest gravestone dating from 1289. At the end of 1301 a dispute arose between a Christian butcher and the Jews; this was settled in early 1302 when six Jews were given limited slaughtering rights. In 1328 Duke Bolko II of Schweidnitz confirmed the liberal privileges granted by his grandfather in 1295, including the right to trade and to lend money without restriction, thus protecting the moneylending Jews after they were excluded from other trades by the guilds. A commission was constituted of four Jewish community leaders ("der Viere") which possessed wide powers; among other accomplishments, it foiled the town's attempt to open a brothel on the Jews' street. During the *Black Death the community was annihilated. In 1370 the new community was permitted to open a synagogue. Swidnica maintained an important yeshivah at which R. Israel *Isserlein and David Falkind, teacher of R. Israel *Bruna, were active. In 1453 John of *Capistrano appeared at Swidnica and accused the Jews of desecrating the *Host; 17 were burnt and the rest expelled. There was no community for three centuries and the synagogue was converted into a chapel.

A new community, organized in 1859, increased from 137 to 339 in 1880, and a synagogue was consecrated in 1877. The community declined to 130 by 1925 and came to an end under the Nazis.

After World War II the community was renewed by Polish Jews; in 1962 a Jewish producers' cooperative was recorded. After the Six-Day War (1967) communal life practically ceased to exist.

BIBLIOGRAPHY: M. Brann, *Geschichte der Juden in Schlesien*, 6 vols. (1896–1917), passim; FJW, 95; A. Grotte, *Synagogenspuren in schlesischen Kirchen* (1937), 25–36; AJYB, 63 (1962), 376–7; Germ Jud, 2 (1968), 754–5; PK, Germanyah.

SWIFT (Heb. סִיס, *sis*), a bird of the genus *Apus* of which three species are found in Israel, the most common being *Apus apus pekinensis*, a small black bird similar to the swallow. Large flights of swifts reach Israel at the end of February and frequent the populated places where their food – flies and mosquitoes – is to be found, filling the air with their cry of "sis-sis," whence their Hebrew name. Their cry sounds like that of a person in pain and to it King Hezekiah compared his groans during his illness (Isa. 38:14). Jeremiah (8:7) notes that the bird arrives in the land at a fixed date. In Israel the swift nests in the interstices of walls and roofs until, at the beginning of July when the fledglings are grown, it returns to South Africa.

BIBLIOGRAPHY: Lewysohn, Zool, 209, no. 258; F.S. Bodenheimer, *Animal and Man in Bible Lands* (1960), 58; J. Feliks, *Animal World of the Bible* (1962), 89.

[Jehuda Feliks]

SWIG, BENJAMIN HARRISON (1893–1980), U.S. businessman and philanthropist. His father, Simon Swig, an immigrant from Lithuania, rose from an ordinary peddler to become a Republican member of the Massachusetts State Legislature and founder of the Tremont Trust Company of Taunton, Mass., for which Benjamin went to work in 1914. He remained with the company until 1920, when it went bankrupt in consequence of the Ponzi postal-coupon scandal. Swig then ventured into the real estate business, in which he prospered until the stock market crash of October 1929, which ruined him financially. He recouped his fortune, however, and in 1937 joined forces with his brother-in-law, J.D. *Weiler, a real estate broker from New York. By the 1940s Swig and Weiler had become one of the largest real estate firms in the United States. In 1945 Swig settled in San Francisco, a city with which his commercial and civic activities were thereafter largely identified. Among the properties acquired by him there were the Fairmont Hotel and the St. Francis; the Bankers Investment Building; and the giant Merchandise Mart.

He began to take an interest in Democratic Party politics, to which he contributed handsomely, was active in the Stevenson campaigns of 1952 and 1956, and was an early supporter of John F. Kennedy, and later, Robert Kennedy. He was a founding member of Brandeis University and gave generously to the State of Israel, as well as a large number of general and Jewish charities, especially the United Jewish Appeal, Israel Bonds, the Hebrew University of Jerusalem, and the national Reform movement. He also gave to many Catholic institutions, including the University of Santa Clara. In 1988, the Mae and Benjamin Swig Fund for Jewish Community Involvement was established as part of the Jewish Community Endowment Fund of the Jewish Community Federation of San Francisco, the Peninsula, Marin and Sonoma Counties. It is dedicated to seed funding programs that provide innovative models for the involvement of individuals in the Jewish community.

Swig's son RICHARD (1925–1997) managed the Fairmont Hotel from 1946. As chairman of the Fairmont Hotel Management Company, he expanded the Fairmont hotel chain into seven major U.S. cities. Following in his family's philanthropic footsteps, he served on numerous boards encompassing all religious, political, and cultural arenas, contributing generously to a wide array of causes. In 1998 the Swig Company sold its interests in three of its Fairmont hotels (in San Francisco, Dallas, and New Orleans), as well as its 50 percent interest in the Fairmont Hotel Management Company, to a hotel investment fund run by Maritz, Wolff & Co.

BIBLIOGRAPHY: W.J. Blum, *Benjamin H. Swig: the Measure of a Man* (1968). **ADD. BIBLIOGRAPHY:** B. Scharlach, *Dealing from the Heart: A Biography of Benjamin Swig* (2000).

[Hillel Halkin / Ruth Beloff (2nd ed.)]

SWITZERLAND, central European republic.

The Medieval Community

Since the frontiers of Switzerland have undergone a long process of evolution, it is difficult to determine where and when the Jews appeared for the first time.

In Kaiseraugst a finger-ring with a carved *menorah*, a *shofar*, and an *etrog* were found in Roman ruins. They are dated to the end of the fourth century. From then on there is no evidence of Jewish life until the 13th century.

Jews are first mentioned in *Basle from 1213, when the bishop of the town ordered the return of the pledges which he had deposited with a Jewish moneylender. In the list of the taxes due from the most important Jewish communities of the Holy Roman Empire (1241), Basle is mentioned as liable for 40 silver marks and 20 silver marks. In the course of the 13th century the first Jewish communities appeared in *Lucerne (1252), *Berne (1262–63), *St. Gall (1268), Winterthur (before 1270), *Zurich (1273), *Schaffhausen (1278), Zofingen and Bischofszell (1288), and Rheinfelden (1290). The number of communities increased in the succeeding century, when there were some 30 communities in the German-speaking part of Switzerland. At the same time, increasing numbers of communities were established in what has become the French-speaking area of Switzerland, then part of the region where the house of Savoy held sway: besides *Geneva, where the first Jewish settlement is mentioned in 1281–82, 14 communities were formed at the end of the 13th and beginning of the 14th centuries.

It is apparent that most of these Jews came from Alsace and southern Germany on the one hand and from France on the other, the stream of immigration gaining in intensity after the expulsion of the Jews from France in 1306. The taxes of the Jews were paid to the counts of Hapsburg in the north and to the dukes of Savoy in the south, with the towns often securing a portion of these revenues for themselves. On occasion, the Jews received the freedom of a city in the north, but this was of limited duration. The principal occupation of these groups of Jews was moneylending. The most important communities in Switzerland proper were those of Berne, Zurich, and Lucerne.

In Zurich a beautiful reception hall of a Jewish moneylender has been discovered. He painted the coat of arms of his noble clients with Hebrew inscriptions on the walls.

By the middle of the 14th century the right to authorize the existence of a community had been transferred to the towns. The communities appear to have been relatively small; Berne, Zurich, and some other communities seem to have owned cemeteries. The life of the Jews until the middle of the 14th century appears to have been free of any major upheavals, with the exception of Berne, where as the result of a *blood libel (c. 1294) some Jews were executed and the rest expelled. The tomb of the supposedly martyred child in the blood libel case was for a long time a place of pilgrimage for Christians. In 1403 another libel was voiced in Diessenhofen, leading to persecutions in Schaffhausen. In 1348 the whole of Swiss Jewry was threatened with extermination. The *Black Death having reached Savoy, a number of Jews of Chillon were tortured to confess to having caused the plague by poisoning the wells. As news of this spread to other communities on Lake Geneva, to German-speaking Switzerland, and to northern Europe, a wave of anti-Jewish persecutions ensued; as each town was struck by the plague, the Jews were burnt at the stake. This was the fate of almost all the communities on the shores of Lake Geneva. When the municipality of Berne learned of these accusations, it requested a copy of the confession, and soon after, the Jews of Berne too were burnt at the stake (November 1348). One local Jew was even accused of having sent poison to the Jews of Basle, and the municipality warned various towns to beware of the Jewish poisoners. Practically all the towns of Switzerland took up the accusation, burning or expelling the Jews, particularly Zurich (Feb. 22, 1349) and Lucerne. These persecutions also spread to Alsace and Germany. The community of Switzerland was thus dispersed, if not annihilated. A few years later, however, the survivors, together with newcomers, had reestablished themselves and reconstituted the former communities. However, as a result of the competition of the Lombards and the Cahorsins, the usefulness of the Jews as a source of credit soon diminished and they were expelled from those towns which required residence permits (Berne, 1427; *Fribourg, 1428; Zurich, 1436; Geneva, 1490). From Basle they fled out of fear of persecution (1397). Soon, only a few Jewish physicians were allowed to live in the Swiss towns. After expulsions from the big cities, Jews found refuge in small towns such as Bremgarten, Kaiserstuhl or the monastery village of Rheinau (1475). After then, their traces disappear.

The only Jewish scholar of note in Switzerland during the Middle Ages was Moses of Zurich, who, at the beginning of the 14th century, wrote notes and additions on the SeMaK (*Sefer Mitzvot Katan*).

In the 1560s the first Jewish families reappear in the region of Basle/Southern Alsace (Kembs, Weil), Waldshut (Tiengen), and possibly the Bodensee region (Rheineck). They lived at various places, e.g., Rapperswil, Mammern, Andelfingen, etc. In 1560, a Hebrew printing press was established in Tiengen, north of Zurzach. In the 17th century stable rural communities came into being. Most of the Jews resided on the border of Switzerland from western Alsace to the Rhine valley, from Basle to Hohenems in Vorarlberg, trading in cattle and peddling during weekdays. In Switzerland they were expelled from the bishopric of Basle (1694) and from Dornach (1736). In the territory of the "county of Baden," administered after 1711 by Berne, Zurich, and Glarus, the Jews concentrated themselves in the two villages of Endingen and Lengnau, having a full Jewish infrastructure and building representative synagogues in the 1750s. In Neuchâtel some Jews already tried to settle in the 1770s. The duke of Savoy attracted Alsatian Jews to Carouge, near Geneva. In 1780, some Jews also resided in Porrentruy and slowly the Jewish landscape of Switzerland began to change.

Slow Steps Toward Emancipation

The proclamation of the Helvetian Republic (1798) was a turning point in the history of the Jews in Switzerland. A year earlier, the Swiss confederation had been compelled to refrain from any discriminatory measures against French Jews. As the influence of the ideas of the French Revolution made itself felt, the problem of the rights of the Jews arose. During the ensuing debates, a majority emerged which refused to grant the Jews total *emancipation on the grounds that the Jews were a political rather than a religious body, insistent on preserving their particularism. Following protests by the Jewish communities, a new debate was held, but no conclusions were reached. In the meantime, the status of the Jews resembled that of the aliens residing in Switzerland. They were granted freedom of movement, residence, and trade.

Some Jews managed to receive a settlement permit in Basle (after 1799), Berne (before 1820), Zurich (1817), La Chaux de Fonds (1818), Avenches (1827), and elsewhere.

The publication of *Napoleon's "Infamous Decree" in 1808, which constituted a check to the civil rights of the Jews, strengthened the hand of their Swiss adversaries. The canton of Aargau dealt with the problem of the Jews in the following manner (May 5, 1809): They were subject to all laws and ordinances of the canton without receiving citizenship; their commercial activities were regulated and limited; and they were advised to engage in useful professions. They were also required to obtain a special authorization before marrying. This was obviously a serious lowering of their status, which also encouraged discriminatory police measures. In 1824, the canton reorganized the Jewish community: It was authorized to retain funds for education and worship, and the Jews were also ordered to provide for the needs of their destitute coreligionists without the assistance of the public authorities. The administrative body was to be nominated by the government of the canton. The freedom of the cities was still refused to them, but instead of being considered as aliens, they became dependents of the canton. In the meantime the situation of the Jews in Switzerland became increasingly paradoxical as certain foreign governments, especially that of France, became interested in safeguarding the rights of their citizens of Jewish religion who were discriminated against in Switzerland. The case of the Jews of Alsace, who were already numerous in Switzerland, was of profound importance for the situation of the Jews in the country. Finally, the revision of the federal constitution of 1866 granted the Jews freedom of residence throughout Switzerland, which henceforward was no longer

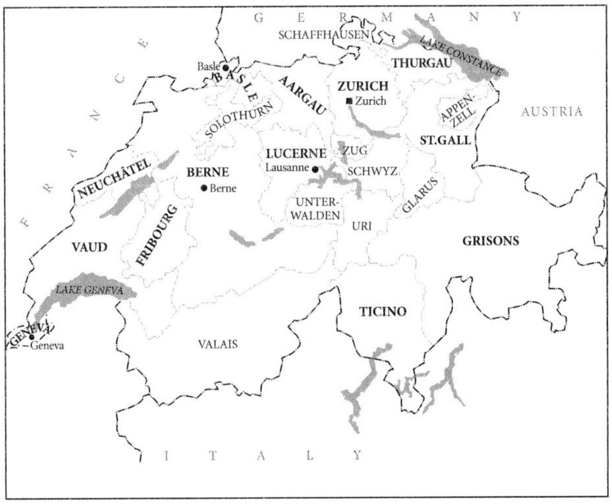

Major Jewish communities in Switzerland, 2004.

dependent on adherence to one of the recognized Christian sects. Federal intervention had become necessary as a result of contradictory votes in which the Jews of Aargau had been granted and then subsequently refused civic rights. In fact the regional Great Council had voted for their emancipation on May 15, 1862, but had been dismissed by a popular vote which had been solicited after a deliberate and active agitation. The emancipation decree having thus been repealed, a new law reintroduced most of the former conditions one year later. It abolished the discriminatory measures concerning residence and marriage and granted the communities the right of electing their own administrative bodies. There had thus been a very slight progress. Other cantons had already previously granted equal rights to their inhabitants and most other cantons followed suit from 1862, with the exception of Aargau, which did not grant full local citizenship rights until Jan. 1, 1879, following a campaign led by the famous historian Meyer *Kayserling, rabbi of Endingen and Lengnau between 1861 and 1871, and the intervention of the federal council, the high court and the diet (Bundesversammlung). Therefore the one canton which inherited two rural communities at its founding in 1803 was the last to grant them emancipation. However, the religious liberty of the Jews was incomplete. After a campaign against cruelty toward animals, in which the influence of the antisemitic movements of the end of the century could be detected, a popular vote decided to include prohibition of *sheḥitah* in the federal constitution (1893). As this decision was taken by plebiscite, it could only be abrogated by another plebiscite, and so the practice of *sheḥitah* on quadrupeds – the legislator neglected the case of fowls – is still prohibited in Switzerland.

Population

The Jewish population of Switzerland increased steadily. Southern Alsatian and south-Baden rural Jews could finally settle in the areas of commerce which they had already frequented from the end of the 16th to the middle of the 17th centuries. In 1888 8,069 persons declared themselves as Jewish; in 1910 20,797 were registered as such. After the 1870s immigration of Jews from Eastern Europe began. Students were attracted by Swiss universities. Women were allowed to study at the University of Zurich from 1867. Rosa *Luxemburg earned her Ph.D. in Zurich, Chaim *Zhitlowsky was active and Vladimir *Medem organized the BUND from Geneva. Jews were welcomed as university teachers, so Chaim *Weizmann taught chemistry, Moritz *Lazarus was university rector in Berne, Max *Buedinger dean in Zurich in 1863. A circle of Jewish students existed around the Hungarian-Jewish philosopher Ludwig *Stein in Berne. Most of the East European Jewish students left Switzerland between 1914 and 1917.

After granting freedom of residence in 1864/66 the communities of Endingen and Lengnau (where the synagogues, reconstructed during the middle of the 19th century, are to be seen and are still used for marriages and some Rosh Ḥodesh prayers) were broken up, and with the exodus from rural communitites of nearby Alsace and Baden, many new communities were formed in cities (Basle 1805, Avenches 1827, La Chaux de Fonds 1833, Berne and Bienne 1848, Geneva 1852, Yverdon 1850, Baden 1859, Zurich 1862, St. Gall 1863, Lucerne 1867, Lausanne 1868). However the number of Jews has remained small in relation to the general population (1920: 0.54%).

Jews were prominent in cattle trading but did not dominate it, constituting only one seventh of all dealers. Many entered the textile trade; some built up firms. Yet Protestant families had already established an international textile industry, when the Jews still were forced to be peddlers. Most banks were in Protestant hands, only the Dreyfus bank of Basle and Julius Bär of Zurich gained some importance. After the 1870s Swiss Jews began to enter liberal professions. They were prominent in founding department stores (Julius Brann of Berlin, the Maus. Nordmann and Loeb families) and held a good part of the St. Gall embroidery industry (until 1912). With the general crisis of the textile industry in Switzerland, the branch lost its importance. The regime of government rationing of food and its preference for peasants' organizations during World War II ruined the private cattle trade in general. In the beginning of the 21st century Jews were concentrated in white collar jobs.

As of 2000, 18,000 Jews were registered in Switzerland. The most important Jewish groups were in the cantons of Zurich (6,461), Geneva (4,356), Basle (city and canton, 1,739), Vaud (2,062), and Berne (807). Most of the Jews had received Swiss citizenship, so that the percentage was finally the same as among the non-Jews (80%).

They mostly lived in city agglomerations. Orthodox families had more children, but many of them remained at their later places of education (e.g., Israel) and left Switzerland. The Jews are no longer the only non-Christian minority. The Muslims surpass them by far (310,800 persons in 2000).

In 1904 13 communities, then consisting of about 1,500 heads of families, formed the Schweizerische Israelitische Gemeindebund (SIG) or Fédération Suisse des Communautés Israélites (FSCI). The SIG is the central body of Swiss Jewry, but all member organizations retain complete autonomy in their own affairs, notably in religious and administrative matters. Four ultra-Orthodox (*ḥaredi*) communities do not participate, two liberals were not accepted. In 2005 there were 23 communities with about 13,500 members. Some 4,500 others are not attached to any formal community, but often participate in other Jewish associations, such as B'nai B'rith.

In 1956, after the Hungarian uprising and Suez war, SIG looked after Jewish refugees from Egypt and Hungary. It also attended to the needs of Jews who had fled to Switzerland from Czechoslovakia after August 1968.

In the 1970s and 1980s Anglo-Saxon families moved to Geneva and Zurich/central Switzerland, thus giving impetus to founding liberal Jewish communities.

Well-to-do Sephardi Jews of North African origin immigrated to the region of Geneva and Lausanne between the 1950s and 1970s. In Geneva, in 1965 the Groupe fraternel séfaradi (est. in 1925) merged with the Communauté Israelite, having its own services in their "Hekhal ha-Ness." In Lausanne once a month a Sephardi service is held.

With the former Alsatian families of French Switzerland turning completely francophone and the Sephardi not knowing German at all, a huge cultural gap exists between the two groups in Switzerland.

[Simon R. Schwarzfuchs / Uri Kaufmann (2nd ed.)]

Jewish Attitudes 1933 to 1945

The SIG had to organize the import of kosher meat. At the end of the World War I *sheḥitah* was permitted, but banned again after 1920. The fight against antisemitism occupied the Jewish communities in the 1920s and after 1933. On April 1, 1933, hundreds of Jews fled to Switzerland from Germany (the day of the "*Judenboykott*"). In Lucerne, the synagogue was attacked and the Swiss government felt obliged to declare that it would respect all rights of Swiss Jews. After 1935 Swiss fascism lost its popularity since the Swiss recognized that they would lose sovereignty in a Nazi Europe. In the following years the Swiss government maintained a strict attitude toward Jewish refugees: only "politically" and not "racially" persecuted ones were welcomed, i.e., social democrats and many fewer communists, who could prove their direct personal danger. The Swiss government ruled that the SIG had to organize the funding for the costs of Jewish refugees. The very acculturated German Jews were perceived as a foreign danger for Swiss society ("*Ueberfremdung*"). After the annexation of Austria to Nazi Germany in March/April 1938 some 2,000 Jews fled to Switzerland. Thus the chief of Federal Foreigner's Police, Heinrich Rothmund, asked the Nazi authorities in October 1938 to mark the passports of all German Jews with a "J" for "Jude," so that Swiss border authorities could deny entry to Jews. Many of the accepted refugees, e.g., Kurt Tucholsky and Else Lasker-Schüler, were forced to leave by the Federal Foreigner's Police. After the outbreak of the war, Jewish refugees were engaged in "productive" labor, laying out streets, draining swamps, or helping the peasants. They had to live in military camps. Families were separated and local authorities forbade "émigrés" to visit parks and other public places.

In April/May 1942, as the first rumors of the Holocaust were spreading, a massive public outcry forced the Swiss government to soften its attitude on the Jewish refugees. The debate on how to respond led to bitter internal debate in the SIG, its president, Saly *Mayer, resigned in 1943. Some 20,000 refugees who managed to approach the Swiss border were turned back. Some 25,000 were welcomed and could survive with the 20,000 local Jews. Even if the *American Jewish Joint Distribution Committee helped support the refugees (52 million Swiss francs), the 4,000 wage-earning Jews had a heavy burden to shoulder supporting thousands of refugees, donating 18,5 million Swiss francs between 1933 and 1952.

After the war the Federal Foreigner's Police continued its harsh policy. The responsible Bundesrat, Eduard von Steiger, a member of the old Bernese patriciate, felt no pangs of conscience at all and resigned only as late as 1953. He is believed to be responsible for destroying files on the denial of admittance to Jews. Only about 2,500 refugees were allowed to stay. Swiss Jews felt very much obliged to help the survivors. Material aid was sent to Germany. Even a teachers' seminary was established in Basle but dissolved in 1948.

The Christlich-Juedische Arbeitgemeinschaft in der Schweiz (Swiss Conference of Christians and Jews) has played an important role in the struggle against antisemitism and neo-Nazism. The "assertions of Selisberg" (Selisberger Thesen), formulated in 1946, were crucial for building a new relationship between Christians and Jews in postwar Western Europe.

Debate on the Past

The first public debate on Swiss refugee policy began in 1953. A detailed report was written by Carl Ludwig, himself a police official in Basle, and published in 1957.

Following a series of representations made by the SIG, the problem of heirless property left in Switzerland by victims of the Nazis was legally resolved in a first step (1955/1962): Jewish social institutions in Eastern Europe, the Maghreb, and Israel received some funds.

In 1969 Alfred Häsler published his popular, moving book, *The Lifeboat is Full.* It was widely discussed, but most politicians were not interested in a debate then.

In his address at the dedication ceremony of a memorial to the victims of the Holocaust in Berne's Jewish cemetery on November 9, 1988, Flavio Cotti, a member of the Swiss federal government, gave what amounted to its first, although guarded, official apology for Switzerland not having saved more Jews during the Holocaust. In 1995, on the 50th anniversary of the end of the War, Swiss president Kaspar Villiger apologized to Jews in the name of the Swiss government for neglect towards Jewish refugees before and during the war years.

But only after 1995 did a debate begin, which ended with the establishment of an Independent Historian's Commission (1996), which published its findings in 2002 in 24 volumes and over 10,000 pages. No other European country made such a serious attempt at investigating national history.

Research by historians in Swiss archives found that at least 20,000 refugees were turned away by Switzerland during the War.

Many Swiss were embittered that their memory of Swiss resistance against Nazism was challenged. Nationalist resentment arose in the public. The SIG took a very hard line and demanded "justice for the Jewish people and fairness for Switzerland." Some of the American-Jewish attacks were not substantiated by facts, since Swiss politics is characterized by the compromises of a "Konkordanz-Demokratie" and is not accustomed to harsh public polemics as in the U.S.

Under strong pressure, the Swiss banks agreed to search for deposits made by Jews prior to World War II and during the Holocaust. It is thought that many of the depositors perished in the Holocaust and left no survivors. In February 1966, the Swiss banks claimed that they had found only some $32 million of such deposits. The international Jewish organizations dealing with the subject (World Jewish Congress and the World Jewish Restitution Organization) felt that this sum was only a small fraction of what really lies hidden. In May 1996, a memorandum of understanding was reached and Swiss banks paid over one billion dollars to the World Jewish Restitution Organization.

In addition, a special Swiss foundation for victims of Nazi persecution (non-Jews and Jews alike) was established in 1997; 273 million. Swiss Francs were donated to it by the Swiss national bank, three private banks, and private industry. Out of 312,000 victims, 255,000 were Jews. Until 2001, some 124,000 people living in Israel, 97,000 in Eastern Europe, and 70,000 in North America had received financial help from this Swiss foundation.

Antisemitism

Though there were some manifestations of antisemitism (attacks on *kippah*-wearing Jews in Zurich, desecrations of Jewish cemeteries and the synagogue of Lugano (2005)), the majority of the Swiss population felt more threatened by Muslim and Third World immigrants. Still antisemitic graffiti do occur, as do revisionist statements, to which the authorities tend to react quite strongly. A new anti-racist legislation, passed by parliament in June 1993, makes antisemitic propaganda and the denial of the Holocaust a criminal offense. Some right-wing politicians attacked the law as being a limitation of freedom of speech and called for a referendum in 1994. The fight to gain a majority of the votes was very hard for the SIG. In 2005 some populist politicians tried to vote down the law through another popular referendum.

From its inception, SIG also attempted to bring about the abolition of the ban on ritual slaughter. The Swiss government removed the ban against *sheḥitah* from the Swiss constitution and added a new law for the protection of animals (1973). When it tried to introduce an exception clause for the Jews, strong opposition was voiced in the Swiss media. The SIG abstained from fighting further in order to safeguard "confessional peace in Switzerland," as formulated by its president Alfred Donath in 2004. The animal protectors were so thoroughly scandalized that they gathered the necessary signatures for an initiative to ban even the import of kosher meat. However, the World Trade Organization prohibits import restrictions of this kind.

Internal Jewish Life

The Swiss Jewish community maintains care of the aged, in which it follows the most up-to-date methods, and promotes youth education through, inter alia, summer camps, meetings of young people and organized trips to Israel, and support for the youth movements. Swiss Jewry has also maintained since 1968 a museum in Basle (Juedisches Museum der Schweiz) which has an important collection of cultural and religious objects. In 1964, SIG participated in the Swiss Exhibition at Lausanne with a pavilion designed to express the basis tenets of Judaism, but the presentation of recent history was neither allowed nor desired by the organizers (i.e., refugee policy). After 1982 an exhibition on the history of Swiss Jewry was shown at various places and translated into French.

The SIG is a founding member of the *World Jewish Congress, and a member of the European Council of Jewish Community Services and maintains active contact with all world Jewish charitable organizations. Inspired by the American Young Leadership program, Swiss-Jewish youngsters are coached in how to represent Judaism and Jewish history to their non-Jewish peers.

After 1955 a movement establishing Jewish schools, inspired by the American example, was led first by the Orthodox community of Zurich. Basle followed (1961) and after 1970 Jewish schools were established in Geneva and Lausanne, a second one in Zurich (1979) and Basle, where there even is a small Jewish high school. Thus 53% of all Jewish children in Switzerland (1st to 4th grade) attend a Jewish school (2000). Some 30% frequenting general schools receive religious lessons, so that more than 80% of all Jewish children receive some kind of Jewish education.

Jewish youth movements have also made an impression. A wide range is active from the Aguda Youth (Zurich), to Bnei Akiva (Zurich), to centralist Ha-Goshrim (Zurich), Emuna (Basle) and Ha-Noar ha-Bone (Berne) to Ha-Shomer ha-Ẓa'ir (Zurich).

In 1952 a small yeshivah was established in Lucerne (later moving to nearby Kriens), parallel to the Lithuanian-type yeshivah of the Botschko family in Montreux (est. in 1927), which functioned until 1985. According to a 2002 Gallup poll, 27% percent of the Jews visit a synagogue at least once a week.

Polarization of Jewish life caused a breakup of Orthodox groups. New *minyanim* were founded. The Lubavitch movement established itself in Switzerland after 1982. Liberal communities came into being in Geneva (1970) and Zurich (1978). Egalitarian groups were also active in the Zurich Cultusgemeinde (Schabbat acheret) and Ofek in Basle. The "Einheitsgemeinde," combining all Jewish currents, is being seriously challenged. After 16 years of discussion, the SIG nearly split over the admission of liberal communities (2004); the Orthodox groups threatened to pull out. A majority did vote for admission but not the necessary two-thirds, so a liberal "faction" was established, which coexists with the SIG on equal footing.

Swiss Jews were definitely more integrated into Swiss society after 1945. They were very proud that the first Jewish member of Swiss government was elected in 1993, Ruth *Dreifuss, being of old Endingen-Jewish ancestry (in office until 2002). Still the number of mixed marriages went up to 60%. Many Jews moved to suburbs far from the Jewish communities. Since being Jewish became more socially accepted, the rate of membership in the communities rose from 50% (1960) to 75% (2000). Many Jewish communities received state recognition, Basle being the first in 1973. This is a matter dealt with by each canton individually.

In February 2005 a new constitution was adopted in Zurich and the way to recognition of the two democratically operating Jewish communities is now open. The first bid for recognition had been turned down in 1877.

Jewish studies were integrated in university curricula, the first being Geneva with a lectureship for Jewish thought held by Chief Rabbi Alexandre *Safran (after 1948). In 1981 the only cathedra of Jewish studies at a Catholic faculty in Europe was founded in Lucerne with Clemens Thoma, a specialist in rabbinic literature. Basle University opened its Institute for Jewish Studies in 1998, a cathedra is now active in Lausanne, and lectureships exist at the universities of Fribourg and St. Gall. Thus every Swiss university with the astonishing exception of Zurich has at least a lectureship in Jewish studies.

The Jewish press, which receives no state subsidies, was firmly established. To the *Israelitische Wochenblatt fuer die Schweiz*, the *Juedische Rundschau Maccabi* of Basle was added in 1942, and the (bi-)monthly *Das neue Israel* (1948–86), edited by the late Veit Wyler. In 2001 the *Rundschau* and the *Wochenblatt* merged into *Tachles*, which bought the American-Jewish *Aufbau* and tries to continue it as a monthly (2005). The French-speaking have their *Revue Juive*. Community bulletins have become much more professional.

Since 1980 there has been nearly no Jewish immigration to Switzerland, resulting in the problem of an aging community.

The situation of Swiss Jewry has been characterized by two seemingly contradictory developments: a strengthening of its institutions and a weakening of its demographic base. Yet Jewish life in Switzerland is quite active and stable, even if the future existence of small communities like St. Gall, Baden, Winterthur, and Fribourg is not secure.

Swiss Jews and Israel

Swiss Jews maintain active contact with Israel. Compared to 20,000 Jews in Switzerland, a high proportion of some 6,800 Swiss citizens are living in Israel. The Swiss-Israel Society is dedicated to the strengthening of relations between the two countries, and on the eve of the Six-Day War (1967) it took the lead in a spontaneous expression of solidarity with Israel on the part of all sectors of the Swiss people.

[Benjamin Sagalowitz / Uri Kaufmann (2nd ed.)]

Relations with Israel

Switzerland does not play any political role in Middle Eastern affairs and is wary of any move that might be interpreted as a breach of her neutrality. Nonetheless, Switzerland has frequently expressed support for Israel – first demonstrated by the holding of *Zionist Congresses on Swiss soil – and this feeling is shared by broad sectors of the Swiss public. These expressions of support reached their height during the Six-Day War (1967). Especially important in this context was the behavior of the Swiss press, cultural organizations, and mass media toward the incident of an Arab terrorist attack on an El Al plane in Zurich in 1969 and the objectivity of the Swiss authorities on all levels – political, legal, and judicial – by placing the responsibility for the attack on the governments of the Arab countries from which the terrorists operated. An act of sabotage in 1970 on a Swissair plane bound for Israel evoked a similar angry reaction. Diplomatic relations existed between the two countries from 1949 and were elevated to ambassadorial level. In addition to the embassy in Berne, Israel maintains a consulate in Zurich and a representative attached to the European office of the United Nations in Geneva.

Formal agreements over air transportation exist between the two countries, as do general scientific and cultural ties. When most of the communist countries severed diplomatic relations with Israel after the Six-Day War, Switzerland represented Israel's interests in Hungary and Guinea.

The broad solidarity with Israel dissipated by 1973, when of all public figures only Friedrich Dürrenmatt spoke out for Israel. The negative image of Israel in the Swiss mass media furthered this process. For many right-wing citizens, Jews are perceived as being enemies of Switzerland after the debate on refugee policy, lost property, and bank accounts. The important Swiss People's Party (Schweizerische Volkspartei, a bourgeois populist right-wing organization) withdrew its earlier ardent support of Israel.

Swiss Foreign Minister Mrs. Calmy-Rey hosted the Geneva conference trying to find a way out of the blocked peace process in 2004. In the Swiss parliament a boycott of weapons from Israel was discussed in the same year, thus marking a remarkable shift in foreign policy from the deep sympathy of 1967 to today's hostility.

[Uri Kaufman (2nd ed.)]

BIBLIOGRAPHY: J.C. Ulrich, *Sammlung juedischer Geschichten…* (Basle, 1768); F. Guggenheim-Gruenberg, *Geschichte der Juden in der Schweiz* (1961); A. Weldler-Steinberg, *Geschichte der Juden in der Schweiz* 2 vols. (1966/1970); Germ Jud, 2 and 3 (1968/1993), index s.v. *Schweiz*; W. Guggenheim et al, *Juden in der Schweiz* (1982); A.A. Haesler, *The Lifeboat is Full: Switzerland and the Refugees 1933–1945* (1969); Schweizerischer Israelitischer Gemeindbund (= SIG), *Festschrift zum 50-jaehrigen Bestehen* (1954); C. Ludwig, *Die Fluechtlingspolitik der Schweiz seit 1933 bis zur Gegenwart* (1957); R. Swiss Jewish Relief Union, *Dix années d'activité de l'Aide juive aux réfugiés en Suisse, 1933–1943* (1944); S.M. Stroock, in: A.J. Karp (ed.), *The Jewish Experience in America*, 3 (1969), 77–122; Kamis-Mueller et al, *Vie Juive en Suisse* (1992); M. Marcus, in: *European Judaism*, 44 (1990); R. Weill, "Wie lange noch Juden in der Schweiz," in: *Judaica*, 1 (1986), 48–57. **ADD. BIBLIOGRAPHY:** U. Kaufmann, *Bibliographie zur Geschichte der Juden in der Schweiz* (1993); U. Altermatt, *Katholizismus und Antisemitismus. (…) Zur Kulturgeschichte der Schweiz 1918–1945* (1999); D. Eppelbaum, "Die Wandmalereien im Haus 'Zum Brunnenhof,' Zuerich. Ein Beispiel juedischer Kunst aus dem 14. Jh. Im Spannungsfeld zwischen Adaption und Abgrenzung," in: *Judaica*, 4 (2002), 261–80; W. Hochreiter, *Sport unter dem Davidstern. Geschichte des jüdischen Sports in der Schweiz* (1998); A. Kamis-Mueller, *Antisemitismus in der Schweiz* (2000²), U. Luethi, *Der Mythos von der Weltverschwörung* (1992); A. Mattioli (ed.), *Antisemitismus in der Schweiz* (1998); P. Krauthammer, *Das Schaechtverbot in der Schweiz* (2000); A. Mattioli (ed.), *Antisemitismus in der Schweiz* (1998); B. Meier: "Zur Geschichte des spaetmittelalterlichen Judentums," in: *Judaica*, 1 (1986), 2–16; D. Neumann, *Studentinnen aus dem Russischen Reich in der Schweiz (1867–1914)* (1987); P. Niederhaeuser et al. (eds.), "Fremd in Zuerich – fremdes Zuerich?" Miteilungen der Antiquarischen Gesellschaft, in: *Zuerich*, 72 (2005), 10–37; J. Picard, *Die Schweiz und die Juden* (1994²), H. Roschewski, "Auf dem Weg zu einem neuen juedischen Selbstbewusstsein?" in: *Geschichte der Juden in der Schweiz 1945–1994* (1994); H. Roschewski, *Rothmund die Juden* (1997); SIG (ed.), *Juedische Lebenswelt Schweiz. 100 Jahre Schweizerischer Israelitischer Gemeindebund* (2004); S. Maechler, *Hilfe und Ohnmacht. Der Schweizerische Israelitische Gemeindebund und die nationalsozialistische Verfolgung 1933–1945* (2005).

SWOPE, GERARD (1872–1957), U.S. electrical engineer and industrialist. Born in St. Louis, Missouri, where his father was a watchcase manufacturer, Swope became fascinated with electricity as a child. He graduated from the Massachusetts Institute of Technology in 1895 and rapidly rose to the post of general sales manager of Western Electric, where he became responsible for opening additional branches in the United States as well as in China and Japan. In 1913 he was elected vice president and director of the company. During World War I, Swope was a member of the U.S. Army's general staff and was decorated. He also received medals from France and Japan. In 1919 he was named president of International General Electric and, in 1922, chairman of its board. From 1922 to 1939 he served successively as president and chairman. Under his leadership the company's success reached unprecedented levels. Swope was also associated with the development of radio and radio parts, and was a director of the National Broadcasting and Radio Corporation of America. In 1939 he retired from General Electric and became chairman of the New York City Housing Authority, one of many offices he filled in voluntary public service. In 1931 he published the "Swope Plan." This plan called for stabilizing industry and emphasized industry's responsibility for preventing unemployment and mitigating its results. He received a number of honorary degrees, the Hoover medal, and the gold medal of the National Academy of Social Sciences. He visited Israel in 1957 and bequeathed several million dollars to the Haifa Technion. He was the brother of Herbert Bayard *Swope.

[Joachim O. Ronall]

SWOPE, HERBERT BAYARD (1882–1958), U.S. journalist and public official; brother of Gerard *Swope. One of the leading newspapermen of his time, he continued to exert wide influence for 30 years after his retirement from journalism. A man of colorful personality and with a variety of interests, he was equally at home in journalism, business, politics, sports, the theater, and society. Born in St. Louis, he joined the staff of the liberal New York *World* in 1909 after short periods on other papers and was soon recognized as one of New York's outstanding reporters. When the Pulitzer prizes were established in 1917, he won the first award for reporting with his war dispatches from Germany. These were collected in the book *Inside the German Empire* (1917). In 1920 he became executive editor of the *World*, and directed a number of exposés, among them the Ku Klux Klan, working conditions in Florida, and crime in New York. Retiring in 1929, he became a policy consultant to corporations, individuals, and government agencies. He was also a member of the first State Racing Commission of New York, served as a consultant to the U.S. secretary of war from 1942 to 1946, and as an alternate United States representative to the United Nations Atomic Energy Commission.

BIBLIOGRAPHY: E.J. Kahn, Jr., *World of Swope* (1965), incl. bibl.

[Irving Rosenthal]

SYCAMORE (Heb. שִׁקְמָה), the *Ficus sycomorus*, of the same genus as the fig tree. There is no connection between it and the *plane tree, whose biblical name is *armon* and which is popularly called the sycamore. The sycamore is frequently mentioned in the Bible and in rabbinical literature. It is a tropical evergreen with a tall trunk, its tree top having long branches. The fruit resembles the fig, but is less sweet. Nowadays it grows wild in the Israeli coastal plain and the Negev, and the fruit is rarely eaten. In biblical and talmudic times the sycamore was one of the most valuable trees in the Ereẓ Israel Shephelah. David appointed an overseer "over the olive trees and the sycamore trees that were in the Lowland" on the royal estates (I Chron. 27:28). Its chief value was its wood which was used as building timber. Ordinary buildings were constructed of it, cedar being used for palaces and luxury edifices (I Kings 10:27; Isa. 9:9). The wood of the sycamore is light and porous compared with the heavy cedar, and it was therefore preferred for making ceilings (Tosef., BM 8:32; TB, *ibid.* 117b). This wood does not absorb damp and withstands rot; proof of this are the coffins of Egyptian mummies, which were mostly made from it and have been well preserved to the present day. The sycamore fruit, called *benot shikmah* or *gimziyyot*, was less valued than its timber (Tosef., Pes. 2:19; Men. 7 la). Special care had to be taken for its fruit to be edible: a few days before it ripened it was punctured. Fruit which has not undergone this process falls prematurely to the ground, and is therefore regarded as ownerless (Dem. 1:1; TJ, Dem. 1:1, 21d). The Bible refers to this puncturing as *belisah*, and the prophet Amos testifies of himself: "I am a herdsman and a *boles* [AV, "dresser," LXX, "piercer"] of sycamores" (Amos 7:14).

In the mishnaic period sycamores were widespread in the Shephelah, and Rabban Simeon b. Gamaliel makes the sycamore characteristic of the low-lying country (Tosef., Shev. 7:11; Pes. 53a): "Wherever sycamores do not grow is Upper Galilee ... wherever sycamores do grow is Lower Galilee" (Shev. 9:2). The Mishnah (Shev. 4:5) describes the methods used for felling sycamore beams so that they should grow anew after a few years. A sycamore that had never been felled was called "a virgin sycamore" (Tosef., Shev. 3:15). Its roots spread sideways and "penetrate downward to the waters of the abyss" (TJ, Ta'an. 1:3, 64b). It is long-lived: "like the sycamore that lives 600 years" (Gen. R. 12:6), and the verse "as the days of a tree shall be the days of my people" (Isa. 65:22) was interpreted as relating to it.

BIBLIOGRAPHY: Loew, Flora, 1 (1928), 274–80; J. Galil, in: *Teva va-Areẓ*, 8 (1966), 338–55 (incl. bibl.); J. Feliks, *Olam ha-Ẓome'aḥ ha-Mikra'i* (1968²), 52–55; H.N. and A.L. Moldenke, *Plants of the Bible* (1952), index. **ADD. BIBLIOGRAPHY:** Feliks, Ha-Ẓome'aḥ, 166.

[Jehuda Feliks]

SYDNEY, capital of New South Wales, *Australia. Founded in 1788 as a British penal settlement, it was the cradle of Australian Jewry. Several Jews were sent there from England as convicts in the first transport and others subsequently. After release they played their part, at times under conditions of great hardship, in the colonization of the country. Some of them prospered and became leading citizens. When in 1817 a Jew died in Sydney there was no Jewish cemetery, but a religious service was held and a *ḥevra kaddisha* formed. P.J. Cohen may be considered the founder of the religious community. He carried the chief rabbi's authority to perform marriages, one of the first being that of Samuel Cohen, founder of a family prominent in both Jewish and general affairs for three generations. When the first congregation was organized in 1832, Joseph Barrow Montefiore – a cousin of Sir Moses *Montefiore – who played a pioneering role also in Melbourne, Adelaide, and New Zealand, was elected president. Services were held in private homes and hotels which were often owned by Jews; in 1837 a house was hired and converted into a synagogue. Soon the congregation was again homeless, until in 1844, when the Jews in New South Wales numbered about 900, the Sydney Synagogue, the first to be specifically built as such, was opened. The Great Synagogue, still in existence, was opened in 1878, when some 3,000 Jews lived in the state.

In the 1850s there was an influx of Jews to New South Wales, still mainly from England but including a number from Germany. Many first settled in the rural areas, often to keep the local store, and in 1861 only 61% of the Jews in New South Wales lived in the metropolis; a century later, however, only 4% lived outside Sydney. The obstacles to religious life were formidable: lack of ministers, difficulty in maintaining observance, and scarcity of women; intermarriage was thus the gravest danger. A.B. Davis served as minister at the Great Synagogue from 1862 to 1905, and Rabbi F.L. Cohen, author of a standard work on synagogal music, from 1905 to 1934. Immigration from 1933 on did much to change the pattern of the community, in which Western European and British immigrants predominated. In 1933 Sydney had four congregations, all Orthodox, and in 1970, 17 Orthodox and two liberal congregations; the *bet din* was under the chairmanship of Rabbi I. Porush. The Rabbi L.A. Falk Library at the Great Synagogue with its 7,000 volumes is the largest Judaica library in Australia.

[Israel Porush]

From the 1930s until the late 1950s Sydney experienced the same patterns of growth as did *Melbourne and other centers of Jewish life in Australia, but with significant differences. More Holocaust refugees and survivors came to Melbourne than Sydney, and, during the second half of the 20th century, Melbourne was clearly the leading Jewish community in Australia, with Sydney a close but perceptible second. Victoria (Melbourne) overtook New South Wales (Sydney) in population around 1939. By 1961, 23,106 declared Jews by religion lived in Sydney, according to the Australian census, compared with about 28,000 in Melbourne. In recent years this gap has remained. In 1996 there were 31,450 declared Jews in Sydney compared with 35,383 in Melbourne, and, in 2001, 32,941 in Sydney and 37,779 in Melbourne. The sources of immigration to the two centers of Jewish life also differed, with Melbourne taking in many more Polish Holocaust survivors and Sydney more Hungarians (following the 1956 Revolution) and also more British emigrées for normal professional reasons. The Jewish presence is also more marked in Melbourne than in Sydney. Sydney has a larger population than Melbourne, 4.2 million compared with 3.5 million, while Melbourne has a much larger, highly visible strictly Orthodox community. Although there are recognizable Jewish neighborhoods in Sydney, Melbourne's community is clearly centered in the Caulfield–East St. Kilda area, while Sydney's is dispersed in two geographically distinct areas, the Eastern suburbs (Bondi–Vaucluse–Rose Bay) south of Sydney harbor, and areas of the North Shore such as St. Ives and Bellevue Hill north of the harbor. Of the 17 postal districts in Australia with more than 1,000 declared Jews in 2001, seven were in Sydney and nine in Melbourne. Sydney's Eastern suburbs were home to nearly 13,000 declared Jews.

In recent years the cultural and political ambiance of the two communities also differed, with Sydney's Jewish community more moderate and conciliatory in its dealings with the government, Melbourne's more forthright and even militant. Sydney itself has also differed socially from Melbourne, the former a cosmopolitan harbor and metropolis well-known for its hedonism, the latter more conservative and containing a larger ideological left. As well, Judaism in Sydney has also been more moderate and centrist than in Melbourne, with stronger Anglo-Orthodox synagogues and, until recently, a weaker strict Orthodoxy.

Because of these factors, full-time Jewish day schools were founded later in Sydney than in Melbourne, and, until the 1980s, attracted smaller enrollments. Sydney had six full-time Jewish day schools: Moriah College (Orthodox), Yeshivah and Yeshivah Girls' High School (Lubavitcher), Masada (Orthodox) on the North Shore, Mount Sinai (Orthodox, in Sydney's southeast), and Emanuel (Liberal). Enrollments totaled nearly 4,000. In general, the evolution of Sydney in the postwar period may be seen as a process of "catching up" to Melbourne, an evolution reflected in increasing Jewish day school numbers in Sydney. It has also been reflected in the growth of Sydney's synagogues, which increased from around ten in 1960 to 25 in the mid-1990s and 33 by 2005. Of today's 33 synagogues in Sydney, 18 are mainstream Orthodox, nine strict Orthodox/Lubavitcher (including Chabad houses), four Sephardi, and two Liberal. Recent notable rabbis in Sydney include Israel *Porush and Raymond *Apple of the Great Synagogue in central Sydney, Brian Fox of Temple Emanuel, and Selwyn Franklyn of the Central Synagogue.

The representative body of the Jewish community in Sydney is the New South Wales Board of Deputies. Half of its members are selected by member bodies and half by a community-wide poll. Sydney has its own edition of the Australian Jewish newspaper, *The Australian Jewish News*, and there are Jewish community broadcasting slots on public radio. There is a well-presented Sydney Jewish Museum, opened in 1992, at 148 Darlinghurst Road, with exhibits on the Holocaust and on Australian Jewish history. The historic Great Synagogue, at 166 Castlereagh Street, offers guided tours to visitors.

[William D. Rubinstein (2nd ed.)]

ADD. BIBLIOGRAPHY: S.D. Rutland, *Edge of the Diaspora: Two Centuries of Jewish Development in Australia* (1998; rev. ed. 2001); H.L. Rubinstein and W.D. Rubinstein, *Jews in Australia*; S.D. Rutland and S. Caplan, *With One Voice: A History of the New South Wales Jewish Board of* Deputies (1998); S. Encel and B. Buckley (eds.), *The New South Wales Jewish Community: A Survey* (1978); S.D. Rutland, *Pages of History: A Century of the Australian Jewish Press* (1995); idem., *If You Will It, It is No dream: The Moriah Story, 1943–2003* (2003); I. Porush, *The House of Israel: A Study of Sydney Jewry…* (1977); L. Cohen, *Beginning with Esther: Jewish Women in New South Wales from 1788* (1987); A. Andgel, *Fifty Years of Caring: A History of the Australian Jewish Welfare Society, 1938–1986* (1988); G.B. Levey and P. Mendes (eds.), *Jews and Australian Politics* (2005).

°**SYKES, SIR MARK** (1879–1919), British traveler and diplomat. Sykes was born in London and educated in Monaco, Brussels, and Cambridge. He served as a soldier in the Boer War (1902) and traveled for some time in Syria, Mesopotamia, and Kurdistan. Several years later he was appointed honorary attaché to the British embassy in Constantinople. In 1915 his special knowledge and qualifications, particularly with regard to the Middle East, won him an appointment as one of the two assistant secretaries to the British War Cabinet, a position in which he prepared regular intelligence summaries on the Middle East for the Cabinet's information. Thus, too, he came to participate in the Anglo-French talks in London on the "Syrian" question, talks that culminated in the *Sykes-Picot Agreement of 1916.

It was at some time between the provisional signing of the agreement in January 1916 and its official ratification in May of that year that Sykes first read the memorandum sent by Sir Herbert *Samuel to all members of the Cabinet the year before, suggesting British sponsorship of the Zionist cause. With the encouragement of Samuel, Moses Gaster, the chief Sephardi rabbi, began an exchange of views on Zionism with Sykes. Eager to see Britain gain a firm foothold in Palestine, Sykes felt that if Britain were to show active sympathy for the Zionist cause, it might be able to extricate itself from the Palestine provisions of the Sykes-Picot Agreement by pointing out that the Jews were overwhelmingly in favor of British trusteeship in the Holy Land.

In 1917 he first met Chaim *Weizmann and Nahum *Sokolow. By that time he had become attracted to Zionism per se, because he viewed it as a movement that would lead the Jews away from urban commerce and back to what he considered the healthier life and attitude of the tiller of the soil. He envisioned an eventual partnership between the Zionists and the Arabs and Armenians (whom he considered friendly toward the Entente) to preserve the stability of the Middle East after the collapse of the Ottoman Empire. At his first important meeting with nine Jewish and Zionist leaders in London on February 7, 1917, Sykes stated his conviction that the Arabs would come to terms with Zionism, particularly if they received support from the Jews in other matters. While in Rome in 1917, Sykes used his influence as a distinguished Catholic layman to explain to the Vatican authorities that Zionism would not clash with Christian or Catholic wishes concerning the holy places in Palestine. He participated in the drafting of the *Balfour Declaration; the final Zionist draft, submitted on July 18, 1917, had his approval, and Leopold S. Amery, a secretary of the War Cabinet, was to stress in future speeches and writings that the issuance of the declaration was due in large measure to Sykes's faith and energy.

Sykes addressed many Zionist meetings and, in a speech on December 2, 1917, said: "It might be the destiny of the Jewish race to be the bridge between Asia and Europe, and to bring the spirituality of Asia to Europe and the vitality of Europe to Asia." At the same time, he was on friendly terms with the Arabs. As a staff member of the Foreign Office he went on several missions to Egypt. In 1918 he went to Aleppo with the hope of reconciling French and Arab aims. His death, from influenza, at the Paris Peace Conference was greatly mourned by Zionists the world over.

BIBLIOGRAPHY: L. Shane, *Mark Sykes* (1923); C. Sykes, *Two Studies in Virtue* (1953); L. Stein, *The Balfour Declaration* (1961); R. Adelson, *Mark Sykes. Portrait of an Amateur* (1975); I. Friedman,

The Question of Palestine, 1914–1918. British-Jewish-Arab Relations (1973, 1992).

[Isaiah Friedman (2nd ed.)]

SYKES-PICOT AGREEMENT (in official terminology, **the 1916 Asia Minor Agreement**), secret agreement reached during World War I between the British and French governments pertaining to the partition of the Ottoman Empire among the Allied Powers. The terms were specified in a letter dated May 9, 1916, which Paul Cambon, the French ambassador in London, addressed to Sir Edward Grey, the British foreign secretary. It was ratified in a letter from Grey to Cambon on May 16. Russia was also privy to the discussions and consented to the terms. The agreement became official in an exchange of notes among the three Allied Powers on April 26 and May 23, 1916. In a subsequent stage Italy, too, gave her consent and the notes, which had been exchanged between April 10 and September 27, 1917, and were confirmed in the Treaty of St. Jean de Maurienne.

Background

When Sir Henry McMahon, the British high commissioner in Egypt, had reached a crucial stage in his negotiations with Sharif Hussein of Mecca (see *Israel State of: Historical Survey), Grey expressed concern that the advocated support of Arab demands on Syria would create the impression in France that the British merely intended to establish their own interests at the expense of the French. "Our primary and vital object," he emphasized, "is not to secure a new sphere of British influence, but to get the Arabs on our side."

An agreement with France was indispensable to avoid the impression that Britain had acted in bad faith. France regarded Syria as a dependency, and a separate arrangement with the sharif without France's participation could have had a chilling effect on the cordiality of the *entente*. Grey therefore suggested that Paris send a competent representative to discuss the matter.

The first round of discussions took place in London on November 23, 1915. The French government was represented by François-Georges Picot, a professional diplomat with extensive experience in the Levant, who before the war had been consul-general in Beirut. The British delegation was led by Sir Arthur Nicolson. Picot was uncompromising; he insisted that Syria was a purely French possession, and by Syria he meant the region bounded by the Taurus ridges in the north and the Egyptian frontier on the south.

The second round of discussions took place on December 21. The British were represented by Sir Mark *Sykes, a leading expert on the East. This time Picot was in a more accommodating mood. Having juxtaposed the desiderata of all the parties concerned, the British, the French, and the Arabs, the two statesmen worked out a compromise solution.

Terms of the Agreement

It was agreed that France was to exercise direct control over Cilicia, the coastal strip of Syria, the Lebanon, and the greater part of Galilee, up to the line stretching from north of Acre to the northwest corner of Lake Kinneret (Sea of Galilee), referred to as the "blue zone." East of that zone, in the Syrian hinterland, an Arab state was to be created under French protection (Area "A"). Britain was to exercise control over southern Mesopotamia (the "red zone"), the territory around the Acre-Haifa bay in the Mediterranean, with rights to build a railway from there to Baghdad. The territory east of the Jordan River and the Negev, south of the line stretching from Gaza to the Dead Sea, was allocated to an Arab state under British protection (Area "B"). South of France's "blue zone," in the area covering the Sanjak of Jerusalem, and extending southwards toward the line running approximately from Gaza to the Dead Sea, was to be a "brown zone" under international administration.

Assessment

In the years that followed, the Sykes-Picot Agreement became the target of bitter criticism, both in France and in England. Lloyd George referred to it as an "egregious" and a "foolish" document. He was particularly indignant that Palestine was inconsiderately mutilated. As seen from the perspective of 1917 this was, perhaps, true, but in the winter of 1915–16, when negotiations were in full swing, the strategic importance of Palestine had not yet been fully appreciated in British official circles. The overriding aim was to make an Arab uprising possible, and this hinged on French concessions to Arab demands in the Syrian hinterland. Nor could military operations on the eastern front take place without French concurrence. Without a British offensive, there could have been no Arab revolt, and without the Sykes-Picot Agreement there would have been no British offensive. The compromise solution with the French was the price that the British had to pay. The true progenitor of the Sykes-Picot Agreement was the McMahon-Hussein correspondence.

From this point of view Arab criticism is even less justified. The two negotiations showed meticulous consideration for Arab interests and blended it with healthy realism. The power vacuum created by the destruction of the Ottoman Empire had to be filled by a new authority; the alternative was chaos. Absolute independence for the Arabs would have invited anarchy or an outside invasion. There was no material incompatibility between the agreement and the pledges made to Sharif Hussein.

The Agreement and Zionism

During the discussions Sykes and Picot took note that the Jews throughout the world have "a conscientious and sentimental interest" in the future of the country. Zionist aspirations were passed over. This lapse was severely criticized by William R. Hall, head of the Intelligence Department of the British Admiralty. He pointed out that the Jews have "a strong material, and a very strong political interest in the future of the country and that in the Brown area the question of Zionism… [ought] to be considered."

It took Sykes several months to appreciate the fact that he had committed a blunder. The growing awareness of Germany's ambition to dominate the Middle East was the decisive factor that prompted him to embrace the concept of a Brit-

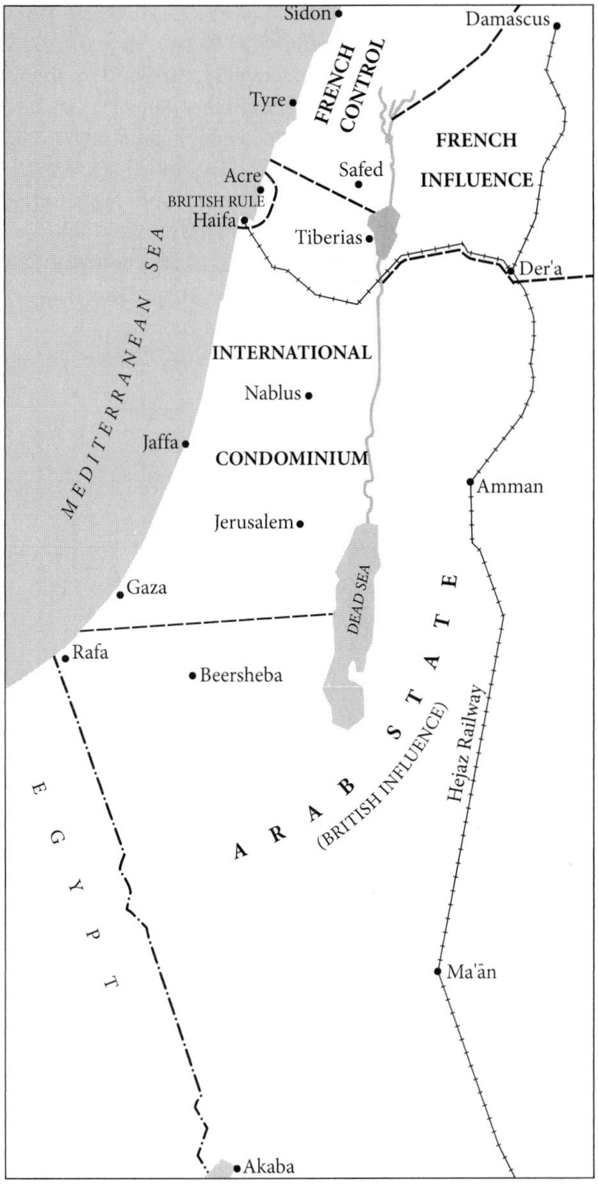

Proposed partition of the Middle East under the Sykes-Picot Treaty, 1916. Based on Zev Vilnay, New Israel Atlas, *Jerusalem, 1968.*

ish-controlled Palestine. A condominium with France in Palestine was fraught with danger, since the very principle of an international regime left the door open to Germany. Hence, as the historian Sir Charles Webster put it, "a situation had to be created in which the worst features of the Sykes-Picot Agreement could be got rid of without breaking faith… In these circumstances Dr. Weizmann's offer was an attractive one." Herein lay the *raison d'être* of the alliance with British Zionism. It provided a way to outmaneuver the French without a breach of faith, and was a useful card at the future peace conference to play against any move by Germany.

The agreement was officially abrogated by the Allies at the San Remo Conference in April 1920, when the Mandate for Palestine was conferred upon Britain.

BIBLIOGRAPHY: L. Stein, *The Balfour Declaration* (1961), 237–69, index; E. Kedourie, *England and the Middle East* (1956), 29–66, 102–41; J. Nevakivi, *Britain, France and the Arab Middle East* (1969), 35–44, index; C. Sykes, *Two Studies in Virtue* (1953), index; H.F. Frischwasser-Ra'ana, *The Frontiers of a Nation* (1955), 5–73; I. Friedman, *The Question of Palestine, 1914–1918. British-Jewish-Arab Relations* (1973, 1992²), 97–118; idem, *Palestine: A Twice Promised Land? The British, the Arabs and Zionism, 1915–1920* (2000), 47–60.

[Isaiah Friedman (2nd ed.)]

SYLVESTER, JAMES JOSEPH (1814–1897), British mathematician. Sylvester was "second wrangler" at Cambridge in 1837, but as a Jew, he was unwilling to subscribe to the Thirty-nine Articles and thus could not obtain a degree or fellowship. He was elected a Fellow of the Royal Society in 1839. Sylvester held a chair at the University of Virginia, U.S. (1841), but his outspoken sympathy for the slaves made it impossible for him to remain in Virginia. He accepted a chair at the Royal Military Academy, Woolwich, England (1855–70), then at John Hopkins (Baltimore, U.S. 1877–83), and at Oxford (1883). Sylvester and his colleague Arthur Cayley were considered the two leaders of pure mathematics in England during the 19th century.

Sylvester dominated the development of the theories of algebraic and differential invariants, and many of the technical terms now in use were coined by him. He was well versed in many languages. He founded, edited, and contributed to the *American Journal of Mathematics*. The Sylvester Medal established by the Royal Society commemorates his valuable services to the advancement of science. His collected mathematical papers were published in four volumes in New York during the years 1904–12.

BIBLIOGRAPHY: DNB; *Proceedings of the Royal Society, London*, 63 (1898), ix–xxv.

[Barry Spain]

SYLVIA, SARAH (1890–1976), South African actress and producer. Born in London, she was taken to Johannesburg as a child, and at the age of 12 played the lead in Goldfaden's *Shulamis*. In London, in 1912, she played opposite Maurice Moscovitch in his Yiddish production of *The Merchant of Venice*. Later in South Africa she organized Yiddish seasons, imported companies, and appeared in many plays including works of Gordin and Sholem Aleichem. Some of her outstanding performances were in English, in *Death of a Salesman* with Ben-Ami (1953) and *The World of Sholem Aleichem* (1960).

SYMMACHUS BEN JOSEPH (late second century C.E.), *tanna*. His patronymic is given only once in the aggadic statement, "Symmachus b. Joseph says: whoever prolongs the word *eḥad* ["one" in the *Shema*] has his days and years prolonged" (TJ, Ber. 2:1; cf. also TB, Ber. 13b). He was a disciple of *Meir, in whose name he transmitted two *halakhot* (BM 6:5; Ḥul. 5:3), and it was stated that he could adduce 48 reasons to support every rule of ritual cleanliness or uncleanness. Such attention to detail and keen legal reasoning, characteristic of

Meir's disciples, was apparently not fully appreciated by all his contemporaries. According to a talmudic *aggadah*, "after Meir died *Judah issued a decree to his disciples not to allow the disciples of R. Meir to enter, for they are disputatious and do not come to learn Torah, but come to embarrass me…." Symmachus nevertheless forced his way through and entered quoting a halakhic saying of R. Meir. R. Judah became angry, and *Yose commented: "People will say, 'Meir is dead, Judah is angry, Yose is silent; what is to become of the Torah?'" (Naz. 49b; Kid. 52b). That he was a recognized legal authority is evidenced by the fact that R. Nathan turned to him for a ruling (Ket. 52a). He is the author of the famous principle in monetary cases: "Money, the ownership of which cannot be decided, has to be equally divided" (BK 46a; et al.) which, however, is not accepted in practice. Although he apparently knew some Greek (Naz. 8b), he is not to be identified with the Symmachus who translated the Bible into Greek. Symmachus may have lived to old age, since the Talmud reports that *Rav, during a visit to Ereẓ Israel probably in the mid-third century, put a question to him (Ket. 81a).

BIBLIOGRAPHY: Hyman, Toledot, 959–60.

[Michael Graetz]

SYMONDS, SAUL (1894–1952), Australian communal leader. Symonds was born in Sydney, the son of a Russian-born furniture dealer, and was educated at Sydney Grammar School and Sydney University. He was a barrister from 1921 to 1939 when he became head of his family's furniture business. Symonds was among the most important communal leaders in New South Wales of the immediate postwar era, when Australia's Jewish community was being transformed by the arrival of thousands of Holocaust survivors. He served as president of the New South Wales Jewish Board of Deputies from 1945 to 1952 and was president of the Executive Council of Australian Jewry in 1946–48, but is best known as president of the Australian Jewish Welfare Society from 1948 to 1952, which (despite its name) was the main body responsible for Jewish immigration. Symonds oversaw the successful arrival and acculturation of thousands of survivors, but was criticized at the time for an officious manner, in contrast to the allegedly more welcoming attitude of Melbourne's immigration leaders.

BIBLIOGRAPHY: ADB, 12, 158; I. Porush, *The House of Israel* (1977), index; W.D. Rubinstein, Australia II, index; A. Andgel, *Fifty Years of Caring: The History of the Australian Jewish Welfare Society, 1936–1986* (1988); S. Rutland and S. Caplan, *With One Voice: A History of the New South Wales Board of Deputies* (1988).

[William D. Rubinstein (2nd ed.)]

SYMONS, JULIAN (1912–1994), British writer and critic. Born in London, the son of a Polish-born Jewish auctioneer, Symons left school at 14 and became one of the best-known writers and critics of detective stories of his day. Beginning with *The Thirty-First of February* (1950), Symons wrote many detective novels such as *The Man Who Killed Himself* (1967) and *Death's Dark Face* (1990). He also produced histories of the detective story such as the influential *Bloody Murder* (1972). Symons also wrote numerous biographies and works on recent history. From 1958 he was chairman of the Crime Writers Association and, from 1976 to 1985, succeeded Agatha Christie as president of the Detection Club. His elder brother, ALPHONSE JAMES ALBERT SYMONS (A.J.A. Symons, 1900–1941), was a noted book collector who founded the First Edition Club and, in 1930, *The Book-Collectors' Quarterly*. In 1934 he wrote *The Quest For Corvo*, a study of the literary eccentric Baron Corvo. A.J.A Symons died of heart failure at the age of 41.

BIBLIOGRAPHY: ODNB; J. Symons, *A.J.A. Symons: His Life and Speculations* (1950).

[William D. Rubinstein (2nd ed.)]

SYNAGOGUE. This article is arranged according to the following outline.

ORIGINS AND HISTORY

The synagogue, together with the *Temple, is the most important institution in Judaism. It has had a decisive influence not only on Judaism throughout the ages, but on organized religion as a whole. As C. Toy points out (*Introduction to the History of Religions* (1913), 546) "their [the Jews'] genius for the organization of public religion appears in the fact that the form of communal worship devised by them was adapted by Christianity and Islam, and in its general outlines still exists in the Christian and Moslem world." Nevertheless, there are almost no historical dates concerning its origin. As its birth is lost in the mists of antiquity and apparently took place unheralded, so it grew to maturity in conditions of obscurity, and makes its definite appearance about the first century of the Christian era as a fully grown and firmly established institution. There is, however, an almost universal consensus of opinion as to the place and origin of its birth and these best present the conditions under which its birth can be most naturally explained. It is natural that when the synagogue had become the central institution of Judaism, the ancient authorities ascribed it as going back to the very beginnings of Judaism. The Targum (Pseudo-Jonathan to Ex. 18:20), the Midrash (Yal., Ex. 408), and Josephus (Apion, 2:175), as well as the New Testament (Acts 15:21), all ascribe its origin to Moses. Basing itself on a passage in the Talmud (Shab. 32a) which castigates those who refer to a synagogue as "Bet Ha-Am," a Midrash, quoted by Rashi and Kimḥi, applies this phrase in Jeremiah 39:8 to the synagogue. Some have seen in Psalms 74:8 "they have burnt up all the meeting places (the A.V. actually has "synagogues" and it was so rendered by Aquila and Symmachus) in the land" as a reference to synagogue and, on this basis, ascribe the Psalm to the Maccabean period (but see below). All these references, however, must be regarded as merely homiletical attempts to push back the date of the origin of this important institution, and, with the exception of the reference in Ezekiel (see below), they can be disregarded from the historical point of view. It is to the period of the Babylonian Exile that one must look for the origin of the synagogue. Not only has it been assumed that the Exiles, deprived of the Temple, in a strange land, feeling the need for consolation in their distress, would meet from time to time, probably on Sabbaths, and read the Scriptures, but it is in Ezekiel, the prophet of that Exile, that one finds the first probable references to it. It has been suggested that in the repeated mention of the assembly of the elders before Ezekiel (8:6, 14:1, 20:1) one can point to the actual beginning of the synagogue. More definite, however, is the reference to the "little sanctuary" in 11:16, and it may have been a true instinct which made the Talmud (Meg. 29a) apply it to the synagogue. The Jews who had remained in Judea after the Exile of Jehoiachin taunted the Exiles that they were removed from the Temple, which still stood, and Ezekiel answered, "Thus saith the Lord God, Although I have removed them far off among the nations, and although I have scattered them among the countries, yet I have been to them as a little sanctuary in the countries where they are come." And although, as will be seen, there was an organic relation between Temple and synagogue during the period of the Second Temple, from the moment the Temple was destroyed, and in the Diaspora before then, the phrase "little sanctuary" faithfully indicates the role of the synagogue in the thoughts and lives of the people. There is in rabbinical literature no tradition or legend of any building in their time having been a synagogue during the period of the First Temple; in Babylonia there was a strong tradition that the famous synagogue Shaf Ve-Yativ in *Nehardea had been established by the Exiles of Jehoiachin, and that its name actually meant "that which has been moved and established" (Meg. 29a).

This view of the Babylonian Exile as the time and place of the emergence of the synagogue is not, however, universally accepted. Some have persisted in dating back its beginnings to the First Temple period (see Levy, bibliography, 7–14); Weingreen, basing himself on such passages as Psalm 116:17 and Isaiah 1:11, 15, which indicate that sacrifice in the First Temple was accompanied by prayer, that the prayer of Hannah at Shiloh (I Sam. 1:10ff.) was unaccompanied by sacrifice, and that Solomon's prayer at the dedication of the Temple makes no mention of sacrifice, comes to the conclusion that in them one can see evidence that the synagogue originated during the First Temple. Similarly, according to him, sacrificial acts at the local shrines were accompanied by prayer; when Josiah banned sacrifices at those shrines (II Kings 22 and 23), religious worship without sacrifice continued. He finds the origin of all the elements of the synagogue – prayer, Scriptural readings, and the sermon – in the history of the First Temple. Friedlander regards it as an invention of the Hellenistic Diaspora, while S. Zeitlin dates it to that, or the Maccabean period.

Until the First Century

Although there is no mention of the synagogue in Ezra and Nehemiah and the post-Exilic prophets, it can be assumed that the returned Exiles brought with them the rudiments of that institution to which they had given birth during their exile. In this connection it is germane to draw attention to the fact that the establishment of the synagogue implies the evolution of standard forms of service, and the Talmud ascribes the formulation of the earliest prayers (the **Amidah*, **Kiddush*, and **Havdalah*) to Ezra and his successors, the Men of the Great Synagogue (Ber. 33a). Weingreen, however (bibliography, 69–70), draws attention to an ostracon discovered by N.

Glueck at Elath (Basor 82, 7–11), belonging, according to Albright, to the sixth century B.C.E., which C.C. Torrey (ibid., 84, 4–5) reads as Bet Kenisa bi-Yrushalayim ("the Synagogue in Jerusalem"). There is no mention of synagogues or their destruction during the persecutions of Antiochus Epiphanes which led to the Maccabean Wars, but this is possibly due to the fact that the main interest of the Books of Maccabees is the Temple in Jerusalem. The suggestion has been made that the reference to Mizpeh in I Maccabees 3:46 as "a place of prayer" τόπος προσευχῇ "where they prayed aforetime" is not to an altar or shrine, but to a synagogue, but this is probably another example of the tendency to ascribe to the shrines of old the function of the contemporaneous synagogue. However, there is mention of the fact of public readings from the scrolls of the Torah (I Macc. 3:48) and to the singing of hymns to the refrain "His mercy is good and endureth forever" (4:24). That it does not refer to the Psalms with this refrain is indicated by a whole hymn on this pattern in Ben Sira 51.

It is natural that in the Diaspora the need for local places of worship was much more keenly felt than in Ereẓ Israel, despite the huge throngs of Diaspora Jews who made the pilgrimages to Jerusalem on the festivals (see *Pilgrimages). In Ereẓ Israel the Temple attracted the main religious loyalties and affections of the people; no such rival existed in the Diaspora. It is true that there existed in Egypt the Temple of *Elephantine and of Onias (see *Onias, Temple of) but these did not have the sentimental hold exercised by the Temple in Jerusalem. It is therefore not surprising that it is in the Diaspora, and particularly in Egypt, that archaeological discovery has revealed the remains of the earliest synagogue. In 1902 there was discovered in Shedia, 26 km. from Alexandria, a marble slab stating that the Jews dedicated this synagogue to Ptolemy III Euergetes (246–221 B.C.E.) and his queen Berenice. The inscription gives the impression of an institution already long established. To the same period and country belongs a dedicatory inscription found in Lower Egypt granting rights of asylum to the synagogue (REJ45 (1902), 163–4). The mention in III Maccabees 7:20 of the founding of a synagogue at Ptolemais during the reign of Ptolemy IV (221–204) is therefore entirely credible.

First Century C.E.

It is in the first century C.E., however, that the synagogue suddenly emerges as a well established and ancient institution, the very center of the social and religious life of the people, unrivaled in the Diaspora, and harmoniously cooperating with the Temple in Ereẓ Israel. It is a remarkable literary phenomenon that all sources, Talmud, Philo, Josephus, the New Testament and, to some extent archaeology, afford evidence of the existence of the synagogue, with every indication that it is anything but a new institution. Philo (see Legatione ad Gaium, 132f.) states that the large population of Alexandria had many synagogues in many quarters of the city; a great synagogue there, where the members of the various craft guilds sat together and which was so huge that the voice of the precentor was inaudible and flags had to be waved to indicate to the worshipers when they should make the responses, is described in the Talmud (Suk. 51b; TJ, ibid. 5:1, 55a; Tosef., ibid. 4:6). It was destroyed during the reign of Trajan (98–117) and could not therefore be later than the first century.

In Ereẓ Israel Josephus mentions synagogues in Tiberias (Life, 280), Dora (Ant., 19:305), and Caesarea (Wars, 2:285–9). The New Testament adds those of Nazareth (Matt. 13:54) and Capernaum (Mark 1:21); the Talmud adds the synagogue in Jerusalem of the Alexandrians (Tosef., Meg. 3 (2): 6; TJ, Meg. 3:1, 73d) and of the "Tarsians" (Meg. 26a). (It has been suggested, however, that the two are identical, "Tarsians" meaning filigree workers and refers to the Tarsian carpet industry which flourished in Egypt. Synagogues of the Tarsians existed also in Tiberias and Lydda (see Krauss, *Synagogale Altertuemer*, 201).) One passage (TJ, Meg. 3:1) gives the number of synagogues in Jerusalem at the time of the destruction of the Temple as 480, another (Ket. 105a) gives what looks like an exact figure of 394. Most authorities dismiss these figures as "doubtless gravely exaggerated," but it must be borne in mind that archaeological investigations have proved beyond question that the synagogues of Israel were small (cf. Baron, Community, 1, 92). (The same applies to modern Israel, and Jerusalem today has more than the larger number quoted above and there seems no reason to dismiss the number as fanciful.) Most significant of all, however, was the existence of a synagogue on the Temple Mount itself (Sot. 7:7–8; Yoma 7:1).

Outside Ereẓ Israel, in addition to the above-mentioned synagogues of Shaf Ve-Yativ in Nehardea and the synagogues in Egypt, Philo refers to the synagogues of Rome (loc. cit., 156), and inscriptions have been found of no less than 13 of these synagogues (for details see Baron, Community, 1, 81–82). In 1963 the ruins of a fourth-century synagogue in Ostia built on the ruins of an earlier one, probably dating from the first century, were discovered. The most extensive evidence of synagogues in every community in the Diaspora is given in the New Testament. Paul preached in many synagogues in Damascus (Acts 9:20, 22), and he refers to synagogues in every city he visited in Asia Minor (Acts 13:5, 14, 14:1, 15:21, 17:1, 10, 18:4, 7), including a number in Salamis in Cyprus. Baron enumerates the following list of known ancient synagogues in the Diaspora, compiled about 1922, to which discoveries since then can be added: Syria and Phoenicia, Asia Minor, including Cyprus – 31; the Balkan Peninsula, including Greece and the Aegean Islands – 19; Italy, including Sicily – 181; Spain, Gaul, and Hungary – 5; North Africa – 21. The synagogue in Stobi, Macedonia, dates from 65 C.E. (Baron, Community, 1, 80; A. Marmorstein, JQR, 27 (1936–37), 373–38). In Delos, Greece, was a synagogue dating from the second pre-Christian century (Sukenik, bibliography, 37, and see below, Architecture). There is therefore no doubt but that by the first century the synagogue was a firmly- and well-established institution in every community, both in Ereẓ Israel and in the Diaspora. While the Temple stood there was an organic relationship between synagogue and Temple. The Mishnah (Sot. 7:7) gives full details of the service in the synagogue on the Temple Mount on the Day of Atonement: "The *ḥazzan* of the synagogue [see below] used to take the scroll of the Torah and hand it to the chief of the synagogue, who handed it to the prefect, who handed it to the high priest, and the high priest received it standing and read it standing, etc." Similarly, in his vivid description of the festivities during the Festival of Water Drawing (see *Sukkot), Joshua b. Hananiah describes the manner in which the day was spent, attending the sacrifices in the Temple alternating with prayer in the synagogue (Suk. 53a). In addition to this, however, the arrangements of the **mishmarot* and *ma'amadot* were that, while the *mishmar* of priests and levites and the Israelite representatives were present during the weekly rota of service of their *mishmar* in the Temple, the remaining members of the *ma'amad* who did not accompany the members of the *mishmar* to Jerusalem gathered in their local synagogues for prayer and fasting (Ta'an. 4:2; and see *Liturgy).

With the destruction of the Temple, however, and the consequent automatic cessation of the sacrificial service, the synagogue remained without a rival as the focus and center of Jewish religious life. Many of the customs and rituals of the Temple were deliberately and consciously transferred to the synagogue, and on the other hand, some of these rituals were forbidden just for the reason that they belonged to the Temple and the Temple only. Prayer was regarded as the substitute for sacrifice, and it was no accident that the word *avodah*, referring to the sacrificial system, was now applied to prayer which was the "*Avodah* of the heart" (Sif. Deut. 41). The service, functions, and the functionaries of the synagogue have remained remarkably consistent throughout the 2,500 years of its history. The order of service laid down in the first chapters of tractate *Berakhot* for daily and Sabbath service, and *Megillah* (3:4–end) for festivals, remains unchanged as the fundamental order of service, to which, in the course of the ages, only additions have been made. The function of the synagogue as a center not only for prayer and instruction, but as the communal center, dates from the earliest period. To the one permanent official of the synagogue in Temple and talmudic times, the *ḥazzan ha-keneset*, the beadle, there were added the professional cantor who was unknown in early times; the *ba'al keri'ah* who read the scriptural portion where previously the person called up read his own portion; and particularly in western countries, the preacher and/or rabbi of a synagogue, as distinct from the rabbi of the community. Owing to special circumstances, greater emphasis was laid on certain aspects of the synagogue in the Middle Ages and in the modern era. For instance, the function of the synagogue as a communal center is already to be noted in talmudic times, but under ghetto conditions, voluntary or enforced, it assumed much greater proportions. Similarly, social needs of the present day, especially in the United States, have tended to turn the synagogue with its ancillary institutions into an all-embracing social center.

Middle Ages

The Talmud justifies the reciting of the **Kiddush* in the synagogue, despite the fact that "*Kiddush* is recited only at a meal" (Pes. 101a; the custom is still universal except in Israel), on the grounds that it was recited for the benefit of visitors and wayfarers "who eat, drink, and sleep in the synagogue" (Pes. 101a). That the reference is not to the synagogue proper is clear from the explicit prohibition of eating and drinking in it (Meg. 28a), but to annexes provided for that purpose, and there has been discovered an inscription from a first-century synagogue recording the name of Theodotus son of Vettenos who built a synagogue "for the reading of the Torah and teaching of the commandments and also built the hospice and chambers and water installations for lodging needy strangers" (Sukenik, bibliography, 70). This aspect of the synagogue was greatly increased during the Middle Ages. There was practically no activity in the daily life of the Jews which was not reflected in the life of the synagogue. Any person having a private complaint could have the service interrupted, until he was promised redress (see **Bittul ha-Tamid*) and the results of lawsuits were announced, as were articles lost and found. Even the announcements of certain properties on the market were included in some synagogues. In Italy any man intending to leave the community had publicly to announce the fact, so that any claims against him could be put forward. Proclamations were made of stolen goods (that this was the practice in talmudic times is mentioned in Lev. R. 6:2). Announcements whose purpose was to enforce moral and conjugal virtues were included. In the synagogue mourners were officially and publicly comforted, a custom which prevails to the present day, and the appearance of bridegrooms on the Sabbaths preceding and following the wedding made occasions for congregational rejoicing. The most powerful social sanction was the **ḥerem* which, inter alia, banned the person against whom it was issued from participation in congregational worship.

[Louis Isaac Rabinowitz]

Modern Period

In the 18th century the rise of *Ḥasidism had a definite effect on the synagogue. The Ḥasidim downgraded the formality of the synagogue service, stressing in its stead the fervor and excitement which should accompany prayer. Their synagogues were much smaller and devoid of elaborate furnishings and decorations; in fact, they were more of the *bet ha-midrash* type, being places for meetings and study as well as for prayer. Communal meals, particularly the **se'udah shelishit*, were held there, and indeed the synagogue was known in ḥasidic parlance as the *shtibl* ("small room") or *Klaus* ("close," in the archaic sense). The ḥasidic synagogue did away with salaried officiants; members of the congregation led the prayers themselves, and generally the whole atmosphere was very informal. By and large pews were replaced by tables and benches, and the internal appearance was very much more austere than that of the regular synagogue.

With the *Reform movement a century later, the synagogue took a turn in the opposite direction. The Reform synagogues were elaborate, dignified, buildings, lavishly and formally furnished. Unlike the ḥasidic synagogue buildings, which were rarely constructed for that purpose but were existing buildings made over, the Reform synagogues were usually designed and built for the specific purpose for which they were to be used. The *ark was an impressive edifice within the sanctuary, as were the *almemar* and the pulpit. Most Reform synagogues, which were known as "temples," included an organ and choir loft, and the almemar was at the front of the auditorium (see below and **Bimah*). Pews were arranged in straight rows with no special section for the women. Officiants in such synagogues were salaried employees of the congregation. There can be no doubt that the Reform synagogues were influenced both in structural style and internal organization by prevailing trends in the various Christian churches. Decorum, dignity, and contemporary aesthetic values became important aims in the planning of the synagogues. These were achieved at the cost, to a large degree, of warmth, excitement, and spontaneity.

Orthodox congregations in western Europe, England, and the U.S. also began to erect elaborate synagogues, with the proviso, of course, that the halakhic requirements were met. A gallery was usually provided for the women from which they could see, as well as hear, the service in progress. Salaried officials led the services and great importance was placed on decorum and dignity. Most synagogues had, in addition to the main sanctuary which was used for sabbaths and festivals, a smaller, less lavish, synagogue, variously called a *bet ha-midrash* or chapel, for weekday services. In the chapel the service was less formal and usually conducted by the congregants. Most synagogue buildings began in the 20th century to have facilities attached for the synagogue school or *talmud torah*, as well as halls for meetings or banquets. These halls are, in many cases, utilized for "overflow" services on the High Holidays, when the seating in the main auditorium is inadequate. Many synagogues also have a "bride's room," in which the bride prepares herself for the wedding ceremony and in which the *yiḥud* takes place afterward (see *Marriage). Some ultra-Orthodox congregations include, in the synagogue building, a **mikveh*. An interesting development in modern times, particularly in the U.S., is the "expanding" synagogue; a hall is immediately adjacent to the main sanctuary divided from it by a movable wall. For the High Holidays the wall is removed, thus increasing, sometimes even doubling, the seating capacity and obviating the need for extra personnel to lead the "overflow" services. However, side by side with these large, formal synagogues, there continued to exist smaller, less elaborate prayerhouses and indeed, in attempting to establish statistical information, one is faced with the difficulty of defining what a synagogue is (see below).

DESECRATION AND DESTRUCTION OF SYNAGOGUES (HOLOCAUST PERIOD). The desecration of synagogues and Jewish cemeteries during World War II by the Germans and their collaborators was a carefully planned operation, executed with utmost thoroughness. It was accompanied not only by vandalism and looting, but by cruelty and malice. In many cases Jews were ordered to burn down their houses of worship for which they were afterward blamed, while those who refused to obey were punished. "Fire Brigades" were formed in some Polish towns, their task being to set fire to synagogues and religious articles, and sometimes even the worshipers, who were forced inside the building to be burned alive. It is impossible to ascertain the vast number of art and religious treasures destroyed or stolen by the Nazis and their fellow travelers and collaborators in the non-Jewish population. Synagogues were destroyed in thousands of communities in eastern Europe, in the large Jewish settlements in Poland, Lithuania, Latvia and Estonia, the Ukraine, Belorussia and such central European countries such as Germany, Austria, Czechoslovakia, and the Balkans. The religious art treasures of these synagogues ran into hundreds of thousands of items, for every synagogue was virtually a repository of ritual and traditional objects. These included Torah scrolls, Torah mantles, Torah shields and pointers, and Holy Arks, often made of carved wood or stone, with their curtains; there were also Chairs of Elijah, chandeliers, candlesticks, prayer books, and *megillot*. The comparatively sparse documentary evidence on the destruction to be found in various archives includes actual destruction orders, the names of those who issued and executed them, and the dates of destruction.

The first attempts to describe the extent of this destruction were made during the war by eyewitnesses, such as Emanuel *Ringelblum and Rabbi Simon Huberband. The latter participated in Ringelblum's "Oneg Shabbat" (code name for secret documentation work of the Warsaw Jewish underground movement). Huberband listed the destruction of Polish synagogues and Jewish cemeteries. According to data in the *Yad Vashem archives, the deportation and liquidation of the Jewish population of Europe was accompanied by the destruction of 33,914 Jewish communities, of which a few thousand were in Poland. It is estimated that 98% of movable Jewish art treasures in Poland, which had been preserved in synagogues or art collections, disappeared during the war. The first official attempt to list the losses in the domain of ritual art objects throughout Poland was made by the Ministerstwo Kultury i Sztuki (Ministry of Culture and Art) in a series of publications of the Claims and Reparations Office. A few of the synagogues in Poland were restored and converted by the authorities for cultural needs (libraries, museums, movie theaters, and cultural centers) or became cooperative grain stores. The architecturally interesting wooden synagogues in Poland were all destroyed by the Germans (see *Poland, and below, Architecture).

Testimony on the destruction of synagogues in Germany and Austria, especially with regard to **Kristallnacht* (1938), was given at the *Eichmann trial. On *Kristallnacht*, about 280 synagogues were destroyed and burned in Germany alone. Of the 23 Viennese synagogues that had existed before the *Anschluss*, the only remaining one was restored in 1964, and two *battei* *midrash* were left. The monetary value of 56 synagogues destroyed in Austria on November 10, 1938, alone, is estimated at 5,000,000 dollars.

[David Davidovitch]

ORIENTAL SYNAGOGUES. In Oriental countries and in Oriental communities in Israel the synagogue has hardly changed throughout the centuries. Low seating is generally provided around the walls of the room and the almemar is always in the center. Occasionally a special chair, of Moses or Elijah, is attached high up on the wall. Prayers are usually led by congregants, although in some of the modern Sephardi synagogues in Israel salaried officials are employed. In Europe and the United States the Sephardi synagogues are much as the Ashkenazi, except for the liturgical rite. (For further information, see *Ottoman Empire: Restrictions on Building New Synagogues.)

IN THE UNITED STATES. While the situation described above holds good for the United States, a further development took place there which in turn influenced the synagogue in the whole western world. Mordecai *Kaplan formulated the concept of the "synagogue center." He felt that the synagogue, if it were to continue to play its role in Jewish life, had to be more than a prayerhouse and, in view of the disintegration of traditional Jewish values in the U.S., more than a house of study. He therefore advocated that the synagogue become an all-embracing center of Jewish social and cultural activity, with the aim that the Jew spend a great deal, if not most, of his leisure time within the confines of the synagogue building. Such a building would no longer be a synagogue but a "Jewish center" and "instead of the primary purpose of congregation organizations being worship, it should be social togetherness.... The history of the synagogue... is a striking illustration of the importance of creating new social agencies when new conditions arise that threaten the life of a people or of its religion" (Mordecai M. Kaplan, "The Way I Have Come," *Mordecai M. Kaplan: An Evaluation* (1952), 311). According to Kaplan, the Jewish center should contain a swimming pool, gymnasium, library, club rooms, public hall, and classrooms, in addition to facilities for worship. It should provide professional club leaders to supervise groups for adults as well as children, and they should include all the activities in which the membership is likely to be interested, and not only of a Jewish nature, but such activities as photography, drama, music, sport, etc. Although most congregations were unable to provide this comprehensive program, both because of financial inadequacy and the fact that other existing organizations such as the YMHA already provided some of them, it remained the ideal for which to aim, with the results varying from synagogue to synagogue. The "center" idea, which was in fact a reformulation of what had always been the synagogue's role, has been generally accepted, and most synagogues provide such activities for their congregants.

According to a 2001 study published in the *American Jewish Year Book*, there were 3,727 synagogues in the United States, among them 1,501 Orthodox, 976 Reform, and 865 Conservative. New York City had 995 synagogues, followed by California with 425.

ISRAEL. Because of the fact that it is a "Jewish" country, many of the functions performed by the synagogue in other countries are provided in Israel by other agencies, often governmental. The nature of the country also obviates the need to affiliate with a synagogue to express one's Jewish identity. Education, including religious, is the concern of the state; burial is the concern of independent burial societies; *kashrut* is supervised and arranged by the *Rabbinate, at its different levels, which institution is financed by the government and independent of the synagogue. Thus, in the Jewish country, a paradoxical situation has arisen; one would have thought that the synagogue would flourish and expand its influence, when in fact it has become little more than a house of prayer. The population, even the religious section of it, finds its expression within other frameworks (see *Israel, State of; Religious Life).

[Raphael Posner]

While the main function of synagogues in Israel is to serve as places of worship, many also organize daily or weekly lectures or classes for their congregants. A vast variety of synagogue services can be found throughout the country, each community of the Diaspora bringing to Israel its own customs and manners. The multiplicity of traditions presents a peculiar problem for the army, since there is no possibility of establishing synagogues suited to the specific customs of diverse communities in every military camp and base. Nor can the army "melting pot" permit soldiers to be divided in prayer. Thus, by force of circumstances, a uniform type of synagogue has emerged, encouraged also by the way in which children from different communities join in prayer and study at religious schools and *yeshivot*.

This pattern has been followed by the younger generation in civilian life, and about 300 synagogues of a unified type have been set up, combining elements from the rituals of Ḥasidim and *Mitnaggedim*, and from Ashkenazim and Sephardim. Before the establishment of the State, there were few distinguished synagogue buildings in the country. Baron Edmond de *Rothschild erected a synagogue in every settlement that he endowed, and the buildings are still to be seen in Zikhron Ya'akov, Rishon le-Zion, Mazkeret Batyah, and elsewhere. The old *yishuv* in Safed, Tiberias, and Hebron had a number of poor synagogue buildings. The Jewish Quarter of Old Jerusalem contained 58 synagogues which had served the Sephardi and Ashkenazi communities from the time when *Naḥmanides renewed Jewish life in Jerusalem after the Crusades. Among them was the Sephardi Great Synagogue of Rabban Johanan ben Zakkai, which included four synagogues in a single large block. The largest synagogue of the Ashkenazi community was called the Ḥurvah ("Ruin"), since it was built on the ruins of the House of Study of Rabbi *Judah Ḥasid. Other notable synagogues were the Bet El synagogue of the kabbalists and the Tiferet Israel synagogue, also called Nisan Bak, after its founder. The oldest synagogue was that of the *Karaites, ascribed to the tenth or eleventh century. During and after the 1948 War of Independence, 55 of these synagogues were destroyed by the Arabs, but some others (Ramban, Ḥabad) were restored after the liberation of the Old City in June, 1967 (see *Jerusalem).

During the British Mandate (1917–48) synagogue building proceeded slowly, principally in the larger cities and with the financial assistance of the local community. Thus in 1923–24 the Great Synagogue and the Sephardi Synagogue Ohel Mo'ed in Tel Aviv, and Yeshurun in Jerusalem, were established, and in the 1930s the Central Synagogue of Haifa was founded. At the time of the establishment of the State in 1948, there were about 800 synagogues of all kinds throughout the country, serving a Jewish population of 650,000. The rapid growth of immigrant housing and the development of townships necessitated new synagogues, particularly where there were liturgical and ritual differences. New buildings were also erected to replace the provisional structures in the veteran religious settlements.

By 1970 there were about 6,000 synagogues. These new synagogues were jointly financed by the Ministry for Religious Affairs, the Ministry of Housing, the Jewish Agency, the Jewish Restitution Successor Organization, the Silverman Fund, the Wolfson Trust, and other agencies. The complete interior furnishing of nine synagogues from Jewish communities destroyed during World War II, and 28 arks from old synagogues in Italy, were transferred to Israel and reconstructed in various places throughout the country. The first of these came in 1952 from Coneglia, near Venice, and was reestablished as the Synagogue of *Benei Roma* in Jerusalem. Others came from Mantua, Padua, and Florence.

There is no distinctive form of synagogue architecture in Israel. Some local congregations have, however, evolved an architecture suited to their specific needs or exploiting local building materials – eucalyptus, olive wood, and marble from the Negev and Galilee. A modern Israel style seems to be emerging gradually, one of its features being the exterior *menorah* (candelabrum), which symbolizes the light of the Torah and is also the emblem of the State of Israel. The synagogue interiors usually conform to the pattern of the congregation's place of origin, and contain carpets and rugs and European or Oriental furniture. There is some new artistic expression in adornments by famous artists, such as Marc Chagall's stained-glass windows at the Hadassah Medical Center Synagogue in Jerusalem. The vast majority of synagogues in Israel are Orthodox, and the traditional partition between the main hall and the women's gallery (see **Meḥiẓah*) prevails in all of them, with variations as to the form and height of the grate or curtain. The *bimah* (platform) is situated in the middle of the synagogue, while the *ammud* (precentor's lectern) is close to the ark at the front wall. Sephardi synagogues, however, have no lecterns, and the entire service is conducted from the platform. In 1963, a Union of Israel Synagogues, embracing all the Orthodox synagogues, was established by Hechal Shlomo, Jerusalem. In 2005 there were about 50 Conservative and Reform synagogues in Israel. The most prominent of these is the *Hebrew Union College's synagogue in Jerusalem. The Karaites, who number about 25,000, have their own houses of prayer. They are concentrated mainly in Ramleh, but are also to be found in Ashdod, Ofakim, Beersheba, Ra'ananna, Maẓli'aḥ, Beth-Shemesh, and Acre.

[Benjamin Zvieli]

IN THE SOVIET BLOC. In the Soviet Union, where the constitution guarantees "freedom of religious worship and anti-religious propaganda," a group of 20 citizens was legally entitled to apply for permission to organize a religious congregation and to acquire a building or a plot for the erection of a building to serve as a place of prayer. Thus, those synagogues which still existed in the U.S.S.R. were each a separate society, not belonging to any federative or other country-wide framework (see below, Synagogue Organizations). Each of them was administered by a "committee of twenty" (in Soviet usage, *Dvadsatka*), which was responsible to the local authorities concerned with religious affairs that it should not engage in any illicit activity, such as "religious propaganda" (propaganda was explicitly reserved only for anti-religious purposes), religious education of children, social welfare work, etc.

In the early period of the Soviet regime, and particularly during the existence of the Jewish section (*Yevsektsiya) of the Communist Party, when suppression of the Jewish religion was regarded as part of the revolutionary remolding of Jewish society, the closing of synagogues and their transformation into "workers' clubs," cinemas, etc., became a mass phenomenon. In a matter of a decade or so, innumerable synagogues and other prayerhouses (of the *shtibl* or *minyan*-type) disappeared, and the meeting of Jews, particularly of the younger generation, for organized prayer or Torah study became a hazardous enterprise. After World War II, and especially during the rule of Khrushchev (1957–64), a drastic reduction of the remaining number of synagogues took place (from over 400 to about 60–65), some of them, mainly in Moscow and other larger cities, remaining intact in order to serve both as showplaces for visitors from abroad as well as centers for the supervision of the remnants of Jewish traditional life by the secret police. At the same time the authorities manipulated from behind the scenes the election of the congregation boards by the *Dvadtsatka*, so as to infiltrate them by agents or collaborators.

Paradoxically, at the same time in the early 1960s, while synagogues were closed down en masse – their congregants vilified in the press as "speculators" and criminals, and even previously tolerated *minyanim*, congregating in private homes on the High Holidays, brutally dispersed by the police – thousands, and later tens of thousands, of Jewish youth, reawakened to Jewish national consciousness, chose the synagogues and their courtyards and surroundings to demonstrate their Jewish identity by singing and dancing on Simḥat Torah and other holidays. These spontaneous gatherings in and around the few remaining synagogues, which at first were dispersed by the police, later became a constant feature of Soviet Jewish life, followed closely by diplomatic and press observers from abroad, which thus gave them, indirectly, some measure of immunity from persecution.

There were three synagogues in Moscow under the Soviet regime: the central Great Synagogue at Arkhispova Street and two small ones, in wooden houses, in the suburbs, Maryina Roshcha and Cherkizovo. In addition, a town near Moscow, Malakhovka, also had a synagogue of its own. There was no official connection whatsoever between these three, or four, synagogues, as no Jewish body of any character was allowed to exist in the U.S.S.R. outside its strictly circumscribed local function. Some cities in Georgia, Daghestan, and Uzbekistan also had more than one synagogue – one for the local, non-Ashkenazi community (Georgian Jews, Bukhara Jews or *Mountain Jews) and one for the Ashkenazi ("Russian") Jews who settled there, mostly as evacuees or refugees during World War II. There was a conspicuous difference in character between these two categories of synagogues.

Whereas the non-Ashkenazi synagogues served as prayer and meeting houses for the local Jewish population as a whole, comprising entire families and teeming with children and young people (similar to the prayer houses of their non-Christian neighbors), the Ashkenazi synagogues were, as in the European U.S.S.R., only visited by some elderly men and women (except sometimes for the demonstrative Simḥat Torah gatherings of the young). In all other places (such as, e.g., Leningrad, Kiev, Odessa, Riga, Vilna, Cemauti, Minsk, Novosibirsk, and others), there was only one synagogue in each. In some of them, such as Leningrad, Kiev, or Riga, the prerevolutionary buildings were still in use, and in addition to the large hall, used on holidays, there were also *shtibl*-type prayer rooms attached for weekday and Sabbath services. In others, such as Odessa or Minsk, shabby buildings at the outskirts of the town served this purpose. There were cities with large Jewish populations, such as Kharkov, in which the last synagogue was closed down some time after World War II and no other allowed to be established. There the militia (police) systematically persecuted Jews who congregated "illegally" on the High Holidays in private houses for prayer, but on the whole these persecutions did not succeed in deterring Jews from repeating this "misdemeanor" every year anew.

A specific trait of almost all the synagogues in the U.S.S.R. was the heavy atmosphere of fear of the secret police which was generally believed to listen to all conversations and keep a sharp eye on any contact between Soviet citizens and visitors from abroad. In many synagogues, including the central synagogue of Moscow, foreign visitors, including (until 1967) Israeli diplomats, were physically segregated from the rest of the congregation by specially erected wooden partitions, the *gabba'im* being responsible for preventing any contact with them. In other Communist countries in eastern Europe, the limitations imposed on the remaining synagogues were less stringent than in the U.S.S.R. In most of them countrywide federations of Jewish congregations, or religious communities, were allowed to exist and to cater to religious needs (baking of *mazzot*, distributing prayer books, etc.) through the synagogues. In Prague the famous Altneuschul was maintained by the authorities as a historical monument, at the same time still serving as a meeting place for prayer. In other Communist capitals possessing modern, imposing synagogue buildings from the 19th or early 20th century, such as Budapest, Bucharest, or Sophia, they were in use, and the atmosphere prevailing in them was less suffocating than in the synagogues of the Soviet Union, though the authorities supervised all of them for all kinds of "security" reasons. Most of them also served as showplaces for visitors from abroad.

With the collapse of Communism, Jewish religious life revived in a freer atmosphere, and numerous synagogues with officiating rabbis, often from Chabad, opened throughout the Russian Federation as well as in other former Communist countries. In 1992 a Rabbinical Alliance was formed, which by 2006 had 90 rabbis as members in 13 countries. In addition, 94 synagogues were affiliated with the Federation of Jewish Communities, which had purchased and restored 80 buildings for use as synagogues.

See also *Russia.

SYNAGOGUE ORGANIZATIONS. A modern phenomenon has been the organization of synagogues of a like type into a Synagogue Union. In the past, particularly in central and eastern Europe, there were periods in which *kehillot* were so organized (see *Councils of the Lands), but the organization of actual synagogues is comparatively new. The reason for this "unionization" is the fact that an individual synagogue is not able by itself to provide adequate educational and religious facilities, whereas several synagogues together have enough resources to take care of such things as religious education, *kashrut*, burial, etc. Another reason might be the influence of the Christian churches which are affiliated to different church organizations.

The *United Synagogue of England has a chief rabbi, a *bet din*, a *kashrut* division, and a religious educational framework. Salaries of the officials in its constituent synagogues are scaled, and candidates for such positions are required to obtain a certificate of competence from the chief rabbi. The rabbinical school, Jews' *College, is under its auspices and the chief rabbi is, ex officio, president of it. There are two other Orthodox synagogue organizations: The Federation of Synagogues, and, more extreme, the Union of Orthodox Hebrew Congregations (Adath Yisroel). Both these latter organizations provide services for their constituents, though not on the same scale as the United Synagogue. The Reform synagogues of England are organized, as are the Liberal synagogues.

In the United States there is a "Union of Orthodox Jewish Congregations," a "United Synagogue" (Conservative), and "Union of American Hebrew Congregations" (Reform). Besides the above, orthodoxy in the U.S. has several other synagogue organizations varying in their degrees of orthodoxy.

A more recent development has been the creation of international synagogue organizations. The Conservative movement is organized into a "World Council of Synagogues," which embraces Conservative-type synagogues in several countries and meets every two years to discuss problems of mutual interest; there is also considerable movement of Conservative rabbis to synagogues in other countries due to the existence of this organization.

In Israel synagogues are organized into the "Union of Synagogues in Israel," and the Conservative and Reform synagogues have their own organizations. Most other countries with a sizable Jewish population have similar organizations to those described above.

Women and the Synagogue

Evolving redefinitions of women's place and role within the synagogue are an integral part of the institution's long history. Recent scholarship demonstrates that women were a regular presence in the ancient synagogues of the Hellenistic Diaspora during the first centuries of the Common Era, and that they were not separated from men during public worship. Greek, Aramaic, and Hebrew inscriptions identify women as regular donors and sometimes as synagogue officers, although scholars still debate whether these titles referred to honorary or actual posts. Although rabbinic sources indicate that women were not unknown as participants in synagogue ritual, the overwhelming tendency in rabbinic literature is against granting women active roles in communal worship.

Cairo **Genizah* documents describe the separation of men and women in 10th- and 11th-century Egyptian synagogues, but also reveal the full engagement of women in their synagogues as worshipers, community members, and contributors. Early medieval European synagogues, built without specific women's areas, do not give evidence either of women's presence or absence. In the 12th century, however, women's sections adjoining the sanctuary began to be added to existing buildings. It is unclear whether these new women's annexes, in spaces such as attached rooms, grilled balconies, and basements, represented greater inclusion of women or an expulsion from the main sanctuary, perhaps because of growing anxiety over the threat of women's ritual impurity (see **Niddah*).

Integration of women into the synagogue space came with the 1639 and 1675 synagogue buildings of the Spanish Portuguese Jews in Amsterdam. These synagogues, built as galleried halls, used their balconies as women's sections, thus integrating women's space into the buildings' symmetrical design. This influential architectural model found imitators around Europe resulting in many synagogues with women's galleries overlooking the sanctuary, although ubiquitous opaque screens, grilles, or lattice work obstructed the view of those within. In these women's sections, beginning in the Middle Ages, the **firzogerin* would lead other women in prayer, either by relaying the prayers and hymns recited in the sanctuary or by using Yiddish devotional prayers that paralleled the Hebrew liturgy. Although attendance at regular communal worship was not central to a Jewish woman's religious obligations, many married women did traditionally attend synagogue on Sabbath mornings and during festival services. Unmarried women were less likely to be present.

As Enlightenment ideas began to undermine traditional Jewish communities in western societies, a growing desire to demonstrate Judaism's bourgeois respectability brought accepted models of Jewish female religiosity into question. Jewish reformers assailed what they saw as Judaism's undignified treatment of women. Nineteenth-century German reformers, especially, lamented the demeaning nature of women's treatment in the traditional synagogue and championed new models of worship, including vernacular sermons, in which women could see themselves as welcome participants. When the pioneer Reform congregation, the Hamburg Temple in Germany, opened in 1818, its open women's gallery was also meant to integrate women into the congregation. It was chiefly in North America, however, that structural changes in women's place became fundamental elements in an evolving redefinition of the synagogue.

Colonial America's earliest synagogues adopted the women's gallery modeled in Amsterdam, yet the second synagogue built in what was to become the United States – in Newport, Rhode Island in 1763 – dispensed with the additional grilles and curtains that surmounted the balustrades of European versions of this space. The almost universal repetition of this innovation in subsequent American synagogues was not, however, a mark of reform; open galleries occurred in congregations which saw themselves as settings for traditional worship. Eighteenth-century American synagogue records indicate the growing presence of young unmarried women assertively attending worship services and suggest that many women began to see synagogue attendance as a central aspect of their Jewish identity. As these women adapted to a religious context where women were highlighted for their public piety, the closed-off women's gallery became increasingly problematic and was quickly abandoned.

By the mid-19th century, many traditionally inclined synagogues in western Europe had adopted open women's galleries. American synagogues, where women were an increasing proportion of the congregation, were moving on to mixed seating of men and women. First introduced in reforming congregations in Albany in 1851, and then in New York City in 1854, family pews had become an almost universal feature in the new synagogues of acculturated American Jews by the 1870s, resisted only by a few of the colonial-era Sephardi congregations.

Seats in the main sanctuary, however, did not confer additional religious agency upon women in the late 19th century. Religious and lay governance remained exclusively male prerogatives. Even the female mutual aid societies which animated female charitable activism before the Civil War faded in importance. It took the arrival of the first waves of what would become two million Jewish immigrants from eastern Europe and Russia between the 1880s and 1920 to spark meaningful public activism among acculturated American Jewish women. The first Jewish synagogue sisterhood groups emerged in the 1890s in Reform, Conservative, and Orthodox congregations to address the needs of, and to Americanize, immigrant coreligionists. Many of these groups also addressed the physical and social needs of their own congregations. This infusion of women's energy is reflected in the construction of large synagogue complexes in the 1890s and early 20th century – suddenly necessary to house the expanded institutional life significantly fueled by female activism.

Meanwhile, immigrant Jews established religious communities of their own, often storefront *shuls* that generally excluded women. But as immigrant synagogues Americanized, they understood that attracting and retaining members meant incorporating women and children into institutional life. The earliest grand immigrant *shul* buildings boasted large and open women's galleries – preserving traditional gender separation, but conveying the American message that women were expected to be present and seen in the synagogue.

As immigrant Jews moved away from their initial neighborhoods, many joined synagogues associated with the Conservative movement. Most of these synagogues adopted mixed seating as a key marker separating them both from the Old World and the ghetto. Another sign of the Americanized synagogue, whether Reform, Conservative, or Orthodox, was the presence of women's organizations as facilitators of congregational sociability and activity. National coordination of such synagogue groups was initiated with the founding of the *National Federation of Temple Sisterhoods within the Reform movement in 1913. This was followed by creation of the *Women's League for Conservative Judaism in 1918, and an Orthodox counterpart in 1926. For decades, these groups contributed energy and money that enabled a vital congregational life.

While American synagogues evolved in continuous dialogue with women's changing roles, synagogues elsewhere in the world did not share in the conversation. They generally maintained more traditional patterns of public worship, including gendered spaces and roles. Even highly acculturated European Jewish communities felt less compelled than their American counterparts to sweep away basic structures like the women's gallery. Mixed seating, even in Reform congregations, remained rare well into the 20th century, and only a few British and German synagogues featured this innovation prior to World War II. Postwar attempts to reconstitute a tiny fraction of the synagogue communities eradicated during the Holocaust have rarely reconsidered traditional gender roles in public worship. Similarly, in the Jewish settlement in Palestine, and then in the new State of Israel, the emphasis on creating a traditional religious establishment precluded efforts to consider women's changing roles.

In North America, however, women's engagement in the work and life of their congregations and growing equality in the religious education of boys and girls raised questions about limitations on Jewish women's religious opportunities. Progress toward equality for women in Reform and Conservative congregations advanced sporadically through the 1950s and 1960s. While Conservative leaders acted to remove some of the formal restrictions on women's ritual participation, Reform leaders discussed the possibility of female religious leadership. A few women did find their way into lay and spiritual congregational leadership during the 1940s and 1950s, but in general, apart from the increasing prevalence of *bat mitzvah ceremonies in the 1960s, little changed until the entry of women into the rabbinate and cantorate beginning in the 1970s (see **Hazzan*; **Semikhah*; *Rabbi, Rabbinate). Women's assumption of religious leadership had profound symbolic and practical implications for every variety of Judaism, reconfiguring expectations of what women should be allowed and encouraged to do. The influence of female rabbis ranges from a deepening emphasis on spirituality, a turn to the healing possibilities of Jewish tradition, challenges to continued exclusions within Jewish tradition and life of marginalized communities, including single people and gays and lesbians, and a general democratization of access to ritual participation, education, and leadership.

Orthodox congregations continue to segregate men and women and to prohibit women rabbis, but some of the most dynamic creativity in contemporary Jewish life can be found in Orthodox feminism. Recent decades have brought transformations in the Jewish education of traditional girls and young women. Unprecedented female engagement in advanced textual study has intensified challenges to what remains the largely male domain of Orthodox public worship. The first International Conference on Feminism and Orthodoxy held in New York City in 1997 led to the creation of the Jewish Orthodox Feminist Alliance, which continues to assert that traditional Jewish legal processes should be pushed to deal with questions of Jewish women's leadership and participation. Although these ideas and regular women's *tefillah* (prayer) groups face strong opposition from within Orthodoxy, they have nonetheless done much to shift both possibilities and realities in the traditional synagogue.

Great Britain's Reform movement ordained its first woman rabbi in 1975. Since then, the Liberal and Reform movements (representing a minority of British synagogues) have embraced the principle of gender equality, though they face the same struggles as North American synagogues in translating this commitment into true access for women to positions of status and authority as religious leaders. Among Britain's Orthodox Jews, women's prayer groups with the support of the chief rabbi have become an active mainstream movement. Women rabbis are just beginning to serve in small numbers of congregations in western Europe, and little change in women's roles has been seen in congregations further to the east. Yet as Jewish communities struggle with the continuing task of reconciling patriarchal traditions with contemporary values, it seems a certainty that the challenge of finding a place for women will continue to define the evolving shape of synagogues around the world.

[Karla Goldman (2nd ed.)]

IN HALAKHAH

Halakhah regulates the following aspects of synagogue construction and use: design and location of the building; furnishings and interior design; proscribed uses of the synagogues and its contents; and ownership and disposal of the building.

Design and Location

Halakhah governs only very specific components of synagogue design and makes no stipulations for the building's general external appearance. Historically, there does not seem to have been a conventional style of synagogue architecture. Synagogues, after satisfying the halakhic structural requirements discussed below, have been built in nearly every conceivable form, usually in the architectural styles prevailing at a particular time and place (see below, Architecture).

The synagogue must have windows, a requirement stemming from Daniel 6:11 which describes how Daniel prayed by windows facing toward Jerusalem. The Talmud (Ber. 34b) warned against praying in a room without windows and the *halakhah* (Sh. Ar., OḤ 90:4, from the Zohar, Parashat Pekudei), perhaps symbolic of the twelve tribes, states that a synagogue should have 12 windows – a stipulation that is rarely met because of architectural and other problems. Rashi commented that windows are required because they allow the supplicant to see the sky, the sight of which inspires reverence and devotion during prayer (Ber. 34b). Indeed, if a wall was built in front of the synagogue windows, it was not only demolished, but the usual requirement of its removal six feet (four cubits) away was insufficient because "… the synagogue needs a lot of light" (Sh. Ar., OḤ 150:4). The entrance to the synagogue, according to the Tosefta (Meg. 4:22), should be on the side of the building facing Jerusalem, i.e., the east side, reminiscent of ancient practice in Ereẓ Israel.

Excavations of early synagogues in the northern part of Israel have revealed that the main entrances are located in the southside, i.e., toward Jerusalem (see below, Architecture). The halakhic codes, however, require that the very opposite should be done because the Holy Ark is placed on the side facing Jerusalem, and it would be unfitting to enter the sanctuary from the same side on which the ark stands. In addition, doors thus located allow the supplicant to bow to the ark as he enters. This difference in the law can perhaps be explained by the institution of a fixed ark inside the synagogue (see below). When possible, it is required that one should go through a vestibule to the main sanctuary to preclude entering directly from the street (Ber. 8a).

In the vestibule, Judah Loew b. Bezalel (Maharal) of Prague explained, the thoughts and cares of the outer world are shed before entering the holiness of the inner sanctuary. Solomon's inaugural prayer (I Kings 8:30) and the fact that Daniel prayed facing Jerusalem (Dan. (Dan. 6:11) are the sources for the requirement that synagogues be oriented toward Jerusalem, and that those in the Holy City itself face in the direction of the Temple. The Talmud clearly demands this orientation for the recitation of the *Amidah* (Ber. 30a). Since it has not always been possible to orient the building in this direction, it became acceptable for the synagogue to be orientated as close to the ideal direction as circumstances would allow. The site on which the synagogue is to be built, according to the Tosefta (Meg. 4:23) and codified by the *posekim* (Sh. Ar., OḤ 150:2), should be the highest spot in the city, and the synagogue should also be the highest building. Jews have been unable to comply with this law in many times and places. As a result, Jews in the Middle Ages attempted to fulfill this law by erecting on the roof of the synagogue a pole or rod which would rise higher than the surrounding buildings. As long as the extension was a "built one" rather than just a simple attachment, this method of compliance was acceptable (Sh. Ar., OḤ 150:2, see Ba'er Heitev, ad loc., and Mishnah Berurah, para. 8). Rav said (Shab. 11a) that "any city whose roofs are higher than the synagogue will be ultimately destroyed, for it is written 'to exalt the house of our God' [Ezra 9:9]."

Jews generally construct their synagogue within the areas they inhabit. But as early as talmudic times some synagogues were built outside the city (see Kidd. 73b), which created a problem of personal safety. For this reason special prayers were inserted to lengthen the service, so that those who came in late could finish with the congregation and thus not have to return home alone. Among these prayers are "Blessed be the Lord for evermore…" recited during the weekday *Ma'ariv* service and the reading of *Ba-Meh Madlikin* during the Friday evening service.

Often synagogues were constructed near bodies of water. Josephus (Ant. 14:258) speaks of a custom of Hellenistic Jewish communities "who make their places of worship near the sea." Paul refers to prayer meetings held by a river where "prayer was usually made" (Acts 16:13). Perhaps the same idea which motivated the institution of the *Tashlikh* ceremony on Rosh Ha-Shanah also lay behind this custom, although the site may have been chosen to obviate the need for a *mikveh*. It has also been suggested that synagogues were built near water because the "contaminated" soil of the Diaspora would be "cleaner" near a body of water. (See Isaac Levy, bibl., p. 31 and n. 7, p. 48.)

Furnishings and Interior Design

The requirement to house the *Torah* scrolls was usually met in the form of an enclosure or closet known as the *aron kodesh* ("holy ark"). In ancient synagogues there was no permanent ark, and if there was one at all it was of a portable nature. There is evidence that the ancient custom was to house the scrolls either outside the building entirely – for reasons of safety – or in an adjoining room.

The reader's desk was placed immediately in front of the ark and sometimes below the floor level (see below, Architecture); since the ark was in an elevated position, the Talmud describes the prayer leader as *yored lifnei ha-tevah* ("he who goes down before the ark," Ta'an. 2:2).

The Torah should be read from the *bimah*, sometimes called *almemar*, an elevated platform, surrounded by a railing for safety, located at the center of the synagogue to enable the entire congregation to hear the reading and sermon properly (Sh. Ar., OḤ 150:5). The modern custom of placing the bimah at the front of the synagogue in order to create more seating space aroused much opposition (Responsa Ḥatam Sofer, OḤ 28; Meishiv Davar, OḤ, Be'ur Halakhah 150:5). In 1886 the rabbis of Hungary and Galicia issued a *ḥerem* against this practice. Nevertheless, the practice spread, especially in the U.S., even among the Orthodox who found a *hetter* ("permit") in Joseph Caro's remark that the position of the *bimah* may change "according to the place and time" (Kesef Mishnah to Yad, Tefillah, 11:3).

The Shulḥan Arukh (OḤ 150:5) specifies that the seating arrangement in the synagogue should provide for the elders to sit adjacent to the ark and facing the congregation, an arrangement which gave rise to the general desire to sit near the *mizraḥ vant* – the eastern wall – because it was the most prestigious place in the synagogue. However, commentators have since decided that this seating plan is no longer valid because people now buy seats, with the best seats going to those who can afford them. It was ruled that this provision of the Shulḥan Arukh applied when the seats were not sold but rather allocated by the community.

For the seating of women in the synagogue see **Meḥiẓah*.

Proscribed Uses of the Synagogue and Its Contents

Although not possessing the same holiness as the Temple, the rabbis have ascribed to the synagogue a holiness patterned after that of the Temple. Accordingly, the Shulḥan Arukh (OḤ 151) proscribes certain kinds of behavior in the synagogue; for example, frivolity, gossiping, eating, drinking, beautifying oneself, sleeping or napping, entering with an unsheathed knife, or to escape bad weather, or as a short cut, transacting business (other than charity and the redemption of captives), and delivering eulogies (unless for one of the city's great men). One may run going to synagogue, but on leaving one must walk, so as not to indicate a desire to get away from it (Ber. 6b).

Dirt and rubbish are not permitted to collect in the synagogue, and although one may enter with one's staff and satchel, it is first required that one clean one's shoes of mud. The upper stories of the building may be used only for purposes which do not violate its spirit as a sanctuary, and it is doubtful whether one may live on top of a synagogue. Even after a synagogue has become a ruin these regulations apply, except if specific conditions were made at the time of construction. These exemptions, however, must never result in the use of the ruin for "a degraded purpose" such as transacting business. If a private home is used as a synagogue, many of these stipulations do not hold.

A distinction in the degree of holiness is drawn between a *bet keneset* and a *bet ha-midrash*. Because Torah is studied in the *bet ha-midrash*, its sanctity is greater than that of the *bet keneset*. Yet teachers and students are allowed to eat and sleep in the *bet ha-midrash* because doing so increases the amount of time available for study. The holiness attributed to the synagogue and the analogy to the Temple led some authorities to rule that a menstruant woman (**niddah*) and a person suffering from leprosy be excluded. These views, however, were minority opinions, and the general rule was that such people were to be admitted since the actual laws of ritual impurity apply only to the Temple itself (see *Purity and Impurity, Ritual).

All objects in the synagogue acquire sanctity by virtue of the sacred purposes which they serve; therefore *halakhah* governs their use. The Shulḥan Arukh specifies that bookcases which held sacred books, the ark in which the Torah stood, and the curtain (*parokhet*) which hung in front of the ark are endowed with sanctity and, for this reason, when no longer usable must be stored away rather than destroyed (OḤ 154: 3).

The holiness of objects is determined by their proximity, in space and use, to the *Torah* scroll, the most sacred object in the synagogue. The Talmud forbids using synagogue objects in a way which would cause them to "go down" in holiness. Thus a discarded ark may not be used to make a chair on which to set the scroll – the chair's holiness being considered less than that of the ark. The reverse order of appropriation, to elevate an object in holiness, is permissible.

OWNERSHIP AND DISPOSAL OF BUILDING. The synagogue is owned by the congregation and those who contributed toward its construction. The concept of synagogue ownership in a small village differs from that in a large town or city. In the former it is assumed that there are no donations from outsiders; therefore a decision of the congregation or their representatives – the "seven good men" of the city – is sufficient in order to sell the synagogue building. But in the city the sale of the building is more difficult, it being uncertain as to whether strangers contributed to the building, and selling without their consent would deprive them of what is, in part, rightfully theirs.

Halakhah suggests ways to resolve this difficulty, e.g., selecting, at the time of construction, either a specific rabbi whose decision would be accepted by all, or reserving this power to whichever rabbi is serving when the decision must be made. It is forbidden to demolish a synagogue until another is provided to take its place, to preclude the possibility of being without a synagogue should the construction of the second building be delayed or interrupted. In the event that the first synagogue is in such a state of disrepair that it is in danger of collapsing, however, it is permitted to demolish the building and to begin construction of the new one immediately.

If a congregation decides to split into two, the holy objects must be divided between the two congregations in proportion to their membership. The rabbis, however, debated whether women and children are to be included in working out the proportions (OḤ 154; Mishnah Berurah, 59). Those who donate articles to the synagogue have the right to have their names inscribed on them. Such inscriptions are permitted only for the persons who actually gave money or contributed personal service for synagogue construction, maintenance, or beautification. Synagogue officers during whose term alteration or expansion is undertaken or completed are forbidden to inscribe their names on the improvements or additions.

IN AGGADAH

According to one talmudic tradition (Ber. 26b) *prayer is in place of the sacrificial cult. Even while the Temple was standing, prayer meetings used to take place in synagogues at the times the sacrifices were offered (see *Liturgy; **Mishmarot* and **Ma'amadot*), and after the destruction of the Temple the prayer services became a substitute for the sacrifices.

The rabbis also extended the concept of holiness which originally attached to the Temple to embrace the synagogue as well (for the halakhic manifestations of this, see above) and saw in the synagogue a substitute for that spiritual center. This idea applied even to the synagogues outside Ereẓ Israel which were seen as extraterritorial units in the foreign lands: "In the times to come the synagogues of Babylonia will be transferred to Israel" (Meg. 29a). The verse "Yet I have been for them as a little sanctuary (*mikdash me'at*) in the countries where they are come" (Ezek. 11:16) was taken to refer to synagogues (Meg. 29a), and one sage even went so far as to say that God is to be found in the synagogue (Ber. 6a), notwithstanding the accepted rabbinic theology that the whole world is full of His glory. Another sage interpreted "Lord, Thou hast been our dwelling place" (Ps. 90:1) as referring to the synagogue, thus extending the idea. One of the reasons for the esteem in which the rabbis held the synagogue was its central role in holding the community together and in perpetuating the Jewish people. Talmudic homilies by the score are aimed at encouraging attendance at synagogue. "A man's prayer is only heard in the synagogue" (Ber. 6a) and "anybody who has a synagogue in his city and does not attend there is called 'a bad neighbor' [cf. Jer. 12:14] and brings exile on himself and his children" (Ber. 8a). Furthermore, "a person who usually attends synagogue and misses a day causes God to inquire after him" and "God becomes angry when He comes to synagogue and does not find a quorum" (cf. Is. 50:2; Ber. 6a). One sage attributed the longevity of Babylonian Jews to the fact that they attended synagogue, and another recommended that one should pray simultaneously with the synagogue service if one is unable to attend (Ber. 7a, 8a).

[Raphael Posner]

ARCHITECTURE

Introduction

The synagogue is the longest surviving religious building type in the Western Hemisphere, spanning a history of over two and a half millennia. Still, due to historical circumstances and the nature of Judaism, the synagogue lacks the stylistic continuity and architectural readability of churches and mosques. Judaism was largely indifferent to the visual; its requirements regarding the synagogue were never enough to create a precise architectural program, which spurred the Jews to borrow some elements and solutions from their neighbors. The frequent migration of the Jews across the Mediterranean and the Middle East, as well as the European mainland, and their frequent political subordination to other people (host nations) also contributed to a fragmented architectural history of synagogues, particularly in terms of exterior. The different building customs, materials, and climates, as well as stipulations of the ruling population, resulted in divergent synagogue appearances.

A coherent style and codified interior space arrangement seems to have emerged only in the Polish region between the 16th and 19th centuries, when Jews lived in relative isolation. Attempts were made after the Enlightenment to create a similarly coherent genre, but this effort dissolved in the stylistic variety of 19th-century Europe and America. Twentieth-century modernism, on the other hand, washed away the stylistic particularity of synagogue architecture, and it became again an organic part of gentile architecture in terms of language.

The interior, however, has displayed a number of common features during most of synagogue history: the orientation of the Ark toward Jerusalem or the east; the separation of men and women; the duality of the Ark and *bimah*; the intimacy, relatively modest scale, and unpretentious design; the use of some specifically Jewish symbols or decoration – all of which justify the use of the term synagogue architecture.

[Rudolf Klein (2nd ed.)]

Historical Roots

In contrast to the Temple, in which the ritual was conducted inside the sanctuary by the priests only, while the rest of the worshipers were kept at a distance, the synagogue was a new type of religious building. It was based on the participation of all the faithful in a collective act of worship conducted around a focus inside the building. It had therefore to provide an ample interior space suited to the size of the congregation, well lit so that the Torah could be read and the precentor seen, and providing places for rest during the lengthy services. These considerations explain why the design of the synagogue was not found in any of the existing pagan sanctuaries of the Greco-Roman worlds. But it can be seen in the remains of the assembly hall of the Greek democracies, the *bouleuteria* or *ecclesiasteria*, in which large groups of people could gather and listen to the discussion. A further complication arose from the requirement of special accommodation for women based on a rigorous interpretation of the existence of women's galleries in the "women's court" of the Temple. This could be provided by the basilica plan, in which columns surrounded a central space, with a gallery on top of the interior porticoes. Another consideration which the synagogue architect had to take into account was the positioning of the building and its orientation. According to Tosefta *Megillah* 4:23, synagogues had to stand on the highest point of a Jewish town; another tradition, attested in Josephus (Ant., 14:258) and Acts (16:13), was the building of synagogues on the bank of a river or the shore of the sea. At Gush Halav in Galilee, for instance, one synagogue was built on top of the town hill, the other in a valley near the spring. The synagogue of Chorazin stands on a high terrace, those of Capernaum and Caesarea near the shore of the sea. In the matter of orientation, the rule implied in Daniel 6:11 that one should pray toward Jerusalem was interpreted in various manners.

The Earliest Synagogues

There is epigraphical evidence for the existence of a synagogue at Schedia, near Alexandria, in the time of Ptolemy Euergetes III (246–21 B.C.E.) and in Jerusalem before its destruction (the synagogue of Theodotus, possibly referred to in Acts 6:9 as the "synagogue of the Freedmen"). Archaeological evidence of synagogues has been discovered in the two Herodian fortresses of Masada and Herodium. At Masada the synagogue passed through two stages, the first probably from the time of Herod, the second certainly from the time of Zealot occupation. In the earlier, the E-shaped arrangement of columns is reminiscent of the transverse row of the Galilean synagogues; in the later synagogue at Masada a corner of the building was separated by a wall from the rest, probably to serve as a receptacle for the Torah scrolls. In both stages of development there were stepped benches along three of the walls, leaving the wall opposite Jerusalem for the entrance. The Herodium synagogue is similar in plan.

The Early Synagogues

This group includes the synagogues in the Galilee dating from the third and fourth centuries C.E. Over 15 have so far been identified. They are rectangular in plan, the largest (Capernaum) measuring 360 square meters (428 square yards), the smallest 110 square meters (131 square yards). The usual proportion of length to width is 11:10. The buildings are built of stone ashlars and paved with stone. The gallery, which ran along three sides of the building (excluding the facade), rested on two rows of columns going lengthwise and one row across. A staircase giving access to the gallery was provided outside the building. Some of the synagogues had an annex probably used for the storage of the (movable) Torah ark. Stone benches ran along two or three sides. In some synagogues there was a porch outside the facade, in others a terrace accessible by staircase. In some cases a courtyard surrounded by porticoes was adjacent to the synagogue. This might have served as a place of rest during the services, or as a sleeping place for wayfarers.

With regard to orientation, the early type of synagogue presents a unique feature: the facades of these buildings are toward Jerusalem. It follows that if the worshipers entered through the main doors (usually three) in this facade, and if they had to face the Holy City in prayer, they had to make an about-turn after entering. In these synagogues no trace of a fixed place for the Torah ark has been found, and it can be assumed that it was a movable object, carried or wheeled in for the services. The architectural origins of this type of synagogue, apart from its general basilica character common to the whole Greco-Roman world, are to be found in the Syro-Roman type of buildings. The architects of the synagogues were probably trained in the Syrian schools of architecture. We know from inscriptions the names of a few of them, in particular Yose the son of Levi "the craftsman" who built at Kefar Biram and Almah. In other cases it is not certain whether those who are mentioned as "making" (*abdun*) a synagogue were the builders or the donors. One feature is noticeable in synagogues of all types: no one seems to have been able to afford to donate the whole building. The various parts were offered by separate donors, and the gift of each was duly recorded in a column, lintel, or "chair of Moses." The execution of the buildings was in the hands of local craftsmen, who introduced a strong Oriental element into the classical orders (mainly Corinthian) of the columns ordered by the architect. The architectural ornament of the exterior facade of these buildings was rich and varied. The builders, it seemed, were interested in proclaiming the importance of the building in the life of the community, not only by its lofty position but also by the splendor of its decoration. Thus not only were the door and window lintels decorated with molded profiles, but they were often surmounted by conches set in a gable to which a rich floral decoration was added. The facade of the two-storied buildings was surmounted with a gable of the type

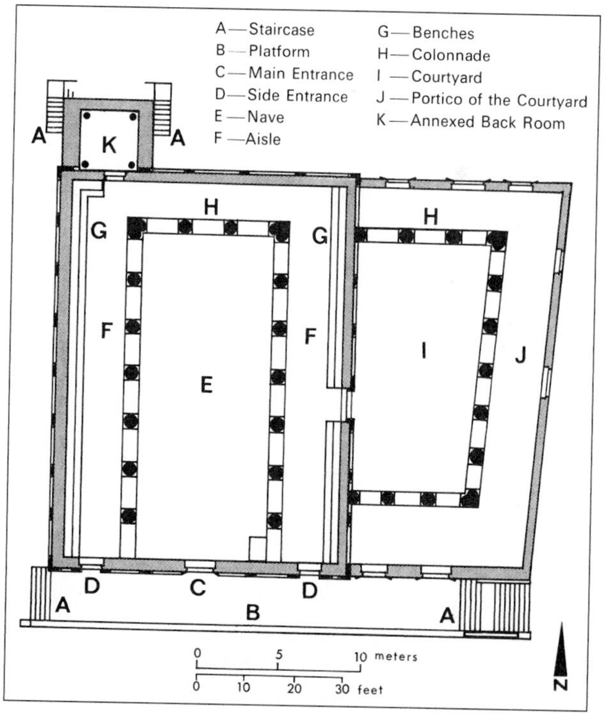

Drawing 1. Early type synagogue at Capernaum, c. third century C.E. After Encyclopaedia of Archaeological Excavations in the Holy Land, *Ramat Gan, 1970.*

known as "Syrian." It consisted of a triangular pediment with its base cut into by an arch. It seems probable that the corners of the building had decorations in the form of lions or eagles. Some of the lintels are of special interest because they had in the center a relief of a wreath held by two winged figures. Occasionally the consoles flanking the doors were made in the form of palm trees. In contrast with this rich, almost flamboyant, exterior, the interior of the building was kept deliberately bare. It was lit by windows above the doors, the one facing the source of all light, Jerusalem, being the largest. The columns within the building were smooth and stood on high pedestals; the double-corner columns at the meeting of the three rows had heart-shaped bases in section. The capitals were of a simplified Corinthian order. The architects, it appears, were interested in avoiding within the synagogue anything which could distract the worshipers while at prayer. One exceptional feature in this respect was the richly decorated frieze; scholars are still discussing the exact position of this architectural feature. Most of them are inclined to place it over the wall of the women's gallery. The frieze usually consisted of a running garland of acanthus or vine scrolls, with various images and symbols set within the medallions. The symbols include a number of Jewish religious objects, such as the *menorah*, the *shofar, etrog*, and *lulav*, and the holy ark. Geometric figures such as the hexagram (Shield of David) or the pentagram (Seal of Solomon), and the fruits of the land, in particular the "seven species" (Deut. 8:8), were also commonly used. Sometimes the tolerant attitude of the communities went so far as to include images derived from the world of Greek mythology. At Capernaum a griffin and a capricorn were included in the decorations, while the artists at Chorazin went still further and featured such pagan elements as Hercules with his club, a centaur, a Medusa, a human face, and a vintage scene. Occasionally, even the symbol of the Romans, the eagle, was represented on synagogue lintels. All these were, however, in relief; the only three-dimensional sculpture depicted lions (found, e.g., at Chorazin). It is clear that these symbols were used in a general and non-pagan sense.

The Transitional Type

In the second half of the third century C.E., architects attempted modifications of various kinds. Sometimes these were made in existing buildings; a typical case is the synagogue of Bet She'arim in which an extra structure was built against the central door, blocking it. The two side doors were left for the entrance, but a new focus of worship was evidently created in the direction of Jerusalem. Other synagogues show a number of architectural experiments. In one of the early-type synagogues, that of Arbel (Irbid), a niche was included in the wall facing the facade, presumably as a fixed receptacle for the scrolls of the Law. At Eshtemoa (el-Samu) in Judea, the problem of the relation of facade versus entrance was solved by changing the traditional plan. One of the long walls of the rectangle faced Jerusalem, while the entrance was through doors made in the short wall. A niche in the wall facing Jerusalem

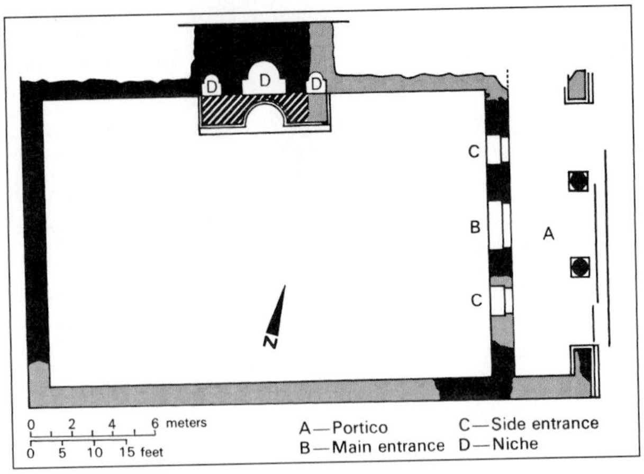

Drawing 2. Synagogue of the transitional period at Eshtemoa, c. fourth century C.E., Ibid.

served as a focal point of worship. The same arrangement was adopted in the earlier of the two superimposed synagogues at Caesarea. At Hammath near Tiberias, two synagogues were excavated. One has a basilica plan, ending in a straight south wall – the direction of Jerusalem – with the entrance from the north. At a later date a square room was attached to the center of the south wall, to serve as Torah ark. Over this fourth-century synagogue a pure basilica type was built in the sixth century. The other synagogue at Hammath (excavated in 1924) also had a basilica plan, ending in a straight wall, with a small niche flanked with small columns in its center. The same arrangement (without the niche, as far as we know) was found at Yafi'a near Nazareth. Here the synagogue was apparently oriented west, with its facade east. If it is assumed that, being in the territory of the Tribe of Zebulun, Yaf'ia was presumed (in accordance with Gen. 49:13) to be in the coastal area, this would mean that the builders followed the earlier plan, with the entrance facing the Holy City. Another synagogue of the transitional type, at Usifiyya (Isfiya) on Mount Carmel, also had a plain back wall with no sign of niche or apse, but its entrance was likewise to the west – with the east wall orientated toward Jerusalem. The transitional type also introduced another innovation in the architecture of the synagogues – mosaic pavements which now replaced the former stone slabs. These pavements were first decorated with geometric designs only, but from the fourth century onward (as we know from a saying of R. Abun recorded in the Jerusalem Talmud (Av. Zar. 3:4, 42d) figurative drawings were permitted. Hammath has the earliest example of the standard type of synagogue pavement, figuring the signs of the Zodiac, with the sun in the center of the circle and the seasons in the four corners. The Zodiac circle was placed in the center of the pavement, with a representation of the ark flanked by two *menorot* beyond it. While the latter image is self-explanatory, it has been suggested that the Zodiac, representing the regular succession of months and seasons, also stood for the fixed holidays and the succession of priestly *mishmarot* and *ma'amadot* in the Temple.

Fifth-Century Synagogues

A new type may be said to have emerged in the fifth century. This dating is confined by the fact that the synagogue of Gerasa was rebuilt as a church in 530 C.E. Once established, this type continued to be built until the eighth century. This later type was based on the pure basilica plan of the same kind as that used in contemporary churches. The building was elongated, with an apse pointing in the direction of Jerusalem. It sometimes had a court (atrium) and forecourt (narthex). The entrance was through three doors in the facade opposite Jerusalem. The interior was divided into a central nave and two aisles by two rows of columns. At the apse end a space was separated from the rest by a chancel screen with columns and chancel slabs. Within, there is sometimes a lower space, probably in order to fulfill the verse "Out of the depths I cry to Thee O Lord" (Ps. 130:1). In the apse, which served as a receptacle for the Torah ark, was another depression, used either as a place for keeping worn-out sacred texts (*genizah*) or for the community chest. The exterior of the building was kept plain and usually had a staircase leading to the women's gallery above the aisles. The lack of external ornament in these later-type synagogues is explained by the fact that they were erected under Byzantine rule, at a time when harsh anti-Jewish laws forbade the erection of new synagogues and only allowed old ones to be repaired when they threatened to collapse. The law was not strictly observed, but certain precautions had to be taken; hence the inconspicuous outer aspect of the synagogues. As far as can be judged, the splendor of the buildings was now concentrated in the interior. This is shown by the mosaic pavements and the elaborate marble capitals and chancel screens. Naturally, plans of these latter synagogues are not identical, but many of them, Bet Alfa, Jericho, Naaran, seem to have followed a standard plan. There were minor changes: at Naaran the porch was altered in shape because of the exigencies of the site; at Gerasa the apse was square in plan, not circular. At Hammat Gader the synagogue was hidden inside a building complex, with indirect entrances from two sides, but the interior of the building was in the basilica plan. At Maon (Nirim), only part of the nave was paved with mosaics, while the aisles and the southern part of the nave had a stone pavement and served as a kind of ambulator. At Gaza the synagogue had apparently a series of additional aisles. In the design of the mosaic pavements of three synagogues of this later type, there is a combination of the Torah ark motif and the Zodiac, with biblical scenes from stories in the Bible: at Bet Alfa there is a representation of the Offering of Isaac; at Gerasa, Noah's Ark; and Daniel in the lions' den at Naaran. In these cases the Jews of that time do not seem to have had any qualms about treading on biblical imagery, including, in one case (at Bet Alfa), a hand symbolizing God. At the same time they seem to have had much more respect for the written explanations added to the figures. At Naaran, for instance, when the images were removed as offensive, the writing accompanying each of them was carefully preserved. Other mosaics in synagogues follow the prevailing Byzantine trend toward a closely knit design that divided the surface into a series of medallions. The basic element is usually an amphora flanked by peacocks; a twisted vine trellis issued from the mouth of the jug, and formed medallions with images of animals inside them. This decoration occurs at Maon and Gaza; both pavements are the product of the same Gaza factory. In the Gaza pavement (508/9 C.E.) the image of King David as Orpheus is added, while at Maon (c. 530) there are representations of animals to which a wedge-shaped part has been added, with specifically Jewish symbols, such as a *menorah* with lions guarding it, a palm tree, a *shofar*, an *etrog* and a *lulav*. In later synagogues (Hammat Gader, Jericho, and En-Gedi), there seems to have been an increasing reluctance to use representations of living beings: at Hammat Gader there are only two lions, and in Jericho all images are absent; at En-Gedi the designs have been replaced by an inscription. The only synagogues which carry actual dates are those of Gaza and Bet Alfa (518–27 C.E.). Of the artists, only the names of the makers of the Bet Alfa pavement have been preserved: Marinos and his son Hananiah. It is interesting to note that the same two artists worked on the pavement of a synagogue which was apparently Samaritan at Bet-Shean, not far from Bet Alfa. As could be presumed concerning the Samaritans, who were restricted in their biblical lore to the Written Law, the ornaments were much more austere than those in the Jewish synagogues: only the ark of the Law and flora or geometric ornaments were allowed. The same is true of the Samaritan synagogue at Shaalbim.

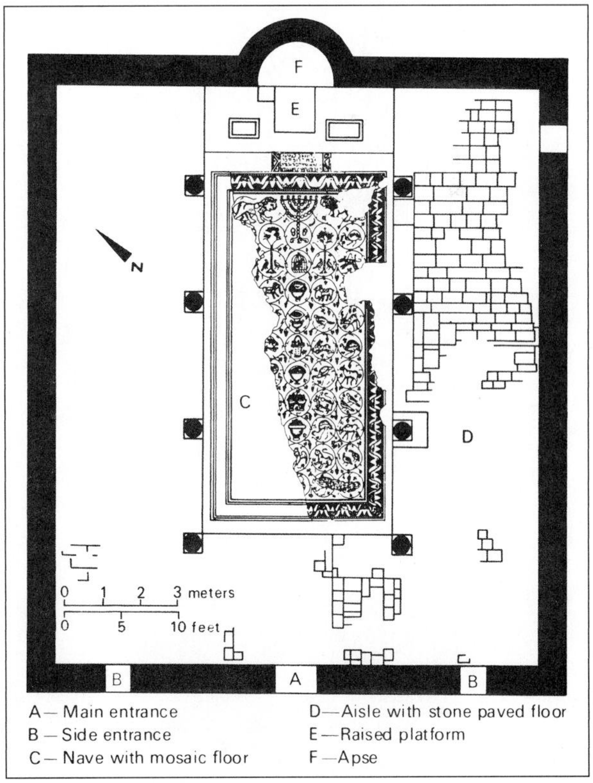

Drawing 3. Late type synagogue at Maon, c. sixth century C.E., Ibid.

Outside Ereẓ Israel

The finds of synagogues in the Diaspora cover a wide geographical and chronological range, from the Hellenistic to the Byzantine. Among the earliest is one at Delos, which must antedate 69 B.C.E., and one of the latest that of Aegina, sixth century C.E. On the whole the development of the Diaspora synagogue follows the same lines as those of Ereẓ Israel. The three earliest of the list, Delos, Priene, and Miletus, follow the basilica plan; at Priene there is a square apse and at Miletus none; in all cases the synagogues are built within a group of buildings and provided with a forecourt. The second-century synagogue of Sardis (Asia Minor), recently excavated, is the largest and most sumptuous of those of the Diaspora, as befits the wealthy community it served. It is integrated within the central marketplace of the town, together with a gymnasium and other public buildings, thus indicating the status of the Jews of Sardis. The synagogue consists of a courtyard and an elongated basilica, with an apse at its western end and the entrances at the east. Thus the elders sitting on semicircular benches within the apse faced Jerusalem, but the position of the rest of the congregation is in dispute. The synagogue had a reading table set in front of the apse and two raised platforms between the doors of the east side. The various ritual objects were beautifully worked. Of the later synagogues, one of the most famous is that of Dura Europos on the Euphrates. Two buildings were found there, one superimposed on the other; the later one is dated 244/5 C.E. They are similar in plan, with a broad central room and three entrances on the east side, a niche for the ark of the Law in the west (facing Jerusalem), and benches round the walls. The synagogue of Dura Europos was hidden between other houses and had an indirect entrance, which was even more obscure in the later building. This synagogue was decorated by famous frescoes; another possible indication of a liberal attitude was the absence of a women's gallery or a special room for the women. Of the synagogues of the fourth century in the Diaspora, three are outstanding: that of Ostia, in which the original arrangements resemble those at Sardis, had a semicircular *bimah* facing Jerusalem. The entrances were later changed by the addition of an aediculum to house the ark. The synagogue of Naro (Hammam Lif, in Africa) was biaxial, with the main entrance on the south and a subsidiary entrance on the west. There was a small interior apse with seats, a special room for the "instruments," a *bimah*, and a room for women. The principal donor was a woman, Julia. This synagogue is distinguished by a richly decorated mosaic pavement with images of animals and plants. The synagogue of Apamea (392 C.E.) was apparently entered from the side, while that at Aegina is a typical basilica.

[Michael Avi-Yonah]

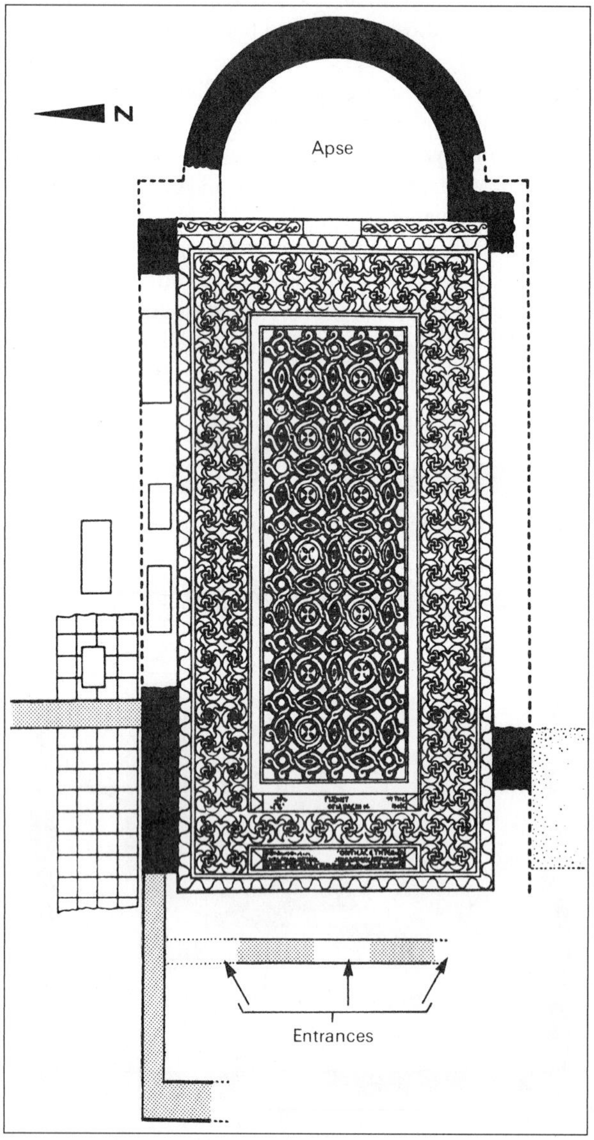

Drawing 4. The Theodoros synagogue in Aegina, Greece, fourth century C.E. From R. Wischnitzer, The Architecture of the European Synagogue, *Philadelphia, 1964.*

From the Middle Ages to the Emancipation

The first synagogues known to modern science in Ashkenazi space emerged concomitantly with the rising prosperity of European lands during the Romanesque period, in the 11th century. This was also the period when Christian-based European antisemitism appeared. In medieval conditions Jews could hardly follow halakhic requirements for the location and design of synagogues. Compromises characterize this period, in which great ingenuity is displayed in creating a space for Jewish worship.

The medieval Jewish communities of the period were small, and this determined the intimate scale of synagogue buildings, which sometimes were hardly more than rooms set aside for public prayer. Moreover, the insecurity of Jewish life, and the frequent threat and fear of the surroundings, were factors which determined building plans. In some places regulations by the Church authority or by the secular government often prohibited the building of new synagogues, and sometimes even the enlargement of old buildings. Further, while Jewish customs decreed that synagogues had to be higher than the surrounding buildings, ecclesiastical regulations required that they be lower than Christian places of worship. Frequently, such laws were spitefully interpreted. It can therefore be assumed that the tradition that grew up of lowering the synagogue floor below ground level was not simply in accordance with Psalm 130:1, referred to above ("Out of the depths I cry"), but was also the result of the need to increase the height of the interior without transgressing the law restricting the external height.

Up until the 18th century the Jews endeavored to retain a degree of external unpretentiousness in their synagogue buildings, however splendid they were internally. This phenomenon is found throughout the lands of the Jewish Diaspora – and the few exceptions (such as the "Altneuschul of Prague) are generally the product of a temporary relaxation on the limitations.

The synagogue interior presents a peculiar duality, the existence of two spatial foci characterized by the interrelationship between the Torah ark and the *bimah*. In many of the Diaspora communities of long standing, the ark appears in the form of a small apse or a niche in the east wall oriented theoretically to Jerusalem. In fact the ark is always facing east, even if Jerusalem is to the south or southeast, unlike the *qibla* in mosques, which strictly follows the direction of Mecca. Jerusalem in the synagogue architecture of Europe becomes a somewhat fictional direction. Although the ark housing the scrolls was one of the most salient features of the building, it did not as yet dominate the interior completely, for the synagogue was also a "house of assembly," a meeting place for the congregation. In the synagogue interior there is another focal item, namely the *bimah* – the dais from which the service is conducted. The relative proximity of two foci in one interior, the ark situated in the east wall and the *bimah* at the center, and the search for a balance between them constitutes the basic feature of the synagogue interior. The relationship between the two and their reciprocal relation to the entire interior space is the principal conceptual and ideological factor in synagogue design. This spatial duality reflects the existential duality of Diaspora Jews who lived between their ancient tradition (and the idea of the return to Ereẓ Israel) and the actual geographical location and indigenous gentile culture.

Later, when Europe was dominated by the late Renaissance and Baroque styles, the ark attained an importance expressed by its size and by the high level of its artistic execution. It was in this period that monumental built-in arks were created, such as can be seen in the Diaspora communities in modern times. Existing synagogues began to be rebuilt and fitted with arks in the new style. Generally, however, European Jewry was conservative in matters of form, still clinging to earlier cultural conceptions, and using medieval idioms while Renaissance architecture was at its height.

The segregation of sexes during prayer, introduced in ancient times and necessitating a women's section, attached but separate, continued in the synagogues of the Middle Ages. In the early synagogues a gallery sometimes served this function. Often the place allotted to women was a separate hall on the same level as the main space, as at Worms. Sometimes the women's section was below the level of the main congregation hall or even actually beneath it as, for example, in Provençal synagogues. In the synagogue of Don Samuel ha-Levi Abulafia in Toledo (subsequently the Church of El-Transito), built in the 14th century, there was an upper gallery alongside the rectangular hall. It was only at the end of the 16th century, when the presence of the woman in the synagogue became an accepted fact, that the women's section acquired full importance. Synagogues began to be built with well-planned women's accommodations, the first such being the major synagogues of Venice, and the Veneto and other Italian communities, and the synagogue of R. Isaac Jacobowicz at Cracow, Poland. Generally, in the medieval period, the *ezrat nashim*, as the women's section was named, was simply added to the existing building as an external "lean-to." The gallery (or galleries) pitched internally over a row of columns is a later development, of which the earliest famous example is the Spanish-Portuguese synagogue of Amsterdam (1685).

The synagogues of medieval Central Europe fall into two main types: synagogues with a twin-naved hall and those with a vaulted or timber-roofed single nave.

Similarly to Antiquity, Jewry borrowed a type of building suitable to its needs not from the Church but from the existing secular forms. The choice was usually a building which was as far as possible removed from the monumental religious character of the Christian church. Jews took as their models town halls or monastic refectories, which were usually vaulted structures with either a single or double nave, the latter distinguished by a row of columns carrying the intermediate portion of the double span. Some scholars pointed out that when copying the ribbed ceilings prevalent at the time, a fifth rib was sometimes added. This helped perhaps to avoid the cruciform vaulting but also contributed to the overall centralizing space-form tendency. However, there are churches to be found having this fifth rib also, but rarely.

THE MEDIEVAL DOUBLE-NAVED HALL IN CENTRAL EUROPE. The oldest building surviving in its original form until *_Kristallnacht_ (November 9–10, 1938) was the renowned synagogue of Worms. Its construction began in 1034, but the structure underwent a fundamental change at the end of the 12th century, when buildings in the city were marked by a transition from the early to the late Romanesque style. The cathedral of Worms was being built in the same period, and some architectural connection exists between the two buildings, especially in the details of the carvings, the column capitals, and the characteristic Romanesque adornments. The internal space arrangement, however, differs radically. While the cathedral shows a tripartite division – a larger nave and two narrower and lower isles – the synagogue avoids this arrangement by having two equal naves. The Worms synagogue is the prototype of the double-naved synagogue, characteristic of medieval central Europe. The ground plan is a simple rectangle in

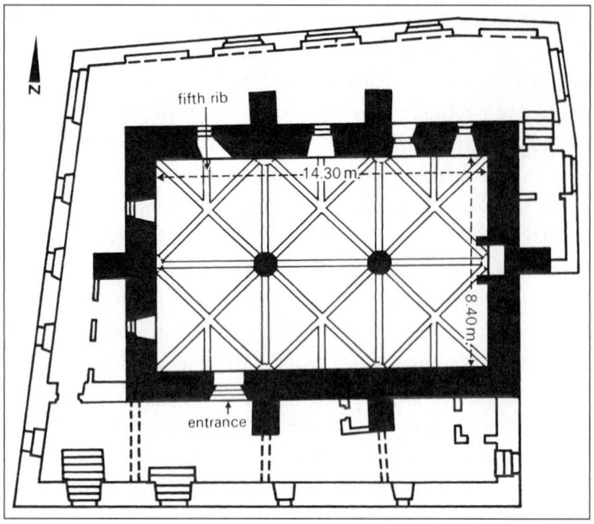

Drawing 5. The Altneuschul of Prague showing the five rib vaulting over each bay, 14th century. From R. Wischnitzer, The Architecture of the European Synagogue, *Philadelphia, 1964.*

which two centrally positioned Romanesque columns support the six groined and cross-vaulted bays. The columns and their capitals, and the portal whose details and decoration are identical with those of the columns (also the chandeliers, known from description only), may have been the work of a Jewish artist. An inscription preserved for nearly 800 years on one of the columns reads: "The pride of the two columns/He wrought diligently/Also the scroll of the capital;/And hung the lamps." The two-naved hall is a centralizing space, the *bimah* being placed midway between the two columns. The women's section attached to the main building's north wall at the same level is smaller and was built in 1213, not long after the completion of the second building of the main hall. This section is also a particular instance of a double-naved hall. The four bays are roofed by four groined cross-vaults, subdivided by the four arches supported on wall-corbels and converging on the capital of the central column. As a *bimah* was not needed in the women's section, it was possible to achieve spatial unity here by using only one column.

A double-naved hall of centralizing design, with four bays around a single pillar, was built in the 14th century for the Eger (today Cheb) synagogue in Bohemia. (It was destroyed in 1856.) In Germany itself few traces of this type remain. The interior and structure of the synagogue and porch at Regensburg, destroyed by order of the town council after the expulsion of 1519, are known from two engravings by the 16th-century artist Albert Altdorfer. The synagogue in Regensburg has three central columns which support eight bays of groined cross-vaults. A similar arrangement characterizes the great synagogue of Buda on the Castle Hill of Budapest, but with ribbed vaults built in the 14th century, severely damaged during the siege of Buda in 1686 when the town was liberated from the Turks and the Jews were expelled. This is the largest medieval synagogue known to modern science, and it was discovered after heavy bombardments during World War II, excavated and reburied in the Cold War era.

The second best-known central European synagogue besides Worms is the old synagogue in Prague, the Altneuschul (literally, the Old New Synagogue, or *Al tenai*, "on condition"). The very narrow windows cast a pall on the interior in keeping with the traditional folk stories woven around this synagogue. The Altneuschul was built in the 13th century and is unique in the Middle Ages for its impressive exterior – so different from the other synagogues of that period. This can be explained by the fact that the building was built in the heart of a large Jewish quarter and there was no fear of offending a hostile environment. It's rectangular plan and double-naved arrangement with two central columns is similar in layout to that of the Worms synagogue, but the vaults and arches are pointed, of rib and panel construction, five ribs to each vault. Only one other synagogue with similar fifth-rib vaulting is known – the double bay, single-nave building at Miltenberg on the Main.

The Old Synagogue (Alte-Schul or Stara Boznica) at Kazimierz, Cracow, was built under the direct inspiration of the Prague Altneuschul in terms of six-bay arrangement, in the second half of the 15th century. This is the largest still-standing medieval synagogue. It is also impressive from the outside with its Renaissance Polish parapet added after the fire in 1557. The *ezrat nashim* is also coupled to the men's prayer room with small windows on the western and northern sides.

THE SINGLE-CELL HALL IN CENTRAL EUROPE. Another type of synagogue building in central Europe in the Middle Ages was the vaulted single-cell hall, i.e., a structure consisting of one nave. There were, of course, timber-roofed synagogues without stone vaults, often with open woodwork, in rare cases with wood panel ceilings. The best-known single-nave synagogue, without stone vault and with visible roof trusses, was at Erfurt. Many were, however, proper stone-vaulted Gothic single-cell buildings. Among the few that still exist, or existed up to World War II, were Bamberg, Miltenberg, Leipnick, and also the still existing Pinkas-Schul in Prague ghetto first mentioned in 1492 and the newly renovated synagogue in Maribor (formerly Marburg a/d Drau) built probably in 1190, in the northeast of present-day Slovenia. The rest of the medieval single-cell hall type synagogues are known from records, drawings, and documents. They developed particularly in Bohemia and Galicia.

In time, throughout central Europe, synagogues began to show the influence of the non-Jewish environment. The ark in particular was influenced by the form of the altar in Catholic churches, and this influence later became common to all the European Jewish communities. German Jewry continued to live and create in earlier cultural conditions. The longitudinal axis was later often enhanced by the addition of the women's accommodation alongside the main building. It usually had small windows along the full length of the interior. These late medieval rectangular synagogues were equipped with built-in arks in a niche or small apse. The *bimah* remained in its central position. Direct descendants of the medieval single-cell hall type synagogue are the Renaissance and Baroque single-cell synagogues, like the ones in Trebic and Holesov in the Czech Republic.

In the central European area the change from the medieval to the Renaissance style exerted a relatively minor influence on the scale and space conception of synagogues and influenced mainly their architectural language.

The Meisel (Meysel) Synagogue in Prague was built in 1592 under a special license granted by Emperor Rudolph II to Mordecai Meisel in recognition of his philanthropic activities. The Meisel Synagogue was burned down completely in 1689 and rebuilt two years later on a basilical plan. The wide nave was barrel-vaulted with lunettes, and the two flanking galleried aisles were cross-vaulted. The building, in which characteristic early Renaissance elements and Gothic forms are intermingled, is a deviation from the previous practice. The Klauz, also in Prague, was built at the end of the 16th century and altered in the 17th. It was barrel-vaulted and stuccoed, with plant scroll and flower ornamentation in the local Renaissance idiom. The stylistic hesitancy of these two examples arose from the architectural setting of Prague, and its outstanding Gothic and Baroque traditions.

The Remo synagogue of Cracow-Kazimierz also falls into the category of the single-cell hall, built on the edge of the Jewish cemetery as a private prayer house in 1553 under special royal dispensation by Israel Isserles, head of the Cracow Jewish community and father of Moses *Isserles (Rema). The initial synagogue, possibly made of wood, burned down and was rebuilt in masonry in 1556–7, standing until 1940, when the Nazis burned it down. It was re-erected and serves as the synagogue of the Cracow Jewish community.

Between 1556 and 1563 the High Synagogue (Wysoka Boznica) was built in Kazimierz over a row of shops. Like the Visoka Sinagoga in Prague, it has no direct access from the ground floor, but via the staircase of the adjacent building.

In 1644 the Isaac synagogue (Ajzykova Boznica) of R. Isaac Jacobowicz was built. The architect was the Italian Francesco Olivieri, who designed many other buildings in Cracow. It had a western women's gallery over the entrance hall, screened off from the main hall by an elegant arcade on Tuscan columns. The structure was barrel-vaulted with high lunettes.

The synagogue of R. Isaac Nachmanovich in Lvov was built in 1582. It is a typical Polish Renaissance synagogue with a square, lunetted, monastic vault. This type of design was repeated in Poland in synagogues at Szczebrzeszyn (end of the 16th century), Zamosc (17th century), and Gusyatin (beginning of 18th century).

In Bohemia and Moravia the same type of square synagogue gained acceptance and spread to Germany (like the timber synagogues from Poland, for which see below) with one of the waves of immigrants at the beginning of the 18th century. These buildings, too, more particularly in Bohemia, were built and decorated in the pronounced Baroque style of south Germany and Austria. In 1757 a synagogue resembling the above was built in the town of Kuttenplan, situated in the center of the Jewish settlement of western Bohemia. The floor of the hall was still below the level of the street, as tradition dictated. A similar synagogue was erected in 1764 at Koenigswart, and other buildings of the same kind were built in many towns of that region. The synagogue in the town of Neuzedlisch (Nove-Sedliste) was built in 1786. It shows the Austro-Bohemian Baroque characteristic of the middle of the century and contained an ark resembling a Catholic high altar. The women's accommodation had two stories built as part of the original plan.

THE FOUR-PILLARED OR NINE-BAY HALL POLISH SYNAGOGUE AND ITS SPREAD TO CENTRAL EUROPE. Unlike the gradual change from the medieval to the Renaissance and post-Renaissance in central and western Europe, in eastern Europe these centuries witnessed the most dramatic change in synagogue design, the introduction of the four-pillared hall, also called the nine-bay arrangement. This type represents the apex of synagogue design before the Enlightenment. This arrangement can be found in stone/brick and also in timber structure. It started to appear in Poland in Renaissance times and spread gradually all over central and central-eastern Europe – Moravia, Hungary – and it was built in the eastern parts of the Hapsburg Empire as late as mid-19th century, as in Huszt, today Ukraine.

In eastern Europe, especially in Poland, the historical circumstances differed from the Renaissance and Baroque conditions of Bohemia and Moravia described above. The isolation of the Jews from the mainstream European environment, already perceptible at the end of the Middle Ages, grew. Jewry created a world of its own in the midst of Polish society. Within this Jewish region an independent art also arose. At first this was of a folk character, which expressed itself in decorative painting and in various arts and crafts, penetrating eventually into the building crafts.

The four-pillared or nine-bay arrangement can be ascribed to the influence of Renaissance central spaces, but in the hands of Jewish craftsmen and rabbis it became a genre of its own, clearly distinguishable from earlier centralized buildings, like Roman and Early Christian mausolea, Byzantine four-pillared churches on a square plan, Crusader "temple-churches," and baptisteries employing the columned or pillared "space-within-space" layout. In synagogue design the principal question was the placement of the *bimah* and giving it architectural emphasis. The advantage of the nine-bay arrangement was the connection of the *bimah* with the building's shell in a firm manner, by placing the *bimah* in the internal space formed by the four pillars. Thus, the bimah was integrated into the structural system of the building – pillars, vaulting, and buttressing – creating a four-pillared sub-space within the shell of the building.

Until mid-19th century this type spread over neighboring countries and is to be found today in Mikulov (Czech

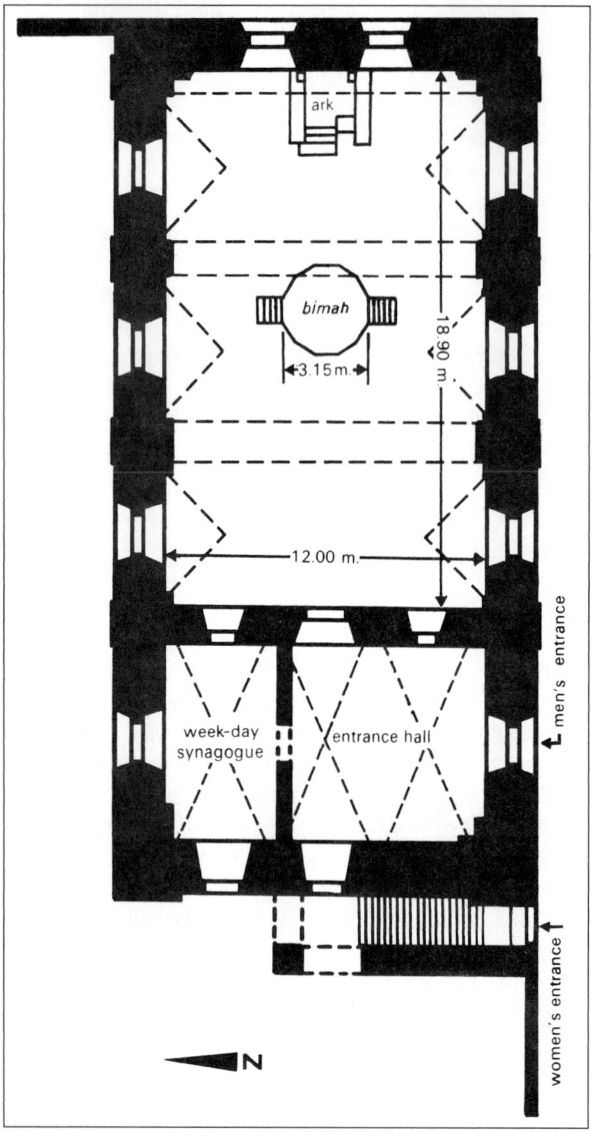

Drawing 6. The Isaac Jacobowicz synagogue at Kazimierz in Cracow, 1644. From R. Wischnitzer, The Architecture of the European Synagogue, *Philadelphia, 1964.*

Republic), Mád, Apostag, Bonyhád (Hungary), etc. The synagogue in Mikulov is an interesting case: it possesses the four columns, but they are very close to each other – there is even no real *bimah* among them and the vaulting has only four Baroque domical bays. This arrangement reinforces speculation, along with the similar timber structure, about the four pillars as representations of the divine throne, because here they are not functional.

In parallel to the nine-bay arrangement with unequal spans (a-b-a rhythm, in which b is smaller than a) described above, a less tightly knit layout type was in use in which the four supporting pillars which contained the *bimah* divided the hall into nine equal bays. The Vorstadt synagogue of Lvov and the synagogue at Zholkva are the most characteristic examples of this type of hall. This type is exemplified by Rzeszow (Reia), Maciejow, Vilna, Nowogrodek, Lutzk, Lancut, and other places.

The four-pillared synagogue can be considered one of the highlights of synagogue architecture. Its validity can be seen in the fact that many of the contemporary and later wooden synagogues were designed with four timber-posts surrounding a *bimah*. This was structurally superfluous, as timber can bridge relatively large spans. It is also interesting to note the prevalence of similar concepts in the vernacular synagogue architecture of far-away North Africa. The four-pillared, stone-vaulted 14th-century synagogue of Tomar, Portugal, has different proportions, but still reflects the basic idea of the four-pillar plan.

The exterior appearance of these buildings reflected both local conditions and influences of the architecture of the period. Many of the nine-bay synagogues, especially those which stood outside the city walls, were built as fortresses, as clearly expressed in the elevations. These included a roof surrounded by a fortified parapet equipped with loopholes and sometimes with small towers, as part of the arcaded attic-story typical of the Polish Renaissance. This exterior appeared in the Vorstadt (suburban) synagogue of Lvov, and in the Zholkva, Lutzk, Pinsk, and other 17th-century synagogues. These features were adopted for the needs of defense against the Cossacks or the Tatars.

Location of the synagogue in medieval and early modern times shows a great variety. When located in the core of a medieval town, it appears usually in the courtyard well hidden from the street façade, like the two synagogues in Sopron (formerly Ödenburg, in Hungary). But if the synagogue stands in a Jewish quarter it may have a quite exposed location like the Altneuschul in Prague. In some cases the synagogue may be

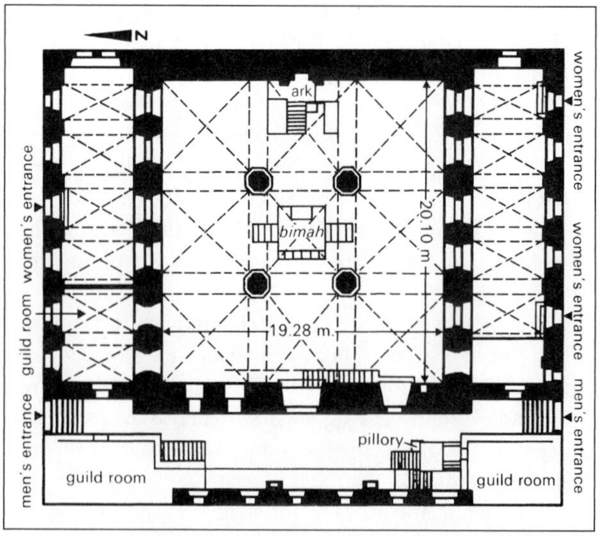

Drawing 7. The fortress-type Vorstadt synagogue in Lvov. Unusual features include two guild rooms on either side of the entrance, and a pillory. After A. Grotte, "Deutsche, boehmische und polnische Synagogentypen vom XI. *Bis Anfang des* XIX. *Jahrhunderts,"* MGEJK, VII–VIII, *Frankfurt on the Main.*

located on the city wall, like the medieval synagogue in Maribor or the Stara Boznica in Cracow-Kazimierz, in which case the synagogue's wall is the city wall at the same time, which may influence the synagogue's fenestration.

The location of the entrance of the synagogue varies according to the building's micro-location and the design of the interior. In the Altneuschul in Prague and the Alte-Schul in Cracow, the entrance is off-center in the southern wall. In other Romanesque and Gothic synagogues (Speyer, Worms, Fuerth, Frankfurt, and elsewhere) the entrance is in the sector furthest from the *bimah*. Only in the 16th century was a firm decision taken on the question of the location of the entrance, following the ruling in Joseph Caro's Shulhan Arukh, although for some time synagogues continued to be built with unorientated entrances. This informal location was typical of small medieval structures, notwithstanding the basic symmetry of the synagogue interior.

WOODEN SYNAGOGUES IN POLAND. The Polish wooden synagogues constitute a unique architectural genre, an expression of a Jewish folk art which developed especially from the mid-17th century under the influence of the Polish vernacular tradition. It spread over the entire Jewish settlement area of eastern Europe side by side with the four-pillar stone synagogues. Many of these synagogues were designed and built by Jewish craftsmen. The Jewish builder, aware of his special theme, began by giving the eaves an upward curve, and piled roof on roof. In a later period the form of building becomes quiet and restrained, but in the 17th century the synagogues were imaginative, dynamic compositions inside and out, of a complex design. The plan was generally simple, a square measuring in the interior about 15 by 15 meters. The women's hall was an annex, or sometimes built as an internal gallery. Characteristic is the special additional "winter room," designed as a shelter for very cold weather, which was generally plastered to facilitate heating.

The oldest known timber building was at Chodorov near Lvov, built in 1651. The roof over the central chamber is internally lined with wooden planks, with the central portion shaped like a barrel-vault. The wall paintings were done

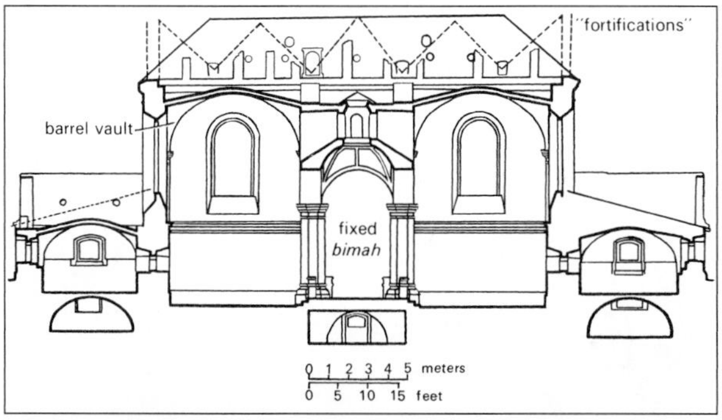

Drawing 8. Section of the fortress-type synagogue of Pinsk, 1640, showing the vaulting, the bimah *structure, and the outside crenellation. From M. and K. Peichotka,* Wooden Synagogues, *Warsaw, 1959.*

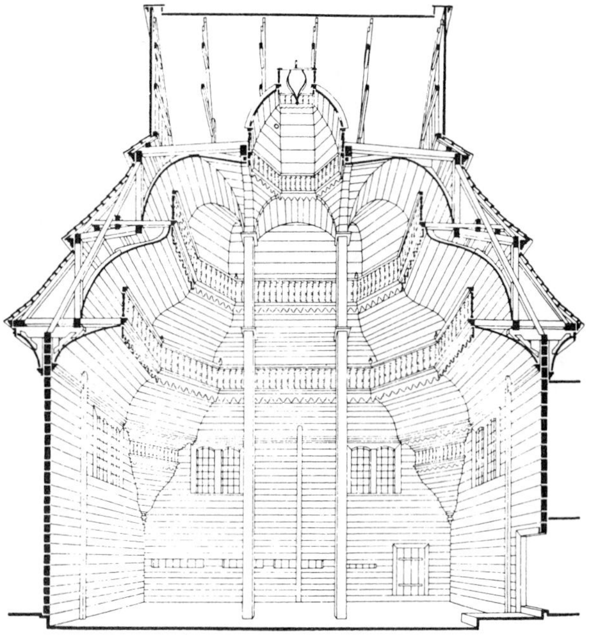

Drawing 9. Perspective section of the synagogue at Wolpa, Poland, built in the early 18th century. The four central timber posts enclose the bimah. *From M. and K. Piechotke,* Wooden Synagogues, *Warsaw, 1954.*

by Israel b. Mordecai and Isaac b. Judah Leib. The same artists executed the drawings in the Gwozdziec Synagogue, which had an octagonal wooden dome over the center. Many other famous wooden synagogues were known, such as Jablonov, Lutomirsk, Zabludow, Wolpa, and countless more. Most of them were built at the end of the 17th or the beginning of the 18th century. The tradition also spread swiftly westward, and in 1767 a wooden synagogue was built at Kurnik near Posen. This synagogue had a quiet and restrained exterior and contained wooden columns in the classical Tuscan order, common in the manor houses of landed gentry in the region. Inside was a very complex timber vaulting, adorned with paintings and wood carvings. The wooden synagogues spread into Germany, the best known among them being at Beckhofen, Horb (presently at the Israel Museum, Jerusalem), and Kirchheim. The construction of the walls in eastern Poland was of horizontal beams of fir or pine, with dovetail joints at the corners and interior plank lining. The normal construction in western Poland was an oak frame covered with pinewood planks. The wooden synagogues built in south Germany according to the Polish tradition changed their exterior appearance due to the half-timber (frame and plaster fillings) system used in Germany. Internally, these buildings retained their traditional form and finish, and their wall paintings.

SPANISH SYNAGOGUES. Historical circumstances created two periods in the history of Spanish Jewry – the medieval period, until the expulsion in 1492, and the "Sephardi" period, associated with the Spanish-speaking communities established in various parts of the world after the expulsions.

A type of synagogue interior was created among Spanish Jewry which made a contribution to the recurring problem of balance between the ark and the *bimah*. This solution much later found further expression and development in Italy.

In terms of architectural language Spanish synagogues followed Islamic forms. Synagogues built during the Golden Age of Muslim Spain did not survive, but even those built in Christian Spain were of Moorish design and reveal only traces of western influence in their "mudejar" decorative schemes. To adorn their synagogue walls the Jews employed verses from the Bible, written in elegant Spanish characters, in emulation of their Muslim neighbors, who adorned their mosques with verses from the Koran. The two best-known synagogue buildings in Spain are at Toledo. One seems to have been built in the second half of the 13th century by Joseph ibn Shushan. It was confiscated at the beginning of the 15th century by the Church authorities and ultimately became known as the Church of Santa Maria la Blanca. Like most medieval synagogues, this building is modest in its exterior and splendid within. Its plan and structure are characteristic of a mosque. Four long arcades, which carry a flat beam-ceiling, divide the interior into five bays. The arches are horseshoe-shaped and the pillar capitals are richly carved. The pillar bases in the two central colonnades are adorned with glazed tiles. Small circular windows in the western wall apparently belonged to the women's hall, which no longer exists. Despite the building's relatively small size (22 × 28 m.) the interior still looks spacious, due to the rhythm created by the horseshoe arches and the columns. The second building (later the El Transito Church) is in the former ancient Jewish quarter of Toledo. It was the synagogue of Samuel ha-Levi Abulafia, minister of Pedro the Cruel, and built about the year 1357. The plan is that of a rectangular hall of long proportions, 9½ × 23 m. The walls are decorated with carved "mudejar" foliage. Lines of verses from the Psalms alternating with decorative patterns surround the hall beneath, and above is the arcaded clerestory. The walls of the women's section are also decorated with ornamental writings, verses from the Song of Miriam. The niche in the eastern wall was initially made for the ark, and inscriptions on each side of it record the erection of the building by Samuel Abulafia. The windows of the clerestory are fitted with alabaster grilles, admitting a diffused light.

The form of the *bimah* in medieval Spain is known from miniatures and 13th-century illuminated manuscripts. At first it seems to have been of minor importance: It was apparently of a light timber construction and found its place ultimately near the western end of the hall opposite the ark. It is possible that in the synagogue of Cordoba the *bimah* was even attached to the western wall. This initiated a longitudinal layout in which ark and *bimah* balance out, a method later fully exploited in Italy. The expulsion of 1492 put an end to any further evolution in Spain itself, but a tradition of an elegantly appointed, well-balanced interior and a memory of juxtaposed ark and *bimah* remained with the exiles.

THE SEPHARDI DIASPORA AFTER THE EXPULSION. The settlement of *Marranos exiled from Spain, who in the 17th century set up new communities in Holland and England, introduced new customs into Jewish religious tradition. Their connection with their Spanish past was broken and they had to build their life anew, and in their synagogue building the influence of local custom was strongly felt. The great synagogue of the Portuguese community at Amsterdam, built in the years 1671–75, was influenced by the building style of the Dutch churches of that time, just as the Spanish and Portuguese synagogue in Bevis Marks, London, built in 1701, resembled meeting houses of the Nonconformists in England. The form of women's gallery in both these buildings later became typical. But the seating layout, and above all the polarized ark-*bimah* relationship, reflected Italian practice and the legacy of Spanish synagogues.

PALESTINE SYNAGOGUES. In Palestine synagogues of the four-column hall type were built by both the Sephardi and Ashkenazi communities. This type was quickly absorbed, and was further modified by the use of the Byzantine internal space concept of four pillars carrying a dome on pendentives. The four-columned synagogues in Palestine are the Ashkenazi synagogue of the "Ari" and the Sephardi synagogue of R. Isaac Aboab at Safed, the Avraham Avinu Synagogue in Hebron (destroyed in 1929), as well as the Elijah and the Istanbul synagogues, both in the Old City of Jerusalem, destroyed in 1948 and rebuilt in 1971. These two synagogues are part of a unique ensemble of four synagogues: Yohanan ben Zakkai Synagogue, the Eliyahu Hanavi Synagogue, the Haistambuli Synagogue, and among them the Emtzai (Central) Synagogue. They occupy an area of 40 meters by 33 meters sharing common features: since at the time the synagogues had been built, the Jews were not allowed to erect structures higher than those of the Arabs surrounding them, consequently their floors are three meters lower than the surrounding street level and their roofs do not protrude in height, but form a continuous whole together with the surrounding roofs. They have no exterior windows, only windows facing the interior courtyards, and

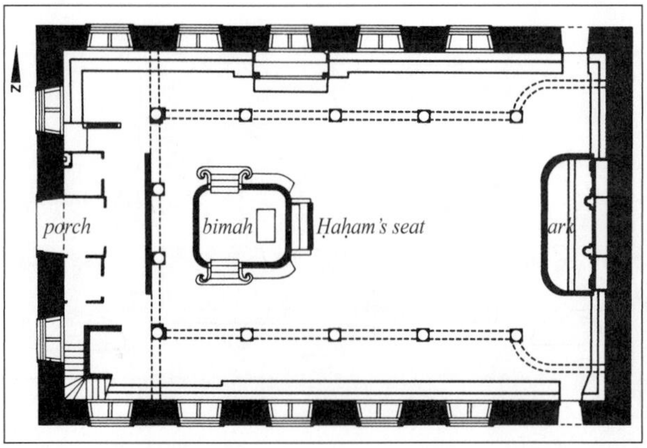

Drawing 10. Bevis Marks, London, built in 1701. From R. Wischnitzer, The Architecture of the European Synagogue, *Philadelphia, 1964.*

their entrances are modestly concealed. From the outside they appear to be an unremarkable agglomeration of buildings. The most important among them, the Yohanan ben Zakkai synagogue, has a double ark in the eastern wall. It has been explained in three ways: 1. As this synagogue is the continuation of the 13th-century Ramban Synagogue, which was a longish hall with two naves, this division called for two arks. 2. Bukharan Jews built double arks, because the Bukharan Emirate obligated the Jewish community to keep the Koran in the synagogue. As they did not want to keep the Torah and the Koran together, they built two arks. 3. The Jerusalem Talmud states that the children of Israel traveled through the desert with two arks in front of them. The second ark contained the broken tablets of the covenant.

The Ashkenazim built their spiritual center a short distance to the north of the old synagogue, in the courtyard later known as the Hurva (Ruin) Synagogue of Rabbi *Judah ha-Ḥasid.

SYNAGOGUES IN TURKEY AND IN THE ARAB COUNTRIES. Many thousands of Spanish Jews were welcomed to the Ottoman Empire in the 16th century. The 68 synagogues of Salonika were mostly destroyed in the great fire of 1917, but it is known that they were without any exterior ostentation. Beit Shaul, the most monumental, had a double-leveled façade with small windows and a segmental pediment over the central bay. The few synagogues in Istanbul, Edirne, and Izmir are similar, a kind of middle way between Byzantine and Sephardi traditions.

Cairo had some 30 synagogues between the two world wars, Alexandria had over 20, including the Eliyahu ha-Navi, the only one existing today, which was enlarged in 1865 by two side-aisles with galleries showing a strong western influence. The francophone Judeo-Egyptian culture created exquisite synagogues, which after 1956 fell into decay as Jews left the country.

In North Africa an autochthonous Jewish culture existed before the arrival of Spanish Jews, who soon became dominant in the region. Still, architecturally, the famous Danan synagogue and the Sadoun synagogue, both in Fez (Morocco), deployed autochthonous forms. The newly restored Danan synagogue, created in the 17th century, has an elongated rectangular floor plan, with three central columns carrying a timber roof. It is characterized by the bipolar arrangement having the ark in the eastern wall and the *bimah* sunk in the western wall, as well as a women's gallery on the southern perimeter wall. The Saba synagogue in Fez, along with a series of other, North African synagogues, displays four central pillars in the manner of Polish synagogues.

The Great Synagogue of Algier (1865, architect Viala du Sorbier) exemplifies European influence with its western-type Oriental style, which returns to its region of origin, but betrays the double condition of its constitutive elements. The synagogue in Rue de Paris in Tunis (1932–37) shows the same tendency, albeit in a 20th-century classicist-deco manner.

The Great Synagogue of Baghdad was described by the traveler Benjamin of Tudela in the 12th century as a building which apparently contained a columned hall opening onto a courtyard, as in a typical mosque, and magnificently adorned with ornamental lettering similar to that of Spanish synagogues. The famous synagogue at Fostat was a Coptic basilica built in the ninth century. In Damascus there existed a vaulted synagogue consisting of a hall with three bays, the only one of this type in eastern countries. The Aleppo synagogue (built in the ninth century and restored for the last time in 1992) resembled in principle the layout of the ancient mosques of Cairo – Amru and Ibn-Touloun – both of the internal courtyard type. The Aleppo synagogue had its separately roofed *bimah* in the middle of the courtyard, where normally the mosque well is placed. The congregation is here seated in the porticoes surrounding the courtyard, and the ark is placed analogically to the "mihrab." This is the most pronounced case of Islamic influence on synagogue design.

ITALIAN SYNAGOGUES. Jews had lived in Italy from the beginning of the Christian era and they preserved ancient local traditions. Italy had also absorbed Ashkenazi Jews who continued to reside there in growing numbers, and after the expulsion of 1492, exiles from Spain. Jews from the Levant also established merchant outposts, notably in Venice. The "bipolar" interior plan, whereby the ark and the *bimah* were placed at the opposing ends of an axial layout, was an important achievement in synagogue design. The synagogues in Italy, as in the other Diaspora centers, generally lacked exterior distinction, and there was nothing novel introduced in the way of structure. The popular methods of construction and covering were the "monastic vault," as in the Ashkenazi synagogue (Scuola Tedesca) at Padua; barrel-vaulting of various types with or without lunettes; coffered ceilings, and other components currently employed in Italy in the 16th, 17th, and 18th centuries.

The synagogue hall sometimes formed part of a large building, which included several additional units such as a *bet midrash*, the offices of the community, etc., and was frequently in the upper story. The decorative schemes were Renaissance, Mannerist, Baroque, or Rococo, the function of the ornamentation being to cover and to fill wall and ceiling surfaces without the use of representational art.

The bipolar hall of the Italian synagogues took final shape only in the 16th and 17th centuries; very little is known about the seating layout and place of the *bimah* in earlier synagogues. The unique contribution of Italian Jewry to architecture was in those intimate spatial schemes with ark and *bimah* at two opposite ends. In some of them highly imaginative variations occurred. In Pesaro and Ancona, the *tevah* (*bimah*) which is attached to the western wall is built on columns one story above the hall floor level, permitting axial entry into the hall facing the ark. (The only two remaining Provençal synagogues, of Carpentras and Cavaillon, both rebuilt in the 18th century in Rococo style, also have a similar layout,

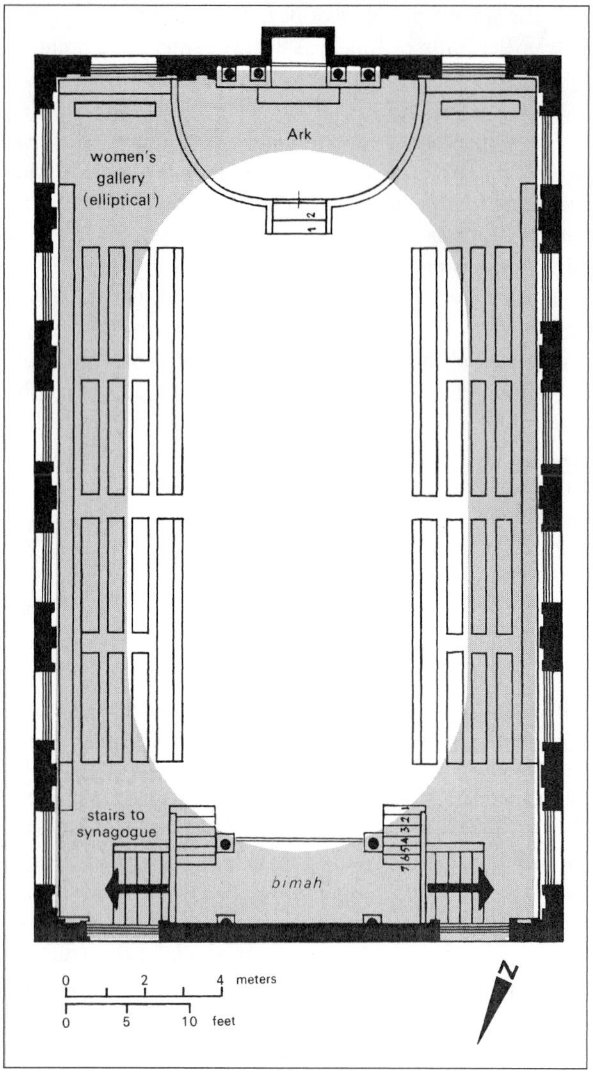

Drawing 11. The Spanish synagogue in Venice, following a bipolar plan. From J. Pinkerfeld, The Synagogues of Italy, *Jerusalem, 1954.*

with the *bimah* elevated on columns high enough to provide enough headroom for axial, direct access underneath.) This resembled the regional practice of placing the church high altars over a crypt.

One of the most beautiful examples was the Sephardi synagogue at Ferrara, built in the middle of the 17th century and later remodeled. Here the *bimah* was placed opposite the ark in the intersection of the main axis with the axis of entrance. But in most cities, especially in the north, a solution took shape which placed the *bimah* against the western wall and elevated it. Frequently it was not regarded as sufficient to place the ark against the wall, but it was placed in a niche or an apsidal space, as in the Canton Synagogue in Venice. The use of a symmetrical layout of two flights of stairs gave an opportunity for varied Baroque *bimah* arrangements. Most important was the almost universally practiced seating layout, like that of the British House of Commons, the congregation being seated in two equal parts facing each other and divided by the aisle or "walk" connecting *bimah* and ark. Thus every worshiper could equally face both foci, and the traditional space conflict was resolved. The most important of the north Italian synagogues is the Spanish synagogue in Venice, Scuola Grande Spagnola. Built in the middle of the 16th century, it was redesigned in the middle of the 17th by the famous Baldassare Longhena, architect of the Baroque church of Santa Maria della Salute and other monuments in Venice. Within the rectangular interior, an elliptical women's gallery surrounds the upper part of the hall. The ark and *bimah* are placed, respectively, at the eastern and western walls, with the typical Italian seating of the congregation on both sides of the aisle, as described above. This work of Venetian Baroque easily outshines other synagogues in Venice. Of a similar layout are the nearby Levantine, the Ashkenazi (Tedesca), the Scuola Canton, and the Italiana, all built in the 17th century in the ghetto.

Italian synagogues left to Jewish art a fine tradition of skilled craftsmanship and furnishing. The Baroque decoration schemes were of a standard equaling the finest Italian gentile work. Torah arks from Italy may be found in several museums in the world. Some of the small Italian communities, now finally dissolved, have transferred all their furnishings to Israel, in order to be set up anew in synagogues there. The furniture of the synagogue of Conegliano Veneto has now been refitted at the Italian Synagogue in Jerusalem; that of Vittorio Veneto has been fully reconstructed in the Israel Museum in Jerusalem.

[Aharon Kashtan / Rudolf Klein (2nd ed.)]

Enlightenment and Haskalah – Synagogues in the 18th Century

The 17th and 18th century Enlightenment brought about profound changes in western societies: the Christian outlook gradually weakened, rationalism came to the fore, and traditional social hierarchy started to lose its significance. All these developments prepared the ground for greater civil liberties for minority groups too – religious and ethnic alike – including the Jews, and eventually the French Revolution and Napoleonic Code granted full civil rights to the Jews for the first time in western history. Although after Napoleon the situation partially reverted to pre-Napoleonic conditions, in the long run the ideas of Liberty, Equality and Fraternity theoretically eradicated racial and religious prejudices. These external changes initiated further changes within Jewish society. The *Haskalah, the Jewish counterpart of the Enlightenment, came into being, bringing about secularism and fostering emancipation.

Although France was the leading country in implementing the aforementioned ideas, large-scale Jewish emancipation started in German lands, as these countries – particularly their eastern regions – had a sizeable Jewish population. The first synagogues emerged here during the early 18th century after the medieval expulsion. In the politically backward, strictly feudal Germany some rulers sought to attract Jewish traders and craftsmen to their territories, feeling they would stimulate economic development. They protected the Jewish communities under their care and sometimes took an interest in the building of synagogues, as in the Heidenreutergasse synagogue, Berlin (1714) and the synagogue at Ansbach, Bavaria (1746). At Woerlitz, Saxony, the Duke of Anhalt-Dessau built a synagogue in his park (1790) in the form of a circular Temple of Vesta. The *Haskalah* and the reform movement also started in Germany, changing slowly the traditional synagogue service, and consequently the interior arrangement of reform synagogues, from the early 19th century. Already in some neo-Classical synagogues the *bimah* was moved to the east, although this would become widespread only in the second half of the 19th century.

The synagogue of Leghorn in Italy was built in 1714 in a graceful southern Baroque style with two tiers of galleries. In England the chief synagogue built during this period was the Great Synagogue, London (1790), by James Spiller, a pupil of James Wyatt. Among the features of this neo-Classic building were rows of Ionic columns and a round-arched niche which contained the ark. Screened by two columns and flanked by Ionic pilasters, this motif was derived from Roman architecture via Andrea Palladio and Robert Adam. Some Georgian synagogues of interest were also built in the United States, such as the Touro Synagogue at Newport, Rhode Island (1763) and the synagogue at Charleston, South Carolina (1797), crowned with a double-tiered octagonal lantern.

19th Century to World War I

In 19th-century Europe more synagogues were built than during all the preceding periods together. This was due mainly to two factors: Jewish emancipation and the urbanization of Europe. Until the 19th century the vast majority of central and eastern European Jews lived in villages and small towns, erecting indistinct synagogues or gathering for prayer in homes. When they moved to major urban settlements, their concentration grew and major places of worship were needed. In many countries the gentiles even liked the idea of having the Jews gathered in fewer places for easier surveillance. The number of urban synagogues rose, their scale and prominence reaching hitherto unseen levels. Still, until the revolutions of 1848 they remained in a restrained framework of neo-Classicism or early Romanticism.

Neo-Classicism is the period which witnesses a breakthrough in synagogue architecture in central and eastern Europe: The famous German neo-Classicist architect, Friedrich Weinbrenner, created his synagogue in Karlsruhe (1798) in the spirit of French revolutionary architecture and quoted the Temple of Solomon, equating implicitly the synagogue with the Temple for the first time in modern central European history. Although the actual synagogue was built in the courtyard, there were two tapering pylons on the street front, recalling Egyptian architecture. The floor plan of the synagogue was an elongated rectangle with a central *bimah*. The adjoining buildings contained a ritual bath; community offices were added in 1810, and they created a monumental ensemble together with the actual synagogue.

Other neo-Classical synagogues of note were those in the Rue Notre Dame in Paris (1819–20), the Seitenstettengasse in Vienna (albeit with some Baroque traces, as the elliptical floor plan which suited the reform service, 1824) and in Munich (1826), the Óbuda Synagogue in the city today called Budapest (1820–21), the ponderous New Synagogue in London (1838), and the Beth Elohim in Charleston (1841), a particularly fine example of the Greek revival. A new flavor was added by Napoleon's campaign in Egypt (1798), which created a fashion for Egyptian details, sometimes combined with the Greek, as in Copenhagen (1833) or in some synagogues in the United States.

As early as 1838, Gottfried Semper, the great 19th-century German architect, created the synagogue in Dresden based on a Byzantine floor plan, a strict neo-Romanesque exterior and an Oriental interior. The exterior architectural language referred to the style of great German Romanesque cathedrals, though the proportions and scale were different. The interior referred to the Oriental origin of the Jews, particularly to the Spanish period before expulsion, to which all Oriental-style synagogues began to refer. This duality depicted the double-layered Jewish identity of the period, which corresponded with the idea of the Jews as the "Asiatics of Europe." Semper, as a theoretician, also paved the way for 19th-century synagogue architecture with his *Bekleidungstheorie* (theory of cladding), which served as a theoretical base for the Oriental-style synagogues, the most widespread genre of architecture created for Jews before modernism. The floor plan of the prayer room in his Dresden synagogue is a square with an eastern *bimah* in front of the ark.

The second half of the 19th century was the heyday of European synagogue building, as a result of a combination of fortuitous factors that contributed to the birth of large-scale representative synagogues almost all over Europe. First, the successful revolutions of 1848 led to full civil rights for the Jews in most of Europe, resulting in spectacular advances for Jewish entrepreneurs and intellectuals and their communities, which wished to display their success in architectural terms. Second, after neo-Classicism elapsed, the emergence of Romanticism and Eclecticism (Free Style) in particular changed the scale of architecture, which lost its previous coherence of style and compactness of form. The hitherto compact masses started to dissolve, the obligatory architectural language to vanish. This milieu amplified the Jewish tendencies toward representation, and synagogues became conspicuous elements of the townscape. The primary concern of synagogue design shifted from the interior to the exterior, becoming a great endeavor to create an appropriate appearance for the gentiles. The interior became more longish with, a *bimah* removed from the center and shifted to the eastern wall, where it created together with the ark an altar-like monumental composition. Consequently seating arrangements in the synagogue changed radically from concentrically placed benches/chairs around the bimah to a longitudinal arrangement in which all benches faced the east as in Catholic churches. Gradually the proportions got even closer to the longitudinal basilical layout of Catholic churches. Abolishing the duality of ark and *bimah* suggested that the duality between a given location in the Diaspora and the Holy Land had ended: Jews were accepted everywhere, they were at home among the gentiles. The wish to return to Jerusalem vanished among Reform Jews. A large altar-like *mizraḥ* uniting the *bimah* and ark answered the needs of the Reform service, with choral and organ music as well as preaching in local language. For the majority of secularized synagogue-goers Hebrew became as exotic as Latin for Catholic worshipers. Besides the basilical plan, the central plan gained ground again, albeit usually without its original raison d'être, the central *bimah*. The large external dome necessitated the central or nearly central floor plan.

In the 1850s major so-called Moorish-style synagogues came into being in German lands and regions under German influence – central and eastern Europe, the Balkans, and overseas. The two most grandiose examples, the Dohány Street synagogue in Budapest (1852–57) and the Oranienburgerstrasse Synagogue in Berlin (1855–66), seated over 3,000 worshipers, mainly middle-class people, as evidenced by period engravings. Although this spectacular development was fueled by the Reform Jews – mainly the very rich and assimilated – the Orthodox gradually followed these trends with a significant time lag. Still, they left the *bimah* in the center.

Nonetheless, synagogue style – so often discussed among 19th-century Jews, architects, and critics alike – has never come into being. This reflects the fact that Judaism cannot be translated into form even in its watered-down, "reform" version. Synagogues were built in a mixture of styles, which sometimes showed more Western revivals – neo-Romanesque, neo-Renaissance, neo-Byzantine – and sometimes more Oriental features – Islamic, Egyptian, Assyrian. The Gothic revival was rarely a factor, being considered Christian, as for instance in the cases of the Meisel Synagogue in Prague, the synagogue in Budweis (Ceškoje Budejovice), or the Gothic synagogues built by Max Fleischer in Vienna. The first, breakthrough generation of 19th-century synagogues was built mainly in Oriental style, as an association with the golden age of Spanish Jewry, like, for instance, the Cologne synagogue (1861), the Central Synagogue, London (1870), the Florence synagogue (1880), and the St. Petersburg (Choral Temple) synagogue (1893). The style was brought by German congregations to the United States, where it was widely adopted, as in Temple Emmanuel, New York (1868), Rodef Shalom, Philadelphia (1869–70), and Plum Street Temple, Cincinnati, Ohio (1866), with its 13 domes and two minarets.

Late in the century the Classical style sometimes returned to favor and was adopted by the U.S. architect Arnold *Brunner on the evidence of the newly published remains of ancient synagogues in Ereẓ Israel. There was a new spate of revivals, including Renaissance, Georgian, Baroque, and in continental Europe neo-Romanesque, propagated by the German Jewish architect Edwin Oppler. He maintained that, as Jews were Germans of Jewish faith and not Asiatics of Europe, they should use the local, national style. Oppler's thinking was influenced by the first major antisemitic waves of the 1870s and 1880s which swept over Europe. In the Hapsburg Empire and neighboring countries to the east and south, this antisemitic wave did not cause major changes in architectural style.

More importantly than style in the second half of the 19th century, composition of masses in synagogues was also a surrogate, an "as if" genre, loosely following forms of different gentile buildings. (A similar influence was at work at the medieval Altneuschul in Prague, but this was a singular case.) Architecturally, the Reform synagogue was a new genre which needed a new expression. In mid-19th-century Germany, for instance, the architects and Jewish community leaders launched competitions to create a suitable typology for the new synagogues, without actual building. These entries were published and served later as guidelines for designing synagogues. Based on these examples and the gentile templates – churches, public buildings, and factory buildings – a wide range of compositional types emerged. Thus, in terms of composition of volume, synagogues in the 19th century can be classified as village-house-type synagogues, burgher-house type, Protestant-church type, Catholic-church/cathedral type, Temple type (references to Solomon's Temple in Jerusalem), factory-hall type, central Byzantine type, palace type, and combinations of these types. The choice between these types depended on the urban location, the intention and standing of the local Jewish community, and the restrictions of the municipality.

Orthodox communities which came into being as a reaction to the rapid reform process in the second half the 19th century clung to older patterns – central *bimah* and somewhat restrained scale and decoration. However, they soon started to compete with the reformers, and by the end of the 19th century Orthodox synagogues often became indistinguishable in the exterior from their Reform counterparts in major cities.

Urban settings also changed remarkably in the 19th century. The hitherto hidden, or at least well-concealed, synagogue appeared on exposed urban locations, close to the town center on major street crossings, or even on the center of squares, sometimes on the main square of the town or city. In the beginning synagogues were still built behind fences – these fences were rather formal, i.e., transparent and richly decorated – but later this tradition was abandoned. In regions where virulent antisemitism was to be expected – numerous Berlin synagogues demonstrate this – the synagogue was in the courtyard, represented on the street façade by the community building.

Between the World Wars

Emerging modernism pushed aside the issue of style, stressing function and clear composition of simple volumes. Modernism can be read as a reaction against highly decorated neo-styles and at the same time seen as the right expression for the Jews – abandoning the visual representation (carved image), establishing universal, cosmopolitan expression by using abstract language.

During the first two decades of the 20th century, a period often labeled proto-modernism, this reaction limited itself to a simplification of design rather than complete abandonment of historical revivals. Later, generally after World War I, architects influenced by the theories of functionalism produced bare and stark synagogues, without conscious reference to any previous period. An early example of simplified design was the Anshe Maariv Synagogue in Chicago (1890–91) by the famous partnership of Dankmar *Adler and Louis Sullivan. Among the outstanding early 20th-century synagogues were those of Essen (1913) and Zurich (1923–24) and two Amsterdam synagogues, which aspired to simplicity and an ingenious use of the local Dutch brickwork: the Linnaeus Straat Synagogue by Jacob *Baars and the Jacob Obrechtsplein Synagogue by Harry *Elte (both 1928).

In his 1924 competition entry for a synagogue in Hietzing, a residential suburb of Vienna, architect Richard J. *Neutra produced one of the first synagogue designs consisting of a flat-roofed building organized around an interior open courtyard. Both Josef Hoffman, the Viennese architect, and Peter Behrens of Berlin submitted proposals in a competition held in 1926 by the Jewish community in Žilina (formerly Sillein or Zsolna) in former Czechoslovakia, today Slovak Republic. Peter Behrens got the commission, and his monolithic, low-domed, square, massive structure was built in 1931. Josef Hoffman made several submissions: one indicates the synagogue as a hemispheric dome resting on a low substructure; another design shows his intention to create a tent-shaped pyramid of glass rising out of an enclosing substructure of rectilinear form. These schemes preceded similar synagogue designs later built in the United States. Important modern synagogues, which were architecturally pioneering and prophetic, were built or proposed in Europe from the 1920s to World War II, when the open flexible plan with the expandable sanctuary space was first being realized.

In this period, once again Germany produced the artistically most advanced synagogues, until the Nazi takeover. Fritz Landauer built the compact and purist synagogue in Plauen (1929–30), which stood in the forefront of modern architecture with its simple monolithic mass, elevated on pillars, and industrial-looking rhythm of small windows and white undecorated walls, as well as a larger asymmetrically positioned modernist oculus containing the Star of David. A bit more conservative was the great Oberstrasse Temple in Hamburg (1931, F. Asher and R. Friedman), with its strict symmetrical massing and windowless walls covered with stone.

Functionalist simplicity characterized the Dollis Hill Synagogue, London (1937) by Sir Owen Williams. The seating arrangement reflected British tradition, and the hexagonal windows refer to the idea of the Star of David and represent a novelty in European architecture of the period. Here the architect dispensed with the gallery supports by means of corrugated walls and ceiling.

The early modern synagogue in Ereẓ Israel is a case in point. A synagogue in Ḥaderah (1935) includes a watchtower and a courtyard to provide shelter for 2,000 people in case of attack. Its architectural language is a combination of pure modernist volumes and traditional arcades, as well as small windows resembling Muslim tradition. The Jeshurun synagogue, Jerusalem (1934–35), features small windows, modernist masses clad with stone.

In America during the period between the two wars functionalist architecture was not very popular. Therefore, Temple Emmanuel in New York City, designed in 1930, possesses a combination of Romanesque portals, Gothic flying buttresses, and Moorish towers.

After World War II

World War II represented a watershed not only in gentile architecture but also in synagogue building throughout Europe. Modernism became officially accepted by the welfare states in Europe and lost its previous elitist aura, often becoming a simplified, cheap common language. War destruction necessitated the building of synagogues, but European Jewry, decimated by the Holocaust, did not need and did not want to erect manifest synagogues. Instead small-scale, modest, functional synagogues came into being. In the Communist Bloc religion was suppressed and very few synagogues were constructed; far more were destroyed – either directly, or by neglect.

These circumstances changed the manner of expression as well, which often concentrated on the correct display of function. Traditional visual symbolism in the circumstances of post-World War II synagogues lost its significance for two reasons: impressing the gentiles in the manner of 19th-century synagogues was pointless after the Holocaust; the significance and the coherence of the urban context which had previously necessitated a manifest synagogue also declined, and the need of declaration disappeared. All these and the puritanism of late modern architecture led to a minimal and austere language in the 1950s and 1960s in Europe.

In America, which became the leading country of synagogue construction after World War II, on the other hand, the large scale prevailed and a certain degree of representation, but on the other hand, suburbanization changed the previous form and expression of synagogues, turning them into multi-purpose buildings. Since 1945 the synagogue has not been merely a house of worship but, in many instances, a community center consisting of a school, administrative offices, a gymnasium, and an assembly hall.

[Rudolf Klein (2nd ed.)]

Later, however, ornament returned in another form. The complementary arts of painting, sculpture, textiles, mosaics, and stained glass were increasingly used in conjunction with architecture. Seeking to represent what the contemporary arts had to offer, the U.S. synagogue engaged the efforts of many eminent artists, who reinterpreted traditional Jewish ritual objects and symbols in a completely modern idiom.

SYNAGOGUES IN AMERICA. Park Synagogue in Cleveland, Ohio, designed by Eric *Mendelsohn in 1948, was conceived as a hemispheric dome enclosing the synagogue proper and rising from a long, low, flat-roofed structure, similar in form to the 1926 design of Josef Hoffman. From the time Mendelsohn went to the United States from Palestine in 1941, until his death in 1959, he designed seven synagogues and community centers, of which only four have been built. The temple and community center for Congregation B'nai Amoona, St. Louis, Missouri (1946), was Mendelsohn's first synagogue and also his first commission in the United States. In this design he expanded the sanctuary space into the entrance foyer and the social hall, thus increasing the Sabbath seating capacity of 600 people to 1,500 for the High Holy Days. First devised by Cecil Moore in Tucson, Arizona (1946), this solution was used by Mendelsohn in a variety of ways. One other example was in the copper-clad, ten-rib steel sanctuary structure for Mount Zion Temple and Community Center in St. Paul, Minnesota, where the rich interior sanctuary space is again expanded into the foyer and assembly hall. Mendelsohn's sketches for synagogues indicate clearly the ideas which are manifested in the distinctive character of each building.

In many synagogues which Percival *Goodman designed, beginning with B'nai Israel Synagogue in Millburn, New Jersey (1951), the strong architectural expression of the ark both on the interior and the exterior of the structure is a dominant recurring theme. In Congregation Shaarey Zedek, in Detroit, Michigan, which Goodman designed in association with Albert Kahn, the sanctuary, dominant because of its location and height (100 feet at the ark), is flanked at the sides by two social halls which form part of the same structure and serve as extensions of the space, since the congregation increases from 1,200 to 3,500 people on the High Holidays. The architects made the social halls triangular in shape and separated them from the sanctuary by folding walls, in order to place the maximum number of congregants in the closest proximity to the *bimah*. When necessary, simultaneous functions can occur without interference; the separation of the side halls permits one to be used as an auditorium while the other is the main dining hall. Both halls may be used for dining, since a separate serving kitchen is provided off the auditorium hall. The three halls are linked by a reception space which allows separate access to each. Just as the sanctuary is the focal point of the building, the ark is the focal point of the sanctuary; thus the seating arrangement of this building is characteristic of the assembly type of plan. Frank Lloyd Wright responded to the idea of creating the synagogue for Beth Shalom in Philadelphia (1954), as a tent on Mount Sinai. His pyramidal, tent-like structure is sheathed in glass, filling the interior with light. The scheme in the plan is capable of variations, so that it can be expanded or contracted as may be desired.

The Reform movement, which began in Germany, produced vital changes in the architecture of synagogues also in the United States. The simplification of the service, the new emphasis on the sermon, the mixed seating of men and women, and the introduction of the organ brought the synagogue closer to the outward forms of Protestant Christianity and resulted in an architectural arrangement similar to that in a church or theater. The *bimah* was consequently taken from its traditional place in the center of the room and put in front of the ark on a platform at one end of it. In the United States this scheme was widely adopted by the Reform and Conservative movements and also by some of the Orthodox congregations. Many later designs, however, have indicated a reaction to the auditorium plan organization of the synagogue with *bimah* placed in the front of the ark, and the seats arranged to face the ark. The above-discussed, difficult problems of the plan arrangement, the double use of the sanctuary space, and the basic disposition of the synagogue interior, perhaps cannot be completely answered by the architect. Kneset Tifereth Israel synagogue in Port Chester, New York, by Philip Johnson, is a well-executed design which directly confronts the problem of an expandable space. The building consists of a symmetrical plan in which the sanctuary and the social hall are actually combined in one large rectangular space, with the entrance at a passage separating the two. A movable screen isolates the sanctuary; the whole space can be opened when necessary. Buildings have been designed which have attempted to combine classrooms and the sanctuary, a social hall and the sanctuary, or a lobby, social hall, and the sanctuary, in order to increase the seating capacity for the High Holidays. This problem, of an expanding and contracting space, is evident in many contemporary synagogues. Those architects who have not had this problem, but instead have been given a single space to design, have usually created a more satisfactory structure, and the ancient central plan has been revived. This arrangement, which clearly provides a better architectural solution, does not provide for expansion of the seating space.

[Richard Meier]

Besides functional innovations in the United States, Louis I. *Kahn, one of the most talented architects in the country, dealt with symbolic aspects of synagogue architecture extensively, although little was constructed from these designs.

After the Enlightenment there were a number of "specialists" in synagogue architecture, such as, for example, the Austro-Hungarian architect Leopold Baumhorn, who created or rebuilt over 40 synagogues, or the American architect Percival Goodman, who was also prolific in the heyday of synagogue construction in the United States; but probably Louis Kahn has been the only world-class modernist architect who devoted major attention to the synagogue. In 1961 Kahn started working for Mikveh Israel and created until 1972 10 versions which demonstrate a transition from traditional boxy modernism, backed by a rational design philosophy, to a highly mystical never-built synagogue fiction: a complex of three detached units, a Sanctuary-House of Study; a Chapel – House of Prayer and School – and a House of the Community. From the fourth version Kahn introduced "light bottles," large cylinders making the building fortress-like from the outside, and in the interior showing up as large dark towers with light-emitting holes. This mystical symbolism was largely absent in post-Enlightenment synagogue history, but particularly in modern times.

The Hurva Synagogue in the Old City of Jerusalem represents Kahn's last word in this genre. He conceived the Hurvah as a new building and not as a ruin: "The new building should itself consist of two buildings – an outer one which would absorb the light and heat of the sun, and an inner one, giving the effect of a separate but related building. The inside building would be a single chamber, resting on four points … there are niches where candle services will be sung during certain ceremonies… the exterior will be visible through the niches which are in the stones. These stones are 16 foot square, the interior chambers are 10 foot square. The stones, like the stories of the Western Wall, will be golden in color; the interior will be rather silver in color. The spaces between them will be such as to allow a sufficient amount of light to enter from the outer chamber, and, completely surrounding the interior chamber, there will be an ambulatory from which people will also be able to witness a service taking place in the interior chamber. The construction of the building is like large leaves of a tree, allowing light to filter into the interior…." Kahn seems to have fallen into the same pitfall as had Herzl some seven decades earlier, the rebuilding of the Temple. No wonder his project was halted. It seems that Kahn has misunderstood Judaism – at least its post-Temple period – and its ambivalence and suspicion toward architecture as the materialization of ideas.

[Rudolf Klein (2nd ed.)]

SYNAGOGUES IN EUROPE. In the postwar period in Europe, few radical changes in planning were generally adopted, though from the late 1950s synagogues began to be constructed with main halls convertible for non-devotional purposes, and were built as part of a social complex including communal centers, old-age homes, and other buildings, as in the United States. Architectural techniques were much developed, however, with the use of reinforced concrete, steel-framed construction, glass walls, and other innovations. The visual effect was generally lighter than in the case of the solid and austere synagogues of the period between the wars. After World War II a number of synagogues were built by the small returning Jewish communities in Germany, where nearly all major synagogues had been destroyed by the Nazis. The synagogues at Offenbach (1956), Dortmund (1956), Duesseldorf (1958), Essen (1959), and Bonn (1959), and the Fasanenstrasse Community House in West Berlin (1959) are of importance. In the case of the last-mentioned building, fragments of the neo-Romanesque synagogue built on the site in 1912 and destroyed by the Nazis were preserved and placed in startling juxtaposition to the new building as a reminder of the tragic fate of the German Jews. In England a synagogue by Harold Weinreich at Woodford, Essex (1954), built out of prefabricated units, attracted attention. A somewhat unusual synagogue is that at the Bernard Lyons Community Center, Leeds (1963), where a paraboloid roof is placed diagonally over the hall. The New Central Synagogue, London (1958), with its round-arched windows, replacing that destroyed by German bombing, should also be mentioned. The largest postwar synagogue in Europe was built by Claude Meyer-Lévy in Strasbourg, France (1958); a traditional structure, it was essentially a classical basilica reinterpreted in terms of reinforced concrete. In Italy the 18th-century Leghorn synagogue, destroyed in bombing raids, was rebuilt by Angelo di Castro in 1962. The new building showed several innovations of plan and structure. The structural skeleton was exposed to view in the manner of Luigi Nervi, and the gallery was a bridge attached to the side walls only and spanning the hall. The seats surrounded the *bimah* on three sides in the shape of an amphitheater. Another interesting postwar Italian synagogue was that built in Milan by Monfredo D'Urbino and E. Gentile in 1954.

[Richard Meier]

In Livorno one of the most creative post-World-War II synagogues in Europe was created. While the commission was more for an American-style community center, Angelo di Castro, the Jewish architect from Rome, restated the concept of the European urban synagogue with a strong architectural identity in 1958. The main architectural feature of the building is a set of bent vertical "buttresses" – actually reinforced concrete frame structure – which project from the wall surface both on the interior and on the exterior. This structural solution created the interior as a single, undivided room in which everyone can hear and see easily, and which recalls the rhythm of pillars from the past. The seats, disposed around several sides of the elongated polygonal interior, give a sense of congregational unity, as do the central placement of the *bimah* and the absence of concealing grilles on the women's gallery. The organic form of the building recalls the tabernacle or Tent of the Wilderness, its billowing form is even more obvious inside, where the vertical lines and the pale-colored wall spaces between them combine with the light-filled interior space to give the impression of an airy and almost weightless tent.

After architectural modernism was eclipsed in the 1970s and 1980s, the austere style of synagogues was abandoned and a new eclecticism emerged in the framework of post-modernism. Many of the strictures of modernism were loosened or abandoned altogether, and architects became free to use elements of the past. Post-modern synagogues were built mainly in the "old countries" of the European Union and in the United States.

The Darmstadt Jewish Community Center, comprising a synagogue with 200 seats and adjacent buildings, was designed by Alfred Jacoby in 1988. It merges modernist purism of form and material with some historic elements – the use of a central dome over the prayer hall and small domes over the entrance, a symmetrical composition of the synagogue and the enclosing buildings, and the use of stone.

SYNAGOGUES IN ISRAEL. Probably the modern State of Israel is the place with the greatest variety of synagogue buildings, greater than the variety of churches or mosques in a Christian or Muslim country. This variety is due to the diversity of immigrant Jewish populations from Europe, Asia, Africa, and the Americas. Some synagogues are indistinct, following the boxy modernist forms and merging with the urban context; others are more visible either through the highlighting of some traditional features, like domes; or by expressively sculptural forms. Thus, the variety runs the spectrum from the tectonic Great Synagogue in Allenby Street to the utterly sculptural, shell-shaped Heikhal Yehudah Synagogue in Arlozorov Street (architects Toledano and Russo, 1980), both in Tel Aviv.

The Hebrew University Givat Ram Campus Synagogue (architects Heinz Rau and David Resnik) is surrounded by lush vegetation and some stones from which its white mushroom-shaped reinforced concrete shell emerges, recalling the tent in the desert. The two-story building contains a sumptuous lobby on the ground floor and in the upper story a windowless synagogue, which, besides artificial light, gets indirect sunshine from downstairs via floor windows. This synagogue is a genuine attempt in the spirit of the postwar modernism to overcome all traditions, to create a new spatial experience, which is unfortunately not suitable for the function of a synagogue.

The synagogue at the Military Academy, Negev Desert (architect Zvi Hecker, 1964–66) has an area of approximately 100 m^2 and accommodates at least 100 people within its polyhedral forms, which create a space progressively narrowing up to the top. The exterior is dominated by cell-like modules, but the interior gives the impression of a harmonious and integrated space. The plan is central, but reflects the double-focus arrangement of traditional synagogues – both Ashkenazi and Sephardi. Seats for the worshipers are placed along the sides of the axis and are inclined, so that both the *bimah* and the Ark can be seen simultaneously. A series of skylights supplies the interior with warm yellow light. The tilted walls render the space abstract, lifting it from its everyday experience. They negate tectonics that might be associated with the tent in the desert.

Ma'alot Synagogue, Jerusalem, Rehavia (architect David Cassutto, 1972) is built on a hexagonal floor plan, with a hexagonal *bimah* in the center. The dominant element of the interior is the set of reinforced concrete pillars and beams. In the center, where the latter meet, there is a hexagonal sculptural element supporting the lighting. Above this element the ceiling is perforated by a grilled skylight, resembling local Islamic architectural tradition.

The Har Nof New Synagogue, Jerusalem (architect David Cassutto, 1993) exemplifies the Israeli type of post-modernist synagogue which recalls the pre-modern language of architecture and a traditional spatial concept. The synagogue is incorporated into a community center, but is visually well distinguishable due to its *kippah*-like flat dome. The facade is covered with Jerusalem-stone, which is pierced through only by narrow slits. On the ground floor the windows are rectangular, on the first floor semicircular. The stern and closed masses are rendered soft by the use of semicircular forms – balconies and projections – recalling forms of the Old City. The approximately 200 m^2 prayer room incorporates the women's gallery. The dome has round glass inlays referring to the local Moslem architectural tradition. The *bimah* is set a little bit westward from the geometrical center of the space, according to the Sephardi tradition. The ark has circular access, with two round wings of stairs recalling the Italian Baroque.

The Cymbalista Synagogue and Heritage Center at the Tel Aviv University Campus (1998), designed by the Swiss architect Mario Botta, highlights Israel's opening to foreign architects. Botta, in the spirit of Italian *racionalismo* – a movement present in Italy since Mussolini – created cubes and cylinders clad with stone using the play of light. The complex is visually divided into three parts, a lower rectangular one from which the two bastion-like volumes grow out, which respond to the dualistic implications of the commission – the secular and religious. The twin fortress-like forms differ only in terms of their interiors: To the west is the Jewish Heritage Center, a lecture hall with its dais set in a small apse; to the east – on the Jerusalem side – is the synagogue, with its centrally located *bimah* and an apse for the Holy Ark. Light is brought into the interior of the paired volumes via series of small windows and a large skylight, spreading over the walls by a square panel set into each cylinder.

RESTORATION OF SYNAGOGUES IN CENTRAL AND EASTERN EUROPE. While in Germany and in the occupied countries during *Kristallnacht* the vast majority of urban synagogues was destroyed or damaged beyond repair, some of them could be still rescued. The Westend Synagogue in Frankfurt, the synagogues in Pestalozzi Strasse and Rykestrasse in Berlin, as well as the Roonstrasse Synagogue of Cologne were restored. From some others only fragments remained, as in the case of Fasanenstrasse, and sometimes quite significant fragments, as in the complete façade section of the Oranienburgerstrasse Synagogue, both in Berlin.

Unlike the great urban synagogues, a certain percentage of the rural ones survived even in Germany and in the occupied lands, and in other central and eastern European countries a substantial number of synagogues were only slightly damaged during the war. Their actual deterioration started in the late 1940s and 1950s, because the Jews had been deported or emigrated, and their synagogues had become exposed to decay and vandalism. Some major synagogues were officially protected from demolition by the local authorities, but little was done to maintain the buildings.

As the tide of intense post-World War II construction receded and the former loathing of modern architectural theory abated, abandoned synagogues started to attract public interest. In the 1980s mainly the synagogues and adjacent community buildings were restored, but with the increasing awareness of the urban context, complete Jewish neighborhoods gradually began to re-emerge, albeit without the Jews. The most

Interior view: "Holy" of the El Ghriba synagogue, Djerba, Tunisia, 1981.
Photo: Jan Parik. By courtesy of Beth Hatefutsoth Photo Archive, Tel Aviv.

The synagogue, a gathering place for the Jews, became a substitute for the Temple of Jerusalem after its destruction (70 C.E.), and the idea of holiness extended to synagogues outside Israel as well. The institution of the synagogue played a central role in preserving the community and perpetuating the Jewish faith. Over the generations, exterior synagogue design varied depending on the location of the Diaspora, with the interior design falling into broad eastern and western styles. The internal appurtenances and decorations became a venue for Jewish artistic expression.

SYNAGOGUES

(opposite page) TOP: Interior of synagogue in Veroia (Veria), Greece. Built originally in the 18th century, the synagogue underwent expansions and alterations as the community grew and dwindled. In this interior view to the northeast we see the Ark under a carved wooden canopy and along the north wall, three plastered rectangles that replaced the grills of the former *mehiza,* or women's gallery. *Photo: Rivka and Ben-Zion Dorfman, Synagogue Art Research, Jerusalem.*

(opposite page) BOTTOM: Third-century synagogue excavated at Capernaum. *Photo: Z. Radovan, Jerusalem.*

(this page): The ruins of the synagogue in Ostin, Italy. *Photo: Z. Radovan, Jerusalem.*

The Magen Aboth synagogue, built in 1910, Alibag, India.
By courtesy of Beth Hatefutsoth, Photo Archive, Tel Aviv. Courtesy of Dorothy Field, Canada.

Synagogue (now an art gallery) in Trencin, Slovakia. This imposing edifice was completed in 1913 to replace a 125-year-old building and to serve the needs of some 1,500 Jews, about 16 percent of the town's population. With lavish dome and Oriental decorative motifs, the synagogue contains a spacious winter prayer-room on the southern side, shown here, where a small *kehillah* of fewer than two dozen members met weekly for Shabbat prayers in the 1990s. *Photo: Rivka and Ben-Zion Dorfman, Synagogue Art Research, Jerusalem.*

Beth Sholom, Elkins Park, Pennsylvania, United States, synagogue designed by Frank Lloyd Wright, 1954. *Photo: Jeffrey Howe, Fine Arts Department, Boston College, USA.*

Part of the painted ceiling of the synagogue in Chodorow, near Lvov, Poland (now Ukraine). The paintings were by Israel Ben Mordechai Lisnicki of Jaryczow in 1714. The synagogue was destroyed during the Holocaust. Reconstruction in Beth Hatefutsoth. *By courtesy of Beth Hatefutsoth Photo Archive, Tel Aviv, Permanent Exhibition.*

The 14th-century Ark of the Law in the Altneushul in Prague. The synagogue is one of the oldest in Europe, dating at least to the 12th century. *Photo: Z. Radovan, Jerusalem.*

ABOVE: Johanan ben Zakkai synagogue, built in the early 17th century by descendants of Jews expelled from Spain, Old City, Jerusalem. *Photo: Z. Radovan, Jerusalem.*

LEFT: Torah scroll niches in a faience-tiled wall from a synagogue in Isfahan, Iran, c. 1550. *Photo: H. R. Lippmann, NY. The Jewish Museum, New York.*

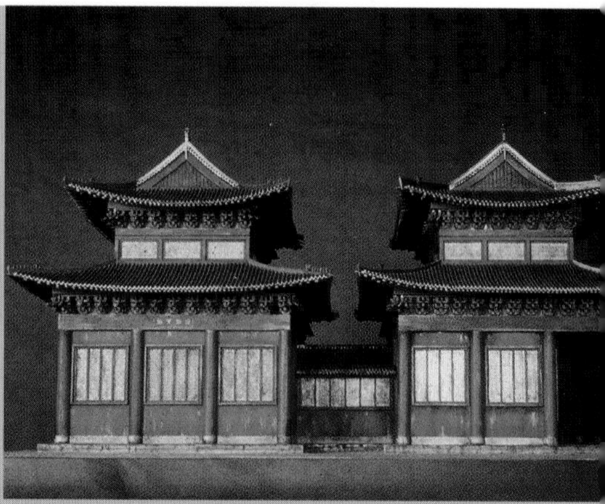

A model of the synagogue of Kai-Feng, China. The synagogue was first constructed in 1163 and rebuilt in 1653. In the 18th century, after the community had disintegrated through assimilation, the synagogue fell into decay. *By courtesy of Beth Hatefutsoth Photo Archive, Tel Aviv. Permanent Exhibition.*

ABOVE and BELOW: Interior and exterior views of the "Zedek Veshalom" Synagogue, founded in 1716, Paramaribu, Surinam. According to beliefs, the floor of sand inside this synagogue remains as such until the community goes back to Jerusalem. *Photo: Micha Bar-Am. By courtesy of Mordechai Arbell.*

important examples of restored Jewish neighborhoods are in Mikulov and Trebic, both in the Czech Republic.

While small and middle-size Renaissance, Baroque, neo-Classical, and some 19th-century synagogues were relatively easily converted to cultural function, major 19th-century synagogues were more difficult to utilize. Unfortunately, in the 1960s and 1970s often the prayer room was divided into two floors by the extension of the women's gallery, and with that the original meaning of the synagogue space was lost, as for instance in the large Arena ut synagogue in Budapest, which functions as a sports club. From the 1980s more strict restorations became the norm by preserving the *bimah* and Ark and adding new functional elements less conspicuously. For instance, the synagogue in Novi Sad (Serbia) was successfully converted into a concert hall. The synagogue in Osijek (Croatia) is a Pentecost Church. The Hungarian synagogues in Baja, Apostag, became municipal libraries, the synagogue in Budapest-Obuda a TV studio, the Pava utca synagogue of Budapest became integrated into the Holocaust Center, the Romantic synagogue in Kecskemet became a house of technology. The early modern synagogue in Kosice (Slovakia) is the seat of the local philharmonic orchestra, the medieval synagogue in Maribor (Slovenia) is an exhibition space.

The Old Synagogue in Holesov, the old synagogue Velke Mezirici, the upper synagogue in Mikulov, all in Moravia (Czech Republic), serve exhibition purposes. The Prague synagogues have been restored. The Meisel synagogue is an exhibition space, and the Pinkas synagogue is a unique Holocaust Museum, with the names of all the victims inscribed on the walls.

In Poland the great synagogue in Zamosc houses a library and reading room, the synagogue of Tykocin houses a museum, Lancut synagogue houses the regional museum and an exhibition of Judaica, in Rzeszow the Old Town Synagogue presently houses archives, and the New Town Synagogue presently serves as an art center.

[Rudolf Klein (2nd ed.)]

BIBLIOGRAPHY: ORIGINS AND HISTORY: I. Levy, *The Synagogue* (1963); M. Friedlaender, *Synagoge und Kirche* (1908); I. Abrahams, *Studies in Pharisaism and the Gospels*, 1 (1917; repr. 1967), 1–17; idem, *Jewish Life in the Middle Ages* (1932²), 1–48; S. Zeitlin, in: PAAJR, 2 (1930/31), 72ff.; E. Sukenik, *Ancient Synagogues in Palestine and Greece* (1934); Baron, Community, 1 (1947), 55–74 and passim; idem, Social², index; I. Sonne, in: IDB, 2 (1962), 476ff.; J. Weingreen, in: *Hermathena*, 98 (1964), 68–84 (Heb. version in: *Hagut Ivrit be-Eiropah* (1969), 253–65); F. Zevi, in: *Scritti in Memoria di Enzo Sereni* (1970), 61–74 (Heb. section). DESECRATION AND DESTRUCTION: E. Ringelblum, *Notes from the Warsaw Ghetto* (1958); D. Davidovitch, *Battei Keneset be-Polin ve-Ḥurbanam* (1960); *Eduyyot*, 1 (1963), 5–82 (evidence at the Eichmann trial); J. Sandel, *Zydowska sztuka kultowa* (1953); A. Kubiak, in: BZIH, 2–3 (1953), 122–70; 4 (1953), 73–96. ISRAEL: *Israel Government Year Book* (1950–), s.v. *Religious Affairs*; J. Pinkerfeld, *Battei ha-Kenisiyyot be-Ereẓ Yisrael* (1946); Jewish Agency, *Iggeret la-Golah*, 55/56 (1955); 60 (1956); Israel Ministry of Religious Affairs, *Beit ha-Keneset Ma'amarim u-Massot* (1955); S. Piker, *Tefillah ba-Areẓ* (1962); M. Piron, in: *Maḥanayim*, 95 (1964), 118–23. IN THE SOVIET BLOC: S.M. Schwarz, *The Jews in the Soviet Union* (1951); W. Kolacz, *Religion in the Soviet Union* (1961); A.A. Gershuni, *Yahadut be-Rusyah ha-Sovyetit* (1961); E. Wiesel, *The Jews of Silence* (1966); Ben-Ami (A.L. Eliav), *Between Hammer and Sickle* (1967); S. Rothenberg, in: L. Kochan (ed.), *The Jews in Soviet Russia Since 1917* (1970), 159–87 (incl. bibl.). ARCHITECTURE: S. Krauss, *Synagogale Altertuemer* (1922); H. Kohl and C. Watzinger, *Antike Synagogen in Galilaea* (1916); E.L. Sukenik, *Ancient Synagogues in Palestine and Greece* (1934); Goodenough, Symbols, vols. 1–3; M. Avi-Yonah, in: Roth, Art, 157–90; B. Kanael, *Die Kunst der antiken Synagoge* (1961); BRF, 1–3 (1949–60); M.I. Rostovtzeff, *Dura-Europos and Its Art* (1938); H.F. Pearson, *A Guide to the Synagogue of Dura-Europos* (1939). MIDDLE AGES TO THE 18th CENT.: G.K. Lukomskii, *Jewish Art in European Synagogues* (1947); W.S. Seiferth, *Synagogue and Church in the Middle Ages* (1970); M. and K. Piechotka, *Wooden Synagogues* (1959); R. Wischnitzer, *The Architecture of the European Synagogue* (1964); F. Cantera-Burgos, *Sinagogas Españolas* (1955); F. Cohn-Wiener, *Die juedische Kunst* (1929); B. Muenzer, *Die Altneusynagoge in Prag* (1932); A. Grotte, *Deutsche, boehmische und polnische Synagogentypen* (1915); R. Krautheimer, *Mittelalterliche Synagogen* (1927); O. Boecher, *Die Alte Synagoge zu Worms* (1960); A. Kashtan, in: Roth, Art, 253–308; J. Pinkerfeld, *Battei ha-Keneset be-Italyah* (1954); idem, "Battei ha-Keneset ba-I Djerba u-Sevivato" in his: *Bi-Shevilei Ommanut Yehudit* (1957), 60–74. CONTEMPORARY: A. Shecket Korros and J.D. Sarna, *American Synagogue History: A Bibliography and State-of-the Field-Survey* (1988); A. Kampf, *Contemporary Synagogue Art* (1966); A. Wischnitzer, *Synagogue Architecture in the United States* (1955); R. Meier (ed.), *Recent American Synagogue Architecture* (1963); Jamilly, in: Roth, Art, 756–95; P. Thiry, R. Bennet, and H.L. Kamphoefner, *Churches and Temples* (1953); Ben-Uri, in: M. Hacohen (ed.), *Beit ha-Keneset* (1955), 195–242. **ADD. BIBLIOGRAPHY:** B.M. Baader, *Gender, Judaism, and Bourgeois Culture in Germany, 1800–1870* (2006); B. Brooten, *Women Leaders in the Ancient Synagogue* (1982); K. Goldman. *Beyond the Synagogue Gallery: Finding a Place for Women in American Judaism* (2000); S. Grossman and R. Haut (eds.), *Daughters of the King: Women and the Synagogue* (1992); P.E. Hyman and D.D. Moore (eds.), *The Jewish Woman in America* (1998), articles on Reform Judaism (K. Goldman), Conservative Judaism (S.R. Schwartz), Orthodox Judaism (J. Gurock); C. Krinsky. *Synagogues of Europe* (1985); L.I. Levine. *The Ancient Synagogue* (2000); J. Wertheimer, *The American Synagogue* (1987), R. Wischnitzer. *The Architecture of the European Synagogue* (1964).

SYNAGOGUE, THE GREAT (Heb. כְּנֶסֶת הַגְּדוֹלָה, *Keneset ha-Gedolah*).

Chronology

The institution of the Great Synagogue, or perhaps, more correctly, the Great Assembly, belongs to that period of Jewish history which is still virtually a complete blank, namely the Persian period. Hence, very little is known of it with real certainty. In the chain of tradition recorded in *Avot* 1:1 it is said to come after the period of the Prophets, and that *Simeon the Just was of its "remnants." *Avot de-R. Nathan* (ARN¹ 1:2) introduces a stage between the Prophets and the "Men of the Great Synagogue," namely that of *Haggai, *Zechariah, and *Malachi. Apparently, they bridged the transition between these two phases. Ezra (identified with Malachi in *Seder Olam*, etc.) was apparently regarded by the rabbis as leader of the Great Assembly, for in *Leviticus Rabbah* 2:11 "Ezra and his companions" are mentioned, while the parallel text in *Song of Songs Rabbah* (to Song 7:14) speaks only of the Men of the Great Synagogue. The Targum to Song of Songs 7:3 further designates *Ezra, *Zerubbabel, *Jeshua, *Nehemiah, *Mordecai, and Bilshan (cf. Ezra 2:2) as members of this assembly (cf. *Seder Olam Rabbah* and *Zuta*. See Ginzberg, Legends, 6 (1928), 447–9). From these and other sources (e.g., Yoma 69b) it appears that traditionally the idea of the Great Synagogue was linked with the narrative in Nehemiah 8–10, where its earliest beginnings are suggested. On the identification and date of Simeon the Just, who stands at the conclusion of this institution's history, opinion is sharply divided. Some identify him with Simeon I, high priest in 310–291 B.C.E., or 300–270 B.C.E., partly on the basis of rabbinic tradition (cf. Yoma 69a), in which case the Great Synagogue came to an end at the close of the Persian period. As rabbinic chronology telescoped this period of some two centuries into 34 years (SOR 30), the whole institution was thought to have lasted only one generation. Hence the rabbinic phrase "generation of the Men of the Great Synagogue" (Gen. R. 35:2). However, this identification raises serious chronological difficulties, especially as *Yose b. Joezer, who in *Avot* comes only two generations later, is firmly dated to the period of Alcimus who executed him about 160 B.C.E. Accordingly, Simeon the Just has been identified with Simeon II, 219–199 B.C.E., and this opinion (convincingly argued by G.F. Moore) is now generally accepted (see, e.g., V. Tcherikover, *Hellenistic Civilization and the Jews* (1959), 437, no. 1). Thus, the statement in *Avot* 1:4 that Yose b. Joezer and *Yose b. Johanan "received from them," and not "from him" – *Antigonus of Sokho (Avot 1:3) – possibly means that they still received traditions directly from the "remnants of the Great Synagogue." The term "remnants" is suggestive of disintegration, and probably this came about in the wake of the major political upheavals of about 201–198 B.C.E. (cf. Tcherikover, op. cit., 75–82).

Character

As noted, tradition associates the Great Synagogue with events recorded in Nehemiah 8–10. Modern scholarship too takes this as its starting point. However, some scholars (notably Kuenen) regarded the whole institution as legendary, its only source being the narrative in Nehemiah. Others (Krochmal) suggest that Nehemiah's assembly served as a model for future ones. L. Loew put forward a curious theory, that the Great Synagogue was identical with the *synagoge megale* of I Maccabees 14:28ff. in which Simeon the Hasmonean, whom he identified with Simeon the Just, was declared king. However, this view is wholly untenable, not least on chronological grounds. Englander interprets the phrase "Men of the Great Synagogue" as "leaders of the Community of Greatness" (*Keneset ha-Gedolah*), i.e., heads of the Jewish community. However, certain sources (e.g., Targ. Song 7:3, and the phrase "remnants of the Great Synagogue") suggest that the members of the Assembly constituted it, and were not merely a part of it. Finally, some (e.g., Finkelstein) regard the *Keneset ha-Gedolah* as a high court, the precursor of the *Sanhedrin ha-Gadol*; but rabbinic evidence (see below) suggests rather "a great legislative and administrative council rather than… a tribunal" (see Baron, Social[2], 1 (1952), 368). What emerges clearly, thus far, is that this institution, whatever it was, had its origins in the organizational framework set up in Ezra 's time. These first-generation developments (cf. Ezra 10: 14–17; et al.) were perpetuated probably in the form of a loosely knit representative body meeting at (irregular?) intervals to pass major enactments.

Enactments

A brief survey of the legislative achievements of the "Men of the Great Synagogue" (or rather those attributed to them) may cast further light on the character of the institution. Traditionally they introduced the *Shemoneh Esreh* (Meg. 17b; et al.), and further "instituted for Israel the *benedictions and prayers as well as the benedictions for **Kiddush* and **Havdalah*" (Ber. 33a). In fact, the traditional view is that the entire liturgy was given a definite form during this period. They established the festival of Purim (Meg. 2a), and they held 24 fasts to pray that *soferim* ("scribes") should not become wealthy, thus assuring a plentiful supply of *sifrei Torah, tefillin* and *mezuzot* for all time (Pes. 50b). They are said to have introduced the classification of the Oral Law into three fields of study, that of Midrash (in the broadest sense of the word), *halakhot*, and *aggadot* (TJ, Shek. 5:1, 48c). They were also active in the field of masoretic studies (Tanḥ. Shemot 17, for *Tikkun Soferim*) and canonization, and to them is attributed the inclusion in the canon of the Books of Ezekiel, Daniel, Esther, and the Twelve Minor Prophets (BB 15a, where "wrote" probably means included in the canon). Achievements such as the formulation of the liturgy, etc., are suggestive of a lengthy progressive development, stretched over a considerable period of time. Furthermore, decisions of such gravity as the canonization of biblical books, etc., could only have been taken by a body of supreme religious authority. These were not the rulings of small local synods (such as are mentioned by Hecateus of Abdera, c. 300 B.C.E.; Reinach, Textes, 17f.), but of a great all-embracing council justly called the "Great Assembly" (but see Yoma 69b, for the rabbinic interpretation of the phrase). There was probably no permanent membership to this council (hence "Men of the Great Synagogue," rather than the "Great Synagogue" itself), nor even a fixed number of participants at its meetings (Zeitlin's view). Thus while R. Johanan taught that "120 elders, including some prophets" instituted the *Shemoneh Esreh* (Meg. 17b), in TJ, Megillah 1:7, 70d, he states that 85 elders, among them about 30 prophets, established the feast of Purim (but see L. Ginzberg, *Perushim ve-Ḥiddushim ba-Yerushalmi*, 1 (1941), 327–30 for harmonistic emendations, following Krochmal). Perhaps out of this body evolved the **gerousia*, which is known to have existed in the time of Simeon (II) the Just (Jos., Ant., 12:142) and over which he probably presided (Tcherikover, op. cit. 81), and subsequent administrative bodies such as the Hasmonean *ḥever*. It probably had combined judicial and administrative authority, and indeed rabbinic tradition (Ḥag. 2:2) ascribes the division of functions to the post-Simeon period of the *zugot* ("pairs").

BIBLIOGRAPHY: L. Loew, *Gesammelte Schriften*, 1 (1889), 399–449; M. Bloch, *Sha'arei Torat ha-Takkanot*, 1 (1879), 107–273; S. Krauss, in: JQR, 10 (1897/98), 347–77; W. Bacher, in: EJ, s.v. *Synagogue, the Great*; H. Englander, in: *Hebrew Union College Jubilee Volume* (1925), 145–69; G. F. Moore, Judaism, 3 (1930), 7–11; L. Finkelstein, in: JBL, 59 (1940), 455–69; idem, *Ha-Perushim ve-Anshei Keneset ha-Gedolah* (1950); E. Bickerman, in: RB, 55 (1948), 397–402; C. Tchernowitz, *Toledot ha-Halakhah*, 3 (1943), 60–81; Baron, Social2, 1 (1952), 367, n. 35; H. Mantel, in: HTR, 60 (1967), 69–91.

[Daniel Sperber]

SYNAGOGUE COUNCIL OF AMERICA, THE, organization formally founded in 1926 on the basis of a suggestion made in 1924 by Rabbi Abram Simon, then president of the Central Conference of American rabbis, that there should be cooperation among the religious elements of American Jewry. In January 1925, Simon offered a resolution at the Union of American Hebrew Congregations calling for a meeting of congregational and rabbinical bodies to consider questions they had in common. Such a meeting was held in June 1925, and as a result the Synagogue Council of America was formed. A constitution was adopted in 1926 and Simon was elected chairman (a title later changed to president). The six organizations making up the Synagogue Council were the Central Conference of American Rabbis, the Rabbinical Assembly, and the Rabbinical Council, representing respectively the Reform, Conservative, and Orthodox rabbinates; and the Union of American Hebrew Congregations (Reform), United Synagogue of America (Conservative), and the Union of Orthodox Jewish Congregations, representing the congregational bodies.

The original declaration of principles provided that the Synagogue Council speak with a united voice in furthering their common religious interests without in any way interfering with the autonomy of any of its constituents. The first project of the Synagogue Council was an exhibit, "Jewish Life in America," at the Sesquicentennial Exposition in Philadelphia. The Synagogue Council at first tried to grapple with religious problems, but the diversity of views prevented any constructive work. From the 1960s onward the Synagogue Council was active almost exclusively in representing the religious Jewish community to the government and Christian religious bodies. It was one of three sponsors of the National Conference on Religion and Race held in January 1963 in Chicago, a participant in the 1960 White House Conference on Children and Youth and in the 1961 White House Conference on Aging, and a sponsor, with the National Council of Churches and the National Conference of Catholic Bishops, of the Interreligious Conference on the Role of Conscience held in May 1967. It also spoke out on social and international issues, voicing the Jewish viewpoint. It also held convocations on matters of concern to the Jewish religious community. As the disappointment in ecumenical dialogue set in, particularly with mainstream Protestant Churches, in the aftermath of the Six-Day War and the perception that the Churches were silent in Israel's hour of need, there was a de-emphasis of the importance of the Synagogue Council and of its actual accomplishments. Other organizations, more narrow in focus and less cumbersome to maneuver, took up the slack and in the aftermath of Vatican II the Catholic-Jewish dialogue intensified but other institutions led the way.

There was always considerable controversy within the Orthodox community as to participation with non-Orthodox rabbis and the issue of the Orthodox granting legitimacy to what some considered non-Orthodox "non-rabbis." Rabbi Soloveitchik had permitted participation – or more accurately, had not forbidden participation – of the rabbis he ordained. When he left public life, even before his death the pressures on the Orthodox participants intensified and many felt more comfortable participating in avowedly secular organizations where similar work was undertaken.

The presidency of the Synagogue Council rotated consecutively among a Reform, Conservative, and Orthodox rabbi. Its role withered, as did its function and even the organization itself. The Council ceased to exist in 1994.

[Sidney L. Regner]

SYNGALOWSKI, ARON (1890–1956), a leader of *ORT. Born in a village near Baranovichi, Belorussia, at the age of 16 he joined the Jewish Socialist territorialist movement, in which he became known as a brilliant orator under the name "Aron Czenstochover." Shortly before World War I he moved to Germany. In 1920, David *Lvovich, a childhood friend, together with Leon *Bramson, arrived in Berlin representing Russian ORT. From that time onward Syngalowski devoted himself to the growth and development of that organization. In 1921, when the World ORT Union was organized in Berlin, he became vice chairman of the executive committee, and after Bramson's death, in 1941, he became chairman of the executive committee. Credit for the reconstruction of the ORT network after World War II and the establishment of its activities in Israel in 1948 is due largely to Syngalowski. He died in Paris and was buried in Geneva. The ORT school in Tel Aviv was named after him.

ADD. BIBLIOGRAPHY: *In Memoriam: En Souvenir du Dr Aron Syngalowski* (1976).

[Vladimir Seev Halperin]

SYNODS, conventions of rabbis, with or without the participation of laymen, held to deliberate and adopt **takkanot* (regulations) and decide on ways and methods of exerting social and moral leadership. The synods originated from, and were activated by, the ideal of reference to a central halakhic authority and a unifying national leadership. The need was felt in the context of the Jewish dispersion and the breakup of the established central institutions, coupled with the diminishing influence of the *geonim* and exilarchs which had become manifestly evident by the second half of the 11th century.

The communities of northern France were the first to inaugurate a long series of synods, which resorted to the sanction of the *ḥerem* ("ban"). The dates on which these synods were held and the identity of their initiators cannot be clearly established because of the tendency to ascribe synodal activity to a single scholar; a whole series of synodal resolutions of a later period were attributed to *Gershom b. Judah and were known as the "*Ḥerem* of R. Gershom." Synods were often held at fairs, like those of Champagne. Like the later fairs in Poland and Lithuania, they were a convenient place to hold conventions.

The first full-fledged Ashkenazi synod should probably be dated around 1150. It was convened at *Troyes by Jacob b. Meir (*Tam) and his brother *Samuel b. Meir (Rashbam). Among questions of Jewish law discussed were those relating to *informers and litigation by Jews in non-Jewish courts. The phrasing of the *takkanot* shows that by "informers" the rabbis also understood ideological opponents who were ready to turn for support to Christian rulers. Another synod took place also at Troyes after 1160. Representatives attended from the communities of the Kingdom of France, and from Normandy and Poitiers. The subject discussed was the dowry of a wife who died within the first year of marriage. The French synods were followed by meetings in the three Rhine cities of Speyer, Worms, and Mainz (Heb. abbr. שו"ם * "Shum"). In 1196 David b. Kalonymus presided over a synod at one of these cities. It dealt with *ḥaliẓah* and other subjects. Some time later an assembly of rabbis adopted resolutions on 20 major legal, moral, and communal matters. In 1220 a gathering at Mainz reaffirmed some of the decisions of the previous synod and added a number of new items. Three years later another meeting at Speyer reenacted the regulations of the two previous conventions. No further synods are known to have taken place until one met at Mainz (c. 1250). Some time later *Meir b. Baruch of Rothenburg, after consulting Jedidiah of Speyer by letter, called a meeting of community representatives at Nuremberg to regulate the problem of wives who deserted their husbands, the so-called "intractable wife" (*moredet*).

In the 14th century the German *Ḥayyim b. Isaac "Or Zaru'a," convened an assembly to rule on the question of offering legal advice to a litigant. In July 1381, at a council in Mainz attended by the local rabbi Moses b. Jekuthiel and other prominent scholars, *ḥaliẓah* was the main topic discussed. Illustrative of the dangers under which synods then convened is the synod of 1386 held in Weissefels, Saxony, consisting of both rabbis and laymen who were to deliberate on religious matters. The travelers had obtained safe-conduct passes from the Saxon princes. Nevertheless a party of German robber-nobles plundered them of their possessions, and held them until a substantial ransom was paid. A complaint to the princes who had issued the safe-conduct brought no redress since all agreed that "the enemies of Christ" deserved no better treatment. Around 1400 a meeting at Erfurt forbade a *Kohen* to pass the city and cemetery at funerals until the dead had been carried through those gates. In 1530 an assembly at Augsburg, convened by *Josel of Rosheim, passed a resolution against usury, besides deliberating many other pressing issues. Twelve years later a synod at Worms, attended by delegates from Frankfurt, Landau, and other towns, renewed the old prohibition on rabbinical bans issued against nonresidents. Not until the synod in Frankfurt in 1603 were questions of Jewish law again discussed. Many significant *takkanot* were enacted there. An investigation by the government of the contents of these ordinances caused serious anxiety among the Jews who had been accused of high treason.

In southern Europe probably the earliest recorded synod took place in 1238 on the island of Crete (Candia). A rabbi Baruch b. Isaac from northern Europe, who visited the Jewish community there on his way to the Holy Land, was amazed at the laxity of religious and moral behavior among the local Jews; he was instrumental in having some 15 prominent Jews of the island adopt a series of ten ordinances to strengthen piety and adapt European *takkanot* to local needs. In 1289 *Hillel b. Samuel of Verona, a philosopher, attempted a very ambitious but abortive Jewish synod to bolster the Maimonidean position on religious issues (see Maimonidean *Controversy). A committee elected two years earlier at a convention in Bologna of delegates from the Papal States, Tuscany, Padua, and Ferrara, adopted in 1418 a number of sumptuary regulations. Several other meetings dealt with general communal problems. The synod at Ferrara in 1554 adopted many significant resolutions, among them a regulation on Hebrew book printing, all of which remained in force until the 18th century.

The French *Sanhedrin of 1807, though it concerned itself with questions of faith, was convened by the secular powers, not by the Jews themselves, and could not therefore exercise any considerable influence on the convictions of the Jewish people. Synods called in the 19th century were animated by the spirit of religious *Reform, such as the Reform rabbinical *conferences in Germany first held in Wiesbaden in 1837. They laid the foundations of liberal thinking on Jewish beliefs and practices.

These synods failed in their purpose of acting as central religious authorities. Each of the Reform groups followed its own course; the Orthodox were hostile to the whole procedure.

BIBLIOGRAPHY: Finkelstein, Middle Ages, index; J. Parkes, *Jew in the Medieval Community* (1938), 246–7; D. Philipson, *Reform Movement in Judaism* (1907), index; N. Bentwich, *Solomon Schechter* (1938), index; Baron, Community, 3 (1942), index s.v. *Councils*; Graetz, Hist, 6 (1967), index s.v. *Rabbinical Synods*; J. Petuchowski, *Prayerbook Reform in Europe* (1968), index; H.H. Ben-Sasson (ed.), *Toledot Am Yisrael*, 3 vols. (1969–70), index.

[Isaac Levitats]

SYRACUSE, city in S.E. Sicily. Inscriptions and other archaeological evidence attest the presence of Jews in Syracuse from Roman times. Toward the middle of the fifth century, the Vandals destroyed the synagogue there, and in 655 the Jews asked the Byzantine authorities for permission to rebuild it. In the 12th century, the Jews of Syracuse received through their rabbi Anatoli b. Joseph a reply by *Maimonides to a legal question. The community was second in importance in Sicily after *Palermo. Two documents from the end of the 14th and beginning of the 15th centuries suggest that the number of Jews in Syracuse exceeded 5,600. The community attained its most prosperous period from the end of the 13th to the end of the 14th centuries, under the rule of the house of Aragon. The administration of the community, whose first regulations dating from 1363 have been preserved, was conducted by 12 *maggiorenti* and 12 *prothi* who had jurisdiction over the religious life of the community and its revenues. The *procuratores et nuncii* represented the community before the government. When in 1395 King Martin I established the office of judge-general for the Jews *(Dienchelele), a Jew of Syracuse, Joseph *Abenafia, was appointed to this office: on his death he was succeeded by Rais of Syracuse.

King Frederick III intervened in favor of the Jews of Syracuse who were harassed by the ecclesiastical authorities in 1375, and the regulations on their behalf were confirmed by King Marlin in 1392. The Jews obtained further privileges in 1399, when they were exempted from the obligation of supplying wax to the court and flags for the castles. When in 1455 various Jews from Syracuse made a clandestine attempt to immigrate to Ereẓ Israel, they were arrested. The community succeeded, however, in obtaining permission for Jews to emigrate in small groups. Among the scholars who lived in Syracuse was Isaac b. Solomon *Alḥadib, astronomer and translator, and Shalom b. Solomon Yerushalmi, for whom several manuscripts were copied. After the edict of expulsion of the Jews from Spanish domains was issued in 1492 it is estimated that about 5,000 Jews left Syracuse. They are said to have represented 40% of the city's population. The "Purim of Syracuse", still observed by some Sephardi Jewish families, probably refers not to Syracuse but to Saragossa in Spain. A number of tombstones dating from the Middle Ages with Hebrew inscriptions have recently been discovered in Syracuse, and the findings published.

BIBLIOGRAPHY: Milano, Bibliotheca, index; Milano, Italia, index; Roth, Italy, index; Orsi, in: *Roemische Quartalschrift*, 14 (1900), 194–7; Simonsen, in: REJ, 59 (1910), 90–95; S. Simonsohn, in: *Archivio storico siracusano*, 9 (1963), 8–20; idem, in: *Sefer Zikkaron le-Izhak Ben-Zvi…* (1964), 273–82; G. De' Giovanni, *L'ebraismo della Sicilia…* (Palermo, 1748); B. and G. Lagumina, *Codice diplomatico dei giudei di Sicilia*, 3 vols. (1884–1909), passim; C. Roth, *Gleanings* (1967), 62–80; Frey, Corpus, 1 (1936), nos. 651–3a.

[Sergio Joseph Sierra]

SYRACUSE, industrial and transportation center in central New York State. The city's Jewish population in 1969 was approximately 13,000 out of a total of 563,000. (For figures for the 2000s, see below.) The first Jew known to have settled in Syracuse was Hesel Rosenbach, who arrived in 1824. Following the completion of the Erie Canal a year later, additional Jews were attracted to the city, and in 1839 a group of German-Jewish immigrants from New York City formed Congregation Keneseth Sholom, whose first rabbi was Abraham Gunzenheimer. More Jews came to settle in the 1840s and a second congregation, consisting of Polish and English Jews, erected a synagogue in 1854, when 184 Jewish families were recorded living in Syracuse. In 1864 a split between Orthodox and Reform factions at Keneseth Sholom led to the formation of a third synagogue, Adath Jeshurun. A local YMHA was organized in 1861 and a chapter of B'nai B'rith in 1867. By then some Jews had already achieved positions of economic importance. Marcus Cone was elected a director of the Merchants Bank when it was founded in 1850, and Joseph Falker was named second vice president of the Syracuse Savings Bank in 1860. A special Jewish company under the command of Captain Solomon Light was formed during the Civil War and served with the 149th Onondoga Regiment from 1862 to 1865.

A large influx of Lithuanian and Polish Jews in the years after 1870 swelled the Jewish population of Syracuse to five or six thousand by 1900. The new immigrants formed a number of charitable organizations such as a burial society, a wayfarers' inn, and a Jewish Ladies Aid Society, all of which were combined into a United Jewish Charities in 1891. The first local Zionist group, the Zion Society, was organized in 1896 and a Hebrew Free School, largely serving the Orthodox community, was established in 1897. The leader of Congregation Adath Jeshurun in the 1890s was Joseph H. *Hertz, later to become Chief Rabbi of Great Britain. During these years Jews began to play an increasingly prominent role in local economic and political life; by the end of the 19th century Sol *Rosenblum & Sons owned a large department store; Gates Thalheimer had one of the largest individually owned wholesale grocery businesses in the state; Moses Oberdorfer was in the process of building the Oberdorfer Foundries; and Danziger Brothers was operating a clothing factory employing over a thousand hands. Jacob Levi was elected a city councilman for four terms starting from 1870 and George Freeman for eight terms from 1880. Joseph Bondy was county supervisor from 1885 to 1890 and was later elected to the New York State Assembly. Louis *Marshall, whose father was an early settler in Syracuse, practiced law there until 1894.

Beginning with the 1900s, the early settlers began moving eastward away from the old Jewish neighborhood. The older synagogues followed them and a number of new ones were later built in the suburbs, such as Beth Israel (1962) and the Suburban Jewish Center of North Syracuse (1954). In 1968 a Jewish community center, which grew out of the original YMHA, had a membership of 5,000 and served the entire Jewish community. Fundraising was undertaken by the Syracuse Jewish Federation, whose Jewish Family Service Bureau helped settle some 200 refugee families from Europe in the city in the years before World War II.

Wage-earners in the Jewish community in 1968 were heavily concentrated in the professions. A study in 1966 showed that over 15% of Syracuse's lawyers and 20% of its doctors were Jewish. Many Jews worked as engineers and scientists in Syracuse's industrial plants. Many others were connected with the faculties of Syracuse University and the Upstate Medical College, both of which also had a high percentage of Jews in their student bodies. Jews continued to be active in local civic life as well.

In early 21st century the Jewish population numbered approximately 9,000.

BIBLIOGRAPHY: Rosenstock, in: AJHSP, 54 (1964), 183–97; Provol, in: AJA, 16 (1964), 22–40; B.G. Rudolph, *From a Minyan to a Community: A History of the Jews of Syracuse* (1970).

[Bernard G. Rudolph]

SYRIA, state in southwest Asia. Although constantly subject to changes, the country's boundaries were primarily: Ereẓ Israel to the south, Asia Minor (Turkey) to the north, Mesopotamia to the east, and the Mediterranean to the west.

Biblical and Second Temple Period

For its earlier history see *Aram; *Aram-Damascus. During the late biblical era the political history of Syria is somewhat similar to that of Ereẓ Israel, as both territories were either subject to the great powers of the east (e.g., Egypt, Assyria, Babylonia) or disputed by two or more prominent empires. (Under subsequent Roman rule the two districts were often considered one entity, with jurisdiction over the area in the hands of the Syrian governor). During the Hellenistic period Syria served as the administrative center of the *Seleucid Empire, with *Antioch as the capital. With the collapse of that empire the country passed briefly into the hands of the Armenians and was eventually conquered by *Pompey (64 B.C.E.). The defense of Syria became strategically vital to the Roman Empire because it was the eastern outpost bordering on the perennial enemy, in the form of the Parthian and subsequently the Sassanid empires. In 616, Syria was briefly controlled by the Persians under Chosroes II and was recaptured by the Byzantines only to fall to the Muslims in 636.

Dating back to biblical times, the Jewish community in Syria developed due to the proximity of the Jewish center in Palestine. Thus, according to Josephus, Ezra was commanded by the Persian Xerxes to appoint judges among the Jews "to hold court in all of Syria and *Phoenicia" (Ant. 11:129). During the Second Temple period, the Jewish community apparently thrived, and even Roman governors of Syria were known to fall under the influence of the Jewish multitudes (cf. Philo, *Legatio ad Gaium* 355–367). Similarly, Josephus, in describing the tribulations of the Jews of Antioch, begins by stressing that "the Jewish race, densely interspersed among the native populations of every portion of the world, is particularly numerous in Syria, where intermingling is due to the proximity of the two countries. It was at Antioch that they especially congregated, possibly owing to the greatness of that city, but mainly because the successors of King Antiochus [Epiphanes, 175–164 B.C.E.] had enabled them to live there in security" (Wars 7:43). These Jews therefore flourished and were in a position to send costly offerings to the Temple at Jerusalem. The community was granted citizen rights equal to those of the Greeks (*ibid.*; cf. Apion 2:39, where these rights were granted by the founder of the city, Seleucus I Nicator), and this probably caused considerable envy of the Jews, which erupted into violence upon the declaration in Palestine of the great war against Rome (66 C.E.). Jewish influence was also felt in *Damascus, where a majority of the female Greek population had strong leanings toward Judaism. This, however, did not prevent the Greeks of that city from slaughtering the entire Jewish population of 10,500 with the outbreak of the Jewish-Roman War (Wars 2:561).

Both the proximity to Ereẓ Israel and the great number of Syrian Jews subsequently convinced the rabbis to consider the area similar to Palestine in certain respects, and thus the *halakhot* "pertaining to the land" (מִצְוֹות הַתְּלוּיוֹת בָּאָרֶץ) were often applied to Syria. The Mishnah states that: "He who buys land in Syria is as one who buys in the outskirts of Jerusalem" (Hal. 4:11); "If Israelites leased a field from gentiles in Syria, R. Eliezer declares their produce liable to tithes and subject to the Sabbatical laws, but R. Gamaliel declares it exempt" (*ibid.* 4:7). Numerous tannaitic traditions discuss the particular halakhic status of Syria (cf. Tosef., Kelim BK 1:5, Ter. 2:9–13; Av. Zar. 2:8), and it appears that the rabbis differentiated between certain districts in Syria (Tosef. Peah 4:6). Nevertheless, the Jews of Syria probably considered themselves part of the Diaspora, and this would explain not only financial support of the Palestinian rabbis, but also the fact that a number of Syrian Jews were brought to *Bet Shearim for burial.

[Isaiah Gafni]

From the Arab Conquest

As far as can be deduced from the writings of Arab historians the Jews of Syria did not occupy a position of prominence at the time of the conquest of the country by the Arabs during the 630s. There is, however, no doubt that they preferred the conquerors, as did most of the population, to the Byzantine rulers. In the history of the conquest related by the Arab historians the Jews are occasionally mentioned among the groups of the population who negotiated with the Arabs; they were included in the surrender treaty of *Damascus in 635. Later, when the inhabitants of *Tripoli fled to Byzantium, the Arabs placed a Jewish garrison in this important coastal town. With the Arab conquest the situation of the Jews was improved in comparison to the former servitude and religious coercion. The Umayyad dynasty, which chose Damascus as the capital of the Muslim empire, treated non-Muslims with tolerance. As the number of Christians in Syria was far greater than that of the Jews, the Arab authors principally mention the Christian officials and counselors of the first *Umayyads; there were, however, several Jews in the royal court of Muʿāwiya. Although the last Umayyads, the descendants of Marwān, emphasized the Muslim character of the kingdom, they did not harass the Jews. With the advent of the *Abbasids (750) there was a decisive change in the attitude of the Muslim kingdom toward Jews and Christians – a situation which was acutely felt in Syria. The burden of the taxes was increased and growing pressure was exerted on non-Muslim groups to convert to *Islam. During this period the Muslim authorities began

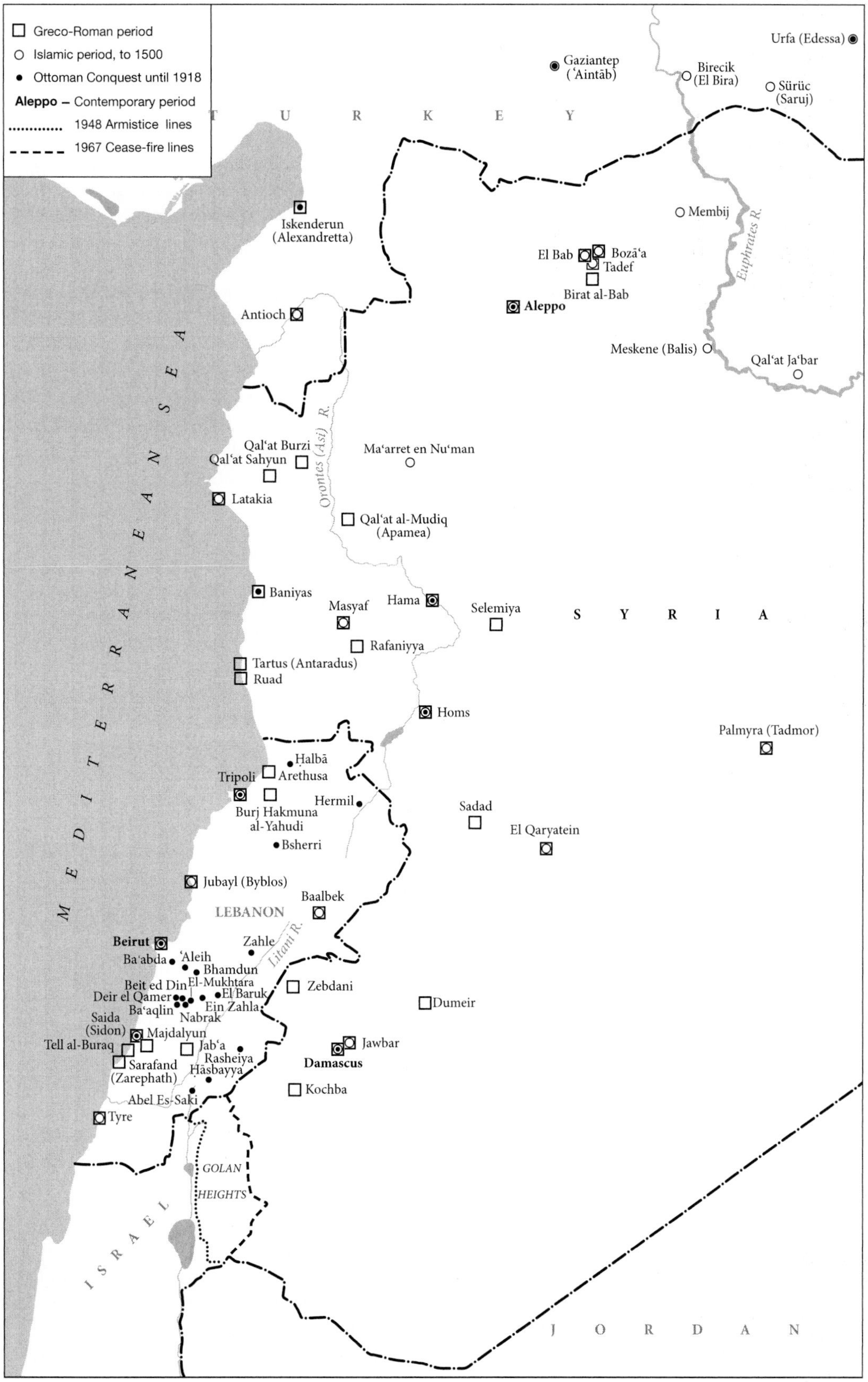

Major Jewish communities in Syria.

to issue decrees against Jews and Christians, e.g., separation from Muslims by wearing distinctive signs on their clothing (see Covenant of *Omar).

The disintegration of the Abbasid caliphate began in the early ninth century. For a period of four centuries Syria became the scene of a struggle between various dynasties and the Jews, like the remainder of the population, suffered greatly. The local rulers and the governors of the caliphs who often regained control over Syria were incapable, for example, of preventing the invasion of the Karmatian hordes from Bahrain or of the Byzantines who penetrated into the country on several occasions and devastated it. In spite of this the tenth century was a period of numerical growth and economic progress for the Jewish population of Syria. The ruin which at the time befell *Iraq as a result of the political chaos prompted many of its Jews to immigrate to other countries, and a considerable number settled in Syria. The emigrants retained their identity and founded their own synagogues in the towns where their numbers were considerable. The Jews then began to play an important role in commerce and banking, even though most of them were craftsmen. The tenth-century Arab geographer al-Maqdisī wrote in his work that "in this land, most of the bankers, dyers, and tanners are Jews."

Immediately after their conquest of Egypt (969) the *Fatimids sent their armies to Syria, which they also succeeded in annexing. Their control over Syria, however, was unstable and the northern regions detached themselves from their authority after a short while. This Shiʿite dynasty, which sought to depose the orthodox caliphs of the Abbasid dynasty, displayed tolerance toward the members of other faiths either because this policy was in accordance with their religious outlook or under the force of circumstances. The period of Fatimid rule over southern Syria was a prosperous one for the Jewish communities. The first vizier of the Fatimids, Jacob *Ibn Killis, a Jew who converted to Islam but remained loyal to his former coreligionists, appointed a Jew, Manasseh b. Abraham al-*Qazzāz, to head the administration of Syria. He utilized his powers on behalf of the Jews and granted many of them positions in government. His son Aṣiya was also a high ranking official in the government. At the beginning of the 11th century the attitude toward the Jews changed for a time when the caliph al-Ḥākim issued various decrees against non-Muslims. In several towns synagogues were destroyed or converted into mosques. After a few years, however, al-Ḥākim reconsidered these moves and the synagogues were returned to the Jews or new ones were constructed. The leading communities in Syria at the time existed in Damascus, *Aleppo, and *Tyre; there were also smaller communities in *Tripoli, *Jubayl, Baalbek, Baniyas, Bazāʿa, and others. The Jews of Syria maintained regular contact with the Palestine academy and were guided by its leaders in all religious affairs. The communities of Syria themselves produced eminent scholars during the 11th century, among them R. *Baruch b. Isaac, who was rabbi in Aleppo during the second half of the century and wrote commentaries on the *Gemara*, as well as other intellectuals who wrote florid poems in Hebrew.

During the 1070s the *Seljuk armies invaded and conquered Syria, with the exception of the coastal strip to the south of *Tripoli. The Seljuk conquest brought disaster to the whole of Syria and Ereẓ Israel and the academy was consequently transferred from *Jerusalem to Tyre and then during the crusader invasion to Ḥadrak near *Damascus, and later to Damascus itself. At the close of the century the crusaders arrived in Syria and conquered the coastal strip. Many Jews fled to towns in the interior of Syria, which remained under Muslim domination. *Benjamin of Tudela, the 12th-century traveler, provides statistics on the number of the Jewish inhabitants in the towns of Syria, many of whom he states were dyers. The Jews of *Antioch and Tyre also engaged in the manufacture of glass, and other sources confirm that many of the Jews of Tyre earned their livelihood in this industry. Jews in Tyre were also engaged in international commerce. The spiritual and religious life of the Jews of Syria was concentrated around the academy, which Solomon, son of the *Gaon* *Elijah ha-Kohen, had transferred to Damascus. The academy continued to exist for several generations and its leaders were known as **geonim*. During the 1140s it was headed by *Abraham b. Mazhir and then by his son *Ezra, whom Benjamin of Tudela met. These heads of academies were the final authority in all matters pertaining to religious life, and the descendants of the Babylonian *exilarchs, who were referred to by the title of *nasi*, also played a role in the leadership of the Jewish population.

During the 1170s Sultan Ṣalāḥ-al-Dīn (referred to as *Saladin by the Christians) succeeded in uniting *Egypt and Muslim Syria under his domination and was thus able to conquer considerable territory from the crusaders. Saladin and his successors, who belonged to the Kurdish *Ayyubid dynasty, were not inclined to persecute non-Muslims and permitted Jews to return to Jerusalem in 1187 after they had conquered the city from the crusaders. Indeed the situation of the Jews improved during this period as a result of the lenient attitude of the Ayyubids and the economic prosperity of the state, owing to the close commercial ties with European countries, notably the Italian commercial colonies of the coastal towns. The Hebrew poet Judah *Al-Ḥarizi, who visited Syria in the late 1210s, mentions a lengthy list of physicians and government officials in the communities of Damascus and *Aleppo.

In 1260 Syria was invaded by the *Mongols, led by Hulagu Khan. They carried out massacres in several towns, but it appears that Jews, like Christians, suffered less than Muslims. In Arab historians' reports of the conquest it is indicated that the great synagogue in the town of Aleppo was one of the refuges which remained untouched by the Mongols and that all the Jews who had escaped to this place were saved. There was no bloodshed in Damascus since the town surrendered to the Mongols. The two largest Jewish communities in Syria thus remained unharmed. The Mongols also advanced into Ereẓ Israel but were defeated at Ayn Jalut (near Ein-Harod) by the Mamluk army coming from Egypt and retreated from Syria (1260). From then until the beginning of the 16th century the *Mamluk sultans ruled Syria. The Mamluks were inclined to accede to the requests of the Muslim theologians and frequently issued decrees against the non-Muslim communities, such as those pertaining to clothing and the dismissal of Jewish (and Christian) officials from government service (1301). The Mamluks, however, were unable to administer their affairs without the assistance of experienced officials and these were therefore restored to their positions after a short while. Yet these decrees intensified conversion to Islam within the non-Muslim intellectual classes.

After the Mamluks conquered *Acre (1291) and the other coastal towns which had remained in the hands of the Crusaders, they destroyed them so that they would not provide a foothold in the event of further invasions from the sea. The ancient communities in these towns, such as the large community of Tyre, thus disappeared. The Jews probably settled in Damascus and Aleppo, where from that time the majority of the Jewish population of Syria resided. The deputy of the **nagid* of Cairo, whose status was recognized by the Muslim authorities, stood at the head of the Jewish community in Syria, as did the *nesi'im* of the House of David, who were known as *exilarchs. On the occasion of the controversy between the kabbalists of Acre and R. David Shimoni during the 1280s, the exilarch of Damascus, R. Jesse b. Hezekiah, supported the Maimonidean faction, and in 1286 he issued a *ḥerem* (ban) against *Maimonides' opponents.

During the second half of the 14th century there were frequent changes in the leadership of the Mamluk State and certain rulers once more found it necessary to resort to decrees against the non-Muslim communities in order to mollify their subjects; in 1354 the decrees of 1301 (see above) were reintroduced in Syria. One of the officials, the Karaite Moses b. Samuel of Damascus, later expressed his experiences in Hebrew poems, particularly on how he went on a pilgrimage to Mecca in the retinue of a Mamluk minister. Non-Muslim officials were returned to their positions after a short while, but Muslim fanatics occasionally induced the authorities to renew the discriminatory decrees and thus caused Jews (and Christians) much suffering.

At the close of 1400 the Mongolian leader, Timur Lank (Tamerlane), invaded Syria with a powerful army, captured Aleppo, massacring its people, and then plundered Hama and Damascus. Before he returned to Central Asia his troops burned Damascus, while many craftsmen were taken captive and exiled to Samarkand. Arabic, Latin, and Hebrew sources indicate that the fate of the Jews was no different from that of the other inhabitants; many of them were killed or exiled. The Jewish population recovered very slowly from these misfortunes. During the 15th century trade in the region prospered once more and European merchants returned to Syria to buy spices and other goods from the Far East. Most Syrian Jews were craftsmen and small merchants, a certain number of whom were living in poverty. Extant information on the size of the Jewish community, which was recorded by Jewish travelers of the late 15th century, confirms its impoverishment during the Mamluk period. According to the writings of R. Joseph de Montagnana, R. Meshullam of Volterra, R. Obadiah of Bertinoro, and an anonymous traveler from Italy, there were about 400–500 families in Damascus (apart from *Karaites and Samaritans). The above-mentioned travelers left no data on other communities, with the exception of R. Obadiah of Bertinoro, who points out that there were 100 families in Tripoli. Thus, the Jewish population of Syria consisted of not more than 1,200 families, or approximately 7,000 persons.

In 1492, Jews were expelled from Spain and many went to countries like *Italy and *Turkey before settling in Syria and bringing about a decisive change in the composition and nature of the Jewish community. Once the number of Spanish Jews in the Syrian towns increased, various problems related to the organization of the communities appeared and the process of their assimilation with the native-born Arabized Jews, the *Mustarabs, raised considerable difficulties. The language spoken by the expellees, their way of life, habits, and outlook were different from the accepted Jewish way of life of Middle Eastern countries. In the large towns – where they resided in greater numbers – the Spanish Jews established their own communities, with independent synagogues, cemeteries, and *battei din*. The wide erudition of their rabbis and the relatively large number of scholars among the Spanish Jews helped them to become leaders of Syrian Jewry throughout the eastern part of the Mediterranean.

A new and significant era in the history of Syria started in 1516 with the defeat of the Mamluks by the Ottoman Turks, who had earlier, in 1453, captured Constantinople and put an end to the Byzantine empire. The 400 years of Ottoman rule (until 1917) greatly contributed to shaping politics, administration, economy, and society in the Syrian lands (including Lebanon and Palestine–Ereẓ Israel), particularly during the 19th century.

One of the largest Muslim empires in history, the Ottoman Sultanate, now controlled major Islamic, Christian, and Jewish centers – Jerusalem, Bethlehem, Damascus – as well as *Mecca, *Medina, and Constantinople-*Istanbul. The majority Muslim-Arabic speaking population and religious leaders developed, by and large, quasi-allegiance to the sultan, who was represented by Ottoman pashas, governors of several provinces – *eyalets* or *vilayets* of Aleppo, Damascus, Sidon, Acre, and *Beirut. These governors, however, controlled only the major cities and their rural neighborhoods, but were periodically challenged by local forces. In the countryside, notably the mountain regions, feudal lords, tribal chiefs, and large families assumed autonomous rule, collected taxes for the sultan and provided tolerable security. Only from the 1830s – under the brief Egyptian rule (1832–40) and the reformed Ottoman administration – was the country gradually put under central control. The growing security facilitated the expansion of foreign activities, diplomatic, economic, and educational, notably by Russia, France, and Great Britain as well as by various missionary organizations. Their main object was the Christian communities in the Syrian lands, some half a million (out of the total population of a million and a half, mostly Sunni Muslims, and small communities of Alawis, Druze, and Jews – some 30,000 by the mid-19th century). Russia supported the (Greek) Orthodox Arabic-speaking Christians – the largest Christian community; France helped the Catholics, mainly the Maronites on Mount Lebanon; while Great Britain backed the newly established Protestant community as well as the Druze in Lebanon and Syria and the Jews in Palestine.

European economic activities that grew significantly during the 19th century benefited mostly Christians (and some wealthy Muslim and Jewish merchants) but damaged the livelihood of Muslim artisans and traders, members of the traditional middle classes. They and members of the lower classes were also badly affected by the newly introduced Ottoman reforms of the Tanzimat in 1839, 1856, and 1876, namely, regular taxation, mandatory recruitment to the army as well as some reduction in the role of Islam and equal status granted to non-Muslims, particularly Christians. All these developments – European intervention, the Tanzimat reforms and periodically provocative Christian behavior – led to Muslim-Christian tension and violence, particularly in Aleppo in 1850 and in Damascus in 1860. In Damascus thousands of Christians were massacred by Muslims, assisted actively by Druze and passively by Jews. Around the same time Druze in Lebanon massacred many Christian Maronites in an ongoing attempt to curb their socio-political ascendancy in Mount Lebanon.

As a result of these events, many thousands of Christians emigrated from Syria and Lebanon to more tolerant places, including Europe and the Americas. Many others, who remained in their homes, sought the protection of foreign powers to enhance their separate communal life. Yet, a small number of Christian intellectuals, mostly educated by American missionaries, tried to find a common ground with their Muslim neighbors in the Arabic language and culture and in secular patriotism centered on Syria. This cultural and patriotic movement constituted a first phase of Arab nationalism that emerged in the early 20th century, but initially it did not attract Muslim intellectuals, let alone Jewish ones.

Some Jews traveled on extended journeys. The strengthening of the ties between the Jews of Syria and Jewish communities in other parts of the empire and the commercial ties as well as the mutual relations between the communities of Syria and Ereẓ Israel resulted in a continued immigration of Spanish Jews to Syrian towns. Aside from the two large communities of Damascus and Aleppo, various 16th-century sources mention the continued existence of smaller communities in ʿAyntāb and Alexandretta (*Iskenderun) in the north of the country and in Hama, Tripoli, Beirut, Sidon, Baalbek, and Baniyas. There were also village settlements in southern Lebanon, to the south of Sidon, where at least some of the Jews engaged in agriculture. The most important community from both the economic and the cultural points of view was that of Aleppo. During the first half of the 16th century the community was headed by R. Meir Anashikon (*Kore ha-Dorot*, 33b) and at the close of the century by R. Samuel *Laniado. The rabbis of Syria during this period maintained regular contact with the rabbis in Ereẓ Israel and exchanged opinions with them in all religious and legal matters. The influence of the *Safed kabbalists was also important, especially in Damascus, where R. Ḥayyim *Vital and R. Moses *Alsheikh lived for a long time. The teachings of the *Kabbalah were propagated with great facility because the Spanish expellees and the first generations of their descendants were carried away by a mood for ecstatic religion. The religious awakening was also expressed in the writing of many homiletical works. Most of the works of the Syrian rabbis were published in Leghorn, Venice, or Istanbul. In 1605 a Hebrew printing press was established in Damascus, but only one book was printed before it closed. At the time there were also intellectuals among the Jews of Syria who wrote secular poems in Hebrew; aside from R. Israel *Najara no other poet of any stature appeared.

The proponents of Shabbateanism succeeded in winning followers in the communities of Syria, and *Shabbetai Ẓevi found many fervent supporters among them. Nathan of Gaza went to Damascus and Aleppo, and even after Shabbetai Ẓevi's conversion, he pursued his activity and received support from within these communities. Due to Aleppo's extensive commerce, Jewish merchants from European countries settled there and by their contributions enabled scholars to devote their lives to the study of the Torah. The literary activity of the rabbis of Aleppo continued as before and for a long time was led by the members of the Laniado family. In the large community of Damascus, however, there were also rabbis who were universally recognized as reliable authorities; these included R. Mordecai Galanté (at the close of the 18th century) and his son R. Moses *Galanté.

During the second half of the 18th century there was great decline in the trade of Aleppo, but on the other hand a wealthy class of bankers emerged among the Jews of Damascus, favored by the authorities and playing an important role in the development of community life. During the middle of the 18th century Saul Farḥi was the banker (*ṣarrāf) of the governor of Damascus; his son *Ḥayyim succeeded him and helped organize the Turkish defenses during Napoleon's siege of Acre (1799). He played an important role in Jazzār Pasha's government in Acre until he was killed in 1820 on the order of ʿAbdallah Pasha.

During the 1830s, the Jewish bankers were led by Raphael Farḥi, brother of Ḥayyim Farḥi, who skillfully protected their positions. The Jewish community in the mountains of Lebanon prospered during this period, particularly in Deir el-Qamar and Ḥāsbayya. In 1832 Ibrahim Pasha, the son of Muhammad ʿAli of Egypt, conquered Syria and introduced modern administration in the country. The direction of the finances of Damascus was entrusted to a Christian, Hanna Bahri, a rival of Farhi. Even though Ibrahim Pasha abolished the discriminatory laws against the non-Muslim communities, he allowed the notorious *Damascus blood libel to occur (1840). Once this traumatic event subsided, the life of the Damascus community, as well as that of Jewish communities in the other towns of Syria, improved under the renewal of Ottoman rule. Most of the Damascus Jews earned their livelihoods in various crafts, and a small class of wealthy Jews engaged in the wholesale and international trade of Persian and local products, as well as in the leasing of taxes. Christians periodically devised more blood libels against the Jews, but with little effect. During the 1860 events the Jewish community of Syria-Lebanon was affected in two ways: in Damascus Christians accused Jews of assisting the rioters and enriched themselves by purchasing the looted property after it was plundered. Some Jews were indeed imprisoned as a result of these accusations until their innocence was proven. In the mountains of Lebanon Jewish communities in Druze villages, such as Deir el-Qamar and Ḥāsbayya, were liquidated.

The end of the 19th century saw a considerable decline in the economic conditions of the Jews in Damascus. Local industries were ruined due to the growing importation of European goods and the opening of the Suez Canal, in particular, which dealt a severe blow to the trade with Persia through the Syrian Desert. Many Jews from Damascus and other places settled in Beirut, which became a large town and a commercial center. Others immigrated overseas, particularly to the Americas. In Damascus, adherence to the values of Judaism was greatly weakened and attempts at the turn of the century to maintain Hebrew schools were unsuccessful. In contrast, the Orthodox Jews of Aleppo kept their traditional educational institutions and a Hebrew press was also established there in 1865. The difference between these two Jewish Syrian communities was also reflected in their attitudes toward the resettlement of Ereẓ Israel. While many of the Aleppo Jews immigrated to Ereẓ Israel and became an active element in its reconstruction, the presence of the Jews of Damascus was almost imperceptible.

After World War I there were three large communities in the French protectorates of Syria and *Lebanon: Damascus, Aleppo, and Beirut. In the first two communities there were about 6,000 Jews and in Beirut about 4,000, while in the other small communities there were about 2,000 persons. There was little public activity among the Jews of Syria. From 1921 a fortnightly newspaper in Arabic, *al-ʿĀlam al-Isrāʾīlī*, was published. In 1946 its name was changed to *al-Salām* (Peace).

[Eliyahu Ashtor / Moshe Ma'oz (2nd ed.)]

Contemporary Period

After World War I, with the collapse of the Ottoman Empire, Syria became, in 1918, a semi-independent state under the leadership of Amir (later King) Faysal, the son of the Sharif of Mecca and commander of the 1916 Arab revolt against the Turks. He worked to create for the first time a Syrian-Arab national community, where Muslims and non-Muslims could live as equals. He also acknowledged the Jewish national home in Ereẓ Israel and in 1919 reached an agreement on this issue with Chaim *Weizmann, head of the Zionist movement. In 1920, however, Faysal was ousted by a military force dispatched by France, which claimed control of Syria and Lebanon. This claim was confirmed by the League of Nations and these two countries were put under French Mandate until World War II. The French endeavored to undermine the Syrian-Arab national community while encouraging local autonomous regions, notably for Druze and Alawis, as well as favoring Christian communities. Jews were treated fairly by the authorities and granted representation in local and regional councils. But they were periodically harassed and some were murdered by Arab nationalists and Muslim fanatics, mainly on account of the Arab-Jewish conflict in Palestine-Ereẓ Israel. Following Syrian independence (1946) and the establishment of Israel (1948), Jews in Syria were subjected to considerable violence (see below).

The independent republic of Syria was initially governed by nationalist leaders and parties who had struggled against the French Mandate. But these failed to tackle the crucial socio-economic problems of the new state and the rebellious minorities as well as to defeat Israel in the 1948 war. Consequently, these civilian politicians were ousted by three military officers in turn, who dominated Syria until 1954. Returning to power, the veteran conservative parties were challenged by radical-secular parties: the communists, Syrian nationalists (PPS), and Baʿthists, who also competed for influence among military officers. These circumstances, compounded by threats of a pro-Soviet or pro-Western takeover, respectively, led Syria in 1958 to create a union with Egypt, the United Arab Republic. However, in 1961 Syria broke away from this union, owing to Egypt's strict domination as well as to discriminatory economic and political measures. In March 1963, Syrian army officers organized another military coup in the name of the Ba'th Party. They established a Ba'thist regime which is still in power (2006), having been headed by four successive leaders: Amīn al-Ḥāfiẓ, a Sunni-Muslim officer, until 1966; Ṣalāḥ Jadid, an Alawi officer, between 1966 and 1970, Ḥāfiẓ al-*Asad, another Alawi officer, between 1970 and 2000, who was succeeded by his son, Bashār, an ophthalmologist by profession. All four leaders were dictators, each developing distinct domestic and foreign policies. Amīn al-Ḥāfiẓ consolidated Ba'thist rule but was caught in a severe conflict between civilian and military factions. Jadīd developed a Marxist-socialist orientation and a militant anti-Israel line which led to the 1967 war. Ḥāfiẓ al-Asad established for the first time a personal-presidential rule that lasted for 30 years, the longest in the modern history of Syria. He continued the socio-economic revolution of his predecessors and the Alawi domination of the military and security apparatuses that had started with Jadīd. He expanded education and other public facilities, but failed to improve the economy and combat corruption. More than his predecessors, he encountered Islamic militant rebellion and put it down with barbaric force, killing some 20,000 people – including women and children

– in the city of Hama (1982). Earlier, he joined Egypt's president, al-*Sadat, in attacking Israel in 1973, but was badly defeated. Subsequently, he tried to maneuver between the Soviet Union, Syria's military supporter, and the U.S., Israel's ally. In the 1990s Asad entered a peace process with Israel with intense American mediation, but peace was not reached after all. Asad died in June 2000 and was succeeded by his son Bashār, who has actually reversed several policies and gains of his father. He has reflected weakness as a leader-ruler, aborted some new political reforms, failed to improve the economy, and lost control of Lebanon, which his father had managed to turn into a Syrian protectorate. Above all he has been more openly involved with Islamic terrorism and with the Iranian Islamic regime. He vehemently opposed the U.S.'s war in *Iraq in 2003 and made some crude antisemitic remarks, even though he suggested renewing the peace negotiations with Israel.

[Moshe Ma'oz (2nd ed.)]

Attitude Toward Israel

Relations between Syria and Israel were marked by political and military tension from the start. Syria's hostility toward Israel was more extreme than that of other Arab states for the following reasons: its ideology of Arab nationalism and its declared aim of destroying Israel and retrieving Palestine. These notions became more influential with the ascension of the Pan-Arab Ba'th Party to power in 1963 and its tendency to achieve a central position in inter-Arab relations. Also, the struggle for power in Syria sometimes found expression in the instigation of clashes on the border with Israel. The 48-mi. (77-km.) border between Israel and Syria differed from Israel's frontiers with other Arab states. The Syrian forces on the Golan Heights (see *Ramat ha-Golan) had topographical superiority over the Israel villages in the Ḥulah and Jordan valleys, which also enabled them to dominate the sources of the Jordan River leading into Lake Kinneret. The *Armistice Agreement between the two countries created demilitarized zones along the major portion of the border, and the struggle over the status of these areas was a constant source of military conflict. The Syrian army was the only Arab force that succeeded in the 1948 war in capturing territories originally apportioned to the State of Israel in the UN Partition Plan (see *Palestine, Partition and Partition Plans). Syria intended to keep these territories, while Israel demanded the complete withdrawal of Syrian forces up to the international border as a condition for signing the armistice agreement. Following a suggestion by Ralph Bunche, the UN mediator, a compromise had been reached: those areas evacuated by the Syrians (as well as additional areas in the sector of Ein Gev and Dardara that were held by Israel) would become demilitarized zones in which "the presence of armed forces of both sides [would]… be absolutely forbidden and no activity of semi-military forces [would]… be permitted" (Israel-Syrian Agreement on a General Armistice, Article 5 (a), v). On both sides of the demilitarized zones were defined areas in which the maintenance of defensive forces was permitted (Article 6); the nature of these forces was defined in an addendum to the agreement; it also assured the revival of normal civilian life in the demilitarized zone, including the return of civilians and the establishment of a local police force (Article 5 (e), v); and a Mixed Armistice Commission was established to supervise the agreement (Article 7). The question of the three demilitarized zones – northern, central, and southern – was a point of military and political contention between Israel and Syria. Israel viewed them as areas under her sovereignty, in which she was free to implement any civilian activity, the only limitation being the above-mentioned military one. Syria, on the other hand, claimed that the sovereignty over these areas was still undecided and protested Israel's right to carry out civilian activities without the approval of the Mixed Armistice Commission and Syria's agreement. Moreover, Syria attempted to prevent any such activity, especially agricultural work and water projects, both by means of military attacks and by presenting complaints to the Mixed Armistice Commission and the UN Security Council. Syria succeeded in gaining control over part of the demilitarized zones, such as al-Ḥimma (after killing seven Israel police in April 1951), the Banyas slopes, the area between the Jordan River and the international border to the east, and on the northeastern shore of Lake Kinneret. A Syrian attempt to gain control over a piece of Israel territory outside the demilitarized zones (near the entrance of the Jordan into Lake Kinneret) in March 1951 was repulsed after a fierce battle at Tel al-Muṭilla. Israel's protest to the Security Council over these moves, like its protests against other Syrian aggressive actions later on, did not succeed in bringing about a denunciation of Syria in the United Nations.

The military and political struggle over the Israel-Syrian border centered on four issues: (1) *Cultivating agricultural areas in the demilitarized zones*. Each time Israeli farmers attempted to cultivate land that the Syrians claimed belonged to local Arabs, Syrian forces interrupted their activity by firing from outposts that overlooked Israel territory, and sometimes major incidents developed, especially in the southern demilitarized zone. On the night of Jan. 31, 1960, units of the Israel Defense Forces carried out an action to wipe out Syrian outposts in Khirbat Tawfiq in the southern zone, but the harassment of Israeli farmers continued, in spite of attempts by the United Nations to mediate the dispute. (2) *Fishing in Lake Kinneret*. In spite of the fact that all of Lake Kinneret was in Israeli territory and outside the demilitarized zones, the Syrians took advantage of their control over the northeastern shore and attacked fishing boats and police boats in this sector. Israeli units retaliated against Syrian outposts northeast of the lake on the night of Dec. 11, 1955 and against the Nuqayb outpost on March 16–17, 1962. The most serious incident in this sector was on Aug. 15, 1966, when Israeli police boats were attacked and, in retaliation two Syrian planes were shot down over the lake. Periodically, Israel would provoke Syria to attack boats in order to carry out fierce punitive actions against Syrian positions. (3) *Development projects in the demilitarized zones*. When Israel began a project to drain Lake Ḥulah in 1951, Syria objected to the implementation of works in the central demilitarized zone, claiming that they provided Israel with a military advantage and that some of the work was done on lands that belonged to Arabs. Armed clashes in March and April 1951, followed by deliberations in the Security Council, led to a stoppage of the work and Israel's leaving the Mixed Armistice Commission. Work was renewed in June 1951 after the chairman of the Armistice Commission ruled that these activities did not constitute a breach of the Armistice Agreement and Israel agreed to avoid using Arab lands; the drainage project was completed in 1957. In September 1953, Israel began digging a canal in the demilitarized zone near the Benot Ya'akov Bridge, as part of the plan for the Jordan-Negev Water Carrier. The Syrians again objected, claiming that this constituted a change in the status of the demilitarized zone, and following its complaint to the Security Council, Israel was requested to stop these activities. Israel then abandoned the original plan and in 1959 began work on the Kinneret-Negev Water Carrier. (4) *The National Water Carrier.* Some Arab states tended initially to accept the principle of sharing with Israel the waters of the Jordan according to the suggestion made by President Eisenhower's special envoy, Eric Johnston, in 1953. But the program was finally rejected by the *Arab League in October 1955. This rejection was influenced by Syrian pressures to prevent Israel's economic development, despite the fact that Syria was apportioned a good amount of water from the Jordan and Yarmuk rivers. When Israel was about to complete the National Water Carrier in 1964, the Syrian Ba'th government demanded that the Arab states declare war in order to prevent the implementation of the project. Syria's demand was rejected by the Arab Summit Conference in January 1964, which decided instead to adopt an alternate plan and divert the headwaters of the Jordan. Syria's role in the diversion plan was to absorb the waters of the Ḥaẓbani (which flowed from Lebanon), combine them with the flow from the Banyas sources, and direct them into the dam that would be built on the Yarmuk River on the Syrian-Jordanian border. Syrian efforts to prevent Israel from also using the Dan River sources led to serious border incidents in November 1964. Israeli attacks against the Syrian diversion works in 1965–66 eventually stopped the diversion project.

Syria was the first Arab state to support the terrorist activities of the Palestinian organization al-Fatḥ, starting in 1965. After the radical wing of the Syrian Ba'th Party – headed by Ṣalāḥ Jadīd – assumed power in February 1966, Syrian support for al-Fatḥ and other terrorist organizations increased; most of their actions were carried out across the Jordanian and Lebanese borders in order to prevent retaliatory action by Israel against Syria. The ideology of the Syrian Ba'th government called for a "popular liberation war" against Israel. The deterioration of Syrian-Israeli relations reached a climax on April 7, 1967, in land and air battles during which many Syrian planes were downed by Israel. Syria's aggressive propaganda, carried on with the support of the Soviet Union, was a decisive factor in the developments leading to the *Six-Day War (1967). Even after the Six-Day War and the occupation of the Golan Heights by Israel, Syria did not abandon the principle of a "popular liberation war," and continued to provide material and political support to the Palestinian terrorist organizations. Syria rejected the Nov. 22, 1967, Security Council resolution, namely, the notion of a peaceful settlement of the Arab-Israel conflict. This extremist position did not change officially when General Ḥāfiẓ al-Asad assumed power in November 1970, although his domestic and foreign policies were in fact more pragmatic than those of his predecessor. The deployment of Israeli troops on the Golan, some 55 kms from Damascus, induced Asad to be cautious and seek a political settlement with Israel. But this strategic predicament also motivated him to try and retrieve the Golan by force. Indeed, in October 1973 he joined Egypt's President Sadat in launching a military offensive against Israel. Syrian troops were able to capture the entire Golan Heights in several days before they were badly defeated and repulsed. In October 1973, Syria accepted UN Security Council resolution 338, which included UN Resolution 242 and the principle of peace with Israel in exchange for territories occupied by Israel in 1967 (and 1973). Subsequently, Asad suggested – mainly in interviews with U.S. media – a "peace agreement" (in fact a non-belligerency agreement) with Israel in exchange for the Golan and the settlement of the Palestinian problem. Israel ignored this offer, but in 1976 reached a tacit agreement with Syria, with U.S. mediation, regarding the deployment of Syrian troops in Lebanon, following the eruption of its civil war. Yet Asad's predicament vis-à-vis Israel grew further, after Sadat signed the Camp David Accords (1978) and the peace agreement (1979) with Begin, Israel's new prime minister, and after Israel officially annexed the Golan Heights in 1981. Asad then adopted a doctrine of strategic balance with Israel, obtaining massive military aid from the Soviet Union, but failing to reach his ambitious goal. Asad sought to improve relations with the U.S., and during the 1990 Kuwait war he dispatched military units to join the American-led coalition that attacked the Iraqi army. Accepting U.S. suggestions, Asad moderated his position and agreed to attend the 1991 Madrid Peace Conference without pre-conditions and to direct negotiations with Israel. Peace negotiations were indeed conducted with active U.S. moderation for some eight years, and in late 1999–early 2000 Syria and Israel almost reached a peace agreement. Asad died in June 2000 and his son Bashār succeeded him and expressed time and again his readiness to resume negotiations with Israel without pre-conditions. But Israel, backed by the U.S., rejected his suggestions due inter alia to his open support of Hizballah and Hamas, Syria's continual occupation of Lebanon, and, from Washington's point of view, Bashār's vehement opposition to America's intervention in Iraq and his indirect help to the Iraqi insurgents. For most Israeli Jews there exist two more reasons to oppose peace with Syria. They refuse to give up the Golan Heights and cannot forget the harsh mistreatment of Jews in Syria since its independence.

[Oded Tavor / Moshe Ma'oz (2nd ed.)]

The Jewish Community in Independent Syria

Following Syria's independence and the events leading to Israel's establishment, Jews in Syria were subject to violent attacks, resulting in many deaths as well as harsh treatment from the authorities. Aleppo in 1947 and Damascus in 1947 and 1948 witnessed many anti-Jewish actions: riots, burning of books and synagogues, bombings of Jewish neighborhoods, as well as killing and looting. Consequently, of about 15,000 Jews in Syria in 1947, only about 5,300 remained in 1957. Most of them left during the 1940s, especially after the 1947 pogroms in Aleppo. Immediately after the establishment of the State of Israel, the stream of Jewish emigration from Syria increased. Most Jews went to Lebanon, but a few were returned to Syria by the Lebanese authorities upon Syrian request. From 1948, the condition of Syrian Jewry continued to decline. The government issued a number of anti-Jewish laws, including a prohibition on sale of Jewish property (1948) and the freezing of Jewish bank accounts (1953). Jewish property was confiscated, and Palestinian refugees were housed in the dwellings vacated in the Jewish quarters of Damascus and Aleppo. Many Jews were put on trial because one of their relatives had succeeded in escaping from Syria, others were compelled to visit the police station daily, and not a few were imprisoned without trial. In addition, various limitations were imposed on them, in particular one forbidding them to leave the country. Only for a while in 1954 were Jews allowed to leave Syria, on condition that they renounce all claims to their property. After the first group had reached Turkey, however, in November 1954, the police forbade others to leave. Immediately after the union with Egypt (United Arab Republic) in 1958, the prohibition on the exit of Jews was again cancelled, on condition that they transferred their property to the government. Frozen bank accounts of Jews were also freed. However, shortly afterwards the frontiers were again closed to them, and in 1959 trials of those accused of helping Jews to leave Syria took place. In March 1964, a decree was enacted which prohibited Jews from traveling more than three miles beyond the limits of their home towns.

After the trial of the Israeli intelligence agent Eli *Cohen and his public hanging in Damascus (1965), Jews were assaulted. They suffered more during the Six-Day War (1967) and afterwards, when many were arrested and others attacked by the Muslim population. Jews were murdered in Damascus, Aleppo, and in Qamishli, near the Turkish border, but because of the strict censorship no precise details were known. Jews made many efforts to leave Syria, and between 1948 and 1961 about 5,000 Syrian Jews reached Israel; in 1968 the number remaining in Syria was estimated at about 4,000. Most lived in Damascus and Aleppo, and belonged to the middle classes and the poor.

The few Jews in Qamishli were not always persecuted since they lived among Muslim Kurds, who were not hostile. The economic situation of the remainder of the Syrian Jewish community worsened. The wealthy generally succeeded in escaping, sometimes even with their capital. The Zilkha Bank in Damascus and the Safra Bank in Aleppo were closed, the former by a government order in 1952.

Most of the Jewish educational institutions were closed. In 1968 only one school, which belonged to the *Alliance Israélite Universélle, functioned in Damascus. The Jews of Syria had no nationwide community organization, and each community had its own governing committee.

[Oded Tavor]

Developments since the 1970s

Approximately 4,000 Jews remained in Syria, of whom 2,500 were in Damascus, 1,200 in Aleppo, and 300 in Qamishli. After the Yom Kippur War the conditions of the Jews in Syria continued to be grim; the Syrian Jewish community was completely cut off from the outside world. The first attempt to break this isolation and escape was undertaken by four young Jewish women, all from Damascus – three sisters, Tony, Laura, and Farah Zaybak, and Eva Saad. They were raped, tortured, and then murdered, and their bodies brought to the Damascus ghetto on March 3, 1974. A week later the corpses of two Jewish boys who had also tried to escape were discovered near the place where the girls had been murdered. Following worldwide protests, the Syrian authorities, anxious to cover up the atrocity, arrested two prominent young members of the Syrian Jewish community, Yosef Shaluh and Azur Zalta, and charged them with murder and smuggling. Moreover, in an attempt to cut all means of escape, 11 Jewish mothers whose children had managed to escape in previous years were arrested, tortured, and interrogated for three successive days in order to extract from them the names of those who had helped their children to leave the country.

On July 3, 1974, an International Conference for the Deliverance of Jews from Middle East Lands, with representatives of 30 nations, convened in Paris at the initiative of the French Council, under the chairmanship of Alain Poher, president of the Senate of France. He called on the Syrian government to comply with the Universal Declaration on Human Rights and to put an end to discrimination against its Jews. The situation, however, continued to be oppressive, with a total ban on Jewish emigration. Even permission for rare cases to go abroad for medical treatment was canceled and Jews had to obtain special permission from the secret police to travel for more than 3 miles from their home. They were frequently searched by the secret police and held for interrogation and torture. A special branch of the secret police oversees the enforcement of anti-Jewish enactments.

Following the peace negotiations between Israel and Egypt, the situation of the Jews did not change much. Agents of the Mukhābarāt, the Syrian secret police, attended synagogue services, possibly also to protect Jews against maltreatment by Muslim fanatics.

At the end of the 1980s, the Jewish population of Syria had declined from about 4,000 in 1983 to about 1,400: 1,180 in Damascus, 150 in Aleppo, and 125 in Qamishli. For virtually the whole of Asad's period, there was no change in the position of the Jewish community. It was denied basic human rights and civil liberties. Mail, telephone, and telegrams were monitored by the Jewish Division of the Secret Police, which kept them under constant surveillance, subjecting them to search and arrest without warrant. Sales of property were prohibited, unless a replacement was being acquired; property belonging to deceased Jews with no surviving family was expropriated without compensation. Identity cards continued to bear the word *Mousawi* (Jew), while non-Jews had no religious identification on theirs. The one Jewish school in Damascus (Ben Maimon) and the one in Aleppo (Samuel) were both supervised by Muslims, and were allowed to teach only biblical Hebrew, limited to two hours a week. Contrary to the Universal Declaration of Human Rights, to which Syria was a signatory, and unlike the rights granted to other Syrian citizens, the Jews were prohibited from emigrating. Except for six months in 1992 (see below), only a few Jews were permitted to travel abroad for medical or business reasons. In addition to paying bribes, large monetary deposits were required and family members had to be left behind, to guarantee the traveler's return.

The *Mukhābarāt* arrested and imprisoned several Jews, without charge or trial, for allegedly attempting to leave Syria or for "security offenses." These prisoners were exposed to torture and deprivation of food, clothing, and medicines. Typical of these were the brothers Elie and Selim Swed of Damascus, held for two years without anyone knowing of their arrest. Subsequently, in 1991, a form of "military trial" was held, where no charges were published and their lawyer was prohibited from addressing the "court." They were sentenced to 6½ years in prison, but were released in April 1992. Earlier, in December 1983, 25-year-old pregnant Lillian Abadi of Aleppo and her young daughter and son were brutally murdered and mutilated in their home. Other Jewish families received threats, but no definitive motive for the killings was ever established and nobody was charged. Nevertheless, the Jewish community believed that if the Asad regime was deposed, their treatment by any successor would be even harsher.

The custom of using *Shabbat Zakhor* as the Sabbath for Syrian Jewry, which originated in 1975 in Toronto, Canada, spread to synagogues throughout North America and other countries, highlighting the plight of Syrian Jews, which, over the years, had been substantially ignored by mainline national and international Jewish organizations.

Criticism of the Syrians' treatment of its Jewish citizens was later raised by several world governments, including Canada, the U.S., and France. The issue was brought before the United Nations Commission on Human Rights. In January 1992, for the first time in responding to the UN body, the Syrian government issued a detailed "accounting" of the "well-being of its Jews," including a listing of students in educational institutions, places of residence outside the ghettos, and occupations of Jews. During the Asad "re-election" campaign of 1992, the Jewish community was obliged to parade in his support, bearing banners in Hebrew – the first time that language had been permitted to be used in public. During Syria's participation in the Madrid Peace Conference in 1992, U.S. Secretary of State James Baker announced that Syrian Jews would be permitted to travel abroad. This change initially did not mean a right to emigrate. The "right to travel" was granted to individuals only under the strict control of the *Mukhābarāt* rather than through the normal channels always available to other Syrians to obtain passports. Permits, when granted, stated that "…the Jew X…" was permitted to travel, and the fortunate applicants were obliged to purchase return tickets.

A large number of Jews, about 2,600, managed to leave in 1992 and joined family in Brooklyn, New York, although some went to other countries. In the U.S., the new arrivals were welcomed by the well-organized long-standing Syrian community. However, the U.S. refused to admit them as refugees, but only as "visitors." Thus, they were denied the governmental resettlement facilities available to immigrants, placing a heavy burden on Jewish communal resources with respect to housing, education, and employment. By 1994, 3,565 Syrian Jews had immigrated to the U.S. The rest went to Israel, including the chief rabbi of Damascus. In 2005, few Jews remained in Syria: according to unofficial figures, fewer than 250.

[Judy Feld Carr / Moshe Ma'oz (2nd ed.)]

BIBLIOGRAPHY: BIBLICAL AND SECOND TEMPLE PERIOD: Schuerer, Gesch, 3 (1909), 10f.; E.G. Kraeling, in: JBL, 51 (1932), 130–60; B.Z. Luria, *Ha-Yehudim be-Suryah* (1957). LATER PERIODS: Ashtor, Toledot; idem, in: HUCA, 27 (1956), 305–26; Rosanes, Togarmah; Mann, Egypt, 1 (1920), 19ff., 27ff., 72ff.; Mann, Texts, 1 (1931), 49–54; 2 (1935), 201–55; S.W. Baron, in: PAAJR, 4 (1933), 3–31; S.D. Goitein, in: *Zion*, 1 (1936), 79–81; Y. Ben Zvi, in: *Tarbiz*, 3 (1932), 436–79; M. al-Maghribi, in: *Majallat al-Majmaʿ al-ʿIlmī al-ʿArabī*, 11 (1929), 641–53; N. Robinson, in: J. Freid (ed.), *Jews in Modern World*, 1 (1962), 50–90. **ADD. BIBLIOGRAPHY:** T. Petron, *Syria* (1972); J.M. Landau, "An Arab Anti-Turkish Handbill," in: *Turcica*, 9:1 (1977), 215–24; idem and M. Maoz, "*Yehudim ve-lo-Yehudim be-Miẓrayim u-ve-Sūriyya*," in: *Pe'amim*, 9 (1981), 4–14; J.F. Devlin, *Syria: Modern State in an Ancient Land* (1983); B. Lewis, *The Jews of Islam* (1984); J.M. Landau, "Ha-Mekorot le-Ḥeker Yehudei Miẓrayim vi-Yehudei Turkiyyah," in: *Pe'amim*, 23 (1985), 99–110; M. Ma'oz, *Syria and Israel: From War to Peace* (1995); A. Levy (ed.), *The Jews of the Ottoman Empire* (1994), index; idem (ed.), *Jews, Turks, Ottomans* (2002), esp. 108–18; M.M. Laskier, "Syria and Lebanon," in: R.S. Simon et al. (eds.), *The Jews of the Middle East and North Africa in Modern Times* (2003), 316–34.

SYRKIN, JOSHUA (**Grigory**; 1838–1922), Hebrew writer and Zionist, born in Shklov. His family moved to Brest-Litovsk when he was an infant. In 1875 he settled in Panevezys, Lithuania, where he became a close friend of Judah Leib *Gordon. He studied at the Moscow Academy of Agriculture and published two scientific works, *Devarim Aḥudim mi-Ma'arekhet ha-Domem* (1868), and *Ma'arekhet ha-Domem* (1869), in which he made the first attempt to create a modern Hebrew terminology in the field of mineralogy. During the 1870s he lost interest in Hebrew letters and went to work in Baron Horace *Guenzburg's gold mines in east Siberia. During the 1880s he became a department head of the Libau-Romny railway and settled in Minsk.

After J.L. Gordon's death Syrkin edited his works for publication. Syrkin joined the Ḥibbat Zion movement and was among the leaders of the Doreshei Zion society in Minsk. He took part in negotiations with barons *Rothschild and *Hirsch in 1891–92 and published a pamphlet entitled *She'erit Ya'akov* (1891), in which he drew up a program to establish a center (Beit Va'ad) to direct Jewish emigration from Russia and settlement in Ereẓ Israel. In 1894 Syrkin traveled to Ereẓ Israel to visit the settlement Ein Zeitim founded by his society. He participated in the first Zionist Congresses. In his book *Ḥezyonot Laylah* (1903) he advanced his views on the history of the Jewish people and closed with a utopian description of the reborn state of Israel.

BIBLIOGRAPHY: Kressel, Leksikon, 2 (1967), 499–500.

[Yehuda Slutsky]

SYRKIN, MARIE (1899–1989), U.S. writer, translator, educator, and Zionist activist. Syrkin was born in Berne, Switzerland, the only daughter of Nachman *Syrkin (1868–1924), theoretician of socialist Zionism, and Bassya Osnos, a feminist socialist Zionist who died in 1914. After sojourns in Germany, France, and Vilna, the Syrkin family immigrated to the United States in 1908. Marie Syrkin, who was fluent in five languages, attended public schools in New York City and received her B.A. and M.A. in English literature from Cornell University. She wrote poetry throughout her life; a collection, *Gleanings: A Diary in Verse,* was published in 1978. Her translations of Yiddish and Hebrew verse were widely anthologized. Twenty years of teaching high school in New York City led to her influential book, *Your School, Your Children* (1944), a study of the American public school system. Between 1937 and 1942, Syrkin reported on Nazi persecutions of Jews; in 1942 she wrote the first editorial in an American journal on Hitler's plans to annihilate European Jewry. After World War II she turned her attention to Jewish resistance movements under the Nazis and wrote an evocative study, *Blessed is the Match* (1947). She also recruited young people in displaced-persons camps to come to the United States as Hillel scholars. Syrkin's authorized biography of her close friend Golda *Meir, *Way of Valor*, appeared in 1955 (revised as *Golda Meir: Woman with a Cause*, 1963; and *Golda Meir: Israel's Leader*, 1969); other works include *Nachman Syrkin: Socialist Zionist* (1961); an anthology of the writings of Ḥayyim Greenberg (1968); and *Golda Meir Speaks Out* (1973). Between 1948 and 1955, she edited the Labor Zionist monthly *Jewish Frontier*. Syrkin became a professor of English at Brandeis University in 1950; she was the first to teach a university course on Holocaust literature, publishing the first theoretical discussion of the subject, "The Holocaust in Literature," in *Midstream* (May 1966). Following retirement in 1966, Syrkin became editor of Herzl Press. She was a member of the Jewish Agency executive (1965–68) and an elected member of the World Zionist Executive. Syrkin received honorary degrees from Brandeis University and the Reconstructionist Rabbinical College and the 1981 Solomon Bublick Prize from the Hebrew University of Jerusalem. Syrkin's first marriage to Maurice Samuel in 1917 was annulled and her second marriage to biochemist Aaron Bodansky ended in divorce. She married the poet Charles *Reznikoff in 1930. After his death in 1976, she spent the rest of her life in California. Her papers are located primarily in the American Jewish Archives in Cincinnati.

BIBLIOGRAPHY: C. Kessner, "Marie Syrkin: An Exemplary Life," in: C. Kessner (ed.), *The "Other" New York Jewish Intellectuals* (1994), 51–70; idem, "On Behalf of the Jewish People: Marie Syrkin at Ninety," in: *Jewish Book Annual* (1988–89), 46; *Jewish Frontier* (Jan/Feb. 1983), containing tributes from colleagues, students, and friends.

[Carole Kessner (2nd ed.)]

SYRKIN, MOSES NAHUM SOLOMONOVICH (1878–1918), writer, orator, and Jewish national leader. Born in Bielsk, Russia, Syrkin completed his studies as a technological engineer at the Polytechnic of Warsaw, where he was among the founders of the first Jewish organization of academic youth, *Kadimah. He became acquainted with the Jewish authors in Warsaw (among them I.L. *Peretz and N. *Sokolow), and wrote political essays, popular scientific articles, and literary criticism for *Ha-Ẓefirah* and the *Sefer ha-Shanah* of Sokolow. He also contributed to *Voskhod and *Budushchnost*. He joined the Zionist movement and was from its beginnings one of the spokesmen for the Russian-Jewish intelligentsia, attending several Zionist Congresses as delegate and correspondent for *Ha-Ẓefirah*. Under the influence of I.L. Peretz, he became a supporter of the Yiddish language and wrote extensively for the Yiddish press. He was among those within the Zionist movement who fought for the preservation of the Yiddish language in Jewish schools and in 1905–06 he edited the daily *Der Telegraf* which was founded by N. Sokolow in Warsaw. In 1907 he moved to Kiev where he held a respected position in the public life of the community, making connections with the Ukrainian nationalist movement and contributing articles (mostly of a technical and scientific nature) to the general Russian press. During World War I he was among the organizers of relief activities for Jewish refugees from the battle areas. He was also one of the few Russian Zionists to support the policies of the Allies. During the 1917 Revolution he was chosen as delegate to the Russian Constituent Assembly on the Jewish National List and to the National Council of Ukrainian Jews. He was elected president of the Kiev community, and a member of the Rada (Ukrainian Parliament); he also edited the Zionist newspaper *Der Telegraf*, which was published in Kiev (1917–18). When head of the delegation of the Jewish community which went to receive *Petlyura in 1918, he caught pneumonia and died.

BIBLIOGRAPHY: S.L. Zitron, *Leksikon Ẓiyyoni* (1924), 463–5; Rejzen, Leksikon, 2 (1927), 647–50.

[Yehuda Slutsky]

SYRKIN, NACHMAN (1868–1924), first ideologist and leader of Socialist Zionism. Born in Mogilev, Belorussia,

Syrkin received a thorough Jewish education by private tutors, and when he moved with his family to Minsk (1884), he completed his studies at a Russian high school. There he joined Ḥovevei Zion (see *Ḥibbat Zion), while maintaining contact with Russian revolutionary circles. He was placed under arrest for several weeks, after which he went to London and then to Berlin (1888), where he studied psychology and philosophy. In Berlin he was a founder of the Russian-Jewish Scientific Society, from whose ranks a number of Zionist leaders emerged (Shemaryahu *Levin, Leo *Motzkin, Chaim *Weizmann, and others). His writing career began at the age of 19 as a contributor to *Ha-Meliẓ* while in Minsk; his first booklet, *Geschichts-Philosophische Betrachtungen* ("Reflections on the Philosophy of History," Berlin, 1896), in which he criticized Marx's concepts and stressed the voluntary element in historical processes.

Syrkin participated in the First Zionist Congress in 1897, leading the few representatives of Socialist Zionism. In 1898, two years after the appearance of *Herzl's *Der Judenstaat*, he published an article in the Austrian Socialist monthly *Deutsche Worte* and enlarged it in the same year into a pamphlet *Die Judenfrage und der sozialistische Judenstaat* ("The Jewish Question and the Socialist Jewish State"), in which he outlined for the first time the idea to which he adhered throughout his life: the realization of Zionism through cooperative mass settlement of the Jewish proletariat. In the press, as well as from the rostrum of the Zionist Congresses, Syrkin forcefully attacked the preponderance of "bourgeois and clerical" elements in the Zionist Organization, as well as Herzl's diplomatic overtures to "reactionary monarchs" (William II) and "tyrants" (Nicholas II). His speeches often caused loud protests and even scandals in the Congress sessions.

Syrkin was an early sponsor of the idea of the *Jewish National Fund and submitted a resolution to this effect to the Second Zionist Congress (1898). Herzl, who seemed to like Syrkin in spite of his provocative speeches, called him "that *exaltado*." From 1901 Syrkin worked for the establishment of Socialist Zionist groups in Germany, Austria, and Switzerland and attained modest results, such as Hessiona (1901, named after Moses *Hess) and Heirut ("Freedom," 1902). He founded short-lived journals in Yiddish (*Der Hamoyn*, 1901) and Hebrew (*Ha-Shaḥar*, 1903) and wrote Socialist-Zionist pamphlets (such as the "Call to Jewish Youth" in Russian), which were often smuggled illegally into czarist Russia. For some time Syrkin tried to support himself and his family by literary work, translating Tolstoy into German and publishing political and sociological articles in leading German magazines. His public activity, however, prevented him from persevering in this career. After an abortive attempt to study medicine he returned to philosophy and published his doctoral thesis, *Empfindung und Vorstellung* ("Sensation and Idea") in Berne in 1903.

In 1904 Syrkin was banished from Germany and spent some time in Paris and then, after the 1905 revolution, in Russia. At the Sixth and Seventh Zionist Congresses (1903, 1905) he strongly supported Herzl's *Uganda Scheme, eventually seceding from the Zionist Organization and for several years becoming a leader and spokesman of the socialist *territorialists, who, in Russia and among some Russian-Jewish émigré circles, insisted on calling themselves Zionist-Socialist (Russ., Sionisty-Sotsialisty, or SS). In 1907 he emigrated to the United States, where in 1909 he joined the Palestine-oriented *Po'alei Zion and returned to the Zionist Organization, having arrived at the conclusion that the revolution of the Young Turks had opened new perspectives for Jewish nationhood in Ereẓ Israel. He was the leader of American Po'alei Zion until his death.

During World War I Syrkin worked for the convention of the Jewish Congress in America, and supported the idea of the *Jewish Legion to fight with the Allies for the liberation of Palestine, at a time when his party still opposed it. In 1919 he became a member of the American Jewish delegation to the Versailles Peace Conference, which joined the *Comité des Délégations Juives. In 1919 Syrkin was the key figure at the world conference of Po'alei Zion in Stockholm, which elected him to head a study commission charged with visiting Palestine and drawing up a plan for mass settlement on a cooperative basis. He toured Palestine with the other members of the commission (whose secretary was Zalman (Rubashov) *Shazar) and was the principal author of the plan, which expressed the basic ideas later implemented by the Zionist labor movement.

Returning to the U.S., he founded a short-lived Po'alei Zion daily *Di Tsayt*, edited by David *Pinski, which existed for only about a year. Syrkin, who had always neglected his own economic interests and had lived as a "professional revolutionary," mainly by writing and lecturing, then intended to settle in Palestine, but he died suddenly in New York of a heart attack. In 1951 his remains were taken to Israel and buried at kevuẓat Kinneret, alongside the graves of other founding fathers of labor Zionism.

Syrkin was a prolific writer in Hebrew, Yiddish, Russian, German, and English. He wrote a political play in Yiddish, "The Jewish People," and began to write a monumental history of the Jews, but, except for brief chapters published during his lifetime, the manuscript has apparently been lost. His selected works were published in Yiddish (*Geklibene Tsionistish-Sotsialistishe Shriften*, 2 vols., 1926), Hebrew (*Kitvei Naḥman Syrkin*, edited by B. Katzenelson and Y. Kaufman, vol. 1, 1939), and English (preceded by a biography written by his daughter Marie *Syrkin, 1961). The moshav Kefar Syrkin and streets in various Israel towns are named after him. During World War II an American Liberty Ship was named "Nachman Syrkin" by the Jewish National Workers' Alliance (Farband) in the U.S.

At no later than the age of 20 (1888), Syrkin conceived the idea which became his lifelong creed and which at first seemed paradoxical: a complete synthesis of socialism with Jewish nationalism, as embodied in Zionism (or, for a while, territorialism). In his youth Syrkin attacked "the wealthy Jewish plutocrats of St. Petersburg, the Poliakovs, and the Guenzburgs, and others of their class who opposed Jewish emigration from Russia." In his early writings (1898) he postulated that "a classless society and national sovereignty are the only means of completely solving the Jewish problem." He criticized Jewish socialists to whom "socialism meant, first of all, the abandonment of Jewishness, just as the liberalism of the Jewish bourgeoisie led to assimilation.... Jewish socialism used internationalism as a cloak to cover its nakedness." He also attacked *Aḥad Ha-Am's concept of a "spiritual center" in Ereẓ Israel because it disregarded social realities like antisemitism and Jewish mass migration, which were the real forces pressing for a Zionist solution. In resolutions of his group Heirut and in articles in *Der Hamoyn* (1902), Syrkin expounded his ideas in unequivocal terms: "The Jewish masses consist chiefly of a proletariat which does not live from labor; only a small proportion belongs to the labor-proletariat ..." Therefore, the Jews "bear the whole yoke of the 'slave of slaves,' the 'proletariat of the proletariat' – persecuted, driven from land to land, destined to perish physically and spiritually." This "proletariat" includes the miserable shopkeepers, peddlers, tailors and shoemakers, and their "sole redemption lies in Zionism." He warned (in 1903) that "emigration to free lands" will eventually be restricted, "even in democratic countries like America." But, though "the masses may be helped" by such emigration and the securing of equal rights in Russia, "it would be only momentarily, not historically." Therefore the Jewish proletarian masses are the "natural fulfillers of the Zionist idea," and their Zionism "is more than the colonization projects of Ḥovevei Zion with its bourgeois limitations; more than the longing for a spiritual center of the *maskil*; more than the philanthropic Zionism of the West Europeans. Their Zionism is social and bound up with the idea of a new society."

Syrkin differed in some fundamental respects from many of the later Socialist Zionists. He was not an orthodox Marxist, and his socialism was more the concept of a moral-voluntary effort than the necessary outcome of the class struggle. He also criticized *Borochov's Marxist analysis of Zionism and his concept that the "elemental" ("stychic") process of mass migration will by objective necessity produce a concentration of the Jewish masses in Palestine. He was a supporter of Hebrew (which he mastered perfectly) as the sole Jewish national language, and rejected Yiddish for this role (though he used it extensively in writings and speeches). On current issues – such as the question of taking sides in World War I and the question of the Jewish Legion, or the idea of co-opting "Jewish plutocrats" to the Jewish Agency (1923) – he often differed from the majority of his comrades. During the 1920s split in Po'alei Zion between those who remained faithful to the Zionist Organization and those who sought to affiliate with the new Communist Third International, Syrkin tried to reconcile both views by maintaining that only the "un-Jewish Jews" among the Communists were the cause of the Communist rejection of Zionism; but he never again abandoned his clear stand in favor of the adherence to the Zionist Organization. Even in matters of religion he went his own way. Though opposed to the "petrified" form of rabbinical practice, he was apparently a deeply religious man. On his death-bed, he called Chaim *Tchernowitz ("Rav Ẓa'ir") and recited with him the *viddui*, the traditional confession before death. Two days before he died, he even wrote a Hebrew prayer, *Birkat ha-Mavet* ("Blessing of Death"), in which his metaphysical sense found poetic expression.

BIBLIOGRAPHY: M. Syrkin, *Nachman Syrkin, Socialist Zionist: a biographical memoir and selected essays* (1961); B. Katznelson, *Ha-Eḥad ba-Ma'arakhah* (1939; LNYL, 6 (1965), 433–42.

SYRKIN, YAKOV KOVOVICH (1894–1974), Russian physical chemist. Syrkin was a professor at the Ivanovo-Voznesensk Polytechnic Institute (1925) and at Institute of Fine Chemical Technology (1931). He was scientific chairman of molecular structure department at Karpov Physico-Chemical Institute (1931–52). He did research in chemical thermodynamics, kinetics of reactions in solution and in gas phase, molecular structure, and chemical bonds. Syrkin wrote *Khimicheskaya svyaz i stroyeniye molekul* ("Chemical Composition and the Structure of Molecules," 1946).

SZABÓ, IMRE (1882–1958), Hungarian author, playwright, and journalist. Szabó was born in Ersekujvar. He began his career as a journalist writing for the German-language daily *Neues Politisches Volksblatt*, and later worked on Hungarian and Jewish newspapers. After World War I Szabó settled in Kolozsvár (Cluj), Transylvania, and devoted himself to literature.

He wrote plays, novels, and biographies, mainly on Jewish subjects, and was strongly influenced by the major Hungarian writers, notably Kálmán Mikszáth. Szabó also published translations of plays from the Yiddish. His works include the story *A pozsonyi zsidó utca* ("The Jews' Street in Pressburg," 1938), a faithful picture of pre-World War I Jewish life; *Zsidó komédiások* ("Jewish Comedians," 1925); and *Kelet kapujában* ("At the Gate of the East," 1937). *Uj zsidók* (1937) contained biographies of Theodor *Herzl and other modern Jewish leaders. Szabó also published a Hungarian version of Louis *Golding's novel *Magnolia Street*. Two later works were *Erdély zsidói* ("The Jews of Transylvania," 1938) and *Róma és Judea* (1943).

BIBLIOGRAPHY: *Magyar Irodalmi Lexikon*, 3 (1965), 116.

[Baruch Yaron]

SZABOLCSI, BENCE (1899–1973), Hungarian musicologist. Born in Budapest, he was the son of Miksa *Szabolcsi and brother of Lajos *Szabolcsi, and studied at Budapest with Kodály. He was the first to collect the notated relics of old Hungarian music from manuscripts and prints, and began publishing them in 1929. From 1929 to 1930 he was the coeditor of *Zenei Szemle* ("Musical Review") and in 1930 edited, with A. Tóth, the first scholarly dictionary of Hungarian music. He was professor of music history at the Budapest Academy of Music from 1945 and director of the Bartók Archives there from 1961.

His research and publications were devoted to European art music; the history of music in Hungary; Hungarian national music; and the comparative study of folk music styles of the world. Szabolcsi's interest in Jewish music was expressed in three studies on Hebrew melody. During the difficult period of 1936 to 1944 he took part in the efforts of Hungarian Jewry to foster cultural activities within the community, and collaborated in the publication of numerous music booklets for Jewish youth. He also edited the music supplement to the *Haggadah* with a Hungarian translation which was published in Budapest in 1942 (Yaari no. 2293). His works include *A XVI. század magyar históriás zenéje…* ("History of 16th-Century Hungarian Music…" 1931); *A zene története* ("History of Music," 1940, 1968[4]); and *A melódia története* (1950, 1957[2]), reworked as *Bausteine zu einer Geschichte der Melodie* (1959).

BIBLIOGRAPHY: MGG, S.V., incl. bibl. to 1962; Grove, Dict, s.v., incl. bibl. to 1947; M. Berlász and I. Homolya, in: *Studia Musicologica Academiae Scientiarum Hungaricae*, II (1969), 7–25 (entire volume dedicated to Szabolcsi on his 70th birthday and includes a bibliography of his writings).

[Andre Hajdu]

SZABOLCSI, LAJOS (1889–1943), Hungarian poet, author, and editor. The son of Miksa *Szabolcsi, he was born in Budapest. From the age of 18, he wrote for his father's newspaper, *Egyenlőség*. In 1915 he succeeded his father as editor in chief and retained the position until the paper ceased publication in 1938. Lajos Szabolcsi continued his father's fight for full Jewish participation in Hungarian life and tried to root out antisemitism by publicizing any violation of Jewish rights. He was in the vanguard of the liberal movement and violently attacked persecution, showing considerable personal courage, particularly during the period of the "White Terror" (1919–22). Szabolcsi was a protagonist of the official line of Hungarian Reform (*Neolog) Jewry, and was violently and vocally anti-Zionist. Several of his works dealt with Jewish themes.

He published *Az új héber költészet története* ("A History of Modern Hebrew Poetry," 1908) and translations of medieval and modern Hebrew verse. Szabolcsi also wrote fiction on Jewish subjects, including the historical novel *A csillag fia* (1918), on *Bar Kokhba; *A levelekimenyegző* ("The Wedding in Levelek," 1920), and the historical drama, *Az áruló* (1923), on *Josephus. Another of his works was *Az emancipáció hatvan éves története* ("The 60-Year History of Emancipation," 1917).

BIBLIOGRAPHY: *Magyar Irodalmi Lexikon*, 3 (1965), 129.

[Baruch Yaron]

SZABOLCSI (Weinstein), MIKSA (1857–1915), Hungarian author, editor, and journalist. Born in Tura, Szabolcsi studied at yeshivot and spent some time at the Budapest rabbinical seminary. Deciding that he wanted to be a writer, he started working as a journalist. He first became known during the blood libel case at *Tiszaeszlár (1882–83), when he was acting as correspondent for the *Pester Lloyd* and other German-language newspapers. During the trial he succeeded in resolving an important problem, but the hostility and prejudice of the court led to his being expelled from the town in which the trial was being held, and there was even an attempt on his life. For a time he edited the *Pester Juedische Zeitung* and in 1886 bought the newspaper *Egyenlőség*, which in his hands became the main organ of Hungarian *Neolog Jewry. Szabolcsi supported the delivery of synagogue sermons in Hungarian and the Magyarization of Jewish names. He was, however, one of the instigators of the fight that succeeded in gaining official recognition of the Jewish religion in 1895. He campaigned vigorously against antisemitism and against misrepresentations of the Talmud and Jewish literature. He was an outspoken anti-Zionist. During the 1890s Szabolcsi maintained the high standard of his newspaper by bringing into the editorial board such talented young Jewish writers as Hugó *Ignotus, Emil *Makai, and József *Kiss. He was also responsible for the foundation of the Jewish literary society, Izraelita Magyar Irodalmi Társulat and the Hungarian Jewish cultural association Országos Magyar Közművelődési Egyesület.

Szabolcsi edited and largely translated Graetz's *History of the Jews*, which appeared in a popular Hungarian edition in 1906–08. His other works include *Olasz zsidók között* ("Among Italian Jews," 1904), *Német zsidók között* ("Among German Jews," 1903), and *Gyöngyszemek a Talmudból és a Midrásból* ("Pearls from the Talmud and Midrash," 1938).

BIBLIOGRAPHY: *Magyar Zsidó Lexikon* (1929), 818–9.

[Baruch Yaron]

SZAJKOWSKI, ZOSA (**Szajko Frydman**; 1911–1978), historian and bibliographer. He was born at Zareby, Poland and lived in France from 1927 until 1941. There he was active in Communist circles until 1937 when, influenced by a group of Russian-Jewish emigré intellectuals associated with YIVO, he left the Communist movement. In 1941 he went to the U.S. and served as a paratrooper in World War II. His historical work is noteworthy for its laborious collection of original sources and ample documentation. He wrote especially on French Jewish history but also on the modern history of the Jews in Eastern Europe.

His books include *The Language of the Jews in the Four Communities of Comtat Venaissin* (1948), *Autonomy and Communal Jewish Debts During the French Revolution of 1789* (1959); *Poverty and Social Welfare among French Jews, 1800–1880* (1953); *Franco-Judaica; an analytical bibliography of books, pamphlets, decrees, briefs and other printed documents pertaining to the Jews in France, 1500–1788* (1962); *Analytical Franco-Jewish Gazetter, 1939–45* (1966); and *Jews and the French Revolutions of 1789, 1830 and 1848* (1970).

°SZÁLASI, FERENC (1897–1946), leader of the antisemitic *Arrow Cross Party, chief of state of Hungary (October 1944–March 1945). Upon retirement from the army (1935) he founded the National Socialist "Party of National Will" and later the Hungarist movement. He was sentenced to three years imprisonment for these activities in 1938 but was released in 1940, whereupon he became the leader of the Arrow Cross Party.

Szálasi pressed for anti-Jewish measures, including extermination. He maintained close relations with the German Nazi party and Hitler made him the "Nation's Leader" and head of the government in Oct. 1944 some time after the Germans had occupied Hungary. His government immediately stepped up persecution of the Jews, and all over the country pogroms broke out, in which he sanctioned the atrocities of his Arrow Cross men. Szálasi aimed to remove all the Jews from the country; to this end he collaborated closely with *Eichmann and Veesenmayer on the "Final Solution." He installed additional ghettos in *Budapest and refused to recognize safe conduct passes or to exempt baptized Jews from living in these ghettos. He also stepped up the deportations and expropriated Jewish property. Seized by Americans on German territory, he was handed over to the Hungarian government, tried, sentenced, and hanged in 1946.

BIBLIOGRAPHY: R.L. Braham, *The Hungarian Jewish Catastrophe: a selected and annotated bibliography* (1962), index; J. Lévai, *Black Book on the Martyrdom of Hungarian Jewry* (1948), passim; A. Geyer, *A magyarországi fasizmus zsidóüldözésének bibliográfiája, 1945–1958* (1958), index.

[Jozeph Michman (Melkman)]

SZALIT-MARCUS, RACHEL (1894–1942), painter and book illustrator. She spent her childhood in Lodz. Her parents, simple working people, encouraged her artistic talent, and in 1911 sent her to Munich to study at the Art Academy. Here she met Julius Szalit, a successful Jewish actor, whom she married. Szalit later committed suicide. In 1916 Rachel moved to Berlin, where she exhibited with the artists of the Secession group and became a member of the November group, young avant-garde artists who joined forces after the November Revolution of 1918. When the Nazis assumed power Rachel Szalit-Marcus fled to France. In 1942 she was arrested and sent to a concentration camp where she died. She painted portraits, flower pieces, and still-lifes. Her best-known works consist of lithographic illustrations to books by Mendele Mokher Seforim, Shalom Aleichem, Israel Zangwill, Heinrich Heine, and Martin Buber.

[Elisheva Cohen]

SZÁNTÓ, GYŐRGY (1893–1961), Hungarian novelist and author. Szántó, who turned from art to literature after becoming totally blind, wrote autobiographical novels such as *Fekete éveim* ("My Black Years," 1934) and other prose works, notably *Bábel tornya* ("The Tower of Babel," 1926) and *Mata Hari* (1928). After World War II he conformed in his writings with the requirements of Marxist literature.

SZÁNTÓ, SIMON (1819–1882), educator and writer, born in Nagykanizsa, Hungary. Son of a rabbi, he received a strict religious upbringing in the talmudic schools of Lackenbach and Golcuv-Jenikov, and managed under great difficulties to obtain a secular education in Bratislava and at Prague University, where he studied German literature. He also studied Jewish theology under S.J. *Rapoport, and was ordained a rabbi in 1844. In 1845 he moved to Vienna, where he founded an elementary and secondary school for boys in 1849 which combined Jewishness with modern secular learning. It became the first Jewish school in Austria entitled to issue officially valid diplomas. Szántó taught Bible and Hebrew literature at the Vienna *bet ha-midrash*; he was also appointed inspector for Jewish religious instruction at public schools and official interpreter of the Hebrew language. In 1861 he founded, with Leopold *Kompert, a weekly journal, *Die *Neuzeit*, which he edited until his death. He contributed to the *Jahrbuch fuer Israeliten* and was its editor from 1865 to 1868.

Szántó was a prolific writer with a precise and lively style, writing a large portion of *Die Neuzeit* himself as well as many articles in the Jewish and Vienna daily press, chiefly on education. He wrote a bible commentary (1845), two historic novels, *Bilder aus Alexandrias Vorzeit and Judentum und Romantik*, and many essays on Jewish history, some in Hebrew. He was a devoted follower of Adolf *Jellinek and a forceful fighter for his ideas of Jewish reform. Szántó also participated in the Reform *synods of Leipzig and Augsburg.

BIBLIOGRAPHY: K. Wurzbach, *Biographisches Lexikon des Kaiserthums Oesterreich*, 41 (1880), 161–4; AZDJ, 46 (1882), 93–95; Wininger, Biog, s.v.

[Hugo Knoepfmacher]

SZASZ, THOMAS STEPHEN (1920–), U.S. psychiatrist and writer. Born in Budapest, Hungary, Szasz graduated from the Royal Hungarian Training Institute in Budapest shortly before the Nazi invasion of Austria prompted his family to move to the United States in 1938. He majored in physics at the University of Cincinnati and earned his M.D. degree in 1944. He then chose to specialize in psychiatry and psychoanalysis, training at the University of Chicago.

Szasz remained affiliated to the university's Institute for Psychoanalysis 1950–56, until he was appointed professor of psychiatry at the Upstate Medical Center of the State University of New York.

Szasz was a prolific writer but became well-known and controversial through *The Myth of Mental Illness: Foundations of a Theory of Personal Conduct* (1961), which called into question many of the fundamental assumptions of psychiatry. He contended that conditions conventionally described by psychiatrists as "mental illness" were more properly characterized as "problems of living" and that the concept of "mental illness" was in fact faulty, insofar as labeling a mind as "sick" was a metaphorical imputation of qualities properly reserved for discussion of the body, wherein diagnosis could be based on actual physical evidence of disease.

The "myth" of which Szasz spoke was the mistaking of this metaphor for reality. He argued in *Law, Liberty and Psychiatry* (1963) that the designation of aberrant behavior as an illness facilitated social control and impinged upon individual freedom. Szasz also argued that, on a practical level, involuntary hospitalization discouraged people from seeking help for fear that they might fall victim to it.

Szasz argued that the essence of his work is "that we have to replace a theological outlook on life with a therapeutic one," with analyst and client working together to increase the latter's self-knowledge and understanding. In his *Manufacture of Madness: A Comparative Study of the Inquisition and the Mental Health Movement* (1971), he developed the notion that repressive trends in psychiatry have their parallels in oppressive forces in the past. In 1970 he helped establish the American Association for the Abolition of Involuntary Mental Hospitalization. His critics argue that he underestimates the dangers inherent in allowing complete freedom of choice to mental patients or – another of his concerns – drug addicts.

After he retired from teaching, Szasz was named professor emeritus in psychiatry at the State University of New York Health Science Center. In 1998 he received the Rollo May Award, presented by the American Psychological Association.

Szasz's other books include *Ideology and Insanity: Essays on the Psychiatric Dehumanization of Man* (1970), *Ceremonial Chemistry: The Ritual Persecution of Drugs, Addicts, and Pushers* (1974), *The Second Sin* (1977), *The Theology of Medicine* (1977), *The Myth of Psychotherapy* (1978), *The Therapeutic State* (1984), *Insanity: The Idea and Its Consequences* (1987), *The Untamed Tongue: A Dissenting Dictionary* (1990), *Our Right to Drugs: The Case for a Free Market* (1992), *A Lexicon of Lunacy* (1992), *The Meaning of Mind* (1996), *Faith in Freedom* (2004), and *Words to the Wise* (2004).

BIBLIOGRAPHY: R. Vatz and L. Weinberg, *Thomas Szasz: Primary Values and Major Contentions* (1982); J. Schaler (ed.), *Szasz under Fire* (2004).

[Rohan Saxena and Ruth Beloff (2nd ed.)]

SZCZEBRZESZYN (Rus. **Shchebreshin**; Yid. **Shebreshin**), town in *Lublin province, E. Poland. An organized community existed there from the first half of the 16th century. The Jews in Szczebrzeszyn traded in spices and frequently did business at the Lublin fairs. In 1583 King Stephen Báthory renewed the rights formerly granted to the Jews there to trade in the villages. In 1597 King Sigismund III Vasa prohibited the Jews from leasing tax collections. A magnificent synagogue, built in Renaissance style, was erected at the close of the 16th century. (It was set on fire in 1939.) The Jews of the town suffered at the time of the *Chmielnicki massacres, in 1648–49. Meir b. Samuel of Szczebrzeszyn, who escaped, gave an account of these events in his *Ẓok ha-Ittim* (Cracow, 1650). In 1701 a session of the *Council of the Four Lands was held in Szczebrzeszyn. There were 444 Jews living in Szczebrzeszyn in 1765. After 1815, when Szczebrzeszyn was incorporated within Congress Poland, there were no restrictions on Jewish settlement in the town. The Jewish population numbered 1,083 (31% of the total) in 1827; 1,605 (38%) in 1857; 2,449 (44%) in 1897; and 2,644 (42%) in 1921.

During the 19th century Ḥasidism had considerable influence in the community. The *ẓaddik* of Javorov, Elimelech Hurwitz, stayed there during the 1880s. The Hebrew scholar Jacob *Reifmann lived in Szczebrzeszyn in the first half of the 19th century.

In the municipal elections held in 1931 the General Zionists obtained three seats, Po'alei Zion one, *Agudat Israel one, and the *Bund five.

[Shimshon Leib Kirshenboim]

Holocaust Period

On the outbreak of World War II there were about 3,200 Jews in Szczebrzeszyn. The German army entered the town on Sept. 13, 1939, but withdrew on Sept. 27, when the town was occupied by the Red Army. On Oct. 9, 1939, the Red Army withdrew according to the new German-Soviet agreement on the partition line. Several hundred Jews, mostly young people, left the town for the east together with the Soviet army. The remaining Jews were immediately subjected to persecutions by the Germans. On Aug. 12, 1940, the Germans ordered 300 Jews to register for work in a forced-labor camp. Most of them did not obey the order and fled from the town. On May 8, 1942, the German police murdered about 100 Jews. On Aug. 8, 1942, several hundred Jews were deported to the *Belzec death camp. On Oct. 21, 1942, all Jews who did not manage to escape were transferred to Belzec and perished there. Hundreds of Jews, however, succeeded in escaping into the surrounding forests, where they organized small guerrilla units. Only a few survived until the liberation of the region in July 1944. After the war the Jewish community was not reconstituted.

[Stefan Krakowski]

BIBLIOGRAPHY: M. Balaban, *Zabytki historyczne w Polsce* (1929), 51; *Sefer Hrubieszów* (1962); *Shebreshin Zhurnal*, nos. 4–5 (1954); I. Schiper, *Dzieje handlu żydowskiego na ziemiach polskich* (1937), index; B. Wasiutyński, *Ludność żydowska w Polsce wiekach XIX i XX* (1930), 33; Z. Klukowski, *Dzięnnik 3 lat okupacji* (1959).

SZCZERCOW, village near Belchatow, in Lodz province, central Poland. Eighty-eight Jews were living in Szczercow in 1808 (17% of the total population). During the 19th century there were no restrictions on Jewish settlement in the locality, and the number of Jews grew to 186 (14%) in 1827, 371 (22%) in 1857, 962 (34%) in 1897, and 1,513 (35%) in 1921. In the latter half of the 19th century, Szczercow Jews engaged in crafts (weaving, tanning, tailoring, shoemaking), transportation, and petty trade.

Holocaust Period

In 1939 Szczercow had a population of 3,200 Jews and 1,800 non-Jews. During the first few days of World War II, the town was completely burned down, and the Jews, homeless and bereft of their possessions, escaped to the nearby town of *Zelow, while 150 found shelter in the city of *Belchatow. A small group of Jews apparently returned to the town and, according to one source of information, the Germans deported the remnant of the Jewish community at the end of 1941 or early in 1942.

BIBLIOGRAPHY: B. Wasiutyński, *Ludność żydowska w Polsce w wiekach XIX i XX* (1930), 51; D. Dabrowska, in: BŻIH, no. 13–14 (1955).

[Danuta Dombrowska]

SZEGED, city in S. Hungary. Jews settled there at a relatively late date, at the close of the 18th century. Previously, the Austrian emperor and Hungarian King Charles III had left the choice "whether or not to accept Jews and gypsies" in the hands of the "free royal cities," and these cities, including Szeged, took advantage of this right to exclude them. Hence the first Jewish family settled in Szeged only in 1781; their numbers grew to 18 in 1786; 38 in 1792; 58 in 1799; 62 in 1806; and 681 in 1840. The first house was acquired by M. Pollak in 1788. Houses could be purchased by them in an extremely small area (1813). In 1844 there were 24 Jewish house owners in the town. The first register, of 1799, records two goldsmiths, two tailors, and one distiller among the Jews. The majority of the Jews in Szeged were merchants and peddlers, who were excluded from participation in the fairs. By the 1860s and 1870s Jews were active in the establishment of companies, banks, and industries, or as craftsmen. A number of crafts, such as goldsmithing and upholstery, were mostly in the hands of Jews. From the 1850s Jews also engaged in agriculture.

Throughout the community's existence, particularly when members of the Loew family served as rabbis (see below), it had an exemplary organization. The regulations of the community were drawn up in 1791 and revised in 1863, and remained in force until the Holocaust. The erection of the first synagogue was planned for 1789, but because of opposition from the authorities was not built until 1803. It was replaced by another (the "Old Synagogue") in 1839, which stood until 1905, when the Great Synagogue was erected. Noted for its magnificence, it was built upon the instructions of I. *Loew (it has been declared an architectural monument).

The first rabbi of the community was R. Jehiel (officiated 1789–90); he was followed by Hirsch Bak (1790–1843), and Leopold *Loew (1850–75), leader of the Hungarian Reform movement (see *Neology) who introduced very moderate reforms in his community. After the latter's death, W. *Bacher (1876–77), a prominent figure in the *Wissenschaft des Judentums, served as deputy rabbi and then I. *Loew succeeded his father, who died in Budapest. After World War I, J. Frenkel (who later settled in Israel) was at first acting rabbi and later rabbi of the community (1927–49). He was succeeded by J. Schindler (1950–63), and then by T. Raj.

Although the community of Szeged joined the Neologists after the schism in Hungarian Jewry following the Congress of 1869 (see *Hungary), it remained united out of respect for the Loew family. In contrast to most of the Hungarian communities, the Szeged community also granted a free hand to Zionist activities and allocated considerable sums to the national funds. The school of the community was established in 1844 and remained open until the Holocaust (1944), at first under the supervision of the rabbis of the Loew family, who acted as its principals and maintained its high standard. After World War II it resumed its work in conjunction with the institutions of *Youth Aliyah.

The Jewish population numbered 3,628 in 1869; 3,618 in 1880; 4,731 in 1890; 5,863 in 1900; 6,903 in 1910; 6,958 in 1920; and 5,560 in 1930. M. *Karman, the leading educator in Hungary, and W. Loew (a brother of I. Loew), the talented translator of Hungarian literature in the United States, were born in Szeged. The liberal and tolerant tradition toward the Jews in Szeged was replaced by anti-Jewish agitation after the establishment of the Horthy regime in the town.

Holocaust and Contemporary Periods

There were 4,161 Jews living in Szeged in 1941. After the German occupation (March 19, 1944), the Jews were confined to a ghetto with the Jews of the immediate vicinity. From there around 3,000 were deported to *Auschwitz, and others to Austria when two transports were erroneously sent to Strasshof.

About half returned from deportation, numbering 2,124 in 1946 and 927 in 1958, with a synagogue, school, old age home, and orphanage for 400 Budapest children who had lost their parents in the Holocaust. Only a few hundred Jews remained by the early 1990s.

BIBLIOGRAPHY: I. Lőw and Zs. Kulinyi, *A szegedi zsidók 1785-től 1885-ig* (1885); *Magyar Zsidó Lexikon* (1929), 828–31.

[Baruch Yaron]

SZEKELY, EVA (1927–), Hungarian-born swimmer, member of the International Swimming Hall of Fame. During her 19-year career (1940–58), Szekely set 10 world records, five Olympic records, and over 100 Hungarian national records while winning two Olympic medals, 10 World University Championships, and 68 Hungarian National Championships. At the age of nine, Szekely was inspired to become an Olympic swimmer after hearing the Hungarian national anthem being played in honor of swimmer Ferenc Csik's gold medal performance at the Berlin Olympics. Despite her intense patriotism, Szekely's career was halted by her Hungarian swimming team which, in 1941, ousted her as a "religious undesirable." During the Nazi invasion of Hungary, she found refuge in a Swiss-run safe house in a section of Budapest known as the International Ghetto, an area set up in July of 1944 via the intervention of Raoul *Wallenberg and Swiss consul Charles Lutz. As it was forbidden for Jews to use the public swimming pools in the protected ghetto, Szekely maintained her fitness by running up and down the staircase in her five-story building a hundred times a day. Szekely resumed her career after the war, and three years later she qualified for the first of her three Olympic appearances, the 1948 London Olympics. There, she competed in the 200m breaststroke, the 100m freestyle, and the 400m freestyle, finishing fourth, fifth, and sixth, respectively. In May 1951, Szekely set a world record of 1:16.9 in a race which would not become an Olympic event until 1968, the 100m breaststroke. At the Helsinki Games in 1952, Szekely won a gold medal in the 200m breaststroke in a record time of 2:51.7, and also finished sixth in the 400m freestyle. In 1956, Szekely and her husband, superstar waterpoloist Dezso Gyarmati, left for the Summer Olympics in Australia the day before the Hungarian Revolution against Communist rule, on October 23. Szekely would later write in her memoirs that "we had no word of our two-year-old daughter, or my parents. I didn't get any real sleep for a week before I was due to race, and lost over 12 pounds." Despite the adversity, Szekely won a silver medal in her specialty, the 200m breaststroke, and even improved a notch in the 400m freestyle, to fifth place. After her retirement, Szekely went on to become a successful swimming coach, helping guide her daughter, Andrea Gyarmati, to a silver and bronze medal at the Munich Olympics in 1972.

[Robert B. Klein (2nd ed.)]

SZEKESFEHERVAR (Hung. **Székesfehérvár**; Ger. **Stuhlweissenburg**), city in W. central Hungary; during the early Middle Ages the capital of Hungary. Jews were living there in the 13th century, and the community, an important one during the 14th, played a role in Jewish affairs in the country as a whole. It interceded with the queen on behalf of the Jews of Pressburg (*Bratislava) in 1503. In the 16th to 17th centuries wealthy Jews who had escaped massacre in Buda (see *Budapest) settled in the town. After Buda passed to the Hapsburgs, Jews were not authorized to enter Szekesfehervar. The first Jews to be granted permission to reside there subsequently were members of a family which opened an inn for Jews attending the fairs. In the year following enactment of the law permitting unrestricted residence (1840) 20 Jewish families settled in the town. The first synagogue was erected in 1867, and in 1892 an organ and a female choir were introduced. The community of Szekesfehervar was one of the staunchest supporters of the *Reform movement. A split within the community occurred in 1861 when the Orthodox group was authorized to form a separate organization, even before the official separation within Hungarian Jewry in 1869. The Jewish population numbered 3,024 in 1910; 2,867 in 1920; and 2,450 in 1930. They were mostly merchants but there were also a number of lessees and landowners, as well as members of the liberal professions.

Holocaust and Contemporary Periods

From 1938 the community was affected by the restrictions and disabilities imposed on the Jews in Hungary. After the German occupation (March 19, 1944) about 5,000 Jews were concentrated in Szekesfehervar and with the 2,075 Jews in the town were deported to the death camp at *Auschwitz. Only 250 returned.

BIBLIOGRAPHY: B. Bernstein, in: *Magyar Zsidó Szemle*, 11 (1894), 508f.; *Etudes orientales à la mémoire de Paul Hirschler*, ed. by O. Komlós (1950), 1–15, 137–44 (Hung.); *Magyar Zsidó Lexikon* (1929), 834–6.

[Baruch Yaron]

SZELL, GEORGE (**Georg**; 1897–1970), conductor, pianist and composer. He was born in Budapest but grew up in Vienna, where he studied piano and composition with Richard Robert and Max Reger. As a composer and pianist, dubbed "the new Mozart," he turned to conducting at age 17. Szell assisted Richard Strauss at the Berlin State Opera (1915) and held conducting posts in German opera houses and in Prague, before his appointments as chief conductor of the Berlin State Opera (1924–29) and of the Neues Deutsches Theater in Prague (1929–37). From 1937 he conducted the Scottish Orchestra in Glasgow and the Residentie Orchestra of The Hague. Immigrating to the United States in 1939, he became principal conductor at the Metropolitan Opera, New York (1942–46), and was noted for his performances there of Wagner and Strauss. From 1946 until 1970 he was appointed permanent conductor of the Cleveland Orchestra and built its ensemble to one of world class by combining the profound European orchestral tradition with the brilliance of the great American orchestras. He won repute for his pedantic approach, his extensive repertoire of modern and classical works, and his lucid interpretations of the Viennese classics. Outstanding among his numerous recordings are the five Beethoven piano concertos (with *Fleisher), the four Brahms symphonies, and Dvořák's last three symphonies. His many world premieres included Hindemith's Piano Concerto (1947), Walton's Partita (1958), and Mennin's Symphony no. 7 (1964), and at the Salzburg Festival, operas by Liebermann and Egk.

BIBLIOGRAPHY: Grove Music Online; *Baker's Biographical Dictionary of Musicians* (1997); D. Rosenberg. "George Szell: Portrait of a Perfectionist," in: *Symphony Magazine*, 31:6 (1980), 15–19; B. Surtees, "George Szell: 25 Years Later," in: *Classical Music Magazine*, 18:1 (1995), 30.

[Naama Ramot (2nd ed.)]

SZENDE, PÁL (1879–1935), Hungarian politician. Born in Nyirbátor, Szende joined the "Sociological Society" in 1907 and was secretary of the National Association of Commerce from 1908 to 1918. In 1914 he joined the Radical Party, which favored Hungary's withdrawal from World War I. Szende advocated land reform and the granting of universal suffrage. When the wartime regime ended in October 1918 he was made director general of the Ministry of Finance in the revolutionary coalition government of Michael Károlyi. A month later he was made minister of finance, and within a few weeks succeeded in stabilizing the economy by means of internal borrowing and a new taxation system. In March 1919, however, the communists led by Béla *Kun seized power and Szende followed Károlyi into exile. In his later years Szende lived in Vienna and Paris, where he lectured on sociology and philosophy.

BIBLIOGRAPHY: Z. Horváth, *Irodalom és történelem* (1968), 19–35.

[Baruch Yaron]

SZENDE, STEFAN (1901–1985), Hungarian writer and journalist, who wrote in German and Swedish. Szende's *Den siste* *juden frän Polen* ("The Last Jew from Poland"), published in 1944, was among the first authentic Holocaust accounts. Its American edition was titled *The Promise Hitler Kept* (1945). After the war Szende lived in Sweden. Willy Brandt, the German politician, his lifelong comrade-in-arms, wrote the foreword to his memoirs *Zwischen Gewalt und Toleranz* ("Between Violence and Tolerance," 1975).

[Eva Kondor]

SZENES (originally **Schlesinger**), **BÉLA** (1894–1927), Hungarian author. Szenes was born in Budapest. He joined the editorial boards of various newspapers, and was noted for his feuilletons (known as *"Szenes-ember,"* which, in Hungarian, has the additional meaning of "coalman"). Szenes wrote humorous plays, which were successful on the Hungarian stage and also abroad. In his short life he was a gifted and prolific writer.

His stories include *A Szenes ember könyve* ("The Story of the Coalman," 1916), *Vidám irások* ("Humorous Writings," 2 vols., 1920–21), and *Csibi* ("To Young People," 1919). Among his plays were *A buta ember* ("The Stupid Man," 1921), *A gazdag leány* ("The Rich Girl," 1921), *Az alvó férj* ("The Sleeping Husband," 1926), and *Nem nősülök* ("I Won't Marry," 1927). His daughter was the World War II Palestinian heroine Hannah *Szenes.

BIBLIOGRAPHY: *Magyar Zsidó Lexikon* (1929) s.v.: *Magyar Irodalmi Lexikon*, 3 (1965), s.v.

[Baruch Yaron]

SZENES, ERZSI (1902–1979), Hungarian poet and author. Born in Nagymihály (then in Hungary) she lived in Kassa (Košice) between World War I and World War II but was in contact with literary circles in Budapest, and with the literary periodical *Nyugat*. At the beginning of the Slovakian mass deportations, she fled to Budapest, but was deported to Auschwitz. After World War II she returned to Czechoslovakia and from there moved to Israel in 1949.

Erzsi Szenes wrote verse in the biblical spirit, and Jewish themes were always present in her poetry; from the period of Nazi persecution onward, they formed the only subject of her work. Her writings include the poems *Selyemgombolyag* ("The Coil of Silk," 1924) and *Fehér kendő* ("White Shawl," 1928); and the stories *Nyártól nyárig* ("From Summer to Summer," 1943), and *Van hazám* ("I Have a Homeland," 1956).

BIBLIOGRAPHY: *Magyar Zsidó Lexikon* (1929), s.v.; *Magyar Irodalmi Lexikon*, 3 (1965), s.v.

[Baruch Yaron]

SZENES, HANNAH (1921–1944), poet and *Haganah fighter who parachuted into Nazi-occupied Europe. Hannah was born in Budapest of an assimilated family, daughter of the writer Béla *Szenes. She early revealed a remarkable intellect and literary talent; at 13 she began to write a diary, which she kept up until 1944. Under the impact of the antisemitic atmosphere in Budapest she became an ardent Zionist, and in September 1939 she went to Palestine and began her studies at the Nahalal agricultural school. Two years later she joined kibbutz Sedot Yam, where she wrote some of her most poignant poems (e.g., Toward Caesarea). At the end of 1942, deeply concerned with the fate of European Jewry and of her mother in Budapest, she joined the group of parachutists organized by the Haganah to rescue Allied prisoners of war and organize Jewish resistance. In March 1944 she was parachuted over Yugoslavia, where she stayed among Tito's partisans. In Srdice she wrote the poem *Ashrei ha-Gafrur* (Blessed is the Match). On June 7, at the peak of the deportation of Hungarian Jewry (see *Hungary, Holocaust) she crossed the border into Hungary but was arrested by the Hungarian police. Though cruelly tortured, she did not reveal any information, and after the fascist takeover in Hungary, a secret court hastily condemned her to death. On November 7, 1944 she was executed by a firing squad in a Budapest prison courtyard. Her remains were taken to Israel in 1950 and interred on Mt. Herzl. In Israel and in the Zionist movement her name became a symbol of devotion and self-sacrifice. Various books were written about her as well as a play by Aharon *Megged. Her diary was published in 1971 (in English).

BIBLIOGRAPHY: M. Syrkin, *Blessed is the Match* (1948); D. and P. Bar-Adon, *Seven who Fell* (1947), 81–124; N. Braslavski (ed.), *Hannah Szenes, Ḥayyeha, Sheliḥutah u-Motah* (196610); Y. Palgi, *Ru'aḥ Gedolah Ba'ah* (1956), passim; Y. Lewy (ed.), *Das Leben von Chana Szenes 1921–1944 nach ihren Tagebuechern* (1960); O. Besser, *Ha-Ẓanḥanit she-Lo Shavah* (1969).

[Livia Rothkirchen]

SZENWALD, LUCJAN (1909–1944), Polish poet and translator. Szenwald wrote revolutionary verse on themes such as the Nazi peril and the Spanish Civil War, outstanding for its cultural breadth and technical virtuosity. He also translated many works by leading foreign authors. *Z ziemi goücinnej do Polski* ("From the Friendly Land to Poland," 1944) appeared in the year of Szenwald's death in action with the Red Army. A posthumous selection of his works was *Pisma wybrane* (1955).

SZÉP, ERNŐ (1884–1953), Hungarian poet and author. Born in Huszt, Szép began writing poetry at a very early age and went into journalism, first in Debrecen and later in Budapest. His delicate, refined verse reflects the life of poor rural Jews and sees the world through the innocent eyes of a child.

Szép's works include *Elalvó hattyú* ("Drowsing Swan," 1924), a verse collection; *Lila akác* ("Purple Acacia," 1919), and *Valentine* (1927; *Marriage for One*, 1929), novels. His stories dealt with types that had not previously appeared in Hungarian literature – performers and circus artists, whose slang was accompanied by the rich, varied, and deep-rooted Hungarian of Szép's books. His novel *Dali-dali-dal* (1934) perpetuates the memory of his father. Szép also wrote the plays *Az egyszeri királyfi* ("Once Upon a Time There Was a Prince," 1914), *Patika* ("Pharmacy," 1919), and *Azra* (1930), based on a poem by Heine. His book *Emberszag* ("Human Smell," 1945) tells of the suffering of Jews in Budapest during the Holocaust.

BIBLIOGRAPHY: *Magyar Zsidó Lexikon* (1929), 843–4; *Magyar Irodalmi Lexikon*, 3 (1965), 212–4.

[Baruch Yaron]

SZER, SEWERYN (1902–1968), Polish jurist. Born in Warsaw, Szer was a lawyer and a senior official in the public notary's office. He went into hiding during the Nazi occupation and in 1944 worked in the legal department of the Polish Committee for National Liberation. Later he became head of the civil law department in the ministry of justice. He worked for the unification and codification of Polish civil law and was the author of works on family law. He also wrote the general part of a lexicon of civil law.

In 1947 Szer was appointed professor of civil law at the Warsaw Academy of Political Science. He became professor of law at Warsaw University in 1949 and then served as a High Court Judge until 1955. In 1956 he headed the civil law department at the Polish Academy of Sciences. An outstanding jurist, he left writings covering all branches of civil law, including succession, property, and private international law.

[Israel (Ignacy) Isserles]

SZERB, ANTAL (1901–1945), Hungarian author and literary scholar. Szerb, who was born in Budapest, became one of Hungary's greatest authorities on European literature. He began his career as an author by writing poetry and stories in the literary periodical *Nyugat* and essays on the Hungarian classics of the early 19th century designed for the educated reader. Szerb achieved his peak with his monumental work, *Magyar irodalom történet* ("The History of Hungarian Literature," 2 vols., 1934), which ran into 13 editions. Another important work was his *A világirodalom története* ("History of World Literature," 2 vols., 1941). Free from superficiality or generalization, these books developed an interesting and even exciting literary style. Szerb made a masterly attempt to integrate Hungarian writing into the mainstream of world literature. Three of his other works are *Stefan George* (1926), *Az udvari ember* ("The Courtier," 1927), and *Vörösmarty tanulmányok* ("Vörösmarty Studies," 1930). As a writer Szerb was a combination of the scholar-teacher and artist. His work was a fusion of meticulous accuracy and imagination, and his humor and irony, his lightness of touch, and his perspicacity make his books genuine classics. Szerb converted to Catholicism as a young man, undoubtedly under the influence of his teacher, the priest-poet Sándor Sik, himself a converted Jew. Toward the end of his life, however, according to his associates, he even became a "zealous Jew." During World War II he rejected opportunities of self-preservation and escaping, and late in 1944 was sent to the Balf concentration camp in western Hungary, where he was murdered by guards.

BIBLIOGRAPHY: *Magyar Irodalmi Lexikon*, 3 (1965), 222–4.

[Baruch Yaron]

SZERENCSÉS, IMRE (Fortunatus; 1460–1526?), Hungarian apostate; financial adviser to the royal house. His birthplace is unknown, but some scholars believe that Szerencsés was a Spanish exile whose real name was Solomon Seneor b. Ephraim. When he arrived in Hungary he was compelled to convert to Christianity and he married a Christian woman of aristocratic birth, although many believe that he secretly remained true to Judaism. Certainly he helped Jews on some occasions. The children of his first, Jewish, marriage remained Jews. As confidant of the chancellor Szalkai (later archbishop of Hungary), Szerencsés held important positions as vice treasurer, supervisor of the frontier estates, and counselor of King Louis II and the queen of Hungary. On his advice the king devalued the Hungarian currency to cover the expenses of the war against the Ottoman Empire. The public blamed the subsequent deteriorating financial situation on Szerencsés. When the state assembly demanded his execution in 1525, the king had Szerencsés imprisoned but ordered his release after a few weeks. In reaction the mob sacked Szerencsés' house. A short while later, Szerencsés was reconciled with the nobles and the king. During the summer of 1525, acting on his suggestion, the king confiscated the property of the Fuggers, the highly influential banking family.

BIBLIOGRAPHY: S. Kohn, *A zsidók története Magyarországon*, 1 (1884), 271–86; S. Büchler, *A zsidók története Budapesten a legrégibb időktől 1867-ig* (1901), 67–73; idem, *Szerencsés Imre származása* (1937); *Magyar Zsidó Lexikon* (1929), 845–6; A. Kubinyi, in: *Mitteilungen des Vereins fuer Geschichte der Stadt Nuernberg*, 52 (1963–64) 98–104; L. Zolnay, *Buda középkori zsidósága* (1968), 32.

[Andreas Kubinyi]

SZERESZEWSKI, MOSES DAVID (1844–1915), merchant and leading Jewish banker in Warsaw. His business activities did not begin until the close of the 19th century, when he engaged in wholesale trade and the import of cloth from Russia. When the development of the Polish cloth industry at the beginning of the 20th century made import from Russia no longer profitable, Szereszewski turned to banking. In 1911 he opened a bank in Warsaw which granted loans to industrialists and which enabled him to invest a considerable part of his fortune in construction. The fact that Szereszewski had invested his wealth in such enterprises before World War I saved him from the harmful effects of interrupted credit activities which the war brought to many other less fortunate businessmen. His son RAPHAEL was a Warsaw banker and public official between the two world wars. He and his brother MICHAEL administered the family bank after their father's death. During the 1920s the two brothers set up an industrial compound which included sugar refineries, chemical factories, and textile works. Beginning in 1916, Raphael served six times as a member of the Warsaw municipal council. He was also a member of the *Sejm from 1922 to 1927. For many years he headed the union of Jewish tradesmen in Poland and was active in many Jewish charitable societies. When the "Society for the Propagation of Jewish Sciences in Poland" was established in 1925, Raphael was appointed a member of its executive. He left Poland at the outbreak of World War II in 1939 and in 1943 settled in New York, where he lived until his death.

BIBLIOGRAPHY: J. Shatzky, *Geshikhte fun Yidn in Varshe*, 3 (1953), index; Y. Gruenbaum, in: EG, 1 (1953), index; 6 (1959), index.

SZERMAN, PINCHAS (1887–1942), *ḥazzan*. Born in Staszow, Poland, he sang as a boy with his elder brother, Abraham Isaac, then *ḥazzan* in Krashnik. Szerman studied in A.B. *Birnbaum's school for *ḥazzanim* in Czestochowa, and in 1909 was appointed *ḥazzan sheni* (assistant *ḥazzan*) at the Tłómacka Street Synagogue in Warsaw. Holding this post until the outbreak of World War II, he served together with the chief *ḥazzanim*, Gershon Sirota and Moshe Koussevitzky, and the choral directors Leo Loew and David Eisenstadt. Szerman was held in high esteem not only for his flexible baritone voice and his unaffected style, but also for his learning and character. He was one of the founders of the *Aggudat ha-Ḥazzanim* (Cantors' Association), in Poland, and served as its president and the editor of its journal *Di Khazonim Velt*.

SZERYNG, HENRYK (1918–1988), Mexican violinist of Polish birth. On *Hubermann's advice he studied with Karl *Flesch in Berlin. He also studied with Jacques Thibaud in Paris, starting his career in 1933. From 1933 to 1939 he studied composition with Nadia Boulanger. During World War II he was liaison officer for the Polish government in exile in London, helped to relocate Polish refugees in Mexico, and performed for the Allied forces. In 1946 he was appointed professor of music at the National University of Mexico. Szeryng made his home in Mexico, and consistently championed the music of native Mexican composers. From 1954 he went on annual tours abroad. In 1970 he was made Mexico's special adviser to UNESCO. The Henryk Szeryng Foundation Career Award was created to help develop the careers of outstanding young violinists. A humanitarian and violinist of extraordinary gifts, Szeryng gained widespread admiration for his technical command, stylistic versatility, and musical intellect of rare insight. He gave the premieres of numerous works written for him, including compositions by Chavez and Penderecki and the first modern performance of Paganini's Violin Concerto no.3 (1971). His recordings include the major violin concertos, Bach sonatas and partitas, the complete Mozart works for violin and orchestra and chamber music, notably with Ingrid Haebler and Artur *Rubinstein. Szeryng visited Israel and made several recordings with the Israel PO. He wrote chamber music and edited baroque violin works, especially those of Bach. His article "La tecnica del violin" (1970) was republished in *Pauta Cuadernos de teoria y critica musical*, 9:34 (Apr–June 1990), 84–98.

BIBLIOGRAPHY: Grove Music Online; *Baker's Biographical Dictionary of Musicians* (1997); I. Hermann. "Henryk Szeryng Kuenstler und Weltbuerger (1918–1988)," in: *Das Orchester*, 36 (Sept. 1988), 934–35; R. Klopcic, "Henryk Szeryng: Master of Bach and the Bow," in *Strings*, 8:1 (1993), 32–34.

[Naama Ramot (2nd ed.)]

SZIGETI, IMRE (1897–1975), Australian graphic artist. Born in Hungary, Szigeti was forced out of Budapest University by antisemitism. He studied art in Berlin. Leaving Germany in 1933, he arrived in Sydney, Australia, in 1939 and worked at textile print designing. A fine graphic artist, his spidery, rhythmical lines show great depth. His work is mostly gouaches, pastels, and line drawings.

SZIGETI, JOSEPH (1892–1973), violinist. Born in Sighet, Szigeti studied with Hubay and made his debut at the age of seven. In 1917 he was appointed professor of violin at the Geneva Conservatory, and in 1926 settled in the United States. His playing was distinguished by ease and vigor, although his bow-arm position was very unusual – close to the body. Szigeti toured the world and participated in many festivals of modern music. He gave the first public performance of many modern works, including the violin concertos of Busoni (1912), Prokofiev (First Concerto, 1935) and Ernest *Bloch (1938). He also published numerous arrangements and a cadenza to Mozart's Third Violin Concerto. Szigeti wrote memoirs *With Strings Attached* (1947, 1967^2), *A Violinist's Notebook* (1965), and *The Ten Beethoven Sonatas for Piano and Violin* (1965).

SZILÁGYI, GÉZA (1875–1958), Hungarian poet. A native of Budapest, where he studied law, Szilágyi joined the editorial boards of various newspapers. He was the first poet in Hungary to portray unrestrained passion, and the publication of his first verse anthology, *Tristia*, led to his prosecution in 1896 and to the banning of his book. Szilágyi had a decisive influence on his great contemporary, the poet Entire Ady. Szilágyi belonged to the Hungarian modernist school, which published various periodicals, such as *Nyugat, Szerda, and Figyelő*. In his often satirical works, he tended to emphasize the more grotesque aspects of life. Of all the Hungarian-Jewish poets of the time Szilágyi adhered most closely to Judaism. He translated extracts from the books of Job and Ecclesiastes, and wrote poems on biblical themes.

His verse collections include *Válagatott régi és új versek* ("Selected Old and New Poems," 1948), *Holt vizeken* ("On the Waters of Death," 1903) and *Neked írtam* ("I Wrote for You," 1911). Three of his prose works were *Lepel nélkül* ("Uncloaked," 1910), *Ez Pest* ("This is Budapest," 1913), and *Menny, pokol, háború* ("Heaven, Hell, War," 1917). Szilágyi was also an active journalist.

BIBLIOGRAPHY: *Magyar Zsidó Lexikon* (1929), 851; *Magyar Irodalmi Lexikon*, 3 (1965), 240.

[Baruch Yaron]

SZILARD, LEO (1898–1964), Hungarian physicist and extraordinary polymath. He was born in Budapest and studied at the Minta School and at Budapest Technical University (1916–19). His engineering course was disrupted by World War I service in the Austro-Hungarian army (1917) from which he was discharged because of illness. Horthy's antisemitic policies persuaded him to leave Hungary for Berlin (1920) where he gained his Ph.D. in physics from the University of Berlin (1922). He worked in different departments of the University of Berlin and for the German General Electric Company (1922–33) before leaving for England with the rise of the Nazis. He did research at St Bartholomew's Hospital, London, and the Clarendon Laboratory, Oxford University (1933–38) before immigrating to the U.S. He worked at Columbia University, New York, before moving to the University of Chicago (1942). He was appointed professor of biophysics at the university's Institute of Radiobiology and Biophysics (1946) but changed to biology (1947) and started a molecular biology laboratory (1948–53). After a period without formal affiliation except as visiting professor to Brandeis University, Waltham, Mass., he again returned to the University of Chicago as professor of biophysics at the Enrico Fermi Institute for Nuclear Studies (1956–61). He became a resident fellow of the Salk Institute, La Jolla, California (1964–66). Szilard's scientific career began with an outstandingly original thesis on thermodynamics. In Germany he collaborated with Albert *Einstein (1926–33) in designing a novel domestic refrigerator and induction pump, filed patents on the linear accelerator, cyclotron, and electron microscope, taught quantum physics with John von *Neumann, and published his analysis of Maxwell's Demon. In England he conceived and patented (1934) the idea of a neutron chain reaction despite the skepticism of many physicists and was at once aware of the implications. After Hahn and Strassman's discovery of uranium fission, (with Walter Zinn) he showed that neutrons are emitted during this process. His experiments with Enrico Fermi led to the construction of the world's first nuclear reactor. He advised his colleagues in the Manhattan Project on reactor design and correctly predicted that radiation damage to reactor constituents could release stored energy; this accounted for the accident involving Britain's Windscale reactor (1957). He was later a creative contributor to the work on phages (viruses which infect bacteria) which initiated modern molecular biology and an influential theorist in the field of enzyme regulation. His World War I experience and the Japanese invasion of China made Szilard averse to militarism. However his alarm, shared by Eugene *Wigner and Edward *Teller, that the Nazis might develop nuclear weapons persuaded Einstein to write to Roosevelt, thereby initiating the Manhattan Project. Szilard's opposition to political interference with scientific freedom led to conflict with General Groves, the overall Project commander. After Germany's defeat he also expressed moral reservations over using nuclear weapons against Japan. After the war he was prominent among Project scientists opposing military control of atomic energy. He attended the first Pugwash conference (1957) and participated in the Pugwash movement and other movements for world security. His writings included the elegant essays *The Voice of the Dolphins* (1961). He was elected to membership of the U.S. Academy of Arts and Sciences (1954) and National Academy of Sciences (1961). When he fell ill, he designed the radiation therapy that cured his bladder cancer (1959).

[Michael Denman (2nd ed.)]

SZOBEL, GÉZA (1905–1963), Slovak painter. Szobel held his first exhibition of paintings at the age of eight. In 1927 he settled in Paris. From 1934 his painting became abstract. He spent World War II in England. His paintings on the Holocaust and war themes exhibited in 1944 were acclaimed by critics. He returned to abstract painting in France.

SZOLD, BENJAMIN (1829–1902), U.S. rabbi and scholar. Szold was born in Nemiskert, Hungary, where his family owned land. Although they were the only Jews in town, he received an excellent Jewish education from the rabbis in the area. At the age of 16, or 14 according to family tradition, he was granted the title *morenu* ("our teacher") by Rabbi Benjamin Wolf at the Pressburg Yeshivah. He went on to Vienna for further study but participated in the Revolution of 1848, and was expelled for his activities. He then returned to Pressburg and from 1849 to 1855 tutored privately. He began to study at the University of Breslau and at the newly founded rabbinical seminary in that city, where he came under the influence of Zacharias *Frankel, Heinrich *Graetz, and Jacob *Bernays, and decided to become a rabbi. In 1858, after applying unsuccessfully for a rabbinical post in Stockholm, he accepted an invitation from Congregation Oheb Shalom in Baltimore in the United States. Oheb Shalom was then on the verge of becoming Reform, but Szold led it to a Judaism which allowed for innovations in ritual practice, but not in basic tenets. He recognized and employed the educational potential of the regular Sabbath sermon. He introduced his own prayer book, *Avodat Yisrael* (1867), to replace the previously used *Minhag Amerikah* (1857) by I.M. Wise, and the traditional *siddur.* The *Avodat Yisrael* was widely adopted by congregations throughout the country. Under Szold's leadership Oheb Shalom became one of the foremost American congregations.

Szold's strong liberal and humanitarian convictions found expression in civic and Jewish communal affairs. He took part in founding charitable institutions and aiding the Russian refugees who streamed in during the 1880s. With his daughter Henrietta *Szold, he organized study groups and a library for immigrants. As early as 1893 he publicly advocated Zionism and was an active Hebraist. He published scholarly articles and commentaries on the Bible, especially on the Book of Job (1886).

BIBLIOGRAPHY: A.L. Levin, *Szolds of Lombard Steet: A Baltimore Family* (1960); M. Davis, *Emergence of Conservative Judaism* (1965), 360–2, 525; *National Cyclopaedia of American Biographies*, 13 (1906), 65–66; DAB, 18 (1936), 262.

[Gladys Rosen]

SZOLD, HENRIETTA (1860–1945), founder of *Hadassah, the Women's Zionist Organization of America, and organizational leader and political figure in Palestine. Szold was born in Baltimore, Maryland. Her parents, Sophie (Schaar) and Rabbi Benjamin Szold, had arrived in Baltimore from Hungary in 1859, after her father was appointed rabbi of Congregation Oheb Shalom. Henrietta, the eldest of eight daughters, received the level of attention and education from her father that was usually reserved for a son. She was taught German (the household language), English, French, Hebrew, secular studies, and Judaism. In 1877, Szold graduated from Western Female High School. For nearly 15 years she taught French, German, botany, and mathematics at the Misses Adam's School in Baltimore. She also taught religious school and gave Bible and history courses for adults at Oheb Shalom. Szold attended public lectures at the Johns Hopkins University and the Peabody Institute, and served as Baltimore correspondent of the New York *Jewish Messenger*, signing her articles "Sulamith."

In 1880, Henrietta's father took her to Europe, where she was horrified to see the degrading conditions under which women prayed in Prague's Alt-Neu Shul. Upon her return to Baltimore, she witnessed the emergence of a Russian-Jewish ghetto as a product of mass immigration. Among these immigrants were Hebraists, Zionists, and other intellectuals who went on to organize the Isaac Baer Levinsohn Literary Society in 1888. With them, Henrietta Szold ran a model night school for immigrants, where she taught until 1893. Inspired by the Zionists she had met, she joined the newly organized Hebras Zion (the Zionist Association of Baltimore) in 1897. Because her father had trained her for a life in Jewish scholarship and had used her services for years as his literary secretary, she also began to volunteer for, and then became the paid secretary of, the editorial board of the *Jewish Publication Society (JPS), a position she held until 1916. The sole woman at the JPS, Szold's duties included the translation of a dozen works, writing articles of her own, editing the books, and overseeing the publication schedule. In 1899 she took on the lion's share of producing the first *American Jewish Year Book*, of which she was sole editor from 1904 to 1908. She also collaborated in the compilation of the *Jewish Encyclopedia*.

After her father's death in 1902, Henrietta and her mother moved to New York. In addition to continuing her work for the Jewish Publication Society, she enrolled at the Jewish Theological Seminary to study Hebrew and Talmud, which she hoped would help her edit her father's manuscripts. Henrietta's acceptance was contingent on her signing a formal promise not to study for the rabbinate. She also joined the New York Hadassah Study Circle, whose members prepared papers on Jewish history and held discussions about Zionism. The physical pressures of her grueling work, plus an unrequited emotional involvement with JTS professor Louis *Ginzberg, whose writings she was editing and translating, resulted in a breakdown. In 1909, Henrietta took a six-month leave from her duties, and she and Sophie traveled to Europe and Palestine.

During her tour of the Holy Land, Szold was shaken by the misery she witnessed. Inspired by her mother's suggestion that Henrietta and her reading group devote their energies to practical work, Szold gathered her friends Sophia Berger, Emma Gottheil, Lotta Levvensohn, Mathilde Schechter, Gertrude Goldsmith, and Rosalia Phillips, and issued an invitation to women interested in "the promotion of Jewish institutions and enterprises in Palestine." On February 24, 1912, 38 women constituted the Hadassah Chapter of Daughters of Zion, elected Henrietta Szold as president, and chose nursing as their focus. The name was changed to Hadassah, the Women's Zionist Organization of America, in 1914 at the second convention, by which time chapters in eight cities had already been established.

In 1916, Sophie died; at the same time, Judge Julian Mack and a group of fellow Zionists decided to offer Henrietta a lifetime stipend so that she could do her work unfettered. At the helm of the new organization of 4,000 women, Szold organized the American Zionist Medical Unit, consisting of doctors, nurses, administrators, vehicles, and drugs, which set sail for Palestine in June 1918 with support from the American Zionist Organization, Hadassah, and the Joint Distribution Committee. Szold was also placed in charge of Zionist educational and propaganda work for the Zionist Organization of America (ZOA). At the end of 1919 she agreed to go to Palestine as its representative. Her remaining 25 years were spent working in Palestine, with occasional trips back to the United States. She became the director of the ZOA's medical unit, ran the Nurses' Training School, and directed health work in Jewish schools.

In 1923 Henrietta Szold returned to the U.S. to see her ailing sister and resumed the active presidency of a steadily expanding Hadassah. In 1926 she resigned and became honorary president. A year later she went back to Palestine as a member of the powerful and prestigious three-person executive of the World Zionist Organization, with the portfolio for health and education. In 1930 she again visited the U.S., where, to her dismay, Hadassah celebrated her 70th birthday with great flourish. When the *Va'ad Le'ummi of Palestine Jewry offered her a seat on its executive committee, she returned to accept the social welfare portfolio, through which she achieved a hygiene program, the rehabilitation of juvenile delinquents, and the establishment of vocational schools. When The Hebrew University opened, however, she was denied a seat on the board, because of her sex.

With the Nazi rise to power in Germany, Henrietta Szold understood the threat to Jewish survival. In 1932, a plan called *Youth Aliyah was conceived to send German Jewish adolescents to Palestine to complete their education. Szold became director of this institution, set up by the Jewish Agency in cooperation with a German-Jewish youth organization to train youth between the ages of 15 and 17, for transfer to *kevutzot* in Palestine. She personally greeted the first group, which arrived in 1934, and Hadassah raised funds in the U.S. to support the organization. Despite obstacles in dealing with the British Mandate government in acquiring immigration certificates, and in working with Jewish communities in both Germany and Palestine, by 1948 the program had cared for 30,000 children. Henrietta Szold, who had always wanted to give birth to "many children," had in a sense become the "mother of the *yishuv*."

In October 1934 Szold laid the cornerstone of the new Rothschild-Hadassah-University Hospital on Mount Scopus.

In 1937 she traveled to Berlin in the interest of Youth Aliyah and went on to the Zionist Congress in Zurich to express her views against the British partition plan and in favor of the controversial notion of a bi-national Arab-Jewish state. During the Arab riots of 1936 and the accompanying "strike" against the government, and until the outbreak of World War II in 1939, Szold worked on behalf of Jewish children and local refugees fleeing Arab attacks. On her 80th birthday in 1940, Szold read her will to a group of friends and expressed her desire to provide for a center for research, publication, and coordination of national youth activities. After her death, the bureau was named Mosad Szold. On her 81st birthday, the Va'ad Le'ummi entrusted her with the planning of its Fund for Child and Youth Care. Two years later, with the help of her close associate, Hans Beyth, she supervised the arrival and care of Youth Aliyah children from all parts of Poland who had wandered for three and a half years. By 1944 Henrietta Szold's failing health prevented her from traveling to the U.S. to receive the degree of Doctor of Humanities from Boston University. It was awarded via a two-way radio broadcast. Later that year she contracted pneumonia and died after a prolonged stay in the hospital that she had done so much to build. To Henrietta Szold, Zionism was the balm for the wounds inflicted by history upon the Jewish people, "an ideal that can be embraced by all, no matter what their attitude may be to other Jewish questions."

BIBLIOGRAPHY: I. Fineman, *Woman of Valor* (1961); A.L. Levin, *The Szolds of Lombard Street* (1960); M. Lowenthal. *Henrietta Szold: Life and Letters* (1942). **ADD. BIBLIOGRAPHY:** B.R. Shargel, *Lost Love: The Untold Story of Henrietta Szold* (1997); S. Reinharz and M. Raider (eds.), *American Jewish Women and the Zionist Enterprise* (2005); B. Kessler (ed.), *Daughter of Zion: Henrietta Szold and American Jewish Woman* (1995).

[Shulamit Reinharz (2nd ed.)]

SZOLD, ROBERT (1889–1977), U.S. lawyer and Zionist. Szold, who was born in Streator, Illinois, graduated from Knox College in Illinois (1909). He served as assistant attorney general in Puerto Rico (1915) and assistant to U.S. Solicitor General John W. Davis (1915–18) before returning to private practice. A Zionist from youth, Szold along with Harry *Friedenwald went to Palestine as members of the Zionist commission in 1919. In 1920 he went to London as a member of the Reorganization Commission together with Julius Simon and Nehemia de Lieme. Szold aligned himself with the Brandeis-Mack forces, which were nevertheless ousted by the Weizmann supporters from the Zionist Organization of America administration (1921). In 1930 the ZOA formally recalled the Brandeis-Mack leadership, and Szold served as chairman of the administration until 1932. In 1942 he became treasurer and chairman of the budget committee of the American Emergency Committee for Zionist Affairs. He was among those who opposed the 1937 proposal of partitioning Palestine between Jews and Arabs. Yet at the 22nd World Zionist Congress in 1946, Szold supported Weizmann in his desire to negotiate with the British instead of the more militant position of Abba Hillel Silver, which prevailed. Szold was a member of numerous organizations devoted to the economic development of Palestine, including the Palestine Endowment Funds, Inc. (est. 1922) and the Palestine Economic Corporation (est. 1926). He served for many years as a senior partner in the New York law firm of Szold and Brandwen. The Robert Szold Institute for Applied Science was established at the Hebrew University of Jerusalem.

Szold was the third cousin of Henrietta *Szold, the founder of Hadassah. He wrote *77 Great Russell Street: Recollections of Robert Szold* (1967).

[Simcha Berkowitz / Ruth Beloff (2nd ed.)]

SZOLNOK, city in E. central Hungary. Jews began to settle there around 1830; at first Jewish peddlers were only permitted to enter the city during the day. In 1848 there were 60 Jews in the city. A synagogue was built in 1850 (later used by the Orthodox congregation) and a second one in 1857. A *talmud torah* was founded in 1925. After the schism in Hungarian Jewry in 1868–69 the community of Szolnok joined the Neologists. In 1898 a magnificent synagogue was built. The community numbered 818 persons in 1869; 1,101 in 1880; 1,455 in 1890; 1,952 in 1900; 2,062 in 1910; 2,103 in 1920, 2,098 in 1930, and 2,590 in 1941. The Jews in Szolnok mainly engaged in trade and crafts, but also served as government and municipal officials. Rabbis of Szolnok were E. Klein (from 1854), V.I. Friedlieber (1887–91) and K. Heves (1898–1945), who died in Budapest.

Holocaust and Contemporary Periods

During World War II, after the German invasion on March 19, 1944, the 1,800 remaining Jews in Szolnok were confined in a ghetto and at the end of June deported to *Auschwitz and Austria. After the war 609 Jews returned to Szolnok. They numbered 320 in 1953 and 200 in 1970. The great synagogue was converted into a municipal library.

The mathematician G. Szegö and the author A. *Komor were born in Szolnok.

BIBLIOGRAPHY: BJCE.

[Baruch Yaron and Alexander Scheiber]

SZOMBATHELY (Ger. **Steinamanger**), city in W. Hungary. The Jewish community there was first organized as a branch of the Rechnitz (Rohonc) community. Jews lived there as merchants from 1687, but only in 1840 were they permitted to settle permanently. In 1846 a school was built where instruction was given in German, and after 1861 in Hungarian. The older synagogue was used by the Orthodox congregation. A new synagogue was built in 1880. The Jewish population numbered 59 in 1840; 1,154 in 1869; 1,678 in 1880; 1,639 in 1890; and 2,635 in 1900. They were mainly occupied as merchants and also included artisans, members of the liberal professions, some landowners, and farm proprietors. Rabbis of Szombathely were L. Koenigsberger, who was ordained as rabbi by M. *Banet; Bela *Bernstein (officiated 1892–1901), and J.

Horovitz (1911–52), who returned after being deported by the Germans and continued at his post.

Holocaust and Contemporary Periods

During World War II, after the entry of the Germans on March 19, 1944, the Jews, numbering around 3,000 in 1941, were crowded into a ghetto with Jews from the surrounding villages. On July 13, all were deported to the death camp at *Auschwitz, of whom some 250 returned. With the Jews of the surrounding district they numbered not more than 750 in 1946, and fewer than 80 in 1970 after emigration to Israel. The synagogue of the community was converted into a concert-hall.

BIBLIOGRAPHY: B. Bernstein, *A zsidók története Szombathelyen* (1914).

[Baruch Yaron and Alexander Scheiber]

SZOMORY (Weisz), DEZSŐ (1869–1944), Hungarian author and playwright. Born in Budapest, Szomory studied music and, while still a child, played before Liszt. In 1890 he deserted from the army and fled to Paris, where he lived until 1906, earning his living as a foreign correspondent. While in Paris, he was considered a disciple of the contemporary naturalist movement, but he only developed as a writer after returning to Hungary. Szomory evolved an elaborate and at times overelegant and artificial style in the decadent *fin-de-siècle* tradition. One of Szomory's outstanding prose works was *A párizsi regény* ("Paris Romance," 1929). He also dealt with Jewish subjects, especially Jewish provincial life, but most of his works about Jews, such as the drama *Péntek este* ("Friday Night," 1896), were aimed at Jewish readers only. A successful dramatist, he wrote plays on social problems, themes also reflected in his historical plays. His works include the short story collection *Elbukottak* ("Those Who Failed," 1892); *Az isteni kert* ("Divine Garden," 1910), *A pékné* ("The Baker's Wife," 1916), and *Levelek egy baratnőmhöz* ("Letters to a Lady Friend," 1927). His plays included *Bella* (1913), *Takáts Alice* (1930), and *Szegedy Annie* (1931).

BIBLIOGRAPHY: *Magyar Zsidó Lexikon* (1929), 867–8; *Magyar Irodalmi Lexikon*, 3 (1965), 273–6 (incl. bibl.).

[Baruch Yaron]

°**SZTÓJAY, DÖME** (1883–1946), Hungarian general and statesman, prime minister of Hungary in 1944. Sztójay was an intelligence officer in Horthy's counterrevolutionary army, and later became the Hungarian military attaché in Berlin. From 1935 until March 1944 he was Hungary's minister to Germany. Already in 1942 Sztójay declared himself Hungary's foremost proponent of antisemitism. After the Nazi occupation of Hungary (March 19, 1944), Horthy and the German Foreign office jointly appointed Sztójay prime minister of the Budapest government. Sztójay established a pro-Nazi, anti-Jewish regime. The Nazis considered Sztójay a reliable collaborator, especially for carrying out the "Final Solution" in Hungary. Within a few days of his appointment, Sztójay called on the members of his government to approve formally severe anti-Jewish measures, including ghettoization and deportation. On March 29, the Hungarian information service announced the Sztójay government's decision to promulgate anti-Jewish laws. Among the many rulings signed by Sztójay was a decree obliging all Jews to wear the yellow badge (March 31, 1944). Sztójay was prime minister until Aug. 24, 1944, when conservative elements in Hungary succeeded in removing him from office after Romania broke away from the Axis (Aug. 23, 1944). When the Soviet army approached Budapest in January 1945, Sztójay fled to Germany. In 1945 he was arrested by American Intelligence, extradited to Hungary, and tried by a People's Court as a major criminal. He was given the death sentence and executed in 1946.

BIBLIOGRAPHY: R.L. Braham, *Destruction of Hungarian Jewry*, 2 vols. (1963), index; R. Hilberg, *Destruction of the European Jews* (1961), index.

[Yehouda Marton]

SZWARC, MICHAEL (1909–2000), U.S. physical chemist. Born in Bedzin, Poland, Szwarc graduated from the Warsaw Polytechnic in 1932 and then studied and taught at the Hebrew University of Jerusalem (1935–42) and Manchester University (1947–52). In 1952 he went to the U.S. as professor of physical and polymer chemistry at the College of Forestry of the State University of New York (Syracuse). In 1964 he was awarded a distinguished professorship by the State University of New York and in 1967 he founded and became the first director of the SUNY Polymer Research Center. He became professor emeritus in 1980. After his retirement in 1979, he joined the Loker Hydrocarbon Research Institute at USC.

Szwarc discovered living polymerization, a reaction that allows the resultant polymers to maintain chain-end reactivity even after completion of the reaction. This advance allows the synthesis of polymers with controlled molecular weights, and with functional groups placed at particular positions in the polymer chain. Szwarc also made fundamental contributions to the development of "block polymers," in which two or more different polymer chains are connected to each other through chemical bonds. This has led to the manufacture of a variety of unique polymeric materials, such as thermoplastic elastomers.

Szwarc was elected a fellow of the Royal Society (London) in 1966 and received two awards in polymer chemistry from the American Chemical Society (1969, 1990) as well as the Kyoto Prize for advanced technology in 1991 in recognition of his fundamental contributions to polymer science. He contributed papers to scientific journals, mostly concerning kinetics and mechanisms of organic reactions and polymerizations.

[Samuel Aaron Miller / Bracha Rager (2nd ed.)]

SZYDLOWIEC, town in Kielce province, E. central Poland. As a center of trade, smithery, and production of building materials, Szydlowiec attracted Jewish settlers from the end of the 15th century. By the end of the 17th century there was an organized Jewish community under the jurisdiction of the *Sandomierz-Krakow province. In 1765 the Jewish population of Szydlowiec and its environs numbered 902 persons. Johann Philippe de Carosi, a German in the employ of the Polish king, visited the town in 1779 or 1780 and found a densely populated Jewish quarter whose population constituted about 90% of the total inhabitants of the town. The Jews engaged mainly in commerce of agricultural produce as well as timber, building materials, beverages, hides, and ironware. In 1788 the owner of the town, Duke Radziwill, granted the Jews additional municipal land and the right to erect additional dwelling houses, a synagogue, and a cemetery. Between 1825 and 1862 Jews were not permitted to reside outside their quarter. The Jewish population of Szydlowiec grew considerably from the 19th century, numbering 2,049 (64.8% of the total population) in 1827; 2,780 (73.2%) in 1857; 5,298 (71.3%) in 1897; and 5,501 (77.1%) in 1921. In the second half of the 19th century Jewish contractors developed the building materials and tanning industries. In 1905–06 Jewish workers and youths, led by the *Bund and *Po'alei Zion, actively participated in the struggle against the czarist regime.

After World War I the town quickly developed into a shoe-producing center (with 14 tanneries), completely controlled by Jews, and provided work for many hundreds of shoemakers, fitters, and traveling salesmen. The ten stone quarries also belonged to Jews, and their products were widely distributed. The Jews in Szydlowiec also had a long tradition of trading in hardware. There were several Jewish libraries, trade unions – especially a strong leather workers' union – and groupings of all parties active among Jews in Poland.

Holocaust Period

On the outbreak of World War II there were about 7,200 Jews in Szydlowiec. On Sept. 23, 1942, 10,000 Jews from Szydlowiec and its vicinity were deported to the *Treblinka death camp. On Nov. 10, 1942, the Germans established four new ghettos in the region (at *Sandomierz, Szydlowiec, *Radomsko, and Vjazd). The Jews were encouraged to leave their hiding places in the forests, being promised security in these ghettos. Thousands of Jews, not seeing any possibility of surviving in the forests during the winter, responded to the German appeal. About 5,000 Jews were concentrated in the ghetto of Szydlowiec. The Jewish community was liquidated when the remaining 5,000 Jews were sent to Treblinka. After the war the Jewish community of Szydlowiec was not reconstituted.

BIBLIOGRAPHY: Halpern, Pinkas; N.B. Gelber, in: *Historishe Shriftn*, 7 (1929), 238–9; S. Kalabiński (ed.), *Carat i klasy posiadające w walce z rewolucja 1905–1907 w Królestwie Polskim* (1956), index; B. Wasiutyński, *Ludność żydowska w Polsce w wiekach XIX i XX* (1930), 32; A. Rutkowski, in: BŻIH (1955), no. 15–16; idem, in: *Folks-Shtime* (Yid. Jan. 22, 1958); A. Finkler, *Shidlovtse, fun Letstn Khurbn* (1948), 105–7; *Devar ha-Shavu'a* (Jan. 3, 1964).

SZYK, ARTHUR (1894–1951), illustrator, miniaturist, and cartoonist. Born in Lodz, Poland, he studied at Cracow and in World War I fought in the Russian army and was taken prisoner; afterward he fought under General Sikorski against the Bolsheviks. Subsequently in Paris, he illustrated books, among them *The Book of Esther*, Flaubert's *Temptations of Saint Anthony*, Pierre Benoit's *Jacob's Well*, and Ludwig *Lewisohn's *Last Days of Shylock*. In 1934 the Polish government sent him to the United States, where he exhibited at the Library of Congress, Washington, D.C., and in many museums. His series of miniatures on the history of the American Revolution was sent as a gift by the Polish government to President Franklin D. Roosevelt. In England, at the outbreak of World War II, he turned his pen to caricatures for British papers and periodicals. In 1940 he went to the U.S., where he drew cartoons lampooning the Nazi leaders. These were collected in a volume, *The New Order* (1941). He also illustrated books such as the *Rubáiyát of Omar Khayyam* (1940). Szyk was noted for his refined draftsmanship and calligraphy, in the style of medieval manuscript-illumination, as shown in an edition of the Charter of *Kalisz, in a sumptuous edition of the *Haggadah* (executed 1932–36; published 1940), and in the highly decorated Declaration of Independence for the State of Israel (1948). These were executed in a close imitation of the illuminated manuscripts of the Middle Ages. His colors had the luminosity of Gothic stained glass windows. His Hebrew lettering was superbly decorative and his illuminations sometimes showed a close acquaintance with Jewish legend.

BIBLIOGRAPHY: Roth, Art, 798.

[Alfred Werner]

SZYR, EUGENIUSZ (1915–), Polish economist and Communist politician. Born in Warsaw, Szyr joined the Communist youth movement at the age of 15 and volunteered for the International Brigade in the Spanish Civil War. During World War II he fled to Russia and served as political officer in the Soviet-sponsored Polish army. Szyr returned to Poland in 1945 and held important economic positions in the Polish government. He was vice chairman of the state commission for economic planning from 1949 to 1953 and was its chairman from 1953 to 1956. He became a member of the government economic council in the following year and in 1964 was made a vice premier. Szyr was a leading figure in the ruling Polish United Workers' Party as a member of its central committee and later of its political bureau. During the antisemitic campaign after the Six-Day War he was publicly attacked and was not reelected to the political bureau at the 1968 party congress although he remained vice premier.

[Abraham Wein]

Initial letter "T" of the phrase Temptavit Deus Abraham *in a 14th-century Paris missal. The illumination shows the "sacrifice" of Isaac. Rheims, Bibliothèque Municipale, Ms. 2301, fol. 49v.*

TA-TN

TAANACH (Heb. תַּעְנַךְ, תַּעֲנָךְ), Canaanite city-state, identified with Tell Tiʿinnik, about 5 mi. (8 km.) S.E. of Megiddo. The earliest city flourished during the 27th–25th centuries B.C.E. (end of early Bronze Age II to the first half of Early Bronze Age III). Relations with Egypt may have been established at an early date, as is evidenced by a possible imitation of Egyptian tomb construction of the third dynasty. The city was abandoned in about 2500 B.C.E. and was only reoccupied in the second millennium (Middle Bronze Age II). In the Late Bronze Age, Taanach came under Egyptian domination. A palace, rebuilt several times in this period, attests the continuing prosperity of the city. Taanach appears in the list of cities subject to Thutmosis III (no. 42) and on a contemporary papyrus listing the envoys of the Canaanite kings (Ermitage papyrus 1115/6). Twelve cuneiform tablets, dating to the 15th–14th century B.C.E., were uncovered in the excavations. In them an Egyptian governor named Amenhotep (the pharaoh?) orders the king of Taanach to supply men and materials to Megiddo and Gaza. The city appears again in connection with Megiddo in the *El-Amarna letter no. 248 (as Tahnuka).

The king of Taanach is listed among the Canaanite kings defeated by Joshua (Josh. 12:21). While the city appears among those supposedly held by Manasseh in the territory of Issachar (Josh. 17:11; I Chron. 7:29), it follows from Judges 1:27 that the Israelites did not capture the city at the time of the conquest. The city played an important role in the war of Deborah. From the description in Judges 5:19 – "Taanach by the waters of Megiddo" – Albright has concluded that during an eclipse of the latter city, Taanach was predominant in the Jezreel Valley. Others doubt this interpretation, especially as the latest excavations indicate that the city was destroyed in about 1125 B.C.E. and lay in ruins for most of the 11th century. The city revived in the period of the United Monarchy, when David established it as one of the levitical cities (Josh. 21:25), which served as administrative centers. Solomon included it in his fifth district, administered by Baana the son of Ahilud (I Kings 4:12). To this period possibly belongs the pillared building similar to those found at Megiddo and Hazor, which some have regarded as a stable. Taanach was conquered by Shishak and it appears in his list of conquered cities between Shunem and Megiddo (no. 14).

The city's existence in later times is attested by Eusebius, who variously locates it 3 and 4 mi. (5 and 6 km.) from Legio (Onom. 98:12; 100:7ff.). In the crusader period, it was a *casal* (village) known as Tannoc, which was dependent on Legio and was a subject of dispute between the bishop and abbey of Nazareth. The present-day village of Ti'innik is located near the ancient site.

Tell Ti'innik was excavated by E. Sellin on behalf of the Vienna Academy (1902–04) and by an American expedition under the direction of P.W. Lapp (1963–68). Among the finds of the recent excavations are a cuneiform tablet in Ugaritic script and an early Israelite high place.

[Michael Avi-Yonah]

In Modern Israel

Although the village Ti'innik and the ancient site remained 1.3 mi. (2 km.) beyond the Jordanian border after the 1949 Armistice Agreement, the larger part of the southern Jezreel Valley came into Israel, and a comprehensive development project of the area was carried out from 1955 under the name Taanach Bloc. After the model of the *Lachish region, three clusters of moshavim, each with three villages grouped around a rural center, were established: in the west are Gadish, Mele'ah, and Nir Yafeh around Omen; in the center Addirim, Barak, and Devorah around Ḥever; in the east Avital, Meirav, and Perazon around Ya'el. The town of Afulah functioned as the urban center of the bloc. Farming in the region was based on intensive, mostly irrigated, field and garden crops (e.g., cotton, sugar beets, groundnuts, wheat, fodder plants, tomatoes, flowers, etc.), dairy cattle, poultry, and, in some of the moshavim, deciduous fruit orchards. In 1968 the moshavim of the Taanach Bloc had a combined population of about 3,200. The Arab village Ti'innik, which came under Israeli administration after the Six-Day War (1967), numbered 294 inhabitants in the autumn 1967 census. At the end of 2002 the populations of Taanach's moshavim were as followed: Gadish 280, Mele'ah 333, Nir Yafeh 316, Addirim 239, Barak 249, Devorah 216, Avital 423, Meirav 312, and Perazon 318.

[Efraim Orni / Shaked Gilboa (2nd ed.)]

BIBLIOGRAPHY: E. Sellin, *Tell Ta'annek* (Ger., 1904); idem, *Eine Nachlese auf dem Tell Ta'annek in Palaestina* (1905); Albright, in: JPOS, 4 (1924), 140; idem, in: BASOR, 94 (1944), 12–27; idem, in: JNES, 5 (1946), 9; Mazar, in: *Sefer Klausner* (1937), 44ff.; Lapp, in: BA, 30 (1967), 1ff.; idem, in: BASOR, 173 (1964), 45–50; 185 (1967), 2–39; Aharoni, Land, index.

TA'ANIT (Heb. תַּעֲנִית; "Fast"), tractate of the order *Mo'ed* in the Mishnah, Tosefta, and Jerusalem and Babylonian Talmuds. In manuscripts and the *editio princeps* of the Mishnah, the Tosefta, the Jerusalem Talmud, and the works of the *geonim*, as well as in medieval rabbinic literature, it is called *Ta'aniyyot* ("Fasts").

The Mishnah contains four chapters. The first two discuss fasts decreed because of drought, including the determination of the time when the rain should descend; the prayers for those fasts; those exempt from the fasts; and the days when fasts may not be decreed. Chapter 1, from the middle of *halakhah* 2 onward, derives completely from the Mishnah of *Meir. Chapter 2:6–7 is a source dealing with the men of the **mishmarot* and *ma'amadot*, an account given in its entirety although only the first part is relevant to the subject of fasting. The third chapter discusses fasts decreed for reasons other than drought. Chapter 4:1–5 deals with the recital of the priestly blessings on fast days. Although only the first *halakhah* is devoted to this subject, the whole of the source used by Judah ha-Nasi containing this *halakhah* is given. This too is derived from the Mishnah of Meir and also contains details of the description and the *halakhot* of the *ma'amadot* (4:2–4) during which the priestly blessings were uttered as they were on fast days. In connection with the *ma'amadot*, the times of the wood offerings of the priests and the people are described (4:5). Chapter 4:6–7 deals with the permanent fast days of the 17th of Tammuz and the Ninth of Av, their causes, and the detailed laws of the Ninth of Av and the preceding days. Chapter 4:8, dealing with the ancient ceremonies of betrothal on the 15th of Av and the Day of Atonement, is a supplement to 4:5 where the 15th of Av is mentioned. The tractate closes with a later aggadic addition about the Temple so as to end on a note of comfort.

The Tosefta of *Ta'anit* is greatly dependent upon the Mishnah and without it, it can be understood only with difficulty. Tosefta 1:1–2:7 parallels the first two chapters of the Mishnah, while chapter 3 of the Mishnah is possibly paralleled by Tosefta 2:8–17 (according to Mss. Erfurt and London to 2:8–3:2). Mishnah chapter 4:1–5 is paralleled by Tosefta 3:1–8, containing here *beraitot* in connection with the connotation of the *mishmarot* and the *ma'amadot* with the texts better than that of the Mishnah. There are also details of events that transpired in the time of the Greek kings (3:7–8), possibly in the time of the high priest *Jason. Mishnah 4:6–7 is paralleled by Tosefta 3:9–14, which also concludes with words of consolation. In the Jerusalem Talmud there are interesting references to Hadrian's persecution and particularly to *Bar Kokhba, as well as legends about the destruction of the Temple (TJ, 4:8, 68d–69b). Particularly well known is the third chapter of the Babylonian Talmud, which is almost completely *aggadah* and is called "the chapter of piety" because of the many stories about *ḥasidim* – men of piety and good deeds – that are scattered throughout it. *Ta'anit* is the only tractate of the Babylonian Talmud to be published in its entirety in a critical edition, according to manuscripts and the first edition, together with an introduction and philological notes by H. Malter (New York, 1930). Despite its faults and defects, this edition is of great value. Malter also published an *editio minor* together with an English translation.

BIBLIOGRAPHY: Zunz-Albeck, Derashot, 303; Ch. Albeck, *Untersuchungen ueber die Redaktion der Mischnah* (1936^2), 135; Epstein, Mishnah, 686f.; Epstein, Tanna'im, 45f., 257.

[Moshe David Herr]

TABACHNIK, ABRAHAM BER (1901–1970), Yiddish poet and literary critic. Born in a village near Mohilev-Podolsk (Ukraine), he immigrated to New York in 1921, taught in Yiddish schools, and worked for the Jewish Telegraphic Agency. He wrote his first poems in Russian, before turning to Yiddish. He co-edited the anthologies *Fayln* ("Arrows," 1928–31), and the literary quarterly *Vogshol* ("Scale," 1959). In the 1950s he made sound recordings of more than 20 Yiddish poets reading their works (17 cassettes, now in the National and University Library, Jerusalem). Some of Tabachnik's best studies as a critic dealt with M. *Rosenfeld, J. *Rolnick, *Mani-Leib, Z. *Landau, and A. Stolzenberg. A collection of his literary portraits was compiled in the volume *Dikhter un Dikhtung* ("Poets and Poetry," 1965).

BIBLIOGRAPHY: LSNYL, 4 (1961), 1–3; S. Niger, *Kritik un Kritiker* (1959), 156–62; S.D. Singer, *Dikhter un Prozaiker* (1959), 113–21; J. Glatstein, *In Tokh Genumen*, 2 (1960), 253–8. **ADD. BIBLIOGRAPHY:** I. Oren (ed.), *Kratkaia evreĭskaia entsiklopediia*, 8 (1996), 676–7.

[Sol Liptzin / Jerold C. Frakes (2nd ed.)]

TABAK, SOLOMON LEIB (1832–1908), Hungarian *posek*. Born in Sziget of humble parents, Tabak was a pupil of Abraham Judah ha-Kohen *Schwartz in Beregszasz. He served as head of the *bet din* of Jekuthiel Judah *Teitelbaum and continued in that office for many years after Teitelbaum's death.

He was the author of a number of books, all with the title *Erekh Shai*: a commentary on the four parts of the Shulḥan Arukh (5 vols., 1891–1909); talmudic novellae (1910) on the Pentateuch (2 vols., 1912–1928) and on the Books of the Prophets and Hagiographa (1932); as well as two volumes of responsa, *Teshurat Shai* (2 vols., 1905–10). Nearly all his works were reprinted in a photocopy edition in New York from 1965 on.

BIBLIOGRAPHY: J.J. (L.) Greenwald (Grunwald), *Zikkaron la-Rishonim* (1909), 45f.; idem, *Maẓẓevat Kodesh* (1952), 43f.; N. Ben-Menahem, *Gevilei Sefarim* (1947), 20f.; idem, in: *Sinai*, 25 (1949), 202–4.

[Naphtali Ben-Menahem]

TABEEL, THE SON OF (Heb. טָבְאַל, pausal form of טָבְאֵל, "God is good" (in Aramaic), Ezra 4:7). When Pekah, king of Israel, and *Rezin, king of Aram, formed a coalition of states to resist the growing power of Assyria, Jotham, ruler of Judah, refused to join this coalition. Not wanting a neutral and potentially hostile state in their rear, Pekah and Rezin invaded Judah in 735 B.C.E. (II Kings 15:37). At this time of crisis, Jotham died, and his son Ahaz reigned in his stead. Isaiah the prophet came to the king with the message that the plans of Israel and Aram would not succeed. Their plan was stated by the prophet in this manner: "Let us go up against Judah, and vex it, and let us make a breach therein for us, and set up a king in the midst of it, even the son of Tabeel" (Isa. 7:6). Thus, Ahaz was to be removed from the Judean throne, and "the son of Tabeel," more congenial to Israelite-Aramean interests, was to become king.

Medieval commentators are agreed that the son of Tabeel is an important official of Israel or Aram, but differ on the exact interpretation of the name Tabeel. One view translates the name (following the Targum) as "the one good for us," regarding Tabeel as an abbreviation for *ha-tov ʾelenu* (Rashi, Kimḥi, Ibn Ezra). Another commonly held view explains Tabeel as referring to Pekah son of Remaliah, king of Israel. By the letter permutation *albam*, which exchanges a letter in the first half of the alphabet with the corresponding letter in the second half (א–ל, ב–מ), the name Tabeel yields רמלא (*rmlʾ*), i.e., Remaliah (Kimḥi, Rashi, Saadiah, Ibn Ezra in *Sefat Yeter*; cf. similar usage of the letter permutation *atbash* (אתב"ש) in the case of בָּבֶל for שֵׁשַׁךְ in Jer. 25:26 and 51:41, and לֵב קָמָי for כַּשְׂדִּים in Jer. 51:1). In his commentary to Isaiah, Ibn Ezra interprets the name Tabeel to mean "no good."

Modern scholars are almost unanimous in interpreting Tabeel as a Syrian-Aramean name. It follows the same pattern as the name Tabrimmon (I Kings 15:18; Rimmon is an Aramean deity, II Kings 5:18), combining the Aramaic adjective *ṭāb*, "good," with a theophoric element. H. Winckler identified "the son of Tabeel" with Rezin himself, but the evidence for such an identification is not compelling (so E.J. Kissane). Scholars generally agreed that Tabeel was an Aramean prince whom Pekah and Rezin wished to place on the Judean throne. W.F. Albright, however, published a text from the Assyrian archives at Calah (first published by H.W.F. Saggs), almost contemporary with the events in Isaiah and Kings, which shows that Tabeel is a region, located in northern Palestine or southern Syria. The "son of Tabeel" is thus presumably a Judean prince whose maternal home was the land of Tabeel (cf. II Sam. 3:3 concerning Absalom) – the son of Uzziah or Jotham by a princess of Tabeel. H.L. Ginsberg (in bibl.) rejects Albright's view, pointing to the fact that the "House of David" was thrown into panic by the Israelite-Aramean alliance against Judah (Isa. 7:2), and that Isaiah actually addresses the House of David as such in verse 13 (and verse 9b, where the verbs are in the plural); see his further arguments. Rezin and Pekah wished to depose the Davidic dynasty, and not merely to replace Ahaz with a Davidide who would join the anti-Assyrian alliance. B. Mazar also differs with Albright. He locates the land of Tabeel in southern Gilead and identifies its population as Judeans, from whom descended the famous Tobiads of the Hellenistic period.

BIBLIOGRAPHY: O. Procksch, *Jesaia* (1930), 176; E.J. Kissane, *The Book of Isaiah*, 1 (1941), 78; W.F. Albright, in: BASOR, 140 (1955), 34–35; B. Mazar, in: IEJ, 7 (1957), 137–45, 229–38; H.L. Ginsberg, in: *Oz le-David (Ben-Gurion)* (1964), 338 n. 5; idem, in: *Fourth World Congress of Jewish Studies*, Papers, 1 (1967), 91–93 (Eng. section); L. Koehler and W. Baumgartner, *Hebraeisches und aramaeisches Lexikon zum Alten Testament* (1967³), 352.

[Gershon Bacon]

TABENKIN, YIẒḤAK (1887–1971), Israeli labor leader and one of the founders of *Ha-Kibbutz ha-Meʾuḥad and *Aḥdut ha-Avodah, member of the First and Third Knessets. Born in Bobruisk, Belorussia, Tabenkin attended a *ḥeder* there. Later he went on to study in Warsaw, Vienna, and Berne. He helped to found *Po'alei Zion, belonging to the wing that favored agricultural settlement in Ereẓ Israel and participation in the Zionist organization. He settled in Palestine in 1911. Tabenkin worked on farms and joined *Ha-Shomer. He advocated collective settlement and was a member of Kinneret during World War I and of Gedudei ha-Avodah after the war. He also participated in the foundation of kibbutz *En Harod. Tabenkin favored large kibbutzim which would be open for mass membership.

In Palestine he belonged to the group that joined with Po'alei Zion in 1919 to form Aḥdut ha-Avodah, as a stage in the unification of the labor movement, and gave the programmatic address at its founding conference. He was a founding member of the *Histadrut in 1920 and of *Mapai in 1930. Tabenkin objected to David *Ben-Gurion's agreement with the Revisionists in 1934, opposed the 1937 partition plan for Palestine, advocated settlement in all corners of the country as part of the struggle for keeping Ereẓ Israel united, and fought for political activism, the independence of the Histadrut, the development of the labor economy, and loyalty to pioneering principles. When Mapai split in 1944, Tabenkin led the faction then called Ha-Tenu'ah le-Aḥdut ha-Avodah, which joined with *Ha-Shomer ha-Ẓa'ir in 1948 to form *Mapam, and was elected to the First Knesset on its list. Within Mapam he fought against the left-wing trend of empathy with the Communist bloc. He was not elected to the Second Knesset, but when Mapam split in 1954, he became the political and ideological leader of Aḥdut ha-Avodah-Po'alei Zion, and was elected to the Third Knesset on its list. In the early 1960s he retired from all his political and party activities, and devoted his time to teaching and writing. Following the Six-Day War Tabenkin opposed any withdrawal from the territories occupied during war, and participated in the establishment of Tenu'at ha-Avodah le-Ma'an Ereẓ Israel ha-Shelemah (The Labor Movement for Greater Israel), some of whose members joined the Likud in later years. He was a delegate at every Zionist Congress after World War I. He headed the Seminar Center of Ha-Kibbutz ha-Me'uḥad at Efal.

Tabenkin's son Moshe (1917–79) was a poet, and writer of children's books. Moshe served in the Palmaḥ, and was a teacher in kibbutz En-Harod.

Among his writings are *Ha-Medinah ha-Ivrit ve-ha-Derekh Eleha* ("The Jewish State and the Way Toward It," 1944); *Vegn un Umvegn* (Yid., "Ways and Roundabouts," 1947); *Ha-Ḥevrah ha-Kibbutzit* ("Kibbutz Society," 1954); *Devarim 1918–1934* ("Collected Works 1918–34," 1967); *Ein Le'an Laseget* ("There Is Nowhere to Retreat," 1967); *Devarim* ("Speeches and Writings," 1967); *Lekaḥ Sheshet ha-Yamim: Yishuvah shel Ereẓ Bilti Meḥulleket* ("The Lesson of the Six Day War: the Settlement of an Undivided Land," 1971).

BIBLIOGRAPHY: Yad Tabenkin, *Yom Iyyun: ha-Sozi'alizm shel Yiẓḥak Tabenkin* (1973); Yad Tabenkin, *Sugyot be-Mishnato shel Yiẓḥak Tabenkin: Yom Iyyun bi-Melot Shalosh Shanim li-Fetirato* (1974); Y. Even-Nur (ed.), *Shelilat ha-Golah be-Mishnato shel Yiẓḥak Tabenkin be-Meẓi'ut bi-Shenat 1973* (1974); Y. Tabenkin, *Yiẓḥak Tabenkin ve-Etgarei Tekufatenu* (1986); E. Kafkafi, *Emet o Emunah: Tabenkin Meḥannekh Ḥaluẓim* (1992); B. Kaneri, *Tabenkin ve-Ereẓ Yisra'el* (2003).

[Susan Hattis Rolef (2nd ed.)]

TABERNACLE (Lat. *tabernaculum*, "tent"; *taberna*, "hut"; the word renders the Heb. *mishkan*), the portable sanctuary constructed by the Children of Israel in the wilderness at the command of God. (The word has no connection with the Festival of Tabernacles – Sukkot – which should correctly be called the Festival of Booths.)

Terminology

The Bible designates the Tabernacle by a variety of Hebrew terms, each of which is significant in that it either describes the structure of the shrine or depicts its function. Primarily the names may be divided into two groups, one connected with the term *mishkan* and the other with the designation *'ohel*, as follows:

(a) *Mishkan* ("Dwelling," i.e., God's Dwelling Place among Israel; e.g., Ex. 25:9).

(b) *Mishkan* YHWH ("The Dwelling of the Lord"; e.g., Lev. 17:4).

(c) *Mishkan ha-'Edut* ("The Dwelling Place of the Testimony," i.e., of the Tablets of the Covenant, inscribed with the Decalogue; e.g., Ex. 38:21).

(d) *'Ohel Mo'ed* ("Tent of Meeting," i.e., where the Lord meets with – reveals Himself to – man; e.g., Ex. 28:43). This designation is very common, occurring about 150 times.

(e) The terms are combined in *Mishkan 'Ohel Mo'ed* ("Dwelling Place of the Tent"; e.g., Ex. 39:32). It should be noted that *'ohel* and *mishkan* are synonyms in Hebrew (e.g., Num. 16:26, 27) and also in Ugaritic, and that in both literatures these designations continued to be applied to sanctuaries that were no longer mere tents. In the Bible these words sometimes occur as poetic expressions for residences that are permanent structures (e.g., Isa. 54:2; Jer. 30:18). With reference to the sanctuary, *mishkan* and *'ohel* are used both in a general sense – to denote the entire structure of the Tabernacle – and in a restricted connotation, the former signifying the beautiful inner ceiling of the shrine, and the latter the covering of goats' hair immediately above this.

(f) Finally, the Tabernacle is also called *Miqdash* ("Sanctuary"; e.g., Ex. 25:8) and *ha-Qodesh* ("The Holy Place"; e.g., Ex. 28:29). The innermost sanctuary is known as the *Qodesh ha-Qodashim*, "The Most Holy Place" or "The Holy of Holies."

Sources

The main source for the account of the construction of the Tabernacle consists of two groups of verses: Exodus 25–31 and 35–40. Both groups are ascribed by the documentary hypothesis to P, but whereas the first takes the form of instructions, the second is largely a repetition of the first in the past tense, i.e., it describes the execution of the instructions. The order of the contents, however, is more systematic in the later chapters, and the Septuagint shows considerable divergences here from the Masoretic Text. There are additional references to the components of the Tabernacle and its furniture in Numbers 3:25ff. and 4:4ff. in relation to the duties of the levites (cf. also 7:1ff.). The Temple built by Solomon (I Kings 6ff.) and that envisioned by Ezekiel (Ezek. 40ff.) provide interesting parallels and differences. Post-biblical sources, which nevertheless shed valuable light on the traditional conception of the Tabernacle structure, are to be found in Philo (II Mos. 91), in Josephus (Ant., 3:122ff.), and especially in the *Baraita de-Melekhet ha-Mishkan* (third century C.E.).

Materials

The Tabernacle, its equipment, and the priestly vestments were made of a great variety of materials, which were voluntarily contributed by the people (Ex. 25:2ff.; 35:4ff.). These comprised gold (fine and ordinary), silver, bronze (an alloy of copper and tin), and acacia wood; violet (*tekhelet*), purple, and scarlet stuff; ordinary linen and fine twisted linen; goats' hair, tanned rams' skins, and goatskins; oil (for lighting and for anointing); spices (for the incense and for the anointing oil); and precious stones (for the ephod and the breastpiece). The value of the materials was in direct proportion to the degree of sanctity of the Tabernacle component or furniture for which it was used. In this way the conception of graduated holiness was preserved in every aspect of the shrine.

The Tabernacle Proper

The structure of the sanctuary (Ex. 26 and 36) was marked by a certain dichotomy – it was in part a tent and in part a wooden enclosure. Its appearance was that of a flat booth. It was comprised of ten curtains of violet, purple, and scarlet fabric with inwoven ("embroidered") figures of cherubim; each curtain measured 28 cubits (a cubit is about 1½ feet by 4.) They were joined (i.e., sewn) together, forming two sets of five curtains each. To one edge of each set (on the long side) were attached 50 loops of violet thread, and the two sets were connected by 50 gold clasps.

The curtains were supported by 20 *qerashim* of acacia wood on the north side, 20 on the south, and eight on the west (rear) wall. Each *qeresh* was ten cubits high and 1½ wide, and gold-plated. The thickness is not stated, but is variously estimated by the authorities as four figures (c. 3 inches), ½ cubit, and 1 cubit. The older view regarded the supports as solid boards, but such an assumption would make the structure unwieldy. Most exegetes now accept the view of A.R.S. Kennedy that *qeresh* denotes a light, open frame, consisting of two side arms joined together at the top, the middle, and the foot by cross rungs, with two tenons projecting below. Such frames would have the additional advantage of permitting the beautiful curtaining to be seen from the interior. Each frame was fitted, by means of the tenons, into two silver bases. Thus on three sides (north, south, and west) the frames formed a continuous framework and the bases provided an unbroken silver foundation. The fourth, or east, side, had no frames; it served as the entrance and was closed by a screen. The frames were further strengthened on each side by five bars of acacia overlaid with gold, which passed through gold rings; one bar ran across the whole length of the side, and above it were two bars of half this length, matched by two similar bars below it. It also appears (the instruction in Ex. 26:22–25 is obscure) that two frames were fastened to each corner on the west side, which served as buttresses. In all there were 48 frames and 100 bases.

The curtains were placed lengthwise across the frames, forming a roof over the sanctuary and providing an excess of nine cubits on the north and south sides (9 × 10 × 9 cubits) and completely covering the rear end to the ground (since the shrine runs 30 cubits long and the curtaining 40). It seems that the extremities of the curtains were fastened at each end by clasps or loops to pegs affixed to the frames.

Over the curtaining was spread a "tent" formed of 11 curtains of goats' hair, each measuring 4 × 11 cubits. These were made into two sets of five and six curtains respectively, fastened together by 50 loops (perhaps of goats' hair) and bronze clasps. On the east side the first curtain was doubled and suspended over the front of the Tabernacle; along the three other sides, this covering reached to the ground. Alternatively there were 12 cubits hanging down, like the train of a dress, on the west side and the overlap in front was tucked under the curtaining (see U. Cassuto, in bibl., 353). On top of this entire structure were spread, for protection from the weather, two more coverings (Ex. 26:14), one of rams' skins dyed red and the other of skins of **taḥash* ("dugong" or "dolphin"; the exact meaning is in doubt). Possibly, in view of Exodus 40:19, one covering composed of both kinds of skins is intended.

Veil (Ex. 26:31ff.)

The sanctuary was divided into two unequal parts by means of the veil (or veil of the screen), which was a beautiful portiere, "skillfully worked," made of the same fabric as the curtains. It hung from golden clasps and was draped over four acacia pillars overlaid with gold and set in silver bases. This partition was placed 20 cubits from the entrance of the Dwelling exactly underneath the clasps that joined the two sets of curtains together. This inner room, a perfect cube of ten cubits, was called the "Holy of Holies" or the "Most Holy Place," while the outer room, measuring 10 × 20 cubits, was known as the "Holy Place." In Solomon's Temple the two compartments, designated respectively *devir* (the inmost sanctum) and *hekhal* (the outer sanctuary), were twice the size of the rooms in the Tabernacle, but in the same proportion of one to two.

Screen (Ex. 26:36–37)

The eastern end of the Tabernacle was closed by "a screen for the door of the tent." It was made of less costly material than the veil, the fabric being embroidered but not with cherubim; it was suspended from golden hooks on five pillars of gold-plated acacia set in bronze bases. The fabric and the bases were like those of the court screen.

Court

The sanctuary was surrounded by a rectangular enclosure, measuring 100 cubits from east to west and 50 cubits from north to south (a double square of 50 cubits each); it was called "the court of the Tabernacle" (Ex. 27:9). The area was screened by five white curtains "of fine twined linen" five cubits high, hung on 60 acacia pillars fixed into bases of bronze five cubits apart. Each pillar had a silver fillet at the top and the curtains were attached to the pillars by means of silver hooks. Added rigidity was given to the pillar by cords and bronze pegs. The curtains on the north and south sides were 100 cubits long, that on the west was 50 cubits long, while the east side had two short curtains 15 cubits long, suspended from three pillars, which extended from the corners toward the center. This left an opening of 20 cubits in the middle, which was closed by a screen of fine linen embroidered in colors and hanging from four pillars.

The perimeter of the court was 300 cubits and its pillars numbered 60. It was obviously intended that the pillars should be five cubits apart. Since the corner pillars served both adjacent sides, the number of pillars represents no problem; although the pillar at each corner helped to uphold a curtain on each side it was to be counted only once in the total (see Cassuto, in bibl., 366–7). The *baraita*, however, solves the problem by assuming the pillars to be placed in the middle of each length of curtain of five cubits.

The exact position of the Tabernacle within the court is not stated. The generally accepted view is that it was situated in the western square, its entrance being 50 cubits from the door of the court in the east, while on the north and south sides there was a space of 20 cubits between the Dwelling and the court curtains. This view is supported by rabbinic tradition (*Baraita de-Melekhet ha-Mishkan*, 5) and by Philo (II Mos. 91).

Furniture

The Torah describes the furniture before it depicts the structure of the shrine, because the "vessels" were considered the more important; the Tabernacle and court merely housed them. The Ark of the Covenant, which was the most sacred object, was kept in the Holy of Holies (Ex. 25:10ff.). It was an oblong chest of acacia wood 2½ × 1½ × 1½ cubits, overlaid within and without with pure gold. It had a gold molding running around its sides, and was provided with gold rings at the four corners (probably attached to the short sides, so that the Ark faced the way the camp was journeying) to receive the bearing poles. Within the Ark were placed the Tablets of the Decalogue ("testimony"), and in front of it were put, in the course of time, a pot of manna (Ex. 16:33ff.) and Aaron's rod (Num. 17:25).

On the Ark rested a slab of gold (2½ × 1½ cubits) called the "propitiatory" or "mercy seat" (*kapporet*), from the opposite ends of which – and "of one piece with it" – rose two figures of cherubim made of beaten work of fine gold. The faces of the cherubim were turned toward the mercy seat, while their wings arched overhead, thus covering the propitiatory. The cherubim represented the *Throne of God (cf. I Sam. 4:4; II Sam. 6:2; and see Cassuto, in bibl., 333). In the "Holy Place," on the north side, was placed the "table of the Presence" (Ex. 25:23ff.; Num. 4:7). It was made of acacia overlaid with pure gold. Its top measured 2 × 1 cubits, and it was 1½ cubits high. The legs were connected by a rail or frame one handbreadth wide, to which were attached four gold rings to receive the staves used for carrying the table. Its accessories included plates for the loaves of the Presence, bread (or shewbread), cups for incense (Lev. 24:7), and large and small vessels (flagons and bowls) such as were used for libations.

Although the table bears a resemblance to that used in idolatrous temples for offering food to the gods, there was a vital difference. The bread of the Presence was eaten by the priests each week (Lev. 24:9) and the various vessels remained empty. The offerings to God were reserved for the altar, where they were consumed by fire. The table and its equipment were only a symbol: the Tabernacle was the House of the Lord.

The lampstand (*Menorah; Ex. 25:31–40) stood on the south side of the Holy Place facing the table. It was made "of beaten work" from a talent of pure gold, and consisted of a central shaft (resting on a tripod or feet) from which branched out, at different heights, six arms (three on each side), which curved outward and upward and became level with the top of the shaft. The arms and the shaft formed stands for seven lamps (not apparently of gold). The stem and arms were decorated at intervals with ornamentations resembling almond blossoms (comprising the knob and the flower). The lamps were placed in the seven "cups shaped like almond blossoms" that formed the ends of the shaft and branches and were so arranged that the flames should illuminate the front side of the lampstand, i.e., the side facing the table. Snuffers and snuff dishes, as well as oil vessels (Num. 4:9), were provided and only the purest oil might be used (Ex. 27:20; Lev. 24: 1–4). The lamps were intended to give perpetual light (Ex. 27:20; Lev. 24:2), or were kindled each night only (Lev. 24:3; I Sam. 3:3).

The altar of incense (Ex. 30:1–5; 37:25–28), placed in front of the veil, was made of acacia overlaid with pure gold, and was one cubit long and wide and two cubits high. It had a gold molding, horns, rings, and bearing poles. Incense was offered on it perpetually, night and morning, and an annual atonement was carried on its horns. The description of this altar here, and not in Exodus 25, is considered by many exegetes out of place, but is justified by Cassuto (in bibl., 390). It is not mentioned in Leviticus 16, despite the reference to the Day of Atonement service in Exodus 30:10, and it is not included in the account of Solomon's Temple in I Kings 6ff., or in that envisaged by Ezekiel (Ezek. 40ff.). Hence many modern scholars consider the passage a late addition (but note the references in I Chron. 28:18; II Chron. 4:19). The altar (Ex. 27:1–8), or the altar of burnt offering (Ex. 30:28), or the bronze altar (Ex. 38:30) was a hollow chest of acacia overlaid with bronze, measuring five cubits in length and width and three cubits in height. It had horns at the corners and halfway down a ledge (Lev.

9:22); below the ledge was a grating on all sides against which the sacrificial blood was dashed. To facilitate its transport it was provided with bronze rings and bronze-plated poles. Its equipment included pots, shovels, bases, fleshhooks, and fire pans (Ex. 27: 1–8; 38: 1–7). It stood at the center of the court, its position in the eastern square corresponding to that of the Ark in the western square. To take hold of its horns was believed to afford asylum (1 Kings 1:50–51). It is claimed by many exegetes that the altar as described here – a hollow box covered, it is assumed, by a thin metal top – could not have survived a single day. Moreover, its form appears to contradict the injunction in Exodus 20:24–25 [22–23] calling for an earthen or stone altar. Cassuto (in bibl., 362), however, points out that no top is mentioned and suggests that the chest was filled with earth or stones. Between the altar and the sanctuary a laver was placed (Ex. 30:17–21), which consisted of a bronze bowl resting on a bronze base. It was made of "the mirrors of the women who performed tasks" (Ex. 38:8). The antiquity of this reference is evidenced by the fact that there is no reference to these servingwomen after the destruction of Shiloh (1 Sam. 2:22). Its purpose was to provide water for the ritual ablutions of the priests.

The Tabernacle Completed and in Use

The chief architect of the sanctuary and its furniture was *Bezalel, who was assisted by Oholiab and a number of skilled artisans (Ex. 31:2ff.; 35:30ff.). They also made the priestly vestments (Ex. 28). On the first of the first month in the second year of the Exodus the entire structure was erected by Moses (Ex. 40:17), and as soon as the task was completed, the cloud of the Lord covered the Tent of Meeting (Ex. 40:34). The consecration of the Tabernacle and the dedication of the priests by Moses are described in Exodus 29 and Leviticus 8–10. Once the Tabernacle was erected, it occupied a central position, physically and spiritually, in the midst of Israel. It stood in the center of the camp. On three sides (north, west, and south) resided the levite clans, while Moses and Aaron and his sons occupied the east side. Further away the 12 tribes were stationed, three on each side of the quadrilateral. The priests performed the sacrificial and other ritual services of the sanctuary; the levites (8,580; see Num. 4:48) were in charge of the components of the shrine when it was dismantled for each journey. During the stationary periods the cloud rested on the tent; the lifting of the cloud indicated that it was time for the camp to move (Ex. 40:36–38). A blast from the silver trumpets gave the signal to strike camp (Num. 10:1ff.). The holy furniture was carefully wrapped by the priests, special care being given to the Ark, and the levites – Kohathites, Gershonites, and Merarites – attended to the transport of the sanctuary and its sacred articles in accordance with their respective schedules (Num. 4:4–33). On the march six tribes preceded the levites and six formed the rear (Num. 2:17; cf. 10:17ff.). The functions of the Tabernacle may be divided into three categories:

(a) It was the dwelling place of the Lord among the Israelites (Ex. 25:8). The Children of Israel were compelled by force of circumstances to depart from the holy mountain, where the Lord had revealed Himself; nevertheless He continued to dwell in their midst, a fact of which the sanctuary was the visible symbol.

(b) It was the center of Israel's cultus in all its major aspects. Here sacrifices – both regular and occasional – and incense were offered up; here the lamp and the shewbread played their role; here the ritual of the great Day of Atonement, the one day in the year when the high priest was permitted to enter the Holy of Holies, was carried out. It was even the venue of the ordeal of *sotah* (wife suspected of faithlessness; see Num. 5:16, 17).

(c) It was the place where the Divine *Presence was revealed and where the cloud of the Lord manifested itself – over the propitiatory (Lev. 16:2), or over the Tent of Meeting (Ex. 40:34), or at the entrance to the tent (Num. 16:19). It was here that God spoke with Moses (Ex. 25:22).

Exegetical and Historical Problems

The biblical account of the Tabernacle and its history bristles with difficulties. Some of these have already been mentioned; but many more remain. Bible critics stress that the specifications of both the Tabernacle and its furniture are often obscure and full of omissions. For example, the shape of the cherubim, the nature of the *qerashim* and their thickness, the material of the lamps, and the size of the outer coverings are unknown. It is still a moot question whether the measurements are external or internal. Exegetes cannot understand how the great weight of the curtains could be borne by the wooden supports, or how the clan of Merari, who had but four wagons for the task, could transport more than four tons of silver (Ex. 38:24), hundreds of feet of curtaining, and 300 bronze bases. It is doubted whether the Israelites possessed the requisite skills in the wilderness period; they certainly needed Phoenician help for Solomon's Temple (1 Kings 7:13–14, 40–45). The quantities of material required and their costliness seem beyond the means of a wandering people recently freed from bondage. Even the suitability of the form of the Tabernacle service for desert conditions is queried. Although the Tabernacle plays an important role in the desert, there is relatively little heard about it after the settlement in Canaan. Hence the authenticity of the scriptural account is questioned.

Against these arguments it should be noted that the biblical text does not purport to be a detailed blueprint. This is clearly indicated by the recurring phrase "according to the manner of it that you were shown on the mountain." Many specifications were omitted because they were already well known; others were probably not considered essential. As regards the materials and skills, it should be borne in mind that the Israelites left Egypt with considerable spoil (Ex. 12:35–36), that much could be purchased from passing caravan merchants, and that in Egypt the Hebrews must have been forced to learn, in connection with their building operations, quite a number of handicrafts. It is also noteworthy that the Tabernacle specifications exhibit various archaic features consonant with a desert origin. Thus the structure was essentially a tent; the red rams' skins find a parallel in the pre-Islamic *qubbah* (tent of red leather); the wood was acacia (not cedar, as in the Temple), which could be obtained in the wilderness. The frames recall the trelliswork in El's throne room mentioned in Ugaritic literature, while the cube shape of the Holy of Holies may display Egyptian influence. It is also possible that the three degrees of access to the Tabernacle correspond to the three limits of approach to Sinai (Ex. 19:17; 20:21 [18]; 24: 1–2).

But the crux of the criticism relates to the tent mentioned in Exodus 33:7–11, likewise called the Tent of Meeting, which appears to be of a wholly different character from that of the Tabernacle depicted in the so-called Presence. It is portrayed as an ordinary tent, to which the verb *naṭa* ("to pitch") is applied. It is sited outside the camp. No cultic services or appurtenances are mentioned in connection with it, and instead of priests or levites Joshua is in constant attendance. It was visited by all who sought the Lord, and the pillar of cloud descended at the door of the tent (not within it), where the Lord spoke with Moses. This divine revelation appears to be of an occasional, not of a regular, character. The verbal forms occurring in the passage are regarded by most commentators as frequentative; Cassuto (in bibl., 430), however, discerns a poetic usage here insofar as the initial verbs are concerned. These verses are ascribed to E or EJ, and certain scholars claim that three other texts (Num. 11:16–30; 12:4–13; Deut. 31:14–15), which refer to the Tent of Meeting, have the same essential characteristics; hence they all belong to E and present a concept of the Tabernacle that diverges radically from that of P.

Numerous solutions of the problems have been proposed, some highly fanciful and all necessarily conjectural. An old tradition, found in the Septuagint and supported by medieval Jewish commentators like Rashi, A. Ibn Ezra, and others, regards the tent of Exodus 33:7 as Moses' own dwelling (cf. Ex. 18:7; and see Cassuto, in bibl., 429ff.). It was erected beyond the camp, because the latter had been defiled by the worship of the golden calf, and it was used as an oracle only until the Tabernacle was complete. In modern times J. Wellhausen and his followers advanced the extreme view that the Tabernacle of P is completely unhistorical and is merely a fictional portrayal composed in the post-Exilic period and based on the Temple structure, only smaller and with such adjustments as the wilderness was conceived to require. The tent of E contains a minute nucleus of historical tradition and probably reflects the existence of a wrapped Ark in the early era of Israel's history. Another exegetical school suggests the theory that the Ark originally belonged to the northern tribes and that the tent, outside the camp, served the southern tribes as a place of revelation. It was David who put the Ark in the tent (II Sam. 6:17), thus uniting the tribes. Subsequently the tent came to be regarded as the shrine of the Ark and the dwelling place of the Lord; the designation *'Ohel Mo'ed* finally became *Mishkan 'Ohel Mo'ed* ("Dwelling Place of the Tent of Meeting"). Other scholars are of the opinion that both tents existed at the same time, the tent outside the camp serving as the locale for divine revelation and the tent inside the camp being the Lord's dwelling place; or that the phenomenon of revelation occurred in both sanctuaries, but it had a prophetic, occasional character in the tent outside the camp, where it took place outside the tent (*'Ohel Mo'ed*), while in the Dwelling (*Mishkan*) within the camp the theophany was a regular occurrence inside the sanctuary. There is also the view that there was actually only one tent, but the shrine was placed outside the camp in peacetime and inside, for protection, in an emergency; or that one school of tradition objected to the conception of God's Presence within the camp and another did not. Finally the theory has been put forward that there existed two traditions with regard to the Tabernacle. One emanated from the northern prophetic circles (hence the reference to Joshua) and conceived the Tabernacle to be an ordinary tent (situated outside the camp) where prophetic revelations were periodically vouchsafed. This tradition avoided the use of the term *mishkan* and made no reference to cultic services within it. The other view derived from a southern priestly source, which included the aspects found in the passages attributed to P. This tradition ascribed to the wilderness Tabernacle some of the developments introduced into David's shrine.

Ingenious as these conjectures are, it must be admitted that no completely satisfactory solution has yet been found. In the references to the Tabernacle in the post-settlement era the precise character of the sanctuary still remains in doubt. It was erected – perhaps as an amphictyonic tentshrine – at Shiloh, where the priest Eleazar and Joshua divided the land among the tribes by lot at the entrance of the Tent of Meeting (Josh. 18:1; 19:51). In I Samuel 2:22, in Psalm 78:60 (destruction of Shiloh), and in II Samuel 7:6 it is still a tent. But in I Samuel 1:7 it is called "House of the Lord," while in verse 9 it is termed *hekhal* ("temple") and reference is made to its doorposts. After the destruction of Shiloh, the Ark is no longer mentioned with the Tabernacle; but there is evidence that the tent was continuously in existence from the Exodus to David's time (II Sam. 7:6). The Ark was captured and taken to Philistia; then to Kiriath-Jearim; and finally to Jerusalem. David apparently provided a new tent for the Ark (II Sam. 6:17; I Chron. 16:1; 17:1). It is thought that the expression "in its place" (II Sam. 6:17) implied that the tent had a Holy of Holies, and from I Kings 1:39, 50, and 2:28 is to be inferred that it contained anointing oil and a horned altar. It has even been suggested that possibly II Samuel 7:18 implies that there was a veil to the Ark. The Tabernacle and Ark were undoubtedly moved to various sites in the Land of Israel (II Sam. 7:6; cf. I Chron. 21:29; II Chron. 1:3–6) until they were finally housed, together with the furniture, in the Temple at Jerusalem (I Kings 8:4). From time to time various renovations had to be made to the Tabernacle on account of decay, and at certain stages additions and improvements may have been effected. Nevertheless it was still regarded as the old wilderness shrine and retained its original designations.

The Theology of the Tabernacle

Unaffected by the exegetical and historical problems arising from the description of the Tabernacle ascribed to P and to E, and irrespective of the solutions proposed, is the question of the shrine's symbolism. The sanctuary is the embodiment of Israel's concept of holiness; all the minutiae of the specifications conjoin to illustrate how "the holy nation" and "the kingdom of priests" can serve the One Holy God "in the beauty of holiness."

The Creator of the universe also dwells among men. The problem of reconciling divine transcendentalism with immanence is a challenge to the conceptual reasoning of the philosopher; to the Israelite it was an intuitively accepted truth inherent in the mystery of faith. To God all things were possible (cf. Gen. 18:14; Num. 11:23; Jer. 32:17, 27). The way of holiness, leading to the Divine Presence, was graduated. Man must not approach holy things suddenly or irreverently (cf. Num. 4:19–20; II Sam. 6:6–7); nor could this be done by everyone or at all times (Lev. 10:1–2; 16:17). This truth is symbolically inculcated in various ways: first, by the position of the sanctuary. Within the great family of nations Israel was "a treasured people," the Lord's priests; within the framework of the 12 tribes – the camp – the priests and levites occupied the central position; the Tabernacle stood in the midst of the tribe of Levi. But the gradation did not end there. The court was the outer enclosure of the sacred structure. Within it stood the shrine, which was in turn divided into two compartments – the Holy Place and the Holy of Holies (or Most Holy Place). The Divine Presence rested on the throne of the cherubim in the Holy of Holies (similar concepts were symbolically expressed in Solomon's Temple and in the sanctuary visualized by Ezekiel).

The relativity of holiness was further pointed up by the materials. Fine or pure gold was used for the Ark, the propitiatory, the table of the Presence and its vessels; for the lampstand and its accessories; for the altar of incense; and for the high priest's garments. Ordinary gold was employed for the moldings, the rings, and the staves of the Ark, of the table, and of the incense altar; for the hooks of the curtains; for the frames and bars; for the pillars of the veil and screen; and for other parts of the high priest's vestments. Silver was reserved for the bases of the frames, for the pillars of the veil, and for moldings in the court. Finally there was bronze, of which metal the altar of burnt offering and its utensils, the bases of the court, and the laves were made. The same principle applied to the embroidered stuff and linen.

The theme of gradation was continued in respect of the three divisions of the people. The Israelites could enter the court only; the priests could serve in the Holy Place; the high priest alone could enter the Holy of Holies but once a year – on the Day of Atonement. Certain symbols are self-explanatory. The light of the lampstand, the purifying purpose of the laves, and the fragrance of the incense easily suggest their significance. The polarity between God and man is shown by contrast: the propitiatory, part of God's throne, is of pure gold; the altar, which receives the offerings of the people, is of bronze. No less important is the fact that the materials were voluntary contributions (Ex. 25:2). All parts of the sacred structure were a gift of the human spirit. Symmetry and symbolism are also manifest in many of the dimensions and ratios of the Tabernacle: the Holy Place was twice the size of the Holy of Holies, which was a perfect cube of ten cubits; the court was 100 cubits long and 50 cubits wide. The oft-recurring numbers of seven and ten (and their multiples and fractions) indicate completeness and perfection. Thus the Tabernacle proclaims that the divine design is perfect and that sanctity and size are in inverse proportion.

The sacrificial service, which was the central function of the cultus, embraced both regular and occasional offerings, expiatory as well as freewill sacrifices of thanksgiving and devotion. Man's relationship to God has many aspects; these were reflected in multi-faceted oblations and rites. The sacrificial cult, it should also be noted, was equalitarian: Heaven accepted the poor man's cereal offering on a par with the rich man's animal oblation. In seeking to bridge the gulf between the human and the divine, the cherubim were of particular significance: they symbolized the celestial beings that formed the heavenly throne of the Lord. The earthly sanctuary mirrored the heavenly domain (cf. Yal. Ps. 713). The concept found its highest expression in theophany and prophetic revelation in the sanctuary precincts. Such experiences were independent of ritual and priestly lineage, and in a sense contradicted the underlying idea of the complex cultic system. Ultimately God communicated with man not via the altar and ceremonial but directly. In M. Buber's terminology, it was an "I-Thou" relationship. This is essentially the thought of Exodus 29:42–45, which defines the Tabernacle's purpose. Sanctuary and ritual, priests and laity, merge in hallowed communion with God. He is not only the God of Genesis – of Creation – but the God of the Exodus – of history.

[Israel Abrahams]

In the Aggadah

Moses was mystified by God's command to build a tabernacle since it seemingly contradicted the omnipresence of God. Various justifications are given: God could not part with the Torah, and therefore He commanded that a house be constructed for Him wherein He could on occasion visit with the Torah; the Tabernacle was a sign to the world that God had forgiven the Children of Israel for the sin of the golden calf and that He would not abandon them even if they sinned; He expressed His love for the physical world by descending to dwell among those who are below; God wanted to be with His children (Ex. R. 33, 34). Lastly, the Tabernacle in no way confined God to only a single site. It is comparable with a cave by the sea which is constantly filled by seawater although the sea is not diminished thereby: so the Divine Presence in the world is not diminished by its filling the Tabernacle (PdRK 4). The structure of the Tabernacle symbolically resembles the heavenly abode, and the order of its construction corresponds to the order of the world's creation (Ex. R. 35:6; 34:2; Num. R. 12:13). The Israelites, who had previously answered the summons to fetch gold for the golden calf, now zealously responded to Moses' appeal for contributions for the Tabernacle. They were not content simply to donate objects from their houses and treasures, but forcibly snatched ornaments from their wives and children. In this way they thought they were atoning for their previous sin (Mid. Lek. Tov to Ex. 35:22). They brought all the material necessary for the construction in two mornings (Ex. R. 41:2). The women were also eager to participate and were especially active in producing the woolen hangings. They spun the fabric while it was still upon the goats (Shab. 74b, 99a).

After Bezalel had finished the construction, the edifice could not be erected by the elders or Bezalel and Oholiab. The people grumbled against Moses for this failure, denying that its construction had been commanded by God. Moses finally put his hand on the Tabernacle and it immediately stood erect (Tanḥ. B., Ex. 1:33). Before the building of the Tabernacle, the voice of God would strike Moses' ear as though through a tube. The people recognized only through Moses' reddened face that he was receiving a revelation. With the consecration of the sanctuary, however, Moses was first beckoned to the sanctuary by a sweet, pleasant, and melodious voice, and only in the sanctuary did he actually hear the divine message (Num. R. 12:4). After its erection, prophecy departed from the heathen nations of the world, Balaam alone being permitted to prophesy because his prophecy was for the good of Israel (Lev. R. 1:12).

[Aaron Rothkoff]

BIBLIOGRAPHY: J. Wellhausen, *Die Composition des Hexateuchs* (1899), 134–52; E. Sellin, in: BWANT, 13 (1913), 168–92; R. Hartmann, in: ZAW, 37 (1917/18), 209–44; M. Loehr, in: OLZ, 29 (1926), 6–8; G. von Rad, *Die Priesterschrift im Hexateuch* (1934), 57–83, 214–22; L. Rost, in: BWANT, 76 (1938), 35; idem, in: J. Hermann (ed.), *Festschrift F. Baumgaertel* (1959), 158–65; Y. Kaufmann, Toledot, index, s.v. *Ohel Mo'ed*; J. Morgenstern, in: HUCA, 17 (1942/43), 153–265; 18 (1943/44), 1–52; F.M. Cross, in: BA, 10 (1947), 45–68; Noth, Ueberlief, 262–7; Noth, Hist Isr; A. Kuschke, in: ZAW, 63 (1951), 74–105; M. Haran, in: *Tarbiz*, 25 (1956), 11–20; idem, in: *Sefer Geiger* (1959), 215–21; idem, in: *Sefer Tur-Sinai* (1960), 27–42; idem, in: JSS, 5 (1960), 50–65; idem, in: *Scripta Hierosolymitana*, 8 (1961), 272–302; idem, in: *Sefer... Y. Kaufmann* (1961), 20–42 (Heb.); idem, in: *Tarbiz*, 31 (1962), 317–25; idem, in: JBL, 81 (1962), 14–24; idem, in: *Sefer... Segal* (1965), 33–41; idem, in: HUCA, 36 (1965), 191–226; W. Beyerlin, *Herkunft und Geschichte der aeltesten Sinaitraditionen* (1961), 129–37; R. de Vaux, in: *Memorial A. Gelin* (1961), 55–70; S.E. Loewenstamm, in: IEJ, 12 (1962), 162–3; B.A. Levine, in: JAOS, 85 (1965), 307–18; H. Schmidt, in: ZAW, 75 (1963), 91–92; B. Gemser, in: JSS, 8 (1963), 110. IN THE AGGADAH: Aptowitzer, in: *Tarbiz*, 2 (1930/31), 137–53, 257–87; Ginzberg, Legends, index; M. Levin, *Melekhet ha-Mishkan* (1968).

TABGHA (Ar. *Al-Ṭābigha*), ancient site on the N.W. shore of the Sea of Galilee. Tabgha is an Arabic corruption of the Greek name Heptapegon ("the seven springs"), a site described by various Christian hagiographers and pilgrims as situated 2 mi. (3 km.) both from Magdala and Capernaum on the banks of the Sea of Galilee. According to Cyril of Scythopolis, it was situated between Paneas and Chorazin (*Vita Sabae*, 24). It is possible that the spring described by Josephus as that of Capernaum (Wars, 3:519–520) is really that of Tabgha. In Byzantine times, the miracle of the loaves and fishes and that of the last appearance of Jesus on the shores of the lake (Matt. 14:17; 15:32ff.; John 21) was located there.

At present, five of the springs are identifiable. They rise 164 ft. (50 m.) from the lake and have a temperature of 29–30° C (84–86° F), and were once used to run mills. In excavations at Tabgha in 1932, a church which had been built in two stages was uncovered. The floor of the later church (mid-fifth century) was paved with a mosaic representing two fish and a basket of bread, as well as two panels, first laid down in the earlier building phase (late fourth century), showing the fauna and flora of the Sea of Galilee. These mosaics are among the finest found in the country and mark a complete change in the style of mosaic art in churches. Over these remains and partly using some of the ancient mosaics on its floor is built the modern Church of the Multiplication of the Loaves and the Fishes. Close by is a Benedictine monastery and, overlooking the area, the church and convent of the Mt. of Beatitudes. The present name of the site is Ein ha-Shivah.

BIBLIOGRAPHY: A.M. Schneider. *The Church of the Multiplication of the Loaves and Fishes at Tabgha* (1937). **ADD. BIBLIOGRAPHY:** Y. Tsafrir, L. Di Segni, and J. Green, *Tabula Imperii Romani. Iudaea – Palaestina. Maps and Gazetteer* (1994): 142, s.v. "Heptapegon."

[Michael Avi-Yonah]

TABI (late first–early second century C.E.), the slave of Gamaliel *II. Tabi was known for his learning. During the Festival of Tabernacles he would sleep in the *sukkah* under a bed, and Gamaliel explained: "Tabi, my slave, is a scholar; he knows that the law of Sukkot does not apply to slaves, and therefore sleeps under the bed" (Suk. 2:1). The Jerusalem Talmud adds that he did so to be able to listen in on the discussions of the sages (TJ, Suk. 2:1, 52d). Furthermore, he wore *tefillin*, usually the prerogative of free men, yet no one interfered with him in view of his well-known piety (TJ, *ibid.*; TJ, Er. 10:1, 26a). His master Gamaliel wanted very much to free him, and so when once (accidentally) he put out Tabi's eye he rejoiced thinking that now Tabi would go free (cf. Ex. 21:26–27). When, however, he happily announced this to R. Joshua, the latter replied that he was mistaken as there had been no witnesses, but he had confessed the act himself (BK 74b). In *Midrash Proverbs* to 9:2 (ed. Buber 62–63) it is related that once the elders were seated before Gamaliel, and Tabi stood serving them. Eleazar b. Azariah then said: "Woe to thee, Canaan, who brought guilt upon your descendants [a reference to Gen. 9:25]. In reality Tabi should be seated, and I should be standing..." (cf. Yoma 87a). When Tabi died Gamaliel received condolences, a rare occurrence in the case of a slave (Ber. 2:7).

The name Tabi (from the Aramaic for "deer"; cf. Acts 9:36) was common to all slaves in the house of Gamaliel, as was the name Tabita to all maidservants (TJ, Nid. 1:5, 49b; see also Lev. R. 19:4). Thus the Tabi mentioned in Pesaḥim 7:2 as being the slave of Gamaliel I was almost certainly an earlier one.

BIBLIOGRAPHY: Hyman, Toledot, s.v.

[Daniel Sperber]

TABIB, AVRAHAM (1889–1950), leader of the Yemenite community in Ereẓ Israel. Born in Hawdan, *Yemen, Tabib went in 1907 to Ereẓ Israel, where he worked in agriculture and in the wine cellar of Rishon le-Zion. He was chosen to the settlement's council and represented the Yemenite community in the negotiations with the Zionist executive to establish Yemenite settlements near Rishon le-Zion, Ḥaderah, Petah Tikvah, Zikhron Ya'akov, and Reḥovot. He initiated the foundation of the Association of Yemenites in Ereẓ Israel, which looked after matters concerning settlement, education, and the encouragement of further *aliyah* from Yemen by Yemenite Jews in Ereẓ Israel. Tabib was active in the labor movement and was a delegate to the founding conference of the Histadrut (1920). He was also a delegate to the first Asefat ha-Nivḥarim and a member of the Va'ad Le'ummi. He was elected on behalf of Mapai to the First Knesset of the State of Israel (1949). Tabib published many articles in the press in Ereẓ Israel and in the press of the Yemenite community, and published two books, *Golat Teiman* (1931) and *Shavei Teiman* (1932). He was the father of Mordekhai *Tabib, the author.

BIBLIOGRAPHY: Tidhar, 4 (1950), 1947.

[Abraham Aharoni]

TABIB, MORDEKHAI (1910–1979), Hebrew writer. Born in Rishon le-Zion, Ereẓ Israel, Tabib worked in agriculture, industry, building, and guard duties. During World War II, he served in the British Army and later, during the War of Independence, was engaged in editorial work for the Israel Defense Forces. He was active in the central institutions of the *Histadrut and *Mapai and served in the Arab section of the Histadrut.

His first published poems and prose appeared, respectively, in *Davar* and in *Ittim*, and his stories in various Hebrew periodicals. Of Yemenite origin, his books which deal with the Yemenite community in Israel are *Ke-Esev ha-Sadeh* (1948; 1960), *Derekh shel Afar* (stories, 1953), and *Ke-Arar be-Aravah* (1957). He also wrote the play *Kinnoro shel Yosi* (1959) and a one-act play in the style of Bialik, *Shelomo ha-Melekh va-ha-Devorah* (1960). His book *Massa la-Areẓ ha-Gedolah* (1968) contains ten stories and a poem. Tabib was one of the editors of *Mevo'ot* (1953–56). With M. Ibrahim, he coedited *Mifgash* (1968), a Hebrew-Arabic anthology of essays on literature, art, and philosophy. A volume of stories was published after his death (1985) as well as *Beẓel ha-Yamim* (1987), a collection of poems and letters.

BIBLIOGRAPHY: Kressel, Leksikon, 2 (1967), 1–2. **ADD. BIBLIOGRAPHY:** Y. Halevi, *Temurot Poetiyyot bi-Yẓirato shel M. Tabib (1986)*; H. Barzel, *Mesaprim Ereẓ Yisraeliyyim* (1974); N. Rezler-Berson, *"Bar-Yosef ve-Tabib,"* in: *Hadoar*, 56:26 (1977), 424–25; 27 (1977), 443–44; Sh. Avizemer, *"'Ani Ohev ad Kelot': Al Olamo ha-Penimi shel M. Tabib,"* in: *Teima*, 2 (1990) 143–48; N. Govrin, *Vehu be-shelo*, in: *Moznayim*, 75:5 (2001), 14–17; Y.H. Ben-Zekhariyah Halevi, *Shirat ha-Yeladim Asher le-M. Tabib*, in: *Ma'agalei Keriah*, 21 (2003), 31–38.

[Getzel Kressel]

TABLETS OF THE LAW, the stones on which the *Decalogue was inscribed. In Exodus 24:12 it is stated that Moses was commanded to ascend Mount Sinai in order to receive "the tablets of stone and the Torah and the commandments which I have written." On them were inscribed the Decalogue Ex. 32:15, 16; "on both their sides; on the one side and on the other… and the writing was the writing of God" (32:16). These first tablets of stone were smashed by Moses when he beheld the orgy of the worship of the *golden calf (32:19). Subsequently he was commanded to hew two tablets of stone and with them ascend the mountain a second time. On these previously prepared tablets God wrote the words which had been inscribed on the first tablets (34:1–4). The tablets are also called "the two tablets of testimony" (34:29). The two tablets were housed in the *Ark of the Covenant which Solomon brought into the Temple when it was built (I Kings 8:9).

In the Aggadah

The Tablets of the Law were among the things created on the eve of the Sabbath of creation (Av. 5:6). Both tablets were of identical dimensions (TJ, Shek. 6:1, 49d). The rabbis differ as to the arrangement of the Decalogue on the tablets (*ibid.*). In the spaces between the Ten Commandments all the 613 *Commandments of the Torah were noted. Although they were fashioned out of the hardest stone, the sapphire taken from the throne of glory (see *Throne of God; *Lekaḥ Tov*, Ex. 31:18), the tablets could be rolled up like a scroll (Song R. 5:14). They weighed 40 *se'ah*, but as long as the writing was upon them they supported themselves, so that Moses could carry them. When, however, he saw the Children of Israel worshiping the golden calf, the letters vanished and the tablets dropped from his hands (TJ, Ta'an. 4; 5, 68c). The second tablets differed from the first in that they were the work of man, Moses having engraved them, while the first were the work of God (Deut. R. 3:17). Moreover, the second tablets included the *Oral Law (Ex. R. 46:1). Assuming that the text of the Decalogue in Exodus was that on the first tablets, while that in Deuteronomy 5 is the version on the second tablets, the rabbis point out the word ייטב ("that it may go well") occurs only in the second tablets, so that when the first tablets were broken "well-being" should not be lost to the world (BK 54b–55a). The broken tablets were kept in the Tabernacle and the Children of Israel carried them with them whenever they went to war (Tosef., Sot. 7:18). King Josiah, foreseeing the destruction of the Temple, hid the Holy Ark with the broken tablets in order to guard them against desecration at the hands of the enemy (Yoma 52b).

The two tablets have become a favorite Jewish symbol, which is usually placed over the ark in the synagogue, and is usually inscribed either with the first ten letters of the alphabet, or with the first words of the Ten Commandments.

BIBLIOGRAPHY: AGGADAH: Ginzberg, Legends, 1 (1909), 83; 3 (1911), 118–9, 139–41; 5 (1925), 109; 6 (1928), 49–50, 59–60.

TABOR (Czech **Tábor**), town in S. Bohemia, Czech Republic. Its *Hussite founders named it after Mount Tabor in Ereẓ Israel. The first information about Jews there dates from 1572, when a Christian house owner was punished for harboring Jews. A plot for a cemetery was acquired in 1634, and a synagogue was opened in 1655. In 1675 an agreement on residence was signed between the town and the Jewish community. The community numbered eight families in 1725; 18 families in 1769; 212 persons in 1840; 72 taxpaying members in 1869; 455 persons in 1884; and 683 persons in 1893 (including Jews in 21 neighboring localities). Jiri Fielder, the author of *Jewish Sights of Bohemia and Moravia*, provides different details about Tabor: The earliest record dates from 1548 and mentions "Jew of Tabor," but the first Jewish family is recorded in the town only in 1594 (until that year, Jews were not permitted to stay in the town overnight). Three Jewish families are recorded in Tabor in 1618, eight families in 1653. From 1843 to 1884 Gutmann *Klemperer was rabbi of the community. During that time the community built a new, Reform-style synagogue and opened a second cemetery. From the end of the 19th century the community decreased, numbering 400 in 1921 and 311 in 1930, when most of the Jews identified themselves with the Czech-Jewish assimilationist movement.

During the Holocaust, in November 1942, there were 1,267 Jews in Tabor. They were deported from there to concentration and death camps.

After World War II a small congregation was reestablished in Tabor. A prayer room was dedicated in 1954. In 1955 a memorial to the victims of the Holocaust from Tabor and several nearby communities was unveiled on the site of the previous cemetery, which had been destroyed by the Nazis. A small congregation was still in existence in 1970. The former synagogue served as a storehouse.

BIBLIOGRAPHY: Kroupa, in: H. Gold (ed.), *Die Juden und Judengemeinden Boehmens…* (1934), 625–9. **ADD. BIBLIOGRAPHY:** J. Fiedler, *Jewish Sights of Bohemia and Moravia* (1991), 175–76.

[Jan Herman / Yeshayahu Jelinek (2nd ed.)]

TABOR, DAVID (1913–2005), English physicist. Tabor was born in London and educated at the Quintin Hogg School. He graduated in physics from the Royal College of Science, London University and Caius College, Cambridge University. He joined the staff of the Cavendish Laboratory for Physics and Chemistry of Solids at the University of Cambridge and became deputy director. He worked in Australia (1939 –49) and returned to Cambridge where he became professor (1973). His field of research was tribology, the study of friction and wear between solid surfaces. His work with F.P. Bowden clarified the nature of the interactions between microscopic irregularities that create friction through adhesion between surfaces in contact. Later, in collaboration with Jacob Israelachvili, he developed methods for analyzing these processes on an atomic scale. His papers have become classics in this field and his findings have been of great practical relevance to machine design. In 1939 Tabor and F.P. Bowden set up the Tribophysics Laboratory in the University of Melbourne, Australia, which worked on ball bearings for military use during World War II and subsequently achieved an international reputation for the industrial applications of its research. Tabor was elected to the Royal Society of London (1963), from which he received the Royal Medal (1992) for his seminal contributions to the field of friction and wear between solids. Active in the Habonim movement, he was the first chairman of the Youth Department of the Australian Zionist Federation in Australia. He was a recognised Hebrew scholar.

His brother ISRAEL TABOR (1911–1991) graduated in electrical engineering from Imperial College, London and worked as an electrical engineer. On the invitation of Pinchas Rutenberg, he joined the Palestine (later the Israel) Electric Corporation in 1946, becoming its director of research. He retired in 1983. Another brother, Harry Zvi *Tabor (1917–) was an authority on the harnessing of solar energy.

[Michael Denman (2nd ed.)]

TABOR, HARRY ZVI (1917–), British and Israeli physicist. Tabor was born in London and educated at Quintin Hogg School London, London University and the Hebrew University of Jerusalem. He worked as a research physicist on defense projects in the World War II (1939–45), and was director of the National Physical Laboratory of Israel (1950–74). His main research interest was the harnessing of solar energy. His expertise was recognized internationally as well as in Israel. He served on many committees in Israel and abroad including the Research Council of Israel (1949–74) and UNESCO. He was president of the International Solar Energy Society (1981–83). His many honors include the Royal Society of London's Gold Medal Energy Award (1975) and the Israel Knesset's Quality of Life Award (1995).

[Michael Denman (2nd ed.)]

TABOR, MOUNT (Heb. תָּבוֹר), a dome-shaped mountain in the N.E. part of the Jezreel Valley, N. of the Afulah-Tiberias road. The peak rises approximately 1,750 ft. (563 m.) above sea level and approximately 1,500 ft. (c. 500 m.) above the surrounding plain. The mountain is 2 mi. (3⅓ km.) wide. It stands out in the plain in an isolated position and can be seen from a distance, giving rise to its renown. It is formed of stratified limestone, with a base of Lower Cretaceous in the west and Neogene in the south and east. Near the road on the eastern side of the hill, a stratum of Pleistocene basalt overlaps the Neogene limestone; the beginning of Naḥal Tabor passes along the division line between these strata. The mountain was once covered by an oak forest, of which only parts remain.

The name Tabor appears to be derived from Phoenician and recalls the name of the Semitic god known in Greek as Zeus Atabyrios (the Greek name of Tabor is Itabyrion). A cave near the top of the mountain may have been the original sanctuary of this god. This sanctuary was revived in Israelite times, calling forth the wrath of the prophet Hosea (5:1). Mt. Tabor may be the holy mountain mentioned in the Blessing of Moses (Deut. 33:19). A conspicuous landmark, Mr. Tabor served as a boundary point between the territories of the tribes of Zebulun (Josh. 19:22), Naphtali, and Issachar. There Barak collected the forces of the northern tribes at Deborah's command; when the forces of Sisera approached the hill from the south, the Israelites rushed down the slopes and routed the enemy (Judg. 4). Mt. Tabor is mentioned as a place reached by the Midianites in Gideon's time (Judg. 8:18), but this may refer to Chesulloth-Tabor, which was probably a levitical town (I Chron. 6:62). The mountain is singled out for its beauty in Psalms 89:13, where it is mentioned together with Mt. Hermon, and in Jeremiah 46:18, where it is described as outstanding among mountains and comparable to Mt. Carmel by the sea.

In post-biblical times, Mt. Tabor, called Itabyrion (Gr. Ἀταβύριον or Ἰταβύριον), served as a Hellenistic fortress and probably the capital of Galilee. It was taken by Antiochus III in 218 B.C.E. (Polybius 5:70, 9). In 66 C.E. Josephus fortified Mt. Tabor, which was later captured by Vespasian (Jos., Life, 188; Wars, 2:573; 4:54–61, where the given height of 30 stades (Gr. Λ; c. 16,650 ft.) should be corrected to 4 stades (Gr. Δ; c. 2,220 ft.)). Christian tradition, started by Cyril of Jerusalem (PG, 33:744), located the transfiguration of Jesus on Mt. Tabor (Matt. 17:1, et al.) and consequently a basilica was built there in the Byzantine period. A Benedictine community settled there in 1100 and remained on the site until 1187. The Arabs built a fortress on the hill (Ar. Jebel al-Tūr) which was dismantled in 1218. The Hospitalers held Mt. Tabor from 1255 to 1263. In 1873 the Franciscans began to rebuild the basilica on the old foundations and their church was consecrated in 1924. Near the basilica is a Greek Orthodox monastery. Remains of an earlier (Jewish?) wall are also visible.

Jewish settlements were first founded in the region of the Tabor in 1901 with the establishment of Kefar *Tavor. The region was captured by the Israel army during the War of Independence in a battle lasting from May 10 to May 15, 1948.

BIBLIOGRAPHY: G. Dalman, *Sacred Sites and Ways* (1930), index; Abel, Geog; 1 (1933), 353ff.; Alt, in: ZDPV, 64 (1941), 91–96; P. Barnabe (Meistermann), *La Montagne de la Galilée…* (1901); K. Kopp, *The Holy Places of the Gospels* (1963), s.v. **ADD. BIBLIOGRAPHY:** Y. Tsafrir, L. Di Segni, and J. Green, *Tabula Imperii Romani. Judaea – Palaestina. Maps and Gazetteer* (1994), 246–47, s.v. "Thabor Mons"; D. Pringle, *The Churches of the Crusader Kingdom of Jerusalem. A Corpus*. vol. 2: *L–Z (excluding Tyre)* (1998), 63–85.

[Michael Avi-Yonah / Abraham J. Brawer]

TABOR (Tábori), PAUL (1908–1974), Hungarian-born author and translator. Abandoning his journalistic career in Budapest, Tabor began working as a scriptwriter with Sir Alexander *Korda in England in 1937. He wrote anti-Nazi works, such as *Epitaph for Europe* (1942; U.S. edition, *A Wreath for Europa*, 1942); and his many novels include *Bricks upon Dust* (1945) and *Salvatore* (1951). Tabor also translated English and American writers into Hungarian and wrote accounts of several visits to Israel. He also wrote or edited such works as *The Social History of Rape* (1971) and *The Gazetteer of Scottish and Irish Ghosts* (1973).

TABORI, GEORG (1914–), Hungarian playwright, novelist, screenwriter, and theater director. Tabori was born in Budapest into a non-practicing Jewish family. His father, Cornelius, and his brother were both dedicated journalists subscribing to a liberal cosmopolitanism. In 1932 Tabori received training to become a hotel manager in Berlin and Dresden. After briefly returning to Budapest he immigrated to London in 1934 and became a British citizen. There he worked as a translator, journalist, and tourist guide. From 1939 to 1947 he was a foreign correspondent for the BBC in Bulgaria and Turkey and also worked for the secret service of the British army in the Middle East. In Jerusalem he met his first wife, Hannah Freund, whose family had all been murdered in Auschwitz. Tabori's first novel, *Beneath the Stone* (1944/45), about a German officer, was not well received. The novels *Companions of the Left Hand* (1945), *Original Sin* (1947), and *The Caravan Passes* (1949) followed. These early novels were only translated into German in the 1990s. They owe their background to Tabori's cultural encounter with the Middle East. He delineates the atmosphere of Cairo in *Original Sin*, and *The Caravan Passes* can be seen as a bridge between Europe and the Islamic world. The characters transcend socio-cultural boundaries, the European characters set against the strangeness of a multi-ethnic milieu.

In 1945 Tabori was invited to Hollywood, where he pursued his passion for history, working with Brecht on the English version of *Galileo*. Later, he wrote also film scripts for such directors as Alfred Hitchcock. Meanwhile his own plays were also beginning to be produced on stage, notably *Flight into Egypt* (1952), directed on Broadway by Elia Kazan. In 1953 Tabori married his second wife, the actress Viveca Lindfors. He initiated his own productions and founded a theater group, the Strolling Players, in 1966. His most famous play, *Die Kannibalen* (1969), received frosty reviews on its premiere in Berlin. In this outstanding play Tabori places his characters in an exceptional situation. A group of famished concentration camp inmates kill their comrade Puffy, who had gotten hold of a piece of bread. At first, the inmates are indifferent, then they decide to make a meal out of him. During the preparations stories are exchanged and memories are shared. However, only two of the characters are able to eat the human flesh. They survive and serve as witnesses. The whole play shifts erratically between disturbing and trivial elements and questions of morality, violence, and moments of dignity. Taboos are deliberately broken and the comical is shocking. Tabori's next disturbing play, *Pinkville* (1970), caused an outcry in the United States, as it was seen as an indictment of the war in Vietnam. In the late 1970s he unconventionally adapted pieces like Kafka's *Der Hungerkuenstler* (1977) or *Siegmunds Freude* and produced a series of experimental productions with his Bremer Theaterlabor. In the 1980s Tabori wrote his play *Peepshow* (1984), which contains many autobiographical elements and Tabori's black humor. The poet Willie is obsessed with sex and death. The play deals with the American-Jewish middle-class dream and the pathological condition of the famous. The character of Willie also enters the play *The Voyeur* (1990). The voyeur is an allegory of the Jewish Holocaust survivor. The play portrays the clichés, prejudices, and collective psychosis of minorities, which are embodied in the Jewish character Weisman, his mongoloid daughter Ruth, and the alleged Native American.

Tabori gained his ultimate recognition as a playwright with *Mein Kampf* (1987), which stages the meeting of Adolf Hitler and the Jewish bookseller Schlomo Herzl, another piece of disturbing and provocative theater. The spectator is drawn into the work despite himself. Tabori later took up residence in Vienna, married to his fourth wife, the actress Ursula Hoepfner. He was the recipient of a number of international prizes for his work such as the Kritikerpreis (1976), the Peter-Weiss Prize (1990), and the Buechner Prize (1992).

BIBLIOGRAPHY: A. Feinberg, *George Tabori* (2003); P.W. Marx, *Theater und kulturelle Erinnerung: kultursemiotische Untersuchungen zu George Tabori, Tadeusz Kantor und Rina Yerushalmi* (2003); M. Roth, *Theater nach Auschwitz: George Taboris Die Kannibalen im Kontext der Holocaust-Debatten* (2003); S. Scholz, *Von der humanisierenden Kraft des Scheiterns: George Tabori – ein Fremdprophet in postmoderner Zeit* (2002); B. Haas, *Das Theater des George Tabori: vom Verfremdungseffekt zur Postmoderne* (2000); J. Struempel, *Vorstellungen vom Holocaust: George Taboris Erinnerungs-Spiele* (2000); A. Feinberg, *Embodied Memory: The Theatre of George Tabori* (1999).

[Ann-Kristin Koch (2nd ed.)]

TABRIZ, capital of the Third Province, N.W. *Iran. A Jewish community existed in Tabriz in the Middle Ages. Samauʾal b. Yahya al-Maghribī, 12th-century author of *Ifḥām al-Yahūd*, mentions Tabriz, together with Salmas (Shahpur) and Khoi, as a place where the followers of the pseudo-messiah David *Alroy continued to adhere to his movement. From the time of Hulagu Khan, Tabriz became the capital of the realm of the Il-khan dynasty. There the Jewish physician *Saʿd al-Dawla was appointed vizier of the Il-khan ruler Arghūn, exercising considerable power until his assassination in 1291; and the vizier, historian, and physician *Rashid al-Din served three rulers until his tragic death in 1318. As attested by Hebrew manuscripts written by scholars in Tabriz and the vicinity, the Jewish community consisted of both Karaites and Rabbanites. The *Karaite physician Nafis b. Daud at-Tabrizi moved in 1354 from Tabriz to *Cairo, where he was converted to Islam. In the 16th century the Yemenite traveler *Zechariah al-Ḍāhiri visited Tabriz and described in his *Sefer ha-Musar* the deteriorating conditions of Jewish life there.

The wave of persecutions which swept over the whole of *Persia under the Safavid rulers *ʿAbbas I and ʿAbbas II severely affected the Jews of Tabriz also, as indicated by the Armenian historian Akel and the Judeo-Persian chroniclers *Babai ibn Lutf and Babai ibn Farḥad. However, the Jewish community survived these persecutions, since between 1711 and 1713 R. Judah b. Amram Diwan, an emissary from Hebron, included Tabriz among his visits to Jewish communities in Persia. Between 1790 and 1797, Jews in Tabriz were accused of a blood libel and massacred. When *David d'Beth Hillel visited Persia in 1828, the Jewish community in Tabriz had already ceased to exist.

BIBLIOGRAPHY: Fischel, Islam, passim; idem, in: PAAJR, 22 (1953), 1–21; Mann, Texts, 1 (1931), 477–549. **ADD BIBLIOGRAPHY:** H. Levy, *The History of the Jews of Iran* (in Persian), 3 (1960), 540–2; A. Netzer, "The Fate of the Jewish Community of Tabriz," in: *Studies in Islamic History and Civilization in Honor of Professor David Ayalon* (1986), 411–19.

[Walter Joseph Fischel / Amnon Netzer (2nd ed.)]

°**TABRIZI, MAHOMET ABU-BEKR-AT-BEN MAHOMET** (probably second half of 13th century), Persian Muslim commentator on the 25 propositions appearing at the beginning of the second part of Moses Maimonides' *Guide of the Perplexed*. There is no information concerning Tabrizi's life. In his 25 propositions, Maimonides had presented a summary of the main doctrines of Aristotelian philosophy, which he used as the basis of his proofs for the existence, unity, and incorporeality of God. Tabrizi in his commentary set out to prove these propositions in detail, for Maimonides had presented only the doctrines themselves, indicating that proofs could be found in Aristotle's *Physics* and *Metaphysics* and their commentaries. Tabrizi based his proofs of the propositions on the works of Arabic authors rather than on the original works of Aristotle, but his discussions of the propositions are comprehensive. Written in Arabic, Tabrizi's commentary was translated into Hebrew twice. One translation, in Arabicized Hebrew, is by Isaac b. Nathan of Córdoba, and was probably composed in Majorca around 1347 (Venice, 1574). The other, in native rabbinic Hebrew, is anonymous and extant only in manuscript (Paris, Bibliothèque Nationale, cod. héb., 974). Ḥasdai Crescas relied heavily upon Isaac b. Nathan's translation of Tabrizi's commentary in his critique of Aristotelian philosophy in *Or Adonai*. It was also utilized by Moses b. Joshua of Narbonne.

BIBLIOGRAPHY: H.A. Wolfson, *Crescas' Critique of Aristotle* (1929), index s.v. *Altabrizi*; Steinschneider, Uebersetzungen, 362; G. Sarton, *Introduction to the History of Science* 3, pt. 2 (1948), index s.v. *Muhammad b. Muhammad*; Steinschneider, Cat Bod, 1143.

TACHOV (Ger. **Tachau**), town in W. Bohemia, Czechoslovakia. Jews from Tachov are mentioned in responsa of the 15th century and in documents from 1464 onward. The community had close connections with adjoining Bavaria, where Tachauer was a family name common among Jews. Five Jewish families are mentioned in the town in 1552 and 1570. The municipal records of 1605 include regulations concerning the inner life of the community. There were 17 families and 12 Jewish houses in the town in 1724. In 1749 the Jews formed an independent fire-fighting unit. An outstanding personality of Tachov was

R. Nahum Sofer (d. 1815); the inscription on his tombstone was later interpreted as a prophecy foretelling World War I. Ḥasidim from Eastern Europe visited the grave frequently on their way to nearby *Marienbad or *Karlsbad.

Rabbi Moses ben Hisdai, said to be one of the authors of the prayer *Avinu Malkeinu*, allegedly was born in Tachov in the 13th century.

In 1836 there were 266 Jews living in 15 houses in Tachov. Woodware, glass, and mother-of-pearl factories were founded by Jews in the 19th century. In 1911 the old Jewish quarter burned down and a new synagogue was built. The old community of Nove Sedliste (Neu-Zedlisch), affiliated to the Tachov community, was disbanded in 1914. The Tachov community numbered 273 in 1921 and 180 in 1930 (2.5% of the total population).

Most of the Jews left Tachov at the time of the Sudeten crisis; those remaining were sent to concentration camps. The synagogue was destroyed on November 10, 1938.

BIBLIOGRAPHY: J. Schoen, *Geschichte der Juden in Tachau* (1927); idem, in: *Zeitschrift fuer die Geschichte der Juden in der Tschechoslowakei*, 3 (1932–33), 213–20; A. Grottee, *Deutsche, boehmische und polnische Synagogentypen* (1915), 11, 73, 78; idem, in: AZDJ, 81 (1917), 54f.; B. Brilling, in: *Judaica Bohemiae*, 3 (1967), 26–35 (Ger.). **ADD. BIBLIOGRAPHY:** J. Fiedler, *Jewish Sights of Bohemia and Moravia*, (1991) 176–78.

[Meir Lamed / Yeshayahu Jelinek (2nd ed.)]

°**TACITUS** (c. 55–120), Roman historian. He viewed *Judea as yet another province of the Roman Empire, mentioning it with Syria as asking for a lighter tribute upon *Tiberius' accession (Annals 2: 42) and relating that it was added to Syria after *Agrippa I's death (Annals 12:23). Tacitus seems to think his readers would be interested in the geography of such a remote area (Histories 5:6–7). He describes events leading up to the Jewish War (66–73) as a series of maladministrations, dwelling on the roles of the procurator Antonius *Felix and his successors, and tells of the prosecution of the war by *Vespasian and *Titus against the background of the turmoil of "the year of the four emperors" (68–69 C.E.; Histories 2:1, 4–6, 73, 76, 79, 81–82; 4:3, 51; 5:1). Yet, despite the basically political setting of that war, from Rome's point of view, Tacitus uses the opportunity offered by his discussion of the sack of Jerusalem (Histories 5:11–13) to launch an attack on Judaism.

He gives a bizarre picture of Jewish national and religious origins (Histories 5:2–5), though in referring to traditions which variously make the first Jews Cretan, Egyptian, Ethiopian, or Assyrian exiles, or the nation of the Solymi celebrated by Homer, he is not wholly inaccurate, since the theory of Assyrian origin may fit with the biblical account of Abraham's wanderings from Chaldea. Nor is his account wholly unfavorable, since the Romans, whose own origins were questionable (see the preface to Livy's *History*), admired and envied peoples who had ancient origins. Tacitus agrees with an unspecified majority opinion which saw the Jews as plague-beset Egyptians driven into the desert by their countrymen. Their rituals, devised by their leader Moses (cf. *Hecataeus), are designed to set them apart from all other nations. Tacitus implies that Moses invented imageless monotheism because it differed so radically from polytheistic Egyptian practices. Though elsewhere (Histories 2:78; also reported by *Suetonius, *De vita Caesarum*, Vespasianus, 5:6) he relates without criticism that Vespasian received a favorable oracle from a deity which had an altar consecrated to its worship on Mt. Carmel but had no temple or cult image (probably a local cult of Zeus), here he seems to censure Jewish reverence directed to such a divine presence and not offered even to kings and Caesars (Histories 5:5). According to Tacitus (Histories 5:3), the desert wanderings of the Hebrews lasted only six days; the Sabbath commemorates the end of their tribulations; Moses led them into their new land, where they consecrated an image of an ass in their Temple (Histories 5:4) because asses led them to a spring in the desert (yet in the sketch of Jewish history from Hasmonean times to the Temple's destruction – Histories 5:1–10 – Tacitus notes that Pompey found no image in the Temple). This portrayal is almost certainly not original, but a composite biased picture derived from scandalmongers such as the anti-Jewish Alexandrian writers – *Manetho, *Chaeremon, *Lysimachus, and *Apion.

His basic contention is that Jews are aloof. Dietary laws, circumcision, Sabbath, and the ban against marrying outside their faith set them apart and, to Tacitus, make them hate non-Jews. Because Judaism attracted Romans, Tacitus, like his contemporary *Juvenal, saw this as a weakening of Roman morality since converts were taught to despise the gods, repudiate the fatherland, and disparage parents, children, and brothers (Histories 5:5). Since the Jew's way of life was synonymous with the practice of his religion, Tacitus' antipathy takes the form of an attack on that religion.

The emperors saw rebellious Judea as a political problem; but Tacitus, concerned with Roman morality, sees policy only in moral terms, and thinks a proper Roman political attitude grows out of proper ethical values in the tradition of earlier generations of Rome. Perhaps this is the reason why he cast the political Judean situation into a mold of condemnation of anti-Roman (to him), Jewish ethics. Walser (see bibliography) has shown that in his treatment of the Parthians, Britons, and Germans, Tacitus knew next to nothing about the psychology of the people on the periphery of the Roman Empire and that he hardly cared to know anything. Tacitus did not hesitate to modify or eliminate even facts of historical importance if they in any way impeded his customary dramatic account of events.

BIBLIOGRAPHY: Reinach, Textes; J. Lewy, in: *Zion*, 8 (1942/43), 1–34, 61–84; A.M.A. Hospers, *Tacitus over de Joden, Hist.* 5, 2–13 (1949), extensive Eng. summary; G. Walser, *Rom, das Reich und die fremden Voelker…* (1951).

[Jacob Petroff]

TADEF, village 24 mi. (40 km.) E. of *Aleppo, the site of an ancient synagogue named after *Ezra the Scribe. Popular tradition holds that on his return from Babylonia Ezra stopped in Tadef and wrote the Scriptures. The synagogue walls bear inscriptions relating to the repairs carried out in the last years of the 14th century. Aleppo Jews were accustomed to make a Ziyāra (annual pilgrimage) to the synagogue. A Jewish community also grew up near the synagogue, and according to the traveler Benjamin the Second there were 20 Jewish families living there in the middle of the 19th century.

BIBLIOGRAPHY: M.F. Oppenheim, *Inschriften aus Syrien, Mesopotamien und Kleinasien* (1913), 175ff.; Ashtor, Toledot, 1 (1944), 277–8; 2 (1951), 120; I. Ben-Zvi, *She'ar Yashuv* (1965^2), 488–90.

[Eliyahu Ashtor]

TADMOR (Heb. תַּדְמֹר; **Palmyra**), an oasis city at the point of intersection of the caravan roads in the central Syrian desert and the steppe land between Lebanon and Jabel Bishri, halfway between the Euphrates and the Orontes River in the Mediterranean Sea area. In classical sources it is called Palmyra, a direct translation of its Semitic name *Tadmor*, which is obviously connected with the word *tamar*, "palm tree." Josephus calls it Ταδάμορα (Ant. 8:154). Its modern name is Tadmura.

Tadmor was situated on the crossroads between Syria-Canaan and Mesopotamia, on the one hand, and between these areas and Arabia on the other. Its resulting importance goes back to the Old Babylonian period. Without doubt the rich trade between the "West" and Mesopotamia, well known from the *Mari documents and other sources, flowed through Tadmor.

In periods of "law and order" during the Old and Middle Babylonian periods, Tadmor served as a well-protected central station for commercial caravans, diplomatic envoys, and royal tours, and as a crossroads for cultural influences. Because it was situated in the desert and steppe land, Tadmor was subject to sudden attacks of Western Semitic desert nomads, such as the Sutaeans, or movements of Western Semitic tribes (as can be deduced from the Mari archives and also, indirectly, from Hittite-Babylonian correspondence). During the Aramaic invasion at the end of the second millennium, Tadmor, being the key point of connection between east and west and north and south, was one of the chief sites of clashes between King Tiglath-Pileser I of Assyria and the nomadic Aḫlamû-Arameans: "On the territory which extends from the feet of the Lebanon mountain to the city of Tadmar (!) of the land of Amurru, [to] the [city of] Anat [on the Euphrates] of the land of Suḫi, and to the city of Rapiqu [on the Euphrates] of the land of Karduniaš [= Babylon] I defeated them decisively" (Annals, lines 31ff.; Weidner, in bibl.).

From this inscription it can be learned that Tadmor belonged to Amurru, which here means not simply the "West" but is connected in some way to the (by then dissolved) state of Amurru, founded by the dynasty of Abdasrita in the 14th century (see *El-Amarna Tablets and *Amorites). This territory was inherited by the Arameans.

The place of Tadmor in the history of pre-Exilic Israel is a direct continuation of the situation described above. I Kings 9:18 reads: "King Solomon rebuilt [fortified and reorganized]... Tamar [*kere* Tadmor; cf. below] in the desert [*midbar*] in the land" (see below). In II Chronicles 8:3–4 "Solomon went [in a military-political campaign] to Hamath-Zobah and took it, and he built [see above] Tadmor in the desert and all the store-cities which he built in Hamath." Even if one considers Tamar of I Kings as one of the fortification enterprises of Solomon in the south, in the Judean Desert on the Arabah route (that passed through Tamar, Ein Hasab, and Hasebah), it seems that from the point of view of defense and control it is part of the same plan as that reflected in the II Chronicles passage. The northern enterprise in Syria was at first a political move but later was motivated by economic considerations. The difficulty in the mention of friendly Hamath-Zobah (LXX, Beth Zobah) can be overcome by supposing that Solomon took control over this city as a countermeasure against the renewed independence of Aram-Damascus (I Kings 11:23–25). Tadmor, as a center of routes in every direction including Arabia and Palestine, was all important for Solomon to hold, in order to maintain at least commercial control over the west up to the Euphrates. By holding and rebuilding Tadmor, he assumed control of the flow of commerce for some time, thus giving a new turn to the economic development of the whole "west" that persisted even after his period. Tadmor was no less important to Solomon than it had been to Tiglath-Pileser I; in fact it was even more so because it was a key point in his north-south control plan.

[Pinhas Artzi]

In the Hellenistic-Roman Period

A neutral city located on the borders of two large empires – the Roman and the Persian – it traded with both (Appian, *Historia Romana*, 5:37–38, 42), and levied duty on all entering and departing caravans for the use of its water and lodging facilities. During the rule of *Odenathus and Zenobia in the third century, Palmyra – as it was known at this period – became an important power for a short time after its armies conquered Palestine and Egypt. After Emperor Aurelian entered into battle against it and destroyed the city in 273, however, it lost its importance.

During the period of its efflorescence, Palmyra had a Jewish community, as is clear from various documents and inscriptions of the period. The mention of Miriam of Palmyra in the Mishnah (Naz. 6:11) as a contemporary of the first-century R. Eliezer indicates that a Jewish community may have existed there at an earlier date. In literal obedience to biblical command the *Shema* (Deut. 6:4–9) is carved on the stone lintel of a building in Palmyra which E.L. Sukenik believes to have been part of a synagogue (CIJ no. 821). Other house inscriptions have also been found; they contain the following biblical texts: (a) Deuteronomy 7:15 and 25:5; (b) *ibid.* 28:4b–5; (c) *ibid.* 7:14; and (d) *Shema Yisrael* in large letters (CIJ nos. 821–3).

All of them predate the third century C.E. A number of Jewish funerary inscriptions have also been found (cf. Cooke, bibl., and CIJ no. 820). They are dated second and third century C.E. From them it seems that the Palmyrene Jewish community was fairly large and conscious of its Judaism, although non-Jewish personal names became increasingly common (as in Egypt), e.g., Wahb'allāth ("the gift of [the goddess] Allāt").

In addition, graves of Palmyrene Jews are to be found in *Bet She'arim and Jerusalem although it is not known whether the bodies were brought to Jerusalem for reburial or whether a community of Palmyrene Jews had settled there. The cemetery of Bet She'arim has a large number of graves of Palmyrene Jews, including spacious, decorated burial chambers. This cemetery was in use for about 150 years, until its destruction by Gaulus in 352. Palmyra's brief rule over Palestine during that period may have made the transport of bodies for burial easier.

The Palmyrene pantheon was a syncretism of Canaanite, Greek, and Syrian deities. One of the latter was the moon god, ʿAglibol (i.e., "calf-ba'al"; Gr. Ἀγλίβαλος; cf. Cooke, bibl., nos. 139, 140), who is identified with the Ugaritic god mentioned in the "Hymn to Rpu" called ʾgl-il ("calf god") connected with tr-il ("bull god"; cf. C.F.A. Schaeffer, *Mission de Ras Shamra*, 16 (1968), 551–5). ʿAglibol is thus connected with the ancient calf god which appeared in the Bible as the golden calf (Ex. 32:4). In Palmyra the month of Tammuz is called "Qnyn," just as Tammuz is lamented with *kinah* in Ezekiel (8:3, 14).

The Talmud (Yev. 16a; Nid. 56b; TJ, Kid. 4:1, 65c, and Yev. 1:6, 3b) mentions Palmyrene converts to Judaism. Buechler suggests this is connected with the conversion of the Adiabene dynasty in the first century C.E. Many Palmyrenes also came into contact with Jews while accompanying commercial caravans to the Persian Gulf along a route which led through such large Jewish centers as *Pumbedita, *Nehardea, *Sura, and *Maḥoza. M. Lidzbarski (*Ephemeris fuer semitische Epigraphik*, 1 (1902), 247f., 2 (1908), 295, 298) points out that specifically Jewish phrases had crept into Palmyrene inscriptions. A number of them (Février, Religion, bibl., 120–7) are dedicated to an anonymous god with the words לבריך שמה לעלמא ("May his name be praised forever") which is generally assumed to be a Jewish influence on Palmyrenes against profaning the name of a god. The Talmud reports that the rabbis looked upon converts from Palmyra, who evidently retained customs of idol worship, with suspicion and viewed the city itself with animosity. "The future destruction of Palmyra will be a day of rejoicing for Israel" (Yev. 17a). Aggadic tradition holds that Palmyrenes participated in the destruction of the First and Second Temples. The brief ten-year rule of Palmyra over Palestine was not a peaceful or happy one, and R. Johanan said: "Blessed be he who will witness the downfall of Tarmod (Tadmor)" (TJ, Ta'an. 4:8, 69b). The Babylonian rabbis also suffered from the Palmyrenes, who, during the reign of Odenathus, fought with Rome against Persia and destroyed Nehardea in the process. The Talmud refers to Odenathus as Ben Naẓer and also mentions Queen Zenobia, who was considered to be sympathetic to the Jews. (For a discussion on the alleged Judaism of Zenobia and of a number of inscriptionary Palmyrene names which are preceded by בת see Février, Religion, bibl., 220).

BIBLIOGRAPHY: BIBLICAL: E.F. Weidner, in: AFO, 18 (1957–58), 343–4; J.R. Kupper, *Les nomads en Mésopotamie* (1958), 47, no. 2, 89; Bright, Hist, 192, 193; A. Malamat (ed.), in: *Bi-Ymei Bayit Rishon* (1962), 31–33; A.L. Oppenheim, *Ancient Mesopotamia* (1964), 60–61, 167, 392; Du Mesnil du Buisson, in: *Bibliotheca Orientalis*, 24 (1967), 20ff.; H. Klengel, *Geschichte Syriens*, 2 (1969), s.v. *Palmyra*. POST-BIBLICAL: C. Moss, in: PEFQS (1928), 100–7; G.A. Cooke, *A Text-Book of North-Semitic Inscriptions*... (1903), 263–340; J.G. Février, *La religion des Palmyréniens* (1931); idem, *Essai sur l'histoire politique et économique de Palmyre* (1931); H.P. Chajes, in: RI (1904), 171–80; M.A. Levy, in: ZDMG, 18 (1864), 65–117; A. Champdor, *Palmyre* (Fr., 1934); L. Berger, in: *Memoires de la Société le Linguistique*, 7 (1892), 65–72; Buechler, in: *Festschrift Adolf Schwarz* (1917), 150ff.; Pauly-Wissowa, 36, pt. 2 (1949), 262–770; J. Starcky, *Palmyre* (Fr., 1952). **ADD. BIBLIOGRAPHY:** A. Bounni, "Palmyra," in: *The Oxford Encyclopedia of Archaeology in the Near East*, vol. 4 (1997), 238–44.

TADMOR, HAYIM (1923–2005), Assyriologist and historian of the Ancient Near East. Tadmor was born in Harbin, China, and arrived in Palestine with his family in 1935. He studied at the Hebrew University where he received his doctorate in 1954 for his dissertation on problems in chronology of the Ancient Near East. His postdoctoral studies took him to the Oriental Institute of the University of Chicago where he studied Assyriology under Benno Landsberger.

From 1958 he lectured at the Hebrew University – until 1965 in the Department for Ancient and Near Eastern Studies and then in the Department of Assyriology. In 1971 he was appointed professor of Assyriology and history of the Ancient Near East.

Tadmor was a foremost authority on the history of the first millennium B.C.E. who made notable contributions to the study of chronology, historiography, and institutions in antiquity as well as to understanding the interrelations between Assyria and the West and the place of Israel in the Ancient Near East.

He applied canons of criticism to inscriptions and historical texts, viewing texts in their broad cultural perspective and emphasizing the value of historiography and literary forms of historical texts. One of his major contributions was his work on Assyrian and Babylonian royal inscriptions.

He edited, with Moshe Weinfeld, and was a contributor to *History, Historiography and Interpretations – Studies in Biblical and Cuneiform Literature* (1983). He edited *The World History of the Jewish People*, volume 5 (The Restoration, The Persian Period). Tadmor served as a chief editor of the *Enẓiklopedya Mikra'it* (1971–82) and was a major contributor to *A History of the Jewish People* (edited by H.H. Ben-Sasson, 1969) and the Russian version (edited by S. Ettinger, 1967). He collaborated with M. Cogan to produce a *Commentary on Kings* (1988) and served as an editor of the *Shorter Jewish Encyclopedia in Russian.*

ADD. BIBLIOGRAPHY: M. Cogan and I. Ephal (eds.), *Ah, Assyria ... Studies ... Tadmor* (Scripta Hierosolymitana 33; 1991); bibliography of Tadmor in: ibid., 341–47; additional bibliography in Er Isr, 27 (Hayim and Miriam Tadmor Volume, 2003), 17–22.

[Elaine Hoter]

TADZHIKISTAN, one of the independent states of the CIS. In 1989 the Jewish population was 14,800, mainly in the capital, Dushanbe. A large proportion of the republic's Jews belonged to the Bukharan Jewish community. Almost all left for Israel during the mass exodus of the 1990s. The rise of Islamic fundamentalism in the republic, which led to civil war, was the major factor in Jewish emigration.

[Michael Beizer]

TAENZER, ARNOLD (**Aaron**; 1871–?), rabbi, author, and historian. Taenzer, born in Pressburg, served as *Landesrabbiner of Tyrol and Vorarlberg at Hohenems (1896–1904) and at Merano (1904–07), and at Goeppingen, Wuerttemberg (from 1907), where from 1910 to 1914 he edited the *Israelitische Wochenschrift.*

His published works include *Die Religionsphilosophie Joseph Albos* (1896), *Der israelitische Friedhof in Hohenems* (1901), *Judentum und Entwicklungslehre* (1903), *Geschichte der Juden in Tirol und Vorarlberg* (1905), *Mischehe in Religion, Geschichte und Statistik der Juden* (1913), *Geschichte der Juden in Brest-Litowsk* (1918), *Geschichte der Juden in Jebenhausen und Goeppingen* (1927), and *Geschichte der Juden in Wuerttemberg* (1937). Taenzer also wrote a *Gedenkschrift* for J. and F. Strassburger (1928) and published sermons and some humorous plays.

BIBLIOGRAPHY: Wininger, Biog, s.v.

TAEUBLER, EUGEN (1879–1953), historian and classical and biblical scholar. Taeubler, born in Gostyn (Poznan), went to school at Lissa; he studied bible and talmud at the rabbinical seminary and the Lehranstalt (Hochschule) fuer die Wissenschaft des Judentums in Berlin. At the University of Berlin he studied classical philology and Semitics under Wilamowitz-Moellendorf, and ancient history and archaeology under T. Mommsen, Eduard Meyer, and Norden. During Mommsen's last years Taeubler served as his scientific secretary. Founder of the *Gesamtarchiv der deutschen Juden* (1906; see *Archives), Taeubler served as its director during 1906–18 and edited its *Mitteilungen* (1908–11). From 1910 to 1916 he lectured on ancient Jewish history at the Lehranstalt until he was called up for military service in 1916; during 1919–22 he directed the research section of the *Akademie fuer die Wissenschaft des Judentums, having played a prominent role in its establishment. During the same period he lectured at the University of Berlin on ancient history. He was assistant professor at Zurich (1922–25) and full professor at Heidelberg (1925–33), becoming a member of the Heidelberg Academy of Sciences in 1929. When the Nazis came to power, Taeubler returned to the Lehranstalt; in the spring of 1941 he gave his last lesson in Berlin. Later that year he immigrated to the United States with his wife Selma *Stern-Taeubler. He became research professor at Hebrew Union College, Cincinnati, teaching Hellenistic Jewish literature until 1953

Among his important works on ancient history are: *Imperium Romanum* (1913); *Die Vorgeschichte des zweiten punischen Kriegs* (1921); and a collection of essays, *Tyche* (1926/27). He wrote numerous studies and essays in Jewish history. *Biblische Studien*, dealing with the period of the Judges, appeared posthumously in 1958, as did *Aufsaetze zur Problematik juedischer Geschichtsschreibung 1908–1950* (1977), essays on Jewish historiography, and *Ausgewaehlte Schriften zur Alten Geschichte* (1987). Taeubler's influence on modern Jewish historiography was considerable. His mastery of ancient history and the methods of historical scholarship was reflected in his understanding of the geographical and geopolitical elements in early Jewish history, the relations between Jews and the lands in which they lived, and the nature of Jewish autonomy in the Diaspora.

BIBLIOGRAPHY: E. Taeubler, *Biblische Studien* (1958), ix–xii (bibliography); S.W. Baron and R. Marcus, in: PAAJR, 22 (1953), xxxi–xxxiv; I.F. Baer, in: *Zion*, 19 (1953/54), 71–74; B. Dinur, *ibid.*, 75–83; idem, *Bnei Dori* (1963), pp. 35–52; S. Stern-Taeubler, in: YLBI, 3 (1958), 40–59; G. Herlitz, *ibid.*, 9 (1964), 83–90. **ADD. BIBLIOGRAPHY:** E. Auerbach, *Pionier der Verwirklichung* (1969), 136–37; H. Scharbaum, *Zwischen zwei Welten … Eugen Taeubler* (2000).

[Benzion Dinur (Dinaburg) / Archiv Bibliographia Judaica (2nd ed.)]

TAGANROG, city in S.W. Rostov district, Russia. Jews first settled in Taganrog at the beginning of the 19th century, when "New Russia" was settled by Jewish immigrants from the northwest area of the *Pale of Settlement. In the 1860s a synagogue with a choir was built. In 1887 Taganrog was incorporated in the administrative region of the Don army, which was beyond the Pale of Settlement; consequently, Jews were henceforth forbidden to live in Taganrog, excepting those who had been living there previously. In 1897 there were 2,960 Jews in Taganrog (6% of its total population); in 1926 they numbered 2,673 (about 3%). In 1939 there were 3,124. Under the Soviet regime the Jewish community and institutions were abolished. When the Germans occupied the city in World War II, all the Jews who did not manage to escape were killed.

By 2005 the new Jewish community of Taganrog had established a community center, a youth club, a women's club, a veterans' club, a Sunday school, and a burial society, as well as a Holocaust Scientific Educational Center.

[Yehuda Slutsky / Ruth Beloff (2nd ed.)]

TAGGER, SIONAH (1900–1988), first Israeli-born woman artist. She was born in Jaffa, daughter of Shmuel and Sultana Tagger. The family had immigrated to Ereẓ Israel from Bulgaria in 1880, and her parents were among the founders of Aḥuzat Bayit. After her attendance at evening classes at Constant's Studio in Tel Aviv, Tagger turned to study in the Bezalel School of Art and Design in Jerusalem (1921). Two years later she traveled to Paris, studied at the Academie L'hote, and participated in the exhibition of the *Salon des Independents*. When Tagger returned to Israel, she took part in the main exhibitions of the young modern artists, such as the Tower of David exhibition in Jerusalem as well as three of the Ohel exhibitions in Tel Aviv. Over the years Tagger continued to exhibit her paintings in Israel as well as outside of the country. From 1940 to 1942 she volunteered to serve in the British ATS, and later joined the Haganah.

In 1948 at the Venice Biennale Tagger represented Israel. In 1952 she settled in the Artists Colony in Safed.

Tagger's art style was created of dialectical tendencies – on one hand, a quest for the universal, turning to the European Modern Art, and on the other, a return to her own roots and to the local. Tagger remained a figurative painter; even in her most abstract phases she remained loyal to practicality.

Tagger's best-known genre was portrait painting. The portraits she painted in the 1920s were created from many sketches. Their artistic style was a combination of Cubistic and Naïve art. A three-dimensional attention to volume, with powerful light-dark contrasts and well-defined stains of color, together magnified the emotional impact of the work (*Portrait of a Boy in White*, 1926, Israel Museum, Jerusalem).

A similar artistic style was a component of her landscape paintings. Tagger liked to draw the view of Tel Aviv and until the 1960s she chose to rent penthouses in Tel Aviv, in order to watch the city's vista, seashore as well as skyline. The exaggeration of the colors, the perspectives as well as the compositions of those paintings expressed the extreme feelings that rose from her gazing. The train movement and tempo in one of her paintings reminds one of the Futuristic's excitement regarding this vehicle (*The Train Passing through Neve Tzedek*, 1928, Collection of Joseph Hackmey, Tel Aviv).

During the 1960s Tagger painted on the matte side of shining transparent Plexiglas sheets. The products of that special technique looked like paintings on glass. Tagger was drawn to this technique owing to her perception of traditional ethnic and folk art. She used bright Oriental colors and a shiny Mediterranean light. The decorative style was dominant in those works and the subjects were usually traditional Jewish themes: the Tablets of the Covenant, Sukkot, Purim, and so on.

BIBLIOGRAPHY: Tefen, The Open Museum, *Sionah Tagger (1900–1988) Retrospective* (1990); Tel Aviv, Tel Aviv Museum of Art, *Sionah Tagger Retrospective* (2004).

[Ronit Steinberg (2nd ed.)]

TAGIN (Aram. תָּגִין; sing., *tag*), special designs resembling crowns placed by a scribe on the upper left-hand corner of seven of the 22 letters of the Hebrew alphabet in a Torah, *tefillin*, or *mezuzah* scroll. A *tag* is generally composed of three flourishes or strokes, each of which resembles a small "*zayin*" – thick on top with a thin line extending downward to the letter. The center stroke is slightly higher than the two end ones. The letters which receive the *tagin* are שעטנזגץ (Men. 29b), including the final ן and ץ (Rashi ad loc.). According to Maimonides the omission of *tagin* does not invalidate the scroll since its inclusion is considered as an "exceptionally beautiful fulfillment of the *mitzvah*" (Yad, Sefer Torah 7:9). Ashkenazi custom, however, holds that the scrolls are invalid without the appropriate *tagin* (*Magen Avraham* and *Ba'er Heitev* to Sh. Ar., OḤ 36:3).

Kabbalah places great stress on the mystical meanings of the *tagin*. Together with the letters and words of the Torah, every additional stroke or sign is a symbol revealing extraordinary secrets of the universe and creation. The importance of the *tagin* is already emphasized by the Talmud in its vivid description of Moses ascending on high to find God engaged in affixing *tagin* to the letters of the Torah (Men. 29b).

Simḥah b. Samuel, a disciple of Rashi, copied a *Sefer Tagin* into his *Maḥzor Vitry* (ed. by S. Hurwitz (1923^2), 674–83). According to tradition, this *Sefer Tagin* authored by Joshua recorded the proper usage of the *tagin* as they appeared on the 12 stones which he first set up in the Jordan River and later transferred to Gilgal (Josh. 4:9, 20). On these stones were inscribed the books of Moses with the required *tagin* (Naḥmanides to Deut. 27:8). An annotated edition of the *Sefer Tagin* was issued by S. Sachs in 1866.

The *tagin* are the "tittles" mentioned in the New Testament (Matt. 5:18; Luke 16:17, translated as "stroke" in the New English Bible).

BIBLIOGRAPHY: Eisenstein, Dinim, 300f., 433.

TAGLICHT, DAVID ISRAEL (1862–1943), Austrian rabbi and scholar. Born in Nagy Berzna (now Veliki Berezny, Ukraine), Taglicht attended yeshivot before going to Berlin, where he studied at the university and at the Orthodox rabbinical seminary. After a tenure (1889–93) in Ungarisch-Ostra (Uhersky-Ostroh), he received a post in Vienna; in 1910 he succeeded to Max *Grunwald's rabbinical office and was able to devote himself to historical studies, the most important of which were *Nachlaesse der Wiener Juden im 17. und 18. Jahrhundert* (1917; continued in 1936), on the wills and testaments of Vienna's leading Jewish families (the *Arnsteins, *Eskeles, *Wertheims, *Oppenheimers, etc.). In 1932 he became rabbi of Vienna's main synagogue, the Leopoldstadt Tempel, and was noted for his oratorical talents and his stand above party struggles. After the Anschluss, Taglicht was forced to scrub the sidewalks and to carry a placard on which was written "I am a Jew." He was humiliated and beaten. He was allowed to leave as a result of foreign pressure and went to England, where he died at Cambridge.

BIBLIOGRAPHY: M. Bloch, in: YIVO *Bleter*, 23 (1944), 249ff.; N.M. Gelber, in: S. Federbush (ed.), *Ḥokhmat Yisrael be-Ma'arav Eiropah*, 2 (1963), 111–5.

TAHAL (Heb. תַּהַ"ל), a corporation whose name is compounded from the initials of the Hebrew words for Water Planning for Israel (*Tikhnun ha-Mayim le-Yisrael*). Established by the government of Israel in 1952 by merging the water resources department of the Ministry of Agriculture with the engineering division of the *Mekorot water company (Israel's national water supply agency), Tahal was founded under Israel's company law. The majority of shares (52%) are held by the government; the remainder are divided equally between the *Jewish Agency and the *Jewish National Fund. The policy of the company is determined by a board of directors. In 1961 the company established a subsidiary, Tahal Consulting Engineers Ltd., to undertake work on a commercial basis in Israel and abroad.

Tahal draws up long-, medium-, and short-term plans for the development of Israel's water resources and drainage facilities. It plans and designs the country's main water supply, irrigation, and drainage works, and advises the government on all issues connected with water resources. In this capacity, Tahal has planned and designed Israel's major groundwater developments, river-water projects, and flood and sewage reclamation projects, including all the installations incorporated in Israel's National Water Carrier (the Jordan Project). It has also carried out extensive research programs on water conservation, including cloud seeding to increase rainfall, evaporation suppression, increase of the water obtainable from uncultivated areas, improved management of groundwater basins, and the utilization of surface and groundwater resources.

In 1968 Tahal designed the last phase of the development of Israel's natural and reclaimed water resources, and studied the engineering and economic aspects of the construction of a large-scale plant for desalting sea water. In 1956, the company was entrusted to design the first crude-oil pipeline (between Eilat and Haifa). Since then, oil and gas transportation and storage have remained one of Tahal's activities, and in 1967 it carried out all engineering studies for the major international pipeline from Eilat to Ashkelon, which was completed and operative in 1970. Over the years, the company has entered other fields such as highway and industrial engineering.

From the early 1960s, Tahal extended operations to an increasing number of developing countries in the Middle East, Africa, Latin America, and Southeast Asia. Its projects, sometimes supported by other Israel agencies, include national and regional development plans for water supply and irrigated agriculture, major water supply, irrigation and drainage projects, the planning and management of regional irrigation schemes, and groundwater development and management. A number of foreign branch offices and partially owned subsidiaries were set up in the company's principal areas of activity. In the early 2000s, Tahal employed approximately 500 engineers, agronomists, scientists, technicians, and administrative workers. Its areas of specialization continued to cover a wide spectrum, encompassing water management, agricultural planning, wastewater treatment, environmental engineering, civil engineering and infrastructure, industrial engineering and energy as well as turnkey projects in the water and sanitation sectors. Tahal's operations are divided as follows: 27% of projects in Israel, 24% in Latin America, 21% in the Mediterranean basin, 21% in Europe, and the rest in Africa and Asia. The total value of projects undertaken by TAHAL in 2001 amounted to US $1 billion.

BIBLIOGRAPHY: Tahal, *Tahal, the Company and Its Activities* (1965); Tahal Consulting Engineers Ltd., *History, Organization, Activities* (1967); Tahal, *Jordan Project* (1963); idem, *Yarkon-Negev Project* (1956); idem, *Dan Region Sewage Reclamation Project* (1962), Tahal publications, nos. 243, 244–48, 250–52; A. Wiener, *Irrigation Water System – Israel's National Water Grid* (1967). **WEBSITE:** www.tahal.co.il.

[Aaron Wiener / Shaked Gilboa (2nd ed.)]

TAḤANUN (Heb. תַּחֲנוּן; "supplication"), name of a prayer which is a *confession of sins and a petition for grace. It forms part of the daily morning and afternoon services and is recited after the *ḥazzan's* repetition of the **Amidah*. The *Taḥanun* begins with a silent recital of David's utterance after being rebuked by the prophet Gad for his sin of numbering the people (II Sam. 24:14), "let us fall, I pray thee, into the hand of the Lord, for His mercies are many, but let me not fall into the hand of men." It is, therefore, also called *nefilat appayim* ("prostration prayer," lit. "falling on the face"). Since prostration during petitions is mentioned in the Bible (Deut. 9:18; Josh. 7:6), it was customary to recite the *Taḥanun* prostrated. In modern times, however, the prayer is recited in a seated position with lowered head and face buried in the bend of the arm. This position is assumed only where there is a Torah Scroll to designate the sanctity of the place. In the Sephardi ritual, it is customary to start the *Taḥanun* with a silent confession of sins (*Viddui*), followed by II Samuel 24:14 (as in the Ashkenazi ritual). The central part of *Taḥanun* is a penitential psalm, Psalm 25 in the Sephardi, and Psalm 6 in the Ashkenazi ritual. The *Taḥanun* is supplemented by additional penitential prayers and *piyyutim*. In the Ashkenazi rite there follows part of a *piyyut* (*Shomer Yisrael*) which also occurs in the **seliḥot* liturgy. The last passage of the *Taḥanun*, starting with a quotation from II Chronicles 20:12 (*Va-anaḥnu lo neda mah na'aseh*), is a shortened form of the whole prayer and was instituted so that latecomers to the morning service could attend the reading from the Torah. The *Taḥanun* prayer is omitted on Sabbaths, festivals, semiholidays, New Moons, from the *Minḥah* service preceding these special days, during the month of Nisan, and on the Ninth of Av. At a circumcision in the synagogue, when a bridegroom attends the service during the first seven days after his wedding, and at prayers held at the homes of mourners, the *Taḥanun* is also omitted.

The origin of the *Taḥanun* dates back to the talmudic period in Babylonia. Although the prayer was known as *nefilat appayim*, many rabbis, such as Eleazar b. Hyrcanus (BM 59b), *Abbaye, *Rava, and especially *Rav refused to prostrate at this prayer, either because they considered complete prostration forbidden outside the Temple in Jerusalem or because they regarded it as not obligatory for a distinguished personage (Meg. 22b; Ta'an. 14b). By the time of the *geonim* the posture had already been modified to sitting (or half-sitting), with the head inclined on the arm. The exact date of the various parts making up the *Taḥanun* cannot be established with certainty. The view that the *Taḥanun* was originally a supplication supplemented by confession of sins recited in private without fixed form is strengthened by the fact that there is considerable variety in the versions given in the various prayer books (e.g.,

*Saadiah Gaon, *Maimonides, etc.). Its final version evolved only in the 16th century.

BIBLIOGRAPHY: Eisenstein, Dinim, 270, 435–6; Baer, S., Seder, 112–9; Elbogen, Gottesdienst, 73–81; Hertz, Prayer, 168–87; E. Levy, *Yesodot ha-Tefillah* (1952²), 177–9; E. Munk, *The World of Prayer*, 1 (1961), 161–70; Abrahams, Companion, lxxviff.

[Meir Ydit]

TAHARAT (Tohorat) HA-MISHPAḤAH (Heb. טָהֳרַת הַמִּשְׁפָּחָה; lit. "family purity"), the term popularly given to the laws of *niddah*, which involve a married couple's abstinence from sexual relations during the period of menstruation until the wife's immersion in the *mikveh*. These regulations are considered by the Orthodox to be basic to the Jewish way of life, and R. Akiva went so far as to declare the son of a *niddah* a *mamzer* (Yev. 29b). Although his viewpoint is not accepted as the *halakhah*, it nevertheless indicates the importance of these laws. In more modern times, many psychological, medical, and physiological reasons have been given for the observance of this precept, and all of them stress the benefits that are gained by the couple practicing abstinence during part of each month. Societies have been organized in many communities for the purpose of instructing people in these laws and supervising the daily functioning of the *mikveh*.

BIBLIOGRAPHY: I.J. Unterman, *Tohorat ha-Mishpaḥah ve-Heikef Hashpa'atah* (1970); D. Miller, *The Secret of the Jew* (1930); N. Lamm, *A Hedge of Roses* (1966); K. Kahana, *Tohorat Bat Yisrael* (1963³).

TAḤASH (Heb. תַּחַשׁ), animal mentioned in the Bible. The skins of the *taḥash* were used as a covering for the Tent of Meeting (Ex. 35:23; 36:19; et al.). According to Ezekiel (16:10) the Children of Israel made shoes of *taḥash* while journeying in the wilderness. Many conjectures have been made as to its identity. In Egyptian *tḥs* means well-tanned leather, and on this basis some are of the opinion that *taḥash* too was merely leather tanned in a certain way. The *tanna* Judah thought it to be skin dyed *altinon* (Greek ἀληδινον) seemingly purple (Eccles. R. 1:9). R. Meir maintained that the *taḥash* was a legendary creature that existed in the time of Moses and was afterward hidden: "The *taḥash* of Moses' day was a separate species and sages could not decide whether they were beasts or domestic animals, and it had one horn on its forehead" (Shab. 28b). Some gave additional signs: that it was a clean animal, that it had multicolored skin, and that it was identical with the *keresh*, the legendary unicorn (*ibid.*; Eccles. R. loc. cit.). Based on these indications, many suggested identifications for the *taḥash* have been proposed, such as the fleet-footed antelope (taking *taḥash* from *ḥish*, "fleet"), or the giraffe, which has many of the signs given by R. Meir, multicolored skin, a horn-like protrusion on its forehead, and some of the signs of a clean animal. Because the Arabic *tukhesh* means the sea mammal *Dugong hemprichi*, some endeavor to identify it with the *taḥash*. This appears at intervals on the shores of Sinai and is hunted by the Bedouin, who make curtains and shoes from its skin. Others identify the *taḥash* with another sea mammal, *Monodon monoceros*, which occasionally reaches the shores of the Red Sea. It has mottled skin and a single tooth-horn on its forehead. These, however, are all conjectures and the identity of the *taḥash* remains obscure. The AV and JPS translation of "badger" has no basis in fact.

BIBLIOGRAPHY: I. Aharoni, in: *Tarbiz*, 8 (1936/37), 319–39; J. Furman, *ibid.*, 12 (1940/41), 218–29; J. Feliks, *Animal World of the Bible* (1962), 50.

[Jehuda Feliks]

TAILORING. The Hebrew word for "tailor," חַיָּט, first appears in mishnaic and midrashic literature. Tailors are mentioned more frequently in the Talmud (Shab. 1:3, 11b; BK 10:10), and Jewish tailors were to be found in Muslim countries at this period, but rarely in significant numbers. Almost every Jewish community had its own tailor whose presence was necessitated by the obligatory ritual commandments such as *sha'atnez*. The Church was also interested in enforcing the wearing of special Jewish garments. Moneylending entailed some knowledge of tailoring since it was necessary to keep pawned clothes in good repair. Although both Church pressure and moneylending were absent in Islamic countries, tailoring on a small and medium scale became an important element in Jewish society. In *Yemen entire Jewish villages subsisted on weaving and tailoring until 1948 (S.D. Goitein, in: JSOS, 17 (1954), 3–26). The main obstacles to Jewish tailors in medieval Europe were raised by the guilds, who continuously tried to restrict their activity to producing their own distinctive clothing for Jewish clients alone. However, in Christian Spain, where there were many Jewish tailors as the Christian guilds were comparatively weak, the rulers often intervened on their behalf when their livelihood was threatened by the encroachment of local guilds and authorities. In 1489 Ferdinand and Isabella of Spain annulled an ordinance enacted in *Burgos which prohibited Jewish tailors and other craftsmen from plying their trade outside the Jewish quarter. The connection between tailoring and the trade in *secondhand goods and old clothes, which had to be repaired and resold, was most clearly in evidence in Italy, especially in *Rome, where a Jewish tailors' guild existed from the 15th century and between one-quarter and one-half of the Jewish community was engaged in various branches of the clothing trade in the 16th century. Bernardino Ramazzini (1633–1714), an early authority on occupational diseases, noted that many Jews suffered from weak eyesight, legs, and lungs, caused by repairing old clothes in poorly lit and badly ventilated rooms. Many Italian cities tried to prohibit Jews from refurbishing old clothes because this often provided a springboard for the prohibited manufacture and sale of new garments. The nexus of tailoring and trading in old clothes remained important in Italian Jewry until the 20th century.

Jewish tailoring in central Europe, as elsewhere, was conditioned by *sha'atnez* laws and the tie with the repair and sale of used clothing, but it grew in scope wherever conditions became more favorable. In *Prague a continuous struggle was waged between the Christian and the Jewish guilds because the Jewish tailors were accused of illegally selling new clothes. The banner of the Jewish tailors' guild, a colorful patchwork of cloth, bore a pair of scissors embroidered in gold. These conflicts were operative in the expulsion of the Prague community (1745), but the move affected the Christian tailors since the expelled Jews now produced wares for the countryside and nobody came to Prague to buy new clothes. Among the 1,418 Jewish families who returned to Prague were 91 tailors and tailoresses, eight trouser sewers, seven linen menders, and 37 button makers, as well as dozens of artisans and merchants dealing in a variety of haberdashery and clothing articles. In rural Bohemia in 1724 there were 182 tailors among 3,093 heads of Jewish households (butchers were the second largest craft with 179); many of these were *peddlers who plied their trade in villages. In *Moravia Jewish tailoring developed along different lines. In 1673, in *Mikulov (Nikolsburg), there were eight Jewish master tailors, each with one apprentice and assistant, and around 1713, in *Prostejov (Prossnitz), there were 12 Jewish tailors (and 18 Christian ones), though they were mainly engaged in selling articles produced by Christians. This activity grew during and after the Thirty Years' War (1618–48) when Jewish military *contractors supplied thousands of uniforms. The number of Jewish tailors in Moravia increased from between one and three in each community at the beginning of the 18th century to between four and 12 at its end. The development from selling old clothes to a modern clothing industry is best demonstrated by the Mandel family of Prostejov. Abraham Mandel (d. 1836) was a dealer in old clothes who specialized in converting uniforms into suits. His son Moses (1792–1862) opened his own old clothes shop and around 1840 began selling new clothes as well. Moses' son, Mayer Mandel (1820–1888), though employing dozens of tailors, had to buy membership in the Plumenau tailors' guild. In 1859 he opened the first clothing factory in Europe and was able to supply uniforms to the whole Turkish army as well as to those of other Balkan states. Jewish enterprise made Prostejov the center of the modern clothing industry in Czechoslovakia.

In *Poland-Lithuania tailoring was one of the first crafts plied extensively in the 16th and 17th centuries and the earliest in which independent guilds were formed by Jews. Their ranks were reinforced by the embroiderers and cap makers, almost exclusively Jewish crafts. Jewish tailors were soon locked in fierce and often bloody competition with their Christian competitors, particularly in *Lublin. Riots were often provoked by artisans who accused Jews of selling ready-to-wear clothing or of selling to Christians. In *Warsaw in 1795 there were 74 Jewish tailors supplying custom-made garments and 53 tailors and 36 sellers of ready-to-wear clothing. The number of tailors in other cities was also large: *Vilna had 88 in 1765 and Lublin 90 in 1759. In *Poznan province they were particularly numerous: in the late 18th century 48 of the 50 tailors in *Krotoszyn were Jews, as were 32 of 51 in *Leszno (Lissa), 31 of 46 in Ostrow Wielkopolski, and 56 of 57 in Rogozno. In the *Pale of Settlement tailoring both at home and as an itinerant craft in the villages became the mainstay of a growing section of the impoverished population of the shtetl. The life-style, songs, and folklore of the *amkho sher un ayren* ("the simple people of the scissors and ironing board") became in Yiddish literature the expression of the joys and sufferings of Jewish workers. This way of life was carried overseas in the mass emigrations to France, England, and the U.S. (see below). In Poland in 1931, 504,570 Jews constituted 44.1% of all those active in the clothing industry; these were fairly evenly divided into employed manual and white-collar workers and home workers. About 52% of the independent employers in the clothing industry were Jews, though most Jewish firms were small or medium sized. Polish antisemitic policy in the 1930s compelled them to adopt new forms of work and organization.

In Germany – except for the production of clothes for Jewish needs and the repair of clothing held in pawn – Jews entered the general field of tailoring as sellers: 41 Christian tailors were employed by Jews in *Frankfurt on the Main in 1611. During the 17th century protests were heard throughout the country that Jewish peddlers were selling new clothes, above all at the *Leipzig fairs and other such *markets. With the growth of cities in the 19th century Jews gradually established stores for haberdashery and the like, then moved into large-scale wholesale clothing manufacture. Between one-third and one-half of the manufacturing firms in the German clothing industry were owned by Jews, and the same proportion of wholesale houses; their share in this trade was highest in Berlin. The production of hats and caps was almost entirely Jewish owned. Various Jewish clothing stores were set up in different places, forming the basis of the later *department stores. In 1644, in Vienna, Christian tailors complained that Jewish tailors were making ready-to-wear garments and employing Christian tailors (A. Pribram, *Urkunden und Akten*, 1 (1918), 143 f.), but in fact Jewish tailors did not become significant until the 19th century. The sale of used European clothing to the Balkans and the Near East, which was centered on Vienna, was managed by Jews. The production of hats, caps, and umbrellas was almost exclusively Jewish, as was that of underclothes, which had been freed of guild restrictions by *Maria Theresa.

Though Jews in France (*Avignon, *Bordeaux, and *Alsace) had long been engaged in buying, repairing, and selling old clothes, this activity declined after the French Revolution. The mass emigration of Jews from Eastern Europe after the pogroms of 1881–83 and 1903–05 and between the world wars brought to *Paris thousands of impoverished Jews who, driven by both experience and necessity, turned en masse to certain sectors of the clothing industry, particularly hat- and cap-making. Since they worked for low pay in "sweatshops" and doing piecework at home, Jews were in the forefront of the unionization of Parisian clothing workers. When 55 Jewish hat makers wanted to found a union in 1892, they had to wait until some of them were naturalized for none of these workers were French. This union remained entirely Jewish

(289 members) until 1936, when the proportion of Jews became 53.6% of the 1,445 members. In the hosiery union their percentage – 90.9 (200 out of 220) before 1936 – declined to 39.6 (720 out of 1,820). The handbagmakers' union was 80% Jewish (160 out of 200) before 1936 and remained so afterward as well (2,400 out of 3,000). After World War I Polish Jews gained a prominent share of the knitware and hosiery industries. However, the role of Jews in the French clothing industries, particularly in production in small family firms, declined after World War II. Jews did not penetrate the field of haute couture in Paris.

[Henry Wasserman]

England

Jews were first connected with the clothing trade in England to a substantial degree as secondhand clothes dealers in the 18th century. At the end of the 18th century there were 1,000–1,500 Jewish dealers in old clothes and even in 1850 between 500 and 600 were still active. They either sold complete garments, or, where these were too worn, cut them up into smaller articles, such as waistcoats. That Jews in this period were particularly concerned with cheap clothing is confirmed by their activity as buyers at the East India Company's auctions of imported cloth, where they seem to have dominated the market in cheap or damaged cloth. Their activity as navy agents (supplying ships with stores at a time when the governments left such matters to contractors) naturally made them suppliers of "slop clothing" for sailors' dress – a connection with the supply of uniforms which persisted to contemporary times. Jews were also prominent in the hat trade, both as sellers and makers.

As the community grew, efforts were made by the communal authorities to cut down the number of hawkers and to apprentice Jewish youth to trades, particularly tailoring, hat-making, and shoe-making. Thus by 1850 *London (perhaps the first large city to do so) had developed an indigenous Jewish artisan class, as well as middle-class clothing entrepreneurs, contractors, and middlemen. By enabling the working classes to buy new clothing in the same styles – although not of the same quality – as those worn by the rich, they began a social revolution. Two firms especially, Hyam, which employed 6,000 people and had a payroll of £200,000 a year, and E. Moses & Son, famous for its advertising techniques, pioneered the new development. These and similar firms supplied outfits for emigrants to the colonies. To supply the needs of these firms small tailoring workshops proliferated, encouraged by the import of the Singer sewing machine in the 1850s and 1860s. The waves of immigrants from Eastern Europe from the 1880s increased the number and concentration of Jews in tailoring. The 1901 census figures of Russian-Polish immigrants show that about 40 out of every 100 men (and 50 out of every 100 women) who were gainfully employed worked in tailoring and 12 or 13 in the boot, shoe, and slipper trades.

Cap-making in London and *Manchester was almost exclusively a Jewish immigrant trade. In Manchester, too, waterproofing had been developed by earlier Jewish immigrants, first in workshops and then in factories, but waterproofing was superseded by the technologically superior rainproof garment. The immigrant tailors had no effect on the bespoke trade; in London, they supplied ready-made garments for merchants and wholesale clothiers and they virtually introduced the ladies' jacket and mantle-making industry to Britain. The principle was subdivision of labor, whereby each operative's task was graded to his skill (or lack of it). Working long hours in small, badly ventilated workshops, the immigrant employees strove to become masters in their turn. This pattern delayed in London and Manchester the introduction of a factory system such as had operated from about 1860 in *Leeds, where at the beginning of the 20th century Montague *Burton adapted bespoke tailoring to factory production and opened a chain of shops for retail distribution. In this he anticipated the Jewish role in the clothing trade of the 20th century with its tendency toward the organization of mass production and of distribution. The Marks & Spencer chain of stores may be cited as an outstanding example (see Simon *Marks and Israel *Sieff). Jews were also active in large-scale distribution in the textile trade, as clothing retailers, and as manufacturers of a wide range of women's ready-made garments. It is noteworthy, however, that Jewish women and girls who before 1939 worked as dressmakers or in tailoring, in the mid-20th century preferred office work. For two centuries, Anglo-Jewry has been connected with the clothing industry. Only the roles have changed: from hawker to retailer, from operative to manufacturer, and from merchant to wholesaler.

[Vivian David Lipman]

United States

Before 1880 Jews from Germany had already become the leading manufacturers of ready-made clothing. German Jewish immigrants had often been connected with the secondhand clothing business in Europe, and many moved into the same occupation upon arriving in America. After the Civil War the market for ready-made clothing expanded among the increasing number of urban dwellers, and the mechanical cutting knife of the 1870s permitted more rapid production of the basic portion of the garment. Ready-made clothing was distributed through secondhand garment merchants, many of whom were German Jews. Some of these men soon began to manufacture ready-made clothing as well as to distribute it. However, it would be erroneous to make too close a connection between the movement of Eastern European Jews into the clothing industry after 1880 and the presence of German Jewish employers in this area. In *Chicago, Bohemian immigrants were the first workers in the ready-made clothing industry. The entry of Eastern European Jews into the clothing industry was primarily the result of their need for work immediately after their arrival in America – a condition shared by all immigrant groups – and the availability of the clothing industry because of its rapid growth in the late 19th century and its particular manufacturing methods.

Unlike many American industries, the garment trades were not mechanized. Manufacturers quickly discovered that clothing could be finished through a series of simple processes that could be learned easily even by inexperienced workers. As the demand for ready-made clothing grew, the East European Jew who arrived in America found the clothing industry to be a source of immediate work, especially since many immigrant Jews often had had some experience in tailoring. Italians, Poles, Lithuanians, and Bohemians who entered the United States from 1894 to 1914 also entered the clothing industry and competed with the Jewish worker. The lack of expensive equipment allowed the clothing industry in most cities to fragment into numerous small shops, most of which finished the goods supplied by the manufacturers. These shops appeared throughout the ghetto areas as they followed the labor supply, and within them developed the "sweatshop" conditions that marked this industry for many decades. These small, overcrowded, poorly maintained shops were operated by a contractor who secured the unfinished garment from the manufacturer and completed the work. The contractors competed with each other for work from the manufacturers, and they in turn tried to make a profit by subdividing the finishing of the clothing and lowering the cost per piece to a minimum. This produced continuous pressure on the piece rates, and long hours of hectic labor in the "season," followed by stretches of unemployment. There was constant friction between the worker and the contractor over the piece rate and the amount of work required to earn the rate. Contractors often sought out the newly arrived immigrants in the expectation that they would accept lower wages. In addition, many contractors gave out part of the finishing work to be done in the homes of the workers. This encouraged the conversion of overcrowded tenement apartments into extensions of the shop, resulting in child labor and continuous work by entire families for minimal piece rates.

Although the older trade unions in the clothing industry opposed these developments, they represented only small groups of skilled workers, and it was not until the formation of unions such as the International Ladies' Garment Workers' Union in 1900 and the Amalgamated Clothing Workers' Union in 1914 that the efforts to organize the immigrant workers achieved any permanent success. These labor organizations, which had a strongly Jewish leadership, were divided on political grounds as moderate trade unionists, Socialists, and Communists contended for control. The dominant tendency was for a mildly Socialistic rhetoric to be combined with trade unionist bargaining procedures. The garment unions also became social and educational institutions, and this contributed significantly to the Americanization of the immigrant membership. As immigrant Jews from Eastern Europe accumulated some experience in America, and a small amount of capital, they attempted to become employers within the garment industry. By World War I East European Jews dominated the ranks of the employers, particularly among the contractors and jobbers where capital requirements were minimal. This persisted until the 1970s, but the character of the work force did not remain ethnically stable. Jewish workers still comprised a significant portion of the employees, but few young persons from Jewish families entered these trades. Thus the proportion of Jewish workers declined steadily as older workers left the industry. Italian workers had become a major group in the needle trades by World War I, but their percentage of the work force also declined as African-American and Puerto Rican workers were increasingly employed in New York City and some of the other metropolitan centers. In addition, as the ladies' garment industry decentralized in search of cheaper labor its ethnic character became more diverse. Thus despite the continued participation of Jews in the garment trades, by 1970 the crucial role of the clothing industry in the lives of American Jews was past.

[Irwin Yellowitz]

In Israel

Tailoring and allied industries developed rapidly in Israel, particularly because of (1) the fast increase in local demand as a result of the increase in population and purchasing power; (2) restrictions on imports, especially in the 1950s and early 1960s, which opened up the market for local manufacturers; and (3) large-scale government aid in financing investments, guaranteeing prices, etc.

Since the market demanded more than it was in the power of this industry to offer, it was in its early stages characteristically a sellers' market. The manufacturers did not endeavor, therefore, to promote new models in order to attract buyers, but were content to copy foreign models. The quality, too, was not always up to the required standard.

In the early 1960s a number of developments occurred, mainly in the policy of the government, which encouraged a change in the manufacturers' outlook and in their general attitude, as regards both fashion and quality. The main change in governmental policy took place in 1962, and allowed for the gradual import of competitive goods from abroad, as well as encouraging more extensive exports. The competition for the local market and the need to export provided an impetus for improving quality, and increasing fashion consciousness and internal efficiency. In relatively few years Israel succeeded in achieving a position in the world fashion industry with a considerable number of products: swimsuits and beach wear, knits, women's underclothes (brassieres, panty hose, panties, etc.), men's neckties, sports clothes, raincoats for men and women, leather coats, etc.

Most Israeli fashions are the work of Israeli fashion designers, and Israel has succeeded in penetrating the world fashion centers of France, Italy, and the American continent. Israel regularly takes part in fairs and fashion weeks both at home and abroad. Sales offices have been opened in the chief exporting countries (e.g., U.S., Germany, France, and Scandinavia). In order to increase exports and ensure the quality of the products, a fashion center has been established by the Export Institute. The center especially tries to increase the manufacturer's know-how, create contacts among importers, buyers, and manufacturers, and guide foreign investors. In the early 2000s Israel's fashion exports reached $670 million a year.

BIBLIOGRAPHY: M. Wischnitzer, *A History of Jewish Crafts and Guilds* (1965); M. Hendel, *Melakhah u-Va'alei Melakhah be-Am Yisrael* (1955), index. ORIENT: S.D. Goitein, *A Mediterranean Society* (1967); idem, in: JSOS, 17 (1955), 3–26; A. Bauer, *Yehudei Kurdistan* (1948), 183; H. Bentov, in: *Sefunot*, 10 (1966), 431f.; M.S. Goodblatt, *Jewish Life in Turkey* (1952). ITALY: M.A. Shulvass, *Ḥayyei ha-Yehudim be-Italyah* (1955), 130–2; J. Donath, in: MGWJ, 72 (1928), 574f.; Roth, Italy; idem, *History of the Jews in Venice* (1930), index; S. Simonsohn, *Toledot ha-Yehudim be-Dukkasut Mantovah* (1964), index, s.v *hayyatim*. CZECHOSLOVAKIA: H. Flesch, in: MGWJ (1930); B. Heilig, in: JGGJC, 3 (1931), 307–448; idem, in: *Zeitschrift des deutschen Vereins fuer die Geschichte Maehrens und Schlesiens*, 31 (1929); idem, *Urkundliches zur Wirtschaftsgeschichte der Juden in Prossnitz* (1929); T. Jakobovitz, in: JGGJC, 8 (1936), 108–11; R. Kestenberg-Gladstein, in: *Zion*, 9 (1944), 1–26; 12 (1947), 47–65; J. Pick, in: *Jews in Czechoslovakia* (1968). POLAND: J. Jacobson, in: MGWJ, 65 (1921), 43ff.; I. Halpern, in: *Zion*, 2 (1937), 72ff.; idem, *Yehudim ve-Yahadut be-Mizraḥ Eiropah* (1969), passim; I. Goldberg and A. Wajn, in: *Bleter far Geshikhte*, 15 (1962/3), 155–205; M.M. Zarchin, *Jews in the Province of Posen* (1939), 31–42; idem, in: JQR, 27 (1937/38), 47–56; M. Hendel, in: *Reshumot*, 5 (1953), 131–45; E. Ringelblum, in: *Ekonomishe Shriften*, 2 (1932), 20–31; M. Balaban, *Der Judenstaat von Lublin* (1919), 63ff.; R. Mahler, *Yehudei Polin Bein Shetei Milḥamot Olam* (1968). LITHUANIA: *Di Yidishe Hantverker in Lite in Tsifern* (1938); M. Linder, in: *Yidishe Ekonomik*, 3 (1939), 1–18; *Der Shnayder*, 1, 1936. GERMANY AND AUSTRIA: A Marcus, *Die Wirtschaftliche Krise der deutschen Juden* (1935), 70–96; idem, in: *YIVO Annual*, 7 (1952), 195–9; J. Lestschinsky, *Das wirtschaftliche Schicksal des deutschen Judentums* (1932); B. Daehn, *Berlin Hausvogteiplatz* (1968); E. Landsberg, in: *Der Morgen*, 3 (1927), 111–3; S. Mayer, *Die Wiener Juden* (1912). FRANCE: M. Lanzel, *Ouvriers juifs de Paris: Les Casquettiers* (1912); M. Roblin, *Les Juifs de Paris* (1952), 97ff.; A. Hertzberg, *The French Enlightenment and the Jews* (1968), index; Z. Szajkowski, in: *Yidishe Ekonomik*, 2 (1938), 232–49; J. Klatzmann, *Le Travail à domicile dans l'industrie parisienne des vêtements* (1957); *Der Trikofabrikant*, 1 (1958–); S. Friedmann, *Etuden tsu der Geshikhte fun Eyngevanderten Yidishn Yishuv in Frankraykh* (1936); idem, *Di Profesionale Bevegung Tsvishn di Yidishe Arbayter in Frankraykh biz 1914* (1937). ENGLAND: V.D. Lipman, *Social History of the Jews in England 1850–1950* (1954); idem, in: JJSO, 2 (1960), 202–18; L.P. Gartner, *Jewish Immigrant in England 1870–1914* (1957); M. Freedman (ed.), *A Minority in Britain* (1955); J. Gould and S. Esh (eds.), *Jewish Life in Modern Britain* (1964). U.S.: O. Schmelz, *Jewish Demography and Statistics Bibliography for 1920–1960* (1961); L. Levine, *Women's Garments Workers* (1924); J.M. Budish and G. Soule, *New Unionism in the Clothing Industry* (1920); J. Seidman, *Needle Trades* (1942); M. Epstein, *Jewish Labor in U.S.A.*, 2 vols. (1950–53); M. Rischin, *The Promised City* (1962); R. Glanz, *Jews in American Folklore* (1961), chap. 16; idem, in: *YIVO Annual*, 9 (1954), 308–31; J. Greenfeld, *ibid.*, 2/3 (1947/48), 180–204; E. Feldman, in: AJA, 12 (1960), 3–14; N. Goldberg, in: *YIVO Bleter*, 23 (1944), 178–205; *Jews in America* (1938), 50–52; J. Loft, in: JSOS, 2 (1940), 61–78; W. Herberg, in: *Jewish Frontier*, 20 (1953), 24–29; M. Josephson, *Sidney Hillman: Statesman of American Labor* (1952), index; M. Hall (ed.), *Made in New York: Case Studies in Metropolitan Manufacturing* (1959).

TAITAẒAK, JOSEPH (16th century), talmudist, Bible scholar, and kabbalist of *Salonika. The dates of his birth or death are not known. The dates usually given, 1487/88–1545, are based on Rosanes (see bibl.), but *Scholem is of the opinion that he was born at least ten years earlier, and there is evidence that he died considerably before 1545. Joseph's father Solomon, himself a talmudic scholar and one of the exiles from Spain, had settled with his family in Salonika. There are no biographical details of Joseph's early life, but from the year 1520 he rose to eminence as an outstanding scholar and the halakhic authority of Salonika. Joseph Caro addressed a question to him merely to inquire as to the rulings of previous scholars of Salonika validating a *mikveh* which Caro considered invalid. Taitaẓak replied that he had not been in Salonika at the time, but gave his reasons for supporting their view. Caro seems to have been greatly impressed by Taitaẓak's learning, and, although he did not accept his view, in his reply refers to Taitaẓak in terms of the greatest esteem and respect, "the light and the holy one of Israel, the crown of the Diaspora," etc. Henceforth Taitaẓak was regarded as an authority, and contemporary scholars addressed their problems to him and gave full weight to his views (for the above, see Caro's responsa *Avkat Rokhel*, nos. 50–51). In his *Maggid Meisharim* Caro refers in laudatory terms not only to his "scholarship and saintliness" but to the fact that "he deserved well of the community by raising many disciples" (see below); among the many students attracted to his yeshivah were Isaac *Adarbi, Samuel de *Medina, Eliezer *Ashkenazi, Isaac *Arollia, and Solomon *Alkabeẓ. Taitaẓak can also be regarded as one of the founders of the kabbalistic circle established by his disciples in *Safed. About 1531 he was in Constantinople, where he was involved in a violent controversy (Rosanes, Togarmah, 2 (1937–38), 23f.) and where he may possibly have met Caro. He later returned to Salonika, however, where he remained for the rest of his life.

Taitaẓak's extant halakhic works are confined to his responsa which appear in the works of his contemporaries – the *Avkat Rokhel* of Joseph Caro (who also refers to him in his *Beit Yosef* to YD 65 and 201), the *She'erit Yehudah* of Taitaẓak's brother Judah (p. 70) – and an unpublished commentary by him on the *Halakhot* of Isaac Alfasi is mentioned, as well as a commentary on *Avot*. His main published works are his biblical commentaries *Porat Yosef* on Ecclesiastes (Venice, 1529) and *Leḥem Setarim* on Daniel and the Five *Scrolls (*ibid.*, 1608), while others remain in manuscript.

Porat Yosef is a philosophical commentary and it is remarkable in the fact that in the philosophical views the author follows the scholastic philosophical system of Thomas Aquinas and Aegidius Romanus (sometimes referred to as Aegidius of Colonna; 1247–1316). He quotes Aquinas by name or as "the sage" and even refers to one of his interpretations as "a fine exposition" (*derush na'eh*). So completely does he follow him that, unlike Ḥasdai Crescas, he accepts none of the development of Aristotelianism in Christian theology by later authorities such as Duns Scotus and William of Ockham, or the Paris school. He accepts the doctrine of Aristotle as expounded by Aquinas. Taitaẓak's thorough familiarity with the subject gives the impression that he knew Latin and possibly studied it in Spain, but it is equally possible that he used the translation of the 14th-century translator of Aquinas, Judah *Romano, which was known particularly in Greece.

Taitaẓak's chief importance, however, is as a kabbalist. He indulged in ascetic practices and is said never to have slept in a bed for 40 years, apart from Sabbaths (Elijah de Vidas, *Reshit Ḥokhmah*, Sha'ar ha-Kedushah 7). He gathered around him a circle of scholars of the Kabbalah. It has hitherto been assumed that it was the visit of Solomon *Molcho to Salonika in 1529 and the messianic sermons which he delivered and published in that year (later called *Sefer ha-Mefo'ar*) which attracted Taitaẓak to esoteric study (cf. Werblowsky, bibl., p. 97f.) but Scholem tends to the contrary opinion that Taitaẓak was already a renowned kabbalist when Molcho arrived in Salonika and this attracted Molcho to him and his circle. Molcho corresponded with Taitaẓak after he left Salonika, informing him of his visions. His famous epistle from Monastir, later published as *Ḥayyat Kaneh* (Amsterdam, 1658), was sent to Taitaẓak.

To Taitaẓak is ascribed the first crystallization of the idea of the **maggid*, a divine voice which spoke or dictated to scholars, the *Maggid Meisharim* of Joseph Caro being the best known example. That Taitaẓak had such a *Maggid* is attested by Joseph Sambari (*Divrei Yosef*, in: A. Berliner, *Quellenschriften zur juedischen Geschichte und Literatur* (1896), 70f.) and by Ḥ.J.D. Azulai in the name of his grandfather (Azulai, 1 (1852), 79 no. 134). However, a manuscript has been discovered which purports to be the revelation of the *maggid* to Taitaẓak. Although more research must be undertaken before it can definitely be ascribed to him, there are grounds for accepting its authority. Taitaẓak's *maggid* differs from that of Caro in that it claims to be the Divine Voice itself and not an angelic personification of the Mishnah, as was the case with Caro, and its language is Hebrew and not Aramaic. Joseph Caro's *maggid*, while praising Taitaẓak for his scholarship, piety, and for the fact that he gathered many disciples (see above), makes the statement that a *maggid* does not communicate "in this manner" with Taitaẓak because of his "love of money" and his "lust for authority" (*Maggid Meisharim* (Amsterdam, 1708), 34a–b). Werblowsky regards the words "in this manner" as an acknowledgment by Caro that Taitaẓak did have a *maggid* but that it was of an inferior order, since the communications came to him through automatic writing. Scholem, however, regards it as denying that he had a *maggid* and that all one can deduce from the statement is that Caro was unaware of Taitaẓak's *maggid*. Caro's statement regarding Taitaẓak's failings is so out of keeping with other information about him that it is not impossible that there was a personal element involved.

BIBLIOGRAPHY: Rosanes, Togarmah, 2 (1937–382), 21–26; M. Benayahu, in: *Scritti in Memoria di Sally Mayer* (1956), Heb. pt. 34 n. 62; R.J.Z. Werblowsky, *Joseph Karo, Lawyer and Mystic* (1962), index.

[Louis Isaac Rabinowitz]

TAKKANOT (Heb. תַּקָּנוֹת pl.; sing. תַּקָּנָה). This article is arranged according to the following outline:

Definition and Substance

A *takkanah* is a directive enacted by the halakhic scholars, or other competent body (see **Takkanot ha-Kahal*), enjoying the force of law. It constitutes one of the legal sources of Jewish law (see **Mishpat Ivri*). A law which has its creative source in *takkanah* serves as the motivated addition of a new norm to the overall halakhic system, whereas a law originating from the legal source of *midrash* (exegesis, i.e., from construing a biblical passage or other existing law; see *Interpretation) serves to reveal the concealed content of existing law within the aforementioned system. The consequence of this substantive difference between these two legal sources of Jewish law is that a law created by means of Bible exegesis mostly belongs to the category of laws called *de-oraita*, whereas a law deriving from *takkanah* always belongs to the category called *de-rabbanan* (see *Mishpat Ivri*). The *takkanah* in Jewish Law is akin to that part of legislation which in other legal systems is termed subordinate. The Written Torah is the constitution – the supreme legislation – of Jewish law, and in the Torah itself power is delegated to the halakhic scholars to enact *takkanot*. Similarly, in the primary legislation of other legal systems, authority is delegated to certain bodies to be subordinate legislators (e.g., to cabinet ministers by way of regulations, to municipal councils by way of by-laws, etc. – see Salmond, 12th ed., 116–124). The authority of the halakhic scholars to enact *takkanot* is said to derive from the Pentateuchal enjoinder, "According to the law which they shall teach thee and according to the judgment which they shall tell thee, thou shalt do; thou shalt not turn aside from the sentence which they shall declare unto thee, to the right hand, nor to the left" (Deut. 17:11), or, according to another opinion, to the enjoinder, "Ask thy father and he will declare unto thee, thine elders, and they will tell thee" (*ibid.*, 32:7; Shab. 23a; Yad, Mamrim 1:1–2; *Hassagot Ramban le-Sefer ha-Mitzvot*, Principle 1). The authority of the scholars to impose *gezerot* (decrees, see below) is held to have been entrusted to them in the enjoinder, "Therefore shall ye keep My charge" (Lev. 18:30), interpreted to mean, "Make a safeguard to keep My charge" (Sifra, Aḥarei Mot 10:22; Yev. 21a).

The legislative activity of the halakhic scholars is sometimes termed *takkanah* and sometimes *gezerah*. The term *gezerah* is generally applied to the determination of directives aimed at deterring man from the prohibited, at making "a fence around the Torah" – i.e., directives of a negative nature prohibiting the performance of a particular act. The term *takkanah*, on the other hand, generally refers to directives aimed at imposing a duty to perform a particular act, i.e., directives of a positive nature enjoining the doing of a particular matter (Maim., Comm. to Mishnah, Intr.). This distinction is not, however, consistently observed in the use of the two terms (see, e.g., Git. 4:2; Shab. 15b). Sometimes a *takkanah* is termed a *tenai bet din* or simply *tenai* (Ket. 4:12; BK 80b), because the *bet din* (court) circumscribes – "conditions" as it were – a particular directive in the manner of a *takkanah* and because sometimes the creation of a *takkanah* is preceded by a condition imposed between the parties to a matter. Sometimes a *takkanah* is also termed *minhag* (see RH 4:1, and cf. Tosef., RH 4:3; Beẓah 4b, etc.). The two terms share in common the factor of legislation save that in the case of *takkanah* the legislative activity is deliberate and open whereas in *minhag* it is anonymous and undirected (see **Minhag*).

Legislation in the Halakhah

Halakhic legislation generally functions with two principal objectives:

(1) to fill a lacuna in the law created in consequence of changed social and economic realities and the emergence of problems which find no answer in the existing *halakhah*; in this event the *takkanah* generally serves to add to the existing *halakhah*;

(2) to amend and vary the existing *halakhah* to the extent that this is dictated by the needs of the hour; in this event it cannot be said that the existing law fails to provide guidance but, on account of changed circumstances, the law as it stands creates difficulties of a social, economic, or moral nature, which the *takkanah* seeks to rectify and resolve.

These two objectives are pursued by legislation, whether *takkanah* or *gezerah*, in all the different fields of the *halakhah* – certain areas whereof are wholly founded on such legislation while in other areas its influence is felt to a greater or lesser degree. The latter phenomenon is largely a reflection of the extent to which it proved possible to resort to interpretation (*midrash*) for a solution to the problems that arose. In seeking the solution to a problem that arose the scholars had recourse, first and above all, to the legal source of interpretation, since by so doing the solution would be forthcoming from scriptural passages or from existing *halakhah*. Only when interpretation was not a means to a solution did the scholars resort to *takkanah* – which represented an innovation in the world of the *halakhah*. Thus a substantial part of the laws of tort, of unlawful possession (*gezelot*), and bodily injury (*ḥavalot*), originate from *midrash*, since these matters are extensively dealt with in the Torah. On the other hand, the laws of property and obligations – which are scantily dealt with in the Torah – developed mainly through the legal source of legislation. At times exegesis and legislation functioned with more or less equal efficacy in the development of a particular field of the law, as for instance in the area of family law.

The scholars dealt extensively with the question how to reconcile the aforementioned objectives of legislation with the fundamental norm of the Torah that "ye shall not add unto the word which I command you, neither shall ye diminish from it" (Deut. 4:2 and 13:1). Did not a rule derived by means of a *takkanah* or *gezerah* in some manner add to or detract from the laws of the Torah? Two of the principal answers given by the scholars to this question may be mentioned. In Solomon b. Abraham *Adret's opinion, the enjoinder against adding to or subtracting from the Torah law is directed against any addition to the precepts of the Torah on the part of an individual acting without due authority, but not against the halakhic scholars acting under the authority entrusted to them as regards the interpretation and continued creativity of the *halakhah*; that, as regards the latter, they are expressly enjoined (Deut. 17:8–11) to solve new problems, also by way of legislation, and once they have done so the individual must not depart from their enactments (Nov., Rashba, RH 16a). A different answer was given by *Maimonides, and other scholars sharing his view, in holding that the aforementioned Pentateuchal prohibition is directed against the individual as well as the halakhic scholars and the courts, and that the solution to the problem posed lies in the strict care taken by the halakhic scholars as regards their manner of exercising the legislative function. According to these scholars, the enjoinder against addition to, or subtraction from, the law of the Torah applies to circumstances in which it is sought to hold that a particular law is one which also has its origin in the Torah and is equal in standing to a law of the Torah; however, when the scholars expressly state that according to the Torah the law is so, and that they, by virtue of the authority entrusted to them, are enacting or decreeing such and such as a law of the rabbis, the matter is permissible (Yad, Mamrim 2:9; Intr. to *Mishneh Torah*) – "for 'ye shall not add' only applies to an addition to the Torah meant to be equal therewith, but making fences and restrictions is not an addition, for these are not to be equated with the Torah" (*Ramban*, Deut. 4:2). Thus in making their enactments the scholars are prohibited from acting within the sphere of primary legislation since this is the domain of Pentateuchal enactment alone, which is everlasting and stands for all time. The legislative activity of the scholars is operative only in the area of subordinate legislation, in which area they are authorized and enjoined to make enactments and decrees of a transient nature – "as a temporary measure" (*le-fi sha'ah; hora'at sha'ah*, etc.) – but not to lay down immutable directives (although this distinction is theoretical only, having regard to the very many *takkanot* which have become transformed into an integral part of the laws comprising the halakhic system and have been accepted as decided law in the Talmud and codificatory literature).

Nature of Halakhic Legislation

The basic principle underlying the legislative activities of the halakhic scholars also serves as the basis for the other legal sources of the *halakhah*, namely, that the Torah and its continuing creativity was entrusted to the authority of the halakhic scholars (*Ramban*, Deut. 17:11; see also Interpretation; **Ma'aseh*; *Authority, Rabbinical; **Sevarah*). This exclusive authority led the halakhic scholars to a complete identification with the spirit and purpose of the Torah. Such an identification at once obliged them to act with great care and responsibility in their exercise of the legislative function, while also rendering possible their enactment of daring and decisive *takkanot* when persuaded that these indeed reflected the spirit and purpose of the Torah. With the sense of responsibility of a physician, entrusted with the well-being and perfection of the *halakhah* (Yad, Mamrim 2:4), the halakhic scholars made penetrating and far-reaching statements which have become well-known maxims of the *halakhah*. An illustration is their interpretation of the verse, "It is time for the Lord to work; they have made void Thy law" (Ps. 119: 126), as meaning: "it is better that one letter of the Torah should be uprooted than that the entire Torah become forgotten to Israel" (Tem. 14b; see also Ber. 9:5, Yoma 69a, and Rashi, ad loc.); similarly, "there are times when the disregard of the Torah may be its foundation" (Men. 99a/b), and – "that he shall live by them and not die because of them" (Sanh. 74a; Yoma 85b), and so on.

No discussion concerning the measure of the scholars' legislative authority, or the determination of rules for their exercise of the legislative function, is to be found until the end of tannaitic times. The sole explanation accompanying many *takkanot* is the factual background and circumstances leading to their enactment. Thus the defilement of oil by the Greeks is the background to the *takkanah* relating to the festival of Ḥanukkah (Shab. 21b). Natural disasters and war are the background to the *takkanot* of the **agunot* ("deserted wives"; Yev. 16:7). Abstention from giving credit explains the institution of the *prosbul (Shev. 10:3–4). "For the sake of good order" (*tikkun olam*) or "for the sake of peace" (*darkhei shalom*) is the general explanation for many other *takkanot* (e.g., Git. 4:2–7; 5:3 and 8–9). When the halakhic scholars were persuaded of the need of the hour they enacted and decreed accordingly, in order that the Torah, its ways and precepts, should not become strange to the Jewish people.

Rules of Legislation

Besides the above mentioned basic principle, the *amoraim* laid down a number of rules and guidelines which determined the scope and authoritative force of the legislative activities of the halakhic scholars.

(1) ABSTENTION FROM FULFILLING A MITZVAH. The rule was established that the court may determine by *takkanah* that a (positive) precept prescribed by the law of the Torah shall not be fulfilled, i.e., that it may direct to abstain from performing an act – "sit and do not do" (*shev ve-al ta'aseh*). A commonly quoted example is the *takkanah* to abstain from blowing the *shofar* on Rosh Ha-Shanah falling on a Saturday (RH 29b, and see Yev. 89a–90b for other examples). In R. Ḥisda's opinion the court is even entitled to enact a *takkanah* which entails the uprooting (*akirah*) of a Pentateuchal prohibition, i.e., that the scholars may direct to "arise and do" (*kum va-aseh*) an act the doing whereof is prohibited in the Torah. Rava expressed a contrary opinion and the *halakhah* was decided that "the court may not make a provision uprooting a matter in the Torah by way of a direction to "arise and do." In the talmudic discussion centering on the above difference of opinion a number of exceptions to the stated rule are laid down, each of which constitutes a self-standing rule of legislation (Yev. loc. cit.).

(2) HEFKER BET DIN HEFKER. This rule lays down that in matters of the civil law (*dinei mamonot*), and in every other matter – even in the field of ritual prohibitions and permissions – which is based on the ownership of property, the scholars have authority to enact even such *takkanot* as involve the uprooting of a law of the Torah by directing to "arise and do." The scholars deduced from the passage, "and that whosoever came not within three days, according to the counsel of the princes and the elders, all his substance should be forfeited, and himself separated from the congregation of the captivity" (Ezra 10:8), that the court has authority to divest the individual of his rights of ownership in property (TJ, Shek, 1:2, 46a; TJ Pe'ah 5:1, 8d). This authority was interpreted to extend not merely to a divestment of proprietary rights but also to the transfer of such rights to new owners of the same property – a conclusion based also on Joshua 19:51 (Yev. 89b; Nov. Rashba, Git, 36b). The principle was the basis for the enactment of very many *takkanot* in different fields of civil law – property, tort, succession, and wills – in terms whereof the ownership of property due to a person according to the law of the Torah was shorn from the latter and vested in favor of another. Thus by virtue of the rule of *hefker bet din hefker* the scholars enacted that a woman validly married in accordance with *derabbanan* enactment, but not the strict law, is inherited by her surviving husband – thereby divesting her father's kin, her legal heirs under the strict law in the absence of a valid marriage, of their ownership of the estate in favor of the husband (Yev. loc. cit.). This is likewise the explanation for the validity of all those modes of *acquisition instituted in the enactments of the scholars. According to the strict law such a mode of acquisition would not avail to extinguish the transferor's title, but the scholars enacted that ownership should nevertheless pass to the transferee by the use of such mode – the authority for such a transfer of ownership deriving from the rule of *hefker bet din hefker.*

This rule is also the basis on which the *amoraim* explained the institution of the prosbul. The Torah enjoins the remission (*shemittah*) of monetary debts in the seventh year, forbids the lender from claiming his debt thereafter, and expressly adjures him not to refrain from lending money for fear that the debt will be wiped out in the seventh year (Deut. 15:1–6). Hillel the Elder, when he saw that the people transgressed the law by refraining from lending to each other, enacted that the lender should write out a prosbul, whereupon the debt would not be wiped out in the seventh year and the lender remain entitled to recover it even thereafter (Shev. 10:3–4). In the Talmud it is asked how it was possible for Hillel to enact a *takkanah* contravening a law of the Torah by prescribing permission to do that which was prohibited. One of the given answers is that Hillel had authority to ordain thus by virtue of the rule of *hefker bet din hefker*, that is the scholars laid down that the money of the debt in the ownership of the borrower passes into the ownership of the lender so that the question of claiming a debt exposed to the Sabbatical year does not arise because the lender seeks to do no more than claim money of which he has already acquired ownership (Git. 36b, *Rashi* and Nov. Rashba thereto). The latter example is an illustration of the use of the said rule in relation to a matter of ritual prohibition – i.e., the lender's claim for the money – based on the factor of property ownership. Another example of a *takkanah* of this kind is the annulment of a woman's marriage in certain circumstances on the basis of a retrospective change in the husband's ownership of the *kiddushin* ("marriage") money (see *Marriage; Yev. 90b and *Rashi* ad loc.; BB 48b and *Rashbam* ad loc.).

(3) IN CRIMINAL LAW. The halakhic scholars are entitled to enact *takkanot* in the area of the criminal law even though they involve the uprooting of a law of the Torah by way of "arise and do," when this need is dictated by the exigencies of the time, that is when such enactment amounts, in the words of the Babylonian *amoraim*, to making a safeguard for the Torah (*migdar milta*). The rule is transmitted in the name of Eleazar b. Jacob: "I have heard that the *bet din* imposes flogging and punishment not prescribed in the Torah (*bet din makkin ve-onshin she-lo min ha-Torah*); not to transgress the law of the Torah but to make a fence for the Torah" (Yev. loc. cit.; Sanh. 46a). By virtue of this rule it was held permissible to lay down punishment by *flogging, and even the capital sentence, when rendered necessary by the prevailing social and moral realities (Sanh. loc. cit.). This was so despite the fact that the Torah law prohibits the flogging of any person for whom such punishment was not reserved (Yad, Sanhedrin 16:12) and that certainly it is prohibited to kill a person not liable to the death sentence according to Torah law since it involves a transgression of "Thou shalt not murder" (Radbaz, Mamrim 2:4). Thus in terms of this rule there were prescribed special punishments (such as incarceration – Sanh. 9:5; see *imprisonment) and procedural rules (for instance, admitting circumstantial evidence and dispensing with the need for prior warning – see TJ Ḥag. 2:2, 78a), when this was necessary for the preservation of good order and the public weal. This legislative guideline served the halakhic scholars throughout the ages as a valuable means toward the ordering of Jewish society. It was instrumental in the development – insofar as the judicial autonomy extended to the different Jewish centers allowed for it – of a proliferous legislation in different fields of the Jewish criminal law and procedure answering the social needs of the time (see, e.g., the statements of Judah b. Asher in *Zikhron Yehudah*, no. 79). At the same time the scholars stressed the need to guard, in the exercise of such wide legislative authority, against doing undue injury to man's image and dignity: "all these matters apply to the extent that the *dayyan* shall find them proper in the particular case and necessitated by the prevailing circumstances; in all matters he shall act for the sake of Heaven and he shall not lightly regard the dignity of man…" (Yad, Sanhedrin 24:10; see also Resp. Rashba, vol. 5, no. 238).

(4) EMERGENCY MEASURES TO RESTORE THE PEOPLE TO THE FAITH. This legislatory guideline, operative also in the area of ritual prohibitions and permissions even as regards enactments involving the uprooting of a law of the Torah by directing to "arise and do," is derived from the act of Elijah in offering a sacrifice on the Mount of Carmel in order to bring back the people from the worship of Baal to worship of the Lord (I Kings 18:19–46), notwithstanding that the Torah prohibits such sacrificial offerings except at the Temple in Jerusalem and that sacrificial slaughter elsewhere is a transgression of two Pentateuchal prohibitions (Yev. 90b, *Rashi* and Tos. ad loc.). Legislative authority of this kind is summarized by Maimonides as follows (Yad, Mamrim 2:4): "And if they (the *bet din*) have seen fit for the time being to abrogate a positive precept or to transgress a negative precept so as to bring back the public to worship of the faith, or to save many in Israel from stumbling in other matters – they do according to the need of the hour. Just as the physician severs a person's hand, or foot, so that he shall survive at all, so the *bet din* at times instructs temporarily to transgress some of the precepts in order that all of them shall be fulfilled, as it was laid down by the early scholars (Yoma 85b); 'Profane on his account one Sabbath so that many Sabbaths shall be observed.'"

(5) ENACTMENTS FOR WHICH "THERE IS REASON AND JUSTIFICATION" (IN MATTERS OF RITUAL PERMISSIONS AND PROHIBITIONS). A study of the rabbinical enactments reveals that the rules of legislation enumerated above do not exhaust the full measure of the halakhic scholars' legislative authority. From time to time there is found a *takkanah* which the former were unable to relate to any of the stated rules and they explained them on special legal and social grounds. Classic examples thereof are the *takkanot* of the *agunot* ("deserted wives") – some of the most important *takkanot* in Jewish law, from the aspect both of their social and humanitarian implications and of the conclusions deriving therefrom as regards the substance of legislation in the *halakhah*. The *takkanot* concern the matter of a married woman whose husband is missing and cannot be traced, and there is lacking sufficient evidence as required by the Torah – two witnesses at least (Deut. 19:15; Git. 26) – to establish the husband's death, so as to permit her to remarry. In ancient times this legal situation

had already created many practical difficulties since it happened more than once that a married man lost his life in circumstances of natural disaster or war but the fact could not be confirmed by the testimony of two witnesses, thus leaving the wife an *agunah* for the rest of her life. The halakhic scholars sought the answer to the problem by resorting to the different legal sources of the *halakhah*, above all through institution of a series of *takkanot*.

The earliest of the series appears to be the one laying down that the wife is believed – and permitted to remarry – if after having gone abroad with her husband she returns alone and declares his death (Yev. 15:1; Eduy. 1:12). Quoted as the factual background to the enactment of this *takkanah* is the case of a woman who returned reporting the death of her husband, it being mentioned that the court investigated the facts finding her report to be true (Yev. and Eduy. *ibid.*; Yev. 116b and Tos.). This *takkanah* failed to meet the existing exigencies, since often, and particularly in times of war, the wife did not accompany her husband and therefore was not in a position to testify to the circumstances of his death. Hence a further *takkanah* was enacted – dating to the time of Gamaliel the Elder in the first half of the first century C.E. – prescribing the testimony of a single witness to the husband's death to suffice in order to permit the wife's remarriage. This *takkanah* apparently was not generally accepted, and even two generations later – in the time of Gamaliel of Jabneh, grandson of Gamaliel the Elder – the *tannaim* were still divided on the matter of permitting the wife's remarriage on the testimony of a single witness to her husband's death. Yet the increasing number of *agunot* left behind by the frequent wars led in the end to the general acceptance of this *takkanah* (Yev. 16:7; Eduy. 6:1 and 8:5).

The *amoraim* were much occupied with the legal substantiation of these *takkanot* which directed to "arise and do" in disregard of the law of the Torah on a matter of ritual prohibition – by permitting a woman, regarded in strict law as still married to her first husband, to marry another. The general explanation of the *amoraim* is that the rabbis relaxed the law in favor of an *agunah* (Yev. 88a). The legal explanations offered are that a woman is presumed to be careful herself to make sure that her husband is dead before remarrying (Yev. 25a; 93b; 115a; 116b), and that it need not be feared that people will lie about a matter the truth whereof is bound to be discovered (*ibid.*). These explanations nevertheless do not suffice in themselves to render permissible the remarriage of an *agunah*, i.e., in accordance with the law of the Torah. The halakhic reason given for the authority of the scholars to so enact concerning *agunot* is this: "For even if the scholars lack authority to uproot a law of the Torah by way of 'arise and do' – certainly all agree that there is such authority to uproot when there is reason and justification for the matter" (Tos. to Naz. 43b; Tos. to Yev. 88a; some of the *rishonim* base their explanation of the *takkanah* on the principle that anyone who married does so subject to the consent of the scholars and the scholars annulled the marriage of a missing husband (see below), but this does not appear to be correct in view of the opinion that the *agunah* who has remarried must be divorced from her second husband if the first should appear – Rashba, quoted in *Shitah Mekubbeẓet*, Ket. 3a). The laws concerning *agunot* were added to in many other enactments. In tannaitic times, and later in amoraic and post-talmudic times, numerous other relaxations of the law were laid down, such as the admission of hearsay evidence, of the testimony of various kinds of disqualified witnesses, and so on (Yev. 16:6–7; Tosef., Yev. 14:7–8; TJ, Yev. 16:1. 15c; RH 22a and Codes; see also **agunah*) – "so that the daughters of Israel shall not remain fettered (*agunot*)" (Yad, Gerushin 13:29; for further instances of *takkanot* of this kind, see Av. Zar. 13a and Tos. thereto; Yad, Nedarim 3:9 and *Kesef Mishneh* thereto).

Role of the Public

The main legislative factor in Jewish law is the authority exercised by the courts and the halakhic scholars in all succeeding generations. Another factor is the legislative authority of the public and its representatives. The source of legislative authority exercised by other than halakhic scholars is to be found in the powers conferred on the king (Deut. 17:14–20; I Sam. 8; see also *Ramban*, Lev. 27:29), which, among others, embrace also legislative activity in different fields of civil and criminal law (Sanh. 20b; Yad, Melakhim, 3 and 4; Gezelah, 5:9–18, Roẓe'aḥ 2:4, Sanhedrin 4:2, and 18:6; see also **Mishpat Ivri*). The earliest manifestations of legislative activity on the part of the public and its representatives are to be found in ancient *halakhot* relating to "the townspeople" (*benei ha-ir*). With the rise of the Jewish community from the tenth century onward and the enactment of *Takkanot ha-Kahal*, this legislative activity became a factor of wide scope and importance in Jewish law. Its field of operation extended to the residents of a particular community or federation of communities, or particular districts, and it functioned in the areas of civil, criminal, and public law, but not in that of ritual prohibitions and permissions.

It is true that the public also exercises a decisive influence on legislation emanating from the halakhic scholars. However, in this case the influence is exercised after the legislative act, whereas in the case of communal enactments – and legislation in other legal systems – the public initiative precedes the legislative act. This conception finds expression in the two Talmuds in different versions: in the Babylonian Talmud – "no decree (*gezerah*) is imposed on the public unless the majority is able to abide thereby" (Av. Zar. 36a); in the Jerusalem Talmud (Av. Zar. 2:9, 41d) – "any decree (*gezerah*) which is imposed by the *bet din* and not taken upon themselves by the majority of the public is not a decree." In a combination of the two versions the principle is summarized by Maimonides thus: "A court which sees fit to institute a decree or enact a *takkanah* or introduce a practice must consider the matter and know beforehand whether or not the public is able to abide thereby… If the court has instituted a decree believing the majority of the public able to abide thereby, and thereafter it is found to be scorned by the people and not followed by a majority of the public – it will be void, and it will not be permissible to compel the people to its observance" (Mamrim 2:5–6, and see commentaries thereto).

Annulment of Takkanot

In the Mishnah the rule was laid down that "one *bet din* may not overrule the statements of another unless it exceeds the other in wisdom and number" (Eduy. 1:5). This rule was construed as applying to a court in its exercise of the legislative function, but in its exercise of the interpretative function the second court has authority to arrive at a different conclusion through an alternative interpretation of a biblical passage or ancient *halakhah* (Yad, Mamrim 2:1). However, a number of exceptions were laid down in terms whereof one court may annul the *takkanah* of an earlier court even though lacking the attributes specified in the above rule. The main exceptions are the following:

(1) if at the time of making its enactment the court expressly prescribed that it could be annulled by any court wishing to do so (Ma'as. Sh. 5:2; MK 3b; see also Tos. to BK 82b);

(2) when an enactment believed to have spread among all of Jewry is later found not to have spread among the majority of the Jewish people (Yad, Mamrim 2:7);

(3) when the original reason and justification for the enactment have ceased to be valid (Beẓah 5a/b; *Hassagot Rabad* on Yad, Mamrim 2:2; *Rashi* and *Beit ha-Beḥirah*, cf. the contrary opinion of Maimonides, loc. cit.).

The rule precluding one court from overruling another has the effect of lending the enactments of the scholars a stability and validity equaling, but not exceeding, that of the laws of the Torah itself. Hence, all the rules and guidelines concerning the authority of the halakhic scholars as regards legislating in connection with a law of the Torah obviously apply also as regards their authority to legislate in connection with a rule originating from earlier enactment by the halakhic scholars: "And if circumstances require it is seeming for the *bet din* to uproot even such matters (enactments and decrees of other courts) – even though it be of lower standing than the earlier (*battei din*) – so that such decrees shall not be of greater stringency than the laws of the Torah itself, since even the latter may be uprooted by any *bet din* as an emergency measure" (Yad, Mamrim 2:4).

Takkanot until the End of the Tannaitic Period

Jewish law has experienced legislative activity in all periods of its history, although in varying degrees of intensity. It should be stressed that the actual number of laws originating from legislative activity by the scholars greatly exceeds the number of laws expressly stated to have been derived from *takkanah*. When a particular law is quoted without designation of its legal source, it is only rarely possible to ascertain such a source – by comparing the statement of the same law in other literary sources – and it may reasonably be assumed that *takkanah* is the legal source of a substantial proportion of such laws. It is possible that even laws construed by way of *midrash Torah* (Bible exegesis) had their creative source in *takkanah*, and that such *midrash* served only to integrate such laws with the relevant Pentateuchal passages (see *Interpretation). Sometimes the halakhic scholars themselves mentioned this possibility (see, e.g., TJ, Shev. 10:1–2, 39b, c, concerning the prosbul); at other times it may be gathered from comparison with other sources dealing with the same subject matter. It is likewise possible that laws presented as having their legal source in *minhag, ma'aseh* or *sevarah* may have had their original source in *takkanah*.

(1) IN THE SCRIPTURAL PERIOD. Talmudic tradition attributes various *takkanot* to most ancient times, for instance to the Patriarchs (their institution of prayers – Ber. 26b); to Moses and Joshua (various enactments concerning relations between the individual and the public in matters of property – BK 80b–81b and cf. Joshua 24:25); to Samuel, Boaz, David, Solomon, Jehoshaphat, Haggai, Zechariah, Malachi, and others. Certain *takkanot* are expressly designated in the Books of the Prophets and the Writings (see, e.g., the ordinance of King David in the area of military law – I Sam. 30:24–25).

(2) THE KENESET HA-GEDOLAH ("GREAT ASSEMBLY"). One of the principal tasks of the men of the Great Assembly was to make legislation "… and make a fence around the Torah" (Avot 1:1). Talmudic tradition attributes to the times of Keneset ha-Gedolah numerous *takkanot* in different fields of *halakhah* – benedictions and prayers (Ber. 33a; BB 15a), family law (incest in the second degree – Yev. 2:4; Yev. 21a). *Takkanot* pertaining to procedural rules and other fields of the *halakhah* are attributed to Ezra the Scribe (BK 82a; TJ, Meg. 4:1, 75a).

(3) THE SANHEDRIN AND THE PERIOD OF THE TANNAIM. The Great *Sanhedrin fulfilled the function of a legislative body. The *takkanot* it enacted in the Temple period, as well as those enacted by the **nasi* and his *bet din* after the destruction of the Temple, are of material importance and served to prescribe the modes for the development of the *halakhah*, fashioning its character and evolutionary path for generations to come. A very substantial part of these *takkanot* are embraced in the different fields of Jewish law – civil, criminal, and public. The overwhelming majority of the *takkanot* of the Sanhedrin have come down anonymously, having been ordained by the Sanhedrin as a legislative body. In restricted cases the name of the halakhic scholar heading the Sanhedrin is recalled – for instance Simeon b. Shetaḥ (in *takkanot* concerning family and criminal law, etc. – Shab. 14b–16b; Ket. 82b; TJ, Ket. 8:11, 32c), Hillel the Elder (concerning the prosbul – see above, and others), Gamaliel the Elder (particularly in the area of family law – Git. 4:2–3, and concerning the *agunot*, see above), Johanan b. Zakkai, Gamaliel of Jabneh, and so on. The aforementioned *takkanot* were also enacted by the Sanhedrin as a body, but they have been traditionally transmitted in the name of the contemporary head of this body. Around the middle of the second century the Sanhedrin sitting at Usha in Galilee enacted a number of *takkanot* known as the "*Takkanot Usha*." This was a time of warfare and hardship following on the decrees of the emperor Hadrian,

and it brought in its train a certain disintegration of family life. A large number of the Usha *takkanot* are concerned with the determination of different family law directives in the area of rights and obligations between spouses and between parent and child (Ket. 49bf.; BK 88b; BB 139b). There are also *takkanot* dating from the end of the tannaitic period attributed to particular scholars, such as Yose b. Ḥalafta of Sepphoris and Judah ha-Nasi.

A decisive majority of the *takkanot* known to have been enacted until the end of tannaitic times have not come down in the names of the bodies or scholars who enacted them. Consequently it is difficult, as regards a large proportion of the *takkanot*, to establish their exact stage of enactment during this long and significant period. These anonymous *takkanot* embrace whole areas of Jewish law, such as family law, property and obligations, labor law, tort, procedure and evidence – in which fields the directives thus laid down constitute basic principles of the aforesaid legal system (see Bloch, bibliography).

In the Amoraic Period

In addition to the already mentioned rules of legislation laid down by the *amoraim*, in which they circumscribed the legislative authority of the halakhic scholars, they also enacted many *takkanot* in all fields of the *halakhah*, laying down additional legislative guidelines in this connection. An illustration is their adoption of the enjoinder to "do that which is right and good" (Deut. 6:17–18) as a legislative guideline decreeing the need, at times, to supplement the law – "His testimonies and His statutes" (*ibid.*) – through the enactment of directives answering the demands of social and economic justice (cf. Ramban, Deut. 6:18). On this principle the *amoraim* based their institution of the law of the abutter's preemptive right (BM 108a), which gives the abutter the right of not only preempting neighboring land put up for sale, but also of claiming such land from a third party purchaser in return for the amount paid by the latter to the seller; "…even if the purchaser is a scholar or a neighbor or relative of the seller and the abutter is an ignorant person and not related to the seller, the latter nevertheless takes priority and evicts the purchaser; this because it is said, 'thou shalt do that which is right and good' and the scholars have held that since the sale is the same, it is right and good that the owner of the abutting land rather than an outsider should buy this place" (Yad, Shekhenim 12:5). It was laid down that for the very reason of doing "right and good," constituting the foundation of the abutter's right, the latter right is not available in certain cases. This applies, for instance, when the purchaser is an orphan – "because greater right and good is done by kindness to these rather than the abutter" – or a woman – because she is not in the habit of constantly exerting herself to buy and therefore once she has bought the land, it is a kindness to let the land remain with her" (Yad, Shekhenim 12:13–14, based on BM *ibid.*). The principle of "right and good" is also the basis of the *takkanah* (concerning matters of *execution (civil)) laying down that property assessed in satisfaction of a debt is always returnable to the debtor against payment (BM 35a; Yad, Malveh 22:15–16).

Another legislative principle of the *amoraim* is that stated by them in matters of marriage and divorce that "a man who marries a woman does so subject to the conditions laid down by the rabbis and his marriage is annulled by the rabbis." The meaning of this is that since every marriage takes place according to "the law of Moses and Israel," it takes place subject to the consent of the scholars who laid down the relevant laws and therefore the scholars have the power, in circumstances deemed proper, to annul the marriage and hold it to have been invalid *ab initio*. The *amoraim* relied on this principle in explaining an earlier *takkanah* of Gamaliel the Elder. According to the strict law, the husband who dispatches a bill of divorcement to his wife may cancel it any time before actual delivery thereof to the wife – it being permissible for him to do so before the court even in the absence of his wife. However, Gamaliel the Elder enacted, "for the general good," that there should be no cancellation of the *get* ("bill of divorcement") in the wife's absence (Git. 4:1–2), because the wife might receive the bill without learning of its cancellation and perhaps marry again, at a time when she is in fact still a married woman so that the children of her second marriage will be *mamzerim* (Get. 33a). Simeon b. Gamaliel held the husband's act of canceling a *get* in the wife's absence contrary to the *takkanah* of R. Gamaliel to be ineffective, i.e., that the divorce is valid and the wife free to remarry. In the talmudic discussion on the matter it is asked how the scholars could possibly rule that a *get* ineffective according to the strict law (because of its valid cancellation as aforesaid) should nevertheless be effective and thereby render the wife free to remarry. In answer to this question it was stated that "a man who marries a woman does so subject to the conditions laid down by the rabbis, and his marriage is annulled by the rabbis" – i.e., since in such case the husband has disregarded the enactments of the scholars by canceling the *get* contrary to their directives, therefore they retrospectively annul the *kiddushin* so as to obviate any need at all for the wife to receive a *get* (Git. loc. cit.). Basing themselves on this principle the scholars laid down various rules in the area of marriage and divorce (see, e.g., Ket. 2b–3a) and even, in a case involving no question of a prior *get*, annulled the *kiddushin* celebrated between a man and a woman forcefully "snatched" by him (Yev. 110a).

In the Geonic Period

In geonic times Jewish life in Babylonia was overtaken by significant social and economic changes. The central authorities imposed heavy taxes on land held by Jews, often even expropriating such land, with the result that cultivation was steadily abandoned by Jews in favor of commerce and the trades. This in turn gave rise to many new problems in different fields of Jewish law, the answers to which – when they were not forthcoming by way of interpretation – were found by the *geonim* through resorting to the legal source of *takkanah*. Thus the *geonim* enacted that a debt is recoverable out of the debtor's personal as well as his real estate – contrary to the talmudic law that it is recoverable out of the real estate only, "since here most of the people (i.e., Jews) have no land and the later scholars made a *takkanah* so that the door should not be bolted before borrowers" (*Ḥemdah Genuzah*, no. 65). With the development of commercial life it was found expedient to enact a *takkanah* creating the possibility of the plaintiff's giving a power of attorney extending to litigation with the defendant on all manner of claims – a possibility which is restricted under the talmudic law (Yad, Sheluḥin 3:7). Many other *takkanot* were enacted in different fields of the law, such as property, obligations, family law, evidence, and civil execution (for particulars see Tykocinski and Schipansky, bibliography, see also *Execution (civil)). In the geonic period there was expressed a solitary opinion – the first recorded – casting doubt on the authority of the post-talmudic halakhic scholars to make enactments expressly contrary to the existing law on matters affecting the validity of a marriage or divorce. This was in connection with the *takkanah* enacted at the beginning of the tenth century by Judah Gaon, requiring the *kiddushin* ceremony to be performed in public along with the recital of the *erusin* ("betrothal") benediction (see *Marriage) and signing of the *ketubbah* ("marriage deed") by witness. The enactment was designed to avoid the doubtful validity of marriages which were hastily contracted on festive occasions by placing a ring on the woman's finger with the object of *kiddushin*. This *takkanah* quoted the amoraic principle that a marriage takes place subject to the conditions laid down by the rabbis (see above), in laying down that a marriage not celebrated in the manner prescribed by the *takkanah* need not give rise to any apprehension (of possibly being valid), since any such marriage contradicted the requirements of the contemporary scholars. Against this sanction there is recorded the aforementioned solitary opinion holding that the authority of the scholars to annul a marriage by virtue of the principle stated by the *amoraim* is confined solely to those cases mentioned in the Talmud (see Freimann, bibliography, p. 20).

A like opinion was expressed in the 12th century by Jacob Tam. In an early geonic *takkanah* it had been laid down, contrary to the talmudic *halakhah*, that the husband could be compelled to give his wife an immediate *get* when the latter claimed such on a plea of *ma'us alai* ("he is repulsive to me"). The background to this *takkanah* was caused by the socio-moral realities of the time, since the wife would invoke the aid of the gentile courts toward compelling her husband to grant her a *get* the effect whereof was to render such a divorce invalid in Jewish law as an unlawful *get me'usseh* ("coerced" *get* – i.e., not falling within one of the halakhically recognized cases of *get* by coercion, see *Divorce). The *geonim* consequently enacted that the case of *ma'us alai* should also be included among the cases of lawful *get* by coercion. R. Tam negated the validity of this *takkanah* because, in his opinion, no authority had been carried over to the post-talmudic scholars to enact a *takkanah* serving to validate a *get* invalid according to talmudic *halakhah*, the post-talmudic legislative authority in the area of family law being confined solely to the pecuniary aspects such as the manner of recovering the *ketubbah* and the like (*Sefer ha-Yashar*, Resp. no. 24). However, the majority of the other *rishonim* – including Naḥmanides and Asher b. Jehiel – did not question the stated legislative authority in matters of marriage and divorce as a matter of principle. They held the *geonim* to have relied on the principle that a marriage is subject to the requirements of the halakhic scholars and the latter consented to annul a marriage on a plea of *ma'us alai* (Resp. Rosh, 43:8). Yet the former too were opposed to applying the above *takkanah* in their own times – but for different reasons. The special background giving rise to enactment of the *takkanah* by the *geonim* had ceased to exist, and its application had not spread among the majority of the Jewish people (Nov. Ramban (Rashba), Ket. 63; Resp. Rosh loc. cit.; cf. also Yad, Ishut 14:8).

In Post-Geonic Times

A material change in the historical reality of the Jewish dispersion asserted itself from the tenth century onward. A Diaspora had existed even in most ancient times, but there had always been one predominant Jewish center exercising spiritual hegemony over all the other centers of Jewish life. Its first location was Ereẓ Israel. Afterward Babylonia enjoyed this standing until the close of the geonic period. The close of this period saw the decline of the Babylonian Jewish center with no other center assuming its predominant influence. Instead there had come into being, and there continued to develop, a number of small centers existing and functioning alongside each other. Beside the North African Jewish centers there arose in the course of time centers of Jewish life in Spain, Germany, France, Italy, Turkey, the Balkan countries, Poland, Lithuania, and elsewhere. From time to time outstanding scholars were still able, by force of their personal standing and influence, to link one center with another or more, but there was no longer one single center recognized by all the others as exercising authoritative influence. This new historical reality found expression in different fields of Jewish life, also as regards the substantive nature of law-making in the *halakhah*. Whereas legislation until this time – whether in Ereẓ Israel or in Babylonia – had enjoyed a national dimension as being applicable to the whole of the Jewish people, it was now to assume a local character and extend only to the particular center of activity of the halakhic scholar or court enacting the *takkanah*. This phenomenon is classically illustrated through the well-known *takkanah* of R. Gershom b. Judah (and see below), prohibiting polygamy (see *Bigamy), which although introducing a decisive change in Jewish family law was not accepted – until comparatively recent times – in a number of sizeable Oriental Jewish centers. The post-geonic enactments, despite their local character, nevertheless became, like the decree of R. Gershom, an integral part of the overall system of Jewish law. This body of local legislation is at the same time indicative of the vitality of Jewish law, of its sensitivity and adaptation to the changing needs of the place and hour. This too can be learned from the enactment of R. Gershom, which was influenced by the prevailing conditions in Germany and the surrounding countries and the fact that in these countries polygamy was prohibited under the general law, whereas the prevailing conditions and outlook in the Muslim countries of the East were different, and there polygamy was a customary and lawful practice. Another material phenomenon in post-geonic Jewish legislation was the gradual consolidation of the view that the legal source of *takkanah* should not be resorted to in order to affect, in any manner contrary to the existing *halakhah*, the validity of a marriage or divorce. The already mentioned isolated opinions to this effect were reinforced, from the 14th century onward, by numerous other opinions holding that the operation of the guiding principle stated by the *amoraim* (on marriage subject to rabbinical requirements and its retrospective annulment) should be confined to the cases of its application in talmudic times. Also, this phenomenon is largely attributed to the fact that the *takkanot* of this period were of a local character, obliging only a limited and defined public, a fact fostering the apprehension that this sensitive area of Jewish family law might come to be governed by many different laws lacking in uniformity.

Legislation in Different Centers

Commencing from the 11th century it is possible to distinguish two main legislative directions in Jewish law:

(a) legislation invested with halakhic authority, i.e., enactments by the courts or halakhic scholars; and

(b) legislation by the public, i.e., communal enactments (*Takkanot ha-Kahal*).

Often there was close cooperation between the two legislative bodies – the halakhic scholars and the public – and many *takkanot* were jointly enacted by them. This was a natural and understandable phenomenon considering that Jewry as a whole represented a traditional society which looked upon the *halakhah* as the supreme value governing its way of life.

A brief outline of legislative activity on the part of the two stated bodies, acting either separately or in cooperation, is given below.

(1) IN GERMANY AND FRANCE. Among the earliest *takkanot* enacted in the above centers are those of the late 10th- and early 11th-century German scholar, Rabbenu Gershom b. Judah – known as the "Light of the Exile" (*Me'or ha-Golah*), because "he brought light to the eyes of the exile through his enactments." To him are attributed many *takkanot* which have left a lasting imprint on Jewish law, particularly in the area of family law. Whether all the *takkanot* attributed to R. Gershom were in fact enacted by him is a matter of dispute among research scholars. The prevailing opinion is that at least two of these, both of substantive importance, were indeed enacted by him. One is the *takkanah* prohibiting a married man from taking another wife. In talmudic times it had already been hinted that polygamy was an undesirable phenomenon in Jewish life, and some scholars of this period even made the husband's right to take a second wife conditional on the consent of his first wife. However, the prohibition of polygamy as a matter of law was first instituted by R. Gershom – on pain of ban, hence the *Ḥerem de-Rabbenu Gershom*, by which name the *takkanah* is known. In so doing he put the stamp of monogamy on the Jewish family save, as already mentioned, in certain Oriental communities where the *takkanah* was not accepted. The second *takkanah* is that in which R. Gershom, contrary to the ancient *halakhah*, prohibited the husband from divorcing the wife against her will.

Some time after R. Gershom's death there were enacted various *takkanot* which are attributed to Rashi. Later, in the 12th century, two great rabbinical conferences took place in Troyes, each headed by Rabbenu Tam (the first also by his brother, Samuel b. Meir (Rashbam)) – at which were enacted important *takkanot* in different fields of Jewish law. At the commencement of the 13th century the outstanding scholars of the generation participated in a number of *synods held in Germany at which were again promulgated *takkanot* on matters of basic principle in different areas of the law. These *takkanot*, known as the "*Takkanot Shum*" (שו"ם = Speyer, Worms, Mainz), were accepted by all the Jewish communities of France and Germany, and later also by those of Poland and other Eastern European countries. Thereafter many more *takkanot* were enacted at various other synods, for instance, at Mainz toward the end of the 14th century, and by individual scholars – among others Meir of Rothenburg and Perez of Corbeil in the 13th century, Jacob Weil and Israel Bruna in the 15th century, and others. Various *takkanot* were also enacted by the great synod at Frankfurt at the beginning of the 17th century, the last of its kind held in Germany. From then on Poland replaced Germany as the main center of Ashkenazi Jewry.

(2) IN SPAIN, ITALY, ETC. From the 11th to the 13th centuries legislative activity in the Spanish Jewish center was mainly initiated by the outstanding contemporary scholars or by individual communities, and not – for various political and social reasons – at inter-regional or wider synods as with Ashkenazi Jewry (see Finkelstein, bibliography, pp. 99ff.). The *takkanot* thus enacted also laid down important matters of principle, and among others may be mentioned those of Toledo and Molina relating to family law. Toward the middle of the 14th century numerous *takkanot* were adopted at a conference attended – apparently in Barcelona – by representatives of the communities in Aragon. A complete collection of *takkanot* resulted from a conference of Castilian communal representatives held at Valladolid in 1432, initiated and headed by the Castilian court rabbi, Don Abraham Benveniste. The collection is divided into five parts, approximately one-half consisting of *takkanot* having an important bearing on different legal matters. Extant too is a collection of *takkanot* of the Spanish exiles in Fez, North Africa, enacted during the period from the end of the 15th century until the end of the 17th century in connection with different aspects of Jewish law (the collection is to be found in *Kerem Ḥamar*, vol. 2).

In Italy many *takkanot* were enacted at different national Jewish conferences called during the 15th century (Forli, Florence, etc.) and the 16th (Ferrara). *Takkanot* were also enacted in other smaller centers such as Crete (see Artom and Cassuto, bibliography), Corfu (see Finkelstein, bibliography, p. 96), and others.

(3) IN POLAND, LITHUANIA, ETC. Toward the end of the 16th century there came into being the Council of Four Lands (*Va'ad Arba Araẓot*; see *Councils of the Lands), the central communal and legislative body of the Polish Jewish center for some 200 years (for details, see Halpern, Pinkas, bibliography). The meetings of the council were attended by delegates and leading scholars representing the Jewish communities in each of the participating regions or lands. As such the Council was, among its other functions, the supreme legislative body of Jewish autonomy in Poland.

The central body of Jewish autonomy in Lithuania was the *Va'ad Medinat Lita*, from early in the 17th century. Whereas very few of the *takkanot* of the Polish council are extant, there has come down a full collection of *takkanot* of the *Va'ad Medinat Lita*, covering the period from 1623 to 1761 and constituting a detailed repository of laws and decisions embracing the different fields of Jewish law (see Dubnow, bibliography). A similar central body of Jewish autonomy, though of smaller scope compared with the other two, was that representing the Jewish communities of Moravia. This body too engaged in a ramified legislative activity of which there is extant a collection of *takkanot* over the period 1650–1748 (see Halpern, bibl.).

Over and above the aforementioned central legislation, there was also legislative activity on the part of the local courts and individual communities (inter alia, the *takkanot* of the communities of Cracow, Nikolsburg (Mikulov), Tiktin (Tykocin), etc., see, e.g., M. Elon, *Ḥerut ha-Perat…* (1964), 280). Much of this great mass of material is scattered, and recalled in various ways, in the different branches of halakhic literature, particularly in the literature of the *responsa and in historical material. In this connection it may be mentioned that special attention to this matter is devoted in the indices to the responsa literature published by the Hebrew University's Institute for Research in Jewish Law.

Post-Geonic Legislation in Family Law

(1) DIFFERENT BRANCHES OF THE LAW. The post-geonic legislative activity comprehended the civil law, family law and succession, administrative law, and evidence and procedure. There was also wide legislative activity, though in lesser measure, in criminal law, its scope having greatly depended on the measure of judicial autonomy enjoyed by the different communities in criminal matters. (For particulars of enactments in various branches of the law, see bibliography, and see under the relevant branch as enumerated in the article *Mishpat Ivri*.)

(2) SPECIAL TREND IN FAMILY AND SUCCESSION LAW. Legislation in the area of family and succession law reflects a special trend. On the one hand a very wide legislative activity is evidenced as regards the pecuniary aspects of these legal branches, including the enactment of *takkanot* contradicting existing law. On the other, scholars came to restrict authority to make enactments contradicting existing law on matters affecting the validity of a marriage or divorce.

The position is illustrated in the following examples: according to talmudic law the husband inherits his wife's entire estate in preference to all other heirs. In answer to the prevailing social realities in different centers, the husband's rights to his deceased wife's estate were restricted in a long series of *takkanot* of Troyes. The "*takkanot Shum*" (see above) laid down that the property brought by the wife at the time of her marriage should be returned by her husband to the person who gave her the property, or to her heirs, in the event of her dying childless within a year of the marriage – if within the second year, the husband to return half of such property. In the Spanish *takkanot*, as expressed in the *takkanot* of Toledo and Molina, the husband's right was restricted to one-half of the estate of his deceased wife, regardless of how long after the marriage she died, the other half to go to the children of the marriage – and if none, to the wife's relatives. In dealing with the substance of these *takkanot* Simeon b. Ẓemaḥ Duran held as follows; "By this *takkanah* the husband's right of inheritance, which is *de-oraita*, is infringed, yet they are entitled to do so for it is found that the scholars instituted the *ketubbat banin dikhrin* [Ket. 52b; see *Succession], so as to encourage a person to give to his daughter as to his son, and since it has been the custom to be generous in giving a dowry, they made the enactment infringing somewhat the husband's right of inheritance" (*Tashbeẓ* 2:292).

A different trend is evidenced as regards legislative authority to annul a marriage. By the commencement of the rabbinical period some scholars held that the principle, already mentioned, of the authority of the scholars of the talmudic period to annul a marriage should not be applied in relation to a marriage valid according to the talmudic law but not conforming to requirements laid down by the scholars in post-talmudic times: "if the rabbis (in the talmudic period) had authority to annul a marriage, we for our part have no authority to do so" (opinion of the Mainz scholars, see *Raban* (= *Even ha-Ezer*), part 3, p. 47; see also the opinion of R. Tam, above). However, the majority of the scholars held that the post-talmudic scholars also enjoyed such authority (opinion of the scholars of Worms and Speyer, see *Raban*, loc. cit., see also the opinions of Naḥmanides and Asher b. Jehiel, under the Geonic Period, above). Later the opinion was expressed that while the authority of the post-talmudic scholars to annul a marriage was not the same as in the talmudic period, yet if the manner of celebrating a marriage be prescribed in a *takkanah* specially enacted for this purpose – for instance with a view to the prevention of deceit and bad faith, by requiring the presence of at least ten persons and the consent of the bride's parents – in which it is expressly provided that a marriage not celebrated in the prescribed manner shall be invalid, then a marriage so celebrated will be invalid (Resp. Rosh, 35:1–2; Resp. Rashba, vol. 1, nos. 551, 1162, 1185; *Sefer Teshuvot ha-Rashba ha-Meyuḥasot le-ha-Ramban*, 125, 142). It was added that a marriage would be invalid not only when celebrated contrary to a *takkanah* of the court but also when contrary to a communal enactment (Rosh and Rashba, loc. cit.; *Toledot Adam ve-Ḥavvah*, Ḥavvah 22:4). This was in fact the practice in different communities. Some 100 years after the above opinion was expressed, it was held by Isaac b. Sheshet Perfet that though this was the law in theory, "in practice I would tend toward greater stringency and because of the stringency of the matter I would not rely on my own authority alone to hold her unmarried without a prior *get*, but do so only if all the scholars of the regions consent thereto and share the responsibility" (Resp. Ribash, no. 399). This distinction between the theoretical statement of the law and decision in a practical case came increasingly to be accepted by the halakhic scholars (see, e.g., Resp. *Yakhin u-Vo'az*, Pt. 2, no. 20). The *halakhah* was decided in this special way: "If a community has made assent and enacted that no person shall marry save in the presence of ten, or the like, and a person nevertheless marries in transgression thereof – it is apprehended that his marriage is valid and the wife requires a *get*; even though the community may expressly have provided that the marriage shall be invalid and have nullified [ownership of] his money [i.e., with retrospective effect so that the *kiddushin* money was not that of the bridegroom and the marriage therefore invalid – see above], nevertheless it is necessary that the greatest stringency be applied in a practical case" (*Rema*, EH 28:21). After this ruling *takkanot* decreeing a marriage to be invalid unless celebrated in a prescribed manner were still enacted from time to time in the Oriental Jewish centers, but there too it was generally decided that the marriage was not invalid.

It appears that the development of the trend toward restriction of legislative authority as regards marriage annulment is connected with the substantive nature of legislation in the post-geonic period. The fact that legislation had a mere local scope led to a proliferation of laws on the same legal subject, enacted by each Jewish center – and even community – acting independently of the others. In general this variety of laws created no insurmountable difficulties, and even greatly stimulated the development of the Jewish law rules of the *conflict of laws. The position was different, however, in the case of laws affecting matters of marriage and divorce. The possibility that a woman regarded in one place as married could be regarded elsewhere as unmarried – in terms of a local *takkanah* – entailed an inherent serious threat to the upholding of a uniform law in one of the most sensitive spheres of the *halakhah*, that of the *eshet ish*. The only way for its prevention was through a restriction of legislative authority in this area (see Resp. Ribash, loc. cit.; Resp. Maharam Alashkar, no. 48).

Takkanot of the Chief Rabbinate of Ereẓ Israel

The spread of the Emancipation and the abrogation of Jewish judicial autonomy, from the end of the 18th century onward, saw a sharp decline – almost to the point of complete cessation – in the resort to the legal source of *takkanah*. This was a natural outcome of the new Jewish historical reality following on the Emancipation. Since the legislative function is a natural accompaniment to governmental organization and judicial autonomy, the loss of the one obviated the need for the other (see **Mishpat Ivri*).

A certain change took place as from the 1930s, coinciding with the establishment of the organizational institutions of the Jewish settlement in Ereẓ Israel, notably the Chief Rabbinate Council. The Jewish judicial authority in matters of family and succession introduced a period of legislative activity on the part of the halakhic institutions. The Rabbinical Supreme Court of Appeal had been established in 1921. When it was later contended before this body that the *halakhah* did not allow for lodging an appeal against the judgment of a court, it was held that "the matter of an appeal has been accepted as an enactment of the scholars, the validity whereof is as that of the law of our holy Torah" (OPD, 71). In 1943 procedural *takkanot* were enacted, most of them based on the *halakhah* and "some of them enacted by the Chief Rabbinate Council for the purpose of ordering procedure in the courts of Ereẓ Israel and for the public good" (introductory note to the *takkanot*). Thus payment of court fees was imposed in connection with litigation – contrary to the existing *halakhah*. Similarly, the introduction of adoption as a legal institution represented an innovation in Jewish law (see *Adoption). Another important innovation introduced by *takkanah* was the engagement by the rabbinical courts to hold equal the rights of sons and daughters and those of husband and wife for purposes of intestate succession. In 1944 the following three matters were enacted in different *takkanot*: the minimal amount of the *ketubbah* was increased "having regard to the standard of living in the *yishuv* and economic considerations"; the levir refusing to grant the widow of his deceased brother *ḥaliẓah* was rendered obliged to maintain her until releasing her; the legal duty was imposed on the father to maintain his children until reaching the age of 15 – not merely until the age of six years as prescribed by talmudic law. Included in the matters laid down by *takkanah* in 1950 was the prohibition against the marriage of a girl below the age of 16. The introductory remarks to the *takkanot* of 1944 emphasize the twofold basis of their enactment, halakhic authority and the assent of the communities of the *yishuv* and their representatives.

Since then there has been no further legislative activity on the part of the bearers of the *halakhah* in the State of Israel. This may be regarded as regrettable since there still remain diverse halakhic problems awaiting solution by means of the legal source of *takkanah*. There is particular need to give attention to a number of problems concerning the *agunah* and other cases involving hardship to women – among others, of the married woman whose husband is unable to give her a *get* on account of his mental illness and cases in which difficulties arise in connection with the granting of *ḥaliẓah*. Solutions to these problems are capable of being found through the enactment of *takkanot* leading to an annulment of marriage in special cases, in the manner and by virtue of the talmudic principle described above in some detail. The already mentioned threat of a proliferation of laws and lack of uniformity on a matter of great halakhic sensitivity, which inhibited past generations from acting on the stated principle, has much abated in modern times in the light of the central spiritual standing which may be allocated to the halakhic authority in Israel in its relations with other centers of Jewry in the Diaspora.

[Menachem Elon]

Status of Knesset Legislation as Enactments for the Public Welfare

In recent generations, halakhic authorities have occasionally expressed their opinion that laws legislated by the Israeli Parliament (Knesset), may also be valid under Jewish Law, subject to the fulfillment of certain necessary requirements, for example, that the legislation enhances public welfare, and is approved by a halakhic scholar (*adam ḥashuv*). Under these conditions, such Israeli legislation has standing similar to that of *Takkanot ha-Kahal* (enactments of the public) in Jewish law (see **Takkanot ha-Kahal*). For example, Rabbi Ovadia Hadaya wrote in one of his responsa that a law of the Knesset – the Tenants Protection [Consolidated Version] Law, 5732 – 1972, promotes the welfare of protected tenants in Israel, and hence the legal arrangements it prescribes have the status of a *Takkanat Kahal* (public enactment) made for the public welfare (see Resp. Yaskil Avdi, Pt. 6, *Ḥoshen Mishpat* 8). This outlook found expression in a ruling of the Rabbinical Court of Appeals, cited in the *Wiloszni* decision of the Israeli Supreme Court. (HC 323/81 (App. 533/81) *Wiloszni v. Rabbinical Court of Appeals et al*, 36 (2) PD 733, 740). The *Wiloszni* case concerned a husband's petition to the High Court of Justice against a decision of the Rabbinical Court of Appeals, which the husband claimed contradicted the Tenants Protection [Consolidated Version] Law 5732 – 1972. In adjudicating the husband's claim, Justice Elon focused on the statement of the Rabbinical Court whereby tenants protection legislation, "is given halakhic validity like any *sitomta* (i.e., customary practice) or *massi'in al-kiẓatan* (i.e., enforcement of communal enactment)." As such the Rabbinical Court of Appeals had taken the provisions of this law into account in its ruling (see **Mishpat Ivri* in the State of Israel). In his decision Justice Menachem Elon commented that the principles of this law could apply in Jewish law by virtue of their having been accepted as a custom, or because they have been accepted by the public as a binding norm, analogous to *Takkanat Kahal.* Justice Elon commented on the status of public legislation in Jewish law, and stated that by virtue of public legislation in Jewish law various laws from the Israeli legal system, in the fields of civil, criminal and public law, could become part of the system of rules of Jewish law with a similar status to that of *Takkanot Kahal* that are recognized by halakhic authorities (see also **Minhag*).

Procedural Regulations in the Rabbinical Courts

The legislation of the Council of the Chief Rabbinate of Israel and of the members of the Rabbinical Court of Appeals also finds expression in the Rules of Procedure for the Rabbinical Courts in Israel. The updated version of these regulations was enacted in 5773 – 1993, during the period of Chief Rabbis Avraham Kahana-Shapira and Mordechai Eliyahu. These regulations prescribed arrangements for a number of issues, such as place of adjudication, summons of litigants, power of attorney to represent litigants in Rabbinical Courts, conduct of court sessions, testimony, oaths, non-appearance of litigants or witnesses, postponement, lien and temporary injunctions, compromise, *ex parte* proceedings, nullification of verdict and rehearing a case, appeals, divorce, confirmation of marriage and divorce, *ḥaliẓah*, ameliorating the plight of *agguno*t, permission to marry a second wife, probate, estates, guardianship, endowments, adoption, conversion (See extensive discussion under *Practice and Procedure.)

Legal Status of Women

In 1951 the Knesset enacted the Woman's Equal Rights Law, 5711 – 1951. In the amendment of the law in 2000, a number of significant new rules and principles were added. Under Section 1B, titled "Permitted Distinction and Affirmative Action," the following situations will not be regarded as infringement of equality or prohibited discrimination: (1) distinction between a man and a woman where the distinction is dictated by substantive differences between them, or the nature of the matter; (2) a directive or act intended to rectify prior or existing discrimination, or a directive or act intended to promote women's equality [...]. Section 6C, titled "Appropriately Representation" provides that all tenders and appointments in public bodies must give expression to the appropriate representation of woman. Section 6D titled "Equality in the Security Forces" states that all women who are candidates, or currently in the Security forces, shall have a right equal to that of a man, to serve in any position...[...] The main purpose of this legislation was to ensure statutory anchorage of equality between men and women with regard to various legal rights and other matters. Some scholars held that the provisions of this law conform with the Jewish Law as it has evolved over the generations. They held that where contradictions between traditional Jewish Law and the needs of contemporary society still remain, the halakhic authorities are empowered to enact appropriate *takkanot* to meet those needs. However, they argued that with respect to the contemporary imperative of equalizing woman's status, the Chief Rabbinate did not adequately respond to the situation and failed to enact detailed and comprehensive *takkanot* (see Menachem Elon, *Jewish Law – History, Sources, Principles* (1994), 1656–1657). These scholars likewise noted that Rabbi Abraham Isaac ha-Kohen Kook, the first chief rabbi of the Land of Israel, desired to see the continued creativity of Jewish law in the rabbinical courts, by utilizing two major legal sources that contributed to the development of the *halakhah* in every age: (1) midrash – in the expanded sense of interpretation and application of traditional law to actual cases so that the law continues to develop, and as Rabbi Kook expressed it, "within the category of received laws," finding new legal solutions through the interpretation of existing law (see *Interpretation), and (2) *takkanah*, i.e., legislation, by which Jewish law meets the needs of new legal and social situations through the enactment of new laws that are added to existing law. These scholars held that the legislative activities of the Council of the Chief Rabbinate and the Rabbinical Courts prior to the establishment of the State of Israel in the areas of judicial procedure and personal status (regarding which the government granted jurisdiction and enforcement powers to these courts), yielded a number of creative and positive results. However, even in these branches of the law creative development was sporadic, fragmentary, and overly cautious, and did not achieve the progress that might have been possible had the halakhic leaders fully exercised their authority and power to meet the needs of the time. Regarding all other areas of Jewish law, particularly in the various branches of civil law, almost nothing was accomplished (ibid, *Jewish Law*, 1598). Justice Elon held that the refusal of the Rabbinate and the rabbinical courts to innovate in the field of equality of woman, and specifically with respect to spousal property relations, yielded unfortunate results in the *Bavli* case. (See HC 1000/92 *Bavli v. Rabbinical Court of Appeals*, 48(2) PD, 221; M. Elon, *The Status of Woman* (Tel Aviv, 2005), 248–250).

The Plight of the Agunah

Numerous members of Israel's parliament, the Knesset, looked to the Chief Rabbinate to exercise its traditional halakhic legislative authority by adopting, at its own initiative, appropriate *takkanot* to resolve a number of problems connected with the refusal of husbands to grant a divorce writ or that of the wives to accept such a writ (see **Agunah*; cf. Menachem Elon, *Jewish Law – History, Sources, Principles* (1994), 1657–1658). Although these *takkanot* were not enacted, the Chief Rabbinate did support Knesset legislation intended to ameliorate, insofar as possible, the plight of the refused spouse.

The legal arrangement that applied until 1995 regarding the enforcement of divorce judgment in Israel is set forth in Section 6 of the Rabbinical Courts Jurisdiction (Marriage and Divorce), 5713 – 1953. The original wording of Section 6 of the law was as follows: "Where a rabbinical court, by final judgment, has ordered that a husband be compelled to grant his wife a *get* or the wife to accept such a document from her husband, the district court may, upon expiration of six months from day of the making of order, on application of the Attorney General, compel compliance with the order by imprisonment." This legislation was viewed as desirable in the writings of a number of leading halakhic authorities, inter alia Chief Rabbis Herzog and Yosef (see Rabbi Herzog's letter in Z. Warhaftig, "Coercion To Grant a Divorce in Theory and in Practice," in: *Shenaton ha-Mishpat ha-Ivri*, 3–4 (1977), 153, 174–175 (in Hebrew), and the responsum of Rabbi O. Yosef, Resp. *Yabi'a Omer*, vol. 3, Even ha-Ezer 20).

The Rabbinical Courts Law (Enforcement of Divorce Judgments), 5755 – 1995, authorizes the rabbinical courts to issue a variety of restrictive orders against a recalcitrant spouse, including limitations on the following: (1) leaving the country; (2) obtaining an Israeli passport or transit pass, holding these travel documents or extending their validity; (3) obtaining, maintaining, or renewing a drivers license; (4) appointment or election to, or service, in an office regulated by law, or in an office in a supervised authority; (5) working in a profession regulated by law, or legal operation of a business requiring a license or legal permit; (6) opening or maintaining a bank account or drawing checks from a bank account. It also included: (7) denying various privileges to a prison inmate; (8) imprisonment to compel compliance; (9) solitary confinement of a prison inmate.

These restrictive orders were mentioned in Israeli legislation after consultation by the legislating organs in Israel with several prominent rabbis in Israel, including Chief Rabbis Avraham Kahana-Shapira and Mordekhai Eliyahu. They are, in essence, an attempt to implement in Israel the principles first suggested by Rabbenu Tam, who held that in suitable circumstances isolating measures (*harḥakot*) be implemented against a recalcitrant spouse (see *Sefer ha-Yashar*, Responsa, 24). The draft law that preceded enactment of the Rabbinical Courts Law (enforcement of Divorce Judgments), 5755 – 1995, explicitly noted that the law was aimed at harnessing a halakhic tool – Rabbenu Tam's *harḥakot* – in order to alleviate the plight of a spouse who was refused a *get*. (See the explanation of the goal of the Draft Bill: Legislative Proposals of the State of Israel – 5754, no. 2281, p. 493.)

[Yehiel Kaplan (2nd ed.)]

BIBLIOGRAPHY: Z.H. Chajes, *Torat Nevi'im…* (1958); idem, *The Student's Guide through the Talmud* (19602), 35–110; Weiss, Dor, 2 (1904[4]), 49–65; Halevy, Dorot, 1, pt. 3 (1923), 46ff.; M. Bloch, *Sefer Sha'arei Torat ha-Takkanot*, 3 vols. (1879–1905); Ch. Tchernowitz, *Toledot ha-Halakhah*, 1 (1934), 174–88; Ḥ. Albeck, in: *Zion*, 8 (1942/43), 165–78; I.Z. Kahana, *Sefer ha-Agunot* (1954), passim; J.M. Ginzburg, *Mishpatim le-Yisra'el* (1956), 45–55; *Pinkas ha-Medinah* (Lita), ed. by S. Dubnow (1925); *Takkanot Kandia ve-Zikhronoteha*, ed. by A.S. Artom and M.D. Cassuto (1943); *Takkanot Medinat Mehrin*, ed. by I. Halpern (1951); Halpern, Pinkas; A.H. Freimann, *Seder Kiddushin ve-Nissu'in…* (1945); I. Schipansky, in: *Hadorom*, 24 (1966), 135–97; 26 (1967), 173–97; 28 (1968), 145–59; I.D. Gilat, in: *Sefer Bar-Ilan*, 7/8 (1970), 117–32; M. Elon, *Ḥakikah Datit…* (1968), 158–65, 182–4; ET, 1 (1951[3]), 279–82; 3 (1951), 325–30; 5 (1953), 529–46; 10 (1961), 95–110; Finkelstein, Middle Ages; Ḥ. Tykocinski, *Takkanot ha-Ge'onim* (1959). See also bibliography of **Takkanot ha-Kahal*. **ADD. BIBLIOGRAPHY:** M. Elon, *Ha-Mishpat ha-Ivri* (1988), 1:391–712, index; ibid, *Jewish Law* (1994), 2:477–879, index; idem, *Jewish Law (Cases and Materials)* (1999), 71–75, 50ff., 145ff.; idem *Ma'amad ha-Ishah, Mishpat ve-Shipput, Masoret u-Temurah, Arakheyah shel Medinah Yehudit ve-Demokratit* (2005), 247–50; idem, "Authority and Power in the Jewish Community: A Chapter in Jewish Public Law," in: *Shenaton ha-Mishpat ha-Ivri*, 3–4 (1976–77), 7–34; M. Elon and B. Lifshitz, *Mafte'aḥ ha-She'elot ve-ha-Teshuvot shel Ḥakhmei Sefarad u-Ẓefon*

Afrikah (1986) (II), 540–43; B. Lifshitz and E. Shochetman, *Mafte'aḥ ha-She'elot ve-ha-Teshuvot shel Ḥakhmei Ashkenaz, Ẓarefat ve-Italyah* (legal digest) (1997), 361–66, 386–92; Y.S. Kaplan, "Continuing Validity of Public Norms," in: *Shenaton ha-Mishpat ha-Ivri*, 18–19 (1992–94), 329–96; idem, "Enforcement of Divorce Judgments by Imprisonment: Principles of Jewish Law," in: *Jewish Law Annual*, 15 (2004), 57–145; E. Shochetman, "The *Halakhah*'s Recognition of the Law of the State of Israel," in: *Shenaton ha-Mishpat ha-Ivri*, 16–17 (1991), 417–500 (in Heb.).

TAKKANOT HA-KAHAL (Heb. תַּקָּנוֹת הַקָּהָל).

Legal Aspects

THE CONCEPT. The *Takkanot ha-Kahal* embrace that part of legislation in Jewish law which is enacted by the public or its representatives in contradistinction to the *takkanot* enacted by a halakhic authority, i.e., by the court and halakhic scholars (see **Takkanot*). The enactment of legislation by the public is already to be found in ancient *halakhah*. Thus it was stated that the *benei ha-ir* ("townspeople") have authority to pass enactments obliging all residents of their town in matters such as the prices of commodities, weights and measures, and laborer's wages, and to impose fines on those transgressing their enactments (Tosef. BM 11: 23; BB 8b). The same sources (Tosef. BM 11:24–26) disclose that legislative authority was entrusted also to more restricted bodies, such as various artisans' and traders' associations within the town, such regulations obliging only the members of the particular association.

For as long as a single Jewish center – first Ereẓ Israel and later the Babylonian Jewish center – exercised hegemony over the entire Diaspora, there was little legislative activity of a local nature, both from the aspect of quantity and in the degree of authority carried. The great impetus to legislation by the public came at the end of the tenth century with the emerging stature of the Jewish community. The community enjoyed a substantial degree of autonomy. It had its own internal governing bodies, saw to the social and educational needs of its members, maintained a *bet din* possessing jurisdiction in the areas of civil, administrative, and ritual law, and to some extent also criminal jurisdiction. It also imposed and collected taxes, both to satisfy the fiscal demands of the ruling power and to finance communal services. The legal order governing the fulfillment of these manifold tasks was in large measure derived through the enactment of *takkanot* by the community. To ensure that the communal enactments be capable of fulfilling their envisaged objectives, the halakhic scholars saw the need to found these *takkanot* on principles belonging to the sphere of the public law and, from the aspect of their legal validity, to free them from the requirements and restrictions found in the private law. In consequence the scholars evolved basic principles in the area of Jewish public law constituting an impressive part of their wide legal creativity in this field, against the background of the social and economic realities of Jewish autonomy (see **Mishpat Ivri*; *Public Authority; **Takkanot*; *Taxation; **Hekdesh*).

SOURCE OF AUTHORITY. The earliest manifestations of non-halakhic legislative authority are to be found in the powers vested in the king (see *Mishpat Ivri*) and in the already mentioned *benei ha-ir*. The authority of the community to make enactments was substantiated by the scholars thus: "In respect of each and every public the position is that the individuals are subject to the majority, and according to the latter they must conduct themselves in all their affairs; and they [i.e., the majority] stand in the same relationship to the people of their town as the people of Israel to the great *bet din* or the king" (Resp. Rashba, vol. 3, no. 411; also vol. 1, no 729; vol. 5, no. 126, et al.). It was held that just as the court is competent to enact *takkanot* in the area of civil and criminal law, even though their content contradict a particular rule of the *halakhah*, so the community too is competent to make enactments in these areas, even though contrary to existing law (Resp. R. Gershom Me'or ha-Golah, ed. Eidelberg, no. 67; Responsum of Joseph Tov Elem quoted in Resp. Maharam of Rothenburg, ed. Lemberg, no. 423; idem, ed. Berlin, no. 220, p. 37; idem, ed. Prague, no. 368; Resp. Rashba, vol. 4, no. 311; Resp. Rosh, 101:1; Resp. *Yakhin u-Vo'az*, pt. 2, no. 2). Sometimes the scholars are found to have employed the expression *hefker ẓibbur hefker*, as an alternative parallel to the rule of *hefker bet din hefker*, in terms whereof legislative authority is conferred on the courts and halakhic scholars (see **Takkanot*; Resp. Rashba, vol. 4, no. 142; Resp. Ribash, no. 399). This parallel between the public and the court was not, however, meant to have application to legislative authority in matters of ritual prohibitions and permissions. In this area the community has no authority to enact a *takkanah* contradicting the *halakhah* (Resp. Rashba, vol. 3, no. 411; *Tashbeẓ*, 2:132 and 239). Here the community was likened to the individual. Just as the individual may contract out of the law of the Torah in matters of the civil law (*mamon*) but not in those of ritual prohibition (see *Contract), so the community cannot make an enactment which is contrary to the law of the Torah on a matter of ritual prohibition, legislative authority on matters of the latter kind being entrusted to the halakhic scholars alone (Resp. Ribash, no. 305).

MAJORITY AND MINORITY. From 11th-century responsa it may be gathered that at that time communal enactments were passed by the majority of the community, thereupon binding also the minority opposed to their passage (Resp. Rif, ed. Leiter, no. 13; idem, ed. Biadnowitz, no. 85; Responsum of Joseph Tov Elem, quoted in Resp. Maharam of Rothenburg, ed. Lemberg, no. 423). In the 12th century Rabbenu Tam held that the majority was not empowered to impose a *takkanah* on the minority opposed thereto and only after the latter's acceptance of it – expressly or by implication – could the majority compel the individual by fine and punishment to compliance therewith (*Mordekhai*, BK no. 179 and BB no. 480; Resp. Maharam of Rothenburg, ed. Cremona, no. 230; *Teshuvot Maimuniyyot*, Shofetim, no. 10). This view was not accepted by the majority of the scholars (Resp. Ḥayyim Or Zaru'a, no. 222; *Mordekhai*, BB no. 482; Resp. Rashba, vol. 2, no. 279; vol. 5, nos. 270, 242; Resp. Re'em, no. 57). Some of the scholars distinguished between *takkanot* of the community enacted by majority opinion and the *takkanot* of professional associations, for which the consent of all members was required. This distinction was explained on the ground that the latter associations involved only a restricted public not having the responsibility of a community, and because of the serious likelihood that the professional interests of the minority might be prejudiced by the majority (Nov. Ramban, BB9a; *Beit Yosef*, Tur ḤM 231:30; Sh. Ar., ḤM 231:28; *Leḥem Rav*, no. 216). The doctrine that the majority prevails derives from the exegesis of the words *aḥarei rabbim lehatot* ("to follow a multitude") in Exodus 23:2 (see *Majority Rule). In talmudic *halakhah* the above passage is interpreted in relation both to a majority judgment of the court (Sanh. 2a–3b) and to a majority as a matter of legal presumption (Ḥul. 11a). From neither case can it be deduced that the majority of the public may impose its enactment on the opposing minority. The scholars did, however, conclude that "in respect of a matter concerning the public the Torah enjoined to follow a multitude and in any matter assented to by the public the majority is followed and the individuals must uphold all that is assented to by the majority" (Resp. Rosh. 6:5). This wide interpretation was held to be a matter of practical necessity "because if it were not so and the minority had the power to set aside the assent of the majority, the community would never agree on anything… for when would the community ever be in unanimous agreement?" (Resp. Rosh, 6:5, 7; see also *Kol Bo*, no. 142). It was similarly decided by a majority of the scholars that a *takkanah* enacted by majority opinion also binds the minority, even though it has not participated in the enactment of the *takkanah*, since those absent at the time thereof are deemed to have implicitly consented to it and because such is the accepted custom (Resp. Mabit 1:264; *Mishpat Shalom*, no. 231, letter *Vav* and references there quoted). Here again the explanation was given that "they must perforce bow to the majority and bear the burden of its enactment, for otherwise no room would be left for applying the rule, to follow a multitude, if those who dissent were to absent themselves [at the time of enactment of the *takkanah*]… a possibility that reason rejects" (Resp. Abraham Alegre, ḤM no. 5; see also Resp. Ribash, no. 249; Resp. Ḥatam Sofer, ḤM no. 116).

THE ROLE OF THE COMMUNAL REPRESENTATIVES. The Jewish community was headed by its duly appointed or elected representatives, called by various names such as *tovei ha-ir* (lit. "good citizens"), *parnasim*, and so on, and sometimes also *shivat tovei ha-ir* (lit. "seven good citizens") – a concept already known in talmudic times (Meg. 26a; see also Jos., Ant., 4:214) – although their number varied from time to time. The *tovei ha-ir* were required to be "… persons chosen not on account of wisdom, wealth or honor, but simply… persons sent by the public to be in charge of public matters" (Resp. Rashba, vol. 1, no. 617; see also *Public Authority; *Taxation). Some scholars held it necessary that the enactment of *takkanot* by the *tovei ha-ir* take place in the presence of the public as the only means of ensuring their enactment with the consent of a majority of the local public (*Mordekhai*, BB no. 480). However, the majority of the scholars took the view that public representatives chosen to be in charge of all public matters are deemed to represent a majority of the public, "by virtue of being sent by the majority of the public which has elected them," and therefore may enact *takkanot* in the public absence (Rashba, loc. cit.; Resp. Mabbit, 1:84); but representatives chosen for limited purposes only cannot always be said to represent the majority and their enactments must be made in the public presence.

SCOPE OF THE TAKKANOT. A problem facing the halakhic scholars was how to invest the communal enactments with the legal efficacy to bind also the classes of persons incapacitated by the rules of the private law from being party to a legal obligation – such as minors and those yet to be born – efficacy without which the *takkanot* would have little practical value. The solution was found through an assimilation of the *takkanot* to the case of customs on various matters instituted by past generations (e.g., concerning festivals, fasts, etc.) – the observance whereof is enjoined also on sons, i.e., succeeding generations (Pes. 50b) since "the fathers are the source of their children" (Resp. Rashba, vol. 3, no. 411; Resp. Ribash, no. 399). The matter was also substantiated with the aid of other analogies from the laws of the oath, and so on (Rashba and Ribash, loc. cit.; see also Resp. Maharam Alashkar, no. 49; *Tashbeẓ* 2:132). At the root of these analogies lay the conviction that the orderly operation of communal enactments demanded their general applicability and continuity, "for if not so… it would become necessary to renew them daily since every day there are minors who reach their majority, and that is an unacceptable matter" (Ribash, loc. cit.). So too it was held that those taking up residence in a particular community are subject to all its existing communal enactments, since "they are deemed to have expressly taken upon themselves all the enactments of that town… when coming to live there, hence they are the same as the other townspeople and embraced by their *takkanot*" (Ribash, loc. cit.). The stated three factors – the rule that in enacting a *takkanah* the majority also binds the minority opposed thereto, investment of the communal representatives with legislative authority, and investment of the communal enactments with validity even in relation to persons lacking in legal capacity – jointly operated to confer fully on the communal enactments the standing of norms of the public law just as legislation is part of the public law in other legal systems. Consequently the validity of the communal enactments was not measured by the standards and requirements applying to a matter of the private law.

HALAKHAH AND THE TAKKANOT HA-KAHAL. The communal enactments share the general objective of all other *takkanot* – to add a directive in answer to a problem which finds no solution in the *halakhah*, or to sanction a departure from the *halakhah* when dictated by the needs of the hour (see *Takkanot*). The halakhic scholars endowed communal enactments with full legal sanction, whether these added to existing *halakhah* or provided contrary thereto. Reference to the halakhic sources, particularly the responsa literature, will reveal a most extensive range of directives on matters of the civil as well as criminal law, laid down in communal enactment, and accepted even when contrary to the *halakhah* on such matters. The following are a few examples (others are mentioned above, s.v. under the heading Source of Authority).

In matters affecting communal property, or other public matters, such as taxation, charitable endowment, and so on, communal enactments made provision, contrary to talmudic *halakhah*, for admitting also the testimony of witnesses residing within the community concerned. This applied notwithstanding the fact of their own pecuniary interest in the matter since, for instance, the tax exemption of one member of the community served to increase the burden on his fellows, and despite the frequent fact of their kinship with the litigants, on account of communal intermarriage (Resp. Rashba, vol. 5, nos. 184 and 286; vol. 6, no. 7; Resp.Rosh, 5:4). This legal situation was accepted as *halakhah* in the codes (Sh. Ar., ḤM 7:12, 37:22; see also *Taxation).

In different communities *takkanot* were enacted whereby the signature of the town scribe on various kinds of deeds was imparted the same efficacy as the signature of two competent witnesses. Such enactments were designed to prevent a number of possible complications, among others the impossibility of verifying deeds on account of the death, or absence abroad, of the witnesses thereto. Deeds signed by the town scribe were held fully valid, since "the public is entitled to assent [i.e., enact] in any wise on a matter pertaining to the civil law *[mamon]*, and it is accepted and valid as if it were an absolute law, for the duly given assent of the public on a matter renders it law" (*Sefer Teshuvot ha-Rashba ha-Meyuḥasot le-ha-Ramban*, no. 65; Resp. Rashba, vol. 3, no. 438). The possibility of illiteracy on the part of a witness was the background to communal enactments which laid down that the town scribe could sign in the name of a witness, on the latter's instructions (Resp. Rashba, vol. 2, no. 111; see also vol. 4, no. 199).

Another communal enactment made provision for the court to proclaim a specified period within which any interested party could submit his claims in respect of a particular asset put up for sale, failing which he would forfeit his rights to such property. This *takkanah* was required to ensure the more efficient transaction of business. Although amounting to a departure from the law – since no support is found in the *halakhah* for the proposition that a person should forfeit his rights on account of failure to lodge his claims thereto within a specified period (see *Limitation of Actions) – it was nevertheless held valid because "an enactment of the community sets aside the *halakhah*, for the townspeople are entitled to stipulate among themselves as they please" (Resp. Rashba, vol. 4, no. 260). Many examples of communal enactments of this kind are to be found in the area of tax law (see *Taxation), and the laws concerning the legal standing of a public authority and its relationships with its employees and the community in general (see Public *Authority). They are also found in the laws pertaining to the administration of consecrated and other public property (see *Hekdesh*). These legal branches developed particularly from the tenth century onward in the different Jewish centers, and communal enactments provided the answer to many of the legal problems arising in connection therewith.

TAKKANOT HA-KAHAL AND HALAKHIC AUTHORITY. That communal enactments whose contents contradicted the *halakhah* could be laid down with a large measure of independence, as already described, held out the possibility that these enactments might become divorced from the living body of the *halakhah*. On the surface, there existed the likelihood that the legal directives originating from communal enactments might, if uncontrolled, evolve into a legal system parallel to the halakhic legal system, leading inevitably to the exclusion of the former directives from the regular framework of the halakhic system. This threat was countered through the development in Jewish law of a number of safeguards serving to link the communal enactments to halakhic authority. These safeguards were not calculated to prejudice the community's legislative independence as regards the possibility that its enactments might conflict with one or other rule of the *halakhah*, yet they served to subjugate such enactments to the spirit and objective of the overall halakhic system. There were three such safeguards, each of which is outlined below, one functioning prior to the enactment of a *takkanah* and the other two thereafter.

APPROVAL BY "A DISTINGUISHED PERSON." The first safeguard, accepted by the majority of the halakhic scholars, was the need for a *takkanah* to be approved – prior to its enactment – by "a distinguished person" (*adam ḥashuv*) residing within the community concerned. The need for such approval was designed to ensure the halakhic scholars some measure of control, even if qualified, over the communal enactments (see below). Support for the need for a distinguished person's approval was found in the talmudic law pertaining to the enactment of a *takkanah* by a professional association. The butchers of a certain town made a *takkanah* to regulate their workdays in a particular manner, enforceable by imposition of a fine in the form of tearing the hide of the animal slaughtered by the offending butcher. In a case where this punishment was carried out, the offending butcher instituted an action against his fellows to recover compensation for the damages resulting therefrom. His claim was upheld by Rava on the ground that there was present a distinguished person in that town but no approval of the regulation had been obtained from him, and it was therefore invalid (BB 9a). Some of the scholars held the need for the aforesaid approval, apparently innovated by the *amoraim*, to exist only with reference to a *takkanah* enacted by a restricted section of the public, such as a professional association, this for the reason of preventing the adoption of resolutions calculated to cause loss to the consumer public, and so on (Nov. Ramban, BB 9a; Nov. Ran, BB loc. cit., Resp. Ribash, no. 399; Resp. Maharam Alashkar, no. 49). However, the majority of the scholars took the view that the stated approval must be also obtained in respect of communal enactments, since the fact of such approval would serve to stress the link between the *takkanah* and halakhic authority, and the *halakhah* was decided accordingly (Resp. Rashba, vol. 1, no. 26; vol. 4, no. 185; *Piskei ha-Rosh*, BB 1:33; Sh. Ar., ḤM 231: 28 – *Rema, Sma* and *Siftei Kohen*, ad loc.). Presumably this safeguard was actually practiced in the different Jewish communities, and sometimes a special directive on the matter is to be found in the body of a *takkanot* collection (see, e.g., J. Halpern (ed.), *Takkanot Medinat Mehrin*, nos. 176, 286, 335). There are, however, also references to the fact that certain communities (see, e.g., Resp. Maharalbaḥ, no. 99), and even a representative body such as the *Council of Four Lands (see Resp. Bah Ḥadashot, no. 63), did not consistently observe the need to obtain the approval of a distinguished person to their *takkanot*. The halakhic scholars were at pains to convince the communal leaders of this need (see Resp. Maharalbaḥ, no. 99 and Resp. Baḥ Ḥadashot, no. 3). Yet at the commencement of the 19th century it was still held by Moses *Sofer that the stated approval was a requirement not of the strict law but of the custom followed by the communities (Resp. Ḥatam Sofer, ḤM 116).

Different opinions were expressed as regards the attributes of "a distinguished person" from whom approval of a *takkanah* must be obtained. One opinion held that he may be either a *talmid ḥakham* ("scholar") or a *parnas* appointed by the community, and the presence of either in the town serves to withhold validity from a *takkanah* until his approval thereof can be obtained (Resp. Rashba, vol. 4, no. 185, et al.). According to another opinion, "a distinguished person" is "a *talmid ḥakham* who is also in charge of the public" (opinion of Ibn Migash, quoted in *Shitah Mekubbeẓet*, BB 9a and in Resp. Rashba, vol. 5, no. 125) – i.e., a person who combined in himself the qualities both of being a learned scholar and of having been accepted as a leader of the public. This opinion was accepted by a majority of the halakhic scholars who interpreted "a distinguished person" thus: "a distinguished scholar able to order the affairs of the community concerned and help its inhabitants to prosper in their ways" (Yad, Mekhirah 14:11); "a learned scholar and leader" responsible for public affairs (*Piskei ha-Rosh*, BB 1:33; Tur ḤM 231:30; Sh. Ar., ḤM 231:28). Thus if locally there be present no person blessed with both these qualities, then the communal enactment should be fully valid even without the approval of a distinguished person (*Yad Ramah*, BB 9b, no. 103; *Maggid Mishneh*, Mekhirah 14:11).

PRINCIPLES OF JUSTICE AND EQUITY. The decisive factor in the integration of communal enactments within the overall framework of Jewish law has been the supervisory authority exercised by the halakhic scholars so as to ensure that the enactments, even when contradicting the contents of a specific halakhic directive, should not depart from the general principles of justice and equity underlying the entire Jewish legal system. These substantive principles served as the common basis of the *halakhah* and of the communal enactments, the zealous preservation of these principles ensuring that the latter become an integral part of the overall Jewish legal system.

These principles find expression in various ways. Thus, for instance, Solomon b. Abraham *Adret stated with reference to a particular communal enactment, "if it is a matter which makes no fence to the law and brings no real good, then even if it was instituted by the representatives and leaders of the public – the public will not need to act in accordance with their wishes" (Resp. vol. 7, no. 108; also vol. 5, no. 287 and vol. 7, no. 340). In another case the communal leaders enacted a *takkanah* serving to enjoin a member of the community from obtaining the ruling power's permission to continue his duties or supervising against the commission of various offenses; a sector of the public objected to the *takkanah* as opening the door to moral laxity on the part of the public. In his responsum on the matter, Adret held that the *takkanah* would have been valid if it had made provision for the position itself to remain but prescribed its entrustment to someone else; however, since the *takkanah* purported to abolish entirely a position of such vital nature, it had to be regarded as of no effect; "and even if the *takkanah* was enacted by the people responsible for most of the needs of the public, yet the fact is that they have to make enactments which enable the community to uphold and not breach the law, and they may not breach the fences of the Torah" (Resp., vol. 2, no. 279). Just as it is forbidden that a *takkanah* should contain anything tending to encourage moral laxity on the part of the public, so it is forbidden that a *takkanah* should be unduly onerous – even though it serves a laudable purpose and remedies a particular situation; hence, according to Adret, in the same way as there had been laid down the principle that a *takkanah* of the halakhic scholars must not be imposed on the public unless the majority is able to abide thereby (Av. Zar. 36a; see **Takkanot*), so too the community may not enact a *takkanah* by which the majority of its members is unable to abide (loc. cit.; also vol. 7, no. 108).

A material principle guarded by the halakhic scholars with the utmost care was that ensuring the right of the minority in general, and of the individual in particular, not to be prejudiced by the majority in arbitrary manner and without justifiable cause. In several centers it happened that the community sought to enact a *takkanah* purporting to impose tax on a local resident in respect of his property situated elsewhere, thereby rendering him liable for double taxation since he was also liable for tax at the place of situation of his property. In this regard it was held by Adret that it was not within the power of the minority to make an enactment – notwithstanding the consent thereto of the majority – imposing an obligation that involved a "robbing" (*gezel*) of the individual, which would be the inevitable but unacceptable result of the individual having to pay tax twice on the same property (Resp., vol. 1, no. 78; vol. 5, no. 178; Resp. Maharam of Rothenburg, ed. Prague, no. 106; see in detail under *Taxation). A like conclusion was stated by Isserles in unambiguous manner: "It is an accepted matter that the *tovei ha-ir* are not authorized to deal high-handedly with the individuals, nor may the majority forcefully dispossess [lit. "rob"] the individual… since the townspeople have no power to make enactments except as conferred on them by law; but to do as they please, that is something that never was nor ever will be!" (Resp. Rema, no. 73). There was also applied to communal enactments the principle that they must apply equally to all and not single out particular persons (*Sha'arei Ẓedek*, no. 16, p. 57a). The rule was formulated that a *takkanah* is valid when two conditions are fulfilled: it must be "a *takkanah* [i.e., to mend matters] for the public, and it must apply equally to all" (Nov. Ritba, Av. Zar. 36b; cf. the principle of equality before the law in relation to the doctrine of **dina de-malkhuta dina*; see **Mishpat Ivri*).

The requirement that legislation accord with the principles of justice and equity led to the observance of the further rule that the provisions of communal enactments should only be made to take effect from the time of their enactment onward, and not retroactively to any earlier period. There was frequent application of this rule in relation to tax laws (see, e.g., Resp. Ribash, no. 477; see also *Taxation), and also in other legal fields (see, e.g., *Zikhron Yehudah*, no. 78).

INTERPRETATION OF TAKKANOT HA-KAHAL. The third factor which safeguarded the integration of communal enactments into the overall Jewish legal system was the fact that the authoritative interpretation of these enactments was usually entrusted to the same body or persons who interpreted the rules of the *halakhah* in general, namely the competent halakhic scholars. In their interpretative activities the latter relied on the different Jewish law rules of interpretation, and examined the content and formulation of a *takkanah* before them by analogy to the talmudic *halakhah* and codificatory literature. In consequence the integration of the communal enactments into Jewish law was affected not only as regards subject matter but also from the literary aspect, as expressed in the responsa literature. For particulars, see *Interpretation.

TAKKANOT HA-KAHAL AND THE JEWISH LEGAL SYSTEM. The phenomenon of a community enacting a *takkanah* which remained subject to halakhic scrutiny and became integrated with the *halakhah*, even though it did not always accord with one or another rule of the *halakhah* itself, is understandable and in keeping with the image of Jewish society until the coming of the Emancipation at the end of the 18th century. Both the community and the bearers of the *halakhah* acknowledged the existence of a single ultimate and guiding value – the authority of the Torah and the *halakhah*. The communal leaders never regarded their enactments as a means of undermining or evading in any way the sanctity of the *halakhah*. On the contrary, they saw their enactment as a special means – adapted to the needs of their time and place – toward modeling public and private life in their community on the principles, objectives, and spirit of Jewish law. These enactments not only constituted a means of ordering – within the wider framework of the *halakhah* – special legal problems arising from particular social and economic trends in the different periods and centers of the Jewish dispersion. They also served toward the evolution of basic principles pertaining to the modes of legislation by a Jewish public in accordance with Jewish law, and toward the development and crystallization of principles of justice and equity, of safeguarding minority rights, and equality before the law, as well as other principles to which the communal enactments were required to conform. For further general details see **Takkanot*.

[Menachem Elon]

Historical Aspects

In the Middle Ages and early modern times the term *takkanah* denoted both a constitution or a statute proposed or adopted by a competent authority in the Jewish community as a general framework of behavior, and also a resolution relating to a single issue adopted by such an authority. In Sephardi communities the terms *haskamah* or **ascama* were used for such enactments. *Takkanot* were issued by synods and councils of scholars or laymen or both: the local community, **ḥevrah*, a synagogue congregation, and a **bet din*. They were also issued on the authority of a leading scholarly personality and obeyed by reason of this authority. All aspects of social, economic, political, and religious life of the Jews were embraced by *takkanot*.

GEONIC PERIOD. During the geonic period the *exilarchs and **geonim* enacted numerous *takkanot* in such areas as civil, family, and liturgical law, which were not only verification of evolving customs but in fact were very often departures from talmudic law. Many customs were made law as a means of counteracting the schismatic teaching of the *Karaites: for example, although the Talmud never mentions a benediction over the Sabbath candles, the *geonim* made this obligatory to demonstrate that the *Rabbanites not only considered the use of candles lit before the Sabbath permissible but also festive and sacral. The use of the ring as a specific symbol of betrothal, instead of cash or "money's worth," as prescribed in the Talmud, was also a geonic innovation. A clear-cut example of a geonic ordinance *takkanah* reflecting a socioeconomic change relates to debts inherited by an orphan not yet of age.

SPAIN. Judah b. Barzillai al-Bargeloni's *Sefer ha-Shetarot* contains a formula expressing the accumulated experience of enactment of *takkanot* in 11th-century Spain. This is a *takkanah* writ to be used when a group (*edah*), community (*kahal*), yeshivah, or the fellows of a *bet midrash* (*benei midrash*) or a synagogue (*keneset*) have agreed to enact a *takkanah* in their yeshivah, synagogue, or *bet midrash*, or the heads of the yeshivah have agreed to enact a *takkanah* "for [all] Israel." In these cases all the abovementioned write a *takkanah* writ in unambiguous terms and sign it, and, if they are so agreed, write that anyone who transgresses this *takkanah* will be excommunicated (ed. S. Halberstam, 1858, 132). In the same collection there is a *takkanah* by a craft guild containing detailed agreements on preventing competition and including financial sanctions against any transgressor (p. 190). *Takkanot* continued to be made mainly by local communities. Statutes adopted at Tudela in 1305 invested power in the community in eight prominent families; no enactment was valid unless eight men representing these families concurred. They decreed that "all judicial decisions rendered in this city shall be based upon the code of R. Moses (Maimonides), of blessed memory." Various 14th-century *takkanot* from *Barcelona reflect the bitter social and political struggle in the community between the rich and the poor, mainly over the composition of the community councils and commissions. Similar problems and *takkanot* are found from *Saragossa. In *Majorca, which was a major maritime center, the *aljama* (*kahal*) adopted *takkanot* in 1356 concerning marriage, inheritance, and commerce which were a compromise between talmudic law and the laws and customs of the country. In 1354 representatives of the province of Valencia and of all the Jewish communities of Catalonia met in Barcelona and proposed many organizational *takkanot*. These proposals reveal the motivations and arguments for centralized leadership as well as those of the diplomatic activity of the communities (see **Shtadlan*). A conference in Valladolid in 1432 proposed a group of *takkanot* for the communities of Castile. Its five sections, regulating education, communal officialdom, punishment of informers, taxation, and sumptuary behavior, were drawn up with the aid of Don Abraham *Benveniste, *rab de la corte* of the kingdom of Castile. *Takkanot* were often copies of rules of a neighboring *aljama*. Some followed the *fueros*, or constitutional charters, of municipalities, and the Spanish rulers played a part in drafting or approving Jewish statutes. *Isaac b. Sheshet Perfet defined the relation between the communities' *takkanot* legislation and royal assent: "no doubt, without the approval of our lord, the king… according to the law of our Torah the community may enact the *takkanot* on its own authority, and also excommunicate and punish the transgressor" (Resp., no. 228). Royal assent was requested only to avoid an accusation of infringing on the sovereignty of the king and also to provide an additional sanction. These *takkanot* were validated through their being inscribed in a minute book (see **pinkas*), by the signatures of scholars and communal leaders, and by proclamation. Rabbinic authorities usually gave unhesitating support to the communal *takkanot*. R. Solomon b. Abraham *Adret (13th century) stated that "no man is entitled to withdraw and disregard a communal ordinance by saying 'I shall not take part in the promulgation of the statutes,' and the like, because the individual is subject to the majority will." The language of the *takkanot* is generally Hebrew. In the Muslim period Arabic, with an admixture of Hebrew, was used. In Toledo Arabic was used as late as the 14th century. Most of the 1432 Valladolid constitution is written in Castilian. When the adopted resolutions were proclaimed before the entire congregation in the synagogue, they usually responded with "Amen." When the *takkanot* were inscribed in the *pinkas* they were generally organized into sections and articles. *Takkanot* were designed to be permanent or temporary: a Saragossa regulation concerning tax exemption was to remain in effect for 50 years; Toledo adopted an ordinance to be effective for 20 years; the Valladolid statutes of 1432 were to be valid for ten years. If no definite period of time was stated, a *takkanah* was to be permanently binding. Interpretation of *takkanot* was the province of either the legislating body or an accepted rabbinical authority. The proclamation of a *ḥerem* as an integral sanction clause of the *takkanot* was a customary procedure, and in early texts *ḥerem* is synonymous with *takkanah*. The conception of the *ḥerem* as divine expulsion from God's grace sufficed to make most Jews obey such *takkanot*, even when, in practice, the offender against communal enactments was often not treated as an excommunicate. Solomon b. Abraham Adret reported: "When I observed the practice of the communities to include the clause of the *ḥerem* in their various *takkanot*, and yet, in all my observations, they never treated the transgressor as an excommunicate, I put the question to my teachers whether such a person was really under the ban or not, and they made no reply." In serious matters the community did not hesitate to make the violator liable to various penalties.

ASHKENAZ AND ẒAREFAT (FRANCE). *Takkanot* appear in the Rhineland and in districts to the west of it early in the history of Jewish settlement in the area. In Ashkenaz in the 11th and 12th centuries *takkanot* sometimes stem from a community to include both itself and its environs (e.g., *Troyes in the time of Rashi), sometimes from a central community attempting to assert its authority over minor communities (a practice sharply rejected by Joseph b. Samuel *Bonfils in the 11th century). They were sometimes adopted by *synods (in France in the 12th century, in Germany in the 13th, and on several occasions in Germany right down to the 17th century). French *takkanot* of the 12th century are sometimes called after Jacob b. Meir (Tam). The topics dealt with in these *takkanot* are as variegated as the problems of Jewish life and autonomy current in those centuries.

MEDITERRANEAN LANDS. *Maimonides enacted a series of *takkanot* directed against *Karaite practices. The community of the island of Crete (Candia) had sets of detailed *takkanot* from the 13th century onward. *Takkanot* were also enacted in Italy. A conference of north Italian communities meeting in Forli in 1418 adopted a set of far-reaching regulations relating to *sumptuary laws. Other conferences of the 15th and 16th centuries confirmed this activity. After the expulsion from Spain (1492) the communities of the Sephardi Diaspora shaped many *takkanot* (*ascamot*) to solve problems specific to their new settlements.

EASTERN EUROPE. In the communities of Eastern Europe and the Councils of the Lands, *takkanot* continued creatively on a greater scale. The *takkanot* of *Moravia embody a codification of a series of enactments, touching on most aspects of social and communal life. This is true to an even larger degree of the resolutions of the Councils of Lithuania and of Poland. The communal authorities (*kesherim*) of *Poznan consistently noted down over the years their proposals for *takkanot* as well as their criticisms of the mode of their implementation. In 1595 the Cracow community codified *takkanot* covering a wide range of problems. Although, as in all cases, they based their *takkanot* on the *halakhah*, they introduced sweeping changes. The court system and method of payment of judges established in Cracow and Poznan reflect a great deal of the social and financial practices of the leading circles of large Jewish communities but little of halakhic principles. The right of **arenda*, in particular, and many other comprehensive economic arrangements, were established by *takkanot*. In 1607 a means of permitting a Jew to take interest from a Jew – *hetter iska* – was introduced in Poland and empowered in many communities by *takkanot*. In Moravia it was arranged that their *takkanot* "shall be in force so long as they are not abrogated by the unanimous decision of the heads of the council (*rashei medinah*) and the fifteen elected officers or by the nine guardians of the *takkanot* then in office, provided it is done with the consent of the chief rabbi *[*Landesrabbiner]* or a scholarly leader, in the event that there is no chief rabbi." The Councils of Four Lands resolved in 1671 that "in any controversy arising between an individual and his *kahal* it shall be resolved in accordance with the provisions of their own *takkanot* and *pinkasim* without interference by the council." In 17th-century Poland-Lithuania Samuel Eliezer b. Judah ha-Levi *Edels voiced opposition to the use of the *ḥerem* as an integral part of a *takkanah*. Some of the first leaders of Ḥasidism – e.g., Aaron of *Karlin – tried to use *takkanot* to effect social amelioration but this trend was not continued. The *Sanhedrin convened by Napoleon enacted radical *takkanot*. In the main, the spread of the *Haskalah and the break-up of traditional autonomy structures combined with a weakening of the authority of the *halakhah* to bring about a gradual cessation of the enactment of *takkanot* in modern times, beginning in Western and Central Europe and spreading to Eastern Europe. It was only in scattered communities in Eastern Europe or the Near East that *takkanot* appeared in the 20th century. The association or *ḥevrah*, however, continued to make use of the *takkanah* to regulate its actions and the life style of the group.

See also *Autonomy; *Community.

[Isaac Levitats]

Research into Takkanot ha-Kahal

Since the very beginning of (modern) research in Jewish studies and Jewish law, various scholars have engaged in the study of *takkanot ha-kahal*, communal enactments. Initially, attention was paid primarily to the historical material found in this literature. In recent times, great attention has been given as well to the vast quantity of legal material found in this literature. The publication of entire collections of public enactments from various centers and different periods – such as the communal ledgers (*pinkasim*) from Italy (see Boxenbaum; Hartom-Cassuto; Carpi; Simonson; Hacohen, Livorno, in the Bibliography below); the Balkan countries, Greece and Turkey (among them see Bornstein); Poland, Germany, Bohemia and Lithuania (see Evron, Heilprin, Roth), and North America (see Amar) – most of them in manuscript, created a fitting infrastructure for study in greater depth. The various legal researchers (Elon, Naḥlon, Hacohen, Kaplan) focused on the study of legal institutions and arrangements as reflected in the communal enactments. In this context, the issue of the authority to make enactments, the mode of their enactment, the scope of their applicability, and the means of their interpretation were all considered. The appearance of detailed legal indexes to the responsa literature, in which a special place is given to the communal enactments, made a special contribution in this field (see Bibliography: Elon-Lifschitz, Lifschitz-Shochetman).

Contribution of the Takkanot ha-Kahal to the Formulation of Israeli Law

The multiplicity and variety of communal enactments and the fact that they were living law and actual practice, and not merely just theory, make them a source of primary importance for the integration of Jewish law into that of the State of Israel. This is particularly prominent in the sphere of public law. In the absence of extensive legislation in the matter, the field of public law in the State of Israel – both legislative law and administrative law – remains based to a great extent not on *legislation* but on *court rulings*, a sort of Israeli version of "common/conventional law." This situation provides abundant room for anchoring many rules in the field of public law on the principles of "justice, freedom, integrity and peace of the Jewish heritage" (in the words of the Foundations of Justice Law, 5740 – 1980, cf. **Mishpat Ivri*) and on "the values of a Jewish state" (in the words of the Basic Law: Human Dignity and Freedom), as expressed in Jewish law in general and in the public enactments in particular.

Reflecting as they do autonomous Jewish community life, with its plethora of styles, there exist in the communal enactments many varied arrangements for the conduct of community life and the modes of decision-making therein, vis-à-vis, for example, issues of majority and minority, manners of elections, appointments to public office, and ousting of a public official from his position, as well as the various basic rights, such as freedom of expression, freedom of movement, and the like (see *Rights, Human: Public Authority).

Furthermore, there are some who wish to view the laws of the Knesset as a kind of *takkanat ha-kahal* and are consequently prepared to grant them halakhic validity (Shochetman, *Hakarat ha-Halakhah*). In one case, the Supreme Court (as expressed by Justice Elon) pointed to the tenant protection laws as valid in Jewish law by virtue of their being viewed as "communal enactments" (HC 323/81 *Vilozhny v. Rabbinical Court of Appeals*, PD 36 (2) 740–743) (see at length under **Takkanot*).

In the Courts in Israel

On more than one occasion, the courts in the State of Israel have made use of communal enactments as a source for interpretation of Israeli law and for the creation of legal arrangements in various spheres. Thus, for example, the Supreme Court (as expressed by Justice Silberg) pointed to various arrangements made in the *takkanot ha-kahal* and intended to share the damage caused as the result of the depreciation of the currency between lender and borrower (CA 248/53 *Rozenbaum v. Zeger*, PD 9, 533). In another case, the Supreme Court (per Justice Kister) used the *takkanot ha-kahal* as a possible source for allowing a judge in a religious court to deal with a certain matter, even though it was liable to concern his own interests (e.g., determination of the tax rate for which members of the community, he among them, would be liable; see HC 21/66 *Katabi v. Chairman of the Kiryat Ekron Local Council*. PD 20 (2) 108). In another case, the Supreme Court (Justice Elon) noted the great power of communal enactments in formulating the material relationships of a couple in view of the changing economic and social reality (CA 2/77 *Ezogi v. Ezogi*, PD 33 (3) 16–17), as well as in creating arrangements allowing daughters to receive a portion in their father's inheritance (Motion 427/78 *Sobol v. Goldman*, PD 33 (1) 800–803). In yet another case, the Supreme Court (Justice Elon) based its interpretation of tax legislation on the principles of interpretation of *takkanot ha-kahal* in Jewish law. The court concluded that the law should be construed according to its actual language rather than from the intention of the legislator, which is not clear from the explicit language of the law (HC 333/78 *Trust Company of Bank Leumi v. Director of Estate Duty*, PD 32 (3) 212–13; see at length *Interpretation). On yet another matter, the Supreme Court (Justice Elon) upheld the conviction of a person on a criminal charge on the basis of a confession given outside the courtroom, inter alia, on the basis of communal enactments from Spain that recognized the need to deviate from the usual laws of evidence under certain circumstances in order to punish the offender (according to 543/79 *Najar et al. v. State of Israel*, PD 35 (1) 163–170; see at length *Capital Punishment). Finally, in another case, the Supreme Court (Justice Elon) made use of an interpretation given by the Ribash to a public enactment from Catalonia in Spain concerning the delegation of powers (see *Public Authority), to construe the limits of the mayor's right to delegate his authority in a matter requiring use of judgment (HC 702/79 *Goldberg v. Head of the Ramat Hasharon Council*, PD 34 (4) 85).

[Aviad Hacohen (2nd ed.)]

BIBLIOGRAPHY: LEGAL ASPECTS: Baron, Community; L.I. Rabbinowitz, *The Ḥerem Hayyishub* (1945); A. Karlin, in: *Ha-Torah ve-ha-Medinah*, 1 (1949), 58–66; B. Lipkin, *ibid.*, 2 (1950), 41–54; idem, in: *Sinai* 25 (1949), 233–53; J. Baer, in: *Zion*, 15 (1949/50), 1–41; ET, 3 (1951), 180, 376–8; J.A. Agus, in: JQR, 43 (1952/53), 153–76; S. Albeck, in: *Zion*, 19 (1953/54), 128–36; 25 (1959/60), 85–121; A.H. Freimann, in: *Yavneh*, 2 (1947/48), 1–6; M. Elon, in: *Meḥkarei Mishpat le-Zekher Avraham Rosenthal* (1964), 1–54; Elon, Mafte'ah, 251–67, 413–24. See also bibliography of **Takkanot*. HISTORICAL ASPECTS: Weiss, Dor, 4–5 (1891); I. Abrahams, *Jewish Life in the Middle Ages* (1920); Finkelstein, Middle Ages; Ch. Tykocinski, *Gaonaeische Verordnungen* (1929); S. Dubnow, *Pinkas Medinat Lita* (1925); M. Frank, *Kehillot Ashkenaz* (1937); Baron, Community, 3 (1942), index; Neuman, Spain, 2 (1942); I. Levitats, *Jewish Community in Russia* (1943); Halpern, Pinkas; idem, *Takkanot Medinat Mehrin* (1952); J. Katz, *Tradition und Crisis* (1961); A. Rechtman, *Yidishe Etnografye un Folklor* (1958); Baer, Spain, 2 (1966), index; H.H. Ben-Sasson, *Perakim be-Toledot ha-Yehudim bi-Ymei ha-Beinayim* (1962); idem (ed.), *Toledot Am Israel*, 3 (1969), index; idem, *Hagut ve-Hanhagah* (1959), index; idem, in: *Zion*, 21 (1956), 183–206; I. Agus, *Urban Civilization in Pre-Crusade Europe*, 2 (1965); M. Zuker, in: *Sefer ha-Yovel le-Rabbi Ḥanokh Albeck* (1963), 378–401; Ashtor, Korot, 2 (1966); A.S. Artom and M.D. Cassuto, *Takkanot Kandia ve-Zikhronotehah* (1943); A.H. Freimann, *Seder Kiddushin ve-Nissu'in* (1945); D. Avron, *Pinkas ha-Kesherim shel Kehillat Posna* (1967). **ADD. BIBLIOGRAPHY:** M. Elon, *Ha-Mishpat ha-Ivri* (1988), 1:391–557, index; idem, *Jewish Law* (1994), 2:477–879, index; idem, *Jewish Law (Cases and Materials)* (1999), 77–85; M. Elon and B. Lifshitz, *Mafte'aḥ ha-She'elot ve-ha-Teshuvot shel Ḥakhmei Sefarad u-Ẓefon Afrikah* (1986), 2:544–61, 581–91; B. Lifshitz and E. Shochetman, *Mafte'aḥ ha-She'elot ve-ha-Teshuvot shel Ḥakhmei Ashkenaz, Ẓarefat ve-Italyah* (legal digest) (1997), 235, 367–72, 386–92; M. Elon, *Kevod ha-Adam ve-Ḥeruto be-Darkei ha-Hoẓa'ah le-Fo'al* (2000); idem, *Ma'amad ha-Ishah*; idem, "*Le-Mahutan shel Takkanot ha-Kahal be-Mishpat ha-Ivri*," in: *Meḥkarei Mishpat le-Zekher Avraham Rosenthal* (1984), 1–54; idem, "*Le-Mahutan shel Takkanot ha-Kahal u-Mashma'utan la-Ḥevrah ha-Kibbutzit*," in: *Amudim – Ḥok u-Mishpat ve-ha-Ḥevrah ha-Kibbutzit* (1984), 26–61; idem, "*Ekronot Yesod be-Darkhei ha-Ḥakikah ba-Mishpat ha-Ivri*," in: *Reuven Bareket Volume* (1977), 130–38; idem, "*Darkhei ha-Yeẓirah ha-Hilkhatit be-Fitronan shel Be'ayot Ḥevrah u-Mishpat ba-Kehillah*," in: *Y. Baer Memorial Volume* (= *Zion*, 44 (1979)), 241–64; idem, "*Demokratyah, Zekhuyot Yesod u-Minhal Takin bi-Fesikatam shel Ḥakhmei ha-Mizraḥ be-Moẓa'ei Gerush Sefarad*," in: *Jewish Law Annual*, 18–19 (1992–94), 9–63; M. Amar, "*Le-Takkanot Makhnes ba-Me'ot ha-18–19*," in: A. Chaim (ed.), *Ḥevrah u-Kehillah* (1991), 35–45; E. Bashan, "*Takkanot le-Hagbalat Motarot: Ha-Reka ha-Ḥevrati ve-ha-Hilkhati*," in: *Hagut*, 3 (1980), 41–68; M. Benayahu, "*Takkanot Ḥezkat ha-Ḥaẓerot, ha-Batim ve-ha-Ḥanuyyot be-Saloniki u-Fiskeihem shel Rabbi Yosef Tiataẓak ve-Ḥakhmei Doro*," in: *Mikhael* 9 (1985), 55–146; L. Bornstein-Makovetski, "*Seridim mi-Pinkas Beit Din Bialata be-Kushta, Shenat* 5699 (1839)," in: *Sefunot*, 68:4 [19] (1989), 53–121; Y. Boxenbaum (ed.): *Pinkas Kahal Verona* (1989); D. Carpi, *Pinkas Kehillah-Kedoshah Padova* (1974–80); Sh. Eidelberg, "*Pinkas Shnadua*," in: *Galed*, 3 (1976), 295–313; D. Evron, *Pinkas Hekhsherim shel Kehillat Pozna* (1967); idem, "*Ha-Berirah bi-Kehillat Pozna ba-Meot ha-17–18*," in: *Galed*, 1 (1973), 51–62; S. Goldin, "*Tafkidei ha-Ḥerem ve-ha-Takkanot ba-Kahal*," in: *Proceedings of the Eleventh World Congress for Jewish Studies*, vol. 12 B1 (1994), 105–112; A. Hacohen, *Parshanut Takkanot ha-Kahal be-Mishpat ha-Ivri* (2003); D. Hacohen, "*Hakehillah be-Livorno u-Mosdoteha (ba-Meah ha-17)*," in: R. Bonfil et al. (eds.), *Memorial Volume for Sh.A. Nakhon* (1978), 107–28; A.S. Hartom and M.D. Cassuto, *Takkanot Kandyah ve-Zikhronoteha* (1943); I. Heilprin, *Takkanot Medinat Mehrin* (1952); M. Hildesheimer, *Pinkas Kehillat Sheintakh* (1992); A. Nahlon, *Kahal ve-Takkanot Kahal ve-Toratam shel ha-Geonim* (2001); A.N.Z. Roth, *Sefer Takkanot Nikelsburg* (1963); I. Shatzipanski, *Ha-Takkanot be-Israel* (1993); E. Shochetman, "*Rubbo Mitokh Kullo*" – *Tokpam shel Ḥukim ha-Mitkabbelim bi-Mele'at ha-Knesset she-eina Mele'ah*," in: *Teḥumin* 9 (1988), 82–102; Sh. Simonson, *Toledot ha-Yehudim be-Dukkasut Mantovah*, 2 vols. (1963–65).

TAKU, MOSES BEN ḤISDAI (13th century), tosafist, commentator on *piyyutim*, and author of the polemical treatise, *Ketav Tammim*. Taku probably wrote in the fourth and fifth decades of the 13th century. The surname "Taku" has not been explained satisfactorily; it may be derived from the town Dachau; or it may be assumed that it comes from Tachov (Tachau) in Bohemia, but neither conjecture has been proved. There have been some doubts whether the same Moses b. Ḥisdai wrote all the halakhic, exegetical, and polemical works ascribed to him. It has been suggested that there was more than one writer of this name in the 13th century. However, comparison of the quotations from his writings in the *Arugat ha-Bosem* of *Abraham b. Azriel prove conclusively that the writer in the three fields of scholarship is the same person. Only one fragment of *Ketav Tammim* has survived, the end of the second part of the work and the beginning of the third. Quotations from the book are also found in Ashkenazi literature of the 13th century. Taku's polemic is unique in medieval European Hebrew literature. He fiercely opposed any innovation in the realm of beliefs and theology, rejecting both philosophy and the esoteric doctrines of the Ḥasidei Ashkenaz, and stated his unqualified acceptance of talmudic tradition at its face value. The main target of his attack was *Saadiah Gaon. He quoted extensively from his *Emunot ve-De'ot* and from his commentary on **Sefer Yeẓirah*, to prove the heresy inherent in the Saadianic doctrine of the revelation of the Divine Glory. Taku thought that Saadiah's teachings were the source of the doctrines of the Ashkenazi Ḥasidim, Abraham *Ibn Ezra, and *Maimonides, which include ideas which seem to him to threaten Orthodox belief – especially the doctrine of the immanence of God, which he understood to approach pagan pantheism. He mourns the new phenomenon of theological study in Judaism, and points at the catastrophic results for Judaism of previous theological inquiry – namely, Christianity and Karaism. His opposition to theological speculation caused him to suspect the authenticity of some parts of the traditional literature on the subject, mainly the **Shi'ur Komah* and other early speculative and mystical works. He calls upon the reader to accept literally the main body of talmudic tradition, to believe in what is explicitly stated there, and to reject any speculation about what is not explicit. It is unknown whether Taku's polemical work had any direct results on Ashkenazi Jewry. However, it is very probable that his arguments reflect the attitude of a considerable segment of the Jewish people of the time, who took no part in the then current controversies.

BIBLIOGRAPHY: R. Kirchheim, in: *Oẓar Neḥmad*, 3 (1860), 54–99; E.E. Urbach, in: *Tarbiz*, 10 (1938/39), 47–50; Urbach, Tosafot, 348–52 and passim; idem, in: *Zion*, 12 (1947), 150–4; idem, *Arugat ha-Bosem*, 4 (1963), 78–81, 177–9; Scholem, Mysticism, 109, 114; idem, in: *Tarbiz*, 28 (1959), 60; Y. Dan, in: *Kovez al Yad*, 6 pt. 1 (1966), 201–2; J.N. Epstein, in: REJ, 61 (1911), 60–70.

[Joseph Dan]

TAL (Gruenthal), JOSEF (1910–), composer, pianist, and teacher. Born in Pinne (Pniewy), Poznania, where his father was rabbi of the community, Tal studied at the Hochschule für Musik in Berlin, with Tiessen, Hindemith and others. He settled in Palestine in 1934 and after a short stay in Kibbutz Gesher, he moved to Jerusalem, where he taught at the Palestine Conservatoire (founded 1933) and was among the founders of the Academy of Music there. He also performed frequently as piano soloist with the Palestine Orchestra (later the Israel Philharmonic Orchestra) as well as playing there as substitute harp player. In 1950 he was appointed as the first lecturer on music at the Hebrew University of Jerusalem. In 1965 he was among the founders of the Department of Musicology at the Hebrew University, which was the first in the country.

Tal was the pioneer of electronic music in Israel, having won a UNESCO fellowship in this field. He set up a studio at the Hebrew University where in addition to composing he conducted an extensive research project on the notation of computer music. As one of the founders of Israeli art music (see *Music: In Modern Ereẓ Israel), Tal was consistent in maintaining his close association with the music of *Schoenberg and his school. He strongly opposed any external ideological pressures in the direction of the artificial concoction of a supposed "national style," maintaining his conviction that the very fact of his living and creating in Israel made him a genuine Israeli composer. An early manifestation of this attitude may be found in the second movement of his Piano Sonata (1952), which is based on an ostinato quote of a simple modal folk song by his friend Yehudah *Sharett, on which a set of atonal, chromatic variations is superposed. Tal kept abreast of all subsequent developments in western music, including serial techniques. His musical style has always been sincere, intense, extremely elaborate, and dominated by powerful individual expression, especially salient in his five symphonies. From 1970 Tal concentrated on the composition of operas, most of them, including *Ashmedai* and *Das Experiment*, commissioned by the Hamburg and Munich Opera Houses, whereas *Yosef* was commissioned by the Israel Opera. Tal used electronic sounds always in conjunction with instruments, such as in his concertos for piano and tape, or with voices, such as in his opera *Massada* and the choral work *Death Came to the Wooden Horse Michael* (poem by Nathan *Zach).

In 1970 Tal was awarded the Israel Prize. In 1981 he was honored with a certificate and honorary membership in the American Academy of Arts and Letters as an individual who had made an outstanding contribution to music. He wrote an autobiography, *Der Sohn des Rabbiners* (1985), and *Ad Yosef – Zikhronot, Hirhurim, Sikumim* ("Memories, Reflections, Summations"), with Ada Brodsky (1997)

BIBLIOGRAPHY: Grove online; P.E. Gradenwitz, *The Music of Israel* (1949, 1996^2); J. Hirshberg, *Music in the Jewish Community of Palestine 1880–1948* (1995); R. Fleisher, *Twenty Israeli Composers* (1997).

[Jehoash Hirshberg (2nd ed.)]

TAL, MIKHAIL (1936–1992), Soviet chess master. Born in Latvia, Tal showed promise at an early age. By the time he was 21 he had already won the Soviet championship (1957). He followed this by winning the series of zonal, interzonal, and candidates' tournaments which qualify a challenger for the world championship. In 1960 he qualified to play *Botvinnik and secured the title by winning six games, losing two, and drawing 13. The match was followed by a year of serious illness, which might have partially accounted for Botvinnik's recapture of the title in the return match. Playing brilliantly, Botvinnik won ten games, lost five, and drew six. In 1965 Tal won matches against the Hungarian chess master Laios Portisch and the Danish Bengt Larsen in the new type of candidates' tournaments, but was defeated by Boris Spassky in the final. In 1968 he again qualified to participate in the Candidates' Match tournament. Tal's play was characterized by a remarkable awareness of balances and imbalances. He exploited the imbalances repeatedly in extraordinary long-range combinative attacks. As a result, his chess suggested the tradition of Emanuel *Lasker and Alekhine rather than the more patient playing styles of Capablanca and Botvinnik. Tal's chess articles in the Soviet press contained some profound analyses of opening variations and of endgame position.

Tal went on to win the International Chess Tournament in Tallinn five times (1971, 1973, 1977, 1981, 1983) and tied with Karpov for first place in Montreal's Tournament of Stars in 1979.

BIBLIOGRAPHY: D.J. Richards, *Soviet Chess* (1965), index; P. Clarke, *Tal's Games of Chess* (1968).

[Gerald Abrahams]

TALAVERA DE LA REINA, city in central Spain. The importance of the Jewish community there lay mainly in its connections with nearby *Toledo, the capital of the kingdom of Castile. When the Jewish settlement was established in Toledo, Jews probably settled in Talavera also; its community was under the jurisdiction of Toledo Jewry until the 13th century, achieving independence in the 14th century when it prospered and increased in size. Of the Jews of Talavera during the 13th century, noteworthy was Don Çulema Pintadura, who was *alfakim* in the service of King Alfonso X. Don Joseph Pimetiela, the royal *alfakim* who signed the agreement with the town of Burgos in the king's name in 1279, came from Talavera. It was also the home of Abu Amar (Joseph) b. Abi Elhassan, a friend of Todros b. Judah ha-Levi *Abulafia, who invited R. Todros to settle in Talavera. After 1280 R. Todros settled in Talavera in order to live at a distance from politics and within proximity of the kabbalists. *Isaac b. Samuel of Acre, who arrived in Spain after 1291, encountered him there. In 1291 the community paid 24,771 maravedis in annual tax; it was then a medium-sized community.

The fate of the community during the persecutions of the Jews in Spain of 1391 is not known. However, *Conversos were living in Talavera whose descendants were tried by the *Inquisition when its tribunal was transferred to Toledo in 1485 (see below). Documents concerning the debts owed by Jews to Christians for the purchase of houses and grain bought from the archbishop of Toledo are extant from 1432. Apparently after 1449 Jews of Toledo settled in Talavera, whose community subsequently did much to assist the inhabitants of the capital. Between 1477 and 1487, 168 families lived there. A precise description of the community's economic structure during that period has been recorded: 13 of the "wealthy" Jews owned property valued at more than 30,000 maravedis, the majority of them earning their livelihood from basket weaving; three were goldsmiths; two were shopkeepers; some were physicians or contractors; most, however, were craftsmen and included a blacksmith, a shoemaker, a tailor, and a cobbler. Only 37 of those who paid taxes had capital of more than 10,000 maravedis; 70 disposed of 1,000–10,000 maravedis, and 60 disposed of 100–500 maravedis. The files of seven Conversos from Talavera who were tried by the Inquisition of Toledo are extant. Some were sentenced to expulsion, with Jews also being called upon to testify against them. The close relations between the Jews and the Conversos there are evident in all the trial proceedings. The Jews of Talavera left Spain when the Jews were expelled from the country in 1492.

BIBLIOGRAPHY: Baer, Spain, index; idem, in: *Tarbiz*, 5 (1934), 236; idem, in: *Zion*, 2 (1937), 46; Newman, Spain, 2 (1942), 245; F. Cantera, *Sinagogas españolas* (1955), 309–10; L. Suárez Fernández, *Documentos acerca de la expulsión de los Judiós* (1969), index; Ashtor, Korot, 2 (1966), 144–5; idem, in: *Zion*, 28 (1963), 40–41; H. Beinart, in: PIASH, 2 (1967), 216–20.

[Haim Beinart]

TALHEIM, village in Wuerttemberg. Jewish refugees from *Heilbronn settled in Talheim in 1437. At the end of the 15th century, Jews from Talheim were permitted to trade at markets in Heilbronn, although they were not allowed to stay overnight. In the middle of the 16th century Jews were permitted to settle in Heilbronn; a number remained in Talheim, where most made their living as moneylenders. Their major occupation later became trading in livestock, although in 1729 the Count of Flein prohibited his subjects from trading in livestock with Jews from Talheim. The effects of the Thirty Years' War depleted the number of Jews, but Jews continued to live in Talheim until the middle of the 18th century.

In 1778 four Jewish families came to the village from nearby Horkheim and established themselves in an old castle (thereafter termed "*Judenschloss*") in the western part of the town. The Jewish settlement was under the jurisdiction of the dukedom of Wuerttemberg, then liberally disposed toward the Jews. Their entry was resented by the burghers in the eastern portion of the town, under the separate jurisdiction of Christopher von Gemmingen. When a new prayer room for the Jewish community was to be dedicated in 1793, they stormed the building, confiscated the sacred objects, and held them until 1803. The entire town came under the jurisdiction of Wuerttemberg in 1806, and Jews were no longer restricted to their small area of settlement. The number of Jews had grown to 40 in 1790, to 62 in 1828, and 122 in 1860. In 1832 the Jewish community of Talheim was included in a district that encompassed Sontheim and Horkheim. From 1849, the community was independent until its dissolution in 1939. The building that housed the prayer room was enlarged and converted into a synagogue in 1836. A *mikveh* and a school were added in 1851, and a school building was constructed in 1857.

From 1873 on, the community began to decline, partly due to a large emigration to the United States. There were only 82 Jews left in 1933. Nazi discriminatory legislation stimulated emigration still further. On Nov. 10–11, 1938, storm troopers demolished the interior of the synagogue. In 1941–42 the 32 Jews left in the town were deported to concentration camps; none returned after the war. During the war the synagogue was used as a prison, and in 1952 it was finally demolished. In 1983 a plaque was mounted to commemorate the former Jewish community and the synagogue.

BIBLIOGRAPHY: T. Nebel, *Die Geschichte der juedischen Gemeinde in Talheim* (1963); P. Sauer, *Die juedischen Gemeinden in Wuerttemberg und Hohenzollern* (1966), 173–6. **ADD BIBLIOGRAPHY:** W. Angerbauer and H. Frank, *Juedische Gemeinden in Kreis und Stadt Heilbronn* (Schriftenreihe des Landkreises Heilbronn, vol. 1) (1986) 230–35; *Germania Judaica*, vol. 3 (1987), 1448–49; T. Nebel and S. Daeschler-Seiler, *Die Geschichte der juedischen Gemeinde in Talheim* (1990^2). **WEBSITE:** www.alemannia-judaica.de.

[Alexander Shapiro]

TALION, a concept of punishment whereby the prescribed penalty is identical with, or equivalent to, the offense. Identical (or "true") talions are death for homicide ("Whosoever sheddeth man's blood, by man shall his blood be shed": Gen. 9:6), wounding for wounding ("an eye for an eye": Ex. 21:23–25; Lev. 24:19–20), and doing to the false witness "as he had purposed to do unto his fellow" (Deut. 19:19). Equivalent talions conform to some feature characteristic of the offense, but not to its essence or degree: the hand that sinned shall be cut off (Deut. 25:12) – not a hand for a hand, but the hand for what it had done. In the case of the adulteress, it is that part of her body with which she is suspected of having sinned that will be visited with divine punishment if she is guilty (Num. 5:21 as interpreted in Sot. 8b–9a, and see *Adultery). (For further biblical equivalent punishments see Ex. 32:20; Judg. 1:7; II Sam. 4:12; II Kings 9:26; Dan. 6:25.) While most identical talions were abolished by talmudic law (see below), equivalent talions survived through talmudic times (cf. Sanh. 58b; Nid. 13b) into the Middle Ages (cf. Rosh, Resp. 17:8 and 18:17; *Zikhron Yehudah* no. 58; et al.), and traces can even be found in modern law (e.g., the confiscation, mostly as an additional punishment, of firearms, vehicles, or other objects by means of which an offense was committed, or of smuggled goods; or the suspension of trading or driving licenses for trading or driving offenses).

True talionic punishments were undoubtedly practiced in biblical and post-biblical times. To retaliate measure for measure is God's own way of meting out justice (cf. Isa. 3:11; Jer. 17:10; 50:15; Ezek. 7:8; Obad. 15; et al.), and is defended by Philo as the only just method of punishment (Spec. 3:181–2). The account of the talion in Josephus (Ant. 4:280) supports the theory that, as in ancient Rome (Tabula 8:2), the victim had the choice of either accepting monetary compensation or insisting on talion (cf. Ex. 21:30 for an analogous case). Even in the talmudic discussion on the talion, one prominent dissenter consistently maintained that "an eye for an eye" meant the actual physical extraction of the offender's eye for that of the victim (BK 83b–84a). The majority, however, settled the law to the effect that talion for wounding was virtually abolished and replaced by the payment of damages (BK 8:1), primarily because the justice of the talion is more apparent than real: after all, one man's eye may be larger, smaller, sharper, or weaker than another's, and by taking one for the other, you take something equal in name only, but not in substance. Not only is the ratio of talion thus frustrated, but the biblical injunction that there should be one standard of law for all, would also be violated (Lev. 24:22). Also if a blind man takes another's eye, what kind of eye could be taken from him? or a cripple without legs who did injury to another's leg, what injury can be done to his? Nor can an eye or any other organ be extracted from a living man's body without causing further incidental injury, such as making him lose vast amounts of blood or even endangering his life; "and the Torah said, an eye for an eye, and not an eye and a soul for an eye" (BK 83b–84a). The very risk, unavoidable as it is, of exceeding the prescribed measure, is enough to render talion indefensible and impracticable (Saadiah Gaon, quoted by Ibn Ezra in his commentary on Ex. 21:24).

The monetary compensation replacing talion was not wholly in the nature of civil damages, however, but had a distinctly punitive element. This is clear from the rule that the penalty for inflicting injuries not resulting in pecuniary damage was *flogging (Ket. 32b; Sanh. 85a; Mak. 9a). The only reason why flogging could not be administered where any damages were payable was that two sanctions could never be imposed for any one offense (Ket. 37a; Mak. 13b; et al.).

While talionic practice was effectively outlawed, the talionic principle, as one of natural justice, was reaffirmed in the Talmud: the measure by which a man measures is the measure by which he will be measured (Sot. 1:7; Tosef. Sot. 3:1 as to punishments and 4:1 as to rewards). The famous precept of Hillel's, said to embody the whole of the Torah, that you should not do to another what you would not like to have done to you (Shab. 31a) is derived from the same principle.

BIBLIOGRAPHY: E. Goitein, *Das Vergeltungsprincip im biblischen und talmudischen Strafrecht* (1893); D.W. Amram, in: JQR, 2 (1911/12), 191–211; J. Horovitz, in: *Festschrift...Hermann Cohen* (1912), 609–58; J. Weismann, in: *Festschrift...Adolf Wach* (1913), 100–99; E. Merz, *Die Blutrache bei den Israeliten* (1916); S. Kaatz, in: *Jeschurun*, 13 (1926), 43–50 (Germ.); J. Norden, *Auge um Auge, Zahn um Zahn* (1916); J.K. Miklisanski, in: JBL, 66 (1947), 295–303; ET, 12 (1967), 693–5. **ADD. BIBLIOGRAPHY:** M. Elon, *Ha-Mishpat ha-Ivri* (1988), 1:185, 331ff.; ibid, *Jewish* Law (1994), 1:207, 397ff.; M. Elon and B. Lifshitz, *Mafte'aḥ ha-She'elot ve-ha-Teshuvot shel Ḥakhmei Sefarad u-Ẓefon Afrikah* (legal digest) (1986), 2:322; B. Lifshitz and E. Shochetman, *Mafte'aḥ ha-She'elot ve-ha-Teshuvot shel Ḥakhmei Ashkenaz, Ẓarefat ve-Italyah* (legal digest) (1997), 223.

[Haim Hermann Cohn]

TALKER, EZEKIEL SAMUEL (1836–1929), Indian Jewish scholar. Talker, who belonged to the *Bene Israel community, was born in Bombay, and in 1867 published in Hebrew and Marathi (the vernacular of the Bene Israel) a book of prayers to be recited on all occasions, from birth to death, and a listing of the dietary laws. The title of the book, translated from Marathi, is *The Book of Ceremonies*, and was the first Hebrew book printed in India from type imported from England. The book became indispensable to all Indian Jews. Talker moved to Karachi where there was a small Bene Israel community and was instrumental in enlarging and rebuilding the Karachi synagogue, built in 1893. He gave it the name Magen Shalom. He served as *ḥazzan* and trained several assistants in order that "the eternal light should be kept burning continuously and eternally." Talker was buried in Karachi.

ADD. BIBLIOGRAPHY: S.B. Isenberg, *India's Bene Israel: A Comprehensive Inquiry and Sourcebook* (1988).

TALLAHASSEE, Florida's capital city, about 160 miles west of Jacksonville in north Florida. The earliest record of a Jew in Tallahassee is 1837 when Raphael Jacob Moses had a store. By 1860 Tallahassee had 15 Jews, according to the *American Israelite*. Three were merchants, two were harness makers, and two were bookkeepers. After the Civil War (1865), Robert Williams and his wife Helena Dzialynski of Jacksonville moved to Tallahassee from nearby Jasper. Williams bought a store, and started three cotton plantations. A traditional Jew, Robert Williams provided the Torah and was civically active as well. The couple had five daughters and all of them found Jewish spouses. In 1877 when Rachelle Williams married Jacob Raphael Cohen of Orlando, a rabbi was brought from Charleston, South Carolina, and Jews from throughout the south attended. Henrietta married Tallahassee merchant Julius Diamond and their daughter Ruby Diamond was born in 1886. She graduated from Florida State College for Women (now FSU) in 1905 with a B.A. in chemistry. Miss Ruby was a legend in her lifetime, Florida's "Miss Daisy." Another daughter, Mena, was the first Miss Florida in 1885.

William Levy, who arrived in 1872, operated a store. In his memory, his wife Sarah gave the property for Temple Israel's first building (1937). Jacob Burkeim and his wife came in 1873 and two years later Jacob started a Sunday school. In March 1878, a Purim Ball was held when there were nine Jewish families and nine single men in town. Alfred Wahnish of Morocco and his wife Carrie came to Tallahassee in the 1880s. He began a 3,600-acre tobacco plantation; today there is a Wahnish Way (street) that designates the site. One of the Wahnishes six children was Sam, president of the American Legion and the Elks, who was elected mayor of Tallahassee in 1939. By the 1890s two lots were designated for Jewish burial in the Old City Cemetery and the Hebrew Benevolent Society was founded (1896). Peddler Sam Mendelson of Romania settled in Tallahassee with his wife Jennie and four children around 1910 because "it was a larger town than Miami." Sam was the founding president of Temple Israel in 1937. Jews living in outlying towns such as Quincy, Live Oak, Monticello, and Perry were mostly involved in dry goods stores or growing tobacco and were closely tied to the Jews living in Tallahassee. The Fleets and Mendelsons are examples of Live Oak Jewish families from 1903 who had some members settle in Tallahassee in later years. In the early 1920s Hyman Myers was a fur and hide trader who also sold pecans and scrap metal. Rose Printing, established in 1932 by Sam and Fannye Rosenberg, is one of the largest specialty printers and book manufacturers in the southeast. Albert Block who married Evelyn Rosenberg, the founders' daughter, was one of the fathers of the state's Minimum Foundation Program guaranteeing a basic level of education for every Florida school child and helped develop the state's community college system.

David Sholtz of Daytona Beach was inaugurated in Tallahassee as Florida's 26th governor on January 3, 1933. He had served in the legislature in 1917 and to date is the only Jew to have served as governor of Florida.

In the early days religious services were held in the Masonic Temple.

Temple Israel was founded in 1937 when Tallahassee's population was 16,000 with fewer than 30 Jewish families. Rabbi Max Eichorn was engaged for Temple Israel and for the 100 female students on the campus of FSCW. In 1939, there was a front-page story in the local paper, "The Grand Lodge of Florida Masons yesterday laid the cornerstone of the first Jewish place of worship to be built here."

B'nai B'rith Lodge 1043 was founded in 1938. The first Jewish cemetery in Tallahassee was established in 1942. During the WW II period, Tallahassee Jewry hosted Jewish soldiers from military bases in the area.

After World War II, Tallahassee grew quickly. Drawn by state government, universities, and the military, the Jewish population also expanded. Shopping in downtown Tallahassee in the 1950s, you could find many "Mom and Pop" Jewish businesses – Turners, Fleets, Mendelsons. and Gilbergs. Groundbreaking for Temple Israel's religious school building was in 1955. Albert B. Block donated the site and Rabbi Stanley Garfein served the congregation for 30 years beginning in the late 1960s. In the 1950s and 1960s Jews were involved in the Civil Rights movement and in anti-discrimination legislation. Gene Berkowitz served as mayor twice (1968 and 1972) and was instrumental in laying the groundwork for the Civic Center. Many Jews throughout Florida have been elected to state government, moved to Tallahassee, and become active in the Jewish community. Richard Stone was secretary of state from 1972 to 1974. He and his wife, Marlene, strongly supported and encouraged Jewish community life. Florida State University also brought many Jews to the community; for a quarter century Richard L. *Rubenstein, the post-Holocaust theologian who authored the controversial work *After Auschwitz*, made Tallahassee his home.

The Jewish population has grown with Jewish faculty at Florida State University and state government. In 2005 Tallahassee, a city of 151,000, had a Jewish population of approximately 4,400. It supports three congregations: Temple Israel

(Reform with about 360 families), Shomrei Torah (Conservative) and Chabad; Hillel and several Jewish organizations: National Council of Jewish Women, Hadassah, and B'nai B'rith. Since the Tallahassee Jewish Federation's inception in the 1980s, the Ruby Diamond Foundation has been the single largest contributor to its campaigns.

[Marcia Jo Zerivitz (2nd ed.)]

TALLINN (Ger. **Reval**; Rus. **Revel**), capital of Estonia. Jews are mentioned in municipal documents from the 14th century. In 1561, when Tallinn was captured by the Swedes, Jewish settlement was prohibited and remained so until 1710, when the city was annexed by Russia. Although outside the *Pale of Settlement, Jewish merchants visited Tallinn and some even settled there, only to be expelled subsequently. In 1828 Jewish conscripts were brought there to be educated in a *Cantonist institution. These youths, as well as other Jewish soldiers stationed in Tallinn, founded the local Jewish community. There was a synagogue founded in 1856 as well as a Jewish cemetery. At that time there were about 60 families of Jewish soldiers in the city. After 1856 they were joined by other Jews permitted to reside outside the Pale of Settlement, and thus the Jewish population grew considerably. In 1897 it numbered 1,193 (2% of the total). The community continued to develop after the establishment of independent Estonia, numbering 1,929 in 1922, and 2,203 in 1934. By that time there was a network of Hebrew educational institutions from kindergarten to secondary school. With the annexation of Estonia to Soviet Russia in 1940, organized Jewish life came to an end (see *Estonia). In 1959, 3,717 Jews were registered in Tallinn (1.3%), of whom 25% declared Yiddish to be their mother tongue. In 1970 there were 3,754 Jews, dropping to around 1,000 in 2005 due to emigration mainly to Israel. In 2005 the Jewish community of Tallinn had a synagogue, community center, kindergarten, Sunday school, summer camp, and burial society. In September of 2005, ground was broken in Tallinn to build the first new synagogue in Estonia in almost a century

BIBLIOGRAPHY: K. Yoktan, *Di Geshikhte fun di Yidn in Estland* (1927); N. Genss, *Zur Geschichte der Juden in Eesti* (1933); idem, *Bibliografia judaica Eestis* (1937).

[Yehuda Slutsky / Ruth Beloff (2nd ed.)]

TALLIT (Heb. טַלִּית, pl. *tallitot*; Yid. *tales*, pl. *talesim*), prayer shawl. Originally the word meant "gown" or "cloak." This was a rectangular mantle that looked like a blanket and was worn by men in ancient times. At the four corners of the *tallit* tassels were attached in fulfillment of the biblical commandment of **ẓiẓit* (Num. 15:38–41). The *tallit* was usually made either of wool or of linen (Men. 39b) and probably resembled the *abbayah* ("blanket") still worn by Bedouin for protection against the weather. The *tallit* made of finer quality was similar to the Roman *pallium* and was worn mostly by the wealthy and by distinguished rabbis and scholars (BB 98a). The length of the mantle was to be a handbreadth shorter than that of the garment under it (BB 57b). After the exile of the Jews from Ereẓ Israel and their dispersion, they came to adopt the fashions of their gentile neighbors more readily. The *tallit* was discarded as a daily habit and it became a religious garment for prayer; hence its later meaning of prayer shawl.

The *tallit* is usually white and made either of wool, cotton, or silk, although *Maimonides and *Alfasi objected to the use of the latter. Strictly observant Jews prefer *tallitot* made of coarse half-bleached lamb's wool. In remembrance of the blue thread of the *ẓiẓit* (see **tekhelet*), most *tallitot* have several blue stripes woven into the white material (see Zohar, Num. 227a). Until a few decades ago, however, they only had black stripes.

Frequently the upper part of the *tallit* around the neck and on the shoulders has a special piece of cloth sewn with silver threads (called *atarah*, "diadem"), to mark the upper (i.e., the "collar") and the outer parts of the four-cornered prayer shawl. Some *tallitot* have the benediction, recited when putting on the *tallit*, woven into the *atarah*. Others, especially those made of silk, are often richly embroidered and some have the benediction woven into the entire cloth of the *tallit*. The minimum size of a *tallit* is that which would suffice to clothe a small child able to walk (Sh. Ar., OḤ 16:1).

The *tallit* is worn by males during the morning prayers (except on the Ninth of *Av, when it is worn at the afternoon service), as well as during all *Day of Atonement services. The *ḥazzan*, however, according to some rites, wears the *tallit* also during the afternoon and evening services (as does the reader from the Torah during the *Minḥah* prayer on fast days). Before putting on the prayer shawl, the following benediction is said: "Blessed art Thou, O Lord, our God, King of the universe, Who hast sanctified us by Thy commandments, and hast commanded us to wrap ourselves in the fringed garment." When the *tallit* is put on, the head is first covered with it and the four corners thrown over the left shoulder (a movement called *atifat Yishme'elim*, "after the manner of the Arabs"). After a short pause, the four corners are allowed to fall back into their original position: two are suspended on each side. On weekdays, the *tallit* is donned before putting on the **tefillin*. Among strictly observant Jews, it was the custom to put on *tallit* and *tefillin* at home and to walk in them to the synagogue (Isserles, to Sh. Ar., OḤ 25:2). They also pray with the *tallit* covering their head; to be enfolded by the *tallit* is regarded as being enveloped by the holiness of the commandments of the Torah, denoting a symbolic subjection to the Divine Will (see also RH 17b). Generally, however, people pray with the *tallit* resting on their shoulders only. The *kohanim*, however, cover their heads with the *tallit* during their recital of the *Priestly Blessing. It is customary in the morning service to press the fringes to the eyes and to kiss them three times during the recital of the last section of the **Shema* (Num. 15:37–41) which deals with the commandment of *ẓiẓit* (Sh. Ar., OḤ 24:4).

The custom of wearing the *tallit* differs in many communities. In the Ashkenazi ritual, small children under bar mitzvah age dress in *tallitot* made according to their size, whereas in the Polish-Sephardi ritual only married men wear them (Kid. 29b). In most Oriental rites, unmarried men wear *tallitot*.

In *Reform synagogues, the *tallit* is part of the synagogue service garments of the rabbi and the cantor. For male congregants, the wearing of a small prayer shawl, resembling a scarf and worn around the neck, is optional. Those called to the reading from the Torah, however, always don a *tallit*.

In some communities, it is customary for the bridegroom to dress in a *tallit* during the **ḥuppah* ceremony. It is likewise customary to bury male Jews in their *tallit* from which the fringes have been removed or torn (see *Burial).

The **ẓiẓit* worn by men with their daily dress is known as **tallit katan* ("small *tallit*").

BIBLIOGRAPHY: Eisenstein, Dinim, s.v.; Gunzbourg, in: REJ, 20 (1890), 16–22; M. Higger, *Seven Minor Treatises* (1930), 31–33; D.B. Abramowitz, *Law of Israel*, 1 (1900), 11–16; G. Friedlander, *Laws and Customs of Israel* (1927), 5–7.

TALLIT KATAN (Heb. טַלִּית קָטָן; "small *tallit"; Yid. *tales koten, arba kanfot*, or *arba kanfes*; and *tsidekel*, from the Ger. *Leibzudeckel*), a rectangular garment of white cotton, linen, or wool with *ẓiẓiyyot* ("fringes") on its four corners. Whereas the ordinary *tallit* is worn only at the morning service, strictly observant Jews wear the *tallit katan* under their upper garment the whole day, so as constantly to fulfill the biblical commandment of **ẓiẓit* (Num. 15:39), a reminder to observe all the comandments of the Torah. The *tallit katan* is, therefore, often worn in a manner that it may be seen; if not, that at least the *ẓiẓiyyot* hang freely and are visible (Sh. Ar., OḤ 8:11). The minimum size of a *tallit katan* ought to be ¾ ell long and ½ ell wide (15 in. × 10 in.). According to another opinion, it should be one square ell (20 in. × 20 in.). The *tallit katan* is put on in the morning, and the following benediction is said: "Blessed art Thou, O Lord our God, King of the universe, Who hast sanctified us by Thy commandments and commanded us [to wear] the *ẓiẓit*." The *tallit katan* must always be clean and, in reverence for its sanctity, should not be worn on the bare flesh but over an undershirt. If one of the *ẓiẓiyot* is torn, the whole *tallit katan* becomes ritually unfit (*pesulah*) until the torn *ẓiẓit* is replaced.

BIBLIOGRAPHY: Shulḥan Arukh, OḤ 8:3, 6; Eisenstein, Dinim, 151–2.

TALMACIU (Rom. **Tălmaciu**; Hung. **Bántolmács**), village in central Romania; until the end of World War I within Hungary. Its name is connected with a theory concerning the ancient Jewish settlement in Transylvania, which supposedly existed during the reign of Decebalus, king of Dacia (d. c. 107). Some have attempted to derive the name Talmaciu, without any philological basis whatsoever, from the word "Talmud." This theory originated in an epos entitled *De oppido Thalmus*, written in Latin by Joannis Lebel, a Christian priest who held office in Talmaciu in the mid-16th century. The work was written in 1542 but was published for the first time in Sibiu in 1779. However, it was known to scholars while still in manuscript and upon the basis of the data it contained, historians and authors began to propagate information on the ancient Jewish settlement. In the epos itself, it is said that a Jew of the tribe of Dan, with several other Jews, came to the assistance of King Decebalus in his struggle against the Romans so as to avenge in this fashion the Roman conquest of Jerusalem. In appreciation for their support, these Jews, of whom Decebalus was very fond, received authorization to settle in the above village. They established a settlement in which there was a thriving Jewish life.

Even though there is so far no substantiation for this theory in any source, or any historical proof, the argument has been repeated since 1557, and particularly after the publication of the work, to the present time. Among historians who seriously discussed this theory were Sulzer in *Geschichte des transalpinischen Daciens* (vol. 2, p. 148) and S. *Kohn, the leading Jewish historian in Hungary, in *A zsidók története Magyaroszágon* ((1884), 6–7). An attempt to investigate the theory and refute it was published by the Romanian Jewish historian Carol Blum in *Evreii din Thalmus* (Sinai Anuar (1928), 73–77). The theory nevertheless lives on and is mentioned in general articles, as well as in publications which deal with the history of the Jews in Transylvania, Romania, and other places.

[Yehouda Marton]

TALMI, IGAL (1925–), Israeli physicist. He was born in Kiev, Ukraine, in the former Soviet Union and immigrated to Palestine the same year. On leaving school he joined the Palmaḥ after which he studied physics under G. *Racah. Sponsored by the newly formed Israel Atomic Energy Commission, he worked with W. Pauli at the Federal Institute of Technology in Zurich (1949–52) followed by a research fellowship at Princeton University, U.S. (1952–54). From 1954 he was a member of the department of nuclear physics of the Weizmann Institute of which he was appointed director (1967); he became professor emeritus. Talmi's research concerned nuclear structure and the manner in which protons and neutrons of nucleons are held together despite the electrostatic repulsion of the positively charged protons. He developed the shell model in which nucleons move in orbits within the core of the nucleus determined by interactions with other nucleons. This model is supported by theoretical and experimental data in good agreement. He continued to work to support his description of the shell model with further physical data. He was awarded the Israel Prize for exact sciences (1965), jointly with his collaborator Amos *De-Shalit, and was elected to the Israel Academy of Sciences. He was a member of the Israel Atomic Energy Commission.

[Michael Denman (2nd ed.)]

TALMID ḤAKHAM (Heb. תַּלְמִיד חָכָם; pl. *talmidei ḥakhamim*; lit. "a disciple of the wise" rather than "a wise student"), the appellation given to a rabbinical scholar. The Talmud expresses the preference of the aristocracy of learning over that of distinguished descent or position by stating that "a *talmid ḥakham*, even though a *mamzer [who is on the lowest rung of the ladder of descent] takes precedence over the high priest [who represents the highest degree of aristocratic descent] who is an ignoramus" (Hor. 3:8, TJ, *ibid.*, 48c, end). The Jerusalem Talmud (Hor. loc. cit.) in extending that list of precedences puts the *talmid ḥakham* (though the word *ḥakham* alone is used) at the top of the list of protocol, preceding the king.

The *talmid ḥakham*, however, represented not only the aristocracy of learning, but much more significant, the learned aristocrat. Although his basic qualification was a comprehensive knowledge of the whole Bible ("the 24 books," Ex. R. 41:5) and the whole of the Oral Law ("Mishnah, Talmud, *halakhah*, and *aggadot*," Song R. 5:13), scholarship alone did not suffice. There were two essential additional qualifications – one was *shimmush*, attending upon, and thus coming under the personal influence of, his teacher and learning from his deportment (Yoma 86a). It was conceivably this duty which lay behind the connotation "disciple of the wise." The other qualification was piety, "Woe unto the enemies of the *talmidei ḥakhamim* (a euphemism for *talmidei ḥakhamim*) who occupy themselves with the Torah and do not possess the fear of heaven" (Yoma 72b).

In Babylonia Rav attempted to lay down a list of attainments that the *talmid ḥakham* should acquire. R. Judah said in his name that they should include a knowledge of writing (a scroll), *sheḥitah*, and circumcision, while Hananiah b. Shelemiah added, also in the name of Rav, the ability to tie the knot of *tefillin* and of *ẓiẓit*, as well as the blessings of the marriage ceremony (Ḥul 9a) – these are not to be regarded as qualifications for being a *talmid ḥakham*, but accomplishments which it was desirable that he should possess. The whole conception of the *talmid ḥakham* in rabbinical literature is based upon the principle of *noblesse oblige*. If on the one hand the rabbis insisted upon the privileges, both material and of status to which the *talmid ḥakham* was entitled, on the other hand they equally insisted upon his maintenance of a rigid and exalted standard of conduct and ethical behavior which was not demanded of the ordinary person.

The material advantages which accrued to the *talmid ḥakham* were considerable. Whereas the Jerusalem Talmud makes the list of preferences which puts the *talmid ḥakham* first apply to both social precedence and such material benefits as redemption from captivity, providing for his means, including clothing, the Babylonian Talmud confines it to the latter. He was exempt from communal taxation, and from all corvées or levies of manpower. One *amora*, interpreting the *ḥanikhim* of Gen. 14:14 as referring to *talmidei ḥakhamim*, states that exile was decreed on the descendants of Abraham because he pressed them into the *angaria* (Ned. 32a), a word which, though in the context refers to military service, applies to all forced labor. As long as he devoted himself only to study, "his stint was performed by the other citizens of the town" (Shab. 114a). He was even exempt from, or forbidden to, indulge in fasting, since "he thereby reduces his toil for the sake of heaven" (Ta'an. 11b). Where an ordinary claimant of lost goods had to produce evidence of identification, the *talmid ḥakham* could claim it solely on his assurance that he recognized it as his (Shab. 114a – this is the real meaning of the phrase, which is often wrongly explained as meaning that he had a "discerning eye"). He was appointed to communal positions (Shab. 114a; Git. 60a).

All the regulations and injunctions with regard to the *talmid ḥakham* bear the unmistakable stamp common to every conscious aristocracy, which finds its expression not only in a rigid standard of ethical conduct (and, of course, in this case the requirements of the ceremonial and ritual law), but a whole host of regulations which belong to the sphere of etiquette and even elegance. To this category, for instance, belong the injunctions that he should be moderate in his sexual life, not "frequenting his wife like a cock" (Ber. 22a) but limiting himself to once a week, on the eve of Sabbath (Ket. 62b). Not only should he wear a distinctive dress; his undergarment should be such that his skin is not visible, his upper garment so long that only a handbreath of his undergarment is visible (BB 57b). He had to be immaculate in his dress, and so insistent were the rabbis on this that they actually stated that "a *talmid ḥakham* on whose garment there is a stain is deserving of death" (Shab. 114a). He should not wear patched shoes, indulge in casual conversation with women in the marketplace, or be found in the company of ignoramuses (Ber. 43b), nor eat in the street or marketplace (TJ, Ma'as. 3:5, 50d). Whereas the *am ha-areẓ* put so many things under his bed that it was like "a packed storehouse," the *talmid ḥakham* kept under it only his sandals in summer and shoes in winter (BB 58a), and whereas the table of the *am ha-areẓ* was like "a hearth with pots all round it," that of the *talmid ḥakham* had to be only two-thirds covered, the other third should be cleared for placing on it the dishes and vegetables (*ibid.*, 57b). Although it was regarded as praiseworthy to bring him gifts (Ber. 54b; Ket. 105b, 111a), the *talmid ḥakham* was enjoined to refrain from benefiting from the public (*Tanna de-Vei Eliyahu* 18). In general he had to be "externally as he was internally" (Yoma 72b), and he had to be entirely beyond reproach (Song R. 6:2 no. 2). He was permitted an "eighth part of an eighth part of pride" (Sot. 5a). It is therefore not surprising that the most compact and comprehensive of the qualities expected of the *talmid ḥakham* are to be found in the post-talmudic tractate *Derekh Ereẓ Zuta, which treats of etiquette. "The *talmid ḥakham* should be modest in his deportment but renowned for his actions; pursuing truth and not falsehood, faithfulness and not violence, humility and not arrogance, peace and not war, following the counsel of the elders and not of children, a lion rather than a woman" (ch. 7, cf. also ch. 1 which is more comprehensive and poetical).

The praise of the *talmidei ḥakhamim* is unbounded. They are the builders who "occupy themselves with the building up of the world during their whole life" (Shab. 114a); they "increase peace in the world" (Ber. 64a); this passage too is connected with the idea of the *talmid ḥakham* as a "builder"); they are compared to the prophets (Shab. 119b). The *talmid ḥakham* had to be held in the utmost respect. R. Akiva went so far as to interpret the "*et*" (אֶת) of Deut. 6:13, "thou shalt have reverence for (*et*) the Lord," to include the *talmidei ḥakhamim* (Pes. 22b). He had to be provided with an escort when going out at night (Ber. 43b), and one of the reasons put forward for the destruction of the Temple was that they held the *talmidei ḥakhamim* in light esteem (Shab. 119b). If in the sphere of social status the lowest rung of the ladder was the *mamzer*, in the social and intellectual sphere he was represented by the *am ha-areẓ*, and "he is an *am ha-areẓ*" (e.g., "he who has studied Bible and Mishnah but has not done *shimmush*") is a synonym for "he is no *talmid ḥakham*" (Ber. 47b; Suk. 22a). There is ample evidence of a tension and even enmity between the *am ha-areẓ* and the *talmid ḥakham*, and similar expressions of hatred for the *am ha-areẓ* on the part of the *talmidei ḥakhamim*, especially in later traditions of the Babylonian Talmud (Pes. 49b). In the Palestinian rabbinic tradition we often find a different tone, such as in the passage where the *talmid ḥakham* who "enters the houses of the *amei ha-areẓ* and delights them with words of Torah" is praised (Lev. R. 34:13). These contradictions have long been the subject of scholarly debate (see: *Am ha-Areẓ). In general, however, it was clear that the *talmid ḥakham* should not associate with the *amei ha-areẓ*, by sitting in their company (Ber. 43b) and, all the more, by dining with them (Pes. 49a). If one could not belong to this aristocracy by virtue of one's attainments, at least one could follow the time-honored practice of "marrying into the aristocracy," and with unusual frequency the advice is given to "marry one's daughter to a *talmid ḥakham*" (cf. Ket. 111b; Pes. 49a) and even the purpose of this "marrying into the aristocracy" would be fulfilled; "the children will be *talmidei ḥakhamim*" (*Tanna de-Vei Eliyahu R.*, 5).

Especial consideration was given to the apparent incongruity of the *talmid ḥakham*, who was supposed to "increase peace in the world," indulging in wordy and often heated controversy with his colleagues in debate. The many references to it are evidence of the desire to solve this apparent contradiction. They point to the fact that whereas the scholars in Ereẓ Israel conducted their debates in an atmosphere of pleasantness, those of Babylonia conducted them with vehemence, not sparing one another's feelings, and "wounding" one another (Sanh. 24a), and it was a Palestinian scholar who taught that "when two *talmidei ḥakhamim* are amiable to one another in their halakhic debates, the Holy One, blessed be He, gives heed to them" (Shab. 63a). The Babylonian scholars, however, while admitting the sharpness and vigor of their discussions, regarded it as a virtue (Ta'an. 7a). Despite the opposition between them they were permitted to combine to form a *zimmun* (the minimum of three for reciting the Grace After Meals in unison) which presupposes a harmony of mind between those participating, and both R. Ḥisda and R. Sheshet who, representing two different trends, the one a reliance on tradition and the other the method of keen dialectics (Er. 67a), cited themselves as examples of halakhic disputants who nevertheless were of common mind (Ber. 47b). In fact, it was insisted that *talmidei ḥakhamim* (the text has "even a father and son" and "a master and a disciple," but the reference is obviously to *talmidei ḥakhamim*) who "study together and become enemies to one another, at the end come to love each other" (Kid. 30b).

An idealized picture of the *talmid ḥakham* is presented; but there is ample evidence that the sages consciously strove to live up to these exalted ideals. In a discussion on what constitutes *ḥillul ha-Shem* (see **Kiddush ha-Shem* and *Ḥillul ha-Shem*), Rav stated that "in my case [i.e., because he was a *talmid ḥakham*] it would constitute *ḥillul ha-Shem* if I took meat from the butcher and did not pay him on the spot," while R. Johanan applied it to personal deportment, "walking four cubits without speaking in Torah or wearing *tefillin*" (Yoma 86a). R. Eleazar rejected gifts sent to him by the *nasi* and refused invitations to be his guest, excusing himself wittily by saying, "Do you not want me to live? – as it is written (Prov. 15:27), 'He that hateth gifts shall live'" and R. Ze'eira and R. Neḥunya b. ha-Kanah did likewise (Meg. 28a; Ḥul. 44b). Innumerable examples could be given of each and every one of these virtues and manners of deportment being not only preached but practiced. The significance of the *talmid ḥakham* as the ideal type of the aristocracy of Judaism is reflected in the fact that the *Oẓar ha-Aggadah* of H.D. Gross lists no less than 281 dicta from the Talmud and Midrashim in which the *talmid ḥakham* is mentioned, yet the list is incomplete, and it can also be supplemented, as he indicates, by those on the synonymous terms, or related subjects of *ẓurva mi-rabbanan*, *ḥakham*, *rav* and *talmid*, etc.

In the modern vernacular the term *talmid ḥakham* merely conveys the person who is learned in Talmud.

See also *Sages.

BIBLIOGRAPHY: L. Ginzberg, *Students, Scholars, and Saints* (1928), 35–58; A. Buechler, *The Political and Social Leaders of the Jewish Community of Sepphoris in the Second and Third Centuries* (n.d.); M. Beer, in: *Bar Ilan*, 2 (1964), 134–62; E.E. Urbach, *Ma'amad ve-Hanhagah be-Olamam shel Ḥakhmei Ereẓ Yisrael* (1965).

[Louis Isaac Rabinowitz]

TALMON, JACOB LEIB (1916–1980), Israeli historian. Born in Rypin, Poland, Talmon went to Ereẓ Israel in 1934 and in 1939 graduated from the Hebrew University, later studying at the Sorbonne, and the London School of Economics. From 1944 to 1947 he was secretary to the Palestine Committee of the Board of Deputies of British Jews. In 1949 Talmon was appointed lecturer at the Hebrew University and in 1960 professor. Talmon is best known for his contribution to the history of ideas, the analysis of the intricate texture of political and social trends in 19th-century Europe, which contained the roots of the apparently new ideological phenomena of the 20th century, particularly totalitarianism.

His main work is contained in his *The Origins of Totalitarian Democracy* (1952) and *Political Messiahism: The Romantic Phase* (1960). Its theme is the struggle between the empirical-liberal and the totalitarian-messianic types of democracy. Both are shown to stem from 18th-century philosophical premises and the clash in the French Revolution. The political and ideological currents since 1800 are seen as variations of these types. Modern revolutionary movements including Marxism and its offshoots are thus presented as expressions of political messianism which still dominates a large part of the world. In another work, *Romanticism and Revolt* (1967), Talmon portrays the age of Romanticism. He delineates the movement of the forces released by the revolution of 1789 toward the tragic clash and denouement of 1848. *The Unique and the Universal* (1965) is a collection of essays designed to bring out the significantly modern tensions between those developments – technological, social, and ideological – which lead to universal uniformity on the one hand and the self-assertion of racial and national peculiarities on the other. In these essays the Jewish phenomenon is highlighted as the outstanding sample of this dilemma, "ultimately a sample of the great human condition."

In his books as well as in numerous essays, articles, and public debates, Talmon proved himself an outstanding interpreter of Zionism in a changing world context. His exchange with Toynbee attracted the attention of the intellectual world. Talmon took an active and determined stand on topical questions of Jewish life such as the Arab-Israel conflict, religion and state, Jewish and Israel identity, continuity and innovation, and Jews and revolution. He showed himself a confirmed believer in the principles of political liberty, freedom of conscience, religious toleration, self-determination, and mutual respect among nations.

After the *Six-Day War (1967) Talmon resolutely advocated a compromise solution of the conflict based on territorial concessions and primarily on the mutual recognition of the Jewish and Palestinian-Arab right of self-determination. Talmon received the Israel Prize for social sciences and law in 1956. He was a member of the Israel Academy of Sciences and Humanities.

TALMON (Zalmonovitch), SHEMARYAHU (1920–), Bible scholar. Born in Skierniwice, Poland, Talmon received his primary and high school education at the Jüdisches Reform-Real Gymnasium in Breslau, Germany. He immigrated to Palestine in 1939, after being interned for three months in Buchenwald concentration camp.

Talmon obtained his doctorate from the Hebrew University in Jerusalem in 1946, focusing in his doctoral thesis on the text and versions of the Hebrew Bible and in particular on "double meanings" in biblical texts. He refined and supplemented these studies over the years, contributing to many areas of biblical study, applying text-critical procedures to the cultural and literary history of ancient Israel.

His sociological approach to text history advanced the understanding of various aspects of the biblical text, especially with regard to the Qumran scrolls found in the Judean Desert. His interests in the texts found in Qumran and in sociological research were combined in the study of the nature and history of the Qumran monastery.

Talmon was active in the field of biblical education both in Israel and elsewhere. He held the position of director for educational institutions in the "Illegal" Immigration Camps in Cyprus (1947–48). He taught at the major Israeli universities and served as a visiting professor at many institutions throughout the world. He was the dean at Haifa University and of the Faculty of Humanities at the Hebrew University and rector of the Institute of Judaic Studies in Heidelberg.

Talmon was also involved in forging cultural and intellectual links with the World Council of Churches and the Vatican and was prominent in international Jewish-Christian dialogue.

He held various editorial positions, published hundreds of articles, and edited numerous books, including *Qumran and the History of the Biblical Text* (1975). His books include *King, Cult, and Calendar* (1986), *Gesellschaft und Literatur in der Hebräischen Bibel* (1988), and *The World of Qumran from Within* (1989). A Festschrift written in his honor, *Sha'arei Talmon*, appeared in 1990.

[Elaine Hoter]

TALMON, ZVI (1922–), *ḥazzan*, composer, conductor. Born in Jerusalem, Talmon obtained his basic cantorial education in the *Shirat Israel* choir there with Cantor Solomon Zalman *Rivlin. He studied at the Eẓ Ḥayyim yeshivah and at the Mizrachi teachers' seminar, both in Jerusalem. He learned composition and conducting at the Jerusalem Institute of Music and at the Academy of Music. He set to music scores of selections from the prayers, biblical passages, Hebrew songs and also arranged the music for the Yad Vashem memorial services for *Yom ha-Shoah* (Holocaust Remembrance Day). He led synagogue choirs, including that of the Hekhal Shelomo synagogue in Jerusalem. His melodies for Sabbath prayers appeared in the *Rinat ha-Heikhal* anthology published by the Cantors Assembly in America. These works are based on traditional chants for prayers and cantillations for Torah reading interwoven with original Israeli tunes. Among his publications are *La-Menaẓeiah Mizmor*, biblical songs, and *Mizmorei Shem ve-Yefet*, Israeli, Jewish, and Italian songs for choirs, and an additional volume of his works for the Sabbath and the Festivals. He has written linguistic studies on the Hebrew and Aramaic languages for which he received his academic degree. Talmon served as an instructor in cantorial music and texts of the prayers at the cantorial school affiliated to the Great Synagogue in Jerusalem.

[Akiva Zimmerman]

TALMUD (Heb. תַּלְמוּד). The word "Talmud" means primarily "study" or "learning" and is employed in various senses. One refers to the opinions and teachings which disciples acquire from their predecessors in order to expound and explain them (*Seder Tanna'im ve-Amora'im*; cf. Rashi to Suk. 28b; BM 32a–b, et al.). Another sense comprises the whole body of one's learning; e.g., "He from whom one has acquired the greater part of his Talmud is to be regarded as one's teacher" (BM 33a). A third meaning is in the technical phrase *talmud lomar*, which is used to indicate a teaching derived from the exegesis of a biblical text. A fourth meaning is the analytical aspect of the commandment of Torah study (cf. Maim., Yad, The Laws of Torah Study 1:11). The word "Talmud" is most commonly used, however, to denote the bodies of teaching consisting largely of the traditions and discussions of the *amoraim* organized around the text of the *Mishnah of R. *Judah ha-Nasi (see *Talmud, Babylonian, and *Talmud, Jerusalem).

In popular parlance two other phrases are used as alternative names for the Talmud. The first is **Shas*, an abbreviation consisting of the initial letters of *Shishah Sidrei* (Mishnah), i.e., the "Six Orders" (of the Mishnah) which serve as the literary foundation for the *talmudim*. The second is **Gemara* (for a full discussion see Albeck, *Mevo ha-Talmud* (1969), ch. 1).

[Eliezer Berkovits / Stephen G. Wald (2nd ed.)]

TALMUD, BABYLONIAN (Heb. תַּלְמוּד בַּבְלִי), a literary work of monumental proportions (5,894 folio pages in the standard printed editions), which draws upon the totality of the spiritual, intellectual, ethical, historical, and legal traditions produced in rabbinic circles from the time of the destruction of the Second Temple in the first century until the Muslim conquest at the beginning of the seventh century. The Babylonian Talmud (Bavli) is often described as being a commentary to the *Mishnah of Rabbi *Judah ha-Nasi, but the actual relationship between these two works is far more complex. The external form of the Bavli is indeed organized in the shape of a vast literary superstructure which rests on the firm foundation of the Mishnah (see *Mishnah, The Mishnah as a Literary Work) – or more precisely on four of the six orders of the Mishnah: *Mo'ed*, *Nashim*, *Nezikin*, and *Kodashim*, there being no Talmud Bavli to the first order of the Mishnah, *Zeraim* (with the exception of *Berakhot*), or to the sixth order of the Mishnah, *Tohorot* (with the exception of *Niddah*). Moreover, the long dialectical arguments called *sugyot*, which make up much of the literature of the Bavli, often take the text of the Mishnah as their starting point. On the other hand, the Bavli includes and discusses two additional bodies of rabbinic sources: (1) *baraitot* – tannaitic sources which were not incorporated in the Mishnah of Rabbi Judah ha-Nasi, deriving for the most part from the same tannaitic period as the sources of the Mishnah (1st–2nd centuries), and almost equal to them in authority (see **Baraita*); (2) the teachings of all the generations of the **amoraim* (3rd–5th centuries), both Babylonian and Palestinian. The Bavli cites and discusses these sources for their own sake, and not merely insofar as they enlighten some obscure point in the Mishnah. The inclusion of these different strata of authoritative religious sources in the Bavli, together with the anonymous and largely post-amoraic editorial literary level of the Bavli – the so called *setam ha-talmud* – make the Bavli into an autonomous and comprehensive work of *halakhah* and *aggadah* (see: Mishnah, *Halakhah* in the Mishnah, *Aggadah* in the Mishnah). In effect, the Bavli incorporates both of the fundamental levels of rabbinic tradition which are represented in the two similar works of talmudic literature which were redacted in Ereẓ Israel – the *Tosefta and the *Jerusalem Talmud (Yerushalmi) – and in so doing both comprehends and transcends these earlier works.

The Talmud Bavli represents the crowning literary achievement of this entire period of Jewish history – which is in fact often simply referred to as the "talmudic period." It was ultimately accepted as the uniquely authoritative canonical work of post-biblical Jewish religion (see: *Talmud, Jerusalem – Acceptance of the two Talmuds), providing the foundation for all subsequent developments in the fields of *halakhah* and *aggadah*, up to the time of the Shulḥan Arukh (16th century) and beyond. Despite manifest difficulties of language and content, the study of the Bavli has also achieved an unparalleled place in the popular religious culture of the Jewish people. It has served as the primary vehicle for the education of countless Jews over the centuries, professional scholars and laypeople alike. Recently it has even filled sports arenas both in the United States and in Israel with devotees, celebrating the conclusion of the 7-year cycle in which the study of the entire Bavli is regularly completed.

The Bavli as a Literary Work

The literary form which is most characteristic of the Bavli as it stands before us today is the *sugya*. The *sugya* is a kind of freewheeling dialectical argument, conducted in a dialect of Eastern Aramaic, in which various tannaitic and amoraic sources are brought and analyzed, and other similar sources are cited in order to prove some point which came up in the course of the discussion. The Aramaic language of the *sugya* is often long-winded and repetitive. It weaves its way in-between these various well defined literary sources, joining them together into an interconnected series of questions, objections, answers and justifications. The resulting literary structure is a continuous dialectical chain of reasoning in which the distinct literary components imbedded within it often lose their individual identities. The anonymous literary level of the Bavli – the *stam ha-talmud* – favors discursive language and even abstract conceptual formulations. The *sugya* often engages in far-reaching comparisons and analogies between issues and concepts drawn from widely disparate and often apparently unrelated areas of *halakhah*. As they stand, the *sugyot* of the Bavli represent the absolute antithesis of the Mishnah in virtually every respect. The *halakhot* and *aggadot* of the Mishnah are expressed in succinct and concrete language. They are arranged as a series of discrete statements, and organized neatly by topic into chapters and tractates. The *sugya* in its final form, on the other hand, is discursive and abstract, continuous and associative, jumping from topic to topic, as the flow of the argument dictates. As antithetical as these two literary forms may seem, the roots of the full-blown Babylonian *sugya* lie deep within earlier forms of rabbinic discourse, and the transition from the one to the other was in all likelihood a gradual one.

The *Sugya* as a Literary Construct

The *sugyot* of the Bavli are often described as records of discussions and debates between the *amoraim* which took place in the Babylonian and Palestinian rabbinic academies during the talmudic period. This description is, however, not entirely accurate. The many extended halakhic and aggadic *sugyot* which fill the Bavli are not transcriptions or protocols of amoraic debates as they actually occurred in the Babylonian or Palestinian academies. Rather, they are carefully crafted literary creations, idealized reconstructions of these debates as remembered, redacted, and reformulated in the process of integrating them into the official curriculum of one or many of the amoraic and post-amoraic academies, both in Babylonia and in Ereẓ Israel. Moreover, the almost universally dialectical character of the Babylonian *sugya*, as described above, is often a literary façade, superimposed by later secondary redactors upon earlier quite different forms of talmudic discourse, which did not always possess a dialectical character. In order to understand this phenomenon more fully it is necessary to distinguish between several distinct literary levels which are found in the talmudic *sugya*, which probably also represent distinct historical stages in the evolution of the literature of the Babylonian Talmud.

The Elements of the *Sugya* (1): Tannaitic Sources

The most fundamental building blocks of Babylonian talmudic literature are the extra-mishnaic tannaitic sources – the *baraitot* – which may be associated in one way or another with some particular *mishnah*. That *baraitot* were already collected and arranged in the order of the Mishnah at a very early period – as a sort of proto-Talmud to the Mishnah of Rabbi Judah ha-Nasi – is clearly demonstrated by the example of the Tosefta. Like the Tosefta, the *baraitot* of the Bavli can relate to text of the Mishnah in a number of different ways. In the Bavli a given *baraita* may be literarily dependent on the *mishnah* with which it is associated, presupposing the specific language of the *mishnah* and expanding or commenting upon it. Alternatively, it may represent an independent but parallel tradition, addressing or formulating the *halakhah* of the *mishnah* in a different language, or reporting alternative or even contradictory opinions on the same halakhic or aggadic issue. It can even contain an earlier and more original version of the very same tradition which has been included in the Mishnah in an abbreviated or revised form (Friedman, *Tosefta Atiqta*). Unlike the Tosefta, *baraitot* in the Bavli regularly transmit **midrashei halakhah*, which derive the *halakhah* of the *mishnah* (or an alternative but related *halakhah*) from the text of the Torah by means of one of the traditional hermeneutical rules. Again like the Tosefta, a *baraita* in the Bavli need not relate directly to the specific halakhic or aggadic content of the *mishnah* at all, but rather may transmit some other tannaitic tradition, which may be intimately related to the issue discussed in the *mishnah*, or alternatively loosely connected to this particular *mishnah* in an associative fashion.

Taken by themselves, the *baraitot* of the Babylonian Talmud are not arranged in a question and answer format, and do not constitute a *sugya*. This is not to say that individual tannaitic sources do not possess any explicit dialectical character. In fact *mishnayot* and *baraitot* sometimes report brief or extended discussions and debates between the *tannaim*, in which objections to particular positions are raised and justifications are offered in their defense. *Midrashei halakhah*, especially those which parallel the *midrashim* of the *Sifra, often contain extended dialectical analyses of both actual and hypothetical halakhic positions. A group of *baraitot* may build one upon the other, representing an extended examination of a single unified issue or set of issues.

All of these phenomena anticipate different aspects of the talmudic *sugya*. Nevertheless, the familiar technical terms which serve to define the role of a *baraita* within the talmudic *sugya* – e.g., *hatanya* (= objection), *detanya* (= proof), etc. – all belong to the amoraic and post-amoraic editorial framework of the talmudic text. Taken by themselves, the *baraitot* which are imbedded within a particular talmudic *sugya* have no more dialectical structure than the parallel group of *baraitot* included in the Tosefta. For the historical relation between the *baraitot* of the Bavli and the Tosefta, see below.

The Elements of the *Sugya* (2): Amoraic Sources

The second major family of constitutive elements which make up the talmudic *sugya* is composed of those sources which report the teachings of the post-tannaitic *Amoraim*. These teachings are transmitted in the Bavli in a number of different literary forms, each of which represents an outgrowth of elements which already existed within tannaitic literature. We can group these literary forms under four headings: (1) *memrot* – the direct statements of the *amoraim* in *halakhah* and *aggadah*; (2) *ba'yot* – formal questions posed in the amoraic academies; (3) *'uvdot* – stories or precedents which report (in the third person, and usually in Aramaic) the actions or decisions of the *amoraim*; (4) amoraic *sugyot* – brief debates between the *amoraim*.

The first literary category – the *memrot* of the *amoraim* – shows the highest degree of continuity with the earlier tannaitic halakhic and aggadic literature. These *memrot* are relatively succinct, discrete statements, usually expressed in a characteristic dialect of mishnaic Hebrew. In many cases these *memrot* are virtually indistinguishable in form and content from similar tannaitic statements included in the Tosefta and in the talmudic *baraitot*. In fact we often find a statement transmitted in the Yerushalmi as a *memra*, while in the Bavli the same statement appears as a *baraita*. Alternatively we find tannaitic statements which are included in the Tosefta, but which are cited in the Bavli as amoraic *memrot*. (For these and similar phenomena see **Baraita*, The *Baraita* as a Literary Source within the Talmudic Sugya; *Baraitot* and *Memrot*.) Like talmudic *baraitot*, *memrot* also can be categorized as either directly dependent on an earlier (usually tannaitic) literary source, or as independent *memrot*, which introduce new halakhic or aggadic topics.

The second literary category – the amoraic *ba'ya* – is rooted in the logical structure of the tannaitic *halakhah* it-

Orders and Tractates of the Mishnah and Talmud

		Mishnah	Babylonian Talmud[1]		Jerusalem Talmud[2]	
		No. of Chapters	No. of Folios	Folios Munich Ed.	No. of Folios	Subject matter
ORDER ZERA'IM	Berakhot	9	64	19	14	Benedictions
	Pe'ah	8	–	3	7	Gleanings (Lev. 19:9–10)
	Demai	7	–	3	6	Doubtfully tithed produce
	Kilayim	9	–	4	7	Diverse kinds (Deut. 22:9–11)
	Shevi'it	10	–	4	7	The Sabbatical Year (Ex. 23:10–11)
	Terumot	11	–	4	9	Heave offering (Lev. 22:10–14)
	Ma'aserot	5	–	2	5	Tithes (Num. 18:21)
	Ma'aser Sheni	5	–	3	5	Second tithe (Deut. 14:22ff.)
	Ḥallah	4	–	2	4	Dough offering (Num. 15:17–21)
	Orlah	3	–	2	4	The fruit of young trees (Lev. 19:23–25)
	Bikkurim	3	–	3	3	First fruits (Lev. 26:1–11)
ORDER MO'ED	Shabbat	24	157	28	18	The Sabbath
	Eruvin	10	105	17	9	The fusion of Sabbath limits
	Pesaḥim	10	121	18	11	Passover
	Shekalim	8	–	6	7	The Shekel dues (Ex. 30:11–16)
	Yoma	8	88	16	8	The Day of Atonement
	Sukkah	5	56	9	5	The Feast of Tabernacles
	Beẓah	5	40	11	5	Festival laws
	Rosh ha-Shanah	4	35	7	4	Various new years, particularly Rosh Ha-Shanah
	Ta'anit	4	31	8	7	Fast days
	Megilah	4	32	9	7	Purim
	Mo'ed Katan	3	29	7	4	The intermediate days of festivals
	Ḥagigah	3	27	6	5	The festival offering (Deut. 16:16–17)
ORDER NASHIM	Yevamot	16	122	24	16	Levirate marriage (Deut. 25:5–10)
	Ketubbot	13	112	20	12	Marriage contracts
	Nedarim	11	91	10	7	Vows (Num. 30)
	Nazir	9	66	8	8	The Nazirite (Num. 6)
	Sotah	9	49	11	9	The suspected adulteress (Num. 5:11 ff.)
	Gittin	9	90	16	7	Divorce
	Kiddushin	4	82	14	9	Marriage
ORDER NEZIKIN	Bava Kamma	10	119	22	7	Torts
	Bava Meẓia	10	119	20	6	Civil law
	Bava Batra	10	176	21	6	Property law
	Sanhedrin	11	113	24	14	Judges
	Makkot	3	24	5	3	Flagellation (Deut. 25:2)
	Shevu'ot	8	49	9	7	Oaths
	Eduyyot	8	–	4	–	Traditional testimonies
	Avodah Zarah	5	76	13	7	Idolatry
	Avot[3]	5	–	2	–	Ethical maxims
	Horayot	3	14	4	4	Erroneous ruling of the court (Lev. 4:22 ff.)

		Mishnah	Babylonian Talmud[1]		Jerusalem Talmud[2]	
		No. of Chapters	No. of Folios	Folios Munich Ed.	No. of Folios	Subject matter
ORDER KODASHIM	Zevaḥim	14	120	21	–	Animal offerings
	Menaḥot	13	110	21	–	Meal offering
	Hullin	12	142	25	–	Animals slaughtered for food
	Behorot	9	61	13	–	Firstlings (Deut. 15:19 ff.)
	Arakhin	9	34	9	–	Vows of valuation (Lev. 27:1–8)
	Temurah	7	39	8	–	The substituted offering (Lev. 27:10)
	Keritot	6	28	9	–	Extripation (Lev. 18:29)
	Me'ilah	6	22	4	–	Sacrileges (Lev. 5:15–16)
	Tamid[3]	7	9	4	–	The daily sacrifice (Num. 28:3–4)
	Middot[3]	5	–	3	–	Measurements of the Temple
	Kinnim[3]	3	–	2	–	The Bird offering (Lev. 5:7 ff.)
ORDER TOHOROT	Kelim[3]	30	–	11	–	Uncleanness of articles
	Oholot (Ahilot)	18	–	7	–	Uncleanness through overshadowing (No. 19:14–15)
	Nega'im	14	–	7	–	Leprosy (Lev. 13, 14)
	Parah	12	–	5	–	The Red Heifer (Num. 19)
	Tohorot	10	–	5	–	Ritual cleanness
	Mikva'ot	10	–	5	–	Ritual ablution
	Niddah	10	73	14	4	The menstruant
	Makhshirin	6	–	3	–	Liquid that predisposes food to become ritually unclean (Lev. 11:37–38)
	Zavim	5	–	2	–	Fluxes (Lev. 15)
	Tevul Yom	4	–	2	–	Ritual uncleanness between immersion and sunset (Lev. 22:6–7)
	Yadayim	4	–	3	–	The ritual uncleanness of the hands
	Ukẓin[4]	3	–	2	–	"Stalks"; parts of plants susceptible to uncleanness

1 The number given is the last page number. The pagination, however, always begins with page 2; one page should therefore be deducted.
2 The number of pages is given in accordance with the Krotoschin edition.
3 There is Tosefta to all the tractates with the exception of *Avot, Tamid, Middot, Kinnim, Kelim.* In the Tosefta, *Kelim* is divided into three sections, respectively called *Bava Kamma, Bava Meẓia* and *Bava Batra.*
4 As will be seen, the tractates are generally arranged in the orders according to the descending numbers of chapters. For departures from this rule see the articles on the individual tractates concerned.

self. Tannaitic *halakhot*, while formulated in terms of specific and concrete cases, almost always involve an implicit judgment concerning some conceptual distinction which underlies its specific rulings (see: Mishnah, The Structure of Tannaitic *Halakhah*). During the amoraic period, the analysis of these tannaitic *halakhot* was often expressed in the form of explicit questions – *ba'yot* – which examine the way in which these conceptual distinctions would apply in closely related but nevertheless slightly different cases. In its simplest form the *ba'ya* merely states the new case to be considered and posits the bare question: *mahu?* – i.e. what should the ruling be in such a case? In a slightly more developed format, the *iba'ya lehu* also explicitly states the different alternative rulings which could apply to this case. In the most developed and elaborate form it also examines in detail the alternative conceptual principles which could be used to decide the issue in one direction or another. These *iba'ya lehu* passages can be quite lengthy, representing highly ramified conceptual analyses of entire areas of *halakhah* (e.g., Ket. 5b–6a). At the same time they almost always remain within the concrete framework of specific cases and rulings, and rarely engage in abstract generalization. Despite the intimate interconnection between the three elements of the talmudic *iba'ya lehu* – (1) the question itself; (2) the statement of alternative possible answers; (3) the reasoning involved in adjudicating the question – only the first element, usually formulated in mishnaic Hebrew, should be counted among the amoraic sources of the Bavli. The second and third levels, which are almost always expressed in Aramaic, probably belong to the anonymous literary level of the Bavli, the *stam ha-talmud* (see below).

The third literary category, the *'uvda*, is in many ways parallel to the tannaitic *ma'aseh* – a story which serves as a legal precedent, either supporting or contradicting a formal halakhic statement quoted earlier. This phenomenon is more highly developed in the Bavli, which often brings an individual *'uvda*, or a series of *'uvdot* – almost always in Aramaic – in order to examine how the abstract halakhic content of a *memra* or *baraita* can be translated into practical terms in the context of specific cases (e.g., Pes. 49a). Since the black and white distinctions of the formal *halakhah* often must give way to a variety of shades of gray (or other brighter colors) when applied in practice, these *'uvdot* often break out of the limited framework of halakhic precedents, growing and expanding into a full-blown aggadic exposition of the ethical and spiritual principles which underlie the *halakhah* (e.g., Ket. 61b–63a, and see: Mishnah, *Aggadah* in the Mishnah).

The fourth literary category – the amoraic *sugya* – also has clear precedents in tannaitic sources. The Mishnah and Tosefta transmit scores of brief formal debates, usually presented as face-to-face discussions between the parties to a dispute which was presented earlier. In these debates, one side attempts to convince the other of the correctness of its opinion, either by force of reason, or by relying upon some accepted and authoritative *halakhah*. After each side has taken its turn in the debate, one side may concede defeat, in whole or in part, or the two sides may remain unconvinced and continue to maintain their respective positions. Starting from the 2nd–3rd generations of *amoraim*, this "*memra* plus debate" format becomes an increasingly prominent form of amoraic literature. After citing a *memra*, which either reports a halakhic dispute between two *amoraim*, or the opinion of an individual *amora* which is then attacked by a colleague, the Bavli will often analyze the dispute by means of a formal debate presented as a face-to-face discussion between the disputing parties. Each side brings proofs for its own positions and objections against the opposing side, defends itself and responds with counterattacks. Unlike their tannaitic counterparts, the *amoraim* had at their disposal an almost unlimited body of authoritative sources which could be exploited in order to attack the positions of their opponents – the entire corpus of *mishnayot* and *baraitot*. According to the accepted canons of talmudic jurisprudence, *amoraim* may not in principle disagree with *mishnayot* and *baraitot*. This formal legal principle no doubt encouraged the *amoraim* to search far and wide for any tannaitic source which could serve – either directly, or indirectly by analogy – to support their own positions or to refute the positions of their opponents. In this way the amoraic *sugya* introduces a second set of tannaitic sources (both *mishnayot* and *baraitot*) into the discussion of a given *mishnah* which were not originally associated with it in the pre-amoraic tannaitic stratum of the Talmud. Whether these debates actually took place in fact, or are themselves literary constructs of the amoraic academies, this kind of discussion provided the impetus for a more abstract form of conceptual analysis – one which looks for common principles of law underlying radically different spheres of *halakhah*.

Despite the importance of the *sugya* for the later development of talmudic literature as a whole, it must be emphasized that at this stage the amoraic *sugya* is still relatively limited in length, and it is only one among a number of different forms of literary sources which are found in the amoraic stratum of the Bavli. Individual *memrot*, or groups of *memrot* organized by topic, standing either by themselves or attached to *mishnayot* or *baraitot*; collections of *memrot* associated with the name of a particular *amora*, often appearing in groups of three, seven, or even ten; *'uvdot* and *ba'yot* – all these literary forms continue to exist *beside* the amoraic *sugya*, not as part of it.

The Framework of the *Sugya*: Stam ha-Talmud

These tannaitic and amoraic literary sources are the building blocks out of which the literature of the Talmud is constructed. No less important, however, to an understanding of the Talmud is an appreciation of the highly creative and pervasive activity of the generations of redactors who combined these elements into more and more complex, lengthy, and continuous dialectical literary structures. As noted above, an amoraic *memra* may often contain an interpretation of a tannaitic source, to which it is immediately appended. The anonymous talmudic editor (*stam ha-talmud*) will interpose a question (in Aramaic) between the *memra* and the tannaitic source (both in Hebrew). This practice serves to highlight a problem in the text of the tannaitic source which may have prompted the amoraic comment. It also turns a non-dialectic structure (text plus comment) into an explicitly dialectical one (question plus answer). Sometimes it affords the *stam ha-talmud* an opportunity to redefine the issue of the *sugya* in line with an agenda which may not have been shared by the amora who authored the original *memra* (cf. Wald, Pesaḥim III, 215–221). The *stam ha-talmud* also introduces editorial comments and technical terms which explicitly define the function of individual sources within the *sugya* (e.g., as questions, objections, proofs, or additional supports), thus creating a continuous line of discussion out of what were originally discrete and unconnected *baraitot, memrot, ba'yot, 'uvdot*, etc.

The *stam ha-talmud* augments the relatively brief amoraic *sugyot* by appending additional objections, justifications, counter-objections, etc. to the original discussion. These additions may not be ascribed directly to the original amoraic disputants, but rather obliquely (e.g., "R. Johanan could have said in response" etc.) or anonymously ("they objected" etc.). Another common way in which the *stam ha-talmud* augments a *sugya* is by transferring existing blocks of talmudic dialogue – either amoraic or "stammaitic" – from place to place in a given chapter, tractate, or even from tractate to tractate (e.g., Wald, Shabbat VII, *sugyot* 3, 7, 10). Certain textual difficulties (*kushiyot*) are often caused as a by-product of the moving of entire passages from place to place, since the language of a passage may be in certain respects context-specific, being more appropriate in the original context, and less appropriate in the new context into which it was introduced secondarily. Other techniques characteristic of the *stam ha-talmud* include the addition of editorial links between a number of originally distinct *sugyot*, thus transforming them into a "super-*sugya*" (Friedman, BM VI, Text, 101–159), or alternatively combining a number of distinct amoraic *sugyot*, which originally dealt with a family of related halakhic issues, thus giving the impression of a single extended amoraic debate on a unified topic (Wald, Pesaḥim III, 137–168).

One of the most prominent tendencies of the *stam ha-talmud* is to employ isolated technical terms – e.g., *gererah* (Shabbat 70b–71b), *ho'il* (Pes. 46a–48a) – as explanations for the concrete *halakhot* of the tannaim and the amoraim. These terms – which have little meaning on their own (*gererah* = dragging; *ho'il* = since) – serve as names for abstract principles which tend to replace the more concrete and implicit form of case-oriented conceptualization characteristic of the earlier *halakhah* (see: Mishnah, The Structure of Tannaitic *Halakhah*). This striking intellectual trend of the *stam ha-talmud* has been singled out for extensive analysis, both for its own sake, and as a possible historical precedent for much of the later brilliant intellectual achievements of post-talmudic halakhic scholarship (Moscovitz). All the same, it should be noted that this use of isolated abstract phrases by the *stam ha-talmud* can also lead to the extension of specific halakhic notions beyond the concrete contexts in which they were originally formulated and originally made sense. In this way the *stam ha-talmud* sometimes introduces conceptual problems into the halakhic framework of the talmudic discussion (Wald, Pesaḥim III, 168–72).

The Place of the Bavli in Rabbinic Literature

An examination of the Bavli reveals that it contains at least two distinct strata of defined literary sources – tannaitic and amoraic – as well clear evidence of multiple layers of redactional activity. This literary analysis, important in its own right, also has important consequences for our understanding of the place of the Bavli in the history of rabbinic literature as a whole. Prior comparisons of the Bavli to the other extant works of ancient talmudic literature, especially the Yerushalmi, have tended to emphasize the striking differences between them, concentrating on the dialectical, discursive and conceptual character of the Bavli, as opposed to the more discrete, concise, concrete, and reserved character of these parallel talmudic texts. Once it is made clear that most of these dialectical, discursive, and conceptual elements belong primarily to the latest literary stratum of the Bavli – the *stam ha-talmud* – it becomes essential to reexamine the historical relationship between the earlier literary strata of the Bavli and these parallel works of Palestinian rabbinic literature.

THE BAVLI AND THE EXTANT TANNAITIC WORKS. It has often been noted (see above) that the *baraitot* of the Bavli bear a striking resemblance to the parallel sources found in the ancient tannaitic collections – the Tosefta and the *Midrashei Halakhah*. On the other hand, there are also significant differences between the language and content of the talmudic *baraitot* and the parallel texts found in our tannaitic collections. The question has naturally arisen whether these extant tannaitic collections served as the sources for the *baraitot* of the Babylonian Talmud, or whether the Bavli used other collections of tannaitic sources otherwise unknown to us. Scholars have offered very different answers to this question, and their disagreement is ultimately rooted in a single issue: whether later talmudic scholars intentionally modified the original text of ancient tannaitic sources. Some scholars have rejected this notion out of hand, and seem to view its rejection almost as an article of faith (see: Mishnah, The Redaction of the Mishnah). Others scholars have brought considerable evidence in support of this notion.

Those who assert that later sages did not allow themselves to interfere in any way with the internal composition of their authoritative tannaitic sources explain the differences between the talmudic *baraitot* and the parallel tannaitic texts by positing that the Bavli drew upon alternative collections of *baraitot* – both *halakhot* and midrashim – which are not to be identified with the extant collections which we possess today. A corollary of this position drawn by many of these scholars is that the extant tannaitic collections – the Tosefta and the extant *Midrashei Halakhah* – were unknown to the redactors of the Bavli. This view asserts, in effect, that our extant collections of tannaitic literature, which were apparently all copied and studied in the geonic Babylonian academies during the period following the final redaction of the Babylonian Talmud, were for some reason unavailable to these same Babylonian redactors. At the same time it asserts that the alternative collections of tannaitic *halakhah* which were actually used (according to this theory) to the very end in the talmudic Babylonian academies were all, for some equally unexplained reason, totally lost, leaving no tangible trace behind among the Babylonian *geonim* who immediately succeeded the final redactors of the Bavli.

The alternative position holds that the final versions of the *baraitot* in the Bavli are the end-product of a long process of study and interpretation, emendation, and reformulation, evidence for which can usually be found within talmudic literature itself. As a result, the scholars who hold this position find no compelling reason to posit the wholesale existence of entire collections of ancient tannaitic sources which have not survived in our hands today. Rather they consider that the extant collections, or other very closely related versions of the same, are the actual sources for the *baraitot* of the Bavli, and that the explanation of the differences between the existing versions of a given tradition is more likely to depend on an analysis of the history of talmudic *halakhah* and *aggadah*, rather than on the chance rediscovery of some hypothetical long-lost work.

One cannot overestimate the depth of this scholarly dispute. The first approach leads to a profoundly pessimistic attitude toward the entire history of talmudic literature. According to this view the vast majority of the ancient tannaitic sources which once existed, and which were actually studied in the academies of the *amoraim*, are almost certainly irretrievably lost. It also leads to a highly skeptical attitude toward higher critical talmudic methodology, since this methodology involves a comparison of the tannaitic traditions preserved in amoraic works with the supposedly more original parallel traditions preserved in the ancient tannaitic collections, in order to understand the ways in which the *amoraim* interpreted and reworked their sources. Since, according to this first view, the tannaitic collections which we possess today were not in fact used by the *amoraim*, they are quite useless in this regard. In any case this view is convinced that the *amoraim* never actually reworked or reformulated any of their ancient and authoritative sources.

According to the second view, the overwhelming majority of the tannaitic sources which were redacted by the central rabbinic yeshivot at the end of the tannaitic period are still in our possession and have been preserved more or less in their original tannaitic form. Moreover these extant collections provide fairly reliable evidence for the form and content of authoritative tannaitic sources which were studied in the amoraic academies. Against this background, it then becomes possible to identify and to analyze the later amoraic and post-amoraic developments of each tradition, as documented in the Yerushalmi (Jerusalem Talmud) and the Bavli.

Finally, it should be noted that the collections of *baraitot* which are embedded in a given *sugya* in the Bavli frequently closely resemble – in number, in order, in form, and in content – the parallel groups of *baraitot* associated with the same *mishnah* in the Tosefta (e.g., Wald, Pesaḥim III, 97–99). This phenomenon gives further credence to the historical hypothesis that at the root of the *sugyot* of the Bavli lies a tannaitic literary stratum which is intimately connected to the tannaitic traditions preserved in our Tosefta. For an authoritative and exhaustive treatment of this issue, see: Friedman, Baraitot; *Tosefta Atiqta*.

THE BAVLI AND THE YERUSHALMI. It has also long been noted that there is a considerable overlap between the amoraic traditions preserved in the Talmud Bavli and those preserved in the Talmud Yerushalmi. These parallel traditions were pointed out for every page of the Bavli by R. Aryeh Leib Yellin in his commentary, *Yefeh Enayim*, which is printed in the Romm edition of the Bavli (see below). When, however, the tannaitic and amoraic literary strata of the Bavli are isolated from the anonymous literary level of the *stam ha-talmud*, this striking and fundamental similarity between the Bavli and the Yerushalmi becomes even more pronounced (Friedman, Yevamot X, 283–321). Detailed analyses of extended portions of the Bavli have revealed that at the root of virtually every *sugya* of the Bavli lies some earlier, more primitive amoraic *sugya* which is documented somewhere in the Yerushalmi (see: Wald, Pesaḥim III). Sometimes this literary dependence extends to an entire chapter, where *sugya* after *sugya* in the Bavli is built on the foundation of an identical series of earlier and simpler parallel *sugyot* found in the same chapter in the Yerushalmi (see: Wald, Shabbat VII). These earlier and simpler *sugyot*, however, do not consist of the *memrot* and discussions of Palestinian *amoraim* only, but rather as often as not include alternative versions of the *memrot* and discussions of early Babylonian *amoraim* as well. The relation between these two Talmuds is not, therefore, one of a later Babylonian tradition building on an earlier Palestinian tradition. Rather, the Yerushalmi regularly provides clear evidence for the earlier and more primitive state of a *common Babylonian-Palestinian talmudic tradition* shared by both of these major centers of rabbinic culture – one which preceded the pervasive additions and revisions of the anonymous redactors of the Bavli.

Moreover, the Yerushalmi itself preserves an even earlier redactional level of this shared talmudic tradition – in the three tractates (BK, BM, BB) commonly referred to as Yerushalmi *Nezikin* (see: *Talmud, Jerusalem – Yerushalmi *Nezikin*). Yerushalmi *Nezikin* not only is free of the discursive and conceptual discussions characteristic of the *stam ha-talmud* in the Bavli; it also lacks much of the extended amoraic *sugya* structure common to both the Bavli and the rest of the Yerushalmi. Instead Yerushalmi *Nezikin* consists mostly of *baraitot*, *memrot*, and other brief amoraic literary sources. Formerly, the explanation of the difference between Yerushalmi *Nezikin* and the rest of the Yerushalmi was sought in a different *place* of redaction. More recently, it has been sought in a different *time* of redaction – reflecting an earlier stage in the development of the shared talmudic tradition, prior to the combination of the isolated amoraic sources (see above) into larger, more involved and elaborate *sugya* structures. At the same time, even the radically different redactional form of Yerushalmi *Nezikin* cannot obscure the common elements of tradition which it shares with the fully elaborated parallel versions of the Bavli (Sussmann).

The relationship between the parallel traditions held in common by both the Bavli and the Yerushalmi is somewhat more complex than that which holds between the *baraitot* in the Bavli and in the Tosefta. On the one hand, the literary evolution of the Bavli and that of the Yerushalmi overlap to a very large extent. So it is to be expected that the Bavli preserved versions of amoraic traditions that are not found in the Yerushalmi as it stands today. On the other hand, later Babylonian *amoraim* (and anonymous redactors) are unlikely to have treated the words of their amoraic predecessors with the same respect that they accorded to ancient tannaitic traditions, and so are more likely to have revised and reformulated them. Therefore, while the Yerushalmi's version of a shared tradition is usually more original than the parallel version found in the Bavli – and so can be used to reconstruct the internal development of amoraic talmudic tradition – this is by no means a hard and fast rule. The Bavli sometimes preserves the more ancient and original version of an amoraic tradition, or of a *sugya*, while the version in the Yerushalmi reflects later developments of the tradition, which were not incorporated into the Bavli.

THE FOUR STAGES OF TALMUDIC TRADITION. Beneath the discursive and conceptual surface structure of the *stam ha-talmud*, one can distinguish three cumulative literary levels within the text of the Bavli: (1) the *baraitot*; (2) the *baraitot* plus the isolated amoraic sources; (3) the *baraitot*, the amoraic sources, plus the expansion and combination of these elements into more or less continuous *sugyot*. To these three literary levels correspond three earlier bodies of talmudic tradition. To the first level in the Bavli, consisting of *baraitot* alone, correspond (more or less) the extant collections of tannaitic sources – Tosefta and the *Midrashei Halakhah*. To the second level, consisting of *baraitot* plus the isolated amoraic sources, corresponds (more or less) the redactional level represented by Yerushalmi *Nezkin*. To the third level of the Bavli, consisting of *baraitot*, the amoraic sources, plus the expansion and combination of these elements into more or less continuous *sugyot* – without extensive additions and explanations by the anonymous redactor – corresponds (more or less) the redactional level represented by the rest of the Yerushalmi. The fourth and final stage in the development of the Bavli is, of course, represented by the editorial and literary activity of the anonymous redactors of the Bavli in its final form – the *stam ha-talmud*.

However one wishes to explain the differences between these three earlier redactional levels and the parallel bodies of tradition, the most striking feature is the surprising degree of uniformity between them. The overall impression made by the Tosefta, the Yerushalmi, and the Bavli is one of successive stages in the literary development of a single common talmudic tradition, rather than independent and distinct traditions. This impression of relative uniformity stands in sharp contrast to the radical multiplicity of master-disciple circles and competing academic centers which are described in the talmudic texts themselves, and testifies to a large degree of centralization in the preservation and distribution of the talmudic traditions which were produced by the many different personalities and centers described in the sources.

The Textual Transmission of the Bavli

Unlike the Tosefta and the Yerushalmi, which during most of the Middle Ages were studied only by professional scholars, the Bavli was widely studied by countless Jews throughout the centuries. It is therefore not surprising to find that the text of the Bavli is preserved in scores of medieval manuscripts, whereas the medieval manuscripts of the Tosefta and the Yerushalmi taken together can almost be counted on the fingers of a single hand. Aside from the relatively large number of extant manuscripts in which the Bavli is preserved (many of which include a single tractate, some more than one, and only one manuscript – Munich 95 – the entire Bavli), the text of the Bavli is characterized by the large number of significant variant readings which are preserved in these manuscripts.

For years it was tacitly assumed – apparently under the influence of European classical scholarship – that these variant readings were caused by the errors of ignorant or careless scribes, and that they entered into the textual tradition of the Bavli during the process of copying and distributing the Talmud, especially in medieval Europe. While no manuscript of the Bavli is free from scribal errors, the phenomenon of progressive accumulation of shared scribal errors (so important in the methodology of classical philology) is almost totally absent in manuscripts of the Bavli. Unlike their gentile counterparts, the scribes who copied the Bavli seem to have been familiar with both the language and the content of the Bavli. This situation gave rise to certain very striking and unexpected forms of "scribal errors," such as copying (part of) a sentence which occurs in another tractate from memory, in place of the similar sentence which actually stood before the scribe in the text from which he was copying. Alternatively we find the annoying scribal practice of "serial abbreviations" which the scribe assumes that the reader will easily be able to decipher on the basis of his familiarity with the terminology and content of the Talmud. In any case, simple scribal errors, which usually yield a corrupt and unintelligible text, are regularly corrected (more or less successfully) by attentive scribes, and rarely are they passed on to the next generation of talmudic copies. Today these isolated scribal errors can easily be identified by means of a simple comparison to other manuscript traditions.

Far more important for an understanding of the Bavli is another totally different category of variant readings, one which does not reflect isolated errors in the transmission of a fixed and final text, but rather fundamentally divergent versions, i.e., different parallel formulations of extended passages within the text as a whole. The first scholar who addressed this issue seriously was E.S. Rosenthal, who correctly concluded that the text of the Bavli must have retained a certain element of fluidity well into the 6th–7th centuries (and perhaps even beyond), in order to explain the presence of such divergent readings in the medieval manuscripts of the Bavli. One of the most striking features of these extended "alternative versions" is that they often reflect the same or similar content, expressed in significantly different language. They seem to reflect an attitude of relative freedom and independence toward the talmudic text, one which allows itself to rephrase or reformulate the language of the tradition. These important and extensive textual variants therefore in all likelihood derive from a relatively early period in the history of the transmission of the Talmud, before the exact wording of the Talmud became sanctified in the eyes of the scholars and the students. It is therefore also highly likely that these variants do not derive from careless scribes who operated on the periphery of the talmudic world, but rather represent authentic alternative traditions which were originally propagated at the very center of talmudic authority – the Babylonian yeshivot themselves. This suggestion has been confirmed somewhat by the surprising discovery that "eastern" (Yemenite) manuscripts and *ge-*

onic traditions, rather than representing the earlier and more original talmudic texts, often reflect the latest and most "up to date" traditions, while isolated medieval manuscripts from the periphery of the talmudic world, in Spain or France, often preserve the more original and "unrevised" talmudic textual tradition (Wald, Pesaḥim III, 319, 336–46).

Rosenthal held that these extended alternative textual variants must have derived from an early period, before the text of the Bavli was formulated in exact language, and almost certainly while its transmission was still oral – and not by the medium of fixed written documents. However, Shamma Friedman's comprehensive studies in this field have shown conclusively that even these extended alternative textual variants are universally limited in extent – they are always localized modifications which have been introduced at a specific point into an otherwise fully formed and stable textual tradition. Since these changes in all likelihood represent a conscious process of intentional editorial revision of a fixed text, the much bandied question of "oral" vs. "written" tradition in the transmission of talmudic literature is relatively insignificant in explaining this phenomenon. (For an examination of the broader cultural significance of the tension between written and oral transmission of rabbinic texts, see: Friedman, Printing the Talmud.)

The systematic recording of the variant readings of the Babylonian Talmud began in the 19th century, with the *Diqduqei Soferim* of R. Rabbinovicz, continued in the second half of the 20th century with the ongoing *Diqduqei Soferim Hashalem* of the Institute for the Complete Israeli Talmud (Yad Harav Herzog), and has culminated today in the complete computerized databank of all extant manuscripts and early editions of the Babylonian Talmud, produced and regularly updated by the Saul Lieberman Institute of Talmudic Research of the Jewish Theological Seminary of America. Facsimile editions of many talmudic manuscripts, which are still of value in confirming the transcriptions in these various works, are available, as are digital images of many manuscripts, on the web-site of the Jewish National and University Library in Jerusalem.

The Redaction of the Bavli

The Bavli states, in its characteristically laconic style (BM 86a): "R. Nathan and R. Judah ha-Nasi are the end of Mishnah; Rav Ashi and Ravina are the end of instruction (הוראה)." Whatever the exact meaning of this rather obscure statement may be, the parallelism between its two halves has led various scholars to ascribe to Rav Ashi and Ravina a role in redacting the Bavli analogous to the role which R. Judah ha-Nasi played in the redaction of the Mishnah. From the preceding discussions it should be clear, however, that there is very little basis for this analogy – for the simple reason that the Bavli never was subjected to a single authoritative, comprehensive, and decisive revision comparable to R. Judah ha-Nasi's redaction of the Mishnah. As noted above, the tannaitic and most of the amoraic literary strata of the Bavli had probably already been formulated to a large degree and accepted as authoritative by many yeshivot in Bavel and Ereẓ Israel long before the time of Rav Ashi. Similarly, many *amoraim* are mentioned in the Bavli whose activity must have extended into the period after Rav Ashi. Moreover, most of the literary activity of the *stam ha-talmud ha-bavli* took place in all likelihood long after Rav Ashi's time. To this we must add the evidence mentioned above which indicates that extensive editorial revision of the text of the Talmud was still going on into the 6th–7th centuries at least. In line with all this evidence we must understand the literary formation of the Babylonian talmudic tradition as an ongoing process which took place over many centuries and in many yeshivot, both prior to and subsequent to the time of Rav Ashi. As such, the impact of any individual scholar – even one of the stature of Rav Ashi – on this process as a whole should not be seen as amounting to a "redaction" of the Bavli in the sense in which we ascribe this term to R. Judah ha-Nasi and his Mishnah.

The *Aggadah* of the Bavli

It has been observed that most of the aggadic material in the Babylonian Talmud is predominantly of Palestinian origin. The contribution of the Bavli in the field of *aggadah* consists largely of the extensive reworking of these earlier Palestinian aggadic themes, often achieving new levels of imagination and originality, which are frequently striking, engaging, and earthy. Sometimes a "mere" linguistic clarification can be the occasion for developing and elaborating a fragmentary tradition in new and unexpected directions (see: Friedman, BT Bava Meẓi'a VI, Commentary, 148). In the area of rabbinic cosmology, the Bavli constructs, out of fragmentary traditions preserved in earlier Palestinian sources, a continuous description of the world order, starting from the lowest levels underlying the earth, proceeding through the seven celestial spheres, and culminating with the highest heaven and the Throne of Glory, including a description of the various populations which inhabit each sphere, and the activities with which they occupy themselves (Ḥag. 12a–b). In the area of historical *aggadah*, the Bavli takes the earlier and rather brief traditions concerning a dispute between R. *Eliezer ben Hyrcanus and the sages over a matter of ritual purity, combines them with the merest suggestion that the sages once considered excommunicating R. Eliezer (TJ MK 3:1, 81c–d), and transforms these story-fragments into an elaborate and continuous narrative: the justly famous drama concerning the "oven of Akhnai" (BM 59b), in which R. Eliezer calls upon supernatural forces in order to decide the *halakhah* in his own favor, while R. Joshua boldly defends the autonomy and integrity of the earthly halakhic process in the face of such heavenly intimidation, and finally, almost against their wills, the sages are forced to excommunicate Eliezer, the resultant affront to Eliezer's honor almost resulting in R. Gamaliel's death at sea, and in fact finally leading to the death of R. Gamaliel, who according to the Bavli is also Eliezer's brother-in-law. Similarly, out of two laconic and fragmentary Palestinian traditions concerning R. *Meir

(TJ Bik. 3:3, 65c, MK 3:1, 81c), the Bavli constructs an elaborate, continuous narrative concerning a plot concocted by Meir and *Nathan to depose the *nasi*, Rabban *Simeon ben Gamaliel, because of the latter's desire to enhance his own honor and status at the expense of the honor of these two sages. The *aggadah* of the Bavli is capable of constructing colorful narratives concerning individuals whose very existence is hardly attested in earlier Palestinian sources. For example, a women named *Beruryah is mentioned in Tosefta *Kelim* (BM 1:6) as having expressed a halakhic position – which was approved by R. *Joshua (!) – in response to the opinion of R. *Tarfon. A similar story is told, also in Tosefta *Kelim* (BK 4:17), concerning a daughter of R. *Hananiah ben Teradyon, who clearly lived two generations after the previously mentioned Beruryah, and who, according to another tannaitic tradition (Sifre Deut. 307), was apparently also taken captive at the time of her father's martyrdom. A third, later midrashic tradition makes mention of the profound wisdom of R. Meir's (unnamed) wife (Midrash Proverbs 31). Out of these three apparently unconnected learned women the Bavli forges a single figure, the famous woman-scholar, Beruryah, who was also the daughter of Hananiah ben Teradyon, and also the wife of Meir. At the same time, the Bavli does not identify Beruryah with the daughter of Hananiah ben Teradyon who was taken captive at the time of her father's martyrdom, and so posits that he also had another daughter, and identifies this second daughter as Beruryah's sister (AZ 18a–18b). The creative and synthetic force of the Babylonian *aggadah* is felt even with respect to characters which have already undergone significant literary development in the earlier Palestinian aggadic tradition. Thus the figure of the arch-heretic *Elisha ben Avuya – whose historical existence is highly questionable – is developed by the Palestinian aggadic tradition in two contradictory directions. According to one tradition (TJ Ḥag. 2:1 77b, and cf. Song R. 1) he is described as an arch-villain who intentionally forces Jews to desecrate the Sabbath and prevents Jewish children from learning Torah, or even – according to an extreme version of this tradition – kills children who learned Torah. This figure is so evil that it is even forbidden to mention his name, and so he is called *aḥer*, "the other." According to a second tradition (TJ Ḥag. 2:1 77b–c; Ruth R. 6; Eccles. R. 7), Elisha was a tragic figure, a great scholar and the teacher of Meir, who lost his faith, and so himself stopped observing the Sabbath and stopped learning Torah. This latter figure – who is still called by his proper name, Elisha – is the focus of a debate whether a sage who has abandoned the Torah can repent (cf. Tosef. Dem. 2:9). According to this tradition, R. Meir continues to maintain a relationship with his former master in the hope of convincing him to repent. In the Bavli these two traditions are fused together, such that the evil arch-villain whose name is not mentioned is the very same figure with whom Meir maintains a relationship and from whom he continues to learn. This paradoxical (or contradictory) figure is obviously far more complex than either of the two distinct figures described in the Palestinian tradition, and the theological and dramatic issues which the Babylonian version of the story raises are far richer than those which emerge from the separate Palestinian traditions out of which the Bavli built its narrative. One who is already familiar with the literary character of the Bavli as a whole and its place in the development of rabbinic tradition (as described above) should have no difficulty in recognizing the nature of the *aggadot* of the Babylonian Talmud: on the one hand they are clearly dependent literarily on the earlier and simpler parallel Palestinian traditions; on the other hand the creative and synthetic editorial techniques which their Babylonian redactors used in revising and reformulating them yield, as often as not, what could easily be seen as new and original creations. This double insight offers a challenge to the literary critic, on the one hand, and should serve, on the other hand, as a warning to the historian not to assume that these Babylonian *aggadot* represent reliable sources for the history of the 1st–3rd centuries in Ereẓ Israel, or for the biographies of the tannaitic and early amoraic figures mentioned in these *aggadot*, unless their contents can first be corroborated by a comparison to earlier, independent Palestinian traditions.

The History of Interpretation

From the time when the *halakhah* and the *aggadah* of the Bavli first took on the final literary form in which we recognize it today, there has never been a generation in which it was not studied and interpreted, and the history of its interpretation would in many respects coincide with much of the history of post-talmudic *halakhah*, *musar* (ethics), Jewish philosophy, *Kabbalah*, and so on. Nevertheless, an overview of the main tendencies of post-talmudic Talmud interpretation would not be totally out of place here. Post-talmudic Talmud interpretation is usually divided into three periods: *geonim* (up to about the 10th century); **rishonim* (11th–15th centuries); **aḥaronim* (16th–20th centuries), to which we add a fourth category: the *ḥokerim* – the modern historical interpreters of the Talmud who have been active since the end of the 19th century.

GEONIM. The activity of the *geonim* was concentrated in the old Babylonian yeshivot, which, despite changes in organization and location, continued to exist. The *geonim* who stood at the head of these academies claimed to have inherited the mantle of religious authority from their amoraic predecessors. From this center they exercised a significant degree of influence over the rapidly developing Jewish communities in Christian Europe, Moslem Spain, North Africa, and the Levant. The *geonim* did not publish (and apparently did not compose) any comprehensive commentaries to the Talmud, but rather kept their tradition of interpretation primarily within the institutional framework of their own academies. Nevertheless many of their individual responsa containing explanations of specific passages and difficult phrases in the Talmud have been preserved, and these, together with certain fragmentary *geonic* commentaries and explanations to the Talmud, have been collected and organized in the order of the text of the Bavli by B.M. Lewin in his *Oẓar ha-Ge'onim*, and by others in similar works which have been published since his death. Prior to these relatively recent publications, the writings of the *geonim* were largely known indirectly, through the citations and discussions of their views in the writings of the *rishonim*.

RISHONIM. Following the decline of the centers of Babylonian scholarship in the 10th century, new centers of Talmud scholarship began to form in Western Europe and in North Africa, and afterwards in Moslem Spain – the academies of the *rishonim*. The most prominent names of the European school are Rabbenu *Gershom b. Judah of Mainz in the tenth century, *Rashi in France in the 11th century, and the *ba'alei ha-tosefot* – "the men of the additions" (**tosafot*) – in the 12th and 13th centuries, the most famous of whom were Rashi's grandsons, Samuel b. Meir (Rashbam), and Jacob *Tam, and his great-grandson, R. Isaac the Elder (the Ri Hazaken). The most prominent names of the North African-Spanish school are Rabbenu *Hananel b. Ḥushi'el and Rabbenu Nissim ben Jacob in Tunisia at the beginning of the 11th century, R. Isaac Alfasi in Algeria and afterwards in Spain who was active during almost all of the 11th century and into the very beginning of the 12th century, and Moses Maimonides at first in Spain and then finally in Egypt during the 12th century. While drawing on common *geonic* traditions, these two schools developed independently and in relative isolation from each other over a period of some 200 years. As a result they formed significantly different approaches to the interpretation of the Bavli.

The major literary works of the European school – the comprehensive commentary of Rashi and the additional localized comments of the *tosafot* – have been printed on the page of the Talmud itself ever since the first complete edition of the Talmud was published in Venice in 1520–23, and have therefore had an extraordinary impact on the basic assumptions of generations of students. The most striking tendency of this school is the assumption that the Bavli is a complete, thoroughly edited, self-contained and self-consistent work of law and literature. This school does not distinguish between different literary levels within the text of the Bavli, nor does it engage in any systematic comparison of the Bavli to the parallel traditions in the Tosefta, the Yerushalmi, or the midrashic collections. On the other hand it seeks out every single real or supposed parallel within the Bavli itself in order to "resolve" – by means of ingenious interpretations and subtle distinctions – any contradictions which might be found to exist between these parallel texts. The result of this school of interpretation is a comprehensive and close analysis of even the smallest details of each and every passage in the Talmud, with the aim of demonstrating an essential unity of thought within the Bavli as a whole. This unity is often left unexpressed in the actual text of the Talmud, but this school is convinced that it does exist implicitly, remaining hidden beneath the semblance of a chaotic collection of disparate opinions which the Talmud presents to the superficial reader, and waiting to be revealed to the eye of reason, after exhaustive analysis and comparison of the relevant parallel texts in the Bavli.

The North African-Spanish school adopted from the very beginning a totally different approach to the interpretation of the Talmud. From its inception this school engaged in a systematic comparison of the sources and *sugyot* of the Bavli to the parallel *sugyot* in the Yerushalmi and to the parallel sources in the ancient tannaitic collections (Rabbenu Ḥananel and Rabbenu Nissim). This tendency toward critical comparison of alternative traditions was carried forward by Alfasi and Maimonides, who not only refrained from harmonizing alternative traditions, but even sought to clarify and to highlight both explicit and implicit contradictions. Their purpose in this endeavor was mostly halakhic, and not literary. They sought to construct a consistent body of Jewish law based on the most convincing interpretations of the most reliable opinions. To this end they needed to unravel the web of contradictory views preserved in the totality of talmudic literature (primarily but not only the Bavli), to single out these most reliable traditions (*ṣaḥaiḥ* in Arabic), and to reject the others, whether they expressly contradicted the views explicitly contained in these select traditions, or whether they tacitly assumed some abstract legal principle which stood in contradiction to one of the legal principles presupposed by one of these accepted *ṣaḥaiḥ* traditions. Alfasi and Maimonides also seem to have regularly distinguished between the various literary levels within the text of the Bavli itself, interpreting tannaitic and amoraic sources by themselves, without necessarily accepting the interpretation of the *stam ha-talmud*, or even tannaitic sources by themselves, without necessarily accepting the interpretation of some particular *amora*. The result is often a remarkably critical and philologically accurate interpretation of *a portion* of the talmudic traditions contained in the Bavli, an achievement unfortunately gained at the cost of the elimination of the rest of the competing and contradictory views from the field of vision.

A third school of Talmud interpretation developed during the latter period of the *rishonim* (13th–14th centuries). This school is associated with the name of Moses Naḥmanides in Christian Spain, who synthesized the achievements of these two earlier schools, combining the detailed and comprehensive literary analysis of Rashi and Tosefot, with the source-comparison and philological criticism of Rabbenu Ḥananel and Alfasi. This school is responsible for some of the most insightful and brilliant interpretations of the Talmud ever produced.

AHARONIM. The transition from the period of the *rishonim* to that of the *aḥaronim* is marked by the publication of the Shulḥan Arukh (1565) of Joseph *Caro. From this point on the development of the normative halakhic tradition was no longer centered on the independent interpretation of the Talmud itself, but rather focused its attention on the determination of the consensus of the halakhic views of the *rishonim*, as expressed in the Shulḥan Arukh and the literature which developed around it. One the one hand, this new situation led to a devaluation of the independent study of the Talmud text itself, which only rarely would be brought to bear in a normative halakhic debate. On the other hand, it freed the study of the Talmud from the artificial limitations of practically oriented normative halakhic interpretation. The Talmud interpretation of the *aḥaronim* moved in various directions. Super-commentaries were composed to the commentaries of Rashi and Tosefot. Works of abstract conceptual jurisprudence were composed, usually as super-commentaries to some highly regarded systematic halakhic work from the period of the *rishonim* (such as Maimonides' Code), or even to the Shulḥan Arukh itself. At the same time the liberation of talmudic scholarship from the narrow restraints of normative halakhic discourse gave impetus to a broadening of the range of talmudic studies, which now included Tosefta, Yerushalmi, *Midrashei Halakhah* and *Midrashei Aggadah* – not merely the Bavli itself.

ḤOKERIM. At first these new directions did not directly influence the interpretation of the Bavli. Starting, however, at the end of the 19th century the increased interest in and familiarity with these earlier documents of talmudic tradition began to arouse a new interest in their possible significance for the understanding of the Bavli itself. The *Yefeh Enayim* of Aryeh Leib Yellin, published in the Romm edition of the Bavli, made available for the first time an easily accessible listing of parallel traditions in the Yerushalmi and Tosefta, the *Midrashei Halakhah,* and *Midrashei Aggadah.* The *novellae* of R. Joseph Ẓvi Dünner attempted an integrated reconstruction of the historical evolution of the parallel versions of talmudic *sugyot,* and together these works can be seen to mark the beginning the period of the *ḥokerim.* Building on the achievements of such giants as Ḥanokh *Albeck, J.N. *Epstein, and Saul *Lieberman, the historical interpretation of the Bavli has been carried forward since the 1970s by the two great *ḥokerim* of the Bavli, David Weiss *Halivni and Shamma Friedman. The work of Halivni and Friedman was of course preceded by the critical literary and historical research of scholars like Julius Kaplan, Hyman Klein, and most especially by the monumental studies of Abraham Weiss. In their critical commentaries both Halivni and Friedman at first emphasized the same central point: the necessity of separating the tannaitic and amoraic sources of the Bavli from the literary framework of the *stam ha-talmud* in which they are imbedded, in order to interpret each level of the Bavli in its own right. While Halivni has remained largely within the framework of this original insight, applying this method over the years to a wide range of talmudic texts (extending over half of the Bavli), Friedman has expanded the critical field of Bavli study to include the lower-critical problems of textual criticism, the higher-critical problems of the synoptic relations between parallel versions of the same tradition, issues of talmudic lexicography, Babylonian Aramaic grammar, and so on. In the early 1990s, Friedman established the Society for the Interpretation of the Talmud, a collaborative venture in which a group of scholars has undertaken the preparation of an edition of the Babylonian Talmud with commentary based on modern scholarly standards and aimed to a wide reading audience.

BIBLIOGRAPHY: Samuel ha-Nagid, *Mavo ha-Talmud* (in the editions of the Babylonian Talmud at the end of tractate *Berakhot*); Frankel, Mishnah; Weiss, Dor, vol. 3; Halevy, Dorot, vol. 2; E. Deutsch, *Der Talmud* (1880); M. Mielzner, *Introduction to the Talmud* (1925); H.L. Strack, *Introduction to the Talmud and Midrash* (1931); D. Wright, *The Talmud* (1932); R.N.N. Rabbinovicz, *Ma'amar al-Hadpasat ha-Talmud* (1952); Epstein, Mishnah; Epstein, Tanna'im; Epstein, Amora'im; E. Schechter, *Ha-Mishnah ba-Bavli u-va-Yerushalmi* (1959); E.L. Berkovits, *Was ist der Talmud?* (1963); B. de Vries, *Meḥkarim be-Safrut ha-Talmud* (1968); H Albeck, *Meḥkarim be-Baraita uva-Tosefta* (1944); idem, *Mavo la-Talmudim* (1969); H. Klein, in: JQR, 38 (1947/48), 67–91; 43 (1952/53), 341–63; 50 (1959–60), 124–46; J. Kaplan, *Redaction of the Babylonian Talmud* (1933); Z.H. Chajes, *Student's Guide Through The Talmud* (1960²); A. Weiss, *Le-Ḥeker ha-Talmud* (1955); idem, *Al ha-Yezirah ha-Sifrutit shel ha-Amora'im* (1962); idem, *Hit'havvut ha-Talmud bi-Shlemuto* (1943); idem, B.M. Lewin, in: Y.L. Fishman (ed.), *Azkarah le... A.Y. Kook,* 2 pt. 4 (1937), 145–208. **ADD. BIBLIOGRAPHY:** M. Sokoloff, *A Dictionary of Jewish Babylonian Aramaic* (2002); Strack-Stemberger, *Introduction to the Talmud and Midrash* (1996), 190–224; A. Goldberg, in: S. Safrai (ed.), *The Literature of the Sages* (1987), 323–66; D. Goodblatt, in: D. Neusner (ed.), *The Study of Ancient Judaism II* (1981), 120–99; D. Halivni, *Sources and Traditions: A Source Critical Commentary of the Talmud,* 5 vols. (1975–2003); S. Friedman, *A Critical Study of Yevamot X with a Methodological Introduction* (1978); idem, *Talmud Arukh,* BT *Bava Mezia VI, Commentary* (1990), *Text* (1996); idem, *Tosefta Atiqta* (2002); idem, in: *Saul Lieberman Memorial Volume,* ed, S. Friedman (1993), 119–64; idem, in: *Sidra,* 7 (1991) vi–vii, 67–102; idem, "Baraitot," in: D. Boyarin et al. (eds.), *Ateret LeḤaim* (2000); idem, S. Liberman and G. Goldstein (eds.), in: *Printing the Talmud* (2005), 143–54; S. Wald, BT *Pesaḥim III* (2000); idem, BT *Shabbat VII* (2006); R. Kalmin, *The Redaction of the Babylonian Talmud: Amoraic or Savoraic?* (1989); D. Kraemer, *The Mind of the Talmud: an Intellectual History of the Bavli* (1990); L. Moscovitz, *Talmudic Reasoning* (2002); J. Sussman, in: *Meḥkare Talmud,* 1 (1990), 55–133; D. Halivni, "Aspects of the Formation of the Talmud," in: *Sidra,* 20 (2005), pp. 69–117 (Heb.); J. Hauptman, *Development of the Talmudic Sugya: Relationship between Tannaitic and Amoraic Sources* (1988); M. Benovitz, TB *Shavuot III* (2003); S. Friedman (ed.), *Five Sugyot from the Babylonian Talmud* (2002).

[Stephen G. Wald (2nd ed.)]

TALMUD, BURNING OF. Despite the mass of restrictions imposed on the Jews by the Church in the political, social, and economic spheres, and the attacks on the Oral Law by Christian theologians, the campaign to proscribe Jewish literature was not launched until the 13th century. An attempt had been made to prevent teaching of the "second tradition" (δευτέρωσις) by Emperor *Justinian in 553 (novella 146), and in 712 the *Visigoths in Spain forbade converts to Christianity to read Hebrew books. The first condemnation of the Talmud to burning was preceded by a period in which new forces of rationalism had made their appearance in Western Europe as well as an upsurge of sectarian movements such as the Cathari or *Albigenses. Such trends were countered with strong measures by the Church. In 1199 Pope Innocent III declared that since Scripture contained lessons too profound for the layman to grasp, Christians should rely wholly on the clergy for its interpretation. The Church also directed its attention to Jews as potential subversive elements. One outcome of the suppression of rationalistic tendencies was the burning of *Maimonides' *Guide of the Perplexed* at Montpellier, southern France, in 1233. The *Guide* was originally denounced to the Dominican inquisitors by Jewish leaders who opposed the study of Maimonides' works. Although the connection between the burning of the *Guide* and the subsequent burning of the Talmud is tenuous, it set a dangerous precedent.

Paris

In 1236 a Jewish apostate, Nicholas *Donin, submitted a memorandum to Pope *Gregory IX listing 35 charges against the Talmud. These included allegations that it contained blasphemies of Jesus and Mary, attacks on the Church, pronouncements hostile to non-Jews, and foolish and revolting tales. They asserted that the Jews had elevated the Oral Law to the level of divinely inspired Scripture, and that this impeded the possibility of their conversion to Christianity. Gregory thereupon ordered a preliminary investigation, and in 1239 sent a circular letter to ecclesiastics in France summarizing the accusations and ordering the confiscation of Jewish books on the first Saturday of Lent (i.e., March 3, 1240), while the Jews were gathered in synagogue. Any other persons having Hebrew books in their possession who refused to give them up were to be excommunicated. He further ordered the heads of the Dominican and Franciscan Orders in Paris to ensure that "those books in which you find errors of this sort you shall cause to be burned at the stake." Similar instructions were conveyed to the kings of France, England, Spain, and Portugal. It was in response to Gregory's circular that the first public religious *disputation between Jews and Christians was staged in Paris on June 25–27, 1240. The chief Jewish spokesman was R. *Jehiel of Paris, the most eminent French rabbi of the period. An inquisitorial committee condemned the Talmud two years later. In June 1242, 24 wagon loads of books totaling thousands of volumes were handed to the executioner for public burning. Copies may also have been seized and destroyed in Rome.

Subsequently the burning of the Talmud was repeatedly urged by the popes. In France, Louis IX ordered further confiscations in 1247 and 1248 and upheld the principle in an ordinance of December 1254. It was confirmed by Philip III in 1284 and Philip IV in 1290 and 1299. A further burning was ordered in Toulouse in 1319 by the inquisitor Bernard Gui and in Perpignan. In his manual for inquisitors Gui also singled out the works of *Rashi, David *Kimḥi, and Maimonides for condemnation. The conflagration in Paris was compared by the contemporary scholar *Meir b. Baruch of Rothenberg to the destruction of the Temple in an elegy *Sha'ali Serufah* ("Ask is it well, O thou consumed in fire") included in the *kinah* of the Ninth of Av. *Jonah Gerondi, who had led the anti-Maimonists, is said to have connected the burning of the Talmud with the burning of the *Guide* in Montpellier and to have bitterly repented his attacks on Maimonides.

Outside France little action was taken in response to the papal appeals. Confiscations may have taken place in England and were ordered in Sicily. There seems to have been widespread destruction in southern Italy in 1270. After the disputation of *Barcelona in 1263, James I of Aragon ordered the Jews to delete all blasphemous references to Jesus and Mary from their copies of the Talmud under penalty of burning the work. Condemnations of the Talmud were issued by popes *Innocent IV in his bull of 1244, *Alexander IV, John XXII in 1320, and *Alexander V in 1409. The restrictive legislation imposed on Aragonese Jewry after the disputation of *Tortosa, 1413–14, contained a condemnation of the Talmud. Pope *Eugenius IV issued a bull prohibiting Jews from studying the Talmud following the Council of Basle (see *Church Councils), 1431–43.

Although the orders of the popes were not effectively upheld by the secular authorities, copying of the Talmud and its study could not be carried out openly and proceeded with difficulty. However, in the new spirit of liberty engendered by the Renaissance, the great German humanist Johann *Reuchlin defended Jewish learning and the Talmud, which had again been condemned to destruction by the emperor in 1509 because of charges leveled against it by the apostate Johann *Pfefferkorn. The polemical battle which ensued between supporters of the humanists and the obscurantists involved leading Christian scholars, and was a prelude to the Reformation.

Rome

It was during the Counter-Reformation in Italy in the middle of the 16th century that the attacks on the Talmud had the most far-reaching consequences. In the reactionary climate, a quarrel broke out between rival Christian printers of Hebrew books in Venice. One of them, with the connivance of certain apostates, denounced the works produced by his competitor as containing matter offensive to the Holy Catholic Church. It developed into a wholesale attack on Hebrew literature. After a council of cardinals had examined the matter, the pope issued a decree (August 1553) designating the Talmud and related works as blasphemous and condemning them to be burned. On Sept. 9, 1553, the Jewish New Year, a huge pyre was set up in the Campo de' Fiori in Rome of Hebrew books that had been seized from Jewish homes. Subsequently the Inquisition ordered all rulers, bishops, and inquisitors throughout Italy to take similar action. The orders were obeyed in the Papal States, particularly in Bologna and Ravenna, and in Ferrara, Mantua, Urbino, Florence, and Venice, the center of Hebrew printing, and also in 1559 in Cremona. Representations by the rabbis gained a reprieve of the indiscriminate destruction. A papal bull issued on May 29, 1554, specified that while the Talmud and works containing blasphemies of Christianity were to be burned, other Jewish works were to be submitted for *censorship. The Talmud was included in the first *Index Expurgatorius* in 1559. The ban against publication of the Talmud, with certain excisions or without them, under a different name, was temporarily lifted (1564) by Pius IV. However, confiscation of Hebrew works continued in Italy, especially in the Papal States, down to the 18th century. The same was the case in Avignon and the papal possessions in France. Renewed interdictions were issued by popes Gregory XIII (1572–85) and Clement VIII (1593). The burning in Rome was commemorated by an annual public fast day observed on the eve of Sabbath of *ḥukkat* (*Shibbolei ha-Leket* 263).

The events in Italy were described by the contemporary chronicler *Joseph ha-Kohen in *Emek ha-Bakhah* and by a number of other writers. Mattathias *Delacrut, who managed to escape with his own books to Brest-Litovsk, relates that in Venice over 1,000 complete copies of the Talmud, 500 copies of the code of Isaac *Alfasi, and innumerable other works were burned. Judah b. Samuel *Lerma lost all the copies of his newly printed *Leḥem Yehudah* in Venice and had to rewrite it from memory. The burning also aroused protest in Christian circles. The Hebraist Andrea Masio openly voiced his resentment of the pope's ruling, saying that the cardinals' report condemning a literature of which they knew nothing was as valueless as a blind man's opinion of color. The proscription of the Talmud in the main center for Hebrew printing was felt throughout the Diaspora. The Jewish centers in Poland and Turkey were prompt to answer the challenge, and printing of the Talmud commenced in Lublin in 1559 and shortly afterward in Salonika. Scholars in Italy subsequently turned to other branches of Jewish learning, and the study of *Kabbalah in particular spread rapidly in Italy after the Talmud had been condemned.

The last auto-da-fé of the Talmud took place in Poland, in Kamenets-Podolski in the fall of 1757, following the spread of the *Frankist movement in Podolia. Bishop Nicholas Dembowski intervened in the controversy between the Frankists and Jewish leaders and ordered a disputation to be held between them. He subsequently condemned all copies of the Talmud found in his diocese to be seized and burned after they had been dragged through the streets in mockery. A search was made with the aid of the clergy, the police, and the Frankists for the Talmud and other rabbinical writings. Nearly 1,000 copies of the Talmud were thrown into a pit at Kamenets and burned by the hangman.

BIBLIOGRAPHY: Loeb, in: REJ, 1 (1880), 247–61; 2 (1881), 248–70; 3 (1881), 39–57; J.D. Eisenstein (ed.), *Oẓar Vikkuḥim* (1928), 81–86; A.M. Habermann (ed.), *Sefer Gezerot Ashkenaz ve-Ẓarefat* (1945), 183–5, 263–4; Roth, Italy, 289–94; R.N. Rabbinovicz, *Ma'amar al Hadpasat ha-Talmud*, ed. by A.M. Habermann (1952); Rosenthal, in: JQR, 47 (1956/57), 58–76, 145–69; A. Ya'ari, *Meḥkerei Sefer* (1958), 198–234; Baer, Spain, 1 (1961), 155; 2 (1966), 15–16, 224–9; Baron, Social², 9 (1965), 55–96; S. Grayzel, *Church and the Jews in the XIIIth Century* (1966), 29, 241; Merhavya, in: *Tarbiz*, 37 (1967/68), 78–96, 191–207 (and Eng. summary).

[Yvonne Glikson]

TALMUD, DAVID L. (1900–), Russian physical chemist, educated at the Odessa Chemical Institute; Talmud joined the Leningrad Institute of Chemistry and Physics in 1930 and from 1934 worked at the Institute of Biochemistry of the U.S.S.R. Academy of Science. In 1934 he became a corresponding member of the Academy, and in 1943 was awarded the Stalin Prize. He wrote extensively, mainly on surface chemistry, colloids, and proteins.

TALMUD, JERUSALEM (תַּלְמוּד יְרוּשַׁלְמִי), also called the Palestinian Talmud, *Talmud di-Venei Ma'arava* (The Talmud of the West), or *Talmud de-Ereẓ Yisrael*. Like its better known "eastern" counterpart – the Babylonian Talmud (Bavli) – the Yerushalmi is an extensive literary work consisting of both *halakhah* and *aggadah* (see: *Talmud, Babylonian), built upon the foundation, and in the order, of the *Mishnah of Rabbi *Judah ha-Nasi (see *Mishnah, The Mishnah as a Literary Work, *Halakhah* in the Mishnah, *Aggadah* in the Mishnah). Neither the Bavli nor the Yerushalmi encompass the entire Mishnah, but rather only four of its six orders – though not the same four. There is both Talmud Bavli and Talmud Yerushalmi for *Moed*, *Nashim*, and *Nezikin*. Unlike the Bavli, however, the Talmud Yerushalmi includes the entire first order of the Mishnah, *Zeraim*. Again, unlike the Bavli, which has *talmud* for most of the fifth order of the Mishnah, *Kodashim*, the Yerushalmi has none. Neither the Bavli nor the Yerushalmi possess a fully edited and organized *talmud*, redacted according to the order of *seder Tohorot* (with the exception of *Niddah*), though both works contain many talmudic discussions (*sugyot*) which deal at length with the sources and issues of *seder Tohorot*. Several chapters of the Yerushalmi are missing from our editions – Shabbat 21–24, Makkot 3, Niddah 4–10) – but these were probably lost in the early middle ages.

Like the Bavli, the Yerushalmi is not primarily a commentary to the Mishnah of R. Judah ha-Nasi. Rather it is an autonomous and comprehensive work of *halakhah* and *aggadah*. Building upon the text of the Mishnah, it includes two additional strata of rabbinic sources: (1) *baraitot* – tannaitic sources which were not incorporated in the Mishnah of Rabbi Judah ha-Nasi, deriving for the most part from the same tannaitic period as the sources of the Mishnah (1st–2nd centuries), and almost equal to them in authority (see *Baraita*); (2) the teachings of five generations of Palestinian **amoraim* (and a few sixth generation scholars), and the first three generations of Babylonian *amoraim*. Like the Bavli, the Yerushalmi cites and discusses these sources for their own sake, and not merely insofar as they enlighten some obscure point in the Mishnah.

Also like the Bavli, the predominant literary form in the Yerushalmi is the *sugya* – a continuous, and sometimes quite lengthy, series of questions and answers, objections and justifications, in which the isolated tannaitic and amoraic sources of the Yerushalmi are combined and unified into a synthetic and dialectical whole. However, unlike the Bavli, the *sugyot* of the Yerushalmi do not contain a great deal of anonymous editorial additions, comments, interpretations, and explanations. It is reasonable, therefore, to assume that the Yerushalmi was redacted at about the time of the latest *amoraim* that are mentioned in it, or about the year 400 C.E. There are no explicit traditions concerning the place of the Yerushalmi's redaction, though it is usually assumed that it was redacted in Tiberias, perhaps with material deriving from Sepphoris and Caesarea also included.

Bavli and Yerushalmi – Similarities and Differences

In comparing the Bavli to the Yerushalmi, scholars have frequently pointed out that the discussions in the Bavli are more long-winded and discursive, involving extensive explanation and abstract conceptualization, forced interpretations of early sources, and so on. The *sugyot* of the Yerushalmi by comparison are more focused, concrete, and succinct. This comparison, while true insofar as the final texts of these two works are concerned, is nevertheless extremely misleading. As later critical scholarship has pointed out, the Bavli is composed of several distinct literary levels – (1) tannaitic; (2) amoraic; (3) *stam ha-talmud* – i.e. the literary work of several generations of anonymous redactors (cf. Talmud, Babylonian, The Babylonian Talmud as a Literary Work). Nearly all of the most prominent features which differentiate the Bavli from the Yerushalmi belong to the largely post-amoraic *stam ha-talmud* stratum of the Bavli. As scholars have pointed out, if one isolates the tannaitic and amoraic strata of the Bavli from the literary embellishments of the *stam ha-talmud*, the Bavli turns out to be remarkably similar to the Yerushalmi. A comparison of these two works as they stand, therefore, cannot contribute much to an understanding of the difference between two different, but contemporary, talmudic traditions, one in Babylonia and the other in Ereẓ Israel. Rather, such a comparison would primarily serve to highlight the difference between two different stages in the development of a single shared talmudic tradition, which was preserved both in Babylonia and in Ereẓ Israel. Since the Yerushalmi was redacted at least one hundred years before the Bavli, it preserves (by and large) a more original form of this shared talmudic tradition, closer in time and in form to the Talmud of the early and middle *amoraim* (both Babylonian and Palestinian). The Bavli, on the other hand, represents a later version of this same shared talmudic tradition, one which has incorporated later (mostly Babylonian) amoraic traditions and interpretations, as well as additions, interpretations, and revisions of the *stam ha-talmud* – all of which stem from the period following the redaction of the Yerushalmi (see Talmud, Babylonian, The Place of the Babylonian Talmud in Rabbinic Literature).

There are, nevertheless, a number of real differences between these two talmudim. First of all, the textual tradition of the Mishnah which is presupposed by the *sugyot* of the Bavli is often different from that presupposed by the Yerushalmi (see: Mishnah: The Later Development of the Text of the Mishnah; and cf. Epstein, Mishnah, 18–25, 195). Second, the Aramaic language of the Yerushalmi differs from that of the Bavli. The language of the Bavli, which is familiar to most Talmud students, belongs to the eastern branch of Aramaic (which includes Mandaic and Syriac). The language of the Yerushalmi, on the other hand, belongs to the western branch of Aramaic (which includes Samaritan and Palestinian Christian Aramaic), and is unfamiliar to most students trained in the Bavli. This dialect was thoroughly investigated by Dalman, whose work was criticized by Kutscher. However, given the fragmentary nature of Kutscher's own contributions in this field, it would seem that his criticism of Dalman was somewhat exaggerated (Macuch, xxxvii). Stevenson's popular grammar of Palestinian Jewish Aramaic is largely based on Dalman's work, and though it too was dismissed by Kutscher, his judgment is relevant primarily for the professional linguistic scholar, and does not relate to the value of this small book for teachers and students. In the field of lexicography, the situation has been vastly improved by the publication of M. Sokoloff's *Dictionary of Jewish Palestinian Aramaic* (1990). Third, the technical terminology of the Yerushalmi is very different from the far more familiar and well-documented terminology of the Bavli. L. Moscovitz has already made a significant contribution toward the clarification of the technical terminology of the Yerushalmi, and it is to be hoped that his continued efforts in this field will soon become available to a wider community of Talmud students.

Only about one-sixth of the Jerusalem Talmud consists of **aggadah*, compared with one-third of the Babylonian. This may be due to the fact that in Ereẓ Israel the aggadic element was assembled in special collections, out of which the later Midrashim evolved. There are in fact many aggadic passages in the Yerushalmi which closely resemble parallel passages found in the classic aggadic collections – **Genesis Rabbah*, **Leviticus Rabbah*, **Pesikta de-Rav Kahana*, etc. – though the precise literary and historical relationship between these parallel texts is not always clear (see **Genesis Rabbah*). For the relative originality and historical reliability of the Palestinian aggadic tradition as a whole, in comparison with the *aggadah* of the Bavli, see: Talmud, Babylonian – The *Aggadah* of the Babylonian Talmud. In the Yerushalmi there is a marked lack of demonology or angelology which looms so large in the Babylonian Talmud, although, contrary to the statement of Ginzburg, *shedim* ("devils") are mentioned (TJ, Shab. 1:3, 3b; Git. 6:8, 48b). There are many references to sorcery (cf. Sanh. 7:13, 25c and even in a halakhic context, Naz. 7:1, 57a); magic (Shab. 6:9, 8d; cf. TB, Shab. 66b) and astrology (Shab. 6:9, 8d) are also mentioned. There is reference only to the two biblical angels Michael and Gabriel.

Yerushalmi Nezikin

It is immediately evident that the text to the three tractates of *Nezikin* ("Damages") – *Bava Kamma, Bava Meẓia*, and *Bava Batra* – differ in a fundamental and striking way from the remainder. The difference extends to style, terminology, and even to the names of the *amoraim* who are mentioned there. The vast majority of *amoraim* quoted belong to the first and second generations; those of the next two generations are hardly mentioned at all; and many of those mentioned in this order are rarely mentioned in the other orders. *Nezikin* has a different terminology and includes old Hebrew words which do not occur elsewhere. It is distinguished by its brevity and shows every sign of being in an unfinished state. Where discussions are found on an identical passage in this and the other orders, that in *Nezikin* often comes to an entirely different conclusion, or gives different answers to those given in the other discussion. Moreover, discussions left incomplete in this order are found completed in the others.

That the Talmud to *Nezikin* is fundamentally different from the rest is universally accepted. Originally explanations of this phenomenon focused on identifying a different location for the redaction of these three tractates. The first to suggest that it emanated from a different source was I. Levy (*Jahresbuch des juedischen theologischen Seminars*, Breslau, 20/21 (1895)). Although it was previously maintained that it was compiled in Tiberias and represents the teachings of the school there, the brilliant research of S. Lieberman argued vigorously against this conclusion. In his opinion, the Jerusalem Talmud to *Nezikin* represents the school of Caesarea, where it was compiled about the middle of the fourth century C.E., half a century before the compilation of the rest. Among the evidence put forward by Lieberman the following may be mentioned. In the Jerusalem Talmud to tractate *Shabbat* (which emanates from Tiberias), the "rabbis of Caesarea" are contrasted with "the local rabbis"; R. Nasa, who is elsewhere (Est. R. 2:9; TJ, Shab. 7:1, 9b; Pes. 2:2, 29a, etc.) mentioned as hailing from Caesarea, is mentioned no less than 14 times in *Nezikin*; the only time the word "here" is mentioned in *Nezikin* (BM 6:3, 11a) the reference is clearly to Caesarea; and lastly, statements attributed in the three *Bava* tractates to *amoraim* without any qualification are in other parts of the Jerusalem Talmud attributed to "the rabbis of Caesarea" (cf., e.g., BB 3:1, 13d with Kid. 4:2, 65d; BK 8:4, 6b with Ket. 5:5, 30a). Recently, however, the focus has moved away somewhat from the aspect of location, and more attention has been given to the aspect of time – that the redaction of Yerushalmi *Nezikin* represents an earlier stage in the development of the talmudic tradition, before the isolated *memrot* and *baraitot* were incorporated into extended synthetic and dialectical compositions (Sussmann, *Meḥkare Talmud 1*).

Acceptance of the Two Talmuds

The Jerusalem Talmud was completed at least a century before the compilation of the Babylonian Talmud – c. 400. Its close was probably due to the situation which prevailed in Ereẓ Israel. In 351 the Roman commander Ursicinus wreaked vengeance on the Jews of Tiberias, Sepphoris, and Lydda, the seats of the three academies, because of their revolts against the army. It was the beginning of the end of organized Jewish learning in Ereẓ Israel. The activities of the main school, that of Tiberias, came to an end with the extinction of the patriarchate in 421, as a result of the troubles and persecution which followed the Christian domination. Although study of the Torah did not cease entirely, conditions were not conducive to the flourishing of *halakhot* or the creation of halakhic works. It was, in fact, almost a miracle that the Torah of Ereẓ Israel was not forgotten entirely. Until the rise of Islam each Talmud was probably authoritative in its own sphere. With the spread of Islam and the establishment of the caliphate at Baghdad in the eighth century, however, the *geonim* of Babylon succeeded in establishing the authority of the Babylonian Talmud throughout Europe. Students flocked to the academies of Babylon from Spain, Provence, Italy, North Africa, and the Byzantine Empire. Hai Gaon (d. 1038) had already laid it down that decisions of the Jerusalem Talmud are to be disregarded when they conflict with those of the Babylonian (*Teshuvot ha-Ge'onim*, ed. Lyck, no. 46; *Sha'arei Teshuvah*, no. 39; cf. *Ha-Eshkol*, Hilkhot Sefer Torah, 60b). It was in North Africa that the relationship of the Babylonian Talmud to the Jerusalem Talmud was finally determined. The Jerusalem Talmud was studied intensively in the school of *Nissim b. Jacob ibn Shahin and *Hananel b. Ḥushi'el. It has been suggested, but without any corroborative evidence, that Ḥushi'el, the father of Hananel, brought it from his native southern Italy, where Palestinian influence was strong. Nissim maintained that many passages in the Babylonian Talmud could be understood only when compared with the parallel passage in the sister Talmud. But it was Isaac Alfasi, the most prominent halakhic figure in North Africa following Hananel, who formalized the role of the Jerusalem Talmud in the emerging world of the **rishonim*. On the one hand, in his classic and decisive work *Hilkhot ha-Rif* he quotes the Jerusalem Talmud extensively, yet at the same time he states unequivocally (Er. 104b) that "since our Talmud [the Babylonian] permits it [the causing of sound on Sabbath] it is of no concern to us that the Talmud of the west forbids it, because we rely upon our Talmud since it is later (*batra'ei*) in time, and they were more versed in that Talmud than we are. Were they not convinced that one need not rely upon that statement of the Jerusalem Talmud they would not have permitted it." The Jerusalem Talmud was not extensively used by Rashi; his quotations from it are very often secondhand, culled from other works. It was, however, better known among some of the tosafists. For example, Solomon ibn Adret and Simeon b. Ẓemaḥ Duran both state that Judah b. Yakar, who lived in France around 1200, wrote a commentary on it. In the 13th century, the talmudic school of Naḥmanides, following the precedents of Hananel and Alfasi, continued to study the Yerushalmi in conjunction with their exposition of the Bavli.

Manuscripts and Editions

The editio princeps of the Jerusalem Talmud is the Venice edition printed by Daniel Bomberg (1523–24), published after the completion of the printing of the Babylonian Talmud (1523) and before he undertook the printing of the Yad of Maimonides which was completed the following year. This edition is based upon the sole extant manuscript of the Jerusalem

Talmud, the Leiden manuscript, which was written by Jehiel b. Jekuthiel b. Benjamin ha-Rofe in 1289. The scribe explicitly states that he copied it from a woefully corrupt text, full of errors; although he had attempted to correct it as much as possible, "I know that I have not corrected even half of the mistakes," and he begs the indulgence of his readers. In addition to those mistakes, it is evident from statements and quotations of the *rishonim* that the scribes in many cases freely changed the orthography characteristic of the original text to make it accord with the accepted spelling and terminology of the Babylonian Talmud. For instance it is specifically stated that in the Jerusalem Talmud אדם is spelled אדן, yet those differences have been eliminated from the manuscript.

This manuscript was the basis of the printed text, but its editor, Jacob b. Ḥayyim ibn Adoniyahu, had at his disposal three other manuscripts, which he calls "accurate" ones. All of these have been completely lost, with the exception of the Yerushalmi to tractate *Horayot*, which was printed by Bomberg in his edition of the Babylonian Talmud and which, according to Lieberman, is the text of one of those three manuscripts. Jacob b. Ḥayyim was not conversant with the language and style of the Jerusalem Talmud and in many places spoiled the text by amendments due to his lack of understanding. It is clear that he did not examine the text before him with sufficient care, or correct it when necessary. Nor did he hesitate to omit passages which he did not understand or add sentences which are not found in the Leiden manuscript (though possibly their source is the other manuscripts mentioned; see J.N. Epstein, in: *Tarbiz* (see bibl.) (with additions by E.Z. Melamed), and his *Amora'im*, pp. 335ff.). An examination of the Leiden manuscript reveals glosses by the scribe and by the editor – both of which have been included in the printed text – and glosses from a third hand which did not find their way into it. When added that printing errors are not lacking, it will be realized that the existing text is hopelessly corrupt.

The task of establishing a correct text is almost an impossible one. Two sources are available. One can be obtained through a collation of all texts in the works of the *rishonim*, as was done by B. Rattner in his valuable *Ahavat Ẓiyyon vi-Yrushalayim*. The other is the fragments on the orders *Zera'im, Mo'ed*, and *Nezikin* of the Jerusalem Talmud in the Cairo *Genizah*. These were collected by S. Schechter who gave them to L. Ginzberg; the latter published them in *Seridei Yerushalmi*, and some in Volume I of *Ginzei Schechter*. In addition, J.N. Epstein and especially S. Lieberman have done valuable work in the reconstruction of the original text of part of the Talmud.

In addition to the Leiden manuscript and the *Genizah* fragments there exists a manuscript in the Vatican of *Zera'im* (except *Bikkurim*) and tractate *Sotah*, in all comprising about one-quarter of the Leiden manuscript. It is full of scribal errors. In 1976 E.S. Rosenthal discovered in the margins of the Escorial Manuscript of the Bavli, an almost complete copy of Yerushalmi Nezikin. This important find was eventually edited and published with a commentary by S. Lieberman in 1984. Later, the Academy of Hebrew Language published an exact transcription of the Leiden manuscript of the Yerushalmi, with carefully annotated corrections and an introduction by J. Sussmann.

Commentaries

Until recently the earliest commentator on the Jerusalem Talmud whose work has been preserved was Solomon Sirilio. There has also been published by A. Sofer a commentary to *Shekalim* by R. Meshullam, who lived in the 12th–13th century and another to the same tractate and belonging to the same period, by "the disciples of Samuel b. Shneor" (New York, 1954). Sirilio was a native of Spain who emigrated to Ereẓ Israel after the expulsion in 1492 and composed his commentary in Ereẓ Israel about 1530, seven years after the first edition was printed in Venice. He apparently never saw that, however, and his commentary is based on a manuscript. His commentary to the order *Zera'im* and some other tractates was published separately by Dinkels; that to *Berakhot* and *Pe'ah* are included in the Romm edition. During the next century only desultory commentaries were written on the Talmud. In 1590 Samuel Jaffe Ashkenazi wrote a commentary on the aggadic portion of the Jerusalem Talmud only, which is valuable for the variant readings he gives from manuscripts in his possession, and for his emendations. An older contemporary, Eleazar *Azikri, wrote one on *Berakhot* and *Beẓah* (the latter published in 1967) and possibly on *Pesaḥim*, which has been lost. R. Yom Tov Lipman *Heller, the famous commentator on the Mishnah, states that his son Abraham wrote a commentary on it, but not a trace of it has been found.

The first extensive commentary was that of Joshua Benveniste of Turkey who commentated on the legal portions of only 18 of the tractates. Part of this was published with the text during the author's lifetime (Constantinople, 1662) and the rest nearly a century later. The revival in the study of the Jerusalem Talmud, especially in Eastern Europe, is due to Elijah b. Loeb of *Fulda. His commentary (Amsterdam, 1710) covers 15 treatises. It stimulated the marginal notes by David *Oppenheim which are clearly a supplement to and a criticism of Elijah's work. Moreover only a few years were to pass before two major commentaries appeared. David b. Naphtali Fraenkel of Berlin (1704–1762) commented on practically the whole of the Talmud which was not covered by Elijah of Fulda (but including *Shekalim*, on which Elijah also wrote: vol. 1, Dessau, 1743; vol. 2, Berlin, 1757; vol. 3, *ibid.*, 1760–62); his work is entitled *Korban ha-Edah* with additions entitled *Sheyarei Korban*.

The first to publish a commentary to the whole of the Jerusalem Talmud was Moses *Margoliot (d. 1780) of Kaidan (Kedainiai), Lithuania. Half was published in his lifetime (vol. 1, Amsterdam, 1554; vol. 2, Leghorn, 1770; vol. 3 (part, no place)) and the remainder in the Zhitomir edition under the title *Penei Moshe* and *Mareh ha-Panim*. The commentaries of Fraenkel and Margolies are regarded as the two standard commentaries to this Talmud, and paved the way to an understanding of the text. They fulfill the same function as Rashi's commentary to the Babylonian Talmud. The commentary of Elijah Gaon of Vilna is invaluable.

The *No'am Yerushalayim* of Joshua Isaac of Slonim contains some brilliant interpretations but it is interspersed with casuistic discussions. A valuable contribution was made by Ephraim Dov Lapp of Jaroslaw who provided a digest of this work which, like all the above commentaries and many others, is published in the Romm edition of the Jerusalem Talmud (1922) under the title *Gilyon Efrayim*, as is the penetrating commentary of Jacob David *Willowski (the Ridbaz). The *Netivot Yerushalayim* of Israel Ḥayyim Daiches (BK, Vilna, 1880; BM, London, 1926; BB, *ibid.*, 1927) combines profundity and learning with a highly developed critical sense. Appended to the photostat edition of the Krotoschin Talmud (1969) is what purports to be a complete list of the commentators on the Jerusalem Talmud, compiled by Rubinstein. The list, however, is largely of works in which commentaries on passages in the Jerusalem Talmud occur incidentally. Special mention, however, should be made of two excellent commentaries in the last century, the *Sefer Nir* of R.M. Kobrin to *Zera'im* and *Mo'ed* and part of *Nashim*, and that of Joseph Engels (1859–1919) in his *Gilyonei ha-Shas*. Most important is Lieberman's *Yerushalmi ki-Feshuto*, and his commentary to *Yerushalmi Nezikin*, mentioned above, as well as the numerous explanations of difficult passages from the Yerushalmi that can be found in Lieberman's monumental commentary to the Tosefta, *Tosefta Kefshuta*.

BIBLIOGRAPHY: S. Lieberman, *Al ha-Yerushalmi* (1929, 1969[2]); idem, *Talmudah shel Keisarin*, Suppl. to *Tarbiz*, 2, issue 4 (1931); idem, *Yerushalmi ki-Feshuto* (1934); idem, in: *Tarbiz*, 20 (1949), 107–17; idem, in: *Sefer Yovel… Alexander Marx* (1950), 287–319 (Heb. sect.); idem, *Yerushalmi Nezikin* (1984); idem, *Studies in Palestinian Talmudic Literature*, (1991); Frankel, Mevo; J.N. Epstein, in: *Tarbiz*, 5 (1933/34), 257–72; 6, issue 1 (1934/35), 38–35; *Sefer ha-Yovel… Ḥ. Albeck* (1963), 283–305; H.J. Dinkels (ed.), *Talmud Yerushalmi…*, 11 vols. (1934–67); L. Ginzberg, *Perushim ve-Ḥiddushim ba-Yerushalmi*, 1 (1941), introduction (Heb. and Eng.); the Eng. text reprinted in his: *On Jewish Law and Lore* (1955), 3–57; J. Rubinstein, *Kunteres ha-Shalem shel Mefarshei ha-Yerushalmi*, in: *Talmud Yerushalmi* (1949). **ADD. BIBLIOGRAPHY:** L. Moscovitz, *The Terminology of the Yerushalmi – Studies in the Dialectical Terminology of the Amoraim* (Heb.) (1988); idem, in: JQR, 91:1–2 (2000), 101–42; idem, in: AJS *Review*, 27:2 (2003), 227–52; idem, in: *The Talmud Yerushalmi and Graeco-Roman Culture I* (1998), 83–125; idem, in: *Proceedings of the Eleventh World Congress of Jewish Studies*, 3a (1994), 22–53; idem, in: *Sidra*, 10 (1994), 69–82; idem, in: D. Boyarin et al. (eds.), *Ateret Le-Ḥaim* (2000), 129–44; idem, in: *Tarbiz*, 66:2 (1997), 187–221; idem, in: *Asufot*, 11 (1998), 197–209; idem, in: *Tarbiz*, 64:2 (1995), 237–58; idem, in: *Sidra*, 8 (1992), 63–75; idem, in: *Tarbiz*, 60:1 (1991), 19–66; idem, in: *Teudah*, 10 (1996), 31–43; idem, in: *Tarbiz*, 60:4 (1991), 523–49; J. Sussman, in: *Meḥkare Talmud I* (1990), 55–133; idem, in: *Meḥkare Talmud II* (1993), 220–83; M. Sokoloff, *A Dictionary of Jewish Palestinian Aramaic* (1990): G. Dalman, *Grammatik des Judisch-Palästinischen Aramäisch* (1905); Wm. B. Stevenson, *A Grammar of Palestinian Jewish Aramaic* (1924); E.Y. Kutscher, *Studies in Galilean Aramaic* (1976); R. Macuch, *Grammatik des Samaritanischen Aramäisch* (1982); Strack-Stemberger, *Introduction to the Talmud and Midrash* (1996), 164–89; A. Goldberg, in: S. Safrai (ed.), *The Literature of the Sages* (1987), 303–22; B.M. Bokser, in: J. Neusner (ed.), *The Study of Ancient Judaism II* (1981), 1–119; M. Assis, in: *Tarbiz*, 56:2 (1987), 147–70; idem, in: *Tarbiz*, 53:1 (1984), 97–115.

[Louis Isaac Rabinowitz / Stephen G. Wald (2nd ed.)]

TALMUD, MUSICAL RENDITION. The Mishnah and *Gemara* were called the Oral Law (*Torah she-be-al Peh*) and continued to be called thus even after they had been put in writing. The transmission of an unwritten text depends on constant repetition (one of the meanings of the term Mishnah), and the more formal such a text becomes, the more its rendition will tend to develop into a formal – and soon also formulaic – sequence of quasi-melodic phrases. According to the Tosefta, R. Akiva enjoined the students to "sing it, constantly sing" (*zemer bi tadira zemer*; Tosef., Oho, 16:8 and Par. 4:7; also Sanh. 99a–b). The most explicit reference found is (Meg. 32b; also Sof. 3:13): "He who reads without melody (*ha-kore be-lo ne'imah*) and studies without a tune (*ve-shoneh be-lo zimrah*), about him the Bible says 'And I also have given you laws that are not good.'" This seems to refer first to biblical cantillation and then to the study of the Oral Law. The two terms *ne'imah* and *zimrah* might imply that the musical character of the two was not identical (*zammer* is also the term in R. Akiva's saying, above); and since *zammer* in the Talmud is usually connected with true singing it is reasonable to assume that the sentences of the Oral Law were rendered then, as they still frequently are, to a set melodic phrase, which was thus felt to be more in the nature of a "tune" than the constantly changing sequence of little motives which make up the cantillation of a biblical text. The warnings against making the Law "as a mere song" may therefore not be wholly metaphorical (Shab. 106b, 113a; Er. 60a). Even after the Mishnah had been put into writing it was studied aloud – as all books were in antiquity; silent reading seems to have been almost inconceivable at that time (cf. M. Hadas, *Ancilla to Classical Reading* (1954), 50–52). The "learning tune" could thus continue in use and be immediately applied to the additional body of oral commentary and discussion which accrued around each

Opening section of Ludas Paschalis *by André Hajdu (1970). This reproduces, with only slight stylization, the typical individual and comulative melodic pattern created in the East Ashkenazi tradition of collective Talmud study. Courtesy Israel Music Institute, Tel Aviv.*

mishnaic passage and was finally codified in writing as the *Gemara*. Other factors which strengthened this practice were the formal connection of the Talmud with the Bible, which was cantillated (cf. *Masoretic Accents, Musical Rendition), and its practical connection with the *derashah* ("homily"), in which at least a quasi-musical delivery always tends to appear as the structure acquires a set rhetorical pattern. A few passages in manuscripts and even prints appear furnished with masoretic accents, such as a *genizah* fragment of the Jerusalem Talmud's *Avodah Zarah* (see J.N. Epstein, *Li-Seridei ha-Yerushalmi*, in: *Tarbiz*, 3 (1931)) or the mishnaic passages in the Babylonian Talmud's *Kiddushin* (Sabbioneta edition 1553), but these have not yet been investigated with a view to discovering whether they represent mere experiments to make precise the divisions of the sentence or have some connection with the "learning tune." Neither have the living traditions of the "learning tune" been investigated and compared.

The developments outlined above only support the contention that the study of the Talmud was carried out from the earliest times by melodic (or rather melodized) rendition; but whether a certain pattern was the standard one, and how and where it survived cannot be stated. The "learning tune" is mentioned in several rabbinical works but here too the evidence has not as yet been collected (Idelsohn, *Melodien*, vol. 8, preface xvii, states that it is often mentioned, but gives only one source – Isaiah Hurwitz's *Shenei Luḥot ha-Berit*, fol. 256b in the Amsterdam edition of 1698). The melody also became customary for talmudic passages used in the liturgy (such as *Ba-Meh Madlikin*). It seems, however, that in many communities these liturgical renditions of a talmudic text acquired a special melody or at least a more elaborate form of the ordinary "learning tune." In Ashkenazi parlance it is called *lernshtayger*, although it cannot properly be classified among the **shtayger* patterns. Owing to their having a place in the liturgy, certain of these talmudic passages also became vehicles for individual cantorial elaboration. The earliest notated evidence of the "learning tune" is featured in the form of a parody – a haggling dialogue between a Jew and a herring seller – in *Chelec oder Thalmudischer Juedenschatz* by the convert Christian Gerson von Recklinghausen (Helmstedt, 1610). Very few specimens were notated in later times or recorded and transcribed in the modern period. Idelsohn's *Melodien* includes some from Yemen (vol. 1, nos. 4, 23, 35, 37, 92), Morocco (vol. 5, nos. 58, 72, 75), and Eastern Europe (vol. 8, nos. 234–6, the last two numbers being cantorial creations; see also in his *Music*, example 17 on p. 189 and pp. 191–2). A rendition from Djerba – the special intonation for the study of *Pirkei Avot* between Pesaḥ and Shavu'ot – was recorded and transcribed by A. Herzog (*Renanot*, facs. 8 (1961), 9–11).

[Bathja Bayer]

TALMUD AND MIDDLE PERSIAN CULTURE.
Jews and Persians lived in close proximity in Mesopotamia for over 12 centuries; for nearly all that time one or another Iranian dynasty ruled the country as a province of its empire. For nearly the entire amoraic period (220–500 C.E.), Babylonia was ruled by the Sasanian dynasty (224–651 C.E.) (Frye). By and large, the two communities coexisted peacefully; as the late third-century R. Huna put it, the Babylonian "exiles" were at ease in Babylonia, as the other exiles – those in the Roman world – were not (Men. 110a). The Persian king of kings wanted it that way. The Jews were a large minority in a vital province; Mesopotamia was both the breadbasket of the Empire and the province most vulnerable to Roman invasion. Jews, unlike the Christians who could become a fifth column once Christianity became the state religion of the Roman Empire in 317, would support the regime if they were satisfied. Indeed, Mesopotamia was so important that the capital was at Ctesiphon, right across the River Tigris from Babylonia. The Jews were thus a bulwark of the Empire – if they were kept satisfied and politically quiescent. As a result, the Sasanians resisted pressure from the Zoroastrian Church to persecute these minorities.

Again, the official religion of the Persian Empire, Zoroastrianism, was comfortable and even familiar to the Jews, with its theological doctrines of creation by the benevolent and omniscient Ohrmazd, reward and punishment, heaven and hell, judgment, creation, the fight against evil, the coming of the messiah, the ultimate defeat of evil, the renewal of creation, and the resurrection of the dead. This was true of its ethical system as well, with its emphasis of right thought, right speech, and right action, and its ritual system with the stress on the avoidance of idolatry, its hatred of sorcery, sodomy, and contact with menstruant women and dead bodies, as well as its valorization of such rabbinic doctrines as the importance of oral transmission and the authority of the rabbis. True, the operation of the sociological/psychological principle of the narcissism of small differences would have meant that leaders of both religions would have stressed their differences rather than similarities, but as the evidence preserved in the Babylonian Talmud indicates, Jewish acculturation to Persian religion, mores and culture was high. Its positive valuation of life in this world – procreation, agricultural and economic activities, as opposed to the world-denying views of Gnosticism and Manichaeism, was also in tune with Jewish values.

As a result of this long-term peaceful coexistence and basic similarity in world-view, we might well have expected what in fact we find: a large number of parallels, mutual and one-way influences and borrowings, etc. These manifest themselves in several areas of Babylonian-Jewish rabbinic life: in lifestyle, in legal and theological borrowings, and in sensibility.

Thus, two prominent Babylonian rabbis – Rav and R. Nahman – adopted the Iranian institution of temporary marriage in their own lives, and contracted such marriages when away from home (Yoma 18b, Yev. 39b), without a trace of moral disapproval from colleagues or the Babylonian Talmud's redactors. Rav and Rava and others permitted polygyny in a much more positive way than do Palestinian sources (Yev. 65a, Pes. 113a), and in general, Babylonian sources betray a much more positive, less ascetic attitude to sex than do Palestinian ones.

However, cultural influences are much more complicated than mere influence one way or another. As James Russell has observed, "influences from one quarter...do not preclude promiscuous intermingling with material from another tradition...; influences need not be a graft, but can be also a stimulus that brings into prominence a feature that had been present previously, but not important" (Russell, 6). Thus, the Babylonian Talmud's attitude to women, as expressed by some of its most influential figures, such as Abaye and R. Papa, echoes exactly the sentiments of a Middle Persian wisdom text, the Book of *Joisht i Friyan* (70–71, ll. 252–256): "It is not what you think, but what I think. You think that wives have great joy from various sorts of clothes and the suitable station as mistress of the house, if she can call such a thing her own. Now, it [is] not so. Wives [have] great joy being with their husbands." The last is later identified with sex. Compare the Babylonian Talmud: "Abaye said: With a husband [the size of] an ant her seat is placed among the great. R. Papa said: Though her husband be a flax beater she calls him to the threshold and sits down [at his side to show her married status]. R. Ashi said: Even if [her husband] has a demeaning family name [she accepts it and] requires no lentils for her pot. And all of them fornicate and attribute [the offspring] to their husbands" (Yev. 118b and Ket. 75a). "A man is obligated to make his children and household happy on the festival, as it is written, 'You shall rejoice on your festival' (Deut. 16:14). How does he make them happy? With wine. R. Judah says: Men with what is suitable for them and women with what is suitable for them. Men with wine, and women – with what? R. Joseph taught: In Babylonia with colored garments, and in the Land of Israel with linen garments"(Pes. 109a). Finally, there is the famous statement recorded in the Mishnah in the name of R. Joshua: "A woman prefers a *kab* [of food] and nine *kabs* of sex to nine *kabs* [of food] and abstinence" (M. Sot. 3:4; see TB Sot. 20a). Whether or not these statements are "merely" folk-sayings transmitted by these authorities, or their own, or falsely attributed to them, is irrelevant. The redactors thought enough of the statements to transmit them in the names of three of the most prominent *amoraim* in the Babylonian Talmud, whose immense prestige then lay behind them, and R. Joseph adds clothes to the mix in a halakhic context. This conglomeration of statements expresses the same mindset as the Middle Persian text. In the end, the "truthful Hifrih" adds R. Joshua's observation to the mix. Women want clothes, social position – but without sex, the others are hardly worth it. Both these texts relate to the same social context.

In this context we may note the rabbinic institution of the "rebellious wife," the *moredet* (Ket. 62a–b), which finds its exact counterpart in the Sasanian *atarsagāyīh*, "insubordination," to which an entire chapter of the Sasanian Law Book is devoted, with similar definitions (refusal of marital relations and domestic "work" and personal spousal service) and penalties (Macuch II, 25–29, 97–120, Perikhanian, 252–259). In this case, as in others, the differences are sometimes as illuminating as are the similarities, and historians of Jewish and Sasanian law ignore them at their peril (see: Elman, "Marital Property in Rabbinic and Sasanian Law"). The rabbinic concept of *ona'ah*, "overreaching" in sales, may be paralleled by MHD 37:2–10, with the same three-day period stipulated, but with a quarter rather than a sixth of the price (TB BM 49b–51a, 69a). Then there is the institution of *me'un* ("refusal"), whereby a underage girl could be married off by her mother or brothers, but could, upon reaching her majority, leave her husband (M. Yev. 13:1, 4, 7 and TB Yev. 107a); for the parallel, see MHD 89:15–17. Examples could be multiplied, and the reader is referred to the studies referred to above.

In the legal sphere we find the same phenomenon. Some parallels involve matters with which every legal system must deal, and are most likely the result of independent development. Similar conditions – economic, social, and religious – produce similar concerns. But studying each in isolation prevents us from gaining a complete picture of the conditions under which each system developed, and the way that each responded to common problems. Is it not unlikely that the rabbis and the Iranian jurisconsults were faced with a rash of fraudulent land-sales, with people claiming to own land they did not, as evidenced by TB BM 14a–b and the Sasanian Law Book 8:13–9:5 The hunger for arable land, certainly in short supply in the Persian Empire, would likely yield such a scheme in Jewish Babylonia (because of the density of population) and Iran (because of the arid conditions of its plateaus and mountains).

The adoption into the rabbinic system of the Sasanian institution of temporary gifts is another noteworthy event. According to both Talmuds (Suk. 41a and TJ Suk. 3:10 [54a]), this innovation was introduced by R. Nahman, who is criticized elsewhere in the Babylonian Talmud for being too Persianized by half (see Kid. 70a–b). It is not surprising that even his close disciple, Rava, expressed hesitations in this regard (Kid. 6b and BB 137b).

This influence extended to the theological realm as well. Thus, the Babylonian Talmud is much more concerned than the Jerusalem Talmud with the vexatious problem of theodicy, with the influential amora, Rava, taking the lead, as Y. Elman has demonstrated in a series of studies published in the early 1990s. The reason for this seems clear. Zoroastrianism's dualistic theology would seem to provide a relatively simple solution to the problem. Why do the righteous suffer? It is the doing of the Evil Spirit, Ahreman. The Babylonian Talmud, in the person of Rava, provides us with a portrait of his highly acculturated hometown, Mahoza, a suburb of the Persian capital, Ctesiphon, whose inhabitants were skeptical of rabbinic authority (see Sanh. 99b–100a, Mak. 22a). Rava himself seems to have fashioned a theological response to the problem, one which included at least one borrowing of a popular Zoroastrian theme, the dependence of vital elements of human life on fate, and not mitzvoth.

One of Rava's most radical statements on the topic fits perfectly within the context of the Middle Persian debate on "fate" and "works." Rava attributes to the workings of fate –

mazzal – the three elements that we may see as components of individual contentment: "[length of] life, [surviving] children, and sustenance" (MK 28a). Rava asserts that these three aspects of human life are astrologically determined and are not dependent on religious merit; he proves this by contrasting the lives of two great – "righteous" – authorities of the previous generation, Rabbah, the head of the Pumbeditan school, and his own father-in-law, R. Hisda.

Rava said: [Length of] life, children, and sustenance depend not on merit but [rather on] *mazzal.* For, take Rabbah and R. Hisda [as examples]. Both were absolutely righteous rabbis; [the proof of this righteousness is that] each master prayed for rain and it came. [Despite this,] R. Hisda lived to the age of 92; Rabbah only lived to the age of 40. In R. Hisda's house – 60 marriage feasts, in Rabbah's – 60 bereavements. At R. Hisda's house there was purest wheat bread for dogs, and it went to waste; at Rabbah's house there was barley bread for humans – and that could not be found.

This statement is not Rava's sole contribution to the matter, however. Rava reshapes R. Joseph's statement in Sot. 21a as to the limited utility of Torah-study and the performance of *mitzvot*; he asserts (in Ber. 5a) that in some cases one's merit may bring upon him yet more suffering, albeit "sufferings of love." As if all this were not enough, he reflects on the perilous nature of Israel's life in exile as played out in his own life (Hag. 5a–b). All of these (the limited protection from the exigencies of human existence afforded by Torah study and the performance of *mitzvot*, humanity's own frail nature, and the "sufferings of love") contribute to the tragic dimensions of the human condition – a recognition that lies at the heart of Zoroastrianism's dualistic view of the universe.

Rava's saying fits extremely well with the situation in Zoroastrian thought, where the theme of astrology versus merit, or "works," as the Middle Persian phrase has it, appears in many Middle Persian compilations, though, as usual, preserved only in post-Sasanian compilations. Still, Rava's apparent citation of a Babylonian Aramaic proverb has a striking parallel in a Middle Persian one. A saying attributed to Ādurbād ī Mahraspandān, the high priest roughly contemporary with Rava, but also transmitted anonymously, provides a striking parallel, though, of course, parts of the following may well include folk sayings, and statements taken from oral tradition but attributed to the high priest: "They say that the blessed Adurbad, son of Mahraspandan, divided the things of the material world into twenty-five parts: five (he assigned) to fate, five to action, five to habit, five to substance, and five to heredity. Life, wife, children, authority, and wealth are mostly through fate. Righteousness and wickedness and being a priest, warrior, and husbandmen are mostly through action. …" (Shaked, *Wisdom*, 174–175). Thus Rava's dictum has its direct referent in a Middle Persian saying. Moreover, while Rava's position is a *novum* in the Babylonian Talmud and in rabbinic literature in general, it is common in Iranian sources. Whether personal reflection impelled Rava's theological musings in this direction, or whether it was the pressure of the more acculturated members of his community, or whether his own encounters with Zoroastrian theology that motivated this conclusion – or, more probably, a combination of all of these – it is clear that Rava's statement, and the many later passages that follow this line in the Babylonian Talmud, relate to this interdenominational discussion In fine, then, the stark difference between the Babylonian Talmud and the Jerusalem Talmud, to which Elman called attention then also, must be laid at the door of the Middle Persian background of the Babylonian Talmud.

Middle Persian attitudes and doctrines made inroads in the Babylonian rabbinic elite culture, in law, in theology, and in general cultural attitudes, as well as in non-rabbinic Jewish attitudes. If anything, the ease that Babylonian Jews felt in the Iranian Exile extended to language as well, but an evaluation of the evidence requires a somewhat different paradigm than historians have developed for the Jewish encounter with Graeco-Roman culture. In any case, the Babylonian rabbinic elite display the influence of Persian culture, law, theological and general *Weltanschauung*. This is all to be expected, not only because of their long, relatively peaceful sojourn in Mesopotamia, but also because Zoroastrianism was, if anything, on the whole, a more benign presence than either Roman paganism or Christianity. Moreover, its theological and ritual structure was more in tune with that of Rabbinic Judaism than Roman paganism was, and while it shared an expectation of a messianic advent with Judaism, that advent was in the future, and therefore not a subject for acrimonious debate as it was with Christianity.

BIBLIOGRAPHY: R.N. Frye, *The History of Ancient Iran* (1983), 287–339 ("The Sasanians"); I. Gafni, *Yehudei Bavel bi-Tekufat ha-Talmud: Ḥayyei ha-Ḥevrah ve-ha-Ru'aḥ* (1990); A. Oppenheim, *Babylonia Judaica in the Talmudic Period* (1983), 179–235; Y. Elman, "Between Rabbi and *Dādwar*: R. Nahman of Mahoza," Thirty-fifth AJS Convention, Chicago, December 20, 2004; M. Boyce, *Zoroastrians: Their Religious Beliefs and Practices* (1979), 118; M. Shaki, "The Denkard Account of the History of the Zoroastrian Scriptures," in: *Archiv Orientalni*, 49 (1981), 114–25; S. Shaked, *Dualism in Transformation: Varieties of Religion in Sasanian Iran* (1994), 11–12; J.R. Russell, "Ezekiel and Iran," in: S. Shaked and A. Netzer, *Irano-Judaica*, 5 (2003); M.L. Satlow, *Tasting the Dish: Rabbinic Rhetorics of Sexuality* (1995); F.M. Kotwal and P. Kreyenbroek, with contributions by J.R. Russell, *The Hērbedestān and the Nērangestān*, vol. 1: *Hērbedestān* (Studia Iranica 10) (1992); A. Schremer, in: PAAJR, 63 (1997–2001), 181–223; S. Shaked (ed.), *The Wisdom of the Sasanian Sages (Dēnkard VI) by Aturpāt-i Ēmētān* (Persian Heritage Series 34); Y. Elman, "Acculturation to Elite Persian Norms in the Babylonian Jewish Community of Late Antiquity," in: E. Halivni, Z.A. Steinfeld, and Y. Elman (eds.), *Neti'ot David* (2004), 31–56; M. Beer, "*Gezerotav shel Kartir al Yehudei Bavel*," in: *Tarbiz,* 54 (1981), 525–37; M. Macuch, *Das sasanidische Rechtsbuch "Mātakdān i Hazār Dātistān" (Teil II)* (1981); idem, *Rechtskasuistik und Gerichtspraxis zu Beginn des siebenten Jahrhunderts in Iran: Die Rechtssammlung des Farrohmard i Wahrāmān* (1993); A. Perikhanian, *The Book of a Thousand Judgements*, trans. N. Garsoian, (1997); S. Secunda, "On the Importance of a Zoroastrian *'Sugya'*: Sasanian Rabbinic and Zoroastrian Study," presented at the AJS Thirty-Sixth Annual Convention, December 29, 2004; "Scripture Versus Contemporary Needs: A Sasanian/Zoroastrian

Example," in: *Cardozo Law Review*, 28 (2006); Y. Elman, "Marriage and Marital Property in Rabbinic and Sasanian Law," in: C. Hezser (ed.), *Rabbinic Law in Its Roman and Near Eastern Context* (2003), 227–76; idem, "Returnable Gifts in Rabbinic and Sasanian Law," in: *Irano-Judaica*, 6 (2004); idem, "'Up to the Ears' in Horses' Necks: On Sasanian Agricultural Policy and Private 'Eminent Domain,'" in: JSIJ, 3 (2004), 95–149; idem, "Cultural Aspects of Post-Redactional Additions to the Bavli," in: J. Rubenstein (ed.), *Creation and Composition: The Contribution of the Bavli Redactors (Stammaim) to the Aggadah* (TSAJ 114) (2005), 383–416; idem, "Middle Persian Culture and Babylonian Sages: Accommodation and Resistance in the Shaping of Rabbinic Legal Tradition," in: C.E. Fonrobert and M.S. Jaffee (eds.), *Cambridge Companion to Rabbinic Cambridge Literature* (2006); idem, "The Babylonian Talmud in Its Historical Context," in: *The Printing of the Talmud* (2005), 19–28; idem, "'He in His Cloak and She in Her Cloak': Conflicting Images of Sexuality in Sasanian Mesopotamia," in: R. Kern-Ulmer (ed.), *Discussing Cultural Influences: Text, Context, and Non-Text in Rabbinic Judaism: Proceedings of a Conference on Rabbinic Judaism* at *Bucknell University* (2006); idem, "*Yeshivot Bavliyot ke-Vatei Din*," in: E. Etkes (ed.), *Ha-Yeshiva* (2006); idem, "R. Yosef be-cIdan Ritha," in: *Memorial Volume for Prof. M.S. Feldblum* (2006), 93–104; M. Weinreich, "*Die Geschichte von Jōišt ī Frīyan, Altorientalische Forschungen*, 19 (1992), 44–101.

[Yaakov Elman (2nd ed.)]

TALNOYE, city in Kiev district, Ukraine. In 1847 there were 1,807 Jews in Talnoye. By 1897 their number reached 5,452 (57% of the total population). During the 19th century, R. David *Twersky lived in Talnoye. Thousands of Ḥasidim in Ukraine adhered to Twersky and subsequently to his sons. The melodies of the *ḥazzan* of the ḥasidic court, R. Yossele Tolner, became popular among the masses in Russia and Poland. The city suffered severely from bands of peasants who ravaged the region in 1919–20. The soldiers of the White Army who passed through Talnoye during the summer of 1919 rioted and burnt down a large part of the city. In 1926 there were 4,169 Jews (39% of the population) in Talnoye. The Jewish settlement was destroyed after the region was taken by the Nazis in 1941.

BIBLIOGRAPHY: A.D. Rosenthal, in: *Reshummot*, 3 (1923), 31121; M. Osherowitch, *Shtet un Shtetlekh in Ukraine*, 1 (1948), 146–64.

[Yehuda Slutsky]

TALPIR, GABRIEL JOSEPH (1901–1990), Hebrew art critic and poet. Talpir was born in Stanislav, Galicia, and after teaching in secondary schools in Vilna and Zamosc immigrated to Palestine in 1925, and from 1932 became editor of *Gazit*, a periodical for art and literature.

He published poems in Israel's newspapers and literary journals, as well as essays and articles on literature and art, mostly in *Gazit*, perhaps the first periodical in Hebrew devoted to the plastic arts. His volumes of poetry include *Jazz Band* (1927) and *Ra'av* (1928). Among his works in the field of art are: *Ḥannah Orloff, Ḥayyeha vi-Yẓiratah* (1950) and *Ommanut Bereshit* (1952). He also published two art albums, with introductions: *Ẓayyarim Yehudiyyim bi-Zemanneinu* (1937) and *Ẓayyarim be-Yisrael* (1964). In addition, Talpir translated several books on art into Hebrew.

BIBLIOGRAPHY: Kressel, Leksikon, 2 (1967), 22–23.

[Getzel Kressel]

TAL SHAḤAR (Heb. טַל שַׁחַר), moshav in central Israel east of Ḥuldah, affiliated with Tenu'at ha-Moshavim. Tal Shaḥar was founded in 1948 by a group from Romania as one of the first settlements established to secure the Jerusalem Corridor. The moshav, which absorbed immigrants from many different countries, had 400 inhabitants in 1970 and 729 in 2002. Its farming was partly intensive. Tal Shaḥar ("Morning Dew") is named after the U.S. leader Henry *Morgenthau, Jr.

[Efraim Orni]

TAM, JACOB BEN MEIR (**Rabbenu**; c. 1100–1171), tosafist and leading French scholar of the 12th century. Rabbenu Tam was the grandson of *Rashi and the son of Meir b. *Samuel, Rashi's son-in-law. His teachers were his father, his brother *Samuel, and Jacob b. *Samson, a pupil of Rashi. Little is known of the members of his family, save that his wife Miriam was the sister of R. Samson b. Joseph of *Falaise and that four of his sons were named Joseph, Moses, Solomon, and Isaac, about whom nothing is known. R. Tam lived in Ramerupt where he engaged in moneylending and viticulture, typical occupations of the Jews there at that time, and became well-to-do. His business affairs brought him into contact with the nobility and the authorities, who occasioned him much trouble. To a great extent his attitude toward non-Jews in various halakhic questions was conditioned by his direct contact with them and his knowledge of their character. During the Second Crusade he was attacked by Crusaders who were passing through, and was miraculously saved from death (1146). After this experience R. Tam left Ramerupt.

Tam was recognized by all contemporary scholars, even by those in remote places, as the greatest scholar of the generation. Abraham *ibn Daud of Spain, and *Abraham b. Isaac and *Zerahiah ha-Levi of Provence, refer to him with great esteem, while the scholars of southern Italy, some his senior in years, submitted their halakhic problems to him. Pupils came to his *bet midrash* from as far away as Bohemia and Russia, and took Tam's teachings back with them on their return to these lands. He won this great renown although he never moved or traveled far from his place of residence in northern France. Nor was he unaware of his outstanding reputation as a scholar, for on it he based the claim that his *bet din* had the authority to issue decisive pronouncements. He even "wrote a prosbul declaring that it had to be done by the foremost *bet din* of the generation" (Tos. to Git. 36b, s.v. *de-allimei*). Tam violently attacked scholars, even in distant places, who refused to accept his decisions and pronouncements, revealing a desire to impose his halakhic authority also on Provence and Germany, a tendency which R. Abraham b. David of Posquières vehemently opposed.

His attitude on this is reflected in the correspondence between him and *Meshullam b. Nathan of Melun. The original subject at issue was not of the greatest halakhic and practical importance, but it gradually developed into a controversy about several customs followed and instituted by Meshullam in his community, that differed from those of Tam. Writing in an extremely aggressive style, Tam threatened to excommunicate anyone who adopted the customs of Meshullam, and severely rebuked the latter for the lack of respect he had shown toward the French scholars including Rashi, and for what Tam regarded as his irresponsible attitude in emending talmudic texts. The extant correspondence is fragmentary and its chronological order cannot be established, but from it as a whole there emerges a clear picture of Tam's bitter fight against Meshullam and his aggressive attempt to impose his own views and decisions on him. Of a similar nature was the correspondence between Tam and Ephraim b. Isaac of Regensburg.

R. Tam proved to be a high-handed leader of his generation who did not refrain either from abolishing several customs which did not appeal to him or from introducing important ordinances and legal permissions dictated by the times. Despite this, he was in principle extremely conservative on questions of custom as is clearly evident from his correspondence with Meshullam. Among later scholars these decisions of Tam at times occasioned great surprise, while some of the earlier authorities contended that they had merely a theoretical character, and that he himself never applied them in practice. On the basis of these lenient pronouncements by him, some scholars of the Haskalah even sought to make him a "reform" rabbi in the spirit of the later Haskalah, but in doing so they completely ignored the sources which indicate that he adopted a strict approach especially as regards unimportant customs observed by ignorant people or women, and that there are no grounds for maintaining he adopted a systematically lenient or a strict attitude. The leader of his generation, he was permeated with the consciousness of this leadership and animated by a desire to maintain communal unity and peace through a life based on the teachings of the Torah and on faith. R. Tam had many pupils and some of his contemporaries, among them also those older than he, regarded themselves as his disciples although never taught by him. Among his best known pupils were *Ḥayyim b. Hananel ha-Kohen, *Moses b. Abraham of Pontoise, Joseph *Bekhor Shor of Orleans, *Yom Tov b. Isaac of Joigny, and *Eliezer b. Samuel of Metz.

The *tosafot* of the Babylonian Talmud are based on Tam's explanations, glosses, and decisions, and are pervaded throughout by his statements. In addition to this, his literary production was large and ramified. His principal work is *Sefer ha-Yashar* (Vienna, 1811) which consists of two parts, the one, responsa (issued in a scholarly edition by S.P. Rosenthal, Berlin, 1898), and the other, novellae on the Talmud (a scholarly edition was published by S. Schlesinger, Jerusalem, 1959). But this work contains only a small part of his responsa, others being scattered throughout the entire literature of the earlier halakhic authorities and in various manuscripts. There is still no complete edition of his responsa. The main trend of his novellae is to corroborate the talmudic texts and to prove that nothing is to be emended, either by deletions or by addenda, whether on the basis of logical argument or on that of other works or parallel sources. Preserved in an extremely corrupt state, *Sefer ha-Yashar*, even after the great labor expended on editing it, still contains many obscure and inexplicable passages. In its present form it comprises excerpts collected in the days of the earlier halakhic authorities and represents the work of many hands, including that of Tam himself, who repeatedly emended and improved much of it. The earlier authorities also refer to Tam's *Sefer ha-Pesakim*, which is no longer extant. It is doubtful whether he wrote a special commentary on the Pentateuch, although biblical comments of his are quoted by the earlier tosafists. It is, however, clear that he composed a commentary on the Book of Job. His *Hilkhot Sefer Torah* are printed in *Maḥzor Vitry* (1923), 651–73.

Tam was also the first French scholar to compose rhymed poetry, in which he was undoubtedly influenced by the Spanish and southern French scholars with whom he came into contact. He exchanged poems with Abraham *ibn Ezra. His *piyyutim* were written largely in the Franco-German style.

[Israel Moses Ta-Shma]

Tam also devoted himself to Hebrew grammar. His *Sefer ha-Hakhra'ot* (1855), the purpose of which was to decide the points of dispute in grammar between *Menahem ibn Saruk and *Dunash b. Labrat, is particularly well known. Tam defended Menahem against the 160 criticisms of Dunash and mostly decided in his favor. Tam's knowledge of grammar was far from perfect, and it is difficult to assume that he discovered the triliteral nature of the Hebrew root himself, independently of Judah b. David *Ḥayyuj, as suggested by some scholars. Joseph b. Isaac *Kimḥi wrote his *Sefer ha-Galui* in answer to the *Sefer ha-Hakhra'ot* justifying the criticisms of Dunash. Tam also wrote a didactic poem on the cantillation of the Torah. *Sefer ha-Yashar ha-Katan*, which deals with ethics, was wrongly ascribed to Tam.

[Nisan Netzer]

BIBLIOGRAPHY: S.D. Luzzatto, in: *Kerem Ḥemed*, 7 (1843), 33ff.; I.H. Weiss, *Toledot Rabbenu... Tam* (1883), also in: *Beit Talmud*, 3 (1882), 33–36, 129–38, 161–9, 193–201, 225–33, 257–61, 289–95; Weiss, Dor, 4 (1904–), index; A. Deutscher, *Toledot Rabbenu Tam* (1884); S.A Wertheimer. *Ginzei Yerushalayim*, 1 (1896), 10–19; Finkelstein, Middle Ages, index; Davidson, Oẓar, index; F. Baer, in: MGWJ, 71 (1927), 392–7; V. Aptowitzer, *Mavo le-Sefer Ravyah* (1938), 357–66; Urbach. Tosafot, index; idem (ed.), *Arugat ha-Bosem*, 4 (1963), index; S. Abramson, in: KS, 37 (1962), 241–8; Y. Kafaḥ, in: *Kovez al Yad*, 7 (1968), 81–100; T. Preschel, in: JBA, 28 (Heb. 1970/71). AS GRAMMARIAN: H. Filipowski, *Teshuvot Dunash ben Labrat im Hakra'ot Rabbenu Ya'akov Tam* (1855); H. Englander, in: HUCA, 15 (1940), 485–95; Urbach, Tosafot, 92–93.

TAMAKH, ABRAHAM BEN ISAAC HA-LEVI (d. 1393), Spanish paytan, talmudist, and philosopher; d rabbi of Gerona. Abraham may have come from Provence, although according to some he originated from Barcelona. Abraham with other scholars was requested by Pedro IV of Aragon to decide on the family purity of the family of one Isaac Castellon. He lived in Gerona, where he was one of the leaders of the community. He was a contemporary and colleague of Profiat *Duran who eulogized him after his death in a letter written to Tamakh's son Joseph which was intended to be read publicly at the memorial service for his father. The academy he headed in Gerona and its library were destroyed in the wave of anti-Jewish violence in 1391. He fled from Gerona, passed through Narbonne, and made his way to Ereẓ Israel. It is known that during his journey he stayed in various communities in Italy and Egypt and also held office in these towns. After reaching Ereẓ Israel, he returned for unknown reasons to Spain, where he died. His fame rests mainly on his commentary to the Song of Songs, published with the biblical text (Sabbioneta, 1558; Prague, 1611). In modern times it has been published with variae lectiones from manuscripts and printed editions by L.A. Feldman (1970). In his commentary Abraham cites by name only Maimonides and Naḥmanides, and the influence of the former's *Guide of the Perplexed* is especially noticeable. There is also a substantial affinity between it and Joshua *ibn Shuaib's homily on the Song of Songs that was included in his large book of sermons. Abraham belonged to the circle of *Nissim b. Reuben Gerondi and *Isaac b. Sheshet Perfet and exchanged letters and poems with them. Abraham's correspondence with Nissim Gerondi and his circle has also been published by Feldman in *Koveẓ al Yad* (see bibliography). There are different views as to the meaning of the name Tamakh. It may have been an acrostic of the words showing respect for the dead, *Tehei Menuḥato Kavod* ("may he rest in honor"), or it may be an ordinary family name, found among many families of levites.

BIBLIOGRAPHY: L.A. Feldman, in: *Koveẓ al Yad*, 17 (1968), 127ff.; idem (ed.), R. Abraham b. Isaac ha-Levi Tamakh, *Commentary on the Song of Songs* (1970), introd. 3–35; idem, in: *Hadorom*, 25 (1967), 186–94; 28 (1969), 222–37; idem, in: *Samuel K. Mirsky Memolrial Volume* (1970), 85–103; Joshua ibn Shuaib, *Derashot* (1969), introd, by S. Abramson, 41–43; Zunz, Lit Poesie, 512; Graetz, Gesch, 8 (1909), 408; Neubauer, in: REJ, 9 (1884), 117; Gross, Gal Jud, 429; Davidson, Oẓar, 1 (1924), 165:2226, 170:3656, 406:8949; Baer, Spain, 2 (1966), 106, 152, 156, 475.

[Leon A. Feldman]

TAMAR (Heb. תָּמָר), locality on the borders of Judah, appearing as Hazazon-Tamar in Genesis 14:7, where it is described as a dwelling place of the Amorites between Kadesh and Sodom. This precludes the identification with En-Gedi attempted in II Chronicles 20:2. According to the Masoretic Text of I Kings 9:18, Solomon built "Tamar in the wilderness," but this reading is not certain as the parallel verse in II Chronicles 8:4 has Tadmor (Palmyra). Ezekiel lists it as a boundary point of the land of Israel, together with Meribath-Kadesh (47:19; 48:28). A Roman fort called Thamara is indicated on the Tabula Peutingeriana, a Roman road map, and is also mentioned by the geographer Ptolemy and by Eusebius (Onom. 8:6ff.), who places it one day's journey from Mampsis (Kurnub). It is also shown on the *Madaba Map. Alt has identified the fort of Tamar with Qaṣr al-Juhayniyya (present-day Mesad Tamar), but Aharoni has argued convincingly for an identification with ʿAyn al-Ḥuṣb (En Hezeva), where there are remains of a Roman fort garrisoned by Cohors I Centenaria. Excavations were made at the site of the *castellum* by M. Gichon in 1973–76. The fort was apparently founded prior to the Roman annexation of the area from the Nabateans in 106 C.E., with the corner towers added at the time of Trajan. Abandoned during the time of Hadrian, the fort was seized at the time of Aurelian's conquest of the Palmyran Empire in 271–73 C.E. The fort was in use, with minor repairs, until the Muslim conquest of 635 C.E.

BIBLIOGRAPHY: Aharoni, *IEJ*, 13 (1963), 30–42. **ADD. BIBLIOGRAPHY:** Roll, IEJ, 39 (1989), 260; Y. Tsafrir, L. Di Segni, and J. Green, *Tabula Imperii Romani. Iudaea – Palaestina. Maps and Gazetteer.* (1994), 247, s.v. "Thamara."

[Michael Avi-Yonah / Shimon Gibson (2nd ed.)]

TAMAR (Heb. תָּמָר; "date palm"), the name of three biblical figures.

(1) Judah's daughter-in-law, the wife of his firstborn son, Er (Gen. 38:6; II Chron. 2:3–4). After *Er's early death, Tamar became the wife of his brother, *Onan, in accordance with the custom of levirate marriage (Deut. 25:5ff.). But because the firstborn son of such a marriage would not count as his (Deut. 25:6), Onan, when cohabiting with her took measures to prevent her from becoming pregnant (Gen. 38:9). When Onan also died young, Judah, fearing now that marriage to Tamar was unlucky, told her to go and live in her father's house until his third son, Shelah, grew to manhood, but did not give her to Shelah even when he had grown up. Tamar therefore laid aside her widow's weeds and sat, veiled so as not to be recognized by Judah, in the gate of a town that she knew Judah would have to pass. A woman sitting in the city gate was bound to be taken for a prostitute, and Tamar supposed that Judah, who had recently been widowed, would probably be attracted. He was, and he offered her a kid for her favors. As pledge of payment, he left with her his seal, cord, and staff. Tamar became pregnant by Judah, but he, thinking that she had become pregnant through harlotry, ordered her to be burned to death. Tamar thereupon sent the seal, cord, and staff to Judah with the message that she was pregnant by the man to whom they belonged. Judah thereupon declared "She is more in the right than I, inasmuch as I did not give her to my son Shelah" (Gen. 38:26). Tamar duly gave birth to twin boys, *Perez and *Zerah. According to Ruth 4:1822, *David was descended from Perez.

[Harold Louis Ginsberg.]

In the Aggadah

Tamar was the daughter of Shem (Gen. R. 85:10). Endowed with the gift of prophecy, Tamar knew that she was destined to be the ancestress of David and of the Messiah, and therefore determined to ensure the fulfillment of her destiny (Zohar, Gen. 188a–b). Judah failed to recognize her because in her modesty she always kept her face covered in his household (Sot. 10b). As a reward for this she became the mother of the royal line of David and the ancestress of Isaiah (ibid.). When she became pregnant she boasted to all that she would be the mother of kings and redeemers (Gen. R. 85:10). Charged with unchastity before a tribunal made up of Isaac, Jacob, and Judah (Tanḥ. B, Va-Yeshev 17), she refused to reveal the name of Judah in order not to humiliate him, preferring to die rather than incriminate him publicly (Ber. 43b). She was condemned to be burned to death as her father Shem was a priest (Gen. R. 85:11). Only at the moment of ultimate danger to her life did she try to save herself. However, when she searched for Judah's pledges, she could not find them, as the evil angel *Samael had taken them away in order to prevent the birth of David, but the angel *Gabriel restored them (Sot. 10b). Judah subsequently married her.

(2) A daughter of David and Maacah, and full sister of *Absalom (II Sam. 13). Her half-brother *Amnon conceived a passion for Tamar and by a ruse got her to come to his room and forced her to lie with him. Then his love turned to loathing and he drove her from his house (II Sam. 13:15). She was later avenged by Absalom, who had Amnon murdered (*ibid.* 13:23–29).

(3) The daughter of Absalom, famed for her beauty (II Sam. 14:27). In the Septuagint version (*ibid.*), Tamar was given in marriage to *Rehoboam, the son of Solomon, to whom she bore *Abijah (but cf. I Kings 15:2; II Chron. 13:2).

[bustanay Oded]

BIBLIOGRAPHY: TAMAR (1): E.A. Speiser, *Genesis* (1964), 297–300. IN THE AGGADAH: Ginzberg, Legends, 2 (1910), 32–36; 5 (1925), 333–5.

TAMARES, AARON SAMUEL (1869–1931), rabbi, writer, and philosopher. Born near Maltsh in the district of Grodno, Tamares became known as the "prodigy from Maltsh." Upon the death of his father-in-law (1893), he inherited his post as rabbi in the village of Milejczyce (Grodno district), which he occupied until his death. With the emergence of political Zionism, Tamares joined the new movement and responded to rabbinical opposition in a series of articles entitled "*Shillumim le-Riv Ẓiyyon*" (*Ha-Meliẓ*, nos. 56–70, 1899). He said that the religious leadership of the people was becoming petrified and incapable of moving with the spirit of the times; this, he argued, was the reason for its loss of mass support.

Tamares participated in the Fourth Zionist Congress in 1900 but returned disillusioned with Zionism, especially its political aspects, and was also unable to find his place in the *Mizrachi movement, which he considered essentially no different from political Zionism. He began to denounce nationalism, and to preach pacifism. This was the subject of his first book *Ha-Yahadut ve-ha-Ḥerut* (1905). At the core of Tamares' outlook was his concept of Judaism as a moral code. He preached acceptance of the *galut* because of its "spiritual purification of our people" by liberating it from the urge for power and war. He also attacked the rabbis for clinging to the superstitions of the masses. These views were expounded in his books *Ha-Emunah ha-Tehorah ve-ha-Dat ha-Hamonit* and *Musar ha-Torah ve-ha-Yahadut* (both in 1912), as well as in many articles in Hebrew and Yiddish signed "Aḥad ha-Rabbonim ha-Margishim." With the outbreak of World War I the attainment of world peace, which he saw as the mission of the people of Israel, became his central concern (expounded in his books *Keneset Yisrael u-Milḥemot ha-Goyim* (1920) and *Sheloshah Zivvugim Bilti-Hagunim* (1930)). He stepped up his attacks on Zionism for its aspirations to make the people of Israel "a nation like other nations," and for its objectives to attain statehood and military power. He also published a book on *halakhah, Yad Aharon* (1923). Tamares was an unusual figure in the rabbinical world: an Orthodox rabbi who fought against the fossilized *halakhah* in a completely original style and who attacked nationalism and political Zionism as anti-Jewish phenomena.

BIBLIOGRAPHY: Rejzen, Leksikon, 4 (1929), 897–902; Kressel, Leksikon, 2 (1967), 989–90.

[Yehuda Slutsky]

TAMARISK (Heb. אֶשֶׁל, *eshel*). Several species of the genus *Tamarix* grow wild in Israel. The tree resembles the *cypress in that its leaves are very small and in one species are barely visible. Unlike the cypress, however, the tamarisk belongs to the Angiospermae, having seeds in a closed ovary. Since in Arabic the tamarisk is called *athl*, which corresponds to the biblical *eshel*, the tree planted in Beer-Sheba by Abraham (Gen. 21: 33), the *eshel* has so been identified. Saul judged the people beneath an *eshel* (I Sam. 22:6), and the bones of Saul and his sons were buried under this tree in Jabesh in Transjordan (I Sam. 31:13; in I Chron. 10:12 the reading is *elah*, a *terebinth). Some rabbis understood *eshel* to be a general name for a tall tree, and some took it to be the *shittim* trees from which the tabernacle was constructed (Yal., Song 985). The tamarisk trees of Israel grow in the warmer regions. Some, like the *Tamarix jordanis* which covers extensive stretches in the thickets of Jordan, grow near water, whereas the *Tamarix tetragyna* grows extensively in the swamp in the vicinity of the Dead Sea. Other species grow in the coastal lowlands and in the sandy stretches of the Negev. In the Sinai Desert grows the species *Tamarix mannifera*, upon which is found a sweet extract of insects that some believe to be the biblical *manna. It would appear that the biblical *arar*, mistakenly identified with the *juniper, is in fact the tamarisk growing in the desert or in salty soil, and it is called *ʿarʿar* in Arabic. The name *arar*, from the root ערה meaning "empty" or "naked," fits the tamarisk for it has only tiny leaves covered with a gray coating of salt which exudes from them. Jeremiah compares a person who puts his trust in man and not in God to "an *arar* in the desert." The tree appears to be suffering and "shall not see when good cometh" (Jer. 17:6). In contrast to the pessimistic Jeremiah, the psalmist (Ps. 102:18) sees hope even for it, for "He hath regarded the prayer of the *arar*" ("destitute"). It has been suggested that this reference is to the brief period of the tree's flowering when it is covered with thousands of pinkish-white blossoms as if wrapped in a *tallit* and praying for the improvement of the hard conditions of its life in the desert.

BIBLIOGRAPHY: Loew, Flora, 3 (1924), 398ff.; H.N. and A.L. Moldenke, *Plants of the Bible* (1952), index; J. Feliks, *Olam ha-Ẓomeʾaḥ ha-Mikraʾi* (1968²), 82–83, 94–95.

[Jehuda Feliks]

TAM IBN YAḤYA, JACOB BEN DAVID (c. 1475–1542), Turkish rabbi and codifier. Leaving Lisbon with his father after the expulsion from *Portugal in 1496, he settled in Constantinople where he achieved a reputation for his comprehensive talmudic knowledge (responsa, *Oholei Tam*, 142). He was appointed a member of the *bet din* presided over by Elijah *Mizraḥi, chief rabbi of *Turkey, and after the latter's death Ibn Yaḥya was recognized, even beyond his own country, as the spiritual leader of Turkish Jewry (*ibid.*, 110 and 147). In his responsa he adopted "the clear and concise style characteristic of the French and German rabbis … who weigh every word" (*ibid.*, 36 and 147). Ibn Yaḥya adopted a rigid attitude in his decisions, but at the same time went to great lengths to seek relief for an *agunah* (*ibid.*, 142). He opposed the view that the *Karaites were not to be regarded as Jews, but a group whose place, halakhically speaking, was intermediate between that of Jews and non-Jews, maintaining that they were to be regarded as Jews upon whom the precepts of Judaism were binding (*ibid.*, 127). Although he had a knowledge of *Kabbalah, he opposed its being taught. He also studied medicine and had a knowledge of Arabic, Turkish, and Spanish, while "his knowledge of Islamic law was so great that their judges frequently consulted with him with regard to their decisions" (G. ibn Yaḥya, *Shalshelet ha-Kabbalah*). Ibn Yaḥya was a prolific writer, but most of his works were destroyed in the conflagration which overtook Constantinople a year before his death. The remnants of his responsa were collected and published after his death in the *Tummat Yesharim* collection (Venice, 1624), under the title *Oholei Tam*, along with his glosses to Alfasi, entitled *Derekh Tamim*.

BIBLIOGRAPHY: E. Carmoly, *Divrei ha-Yamim li-Venei Yaḥya* (1850); Graetz, Gesch, 9 (1891³), 33, 394; Rosanes, Togarmah, 2 (1937/38), 6ff.

[Ephraim Kupfer]

TAMID (Heb. תָּמִיד), the ninth or tenth tractate of the order *Kodashim* in the Mishnah and the Babylonian Talmud. *Tamid* is an abbreviated form for *olat tamid* ("daily burnt-offering") and refers to the daily (morning and evening) sacrifices as set out in Exodus 29:38–42 and Numbers 28:1–8 (cf. II Kings 16:15; Ezek. 46:13–15; Neh. 10:34, and II Chron. 13:11). This tractate is not actually concerned with these sacrifices; it gives a description of the morning work in the Temple, from the moment the priests set about their work early in the morning until after the *tamid* sacrifice was organized later in the morning. Little controversy is recorded here in the Mishnah, a sign of an early redaction, probably from just before or soon after the destruction of the Temple. In current editions of the Mishnah and Talmud, *Tamid* has seven chapters, but originally it seems to have had only six, the present seventh being included in the sixth, and this explains its position after *Keritot* and *Me'ilah,* which also have six chapters each.

Chapter 1 discusses the priestly night watches and the preparations for the morning sacrifice, in particular the clearing of the ashes of the previous day's offerings from the altar. Chapter 2 deals mainly with laying a new fire on the altar. Chapter 3 deals with casting lots to determine which priests have to perform the various sacrificial duties. Chapter 4 describes in detail how the lamb was slaughtered and prepared for the sacrifice. Chapter 5 states that the recital of the *Shema prayer in the Temple was preceded by a blessing and was followed by three others, including the biblical priestly benediction. Chapter 6 treats of the offering of incense. Chapter 7 first discusses the high priest's entry, his prostration and the accompanying ceremonials, and the way in which the high priest and common priests administered the priestly benediction. Then follows a long paragraph setting out in detail the special ceremonial, when the high priest himself participated in the sacrificial service. At the end of the chapter is the phrase, "this is the order of the *Tamid*…," which seems to conclude the tractate. Yet, in current editions, there is an additional passage giving the list of psalms sung by the levites on different days of the week. The Mishnah of *Tamid* is that of *Simeon of Mizpah as is established by the Talmud (Yoma 14b). The Mishnah of *Yoma* 2:3–4 derives from that of *Tamid*, and a comparison between them indicates that the text in *Tamid* is a later compilation. The Mishnah of *Tamid* has a distinct Hebrew style containing expressions not found elsewhere in the Mishnah. *Tamid* was translated into English by M. Simon in the Soncino edition (1948).

BIBLIOGRAPHY: Epstein, Tannaʾim, 27–31; Ḥ. Albeck, *Shishah Sidrei Mishnah, Seder Kodashim* (1959), 291f.

[Arnost Zvi Ehrman]

TAMIR (Katznelson), SHMUEL (1923–1987), Israeli lawyer and politician, member of the Sixth to Ninth Knessets. Tamir was born in Jerusalem, the son of Dr. Reuben Katzenelson, but later adopted the name he had assumed while a member of the *Irgun Ẓevaʾi Le'ummi. He grew up under the influence of the atmosphere that followed the massacre of Jews in *Hebron in 1929, and believed that those accused of Haim *Arlosoroff's murder were innocent. Tamir joined the IẒL in 1938. He was a radio announcer on the Voice of Jerusalem but was fired in 1944 when his membership in the IẒL was discovered, after he had commanded an operation to blow up the income tax office in Jerusalem. In 1946 he was appointed deputy commander of the IẒL in Jerusalem, and the following year was arrested by the British authorities for the third time, and deported to Kenya, where he was allowed to study for his final law examinations. In July 1948 Tamir was returned to Israel, but was not mobilized to the IDF in the War of Independence. He joined the *Ḥerut Movement when it was founded in 1948, and belonged to the La-Merḥav faction that supported unity with the General Zionists. Tamir left the Ḥerut Movement in 1952 and concentrated on his legal career. Among the important cases in which he was involved was the Ẓerifin trial in 1953, in which he defended an underground group called "Loḥamei Malkhut Yisrael" responsible for an explosion in the Soviet Embassy in February 1953. In 1954 Tamir defended Malki'el Grunwald, in a libel suit brought against him by Israel *Kasztner, whom he had accused of collaborating with the Nazis. In 1962 he represented the Herzliya film studios in an appeal against the decision of the censorship to prohibit the screening of a newsreel showing a demonstration in the Arab village of Sumayil that was crushed with violence. In 1957 Tamir was one of the founders of a movement called "Ha-Mishtar he-Ḥadash" that sought to bring about changes in the Israeli political system. In 1964 he returned to the Ḥerut movement, and participated in the founding of *Gaḥal, on whose list he was elected to the Sixth Knesset in 1965, but he was expelled from the Ḥerut movement after criticizing the leadership of Menaḥem *Begin. In March 1967, together with two additional members who broke away from Gaḥal, he established the Free Center Party, which ran in the elections to the Seventh Knesset in 1969 and won two seats. The Free Center joined the Likud when it was formed in 1973 prior to the elections to the Eighth Knesset, and the following year Tamir called upon the Likud to accept the principle of territorial compromise in a settlement with the Arabs. It was against the background of this initiative that the Free Center fell apart. In January 1977 Tamir resigned his Knesset seat, and joined the new *Democratic Movement for Change, which won 15 seats in the elections to the Ninth Knesset. After the DMC joined the government, Tamir was appointed minister of justice. After the DMC disintegrated in September 1978 Tamir became part of the Democratic Movement parliamentary group. In August 1980 he resigned from the government, since he felt that the Democratic Movement, with only four Knesset members remaining, ought not to have three portfolios in the government. In March 1981 he left the Democratic movement and remained in the Knesset as a single MK. He did not run in the elections to the Tenth Knesset in 1981, and returned to his law practice. In the years 1983–85 he was head of the team that negotiated the exchange of prisoners deal with the PLO, in the aftermath of the Lebanese War.

His autobiography *Ben ha-Areẓ ha-Zot* appeared in 2002.

[Susan Hattis Rolef (2nd ed.)]

TAMIRIS, HELEN (née **Becker**; 1905–1966), U.S. choreographer and pioneer in the development of modern dance. Helen Tamiris, who was born in New York, made her debut as a concert dancer in 1927. Her interest in American themes and rhythms was expressed in her *Negro Spirituals* in the 1930s and in her works of social protest. In 1930 Helen Tamiris, together with Martha Graham, Doris Humphrey, and Charles Weidman, formed the Dance Repertory Theater. She served as dance director for the Group Theater in 1932. As chief choreographer of the W.P.A. Federal Dance Theater, she created *How Long Brethren?* (1937). She did the choreography for Broadway musicals including *Annie Get Your Gun* (1946). In 1957 she returned to the concert dance field. She established a company in 1960 with her husband Daniel Nagrin, who was noted for his solo portrayals and had appeared in several Broadway shows.

BIBLIOGRAPHY: *New York Times* (Aug. 5, 1966), 31.

[Marcia B. Siegel]

TAMM, IGOR YEVGENYEVICH (1895–1971), Russian physicist and Nobel Laureate. Tamm was born in Vladivostok and graduated in physics from Moscow University (1918). He worked in different universities and institutes in Moscow and the Crimea including the Moscow State University (1924–37). He was appointed professor and head of the theoretical division of the P.N. Lebedev Institute of Physics of the (then) U.S.S.R. Academy of Sciences (1934–71). Tamm was a theoretical physicist whose early work concerned light and quantum theory. He is best known for his explanation of the Cerenkov effect, the blue glow produced by charged particles from radioactive decay when these penetrate fluids. Tamm showed that the effect is attributable to a "bow wave" of photons created by fast particles exceeding the speed of light in a fluid medium. This explanation did not simply explain an aesthetically beautiful phenomenon but had implications for the subsequent progress of particle physics including the discovery of anti-protons. He was awarded the 1958 Nobel Prize in physics for this discovery, shared with Pavel Cherenkov and Il'ja Frank. Subsequently he continued his work on the theory of light, transistors, the nature of showers in cosmic rays, and, in collaboration with Andrei Sakharov, methods for controlling thermonuclear fusion reactions. He also collaborated closely with Professor L. Mandelstam between 1920 and 1944. Tamm's honors include election to the (then) U.S.S.R. Academy of Sciences (1953), the American Academy of Arts and Sciences, and the Swedish Physical Society, and also the State Prize of the former U.S.S.R. (1946) and the title of Hero of Socialist Labor.

[Michel Denman (2nd ed.)]

TAMMUZ (Heb. תַּמּוּז; from Sumerian *Dumuzi*, "Invigorator of the Child"), the Sumerian-Babylonian fertility god. He is the invigorating power in dates, grain, and milk, and hence his role as a shepherd in Sumerian literature (Th. Jacobsen).

In ancient Mesopotamia sacred marriage rites were conducted in the spring to ensure Tammuz' presence as manifest in the fertility of flocks and earth. The climax of the rites was the performance of the marriage act between the king or governor and the chief priestess. Depictions on seals from the Proto-Literate period (3500–3200 B.C.E.) indicate the great antiquity of this rite. Numerous sacred marriage texts revolving around fertility rites have survived from later periods.

The death of vegetation in the intense heat of the summer was interpreted as Tammuz' departure to the netherworld. It is described in the Sumerian myth "Inanna's Descent into the Netherworld," which is also extant in an Akkadian version.

During the Babylonian Exile the Jews named the fourth month of the Hebrew calendar (c. July) after Tammuz (see next entry). In pre-Exilic Judah, Isaiah (17:10–11) has been supposed (very questionably) to allude to the Tammuz rites, which included planting of anemone seeds. Ezekiel (8:14) in a vision of the Jerusalem Temple, which he had in his Babylonian exile, saw women, at the gate of the inner forecourt, weeping for Tammuz.

Tammuz' summer departure was also mourned by the Phoenicians, who called him Adon, i.e., "Lord." They passed the ritual on to the Greeks who Grecized the name into Adonis.

BIBLIOGRAPHY: A. Moortgat, *Tammuz*, (1949); Th. Jacobsen, in: H. Frankfort et al. (eds.), *Before Philosophy* (1949), 213–6; idem, in: *History of Religions*, 1 (1962), 180–213; S.N. Kramer, in: Pritchard, Texts, 41–42, 52–57, 106–9; *ibid* (1969^3), 637–45; idem, *The Sumerians* (1963), 153–60; idem, in: *Proceedings of the American Philosophical Society*, 107 (1963), 485–527; idem, *The Sacred Marriage Rite* (1969); E.Y. Kutscher, *Millim ve-Toledoteihen* (1961), 59–61; O.R. Gurney, in: JSS, 7 (1962), 147–60.

[Raphael Kutscher]

TAMMUZ (Heb. תַּמּוּז), the post-Exilic name of the fourth month of the Jewish year. The word, but not the month, occurs in Ezekiel 8:14 and is held to be identical with the Babylonian Dumuzi corresponding to Adonis of the Greeks. Tammuz as the name of the fourth month occurs frequently in rabbinic literature, as in *Megillat Ta'anit. Its zodiacal sign is Cancer. In the present fixed Jewish calendar it invariably consists of 29 days, the first of Tammuz never falling on Monday, Wednesday, or the Sabbath (see *Calendar). In the 20th century Tammuz in its earliest occurrence extended from June 10th to July 8th and in its latest from July 9th to August 6th. Traditionally historic days in Tammuz are: (1) the festive 14th of Tammuz, the anniversary of a Pharisaic victory over the Sadducees (Meg. Ta'an. 331); (2) the 17th of Tammuz, a fast commemorating five calamities which befell Israel (see *Tammuz, Fast of). With the 17th of Tammuz commences the three-week mourning period over the destruction of Jerusalem which ends with the Ninth of *Av.

[Ephraim Jehudah Wiesenberg]

TAMMUZ, BENJAMIN (1919–1989), Israeli writer and journalist. A native of Kharkov (Russia), Tammuz went to Ereẓ Israel in 1924. He studied at a yeshivah while attending the Herzlia secondary school in Tel Aviv. Later he worked as a laborer in British army camps, a press censor for the Mandatory government, and a reporter for *Mivrak*, the *Loḥamei Ḥerut Israel newspaper. He was also a member of the Palmaḥ. Tammuz spent a year living among the Bedouin, an experience which left a deep impression upon him. In 1950–51 he studied art history at the Sorbonne in Paris, further developing his talent as a sculptor. From 1965 he was editor of the weekend literary supplement of **Haaretz*, and wrote occasional art criticism. Tammuz was appointed cultural attaché at the Israel embassy in London in 1971.

He gained literary acclaim with his first book, *Ḥolot ha-Zahav* ("Golden Sands," 1950), a collection of lyrical, impressionistic short stories of childhood, and the stories in *Gan Na'ul* ("A Garden Enclosed," 1957). In his subsequent works, emotional and even sentimental elements vie with his penchant for satire and social criticism. His picaresque sequence, the trilogy *Ḥayyei Elyakum* (1965, 1966, 1969) recounts the adventures of an anti-hero, who remains an outsider in Israeli society, follows his beloved to Spain and returns to his homeland only to find himself in an institution for the mentally ill. While the novel *Pundako shel Yirmiyahu* ("Jeremiah's Inn," 1984) is written in the genre of the grotesque, some of Tammuz's later novels are distinctly symbolic. Thus, for instance, *Yaakov* (1971) and the novella *Ha-Pardes* ("The Orchard," 1973), which tells the story of two brothers, sons of a Jewish father and two mothers, one Jewish, the other Muslim. The brothers' struggle over the love of Luna, the beautiful daughter of a Turkish effendi, symbolizes the struggle of Jews and Arabs over the land of Israel. *Requiem le-Na'aman* (1978) is a satirical dystopia, a family saga which stands for the hopes and disillusionment in Israel. The founder of the Abramson dynasty represents the revolutionary change in Jewish history, as he leaves the Diaspora behind and settles in Palestine as an ardent believer in Zionism. His son, Na'aman, a sensitive musician, points to the decadent disintegration of the family, as he chooses to live in France and goes mad. Grandson Elyakum is killed in the War of Independence while great-granddaughter Bella-Yaffah loses her mind. *Minotaur* (1980) is the intriguing story of Alexander Abramov's obsessive, platonic love for Thea, an embodiment of the ideal of beauty and of European culture. Many of Tammuz's prose works have been translated into English, among them: *A Castle in Spain* (1973), *Minotaur* (1981; 1982), *Requiem for Naaman* (1982), *The Orchard* (1984), and *A Rare Cure* (1981). Information about translations is available at the ITHL website at www.ithl.org.il.

ADD. BIBLIOGRAPHY: A. Feinberg, "*Mishlei Bakbukim*," in: *Al ha-Mishmar* (December 12, 1975); G. Ramras-Rauch, "*Shayyakhut le-lo Hizdahut*," in: *Shedemot*, 64 (1977), 66–69; Y. Ben Yosef, "*B. Tammuz*," in: *Turim*, 9–10 (1979), 59–63; B. Ziffer, in: *Haaretz* (August 22, 1980); O. Bartana, in: *Davar* (October 24, 1980); Y. Oren, in: *Yedioth Aharonoth* (September 19, 1980); A. Feinberg, "*Minotaur*," in: *Modern Hebrew Literature*, 6 (1981), 3–4; Y. Barzilai, *Mi-Kana'aniyyut le-Kosmopolitiyyut*, in: *Hadoar*, 61:16 (1982), 244–47; R-S. Sirat, "La Société israélienne après la guerre de Kippour, B. Tammuz 'Requiem le-Naaman,'" in: *Permanences et mutations dans la société israélienne* (1996), 181–88; H. Zakai, "*Ḥayyei Elyakum*," in: *Mi-Bayit u-mi-ba-Ḥuẓ* (1996), 59–71; G. Shaked, *Ha-Sipporet ha-Ivrit* (1998), 108–19.

[Gitta (Aszkenazy) Avinor / Anat Feinberg (2nd ed.)]

TAMMUZ, FAST OF, communal fast occurring on the 17th of Tammuz, commemorating the breaching of the walls of Jerusalem by Nebuchadnezzar (586 B.C.E.) and Titus (70 C.E.). The Jerusalem Talmud (Ta'an. 4:8, 68c) maintains that both catastrophes occurred on this date, and that Jeremiah's sorrow caused him to err when writing that "the city was broken up" by Nebuchadnezzar on the 9th of Tammuz (Jer. 52:6–7).

This, however, is not the view of the Babylonian Talmud (Ta'an. 28b), which accepts Jeremiah's dating as correct, and simply considers the destruction of the Second Temple more important (Sh. Ar., OḤ 549:2). According to the Mishnah (Ta'an. 4:6), four other calamities happened on the 17th of Tammuz: the tablets of the law were broken by Moses; the daily offering ceased in the First Temple; the heathen *Apostomos burned the Torah in the sanctuary, and erected an idol there (but some texts read "an idol was set up," Rashi, Ta'an. ad. loc.).

The Fast of Tammuz is closely linked with that of the 9th of Av. The Midrash commenting on the verse "all her persecutors overtook her between the straits" (Lam. 1:3) says, "these are the days of distress from the 17th of Tammuz to the 9th of Av." These 21 days are known as *bein ha-meẓarim* ("between the straits") or as the three weeks of mourning. However, the Fast of Tammuz is also traditionally associated with "the fast of the fourth month" mentioned by Zechariah (8:19; TJ, Ta'an. 4:8, 68c) which in the messianic era "shall be to the house of Judah joy and gladness and cheerful feasts" (see Maim. Yad., Ta'anit, 5:4 and 19). The liturgy for the day is similar to that of the other fast days, i.e., **seliḥot* are recited, the Torah is read, and a special insertion is made in the **Amidah*.

See *Fasting and Fast Days; *Av, the Ninth of; *Three Weeks.

BIBLIOGRAPHY: Ḥ. Pearl, *Guide to Minor Festivals and Fasts* (1963), 57–60; Eisenstein, Dinim, 394; Y.T. Lewinski, *Sefer ha-Mo'adim*, 7 (1957²), 157–65.

TAMPA, city in Hillsborough County, located on the west coast of Florida on Tampa Bay. Tampa was graced by early Spanish explorers in the 16th century. It has its origin in 1824 when Fort Brooke was erected to keep watch on the Seminole Indians. Probably the first permanent Jewish settler in the area was Emmaline Quentz Miley in 1846, whose husband was a Scotsman whom she made sell his slaves before their marriage. They had 12 children; she died in Hillsborough County in 1907. With the arrival of Henry Plant and the South Florida Railroad in 1884, the discovery of vast deposits of phosphates, and the relocation of the cigar industry from Key West in 1886, Tampa became a center of growth. Glogowski, Maas, Kaunitz, Brash, Oppenheimer, Wolf, and Wohl are some of the Jewish families who settled during this boom period. Most lived in Ybor City and were active in commerce, a few in the cigar industry. Herman Glogowski, a Jew who served as mayor for four terms, officiated in 1888 at the cornerstone ceremony for the Tampa Bay Hotel that opened in 1891. Glogowski had emigrated from Germany and established a clothing store in Tampa by 1884. He became "permanent president" of the first congregation. In 1894, 31 men and women met in the home of M. Henry Cohen to organize Schaarai Zedek as an Orthodox congregation; a Torah was purchased for $75. Rabbi D. Jacobson became the first spiritual leader and Abe Maas was among the founders. The Maas family came from Germany in the 1880s. The first store of Abe and Isaac Maas in Tampa opened in 1886, marking the beginning of one of the largest department store chains in Florida that lasted 105 years. Morris Wolf of Germany immigrated to Tampa in 1895. He worked at Maas Brothers until 1898 when he left to open a custom clothing store that became Wolf Brothers in 1899; his brother, Fred, joined him. The Cuban War of Independence in 1898 brought prosperity to local businessmen. Relatives from Key West, Ocala, and Jacksonville gravitated to Tampa, many from Romanian background. Isadore Kaunitz who opened Blanco Clothing Store in 1891 in Ybor City first employed most Romanian Jews. The Rippa family emigrated from Romania to Key West, then to Tampa when the cigar industry declined in Key West, and opened their own cigar factory in Ybor City in 1904. German-born Henry Brash came with his family first to Marianna, FL, where in 1879 he was elected mayor (Florida's earliest known Jewish mayor). Henry married Sarah Zelnicker in 1888 and they settled in Tampa in 1894. He opened a haberdashery store and was a founder of Congregation Rodeph Sholom in 1903, when there was dissension between the Reform and Orthodox members of Schaarai Zedek. A 1902 lawsuit brought by the Orthodox faction of the congregation regarding "dirty tricks" used by the "Reformers" to take control of the congregation and the building resulted in Schaarai Zedek becoming Reform and a new Orthodox congregation, Rodeph Sholom. Sarah Brash organized the Tampa section of the National Council of Jewish Women in 1924. Max Argintar, another Romanian, arrived in Tampa in 1902, opened his store in 1908; son Sammy continued what was to be a 96-year-old operation in the same location.

By the end of World War I, Tampa's Jewish community was the second largest in the state, partly as a result of a dizzying real estate boom. Growth propelled the Jewish community to dedicate new synagogues, expand their synagogue school programs, and inaugurate youth clubs. Jews were active in civic affairs and held leadership positions. "Salty" Sol Fleischman, "The Dean of Florida's Sportscasters," got behind a microphone on radio WDAE in 1928, wrote sports columns for the *Tampa Tribune* and went on television in 1957. He broadcast almost every sports event in the area for more than 50 years. With the advent of World War II, Tampa's shipyards were reactivated and MacDill Air Force Base was established, as was Drew Field, now Tampa International Airport. Tampa's Jews patriotically joined the war effort. The Young Men's Hebrew Association had been started in 1906 and after the war, the YMHA became the Jewish Community Center. Hadassah began and the Dictators Club was one of the Jewish fraternities in Tampa in the 1930s. It became the Tampa chapter of AZA, a youth group of B'nai B'rith. Rabbi David L. Zielonka served Congregation Schaarai Zedek from 1930 to 1970. He and Clarence Darrow joined with other religious leaders in 1931 in an interfaith debate. When the University of Tampa opened in 1931, Rabbi Zielonka served on the faculty, and in 1963 he became head of the department of Religious Studies. B'nai B'rith Women began in the mid-1940s to work on projects to aid Israel and the local community. Post-World War II development and migration from the north spurred growth in the Jewish community. During the 1950s and 1960s, civil rights led to intense debate within the Jewish community while Zionism received near unanimous support. The full impact of the Holocaust intensified educational programs in synagogue and organizational life. In 1958 Stanford and Millard Newman bought a cigar factory and actively participated in the resurgence in cigar manufacturing in the 1960s. Dr. Richard Hodes was elected to the Florida House of Representatives in 1966, where he served for 16 years and gave the nominating speech for Jimmy Carter at the Florida Democratic Convention in 1975. Attorney Harry N. Sandler served in the Florida legislature from 1932 to 1935 and was a sponsor of the Homestead Exemption Amendment. Appointed to the Thirteenth Judicial Circuit Court in 1935, he served until 1964. Sandra Warshaw Freedman entered politics in 1974 as a city councilwoman and became the chair in 1983. In 1986, Sandra Freedman was elected the first woman mayor of Tampa. Jerome Waterman played a major part in the growth of aviation in Tampa, was an associate of Capt. Eddie Rickenbacker in the formation of Eastern Airlines and wrote books and newspaper columns. The Tampa Jewish Welfare Federation served as the coordinating agency for charitable and philanthropic work in the Jewish community under the Tampa Jewish Community Council, which was formed in 1969. By the 1970s, the Jewish community dedicated new congregations (Beth Am, Kol Ami, Temple David, Jewish Congregation of Sun City Center, Chabad Lubavitch, and Young Israel), established Hillel Day School and built facilities for the elderly (Mary Walker Apartments, Jewish Towers, and Menorah Manor). A Fred Shochet publication, *The Jewish Floridian*, made its Tampa debut on April 6, 1979; the local editor was Judy Rosenkranz. Jews have remained in the forefront of political life and have rallied to support all civic and cultural causes. Frank Weaner sued the Ku Klux Klan in 1977. Helen Gordon served in the Florida Legislature beginning in 1974 both in the House and Senate. Ron Glickman won his first election in 1984 as a Hillsborough County commissioner, then was elected to the Florida House of Representatives in 1986. James Shimberg was inducted into the National Housing Hall of Fame in 1985. Native Tampa brothers Martin and Myron Uman have made significant contributions in science. Martin is an internationally known expert in lightning research at the University of Florida. Myron joined the National Research Council in 1975, and in 1986 was appointed executive director of the research panel advising NASA on the redesign of the shuttle's booster rockets. Growing up in Tampa in the 1930s, Elinor Rosenthal Ross advanced to stardom at the Metropolitan Opera in New York; among her famous performances was the lead in *La Traviata* in 1965. In 1984, J. Leonard Levy was chair of the Super Bowl XVIII Task Force; in 1991 he served as co-chair of Super Bowl XXV. Malcolm Glazer, who owns the NFL team, the Tampa Bay Buccaneers, in May 2005 purchased the world's largest soccer team, Manchester United, and has attracted to Tampa the 2009 Super Bowl. Many of the families who settled over a century ago have fourth generations living in Tampa. In the early 21st century the Jewish population was approximately 25,000 in a general population of about 330,000. In 1995 the Jewish Community Center and the Jewish Federation merged on the 21-acre campus that also houses the Weinberg Village Senior Residences. *The Jewish Press of Tampa*, established in 1985, is published in cooperation with the Jewish Federation. The community is growing and new congregations are forming in areas outside the core of the city. Current congregations include Schaarai Zedek (Reform), Rodeph Sholom (Conservative), Bais David (Orthodox), Bais Tefilah (Orthodox), Beth Am (Reform), Kol Ami (Conservative), and Young Israel (Orthodox). In operation are a Hillel at University of South Florida, two day schools, two *mikva'ot*, and branches of many national and Israeli organizations.

[Marcia Jo Zerivitz (2nd ed.)]

TANAKH (Heb. תַּנַ"ךְ), the usual Hebrew collective term for the Old Testament. The term is composed of the initial letters of the words *Torah* ("Pentateuch"), *Nevi'im* ("Prophets"), and *Ketuvim* ("Hagiographa"). This threefold division of the Bible is commonly found in the Talmud (e.g., Shab. 88a; Sanh. 101a; Kid. 49a; MK 21a), and arguments are often supported by quoting individual verses from each of the sections (e.g., Meg. 31a; Mak. 10b).

TANDLER, JULIUS (1869–1936), anatomist and social politician. Born in Iglau, Moravia, Tandler studied medicine in Vienna, receiving his M.D. degree in 1895. He was an assistant at the Anatomical Institute of Prof. Emil Zuckerkandl in Vienna and succeeded him as head of the institute in 1910, remaining there until 1934. He was dean of the medical faculty from 1914 to 1917 and developed ideas toward the reform of medical education. Tandler conducted research in various fields of anatomy, such as the heart, the prostate, and the uterus, and was interested in the close connection between anatomy and clinical work. Among his publications are *Topographie des weiblichen Ureters* (1901) and *Anatomie und Ätiologie der Genitalprolapse beim Weibe* (1907), both of which were written together with Joseph Halban; *Die Biologischen Grundlagen der sekundaren Geschlechtsmerkmale* (1913); and his well-known, four-volume *Lehrbuch der systematischen Anatomie* (1918–1929).

In 1919 Tandler, as a social democrat, became under-secretary of state in the Ministry of Social Administration of the Republic of Austria and reorganized hospital legislation. From 1920 to 1934, he was a city councilor in Vienna and made significant contributions to modern social medicine by creating a new system of welfare which became known the world over. His system was based on the idea that it is society's duty to help, on the right of those in need to receive welfare, and on social responsibility. All kinds of welfare were included with advisory boards being set up to deal with problems of young couples, pregnant women, mothers, war invalids, babies, and the elderly. He was responsible for the building of new kindergartens as well as the Kinderübernahmsstelle, the largest children's home in Europe.

Having earned an international reputation, he was a participant on the Health Committee of the League of Nations (1929–1933). In 1933 he responded to a call to China, where he helped develop modern social medicine. Frequent antisemitic riots in his Anatomical Institute as well as his advancing age prompted him to continue his work outside Austria. After the Austrian Civil War (1934) he had to retire. He again went to China and then on to Moscow, to reorganize the hospital system. He died in Moscow.

BIBLIOGRAPHY: A. Goetzl and R.A. Reynolds, *Julius Tandler* (1945); K. Sablik, *Julius Tandler, Mediziner und Sozialreformer* (1983).

TANENBAUM, family of three generations of Canadian entrepreneurs and philanthropists. According to family lore, the family's patriarch, ABRAHAM TANEBAUM (1877–1957) left Parczew, Poland, north of Lublin, for New York in 1911. Instead of going to New York, two Toronto-bound acquaintances from Parczew convinced Abraham to join them. Soon after arriving in Toronto, Abraham was driving a horse and cart through residential and industrial areas of the city in search of scrap metal. By 1914, on the eve of war in Europe, Abraham had saved enough to bring his wife, Chippa Sura, and two young sons, JOSEPH TANENBAUM (1906–1992) and MAX TANENBAUM (1909–1983), to join him in Toronto. Two daughters were born there.

Industrious and hard-working, Abraham progressed from peddling for scrap metal to recycling of scrap metal from demolition sites and eventually building his Runnymede Iron and Steel Company into a major steel fabrication firm and real estate empire. An observant Jew, Abraham Tanenbaum also remained close to his roots. He was a founder of Knesset Israel Synagogue, house of prayer to many in the small working-class Jewish community in the junction area of then northwest Toronto, and was an active supporter of Toronto's Eitz Chaim Talmud Torah.

While his two sons were still only boys, Abraham brought them into the family business, Joseph just twelve and with only a six-grade education and Max after finishing eighth grade and only two days beyond his bar mitzvah. They learned the business from the ground up, and as Runnymede Steel expanded rapidly though the war years and into the postwar era, the two brothers assumed control of the firm from their father. In 1951 the two brothers parted company. Joseph, or JT as he was popularly known, stayed on as head of Runnymede while Max established his own company, York Steel. Each was soon a major and successful industrialist in his own right and involved in major public construction projects that underpinned the rapid economic expansion of Toronto and southern Ontario in the 1950s and 1960s. Joseph's firm, Runnymede, was especially prominent in high-level bridge building including the mammoth Burlington Skyway Bridge project completed in 1958. Max also profited from the stream of public and private infrastructure projects. For example, Max landed the contract to supply fabricated steel for an upgrading and expansion of the Toronto Airport, at that time the largest contract of its kind let out by the Canadian government.

As their separate business holdings grew larger and more diverse, the brothers were also influential in Jewish community affairs, giving generously to Jewish and non-Jewish causes. In Toronto, which both men called home, their altruism helped ensure the growth of Jewish parochial education, comprehensive care for the Jewish elderly, and expanded funding for university-based health care research. Their generosity was also directed to a number of Jewish religious institutions. Although the brothers often demonstrated different funding priorities, their generosity left its marks on Jewish institutions in the United States and Israel as well. This tradition of community engagement continued to the next generation.

Among Max's children are JOEY TANENBAUM (1932–) and LARRY TANENBAUM (1945–). Joey was born in Toronto. A graduate in engineering from the University of Toronto, as president and CEO of Jay-M Holdings, he had a successful career in real estate development and construction. Joey and his wife, Toby, have also been prominent in the Jewish and non-Jewish communities. In addition to their generous support of health care research, they are highly regarded and influential patrons of arts and culture in Canada. Their financial contribution was critical to the construction of a new opera house in Toronto named in their honor. Avid art collectors, they have donated major art collections to the Art Gallery of Ontario, the Royal Ontario Museum, and the Art Gallery of Hamilton. Interested in his family's history, Joey also funded the restoration of his grandparents' Knesseth Israel Synagogue in Toronto. It is now Ontario's oldest purpose-built synagogue still in use.

Joey's brother, Larry, who earned a B.Sc. in economics from Cornell University, had a successful career as chairman and CEO of Keler Van Nostrand, a private investment holding company with diversified interests in construction and infrastructure, electronics and technology and sports and entertainment, including a controlling interest in several major league sports franchises. Larry was also deeply involved with the United Jewish Appeal of Greater Toronto, Toronto Mount Sinai Hospital, the Canadian Council of Christians and Jews, and the Baycrest Centre for Geriatric Care. In 2004 he helped organize the Canadian Council for Israel and Jewish Advocacy to conduct and direct a wide range of non-partisan public advocacy initiatives on behalf of the Canadian Jewish Community.

BIBLIOGRAPHY: H. Teller, *Bridges of Steel – Ladders of Gold* (1990); R. Sharp et al., *Growing Up Jewish. Canadians Tell Their Own Stories* (1997), 143–49.

[Harold Troper (2nd ed.)]

TANENBAUM, SIDNEY HAROLD ("Sid"; 1925–1986), U.S. basketball player, New York University first team All-American 1946–47, two-time winner of the prestigious Haggerty

Award (1946–47), recipient of the Bar Kochba Award for the best Jewish athlete of 1947. A native of Brooklyn, NY, Tanenbaum was a gifted shooter and ball handler first at Thomas Jefferson High School and then NYU, which he helped lead to two NCAA tournament appearances, including a trip to the championship game in 1945. After completing his career as NYU's all-time leading scorer (992 pts.), Tanenbaum played in the NBA's precursor, the BAA, for two seasons, appearing in a total of 70 games with the New York Knicks and Baltimore Bullets. He showed promise, scoring nine points per game while shooting 83 percent from the free throw line, but Tanenbaum – who married right after graduating – chose to cut his professional basketball career short due to the excessive travel. Tanenbaum found work in his father-in-law's metal spinning and stamping shop, eventually becoming the owner, and managed to turn it into a very successful business. It was in this very shop that Tanenbaum was tragically stabbed to death. Bob Gottlieb, long-time friend and coach of the Branch West Recruiting Service, said that "Sid was just a peach of a person; great two-hand set shooter, but an even greater human being. God did not make better people than Sid." Each year, NYU awards its top student-athlete the Sid Tanenbaum Memorial Award. An annual half-court basketball tournament is held in Woodmere, N.Y., in memory of Tanenbaum, who continued to play in pick-up games until his death. A plaque at the entrance to the courts used in the tournament reads: "Sid Tanenbaum Memorial Courts. NYU All-American, New York Knicks. He touched us all."

[Robert B. Klein (2nd ed.)]

TANGIER(S) (Tanja), Moroccan town situated at the entrance of the Straits of Gibraltar; known in antiquity as Tingis. Tangier's site was inhabited by the Phoenicians and then by the Carthaginians. A number of historians believe that a Jewish community existed in Tingis, an opinion corroborated by ceramic finds with *menorah* stamps. Abraham ibn Daud mentions that the Jews were wiped out by the *Almohads (c. 1148) from Tangier to Mahdia (*Sefer ha-Kabbalah*, 96). Many refugees arrived after the expulsion from *Spain. The *Rote family maintained a commercial house in the town about 1535. In 1541, when the town was ruled by the Portuguese, small sections of the communities of Azemmour and *Safi settled there; the Inquisition, however, outlawed their presence and their stay was thus of brief duration. In 1661, when the Portuguese ceded Tangier to England, the British attracted Muslim and Jewish inhabitants from the neighboring towns of Larache and Ksar el-Kabir. The Jewish community was composed of these new elements, in addition to Jews from the *Netherlands. In 1675 a serious controversy broke out between the Moroccan-born Jews and those of foreign origin; a *ḥerem* ("ban") was issued against the latter by the rabbis of *Tetuán, to whom the community of Tangier was subordinate. In 1677 the Jews were expelled from the town, not returning until 1680. The principal adviser and interpreter to four successive governors, however, was Solomon *Pariente. Samuel de Paz, a diplomat in the service of the British, lived in Tangier and Jacob Falcon, leader of the Tetuán community, was entrusted with delicate missions by the governors of Tangier. The Jews carried on an extensive trade in the town. However, when the English abandoned the town (1684), this trade came to an end and, with the exception of a few craftsmen, all the Jews left.

In 1725 there was only one important Jewish merchant, Abraham Benamor of *Meknès, who organized a new community of about 150 people, most of whose members were of the same origin as himself; the community appointed R. Judah Hadida, the first *dayyan* of Tangier, as its leader in 1744. Moses Maman of Meknès, the treasurer of the sultan, encouraged a number of important Jewish merchants of Tetuán, and particularly of *Salé-Rabat, to settle representatives in Tangier, where they were exempted from certain taxes. When Christians were excluded from Tetuán in 1772, a number of European consuls established their consulates in Tangier. They were followed by their Jewish interpreters who enjoyed certain privileges in that capacity. The majority of the community, however, lived in poverty. It was headed by the *dayyan* R. Aaron *Toledano, who was succeeded by his son R. Moses Toledano and his grandson R. Abraham Toledano. As a result of the presence of delegates of the European nations in Tangier, a number of the Jewish advisers of the sultans were required to reside there: Samuel *Sumbal died there during one of his stays (1783); Jacob Attal was executed there by the sultan Mūlāy Yazīd. This sultan imposed a fine on the poor community which it was incapable of paying. There were fewer than 800 Jews living in Tangier in 1808 and over 2,000 in 1835. The community, however, continued impoverished, in spite of the presence of the *Nahon family, who were engaged in the wax trade on a large scale; Joseph *Chriqui of Mogador, the most influential member of the community; and the *Abensur, Sicsu, Anzancot, and *Benchimol families, who were supported by the European powers to whom they rendered important services. In commemoration of its escape during the French bombardment of Tangier in 1844, the community celebrated a *Purim known as *Purim de las bombas*, since it did not suffer any losses. By 1856 the situation of the 2,600 Jews in Tangier was still generally distressing, but a definite improvement occurred with the arrival of a new group of Jews from Tetuán. By 1867 the community had increased to 3,500 persons and was headed by the *dayyan* R. Mordecai Bengio. A wider and more prosperous middle class financed the establishment of the schools of the *Alliance Israélite Universelle (1864).

The Spanish influence, however, which was exerted by the Jews of Tetuán, left a decisive imprint on the community: Spanish was the language spoken by all. The Moroccan press, whose sole center was in Tangier, was controlled by dynamic Jewish elements among whose characteristic personalities were Ben-Ayon, editor of the first newspaper in Tangier (1870); Levy *Cohen, founder and editor of the second newspaper, *Le Réveil du Maroc* (1884); Phinehas Assayay; Abraham Pimienta; and Isaac Laredo. Other newspapers made their appearance after 1886. This press, which was published in English, Spanish, French, and Arabic, called for the Europeanization of *Morocco and supported the "Junta" (the committee of the Jewish community). Jewish authors and poets, especially those writing in the Spanish language, flourished in Tangier. In December 1923 Tangier was declared an international zone. It was governed by a commission composed of representatives from Great Britain, France, Spain, Portugal, Belgium, the Netherlands, Sweden, and, later, the United States. There were then over 10,000 Jews living there. Many, however, had emigrated to South America or settled in *Casablanca. In Tangier the Jewish middle class founded hospitals and numerous welfare institutions. The Jewish intelligentsia brought about a revival of a distinctively Jewish culture. The initiators of this revival were José *Benoliel, the learned historian and last leader of the community, Abraham Laredo (d. 1969), and the kabbalist Samuel Toledano. *Zionism was well represented in this revival. During 1939–40 many Jews of Eastern European origin took refuge in Tangier, and the community made great efforts to assist them to settle there. A number established themselves permanently. In 1940, Tangier lost its international status following Spain's temporary annexation of the Zone. This spelled anxiety for the Jews although, in contrast to what had happened in French Morocco, no racial laws, Vichy-style, were enacted against them. During World War II, Nazi propaganda and pro-Franco fractions dominated Tangier's political scene but, once again, despite some anger vented against Jews no particular harm came to them.

Approximately 12,000 Jews lived in the International Zone of Tangier in 1948, and by 1950 about 2,000 Spanish Moroccan Jews joined them, bringing their total to about 15,000 in 1951. Pre-1956 Tangier also had a highly heterogeneous population that included 40,000 Muslims, 20,000 Spanish, 6,000 French, and 5,000 other Europeans. The Jews of Tangier had the highest proportion of bearers of foreign passports in comparison to the rest of the Moroccan Jewish communities. In fact, politically, during the colonial era, the Jews of Tangier enjoyed an autonomy unheard of throughout the country. They possessed rights granted by the international zone's legislative assembly and approved by Morocco's sultan. After Morocco gained independence in March 1956, Tangier still retained its international zone status until October of that year before being annexed into a unified Moroccan Kingdom. Several Jewish personalities of Tangier, including Solomon M. Pinto, attempted to preserve the community of about 17,000 persons. A powerful movement for emigration had, however, already been set in motion. During the 1950s and early 1960s, when Morocco prevented Jews from leaving, suspecting that their final destination was Israel, the Israeli Mossad in conjunction with local activists used Tangier as an underground center to smuggle people – by land and sea routes – to Algeciras (southern Spain) and Gibraltar. Jews from Tangier helped build up a new Jewish community in Madrid, while others settled in Geneva, Canada, or the United States. Only a few hundred emigrated to Israel. After Tangier had been annexed by Morocco the number of Jews fell to about 4,000 in 1968. Before the annexation, the Jewish community had three representatives on the Tangier Legislative Assembly; the head of the rabbinical court was the officially recognized representative of the community. In the 1950s and 1960s the *Alliance Israélite Universelle and the Oẓar ha-Torah maintained schools there. A vocational school was supported by the American Joint Distribution Committee. The community also had a rabbinical seminary and social welfare institutions. There were only about 250 Jews in Tangier in 1970. Since then Jewish institutions have gradually disappeared. Even though a campus of the American University was established there, Jewish schools closed down. Tangier of the post-1970 period was no longer the cosmopolitan international zone of the Maghreb. This period saw the rise of Islamic radicalism, abject poverty, and the departure of most Europeans. Antisemitism was on the rise in the 1990s. With the outbreak of the second Palestinian Intifada (uprising) in September 2000, an angry mob marched in the streets, chanting for a holy war against the Jews and the U.S. King Muhammad VI responded and warned Muslims not to abuse Jews, placing armed guards around remaining Jewish institutions. In 2005 fewer than 150 Jews remained in Tangier, most of them elderly persons. It is likely that within a decade no Jews will remain there.

BIBLIOGRAPHY: C. de Nesry, *Le Juif de Tanger et le Maroc* (1956); J. Abensur, *Mishpat u-Ẓedakah be-Ya'akov*, 1–2 (1899–1901), passim; CH Firth, in: JHSET, 4 (1899–1901), 198–201; A.I. Laredo, *Memorias de un Viejo Tangerino* (1935); J.M. Toledano, in: HUCA, 8–9 (1931–32), 481–92 (Heb.); D. Corcos, in: *Sefunot*, 10 (1966), passim; Hirschberg, Afrikah, index; idem, in: *Essays Presented to Chief Rabbi Israel Brodie…* (1967), 155–7; Miège, Maroc, passim. **ADD. BIBLIOGRAPHY:** M.M. Laskier, *The Alliance Israélite Universelle and the Jewish Communities of Morocco: 1862–1962* (1983); M. Serels, *A History of the Jews of Tangier in the Nineteenth and Twentieth Centuries* (1991); S. Graham, *The International City of Tangier* (1955).

[David Corcos and Haim J. Cohen / Michael M. Laskier (2nd ed.)]

TANḤUMA BAR ABBA (second half of the fourth century C.E.), Palestinian *amora*. Tanḥuma, to whom the *Tanḥuma Midrash has been ascribed, was one of the most prolific aggadists. His principal teacher in *halakhah* and *aggadah* was R. *Huna. Nothing is known of his private life. In his public activities he was distinguished for his defense of Jews and Judaism against non-Jews. In one of Tanḥuma's conversations with non-Jews, the emperor suggested that Jews and non-Jews become one nation. To this Tanḥuma replied, "But we who are circumcised cannot possibly become like you." The emperor answered, "You have spoken well. Nevertheless, whoever gets the better of the emperor in debate must be thrown into the *vivarium*" ("arena of wild beasts"). Tanḥuma was thrown in, but came out safely (the well-known motif of Daniel). A heretic who was present maintained that this was because the animals were not hungry, whereupon he was thrown in and was eaten (Sanh. 39a). Its contents indicate that this conversation was between Tanḥuma and a Christian: thus in Yalkut, Zephaniah 567, the emperor bases his remarks on the verse (Zeph. 3:9): "For then will I turn to the peoples a pure language, that they may all call upon the name of the Lord, to serve Him with one consent"; this verse has significance only when quoted by a Christian and not a pagan ruler. (For another conversation between Tanḥuma and non-Jews on matters of faith, see TJ, Ber. 9:1, 13b). In Antioch he argued with those who believed in dualism (Gen. R. 19:4). It has been suggested that the title "pleader" (σχολαστικός), given Tanḥuma, refers to this activity (TJ, Ber. 4:2, 7d).

Tanḥuma is noted especially for the proems with which he introduced his discourses. The phrase "R. Tanḥuma began his discourse with this biblical text" occurs frequently in the Midrashim (particularly in *Pesikta Rabbati*). The structure of his discourses was as follows: after a halakhic question, which he did not answer immediately, he quoted a biblical verse, usually from the Hagiographa, which he then connected with the first verse of the current Sabbath's portion of the Pentateuch and only reverted at the end of his discourse to the question that had been raised at the outset. Among the principal ideas that distinguished his many discourses are the signal value of studying the Torah and of charity, and the future redemption of the nation. The following is an example of his teaching: "'Who deliverest the poor from him that is too strong for him' (Ps. 35:10). This applies to Israel, who falls into the hands of the nations of the world, and God delivers them. For 'the poor' refers to Israel…. David said, 'A sheep among 70 wolves, what can it do? Israel among 70 powerful nations, what can Israel do, were it not that You stand by them every hour'" (PR 9:2).

BIBLIOGRAPHY: Frankel, Mevo, 131a–b; S. Buber (ed.), *Midrash Tanḥuma* (1885), introd.; Bacher, Pal Amor; Zunz-Albeck, Derashot, 108–16; Ḥ. Albeck, *Mavo la-Talmudim* (1969), 401f.; Hyman, Toledot, 1243.

[Moshe Beer]

TANḤUMA YELAMMEDENU (תַּנְחוּמָא יְלַמְּדֵנוּ), a category of midrashic literature, including the following works: *Tanḥuma* (to the entire Pentateuch), extensive parts of *Exodus Rabbah, Numbers Rabbah, Deuteronomy Rabbah* and *Pesiqta Rabbati*. Many medieval quotations (often citing "*Tanḥuma*" or "*Yelammedenu*") and fragmentary manuscripts (many from the Cairo *Genizah*) of other partially preserved versions, testify to the diversity and popularity of this type of midrashic work.

Tanḥuma-Yelammedenu Midrash consists primarily of literary homilies to the triennial cycle of weekly biblical lections. Unlike structurally similar works such as *Leviticus Rabbah* and *Pesiqta de-Rav Kahana, Tanḥuma-Yelammedenu* Midrash has relatively little Aramaic, being written in late Rabbinic Hebrew though still employing many Greek and Latin loan-words. Another distinguishing feature is the special halakhic proem (often beginning with the expression *yelammedenu rabbenu* "Let our master teach us") which precedes the series of proems, each beginning with a different verse, with which each composite homily normally begins. Many passages are attributed to the renowned homilist, Rabbi Tanḥuma bar Abba, who was active during the second half of the fourth century in Palestine.

Earlier scholars made conflicting claims about the date and identity of the "early" *Tanḥuma* or *Yelammedenu* which was thought to be the "original" source of the all the surviving works of this type. Later research tends rather to distinguish relatively early traditions and sources within early, middle, and late redactional strata running through the various works. *Tanḥuma-Yelammedenu* literature is best regarded as a particular midrashic genre which began to crystallize toward the end of the Byzantine period in Palestine (5–7th century C.E.), but continued to evolve and spread throughout the Diaspora well into the middle ages, sometimes developing different recensions of a common text. For example, *Tanḥuma* (printed version, first published in Constantinople, 1520–22) seems to have undergone final redaction in geonic Babyonia. While *Tanḥuma* Buber (first published by Solomon Buber, Vilna 1875), which is considerably different in the books of Genesis and Exodus, seems to be a European (Italian-Ashkenazi) recension of similar midrashic material. We find a similar phenomenon with regard to *Deuteronomy Rabbah*, which survives in at least two different versions both of which belong to the *Tanḥuma-Yelammedenu* category of midrashic literature. *Deuteronomy Rabbah* (regular or printed version) found in the printed editions of *Midrash Rabbah*, MS. Parma De Rossi 1240 and fragments, circulated primarily in France and Germany; it contains 27 literary homilies on the triennial cycle weekly lections of Deuteronomy. On the other hand, *Deuteronomy Rabbah* Liebermann (as published by Saul Liebermann) found in most manuscripts of *Midrash Rabbah*, contains alternate or additional midrashic material (the extent of which varies in different manuscripts) of the *Tanḥuma-Yelammedenu* type that circulated primarily in Spain and North Africa.

An English translation of *Tanḥuma* "Printed Version" was published by Samuel A. Berman: *Midrash Tanhuma-Yelammedenu: An English Translation of Genesis and Exodus from the Printed Version of Tanhuma-Yelammedenu With an Introduction, Notes, and Indexes* (1996), and an English translation of *Tanḥuma* Buber by J.T. Townsend, *Midrash Tanhuma*, vols. 1–3 (1989–2003). An English translation of the printed version of *Devarim Rabbah* was published by J. Rabbinowitz, in the Soncino edition of *Midrash Rabbah* (1939; reprinted 1961).

BIBLIOGRAPHY: Zunz-Albeck, Derashot, 108–16, 366–75; J. Mann, *The Bible as Read and Preached in the Old Synagogue*, 1 (1940); idem and I. Sonne, *ibid.*, 2 (1966); E.H. Gruenhut, *Sefer ha-Likkutim*, 2 (1904²); 6 pt. 2 (1903); L. Ginzberg, in: *Ginzei Schechter*, 1 (1928), 449–513; A. Epstein, in: *Beit Talmud*, 5 (1887), 7–23; M. Stein, in: *Sefer ha-Yovel… Moshe Schorr* (1935), 87–112; E.E. Urbach, in: *Kovez al Yad*, 16 pt. 1 (1966), 3–54; J. Theodor, in: MGWJ, 35 (1886), 559ff.; 36 (1887), 35ff.; S.A. Wertheimer, *Battei Midrashot*, 1 (1950²), 139–75; S. Lieberman, *Midrash Devarim Rabbah* (1940), index; G. Stemberger, *Introduction to the Talmud and Midrash*, translated and edited by M. Bockmuehl (1995), 303–7, 333–35; M. Bregman, "Stratigraphic Analysis of a Selected Pericope from the Tanhuma-Yelammedenu Midrashim," in: *Proceedings of the Tenth Congress of Jewish Studies*, Division C, vol. 1: Jewish Thought and Literature (1990), 117–124 (Heb.); idem, *The Tanhuma-Yelammedenu Literature – Studies in the Evolution of the Versions* (2003) (Hebrew with English abstract).

[Marc Bregman (2nd ed.)]

TANḤUM BEN ELIEZER (1746–1819), Lithuanian rabbi. Tanḥum was the son of Eliezer b. Ẓevi Hirsch (d. 1791) of Orla, the author of *Mahadura Kamma u-Vatra*, talmudic novellae. When his father relinquished the rabbinate of Orla, Tanḥum was appointed *av bet din* there, and when his father was subsequently appointed rabbi in Grodno, he became *av bet din* in Grodno. When he failed to be appointed to succeed his father as rabbi after his death, he decided to engage in business. His signature appears first on a *takkanah* of 1818 in connection with the election of three delegates who were to be stationed permanently in St. Petersburg to defend Jewish rights before the czarist government.

Tanḥum left three works, the manuscripts of which were in the possession of his grandson Elijah Perez of Vilna: a kabbalistic commentary on the Pentateuch, entitled *Menuḥat Emet; Menuḥat Shalom*, consisting of casuistic expositions and halakhic novellae; and *Neḥamat Ẓiyyon*, notes on the talmud. Tanḥum's son, Issachar *Baer (1779–1855), served from 1819 until his death as *dayyan* of Vilna.

BIBLIOGRAPHY: S.E. Friedenstein, *Ir Gibborim* (1880; repr. 1969), 54, 69–70; S.J. Fuenn, *Kiryah Ne'emanah* (1915), 277, n. 37; *Yahadut Lita*, 3 (1967), 266, 270.

[Yehoshua Horowitz]

TANḤUM BEN ḤANILAI (Ilai or **b. Hanila** in the Jerusalem Talmud), Palestinian *amora* of the second half of the third century. The name Ḥanilai suggests a Babylonian origin. He was a pupil of Joshua b. *Levi (BK 55a). A prominent aggadist, his teachings were of a high ethical and moral character. He taught that God says to Israel, "My daughter [the Torah] is in thy hands; thy daughter [the soul] is in My hands. If thou protect Mine, then I shall protect thine" (Tanḥ. Ki Tissa, 28). At meals he would remind his family "to set aside a portion for the poor" (Tanḥ. Mishpatim, 8). "A man who has no wife," he stated, "lives without joy, without blessing, and without goodness" (Yev. 62b). "One should never break away from the accepted custom," for when Moses ascended to the angels, he ate no bread, but when the angels visited Abraham, they appeared to eat and drink (BM 86b). A characteristic of his *aggadah* is a system of connecting the last words of one Bible verse with the opening words of the next. Thus by connecting Leviticus 1:16 with 2:1, he deduces that the crop of a bird-offering is unworthy of the altar, since the food in it is obtained by robbery and violence (Lev. R. 3:4). R. Tanḥum died on Ḥanukkah (TJ, MK 3:9, 83d).

BIBLIOGRAPHY: Bacher, Pal Amor, 1, 3; Hyman, Toledot, s.v.; Ḥ. Albeck, *Mavo la-Talmudim* (1969), 192.

TANḤUM BEN ḤIYYA (end of the third and beginning of the fourth centuries C.E.), Palestinian *amora*. In Babylonian sources he is referred to as Tanḥum "of Kefar Akko" (MK 16b; Yev. 45a), which, according to S. Klein (*Ereẓ ha-Galil*, 42), is in Lower Galilee. Elsewhere, however (Gen. R. 100:7), his birthplace is given as Kefar Agin (today Umm Jūnī, south of the Sea of Galilee), which was, apparently, not well-known in Babylon and was therefore referred to as Kefar Akko. He also seems to have spent some time in Tiberias, and on one occasion he and Aḥa, the trustee of the local castle, ransomed some captive Jewish women who had been taken there from Armenia, probably by Roman troops (Yev. 45a, see Dik. Sof.). While in Galilee, he was appointed a member of the commission which determined the intercalation of the calendar (TJ, Sanh. 1:2, 18c). Tanḥum was wealthy and charitable, and it is related that whenever his mother purchased meat for her household, she would also purchase an equivalent amount for distribution among the poor (Lev. R. 34:5). Among his colleagues was Ḥanina b. *Papa (TJ, MK. 3:7, 83c), and he transmitted sayings in the name of Joshua b. Levi (TJ, Shek. 3:1, 47b), and Johanan (TJ, Ta'an, 2:1, 65b), Three of his explanations of *halakhot* are recorded (Bek. 57b; TJ, Meg. 4:1, 75a twice), and among his many aggadic sayings are: "When one who has learnt, taught, and observed the Law fails to prevent evil when it is in his power to do so, he shall be smitten with the curse: 'cursed be he that confirmeth not all the words of the Torah, to do them'" (Deut. 27:26; TJ, Sot. 7:4, 21d). The *aggadah* relates that when he died, "all human statues were dislodged" (MK, 25b).

BIBLIOGRAPHY: Hyman, Toledot, s.v.; Ḥ. Albeck, *Mavo la-Talmudim* (1969), 271–2.

TANḤUM BEN JOSEPH (Ha-)YERUSHALMI (c. 1220–1291), philologist and biblical exegete. Few biographical details are known of him. As his name indicates, either he or his family originated from Jerusalem, and according to Bacher, he lived for some time in Ereẓ Israel and subsequently went to Egypt, where he died. Tanḥum had an extensive knowledge of philosophy, and knew a number of languages, including Arabic and Greek, and it would appear that he knew medicine (*Al-Murshid al-Kafi*, s.v. *tavlul*). He had a profound knowledge of all the biblical exegetes and grammarians who had preceded him (there are more than 250 references in the section of his *Al-Murshid al-Kafi* to the letter *tav* alone, many of which are not identifiable). He was the last representative of the rational school of biblical exegetes in the East, but the "central pillars" upon which he based his works were "the words of the revered Rabbi Moses b. Maimon in his scientific outlook and his religious beliefs, and the words of R. Jonah *Ibn Janaḥ in grammar and philology."

One of his works which has survived is *Kitab al-Bayān*, consisting of commentaries on the books of the Bible, with an introduction (or first part) called *Al-Kaliat* ("General Principles"), a work which earned him the title of "the Ibn Ezra of the East." Portions of this commentary are scattered in various libraries, such as the Bodleian and the Guenzburg libraries. In addition to fragments which have been published in various learned periodicals, there have appeared his commentary on Judges, Samuel, Kings, and Jonah (T. Haarbruecker, 1842–62); Habakkuk (S. Munk, 1843); Lamentations (G. Cureton, 1843); Ecclesiastes (S. Eppenstein, 1888); and Psalms (idem, 1903). Another extant work is the above-mentioned *Al-Murshid al-Kafi*, a lexicon giving in alphabetical order the nouns and verbs in Maimonides' *Mishneh Torah*. This work is of considerable importance on account of the new Hebrew terms which he coined, and it constitutes the greatest codex of Maimonides' work. Most of the introduction, as well as a number of entries in the work, was published by W. Bacher under the title *Aus dem Woerterbuche Tanchum Jeruschalmi's* (1903).

Joseph b. Tanḥum *ha-Yerushalmi was his son.

BIBLIOGRAPHY: I. Goldziher, *Studien ueber Tanchum Jerúschalmi* (1870); B. Toledano, in: *Sinai*, 42 (1961), 339–55; H. Shy, in: *Leshonenu*, 33 (1969), 196–207, 280–96; S. Poznański, in: REJ, 40 (1900), 130–53; 41 (1900), 45–61; Steinschneider, Arab Lit, 234–6; E. Ashtor (Strauss), *Toledot ha-Yehudim*, 1 (1944), 144ff.; 3 (1970), index.

[Ephraim Kupfer]

TANNA, TANNAIM (Aram. תַּנָּא, תַּנָּאִים), the sages from the period of *Hillel to the compilation of the *Mishnah, i.e., the first and second centuries C.E. The word *tanna* (from Aramaic *teni*, "to hand down orally," "study," "teach") generally designates a teacher either mentioned in the Mishnah or of mishnaic times (Ber. 2a). It was first used in the Talmud in this sense to distinguish such teachers from later authorities, the *amoraim. However, not all teachers mentioned in the Mishnah are called *tannaim*; the frequently found phrase *zekenim rishonim* ("former elders"; Shab. 64b, Naz. 53a, etc.) probably refers to scholars who precede the schools of Hillel and Shammai, i.e., the *zugot*, etc. Thus, the tannaitic period covers a period from about 20 to about 200 C.E., the approximate date of the final redaction of the Mishnah by Judah ha-Nasi. These two centuries are generally divided into five generations – corresponding to the five generations of *zugot* (Avot 1), also spanning some two centuries – with a sixth transitional generation of semi-*tannaim*, contemporaries of Judah I, who, while not appearing in the Mishnah, are mentioned in the Tosefta or *baraita*. Of course, such a division is necessarily arbitrary, and many *tannaim* cannot be easily fitted into their rigidly compartmentalized periods. Often they span two or more successive generations. Nevertheless, the "five-generation grid" is a useful frame of reference and has been used by successive chronographers since it was first introduced by Ibn Daud in his classic *Sefer ha-Kabbalah* (second half of 12th century; see, *Sefer ha-Qabbalah*, ed. by G. Cohen, 1967, LVI).

In this somewhat artificial system of division there are two major landmarks: 70 C.E., the year of the fall of Jerusalem, and 135, the year of the fall of Betar. The first marks the end of the Temple period, and is followed by one of reconstruction. Johanan b. Zakkai established a flourishing center at Jabneh, and his most important disciples were Eliezer b. Hyrcanus (who founded a school at Lydda), Joshua b. Hananiah, Yose ha-Kohen, Simeon b. Nethanel, and Eleazar b. Arakh (Avot 2:8). Among their younger contemporaries were Ishmael (b. Elisha), Tarfon, and Johanan b. Nuri, but undoubtedly the most outstanding of them was Akiva (whose school was at Bene-Berak). This highly creative phase came to a savage end around 130. It remained to the pupils of Ishmael (e.g., Josiah and Jonathan) and of Akiva (Judah b. Ilai, Yose b. Ḥalafta, and Simeon b. Yoḥai) to regroup, moving the centers of learning to Galilee (Usha, Tiberias, etc.). In this second period, Meir, a pupil both of Ishmael (first) and (then) Akiva, emerges as the most prominent personality, and it is primarily his tradition that is continued by Judah I (at Bet She'arim and Sepphoris). Judah's death (c. 220) brings to a close the tannaitic period.

The crippling defeats of 70 and 135 were both followed by a period of military oppression and spiritual repression, and by a general depression, and both periods of reconstruction had to contend with a society splintered by shifts of population from Jerusalem to other Judean centers (c. 70–130) and from Judea to Galilee (135 onward). Furthermore, not only was there social disintegration in the communities and their administrative bodies, but also a serious danger of the collapse of a central Jewish authority. Both the destruction of the Temple and later that of Jabneh left a vacuum of authority that had to be replaced rapidly. Thus, Johanan b. Zakkai had to contend with considerable initial antagonism on the part of several strata of society – the priestly faction, elements of the aristocracy, and a number of rabbis (see Alon, Meḥkarim, 1 (1957), 253–73). He and, after him, Gamaliel of Jabneh made it their prime objective to consolidate their authority, to make it accepted by the whole populace, and at the same time to gain the recognition of the Roman civil authorities. When Simeon b. Gamaliel set up his academy at Usha in the middle of the second century, he followed much the same policy.

The establishment of such a centralized authority, in the form of a great Sanhedrin that would convene on special occasions to discuss and give rulings and directives on basic issues, brought together scholars from varying backgrounds and differing traditions. A period of political calamity and spiritual depression is also one in which there is a grave danger of the loss of traditional knowledge; leading scholars are killed, there is a diminution of study, established bodies of learning – the yeshivot or *battei midrashot* – are dismantled, and their members scattered. Thus the central authorities appreciated the urgent need to collect the different strands of tradition and weave them into organized bodies of material. In this way, out of chaos and destruction there arose a new order, in the form of the great bodies of halakhic tradition. These, the literary production of the *tannaim*, may be roughly grouped under two main headings: that which belongs to the genre of the codex, i.e., succinct halakhic formulations arranged under abstract legal categories, or other mnemonic devices; and *Midreshei Halakhah*, halakhic Midrashim arranged as some kind of extended exegetical commentaries to the books of the Pentateuch.

In the former category comes, first and foremost, the Mishnah. This began as a collection of "evidences" (*eduyyot*) on different legal topics, which was put together during the Jabneh period. During this time also, certain primary editorial guidelines were drawn up (Eduy. 1:4–6). Akiva was a key figure in the continued collection, collation, and classification of the *halakhot*, or *mishnayot*, which at times came together in groups, linked to one another by mnemonic devices, such as a common catchword, parallel structure, etc. (see *Mnemonics). The work was continued by Akiva's pupils, the most important among them being Meir, until it reached its consummation in the final editorship of Judah ha-Nasi in the early third century. This superb work of codification forms the basis of that vast corpus of amoraic law and lore known as the *Talmud or *Gemara*, and indeed of all subsequent codices. It remains the supreme monument to the tannaitic achievement. Judah ha-Nasi was selective in his editorship, excluding a great many *halakhot* from his Mishnah codex. These were subsequently assembled about a decade or two later by the semi-*tannaim* Ḥiyya and Oshaiah and arranged in a parallel corpus titled the *Tosefta. Even so, a great many *halakhot* were omitted from this secondary collection too, and they subsequently appear in the Talmud. They are termed *beraitot* ("excluded" or "external" *halakhot*; see Epstein, Tanna'im, 13–262).

Now while the Mishnah and to a slightly lesser extent the Tosefta represent material reflecting in the main the Akiva tradition, as passed on by his pupils and taught in his academies, the other major body of tannaitic literature, the halakhic Midrashim, reflect to a great extent the tradition of Akiva's great contemporary opponent, Ishmael, and the latter's pupils. A number of such compilations survive to this day: the *Mekhilta de-R. Ishmael* and one of Simeon b. Yoḥai to Exodus; the *Sifra* (or *Torat Kohanim*) to Leviticus; the *Sifrei* (edited by the school of Rav) and the *Sifrei Zuta* (cf. the school of Lydda) to Numbers; and the *Sifrei* and *Midrash Tannaim* to Deuteronomy. Each of these works is individual in style, character, and halakhic tendency, but they are all unified in the basic form, that of an exegesis from the verse to the abstract halakhic formulation. As such they form a valuable complement to the Mishnah and are frequently cited in the Talmud to help elucidate the Mishnah's sources (see Epstein, Tanna'im, 495–746). The basis of these exegetical Midrashim were the various hermeneutical rules (see *Hermeneutics) laid down at different times by a number of leading authorities – Hillel, Naḥum of Gimzo, Akiva, and Ishmael, It has been suggested that the 32 rules of interpreting the Bible for aggadic purposes, attributed to Eliezer b. Yose Ha-Gelili, are also of the tannaitic period.

Finally mention should be made of a very particular kind of work, the **Seder Olam Rabbah*, compiled (for the main part) by the great *tanna* *Yose b. Halafta in the middle of the second century. This is a systematic chronology of world history from the time of Adam till the destruction of the Second Temple. In parts it is an exegesis of biblical verses and in parts engenders ancient chronological oral traditions. It has already been pointed out that the greater part of the tannaitic period was one of extreme economic hardship, when poverty was rife and taxation a crippling burden. One might expect that under such circumstances scholars would have been deterred from learning, especially since the community could ill-afford to support them. However, quite to the contrary, the study of Torah became even more intensive in the period after Bar Kokhba. While in Temple times scholars had either supported themselves, or been paid a pittance out of Temple funds, during the Jabneh period a policy emerged of encouraging the community to regard the support of the sages as a religious-communal function. Nonetheless, many scholars still plied their crafts as cobblers, smiths, scribes, etc., supporting themselves in this way in their spare time. In the aftermath of the Bar-Kokhba war, Simeon b. Yoḥai developed the doctrine that scholars should devote themselves to the study of Torah to the exclusion of all else. By the amoraic period public support of poor scholars through regular and generous contributions to the academies was already an established custom (see M. Beer, in: *Sefer ha-Shanah*, Bar Ilan (1968), 167–80).

The *tannaim* were both scholars and teachers. They expounded the law and taught it to the people in academies and synagogues. They encouraged the people, raised their spirits, and exhorted them to higher moral aims. Numerous fragments from the homilies of the *tannaim* survived in the later aggadic compilations. Furthermore, the leaders among them represented the people before the Roman civil authorities, even going to Rome to plead their causes and bring ease to their hardships. Thus their involvement was not merely with the spiritual but also with the social and political developments of the nation. Their achievements in all these spheres in the face of overwhelming objective difficulties are eloquent testimony to their great spirit and ability (for creative activity of the *tannaim* and their importance, see *Sages and *Mishnah).

The term *tanna* has a secondary meaning of someone of the amoraic period, who hands down tannaitic statements, knows and memorizes them, and teaches them in the *bet ha-midrash* (e.g., Pes. 100a). These later *tannaim* served as living libraries, and were spoken of as "baskets full of books," in contrast to the eminent scholars. It was said of them that they ruin the world (*ha-tannaim mevalleh olam*, Sot. 22a) in that they give decisions based on traditions they have learned without knowing their reasons and their application to practical cases.

For a list of the more important *tannaim* see Chart: Tannaim.

For the issue of biographical historicity, see **Aggadah*; *Talmud, Babylonian.

BIBLIOGRAPHY: J. Bruell, *Mavo ha-Mishnah*, 1 (1876), 43–253; Frankel, Mishnah, 47–219; Ḥ. Albeck, *Mavo la-Mishnah* (1959), 216–33; H.L. Strack, *Introduction to the Talmud* (1931).

[Daniel Sperber]

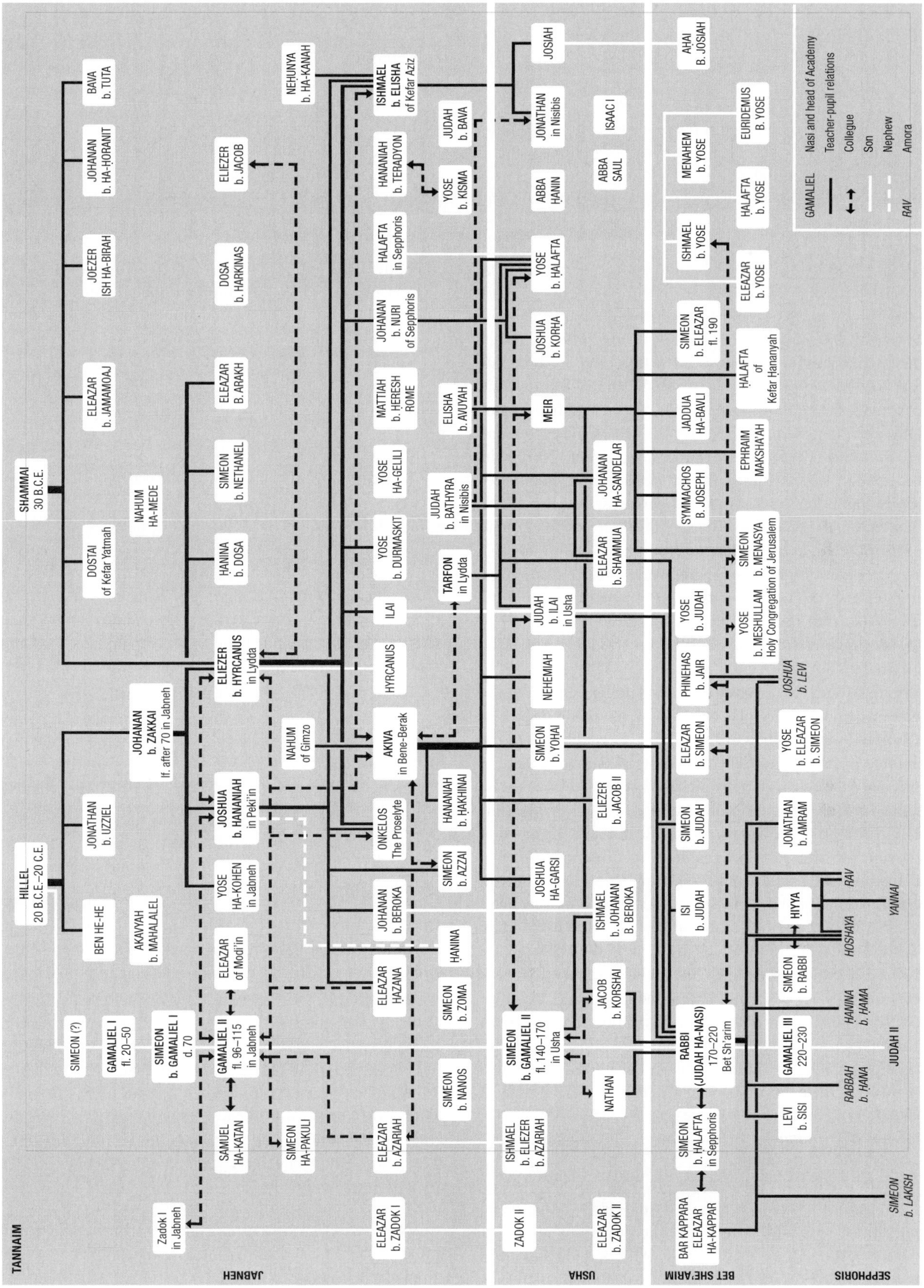
TANNAIM
JABNEH
USHA
BET SHE'ARIM
SEPPHORIS
HILLEL 20 B.C.E.–20 C.E.
SHAMMAI 30 B.C.E.
BEN HE-HE
JONATHAN b. UZZIEL
DOSTAI of Kefar Yatmah
ELEAZAR b. JAMAMOAJ
JOEZER ISH HA-BIRAH
JOHANAN b. HA-HORANIT
BAVA b. TUTA
AKAVYAH b. MAHALALEL
NAHUM HA-MEDE
SIMEON (?)
GAMALIEL I fl. 20–50
SIMEON b. GAMALIEL I d. 70
JOHANAN b. ZAKKAI fl. after 70 in Jabneh
Zadok I in Jabneh
SAMUEL HA-KATAN
GAMALIEL II fl. 96–115 in Jabneh
ELEAZAR of Modi'in
YOSE HA-KOHEN in Jabneh
JOSHUA b. HANANIAH in Peki'in
ELIEZER b. HYRCANUS in Lydda
HANINA b. DOSA
SIMEON b. NETHANEL
ELEAZAR B. ARAKH
DOSA b. HARKINAS
ELIEZER b. JACOB
NEHUNYA b. HA-KANAH
SIMEON HA-PAKULI
ELEAZAR b. ZADOK I
ELEAZAR b. AZARIAH
ELEAZAR HAZANA
JOHANAN b. BEROKA
ONKELOS The Proselyte
NAHUM of Gimzo
HYRCANUS
ILAI
YOSE b. DURMASKIT
YOSE HA-GELILI
MATTIAH b. HERESH ROME
JOHANAN b. NURI of Sepphoris
HALAFTA in Sepphoris
HANANIAH b. TERADYON
ISHMAEL b. ELISHA of Kefar Aziz
SIMEON b. NANOS
SIMEON b. ZOMA
HANINA
SIMEON b. AZZAI
HANANIAH b. HAKHINAI
AKIVA in Bene-Berak
TARFON in Lydda
JUDAH b. BATHYRA in Nisibis
ELISHA b. AVUYAH
YOSE b. KISMA
JUDAH b. BAVA
ISHMAEL b. ELIEZER b. AZARIAH
ZADOK II
SIMEON b. GAMALIEL II fl. 140–170 in Usha
JOSHUA HA-GARSI
SIMEON b. YOHAI
NEHEMIAH
JUDAH b. ILAI in Usha
MEIR
JOSHUA b. KORHA
YOSE b. HALAFTA
ABBA HANIN
JONATHAN in Nisibis
JOSIAH
ELEAZAR b. ZADOK II
NATHAN
JACOB b. KORSHAI
ISHMAEL b. JOHANAN B. BEROKA
ELIEZER b. JACOB II
ELEAZAR b. SHAMMUA
JOHANAN HA-SANDELAR
ABBA SAUL
ISAAC I
BAR KAPPARA ELEAZAR HA-KAPPAR
SIMEON b. HALAFTA in Sepphoris
RABBI (JUDAH HA-NASI) 170–220 Bet Sh'arim
ISI b. JUDAH
SIMEON b. JUDAH
ELEAZAR b. SIMEON
PHINEHAS b. JAIR
YOSE b. JUDAH
YOSE b. MESHULLAM
SIMEON b. MENASYA
Holy Congregation of Jerusalem
SYMMACHOS B. JOSEPH
JADDUA HA-BAVLI
SIMEON b. ELEAZAR fl. 190
ELEAZAR b. YOSE
ISHMAEL b. YOSE
MENAHEM b. YOSE
AHAI B. JOSIAH
LEVI b. SISI
GAMALIEL III 220–230
SIMEON b. RABBI
HIYYA
JONATHAN b. AMRAM
YOSE b. ELEAZAR b. SIMEON
EPHRAIM MAKSHA'AH
HALAFTA of Kefar Hananyah
HALAFTA b. YOSE
EURIDEMUS B. YOSE
SIMEON b. LAKISH
RABBAH b. HANA
JUDAH II
HANINA b. HAMA
HOSHAYA
YANNAI
RAV
JOSHUA b. LEVI
GAMALIEL Nasi and head of Academy
Teacher-pupil relations
Collegue
Son
Nephew
RAV Amora

TANNA DE-VEI ELIYAHU or **Seder Eliyahu** (Aram. תַּנָּא דְבֵי אֵלִיָּהוּ or Heb. סֵדֶר אֵלִיָּהוּ), a midrashic work. Unlike all the other Midrashim it does not consist of a compilation or collection of individual homilies but is a uniform work stamped with a character of its own. The work, which is characterized by original expressions and rhetorical constructions couched in poetic and even flowery language, is distinguished by its didactic moral aim: the author deals with the divine precepts and the reasons for them, and the importance of knowledge of Torah, prayer, and repentance. He is especially concerned with the ethical and religious values which are enshrined in the Bible and in the trials and lives of the patriarchs.

The problem of the date and place of composition of *Seder Eliyahu* has not yet been resolved. It has been variously dated almost anywhere between the third and tenth centuries. S.J. *Rapoport suggested the tenth century, on the basis of three considerations: the number of its chapters does not tally with that given by the *Arukh*, which he believed to be the *Tanna de-Vei Eliyahu* mentioned a number of times in the Talmud (e.g., Ket. 106a; from the collection of geonic responsa published by S. Assaf, it is now clear that the *Arukh* quoted Natronai Gaon, who lived in the ninth century); some of the quotations in the Talmud from the *Tanna de-Vei Eliyahu* are not found in the present work; and the dates given in the work (chap. 2, p. 6; chap. 7, p. 37; chap. 29, p. 163) indicate the tenth century. While Zunz agreed with Rapoport, M. Friedmann refuted two of his arguments; proving that the original number of chapters in the manuscripts conforms to that mentioned in the *Arukh* and maintaining rightly that the dates were altered by later copyists. However, he conceded the third point and held that the *Tanna de-Vei Eliyahu* of the Talmud is distinct from the present work. In his view, in its original form it dates from the third century but contains late additions. Despite the determined attempt of Margalioth to prove that the two works are identical and the fact that the nine passages from the *Tanna de-Vei Eliyahu* cited in the Babylonian Talmud do in fact occur in the present work, an examination of the sources of the Midrash as a whole makes it clear beyond question that it utilizes both the Babylonian Talmud and Midrashim which are later than it (Urbach, see bibl.). The other proofs which Margalioth puts forward as indicating an early date (in his view, the first half of the third century) – the names of the scholars mentioned, all of whom are *tannaim*, as well as the expressions used, which he believes are all tannaitic – are not decisive. As the author often omits to mention the name of the sage who delivered the homily, it is therefore possible that he gave only the names of the most famous of the *tannaim* to whom he ascribes his statements. Margalioth's conclusions with regard to expressions are also far from irrefutable (Urbach).

Similarly all attempts to infer the date from the historical references are inconclusive. Mann and Epstein fix its date at the end of the amoraic era (Epstein is of the opinion that it was arranged then.) Aptowitzer fixes the date of its composition as the ninth century. All that can be stated with certainty is that the Midrash was compiled before the ninth century (Albeck), and that Natronai Gaon refers to the present work and not, as Rapoport and Zunz thought, to the talmudic.

Eliyahu is the speaker in the work but there is no suggestion of a pseudepigrapha, nor should it be inferred that its author is a certain Abba Eliyahu. The name is mentioned only in chapter 15 of *Seder Eliyahu Zuta* and this chapter is a later addition by a copyist. The author relates that he came from Jabneh, that he resided in Jerusalem, and that he wandered in Babylon. He disputes with a fire worshiper and with those who accept the Bible but not the Mishnah (whether he was referring to Christians or to Karaites is a disputed point). His halakhic conclusions, which contain interesting deviations from accepted *halakhah*, constitute a problem on their own, but in general his *halakhah* approximates to that of Ereẓ Israel.

The work is in two sections: *Seder Eliyahu Rabbah* and *Seder Eliyahu Zuta*, and the original parts of the second appear to be by the same author as the first. There are a number of editions: Venice, 1598; Prague, 1676–77 with Samuel Heida's commentaries *Zikkukin de-Nura* and *Bi'urin de-Esha*, according to which there were many other editions; Vienna, 1901 with introduction and notes by M. Friedmann, from a Rome manuscript of 1073; *Tanna de-Vei Eliyahu Zuta* (19 chapters) edited by H.M. Horowitz from a Parma manuscript and published in part 2 of *Beit Eked ha-Aggadot*; appendixes to *Seder Eliyahu Zuta*, being three chapters of *Derekh Ereẓ* and seven of *Pirkei de-R. Eliezer* (Vienna, 1904) by M. Friedmann; and *Likkutei Seder Eliyahu Zuta* from a *Genizah manuscript, published by L. Ginsberg in *Ginzei Schechter* part 1, 238–45.

BIBLIOGRAPHY: M. Friedmann (Ish-Shalom) (ed.), *Seder Eliyahu Rabbah ve-Seder Eliyahu Zuta* (1904), introd.; Zunz-Albeck, Derashot, 55–57, 292–98; J. Mann, in: HUCA, 4 (1927), 249–51, 302–10; M. Kadushin, *The Theology of Seder Eliahu* (1932); V. Aptowitzer, in: *Jewish Studies in Memory of G.A. Kohut* (1935), 5–39; Epstein, Mishnah, 762–4, 1302f.; M. Margalioth, in: *Sefer Assaf* (1953), 370–90; R.J.Z. Werblowsky, in: JJS, 6 (1955), 201–11; E.E. Urbach, in: *Leshonenu*, 21 (1957), 183–97; S.K. Mirsky, in: *Shanah be-Shanah* 5725 (1964), 215–22.

[Jacob Elbaum]

TANNENBAUM, FRANK (1893–1969), U.S. economic historian. Born in Austria, Tannenbaum was taken to the United States in 1905. He was a member of the research staff of the Institute of Economics in Washington (1925) and subsequently made economic and social surveys of Puerto Rico (1928–30) and Mexico (1931). In 1939 he was appointed professor of history at Columbia, where he taught economic history until his retirement in 1961. Tannenbaum's numerous writings include: *Peace by Revolution* (1933), *Crime and the Community* (1937), *Mexico: The Struggle for Peace and Bread* (1950), and *Ten Keys to Latin America* (1962).

TANSMAN, ALEXANDER (**Alexandre**; 1897–1986), composer, pianist, and conductor. Born in Lodz, Poland, Tansman studied at the conservatories of Lodz and Warsaw. In 1919 he submitted two works in competition for the Polish National Prize and won the first and second prizes. He settled in Paris in 1921 and appeared as pianist and conductor. His works of the 1920s retained Polish features such as Mazurka rhythms and Polish folk melodies. In the same years he was strongly influenced by the neo-classicism of Igor Stravinsky. From 1941 to 1946 Tansman lived in the U.S., where he wrote music for films, until he returned to France in 1946. His music evinces a strong lyrical feeling and is moderately modern in style. Many of his works were inspired by his Jewish origin, among them Isaïe le prophète (1950), an oratorio; Sabbataï Zévi, le faux messie (1958), an opera; and many others. He also wrote *Igor Stravinsky, ouvrage…* (1948, *Igor Stravinsky, the Man and His Music*, 1949). His honors included the Coolidge Medal (1941), election to the Académie Royale of Belgium (1977), and the Polish Medal of Cultural Merit (1983).

ADD. BIBLIOGRAPHY: NG^2; MGG, s.v.; J. Segiella, *Child of Fortune: Alexander Tansman and His Life and Times*, 1–2 (Pol., 1996).

[Claude Abravanel / Yulia Kreinin (2nd ed.)]

TANTA, town in Lower *Egypt, situated between *Alexandria and *Cairo. A prosperous Jewish community, noted for its loyalty to Jewish tradition, existed in Tanta at least from the beginning of the 17th century and it is possible that the community was founded in earlier times and grew considerably during the second half of the 19th century. At one time, it was the third-largest Jewish community in Egypt, after Cairo and Alexandria. A document from the Muslim court of law in Tanta from 1871 deals with the case of the merchant Joseph Levi of Cairo, who purchased real estate in the vicinity of Tanta. In 1897 there were 883 Jews in Tanta and in 1917, 1,183. Most of the Jews in Tanta were of North African origin. During the period of the community's prosperity, there were three synagogues, a Jewish school, and a women's charitable society. The Jewish population in the city grew because of its location on the railroad line connecting Alexandria and Cairo. The *Alliance Israélite Universelle founded a school in Tanta in 1903 and in 1905–6 232 students of both genders were enrolled, some of whom were Muslims. This school remained after the Alliance Israélite Universelle had left Egypt in 1922. After World War I, the number of Jews decreased when many of them left for Cairo and Alexandria and others went to Ereẓ Israel. Only the poor remained and they too eventually died or departed. In 1912 the Jews of the town contributed to the Kuppat Pidyon Shevuiim of Jerusalem for the young Jews who joined the Ottoman army. The rabbi of Tanta at the end of the 19th century and the beginning of the 20th was David Nahmias, who submitted a number of halakhic questions to R. Raphael Aaron ben Simeon. He received one answer in 1900 about an ice factory which had been opened. In 1901 the rabbis of Cairo traveled to Tanta to publish there the new *kiddushin* regulation. Emile *Suarez was the president of the Tanta community in 1938.

ADD. BIBLIOGRAPHY: J.M. Landau, *Jews in Nineteenth-Century Egypt* (1969), index; S. DellaPergola, in: J.M. Landau (ed.), *Toledot ha-Yehudim be-Miẓraim ba-Tekufah ha-Otmanit (1517–1914)* (1988), 41–42; Z. Zohar, in: ibid., M. Winter, in: ibid., 408. G. Pozailov, *Ḥakhmeihen shel Arbaʿ Arei ha-Kodesh*, 2 (2001), 601.

[Eliyahu Ashtor / Leah Bornstein-Makovetsky (2nd ed.)]

TANUJI, family in Tunis. Ishmael Ha-Kohen *Tanuji, was a rabbi in Tunis. Joseph *Tanuji wrote *Benei Yosef* (1793) for his nephew JUSTO COHEN, the leader of the Tunisian community in Leghorn. His son SHALOM was a rabbi and a commentator on the Talmud. JOSHUA COHEN (mid-late 18th century) was caid, official tax collector, and leader of the Jewish community in Tunis. Ḥ.J.D. *Azulai who stayed in Tanuji's home, located outside the ghetto, during his visit in Tunis, drew a vivid picture of both Joshua and his son MOSES, describing the great wealth and hospitality of the Tanujis and their respect for learning. A Talmud class met in their home every Sabbath in which rabbis and dignitaries participated. Joshua Tanuji ordered and financed the shipping of a Hebrew printing press from Leghorn to Tunisia. The Tanujis led the struggle against the Leghorn community in Tunis and opposed the study of Kabbalah. Joshua Tanuji even had R. Solomon Uzan imprisoned in a dispute over taxes. JUDAH COHEN (d.c. 1835), rabbi in Tunis, was known for his piety.

He wrote ten works, mainly commentaries on tractates of the Talmud; his major compositions were *Ereẓ Yehudah* (Leghorn, 1797) and *Admat Yehudah*, the latter published with David *Najar's *Ẓemaḥ David* (Leghorn, 1828).

BIBLIOGRAPHY: D. Cazès, *Notes bibliographiques sur la littérature juive-tunisienne* (1893), 117–36; Hirschberg, Afrikah, 2 (1965), 135–7, 155–7.

TANUJI, ISHMAEL HA-KOHEN (16th century), Tunisian rabbi and author. Ishmael was apparently the first rabbinic scholar and author in *Tunis. As a result of the difficult political situation prevailing there, he left Tunis and went to *Egypt. From his approbations to the works of others it would appear that he was chief rabbi of Egypt (cf. Responsa Elijah b. Ḥayyim, pt. 2, no. 55). Ḥ.J.D. *Azulai states that there was a synagogue in Egypt in his time where Ishmael used to pray which was called after his name. He completed his well-known book, *Sefer ha-Zikkaron* (Ferrara, 1555) in 1543. It is a collection of rulings and laws selected from the early halakhic authorities and arranged in the order of the talmudic tractates. While he was engaged in the writing of this work, the rulings of *Jacob b. Asher, author of the *Turim*, came to his notice, and realizing that they followed the same pattern as his work he quoted them frequently.

BIBLIOGRAPHY: Azulai, 1 (1852), 56a; D. Cazès, *Notes bibliographiques sur la littérature juive-tunisienne* (1893), 117–20; Hirschberg, Afrikah, 2 (1965), 155.

TANUJI, JOSEPH BEN SHALOM HA-KOHEN (early 18th century), Tunisian rabbi. Both he and his father bore the title of caid. Tanuji studied under Abraham Tayyib. He was the author of *Benei Yosef*, which was published 70 years later

(Leghorn, 1793) at the expense of a member of his family, the caid Judah Tanuji.

It consists of a brief commentary on parts of the tractates *Bava Kamma, Bava Mezia, Avodah Zarah*, and *Me'ilah*, together with notes on the *Mishneh Torah* of *Maimonides and on Elijah *Mizraḥi. The editor appended (p. 35a–b) some notes by Abraham Tayyib on Maimonides and by Ẓemaḥ Sarfati on *Sanhedrin*.

BIBLIOGRAPHY: D. Cazès, *Notes bibliographiques sur la littérature juive-tunisienne* (1893), 121–8.

TANZHAUS ("dance hall"; Heb. *bet ḥatunnot* or *bet nissu'im*, "wedding hall"), a communal institution mainly in Germany. It served as a place for wedding festivities. The sexes never mixed in dances, except for a modest ritual of dancing with a bride. During the 15th and 16th centuries, debates on mixed dancing took place in different communities and at times even contributed to a split between the community and its leaders. Dancing was a favorite entertainment, and although the *Tanzhaus* was designated only for weddings, many towns used it as a public dance hall and held celebrations there from time to time. Most Jewish quarters in Germany and France had a *bet ḥatunnot.* (See also *Dance.)

BIBLIOGRAPHY: I. Abrahams, *Jewish Life in the Middle Ages* (1920), 75, 380; H.H. Ben-Sasson, in: *Zion*, 27 (1962), 189–94.

[Natan Efrati]

TAPPUAH (Heb. תַּפּוּחַ, תַּפֻּחַ)

(1) a city of the tribe of Judah, located in the district of the northern Shephelah with Zanoah and Enam (Josh. 15:34). The Tappuah listed with the sons of Hebron (I Chron. 2:43) is perhaps identical with the Beth-Tappuah of Joshua 15:53. Its assumed identification with post-biblical Bethletepha (present-day Beit (Bayt) Nattīf) is doubtful.

(2) A city in Ephraim, the territory of which was in Manasseh. It was situated south of Shechem near the brook of Kanah (Josh. 16:8; 17:7, as En-Tappuah; 17:8). Although the king of Tappuah is listed among the kings defeated by Joshua (Josh. 12:17), and his territory fell to Manasseh, the stronger Ephraim was needed to capture the city itself. The suggested identification with the Tappuah fortified by Bacchides (I Macc. 9:50) is based on a misreading (see *Tekoa). The accepted identification is with Sheikh Abu Zarad near a spring called ʿAyn al-Tuffūḥ in the vicinity of the village of Yāsūf (the Yashub of LXX and perhaps of the Samaria Ostraca). Late Bronze and Iron Age pottery has been found on the site.

BIBLIOGRAPHY: F.M. Abel, in: RB, 45 (1936), 103ff.

[Michael Avi-Yonah]

TARAGAN, BEN-ZION (1870–1953), writer, teacher, and journalist in Ereẓ Israel and *Egypt. Born in Jerusalem, he received a traditional education at the Bet-Midrash Doresh Zion and yeshivot, learned printing, and began to work in the printing press of E. *Ben-Yehuda. When the latter was imprisoned, Taragan became manager of the press, and, after Ben-Yehuda was freed, helped him in preparing his dictionary. Taragan also contributed to Ben-Yehuda's periodical *Hashkafah*. In 1906 he left for *Alexandria, where he worked as secretary of the rabbinate and as a teacher of Hebrew in the first school to use the teaching method of Ivrit be-Ivrit (Hebrew in Hebrew) in Egypt. Taragan took an active part in Jewish communal life, especially among the youth of Alexandria. He also served as a reporter-correspondent for Hebrew periodicals in the Diaspora. Taragan published textbooks on teaching Hebrew. However, more important are his histories of the Alexandria community – *Les communautés israélites d'Alexandrie; aperçu historique depuis les temps des Ptolémées jusqu'à nos jours* (1932) and *Korot ha-Kehillah ha-Yehudit be-Alexandria, 1906–1946* (1947) – as an eyewitness record of contemporary trends and developments there.

BIBLIOGRAPHY: J.M. Landau, *Jews in Nineteenth-Century Egypt* (1969), 14–15.

[Haïm Z'ew Hirschberg]

TARANTO, city in Apulia, S. Italy. A series of tombstone inscriptions in Hebrew, Latin, and Greek from the third century until the 12th testify to the existence of a Jewish colony in Taranto. The chronicle of *Josippon (tenth century) states that Titus settled Jewish prisoners from Palestine in Taranto. During the Middle Ages Taranto became one of the most important Jewish centers of southern Italy, although the city suffered from Arab raids in 839 and 925, when Shabbetai *Donnolo was ransomed there. *Benjamin of Tudela, who passed through Taranto c. 1159, found approximately 300 Jewish families whose economic condition was good. During the anti-Jewish persecutions of 1290–94, 172 families of Taranto Jews converted to Christianity. In 1411 the people attacked the Jews, sacked their houses, and killed the town captain when he came to their rescue. In 1463 King Ferrante I approved the city's demands, among them a request that the Jews should live separately from the Christians, and that the New Christians be allowed to postpone the payment of their debts and not be persecuted by the Inquisition. In 1464 the king, responding to the city's demand, ordered that the Jews wear a distinctive sign, as they did in Lecce. But in 1465 the king approved the Jews' request to renew their privileges, promised to refrain from inquisitorial procedures, pardoned past transgressions, and forbade the painting of the images of saints in the Jewish quarter; the king also promised not to permit New Christians to exercise authority over Jews. In 1474 in response to the city's requests the king imposed restrictions on the Jews' usury. Several copyists operated in Taranto, among them the physician Samuel ben David Samuel Ibn Shoham il Medico, Burla of Corfu, Menahem ben Joseph Vivante, Isaac Cohen ben Nathan. The latter copied the *Be'ur Sitrei Torah* of Naḥmanides. Among the privileges granted the city council of Martina in 1495, King Frederick of Aragon forbade New Christians to press charges against those who robbed them (probably during the riots of 1494–1495 during the French invasion of the Kingdom of Naples) and prohibited their coming to live in that city. In 1510–11 Taranto's Jews and New Christians were expelled together with those of the entire kingdom of *Naples. A small number returned in 1520, but in 1540 they were expelled again.

BIBLIOGRAPHY: Milano, Italia, index; Vacca, in: *Rinascenza Salentina*, 4 (1936), 221–9; Antonucci, *ibid.*, 3 (1935), 103–5; N. Ferorelli, *Ebrei nell'Italia meridionale…* (1915), passim; Adler, in: JQR, 14 (1901/02), 111–5; Frey, Corpus, nos. 620–31. **ADD. BIBLIOGRAPHY:** D. Abulafia, "Il mezzogiorno peninsulare dai bizantini all'espulsione," in: *Storia d'Italia. Annali 11, Gli ebrei in Italia. Dall'alto Medioevo all'età dei ghetti, ed. Corrao Vivanti* (1996), 5–44; C. Sirat and M. Beit Arié, *Manuscrits médiévaux en caractères hébraiques portant des indications de date jusqu'à 1540* (1972–1986), 1; C. Colafemmina, "Copisti ebrei a Taranto in XV," in: *Cenacolo*, 19 (1995), 53–62; C. Colafemmina, *Gli ebrei a Taranto* (2005).

[Arial Toaff / Nadia Zeldes (2nd ed.)]

TARASCON, town in S. France, south of Avignon. The earliest evidence of Jews in Tarascon is a fragment of a Hebrew inscription dating from 1193, probably from a tombstone, encased in the St. Gabriel Tower. The oldest written document concerning the Jews of Tarascon dates from 1283, but the community essentially gained in importance with the influx of Jews expelled from the kingdom of France. The Jews enjoyed complete commercial freedom and were authorized to possess real estate and hold the public office of toll gatherer, broker, or seller at auctions. A relatively large number of Jewish physicians lived there; at least four at the beginning of the 14th century, and at least six at the beginning of the 15th century. The Jews made up almost 10% of the total population, with about 100 families at the close of the 14th century and possibly more than 150 families in 1487. The present-day Rue des Juifs commemorates the old Jewish quarter – the *carrière* or *Carrieyra dels Jusieus* or *Juzataria* – which from 1378 became the compulsory quarter for the Jews. The community owned a synagogue, a slaughterhouse, and a cemetery.

The charter (or *coutumes*) of Tarascon of 1345 which was ratified by Queen Jeanne already points to a deterioration in the condition of the Jews; although it prescribes that the Jews would only pay for the local taxes, it was, on the other hand, forbidden to them to sell meat slaughtered according to the Jewish law on the general market (compared here to the meat of animals which had died of disease, or to contaminated meat!) or to slaughter animals for Christians; lastly, they were not allowed to work on Sundays and on Christian festivals. When accused of having propagated the *Black Death (1348–49), the Jews of Tarascon were the victims of bloody persecutions. From 1382 they were no longer authorized to possess land and vineyards, and from the second half of the 15th century they were excluded from public office.

As a result of the vigorous protective measures taken by the municipal council, the Jews of Tarascon were spared the anti-Jewish persecutions which broke out in several towns of *Provence from 1484. However, after the example of other towns of Provence, the inhabitants of Tarascon accused the Jews in 1496 not only of being the enemies of the Christian faith but also of having committed usury and robbery. Charles VIII, king of France – who had acquired Provence a short while before – reacted with an expulsion order which came into force on July 15. Almost all the Jews of Tarascon took refuge in *Comtat Venaissin. Only a few converted so as to remain in Tarascon. Scholars of great renown had stayed in Tarascon for periods of various length, including Joseph b. Abba Mari *Kaspi (1297–1340), the philosopher, exegete, and author of *Sefer ha-Sod* and *Adnei Kesef.* During the 18th century Jews who had chosen to settle in Tarascon were expelled by the Parliament of Provence of December 11, 1775. By 1970 there was no Jewish community in Tarascon.

BIBLIOGRAPHY: Gross, Gal Jud, 248–50; S. Kahn, in: REJ, 39 (1899), 95–112, 261–98; D. Siderski, *ibid.*, 99 (1935), 123–6; B. Blumenkranz, in: *Bulletin philologique et historique … congrès 90* (1965, pub. 1968), 622; A. Drouard, in: *Archives Juives*, 4 (1967/68), 15–18; Z. Szajkowski, *Franco-Judaica* (1962), no. 339.

[Bernhard Blumenkranz]

TARAZONA, city in Saragossa province, N.E. Spain. Its Jewish community was one of the most important in the kingdom of Aragon. The proximity of the town to the border of the kingdoms of Castile and Navarre offered its inhabitants extensive commercial opportunities, and the community had lengthy periods of prosperity and expansion. There were two Jewish quarters: an old and a new, each having a synagogue and located near one another; the new was really an extension of the old among houses of Christians. The old quarter was situated between the Conde and Rua Alta Streets up to the Iron Gate; a street there is still known as the "Street of the Jews." The new one began to form in 1371 between the Aires Street, the town square, and the Rebate Square (at present known as de la Merced). The Jewish cemetery was in its vicinity.

The Jewish settlement in Tarazona was an ancient one; in 1123 Alfonso I granted the bishop of Tarazona a tithe from the taxes of the Jews of his bishopric. However, it began to increase in importance in the 13th century, and members of the *Portella family were active there during that period; Don Musa de Portella acted as the bailiff of the town during the reign of James I until being appointed bailiff of the kingdom; after him, Ishmael de Portella acted as the executor of the infante Pedro, son of Alfonso III. Baer states that this family was capable of financing the taxes and budget of the whole community (see bibliography).

Pedro III took a special interest in the organization of the community and in 1285 ratified a communal regulation which established procedure for the payment of taxes on real estate and movable property, as well as stipulating persons exempted from such payments, the declaration of the assessed serving as the basis for taxation.

After the *disputation which he conducted in Pamplona with Cardinal Pedro de Luna (1375), R. Shem Tov b. Isaac Shaprut settled in Tarazona, where he probably wrote *Even Boḥan* during the early 1380s and served as physician. However, he became involved in a controversy, of which the details are unknown. A number of Jews in Tarazona engaged in moneylending and provided loans for the municipal council and to the inhabitants of nearby towns in Navarre and Castile.

After the Persecutions of 1391

The community of Tarazona was unaffected by the persecutions of the Jews in Spain in 1391, through the energetic protection given by the crown. The wave of conversions among the Jews in Spain in this period also affected this community, and after the disputation of *Tortosa (1413–14) many of its members abandoned the Jewish faith, including some of the most prominent local Jews. There were other members of these families, however, who remained loyal to Judaism and continued to take important roles in the community administration.

The community had apparently regained its strength by the 1430s. Jews built houses there, the building contractors being apostate Jews and Moors. To assist the community further, in 1457 Alfonso v granted its request for alleviations and exempted it from payment of taxes and other levies. Alfonso's favorable attitude was guided by his desire to rehabilitate the communities in the kingdom as a whole (as in Saragossa, Jaca, Teruel, etc.). John ii also adopted this policy with regard to the Jews of Tarazona. However, like the rest of the Jews in the kingdom, Tarazona Jewry suffered from the internal policy of Ferdinand v. In 1484 Ferdinand ordered the Jews of the town to testify before the *Inquisition if they knew of any *Conversos who observed the Jewish precepts. In 1491 several members of the Santa Fé (Asniel) family were burned at the stake; others were sentenced in 1497 and 1499.

When the Jews were expelled from Spain in 1492, those of Tarazona probably left for nearby Navarre. The collection of their outstanding debts was entrusted to Luis de Alkalá and Fernando Núñez Coronel (Abraham *Seneor).

BIBLIOGRAPHY: Baer, Spain, index; Baer, Urkunden, 1 (1929), index; J.M. Sanz Artibucilla, *Historia de la Ciudad de Tarazona*, 2 vols. (1929–30); idem, in: *Sefarad*, 4 (1944), 73–98; 5 (1945), 337–66; 6 (1946), 374–6; 7 (1947), 63–92; 9 (1949), 393–419; F. Cantera, *ibid.*, 3 (1943), 240f.; L. Piles Ros, *ibid.*, 10 (1950), 107ff.; F. Cantera, *Sinagogas españolas* (1955), 311–3; Suárez Fernández, Documentos, 30, 486.

[Haim Beinart]

TARBIZ, Hebrew quarterly for Judaic studies; published since 1930 by the Hebrew University, Jerusalem. *Tarbiz'* founder and first editor was J.N. *Epstein (1930–52), who was assisted by E.Z. *Melamed, under whom articles in the general humanities were also accepted. Epstein's successor was Ḥ. *Schirmann (1954–69), who edited the quarterly with the assistance of E.J. Goleh (Fleischer), J. Heinemann, and I. Yeivin. From 1970 the editorship was taken over by E.E. *Urbach, assisted by Goleh. Subsequent editors were J. Dan, M. Haran, and M.D. Herr (1982–86); M. Idel, D. Rosenthal, and J. Yahalom (1987–91); W.Z. Harvey, Y. Kaplan, and I.M. Ta-Shma (1992–96); M. Ben-Sasson, M. Kahana, and C. Turniansky (1997–2001).

Several larger monographs appeared as supplementary volumes to *Tarbiz*, e.g., S. Assaf, *Sefer ha-Shetarot le-Rav Hai Ga'on* (1930); J.N. Epstein, *Perush R. Yehudah b. Nathan li-Ketubbot* (1933); and S. Lieberman, *Talmudah shel Kisrin* (1931).

[Baruch Yaron]

TARBUT (Heb. "culture"), Hebrew educational and cultural organization maintaining schools in most Eastern European countries between the two world wars. Especially active in Poland, it maintained there 183 elementary and nine secondary schools, 72 kindergartens, four teachers' seminaries, an agricultural school, and four evening schools (1934–35), and published periodicals, curricula, and textbooks. Instruction was given in Hebrew, and biblical and modern Hebrew literature, and the education was Zionist oriented, promoting pioneer settlement in Ereẓ Israel. Tarbut started activities in Russia, particularly after the February 1917 Revolution, but was soon proscribed, with all Hebrew activity, by the Soviet authorities.

TARES (Heb. זוּנִים, *zunim*), the darnel – *Lolium temulentum*, weed which grows among grain, particularly wheat. The grains resemble those of wheat so that it is very difficult to separate them by sifting, and as a result they are sown together with the wheat and grow with it in the field. Darnel flour is poisonous and gives a bitter taste to bread in which it has been mixed. The tares do no harm to birds, especially to doves (TJ, Kil. 1:1, 26d). Nobody would consciously sow tares in his field. Hence the parable in the New Testament about the peasant "who sowed good seed in his fields… and his enemy came and sowed tares in the midst of the wheat" (Matt. 13:24–30). According to the *halakhah* wheat and tares do not constitute **kilayim* with one another (Kil. 1:1). The Jerusalem Talmud (*ibid.*) quotes a view that tares are called *zunim* because as a result of them the wheat *mezannot* ("commit[s] adultery"), i.e., it changes its characteristics and is turned into tares. This view had already been propounded by Galen (*De Alimentis*, 1:27), but Basilius argued with him: "Tares and other wild weeds are not formed by cultivated species changing into wild species" (*Hexameron* 5:5a). It has been demonstrated that by a thorough separation of the darnel seeds from the wheat seeds tares do not grow.

BIBLIOGRAPHY: Loew, Flora, 1 (1928), 723–9; B. Cizik, *Oẓar ha-Ẓemaḥim* (1952), 802–3; J. Feliks, *Kilei Zera'im ve-Harkavah* (1967), 22–23.

[Jehuda Feliks]

TARFON, *tanna* in the generation after the destruction of the Temple in 70 C.E.; one of the leading scholars of *Jabneh. Tarfon was a priest. The Temple was still standing in his youth, and he recounts what he saw there (TJ, Yoma 1:1; 3:7; et al.). He may have studied under *Johanan b. Zakkai, but in any case it is certain that he already occupied an honored place among the scholars of the second generation of *tannaim* (Yad. 4:3), and his greatness is expressed in the designations given him: "the father of all Israel" and "the teacher of all Israel." On several occasions he appears as chief spokesman among the contemporary scholars (Yoma 76a; et al.). His place of residence was *Lydda, where he taught and judged monetary cases (BM 4:3; Ta'an. 3:9; et al.). Tarfon's main disputant was *Akiva and many halakhic discussions between them are recorded. He is also mentioned among the scholars who were with Akiva in Bene-Berak on the night of Passover "and spoke about the Exodus from Egypt the whole of that night" (according to the Passover *Haggadah*, cf. Tosef. Pes. 10:12). Akiva esteemed Tarfon as "a publicly recognized expert" (Sanh. 33a), and was most particular about his dignity, calling him *ha-zaken* ("the elder"; Sif. Num. 148; Men. 68b). This esteem was mutual, and Tarfon addressed Akiva as "my teacher and master" (Kal.) and said to him: "anyone who is separated from you is as if he is separated from life" (Sifra, Nedavah 4:5; et al.). On the other hand there is a difference of opinion in the Talmud (Ket. 84b) as to whether Tarfon was the teacher or the colleague of Akiva. Among Tarfon's pupils were Judah b. Ilai who transmitted dicta in his name, Yose ha-Gelili, Eleazar of Modi'in, and Ishmael; Simeon b. Yoḥai quoted his sayings (TJ, Meg. 1:6).

Much is told of Tarfon's humane character. Possessed of considerable means (Ned. 62a), he betrothed 300 women during a year of drought in order that they should be able, as the wives of a priest, to eat **terumah* (Tosef., Ket. 5:1). It is also related that on one occasion, when he went to eat figs on his own property, the watchmen, failing to recognize him, struck him. When they discovered his identity and asked forgiveness he replied: "As each stick came down on me I pardoned you for each successive blow" (TJ, Shev. 4:2). On one occasion he saved himself from assault by revealing his identity, and as a result was distressed all his life and used to say, "Woe is me that I made use of the crown of the Torah." He distinguished himself in the exemplary manner in which he honored his mother (TJ, Kid. 1:7, see also Kid. 31b) and his care to avoid transgression (Kid. 81b). In several matters he acted strictly in accordance with Bet Shammai, for which he was punished (Ber. 1:3; et al.). Tarfon was distinguished by his great erudition: "When a scholar came to him and said, 'Teach me' he would cite Scripture, Mishnah, Midrash, *halakhot* and *aggadot*; when he left he was full of blessing and goodness" (ARN[1], 18, 67). He was methodical in his learning and once remarked to Akiva: "How long will you rake words together and use them against us, Akiva? I cannot bear it" (Sif. Num. 75; cf. his statement to Eleazar of Modi'in, Yoma 76a), but when he was convinced, he praised him greatly (*ibid.*). In his teaching he used the method of instructive dialogue; he put a question to his pupils who replied, "teach us, Sir," and Tarfon retorted: "You answer." Occasionally he began with "I shall ask" (Tosef., Ber. 4:16–17). A number of phrases were coined by Tarfon. When he wished to express his approval of a statement, he would exclaim, "*kaftor va-feraḥ*" ("knob and flower"; cf. Ex. 25:33); for disapproval, "my son shall not go down with thee" (Gen. 42:38); to express distress, "your ass has gone, Tarfon"; for an oath he would say, "May I ruin my son." His best known aggadic saying is: "The day is short, and the work is great, and the laborers are sluggish, and the reward is much, and the Master is urgent. It is not your duty to complete the work, but neither are you free to desist from it" (Avot 2:15). He also stated: "God did not cause His divine presence to rest upon Israel until they had worked" (ARN[1] 11, 45). On the question of whether study or observance is greater, he decided in favor of the latter (Kid. 40b).

There is no information about his death, but according to one *aggadah* (Lam. R. 2:4), he was one of the *ten martyrs. The Tarfon to whom *Judah Nesiah brought the firstborn of an ass (Bek. 11a) was not the *tanna* but a later *amora* of that name, nor is he to be identified with the Jew Tryphon who appears in the dialogue of the Church Father *Justin. For Tarfon's descendants, see *Bava Meẓia* 85a (with caution).

BIBLIOGRAPHY: Frankel, Mishnah (1923[2]), 107–12; Hyman, Toledot, s.v.; A. Orenstein, in: *Sinai*, 39 (1956), 182–8; J.L. Maimon (ed.), *Yiḥusei Tanna'im ve-Amora'im* (1963), 482–5; J. Neusner, in: *Judaica*, 17 (1961), 141–67.

[Zvi Kaplan]

TARGUM. In its verb form the Hebrew root *tirgem* means both "to explain" and "to translate." The nominal form means "translation." Although technically it can apply to translation into and from any language, the word is employed in rabbinical literature almost exclusively for Aramaic biblical text, both the Aramaic translation of the Bible's Hebrew (cf. Meg. 3a) and the originally Aramaic portions, including individual words (e.g., Gen 31.47; cf. Shab. 115a; Yad. 4:5). The Targum, i.e., the Aramaic translation par excellence, is the Targum *Onkelos, which was regarded as so authoritative that worshipers were enjoined to read the weekly portion privately "twice in the original and once in the Targum" (Ber. 8a), a custom which is still maintained in orthodox circles. To such an extent was "targum" regarded as synonymous with Aramaic that the Kurdistani Jews, who speak Aramaic, refer to their language as "Targum."

For the language, see *Aramaic; for the Aramaic Bible translations, see *Bible, Translations.

TARGUM SHENI (Heb. תַּרְגּוּם שֵׁנִי; lit. "Second Translation"), a collection of homilies in Aramaic on the Book of Esther (*Scroll of Esther). It is so extensive that despite its name it can hardly be regarded as a translation. Only about 75 of the verses have been translated literally, the remainder being an extensive midrashic paraphrase. The author makes free use of the *aggadot*, adapting them and embellishing them with his own additions. Hai Gaon writes: "Here in Babylon there are several Targums of Esther which differ from one another. One has many additions and Midrashim, and the other none" (L. Ginzberg (ed.), *Ginzei Schechter* (1929), 86). The former refers to the *Targum Sheni*, while the latter to the *Targum Rishon*. Rashi (to Deut. 3:4) and the *Arukh* of Asher b. Jehiel both quote it.

Outstanding among the stories interwoven into the *Targum Sheni* is the variegated description of Solomon's throne (1:2). Mention is made, in incorrect chronological order, of

Nebuchadnezzar, Alexander, Shishak, and Antiochus, all of whom wanted to sit upon this splendid throne but did not succeed and were punished. In the end Cyrus, king of Persia, "as a reward for occupying himself with the Temple succeeded in occupying it." This description is intended to call to mind the glorious past of the people of Israel, and there is substance for the view that its purpose was to provide a story for home reading on Purim, with the aim of strengthening Jewish national pride (G. Salzberger, *Salomos Tempelbau und Thron* (1912), 70f.). Some of these motifs are also found in the Koran (27:20–40), and it has been suggested that the author also made use of Arabic sources.

Summary

The following passages may be mentioned as examples of the homilies. Ahasuerus was one of ten kings who reigned or who were to reign over the world (cf. PdRE 11). There were four kings who reigned over the whole world: Solomon and Ahab of Israel, and Nebuchadnezzar and Ahasuerus among the gentiles (1:1). There are eulogies of Solomon: all kings feared him, and every type of demon was in his power. Solomon's throne is described: in front of it stood 12 golden lions and 12 golden eagles, and it had six steps of gold. On the first step crouched a golden ox together with a golden lion, on the second a golden wolf together with a golden sheep, and so on with each step. Above the throne stood a golden candelabrum, from one side of which protruded seven arms upon which were depicted the seven patriarchs – Adam, Noah, Shem, Abraham, Isaac, Jacob, and Job – and the other side depicted seven pious men – Kehat, Amram, Moses, Aaron, Eldad, Medad, and Hur (1:2). The *Targum Sheni* contains the most detailed description of the Queen of Sheba found in aggadic literature (cf. W. Herz, *Gesammelte Abhandlungen*, pp. 413–55), and also has *aggadot* on the destruction of the Temple.

Ahasuerus demanded that Vashti appear naked wearing only her crown. Vashti refused to comply as she was a king's daughter and moreover her consent would endanger his life because the other kings would kill him (1:11–12). Ahasuerus regretted killing Vashti and ordered those who had counseled it to be executed (2:1). The genealogy of Mordecai is given (2:5). Mordecai concealed Esther from the king's officials, and when this became known to the king, he issued an order that whoever hid Esther was to be put to death (2:8). The reason the virgins were assembled a second time was that the ministers advised the king that if he wanted to know Esther's birthplace he must make her jealous through other women (2:19). Haman's descent is from Eliphaz, the firstborn of Esau (3:1). The accusations made by Haman against the Jews are quoted at great length (3:8). They include interesting details of the manner in which the Jews celebrate the Sabbath and festivals: e.g., on Shavuot, Jews ascend to the roofs of their synagogues and throw down apples, and when these are picked up, they say: "Just as these are gathered so may our children be gathered from among the gentiles"; on Sukkot they "go into gardens and orchards … ruthlessly tear the branches, rejoice, make a circuit crying 'Save, O Lord' [*hoshanah*] and dance like goats." The work says that on the Sabbath and festivals the Jews read their books and translated their prophets, which proves that at the time the *Targum Sheni* was compiled it was customary to read the Targum of the prophets.

In 4:1 Ahasuerus tells the people that Haman offered him 600,000 shekels for the sixty myriads who left Egypt, and that he accepted this in agreement to slay the Jews. In 4:13 Mordecai's call to Esther to entreat God's mercy gives a large number of examples from Jewish history that God is stronger than Israel's oppressors. In 5:1 Esther's prayer is given, and in 5:14 it is told how Zeresh proposed that Mordecai should be hanged, because Abraham was saved from fire, Isaac from the sword, Moses and the Israelites from water, and Daniel from the lions. In 6:1 the cry of the Israelites reached Heaven, and even the angels were alarmed, saying that the end of the world had come. The attribute of mercy intervened with God on Israel's behalf, whereupon God yielded and immediately sent the angels appointed over confusion and panic to alarm Ahasuerus in a dream. In 6:9 it is related that when the king heard Haman's proposal of what should be done to the man faithful to the king, the suspicion arose in his mind that Haman wanted to take his life. In 6:11 there is a long dialogue between Haman and Mordecai. Haman admits to Mordecai that "your sackcloth and ashes have been more powerful than the 10,000 talents of silver I promised to bring to the king's treasury." When Mordecai mounted the horse, 12,000 chosen youths, each holding a cup and goblet of gold in their hands, called by order of the king: "Thus shall be done to the man…." In 6:13 Haman is told by the wise men and by Zeresh that Mordecai is a descendant of Hananiah, Mishael, and Azariah, and that just as their calumniators were destroyed, so would Haman be. In 7:10 the trees meet in council, and all refuse to have Haman hanging from them, but finally the cedar agrees.

The author of the *Targum Sheni* knew the Targum of Onkelos, the Targum of Jonathan to the prophets, and the *aggadot* of the Talmud and the Midrash, which he quotes. *Targum Sheni* has a number of points in common with the *Midrash Panim Aḥerim*, version 2 (Buber's ed. 1886), and with the *Midrash Abba Guryon* (*ibid.*). The author of the *Targum Sheni* was fond of long speeches and also integrated into the Targum extensive prayers with biblical verses and with examples from the past. A poetic tone is also noticeable in his words (cf. 3:2; 4:1, 17; 5:1; 6:11; 7:9; 8:18), and the work's poetic character is also testified to by the alphabetic acrostic (1:2; 5:1, 7, 10). The language of the Targum is close to Western Aramaic, and contains many Greek words. D. Heller distinguished in it several narrative motifs (see MGWJ, 70 (1926), 485).

Date

The date of the work cannot be determined exactly. The view of S. Gelbhaus (see bibl.) that it belongs to the amoraic period, in the fourth century, is disproved by the fact that it contains later material. P. Cassel (see bibl.) dates it in the sixth century and explains its mention of Edom to be the rule of Justinian

(527–565). However, this view of Edom can also apply to other periods. A basis for dating was also found among the accusations made by Haman: "They come to the synagogue … and curse our king and our ministers." This statement is regarded as an allusion to the suspicion that Jews combine a curse with the prayer said in the synagogue for the welfare of the kingdom. Since this prayer is thought to have been composed in the eighth century it is conjectured that the *Targum Sheni* postdates that century. L. Munk (see bibl.) puts its date still later, in the 11th century, but he gives no proof. It seems that the most acceptable view is that which places its composition at the end of the seventh or the beginning of the eighth century, a view that is strengthened by its relationship to the *Pirkei de-R. Eliezer.* Regarding its relationship to the *Targum Rishon*, there are features common to both Targums, but there are also many differences, and there are many *aggadot* in the *Targum Rishon* not included in the *Targum Sheni.* The view of P. Churgin (see bibl.) may be accepted that they are two independent compositions.

BIBLIOGRAPHY: TEXT PUBLICATIONS: L. Munk (1876); P. Cassel (1885); M. David (1898); *Patshegen ha-Ketav* (with Heb. transl.) (1837). ABOUT THE BOOK: Aaron b. Mordecai, *Meẓah Aharon* (1815); A. Posner, *Das Targum Rischon zum Buche Ester* (1846); J. Reiss. in: MGWJ, 25 (1876), 400ff.; 30 (1881), 473ff.; S. Gelbhaus, *Das Targum Scheni zum Buche Esther* (1893); B. Edelstein, *Az Eszter Midrások* (1900); G. Salzberger, *Salomos Tempelbau und Thron* (1912), 70ff.; E. Cohn, in: *Maybaum-Festschrift* (1914), 173–8; A. Sulzbach, *Targum Scheni zum Buch Esther* (Ger. tr.) (1920); B. Heller, in: MGWJ, 70 (1926), 485–7 (recension of the preceding work by A. Sulzbach); Ginzberg, Legends, 6 (1928), 450ff.; P. Churgin, *Targum Ketuvim* (1945), 214–35.

[Yehuda Komlosh]

TARGU-MURES (Rum. **Tîrgu-Mureş**; Ger. **Neumarkt**; Hung. **Marosvásárhely**), town in Transylvania, central Romania; until the end of World War I and between 1940 and 1945 within Hungary. As Jewish residence in Targu-Mures was prohibited from 1650, Jews at first established themselves in the neighboring villages of Náznánfalva (Nasna) and Marosszentkirály. Beginning in the 16th century, and more so in the 17th, Jews from the Ottoman Empire (Sephardim) arrived in large numbers. In 1836 Jews began to settle in the town itself, most of them coming from these villages. There were 23 Jews living in Targu-Mures in 1837, and 36 in 1841. During the period of the 1848–49 revolution, their number increased to 169. An organized community was founded in 1851. After the legal emancipation of the Austro-Hungarian Jews the majority of Targu-Mures Jews used Hungarian as their everyday means of communication, making a marked contribution to Hungarian culture. Between 1869 and 1879 there was a *Neologist community. An *Orthodox community was established in 1871. The original community decided to remain *status quo ante. The Great Synagogue, later taken over by the Orthodox congregation, was erected in 1873. Another large and magnificent synagogue was opened in 1899. A school maintained by the community was open between 1880 and 1940. There was also a yeshivah maintained by the Orthodox community. The Jewish population numbered 802 (6.1% of the total) in 1869; 1,036 (7.1%) in 1890; 2,755 (10.8%) in 1910; 3,246 (10.7%) in 1920; and 5,193 (13.6%) in 1930. One of most important characteristics of the Jews in Targu-Mures was their openness toward cultural innovation.

A Jewish club was organized in the town between the two world wars where a variety of cultural activities took place. Zionist organizations were active, and the national headquarters of the Zionist youth movement Avivah-Barisia was situated for a while in Targu-Mures.

Holocaust and Contemporary Periods

During World War II the Jewish population, which numbered 5,963 (12.7%) in 1941, increased when a number of Jews from the surrounding area, including a small number of proselytes from nearby villages, were concentrated in a ghetto there. Around 1,200 Jewish men were drafted into labor battalions, over half dying. The remaining Jews were ghettoized. Starting in late May 1944, 7,000 of them were deported to Auschwitz; 1,200 survived. Among those murdered in Auschwitz were the two rabbis of the town, the Orthodox rabbi Menahem Emanuel Sofer, who had held office from 1918, and Dr. Ferenc Loewy (b. 1869) who had held office from 1903, and who wrote a number of studies on the history of the Jews of Transylvania.

After the war, in 1947, 820 survivors of the camps or former inhabitants of the surrounding region gathered in the town. Their number gradually declined as a result of emigration to Israel and other countries. In 1971 about 200 Jews remained in Targu-Mures. There was still limited community life but no rabbi. In the beginning of the 21st century the remnants of the Targu-Mures Jewish community inaugurated a splendid monument consecrated to the memory of those who disappeared in the Holocaust.

BIBLIOGRAPHY: M. Berner, *Oh, kiválasztott népem* (1947).

[Yehouda Marton / Paul Schveiger (2nd ed.)]

TARIF, AMIN (c. 1898–1993), Druze leader. Tarif was the spiritual leader of the Druze community in Israel and the president of its High Court. He was born in Julis, a Druze village in the Galilee, and became a sheikh in 1928 after his father's death. He became head of the Druze community after the *War of Independence, head of the Druze religious council in 1957, and head of the Druze court of appeals in 1963. He was an outstanding spiritual leader and a fine personal example for his community and Israeli society at large. He was awarded the Israel Prize in 1990 for his special contribution to national and social life.

[Fern Lee Seckbach]

TARN, NATHANIEL (1928–), English poet and anthropologist. Tarn was born in Paris and in 1960 became a lecturer in anthropology at London University, specializing in the culture and ethnology of Latin America and the Pacific islands. In his early poetry, primitive peoples and rituals play an important part, often being identified by means of biblical symbolism or by its evocation of Eden as a contrast to the savagery of modern life. His first volume of verse, *Old Savage/Young City*, appeared in 1964. In 1967 he became an editor at the London publishing house of Jonathan Cape.

Tarn's poetry which displays a certain metaphysical quality is deeply influenced by *Ḥasidism and the *Kabbalah. This is apparent in poems on R. Abraham *Abulafia, R. *Simeon Bar Yoḥai, and *Israel b. Eliezer the Ba'al Shem Tov. Tarn sees in Jewish mysticism a means of defining and, perhaps, assuaging the existential crisis of modern man. In "Where Babylon Ends" he visualizes the 20th-century situation in terms of a confrontation between Babylon and Jerusalem, and in "Noah on Ararat Again" he finds in the Bible story an image of survival after flood and holocaust which is pointedly relevant to mid-20th-century experience. His *Selected Poems: 1950–2000* was published in 2002 and another book of poetry, *Recollections of Being*, in 2004. In later years Tarn lived in Santa Fe, New Mexico.

BIBLIOGRAPHY: H. Fisch, in: *Judaism*, 14 (1965), 479–90.

[Harold Harel Fisch]

TARNOBRZEG (**Dikow**), town in Rzeszow province, S.E. Poland. The city is referred to as Dzikow in the 1765 census. At that time 569 Jews paid the poll tax in the city and the surrounding villages. In 1655 all the Jews of Tarnobrzeg were massacred. A special prayer was recited annually in the synagogue at *Sandomierz on the anniversary of their death. There were 2,768 Jews (80% of the total population) in 1880; 2,840 (80.7%) in 1890; 2,537 (78%) in 1900; 2,642 (96.3%) in 1910; and 2,146 (67.7%) in 1921. In the latter half of the 19th century, Ḥasidism had considerable influence in the community. Outstanding in the spiritual leadership of the community at that time was R. Meir Horowitz, author of *Imrei No'am*. The *Baron de Hirsch Fund established a school in Tarnobrzeg before World War I.

[Nathan Michael Gelber]

Holocaust Period

At the outbreak of World War II there were about 3,800 Jews in Tarnobrzeg. The Germans occupied the town on Sept. 17, 1939, and immediately instigated pogroms. In October 1939 the Germans concentrated the Jewish population in the town market. They robbed the Jews of all their possessions and expelled them to the newly established German-Soviet border. Many were killed on the way but some succeeded in crossing into Soviet-occupied territory. In August 1941 part of the Jewish population returned to Tarnobrzeg. The final liquidation of the Jewish community took place in July 1942. After the war the Jewish community of Tarnobrzeg was not reconstituted.

BIBLIOGRAPHY: R. Mahler, *Yidn in Amolikn Poyln in Likht fun Tsifern* (1958), index; E. Heller (ed.), *Żydowskie przedsiębiorstwa przemysłowe w Polsce według ankiety 1921 roku*, 5–6 (1923), 117, 142; I. Lewin, *Przeczynki do historji literatury zydów w Polsce* (1935), 15.

TARNOGROD (Rus. **Tarnograd**), village near Bilgoraj, Lublin province, E. Poland. Tarnogrod was founded in 1567. In 1569 King Sigismund II Augustus granted the village a charter which banned Jews. In 1580 King Stephen Báthory allowed Jews to settle in the village, buy houses, and run businesses, especially in the liquor and beer trade, justifying this permission as essential to the development of the locality. In 1648 the Cossacks massacred all Jews in Tarnogrod. The community was later renewed, and by the end of the 17th century there were Jewish merchants from Tarnogrod who traveled to fairs at *Leipzig. In 1686 an attractive stone synagogue was erected which still stands. In the 17th and early 18th centuries representatives of Tarnogrod held important positions in the *Councils of the Lands. They included Solomon, Abraham b. Isaac, and R. Azriel b. Moses ha-Levi Ashkenazi, author of *Naḥalat Azri'el* (Frankfurt, 1691). Azriel's successor in the rabbinate of Tarnogrod, R. Nathan Nata b. Jacob of Lublin, participated in council meetings from 1718 to 1733. In the 1750s Aryeh Leib b. Samuel served as rabbi of Tarnogrod. The 1765 census records 1,606 poll-tax paying Jews in Tarnogrod and neighboring villages.

The village passed to Austrian rule in 1772, and in 1815 it was included in Congress Poland. The Russian government limited Jewish settlement in Tarnogrod between 1823 and 1862. In the early 19th century Moses Joshua Heshel b. Mordecai Orenstein, author of *Yad ha-Talmud* (Lvov, 1827/28), was rabbi of the community. Some 1,260 Jews lived in Tarnogrod in 1827 (32% of the total population); in 1857 there were 1,673 Jews (41%); in 1897 there were 1,635 (32%); and in 1921 there were 2,238 (47%). All the Jewish parties were active in Tarnogrod between the two world wars.

[Nathan Michael Gelber]

Holocaust Period

On the outbreak of World War II there were about 2,500 Jews in Tarnogrod. The Jewish community was liquidated on Nov. 2, 1942, when 3,000 Jews from Tarnogrod and its vicinity were deported to the *Belzec death camp. After the war the Jewish community was not reconstituted.

BIBLIOGRAPHY: Halpern, Pinkas, index; B. Wasiutyński, *Ludność żydowska w Polsce w wiekach XIX i XX* (1931), index; M. Berensohn, *Dyplomataryusz dotyczący żydów w Polsce* (1910), no. 184; M. Baliński and T. Lipiński, *Staro zytna Polska*, 2 (1845), index; I. Schiper, *Dzieje handlu żydowskiego na ziemiach polskich* (1937), index.

TARNOPOL (Rus. **Ternopol**), city in Ukraine, formerly in the province of Lvov, Poland. Jews began to settle in the city shortly after its foundation in 1540. They were granted special privileges by the lord of the city, the hetman Jan Tarnowski, as Jewish residents of his personal domain. The charter granted to Tarnopol in 1550 indicates that Jews were permitted to live in all parts of the city, apart from the marketplace. An organized community had already formed before 1648–49. Jews took an active part in the defense of the city during the many attacks to which it was subjected in the mid-17th century. The royal grant authorizing the erection of a fortified synagogue – already constructed by this time – stipulated that the community was to install artillery loopholes on all sides and to acquire cannon. The members of the community, among whom artisans were singled out, were required to defend the synagogue under the direction of a "Jewish hetman." During the attacks by *Chmielnicki, however, most of the Jews fled, and those who remained were massacred.

Privileges renewed in 1740 allowed the Jews of Tarnopol to live in, and conduct trade in, any part of the city. Jews were permitted to purvey alcoholic liquor and to keep taverns on payment of a liquor duty to the manorial lord. Jewish artisans could engage in crafts, provided that they observed the rules of the Christian guilds and paid a specified sum into the guild funds. The charter also regulated Jewish judicial jurisdiction. The Tarnopol community built up a flourishing economy, controlling the grain and cattle trade, with Jewish business predominating in the city fairs. It also played an important role in Jewish *autonomy in 18th-century Poland-Lithuania (see *Councils of Lands).

Noted rabbis of Tarnopol of this period included Joshua Heshel Babad, who was deposed from the rabbinate in 1718 and returned to office in 1724. He was followed by Jacob b. Isaac Landau, in office until 1777, and Joshua Heshel b. Isaac *Babad between 1809 and 1838.

The position of the Jewish community deteriorated after Tarnopol passed to Austria in 1772. The authority of the manorial lord diminished, and was eventually terminated. Taxation became increasingly burdensome. The census for 1788 registered 6,380 Jewish males and 6,374 females for the district of Tarnopol, including eight subsidiary communities. The Jews were mainly occupied as taverners and retailers, with a considerable number of artisans.

In 1788 Naphtali Herz *Homberg founded the first modern Jewish school in Tarnopol, in which Hirsh Eisenstaedter taught, but it was closed down with similar institutions in 1806. At this time Joseph *Perl began his efforts to establish a Jewish school along his own lines with emphasis on instruction in German and secular subjects, with the assistance of the *maskil* Dov Ginzburg, and others. Perl only succeeded in 1813, when Tarnopol was under Russian rule (1809–15), and then mainly by financing it himself, and donating the building. From 1814 to 1816 Perl also published a Hebrew periodical, *Ẓir Ne'eman* (1814–16), in Tarnopol. Perl transferred the school and its prayer house to the community in 1818. It received official recognition as a public school, and its syllabus was revised to conform to that of the general school system. The school met violent opposition from Orthodox circles. It was banned along with the school at *Brody in 1816 by the rabbi of Lvov, Jacob *Ornstein. The *Ḥasidim also opposed it.

About 1813 a Hebrew printing press was set up in Tarnopol by Naḥman Pineles and Jacob Auerbach, the type as well as some of the personnel coming from *Zbarazh. In all, some 25 works were printed in Tarnopol. This printing venture came to an end about 1817, due apparently to the boycott by the Orthodox of a press supporting Haskalah.

In 1838 a bitter conflict flared up in the community between the *maskilim* and the Orthodox members over the choice of a rabbi. The candidate put forward by the *maskilim*, S.J. *Rapoport, was nominated with the support of the authorities. However, Perl died in 1839, and Rapoport relinquished the office a year later. The circle of *maskilim* who had gathered around Perl found increasing adherents, and gained a new intellectual leader in Nachman *Krochmal, who moved to Tarnopol in 1838. Other *maskilim* were Samuel Leib Goldberg (1807–46), Bezalel *Stern, Isaac Michael Munis, Moses Ḥayyim Katz, Nathan Horowitz (Krochmal's son-in-law), and many more.

In 1843–44 a change in Jewish civic status accorded Tarnopol Jewry electoral and elective rights in the municipality. In the elections to the Austrian parliament following the revolution of 1848 Tarnopol Jews elected one of their number as a delegate. The community was headed by Jacob Atlas, a doctor, from 1846 to 1849, and until 1858 the community was led by the *maskilim*, to be subsequently replaced by the Orthodox. The school founded by Joseph Perl was extended after 1848, and a girls' school was added.

From the 1860s, the *maskilim* in Tarnopol, as in the whole of Galicia, showed a growing tendency to assimilate into Polish national life and culture. Simon Dankowicz, a major advocate of *assimilation who had taken part in the Polish uprising of 1863, was nominated in 1890 as preacher in the synagogue founded by Perl. During the 1860s a number of welfare and philanthropic institutions, hospitals, and orphanages were founded in Tarnopol. The rabbi in this period was Joseph *Babad. In 1894 a Zionist society was formed.

The Jewish population of Tarnopol numbered 1,161 in 1765. In the district of Tarnopol it numbered 11,997 in 1827 (out of 197,296); all but one of the 76 commercial establishments were Jewish-owned; 205 Jews were occupied as taverners, and 364 as shopkeepers, while a considerable number were artisans. There were 11,000 Jews living in Tarnopol (52% of the total population) in 1869; 13,842 (50.5%) in 1890; 13,490 (44.2%) in 1900; 14,000 in 1910 – the last official census conducted by the Austrian government – 16,320 in 1921, and 14,000 in 1931.

Tarnopol Jews suffered severely during World War I, as the city changed hands seven times in the fighting. With the dissolution of the Hapsburg monarchy, a Ukrainian government was organized in Tarnopol, and in December 1918 a Jewish militia of 800 men was formed. In the elections to the Jewish National Council in Western Ukraine, held in March 1919, the Zionists won a clear majority. The council was active until Tarnopol was taken by the Poles, who encouraged the Polish assimilationists within the community and turned over the leadership to them. Between 1922 and 1932 the community was led by representatives of the national lists. Pressure was exerted by the regime in Poland, and commissars were nominated in the leadership.

[Nathan Michael Gelber]

Holocaust and Postwar Periods

According to an unofficial source, *Bleter far Geshikhte*, there were 18,000 Jews in Tarnopol in 1939. As in other communities under Soviet occupation (1939–41), the Jewish community organization was dissolved, political parties were prohibited, Hebrew education was discontinued, and the Yiddish schools were nationalized. After the outbreak of the German-Soviet war (June 1941), a few days after Tarnopol was occupied by the German army, 5,000 Jews were massacred (July 4–11). The Germans fined the Jewish community 1,500,000 rubles. Sixty-three Jews belonging to the intelligentsia were invited to the *Gestapo on the pretext of receiving public appointments, but were all murdered in the Gestapo office. The ghetto established in Tarnopol in September 1941 was the first to be set up in Galicia. Over 12,500 people were crowded into a small area, and for a while it seemed that Jewish life, though extremely difficult, would continue. Attempts were made to renew the Jewish school system, and several orphanages and old age homes were established in the ghetto. The *Judenrat was headed by Gustav Fischer, who was succeeded by Karol Pohoryles. At the same time the ghetto inmates were gradually murdered; on March 25, 1942, 1,000 Jews were shot in the nearby forest. Thousands of Jews were seized in the streets or taken from their homes for forced labor at labor camps in the Tarnopol district. On August 29–31, 1942, over 4,000 Jews from Tarnopol were sent to the *Belzec death camp. On Sept. 30, 1942, a further 1,000 Jews were sent there. During the following winter the remaining able-bodied Jews were separated and put into a labor camp near the ghetto. The final liquidation of the ghetto took place on June 20, 1943, followed by that of the nearby work camp (Aug. 6, 1943). Small numbers of Jews fought from bunkers or joined the partisan fighters in the district.

When the Soviet forces recaptured Tarnopol, about 150 Jews came out from hiding and 200 returned from the Soviet Union, where some of them had served in the Soviet army. A memorial book to Tarnopol Jewry was published as volume 3 of the *Enẓiklopedyah shel Galuyyot* (1955; Heb; partly Yid; Eng. summary). Tarnopol societies were established by former Jewish residents in Israel and the United States.

A monument erected to the memory of the Jewish martyrs in the Holocaust was completely destroyed in the 1950s. In the late 1960s there were about 500 Jews in Tarnopol. The old Jewish cemetery served as a building site and the later cemetery housed nine garages.

One of the main administrative centers in western Ukraine, by 2005 Tarnopol had a Jewish community center, a Jewish Sunday club, and a women's club.

[AharonWeiss]

BIBLIOGRAPHY: N.M. Gelber, in: EG, 3 (1955), 22–108; Ph. Friedman, in: YIVO *Bleter*, 31–32 (1948), 131–90; J. Letschinsky, *Rządy rosyjskie w kraju tarnopolskim 1809–1815* (1903); M. Balaban, *Spis Żydów i Karaitów* (1909); J. Leniek, *Przwileje króiówascicieli miasta Tarnopola* (1932); Habermann, in: *Alim le-Bibliografyah*..., 2 (1935/36), 24ff.; S. Katz, in: KS, 15 (1938/39), 515f.; H.D. Friedberg, *Toledot ha-Defus ha-Ivri be-Polanyah* (1950²), 148f.

TARNOPOL, JOACHIM ḤAYYIM (1810–1900), *maskil* in *Odessa, author, communal worker, and wealthy merchant. At the beginning of the reign of Alexander II, he began his endeavors for the emancipation of the Jews and their reconciliation with the Russian people. In 1855 he published his pamphlet *Notices historiques et caracteristiques sur les Israélites d'Odessa*. In 1856, together with his friend Y. *Rabinowitz, he approached the Russian authorities and requested permission to publish a Jewish periodical in Russian which would propagate the ideologies of the Haskalah and reconciliation with the Russian people. In May 1860, Tarnopol, together with Rabinowitz, edited the first Russian-Jewish newspaper, **Razsvet* ("The Dawn"). A dispute, however, immediately broke out between them as to whether a Jewish newspaper in the country's language should publicly condemn the internal deficiencies of the Jewish people and thus arm the hands of its enemies outside the community and estrange the youth that had received a foreign education. Tarnopol, who was against criticizing Jewish internal affairs before outsiders, resigned from the editorship of the newspaper (from the 20th issue). He published his reasons for this step in a letter to the editorial board of **Ha-Maggid* (nos. 45–46, 1860). In 1868 his book on "an attempt at cautious reform within Judaism, meditations on the internal and external way of life of Russian Jews" was published in Odessa in Russian. It was a summary of his outlook on the road to be followed by Russian Jewry.

BIBLIOGRAPHY: Yu. I. Gessen, in: *Perezhitoye*, 3 (1911), 38–52; S. Zinberg, *Istoriya yevreyskoy pechati v Rossii* (1915), 39–48, 257–60; B. Shoḥetman, in: *He-Avar*, 2 (1954), 61–66; Y. Slutsky, *Ha-Ittonut ha-Yehudit-Rusit ba-Me'ah ha-XIX* (1970), 40–44.

[Yehuda Slutsky]

TARNOPOLSKY, SAMUEL (1908–), Argentinean physician, historian, and novelist. Born in the town of Bernasconi, province of La Pampa, to Russian immigrants, Tarnopolsky studied medicine in Buenos Aires, becoming a professor of rheumatology and founder of the Argentine Society for the Study of Rheumatology. He was listed by the World Health Organization as one of the world's best rheumatologists. The author of numerous medical textbooks, including *Reumatismo y Enfermedades Relacionadas* ("Rheumatism and Related Diseases," 1950), Tarnopolsky expanded the conventional borders of his discipline by writing several books on the indigenous medicines (and medicine men) of his native province, most prominently in *Los Curanderos, Mis Colegas* ("The Witch Doctors, My Colleagues," 1994).

Tarnopolsky's identification with the rural, gaucho roots of Argentinean history resulted in several texts on the war between Spanish *conquistadores* and the Pampa Indian tribe, the prologue to Dionisio Schoo Lastra's groundbreaking book *El Indio del Desierto* ("The Indian of the Desert," 1928), the fictionalized stories *Alarma de Indios en la Frontera Sud – Epi-*

sodios de la Conquista del Desierto ("Indian Alarm on the Southern Frontier: Episodes from the Conquest of the Desert," 1952), and *La Rastrillada de Salinas Grandes* ("The Path of Salinas Grandes," 1944) garnered him the first invitation presented to any Jew to address the Círculo Militar, Argentina's military academy.

He dedicated his intellectual output to the three peoples who shared his loyalty: the Spanish conquerors, whose prowess he admired, the Pampa Indians whom he revered, and the Jewish nation, to which he belonged. He wrote a prize-winning study *Indios pampas y conquistadores del desierto en la novela* ("Pampa Indians and Conquerors as Literary Figures," 1996), and numerous works relating to Jewish life in Argentina, including a study of antisemitism among the Argentinean elites and intellectuals, *Los Prejuiciados de Honrada Conciencia*, ("The High-Minded Bigots," 1971), an essay titled *Nosotros, los judios que colonizamos el desierto Pampa* ("We, the Jews who Conquered the Pampa Desert," 1992), and the novel for which he is best known, *La Mitad De Nada* ("Half of Naught," 1969), a meditation on the predicament of young urban Jews in the 1960s Buenos Aires.

[Noga Tarnopolsky (2nd ed.)]

TARNOW, city in Poland, 45 mi. (72 km.) E. of Cracow. Jewish merchants in Tarnow are mentioned in a few sources of the 15th century. The growth of the community and development of its institutions in the 1630s was based on grants of privileges successively endorsed by the magnates who owned Tarnow as their private domain (see *Poland-Lithuania). Its first privilege dating from 1581 exempts Tarnow Jewry from the municipal jurisdiction, entitles Jews to engage in trade in their own buildings and shops, and to distill and deal in alcoholic liquor. They were to pay taxes directly to the magnate and might own a cemetery near the city. The municipality was responsible for securing the synagogue and cemetery from attack. This grant met with strong opposition from the townsmen.

The ravages of the Swedish invasion in 1655 and a fire which broke out in 1663 caused much suffering to the community. As a result of the decrease of population and general economic deterioration, the Christians reached an agreement with the Jews in May 1670 to settle matters in dispute, including the question of importation of goods purchased outside the city bounds at the fairs. The agreement allocated to the Jewish community between 25% and 30% of the total tax paid by the townspeople. It prohibited the community from allowing newcomers to settle in Tarnow, excepting religious functionaries it was deemed necessary to invite from elsewhere (after informing the municipality), and assured the Jews of a water supply from the city wells. The Christian guilds on their part reached an understanding with the Jewish artisans. These agreements helped to mitigate the tensions existing between the Jewish and Christian populace. The same year (1670) the city overlord ratified the former privileges granted to the Jewish community; they were endorsed in 1676 and again in 1684.

There were four conflagrations in Tarnow in the first half of the 18th century: during the first, in 1711, all 23 buildings in the Jewish street and goods in the Jewish-owned shops were destroyed, and the community was exempted from the poll tax for four years to alleviate its plight. The lord of Tarnow was subsequently persuaded to allow Jews to reside and construct buildings outside their designated area. Jewish *guilds were established in 1740 which reached an agreement with their Christian counterparts on payment of special dues. The Tarnow community belonged to the Land of Lesser Poland (Kracow-Sandomierz) in the framework of the *Council of the Four Lands. The *parnas* of the community, Benjamin Ze'ev Wolf b. Ezekiel Landau, took an active part in the conventions of the council and represented Jewish interests before the secular authorities between 1718 and 1737. The census of 1765 records 900 Jews in Tarnow and 1,425 living in the villages within its communal jurisdiction.

Tarnow's annexation to Austria after the first partition of Poland in 1772 created new political conditions and weakened the authority of the manorial lord. In 1788 a Jewish school with secular educational trends under the direction of Naphtali Herz *Homberg was established in Tarnow, which continued until 1806. In 1833 the community asked the governor of Galicia for permission to widen the Jewish street and allow Jews to reside on the market square. Their request was strongly opposed by the municipal council which countered by suggesting the establishment of a *foermliche Judenstadt*, the setting up of an official Jewish quarter outside the city where the Jews were to move. No specific instructions followed, and Jews began to move beyond the old quarter shortly afterward, despite resistance from the citizens. *Blood libels were leveled against Jews in Tarnow in 1829 and 1844, but the accused were later released. A Jewish hospital was founded in 1842; in the 1890s the *Baron de Hirsch foundation established a school in Tarnow which continued in existence until 1914.

The majority of the Tarnow community were Ḥasidim, but in the 19th century the influence of the Enlightenment (*Haskalah), made itself felt in Tarnow, where the Hebrew writer Mordecai David *Brandstaedter was prominent. Zionism spread among the youth and a number of *maskilim* in the 1890s, and a society of Ahavat Zion was founded in Tarnow in 1891 with the object of immigrating to Ereẓ Israel and founding a Galician settlement there; the Zionist movement was headed by Abraham *Salz up to 1914. The community numbered 1,200 in 1772 (34% of the total population), 7,914 in 1846, 11,677 in 1890 (42.4%), 15,108 in 1910 (41.2%), 15,608 in 1921 (44.2%), and 19,330 in 1931. Around the beginning of the 20th century the expanding cloth and hat industry in Tarnow occupied 300 Jewish workers.

In 1921, of the 593 Jewish-owned workshops and light industrial plants in Tarnow, 320 employed hired labor and 261 were owner-operated; the total of Jewish hired workers was 830 (555 males, 227 females, 48 minors). The majority of enterprises were garment-manufacturing, mainly hats (360, employing 1,088 persons, 573 of them Jews). Economic conditions deteriorated for the Jewish sector after Poland regained its independence in 1919, and the community was eventually forced to provide social assistance. The income of the community in 1928 was 271,890 zlotys and the expenditure 396,264 zlotys. The Polish authorities intervened in communal affairs; elective offices were abolished and commissars appointed who administered communal matters for over six years. The Zionist movement in Tarnow was headed by Shmuel Shpan and Ḥayyim Neiger. Communal elections were held in February 1937, and a Zionist leadership was returned, of which Abraham Chomet was elected chairman, the last to hold this office.

[Nathan Michael Gelber]

Holocaust Period

Before the outbreak of World War II there were over 25,000 Jews in Tarnow. The German army entered on Sept. 8, 1939, and terrorization of the Jewish population began. In May 1940 leading Jewish personalities (the lawyers Emil Wieder and Isaac Holzer and the director of the local Hebrew school, Maximilian Rosenbusch) were deported to *Auschwitz; they were among the first Jewish victims of that camp. In March 1941 a decree proclaiming the establishment of a ghetto was issued. At the beginning of June 1942 Jews from all surrounding smaller places were concentrated there. A few days later, on June 11–13, 1942, about 12,000 Jews from Tarnow were deported to the *Belzec death camp and exterminated there. After that deportation the ghetto was divided into two parts: Ghetto A, which became a forced-labor camp; and Ghetto B, a family camp, where many died from hunger.

On Sept. 10, 1942, the second deportation took place and another 8,000 Jews met their deaths in Belzec. On Nov. 15, during the third deportation, about 3,000 Jews died. The last deportation took place on Sept. 2, 1943, when 5,000 Jews were sent to Auschwitz and another 3,000 to the Plaszow concentration camp. Almost all of them perished. Over 500 Jews who tried to hide were shot and another 700 were shot on the way to the Szebnia camp. Only 300 Jews were left in Tarnow in a newly established forced-labor camp (so-called *Saeuberungskommando*), but in December 1943 they were transferred to the Plaszow concentration camp, where almost all of them were murdered. After the war over 700 Jews settled in Tarnow but soon left the city due to the inimical attitude of the local Polish population. In 1965 only 35 Jews lived there. Organizations of former Jewish residents of Tarnow are active in Israel, the United States, France, and Canada.

[Stefan Krakowski]

BIBLIOGRAPHY: *Torne: Kiem un Khurbn fun a Yidisher Shtot* (1954); Halpern, Pinkas, index; R. Mahler, *Yidn in Amolikn Poyln in Likht fun Tsifern* (1958); I. Schiper, in: *Kwartalnik historyczny*, 19 (1905), 228–39; *Tarnow-Sefer Zikkaron*, ed. by A. Chomet and J. Cornillo, 2 vols. (Yid. and Heb., 1968).

°**TARONJI Y CORTÉS, JOSÉ** (1847–1890), Spanish priest and poet. Born of *Chueta parents in Palma, Taronjí y Cortés was descended from an old Jewish family, several members of which had been martyred by the Inquisition during the late 17th century. Though ordained in 1872, he was denied a position in the cathedral of Palma de Mallorca because of his Jewish ancestry.

From 1876 to 1877 Taronjí y Cortés launched a series of attacks on the racial prejudices of the island's ecclesiastical hierarchy, in articles published in the *Almanaque Balear* and in his book *Una mala causa a todo trance defendida* (1877). These were reprinted in 1967 with introductory notes which suggest that anti-Chueta prejudice was still alive in the mid-20th century. His *Algo sobre el estado religioso y social de la isla de Mallorca* (1877) created a nationwide furor and resulted in some liberalization of official policies in Majorca. Taronjí y Cortés also gained renown as a Catalan poet.

BIBLIOGRAPHY: B. Braunstein, *The Chuetas of Majorca* (1936), index s.v. *Taronjí; Homenaje al Josée Taronjí y Cortés* (1967); A.L. Isaacs, *The Jews of Majorca* (1936), 8–9, 210.

[Kenneth R. Scholberg]

TARRAGONA, Mediterranean port in Catalonia, N.E. Spain. The Jewish settlement there was of ancient date; Jews apparently established themselves in the harbor town during the Roman era. A laver discovered there bearing the inscription "Peace over Israel, over ourselves, and our children" probably belongs to this period. Coins with Hebrew inscriptions also testify to the existence of a Jewish settlement under the Visigoths. During the period of Arab rule, Jews in Tarragona engaged in commerce and agriculture, and some owned lands and properties. Apparently for this reason it was known as a "Jewish city" (al-Idrisi, 1152). In 850, the Jews of Tarragona aided the Arabs in the capture of Barcelona, but it was later reconquered for the Christians by Ramón Berenguer. Tarragona passed to Christian rule in the 11th century. Its proximity to *Tortosa must have influenced the size of the Jewish population in Tarragona since a number of Jews had already moved to Tortosa under Arab rule.

Jewish Quarter

Most of the Jewish population lived in the upper town which was surrounded by a wall, to the northeast of the present built-up area. In the course of time, the quarter was transferred to the southern part of the town, to the streets now called En Granada, and En Talavera, including some of the alleys in this area, and the square now known as Plaza de los Angeles. The square of the Jewish quarter is in the central part of En Talavera. This district was recently restored. In 1239 there were 95 houses in the quarter. Deeds of sale drawn up in Hebrew for lands situated in the "Quarter of Israel" near the city wall, and for lands and houses beyond the wall, have been preserved. On the road known as dels Fortins in the vicinity of the "Beach of the Miracles" (Playa de los Milagros), a Jewish cemetery existed for many generations; several of its tombstones have been preserved from the 13th to 14th centuries. Apparently the stone of a washing well which was probably situated in the courtyard of the synagogue should also be attributed to this period;

it bore the inscription: "He brought streams out of the rock [cf. Ps. 78:16] to minister in the sanctuary [cf. Ezek. 44:27]." A unique seal for endorsing the *kashrut* of *maẓẓot shemurot* was discovered in the neighborhood of Tarragona.

After the Reconquest

In Tarragona, as in other places of Catalonia, Jews held the position of bailiff (Vidal bar Judah, 1187; Bonafos bar Judah, 1192); several deeds of sale bearing their signatures are extant. In 1235 delegates of the Church convened in Tarragona to discuss the interest rates charged by Jewish moneylenders. At this convention the rates which had been fixed in 1228 (20%) were ratified, but Christians were still authorized to take an interest rate of 12%. Any Jew who disobeyed this order was to be condemned to servitude and confiscation of his property. It was then also decided that any Jew who adopted Islam would be condemned to servitude for life; the same sentence would be applied to a Muslim who adopted Judaism. This anti-Jewish policy is also expressed in a bull which Benito de Rocaberti, archbishop of Tarragona, obtained from Pope Urban IV in which the Jews were ordered to wear a *badge to distinguish them from Christians. On frescoes in the cathedral of Tarragona paintings are found in which Jews are distinguished from the other personalities by a white circular sign. In 1267 Pope Clement IV ordered the archbishop of Tarragona to collect the books of the Jews throughout the kingdom of Aragon and to hand them over to the Dominicans and Franciscans; Pablo *Christiani was proposed as his assistant in this activity.

In its relations with the monarchy, the community of Tarragona obtained from James I in 1260 an exemption from the obligation to accommodate the royal house and to provide it with linen and other objects at the time of his visit to the city. The king even authorized the community to close the gates of its quarter. In taxation matters, Tarragona belonged to the *collecta* of Barcelona; the regulations by which the community was governed were also modeled on those of Barcelona (Solomon b. Abraham Adret, Responsa, pt. 3, no. 411).

In 1313 the archbishop of Tarragona and the inquisitor Juan Llotger issued a decree ordering that Jews of Tarragona and Montblanch who had been involved in assisting proselytes and Conversos to return to Judaism should have their properties confiscated and be banished for life from the kingdom. However, the expulsion order was limited by James II to the region of Tarragona. The order was issued against ten Jews. A heavy fine was imposed on the community and one of its synagogues was confiscated and converted into a church. Even Jews who had been forcibly converted at the time of the *Pastoureaux persecutions (1320–21) and later returned to Judaism were called to account by the *Inquisition. Many of them fled, while others were condemned to death and their houses to be destroyed by fire. The king, however, ordered an alleviation of their punishment; he fined them and permitted their heirs to redeem their confiscated property for a sum of 15,000 sólidos.

In the persecutions which followed in the wake of the *Black Death in 1348, 300 Jews of Tarragona and neighboring Solsona were massacred. The Jews of the town were nevertheless ordered to pay 150 sólidos in Barcelona currency to the royal treasury. In 1363 Pedro IV demanded a further 1,000 livres in Barcelona currency. Despite this grave situation, a Jew was still holding the position of municipal physician in 1374. In 1388 King John I of Aragon granted the community of Tarragona the same rights as those of Barcelona.

The 1391 Persecutions and Subsequent Period

Shortly before the outbreak of the anti-Jewish persecutions which swept Spain in 1391, the archbishop of Tarragona instituted legal proceedings against a number of works of *Maimonides "because it is said that certain errors against the Christian faith had been found in them." When the persecutions broke out, the Jews of Tarragona took refuge in the citadel in fear of attack by the rioters. They addressed a letter of appeal to the king, asking for his protection, and John I notified the community (July 24) that he had placed them under special protection of the archbishop, the royal officials, and the municipality, and ordered that rioters and agitators be tried and condemned as rebels against the royal authority. On September 22, however, he commanded the *vicarius* of Tarragona to gather information on the heirless Jewish property which had remained after the disorders and to transfer it to him. He expressed a particular interest in the property of those who had been martyred and the property of the community.

After the persecutions, measures were taken to reestablish the Jewish settlement in Tarragona. Queen Violante promised the Jews "who lived there or who would settle there in the future" a tax exemption for a duration of five years (Aug. 13, 1393). On October 27 she authorized the Jews who had settled there to raise funds in other communities for the erection of a synagogue, the purchase of a Torah scroll and other books, and for the redemption of the cemetery.

During the second half of the 15th century – a difficult period for the Jews of Aragon, as for the whole of Spanish Jewry – Isaac *Arama held rabbinical office in Tarragona. He maintained a yeshivah and fostered observance of the precepts within the community. At the time of the expulsion of the Jews from Spain in 1492 Tarragona was a port of embarkation for the exiles from the kingdom of Aragon.

BIBLIOGRAPHY: MUSLIM PERIOD: B. Hernández Sanahuja, *Tarragona bajo el poder de los árabes* (1882). CHRISTIAN PERIOD: Baer, Spain, index; Baer, Urkunden, index; Neuman, Spain, index; H.C. Lea, *A History of the Inquisition of Spain*, I (1906), 553; J.M. Millás Vallicrosa, *Documents hebraics de Jueus Catalans* (1927), 7ff; J. Sánchez Real, *Boletín Arqueológico de Tarragona*, 49 (1949), 15–39; idem, in: *Sefarad*, 9 (1949), 476ff. (includes plan of the quarters); 11 (1951), 339–48; F. Cantera-Burgos, *ibid.*, 15 (1955), 151–4; J.M. Millás Vallicrosa, *ibid.*, 26 (1966), 103–6; Cantera-Millás, Inscripciones, 264ff., 350ff.

[Haim Beinart]

TARRASCH, SIEGBERT (1862–1934), German chess master. Born in Breslau, Tarrasch became a physician and practiced in Nuremberg. A man of great culture, he became one of the most successful chess players of his period. His tremendous ability was proved by his many victories in tournaments. In matches he defeated Frank James Marshall and Jacques Mieses and drew with Mikhail Tchigorin and Carl Schlechter. But he was overshadowed by Emanuel *Lasker and when in 1908 he played Lasker for the world championship he was convincingly defeated. His doctrine, which he expressed in his book *Die moderne Schachpartie* (1916), was influenced by *Steinitz. The difference is that he laid greater emphasis on the strong center and maneuvering space. His other important books were *Dreihundert Schachpartien* (1909) and *Das Schachspiel* (1931; *The Game of Chess*, 1935).

BIBLIOGRAPHY: F. Reinfeld (ed.), *Tarrasch's Best Games of Chess* (1947). **ADD. BIBLIOGRAPHY:** W. Kamm, *Siegbert Tarrasch. Leben und Werk* (2004).

[Gerald Abrahams]

TÁRREGA, town in Catalonia, N.E. Spain. Like others in that region, the community of Tárrega reached its greatest prosperity in the 13th century. There is little data on the Jews of Tárrega up to the days preceding the *Black Death (1348–49). In 1346 a new synagogue was built there, but the community then suffered heavily from the Black Death persecutions. In his book *Emek ha-Bakha* Joseph *ha-Kohen tells of the riots which broke out there on the tenth of Av. Three hundred Jews fell on that day, and the survivors were left destitute after giving all their money in exchange for shelter. Pedro IV strove with the utmost energy to quell the rioting and punish its instigators, but he pardoned all the rioters in April 1350. The same month the town council was requested to build the Jewish quarter anew within two years at the place called La Font. In order to defray the expenses caused by the riots, Pedro allowed the town council to impose a special tax on foodstuffs. Also in 1350 the community of Tárrega paid 400 sólidos in Barcelona currency as annual tax. As the Black Death epidemic did not cease for a long time, the Jews of Tárrega continued to be in danger. In 1362 Pedro ordered that measures be taken to protect the community, with guards being selected by the community's trustee (*ne'eman*). No data are available concerning the condition of the Jews in Tárrega following the persecutions of 1391. At any rate, there was a Jewish community there throughout the 15th century, probably existing until the general expulsion from Spain in 1492, as shown by the fact that in the late 1470s the physician Abraham Shalom was asked to come and settle in Tárrega from nearby *Cervera.

BIBLIOGRAPHY: Baer, Urkunden, 1 (1929), index; A. López de Meneses, in: *Sefarad*, 19 (1959), 115–26, 321–62.

[Haim Beinart]

TARSHISH (Heb. תַּרְשִׁישׁ),

(1) A distant port from which silver, iron, tin, lead, ivory, monkeys, and peacocks were brought to Palestine (cf. I Kings 10:22; Jer. 10:9; Ezek. 27:12). The location of Tarshish is uncertain, since the biblical references to it are vague and apparently contradictory. (The word may mean a "refinery," from the Akk. *rašāšu*, "to be smelted.") According to Genesis 10:4 (cf. Isa. 23:1), it must be a Mediterranean port, since Tarshish is said to be a "son of Javan" (Greece). Some identify it with the mining village in southwestern Spain called Tharsis (Tartessus, which was, according to Herodotus 4:152, "beyond the Pillars of Heracles," and according to Plinius and Strabo, in the Guadalquivir Valley; this is very probable). Jonah, fleeing from his mission in the east (Nineveh), took, from the Jaffa port, a boat going to Tarshish, i.e., westward (Jonah 1:3). On the other hand, Solomon had a "fleet of Tarshish," whose home port was Eẓion-Geber on the Red Sea (I Kings 10:22); some explain the expression "fleet of Tarshish" as a fleet composed of big and strong ships, capable of long voyages (cf. Isa. 60:9), but not necessarily to Tarshish – Solomon's fleet went to *Ophir as well. According to II Chronicles 20:36, however, the fleet of Jehoshaphat intended to sail to Tarshish from the port of Eẓion-Geber, in which case Tarshish would lie somewhere along the Red Sea or the Indian Ocean (cf. II Chron. 9:21; I Kings 22:49).

(2) Tarshish is also the name of a Benjamite, son of Bilhan (I Chron. 7:10), and of one of the "seven princes of Persia and Medea" in Esther 1:14.

TARSKI, ALFRED (1902–1983), mathematical logician and founder of logical semantics. Born Teitelbaum in Warsaw, Poland, he studied logic at Warsaw University, a course disrupted by the events of World War I. In 1923 he changed his name to Tarski and became a Roman Catholic. Despite his growing international reputation, his academic advancement in Poland was slow. The Germans invaded Poland while he was attending a Harvard conference; he remained in the U.S. After prestigious but temporary appointments, he joined the University of California at Berkeley in 1942, becoming professor of mathematics in 1949. He remained at Berkeley for the rest of his career. Tarski was a logician ranked by his peers as the equal of Aristotle, Frege, and Godel. He pioneered the field of metamathematics. His most important contribution to logic is the semantic method, which allows a more exacting study of formal languages and especially the concept of truth. He also contributed to algebra and measure theory. His precise, energetic but at times acerbic teaching was enthusiastically received in the department he established at Berkeley and internationally as a visiting professor. His publications include *An Introduction to Logic*, which has been translated into many languages including Hebrew in 1957, and many monographs on basic mathematics and mathematical logic, as well as his collected papers (edited by Steven R. Givant and Ralph N. McKenzie). His many honors include election to the U.S. National Academy of Sciences and the British Academy.

[Michael Denman (2nd ed.)]

TARTAKOVER, SAVIELLY GRIGORYEVICH (1887–1956), chess master. Born in Rostov-on-Don, Russia, Tartakover, a lawyer, spent most of his life as a chess player, living in

France. In World War II he served in the Free French Forces. After the war he represented France in chess tournaments. He was an original and creative player. Tartakover attained master rank at Nuremberg in 1906 and established himself as an experimentalist of genius. He became associated with Nimzovitch, Breyer, Reti, and Alekhine in the development of modern subtleties of strategy. Tartakover won several prizes before World War I, but most of his tournament successes were achieved between the world wars. After World War II he won at Venice, Hastings, Beveryk, and other places. He contributed to opening theory, to endgame techniques, and created many fine combinations. A very witty and cultured man, Tartakover is renowned for his epigrams, one of which is: The mistakes are all there, waiting to be made.

He wrote several books on chess, the best known being *Die Hypermoderne Schachpartie* (1924), *Schachmethodik* (1928), *500 Master Games of Chess* (with J. Du Mont, 1952), *My Best Games of Chess 1905–1930* (1953), and *My Best Games of Chess, 1931–1954* (1956).

[Aharon Weiss]

TARTAKOWER, ARIEH (1897–1982), sociologist, demographer, and communal leader. Tartakower was born in Brody, E. Galicia. He lectured on the sociology of the Jews at the Institute of Jewish Sciences in Warsaw. Tartakower was founder and chairman of Hitaḥadut, the Labor Zionist organization in Poland, and also served as an alderman of the city of Lodz during 1938–39. He was a member of the World Zionist Actions Committee from 1927. Emigrating to the United States in 1939, he served as director of relief and rehabilitation of the *World Jewish Congress and deputy director of its Institute of Jewish Affairs. Tartakower settled in Palestine in 1946 and lectured on Jewish sociology at the Hebrew University. From 1948 until 1971 he was chairman of the Israel section of the World Jewish Congress, and from 1959, of the executive committee of the World Hebrew Confederation. In 1971, he headed the World Jewish Congress' Cultural Department. He was a founding member and president of the Israel Association for the United Nations. He was one of a small group of scholars, including A. *Ruppin and J. *Lestschinsky, who developed the study of Jewish sociology. Tartakower wrote many books in Hebrew, Yiddish, Polish, and English and frequently contributed to periodicals in different languages.

Among his main works are *Toledot Tenu'at ha-Avodah ha-Yehudit*, 3 vols. (1929–31), *Nedudei ha-Yehudim ba-Olam* (1947^2), *Ha-Adam ha-Noded* (1954), *Ha-Ḥevrah ha-Yehudit* (1957), *Ha-Ḥevrah ha-Yisre'elit* (1959), *In Search of Home and Freedom* (1958), *Ha-Hityashevut ha-Yehudit ba-Golah* (1959), *Am ve-Olamo* (1963), and his survey of contemporary Jewish communities *Shivtei Yisrael*, 3 vols. (1963–69).

BIBLIOGRAPHY: A. Manor, *Aryeh Tartakower, ha-Sozyolog ha-Ivri* (1962), incl. bibl.; *Bi-Netivei Hagut ve-Tarbut, Koveẓ… le-Aryeh Tartakower* (1970), incl. bibl.

[Natan Lerner]

TARTAN (Heb. תַּרְתָּן; from Akk. *turtānu* or *tartān*), title of the Assyrian commander in chief who came immediately after the king. The title is attested as early as the reign of Adad-nirari II (911–891 B.C.E.). A general bearing the title *tartan* was sent by Sargon II in 711 against Ashdod (Isa. 20:1); another *tartan* headed a delegation sent by Sennacherib to Hezekiah (II Kings 18:17).

BIBLIOGRAPHY: E. Ebeling and B. Meissner, in: *Reallexikon der Assyriologie*, 1 (1932), 460.

TARTU (Ger. and Swed. **Dorpat**; Rus. **Yuryev**), city in E. Estonia. A small Jewish community was founded there by demobilized soldiers from the army of *Nicholas I in the 1860s. A synagogue was erected in 1876. The community numbered 1,774 (4% of the total population) in 1897, 1,115 in 1922, and 920 in 1934. There were both Jewish elementary and secondary schools in the city. Jews studied at the University of Tartu from the 1840s; there were 235 Jewish students in 1886 (14.8% of the total number of students). With the Russification of the university and the introduction of a *numerus clausus, the number of Jewish students was reduced, and a further reduction occurred after the establishment of independent Estonia following World War I; from 188 Jewish university students in 1926 their number decreased to 96 in 1934. In 1934 a seminary for Jewish studies was opened at the university under the guidance of the scholar L. Gulkowitsch. He was succeeded by the scholar and educator M.J. Nadel (1893–1936) and by the Hebrew author H.J. Port (1892–1940). The Association for the Study of Jewish History and Literature, founded in 1884, held an important place in the life of the Jewish students. Among the association's first members were Jacob *Bernstein-Kogan (Cohan) and A. Broide; it became a center particularly for the national minded and Zionist students. When Estonia was incorporated in the Soviet Union in 1940, Jewish communal life in Tartu was brought to an end. After the German occupation in 1941 the Jews who did not succeed in escaping from Tartu were murdered.

Some 200 Jews returned to Tartu from the Soviet Union, later joined by Russian-born Jews. In 1967, many of them immigrated to Israel. The city has a Jewish community center.

BIBLIOGRAPHY: K. Jokton, *Di Geshikhte fun di Yidn in Estland* (1927), 25–57. J. Bernstein-Cohen, in: *Sefer Bernstein-Cohen* (1946), 84–91.

[Yehuda Slutsky / Ruth Beloff (2nd ed.)]

TARUSKIN, RICHARD (1945–), U.S. musicologist and critic born in New York. He graduated from Columbia University with the M.A. thesis "Vladimir Vasilievich Stasov: Functionary in Art" (1968). He studied at the Moscow State Conservatory (1972) and continued his Russian studies, receiving a Ph.D. in 1975. He published thereafter articles and books on Russian music, including *Opera and Drama in Russia as Preached and Practiced in the 1860s* (1981; 1993^2); *Musorgsky: Eight Essays and an Epilogue* (1992); *Stravinsky and the Rus-*

sian Tradition: A Biography of Works through Mavra* (1996); and *Defining Russia Musically: Historical and Hermeneutical Essays* (1997). He developed parallel studies in the history of Western music and wrote a masterwork in six volumes, *The Oxford History of Western Music* (2004), in which he focused on the history of musical culture rather than on the selected classic repertoire as the traditional German concept taught. In his other activity as performer he was a choral conductor (director of the Columbia University Collegium Musicum and Cappella Nova) as well as viola da gamba soloist. He also recorded and edited numerous compositions of early and Renaissance music and wrote critical essays collected in his book *Text and Act: Essays on Music and Performance* (1995). His teaching career developed first at Columbia University (from 1973 to 1987), then at the University of California, Berkeley, where he was appointed professor of music in 1997. Taruskin was a constant contributor to the *New York Times*, *New Republic*, *Opus*, *Atlantic Monthly*, and *Opera News*. His phenomenal erudition, consistent historical thinking, and writer's gift made him unrivaled in the musicology of our time. He was awarded the Greenberg Prize (1978); the Alfred Einstein Award (1980), the Dent Medal (1987), and the Kinkeldey Prize (1997). He was a member of the American Philosophical Society.

BIBLIOGRAPHY: Grove Music Online.

[Marina Rizarev (2nd ed.)]

TARUTINO, village in *Bessarabia, Ukraine. Tarutino was founded as a German colony at the beginning of the 19th century. As a result of Jewish emigration to Bessarabia in the first half of the 19th century Jews began to settle in Tarutino despite the fact that after 1839 the law prohibiting Jews from settling in border regions applied there. The *May Laws of 1882 forbidding Jews to reside in rural areas also applied there. Occasionally Jews were expelled on the grounds that they were living there illegally. Nevertheless, the Jewish community continued to grow and in 1897 there were 1,873 Jews (36% of the total population) in Tarutino, most of them engaged in business. In 1925 the 285 members of the local loan fund included 17 farmers, 57 artisans, and 172 tradesmen. There were 1,546 Jews (26.7% of the total population) in 1930. The community was destroyed in 1941 when the Germans and Romanians entered Bessarabia during World War II.

[Eliyahu Feldman]

TASHKENT, capital of Tashkent district, Uzbekistan. Tashkent was conquered by the Russians in 1865. Previously there was a small community of Bukharan Jews living in a special quarter there. Russian rule improved the legal status of the Jews, and many Jews from neighboring *Bukhara consequently settled in Tashkent. Although Jews from European Russia were prohibited from settling in Tashkent under czarist rule, a small community of Russian Jews who belonged to categories permitted to settle outside the *Pale of Settlement was formed there during the second half of the 19th century. In 1897 there were 1,746 Jews in the region of Tashkent, most of whom lived in the town itself. On the eve of World War I about 3,000 Jews lived there and maintained Jewish educational and cultural institutions in which the language of instruction was Hebrew. A Tajiki-language Zionist newspaper, *Raḥamim*, was published. With the establishment of the Soviet regime, the Jewish cultural and religious institutions were gradually liquidated and the Zionist newspaper was replaced by a Communist one, *Bairaki Huriet* ("The Flag of Freedom"). During the 1920s and 1930s Tashkent became one of the centers to which active members of the Zionist Organization and members of the pioneering youth movements were exiled. During World War II Tashkent became one of the most important absorption centers for refugees from the German-occupied regions. Many remained in the town after the war, and a large Jewish settlement was thus created.

Contemporary Period

In the 1959 census 50,445 Jews were registered in Tashkent (5.5% of the total population), most of them newly arrived Ashkenazi Jews and a minority of old-time Bukharan Jews. There was one synagogue for Ashkenazim and two for Bukharans all in the same compound. In 1963 the organized baking of *maẓẓot* was prohibited, but Jews continued to bake them at home. The synagogue buildings were damaged in the 1966 earthquake in the area; the Bukharan Jews repaired their synagogue, while Ashkenazim moved to a new synagogue building. Tashkent Jews applied for exit permits to Israel, particularly from 1968. After the mass exodus of the 1990s only a few thousand Jews remained in Tashkent, which maintained an active community center as part of the general revival of Jewish life.

BIBLIOGRAPHY: *Voskhod*, 5 (1885), 1413–14; 6 (1886), 450–1; A. Neimark, in: *Ha-Asif*, 5 (1889), 74–75; E. Tcherikower (ed.), *In der Tkufe fun Revolutsye* (1924), 356–66; A. Rudnitski, *Shanah be-Rusyah* (1945), 193–7; I. Ben-Zvi, *Niddeḥei Yisrael*, ed. by A. Reuveni (1965), 165–6, 175 (= *The Exiled and the Redeemed*, 1957).

[Yehuda Slutsky]

TASHLIKH (Heb. תַּשְׁלִיךְ; lit. "thou shalt cast"), ceremony held near a sea or a running stream on the first day of *Rosh Ha-Shanah, usually late in the afternoon. When the first day occurs on the Sabbath, the ceremony is deferred to the second day, to ensure that no prayer book be carried to the riverside on the Sabbath (*Peri Megadim* to Sh. Ar., OḤ 583:2). The term itself is derived from Micah 7:19: "Thou wilt cast all their sins into the depths of the sea." The core of the ceremony is the recitation of Micah 7:18–20. Psalms 118:5–9; 33; 130; and Isaiah 11:9 are added in some rites. Kabbalists added quotations from the Zohar and there were other variants in different communities (e.g., in Kurdistan Jews actually entered the water; in certain parts of Bulgaria the ceremony was performed on the afternoon of the Day of Atonement).

The origin of the custom – not mentioned by talmudic, geonic, or early authorities – is uncertain. J.Z. Lauterbach (*Rabbinic Essays* (1951), 299–433) suggests a pagan origin, and Schulman (*Ha-Meliẓ*, 8 (1868), 106–7) even claims that Josephus hints at the custom (Ant., 14:10–23). There is no direct reference to the custom, however, until Jacob *Moellin (d. 1425), in his *Sefer Maharil* (Warsaw ed. (1874), 38a), explains it as a reminder of the midrashic tale (Tanḥ. Va-Yera, 22) of Abraham's refusal to be deterred from his mission to sacrifice Isaac even after Satan had transformed himself into a brook obstructing his path. Other authorities suggest that, as fish never close their eyes, so the ceremony is symbolic of God's eyes, ever-open (Isaiah Horowitz, *Shenei Luḥot ha-Berit* (Josefow ed. (1878), 139); or, as the fate of fish is uncertain, so is the ceremony illustrative of man's plight (cf. Eccles. 9:12; Moses of Przemysl, *Matteh Moshe*, Warsaw ed., 1876, 166). Moses Isserles (*Torat ha-Olah*, 3:56, Lemberg, 1858 ed., part 3, 48b) saw the ceremony as a tribute to the Creator, to Whose work of creation (this actually starting on Rosh Ha-Shanah) the fish were the first witnesses. Thus it was recommended that the ceremony be performed on the banks of a river where living fish are found (*Magen Avraham* to Sh. Ar., OḤ 583:2). However, when this is impossible, the ceremony is performed even by a well of water as is customary in Jerusalem.

The custom of shaking the pockets of one's garments during the ceremony is popularly taken as a rite of transferring the sins to the fish, but other authorities connect it with the talmudic saying that cleanliness of garments is a sign of moral purity (see Shab. 153a). To feed the fish during the ceremony is forbidden (Maharil, loc. cit.).

Oriental-Sephardi Jews have practiced the custom since the time of Isaac *Luria.

BIBLIOGRAPHY: J.Z. Lauterbach, *Rabbinic Essays* (1951) 299–433; Schulman, in: *Ha-Meliẓ*, 8 (1868), 106–7; Abrahams, in: JC (Sept. 27, 1889), 15–16; E. Munk, *The World of Prayer*, 2 (1963), 212–5; S.Z. Ariel, *Enẓiklopedyah Me'ir Nativ* (1960), 454–5.

TA-SHMA, ISRAEL MOSES, (1936–2004), a prominent Israeli scholar of talmudic and rabbinic literature. Ta-Shma was born in Tel Aviv into a Religious Zionist family. He attended the Yeshivat ha-Yishuv he-Ḥadash high school, afterwards studying at the Hebron Yeshivah in Jerusalem. At the age of 21 he received rabbinic ordination and left the yeshivah world to study at the Hebrew University where he received his B.A. and M.A. He received his doctorate from Bar-Ilan University in 1973. He taught at Bar-Ilan in the Talmud Department until 1981 when he was hired to teach at Hebrew University and to be the director of the Institute of Microfilmed Hebrew Manuscripts at the Jewish National and University Library on the Givat Ram campus, Jerusalem. At the same time, Ta-Shma was the academic secretary of Mekiẓe Nirdamim, the 200-year-old organization that publishes Jewish scholarship from manuscript. Throughout his academic career, Ta-Shma used manuscripts as the basis of his work. He was one of the first modern scholars to do so, thus forging new paths in Jewish academic research. Beginning in 1963, for 18 years, Ta-Shma was one of the editors of the *Hebrew Encyclopedia*. In 1984 he founded the journal, *Alei Sefer*, at Bar-Ilan University. He was the journal's editor for ten years. In 1991, he received tenure from Hebrew University and retired from teaching in 1999. In 2002 he received the Bialik Prize. In 2003, he received both the Prime Minister's EMET Prize and the prestigious Israel Prize for his work in Talmud.

Along with over 150 articles and numerous collections that he co-edited with others, Ta-Shma wrote a number of important works including *Rabbi Zeraḥya Ha-Levi: Ba'al ha-Ma'or u-Venei Ḥugo*, based on his Ph.D. dissertation (1992); *Halakhah, Minhag u-Meẓi'ut be-Ashkenaz 1000–1350* (1996); *Minhag Ashkenaz ha-Kadum: Ḥeker ve-Iyyun* (1999); *Ha-Sifrut ha-Parshanit le-Talmud be-Eiropa u-vi-Ẓefon Afrika: Korot, Ishim ve-Shitot – Ḥelek Alef 1000–1200* (1999); *Ha-Sifrut ha-Parshanit le-Talmud be-Eiropa u-vi-Ẓefon Africa: Korot, Ishim ve-Shitot – Ḥelek Bet 1200–1400* (2000); *Ha-Niglah she-be-Nistar: Le-Ḥeker Sheki'ei ha-Halakhah be-Sefer ha-Zohar* (expanded edition, 2001); *Rabbi Moshe ha-Darshan ve-ha-Sifrut ha-Ḥiẓonit* (2001); *Ha-Tefillah ha-Ashkenazit ha-Kedumah: Perakim be-Ofyah u-ve-Toldoteha* (2003); and a collection of his articles edited by Y. Hovav, *Knesset Meḥkarim: Iyyunim be-Sifrut ha-Rabbanim bi-Yemei ha-Beinayim* (2004). It is interesting to note that his first publication was a religious song book for IDF soldiers (1960) issued by the Chief Rabbinate of the IDF.

The judges of the 2003 Israel Prize said, "Ta-Shma was graced with very broad knowledge in all aspects of Talmudic and rabbinic literature both in print and in manuscript, brilliant ability and a sharp intuition for creating an integration between various and different fields of knowledge, and a voluminous output of research."

[David Derovan (2nd ed.)]

TASHRAK (Heb. 1926–1872 ;תשר"ק), most common pseudonym of **Israel Joseph Zevin**, a humorist and pioneer of the Yiddish press in America. Born in Horki (Belorussia), Zevin immigrated to the U.S. in the late 1880s. From 1893 until his death he was on the staff of the Orthodox daily *Yidishes Tageblat* in New York, and wrote under his own name and the pseudonym Yudkovitch. He became a member of the paper's editorial board and for a time served as its editor-in-chief. From 1924 he wrote, under the names Dr. A. Adelman and Meyer Zonenshayn, for the *Morgn Zhurnal*, also in New York. His writings – stories, feuilletons, and articles on current affairs – appeared in other American newspapers and in the foreign press. He won recognition principally for his humorous tales about the typical Jewish immigrant's adventures in the U.S. (later these appeared in book form as *Y.Y. Zevins Geklibene Shriftn* ("Selected Works of Y.Y. Zevin," 1906); *Geklibene Shriftn* ("Selected Works," 1909); and *Tashraks Beste Ertseylungen* ("Tashrak's Best Stories," 4 vols., 1910). He also published anthologies of *aggadot*, *midrashim*, and proverbs (*Ale Mesholim fun Dubner Magid* ("The Complete Proverbs of the *Dubner Maggid*," 2 vols., 1925); *Ale Agodes fun Talmud* … ("The Complete *Aggadot* of the Talmud," 3 vols., 1922); *Der Oytser* *fun Ale Medroshim*, ("The Complete Treasury of Proverbs," 4 vols., 1926)), which he had collected and translated into Yiddish toward the end of his life. Zevin wrote children's stories (*Mayselekh far Kinder*, "Stories For Children," 1919), a number of stories in Hebrew, and a posthumously published novel. From 1905 he began to write in English, mainly translating his own stories which appeared in the English section of the *Tageblat* and in the weekly *American Hebrew*. Between 1914 and 1917 he was a regular contributor to the Sunday issue of the *New York Herald*, and became known for his essays, interviews, and humorous pieces on New York Jewish life.

BIBLIOGRAPHY: Rejzen, Leksikon, 4 (1929), 902–12.

[Chava Turniansky / Benjamin Sadock (2nd ed.)]

TASMANIA, island S. of Australia and Australian state; established as a penal colony in 1803. Jewish names appear in its early history. Solomon, reported to be in safe custody (1819); a land grant to Emanuel Levy (1820); the charter granted for the Bank of Van Diemen's Land with Judah and Joseph Solomon among the shareholders (1823); a letter of recommendation as a settler to A. Aaron (1824). A petition from Bernard Walford was granted for a Jewish burial ground (1828). Ikey Solomons, a famous convict, may have been the model for Fagin in Dickens' *Oliver Twist*. In 1837 there was a total of 132 Jews, of whom 124 were free. By 1854 the Tasmanian Jewish population was 435, of whom 259 were free. In 1847 it was arranged that all Jews in Hobart and Launceston prisons should have the privilege of attending synagogue and refraining from work on the Sabbath. Pass holders were permitted to be counted in a *minyan*, but they could not have honors bestowed on them. By 1891 the number of Jews had fallen to 84. Most of the early settlers were illiterate and stated their occupation as farmers. Some, however, rose to prominence. Samuel Benjamin, born in southern Tasmania in 1839, attained the position of an alderman of Hobart City in 1897; John William Israel, born in Launceston in 1850, became auditor-general in 1895 and was elected president of the Civil Servants' Association at its foundation in 1897.

With the arrival of Orthodox newcomers from England, and spurred on by the need to distribute charity, the community consecrated its first synagogue in Hobart on July 4, 1843. In March 1864 the Hebrew Proprietary School was permanently incorporated with the synagogue. The first *bet din* in the city dates from 1911. The Hobart synagogue is the oldest standing synagogue within the British Commonwealth outside of England. The Tasmanian Hebrew Benevolent Society was formed in 1847. The Hobart synagogue celebrated the 120th anniversary of the laying of its foundation stone in 1963. The community remained small and has been constantly reduced by intermarriage. The Launceston synagogue was consecrated in 1846, with D. Benjamin as its president. It flourished for some years, serving about 100 families, but eventually the Jewish population of the town dwindled, the trustees died, and the religious articles were removed to Hobart. The synagogue was closed down in 1871, but it was reopened in 1939.

Tasmania failed to benefit from the arrival of thousands of refugees in Australia during and after the Nazi period, and its Jewish population steadily declined during the first post-1945 decades. The number of declared Jews in Tasmania, according to successive Australian censuses, totaled 158 in 1954, 136 in 1961, and only 98 in 1971. Since the 1970s, however, the community has grown again, thanks to migration from the mainland and from overseas, and stood at 145 in 1981, 160 in 1986, 167 in 1996, and 180 in 2001. An Orthodox and Reform synagogue currently exist in Hobart, as well as an Orthodox synagogue in Launceston, and a Chabad House in Sandy Bay.

BIBLIOGRAPHY: M. Gordon, *Jews in Van Diemen's Land* (1965); Australian Jewish Historical Society, *Journal and Proceedings*, 1 pt. 3 (1940), 72; 2 pt. 8 (1947), 413–8; 3 pt. 5 (1951), 209–37; 5 pt. 8 (1964), 428–33. **ADD. BIBLIOGRAPHY:** H.L. Rubinstein, Australia I, index; W.D. Rubinstein, Australia II, index.

[Shmuel Gorr / William D. Rubinstein (2nd ed.)]

TATLIN, VLADIMIR E. (1885–1953), Russian painter, sculptor, and architect. Tatlin was born in Moscow. He is chiefly remembered for his design for a memorial to the Third International (1920), a leaning steel and wire spiral of 1,300 ft. The design is regarded as an early example of constructivism.

TATTENAI (Aram. תַּתְּנַי; I Esd. 6:3, 7, 26, Sisinnes), governor (*peḥah*) of the territory known as "Beyond The River" (*eber nahara* in Aramaic; Coele-Syria and Phoenicia in I Esd.) under Darius I. Tattenai was subordinate, at least at first, to Ushtannu (Hystanes), governor of Babylon and "Beyond The River." Learning that work had been resumed on the Jerusalem Temple in 520 B.C.E., he came, together with Shethar-Bozenai and his colleagues the investigators, to inquire as to the Jews' right to build. They informed the officials that permission had been granted by Cyrus. The permit was confirmed and renewed by Darius who wrote to Tattenai and his colleagues, "Keep away from there! Let the work on this Temple alone!" Tattenai and his men withdrew and the Temple was completed (Ezra 5:3ff.; 6:13ff.).

BIBLIOGRAPHY: A.T. Olmstead, in: JNES, 3 (1944), 46; A.F. Rainey, in: *Australian Journal of Biblical Archaeology*, 1 (1969), 53.

[Bezalel Porten]

TATTOO (Heb. *ketovet ka'ka*), a sign made by puncturing the skin and inserting pigment. A mark of slavery or of submission to a deity (Isa. 44:5, although tattooing is not explicitly mentioned) in the ancient Near East, Greece, and Rome, tattooing is prohibited in Leviticus 19:28. The anonymous Mishnah in *Makkot* (3:6) states that one is culpable of the transgression of tattooing only if it consists of writing and is done with indelible ink. However, R. Simeon b. Judah in the name of R. Simeon, in accepting this view, states that one is guilty only if he tattoos the name of an idol (according to the interpretation of the Talmud; Mak. 21a). In this way he explains the last words of Leviticus 19:28, "I am the Lord." The *halakhah* is in accordance with the anonymous Mishnah (Sh. Ar., YD 180:1). Maimonides agrees but adds that although all tattooing is forbidden, the origin of the prohibition is that it "was the custom of idolaters to inscribe themselves [by tattooing] to an idol, to indicate that they were bondslaves to it and devoted to its service" (Yad, Avodah Zarah 12:11).

TAU, MAX (1897–1976), publisher and author. Tau, who was born in Beuthen, Upper Silesia, was for many years the literary director of the publishing house of Bruno Cassirer and a book reviewer for the *Frankfurter Zeitung* and other journals. In 1938 he immigrated to Norway and in 1942, during the persecution of the Jews there, he took refuge in Sweden. After World War II he attained an important position in Norwegian publishing. Among the important authors he introduced in Norway, there were many Jews and some Israelis. He also introduced Norwegian authors in Germany (even before the war). Among his most significant achievements was the creation of a "Peace Library" which, he hoped, would become internationally important and would help revive respect for the human being. His many honors included the first award of the German publishing trade's peace prize (1950), and a school in Kiel, Germany, that was named after him.

Tau himself wrote several novels and autobiographical books in German, published in Norwegian and German, in which he described his parental Jewish home, German-cultural life, his absorption into Norwegian society and, above all, his faith in humanity. They include *Tro på mennesket* (1946; *Glaube an den Menschen*, 1948), *Denn ueber uns ist der Himmel* (1955), *Das Land, das ich verlassen musste* (1961), *Ein Fluechtling findet sein Land* (1964), and *På forsoningens vei* (*Auf dem Wege zur Vesoehnung*, 1967).

BIBLIOGRAPHY: *En Mosaikk – Max Tau* (Norwegian, 1967); *Baumeister einer bruederlichen Welt. Max Tau: Dokumente einer Ehrung* (1966).

[Oskar Mendelsohn]

TAUBE, MICHAEL (1890–1972), conductor. Born in Lodz, Poland, Taube conducted in Bonn and Cologne, in 1924 became assistant to Bruno Walter at the Berlin Opera, and in 1926 founded the Taube Chamber Concerts. In 1933 Taube was among the founders of the Juedischer Kulturbund. He emigrated to Palestine in 1934 and led a symphony orchestra in Jerusalem, which was later disbanded with the founding of the Palestine (later Israel) Philharmonic and the Palestine Broadcasting Service orchestras in 1936, which he frequently conducted. In 1956 Taube established the Ramat Gan Chamber Orchestra. He also organized the Israel Bach Society and the Israel Mozart Society which were active for several years.

TAUBE, MOSHE (1927–), *ḥazzan*. Born in Cracow, at the age of eight he had already absorbed the traditional cantorial melodies from the cantors Samuel Kaufman and Joseph Mandelbaum. As a youth he began to study music and piano at the Cracow Conservatory. These studies were abruptly interrupted by the Holocaust which he survived. After World War II he immigrated to Palestine and joined the Haganah. He was drafted into the Israel army as soon as the state was declared and fought in the battles to liberate Jerusalem. Taube resumed his musical education at institutes in Jerusalem and Haifa and also appeared in concerts and led services throughout Israel. He took part in Kol Yisrael and Kol Ẓiyyon la-Golah and became chief cantor at the Bograshov Street Synagogue in Tel Aviv. He developed a special cantorial style combining traditional and innovative approaches and composed melodies for prayers. In 1957 he went to the United States and became senior cantor at the Shaarey Ẓedek congregation in Manhattan, serving there until 1965, when he became chief cantor at Beth Shalom in Pittsburgh. Taube studied at Juilliard School of Music and taught at the cantorial school of the Jewish Theological Seminary as well as the University of Pittsburgh. He produced records of his original cantorial works and belonged to the Cantors Assembly.

[Akiva Zimmerman]

TAUBE, SAMUEL BARUCH (1914–), *ḥazzan*. Taube was born in Zelov, near Lodz in Poland. His family moved to Austria when he was a child. In Vienna he studied cantorial liturgy and music; among his teachers was the cantor Emmanuel Frenkel. His first cantorial position was in the Montefiore Synagogue in Vienna. He then went to Paris, where he held the position of cantor in the Synagogue de la Rue Montevideo. During World War II he was deported to a concentration camp, but his talents saved him. After the war he served as cantor to the Jewish community of Goeteberg in Sweden. He held cantorial positions in London from 1947 until 1958 when he moved to Washington, to the Beth Sholom Synagogue. In 1963 Taube moved to Montreal, Canada, where he was cantor to the Beth Orah Congregation until 1975, when he moved to Israel, where he trained cantors. For over a decade, he was also a faculty member of the Tel Aviv Cantorial Institute. He made recordings of cantorial music available through Musique Internationale Chicago. The hundreds of cantorial recitatives that Taube has transcribed over the decades are models of perfection in this art.

[Akiva Zimmerman / Raymond Goldstein (2nd ed.)]

TAUBENSCHLAG, RAPHAEL (1881–1958), papyrologist and legal historian. Born in Galicia, in 1913 Taubenschlag began to lecture at the University of Cracow, from 1921 as professor of Roman law. He devoted most of his research to Egyptian legal documents and Greek inscriptions, also making important contributions to the study of Roman law and research on Polish law during the Middle Ages. When World War II broke out, he fled to France and then to the United States. There he wrote his main work, *The Law of Greco-Roman Egypt in the Light of the Papyri 332 B.C.–640 A.D.* (1944, 1955[2]). He served as chair of papyrology at Columbia University. During that time he founded the *Journal of Juristic Papyrology* (JPP) in 1946, which he edited until his death. In 1947 he returned to

Poland and was appointed professor of Roman law and ancient codes at the University of Warsaw. Since 1947 the JPP has been published annually in Warsaw under the auspices of the Department of Papyrology at Warsaw University.

Some of his numerous publications were collected posthumously by his students and published as *Opera Minora* (2 vols., 1959).

[Reuven Yaron / Ruth Beloff (2nd ed.)]

TAUBER, RICHARD (Ernst Seiffert; 1892–1948), singer. Born in Linz, Austria, Tauber studied at Frankfurt. In 1913 he was engaged under a five-year contract by the Dresden opera, where he sang leading tenor parts. He also sang at various other renowned opera houses in Germany and Austria, and at the Salzburg Mozart festivals. From about 1925 he turned to light opera, especially the Lehar operettas (e.g., *Land of Smiles*) in which he became internationally famous; and after 1928, also appeared in musical films. In 1938 he settled in England, where he appeared at Covent Garden. His voice charmed audiences by its tenor quality, pleasant tone, and graceful inflections. Tauber composed an operetta, *Old Chelsea* (1942), and appeared in its leading role.

TAUBERBISCHOFSHEIM (Bischofsheim on the Tauber), town in Baden, Germany. The first documentary evidence for the presence of Jews in Tauberbischofsheim dates from 1235 when eight Jews of Lauda and Tauberbischofsheim, accused of murdering a Christian, were tortured and executed. The city had an established community by the end of the 13th century when 120 Jews were martyred during the *Rindfleisch disturbances of 1298. The community recovered relatively soon, only to suffer again during the *Armleder persecutions of 1337. The community was annihilated in the *Black Death persecutions (1348–49). Jews resettled in Tauberbischofsheim in 1373; in later centuries, however, Jews are only briefly recorded. A synagogue is mentioned in the 18th century, but the Jewish community was then very small. It increased from 109 in 1825 to 200 by 1880 (6.51 percent of the total population) but decreased to 106 by June 1933. In 1827 the community was affiliated with the district rabbinate of Wertheim. Until 1875 the cemetery of Kuhlsheim was used by the Tauberbischofsheim community. Jewish industrialists and merchants contributed significantly to the economic life of the city. In 1931 the cemetery was desecrated. On *Kristallnacht*, Nov. 9–10, 1938, the synagogue was not among those burnt down in Germany because it abutted on houses owned by Christians. The interior of the synagogue was desecrated, although the Torah scrolls were rescued by Christian clergy. Many of the Jews had left the town before the outbreak of World War II. On Oct. 22, 1940, 22 Jews there were deported to *Gurs, only four of whom survived the war; another ten died in *Auschwitz.

The building of the synagogue was transformed into a residential building after 1950.

BIBLIOGRAPHY: Salfeld, Martyrol, index, s.v. *Bischofsheim*; F. Hundsnurscher and G. Taddey (eds.), *Die juedischen Gemeinden in Baden* (1968); *Germania Judaica*, 1 (1963), 372–3; 2 (1968), 815–6; 3 (1987), 1450–53; PK, Germanyah. **ADD BIBLIOGRAPHY:** F.-J. Ziwes, *Studien zur Geschichte der Juden im mittleren Rheingebiet waehrend des hohen und spaeten Mittelalters* (Forschungen zur Geschichte der Juden. Abteilung A, Abhandlungen, vol. 1) (1995); F. Gehrig and H. Mueller, *Tauberbischofsheim. Beitraege zur Stadtchronik* (1997), 285–97. **WEBSITE:** www.alemannia-judaica.de.

TAUBES, AARON MOSES BEN JACOB (1787–1852), Polish and Romanian rabbi. Taubes was a pupil of Jacob *Ornstein of Lemberg. After serving as rabbi of Snyatyn, he was appointed rabbi of Jassy and district in 1841, in which office he exercised considerable influence on Romanian Jewry. The historian Ḥ.N. Dembitzer praises him as the outstanding rabbinical authority of his time to whom the most famous rabbis turned with their problems.

His published works are *To'afot Re'em* (1855), responsa; *Karnei Re'em* (1864), novellae and notes on the Talmud and its commentators, published in the standard editions of the Talmud, together with notes by his son Samuel; and *Karnei Re'em* (1881) on the Pentateuch with additions by his grandson Isaac Eisik (Shor). This work makes considerable use of Kabbalah. Many of Taubes' descendants served as rabbis in Jassy and in other communities in Romania. His sons Samuel Schmelke and Jacob, after serving in other communities, succeeded their father in Jassy.

BIBLIOGRAPHY: S. Buber, *Anshei Shem* (1895), 27; EIV, 18 (1966), 380–1.

[Itzhak Alfassi]

TAUBES, ḤAYYIM ẒEVI (1900–1966), rabbi and scholar. Born in Chernelitsa, Ukraine, Taubes served as rabbi in Odesburg, at the Pasmaniten Temple in Vienna – lecturing also at the teachers' seminary – and in Zurich, Switzerland. In 1965 he settled in Israel. A pupil of H.P. *Chajes, Taubes was an ardent Zionist from his youth and prominent in the Mizrachi movement.

Among his published works are *Lebendiges Judentum* (1946); *Ha-Nasi ba-Sanhedrin ha-Gedolah* (1925); *Likkutei Yiẓḥak ibn Ghayyat* (1952), an annotated edition of a work by the 11th-century Spanish talmudist; and *Ma'amad Hakhel be-Tifarto* (1953). Taubes edited the geonic material on the tractate *Sanhedrin* in his *Oẓar ha-Ge'onim al Massekhet Sanhedrin* (1966).

His son JACOB TAUBES (1923–), historian of religion, was born in Vienna, and became professor of Jewish studies and the sociology of religion at the Free University of West Berlin in 1959.

He published *Abendlaendische Eschatologie* (1948), *Psychoanalysis and the Future* (1957), and *Religious Experience and Truth* (ed. S. Hook, 1961), and edited the *Review of Religion* (1957–60), and the *Journal for the Scientific Study of Religion* (from 1961).

TAUBES, LOEBEL (1863–1933), pioneer Galician Zionist. Born in Bendery, Bessarabia, Taubes was raised in Galicia, where his father was the rabbi of Otynya. His Zionist activities began at the end of the 1880s, and in 1890 he began publishing the first Yiddish newspapers in Galicia (*Di Yidishe Folkstsaytung*, and later *Der Folksfraynd*, first in Kolomiyyo and then in Czernowitz). He was one of the first to fight for the Austrian government's recognition of Yiddish as the spoken language of the Jews of Galicia. For decades Taubes was the best known Zionist propagandist in Galicia and Austria, where his speeches in hundreds of towns and villages attracted mass audiences and did much to spread Zionism, especially among Orthodox circles. He was closely associated with *Herzl and published a Yiddish translation of *Der Judenstaat* (1897). He was one of the initiators of the Conference for the Yiddish Language and Culture, which met in Czernowitz in 1908. He lived in Kolomyia, in Czernowitz, and from 1914 in Vienna. In 1920 Taubes published the Hebrew version of the proceedings of the *Kattowitz Conference and his memoirs, and in 1928 he brought out a book on talmudic motifs in Yiddish proverbs.

BIBLIOGRAPHY: LNYL, 4 (1961), 44–45; N.M. Gelber, *Toledot ha-Tenu'ah ha-Ẓiyyonit be-Galiẓyah* (1958), 270 and index; G. Bader, *Medinah va-Ḥakhameha* (1934), 108–9.

[Getzel Kressel]

TAUBMAN, A. ALFRED (1924–), U.S. entrepreneur. Taubman, who was born in Pontiac, Mich., attended the University of Michigan without graduating and the Lawrence Institute of Technology, where he studied architecture. He became a store designer. In 1950, with a $5,000 loan, he formed the Taubman Company, a real-estate development and property management concern, and built it into one of the most prominent developers and managers of giant regional shopping malls in the United States. His first project in 1953 was a 26-store open-air shopping center in Flint, Mich. A few years later, he built an enclosed mall in Hayward, Calif., and then put together what was widely considered one of the finest collections of shopping malls in the world. In 2004, the average American mall had annual sales of around $340 a square foot. Taubman's malls, with high-end stores, averaged close to $500 a square foot. One of his prize malls was in Short Hills, N.J., which he bought in 1980 when there were only seven stores that were still in business. He renovated it four times until he got the right store mix: Neiman Marcus, Saks, Nordstrom, and Macy's. The mall had average annual sales of $800 a square foot. By the early years of the 21st century Taubman operated 19 shopping malls in nine states, including five in the Detroit area. In the 1970s Taubman went into business with Max *Fisher, the Detroit financier and adviser to Republican presidents. He had been Taubman's mentor since the 1950s, when he asked him to develop a chain of Speedway gas stations. Fisher and Taubman bought the Irvine Ranch in Southern California, which became one of the most profitable residential and commercial ventures in American history. It allowed Taubman, along with a group of investors that included Henry Ford II, to buy the majority share in Sotheby's, the famed auction house, in 1983 for $130 million. The move gave Taubman entrée to the art world and to European society. In 1993 Taubman became chairman and a director of Sotheby's but in 2001 he stood trial on charges that from 1993 to 1999 he had colluded with his chief rival, Christie's, to fix sellers' commissions, violating antitrust laws and cheating customers out of $400 million. A year earlier, to settle a civil class-action suit, Taubman stepped down from his Sotheby's post and paid one-third of the more than $500 million settlement made to former clients out of his own pocket. In the criminal trial, Taubman was convicted and spent a year in prison. Taubman was a major philanthropist, giving to educational and Jewish causes. A part-time resident of Bloomfield Hills, outside Detroit, Taubman was one of the two largest all-time contributors to the Jewish Federation of Metropolitan Detroit, mostly anonymously. In 1999, the federation named one of its Jewish community center campuses after Taubman, a member of Shaarey Zedek, a Conservative congregation in Southfield, Mich. With a $30 million gift, Taubman endowed the program in architecture and urban affairs at the University of Michigan, where a wing of the hospital is named after him. Brown University boasts the A. Alfred Taubman School for Public Policy and American Institutions, while Harvard University has the Taubman Center for State and Local Government.

[Stewart Kampel (2nd ed.)]

TAURAGE (Ger. **Tauroggen**), town in W. Lithuania (referred to by Jews as Tavrig). From 1795 until the establishment of independent Lithuania after World War I, it was a town in the province of Kovno within the limits of the *Pale of Settlement. In 1847 there were 410 Jews in the town; after 1850 the community increased and in 1897 numbered 3,364 (54.6% of the total population). At the beginning of the 20th century the local rabbi, Abraham Aaron Burstein, founded a yeshivah which existed until World War I. When the Jewish population was expelled from the battle zone during the war the Jews of Taurage were also evacuated (May 1915) to inner Russia, and the community ceased to exist. After the war the community did not recover its former status. In 1923 there were 1,772 Jews (32.5% of the population) and the community supported a Hebrew secondary school. In 1936 a *blood libel was circulated and riots were prevented only because of the community's *self-defense organization. When the Germans occupied Taurage during World War II, the Jews were concentrated in a ghetto, and after a few months they were massacred. S.P. *Rabbinowitz was born in Taurage.

BIBLIOGRAPHY: *Lite*, 1 (1951), 1221–23, 1584–85; *Yahadut Lita* (1959), 61.

[Yehuda Slutsky]

TAUSIG, KARL (1841–1871), pianist. Born in Warsaw, Tausig first studied with his father, Aloys Tausig, who had been a pupil of Sigismund *Thalberg, then from the age of 14 with Liszt and became his favorite pupil. In 1865 Tausig settled in Berlin, where he opened the Schule des hoeheren Klavierspiels (School of Advanced Piano Playing). His playing was in a grand and impassioned style with remarkable tone and technique described by Liszt as "infallible." He wrote *Taegliche Studien* and also composed some virtuoso pieces and arrangements.

TAUSK, VIKTOR (1877–1919), Austrian psychiatrist, and one of Sigmund *Freud's early pupils. Tausk, already a judge in Croatia, went to Vienna in 1908 to study medicine and psychiatry. He became a member of the group around Freud, and in spite of his involvement in the dissension in the group, Freud had a high opinion of him. In 1914 Tausk read a paper on melancholia to a meeting of the Vienna Psychoanalytic Society. As an army psychiatrist in World War I he used psychoanalytic methods in the treatment of war neuroses. In 1918 he returned to Vienna, where Freud refused to psychoanalyze him himself and arranged for his analysis by one of his pupils, Helene Deutsch. The treatment was not a success and shortly after Tausk committed suicide.

Tausk published a number of papers in 1913–14 on infantile sexuality and dreams. His outstanding contribution was in the psychoanalytic interpretation of schizophrenia which he published in 1919, *Ueber die Entstehung des "Beeinflussungsapparates" in der Schizophrenia* ("On the Origin of the 'Influencing Machine' in Schizophrenia," 1933). In 1991 a collection of his psychoanalytical papers was published in English as *Sexuality, War, and Schizophrenia.*

BIBLIOGRAPHY: P. Roazen, *Brother Animal: The Story of Freud and Tausk* (1969); K.R. Eissler, *Talent and Genius: The Fictitious Case of Tausk contra Freud* (1971).

[Louis Miller / Elisabeth Dessauer (2nd ed.)]

TAUSSIG, family of U.S. naval officers. EDWARD DAVID TAUSSIG (1847–1921) was born in St. Louis, Missouri, and was appointed to the U.S. naval academy in 1863. He fought in the Union Navy during the Civil War and served on a number of ships between 1867 and 1898, when he was given command of the gunboat *Bennington.* Taussig retired as a rear admiral in 1908. A destroyer was later named in his honor. His son, JOSEPH KNEFLER TAUSSIG (1877–1947), who was born in Dresden, Germany, fought in the Spanish-American War of 1898 as a naval cadet and was given his first command in 1911 on the USS *Amen.* During World War I he commanded escort vessels protecting convoys in submarine-infested waters. From 1933 until 1936 Taussig was assistant chief of naval operations. He then commanded the flagship USS *Idaho* for a year. He retired with the rank of vice admiral in September 1941 but was recalled to service in 1943. After his death a warship was named in his honor.

TAUSSIG, FRANK WILLIAM (1859–1940), U.S. economist, born in St. Louis, Missouri. Taussig's father was an immigrant from Prague, who had become president of a successful railroad company, and his mother was a daughter of a Protestant teacher from the Rhineland. In 1885 Taussig began a teaching career at Harvard, where he became professor of economics in 1901. He served as the first chairman of the United States Tariff Commission in Washington from 1917 to 1919 and was a close adviser to President Wilson.

Taussig's principal field was the theory, history, and practice of international trade and trade policy. His major work *Principles of Economics* (1911) was for many years a standard textbook. Other writings include *The Tariff History of the United States* (1888), *Wages and Capital* (1896), and *International Trade* (1927).

BIBLIOGRAPHY: J.A. Schumpeter, *Ten Great Economists From Marx to Keynes* (1951), 191–221.

[Joachim O. Ronall]

TAUSTE, town in Aragon, N.E. Spain, close to the border of the former kingdom of Navarre. The earliest information about the community of Tauste is from about 1271. It concerns the payment of 600 sólidos as yearly tax, which attests to a certain prosperity. This decreased to 332 sólidos in 1304 and further dwindled during the 14th century. In 1357 the Inquisition held trials in Tauste, and several Jews were condemned to life imprisonment. The nature of their offenses is not known. Nothing is known of the fate of the community during the persecutions of 1391. In 1402 the Jews of Tauste were requested to give a loan to the king. In 1405 there was an attempt to set up a burial society for the community. In 1414 the infante Alfonso (later Alfonso V) confirmed a royal decree restricting the area of the Jewish quarter; a time limit of six months was set for carrying out the resulting changes of residence. In 1458 this community figured among those granted a series of concessions by John II. Toward the end of the century, however, the community dwindled and experienced great poverty. In 1483 Ferdinand of Aragon appointed the surgeon Yuce Atorcar to head the community, which was placed under the supervision of the *merino* of *Saragossa.

BIBLIOGRAPHY: Baer, Urkunden, index; Neuman, Spain, index; I. de las Cagigas, in: *Sefarad*, 6 (1946), 74; L. Piles Ros, *ibid.*, 10 (1950), 105, 372f., 383f.

[Haim Beinart]

TAV (**Taw**; Heb. תָּו ;ת), the twenty-second and the last letter of the Hebrew alphabet; its numerical value is 400. The basic pictographic shape of this letter consisted of two strokes crossing each other × or +, i.e., the simplest mark and hence its name *taw.* While in the Proto-Canaanite and in the early Phoenician scripts, until the tenth century B.C.E., both the x-shaped and the cross-shaped *taw* were used; in the ninth century B.C.E. the letter's stance was stabilized. The Hebrew script preserved the x-shaped × and did not alter its form, but in the Samaritan script it became ࠕ. On the other hand, the late Phoenician script adopted and developed the cross-shaped *taw* † → † → 𐤕. and in the Aramaic script it evolved as follows: 𐡕 → 𐡕 → 𐡕. The last form was the prototype of the Jewish *taw* ת and Arabic ت which developed through the Nabatean 𐢞 → 𐢞 → 𐢞. The Greek (and Latin) "T" is a variation of the cross-shaped *taw.* See *Alphabet, Hebrew.

[Joseph Naveh]

TAVUS, JACOB BEN JOSEPH (16th century), author of a Judeo-Persian translation of the Pentateuch, written in Hebrew characters. This work was included in one edition of the polyglot Bible printed in Constantinople in 1546 by Eleazar b. Gerson *Soncino together with the Hebrew original, the Aramaic Targum, and the Arabic version of *Saadiah Gaon. Another edition comprises Judeo-Greek and Judeo-Spanish. It has not been established whether Tavus actually worked in Constantinople, for nothing else is known of his life. The Tavus Pentateuch translation was based on a long tradition of Judeo-Persian Bible translations. Transcribed into Persian characters, it was incorporated in Bishop Walton's polyglot Bible (London, 1654–57).

BIBLIOGRAPHY: S. Munk, *Notice sur R. Saadia Gaon… et sur une version persane* (1838), 62–87; A. Kohut, *Kritische Beleuchtung der persischen Pentateuch-Uebersetzung des Jacob ben Joseph Tawus* (1871); Fischel, in: HTR, 45 (1952), 3–45.

[Walter Joseph Fischel]

TAWIOW, ISRAEL ḤAYYIM (1858–1920), Hebrew author. Born in Druya, Belorussia, he moved with his parents to Riga, where he remained most of his life. In 1889 he began publishing serials in *Ha-Meliẓ* which excelled in their biting satire and wit. Tawiow quickly acquired a reputation as a brilliant essayist. He became a regular contributor to the weekly *Ha-Dor* and during 1905–08 lived in Vilna, serving on the editorial staff of the daily *Ha-Zeman*. He also published a vocalized daily Hebrew newspaper for children called *He-Ḥaver* (1908).

Tawiow's many essays on language and folklore, displaying both erudition and acuity, were posthumously published under the title *Kitvei I.Ḥ. Taviov* (1923). Of significance is his book *Oẓar ha-Meshalim ve-ha-Pitgamim* ("Treasury of Proverbs and Sayings," 1919, 1922^2), in which he collected, explained, and annotated over 3,000 Hebrew and Aramaic proverbs. He also wrote a number of textbooks on the Hebrew language and literature which were widely used. Among them are *Eden ha-Yeladim* (1896 and over 15 subsequent editions), a chrestomathy; *Moreh ha-Yeladim*, rules of the Hebrew language; *Ha-Mekhin* (1899), a beginner's text in the Hebrew language; *Mivḥar ha-Sifrut* (1899); *Oẓar ha-Shirah ve-ha-Meliẓah* ("Treasury of Verse and Metaphor," 1922); *Moreh ha-Signon ve-Shimmush ha-Lashon ha-Ivrit* ("Instructor in Hebrew Style and Usage," c. 1890), and others; and *Torat ha-Nikkud* ("Laws of Vocalization," 1904). Tawiow also tried his hand at belles-lettres, writing, among other works, a comedy called *Ha-Sorer be-Veito* (1900). He also translated works by Berthold Auerbach, Oscar Wilde, and Charles Dickens.

BIBLIOGRAPHY: M. Bobé, in: *He-Avar*, 16 (May 1969), 141–63; N. Slouschz, *Renascence of Hebrew Literature* (1909), 281; Waxman, Literature, 4 (1960^2), 85. **ADD. BIBLIOGRAPHY:** G. Shaked, *Ha-Sipporet ha-Ivrit*, 1 (1977), 219–50.

[Gedalyah Elkoshi]

TAWRIZI, JUDAH MEIR BEN ABRAHAM (d. before 1646), Karaite physician and author living in Jerusalem. His works comprise an Arabic commentary on the Book of Esther, in which he frequently quotes *Rabbanite authors and cites Rabbanite customs, and mentions the *blood libel; and glosses to the code of Karaite law (entitled *al-Murshid*) of *Samuel al-Maghribī, in which he too refers to Rabbanite codes. He also composed Hebrew liturgical hymns. The appellation Tawrīzī (less correctly Taurīzī) is said to be a dialectal form of Tabrīzī, indicating that the family originated in the Persian city of *Tabriz. Judah Meir's son, ABRAHAM MEIR, also practiced medicine and wrote liturgical poetry.

BIBLIOGRAPHY: Steinschneider, Arab Lit, 258; Mann, Texts, 2 (1935), 70f., 106–8.

[Leon Nemoy]

TAX, SOL (1907–1995), U.S. anthropologist. Born in Chicago, Illinois, Tax received a Ph.B. from the University of Wisconsin (1931) and a Ph.D. from the University of Chicago in 1935. He joined the faculty of the University of Chicago in 1940, where he taught until his retirement in 1974. He was appointed chairman of the anthropology department in 1955 and served as dean of the adult education extension school from 1962 to 1968. He served as editor of *American Anthropologist* (1952–55). In 1957 he founded the international journal *Current Anthropology*, which he edited until 1974. He served as director of the Fox Indian Project in Iowa (1948–62). He did fieldwork among the Mescalero Apache (1931), the Guatemalan Indians (1934–41), and the Chukas Indians of Mexico (1942–43). In 1961, Tax coordinated the American Indian Chicago Conference, which assembled 700 Native Americans from more than 80 tribal groups at the University of Chicago. They prepared a Declaration of Indian Purpose, which sought to present a unified position on the relation of native people to the American government. In the 1960s and 1970s, Tax's work included research in developing countries and the former Soviet Union.

Tax was an acknowledged head of the "action anthropologists," a school that holds that the task of the field worker is not just to undertake research but also to assist in the acculturation of the native populations he studies. He repeatedly called for the improvement of living conditions on American Indian reservations in accordance with the Indians' own desires and aspirations.

In another vein, Tax organized a conference on the military draft in 1968, bringing together military leaders and political figures to discuss the issue of the draft and its alternatives.

Tax was president of the American Anthropological Association (1958–59). He also served as director of the Smithsonian Institution's Center for the Study of Man; served on the U.S. National Commission for UNESCO; and served on President Johnson's special task force on American Indian Affairs. Tax was a consultant for the U.S. Office of Education; the U.S. Bureau of Indian Affairs; the National Institute of Mental Health; and the Smithsonian Institution. In 1962 he received the Viking Fund Medal and Award from the Wenner-Gren Foundation for Anthropological Research.

Among his books are *Acculturation in the Americas* (1952), *Penny Capitalism: A Guatemalan Indian Economy* (1953), *The Evolution of Man* (1960), *Acculturation in the Americas* (1967), *Heritage of Conquest* (1968), and *Cultures beyond the Earth* (1975). The books he edited include *An Appraisal of Anthropology Today* (1954), *Evolution after Darwin* (1960), *The Draft* (1967), *The People vs. the System* (1968), and *Horizons of Anthropology* (1977).

ADD. BIBLIOGRAPHY: *Representative Papers of Sol Tax, 1937–1977* (1977); R. Hinshaw (ed.), *Currents in Anthropology: Essays in Honor of Sol Tax* (1979); R. Rubinstein (ed.), *Fieldwork: The Correspondence of Robert Redfield & Sol Tax* (1991).

[Ephraim Fischoff / Ruth Beloff (2nd ed.)]

TAXATION. This article is arranged according to the following outline:

Special taxation imposed on the Jews by the state or ruler of the territory in which they were living has played a most important part in Jewish history.

HISTORICAL ASPECTS

It is self-evident that a section of the population of a country which pays special taxes must receive special organization and hold a special status (see *autonomy). On the other hand, the abolition of such special taxation implies an approach at least to parity of status and ultimate *emancipation. The state generally tended to impose the tax burden on the Jews by as simple and mechanical a means as possible – per capita, on houses, and the like. Hence the Jewish community body, which had the collective responsibility for the tax, usually tried to redistribute the amount to be paid on more equitable and less mechanical principles; this led to constructive social developments as well as tensions within the community.

Talmudic literature is filled with complaints against the severity of the taxation in Ereẓ Israel during the period of Roman domination. However intolerable this may have seemed, it was not discriminatory, and the pagan population of the area doubtless had similar complaints. On the other hand, the **Fiscus Judaicus* introduced after the fall of Jerusalem in 70 C.E., diverting to the temple of Jupiter Capitolinus in Rome the half-shekel formerly paid voluntarily each year by every Jew to the Temple in Jerusalem, was definitely discriminatory, paid by no other than Jews. It was thus the forerunner of the discriminatory taxation of the Jews in Europe in the Middle Ages, and it was precisely imitated in the **opferpfennig* poll tax exacted by the Holy Roman Emperors in Germany, as successors to the Roman caesars, from 1342. On the other hand, the Temple tax was in a way revived in the semi-voluntary **aurum coronarium* levied by the Palestinian patriarchs from the Jewish communities to which their authority reached.

In the Dark Ages, especially in south Italy and Sicily, the Jews were so far identified with the dyeing industry that the special dye tax was known as the *tincta judeorum*, etc., implying that it was paid in effect only by Jews: this, which was claimed by the local bishops as their perquisite, thus became in effect a discriminatory Jewish tax. The Muslim world meanwhile imposed on the Jews, as on other nonbelievers, two special taxes – the **kharaj*, a land tax in lieu of military service, calculated according to the productivity of the holding, and the *jizya*, a poll tax levied on unbelievers as the price of the free exercise of their religion. It is a moot point long discussed whether Jews paid special taxes in the Byzantine Empire. But when *Benjamin of Tudela was in Rome around 1169 he recorded as noteworthy that the Jews there paid no special tax to any authority.

With the development of Jewish finance in northern Europe the special taxation of the Jews entered on a new phase. One of the reasons for the toleration and protection they now received from the authorities was, precisely, their utility to the treasury. Every financial transaction was now subject to a tax in order to regularize it. Every phase in daily life – such as marriage or betrothal – required the royal license. Death duties ("reliefs") of as much as one-third were imposed on the estates of wealthy financiers. Fines were imposed on individuals, on communities, or on the entire body of Jews of a country to atone for misdemeanors, real or fictitious. In due course, in countries such as England, the system of "tallage" was introduced: theoretically an impost to meet some special contingency, it became, so far as the Jews were concerned, a regular source of royal revenue. Most detailed information regarding the method of exaction is available from England. The heads of the community were assembled and the royal demands intimated to them. The total amount would be divided among the various communities, which in turn would apportion the assessment among individuals. The so-called Jewish Parliament of *Worcester (1240–41) under Henry III consisted of from two to six representatives of every community of England, convened to apportion a tallage of 20,000 marks imposed on them. With the development of the financial organization of the *Exchequer of the Jews, a preliminary to the imposition of a tallage would be the closing of the **ar-chae*, or chirograph chests, which would be sent to the Exchequer for their contents to be investigated and the capability of each individual to pay determined; on some occasions this would be accompanied by wholesale arrests among the Jews to forestall evasion.

The systematic cancellation of debts due to the Jews in return for some immediate monetary payment from the debtors, especially in Germany from the close of the 14th century, was in effect an indirect method of taxation. In the same country a special poll tax similar to that levied on animals, and included in the same list of tolls, had to be paid by Jews at the entrance to every town and state. Even when dead, there was a special toll to be paid at the city boundary on the way to the cemetery. In *Frankfurt, no fewer than 38 different imposts were levied on the Jews, mostly additional to those payable by the other townsfolk. Any Jew encountered on the highway could be compelled to pay the dice tax to atone for the casting of lots for the garments of Jesus at the crucifixion. The tolls on the road, known as the *impôt du pied fourchu* ("toll of the cloven hoof"), were abolished in the eastern provinces of France only in 1784.

In medieval Spain, taxation covering both payments due to the treasury and those for the maintenance of communal institutions was levied generally on incomes, estimated either by assessors (*posekim*) or by individual declaration under oath. As a result of complaints, in 1300 James II of Aragon imposed the method of declaration in his dominion. Henceforth, all taxes both communal and royal were to be apportioned by a board representing the three economic strata of the community (*manus*) before whom every taxpayer was to declare his income under oath. Groups of small Spanish communities were combined by the treasury as a *collecta* for taxation purposes. For the system as it applied in a typical Spanish community see *Huesca.

In *Sicily there were a large number of special levies – apart from the poll tax (*jizya*) still retained from Saracenic times – on animals slaughtered in the Jewish fashion, on wine and cheese prepared for Jewish use, on cloth of Jewish manufacture, a "beam tax" on the sale of houses, a tax for permission to have musicians at weddings, and even a tax on childbirth. This was apart from the obligation to provide banners for the royal galleys and similar exigencies. A "Jewish Parliament," for the purpose of allocating taxation among the Jewish communities, similar to that held at Worcester in England in 1240–41, was convened at *Palermo in 1489 (Lagumina 754). In the ghetto period in Italy a graduated tax was originally levied on income or capital, it being left largely to the individual to assess the contribution he should make. In Venice, Padua, and other cities the assessments were made by a secret commission of *transadori*, whose identity was concealed from the contributors. At the close of the 17th century, a new system was widely introduced, known as the "*cassella*," or chest, in which the amounts were deposited at stipulated times in the presence of officials sworn to secrecy. A sermon would be delivered by the rabbi on the previous Sabbath emphasizing the moral duty of meticulous honesty. In some places money boxes were to be found also in certain buildings, where the prescribed percentage on brokerage could be deposited immediately. The conditions governing the system, which differed widely in details from place to place, were usually printed at intervals, in Italian or in Hebrew, for the guidance of the contributors. In Rome, in addition to the extraordinary impositions, regular taxes included a levy for the upkeep of the House of *Catechumens, another for the expenses of the carnival, and so on. Here as elsewhere in the Papal States the basis of the financial system was a tax not on income but on property, fixed for *Rome at 5 percent; at *Ferrara at 3 percent; at *Ancona at 1 percent, ultimately raised to 1¼ percent.

A meat or *sheḥitah* tax was very common throughout the Jewish world, sometimes payable not in currency but in tokens (see *medals). In effect, this was also in its way a tax graduated according to means, it being assumed that the wealthy ate more luxuriously than the poor. Where the system of voluntary assessment was used in Italy, it was reinforced by a ban of excommunication on any person who knowingly made a fraudulent declaration of his income, and he would thus bear a constant burden of sin of which he alone was aware. Throughout the Jewish world, rabbis and scholars were supposed to be exempt from communal taxation, this often leading to complications and internal disputes. The Council of the Four Lands in Poland-Lithuania (see *Councils of Lands) owed its origin to the need for having a recognized and authoritative body for the assessment of the state taxes on the Jewish population, and, formally, this was the sole function of the council in the eyes of the state. The overall sum was distributed among the "provinces" which in turn divided their quotas among the individual communities. In the first half of the 19th century special taxation, e.g., on *kasher* meat (**korobka*) and the Sabbath candles (*candle tax), was used in Russia as an instrument to discourage traditional observances in the Jewish communities.

After the Resettlement of the Jews in England, various proposals were made for the separate taxation of the Jews for the benefit of the Exchequer. None however was implemented, and this was of great importance in establishing for the Jews the equality of status which was the preliminary to emancipation. The example of the mother country, with the same implications, was imitated in the American colonies; though in *Jamaica and the *West Indies special taxation of the Jews was the rule until the early 19th century. The abolition of special taxation was a corollary to the admission of the Jews to civil rights in France and elsewhere on the continent of Europe at the end of the 18th and beginning of the 19th centuries.

After the emancipation and the end of the special levies on the Jews, some sort of communal taxation remained necessary to defray the cost of communal institutions. The synagogues were generally maintained by membership dues, pew rentals, and voluntary offerings. In the Sephardi communities of northern Europe, etc., the system of *finta* assessed on estimated income by *fintadores* was widely used. The United Synagogue in London imposed a heavy levy on tombstones in order to defray the costs of education. In countries such as Germany and Italy, where the officially recognized Jewish communities were regulated by law, they had the right to impose taxation on all members, which was exacted by the governmental agencies, for the maintenance of essential institutions: refusal to pay hence became equivalent to withdrawal from the Jewish community. In *Argentina the Ashkenazi community paid a small due fee and most of the money for community affairs came from the high taxes on tombstones, whereas in the Sephardi community the percentage of intake was almost reversed. The situation was not much different in other South American communities.

For taxation in modern Israel see *Israel.

[Cecil Roth]

LEGAL ASPECTS

The Biblical Period

Although no detailed description has come down of the taxation system practiced during this period, various particulars of it can be gathered from a number of scriptural references to the subject. Thus the prerogatives enumerated in I Samuel 8:11–17 give an indication of the servitudes, levies, and obligations which the king was entitled to impose on the population, including the following: a tenth of the yield of the field and of the vineyard and the flock, a levy on the vineyard and the olive grove, and compulsory personal service. The biblical description reflects the fiscal system in operation in the Canaanite city kingdoms. The First Book of Kings (4:7–15) tells of King Solomon's division of the kingdom into 12 administrative units, each under the charge of an officer responsible for providing the king and his household with victuals for one month in the year.

TERMINOLOGY. Matters of taxation are mentioned in the Bible under a variety of terms, a number of which continued to be in use in later times. One of these, *mekhes* (Num. 31:28, 37–41), is mentioned in connection with the tribute paid to the priests from the spoil of the war with the Midianites. The like term in Akkadian, *miksu*, described both a tribute from the yield of the fields and a toll levied on travelers and their goods (EM, 4 (1962), 964f.), and in the latter sense the term *mekhes* was employed by the sages of the Talmud (see, e.g., Kil. 9:2; Shab. 8:2, Sem. 2:9) and is still in use in modern Hebrew in the State of Israel. It is clear that a toll of this kind was levied by the kings of Israel on goods imported from abroad or those in transit (cf. I Kings 10:15). In the Bible the term *mas* (mod. Heb. for "tax") occurs in the sense of compulsory labor in the king's service (Ex. 1:11; II Sam 20:24; I Kings 4:6 and 5:27), and is synonymous with the term *mas oved* (JPS, "taskwork"). The main taxes imposed for the benefit of the Persian kingdom were the *mindeh, belo,* and *halakh*, which are mentioned in the letter of the Persian king to the scribe Ezra, exempting all the priests, levites, and other servants of the "house of God" from their payment (Ezra 7:24). The *mindeh* was a general tax payable in money, the *belo* a tax in specie, and the *halakh* apparently a tax on land. Besides the regular taxes, the king apparently from time to time imposed taxes on the people for special purposes, such as those exacted by Menahem and Jehoiakim for payment to the conquerors (II Kings 15:19–20 and 23:35).

Some of the tax alleviations mentioned in the Bible include exemptions given to "the father's house" in reward for a person's act of special bravery (I Sam. 17:25), the general release granted in celebration of a special occasion – as in the case of Queen Esther's coronation (Esth. 2:18) – and the exemption given to the servants of the Temple. At times the tax burden weighed heavily on the people and the oppressive fiscal policy followed in the time of King Solomon was a cause of the rebellion against his son Rehoboam (I Kings 12) and led to the killing of Adoram, the officer in charge of the levy. In a sense the concept of tax, as an imposed duty to contribute toward the needs of an individual, or of the public, is reflected also in the laws relating to matters of **terumah* ("heave offering"); *ma'aser* ("tithe"); **leket*, **shikhḥah*, and **pe'ah* ("gleanings," "the forgotten sheaf," and "the corner of the fields," respectively); **ẓedakah* ("charity"), the half-and third-**shekel*; *shemittah* ("the year of the release"); and *yovel* ("*Jubilee").

The Talmudic Period

The Talmud discusses both those taxes imposed by the Jewish local authorities on the Jewish town residents and those imposed by the central governmental authority on the Jewish public. The material on the laws of taxation during this period is scant, but the laws discussed nevertheless formed the basis of a number of post-talmudic tax rules.

JEWISH MUNICIPAL TAXES. "The resident of a town may be compelled to contribute to the building of a [town] wall, doors, and a crossbar" (BB 1:5), and to the building of a prayer house, to the purchase of the Scrolls of the Law and of the Prophets (Tosef., BM 11:23), and to the hire of the town guards (BB 8a). Similarly, he may be compelled to contribute toward the cost of the town's water supply and drainage system, an expense which must also be borne by a person who owns a dwelling in the town even though he is not resident there (Tosef., BM 11:17 according to the Vienna MS; see also Yad, Shekhenim 6:3; Resp. Maharam of Rothenburg quoted in *Mordekhai*, BB 475; Sh. Ar., ḤM 163:2). In the same way the townsmen have to contribute toward the cost of providing the poor with food and clothing and toward the communal charity box and *ma'ot ḥittin* (money for the poor to buy wheat on Passover; BB *ibid.*; TJ, BB 1:4, 12d). For the purpose of liability for some of these taxes – namely for repair of the wall or *ma'ot ḥittin* – a person is regarded in the Talmud (TJ and TB, *ibid.*) as a resident if he has lived in a town for 12 months; if he has bought a dwelling there he immediately becomes liable; as regards certain contributions, e.g., to the charity box, he becomes liable upon shorter periods of residence (*ibid.*, see also *Domicile; with regard to *ma'ot ḥittin* on Passover, see further *Or Zaru'a*, Hilkhot Pesaḥim, no. 255).

The *amoraim* of Ereẓ Israel discussed the principle of yardsticks for determining the rate of such taxes, deliberating whether a tax should be levied as a poll tax (according to the number of persons in the family), or according to financial means, or "according to the proximity of the dwelling" (that is according to the measure of benefit the taxpayer derived from his relative proximity to the wall), the first method being rejected in favor of one of the other two (BB 7b). The majority of the *posekim* held that these two yardsticks should be combined in such a manner that the rate of contribution would first be apportioned according to the financial means of each resident and then according to the measure of benefit derived from his relative proximity to the wall, so that "a poor man nearer the wall shall pay more than one further away; a rich man nearer the wall shall pay more than one further away, but a rich man further from the wall shall pay more than a poor man nearer the wall" (Tos. to BB 7b; Tur and Sh. Ar., ḤM 163:3; for a different opinion, see Yad, Shekhenim 6:4 and R. Hananel, BB *ibid.*). A similar problem is discussed in the Talmud in connection with a caravan in the wilderness threatened by a band of robbers and it is stated that: "the contribution to be paid by each [for buying them off] shall be apportioned in accordance with the amount of money which each has and not in accordance with the number of persons there"; but if they hire a guide to go in front of them, the calculation will have to be made "also according to the number of souls" in the caravan since a misstep could involve danger to life (Tosef., BM 7:13; BK 116b; in the TJ, BM 6:4, 11a the word "also" is omitted before the words "according to the number of souls"); however all this only applies if the manner of apportionment of the contribution is not determined by local custom, since this always prevails (BK 116b; see also Tosef., BK, and TJ, loc. cit.).

TAXES OF THE CENTRAL GOVERNMENT. The tannaitic and amoraic sources mention various kinds of taxes imposed by the general government. Some of those imposed by the Roman authorities in Ereẓ Israel included the *tributum soli*, a land tax, the *tributum capitis* or poll tax, *arnona*, and a customs toll on the transit of goods, as well as a toll on highways and bridges (see Alon, bibl.). Among the taxes levied by the Persian authorities were the *taska*, a land tax, and the *karga*, a poll tax (see J. Newman, bibl.).

The Persian Government in Babylonia. The Babylonian halakhic scholars upheld the various taxes imposed by the governmental authorities, in reliance on the rule of **dina de-malkhuta dina* ("the law of the land is law," BB 55a, et al.), even giving effect to certain acts which were valid under general law but not in Jewish law. Thus under Persian law a person's land became charged in the king's favor for payment of the *taska*, and if it was not paid the land could be sold by the royal officials to anyone paying the tax in the landowner's stead. The *amora* Samuel upheld the validity of such a sale on the basis of the above-mentioned rule (BB 55a; see also BM 73b); Similarly upheld was the rule of Persian law that not only the king could enslave a person who failed to pay the *karga* but anyone else paying the tax in the debtor's stead (Yev. 46a; BM 73b) – except that in Jewish law "he shall not treat him as a slave" (Yad, Gezelah, 5:16; Sh. Ar., YD 267:16).

The Roman Government in Ereẓ Israel. The scholars of Ereẓ Israel, however, looked upon the Romans as foreign conquerors whose rule should be rebelled against and whose taxes were an instrument of robbery and extortion leveled against the Jews. Hence tax evasion was customary in Ereẓ Israel (Ned. 3:4; TJ, Sot. 5:7; BB 127b, R. Johanan) and there the *tannaim* discussed the question of whether or not it was permissible to avoid paying customs in certain circumstances (BK 113a). A certain change of attitude is manifest at the time of R. Judah ha-Nasi, who, like some other men, instructed his sons not to elude customs (lest they be detected and the authorities confiscate everything they had; Pes. 112b; cf. TJ, Ket. 12:3). Regarded in a similarly unfavorable light were the *gabba'im* and *mokhesim* – Jewish officials and publicans who collected taxes and imposts on behalf of the Roman authorities – who were looked upon as robbers and disqualified from being witnesses or judges (Sanh. 25b), whose money could not be taken for charitable purposes (BK 10:1), and who were not acceptable as **ḥaverim* (Tosef., Dem. 3:4; TJ, Dem. 2:3). At a later time the opposition to Roman rule became less intense and the *halakhot* permitting customs evasion came to be interpreted as applying to customs dues imposed without any specified limit or those imposed without the authority of the ruling power (but by the customs collector himself) – in which case it was held that the rule of *dina de-malkhuta dina* did not apply (BK 113a; Ned. 28a). Customs evasion eventually became strictly prohibited: "a person who evades customs is as one who has shed blood – and not only shed blood, but also worshiped idols, committed acts of unchastity, and profaned the Sabbath" (Sem. 2:9). Similarly, it was laid down in the codes: "If the king fixes a tax of, say, a third or a quarter or another fixed measure and appoints to collect it on his behalf an Israelite known to be a trustworthy person who would not add to what was ordered by the king, this collector is not presumed to be a robber, for the king's decree has the force of law. Moreover, one who avoids paying such a tax is a transgressor, for he steals the king's property, whether the king be a gentile or an Israelite" (Yad, Gezelah, 5:11; cf. Sanh. 25b).

TAX IMMUNITY. Just as the Persian rulers exempted priests, levites, and other servants of the Temple from the payment of taxes, so the sages of the Talmud laid down that *talmidei ḥakhamim* should be exempted from contributing toward the upkeep of the town guard – for the reason that they did not need any protection since the Torah was their guard (Ned. 62b; BB 7bff.). However, some of the sages did not exempt rabbinical scholars from such imposts (R. Judah ha-Nasi and R. Naḥman b. Ḥisda, BB *ibid.*) and the fact that there were scholars who paid these is confirmed in several talmudic sources (see e.g., Yev. 17a; Sanh. 27a–b; Yoma 77a – expunged by the censorship and quoted in *Ein Ya'akov* and *Dikdukei Soferim*, Yoma 77a). Exemption of scholars from tax payments was known in other contemporary legal systems (see S. Lieberman, in: JQR, 36 (1945/46), 360–4) and was also a practice in later times (see below). It was laid down that rabbinical scholars must pay taxes levied for the upkeep of roads and streets (BB 8a; Yad, Shekhenim, 6:6; Sh. Ar., YD 243:2, and ḤM 163:4). *Orphans (whose liabilities are lightened in a number of respects in Jewish law) must contribute taxes for purposes of the town guard, the digging of a well, the supply of water to the town and fields, and toward all other matters from which they derive benefit; if the expenditure fails to bring about the desired result, the orphans will be entitled to a refund of whatever they paid, since in the absence of a benefit such payment amounts to a waiver of their money, an act beyond their legal capacity (BB loc. cit. and *Rashi* thereto; Yad, and Sh. Ar., loc. cit.). In the case of an unemployed person who has no income (a *pardakht*) the town residents may approach the government tax collector to release him from his tax contribution; sometimes he is held liable like all other residents and sometimes released (BB 55a; see also *Rashbam*, Tos., *Beit ha-Beḥirah* and *Shitah Mekubbeẓet* thereto; Kohut, Arukh, s.v. "אנדיסק" and supplement thereto s.v. "פרדכש"; M. Beer, bibl., pp. 250f.).

The Post-Talmudic Period in General

The main development of Jewish tax law came in the post-talmudic period, both as regards the determination of general principles and detailed rules and as regards the volume and compass of the material. At the same time this development was an important factor in the evolution of Jewish public law and a number of basic principles in this field evolved from the discussions on the laws of taxation. Therefore a comprehensive discussion of the laws of taxation offers some insight into the evolution of Jewish public and administrative law (see also *Public Authority).

In the post-talmudic period the distinction between Jewish municipal taxes and those imposed by the government was maintained as the basis for discussion of the laws of taxation, and the great development in this branch of the law is mainly to be ascribed to two historical factors affecting the Jewish people, one internal, the other external. From the close of the geonic period onward, Jewish autonomy found its main expression in the various Jewish communal organizations or in a roof organization embracing a number of communities. Starting from this time Jewish life was molded by the new historical reality that hegemony was no longer exercised over the whole Jewish dispersion by a single center – as previously in Ereẓ Israel and Babylonia – and different centers, functioning alongside or in succession to one another, came into existence in Spain, Germany, North Africa, the Balkan countries, Poland, Western Europe, and so on. The result was the strengthening of the individual community and the development of its organizations, and this led in turn to great development in the fields of administrative law and communal enactment (see *Takkanot ha-Kahal*), and to the creation of a proliferous collection of decisions concerning relations between the citizen and the public. The community provided various social services and maintained religious, educational, and judicial institutions, as well as its own administrative and governing bodies, all of which had to be financed through various methods of taxation.

The decisive external factor was that the central governments of the various countries of Jewish settlement in the Middle Ages imposed heavy taxes on the Jews (as "toleration money") in return for their right to live in these countries, and the halakhic scholars stressed their factual purpose so far as the Jewish community was concerned: "the various taxes are for the purposes of protection and they guard us amid the nations; for what reason would the nations have to protect us and to settle us in their midst if not for the benefit they derive by exacting taxes and imposts from the Jews?" (Resp. Ran, no. 2; *Piskei ha-Rosh*, BB 1:29). These taxes were not imposed on the individual directly, but collectively on all the communities in a particular area or on a specific community, and the authorities held the communal leaders responsible for payment of the overall amount. Thus "in all matters of taxation each community has been obliged to make a partnership of its members… since the king makes a general demand and not from the individual" (Resp. Rashba, vol. 5, no. 270). Normally the central authority periodically imposed a "fixed tax" of a comparatively reasonable amount. Sometimes however – on account of special circumstances such as war – an "unlimited tax" of a very large sum of money was imposed, and in these cases the scholars laid down different rules from those governing the regular tax (see illustrations below; on the two types of taxes, see, e.g., *Terumat ha-Deshen*, beginning of Resp. no. 341 and conclusion of no. 342). The fact that taxes were collected by the community both for its own purposes and on behalf of the central authority was instrumental in the development of a refined tax law system governing matters such as determination of the rate of contribution to the tax and tax classification, assessment adjudication and collection, and determination of tax alleviations and exemptions, a system which was evolved in close cooperation between the halakhic scholars and communal leaders.

LEGAL FOUNDATIONS OF THE TAX LAW SYSTEM. In part, the tax law of this period was based on the legal principles determined by the scholars in talmudic times, but in the main it was derived from additional legal sources.

Dina de-Malkhuta Dina. This doctrine was relied upon and its application extended to meet the new and changing needs of the time. Thus, for instance, many scholars found it necessary to decide – contrary to the rule in the Talmud that the doctrine of *dina de-malkhuta dina* does not apply to an unlimited tax – that a tax exacted for the waging of war and "other costly needs" should be heeded even if it was an unlimited tax (R. Isaac the Elder, quoted in *Haggahot Mordekhai*, BB no.

659 end, and in *Teshuvot Maimuniyyot*, Gezelah, no. 9). This change resulted from the strong hand displayed by the ruling power, particularly in the case of German Jewry: "even if our taxes at the present time have no fixed rate but are imposed at the will of the ruler, it is necessary that they be paid and whoever fails to do so is liable to suffer punishment of death, plunder, or imprisonment… for in these times these are all called taxes" (*Mordekhai*, BK no. 190, in the name of Meir of Rothenburg; see also Resp. Ḥayyim Or Zaru'a, no. 253, and cf. his criticism, no. 110; Resp. Maharil, no. 71; Resp. Maharyw (Jacob Weil), no. 38). In Spain, too, in the 14th century, a similar opinion was expressed although in a different context: "all government decrees concerning Jews, even as regards a monetary fine, are a matter of *pikku'aḥ nefesh*" (Resp. Ribash, no. 460). From the legal standpoint this approach was justified by the scholars on the grounds that since it was known that the ruling power behaved in the manner described and that with that knowledge "we establish residence under them and take upon ourselves the hardships and burdens they impose, all of these shall henceforth fall under the rule of *dina de-malkhuta dina*" (*Terumat ha-Deshen*, Resp. no. 341; see also Resp. Maharam Mintz, no. 1; Resp. Maharik, no. 4; for further illustrations see below).

Tax Rules from the Talmudic Period. The principle that the town residents must contribute toward the costs of their security needs, the provision of social and religious services, sanitation, and so on, was applied and extended in post-talmudic times to the payment of various other taxes (Meir of Rothenburg, quoted in *Mordekhai*, BB, 478) and generally to "any matter of the town's needs" (*Mordekhai*, loc. cit.; Resp.Rosh, 6:22) so as to cover the whole spectrum of the community's requirements (Sh. Ar., ḤM 163:1, and see below).

The Community as Partnership. In addition, the post-talmudic scholars applied to the legal relationship between different members of the community the law of *partnership, and by virtue of this deduced a number of conclusions pertaining to the field of tax law. Thus, for instance, they based the legal right to oblige a community member to swear that his declaration of taxable assets was correct (see below) on the rule that one partner may oblige his fellow to swear an oath even in the case of a "doubtful" plea (*ta'anat shema*; *Terumat ha-Deshen*, Resp. no. 341). The rule that a community member might not secure a personal tax waiver except through the mediation of the community was justified likewise on the principle of partnership law restricting a partner's right to enjoy personally a benefit which should be enjoyed by the whole partnership without the consent of his partners (Resp. Maharam of Rothenburg, ed. Prague, no. 918, 932). Similarly, the scholars followed the rule that partners are jointly liable for the whole of a partnership debt in laying down that all members of the community bore collective responsibility for the whole amount of the tax imposed (Resp. Rosh 5:9; for further illustration see, e.g., *Mordekhai*, Ket. no. 239; *Rema*, ḤM 163:3, 6 and 176:25; *Noda bi-Yhudah*, Mahadura Tinyana, ḤM no. 40, and see below).

Communal Enactments (Takkanot ha-Kahal) and Custom. The scholars found the methods outlined above insufficient to overcome the wide array of tax law problems with which they and the communal leaders were confronted. Application of the private law rules of partnership offered no comprehensive basis for solving the myriad tax law problems that arose and belonged, by their very nature, to the field of the public law – not only because partnership law offered no analogy for the overwhelming majority of tax law matters but also because a legal arrangement governing relationships between two or three partners was often unsuited to regulation of the legal relationships between all the different units comprising the community. They found the way to settling most of the laws of taxation through using the authority vested in the public to make enactments (see **Takkanot ha-Kahal*), and by means of the legal source of custom (see **Minhag*). A certain initial hesitation over the binding nature of a custom when it was contrary to "an established and known *halakhah*" of the Talmud on a matter of tax law (see the statement of R. Baruch of Mainz in the 13th century, quoted in *Mordekhai*, BB no. 477) was overcome, and every rule and usage deriving from communal enactment or custom was given full legal recognition. The fact that these two legal sources were instrumental in the development of most of the post-talmudic tax laws accounts, therefore, for the great diversity found in Jewish tax law, which reflects the *takkanot* and customs of the various Jewish communities.

The existence of this fact was constantly stressed by the halakhic scholars of all communities. Thus Solomon b. Abraham *Adret, leader of Spanish Jewry in the 13th century and one of the main formulators of Jewish public law, stated: "Nowhere are the tax laws founded on talmudic sanctity and everywhere there are to be found variations of such laws deriving from local usage and the consent of earlier scholars who 'set the landmarks,' and the town residents are entitled to establish fixed *takkanot* and uphold recognized customs as they please even if they do not accord with the *halakhah*, this being a matter of the civil law. Therefore if in this matter they have a known custom it should be followed, since custom overrides the *halakhah* in matters of this kind" (Resp. Rashba, vol. 4, nos. 260, 177; vol. 3, nos. 398, 436; vol. 5, nos. 180, 363, 270; vol. 1, no. 664, et al.). A similar view was expressed by R. *Meir b. Baruch of Rothenburg, a contemporary of Adret and leader of German Jewry: "tax matters are dependent neither on analogy from nor on express talmudic law, but on the custom of the land… since tax laws are part of the law of the land… and the product of many different customs" (Resp. Maharam of Rothenburg, ed. Prague, nos. 106, 995; see also the statements of R. Avigdor Kohen Ẓedek, quoted in *Mordekhai*, BB, 477). R. Israel *Isserlein added the following explicit remarks: "In all matters affecting the public, their custom shall be followed in accordance with the order they set for themselves, as dictated by their needs and the matter under consideration – for if they be required to follow the strict law in every matter, there will always be strife among themselves; furthermore, at the outset they allow each other to waive the strict law and make up their minds to follow the imperatives of their own custom" (*Terumat ha-Deshen*, Resp. no. 342). This idea was restated in a responsum of the 16th-century Greek halakhist, Benjamin Ze'ev (*Binyamin Ze'ev*, 293), who added: "a custom of the town residents overrides [a decision of] a court of talmudic scholars, even though it has relied on Scripture, and not merely the custom of scholars but also the custom of ass drivers is to be relied upon" (see also Resp. Maharashdam, ḤM nos. 369 and 404; *Noda bi-Yhudah*, Mahadura Tinyana, ḤM no. 40).

In the context of tax law, important principles pertaining to custom in general were laid down. These included the stipulation that a custom must be established and widespread: "that the town residents practiced the custom at least three times, for often the public reaches a conclusion according to need without intending to establish a custom at all" (*Terumat ha-Deshen*, Resp. no. 342). Similarly, it was decided that the established existence of a custom need not be proved in the formal ways prescribed by the laws of evidence: "although it is necessary to inquire whether a custom is established or not, the inquiry itself need not be overly formal and hearsay evidence as well as the evidence of disqualified witnesses is admissible" (*ibid.*). These principles were accepted as decided law (*Darkhei Moshe*, ḤM 163, n. 7; *Rema*, ḤM 163: 3). (For validity of a "bad custom" in the tax law field, see *Minhag.)

An exaggerated proliferation of local *takkanot* and customs was prevented by the fact that these were usually enacted for or adopted by all the communities in a particular region. Thus Solomon b. Abraham Adret relates that the Jewish community of Barcelona and its environs enacted uniform *takkanot* in the matter of taxes, their assessment and collection – "one chest and one pocket for us all" – and he describes how the community of Barcelona proper, the largest in the region, first consulted with all the surrounding communities on the *takkanot* to be enacted, although in other areas the main community sometimes neglected such prior consultation (Resp. Rashba, vol. 3, no. 412). Other regional enactments of this kind are evidenced in the *takkanot* of Vallidolid (of 1432) and those of the German communities (see Finkelstein, bibl.; also Halpern, Pinkas; *Takkanot Medinat Mehrin; Pinkas ha-Medinah*, bibl.; see further Resp. Maharam of Rothenburg, ed., Prague, no. 241; *Massa Melekh*, 5: 1, 1–3).

INTEGRATION OF TAX LAW INTO THE JEWISH LEGAL SYSTEM. The creation of tax laws in this manner carried with it the danger that the link between this branch of the law and the overall system of Jewish law, which was based on the talmudic *halakhah* and its evolution, might become weakened. This aspect was stressed by the halakhic scholars, and Solomon b. Abraham Adret, for instance, pointed out the diversity in tax laws and noted that this was because the communal enactments were not based on binding talmudic law, "for if so there would be one measure for all the communities, as there is in regard to all other laws of the Torah" (Resp. Rashba, vol. 5, no. 270; and see also vol. 3, no. 412). The scholars and communal leaders nevertheless succeeded in preserving the proliferous body of the tax laws that developed in the Diaspora during this period as an integral part of the Jewish legal system, mainly through adherence to the principles enumerated below.

Reliance on Halakhic Sources. The halakhic scholars were understandably anxious to establish a link between the various *takkanot* and customs and the strict law: "even though it has been said... that in tax matters custom overrides the law, it is at any rate desirable and proper to examine carefully whether we can reconcile all the customs with the strict law, and even if not entirely so it is yet preferable that we find support in the teachings of the scholars and substantiate them with the aid of reason and logic" (*Terumat ha-Deshen*, Resp. no. 342). Thus, for example, support in the form of several talmudic references, was found for the widely accepted custom that a person appealing against a tax assessment has first to pay as assessed before the legal hearing could take place, even though this custom was in contradiction to the Jewish law principle that the burden of proof is on the claimant (see below). Similarly, a *takkanah* aimed at extending the creditor's lien to cover also a tax debtor's money in the hands of a third party even when it was no longer held in specie – and contrary to a rule of the Talmud – was justified by R. Nissim by way of an interpretation which lent a specific legal character to a tax debt (see below). An interesting expression of this general trend is found in two responsa of the 17th-century German halakhic scholar Jair Ḥayyim *Bacharach (Resp. *Ḥavvot Ya'ir*, nos. 57, 58), who was consulted in both cases by the communal leaders on the procedure to be followed upon their discovery that the taxpayer's assets in fact far exceeded the amount on which he had been assessed. After giving a detailed exposition of the talmudic law and existing custom concerning tax assessment, Bacharach went on to describe his approach to the question of integrating law and *takkanot* in the field of taxation: "although certainly in assessment and related matters the community has authority to act as it thinks proper, and it is not necessary to hearken to the voice of a person who seeks to find the original approach of the law [on these matters], yet you should endeavor to examine the reasoning of our scholars and call it to your aid... and thereafter do as you see fit, keeping close to the law of the Torah." Having dealt with the attitude of the *halakhah* and with the existing *takkanot* and customs, Bacharach concluded by stating: "So my humble opinion tends to be like the decisions which are given by lay tribunals [*piskei ba'alei battim*; see *Mishpat Ivri*] together with some measure of application of the strict law."

Legal Interpretation by the Halakhic Scholars. Another reason for the orderly integration of tax enactments and customs into the Jewish legal system was the fact that in most cases the problems and disputes arising from them were brought before the halakhic scholars. In answering these problems and in their interpretation of the various *takkanot* and customs, the scholars applied the accepted rules of interpretation as well as the general principles of Jewish law normally applied in the courts (see below) and a problem that fell outside the purview of an existing custom or *takkanah* was dealt with according to talmudic law and the codes (see, e.g., Resp., Rashba, vol. 4, no. 260; Resp. Maharam of Rothenburg, loc. cit., and further illustration below), since "in all matters that have not been explicitly stated [in communal enactments] we are obliged to adhere as close as possible to the law of the Torah" (Resp. Rama da Fano, no. 43; Resp. Maharashdam, ḤM no. 442).

Principles of Equity and Justice. Also instrumental in the maintenance of an organic link between tax laws and the general system of Jewish law was the scholars' practice of scrutinizing customs and enactments and invalidating them when they were contrary to Jewish law principles of equity and justice. Thus a *takkanah* aimed at rendering the taxpayer liable for double taxation on the same property – both at his place of residence and at the place where the property was situated – was rendered null since "this is nothing but robbery, and it is not possible to stipulate contrary to the law of robbery" (Resp. Rasba, vol. 5, no. 178; vol. 1, no. 788; see also Resp. Maharam of Rothenburg, ed. Prague, no. 106). On the strength of the said principles the scholars also invalidated another *takkanah* which purported to lend a tax obligation retroactive effect, and further, excluded the possibility of combining two methods of tax assessment in a manner drastically increasing the taxpayer's burden (see below). Similarly, a tax custom whose purpose was "to extract vengeance from an individual or individuals" was held to be of no force and effect (*Massa Melekh, Ne'ilat She'arim, Minhagei Mamon*).

Accumulation of Tax Takkanot and Customs in Halakhic Literature. Another reason for the close link between the tax law and the general halakhic system is to be found in the fact that a very substantial part of tax customs and *takkanot* were quoted, often in full, and discussed in the vast responsa literature and other compilations of the halakhic scholars (see below).

Yardsticks of Tax Assessment

The problem of the yardstick to be applied in the assessment of an individual's tax liability continued to occupy the attention of the post-talmudic halakhic scholars.

POLL TAX. This tax, apparently imposed throughout the post-talmudic period, was "a fixed per capita allocation" (Resp. Rashba, vol. 5, no. 220) and was often referred to during this period by its talmudic name, *karga* (Resp. Rashba, vol. 5, no. 178, et al.).

ASSESSMENT ACCORDING TO FINANCIAL MEANS. Generally, most taxes were levied in accordance with the taxpayer's means, a principle the scholars regarded as fundamental to Jewish law. Thus it was decided that the individual members of the community should contribute according to their means toward a specified sum required for their own security needs, contrary to the practice in the case of an amount collected by the central authority: "and if at first, when the gentiles were appointed to be in charge of the guards, they departed from Jewish law in equating the poor with the rich, yet now that they entrusted this matter to ourselves we should not change the law of the Torah that in matters dependent on money the calculation must be made according to means… and it may not be said… that the rich shall not make increase, nor the poor decrease" (*Mordekhai*, BB no. 475 in the name of Maharam of Rothenburg, and no. 497). This approach was fortified by a legal explanation with an interesting historical background: "whatever new decrees and afflictions the gentiles may impose on Israel, even if they should be minded to afflict us by having us refrain from food and drink, yet all is collected according to financial means, for their main concern is the money" (*Piskei ha-Rosh*, BB 1:22; cf. also *takkanot* of the Saragossa community, in Dinur, Golah, 2, pt. 2 (1966^2), 366f.).

ASSESSMENT IN ACCORDANCE WITH THE TAX PURPOSE. Some scholars held that individual tax liability should be assessed in accordance with the purpose for which the tax was imposed. Thus if the purpose was to raise a specific sum in order to bribe the authorities to prevent riots against the Jews on the eve of their festivals, "the law holds that they should pay [tax] according to means as well as souls, since on these days both persons and property are endangered – all this in accordance with the need of the hour and the local situation." In the case of regular taxes imposed by the authorities, means alone was to be the criterion: "for the kings and governments only impose taxes on people with means, and they protect their means by payment of the taxes." If a specified sum was to be raised for the purpose of bribing the authorities not to forbid ritual slaughter or the sale of bread to Jews, assessment was to be according to souls alone, since in this case rich and poor would suffer equal harm. All these distinctions, however, were to remain subject to local custom and enactment (Resp. Rashba, vol. 3, no. 401). All were not consistently observed, and in another responsum Solomon b. Abraham Adret himself (*ibid.*, no. 381) laid down that the cantor's emolument was to be paid out of the community chest; although he fulfills the duty for rich and poor alike the poor cannot afford as much as the rich, and in all matters of the public weal which are dependent on money the contribution must be made according to means. On the other hand, in a later period the opinion was expressed that in the case of the cantor's emolument, the assessment required a combination of two methods – one-half according to souls – for although the poor had as much need of the cantor as did the rich, yet the rich were prepared to pay more to a cantor with a better voice, and "therefore they made this compromise" (Sh. Ar., OḤ, 53:23 and Taz, *ibid.*, no. 14). As a result of the multiplication of possible distinctions of this nature, it was laid down that these matters had to be decided "on the merits of each case, as the judges see fit" (*Rema*, ḤM 163:3); "since these matters are not clearly dealt with in the *halakhah* as found in books only, but must be dealt with by the judges... in taking account of the abnormal and emergency situation and the decrees of the authorities" (*Terumat ha-Deshen*, Resp. no. 345). It was held that liability for tax existed even when the taxpayer had no need for the services financed thereby and therefore could not expect any return consideration. Thus it was decided that the cost of educating children – if this was beyond their fathers' means – should be borne by the whole community, each member contributing according to his means (Resp. Ramah, no. 241; Sh. Ar., loc. cit.); moreover, it was held to be the rule that all the needs of the town must be financed by the whole community, even if some were not in need of certain services, such as a wedding hall or ritual bath, and so on (Resp. Mahari Mintz, no. 7: Sh. Ar., loc. cit.). At different times when the rich sought to evade their tax duty, the halakhic scholars responded in various ways (see, e.g., Dinur, Golah, 2, pt. 2 (1966), 393–5).

TAX PURPOSES. The purposes for which taxes were levied during the post-talmudic period embraced a wide spectrum of municipal needs – such as maintaining the town guard, providing health, educational, and religious services, and for judicial and civil execution institutions, funds for combating informers, funds for charity to the poor, for hospitality, and for *ma'ot ḥittin* on Passover – in addition to various taxes, fixed or otherwise, imposed by the central authorities on the Jewish community and collected by the communal authorities from its members (see illustrations cited and see also Tur, Sh. Ar., ḤM 163, and standard commentaries). These taxes were known by various names, some corresponding to those mentioned in the Talmud, and other taxes were called by the names customary in the various countries of Jewish settlement.

Taxable Property

Taxes were mainly direct and based on income from property, movable or immovable: "for property which cannot be utilized and earned from is not properly taxable" (Resp. Ran, no. 2:21). Non-income-bearing property was subject to tax reduction in the case of a special property tax or a non-recurrent "unprescribed" tax imposed in a very large amount in the event of a special false accusation or other emergency. The increasingly severe fiscal burden imposed by the ruling power, particularly in the case of German Jewry, fostered the tendency toward imposing taxes on non-income-bearing property also, as will be detailed below.

LAND. "It was accepted in ancient times that taxes should not be imposed on land, for tax derives only from a business transaction" (Maharam of Rothenburg, quoted in *Mordekhai*, BB no. 481), and this continued to be the practice in 13th-century Germany although unsuccessful efforts had been made to bring about a change (*ibid.*). A land tax, in Meir b. Baruch's opinion (*ibid.*), could exist only in the event that "the land itself is tax-burdened," that is if the tax was expressly imposed as a property tax on land, or if the tax was imposed in a time of emergency when there was reason to fear "the plunder of courtyards and land, and the burning and destruction of houses" (Sh. Ar., ḤM 163:3). Similarly, in the case of a person buying and selling land, "it is the universal custom that tax is payable on everything that a person may wish to sell, whether household articles or land... for anything that is for sale is like merchandise" (Resp. Maharyw, no. 84, and see below).

HOUSES. In the case of houses it was decided that local custom should be followed, and when there was no such custom the issue depended on the nature of the tax: if imposed to finance the expenses of the town guard the tax would extend also to houses, i.e., to owners of houses in the town even if they did not reside there (see below); however, if the tax "be like all other fixed taxes payable annually – to the ruling power or municipal authorities – on account of the income earned in the town, houses will not be subject to tax; yet if a person should own two or three houses, he must pay tax on them for this is no different to any other income, but he shall not pay tax on his own dwelling, save in the case of a tax in a large amount or when the ruler has determined that they shall pay tax on everything they own" (Maharam of Rothenburg, quoted in *Mordekhai*, BB no. 475 and see Resp. Maharyw, no. 84).

In certain areas of Spain in the 13th century, tax was payable on land even independently of its sale (Resp. Rashba, vol. 5, no. 182). In one case it was decided that on land and all else from which no income was derived, tax was payable at one-quarter of the regular rate (*Teshuvot ha-Rashba ha-Meyuḥasot le-ha-Ramban*, no. 184); this was apparently a property tax expressly imposed as such. On houses, however, no tax was imposed (Resp. Rashba, vol. 5, no. 179, 182).

VINEYARDS AND FIELDS. The rule was established that even income-bearing movable property from which a loss could more commonly be anticipated than a profit – such as the yield from a field or vineyard – should not be taxable. Hence it was decided as early as the 11th century that a tax which the town residents sought to impose on a woman's vineyard was contrary to law because the great effort and expense involved in the vineyard's cultivation did not necessarily assure an income, and it was wrong that an asset should be consumed by the tax levied on it (Resp. Joseph Tov Elem (Bonfils), quoted in Resp. Maharam of Rothenburg, ed. Prague, no. 941 and in *Mordekhai*, BB no. 481; see also *Takkanot Rashi*, quoted in Resp. Maharam of Rothenburg, ed. Berlin, no. 866 and in Finkelstein, bibl., p. 149). However, in 15th-century Germany there was a change in the profitability of vineyards: "in these countries, in the main the people sustain themselves by their vineyards and derive their wealth from them." Thus a situation arose in which there was no possibility of exempting vineyards entirely from taxation yet frequent heavy losses from such property could nevertheless be anticipated. It was decided, therefore, that tax was to be assessed on one-half of the value of the property, but that no exemption was to be granted in the case of a "very large and exaggerated" emergency tax (*Terumat ha-Deshen*, Resp. no. 342). In Salonika, in the 17th century, tax was payable on the full value (*Massa Melekh*, 3: 2, 1).

MONEY LOANED ON INTEREST. This was an obvious category of taxable property: "there is no more convenient class of merchandise; since the lender holds his pledge and his money grows, he benefits without effort or strain, or any need to supervise, nor does he have any expense…" (R. Yom Tov Elem, quoted in Resp. Maharam of Rothenburg, ed. Prague, no. 941). In the course of time, when it became increasingly likely that money loaned to non-Jewish borrowers would never be repaid, it was decided that the interest was not to be taxed (as in the case of vineyards), except that exemption was not to be granted on the whole amount of the loan, for since "in our time we mostly earn our livelihood from lending money on interest, what other source of taxation is there?" If interest was reflected as capital and compounded thereon, the interest was to be regarded as capital and taxable (*Terumat ha-Deshen*, Resp. no. 342). A person was held to be liable for tax on income derived not only from his own property but also from the property of others held in his possession (*Mordekhai*, BB no. 481; *Nimmukei Menahem* of Menahem Merseburg, Din. 5; see also various opinions in *Terumat ha-Deshen*, Resp. no. 342 and *Rema*, ḤM 163:3). It was held that a debt which the creditor despaired of recovering might be excluded from his list of taxable property provided that he assigned his right in the matter to the communal trustee; if the debt was recovered by the community, two-thirds of it had to go to the community and the remainder to the creditor (*Terumat ha-Deshen*, loc. cit.; for a different ratio, see Resp. Maharyw, nos. 84 and 133). In another *takkanah* debts were declared completely tax-free (Resp. Rama da Fano, no. 43).

MONEY IN DEPOSIT OR TRUST. It was *Hai Gaon's opinion (quoted in *Terumat ha-Deshen*, Resp. no. 342) that money deposited with a trustee was not taxable, since no profit was derived from it by its owner. From the 13th century onward, the majority of the German *posekim* came to hold the converse opinion (Resp. Ḥayyim Or Zaru'a, no. 253; *Terumat ha-Deshen*, loc. cit.; Resp. Maharyw, no. 133; cf. the contrary opinion in *Nimmukei Menahem* of Menahem Merseburg, Dinim 10, 18), and it was stated: "Our custom is that a person is liable on all that he owns, whether openly or concealed" (Resp. Maharil, no. 121). In a special *takkanah* of the Mantua community in the 16th century, even a "hidden portion [*maneh kavur*] earning no income" was declared taxable. It was necessary to decide that no tax was payable for the period of the theft on a sum of money stolen and later returned to its owner, since the particularly stringent nature of the rule which – contrary to the general law and custom – rendered taxable such money "from which its owner certainly derives no income," required that it be narrowly interpreted and its operation confined to the case of an asset "guarded in the owner's possession" (Resp. Rama da Fano, no. 43; see also *Rema*, ḤM 163:3).

RIGHTS AND OBLIGATIONS. Some scholars held that a property right recoverable by action, such as a right to payment of a dowry, was taxable (Resp. Maharyw, no. 82), but not a right which its owner was uncertain of recovering; nor were the unpaid wages of a teacher, laborer, or employee taxable – even if already due – until they were actually paid (*Terumat ha-Deshen*, Resp. no. 342). A debt was held to be deductible from the amount of a person's taxable assets (Resp. Rashba, vol. 1, no. 1074, et al.), and apparently the deduction was allowed only after the debt had matured, although in 15th-century Germany it was allowed even before maturity of the debt (*Terumat ha-Deshen* and *Rema*, loc. cit.).

JEWELRY, GOLD, AND OTHER VALUABLE ARTICLES. It was deduced from the statements of "some of the *geonim*" (quoted in *Terumat ha-Deshen*, loc. cit.) that no tax was payable on property of this kind since no profit was derived from it; an 11th-century *takkanah* nevertheless records the assessment of such articles at half value for tax purposes (*Takkanot Rashi*, quoted in Resp. Maharam of Rothenburg, ed. Berlin, no. 866), and in the 15th century it was the practice to assess these articles at their full value on account of the "swindlers" who used to invest the money they earned in precious stones and jewels in order to gain tax exemption (*Terumat ha-Deshen*, loc. cit.).

BOOKS. Solomon b. Abraham Adret ruled that book manuscripts which were of very great value, were taxable at one-quarter of their value, i.e., at the same rate as land, even though they were not income producing (*Teshuvot ha-Rashba ha-Meyuḥasot le-ha-Ramban*, no. 184); however the majority of the scholars exempted them entirely – both because books were not income producing and "lest in future people refrain from hiring scribes to write books" (*Terumat ha-Deshen*, loc. cit.).

MEAT AND WINE. A tax on the purchase and sale of wine and meat is mentioned in various medieval *takkanot* and responsa (Resp. Rashba, vol. 2, no. 213; Resp.Rosh, nos. 6: 14, 102:6; Resp. Ritba, no. 44; *Takkanot Castile*, in Finkelstein, bibl., p. 371).

TAX CEILING. At first it was considered that there was no ceiling on the amount of a person's tax liability: "it has been the custom since ancient times… that a person is liable for tax, however high the amount, on all of his business transactions" (Resp. Maharam of Rothenburg, ed. Berlin, no. 127). Later, in certain areas, such a ceiling was provided for, but was only applied in respect of regular taxes and not of those specially imposed in times of emergency or in other special circumstances (*Massa Ḥayyim, Missim ve-Arnoniyyot*, nos. 27, 61).

CONSECRATED PROPERTY. Property dedicated to the needs of the poor, or to religious and educational needs, and the like (see *Hekdesh*) was regarded as exempt from tax on various grounds: since consecrated property was deemed to belong to the community it was not logical for the community to tax its own assets (Resp. Ran, no. 2); such property was not intended for profit-making purposes – a precondition to taxation (*ibid.*); and in order to encourage the consecration of property (to strengthen the hands of those "who perform a *mitzvah*" (*ibid., Terumat ha-Deshen*, Resp. no. 342). It was decided that the exemption only applied in respect of property that had already been dedicated and set aside at a particular place, but not otherwise, in order to discourage fraudulent acts (Resp. Rashba, vol. 5, nos. 142 and 141, 143; vol. 2, no. 57; Resp. Rosh. 13:6; Sh. Ar., ḤM 163:3; for further particulars, see *Massa Melekh*, pt. 3).

Place of Residence, Business, or Situation of Property

It was laid down that tax was payable at the place where the taxpayer was resident. In general, a person was regarded as a resident of the town in which he had lived for a period of 12 months or more; a lesser period entailed the duty to contribute toward some of the town's needs, and a person immediately became the resident of a town in which he purchased a dwelling (see above). In the 12th century the *posekim* disagreed on the criteria of residence for purposes of tax liability. According to one view, "even if he has rented a house he is not to be likened to one who has purchased a dwelling there [in the town], since in the latter case the *kinyan* proves that he has made up his mind to settle, but if a dwelling is rented it may not be his intention to settle and he should not be held liable"; another opinion was that "a person who comes to dwell and settle there is like one who purchases a dwelling there" (opinions quoted in *Mordekhai*, BB no. 477 and in Resp. Maharyw, no. 124), and this latter became the accepted opinion (*Terumat ha-Deshen*, Resp. no. 342; Resp. Maharik, no. 17). It was held that at all events a fixed local custom to impose tax liability, even upon residence in the town for a period of less than 12 months, was to be followed (*Mordekhai*, loc. cit.), and in various places other periods were prescribed (see, e.g., *takkanot* of the Saragossa community, 1331, in Dinur, Golah, 2, pt. 2 (1966^2), 345f.; Resp. Rashba, vol. 3, no. 397; see also Sh. Ar., ḤM 163:2; for further particulars, see *Massa Melekh*, pt. 1).

SITUATION OF PROPERTY. A property tax was regarded as payable at the place where the property was situated regardless of the owner's place of residence (Resp. Rashba, vol. 5, 178; Resp. Ritba, no. 157). This principle was deduced from the talmudic rule that a person owning property (a *ḥaẓer*) in a town of which he is not a resident must contribute toward the costs of the town's water supply (Maharam of Rothenburg, quoted in *Mordekhai*, BB no. 475, on the authority of Tosef., BM 11:18). Meir of Rothenburg's reasoning in this matter is interesting. Starting from the mishnaic *halakhah* that "the [upkeep of the] water channel, the city wall, and the towers thereof and all the city's needs… were provided from the residue of the shekel-chamber" (i.e., from the money of all Israel; Shek. 4:2), he poses the question, "and why shall the city not be built by the Jerusalemites themselves, on their own?" His answer is "because no tribal division was made of Jerusalem and it is a dwelling place for all the house of Israel, therefore the funds come from the residue of the shekel-chamber, contributed by all Israel" (*ibid.*).

PLACE OF BUSINESS TRANSACTION. Tax on profits derived from a business transaction was likewise held to be payable at the place where the business was transacted and the profit made (Resp. Rashba, vol. 5, no. 263), for the reason of *dina de-malkhuta dina*, since according to the general law of the land the king may "decree that no person shall carry on business in his country unless he pay so-and-so much" (Resp. Rashba, vol. 3, no. 440; vol. 1, no. 664; vol. 5, nos. 263, 286); even talmudic law entitled the residents of a town to call upon a person not to carry on his business there "in order not to diminish their profit" unless he paid them tax on his profits, and his refusal to do so gave the townspeople authority to restrain him from carrying on business in their community (Resp. Rashba, vol. 5, no. 270; see also Resp. Ritba, no. 157). The community was at all events held to be entitled to enact a *takkanah* that anyone carrying on business in their town should pay them tax on this, since "on this matter all communities have rules and *takkanot* not derived from talmudic law" (Resp. Rashba, vol. 3, no. 397). Moreover, even people coming to a particular town in circumstances of **ones*, for instance when fleeing from the enemy, with the intention of returning to their own town once the danger had passed, could be liable to contribute toward the taxes of that town after they had sojourned there for more than 12 months and transacted business like the townspeople, although perhaps not at the same rate as the permanent residents of the town (*Binyamin Ze'ev*, no. 293, with detailed discussion and quotation of different opinions; for further particulars, see *Massa Melekh*, 1:2, 1–2).

DOUBLE TAXATION. It was held to be clear that a person who was not resident in the town where he transacted business could only be taxed by that community on business transacted locally and not on business transacted in the town of his residence or on property he owned there (Resp. Rashba, vol. 3, no. 440). Furthermore, even the community where he lived could not tax him on business transacted in another community, "for if this be permitted an injustice will be done in that he is made to pay twice" (*ibid.*), and it was an important principle that "the same asset cannot be taxed in two different places" (Resp. Rashba, vol. 5, no. 270). In one instance the leaders of a certain community sought to enact that a resident of the local community was to be taxed also on his property situated in the area of another community because "the community has authority to make enactments and rules so that no one shall escape liability." Notwithstanding the right of a community to make enactments in tax matters even if they were contrary to a rule of the *halakhah*, Solomon b. Abraham Adret rejected the validity of this *takkanah* because it was "nothing less than robbery and it is not possible to contract out of the laws of robbery… for the community has no right to rob an individual of his money and take it for itself" (Resp. Rashba, vol. 5, no. 178). This decision of principle led to the enactment, in certain communities, of *takkanot* aimed at one and the same time at avoiding double taxation while minimizing, as far as possible, loss of tax income to the community in which the taxpayer resided. Thus the *takkanah* of a certain community rendered local residents liable for tax even on their property situated elsewhere, but as they were allowed first to deduct from their tax assessment the tax payable to the other community and the balance went to the local community, the *takkanah* apparently brought little benefit to the local community (Resp. Rashba, vol. 5, no. 282, also no. 178). This distinction between property situated at the taxpayer's place of residence and property situated elsewhere naturally also influenced the laws concerning the declaration of assets for purposes of tax payment. Thus it was laid down that a taxpayer owning property in another country where he also had a creditor was to deduct the debt in question from the property declaration he submitted to the foreign country and not from the declaration he submitted to the authorities at his place of residence (Resp. Rashba, vol. 1, no. 1074).

The objection in principle to double taxation was apparently not always generally accepted in the Jewish community in Germany. In the 14th century it was stated: "some hold that money which is retained by a person outside the town of his residence… is tax exempt… and others say that a person who has money outside his town, even abroad, must pay tax on all his money, and must also pay tax in the other place on the same money, even if the money has never come into his hands, and this is the custom of the majority of the people" (Menahem of Merseburg, quoted in Resp. Maharyw, no. 133). This was still the case in the 15th century: "It is the custom in all these countries that taxes and impositions are payable also on property that has always remained outside the country, and I am accustomed to dealing accordingly" (*ibid.*).

Date of Accrual of Liability

The halakhic scholars were much occupied with the question of whether liability for a tax obligation accrued on the date when the basis for its existence came into being or on the date when the tax payment became due for collection. The difference related mainly to two events of common occurrence in daily life: firstly, when a resident left or joined a community after imposition but before collection of the tax; secondly, when the taxpayer's financial position changed between the time of imposition of the tax and the time of its collection.

LEAVING OR JOINING THE COMMUNITY. *Leaving the Community.* A minority opinion held a person to be exempt from paying tax to the community which he left after the imposition but before the collection of such a tax (R. Tam, quoted in *Mordekhai*, BB nos. 475–476 and in Resp. Maharik, no. 2; see also *Massa Melekh*, 1:2; 3:2). However, the majority of the *posekim* disputed this view: "It seems to me to be as a law of the Torah that when the king has called for a tax… everything that one possesses becomes charged in the king's favor, and, even if one should run away before collection of the tax, everything is already so charged – for the law of the land is law and even the measure that is within the jar becomes charged in favor of the *karga*" (Isaac the Elder, quoted in *Mordekhai*, BB no. 476 and in *Teshuvot Maimuniyyot*, Gezelah, no. 9; Judah of Paris, quoted in *Mordekhai*, BB no. 659); similarly, "the *geonim* of France decided that when a man leaves his city, he must pay the tax imposed on him" and, in any event, "such is the custom in all the communities that a person cannot, upon leaving the city, gain exemption from a tax for which he has already become liable" (see *Mordekhai*, BB nos. 656 and 476).

This question was also disputed in Spain in the community of Solomon b. Abraham Adret, and there the matter was decided in accordance with the above-mentioned principle, after "they investigated and inquired from other communities and ascertained from all the communities and their leaders that they follow the opinion of those who exempt persons who come into the community [after imposition of the tax] and hold liable those who leave the community; since then the dispute has become resolved and in accordance with this we apply the law in all the communities in our area" (Resp. Rashba, vol. 5, no. 179). In other places *takkanot* were enacted to the express effect that anyone intending to leave the city had first to pay all the taxes for which liability had already accrued (*ibid.*, vol. 3, no. 406; see also vol. 3, no. 405 and vol. 4, no. 260) and the *halakhah* was thus decided in all later periods: "The law obliges him to pay in full, on all his property, the taxes that have already been imposed, along with all the expenses involved, since he has already become liable for them as one of the taxpayers and he cannot rid himself of them by departing from the city" (Resp. Ritba, no. 157). A similar decision was given by Joseph Colon in Italy in the 15th century: "The prevailing *halakhah* among the Jewish people is that those who run away after imposition of a tax are not thereby exempt from paying their share of the tax" (Resp. Maharik, no. 2); moreover, "anyone escaping from the tax so as not to contribute along with his neighbor will not in the long run, if he returns to the country, derive any reward from his action" (*Leket Yosher*, OḤ, p. 139; see also Sh. Ar., ḤM 163:2). Since a person leaving a city was liable for the payment of his share of the tax, it was held, in a certain case where the authorities refunded part of the tax collected to residents of the community that such person was also entitled to claim his share of the amount refunded by the authorities (Resp. Rashba, vol. 3, no. 405).

In the German community the scope of tax liability of a departing resident was even extended. It was laid down that the tax liability existed not only if the amount payable had been finally determined at the time of the resident's departure, but it sufficed if it had been known that a tax was going to be imposed, even though the amount had not yet been settled between the community and the authorities (Resp. Ḥayyim Or Zaru'a, no. 80). In the 15th century the matter was more precisely defined: "A person leaving the city or the country to settle in another country must share equally with the residents of his former place of domicile the burden of any new tax imposed on them within 30 days of his departure" (*Terumat ha-Deshen*, Resp. no. 342); this was because it had to be assumed that the tax had been "under preparation" for some time prior to its imposition, at which time the departing resident was included in the reckoning, and also that the tax was under discussion in the community for some time prior to its imposition; therefore to exempt from such a tax any person leaving the city a few days before the imposition of the tax would amount to encouraging many to evade taxes by leaving the city and returning there in due course (*ibid.*; see also *Rema*, ḤM 163:3; *Massa Melekh*, 1:2, 3–4).

Joining the Community. The natural corollary of this rule was to exempt a person from liability for a tax imposed before he had joined the community even though the tax fell due for collection after his arrival, "since it is not possible to burn the candle at both ends by holding newcomers liable at the time when the tax is collected and departing residents liable at the time when the tax obligation is created" (Resp. Rashba, vol. 5, no. 179). This was also the custom followed in various other communities ("the custom of the community in Crete is not to reduce the tax for the departing resident nor to exact it from the newcomer," quoted in *Mordekhai*, BB no. 656). It was further decided that a community could not demand that a newcomer contribute toward the payment of any particular tax imposed for a reason clearly connected with an event preceding his arrival – as in the case of a tax imposed by one authority because the community had made a similar tax payment before to another authority, at a time when the newcomer was not yet a resident of the community (Resp. Rashba, vol. 4, no. 260).

Retroactive Tax Liability. The majority of the halakhic scholars held that the imposition of retroactive tax liability – that is imposition of liability on a person not resident in the community at the time of creation of the underlying tax obligation – -was invalid even though it was sanctioned by custom or express *takkanah*. In a certain case it was held that a tax imposed by the community for the purpose of repaying an existing loan could not be exacted from a person who came to live in that community after the loan had been taken, even though he came there before the imposition of the tax: "for why should he repay that which he has not borrowed and how shall he restore that which he has not himself taken ['robbed']?" (Rashba, quoted in Resp. Ribash, no. 477). Moreover, this principle could not be set aside even by an express communal enactment, since "the community cannot make any law or *takkanah* to the detriment of an individual member and contrary to the accepted law, except with the latter's consent, because the community cannot stipulate to 'rob' others" (Ribash, *ibid.*; see also Resp. Rashba, vol. 3, no. 412). On the other hand, the German scholars regarded as valid "a *takkanah* that anyone coming to live with us in the city within a given year shall pay retroactively the tax paid by the others at the beginning of that year" (Resp. Ḥayyim Or Zaru'a, no. 226; in this particular case the individual concerned was exempted because he came to live not in the city itself but in a nearby village; cf. however Resp. Rashba, vol. 4, no. 260 where the validity of an express *takkanah* of the type mentioned above was apparently recognized in certain cases).

CHANGE IN THE TAXPAYERS' FINANCIAL POSITION. In principle, the date of creation of the underlying tax obligation was recognized as the crucial time for the purpose of determining the measure of individual liability for the tax. Hence the taxpayer had to be assessed according to his financial position at that time, regardless of any change in his financial position at the time of collection of the tax. The halakhic scholars justified this rule by likening the residents of the community to partners, who remain liable for repayment of the debt according to the rate of individual participation in the original obligation and not according to their respective financial positions at the time of repayment. However, while the community had no authority to determine by *takkanah* that the time of the collection of the tax and not the time of its imposition was to be deemed the crucial date for purposes of the essential liability for the tax obligation, it was held that so far as the measure of individual contribution toward the tax was concerned the community was entitled to enact by *takkanah* that the individual taxpayer be assessed according to his financial position at the time of collection, and this was the practice followed (Rashba, quoted in Resp. Ribash, no. 477). This *takkanah* was explained on the basis of the difference between the rules of private law concerning a loan taken by individual partners and the rules of public law concerning a loan taken by the community: "for the community that borrows for communal purposes is not like those who borrow for themselves personally, but it borrows for the community chest" (*tevat ha-kahal*; for particulars of this concept, see Resp. Rashba, vol. 3, nos. 400, 411; vol. 4, no. 309 and other references to it in this article), "and this debt it has to repay from whatever is available in the chest at the time of payment; such is the custom all over, and neither the poor who have become rich nor the rich who have become poor… pay except according to their means at the time of payment; this is also our practice and in any event it is impossible to do otherwise" (Resp. Rashba, vol. 3, no. 412; for particulars of this development from private to public law, see Public Authority; *Takkanot ha-Kahal*). However, it was pointed out that this explanation lacked validity in the case of a person who was not a resident of the city at the time when the loan was taken, since he could in no way be said to have borrowed "for the community chest" (Rashba and Ribash, loc. cit.).

Other scholars determined the crucial date for purposes of tax liability according to the substantive nature of the tax in question. Thus, in the case of a tax of the kind that was regularly imposed from year to year by the authorities, it was held that a person coming to live in the community in the middle of the tax year should be liable for payment of a share pro rata to the remainder of the tax period, since for the duration of that period he would benefit on account of the tax imposed; hence there was all the more reason why a resident who became rich in the course of the tax period had to contribute in accordance with his current means. However, in the case of a nonrecurring tax only those who were resident in the city at the time it was imposed had to contribute (Resp. Rosh 6: 12; see also *Rema*, ḤM 163:3).

Tax Relief and Immunity

Tax relief on a personal basis is recognized in Jewish law, sometimes for financial reasons and sometimes for social or demographic reasons.

PERSONS OF LIMITED MEANS. It was held that the poor had no obligation whatsoever to pay tax (Resp. Rosh, 6:4, 12), neither on their income from business transactions nor in the form of a poll tax (see *takkanot* of the Saragossa community in Dinur, Golah, 2, pt. 2 (1966^2), 366f.). Elsewhere it was laid down that widows, unmarried orphans, and the disabled were not to be taxed unless their property exceeded a certain amount, and then on the excess only (*Takkanot* Castile (Finkelstein, bibl. p. 371)). A 15th-century German *takkanah* exempted from tax all persons who owned less than a certain amount, but rendered those who owned more than the specified amount liable for tax on all their property (*Terumat ha-Deshen*, Resp. no. 342). In 13th-century Germany it had been the practice to exempt orphans until their majority and marriage (Or Zaru'a, quoted in *Terumat ha-Deshen*, loc. cit.), but in the time of Israel Isserlein orphans also were taxed in accordance with their financial means, on account of the increased tax burden and because tax payment was a matter of safeguarding the security of the community, an obligation regarded as devolving on orphans also (*ibid.*); however, it was laid down that orphans were exempt from the duty of contributing toward the building of a synagogue (*Rema*, ḤM 163:4).

In cases where persons of limited means were held liable for tax, the communal leaders and halakhic scholars sought legal ways to ease their burden (see, e.g., Resp. Rashba, vol. 5, no. 220). An interesting illustration of this can be found in the *takkanot* of the Huesca community of 1340. These prescribed a detailed and onerous list of diverse taxes, apparently aimed at financing communal services as well as raising the amount levied by the crown. The list included poll tax; property tax on houses, vineyards, fields, and gardens; a business and profits tax on wine and various other commodities; and taxes on leases and loans, on gold and silver jewelry, expensive garments, and the like. At the same time, "50 Jews who do not today own property to the value of 50 solidos" were exempted from the poll tax; also exempted were "those who study day and night and have no other occupation" (Dinur, loc. cit., pp. 349–53, and see below with reference to exemptions granted to scholars). On the other hand, the scholars were opposed to exempting a person from tax liability on the grounds of alleged straitened financial circumstances when in fact there was no more at stake than the interests of a man of means under whose patronage such a person was working. Thus Isserlein mentions that in Germany in the 15th century "some of the *ba'alei battim* ['householders'] have to some extent been forcing the custom of having their servants made exempt even though they have money on which they earn, because they eat at the table of the *ba'alei battim*." Criticizing this custom, he declared "that it ought not to be followed" (*Terumat ha-Deshen*, Resp. no. 342; for further particulars, see *Massa Melekh*, 4:4; as regards tax liability and exemption of "an idle person transacting no business in the city," see Tur and Sh. Ar., ḤM 163:6 and standard commentaries; *Massa Melekh*, 1:1, 4; this case was one that had become of little practical importance, "to be in the position of an idler is something that is not so common – I have skimmed over it" (loc. cit.)).

ENCOURAGING SETTLEMENT IN EREẒ ISRAEL. In Germany in the 12th century it was decided that a person remained liable for a tax imposed before he left his place of residence, even though he intended to settle in Ereẓ Israel, since "the upholding of life (*pikku'aḥ nefesh*) is a more important *mitzvah* than settling in Ereẓ Israel… and the tax for which he is liable should not be imposed on the public for the sake of the *mitzvah* of settling in Ereẓ Israel" (quoted in *Mordekhai*, BB no. 656). It is possible that in this case the tax was required in circumstances of special urgency. On the other hand, it is mentioned that in the Turkish countries in the 16th century – the period following the expulsion from Spain and the mass immigration to and consolidation of the Jewish settlement in Ereẓ Israel – it had been the fixed custom for many years in the city that "anyone migrating to Israel to take up residence there had his property exempted from all kinds of taxes, even if it was left behind in that city" (quoted in *Paḥad Yiẓḥak*, s.v. *Missim zeh Yammim*). In one case the residents of the city sought to abrogate the custom in question by an express *takkanah*, but it was decided that they had no authority to do so "especially because by enacting such a *takkanah* they would deter the public from fulfilling the *mitzvah* of living in Ereẓ Israel" (*Paḥad Yiẓḥak*, loc. cit.; *Massa Melekh*, 1:2:3, 4; 5:2, 6; see also *Massa Ḥayyim Missim ve-Aroniyyot*, no. 2).

LARGE FAMILIES. Another kind of tax exemption was that granted to "a person who has 12 children" (quoted in *Paḥad Yiẓḥak*, s.v. *Missim, Mi she-Hayu Lo*). In a certain case in Italy it was decided that the father of such a large family was to be entirely exempted from tax payment and that the tax collected from him had to be returned, "since this is not something decreed by the king contrary to law, but it is the law of the land" (*ibid.*). This exemption apparently had its roots in the general law of taxation in Italy.

TALMIDEI ḤAKHAMIM (HALAKHIC SCHOLARS). The circumstances of a scholar's immunity from taxation, based on the talmudic *halakhah* (see above), remained a subject of much discussion in post-talmudic times. As in talmudic times, there continued to be a measure of reciprocity on this subject between Jewish law and the surrounding legal systems. Influenced by Roman law, tax immunity was customary in the case of scholars and the Catholic clergy and such immunity was also extended in the Muslim countries, although in a more restricted manner (see Baron, Social², 5 (1957), 76; idem, Community, 2 (1942), 14f., 274; cf. *Tashbez* 3:254).

Reservations. In the geonic period it was laid down that rabbis were to be exempted from taxes imposed on the community by the king and his ministers (*Zikkaron la-Rishonim*… 1, pt. 4 (1887), ed. Ḥarkavy, no. 537), an exemption which apparently extended to all kinds of taxes. Starting from the tenth century, some of the scholars greatly reduced the scope of this exemption in holding that it should apply only in the case of an inclusive tax imposed on the community as a whole; a tax imposed on an individual basis was to be borne by halakhic scholars also and the community had no obligation to pay for them (R. Hananel, quoted in Nov. Ramban, BB 8a; *Beit Yosef*, ḤM 163:11). Notwithstanding his earlier ruling, which ran counter to the view prevailing in his day that a scholar was forbidden to seek sustenance from the public in order to devote himself to study (as this amounted to a profanation of God's Name), Maimonides decided that in the matter of taxation, "the Torah has exempted all *talmidei ḥakhamim* from all governmental dues, such as a levy, *arnona*, or special personal tax… which must be paid for them by the community, including [a tax for] the building of a wall and the like; and even if the *talmid ḥakham* be a man of great financial means he is not to be held liable for any of these" (Comm. Avot 4:5). To exact a tax payment from a *talmid ḥakham* would amount to "robbing" him (idem, Resp. (ed. Blau) no. 325; cf.Yad, Talmud Torah, 6:10). Many of the scholars followed the opinion of R. Hananel (Nov. Ramban, *Beit ha-Beḥirah* and Nov. Ran, BB 8a), but others accepted Maimonides' view (*Yad Ramah*, BB 8a; *Sefer ha-Ḥinnukh*, no. 222), as did the majority of the *posekim* (Resp. Rosh 15:7–8; Tur and Sh. Ar., YD 243:2–3; ḤM 163:4–6; R. Jeroham, *Sefer Meisharim* 32:2). Asher b. Jehiel averred: "In these generations I see the need, *a fortiori*, to apply this rule; in the time of the talmudic sages, *talmidei ḥakhamim* – of whom there were thousands – were exempt from various burdens and taxes; all the more reason in these generations – when it is hard to find one in a city and two in the same family – to exempt them from such burdens" (Resp. Rosh, loc. cit.). This was indeed the practice followed and even where the most onerous tax burden was imposed, "those who study day and night and have no other occupation" (*Takkanot* Huesca of 1340, in Dinur, loc. cit. p. 349) were exempted even from poll tax. In the Castilian *takkanot* of 1432 the widows of certain scholars and communal leaders were also exempted from tax, a concession partly based on the rule that "the wife of a *ḥaver* is as a *ḥaver* himself" (Av. Zar. 39a), and because the widow of a *ḥaver* remained entitled to some of the rights formerly enjoyed by her husband (Finkelstein, see bibl. p. 369).

"The Torah is his Occupation" (Torato Omanuto). In the Talmud the term *rabbanan*, in the context of tax exemption, is employed without qualification, but the *geonim* established the requirement of "*torato omanuto*" (quoted in *Terumat ha-Deshen*, Resp. no. 342). Differing opinions were expressed on the interpretation of this phrase. One view was that it meant, "they fulfill *ve-hagita bo yomam va-laylah* with all their strength and ability, and do not leave off studying the Torah except to fulfill a *mitzvah*, to seek a livelihood and sustenance for themselves and their families" (Responsum of Meir ha-Levi in: *Sefer Kol Bo*, 108b; see also Naḥmanides and *Piskei ha-Rosh*, BB 1:26; *Terumat ha-Deshen*, Resp. no. 341; Resp. Israel of Bruna, no. 102). Other scholars held it to be a precondition of the exemption of a *talmid ḥakham* that "he is not occupied at all with worldly needs" (*Beit ha-Beḥirah*, BB 8a; *Sefer Ḥasidim*, no. 293; see also *takkanot* Huesca, above).

The Role of Custom. It was decided that although the law concerning a *talmid ḥakham* was no longer practiced with regard to certain matters (e.g., the special fine imposed on a person who shamed him), it still remained in effect as regards his exemption from taxation (*Terumat ha-Deshen*, Resp. no. 341). The exemption was taken to apply not only to a scholar holding office as a rabbi or head of a yeshivah, but also, as appeared from the talmudic source from which the exemption was derived, to scholars who "'trudge from city to city and from country to country'… those are scholars who go from yeshivah to yeshivah, because it is not customary for one who is qualified to be at the head to trudge from city to city" (*Terumat ha-Deshen*, Resp. no. 342; Resp. Maharit, vol. 2, ḤM no. 59 et al.). However, by the 15th century there were places where no scholars except those serving as the heads of yeshivot were exempt from taxation (*Terumat ha-Deshen*, loc. cit.) and, in consequence, the *halakhah* was decided that "there are places where it has been the practice to exempt *talmidei ḥakhamim* from taxation and other places where the practice has been not to exempt them" (Sh. Ar., YD 243:2).

Cantor of the Synagogue. Differences of opinion were also expressed concerning the position of a synagogue cantor, who usually also served as teacher of the children and therefore could be regarded, to some extent, as a scholar. Isaac b. Sheshet Perfet held that he was exempt from tax but other scholars disagreed (Resp. Ribash, nos. 475–7); Isserlein testifies that "in no community have I found them to hold their cantor liable for tax, even if he should have some means, and this is a worthy and proper custom" (*Terumat ha-Deshen*, loc. cit; see also *Rema*, ḤM 163:5).

In the State of Israel. The tax liability of a *talmid ḥakham* has been discussed under existing circumstances in the State of Israel. It was held that since rabbis and heads of yeshivot receive full salaries and a substantial proportion of the taxes of the state went toward the provision of various services to which *talmidei ḥakhamim* also had to contribute, and since tax exemption was a matter of custom, it was necessary that "the custom be upheld to exact tax, at the appointed rate, from rabbis, heads of yeshivot, and *talmidei ḥakhamim* who earn salaries" (see K.P. Tekhorsh, bibl., p. 279. For further particulars concerning taxation of scholars, see *Massa Melekh*, 4:1–3; 5:2, 5).

GOVERNMENTAL OR COMMUNAL EXEMPTION. A common problem in post-talmudic Jewish life was that which arose when individuals, generally those who were influential in governmental circles, gained for themselves a personal tax immunity from the authorities. The halakhic scholars and communal leaders fought against this phenomenon although German and Spanish Jewry differed in their approaches to the matter.

Governmental Exemption in Germany. As early as the 11th century a German *takkanah* decreed, on pain of ban, that "no local male or female resident shall be entitled to secure his/her exemption from the public burden" (*Takkanot Rashi*, quoted in Resp. Maharam of Rothenburg, ed. Berlin, no. 866). A 13th-century *takkanah* laid down that "no person shall secure exemption from the tax because he moves in the royal court" (Finkelstein, bibl., p. 226). In one of his responsa, R. Simḥah of Speyer – after discussing the tannaitic *halakhah* concerning a customs waiver granted to partners (Tosef., BM 8:25–26) – laid down that as far as the community was concerned any governmental exemption had to be shared equally between all its members (as was the custom followed by his uncle, Kalonymus b. Meir), since "all Israelites are sureties for each other to accept the burden of their exile and will share with each other in their comfort and redemption" (quoted in *Or Zaru'ah*, BK no. 460, and in Resp. Maharam of Rothenburg, ed. Prague, no. 932). Similarly, the case was cited of "R. Eliakim, who was close to the royal court and shared with the community any exemption given him by the king" (Resp. Maharam of Rothenburg, ed. Prague, no. 930).

Meir of Rothenburg strongly criticized those who secured any form of tax relief without sharing the benefit of this with the community. In a case where a person acted on his own initiative and came to an arrangement with the authorities "to pay tax independently [of the community]" he laid down that all members of the community had to be regarded as partners for all tax purposes, and a partner could not enjoy personally a benefit due to the whole partnership without the approval of his other partners even if this was not the law of the Torah, "since it has been the custom in the whole kingdom for them to be partners, they are not entitled to act separately, for if everyone were to do so it would lead to evil consequences because everyone would throw off the burden from himself and impose it on his neighbor and endless quarrels shall come about… therefore it is necessary to protest against Reuben who saw fit to act separately" (Resp. Maharam of Rothenburg, ed. Lemberg, no. 108). In a similar case he added that the consent of the authorities was of no effect because "it is not *dina de-malkhuta* but *gezelah de-malkhuta*, like a tax collector exacting a tax in an unspecified amount… since it is the custom in the city for all the Jews to participate in the tax"; he held that the person who made the separate arrangement was to return to the authorities and explain that it was the law of the Jews not to act separately but to carry the burden jointly, that all his fellow-Jews were quarreling with him on this account, and that he no longer wished to pay tax independently. In R. Meir's opinion it was necessary to take a more stringent approach in such matters, even if there was no support for this in the Talmud (Resp. Maharam of Rothenburg, ed. Cremona, no. 222; idem, ed. Prague, no. 915). At the same time he ruled that the prohibition was only to apply when the individual was granted an exemption prior to the final determination of the amount of the tax imposed on the community, for in this case it could be assumed that the reduction granted to the individual would have to be made up by the community in general; if, however, an individual exemption was granted after the final determination and it was known that this fact had in no way increased the amount of the tax for others, the individual concerned could not be required to participate with the others (Resp., ed. Prague, no. 134; ed. Lemberg, no. 358; *Mordekhai*, BK no. 177; *Teshuvot Maimuniyyot*, Kinyan, no. 1). This distinction of principle was accepted, with slight modifications, by the majority of the *posekim* (Resp. Ḥayyim Or Zaru'a, nos. 80 and 206; Resp. Ribash, no. 132; Resp. Maharil, no. 71; Resp. Maharyw, no. 38; *Terumat ha-Deshen*, Resp. no. 341 and *ibid.*, *Pesakim u-Khetavim*, no. 144).

Governmental Exemption in Spain. The Spanish halakhic scholars apparently took a less stringent view of personal exemption from taxation. In one case Solomon b. Abraham Adret dealt with the scope of a tax exemption granted to an individual by the authorities and concluded that it did not extend to taxes connected with the protection and security of the Jewish public; on the question of individual tax exemption itself, he stated: "I do not put myself forward in the matter – this has been and remains a disputed topic – until the court asks for my opinion" (Resp. Rashba, vol. 5, no. 183; vol. 1, no. 644; but cf. vol. 5, nos. 279, 281). A 14th-century *takkanah* of the Alcolea community ruled that a ban of one year could be imposed on any person seeking from the authorities exemption or relief from taxation, and this was also applicable to a person availing himself of such a privilege which had been arranged by a friend, "even without his knowledge" (Resp. Ribash, no. 460; see also *Rema*, ḤM 163:6; for further particulars, see *Massa Melekh*, pt. 2; 4:8).

Exemption by the Community. Clearly, the reasons for objecting to a personal tax privilege granted by the authorities had no relevance in the case of a personal exemption granted by the community itself. The scope of this kind of exemption, however, was discussed in a number of instances (see, e.g., Resp. Rashba, vol. 1, no. 967; vol. 5, no. 281; Resp. Rosh, 6: 19). In these cases the problem of the legal validity attaching to the act of waiver arose and it was ruled that the matter depended on local tax usage (Resp. Rashba, vol. 5, no. 180). It was decided that since a waiver of this kind was effected by the public, it had to be regarded as fully valid: "all matters agreed to by the community or its duly appointed representatives require no *kinyan* or deed, but the statements of the former are regarded as written and delivered" (Resp. Rosh, 6:21; see also *Rema*, ḤM 163:6; *Public Authority; **Takkanot ha-Kahal*; for further particulars, see *Massa Melekh*, 5:1, 4–8).

Methods of Tax Assessment

The halakhic scholars were greatly preoccupied with the problem of the method of assessing the taxpayers' assets, which formed the subject matter of many communal *takkanot*. Two principal methods were followed: the first based on a declaration of assets submitted by the taxpayer, called a *hoda'ah*, and the second on an evaluation of assets by communal assessors or trustees, which was called a *pesak*, the assessors being referred to as *posekim* (for a comparison, see, e.g., Resp. Rashba, vol. 3, no. 411, and Resp. Ribash, no. 457). These two methods had much in common and other variations were also in use (Ribash, loc. cit.).

DECLARATION BY THE TAXPAYER (HODA'AH). Detailed descriptions of this method of assessment are to be found in a number of responsa. In Spain a date was fixed for submission of the declaration to the trustees (*ne'emanim*; for particulars of this office see below), as well as a later date for submission of a supplementary declaration (Resp. Ritba, no. 114). In another Spanish responsum it is indicated that the community used to appoint 12 persons to determine procedure and supervise submission of the declaration. Among their tasks was determining the date, place, and person to whom the declaration had to be submitted, and in what language it should be made. These 12 persons were given authority to make occasional changes in the details concerning completion and submission of the declaration, but not to change the essential method itself: "they may not change from the method of the *hoda'ah* to that of the *pesak* or to any other method" (Resp. Ribash, no. 457, also nos. 458, 459). The taxpayers (*pore'ei ha-mas*) were required to set out in the declaration full details of their property, business transactions, debts, pledges, and the like (Resp. Rashba, vol. 3, nos. 383, 396, 399, 408; Resp. Ribash, loc. cit.).

It was required that a reasonable and uniform period be prescribed for completion and submission of the declaration, "since some may arrange this in a day and some need ten days or more" (Resp. Ribash, nos. 458 and 459). The taxpayer would bring his declaration form (*pinkas hoda'ato*) to the trustees for them to examine its contents in his presence and then to record the total amount declared in the communal register (*pinkas ha-kahal*); they then returned to the taxpayer "a token of his declaration" (*mazkeret hoda'ato*; Resp. Rashba, vol. 1, no. 1074; vol. 3, no. 383). The amount that each individual had to contribute toward the tax could be ascertained from the communal register; the names of those who did not have to pay were followed by a blank space and no mention of any amount (Resp. Rosh, 5:9; 6:4). From time to time a new declaration of property had to be submitted and, in case of increase, tax had to be paid on the increment (Resp. Rashba, vol. 3, no. 407); in the event that there was a large decrease as compared with the amount previously declared, the trustees would inquire into the matter, which often led to acrimonious dispute (Resp. Ritba, no. 114).

EVALUATION OF ASSETS BY TAX ASSESSORS. There is early testimony that the community appointed trustees for the purpose of faithfully assessing each member of the community, so as to avoid complaints of an unjust apportionment of the tax (Yom Tov Elem, quoted in Resp. Maharam of Rothenburg, ed Lemberg, no. 423). These had to be "knowledgeable in the tax" so as to assess each individual according to his assets (*Teshuvot Ge'onei Mizraḥ u-Ma'arav*, no. 205). Sometimes the city elders and judges who were knowledgeable in all local transactions would prepare a "deed of comparison" (*shetar hash-vayah*) so as to "compare between them and see how much tax or charity each would have to pay and thereby avoid dispute among the taxpayers" (*Sefer ha-Shetarot* of Judah b. Barzillai, ed. by S.J. Halberstam, p. 137f.). After assessment of the tax a *shetar pesika* would be written to the effect that the communal leaders had determined that X was to pay so-and-so much tax each year and that no one, not even the court or the communal leaders, should have the authority to vary such a determination (*ibid.*, p. 75).

In various responsa of a later period details are given of the functions of these assessors (*posekim*) and of the *pinkas ha-pesika* they kept (see, e.g, Resp. Rashba, vol. 5, no. 279, 281). The assessors recorded the assessed amount of each taxpayer – based on their estimate – in the communal register (*pinkas ha-kahal*; Resp. Rosh, 6:4). Without doubt this assessment too was based on various particulars available to the assessors, although at times they erred grossly in their estimates (Resp. Rosh, 6:4) and on occasion their assessment was followed by protracted argument with the taxpayer which occasionally ended in a very substantial correction of the original assessment (e.g., from 800 *zehuvim* to 150: Resp. Maharyw, no. 124). When a person was assessed as having no taxable assets, a blank space was left beside his name in the communal register (Resp. Rosh, 6:4).

THE TRUSTEES. The number of tax assessors (called trustees and by several other names) varied from place to place (the responsa collections of various scholars mention the figure of three, four, ten, and so on) and they were generally chosen by lot from a number of candidates (Resp. Rashba, vol. 3, no. 417). They were required to have expert knowledge of the tax system and to perform their duties faithfully: "and it is the custom in the communities that they appoint the shrewd… they examine minutely to impose justly on everyone, according to the efforts and activities of each, and they must judge others as they would themselves as it has been said (Shab. 31a) 'do not unto your neighbor that which is hateful to you'" (Joseph Tov Elem, quoted in Resp. Maharam of Rothenburg, ed. Prague, no. 941). Those who assessed the tax liability of each according to evaluation of his assets were warned "to guard against favoring one who is liked or dealing onerously with one who is disliked, in order not to be disqualified from testimony or the oath" (Or Zaru'a, quoted in Resp. Maharashdam, ḤM 442).

Generally, such an appointment was looked upon as an honorable one: "all families in the city would like one of their members to be appointed, for the honor of the family alone" (Resp. Rashba, vol. 3, no. 399), but there is no doubt that such an appointment also served personal economic interests. In a case where the wealthy families insisted that their interests be represented by two of the five appointees, Israel Isserlein saw fit to accede to their request since the other three would still compose an impartial majority; also, letting the rich have their representatives would show them that their contentions were being taken into account and they would therefore refrain from strictures and appeals; this was possible, however, only if the two men chosen by the rich were "men of truth, certainly not those reputed to be swindlers and cunning men" (*Terumat ha-Deshen*, Resp. no. 342). Sometimes a candidate for election would give notice of his unwillingness to accept the position, and in a case where such a person was nevertheless elected, Solomon b. Abraham Adret held that "his withdrawal from the assent is of no effect, and he is obliged to take up his trusteeship since the community has seen fit to disregard his wishes" (Resp. Rashba, vol. 3, no. 417; see also vol. 4, no. 309). At times an appointee sought to be released from his position after having served for a period (Resp. Ribash, no. 461).

This dual attitude toward appointment as a trustee found legal recognition in the determination that the trustee's liability for any damage he himself caused had to be equated with that of a gratuitous bailee and not a bailee for reward (see **Shomerim*; Resp. Rashba, vol. 5, no. 10). Cases of refusal to accept appointment as a trustee are mentioned in particular in circumstances where the central authorities imposed special emergency taxes on the community – e.g., for the purpose of waging war – and the latter found itself unable to bear the burden of the tax and the means employed for its collection (as in the case of the tax imposed in Prague in 1751: see Elon, *Ḥerut ha-Perat*, pp. 221f.).

In a case where one of the three trustees was unable to read the contents of the declarations, he was nevertheless held to be fit for his position on the ground that the other two could read the contents to him and that they could be trusted to do so without distortion; since the main task of the trustees was to apply the same standards to all, it was held that the trustees who could not read remained as competent as the other two, and sometimes more so, as far as expertise in matters of collection, payment, loans, and the accumulation of other related knowledge was concerned (Resp. Rashba, vol. 3, no. 399). This was an expression of Solomon b. Abraham Adret's general objective of involving all members of the public in communal administration; elsewhere he added: "in many places individuals are not so literate, yet they are appointed along with those who are knowledgeable" (a similar view was taken with regard to signature by the town scribe in place of a witness who could not sign his own name: Resp. Rashba, vol. 2, no. 111; the same held good even for the appointment of a judge from among the residents of a village where "there is no one who knows even one letter" if the man was accepted by the public: *ibid.*, no. 290). The trustees were enjoined to observe total secrecy concerning details which came to their knowledge in the execution of their duties (*Avodat Massa*, no. 1:2). Apparently this office led to the emergence, in the course of time, of special experts in tax matters. Thus in one of his responsa Asher b. Jehiel mentions that he was asked to give his decision "after consulting with tax specialists" and that he saw fit to do so and to uphold their conclusion (Resp. Rosh, 6:4). This phenomenon is probably to be attributed to the fact that the tax laws were based largely on the various *takkanot* and customs in this field, an area in which the experts had gradually acquired special knowledge.

DOCUMENTARY EVIDENCE. In various *takkanot* provision was made concerning the right or otherwise of the assessors to demand documents from the taxpayer. In one instance it was laid down that the ten trustees were sworn "to act faithfully and truthfully to the best of their knowledge and not to seize the records (*kitvei zikhronot*) of any individual" unless it was agreed by a majority of the ten "to inquire into the affairs of such an individual and to punish him" (Resp. Rashba, vol. 5, no. 126; vol. 3, no. 411).

Erroneous Assessment. Asher b. Jehiel held that in the case of error, even gross error, made by the assessors in the taxpayer's favor – for instance "if they taxed Reuben on 1,000 *zehuvim*,... and later ascertained that he had 10,000 *zehuvim*" – the taxpayer was to benefit from the erroneous assessment and did not have to add to it since he had paid according to the estimate and "had divine assistance" (Resp. Rosh, 6:4). Samuel di Medina, the 16th-century scholar of Salonika, found this decision difficult to comprehend but followed it nevertheless, out of high regard for his predecessor (Resp. Maharashdam, ḤM 442). Around 100 years later a different decision was given in Germany in a case where an assessment of property had been made for tax purposes, and on the taxpayer's death two years later "many times this amount was found in his estate" (Resp. *Ḥavvot Ya'ir*, no. 57). The question that arose was whether to deal with the matter in a manner favoring the assessed party "and say that during the two years in question he had prospered greatly or had an unexpected windfall," or to hold that he had "deceived" for purposes of the assessment and therefore additional tax had to be exacted from him. In his decision Jair Ḥayyim Bacharach reviewed at length the *halakhah* and contemporary customs concerning tax assessment and laid down that the decision in a matter of this kind had to take into account a number of factors, such as the nature of the business carried on by the assessed (that is, whether or not it allowed for the possibility of such sudden enrichment), his previous conduct in tax matters, and the general position as regards the prevalence of tax fraud and concealment. (The same approach was followed in another case, *ibid.*, no. 58.)

Information under Oath and Ban. In order to ensure the veracity of the taxpayer's declaration, it was customary in many places to impose a ban on a person filing an inaccurate declaration, or to require the taxpayer to take an oath on the truth of his declaration. Solomon b. Abraham Adret decided that in strict law an individual could not be compelled to swear to the truth of his declaration: "as in the case of a debtor pleading a lack of means to pay his creditor, when the court cannot, in law, ban or compel him to take an oath, and instead tells the claimant: 'go seek him out and recover from him'!" However, in the same way as it had been ordinated that a ban could be imposed on a debtor pleading a lack of means (*ein li*: see *Execution (Civil); Yad, Malveh, 2:2), in this case too "the ban may be imposed without any qualification… so that everyone who has some means shall pay his proportional share to the community chest." Since the *geonim* had ruled that a debtor pleading a lack of means could be made to take a solemn oath to this effect, "it is possible that in this matter too [i.e., the taxpayer's declaration] the same may be done on the basis of a *takkanah*" (Resp. Rashba, vol. 3, no. 392).

The practice of swearing such an oath in accordance with various *takkanot* came to be expressly recognized by Solomon b. Abraham Adret (see, e.g., *ibid.*, no. 408). Asher b. Jehiel was opposed to an individual's swearing an oath of this kind in tax matters, distinguishing between such an oath and that which one partner could require from his fellow partner even in the case of *ta'anat shema* ("doubtful plea"; see *Oath); he was only prepared to recognize the custom whereby in communal enactments of this kind, "they impose a ban on the whole community to observe them, but do not require an oath from each individual" (Resp. Rosh, 6:13). This ban was imposed in general terms in the presence of all persons above the age of 15 who were called upon to make payment honestly (Resp. Rashba, vol. 5, no. 222). However, Asher b. Jehiel's opinion was not accepted and in the 15th century Isserlein based the community's right to require an individual to swear an oath to the truth of his tax declaration on the premise that the members of a community were comparable to partners and one partner could require an oath from his fellow even on a *ta'anat shema* (Terumat ha-Deshen, Resp. no. 344 and see below). This was also the decision of Isserles (*Rema*, ḤM 163:3) and of later *posekim* (see, e.g., *Noda bi-Yhudah*, Mahadura Tinyana, ḤM no. 40). Bacharach expressed the opinion that after the conduct of the taxpayer and the general position as regards honesty in tax payment were taken into account, it was in the absolute discretion of the community "to prevent one from taking an oath even if he should wish to do so, and to require an oath, according to their discretion, from one who should wish to do so; and no explanation is called for, provided only that their hearts shall be turned toward heaven" (Resp. *Ḥavvot Ya'ir*, no. 57 and see particulars cited there of cases in which the oath was taken).

ALTERNATING BETWEEN DIFFERENT TAX METHODS. It was held that where it was customary for the whole community to follow the self-assessment method (i.e., by way of a declaration) an individual had to be refused a request that his liability be assessed by assessors: "impose on me as you see fit, and I shall do as you wish" even if he made his request because "I am afraid I shall not on my own be able to do as required by law." The reason for this was that an individual was not entitled to choose his own method but had to follow the one agreed upon by the public (Resp. Rashba, vol. 3, no. 392). The trustees too were held to have no power "to change from the method of declaration to that of assessment *pesak* or to any other method" (Resp. Ribash, no. 457); only the community itself could do so (*Terumat ha-Deshen*, Resp. no. 343, and see below; *Rema*, ḤM 163:3) and sometimes it exercised this power. This fact is illustrated, for instance, in the extant records of the tax system practiced in the Mantua community from the end of the 16th century until the beginning of the 18th. The tax code of this community, the "order of assessment" (*seder ha-ha'arakhah*), dating from the end of the 16th century, deals in detail with the various kinds of taxable property and income, and sets out the order of assessment of property and tax by the assessors, the manner of their election, and so on. Yet it appears that from the end of the 18th century this community practiced the *casella* system – named after the case or box into which the tax payment was deposited – which introduced many changes into the tax collection procedure, mainly a changeover to the method of individual self-assessment (see Simonsohn, bibl. vol. 1, pp. 272–301).

The community, however, was not entitled, when it varied the tax method, to adopt indiscriminately the stringencies of different methods in determining the taxpayer's liability: "so far as concerns the wish of his community to do something that is new and completely unheard of, namely to combine the stringencies of two systems by both assessing and imposing a ban, and then not allowing him any reduction in the assessed amount while obliging him to pay the difference (if he be under-assessed at a time when he himself knows that he owns more than the assessed amount) this is robbery and extortion, and a person is not put to death in two ways… we must not innovate further stringencies and once they have made their assessment they cannot any more impose a ban on him and there is no substance in the statements of those who would insist on combining the stringencies of both systems" (*Noda bi-Yhuda*, loc. cit.). This is one more illustration of a restriction on the community against departing from the general principles of equity and justice (see above).

TAX METHODS AND SOCIO-ECONOMIC CLASS DISPUTE. To a large extent both the choice of tax method and the desire to change from one to the other were an outcome of communal dispute of a social and economic nature, and it was no easy task for the halakhic scholars to conciliate between the conflicting class interests. Isserlein, who in a certain case saw fit to uphold the demand of the wealthy that two out of the five trustees be their own representatives (see above), gives a further interesting description of the manner in which the actual tax method was determined (*Terumat ha-Deshen*, Resp. no. 343).

A "heavy tax" had been imposed on the community; for the purpose of its collection, the community prescribed the method of individual self-assessment, by declaration, the latter to be affirmed under oath. A wealthy section of the community (*ba'alei kissin*) objected to this method and demanded that the assets and tax liability of each be determined by assessors, "as has been the custom for some years." Alternatively, they demanded that even if the declaration method was applied the taxpayer should not be required to detail all particulars of his assets in the declaration: "out of concern for the fact that this might cause them harm in a number of ways"; instead the taxpayer should merely have to specify the general amount at which he assessed his assets and affirm under oath that he had no more. This time Isserlein rejected the demands of the wealthy. As regards the first, he held that the community members had to be regarded as partners and since each partner had the right to require an oath from his fellow partner even on a doubtful plea (because otherwise a partner would permit himself to depart from the truth by reason of his activity on behalf of the partnership business), therefore there certainly existed grounds for the same reasoning in respect of the wealthy members of the community, who were likely to permit themselves an untruthful declaration because they were active on behalf of the community and represented it before the authorities, and because each of them would assume that none of the others submitted a truthful declaration. Furthermore, if assessment were to be made by assessors without the oath of the taxpayer, it would be impossible to ascertain the true state of affairs: "human beings are not prophets who are able to know what the next man has in his money-box... a person may become rich unbeknown to anyone else... and people are likely to conceal their assets so as to avoid being regarded as having reached satiety." So far as the alternative demand was concerned, Isserlein held that it was indeed proper according to talmudic law, but that it had already been laid down by the *geonim* and later scholars that a person taking any oath was required to give details of the matter sworn to, so as to avoid error or deceit; this was all the more so in tax matters, when "people are in the habit of employing all kinds of stratagems to evade payment." Therefore if the taxpayer were allowed a general oath without providing details, it would open the way to error and abuse: "hence it is necessary to set out in detail and explain clearly all the assets, their quality and substance... and this has been the practice since long ago in all our borders."

It may be noted that this reasoning provided a basis not only for the determination of a method of tax assessment where none had previously existed, but also for the variation of a method of tax collection practiced for some time (this was also the conclusion of *Rema*, ḤM 163:3. For further particulars of tax assessment methods, see *Massa Melekh*, 5:2).

Tax Appeals

The communal fiscal system allowed for the taxpayer to appeal against his assessment to a higher instance, on both the amount and questions of law. In many communities there were special tribunals for this purpose (e.g., in the Mantua community: see Simonsohn, bibl., vol. 1, pp. 283 f.) and often appeals of this nature would be aired before the halakhic scholars, who dealt with the matter at issue according to the *halakhah* and the pertinent customs and *takkanot*.

PRESUMPTION OF POSSESSION (DIN MUḤZAK) IN FAVOR OF THE COMMUNITY. In this connection a fundamental problem with an important bearing on the relationship between the community and the individual in Jewish law was discussed. A *takkanah* attributed to R. *Gershom b. Judah laid down that a person could not object before the courts in respect of a tax imposed on him, "until he pays what was imposed on him, either in cash or in pledges." This rule was equated with the general rule applicable to all appeals against a judgment, namely that payment is not to be delayed until the appeal is heard (*Binyamin Ze'ev*, no. 295; cf. *Takkanot Medinat Mehrin*, no. 214). It was laid down that only in the event that the city elders agreed with the individual that the tax imposed on him was unlawful would the legal hearing have to be disposed of first (*takkanah* quoted in Resp. Maharik, no. 17 (cf. also nos. 1, 2) and in *Binyamin Ze'ev*, no. 295). Meir of Rothenburg thought that this presumption in favor of the community had no talmudic basis, but on further consideration he concluded that this was "a custom according with the Law of the Torah." On the basis of the doctrine of *dina de-malkhuta dina* (BM 73b; and see above), he held that the king was "presumed to be in possession of [*muḥzak*] the tax [demanded] of each individual" and therefore "also the community wishes to be presumed in possession, to be defendants and not plaintiffs... with regard to the rule that the burden of proof is on the person who seeks to recover from another... for thus it will at all times have the upper hand" (Resp. Maharam of Rothenburg, ed. Prague, nos. 106, 915; ed. Lemberg, no. 371). He also held that his reasoning contributed to the good order of the public, "for if we were to hold otherwise, everyone would reply to the community, saying: 'I am exempt from the law' or 'I have already paid my tax'... everyone would do wrong and think in his heart 'who shall sue me?'... since a shared pot is neither hot nor cold" (see BB 24b). In his opinion this additional substantiation could also be based on various analogies from the talmudic law (idem, ed. Prague, no. 106; *Mordekhai*, BB no. 552). However, the presumption only operated in the community's favor in case of doubt about the true legal position; if *prima facie* it appeared that the law was against the community, the individual would not have to comply except after conclusion of the legal hearing: "justice shall not be perverted against the individual for the sake of the public, nor is robbery permissible because it is committed by the public" (Maharam, loc. cit., and cf. BB 100a). Therefore, if the individual pleads, "this is the law of the community and this has been their practice until now," while the community contends otherwise, and the matter is uncertain, "then why should the community be in a stronger position? And the position of the claimants is not worsened even if they are not many, since they are representative of the community" (*Nimmukei Menaḥem* of Menahem Merseburg, Din 37).

Solomon b. Abraham Adret reached the same conclusion, except that he emphasized that in law the principle which placed the burden of proof on the claimant was also applicable between the community and the individual; however, "it is an ordinance for the sake of good public order, that it shall not be possible for every person to say, 'I shall not pay until adjucation of my plea that I am not liable,' otherwise everyone shall do so with the result that the tax will never be collected, and only the swindlers shall be encouraged. We here [in Barcelona] have also ruled that any person who denies liability must first make payment before the matter can be adjudicated upon." In such a case it did not suffice for the individual to provide a surety for the amount in dispute (Resp. Rashba, vol. 3, nos. 398 and 406).

PRESUMPTION AND THE RIGHTS OF THE INDIVIDUAL. Later the scholars became concerned that this presumption, which was necessary as an effective deterrent against tax evasion, should not prejudice the rights of the individual in disputes with the community. Thus, for example, it was decided that in a case where there were two differing halakhic opinions, one rendering the individual liable for tax and the other exempting him from it, the law had to be applied in favor of the community which is presumed to be in possession – as is the law in any other case of actual possession (see *Extraordinary Remedies; also *Codification of Law, s.v. the plea of *kim li*; Resp. Maharyw, no. 133). Similarly, it was decided that in a dispute between the individual and the tax trustees concerning the statements made by the former in his deliberations with them, the trustees had to be believed because they were representatives of the community, "and the community is [presumed to be] in possession… and because of this they are believed" (Resp. Maharyw, no. 84). Concern that the operation of the presumption might prejudice the rights of the individual was particularly real because, theoretically, the justification for affording the community a favored status in this respect was capable of being applied in every case of dispute between the community and the individual and not necessarily in tax matters only, as in fact could be deduced from the talmudic sources quoted as an analogy for the presumption (see *Terumat ha-Deshen*, Resp. no. 341).

LIMITING THE SCOPE OF THE PRESUMPTION. As a way of safeguarding the rights of the "defenseless" individual in disputes with the "powerful" community, the scholars laid down several material reservations, by means of which the presumption that the community was in possession was restricted. First was that the presumption only operated in favor of the community in respect of a tax imposed by the ruling power and "all other payments for governmental purposes" embraced within the rule of *dina de-malkhuta dina*, so far as "all other public matters and needs" was concerned the presumption did not apply. With a view to safeguarding the interests of the public, it was held to be sufficient if the individual gave a *pledge for the amount in dispute, "so that he shall be the plaintiff and the one in pursuit of justice, and the public not be occasioned loss." It was also laid down that the presumption could not be held to operate in favor of the public with regard to the plea of *kim li* (see above; *Terumat ha-Deshen*, loc. cit.). Secondly, since the explanation for the presumption in favor of the community was based on the theory that the king was presumed to be in possession of the tax by virtue of the rule of *dina de-malkhuta dina* (the community being the agent of the king), therefore if the community had already paid the tax to the government and then sought to collect the tax from individual members of the community, it could no longer rely on the operation of the presumptions in its favor, since on making payment to the king it had ceased to be his agent (*Nimmukei Menaḥem* of Menahem Merseburg, Din. 37). On the basis of this distinction Joseph b. Ezra, the 16th-century scholar from Salonika, concluded: "accordingly we learn at this time, when the communities do not distinguish between the king's taxes and other taxes, that there is no room for presuming in favor of the public unless there is a custom to this effect and such custom is not called into question" (*Massa Melekh*, pt. 6, 3rd *Tenai*). Thirdly, if there was still time for it the individual was entitled to have the legal hearing take place prior to the due date of the tax payment and in this event no pledge was to be taken from him (*Massa Melekh*, pt. 6, 3rd *Tenai*; see also *Terumat ha-Deshen*, Resp. no. 341). Fourthly, in the 16th century it was concluded, from the thesis that the community acted as the agent of the government, that in circumstances where it could be assumed that the community made its plea in order to safeguard its own interests and because it acted as the agent of the government, the presumption would not avail the community: "and there is no distinction between the kings' due and other public needs – they [the community] are the ones who claim and seek to cover payment and the burden of proof is theirs." The only difference between the community and the individual, in case of a dispute between them, lay in the fact that the former could demand a pledge from the individual in order to ensure a legal hearing of their dispute (Resp. Menahem da Fano, no. 43; already in R. Gershom's *takkanah* the matter of taking a pledge was mentioned, although apparently in satisfaction of the debt and not only for the purpose of securing its repayment. For further particulars see *Massa Melekh*, pt. 6).

Adjudication and Evidence

The special circumstances which formed the background to the development of the tax law system led to the appearance of *takkanot* and customs which introduced into this field of the law far-reaching changes that also affected matters of adjudication and the laws of evidence. Apart from the fact that special tax courts, composed of communal leaders adjudicating "in accordance with their own custom" (Resp. Rosh, 7:11; and see below), existed in many places, significant changes were introduced into the *halakhah* concerning *dayyanim* and witnesses even in the courts presided over by the halakhic scholars.

DISQUALIFICATION OF WITNESSES AND JUDGES. Jewish law lays down stringent requirements governing the competency of *witnesses, and disqualifies relatives of the litigants as well as other interested parties from acting as witnesses in a suit (Tur and Sh. Ar., ḤM 33 and 37 and standard commentaries). Hence in strict law the testimony of a member of the community was inadmissible in any matter connected with local taxes, since any tax ruling for or against an individual member of the community inevitably affected the tax rate for the rest of the community also. According to talmudic law, a town resident was disqualified from testifying in a matter concerning the property common to the residents in his town, such as the public baths, unless he renounced all benefit from the particular property (BB 43a; Sh. Ar., ḤM 37:18ff.). In post-talmudic times, however, the existing realities of Jewish life made the strict observance of this rule impossible, certainly as regards a number of public matters (see **Takkanot ha-Kahal*), particularly the adjudication of tax disputes. As late as the 12th and 13th centuries it was still decided in Germany that the testimony of communal leaders to the effect that a person had made a declaration before them in regard to a tax matter was not to be admitted, "as long as they [the communal leaders] have not paid their share of the tax," in view of their interest in the matter (*Mordekhai*, BB no. 483, in the name of Avi ha-Ezri and of Meir of Rothenburg). In one instance Asher b. Jehiel decided that a member of the community was not competent to testify unless he "genuinely" renounced all personal benefit in the matter concerned (Resp. 58:1, 3), and in another case he went to the extent of holding that so far as tax was concerned, it was quite inconceivable for a member of the community to renounce effectively (or exclude himself from) all benefit deriving from his testimony: "for this matter of tax payment will ever be customary, and it is impossible for them to effect a renunciation in such manner as never to benefit from the tax that will be paid" (*ibid.*, 6:15, also 6:21). In addition, the question of the disqualification of witnesses on the grounds of their kinship with one or other of the parties, or with the judges, often presented problems, since members of the community intermarried and created ties of affinity with each other. For all these reasons judges themselves were often in a similar position of being disqualified by law from hearing a matter (BB loc. cit.; Tur and Sh. Ar., ḤM 7:12; *Beit Yosef* and other standard commentaries).

ABROGATION OF DISQUALIFICATIONS. The problems outlined above were overcome by means of communal enactments which expressly qualified members of the community as witnesses and judges in matters concerning their fellow-residents. The question of the validity of a *takkanah* of this kind was raised before Solomon b. Abraham Adret, and answered in the affirmative: "This too is clear, that the enactment of the community is conclusive; in tax matters it has been the practice of all the communities to adjudge the town residents and to gather testimony from them, even though they be relatives of the judges or the litigants; moreover, it may be that the interests of the court and of the witnesses are at stake in their judgment and testimony, but they nevertheless testify for themselves; all this derives from the law of communal enactment" (Resp. Rashba, vol. 6, no. 7). He held that a *takkanah* of this kind was vital for the proper administration of justice in tax matters in particular and in matters of the public domain in general, "for otherwise you annul all communal enactments, yet the custom of the communities is law and in all matters of this kind it must be held that custom overrides the *halakhah*" (*ibid.*, vol. 5, no. 286); furthermore, *takkanot* of this nature were common "and no community has ever called this matter into question" (*ibid.*, no. 184; cf. the like opinion in Resp.Rosh, 6:15).

The impact of these *takkanot* became part of the fixed law: "Tax matters are not dealt with by the local judges, since they and their relatives have an interest therein… but if they have made a *takkanah* or the local custom is that the local judges deal also with tax matters… then this is the law" (Sh. Ar., ḤM 7:12); likewise as regards witnesses: "in these times it has been the practice to accept witnesses from among members of the [local] community… in regard to all their matters, and they are competent even in matters involving their relatives, for the reason that they [the communities] have accepted this for themselves" (ḤM 37:22). This *halakhah* became so widely accepted that at the beginning of the 20th century it was stated: "In our time we have never seen or heard that a matter affecting the community shall not be adjudged by the local *dayyanim*… and the local *dayyanim* are competent to deal with all matters of the community" (*Arukh ha-Shulḥan*, ḤM 7:22. For further particulars see **Minhag*; **Takkanot ha-Kahal*; *Massa Melekh*, pt. 7.).

Principles of Interpretation

The fact that a substantial part of the Jewish tax law system became based on written *takkanot* enacted in the various communities, contributed toward great creativity in the field of the interpretation of laws. In tax disputes between the individual and the community, and between different communities, the halakhic scholars were frequently called upon to interpret these *takkanot* and in so doing they not only decided the concrete matter before them, but also established guiding principles of interpretation of importance to Jewish law in general (see *Interpretation). It may be noted that the scholars based the principles they applied in the interpretation of the communal enactments on a wide discussion of and reliance on various analogies from talmudic law, as can be seen from the responsa mentioned below.

INTERPRETATION OF COMMUNAL ENACTMENTS. Interpretation of the communal enactments was, in the main, the task of the halakhic scholars before whom a particular matter was brought, and very many of the responsa concerning tax matters include detailed discussions on such interpretations (see, e.g., Resp. Rashba, vol. 5, nos. 277, 279; Resp. Ritba, nos. 114, 120; Resp. Maharyw, no. 84; and see illustrations below). Sometimes, however, a *takkanah* included an express provision that any doubt concerning the meaning of a matter mentioned in it was to be resolved by the interpretation of the incumbent communal leaders (called *muqaddimūn* or *berurim*), and the scholars decided that in this event the interpretative authority was entrusted to the aforesaid leaders (Resp. Rashba, vol. 3, no. 409; vol. 5, no. 221). Notwithstanding such an express provision there remained the possibility that in certain cases the issue had to be left to the decision of the halakhic scholars. This happened, for instance, in a case (Resp. Ritba, no. 134) which arose from a *takkanah* laying down that a person giving in marriage "a daughter or sister" to someone who did not pay tax in that community was liable, in certain circumstances, to pay tax on the amount given as a dowry. A resident of the community gave his granddaughter in marriage and the community demanded tax from him, contending that this case too was covered by the *takkanah* since "grandchildren are as children." The grandfather challenged this demand, pleading that such a construction was valid "in the language of the Torah" (see, e.g Yev. 62b with reference to the *mitzvah* of procreation), "... but in human parlance and dealings, grandchildren are not called children," and therefore when a person bequeathed his property to his "children" his grandchildren were not included in the bequest (BB 143b). The communal leaders rejected this plea and, on the basis of the provision that anything in the *takkanah* whose meaning was doubtful must be interpreted as the communal leaders saw fit, contended that their own interpretation was binding. In his responsum Yom Tov b. Abraham Ishbili (Ritba) proved from talmudic law that in all matters concerning business transactions, vows, and communal enactments, the standards of "human parlance" had to be applied, and by these standards grandchildren were not to be equated with children (cf. also Yad, Nedarim, 9:23; Sh. Ar., YD 217: 46). On this basis he held that there was no further room for the communal leaders to interpret the term under dispute, "since the language used is not doubtful but clear" and the communal leaders' interpretative authority was confined solely to a case where doubt existed about the meaning of a particular term.

AMBIGUITY IN TAX ENACTMENTS. In a case of conflicting provisions in a *takkanah* dealing with tax liability, it was held that the *takkanah* in question had to be interpreted in favor of the taxpayer (Resp. Rashba, vol. 5, no. 281) and so too if the text of the relevant provision allowed for alternative interpretations. The basis for this statement was as follows: since the *takkanah* purported to impose on the individual a payment for which he would not otherwise be liable, therefore "everything that falls outside the ambit of the strict law cannot be made to apply to him except when this is clearly justified, and until this is so talmudic law has to be applied... because the burden of proof is on the plaintiff" (Resp. Rashba, vol. 3, no. 397; Ritba, no. 157). For the same reason an ambiguity in the text operated to the disadvantage of the individual if in strict law he was liable for the tax. In a case where the community had agreed to grant one of its members a tax exemption without specifying the period of its duration, Asher b. Jehiel rejected the member's plea that his had been an exemption for life and held that the law was in favor of the community if it pleaded that the exemption had been intended for one year only: "since he is obliged to pay along with the others but seeks to escape liability on the plea that he was granted an exemption, therefore he is at a disadvantage... and since he was given an undefined exemption, we have to interpret this exemption as restricted to the minimum that we have to adjudge him" (Resp. Rosh, 6:19).

LANGUAGE OF THE TAKKANAH AND INTENTION. It was held to be a basic principle that a *takkanah* must be interpreted in accordance with the knowledge and understanding of those who had authority to do so – the halakhic scholars or the communal leaders (*muqaddimūn*), as the case might be – and not according to "the intention of those who enact the *takkanah*" (Resp. Rashba, vol. 3, no. 409; in this particular case authority was entrusted to the *muqaddimūn*). However, exaggerated adherence to this principle was to be avoided, since "at all events there are times when the intention is common knowledge and is like a stake that cannot be uprooted, so that all know that a certain condition or matter was instituted, beyond any doubt, with a specific intention, even though the language allows for a contrary interpretation" (*ibid.*). This rule was illustrated in a dispute involving the interpretation of a *takkanah* stating that tax declarations had to be brought to the synagogue on a particular day of the week. In actual fact, however, the tax trustees sat in the courtyard (*ḥaẓer*) in front of the synagogue and on one of the upper floors (*aliyah*) but not inside the synagogue itself. Therefore it was averred that this was not in keeping with the language of the *takkanah* since places such as the *ḥaẓer, aliyah, azarah*, and so on had their own separate names and identities. This contention was rejected out of hand by Solomon b. Abraham Adret, for the reason that the relevant text had to be interpreted, in each case, in its own substantive context; thus if the *takkanah* in question had been concerned with prayer, the intention would have been to refer to the synagogue itself, that is the place where the congregation was led in prayer, but in a *takkanah* concerned with the submission of tax declarations, "the intention was not that they should actually be inside [the synagogue], for what need is there for them to be inside? On the contrary, no more was intended than that they should be in one of its areas, so as to be available to all" (Resp. Rashba, vol. 5, no. 222).

Various kinds of formalistic sophistry in interpreting the text were rejected. A certain *takkanah* stated: "If at the time of accounting it shall be found that a person shows an increase in his capital and money and all his property, beyond what was shown at the time of accounting in the previous year, he shall pay so-and-so much on such increase." A member of the community who showed an increase in respect of some items but not in respect of "all his property" therefore contended that his case fell outside the ambit of the *takkanah*. Again Solomon b. Abraham Adret rejected this as "an idle plea… devoid of all reason or substance," since the meaning of the *takkanah* was not that the taxpayer had to show an increase in everything actually mentioned, but merely in one or other part of his assets, "and it is the way of the world to speak in this manner… the intention is plain, that everyone shall every year supplement his account with the increase over the previous year" (Resp. Rashba, vol. 3, no. 407). In the case of another *takkanah*, enforced by ban, it was provided that the taxpayer had to submit an annual declaration affirmed under oath, "and he shall not add thereto nor detract therefrom in any event whatever," until submission of the next annual return. A member of the community discovered in the middle of the year that he had forgotten to declare a certain asset but voiced his fear of rectifying the matter in view of the ban accompanying the stated provision. Solomon b. Abraham Adret replied that it was inconceivable for a person to escape tax liability on account of his own forgetfulness: "this is something which the ear, the heart, and reason all reject," hence the said condition could not reasonably be given its plain meaning, namely that nothing at all could be added to the declaration: "how does it matter to them [the community] that he shall not add when he wishes to do so?" There was no choice, he held, but to say that principally it was intended that there should be no detraction, and that the words "he shall not add thereto," represented no more than a routine and customary form of expression (loc. cit., no. 408).

Tax Collection Procedure

SECURING AND RECOVERING A TAX DEBT. It was laid down that a tax debt, "from the moment of its assessment by the trustees," must be regarded in the same way as a debt "by deed" and was to be recovered out of the debtor's "free" property (*nekhasim benei ḥorin*), and failing this from his "alienated and encumbered" property (*nekhasim meshu'badim*), that is from property which the debtor had transferred to a third party after becoming liable for the tax (see *Lien; Resp. Rashba, vol. 5, no. 136; vol. 4, nos. 64, 65). The free property included all the property, movable or immovable, in the debtor's possession, except that he had to be left with his basic needs for survival (Resp. Rashba, loc. cit.; see also *Execution (Civil)) and except as otherwise provided in any *takkanah*. An instance is recorded in which the community enacted that a debtor's seat in the synagogue could not be attached in payment of a debt, not even a tax debt; later a special *takkanah* was enacted in connection with an extraordinary tax imposed by the central authorities, to the effect that even a synagogue seat could be taken in satisfaction of such an unpaid tax debt (Resp. Rosh, 5:4; at that time a synagogue seat entailed a proprietary right: see **Ḥazakah*).

For the purposes of recovering a tax debt, the concept of *nekhasim meshu'badim* had a wider scope than in the case of a regular debt. Thus it was held: "It has been the custom of all the communities… that when a person's money is subject to a debt owed to the community and this money is given to another, then the party becoming entitled to it takes the place of the first owner"; therefore the tax could be exacted from such money – even though this was not the law in case of any other debt – since "the tax obligation is imposed on the money, and all money which is so obligated and acquired by the second owner is still subject to the obligation of the first owner" (Resp. Ran, no. 10). It was also the practice to oblige the tax debtor to provide a surety or pledge for repayment of the debt (see, e.g., Resp. Rashba, vol. 3, no. 398; Resp. Rosh, 6:29; 7:11).

FINE, BAN, OR IMPRISONMENT. The customary means of coercion in post-talmudic times, a fine or ban (*niddui* or *ḥerem*), were also adopted against errant taxpayers (see, e.g., Resp. Ramah, no. 250; Resp. Rosh, 6:29, 28:4). Another means of enforcing a tax debt was imprisonment. Originally, in Jewish law imprisonment was not employed as a means of enforcing repayment of a debt, no matter what kind, since this was looked upon as prejudicial to the debtor's personal freedom and inimical to the fundamental principles of Jewish law governing the creditor-debtor relationship. It was only from the 14th century onward – in consequence of changed socio-economic conditions and influenced by the surrounding legal systems – that the Jewish communities came to adopt imprisonment for debt, and then with material reservations designed to protect an impoverished debtor (see *Imprisonment for Debt). However, in the case of a tax debt, imprisonment as a means of coercion had come into practice at an earlier date, apparently as early as the 11th century (see Rashi to Pes. 91a and Elon, *Ḥerut ha-Perat…*, p. 113). At any rate, it is recorded that in the 13th century it was "the custom of the communities to imprison any person who failed to pay the king's tax because the law of the land is law" (Resp. Rosh, 68:10). Some scholars explained this law on the basis that since the tax in question went to the government and since the general law of the land required that the debtor be imprisoned until he paid the tax, it followed that the community had to do likewise as "the king's agents" (Resp. Ranaḥ, no. 58; cf. the same concept above). However, as regards a tax debt, imprisonment was customary, not only in respect of "the king's tax," but also in respect of a communal tax: "The custom is widespread, in all countries of the Diaspora, that a person who owes [and fails to pay] tax to the community is incarcerated in prison; he is not brought before the court, but the communal leaders adjudge him in accordance with their custom, and he is not set free until he pays or until he provides a surety or binds himself by deed… for such is the tax law" (Resp. Rosh, 7:11). This continued to be the practice in the following century (see, e.g., *Zikhron Yehudah*, no. 79; see also the charter of rights for Majorcan Jewry, of 1315, in Dinur, loc. cit., vol. 2, pt. 2, p. 354).

After imprisonment had become an accepted means of enforcement in the case of regular unpaid debts, that is from the 14th century, it continued to be used, sometimes with increased severity, in respect of tax debts. Joseph Colon, the 15th-century Italian halakhic scholar, stated that it was permissible to have a recalcitrant tax debtor imprisoned and compelled to pay his debt, even through intervention of the gentiles; this he explained on the basis that a Jew who refused to submit to the internal Jewish government was as one who refused to be adjudged before a Jewish court and whom it was permissible to sue in the civil courts, and under the general law of the land it was the practice for debtors to be imprisoned (Resp. Maharik, no. 17; here this rule was attributed to R. Gershom b. Judah; see also *Rema*, ḤM 163:1). Even in such a case, however, it was forbidden for all of the debtor's property to be handed to the civil authorities in a manner that caused him loss far beyond the measure of his tax liability (Resp. Maharik, no. 127); furthermore, it was forbidden to coerce, through the general authorities, any individual who was not a resident of the community claiming the tax from him, since such an individual was not subject to the jurisdiction of that community: "shall robbery be permitted because it is committed by the public?" (Resp. Maharik, loc. cit.). From the end of the 16th century onward, there are instances of particular severity in the enforcement of tax collection methods. Tax evasion had become a severe hindrance to the effective organization of autonomous Jewish life and to the maintenance of proper relations with the central government. Thus, for example, the following procedure was adopted: if a tax debt remained unpaid for three days, the debtor was declared "obdurate" (*sarvan*); if he persisted in his refusal, a ban was imposed, with various degrees of severity (see *Ḥerem); if thereafter the debt remained unpaid for a specific period of time, the debtor was imprisoned until the debt and the expenses involved were paid. This procedure was justified thus: "therefore we have taken such a stringent approach as concerns the tax *takkanah* because we see that many stumble in this respect and permit themselves latitude in tax matters, without taking to heart that this amounts to robbery of the public; hence we very carefully warn the public about this matter" (see *takkanot* of the Cracow community and of Moravia in the 17th century in Elon, *Ḥerut ha-Perat…*, pp. 178–80, 195f.). In another *takkanah* provision was even made for various sanctions, including imprisonment, to be adopted against communal leaders in the event of their failure to transfer the tax monies ("*Toleranzgelder*") to the proper destination in time, so as to avoid "great wrath" on the part of the government (Elon, *ibid.*, p. 221). A similar detailed description has come down of the onerous tax collection procedures which, in the middle of the 18th century, the leaders of the Prague community were compelled by the government to adopt in order to raise the amount the latter prescribed for financing a war (see Elon, *ibid.*, pp. 221f.).

Ethics of Tax Payment

At all times the halakhic scholars sought to educate members of the public toward genuine payment of their taxes, and emphasized the basic premise that anyone who evaded payment of his share of the tax increased the burden of the remaining members of the community by obliging them to pay more than their due share, and that this was the case whether the tax went to the government or toward financing the various services provided by the community. Hence it was held that tax evasion entailed not only ordinary robbery, but also "robbery of the public" (*gezel ha-rabbim*), which had to be most severely punished (see BB 35b, 88b). This transgression is repeatedly warned against (see, e.g., *Sefer Ḥasidim*, nos. 671, 1386, 1451), and not only the offender was held to be subject to punishment but also the communal leaders (even when they had paid their own due share of the tax) who failed to enact suitable *takkanot* designed to discourage others from tax evasion (loc. cit., no. 671). Samuel di Medina concluded that tax evasion rendered a person "a robber and disqualified as a witness and profit gained in consequence is to be weighed against the loss of the world to come" (Resp. Maharashdam, ḤM no. 442).

The multiple exhortations against tax evasion were aimed at counteracting a common human weakness to justify such conduct on a variety of grounds (see, e.g., *Terumat ha-Deshen*, Resp. no. 343). Hence in various *takkanot* a strict ban was imposed on all persons evading tax payment or aiding and abetting the evasion (see, e.g., *takkanot* of Valladolid of 1432, in Finkelstein, loc. cit., p. 371). Indeed, many were most careful to meet their tax liability in full, and often, after having submitted declarations of their taxable property, they returned to advise the trustees of any particulars they had forgotten to mention, in order to fulfill "the duty toward Heaven" and pay the true amount that was due (Resp. Rashba, vol. 3, no. 408). However, there were also instances where means of special severity had to be adopted to cope with tax evasion: "In these times fraud is prevalent and it is right to act with great severity so as not to encourage those who practice it" (Resp. Maharil, no. 121 and see above). A detailed and instructive illustration of the demand for integrity in tax payment is to be found in the "order of assessment" of the Mantua community of 1695. After it is stressed that the individual must faithfully render his tax "report" in all its details – lest he commit "robbery of the public" and his transgression be "beyond bearing" – it is stated: "for he shall not permit himself to do so and think that others too do not submit their report honestly and justly, and therefore he may act like them and withhold for himself… it is forbidden to do so for two reasons: firstly, this is simply a vain answer and an unfounded judgment, for how can he have clear information about the others… and secondly if it were true as he thinks, I would be surprised to know who permitted the robbery of those of good and upright heart because of someone who acts dishonestly, or who permitted a man to forfeit his right in the world to come because of that sinner or sinners?" (ch. 15; see further *Massa Ḥayyim, Missim ve-Arnoniyyot*, no. 16).

Halakhic Compilations of Tax Law

The special development that took place in the field of tax law also left its mark on the literary sources of Jewish law. The fact that this development took place mainly in the 12th and 13th centuries can be clearly deduced from a review of the classic halakhic compilations of Jewish law. Thus, for example, there is very little mention of tax law in Alfasi's *Sefer ha-Halakhot* or in Maimonides' *Mishneh Torah* (11th and 12th centuries respectively). The subject is discussed more widely in Jacob b. Asher's *Turim* (ḤM 163) from the 14th century, and the scope of the discussion is progressively wider in Joseph Caro's *Beit Yosef* and Shulḥan Arukh, in Moses Isserles' *Darkhei Moshe* and glosses (ḤM 163) from the 16th century in Ereẓ Israel and Poland respectively, and in Ḥayyim Benveniste's *Keneset ha-Gedolah* to the *Tur* and *Beit Yosef* in the 17th century in Turkey. In the responsa collections also, particularly those dating from the 13th century onward, whole sections are devoted to tax law, which provide a great deal of informative material on this field of Jewish law (see indexes to the responsa collections; for particulars of all the above-mentioned works, see *Codification of Law).

The emergence of compilations specially devoted to the subject of tax law is of interest. As early as the 11th century a small work of this kind was compiled by Joseph Tov Elem (quoted in Resp. Maharam of Rothenburg, ed. Prague, nos. 940, 941). In the 14th century some 50 tax *halakhot*, in summary form, were quoted in the *Nimmukim* of Menahem of Merseburg (printed as an addendum to Resp. Maharyw). The most comprehensive and interesting compilation of this nature is the *Massa Melekh*, written by the 16th-century scholar from Salonika, Joseph b. Isaac ibn Ezra. Divided into seven parts, the work is a comprehensive review of tax law, titled and subtitled according to subject matter. At the end of these seven parts the author added a concluding section, *Ne'ilat She'arim*, containing a detailed exposition of the laws of custom with the author's explanation that tax law was based, first and foremost, on the legal source of custom. An interesting literary feature is the author's condensation of his own detailed discussions within the body of his work, into brief summarized *halakhot*, each containing the conclusion drawn from the preceding discussion (see summaries of the seven parts, pp. 65, 1–70, 2 and of the *Ne'ilat She'arim*, pp. 70, 2–72, 4). This method corresponded to that adopted by Joseph Caro, whose Shulḥan Arukh contains the summarized conclusions of the discussions in his *Beit Yosef*. Another such compilation is the *Avodat Massa*, written by the 19th-century scholar from Izmir, Joshua Abraham Judah. His book is composed of 24 sections subdivided into paragraphs and contains collections of tax *takkanot* and customs from Joseph Escapa, a rabbi of Izmir in the 17th century, and subsequent scholars. Some time later a work called *Massa Ḥayyim* was compiled by Ḥayyim *Palache, also of Izmir. It is divided into three parts, the first containing a very large collection of diverse *takkanot* and customs, particularly in the tax law field, the second dealing with various laws concerning tax matters, and the last part with the law of custom in general; each part is arranged in alphabetical order. In addition, tax laws are dealt with in detail in the *takkanot* collections of the various communities (see bibl.).

In the State of Israel

For a discussion of the sources and details of the tax laws in the State of Israel see *Israel, State of: Taxation, as well as the work of Witkon and Ne'eman (bibl.). It may be noted that terms such as *mas, mekhes, belo,* and *arnona* are still current in the State in the context of tax matters, although they generally have a different meaning from that attributed to them in the course of this article (see Witkon-Ne'eman, pp. 4–8, et al.). In 1964 a tax museum was established in Jerusalem for the preservation of historical material relating to Jewish tax law and all matters touching on taxation in Ereẓ Israel in its earlier and later periods and in the State of Israel. In addition to various research projects, a periodical, *Rivon le-Inyenei Missim*, devoted to tax matters, is published regularly under the auspices of the museum.

[Menachem Elon]

ARTIFICIAL TRANSACTIONS. Article 86 of the Income Tax Ordinance (New Version) stipulates that when a tax official concludes that a particular transaction which effectuates a reduction in the tax due is "artificial or invented," that transaction may be disregarded in fixing the amount of tax to be paid. In interpreting the term "artificial transaction," the Israel Supreme Court relied on Jewish Law (CA 265/67 *Mapi Ltd. v. the Tax Assessor for Large Businesses, Tel Aviv*, 21 (2) PD 593, per Justice Moshe Silberg).

Justice Silberg noted that Jewish Law holds a rather liberal attitude toward circumvention of the law through means of the law itself, in order to maintain the "flexibility and vitality of the ancient law, so as to enable it to incorporate changing patterns of life." Circumvention of the law by using the law is referred to in *halakhah* as *ha'aramah*, and there are various instances of its practice in Jewish law: for example, *ha'aramah* to circumvent the prohibition against taking interest on a loan (see *Usury). In some instances, the *halakhah* upheld *ha'aramah;* in others, it was rejected.

In his opinion, Justice Silberg discusses two examples, one of which was halakhically accepted, the other rejected. The first example involves the second tithe (*ma'aser sheni*). The Torah provides that one-tenth of an individual's yearly produce is to be set aside and taken to Jerusalem to be consumed there (Lev. 27:30–31; Deut. 14:22). The Torah likewise provides that the tithe may be redeemed for an amount of money equal in value to the produce, which is then taken to Jerusalem where it is used to purchase food; however, in that case an additional sum of money equal to one-fifth of the value of the produce must be added. The Mishnah, however, considers various methods for avoiding payment of the extra fifth. One such method is to give a sum of money equal to the value of the produce as a gift to a friend, who then uses the money to redeem the produce, after which he returns the money to the owner, relying upon the rule that if the tithe is redeemed by someone other than the owner of the produce, the additional fifth need not be given. Thus, through this fictive gift, the owner of the produce circumvents his obligation to add a fifth to the redemption money. This result was planned in advance, as the purpose of the gift of the money was to evade the obligation to add the fifth. The Mishnah itself cites this method as achieving this result.

The second example discussed by Justice Silberg, one rejected by the *halakhah*, involves the first tithe (*ma'aser rishon*). This tithe, also a tenth of the produce, is set aside prior to the second tithe and given to the Levites. According to an interpretation of the biblical passage (Num. 18:21f.), the obligation to set aside the first tithe only applies to that produce that is brought into the house through its entrance. If it is brought in by a circuitous way, such as through the roof, the first tithe need not be given. However, this method of evading the obligation was rejected.

Justice Silberg analyzes the difference between the two cases: viz. the acceptance of the *ha'aramah* involving the second tithe, and the rejection of that involving the first tithe. He concludes that "with regard to the second tithe, although the purpose was to obviate the obligation to give the additional fifth, the mechanism used and its legal effects are much broader and deeper. The ownership of the object (i.e., the money used to redeem the produce) must actually be transferred to the recipient (i.e., the one who actually performs the redemption) and all the necessary requirements must be satisfied. If anything related to the substance or scope of the transfer is omitted… the *ha'aramah* does not achieve its purpose." On the other hand, bringing the produce through the roof involves nothing beyond the exemption from paying the tithe. This act has no other significance.

Using the same standard, Justice Silberg concluded that the term "artificial transaction" in the tax law should be interpreted as referring to a transaction that has no substance or purpose other than the desired reduction in the amount of the tax. (See also Cr. A. 1182/99 *Hurvitz v. State of Israel* 54 (4) PD 85–88, per Justice Yitzhak Englard).

INTERPRETATION OF TAX LAWS. An example of the rule that communal enactments (*takkanot ha-kahal)* in the area of tax law be interpreted according to their language and not according to their intention which did not receive expression in the *takkanah,* appears in a responsum of R. Solomon b. Abraham Aderet. The question submitted concerned a communal enactment whose purpose was to increase the amount of taxes collected by the community. However, application of the terms of the enactment had the unforeseen result that a particular taxpayer's obligation was reduced. Rashba ruled that the clear language of the enactment must be applied (Resp. Rashba vol. 5 no. 282). The Israeli Supreme Court relied on this ruling as to statutory interpretation in general, and to tax law in particular (HC 333/78 *Trust Association of Bank Leumi of Israel v. Administrator of Estate Taxes*, 32 (3) PD 202, Justice Menachem Elon; for extensive discussion, see *Interpretation).

[Menachem Elon (2nd ed.)]

BIBLIOGRAPHY: HISTORICAL ASPECTS: Baron, Community, index: 550–4; Baron, Social², index; U. Heyd, *Ottoman Documents on Palestine, 1552–1615* (1960), 117–27 and index (translated into Hebrew by A. Givati and published by Ha-Muze'on le-Missim, Jerusalem, *Firmanim be-Inyenei Missim be-Ereẓ Yisrael me-ha-Shanim 1560–1585* (1965); B. Lewis, *Notes and Documents from the Turkish Archives* (1952); Israel, Misrad ha-Oẓar, *Hitpatteḥut ha-Missim…* (1954); Ha-Muze'on le-Missim, Jerusalem, *Hitpatteḥut ha-Missim be-Ereẓ Yisrael*, ed. by A. Mendel (1968); J.A. Judah, *Sefer Avodat Massa* (Salonika, 1846, Jerusalem, 19642); A. Suessmann, *Judenschuldentilgungen unter Koenig Wenzel* (1907); Kisch, Germany, index; Baer, Spain, index; Roth, England, index; H.G. Richardson, *English Jewry under Angevin Kings* (1960), index; B. and G. Lagumina, *Codice Diplomatico dei giudei di Sicilia*, 3 vols. (1884–1909); C. Roth, *History of the Jews in Venice* (1930), 124–7; idem, *Gleanings* (1967), 214–8; A. Milano, *Il Ghetto di Roma* (1964); S. Luce, in: REJ, 2 (1881), 15–23; L. Lazard, *ibid.*, 15 (1887), 233–61; *ibid.*, index vol. 50 (1905), s.v. *Taxes imposées aux Juifs*; Dubnow, Hist Russ, 3 (1920), index s.v. *Tax*; I. Levitats, *Jewish Community in Russia 1772–1844* (1943), index; L. Greenberg, *Jews in Russia*, 1 (1944), index; *Rivon le-Inyenei Missim*, 1 (1965–to date). LEGAL ASPECTS: *Seder ha-Ha'arakhah li-Kehillat Mantovah* (1695, reprint 1963); Finkelstein, Middle Ages, index s.v. *Taxes; Pinkas ha-Medinah… Lita…*, ed. by S. Dubnow (1925), s.v. *Missim*; Gulak, Oẓar, 337–44; idem, in: *Sefer Magnes* (1938), 97–104; idem, in: *Tarbiz*, 11 (1939/40), 119–22; J. Newman, *Agricultural Life of The Jews in Babylonia* (1932), s.v. *Taxation*; B.D. Weinryb, in: HUCA, 16 (1941), 187–214 (Germ.); Baron, Community, 2 (1942), 246–89, and index (in vol. 3) s.v. *Taxes* and *Taxpayers*; Neuman, Spain, 1 (1942), 60–111; 2 (1942), index s.v. *Taxation; Takkanot Kandia ve-Zikhronoteha*, ed. by E.S. Artom (= Hartom) and U.M.D. Cassuto, 1 (1943); Halpern, Pinkas, s.v. *Missim*; M. Benayahu, in: *Kobez al Jad*, 4 (14; 1946), 193–228; ET, 2 (1949), 194–6; 5 (1953), 46–51; *Takkanot Medinat Mehrin*, ed. by J. Halpern (1951), index s.v. *Missim*; I.M. Horn, *Meḥkarim* (1951), 73–91; K.P. Tekhorsh, in: *Ha-Torah ve-ha-Medinah*, 5–6 (1952/54), 233–82; M. Beer, in: *Tarbiz*, 33 (1953/54), 247–58; S. Baron, *Historyah Ḥevratit ve-Datit shel Am Yisrael*, 1, pt. 3 (1957), 50f.; 2, pt. 4 (1965), 138–45; J. Katz, *Masoret u-Mashber* (1958), s.v. *Missim*; Alon, Toledot, indexes s.v. *Missim* in both vols.; B.Z. Benedikt, in: *Ha-Torah ye-ha-Medinah*, 11–13 (1959/62), 590–8; D.J. Kohen, in: *Sefer Yovel le-Y. Baer* (1960), 364–8; Baer, Spain, index in vol. 2 s.v. *Taxation*; S. Simonsohn, *Toledot ha-Yehudim be-Dukkasut Mantovah*, 2 vols. (1962–64), index s.v. *Mas; M. Elon, Ḥerut ha-Perat be-Darkhei Geviyyat Ḥov…* (1964), 15–17, 75, 81, 85, 113f., 127–31, 136, 152, 164, 178–80, 195f., 221f.; idem, in: *Meḥkerei Mishpat le-Zekher Avraham Rosenthal* (1964), 25, 28–31, 42–51; idem, Mafte'aḥ, 132–8, 649; J. Bazak, *Hilkhot Missim ba-Mekorot ha-Ivriyyim* (1964); EM, 5 (1968), 13, 51–55; *Toledot Am Yisrael*, ed. by H.H. Ben-Sasson, 3 vols. (1969), index in vol. 3 s.v. *Mas*; A. Witkon and J. Ne'eman, *Dinei Missim* (1969⁴). **ADD. BIBLIOGRAPHY:** M. Elon, *Ha-Mishpat ha-Ivri* (1988), 1:347ff., 372ff., 379ff., 566ff., 585ff., 602ff., 745ff., 617–629, 746ff., 2:1204ff., index; idem, *Jewish Law* (1994), 1:416ff., 450ff., 459ff.; 2:688ff., 720ff., 763–78, 920ff., 3:1444ff., index; M. Elon and B. Lifshitz, *Mafte'aḥ ha-She'elot ve-ha-Teshuvot shel Ḥakhmei Sefarad u-Ẓefon Afrikah* (legal digest) (1986), 234–44; B. Lifshitz and E. Shochetman, *Mafte'aḥ ha-She'elot ve-ha-Teshuvot shel Ḥakhmei Ashkenaz, Ẓarefat ve-Italyah* (legal digest) (1997), 170–77; *Enzyklopedia Talmudit*, vol. 2, s.v. "*arnona*," 194–96; vol. 5, s.v. "*gabai*" 50–51; vol. 9 s.v. "*ha'aramah*," 697ff; Index.

TAX GATHERERS. In Jewish history in the period of Roman rule two categories should be distinguished under this heading: (1) *mokhesim*, farmers-general (see *publicani*), by preference of the equestrian order, and (2) *gabba'im*, their agents employed in collecting the taxes (sometimes also called *pub-*

licani, as in the New Testament). The first Roman organization of taxes in Syria and Palestine was begun by Pompey (c. 65 B.C.E.). Under Gabinius' administration there was almost no place for the *publicani* in Judea, as Gabinius was their bitter enemy and tried in every way to eliminate them from the tax gathering in his province. However, during the Herodian period, Julius Caesar made the rulers of the new Jewish state responsible for the taxes (Jos., Ant., 14:163ff., et al.). The Herodian rulers farmed the taxes out to individual farmers or to associations. In the period of the Roman principate poll taxes and land taxes were collected directly by officials (cf. Tosef., Dem. 6:3) and only customs, tolls, and similar taxes were farmed out to *publicani*. In the second and third centuries the *bouleutai* (= *curiales*), and the *decemprimi* of the towns and villages, and notable persons of the *strategiae* had to answer for the full payment of taxes imposed on their districts (see BB 143a). Often, to evade these duties, they took to flight. R. *Johanan even advised crossing the Jordan and leaving Ereẓ Israel rather than assuming such duties (TJ, MK 2:3, 81b).

As the burdens of taxation became ever more intolerable, so did the tax farmer or collector become a more hateful and dreaded personality (cf., Sanh. 92b, where a *gabbai* is likened to the bear in Amos 5:19). At times they even contrived to extract payments by torture (see Num. R. 17:5; cf. Philo, Spec. 3, 153–63). Being so unpopular, the collector's job was no easy one; indeed at times he ran great personal risk, as an enraged populace was quite likely to lynch him (Gen, R. 42:4). Since both *mokhesim* and *gabba'im* were classed with "robbers," talmudic law disqualified them from acting as witnesses (Sanh. 25b). Neither was their money accepted for charity (BK 10:1). Sometimes however, tax collectors were unwilling agents of the *publicani*. Thus, Tosefta Demai (3:4, et al.) reads: "At first [the sages] said, 'A *ḥaver* who becomes a *gabbai* is expelled from the order.' Subsequently they declared, 'As long as he is a *gabbai* he is not trusted, but if he withdraws from being a *gabbai* he is [again] trusted.'" A number of Jewish tax collectors and farmers are mentioned, e.g., Johanes from Caesarea (Jos., Wars, 2:287), Zechariah on the Jordan near Jericho (Luke 19:2), the tax gatherers at Capernaum on Lake Tiberias, probably responsible for customs, port duties, and fishing tolls (Matt. 9:9), etc. Tax collectors formed themselves into companies (*societas publicanorum*), each member taking a share (a quarter or less) of the collection and its profits, according to the capital invested.

BIBLIOGRAPHY: F.M. Heichelheim, in: *An Economic Survey of Ancient Rome*, ed. by T. Frank, 4 (1938), 231–45; ET, 5 (1953), 46–51; A. Schalit, *Koenig Herodes* (1969), 290ff.; A. Inlak, in: *Tarbiz*, 11 (1940), 114–22; idem, in: *Sefer Magnes* (1938), 97–104.

[Daniel Sperber]

TAYLOR, ELIZABETH (1932–), U.S. actress. Taylor was born in London, England, to American art dealer Francis and actress Sara Taylor (stage name Sara Sothern). The family moved to Los Angeles in 1939, where with her mother's encouragement, Elizabeth appeared in her first film, *There's One Born Every Minute* (1942). A year later she signed with Metro-Goldwyn-Mayer, where she appeared in *Lassie Come Home* (1943). In 1943, she starred in *National Velvet* with Mickey Rooney; during the filming a horse riding accident left her with a broken back and the pain would plague her for the rest of her life. Critical acclaim for the film led to roles in *Little Women* (1949), *Father of the Bride* (1950), and *A Place in the Sun* (1951). In 1950, she married hotel heir Conrad Hilton Jr., divorcing him less than a year later in 1951. In 1952, she married British actor Michael Wilding, divorcing him in 1957. In 1956, she starred opposite James Dean in *Giant*, and received her first Oscar nomination for *Raintree Country* (1957). She married producer Michael *Todd in 1957. Taylor turned to Todd's rabbi, Max Nussbaum of Temple Israel of Hollywood, to convert her to Judaism in early 1959, taking the Hebrew name Elisheba Rachel. On March 24, 1958, Todd was killed in a plane crash in New Mexico. A grief-stricken Taylor poured her emotions into playing Maggie in *Cat on a Hot Tin Roof* (1958), which earned her a second Oscar nod. While on the set, she met Eddie *Fisher, and following Fisher's divorce from Debbie Reynolds, the two were married by Rabbi Nussbaum at Temple Beth Shalom in Las Vegas on May 12, 1959, with Mike Todd, Jr., as best man. *Suddenly Last Summer* (1959) earned her a third Academy Award nomination. One year later, her turn as a call girl in *Butterfield 8* (1960) won Taylor her first best actress Oscar. In 1961, Taylor signed with 20th Century Fox for $1 million to star in *Cleopatra* (1963). Taylor had an affair with co-star Richard Burton during the shoot that the Vatican even addressed. In 1962, a distraught Taylor attempted suicide. But following a divorce from Fisher, Taylor married recently divorced Burton on March 15, 1964. *Who's Afraid of Virginia Woolf?* (1966) earned Taylor her second Oscar. Taylor divorced Burton in 1974, remarried him in 1975, but divorced again a year later. She married Republican Senate hopeful John Warner in 1976, but the two divorced following media scrutiny of her weight gain. Taylor turned to Broadway, where she appeared in *Little Foxes* (1981) and later in *Private Lives* (1983) with Burton. In 1983, Taylor admitted herself to the Betty Ford Clinic for alcohol addiction. After many of her friends, including Rock Hudson, died of AIDS, Taylor became the first celebrity to support AIDS research and co-founded the American Foundation for AIDS Research. In 1988, she returned to the Betty Ford Clinic, where she met 40-year-old construction worker Larry Fortensky, whom she married in 1991 and divorced in 1996. In 2000, Queen Elizabeth dubbed Taylor Dame Commander of the Order of the British Empire.

[Adam Wills (2nd ed.)]

TAYLOR, SIR PETER MURRAY, Baron Taylor of Gosforth (1930–1997), British jurist. Born in Newcastle-on-Tyne, Taylor was educated at Tyne Royal Grammar School and Pembroke College, Cambridge. He served as a captain in the Army Education Corps and captained Northumberland at rugby. Called to the bar in 1954, he was appointed a Queen's Counsel in 1967 and was a prominent prosecutor, involved in the high-profile cases of John Poulson and Jeremy Thorpe. He served as recorder of Huddersfield and of Teesside. In 1979–80, he was elected chairman of the Bar. Taylor became a judge of the High Court of Justice in 1980 and was a Lord Justice of Appeal, 1988–92. He achieved national prominence when he conducted the inquiry into the 1989 Hillborough (Sheffield) Football Stadium Disaster, and his findings led to the establishment of the Football Licencing Authority. In 1992 he was created Lord Chief Justice of England, the first Jew to hold the post since Rufus Isaacs (Lord *Reading) in 1921, serving until his death. He was a member of the United Hebrew Congregation of Newcastle and was active in the Soviet Jewry campaign in the late 1970s. Taylor was knighted in 1980 and made a life peer in 1992.

ADD. BIBLIOGRAPHY: ODNB online.

[David Cesarani / William D. Rubinstein (2nd ed.)]

TAYLOR, SYDNEY (1904–1978), U.S. author of the *All-of-a-Kind Family* children's book series; a founder of American Jewish children's literature. Born Sarah Brenner, Taylor was the third child of Morris and Cecilia Marowitz Brenner, who immigrated to New York City in 1900. The Brenners raised their seven children in an Orthodox Jewish home. As a teenager, Sarah began to assimilate, and by the time she began writing in the 1940s, she was no longer an observant Jew. However, she always maintained her Jewish identity.

As a young woman, Taylor became involved with the performing arts, acting on stage with the Lenox Hill Players and dancing with Martha Graham's modern dance troupe. She married Ralph Taylor in 1925 and had a daughter, Joanne, in 1935. Taylor began to record stories of her childhood when Joanne asked her why the books she read had only gentile characters. *All-of-a-Kind Family* was published in 1951 after it won a contest sponsored by Follett Publishing.

Although children's books with Jewish themes and characters had been published since the early 20th century, Taylor's were the first to reach a large, mainstream audience comprised of both Jewish and non-Jewish readers. She was also the first American author to depict observant Jewish children in realistic situations. Published until 1978, Taylor's *All-of-a-Kind Family* books were in wide circulation throughout the country.

The books presented Jews, the Lower East Side, and, in later books, the Bronx, in positive terms and a warm light. While at times Taylor elided the difficulties her family experienced or made writing decisions that romanticized actual incidents, she also depicted real pressures and conflicts that she and her family went through, such as poverty, inter-generational disagreement, and even the beginnings of assimilation. To millions of readers, she provided a bridge between the present and the past and supplied them with role models for a strong and proud American Jewish identity.

In addition to publishing the five novels that comprised the *All-of-a-Kind Family* series (*All-of-a-Kind Family* (1951); *More All-of-a-Kind Family* (1954); *All-of-a-Kind Family Uptown* (1958); *All-of-a-Kind Family Downtown* (1972), and *Ella of All-of-a-Kind Family* (1978)), Taylor also wrote several other children's books and short stories. She was the dance and drama director at Camp Cejwin in Port Jervis, New York, for over 30 years and wrote dozens of plays for the Cejwin campers, who performed them every summer from the late 1940s to the early 1970s. Today, the Association of Jewish Libraries gives out two awards for outstanding Jewish children's literature in Sydney Taylor's name.

BIBLIOGRAPHY: S.P. Bloom. "Sydney Taylor," in: P.E. Hyman and D.D. Moore (eds.), *Jewish Women in America*, vol. 2 (1997), 1381–82.

[June Cummins (2nd ed.)]

TAYMA (Tema), an oasis in northwest *Arabia, already mentioned in the Bible (Isaiah 21:14; Jeremiah 25:23; Job 6:19) with another close oasis, Dedan, as a center of water and food in Arabia, through which the caravans made their way from South Arabia (Sheba) to the Land of Israel and to Mesopotamia. Tema is mentioned as well as a descendant of Ishmael (Genesis 25:15; I Chronicles 1:30) and with the same function in an Assyrian text from the eighth century B.C.E. Tema was one of the oldest Jewish communities in northern Arabia. Nabonidus, the last Babylonian king (539–555), recounts in one of his inscriptions that he built his house in Tema (542–552); this raised the conjecture that some of the Jewish exiles in *Babylonia settled with him in Tema. This conjecture was supported by Nabonidus' prayer found with the *Qumran Scrolls. According to inscriptions, Arabs settled among the Jews in Tayma in about the mid-fifth century, and many of them adopted Jewish ways, as Jews owned most of the land and the date palms in the area. Tema became the central Jewish settlement in northwest Arabia in the two or three centuries before Islam, alongside two other oases: Dedan (al-'Ulā) and Hajrah (Madā'in Ṣāliḥ). It seems that Tema was the place where the first Judeo-Arabic biblical translation was produced for the Arabic-speaking Jewish communities in pre-Islamic Arabia. In that area the earliest Judeo-Arabic inscriptions were found, from the fifth or the sixth century B.C.E. About the importance of Tema as a Jewish settlement during that time we can learn from the verse of the 6th–7th century Arab poet A'shā Maymūn who called the town "Taymā; of the Jews." The most famous Jew of the pre-Islamic era is the poet *Samuel ibn Adiya who built his castle, al-Ablaq, near Tema; his name is still known for his faithfulness. Because of their special status among the Arabs, the Jews of Tema were allowed to retain their land even after *Muhammad's conquest. The results of the extensive excavations carried out recently in Tema and its vicinity may uncover new information about Jewish settlements.

BIBLIOGRAPHY: M. Liverany, "Early Caravan Trade between South Arabia and Mesopotamia," in: *Yemen, studi archeologici, storice e filolgici sull'Arabia meridionale*, 1:111–15; Baron, Social², 3 (1957), index; H.Z. Hirschberg, *Yisrael ba-Arav* (1946), index; Sergio Noja, "Testimonianze epigraphiche do Giudei nell'Arabia settentrionale," in: *Bibbia e Oriente*, 21, 283–316; idem, "L'Arabie sédentaire et nomade," in: S. Noja (ed), *L'Arabie avant l'Islam*, 19–92; B. Chiesa, "Les commnautés juives en Arabie," in: *ibid.*, 167–97; Y. Tobi, *Bein Ever* *la-Arav*, 2 (2001), 17–60; G.D. Newby, *The History of the Jews in Arabia* (1988).

[Yosef Tobi (2nd ed.)]

TAYMOR, JULIE (1952–), U.S. director. Born in Newton, Mass., Taymor had a passion for theater beginning at age seven with backyard performances of *Cinderella*. She began working with masks at 16 when studying at L'Ecole de Mime in Paris. Then she went to Oberlin College, where she joined Herbert Blau's experimental theater company and also studied folklore and mythology. After graduation, she went to Indonesia, staying for four years on fellowships, and developed a mask-dance troupe, Teatr Loh, living with one of the actors in a small compound with a dirt floor and no running water or electricity. The tensions she witnessed as a slow-moving individualistic culture confronted the fast pace of consumer-driven change inspired her first major theater work, *Way of Snow*, performed by an international company of actors, musicians, dancers, and puppeteers. Taymor designed her first American production, *The Odyssey* (1979), at the Baltimore Stage and achieved her first acclaim in New York City as production designer for Elizabeth Swados' *The Haggadah* (1980), creating a giant seder tablecloth that billowed up, Beijing Opera-style, to become the Red Sea, not to mention life-size puppet rabbis debating Passover scholarships, and alarmingly graphic plague effects projected through shadow puppets. She and a composer, Elliot Goldenthal, who later became her companion, collaborated on *Juan Darien, A Carnival Mass* (1988), which was revived at Lincoln Center in 1996, giving Taymor her first Broadway credit. From there, Taymor was engaged by the Disney company to take a story that many people know, *The Lion King*, a 1994 film that grossed $450 million worldwide, and elevate it to a theatrical event of enduring magnitude. The musical blended actors in masks and African costumes and life-size animal puppets operated by actors in full view of the audience. A giraffe is actually an actor wearing a conelike giraffe neck and head, balanced on arm and leg stilts. The show opened in 1997 and was a huge hit. It received 11 Tony Award nominations, including best musical, book, score and direction. Taymor won in two categories, direction and costume design. Besieged with opportunities after her overwhelming success, Taymor turned to film, directing *Titus* (1999), an adaptation of Shakespeare's *Titus Andronicus*, starring Anthony Hopkins and Jessica Lange. Taymor's edgy and avant garde take on Shakespeare's early drama, with music video-style editing, offended some by its goriness and supposed lack of reverence for the source material. The film was not a success, but Taymor triumphed with her next film, *Frida* (2002), a biographic portrait of the half-Jewish Mexican artist Frida Kahlo starring Salma Hayek. The film won six Academy Award nominations and won in two categories, for best makeup and original score.

[Stewart Kampel (2nd ed.)]

TAY-SACHS DISEASE (Amaurotic Familial Idiocy). Amaurotic Familial Idiocy, known as the Tay-Sachs Disease after W. Tay, an English ophthalmologist who discovered it in 1881, and B. Sachs, a U.S. neurologist who followed in 1887, is a hereditary disease, characterized by the onset during the first year of life of progressive retardation of development, followed by dementia, blindness, and paralysis. The outcome is invariably fatal by the third or fourth year of life.

The disease has a predilection for children of Ashkenazi Jewish families, with about 90 percent of all cases occurring in Jewish children whose antecedents are from families originating in the Polish-Russian provinces of Grodno, Suwalki, Vilna, and Kaunas (Kovno).

The disease is carried by autosomal recessive genes and occurs only when both parents are carriers. The combination of both affected genes in the child occurs, according to Mendelian Theory, in 25% of cases, with all these children developing the disease.

The eponym Tay-Sachs, while originally all-inclusive, is today restricted to the infantile type of amaurotic idiocy, while five other variants of this disease which have been described are associated with other eponyms.

The clinical signs and symptoms primarily affect the central nervous system. Recent research has demonstrated that the disease is caused by a genetically determined metabolic defect, leading to the accumulation within cells of the brain of abnormal quantities of gangliosides, complex fatty substances of the sphingolipid family. The genetic defect is caused by the deficient activity of a specific enzyme (Hexosaminidase A) required in biochemical reactions for the breakdown of a ganglioside, GM_2. This deficiency leads to accumulation of these fatty substances in the blood and their deposit in the tissues, subsequently associated with degenerative changes.

The Kingsbrook Jewish Medical Center (formerly the Jewish Chronic Disease Hospital) in New York City has been a center for research and treatment of the disease and has the largest experience in caring for its victims. There is no specific treatment of the disease, but supportive care in units especially skilled in handling such children provide considerable help to parents and temporarily improve the immediate prognosis of the affected child.

The development of methods for the assay of blood serum Hexosaminidase A activity has led to the introduction of tests which make it possible to discover carriers of the gene causing the disease. Jewish community organizations and health centers in various parts of the United States and in Israel have sponsored screening programs for the detection of the carrier state in couples considering marriage. When both are carriers, they may be counseled to avoid marriage or not to have children.

Similar biochemical studies are possible on the amniotic fluid of pregnant women to determine if the fetus is affected by the disease. This test permits near-accurate prenatal diagnosis of the disease. In such cases abortion is often advised.

Since Tay-Sachs disease is primarily a disease of Jews and the performance of abortion has religious and moral aspects, the permissibility of abortion where the disease has been diagnosed in the fetus has been discussed by rabbinic authorities. Rabbinical responsa in general oppose abortion in Tay-Sachs. As the detection of the disease in the fetus is still very difficult before the completion of three months of pregnancy, those rabbinical authorities who limit interruption of pregnancy in cases of fetal malformation (German measles) to the first three months of pregnancy, do not consent to an abortion in Tay-Sachs disease.

Rabbi E.J. Waldenberg, however, permits abortion because of Tay-Sachs up to seven months of pregnancy, in view of the tragic nature and inevitable effect upon a child born with this disease.

BIBLIOGRAPHY: Stanbury, Wyngaarden and Fredrickson, *The Metabolic Basis of Inherited Disease* (1972); R.H. Post, in: *Lancet* (June 6, 1970) 1230–1.

[David M. Maeir]

TAYYIB, ISAAC BEN BENJAMIN (d. 1830), rabbi, kabbalist, and author from *Tunis. No biographical details are known of him and his reputation rests on his works.

They are: (1) *Erekh ha-Shulḥan*, a commentary on the Shulḥan Arukh: *Oraḥ Ḥayyim* (1791), *Yoreh De'ah* (1798), *Ḥoshen Mishpat* (1815), *Even ha-Ezer* (1844), all published at Leghorn; (2) *Vavei ha-Ammudim* (1858), a commentary on the *Sefer Yere'im* of *Eliezer of Metz; (3) *Ḥukkat ha-Pesaḥ* (1853), a commentary on the Passover laws in the Shulḥan Arukh; (4) *Sefer ha-Zikkaron* (2 parts, 1892). Part 1 consists of novellae and part 2 is a kabbalistic commentary on *Avot* and the Passover *Haggadah*; (5) *Ḥelev Ḥittim* (1896), talmudic novellae; (6) *Va-Yizra Yiẓḥak* (Djerba, 1941), novellae to Genesis.

BIBLIOGRAPHY: D. Cazès, *Notes bibliographiques sur la littérature juive tunisienne* (1893), 311–23.

ṬAYYIBA, AL-, Muslim-Arab community, with municipal council status in central Israel, bordering on the Samarian hills. Al-Ṭayyiba, the largest village of the "Little Triangle" was included in Israel's borders following the armistice agreement with Jordan in 1949. It quickly expanded, reaching a population of 10,000 in 1968 and 30,400 in 2002, with an area of 7.3 sq. mi. (19 sq. km.). It received municipal status in 1990. Its farming progressed considerably, consisting mainly of field crops, vegetables, and fruit orchards. It also had a number of small industrial enterprises, mainly in the food and agricultural service branches. The site is possibly identical with a village Tivata (טִיבָּתָא), mentioned in the Talmud (TJ, Dem. 2:1, 22c).

[Efraim Orni]

TCHERIKOVER, VICTOR (**Avigdor**; 1894–1958), historian. Tcherikover was born in St. Petersburg, Russia, into a family of *maskilim*. Graduating from the humanistic high school in Moscow, he studied philosophy and later ancient history at the University of Moscow, then left for Germany in 1921 and studied ancient history at Berlin University. Emigrating to Palestine in 1925, Tcherikover became one of the first teachers at the Hebrew University, and the first professor of ancient history. During the 1950s he headed the departments of general history and classical studies.

A general historian by training, Tcherikover first wrote in the field of Hellenistic history; his *Die Hellenistischen Staedtegruendungen von Alexander dem Grossen bis auf die Roemerzeit* (1927) became the basic work in this field. Later he devoted himself entirely to the study of Jewish history during the Graeco-Roman period and became one of the most distinguished scholars in the field. His two special interests were the history of Palestine from the Macedonian conquest until the establishment of the Hasmonean state and the history of the Jewish Diaspora in Egypt during the Hellenistic-Roman period. Tcherikover's fundamental research in the first field was *Palestine under the Ptolemies* (1937). In this study papyri relating to Palestine were fully utilized and analyzed for the first time, giving a new insight into the administration of Ptolemaic Palestine, methods of trade, the non-Jewish population, and the Greek towns. In addition, in his *Ha-Yehudim va-ha-Yevanim ba-Tekufah ha-Helenistit* (1931; *Hellenistic Civilization and the Jews*, 1959; second revised and enlarged Hebrew ed., 1963) Tcherikover gave a general picture of the Jewish history of the Hellenistic period – including the period of the Seleucid rule, the revolt of the Maccabees, and the rule of the Hasmonean dynasty. The second edition of this work contains a general synthesis of Tcherikover's views on the relationship between the Jews and the Greeks.

The other important field of Tcherikover's work on the history of the Diaspora in Egypt was based on his research of papyri. Among the tens of thousands of Greek papyri found in Egypt from the end of the 19th century onward, papyri which mentioned Jews or matters connected with Jews were also discovered. Tcherikover initiated systematic research of the Jewish papyri, publishing many studies and a comprehensive research work, *Ha-Yehudim be-Miẓrayim ba-Tekufah ha-Helenistit-ha-Romit le-Or ha-Papirologyah* ("The Jews in Egypt in the Hellenistic-Roman Age in the Light of the Papyri," 1945, 1963^2, with Eng. summary). At the outset of his work on papyrology, Tcherikover realized that without a complete collection of the documents concerning the Jews there would be no solid basis to research on Jewish papyri. Consequently, starting in 1935, the preparation of his *Corpus Papyrorum Judaicarum* held a central place in Tcherikover's work. The first volume of the work was published in 1957, while volumes two and three were published posthumously in 1960 and 1964. Nearly 600 documents pertaining to Egyptian Jewry during the Hellenistic, Roman, and Byzantine periods are reproduced in the Greek original, accompanied by a translation and a scholarly commentary. Tcherikover's general introduction is a book in itself, reconstructing the millennium of the Egyptian Diaspora's existence with much historiographic expertise. Tcherikover's scholarly work is outstanding for construction, clarity of thought, lucidity of presentation, precision of detail, and general historic perception.

[Alexander Fuks]

TCHERIKOWER, ELIAS (1881–1943), historian. Tcherikower was born in Poltava, Ukraine, where his father was a pioneer of the Ḥibbat Zion movement. Graduating from the art school in Odessa in 1904, he decided to give up painting for writing. While in Odessa he joined the Zionist-Socialist circle, and after the 1905 Revolution, while a student at the University of St. Petersburg, he was arrested for participating in an illegal Russian Social-Democratic Labor Party conference, spending nearly a year in prison. In 1905 Tcherikower published his first study, a Marxist interpretation of *Mendele Mokher Seforim, in *Yevreyskaya Zhizn*. He contributed to the Russian-Jewish press and to the *Yevreyskaya Entsiklopediya*, and edited the pedagogical *Vestnik* OPE (1910–14). In 1914 his first book was published, the first volume of a history of the *Society for the Promotion of Culture among the Jews of Russia. In 1915 Tcherikower moved to New York, where, influenced by Ber *Borochov, he began to write in Yiddish. He was also active in the Jewish Congress movement.

Returning to Russia after the February Revolution, he settled in Kiev and became the leading spirit of a small group of Jewish intellectuals who, despite the many dangers, compiled many thousands of eyewitness reports and documents on pogroms and other phases of Jewish life in the Ukraine. In 1921 Tcherikower and the other members of the group left for Berlin, where they founded the Ostjuedisches Historisches Archiv with the plan to publish a seven-volume history of the pogrom movement in the Ukraine in the years 1917–21. Among the volumes published simultaneously in Yiddish and Russian was Tcherikower's *Anti-semitizm un Pogromen in Ukraine 1917–1918* ("Antisemitism and Pogroms in the Ukraine 1917–1918," 1923), with an introduction by S. Dubnow. Tcherikower completed a second volume during the 1930s, *Di Ukrainer Pogromen in Yor 1919* ("The Pogroms in the Ukraine in 1919"), which was published in 1965. One of the founders of the YIVO Institute in 1925, Tcherikower established its history section and edited three acclaimed volumes of *Historishe Shriftn* (1929–39) published by it.

Together with his wife Rebecca (1884–1963) he was a key figure in the preparation of the defense for Shalom *Schwartzbard during 1926–27; in the Berne trial on the *Protocols of the Elders of Zion (1934–35); and in the defense for David *Frankfurter (1936). Moving to Paris after Hitler's rise to power, Tcherikower, with Israel *Yefroykin, published the periodical *Oyfn Shaydveg*, which aimed at fostering a reappraisal of Jewish emancipation among Jewish intellectuals. He arrived in New York in 1940, continuing his activities with YIVO. He edited *Yidn in Frankraykh* (1942; *The Jews in France*, 1942), and the two-volume *Geshikhte fun der Yidisher Arbeter Bavegung in di Faraynikte Shtatn* ("History of the Jewish Labor Movement in the United States," vol. 1, 1943, vol. 2, 1945). A one-volume version of this work in English was published in 1961 as *The Early Jewish Labor Movement in the United States*. The bibliography of Tcherikower's works, compiled by A. Kin and Z. Szajkowski (1948, suppl. 1951) contains 470 titles.

TCHERNICHOWSKY, SAUL (1875–1943), Hebrew poet. Born in the village of Mikhailovka, Russia, Tchernichowsky grew up in the home of pious parents who were, however, open to the influences of the *Haskalah and *Ḥibbat Zion. He attended a modern Hebrew school, where he studied mainly Hebrew and the Bible, and at ten entered a Russian school. The many-sidedness of his education left a distinctive mark on his poetry in which the village, its life, and its landscape are also intrinsic components. Opening wide intellectual vistas for the young poet, his learning and knowledge were a source of inspiration as well as a wealth of material which Tchernichowsky transformed into aesthetic experiences. His education developed and nourished his critical attitude toward Diaspora Jewish culture and the yoke of the Jewish exile; cultivated his interest in other cultures; inspired his devotion to the Hebrew language, Jewish nationalism, and Zionism; and influenced his attitudes toward the traditional Jewish way of life.

His literary life may be divided into five periods:

The Odessa Period (1890–99)

At 14, Tchernichowsky was sent to Odessa to further his education: first in commercial secondary schools, and later through independent study in preparation for entry into the university. He was especially interested in languages and his studies of German, French, English, Greek, and Latin later stood him in good stead when he translated poetry from these languages into Hebrew. An avid reader of poetry, he was particularly influenced by the works of Pushkin, Lermontov, Goethe, Heine, Shakespeare, Byron, Burns, Longfellow, and later the Greek classics. In Odessa, Tchernichowsky was drawn to Zionist circles as well as to the younger Hebrew literary circles; the latter stimulated his interest in modern Hebrew literature, especially in the poetry of M.J. *Lebensohn, J.L. *Gordon, Ḥ.N. *Bialik, and the stories of S.Y. *Abramovitsh (Mendele Mokher Seforim). These left their mark on the writings of the young poet who at that time started publishing in various periodicals. His first two poems were "*Masat Nefesh*" in *Ha-Sharon* (Cracow, 1892/3) and "*Ba-Ḥalomi*" in *Ha-Pisgah* (Baltimore, 1892/3); and his first published book of verse – *Ḥezyonot u-Manginot* ("Visions and Melodies," 1898). This full-length work reflects the poet's deep involvement with the poetry of different nations and the influence it had on both the form and the content of his original poems, as well as his translations.

Characterized by a variety of classical poetic forms and complex rhythms, Tchernichowsky's poetry reveals his sensitivity to the sound and rhythm of language and his flair for accurate epithets. In this first collection of poems, the Tchernichowsky style is already clearly expressed. While most of his contemporaries developed their style through a struggle with classical Hebrew sources, Tchernichowsky put special emphasis on formal elements in both the choice of language and forms of verse. He drew his images from direct observation. Though his style has a biblical flavor and is replete with biblical imagery, he did not draw on the multifarious traditional implications and overtones that Hebrew terms and stock phrases could yield. Tchernichowsky's concept of love and nature, major themes in *Ḥezyonot u-Manginot*, is in the spirit of the Romantic poets. This quality added a new dimension to contemporary Hebrew poetry. The ideological concepts of his poetry may be traced to the poet's early Haskalah education and to the influence of Zionist and Hebrew literary circles with which he associated in Odessa. His reflective poems strongly call for a revolt against the fate of the Jewish people in exile, and even more, against the futility of the people's struggle for freedom. Criticism of Diaspora Jewish culture, an important motif in Tchernichowsky's later poetry (see "*Be-Leil Ḥanukkah*," "*Ḥarbi Ei Ḥarbi?*" and others) is already anticipated in this early work. The socialist influence (as in "*Ani Ma'amin*" and "*Me-Ḥezyonot ha-Navi*"), although found in these poems, was to remain marginal.

The Heidelberg-Lausanne Period (1899–1906)
Failing to gain admission to a Russian university, Tchernichowsky studied medicine in Heidelberg. He completed his medical studies in Lausanne in 1905. During this period, the poet came under the influence of the works of Goethe and Nietzsche. His own writings at that time are contained in two volumes: *Ḥezyonot u-Manginot* (Book 2, 1900), and the first part of *Shirim* ("Poems," 1910, which subsequently appeared in four enlarged editions). The motifs and stylistic peculiarities of the first volume of *Ḥezyonot u-Manginot* are also basic to the second, but the work is characterized by a more profound insight. Formalistically, the poet experiments with the long poem (the ballad and the epic). The form and structure of "*Bein ha-Meẓarim*," "*Amnon ve-Tamar*," and "*Barukh mi-Magenẓah*" are an extension of the ballad; while "*Levivot*," "*Berit Milah*," and "*Ke-Ḥom ha-Yom*" are narrative poems of wide scope. These poems are marked by the poet's close involvement expressed through his identification with his protagonists (spiritual personages in Jewish history) whose victory in defeat epitomizes the tragedy of the Jewish destiny.

In his narrative poems (the idylls), he lovingly describes the traditional Jewish way of life as he remembers it from his village childhood. His reflective poems, influenced by Nietzsche, are a criticism of Diaspora Jewish culture and Jewish religion which he contrasts with the Hellenic ideal of beauty, advocating an absolute response to the life impulse which imbues earthly existence (e.g., in "*Le-Nokhaḥ Pesel Apollo*," "*Me-Ḥezyonot Nevi'ei ha-Sheker*," and "*Le-Nokhaḥ ha-Yam*"). The motifs of enjoyment of the life of the senses and corporeal existence, whose tragic undertones are already felt in these early poems, are also dominant in the love and nature poems of the period ("*Ha-Navah mi-Dilsberg*," "*Lenchen*," "*Aggadot ha-Aviv*," "*Si'aḥ Kedumim*," and "*Mi-Tokh Av he-Anan*"). Tchernichowsky's romantic tendencies evidenced in the poems in the first collection are here replaced by an outspoken and consistent pantheistic and worldly view of life. His poetry at this time, infused with an underlying tension between two extreme yet mutually complementary motifs, embodies two different, possibly contradictory attitudes to reality. Ideologically, this tension is manifest through the poet's ambiguous attitude toward the Jewish heritage and the Jewish destiny. In terms of poetic experience and style, it is marked by a simultaneous double play of expression – sentimental lyricism and the restrained epic narrative.

The Russian Period (1906–22)
His personal experiences and the contemporaneous historical events left a deep impact on the poet; they form the subject of many of his works, and are a crucial factor in the molding of his outlook during these maturing years. Upon completion of his studies in Lausanne, he returned to Russia but had difficulty in finding a permanent post since he did not have a medical degree from a Russian university. He wandered from place to place, holding various posts. In Melitopol, he was arrested as a "political agitator" (1907). He settled in St. Petersburg in 1910, after his medical degree had finally been recognized. At the outbreak of World War I, he was drafted and served as an army doctor. After the Bolshevik revolution his economic situation deteriorated and in 1919, he settled in Odessa after a long journey through the Crimea. There he earned a scanty livelihood as a physician, and after three years of hardship left Russia.

Despite the years of adversity, there was no letup in Tchernichowsky's literary creativeness. In addition to poems, most of which were written in the latter part of the period, he composed stories, a number of scholarly essays and, of particular importance, translated a number of literary works from the Greek: Anacreon's lyrics (1920), Plato's *Symposium* (1929), and part of Homer's *Iliad*; and various English works, including Longfellow's "Evangeline" (he had previously translated the "Song of Hiawatha" which appeared in Odessa in 1912–13).

His poems of this period were collected and published under the title *Shirim* (Part 2) and *Shirim Ḥadashim* ("New Poems," 1923). Few of the poems in this volume, however, directly reflect the contemporaneous events that agitated the world; they are rather marked by Tchernichowsky's deliberate tendency to evade a confrontation with his time. In *Shirim Ḥadashim*, the poet expresses himself mostly in the rigorous form of the sonnet, but the poetic content does not complement the form. In his long narrative poems, especially those written in the later part of the period ("*Ba-Goren*" and "*Ḥatunnatah shel Elkah*"), he reverts back to the past and its tranquility, particularly his childhood years. These poems are free of the tragic undercurrent that lurked in his early "idylls," instead they highlight the comic ("*Ma'aseh be-Mordekhai ve-Yukhim*," "*Eli*," and "*Simḥah Lav Davka*").

Tchernichowsky also continued to write in the vein of the nature poetry of the Heidelberg period ("*Kismei Ya'ar*") with his detailed and minute descriptions of landscape (the Crimea sonnets) and the recrudescence of his "pagan" motifs, especially in the first part of the period ("*La-Ashtoret*

Shir ve-la-Bel," "*Olat Regel*," and "*Mot ha-Tammuz*"). Through withdrawal and by delaying and restraining his reaction he responded to contemporary historical events, which had undermined his naive attitude toward reality; they were reflected in a literary retrogression (e.g., in "*Al Tivez li-Meshorer*"). The shock finally finds direct expression in "*Ha-Kaf ha-Shevurah*" where for the first time he describes the experience of his arrest; in some of his stories based on his experience as an army doctor; and, especially, in the two sonnet sequences "*La-Shemesh*" (1919) and "*Al ha-Dam*" (1923). The aesthetic moment in these sonnets is kindled by a powerful tension between two diametrically opposed, incompatible, and irreconcilable attitudes. In "*La-Shemesh*," Tchernichowsky affirms life in all its manifestations, despite the disease and death that surround him; he accepts civilization: religion, art, and philosophy, despite fading ideals and the degeneration of the times. This is a crystallization of the ideal of the poet's cultural universalism which characterizes his previous works and now also includes the religious aspects of Jewish culture. In "*Al ha-Dam*," however, civilization is seen as a manifestation of the degeneration of the creative life force and is rejected with the same vigor as it had been affirmed in "*La-Shemesh*." The poet spurns any ideology which claims to bring salvation to the world but which, in fact, only leads to more bondage and death. The redemptive power of art is man's only hope and the poet's only asylum in the wreckage of his universe.

The Berlin Period (1922–31)

After a brief stay in Constantinople where he tried in vain to secure a position as a doctor in Palestine, Tchernichowsky moved to Berlin. He visited Palestine (1925) on behalf of the newly founded World Red Magen David Organization and tried to find permanent employment there; unable to do so, he returned to Berlin. In 1928, he visited the United States. In Berlin he earned a meager living from his literary work. For some time he edited the natural sciences and medicine section of the *Eshkol Encyclopaedia* and the literary section of the quarterly *Ha-Tekufah*. During this period, he wrote stories and articles which were published in the collection *Sippurim* (including also works he had written in Odessa, 1921–22) and in *Sheloshim u-Sheloshah Sippurim* (1941–42). In the main, he devoted himself to translation. Among the works he rendered into Hebrew are Goethe's *Reineke Fuchs*; Molière's *Le Malade Imaginaire*; Shakespeare's *Twelfth Night* and *Macbeth*; the Babylonian epic *Gilgamesh*; the Finnish epic *Kallevvallach*; Sophocles' *Oedipus Rex*; and he completed the translations of Homer's *Iliad* and *Odyssey*. Tchernichowsky also wrote children's poems, published in the collection *He-Ḥalil* (1922–23), a literary study of *Immanuel of Rome (1925), and a play *Bar Kokhva*. Many of his writings of the period were collected in a ten-volume jubilee edition of his works (1928/29–1933/34). These were edited by him and published by the Zionist General Council as a mark of appreciation to Tchernichowsky. Most of Tchernichowsky's poems of the period were printed in the third volume of his collected works.

"*Mayim she-Lanu*" ("Stale Water"), a narrative poem which bears a thematic link with the poet's earlier literary periods, has for its subject an episode that occurred during his stay in Odessa after the revolution. It describes the physical but mostly the spiritual distress of an intellectual who had become superfluous in the new social order and seeks escape in his memories of the distant, stable, and peaceful past. The keen awareness of historical perspective, missing from the earlier work "*Ḥatunnatah shel Elkah*," is one aspect of a general tendency in Tchernichowsky to retrospect now through a tragic consciousness. This casts his themes in a new light. His despair "of God and of gods," the general theme of "*Al ha-Dam*," also forms a background to his love poems "*Shirim le-Ilil*" and "*Ha-Na'ar ha-Kushi*"; the motif of the poems is the tragic nature of a fateful, ephemeral chance meeting expressed through desire and longing for another and fateful dependence on him. This motif does not form part of the exultant and egocentric love lyrics of his earlier works. Love now takes the place of faith and has become almost a cult. His serious poetry on nature and the theme of sensual existentialism have taken a mystical bent. The affirmation of the redemptive mission of art and of the gospel of beauty are the subject of several poems in this collection. This affirmation the poet has also filtered through his tragic consciousness in which he has come to realize that total achievement is impossible (see "*Ha-Pesel*"). His tragic ballads are an external expression of this mood.

Tchernichowsky also develops the tragic theme in his nationalist poetry of this period. At the beginning of his career, he had expressed sorrow at his alienation from his people and its culture, brought on by the futility of their struggle for freedom; now his sorrow is caused by his inability to be in Ereẓ Israel and to participate in the national rebirth to which he was so committed. During this period, he wrote some of his most fervent Zionist poems ("*Omerim Yeshnah Ereẓ*," "*Ẓedaktem ha-Bonim ha-Ẓe'irim*," and "*Al Harei Gilbo'a*). In his tragic absence he recognizes the inexorable fate of the eternal wanderer. Only through acceptance of his fate and identification with it, is he able to overcome its tragedy. The entire universe now becomes the scene of his wanderings (see "*Ha-Adam Eino Ella*").

The Ereẓ Israel Period (1931–43)

In 1931 Tchernichowsky was commissioned to edit (in Latin, English, and Hebrew) *Sefer ha-Munnaḥim li-Refu'ah u-le-Madda'ei ha-Teva* ("The Book of Medical and Scientific Terms") on the basis of material collected by A.M. Masie, and was thus able to settle in Ereẓ Israel. Upon completion of the work (1934), he was appointed physician of the municipal schools in Tel Aviv. In 1936, he signed a contract with Schocken Publishing House, and moved to Jerusalem where he lived until his death in August 1943.

Despite economic and social difficulties which led to his silence during his early years in Ereẓ Israel, he soon found himself at home in the country and its public life. Three times he was elected to represent the Hebrew branch of the PEN

Club, an international literary organization, at its world conference, and he expressed his opinions freely on current political questions. During this volatile period of Arab rioting, the struggle for Jewish labor and land settlement, controversy over defense policy and partition, World War II, and the beginning of the Nazi Holocaust, Tchernichowsky supported the Jewish maximalist-nationalist position. His poems were imbued with deep nationalist pathos (see the one-volume *Kol Shirei Sha'ul Tchernichowsky*, 1937); the collection *Re'i Adamah* (1940); and his last volume of poetry *Kokhevei Shamayim Reḥokim* (1944), many of them expressing his direct reaction to the struggle of the Jewish *yishuv* for its rights. This change in the poet's outlook is also discernible in the development of constantly recurring themes in his poetry on love, on nature, and of contemplation. Tragic retrospection gives way to direct and optimistic identification with contemporary life, in many respects recalling Tchernichowsky's early poetry with its critical attitude to religion and its "pagan" credo. This apparent retrogression to his earlier view, however, seems to have been prompted by an attempt at identification with the life in Ereẓ Israel which he saw as a regeneration of the ancient myth of settlement in the homeland.

In this last period, the poet, retracing his literary path, arrives at a second culmination: a more comprehensive and balanced tragic retrospection. With the outbreak of World War II and the Holocaust of European Jewry, he relives the shock of the World War I period and the Bolshevik revolution. As in his earlier works, Tchernichowsky reacts with ballads whose themes were taken from the tragic history of Jewish persecution in the Diaspora ("*Harugei Tirmunya*," "*Nisset ba-Olam*," and "*Balladot Vormaiza*"), seeking in the past an explanation for the tragedy of the present. No less characteristic is his return to early narrative poetry ("idylls") describing his childhood and village life. These poems served as a vehicle both to express the poet's present emotional state and, in a way, to escape it. His identification with the tragic Jewish fate, emphasized by the moral victory of the innocent victim devoted to truth and righteousness, however, overpowers pagan triumph. There is also a recrudescence of the idyllic love for the traditional Jewish way of life. This return to memories of a European childhood may possibly explain the poet's sense of estrangement from the renascent Jewish life in Ereẓ Israel. This tragic consciousness is apparent in many of Tchernichowsky's later poems ("*Ani-Li mi-Shelli Ein Kelum*," "*Amma de-Dahava*," his most comprehensive epic work, and his last poem "*Kokhevei Shamayim Reḥokim*") which bear parallels to the poet's tragic retrospective poetry of the Berlin period. For the third time, the poet comes to feel alienated from his people, due to his culture, his emotional reactions, and his national and social outlook. Though he reverted to the tragic evaluation of the national and individual destinies, Tchernichowsky's later poetry also shows a tendency toward reconciliation and acceptance. In "*Amma de-Dahava*" there is an attempt to bridge the gaps between the experiences of the child and those of the aging poet, and between the experiences of the alien homeland and that of alienation in the historical homeland.

Tchernichowsky's work, as a poet and as a translator, reveals a consistent tendency to break the constricting bonds of Hebrew literature and expand its content and form. In his translations, the poet presented the Hebrew reader with some of the finest classics of world literature: in the fields of epic and lyric poetry, of folk literature and drama. In this way, he realized the logical consequence of his proclivity for a universal culture which does not contradict one's national loyalties. His work as a translator had a direct influence on his original poetry which, with every successive collection of poems, showed a greater command of form; it was in consonance with his avowed program for widening the horizons of Hebrew poetry through the mastery of classical poetic forms (see his critical essay on the poetry of Immanuel of Rome). Tchernichowsky's concern with the aesthetic form is one of his important contributions to modern Hebrew poetry. This deliberate program to come to grips and to control the classic poetic form and structure was undoubtedly connected with the poet's national, social, and cultural outlook with which every critical evaluation of his work must contend. It is easy to perceive the connection between his criticism of stagnant Jewish culture in the Diaspora and his admiration for the ideal of Hellenic beauty or paganism on the one hand, and his concern with aesthetic form on the other. It is also easy to understand the effect that these extreme ideological criticisms had on the Hebrew reading public. This inconsistent and often self-contradictory ideology is, however, one of the fundamental premises which underlie the total poetic experience in Tchernichowsky. The national, social, or cultural ideology is not merely a central characteristic which may be isolated and separately recorded; it is an integral and consistent feature of all his poetry. Tchernichowsky's "ideology" is, in effect, a rejection of life bound by ideology; its aim is to justify the unmediated expression of experience by its own inner logic. His sensitivity to sound and rhythm, and his predilection for realistic narrative stem from this view. This "ideology" is the basic motif in his earthy love and nature poetry in which he expresses the feelings of a Jew of his time. This poetry among all his works is his most individual and characteristic contribution to modern Hebrew literature, and it produced a lively and enthusiastic reaction among his younger contemporaries.

His aspiration for an unmediated expression of the totality of existence, of which man is a part, also explains the poet's vacillation between idyllic contemplation, which conceives man as a being who belongs to the universe, and tragic contemplation, which sees man as a stranger in the universe. One view or the other may at times be emphasized, but each element (tragic or idyllic) is alternatively present in the poetry of the other. The duality, inherent in a view of reality where the idyllic and the tragic are components, apparently explains Tchernichowsky's changing evaluation of Jewish and world cultures. The interchangeability of the sense of belonging and the sense of alienation, which ideologically is contradictory, in the sphere of experience is a fluctuation between extremes. Tchernichowsky comes to accept his people's heritage within the framework of human culture. In *"Amma de-Dahava"* and *"Kokhevei Shamayim Reḥokim,"* the poet welded out of the contradictory experiences and evaluations that constituted his universe as a Jew who is devoted both to the culture of his people and to European culture a balanced and harmonious acquiescence. These two works are among his most complete artistic achievements, and his most important contributions to Hebrew poetry. Various editions of Tchernichowsky's work were published through the close of the 20th century. In 1990 a new edition of *Kol Kitvei S. Tchernichowsky* appeared. A list of the English translations of his works appears in Goell, Bibliography.

BIBLIOGRAPHY: E. Silberschlag, *Saul Tschernichowsky* (1968; containing translations and bibliography); *Ha-Shiloaḥ*, 35 (1918), 97–222 (autobiography and articles about him); J. Klausner, *Sha'ul Tchernichowsky, ha-Adam ve-ha-Meshorer* (1947); J. Lichtenbaum, *Sha'ul Tchernichowsky, Ḥayyav vi-Yẓirato* (1953); D. Sadan, *Bein Din le-Ḥeshbon* (1963), 14–34; B. Kurzweil, *Bialik ve-Tchernichovsky* (1967²), 211–344; E. Schweid, *Ha-Ergah li-Mele'ut ha-Havayah* (1968), 85–194; Shunami, Bibl, nos. 4376–4386; M. Ribalow, *The Flowering of Modern Hebrew Literature* (1959); Waxman, Literature, index; Kressel, Leksikon, 2 (1967), 44–58. **ADD. BIBLIOGRAPHY:** Y. Haefrati, *Disjunctive Structure in the Poetry of S. Tschernichowsky, with Special Emphasis upon his Idyll* (1974); idem, *Mivḥar Ma'amrei Bikkoret* (1976); Sh. Avnery, *Sheloshah She'arim: Ma'amarim be-Vikkoret Shiratenu* (1978); Sh. Yaniv, *Hitpatteḥut ha-Baladah ba-Sifrut ha-Ivrit* (1981); A. Shaanan, *S. Tshernichovski: Monografiyyah* (1984); Ch. Shoham, *Be-Darkhei ha-Idiliyah* (1989); Y. Mazor, *Tshernichovski ha-Aḥer: Tavnit Nof Sippuro* (1992); H. Barzel, *Shirat ha-Teḥiyyah* (1992); B. Arpaly, *S. Tshernichovski: Meḥkarim u-Te'udot* (1994); Z. Luz, *La-Shemesh* (1996); M. Zohori, *Pirkei Lashon: Shirat Tshernichovski ve-ha-Tanakh* (1997); B. Arpaly, *Tom u-Tehom: Ha-Idiliyah shel Tshernichovski* (1998).

[Eliezer Schweid]

TCHERNOWITZ, CHAIM (pseudonym **Rav Za'ir**; 1871–1949), talmudic scholar and Hebrew author. Tchernowitz, born in Sebesh (district of Vitebsk), Russia, studied in Lithuania and obtained *semikhah* from Isaac Elchanan *Spektor of Kovno in 1896. Moving to Odessa the following year, he founded his own yeshivah, eventually transforming it into a rabbinical seminary (1907) which attracted many students from the Jewish intelligentsia in Russia, including Ḥayyim Naḥman *Bialik and Joseph *Klausner. Tchernowitz's ambition was to combine traditional study with modern research in order to rejuvenate Jewish learning. His pseudonym Rav Ẓa'ir (young rabbi) reflects his aims. Tchernowitz received a Ph.D. from the University of Wuerzburg in 1914. Settling in the United States in 1923, he taught Talmud at the Jewish Institute of Religion in New York.

Tchernowitz's writings may be classified under two headings: scholarly and publicistic. His first scholarly article appeared in *Ha-Shiloaḥ* 3 (1898), entitled, *"Ha-Sanegoryah be-Vattei Dinin shel Yisrael."* He subsequently published studies on the codes of literature preceding R. Joseph Caro, *"Le-Toledot ha-Shulḥan Arukh ve-Hitpashetuto"* (*Ha-Shiloaḥ*, 4 (1898); 5 (1899); 6 (1899)). In a more popular vein he wrote a series of general articles on the Talmud, *"Ha-Talmud"* (*Ha-Shiloaḥ*, 7 (1901); 8 (1901–2); 10 (1902)), His first books were methodological studies aimed at modernizing the teaching of Talmud: *Shi'urim be-Talmud* (2 vols., 1903), on Bava Kamma, and *Kiẓẓur ha-Talmud* (vol. 1, 1919; vol. 2, 1922). Tchernowitz's primary interest was to produce a full historical account of the development of the *halakhah*. Although he did not discount the works of his predecessors, I.H. *Weiss and I. *Halevy, he thought that they neglected the long era preceding the late Second Temple period and that they overlooked sociological, ideological, and political factors. His concern was to present the *halakhah* not in its final crystallization but in its development beginning in pre-Mosaic times. His *Toledot ha-Halakhah* (4 vols., 1935–50) covers the period up to the destruction of the Second Temple, and *Toledot ha-Posekim* (3 vols., 1946–47) deals with the post-talmudic, geonic, and medieval periods. These works are widely used by students of the history of Jewish law.

As a publicist, Tchernowitz showed deep interest in the Zionist movement and in contemporary Jewish problems. He published articles and essays, many of them controversial and polemic, in scores of Hebrew and Yiddish periodicals which appeared later in book form: *Be-Sha'arei Ẓiyyon* (1937). *Ḥevlei Ge'ullah* (1949) is a collection of his essays on the struggle for Jewish political independence. In 1940 Tchernowitz founded the Hebrew monthly *Bitzaron* in New York, which he edited until his death. Toward the close of his life he published a series of vivid autobiographical articles in *Bitzaron*, posthumously issued under the title *Pirkei Ḥayyim* (1954). His *Masekhet Zikhronot* (1945) is a collection of essays on Mendele Mokher Seforim, Aḥad Ha-Am, Bialik, and other well-known personalities with whom he associated during the early stages of his career.

BIBLIOGRAPHY: A.R. Malachi, *Peri Eẓ Ḥayyim* (1946), bibl. of the works of Tchernowitz and literature about him; *Bitzaron* (April 1948), Rav Ẓa'ir jubilee issue; *ibid.* (May 1949), memorial issue.

[Jacques K. Mikliszanski]

TCHERNOWITZ, SAMUEL (1879–1929), Hebrew journalist, brother of Chaim *Tchernowitz. Born in Sebesh, Samuel Tchernowitz participated there in Zionist activities. In 1903, he moved to Warsaw, where he became the secretary of the children's weekly *Olam Katon*, and then joined the editorial board of *Ha-Zeman*. With the renewed publication of *Ha-Ẓefirah* in 1910, he joined its editorial board, replacing Sokolow as editor, and was active in the Hebrew movement and at the Congress of the Hebrew Language and Culture Organization in Vienna (1913). When *Ha-Ẓefirah* ceased publication during World War I, he returned to Russia, and became one of the editors of the daily *Ha-Am*. He emigrated to Palestine in 1921, served on the editorial board of *Haaretz*, and was secretary of the Va'ad Le'ummi. He began to write in *Ha-Meliẓ* in 1897 and until his death contributed to Hebrew periodicals. His chief contribution was to *Ha-Zeman* and *Ha-Ẓefirah*, and he was one of the first modern correspondents of the Hebrew press. *Ha-Ẓefirah* published in serial form his monograph on the *Benei Moshe, which was later published as a book, *Benei Moshe u-Tekufatam* (1914). Of his numerous essays and articles, only one small collection, *Im Shaḥar*, was published (1927). His son was the Israeli diplomat Jacob *Tsur and his daughter was the Hebrew writer Yemimah *Tchernowitz-Avidar.

BIBLIOGRAPHY: Kressel, Leksikon, 2 (1967), 43–44; J. Tsur, *Sunrise in Zion* (1968), index, s.v. Tsur, Samuel and Tsur, family.

[Getzel Kressel]

TCHERNOWITZ-AVIDAR, YEMIMAH (1909–1998), Israeli author of children's books, daughter of Samuel *Tchernowitz. Born in Vilna, she immigrated to Palestine in 1921. She published stories, poems and legends for children in *Eden* (ed. by D. *Persky), as well as stories about Argentinian Jewry. She wrote a regular column for children in the newspaper *Davar* and many popular books for children. Among these are *Muki* (1943); *Eḥad Mishelanu* (1947), *Shemonah be-Ikvot Eḥad* (1945). Rama Zuta edited Tchernowitz-Avidar's diaries of the years 1919–1936 (2004). For English translations of her work see Goell, Bibliography, 2575–2580, 3139–42.

Her husband, Yosef Avidar (1906–1995), was deputy chief of the General Staff of the Haganah in 1946 and later deputy chief of staff of the Israel Defense Forces. He was Israel ambassador to Moscow (1955–58) and Buenos Aires (1960–65), and controller of the Histadrut (1968–71). He is author of the book *The Party and the Army in the Soviet Union* (1985).

ADD. BIBLIOGRAPHY: R. Gefen-Dotan, "*Al Ḥavurot ha-Yeladim shel Y. Tchernowitz-Avidar*," in: *Sifrut Yeladim ve-No'ar*, 10:3–4 (1984), 55–58.

[Getzel Kressel]

TEACHER OF RIGHTEOUSNESS (Heb. מוֹרֶה צֶדֶק *moreh ẓedek*), the organizer of the *Qumran community or *Yaḥad. His designation may have been derived from such biblical passages as Hosea 10:12, "it is time to seek the Lord, till He come and cause righteousness to rain [*yoreh ẓedek*] upon you," or Joel 2:23, "rejoice in the Lord, your God; for He giveth you the former rain in just measure" – *et ha-moreh li-ẓedakah*, which has sometimes been translated "teacher of righteousness" (see AV margin). He is never indicated by his personal name, so far as can be told from surviving records; it has been suggested that his name was Zadok, and that it was for this reason that his followers were called *Zadokites (so H.J. Schoeps, *Urgemeinde, Judenchristentum, Gnosis* (1956), 74); but this is uncertain. Knowledge of him is derived from two principal sources – the Zadokite Fragments (or Book of the Covenant of *Damascus) and various Qumran commentaries on books or sections of the Bible.

(1) The Zadokite Fragments

At the beginning of the Zadokite Admonition in a time of apostasy, God "remembered the covenant of the forefathers and caused a remnant to remain for Israel." For 20 years this remnant groped for a way like blind men, "and God took note of their deeds, for they sought Him with a perfect heart; and He raised up for them a teacher of righteousness to direct them in the way of His heart, that He might make known to the last generations what He was about to do to the last generation" (CD 1:4–12). While the godly remnant had a distinct existence of 20 years before the Teacher of Righteousness arose, he was the effective founder of the community, for they appear to have had no leader before him.

To the community which he organized, the voice of the Teacher of Righteousness was as the voice of God; the reward of ultimate salvation and victory is held out to those who "listen to the voice of the Teacher of Righteousness" (CD 20:28, 32). The Zadokite Admonition, in the form in which it has survived, apparently dates from a period after the death of the Teacher of Righteousness: an interval of indefinite duration runs "from the day when the Unique Teacher was gathered in until a Messiah stands up from Aaron and from Israel" (CD 20:1). It has been suggested that "Unique Teacher" (*moreh ha-yaḥid*) should be emended to "Teacher of the Community" (*moreh ha-yaḥad*), but this is probably unnecessary. If the Unique Teacher is identical with the Teacher of Righteousness – and it is difficult to think that anyone else could have been so designated by the community – he was evidently thought of as a preparer of the way for the messianic age but not as a messianic personage himself. There is a further passage in the Admonition which interprets the "nobles of the people" in the Song of the Well (Num. 21:17ff.) as "those who have come to dig the well with the staffs which the Staff [lawgiver] instituted [*bi-meḥokekot asher ḥakak ha-meḥokek*] to walk thereby… and without which they will not grasp instruction until there stands up one who teaches righteousness [*yoreh ha-ẓedek*] in the latter days" (CD 6:8–11). If the section in which these words appear is of the same date as the other passages quoted, then the community evidently expected at the end-time either another teacher of righteousness to arise or else the first Teacher of Righteousness to return to earth – in the latter case a comparison may be made with the similar expectation of the return of Elijah cherished in other Jewish circles.

In the Qumran texts themselves a parallel to the past and future Teacher of Righteousness is provided by the past and future Expounder of the Law (*doresh ha-Torah*). The "Staff" (*meḥokek*) in the Song of the Well is "the Expounder of the Law" who ordained the rules by which the men of the covenant live (CD 6:7); he is conceivably identical with the Teacher of Righteousness who organized the community. Later in the Zadokite Admonition the "star" of Amos 5:26 and (more especially) Numbers 24:17 is "the Expounder of the Law [*doresh ha-Torah*] who is to come to Damascus" (CD 7:18ff.). This coming Expounder of the Law is mentioned also in 4Q *Florilegium*, in an interpretation of II Samuel 7:11–14. In both of these passages he is to be accompanied by the Davidic Messiah, called "the prince of all the congregation" in CD 7:20 and "the shoot of David" in 4Q *Florilegium*. Since Torah is to be sought from the priest's lips (Mal. 2:7), this coming Expounder of the Law may be the great priest of the new age who will act as colleague to the great king; he may also be tentatively identified with the Teacher of Righteousness who is to stand up in the latter days (CD 6:11).

(2) The Commentaries

In the very fragmentary commentary on Micah from Cave 1 (1Qp Micah) the words "What are the high places of Judah? Are they not Jerusalem?" (1:5) are interpreted of "the Teacher of Righteousness, the one who [teaches the law to his] [council] and to all who volunteer to join the elect ones [of God, who keep the law] in the council of the community, who will be saved from the day [of judgment]."

Some fragmentary comments on Psalm 37 found in Cave 4 interpret certain statements in that psalm with reference to the Teacher of Righteousness. Verse 23, "It is of the Lord that a man's goings are established..." is said to concern "the priest, the Teacher of [Righteousness,... whom God] established to build for himself the congregation..."; and verses 32ff., "the wicked watcheth the righteous and seeketh to slay him...," are interpreted of "the Wicked [Priest] who [rose up against the Teacher of Righteousness] to put him to death [because he taught...] the law... He laid hands on him, but God 'will not abandon [him into his hand or let him be condemned when he is] brought to trial.'" Parallel to this last comment is one from another fragment, in which Psalms 37:14ff., "the wicked have drawn out the sword, and have bent their bow; to cast down the poor and needy...," is read as a reference to "the wicked of Ephraim and Manasseh, who will seek to lay hands on the priest and the men of his council in the hour of trial which is to come upon them. But God will redeem them out of their hands." From these fragments it is learned that the Teacher of Righteousness was a priest and that among his opponents was one outstanding figure called the *Wicked Priest.

These two facts are confirmed, and further information is supplied about the Teacher, in the commentary on Habakkuk from Cave 1 (1Qp Hab.). From the prophet's complaint in Habakkuk 1:4 that "the wicked doth beset the righteous" (interpreted of [the Wicked Priest] and the Teacher of Righteousness) onward, the Teacher plays a prominent part in the exposition. Those among the nations who are called upon in Habakkuk 1:5 to wonder and be astonished at the work which God is about to do, which they "will not believe though it be told," are the unfaithful ones who paid no heed to the words which the Teacher of Righteousness spoke from the mouth of God, refusing to believe "when they hear all that is [coming upon] the last generation from the mouth of the priest into [whose heart] God put [wisdom] to interpret all the words of his servants and prophets" (1Qp Hab. 2:7–9). This is in line with what is already known about the Teacher's mission from the Zadokite Admonition. The Teacher understood the course of future events by divine illumination: on Habakkuk 2:1ff. the commentator states that "God commanded Habakkuk to write the things that were coming on the last generation," but did not inform him when the epoch would be fulfilled. And as for the words, "so he may run who reads it," their interpretation concerns the Teacher of Righteousness, to whom God made known "all the mysteries of the words of His servant the prophets" (1Qp Hab. 7:1–5). The words of the prophets remained mysteries (*razim*), even to the prophets themselves, until the interpretation (*pesher*) was revealed to the Teacher; after that, the mysteries were mysteries no more, at least to those who heard and believed him. Of them the words of Habakkuk 2:4 ("the righteous shall live by his faith") were spoken: "Their interpretation concerns all the doers of the law in the house of Judah, whom God will save from the house of judgment because of their toil and their faith in the Teacher of Righteousness" (1Qp Hab. 8:1–3).

Of the occasions when "the Teacher of Righteousness and the men of his council suffered iniquity" at the hands of the Wicked Priest (1Qp Hab. 9:9, cf. 8:17) one is singled out for special mention. This was when "the Wicked Priest pursued after the Teacher of Righteousness to swallow him up in his hot fury, even to his place of exile, and on the occasion of the sacred season of rest, the Day of Atonement, appeared among them to swallow them up and to make them stumble on the fast-day, their Sabbath of rest" (1Qp Hab. 11:4–8, on Hab. 2:15). It is usually held that this implies that the Teacher and his followers observed the Day of Atonement according to a different calendar from that followed by the official priesthood in Jerusalem, and there is other evidence to confirm this (see *Calendar). The reference to "swallowing them up" recalls Habakkuk 1:13, "wherefore lookest Thou when they deal treacherously and holdest Thy peace when the wicked swalloweth up the man that is more righteous than he?" – a passage which the commentary interprets of "the house of Absalom and the men of their council, who were struck dumb when the Teacher of Righteousness was chastised, and did not aid him against the *Man of Lies who rejected the law in the midst of all their congregation." This occasion may not be the same as the last, for the Man of Lies is probably not the Wicked Priest, and the problematic house of Absalom figures here but does not in the comment on Habakkuk 2:15. The Teacher of Righteousness, then, was persecuted by the Wicked Priest, but (as the commentary on Ps. 37:14ff., 32ff. suggests) was delivered from his malice.

(3) Attempts to Identify the Teacher

It has been argued that the title "Teacher of Righteousness" designates a succession of leaders of the Qumran community, but even so, it is apparently used especially of the community's first organizer. As for his identity and date, suggestions range from Ezra (so T.H. Gaster, *The Dead Sea Scriptures* (1956), vi *et passim*; C.T. Fritsch, *The Qumran Community* (1956), 83ff.) and Nehemiah (so L. Rabinowitz, in JBL, 73 (1954), 11ff.) at one end, and Menahem son of Judah the Galilean (or his kinsman and successor, Eleazar b. Jair) killed by Eleazar captain of the Temple in 66 C.E. at the other (so C. Roth, *Historical Background of the Dead Sea Scrolls* (1958), 12ff.; G.R. Driver,

The Judaean Scrolls (1965), 267ff.). A number of scholars have identified him with Onias III, the last legitimate high priest of the house of Zadok, assassinated at the instance of the illegitimate high priest Menelaus in 171 B.C.E. (so H.H. Rowley, *Zadokite Fragments and the Dead Sea Scrolls* (1952), 67ff.; M. Black, *The Scrolls and Christian Origins* (1961), 20); others have suggested Onias the rain-maker, killed by partisans of Hyrcanus II in 63 B.C.E. (so R. Goossens, *La Nouvelle Clio*, 1–2 (1949–50), 336ff.; cf. A. Dupont-Sommer, *Essene Writings from Qumran* (1961), 359 with notes 2, 3), or Judah b. Jedidiah, one of the sages massacred by Alexander Yannai (so W.H. Brownlee, in: BASOR 126 (1952), 10ff., where this Judah is further identified with Judah the Essene, contemporary of Aristobulus I). The mention of "the house of Absalom" in 1Qp Hab. 5:10ff. does not help much, because, even if "Absalom" be a real name of the period and not a figurative one, an "Absalom" can be produced from contemporary history to suit almost every suggested identification of the Teacher. Perhaps the Teacher of Righteousness is not mentioned outside the Zadokite and Qumran literature and must be thought of as an otherwise unknown religious leader who had his following in or after the time of the Hasmonean dynasty. If, as is not unlikely, it is his voice that can be heard speaking in the first person in some of the Qumran *Thanksgiving Psalms, they throw further light on his devotion and struggles.

BIBLIOGRAPHY: A. Michel, *Le Maître de Justice* (1954); G. Jeremias, *Der Lehrer der Gerechtigkeit* (1963); J. Carmignac, *Christ and the Teacher of Righteousness* (1962); F.F. Bruce, *The Teacher of Righteousness in the Qumran Texts* (1957); Roth, in: VT, 13 (1963), 91ff.

[Frederick Fyvie Bruce]

TEACHERS' ASSOCIATION IN ISRAEL, organization founded in 1903 at a meeting of teachers in Zikhron Ya'akov, convened by Menaḥem *Ussishkin, who was then visiting Ereẓ Israel. It was attended by 59 of the approximately 100 teachers in the country. The aims of the association were declared to be:

(a) Improvement of educational facilities in Ereẓ Israel and standardization of the schools;

(b) Revival of the Hebrew language and the instilling of a national Jewish spirit into schools;

(c) Improvement of teachers' conditions.

During the first decade of its existence, the Teachers' Association contributed greatly toward the foundation of the Hebrew school system. It decided in favor of using the Sephardi pronunciation of Hebrew, and formed a committee of linguists whose task was to establish the new Hebrew terminology for the teaching of various academic subjects. The association also organized training courses for unqualified teachers, determined a syllabus for eight-grade elementary schools, devised teachers' qualifying examinations, and published textbooks and teaching manuals. Its organ, *Ha-Ḥinnukh* ("Education"), founded in 1910, reached a circulation of 18,000 (1968).

The outstanding achievement of the Teachers' Association was the establishment of Hebrew as the language of instruction in the schools of Ereẓ Israel. The first attempt to teach in Hebrew was made by Eliezer *Ben-Yehuda in 1889, and teachers in the early settlements followed his example. However, urban schools, maintained by the *Hilfsverein der deutschen Juden and the *Alliance Israélite Universelle, refused to use Hebrew for instruction. When the central committee of the Teachers' Association learned that the Board of Governors of the Haifa *Technion, controlled by the Hilfsverein, had decided that the language of instruction in the new institution would be German, they declared a boycott of Hilfsverein institutions in Ereẓ Israel (1914). The association proceeded to assist in establishing Hebrew schools which formed the nucleus of a national school system.

During the 1920s the association began campaigning for better working conditions for teachers. At the time, the Jewish community in Palestine had gained a large measure of autonomy under the British Mandate; but, as a result of the financial difficulties of the Zionist Organization, which was responsible for Hebrew education, and the lack of material support from the Mandatory authorities, teachers' salaries were paid belatedly. The Teachers' Association called its first strike in 1925, in order to ensure prompt payment of salaries. When the State of Israel was established in 1948, kindergartens and elementary schools became state-controlled, and their teachers became state employees. Nevertheless, the struggle for an improvement in working conditions continued for many years, and only in the second decade after the establishment of the state was there a significant improvement in conditions. Among the important achievements of the association are the linking of teachers' salaries to those of other university graduates in Israel, the reduction of overcrowding in classes, compensation for teachers on extension courses, and the application of the Pensions Law to teachers.

In the 1930s the association set up branches all over Israel, and specialized affiliated bodies were established (organizations of kindergarten teachers, secondary school teachers, headmasters, etc.). In 1951 Arab teachers joined the association, and a special department was opened for them. The issue of whether the association should join the Histadrut was debated for 27 years. However, in 1950 a majority decided in favor of joining the Histadrut, provided the association retained a large measure of autonomy.

When education became state-controlled, the association increased its pedagogic activities. It began by organizing its own in-service training for kindergarten and other teachers; in 1957 a joint committee was formed by the Teachers' Association and the Ministry of Education to plan teachers' extension courses, and their administration and inspection. In 1959 the association set up a central archive documenting the history of Hebrew education and the Teachers' Association. *Hed ha-Ḥinnukh* ("Education Echo"), first published by the association in 1927, became a weekly publication in 1949. In 1967 it had a circulation of 22,000. A quarterly on kindergarten education, *Hed ha-Gan* ("Kindergarten Echo"), was also published. The association's publishing house, Oẓar ha-Moreh, began activities in 1950, and has since published numerous teachers' aids, teaching manuals, anthologies and studies in psychology and education.

In 1951 the association established contacts with international teachers' associations, and, in 1961, it was host to the Conference of the Federation of Teachers' Associations.

In 1968 it had a membership of approximately 20,000 elementary-school teachers, 3,000 kindergarten teachers, 3,000 secondary-school teachers, 700 instructors at teachers' training colleges, and 500 school inspectors. It also had 2,000 Arab members. In 2005 it had 100,000 members, making it the largest trade union in Israel. In 1990 the Association established the Association of Teachers for the Advancement of Teaching and Education. Its activities include study weekends, workshops, conventions, educational tours in Israel and overseas, theater evenings, lectures, the creation of a code of ethics, surveys, and research; it had 65,000 members.

BIBLIOGRAPHY: Sh. Levin, *Teachers Union in Israel* (1961), publ. by ITU; *Jubilee Book of the Teachers' Association in Israel, 1903–1953* (Heb., 1956); H. Shifroni, *Histadrut ha-Morim* (1954), publ. by ITU. **WEBSITE:** www.itu.org.il.

[Shalom Levin]

TEC, NECHAMA (1931–), U.S. sociologist and authority on rescue and resistance during the Holocaust. Tec devoted her scholarly career to understanding altruistic and cooperative behavior under extreme conditions. Her path-breaking research, which emphasizes the matrix of personal, social, and cultural contexts that motivated instances of altruism, questions earlier attributions of such behavior to class, politics, or religion. Drawing from sources including memoirs, interviews, and archival documents in German, Polish, and Yiddish, Tec suggests that factors such as social marginality, independent-mindedness, and empathy for the vulnerable were critical to Jewish and Christian rescuers and resisters.

Tec's research originated in her family's World War II experiences. Born in Lublin, Poland, to Roman Bawnik, a businessman, and Esther (Hachamoff) Bawnik, Tec lived for three years during the war under an assumed Christian identity. With the aid of Catholic Poles, her sister and parents also survived by passing as Christians. She married Leon Tec, a child psychiatrist, in 1950 and immigrated to the United States in 1952, where she had two children. Educated at Columbia University, she received her B.A. (1954), M.A. (1955), and Ph.D. (1963) in sociology.

A thematic continuity weaves through Tec's numerous articles and books; each research project grows out of the previous one. Tec's first books on gambling and drug use reflected her early interest in fringe behavior. With the 1984 publication of her memoir, *Dry Tears: The Story of a Lost Childhood*, Tec began to integrate this interest with the nascent field of Holocaust studies. In *Dry Tears* and her subsequent books (*When Light Pierced the Darkness: Christian Rescue of Jews in Nazi-Occupied Poland* (1986); *In the Lion's Den: The Life of Oswald Rufeisen* (1990); *Defiance: The Bielski Partisans* (1993); and *Resilience and Courage: Women, Men, and the Holocaust* (2003)), Tec explored marginal behavior in the context of World War II. Her studies illuminate the rare but vitally important phenomenon of Jews and Christians risking their lives, and often those of their families, to help others escape Nazi persecution. In the critically acclaimed *Resilience and Courage,* Tec considers these and other aspects of the Holocaust from the perspective of gender, noting that, "even though the Germans were committed to sending all Jews to their deaths, for a variety of reasons women and men traveled toward that destination on distinct roads" (12) and often employed different coping strategies.

Tec received numerous awards, honors, and prizes, including appointment to the Council of the United States Holocaust Memorial Museum; two Pulitzer Prize nominations; a National Jewish Book Award; a First Prize for Holocaust Literature by the World Federation of Fighters, Partisans and Concentration Camp Inmates; and an International Anne Frank Special Recognition Prize. She served on the sociology faculty at the University of Connecticut for over three decades, and held several senior research fellowships, scholar-in-residencies, and international lectureships.

BIBLIOGRAPHY: J.T. Baumel, Review of *Resilience and Courage*, in: *Yad Vashem Studies*, 32 (2004), 479–86; D.H. Hirsch, Review of *Defiance: The Bielski Partisans*, in: *Shofar,* 13 (Summer 1995), 91–94.

[Rona Sheramy (2nd ed.)]

TECHNION, ISRAEL INSTITUTE OF TECHNOLOGY, Israel's major engineering university; situated in Haifa. Paul *Nathan of Berlin, one of the leaders of the *Hilfsverein der deutschen Juden, was the father of the plan for a technical school in Haifa. Aided by a 100,000 ruble gift from the heirs of Kalonymus *Wissotzky of Moscow and a $100,000 contribution from Jacob *Schiff of New York, the Hilfsverein proceeded to construct a building, with Alexander *Baerwald as architect. The cornerstone was laid on the slopes of Mt. Carmel in 1912. Zionist personalities like *Aḥad Ha-Am, Jehiel *Tschlenow, and Shmarya *Levin sat on the governing board, in addition to leaders of the Hilfsverein.

As the date approached for the opening of the school, then known by the German name Technikum, a struggle broke out in the governing board over the language of instruction. The Zionist minority insisted on Hebrew, but the majority voted for German. The decision aroused a storm of controversy, in which the Hebrew *Teachers' Association took the lead. Meetings were held throughout the country; resolutions of protest were passed by practically all Jewish institutions and organizations; the Teachers' Association issued a ban against the acceptance of posts or the registration of students in the Technikum; pupils at the Hilfsverein's other schools struck in support of a demand to institute Hebrew as the sole language of instruction, and many of the teachers resigned. This "language conflict" helped to accelerate the establishment of a network of national Hebrew schools. The opening of the Technion was delayed, and before the controversy could be settled, World War I broke out. The unoccupied building served as a military hospital, first for the Turkish forces and later for the British. After the war, the Zionist Organization acquired the property from the Hilfsverein and the first classes on a university level were held in December 1924.

In the period preceding the establishment of the state, and especially during the administration of Shlomo *Kaplansky as head of the institution (1931–50), the school developed as a technological university training engineers on Central European standards. Yaakov *Dori, who was president from 1951 to 1965, with the assistance of Sydney Goldstein, who was vice president for some years, altered the educational patterns of the Technion, modeling it more on similar institutions in Western Europe and the United States. In addition to the faculties of engineering and architecture, a faculty of natural sciences and mathematics was opened in 1953. In 1952 the Technion began conferring masters' and doctors' degrees, in addition to those of bachelor and ingénieur. A school of graduate studies was formally established in 1957. In 1953 the Technion began its move from the original building in midtown Haifa to a 300-acre campus on Mt. Carmel, popularly known as Technion City. Dori was succeeded as president by Alexander *Goldberg in 1965. Successive presidents have been Gen. (Res.) Amos Horev (1973–82), Prof. Josef Singer (1982–86), Dr. Max W. Reis (1986–90), Prof. Zeev Tadmor (1990–), Amos Lapidot (1998–2001), and Yitzhak *Apeloig (2001–).

The following faculties and departments exist at the Technion: Aerospace Engineering, Agricultural Engineering, Architecture and Town Planning, Biology, Biomedical Engineering, Chemical Engineering, Chemistry, Civil and Environmental Engineering, Computer Science, Education in Technology and Science, Electrical Engineering, Food Engineering and Biotechnology, General Studies, Industrial Engineering and Management, Materials Engineering, Mathematics, Mechanical Engineering, Medicine, and Physics, and Teacher Training.

Research is carried on in all faculties and departments. Projects are sponsored by industry, the government of Israel, and foreign governments and foundations through the Research and Development Foundation. The Foundation operates field laboratories and offers consultant services, testing facilities, quality control, and technological surveys. Important research institutes on the campus are the Samuel Neaman Institute for Advanced Studies in Science and Technology, the Rappaport Family Institute for Research in the Medical Sciences, the Asher Space Research Institute, the Solid State Institute, and the Transportation Research Institute. In 1994–95 there were 10,581 students, comprising 7,763 in undergraduate studies and 2,818 in the Graduate School. In addition, some thousands are enrolled in external studies and extension courses given in various parts of the country. In 2005 the Technion had 12,818 students, among them 9,306 undergraduates, 2,683 studying for a master's degree, and 829 for doctoral degrees. In 2005 it had 76,510 alumni. The vast majority of engineers and architects practicing in Israel are graduates of the Technion. This is the chief reservoir of skilled manpower for Israel's burgeoning high-tech industries. Over 70% of Israel's founders and managers of high-tech firms are Technion graduates and 74% of the managers in the electronic industries hold Technion degrees. An innovation was the establishment of a medical school in 1970; by 1995 close to 500 M.D. degrees had been granted. Among the medical school faculty are Avram *Hershko and Aaron *Ciechanover, the Nobel Prize laureates who received the prize in 2004 for their discovery of the crucial role of ubiquitin in the process of protein breakdown in cells. The Technion also has a special program for students to design, build, and launch their own satellite. Student facilities on campus include dormitories, a sports center, student union building, swimming pool, and a network of libraries. The language of instruction is Hebrew, but foreign students often get along with English, especially in the Graduate School. Over the years the Technion has offered many degree programs in English for students from developing countries in Africa and Asia. The Technion serves as a venue for national and international conferences and symposia on technology and science.

The Technion is an independent institution under the authority of its Board of Governors, which includes civic and industrial leaders, representatives of the teaching staff, the alumni, the government, and Technion Societies in various parts of the world. It is recognized for the conferment of academic degrees by the Israel Council for Higher Education. The executive body is the council, which meets monthly, and the chief executive officer is the president, appointed by the Board of Governors. Academic authority is vested in the senate, composed of the president, the vice presidents, all full professors, and other representatives of the academic staff.

BIBLIOGRAPHY: C. Alpert, *Technion, the Story of Israel's Institute of Technology;* N. Levin, *Ma'avak ha-Rishonim al Yi'ud ha-Technion* (1964); *Toledot ha-Technion be-Reshito* (1953); *Technion; A Bi-Monthly of Features, News and Events*, 1 (1965–to date); *Technion Bulletin*, 1–8 (1941–48) superseded by: *Technion, Israel Institute of Technology*, 1–17 (1949–66); *Technion Yearbook*, 1–23 (1942–66); *Technion Catalogue…* (1955–66); *Technion – The President's Report and Reports of Other Officials* (1954–69). **WEBSITE:** www.technion.ac.il.

[Yaakov Dori]

TECHNOLOGY AND HALAKHAH. *Halakhah* deals with the prescription of the behavior of the individual, the family, the community, and a Jewish state. It encompasses all the actions in one's life. It sets forth both the principles and the guidelines along which day-to-day problems, both legal and ethical, have to be solved. Until the 19th century, rabbis well versed in *halakhah* were able to apply these legal principles to the ever-changing environment in which Jews lived. For instance, new methods of financing brought about the widespread application of *hetter iskah*, in which a legal way was found to use modern banking concepts which include interest, without transgressing the law forbidding the use of interest (see *Moneylending). The economic necessity to compete with non-Jews in the industrial and commercial fields resulted in the rather widespread use of non-Jews as Shabbat *goyim*, so that legally a business or factory could operate and produce on the Sabbath, for example, by having the non-Jew as an official legal partner. These solutions were all developed within religious communities in the Diaspora, and involved no special strain on the main body of the *halakhah*.

During the 19th and 20th centuries, modern technology advanced rapidly. This advance brought about many problems and many strains. These were particularly felt in the State of Israel where none of the solutions that are applicable in the Diaspora could be easily applied.

Modern technology affects the life of every individual. It creates not only ideological and ethical problems but poses real problems in keeping the commandments expounded in detail in the Shulḥan Arukh and amplified further by generations of rabbis in their responsa. The main problems are in the observance of the Sabbath, in *kashrut*, in personal and family life, e.g., birth control and other medical problems. Of course, educational and philosophical problems occur as well, since any new technological advance brings about a reorientation of thought and concepts of large segments of the population, concepts which sometimes are seen to be in conflict with stated precepts of ethical principles exposed by the leading religious ethical thinkers of previous generations. During the last 150 years, many responsa have been written trying to find solutions, sometimes technical and sometimes halakhic, to the problems that modern technology has brought about. Most of these responsa deal with the adaptation of the individual to changing situations. These responsa are, in general, marked by a greater restraint than those of previous generations. They have, therefore, given the impression that the *halakhah* does not keep up with the times. Some of the reasons for this impression, however, are the following:

Communication and Language Problem

Modern technology has advanced rapidly in nearly all fields of human activity. The rabbi, who until the 18th century may have been familiar with all the major aspects of science and life, cannot be expected today to have this knowledge or even keep up with the rapid advances of knowledge in a particular field. He needs, therefore, an "interpreter" to explain the technology to him so that he can interpret the legal halakhic implications concerned with the observance of the *mitzvot* in modern society. Since each field of science or technology has its own language, communication between those who interpret the *halakhah* and the specialists in technology has been difficult and has often led to incorrect evaluation of details. This problem is particularly acute in the understanding of new instruments utilizing all forms of new energy sources such as electricity or nuclear energy (and hence the permission or prohibition to use these instruments on the Sabbath).

Fear of Cultural Assimilation

Accommodation of religious individuals to changes in their standard of living may bring about acceptance of the cultural milieu of the community in which the technological advances are made. Halakhic solutions may be found which render it possible to use modern technology and keep all the religious commandments. However, the fear of undermining Jewish faith through the cultural influence emanating from the non-Jewish communities by the vehicle of technology sometimes underlies the reluctance to find solutions to technological problems.

Religious Minority

Responsa in general were written for a Jewish religious community, or for an individual living within a religious community. However, religious congregations in the Diaspora often set themselves apart from those of non-observant Jews. Response to technological changes might be readily acceptable to a religious community which fully accepts the *halakhah*, but not so much to a mixed community of which the majority are not observant. Halakhic solutions must be fulfilled in every detail. Small deviations, sometimes for the convenience of the consumer, may lead to wider prohibitions than were imposed before such a solution was found. Only persons well versed, trained, and used to the legal framework of the *halakhah* may be willing to accept these solutions, but new halakhic regulations may lead to friction within the community. This fear of either causing additional friction or non-observance of all the details often acts as a deterrent to publication of halakhic solutions in response to changes in technology. The last reason is probably the most dominant factor as to why the rabbis have not concerned themselves with the problems of application of the *halakhah* to the Jewish secular state. It has been felt, and probably correctly, that a secular legal arm of the state may adopt only part of these regulations. The result would be a secularization and adulteration of the *halakhah* in such a way as would be palatable to a majority of Jews but not conforming to the exact prescription of the *halakhah*.

A few major aspects of these problems will be considered here: (a) Sabbath observance; (b) *kashrut*; (c) medical problems; (d) agriculture.

SABBATH OBSERVANCE. Probably the major problem facing the religious Jew in the State of Israel and abroad is that of Sabbath observance. In Israel it is relatively easy for a factory to obtain a license to operate on the Sabbath. The result of this is that employment of religious Jews in certain well-defined areas in industries becomes a problem. An objective employer naturally prefers the worker or engineer who is available all days of the week. Additionally, even if the religious Jew could overcome this natural bias, he would be reluctant to work until Friday with the knowledge that his fellow workers would continue his work on the Sabbath. According to the *halakhah* even preparation of work for another Jew to work on the Sabbath is forbidden. The result of all this is the beginning of an economic ghetto for religious Jews in Israel. In selective occupations in heavy and light industries, or in the communication industry, one cannot find many Orthodox Jews, certainly much fewer proportionately than their percentage in the population. The situation is likely to become more acute with the increase of the industrial capacity of Israel.

Institute for Science and Halakhah

The Institute for Science and Halakhah (Makhon Madda'i Tekhnologi li-Ve'ayot Halakhah) was founded by four organizations – the Orthodox Scientists of Israel, the Religious Engineering Association, the Harry Fischel Institute and the Yad ha-Rav Herzog in Jerusalem – with the aim of rectifying this situation. As an independent organization with no political affiliations, it is dedicated solely to solving the basic problems of a modern religious society in a modern technological state, without compromising halakhic principles.

The institute was established to engage in research and development. The research unit defined the main problems regarding Sabbath observance in industry and agriculture. These current problems center around general maintenance and repairs on the Sabbath for plants operating on that day. The problems that have been considered by this Institute are (a) the use of automation and servomechanisms; (b) the problem of transmitting information (writing not being permitted on the Sabbath); exploratory work on the use of tape recorders and magnetic recording has been instituted; (c) the possibility of using hot water systems on the Sabbath; (d) problems connected with the use of photoelectric cells, with microphones, and with electric switches. Though a five-day work week could easily solve most of the problems, in the early 21st century Israel had not shifted completely to it. (On-line maintenance is not sufficiently known or utilized in industry.) The institute was faced with formulating a more exact definition of "work" and "causation" as far as the Sabbath is concerned. The utilization of these concepts and the subsequent development of computer technology has wide implications for work in defense, for police work and for hospitals, and may make it possible for observant Jews to be employed more widely in these fields without being obliged to transgress fundamental religious principles.

After two or three years' work, members of the Institute felt that they had established enough halakhic and technological know-how to apply this knowledge to such industries as demand it and have the goodwill to utilize it.

THE HALAKHIC DEFINITION OF WORK. The basic aspects and halakhic interpretation dealing with the definition of direct and indirect (גורם, *gorem*) work (מלאכה, *melakhah*) on the Sabbath have been evolved. On the Sabbath only certain types of work are not forbidden and these must be performed in a certain manner with a good purpose and under certain conditions. Physical work is not always forbidden. Hence it is necessary to have a clear definition of the traditional 39 categories of work and their derivatives, and a sort of compendium of the law with application to modern technology. The *halakhah* does not forbid the performance of work on the Sabbath *per se*; it forbids the performance of constructive work by a Jew. The main emphasis is on "*Thou* shalt not work," i.e., on the person who performs the action. This is the basis of the permission to use electric lights or place cooking food on the stove before the Sabbath and keep it there on the Sabbath. It is also the basis for permitting the use of an automatic switch ("the Sabbath clock") for turning electricity on and off on the Sabbath. The principle of the Sabbath clock can be generalized to micro- and mini-computers to perform many functions on the Sabbath, provided the program is already set before the Sabbath. This generalization has been worked out by the institute and successfully applied to a number of industrial systems

The practical implications of the definition of the concept of "work" or "causation" are enormous. They clearly imply a new type of Sabbath technology which would enable automated operation of factories in which an absolute shutdown is not feasible.

However, the institute is also engaged in technological innovations which will benefit the individual family, of which the following are examples:

(1) Cooking with Gas on the Festivals: The lighting of fire from an existing flame is permitted on the Festivals (but not on the Sabbath) in order to heat or cook food. It is forbidden, however, to extinguish the flame, under normal conditions. The institute has developed an inexpensive device to extinguish the gas flame at any desired interval, and to kindle the flame whenever desired.

(2) Use of Hot-Water Heaters on the Sabbath: The use of hot water from hot-water heaters on the Sabbath presents problems of *halakhah*. Commercial water heaters are so constructed that by opening the hot-water faucet, cold water automatically enters the heater. The inflow of cold water is again heated by the heating element and also by the hot water remaining in the boiler. In many cases the inflow of cold water triggers a thermostat which in turn ignites the heating element. The institute has developed a system whereby the inflow of cold water is regulated automatically and is independent of the outflow of hot water. Hence, the person who uses the hot water is not the direct cause of activating the heating of cold water. The method is particularly useful for hotels and other large institutions.

(3) Operation of Automatic Elevators on the Sabbath: There are two schools of thought on the question of use of an automatic elevator on the Sabbath. One school disregards the influence of the weight of the individual on the functioning of the elevator. When the elevator ascends, the individual's weight necessitates increased electric consumption, and when it descends it may also require generation of electricity. Nevertheless, this school of thought does not consider the influence of the individual's weight as a direct action prohibited in the commandment, "Thou shalt not perform (constructive) work." The other school of thought feels that the influence of the individual's weight cannot be disregarded, and it is as though the person himself actually generated the electricity. The institute has taken all those points into consideration with regard to various types of elevators and has developed modifications which can be built into commercial elevators to permit their use on the Sabbath.

(4) Transmission of Vital Records and Information on the Sabbath: Communication in one form or another is essential in increasing areas of modern life. In a number of institutions, such as the police force and in hospitals, careful records must be kept. Writing on the Sabbath is forbidden according to the *halakhah*. The institute has therefore developed automatic record-keeping devices connected to tape recorders or other small computers.

In addition, the institute deals with many problems in the field of the dietary laws (*kashrut*).

Two important research monographs on the halakhic definition of work were published in the late 1970s: *Action and Causation* by Rabbi L.I. Halperin (1977) and *Primary, Secondary and Chains of Action* by Prof. W.Z. Low (Mosad ha-Rav Kook, 5738).

KASHRUT. Modern foods contain many types of synthetic ingredients. The purpose of these ingredients is sometimes medical but more frequently to permit the on-line production of preserved foods. Some of these ingredients are not *kasher* and even the admittance of minute quantities may in certain cases cause the whole food to be non-*kasher*. In the Diaspora, the tendency has been to induce major food manufacturers to find substitutes which are *kasher*. In the United States *kasher* food may have a U sign surrounded by a circle, Ⓤ. (the sign of the supervision of the Union of Orthodox Congregations of America), the letter K in combination with other letters or geometric symbols (circle, triangle), and so forth, depending on whether the *kashrut* supervision is under any one of a number of national or local rabbinic bodies. Large U.S. food companies have met the demand of Orthodox Jewry because of the fear of losing sales of their products. In Israel there is no law at present which demands the food producer to list exactly all the ingredients contained in his product, and the penalties for stating that non-*kasher* food is *kasher* are not very severe. There is no control mechanism, apart from the interest of the individual rabbi, for finding out whether the ingredients are really *kasher* or not, nor are there laboratories advanced enough to test these ingredients. The technological problems in this case are, on the whole, far simpler than the Sabbath problem, since the difference in cost between *kasher* and non-*kasher* ingredients for such minute additives is small.

MEDICAL PROBLEMS. Here again this problem involves both the individual and the total community.

On the subject of *birth control, the rabbis in the last 150 years have been divided into two camps – those who do not permit birth control under any circumstances and those who permit the women to practice birth control under certain circumstances. To a large extent most responsa since the 1950s have dealt with permission to use certain birth control techniques for individual cases. The general rule is that each individual case should be judged on its merits. Under certain circumstances, the rabbi may give permission to use birth control not only because of direct medical reasons but also because of psychological needs. There is a certain amount of conservatism in halakhic rulings in permitting the use of new contraceptives such as the "pill," since the medical problems involved have not been sufficiently explored. A halakhic decision to use the pill may, in certain selective cases, lead to sickness and possibly even death and few rabbis would permit this unless the demand is advocated by the family doctor. Here, also, is an inherent fear that the widespread use of contraceptives may undermine, to some extent, Jewish family life. This is buttressed by the feeling that after the Holocaust in Europe, the natural increase of the Jewish people should be encouraged rather than discouraged.

The question of *artificial insemination has been extensively dealt with by many rabbis and the consensus of opinion today is that artificial insemination using the semen of the husband is permitted but using the semen of unknown donors causes considerable controversy, and the majority of rabbis oppose it. In general, it can be said that the technological innovations of family planning have been adequately dealt with in the responsa of rabbis all over the world, since these involve day-to-day problems affecting both the religious and nonreligious Jew alike. The new medical technologies of the last decades of the 20th century, from *transplants to surrogate motherhood and genetic engineering, have posed new halakhic challenges and are the subject of ongoing debate. (See also *Medicine and the Law.)

AGRICULTURE. Technological problems connected with agriculture arise because of new types of hybrid seeds and foods which have been developed. Jewish law does not permit *kilayim* such as the sowing of two different types of seeds in a given field or the crossbreeding of two different types of animals (see *Mixed Species). Many types of hybrid grains and foods are, of course, very popular but many of these cannot be produced by a religious person. Religious kibbutzim and moshavim in Israel strictly adhere to these prohibitions. An additional problem is the observation of the seventh year of rest (*Shemittah*, see *Sabbatical Year). Here the rabbinical authorities have adopted the attitude that the best solution is to sell the agricultural land to non-Jews during this seventh year and, under these circumstances, a large fraction of the work in the field can be performed and the produce eaten. Other rabbis, however, feel that the land should lie fallow and only work should be performed which would preserve the earth and the trees and prevent their deterioration. This prohibition has resulted in considerable experimentation in hydroponics, to which the prohibition does not apply. It is employed, for example, in kibbutz Ḥafeẓ Ḥayyim. It is not impossible that the implications of this research may be of importance to Israeli agriculture in the future. Similarly the prohibition of milking by hand on the Sabbath – the selective crossbreeding of cows renders daily milking imperative – causes religious kibbutzim to use milking machines which, with certain changes dictated by the *halakhah*, can be used on the Sabbath. This, again, was a spur to nonreligious kibbutzim to use milking machines both on the Sabbath and during the week. However, without technical adaptation the milking machine is not permitted to be used on the Sabbath.

Service in the armed forces has also given rise to many technological problems.

There is a general feeling that the *halakhah* has not kept pace with the demands of modern technology. Solutions have been found and numerous responsa all over the world have been written in cases where technology infringes on prohibitions of the Jewish law, but in most, partial solutions have been found for the individual. In some cases, the *halakhah* has anticipated such problems as the question of the definition of death or the question of whether the computer should be regarded in the same light as a person insofar as some Jewish commandments are concerned. In most cases these responsa came as answers to individual inquiries. There has also been, to some extent, a lack of caution in these responsa in defining the prohibition of or permission for using a modern technological device by not stating clearly the brand name, the manufacturer, and a detailed description of the instrument itself. Since modern technology advances very rapidly, the lifetime of such a gadget may be very brief. Small changes in the internal parts may even result in a halakhic transgression which did not apply to a previous model. The converse may hold true as well. The *halakhah* has not yet produced a body of scholars who systematically analyze the needs of a modern society as distinct from the individual and the applications of the *halakhah* to such a society. The demand for such work would only arise if a community should come about in which the majority observed the *halakhah*.

The Secular State of Israel and the Day of Rest: Sabbath

The establishment of a secular modern Jewish State of Israel brought into sharp focus a number of central problems, such as the identity, the ideological content of the State, and its relationship to *halakhah*. These problems had already existed during the Mandatory period; however, the state had to enact new laws. Very often the laws were copies of the laws of other democratic countries to which only some religious Jewish overtones or content were added, and such laws were often in conflict with the *halakhah*. While the main issue centered on the problems of personal status, such as a definition of "Who is a Jew," other issues, such as the nature of the Sabbath – the day of rest – also brought the secular and religious elements into conflict. Traveling on the Sabbath may be taken as an example.

Whereas the secular law merely declares the Sabbath as a day of rest for Jews, with provision for exemption, the *halakhah* forbids not only all constructive work (*Melekhet Maḥshevet*) on the Sabbath, but also traveling, even for pleasure and recreation. Public transportation in most of the country is forbidden (except for bus transportation in Haifa and some other places). However, affluence has brought about an increase in private travel and in concomitant work in the operation of various leisure and recreational services on the Sabbath. The increase in the number of tourists also increased the pressure to provide them with entertainment on the day of rest. However, the most serious problem revolved around work on the Sabbath in various essential industries.

The Knesset Law of Work Permits on the Day of Rest

The Knesset enacted a number of regulations which established norms as to which workers and places of employment would be permitted to operate on the Sabbath and Jewish holidays. The law equivocally states that the day of rest of 36 hours must include the seventh day – the Sabbath – for Jewish workers. (For non-Jewish workers the day of rest is the day chosen by each denomination.) The minister of labor is empowered by law to grant permission to factory owners to operate on the Sabbath and to employ workers, provided the work is related to defense of people or of property, or if shutting down would cause considerable damage to the economy of the country or disrupt services considered by the minister of labor to be essential to the public or part of it. The ministry of labor had been dominated by the Labor Party, with its various nuances, for 30 years, and during the period of its hegemony the tendency was to interpret the law liberally so as to classify many important services as either essential or of such a nature as to qualify them as being of significance to the economy of the country. As a result, many industries received permits to operate on the Sabbath even though relatively simple technological innovations exist which would render it unnecessary. In addition, the Knesset enacted specific laws exempting a number of cooperatives, particularly those engaged in public transport, as well as companies engaged in oil prospecting and drilling, from the above ordinances.

The new coalition government, appointed after the elections in May 1977 and headed by Begin and the Likud, effected a change in atmosphere. The new coalition agreement on these issues provides for a review of all Sabbath work permits granted in the past and intends to use a narrower interpretation of the phrases "essential services" and "economic necessity." The Institute of Science and Halakhah which, under the chairmanship of Prof. W.Z. Low, had in the past specialized in finding technical and halakhically acceptable solutions for such problems, was given official status by the new government and was appointed to design alternative solutions in order to obviate the need for workers to be employed on the Sabbath.

BIBLIOGRAPHY: Articles on these subjects regularly appear in the following periodicals: *Jewish Life* (1933–); *Hadorom* (1957–); *No'am* (1957–); *De'ot* (1957–); *Tradition* (1958–); Makhon Madda'i Tekhnologi li'Ve'ayot Halakhah, *Yedi'ot ha-Makhon* (1967–); *Proceedings of the Association of Orthodox Jewish Scientists* (1970–); and in various rabbinical journals. Some of these articles were summarized in I. Jakobovits, *Jewish Law Faces Modern Problems* (1965); J. Bemporad et al. (eds.), *Focus on Judaism, Science, and Technology* (1970).

[William (Ze'ev) Low]

TEDESCHI (**Tedesco**, "Ashkenazi"), name of several Italian families whose members were found particularly in Ancona,

Rovigo, Veneto, Piedmont, Rome, and Ferrara. The Tedeschi families, however, did not originate from a single stock, and the name is also common among Christian families, especially in Sicily. ISAAC and MOSES TEDESCO were among the representatives of the Catalan School in Rome in 1581. From the 18th to the 20th centuries the family produced some distinguished rabbis, jurists, physicians, and writers, among them NATHAN TEDESCHI, author of a *ḥidah* (enigmatical poem) for Purim (1765).

MARCO TEDESCHI (1817–1869) was rabbi in Nizza-Monferrato, Saluzzo, Asti, and Trieste, having been appointed to the last position by Cavour in 1858. He was a preacher of renown and translator of prayers into Italian (*Le preghiere di un cuore israelita*). His poems were published by Rabbi V. Castiglioni as *Yelid Kinnor* (1886).

DAVID VITA TEDESCO (1820–1849), of Venice, edited a text of prayers for the five fast days with an Italian translation (1845); he also translated and wrote commentaries on several books of the Bible, which were not published, and was among the disciples of Samuel David *Luzzatto. Moses Isaac *Tedeschi (Tedesco), was a teacher, translator, and biblical commentator. ELIEZER LAUDE TEDESCHI, rabbi of Turin, was the author of a chant for the inauguration of the Hebrew school there (Scuola ebraica), in 1884.

ISAAC REFAEL TEDESCHI (1826–1908) was born in Ancona and became the first rabbi of the Jewish community (Universita ebraica) of Bologna after its reestablishment in 1860. He was a propagator of pre-Zionist ideas from as early as 1871. He was appointed rabbi at Corfu in 1865 and succeeded Rabbi David Vivanti in Ancona in 1877. Tedeschi energetically defended Jewish Orthodoxy, often polemizing with Italian rabbis of liberal tendencies. He contributed to the main Italian Jewish newspapers and *Ha-Ẓefirah*. Some of his works were collected by his disciple, Rabbi H. Rosenberg, and were published (in Italian, 1929; as *She'elot u-Teshuvot*, 1932). However, many remained unpublished, among them a commentary to the Torah and an addition to Isaac Lampronti's *Paḥad Yiẓḥak* (*Avnei Zikkaron*).

Gad (Guido) *Tedeschi (1907–1992) was professor of civil law at the Hebrew University in Jerusalem.

BIBLIOGRAPHY: Mortara, Indice, 64; C. Roth, *Venice* (1930), index; G. Bedarida, *Ebrei d'Italia* (1948), index; H. Rosenberg, *Saggio degli Scritti dei Rabbini Vivanti e Tedeschi* (1929); idem, *Saggio degli Scritti in lingua ebraica dei Rabbini Vivanti e Tedeschi* (1932); V. Castiglioni et al., *I.R. Tedeschi* (1909); A. Milano, *Il ghetto di Roma* (1964), index; idem, *Storia degli Ebrei Italiani nel Levante* (1949), 191.

[Alfredo Mordechai Rabello]

TEDESCHI (Tedesco), MOSES ISAAC BEN SAMUEL (1821–1898), translator, and teacher. Tedeschi was born in Trieste. He engaged in teaching most of his life except for a short period (1861) when he served as a rabbi of Spoleto. During his 34 years as a teacher he compiled his *Ho'il Moshe*, consisting of expositions of most of the books of the Bible (published between 1870 and 1892). This commentary was based both upon traditional commentaries and the modern commentaries from the era of *Mendelssohn to Samuel David *Luzzatto (with whom he was on friendly terms). In his introduction Tedeschi points to the difference of approach in the various commentaries which were written at different times of his life "but there is no absolute contradiction between them and they can be regarded as one corpus."

He also published *Musar Melakhim* (1878), ethical sermons based upon the tractate, *Avot; Zekher Rav* (1878), of Benjamin *Mussafia with an Italian translation and a dictionary called *Mafte'aḥ ha-Shorashim; Oẓar Nirdefei Leshon Ivri* ("Hebrew synonyms," 1879); *Simḥat ha-Regel* (1886), sermons for the festivals and notes on the Targum of Proverbs, includes his autobiography (pp. 51–61); and *Ru'ah Yisrael* (1894), a translation from Italian to Hebrew of a collection of studies by Mordecai (Marco) *Mortara, rabbi in Mantua.

BIBLIOGRAPHY: *Sefer Zikkaron le-Soferei Yisrael* (1889), 6f.; Zeitlin, Bibliotheca, 394f.; Kressel, Leksikon, 1 (1965), 163.

[Yehoshua Horowitz]

TEFILLIN (Heb. תְּפִלִּין; usually translated "phylacteries"; sing. *tefillah* – see Men. 4:1; Mik. 10:3), two black leather boxes containing scriptural passages which are bound by black leather straps on the left hand and on the head and worn for the morning services on all days of the year except Sabbaths and scriptural holy days (see below). In four passages of the Bible (Ex. 13:1–10 and 11–16; Deut. 6:4–9 and 11:13–21) there occurs the almost identical passage requiring the Jew to put "these words" (of the Law) for "a sign upon thy hand and a frontlet between thine eyes." (Only in the first does "*zikkaron*" – "memorial" – occur instead of *totafot* – "frontlets.") Both the passages of Deuteronomy state explicitly, "and thou shalt bind them," while the two passages in Exodus merely say, "and they shall be."

Of all the commentators on the Bible only the 12th-century commentator Samuel b. Meir takes this command as a figurative one. In his commentary on Exodus 13:9 he says: "according to the essence of its literal meaning it means 'it shall ever be as a memorial as though it were written upon thy hand,' as in the verse: 'Set me as a seal upon thy heart as a seal upon thine arm.'" (Song 8:6; Abraham ibn Ezra suggests the same explanation but rejects it.) Apart from this, it was accepted that the verse had to be taken literally and that the words of the Scripture had to be bound on the hand and placed (on the forehead) between the eyes. The portions selected for the fulfillment of this commandment were the four above-mentioned passages which constitute the *tefillin*.

The rabbis were aware of the fact that apart from these verses there is no explicit reference to this ceremony or the manner in which it was to be fulfilled in the Bible, and they regarded it as the classic example of a biblical law whose details are wholly "of the Scribes" and immutable (Sanh. 88b); it is, indeed, a perfect example of an injunction whose method of performance is the result of the Oral Law. The Samaritans did not wear them (Men. 42b).

The *tefillin* are first mentioned in the Letter of *Aristeas (159), but only the *tefillah* of the hand: "and upon our hands too, He [God] expressly orders the symbols to be fastened." Josephus (Ant. 4:213) mentions both, that of the head before the hand. The rabbis regarded them as having been instituted at the earliest times, and in a discussion as to whether the incident of Ezekiel in the Valley of Dead Bones was a vision or a fact, "Judah b. Bathyra stood up and said, 'I am one of their descendants and these are the *tefillin* which my grandfather handed down to me from them'" (Sanh. 92b).

Tefillin are mentioned once in the New Testament under the peculiarly inappropriate name of "phylacteries" (Gr. φυλακτήριον, "amulet"), and this name has been universally adopted as the English equivalent of the word. (For the meaning of the word, see later.) It is part of the diatribe against the Pharisees, "But all their works they do to be seen of men; they make broad their phylacteries" (Matt. 23:5). This charge of the demonstrative nature of the commandment is, in fact, confirmed by the rabbis, who interpret the verse "and all the peoples of the earth shall see that the name of the Lord is called upon thee" (Deut. 28:10) to refer to "the *tefillin* of the head" (Ber. 6a).

The *tefillin* were worn by day, but not at night; it is even stated that "he who wears *tefillin* at night transgresses a positive commandment" (TJ, Ber. 2:3, 4c), but it is doubtful whether they were generally worn all day. Both of Rabban Johanan b. Zakkai (Suk. 28a) and his disciple Eliezer b. Hyrcanus (TJ, Ber. 2:3, 4c) in Ereẓ Israel, as well as of Ada b. Ahavah in Babylon (Ta'an. 20b), it is stated that they "never walked four cubits without wearing phylacteries," suggesting that this was an act of special piety. They were worn only by men, but according to a *baraita*, "Michal the daughter of the Cushite [i.e., Saul, cf. MK 16b] wore *tefillin* and the sages did not protest" (Er. 96a).

There is evidence of a certain laxity in the fulfillment of this commandment during the talmudic period. It is stated that because the Jews did not risk martyrdom for them during the Hadrianic persecution "the precept is still weak with them" (Shab. 130a). It is, however, certain that the injunction was largely disregarded both in France and in Spain in the 12th and 13th centuries. This is specifically stated (Tos. Shab. 49a), and Jacob Tam actually quotes the talmudic passage in extenuation of this laxity (*ibid.*), contending that the statement that "a head which does not wear *tefillin* is of a willful sinner of Israel" (RH 17a) refers only to one who refuses to wear them out of defiance or contempt. Little more than half a century later Moses of Coucy states: "In the year 1236 I was in Spain to reprove them…and there was a wholesale repentance and thousands and tens of thousands accepted the duty of donning *tefillin*… and so it was in other lands, and afterward my admonitions were accepted in all these places" (*Sefer Mitzvot Gadol*, Positive Commandment 3).

Nevertheless, it would be erroneous to regard the difference of opinion between Rashi and his grandson Tam as to the correct order of the paragraphs in the *tefillah* of the head as proof that it was a re-innovation at the time, as the discovery of the *tefillin* in the Dead Sea area shows (see later).

Order of Passages

As stated, both the *tefillin* of the hand and of the head contain the four paragraphs. Whereas in the *tefillah* of the hand they are written on one piece of parchment and in the order of their occurrence in the Bible, the *tefillah* of the head is instead divided into four compartments, and the four paragraphs – each written on a separate piece of parchment and tied – are inserted in them. Only according to Rashi are they inserted in the order of their occurrence; according to R. Tam, the passage from Deuteronomy 11:13–21 precedes that of Deuteronomy 6:4–9.

This is practically the only difference of opinion found with regard to the *tefillin*. Rashi's order has been universally accepted, although a small but diminishing number of individuals of especial piety, in view of possible doubt, substitute "R. Tam's *tefillin*" for those "of Rashi" for the concluding part of the service. Apart from that there is a remarkable uniformity of custom and procedure which applies to all rites and communities, and, with a few differences which will be noted, the details which follow are universal.

Both the *tefillin* are cubical boxes ("square") of leather painted black (Men. 35a). The parchment must be made from the skins of ritually clean animals (*ibid.*, 42b, Sanh. 48b), preferably of a calf (OḤ 32:44), and the scriptural passages written on them in square ("Assyrian") script, like that of the *Sefer Torah*. The aperture into which the parchment is inserted is closed with a square piece of thick leather (*titora*) and stitched with 12 stitches of gut made from clean animals (Shab. 8b). Protruding from the back of the *tefillin* case is a hollow extension (*ma'barta*) through which the straps are passed. These straps must also be made from the hide of clean animals and be black on the outside.

The arrangement of the straps is conditioned by the purpose to which they are put. That of the hand *tefillah* is in the form of a noose to enable it to be tightened on the arm; that of the head has a circlet, tied with a knot, its size adjusted to the circumference of the head, the two ends hanging loosely.

Under the influence of the Kabbalah the word שַׁדַּי (*Shaddai*; Almighty) is represented on both *tefillin*. In the case of the *tefillin* of the head it is represented by the letter ש inscribed on the box on both sides, that on the right having the normal letter with three strokes, that on the left with four. The knot is made in the shape of a ד while the י is represented by the end of the strap. In the case of the hand *tefillah* the strap is wrapped on the hand in the shape of the ש and the ד and the knot at the end is in the shape of the י.

The order of donning the *tefillin* is meticulously laid down. They are put on after the *tallit*. That of the hand is put on first, placed on the upper arm ("opposite the heart"), and the noose is tightened when the blessing to lay the *tefillin* is recited. The plain spelling of the word "thy hand" (יָדְכָה) in Exodus 13:16 was interpreted to mean "the weak hand" (יָד כֵּהָה), and a left-handed person therefore places it on his right hand, though it is not "opposite the heart"; the strap is wound seven times round the arm between the elbow and the wrist. The Ashkenazim wind it anti-clockwise, in an inward manner, the Sephardim (followed by the Ḥasidim) clockwise. The head *tefillah* is then put on, care being taken that it lies above the middle of the forehead and all on the hair of the head, the knot resting on the nape of the neck, the two loose ends being made to hang down in front. The blessing "on the commandment of the *tefillin*" is recited at the time. Since, however, according to one opinion, the second blessing is superfluous, it was instituted that after reciting it, it be, so to speak "neutralized" by adding the words "blessed be the name of His glorious kingdom for ever." The remaining part of the strap of the hand *tefillah* is then wrapped in a prescribed manner on the hand and the middle finger of the hand to form the abovementioned ש and ד, while Hosea 2:21–2 is recited. Palestinian scholars in the talmudic period were accustomed to recite a benediction (*Lishmor ḥukkav* – to observe His commandments) when they took off the *tefillin* (Ber. 44b). However, *tosafot* (*ibid.*) point out that they used to wear *tefillin* all day and recite the benediction at night.

Tefillin are worn on all weekdays, but not on Sabbaths and festivals. The reason given in the Talmud (Men. 36b) is that they are called "a sign," but the Sabbath itself is so called (Ex. 31:17), and the same rule was applied to festivals. In the Diaspora, Ḥasidim do not don *tefillin* during the intermediate days of the festivals while *Mitnaggedim* do; in Israel, it is the universal custom not to wear them on the intermediate days.

The duty of laying *tefillin* begins when a boy reaches his religious majority, i.e., at the age of 13 years and a day, but he usually begins to do so a few weeks earlier for practice. Among Oriental communities a special ceremony is held to celebrate it. Since the *tefillin* are a "*pe'er*" (a "diadem of glory"; see later) they are not worn on the morning of Tishah be-Av, their donning being postponed to the *Minḥah* service (in some German congregations this applies to other fast days also), nor by a bereaved person before the burial; various other categories are temporarily exempt, either because of inability to concentrate (e.g., a bridegroom on his wedding day) or because the body is unclean (Shab. 49a). Similarly, they must not be worn in a cemetery, in an unclean place (Ber. 18a), or while asleep.

The Talmud stresses the supreme importance of the *tefillin*. Even God dons them (Ber. 6a), hearing the verse, "who is like thy people Israel, one people on earth (I Chron. 17:21)" (Ber. 62). A person who does not put them on is a willful transgressor. God surrounded Israel with seven precepts, including "*tefillin* on their heads, *tefillin* on their arms," and "whosoever has the *tefillin* on his head, the *tefillin* on his arm, *ẓiẓit* on his garment and the *mezuzah* on his doorpost is fortified against sinning" (Men. 43b). Their sanctity was stressed by regarding them as "rendering the hands unclean" as is the case with the *Sefer Torah* (Yad. 3:3), and if they are accidentally dropped, the person responsible is obliged to fast for that day.

The wearing of *tefillin* induces a serious frame of mind, preventing levity (Ber. 30b). According to Bet Hillel the *tefillin* had to be examined every year, but Bet Shammai disagreed (Mekh., Pisḥa, 17, p. 157, vol. 2; cf. TJ, Er. 10:26a, where other rabbis are mentioned). The law was later established to examine them once (or twice) every seven years (Tos. Men. 43a).

The kabbalists instituted a meditation before putting on the *tefillin* which is a perfect example of the spiritualization of a ceremonial precept. It includes the statement, "He hath commanded us to lay the *tefillin* upon the hand as a memorial of His outstretched arm; opposite the heart to indicate the duty of subjecting the longings and designs of our heart to His service; and upon the head, over against the brain, thereby teaching that the mind, whose seat is in the brain, together with all senses and faculties, is to be subjected to His service."

The word *tefillah* is identical with the word for prayer, but it may be a homonym, and some have interpreted it as derived not from the root of this word פלל ("to intercede") but from פלה (to "separate", "distinguish") indicating that thereby the Jew is distinguished from the non-Jew. One *mishnah* (Mik. 10:2) mentions the *tefillah* together with an amulet but does not suggest any connection between them. Some scholars have suggested that the phylacteries derive from some form of amulet or charm (see Trachtenberg, *Jewish Magic and Superstitions* (1961^2), 145–6), but others feel that there is no evidence that it was regarded as an amulet, as the word "phylacteries" suggests.

The main exposition in the Talmud on the laws of *tefillin* is found in Men. 34a–37b, in a discussion of the statement of the Mishnah 3:7 that if one of the four paragraphs is missing the *tefillin* are invalidated. All references, except where otherwise stated, are from this passage. The small tractate called *Tefillin* is a late composition which merely assembles the material scattered in the Talmud and belongs to the geonic period.

The Tefillin of the Dead Sea

Before 1968 a number of fragments of *tefillin* found in the various caves of the Dead Sea were published (for a list see bibl., Yadin, 7, n. 1). All apparently belonged to the *tefillin* of the hand and were found without their original containers or capsules. (Previous fragments, however, include *tefillin* of the head, and some empty capsules of head *tefillin* have been found.) They did, however, reveal one important point, namely that the difference of opinion between Rashi and his grandson Jacob Tam as to the order of the scriptural passages did not originate with them, but they transmit different traditions which go back to the first century at least, both systems being found among those fragments, and both were therefore in use concurrently. In point of fact the *Piskei Tosafot* to Men. 34b has the statement that "In Nehardea and in Jerusalem they found two sets of *tefillin*, one according to the order of Rashi and the other according to that of Tam."

In 1968, however, Yigael Yadin acquired the only known capsule of the head *tefillin* of this period, found together with the portions of the text. It was almost certainly found in one of the Qumran caves, probably Cave 4, and its importance lies in the fact that exhaustive scientific tests proved that of the four passages, all tied, three were in the original positions in the capsules in which they were found, and they thus afford undeniable evidence of both the manner in which the slips had been folded and tied, and the materials used for the tying. Of additional importance is the fact that they include the text of the Decalogue. This last discovery confirms an assumption which was made on the basis of certain passages in the Talmud. According to the Mishnah (Tam. 5:1), in the Temple the priests used to recite the Decalogue together with the three paragraphs of the *Shema, but the addition of the Decalogue to the *Shema*, which "according to the law should be part of the daily service," was discontinued "because of the errors of the sectarians that they should not say 'these alone were given to Moses in Sinai'" (TJ, Ber. 1:8, 3c; cf. also TB, *ibid.*, 12a). The *Nash Papyrus of the second century (JQR, 15 (1902–03), 392–408) contains the Decalogue with the first paragraph of the *Shema*. The *Sifrei* to Deuteronomy 4:6, which deals with the *tefillin*, used two exegetical interpretations to justify the exclusion of the Decalogue from the *tefillin*, and it was plausibly assumed that originally, or in some quarters, the *tefillin* actually included the Decalogue, but it was excluded for the same reason as from the daily service, the exegetical justifications for the exclusion being merely a rationalization. The order of the passages in those *tefillin*, apart from their additions, follow the order given by Rashi, with one exception, that the order given by him for the second and third paragraphs is transposed, a change which is expressly permitted in the Talmud (Men. 34bf.).

S. Goren (see bibl.) has examined the *tefillin* of the Dead Sea Scrolls from the point of view of the *halakhah*, and has established that whereas the *tefillin* of Murabba'at accord with the *halakhah*, those of Qumran 1 and 4 are sectarian in nature.

It therefore seems probable that during the first century there were considerable variations and differences of custom as to the order, and additions to, the four basic paragraphs of the *tefillin*, but by the beginning of the second century, uniformity was established as to the text, while two traditions remained and persisted as to the order in which these paragraphs were to be written.

The form of the *tefillin* and the materials used, both the parchment and the tendons used for tying the passages, not only confirm the regulations given in the Talmud but in many cases throw new light on obscure passages.

BIBLIOGRAPHY: M.L. Rodkinssohn, *Tefillah le-Moshe... Toledot ha-Tefillin ve-Koroteihen* (1883); A.D. Bloch, *Keter Tefillin* (1914); M. Higger (ed. and tr.), *Seven Minor Treatises* (1930), 24–30; Eisenstein, Dinim, 443–6; *Kunteres Ẓiyyurim le-Limmud... Dinei Hanaḥat Tefillin* (1957); A. Cowen, *Tefillin* (Eng., 1960); Israel, Ministry of Religions, *Leket Dinim bi-Khetivat SaTaM* (1960); A.M. Breitstein, *Seder Parashiyyot ve-Oẓar Inyenei Tefillin de-Rabbenu Tam* (1966); A. Kon, *Si'aḥ Tefillah* (1966^2), 209–65; Ẓe'irei Aguddat Ḥabad, Israel, *Tefillin* (1968); S. Rozman, *Zikhron Kedoshim Carpentras-Marmaresh* (Yid., 1968), 347–8; T. Reik, *Pagan Rites in Judaism* (1964), 103–52. TEFILLIN OF THE DEAD SEA SCROLLS: Y. Yadin, *Tefillin from Qumran* (Heb. and Eng., 1969), includes a list of all the *tefillin* of the Dead Sea hitherto published; idem, in: *Ḥadshot Muze'on Yisrael*, 4 (1969), 36–45: S. Goren, in: *Maḥanayim*, 62 (1961), 5–14.

[Louis Isaac Rabinowitz]

TEHERAN, capital of *Iran. Situated near the ancient biblical site of Rages (mentioned in the Book of Tobit), Teheran did not rise to prominence until the Kajar dynasty established its capital there about 1788. It soon attracted Jews from many provincial villages and towns, and according to the Jewish traveler *David d'Beth Hillel the Jewish population in Teheran amounted to about 100 families in 1828. Travelers, *sheliḥim*, missionaries, and other European visitors (including J. *Wolff, *Benjamin II, E. *Neumark, and G.K. Curzon) who came throughout the course of the 19th century, all indicate the growth of the Jewish community in Teheran. At first the Jews lived in a very poor, unsanitary quarter (*mahallah*), where they established synagogues and other religious and social institutions. The development of their economic life was greatly hampered by the concept of the ritual uncleanliness of non-believers (Jews and Christians alike) held by Shiʿite Islam, the religious basis of the dynasty. The Jews engaged in handicrafts and small businesses, and were itinerant peddlers dealing in carpets, textiles, antiquities, and luxury articles; very few of them were able to reach positions of economic importance. Some native Jewish physicians in Teheran in the time of Shah Nasr-ed-Din achieved a measure of prominence even before the shah appointed the Austrian Jew J.E. *Polak as professor at the Teheran Medical College, and his personal medical adviser (1851–56).

The political and legal status of the Jews improved in the second half of the 19th century thanks to the intervention of European Jewry under the leadership of Sir Moses *Montefiore and A. *Crémieux, who during the shah's visits to Europe in 1873 and 1889 presented petitions and demands for the amelioration of the life of their coreligionists. This intervention led to the establishment of Jewish schools by the *Alliance Israélite Universelle; the first Alliance school in Teheran was opened in 1898 with J. Cazès as director. As a result of the constitutional reforms under Shah Muzaffar-ed-Din in the early decades of the 20th century, the Jews were granted citizenship in 1906, though they were not permitted to elect their own representative to the Persian parliament until a few years later. Under the Pahlevi dynasty (1925–1979), the position of the Jews throughout Iran improved considerably. In Teheran they were assisted not only by the Alliance, but also by *ORT, *Oẓar ha-Torah, and above all by the American Jewish *Joint Distribution Committee, which in 1947 laid the foundation for all social, medical, and educational activities of the Jews of Teheran and Iran as a whole. A Zionist organization was established in Teheran a year after the Balfour Declaration (1917). A cultural and spiritual revival also led to a considerable *aliyah* to Ereẓ Israel in the early decades of the 20th century. Among Teheran's prominent leaders were Solomon Kohen Ẓedek, author of the first Hebrew grammar for Persian Jews (1918); Mullah Elijah Ḥayyim Moreh, author of three *Judeo-Persian books on Jewish tradition and history (1924–27); Shmuel Ḥayyim, editor of a Jewish newspaper in the Persian language and an ardent Zionist; Aziz Naim, author of the first history of the Zionist movement in Persian; Kermanyan, translator into Persian of A. Bein's biography of Theodor Herzl; and Soliman Hayyim, a great Jewish-Iranian lexicographer and author of several Persian dictionaries. One of the earliest immigrants to Ereẓ Israel was Mullah Ḥayyim Elijah Mizraḥi, whose son, Ḥanina Mizraḥi, wrote several books on Persian Jews in Ereẓ Israel and other monographs.

[Walter Joseph Fischel]

Contemporary Period

The Jewish population of Teheran in 1948 consisted of approximately 35,000 persons and constituted 37% of the total Jewish population of Iran. Although there was considerable emigration to Israel, the number remained stable, as Jews from the provinces migrated to the capital. Much poverty continued to exist in the Jewish quarter (*mahallah*), although with the economic development of the country generally improved, the economic situation of Jews there improved. Teheran had a network of schools run by the Alliance Israélite Universelle; 15 elementary and two high schools, as well as schools run by Oẓar ha-Torah and ORT. In 1961, 7,100 pupils attended the Alliance Israélite Universelle and Oẓar ha-Torah schools. Hundreds of Jews (700–800 in 1949) studied also in Protestant mission schools, and approximately another 2,000 in government schools. In 1961 the number of Jewish students at Teheran University was estimated at 300; however, in 1957 it was estimated that about 3,000 Jewish children in Teheran were receiving no education, although this number probably dropped in the 1960s. The community ran the Kanun Kheir Khah Hospital for the needy (founded in 1958), and a Jewish soup kitchen financed by the American Jewish Joint Distribution Committee. The headquarters both of the youth organization, Kanun Javanan, which extended aid and sponsored lectures to poor children, and of the Jewish women's organization were located in Teheran. Community affairs were run by a council, elected by prominent members of the community, which was headed by Enayatollah Montakhab in 1951 and by Arieh Murad in 1959. The head of the rabbinical court in 1959 was Rabbi Jedidiah Shofet. His judge's salary was paid by the government, and his judgments put into effect by government law courts.

Under the Pahlevi dynasty, the Jews in Teheran enjoyed complete freedom and equality, and many rose to positions of influence in the social and economic spheres. In 1957 the first Iranian-Jewish Congress was organized in Teheran and branches of the World Jewish Congress were established. In 1970, 40,000 Jews (55% of the total Jewish population of Iran) lived in Teheran, and the community was composed of Jews from various Iranian provinces including *Meshed, and from *Bukhara, *Baghdad, and other Oriental communities, as well as of Ashkenazim from Russia, Poland, and Germany. In the early 21st century a large proportion of Iran's estimated 11,000 or so Jews lived in Teheran.

[Hayyim J. Cohen / Walter Joseph Fischel]

BIBLIOGRAPHY: M. Abeshus, in: MJV, 20 (1906), 121–54; W.J. Fischel, in: JSOS, 12 (1950), 119–60; H. Mizraḥi, *Yehudei Paras* (1959), passim; J.B. Schechtman, *On Wings of Eagles* (1961); I. Ben-Zvi, *Meḥkarim u-Mekorot* (1966), index; E. Spicehandler, *Yahadut Iran, Kiyyumah u-Ve'ayoteha* (1970; incl. bibl.). **ADD BIBLIOGRAPHY:** A. Netzer, *"Ha-Kehillah ha-Yehudit be-Tehran mi-Reishitah ad ha-Mahapekhah ha-Ḥukatit 1906,"* in: *Shevet va-Am* (1980), 248–82; idem, "Jews of Teheran," in: *Padyavand: Judeo-Iranian and Jewish Studies* (in Persian), 3 (1999), 145–204.

TEḤINNAH (Heb. תְּחִנָּה), a *piyyut* form which originated in the *taḥanun* prayer for the fasts of Monday and Thursday. The term was also transferred to *piyyutim* for the *seliḥot* days, and indeed both the construction and subject of the *teḥinnah* are similar to *seliḥot*. The *teḥinnah* is usually said quietly, its subject being the relationship between God and the people of Israel. It is sometimes constructed in rhymed verses, sometimes in rhymed rhetoric, or even unrhymed, in the style of a *bakkashah*. In addition to Hebrew *teḥinnot*, there were early modern Yiddish **tkhines* for women published in small brochures from the beginning of the 17th century in Bohemia (Prague), Switzerland (Basle), Germany (Sulzbach, Fuerth, Roedelheim), and many towns of Russia and Poland. Occasionally *teḥinnot* were added as appendixes to editions of the prayer book.

BIBLIOGRAPHY: Elbogen, *Gottesdienst*, 229; Schirmann, *Sefarad*, 718.

[Abraham Meir Habermann / Chava Weissler (2nd ed.)]

TEHOMI (Zilberg), AVRAHAM (1903–1990), Zionist underground fighter. Tehomi was born in Odessa, Ukraine, and in 1919 joined *He-Ḥalutz, and participated in the defense of the Jewish population in Odessa during its civil war. In 1922 he escaped from Russia, and arrived in Palestine the following year where he worked as a laborer and joined the *Haganah. From 1929 to 1931, he was Haganah commander for the Jerusalem district. In 1931 he formed the Irgun Ẓeva'i Le'ummi (IZL), and was its commander-in-chief until 1937. During this period he was also active in smuggling into Palestine huge quantities of arms from Finland and Poland. In 1937 he rejoined the Haganah, and was appointed to the High Command, in charge of training. In 1939 he was involved in bringing into Palestine Jewish "illegal" immigrants, and during World War II, he organized a Jewish Intelligence group working for the Allies. After World War II, he was active in the Hebrew Committee for National Liberation headed by Hillel Kook (Peter Bergson) in the U.S.

BIBLIOGRAPHY: Tidhar, 5 (1952), 2127–28; A. Tehomi, *The Dream and the Awakening* (1977); Dinur, Haganah, 1–3 (1954–72), index; D. Niv, *Ma'arkhot ha-Irgun ha-Ẓeva'i ha-Le'ummi*, 2 (1965), index.

[Joseph Nedava]

TEICHOLZ, BRUCE B. (1914–1993), U.S. communal worker. Teicholz was born in Rzeszow, Poland, and from 1936 to 1939 was director of Polski-Lloyd, AG. After the Nazi invasion of Poland he joined the Polish underground, fighting in a partisan group called Skole-Lawdezne. He reached Budapest in 1942, where he worked with the Polish Rescue Committee, and subsequently became president of the Committee for Jewish Inmates of the Concentration Camps, Austria (1945–51) and president of the Zionist Organization of Austria (1948–50). He immigrated to the U.S. in 1952 and devoted himself to communal work, particularly in ORT, of which he had been president in Vienna from 1945 to 1948. In 1970 he became president of the National ORT League and vice president of the American ORT Federation.

In 1988 a Holocaust memorial was dedicated at the Dohany Utca Synagogue in Budapest, where Teicholz received an award for his work on behalf of Hungarian Jewry.

BIBLIOGRAPHY: S. Szende, *Der letzte Jude aus Polen* (1945), 185–6; Y. Bauer, *Flight and Rescue* (1967), 158–62, 189, 301; E. Dekel, *Bricha* (1971), 131–4.

TEIF, MOSHE (1904–1966), Soviet Yiddish poet. Born in Minsk, he contributed to Soviet Yiddish journals from 1924. His most prolific period was in the years immediately preceding the first purge of the Minsk writers (1937), when he published poems and short stories for children, his collection of lyrics *Lider un Poemes* ("Songs and Poems," 1933) for adults, and translations of Schiller's *Wilhelm Tell* (1935) and Scott's *Ivanhoe* (1937). His *Milkhome-Lider* ("War Poems," 1947) mirrored his experiences at the front in World War II. He was imprisoned from 1937 to 1941 and from 1948 to 1953 but survived. After the death of Stalin, his poems appeared in Russian translation, in 1958, and again in Yiddish in 1965. He participated in **Sovetish Heymland* from its inauguration in 1961. His translation of the Song of Songs and his autobiography appeared posthumously in 1967.

BIBLIOGRAPHY: LNYL, 4 (1961), 79ff.; *Sovetish Heymland* (Dec. 1967), 128–36. **ADD. BIBLIOGRAPHY:** *Korni* (Moscow and Kiev), no. 22 (2004), 5–128.

[Sol Liptzin]

TEITEL, JACOB (1851–1939), jurist and communal worker. Teitel, the son of a wealthy family of *maskilim*, was born in Cherny Ostrov, Podolia. He graduated in law at the university of Moscow in 1875 and was appointed examining magistrate in the region of *Kuibyshev (Samara) and, in 1904, judge of the district tribunal of *Saratov, and was one of the first Jews in Russia to be employed in the judicial service during the czarist regime. He was often urged to convert. He was compelled to resign (1912), but continued to participate in the public life of the Volga region and maintained contact with the Russian intelligentsia, authors and artists, many of whom praised him in their works and memoirs (including M. *Gorki). He devoted himself to communal and philanthropic work, especially in assisting Jews oppressed by the authorities, and was among the founders of a large relief enterprise which supported the Jewish youth who felt compelled to leave to be able to pursue their studies at higher institutions in Western Europe. Teitel left the Soviet Union in 1921. He became president of the Union of Russian Jews in Germany, and collaborated with the relief organization for Russian-Jewish refugees. When the Nazis came to power, Teitel transferred his activities to France, where his memoirs, *Iz moyey zhizniza sorok let*, were published in 1925. A festschrift, edited by N.L. Aronson and others, was published for his 80th birthday in 1931.

BIBLIOGRAPHY: A.A. Goldenweiser, *Ya. L. Teitel*, 1850–1939 (1944 = *Yevreyskiy Mir*, vol. 2, 1944); O.O. Gruzenberg, *Ocherki i rechi* (1944), 164–8.

[Yehuda Slutsky]

TEITELBAUM, family of rabbis and dynasty of *ẓaddikim* in Hungary and Galicia. Its founder, MOSES BEN ẒEVI OF UJHELY (*Satoraljaujhely in Hungary; 1759–1841), was born in *Przemysl, Galicia. A pupil of *Jacob Isaac ha-Ḥozeh (the Seer) of Lublin, he first served as rabbi at Sieniawa (Galicia) and from 1808 at Ujhely. Moses was among the first to spread Ḥasidism in the northern and central districts of Hungary. He won renown as a learned man and a wonder-working *ẓaddik* among all sectors of the Jewish community, both Ḥasidim and others. He wrote *Yismaḥ Moshe* (Lemberg, 1848–61), considered one of the classic homiletic works of Ḥasidism, and responsa, *Heshiv Moshe* (Lemberg, 1866).

His only son, ELEAZAR NISAN OF DROGOBYCH (1788–1855), served as rabbi at *Sighet (Marmaros-Sziget), Hungary, and for 15 years at *Drogobych. He wrote no works himself, but his teachings are recorded in works written by his father and one of his sons. Of these SAMUEL was rabbi at Gorlice, and Nahum Ẓevi succeeded his father as rabbi at Drogobych; the best known, Jekuthiel Judah of Sighet (1) (1808–1883), became one of the greatest *admorim* in Hungary. Born in Drogobych, he studied with his grandfather, Moses, and served first as rabbi at Stropkov. After his grandfather's death in 1841 he was rabbi in Ujhely, but was forced to leave under pressure by the *Mitnaggedim. He then officiated in Gorlice and Drogobych. However, he became known chiefly as rabbi at Sighet, where he moved in 1858; he subsequently gathered around him many Ḥasidim, and also founded a yeshivah. Jekuthiel Judah wrote many works, among them *Yitav Lev*, on the Torah (in five parts, 1875); *Yitav Panim*, on the festivals (in two parts, 1881–83); responsa *Avnei Ẓedek* (in two parts, 1885–86); and *Rav Tov* on the Torah (1889).

His sons were ABRAHAM AARON (d. 1910), rabbi at Kolbuszowa; MOSES JOSEPH (d. 1897), rabbi at Ujhely; ELIJAH BEZALEL (d. 1918), rabbi at Havasmezö and Tecsö (Tyachevo); the best known was HANANIAH YOM TOV LIPA OF SIGHET (b. in the 1830s–1904) born in Stropkow. At first he served as rabbi at Tecsö, but after his father's death in 1883 left for Sighet, where he became involved in the dispute which broke out in the community over the question of joining the national organization of Orthodox congregations of Hungary which had its headquarters in Budapest. Like his father he became known as a learned man and *ẓaddik*, and many sought him out. He wrote *Kedushat Yom Tov*, on the Torah and festivals (in two parts, 1895). His son, ḤAYYIM ẒEVI OF SIGHET (b. in the 1870s–1926), born in Sighet, was also a rabbi and *ẓaddik*. He wrote *Aẓei Ḥayyim* on the Torah and the festivals (in three parts, 1927–34); responsa *Aẓei Ḥayyim* (in two parts, 1939); and *Aẓei Ḥayyim*, on tractate *Gittin* (1939). His son, JEKUTHIEL JUDAH OF SIGHET (2), the last rabbi to serve in Sighet, perished in the Holocaust at *Auschwitz in 1944.

JOEL(ISH) TEITELBAUM OF SATMAR (1888–1979), son of Hananiah Yom Tov Lipa Teitelbaum, served in communities in the Carpathians and northern Transylvania, and from 1928 at Satmar (*Satu Mare). He became involved there in fierce controversies with both Zionist circles and Ḥasidim attached to other *ẓaddikim*, who violently opposed him. During the Holocaust, in 1944, he was saved in the rescue train arranged through R.R. *Kasztner and from *Bergen-Belsen reached Ereẓ Israel. In 1947 he settled in the Williamsburg quarter of Brooklyn, New York, which was the center of a ḥasidic congregation that continued the way of life of a ḥasidic town in Hungary. In 1953 Teitelbaum became rabbi of the ultra-Orthodox *Neturei Karta community in Jerusalem, although he remained in New York and only visited Israel every few years. Later his ties with the community weakened and it ceased to regard him as rabbi.

Teitelbaum continued to be one of the most vigorous opponents of Zionism and the State of Israel, and engaged in intensive activity against the latter both in Israel and abroad, in his writings and sermons, and by demonstrations. While his opposition to Zionism and the State of Israel was based on halakhic grounds, most of which had been raised from the beginning of the Zionist movement, he added objections to the way of life and the social and political order in Israel, which in his opinion contradict the principles of *halakhah*. According to Teitelbaum, Zionism and the establishment of the State of Israel constitute a violation of the three oaths which the people of Israel were made to swear (see Ket. 3). This has delayed the coming of the Messiah and complete redemption, and resulted in all the troubles affecting the Jewish people in the 20th century. The Holocaust also was a punishment for the sins of Zionism and the State of Israel. Hence Teitelbaum denounced the secular character of the state, objecting to its democratic regime and legislature as not being founded on *halakhah*.

Teitelbaum also opposed the use of Hebrew as the spoken language, since this has secularized the holy tongue, and the adoption of the Sephardi pronunciation instead of the Ashkenazi. However, Teitelbaum did not express opposition to settlement in Israel provided that it was not through a mass *aliyah* movement but carried out by individuals only, from this point of view Ereẓ Israel being no worse than other countries. *Naḥmanides' opinion that to settle in Ereẓ Israel is a positive commandment is interpreted by Teitelbaum as referring to those who live in the country and observe the commandments of the Torah. If, however, a person living in the country does not observe the commandments, but is sinful, he defiles it, and those who fear the word of the Lord have a duty to see that he leaves. Teitelbaum forbade the Ḥasidim living in his community to cooperate with state institutions, while ordering those living in Israel not to take the oath of loyalty to the state, not to take part in the elections to its parliamentary institutions, and not to make use of its law courts or legal system.

An eminent scholar and sharp polemicist, Teitelbaum combined extreme fanaticism with a forceful personality. His public stand and at times his actions gave rise to much dissension and opposition. He succeeded in gathering round him a large ḥasidic community, exercising authority over his Ḥasidim even in matters which were really political. His discourses and sermons, mainly devoted to an explanation of his position on various matters, could be regarded for the most part as polemics against the State of Israel.

In 1970 Teitelbaum founded *Kiryas Joel in Monroe, New York, where many of his tens of thousands of Satmar followers moved. After his death he was succeeded by his nephew Moshe Teitelbaum (1914–2006), who divided the control of the Williamsburg and Monroe Satmar communities between two of his sons: Rabbi AARON TEITELBAUM (1948–), chief rabbi of Satmar-Kiryas Joel, his eldest son, and Rabbi ZALMAN LEIB TEITELBAUM (1952–), chief rabbi of Satmar-Williamsburg, his third son.

BIBLIOGRAPHY: J.J.(L.) Greenwald (Grunwald), *Ha-Ẓofeh me-Ereẓ Hagar* (1911); idem, *Maẓẓevet Kodesh* (1952); A.Y. Bromberg, *Mi-Gedolei ha-Ḥasidut*, 8 (1952); P.Z. Schwarz, *Shem ha-Gedolim me-Ereẓ Hagar* (1914); N. Ben-Menahem, in: *Sinai*, 25 (1949); *Sefer Milḥemet Mitzvah he-Ḥadash* (1929); J. Sperber, *Sefat Emet* (1929); H. Lieberman, *Der Rebbe un der Sotn* (1959); G.G. Kranzler, *Williamsburg, a Jewish Community in Transition* (1961); S. Poll, *The Hassidic Community of Williamsburg* (1962); S. Rozman, *Sefer Zikhron Kedoshim li-Yhudei Carpatoruss-Marmarosh* (Yid., 1968), 84–87, 92–100.

[Avraham Rubinstein]

TEITELBAUM, AARON (1890–1950), U.S. rabbi and communal worker. Teitelbaum was born in Jerusalem but was a citizen of the United States since his father had acquired American citizenship before Aaron's birth. After being ordained by R. Ḥayyim *Berlin and Rabbi A.I. *Kook in 1911, Teitelbaum proceeded to the United States and in 1914 was appointed secretary of the Union of Orthodox Rabbis of the U.S. and Canada. In this capacity he arbitrated in a labor dispute between the garment workers and their employers. On the outbreak of World War I Teitelbaum took the initiative in establishing the Central Relief Committee for relief work on behalf of rabbis and Orthodox institutions. Simultaneously the American Jewish Relief Committee was formed for general relief, and in November 1914 these two bodies, together with the Peoples' Relief Committee, amalgamated to form the *American Jewish Joint Distribution Committee (the "Joint"), with Teitelbaum appointed to its executive. From this time until his death he was regarded as the representative of Orthodox Jewry in the Joint, and later in the Jewish Agency, being appointed a member of the Jewish Agency Council on its foundation in 1929 and a member of its Administrative Committee from 1929 to 1931. In 1918 he was appointed by Woodrow Wilson as the only Jewish member of the Hoover Commission, set up to investigate conditions in Europe and the Near East, serving as commissioner of relief, Near East Relief Mission. He used the authority of this position, and the large amounts of money made available to the Joint, to reestablish the yeshivot in Eastern Europe which had been destroyed during the war. Teitelbaum was responsible for persuading the State Bank of New York to buy up the whole issue of $150,000 in bonds issued by the municipality of Tel Aviv, the first transaction of this kind. In 1930 he returned to Jerusalem, but on the outbreak of World War II he returned to the United States to set up relief programs for European Jewry. He returned to Jerusalem in 1950, where he died the same year.

TEITELBAUM, ABRAHAM (1889–1947), Yiddish and English actor. Born in Warsaw, Teitelbaum worked in London with Maurice *Moscovitch. This led to his appearance in English in a West End production of *Cumberland's *The Jew*, and *Daughters of Shem* by Samuel Gordon and Carmel Goldsmid. After World War I he joined the *Vilna Troupe, and staged Eugene O'Neil's *Desire under the Elms* and Strindberg's *The Father*. In 1919 he went to New York and the rest of his career was spent at Schwartz's Jewish Art Theater.

ADD. BIBLIOGRAPHY: D. Mazower, *The Yiddish Theatre in London* (1987).

TEITELBOIM VOLOSKY, VOLODIA (1913–), Chilean politician. Born in Chillan, he became a lawyer in 1945 and was also a journalist and writer. He was editor of the Catholic daily *El Diario Ilustrado de Santiago*. He was active in the Communist Party from his youth and was one of the founders of the party's daily, *El Siglo*. He was a member of the Central Committee of the Chilean CP from 1946 and acted as a member of its Political Delegation for many years.

Between 1961 and 1965 he was an MP for Valparaíso.

Teitelboim was a poet, novelist, and author of several books. He was elected to the Senate in 1973 and following the fall of Allende settled in Moscow where he directed subversive activities against Pinochet. He returned to Chile when democracy was reestablished (1989). In the new democratic era, he wrote many books, including a biography of Pablo Neruda, of whom he was an intimate friend, and a two-volume autobiography.

[Moshe Nes El (2nd ed.)]

TEITLER, SAMUEL (1900–1990), Swiss jurist. Teitler, born in St. Gall into a family of Polish-Jewish origin, he graduated as a lawyer and lectured in law at the St. Gallen School (today university) for Economics and Political Science and was a prominent figure in the Swiss Social Democratic Party. A judge of the State Court of Appeals, he was appointed alternate judge of the Swiss Supreme Court in 1957. He was president of the St. Gallen Jewish community and a member of the central committee of the Swiss Zionist Federation. He was also president of the Swiss Friends of the Hebrew University. He established a philanthropic foundation in St. Gall. His bequest is in the Archiv fuer Zeitgeschichte, Zurich.

[Uri Kaufmann (2nd ed.)]

TEITSH, MOYSHE (1882–1935), Yiddish journalist, poet, novelist, and dramatist. Born near Vilna, Teitsh began his Yiddish career in 1902 under Abraham *Reisen's influence, becoming a journalist in Warsaw in 1904. His sad, autumnal lyrics and his short stories were popular before World War I, while after the 1917 Revolution he wrote proletarian lyrics and tales, a biblical drama, *David un Bathsheba* (1920), articles for the Moscow Yiddish daily *Emes*, and was the Moscow correspondent of the New York daily *Frayhayt* and the Buenos Aires daily *Di Prese*. From the mid-1920s, he reinvented himself as a prose realist devoted to pre-1917 Jewish life and contemporary events. His most significant books were *A Hoyf oyf Tshebotarske* ("A Courtyard on Tshebotarske," 1926) and *Der Toyt fun Khaver Vili* ("The Death of Comrade Willie," 1931); a selection of his 1903–23 writings, *Far Tsvantsik Yor* ("Twenty Years Ago") appeared in 1927; his selected works appeared posthumously in 1936.

BIBLIOGRAPHY: Rejzen, Leksikon, 1 (1926), 1174–7; LNYL, 4 (1961), 72–6. **ADD. BIBLIOGRAPHY:** G. Estraikh, in: *Jews in Eastern Europe* 2 (2000), 25–55; idem, in: *East European Jewish Affairs* 2 (2002), 70–88.

[Sol Liptzin / Gennady Estraikh (2nd ed.)]

TEITZ, (MORDECHAI) PINCHAS (1908–1995), U.S. rabbinic leader. Born in Subat, Latvia, where his father was the rabbi, Teitz studied at yeshivot of Slobodka and Telz, being ordained in 1931. He was active in communal work in Latvia, founding the Yavneh Yeshiva in Livani and the Yavneh youth movement in Latvia, and editing a newspaper, *Unzer Shtime*. He worked with Mordechai Dubin, a member of the Latvian parliament, and for a year with Rabbi Joseph Rosen, the Rogachover, in Dvinsk From his father, whose synagogue had a room for ḥasidim on one side, a room for *mitnaggedim* on the other, with the rabbi and his family living in rooms between the two, he learned to unite the community. From Dubin he learned how to get Jews and non-Jews to work together for shared benefit. From his father's brother, Rabbi Eliyahu Akiva Rabinowich, editor of *Ha-Peles* and *Ha-Modi'a*, with whom his family found refuge during WWI, he learned to analyze problems, to think of solutions and to turn them into reality.

A charismatic speaker, he came to the U.S. in 1933 with Rabbi Elijah M. Bloch to spend a year visiting major Jewish centers in behalf of Telz Yeshiva. Soon after he became rabbi of Elizabeth, N.J. He and his wife built a classic *kehillah*, starting with a *talmud torah*, a *mikveh*, and a day school in 1940, one of the first outside a major city. They united the various entities under the title Jewish Educational Center (JEC), which grew to include yeshivah high schools for boys and girls and a *kollel* for college students. In a unique structure for an American community, one rabbi led five synagogues and the JEC, all joined in one *kehillah*. He helped Princeton students found the Yavneh kosher dining hall at their university. He built two synagogues in Elizabeth, one in 1947, the second in 1955.

In 1953 he founded *Daf Hashavua*, a weekly radio broadcast of Talmud that continued until 1988. Tapes of the broadcasts were aired in other cities in the U.S. and Canada, and reached the U.S.S.R. on *Kol Zion la-Golah*. He also pioneered the use of long-playing records to teach Talmud with *Bas Kol*.

He was active in Va'ad Hazzalah, trying to rescue Jews during the Holocaust, spending two months in London and Paris in 1945 helping refugees. Beginning in 1944 he urged the American Jewish community to forge ties with Jews in the U.S.S.R. In 1964 he and his wife made the first of 22 trips to the Soviet Union. He raised money privately to bring physical and religious necessities to Jews behind the Iron Curtain, including special *siddurim* that would enable a Jew in Russia to learn to read Hebrew and to observe *mitzvot*. He obtained permission to bring in *tefillin* as long as one side would be transparent. He taught Rabbi Eliyahu Essas and worked with him and others to preserve cemeteries and restore the graves of great scholars.

He was treasurer of Ezras Torah for over 30 years and co-founder in 1980 of Merkaz Harabbanim, an effort to move young rabbinic couples out of the yeshivah and into the communities that needed them. His son, Rabbi Elazar Mayer Teitz, succeeded him as rabbi of the *kehillah* in Elizabeth.

BIBLIOGRAPHY: R. Blau, *Learn Torah, Love Torah, Live Torah: Harav Mordechai Pinchas Teitz, the Quintessential Rabbi* (2001).

[Rivka Blau (2nd ed.)]

TEIXEIRA, PEDRO (c. 1570–c. 1650), Portuguese Marrano explorer and author. Born in Lisbon, Teixeira was one of the greatest travelers of his age, circumnavigating the globe during the years 1585–1601. His first journey, begun in 1585–86, took him to China and the Philippines, from there to the Americas, and finally back to Lisbon, in 1601; his second took him to India, Persia, and other parts of the Orient between the years 1603 and 1609, when he is thought to have settled in Antwerp. Teixeira published a detailed account of these travels, *Relaciones de Pedro Teixeira…* (Antwerp, 1610), containing data long considered authoritative. It was translated into French in 1681 and the first English version appeared in 1708–10. A complete English translation, *The Travels of Pedro Teixeira*, was published in 1902. The book is still held to be one of the most important sources of information about the Orient at the beginning of the 17th century. Apart from the descriptive material, it contains a history of the rulers of Persia and demographic information about the Jews of Baghdad, Aleppo, and Persia. In Baghdad, Teixeira found two or three hundred Jewish families, mainly poor people, living in a district of their own. Aleppo had a larger and wealthier community of a thousand families, for the most part merchants, but including also craftsmen, silversmiths, and lapidaries. The Jews managed the Aleppo mint and customs house and possessed an impressive synagogue. In the provinces of Persia, Teixeira located some 8,000–10,000 Jewish families. Teixeira is said to have arrived in Brazil in the early 1620s and to have led successful forays against the English and the Dutch. In July 1637, at the request of Philip III of Portugal (Philip IV of Spain), he undertook a journey of exploration in the country. In what was to be his last expedition, Teixeira set out from Pará (Belém) with a party of 2,000 men and made the first continuous voyage up the Amazon, finally reaching Quito after an adventurous trip lasting ten months. In the course of this journey he extended the boundaries of Brazil and established a line of demarcation between the Spanish and Portuguese possessions in South America. There are conflicting accounts of the last years of Teixeira's life. Some authorities claim that he finally became governor of Pará and died there; others maintain that he returned to Europe and settled in Antwerp, where he reverted to Judaism. A description of his expedition to the source of the Amazon is found in the *Nuevo descubrimiento del Gran Rio de la Amazonas* (1641).

BIBLIOGRAPHY: M. de Saavedra y Guzmán, *Viaje del capitán P. Teixeira…* (1889); Roth, Marranos, 76; J. Amador de los Rios, *Estudios históricos, politicos y literarios, sobre los Judíos de España* (1848), 554–8; P. Teixeira, *The Travels of Pedro Teixeira*, ed. and tr. by W.F. Sinclair (1902), introd. by D. Ferguson.

[Kenneth R. Scholberg]

TEIXEIRA DE SAMPAIO, ABRAHAM SENIOR (formerly Diego; 1581–1666), Portuguese Marrano nobleman. Born in Lisbon, Teixeira was the son of Dom Francisco de Melo, a gentleman of the Portuguese royal house, and Dona Antonia de Silva Teixeria, lady-in-waiting to the queen. In 1643 he moved to Antwerp, where he was appointed consul and paymaster for the government of Spain. After the death of his first wife, he married Dona Anna (Sarah) d'Andrade, a noblewoman who had borne him a son, Manoel, 20 years before. Soon after, Teixeira and, even more, his wife felt a compelling need to practice Judaism. They moved to Hamburg and there Teixeira and his sons were circumcised (c. 1648), creating a scandal in the Catholic world. The imperial Viennese court indignantly demanded the confiscation of Teixeira's property, assessed at over 250,000 crowns. The Hamburg senate, however, objecting to the loss of this new-found capital, thwarted its confiscation. Teixeira prospered, founding the international banking house that became known as Teixeira de Mattos. Taking a prominent part in Jewish public affairs, Teixeira in 1657 interceded with King Frederick III of Denmark to secure civil rights for the Jews of Glueckstadt, a Danish port on the Elbe. For a time he headed Hamburg's Sephardi congregation and in 1659 arranged for the construction of a new synagogue. When the officials of Hamburg's St. Michael Church asked him to acquire the copper sheets they needed for roofing, he did so and refused to accept payment. Called "the rich Jew," he maintained an aristocratic home, traveling in a luxurious carriage attended by a retinue of liveried servants. Whenever Queen Christina of Sweden visited Hamburg after 1654, she stayed in his home. From 1655 until his death he was resident diplomatic and financial minister for the Swedish crown, a post inherited by his son Manoel. Two charities founded by Teixeira and Sarah, one for poor brides and the other for captive Jews, continued to function in Hamburg into the 20th century.

BIBLIOGRAPHY: H. Kellenbenz, *Sephardim an der unteren Elbe* (1958), 278–300, 483; Graetz, Gesch, 4 (1894), 690; Roth. Marranos, 301; I. da Costa, *Noble Families among the Sephardic Jews* (1936), 81, 110.

[Aaron Lichtenstein]

TEIXEIRA PINTO, BENTO (c. 1545–1600), Portuguese Marrano author and martyr. The son of a New *Christian, Manoel Alvares de Barros, Teixeira Pinto was born in Oporto and educated at a Jesuit college. He evidently left Portugal as a youth and spent about 30 years in Brazil, where he became a teacher. In 1565 he accompanied Jorge de Albuquerque Coelho, the governor of Pernambuco (Recife) on a voyage to Lisbon in the course of which the two men were shipwrecked. This experience is described in Teixeira Pinto's *Relaçâo do naufrágio*... (1601), which was later republished in the *História Trágico-Marítima*, 2 (1736), and again in 1872. From 1584 he lived in Ilheús, Bahia. Teixeira Pinto was first denounced to the Inquisition in 1591–92 and again in January 1594, the charges including Judaizing and possessing of a copy of the pastoral novel *Diana* by the Converso author Jorge de Montemayor (see *Spanish and Portuguese Literature). After his arrest in August 1595, Teixeira Pinto was sent from Brazil to Lisbon. He appeared at an auto-da-fé in 1599 and died at the hands of the Inquisition the following year.

Teixeira Pinto is best known for his epic poem glorifying the city of Pernambuco, *Prosopopéa* (1601; ed. A. Peixoto, 1923). Though clearly influenced by the Portuguese poet Camões, it was the first literary work of note to be written in Brazil and was dedicated to Teixeiro Pinto's old traveling companion, the governor of Recife. Printed at the end of this volume is the emblem of a phoenix and a telling quotation from Song of Songs 8:6. The phoenix arising from its own ashes was the symbol of the Portuguese synagogue *Neveh Shalom* in Amsterdam, and its use in this book, published in Lisbon a year after the writer's death, would seem to have been intended as a gesture of defiant mockery of the Inquisition. Teixeira Pinto has been falsely credited with the authorship of the *Diálogos das Grandezas do Brasil*, which was probably the work of his contemporary and fellow-Marrano, Ambrósio Fernandes *Brandão.

BIBLIOGRAPHY: A. Wiznitzer, *Jews in Colonial Brazil* (1960), 20, 25, 28–32.

[Godfrey Edmond Silverman]

TEKA (**Tecanus**; **Techanus**), moneylender of diplomatic standing in Vienna at the beginning of the 13th century. In the peace treaty between Duke Leopold VI of Austria and King Andrew II of Hungary of 1225, Teka appears as the sole guarantor (*fideiussor*) of Leopold VI for the sum of 2,000 marks. In 1232 he is mentioned as "*comes camerae*" (royal fiscal agent) and possessor of a manor in Hungary. In 1235 real estate which had been donated to a monastery was designated as collateral in a loan he negotiated in conjunction with some Viennese burghers. At the time Teka had a house in Vienna.

BIBLIOGRAPHY: J.E. Scherer, *Rechtsverhaeltnisse der Juden in den deutsch-oesterreichischen Laendern*, 1 (1901), 126–7; MHJ, 1 (1903), index s.v. *Tekanus*; H. Gold (ed.), *Gedenkbuch der untergegangenen Judengemeinden des Burgenlandes* (1970), 7–9.

[Meir Lamed]

TEKHELET (Heb. תְּכֵלֶת; "blue"), *argaman* ("purple"), and *tola'at shani* ("*crimson worm") are frequently mentioned together in the Bible as dyestuffs for threads and fabrics, including the curtains of the Tabernacle (Ex. 26: 1), the veil (Ex. 26:31), the veil for the tent (Ex. 26: 31) and the ephod (Ex. 28:6). A thread of *tekhelet* had to be included in the fringes (Num. 15: 38). Princes and nobles wore garments of *tekhelet* (Ezek. 23:6) and it was used for the expensive fabrics in the royal palace (Esth. 1:6). The Tyrians were expert dyers with these materials (II Chron. 2:6; cf. Ezek. 27:7). According to the talmudic *aggadah*, the dwellers in Luz (a legendary locality) were experts in dyeing *tekhelet* (Sanh. 12a; Sot. 46b). *Tekhelet* was extracted from the *ḥillazon* – a snail found in the sea between the promontory of Tyre and Haifa (Shab. 26a; Sif. Deut. 354). Members of the tribe of Zebulun engaged in gathering it (Meg. 6a), and according to the Midrash, it is this which is referred to in that tribe's blessing that their inheritance would include "the hidden treasures of the sands" (Deut. 33: 19). The *baraita* notes that the *tekhelet* multiplies like fish, i.e., by laying eggs, "and comes up once in 70 years, and with its blood *tekhelet* is dyed, and that is why it is expensive" (Men. 44a; cf. Sif., *ibid.*). The statement reflects the fact that the snail reaches the shore in shoals infrequently and the extraction of the dye is a very expensive process. For this reason "a garment made wholly of *tekhelet*" was considered expensive and rare (Men. 39a, etc.).

The color of *tekhelet* was between green and blue and was thus described: "*Tekhelet* resembles the sea, the sea resembles grass, and grass resembles the heavens" (TJ, Ber. 1:5, 3a). It is like the color of the *leek. *Tekhelet* was usually dyed on wool (Yev. 4b). The color was fast and withstood oxidization (Men. 42b–43a). The best dye was obtained when extracted from live snails (Shab. 75a) and to make it fast various materials were added (Men. 42b). In the time of the Mishnah another dye, *kela ilan*, extracted from the Indian indigo plant, was introduced into Ereẓ Israel. This dye is very similar in color to *tekhelet* but is much cheaper. Thenceforth indigo was frequently used to counterfeit, and was sold as, *tekhelet*. Ways of testing to distinguish them were indeed suggested, but the *baraita* concluded that "There is no way of testing the *tekhelet* of *ẓiẓit*, and it should be bought from an expert" (Men. 42b). It is worthy of note that dyed *ẓiẓit* were discovered in the Bar Kokhba Caves. The testing of them by modern methods proved almost with certainty that they were in fact dyed with indigo – the aforementioned *kela ilan*. For all these reasons –

the high cost of *tekhelet*, the difficulty of gathering the snails and extracting the dye, and because of the fear of counterfeiting with *kela ilan* – some *tannaim* permitted *ẓiẓit* made without a thread of *tekhelet* (Men. 4:1; cf. Men. 38a). It is probable, however, that many continued to fulfill the biblical precept. In the time of the *amora* Abbaye, Jews still engaged in dyeing with the *tekhelet* and Samuel b. Judah, a Babylonian *amora* who had resided in Ereẓ Israel, explained the dyeing process to him. In the time of the *savora* Aḥai the differences between *tekhelet* and *kela ilan* were tested (Men. 42b). The Midrash, however, notes that "nowadays we only possess white *ẓiẓit*, the *tekhelet* having been concealed" (Num. R. 17:5).

Gershon Ḥanokh Leiner, the ḥasidic rabbi of Radzin, proposed in his books *Sefunei Temunei Ḥol* (1887) and *Petil Tekhelet* (1888) that the precept of the *tekhelet* in *ẓiẓit* be reintroduced. He came to the conclusion that *tekhelet* had been extracted from the cuttlefish, *Sepia officinalis* (*vulgaris*), which has a gland in its body that secretes a blue-black dye, and his suggestion was adopted by his followers. From the sources, however, it seems that the *tekhelet* dye was much lighter, and the descriptions of *tekhelet* in rabbinical literature do not fit this creature, which is common on the shores of Israel, its dye being neither expensive nor fast. It is also difficult to identify it with the *ḥillazon*. *Ḥillazon* in rabbinical literature is a land or sea snail (Sanh. 91a). Among the latter there are species in whose bodies is a gland containing a clear liquid, which when it comes into contact with the air becomes greenish: this is *tekhelet* which, after the addition of various chemicals, receives its purple color, the "royal purple" of literature. The Phoenicians in particular specialized in it, Phoenicia in Greek meaning the land of purple. Around Tyre and Ras-Shamra – the site of ancient Ugarit – large quantities of shells of the purple snail have been found. These belong to the species *Murex trunculus* and *Murex brandaris*, which are found along the length of the eastern shore of the Mediterranean and whose quantities change from time to time. A modern investigator extracted 1.4 gram of the purple dye from 12,000 such snails, thus explaining the high cost of the *tekhelet* and purple dyes. Isaac *Herzog, in a study of *tekhelet* ("The Dyeing of Purple in Ancient Israel," 1919; see bibliography), reached the conclusion that it was extracted from the snails *Janthina pallida* and *Janthina bicolor* that are found a considerable distance from the shore and only reach it at long intervals. This in his opinion explains the statement that the *tekhelet* comes up once in 70 years (Men. 44a). The dye extracted from these snails varies between violet blue and the blue of the heavens. Most investigators incline to the view that *tekhelet* and *argaman* were extracted from the *Murex* snails.

BIBLIOGRAPHY: Krauss, Tal Arch, 1 (1910), 146–7; S. Bodenheimer, *Ha-Ḥai be-Arẓot ha-Mikra*, 2 (1956), 305ff.; M.M. Kasher, in: *Sefer ha-Yovel ... Eliyahu Jung* (1962), 241–58; J. Feliks, in: *Talmud El-Am – Berakhot* (1965), 173–4; I. Frenkel, *Men of Distinction*, 1 (1967), 51–57. **ADD. BIBLIOGRAPHY:** Feliks, Ha-Ẓome'aḥ, 230, 284, 285; I. Herzog, *The Royal Purple and the Biblical Blue: The Study of Chief Rabbi Isaac Herzog and Recent Scientific Contributions*, ed. E. Spanier (1987).

[Jehuda Feliks]

TEKI'ATA (**Teki'to**; Heb. תְּקִיעֲתָא, תְּקִיעוֹת), three series of scriptural verses included in the *Musaf* service of Rosh Ha-Shanah, designated **malkhuyyot*, **zikhronot*, and **shofarot*, and concerned respectively with the Kingdom of Heaven, the remembrance of the Covenant, and the sounding of the horn of Redemption. Each series of verses concludes with an appropriate benediction: "Blessed art Thou ... King of the whole earth...," "... Who remembers the Covenant," and "... Who hears the sound of the horn of his people Israel."

The *teki'ata* are first mentioned in the Mishnah of Rosh Ha-Shanah (4:5–6). According to the first opinion of the Mishnah, each of the series comprises ten verses – three from the Pentateuch, three from the Prophets, three from the Hagiographa, and a final verse from the Prophets. Another view expressed in the Mishnah, that of *Yose b. Ḥalafta, is that the final verse may also be from the Pentateuch. R. *Johanan b. Nuri maintained that each *teki'ata* should contain only three verses – one from the Pentateuch, one from the Prophets, and one from the Hagiographa. Halakhic practice conforms to Yose b. Halafta's opinion; and each *teki'ata* contains ten verses, the final one being from the Pentateuch. The Ashkenazi and French custom differs, however, in that the hagiographic verses in each series precede those from the Prophets. In the course of time, introductory *piyyutim* were added to the *teki'ata: Aleinu le-Shabbe'aḥ* and *Ve-Al Ken Nekavveh* before the *malkhuyyot, Attah Zokher* before the *zikhronot*, and *Attah Nigleita* before the *shofarot*. These introductions are attributed to *Rav (second and third centuries C.E.) and are therefore called *Teki'ata de-Rav* or *Teki'ata de-Vei Rav*.

In the age of the *paytanim* more *piyyutim* were added, corresponding to the theme of each *teki'ata*. It may be assumed that these *piyyutim* were first used as alternatives to those of Rav, but eventually both old and new were incorporated jointly into the liturgy. The oldest *piyyutim* are those of *Yose b. Yose (*Ahallelah* ... Davidson, Oẓar, 1 (1924), 69 no. 1494). Saadiah b. Joseph Gaon praised them in his *siddur* (ed. by I. Davidson et al. (1941), 225), stating that he chose them in preference to all others. They have been adopted into the Ashkenazi and French rites; and so also have the *piyyutim* of Eleazar *Kallir. *Teki'ata* by Solomon ibn Gabirol beginning *Ansikhah malki* (Davidson, *ibid.*, 310 no. 6823) are also well known. Several *teki'ata* were discovered in the Cairo *Genizah*, outstanding among them being those composed by a Palestinian *paytan*, Mishael, who lived after Kallir; and still other *teki'ata* exist in manuscript.

BIBLIOGRAPHY: Elbogen, Gottesdienst, 142, 216, 264; D. Goldschmidt (ed.), *Maḥzor le-Rosh Ha-Shanah* (1970), introd. 44–48.

[Abraham Meir Habermann]

TEKINALP, MUNIS (1883–1961), pseudonym and later officially adopted name of **Moiz Kohen**, political ideologue and economist. Born into an Orthodox Jewish family in Serres, Macedonia, he devoted his life and writings to promoting the political interests of the *Ottoman Empire, then those of the Republic of *Turkey. As a youngster, he went to *Salonika to study at the school run by the *Alliance Israélite Universelle, later in the Jewish Teachers' College (where he was ordained as a rabbi, although he never practiced), finally at the École Impériale de Droit. He lived in Salonika until 1912, when it was conquered by the Greeks; thereupon, he moved to *Istanbul, where he remained for most of his life.

Salonika and Istanbul were then hotbeds of intellectual activity and Moiz/Munis became involved in political writing for various Turkish newspapers, focusing on socioeconomic issues, socialism, nationalism and (briefly) Zionism; he even attended, as a delegate, the World Zionist Congress in Hamburg. He preached fraternization between Muslims and Jews via the complete Ottomanization of the latter, e.g., by urging Jews to adopt and employ Turkish rather than their communal languages (a subject to which he reverted frequently).

In addition to the above propaganda for the Turkification of Jews in the Ottoman Empire, then in the Republic of Turkey, Tekinalp's main writings were devoted to serve the advance of the empire, or of Turkey. Besides numerous newspaper articles in Turkish, French, and German, he wrote several books. *Türkismus und Pantürkismus* (1915), of which Turkish and English versions also exist, was an impassioned plea for saving the embattled Ottoman Empire through the mobilization of support by all peoples and groups of Turkic origins. *Türkleştirme* (i.e., Turkification) (1928; 2001^2) appealed to all ethnic minorities – and, most especially, to Jews – to integrate into the recently founded Republic of Turkey. *Kemalizm* (1936), translated a year later into French as *Le Kémalisme*, was the first detailed systematic analysis of Kemalism, the republic's new official ideology. Finally, *Türk Ruhu* (i.e., the Spirit of the Turks, 1944) presented his views on the Turkish past, present, and future.

BIBLIOGRAPHY: J.M. Landau, *Tekinalp, Turkish Patriot 1883–1961* (1984; Turkish translation 1996), includes bibliography; idem, *Pan-Turkism* (1881; 1995^2), index; L. Behmoaras, *Bir kimlik arayişinin hikâyesi* (2005).

[Jacob M. Landau (2nd ed.)]

TEKOA (Heb. תְּקוֹעַ), city of Judah connected with the family of Hezron, the son of Perez (I Chron. 2:24; 4:5). It was the birthplace of Ira the son of Ikkesh, one of David's "mighty men" (II Sam. 20:26; I Chron. 11:28; 27:9). From Tekoa came the wise woman who, at the instigation of Joab, persuaded David to pardon Absalom (II Sam. 14). Rehoboam included it in his line of fortifications; it is mentioned together with Etam and Beth-Zur (II Chron. 11:6). In this way, he hoped to safeguard the road leading from En-Gedi to Jerusalem; it proved effective later when Jehoshaphat warded off there an invasion of the Moabites and Ammonites who came from the Dead Sea (II Chron. 20:20). Jeremiah refers to Tekoa as being on the southern approaches to Jerusalem (6:1). It was renowned, above all, as the birthplace of the prophet Amos (1:1); in later times, his tomb was worshiped there and in the Byzantine period, a church was built in his honor, remains of which are still visible. According to the Greek version of Joshua 15:59, it was in the district of Beth-Lehem in Judah. After the return from the Babylonian exile, it was possibly the capital of one of the districts of Judah. The people of Tekoa – but not its nobles – repaired sections of the walls of Jerusalem, one part near the Old (Yeshanah) Gate, the other on the Ophel (Neh. 3:5, 6, 27). In the time of the Maccabean revolt, Bacchides fortified it (Jos., Ant., 13:15; I Macc. 9:50, as Tepho (Tappuah), which should be corrected to Theko). In the First Jewish War, it served as an encampment for Simeon Bar-Giora (Jos., Wars, 4:518) and later for Cerealis, the Roman commander (Jos., Life, 420). Eusebius places the village 12 mi. (c. 19 km.) from Aelia. It was a benefice of the Holy Sepulcher in Crusader times. It is identified with Khirbet et Tuqu', a ruin southeast of Bethlehem and 2,760 ft. (850 m.) above sea level. The site was surveyed by M. Kochavi in 1968 and by Y. Hirschfeld in 1981–82. The ruins cover an area of about 17 acres and overlook an ancient road leading to En Gedi. The visible ruins are mainly from the Byzantine period, with two churches, houses, and hostels or markets. Pottery found dates from the Hellenistic to medieval times.

[Michael Avi-Yonah / Shimon Gibson (2nd ed.)]

The modern Taqqū' is a Muslim-Arab village on the edge of the Judean Desert south of Bethlehem. In 1967 there were 1,362 inhabitants, growing to 4,890 in 1997. The nearby Jewish village of Tekoa was founded in 1975 as part of Gush Eẓyon and had a population of 1,179 in 2004.

[Efraim Orni]

BIBLIOGRAPHY: Suetterlin, in: PJB, 17 (1921), 31–46; Beyer, in: ZDPV, 54 (1931), 219; Avi-Yonah, Land, index. **ADD. BIBLIOGRAPHY:** Y. Hirschfeld, *Archaeological Survey of Israel: Map of Herodium (108/2)* (1985), 39*: Site No. 37; Y. Tsafrir, L. Di Segni, and J. Green, *Tabula Imperii Romani. Iudaea – Palaestina. Maps and Gazetteer.* (1994), 248, s.v. "Thecoa I."

TEKOAH (Tuckachinsky), YOSEF (1925–1991), Israeli diplomat. Tekoah was born in Belorussia, but emigrated as a child with his family to Shanghai, where he graduated in law. He joined the Israel Foreign Service at the inception of the State and held the posts of deputy legal adviser to the Ministry for Foreign Affairs, legal adviser to the Israel Defense Forces on Armistice Affairs, and director of armistice affairs. In the last capacity he headed Israel's delegations to the Mixed Armistice Commissions with Egypt, Lebanon, Jordan, and Syria from 1948 to 1958.

In 1958 he was appointed deputy permanent representative of Israel to the United Nations with the rank of minister plenipotentiary, and from May 1959 was acting permanent representative. He served as ambassador of Israel to Brazil in 1960–62, and to the U.S.S.R. from 1962 to 1965. In 1966 he was appointed assistant director-general of the Ministry for Foreign Affairs, and in January 1968 permanent representative to the United Nations. On his retirement in 1975 he was appointed president of the Ben-Gurion University of the Negev.

TEKUMAH (Heb. תְּקוּמָה; "Resurrection"), moshav in Israel's western Negev, 3 mi. (5 km.) N.W. of Netivot, affiliated with the Moshav Association of Ha-Po'el ha-Mizrachi. Tekumah was founded on Oct. 6, 1946, by survivors of the *Holocaust in Poland and Hungary, on a site 5 mi. (8 km.) further south, as one of the 11 settlements established in the same night in the South and the Negev. In 1949, the moshav moved to its present locality while the former site was taken over by moshav Sharsheret ("Chain"), also affiliated with Ha-Po'el ha-Mizrachi and composed of newcomers from Tunisia. In 1970 Tekumah had 248 inhabitants (including families from Romania) and Sharsheret 545; by the mid-1990s, Tekumah's inhabitants numbered 343, while Sharsheret's population dropped to 248, and at the end of 2002 the population of Sharsheret was 283 and Tekumah's 421. Farming in both settlements was partly irrigated and in Tekumah it included vegetables, flowers, citrus groves, sheep, and poultry, while Sharsheret's farming was based on honey production, vegetables, flowers, and citrus. One of the main pumping stations of the *Yarkon-Negev water pipeline was located nearby. Both moshavim had begun to expand and absorb newcomers.

[Efraim Orni / Shaked Gilboa (2nd ed.)]

TEL ADASHIM (Heb. תֵּל עֲדָשִׁים), moshav in northern Israel, in the Jezreel Valley 3 mi. (5 km.) north of Afulah, affiliated with Tenu'at ha-Moshavim. In 1913, the site became Jewish property and members of *Ha-Shomer set up a camp there. In 1923 pioneers from Eastern Europe and Ha-Shomer veterans founded the moshav, which expanded after the *War of Independence (1948) with the settlement of new immigrants. In 1970 Tel Adashim numbered 400; in 2002, 477, with expansion subsequently underway. Farming consisted principally of flower growing. Other sources of livelihood were guest rooms, an events garden, and a hydraulic equipment plant. The name, literally "hill of lentils," was adapted from the Arabic name of the site.

[Efram Orni / Shaked Gilboa (2nd ed.)]

TEL AVIV-JAFFA (Heb. תֵּל־אָבִיב־יָפוֹ), second biggest city in Israel, in the central part of the Coastal Plain, created in 1949 by the merger of Tel Aviv and *Jaffa. Tel Aviv itself, the "first all-Jewish city" (הָעִיר הָעִבְרִית הָרִאשׁוֹנָה) in modern times, was founded in 1909, originally as a garden suburb of Jaffa, but it evolved over several decades, particularly beginning from the 1930s, to become the largest urban settlement of the new *yishuv* and the core of conurbation which is, in fact, a kind of "megalopolis" stretching from *Herzliyyah in the north to *Reḥovot in the south. Tel Aviv-Jaffa is a bustling city, with 384,000 inhabitants in 1970 and 360,500 in 2002. The municipal area is around 20 sq. mi. (50 sq. km.). Tel Aviv-Jaffa serves as the business, entertainment, press and publishing center of the country. Despite efforts to transfer more and more government and administrative offices to Jerusalem, it remained the site of the Ministry of Defense and of the *Histadrut executive, and also contained, in the large perimeter of its conurbation, the towering diamond-exchange building and a great number of medium and small industries and workshops. It lacks a homogeneous character. Its oldest central part, originally (before World War I) an idyllic cluster of one-story family houses surrounded by gardens, with the Herzlia High School (the Gymnasia) as their center, is now an agglomeration of overcrowded, narrow streets of a typically Mediterranean character, whose old houses have disappeared to make room for office buildings, including several skyscrapers, among them what was once the tallest building in the Middle East – Migdal Shalom, on the original site of the Gymnasia. The southern parts of Tel Aviv are the poorest, housing – often in slum like buildings – tens of thousands of old-time immigrants, mostly from Afro-Asian countries. These immigrants streamed to Tel Aviv en masse in the early 1950s, due to their inability to adjust to the initially harsh conditions of agricultural settlement in the outlying parts of the country.

On the other hand, there are the newer parts of the city, from Allenby Road northward, and particularly the quarters and suburbs erected in the later 1950s and the 1960s. Among these are Ramat Aviv, which also houses *Tel Aviv University. These sections have had a Central and Western European, and often somewhat "Americanized," character. Tel Aviv's commercial and bohemian center was Dizengoff Street and it was, on the whole, the only place in Israel with a pronounced "metropolitan" rhythm of life. During the 1990s the bohemian center of Tel Aviv shifted to Shenkin Street and its surroundings farther south, where a diversified population of artists and secular and religious people lived together.

Tel Aviv has struggled with the typical problems of a city of its kind: sea and air pollution (an outmoded sewage system and the enlargement of its power station, "Reading D," whose character changed from an old, peripheral, out-of-town building into a modern plant with a huge chimney dominating large parts of the city), traffic jams, juvenile delinquency, beggars, etc. Politically, control of the municipal government of Tel Aviv was always a major objective of the contending parties, mainly in the tug-of-war between the Labor and non-Labor camps. Tel Aviv's main period of development from a suburb into a city occurred under the mayoralty of moderate non-Labor personalities, General Zionists such as Meir *Dizengoff and Israel *Rokach. However, in the 1960s its elections resulted in a Labor-dominated municipal council, with labor leaders such as Mordekhai *Namir occupying the post of mayor. Tel Aviv often evokes extremely contradictory feelings. There are people who flee from its noise and heat into quieter suburbs (thus diminishing the number of its inhabitants, though not of the conurbation as a whole), or those who regard it as a drab "upstart" in comparison with the eternity and beauty of Jerusalem. On the other hand, it has its devoted local patriots, including well-known poets, who have regarded it as a realistic embodiment of the renewed Jewish nation, consisting of the "ingathered exiles from all corners of the earth" and who are attracted by its very life and liveliness.

Background to Tel Aviv's History and Development

Tel Aviv attained its preeminent position in less than three decades after its founding. Its progress is particularly striking because modern conditions deprive it of most of the advantages which allowed Jaffa to thrive in antiquity: its straight, shallow shore is unsuitable for the construction of a modern port, and low, narrow sandstone ridges bar the cooling sea breeze, making the summer climate sultry, and impeding the drainage of rainwater from certain sections of the city. Only its location at a focal point of the country's communications network can be valued as a positive factor. Tel Aviv's phenomenal growth is therefore to be attributed to historical circumstances rather than to geographical assets. The fact that until 1948 Tel Aviv constituted the first and only modern all-Jewish city, while all the country's other towns had either a mixed or a totally non-Jewish population, gave the city its special character and imposed on it unique tasks in the *yishuv*'s social and cultural life – eventually making it the principal workshop for preparing Israel's independent statehood.

Tel Aviv's beginnings go back to the revival of the Jewish community of Jaffa in 1820. In that year, a Jewish traveler from Constantinople named R. Yeshaya Adjiman brought the first house in Jaffa into Jewish possession (among the local Arabs it soon became known as "Dār al-Yahūd," i.e., "the Jewish house," and it served as a temporary hostel for newcomers). The Dār al-Yahūd served as the nucleus around which grew the new Jewish community at the beginning of the 19th century. The first Jewish settlers were merchants and artisans originating from North Africa who preferred living from their own handiwork instead of being dependent on **ḥalukkah* in Jerusalem. In the second half of the 19th century, Jews coming from Europe attached themselves to the Sephardi community and laid the ground for the Ashkenazi community; the two communities were amalgamated in 1891. After the city wall was completely demolished in 1888, Jews began to live beyond the confines of Jaffa's Old City.

Throughout the ages, Jaffa served as the "gate to Zion," even in periods when it had no permanent Jewish inhabitants. Travelers and immigrants intending to settle in Jerusalem and the country's other "holy cities" entered the country via its port, which continued to constitute the gateway for the first two large waves of Zionist immigration, from 1882 onward. The First Aliyah caused a profound change in Jaffa's Jewish community. It was there that the first signs of "political Zionism" appeared, that the first Zionist public institutions were established, and that foundations were laid for both Hebrew education and Jewish industry. While Jaffa's Jewish community previously totaled about 1,000 persons, 5,000 new immigrants settled there, thronging the narrow and dirty lanes of the town and living in alien and often hostile surroundings where they were dependent on the whims of Arab landlords.

To alleviate their lot, the Jerusalemite Shimon *Rokach founded a welfare society named Benei Ẓion in 1884, simultaneously establishing (together with his brother Eliezer) a second society, Ezrat Israel, whose functions went beyond giving alms: it aided in establishing a hospital, and also initiated the building of Jaffa's first Jewish quarter, Neveh Ẓedek, in 1887. For this purpose, an area of about 14,000 sq. yds. was acquired from Aharon Chelouche, one of the founders of Jaffa's Jewish community. Jaffa Jews were delighted with this quarter, dubbing it "the Parisian houses," although with its narrow lanes, tightly packed houses, and absence of sanitary facilities, it differed little from Jaffa's other quarters. Its importance, however, lay in the fact that it assembled Jews in a geographical community framework based on fraternal relations. Jaffa's second Jewish quarter, Neveh Shalom, was founded in 1891 by Zeraḥ *Barnett. It extended over about 10,000 sq. yds., and was acquired from Arabs. The homes put up for sale remained empty until the rabbi of the Jaffa community, Naphtali Herz Halevi, bought the first house. Others followed him, and a *talmud torah*, Sha'arei Torah, was opened there in 1896 by the Ashkenazi community. The quarters soon combined their religious character with the new national spirit. Absorbing more inhabitants from among the Sephardi Jews, they expanded and linked up with each other and with Arab Manshiyeh. More Jewish quarters were added to Jaffa in 1904–05, including Maḥaneh Yosef, Kerem ha-Teimanim, and Ohel Moshe. The lands for this purpose had been secured by the founding families of the Jaffa Jewish community, such as Matalon, Moyal, and others.

The Second Aliyah arriving in those days swelled the community's numbers to 7,000, again making dwellings scarce in both the Arab and Jewish sectors and apartment rents excessive. This provided the impetus for founding another Jewish suburb within the boundaries of Jaffa's precincts. The idea had been in the air for a time and was forwarded from various sides, but practical results were achieved only in a meeting on July 5, 1906, which took place in the Yeshurun Club, Jaffa. It was attended by more than 100 Jaffa Jews, both veterans and new immigrants, including merchants, artisans, teachers, and members of other free professions. On the spot they founded an Aguddat Bonei Battim (House Builders' Society), elected a steering committee, and drew up a membership list. Later in the same year, with the number of members reaching 60, the society was renamed Aḥuzzat Bayit (Housing Property). Meanwhile, the Jaffa Jewish community had increased to 8,000, out of a total population of 47,000. The Anglo-Palestine Bank had opened its Jaffa office, as had the Palestine Office of the Zionist Organization under Arthur Ruppin (1908), and the E.L. Lewinsky Seminary for women teachers, all strengthening the middle-class and intellectual element in the community.

The founders' idea was to establish a garden suburb where they could retire every evening after their day's work in noisy Jaffa. It was to be modeled after similar suburbs of European cities, and was not regarded as an extension of the original Jaffa as the earlier Jewish quarters had been. This firm resolution ultimately transformed the small garden settlement of Aḥuzzat Bayit into the "first all-Jewish city." When the founders prepared the basis for urban development, they could hardly hope to be reckoned as Zionist pioneers, as the Zionist Movement then directed its resources exclusively toward agricultural settlement. They also had to overcome the numerous obstacles placed in their path by the Turkish authorities. The members deposited the sum of 100,000 francs with the Anglo-Palestine Bank in order to purchase the "Karm Jabali" land northeast of Jaffa. The society also obtained a loan of 300,000 francs from the Jewish National Fund Head Office in Cologne, in order to construct the first 60 houses. On April 11, 1909, the housing plots were portioned out by lottery, at a meeting on the Aḥuzzat Bayit land which was henceforth regarded as Tel Aviv's founding day.

Within a year, the suburb's main streets – named after *Herzl, *Aḥad Ha-Am, *Judah Halevi, *Lilienblum, and *Rothschild – were laid out, the first 60 houses were completed, and the foundations were prepared for the Herzlia Gymnasia. On May 21, 1910, the suburb's name was changed to Tel Aviv, based on the name of a Babylonian city mentioned in Ezekiel 3:15, and chosen by Nahum Sokolow as the title of his Hebrew translation of Herzl's novel *Altneuland*.

1909–1917

Until World War I, Tel Aviv grew as more small suburbs came into being around the first nucleus: in the east, Naḥlat Binyamin (named after Edmond de Rothschild) and Merkaz Ba'alei Melakhah (Artisans' Center), and in the north, Ḥevrah Ḥadashah (New Society, later becoming Allenby Street) and Ge'ullah. The last brought Tel Aviv's area up to the seashore, and the former created the contact with the Neveh Ẓedek and Neveh Shalom quarters. Until 1914, Tel Aviv's area had increased 20-fold to over 1,000 dunams, and its population had grown from 300 to 2,026. There were 182 houses, mostly one-story. Zionist institutions began to move out of Jaffa to Tel Aviv.

The war halted the town's progress. The attitude of the Turkish authorities deteriorated from suspicion to open hostility. Tel Aviv's local council tried to meet emergencies by providing food for local and other Jews, speeding their naturalization as Turkish citizens, regulating their mobilization for the Turkish army, etc. Official hostility culminated in the wholesale expulsion of the Jews from both Jaffa and Tel Aviv on March 28, 1917. The evacuees were absorbed in the moshavot of the country's interior, and some of them migrated as far as Damascus and Egypt. The few people remaining in Tel Aviv set up an "emigrants' committee," and formed a guardsmen's group to protect the evacuees' property.

1918–1939

On Nov. 16, 1917, Jaffa and Tel Aviv were occupied by British forces. Soon after the Jews could return, and a year later they joyfully celebrated the end of the war. In 1919, young penniless immigrants of the Third Aliyah came to Tel Aviv but found neither housing nor work. Tents were put up for them on the seashore and elsewhere. The Arab riots which broke out in Jaffa on May 1, 1921, caused many Jews to abandon their homes and shops and seek refuge in Tel Aviv. Hundreds of these families were also temporarily housed in tent camps on newly acquired lands of the later New Commercial Center – the "Merkaz Mishari," the Tschlenow quarter, and the "Homeless' Quarter," or Nordiyah. Jaffa remained without Jewish merchants. On May 11, 1921, Tel Aviv was accorded "town council" status with partial administrative and judicial autonomy, and the right to maintain a local police force. A municipal court was set up, as well as a fire brigade and a first aid station. For municipal transportation, small buses of the "Sunbeam" type were introduced. In 1922, six quarters of Jaffa, among them Neveh Ẓedek and Neveh Shalom, were annexed to Tel Aviv, whose population reached 15,000. A year later a power station was opened by the Palestine Electric Corporation (founded by Pinḥas *Rutenberg), and electric lights replaced hurricane lamps.

In 1924, the Fourth Aliyah composed mostly of middle-class elements from Poland began to arrive, and many of its members took up residence in Tel Aviv, establishing small industries in its southern reaches (Wolowelsky Street, Givat Herzl). In 1925, the town's population had jumped to 34,000, construction of houses progressed rapidly, and the southern Tschlenow, Schapira, and Neveh Sha'anan quarters came into being. Cultural institutions, such as Habimah, the Ereẓ Israel Opera, and the Kumkum satirical theater group were founded. The *Histadrut and its local council (Mo'eẓet Po'alei Yafo) became an important factor in the city's development. The built-up area expanded in two directions, southeast and north, as the first three-story houses began to appear, and a commercial center crystallized along the Tel Aviv-Jaffa and Petaḥ Tikvah roads, and Herzl and Naḥalat Binyamin streets. A break in this quick expansion came with the economic crisis of 1927–30, which affected particularly the middle class of the Fourth Aliyah, caused many of the new enterprises to close down and unemployment to spread, and brought building activities to a halt.

Between the 1920s and 1940s, the city's expansion was constricted in the east and southeast by the Arab villages of Sumeil, Salameh, etc., and the German colony of Saronah, with their plantation belt. The inhabitants of these areas, enjoying mounting prosperity thanks to the expanding market in the nearby city, saw no reason to sell their land even at speculative prices. This left the narrow strip of sand dunes and sandstone ridges in the north as the principal reserve for the city's growth. To overcome the haphazard expansion which had followed opportunities of land acquisition, the British town planner Sir Patrick Geddes was invited in 1925 to prepare a blueprint. Although he knew that the original idea of Aḥuzzat Bayit as a garden suburb had by then become obsolete, he followed the old layout of two north-directed main roads, extending Ben Yehudah and Dizengoff beyond Bograshov Street to the Yarkon River bed, thus bringing the south-north length of Tel Aviv to over 3 mi. (5 km.), while the west-east width measured only a few hundred meters. The short side streets in the latter direction became blind alleys, often ending in tennis and other sports courts. This layout made services (communications, water, electricity) relatively expensive for the city's northern part. The shortage of building ground engendered land speculation, making north Tel Aviv the domain of the relatively well-to-do, who could afford higher apartment rents.

After the economic crisis, a new development arrived with the Fifth Aliyah from Germany, which began in 1933 and reached its high point in 1935. The newcomers brought managerial and technical know-how, as well as financial means. The city's population leaped from 45,564 in 1931 to 120,000 in 1935. The building and industrial prosperity attracted laborers and professionals from the moshavot and from other urban centers to Tel Aviv. The establishment of larger industrial enterprises was aided by the *Haavara agreement, which enabled immigrants from Central Europe to transfer to Palestine part of their capital in the form of goods and machines. The last remnants of the Aḥuzzat Bayit suburb disappeared, with industry taking up more of the city's southern reaches. On May 12, 1934, Tel Aviv was officially recognized as a city, receiving municipal corporation status. It increasingly became the *yishuv*'s economic, financial, political, and cultural center. The Philharmonic Orchestra was founded, the Tel Aviv Museum was opened in the home of the city's long-time mayor, Meir Dizengoff, and the cornerstone was laid for the Habimah building. Tel Aviv severed its last ties with Jaffa. Its growth continued, bringing its population in 1939 to 160,000 inhabitants, who then constituted 35.9 percent of Palestine's total Jewish population.

1939–1948

While World War II paralyzed building, it stimulated the city's industrial development, as enterprises had to be geared to the production of goods for the Allied war effort. Urban and interurban communications improved with the opening of the Central Bus Station in south Tel Aviv in 1942. In 1943 the Palestine high commissioner issued an order doubling Tel Aviv's municipal area from 630 hectares (1,556 acres) to 1,260 hectares (3,112 acres), whereby both the rest of Jaffa's Jewish quarters in the south and vacant land in the north were included in its boundaries. During the same period, the seat of all the country's Hebrew newspapers and of most of its publishing houses also became the center of the *yishuv*'s political life and its defense activities. A "civil guard" was established. The anti-Zionist policy of the British authorities was violently opposed. The first "illegal" immigrant ships (*Patria, Tiger Hill*) anchored off Tel Aviv's shore. The city played a prominent role and suffered much in the struggle with the British authorities after World War II, when both the *Haganah and the dissident underground organizations (IZL and Leḥi) had their headquarters there.

When Israel's *War of Independence broke out, Tel Aviv numbered 210,000 inhabitants. While in the first months of the war the city was incessantly shelled from Jaffa's Arab quarters, which interlinked with Tel Aviv's central sections, the situation changed dramatically after the conquest of Jaffa, the flight of the great majority of its Arab inhabitants, and the signing of its capitulation in the Tel Aviv Haganah headquarters on May 13, 1948. One day later the State of Israel was proclaimed in Tel Aviv's museum building.

From 1949

The city renewed its expansion even before the war ended: on April 24, 1949, Tel Aviv's and Jaffa's areas were amalgamated, and the city's official name became Tel Aviv-Jaffa; one of the world's youngest cities had thus incorporated one of its oldest. Simultaneously, abandoned Arab villages in the east and northeast (Shaikh Muwannis, Jamūsin, Sumail) were also included in the united city's boundaries, whose area thus grew to 4,242.5 hectares (over 10,000 acres). Although the incorporation of Jaffa – with its destitute, empty quarters, dilapidated structures, and winding lanes – demanded great efforts in reconstruction, the new areas added to Tel Aviv opened vistas in rational planning. Building quality improved perceptibly from the 1950s. In that decade the first suburbs north of the Yarkon River came into being (Yad ha-Ma'avir, Ẓahalah, etc.). From the early 1960s, multistoried structures began to go up, particularly in the center of the city. The focus of social and commercial life gradually shifted northward and particularly northeast, from Naḥalat Binyamin Street and Allenby Road to Ben-Yehuda Road, Dizengoff Square, Dizengoff Road, and Ibn Gabirol Road, where the new municipality building was erected. Tel Aviv's waterfront (Ha-Yarkon Street) became, with the construction of large hotels, the country's primary center of tourism.

The flight of most of Jaffa's 100,000 Arab inhabitants (of whom only 4,000 remained in the summer of 1948 – 2,000 of them Muslim Arabs, 1,500 Christians, and the rest Armenians and others) enabled the united city to house, often under difficult conditions, the first great wave of postwar immigration. In the 1950s, 65,000 Jews lived on Jaffa's 6,050 hectares (14,943 acres). A joint body was set up by the government and the municipality in the 1960s to deal with Jaffa's reconstruction. Under its auspices, thousands of families were transferred from its slum quarters to new housing projects; the swampy ground of the Basa and Givat Aliyah quarters was drained; public gardens were planted; and educational, youth, sports, and cultural facilities were installed. The Jaffa Hill ("Ha-Shetaḥ ha-Gadol") was transformed into an attractive tourist, art, and entertainment center, with its ancient structures refitted to house galleries, restaurants, and nightclubs; and a park was planted on the steep hill slope adjoining Jaffa Museum and the churches, mosques, and archaeological excavation grounds of Jaffa Hill.

Among Tel Aviv's ambitious projects begun between 1968 and 1971, the following are outstanding: the "Lamed" project, a housing zone on the poor sandy soil stretching north from the Yarkon River to the outskirts of Herzliyyah; other housing zones in the north, east, and southeast (Tel Kabbir, Givat ha-Temarim, Neveh Afekah, Neveh Sharett); two new industrial zones, one of which, in the north, was reserved for science-based enterprises; and the planting of more parks and recreation grounds, among them one covering 180 hectares (444 acres) in the "Lamed" zone, and another, the Histadrut Park, in the south. Particular attention was paid to easing transportation problems: a huge, seven-story Central Bus Station with 2,691,000 sq. ft. (250,000 sq. m.) of floor space was built in the city's south. An arterial, multilane speed road, called the Netivei Ayyalon (since it makes use of the bed of the Ayyalon) simultaneously serves for rainwater drainage from low-lying areas and thus prevents inundations. Tel Aviv's port was transformed into a recreation and commercial center after the opening of the Ashdod port in 1966.

Over the years, Tel Aviv's population declined due to two main factors: lack of land for new neighborhoods, and the resulting high prices for apartments. In order to solve this problem, the municipality promoted the construction of high-rise apartment buildings, which now dominate the city's skyline.

Tel Aviv-Jaffa in the 21st century continues to maintain its position as the economic and cultural center of Israel. The city's industry moved to other places, but it still serves as a business and commercial center in which economic institutions such as main banking offices and the stock market are located. Each day about a million people work in Tel Aviv-Jaffa. In addition, the majority of foreign embassies are located there. As a cultural center, the city houses four theaters (Habimah, the Cameri, Beit-Lessin, and Gesher); three major museums (Tel Aviv Museum of Art, Eretz Israel Museum, and Beit Hatefusoth) and many small museums and art galleries; the Israel Opera; the Israel Philharmonic Orchestra; and the Suzanne Dellal Center for Dance and Theater. The main newspapers have their main offices in Tel Aviv. The city is also a center for tourism, with 60 hotels and 5,000 rooms.

In July 2003, UNESCO named Tel Aviv a world heritage site, thanks to the city's unique Bauhaus architecture, which has caused it to be called "the white city."

The Tel Aviv Conurbation

Tel Aviv's municipal boundary, contiguous with satellite towns almost in its entire length, merges with them into a solid built-up area for 7 mi. (12 km.) in the east and even larger distances from north to south. In the east, the satellite chain stretches through Givatayim and Ramat Gan and reaches Petaḥ Tikvah. In the south, the cities of Ḥolon and Bat Yam link up with Jaffa. In the southeast only the fields of the Mikveh Israel farming school form a curtain of green between the mother city and the industrial or semi-industrial centers of Azor, Bet Dagan, etc. In the northeast, Ramat ha-Sharon forms the continuation of Tel Aviv's new suburbs and connects them with the town of Herzliyyah. The communities of Ra'anannah, Hod ha-Sharon, Kefar Sava, Petaḥ Tikvah, Yehud, Or Yehudah, Lydda, Ramleh, Rishon le-Zion, Nes Ẓiyyonah, and Reḥovot form the "outer ring." With the relatively small decrease of the population of Tel Aviv proper in the 1960s, there was a simultaneous rapid expansion of the southern satellites in the same decade (Bat Yam 7% annually, Holon 6.2%), while the growth in the east was more modest (Bene-Berak 4.1%, Givatayim 3.6%, Ramat Gan 2.2%). In 1970 the conurbation contained over 30% – and together with the outer ring over 42% – of the State of Israel's population (not including the regions under Israel administration after June 1967). In 2003, the Tel Aviv conurbation included 1,167,500 inhabitants, consisting of 17.3% of Israel's population.

[Hanna Ram / Shaked Gilboa (2nd ed.)]

Tel Aviv's mayors:

Meir Dizengoff (1921–1925)
David Bloch (1925–1927)
Meir Dizengoff (1928–1936)
Israel Rokach (1936–1952)
Chaim Levanon (1953–1959)
Mordechai Namir (1959–1969)
Yehoshua Rabinowitz (1969–1974)
Shlomo Lahat (1974–1993)
Ronnie Milo (1993–1998)
Ron Huldai (1998–)

BIBLIOGRAPHY: G. Hanoch, *Jewish Town Tel Aviv* (1932); A.Z. Ben-Ishai, *Tel Aviv* (Eng., 1936); M. Dizengoff, *Tel Aviv and its Development* (n.d.); M. Kalir, *Tel Aviv-Yafo* (1954); Y. Aricha, *Tel Aviv – 60 Years* (1969); E. Orni and E. Efrat, *Geography of Israel* (1971^3), 331–40; A. Druyanow (ed.), *Sefer Tel Aviv* (1936); A.A. Weis, *Reshitah shel Tel Aviv* (1957); Z. Vilnay, *Tel Aviv-Jaffa…* (1965). **WEBSITE:** www.tel-aviv.gov.il.

TEL AVIV UNIVERSITY (TAU), Israel university. Its name was first established in 1956, but its antecedents go back to 1935, when the Tel Aviv School of Law and Economics was established. In 1953 and 1955 the Tel Aviv municipality founded University Institutes of Biological Studies and of Jewish Studies, which in 1956 referred to themselves as faculties of Tel Aviv University. In the late 1950s, the Tel Aviv School of Law and Economics became a branch of the Hebrew University faculties of Law and Economics. In 1956 this branch, together with the faculties of Biological and Jewish Studies, were combined into Tel Aviv University, first as a municipal institution and, from 1962, as an autonomous body supported by the municipality, the government, and friends in Israel and abroad. The new university grew rapidly from about 1,650 students in 1962–63 to some 29,000 in 2005–06 – the largest in Israel – with an academic staff of around 1,200.

In 2004–05, the university comprised nine faculties, over 100 departments, three super-centers and over 90 research institutes. The faculties were of Humanities (including schools of Jewish Studies, History, Cultural Studies, and Education); of Law; Engineering; Exact Sciences (with schools of chemistry, physics and astronomy, and mathematical sciences); Life Sciences; Faculty of Management (including the Graduate School of Business Administration); Faculty of Social Sciences, including school of Economics and Social Work); Medicine (embodying schools of Medicine, Dental Medicine, the Continuing Medical Education, and the School of Health Professions); and the Faculty of Arts (including the School of Architecture and the Rubin Israeli Academy of Music).

TAU's encouragement of interdisciplinary research is reflected in its three super-centers, involving faculty from various fields. These are the Adams Brain Studies, Cardiac Research and Medical Engineering, and Ecological and Environmental Studies. The university's 220-acre campus at Ramat Aviv comprises faculties and research institutes, students' dormitories and facilities, a sports center, zoological and botanical gardens, an art gallery, and a statue garden. The university owns and operates the Wise Observatory near the Ramon crater in the Negev, and takes part in research at the Steinitz Interuniversity Institute Marine Laboratories in Eilat.

The university encourages communal involvement of students and staff. It operates a clinic providing legal aid in criminal cases, a center for legal advice on human rights, a clinic for ecology legal counseling, and community theater programs. Some 2,000 students were tutoring disadvantaged children, and many provided volunteer services to the elderly and aid the community through several social involvement programs.

TAU has special links with Jewish communities abroad, offering programs of Jewish studies to teachers and students from various countries. It is also involved in Jewish special education, research and teaching worldwide. The university also maintains academic supervision over a few academic institutions in the Tel Aviv area: the Center for Technological Design in Holon, the New Academic College of Tel Aviv-Yaffo, and the Tel Aviv Engineering College. The university also awards each year the Dan David Prize (three prizes, each $1 million) for achievements having an outstanding scientific, technological, cultural or social impact on our world.

The Overseas Student Program gives students from abroad the opportunity to study at Tel Aviv University for limited periods. The program is available in English and Spanish, and offers a wide choice of courses. Students may elect to combine university study with kibbutz experience. Other study opportunities for students from abroad are a Graduate Program in Middle Eastern Studies, a Summer Law Program, the Sackler School of Medicine New York State/American Program, the Medical Elective program, and the Wharton-Recanati-INSEAD-York Project in Management.

The Middle East peace process and ensuing regional cooperation opportunities are important research fields at the university, notably through its research institutes – mainly the Dayan Center for Middle Eastern and African Studies, the Jaffee Center for Strategic Studies, the Steinmetz Center for Peace Research, the Curiel Center for International Studies, and the Hammer Fund for Economic Cooperation in the Middle East.

The university has a Board of Governors, headed by Michael H. Steinhardt in 2005, which has an international membership of scientists, scholars, entrepreneurs, and public figures. The board elects the president (Prof. Itamar *Rabinovich, elected in 2003), vice presidents, chancellor of the university (Sir Leslie Porter), and the executive council, of which Dov Lautman is chairman. The supreme academic body is the Senate, which elects the rector (Prof. Shimon Yankielwics) and vice rector, approves elections of deans, and deals with all major academic issues. Website: www.tau.ac.il.

TELENESHTY (Rom. **Telenești**), town in Central Moldova in the region of Bessarabia. Teleneshty was founded at the end of the 18th century by Jews invited by the estate's owner. In 1794, a *ḥevra kaddisha* was founded, the register of which was preserved until World War II. In 1796 the owner of the estate concluded an agreement with the Jews laying down their privileges and obligations and fixing the amount of taxes to be paid for wine and spirits brought into the place and sold there. The community grew during the 19th century as a result of the large Jewish immigration to Bessarabia. In 1897 there were 3,876 Jews (89% of the total population), many of them engaging in viniculture, wine processing, and tobacco production. The 636 members registered in 1925 in the local fund included 205 tradesmen, 188 artisans, and 156 farmers. In 1930 there were 2,811 Jews in Teleneshty (73.9% of the total population). The communal institutions included a hospital founded in 1870. The community was destroyed when the Germans and Romanians invaded Bessarabia in July 1941. In the late 1960s the Jewish population was estimated at about 800. There was no synagogue. The writer S. *Ben-Zion was born and began his literary activities in Teleneshty which is described in his story "*Nefesh Reẓuẓah*" ("A Crushed Soul", 1952).

[Eliyahu Feldman]

TELEVISION AND RADIO.

In the U.S.

In the U.S. Jews have played a major role in the development of television and radio as they have in other entertainment industries. They have been well represented in all executive and technical aspects of the industry, as well as among performers. As in motion pictures, one factor encouraging their participation was the development of a new field at a time when Jews were available to enter it, and for which they had a penchant. It was not encrusted with fixed traditions and prejudice. In an era when discrimination blocked opportunity for Jews in many other fields, broadcasting had room for those with individual ability and original ideas and initiative.

In the early days of the development of broadcasting, Jewish inventors, experimenters, and promoters already played significant roles. As early as 1877 Emile *Berliner patented a telephone receiver which produced a clear sound and extended the range of communications. This was the forerunner of the microphone and was purchased by the Bell Telephone Company, which engaged Berliner for three years as the company's chief instrument inspector. Berliner also made important inventions for the gramophone, replacing the cylinder with a flat disc made of hardened rubber material that could be produced cheaply in large quantities. The Berliner gramophone was developed into the Victor Talking Machine.

Jews held key positions in the emergence and shaping of the three major U.S. networks. David *Sarnoff started the first U.S. radio chain, the National Broadcasting Company, in 1926 as a service of the Radio Corporation of America. He became president of RCA in 1930. When he retired in 1970, he was succeeded by his son Robert, who had earlier served as president of NBC. Comparable in influence and competitive to NBC is the Columbia Broadcasting System (CBS) which was founded under the presidency of William S. *Paley two years after NBC was organized. Both NBC and CBS pioneered in the introduction of television – black-and-white and later color. The third major network, the American Broadcasting Company (ABC), was an outgrowth of the NBC network. It was bought out by United Paramount Theater, and Leonard H. Goldenson became its president. Apart from the heads of the major networks, many Jews worked at all levels in the organizations as well as in the smaller networks, educational services, local stations, etc.

Many Jews came to the fore as radio and television stars. Such stars as Al *Jolson, Ed Wynn, Eddie *Cantor, Jack Benny, Groucho *Marx, Milton Berle, and Sid Caesar became top entertainment figures in the new media, and personalities such as Walter *Winchell, David Susskind, and Leonard *Bernstein became household names. In addition, there were popular Jewish situation comedies, notably "The Goldbergs," in which Gertrude Berg starred for years. Producers such as David Wolper achieved great influence. Many Jewish communities sponsored their own regular shows which brought local and general Jewish news, reports from Israel, and Jewish music. Another feature in towns with large Jewish populations was the presentation of programs in Yiddish (such as on the New York station WEVD, owned by the *Jewish Daily Forward*) and sometimes in Hebrew.

As part of their responsibility, radio and television outlets devoted part of their time to public service programs, some of which have been religious. In this framework Jewish organizations shared time with representatives of other religions. NBC and ABC worked with the Jewish Theological Seminary to present programs of interest to both the Jewish community and to non-Jews ("The Eternal Light," "Frontiers of Faith") and CBS worked with the New York Board of Rabbis (similar arrangements were made with rabbis in other major towns). The American Jewish Committee, the Anti-Defamation League, and other Jewish organizations maintained relationships with the broadcasting media within the scope of their areas of interest.

By the end of the 20th century and beginning of the 21st, Jews had assimilated into the television and radio industries as the companies became part of larger corporations. At one point, when the Disney Corporation owned ABC, its president was Michael *Eisner. At CBS, Leslie *Moonves, a Jew, held the reigns and at NBC Jeff *Zucker was in the second-highest post at the network. On radio, one personality who emerged was Howard *Stern, who, saying he was fighting censorship, moved his controversial programs to Sirius satellite radio, avoiding governmental oversight.

In Latin America, where the emphasis was more on independent stations than on networks, Jews played a small role in broadcasting of Jewish interest. The type of programming, however, was such that many communities were able to sponsor regular programs in Spanish, Portuguese, and Yiddish.

In Europe

In Europe, regular Jewish broadcasts were directed mainly to Jewish audiences abroad and not to the domestic Jewish population. In fact, these broadcasts could rarely be heard in the countries of origin, their main object being the projection of a particular line of thought or political policy in other regions. The Hebrew Service of the BBC ("Kol London") continued daily for 19 years, from 1949 to 1968. Its main purpose was the projection of British political thought and culture. It was beamed not only to Israel and the Middle East but also to Eastern Europe.

A daily Yiddish broadcast from Bucharest, Romania, to the United States covered current affairs and news and often included matters of specifically Jewish interest. During the period of the Six-Day War, Moscow started broadcasting in Hebrew and Yiddish (15 minutes each). This daily broadcast was listed as transmitted by "Radio Station Peace and Progress." It was beamed to Israel and devoted to promoting official Russian policy on the Middle East. The Yiddish broadcasts were almost the same as those in Hebrew.

Radio Birobidjan also sent out a broadcast in Yiddish, but it could hardly be heard outside its area. It had practically no Jewish content, except for occasional reviews of new editions of **Sovetish Heymland* (the Yiddish monthly published in Moscow) and occasional interviews with Jewish workers in the territory's industry and agriculture on their achievements. Jewish records were also played.

The French Overseas Radio directed its daily Yiddish broadcasts to Eastern Europe. It contained a daily news bulletin and a commentary on current affairs.

All the broadcasts mentioned fell into the category of foreign or external broadcasting. Jewish communities in Europe had few special programs, either on radio or television, devoted entirely to Jewish affairs or matters of Jewish interest. Only now and again was a program of specifically Jewish interest presented, and then it usually came under the heading of "religious broadcasting." One of the best known was a regular program over the French television network.

In Britain, there were very few Jewish names among the radio or television "personalities" appearing regularly before a camera or a microphone. Among those better known was the actor David Kossoff and the compere David Jacobs. Jews who reached important positions in radio or television were engaged mainly in scriptwriting, production, and administration. John Jacobs (David's brother) became head of drama at Anglia Television in 1964. In the field of current affairs, Jeremy Isaacs became known for his work on programs like "This Week" (Rediffusion) and "Panorama" (BBC). Elkan Allan, writer and producer, was head of entertainment of Rediffusion Television from 1962 to 1965. Cyril Bennett (d. 1977) became controller of programs at London Weekend Television and Brian Tessler director and program controller of ABC Television. Among the prominent administrators were Lord (Sidney) Bernstein, chairman of Granada Television Ltd., Sir Lew Grade, joint managing director of Associated Television Ltd., and Bernard Delfont, TV executive and impresario.

[Erwin Bienenstok]

For Israel, see *Israel, State of: Cultural Life (Radio; Television).

BIBLIOGRAPHY: T. Levitan, *Jews in American Life* (1969), 96–99, 199–203, 245–46; IGYB (1950–); G. Wigoder, in: *Gazette, International Journal for Mass Communication Studies*, 7 no. 1 (1961), 129–36; EIV, supplement vol. (1967), cols. 446–48; Givton, in: European Broadcasting Union Review, 93 B (Sept. 1965).

TEL ḤAI (Heb. תֵּל־חַי), settlement in N. Israel, on the N.W. rim of the Ḥuleh Valley, S. of Kefar Giladi. Tel Ḥai, founded in 1918, was originally one of three outposts established in this area to guard outlying Jewish land. The "Shepherd's Group" of *Ha-Shomer Association constituted the first settlers; one year later this group dispersed and another took its place. After the Ḥuleh Valley was marked for inclusion in the French Mandate territory of Syria, Arabs revolting against the French attacked the cluster of small Jewish settlements there. Joseph *Trumpeldor and seven comrades fell in the defense of Tel Ḥai on 11 Adar 5680 (1920). His last words, "It is good to die for our country," are engraved on the pediment of the statue of a roaring lion marking their grave. The defense of Tel Ḥai has become a part of Israel's national lore, and each year Tel Ḥai day is celebrated by youth gatherings and visits to Tel Ḥai and similar sites. In 1926 the settlement compound was merged with *Kefar Giladi. The original quadrangular compound was preserved, and a youth hostel and a *Haganah museum were set up there. The name Tel Ḥai means roughly "hill of life," a hebraicized version of the former Arabic name Talḥa.

[Efraim Orni]

TEL KAẒIR (Heb. תֵּל קָצִיר), kibbutz in northern Israel, S.E. of Lake Kinneret, affiliated with Iḥud ha-Kevuẓot ve-ha-Kibbutzim. Tel Kaẓir was founded in 1949 by members of the Israel Scout Movement on a site which had served during the *War of Independence (1948) as an advanced fortified enemy position in the Syrian attack on the Jordan Valley settlements. Until the *Six-Day War (1967), Tel Kaẓir, lying close to and beneath the Syrian positions beyond the border, was continually subject to Syrian attacks. While the gravest danger was overcome when the Golan Heights fell to Israel's forces in June 1967, the kibbutz continued to lie within artillery range from beyond the Jordanian border in the south. In 1967 kibbutz lands to which the Syrians had barred all access were reclaimed and intensively cultivated. Bananas, fruit orchards, dairy cattle, poultry, and ostrich raising constituted its prominent branches of farming. The kibbutz also developed a tourism industry, including a holiday resort, guest rooms, and organized trips. In the mid-1990s, Tel Kaẓir's population numbered 364, dropping to 225 in 2002. The name, meaning "Mound of Harvest," was adapted from the former Arabic name of the site.

[Efram Orni / Shaked Gilboa (2nd ed.)]

TELLER, EDWARD (1908–2003), physicist, U.S. citizen from 1941. Teller was born in Budapest but left Hungary because of Horthy's quota system for university entrance, ostensibly to study chemistry in the Karlsruhe Technical Institute (1926). He changed to mathematics at Munich University before moving to the University of Leipzig in 1928 after a break occasioned by the loss of most of his right foot in a trolley car accident. Teller received his doctorate in Leipzig (1930), where his career interests were determined by Heisenberg's teaching of quantum physics to extraordinarily gifted students. He held a research appointment at the University of Gottingen (1929–33), where he worked on molecular structure, notably of hydrogen, and collaborated with Niels *Bohr in Copenhagen and Enrico Fermi in Rome. Foreseeing the fate of Jewish scientists in Nazi Germany, he moved to the U.K. in 1933, where he was sponsored by the British scientists Frederick Lindenmann and George Donnan. After further work on nuclear structure in the Institute for Theoretical Physics, Copenhagen, and University College, London, he moved to George Washington University (1935) with support from the Rockefeller Foundation. His work on nuclear structure and particle behavior in radioactive decay (with George Gamow) made him receptive to the momentous consequences of the newly discovered phenomenon of nuclear fission. In 1939 Teller accompanied Leo Szilard to the meeting with *Einstein which resulted in the letter to President Roosevelt and eventually to the Manhattan Project. In 1942 he joined Fermi in Chicago, where the world's first nuclear reactor was constructed and where they discussed the possibilities of a sustained nuclear fusion reaction. In 1943 he was recruited to the Manhattan Project team at Los Alamos. His contribution to the development of fission weapons was often ambivalent but he showed immense insight in helping to solve the problems of his collaborators. He was, however, preoccupied with the problems of nuclear fusion reactions. Teller's contribution to the eventual production of fission weapons was partly political. His experience of antisemitism in Hungary, the Nazi regime in Germany, Communist persecution of fellow scientists accused of disloyalty, and the Communist regime in postwar Hungary convinced him of the necessity to compete with the Soviets in the race for thermonuclear weapons. His views overcame the doubts of many scientists and politicians. His practical contribution was to design (with Stanislaw *Ulam) a fission trigger for sustained hydrogen nuclear fusion. He advocated the establishment of the Lawrence Livermore National Laboratory, which he later directed (1958–60), as a second center for nuclear weapons research. From 1960 to 2003 he held senior, later emeritus positions at Livermore and in the University of California. His interests concerned the practical applications of nuclear technology to power units in ships and submarines, often rather speculative civil engineering projects such as a Red Sea to Dead Sea canal, and anti-missile defense. He was a pioneer of safety measures in nuclear power stations. His passion for science education established the University of California at Davis as a leading school. Temperamentally unpredictable, Teller was shunned by many colleagues who opposed the development of thermonuclear weapons, his opposition to test ban treaties, and his enthusiasm for antimissile defense systems. Many were appalled by his testimony to the Gray Committee (1954), when he opposed *Oppenheimer's access to classified information. Despite this opposition he was a major influence on U.S. defense policy. He was awarded the Fermi Prize (1962), the National Medal of Science, the Herzl Prize given to descendants of Hungarian Jewry who have distinguished themselves on behalf of Israel and the Jewish people, and the Presidential Medal of Freedom (2003).

[Michael Denman (2nd ed.)]

TELLER, ISRAEL (1835–1921), Hebrew writer, grammarian, and teacher. Born in Zolochev, Galicia, he moved to Romania, where for 30 years he was a teacher and a director of Hebrew schools in various Jewish communities. He was among the first to join the Ḥovevei Zion when they became active in Romania; he also contributed to Hebrew periodicals, as well as the Yiddish press. In 1896 he came to Israel and was a teacher in Reḥovot. His works include *Mabbat Ḥofshi ba-Dikduk* (1906), in which he maintains that Hebrew grammar should conform to the modern spoken language, and *Torat ha-Lashon* (1912), in which he expounds his method of Hebrew grammar. Teller's poetry, didactic and tendentious in quality, has slight literary merit. A collection of his articles, entitled *Ben-Oni*, was published in 1914.

BIBLIOGRAPHY: G. Bader, *Medinah va-Ḥakhameha* (1934), 111; I. Klausner, *Ḥibbat Ẓiyyon be-Romanyah* (1958), index; Kressel, Leksikon, 2 (1967), 23–24; Tidhar, 1 (1947), 279.

[Yehuda Slutsky]

TELLER, ISSACHAR BAER (b. c. 1607), physician and surgeon. Teller, a barber-surgeon in the Bohemian capital Prague, was the author of what is believed to be the first printed medical book in Yiddish, *Be'er Mayim Ḥayyim* ("Well of Living Water"). The book was printed in Prague without any date, but it must have been before 1655. This is an extremely rare book: the only complete copy known is the one in the Bodleian Library, Oxford; another copy, with the title-page missing, is in the Rosenthaliana Library in Amsterdam. Teller wrote his book as a practical manual of therapeutics. He chose the Yiddish idiom for readers not sufficiently acquainted with Hebrew. In a rhymed introduction and an epilogue he explained his main object: to help poor people who could not afford doctors' fees. Teller was well-versed in the Latin literature of his time, as his quotations – in Hebrew characters – show, and was progressive enough to oppose the astrological medicine so popular in his time. The small book is interesting not only from a medico-historical point of view, but also as source material for linguistic studies of the Yiddish of the period. The portrait of Teller which appears in the book is probably the only authentic portrait of a Jewish barber-surgeon in existence.

A facsimile of *Be'er Mayim Ḥayyim*, produced in Jerusalem in 1968 with prefaces in Hebrew and English, includes as an appendix the *Aphorisms* of Hippocrates translated into Hebrew by Teller's teacher, Joseph Solomon *Delmedigo.

BIBLIOGRAPHY: Steinschneider, Cat Bod, 1065 – 66; J.O. Leibowitz (ed.), *Be'er Mayyim Ḥayyim* (1968).

[Joshua O. Leibowitz]

TELLER, ẒEVI LAZAR (originally **Hirsch Lazar**; 1840–1914), Hebrew educator and writer. Born in Zolochev, Galicia, he taught in Jewish schools in Romania (1866–86), and later in Galicia. In Romania he was an active member of the Ḥibbat Ẓion movement and upon his return to Galicia became a leader of the Zionist movement there. Beginning in the 1870s, he published poems, translations of poems, and articles on current affairs in the Hebrew press.

His books include *Te'udat Yisrael* (1878); *Leshon Limmudim* (a grammar, 1884); *Za'akat Shever* (1885); *Siftei Renanot* (poems, 1892); *Kol Elohim* (poems and prose, 1897); *Eḥarti Lavo* (novel, 1908); and *Hed ha-Am* (poems, 1913). He also edited and published the first pedagogic periodical in Hebrew, *Eitanim* (3 issues; 1898).

[Getzel Kressel]

TEL MOND (Heb. תֵּל מוֹנְד), moshavah with municipal council status in central Israel, in the southern Sharon, 6 mi. (10 km.) N. of Kefar Sava. Its area is about 3 sq. mi. (8 sq. km.). Tel Mond was founded in 1929 upon the initiative of Sir Alfred Mond (later Lord *Melchett), who planted large citrus groves and enlisted the participation of other British Jews through his Palestine Plantations Company. Tel Mond became the center for a group of smallholder villages (the "Tel Mond Bloc"). After 1948 many immigrants were absorbed there, partly from a **ma'barah* (immigrant transit camp) which was later transformed into a permanent housing scheme. In 1954 Tel Mond received local council status. In 1970 the village had 3,060 inhabitants. Its economy was based principally on citriculture. By the mid-1990s its population had increased to 4,060, rising further to 7,260 in 2002. The majority of residents now worked outside the moshavah.

[Efraim Orni /Shaked Gilboa (2nd ed.)]

TELSIAI (Rus. **Telshi**; Ger. **Telschen**; Yid. **Telz**), city in N.W. Lithuania. Jews began to settle in Telsiai in the 17th century, when they were under the jurisdiction of the community of *Kedainiai. During Russian rule (1795–1915) Telsiai was a district town in Kovno province. J.L. *Gordon, who was a teacher in the state-controlled Jewish school from 1866 to 1872, describes the community in his letters and poems as conservative and attached to tradition. The number of Jews in the community increased from 2,248 in 1847 to 4,204 in 1864. The years of famine in Lithuania in the 1850s and the lack of railroad connections contributed to the decline of Telsiai and emigration from the town. In 1897 3,088 Jews (51% of the total population) lived there.

The community was wiped out when the Germans invaded Lithuania. In July 1941 all the men were brutally tortured and killed by the Lithuanian Fascists and within six months the women too were murdered. In 1970, the Jewish population of Telsiai was estimated at around 150.

Telz Yeshivah

Telsiai became important for the Jews and Jewish history because of the yeshivah which existed there from 1875 to 1941. Established by the community's scholars, it developed into a central institution of traditional Jewish scholarship under the leadership of Eliezer *Gordon, rabbi of the community from 1883 to 1910, and after his death, of Joseph Leib Bloch (1910–30). New methods were introduced in the yeshivah; the division of the pupils into five classes according to their knowledge, periodic tests, and compulsory attendance at classes. The study of **musar* was instituted under Gordon and became especially prominent under Bloch. The reputation of the yeshivah was furthered by Simeon Shkop (to 1904) and Ḥayyim Rabinowitz, who shaped the "way of Telz" in Torah study, which concentrated on the development of acuity and skill in profound logical analysis. After the *Volozhin yeshivah was closed by the authorities in 1892, Telz became one of the central yeshivot in Russia and had 300–350 students. A new building was completed in 1897 (it was rebuilt after the great fire of 1908). When some Telsiai Jews were expelled during the general expulsion from Lithuania in 1915, the yeshivah continued its activities. During the period of Lithuanian independence (1918–40) the yeshivah was one of the three largest in the country, serving as a Torah center for all Orthodox Jewry.

In a community of 1,545 Jews in 1923 (approximately one-third of the town's total population) and 2,800 Jews in 1939, the yeshivah had a decisive influence. A complete educational network was established under its control: an Orthodox kindergarten, an educational institution for boys, a school for girls, an Orthodox secondary school for girls called Yavneh, a seminary for Orthodox teachers, also called Yavneh (transferred in 1924 from Kovno to Telz), headed by Yiẓḥak Raphael Holzberg-Eẓion, and a Hebrew seminary for teachers. Near the yeshivah a *kolel* was established in which graduates of the yeshivah were trained for the rabbinate. The Orthodox Hebrew monthly *Ha-Ne'eman* (1928–31) and the bulletin of *Agudat Israel in Lithuania, *Der Yidisher Lebn*, were issued in the town. Yeshivah students were sent to Lithuanian towns to establish "small yeshivot" (i.e., schools for children) in which they prepared children for study in the Telz yeshivah. In the 1930s Abraham Isaac Bloch and Azriel Rabinowitz, the sons of its first leaders, were the heads of the yeshivah. With the Soviet annexation of Lithuania in 1940 the yeshivah building was confiscated and the students dispersed to several Lithuanian towns, where they continued their studies under their rabbis. A few teachers and students managed to reach the United States.

In 1941 the Telz yeshivah was reestablished in Cleveland, Ohio, under E.M. *Bloch, and in 1971 it had about 400 students and was directed by M. *Gifter. In 1959, a girl's school by the name of Yavneh, counterpart of the yeshivah, was founded in Cleveland, and two years later a teachers' seminary was opened there.

BIBLIOGRAPHY: A.E. Friedmann, *Sefer ha-Zikhronot* (1962), 106–11; *Sefer ha-Yovel le-S. Shkop* (1936), 38–44, 54–56, 63, 73–74; M. Berlin, *Mi-Volozhin ad Yerushalayim*, 1 (1939), 164–71; *Lite* (1951), 1574–76; E.M. Bloch, *ibid.*, 623–30; idem, in: *Ha-Pardes*, 16 (1942), 5–8; E. Asheri, *Ḥurban Lita* (1951), 238–40; S. Assaf, in: *He-Avar*, 2 (1954), 34–45; Gifter, in: *Mosedot Torah be-Eiropah* (1956), 169–88; Alon, Meḥkarim, 1 (1957), 1–11; *B. Dinur, Be-Olam she-Shaka* (1958), 62–78; *Yahadut Lita*, 3 (1967), 315–6; Bialoblocki, *ibid.*, 233–7; D. Katz, *ibid.*, 233–7; S. Kushnir, *Sadot ve-Lev* (1962), 29–36.

[Yehuda Slutsky]

TELUSHKIN, NISSAN (1882–1970), rabbi. Born in Bobrosk, Minsk Province, Lithuania, Telushkin attended yeshivot in Kursov and Slutsk, Lithuania, under some of the leading scholars of the time, including Rabbi Baruch Baer Leibowitz and Rabbi Isser Zalman Meltzer. In 1902 he received ordination from several rabbis, including Rabbi Samuel Moses Shapiro, Rabbi Joseph Bakst, and the Lubavitcher *rebbe*, Rabbi Shalom Dov Schneersohn.

After that, Telushkin served as a congregational rabbi in Europe until 1924, when he immigrated to the United States. There, he assumed the leadership of Congregation B'nai Yitzchak in Brooklyn, where he remained until retirement in 1967.

Telushkin was unusual in his dual support of religious Zionism and Ḥasidism. He was involved with Mizrachi, the religious Zionist organization of America, and the Lubavitch community and functioned on behalf of the Vaad ha-Rabbonim of New York. He became editor of the Vaad's Torah journal, *Hamsiloh*.

Part of his life's work was to improve the conditions of *mikva'ot* in New York. In that realm, Telushkin wrote a book, *Taharat Mayim*, about the laws of *mikveh*. It received wide praise from his colleagues. Telushkin also wrote a three-volume commentary on the Bible titled *Ha-Torah ve-ha-Olam*.

[Lynne Schreiber (2nd ed.)]

TEL YIZḤAK (Heb. תֵּל יִצְחָק), kibbutz in central Israel, near Even Yehudah, affiliated with Ha-No'ar ha-Ẓiyyoni. Tel Yiẓḥak was founded by a group from Galicia in 1938. Since 1963, Neveh Hadassah, a youth village belonging to Hadassah and *Youth Aliyah, has been included in the area of Tel Yiẓḥak. In 1970 Tel Yiẓḥak had 510 inhabitants, increasing to 622 in 2002. Farming branches included irrigated citrus groves, field crops, and avocado plantations. Other sources of livelihood were a small supermarket, a pub, and catering. The kibbutz also operated a factory for building materials. Masoha, an institute for Holocaust studies, and the Zionist Youth Archive were located at the kibbutz. Its name commemorates Yizḥak Steiger, the founder of the Ha-No'ar ha-Ẓiyyoni movement in Galicia.

[Efraim Orni]

TEL YOSEF (Heb. תֵּל יוֹסֵף), kibbutz in northern Israel, in the Harod Valley, 8 mi. (13 km.) S.E. of Afulah, affiliated with Iḥud ha-Kevuẓot ve-ha-Kibbutzim. Named in memory of Joseph *Trumpeldor, Tel Yosef was founded in 1921 as a work camp of *Gedud ha-Avodah ("Labor Legion"), together with *En-Harod, at the foot of Mt. Gilboa. Its members participated in draining the local malaria-infested swamps. In the ensuing years, En-Harod seceded from Gedud ha-Avodah. After 1928 Tel Yosef joined Ha-Kibbutz ha-Me'uḥad. In 1929 both kibbutzim moved to their present site on the slope of the Ẓeva'im Ridge. In the 1936–39 Arab riots, Tel Yosef suffered frequent attacks. In the 1951–52 split in Ha-Kibbutz ha-Me'uḥad, Tel Yosef joined Iḥud ha-Kevuẓot ve-ha-Kibbutzim, and a group from the kibbutz moved to nearby Bet ha-Shittah. In 1970 the kibbutz had 515 inhabitants; in 2002, 400. Its economy was based on irrigated field and fodder crops, mainly cotton and sugar beet; deciduous fruit orchards, carp ponds, etc. It housed the Iḥud ha-Kevuẓot ve-ha-Kibbutzim printing press and was a partner with En-Harod in a truck garage and cooperative. Bet Trumpeldor, containing the archives of Gedud ha-Avodah and other historical documents, was located in Tel Yosef. The kibbutz, together with En-Harod, maintained the regional museum, Bet Sturman, and a regional theater stage. Tel Yosef has educated Youth Aliyah groups.

[Efram Orni / Shaked Gilboa (2nd ed.)]

TEMA (Heb. תֵּמָא, תֵּימָא), son of Ishmael and a locality in Arabia (Gen. 25:15; 1 Chron. 1:30). Tema is identified as Taima, an outlying town and oasis in the Jebel Shammar province of Nejd, a major region of Saudi Arabia, 200 mi. (320 km.) west of Hail. Tema was a caravansary on the junction point of the highways to Damascus and the Persian Gulf (Isa. 21:14; cf. Job 6:19). Jeremiah prophesied against Tema (25:23), as one of the nations among other northern Arabian people (see *Rodanim). Tema became part of the Assyrian (Babylonian) sphere of interest in the Arabian war of Tiglath-Pileser III (732 B.C.E.) when he dispersed the coalition headed by Samsi, the queen of the Arabs. The coalition was comprised of Masʿa (cf. Massa, Gen. 25:14), Tema ((*ālu*) *temaj*) and Haiappa (Ephah of *Midian, Gen. 25:4). One of the gates of Nineveh rebuilt by *Sennacherib was called *katrê Summ'an/il u Têmê quiribša irrub abul madbari*, "'The Gifts of Sumuʿan/il and Têmê, enter through it,' the Desert Gate." Much information about Tema in the neo-Babylonian period has been gained from the publication of the Harran Inscriptions of *Nabonidus, the last king of Babylon before the Persian period (already partially known from the Verse Account of Nabonidus). Nabonidus destroyed Tema (522 B.C.E.), rebuilt it, and made it his residence for about ten years. From there he went further and reached Yathrib (later Medina). Cyrus II conquered the entire region a few years later (c. 540 B.C.E.). Tema around that time was a cosmopolitan town, as is attested by the proper names cited in the Taima Stele (Louvre).

BIBLIOGRAPHY: D.D. Luckenbill, *The Annals of Sennacherib* (1924), 113; T.W. Rosmarin, in: *Journal of the Society of Oriental Research*, 16 (1932), 1ff.; A. Heidel, in: *Sumer*, 9 (1953), 170–71, 8:8–9; C.J. Gadd, in: *Anatolian Studies*, 8 (1958), 35ff.; A. Grohmann, *Arabien* (1963), 22 and index s.v. *Tamima*; H. Tadmor, in: *Studies... B. Landsberger* (1965), 356; V.G. Dossin, in: *Revue d'assyrologie*, 64 (1970), 21, 39 (for a doubtful reference to Tema).

[Pinhas Artzi and Laurentino Jose Afonso]

TEMAN (Heb. תֵּימָן, from יָמִין; "right, south"), grandson of Esau and name of a place in Edom (Gen. 36:11, 15, 34; Amos 1:12). Teman and Bozrah represented the whole land of Edom (Amos 1:12; Obadiah 9). Its inhabitants were famous for their wisdom (Jer. 49:7; cf. Job 2:11).

Teman is identified with Ṭawīlān, below Jebel Heidan, northeast of Elji. A great amount of Edomite Early Iron I–II pottery (1200–600; see Glueck in bibl.) was discovered at its site. One of the "kings who reigned in the land of Edom, before any king reigned over the Israelites," was a Temanite (Gen. 36:34). At least from the period of the *geonim* the term was used for the South Arabian region of *Yemen.

BIBLIOGRAPHY: N. Glueck, in: AASOR, 15 (1934/35), 82–83.

TEMERLS, JACOB BEN ELIEZER (also known as **Jacob Ashkenazi**; d. 1666), rabbi and kabbalist. Temerls was born in Worms, but in his youth went to Poland. He taught in Lublin, but later moved to Kremenets, where he resided for the greater part of his life. He spent his last years in Vienna, where he died. He was greatly revered as an outstanding talmudist and kabbalist; some of Europe's leading rabbis turned to him for advice. It was said of him that "he did not leave the house of study but engaged in the study of the Torah in purity, fasting daily for 40 years."

He was the author of a short kabbalistic commentary on the Pentateuch, *Sifra di-Ẓeni'uta de-Ya'akov* (published by his son Eliezer Lipmann, Amsterdam, 1669). Eliezer Lipmann, who added to the volume rules for the study of the Kabbalah, expressed the hope that it would be vouchsafed him to publish also his father's other writings, which included a larger commentary on the Pentateuch and the Five Scrolls, a commentary on the expositions of passages in the Prophets and the Hagiographa, the Jerusalem and Babylonian Talmuds, and the Zohar, including the *Idrot*, as well as commentaries to the works of Isaac Luria. However, none of these was published; nor was a collection of his responsa, mentioned by Aaron Samuel *Koidanover in *Emunat Shemu'el* (Frankfurt, 1683). An approbation by Temerls, written in 1660, appears in Ḥayyim Bochner's *Or Ḥadash* (Amsterdam, 1771 or 1775).

BIBLIOGRAPHY: H.N. Dembitzer, *Kelilat Yofi*, 2 (1893), 117a–125a; B. Wachstein, *Die Inschriften des alten Judenfriedhofes in Wien*, 1 (1912), 462–5.

[Tovia Preschel]

TEMIANKA, HENRI (1906–1992), U.S. violinist and conductor. Born at Greenock, Scotland, Temianka studied with Blitz in Rotterdam (1915–23), at the Berlin Hochschule fuer Musik in Berlin (1923–34), and with Carl *Flesch and *Rodjinsky (conducting) at the Curtis Institute, Philadelphia. He made his debut as violinist in New York in 1928. He was leader of the Scottish orchestra (1937–38), and the Pittsburgh SO (1941–42), but he essentially devoted himself to a career as a soloist and appeared throughout Europe and the United States. In 1935 he was a prizewinner at the Wieniawski Competition in Warsaw and was invited to play in the USSR. In 1946 he founded the Paganini String Quartet and was its leader and first violinist until 1966; the quartet gave premieres of works by *Castelnuovo-Tedesco, *Milhaud, and Lees, and counted Beethoven's Razumovsky Quartets among its finest recorded performances. In 1958 he founded the Temianka Chamber Symphony Orchestra, which he conducted. He was also musician-in-residence at the University of California and professor of music at California State College. Temianka made a number of educational films, edited several quartets, and published an autobiography, *Facing the Music* (1973). In his elegant interpretations he combined the best elements of the French tradition and the Flesch school.

BIBLIOGRAPHY: Grove Music Online.

[Amnon Shiloah (2nd ed.)]

TEMIN, HOWARD MARTIN (1934–1994), U.S. Nobel laureate in medicine. Temin was born in Philadelphia and graduated in biology from Swarthmore College. He received his Ph.D. at the California Institute of Technology, studying Rous sarcoma virus. His mentors included Renato Dulbecco and Harry Rubin. This work shaped his lifelong interest in animal viruses and their role in cancer induction. In 1960 he moved to the McArdle Laboratory for Cancer Research at the University of Wisconsin, Madison, where he worked for the rest of his life. He formulated the hypothesis that RNA viruses direct virus synthesis in infected cells through a DNA provirus. This contradicted the contemporary central tenet that RNA synthesis is invariably DNA-directed, and it was ignored for six years. His discovery in 1970 of RNA-directed DNA polymerase (reverse transcriptase), confirmed simultaneously and independently by David *Baltimore, indicated the mechanism by which viral RNA directs new viral synthesis. This led to general acceptance of his ideas and has profoundly influenced subsequent animal virology, including HIV research. He was awarded the Nobel Prize in medicine for this work in 1975 (jointly with David Baltimore and Renato Dulbecco). For the rest of his career he studied viral replication and its role in cancer induction, and in particular retroviral sequences which are cellular ("endogenous") components but may be implicated in cancer. Temin's many honors included membership of the U.S. National Academy of Sciences, the National Medal of Science, and the Gairdner and Lasker awards. A nonsmoker, Temin campaigned against smoking in public places. He died of lung cancer in Madison.

[Michael Denman (2nd ed.)]

TEMKIN, family in Ereẓ Israel. MOSHE (1885–1958), Hebrew writer, was born in Siedlce, Poland. He emigrated to Palestine in 1906, where he worked at various trades before becoming a physician in 1922. He was a member of the central committee of Ha-Po'el ha-Ẓa'ir and the secretary of the Galilee (1916) and Samaria (1918) workers' organizations. He began to publish articles and stories during the Second Aliyah, writing also on medical subjects in Hebrew and French.

His books are: *Negu'ei ha-Moledet* (1936, a novel on the *Nili group); *Ha-Holekhim la-Mavet Sho'alim li-Shelomkha* (1943, a novel about *Trumpeldor); *Ha-Na'arah min ha-Emek* (1944, stories); *Neshamah Mefo'eret bi-Kheli Mekho'ar* (1944, on Van Gogh); *Sha'ul Tchernichowsky* (1944); *Sofer ha-Ẓa'ar ve-ha-Za'am* (1945, a work about *Brenner); *Be-Ma'gelei ha-Kesem* (1954, stories).

His brother, MORDECAI (1891–1960) was a Hebrew poet. In 1909, after teaching for two years, he emigrated to Ereẓ Israel but went back to Poland as a result of ill-health. He returned to Ereẓ Israel in 1911, and devoted himself to teaching. After his first poem in *Ha-Po'el ha-Ẓa'ir* (1909), many others were published in *Reshafim* (ed. by. D. *Frischmann) and in the newspapers and periodicals of the country over several decades.

His books of poems are: *Netafim* (selected poems of 1912–26, 1927), *Shirim u-Tefillot* (1934), *Sefer ha-Shirim ve-ha-Tefillot* (1942), *Be-Elem Kol* (1956), *Eged Kat* (selected poems, 1961), and *Shirei Yerushalayim* (1965). He also translated works of Mann, H. von Kleist, Chekhov, and Max Brod and produced a Hebrew translation of Gottfried Keller's novel *Der gruene Heinrich (Heinrikh ha-Yarok*, 1969).

BIBLIOGRAPHY: S. Halkin, *Modern Hebrew Literature* (1950), 139, 194; Kressel, Leksikon, 2 (1967), 25–26.

[Getzel Kressel]

TEMKIN, ASHER (19th century), small trader in Mogilev, converted to Christianity in 1832. His pamphlet defaming the Talmud (*Derekh Selulah*) was published in Hebrew and Russian by order of Czar Nicholas I in the printing house of the Academy of Sciences and distributed free of charge. I.B. *Levinsohn (Ribal) in his work *Yemin Ẓidki* (clandestinely circulated in manuscript and printed only in 1881) argued against the work of Temkin, showing the positive contribution of the Talmud to Jewish ethics. To show their appreciation of Temkin's defamatory work, the Russian authorities first appointed him *psalomshchik* (low-grade clergyman) and then censor.

BIBLIOGRAPHY: J. Raisin, *The Haskalah Movement in Russia*, 6 (1913), 146; Ginsburg, in: *Forward* (Jan. 27, 1935).

TEMPLE

The article is arranged according to the following outline:

In ancient times, a central building for the worship of God in Israel. The most common biblical names for the Temple are: "the House of the Lord" (I Kings 3:1); "the House of God" (Dan. 1:2); "the Holy Temple" (Jonah 2:5[4]); "the Temple of the Lord" (II Kings 24:13); and "the Sanctuary" (Ezek. 45:4). In the Mishnah (e.g., Ma'as. Sh. 5:2) and Tosefta (e.g., Tosef., Ber. 3:16), the name commonly used is *Beit ha-Mikdash* (*Miqdash*), which occurs only once in the Bible (II Chron. 36:7).

FIRST TEMPLE

HISTORY

Following the destruction of Shiloh (c. 1050 B.C.E.), the need for a central Temple was felt. The military defeat suffered by the Israelites at Eben-Ezer, which ended in the capture of the ark by the Philistines, brought about a severance of the ark from the altar. For a generation and more, the ark wandered from place to place until David finally brought it to Mount Zion, where he erected a tent for it (II Sam. 6:17). The high places set up at Nob (I Sam. 21), at Gibeon (I Kings 3:4), and at other sites, e.g., Beth-El and Mizpah, were unable to serve as a unifying center for the divided tribes who were competing for national supremacy. These high places could not, in consequence, become the permanent site for the ark. However, with the capture of Jerusalem and the establishment of the royal palace on Mount Zion, a suitable place for this purpose was found. Jerusalem was situated on the border between the Rachel tribes and the Leah tribes; and on the border between Judah, the tribe to which David belonged, and that of Benjamin, the tribe from which sprang Saul, the first king of Israel. As a newly conquered city, it had not been incorporated into the territory of any one tribe (cf. Meg. 26a). By its very nature it was, therefore, the one and only place likely to satisfy the claims of all the tribes. The threshing floor of Araunah the Jebusite was chosen as the site of the Temple. There it was that David had built an altar to check a plague that had broken out among the people (II Sam. 24; I Chron. 21). From II Chronicles 3:1, it appears that the spot selected for the altar was also the place which tradition had identified as the site of the binding of Isaac. David had wanted to build the Temple there, but, according to the biblical narrative, he was dissuaded by the prophet Nathan (II Sam. 7) on the grounds that it would be more proper to leave the project for his son. Solomon pursued the task and completed it with the assistance of King Hiram of Tyre under the supervision of a craftsman who was the son of "a man of Tyre" and "of a widow of the tribe of Naphtali" (I Kings 7:14; "of a woman of the daughters of Dan," according to II Chron. 2:13 [14]). The copper required for the columns and the vessels came (as the investigations of N. Glueck have shown) from Solomon's copper mines in Edom, on the shores of the Red Sea (I Kings 7:46). It was from Solomon's commercial enterprises and especially from David's war booty that the ample silver needed for the project was acquired. Thirty thousand Israelites took part in the operation (I Kings 5:27–32), together with 150,000 Canaanites who served as porters and quarrymen (II Chron. 2:16, 17; cf. I Kings 9:20–22), and "chief officers who were over the work," who numbered 3,300 men (I Kings 5:30; 3,600 in II Chron. 2:17 [16]). The work was begun in the month of Iyyar in the fourth year of Solomon's reign and was completed in the 11th year of his reign in the month of Bul (= Marḥeshvan, I Kings 6:1, 38). The dedication of the Temple, which took place in the presence of the elders of Israel, the heads of the tribes, the "leaders of the fathers' houses" (I Kings 8:1–2; II Chron. 5:2–3), and "a great assembly, from Lebo-Hamath unto the Brook of Egypt," lasted 14 days (I Kings 8:65; II Chron. 7:8). It was then that the ark was brought to its permanent abode in the Holy of Holies, and Solomon offered up a prayer in the presence of the entire people.

The deterioration in the political situation, which set in at the end of Solomon's days, also had an adverse effect upon the fortunes of the Temple. In order to offset the importance of Jerusalem as a religious center, Jeroboam found it politically expedient to reinstate the shrines at Beth-El and Dan (I Kings 12:26–33). With the political and military reverses suffered after the reign of Solomon (by the Kingdom of Judah), the Temple, as a depository of money and as a sanctuary rich in its ornaments and vessels of gold, was exposed to periodic spoliation. Shishak king of Egypt (I Kings 14:25–26; II Chron. 12:9), Ben-Hadad (I Kings 15:18; II Chron. 16:2) and Hazael (II Kings 12:19), kings of Aram-Damascus, as well as Jehoash king of Israel (II Kings 14:14; II Chron. 25:24), all obtained money from the Temple treasuries, either as plunder or as tribute. It was apparently to send tribute to the king of Assyria that Ahaz removed the lavers from their bases and the "brazen sea" from its support of brazen oxen (II Kings 16:17). Hezekiah, too, stripped the gold from the doors of the Temple and from the doorposts and sent it to Sennacherib (II Kings 18:16). On the other hand, the Temple needed renovation from time to time. Most often referred to are the repairs executed in the days of Jehoash under the supervision of Jehoiada the high priest, which led to the institution of a permanent "chest" for a Temple repair fund (II Kings 12:5ff.; see above), as well as the reconstruction undertaken in the reign of Josiah, when, according to the Bible, the "Book of the Law" (= Deuteronomy; II Kings 22:3ff.; II Chron. 34:8ff.) was discovered.

However, more important changes than these physical changes were those changes introduced into the Temple service as a result of the religious struggle waged throughout that period. Although the service of God continued in the Temple even under Athaliah, that service, as well as the Sanctuary itself, was endangered by the temple of Baal which had been erected by the queen and by the priests of Baal who were active under her protection. This provoked a revolt against the queen under the leadership of the high priest Jehoiada, as a result of which Baal worship was eradicated from Jerusalem (II Kings 11). Under Hezekiah, the Temple at Jerusalem was confirmed as the sole place of worship in Judah (II Kings 18:4–6, 22; Isa. 36:7; II Chron. 32:12), and in a large measure it also served as the religious center for the other Israelite tribes, from among whom pilgrims (after the destruction of the Northern Kingdom) would go up to the Temple for Passover (II Chron. 30:1ff.). Under Manasseh, the use of high places was revived and idolatry penetrated the Temple itself (II Kings 21:2ff.; II Chron. 33:2ff.). However, with the accession of Josiah, the Temple was finally established as the one and only sanctuary for the whole nation. The Passover celebration which was held during his reign, and which, in the words of the Bible, was unparalleled since "the days of the Judges," was a strong demonstration of the nation's religious uniqueness and the preeminence of Jerusalem (II Kings 23:21–23; II Chron. 35:1–18). However, the Temple did not long retain this exalted position. A few years after Josiah's death, Nebuchadnezzar removed from the Temple "the vessels of the house of the Lord… and put them in his palace in Babylon" (II Chron. 36:7; Dan. 1:2; cf. Jer. 27:19–22; Dan. 5:3ff.; Ezra 1:7; 6:5). Eight years later Nebuchadnezzar attacked Jerusalem a second time and took away "all the treasures of the house of the Lord, and the treasures of the king's house, and cut in pieces all the vessels of gold in the Temple of the Lord which Solomon king of Israel had made" (II Kings 24:13; Jer. 28:3; II Chron. 36:10). Eleven more years went by – and then came total destruction. Nebuzaradan, Nebuchadnezzar's captain of the guard, stormed the Temple (586), smashed the pillars of brass and the bases and the brazen sea, and after having stripped the building of all its brass as well as of its sacred vessels of bronze, silver, and gold in order to send them to Babylon, burned the Temple to the ground. The day of the destruction of the Temple is given in one passage as the seventh of Av (II Kings 25:8) and in another (Jer. 52:12) as the tenth of Av. Traditionally (Ta'an. 29a), this discrepancy is reconciled by the statement that "On the seventh [of Av] the heathens entered the Temple and ate therein and desecrated it throughout the seventh and eighth, and toward dusk of the ninth day set fire to it and it continued to burn the whole day." It is further related: "The day on which the First Temple was destroyed was the eve of the ninth of Av, a Sunday, and in a year following the Sabbatical Year, and the course of the family of Jehoiarib were on duty and the levites were chanting the Psalms standing on their dais" (*ibid.*).

The destruction of the Temple marked the end of an epoch in the history of the people and its religion. From the days of Micah (3:12; Jer. 26:18) the prophets had never ceased (cf., e.g., Jer. 7:14; 26:4–6; Ezek. 5:11) to warn the people that, in punishment for its religious and moral transgressions, the Temple would be destroyed, despite the belief, prevalent among the masses, that "the Temple of the Lord" could not but continue forever (Jer. 7:4). The destruction of the Temple and the Exile to Babylon which followed it represented, in some measure, a triumph for the prophetic position. In consequence, the destruction was attended by renewed zeal in the observance of the commandments of the Law, coupled with an awakening of the hope for the rebirth of an independent religious-national life in the spirit of the prophecies of consolation. "In the 14th year after the city was conquered," Ezekiel, the prophet of the Exile, foretold the reconstruction of the Temple and beheld in a vision (Ezek. 40–48) the details of the restored edifice, its service, its procedures, and so on. In that same generation, too, four annual fasts were appointed in commemoration of the destruction of the Temple and the events which accompanied it (Zech. 7:1ff., 8:19; see Tosef., Sot. 6:10–11; Sif. Deut. 31). One of these, the fast of the Ninth of Av (the fast of the fifth month), was instituted for the day on which the Temple was burnt (see above). In memory of this event, lamentations over the destruction (see *Lamentations) were composed, which were apparently recited in public already in the days of the Babylonian Exile (cf. II Chron. 35:25).

[Yehoshua M. Grintz]

STRUCTURE

The two principal sources for the plan of the First Temple erected on Mt. Moriah in Jerusalem between the fourth and the 11th years of Solomon's reign are I Kings 6–8 and II Chronicles 2–4. These differ in several important details; in addition to the Book of Kings, the editor of Chronicles apparently used another source whose description of the Temple plan varied considerably. A third independent description is found in the Book of Ezekiel (40ff.).

The Temple was not originally intended to serve as a place of prayer, but to house (or as an abode for) the *ark of the Lord, symbol of the Covenant between the people and its God (I Kings 8:21). Hence it was called "the House of the Lord," in the same way that one would speak of "the house of the king" or any ordinary domicile. As a tabernacle it was not necessary for it to be large. Its structure had to meet the requirements of a symbolic tabernacle of God and a repository for the sacred furniture and the offerings brought to God by His worshipers. As a place for divine worship the Temple was not judged by its size but by the splendor and massiveness of its construction, and indeed, the dimensions of the main hall of the First Temple, which in II Chronicles 2:4[5] is called "great," did not exceed 40 × 20 cubits (approximately 66 × 33 ft.). It should be noted that the roof of the Temple was not supported by pillars set in the center of the room as was the practice in palaces of this period and its width was the maximum which was structurally possible. Without pillars the rooms were impressive in their spaciousness. The Temple was also relatively high – 30 cubits (about 50 ft.) – much taller than most Canaanite temples. The courtyard of the Temple, however, had to be extensive, for it served as the place of assembly for the public which came to inquire of God, to bring sacrifices, and to pray. The "House of the Lord" was built originally by Solomon as a royal chapel, like the temples which kings in the Near East built adjoining their palaces. The Temple of Solomon, however, was quickly transformed into a national religious center and the symbol of the Covenant between the people of Israel and its God.

The Ground Plan of the Temple

The Temple was oblong in shape and composed of three sections of equal width: a porch or hall (the vestibule, *ʾulam*), a main room for divine service *heikhal* (*hekhal*), and the "Holy of Holies" (*devir*). Attempts to find parallels to this plan in Egypt, Assyria, Babylonia, and in areas of Aegean culture have not been too successful. Most scholars today recognize an affinity between the Temple of Solomon and the Canaanite and Phoenician cultures current in Palestine in the second part of the second millennium and beginning of the first millennium B.C.E. These cultures had a strong influence on the culture and art of the Israelites. The Bible as well stresses the great contribution of Hiram, king of Tyre, to the Temple in supplying building materials and artisans. The most important evidence, however, is derived from excavations of temples of the Late Bronze period. Several temples in Palestine, such as the Late Fosse Temple at Lachish, the temple at Beth-Shean in Stratum VI, and especially the temple at Hazor in Stratum 1b (Area H), while they cannot be compared in size and splendor with the Temple at Jerusalem, already show – several centuries before Solomon – the general scheme of the main elements of the Temple, the porch, main hall, and Holy of Holies (which is often only a niche in which a statue of the deity stands), built one after the other on the long axis of the building.

Original Israelite elements are also contained in the design of the Temple, particularly in the Holy of Holies, which continue the tradition of the early *Tabernacle. The biblical descriptions of the Tabernacle, however, are not clear nor are the dates of the texts.

A shrine found at Arad in southern Judah has been attributed to the ninth-eighth centuries B.C.E. by its excavator, who suggests that its foundations may even date back to the tenth century B.C.E., i.e., to the time of Solomon. These dates, however, have not yet been definitely established. The shrine at Arad consists of a large court containing an altar, a small hall, and a niche with steps leading up to it. Thus it differs from the Temple of Solomon in plan but it is identical in orientation (for details see *Arad).

A small temple discovered at Tell Tainet in northern Syria provides evidence of the wide distribution of the plan of the Temple of Solomon. This is a small royal chapel built adjoining the palace of the king (as was the Temple of Solomon) and although it is much smaller and of a later date (ninth–eighth centuries B.C.E.) than the Temple at Jerusalem there is a striking resemblance between their general plans as well as in many construction details. This method of construction was followed for a long period of time and it can also be seen in the ground plan of the Second Temple whose builders tried to adhere as closely as possible to the biblical source.

Although the physical structure of the Temple was influenced by the design of Near Eastern architecture, in function it differed radically from all other foreign shrines. According to Israelite belief, God did not dwell in His Temple. The Temple was no more than a place wherein He chose to have his *Divine Presence (*Shekhinah*) rest, in order to prevail upon man to direct his heart to his God. Unequivocal expression of this view is already given in "the prayer of Solomon" (I Kings 8).

The Detailed Plan of the Temple

GENERAL DESCRIPTION. According to Ezekiel 41:13–14, the Temple was 100 cubits (about 165 ft.) long and 50 cubits wide (without the platform on which it was built). Adding together the dimensions of the rooms of the Temple, the inner and outer wall, the width of the storehouse – a three-story side structure (*yaẓiʿa*) divided into cells and chambers which surrounded the Temple on three sides – and its walls, brings us almost exactly to the dimensions mentioned by Ezekiel. The 2:1 proportion between the length and width of the outer measurements of the Temple was also followed in the interior: the porch measured 20 cubits in width and ten cubits in length (1:2); the main hall, 40 cubits in length and 20 cubits in width (2:1); while the Holy of Holies was a square (1:1). The 20 cubits width of the Temple was, as stated above, almost the maximum width which could be roofed without supporting pillars. Thus the dimensions are not arbitrary but were arrived at through precise planning.

THE PORCH. The function of the porch (Heb. *ʾulam*; apparently borrowed from Akk. *ellamu*, "front") was to separate the sacred precinct from the profane. The Septuagint version of Ezekiel 40:49 cites the number of steps which led to the Temple: "and they ascended it by ten [*ʿeser*] steps" instead of the original text "and it was by steps that [*ʾasher*] it was ascended." The width of the porch – alongside of which the entrance was located – was 20 cubits, and its depth was 10 cubits. The height of the porch is not certain. The only source which mentions its height – 120 cubits – is II Chronicles 3:4 and the text is apparently corrupt. One proposal corrects this to 20 cubits on the basis of the Syriac translation and largely on conjecture, but this is not accepted by all scholars. Some suggest that the porch rose above the main hall, like a tower, following the description in II Chronicles (this interpretation was followed by the builders of the Second Temple). Others lower the porch and still others conclude from the silence on this point in the main source in the Book of Kings that the height of the porch was the same as the general height of the building (30 cubits). On both sides of the entrance stood supporting pillars (see *Jachin and Boaz), each 3 cubits wide and 5 cubits thick; the width of the entrance gate was 14 cubits (23 ft.).

THE MAIN ROOM (HEKHAL) OR HOLY PLACE. The main room was entered from the porch through a gate, 10 cubits wide, in which two doors of cypress wood were set. The doorposts, made of olive wood, were apparently composed of four frames set one within the other, like those found in the temple of Tell Tainet. The thickness of the walls between the porch and the *hekhal* was 6 cubits. The latter was the largest chamber of the Temple, measuring 40 × 20 cubits (approximately 66 × 33 ft.) × 30 cubits in height. These dimensions were considerable in comparison with those of other Near Eastern temples. The *hekhal* served as the main chamber for divine service. The world *hekhal* is borrowed from the Akkadian (*ekallu* – derived ultimately from the Sumerian *é.gal*, "great house"). W.F. Albright maintains that the ancient Canaanite temples initially consisted of one large hall only, called *hekhal*, and that when porches were eventually added on both ends, the name *hekhal* came to denote the principal middle chamber.

The windows of the *hekhal* were set in its upper part, since the flanking structure mentioned above rose to about half the height of the *hekhal*. In the Bible they are called "windows with recessed frames" (I Kings 6:4), terms which are not entirely clear and which have been variously interpreted. By analogy with ivory reliefs found at Samaria, Arslan-Tash, and Nimrūd, it may be assumed that these windows were of the type common in that period in Syria and Palestine, i.e., wide on the outside and narrowing toward the inside, an effect achieved by the use of window frames set one within the other.

THE HOLY OF HOLIES (DEVIR). The Holy of Holies, the rear part of the Temple, was designed to serve as a tabernacle for the ark of the Covenant and the *cherubim. Its interior measurements were 20 × 20 × 20 cubits. The 10 cubits difference in height between the Holy of Holies and the main hall has been explained in various ways. Busink suggests that the Holy of Holies was laid as an independent unit – the tabernacle – under the main roof of the Temple. According to K. Galling, the floor level of the Holy of Holies was raised 10 cubits, but the most reasonable solution is perhaps the combination of a slight elevation of the floor, as was common in Canaanite temples, and a lowering of the roof beneath the level of the roof of the main hall. It may be assumed that the raised floor of the Holy of Holies served as a sort of platform on which stood the ark and the cherubim (a hint of this may be found in Isa. 6:1).

The jambs of the *devir* gate, in which olive wood doors were set, were constructed like the *hekhal* gate and the Temple windows, that is, of five frames set one within the other (I Kings 6:31). There were no windows in the Holy of Holies.

R. de Vaux maintains that the wall between the main hall and the Holy of Holies was merely a thin partition of cedarwood, since the Bible treats the *hekhal* and the Holy of Holies as one unit and gives their combined length in one figure – 60 cubits, with that of the *hekhal* 40 cubits, and that of the Holy of Holies 20 cubits. Had a dividing wall separated them, their combined length would have exceeded 60 cubits by the addition of the width of that wall. De Vaux accordingly emends the text of I Kings 6:16 to read: "He built twenty cubits on the rear of the house with boards of cedar from the floor to the rafters, and they were a separation (reading ויבדלו instead of ויבן לו, "he built them for himself") within the *devir*, as the most holy place." De Vaux regards the "boards of cedar" as a partition; however, a gate made of five frames would necessitate an extremely thick wall, and evidence of such a substantial wall is provided by the Canaanite and Greek temples and by that of Tell Tainet.

THE ADJACENT BUILDING (YAẒI'AH). This building, whose walls ran parallel to those of the Temple and surrounded it on all sides except the front, was of three stories of varying widths. The inner width of the rooms of the lowest story was 5 cubits and to lay the beams of the roof which formed the floor of the second story, the thickness of the walls was reduced so that the width of the rooms of the second story was 6 cubits and of the third story, 7 cubits. Each story was divided into about 30 chambers. The entrance to this side structure was, according to I Kings 6:8, on the south side, while, according to Ezekiel 41:5–6, it was entered on both sides. The upper stories were reached by *lulim*, i.e., apertures in the shape of holes. In this building the numerous Temple vessels, utensils, and treasures were stored. The building was a little over 15 cubits high with each story 5 cubits (about 8.2 ft.) high. A later date for this building has been proposed by some scholars: K. Galling suggests the period of the later kings of Judah; M. Moehlenbrink, the time of Zerubbabel; but there seems to be no sound reason for not attributing it to the time of Solomon.

The Temple Furniture

THE ALTARS. The small altar (2 × 2 × 3 cubits), made of cedar and overlaid with gold, stood before the entrance to the Holy of Holies. It resembled the altars of the ancient Canaanite temples. The large, main altar for burnt sacrifices and the fat of peace offerings, was made of bronze and stood in the court of the Temple, before the porch (II Chron. 8:12). Somewhat of a parallel can be found in the altars discovered in the shrine at Arad. Two small incense altars were set within the building and a sacrificial altar stood in the courtyard. The large altar at Jerusalem was 10 cubits high and was built in stepped tiers. The lowest tier, which was sunk in the earth and was called "the base on the ground" (Ezek. 43:14), was set off from the floor of the court by a channel, and measured 20 × 20 cubits. The length and width of the three tiers above it were 16 × 16, 14 × 14, and 12 × 12 cubits, respectively; the height of the lowest tier was 2 cubits; that of the middle 4 cubits; and that of the uppermost, called *har'el*, 4 cubits.

Set at the four corners of the *har'el* were "horns," exactly as on small Canaanite incense altars. The altar is described by Ezekiel, who apparently refers to the altar erected by Ahaz which was modeled after the one he had seen at Damascus (II Kings 16:10). Ascent to the altar was by steps on its east side (Ezek. 43:17). The fact that its base was called "bosom of the earth" while its uppermost tier was called *har'el* ("mountain of God"), together with its striking resemblance to the Babylonian ziggurat ("temple tower," "mountain peak"), has led several scholars to conjecture that the plan of the altar expressed something of the cosmic symbolism typical of the religions of the Ancient Near East. W.F. Albright sees a connection between "bosom of the earth" and the Akkadian *irat erṣetim* or *irat kigalli*, which is found in the Babylonian temples and which also means "bosom of the earth," "bosom of the underworld." The same applies to the name *har'el* which, according to him, derives from the Akkadian *arallû*, a poetic name for the netherworld.

THE BRAZEN SEA. This bowl, of huge dimensions, which stood in the Temple court, southeast of the Temple proper, was doubtless one of Hiram's greatest technical achievements. As it was 10 cubits in diameter and 5 cubits high, it could hold (on the assumption that its bottom was flat and its walls vertical) 1,765.78 cu. ft. of water. However, in the light of the statement in I Kings 7:26 that the "sea" held 2,000 bath (II Chron. 4:5 has 3,000 bath), i.e., nearly 2,825.25 cu. ft., it may be assumed that it had sharply convex sides. From the thickness of its walls (approximately 7.5 cm., about 3 in.) its weight can be calculated at some 33 tons. Some scholars believe that both the form and name of the vessel are connected with the mythological "sea," known from the Bible and Canaanite documents. The division of the 12 oxen, on which the "sea" stood, into four groups of three, each of which faced one of the points of the compass, has been interpreted as symbolic of the four seasons. Due to its great weight, the "sea" was eventually dismantled. Ahaz gave the oxen, together with the other Temple utensils, as tribute to the king of Assyria (II Kings 16:17). In 586 B.C.E. the Chaldeans broke the "sea" and carried its metal off to Babylon (II Kings 25:13).

THE COLUMNS. Different views have been expressed concerning the bronze columns, *Jachin and Boaz. Did they support the roof of the porch or were they freestanding columns at the entrance, of purely ornamental or cultic purpose? According to II Chronicles 3:15, the second supposition is the more acceptable, but on the basis of the detailed description of the capitals, the special names given to them, and also their great diameter (4 cubits), which rendered them large enough to block the entrance, some scholars incline to the first supposition. Were they pillars, obelisks, fire altars, "trees of life," or the like? W.F. Albright has suggested that they should be regarded as two huge incense stands. Opinions also differ as to the meaning of their names. An original suggestion is that of R.B.Y. Scott – that the words *yakhin* (Jachin) and *bo'az* (or *be-'oz*) were the first words of inscriptions engraved on the columns: יכין ה' כסא דוד ומלכותו לזרעו עד עולם; "May the Lord establish (*yakhin*) the throne of David and his kingdom for his seed for ever"; and perhaps: בעז ה' ישמח מלך; "In the strength (*be-'oz*) of the Lord shall the king rejoice" (cf. Ps. 21:2).

THE BASES AND THE LAVERS. Archaeological discoveries have helped greatly toward understanding the design of the ten brass bases described in detail in the Book of Kings, especially the Larnaca (in Cyprus) "base" which, in most of its details, resembles the bases of the Temple. The latter measured 4 × 4 × 3 cubits. Their upper parts were shaped like round "collars," into which the "lavers" were fitted. These lavers, which were concave, are also known from excavations at Ugarit and Megiddo.

THE CHERUBIM. In the Holy of Holies there were two "cherubim" of olive wood which hovered over the ark of the Covenant. They were each 10 cubits high and the combined spread of their four wings was 20 cubits. Archaeological discoveries indicate that the *cherub was a form of sphinx, with the body of a lion, the head of a man, and two wings. In ancient mythology it was commonly believed that the cherubim served God (cf. II Sam. 22:11), and that their main task was to guard the ark of the Covenant in the Holy of Holies and the "Tree of Life" in the Garden of Eden (Gen. 3:24). The depictions of the thrones of Ahiram, king of Byblos, of the ruler of Megiddo, and of others, in which the thrones rest upon the cherubim, provide a concrete representation of the concept "enthroned upon the cherubim."

The Temple's Site and Orientation

On the basis of a tradition thousands of years old, the site of the First Temple can be fixed on the "Temple Mount," on the east side of Jerusalem, north of Ophel. From earliest times, the "Rock" (or "Foundation Stone") was regarded as the most sacred object on the mount and was associated with memorable events in history and with manifestations of the Divine Presence. (See also Yoma 5:2, "After the Ark was taken away a stone remained there [in the Holy of Holies] from the time of the early Prophets and it was called *Shetiyyah* ["foundation"].") Nevertheless, scholars are divided on the exact site of the Temple. The main issue is whether the altar, which stood to the east of the Temple, was built on the Rock. Some maintain that the Rock itself served as an altar in ancient times, for, according to II Samuel 24:18, 25, David set up an altar in the threshing floor of Araunah the Jebusite – on the very spot where, according to II Chronicles 3:1, Solomon erected the Temple. Against this others argue that had the altar been situated on the Rock, the area would not have sufficed for the Temple which was the west of it, as has been shown by topographical research on the formation of the mount at the time of the First Temple. Contemporary scholars generally accept the second opinion, according to which the Holy of Holies was erected on the Rock. The Rock itself, whose present height is 5 ft. 9 in. above the floor of the mosque of the Dome of the Rock, may have served as the platform of the Holy of Holies.

There is no doubt that the building was oriented from east to west, so that the porch faced eastward. Evidence of this can also be found in the words of Ezekiel: "And he brought me into the inner court of the Lord's house, and, behold, at the door of the temple of the Lord, between the porch and the altar, were about five and twenty men, with their backs toward the temple of the Lord, and their faces toward the east; and they worshipped the sun toward the east" (8:16). (It may be observed that the temple of Tell Tainet also faces east.) The exact position of the Temple in relation to the royal palace is not certain, although it was south of the Temple.

Building Materials and Ornamentation

Biblical sources provide evidence of the following main building materials: cedarwood, floated down in rafts to the neighborhood of Jaffa, and "finished stones," "stones from the quarry," "costly stones – hewn stones" (I Kings 5:31), which were used for the foundation of the structure. A detailed account is also given of the stones which were used in building the king's palace which were "sawed with saws" as well as of "great stones, stones of ten cubits, and stones of eight cubits" (I Kings 7:9–10) which were used for the Temple foundation. In addition, Solomon is said to have built the inner court of the Temple "with three rows of hewn stone, and a row of cedar beams" (I Kings 6:36). The Bible further tells how the Temple was erected and of the crews of masons and the thousands of laborers which Solomon conscripted for the work.

The method of construction in both stone and timber, whereby the timber was used to brace and strengthen the walls and also to face the interior of the building, was prevalent in Palestine and in the neighboring countries. A building of masonry and timber was found also at Ugarit, and there too a row of timber is inserted between the third and fourth course; the same is true of the buildings found at Megiddo (in Solomon's time) and Senjirli.

The biblical account leaves no doubt that the lower courses of Solomon's building were of large hewn stones, that its exterior walls were also of masonry, and that its interior walls were paneled with cedarwood. Within the courses, beams and cedar planks were set to brace and strengthen the building. The same account mentions various decorations: carvings, cherubim, palm trees, open flowers, and chainwork. All these terms, which were quite obscure up to recent years, have now become comprehensible thanks to archaeological discoveries that uncovered the ivory reliefs at Samaria, Arslan-Tash, Megiddo, and elsewhere.

Conclusion

The general picture of Solomon's Temple is clear in its major outlines. It has been seen that the plan of the Temple, its array of utensils, its decorative motifs, and the method of its construction are to a certain degree rooted in ancient traditions of the Near East. It should not, however, be deduced from this that Solomon's Temple was a stereotyped building, similar in all respects to the Canaanite temples. The distinct Israelite form of divine service also left its mark – both on the general structure of the Temple and on a number of details.

[Yigael Yadin]

RITUAL

The Service in the Temple

In addition to the sacrificial worship (for details see *Sacrifice), it was customary for the levites to sing ("they shall stand every morning, thanking and praising the Lord, and likewise at evening," I Chron. 23:30) to the accompaniment of "lyres with harps, and with cymbals" (I Chron. 25:1; II Chron. 29:25). Many of the psalms in the Book of Psalms are ascribed to these levite singers (the descendants of *Asaph, *Heman, and *Jeduthun). This singing constitutes something of an innovation, for the Pentateuch makes no reference to it (see *Music).

Primarily, however, the Temple was a place of assembly for the entire people for purposes of sacrifice, prayer, and thanksgiving. The people would come to the Temple to bring both sin and guilt offerings as well as burnt offerings and peace offerings and meal offerings with frankincense either in fulfillment of vows, as freewill offerings, or as peace offerings of thanksgiving. These sacrifices, which had to be eaten within a day or two of their slaughter, were apparently brought to the accompaniment of songs (Ps. 26:6–7; 56:13; 100:2, 4; 116:17; 118:19) and in procession ("the voice of those who sing… 'Give thanks to the Lord of hosts, for the Lord is good, for His steadfast love endures for ever,'" Jer. 33:11). Many psalms which call upon man to give thanks to God ("Give thanks unto the Lord," e.g., Ps. 107, 118, 136) and to praise Him ("Praise the Lord," Ps. 113–116, 135, et al.), as well as others (e.g., Ps. 26, 27, 56, 100), were certainly associated with the bringing of these thanksgiving or freewill offerings. Individuals (or the entire community after a war, I Sam. 15:15) would bring objects set apart for sacred use (חֲרָמִים) for sacrifice.

Special importance was attached to public processions in celebration of the festivals. The people would come to the Temple "to worship before the Lord" on Sabbaths and New Moons (Isa. 1:13; 66:23; Ezek. 46:3; cf. II Kings 4:23). Particularly at the appointed seasons and at the three pilgrim festivals, large numbers would stream to the Temple (Isa. 33:20; Ezek. 46:9; Lam. 1:4; 2:6). They would come not only from Jerusalem but also from all of Judah (Jer. 7:26; 26:2; cf. Ps. 122:1–2) and even from beyond, from Shechem, from Shiloh, and from Samaria (Jer. 41:5). The number of pilgrims to Jerusalem increased especially after the destruction of Samaria (II Chron. 30:1ff.; 35:1ff.). The festal crowd would proceed in a "throng… with glad shouts and songs of thanksgiving" (Ps. 42:5 [4]) and would enter the Temple gates "with thanksgiving and… praise" (Ps. 100:4; cf. 95:1–2; 118:19; Isa. 26:1–2). The procession would be accompanied by the playing of musical instruments (with "gladness of heart, as when one sets out to the sound of the flute to go to the mountain of the Lord," Isa. 30:29), and this may also have been the custom at the time of the bringing of the firstfruits (cf. Bik. 3:4). During these pilgrimages, Jerusalem was filled with a multitude of people and animals ("like the flock at Jerusalem during her appointed feasts," Ezek. 36:38). The celebrants would solemnize the festival with singing which would, at times, continue into the night (Isa. 30:29; cf. Pes. 85b). Pilgrims to the Temple were particularly numerous on the Feast of Tabernacles, celebrated at the time of the ingathering of the harvest (e.g., I Kings 8:2; Zech. 14:16; II Chron. 7:9) and at Passover.

The Temple assumed special importance also on fast days. Then too large numbers would flock to it from Jerusalem and the border cities (Jer. 36:6–9). These gatherings would usually be held "in the court of the Lord's house" (Jer. 19:14), in the outer gate (Jer. 7:2), and on these occasions the prophets (see below) would address the people (Jer. 26:2; II Chron. 24:20–21).

The Temple Treasury

The funds for the maintenance of the Temple were kept in permanent *treasuries in the Sanctuary (I Kings 14:26; II Kings 12:19; 14:14; 18:15; 24:13; I Chron. 9:26; 26:20; II Chron. 5:1). The payment of tribute exacted by foreign enemies would be made from these funds. There was, furthermore, "the treasury of dedicated things," which was guarded by a special official of levitical descent. It consisted of war booty and other allocations assigned to the Temple by kings and generals (II Sam. 8:11–12; I Kings 7:51; II Chron. 26:27), as well as dedications made by individuals. The sources enumerate three types of such dedications: the money valuation based on the age of the individual male or female, which would be given to the priest as "holy to the Lord" (Lev. 27); money donations which a man's heart prompts him to bring into the house of the Lord"; and the money "for which each man is assessed" (II Kings 12:5[4]), which according to II Chronicles 24:6 is to be identified with the tax of a half-shekel imposed by Moses on every Israelite from the age of 20 upward, for the building of the Tabernacle (Ex. 30:13). This money would first be handed to the priests who would take it "each [man] from his acquaintance" (II Kings 12:6[5]) and deposit it in the treasury. In the 23rd year of Jehoash's reign, the high priest Jehoiada issued a decree whereby the "money of the dedicated things" was to be deposited, through the medium of "the priests who guarded the threshold," in a special chest by the bronze altar (12:10[9]). He also directed that this money was to be applied exclusively to the repair of the Temple (12:7–16 [6–15]). This regulation remained in force, apparently, to the end of the period of the First Temple (see II Kings 22:4, et al.). The supreme trustee of this money (as of the Temple administration as a whole) appears to have been the king, since the regular sacrifice was offered "from his own possessions" (II Chron. 31:3; cf. Ezek. 45:17).

The Temple treasures seem to have included stores of produce, the tithe (of grain, cattle, and sheep) and the dedicated things which, according to II Chronicles 31:4ff., would be brought to the chambers of the Temple (of this there is evidence particularly in the early period of the Second Temple – see below), and from which allocations would be made to the priests and the levites. The Temple also served as a storehouse for the royal weapons (e.g., the spears and shields of King David – II Kings 11:10; II Chron. 23:9; cf. I Sam. 21:10).

The Ministers in the Temple

The right to serve in the Temple was assigned to the priests who where descended from Aaron (as mentioned frequently in the Pentateuch; see also Ps. 115:10; 135:19). Even before the building of the Temple, the star of the priestly families of Abiathar and Eli had set, and only members of the family of Zadok served as high priests. The levites, "the house of Levi" (Ps. 135:20), included the singers to the accompaniment of instruments, as well as the gatekeepers and those appointed to be "in charge of the treasuries of the house of God and the treasuries of the dedicated gifts" (e.g., I Chron. 26:20). The levites also assisted the priests in various services (for details see *Priests).

In addition to these Israelite functionaries, non-Israelites, Nethinim, also served in the Temple (for details see *Gibeonites and Nethinim). They were descendants of the Gibeonites (cf. Josh. 9:23, 27) and of the "Servants of Solomon" (Ezra 2:58; Neh. 7:60), i.e., members of the other Canaanite peoples whom David and Solomon had made "a levy of bondservants." Ezekiel (44:9) expresses opposition to the service in the Temple of "all the foreigners who are among the people of Israel," but this opposition proved fruitless (see Ezra 2:43–58). The duty of the Nethinim was apparently to perform menial tasks such as the hewing of wood and the drawing of water (see Josh. 9:27).

The king also enjoyed a certain status of holiness in the Temple (I Kings 8:64; 9:25; cf. II Sam. 6:17; 8:18, and see above), but in contrast to the priests, he was not permitted to enter the *hekhal* or to burn incense (II Chron. 26:16). Nevertheless, he had the right to draw up the plan for the building of the Temple (I Kings 6–7; I Chron. 28:11ff.), to determine the celebration of festivals (I Kings 8:65 – 66), to consecrate the inner court when occasion demanded it (I Kings 8:64), to alter the form and position of the altar (II Kings 16:10–16), to add sacrifices for given purposes (II Chron. 29:20–21), and to designate the courses of the priests and the levites (II Chron. 29:25).

THE SIGNIFICANCE OF THE TEMPLE FOR THE PEOPLE

The Temple was regarded as a national center, and since it was, moreover, the abode of the ark, it was considered to be the site of the revelation of the Divine Presence and hence also the preferred place for prayer (I Kings 8:22–53; cf. Josh. 7:6–9; I Sam. 1:10–16; II Sam. 7:18–29). To it, the individual Israelite would direct his supplications even from afar (I Kings 8:44–48; cf. Dan. 6:11), in the belief that man's prayer would reach it even from the most remote places (Jonah 2:5, 8). There the people would gather in times of distress (Joel 2:15–16), when the priests would weep "between the vestibule and the altar" (Joel 2:17).

The growth of the Temple's importance as a religious center was bound up in large measure with the struggle against the high places, which appears to have become intensified in Judah with the political breach in the nation after the death of Solomon. During the reign of the dynasty of Omri the practice of idolatry gained ground in Israel, even as it did in Judah in the days of *Athaliah. By the very nature of things, idolatrous practices were concentrated especially in localities not subject to official supervision, that is, at the local high places. This brought about a sharpening of the conflict, which, in turn, led to an increased emphasis upon the special significance of the Temple in Jerusalem, and, ultimately in the reign of Hezekiah and Josiah, to the prohibition of the use of the high places and to the centralization of worship in the Temple.

This enhanced significance of the Temple in Jerusalem is apparent especially in the statements of the prophets. Although they opposed sacrifices and prayer as "a commandment of men learned by rote" (Isa. 1:10–15; Jer. 14:11–12, et al.), there is not the slightest trace in their utterances of any intention of belittling the Temple itself. The *Temple Mount, Mt. Zion, is, in their words, the mountain of the Lord, the holy mountain (Isa. 11:9; 56:7; 65:11, 25; Joel 2:1; 4:17; Zeph. 3:11, et al.), wherein the Lord dwells (Ps. 74:2), and the Temple is the house of the God of Jacob and the Lord's house (Isa. 2:2–3; Jer. 23:11; Ezek. 8:14, 16; Joel 1:13–16; Micah 4:1–2; Haggai 1:14, et al.). Like its earlier counterpart, Shiloh, the Temple is the place whereon God's name is called (Jer. 7:12, 30; 34:15), "a glorious throne set on high from the beginning" (Jer. 17:12), the habitation of the Divine Presence (Ezek. 9:3; 43:5–9; Joel 4:17, 21; Hab. 2:20, et al.), the place from which the Divine Presence reveals itself to the prophet (Isa. 6:1; Amos. 1:2; 9:1); and in "the end of days" the Temple is destined to be the place of prayer for Israel (Isa. 27:13; Jer. 31:5; 33:10–11) and for all the nations (Isa. 2:2–3; 56:7; 66:20, 23). With the destruction of the Temple, much prophecy begins to center around the vision of its reconstruction. The beginning of this transition is to be found in Ezekiel, who has a vision of the future Temple (chs. 40–48); its climax and culmination are reached in the later prophets, who are the chief advocates of its rebuilding in their own day (Haggai 1–2; Zech. 1:16; 2:15; 6:12; 8:3; 22:23) and of the purification of its worship (Mal. 1–3).

[Yehoshua M. Grintz]

SECOND TEMPLE

HISTORY

The Temple of Zerubbabel

The Jerusalem Temple is a major focus of attention in post-Exilic biblical books. Deutero-Isaiah foretells that Cyrus shall be divinely charged with the task of restoring the Temple (Isa. 44:28). The Chronicler ends his account (II Chron. 36:22–23) and the Book of Ezra begins its account with the fulfillment of this prophecy (Ezra 1:1ff.), referring to the earlier word of Jeremiah (cf. Jer. 29:10). Issued in 538 B.C.E., after his conquest of Babylon, Cyrus' rescript relates the return exclusively to the reconstruction of the Temple. The repatriates were to be aided by the Jews remaining behind and by their gentile neighbors. Temple vessels taken as booty by Nebuchadnezzar were delivered by the treasurer Mithridates to the Davidic prince Sheshbazzar for return to Jerusalem (Ezra 1:7ff.).

Although one source speaks of Sheshbazzar, with the title of governor, as having indeed laid the foundations for the Temple (Ezra 5:14ff.), another credits his nephew (?) Zerubbabel and the priest Jeshua with the honor. Despite intimidation from their neighbors they established an altar in the seventh month (year ?), reinstituted the sacrificial cult, and offered up the special sacrifices required for the festival of Tabernacles. All was performed "as written in the Torah of Moses the man of God" (Ezra 3:1ff.).

Masons and carpenters were engaged for the construction, and cedars from Lebanon were ordered from the Sidonians and Tyrians, to be shipped to Jaffa. Expenses were to be borne by the royal treasury and a memorandum of a royal decree to this effect was recorded in the archives in Ecbatana in Media. It included the dimensions of the Temple and the architectural feature that it was to be built with three courses of stone and one of timber (Ezra 3:7; 6:1ff.). A similar feature was recorded for the courtyard of Solomon's Temple (I Kings 6:36; 7:12). Unfortunately the figures for the dimensions appear to be corrupt; they are "its height sixty cubits, its width sixty cubits" (Ezra 6:3). On the basis of the dimensions of the Solomonic Temple (I Kings 6:2) and the *Peshitta*, the text has been restored, "its height [thirty] cubits, [its length] sixty [cubits], its width [thirty] cubits."

Levites were appointed to direct the work. The laying of the foundations was accompanied by a ceremony, the priests blowing the trumpets and the levites, sons of Asaph, handling the cymbals. They chanted psalms of praise in fulfillment of the word of Jeremiah (Jer. 33:10–11) and the people raised their voices in mixed cries of joy and sounds of weeping (Ezra 3:8ff.). When the neighboring peoples heard that building was actually under way, they asked to participate in the project. They claimed to have been settled on the land by the Assyrian king Esarhaddon (681–669 B.C.E.) and to have been worshiping the God of Israel since then. Their request was rejected on the grounds that to the repatriates only had Cyrus given permission to build. Thus rebuffed, the neighbors turned into enemies and by one means or another brought the building operation to a halt (Ezra 4:1ff.).

The work on the Temple, begun in the second month of the second year of the Exiles' return (Ezra 3:8), was not resumed until Elul 24 in the second year of King Darius (Haggai 1:15). If it is assumed that the chronological calculation in the periphery of Judah was the same as that in the center of the Persian Empire, then this date would have been September 21, 520. Rebellions in the eastern provinces had been put down, but Egypt was still in revolt. On Elul 1 (August 29) Haggai turned to Zerubbabel and Jeshua and rebuked them for listening to the people who said "the time has not yet come to rebuild the Temple." The prophet attributed recent drought and poor economic conditions to failure to build the Temple. Undertaking the task would bring prosperity, he assured them (Haggai 1:1ff.). Shortly after work was begun, a second prophecy of encouragement was uttered on Tishri 21 (October 17 – Haggai 2:1ff.), and the words of Haggai were soon taken up by Zechariah (Zech. 1:1ff.). The laying of the foundation is dated to Kislev 24 (December 17 – Haggai 2:18), and both prophets foresaw the onset of earthshaking events and hinted at the establishment of Zerubabbel's independent rule (Haggai 2:6ff., 20ff.; Zech. 1:16–17; 4:6ff.; 6:12–13).

Connected as it was with thinly veiled messianic aspirations, the renewed building of the Temple aroused the suspicions of Tattenai, governor of Trans-Euphrates and his subordinate Shethar-Bozenai. The two rulers came to Jerusalem with their staff to investigate the situation. They were informed of the decree by Cyrus, and wrote to Darius for corroboration (Ezra 5). Word came back confirming the decree and authorizing the work to continue, now as before at royal expense. Regular sacrifices for the welfare of the king and his family were likewise to be subsidized by the royal treasury. Interference in the building project was subject to the penalty of death (Ezra 6:1ff.). As the work proceeded apace, Jews became anxious to abolish the days of mourning for the Temple's destruction (Zech. 7). Work was finally completed on the third of Adar in the sixth year of Darius (March 12, 515). The dedicatory sacrifices consisted of 100 bulls, 600 small cattle, and 12 he-goats as purificatory sacrifice. The last number signified the unity of the 12 tribes, and the amount of all three sacrificial groups was worked out in proportion to the number of sacrifices offered at the dedication of Solomon's Temple (I Kings 8:63).

Although there is no description of the construction of the Temple or its layout, as there is for Solomon's Temple (I Kings 6–7) and for that projected by Ezekiel (Ezek. 40ff.), scattered references permit a partial picture. Around the Temple there were two courtyards with chambers, and gates, and a public square. The assembly convened by Ezra to dissolve the mixed marriages was held in the Temple plaza (Ezra 10:9). On the Ophel and in the area between the outer Temple wall and the city wall to the east the temple servants (Nethinim) and priests had their dwellings. This northeastern part of the wall, beginning with the Horse Gate, was repaired, under Nehemiah's direction, by the priests, "each one in front of his own house." Among these were Shemaiah son of Shecaniah, keeper of the East Gate (of the Temple courtyard), and Meshullam son of Berechiah who worked opposite his chamber. Malchijah the goldsmith worked across from the Muster Gate of the Temple courtyard (Neh. 3:26ff.).

Temple chambers played a prominent role in the events of the period. Ezra brought with him from Babylon silver, and gold, and vessels for deposit in the Temple chambers (Ezra 8:25ff.). His confessional concerning mixed marriages took place in front of the Temple. Upon conclusion, he repaired to the chamber of Jehohanan son of Eliashib where he spent the night in fasting and mourning (Ezra 10:1–6). Another Eliashib, in charge of the Temple chambers and related to Tobiah, assigned him a large chamber where vessels, meal offerings, and frankincense, tithes of grain, wine, and oil for the levites, singers, and gatekeepers, as well as the priestly offerings were ordinarily stored. The assignment of this chamber had been made during Nehemiah's absence from Jerusalem, and upon his return he expelled Tobiah and his possessions from the chamber, purified it, and once again he stored the Temple vessels, meal offerings, and frankincense there (Neh. 13:4ff.).

The earlier pact to observe the Torah, pushed through by Nehemiah, had sought to provide for the orderly functioning of the Temple cult and the sure support of its personnel. It stipulated an annual contribution of one-third of a shekel to finance the regular daily and festal sacrificial service and obligated everyone to supply, in rotation by lots, wood for the altar. Firstfruits were to be brought to the Temple annually not only from the produce of the soil but also from the orchard. The redemption of the human firstborn and of the impure animals was to be carried out at the Temple. There the priests were to receive the firstborn of the clean animals. Other offerings brought to them and stored in the Temple chambers included the meal offering (cf. Num. 15:17ff.) and the priestly offering from the produce of the soil and from the fruit of the tree (cf. Num. 18:12ff.; Deut. 18:4). The most far-reaching requirement was the tithe offering, formerly voluntary (Num. 18:21ff.) but now obligatory annually, to be given not only to the levites (contrast Deut. 14:22ff.) but also to the singers and gatekeepers. The levite was to go out to the fields and collect the tithe in the presence of a priest. A tenth of the tithe was due the priest and was deposited in the Temple chambers along with the other priestly offerings (Neh. 10:33ff.).

In view of the relatively small number of levites in contrast to the large number of priests (cf. Ezra 2:37ff. = Neh. 7:39ff.; Neh. 10:2ff.; 12:1ff.), it was utopian to have believed that the levitical tithe could be made obligatory. Initial efforts to have the tithe, like the priestly offerings, brought to the Temple chambers (Neh. 12:44) for distribution there failed. The portions of the levites were not being delivered, and out of economic need they and the singers fled Jerusalem to work their fields in the country. During Nehemiah's second tour of duty he sought to rectify the situation by firm action. He rebuked the Jerusalem officials for neglecting the levites, gathered them again into the city, reinstituted the practice of bringing the tithe to the Temple storeroom, and appointed special officials – Shelemiah the priest, Zadok the scribe, Pedaiah the levite, and Hanan son of Zaccur son of Mattaniah – to supervise the collection and guarantee the distribution (Neh. 13:9ff.). Now that all the sacred offerings, of priests and levites, were being brought to Jerusalem, it was necessary to organize these cultic officials into fixed groupings with regular periods of service. Earlier lists of priestly families varied from two (Ezra 8:2) to four (Ezra 2:36ff. = Neh. 7:39ff.) to 21 (Neh. 10:3ff.; 12:1–7). The list of 24 divisions attributed by the Chronicler to David (I Chron. 24–25) may have originated from the organizational activity of Nehemiah. He determined that the regular supply of wood for the altar was to follow a fixed plan and not be determined by lots, and he also organized the manner by which the firstfruits were to be brought to Jerusalem (Neh. 13:30–31).

Nehemiah, then, more than any other person, was responsible for the organization of the Temple cult, and he concluded his memoirs by an appeal to God to remember him favorably (Neh. 13:29–30). A very discouraging picture of the cult, however, is presented by the prophet Malachi, who may have prophesied after Nehemiah. The people are accused of not bringing the tithes and priestly offerings to the Temple storehouse and of bringing to the altar unfit animals, the likes of which they would not dare bring to the governor. The priests are rebuked for betraying their charge (Mal. 1:7ff.; 2:8; 3:8ff.). Intermarriage was considered by him a profanation of the sanctuary and excessive divorce reason for rejection by God of the people's offerings (2:10ff.). But the Lord would appear in His Temple, punish the wicked, and purify the priesthood so that "the offering of Judah and Jerusalem would be pleasing to the Lord as in the days of old and as in former years" (3:1ff.).

The restoration of the Temple cult was closely bound up with the efforts of the repatriates, or at least certain of their leaders, to maintain a sacred exclusivity. Yet the policy that was ultimately to prevail in Judaism was that proclaimed by Deutero-Isaiah on the eve of the Return. The foreigner who observed the covenant of God, especially the Sabbath, would be entitled to sacrifice in His Temple – "for my House shall be called a House of prayer for all peoples" (Isa. 56:6–7).

[Bezalel Porten]

The Hellenistic Period

When Judea came under Greek rule, following the campaign of Alexander the Great, there was a closely knit Jewish population centered around the Temple in Jerusalem. Simeon the Just (Jos., Ant. 12:43, 157, 158), fortified the sanctuary (apparently by the erection of the *Western Wall, which served to defend it from the city side), and dug a large reservoir within the confines of the Temple Mount (Ecclus. 50:2ff.). Ben Sira's description (loc. cit.) of Simeon's officiating in the Temple reflects the early stages of the highly impressive service which in time became customary (see later). The Hellenistic kings respected the Temple and lavished gifts upon it. Antiochus III was particularly generous; he donated wine, oil, frankincense, fine flour, ordinary flour, and salt from his own revenues and also provided wood for the Temple's construction and repair. Like the Persian rulers before him, he exempted all Temple functionaries, including scribes, from the payment of royal taxes (Jos., Ant. 12:140–2). Seleucus IV followed in his footsteps in this respect, covering all the expenses connected with the offering of the sacrifices (II Macc. 3:3); although this did not deter him, when he was later in financial straits, from sending his officer Heliodorus to Jerusalem to seize the contents of the Temple treasury (his design was frustrated: see II Macc. 3:5ff.). The attitude of the Seleucid monarchs changed radically in the days of Antiochus IV Epiphanes. On his way back from Egypt in 169 B.C.E., Antiochus broke into the Temple, and carried off its precious vessels; two years later he erected the "abomination of desolation" on the altar, turning the building into a temple of Zeus. The sacred services were suspended for over three years, being renewed only after the conquest of Mount Zion and the Temple by *Judah Maccabee, celebrated in the institution of the festival of *Ḥanukkah (I Macc. 4:58; II Mac. 1:9; 2:18). Judah also fortified Mount Zion, surrounding it with a wall in order to defend the Temple (I Macc. 4:59), especially from danger from the west, where the Greek-held Acra fortress was situated. From that time on the Temple service continued to be held without interruption, even when the Greeks succeeded in reasserting their control. In the days of Simeon the Hasmonean (141–135 B.C.E.) the Acra was razed, making the Temple henceforward the highest point in the city (Jos., Ant. 13:217). Important innovations were made in the Temple service in the time of John Hyrcanus II (TJ, Sot. 9:11; Tosef., Sot. 10:3).

[Yehoshua M. Grintz]

From the Roman Conquest until the Destruction

When Pompey conquered Jerusalem he entered the sanctuary and penetrated into the Holy of Holies (Jos., Wars 1:152), but left everything undisturbed. However, when Crassus passed through the country on his way to Parthia several years later, he plundered the Temple treasury of 2,000 silver talents (Jos., Ant. 14:105). An important landmark in Temple history is its renovation by Herod. Agrippa II renewed the eastern porticos (Ant. 20:220). During his reign the priests erected a wall on the western side of the inner court, in order to screen the altar service from the eyes of those feasting in the new royal banquet hall which the king had constructed in his palace in the Upper City (Ant. 20:189–92). The Temple porticos were damaged several times during the period of unrest preceding the rebellions against Rome in the days of Varus (Jos., Wars 2:49) and later those of *Gessius Florus (*ibid.*, 2:330, 405); each time, however, they were repaired. In Pontius Pilate's time, the aqueduct which ran from the Hebron area to Jerusalem entered the Temple Mount (Wars 2:175). During the Roman war, in 70 C.E., *John of Giscala fortified himself in the Temple (the inner court was held for a time by Eleazar b. Simeon). In his struggle with Simeon b. Giora, John erected towers at the corners of the Temple (Wars 4:58).

The appointment of the high priests by the civil authorities – a custom which was inaugurated by Herod – led to a decline in the status of the office but also increased the Pharisees' control over the details of the service. The appointment of an honorary guard over the vestments of the high priest, originally made by the royal authorities and then taken over by the Roman governors, was a source of friction between the Roman government and the Temple authorities. A special rescript promulgated by Claudius (c. 46 C.E.) transferred the appointment of this guard of honor to the Temple authorities. The outbreak of the Roman war was signalized by the cessation of the sacrifice offered for the well-being of the Roman emperor (Wars 2:409ff.; Git. 56a).

With the siege of Jerusalem, the Temple became the focus of the whole war. The Romans' first step toward capturing the Temple Mount was their breach of the wall of the Fortress of Antonia (on the third of Tammuz). On the ruins of this fortress, they constructed a ramp which reached the inner wall of the court in four places (Wars 6:150–1). On the 17th of Tammuz the *tamid* sacrifice ceased to be offered (Ta'an. 4:6) – possibly because there were no priests available capable of performing the prescribed service (Wars 6:94). The Temple porticos were destroyed by fire between the 22nd and 28th of Tammuz (*ibid.*, 164–8; 177–9, 190–2). The frequent Roman assaults on the wall of the court were repulsed until the eighth of Av, when Titus gave orders to set fire to the gates of the court (*ibid.*, 241). The next day a council was held at the Roman headquarters to decide upon the fate of the Temple. According to Josephus (*ibid.*), Titus did not want the Temple to be demolished, but a different source, probably based on Tacitus, states that he demanded its destruction. In Josephus' account the burning of the Temple is accidental, resulting from a Roman soldier having thrown a burning torch through a window into one of the Temple chambers on the north side. In spite of Titus' efforts to contain the flames (so Josephus says), another torch was thrown against the Temple gate (apparently the gate of the sanctuary because the entrance hall was not closed by a gate), and the entire building went up in flames, except for two gates (Wars 6:281). The Jewish defenders fought with desperate bravery until the very last, and when they saw the edifice go up in flames many threw themselves into the fire. According to Josephus (Wars, 6:248–50) the catastrophe occurred on the tenth of Av in the year 70 C.E.; according to the Talmud (Ta'an. 29a) on the ninth. Some of the Temple vessels were saved from destruction and fell into the hands of the Romans. They are depicted on one of the reliefs on Titus' victory arch in Rome (see *Titus, Arch of).

[Michael Avi-Yonah]

STRUCTURE

The First Building

Those who returned from the Exile looked upon the Second Temple as a continuation of the First and tried to reconstruct an exact replica of it. Due to their poverty, however, they were not able to adorn it with all its original splendor, and many of the old men who had seen the First Temple in all its glory wept when they saw the modest proportions of the new foundation (Ezra 3:12; Tob. 14:5). At the beginning of the Persian period, therefore, the Temple was of modest proportions and simply adorned, but as the economic position of the Jews in Judea improved and the number of Jews the world over increased, they continued to add to the Temple structure and to beautify it. In Ben Sira (50:1–2) it is related that in the days of Simeon the son of Onias the high priest (first half of the second century B.C.E.) "the Temple was fortified [and]...the wall was built [having] turrets for protection like a king's palace." The Greek text of Ben Sira tells that in the author's day the "Temple Mount" was established – i.e., the open flat area around the Temple proper was created; foundations were laid and earth was piled on top of them until the level of the square surrounding the Temple was increased to twice its original height. A wall was also built along the southern and western perimeters of the Mount. On the east and north it was fortified by the city wall.

At the time of the internecine struggle between the *Hasideans and the Hellenizers, in the days of Antiochus IV and during the period when his decrees forbidding the practice of Judaism were in force, the daily offering was suspended, and the altar was profaned. When Judah the Maccabee and his men succeeded in reentering Jerusalem and reconsecrating the desecrated Temple, they pulled down the altar, and placed its stones in one of the chambers in the Temple precincts (Mid. 1:6). Later the Hellenizing high priest Alcimus (who was appointed in 161 B.C.E. by Demetrius I to succeed Menelaus)

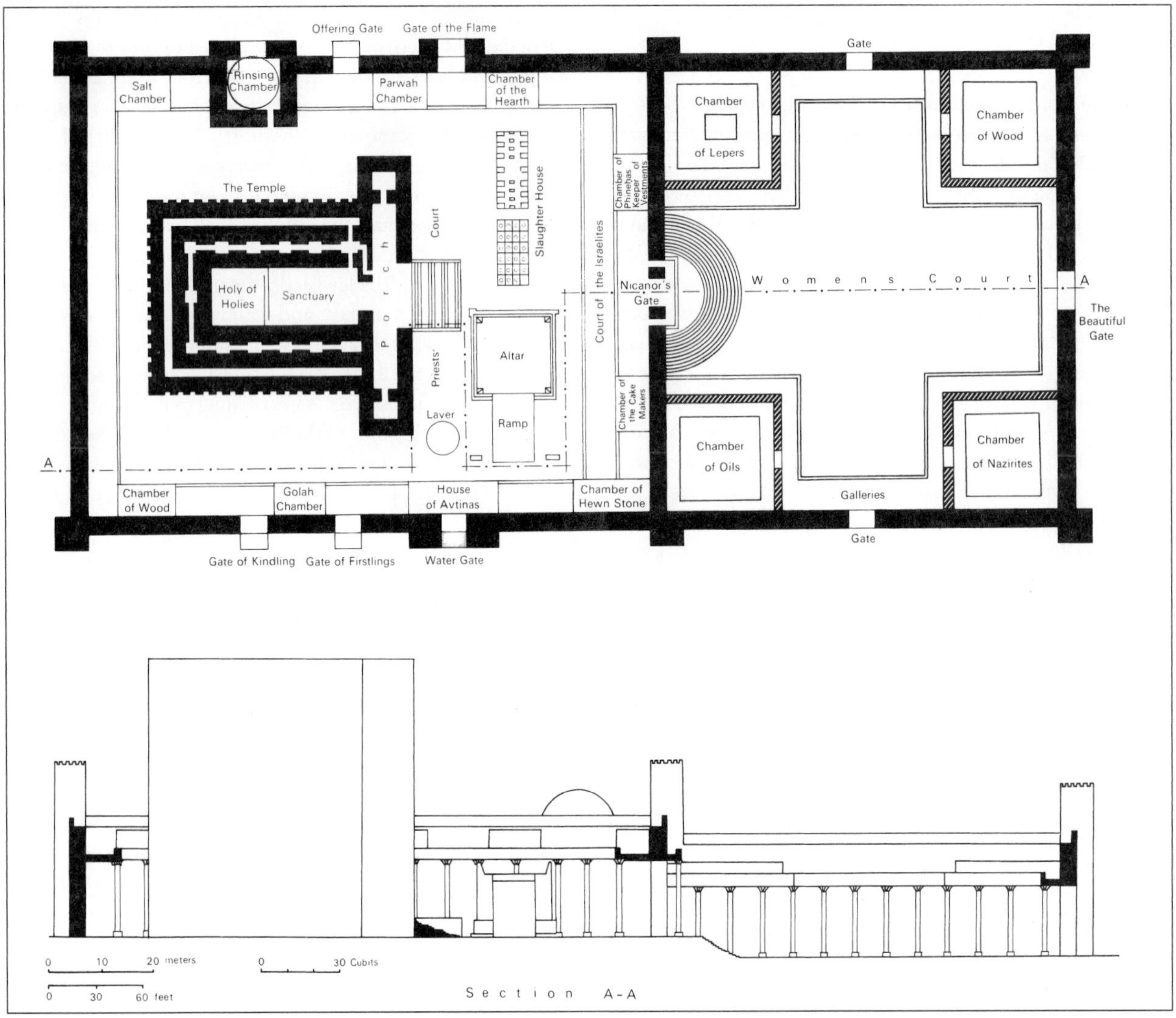

Suggested restoration of the Second Temple, according to Mishnah Middot and Josephus, Jewish Antiquities. *Based on* Atlas of Israel, *Jerusalem, 1970.*

made breaches in the *soreg* – the fence cutting off the portion open to gentiles, beyond which they were forbidden to go – but later, in the days of Jonathan the Hasmonean, the breaches were repaired. (This is the background of Mid. 2:3 "And there were 13 breaches which had been made by gentile kings. They mended them and in connection with them they ordained 13 prostrations.") In Hasmonean times the walls of the Temple Mount were also fortified, so that it became the highest fortification in the city (Jos., Wars 5:245). The first bridge (i.e., the northern one) connecting the Upper City and the Temple Mount was probably also constructed at this time.

Reconstruction by Herod

In the 18th year of his reign, Herod decided to rebuild the Temple (Ant. 15:380), and in order to allay the fears of the people and avoid their wrath, he completed all the preparations for the new building before demolishing the existing structure. A thousand priests were trained to be stonemasons and builders, so that they could do the necessary work in the inner portions of the Temple where non-priests were forbidden to enter, and all the building materials were assembled, as well as around a thousand wagons to transport the stones (Ant. 15:390–1). The Mishnah has preserved various traditions concerning the extreme care with which the *halakhah* was kept in all that related to the Temple's construction in Herod's day. For the erection of the altar and the ramp by which the priests ascended to it, unhewn stones were quarried from under the virgin ground of the Beth-Cherem Valley. No iron touched them in the process (Mid. 3:4). While sacrifices were being offered curtains were drawn before the sanctuary (*hekhal*) and the courts, both so as to enable the worship to continue undisturbed and to conceal the inner portion of the Temple from the eyes of the multitude (Eduy. 8:6). In spite of the large-scale preparations and the diligence of the workmen, the building operations continued for 46 years (John 2:2), and shortly before its destruction various finishing touches were still being put to the edifice (Ant. 20:219). During the Herodian renovation the area of the Temple Mount was doubled. This was accomplished by constructing gigantic supporting walls and filling in the intervening area. Around the forecourt thus created, porticos were built. The second bridge, which connected the southern portion of the Temple Mount with the Upper City, was built at this time. The sanctuary itself was raised 40 cubits and broadened 30 cubits and its facade was renewed. The edifice was built of white stone. Its gates and many of its decorations were plated with silver and gold (Wars 5:223). Talmudic tradition too emphasizes the splendor of the building: "He who has not seen the Temple of Herod has never in his life seen a beautiful building" (BB 4a). The descriptions of the Temple found in Jewish literature, talmudic and other, from the end of the Second Temple period reflect, for the most part, the building as it was after the Herodian reconstruction. There are three main sources for details of the Temple: talmudic literature, particularly the tractates *Middot, Tamid, Yoma*, and *Shekalim*; Josephus' *Antiquities* (15:380–425 and his *Jewish Wars* (5:184–247); and archaeological findings, including especially inscriptions.

The *Temple Mount is surrounded by the remnants of a wall. With the exception of the northern side and northern half of the western side this wall was examined by Warren during 1864–67, and from 1967 by B. Mazar; they reached the conclusion that it dates from Herodian times. Its foundations are at present deep underground (25 meters at the southeast corner and 21 meters at the Western Wall), but in ancient times, too, part of it was below ground level. These lower layers were built of ashlars with wide marginal dressings and protruding surfaces, whereas those visible to the eye while the Temple stood were of stones with low, smooth projections and double margins. The largest stone found in the Western Wall is 12 meters (c. 40 ft.) long, but the most massive is in the 28th layer on the southern side which is the level of the threshold of the gates to the Temple: it is 7 meters (c. 24 ft.) long, 1.85 (c. 6 ft.) high, and weighs over 100 tons. Herod's aim was to create a rectangular platform and this necessitated large-scale changes in the topography of the Temple Mount. In order to level the ground, 5–14 meters (17–58 ft.) of the stone at the northwestern corner were hewn away. On the other hand, a small valley which ran in a southeasterly direction along the length of the old wall of the Temple Mount down to the Kidron had to be filled in. A wall 38 meters (c. 124 ft.) high was constructed and then the pit thus created was filled in with earth. At the southwest corner the direction of the Tyropoeon Valley, which used to cut across the Temple Mount, was deflected. The highest point of the rock at the southeast corner, which faces the Kidron Valley, was 47 meters (c. 154 ft.) lower than the level of the planned Temple area. Herod therefore had this space filled with stones and earth to the height of 30 meters (c. 98 ft.), on top of which he built a vaulted structure 88 meters (c. 290 ft.) long (known today as "Solomon's Stables").

The Mishnah (Mid. 1:3) mentions only five gates to the Temple Mount: the two gates of Huldah on the south, Coponius' Gate in the west (called after *Coponius the first Roman procurator of Judea), the Gate of Tadi in the north, and the Shushan Gate in the east. This description fits the archaeological findings except for the western side. Two gates and a bridge have been found on this side. According to the statement of Josephus there were four gates on the west (Ant. 15:401). On the south the remains of two gates have been found, known today as the "Double Gate" and the "Triple Gate." From these gates vaulted underground passageways lead up to the area on the Temple Mount. Of the "Double Gate" there remains the threshold to the lintel, which is from the period of the Second Temple, and also the entrance hall containing a central pillar and four arches, in two of which some decoration is still discernible; this too apparently dates from Temple times. Of the "Triple Gate" only a portion of the original doorpost remains. The width of the passageways is 5.5 meters (c. 18 ft.), and in the "Double Gate" 11 meters (c. 36 ft.). In the Western Wall an arch and a bridge have been discovered (Wilson's Arch) which connected the Temple Mount with Herod's palace (at the site of the present "citadel"). Another gate, on the southern side of the Western Wall, is now known as Barclay's Gate. The length of its lintel is 7.5 meters (c. 25 ft.) and its height 2.08 meters (c. 7 ft.). The threshold of this gate is lower than all the others and steps apparently led down from it to the Tyropoeon Valley. One of these two gates may possibly be identified with the Coponius Gate of the Mishnah. At the southern end of the Western Wall remains are still visible which are known as "Robinson's Arch" (see *Jerusalem). The Gate of Tadi had no lintel, but consisted of two stones slanting against each other, a triangular form witnessing to the gate's antiquity (Mid. 2:3). On the doors of the Shushan Gate was a picture of Persepolis. This gate, which was undoubtedly on a direct axis with the Temple, was south of the "Mercy Gates" (i.e., the "Golden Gates") which can be seen in the Eastern Wall today. The Eastern Wall was lower than all the others, so as not to obstruct the view of the sanctuary from the eyes of the priest burning the *red heifer on the top of the Mount of Olives (Mid. 2:4).

From the Eastern Gate a bridge supported by arches spanned the Kidron Valley; it was called "the heifer's gangway" (Par. 3:10; Shek. 4:2). A second bridge, called "the scapegoat's gangway," extended from the southern end of the Eastern Wall toward the desert. Remains of it have been found close to the southeastern corner of the Temple Mount (Shek. 4:2).

The length of the walls of the Temple Mount were 281 meters (c. 915 ft.) on the south, 466 meters (c. 1520 ft.) on the east, 488 meters (c. 1590 ft.) on the west, and 315 meters (c. 1,025 ft.) on the north, a sum total of 1,550 meters (5,050 ft.; the area of the Temple Mount is 144,000 sq. m. (c. 169,000 sq. yds). Marks on the inside face of the Western Wall indicate that buttresses divided the upper portion of the wall into niches (like the wall surrounding the Cave of Machpelah at Hebron which is also Herodian). The wall had embrasures, and guards chosen from among the levites were posted at its corners and gates. Around the wall – at least at the southwestern end – was an adjoining plaza whose different levels were connected by steps. Shops were built on the lower levels underneath this plaza.

The Temple Square

The Temple square, which was open to everyone, including gentiles, lay within the wall. It was surrounded by porticos which at the northwest corner joined up with the Fortress of Antonia. The porticos consisted of two rows of columns, each one 25 cubits high, and their roofs were flat. The one on the east was thought to be the most ancient, and Josephus ascribes it to Solomon's day. It was known as "The Street of the House of the Lord," and as early as Ezra's day was used as a place for mass gatherings (Ezra 10:9). The largest and most famous of the porticos was that situated on the southern end of the Temple Mount, known as the "Royal Portico." According to Josephus (Ant. 15:415) it was 185 meters (c. 620 ft.) long. Since the southern wall of the Temple Mount is longer, it was apparently reached by steps leading up to it at either end. The "Royal Portico" had the form of a basilica, i.e., a central oblong hall with a colonnade leading out from each side. Between them ran four rows of columns, 7 meters (c. 23 ft.) high (hewn columns of this height have been found lying on stony terrain in several places in the Jerusalem area, such as have been discovered in Jerusalem in the Russian Compound, Maḥaneh Yehudah and elsewhere; they seem to have cracked in the course of being quarried and were therefore abandoned). The width of the central hall was 15 meters (c. 50 ft.), and its height 30 meters (100 ft.); the colonnades were 10 meters (c. 33 ft.) wide and 16 meters (c. 53 ft.) high. The porticos of the square as far as the *soreg* were thronged with people, and both merchants and *money changers were to be found there. The money changers (whom Jesus tried to remove; see Matt. 21:12; Mark 11:15; Luke 19:45) converted the light Roman coins to the Tyrian shekel which was thought to be equivalent in value to the "Holy Shekel." The merchants sold doves and whatever else was needed for the sacrifices. Here too preachers harangued the multitudes (Matt. 21:23ff.).

At the end of the court was a *soreg* (a stone lattice work) which surrounded the consecrated area – the Temple Mount proper in the narrow mishnaic sense, i.e., the "500 cubits by 500 cubits" (Mid. 2:1). According to the Mishnah (Mid. 2:3) the height of the *soreg* was 10 handbreadths (70 cm. = 28 in.), but Josephus states that it was 3 cubits (1.5 m. = 5 ft.); this latter measurement seems more appropriate for a fence to which were attached plaques written in Greek and Latin forbidding gentiles to pass that point on pain of death. Remains of these inscriptions bearing the Greek text (one complete plaque and one partly preserved) have been discovered in Jerusalem (in 1870 and 1936). Beyond the *soreg* were 14 steps and then the *ḥel* ("rampart"), which was 10 cubits (5 m. = 17 ft.) broad (Mid. 2:3; Wars 5:195–7). Beyond the *ḥel* were the wall of the main forecourt (*azarah*), and the Court of the Women (*ezrat nashim*). In the outer court were the store-chambers for the shekels and the Temple vessels, and also "*shofarot*" (chests in the form of horns, i.e., narrow at the top, where the opening was, and wider lower down) for the donations (*terumot*) of the people (Shek. 2:1).

The Courts

The Court of the Women (Mid. 2:5) was situated at the east of the Temple Court (before the Court of the Israelites and Priests). It was square, each side being 135 cubits long, and was not roofed over. In each of its four corners were square chambers (40 × 40 cubits) also unroofed (but apparently surrounded by porticos as a protection against the rain). At the southeast corner was the Nazirites' chamber, at the northwest the lepers'; the southwestern chamber was used for the storage of oil and that on the northeast for wood. A balcony surrounded the Court of the Women, from which the women used to watch the celebrations of the Feast of the Waterdrawing (*Simḥat Bet ha-Sho'evah*) on the nights of Sukkot. The Court of the Women had four gates: the eastern one was very large (35 m. = c. 115 ft. high) and like the rest of the gates of the Temple (except for "Nicanor's Gate") was overlaid with plates of silver and gold (Wars 5:204–5). Secondary doors led into the Court of the Women from the north and from the south. The western gate was called *Nicanor's Gate. Josephus uses the name Corinthian Gate – apparently because its brass plating was embossed with a highly artistic decoration of Corinthian work, and this is why Acts (3:2, 10) refers to it as the "Beautiful Gate." It was reached by an ascent of 15 steps, which were not rectangular, as were all the other stairs on the Temple Mount, but in the form of a semicircle (Mid. 2:5). On either side of the staircase (whose height was 3.5 m. = c. 12 ft.) were chambers (underneath the Court of the Israelites) in which the levites stored their musical instruments. Nicanor's Gate had two wicket doors. Next to it the *sotah* ("wayward woman") was given the "waters of bitterness" to drink. According to the Mishnah, *Yoma* 3:6, Queen Helena had a golden tablet made on which the biblical passage concerning the *sotah* was engraved, and it was probably set up here.

From the Court of the Women one ascended to the Court of the Israelites, which was actually that portion of the Court of the Priests open to all male Jews. Both of these courts were enclosed by an inside wall 20 meters high, on top of which were exhibited enemy spoils taken by the Hasmoneans and Herod. The Court of the Israelites' was long and narrow (135 × 11 cubits). It was set off from the Court of the Priests by blocks of large polished ashlars and according to others by the levites' stand and stairs leading up to it, so that the Court of the Priests was 2½ cubits higher than that of the Court of Israelites. At the back of the Court of the Israelites, on either side of Nicanor's Gate, were two chambers: the northern one (to the right) was the chamber of Phinehas, keeper of the vestments, and the southern one (to the left) the chamber of the makers of the *ḥavitin* ("cakes"; Mid. 1:4); these chambers seem to have opened on to the Court of the Priests. On the holidays the public used to crowd the narrow area allotted them – particularly on the Festival of Passover, and on the Festival of Sukkot at the close of the Sabbatical Year, when the king used to stand upon a wooden dais erected for the occasion (Sot. 7:8), to read the biblical portion traditionally assigned to him. Non-priests used to enter the Court of the Priests only for the purpose of "laying their hands" on the animal being sacrificed, for its slaughtering, and in the waving of the portions of the sacrificial animal (Kelim 1:8).

Most of the sacrificial rites took place in the Court of the Priests. The measurements of this court were 187 × 135 cubits, and it surrounded the sanctuary proper on all sides. In it stood the large altar which had a square base, each side measuring 32 cubits. It was at least 16 cubits high and at each of its four corners were "horns." The base was whitewashed. At the southwest corner of the altar were two vents – one on each side – through which the blood of the sacrifices drained, flowing from there through a conduit which eventually led to the Kidron. Underneath this corner, a slab a cubit square was set in the floor, which could be raised in order to reach underneath the altar to clean the conduits (Mid. 3:3). At this same corner there were also two cups into which the wine and the water libations were poured (Suk. 4:9). The altar was ascended by means of a ramp on its southern side, which was about half as wide as the altar itself. To the west of the ramp was an aperture where were placed the birds intended for a sin offering which had become disqualified for sacrifice prior to their removal to the place of their burning (Mid. 3:3; Tosef., Zev. 7:6). Between the altar and the front of the sanctuary proper was the laver, a copper appurtenance with twelve spigots, from which the priests washed their hands and feet. North of the altar was the slaughtering area where six rows of four rings were set in the floor, or perhaps four rows of six rings (Mid. 3:5). In front of the rings were light small marble pillars to which cedar beams were attached. Iron hooks were set into these blocks for the purpose of hanging sacrificed animals while they were skinned. Between the pillars were marble tables to facilitate preparing the sacrifices.

As indicated, the Court of the Priests was surrounded by a wall. There is a difference of opinion as to the number of gates which were to be found in it. According to *Middot* 1:4–5, and Josephus, *Antiquities* 15:418, there were seven gates (if one includes the Gate of Nicanor which properly speaking was not found at the entrance of the Court of the Priests, but rather in the Court of the Israelites which was open to the Court of the Priests). However elsewhere, in *Middot* (2:6), in *Shekalim* 6:3, and in Josephus' *Jewish Wars*, 5:198, the number is eight. The smaller number seems more likely. The names of the gates were as follows. From west to east on the northern end were the Gate of the Flame (*bet ha-moked*), the Gate of the Offerings, and the Gate of the Kindling (*niẓoẓ*) which had an upper story where a priestly guard was stationed, whereas the guard below was made up of levites. On the southern side were the Gate of the Fuel, the Gate of the Firstlings, and the Water Gate (which was situated close to the laver within the Court of the Priests and the water conduit on the outside). The chambers of the *azarah* (the Temple Court) were between the gates (and sometimes above them). Their number too is uncertain. According to *Middot* 5:3 there were six. In addition, two "houses" were situated near the outer wall, one of which (the *bet ha-moked*) contained four chambers. Some of the chambers were situated partly inside and partly outside the sanctuary. Others were entirely within its area and some entirely without. If it is assumed that the order of the chambers in the *azarah* coincides with the order of the gates, then to the north were the chamber of the salt, the *parvah* chamber (Jastrow, following Maimonides, takes it to be a Persian proper name; others assume it comes from the Hebrew word *parvah* "animal skin"), and the rinsing chamber. Between the first two chambers stood the *bet ha-moked*, which also served as an entrance to the court, and contained four chambers, two inside and two outside the consecrated area, with blocks of polished stone separating them.

On the southwest was the Chamber of the (Lamb) Sacrifices, on the southeast the Chamber of the Shewbread Makers. On the northeast was the chamber containing the remnants of the defiled altar stored by the Hasmoneans, and on the northwest corner was the descent to the Chamber of Ritual Immersion (*bet ha-tevilah*; Mid. 1:6). The approach to it was through a *mesibbah* (a winding staircase going underground) which is perhaps to be identified with the long cistern (no. 1) that extends northward from under the Dome of the Rock. The Chamber of Ritual Immersion itself may be the cistern (no. 3), which contains several rooms. The *bet ha-moked* was a sizable edifice covered by a dome. Broad slabs of stone were set into the inner circumference of the building, and upon them the priests of the watch slept. From the Rinsing Chamber (*lishkat ha-madiḥim*) another *mesibbah* led to the roof of the *parvah* chamber, where was situated the ritual bath in which the high priest immersed himself on the Day of Atonement. In spite of the fact that it was in an upper story, it was nevertheless on a lower level than the aqueduct reaching the Temple Court from the spring of Etam (Yoma 31a). South of the Temple Court was the Wood Chamber, the Chamber of the Bowl (containing the Cistern of the Bowl), and the Chamber of Hewn Stone, where the Sanhedrin sat (this chamber certainly adjoined the Court of the Israelites). Between these two chambers was the chamber of the house of *Avtinas, where the incense was prepared. It was situated above the Water Gate and the high priest's chamber was outside it. The gates of the *azarah* were 20 cubits high and 10 cubits wide; they were approached from the *ḥel* by means of 12 steps (Mid. 2:3; according to Josephus five steps, but this number seems to be too small). The western side, where the *devir* (Holy of Holies) was, had no gates or steps, but *Shekalim* 6:3 concludes with the statement: "…and two in the west which had no names" (but cf. Mid. 1:4).

The Temple proper had the "form of a lion, narrow in the rear and broad at the front" (Mid. 4:7). The facade was square: 100 cubits wide and 100 cubits high. The rear of the building was the same height but it was only 70 cubits wide. The additional 30 cubits in the front consisted of two compartments, one on each side of the entrance hall. The facade was adorned with four pillars, possibly two stories high. Their capitals were certainly Corinthian. The building had a flat roof. The gate of the entrance hall was open and a large curtain was visible through it. Over the entrance were five wooden beams, narrow at the bottom and widening out at the top, laid between tiers of stone. The height of the entrance was 40 cubits and its breadth 20 (Mid. 3:7). The entrance hall itself was narrow, only 11 cubits. Along the ceiling joists of cedar were set, from which were suspended crowns (*atarot*) of gold, as well as golden chains which the young priests used to climb in order to clean and polish the crowns. Behind the entrance hall was the sanctuary (40 × 20 cubits), all of whose walls were plated with gold. The gate of the sanctuary was the "Great Gate" of the Temple, the turning of whose hinges was heard from afar (Tam. 3:8 "to Jericho"). It was 20 cubits high and 10 cubits broad and was shut by a bolt. It also had two wickets: the southern one was closed up, but the northern one served as a passageway to the compartment (*ta*) which led into the sanctuary. Over the gate of the sanctuary was the golden vine, to which the people used to donate a leaf or a pip of gold, or an entire cluster of grapes, which the priests would attach to it (Mid. 3:8).

Within the sanctuary stood the altar of incense, the table of shewbread, and the golden candelabrum with its appurtenances (the tongs and snuff-dishes). In the floor of the sanctuary was a loose marble slab, the dust from underneath which was used in the preparation of the "waters of bitterness." Around the sanctuary were 38 compartments arranged in three stories. Since the width of the walls diminished as they rose, the compartments in the upper stories were deeper than those below. On the north and south side there were five compartments on each level (i.e., 15 on either side), and on the western side there were eight compartments (three on the ground floor and the first floor, respectively, and two on the upper story). Within the wall against which the compartments were situated, there was a *mesibbah* which was reached through the compartment at the northeastern corner. This *mesibbah* led to the upper story of the sanctuary, which was 40 cubits high and contained wooden columns by means of which the flat roof of the upper story could be reached. With the upper story the height of the entire edifice was brought to the stipulated 100 cubits. The upper story was empty, and a row of polished ashlars (*pesifasin*) indicated the boundary between the sanctuary and the Holy of Holies below. Beyond this line were apertures in the floor of the upper story. When necessary, workmen were let down to repair the walls of the *devir* (Mid. 4:5). The Holy of Holies, which was situated at the western end of the sanctuary, was square (20 × 20 cubits). Two curtains separated it from the sanctuary. It contained no objects at all, and even the high priest entered it only once a year, on the Day of Atonement, in order to offer incense. The Mishnah (Kelim 1:6) defines ten degrees of sanctity which pertained to the different parts of the Temple and its environs: the Temple Mount was holier than the city of Jerusalem as a whole, the *ḥel* was holier than the outer portions of the Temple Mount, and so on in ascending degrees of sanctity, culminating in the Holy of Holies.

[Shmuel Safrai and Michael Avi-Yonah]

RITUAL

Sources

Tannaitic and amoraic literature contains a wealth of material describing the Temple ritual. Several mishnaic tractates, such as *Tamid, Middot*, and *Yoma*, are devoted to the description of the Temple ritual or they are based on the recollection of sages who lived when the Temple still stood, e.g., Simeon of Mizpah and Eliezer b. Jacob I, while priests and levites gave personal testimony as eyewitnesses. Eliezer b. Jacob is quoted as saying: "I forget for what purpose the Wood Chamber was used" (Mid. 5:4). Other rabbis who served as levites and priests in the Temple, such as R. Hanina Segan ha-Kohanim, R. Zadok, R. Johanan b. Gudgadah, and R. Joshua b. Hananiah, also report miscellaneous details. Many rabbinic traditions relating to the Temple ritual have been preserved and transmitted in almost every midrashic work and talmudic tractate. Second only to the Mishnah are Josephus' works: the *Wars*, several of the books of the *Antiquities*, particularly books 3, 5, and 20, and his *Contra Apionem*. Much information is to be found in the New Testament and in early Christian tradition. Because of the Temple's central position in the life of the people, almost all of the literature dating from the Second Temple period, such as the Letter of Aristeas, *Ben Sira (ch. 50), the Books of the Maccabees, the Testament of the Twelve Patriarchs, et al., make at least some mention of the Temple, and many of them treat it at length. The Greek and Roman writers also make passing mention of it in their writings concerning the Jews. Information with details of the Temple ritual dates for the most part from the generations immediately preceding its destruction. However, the general outlines of the ritual were set at the very beginning and the form of the Temple service hardly changed. Evidence of this continuity is the fact that the names of some of the most important functionaries in the Temple, such as the *segan, amarkal*, and the *gizbar* ("treasurer"), are of Persian and Assyrian origin and stem from long before the Hellenistic period.

Functionaries and Participants

PRIESTS. The priests officiated at the daily service. They alone were permitted to enter the sanctuary (*hekhal*) to approach the altar. They offered congregational sacrifices as well as those brought by individuals, burned the incense, lit the lamp in the sanctuary, and blessed the people. Even in respect to the tasks assigned to the levites, such as the singing of psalms and acting as gatekeepers, the priests participated, although maintaining their superior status. It was they who sounded the trumpets at the commencement of the singing and in the intervals between chapters. Wherever both priests and levites stood guard, the priests were stationed above, in the higher story, and the levites below (Mid. 1:5). Even those tasks whose performance was permitted by the *halakhah* to

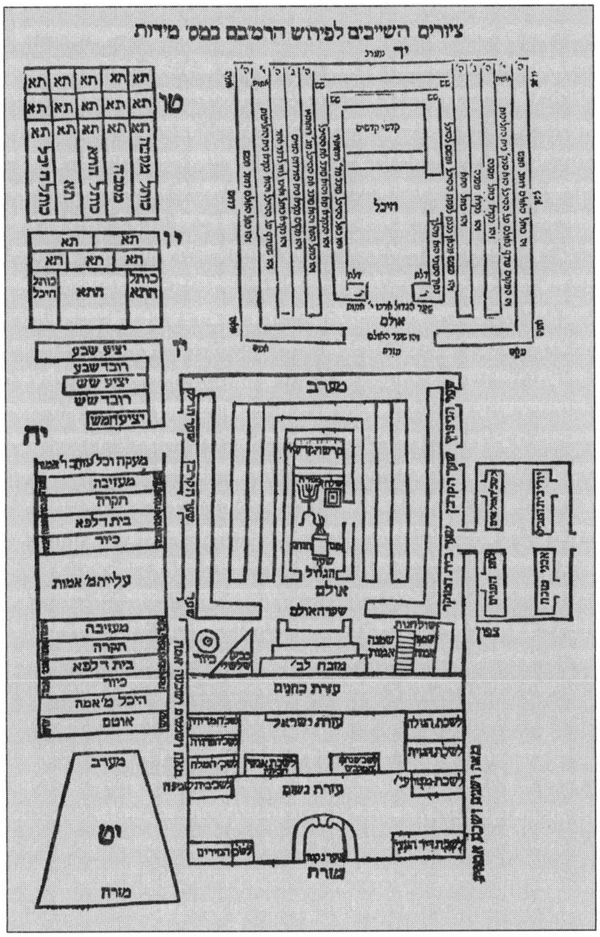

Floor plans of the Temple according to Maimonides. Lower right, general plan showing the various implements; upper right, detailed plan of the inner area. From the Babylonian Talmud, tractate Middot.

levites and Israelites at large – such as ritual slaughter of the animals to be sacrificed, and the accompanying of the scapegoat to the wilderness on the Day of Atonement – were not as a rule given over by the priests to others (Yoma 1:3). The priests were divided into 24 *mishmarot* ("divisions"), each of which served for a week at a time (see **Mishmarot and Ma'amadot*). About 20 priests were chosen by lot – the method used to assign the tasks connected with the Temple service – to offer the daily burnt offering (*tamid*), and in addition many more priests served in connection with offerings of individual sacrifices (Yoma 2; Tam. 3). Priests who came from the Diaspora were permitted to join their *mishmar*, except for those who had served in the Temple of Onias in Egypt (Men. 13:10). According to the letter of the law, a youth might begin to participate in the work of the Temple service as soon as he reached puberty, and was not disqualified "until he became old," no specific age being mentioned. However, "his brethren priests do not permit him to serve until he reaches the age of 20" (Ḥul. 24b; cf. Sif. Num. 63). Priests who were disqualified from participating in the Temple ritual because they had a physical blemish nevertheless went up with their *mishmar*, assisted in the work permitted them, in various secondary services, joined the other priests in the blessing of the people, and received their portion of the sacrifices since they were permitted to eat of them (Mid. 2:5; Tosef, Suk. 4:23). There is a wealth of sources attesting the faithfulness of the priests to the Temple and the Temple service, both in normal times and in hours of emergency. Even in times of famine the altar was served, nor did the priests touch the Temple food stores. When Pompey conquered Jerusalem and besieged the Temple, the priests continued with their ritual tasks in spite of the battering of the rams, and even when the Roman soldiers broke into the Temple and massacred the assembled people they went on with their sacred duties (Jos., Ant. 14:67).

LEVITES. During the Second Temple period all tasks directly connected with the offering of the sacrifices were taken away from the levites. In the descriptions of the Temple service in books dating from the beginning of the period, such as Ezra, Nehemiah, and Chronicles, the levites are always mentioned too, but in similar descriptions in later writers, such as Ben Sira and I Maccabees, the levites no longer appear. During the greater part of the Second Temple period, the only functions of the levites were as singers and gatekeepers; whereas the priests with their trumpets stood right by the altar, the choir of levites was stationed on a dais located on the boundary between the Court of the Priests and the Court of the Israelites (Mid. 2:10). The division of the levites by family, mentioned in I Chronicles 9, into choir members and gatekeepers was strictly preserved until the destruction of the Temple (Ar. 11b; Jos, Ant. 20:218). The gatekeepers were responsible for the supervision of the Temple visitors with a view to forbidding anyone ritually impure from entering its precincts. They also saw to the physical cleanliness and the general servicing of the Temple (Philo, Spec. 156, Praem. 6). They stood guard within the Temple day and night, and locked the Temple gates at the proper times. Shortly before the Temple's destruction, the Sanhedrin ruled that the levites were permitted to wear the priestly linen garb (Ant. 20:216). Like the priests, the levites were also divided into 24 divisions, but the further subdivision into *battei av* ("families") does not seem to have existed.

ISRAELITES. Jews who were neither priests nor levites, namely, Israelites, visited the Temple either:

(a) in order to offer sacrifices and to fulfill other ritual obligations connected with the Temple such as the bringing of gifts and offerings, the stipulated sacrifice after childbirth, or upon the purification from the defilement of leprosy, and so on;

(b) in order to pray there, particularly at the hours of the sacrifices but at other hours as well; or

(c) to serve in the Temple in addition to the priests as members of the *ma'amadot* (divisions of popular representatives deputed to accompany the daily services in the Temple with prayers).

In addition to the offering of the regular sacrifices, and the optional ones, such as those brought in connection with vows and freewill offerings, Nazirites came to the Temple when they completed the period of their vow bringing their sacrifice and cutting their hair; the lepers after their period of defilement brought an offering; and many came to the Temple to become purified from the defilement of contact with a dead person; etc. However, many people came to the Temple, not because of any ritual obligation, but simply to witness the service, most of which was performed in the open court. According to Luke (1:10) the people used to gather for prayer particularly at the time of the offering of the incense in the sanctuary, after the sacrificing of the daily burnt offering (*tamid*), in order to receive the priestly benediction, since the priests blessed the people after offering the incense. They also came to prostrate themselves before God at the time of the intonement of the daily hymn at the completion of the Temple service (Ecclus. 50; Tam. 7). The institution of the *ma'amadot* (see **Mishmarot and Ma'amadot*) was based upon the idea that the daily and festival sacrifices were obligatory upon the community as a whole, and that the priests were the emissaries not of God, but of the people (Sif. Zut., Shelaḥ, beginning). Every individual was obliged to give the half-shekel for the communal offerings and, contrary to the views of the Sadducees, "no individual may donate the daily sacrifice" (Men. 65a), nor could "the sacrifice of an individual be offered if he was not present." For the same reason the members of the *ma'amad* stood by the priests while they offered up the daily sacrifices, and afterward they assembled for prayers and scriptural readings, and also fasted (Ta'an. 4:2; et al.).

Before a non-priest entered the Court he ritually immersed himself even if he was levitically clean (TJ, Yoma 3:3, 40b). A person had to remove his shoes before entering the Temple Mount, and many people made a point of dressing themselves in white (Jos., Wars beginning of Book II et passim). The Temple was open to all Israelites. Only those who had been excommunicated were prevented from entering the Temple (Eduy. 5:6; Jos., Ant. 19:332). Except for perpetrators of particularly heinous sins, sacrifices were also accepted from everyone: "sacrifices are accepted from the hands of transgressors so that they may repent" (Ḥul. 5a). In contrast to the customary practice in the other temples in the Orient, a person coming to the Temple in Jerusalem to offer a sacrifice did not have to make any payment for the privilege of sacrificing. He even received the necessary wood gratis from the Temple's stockpile (Sifra 14; Men. 21b). Those who visited the Temple did not turn their backs upon it when they went out, but rather went round the Temple Mount, keeping to the right and emerging by the gate on the left. On their way they prostrated themselves 13 times. According to one tradition, these prostrations corresponded to the 13 gates, but according to another they corresponded to the 13 breaches which the kings of Greece had made, and in this way they gave thanks to God for the repair of the breaches (Mid. 2:2; Shek. 6:1).

THE OFFICERS OF THE TEMPLE. A regular staff supervised and instructed the divisions of priests and levites, who were relieved every week. These officials distributed the various duties among the priests of the *mishmar* by lot, supervised the watch, announced the opening and locking of the gates, regulated the sale of the libations and the birds for the sacrifices, and directed the details of the service. A partial list of these regular officials has been preserved in *Shekalim* chapter 5 and in the Tosefta chapter 2. The list contains mostly priests, but for the less important tasks levites are also mentioned. The positions seem to have been largely hereditary. Thus it is related that *Bet Garmu, who were appointed over the preparation of the shewbread, and the *Avtinas family, who prepared the incense, kept the technical details a secret within their own clan and refused to divulge them to others (TJ, Shek. 5:2, 49a). Besides those appointed over specific tasks, *gizbarim* ("treasurers") and *amarkalim* ("trustees") are mentioned. They did not deal with the daily work, but were responsible for the general administration of the Temple, as well as for the various Temple magazines and treasuries. In the hands of the *amarkalim* were the keys to the storehouses, and the *gizbarim* assessed the value of people, animals, or objects dedicated to the Temple, for the purpose of their redemption, superintended the collection of the half-shekel, the provision of the requirements for the altar, etc. The *gizbarim* and the *amarkalim* are usually mentioned together in the sources. Constituting a sort of governing body at the head of the Temple, they were related by blood to the high priesthood (Tosef., Men. 13:21), and represented the priestly order as a whole. To the list of Temple officials should be added two *catholici* (controllers of the Temple treasury). In order of importance the *catholicos* was between the high priest and the *amarkal* and the *gizbar* (TJ, Shek. 5:3, 49a), but the sources do not contain any details concerning the functions of this office. The officials served in pairs (except for two offices expressly stated in the Mishnah to have been held by a single official) since "authority may not be exercised over the community [in matters of money] by less that two [officers]": there were never fewer than three *gizbarim* and seven *amarkalim*.

THE HIGH PRIEST AND HIS DEPUTY. At the head of the Temple was the high priest. Since in the days of the Second Commonwealth, the Second Temple enjoyed a central position in the life of the people, the high priest stood at the head of the people during most of this period. His position in the Temple found expression in his unique golden garb (which consisted of eight golden vestments), in the offering of the *ḥavitin* ("cakes") in the name of the high priest together with the *tamid* sacrifice in the morning and in the afternoon, and in his independence of the division of the service among the *mishmarot* and *battei av*, for he could offer animal sacrifices and incense whenever he chose (Tam. 7:3). The high priest officiated at the Temple on the Sabbath and on holidays, particularly on Sukkot, which was celebrated in great pomp with the participation of great masses of people (TJ, Ḥag. 2:4, 78b; Jos., Wars 5:230; I Macc. 10:15–21). Especially striking was the part he played in the service of the Day of Atonement, which was performed entirely by the high priest himself. The most awesome moment of the service was the entrance of the high priest into the Holy of Holies to offer the incense – this being the only time during the entire year that anyone at all entered the Holy of Holies. The high priest also officiated on special occasions, such as the burning of the red heifer, and he read from the Torah at the close of the Sabbatical Year (see *Hakhel*).

Second in importance to the high priest was the *segan*, the chief of the priests. He attended the high priest when he ministered (Tam. 7:3) and supervised the sacrificing of the *tamid* and the regular daily Temple service in general. The *segan* is identical with the *strategos* mentioned by Josephus and the Christian Gospels. At the end of the Second Temple period the Pharisees ensured that the high priests, who were of the Sadducean faction, nevertheless performed the service in the proper Pharisaic manner. One of the means of Pharisaic control was the *segan*, who attended the high priest when he ministered and so could see that he did not deviate from the form prescribed by Pharisaic teaching. The holders of the office of *segan* who are known by name were all Pharisees.

The Daily Service

The essential element of the daily Temple service was the offering of the *tamid* sacrifice of two lambs, one in the morning, with which the service began, and one in the afternoon, with which it concluded. Between the two, sacrifices offered by individuals were brought: freewill offerings (*nedavah*), burnt offerings (*olah*), peace offerings (*shelamim*), thanks offerings (*todah*), and meal offerings (*minḥah*) of various sorts; and obligatory sacrifices: sin offerings (*ḥatta'ot*), guilt offerings (*asham*), and all the various sacrifices connected with the rites of levitical purification of both men and women. The Bible contains no allusion to prayers accompanying the sacrifices. In the Second Temple, prayers, blessing, and Pentateuchal readings were added to the Temple service. After the offering of the incense, the priests gathered together on the steps of the entrance hall and blessed the assembled people with the *Priestly blessing (Tam. 7:2). As the high priest entered the Holy of Holies on the Day of Atonement, he used to say a short prayer, and at the conclusion of his ministration he read certain portions from the Bible. During the offering of the incense the people used to gather in the *azarah* for prayer. The libation of wine at the conclusion of every *tamid* sacrifice was accompanied by levitical singing. After the service the members of the division of Israelites deputed to accompany the daily Temple services gathered for Scripture reading and prayer.

On the Sabbath, new moons, and festivals, a *musaf* ("additional sacrifice") of the day was offered immediately following the morning *tamid*. The number of animals offered at the *musaf* sacrifice differed on the different holidays. Besides the *musaf*, the special ceremonies peculiar to the festival were performed, such as the bringing of the *Omer* on the second day of Passover, the two breads on Shavuot, the procession with the *lulav* ("palm branch") and the libation of water on Sukkot. The special ceremonies performed on the festivals, both those of biblical origin and those which were instituted only during the Second Temple period, were for the most part related to the changing seasons of the year, and the masses of pilgrims who had gathered in Jerusalem for the holiday usually took part in them as spectators if not as actual participants.

THE MORNING TAMID. The daily service began shortly after dawn with the proclamation: priests to their service (*avodah*); levites to their stand (*dukhan*), and Israelites to their post (*ma'amad*) (TJ, Shek. 5:2, 48d). The first act was the removal of ashes of the burnt sacrifices (*deshen*), since the whole night through a fire burned on the altar and consumed the limbs of the sacrifice placed upon it. Those who wished to draw lots for the privilege of performing this service arose early and performed their ritual ablution (*tevilah*) before the appointed official arrived. After the lots were drawn, the officer would open the wicket in the gate leading from the *bet ha-moked* to the *azarah* and the priests entered the court, "and they took with them two burning torches, and they divided into two groups. One went around the *exedra* [covered porch] eastward, and the other westward, seeing to it that all was in order, until they met at the chamber of the makers of the *ḥavitin* [situated at the southern side of the Gate of Nicanor which was at the east]. After both groups arrived and announced: 'All is in order,' they set the makers of the *ḥavitin* cakes to their task" (Tam. 1:3). The priest who had drawn the lot to remove the *deshen* approached the altar alone, but immediately after he began the task his fellow priests ran up and joined him until all the ashes had been removed. The priest who removed the ashes also arranged the wood on the altar for the burning of the sacrifices and the coals for the incense. After placing the wood on the altar, the priests gathered in the Chamber of Hewn Stone, where lots were then drawn for the privilege of performing the different tasks connected with the offering of the *tamid* sacrifice. Of the 13 priests chosen, nine were assigned to the sacrificial animal itself and four to the ancillary tasks of removing the ashes from the inner altar in the sanctuary, the offering of the meal offerings, and the wine libation (Tam. 3; Yoma 2:3). After the sanctification of their hands and feet they awaited the time appointed for the slaughtering. When the priest who had gone up to look out announced that the entire eastern horizon had become light "even unto Hebron," they began to bring the lamb and the necessary instruments and vessels, and at this time too those who had drawn the privilege of performing the necessary tasks within the sanctuary went to perform their appointed duties: to remove the ashes from the inner altar and from the candelabrum and to open the gates of the sanctuary, which remained open during the entire service.

Trumpets were sounded as the gates were opened. The priest whose task it was to remove the ashes from the inner altar and cleanse the candelabrum was first to enter. The priest who removed the ashes from the altar put them into a basket (*tene*) which he set by the side of the altar. The residual matter removed from the candelabrum was placed in a *kuz* (an oil vessel the shape of a large wine cup). If he found the two easternmost wicks burning the priest did not rekindle the rest, since the candelabrum as a whole was filled and lit only in the evening. But if he found them extinguished he cleaned them first, and then lit them from the flame of the other wicks, or, if necessary, from the altar fire, afterward cleaning the rest of the lights and preparing them for lighting in the evening. He then set the *kuz* on the second of the three steps leading up to the candelabrum and departed. It was then that the *tamid* was slaughtered (Tam. 3; Suk. 3:5). After the slaughter of the *tamid* and the preparation of its limbs for offering upon the altar, the priests gathered in the Chamber of Hewn Stone and with the people read the Ten Commandments, the three paragraphs of the *Shema*, and their benedictions (Tam. 5:1; Yoma 37b; and cf. Ber. 11b–12a).

When they finished, the Temple official called out: "New candidates for the offering of the incense come and draw lots." Only those who had never had the privilege of performing this function participated in the drawing. Then the last lot, which was for the privilege of bringing the limbs of the sacrifice to the altar, was drawn. The distribution of all the tasks connected with the *tamid* sacrifice completed, those priests who had not been chosen to take part in the service departed and took off their sacred vestments (Tam. 5). The priest who had drawn the lot for the offering of the incense gave the *maḥtah* ("firepan") to the priest who stood next to him for him to gather coals from the outer altar and help in the preparations for the offering of the incense. When the two priests reached the point between the entrance hall and the altar, one took the *magrefah* (apparently a musical instrument in the Temple, shaped like a shovel) announcing with it to the priests and the assembled multitude in the Temple to be ready for the solemn moment. The priests drew nearer in order to enter the sanctuary and prostrate themselves following the offering of the incense, the levites readied themselves for their choir duties, and the head of the *ma'amad* took the ritually unclean who had come to the Temple in order to be cleansed and brought them to the Gate of Nicanor. Then the two priests ascended the steps of the hall, preceded by those who had cleared the ashes from the altar and the candelabra. They now removed the vessels which they had previously set down. The priest who had cleaned the candelabrum now also cleaned the two easternmost wicks. The westernmost one was left burning – for this was the eternal flame which burned day and night. The priest who had gathered the coals entered the sanctuary first, scattered them over the incense altar, prostrated himself, and departed. Then the priest who was chosen by lot to offer the incense entered, bearing the pan of incense in his hand. He was accompanied by a priest appointed for this task who instructed him in the proper ritual, and he did not offer it until he was told: "Offer the incense!" The officiating priest waited until the space between the hall and the altar was cleared of people, offered up the incense, prostrated himself, and departed (Tam. 6; Kelim end of ch. 1). During the offering of the incense in the sanctuary, the people used to gather in the *azarah* for prayer, and even outside the Temple these times were set aside for prayer (cf. Luke 1:10; Judith 9:1). After the departure of the priest who had offered the incense, all the priests filed into the sanctuary, prostrated themselves, and went out again. Those who had served inside the sanctuary stood with their serving vessels on the steps of the hall while the rest of the priests, upon leaving the sanctuary, stood to their left and blessed the people with the priestly blessing (Num. 6:23–25), with outstretched hands, pronouncing the ineffable name as it is written (Tam. 7:2; Sot. 7:6; Kid. 71a; Philo, Mos. 114; Jos., Ant. 2:275). In earlier times the high priest himself used to bless the people, but at the end of the Second Temple period, even when the high priest was present the blessing was pronounced by all the priests together (Kid. 71a). When the ineffable name was pronounced, the people fell upon their faces (Ecclus. 50:21., Eccles. R. 3:11).

After the priestly benediction came the last part of the service, the lifting of the limbs of the sacrifice on to the outer altar, the offering of the meal offering (*minḥat solet*), and the libation of the wine upon the altar. Before the libation, trumpets were sounded. When they were about to pour the libation, the *segan* signaled with a scarf (as a flag), and Ben Arza sounded the cymbal, and "the levites raised their voices in song." The levites' choir completed the service attendant upon the offering of the *tamid* of the morning (Tam. 7).

THE AFTERNOON TAMID. At the eighth and a half hour the private sacrifices were concluded and the offering of the afternoon *tamid* was begun. The order of the service was the same as that of the morning *tamid*, except for the arrangement of the wood on the altar and the priestly benediction, which took place in the morning only. In the evening two logs were placed upon the altar to keep the fire burning all night, the oil in the candelabrum was replenished, and all seven lights were lit. All those who were chosen by lot for the morning service also served in the evening, except for the priest who had offered the incense (TJ, Yoma, 2:3, 39d; Sif. Zut., Pinḥas, end). Following the afternoon *tamid* the gates of the sanctuary were closed. The exact hour for this is not mentioned but from various talmudic references it may be concluded that it was close to sunset. The gates of the Court were shut, but some priests remained inside to offer the limbs and entrails which had not been consumed during the day. They also replenished the altar with wood so that the flame should not die out. Probably they entered the *azarah* through one of the wickets which led from the *bet ha-moked*, where the priests spent the night (Zev. 9:6; Ber. 1:1). Toward evening the priests partook of their meal of the sacrificial meat and bread. The *tamid* sacrifice was the essential part of the Divine Service. All sections of the populace were most loyal and devoted to the Temple and its service and were willing to go to extreme measures in order that the regular sacrifice of the daily *tamid* should continue uninterrupted – even in the days of the direst distress which fell upon the city and the Temple (Sot. 49b).

The Sabbath

Individual sacrifices were not brought on the Sabbath, but all the work attendant upon the offering of communal sacrifices was permitted; fire was lit on the altar, the *tamid* was slaughtered, the incense was offered, and the lights were lit, but care was taken that whatever could be done beforehand was done on the eve of the Sabbath. In addition to the *tamid* sacrifice, the additional Sabbath sacrifice of two sheep was offered and the shewbread was laid out (Men. 11 and Tosef. ad loc.). On the Sabbath the *mishmar* changed after the *musaf* sacrifice (Tosef., Suk. 4:24), but the priests of the second *mishmar* came to the Temple in the early morning, since in the morning prayer the outgoing *mishmar* blessed the incoming one: "May He Who caused His name to dwell in this House, let dwell among you love and brotherhood, peace and friendship" (Ber. 12a). The daily hymn of the *musaf* sacrifice was the biblical portion "*Ha'azinu*" (Deut. 32), which was divided into six sections, one section being sung each Sabbath (RH 32a). After the *musaf* sacrifice, the shewbread was set out; the new bread being brought in and the old bread removed and distributed among the priests. This was the first task performed by the new *mishmar*. The loaves, baked before the eve of the Sabbath and placed upon a marble table in the entrance hall, were set out by four priests, two of whom held the two sets of loaves (six to each set), and two the two censers of white frankincense (*levonah*). Four other priests preceded them in order to remove the bread and censers from the preceding Sabbath. While one set of priests removed the old shewbread, the other immediately replaced it with fresh loaves. The bread was laid out in two rows and the censers of incense placed next to them. The loaves which had been removed were placed upon a golden table in the entrance hall and the old white frankincense was offered up, which made the old shewbread permitted to the priests for their consumption. The bread was divided among the outgoing and the incoming *mishmar* alike. Legend relates that in olden times, in the days of Simeon the Just, "a blessing was bestowed upon… the shewbread, so that every priest, who obtained a piece thereof as big as an olive, ate and became satisfied, some even leaving something over. From that time on a curse was sent… so that every priest received a piece as small as a bean; the decorous [priests] withdrew their hands from it, while the voracious ones took and devoured it" (Yoma 39a).

The sacrificial meat apportioned to the priest when he officiated, had for the most part to be eaten in the Court by men only; no more than a small portion of it was permitted to be eaten outside the Temple precincts but within the boundaries of Jerusalem, and even some of this could not be brought home for the private consumption of the priest's family. All that he could take with him were the hides, which were distributed among the priests of the officiating division, and the Pharisaic sages contended bitterly with the aristocracy of the priesthood in an attempt to make them deal fairly with the ordinary priests in this matter (Tosef., Men. 13:18–19).

The Pilgrim Festivals

During the festivals, when great multitudes went up to Jerusalem, the order of the service was different because, in addition to the statutory sacrifices, time had to be found for the offering of the many sacrifices brought by the pilgrims. Their obligatory offering (*olat re'iyyah*) was sacrificed on the festival itself, while their voluntary sacrifices were offered during the intermediate days (Beẓah 2:4 and the ensuing discussion in both the Jerusalem and Babylonian Talmuds). To make time for all these sacrifices, the service was begun at an earlier hour. Normally the ashes were removed from the altar when the *gever* (either "cock" or "Temple crier") sounded, or approximately at that time, either slightly earlier or later. On the Day of Atonement they were removed at midnight, and on the festivals at the beginning of the first watch; "by the time the cry of the *gever* was heard, the Temple Court was already teeming with visitors [Israelites]" (Yoma 1:8). Josephus (Ant. 18:29) states that on the festivals the Temple gates were opened for the public from midnight on. In order to encourage uninhibited access to the Temple, a lenient view was taken on the festivals with regard to laws of ritual purity, both in the city and in the Temple itself (Jos., Ant. 18:29; Ḥag. 3:7). During the festival the curtain which normally hung at the entrance to the sanctuary was rolled up to enable the people to view the Holy of Holies, and the holy vessels and appurtenances were even brought out into the *azarah* in full view of the pilgrims (Jos., Ant. 3:128; Yoma 54b; Ḥag 3:7). On the festivals priests of all the *mishmarot* came up to Jerusalem, both from Ereẓ Israel and from the Diaspora, and they were all permitted to partake of the meat from the festival sacrifices (Suk. 5:7; Men. 11:7. For the sacrifices offered on the different festivals see under their respective titles.)

Temple Music

This included both choir singing and musical instruments. Music accompanied the daily *tamid* offering both on weekdays and holidays, the *musaf* sacrifices, the offerings of the people, their processions, and their assemblies. The texts sung were mostly Psalms, selected poetical sections of the Pentateuch such as the *Shirat ha-Yam* (Ex. 15) and *Ha'azinu*. The Pentateuch mentions only two trumpets in connection with divine service. In the later biblical books all the musical instruments are already mentioned, though not in conjunction with the *tamid* sacrifice. The masoretic text of the Bible contains a specific heading for Psalm 92 only, which was "For the Sabbath day," but in the Septuagint similar headings are found to the psalms for all the days of the week except for the psalm for the third day (i.e., Tuesday), which is chapter 82. Mishnaic sources mention lutes, lyres, and a cymbal in conjunction with the offering of the *tamid*, and on festivals flutes were added, particularly on occasions when there was large-scale public participation, such as the slaughtering of the Passover sacrifice, the *Simḥat Bet ha-Sho'evaḥ*, and the bringing of the firstfruits.

In the *baraita* appended to the end of the tractate *Tamid* the daily psalms chanted are enumerated: "The song which the levites used to sing in the Temple: On the first day [i.e., Sunday], they used to say [Ps. 24]: 'The earth is the Lord's and the fullness thereof, the world and they that dwell therein'" (Tam. 7:4), and so on for each day of the week. Other *beraitot* (in RH 31a; Suk. 55a) mention the psalms recited on most of the holidays and some of these are also confirmed by the headings found in the Septuagint. In addition to the daily psalms the *Hallel* (Ps. 113–118) was recited on the three festivals and on the eight days of *Ḥanukkah. On the festivals the *Hallel* was sung during the offering of the sacrifices of the people, and the flute was sounded at the same time. Special psalms were appointed for each festive occasion in the Temple: at the bringing of the firstfruits, Psalm 30; during the *Bet ha-Sho'evah* festivities, the 15 Songs of Ascent (Ps. 120–34); and so on.

The Mishnah states: "There may be no fewer than 12 levites participating on the [levite choir's] stand, and minor children from the families of the elite of Jerusalem were added to them to make the result more melodious." As for the musical accompaniment, the Mishnah states: "There may be no fewer than two lyres (*nevalim*) nor more than six; no fewer than nine harps (*kinnorot*), but as many as desired may be added; there is only one cymbal (*ẓilẓal*)" (Ar. 3:3–6). The flute (*ḥalil*) is always mentioned in the singular.

Gentiles and the Temple

Biblical law expressly permits the acceptance of sacrifices from gentiles (Lev. 22:25), and this was apparently the practice in the First Temple (I Kings 8:41–43). The number of such sacrifices became very large in the days of the Second Temple, and special regulations were made with respect to them. The rule is: "Vow offerings (*nedarim*) and freewill offerings (*nedavot*) are accepted of them" (Shek. 1:5). Gentiles are frequently mentioned as coming to the Temple from near and far in order to bring sacrifices (Pes. 3b; Jos., Ant. end of Book 3; John 12:20). It was decided that if a gentile sent a burnt offering from overseas, without the necessary accompanying libations, these must be provided out of public funds (Shek. 7:6; Sif. Zut. 15:2). The names of various gentile kings and princes who offered sacrifices in the Temple are known: e.g., Ptolemy III (Jos., Apion 2:5); Antiochus VII Sidetes, when he besieged Jerusalem in 133 B.C.E. (Ant. 13:242); Marcus Agrippa who offered up a hecatomb (100 burnt offerings) in the year 15 B.C.E. (Ant. 16:14); and Vitellius, the Roman governor of Syria who went up to Jerusalem especially in order to offer sacrifice in the Temple on Passover (Ant. 18:122). Josephus categorically states that the altar of the Temple in Jerusalem was held in high esteem by all Hellenic and non-Hellenic peoples (Wars 5:17), and the fame of the Temple reached all parts of the world (Wars 4:262; cf. Suetonius, *De Vita Caesarum*, Augustus 93). Besides the sacrifices received from gentiles, from the days that the exiles returned from Babylon a special sacrifice was offered for the welfare of the gentile ruler. Thus, sacrifices were offered for the well-being of the Persian monarch (Ezra 6:9–10), for Hellenistic kings, such as Demetrius I (I Macc. 7:33), and afterward for the well-being of the Roman emperors (Wars 2:197); according to one source (Philo, Embassy to Gaius 317) two lambs and a bull were offered daily (and cf. *ibid.* 157).

The Temple Treasury

The Temple had need of considerable amounts of gold and silver (II Macc. 3:4) for the purchase of the required sacrifices, for the ritual vessels, garments, and other utensils, for the administration, and for miscellaneous public expenses. In the course of time a great treasure accumulated in the store-chambers appointed for this purpose (Wars 6:282). Just as in the period of the First Temple, so during the days of the Second Temple money and precious vessels reached the Temple from various sources. When Judea was subject to foreign hegemony, the gentile kings sometimes covered the Temple expenses from their own treasury, or at any rate presented it with gifts to defray the cost of the upkeep. Darius donated the funds required for the completion of the Temple structure, and for the regular sacrifices, from the taxes gathered from the province "Beyond the River" (Ezra 6:8–17). Details are given of the gifts made by Artaxerxes (Ezra 7:20–23). According to the Letter of Aristeas 33, 40, 52–82, and Josephus (Ant. 12:40 ff.), Ptolemy Philadelphus presented a golden table and beautiful golden vessels to the Temple. Seleucus IV gave enough of his income to defray the entire costs of the sacrifices (II Macc. 3:3), and so did other Hellenistic kings (Ant. 13:78; Apion 2:48). Antiochus III donated 20,000 shekels for sacrifices and in addition great quantities of wheat, flour, and salt and all the materials which were necessary for repairs, including cedars of Lebanon (Ant. 12:140–1). Similarly Demetrius promised the "Jewish Nation" to consecrate the town of Acco (Ptolemaïs) to the Temple in order to defray the expenses from its taxes, and in addition 15,000 shekels from his own income (I Macc. 10:39–45). Roman rulers, like Sosius, who conquered Jerusalem for Herod (Ant. 14:488), Marcus Agrippa (Philo, Embassy to Gaius 37), Augustus Caesar and his wife Julia (Wars 5:562; Philo, Embassy to Gaius 157 ff.), and others (Jos., Wars 4:181; 2:413) gave all manner of gifts to the Temple (golden bowls, golden wreaths, etc.). Among the Jewish donors was Ben Kattin who donated 12 spigots and a machine (a pulley) for the laver (Yoma 3:10). King *Monobaz had the handles of all the vessels used on the Day of Atonement made of gold. His mother, Helena of Adiabene, commissioned a golden candelabrum and set it over the door of the sanctuary. Ben Gamala replaced the boxwood lots cast on the Day of Atonement in connection with the scapegoat which was sent off into the wilderness with gold ones (*ibid.*). The alabarch Alexander, Philo of Alexandria's brother, donated the gold and silver plating of the gates of the sanctuary (Wars 5:53). Nicanor of Alexandria donated the famous copper gates of Corinthian workmanship (Yoma 3:10). At the time of the construction of the Second Temple, Heldai, Tobijah, and Jedaiah from the *golah* (the returning Babylonian exiles) donated the golden crowns which were hung from the ceiling of the Temple (see above). Many people devoted houses and fields to the Temple, but since the Temple at Jerusalem did not keep landed property, it was sold and the proceeds deposited in the Temple treasury (Tosef., Shek. 2:15; Mish., Ar. 8). The Temple treasury also contained the deposits of individuals, such as widows and orphans (II Macc. 3:10), but particularly of the wealthy (such as Hyrcanus the Tobiad: II Macc. 3:11) "who deposited there the entire wealth of their house" (Jos., Wars 6:282). This portion of the treasure house was so vast that Josephus wrote that "it was the general repository of all Jewish wealth" (*ibid.*). However, the most important, or at any rate the steadiest, source of income was the half-shekel tax paid annually by every Jewish adult male from the age of 20 (on the basis of Ex. 30:14–15; cf. Philo, Spec. 1:76–78). These moneys were used to defray the expense of the offerings sacrificed for the entire community and other expenses (see later). The half-shekel was levied upon everyone – except women, slaves, and minors, and even from these it was accepted if offered (Shek. 1:5) – whether they lived in the land of Israel or in the Diaspora, but the wealthy used to give "golden drachmas" (Tosef., Shek. 2:4). In spite of temporary difficulties caused by gentiles on occasion (Jos., Ant. 14:110 ff.) the flow of money never stopped for any length of time. In the Roman period, rulers of cities and governors of provinces attempted to lay their hands on the funds or at least to place difficulties in the way of their collection and remission to Jerusalem, and one of the important privileges granted the Jews in the days of Julius Caesar and Augustus was the permission to collect and send the half-shekels to Jerusalem without hindrance. Augustus even included them in the category of "sacred money" and thus anyone stealing them was subject to the death penalty on the grounds of sacrilege (Cicero pro Flacco, 28; Jos., Ant. 14:215 et al.; 16:163 ff.). Collections made in Babylon were first deposited in the fortified cities of *Nisibis and *Nehardea and later transferred to Jerusalem under armed guard (Ant. 18:310–3). Every year, on the first of Adar, the *bet din ha-gadol* (the high court in Jerusalem) used to send out messengers to the provincial areas (in Judea), to announce publicly the obligation to bring the half-shekels in due time for them to be delivered to the Temple chamber on the first of Nisan (TJ, Shek. 1:1, 45d). On the 15th of Adar tables of money changers were set up in the country at large (Shek. 1:3), and on the 25th day they were set up in the Temple, and pledges were taken from those who could not pay (with the exception of the priests; *ibid.*). Both in the Temple and in the country at large *shofarot* were set up for this purpose. There were 13 *shofarot* in the Temple (Shek. 6:1, 5), each inscribed with the object for which the money collected was to be spent (i.e., "new shekels" for use during the coming year, "old shekels" to defray the expenses of the outgoing year, others for specific types of sacrifice, such as wood for the altar, incense, and the like). The money collected was divided into two parts: three *kuppot* ("large containers") of nine *se'ah* each were set aside as the *terumat ha-lishkah* (contribution to the Temple treasury chamber) and the rest was collected in a special container called the *sheyarei ha-lishkah* ("surplus funds"). The appropriations were made from the shekels in the Temple treasury chamber three times a year, 15 days before Passover, 15 days before Shavuot, and on the 29th of Elul. The money was used mainly for the purchase of the communal offerings and the incense (Shek. 4:1), but it was used as wages for those who watched the aftergrowths in the seventh year, with the object of gathering them for use in the communal offering, and for the women who wove curtains for the gates of the Temple (TJ, Shek. 4:3, 48a; Ket. 106a). In addition, the red heifer, as well as the scapegoat which was sent out into the wilderness on the Day of Atonement, were bought from these funds, as were the vestments of the high priest. The inspectors of animal blemishes in Jerusalem were also paid from the *terumot ha-lishkah*, as were the experts who taught the priests the laws of ritual slaughtering and those who examined the scrolls for mistakes. The money from the *sheyarei ha-lishkah* was used to defray the expenses of the erection of a special bridge across the Kidron Valley, and for the expenses connected with the altar of the burnt offerings, the sanctuary, and the courts (Shek. 4:2; TJ, Shek 4:3; 48a; according to Ket. 106b these expenses were covered by the funds donated for the maintenance of the Temple). The money was also for all the needs of the city of Jerusalem, especially the maintenance of the water system and the repair of the towers (Shek. 4:2; TJ, Shek. 4:3, 48a).

There was another treasury chamber in the Temple, where funds were collected for Temple repair. The income here was from the *arakhin* ("vows of valuations") and the consecrations in general (see Lev. 27 and Ar. 24a). There were also special chambers for freewill offerings. One was the chamber of anonymous gifts for those who wished to give charity anonymously: "sin-fearing persons used to insert their gifts therein secretly, and the poor of good family would be supported therefrom secretly" (Shek. 5:6). Another treasury was the "chamber of vessels" (in which 93 silver and gold vessels were stored which were used in the Temple service: Tam. 3:4) where donations of vessels to the Temple were received. Once every 30 days the treasurers would open it and any vessel they found inside that was of use for the repair of the Temple they left there; but the others were sold and their price went to the chamber of the repair of the Temple (Shek. 5:6).

A special store was created as a result of the obligation which the priests, levites, and people at large took upon themselves in the days of Ezra and Nehemiah (Neh. 10:35; 13:31) to bring "the wood offering at set times, every year, to keep the fire on the altar of the Lord our God, as it is prescribed in the Torah." Particular families undertook the obligation to donate wood on specific days of the year, because, according to tradition, "when the exiles to Babylon returned to Judea they found no wood in the Temple wood-chamber and the families here mentioned came forward and offered wood of their own. The prophets among them thereupon made it a condition that even should the chamber be full of wood at any time they should still continue to bring their offerings" (Ta'an. 28a). When they brought the wood they would offer freewill burnt offerings and that day was a festival for the family – one on which manifestations of mourning, fasting, and work were prohibited (*ibid.*). The Mishnah (Ta'an. 4:5) enumerates nine families who used to bring wood offerings on specific dates (which are also mentioned). Since almost all these families were among the returning exiles listed in the books of Ezra and Nehemiah, the list is based upon a tradition going back to the beginning of the Second Temple. The 15th of Av (Meg. Ta'an. to the 15th of Av; Jos., Wars 2:425) was set aside as the day of the "wood offering," on which all the people brought wood, and the atmosphere of the day was festive: "On that day the felling of trees for the altar fire was discontinued… because [from then on] they would not dry properly" (Ta'an. 31a). Generations after the destruction, the descendants of these families still celebrated the anniversary of their family's bringing the wood offering (Tosef., Ta'an. 4:6). The wood was stored in the wood chamber, and the priests who were physically blemished cared for and sorted the wood, because wormy wood was unfit for setting on the altar (Mid. 2:5).

Provision of the Temple's Needs

It was the duty of the Temple treasurers to purchase the animals for the communal sacrifices and to make animals available for purchase for private sacrifices when the potential donors found difficulty in bringing them themselves. Wine, fine flour, and oil were sometimes bought from the treasuries of the Temple because of the difficulties in bringing them posed by considerations of ritual purity. This was particularly so in respect to those from the Diaspora, since the Diaspora per se is defiling, and for gentiles it was impossible altogether. Many obligatory personal sacrifices consisted of doves, and many people also brought them as a freewill offering. Measures seem to have been taken to lessen the commercial traffic within the Temple precincts. The New Testament relates that Jesus chased the money changers and vendors of doves from the Temple precincts (Matt. 21:12; et al.). Toward the end of the Second Temple period, doves were no longer sold in the Temple precincts. Instead *shofarot* were set up in the Temple and anyone who was obliged to offer a pair of doves or wished to do so as a freewill offering dropped the appropriate sum into it, and each day sacrifices were offered in accordance with the amount in the *shofarot* (Shek. 6:5 and Tosef., Shek. 3:2–3). The Mishnah describes how those who came to sacrifice obtained their libation offerings. The individual came first to Johanan who was appointed over the seals, and gave him the proper sum, for which he received a seal. He then took the seal to Ahijah, who was appointed over the libations, gave it to him and received the libation in exchange (Shek. 5:4).

All sacrifices, whether individual or communal, could be brought either from Ereẓ Israel or from the Diaspora, and from new or old produce, except for the *Omer* (Men. 8:1), which had to be from barley grown in Ereẓ Israel. The Mishnah and Tosefta *Menaḥot* contain detailed traditions concerning the provenance of these communal offerings. The places were chosen either because the crop ripened early there, or because they were famous for the quality of their produce. Fine flour and wine came mainly from Judea, oil from Galilee, rams from Moab, calves from the Sharon, and lambs from the Hebron area. The doves were raised on the Mount of Olives and the King's Mountain (Men. 8, Tosef., Men. 9:13; Men. 87a; TJ, Ta'an. 4:8, 69a). The sources describe the salt as "the salt of Sodom." The Pentateuch mentions only four ingredients for the preparation of the incense (Ex. 30:34), but the tannaitic tradition which was considered to have Mosaic authority mentions 11 elements, to which were further added various other ingredients to make the smoke rise (Ker. 6a). According to a late tradition there were groves in the vicinity of Jerusalem for the cultivation of herbs for the incense (Song R., ed. Gruenhut to 4:13).

THE SIGNIFICANCE OF THE TEMPLE FOR THE PEOPLE

The returning exiles organized their lives around the altar and the Temple in Jerusalem, and, at least officially, the aim of those who returned to Judea in the wake of Cyrus' declaration was merely to restore the Temple (Ezra 1:1–5). In the course of time the Temple worship, which centered around the sacrificial rites, lost some of its position as the sole means by which the religious and communal life of the nation could find expression. To a considerable extent the center of gravity shifted to the study of the Torah, and the *synagogue and *bet midrash* gradually assumed an even greater importance. In the course of time the leadership of the people and the judicial functions ceased to be the sole prerogative of the priestly class. However, since all of these institutions and the basic concepts behind them were organically connected with the Temple service, it was through this channel that they became part of the life of the people. The synagogue, which is first mentioned during the Second Temple period, apparently had its foundation in the assembly called by Ezra (Neh. 9). A synagogue, or at least something very similar to it, was to be found in the Temple Court, and the prayers and Torah readings were woven into the Temple service. The stipulated hours of prayer were set according to the times of the sacrifices, and those who stood in prayer, no matter where they might be, turned their faces to Jerusalem and to the Temple (Ber. 4:5). Other liturgical forms such as the priestly blessing, the waving of the *lulav* on Sukkot, and the blowing of the *shofar*, were also taken from the Temple service, and their practice had already spread to the synagogue both in Ereẓ Israel and in the Diaspora even while the Temple was still standing. In the course of time homiletic Midrash and Torah study, which were also connected with the Temple, were added to the reading of the Torah. On the Sabbath and holidays, the Sanhedrin convened – not as a court of law, since it was forbidden to pronounce judgment on the Sabbath or on a holiday, but as a *bet midrash*, a center of study (Tosef., San. 7:1). Both Josephus and tannaitic tradition clearly reflect the fact that sages used to teach the law to the people in the Temple Courts (Ant. 17:149; Pes. 26a). The Gospels also relate that Jesus taught the law daily in the Temple Courts whenever he was in Jerusalem, and that after his death the apostolic Christian community continued to do so (Luke 21:37; Acts 2–4). The Holy Scriptures and other national historical literature were kept in the Temple, which acted not only as a repository but also as an agency for their careful preservation and dissemination. The redaction of the *Megillat Ta'anit* and the Book of *Megillat Beit Ḥashmonai* took place in the chambers of the Temple, (*Halakhot Gedolot*, ed. Venice, 141d). Whenever a doubt arose about the correct reading of the text of the Holy Scriptures, it was determined on the basis of the consensus of the ancient manuscript kept in the Temple (Sif. Deut. 356), and many scribes and proofreaders were kept in the Temple employ (TJ, Shek. 4:3, 48a). Various sources clearly reflect the existence of a *sefer ha-azarah* – i.e., a manuscript kept in the Temple Court – which was read before the assembled multitude on festive occasions and according to which other texts were regularly corrected (TJ, San. 2:6, 20c, MK 3:4). The Temple authorities also sent copies to the Diaspora communities when they so requested (cf. II Macc. 2:15). The Sanhedrin and the various law courts connected with it sat in the Chamber of Hewn Stone and in the outer courts. The full prerogatives were invested in the Sanhedrin only when it sat in the Temple precincts and while the sacrificial system was in operation (Sif. Deut. 152; Sanh. 14b). These religious elements and values were added to the Temple, but basically it continued to be looked upon as the "dwelling place" of the Divine Presence, and as the only fitting place to bring sacrifices in His name, both communal and individual. The offering of sacrifices and the attendant purification atoned for the sins of the nation as a whole and for those of the individual, and served as a means by which the spiritual purification and uplifting of man was furthered. The Temple and its appurtenances were pictured as symbolizing the entire universe, including the stars of the firmament, and the Temple service was considered to be a source of blessing to all the nations of the world and even to the heavens and the earth and all it contains (Philo, II Mos. 84–93; Jos., Ant. 3: 179–87; Suk. 55b).

[Shmuel Safrai]

IN THE ARTS

The Tabernacle, Temple, and Temple implements provided the background to many literary and artistic works. In literature, one of the earliest instances is "*Le Tabernacle*," a mystical extended section of *L'Encyclie des secrets de l'éternité* (1571) by the French poet and Bible scholar Guy *Le Fèvre de la Boderie. Among Jewish writers the Western Wall of the former Temple has been a chief source of inspiration, as in Heinrich *Heine's poem, "*Jehuda ben Halevy*" (one of the *Hebraeische Melodien* in *Romanzero*, 1851), where he writes of the very stones mourning on the Ninth of Av. Other themes connected with the Temple have attracted the attention of Jewish writers. Edmond *Fleg's story, *L'Adultère*, translated by Louis Zangwill as "The Adulteress," in: J. Leftwich (ed.), *Yisrōel* (1933), is a dramatic and moving account of the "Ordeal of the Bitter Waters" inflicted on an unfaithful wife in the time of the Second Temple. Isaac *Rosenberg's "The Burning of the Temple" was one of the poems published in his posthumous *Collected Works* (1937). A sub-theme is that of the Temple candelabrum or **menorah*. Stefan Zweig's short novel, *Der begrabene Leuchter* (1937; *The Buried Candelabrum*, 1937), recorded that "The Candelabrum we are burying will one day come to life again and give light to the children of Israel when they have found their way back to their homeland..." The search for the "true *menorah*" is also the subject of a modern detective novel by the English writer Lionel Davidson in *A Long Way to Shiloh* (1966, U.S. edition, *The Menorah Men*, 1966).

The Temple has often been portrayed in Christian art, and plans and implements of the Temple have figured in many Jewish manuscripts, where they sometimes symbolize the city of Jerusalem. In Christian sources the Temple forms the setting for the following subjects, taken sometimes from the Hebrew Bible, but more generally from the New Testament: Solomon Constructing the Temple (I Kings 6 and II Chron. 3); the (apocryphal) Presentation of the Virgin in the Temple, which, however, often showed only the steps outside the building; the (apocryphal) Marriage of the Virgin (or *spozalio*), popular with early Renaissance, particularly Umbrian, painters and shown as taking place in the open air outside the Temple, as in the famous painting by Raphael (Brera Gallery, Milan); the Circumcision of Jesus (Luke 7:21) by Mantegna, Bellini, *Rembrandt, and others; the Presentation of Jesus in the Temple (Luke 2:22–40), popular with 15th-century painters, including Rogier Van Der Weyden, Memlinc, Fra Angelico, Mantegna, Bellini, and Carpaccio, and also treated by Rembrandt; the Child Jesus Confuting the Doctors (Luke 2:4–51), by Bosch, Duerer, Veronese, and Ingres among others (in a medieval Spanish version, the interior of the Temple is visualized as a contemporary synagogue interior with a high *bimah*, reached by a flight of steps); and Jesus Casting the Money Changers out of the Temple (John 2), treated by several Renaissance artists including Lucas Cranach, Pieter Breughel, and Jacopo Bassano, but above all by El Greco, who painted several versions. Representations of the Tabernacle and Temple interiors, and of the Ark of the Covenant and *menorah*, are also not uncommon in Christian ecclesiastical art of the 11th–15th centuries. Some of the earlier documents allegorize the structure as the "Temple of Wisdom." A colorful and imaginative evocation of the Temple, notable for its portrayal of Jewish types, is the English pre-Raphaelite William Holman Hunt's *The Finding of Christ in the Temple* (1862; Walker Art Gallery, Liverpool).

The Hebrew Bible was frequently illustrated in engravings of the 17th century, particularly in Holland. Among these were a number representing scenes which included the Temple. There were also engravings of imaginary reconstructions of the Temple. The Dutch rabbi and artist, Jacob Judah Leon (1603–1675), was called "*Templo" on account of his models of Solomon's Temple which he afterward painted and engraved. Since the real appearance of the Temple was unknown, it was often imagined as a round or polygonal domed structure, resembling Dome of the Rock which stood on its site (cf. the printer's mark of Marco Antonio *Giustiniani). It was sometimes represented in this way in Jewish as well as Christian sources. The outstanding feature of the interior of the Temple as imagined by artists was the twisted columns, commonly thought to have existed in the Temple and associated with Jachin and Boaz. These figure in the miniature representation of Pompey's entry into the Holy of Holies from the illustrated *Josephus* by the 15th-century French artist Jean Fouquet. On the other hand, there was always a tendency on the part of artists to represent Jerusalem and the Temple as cities and churches of their own era and country. In Fouquet's *Josephus* the exterior of the Temple is represented as that of a French late Gothic cathedral, and in Renaissance and baroque times it was often visualized in a classical form, or in the style of the period. Rembrandt's painting of the *Woman Taken in Adultery* (National Gallery, London) evokes an exuberant, though dimly lit, baroque interior, heaped with barbaric gold. See also: *Jerusalem in the Arts; *Titus in the Arts; *Zerubbabel in the Arts.

Temple Implements in Illuminated Manuscripts

Full-page miniatures depicting Temple implements were a common feature in Spanish Bible decoration in 13th- to 15th-century *illuminated manuscripts. Illustrations of Temple implements, however, appear in earlier Oriental Bibles as well as in 13th- and 14th-century Ashkenazi and Italian Bibles. In most of these there are two full pages depicting individual vessels arranged decoratively, sometimes on different colored backgrounds. Every vessel is shown in a traditional stylized way and, in most cases, the same vessels are grouped together on one page. Among the most important utensils shown are the seven-branched candelabrum (*menorah*), consisting of a central shaft, branches, bowls, knobs, flowers and a three-legged stand. Next to the *menorah* there are, usually, tongs (*melkaḥayim*) and firepans (*maḥtot*) (Ex. 25:31–40; 37:17–24). Flanking most *menorot* are two small stone steps (*even*). The two rectangular tablets of the Law represent the Ark of the Covenant (*aron*; Deut. 10:5) which has the mercy seat (*kapporet*) and above it an elongated rectangular panel with two stylized cherubim or wings on top (Ex. 25:10–22; 37:1–9). Other essential implements are: the sacrificial altar (*mizbaḥ ha-olah*) with a brass mesh (*ma'aseh reshet*) and a ramp (*kevesh*) leading to it. Also represented are the altar's main implements: firepans (*maḥtot*), flesh-hooks (*mizlagot*), pots (*sirot*), basins (*mizrakot*), and shovels (*ya'im*; Ex. 27:1–8; 38:1–7), as well as the gold incense altar (*mizbaḥ ha-ketoret*) with its incense shovels (Ex. 30:1–7; 37:25–29) and the shewbread table laid with twelve loaves of bread, six on each side (Ex. 25:23–29; 37:10–16). On top, or on the side of the table, are two incense pans (*bazikhei levonah*) which were placed with each row of the shewbreads (Lev. 24:7). Other elements are the jar of manna, Moses' staff, and Aaron's flowering rod, which according to the Bible should be put into the Ark of the Covenant (Ex. 16:33; Num. 17:25), trumpets and horns (Lev. 25:9; Num. 10:2), the laver (*kiyyor*) and its stand (*kan*), usually similar to the manna jar (Ex. 30:18; 38:8).

Most of these implements are mentioned only in respect of the Tabernacle in the desert. There are, however, some manuscripts in which implements are depicted from both the First and Second Temples. Such examples are the two pillars, Jachin and Boaz, of the First Temple (I Kings 7:15–22, e.g., British Museum, Ms. BM King's 1, fol. 4) and the Golden Vine of the Second Temple (Mid. 3:8; e.g., Ms. King's 1, fol. 3v, 4).

The idea of depicting the Temple implements was probably inspired by the messianic hope of rebuilding the Temple. This is shown by the use of a picture of the Mount of Olives, where according to Jewish tradition the Messiah would make his first appearance (Zech. 14:4). The Mount of Olives is usually depicted by a stylized tree on top of a mound. The presentation of implements of the Temple in Bible manuscripts probably originates from the East. A Karaite Bible from Cairo of 930 C.E. (Leningrad, Ms. II, 17) has two full pages with highly stylized plans of the Tabernacle or the Temple. The implements included are the *menorah*, the Ark of the Covenant, the altar, Aaron's rod, the jar of manna, the laver and its stand, pots, shovels, basins, and possibly Solomon's Temple columns and the Golden Vine. As C. Roth has suggested, the origin of the implements in the Oriental Bibles may have been late antique Jewish art either from surviving mosaic synagogue floors (*Bet Alpha synagogue, sixth century) or from illuminated manuscripts which have not survived. The relationship between the illustration of the implements and actual plans of the Temple has not been sufficiently studied. Observing some fragmentary plans both in Hebrew (e.g., British Museum, Ms. Or. 2201, fol. 2, Oxford, Bodleian Library, Ms. Ken. 2, fols. 2v, 3) and Latin manuscripts, mainly Nicholas de Lyra, *Postillae in Biblia* (e.g., Oxford, Ms. Bod. 251) and Petrus Comestor (e.g., Florence, Bibliotheca Laurentiana, Ms. Plut. 2.1), it seems that both the implement illustrations and the plans were drawn from the same source. Similarities can be seen in the sacrificial altar, the *menorah*, and their accessories.

The influence of illustrations of the implements on Spanish Latin Bibles was observed by C. Nordström. Some similar influence can be found in Hebrew Bibles of Ashkenazi and Italian origin. In most cases only the *menorah* is depicted in France (e.g., British Museum, Ms. Add. 11639, fol. 114), in Germany (e.g., Paris, cod., heb. 36, fol. 283v), and in Italy (e.g., British Museum, Ms. Harley 5710, fol. 136), but in some cases there are double-page miniatures of the implements; this is also the case in German manuscripts such as the Regensburg Pentateuch (Israel Museum Ms. 180/52, fols. 155v, 156).

[Bezalel Narkiss]

BIBLIOGRAPHY: FIRST TEMPLE: B. Stade, in: ZAW, 21 (1901), 145–90; T.W. Davies, in: *Hasting's Dictionary of the Bible*, 4 (1902), s.v. *Temple*; M. Nikolsky, in: ZAW, 45 (1927), 171–90; K. Galling, in: JPOS, 12 (1932), 43 ff.; idem, *Biblisches Reallexikon* (1937), 511–9; K. Moehlenbrink, *Der Tempel Salamos* (1932); K. Watzinger, Denkmaeler Palaestinas, 1 (1933), 89 ff.; L. Waterman, in: *American Journal of Archaeology*, 41 (1937), 8 ff.; idem, in: JNES, 2 (1943), 283–94; G.E. Wright, in: BA, 4 (1941), 17–18; idem, in: JNES, 7 (1948), 53; idem, in: BA, 18 (1955), 41–42; W.F. Albright, in: BASOR, 85 (1942), 18–27; H.G. May, *ibid.*, 88 (1942),

19–2/; R. de Vaux, in: *Kedem*, 2 (1945), 48–58 (incl. bibl.); L. Myres, in: PEQ (1948), 14–41; C.C. Wylie, in: BA, 12 (1949), 86–90; M.B. Rowton, in: BASOR, 119 (1950), 20–22; P.L. Garber, in: BA, 14 (1951), 1–24; idem, in: *Archaeology*, 5 (1952), 165ff.; A. Parrot, *Le Temple de Jérusalem* (1954), 1–44; L.H. Vincent, in: *Mélanges Robert* (957), 137–48; M. Haran, in: *Yedi'ot*, 25 (1961), 211–23; idem, in: *Tarbiz*, 31 (1962), 317–19; idem, in: JBL, 81 (1962), 14–17; idem, in: IEJ, 13 (1963), 46–58; idem, in: EM, 5 (1968), 322–28, 340–60; idem, in: *Biblica*, 50 (1969), 251–67; N. Avigad, in: *Beth Mikra*, 8 (1964), 4–25; S. Yeivin, *ibid.*, 26–53; Th. A. Busink, in: *Ex Oriente Lux*, 17 (1964), 165–92; H. Schult, in: ZDPV, 80 (1964), 46–54; G. Bagnani, in: W.S. McCullough (ed.), *Essays in Honor of T.J. Meek* (1964), 114–17; D. Ussishkin, in: IEJ, 16 (1966), 104–10; idem, in: *Yedi'ot*, 3 (1966), 76–84. SECOND TEMPLE: M. de Vogüe, *Le Temple de Jérusalem* (1864); J. Hildesheimer, *Die Beschreibung des herodianischen Tempels…* (1877); K. Schick, *Die Stiftshuette, der Tempel in Jerusalem und der Tempelplatz der Jetztzeit* (1896); G. Dalman, in: PJB, 5 (1909), 29–57; P. Berto, in: REJ, 59 (1910), 14–35, 161–87; 60 (1910), 1–23; F.J. Hollis, *The Archaeology of Herod's Temple* (1934); ET, 3 (1951), 102–6, 149f., 182–87, 213–20, 224–41, 244f., 249f.; 10 (1961), 575–87; L.H. Vincent, in: RB, 61 (1954), 5–35, 398–418; idem, and M.-A. Steve, *Jérusalem de l'Ancien Testament*, 2 (1956), 420–70; M. Avi-Yonah, in: *Sefer Yerushalayim*, 1 (1956), 392–418; idem, in: *Religions in Antiquity (Essays in Memory of E.R. Goodenough)* (1968), 327–35; EM, 5 (1968), 322–60; B. Mazar, in: *Eretz-Israel*, 9 (1969), 161–74; A, Schalit, *Koenig Herodes* (1969), 372–97. IN THE ARTS: A. Yaari, in: KS, 15 (1938/39), 377–82; P. Bloch, in: *Monumenta Judaica* (1963), index (published separately as: *Nachwirkungen des Alten Bundes in der Christlichen Kunst*, 1963); Meyer, Art, nos. 1721 (Metzger, 2207 (Roth), 2515 (Stassof and Ginzburg); C.E. Nordström, in: *Horae Soederbcomianae* 6 (1964); idem, in: *Synthronon*, 2 (1968), 89–105; J, Gutmann, in: *Art Journal*, 27 no. 2 (1967–68), 168–74.

TEMPLE MOUNT, the trapezoid-shaped (approximately rectangular) walled-in area (approx. 140 dunams) in the southeastern corner of the Old City of Jerusalem. The four walls surrounding it (see *Western Wall) date – at least in their lower parts – from the time of Herod's Temple (end of first century B.C.E.; see *Temple: Second). These huge supporting walls, partly buried underground (except for the northern one), were built around the summit of the eastern hill (see *Jerusalem) identified as Mount *Moriah, the traditional site of the **Akedah* and the known location of the two Temples. The gaps between the walls and the mount were filled in to create a large surface area around the Temple. Its eastern wall and the eastern half of its southern wall form part of the city wall on those sides. Deep valleys (now partly filled by debris) run outside the walls (northeast, east, south, west), thus separating the Temple Mount from and elevating it above its surroundings, both inside and outside the city.

The dimensions of the Temple Mount (north, 313 m. (1,020 ft.); east, 470 m. (1,530 ft.); south, 280 m. (910 ft.); west, 485 m. (1,578 ft.)) extend considerably beyond those given in the Mishnah (Mid. 2:1), which describes a square of approximately 250 × 250 m. (815 × 815 ft.), referring only to the sanctified area within the Temple Mount as known today (also known by its Arabic designation Ḥaram al-Sharīf, i.e., the noble sanctuary). The entire enclosure consists of an esplanade or courtyard (the most important structure on its southern side being the Mosque of al-Aqṣā), surrounding an elevated platform (4 m. (13 ft.) higher) occupying approximately 23 dunams and decorated by arched structures around the central structure (the Dome of the Rock). In each of the walls there are a number of gates. Some are ancient gates (see *Temple: Second; *Jerusalem), which are blocked, and some are newer gates, from the Arab conquest (638) onward which are still in service (the latter are only in the northern and western walls).

Within the area of the Temple Mount there are about 100 different structures from various periods, among them great works of art and craftsmanship, including open Muslim prayer spots (some of them with small domes), arches, arched porticos, Muslim religious schools, minarets, and fountains (some for drinking and others for worshipers to wash their hands and feet before prayer). Underneath the present-day surface, in the "artificial" parts of the mount, there are 34 cisterns (the largest of these holds as much as 12,000 cu. m. (168,000 cu. ft.)). There are also other substructures, the largest of which is known as "Solomon's stables."

Caliph Omar prayed on the Temple Mount after he conquered Jerusalem in 638, accompanied by the Yemenite Jewish apostate Ka'ab al-Akhbar. In 684 (or 687) the Ummayyad caliph Abd-al-Malik began to build the Dome of the Rock (wrongly called the Mosque of Omar), a shrine over the rock believed to be the **even shetiyyah* of Herod's Temple, located approximately in the center of the Temple Mount. This monumental piece of architecture of octagonal shape was completed in 690–91. Abd-al-Malik built the Mosque of al-Aqṣā in about 700 on the spot where Omar is supposed to have offered his prayers. (According to some historians, al-Aqṣā was only completed in 795 by his son Al-Walid.) The present building was constructed in 1033. After the conquest of Jerusalem by the crusaders, the Dome of the Rock was converted into a church and called Templum Domini (the Temple of the Lord) and al-Aqṣā became a church called Templum Solomonis (Solomon's Temple). They were reconverted into Muslim houses of worship after Saladin's conquest of Jerusalem in 1187 and have remained so ever since.

[Jacob Auerbach]

In Jewish Law

The special status of the Temple Mount in *halakhah* derives from its being the site of the Temple, which stood approximately in its center. The special status applies not only to the actual site of the Temple and its courts, but to the whole of the mount. Jerusalem, the whole of which is holy, is regarded as equivalent to the "camp of Israel" that surrounded the sanctuary in the wilderness; the Temple Mount as a whole is equivalent to "the camp of the levites," which in the wilderness immediately surrounded the sanctuary; and the Temple with its courts, from the entrance of the court of the Israelites and beyond (see *Temple), is regarded as representing the "camp of the Divine Presence" there, in respect of the *halakhot* applying to each of these "camps" (Sif. Naso 1; Zev. 116b).

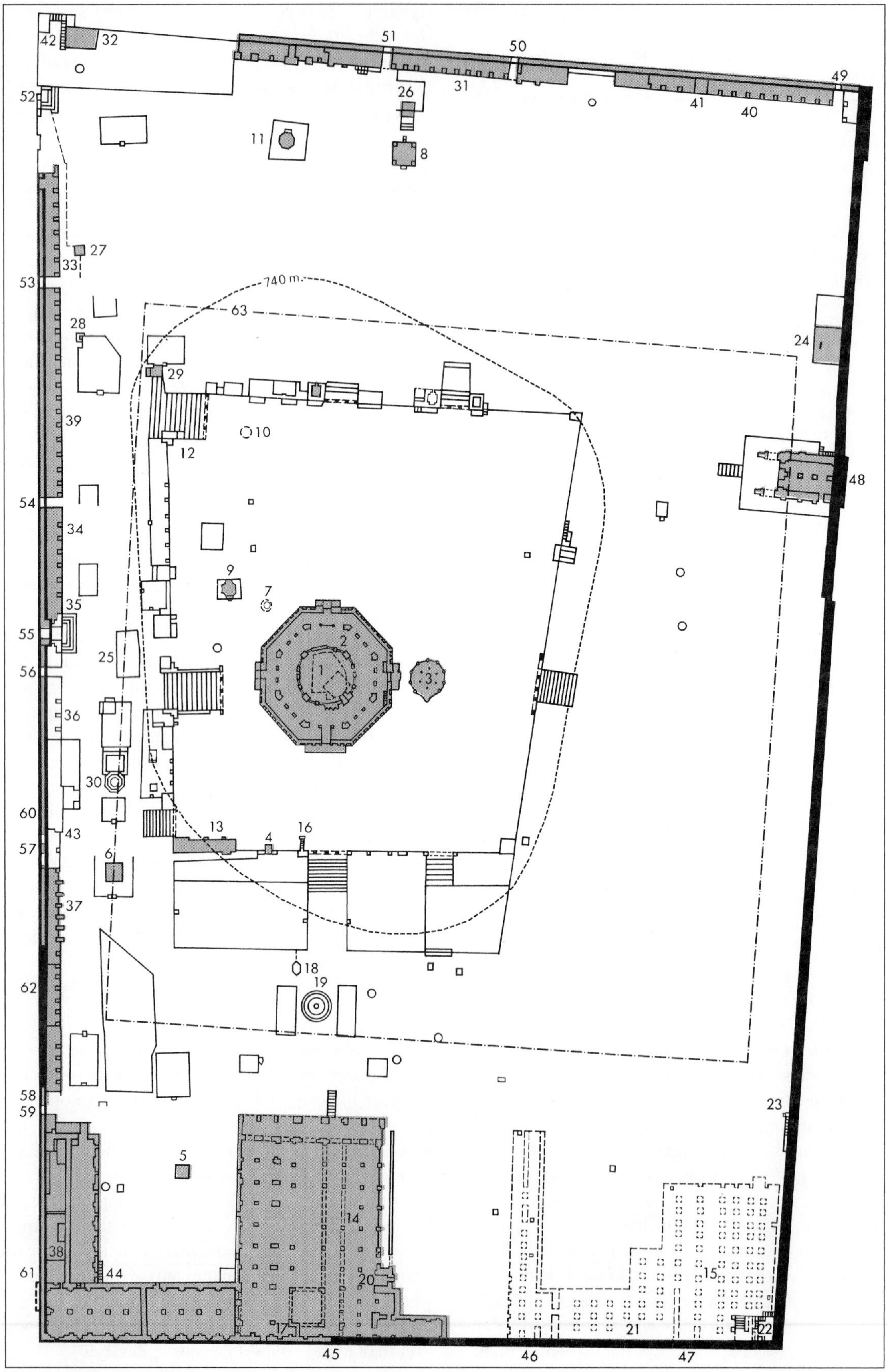

740 m.
1
2
3
4
5
6
7
8
9
10
11
12
13
14
15
16
17
18
19
20
21
22
23
24
25
26
27
28
29
30
31
32
33
34
35
36
37
38
39
40
41
42
43
44
45
46
47
48
49
50
51
52
53
54
55
56
57
58
59
60
61
62
63

Key to plan of Temple Mount

1. "The Rock"
2. Dome of the Rock
3. Dome of the Chain
4. Dome of Joseph
5. Dome of Yūsuf
6. Dome of Moses
7. Dome of the Prophet
8. Dome of Suleiman Pāshā
9. Dome of the Ascension
10. Dome of the Spirits
11. Dome of Solomon
12. Al-Khiḍr (Elijah) Dome
13. Al-Naḥawiyya Dome
14. Al-Aqṣā Mosque
15. Solomon's Stables
16. Summer Pulpit
17. Pulpit of Nūr al-Dīn
18. Olive Tree of the Pophet
19. Al-ka's ("The Goblet")
20. Miḥrab of Zechariah
21. Miḥrab of David
22. Cradle of Jesus
23. Seat of Muhammad
24. Seat of Solomon
25. Fountain of Qāyt-Bāy
26. Fountain of Sultan Suleiman
27. Fountain of 'Alā' al-Dīn al Baṣīr
28. Fountain of Sheikh Budayr
29. Fountain of Sha'lan
30. Fountain of Qāsim Pāshā
31. Al-Madrasa al-Dawīdāriyya
32. Al-Madrasa al-Jāwiliyya
33. Al-Madrasa al-Manjikiyya
34. Al-Madrasa al Arghūniyya
35. Al-Madrasa al Khātūniyya
36. Al-Madrasa al Uthmāniyya
37. Al-Madrasa al Tankiziyya
38. Al-Madrasa al Fakhriyya
39. Western Porch
40. Northern Porch
41. Minaret of Israel
42. Minerat al-Ghawānima
43. Minerat of the Gate of the Gate of the Chain
44. Minerat al-Fakhriyya
45. Double Gate (blocked)
46. Triple Gate (blocked)
47. Single Gate (blocked)
48. The Golden Gate (blocked)
49. Gate of the Tribes
50. Gate of Forgiveness
51. The Dark Gate
52. Ghawānima Gate
53. Gate of the Inspector
54. The Iron Gate
55. Gate of the Cotton Market
56. Gate of the Bath
57. Gate of the Chain, Gate of Peace
58. Barclay's Gate (blocked)
59. Gate of the Mughrebins
60. Wilson's Arch
61. Robinson's Arch
62. Western (Wailing Wall)
63. Balustrade (Second Temple)

During the Period of the Temple

There were differences in degree of sanctity between the different sections of the Temple Mount. Into the most holy section, the Holy of Holies, only the high priest was permitted to enter, and then only once a year, on the Day of Atonement, for the service, and even this was dependent upon definite conditions. Besides this, those who were ritually unclean were forbidden to enter the Temple, as well as the courts of the priests and of the Israelites, by a positive precept (Num. 5:2) and a negative one (Num. 5:3). Those ritually unclean as the result of an unclean issue from their bodies were forbidden by a positive and negative precept from entering any part of the Temple Mount. By rabbinic enactment anyone ritually unclean was equally forbidden to enter the rampart (*ḥel*) and the court of the women. According to one opinion, anyone unclean, whether by biblical law or rabbinic enactment, was forbidden to enter any part of the mount. It was however permitted to enter the Temple, even the Holy of Holies, in order to execute necessary repairs, but under defined conditions. In addition, there are precepts which derive from the respect in which the area is to be held. It was forbidden to enter the area of the Temple Mount in a disrespectful manner or for mundane purposes: "A man should not enter the Temple Mount with his staff or wearing his shoes or with his feet dust-stained; nor should he make of it a short cut, and spitting [is forbidden] a fortiori" (Ber. 9:5). It was permitted to enter the Temple Mount from the right side only and to depart from it on the left side only, except in special circumstances (Mid. 2:2; Maim. Yad, Beit ha-Beḥirah 7:3).

The Status of the Temple Mount After the Destruction of the Temple

This raised a special halakhic problem, as can be gathered from most of the talmudic sources dealing with the subject (Eduy. 8:6; Meg. 10a–b). It appears that the most accepted view – and this too is the view of most commentators and halakhic authorities – is that the sanctity of the Temple site, and of the other parts of the Temple Mount according to their grades, and of Jerusalem as a whole – including any prohibitions against entry arising from these – remained even after the destruction. This is especially stressed by Maimonides (Yad, Beit ha-Beḥirah 6:14–16), but *Abraham b. David of Posquières (the Rabad, *ibid.*) criticizes this view and rules that "one entering there nowadays is not liable for the penalty of **karet*." Some have understood the latter to mean that no part of the Temple Mount is nowadays sacred, and unrestricted entry is permitted; and some acted accordingly, as reported by Menahem b. Solomon ha-*Meiri (*Beit ha-Beḥirah* to Shevu. 16a) that the "the custom is widespread to enter there, as I have heard." However, generally speaking, his statement was understood to refer only to the liability for *karet* but not to the permission to enter. In any case his opinion was not accepted as the *halakhah* (Magen Avraham to OḤ 561:2).

A secondary problem, not discussed, is to what extent the permission to enter which applied in Temple times obtains after the destruction. However, it is held that in general there is no one who has not been rendered ritually unclean by direct or indirect contact with the dead and there is no possibility of becoming cleansed, since there are no ashes of the *red heifer, which are indispensable for such purification. According to the view that all ritually unclean persons are forbidden to enter the entire Temple Mount, the prohibition against entrance is clear-cut. Yet according to the view that the prohibition against entry in the case of one rendered unclean by contact with the dead is restricted to the area within the rampart, while the area outside is forbidden only if the uncleanness could have been avoided or if it is a form of uncleanness from which cleansing is possible even today, there are apparently grounds for permitting entry to that area. The problem remains, however, of identifying that permitted area, since no unequivocal conclusions on this can be derived from the sources. It is discussed by *David b. Solomon ibn Abi Zimra (Responsa, pt. 2, no. 691) on the assumption that the Dome of the Rock is on the exact site of the Temple. With this as a starting point and with the aid of the measurements found in talmudic sources, he established into which area of the Temple Mount entry is forbidden nowadays and into which it is permitted. However, his premise about the exact site of the Temple is not universally accepted and many doubts remain. Most authorities take the view that entry is forbidden today to the entire area of the Temple Mount. In recent generations, the rabbis of Jerusalem – particularly A.I. *Kook – strongly upheld this prohibition.

A vehement controversy on the question of entry into the Temple area took place after the liberation of Jerusalem in 1967. It did not apply to the armed forces who captured and held the site, since their presence there was regarded as a security necessity involving *pikku'aḥ nefesh* in relation to others. The chief rabbi of the Israel army, S. Goren, maintained that on the basis of his study of the sources he had succeeded in identifying an area south of the Temple Mount that was definitely outside the area forbidden to one unclean through contact with the dead. As a result, he stated that in his opinion it was permitted to enter that area after cleansing oneself from other forms of uncleanness, as is possible nowadays, and observing those injunctions applying to reverence for the Temple. Most rabbis disagreed with him, however, and took the accepted view that entry into the whole Temple area is forbidden (except for security reasons). Similarly, a special halakhic problem arose as to whether entry is permitted for the purpose of offering congregational *sacrifices, on the halakhic basis that "they may offer sacrifices although there is no Temple" (Eduy. 8:6), and in accordance with the rule that "uncleanness is superseded [or overridden] by the congregation"; i.e., if the whole congregation have become unclean by contact with the dead and there is no possibility of their being cleansed. Communal sacrifices which are offered at specific times, particularly the paschal lamb (Tem. 2:1; Pes. 79a–80b; Maim. Yad, Bi'at ha-Mikdash 4:10–12; Korban Pesaḥ 7:1), would be permitted. The problem had already been discussed by *Estori ha-Parḥi in his *Kaftor va-Feraḥ* (ch. 6). In the modern period it was examined by S. *Kalischer in his *Derishat Ẓiyyon* (*Ma'amar ha-Avodah*; par. 3 (1964), 124), and he expressed the view that "if permitted by the ruling powers," it would be permissible and even obligatory to offer communal sacrifices nowadays, including the paschal lamb, on the Temple Mount, upon an altar built on the site of the altar at the time of the Temple. Ẓevi Hirsch *Chajes concurred to some extent, but the majority of the authorities, including Akiva *Eger and David Friedmann of Karlin (*She'ilat David*, 1 (1913), 27ff.; *Kunteres Derishat Ẓiyyon vi-Yrushalayim*), rejected the suggestion – either because the exact site of the altar cannot be established, or because precise knowledge of the priestly garments being lacking they cannot be prepared, or because of doubts of the priestly lineage of present-day kohanim (see *Yiḥus*; *Priests and Priesthood). This problem too was revived after the Six-Day War. There were some who favored the offering of at least the paschal lamb on the Temple Mount. Those who rejected the possibility on halakhic grounds were again a majority (quite apart from external considerations) and the suggestion was not implemented.

The rending of garments, obligatory upon one "who sees the ruins of the Temple" for the first time or after a lapse of 30 days without seeing it (see MK 26a; TJ, Ber. 9:2), is discussed in detail by the halakhic authorities. They also discuss to which part of the Temple Mount it applies: whether to a view of the Temple site from a distance without seeing the area of the Temple or of the court, or to the Western Wall, which is a remnant of the wall of the Temple Mount; or if it applies to one who lives in Jerusalem. The accepted custom is that a man living permanently in Jerusalem does not rend his garments even if he has not seen the ruins for 30 days (see Sh. Ar., OḤ 561; *Pe'at ha-Shulḥan* 3:1–7; J.M. Tykocinski, *Ir ha-Kodesh ve-ha-Mikdash*, pt. 2, ch. 17; idem, *Sefer Ereẓ Yisrael* (1955), no. 22). The problem of whether the sanctity of the Temple Mount applies to the Western Wall is also discussed (see A. Bornstein, *Avnei Nezer*, YD pt. 2, no. 450).

[Zvi Kaplan]

Location

Various attempts have been made from time to time to determine the exact location of the Temple. The preservation of a large part of the original external walls of the Temple compound (including the Western Wall) enables the overall area to be determined, for the most part, with precision, but controversy surrounds all suggestions concerning the exact siting of the Temple building within the compound. By popular tradition the *even shetiyyah* over which the Temple stood is now covered by the Dome of the Rock (the Mosque of Omar). However various archaeologists over the past century have questioned this location. In 1975, a Jerusalem physicist, Prof. A.S. Kaufman of the Hebrew University, put forward a new theory, based on technological investigation as well as examination of the sources. His views have evoked widespread interest: some scholars of the period have declared themselves convinced; others have found the theory "not proven." The following summary has been written by Prof. Kaufman:

Method

The principal features of the Second Temple as reconstructed by Herod can be determined by combining a knowledge of Jewish texts, notably Tractate *Middot* of the Mishnah, with information derived from finds in the Temple area and simple calculations. The finds, located in the northwestern part of the area and exposed above ground, consist of a mass of rock hewn and dressed in Herodian style, a hewn rock-ledge, remains of a small stone structure, and rows of dressed stones. The mass of rock, the remains of a small stone structure, and certain rows of dressed stone possess two common features; they are aligned at an angle of 9° south of west and dimensions are an integral multiple of a certain unit of length (see below, Standard Cubit).

Plan

The Temple was of rectangular shape at its eastern side, while by the *heikhal* (sanctuary) it narrowed toward the west. The northwestern corner of the inner court (*azarah*), including the gate there (*Middot* 2:3, 2:6), was built on the rock mass which was hewn in the shape of a right angle. The form of the *heikhal* was similar to that of the inner court in that it was "narrow behind and broad in front" (Middot 4:7), while the porch protruded at both ends. The thickness of the northern wall of the inner court and Court of the Women was five cubits whereas that of the Western Wall (*kotel ma'aravi*) of the inner court was eight cubits.

Conclusion

The Temple was located on a secondary peak of the Temple Mount toward the northwestern corner of the Temple area. The existing platform on which the Dome of the Rock is situated (subsequently referred to as the platform) conceals from view most of the area of the two courts. The Dome of the Rock itself, according to this, is not built on the site of the Temple. The small Dome of the Spirits or of the Tablets which stands on bare rock to the northwest is the existing indication of the position of the Holy of Holies: the rock there would then be identified as the *even shetiyyah* or Foundation Stone (Yoma 5:2). The position of the apex of the inner face of the Western Wall of the inner court is almost coincident with the eastern face of the northwestern archway at the top of the staircase leading to the platform. The axis of the Temple which divided it into two equal parts (the altar excluded) was aligned exactly in the geographic east-west direction. The center of the Dome of the Spirits is situated 1.7 m to the south of the axis, with an estimated uncertainty in position of about 10 cm.

Standard Cubit

The length of the cubit (*ammah*) used in the construction of the Second Temple was 43.7 cm. This was determined from dimensions of the finds on the site, with a correction factor introduced to account for the dimensions of an ancient vault discovered by Warren in 1868.

Confirmation of the Results

Great significance is attached to the existence of a cemented cistern beneath the platform. The position of the Temple axis as determined from the location and shape of this cistern is identical with that determined from the finds above ground (see Method, above). The cistern apparently served several functions. One part suits the description of the water reservoir in the Chamber of the Exile (*Middot* 5:4). The northern portion conforms to the ritual bath for the immersion of the veil (Shek. 8:4), while the western wing was probably the place for overnight immersion of the laver (*Yoma* 3:10).

Location of the Altar

The location of the altar was determined by accepting the tradition of Eliezer ben Jacob (Zev. 59a; Yoma 37a) and from a fundamental understanding of the Temple dimensions as recorded in Tractate *Middot*. There was a space of 5½ cubits between the edge of the ramp leading to the Altar and the inner face of the southern wall of the inner court. Another cemented cistern below the platform conforms to the description of the pit for libation offerings and was situated 1.2 m from the southwestern corner of the Altar (*Middot* 3:3). The platform completely obscures from view the place of the Altar and the ramp, as well as the two cisterns.

Predictions

By superimposing an exact plan of the Temple on a map of scale 1:500, the position of the Temple in relation to existing topography can be determined. For example, just beyond the northeastern edge of the platform, the wild plant growth is stunted across a strip of ground of width five cubits. The position of this strip would coincide with that of the northern wall of the Court of the Women. Moreover, it appears that the same clear strip extending over most of the distance between the northeastern corner of the platform and the rock mass is visible in a German aerial photograph taken in 1918.

Additional Results

The continuation eastward of the Temple axis in a straight line passes over the Mount of Olives at a spot which is compatible with the position of the priest during the ceremony of the burning of the red heifer (*Middot* 2:4). The approximate position of the buried Ark of the Covenant is indicated on the map close to the clear strip of ground referred to above (see Shek. 6:1). Below the inner court there are indications of the existence of a vault which apparently continues under the *heikhal* (Parah 3:3; *Tosefta Kelim* BK 1:1).

Scientific Parameters

The essential features of the plan and location of the Temple can be reconstructed from the following parameters in conjunction with Tractate *Middot*:

(a) standard cubit, 43.7 cm;

(b) direction of the axis, geographic east-west;

(c) coordinates of the apex of the inner face to the western wall of the inner court on the national grid, 131 788.8, 172 318.9;

(d) angle of inclination of the inner court by the *heikhal*, 9.0;

(e) thickness of the partition wall between the two courts, 11 cubits (provisional).

The overall inaccuracy is estimated as that of the map, 1:500, or about 20 cm.

First Temple

There are indications that the First Temple was in the same locality as the Second Temple. Apparently, its axis was inclined at an angle 6° south of west, and the continuation of the axis in a straight line eastward passed through the center of the Golden Gate. The standard cubit used in the construction of the First Temple ("cubits after the first measure" (II Chron. 3:3), and that in use at the time of Moses (Kelim 17:9) was 42.8 cm.

[Asher S. Kaufman]

BIBLIOGRAPHY: A.I. Kook, *Mishpat Kohen* (1966²), no. 96; ET, 3 (1951), 224–41; 10 (1961), 578–87.

TEMPLERS (Tempelgesellschaft), German sect which founded settlements in Ereẓ Israel in the 19th and 20th centuries. The sect, which had its origin in the Pietist movement, was expelled from the Lutheran Church in 1858 and established itself under the name of Tempelgesellschaft ("Temple Society") as an independent religious community. Its aim was to realize the apocalyptic visions of the prophets of Israel by establishing colonies in the Holy Land. In 1860, when it had a membership of 5,000, four of its members went to Ereẓ Israel to study conditions, and six years later several farming families belonging to the Templers made an abortive attempt to settle in what is today the Nahalal area. Two years later, in 1868, several dozen Templer families from Wuerttemberg established a colony in Haifa, at the foot of Mt. Carmel. For some time the leader of the sect, Christoph Hoffmann, tried to persuade the Turkish government to make the sect a free grant of agricultural land, and in 1871, when his attempts had failed, he purchased a tract of land on the site of what is today the Kiryah (government offices' area) in Tel Aviv, and founded an agricultural settlement there, naming it Sarona. Although the settlers suffered great hardship and many (especially infants) succumbed to malaria and the unaccustomed climate, they eventually became prosperous farmers.

Individual Templers also settled in Jerusalem and in 1878 founded a residential quarter (the German Colony) in the Emek Refaim district; others settled in Jaffa and Haifa. In 1875, according to figures given by the founders of the sect, there were 750 Templers living in Ereẓ Israel, who maintained two schools and a hospital. In 1902 they founded a settlement in the Lydda plain, naming it Wilhelma (after the Kaiser), and in 1906 two small villages, Bethlehem and Waldheim, were established in Lower Galilee by Templers who had rejoined the Lutheran Church. In the towns, Templers and ex-Templers (who had returned to Lutheranism) owned hotels, stores, and workshops. By 1914 their number had risen to 1,200. When the British conquered Palestine in 1917/18, the German settlers were deported as enemy aliens, but they were allowed to return after the war. In the summer of 1938 there were 1,500 Germans of Templer origin living in the country, owning a total of 6,700 acres of land. When World War II broke out, they were interned and by 1943 they were repatriated to Germany – in exchange for Palestinians who had fallen into German hands – or deported to Australia. Their property was taken over by the Israel government in 1948, and was taken into account in the *Reparations Agreement concluded with the German Federal Republic.

At no time did the Templers succeed in formulating a uniform religious ideology. In 1845 Hoffmann founded a weekly, *Sueddeutsche Warte* ("South German Lookout"), which acknowledged the divine origin of the prophetic books, but denied the historical authenticity of the Bible stories. The weekly had a large circulation. In the wake of the Crimean War, Hoffmann, like other visionaries of the period, came to believe that the Day of Judgment was at hand, and that the people of Jesus – not the Jews – would inherit the Holy Land. After he had settled in Ereẓ Israel, Hoffmann's views underwent a further development and he gave up his belief in the Trinity, and in the divinity of Jesus and his expiation of man's sins. In Germany itself the sect did not last long, and it continued to exist only in Ereẓ Israel. Even there the Templers, especially those living in the towns, failed to preserve their distinctive character: the second generation, and even more so the third, adopted a levantine way of life. On the other hand, they kept up their ties with Germany and became ardent German nationalists.

[Abraham J. Brawer]

German National Socialist Party in Palestine

Decreasing religious fervor and strong German nationalism made the Templers receptive to the Nazi ideology introduced by the Auslands Organisation der NSDAP (Organization of Nazis Abroad). A Templer in Haifa, Karl Ruff, became the first member and local leader of the Palestine National Socialist Party in January 1932. Fearing economic repercussions from the *yishuv*, few settlers joined the party formally; but sympathy for *National Socialism was widespread, particularly among the younger settlers. By 1934 the seven German colonies in Palestine were linked by a network of officials, and Nazi party activities penetrated all spheres of the community life. Dissension grew among the colonists after the Nazi Party failed in having one of its members elected to the post of president of the Temple Society in January 1935. Cornelius Schwarz, however, a National Socialist from Jaffa, became *Landesgruppenleiter* of the Nazi Party for Palestine in October 1935. Meanwhile local party pressure had secured the dismissal of Heinrich Wolff, the German consul-general in Jerusalem, whose more extreme successor, Walter Doehle, actively supported the local leaders. By September 1939, only about 350 Palestinian Germans were of the Nazi Party, but approximately half had joined the Deutsche Arbeitsfront (the German labor organization created by the Nazis) or similar organizations. By mid-1938 all full-time German teachers in Palestine were enrolled in the Lehrebund (German teachers' organization) which, along with the rest of the educational system and youth organizations, had been pervaded by National Socialism.

Nazi agents distributed antisemitic literature (e.g., Hitler's *Mein Kampf*) in Arabic among the population of Palestine. Some of them actively aided the Arab revolt (1936–39). The younger generation especially identified itself with the aims of the Nazi Party in Germany, and 400 of them entered the German army, some as volunteers. From the outbreak of World War II the colonists were interned as enemies, and, as a result, the party was paralyzed; but they maintained their loyalty to Hitler till the end.

[Ann Ussishkin]

Further Information

The Templers who were deported from Palestine to Australia in 1943 by the British authorities joined the local community, which grew to some 1,350, mostly in Melbourne, Sydney, and Adelaide. In Germany they numbered some 800 with their center in Stuttgart, and continued to issue their periodical, which first appeared in 1845. The Australian group also produced a periodical. The Templers in Russia disappeared after the 1917 Revolution, while those in the U.S. joined the Unitarians.

Some scores of the Templers who remained in Israel were deported in 1950, and the few permitted to remain are no longer associated with the sect. The number of Templers throughout the world has remained comparatively stable during the last decades at some 2,200, with a slight tendency to increase. They have never engaged in missionary activity.

BIBLIOGRAPHY: H. Kanaan, *Ha-Gayis ha-Ḥamishi: Ha-Germanim be-Ereẓ Yisrael ba-Shanim 1933–1948* (1968); Ch. Hoffmann, *Occident und Orient* (1875, 1926²); idem, *Mein Weg nach Jerusalem*, 2 vols. (1881–84); Ch. Rohrer, *Die Tempelgesellschaft* (1920); idem, *Ist die Bibel die Quelle der Gotteserkenntnis?* (1935); Schmidt, in: *International Affairs*, 28 (1952), 460–9; Erez, in: WLB, 17:2 (1963), 25 (includes bibliography); L. Hirszowicz, *Third Reich and the Middle East* (1966). **ADD. BIBLIOGRAPHY:** P.P. Read, *The Templars* (1999).

TEMPLE SCROLL, scroll of the *Dead Sea Sect. In 1967 Yigael *Yadin acquired for the "Shrine of the Book," through the generosity of the Wolfson foundation, a scroll which almost certainly came from the Qumran caves. It is one of the most important of the Qumran finds and has been named the Temple Scroll. The longest scroll hitherto discovered, it measures over 28 ft. (8.6 m.) in length and consists of 66 columns (of text). It has been dated to the end of the second century B.C.E. The author of the scroll evidently believed, or wanted his readers to believe, that it was part of the Torah (given by God to Moses) since he always lets God speak in the first person. Furthermore, the Tetragrammaton is always written in full and in the same (square) script as in the scroll, which was the practice of the Qumran scribes only when copying biblical texts. The scroll is also unique in its contents, which concern four groups of topics:

Halakhot on Various Subjects

The arrangement of these laws – of which the scroll contains a large collection – differs from that in the Torah and many additional rules are given, some of sectarian and polemic nature and others concerning, though at many times disagreeing with, rulings of the Mishnah. Of special interest are the many passages dealing with rules of cleanness and uncleanness, both because they contain quotations from the Pentateuch with interesting variations from the masoretic text and because they manifest greater strictness in these matters than the parallel injunctions in the Mishnah. The scroll also has a special chapter on the rules of burial and regulations with regard to cemeteries.

Festivals and Festival Practice

A considerable part of the scroll is devoted to a detailed prescription of rules concerning the celebration of the various festivals, their sacrifices, and offerings. It decrees, however, the celebration of two festivals additional to those in the traditional Jewish calendar, namely that of the New Wine and that of the New Oil (the latter is known also from other Qumran documents) to be celebrated 50 and 100 days respectively after Shavuot.

Temple Plan and Practice

The commandment to build the Temple and the detailed instructions provided follow the manner and style of Exodus 35ff., which deals with the Tabernacle. The scroll differs, however, from all hitherto known ancient sources concerning the First, Second, and Herodian Temples, and it appears that its author endeavored to supply the "missing" Torah concerning the Temple which was given to David by God (I Chron. 28:11ff.; cf. TJ, Sanh. 29a for reference to such a scroll). The Temple of this scroll is a man-made one to be built as ordained by God until the day that God will create His own Temple. It is particularly in this section of the scroll that the terminology (words like *ris* ("stadium"), *roved* ("a tread of a stair"), *kiyyur* ("entablature"), *mesibbah* ("spiral staircase")), betrays the period of its writing.

The main interest of this section lies, however, in the detailed prescriptions for the courts and the sacrificial machinery, and in the instructions for Temple procedure during festivals, notably Sukkot. There were to be three exactly square courts, one inside another, being respectively about 280, 500, and 1,600 cubits long. The middle and outer courts were to have 12 gates corresponding to, and named after, the 12 tribes of Israel. A considerable portion of the Temple section is devoted to a variety of rules of cleanness and uncleanness to be observed in the city itself, even going into such detail as to prescribe location and architectural details for public toilets.

The Statutes of the Kings

Another section of the scroll deals at first with the king's bodyguard, which is to consist of 12,000 soldiers – 1,000 per tribe. These must be without blemish, "men of truth, God-fearing, hating unjust gain" (cf. Ex. 18:21 where the text concerns judges). The main purpose of this guard is to protect the king against the gentiles. The scroll also prescribes death for acts of espionage. Finally, the scroll gives detailed mobilization plans, the size of the army to be called into action varying from one-tenth to one-half of the nation's force – depending on the seriousness of the threat of war facing the king and the people – while the remainder are to stay in the cities and protect them.

Further Research

Further research on the Temple Scroll, which culminated in its publication with a detailed commentary in three volumes, confirmed the main conclusions given in the original article above. The suggested date of its composition, the second half of the 2nd century B.C.E., is confirmed on paleographic, linguistic, syntactical and historical grounds. It was the formative period of the Hasmonean dynasty, that of John *Hyrcanus I (135–104 B.C.E.), his son *Aristobulus (104–103) and Alexander Yannai (103–76), the last two of whom were High Priests and temporal rulers.

The attainment of independence, the problems raised by this dual role, the need for the reconstruction of the *Temple, the necessity for promoting regulations for the civil administration, the judicial system, the army, relations between the king and the people constitute the background to the two largest portions of the Scroll – the details of the building of the Temple and its practice and the *Statutes of the Kings, details about both of which are sparse in the Bible. To give but one example: the prohibition against the use of foreign mercenaries is to be viewed in the light of the fact that according to *Josephus (Ant. 12:244), John Hyrcanus was the first to employ those mercenaries.

The Scroll can be divided into two parts – editorial and additions.

The first part is characterized by the superb skill of the author in assembling and harmonizing into a whole the different and sometimes contradictory passages in the Bible on a given subject. He does not hesitate to emend the traditional text or to add words and phrases in order to gain his point. In this section biblical Hebrew largely predominates. It is the second part, dealing largely with contemporary matters, that contains post-biblical words, and phrases and syntax which are found only in the Mishnah.

This second part consists of the additions enumerated in the original article: the *halakhah* laid down by the sect; the festivals and their regulations; the plan of the Temple and its rules; the monarchy and its administration.

The Halakhah

All the evidence points to the fact that, unlike the other *Qumran documents, the Scroll was not a sectarian commentary on the Scriptures, but was regarded as a canonical work, part of their Torah, possibly to be identified with the "Book of Hegu" mentioned in the Damascus Covenant (10. 12.14), or even with the *Mishneh Torah* mentioned in the Bible, regarded by the Pharisees as referring to the Book of Deuteronomy, and having the same status as the Pentateuch.

The Scroll thus constitutes what might be called the *halakhah* of the *Essenes, written when the *halakhah* of the *Pharisees, which became normative Judaism, was being transmitted only orally, and its importance lies in the fact that for the first time we have an exposition of Jewish practice other than that of normative Judaism.

Many of its regulations stand in direct conflict with those of the Pharisees and always reveal a more extreme attitude. Thus, where the *Mishnah* (Hul. 4:3) says that a dead fetus in the womb does not render the mother ritually unclean, the Scroll says the opposite; where Pharisaic law limits the contamination from animal carcasses to the flesh, but explicitly excludes "the bones, the teeth, the nails and the hair," the Scroll equally explicitly includes them. Where the rabbis interpret Deut. 21:22 to mean that the body of a criminal on whom the death sentence was carried out was to be suspended from a tree after death (Sanh. 46b), basing themselves on the order of the words, the Scroll deliberately inverts that order to state: "You shall hang him on the tree and he shall die" (Col. 64). It is in the laws of ritual purity and impurity that the extremism of the Essenes is most marked.

The Festivals

As stated in the original article, where normative Judaism provides for only one festival of the first fruits, on the 50th day after "the morrow of the Sabbath" (Lev. 23:15) after which first fruits could be brought regularly, the Scroll provides for four such festivals, at 50-day intervals, for barley, wheat, wine and oil. Since they interpreted the words "the morrow of the Sabbath" not only, like the Sadducees, as Sunday, but as the Sunday after the conclusion of the whole Festival of Passover, i.e., the 26th of the first month, and since according to their calendar the 1st of the first month always fell on Wednesday, all these festivals fell on Sunday: the First Fruit of Barley, Sunday the 26th of the first month; the First Fruit of Wheat, Sunday the 15th of the third month; the First Fruit of Oil, Sunday, the 22nd of the sixth month. In addition there were the festival of the wood offering (cf. Neh. 10:35, and Mishnah Ta'an 4:4, 5) which lasted for six days, and an annual seven-day festival of the ordination of the priests. It was based on the ordination of the priests mentioned in Lev. 6, which normative Judaism regarded as a one-time act.

The Temple and its Regulations

The Scroll deals with the building of the Temple in such exhaustive detail that half of it is devoted to this, justifying the title "Temple Scroll" given to the document as a whole. It was to be an earthly Temple, built by man, as distinct from the Temple to be built by God "at the end of days." Its main aspect was that it was to be surrounded by three concentric squares.

It is in this section that the extremism of the sect with regard to ritual purity is most marked. The Pharisees applied the word "camp" in the Bible, in which ritual purity was to be maintained, to three "camps" of descending order of sanctity: the Temple itself, the Levitical camp, i.e., the Temple precincts, and the "camp of Israel," which was the city, thus permitting leniency in the laws of ritual uncleanness in Jerusalem.

The Essenes, however, declared that the whole city of the Temple constituted that camp, with the result that all acts involving ritual contamination, including sexual intercourse, body evacuation, and the bringing of animal products other than those for sacrifices, were forbidden within the city boundaries. As a protest against the disregard of these laws they refrained from participating in the Temple cult and withdrew to the desert until such time as their rules would be accepted.

The Statutes of the Kings

It is in these statutes that the contemporary historical situation is most strongly in evidence, pointing to the date of the composition of the Scroll. It deals with (1) the king's guard; (2) the obligation of the king to organize an army; (3) the appointment of a judicial council; (4) the number of wives permitted to a king; (5) the relations between the king and the people; (6) regulations for conscription in case the country is attacked; (7) regulations for an offensive war; (8) the division of booty; and (9) the obligation of the king to adhere to the Divine Commandments.

An important aspect of the Temple Scroll is the light it throws on the relations between the Essenes, to whom the Temple Scroll undoubtedly belongs, and early Christianity. It had previously been assumed that the common denominator between them was the rejection of the Temple cult. The scroll, however, reveals beyond question that not only did the Essenes uphold this cult, but they were its most extreme adherents, regarding the Pharisees as heretics.

It is therefore to be assumed that the early Christians came into contact with the Essenes during the later period of their existence when, in rejection of the administration of the Temple of their time, they withdrew from Jerusalem and evolved a theology and a practice which enabled them to live without it. This was, however, only a temporary measure, until such time as the Temple would be rebuilt and their principles put into practice. What was a temporary solution to the Essenes was accepted by the early Christians as their permanent standard.

BIBLIOGRAPHY: Y. Yadin, in: D.N. Freedman and J.C. Greenfield (eds.), *New Directions in Biblical Archaeology* (1969); Y. Yadin, *Megillat Ha-Mikdash*, 3 vols. (1977). **ADD. BIBLIOGRAPHY:** Y. Yadin, *The Temple Scroll*, 3 vols. (1983); G. Brooke (ed.), *Temple Scroll Studies* (1989); M.O. Wise, *A Critical Study of the Temple Scroll from Qumran Cave 11*.

[Yigael Yadin]

TEMPLO, JACOB JUDAH (Aryeh) LEON (1602–1675), Dutch rabbi, teacher and scholar. Born in Portugal in the area of Coimbra to a Marrano family and educated under Isaac Uziel, together with the future leaders of the Amsterdam Sephardi community Isaac *Aboab da Fonseca and *Manasseh Ben Israel, Templo was his nickname at the end of his life; his descendants adopted it as their family name. He went to Hamburg, where in 1628/29 he became a rabbi of the house-synagogue of the Cardozos. Afterwards he taught in the congregational school in Amsterdam until the union of the three Sephardic communities in 1639. Then he was appointed *ḥakham* at Middleburgh, Holland, where he was financially supported by the Christian Orientalist and collegiant Adam Boreel with whom he collaborated in translating the Mishnah into Spanish, a chiliastic project. In connection with this work he constructed a wooden model of the Temple of Solomon which made him famous. Thanks to a print in a Dutch States Bible of 1682, illuminated by the master illuminator Dirk van Santen, even the colors used in this model are known. In 1643 he returned to Amsterdam to serve as teacher in the Ets Ḥaim academy. There he collaborated at Manasseh Ben Israel's press, punctuating the 1646 Hebrew edition of the Mishnah. While in Middleburgh he published a work in Dutch and Spanish on the Jerusalem Temple, *Afbeeldinghe vanden Tempel Salomonis* (1642, reprinted in 1644 and 1669) and *Retrato del Templo de Selomoh* (1642), some copies being illustrated with copper engravings, which might be the work of Pieter Willemsz and other artists. The book also appeared in Hebrew (*Tavnit Hekhal*, 1650), French (1643), German (1665) and Latin (1665, reprinted in 1674). It was followed by similarly illustrated treatises on the Ark (*Tratado del Arco del Testamento*, 1653), the cherubim (*De Cherubinis tractatus*, 1647 and *Tratado de los Cherubim*, 1653/54), and the Tabernacle (*Afbeeldinge van den Tabernakel*, 1647 and 1669, *Retrato del Tabernaculo de Moseh*, 1654; Eng. tr., 1675). Templo was not only an artist, who illustrated his books himself, but a collector of pictures. For his private museum at Amsterdam where he sold his books and the copper engravings, he also constructed a model of the Tabernacle and a scale model of the Israelites in the desert. Two illustrated posters with information on his exhibits are known, from which it appears that he traveled with his models to other places. His exhibition was visited by many people from the Netherlands and abroad, who sometimes reported about it, such as John Dury, Philipp von Zesen, William Lord Fitzwilliam, Philip Skippon. He showed the temple model to Queen Henrietta Maria of England when she visited Amsterdam in 1643. He took his model with him to England in 1671 with letters of recommendation by the famous Dutch poet and statesman Constantin Huygens, who was instructed in Hebrew literature by him in his youth. The letters were directed, among others, to the Portuguese ambassador, the archbishop of Canterbury, and the architect Sir Christopher Wren; possibly Leon hoped to show the model to King Charles II. (While there, he is said to have designed the coat of arms used by the English freemasons. This, however, seems unlikely.) The model remained on show in London for over a century but is now probably lost. In 1670/71 he published *Kodesh Hillulim* (*Las alabanças de santidad*) in Amsterdam – the Hebrew text of the Psalms with translation, paraphrase, and annotations in Spanish. Among his unpublished works, which mostly dealt with the Temple and its worship, was a series of drawings illustrating the Mishnah, subsequently used by Wilhelm *Surenhuis for his Latin translation. He left behind some polemical materials in manuscript, but his connection to the Latin disputation with Philip Limborch, generally called the *Colloquium Middleburgensis*, is no longer believed. He died on July 19, 1675, in Amsterdam, shortly before the inauguration of the great Sephardi Esnoga. His portrait (in two versions and dating from the 1640s) was drawn and engraved by Salom Italia. A third portrait from 1652 is anonymous. The earliest portrait was copied by the German engraver C. Buno (Baum) for the Latin translation of the book on the Temple. His son, SOLOMON JUDAH LEÃO TEMPLO (d. c. 1733), also taught in the Jewish congregational schools in Amsterdam. He composed a Hebrew grammar in Portuguese (*Reshit Ḥokhmah, Principio de sciencia*, 1703) for their use, besides publishing a number of sermons.

BIBLIOGRAPHY: Brugmans-Frank, 389, 521–3. **ADD. BIBLIOGRAPHY:** J. Zwarts, in: *Nieuw Nederlandsch Biografisch Woordenboek*, 6 (1924), 941–43; idem, in: *Hoofdstukken uit de geschiedenis der Joden in Nederland* (1929), 120–5; idem, in: *Historia*, 4 (1938), 277–82, 307–10, 381–85; 5 (1939), 84–89; H. Rosenau, in: JJS, 23 (1972), 72–81; A.K. Offenberg, in: *De tempel van Salomo. Een terugblik in het nabije en verre verleden* (1976), 54–75; idem, in: *Studia Rosenthaliana*, 12 (1978), 111–32; 26 (1992), 125–31; idem, in: *Jewish-Christian Relations in the Seventeenth Century. Studies and Documents* (1988), 95–115; idem, in: *De Zeventiende Eeuw*, 9 (1993), 35–50; idem, in: *De weergaloze Van Santen* (2000), 21–30; A.L. Shane, in: JHSET, 25 (1977), 120–36.

[Cecil Roth / A.K. Offenberg (2nd ed.)]

TEMUNAH, THE BOOK OF (Heb. סֵפֶר הַתְּמוּנָה), a kabbalistic book whose method represents a particular trend in the *Kabbalah. Written round about the 1270s, when printed it was attributed to Ishmael, a high priest, but in the numerous early manuscripts of the book this attribution is not found. It is clearly recognizable that the author had no pseudepigraphic intentions. *Temunah* is one of the most difficult works in kabbalistic literature, despite the fact that it is written in very good Hebrew. The author concealed his daring opinions behind obscure and solemn phraseology. Some small degree of penetration in understanding the central ideas in the book is made possible by the excellent commentary, written apparently soon after its appearance. One should not exclude the possibility that the anonymous interpreter of the book knew of an oral tradition which enabled him to penetrate its secrets.

There are two editions of the book, published at Korets in 1784 and Lemberg in 1892. But there is evidence from the year 1743 that it had already been printed in Cracow in 1549. In fact, one version was also printed in Casablanca in 1930 without the editors realizing what it was. In a book erroneously entitled *Sefer ha-Malkhut* there are three or four early kabbalistic works, and from page 4b to page 20d one finds a text of the *Temunah*, identical to that printed in the above-mentioned Lemberg edition, under the heading *Nosaḥ shel ha-Ketav Yad*.

The author of *Temunah* is apparently the author of *Sod Shem ha-Meforash* (The Secret of the Tetragrammaton; see *God, Names of), which appears from page 72a to page 75b. Another work following the same trend, and perhaps even by the author of *Temunah*, is the commentary on the 72-lettered Name of God. Like *Temunah*, which contains three interpretations of the forms of the Hebrew alphabet, this work contains three commentaries on the 72-lettered Name. In many MSS these three commentaries appear in synoptic form, each with a different name: *Ha-Gemara, Ha-Pe'ullot, Perush Shelishi*. To the same group belongs the esoteric commentary on the Passover **Haggadah* which can be found in several MSS (such as Bodleian, Cat. Neubauer no. 1557; Parma, Cat. Perreau no. 87, etc.). This work was certainly not written by the author of *Temunah*. Another book of the same trend was *Sod Ilan ha-Aẓilut* of the middle of the 14th century. This text appeared in an abbreviated version entitled *Sefer Sod ha-Shem* at the end of *Zohar Ḥadash*, printed in Constantinople in 1740. The influence of *Temunah* persisted until the spread of the Kabbalah of Moses *Cordovero and Isaac *Luria. In his book *Magen David*, *David b. Solomon Abi Zimra (Radbaz) made extensive use of the *Temunah*. Its renewed influence could be discerned in Shabbatean literature (see *Shabbetai Ẓevi).

The main importance of *Temunah* is in the theory of *Shemittot* (cosmic cycles; see *Kabbalah). This pivotal point of the book takes the form of the commentary on the forms of the alphabet, which is an expression of the manifestation of God in His *Sefirot and His creative power.

BIBLIOGRAPHY: G. Scholem, *Ursprung und Anfaenge der Kabbala* (1962), 407–19; idem, in: *Kovez al Yad*, 5 (1950), 65–102; idem, *Ha-Kabbalah shel Sefer ha-Temunah* (1965); I. Weinstock, *Be-Ma'gelei ha-Nigleh ve-ha-Nistar* (1970), index.

[Efraim Gottlieb]

TEMURAH (Heb. תְּמוּרָה; "exchange"), sixth tractate in the Mishnah order of *Kodashim*, with Tosefta and *Gemara* in the Babylonian Talmud. In seven chapters (the Tosefta has four), it deals with the regulations concerning the exchange of an animal consecrated for sacrifice and with associated problems (based on Lev. 27:9–10).

Chapter 1 considers the persons and sacrifices that are included in the laws of *temurah*. In chapter 2, which lists several differences between congregational and individual sacrifices – one of which is that the law of *temurah* applies to the latter but not to the former – there is a digression on the chronology of the reign of King David. The regulations applicable to the offspring of animals dedicated as sacrifices are covered in chapter 3. In the next chapter there is a discussion of a sin-offering whose owner had died or which belonged to a man whose sin had been expiated by another sacrifice – the first one having been lost, and then found – and similar cases. Chapter 5 covers various formulas of dedication and their effects. Chapter 6 touches on animals which are not only unfit for being offered as sacrifices, but also render unfit those with which they have become mixed. Special consideration is given to the offerings of "the hire of a harlot or the price of a dog," which are specifically prohibited in the Bible (Deut. 23:19). The last chapters deal first with the differences between the dedication of offerings to the altar (i.e., specifically for sacrifices) and those dedicated for the maintenance of the Temple (e.g., building repairs), the law of *temurah* applying only to the former. It then discusses the manner of disposing of things which are forbidden, not only as food but for any use (e.g., meat cooked in milk or bread found on Passover) – whether by burning or burial. Of particular interest are two passages in the Babylonian *Gemara* dealing with the Oral Law and its transmission (14b, 16a).

The final redaction of the Mishnah of *Temurah* took place in the school of Judah ha-Nasi, even though chapter 4 mentions later *tannaim*, including *Eliezer b. Simeon, *Yose b. Judah, and even Judah ha-Nasi himself (4:3; 6:2). Many of its anonymous *mishnayot* represent the views of R. Simeon b. Yoḥai, as a comparison with parallels proves. The Talmud to *Temurah* is composed in the main of tractates that were redacted at an early date. On the other hand, its style resembles that of the tractates *Nedarim, Nazir, Keritot*, and *Me'ilah*, whose editing certainly took place later than that of the rest of the Talmud. Among its stylistic features is the frequent appearance of "alternative readings," which occur in it much more often than "alternative readings" do in other tractates. In the manuscripts the "alternative readings" do not differ from one another in content but simply in elaboration and language and style. This phenomenon is already mentioned in the **tosafot* included in the *Shitah Mekubbeẓet*, which states (ad 17a): "It is difficult to understand wherein all these versions of *Temurah* differ from one another." Different opinions are given to explain this phenomenon. Some hold them to be additions of the **savoraim*, others that they are part of a very late amoraic arrangement of the Talmud and are not supplements but an integral part of the text. The tractate also contains several other unique terminologies, e.g., *tiba'i* instead of *teiku; bazya* instead of *zila* (7a), *lai* instead of *la* (8b), etc. *Temurah* was translated into English by L. Miller in the Soncino edition (1948).

BIBLIOGRAPHY: Epstein, Tanna'im, 457f.; Epstein, Amora'im, 131–44.

[Arnost Zvi Ehrman]

TEN DAYS OF PENITENCE (Heb. עֲשֶׂרֶת יְמֵי תְּשׁוּבָה; *aseret yemei teshuvah*), the first ten days in the month of Tishri, i.e., from *Rosh Ha-Shanah until the *Day of Atonement, inclusive. According to the Talmud (RH 18a; cf. Maim. Yad, Teshuvah 2:6), this is the most appropriate time for repentance. Rosh Ha-Shanah is regarded as the day of annual judgment, on which God opens the "book of life." He "seals" it, however, only on the Day of Atonement and repentance in the intermediate period is therefore held to be particularly timely for obtaining God's pardon to be inscribed in the "book of life."

The concept of repentance is reflected in the following changes in the liturgy during the Ten Days of Penitence: (1) In the third benediction of the **Amidah*, the closing formula is changed from "Holy God" to "Holy King"; in the eighth, from "the King who lovest righteousness and judgment" to "the King of judgment." (A similar change is made in the *Magen Avot* prayer of the Sabbath eve liturgy; Sh. Ar., OḤ 582:1–3). (2) Petitions for inscription into the "book of life" are inserted in the *Amidah* before the closing formulas of the first, second, and last two benedictions (Sof. 19:8). (3) The **Avinu Malkenu* prayer is recited daily, except on the Sabbath, in the morning and afternoon prayers in public worship. (4) Early at dawn (in Sephardi and Oriental communities also after midnight), special penitential prayers, **Seliḥot* (or *Ashmorot*) are recited before the **Shaḥarit* prayer.

It is thought meritorious to fast on these days and to devote oneself in an increased measure to prayer, to study of Torah and to the performance of good deeds (Sh. Ar., OḤ 602–603).

The third of Tishri is the *Fast of Gedaliah, observed as a public fast day (see: *Fasting and Fast Days).

On the ninth of Tishri, the eve of the Day of Atonement, only a small part of the *Seliḥot* is recited in the morning; the greater part is included in the traditional liturgy of the evening prayer after **Kol Nidrei*.

The rabbis prohibited fasting on the eve of the Day of Atonement and declared that "for those who eat and drink on the ninth of Tishri, it is reckoned to them as if they had fasted on both the ninth and the tenth of Tishri (i.e., the Day of Atonement)" (RH 9a–b). Strictly Orthodox Jews observe the ritual of **kapparot* on the eve of the Day of Atonement, the ceremony of absolution from vows (*hattarat nedarim*), and some even the custom of voluntary flagellation.

BIBLIOGRAPHY: Eisenstein, Dinim, 331–2.

TENDLER, MOSHE (1926–), biochemist, professor of Talmud, one of the world's leading experts on medical ethics. He was *rosh yeshivah* at Rabbi Isaac Elchanan Theological Seminary and University Professor of Medical Ethics at Yeshiva University. From 1965 he was the spiritual leader of the Community Synagogue of Monsey.

He received a B.A. from NYU in 1947, and a masters degree in 1950. He was ordained at RIETS in 1949 and in 1957 received his Ph.D. in biology from Columbia.

He married Shifra Feinstein, the daughter of Rabbi Moses *Feinstein. Rabbi Tendler was for more than 35 years the close associate of his father-in-law and a principal interpreter of his views on medical ethics issues; he, in turn, also deeply influenced his father-in-law's view on the issue of death and also of transplants.

Tendler wrote dozens of articles on a broad range of medical ethics. But his greatest contribution to medical ethics has been in his oral lectures and rabbinic decisions on ethical problems. He was the first to teach Medical Ethics as part of a formal university curriculum.

He was a forceful advocate for greater organ donor contribution on the part of the Jewish public on the grounds that saving human life – Jew or Gentile – is halakhically mandated as first priority.

His rulings have not gone without controversy, as for instance in his recommendation after a death from herpes that *meẓiẓah ba-peh*, or oral suction of the circumcision wound, be conducted with a sterile tube.

He was also involved in another medical ethics controversy, being a strong advocate of pre-embryo stem cell research, which he argues is essential for the development of remedies for major illness.

He was also involved in the controversy over the question of definition of death, and objected to the term "brain death." He has argued that the Jewish view is that cessation of cerebral functioning is not sufficient but rather that all brain stem activity must have ceased for death to be determined.

Tendler was chairman of the Bioethical Commission of the Rabbinical Council of America and served on the Medical Ethics Task Force of the Federation of Jewish Philanthropies. He was medical ethics consultant for the American College of Chest Physicians and the National Association of Bioethics of Embryo Research. He was chairman of the Medical Ethics Commission of the Jewish Philanthropies of New York.

With over 50 children and grandchildren living in Israel, Tendler was involved in Israeli political issues. He most strongly criticized the Orthodox Union of America for not taking a stand and opposing Israel's unilateral disengagement from Gaza in August 2005.

He is the author of *Pardes Rimmonim: A Marriage Manual for the Jewish Family* (1977) and co-author of *Responsa of Rav Moshe Feinstein: Translation and Commentary: Care for the Critically ill* (2001). He is co-editor with Fred Rosner of *Practical Medical Halachah* (1997).

BIBLIOGRAPHY: F. Rosner (ed.), *Pioneers in Jewish Medical Ethics* (1997); Jewish Virtual Library Org., "The Brain Death Controversy in Jewish Law, Jewish Whistleblower"; "Rabbi Moshe Tendler Terms of Harassment" (2005); The OCWEB.Org., "Ten Questions for Rabbi Moshe Tendler" (Feb. 2003).

[Shalom Freedman (2nd ed.)]

TENE, BENJAMIN (1914–1999), Hebrew poet. Born in Warsaw, Tene settled in Ereẓ Israel in 1937. His first poems appeared in the Warsaw publication *Ha-Shomer ha-Ẓa'ir* (1933). His subsequent work was published in *He-Atid* and in the Israel press.

Tene's books of poetry include *Mekhorah* (1939); *Massa ba-Galil* (1941); *Temolim al ha-Saf* (1947); *Shirim u-Fo'emot* (1967); and two books of poetry for children, *Dani Dan u-Telat Ofan* (1952), and *Keẓir ha-Pele* (1957). His two books of folktales for children are *Leket Pele* and *Ẓeror Pela'im* (both in 1968). His translations into Hebrew include several books of poetry and collections of Polish and Soviet prose, several children's books, and I. *Manger's *Shirim u-Valladot* (1968). From 1948, Tene was editor of *Mishmar li-Yladim*. His memoir of a childhood in Poland before World War II appeared in English, *In the Shade of the Chestnut Tree* (1981).

BIBLIOGRAPHY: Kressel, Leksikon 1 (1967), 27. **ADD. BIBLIOGRAPHY:** M. Regev, *"Yoman Sheme-Ever la-Zeman,"* in: *Ma'agalei Keriah*, 10–11 (1984), 123–30; idem, *"Al Shetei Yeẓirot,"* in: *Sifrut Yeladim ve-No'ar*, 11:2–3 (1985), 43–46.

[Getzel Kressel]

TENENBAUM, JOSEPH L. (1887–1961), U.S. urologist, Zionist leader, and author. Tenenbaum was born in Sasov, Poland, and in 1919 he was a delegate to the Paris Peace Conference, representing the Jewish National Council of Poland. Immigrating to the United States in 1920, Tenenbaum became a urologist and surgeon, teaching at Columbia University (1922–24) and subsequently working in several New York hospitals. Along with his distinguished medical career, Tenenbaum was a leader in U.S. Jewish life, serving as chairman of the executive committee of the American Jewish Congress (1929–36), as vice president of that organization (1943–45), and as a member of the administrative committee of the World Jewish Congress (1936). He was the founder and chairman of the Joint Boycott Council (1933–41), an organization that promoted the boycott of German materials in the United States before and during World War II. As president of the American and the World Federation of Polish Jews, Tenenbaum twice visited Poland after the war to bring aid to the remaining Jews there.

His writings include *Peace for the Jews* (1945); *In Search of a Lost People* (1948); *Underground* (1952), a book about World War II; and *Nazi Rule in Poland and the Jewish Medical Profession*, which appeared as one part of a three-part work entitled *Martyrdom of Jewish Physicians in Poland* (ed. by Louis Falstein, 1964). His most comprehensive and fundamental work, *Race and Reich* (1956, reprinted and enlarged Hebrew edition, 1960), explains the racial character of the German people, its roots, and its integration into the National Socialist movement. Although dealing primarily with the persecution of the Jews throughout the whole occupied area of Europe, it also deals with the religious and economic policy of Hitler.

[Moshe Gottlieb]

TENENBAUM, JOSHUA (**Shia**; 1910–1989), Yiddish writer. Born near Lublin, Tenenbaum trained as a typesetter and immigrated to Belgium, where he published his first poem, "Mayn Gelibte" ("My Beloved") in 1926). In 1932 he co-edited the journal *Yung Belgye*. From 1934 he lived in the U.S. Tenenbaum wrote widely and in almost every prose genre but is perhaps most admired for his memoirs (in *Yizker Bukh Koriv*, "Koriv Memorial Book," 1955, and *Der Emes Zol Zayn Dayn Shtern*, "May the Truth Be Your Star," 1960) and his impressionistic sketches such as those comprising *In Gots Geshtalt* ("In God's Image," 1951).

BIBLIOGRAPHY: LNYL, 4 (1961), 98–9. **ADD. BIBLIOGRAPHY:** S. Liptzin, *A History of Yiddish Literature* (1985), 459–60; B. Kohen (ed.), *Leksikon fun Yidish-Shraybers* (1986), 284.

[Leonard Prager / Lily O. Kahn (2nd ed.)]

TENENBAUM (Tamaroff), MORDECAI (1916–1943), resistance and ghetto fighter. Born in Warsaw, he went to *Tarbut Hebrew schools and then studied Semitic languages at the Warsaw Oriental Institute. His linguistic skills would later help him pass as a non-Jew on the "Aryan" side of Warsaw. In 1935 he joined the *Po'alei Zion youth movement Frayhayt. From 1938 he was a member of the central committee of *He-Ḥalutz in Warsaw. He trained for kibbutz life and underwent military training in the movement. At the outbreak of World War II he went to Vilna, where he hoped to escape the Germans and immigrate to Palestine. Permits were limited and Tenenbaum gave them to others. He remained behind to help. He participated in the January 1, 1942, meeting at which Abba *Kovner issued his proclamation of resistance. It spoke to Jewish youth, urging them to recognize the situation: "Jewish youth, do not believe those that are trying to deceive you. Out of 80,000 Jews in the 'Jerusalem of Lithuania' (Vilna) only 20,000 are left." The proclamation spelled out what was happening at Ponar, the killing field of Vilna: "All the Gestapo roads lead to Ponar, and Ponar means death." It foresaw the "Final Solution" three weeks before the *Wannsee Conference: "Hitler plans to destroy all the Jews of Europe, and the Jews of Lithuania have been chosen as the first line." And it called for resistance: "We will not be led like sheep to the slaughter. True, we are weak and helpless, but the only response to the murderer is revolt! Brothers! It is better to die fighting like free men than to live at the mercy of the murderers. Arise! Arise with your last breath!"

Tenenbaum had become active in the pioneer resistance movement under the Soviet regime and continued after the German occupation. He obtained forged papers and posed as a Tatar named Tamaroff. He went to Grodno and Bialystok to organize the movement. In March 1942, he returned to Warsaw, bringing with him important information as to what was happening elsewhere. In Vilna and the environs the killing of Jews had begun. Polish Jews were still ghettoized, systematic slaughter had not commenced. Tenenbaum was not quite believed by all, but confirmation was received from Lublin and news of the gassing at Chelmno. Together with Itzhak *Zuckerman, he edited *Yediot*, a clandestine newspaper, and also helped found the Jewish Fighting Organization (ZOB) in the summer of 1942, acquiring weapons and training recruits in the use of arms. In November 1942 he was sent to Bialystok, where he worked to set up a Jewish Fighting Organization within the ghetto underground. He attempted to reach Grodno but was shot by the Germans, who discovered his forged papers. Still he escaped, reached the only remaining ghetto in Grodno, and then returned to Bialystok, where he gained the support of Judenrat chairman Ephraim Baraz for resistance activities. With the help of Ẓevi Marsik, he founded the ghetto archive in Bialystok and kept a diary, *Dappim min ha-Delekah* (1948), thus uniting in his person two forms of resistance, armed and spiritual. As in Warsaw, Vilna, and other ghettos, armed resistance did not begin in Bialystok with the onset of deportations, which had begun in January. It occurred toward the end in a desperate last stand. Tenenbaum united all the underground forces and became their commander. A Communist, Daniel Moszkowicz, was his deputy. Leading the Bialystok Ghetto Revolt (August 16, 1943), his strategy was to break the German siege and enable as many Jews as possible to escape to the forest. It is said that he and his deputy committed suicide when his ammunition gave out after three days of fighting. Sporadic fighting continued for a month. The fighters of Bialystok invoked the memory of Musa Dagh, the stronghold in the Armenian resistance featured in the Franz Werfel novel and which served as an inspiration.

BIBLIOGRAPHY: Klibansky, in: *Yad Vashem Studies*, 2 (1958), 295–330; idem, in: *Yalkut Moreshet*, 9 (1968), 58–70; *Leksikon ha-Gevurah* (1965), 175–7 (incl. bibl.). **ADD. BIBLIOGRAPHY:** *Jewish Resistance during the Holocaust*: Proceedings of the Conference on the Manifestation of Jewish Resistance (1971).

[Nathan Eck / Michael Berenbaum (2nd ed.)]

TEN LOST TRIBES, legend concerning the fate of the ten tribes constituting the northern Kingdom of Israel. The Kingdom of Israel, consisting of the ten tribes (the twelve *tribes excluding Judah and Benjamin who constituted the southern Kingdom of Judah), which fell in 722 B.C.E. and its inhabitants were exiled to "Halah and *Habor by the river *Gozan, and in the cities of the Medes" (II Kings 17:6 and 18:11; for details and conjectures as to their ultimate fate, see Assyrian *Exile), but in general it can be said that they disappeared from the stage of history. However, the parallel passage in I Chronicles 5:26 to the effect that the ten tribes were there "unto this day" and the prophecies of Isaiah (11:11), Jeremiah (31:8), and above all of Ezekiel (37: 19–24) kept alive the belief that they had maintained a separate existence and that the time would come when they would be rejoined with their brethren, the descendants of the Exile of Judah to Babylon. Their place in history, however, is substituted by legend, and the legend of the Ten Lost Tribes is one of the most fascinating and persistent in Judaism and beyond it.

The belief in the continued existence of the ten tribes was regarded as an incontrovertible fact during the whole period of the Second Temple and of the Talmud. *Tobit, the hero of the apocryphal book of his name, was depicted as a member of the tribe of Naphtali; the Testament of the 12 Patriarchs takes their existence as a fact; and in his fifth vision, IV Ezra (13:34–45) saw a "peaceable multitude… these are the ten tribes which were carried away prisoners out of their own land." Josephus (Ant., 11:133) states as a fact "the ten tribes are beyond the Euphrates till now, and are an immense multitude and not to be estimated in numbers." Paul (Acts 26:6) protests to Agrippa that he is accused "for the hope of the promise made unto our fathers, unto which promise our twelve tribes, instantly serving God, hope to come," while James addresses his epistle to "the twelve tribes which are scattered about" (1:1). The only opposing voice to this otherwise universal view is found in the Mishnah. R. Eliezer expresses his view that they will eventually return and "after darkness is fallen upon the ten tribes light shall thereafter dwell upon them," but R. Akiva expresses his emphatic view that "the ten tribes shall not return again" (Sanh. 10:3). In consonance with this view, though it is agreed that Leviticus 26:38 applies to the ten tribes, where R. Meir maintains that it merely refers to their exile, Akiva states that it refers to their complete disappearance (Sifra, Be-Ḥukkotai, 8:1).

Their inability to rejoin their brethren was attributed to the fact that whereas the tribes of Judah and Benjamin (the Kingdom of Judah) were "scattered throughout the world," the ten tribes were exiled beyond the mysterious river *Sambatyon (Gen. R. 73:6), with its rolling waters or sand and rocks, which during the six days of the week prevented them from crossing it, and though it rested on the Sabbath, the laws of the Sabbath rendered the crossing equally impossible. According to the Jerusalem Talmud, however (Sanh. 10:6, 29c), the exiles were divided into three. Only one-third went beyond the Sambatyon, a second to "Daphne of Antioch," and over the third "there descended a cloud which covered them"; but all three would eventually return.

Throughout the Middle Ages and until comparatively recent times there were claims of the existence of the ten lost tribes as well as attempts by travelers and explorers, both Jewish and non-Jewish, and by many naive scholars, both to discover the ten lost tribes or to identify different peoples with them. In the ninth century *Eldad ha-Dani claimed not only to be a member of the tribe of Dan, but that he had communicated with four of the tribes. David *Reuveni claimed to be the brother of Joseph the king of the tribes of Reuben, Gad, and the half-tribe of Manasseh who were settled in Khaybar in Arabia, which was identified with the Habor of II Kings. Benjamin of Tudela has a long description of the ten tribes. According to him the Jews of Persia stated that in the town of *Nishapur dwelt the four tribes of Dan, Asher, Zebulun, and Naphtali, who were then governed "by their own prince Joseph Amarkala the Levite [ed. by N.M. Adler (1907), 83], while the Jews of Khaybar are of the tribes of Reuben and Gad and the half-tribe of Manasseh" (*ibid.*, 72), as was also stated by Reuveni. Persistent was the legend that they warred with Prester John in Ethiopia, a story repeated by Obadiah of *Bertinoro in his first two letters from Jerusalem in 1488 and 1489. The kabbalist Abraham Levi the elder, in 1528, identified them with the Falashas (see *Beta Israel). Abraham *Farissol gives a long account of them based upon conversations with David Reuveni not to be found in the latter's diary, while the most expansive is that of Abraham *Jagel, an Italian Jew of the 16th–17th centuries, in the 22nd chapter of his *Beit Ya'ar ha-Levanon*.

Jacob *Saphir (1822–1888) cherished the hope that he would discover the lost tribes. He tells the story in great detail of Baruch b. Samuel, a Jew of Safed who, sent to seek them, had visited Yemen and after traveling through an uninhabited desert established contact with a Jew who claimed to belong to the "sons of Moses." However, Baruch was murdered before he could visit them (*Even Sappir*, 1 (1866), 41), and in the following chapter Saphir transcribes word for word the evidence given by a certain Baruch Gad to the rabbis of Jerusalem in 1647 that he had met the "sons of Moses" in Persia, who gave him a letter to Jerusalem. He concludes wistfully, "Were I able to give full credence to this letter… I would subject it to a meticulous analysis and would learn from it matters of supreme importance, but the recollection of the fraud of Eldad ha-Dani brings suspicion upon Baruch the Gadite, for one supports the other… I have done my duty by putting the facts down and you may judge for yourselves and I will hear also what contemporary scholars say about it."

Various theories, one more farfetched than the other, have been adduced, on the flimsiest of evidence, to identify different peoples with the ten lost tribes. There is hardly a people, from the Japanese to the British, and from the Red Indians to the Afghans, who have not been suggested, and hardly a place, among them Africa, India, China, Persia, Kurdistan, Caucasia, the U.S., and Great Britain. Special interest is attached to the fantastic traveler's tale told by Aaron (Antonio) Levi de *Montezinos who, on his return to Amsterdam from South America in 1644, told a remarkable story of having found Indians beyond the mountain passes of the Cordilleras who greeted him by reciting the *Shema*. Among those to whom Montezinos gave his affidavit was *Manasseh Ben Israel, then rabbi of Amsterdam, who fully accepted the story, and to it devoted his *Hope of Israel* (1650, 1652^2) which he dedicated to the English Parliament. In section 37 he sums up his findings in the following words:

"1. That the West Indies were anciently inhabited by a part of the ten Tribes, which passed thither out of Tartary, by the Streight of Anian. 2. That the Tribes are not in any one place, but in many; because the Prophets have fore-told their return shall be into their Country, out of divers places; Isaiah especially saith it shall be out of eight. 3. That they did not return to the Second Temple. 4. That at this day they keep the Jewish Religion. 5. That the prophecies concerning their return to their Country, are of necessity to be fulfilled. 6. That from all coasts of the World they shall meet in those two places, sc. Assyria and Egypt; God preparing an easier, pleasant way, and abounding with all things, as Isaiah saith, ch. 49, and from thence they shall flie to Jerusalem, as birds to their nests. 7. That their Kingdom shall be no more divided; but the twelve Tribes shall be joined together under one Prince, that is under Messiah, the Son of David; and that they shall never be driven out of their Land."

The Latin work was translated into English the same year it was published, and ran through three editions in as many years, and Manasseh Ben Israel used this "evidence" of the dispersal of the Jews throughout the world as an argument to Oliver *Cromwell in his appeal to permit the return of the Jews to England, then the only country which had no Jews. As long as this situation existed, the fulfillment of the prophecy that the coming (or the second coming) of the Messiah would take place only when the Jews were scattered in the four quarters of the world (section 35). Both through the translation and the correspondence which the story initiated between Manasseh Ben Israel and theologians in England, it played a significant role in creating the atmosphere which eventually brought about the return of the Jews to England.

BIBLIOGRAPHY: A. Neubauer, in: JQR, 1 (1889), 14–28, 95–114, 185–201, 408–23; A. Hyamson, *ibid.*, 15 (1903), 640–76; C. Roth, *A Life of Menasseh Ben Israel* (1934), 178–93; A.H. Godbey, *The Lost Tribes, a Myth* (1930); L. Wolf, *Menasseh Ben Israel's Mission to Oliver Cromwell* (1901), 17–56; D. Tamar, in: *Sefunot*, 6 (1962), 303–10. **ADD. BIBLIOGRAPHY:** H. Halkin, *Across the Sabbath River: In Search of a Lost Tribe of Israel* (2002); T. Parfitt, *Lost Tribes of Israel* (2003); idem, *Thirteenth Gate, Travels among the Lost Tribes of Israel* (1987).

[Louis Isaac Rabinowitz]

TEN MARTYRS, THE (Heb. עֲשָׂרָה הֲרוּגֵי מַלְכוּת, *asarah harugei malkhut*), name given to ten sages put to death by the Romans. A number of late Midrashim, such as *Elleh Ezkerah* (A. Jellinek, *Beit ha-Midrash*, 2 (1938^2), 64–72; 6 (1938^2), 19–35), relate that the Roman emperor decided to execute ten great Jewish sages, corresponding to the ten sons of Jacob who had sold Joseph. After one of those sages ascended to Heaven and heard that it had been a heavenly decree irrevocably sealed, they accepted it, and by the emperor's orders were, one after another, tortured and executed in various violent manners. Among them were *Akiva and *Hananiah b. Teradyon, who, according to tannaitic sources, were tortured and put to death at the time of the Hadrianic persecutions. There is no mention in early sources, however, of a collective sentence passed upon a group of sages tried together. Moreover, neither tannaitic literature nor the Jerusalem Talmud and the early amoraic aggadic Midrashim know the term *harugei malkhut* in this aggadic connection, while in halakhic sources this term denoted people condemned and put to death by a Jewish king (Sanh. 48b). A list of ten martyrs is first enumerated in *Lamentations Rabbah* (2:2) with no description of the manner in which they were put to death, and without being referred to as *harugei malkhut*, this appellation (with no mention of the number ten), the list, or the story itself being employed, meaning martyrs, in *Song of Songs Rabbah* (8:9) and in the Babylonian Talmud (Sot. 48b; BB 10b). The story of the "ten" appears for the first time in *Heikhalot Rabbati*, composed in the circles of the *"Ba'alei ha-Merkavah"* (the mystics who studied Ezekiel's vision of the Heavenly Chariot, in which circles were, even later still, composed of the particular Midrashim of the Ten Martyrs, including *Elleh Ezkerah*).

The various versions of the legend, all bearing a distinct mystical stamp, contradict one another in certain details and are often at variance with early accounts. For example, the description of the martyrdom of *Judah b. Bava conflicts with the early tradition according to which he was killed by Roman soldiers after ordaining students between Usha and Shefaram (Sanh. 14a). The list of the martyrs differs in practically all of the sources, and not all of the alleged victims are contemporaries. As early as the tenth century the legend could not be accepted at its face value (*Iggeret de-Rav Sherira Ga'on*, ed. Lewin, 74–75). Some of the Jewish chroniclers of the 16th century, such as Abraham Zacuto (*Yuḥasin ha-Shalem*, 38 (ed. Filipowski, 1857), Gedaliah ibn Yaḥya (*Shalshelet ha-Kabbalah*, s.v. *Akiva*), and David Gans (*Ẓemaḥ David*, for the year 3838), who considered the question of the historical veracity of this legend, all came to the conclusion that it does not conform to historical fact or stand up to critical examination (*Shalshelet ha-Kabbalah* states that only some of the sages mentioned were actually put to death). Modern research accords with this view, after the attempts of some scholars to make the legend conform to historical fact have been unsatisfactory.

It seems that the martyrdom of different sages during the times of the Hadrianic religious persecutions served as the themes of different *aggadot*. Over the generations there was a blurring of the boundaries between accounts of events in the time of Hadrian and traditions concerning individuals killed during the War of Destruction and in the time of Trajan. These various traditions were combined. The occupation of some of the martyrs with mystic speculation, a fact which earned for them an important role in the *heikhalot* literature, led the circles of the mystics known as the *"Ba'alei ha-Merkavah"* to create a legendary *aggadah* which entered the later Midrashim and which described the successive tortures and executions of ten martyrs, giving as reason for all this the sin of Jacob's sons in selling their brother Joseph into slavery (Mid. Prov. to 1:13 – the attribution to R. Joshua b. Levi is evidently pseudepigraphic). This legend soon became very important. It was added by copyists of the Middle Ages to several manuscripts of early aggadic Midrashim. It served as a much favored theme for *piyyutim* from the time of *Kallir, the best known being *"Elleh Ezkerah"* (which is found in the liturgy of the Day of Atonement and the Sephardi liturgy of the Ninth of Av) and *"Arzei ha-Levanon Addirei ha-Torah"* (included in the Ashkenazi *kinot* of the Ninth of Av).

In the Middle Ages Jews killed by gentiles were named *harugei malkhut*, and there was even a codifier who learned from the legend the law that martyrs are not to have a funeral oration (Tur, YD 345, but cf. Beit Yosef, ad loc.; cf. also "Chapter of Fast-days" (in *Halakhot Gedolot* et al.)). The legend of the Ten Martyrs mystically united various affairs, creating an artificial harmonization, while obliterating real actual and historical background. This is no wonder, for its creators had no interest in historical accuracy, but were mystics. The creators of this legend meant to create a mystical legend, but in fact handed down to future generations an epic work which filled an important role in the life of the Jews in the Middle Ages. In a world of religious persecution and its attendant acts of martyrdom, the *aggadah* of the Ten Martyrs became most popular, as it set before the oppressed and the persecuted an example of the exalted images of the greatest of the sages, who, though innocent, submitted themselves to martyrdom and in the very extremity of their torture voiced with love the justice of Heaven's decree. Especially from the time of the First Crusade, the Ten Martyrs served as a model for contemporaneous martyrs, who were also called *harugei malkhut*. The Ten Martyrs, along with *Hannah and her seven sons, became the archetypes of Jewish martyrology.

BIBLIOGRAPHY: Zunz-Albeck, Derashot, 66, 312–4 (sources and bibliography); Krauss, in: *Ha-Shilo'aḥ*, 44 (1925), 10–22, 106–17, 221–33; Finkelstein, in: *Essays... L.R. Miller* (1938), 29–55; Zeitlin, in: JQR, 36 (1945/46), 1–16; Urbach, in: *Sefer Y. Baer* (1960), 57–58; J. Katz, Bein Yehudim le-Goyim (1960), 91–92; L. Ginzberg, *Perushim be-Ḥiddushim ba-Yerushalmi*, 4 (1961), 48–49.

[Moshe David Herr]

TENNENBAUM (Tannenbaum), JACOB (1832–1897), Hungarian rabbi. Born in Szendrö, Tennenbaum served in several important communities: Tallya (1858–69), Mezöcsat (1869–73), and Putnok (1873–79). He was the author of *Naharei Afarsemon* (2 vols., 1898–1911), comprising responsa, novellae on talmudic topics and on tractate **Beẓah*, and of *Shemen Afarsemon* (1899), on the *Pentateuch. He was one of the main pillars of Hungarian Orthodoxy, for which he fought strenuously. He conducted a large yeshivah and educated a generation of important scholars. His son MEIR served as rabbi in Fülek (Filakovo) and Torna (Turna), and on his father's death succeeded him as rabbi of Putnok, where he died in 1928. Meir published the books of his grandfather, Ze'ev Wolf Tennenbaum, *Ayyelet ha-Shaḥar* (1876), on the Book of Esther, with his own additions. He was the author of the *Imrei Me'ir* (1929), sermons. Meir's son MENAHEM was also rabbi of Fülek and Torna.

BIBLIOGRAPHY: P.Z. Schwartz, *Shem ha-Gedolim me-Ereẓ Hagar*, 1 (1914), 46b no. 152; 3 (1915), 28a no. 2, 37b no. 53; A. Stern, *Meliẓei Esh al Ḥodshei Kislev-Adar* (1962²), 59b–60b; *Magyar Rabbik*, 3 (1907), 115.

[Naphtali Ben-Menahem]

TENNESSEE, S. central state of the U.S.; general population in 2001, 5,702,000; Jewish population of 18,000. The first known Jewish child was born in 1795. Jewish immigrants, many petty merchants or craftsmen from rural Germany, arrived in Tennessee from Central Europe between 1820 and 1848. They moved to rural areas remote from Jewish life. In 1851 a small group of Jews, the Hebrew Benevolent Burial Society, bought a cemetery in *Nashville. They petitioned for a charter as Kaal Kodosh Mogen David, it was granted in 1854. Their stated their purpose as "establishing in the city of *Mem-

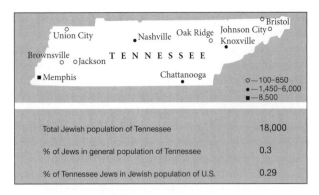

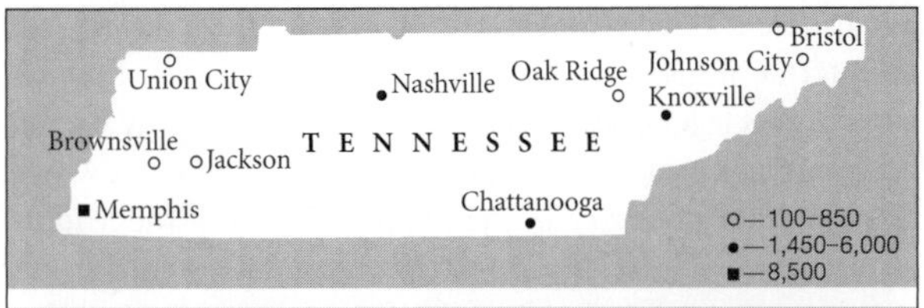

Total Jewish population of Tennessee	18,000
% of Jews in general population of Tennessee	0.3
% of Tennessee Jews in Jewish population of U.S.	0.29

Jewish communities in Tennessee. Population figures for 2001.

phis a church for the worship of Almighty God according to the rites and creed of the Hebrew sect."

The Civil War split Jewish families as it divided the United States. Tennessee Jews were included in *Grant's infamous Order No. 11 expelling all Jews from his military department, quickly rescinded by Lincoln. About 1861 the seven Jewish families of Knoxville received land for a cemetery. A Hebrew Benevolent Association was organized. In 1877 it became a synagogue but without a building or a full-time rabbi until 1922. Chattanooga's Civil War veterans inspired the Jewish community in 1866 to form Chabra Gamilas Chesed, later the Hebrew Benevolent Association, and established a cemetery. In 1882 the first Reform Temple was built. In 1866, the 18 Jews of Murfreesboro organized Kahl Kodesh Bene Sholom. In 1867 a Jewish burial ground was bought in Brownsville, and Congregation Adas Israel was founded. In 1885 a congregation, B'nai Israel, was organized in Jackson.

In 1867 Congregation Mogen David in Nashville merged with Congregation Ohava Emes, and this congregation became Ohavai Shalom and later in 1876 the Vine Street Temple. Adopting Reform Practice in 1876, they became one of the first members of the Union of American Hebrew Congregations.

Congregation B'nai Israel in Memphis was founded in 1858. Their first rabbi, Jacob Peres, moonlighted as a grocer, and kept his store open on Saturday. He was fired, but sued the congregation, He lost his libel suit, but set legal precedent before the Tennessee State Supreme Court, which ruled that "a religious institution is sovereign;…its policies and practices may not be challenged by legal action of a court of law."

There were two yellow fever epidemics in Memphis during the 1870s. Jews from all over the United States contributed $60,000 for relief. The Jewish population of Memphis was reduced from 2,100 to 300 as Jews fled the epidemic or died. Rabbi Max Samfield courageously stayed. Jewish orphans were sent from Memphis to orphanages in Cleveland and New Orleans.

Maimonides Lodge of B'nai B'rith, was founded in Nashville in 1863. By 1878 there were six active lodges: Brownsville, Chattanooga, and Nashville, and three in Memphis.

The second wave of immigration to the state came between 1880 and 1924 from Eastern Europe. Orthodox and Yiddish-speaking, these new arrivals established a whole array of organizations, Zionist groups, newspapers, Yiddish theater, and Yiddish schools. German Jews established Settlement Houses to facilitate their Americanization. Some Jews arrived by choice; others were sent by philanthropists and agencies such as the Industrial Removal Society in an effort to diffuse Jewish immigrants throughout the country. In 1892, a new Orthodox congregation began in Memphis, the Baron Hirsch Benevolent Society; over time it became the largest Orthodox Jewish congregations in the country.

East European immigrants actually formed entirely new communities in the Ti-Cities area, which includes Kingsport, Bristol, and Johnson City. Bristol seemed to have two congregations, one Reform and one Orthodox. It was 1905 before land was purchased for a cemetery. The Oak Ridge community was founded in 1943 by scientists sent in to work on the Manhattan Project. to develop the atomic bomb. By 1944, the young Jewish scientists were hauling cinder blocks to do the actual construction themselves.

The Jewish population increased after World War II as Jewish men who had passed through Middle Tennessee from 1942 to 1944, when the Second Army trained there, married local Jewish women who had run a snack bar with Jewish food for the soldiers. After the War, Jews came to Tennessee as managers and professionals. Their social, political, and organizational skills changed many Jewish communal organizations from immigrant social-service organizations, to organizations active in the political, social, and religious life of the state. Jewish communities in small Tennessee towns disappeared as older members died and the younger generation left for college and careers in larger cities.

Tennessee Jews emulated their Southern brethren. Denied membership elsewhere they established their own clubs, which became a central part of Jewish life. Jews often meet in synagogues and in business, in country clubs and in philanthropic endeavors. In each, leadership overlaps. Living in the Bible belt where church membership was routine most communities have high rates of synagogue membership.

Although Jewish organizations did not officially support civil rights, many individuals did so and individual rabbis spoke out forcefully, not without significant peril. In 1958, the Nashville Jewish Community Center was dynamited. In 1980 a Ku Klux Klan splinter group's attempted to bomb The Temple in Nashville, with Rabbi Falk inside, was averted. A full page ad which included 600 signatures of local leadership decried the attempt.

In the early 21st century, Memphis had about 8,500 Jews, Nashville, some 6,000, Knoxville 1,800, and Chattanooga 1,450. There were also congregations in Bristol, Brownsville, and Jackson.

[Annette Ratkin (2nd ed.)]

TEOMIM, AARON BEN MOSES (c. 1630–1690), rabbi. Teomim was a member of the well-known Teomim-Fraenkel family of Vienna, which had settled in Prague. In 1670 he succeeded Samson *Bacharach as rabbi of Worms. After refusing a call to Lissa in 1677, he accepted one from the Cracow community in 1687. At that time the French army was besieging Worms and it was only with the greatest difficulty that Teomim succeeded in leaving, and for three years he had to travel from place to place before reaching Cracow in March 1690. A few months later, on his way to a meeting of the *Council of the Four Lands, he was arrested at Chmielnik on a Sabbath on the orders of a Polish nobleman, probably in order to blackmail the Cracow congregation. As a result of the ill-treatment to which he was subjected, he died before reaching prison.

Teomim's best-known work is a commentary on the *Haggadah, Matteh Aharon* ("the rod of Aaron"; Frankfurt, 1678) which he wrote in fulfillment of a vow should he recover from a serious illness which had befallen him on Passover 1675. It has been reprinted many times (26 entries in Ya'ari's bibliography of *Haggadot*). Teomim also wrote *Bigdei Aharon* (Frankfurt, 1710), sermons, and a volume of unpublished responsa, some of which are quoted in contemporary works. These writings found a severe critic in Jair Ḥayyim *Bacharach, son of Samson. His motives were probably not disinterested, as he claimed the rabbinate, which had been held by both his father and grandfather. He accused Teomim of distorting the import of the Talmud and falsifying the true meaning of the *aggadah*.

BIBLIOGRAPHY: J.M. Zunz, *Ir ha-Ẓedek* (1874), 128–50; Fuenn, Keneset, 88f.; H.N. Dembitzer, *Kelilat Yofi*, 2 (1893), 71b; D. Kaufmann, *R. Jaïr Chajjim Bacharach* (Ger., 1894), 54f.

TEOMIM, ARYEH LEIB (d. 1831), Galician rabbi and author. In his youth Teomim became famous as a prodigy and while still very young was chosen rabbi of Lyzhansk (Lezajsk) in Galicia. Despite his youth he vigorously opposed Ḥasidism which began to spread in Galicia, with its center at Lyzhansk, headed by *Elimelech of Lyzhansk, author of *No'am Elimelekh*. However, he did not remain there long. After the death of his wife, he married the daughter of Samuel Bick, at that time one of the wealthiest men of Galicia. Teomim moved to Brody, where he occupied no official rabbinic position. In 1815 he was appointed rabbi of the town and, being a man of wealth and property, conducted his rabbinate with great firmness, without fear of the wealthy lay leaders. When in 1818 the grammar school in Brody was established under orders from the emperor of Austria, Teomim was among those who welcomed it, since "the Torah has to be combined with general knowledge." The Ḥasidim were vigorously opposed to this school. In 1827 he became ill and as a result was unable to carry out his rabbinic functions. The community appointed Eliezer Landau as its rabbi, but out of fear of angering Teomim did not inform him. However, the latter died during Teomim's lifetime. According to the tradition in Brody, Teomim saw a large funeral passing by his house. He asked the maid: "Whose funeral is it?" She innocently replied, "The rabbi of the city." Sorely hurt, his condition deteriorated, and he died two months later. He was the author of commentaries on the Torah, Esther, Ruth, and the Passover *Haggadah*; *Ayyelet Ahavim*, novellae on talmudic tractates, and *Ya'alat Ḥen* were both published in Zolkiew in 1802.

BIBLIOGRAPHY: Y.A. Kamelhar, *Dor De'ah*, 2 (1963²), 159–61; N.M. Gelber, *Toledot Yehudei Brody* (= *Arim ve-Immahot be-Yisrael*, vol. 6, 1955), index.

[Itzhak Alfassi]

TEOMIM, JOSEPH BEN MEIR (c. 1727–1792), rabbi, author, and halakhic authority. Born in Steritz (Szczerzec), near Lvov, Galicia. Teomim was educated by his father, who was *dayyan* and *darshan* ("preacher") in Lvov and the author of *Birkat Yosef*. Despite his distinction as a talmudic scholar, which he already evinced in his youth, Teomim had to resort to teaching to eke out a precarious livelihood. For some years he lived in Komarno, but then returned to Lvov, and in 1772 moved to Berlin, where he continued his studies in the well-known *bet ha-midrash* of Daniel Jaffe. This was the most fruitful period of his life. Although he became renowned for his scholarship, he evaded all who turned to him on halakhic or practical affairs, and devoted himself entirely to his studies. In 1774 he was called to succeed his father in Lvov, and in 1781 acceded to the request of the community of Frankfurt on the Oder to accept the position of rabbi, stipulating at the same time that they provide for the maintenance of 10–12 yeshivah students. It was requested that he agree to remain with them for at least six years, but in fact he remained there for the rest of his life.

Teomim's fame rests upon his classic commentary to the Shulḥan Arukh, the *Peri Megadim*, and he is referred to by that name alone. *Peri Megadim* on *Yoreh De'ah* is a supercommentary on the two main commentaries of the Shulḥan Arukh, the *Turei Zahav* and the *Siftei Kohen*, and its parts are entitled, respectively, *Mishbeẓot Zahav* and *Siftei Da'at*. The work was first published in Berlin in 1771–72 and has since appeared in all large editions of the Shulḥan Arukh. The *Peri Megadim* on *Oraḥ Ḥayyim* similarly consists of *Mishbeẓot Zahav* on the *Turei Zahav*, and *Eshel Avraham* on the *Magen Avraham*, and was first published in 1787 in Frankfurt and subsequently in all editions of the Shulḥan Arukh. Three aims can be distinguished in *Peri Megadim*; to explain the *Turei Zahav* and the *Siftei Kohen*, to add to them those laws which they had omitted, and to add forewords and principles to all the *halakhot*. In connection with the first aim he cites all the *rishonim* upon whom these commentators based themselves, subjecting their statements to a thorough and painstaking analysis. Although he decides between differing views, at the same time he emphasizes that his decision is not to be taken as a definitive *halakhah*. His "Introduction and Principles of the *Peri Megadim*" to the literature of the *posekim* is of considerable value, since he collates and presents in a complete form the various principles hitherto scattered in the different works. Of particular importance is the introduction to the laws of the admixture of forbidden and permitted foods in the section *Yoreh De'ah*, entitled *Sha'ar ha-Ta'aruvot*. In it he collects all the scattered *halakhot* on this topic and at the same time summarizes the minutest details to be derived from them. The work became a standard one in the rabbinic world, was accepted by all circles of Jewry, and numerous commentaries have been written on it. Even ḥasidic authorities postulated that "the Heavenly *bet din* too" decided *halakhah* in accordance with Teomim.

In addition to *Peri Megadim*, Teomim compiled other works, all of which went through many editions: *Porat Yosef* (Zolkiew, 1756), novellae to tractates *Yevamot, Ketubbot*, and *Bava Kamma*, as well as expositions of Alfasi's code and of Maimonides' *Mishneh Torah*; *Ginnat Veradim* (Frankfurt on the Oder, 1767), 70 methodological rules for understanding the Talmud – both works compiled in his youth; *Tevat Gome (ibid.*, 1782; *Gome* is derived from the initials of *Gemara*, Midrash, *Aggadah*), a new edition of novellae on the Torah, contained in *Rav Peninnim (ibid.*, 1772), a work by his father on the Pentateuch; *Shoshannat ha-Amakim*, a talmudic methodology, comprising expositions of 24 talmudic principles which appeared first in the *Rav Peninnim* and then separately (*ibid.*, 1782): *No'am Megadim* (in *Seder Hegyon Lev*, 1845), sources for the prayers and their laws; and *Notarikon* (1910), completed in the last year of his life, consisting of ethical sayings, novellae, and sermons. He also wrote *Rosh Yosef* to tractate *Ḥullin* (Frankfurt on the Oder, 1794); to *Berakhot, Shabbat, Megillah, Pesaḥim, Beẓah* (1863); and to the remainder of the order *Mo'ed* (1883). Some of his novellae were also published in his father's work *Birkat Yosef ve-Eliyahu Rabba* (Zolkiew, 1747). Teomim's responsa that appear in his various works were collected and published under the title *Teshuvot Peri Megadim* (1935). A collection was also made of his sayings on reward and punishment, entitled *Mattan Sekharan shel Mitzvot* (1874). He also wrote *Ha-Maggid*, comments on the Pentateuch and **haftarot*; and *Em la-Binah*, a lexicon of Hebrew and Aramaic roots in alphabetic order. Teomim also mentions unpublished works.

BIBLIOGRAPHY: Z.J. Michelsohn, *Toledot Yosef*, appended to J. Teomim, *Notarikon* (1910); S. Buber, *Anshei Shem* (1895), 95–97; L. Loewenstein, in: MGWJ, 57 (1913), 354f.; S. Knoebil, *Toledot Gedolei Hora'ah* (1927), 106–10; S.M. Chones, *Toledot ha-Posekim* (1910), 498f.; Waxman, Literature, 3 (1960^2), 713f.; Y.A. Kamelhar, *Dor De'ah*, 2 (1935), 92–95; A. Freimann, in: *Kobez al Jad*, 3 pt. 2 (1940), 218, 221–4; Ch. Tchernowitz, *Toledot ha-Posekim*, 3 (1947), 193–201; R. Margaliot, in: *Sinai*, 27 (1950), 353–5; B. Yasher (Schlichter), in: *Sura*, 1 (1953/54), 439–42; EG, 4 (1956), 414; A. Blau, *Massu'ot* (1965), 143–51; O. Feuchtwanger, *Righteous Lives* (1965), 57–60.

[Itzhak Alfassi]

TEPLICE (Czech **Teplice-Šanov**, Ger. **Teplitz** or **Teplitz-Schoenau**), city in N. Bohemia, Czech Republic. The Jewish community of Teplice was one of the largest and most important in Bohemia from the 16th century onward, one of the few places from which Jews were not expelled until the Nazi regime. The first evidence of Jewish settlement dates from 1414, when there were 20 Jews in the city. In 1480 the community had a cemetery and a synagogue. In 1570, 23 families resided in Teplice. The old cemetery had to be abandoned in 1669 and a new one was opened. In 1667 there were 262 Jews in Teplice. After the persecutions at the end of the 17th century their number had diminished to 187 in 1702. In 1823 there were 496 Jews dwelling in 50 houses. The community flourished under the benevolent patronage of the Clary family. During the period of industrial development, Jews engaged in the glass, ceramic, and coal-mining industries, as well as in developing the noted spa. Rabbis who served in Teplice included Z. *Frankel (1832–36), who left for Dresden after encountering local opposition; his successor, David Pick (1836–78), who gave sermons in German and was the first in Austria to use the organ during services; Adolf Rosenberg (1878–87); Adolf Kurrein (1887–1919); and Friedrich Weiss (1920–38), who wrote the history of the community. In the second half of the 19th century, the Teplice community became the second largest in Bohemia (after Prague), numbering 1,718 (11.6% of the total population) in 1880, 2,704 (10.1%) in 1910, and 3,213 (10.4%) in 1930, the highest percentage in Bohemia. The increase was due to the influx of East European Jews, who organized their own Orthodox community and reconsecrated the old synagogue for their use in 1925. There was also a strong Zionist center in Teplice.

The rabbi and the majority of the community left in summer and fall 1938, as Teplice was situated in the Sudeten region, scene of bitter Czech-German strife and Nazi agitation. After the Munich agreement, almost no Jews remained. The old cemetery (dating from 1669) was destroyed by the Nazis; the new one, opened in 1862, was still extant in the late 1960s. The synagogue, built in 1883, was also destroyed by the Nazis. After World War II a new community was organized, mainly by refugees from Subcarpathian Ruthenia, and totaled 1,200 in 1948. In 1965 about 500 community members remained, employing a cantor and holding services in the communal center prayer room. After 1967 the community declined.

BIBLIOGRAPHY: P. Wanie, *Geschichte der juden von Teplitz* (1925); F. Weihs, in: H. Gold (ed.), *Juden und Judengemeinden Boehmens* (1934), 646–74; B. Brilling, in: *Zeitschrift fuer die Geschichte der Juden*, 6 (1968), 167–73; idem, in: *Zeitschrift fuer die Geschichte der Juden in der Tschechoslowakei*, 6 (1938); 23–27; J. Diamant and B. Glaser, *ibid.*, 63–68; R. Iltis (ed.), *Die aussaeen unter Traenen…* (1958).

[Jan Herman]

TEPLITZ, SAUL I. (1921–), U.S. Conservative rabbi. Teplitz was born in Vienna, Austria, and was brought to the United States in 1922. He received a B.A. from the University of Pittsburgh in 1941 and was ordained in 1945 at the Jewish Theological Seminary, where he earned a D.H.L. in 1956 and a D.D. in 1971. He served as rabbi of Laurelton Jewish Center in Laurelton, N.Y. (1944–60) and the Jewish Community Center of Harrison in Harrison, N.Y. (1960–63) before becoming rabbi of Congregation Sons of Israel in Woodmere, N.Y. (1963, emeritus since 1991). He also served as chairman of the Board of Education of the Hebrew High School of the Five Towns and president of the Commission on Synagogue Relations, Federation of Jewish Philanthropies of New York. In addition, he was a judge for the Jewish Conciliation Board of America, and associate professor of homiletics at the Jewish Theological Seminary (1981–94). In 1975, he was named chairman of the Rabbinical Advisory Committee of New York UJA-Federation, and chairman of the New York Rabbinic Cabinet of Israel Bonds in 1976. In 1978, he was elected vice president of the New York Board of Rabbis.

At the same time, Teplitz assumed national Jewish leadership positions as well, serving as chairman of the United Synagogue Youth Commission (1974–76), before becoming president of the Synagogue Council of America (1977–79). In 1978, he was elected president of the *Rabbinical Assembly. As president, he met with Israeli Prime Minister Menachem *Begin to protest proposed amendments to the *Law of Return that would deny recognition in Israel of conversions performed by non-Orthodox rabbis anywhere. During his tenure in office, Conservative Judaism's *Passover Haggadah: Feast of Freedom* was published, as well as the second volume in the series *Emet ve-Emunah: Studies in Conservative Jewish Thought*, and a *festschrift* honoring RA executive vice president Wolfe *Kelman. He also created a Blue Ribbon Committee to develop a blueprint for the future of the RA and chaired the Task Force on Halachic Guidance and Conservative Ideology. In 1982, he was the recipient of the Louis Marshall Award from the Jewish Theological Seminary.

Teplitz wrote *Life is for Living* (1970) and *The Courage to Change* (1999). He also edited *The Rabbi Speaks*, two volumes of sermons for the New York Board of Rabbis, and *Best Jewish Sermons*, 11 edited volumes of selected sermons.

[Bezalel Gordon (2nd ed.)]

TEPPER, KOLYA (1879–?), Yiddish writer. Born in Odessa, Tepper became a Zionist in his youth and a member of the circle of *Aḥad Ha-Am and a delegate to the Second Zionist Congress (1898). He lived in Switzerland 1901–3, where he was a propagandist for the Zionist movement. He then returned to Russia, where he renounced Zionism for the ideology of the *Bund. He was arrested later that year in Pinsk but freed a day later by a group of Jewish workers. In 1907 Tepper fled Russia for the United States, where he began writing essays under the pseudonym "Duke D'Abruzzi" in the radical press, including the *Fraye Arbeter Shtime* (publ. as *Zigzagn*, "Zigzags," 1915). He was also a prolific translator of foreign literature, including works by Chekhov, Brandes, and Ibsen. In New York, Tepper befriended several of the poets associated with Di *Yunge and contributed to their literary efforts. Following the 1917 Revolution, he returned to Russia, then lived in Vilna and Warsaw in 1920–22, before moving back to the Soviet Union. It is not known when or how he died.

BIBLIOGRAPHY: Reyzen, Leksikon, 1 (1926), 1183–6; LNYL, 3 (1960), 103–5; M. Ravitch, *Mayn Leksikon*, 1 (1945), 104–6. **ADD. BIBLIOGRAPHY:** R.R. Wisse, *A Little Love in Big Manhattan* (1988), 45–50.

[Melech Ravitch / Marc Miller (2nd ed.)]

TEPPER, MORRIS (1916–), U.S. meteorologist. Tepper was born in Palestine and moved with his family to New York in 1922. He graduated with an M.A. in mathematics from Brooklyn College and gained his Ph.D. in fluid dynamics from Johns Hopkins University, Baltimore (1952). He served as a meteorologist in the U.S. Air Force in the Pacific Theater (1943–45) during World War II. He joined the U.S. Weather Bureau as a research meteorologist in 1946 and was head of a team conducting research on local storms (1951–59). In 1959 he joined the National Aeronautics and Space Administration (NASA) as a meteorologist in the office of space flight development, and later became director of meteorological systems and deputy director of the earth observations programs division. He was a special project officer at NASA's Goddard Space Flight Center (1978–79). In 1979 he left NASA to become professor of mathematical physics at Capitol College in Laurel, Maryland. Tepper's research has concerned the origins and prediction of severe local storms. With NASA he supervised the introduction of satellite systems for forecasting local storms and global weather patterns, essential for terrestrial and space travel. He worked through the UN Committee on Space Research to promote international cooperation on space meteorology.

[Michael Denman (2nd ed.)]

TERAH (Heb. תֶּרַח), father of Abraham, Nahor, and Haran. Terah is mentioned in the Bible chiefly in genealogical lists (Gen. 11:24–28; Josh. 24:2: I Chron. 1:26–27). The only biographical material is contained in Genesis 11:31–32; the Bible tells of Terah's migration from Ur toward Canaan and his stopping at Harran (see *Haran), where he died at the age of 205 (in the Samaritan Pentateuch 145). Since both Ur and Harran were centers of moon worship in Mesopotamia, attempts have been made to connect the personal name Terah to the word *yare'aḥ*, "moon" (Akk. (*w*)*arḥu*), and similar etymological connections with lunar terminology have been sought for the names of other members of Terah's household.

At an early stage of the interpretation of literary texts in Ugaritic, some scholars mistakenly construed the verb *trḥ*, "to take as a wife," as the proper name Terah. Now that it is clear that the proper name Terah – either as moon-god or eponymous hero – does not appear in Ugaritic literature, the only remaining extra-biblical attestation of the name Terah is in the neo-Assyrian place-name *tīl turaḥi*. The latter was situated in the Balikh Valley in Mesopotamia, in the general vicinity of Harran. The correspondence of Terah's name with the name of a site in the Harran area is paralleled by the correspondence of the name Nahor, the name of Terah's father and of one of his sons, with that of the city of Naḥur, and of the name of Terah's grandfather Serug with that of a city called Sarugi in cuneiform sources.

The name Terah also appears in the Bible (Num. 33:27, 28) as the name of a site in the Sinai Peninsula.

[Murray Lichtenstein]

In the *Aggadah*

Terah's wife, the mother of Abraham, was Amathlai, the daughter of Karnebo (BB 91a). Terah was a manufacturer of idols and during his absence he left Abraham to sell them in his place. When, on his return, he discovered that Abraham had destroyed the idols, he delivered him to Nimrod (Gen. R. 38: 12).

Abraham later attempted to convince his father to leave the service of Nimrod and accompany him to the Land of Canaan. Noah and Shem aided Abraham in persuading Terah, and he finally consented to repent and to leave his homeland (Yashar, No'aḥ 27b–28a). For many years Terah continued to witness his son's glory, for his death did not occur until his grandson Isaac was 35 years old (SER 5:28). God accepted his repentance, and when he departed this life he immediately entered into Paradise. He was spared from hell even though he spent the majority of his days in sin (Gen. 11:27; Gen. R. 38:12).

[Aaron Rothkoff]

In Islam

Āzar (Terah) is the name of Abraham's father according to Sura 6:740. It is derived from Elāzār or Elieser. *Muhammad understood that those names were determined by the article *al* (Āzar), Āzar was a heathen (19:43–49). Abraham tried to teach his father the true religion, showing him that his idols were powerless by smashing them (21:53–58). It is clear that the tales about Āzar are connected with those about *Abraham's wars against the heathens.

[Haïm Z'ew Hirschberg]

BIBLIOGRAPHY: W.F. Albright, in: BASOR, 71 (1938), 35–40; Bright, Hist, 70; C.L. Gibson, in: JSS, 7 (1962), 54; Ginzberg, Legends, 1 (1961), 186–217; 5 (1955), 208–18. **ADD BIBLIOGRAPHY:** A. Jeffery in: EIS², 1 (1960), 810 (includes bibliography).

TERAPHIM (Heb. תְּרָפִים), household gods. The etymology of the word teraphim has defied commentators from ancient times until the present. W.F. Albright suggests the possible rendering of "old rags," based on the Canaanite *trp*, "to wear out." L. Koehler and W. Baumgartner also suppose that teraphim has obvious odious connotations and that its root *trp* means to act ignominiously. H.A. Hoffner has pointed to a Hurro-Hittite source for the word (Hittite: *tarpis*, "protective or malevolent spirit"). That these figurines were small and portable is obvious from the way Rachel managed to hide them in the camel cushion (Gen. 31:34). On the other hand, the fact that Michal could deceive her father's messengers by leading them to believe that the teraphim on the bed were David's figure, makes it seem that some were of considerable size (I Sam. 19:13). There is nothing in this incident, however, to show conclusively whether such a figure represented an entire human form or simply a head or bust.

The teraphim are both condoned and condemned in biblical writing. From the story of Rachel's flight and her appropriation of her father's teraphim, it seems to have been the accepted custom among the people in Mesopotamia to have objects of worship in their house and to take them along when going abroad (see Greenberg, in bibl.). Furthermore, in the story of Michal, teraphim seem to be a usual piece of household furniture and were most probably tolerated by the Israelite religion of that time.

The tablets from Nuzi proved to have direct bearing on knowledge of teraphim since the Akkadian term *ilāni*, "gods," was used in Nuzi legal texts in ways that closely paralleled some of the occurrences of the word *ʾelohim* or its interchangeable partner teraphim (Gen. 31:30; cf. 31:19, 34, 35). In an adoption contract from Nuzi it is stated that on the death of the adoptive father the adopted son shall be heir. If, however, a natural son is born, he shall be the primary heir and receive his father's *ilāni* ("gods"); otherwise, the *ilāni* go to the adopted son. In cases where a normal heir was lacking, the possessor of the *ilāni* was entitled to a large share of the inheritance.

Rachel's theft of her father's teraphim may be viewed as an attempt to secure her own right to her father's inheritance. Then again, since Laban had begotten sons, Jacob, who may have been adopted by Laban, would have had no right to the gods, and thus Rachel might have stolen them in order to secure the right of paterfamilias for her husband. The idea that possession of the household gods was in some way connected with rights to property inheritance has found widespread acceptance. M. Greenberg, however, has cast serious doubts on the validity of this interpretation, and maintains that since both the adopted son and the legitimate heir divide the inheritance equally, the possession of these household gods does not determine a title to inheritance but rather leadership of the family, and a claim to paterfamilias.

Apart from the household gods already discussed, a different sort of teraphim is encountered in the Bible; their place is not in the home but in the sanctuary, and they were used by the Israelites in cultic ritual. Teraphim were employed in divination in the period of the Judges (Judg. 17:5; 18:17), like the divining ephod with which they are compared, and their use in divination is particularly obvious in the condemnation of teraphim in I Samuel 15:23, where the iniquity of teraphim is placed on a par with the sin of divination. Josiah, known for his far-reaching cultic reforms, did away with all the cultic objects of abominable idolatry, including teraphim (II Kings 23:24). Zechariah further rejects the teraphim by including them among the sources of false prediction (Zech. 10:2). Divination teraphim are assumed by Ezekiel to have been among the devices consulted by the king of Babylon (Ezek. 21:26).

BIBLIOGRAPHY: C.H. Gordon, in: BA, 3 (1940), 1–12; A.E. Draffkorn in: JBL, 76 (1957), 216–24; M. Greenberg, *ibid.*, 81 (1962), 239–48; N. Sarna, *Understanding Genesis* (1967), 200–1; H.A. Hoffner, in: JNES, 27 (1968), 61–68.

TEREBINTH, a tree of the genus *Pistacia* of which four species grow in Israel (for two of them see *Mastic (Lentisk) and *Pistachio). Most important of them are *Pistacia atlantica* and *Pistacia palaestina*, which are among the largest and most widespread forest trees of Israel. Their biblical name, *elah* – like *allon*, the *oak – is derived from *el*, meaning strong and sturdy. Certain terebinths are singled out for special mention in the Bible because of events associated with them. Jacob buried the idols of Laban's house "under the terebinth which was by Shechem" (Gen. 35:4); the angel of the Lord appeared to Gideon under a terebinth (Judg. 6:11); and the bodies of Saul and his sons were buried beneath one (I Chron. 10:12; in I Sam. 31:13 the reading is *eshel*, *tamarisk). The vale of Elah (I Sam. 17:2), where David slew Goliath, was so called because of the terebinths which grew in the district. These beautiful tall trees also served as sites of idol worship and are mentioned deprecatingly in Hosea (4:13), Isaiah (1:29), and Ezekiel (6:13). The word *elah* also occurs in the Bible as a personal name, and it is possible that the word *elon* also refers to the terebinth (though some identify it with the oak). The *elah* referred to in Scripture as a tall tree is the *Pistacia atlantica*, which develops a tall trunk and widespread foliage and branches; it was by those branches that Absalom was caught by his long hair (II Sam. 18:9). The terebinth is deciduous, shedding its leaves in winter (Isa. 1:29–30). Isaiah compares the remnant of Israel to the *mazzevet* ("trunk") of the oak and the terebinth which grew in the vicinity of the Shallekhet Gate in Jerusalem; though continually felled, the trees renewed themselves, putting forth lowly and fresh branches (6:13; see Rashi ad loc. and Feliks, p. 104, n. 9).

The Mishnah (Shev. 7:5) mentions the terebinth as one of the trees whose *lulavim* ("shoots") were eaten, apparently after being pickled in salt or vinegar. In Arabic the terebinth is called *butm* and in Aramaic *butma*; the Jerusalem Talmud notes that the latter is related to the pistachio (TJ, Kil. 1:4, 27a) and even today it is sometimes customary to graft the pistachio on to the wild terebinth. The *Pistacia atlantica* is among the largest and oldest trees of Israel. Particularly well known is the ancient tree in Tel Dan near the source of the Jordan, which is about 1,000 years old and has a girth of about 20 ft. (6 m.). The species *Pistacia palaestina* is common in the Judean Hills and in Upper Galilee. Since its branches are gnawed by goats, it is mostly stunted and looks like a shrub.

BIBLIOGRAPHY: Loew, Flora, 1 (1926), 191–5; J. Feliks, *Olam ha-Ẓome'aḥ ha-Mikra'i* (1968^2), 104–6; idem, *Kilei Zera'im ve-Harkavah* (1967), 106f. **ADD. BIBLIOGRAPHY:** Feliks, Ha-Ẓome'aḥ, 26.

[Jehuda Feliks]

TEREFAH (Heb. טְרֵפָה; lit. "torn" by beast of prey), an animal whose death is due to physical defects or injuries is said to be *terefah* (Maim. Yad, Ma'akhalot Asurot, 4:8). The biblical prohibition, "Ye shall not eat any flesh that is torn of beasts (*terefah*) in the field; ye shall cast it to the dogs" (Ex. 22:30), applies to a clean animal that has suffered a mortal injury from wild beasts but is not yet dead, since if it is dead it is carrion (**nevelah*). Such an animal, even ritually slaughtered before dying, is forbidden since it would have not recovered from its injury. The rabbis considered the scriptural verse merely as a particular instance of a general principle applying equally in the case of an animal sustaining a mortal injury from any other cause, or suffering from a fatal illness. It is *terefah*, whatever the cause of the defect (Mekh., Mishpatim, 20). The rabbis therefore laid down that "if an animal with such defect cannot live, it is *terefah*" (Hul. 3:1), i.e., any clean animal sustaining an injury from which death must result within 12 months (Rashi, *ibid.*) is *terefah*. An animal which is about to die from natural causes, such as age, is not *terefah* since the defect must be similar to that inflicted by a wild beast (Ḥul. 37a).

This broad concept of *terefah* is very old, being known already in the days of John Hyrcanus (second century B.C.E.). The Mishnah (Sot. 9:10) relates that this high priest abolished the "stunners," who, the *baraita* (Sot. 48a) explains, used to strike the sacrificial calf with clubs to bring it to the ground. Johanan asked them how long they would supply the altar with *terefah* (in that the clubbing might have caused a perforation of the membrane of the brain) and he thereupon installed rings to hold fast the animal's neck.

The Eight Types of Terefah

According to the Talmud, eight types of *terefah* were revealed to Moses at Sinai: clawing, perforation, deficiency, missing organs, severed organs, falling, tearing, fracturing (Ḥul. 43a). Their mnemonic is *DaN ḤaNaK NeFeSh* ("Dan strangled a soul" = *Derusah, Nekuvah, Ḥaserah, Netulah, Keru'ah, Nefulah, Pesukah, Shevurah*). The definitions of the types are as follows: (1) clawing, the clawing of an animal by a wild beast or of a bird by a bird of prey; (2) perforation, a perforation to the cavity of one of the following 11 organs: the pharynx, the membrane of the brain, the heart and its aorta, the gall bladder, the vena cava inferior, abomasum, rumen, omasum, reticulum, intestines, the lung and trachea; (3) deficiency, the absence from birth of one of the lobes of the lung, or one of the feet; (4) missing, the absence of converging sinews in the thigh, or the liver, or the upper jaw; (5) severing, the severing of the membrane covering the spinal cord whether the spinal column be broken or not; (6) falling, the crushing of one of the internal organs of an animal as the result of a fall; (7) tearing, the tearing of most of the flesh covering the rumen; (8) fracturing, such as the fracturing of most of its ribs.

All *terefot* are included in these 8 principal categories. The Mishnah (Ḥul. 3:1) adds 10 subsidiary forms of *terefot*, making 18 in all. They are further subdivided, and Maimonides (Yad, Sheḥitah, 10:9–13) lists in detail all the 70 *terefot* mentioned in the Talmud and concludes: "One may not in any circumstances add to this list of *terefot*, for in the case of any other defect in an animal, beast, or bird, beyond those which the sages of former generations have enumerated, and which the authorities have established, it is possible for the animal to continue to live, even if in the light of our own medical knowledge it cannot survive. Conversely, as regards defects that the sages have enumerated as *terefah*, even if according to present medical knowledge some of these are not fatal and the animal can survive, one must be guided only by what the sages have enumerated, as it is said, 'according to the law which they shall teach thee' [Deut. 17:11]."

See *Dietary Laws.

BIBLIOGRAPHY: J.L. Katzenelson, *Ha-Talmud ve-Ḥokhmat ha-Refu'ah* (1928); J. Cohn, *The Royal Table; an Outline of the Dietary Laws of Israel* (1963); I. Grunfeld, *The Philosophical and Moral Basis of the Jewish Dietary Laws* (1961); H.L. Moled, *The Book of Life; a Treatise on ... the Laws ... relating to the Torah ...* (1956); F.J. Simoons, *Eat not this Flesh* (1961); M.L. Schapiro, *Jewish Dietary Problems* (1919).

[Abraham Arzi]

TERKEL, STUDS (**Louis**; 1912–), U.S. writer and interviewer. Born in New York, the son of immigrant parents, he moved at age eight with his parents to Chicago, a town with which he remained closely associated. His parents opened a boarding house in an Italian district where he went to school. He attended the University of Chicago and then law school. At the time of the New Deal he got a job on a writers' employment program and began to dabble in music, theater, and acting. Gradually he turned to radio and later to television, first as a news commentator and sportscaster, and from the mid-1940s, hosting interview shows. In 1949 he had his own television show, *Studs' Place*, an improvised sitcom where he played himself as a restaurant owner. In 1953 he was investigated by the House Un-American Activities Committee. When he refused to name names, he was barred from appearing on television. The resourceful Terkel eventually found a job at the *Chicago Sunday Times* writing a regular jazz column. During that period he also acted in various plays, such as *Of Mice and Men*.

In 1958 Terkel launched his long-running daily one-hour radio program on Chicago's WFMT-FM, the *Studs Terkel Show*, which was broadcast throughout the U.S. until 1998. In the 1960s Terkel saw the applicability of the tape recorder to social research and utilized oral history as a tool for writing social history. He tracked down everyday men and women and recorded their story, dramatizing the experience of anonymous Americans who would otherwise have remained anonymous.

He made a great impression with *Hard Times: An Oral History of the Great Depression* (1970), following this with other oral histories including *Working* (1974) and *Race* (1992). He also published *Giants of Jazz* (1957); *Division Street: America* (1967); *Talking to Myself: A Memoir of My Times* (1977); *American Dreams* (1980); *Chicago* (1985); *The Great Divide* (1988); *Coming of Age* (1995); *My American Century* (1997); *Will the Circle Be Unbroken?* (2001); *Hope Dies Last* (2003); and *And They All Sang* (2005).

A collection of six CDs, spanning the 1950s to 1997, titled *Voices of Our Time: Five Decades of Studs Terkel Interviews*, was released in 2005. Terkel's book *The Good War* (1985) won the Pulitzer Prize.

[Geoffrey Wigoder / Ruth Beloff (2nd ed.)]

TERNI, DANIEL BEN MOSES DAVID (late 18th–early 19th century), Italian rabbi and poet. Terni came from Ancona, and served as rabbi in Lugo, Pesaro, and Florence. His most important work is *Ikkerei ha-Dat* (a reference to the initials of his name ד"ט), an anthology of halakhic rulings found in the works of the **posekim* and in responsa. It is largely confined to new rulings evolved in the 18th century after the publication of the *Leket ha-Kemaḥ* of Moses *Ḥagiz, and differs from the works which were its predecessors in that Terni also added his own views. The only parts of the work published were on *Oraḥ Ḥayyim* (Florence, 1803) and *Yoreh De'ah* (*ibid.*, 1806). The book has been republished a number of times and was also included in later editions of the Shulḥan Arukh.

Terni also wrote *Se'udat Mitzvah* (Venice, 1791), homilies for the festivals and special occasions; *Mattenat Yad* (Florence, 1794); and *Shem Olam* (Piotrkow, 1929), homilies and novellae on the Torah. He composed *Ketav ha-Dat* (Leghorn, 1791), psalms and prayers of thanksgiving for the deliverance of the Jews of Florence from attack in June 1790, and was the author of secular poetry, as well as a musical play, *Simḥat Mitzvah* (Florence, 1793), on the occasion of the dedication of the synagogue in Florence.

BIBLIOGRAPHY: Ch. Tchernowitz, *Toledot ha-Posekim*, 3 (1947), 322f.; Gorali, in: *Taẓlil*, 2 (1961), 85–92; Schirmann, in: *Zion*, 29 (1964), 107f.; I. Adler, *La pratique musicale savante*, 1 (1966), 124f.

[Abraham David]

TERRACINI, BENVENUTO ARON (1886–1968), Italian philologist. Terracini, who was born in Turin, was a lecturer in Italian at the Akademie fuer Handels-und Sozialwissenschaften in Frankfurt. After serving in the Italian army in World War I, he was in charge of linguistics at the University of Genoa and then held professorships successively at the universities of Cagliari and Padua and the State University of Milan. In 1941 he went to the Argentine as a refugee from Fascism, and served until 1946 as professor of general linguistics and Romance languages at the National University of Tucuman. He returned to Italy in 1947 and was professor of linguistics at the University of Turin until 1961. Terracini was editor of *Archivio Glottologico Italiano* and director of the Instituto per l'Atlante Linguistico. He took an active part in the affairs of the Jewish community of Turin and from 1948 to 1961 served as a member of the board of the Union of Italian Jewish Communities. His published works include *Guida allo studio linguistica storica* (1949), *Conflictos de lenguas y de cultural* (1957), and *Pagine e appunti di linguistica storica* (1957).

TERRACINI, UMBERTO ELIA (1895–1983), Italian Communist leader. Terracini joined the Socialist Party as a youth and became a member of its executive as a representative of the radical wing. In 1921 he joined the newly formed Italian Communist Party. In 1926 Terracini edited the radical newspaper *L'Unità* of Milan and the same year was sentenced to 23 years' imprisonment by the Fascist administration. Pardoned in 1937, he was exiled to a remote part of the country. On his release in 1943 he took refuge in Switzerland. He returned to Italy in 1944 to take a leading part in the resistance in the Ossola Valley. When World War II ended, Terracini became a member of the Consultative Assembly. He was elected a deputy to the Constituent Assembly and after the resignation of Giuseppe Saragat served as speaker from 1947 to 1948. In 1948 he became a senator and distinguished himself as one of the foremost orators in the Communist Party. In 1965–66 he was the party's candidate for the presidency of Italy. He took an independent, sympathetic position in the controversy about the persecution of Jews in the Soviet Union and showed himself favorably disposed toward the State of Israel. He wrote the preface to the reader on Soviet Jewry, *Gli ebrei nell' URSS* (1966).

[Giorgio Romano]

TERRITORIALISM. Jewish movements in the 20th century aiming to establish an autonomous settlement of Jews in a sufficiently large territory "in which the predominant majority of the population shall be Jewish." In contrast to Zionism, Territorialism regarded Ereẓ Israel as one of these territories but not the only one. Any other attempts in the past and present by Jews or non-Jews, by organizations or governments, to assist in finding a refuge for oppressed Jews do not fall within the scope of Territorialism as defined above. They are dealt with under separate headings (see Agricultural Settlement, *Migration, *Jewish Colonization Association (ICA), *Birobidzhan, *Crimea, Baron Maurice de *Hirsch, *Evian Conference, Paul *Friedmann, Davis *Trietsch, *Madagascar Plan).

ITO

Territorialism was a child of the Zionist movement. It came into existence after the death of Theodor *Herzl, during the Seventh Zionist Congress (Basle, July/August 1905), which decided not to proceed with the Guas Ngishu projects in East Africa (commonly called the *Uganda Scheme) offered by the British Government in 1903 for an autonomous Jewish settlement. Twenty-eight delegates who refused to accept the rejection of the British offer withdrew from the congress, and with additional delegates met in a separate conference (July 30 and August 1) where they decided to secede from the Zionist Organization and to establish an independent Jewish Territorial Organization (abbr. ITO). Israel *Zangwill, their leader, at first opposed secession but accepted it after the general meeting of the Anglo-Palestine bank had refused to expand its activities beyond the Palestine area. He became president and remained in that capacity until the dissolution of the ITO in 1925. The first conference in Basle defined the objects of ITO as follows:

> I. To procure a territory upon an autonomous basis for those Jews who cannot, or will not, remain in the lands in which they at present live. II. To achieve this end the Organization proposes (a) to unite all Jews who are in agreement with this object; (b) to enter into relations with Governments and public and private institutions; (c) to create financial institutions, labor-bureaus, and other instruments that may be found necessary.

It appeared at first that a peaceful coexistence of the ITO and Zionist Organization was possible. ITO was one of the few movements which participated in the Brussels Conference (Jan. 29, 1906) called by the Zionist Organization to discuss a constructive solution of the Jewish migration problem. But the conference ended without any tangible results and the two movements quickly drifted apart. Subsequently, in the first few years, ITO constituted a definite threat to the Zionist Organization, and bitter controversies ensued between the two movements in meetings and in the Jewish press.

ITO secured the collaboration of a great number of influential Jews and some leading Zionists all over the world. Among the latter were Israel *Jasinowski, Max *Mandelstamm (Russia), Karl Jeremias, Alfred *Klee (Germany), and Nahum *Slouschz (France). Some anti-Zionist leaders joined, for instance, Lucien *Wolf, obviously with a view to fight Zionism from this newly created platform. Some Socialist Zionists, headed by Nachman *Syrkin and the *Zionist Socialists in Russia (abbr. SS), also known as Zionist Territorialists, also joined the ITO. Within a short time ITO established numerous branches all over the world and, in Russia alone, over 280 emigration centers. The headquarters were in London. It concentrated organizational activities in various commissions among which the international council, consisting of 31 members, attended to political and administrative work, while suitable territories were selected by a geographical commission, consisting of such prominent men as Lord *Rothschild (England), Paul *Nathan and James *Simon (Germany), Max Mandelstamm (Russia), and Daniel *Guggenheim, Judge Mayer *Sulzberger, and Oscar S. *Straus (U.S.).

ITO's first efforts were directed to a continuation of the negotiations with the British Government regarding East Africa. However, notwithstanding the sympathies for ITO expressed publicly by members of the government (as for instance, Winston S. *Churchill, Lord Elgin, Herbert Gladstone), no success accompanied these negotiations. Further attempts were made to procure "ITO Land" in Angola (1907), Cyrenaica (1908), Mesopotamia (1909), as well as in Australia, Mexico, and many other localities. "There was not a land on earth that we did not think about," Zangwill confessed years later. All these attempts ended in failure. The only practical success of ITO was the establishment of an assembly-point in *Galveston (Texas). This, however, constituted an abandonment of the original program which aimed at a compact autonomous settlement, because Galveston served as a transition harbor for individual Jewish immigrants on their arrival from Europe, whence they were sent to southern and western areas of the United States and thus diverted from New York and other crowded centers in the east. The scheme was financed by Jacob H. *Schiff ($100,000), and Lord Rothschild of London and Baron Edmond de Rothschild of Paris ($10,000 each). During World War I, ITO at first declined cooperation with the Zionists in England but after the issuance of the *Balfour Declaration (1917), the ITO delegated David *Eder to join the *Zionist Commission in Jerusalem, simultaneously ceasing any activities of its own. In 1925 it was formally disbanded.

AIKO

Independent of ITO and with less organizational ability and success was the "Allgemeine Juedische Kolonisations-Organisation" (abbr. AIKO) which was initiated by Alfred *Nossig soon after the revolution of the Young Turks in 1908. Nossig also seceded from the Zionist Organization, of whose General Council he was a member, to pursue his activities independently. AIKO rejected the national and political aspect of Zionism and differed from ITO insofar as it sought a compact Jewish settlement in Palestine, Syria, and the Sinai Peninsula only, and did not emphasize the autonomous aspect. On the other hand, it did not reject autonomy should it develop through gradual immigration into the area. AIKO was established in Berlin and was joined by a number of prominent persons in Germany and other countries (primarily in Austria, England, Poland, and Russia). It counted among its members leading Zionists such as the future president of the Zionist Organization Otto *Warburg, Adolf Friedemann, Moses *Gaster, and Selig Eugen *Soskin, as well as some leaders of the Orthodox *Agudat Israel. However, these Zionists soon left AIKO because of its anti-Zionist stance. Unlike ITO, however, AIKO never became a threat to the Zionist Organization. It created subsidiary institutions: the Orient Colonising Company (London, 1909), the Juedisches Hilfskommittee Roter Halbmond fuer Palaestina, and the Deutsch-Israelitisch-Osmanische Union (both in Berlin, 1915). AIKO tried to reopen negotiations with the British Government (1911) regarding settlement in the Sinai Peninsula (contemplated and abandoned in 1902–03 by Herzl), and before (1909) and during World War I with the Turkish authorities for a compact settlement in Palestine; but it failed. AIKO's only practical result was the financial assistance rendered in the land acquisition for *Kefar Uriyyah. An "international Colonization Conference" called by AIKO in 1914 had to be canceled owing to the outbreak of the war. The organization was dissolved in 1920.

After the Balfour Declaration (1917) and in the 1920s the efforts of Jewish settlement centered on Palestine. The economic crises resulting from the world depression in 1929–32, as well as the increase of antisemitic policies, particularly in Central and Eastern Europe, greatly stimulated the urge of Jewish emigration. These conditions and the restricted immigration quotas to Palestine led to a revival of territorialist activities. The ascent of Nazism in Germany considerably speeded up this revival, and in various parts of the world Jewish groups were established which sought to alleviate these conditions by territorialist methods.

International Jewish Colonization Society

Shortly before World War II efforts were made to centralize all territorial and settlement activities into one organization to comprise all groups seeking autonomous or compact Jewish settlements as well as individual settlement schemes. On the initiative of Daniel Wolf in Amsterdam, the "International Jewish Colonization Society" was formed in November 1938. A number of important individuals and organizations, for instance, the "Freeland League" (see below), the ICA, and others, agreed to associate themselves with these efforts. The society's aim was "to finance settlements of Jews in suitable areas in the world." As this also included Palestine, Zionists agreed to cooperate. At a conference in London (Dec. 4, 1938) a representative international board was elected to head the society's activities. A number of prominent non-Jews also agreed to serve on the board. Some substantial amounts were raised, most of which had been used for investigations in various territories throughout the world regarding their suitability for Jewish settlement. The only area that promised certain possibilities was Surinam; but it came to nothing. (This proposal was reopened in 1948 by the Freeland League.) The outbreak of World War II brought the society's activities to an abrupt end.

Freeland League

On July 26, 1935, representatives of a number of societies met in London and established the "Free Land Movement, a League for Territorial Organizations," which subsequently became the Freeland League for Jewish Territorial Colonization. Its purpose was defined as:

> aiming to find and obtain large scale room in some sparsely populated area for the Jewish masses where they could live and develop according to their own views and culture and religion.

The league thus did not expressly demand autonomy, but did not exclude it. Simultaneously the league made its position clear toward Zionism and Palestine, stressing that its work applies "to those Jews who seek a home and cannot or will not go to Palestine." In contrast to pre-World War I conditions, Zionists did not oppose these activities, recognizing a justification of some temporary alleviation of Jewish misery if it was attainable. All the efforts of the league ended in failure. It negotiated for settlements in Angola (1938), Ecuador (1935), Kimberley, Australia (1938–44), and Surinam (1948), and sent out commissions to investigate these and other territories for their suitability for compact settlement. However, in all instances, the governments concerned declined to accept large Jewish immigrant groups in their territories. The Freeland League had its first headquarters in London (1935–41) and since then in New York. Its moving spirits and leaders were *Ben-Adir (Abraham Rosin) and Isaac Nachman *Steinberg. After the latter's death (1957) the leadership fell to Mordkhe Schaechter. Although without an obvious purpose and without pursuing practical settlement efforts, the league still (1971) maintained a central office in New York and published *Oyfn Shvel*, a bimonthly (from 1941); *Freeland* (from 1944); *Boletin* (from 1957); and *Freyland* (from 1957).

BIBLIOGRAPHY: R.J.H. Gottheil, *Zionism* (1914), 135–42; M. Simon (ed.), *Speeches, Articles and Letters of Israel Zangwill* (1937), 231–328; A.G. Duker, in: *Contemporary Jewish Record*, 2 (March–April 1939), 14–30; Ben-Adir, in: *The Jewish People Past and Present*, 2 (1948), 305–22; M. Wischnitzer, *To Dwell in Safety* (1948), index; C. Weizmann, *Trial and Error* (1949), 117, 148–9, 204; O.K. Rabinowicz, *Winston Churchill on Jewish Problems* (1956), 185–95; idem, in: *Herzl Yearbook*, 1 (1958), 30–31, 72–74, 79; J. Leftwich, *Israel Zangwill* (Eng., 1957), 216–39; A. Tartakower, *Ha-Hityashevut ha-Yehudit ba-Golah* (1959); M. Syrkin, *Nachman Syrkin* (Eng., 1961), 86–108; *Yiẓhak Nachman Steinberg Gedenk-Bukh* (Yid., 1961).

[Oskar K. Rabinowicz]

TERTIS, LIONEL (1876–1975), violist. Born in England, Tertis was a viola soloist. This instrument, popular in the 18th century, had been neglected, and it was due to Tertis' exceptional playing that the viola was recognized as a solo instrument. Pieces were written especially for him and he designed a viola that was widely manufactured (the Tertis model).

TERTULIAN, NICOLAE, originally **Nathan Veinstein** (1929–), Romanian literary critic and editor. One of Romania's most respected literary scholars, Tertulian edited the weekly *Contemporanul* (1948–54) and from 1954 was an editor of *Viata Românească*, the organ of the Romanian Writers' Union. He was a prominent figure at many international literary congresses. Tertulian's works include *Probleme ale literaturii de evocare istorica* (1954), *Esseuri* (1968), and *Evolutia spirituala a lui George Lukacs* (1969). From the 1980s he lived in France, where he wrote about Romanian culture. He also published several works on Heidegger there as well as focusing on the literary and esthetic works of Lukacs and on Croce's basic concepts of the role played by culture in the life of a society.

TERUEL, city in *Aragon, E. Spain. No data are available about the beginning of the Jewish settlement in Teruel, which formed one of the most important communities in Aragon. It was already prosperous in the Muslim period and recovered quickly after the conquest of the town by *Alfonso II in 1171. The Jewish quarter was located in the vicinity of the present street called Calle Ainsa, extending toward the city wall, in the northeastern section of Teruel. The excavations in 1925–26 on the site of the old Jewish cemetery revealed several tombstones and a few golden rings engraved with feminine names, one of which was inscribed in Hebrew. The status of the Jews is apparent from the *fuero* (charter) granted by Alfonso II to Teruel (1176), regulating questions pertaining to mixed Jewish-Christian administration and defining the Jews as "slaves of the king, belonging entirely to the royal treasury." In 1285 Pedro III exempted invalids and paupers from taxes but clamped taxes on non-movable property, Muslim slaves, cattle, moneylending, etc.

During the 14th century frequent quarrels broke out within the community concerning the apportionment of taxes and their manner of collection. Between 1310 and 1313 it was agreed that each individual would pay a permanent tax of six dinars and an additional impost estimated according to his property and debts. Shortly before the persecutions of 1391, Queen Violante requested the community heads to carry out a new assessment in view of further taxation, as the indirect taxes already in force did not suffice to cover the community's debts. The community was headed by *muqaddimūn* and *clavarii* ("collectors") who collected taxes and saw to the strict observation of Jewish rites, thus winning the praise of *Isaac b. Sheshet Perfet (Ribash). The wave of anti-Jewish riots of 1321 affected Teruel when the Jews there were accused of poisoning the wells. In July 1348 Pedro III ordered the bailiff of Teruel to shut off the Jewish quarter in order to ward off rioters. The Jewish community was accused of an alleged *Host desecration in 1377. Permission was given in 1382 to the Najari (or Nafari) family to build a synagogue in Teruel. Prior to the 1391 riots the community lent 24,000 sólidos to King Pedro. In August 1391 Queen Violante ordered the town authorities to protect the Jews from hostile villagers. In the days of the *Tortosa disputation the preacher Vicente *Ferrer stayed in Teruel and induced the authorities to issue laws providing for the segregation of Jews from Christians. He was also accountable for the conversion to Christianity of many Jews, among them the Najari family, who at the end of the 14th century leased the crown taxes in Aragon.

In 1417 Alfonso V intervened on behalf of the Jews in Teruel to protect them from the admonitions of overzealous converts. Various privileges and facilities were granted by the king to the Jews of Teruel during the 1450s, especially in 1457 when together with the other communities of Aragon they were exempted from taxes and services. A change for the worse occurred in 1484, with the coming of the inquisitors Juan de Colivera and Marín Navaro to the town, both sent by *Torquemada. Between 1484 and 1486 more than 30 Conversos were condemned to burn at the stake. The activities of the Inquisition came to a climax when Jews were ordered to leave Teruel in 1486. Their expulsion, however, did not take place until 1492, as part of the general expulsion from Spain. Several scores of Jews in Teruel were then pressured by the *Franciscans to convert to Christianity.

BIBLIOGRAPHY: Baer, Spain, index; Baer, Toledot, index; Baer, Urkunden, index; Neuman, Spain, index; M. Serrano y Sanz, *Orígines de la dominación española en América*, 1 (1918), 36–37; A. Floriano, in: *Boletín de la Real Academia de la Historia*, 84 (1924), 560f.; 86 (1925), 546ff.; idem, *La aljama de los judíos de Teruel* (1926); B. Llorca, in: *Sefarad*, 2 (1942), 124ff.; L. Piles Ros. *ibid.*, 10 (1950), 110f.; F. Vendrell, *ibid.*, 13 (1953), 87ff.; D. Romano, *ibid.*, 17 (1957), 144–9; M. Sánchez Moya, *ibid.*, 18 (1958), 283–90; 20 (1960), 163–72; 26 (1966), 273–304; M. Gorosch, *El Fuero de Teruel* (1950); A. Novella Mateo, in: *Teruel*, 10 (1953), 1–5; A. López de Meneses, *Documentos*… (1956), 33, 44, 49, and passim.

[Haim Beinart]

TERUMOT (Heb. תְּרוּמוֹת; "heave offerings"), sixth tractate of the order *Zera'im*, in the Mishnah, Tosefta, and Jerusalem Talmud. There is no Babylonian Talmud on this tractate. It details the laws of *terumah* (the heave offering) to be given to the priest in accordance with the biblical injunctions (Lev. 22:10–14; Num. 18:8, 11, 12, 26, 30; and Deut. 18:4). There were two basic types of *terumah*: one was the regular heave offering or *terumah gedolah* ("great *terumah*") which the Israelites were required to separate from their own crops and to give to the priest; the other was the "tithe heave offering" or *terumat ma'aser* which the levites had to separate for the priests from the tithes they received (see *Terumot* and *Ma'aserot*). The tractate gives a precise definition of these two obligations, although its chief subject is the *terumah gedolah*.

The Mishnah is divided into 11 chapters. Chapter 1 enumerates the five classes of persons who may not set aside *terumah* and the different cases in which the separation is considered valid, although the method utilized in selecting the *terumah* was not the correct one. Chapter 2 consists of further enumeration of cases in which the heave offering is valid, although the method of procedure followed in selecting it was not in consonance with the *halakhah*. An example of this is selecting clean grain as the *terumah* for unclean grain. Chapter 3 quotes some cases where *terumah* had to be given twice. The owner could empower his servant to set aside the *terumah* for him. The order for giving the various dues such as the first fruits, the heave offering, and the tithe is detailed, as is the procedure to be followed when one makes a slip of the tongue while separating *terumah* or taking an oath. Chapter 4 discusses the selection and measuring of the great heave offering and the tithe heave offering. Chapter 5 discusses the mixing of other fruits with ritually clean and unclean *terumah*. Chapter 6 deals with the compensation that must be made by one who has eaten or otherwise derived benefit from a heave offering (cf. Lev. 22:14). Chapter 7 is a continuation of this discussion and gives cases in which only the value of what has been eaten need be paid, without the additional fifth (*ḥomesh*). Chapter 8 deals with how long heave-offering wine and other liquids may be left uncovered and the dangers of their becoming poisoned. Regarding this, Josephus (Apion, 1:165) quotes from a Greek writer of the third century B.C.E. that Pythagoras followed the custom of the Jews in not drinking a certain water. Lieberman suggests that the reference is to this exposed water (cf. Albeck, Mishnah, Zera'im 390). Also discussed is that one may not deliberately defile *terumah*. Chapter 9 outlines the procedure when seeds of *terumah* produce have been deliberately or unwittingly sown. Chapter 10 enumerates the cases in which the flavor of *terumah* prohibits other food and the regulations regarding other cases in which lawful foods become forbidden through the flavor they acquire from prohibited foods. Chapter 11 discusses the usage that may be made of clean and unclean *terumah* in both solid and liquid forms.

Epstein has pointed to several sources and strata in *Terumot. Mishnayot* 4:8–9 and 4:10 record two contradicting traditions concerning a dispute between Eliezer b. Hyrcanus and Joshua b. Hananiah. According to the Jerusalem Talmud, the former represent the teachings of the school of R. Judah and the latter the school of Meir. It is noteworthy that the statements of Eliezer (the last of the school of Shammai) and Joshua were so often interchanged that a prohibition was eventually imposed on any changes of this nature (Sif. Deut. 188).

The Tosefta consists of ten chapters. It corresponds in general to the Mishnah, but there are 26 *mishnayot* which have no corresponding Tosefta. It contains an interesting and extensive definition of the boundaries of Ereẓ Israel (2:12). One of the few aggadic passages in the Jerusalem Talmud to the tractate relates that before *Diocletian became the emperor of Rome (285–305 C.E.), he was originally a swineherd in Tiberias. Whenever he came near the school of Judah II, the young pupils would beat and mock him. When he became emperor he determined to avenge himself on the Jews and their scholars. He went to Paneas, a place at some distance from Tiberias, and from there sent a summons to Judah II, ordering him to appear before him, together with the other scholars, at the conclusion of the Sabbath. He directed his messenger to deliver the summons to Judah on Friday evening so that the scholars, who would not travel on the Sabbath, would be unable to make the journey in time and would therefore be liable to punishment for disobedience. A miracle happened, and the scholars succeeded in appearing before the emperor at the proper time. They appeased his anger by proclaiming that they scorned only the swineherd Diocletian, but obeyed and honored Emperor Diocletian. Diocletian responded that they should be cautious and never insult even a lowly Roman, since he might rise in rank and take revenge (8:10, 46b). A similar story is recorded in *Genesis Rabbah* 63:8. *Terumot* appeared in English in *The Mishnah* (1933, trans. by H. Danby).

TERUMOT AND MA'ASEROT (Heb. תְּרוּמוֹת, "heave offerings," and מַעַשְׂרוֹת, "tithes"), dues given to the priests and the poor. A number of passages in the Bible deal with *ma'aser* and according to the *halakhah* they refer to different categories: the first tithe is given to the levites (Num. 18:21–24); the second tithe is eaten in Jerusalem or redeemed (Deut. 14:22–26); and the tithe that is given to the poor (Deut. 14:28–29 and 26:12). In order to render agricultural produce fit for ordinary consumption (*ḥullin*), *terumot* and *ma'aserot* had to be allocated from it in the following manner: first *terumah* was set aside for the priests, and from the remainder a tenth, the first tithe, was given to the levites. The levites then had to give a tithe of this first tithe, called *terumat ma'aser* or *ma'aser min ha-ma'aser* ("a tithe of the tithe") to the priests. After *terumah* and the first tithe were set aside, a second tithe had to be given of the remainder. In the first, second, fourth, and fifth years of the sabbatical cycle this constituted the second tithe, while in the third and sixth years it became the poor man's tithe. The second tithe had either to be taken up to Jerusalem to be eaten there, or redeemed for money and the money plus an added quarter taken to Jerusalem, where it could be spent at the owner's discretion for his upkeep. The tithe given to the poor is not regarded as sacred. On the last day of Passover of the fourth and seventh years a declaration in line with the biblical injunction (Deut. 26:13–15, called "the declaration of the tithe"), which was applied to all tithes, was made.

Produce from which *terumah* and *ma'aser* have not been set aside is called *tevel* and may not be eaten either by its owner or by priests. The produce of an **am ha-areẓ*, who is "unreliable as to tithes" so that it is uncertain whether its *terumot* and *ma'aserot* have been set aside as prescribed, is called **demai*.

The Bible does not prescribe a given quantity of *terumah*. Hence, according to the letter of the Law, the offer of a single ear of wheat should be enough for the whole. However, the rabbis established a quota: "The proper amount of *terumah*: if a man is liberal it is one-fortieth – Bet Shammai say one-thirtieth – for the average man it is one-fiftieth, and for the niggardly, one-sixtieth" (Ter. 4:3).

Although biblical law confines the duty of giving *terumot* and *ma'aserot* to grain, wine, and oil (cf. Deut. 12:17, "the tithe of the corn, the wine, and the oil"), the sages deduced from the Bible that it applied to other produce and fruits and, according to the *halakhah*, it was further applied to vegetables. The halakhic rule is that "whatever is food and guarded [i.e, does not grow wild] and grows from the earth is liable to tithes" (Ma'as. 1:1). At the close of the tannaitic era the duty of giving tithes was extended to money as well. Similarly there is evidence of *terumah* and *ma'aser* being set aside from all foods, and it would seem that this was "the custom of the pious."

The Bible prescribes a tithe to be set aside from cattle (Lev. 27:32), but this the *halakhah* treated as a sacrifice (Zev. 5:8). On the other hand, a substantial number of sources in the apocryphal *halakhah* indicate that a tithe of cattle was given to the priest (Jub. 32:15, cf. Philo, Virt. 95, etc.; cf. also II Chron. 31:6). Apparently this was the practice at the beginning of the Second Temple era, while the *halakhah* that regards the tithe of cattle as a sacrifice consumed by the owner reflects the practice of a later period. Some of the apocryphal sources (Jub. 32:11; Tob. 1:7; etc.) explain the verses of the Bible as if the second tithe was set aside every year (as does also Targ. Jon.), and that three tithes were set aside in the third and sixth years. It seems, however, that this was written according to their understanding of the verses, without subsequent exegesis, and should not be regarded as reflecting actual conditions.

According to theoretical *halakhah*, the owner of produce can give the *terumah* and *ma'aser* (first tithe) anywhere and to any priest or levite he pleases. This *halakhah* was not in force at the beginning of the Second Temple period. It is seen from the post-Exilic biblical books (Mal. 3:10; Neh. 13:5, etc.), the Apocrypha (Judith 11:13; Tob. 1:6–7; etc.), and Philo (Spec. 1:132–5) that the *terumot* and *ma'aserot* were taken to the Temple in Jerusalem (cf. also LXX, Ex. 1:21). It is almost certain that the regulations concerning the bringing of the priestly and levitical gifts to Jerusalem were made in the time of Ezra and Nehemiah, as part of their general tendency to enhance the national and economic status of Jerusalem. These regulations also seem to be connected with the working procedures of the priests and levites in the Temple, for in this way the priestly and levitical gifts could all be collected at the Temple and fairly distributed among the priests and levites engaged at the time in the divine service.

No definite time was fixed for carrying the *terumot* and *ma'aserot* to Jerusalem, but it may be assumed that they were taken there during the pilgrimage festivals. The second tithe, too, was taken up at that time, as were such other gifts as the firstborn of cattle and the fruit of the fourth-year planting, probably for the purpose of "adorning the streets of Jerusalem with fruit" (RH 31b).

According to the *halakhah*, the first tithe is given to the levites, but there is ample evidence of a practice by which it went to the priests. This is first mentioned in Nehemiah (13:4–13), and the Talmud explains it as a penalty imposed upon the levites because so few of them had returned to Zion (Yev. 86b). The practice of the priests taking tithes continued during the Persian and Hellenistic epochs, and there are echoes of it in the Apocrypha (Judith 11:13; Jub. 13:25–27; etc.). Presumably, however, they were not the only recipients, but the tithes were distributed proportionately among the priests and levites on duty in the Temple. It is possible that the following dictum in a highly problematic *baraita* more or less represents the position with regard to the division of the tithes during these periods: "At first the tithe was divided into three parts, one-third for known priests and levites, one-third for the treasury, and one-third for the poor and to **ḥaverim* who were in Jerusalem" (TJ, Ma'as. Sh. 5:9, 56d).

The Hasmonean kings tried to seize control of the tithes for their own purposes. The edict of Johanan the high priest (Ma'as, Sh. 5:15) must be understood with this in mind as well as the subsequent edict of Julius Caesar to Hyrcanus II stating: "and in addition they shall also pay to Hyrcanus and his sons the tithes that they also paid to their forefathers" (Jos., Ant., 14:203). It may be assumed that the halakhic provision that *terumah* and *ma'aser* could be given everywhere and to any priest or levite was not only congenial to the owner of the produce but also expressed Pharisaic opposition to the use the Hasmonean kings were making of the tithes. The Pharisees wanted to retain the precept of setting aside these dues while preventing their being taken by the Hasmonean rulers in Jerusalem. This *halakhah* seems to have been fairly widely followed and there are sources, both internal and external, from the end of the Temple period, showing that tithes were given at the various localities. It is against this background that the term "priests and levites who stood by the threshing floor" came into being.

Terumot and *ma'aserot* continued to be set aside also after the destruction of the Temple, when tithing became a kind of substitute for the sanctity of the Temple and the sacrificial service. This is evident from the following incident: "Once Tarfon was late in coming to the *bet midrash*. Rabban Gamaliel said to him, What is the reason for your delay? He replied: I was performing the [Temple] service. He then said to him: How come? Is there any service nowadays? He answered: It says in the Bible: 'I give you the priesthood as a service of gift' [Num. 18:7], making the eating of food within the borders of Ereẓ Israel equivalent to the service in the Temple" (Sif. Num. 116).

The dispute on whether tithes should be given to the priests or to the levites also continued after the destruction of the Temple. Toward the end of the tannaitic era a new tendency developed: the tithes were given especially to those priests and levites who were scholars, too, and in the course of time even to scholars who were not priests and levites. The idea behind this is clear: to endow those who held communal appointments and were in charge of the spiritual leadership of the nation with the perquisites which before had belonged to the priests and levites.

The commandment of *terumah* was throughout strictly observed by most sections of the people; but this was not so with the first tithe. The main reasons for the failure to offer the prescribed tithes were (1) the economic hardship involved; (2) their utilization as taxes by the Hasmonean rulers; (3) the fact that many priests and levites were landlords in their own right; (4) the difficulty of carrying the tithes to Jerusalem at the time when this was the common practice; (5) the process of urbanization that began in Herod's time, when the farmers considered themselves discriminated against in favor of the town dwellers who were not tithed; (6) the reduced significance of the tithes after the destruction of the Temple.

The sages themselves appreciated the difficulty of complying exactly with the commandments relating to tithes, and within the framework of the *halakhah* evolved various exemptions and means of evasion. But there also was an opposite tendency. Many sayings of the sages and *halakhot* emphasize the great importance of the commandments and their full observance, as well as punishments incurred by transgressors, and the rewards accruing to the observant. The commandment was no doubt not extolled solely on theoretical grounds, but there must have been many who followed it scrupulously. Observance of tithes was one of the elements that united the groups of *ḥaverim* who tended to be even more strict than the original commandment. In the light of the punctiliousness of these groups, the concept of one "trustworthy in tithes" was created, with whom the *ḥaverim* could have commercial intercourse "without fear of *demai*." In the time of Bar Kokhba, the observance of the tithe rules was well established in wide circles; this can be inferred from the tenancy contracts signed in the name of Bar Kokhba stipulating that the quantity of produce due to the landlord be delivered after deduction of tithes. The great importance attached to the tithes by the sages and the *ḥaverim* on the one hand, and their widespread neglect on the other, resulted in "untrustworthiness in respect of tithes" coming to be considered one of the characteristics of the *am ha-areẓ*. Thus the observance or neglect of the rules of tithing turned into a class distinction.

According to the *halakhah*, the duty of setting aside *terumot* and *ma'aserot* did not apply outside Ereẓ Israel, following the principle: "Every precept dependent on the land [of Israel] is in force only in that land, and one not so dependent is in force both within and without the land [of Israel] except for **orlah* and **kilayim*" (Kid. 1:9). In fact, however, there is ample evidence that *terumot* and *ma'aserot* were set aside in the Diaspora as well – in Egypt, Babylon, and in various places in Asia Minor. It may be assumed that this applied in the Diaspora as a whole (evidence of the practice in Syria is irrelevant since in this respect it was almost considered part of the Land of Israel). It seems that in the Diaspora *terumot* and *ma'aserot* were not, as a rule, given to the local priests and levites but were brought to the Temple in Jerusalem. This was almost certainly done at the time of the pilgrimage when the half shekel was also brought there. Since it was impossible to carry the actual *terumot* and *ma'aserot* to Jerusalem, it may be assumed that they were converted into money, frequently at a symbolic amount, which was then taken to Jerusalem. It may be noted, too, that in the Diaspora it was customary to set aside *terumot* and *ma'aserot* in the Sabbatical year. There is evidence that in Egypt this certainly "applied to the poor man's tithe, that the poor of Israel could be supported by it in the Sabbatical year" (Yad. 4:3).

BIBLIOGRAPHY: A. Oppenheimer, in: *Sefer Zikkaron le-B. De Vries* (1969), 70–83; E.E. Urbach, in: *Zion*, 16 (1951), 1–27; H. Albeck, *Shishah Sidrei Mishnah, Seder Zera'im* (1958), 173f., 217–20, 243f. etc.; idem, *Das Buch der Jubilaeen und die Halacha*, in: *Siebenundvierzigster Bericht der Hochschule fuer die Wissenschaft des Judentums in Berlin* (1930); Alon, Meḥkarim, 1 (1957), 83–92; A. Buechler, *Die Priester in dem Cultus im letzten Jahrzehnt des Jerusalemischen Tempels* (1895); idem, *Der Galilaeische Am-ha-Areẓ des zweiten Jahrhunderts* (1906); idem, in: *Festschfrift … M. Steinschneider* (1896), 91–109; idem, in: *Zikhron Yehudah. Tanulmányok … Blau L. … emlékére* (1938), 157–69 (Heb. pt.); S. Belkin, *Philo and the Oral Law* (1940), 67–78; J. Jeremias, *Jerusalem in the Time of Jesus* (1969), index s.v. *Terumah Tithes*; H. Vogelstein, *Der Kampf zwischen Priestern und Leviten* (1889); S. Safrai, *Ha-Aliyyah la-Regel bi-Ymei ha-Bayit ha-Sheni* (1965); Z. Karl, in: *Tarbiz*, 16 (1944/45), 11–17; A. Schalit, *Hordos ha-Melekh* (1964^3), 138–41, 438–40.

[A'hron Oppenheimer]

TESCHEN (Czech český Těšín, Pol. Cieszyn), town in Silesia. Capital of the duchy of Teschen in the Middle Ages, Teschen was divided between Czechoslovakia and Poland in 1920, incorporated entirely in Poland in 1938, and redivided in 1945. Jews are mentioned in connection with the town at the end of the 14th century. It used to be mistakenly assumed that the oldest tombstone in the Jewish cemetery dated from 1392. The first Jew received permission to settle there in 1575, and in 1640 the Jewish customs collector of the duchess was permitted to acquire a cemetery for the community. In 1785 the cemetery was sold to the 88 *Familiants of the district. The community of *Ostrava buried their dead there until 1872. In 1848 the authorities expelled some of the Jews living in the town, and those living in the vicinity were attacked by the populace. Before the plebiscite determining the future of the town was held in 1918, Polish nationalists threatened the Jews with pogroms if they voted for Czechoslovakia; the Czechoslovakian government dispatched Alfred *Fuchs, then a Czecho-Jewish functionary (see Svaz *čechů-židů) to influence the Jews in favor of the Czechs. There were 1,313 Jews in the town (8.5% of the total population) in 1890; 1,666 (9%) in 1900, 2,063 (10%) in 1910, and 1,148 (10.8%) in 1930. In the Polish part of the town (Cieszyn) the Jewish community numbered 1,591 (10.4% of the total population) in 1921.

Before the outbreak of World War II the community had two synagogues, two cemeteries, and a communal center. Two representatives of the Jewish National Party were returned to the municipal council in May 1938. The community was dissolved in September 1939. The Jews remaining there in 1943 were deported to death camps. A small congregation was reestablished after World War II, affiliated in 1959 to the Ostrava community.

BIBLIOGRAPHY: Bondy-Dworský, no. 880, 660–61; Berger, in: MGWJ, 40 (1896), 37–40; B. Bretholz, *Quellen zur Geschichte der Juden in Maehren im Mittelalter* (1935), index; Y. Toury, *Mehumah u-Mevukhah be-Mahpekhat 1848* (1968), 40–42; *Židovské zprávy* (March 3 and Oct. 10, 1919); B. Wasiutyński, *Ludność żydowska w Polsce…* (1930), 158–61; R. Iltis (ed.), *Die aussaeen unter Traenen…* (1959), 79; B. Brilling, in: *Judaica Bohemiae*, 4 (1968), 105–9, 113–4; PK *Germanyah*.

[Meir Lamed]

TET (Heb. טֵית ;ט), the ninth letter of the Hebrew alphabet; its numerical value is therefore 9. The early, Proto-Canaanite form of this letter has not yet been attested, but in the tenth century B.C.E. it consisted of crossing strokes (compare with the *taw*) surrounded by a circle ⊕, ⊗. In the cursive scripts there was a tendency to open the circle. Thus in the Hebrew script it was drawn 𐤈; in the Samaritan ࠈ; Phoenician 𐤈, 𐤈: Aramaic 𐡈; Jewish ט; Nabatean 𐢋 → ط → Arabic ط. The Greek *theta* preserved the closed circle. See *Alphabet, Hebrew.

[Joseph Naveh]

TETRARCH, Greek term meaning vassal-ruler, given to minor rulers in the provinces of Judea and Syria in the Roman period. The original meaning of the word was "head of the four," and it was used in this sense in Thessaly. However, in the course of time it lost its original meaning and during the Roman era was used for a ruler of a rank lower than that of king. The tetrarchs were appointed by the Roman emperor and were subject to him. The region ruled by the tetrarch was called a tetrarchy. Within the tetrarchy and in all internal affairs the tetrarch had the rights of a king, as well as a fixed yearly income. In all foreign affairs, however, he was subject to Rome. Among the better known tetrarchs of Jewish history were *Phasael, his brother *Herod, later to become king, and the latter's sons – Herod *Antipas, tetrarch of Galilee and Transjordan with a yearly income of 200 talents, and *Herod Phillipus, tetrarch of the Bashan, Argob, and Hauran with a yearly income of 100 talents.

BIBLIOGRAPHY: Jos., Ant., 17:318, 319; Schuerer, Hist, 353 n. 12; G.H. Stevenson, *Roman Provincial Administration…* (1939, repr. 1949).

[Edna Elazary]

TETUÁN (ancient name, **Tamuda**), town and port in N. *Morocco. It was destroyed by the Spanish in 1399 but rebuilt a few years before 1492 by an Andalusian chieftain, al-Mandārī, who used it exclusively as a refuge for Moors and some Spanish Jews. The Jewish community began to grow in importance from 1511. Due to the positive attitude of the rulers of Tetuán, the sea outlet gave great impetus to the development of maritime trade. Trade remained exclusively in the hands of the local Jewish community almost until the beginning of the 20th century. The relations between Jews and Andalusian Muslims always remained excellent. Both communities had occasion to suffer from the incursions of the *Rif Berbers and other elements: in 1610 they were suddenly impoverished by the exorbitant tax which was imposed by the sultan; in 1665 the town was raided by a rebellious army, and the splendid Bibas Synagogue was burned and razed. By 1727 there were seven synagogues in the town. Serious persecutions took place in 1790: robberies, acts of rape, murders of Jewish notables, and other atrocities were perpetrated by order of Mūlāy Yazīd, the new sultan, in an act of revenge against the prosperous community, as it had refused to loan him money some years earlier – he had intended to use the money to raise an army and rebel openly against his father's rule. One of Mūlāy Yazīd's own sons, a pretender to his father's throne, in 1822 looted the Jewish community, whose considerable wealth was found sufficient to keep a considerable army. Another wave of atrocities and lootings took place in 1860 during the Spanish-Moroccan war.

Until 1772 Tetuán was the residence of the representatives of the European nations. After their forced departure for Tangier and the exclusion of all Christians from Tetuán, the Christian representatives were replaced by consuls and consular agents, who were chosen from among the members of the local Jewish community. This community appears to have always been comprised of at least 3,000 persons, and occasionally it soared to 8,000 and more. Its first *av bet din* was R. Ḥayyim Bibas, one of the expellees from *Spain. For many generations the spiritual and temporal leadership of the community was entrusted to members of the same families – *Abudaraham, *Almosnino, Bendelac, *Bibas, Cazès, Coriat, Crudo, Falcon, Hadida, *Hassan, *Nahon, and Taurel.

In the 19th century the community venerated the *dayyan* R. Isaac ben Walid, author of *Va-Yomer Yiẓḥak* (2 vols., Leghorn, 1855), an inexhaustible source of information about the social, economic, and religious history of the Jewish community of Tetuán. In no other community were Jewish descendants of Spanish and Portuguese refugees able to preserve so well their language (Castilian Spanish), the integrity of their customs, and the purity of their traditions. Until the middle of the 18th century the Jews of Tetuán gave shelter to Portuguese Marranos, who returned to Judaism when they settled in the town. In the same century an influx of Jews from other Moroccan communities, attracted by the great prosperity enjoyed by that town, started to flow into Tetuán. Generally, these newcomers were easily assimilated into the original Spanish-Portuguese nucleus, but at the same time they also introduced superstitious beliefs and spread among the Jews throughout northern Morocco a dialect called "Ḥakétie," a mixture of corrupted Castilian, Arabic, and Hebrew.

Although they generally tended to return, the Jews of Tetuán often left their native town. They formed early elements of communities such as Melilla, Oran, Gibraltar, Buenos Aires, Montevideo, Rio de Janeiro, Lima, and Caracas. During the 19th century Tangier owed its own prosperity to Tetuán. Emigration increased drastically when the Jews of Tetuán were consigned to a single quarter of the town (August 1807), the *Juderia*, where they were forced to live until 1912. The community had its own private schools, where subjects were taught in Castilian. There were also several important yeshivot in the town. The first *Alliance Israélite Universelle school was founded in Tetuán in 1862, with the support of R. Isaac ben Walid. The major part of the budget needed for the upkeep of the school was provided by the notables of the community. From 1912 – under the Spanish protectorate and until the present day – several families have maintained a considerable influence on the affairs of the town.

[David Corcos]

Tetuán was the largest Jewish community in Spanish Morocco. Of 14,196 Jews in Spanish Morocco in 1949, 7,630 lived in Tetuán. In 1951, however, after emigration to Israel and to the international zone of Tangier, only about 8,000 Jews remained in Spanish Morocco; 4,122 lived in Tetuán. The 1960 census indicated 3,103 Jews in the town and by 1968 their number had dropped to about 1,000. The Jewish community in Tetuán had three Alliance Israélite Universelle schools, which in 1950 were attended by 746 pupils, but by 1957 the number had dropped to 430. There was also a vocational training school, *Or Yeladim*, at which 250 children studied in 1957. In 1961 the total number of pupils attending Jewish schools was 565. The community's affairs were run by a council, headed by Jacob Benarroch until 1954. In 1955 a new council was appointed by government order, and Jacob Serfaty (d. 1978) was appointed its head, serving in this capacity until his immigration to Israel in 1972. The rabbinical council was headed by R. Judah Halfon. After his retirement R. Abraham Bibas was appointed *dayyan*. By 1968 most of the community's institutions had closed. In the early years of the 21st century only a handful of Jews remained in Tetuán. Those who left settled either in the nearby Spanish enclaves, in parts of Spain, or in Latin America. Others migrated to the community of *Casablanca.

[Haim J. Cohen / Michael M. Laskier (2nd edition)]

BIBLIOGRAPHY: D. Abbou, *Musulmans, Andalous et Judéo-Espagnols* (1953), 401–14; Miège, Maroc, passim; Hirschberg, Afrikah, index; J.B. Vilar Ramirez, *Juderia de Tetuán* (1969); A.N. Chouraqui, *Between East and West* (1968), index. **ADD. BIBLIOGRAPHY:** M.M. Laskier, *The Alliance Israélite Universelle and the Jewish Communities of Morocco: 1862–1962* (1983); idem, *Israel and the Maghreb: From Statehood to Oslo* (2004).

TEUBAL, EZRA (1886–1976), leader of the Aleppan and the general Jewish community in *Argentina. Born in *Aleppo, *Syria, the eldest of the Teubal brothers, Ezra immigrated to Buenos Aires in 1903. He received a traditional religious education and studied French in the *Alliance Israélite Universelle and English in an American Protestant School in Aleppo. No sooner had he established himself in Argentina than he took steps to bring his brothers and all the family to Buenos Aires.

In 1912, he set up, together with his brothers, a textile imports company: Ezra Teubal Hermanos. In the 1920s, when most Syrian Jews were still peddlers and the most successful were importers or merchants, the Teubal brothers' business became one of the most renowned industrial textile factories in Argentina. Among his many activities, Ezra was appointed treasurer of the Textile Section in the Argentine Industrial Union for many years.

Moreover, he took an active role in Jewish communal affairs. He supported and sponsored numerous and different kinds of Sephardi and Ashkenazi religious, philanthropic, cultural, and sports organizations. He participated in the foundation of almost all the early Aleppan institutions, such as the burial society, Hessed Shel Emeth, which changed into the communal organization Asociación Israelita Sefaradi Argentina (AISA), and was its first president in 1924–30. He supported, among others, organizations such as Hospital Israelita, Asilo de Huérfanos Israelitas, Club Náutico Hacoaj, B'nai B'rith, Alliance Israélite Universelle, the Museo Judío, and the local Friends Association of the Hebrew University of Jerusalem.

Furthermore, he was fully committed to anti-Nazi campaigns and to the promotion of the early Zionist activities of the Sephardi Jews. He was very active in the support of the foundation of the State of Israel. He participated in the establishment in 1918 of Geulat Sion, the first Zionist group constituted by Sephardim, and was its first president. In 1936 he was one of the Argentine delegates to the World Jewish Congress elected by DAIA – the roof organization of all the Jewish associations. Teubal was president of the Comité Intercomunal Sefaradi pro "Geulat Haaretz," established to found a Sephardi settlement in Palestine, to be named "República Argentina." He was president of the local Jewish Agency. Like all of his brothers, he was a strong supporter of the Centro Sionista Sefaradí, the JNF, and the Comité Sefaradí Pro-Keren Hayesod. He was the first contributor to the establishment of Beit Harashal Seminary in Jerusalem for the instruction of rabbis and spiritual leaders for the Sephardi communities in Israel and the Diaspora.

In the 1950s and 1960s, as the Aleppans took their first steps toward a process of Orthodox religious revitalization under Rabbi Itzhak *Chehebar, Ezra Teubal, as well as other modern-oriented leaders, began to exert less influence on the community. Afterwards he gave his support to the foundation of Conservative and Reform synagogues in Buenos Aires, such as Bet El and Emmanuel. When he died, the central religious ceremony was organized by more than 30 institutions in an Ashkenazi Temple, the Congregación Israelita de la República Argentina.

[Susana Brauner (2nd ed.)]

°**TEUCER OF CYZICUS** (c. 100–50 B.C.E.), Greek author. He wrote historical works on various subjects, including a Jewish history, as reported by Suidas. None of his works survive.

TEUTSCH, DAVID (1950–), U.S. Reconstructionist rabbi. Teutsch was born and raised in Salt Lake City, the son of refugees from Germany. He received a bachelor's degree from Harvard University and was ordained in 1977 by Hebrew Union College-Jewish Institute of Religion in New York. In 1991 he received a Ph.D. from the Wharton School of the University of Pennsylvania for work in organizational ethics.

From 1974 to 1979 he was rabbi of Ramat Shalom congregation in Spring Valley, N.Y. From 1978 to 1980 he was on the staff of the National Jewish Resource Center (later CLAL). After 1980, his professional career centered on the Reconstructionist movement. In that year he became assistant director of the Federation of Reconstructionist Congregations and

Havurot (later Jewish Reconstructionist Federation), serving as executive director from 1982 to 1986. In 1986 he became a dean, and later vice president, of the Reconstructionist Rabbinical College (RRC) near Philadelphia. From 1990 he chaired the department of contemporary civilization. Teutsch was the fourth president of RRC, serving from 1993 to 2002. After that, he continued as a professor and director of the Center for Jewish Ethics. Teutsch also served as an organizational consultant and leadership trainer for Jewish and non-Jewish organizations.

Teutsch was one of the leading figures in Reconstructionism after the retirement of Ira Eisenstein. In addition to his organizational leadership, he was editor of the *Kol Haneshamah* series of liturgy, including seven volumes, beginning with *Kol Haneshamah: Erev Shabbat* (Sabbath eve) in 1989. This series expressed a contemporary Reconstructionist view, offering modified traditional texts along with interpretations, *kavvanot* (intentions or spiritual guidance), and contemporary readings. Many of the additions were by women. A central feature was a gender-neutral English translation, avoiding masculine terms such as "Lord" and "he." The *Kol Haneshamah* series continued with volumes including Shabbat and Festivals (1994), Weekdays (1996), and High Holy Days (1999).

Teutsch also devoted considerable efforts to Jewish ethics and practice. A major contribution to both was his articulation of values-based decision-making (VBDM), a method for reaching ethical decisions in a Jewish framework for those who do not accept the binding nature of *halakhah*. This framework includes articulating values (for example, *kevod ha-beriyyot* – respecting people; democracy; and *kelal Yisrael*, the wider Jewish people) that might apply, or be in conflict, in a given situation. An individual, family, or community can apply the methodology. Teutsch published a number of booklets on ethics and Jewish practice, some with commentary by rabbis and lay people, eventually to be combined in a larger publication.

David Teutsch is married to Betsy Platkin Teutsch, a Judaic artist. Together they were among the founders in 1986 of Minyan Dorshei Derekh, a Reconstructionist community within Germantown Jewish Centre, a Conservative congregation in Philadelphia. He described his vision and experience in *Spiritual Community* (2005).

BIBLIOGRAPHY: E. Caplan, *From Ideology to Liturgy: Reconstructionist Worship and American Liberal Judaism* (2002); B. Hirsh, "Values-Based Decision Making: Some Second Thoughts," in: *Reconstructionist*, (Fall 2005); R. Langer, Review of *Kol Haneshamah: Shabbat Vehagim*, in: CCAR *Journal* (Winter 1997).

[Robert P. Tabak (2nd ed.)]

TEVET (Heb. טֵבֵת), the post-Exilic name of the tenth month of the Jewish year. Mentioned in Esther 2:16, in Josephus' *Antiquities* (11:148), and frequently in rabbinic literature (e.g., *Megillat Ta'anit*), it is linked with the Assyrian-Babylonian *tebetum*. The root of the name is possibly related to *tava* (Heb. טבע, "to dip" or "to sink"), Tevet being the month of "sinking in" or "the muddy month," because of its abundant rainfall. The zodiacal sign of this month is Capricorn. In the present fixed Jewish calendar it invariably consists of 29 days, 1st of Tevet never falling on Thursday or the Sabbath (see *Calendar). In the 20th century, Tevet, in its earliest occurrence, extended from December 4th to January 1st, and in its latest, from January 2nd to the 30th. Apart from the last two or three days of the festival of *Ḥanukkah coinciding with 1st–2nd or 1st–3rd of Tevet, and 28th of Tevet, commemorating the *Pharisees' success in ousting their Sadducean opponents from the Sanhedrin (Meg. Ta'an. 342–43), all the historical days in Tevet are fasts: (1) 5th of Tevet, when the report of the fall of Jerusalem at the hands of Nebuchadnezzar reached the Judean exiles in Babylonia (Ezek. 33:21); and, according to an antiquated tannaitic view (RH 18b; and see below), the "fast in the tenth month" (Zech. 8:19); (2) 8th of Tevet, marking the completion of the *Septuagint, an event regarded as fateful as the construction of the *golden calf in the wilderness (Sof. 1:7; Meg. Ta'an. 13); (3) 9th of Tevet, the reason for this fast being suppressed in the oldest sources. According to later sources, Ezra and Nehemiah died on that day (*Kol Bo*, Fuerth ed. (1782), 52c no. 63). It is also said to have coincided with *dies natalis* in 3761 A.M. (on the basis of a calculation in Abraham b. Ḥiyya's *Sefer ha-Ibbur*, ed. by H. Filipowski, (1851) 109); (4) 10th of Tevet, commemorating the beginning of the siege of Jerusalem by Nebuchadnezzar (Jer. 42:4, et al.), the "fast in the tenth month," according to the accepted talmudic view (RH 18b, et al.). This fast can never fall on the Sabbath (contrary to JE 12 (1905), 72).

[Ephraim Jehudah Wiesenberg]

TEVET, NAHUM (1946–), Israeli sculptor. Born in Kibbutz Mesilot, Tevet began his art studies at the Oranim kibbutz seminar and later went on to the Avni Art Institute in Tel Aviv. One of his most influential teachers was Raffi Lavie, who taught him for three years (1967–70). In 1979, thanks to a scholarship from the America-Israel Cultural Foundation, he lived for a year in the United States. Tevet lived and worked in Tel Aviv. From 1980 he taught at the Bezalel Academy of Art and Design in Jerusalem. Over the years he was awarded many art prizes.

Tevet's sculptures are recognized by their material – wood – and by their complex assemblage.

In his early works it was clear that Tevet had turned to the language of Minimalism. He used ready-made objects taken from the kibbutz environment. Beds, chairs, and tables were placed at the gallery first as simple objects and later in a more complicated construction. One of the main installations of the early period was at the Bertha Urdang Gallery in New York. Two separate rooms each contained a complex network of thin wood beams that established a basic structure. The linear quality of these wood constructions evoked a drawing in three dimensional space. Tevet noted that in the process of creating this work he began with the idea of a two-dimensional drawing on the floor of the gallery and then it grew to fill the room. This upward movement from the floor was one of the typical features of Tevet's works (*Sound for a Silent Movie*, 1986, Collection of the Artist).

Tevet's works demanded a long process of looking and deciphering. Through the connection of the parts and the repetition of colors, the coherency of the work is clear, but the ready-made details and the other completed forms draw the gaze into its depths.

One of the recurring forms in the sculptures is the table. As a metaphor the table could symbolize the dining table (of the kibbutz dining room for instance), or the desk of the artist, the poet, the teacher, or the philosopher. Through its minimalist form it became a bench or a column. Positioned on its side it became almost figurative and placed one above the other the tables created an open-closed form. The colors of the tables also changed the meanings, and their position on the walls altered all the spaces in the gallery.

As a highly esteemed teacher Tevet influenced young Israeli sculptors (for instance, Drora Dominey and Yehudit Sasportas), and his works became an important part of the heritage of the Israeli art world.

BIBLIOGRAPHY: Tel Aviv Museum of Art, *Nahum Tevet: Painting Lessons – Sculptures 1984–1990* (1991); B. Urdang, *The Disciplined Spirit* (1986).

[Ronit Steinberg (2nd ed.)]

TEVET, SHABBETAI (1925–), Hebrew writer. Born in Tel Aviv, he was associate editor of *Ba-Maḥaneh* during the War of Independence. From 1950 he was a member of the editorial board of *Haaretz*.

His books include *Ha-Mishpaḥah ha-Gedolah shel Shin Tet* (articles, 1954); *Ha-Yeled she-Kare'u Lo Rivkah* (stories for children, 1956); *Massa Ẓahal be-Sinai* (1957); *Ḥamishim Shenot Tel Aviv* (1959); *Shefa va-Ḥaradah* (1963); *Gidonim* (1968); *Kilelat ha-Berakhah* (1969), on the relations between Jews and Arabs after the Six-Day War, particularly on the West Bank; *Sha'ashu'a u-Vitto* (1970). His book on the Six-Day War appeared in English translation as *The Tanks of Tammuz* (1969). Several of his plays were staged but not published. Among his other books are a biography of Moshe Dayan (1972) and of David Ben-Gurion (1977), a study of Ben-Gurion's attitude to the Arabs in Ereẓ Israel (1985), and a study of the first political murder in Ereẓ Israel, that of Chaim *Arlosoroff (1982).

ADD. BIBLIOGRAPHY: E. Shealtiel, in: *Haaretz* (October 10, 1980); A. Doron, in: *Davar* (December 12, 1980); B. Morris, "*Use-farim, ve-Gevilim be-Ziknah Regilim*," in: *Alpayim*, 12 (1996), 73–103; A. Shapira, "*Ha-Historiyyografiyyah shel ha-Mitologiyyah* (Ben-Gurion and the Holocaust)," in: *Alpayim*, 18 (1999), 24–53; Sh. Aharonson, "*Ha-Ittonai ke-Biograf ve-Historyon*," in: *Iyyunim bi-Tekumat Yisra'el*, 11 (2001), 527–33.

[Getzel Kressel]

TEVUL YOM (Heb. טְבוּל יוֹם; lit. "one who has bathed that day"), tenth tractate in the order *Tohorot* in the Mishnah and the eleventh in the Tosefta. There is no *Gemara* either in the Babylonian or the Jerusalem Talmud. In four chapters (two in the Tosefta) it deals with problems arising out of Leviticus 22:6–7, which lays down that a person ritually unclean (or a ritually unclean vessel according to Lev. 11:32) remains unclean until sunset, even after ritual immersion during the day. The degree of impurity of such a person between immersion and sunset (the *tevul yom*) is slight. For example, if he touches food of *ḥullin* (i.e., not holy food), it does not become defiled; yet the priests may not eat holy food (e.g., *terumah* or *ḥallah*) in that state. Nevertheless, though the *tevul yom* defiles the holy food by touching it, if this food touches other food, the latter does not become unclean, as is the case with regard to uncleanness of a higher degree.

The Mishnah contains four chapters. Chapter 1 first considers the case of two portions of *ḥallah* adhering to one another, the *tevul yom* having touched one portion; the question is whether because of the *ḥibbur* ("connection") between the two, both become defiled. A long discussion follows as to what is considered a *ḥibbur* in this respect. Chapter 2 deals with the problems arising from the contact of the *tevul yom* with liquids. Chapter 3 reverts to questions of *ḥibbur* and discusses cases such as one in which vegetables of *ḥullin* cooking in oil of *terumah* are touched by a *tevul yom* as to whether the whole dish becomes defiled or only the part he actually touched. Chapter 4 discusses a great variety of questions, for example, how a woman who was a *tevul yom* and was kneading dough should set aside the *ḥallah* without defiling it. Another case, which has nothing to do with the general subject of this tractate, concerns a man setting out in a caravan who commands, "Write a bill of divorce for my wife," without stating specifically "and hand it to her." The question arises as to whether one may presume that he meant it to be given but forgot to say so because of his excitement. Caravans were fraught with danger, and if he disappeared, his wife would remain an *agunah* unless it was established that he meant the divorce (*get*) to be given to her. The concluding *mishnayot* of the tractate (4:5–7) thereupon deal with the problem of presumption, namely that there is a *tenai bet-din* (a kind of *praesumptio iuris*) to the effect that under certain circumstances, if one intended to make a stipulation, it is considered as having been made even if it was not done explicitly. These *mishnayot* form a group unrelated to the general content. They consist of laws which, according to R. Joshua b. Hananiah, were the work of the *soferim* (Epstein, Tannaim, 63ff.; and Tosafot Yom Tov, who disagrees). Mishnah 1:1 is a combination of two sources recorded unchanged by the editor. Both sources relate to a common dispute between the schools of Shammai and Hillel. In the Tosefta there are several independent groups of *beraitot* such as 1:4–7, similar in content to Mishnah 2:2b. Many of the *mishnayot* of this tractate remain without corresponding Tosefta. *Tevul Yom* was translated into English by H. Danby, *The Mishnah* (1933).

[Arnost Zvi Ehrman]

TEWELES, JUDAH (1808–1869), *rosh yeshivah* in Prague, a watchmaker by profession. He was a grandson of Lipmann Teweles, mintmaster of the kingdom of Bohemia. His father,

David, was a scholar and Judah wrote novellae at the age of 15. After learning his trade as an apprentice to a Christian watchmaker, he was accepted after much opposition as master in the Prague watchmakers' guild. He studied Talmud under Nehemiah *Trebitsch and Samuel *Landau. Although he held no official post, every Saturday he lectured to such Prague scholars as Samson Raphael *Hirsch, Nathan *Adler, Solomon Judah *Rapoport, and Saul Isaac Kaempf, who accepted him as an authority. In 1863 he gave up the watchmakers' trade and accepted an appointment as *rosh yeshivah*. After his death, the *Afike Jehuda society was founded in his honor. Significant of the esteem in which he was held was the remark at his funeral that the Torah itself was being buried. None of his writings was printed.

[Meir Lamed]

TEWI, THEA (1915–), U.S. sculptor. Born in Berlin, Tewi received a degree from the Staatliche Kunstakademie in 1935. She and her husband Charles Kalman Schlachet fled from the Nazis to the U.S. in 1938. Between 1953 and 55, Tewi studied at the Sculpture Center, the Art Students League and, under the tutelage of Seymour Lipton, at the New School for Social Research. She began a custom-made lingerie business and by 1945 was voted the best lingerie designer in the U.S. In 1950 she returned to sculpture, and worked in various media, with an emphasis on marble. She frequently used Jewish subjects and in 1966 won the National Arts Club award for religious sculpture for a work which referred to the forms and shapes of the Hebrew alphabet. The artist's works are quietly emotive. For example, *Three Figures* (1965) is a white marble sculpture depicting three robed and hooded figures of indeterminate gender whose bodies remain fused by the stone. Simple and highly evocative, this work has an elegance and solemnity heightened by the tall black plinth which elevates the work to almost eye-level. Another marble work of 1965, *The Gordian,* suggests the eponymous knot with its depiction of form composed of convolutions and interlacings. In 1969, Tewi was awarded the first prize and medal of honor in the National Association of Women Artists Annual Exhibition. In 1975 and 1979, she won first prizes at two different exhibitions at the National Arts Club. Her *Cactus Couple* (1990), a representation of two cactus plants hewn out of green serpentine marble, is located on the roof of the Arsenal in Central Park, New York. She served as chair of the Sculpture Jury of the National Association of Women Artists (1973), and as president of the Sculptors League (1971–1991). Tewi's work has been exhibited at the Brooklyn Botanic Garden, the Museum of Modern Art, Paris, the National Academy of Design, the National Arts Club, and New York University. Examples of her work are in the collections of the Cincinnati Art Museum, Kew Gardens, New York, the National Museum of American Art, and the Snite Museum of Art, Notre Dame University, among other places.

BIBLIOGRAPHY: V. Watson-Jones, *Contemporary American Women Sculptors* (1986).

[Nancy Buchwald (2nd ed.)]

TEXAS, state in the southwest U.S., the second largest in area and population, with a total estimated population (2000) of 20,851,820. The state's Jewish population was approximately 131,000 (0.6% of the state total), with 22 communities having 100 or more Jewish residents. Approximately 68% of Jewish Texans lived in either the *Houston or *Dallas metropolitan areas, with the remainder in *Austin, *San Antonio, Fort Worth, *El Paso, Corpus Christi, and smaller communities.

While a handful of pioneers with Jewish ancestry passed through or lived briefly in Texas as early as the years of Spanish and Mexican rule, organized Jewish life did not appear until the 1850s, after the region had been annexed into the United States. The state's southern portion, extending as far north as San Antonio, was part of a massive 1590 land grant issued to Luis de Carvajal y de la Cueva, a Spanish adventurer several of whose family members were executed by the Mexican Inquisition as secret Jews; Carvajal himself was a devoted Catholic but was imprisoned until his death for sheltering his crypto-Jewish relatives. Still, no Carvajal settlements existed north of the Río Grande in present-day Texas, and Spanish colonization left no record of Sephardic practice there.

The first North American Jew known to have been in Texas was Captain Samuel *Noah of New York, who commanded a Mexican force against Spain at San Antonio in 1811 though he only remained in the area briefly. After Mexico, then including Texas, achieved independence from Spain in 1821, a small number of individuals (perhaps no more than 10 or 20) of Jewish background appeared in the region, though none practiced the faith openly or consistently. Adolphus Sterne opened a general store in Nacogdoches in 1826 and served as a local official to the Mexican government. Sterne formally converted to Catholicism as required by Mexican law, but was raised in a Jewish home in Germany before immigrating to America. Jacob de Cordova, a land merchant, arrived in 1839 and operated businesses in Galveston and Houston. Like Sterne, de Cordova married a Christian woman, as was common in frontier settings, and he neither practiced the Jewish faith openly nor identified himself as a Jew. The first report of self-identified Jews was in the early 1830s at Velasco, on the Gulf Coast near present-day Freeport, where Abraham Labatt, who had been active in large Jewish communities in the U.S., recognized residents Jacob Henry and Jacob Lyons as fellow Jews.

A handful of Jews from the United States fought in the Texas war for independence from Mexico and remained afterward in the new republic which, with constitutionally guaranteed religious freedom, began to attract more Jewish settlers, mostly Central European immigrants who had lived for a time in the U.S. After Texas joined the United States in 1846, the Jewish population grew still faster, and as Jews gathered in the state's largest cities they began to shape the rudiments of institutional Jewish life. In Galveston, the Dyers and Ostermans formed the core of a growing Jewish merchant class that also included Michael Seeligson, who was elected Galveston's mayor in 1853. When a Dyer child passed away in 1852, the

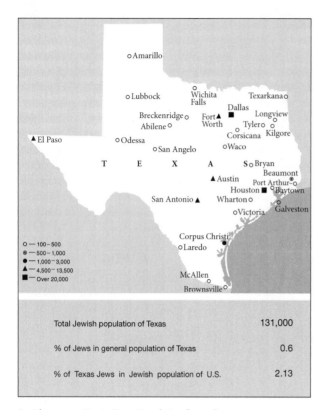

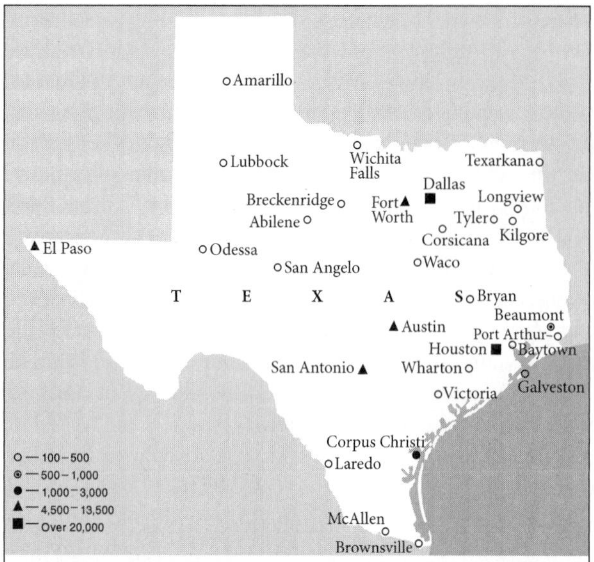

Total Jewish population of Texas	131,000
% of Jews in general population of Texas	0.6
% of Texas Jews in Jewish population of U.S.	2.13

Jewish communities in Texas. Population figures for 2001.

family established a cemetery and invited a New Orleans rabbi to perform the burial, the state's first recorded Jewish religious service. In nearby Houston, the city's first permanent Jewish residents, Lewis A. and Mary Levy, had purchased a plot of land for use as a Jewish cemetery as early as 1844; Lewis Levy later spearheaded the creation of a Hebrew Benevolent Society in 1855. In 1856, San Antonio Jews led by Henry Mayer and Louis Zork began meeting as an informal congregation, and three years later Houston's Beth Israel was formally chartered as the state's first Jewish congregation. B'nai Israel in Galveston was founded in 1868, followed by other Jewish congregations in Victoria (1872), Jefferson (1873), San Antonio (1874), Dallas (1875), Austin (1876), Waco (1879), Brenham (1885), Tyler (1887), Marshall (1887), Fort Worth (1892), and El Paso (1900). Jewish communal institutions flourished alongside the synagogues: B'nai B'rith chapters were active in every major city, and in 1898 the state's first chapter of the Council of Jewish Women was formed in Tyler. In 1908, the *Texas Jewish Herald* was established in Houston. Published today as the *Jewish Herald-Voice*, it is among the longest-running Jewish newspapers in the country.

While most of the state's first congregations observed Reform worship services, there was a strong traditional presence, and many cities also sustained Orthodox synagogues. Congregation Beth Israel in Houston was founded on the Orthodox ritual, though it later changed to Reform, and the state's larger communities also supported *talmud torahs*, *shoḥatim*, and traditional *minyan* services. The predominance of Classical Reform in part explains the anti-Zionist sentiment that prevailed in Texas until World War II, but Zionist organizations were nonetheless strong in many Texas communities, often led by European-educated rabbis and sustained by a growing influx of Eastern European immigrants. In 1905, the Texas Zionist Association was formed to coordinate Zionist efforts across the state, and in 1914 the state's first Hadassah chapter was chartered in Wharton.

As in other southern and western states, Jews were initially attracted to Texas for the enormous commercial opportunities of an expanding region. From the coastal commercial centers of Galveston and Houston, where Jews participated heavily in the cotton trade, Jewish retailers followed the state's burgeoning rail system: by the early 20th century Jews were present in at least 70 communities, many operating the town's only retail establishment. In larger cities, Jews dominated the retail industry and built many of the state's premier retailing institutions including Sanger Bros. and Neiman-Marcus. In several cases, as frontier customers paid in barter rather than cash, retail businesses led Jewish families into the state's signature industries: cattle and oil.

The Galveston Plan, directed from New York but managed locally by Galveston's beloved Rabbi Henry *Cohen, sought to divert the flow of European Jewish immigration to the Texas Gulf Coast, bypassing the overcrowded ghettos of New York, and between 1908 and 1914 some 10,000 European Jews passed through the city to destinations throughout the western states. Of these, about 2,000 settled in nearly 100 Texas communities, providing a burst of social and religious development statewide. Despite this effort, however, and despite the general southerly migration of American Jews to sunbelt states after World War II, relatively few Jews were drawn to Texas. Today, although Texas is the state with the second-highest population, it ranks tenth in Jewish residents. In part this is because the Texas economy remained heavily agrarian even after World War II, leading migrants to seek the greater mercantile opportunities and stronger Jewish communal life of California and Florida. But as the contemporary Texas economy strengthens in fields like electronics, computing, and aerospace, the Jewish population is growing rapidly, especially in high-tech centers like Austin.

Following national trends, Jewish communities in small Texas towns are disappearing as the population clusters in metropolitan areas and their suburban and exurban outgrowths, though congregations remain active in smaller cities including Abilene, Amarillo, Brownsville, Corpus Christi, El Paso, Longview, Lubbock, Odessa, and Tyler. In large cities, Jews maintain a variety of religious and social institutions which sustain virtually every political, social, and worship style. Lubavitchers are organized in Austin, Dallas, Houston, and San Antonio; Holocaust museums and research centers have been established in Dallas (1984), Houston (1996), El Paso (1992), and San Antonio (1990); Jewish newspapers serve the communities of Dallas, Houston, San Antonio, and Fort Worth; the Texas Jewish Historical Society was created in 1980, while Dallas, Houston, and San Antonio support local Jewish historical societies; and all of the major cities and several smaller ones maintain Jewish charitable federations and/or community centers. While Jews remain a much smaller proportion of the Texas population than is the case in other large states, the Lone Star State is home to Jewish life of increasing richness and complexity.

BIBLIOGRAPHY: N. Ornish, *Pioneer Jewish Texans* (1989); R. Winegarten and C. Schechter, *Deep in the Heart: The Lives and Legends of Texas Jews, a Photographic History* (1990); H.A. Weiner, *Jewish Stars in Texas: Rabbis and Their Work* (1999); B.E. Stone, "West of Center: Jews on the Real and Imagined Frontiers of Texas" (Ph.D. Dissertation: The University of Texas at Austin, 2003); H.A. Weiner and K. Roseman (eds.), *Lone Stars of David* (2007).

[Bryan Edward Stone (2nd ed.)]

TEXTILES. In the biblical period garments were produced from both animal and vegetable materials. The most common garments were made of animal furs, especially of the less expensive sheepskin and goatskin, though rarer skins were also used. The pelts were processed to make them soft and hairy. Simple garments were sewn from these skins with the hairy surface worn either against the body or outward. Skins were prepared in two fashions: hard and thick for footwear, and soft, thin, and more delicate for clothing. Skins were also used for military dress and various military accessories. Beginning with the second millennium B.C.E., leather and fur were processed by specialists, who maintained facilities for this purpose. Natural silk, bought from India and Arabia, was used only in the most expensive garments, such as royal raiment. The most common, however, and almost the sole materials used for textiles were wool and linen. (The identification of *meshi* (Ezek. 16:10, 13) with silk, by Rashi, followed by all other commentators, is almost certainly a mistaken one. The first reference to silkworms is by Aristotle in his *De Animalibus Historia*, 5.) The preparation of cloth required several operations. The raw material was cleaned, and if necessary dyed (see *Dyeing). It was then used for the spinning of threads which was done on a spindle – a short, narrow rod at whose end is a circular weight which maintains the rod suspended in a vertical position and serves as a small fly wheel to turn the rod on its axis. By turning the suspended spindle with deft finger motions, the fibers were inwoven into threads of uniform thickness. The threads thus produced were bound about the spindle stick as on a bobbin (H. Gressman, *Altorientalische Bilder zum AltenTestament* (1926²)). Spinning was done by old people or women at home in their spare time (cf. Prov. 41:19). Some excavations have revealed perforated weights, generally made of stone.

The next process in the production of clothing was the weaving of the woolen or flaxen threads into cloth. For this purpose there were vertical or horizontal looms, and for larger cloths, the mobile looms were attached to the ground. The base for the woven cloth consisted of the warp strands that stretched through the length of the cloth. On a vertical loom the warp strands were closely spaced over the two horizontal bars of the fame. Larger vertical looms used only one horizontal bar, with perforated clay or stone weights attached to the other end of the warp strands. On horizontal looms, the tension in the warp was maintained by two bars held in place on the ground or on a table. The woof strands were passed alternately above and below the warp threads. More complex patterns were produced by picking up several warp strands at a time or by multidirectional weaving. The most advanced looms permitted more complex methods such as separating warp groups by attaching them to several upper or lower bars whose positions could be exchanged. The woof thread was bound about a beam, which served as a bobbin that was passed back and forth over the warp all the while unwinding the thread. To make the cloth more opaque, a rough comb was passed along the taut warp strands, to make the woof adhere more thoroughly. The proximity of the threads determined the strength of the cloth, while the thickness determined its coarse or delicate structure. Much use was made of colored threads which could be woven into particular patterns. Clothing was sewn by hand with metal or bone needles, also used for coloring embroidery on the fabric, which was an integral part of its decoration. Clothing was fastened with laces tied to one another by means of special pins. The use of buttons was very rare.

In the Talmud

During the talmudic period wool and linen continued to be the main sources for textiles. Whereas, however, wool was more plentiful in Ereẓ Israel, linen was so abundant and cheap in Babylon that its cheapness was regarded as one of the main material attractions of the country (Ta'an. 29b). To such an extent did the economy depend upon it that public prayers were offered when its value dropped by 40% (BB 91a). There were special districts where flax was soaked and where it was sold (Git. 27a). The difference between Ereẓ Israel and Babylon with regard to those two materials is reflected in the statement that whereas in Babylon colored woolen garments were regarded as the most expensive, in Ereẓ Israel white linen was so regarded (Pes. 109a). During this period a considerable number of new materials appear. However, it is interesting that two passages in which these new materials are mentioned are explicitly connected with this extension.

Mishnah *Kilayim* 9:1 states that "Wool and linen alone are forbidden under the law of *mixed species," and the subsequent *mishnayot* deal with the new textiles common at the time. They are camel hair (cf. Matt. 3:4), hemp (9:1), silk and floss silk (9:2), and a textile made of a mixture of hemp and linen. Garments made of hemp were usually imported (9:7). In Babylonia hemp was even cheaper than linen (Ket. 8b). Similarly, on the law enjoining that the *ẓiẓit* must be attached to one's "garments" (Num. 15:38), the Talmud, acknowledging that the word in the Bible applies only to wool, continues "Whence then can I include camel hair, rabbit hair, goat hair, floss silk [*kallakh*], raw silk [*Sirikon* = Lat. *Sericom*], fine silk (*Shira'in* – Men. 39b; cf. also Sifra, *Tazri'a*, Perek 16)." *Kallakh* occurs in Mishnah *Shabbat* 2:1 as one of the materials forbidden for use as wicks for the Sabbath lamp. The Babylonian *amoraim*, uncertain of its identification, in their discussion mention a number of varieties of silk used in Babylon such as "*metuksa*" (Gr. μέτυξα) and *peranda* silk (Late Gr. πράνδιοι). In addition cotton was extensively used. It should be noted, however, that the talmudic word *kutnah*, or *kitnah*, is not cotton, but linen. The Arabic form of the word *qutn* was adapted by traders for the Arab cottons which they introduced into Europe. The talmudic name for cotton is *ẓemer gefen* ("vine wool"; Kil. 7:2, TJ, Ket. 2:4, 27d).

Home weaving was so essential an aspect of the domestic menage, at least in mishnaic times, that it is stated that even a wealthy woman "even if she brought a hundred maidservants" into the house, should still be obliged to engage in wool-spinning, "since idleness leads to lewdness" (Ket. 5:5); nevertheless, there is ample evidence of the existence of textiles, and specifically woolen goods, manufactured on a commercial scale. "Ben Zoma said, 'how many labors did Adam have to perform before he obtained a garment to wear! He had to shear, wash, comb, spin, and weave (the wool) before he had a garment to wear, whereas I get up early and find all that done for me. All kinds of people come betimes to my house, and ... I find all these ready'" (Ber. 58a).

[Louis Isaac Rabinowitz]

Medieval Period

The prominence of Jews in the manufacture of textiles in the Mediterranean Basin in the Middle Ages was connected with the widespread commerce in textiles, particularly silk and the more expensive fabrics, in general, and with Jewish commercial activity in this sphere in particular. Cheaper types of cloth were also an important article of trade; thus, in the sources of the period, wherever a Jewish merchant is mentioned plying his trade he was most commonly dealing in textiles. In medieval Egypt the silk trade "fulfilled a function similar to that of stocks and bonds in our own society. In other words, it represented a healthy range of speculation, while providing at the same time a high degree of security" (S.D. Goitein, *A Mediterranean Society* (1967), 223).

In Muslim Spain, where many Jews engaged in the silk industry, there "were two brothers, merchants, the manufacturers of silk, Jacob *Ibn Jau and ... Joseph ... they became successful in the silk business, making clothing of high quality and pennants that are placed at the tops of standards of such high quality as was not duplicated in all of Spain" (Ibn Daud, Tradition, 68–69). To King Roger of Sicily was attributed the introduction of the silk industry into his lands by means of captured Jewish craftsmen from the Balkans (1147). *Benjamin of Tudela describes the Jews of Thebes as "the good craftsmen in making silk and purple clothes in the land of the Greeks"; at *Salonika he also noted that "they deal in the craft of silk," while among the Jews of *Constantinople he found "craftsmen in silk" (ed. Adler (London, 1907), 12–16). The occupation of *dyeing, then widespread among Jews and often mentioned by him, was connected with textiles. In Spain woolen cloth, produced from the famed local merino sheep, was produced by Jewish weavers, particularly in *Majorca and the eastern cities of *Barcelona, *Valencia, and *Saragossa. The weaver's guild in *Calatayud had its own synagogue. *Moneylending in Western and Central Europe brought Jews into contact with valuable textiles given in pawn which they had to maintain in good state, and also often to sell.

In the Ottoman Empire

Many of the exiles from Spain and Portugal (1492, 1497) continued their former occupations in the textile trade or crafts in their new places of settlement in the Ottoman Empire, or turned to them when they arrived in the Balkans and came into contact with the old tradition of Jewish occupation in this field. Salonika had been established as a center of the textile industry before the arrival of the refugees, many of whom joined in manufacture of the produce of the Balkan hinterland. Thus in the 16th century thousands of Jews engaged there in all stages of the production of cloth (known as "*abba*"). A textile workshop could be found in almost every Jewish home, where the head of the household worked with his wife and children. Jews also distributed and sold the local cloth. Textile workshops were bequeathed to synagogues and charitable institutions. At Ḥanukkah it was customary to donate pieces of cloth to poor yeshivah students. The scope and problems of the industry and trade in textiles in Salonika is shown in the many communal regulations and rabbinical injunctions issued against price slashing, the sale of wool to foreigners, and the purchase of raw wool with cash (which only the wealthy could afford to do). Locally made garments only could be put up for sale, and every Jew over 20 years old had to wear clothes locally produced. From 1586 the tax on Salonika Jewry levied by the Ottoman authorities was payable by a quota of cloth (1,200 standard pieces of cloth), which was presented to the janissaries.

The most flourishing period for the Jewish textile industry in Salonika was between 1500 and 1580, but afterward it gradually declined. A financial crisis in 1584, and others that succeeded it, forced many Jewish artisans to leave for other textile centers (Verria, *Rhodes, Smyrna). The Ottoman authorities afforded the industry no protection against the superior, foreign-made, European textiles, which swamped the market. Hence the Salonika Jews began to specialize in carpets and other local wares.

At the peak period of activity in the Safed textile center in Ereẓ Israel (1530–60), the majority of earners among the approximately 15,000 Jews there were employed in the manufacture of high-quality woolen cloth, produced from raw, short-fibered wool sent from the Balkans to Safed via *Sidon. All stages of production were carried out in Safed; the fulling mills (known as *batan*) utilized the many local springs; one is still standing. Tales of the leading Safed mystics show that many owned such textile mills. Both the trade and the community itself began to decline rapidly after 1560, for the same reasons as had operated against Salonika and because of transport hazards at sea.

Eastern Europe

Their occupation in *arenda* and their predominant role in the grain and forest produce export trade in Poland-Lithuania, enabled Jews to take an important part in the import trade of textiles there. From the 16th century Jews traded extensively in textiles on every level of the trade and in all types and qualities of cloth. Though never occupied directly in weaving or spinning, Jews were predominant in the trade in raw wool, yarn, and textiles of all types. Three Jewish weavers are mentioned in Plotsk in the 16th century. In *Mezhirech the Christian weavers attacked some Jewish rivals in 1636. The Poznan community declared the trade in raw wool produced in the region to be a *ḥazakah*, and appointed a special wool *parnas* in the 17th century to prevent foreign merchants from buying it up. In the Poznan region Jewish merchants would advance money, or farm out herds of sheep, in order to obtain the raw wool, which they gave out to local Christian craftsmen to make up into cloth for them. This expertise in capitalist entrepreneurship was in modern times transposed by many Jews of this region to Germany after the partitions of Poland-Lithuania at the end of the 18th century. Jewish *peddlers, in particular in the *Pale of Settlement and parts of Austria-Hungary, bought up raw materials in the villages, and supplied them to large-scale Jewish traders, and also sold fabrics and clothes in the villages.

Under Russian rule in modern times Jews were active on various levels in the development of the Polish textile industry, and in its celebrated center at *Lodz. In 1842, 39 of 82 Jews engaged in commerce in Lodz were suppliers of wool or yarn to artisans. In the early 1840s Jewish wool and yarn merchants and cotton importers began founding firms of their own. In 1864 there were more than 50 independent Jewish manufacturers in Lodz. The early 1860s witnessed a growing increase in Jewish investment and industrial ventures in textiles, with Jews leading in technological innovations and business organization methods at Lodz as well as at *Bialystok. In 1867 about 11% of the factory owners in Lodz were Jewish, but these accounted for only 8.5% of the total production. However, entrepreneurs such as Israel Poznanski, Bielchowsky, Joshua Birnbaum, and others forged ahead to become the leading Lodz textile manufacturers. Jewish participation in the textile industry there reached its peak before World War I, when 45.6% of all Lodz textile factories were owned by Jews and almost 27,000 Jewish workers were engaged in various branches of the industry and trade. Of these, one-third were still using manual looms, living in indescribable poverty in the Balut suburb of Lodz. Very few were employed in factories and virtually none in specialized technical work.

In independent Poland between the two world wars, Jewish participation in the Lodz and Bialystok textile industry was hard hit by the anti-Jewish discriminatory policies of the state. Some, however, like Oscar Cohn, managed to develop their factories with foreign capital. By 1931 textile enterprises in Jewish ownership were mainly on a smaller scale, and Jews were employed in the industry in clerical posts rather than as workers. In 1931, 16% of those employed in the textile industry in Poland were Jews, and 71.4% of the independent employers.

Central Europe

Jewish traders, generally from Poland-Lithuania, played a considerable role both as buyers and sellers of fabrics and clothes on *market days and at the fairs in Central Europe. At *Vienna, the entrepôt of all types of textile goods, Jewish merchants from the wool-producing provinces, Hungary, and Galicia, traded there with Jews from the textile-manufacturing areas of *Bohemia and Moravia, while the imperial army, and the city itself, took a large part of the products. Among the Viennese privileged manufacturers were Hermann *Todesco, who developed the silk industry there (further developed by S. Trebitsch and sons), and Michael L. *Biedermann, by whose single-handed efforts Vienna displaced Budapest as center of the wool trade in the Hapsburg Empire. Another privileged merchant manufacturer who was ennobled was M. *Koenigswarter. In 1846, 33 of 133 textile printing firms in Vienna were Jewish-owned, 11 of 72 cotton producers were Jews, as were also 27 of 53 textile commission agents, primarily for the Balkans and the Orient. In 1855 there were 89 Jewish-owned printing and weaving enterprises, about 5% of the total. After the official abolition of all restrictions on Jewish trade (1859; 1867) the participation of Jews in the Viennese textile trade became virtually a monopoly; even after World War I, when each of the Hapsburg successor states developed and protected its own textile industries.

In Hungary

The Hungarian wool trade was conducted almost entirely by Jews, who were thus in a position to establish textile industries. Adolf and Heinrich Kohner, originally Moravian feather merchants, established Hungary's first modern wool textile factories. Other notable textile manufacturers were Robert Szurday (originally Weiss, ennobled in 1899), Leo Buday (originally Goldberger), and Samuel Goldberger (ennobled in 1867).

Bohemia and Moravia

These areas, the most industrialized in the Hapsburg Empire, also produced most of its textiles, and Jews played a prominent role in this industry. From the 17th century Jews had been almost the sole dealers in raw wool, from the peasants together with furs, hides, livestock, and other agricultural produce. The peddler, who maintained immediate contact with the peasant, sold his wares to a Jewish merchant who had the wool washed and bleached, spun by peasants, and woven by artisans, and then sold it at the fairs. One of the earliest cloth manufacturers was Feith Ehrenstamm of Prossnitz (*Prostejov), who supplied the imperial army with large quantities during the Napoleonic wars by organizing the production of hundreds of local weavers.

In *Brno three of the first seven modern steam weaving factories were established by Jews, who had previously been supplying weavers with wool. Among the larger firms was that of L. *Auspitz, inherited and expanded by Phillipp *Gomperz, as well as the *Loew-Baer factories, and those of the Popper brothers and Salomon Strakosch. The textile industry also followed the same pattern in Reichenberg (*Liberec) where the earliest suppliers of wool there were the sons of Jacob *Bassevi of Treuenberg in the 17th century. Jews not only supplied the raw material but sold off the finished goods, primarily in Prague, where almost all the textile merchants were Jews (459 compared with 39 gentiles in 1772). Some of them established factories for cloth printing and other end processes, among them Moses and Leopold Porges, Salomon Brandeis, Simon *Laemel, and many members of leading Prague Jewish families. In Czechoslovakia after World War I Jewish activity in textiles continued and developed. The nationalization of the jute industry after 1918 was organized by Emanuel Weissenstein and Richard Morawitz, who remained president of the "Juta" concern until 1939. In Trutnov, the center of the flax industry, Alexander Videky was chairman of the flax exchange for many years.

Germany

The mercantilist policies of 18th-century Prussia encouraged *Court Jews and other Jewish financiers and purveyors to become entrepreneurs of various branches of the textile industry there. Levi Ulff brought Dutch artisans to Brandenburg in 1714 and founded a ribbon factory, which was soon commissioned to supply all the royal regiments. The elders of the Berlin Jewish community proposed setting up woolen cloth factories in Pomerania at their own cost (and to import 3,000 workers), in return for freeing the Jewish community from a newly imposed silver tax, but their proposal was rejected. Many Jews initiated new factories, some in new branches of textiles, such as Pinthus Levi of Rathenow, a horse and grain purveyor, who set up a canvas factory in 1763, which employed more than 1,000 workers. Isaac Bernhard, who imported silk from Italy, received state support in establishing a factory which soon employed 120 looms (his trusted bookkeeper was Moses *Mendelssohn, whose residence in Berlin depended on his employment). David *Friedlaender was a large-scale silk manufacturer. After the first partition of Poland (1772) Benjamin Veitel *Ephraim utilized the semi-professional local labor of Jewish women and girls in the Netze district, where Jews formed 6% of the total and one-quarter of the urban population. He established schools for teaching pillow-lace manufacture, and by 1785 was employing about 700 Jewish women and girls.

At *Stuttgart, center of the south German textile industry, there were in 1930 about 170 Jewish manufacturers and the same number of merchants; mainly in processing semi-raw products, semi-finished goods, and finishing, and particularly in the manufacture and trade in tricots and knitwear. Jews were also active in the nearby textile centers of Untertuerkheim, Bocholt, Westphalia, and Landeshut, Silesia, where the linen-manufacturing firm of H. Gruenfeld was well known. Jews participated in the trade and import of wool and in the finishing stages of the industry. Generally, Jewish entrepreneurs tended to concentrate in specific sectors, such as the manufacture of jute sacks, and drapery – lace ribbons, suspenders, garters, neckties, etc. – knitwear, and carpets. Between the two world wars the most important Jewish textile merchant in Germany was James *Simon, multi-millionaire philanthropist. A distinguishing feature of the Jewish participation in the German textile trade was its close connection with Great Britain, from which goods were imported, methods followed, and designs imitated, by means of agents and relatives. Jewish participation in the trade in finished textile goods (about 40%) was twice as high as their participation in the industrial sector of the textile industry.

Great Britain

Jews had mainly entered the textile industry and trade in Great Britain after the industrial revolution. One of the first was Nathan M. *Rothschild who established himself as a cotton-goods manufacturer (especially of uniforms) in Manchester in 1797. He was followed by many Jewish buyers from Jewish and non-Jewish firms from Germany and the continent, many of whom became independent exporters of cotton goods. At Bradford, Jacob Behrens became important after 1838, and several other German Jews were active there, as well as in other textile centers. In Scotland, they were prominent in the local jute industry in the last quarter of the 19th century, Sir Otto *Jaffe (see also *Tailoring) was a leading figure in Northern Ireland.

United States

In the United States few Jews entered the textile industry, an outstanding exception being the *Cone family of Carolina. However, Jews became prominent in raw cotton and wool brokerage, as well as in the wholesale and retail trade in fabrics. None of the large producers of synthetic fibers was Jewish-owned.

[Henry Wasserman]

In Israel

In the late 1960s the textile industry became one of the largest industrial branches in Israel, second only to the foodstuff industry. The output in 1969 was 10% of the total industrial output, amounting to IL 925,000,000. At the same time textile products constituted about 12% of industrial exports, totaling $66,000,000, the second largest export branch after diamonds.

By 1937 there were already 86 spinning and weaving plants in Ereẓ Israel, with about 1,500 employees. The necessary capital and technical knowledge were brought by Jewish professionals from Europe, an example of such enterprise being the Ata plant near Haifa. The development of the textile industry received considerable impetus in World War II which cut off the European supply, stimulating local manufacture for army needs. In 1943 the number of factories had grown to 250, employing about 5,630 workers; invested capital had grown fourfold and the output value tenfold.

After the establishment of the State of Israel, during the government's drive to step up industry, the textile industry expanded, and special emphasis was put on its establishment in development areas. By 1965, 25% of the textile workers were employed in the three large cities – Jerusalem, Tel Aviv, Haifa – while the rest were concentrated in new industrial areas, in particular in the development areas of Lachish, Ashkelon, and in the Negev and Galilee. The new plants were equipped with the latest machinery, including improved automatic weaving looms, which gave employment to hundreds of workers. While the older plants located in the central part of Israel employed about ten workers each, plants in the development areas employed an average of 50 workers each. There was a rapid growth in production, which before 1955 was mainly concerned with finishing processes. The products were then processed from the raw cotton stage. Apart from increase in quantity of production, there was an improvement in design and techniques. Export of textiles was expanded, and in 1971 exports had increased to one-fifth of the industry's output. In 1965 there were 1,007 textile factories employing 26,300 workers, including 100 plants employing more than 50 workers each. In 1970 there were 300,000 cotton-spinning machines and 50,000 wool-spinning machines, compared with 55,000 cotton-spinning machines before the outbreak of World War II. The number of mechanical looms grew from 2,000 before 1948 to 6,000 in 1970, more than half of them automatic and up-to-date.

The expansion of Israel's textile industry was also a result of the development of cotton growing in Israel as a profitable agricultural branch. Following successful experiments in 1953, the cotton-planted areas were expanded from 300 dunams in 1953 to 290,000 dunams on irrigated land and 32,000 dunams on unirrigated land, a total of approximately 330,000 dunams. The output of cotton fiber grew from 95 kg. per dunam in 1955 to 130 kg. per dunam in 1969. The total output of cotton grew from 2,000 tons in 1955 to 39,200 tons in 1969, when 21,000 tons of cotton were exported and about 18,000 tons were sold to the local industry. The carding machines were set up in various places in the cotton-growing areas. About 400 tons of wool were produced in 1969 by local sheep, but of this only 100 tons were sold to the local textile industry. The majority of the raw material for Israel's wool industry is therefore imported. Other raw materials for the textile industry are also imported.

[Zeev Barkai]

In the 1990s Israel's textile industry faced a crisis as cheap East Asian labor made it uncompetitive. At that time around 400 Israeli Arab sewing shops handled the brunt of the subcontracting work. These began to close down. The turnaround came when Israeli firms began doing their sewing work in Jordan and Egypt. The giant Delta company led the way, followed by Polgat, Argeman, Kitan, and others. In the early 2000s Israeli companies had 30 plants in Jordan employing 6,000 workers while employment in the industry in Israel dropped from a peak of 45,000 to 38,000. Israel's growing exports reached $370 million a year as it continued to supply such retailers and designers as Marks & Spencer, The Gap, Victoria's Secret, Wal-Mart, Sears, Ralph Lauren, Calvin Klein, and Donna Karan.

BIBLIOGRAPHY: TALMUD PERIOD: Krauss, Tal Arch, 1 (1910), 136–42; J. Newman, *Agricultural Life of the Jews in Babylonia* (1952), 104–5. MEDIEVAL PERIOD: S.D. Goitein, *A Mediterranean Society* (1967); M. Wischnitzer, *A History of Jewish Crafts and Guilds* (1965); O. Schmelz, *Jewish Demography and Statistics. Bibliography for 1920–1960* (1961), 83ff. OTTOMAN EMPIRE: S. Avizur, in: *Sefunot*, 6 (1962), 41–71; 8–12 (Eng.); idem, in: *Oẓar Yehudei Sefarad*, 5 (1962), 101–8; S.A. Rosanes, *Korot ha-Yehudim be-Turkiyyah*, 3 (1938), 384–96; I.S. Emmanuel, *L'Histoire de l'Industrie des Tissus des Israélites de Salonique* (1935); M.S. Goodblatt, *Jewish Life in Turkey* (1952), 47ff.; M. Benayahu, in: *Oẓar Yehudei Sefarad*, 5 (1962), 101–8; S. Schwarzfuchs, in: REJ, 121 (1962), 169–79; Y. Kena'ani, *Ha-Ḥayyim ha-Kalkaliyyim bi-Ẓefat* (1935). POLAND: P. Friedmann, in: S.W. Baron and A. Marx (eds.), *Jewish Studies in Memory of George A. Kohut* (1935), 178–247; idem, in: *Lodzer Tagblatt* (1931), nos. 204, 210, 216, 222, 228, 234, 240, 246, 252; idem, *Lodzer Visenshaftilikhe Shriftn*, 1 (1938), 63–132; R. Mahler, *Yehudei Polin Bein Shetei Milḥamot Olam* (1968), 69–113; W.M. Glicksman, *In the Mirror of Literature* (1966), 43f., 55f., 130–43; A. Yasny, *Geshikhte fun der Yidisher Arbeter Bavegung in Lodz* (1937); B.D. Weinryb, *Neueste Wirtschaftsgeschichte der Juden in Russland und Polen* (1934), index s.v. *Textil, Weber, Tuchmacher*; D. Boim, in: *Yidishe Ekonomik*, 1 (1937), 34–43; 83–91; S.E., *ibid.*, 199–201; M. Linder, *ibid.*, 149–57, 240–51; M. Ashkewitz, *Zur Geschichte der Juden in Westpreussen* (1967), 69ff.; D. Avron (ed.), *Pinkas Hekhsherim shel Kehillat Pozen*, index, s.v. *Soḥer Ẓemer*. CENTRAL EUROPE: S. Mayer, *Die Wiener Juden* (1917); J. Pick, in: *The Jews of Czechoslovakia* (1968), 409–16; E. Hofmann, in: H. Gold (ed.), *Juden und Judengemeinden Boehmens* (1934), 529–69; R. Kestenberg-Gladstein, in: *Zion*, 12 (1947), 49–65, 160–89; B. Heilig, in: BLBI, 3 (1960), 101–22. GERMANY: A. Marcus, *Die wirtschaftliche Krise des deutschen Juden* (1931), 70–96; idem, in: *YIVO Annual*, 7 (1952), 189–99; S. Stern-Taeubler, in: JSOS, 11 (1949), 129–52; E. Landsberg, in: *Der Morgen*, 3 (1927), 99–113; A. Cohn, *Beitraege zur Geschichte der Juden in Hessen-Kassel* (1933), 41–50; M. Zelzer, *Weg und Schicksal der Stuttgarter Juden* (1965), 32ff., 472–7; A. Taenzer, *Die Geschichte der Juden in Jebenhausen und Goeppingen* (1927), 109–50, 431–69; J. Jacobson, in: ZGJD, 1 (1929), 152–62; F. v. Gruenfeld, *Das Leinenhaus Gruenfeld* (1967); I.M. Kulisher, in: *Yevreyskaya Starina*, 11 (1924), 129–61. GREAT BRITAIN: A.R. Rollin, in: JHSET, 17 (1951–2), 45–53; C.C. Aronsfeld, in: YLBI, 7 (1962), 315ff.; V.D. Lipman, *Social History of the Jews in England, 1850–1950* 1 (1954); idem, in: JJSO, 2 no. 2 (1960); M. Freedman (ed.), *A Minority in Britain* (1955); L.P. Gartner, *The Jewish Immigrant in England 1870–1914* (1960); J. Gould and S. Esh, *Jewish Life in Modern Britain* (1964); A.R. Rollin, in: JHSET, 15 (1946). **ADD. BIBLIOGRAPHY:** W. Badarneh, "Marks & Spencer Calls the Shots: Israeli Textiles Flourish in Jordan and Egypt," in: *Challenge* (March 2000).

THAILAND (Prathet Thai), kingdom in S.E. Asia, formerly known as Siam. Jewish merchants occasionally visited the court of Siam. In 1683 the London Jew Abraham *Navarro, sent by the East India Company as interpreter to China, spent several months in Siam. During his travels in the Far East in 1920–21, Israel Cohen tells of meeting a Russo-Jewish diamond merchant from Antwerp on his way there, and of a Jewish musician who had performed before the king. The Siamese foreign minister wrote in 1921 expressing his government's accord with the establishment of a national home for the Jewish people. In the 1920s a few refugees from Soviet Russia arrived from Harbin and settled in the capital Bangkok. The size of the community was temporarily increased after 1933 by some 120 refugees from Nazi persecution, most of whom left after World War II. Communal activities were organized by P.B. Jacobsohn, who became Israel's honorary consul-general in 1953. An Israel embassy was opened in 1958, and friendly relations between Thailand and Israel were expressed through technical and economic cooperation. In 1964 a Jewish Association was incorporated, and in 1966 a Jewish community center with a synagogue was established. A number of Torah scrolls were presented to the community by the *Singapore Jewish Welfare Board in 1960. Sabbath eve services were conducted by a U.S. Army chaplain, who cared for the community's religious needs. There is no Jewish cemetery, and burials are conducted in a corner of the Protestant graveyard. In 1969 the permanent Jewish community of Thailand consisted of some six families in a total population of 31 million, with another 250 temporary residents. In the early 21st century a total of 250 Jews lived in Thailand, comprising Sephardim from Syria and Lebanon and Ashkenazim from Europe, the United States, and Shanghai. The Jewish Association of Thailand was housed in a three-story building in the residential area of Bangkok. It incorporated the Ashkenazi synagogue and the rabbi's home. There were also Sephardi and Chabad synagogues.

BIBLIOGRAPHY: I. Cohen, *Journal of a Jewish Traveller* (1925), 203, 222; M. Wischnitzer, *Die Juden in der Welt* (1935), 299; W.J. Fischel, in: PAAJR, 25 (1956), 45–53.

[Shaul Ramati]

THALBERG, IRVING GRANT (1899–1936), U.S. film producer and executive. Born in New York, Thalberg joined Universal Pictures soon after leaving high school and was the studio's general manager at 24, when he produced *The Hunchback of Notre Dame* (1923). A year later he was Louis B. Mayer's right-hand man, and soon after the Metro-Goldwyn-Mayer merger in 1924 he became the company's production chief. He produced *Ben-Hur* in 1926.

Thalberg guided MGM in its transition from the silent screen to sound, breaking box-office records with the pioneering musical *Broadway Melody* (1929). He was responsible for some of the most celebrated films of his time, such as *Greed* (1924); *The Big Parade* (1925); *Mata Hari* (1931); *Grand Hotel* (1932); *Strange Interlude* (1932); *Bombshell* (1933); *The Barretts of Wimpole Street* (1934); *The Merry Widow* (1934); *China Seas* (1935); *Mutiny on the Bounty* (1935); *San Francisco* (1936); *Camille* (1936); *Romeo and Juliet* (Oscar nomination for Best Picture, 1936); several *Marx Brothers comedies; and the much-acclaimed *The Good Earth* (Oscar nomination for Best Picture, 1937). He brought many performers to fame, among them John Gilbert, Greta Garbo, Clark Gable, Joan Crawford, and Norma Shearer, whom he married in 1927 on her conversion to Judaism. (She returned to Christianity in 1942.)

Thalberg was one of the 36 founders of the Academy of Motion Picture Arts and Sciences, established in 1927. Others were Douglas Fairbanks, Mary Pickford, Harold Lloyd, Cecil B. DeMille, Louis B. Mayer, and the Warner brothers, Harry and Jack.

Thalberg's final project for MGM was *Marie Antoinette* (1938), which was in the early stages of production at the time of his death. The title role went to Shearer, who took a keen interest in the film and considered it an ode to her husband. Dubbed "the boy wonder" early in his career, Thalberg died of pneumonia at age 37.

Although he produced almost 90 films, Thalberg did not permit his name to appear in any of the film credits, believing that "credit you give yourself is not worth having."

After his death, credit was awarded him in the form of the prestigious Irving G. Thalberg Memorial Award. Created by the Academy of Motion Pictures Arts and Sciences, the annual award is presented to acknowledge "creative producers, whose bodies of work reflect a consistently high quality of motion picture production."

BIBLIOGRAPHY: B. Thomas, *Thalberg: Life and Legend* (1969). **ADD. BIBLIOGRAPHY:** M. Samuel, *Mayer and Thalberg: The Make-Believe Saints* (1975); R. Flamini, *Thalberg: The Last Tycoon and the World of MGM* (1994).

[G. Eric Hauck / Ruth Beloff (2nd ed.)]

THALBERG, SIGISMUND (1812–1871), pianist. Thalberg was born in Geneva to Joseph Thalberg and Fortunee Stein of Frankfurt. He himself always claimed to be the illegitimate son of Count Moritz Dietrichstein and Baroness von *Wetzlar (of the ennobled Jewish Viennese family), but the claim is disproved by the birth certificate. At the age of ten he was taken to Vienna by Count Dietrichstein and there studied composition with Sechter and piano with Hummel. He later studied with Pixis and Kalkbrenner in Paris. Between 1830 and 1836 he undertook his first concert tours in Germany, France, and England and became one of the foremost virtuoso pianists of his time; several serious critics even put him above Liszt. He evolved a fingering technique for the brilliant piano pieces composed in the fashion of the period (his own, Liszt's, and others) which separated the melody, bass line, and accompanying voices and arpeggios in a way that gave the impression of a three-handed playing. For this purpose he also elaborated the technique of notating such pieces on three staves.

Thalberg composed two operas, a string trio, a duo for violin and piano, piano duets, songs, and over 80 piano pieces, many of them fantasies, variations, and arrangements based on operatic melodies. They are mostly of the salon-piece genre, and Thalberg himself exemplified the 19th-century figure of the "pianistic lion."

BIBLIOGRAPHY: Grove, Dict; MGG; Riemann-Gurlitt; Baker, Biog Dict (1958⁵), s.v. and VII (preface).

[Bathja Bayer]

°**THALLUS** (Gr. θαλλος), a first century C.E. author (probably heathen) of a lost Greek universal chronicle in three books of which eight fragments survive. Thallus' main theme was Hellenic rather than biblical history. Freudenthal suggested that Thallus was a Samaritan, because his Euhemeristic tendencies resembled those of the Samaritan Pseudo-*Eupolemus and because according to an emended text on Thallus, a Samaritan imperial freedman is said by Josephus to have loaned a million drachmae to King Agrippa I (Ant., 18:167). There is no reason to assume, however, that Euhemeristic tendencies as such indicate Samaritan origin, while the reading "Thallus" in Josephus is an uncertain emendation. The fact that Thallus recorded the eclipse of the year 29 – the year of Crucifixion – does not prove a link with the Christians. It is even probable that Thallus did not mention Moses in his history, though he may have known him from the Oriental chronicles.

BIBLIOGRAPHY: F. Jacoby (ed.), *Fragmente der griechischen Historiker*, 2 D (Text) (1929), 1156–58, no. 256; 2 D (Komm.) (1930), 835–7, no. 256; Wacholder, in: HTR 61 (1968).

[Ben Zion Wacholder]

THANKSGIVING PSALMS, common designation for one of the *Dead Sea Scrolls. It was bought in Jerusalem in 1947 by Eleazar Lipa *Sukenik who, from the contents, designated the scroll *Hodayot* (Heb. הוֹדָיוֹת). Scientifically its registration is 1QH (Cave 1, Qumran, *Hodayot*). It is now in the Shrine of the Book, Jerusalem.

The Scroll

The leather scroll was in two separate parts. One consisted of three sheets, each with four ink-written columns, the other of approximately 70 fragments, of which 5 formed one sheet with 5 columns, while 3 were the main part of one column. When published in 1955 the text appeared in 18 more or less complete columns and 66 fragments. The length of the scroll is uncertain as is the original sequence of the columns. There are several holes in the leather, and the top and bottom of the columns have disintegrated. This sometimes leads to uncertainty about the length of the individual poems of which the text consists, because the end and beginning of poems may have been located in the weathered away parts. Often it is possible with reasonable certainty to reconstruct the missing text, especially by means of fragments from a second manuscript from Cave 4. The scroll was written by at least two scribes working more or less accurately. The change is distinct in col. 11:22. In several cases the text was corrected first by the scribes or by later correctors. The script is Hebrew square characters, except that *El* (God) sometimes is in the old cursive script. Paleographically the scroll is considered to date from the 1st century B.C.E.

Contents

Because of the Scroll's fragmentary character it is impossible to tell the number of poems it contains. In columns 1–18 something like 30–35 poems may be represented varying in length from 8 to 50–60 lines. There are no headings, the division being marked only by a blank space. The majority of the poems begin with the introductory formula: "I thank Thee, O Lord" (or: "my God"), the rest: "Blessed be Thou, O Lord." In col. 5:20 the words: "I thank Thee" have been corrected to "Blessed be Thou." To judge from the contents, the two formulas do not signify different psalm groups. The substance is thanks to God for the salvation He has bestowed upon mankind, which is perceived as totally distinct from God. Radically man is described as sinful by nature; he is formed of clay and kneaded with water (1:21; 3:21), and returns to dust (10:4, 12:36); he is carnal (15:21; 18:23), born of a woman (13:14). The concept of sin does not concern only the external side but comprises man's whole existence, even spirit and heart being perverted (3:21; 7:27). Man cannot justify himself (1:25), and has no right before God (7:28; 9:14ff.). Natural man cannot comprehend God nor proclaim His glory (12:30), his heart and ears being dust and uncircumcised (18:4, 20, 24). Man's destiny is entirely governed by God (15:13, 22), and he can do nothing apart from the will of God (10:5ff.). As distinct from man, God is the almighty creator (1:13f.; 15:13f.). From His foreknowledge and foreordination He has established the activities of creation (1:7), and appointed the destiny of man (15:13f.), even man's thoughts (9:12, 30). His wisdom is unlimited (9:17), though incomprehensible for natural man (10:2). Man's only possibility lies in the revelation of God. Those to whom God from His preordination has revealed Himself are able to get insight into God's mysteries (12:20), to sanctify themselves to God (11:10f.), and to praise His name (11:25). They are not identical with the people of Israel – "Israel" does not occur in the preserved text – but are the remnant who accept the revelation, not by their own will but by God's predestination (6:8); they have been cleansed of their guilt by God (3:21). Mankind is thus divided into two groups: the elected who belong to God and for whom there is hope (2:13; 6:6), and the ungodly who are far from God (14:21) and allies of Belial (2:22); with all their might they war against the righteous (5:7, 9, 25). Naturally salvation is only meant for the chosen, and it is significant that it is talked of as a salvation which has already taken place (2:20, 5:18). This concept of man's situation originates in the existence of the religious community in Qumran, and this becomes especially evident in comparing the poems with other Qumran writings, first of all the *Manual of Discipline with which the psalms have dogmatically close similarities. Acceptance into this community is in itself salvation (7:19f.; 18:24, 28). No wonder, therefore, that there is no clear distinction between this and the eschatological salvation. The idea of the resurrection of the righteous is found (6:34), but does not play a great part. Eschatologically the main subject is not the salvation of the righteous but the final destruction of the ungodly. Neither is any stress laid upon messianic expectations. The phraseology of col. 3:13–18 is greatly influenced by late Jewish messianic expectations, and is often believed to describe the coming into the world of the Messiah. But even here there is no description of any messianic activities, and the main point is the usual description of the ruins of ungodliness.

Relations to the Bible

The dependence upon biblical literature, which is significant for the Qumran literature, is especially valid for the *Thanksgiving Psalms*. They have sometimes been indicated as a mere mosaic of biblical quotations; this is a misinterpretation. Direct references to biblical texts and authors, as in the New Testament, are never found, and only col. 2:29f. can be called a proper quotation (Ps. 26:12). In some cases the wording is so general and frequently found that it is hardly due to literary dependence, but rather to usage of traditional religious language. But apart from this the poems often allude to and rely on biblical passages. Sometimes expressions of similar meaning or wording from scattered places in the Bible are combined into a meaningful piece of writing. This is no dull imitation, but indicates to how great an extent the community in Qumran felt itself tied to biblical tradition. The Bible was read and interpreted from the community's own existence; those enlightened by the revelation of God would understand that the holy writings originally referred to the community and its history. But this point of view should not be misinterpreted; it has often been assumed that from the wording of the texts one could extract an explicit account of the history of the community and its founder and leaders. Col. 4:8f., e.g., reads "But they have expelled me from my country like a bird from its nest, and all my friends and relatives have been driven from me, and they esteem me as a broken vessel"; this has commonly been taken to refer to the author's fleeing from Jerusalem under the persecution of the priesthood. The source in this case is evidently Psalms 31:12f., but similar expressions occur elsewhere in biblical Psalms as traditional material for portrayals of misery. One must avoid reading into the texts. Poetical literature should not be treated like historical or juridical literature; it follows its own regulations, and must allow for biblical phraseology being used to a wide extent as images and symbols. Naturally the poems first of all borrow from the biblical Psalms. Next come the prophetic writings, and especially Isaiah, whereas the Torah is used proportionally rarely. From a stylistic point of view the poems are dependent upon the biblical Psalms with their different motives of complaint, thanksgiving, confidence, repentance, and prayer, but there is a marked loosening of the classical composition, as is also the case in other late Jewish psalm literature, e.g., Psalms of *Solomon. The term "Thanksgiving Psalms" should not be confused with the biblical thanksgiving psalms, which belong in a specific situation and follow fixed stylistic rules. Most of the Qumran psalms may well be termed thanksgivings, or, even better, hymns, but they are strongly influenced by motives of misery, complaint, and prayer as a result of the dualistic attitude to life in the community.

Use of the Psalms

While it is nowadays commonly accepted that the biblical Psalms were originally created for cultic purposes in the Temple, it is mostly assumed that the late Jewish Psalm literature, including the *Thanksgiving Psalms*, had no such function, but was "private" poetry expressing personal misery or happiness, or else was meant for spiritual and didactic edification. This, however, is no necessary alternative; the biblical Psalms were in later times used for edification and instruction along with their use in the Temple service. One has to reckon on the possibility of the Qumran psalms, or at least some of them, being used in the divine services in Qumran. This is especially valid for the poems in cols. 14, 16, and 17, which seem to refer to the community's internal life in an almost "technical" way. They may have been used as liturgies in the annual feast for renewal of the covenant, at which also new members were initiated into the community, which is expressly stated in cols. 1–2 in the *Manual of Discipline*. It is significant that the dependence upon biblical literature is much less marked in these liturgies.

Literary Origin

Neither in the poems themselves, nor in the other Dead Sea Scriptures, is any direct or indirect information given as to the authorship of the psalms or of the time and place of their composition, and one therefore has to judge from the contents. Mostly the whole collection has been considered to be an original literary unit with a single author, whose identity was to be sought in the "I" constantly occurring as the subject, and whose history of misery and suffering was told in the poems (e.g., 2:10f., 4:8ff., 6:19ff). Frequently this person has been identified with the *Teacher of Righteousness, or, possibly, some other leading personality within the community. There are, admittedly, passages in which "I" is talked of in such personal modes of expression in relation to the community (e.g., 4:23f.; 7:20f.; 8:21ff.), that it is reasonable to interpret them in terms of some leading individual. But even in these cases there is no clear indication of such a person being identical with the Teacher of Righteousness. And generally "I" occurs in such a way that it hardly can represent any single historic person, but is to be understood collectively in terms of the community and its individual members. Again in this respect the *Thanksgiving Psalms* belong to a tradition which goes back to the biblical Psalms, in which the "I" is not to be understood as referring to an individual author but to those who at any time take the psalm into their mouth. Nothing indicates that "I" in these late psalms should not be understood in the same way.

It cannot even be proved either that all the psalms originate from the same author, or that they date from the same time and place. Study of these poems shows that their apparent uniformity is not substantial. They express the same doctrines, but in style, phraseology, and vocabulary, as well as in their relation to biblical literature there are so many variations that it is reasonable to assume different authors. The majority of the psalms seem to presuppose the existence of the community; but some of them are so general in their expressions that they could well date from a time when the pious individuals had not yet segregated themselves as a separate religious group in Qumran. The only certainty is that this manuscript dates from the first century B.C.E. But the existence of another manuscript in Cave 4 may indicate that this may not be an original, but copies of earlier manuscripts.

BIBLIOGRAPHY: E.L. Sukenik, *Dead Sea Scrolls of the Hebrew University* (1955); J. Licht, *Megillat ha-Hodayot* (1957); Dupont-Sommer, in: *Semitica*, 7 (1957); S. Holm-Nielsen, *Hodayot, Psalms from Qumran* (1960); M. Mansoor, *Thanksgiving Hymns* (1961).

[Svend Holm-Nielsen]

°THARAUD, JÉRÔME (1874–1953) and **JEAN** (1877–1952), French novelists and essayists. The two are generally spoken of together because they wrote all their books jointly under the name J.-J. Tharaud.

An early Tharaud work on a Jewish theme was *Bar-Cochebas* (1907), but it was not for another decade that they embarked on the series of books that were designed to explain Judaism and traditional Jewish life to the average Frenchman.

From their studies of Jewish life in Central Europe, the Tharauds were inspired to describe, within the framework of loosely constructed novels, the picturesqueness of the ghetto, and the role of the synagogue and the yeshivah. The novels include *L'Ombre de la croix* (1917); *Un royaume de Dieu* (1920), an admiring account of East European Jewry's high ethical and cultural standards; *Quand Israël est roi* (1921); and *La Rose de Sâron* (1927). In *L'An Prochain à Jérusalem* (1924), an enthusiastic survey of Zionism's spiritual and messianic roots, the Tharaud brothers derided those Western Jews who were happy to dispatch their brethren to a Promised Land with which they themselves felt only nominal links. Another work of nonfiction was their *Petite histoire des Juifs* (1927). In 1933 the Tharaud brothers suddenly reversed their attitude in *Quand Israël n'est plus roi*, which presented Jews in an extremely unfavorable light. The Tharauds had finally chosen to adopt the antisemitic view that ancient Israel and modern Jewry were two separate entities, and that the solution to the "Jewish problem" was the enforced physical separation of the Jews from gentile society.

BIBLIOGRAPHY: J. Bonnerot, *Jérôme et Jean Tharaud; leur oeuvre* (1927); D. Halévy, *Eloge de Jérôme Tharaud* (1954); C. Lehrmann, *L'élément juif dans la littérature française*, 2 (1961), 106–8.

[Sidney D. Braun]

°THATCHER, MARGARET, BARONESS (1925–), British prime minister. The daughter of a Methodist grocer in Grantham, Lincolnshire, and an Oxford graduate, Margaret Thatcher entered Parliament in 1959 and served as Conservative prime minister from 1979 to 1990, winning three general elections. Her government was remarkable for the number of Jews she appointed to senior positions and for her respect for the British Jewish community. In the late 1930s her father had taken in a German Jewish refugee as a maid, which Margaret Thatcher credited with raising her awareness of the plight of Jews. At one time Thatcher had five Jews in her cabinet of 20 or so members, among them holders of the very senior positions of chancellor of the exchequer and home secretary. This led former Prime Minister Harold Macmillan to make his famous bon mot that the Thatcher cabinet "had more old Estonians than old Etonians." Thatcher also warmly admired Chief Rabbi Immanuel *Jakobovits, awarding him a peerage, and viewed the upward social mobility of Britain's Jews within a few generations, largely through their own ability and without state aid, as holding wider lessons for British society. It is estimated that up to two-thirds of Britain's Jews voted for the Conservative Party during the Thatcher years, which also coincided with the movement of the Labour Party to a hard-left position on many issues and the growth of an anti-Zionist left hostile to Israel.

The movement of most British Conservatives to the right might also be contrasted with the situation 20 or so years earlier, when Jews had a visible profile in the Labour government of Harold *Wilson.

BIBLIOGRAPHY: G. Alderman, *Modern British Jewry*; W.D. Rubinstein, *Jews in Great Britain*; S. Brook, *The Club: The Jews of Modern Britain* (1989); M. Thatcher, *The Downing Street Years* (1995).

[William D. Rubinstein (2nd ed.)]

THEATER.

ORIGINS
POST-BIBLICAL PERIOD
FROM 1600 TO THE 20TH CENTURY
- England
- France
- Germany
- Italy
- Holland
- Russia
- United States
- Jews in the Musical
- The Jew as Entertainer

YIDDISH THEATER
- Premodern Performance in Yiddish
- Haskalah Drama
- Broder Singers
- The Goldfaden Era
- Westward Exodus
- The Gordin Era
- New York to World War II
- Latin America
- The Art Theater Movement in Eastern Europe
- Interwar Poland
- Soviet Yiddish Theater
- Other Centers
- The Late 20th Century
- Conclusion

ORIGINS

Neither biblical nor talmudic literature contains anything which can be described as "theater" or "drama" in the modern sense of these terms. The Song of Moses (Ex. 15), with its choric refrain in the Song of Miriam, has often been cited as containing the rudiments of drama, which began as a combination of song and dance. The same has been suggested for the Song of Songs, and various attempts have been made with limited success to arrange this book for performance. It would be rash to suggest that writers of the Bible were quite untouched by the Athenian drama which had developed on the fringes of the Israelite world in the fifth century B.C.E. The Book of Job (dating probably from the fifth or fourth century B.C.E.) conforms in a general way to dramatic principles. It is written largely in dialogue, it shows expression of character, and it contains dramatic incidents. If there were in biblical writing tendencies toward formal dramatic composition, they reached their furthest development in Job. However, presentations of the Book of Job on the stage have fallen short of proving that it was written for performance.

POST-BIBLICAL PERIOD

Dramatic intentions are not manifest in post-biblical writing, except in the work of *Ezekiel of Alexandria, who lived in the first century B.C.E. and wrote tragedies on biblical themes. He wrote in Greek, and the known fragments of his work owe their survival to non-Jewish scholars. On the whole, post-biblical literature is without any works intended for performance in a theater. But the rabbis were fully aware of and generally disapproved of the theaters, amphitheaters, and circuses that existed in their Hellenistic-Roman world. They discouraged attendance at the theater except in certain circumstances. The Midrash indicates contemporary opinion when, in reference to the Bible story of Joseph in Egypt, it quotes two rabbis relating how, on the day of the Nile festival, a day of theatrical performances which all flocked to see, Joseph "went into the house to cast up his master's accounts" (Gen. R. 87:7).

The rabbis of the Talmud taught that one should not go to theaters or circuses because sacrifices were offered in honor of the idols. Where no such sacrifices were offered it was still prohibited to be present since persons watching the clowns and buffoons performing would transgress the prohibition against sitting in "the seat of the scornful" (Ps. 1:1). Nevertheless Rabbi Nathan thought Jews should be allowed to attend circuses and shows to watch gladiatorial contests since the members of the audience usually had the right of saving the life of the victim (Av. Zar. 18b).

Other evidence suggests that though the pious kept aloof from the theater, many others did not. It is considered that one of the purposes of Ezekiel of Alexandria in writing his biblical tragedies was to divert Jews from attendance at pagan theaters. This indicates that Jews were regularly to be found among the theater-going public.

Women were forbidden to go to shows of any kind. There is a touching passage in the Midrash (Ruth R. 2:22) in which Naomi tells Ruth that if she insists on conversion to Judaism, she will have to deny herself certain pleasures. "My daughter," she says, "it is not the custom of the daughters of Israel to frequent theaters and circuses."

The theaters that arose in Palestine during the Hellenistic period were largely swept away by the Maccabean War (167 B.C.E.), but a revival of forms of entertainment took place in the next century under Herod, and the larger cities including Jerusalem had theaters, amphitheaters, and hippodromes. These were gentile institutions. There was no attempt at creating a Jewish playhouse.

By the second century of the Christian Era, performance of tragedy had practically vanished from the Palestinian theater, and had been replaced by buffoonery, ribaldry, and coarse comedy which sometimes ridiculed Jews and their customs (Lam. R. 3:13). The hostility of the rabbis was such that they declared it sinful for a Jewish workman to take part even in the building of a stadium or amphitheater (Av. Zar. 16a).

In Rome during the time of Nero (first century C.E.), there were Jews on the Roman stage as well as in the auditorium. A Jewish actor *Aliturus (or Alityros) is known to have been among the emperor's favorites. He is mentioned by *Josephus without any apparent surprise at finding a Jewish actor in high favor in court. The sarcophagus of an actress, Faustina, in the Roman catacombs of the first or second century C.E. displays Jewish symbols and the word "*shalom*" in Hebrew. Another player, Menophilus (first century), lampooned by the Roman epigrammatic poet Martial, appears to have been a Jewish comedian. In the third century the rabbinical scholar Simeon b. Lakish (also known as Resh Lakish) earned his living as a strong man in a circus at Sepphoris, as related in the Talmud (BM 84a; Git. 47a, et al.). All this suggests that Jews were not uncommon in the theatrical profession. As Jews became increasingly unpopular, however, during the Jewish War, they, like the early Christians, tended to conceal their origin.

Jewish theatrical activity at this early period thus remains largely conjectural. The Bible, nevertheless, played a very positive role both as a source of dramatic inspiration and as an influence on content in all forms of theatrical representation. The Bible has had a primary and enduring role in the history of the Western theater. In the first place it provided the starting point of modern theater in the medieval mystery plays, and secondly it continued to provide subjects and ideas to which playwrights, poets, composers, and choreographers have turned again and again. (See *Bible, in Arts.)

In the history of the Jewish theater, the mystery play has great relevance. The two came into contact in Italy in the early Renaissance period when the ducal heads of the city-states often sponsored the entertainments held at ducal weddings or other festive occasions. In their ghettos the cultural life of the Jewish communities tended to follow the gentile pattern. The Purim play was a counterpart to the kind of show the gentiles enjoyed at their carnivals (see *Purim-Shpil). In time it was turned into an elaborate theatrical presentation played by Jewish theatrical companies who acquired considerable fame. (See also below: The Jew as Entertainer.)

In Italy, in the 16th century, Mantua became famous for its court pageantry and was the center of the new Italian drama.

The Jewish community, about 2,000 people, often provided and most likely paid for dramatic spectacles for ducal entertainments. On Fridays, the performances began early since they had to end before Sabbath. The Jewish company of the Mantua ghetto acquired a high reputation as did companies in other Italian cities where there were Jewish communities. The Venetian diarist, Marin Sanudo, records on Saturday, March 4, 1531, the day after Purim, that "there was performed among the Jews in the 'Geto' a very fine comedy; but no Christian could be present by order of the Council of Ten. It ended at ten o'clock at night." This was almost certainly an annual event, which gentiles must have attended in earlier years, thus arousing the disapproval of the Council. In 1489, as a special request, the story of Judith and Holofernes from the Apocrypha was staged in Pesaro by the Jewish community at its own expense as the main show in the elaborate wedding celebrations of Giovanni Sforza, lord of Pesaro, to the sister of the marquess of Mantua.

In 1525 two obviously famous Jewish actors, Solomon and Jacob, were sent for from Ferrara to act in a comedy at a great banquet given by Cardinal Ercole Gonzaga in Mantua. By 1525 participation of Jews in state performances was regarded as a normal thing. In 1549 the Jews presented a comedy at the wedding of Duke Francesco in Mantua. In 1563 they performed Ariosto's *I Suppositi*, in 1568 *Le Due Fulvie* by Massimo Faroni of Mantua. In 1583 they presented a comedy *Gli Ingiusti Sdegni* by Abbé Bernado Pino with dances by the Jewish ballet master, Jacchino *Massarano. Under Duke Vincenzo of Mantua (from 1590) the Jews were required to perform almost annually. As many as 80 members took part in one performance. The success of the Mantuan community's theater company was due in large part to one man, Leone Portaleone Sommi, an impresario, well known all over Europe, who stands at the threshold of modern times and modern theater.

[Lewis Sowden]

FROM 1600 TO THE 20TH CENTURY

The Jew's participation in 17th-and 18th-century theatrical productions was at best insignificant. As a stage character, however, the Jew, portrayed by non-Jewish actors, became a popular figure in the European theater. He was generally a villain, although occasionally, in plays by authors opposed to Jew-baiting, a supernoble being. Jewish actors, until 1900, were isolated figures, facing prejudice and often abuse. It was not until the second half of the 19th century that Jews gained prominence as actors and directors in Europe and in the United States and made their mark as they had in other professions.

England

The bleak period is typified by the theater in England, where the Shakespearean age had made drama the most important art form in the country. Jews, who had been expelled in 1290, were little known in England until their return in the mid-17th century, but they were known on the stage. Early representations of Jews as villains gave way to stage characters who, because they were Jews, were either usurers or fools, and almost always ridiculous.

The first English secular play which included a Jewish character was *The Three Ladies of London* by R.W. (possibly Robert Wilson), published in 1584, in which a Jew, portrayed as decent and honorable, was nevertheless defrauded. Shortly afterward, *Marlowe's *The Jew of Malta* (1591) and *Shakespeare's *The Merchant of Venice* (1596), in both of which a Jew was the villain, set a pattern which was to endure. There are on record 80 plays published in England from 1584 to 1820, in which at least one character was recognizable as being Jewish; most of them were written after 1700. After 1800 plays with Jewish characters appeared at the rate of almost one year. (See *English Literature.)

Shakespeare's Shylock was first played comically, until, in 1741, the Irish actor Charles Macklin caused a sensation by defying tradition and playing him as a tragic character and according to the original text.

When the English theaters, closed by the Puritans in 1642, were reopened after the restoration of the monarchy in 1660, King Charles II extended his protection to Jews, and playwrights were therefore discouraged from lampooning them. More important than mere protection was the fact that King Charles continued Cromwell's benevolent policy of allowing Jews to resettle in England. This meant in fact that Jews could now live and work openly in the country. It was some time, though, before Jews made their way in the theater. Samuel Pepys' Diary for Aug. 12, 1667, refers to a "Mrs. Manuel, the Jew's wife, formerly a player," and praises her as "a mighty discreet, sober-carriaged woman"; but it is probable that Mrs. Manuel was not herself Jewish.

The first Jewess to win a name on the English stage was Hannah *Norsa, daughter of an Italian Jew from Mantua who kept a tavern in Drury Lane. She played the part of Polly Peachum in *The Beggar's Opera* in 1732 with great success. Another popular actor on the London stage was *Leoni (Myer Lyon), a singer who made his debut at Drury Lane on Dec. 13, 1760, in a play called *The Enchanter*. When Leoni played the lead in *The Duenna* by Richard Sheridan it could not be performed on Friday night as Leoni sang in the Duke's Place Synagogue. When it opened in 1775 at Covent Gardens at Leoni's insistence, the name of the principal male singing part was changed from Cousin Moses to Don Carlos.

Both Leoni and another actor who played the part of the rich and absurd Isaac Mendoza in *The Duenna* are reported to have used the exaggerated foreign accent that had become standard for Jewish characters from at least 1715, when the character Mordecai used it in Charles Knipe's *A City Ramble*. Among the leading actors who played accented Jewish roles was Ralph Wewitzer who played in Garrick's and Edmund Kean's companies and who may have been of Jewish birth. The broken accent was considered hilarious by 18th- and 19th-century audiences. From the end of the 18th century on, however, there were several plays of importance that presented

Jews in a favorable light, among them those by C.Z. Barnett (1802–1890), a Jew who was a playwright and an actor.

A small number of Jewish performers who became known as "Astley's Jews" also played at Astley's circuses at the end of the 18th and the beginning of the 19th century. Chief of the troupe was Jacob De *Castro, a comedian, who wrote an autobiography, *Memoirs* (1824).

One book changed the atmosphere for Jews in the arts and profoundly influenced their portrayal. In *Oliver Twist*, Charles Dickens drew Fagin as an unrelieved picture of evil, which set the tone in drama for most of the rest of the 19th century. The first adaptation of *Oliver Twist* reached the stage in 1838, the very year of the novel's publication. Fagin was followed by an almost unrelieved procession of Jewish stage distortions, and even helped to popularize a lisp for stage Jews that lasted until 1914.

Nevertheless, the Jews were beginning to protest. They comprised a considerable portion of theater audiences at the time, and during one performance in 1839 their resentment overflowed into a disturbance that drowned the play completely. A riot stopped Dibdin's *Family Quarrels* at its 1802 opening when the audience took offense at a Jewish reference. Jews often expressed their disapproval of a play by staying away. A revival of *The Jew of Malta* in 1818 led to a Jewish boycott of London theaters for the rest of the season.

In contrast to their portrayal on the stage, Jews were winning distinction as actors, singers, and even writers. Maria Bland, an actress, won fame at Drury Lane toward the end of the 18th century. Mary Anne Goward Keeley (1806–1899), her husband, Robert Keeley (1793–1869), and Henry Sloman (Solomon; 1793–1873) played in London theaters. John *Braham sang at Covent Garden and in 1835 built St. James' Theatre. Edward Stirling (1811–1894) and Morris Barnett were actors and playwrights. Adelaide Neilson (1846–1880) appeared twice on tour in the U.S.

The Jewish stereotype on the London stage was finally broken in 1914 by three plays that treated Jews in some depth: Israel *Zangwill's *The Melting Pot*, Harold F. *Rubinstein's *Consequences*, and Herman Scheffauer's *The New Shylock*. In 1922 came Galsworthy's *Loyalties*, which treated the Jew and the prejudices surrounding him with dignity and objectivity. Leon M. Lion the actor-producer, played in a revival of the play in 1928.

With the rise of the Nazis on the Continent, the Jew became a tragic figure and could no longer be treated on the English stage in a spirit of caricature or ridicule. Jewish actors came to the fore without having to aver or deny their Jewishness, among them Alfred Marks, Alfie Bass (d. 1987), David Kossoff, Yvonne Mitchell, and Leonard Sachs. Among directors the most important was Sir Herbert Beerbohm-Tree (1853–1917).

France

In most 19th-century French plays Jews were either caricatured or romanticized, the men portrayed as ugly, old, and dirty, and the women as noble, beautiful, and heroic, but there were three important exceptions. *Le Juif* by Marc-Antoine-Madelaine Desaugiers (1772–1827) produced in 1823 included the benevolent character Isaac Samuel. The playwright Adolphe Philippe d'Ennery (1811–1899), who had been a public notary and was said to be a Jew named Jacob, criticized the convention that a Jew must be grotesque and repulsive. Catulle *Mendes (1841–1909), whose father was a Jew, painted a sympathetic Jewish character in *Les Mères Ennemies* (1880). But there was no Jewish character in French drama as memorable as the English Shylock or the German Nathan the Wise.

Foremost among France's Jewish actors was Sarah *Bernhardt who, though Roman Catholic by upbringing, was proud of her Jewish heritage; and Eliza (*Rachel) Felix who died young, having become famous as an interpreter of French classic roles.

There were, of course, many more Jewish actors on the French stage: René Alexandre (1885–1945) who was noted for Corneille and Victor Hugo roles; Harry *Baur who began at the Grand Guignol and went over to films; George Berr (1867–1942), an actor, director, and author of fame whose beautiful voice contributed to his success; Marthe Brandes (1862–1930) whose original name was Josephine Brunschwig, and whose grace was famous; Daniel Gelin (1921–2002), a Comédie Française stage actor and director of films; Robert Hirsch (1921–), actor; Romanian-born Edouard Alexander de Max (1862–1930) who became well known in roles of young tragic figures like Schiller's Don Carlos; Simone Simon (1914–2005), equally at home on stage and screen; Gustave Hippolite Worms (1836–1910); the athletic Eugène Silvain (1851–1930), noted for his Roman profile; and Suzanne Reichenberg (1853–1924) who for 30 years specialized in young roles. Jules Claretie (1840–1912), dramatist and journalist, was from 1885 to 1912 the administrator of the Comédie Française. Gustave Cohen (1879–1958) was the great French historian of the theater.

In a special category belong Jean Gaspard Deburau (1796–1846) and his not-quite-so-famous son Jean Charles (1829–1873). Jean Gaspard, whose father Philippe Germain (1761–1826) had a theater of marionettes, was born in Bohemia in 1811 and came to Paris where he became a mime at the Théatre des Funambules ("Theater of the Tightrope-Walkers"), which once had been a circus. He created Pierrot, a new type which, because of its originality and the excellence of the performer, became a sensation overnight. He himself wrote the plays in which Pierrot was the tragic hero, and his art of pantomime was considered unique. His son continued in his father's career with success, but did not equal his reputation.

Germany

In no other country in modern times did the theater play as important a role as in Germany (see *German Literature). And in no other country did the Jew figure so prominently in dramatic literature, in acting or directing. His beginning was early and on a hostile note. In 1573 97 boys, five to 17 years old, performed a play called *Ein Schoen Christlich new Spil von Kinderzucht* in Ensisheim (Upper Alsace). The play, written by Johann Rassern, the parson of Ensisheim, tells the story of two boys, one of whom, spoiled by his mother and corrupted by a Jew, Ulmann, ends his life on the gallows. An unknown artist illustrated the manuscript with 63 woodcuts which depict the action of the play: Ulmann and the boy at a dice game; Ulmann dragged to the gallows; and Ulmann being removed from there by the devil (F.R. Lachman, *Die "Studentes" des Cristophorus Stymmelius und ihre Buehne*, 1926).

In 1616, *Das Endinger Judenspiel*, dealing with the trial and burning of Jews for murder after the disappearance of a Christian family, was performed in Endingen (Baden). Following that Andreas Gryphius (1616–1664) presented his *Horribilicribrifax* (1663; after Plautus' *Miles Gloriosus*) featuring the boasting Jew Issachar; and, decade after decade from 1634, the Bavarian Oberammergau Passion Play has been staged, latterly in the face of energetic Jewish protests. The 17th and 18th centuries produced a considerable number of villainous or at least reprehensible Jewish figures in dramatic literature.

Nevertheless, Germany, at a relatively early time, provided exceptions to the general attitude. *Die Juden* (1749), written by Gotthold Ephraim *Lessing, boldly attacked Christian prejudice. Much more important, however, was Lessing's *Nathan der Weise* (1779) in which Jewish, Christian, and Muslim characters present the idea that virtue is not bound to religion and that all religions are equally important. The play was banned from the stage for a number of years. A considerable number of writers for the stage followed Lessing's example and created sympathetic Jewish figures in their plays. The caricatured Jew remained popular in the 19th and 20th centuries. An example is quoted by S.M. Dubnow (*Die neueste Geschichte des juedischen Volkes 1789–1914*, vol. 2, p. 12): in 1815–16, a very bad comedy, *Die Judenschule* or *Unser Verkehr* had enormous success. A popular actor, Wurm, aping the Jewish "jargon," and mocking Jewish peculiarities, was applauded nightly. When the play was scheduled to be produced in Berlin, Israel *Jacobsohn obtained a prohibition against the performance from Chancellor Hardenberg. The public became furious and held nightly demonstrations until the prohibition was revoked.

It was only toward the end of the 18th century, the time of the Emancipation, that Jewish actors appeared on the German stage. Their number, however, increased rapidly, a fact noted by the German actor and historian of the theater, Eduard Devrient, in his *Geschichte der deutschen Schauspielkunst* (5 vols., 1848–74). It seems that Jacob Herzfeld (1769–1826), who was admired by Goethe and Schiller and corresponded with both, was the first serious Jewish actor on the German stage. He was followed by members of three generations of his family. Eduard Jerrmann (1798–1859) had equal success on the French and on the German stage, Heinrich Marr (1797–1871) was the first Mephisto, Anton Ascher (1820–1884) the first Jewish comedian. Moritz Rott (1797–1867), Ludwig *Dessoir, and especially the Polish-born Bogumil *Dawison, followed by Siegwart Friedmann (1842–1916), Maximilian Ludwig (1847–1906), and the Budapest-born Max Pohl (1855–1935) were outstanding actors in Germany. Adolf von *Sonnenthal, born in Budapest, was the uncontested star of the Vienna Hofburg-theater.

Great stage managers soon began to appear in the German theater. Berlin was without doubt one of the two capitals of world theater, the other being Moscow. Hebrew actors from Palestine who met in Berlin gave the first performance of Henie Rochet's play *Belshazzar* and created the Teatron Ereẓ Yisre'eli. While in other European countries all theaters of importance were concentrated in the capital, in Germany leading theaters existed in more than a dozen cities, many under Jewish managers who often doubled as outstanding stage directors. An important development in stagecraft was brought about by the Jewish director of the theatrical company of Duke George II of Saxony Meiningen (1826–1914), Ludwig *Chronegk, who, when the Meininger toured the country, staged more than 250 plays, introducing new precision, discipline, and natural behavior and creating a closely knit ensemble. In the company were Ludwig *Barnay who later had a theater of his own in Berlin, and Hungarian-born Leopold Teller (1844–1908).

The next step in the development of the German stage was taken by another Jewish director, Otto *Brahm (Abrahamsohn), who became a pioneer of the naturalistic theater. Emanuel Reicher (1849–1924) and Else Lehmann (1866–1940), among others, acted under his direction. Together with two other Jews, the publisher Samuel *Fischer and the critic Alfred *Kerr, Brahm prepared the way to fame of such non-Jewish authors as Frank Wedekind and Gerhart Hauptmann.

The name of Max *Reinhardt, who moved away from Brahm's naturalism and allowed free play to fantasy, became closely associated with a great number of Jews acting under his direction: Victor Arnold (1873–1914), Ernst *Deutsch, Max *Pallenberg, and Rudolph *Schildkraut were among them. At the same time there were actors like Elizabeth *Bergner, Maria Fein (1896–1965), Alexander Granach (1890–1945), Paul Graetz (1890–1966), Ludwig Hartau (1872–1922), Peter *Lorre, Fritzi Massary, Grete Mosheim (1905–1986), Luise Rainer (1912–), Gisela Werbezirk (1875–1956), and many others. The last director who changed the outlook of the theater in Germany before Hitler's rise to power was Leopold *Jessner, pioneer of expressionism on the stage. It was under his direction that actors like Fritz *Kortner reached the zenith of their careers.

During the 19th and at the beginning of the 20th centuries many names of Jewish theater directors in Berlin and elsewhere became widely known. Carl Friedrich Cerf (1771–1845) created the first private theater in Berlin; Victor *Barnowsky, Oscar Blumenthal (1852–1917), and Gustav Lindemann (1872–1960) in Duesseldorf are among them. Alfred Kerr was the most notable representative of a generation of Jewish theater critics who had enormous influence on the development of the theater in Germany and made the reviewing of plays a quasi-independent art form. Romanian born

Ernst Stern (1876–1954) was, during the last pre-Hitler decades, Berlin's and Reinhardt's most honored scenic artist and stage designer. Jewish audiences played an important, sometimes decisive role, as developments after Hitler's take-over illustrate. On April 10, 1933, the Berlin correspondent of the *Daily Telegraph* reported: "The theaters are beginning to suffer from the impoverishment of the Jews, who have always been lavish patrons. A new production at the Deutsches Theater, enthusiastically praised by the entire press, has been taken off after a few performances before a nearly empty auditorium."

When Hitler came to power, there were about 2,400 Jewish actors and theater directors in Germany. On April 1, 1933, an organized anti-Jewish boycott began and Jewish actors were ousted. These actors and the public reacted by forming the *Juedscher Kulturbund ("Jewish Cultural League"). From 1933 on, Jews who fully understood the situation and were able to do so, left Germany; but "the Jewish Cultural League from 1933 to 1938 (in a limited way until 1941) supported three theater ensembles, an opera, two symphonic orchestras, one cabaret, a theater for Jewish schools, some choirs, numerous chamber music groups, and lectures and art exhibits. About 2,500 artists (actors, singers, instrumentalists, poetry readers, directors, dancers, graphic and plastic artists) and lecturers belonged to this organization set-up, and nearly 70,000 people in about 100 cities formed the public, the largest voluntary union of Jews in Germany" (H. Freeden, *Juedisches Theater in Nazideutschland*, 1964, p. 1). The first performance, on Oct. 1, 1933, was Lessing's *Nathan der Weise*. When Allied Powers reopened the Deutsches Theater in Berlin in 1945, the first performance was again *Nathan der Weise*. The director was Vienna-born Fritz Wisten, one of the few surviving members of the Juedischer Kulturbund. Very few Jewish actors and directors returned to Germany after the war; the most important of those who did were Fritz Kortner and Ernst Deutsch.

Italy

Jewish theaters in the Italian ghettos continued their performances until well into the 18th century. Later on, a few Jewish playwrights appeared on the scene. Among the actors, Gustavo Modena (1803–1861) was an interesting personality, a revolutionary who had to flee Italy and was only able to return after an amnesty had been granted. He was especially brilliant in recitation. Giovanni Emanuel (1848–1902) toured in Berlin, Vienna, and Russia, but had his greatest triumphs in Shakespeare and Schiller parts in South America. Claudio Leigheb (1848–1903), who specialized in comedy roles, was an actor's son. Giuseppe Sichel (1849–1934) helped to make French comedy popular in Italy. Enrico Reinach (1851–1929) mostly played the part of the young lover. Virginia Reiter (1868–1937) achieved fame largely thanks to her Jewish features which could give dramatic expression to any kind of emotion and to her beautiful voice. Anche Oreste Calabresi (1857–1915) was equally at home in drama and in comedy. Ugo Piperno (1871–1922) acted on the stage and in a number of films. The great Italian historian of the theater, Alessandro d'Ancona (1835–1914), was a Jew.

Holland

In Holland, writer and dramatist Herman *Heijermans (also Heyermans) dedicated his prose works and his plays to the problems of the proletariat and the lower middle class, especially Jews. In one of his plays, *Ghetto* (1898), the role of Sachel was played by the Jewish actor Louis de Vries (1871–1940) who was also a director and theatrical organizer. He was outstanding in such roles as Shylock, Hamlet, Fuhrmann Henschel, and Higgins in Shaw's *Pygmalion*. Holland's most outstanding actors, however, belonged to the Bouwmeester family which provided actors from the second half of the 18th century to the first half of the 20th. The first acting members of this family were Frederik Adrianus Rosenveldt (1769–1847), a comedian, and his son Frederik Johannes Rosenveldt (1798–1867) who married Louise Francina Maria Bouwmeester. Their children took their mother's name. Louis Frederik Johannes *Bouwmeester (1842–1925) came to be considered Holland's greatest actor. Other acting members of this family include Theodora Antonia Louis Bouwmeester (1850–1939), who acquired fame as Schiller's Maria Stuart, as Madame Sans-Gêne, and in other roles; Frederik Christianus Bouwmeester (1885–?), and Lily Bouwmeester (1901–1993), a stage and film actress.

Russia

In czarist times, Jewish actors on the Russian stage in Moscow and St. Petersburg were usually members of foreign touring companies. But there were Jewish actors in the provincial troupes mostly under Russian names. Some of them had come from the Yiddish theaters when they were closed by czarist edict in 1883 and most of them took Russian names (if not baptism). The lifting of the ban for a few years before the Russian Revolution changed the situation little, though the rising film industry did provide further scope. By 1914, Ossip Runitsch, who had started on the stage, had become a star of the Russian cinema. A well-known Jewish player in czarist companies was Alla *Nazimova, who left for the U.S. in 1905. The revolution brought other Jewish personalities into the open. Zinaida Raikh, the wife of V. Meyerhold, the Russian director, achieved a triumph in Meyerhold's production of *The Lady of the Camellias* in the 1930s. She was murdered in her Moscow flat in 1940 after Meyerhold's arrest and execution by Stalin's agents. After the Stalinist period, the outstanding Jewish actor on the Russian stage was the comedian Arkadi Raykin.

[Lewis Sowden and Frederick R. Lachman]

United States

The theater in the United States, especially on New York's Broadway, was during the 19th and the beginning of the 20th century strongly influenced by Europe and especially by England, but gained independence fast and developed largely under the stimulus of Jewish directors and players. An early if atypical figure was the actress Adah Isaacs *Menken, who created a sensation in the title role of Byron's *Mazeppa* in 1861.

Before the end of the century, the playwright David *Belasco and the producers *Frohmans brothers were important names in the New York theater world, the first of the great line of personalities that was subsequently to arise on Broadway.

Jewish influence in a city with a growing Jewish population was among the sources from which the New York theater was enriched. During the 1890s, Yiddish theater was developing rapidly on Second Avenue and growing into a training ground for actors, among them personalities such as Paul *Muni, who were inevitably to turn their eyes toward Broadway. Another source of trained actors was the music hall or variety theater. It abounded in Jewish comedians and sent much talent to the "legitimate" stage. Derogatory references to Jews were largely absent from the music halls because of the pressure from Jewish performers.

The early and middle years of the 20th century saw the rise of Jews to unequaled prominence on Broadway, where they distinguished themselves as actors, playwrights, songwriters, and composers. Early outstanding figures were the playwrights Clifford *Odets, Elmer *Rice, S.N. *Behrman; the showman Billy *Rose; and the producers *Sam and Jed *Harris. Others were Arthur Leroy Kaser, who wrote monologues, Elmer C. Levinger, who wrote 19 short plays about Jewish history before World War II, and Samson Raphaelson, who in 1925 wrote *The Jazz Singer* about a Jewish boy who had to choose between being a cantor and a musical comedy actor. Al *Jolson made the lead role famous. Later in the century playwrights who were Jewish made a major impact on the drama. (See also *United States Literature.)

Of the hundreds of Jews who achieved fame as actors and actresses in the half-century from 1920, practically none remained basically a stage actor. Writers, producers, directors, and actors divided their time between stage, film, and television, whereby the importance of film and television continuously increased. In addition, on the stage, the musical absorbed a high percentage of the Jewish theatrical people, and a number of them, such as the *Marx brothers or the *Ritz brothers, stayed on the thin borderline between acting and entertaining. There are a few, among the many, who remained equally at home in all the media, Zero *Mostel, Danny *Kaye, and Sid Caesar among them.

Among the producers were Max Liebman, discoverer of Danny Kaye and Sid Caesar; and Alexander H. Cohen, who became known as Broadway's "Millionaire Boy Angel" and produced more than 30 stage shows in New York and London. During the 1960s Mike *Nichols became one of the outstanding stage and film directors. Jules Irving and Herbert Blau, who had founded in the early 1950s the Actors' Workshop, an avant-garde group in San Francisco, became in 1965 co-directors of the Lincoln Center Repertory Theater in New York. Blau resigned that post in 1967. Florenz *Ziegfeld and the *Shubert brothers, Mike Todd, Lee Strasberg, and many others were important and successful producers, directors, and teachers of generations of actors. Boris *Aronson, who began his career in the Yiddish theater when he came to New York in the early 1920s, became America's best-known stage designer. Jean Rosenthal was the leading lighting designer of the theater in the 1950s and 1960s.

[Mark Perlgut]

Jews continued to play a prominent role in the New York theater, particularly on Broadway, largely through the ownership of theaters. The Shubert organization, run by Gerald Schoenfeld and Bernard *Jacobs, controlling the largest houses, which offered the prospect of higher profits, were a significant force in the economics of the theatrical offerings. Despite the absence of Joseph *Papp, who had died, his Public Theater continued to present provocative Shakespeare comedies and dramas and other works. Arthur Miller died in 2005 but his major works, including *Death of a Salesman, All My Sons*, and *A View from the Bridge*, were produced throughout the United States. Younger Jewish playwrights, like Tony *Kushner, Jon Robin Baitz, Richard Greenberg, and Wendy *Wasserman emerged as serious dramatists.

[Stewart Kampel (2nd ed.)]

Jews in the Musical

The musical comedy, later called musical play or simply musical, has its sources in the European operetta and in vaudeville. The musical comedy moved from England to the United States where in the 20th century the genre expanded and underwent its greatest development. Already in the earliest forms of musical theater, the revue or vaudeville, Jews had played an important role: Florenz Ziegfeld with his *Ziegfeld Follies*, which, between 1907 and 1931, introduced many singer-actors and composers like Irving *Berlin and Jerome *Kern. Elaborate revues were presented by the Shubert brothers, theatrical entrepreneurs who, by 1956, owned 17 theaters on Broadway and about half of the nation's legitimate theaters. In the field of operetta, Rudolf Friml and Sigmund *Romberg, both immigrants from Europe, dominated: Friml, born in Prague, with *The Firefly* (1912) and *Rose Marie* (1924), Romberg, Vienna-born, with *The Student Prince* (1924) and *The Desert Song* (1926). Jerome Kern, whose works include the *Princess Theater Shows* (1915–18), was one of the earliest composers for musical comedy. So was Irving Berlin with *Yip, Yip, Yaphank* (1918). He and producer Sam H. Harris built the Music Box Theater in 1920 and here they put on their sophisticated and lavish *Music Box Revues* (1921–24).

The 1920s saw composers such as Richard *Rodgers, George *Gershwin, and Arthur Schwartz (d. 1984), with Lorenz Hart, Oscar Hammerstein II, E.Y. Harburg, Howard Dietz, Ira Gershwin, George S. *Kaufman, and Morrie Ryskind as lyricists and librettists. The team of Rodgers and Hart became one of the most fruitful in American musical history, producing 27 musicals. Dietz wrote the music for the *Grand Street Follies* (1925). George Gershwin, one of the most celebrated composers of the era, wrote, in addition to several large works for orchestra, the music to more than 20 Broadway musicals. His brother, Ira, wrote the lyrics for many of George's shows.

Early important examples of the musical play were *Dearest Enemy* (1925) and *A Connecticut Yankee* (1927), both by Richard Rodgers and Lorenz Hart; still more important was *Showboat* (1927) by Jerome Kern and Oscar Hammerstein II, based on a book by Edna *Ferber, and destined to become a classic of the American musical theater.

Musical plays of the 1930s mirrored the reality of American life, the slump and the Depression; *Of Thee I Sing* (1931), a satire on American politics by Morrie Ryskind (d. 1985), George S. Kaufman, and George and Ira Gershwin, was the first musical to win the Pulitzer Prize for drama. Kurt *Weill was the composer for *Johnny Johnson* (1936), an anti-war comedy, and for *The Eternal Road* (1937), a pageant of Jewish history produced by Max Reinhardt. George Gershwin reached a new high with *Porgy and Bess* (1935). *Pins and Needles* (1937), an amateur revue presented by the heavily Jewish International Ladies Garment Workers, became a Broadway hit. Harold Rome wrote most of the music and lyrics.

In the 1940s the American musical play came fully into its own. *Pal Joey* (1940), a Rodgers and Hart work, was an "adult" musical, one of the first to deal with the seamy side of life. *Lady in the Dark* (1941), dealing with the hitherto theatrically unexplored world of psychoanalysis, had libretto by Moss Hart, score by Kurt Weill, lyrics by Ira Gershwin, and was produced by Sam Harris.

In 1943 Richard Rodgers and Oscar Hammerstein II wrote *Oklahoma*, which fully demonstrated the use of music in telling a story and delineating character. It was followed by other productions equally triumphant in the new form: *Carousel* (1945) and *South Pacific* (1949 Pulitzer Prize winner) both by Rodgers and Hammerstein; *Annie Get Your Gun* (1946; music by Irving Berlin); and *Brigadoon* (1947), with book and lyrics by Alan Jay Lerner.

Jewish writers and composers continued to make brilliant use of the musical play in the same years. E.Y. Harburg wrote the lyrics for *Finian's Rainbow* (1947). Frank Loesser wrote the music and lyrics for *Guys and Dolls* (1950). *The Pajama Game* (1954) and *Damn Yankees* (1955) were hits by the songwriting team of Richard Adler and Jerry Ross. *The Threepenny Opera* (1954) with score by Kurt Weill, and libretto modernized by Marc Blitzstein, had a fabulously successful off-Broadway revival. It ran for over six years. Frederick Loewe composed for Alan J. Lerner's *My Fair Lady* (based on Shaw's *Pygmalion*) in 1956. Leonard *Bernstein, who had had earlier successes such as *Wonderful Town* (1953), introduced new trends in *West Side Story* (1957). *The Sound of Music* (1959), another Rodgers and Hammerstein collaboration, brought a story of the Nazi invasion of Austria to the musical stage. In 1961 *How to Succeed in Business Without Really Trying*, with words and lyrics by Frank Loesser, was the fourth musical play to win the Pulitzer Prize for drama. The 1964 hit *Fiddler on the Roof* emphasized once more the Jewish contribution to the new form in a play based on Yiddish stories by Shalom Aleichem, with a score by Sheldon Harnick and Jerry Bock, and choreography by Jerome Robbins. Zero *Mostel created the role of Tevya and the play had one of the longest runs of the 1960s. *Milk and Honey* (1961), with music and lyrics by Jerry Herman, was a musical with an Israel setting starring Molly Picon. Herman also contributed the smash hit *Hello Dolly*! (1964), *Mame* (1965), and *Dear World* (1968). *No Strings* (1962), about an interracial love affair, had music and lyrics by Richard Rodgers. Among performers, Barbra Streisand skyrocketed to fame as the Broadway singing sensation of the 1960s through her roles in *I Can Get It For You Wholesale* (1962) and *Funny Girl* (1964). Subsequently Julie *Taymor made a significant impact on the Broadway musical with her daringly original staging of *The Lion King*, a musical that had a long life. And the grandson of Richard Rodgers, Adam Guettel, began a promising career as a Broadway composer with *A Light in the Piazza*.

In other countries, too, Jewish talent was attracted by the scope offered in the musical. In England, one of the most successful stage shows of the 1960s was *Oliver!* with lyrics and music by Lionel Bart and the book based on Dickens' *Oliver Twist*. It was followed by the same composer's *Blitz* in 1962. In South Africa, the African musical *King Kong* was produced and directed by Leon Gluckman in 1959 with a story by Harry Bloom. It reached London in 1961.

In Israel too the musical play proved a success in the commercial theater. One of the first such hits was the Chamber Theater's production of *King Solomon and the Cobbler* (1966) based on a play by Sami Gronemann. Giora Godik, after winning the public with American musicals, presented the all-Israel musical play *Casablan* in 1967. Since that time musicals have been a staple of Israeli theater.

[Harvey A. Cooper]

The Jew as Entertainer

From the early Middle Ages on, entertainers were mimes, storytellers, clowns, singers, dancers, acrobats, jugglers, and tamers of wild animals. Beginning in the 13th century, or even earlier, Jews in Italian cities were compelled to participate in the carnival-time buffooneries as mounts for soldiers or for the general populace. The *Corso degli ebrei* ("race of the Hebrews") became a regular carnival feature. Jews played their role as clowns or buffoons for the diversion of powerful men in the Christian world, and from the 16th century on, in the Muslim world (e.g., for the sultan in Constantinople). The role in most cases was not a chosen one. Vagrant mimes, musicians, players, and jugglers began to appear in Europe as early as the 11th century. They were called minstrels in England and France, *Spielleute* in Germany. Jews grouped together and began to entertain predominantly Jewish audiences. Their performances became particularly associated with Purim festivities. The professional jokers were called *leẓim* ("mockers"), or later on, *marsheliks* ("buffoons"). During the 14th and 15th century, some of these *leẓim* gradually developed into actors; their performance evolved into the Yiddish word-drama which originally was based on biblical themes.

For a long time, however, the entertainment performed between the acts of a play was more popular than the play itself. During these interludes the performers were in their element, clowning as rabbis, medical men, pharmacists, midwives, or even as devils, at times severely mocking Jewish peculiarities. The *leẓim-marsheliks* continued, together with the Purim plays, until far into the 19th century. Their name gradually changed to *badḥanim* ("fools"). They appeared in the Jewish settlements in Galicia, later on in the Jewish villages of Russia, the Bukovina, and Romania. A new type of itinerant entertainers assumed the name of the place they had come from and were called *Broder Singers. In comic disguises, they sang, danced, and, occasionally, performed short one-act plays.

In modern times, entertainment has developed into a world of its own, and an extremely high percentage of its population is Jewish. London's music halls produced artists such as Lottie Collins (1866–1910). In Berlin Hermann Haller (1872–1943) became famous as creator of revues and shows. Florenz Ziegfeld in New York with his spectacular *Ziegfeld Follies* gave the first big chance to artists such as Fanny Brice and Eddie *Cantor.

In addition to Jewish professional entertainers in the 20th century in Europe and the U.S. who often were actors as well as entertainers (Jack Benny, Milton Berle, Victor Borge, Danny Kaye, the Canadian comedian team Johnny Wayne and Frank Shuster), there were artists who specialized in forms of entertainment which had very little or nothing to do with acting: the magician Samuel Bellachini; the clown Grock; the athletes Josef and Siegmund Breitbart; Harry *Houdini, escape artist; Harry Reso, the step-dancer; Sophie *Tucker, the last "red hot Mamma," and an immense number of others for whom, more and more, television became an ideal forum.

[Frederick R. Lachman]

YIDDISH THEATER

Theatrical performances in Yiddish have taken place for at least half a millennium, and in modern times have spanned six continents. Yiddish drama and theater absorbed virtually every major trend that emerged in Western drama, and Yiddish playwrights and performers have been deeply influenced by, and have exerted their own influence on, the drama and theater of broad swaths of Europe, the Americas, and to a lesser extent, Australia and South Africa. For millions of Yiddish speakers, theater has long been a lively form of entertainment, but it has always been something more than that as well. Particularly at its height, from the late 19th century to the middle of the 20th, the Yiddish theater provided millions of Jewish theatergoers with a powerful tool to help understand the ever-changing world in which they lived.

Premodern Performance in Yiddish

For many centuries, Judaism placed significant barriers in the way of the development of a full-fledged, professional Jewish theatrical tradition, and as a result the process was slowed significantly. Similar to early Christian commentators like Augustine and Tertullian, the rabbis of the talmudic period and the early Middle Ages harbored a deep suspicion of theater, influenced in no small measure by the excesses of Roman entertainments. In the Christian world, such objections were overcome by pedagogical necessity, as theater came to fill a void left by the illiteracy of the masses in ways that few sermons could. The fact that antisemitic attitudes figured prominently in medieval Christian drama did little to endear the theatrical art to Jewish authorities, however.

Yet long before scripted dramas were written and performed in Yiddish, Yiddish speakers could enjoy the performances of entertainers who performed at Jewish events, particularly weddings. In German-speaking countries arose the figure of the *leyts* or *marshelik* (influenced by the German *Narr*, "fool"), known in Slavic countries as the *badkhn*. This was part of a wider fabric of performers in the medieval Jewish world, including magicians who performed at fairs, wandering troubadours, and wedding musicians (at times interchangeable with the *badkhn*). Over time, the *leytsim* and *badkhonim* developed their own repertoire of wedding songs, riddles, parodies, and serious and comic songs; the *leyts* thus became an important forebear of the Yiddish musical theater. The collections of Menachem Oldendorf and Isaac Wallich preserve examples of the medieval *badkhn*'s repertoire.

Scholars have been unable to determine with precision when formally scripted performances in Yiddish began taking place. A number of texts in Old Yiddish, including some in both the Oldendorf and Wallich collections, seem suitable to performance, but whether they were put to such a use is not clear. Certainly by the end of the 16th century, however – and possibly much sooner – dramatic dialogues were being publicly performed in Yiddish. A short farce, *Dos Shpil fun Toyb Yeklayn, Zayn Vayb Kendlayn, un Zeyere Tsvey Zinlekh Fayn* ("The Play of Deaf Yeklayn, His Wife Kendlayn, and Their Two Fine Children") was performed in Tannhausen in 1598, probably as an interlude within a larger performance. While this play was a farce that commented on contemporary social types, the dominant type of work performed in Yiddish from the Middle Ages to the 19th century was the *purimshpil* ("Purim play"). Extant manuscripts of Yiddish poems about the Purim story date back to the 15th century, and printed versions as early as the 16th; it is generally believed that performances of the *purimshpil* date back as least as early as the late 15th century. The earliest extant manuscript of a performance text of a full-scale *purimshpil* is an *Akhasheyresh-shpil* ("Ahasuerus Play") dating to 1697. This play and many others retell the Purim story in a spirit of earthy irreverence befitting the jovial mood of the holiday; the humor of such plays relied heavily on scatological and sexual jokes and puns, which not infrequently drew the wrath of religious and communal authorities. By no means all Purim plays, however, were based on the Book of Esther; other popular subjects included the sale of Joseph into slavery, the binding of Isaac, David and Goliath, and Samson and Delilah.

The form of the earliest extant *purimshpil* resembles the German *Fastnachtspiel* in many ways, including not only the aforementioned profanity and eroticism, but the central role of a narrator (here known as the *loyfer*, *shrayber*, or *payats*). The traditional *purimshpil* was performed entirely by men and boys – often yeshivah students. Since most performances took place in the homes of wealthy families, the plays needed to be short so that companies could make their rounds. Masks and primitive costumes were the norm, and extant early texts do not tend to indicate changes of costume or scenery. Beginning in the 16th century, *purimshpiln* gradually became more elaborate, and in some places, they expanded beyond the one-day festival itself, with performances being offered for up to two weeks on either side of the holiday. By the early 18th century, *purimshpiln* reflected many trends in the contemporary European theater in literary style, subject matter, and scene design. Most of the extant Purim plays from the period indeed resemble Baroque *Staatsaktionen* far more than they do the folk plays that preceded them: their plots are complex and politically charged, their language ornate (Latinate and French-influenced); one of the plays is identified as an opera; another is provided with a description of the instrumentation of the orchestra that accompanied the performance. Nevertheless, the plays maintained a connection with Purim and were performed during the appropriate season. Though the development of the modern Yiddish theater altered the function of the *purimshpil* among Yiddish speakers, it did not altogether supplant this performance form, which continues to be staged to this day, particularly in many Ḥasidic communities.

Haskalah Drama

The carnivalesque atmosphere that prevailed on Purim was critical for loosening restrictions that made it impossible for theatrical performance to take root in the Jewish community during the rest of the year. Though women could still not perform in public on Purim, that holiday at least suspended the traditional prohibition (from Deut. 22:5) against men wearing women's clothing, and it was common for yeshivah students – whose traditional learning equipped them well to make learned, extempore ad libs – to perform the roles in Purim plays. As long as the Jewish community as a whole adhered to rabbinic law, however, Jewish theatrical performances would have to remain confined to one season only. The sea change that transformed the place of theater in the Jewish world came about in the late 18th century, when the Haskalah movement was born in Germany. In essays, pamphlets, fiction, poetry, and drama, the *maskilim* exhorted their fellow Jews to become less insular, to integrate more fully into European society (at least to the extent that the law and their non-Jewish neighbors allowed), and to reap the fruits of secular thought in politics, philosophy, science, and the arts. While the movement initially met with fierce resistance from religious Jews, it ultimately paved the way to new forms of religious expression and a new orientation toward the non-Jewish world.

Although no professional Jewish theater existed when the Haskalah began, a number of *maskilim* voiced their polemics in dramatic form – possibly with the intention of performances in literary salons or Jewish schools. This phenomenon began with two of the leading figures of the Berlin Haskalah, Isaac Euchel and Aaron Halle-Wolfssohn. Both Euchel's *Reb Henokh, oder Vos Tut Men Damit?* ("Reb Henokh, or What Can Be Done with It?" *ca.* 1792) and Wolfssohn's *Leichtsinn und Frömmelei* ("Frivolity and False Piety," *ca.* 1796) helped set the tone for decades of Haskalah dramas. Both of these satires make rich use of a wide palette of social types and attitudes, and varying levels of language. Almost all subsequent Haskalah plays were comedies; among the most accomplished and influential were the anonymous satire *Di Genarte Velt* ("The Duped World," *ca.* 1810); Solomon Ettinger's comic melodrama *Serkele* (1838), featuring a gallery of comic types ranging across the social spectrum; Avrom Ber Gotlober's grotesque and wickedly anti-ḥasidic *Der Dektukh, oder Tsvey Khupes in Eyn Nakht* ("The Bridal Veil, or Two Weddings in One Night," 1839); several comedies and melodramas by Israel *Axenfeld written in the 1830s and 1840s, including *Der Ershter Yidisher Rekrut in Rusland* ("The First Jewish Recruit in Russia," *ca.* 1840), which in fact expresses considerable ambivalence about the goals and methods of the Haskalah; and S.Y. *Abramovitsh's scathing social satire, *Di Takse* ("The Tax," 1869).

Broder Singers

The 1850s also saw the rise of a type of performer known as the Broder Singer. Taking their name from the Galician city of Brody (or Brod) – the home town of the reputed "father" of the form, Berl Broder (Berl Margulis) – Broder Singers would come to play a direct role in the formation of the modern, professional Yiddish theater. Like the *purimshpil*, the performances of the Broder Singers became more elaborate over time. Initially, songs telling a story – often based on familiar character types and situations from everyday Jewish life – were accompanied by facial expressions and gestures. From there it was a short step to embedding the songs into theatrical situations with a couple of performers, quick changes of costume to suit the characters described in the lyrics, and simple make-up. As the Broder Singers' fame grew, so did their geographical reach. They spread throughout Galicia and Romania, and from there into Russia. The repertoire and performance styles of the most renowned of these figures, including Berl Broder and Velvl Zbarzher, inspired the first generation of professional Yiddish playwrights.

The Goldfaden Era

Though Yiddish companies managed to perform in places like Warsaw (in the 1830s and 1860s) during seasons completely unconnected with Purim, such efforts met with stiff resistance from Jewish community leaders, and left no direct legacy. Abraham *Goldfaden, on the other hand, would earn the title of "Father of the Yiddish Theater" by forming the first relatively stable professional Yiddish troupe and proceeding to write its plays, compose its music, and direct the actors. Goldfaden's background prepared him in many ways for the task. He claimed to have begun composing songs as a young boy and was a published poet and dramatist by the time he completed his rabbinical studies in the 1860s. His first full-length play, *Di Mume Sosye* ("Aunt Sosya," 1869), bore the clear influence of Ettinger's *Serkele* – not entirely surprising, since Goldfaden had played the title role in a production staged at his seminary in Zhitomir in 1862. And one of Goldfaden's early teachers was none other than the noted satirical writer and dramatist Abraham Baer *Gottlober. After trying his hand at various careers, Goldfaden assembled his first company in Jassy, Romania, in 1876. His star performer, Israel Grodner, was a seasoned Broder Singer. Over the next several years, the playwright would turn out a stream of vaudevilles, burlesques, and full-length comedies. His early plays were often crude, but among them are several of his masterpieces: *Shmendrik* (1877), *Di Kishefmakherin* ("The Sorceress," 1879), and *Der Fanatik, oder di Tsvey Kuni-Leml* ("The Fanatic, or the Two Kuni-Lemls," 1880). In these musical comedies, Goldfaden sharply critiqued, in the spirit of the Haskalah, religious hypocrisy, fanaticism, and insularity. He did so with lively music, witty lyrics, deftly drawn characterizations, and the increasingly assured hand of a skilled *farceur.* Within the first year of his company's existence, Goldfaden hired his first actress, and two rival troupes were formed, one led by Joseph Lateiner and the other by self-styled "Professor" Moyshe Hurwitz. These two men would become Goldfaden's lifelong rivals. Though critics would always favor Goldfaden, Hurwitz and Lateiner would become as popular as they were prolific, each with an enormous number of musicals and melodramas to his credit. Lateiner's plays include *Aleksander, Kroyn-Prints fun Yerusholayim* ("Alexander, Crown Prince of Jerusalem," 1892), *Blimele, di Perle fun Varshe* ("Blimele, the Pearl of Warsaw," 1894), *Dovids Fidele* ("David's Violin," 1897), Dos Yidishe Harts ("The Jewish Heart," 1908); Hurwitz's plays include *Tisza Eszlar* (1887), *Ben Hador* (1901). In addition to this trio, other playwrights who contributed to the foundation of the professional repertoire were Nahum-Meyer Shaykevitsh (*Shomer), a prolific writer of melodramas and light comedies, and Yoysef-Yude Lerner, who adapted a number of works on Jewish themes from other languages; these included Karl Gutzkow's *Uriel Acosta*, Jacques F. Halévy and Eugène Scribe's opera *La Juive* (as *Zhidovka*), and Salomon Hermann von Mosenthal's *Deborah*. Other writers active during this period were Sigmund Feinman, Israel Barski, Rudolph Marks, and Reuben Weissman.

Westward Exodus

The pogroms that followed the assassination of Czar Alexander II in 1881 helped spark a Jewish exodus from Russia. Over the next few decades, several million Jews left their homes in Eastern Europe in search of more favorable social and economic surroundings The Yiddish theater moved with the masses. To be sure, this shift was given a firm push by the czarist authorities, who banned Yiddish theater in 1883. Though the ban would turn out to be capricious and inconsistently enforced, it made a difficult business all the more precarious, and many performers and playwrights headed for places where they could pursue their work more freely. Companies were created or expanded in Eastern European cities outside the Russian empire, like Warsaw and Lemberg, while new centers of Yiddish theater arose further west. By far the most important homes of Yiddish theater in Western Europe were Britain and France. In London, performances were staged at such venues as the Whitechapel, Grand Palais, and Pavilion theaters. During the westward exodus from Eastern Europe, London become both a haven in its own right, and a way station for refugees ultimately planning to settle in the U.S. Stars such as Jacob Adler, David Kessler, M.D. and Fanny Waxman, and Sigmund and Dina Feinman made London their home for a time, enriching the quality of performance in the East End theaters – and in Feinman's case, also penning a number of dramas. London was also well positioned to serve as both a destination for visiting companies – both the Vilna Troupe and New York's Yiddish Art Theatre made numerous visits in the 1920s and 1930s – and as a launching pad for performers and companies heading to northern British cities such as Manchester, Leeds, and Glasgow. The most prolific London-based Yiddish playwright was Joseph Markovitsh, while the single most successful work written for the London Yiddish stage was journalist S.Y. Harendorf's *Der Kenig fun Lampeduze* ("The King of Lampedusa," 1943), which ran for months at the Pavilion Theatre before that venue was permanently put out of business by the German bombs that carpeted London during the Blitz. Paris was more of a stopover than a destination in itself for many East European Jews. By the time Goldfaden first visited Paris in 1889 and assembled a company there, the French capital had already hosted Yiddish performances for several years. But the city never developed a distinctive tradition of professional Yiddish theater, although it did provide fertile ground for a number of amateur or semi-professional drama groups tied to specific political movements – for example, the anarchist Frayhayt group, the Labor Zionist Fraye Yidishe Bine, and the Bundist Fraye Yidishe Arbeter Bine. Members of such groups were workers and artisans. While little French Yiddish drama was home grown, Paris was the longtime home of Chaim Sloves, author of notable dramas like *Homens Mapole* ("Haman's Downfall," 1949), *Borekh fun Amsterdam* ("Baruch of Amsterdam," 1956), and *Nekome Nemer* ("Avengers," 1947).

The Gordin Era

The nature of the early professional Yiddish repertoire, as well as the uneven production values by which such plays were staged, sparked ongoing tensions among critics, playwrights, and audiences. Reviewers constantly lamented the "low" taste of the Yiddish audience (pejoratively nicknamed "Moyshe") and the dominance of *shund* (popular theater; literally, "trash"). In common parlance, "Moyshe" was frequently described as "licking his fingers" in delight at such offerings. Yiddish playwrights, for their part, often shrugged off the critics' complaints, suggesting that such niceties as aesthetic ambitions had to take a back seat to practical concerns like putting food on the table. Not all playwrights, however, were so disdainful of social and aesthetic criteria for drama, and when Jacob Gordin emerged on the scene with his first drama in 1891, many critics – along with more serious-minded actors and playwrights – felt that a new era was dawning. Gordin, a new Russian immigrant to New York with a background in utopian politics and intellectual activity, also deplored the existing repertoire, but was pleasantly surprised by the sophistication of performers like Jacob P. Adler, whom he met not long after arriving in New York. Gordin was persuaded to write a play for Adler, and the result was *Sibirya* ("Siberia," 1891), a work with its share of melodramatic touches, but far more naturalistic than anything that had previously been seen on the Yiddish stage. Gordin would be hailed in many circles as the great reformer of Yiddish drama; successes such as *Der Yidisher Kenig Lir* ("The Jewish King Lear," 1892), *Mirele Efros* (1898), *Got, Mentsh un Tayvl* ("God, Man, and Devil," 1900), and *Khasye di Yesoyme* ("Khasye the Orphan Girl," 1903) would become fixtures on Yiddish stages for decades, and their main roles became proving grounds for leading men and women as well as character actors. The effectiveness of Gordin's best plays derives in large measure from the fact that he wrote for outstanding actors like Jacob Adler, Sarah Adler, Keni Liptzin, Dovid Kessler, and Bertha Kalish. Like the European playwrights he emulated, such as Henrik Ibsen, Gerhart Hauptmann, and Maxim Gorky, Gordin often sparked controversy for his treatment of delicate social issues. Both his social engagement and his dramaturgical technique drew a following not only among audiences and critics but also among fellow playwrights. By the time of Gordin's death in 1909, the most obvious heirs to his mantle were Leon Kobrin (*Yankl Boyle* (1913), *Riverside Drive* (1928), *Tsurik tsu Zayn Folk* ("Back to His People," 1914), and *Di Nekst-Dorike* ("The Woman Next Door," 1916)) and Zalmen Libin (Yisroel-Zalmen Hurvits) (*Hanele oder di Yidishe Medea* ("Hannele or the Jewish Medea," 1903), *Tsebrokhene Hertser* ("Broken Hearts," 1903)), though neither would achieve Gordin's level of influence. Other popular contemporaries of Gordin included Nokhem Rakov (*Der Batlen* ("The Idler," 1903), *Di Grine Moyd* ("The Green Girl," 1904), *Khantshe in Amerike* ("Khantshe in America," 1913)); Isidore Zolotarevsky (*Der Yeshive Bokher* ("The Yeshivah Student," 1899), *Di Yidishe Ana Karenina* ("The Jewish Anna Karenina," 1901–2), *Di Vayse Shklavin* ("The White Slave," 1909)); Avrom-Mikhl Sharkanski (*Kol Nidre* ("All Vows," 1896)); the brothers Anshl and Moyshe Shor (*A Mentsh Zol Nen Zayn* ("Be a Decent Person," 1909)); and Moyshe Richter (*Moyshe Khayat* ("Moyshe the Tailor," 1903) and *Sholem Bayis* ("Domestic Tranquility," 1904)). Such works became popular on Yiddish stages worldwide.

For all of Gordin's achievements, he did not manage to drive *shund* from the Yiddish stage, one of his explicitly stated goals. The Yiddish critics tended to attribute this fact to *Moyshe*'s low taste, but they failed to appreciate that *shund* – or to use a less value-laden term, musicals and melodramas – could succeed for positive reasons as well. Though the acting on Yiddish stages was often uneven and overblown, many Yiddish performers possessed extraordinary talent. Audiences worshiped specialists in musical theater like Boris and Bessie Thomashefsky, Sigmund and Dina Feinman, Clara Young, and Regina Prager; comedians like Berl Bernstein and Zelig Mogulesco; and character actors like Boaz Young and Bina Abramovitsh. And because of the importance of music in the Yiddish repertoire, its composers contributed as much to its success as its performers. Among the most important composers of music for the Yiddish theater were Arnold Perlmutter and Herman Wohl (who had many of their greatest successes as a team), Dovid Meyerovitsh, Louis Friedsel, Joseph Rumshinsky, Abe Ellstein, Sholem Secunda, and Peretz Sandler.

New York to World War II

As long as westward migrations continued, New York would continue to assert itself as one of the world capitals of Yiddish theater. Almost all of the most important actors and performers in the American Yiddish theater were foreign-born, many having started their careers in cultural centers like Warsaw and Odessa. Among the playwrights in this category were David Pinski and Peretz Hirschbein. Both men were talented journalists and prose writers, and both generated a distinguished body of dramatic work as well. Pinski could write biting satires, like *Der Oytser* ("The Treasure," 1911), but often wrote in a darker vein, in dramas like *Der Eybiker Yid* ("The Eternal Jew," 1929), *Di Familye Tsvi* ("The Family Tsvi," 1905), and *Ayzik Sheftl* ("Isaac Sheftl," 1904–5). He also wrote popular dramas revolving around tempestuous human passions in works like *Yankl der Shmid* ("Yankl the Blacksmith," 1909) and *Gabri un di Froyen* ("Gabri and the Women," 1905). Hirschbein experimented with various dramatic modes and registers, but is best known for his idylls of village life, relying more on deftly developed characters and convincing dialogue than on plot. These include *A Farvorfn Vinkl* ("A Forsaken Nook," 1918), *Di Puste Kretshme* ("The Idle Inn," 1919), and *Grine Felder* ("Green Fields," 1918). Other accomplished members of this new wave of dramatists working primarily in New York were Osip Dimov (*Shma Yisroel* ("Hear, O Israel," 1907), *Bronx Express* (1919), *Yoshke Muzikant* ("Yoshke the Musician"; the first of numerous versions premiered in 1914 as *Der Gedungener Khosn* ("The Hired Bridegroom")); H. Leivick (*Shmates* ("Rags," 1921), *Shop* (1926), *Der Goylem* ("The Golem," 1925)); Fishl Bimko (*Ganovim* ("Thieves," 1919), *Dembes* ("Oaks," 1922)); Harry Sackler (*Yizkor* ("Remembrance," 1922), *Mayor Noyekh* ("Major Noah," 1928), *Rakhav fun Yerikho* ("Rahab of Jericho," 1928)), and Avrom Shomer (*Aykele Mazil* ("Ikey the Devil," 1911), *Style* (1913), *Der Griner Milyoner* ("The Green Millionaire," 1915)). These playwrights often wrote for companies that joined the assemblage of notable Yiddish troupes. Foremost among these in New York was Maurice Schwartz's Yiddish Art Theater, which subsisted on a diet of Western and Yiddish classics, new Yiddish dramas, and – most lucratively – adaptations of Yiddish novels, like *Shalom Aleichem's *Tevye der Milkhiker* ("Tevye the Dairyman," 1919) and I.J. *Singer's *Yoshke Kalb* (1932), dramatized by Schwartz himself. Schwartz's company was in theory an ensemble, but in practice it belonged very much to the 19th-century star system. For true ensemble acting, New York Yiddish audiences went to Artef (from the Yiddish acronym for Workers' Theater Collective), which opened its doors in 1928 with a production of Soviet Yiddish playwright Beynush *Shteiman's *Baym Toyer* ("At the Gate," 1928). The company established itself as the avant-garde answer to commercial offerings with innovative productions of such works as Israel Axenfeld's *Der Ershter Yidisher Rekrut in Rusland* (aka *Rekrutn* / "Recruits," 1934) and Sholem Aleichem's *Dos Groyse Gevins* ("The Jackpot," 1936; often going by the alternate title *200,000*). Artef never managed to launch any major new playwriting talent, however.

Latin America

Many performers based in the United States regularly made their way to Latin America. While companies were also formed in such places as Mexico City, Uruguay, Chile, and Brazil, Buenos Aires was by far the largest and most significant Latin American hub for Yiddish performers and eventually emerged as a major center for Yiddish theater. Productions of plays from the European repertoire began there by 1901, and soon popular performers from North America and Europe, including Boris Thomashesfky, Maurice Schwartz, Celia Adler, Rudolph Zaslavsky, Zygmunt Turkow and Ida Kaminska, and Joseph Buloff added Buenos Aires and other cities and town in Argentina and neighboring countries to their list of touring destinations. The Yiddish theater in Buenos Aires had a long-standing connection to the seedier side of Latin American life, for pimps and prostitutes in this major center of the "white slave" trade invested heavily in the theater, and had some control over its contents. In his memoirs, Peretz Hirschbein recalls how the many prostitutes in the audience for the Buenos Aires production (*ca.* 1910) of his drama *Miryam* were moved to tears by the plight of his heroine, an innocent *shtetl* girl who falls into a life of prostitution. Leyb Malekh's *Ibergus* ("Remodeling," 1926) hit even closer to home, for that drama specifically addresses the connections and conflicts among different strata of Argentinean society: the respectable folk, prostitutes and gangsters, and actors. The play caused an uproar when it premiered in Buenos Aires in 1926. That city rose to greater prominence as a center of Yiddish theatrical activity in the 1930s, particularly with the founding of organizations like IFT (*Idisher Folks Teater*, "Jewish People's Theatre") in 1932, in the tradition of left-wing, artistically ambitious troupes like its notable contemporaries, Yung Teater in Warsaw and Artef in New York. IFT continued to offer its audiences plays addressing social issues, until demographic changes forced it to switch to Spanish performances in the mid-1950s. Though the Argentinean Yiddish theater enjoyed years of prosperity following World War II, when many talented refugees made their way there, the seeds of its decline had already been sown. Young Argentinean Jews, like their counterparts in North America and Western Europe, were being raised in a native language other than in Yiddish, and one theater after another either closed its doors forever, or abandoned Yiddish in favor of the local language.

The Art Theater Movement in Eastern Europe

In New York, Gordin was often praised for breathing fresh life into Yiddish drama. This was particularly true in the 1890s; later, prominent critics like Abraham Cahan, who had championed Gordin early on, reversed course and harshly attacked his dramaturgy. European critics like I.L. Peretz and Noyekh Prilutski, however, never warmed to Gordin in the way that many American critics had. Peretz regarded Gordin as little better than a *shund* playwright, and felt that a different type of dramaturgy was needed to help Yiddish drama take a seat of honor at the table of Western dramatic literature. Peretz sought to remedy this situation partly by articulating ambitious critical criteria, partly by writing plays himself, and partly by championing new talent. As a playwright, Peretz was influenced most notably by naturalism in his short plays and symbolism in his full-length, poetic dramas. The latter include *Baynakht afn Altn Mark* ("A Night in the Old Marketplace," 1907) and *Di Goldene Keyt* ("The Golden Chain," 1907); among his best-known one-acts are *Shvester* ("Sisters," 1905) and *Es Brent* ("It's Burning," 1901). But Peretz, like other classic Yiddish writers such as Sholem Aleichem, would never achieve the success as a dramatist that he did in prose (at least not during their lifetimes, though many of Sholem Aleichem's plays enjoyed successful revivals in later years). While flashes of brilliance frequently make their presence felt in Peretz's plays, they often lack an effective dramatic structure to give the action a focus and propel it forward.

Whatever Gordin's shortcomings, he showed a far surer hand as a dramatist, and actors loved to play his characters. One sign thereof is the fact that even in Eastern Europe, with different sorts of commercial pressures and audiences quite different from those in the U.S., Gordin's plays featured prominently in the performed repertoire, while Peretz's tended to be invisible. This was true of the first ensemble companies to try to elevate the level of artistry in Yiddish drama and theater, starting with the troupe led by Esther-Rokhl Kaminska in the early 1900s. Gordin's plays were the bread and butter of the Kaminska Troupe (later known as *Di Fareynikte* – "the united ones"). When Kaminska left Europe to tour in the U.S. in 1909, she left a void that could not be filled, but both as performer and as matriarch of a theatrical dynasty, she continued to help shape Yiddish theater as well as film for many decades.

As a mentor of young talent, Peretz left an indelible mark on the development of Yiddish drama. Sholem *Asch, for example – arguably Peretz's most successful protégé – penned a number of plays, most notably *Got fun Nekome* ("God of Vengeance," 1907), though he would become far better known as a novelist. Another student of Peretz's, as well as of Polish playwright Stanislaw Przybyszewski, was Mark Arnshteyn, who would write and direct productions in both Polish and Yiddish, including his most successful work, *Der Vilner Balebesl* ("The Little Householder of Vilna," 1908). In 1907, Arnshteyn and Avrom-Yitskhok Kaminski, in an effort to infuse 'literary' plays into the Yiddish repertoire, founded the *Literarishe Trupe* ("literary troupe"), with which they toured with plays by Gordin, Arnshteyn, David *Pinski, and Sholem Aleichem. A similar effort was undertaken a couple of years later by yet another of Peretz's protégés, Peretz *Hirschbein. Having earned the blessing of figures like Peretz and Bialik at the outset of his career, Hirschbein founded a company in Odessa in 1908 that became known as the Hirschbein Troupe. His company, which performed works by its founder, as well as by Asch, Pinski, Gordin, and Sholem Aleichem, stayed in business for only two years, but achieved an impact out of proportion to its short life through its earnest striving for higher artistic standards in Yiddish drama and theater. During this same period, other notable companies in Russia and Poland included those led by Aba Kompanayets, Misha Fishzon, Dovid-Moyshe Sabsay, and Yankev-Ber Gimpel.

Interwar Poland

Hirschbein's troupe served as a forerunner for the *Vilna Troupe, founded in 1916 with the express purpose of carrying on Hirschbein's reforms. The Vilna Troupe brought to light what was to become the most famous play in the Yiddish repertory, S. Anski's *Der Dibek* ("The Dybbuk," 1921), directed by Dovid Herman, who had encouraged Hirschbein to write in Yiddish. The play caused a sensation at its Warsaw premiere, just weeks after the author's death. It has been translated into and performed in many languages, and inspired several adaptations as well. The company's further successes included Osip Dimov's *Yoshke Muzikant* ("Yoshke the Musician," or "The Singer of His Sorrow"), Asch's *Kiddush ha-Shem* ("Sanctification of the Name," 1928), Peretz's *Baynakht afn Altn Mark* ("A Night in the Old Marketplace"), and *The Merchant of Venice*. Although the Vilna Troupe suffered the loss of many talented performers who left for other opportunities, it continued to be vital until the Holocaust, when its remaining members were trapped in the Vilna Ghetto and liquidated along with their neighbors. Before that, however, interwar Poland became as rich a breeding ground for significant new ventures in Yiddish theatrical performance as any that had ever existed. The 1920s brought the creation of such companies as VYKT (*Varshever Yidisher Kunst Teater* "Warsaw Yiddish Art Theatre"), founded in 1924 and led by Zygmunt Turkow and his wife Ida Kaminska; VNYT (*Varshever Nayer Yidisher Teater* "Warsaw New Yiddish Theatre"), founded by Zygmunt's brother, Jonas Turkow, in 1929; and *Yung Teater* ("Young Theater"), established by Mikhl Weichert in 1932. VYKT used modern techniques for to stage both new and classic plays from the European repertoire, and Yiddish classics by Ettinger and Mendele. Turkow and Kaminska put their stamp on roles from within and beyond the Yiddish repertoire – he in such parts as Molière's Harpagon to Sholem Aleichem's Tevye, she in Yiddish standards like *Mirele Efros* (continuing in her mother's footsteps) and roles from the world repertoire, like Bertolt Brecht's *Mother Courage*. More political and experimental was Mikhl Weichert's *YungTeater*, whose first production, *Boston*, used innovative environmental theater techniques to tell the story of the Sacco and Vanzetti trial. *Yung Teater* commented further on American travesties of justice with Leyb Malekh's effective agitprop drama *Mississippi*, based on the Scottsboro affair. Weichert's politics often made him run afoul of the censors, a situation he commented on obliquely in the production of his own play, *Trupe Tanentsap* (1933), a play-within-a-play that used a production of Goldfaden's *Two Kuni-Lemls* to comment on contemporary censorship. Other notable productions included Jacob Preger's *Simkhe Plakhte* (1935), and Georg Büchner's *Woyzeck* (1936), in a Yiddish translation by Itsik Manger. Those with less experimental tastes had many other options in cities like Warsaw, including the Theater for Youth – founded in 1926 under the direction of Thea Artishevski and the producer David Herman – which became the most popular of the music theaters. Adding to the vitality of the Polish Yiddish theater scene between the two World Wars was *kleynkunst*, "a sort of cabaret revue, witty, gay, and irreverent, rapidly winging from music to dance to monologue to sketch" (Sandrow, 323). *Kleynkunst* theaters included Azazel in Warsaw, Ararat in Lodz, led by writer/performer Moyshe Broderzon, who discovered such talents as the comedians Shimen Dzigan and Yisroel Shumakher, who would enjoy a long career together – the most successful double act of its kind in the Yiddish language – in sketches filled with political and social commentary.

Poland had become arguably the world's richest soil for Yiddish theater by the 1930s, so the annihilation of Polish Jewry by the Nazis destroyed a particularly vibrant theatrical culture. Yet during the war, performers made valiant efforts to carry on their activities in the face of the gravest danger. Warsaw ghetto leader Emmanuel Ringelblum's diaries chronicle all measure of cultural undertakings, from journalism to the visual arts to musical and theatrical performance. Jonas *Turkow gave a list of 138 performers who perished in the Warsaw ghetto, including Mazo, director of the Vilna Troupe, and his wife Miriam Orleska. As the Nazi ghettoes were liquidated and the survivors were sent to concentration camps, they continued to perform, when possible, even in the camps. After the war, surviving actors resumed activity, first in DP camps, and then to the many places to which the performers dispersed.

Soviet Yiddish Theater

After the Russian Revolution, state-sponsored Yiddish theaters were founded in a number of major cities of the Soviet Union. Some were established quickly, as in Vilna and Odessa. Others were created later, after the political situation stabilized. A total of 14 state Yiddish theaters were ultimately established; the most noteworthy included the Minsk State Theater (*Bilgoset*), directed by M. Rafalski, and the Yiddish State Theater in Kharkov, directed first by Ephraim Loyter, and later by M. Norvid.

Other companies were established in such cities as Tarnopol, Lviv, Zhitomir, Dnepropetrovsk, Bialistok, Grodno, Vilna, Kovno, Riga, and Czernowitz. In addition, many of these companies traveled widely, so that Yiddish theater reached communities throughout much of the Soviet Union. The most celebrated Soviet Yiddish theater company was the Moscow State Yiddish Theater (best known by the Russian acronym for "state Jewish Theater," GOSET). Starting as a small studio in St. Petersburg just after the revolution, and moving to Moscow a couple of years later, GOSET revolutionized Yiddish theater with avant-garde productions of Yiddish classics, new Yiddish plays, and works from the European repertoire. The company's founder, and its leader for much of the 1920s, was Alexander Granovsky, who put his mark on Yiddish standards like Goldfaden's *Di Kishefmakherin*, Sholem Aleichem's *Dos Groyse Gevins*, and Peretz's *Baynakht afn Altn Mark*. Marc *Chagall was also briefly involved with the company as designer, but made an impact all out of proportion to the time he spent with GOSET. The company also had the input of significant musical talent in Joseph Achron and Leyb Pulver. After Granovsky defected to the West in 1928, actor Solomon Mikhoels took the reins and guided the company ably, focusing for a while on new works like Moyshe *Kulbak's *Boytre* (1936) and Dovid *Bergelson's *Der Toyber* ("The Deaf Man," 1930) and *Prints Ruveyni* (1945). When the Soviet authorities used Kulbak's underworld drama as an excuse to crack down on the troupe – Kulbak was arrested and disappeared into the gulag – GOSET responded with politically correct versions of Goldfaden's *Shulamis* (1938–9) and *Bar Kokhba* (1939). This strategy may have bought the troupe some time, but it did not avert disaster forever. Mikhoels was murdered in a staged accident in 1948, and Benjamin Zuskin was killed in a purge of Jewish intellectuals in 1952.

Other Centers

As Yiddish speakers spread across the globe in search of most hospitable environments, they established theatrical activity on six continents. For every major metropolis with multiple theaters and cabarets, there were numerous smaller cities and towns with less sizable and diverse offerings, but which helped provide a lifeline for performers and companies who needed audiences beyond their local ones in order to make a decent living, and which brought Yiddish theater to avid theatergoers living off the beaten path. The American "provinces," for example, included cities like Philadelphia, Chicago, and Baltimore, and countless cities and towns between and beyond. Among the places where Yiddish theater was performed, several important secondary hubs are worth noting: South Africa, where Sarah Sylvia reigned as the leading star, and where visitors like Maurice *Schwartz, Molly *Picon, and Meir Tselniker sojourned; Australia, dominated for decades by the artistic leadership of Polish immigrants Yankev Weislitz and Rochl Holzer, and playing host to numerous guest artists, from Shimon *Dzigan to Dina Halpern to Ida Kaminska and Zygmunt Turkow; and Montreal, which had long served as a "provincial" theater on the North American circuit. The leading figure of the Montreal Yiddish theater in the second half of the 20th century was Ukrainian-born Dora Wasserman, who established the Yiddish Drama Group in the 1950s; later renamed the Dora Wasserman Yiddish Theatre, control of the company passed to her daughter Bryna after Dora Wasserman's death in 2003. Israel became home to countless native Yiddish speakers, but proved problematic for Yiddish theater. The language wars that raged in Mandate Palestine and later in the State of Israel made public theater performances in Yiddish difficult to stage; so despite an abundance of talent, Yiddish theater was often suppressed. Nevertheless, it played a role in Israeli life. Yiddish performances in Palestine began as early as the 1890s, and in spite of both widespread scorn for Yiddish and special taxes imposed on "foreign-language" theaters, Yiddish theater was performed regularly in the early decades of the state. Immigrants from Eastern Europe like Shimon Dzigan, Mary Soriano, Max Perlman, Eni Litan, and Gita Galina were popular with Israeli audiences, who also welcomed visitors like Avrom Morevsky, Ida Kaminska, Joseph Buloff, and Maurice Schwartz. As of the early 21st century, little regular activity remains, but Shmuel Atzmon's *Yiddishpil* company, based in Tel Aviv, continues to carry the flame.

The Late 20th Century

In spite of social and economic pressures that drove millions of Jews westward, Yiddish theater continued to thrive in Poland, Romania, and the Soviet Union up to the outbreak of World War II. After the war, though, the soil that had been so fertile for such performances was largely scorched earth. Yet until a new wave of antisemitism broke out in Poland in the 1950s, many Polish Jews attempted to rebuild their lives in their native land, and two companies arose in Poland in 1946. The Nidershlezis Yiddish Theater, directed by S. Zack, produced Hirschbein's *Grine Felder* and Sloves's *Homens Mapole*. The Lodz Theater, directed by Moyshe Lipman, presented Dzigan and Schumacher and Ida Kaminska. In 1950 these two companies joined forces as the Jewish State Theater, working with a government subsidy under Kaminska's direction. It achieved success with the Manger-Fenster adaptation *A Goldfaden Kholem* ("A Goldfaden Dream," 1950) and Gordin's *Mirele Efros*, with Kaminska in the title role.

While Yiddish culture was decimated by Hitler and Stalin, it did not always fare well in countries where its speakers were free to perpetuate it – for they were also free *not* to. Everywhere that Ashkenazim went in search of greater economic opportunity and religious freedom, they faced ongoing dilemmas about how to strike a desirable balance between maintaining a connection to their religious roots and adapting to new surroundings. More often than not, they pursued the latter at the expense of the former, and Yiddish was often neglected as part of the bargain. What allowed the Yiddish theater to continue developing in places like New York was a steady supply of new immigrants. When the U.S. Congress enacted strict immigration quotas in the early 1920s, that supply largely dried up, and the American Yiddish theater began a slow but steady decline (which might have happened anyway, given the rise of new competition like film, radio, and television). Yet many of the stars of this period continued performing for a long time. Artef was an important force throughout the 1930s, as was the Yiddish Art Theatre in the 1930s and 1940s. By the 1930s, more performers who had started their careers in the Yiddish theater were crossing over successfully to Broadway and Hollywood than had actors in earlier generations. English-language audiences embraced such actors as Paul Muni (born Muni Weisenfreund) and Joseph Buloff, and numerous Yiddish actors enjoyed success in character roles. With the graying and shrinking of the Yiddish-speaking audience, Yiddish theater in the late 20th century increasingly became more a labor of love than a business. The one American company continuing to offer Yiddish performances on anything like a regular basis as of the early 21st century is the Folksbine. Elsewhere, Jewish theaters make occasional forays into producing Yiddish drama in English, just as some of the Yiddish classics have made their way into the repertoire in Hebrew, Polish, German, and other languages.

Conclusion

For hundreds of years, the *purimshpil* provided a Jewish counterpart to the dramas of the medieval Church, and as different as the contents and purposes of such performances were, Yiddish theater absorbed influences from its Christian neighbors from the very beginning, while putting a distinctly Jewish mark on the proceedings. That combination continued to lend the Yiddish theater its special character well into the modern era. The *purimshpil* and other performance forms originating in pre-modern times set other precedents as well: the centrality of music to much of Yiddish theatrical performance, the roots of Yiddish theater in Jewish texts and traditions, and challenges that Yiddish performances often presented to communal authorities. Jewish law kept the Yiddish theater from growing into a professional, year-round phenomenon for several centuries, by which point other European cultures had long-standing secular theatrical traditions. The Yiddish theater had a great deal of catching up to do, and it took to this process with relish. Pioneers like Goldfaden poured their knowledge of both Jewish materials and non-Jewish texts, music, and theatrical techniques into their work. Yiddish actors learned their craft partly from watching their counterparts perform in Russian, Romanian, Polish, German, and other languages, and partly from simply rolling up their sleeves and going to work. The most talented figures of the first generation of modern Yiddish theater could hold their own with contemporaries coming out of cultures with much more extensive theatrical traditions. The development of Yiddish theater and drama turned out to be remarkably compressed. Joining other European theatrical cultures only late in the 19th century, Yiddish theater took little time to diversify its repertoire, from the early musicals and melodramas that dominated the marquees to the many theatrical styles that would arise in the 20th century: naturalism, symbolism, expressionism, constructivism, etc. The combined forces of annihilation and persecution in Europe, and acculturation and assimilation of Yiddish speakers worldwide, conspired to cut short the remarkably rapid maturation of Yiddish theater and drama. It seems impossible to imagine a world in which Yiddish theater will ever play as vital a role in Jewish life as it did at its height, yet performers, scholars, and audiences continue to explore its legacy in many ways. Several of the best-known Yiddish dramas (for example, An-Sky's *Der Dibek* and Asch's *Got fun Nekome*, in many different translations as well as in adaptations by playwrights like Paddy Chayefsky, Donald Margulies, and Tony Kushner) have a long history of performances – some of them quite distinguished – in multiple languages. There is reason to believe that as translators make additional works available for non-Yiddish-speaking readers and audiences, other Yiddish plays will take their proper place in the world repertoire. The Yiddish theater has also attracted the attention of a number of distinguished historians and literary critics, including Yitskhok Schiper, Max Erik, Shmuel Niger, Jacob Shatzky, Noyekh Prilutski, and Zalmen Zylbercweig. The late 20th century witnessed a dramatic increase in scholarly books and articles on Yiddish theater and drama, a trend that shows no sign of abating in the early 21st century. The confluence of scholars, translators, playwrights, and audiences willing to give the Yiddish theater a fresh look suggests that long after the Yiddish theater's most vital period has passed, our understanding of the phenomenon it represented continues to grow.

For theater in Israel, see *Hebrew Literature, Modern (Drama); *Israel, State of: Cultural Life (Theater).

[Joel Berkowitz (2nd ed.)]

BIBLIOGRAPHY: GENERAL: *Enciclopedia dello Spettacolo* (1954–62); J. Gregor, *Weltgeschichte des Theaters* (1933); G. Freedley and J.A. Reeves, *A History of the Theater* (1955^2); C. Roth, *Jewish Contribution to Civilization* (1938); idem, *Jews in the Renaissance* (1959); V.I. Zoller, in: *Mitteilungen zur juedischen Volkskunde*, 29 (1926); S. Salomon, *Jews of Britain* (1938); E.D. Coleman, *Jews in English Drama* (1943); R. Craig, *English-Religious Drama of the Middle Ages* (1955); E. Chambers, *The Mediaeval Stage*, 2 vols. (1903); H. Carrington, *Die Figur des Juden in der dramatischen Litteratur des XVIII. Jahrhunderts* (1897); M.J. Landa, *The Jew in Drama* (1969^2); H. Freeden, *Juedisches Theater in Nazi-Deutschland* (1964); G. Weales, *American Drama Since World War II* (1962); F. Ewen, *Complete Book of the American Musical Theater* (1959^2); idem, *The Story of the American Musical Theater* (1968^2). YIDDISH THEATER: D.S. Lifson, *The Yiddish Theatre in America* (1965); B. Gorin, *Di Geshikhte fun Yidishen Teater*, 2 vols. (1918, 1923^2); Z. Zylbercweig, *Leksikon fun Yidishn Teater*, 6 vols. (1931–70); Y. Schiper, *Geshikhte fun Yidisher Teater-Kunst un Drame*, 3 vols. (1923–28); J. Shatzky (ed.), *Arkhiv far der Geshikhte fun Yidishn Teater un Drame* (1930); M. Litvakov, *Finf Yor Melukhesher Yidisher Kamer-Teater* (1924); **ADD. BIBLIOGRAPHY:** M. Altshuler, *Ha-Te'atron ha-Yehudi bi-Vrit ha-Mo'aẓot* (1996); A. Belkin, *Ha-Purim Shpil: Iyyunim ba-Te'atron ha-Yehudi ha-Amami* (2002); Y. Berkovitsh, *Hundert Yor Yidish Teater in Rumenye* (1976); J. Berkowitz, *Shakespeare on the American Yiddish Stage* (2001); J. Berkowitz (ed.), *Yiddish Theatre: New Approaches* (2003); B. Gorin, *Di Geshikhte* *fun Yidishn Teater* (1923); N. Bukhvald, *Teater* (1943); E. Bützer, *Die Anfänge der jiddischen purim shpiln in ihrem literarischen und kulturgeschichtlichen Kontext* (2003); B. Dalinger, *'Verloschene Sterne'. Geschichte des jüdischen Theaters in Wien* (1998); Y. Dobrushin, *Di Dramaturgye fun di Klasiker* (1948); J. Hoberman, *Bridge of Light: Yiddish Film Between Two Worlds* (1991); A. Krasney, *Ha-Badkhan* (1998); A. Kuligowska-Korzeniewska and M. Leyko (eds.), *Teatr żydowski w Polsce* (1998); J-M. Larrue, *Le Théâtre yiddish à Montréal* (1996); Y. Lyubomirski, *Melukhisher Yidisher Teater in Ukrayne* (1931); J. Mestel, *70 Yor Teater-Repertuar* (1954); idem, *Undzer Teater* (1943); A. Mukdoiny, *Yitskhok Leybush Perets un dos Yidishe Teater* (1949); E. Nahshon, *Yiddish Proletarian Theatre: The Art and Politics of the Artef, 1925–1940* (1998); B. Orshanski, *Teater-Shlakhtn* (1931); S. Perlmutter, *Yidishe Dramaturgn un Teater-Kompozitors* (1952); B. Picon-Vallin, *Le Théâtre juif soviétique pendant les années vingt* (1973); N. Sandrow, *Vagabond Stars: A World History of Yiddish Theater* (1977, 1999^2); Kh. Shmeruk, *Meḥazot Mikrayim be-Yidish (1697–1750)* (1979); Y. Tsinberg, *Di Geshikhte fun Literatur bay Yidn*, 8 vols. (1943); J. Veidlinger, *The Moscow State Yiddish Theater* (2000); M. Viner, *Tsu der Geshikhte fun der Yidisher Literatur in 19tn Yorhundert*, 2 vols. (1945); I. Manger, J. Turkow, and M. Perenson (eds.), *Yidisher Teater Tsvishn Beyde Velt-Milkhomes*, 2 vols. (1968); A. Zable, *Wanderers and Dreamers: Tales of the David Herman Theatre* (1998).

THEBEN (Mandl), JACOB KOPPEL (1732–1799), head of the community of Pressburg and renowned **shtadlan* (the name of Theben is derived from the town of Devin (Ger. Theben) situated near Pressburg). Born in Pressburg, Theben inherited from his father the exclusive representation of the textile industry and the status of **parnas* and delegate of the Jews at court. He maintained relations with the court of the Austrian emperor and the noblemen of his retinue. Theben was elected *parnas* of the community of Pressburg in 1783. He waged a struggle against the decrees of Empress *Maria Theresa and the degrading projects of *Joseph II, which included shaving off the beards of the Jews. When the bridge toll was raised for Jews only, he acquired a lease of the collection of custom duties and reduced the fee. He was particularly renowned for his political struggle against compulsory military service by the Jews (one of the decrees of Joseph II). He did not demand the abolition of this service in exchange for a payment, but equal rights in exchange for equal obligations. He regarded military service and sacrifice by those deprived of rights as absurd. In 1796 Theben presented Emperor Francis I with a gift of 20,000 gold ducats in the name of the Jews and thus obtained the exemption from military service, but no rights, for them. In his private life he was the typical wealthy Jew of his period; his house was frequented by the poor and his table was always ready to welcome them. When he was received in audience by kings, his *takhrikhim* (funeral shrouds) were among his personal objects. His father ABRAHAM THEBEN (d. 1768) carried the Hebrew title *Manhig u-Farnas ha-Medinah*. He exploited his wide influence for the benefit of the Jews and interceded in favor of those tortured as a result of the *blood libel in the village of Orkuta (1764).

BIBLIOGRAPHY: I. Reich, in: Beit El, 2 (1868), 362–81.

[Baruch Yaron]

THEBES, ancient city in Upper *Egypt. A provincial backwater during the Old Kingdom, the small town of Wase rose to national prominence as the city of the 11th-Dynasty kings who founded the Middle Kingdom (c. 2134–1786 B.C.E.). The cult of the god Amun (biblical, *Amon) took root and flourished there after its introduction by succeeding kings of the 12th Dynasty, although they transferred their own residence to the north. At the outset of the 18th Dynasty (c. 1575) and, simultaneously, of the Egyptian Empire, the city became an international metropolis and Amun became the most important deity in the Egyptian pantheon. Amun granted victory to the pharaohs of the New Kingdom, and in gratitude they built splendid temples to him. When the Greeks first visited the city, its numerous temples and palaces so reminded them of their own storied "Thebes of the Hundred Gates" that they bestowed that name on the Egyptian city. To the Egyptians, however, from the New Kingdom on, Thebes was called either Wase, or more frequently simply "the City" (*niwe*) or "the City of Amun" (*niwe Amun*) whence the biblical No (Jer. 46:25 and Ezek. 30:14–16) and No-Amon (Nah. 3:8). The brutal sacking of this city by the Assyrians in 663 B.C.E. made such an impression that 50 years later, likening the forthcoming fate of Nineveh to it, the prophet Nahum (3:810) declared "Are you better than No-Amon that was situated among the rivers, that had the waters around her?… Cush and Egypt were her strength, and it was infinite;… Yet was she carried away."

BIBLIOGRAPHY: A.H. Gardiner, *Ancient Egyptian Onomastica*, 2 (1947), 24ff.; C.F. Nims, *Thebes of the Pharaohs* (1965).

[Alan Richard Schulman]

THEBES, city in E. central Greece. Benjamin of Tudela, the 12th-century traveler, found 2,000 Jews in Thebes. They worked in silk dyeing. The city was renowned throughout Greece for these artisans and for its weaving mills. Judah Al-Ḥarizi, who visited the city in 1218, mentions the poet, Michael b. Caleb, a native of Thebes. The community was led by five officials (*ephori*) and was famous for its scholars. Jewish tombstones of the 14th–16th centuries have been discovered there. In 1613 anti-Jewish agitation took place in the city. During the 17th century an agreement was reached not to wear silken clothes for seven years in order to prevent the jealousy of the gentiles. As a result of the Greek rebellions against the Turks during the 18th century, the Jewish community was destroyed.

BIBLIOGRAPHY: Andréades, in: *Economic History*, Supplement, 3 (1934–37), 1–23.

[Simon Marcus]

THEBEZ (Heb. תֵּבֵץ), city attacked by Abimelech, the son of Gideon, after suppression of the revolt of the Shechemites. It may therefore be assumed that the place was not far from Shechem and was perhaps under its jurisdiction. Abimelech captured the city and attacked the tower (citadel or *migdal*) by burning the doors of the gate; there he was killed by a millstone thrown on him by a woman (Judg. 9:50–57). This event was remembered even in the time of David (II Sam. 11:21; cf.

Jos., Ant., 5:251–53; 7:142). Eusebius locates the village of Thebez 13 mi. (c. 21 km.) from Neapolis in the territory of that city, on the way to Scythopolis (Onom. 100:11ff.). This place was called Thopas under the Crusaders (1108 C.E.). It is the present-day Arab village of Ṭūbās (see below). However, the identification of this village with the biblical Thebez is doubtful, as no remains of that time were discovered there and as the similarity of the names is only superficial. Some scholars view Tirzah as a corruption of Thebez.

[Michael Avi-Yonah]

Ṭubas

Tubas (Tevez; Heb. תֵּבֵץ) is a Muslim-Arab village with municipal council status in Samaria, near Nablus (Shechem). The village, which had served in the 1936–39 Arab riots as a center for armed bands, was taken in the *Six-Day War by Israeli forces (June 7, 1967). According to the 1967 census, it had 5,262 inhabitants. By 1997 its population had grown to 11,760, including 6% refugees. Its economy was based on field crops, vegetables, fruit orchards, and sheep and goat flocks. The inhabitants of Ṭūbās owned large tracts of land on the eastern slopes of Samaria and in the lower Jordan Valley, which were worked by tenants.

[Efraim Orni]

BIBLIOGRAPHY: Conder-Kitchener, 2 (1882), 229, 247, 249; Abel, Geog, 2 (1938), 477; Aharoni, Land, 241.

THEFT AND ROBBERY (Heb. גְּנֵבָה וּגְזֵלָה). An object which is in the possession of a person without the consent of its owner or any other person having a right thereto, when that person knows – or should know – that the latter does not consent, is considered to be stolen or robbed by him, regardless of whether the person holding it intends to restore it to the possession of the person entitled to it after a time or not at all (Sh. Ar., ḤM 348:1). The thief differs from the robber in the fact that the former steals furtively, when unobserved, whereas the robber takes openly and forcefully (BK 79b). This distinction is of practical significance for criminal law only; in dealing with civil cases the law relating to a robber applies equally to a thief and vice versa.

Civil Aspects

To establish that the object is in his possession, it is necessary for the thief or robber to perform an act of *acquisition (*kinyan*), such as a "lifting up" or "pulling" thereof, in the same manner as a person who wishes to acquire ownership of ownerless property; without this the object does not enter his possession and no theft or robbery is committed (BK 79a and Tos. thereto). In terms of this definition, land is never robbed (Suk. 30b), as it remains in the possession of its owner and never of the robber because it cannot be carried away, and the owner, who can always restore it to his possession by judicial means (BM 7a and Tos. to BM 61a), retains control thereof. On the other hand, a bailee who, without the owner's consent, overtly converts an object to his own use or denies the ownership of the bailor is thereby stealing it (Yad, Gezelah 3:11 and 14). This rule applies in the case of any person, such as a borrower or hirer, who has acquired possession of property with the owner's consent and thereafter refuses to return it (*Maggid Mishneh*, Gezelah 1:3). Many of the scholars of the Talmud are of the opinion that anyone who borrows a thing without the owner's consent is a robber (BB 88a). Moreover, some of them hold that anyone into whose hands a thing comes with the consent of its owner who afterward changes or departs from the use intended for it by the owner is a robber (BM 78a), for his possession thereof is contrary to the owner's wishes. Similarly, a man who finds a lost article and takes it with the purpose of keeping it is a robber (BM 26b), but a bailee who fails to return a thing, falsely pleading that it was stolen from him, is a thief and not a robber (BK 108b).

Certain things are not subject to the law of robbery because people do not mind their being taken; therefore a man who takes them without permission becomes entitled to them, as in the case of a tailor appropriating part of the thread with which he sews a suit, or a carpenter appropriating the sawdust from timber (BK 119a), or a son supported by his father who gives a morsel of food to a friend (Tosef., BK 11:4). In some cases the rabbis, for the sake of peace and order, regulated for the extension of the laws of robbery to property not legally subject thereto, because the ownership is not effective in law – as in the case of property found by a deaf-mute, idiot, or minor – as well as animals, birds, and fishes caught in certain snares set for them (Git. 59b).

RESTITUTION. The thief or robber is obliged to restore the stolen property itself (in specie) to the owner. The obligation comes into being from the time that the robbery is committed and is not fulfilled until the stolen property is returned in such a manner as to enable the owner to know that it has been restored to his possession (BM 31a).

SHINNUI. If the thing robbed is damaged while in the robber's possession, he is obliged to compensate the owner for the loss in accordance with the law applicable to a tort-feasor (see Tashba in: *Shitah Mekubbeẓet*, BK 97a); if improved while in the possession of the robber, it must be returned with all improvements, for which the robber is entitled to be compensated. If the thing is lost or destroyed while in the possession of the robber (cf. Sanh. 72a), or is changed to such an extent that it can no longer be put to its former use and is not fit for the owner's purpose (Rashba and Ramah in: *Shitah Mekubbeẓet*, BK 96a), the robber must pay the value of the thing robbed at the time of the robbery. The Talmud records disputing opinions on the law of *shinnui*. As indicated, *shinnui* ("transmutation," "*specificatio*") is constituted when the stolen property has undergone a change, whether an improvement or deterioration, to the extent that it is no longer fit for its former use, such as wood converted into utensils, wool into clothes, stones which are cut (BK 93b), an animal which has grown old, a coin which has cracked and is not fit to be used, fruit which has rotted, and wine that has gone sour (BK 96b). An accepted criterion for testing whether the *shinnui* is such that the stolen property is rendered unfit for its former use is to examine whether it has undergone a change of name (BK 65b), for people customarily call something which has a specific use by a particular name, so that a change of name denotes a *shinnui*. Yet some scholars are of the opinion that *shinnui* is subject to no special law: the robber must restore the changed object itself; if it is damaged by the change, he must compensate for it; if improved, he is entitled to compensation. However, most scholars hold that the return of the changed stolen property does not serve to restore the owner to the position he held prior to the robbery, inasmuch as the thing is no longer fit to be used by the owner as before and is therefore as if lost to him; thus the robber has to compensate for the thing according to its value at the time of the robbery, thereby acquiring ownership of the changed article. A third opinion is that in law the robber must restore the changed thing itself, but the rabbis – in order to encourage contrition on the part of the robbers – regulated that stolen property, if improved, need not be returned and the robber must only pay compensation for it (BK 66a, 93b, 94a). Again, others are of the opinion that even when the possibility of restoring the thing to its prior use remains – and therefore by law the *shinnui* does not transfer title – still if the loss which the robber would sustain in restoring the thing to its former use exceeds the benefit which the owner would derive from it, then the rabbis regulated that the robber need not restore it. In such an event the robber need only compensate for its value. An example of such a case is where the robber would have to demolish a whole structure in order to return a stolen beam which he had built into it (BK 95a).

Any profits which the stolen property may yield while detained by the robber belong apparently to the robber and he is not required to account for them to the owner (see *Rema*, ḤM 354:1). Moreover, any loss suffered by the owner as a result of being deprived of the use of the stolen property while it was detained by the robber is an economic loss, for which the robber is not required to compensate him (ḤM 363:3 and *Sma* thereto). Similarly the robber does not pay for a sickness from which a beast recovers (ḤM 363:1).

YE'USH. Apart from *shinnui* the robber may also acquire ownership of the stolen property and be required merely to pay compensation for it in the event of the owner's **ye'ush* ("despair"). Once the owner has lost all hope of the stolen property being restored to his possession, his ownership thereof is extinguished and title thereto is acquired by the robber, who is required only to pay its value at the time of the robbery. Opinions are divided in the Talmud on the question as to when exactly *ye'ush* is constituted and title conferred on the robber. Some scholars hold that *ye'ush* follows mere theft but not mere robbery: some hold the opposite view; and still others aver that *ye'ush* follows either (BK 114a–b). Another view is that despair alone does not suffice as it cannot be ascertained whether the owner has truly abandoned hope; to be recognized as real, *ye'ush* must therefore be accompanied by something more: either *ye'ush* with a change of possession, the stolen property having passed from the robber to a third person, or *ye'ush* accompanied by a change in the name by which the stolen article is called, i.e., when it has changed to such an extent, that people will incline to call it by another name even if it were possible to restore the article to its prior name. Mere *ye'ush* is nevertheless held by some scholars to suffice and to confer title to the stolen property on the robber (BK 66a–67a, 115a).

In strict law, when the thief delivers the stolen property into the possession of a third party prior to the owner's *ye'ush,* the latter may recover possession of his property from the third party without payment, for he has remained owner thereof. This law, if unamended, would have caused hardship to a bona fide purchaser on the open market, who could never be certain that he would not be deprived of his purchase by its true owner; as a result, since they had no means of taking precautions, people would never be in a position to buy anything with certainty. The rabbis accordingly enacted the *takkanat ha-shuk* ("open market rule") to protect both the purchaser in good faith and the owner. It provided that a man who purchases and pays for an article in the market without being in a position to know that it was stolen, while obliged to return it to the owner, is also entitled to demand a refund of the price from the latter. The owner accordingly recovers his pro-perty without causing the purchaser any loss (BK 115a).

In a case where the robber has transferred the stolen property into the possession of a third party and it is consumed by the latter prior to the owner's *ye'ush,* the Talmud records a dispute over whether the owner may demand compensation from one or the other at his option or from the robber only (BK 111b). Again, opinions are divided on the question of whether the heirs (of the robber) are considered as strangers, in the same position as a third party into whose possession the stolen property has come, or whether their possession is as that of the robber from whom they inherited (*ibid.*). In the post-talmudic period, the courts adopted the practice of restoring the stolen property itself to the owner even after *ye'ush* and a change of possession (*Rema*, ḤM 356:7).

[Shalom Albeck]

The Criminal Law

Stealing is repeatedly prohibited in the Bible. As the prohibition contained in the Decalogue (Ex. 20:13; Deut. 5:17) appears in the context of capital offenses, such as murder and adultery, it has been held to constitute the capital offense of man-stealing (see *Abduction), while the prohibitions of theft (Lev. 19:11) and robbery (Lev. 19:13), which appear in the context of fraudulent and oppressive dealings with men, were held to constitute the non-capital offense of larceny of money or chattels (Mekh. Yitro 8; Sanh. 86a; BM 61b; Yad, Genevah 1:1). The differentiation between theft and robbery is the same as in civil law (see above): theft is committed clandestinely, robbery openly (Yad, Genevah 1:3). It does not matter whether or not the thief (or robber) intended to enrich himself, permanently or at all, or whether he committed the offense only to annoy the owner or as a practical joke, or with the intention of borrowing and returning the thing taken, or with the resolve to pay all damages and penalties (BM 61b; Tosef., BK 10:37; Sifra Kedoshim 2); and it is said that the prohibition extends also to stealing one's own from the thief (BK 27b; Tosef., BK 38).

Criminal misappropriations are classified as falling into seven categories:

(1) *Fraud, that is, "stealing another man's mind";

(2) stealing by way of falsifying *weights and measures;

(3) stealing things which are useless or the use of which is forbidden to their owner, which is not punishable;

(4) misappropriating bills, lands, or consecrated property – for which only restitution has to be made;

(5) stealing chattels, for which the penalty is double payment (Ex. 22:8);

(6) stealing and selling or slaughtering oxen or sheep, for which the penalty is five or fourfold (Ex. 21:37); and

(7) man-stealing for which the punishment is death (Mekh. Mishpatim 13; Tosef., BK 7:8–17).

Although stealing and robbery constitute violations of negative injunctions by overt acts, they are not punishable by *flogging, because they entail monetary sanctions and one species of sanction always excludes all others (Yad, Genevah 3:1, Sanhedrin 18:2). But flogging was administered to a thief where the thing stolen had already been returned by him prior to his conviction and he has committed the theft for purposes other than self-enrichment (cf. *Minḥat Ḥinnukh*, no. 224); or where the offender (e.g., an infant or slave) was not capable of owning property from which reparation could be made (Yad, Genevah 1:10). Where the offense of stealing is merged in a graver offense, as for example where stealing is committed by slaughtering on the Sabbath an animal belonging to another, the capital punishment for the violation of the Sabbath absorbs and nullifies any monetary liability for stealing (Ket. 31a; Yad, Genevah 3:1–2); but where the offense is completed before the graver offense is commenced, as where pork is first stolen and then eaten, the monetary penalties for the theft are incurred in addition to the liability to be flogged for eating pork (Ket. 31b; Yad, loc. cit.).

The main difference between civil and criminal misappropriation is that while the civil remedy is restoration *in statu quo ante*, the criminal sanction is the payment of "double" (Ex. 22:8) or quadruple or quintuple (Ex. 21:37). While restitution may be ordered even where no witnesses are available to testify to the theft and to the previous warning administered to the thief (see *Penal Law), as, for example, on the *admission of the thief himself, the sanction of double, fourfold, or fivefold payment may not be imposed on him otherwise than upon judicial conviction (Ex. 22:8) on the strength of the testimony of witnesses (BK 64b; Yad, Genevah 1:4–5). The purpose of imposing the penalty of double restitution has been said to be that the thief should lose what he had intended his victim to lose (Yad, loc. cit.), and the reason for quadruple or quintuple that he who not only steals, but also sells or slaughters the animal stolen, has proved himself a persistent offender (Tosef., BK 7:2).

Payments recovered as penalties for theft are paid over to the victim ("he shall pay double unto his neighbor": Ex. 22:8). Execution is levied on the chattels of the thief first; if these are found insufficient, then execution proceeds to the best of his lands (Ex. 22:4; BK 7a–b). If he has neither movable nor real property, then the court orders that the thief be sold into slavery ("if he have nothing, then he shall be sold for his theft": Ex. 22:2) and the proceeds of the sale be paid out to the victim; but no such sale is ordered where only the penalties exceeding the value of the thing stolen are irrecoverable: once restitution has been made, the court waits for recovery of penalties until the thief attains the means to make the payments (Kid. 18a). Nor is a woman thief ever sold into slavery (Sot. 3:8). As the thief is sold "for his theft" only (Ex. 22:2), he may not be sold where his value exceeds that of the thing stolen; but where the value of the thing stolen exceeds the proceeds of the sale of the thief, he remains indebted for the balance, which may be recovered from him as a civil debt if and when, after his release (Ex. 21:2; and see *Slavery), he acquires property of his own (Yad, Genevah 3:11–14). A thief sold for several thefts from different victims may be held in partnership by all of them, or the proceeds of his sale will be distributed among them *pro rata* (*ibid.* 3:16).

In later talmudic and post-talmudic times, the sale of thieves into slavery became, of course, obsolete. Already in the seventh and eighth centuries, convicted thieves were flogged (*Halakhot Pesukot min ha-Ge'onim*, no. 94), presumably because nothing could be recovered from them. Later, there are ever-increasing indications to the effect that thieves became a grave menace to society, not so much because of the monetary damage they caused within the community, but because of the ill-repute their misconduct brought upon the Jews at large: they were ostracized and expelled from their cities (see **Ḥerem*), and delivered to non-Jewish authorities for adjudication and punishment (cf. e.g., *Takkanot Medinat Mehrin*, no. 265; *Pinkas Hekhsherim shel Kehillat Pozna*, nos. 1614 and 1655) quite apart from such routine punishments as floggings, *fines (*Takkanot Medinat Mehrin*, no. 263) and *imprisonment (*Tashbeẓ* 3:168) administered to them.

[Haim Hermann Cohn]

State of Israel

The law appertaining to theft and robbery is the Criminal Code Ordinance of 1936. The Ordinance is based on the rules of English criminal law and provides for a maximum penalty of three years imprisonment for theft while robbery, which is defined as the use or threat of force in the course of theft, is punishable by 14 years imprisonment.

Distinction between Theft and Robbery

The Talmud states that the distinction between theft and robbery is that the thief steals surreptitiously while the robber takes overtly and by the use of force (BK 79b). In the *Gali* case (*Gali v. State of Israel* (40 (4) PD 169, 1986), the defendant approached the victim and, without warning, snatched a box containing jewelry worth half a million dollars from the victim's hand. The defendant then quickly escaped and disappeared. The issue in this case was how to classify this act. In his opinion, Justice Elon discussed the question in terms of both Jewish Law and the Israeli statutes, arriving at the conclusion that, under both systems, such an act constitutes robbery, even though forceful power was not used in the taking. In such instances, he held, the deciding factor in classifying the act is the victim's perception. If the victim is aware of the snatching, the act is robbery, as there is perforce an element of violence, even if slight. If the victim is unaware of the snatching, as when he or she is pick-pocketed, there is no element of violence, and the act is considered as theft.

The opinion commends the lower court judge, and the attorney who appeared there, for relying on Jewish Law, in compliance with the Foundations of Law Act, 1980. The opinion states:

> The laws of theft and robbery in Jewish Law are numerous, and many of them are particular to this legal system and extremely instructive. Concerning the question at hand, the position of Jewish Law is concise and well defined. Let us examine Maimonides' illuminating words in his *Mishneh Torah*:
>
> Who is a thief? One who takes someone's money secretly, without the knowledge of the owner, such as one who puts his hand into the purse of his neighbor and takes money without the owner seeing it, and similar cases. But if he takes it openly and publicly by force, he is considered not a thief, but a robber (Yad, Genevah 1:3).
>
> Who is a robber? One who takes someone's money by force, such as snatching an object from his hand (Yad, Genevah 1:3)

The opinion concludes with the following remarks:

> These words of Maimonides, which summarize the position of Jewish law as it emerges from the talmudic sources (BK 57a, 79b), and as it was subsequently formulated in the codes (Sh. Ar., ḤM 348:3, 359:7) define the act of robbery as theft which includes an element of force… This occurs when the act is done openly, i.e., when the victim from whom the object is snatched is aware of the snatching.

Penalties for Theft

Under Jewish law, there is a penalty of double and sometimes quadruple or quintuple payment for theft. In post-talmudic times, other penalties were imposed, as the situation required.

The case of *Anon. v. State of Israel* (35 (4) PD 438, 1981) dealt with the proper punishment for acts of embezzlement that occurred over a three-year period. The defendant was a member of the foreign service of the State of Israel who embezzled a sum of $80,000 dollars by means of an elaborate scheme of fraudulent practices. Upon conviction, the trial judge sentenced the defendant to imprisonment for three years. The defendant argued before the Supreme Court, inter alia, that prior to these acts he had been a constructive member of society, that he had returned the embezzled funds, and that he would not commit such acts in the future. Therefore, he argued, a prison sentence should not be imposed on him.

In his opinion, Justice Elon asserted that, "Crimes in which the criminal takes advantage of the authority and trust reposed in him by deceiving those who relied upon him are counted among the most serious crimes which undermine the foundations of civilized society." In particular, he added, "One who embezzles the funds of the general public is guilty of a more serious crime than one who embezzles funds belonging to an individual."

Jewish law emphasizes the distinction between stealing from the public and stealing from a private individual: "Theft from the public is more severe than theft from an individual, for one who steals from an individual can compensate him by returning what he has stolen, while one who steals from the public cannot compensate them by returning what he has stolen" (Tosefta, BK 10:14, ed. Zuckermandel). In light of the great damage to the public, the serious nature of the defendant's acts, and in order to deter potential criminals, the Supreme Court upheld the sentence imposed by the lower court.

The Rabbinic Law of Robbery

"The Rabbinic Law of Robbery" refers to various acts which are considered theft by force of rabbinic enactment, even though in terms of biblical law these acts did not constitute theft, and were not prohibited. A prime example of the rabbinic law of robbery is money taken by means of gambling. Under biblical law, taking such winnings is not theft, since the loser has consented to the taking. However, the Rabbis enacted that, inasmuch as the winner takes money without giving anything in return, and there is actually no unreserved consent by the loser, such taking is regarded as theft.

One of the differences between robbery under rabbinic law and robbery under biblical law is that, in the former, a court does not have the power to effect a restoration of the money taken (Yad, Gezelah va-Avedah 6:16).

A responsum by *David ibn Zimra (Resp. Radbaz 1:503) explains that in such cases, none of the parties acted with the intent of following the rabbinic law. In this respect, the rabbinic law of robbery differs from other rabbinic enactments, such as the methods instituted by rabbinic law for acquiring property, in which the parties act in reliance on rabbinic law and its enforcement. In such instances, a court enforces the enactments of rabbinic law.

David ben Solomon ibn Abi Zimra (Radbaz) ruled that the rabbinic law of robbery is subject to the sanction of a ban as well as other religious and moral sanctions.

For example, a gambler who lives by gambling is disqualified as a judge or a witness in court, and in order to have the disqualification removed he must pay back or give to charity the money he has accumulated from his gambling (see *Gambling).

[Bernard Auerbach (2nd ed.)]

Robbery by the State

Halakhic authorities expanded the application of the law governing robbery, so that in addition to the private law concerning robbery of one individual by another, the law also included robbery from the individual by a public authority, as a matter of constitutional and public law.

In connection with the doctrine *dina de-malkhuta dina* ("the law of the state [lit. the kingdom] is law"), by which the *halakhah* acknowledges the binding nature of the laws of the state, a basic distinction was established. This doctrine applies to the expropriation of property by the king under general legislation that applies to all inhabitants of the state equally and in a non-discriminatory manner. Such expropriation is within the king's power. But the doctrine does not apply if the expropriation does not conform to a general law promulgated by the state, and such a situation is considered as theft.

Maimonides states (Yad, Gezelah va-Avedah 5:14): "The principle of the matter is this: Any law enacted by the king that applies generally and not only to a single individual is not robbery; but whenever he takes discriminatorily from a particular individual only, and not by law applicable to everyone, he acts lawlessly against that individual, and this is robbery."

Maggid Mishneh (by *Vidal Yom Tov of Tolosa, fourteenth century) comments: "The *law* of the land is law, but *thievery* by the 'land' is not law." The practical application of this distinction mainly concerns whether one may derive any benefit from property expropriated by the government, such as purchasing it. If the property has been taken lawfully by the state, one may obtain the property and benefit from it. But if it has been taken unlawful ly, by thievery, it may not be obtained or used, "for anyone who does these or similar things strengthens the hands of law violators." (Yad, Gezelah va-Avedah 5:1; Sh. Ar., ḤM 369).

Similarly, R. *Isaac b. Sheshet Perfet (Resp. Ribash ha-Ḥadashot, 9) ruled that a fine levied against all Jews in a particular locality, due to the acts of a few Jews who were guilty of monetary fraud, was "utter robbery," as it was collective punishment. This could not be seen as falling under the rubric of "the law of the land is law" in the same way as does ordinary tax law.

Robbery by the Community

From the 11th century onward, with the rise in the authority of the *kehillah* (the Jewish community) in the various diasporas, the monetary relationship between the individual and the community became a subject of discussion. Responsa on this question emphasize that unlawful seizure by the community of individual property is robbery.

A responsum by the halakhic authority of 12th-century Mainz (Resp. Or Zaru'a, 222) rejected the community's claim that it may require the members of the community to pay the taxes assessed against them, without giving them the opportunity to declare under oath the value of the property that they possess. This ruling rested on the ground that the community is subject to the same laws concerning robbery as the individual. As the community may not rob the individual, the communal enactment was therefore void.

The responsum relies on the talmudic dictum, "Does the fact that they are many give them a license to be robbers?" This maxim was stated to support the rule that the public may not establish a path through the property of an individual without his consent (BB 100a).

A similar ruling concerning the obligation to pay a tax (Resp. Maharam of Rothenburg, ed. Prague, 106) held that where it is clear that a tax assessment is incorrect, we do not apply the principle that the tax payer must first pay and only afterwards litigate his right to a refund. Maharam also relied on the Talmudic dictum referred to above, and concluded that the arbitrary infringement by the community on the individual's rights constitutes robbery.

A responsum by Ribash (Resp. Ribash, 477) held that a community may not require an individual to pay a tax that was levied to cover expenditures incurred before the individual became a resident of the community. Ribash concluded that such a requirement would entail robbery. The community has no authority to adopt an enactment that would unjustifiably take an individual's property, as "the public may not legislate to rob others" (see *Takkanot ha-Kahal*).

Ḥamas (Violence)

The Bible makes no distinction between the terms *ḥamas* and *gezel* (robbery). God tells Noah, "the end of all flesh has come before me, for the earth is filled with *ḥamas* on account of them" (Gen. 6:13). The Sages and biblical commentators interpret *ḥamas* to refer to robbery. The prophets often referred to *ḥamas* in conjunction with the term *shod* (robbery, plunder). However, the two terms were differentiated in the tannaitic period and the term *ḥamas* was used to connote an act that borders on robbery, although biblically permitted.

The Babylonian *amoraim* interpreted the term *ḥamsan* to refer to one who forcefully takes someone else's property against his will, but pays him for the property (BK 62a). The Jerusalem Talmud states that a *ḥamsan* is one who intentionally steals property that is worth less than a *perutah*, so that a court will not hear the action (TJ, BM 4:2)

The act of a *ḥamsan* is not robbery under biblical law, but it is a violation of the commandment, "You shall not covet" (Yad, Gezelah va-Avedah 1:9, cf. Rabad's gloss, ad loc.). However, the act constitutes robbery under rabbinic law. A *ḥamsan* may therefore not be a witness, although he is competent to be a witness under biblical law (Sanh. 25b; Yad, Edut 10:4).

If the victim of an act of *ḥamas* states that he consents to transfer the property to the *ḥamsan* or he indicates this by his conduct, the transfer is legally valid (see *Ones*). However, if the victim does not so state or indicate, the transfer is invalid. According to some halakhic authorities, a transfer under compulsion is invalid only under rabbinic law; therefore, a court does not have the power to effect a restoration of the property (*Biur ha-Gra*, Sh. Ar., ḤM 205:1)

[Menachem Elon (2nd ed.)]

BIBLIOGRAPHY: Ch. Tchernowitz, in: *Zeitschrift fuer vergleichende Rechtswissenschaft*, 25 (1911), 443–58; idem, *Shi'urim be-Tal-*

mud, 1 (1913), 63–121; I.S. Zuri, *Mishpat ha-Talmud*, 6 (1921), 50–58; S. Assaf, *Ha-Onshin Aḥarei Ḥatimat ha-Talmud* (1922), index; Gulak Yesodei, 2 (1922), 219–25; M. Jung, *Jewish Law of Theft* (1929); Herzog, Instit, 1 (1936), 101–5; ET, 5 (1953), 454–86, 517–29; 6 (1954), 199–225; EM, 2 (1954), 464f.; S. Loewenstamm, *ibid.*, 536f.; B.Z.M. Ouziel, in: *Berakhah li-Menaḥem Z. Eichenstein* (1955), 64f.; N. Rakover, in: *Sinai*, 49 (1961), 17–28, 296–307; Elon, Mafte'aḥ, 23–25; B. Cohen, in: *Jewish and Roman Law*, 1 (1966), 159–78; 2 (1966), 472–537, 772–5, 786f.; S. Albeck, in: *Bar-Ilan*, 4–5 (1967), 117–31. **ADD. BIBLIOGRAPHY:** M. Elon, *Ha-Mishpat ha-Ivri* (1988), 1:59f., 65f., 97, 105, 119, 120, 132, 175, 194f., 202, 208, 258, 276f., 293, 331f., 338, 346, 405, 420, 433, 481, 484, 486f., 490f., 492f., 494, 498, 502, 505, 512, 518, 521, 525, 532, 534, 564, 566, 571, 618, 621f., 627f., 644, 694f., 701f., 724, 786; 2:950, 1002f., 1075, 1078; 3:1437f., 1469; idem., *Jewish Law* (1994), 1:65f., 73, 109, 118, 134, 135, 149, 194, 218f., 228, 234, 302, 325f., 348, 397f., 406, 416; 2:495, 513, 528, 586, 589, 591f., 596, 599f., 601, 607, 611, 615, 623, 631, 640, 648, 651, 685, 688, 703, 764, 768f., 776f., 797, 856f., 865f., 894, 965; 3:1151, 1212, 1296, 1300; 4:1710, 1747; idem, *Jewish Law (Cases and Materials)* (1999), 213, 244; M. Elon and B. Lifshitz, *Mafte'aḥ ha-She'elot ve-ha-Teshuvot shel Ḥakhmei Sefarad u-Ẓefon Afrikah* (legal digest) (1986), 2:48–53; B. Lifshitz and E. Shochetman, *Mafte'aḥ ha-She'elot ve-ha-Teshuvot shel Ḥakhmei Ashkenaz, Ẓarefat ve-Italyah* (legal digest) (1997), 34–36, 48–49; *Enẓiklopedyah Talmudit*, s.v. *Gezel*, 5:454–529; s.v. *Hamsan*, 16:52–57.

THÉMANLYS, PASCAL (1907–), French author. Descended from an old Bordeaux family, Thémanlys was born in Paris. A Zionist and a mystic, he believed in the reestablishment of Ereẓ Israel as Jewry's spiritual center. Settling in Israel in 1949, Thémanlys was cofounder with Joseph Milbauer of the Association des Amitiés Israël-France. His works include *Figures passionees* (1930), *Les merveilles du Becht* (1934), *Grands d'Israël, des Pharisiens à nos jours* (1938), *Influences* (1949), and *Un itinéraire de Paris à Jérusalem* (1963).

°**THEMISTIUS** (317–c. 388 C.E.), statesman, rhetorician, and philosopher, known to medieval Jewish philosophers as a major interpreter of Aristotle; the author of commentaries which Maimonides recommends highly (see Maimonides' letter to Samuel ibn Tibbon, in S. Pines' introduction to his translation of *The Guide of the Perplexed* (1963), lix).

Themistius lived in Constantinople most of his life. A pagan, he held the office of senator and even prefect in the new Christian capital, and celebrated its emperors in several panegyrics. The pliant nature of Themistius' personality is also evident in his philosophical writings, in which he shows familiarity with the various currents of Greek philosophy and, in the tradition of late Greek thought, he believes Plato and Aristotle to be in substantial agreement.

Only two of Themistius' commentaries were translated into Hebrew (from earlier Arabic translation): his paraphrase of Aristotle's *De caelo* by Zerahiah b. Isaac *Gracian, in 1284; and his paraphrase of Book 12 of the *Metaphysics* by Moses ibn *Tibbon, in 1255 (both edited by S. Landauer, *Commentaria in Aristotelem Graeca*, 4 (1902), 1–167; 5 (1903), 1–35). Themistius' other commentaries, to the *Prior* and *Posterior Analytics*, the *Physics*, and *De anima*, were known either through Arabic translations or through secondary sources. He is often quoted by other late Hellenistic writers, notably John Philoponus, and by Islamic philosophers, particularly *Averroes. It is through supercommentaries to Averroes' writings that Themistius' views often find expression in the works of such late medieval Jewish figures as Levi b. Gershom and Moses of Narbonne.

Themistius' own contribution to Peripatetic philosophy lies in the interpretation, not completely consistent, which he gave to Aristotle's doctrine of the *intellect. He considered the "potential intellect" of Aristotle to be an independent, separate substance, though closely related, as matter is to form, to the similarly separate "agent intellect." He saw the intellect's bridge to corporeal forms and to man as accomplished through a "common," "passive intellect," neither separate nor immortal. Averroes was later to build upon this notion of an independent political intellect, identifying its substance completely with the universal Agent Intellect.

BIBLIOGRAPHY: Pauly-Wissowa, 2nd series, vol. 5 (1934), s.v. *Themistes*; Steinschneider, Uebersetzungen, 125, 176; F.E. Peters, *Aristoteles Arabus* (1968), 16, 18, 34, 36, 42, 52; O. Hamelin, *La théorie de l'intellect* (1953), 38–43, 58–72.

[Alfred L. Ivry]

THEOCRACY, literally the "rule of God," but generally applied to mean a state ruled by religious law. In the first century C.E. Josephus created the term "theocracy" to describe the people of Israel's polity. "Some peoples have entrusted the supreme political power to monarchies, others to oligarchies, yet others to the masses. Our lawgiver, however… gave to his constitution the form of what – if a forced expression be permitted – may be termed a 'theocracy,' placing all sovereignty and authority in the hands of God" (Apion, 2:165). That description is entirely accurate, if taken literally. The Torah repeatedly refers to God as the immediate ruler of the Jewish people and gives only passing attention to human self-rule in the form of a monarchy (Deut. 17:14–20). The Book of Joshua and particularly the Book of Judges depict a pure theocracy.

The period of such direct divine rule was, however, limited. Divine sanction was given to the new monarchy, although the latter was said to imply a rejection of God's direct kingship (I Sam. 8:7). From that time on, what is in effect Jewish theocracy is understood to be one of various forms of indirect divine rule, which generally acted through the official religious institutions. Thus, in the Second Temple era there were times when the high priesthood united political and religious power, as in the Hasmonean rulers. In such priestly rule, theocracy was transformed into heirocracy, a priestly rule. It may be contrasted with the nomocracy, in this instance rule by sacred law, of the post-Temple period. Josephus seems to have recognized this when he wrote, describing Torah law, "be content with this, having the laws for your masters and governing all your actions by them; for God sufficeth for your ruler" (Ant., 4:223).

In the talmudic period and the Middle Ages the polity of the Jewish community, though built on religious law, was not strictly speaking a theocracy since it was not ruled exclusively by the rabbis. In fact, there was continual tension between the rabbis and the lay leadership.

Contemporary Israel

The question of the character of the Jewish polity, largely theoretical for nearly two millennia, became a matter of practical concern with the establishment of the State of Israel. Secularists and most non-Orthodox theoreticians have maintained that religious institutions in Israel should refrain from exercising a direct role in the government. The overwhelming majority of Orthodox thinkers have been willing to accept the essentially non-religious structure of the Jewish state, provided that Orthodoxy has certain political rights and power. A tiny minority, insisting upon a rigorous interpretation of God as sole ruler, rejects the present State of Israel as blasphemous and insists that a Jewish state can be established only with the coming of the king-messiah.

BIBLIOGRAPHY: Baron, Community, 2 (1942), 52–168; E. Borowitz, *How Can a Jew Speak of Faith Today?* (1969), 90–107; N. Rotenstreich, in: *Judaism*, 15 (1966), 259–83; A. Lichtenstein, *ibid.*, 15 (1966), 387–411.

[Eugene B. Borowitz]

THEODOR, JULIUS (1849–1923), rabbi and researcher of the *aggadah* and Midrash. Theodor, born in Schalleninken, E. Prussia, studied at Breslau Rabbinical Seminary under Z. Frankel and H. Graetz. After teaching religion in Tarnowitz and Bromberg (Bydgoszcz), he served as rabbi in Brant and in *Bojanowo (1888–1919). He was active in communal life and rabbinical organizations, following a traditional line. After World War I he moved to Berlin. His scholarly work was devoted almost entirely to research in the *aggadah*, in which field he published articles in Hebrew and German. His life work was the publication of the *Midrash Bereshit Rabbah* in a scholarly edition entitled *Minḥat Yehudah*, based upon manuscripts and first editions with variant readings and a comprehensive commentary. Theodor did not succeed in preparing the entire Midrash, but more than half was published during his lifetime (1903–17); the remainder of his literary estate was published in 1926 by Ḥ. Albeck, who also published the last part of the Midrash with a comprehensive introduction (1928–36). Theodor had the distinction of being the first to publish a text of rabbinic literature in a scientific and amended edition in accordance with the philological methods then current. This edition, in which both his talmudic scholarship and classical philological knowledge found expression, serves as an instructive example of accuracy and care and is a most important contribution to the study of the *aggadah*.

BIBLIOGRAPHY: A.B. Posner, in: S. Federbush (ed.), *Ḥokhmat Yisrael be-Ma'arav Eiropah*, 2 (1963), 289–90.

[Moshe David Herr]

°**THEODORE OF MOPSUESTIA** (c. 350–428 C.E.), Christian Bible exegete and theologian. Born in Antioch, Theodore was bishop of Mopsuestia in Cilicia from 392 C.E. until his death. Of all his commentaries, only that on the minor prophets is wholly extant. Theodore interpreted the biblical narrative as historical and not allegorical, but always in the light of Christian salvation history. He recognized few direct messianic prophecies, and he showed little regard for the Books of Esther and the Song of Songs. His commentary on Psalms is considered his most important exegetical work.

BIBLIOGRAPHY: R. Devreesse, *Le Commentaire de Th. de Mopsueste sur les Psaumes* (1939); Zahh, in: *Neue kirchliche Zeitschrift*, 11 (1900), 788–806; Abramowski, in: *Zeitschrift fuer Kitchengeschichte*, 72 (1961), 263–93; U. Wickert, *Studien zu den Pauluskommentaren Theodors von Mopustia* (1962); Sullivan, in: *The New Catholic Encyclopedia*, 4 (1967), 18–19 (incl. bibl.); *The New Schaff-Herzog Encyclopedia of Religious Knowledge*, 11 (1953), 320–2 (incl. bibl.).

[Zev Garber]

THEODOSIUS, spokesman for the Samaritan community of *Alexandria in the second century B.C.E. During the reign of Ptolemy VI Philometor (180–145 B.C.E.) a dispute arose between the Jews and Samaritans of Alexandria. The quarrel centered around the respective temples in Jerusalem and Mount Gerizim, and appears to have been a continuation of an earlier dispute (Jos., Ant., 12:10). Whereas the Jews wished to send sacrifices to the Temple at Jerusalem, the Samaritans held that their temple on Mount Gerizim was the only legitimate one. Both sides agreed to bring the dispute before Ptolemy Philometor, and Theodosius was among those appointed to present the Samaritan case. The Jewish party, however, represented by one Andronicus the son of Messalamus, succeeded in persuading the king "that the Jerusalem Temple alone was built in accordance with the laws of Moses." As a result, Theodosius and the other Samaritan participants are said to have been put to death (Jos., Ant., 13:74–79).

[Isaiah Gafni]

°**THEODOSIUS I**, Roman emperor, 379–395 C.E. Although Theodosius, an orthodox Christian, was responsive to the influence of the church, he subordinated it to his authority. During his reign, and in the reigns of his sons Arcadius and *Honorius, the civil position of the Jews greatly deteriorated. In 388 the bishop of Callinicus on the Euphrates incited a crowd to burn a synagogue; the emperor commanded the governor of the East to punish the culprits and have the bishop rebuild the synagogue. *Ambrose, bishop of Milan, however, by his spiritual influence and by threats of damnation, persuaded the emperor both to reconsider his decision and repeal it (Ambrose, Epistula XL). In 393 Theodosius prohibited polygamy for Jews. Although this law corresponded with actual practice, it constituted an imperial intervention in the private life of the Jews (C. Justiniani 1:9, 7). The same year Theodosius asked the governor of the East to suppress with due severity the excessive zeal of those who usurped rights for themselves in the name of the Catholic religion. He stressed that Judaism was a lawful sect and forbade destruction of its synagogues (C. Th. 16:8, 9). From 393 to 426 there were at least ten imperial interventions against damaging synagogues, which indicates clearly the actual position of the Jews.

BIBLIOGRAPHY: F.-M. Abel, *Histoire de la Palestine*, 2 (1952), 300ff.; M. Avi-Yonah, *Bi-Ymei Roma u-Bizantiyyon* (1970), 180, 182f.; Baron, Social², index.

[Alfredo Mordechai Rabello]

°THEODOSIUS II (Flavius Theodosius Junior), Roman emperor of the East, 408–450 C.E. Theodosius II edited the first official collection of the imperial statutes from the time of Constantine to the year 438, the year of publication of the Theodosian Code (C. Th.). The Code was accepted and published by Emperor Valentinian III also in the West, where it enjoyed wide circulation. The Jews are dealt with particularly in chapters 8 and 9 of book 16: (*"De Judaeis, Caelicolis, et Samaritanis"*; *"Ne Christianum mancipium Judaeus habeat"*). The reign of Theodosius II marks a serious deterioration in the position of the Jews. His first law, of May 408, is directed against the feast of Purim, since it was believed that the Jews then burned images of the cross (C. Th. 16:8, 18). In 415 the patriarch Gamaliel was deposed (C. Th. 16:8, 22); construction of new synagogues was forbidden and destruction of the existing ones ordered, provided this did not result in disorder. The office of patriarch disappeared in the subsequent years, and in 429 the emperor took advantage of this by imposing a new tax which was to be paid by the community (a much easier and safer system for the treasury; C. Th. 16:8, 29; see *Honorius). Nevertheless, Judaism was proclaimed a tolerated cult in 423 (C. Th. 16:8, 26), provided it did not offend the Christian religion. Synagogues were protected, the reconstruction of synagogues that had been destroyed was ordered, and observance of the Sabbath was permitted (C. Th. 16:8, 10, 25, 27). However, in 438 an important statute was issued in which the Jews were defined as "enemies of the Roman laws and of the supreme majesty." Consequently they were forbidden to hold any high office, military or civil, and they lost all jurisdiction over Christians; the prohibition to build new synagogues was reinstituted, and the destruction of those that were unsafe was ordered. Jews, however, were not to be exempted from the burdensome curial offices. The civil inferiority of the Jews and discrimination against them were thus legally sanctioned.

BIBLIOGRAPHY: Juster, Juifs, 1 (1914), 162–6, 237; 2 (1914), 101–3; F. Nau, in: REJ, 83 (1927), 184–206; C. Pharr et al. (eds. and trs.), *The Theodosian Code* (1952); Baron, Social², index; J. Gaudemet, *L'Eglise dans l'Empire Romain* (1958), 623ff.; M. Simon, *Verus Israel* (Fr., 1964²) J.W. Parkes, *Conflict of the Church and the Synagogue* (1964).

[Alfredo Mordechai Rabello]

THEODOSIUS OF ROME ("Todos Ish Romi"; see Jastrow Dict. 1650), the spiritual leader of the Roman Jewish community some time during the late first century C.E. Yose b. Ḥalafta relates that he instituted in Rome on the nights of Passover the eating of "helmeted goats," i.e., goats roasted with entrails and legs on the head, like a helmet, the manner in which the paschal lamb was sacrificed. They (i.e., the sages, not Simeon b. Shetaḥ, as in Ber. 19a) sent to him, declaring that were he not Theodosius, they would have declared a ban against him, because he was "making Israel eat sacred flesh outside[the Temple]" (Pes. 53a; cf. Tosef., Beẓah 2:15). This story demonstrates the degree to which the central religious authorities in Palestine (probably Gamaliel and the *bet din* at Jabneh) kept a strict check on Diaspora Jewry. In the amoraic period, the question arose whether Theodosius was a "great man" (*gavra rabba*) or merely a "powerful man" (*ba'al egrofin*). They proved that he was a "great man," citing a teaching of his: "What did Hananiah, Mishael and Azariah see that they delivered themselves for the Sanctification of the[Divine]Name into the fiery furnace…–" It is surely indicative that the only teaching recorded of this prominent Diaspora leader deals with the problem of "the sanctification of the Name" (implying martyrdom), one no doubt of very topical import. According to another amoraic tradition, Theodosius gave financial support to scholars (Pes. 53b).

BIBLIOGRAPHY: M. Vogelmann, in: *Sefer Zikkaron li-Shelomo S. Mayer* (1956), 196–200; M. Beer, in: *Zion*, 26 (1961), 238–40; S. Lieberman, *Tosefta ki-Feshutah*, 5 (1962), 959–60.

[Daniel Sperber]

THEODOTUS (second century B.C.E.), Samaritan author of an epic on the rape of Dinah (Gen. 34). The long fragment extant preserves a summary together with 47 lines of the original poem (Eusebius, *Praeparatio Evangelica*, 9:22, quoting Alexander Polyhistor). The epic's title is not known; the heading *On the Jews* is not the author's. It is not specific enough nor would Theodotus, a Samaritan, have given it this title. Modern writers sometimes refer to it, without evidence, as *On Shechem*. Theodotus' reference to Shechem as "the holy town" makes it certain that he was a Samaritan. It is unlikely, therefore, that this is the Theodotus to whom Josephus referred in his list of pagan authors who wrote about the Jews (Jos., Apion, 1:216). Neither is it reasonable to identify him with the Phoenician writer by the same name mentioned by the second-century church father Tatian (*Oratio ad Graecos*, 37).

The epic opens with a panoramic view of Sicima (Shechem) and its majestic surroundings, followed by an introduction of Jacob as he is received hospitably into the city. The epic here reverts to the patriarch's journey to Mesopotamia to escape from his brother's wrath. As he crosses the Euphrates, rich in cattle, Laban welcomes him, but then proceeds to cheat him. After Dinah, fair and noble, is born, Jacob recrosses the river and becomes a landowner in the vicinity of Shechem. His sons are shepherds and Dinah joins the women in weaving wool. Dinah is curious to see the city during a festival; there she is raped by Sychem (Shechem), who later asks Jacob for her hand; Jacob agrees on condition that all inhabitants of Shechem be circumcised. Again and again the significance of this rite is stressed, suggesting that the author was attempting to combat intermarriage. Meanwhile, Symeon (Simeon) recalls God's promise to Abraham that his seed would inherit the land of ten nations, inciting Levi to avenge their sister's shame from this Sodom-like city, where guests are ravished. The last nine lines depict vividly the slaying of Emmor (Hamor) and Sychem. The epic ends with a description of how the brothers joined in the sacking of the city and how Dinah was restored to her father.

Theodotus was a master of the classical epic, with a touch of the real poet. The poem was rooted in Homer, whose lines are sometimes paraphrased. But he was not necessarily a syncretist like Pseudo-*Eupolemus. The manuscript's reading that the father of Sicimius (Shechem) was Hermes (which lends credence to Theodotus' syncretism) is usually emended to Emmor (Hamor).

BIBLIOGRAPHY: Schuerer, Gesch, 3 (1909[4]), 499–500 (includes bibliography); J. Guttmann, *Ha-Sifrut ha-Yehudit ha-Hellenistit*, 1 (1958), 245–61.

[Ben Zion Wacholder]

THEOLOGY.

Introduction

Defined by Richard Hooker, the Renaissance theologian, as "the science of things divine," theology (from the Greek word *theos*, "God," and *logos*, "word," "doctrine") is a sustained, rational discourse on *God, His nature, His relationship to man and the universe, the manner in which He communicates His will to mankind, including such kindred topics as providence, *miracles, prayer, worship, *free will, *sin, *repentance, the problem of *evil, immortality, and angelology. Theology has been particularly prominent in Christian thought, the Christian thinkers having devoted a good deal of reflection to the implications of their faith. For historical reasons (the heritage of the Bible with its strong practical emphasis; the influence of the Talmud, in which the ideal of law is paramount; the absence of doctrines such as the Trinity calling for precise definition; the dispersal of Jews in many different communities with varying patterns of thought), the genius of Judaism has been directed more toward the practices of the faith than toward abstract speculation, more to what God would have men do than to what God is. Therefore it has been frequently asserted that Judaism has no theology. Attempts at constructing a Jewish theology have sometimes been met with fierce opposition both by secularists, who object to the *theos* of theology, seeing it as retrogressive and as leading to heresy hunting, and by the Orthodox, who object to the *logos* of theology as harmful to faith, which, they claim, demands only obedience to the law and which can only be disturbed through an inquiry into its roots. Some declare, therefore, that the whole theological exercise is un-Jewish. While there may be some truth to the contention that Judaism does not know of any systematic theology (even this is belied by the efforts of the medieval Jewish thinkers), it is obvious that God has been at the center of Jewish life and thought since the beginnings of Judaism. Jews have thought profoundly about God and there is a Jewish theology even if some prefer to call it by some other name. There is the further point that the halakhic approach can only be defended on non-halakhic grounds. "Pan-Halakhism," to use a phrase coined by A.J. *Heschel, is self-defeating.

Theology in the Bible

The whole of the Hebrew Bible has God as its concern: the only biblical book containing no direct reference to God is the Book of Esther. The Bible does not, however, stand on its own in the Jewish tradition. The Torah is the Bible as interpreted in and by the historical experiences of the people of Israel. This goes a long way toward explaining why there have been no serious attempts among Jews at writing a biblical theology. For example, in discussing the theological difficulties of God "…visiting the iniquity of the fathers upon the children unto the third and fourth generation…" (Ex. 20:5), the Jewish theologian will not be content with this text on its own but will seek to discover how it ties up with other texts, such as Deuteronomy 24:16 and Ezekiel, chapter 18. Above all, he will wish to know how the biblical doctrines fared at the hands of their Jewish interpreters throughout Jewish history. The modern Jewish theologian also accepts the insights provided by biblical criticism, archaeology, and philology. He recognizes the developing nature of biblical thought. His theology builds on the Bible but utilizes all the tools provided by modern scholarship for the understanding of the Bible. The study of biblical theology is, then, for him not a means of acquiring a ready-to-hand series of infallible texts, but a method of discovering how it all began, how the impact of the Divine first made itself felt in Israel's collective life, how man quested for God, and how God allowed Himself to be found. While biblical theology has succeeded in establishing itself as a legitimate branch of biblical studies (H.H. Rowley (ed.), *Old Testament and Modern Study* (1951), 311–45; E. Jacob, *Theology of the Old Testament* (1958), 11–26) those who engage in it, all of them Christian scholars, generally approach the Old Testament from the point of view of the "New" and the interpretations of the Church. The criteria for determining the "permanent values" inherent in the biblical record, adopted by the Jewish theologian, are those provided by the Jewish tradition.

The key theological idea in the Bible is the sovereignty of God. He is the "living God," Creator of the world and all that is in it: One, All-powerful, All-good and Holy, demanding of His creatures that they practice justice and righteousness. He chooses Israel to be a "light to the nations." He is both transcendent and immanent, uncontained by the highest heavens and yet "tabernacling" (i.e., dwelling as in a tent; see Cross, in: *Biblical Archaeologist Reader*, 1 (1961), 201–28) in the midst of the Children of Israel. He has many names but His special name is YHWH. Myths are not attached to Him as they are to pagan gods. He has no feminine partner and there is no name in the Bible for "goddess." He is beyond birth and death and all similar human manifestations, though He is frequently described in anthropomorphic terms. These terms are, however, in no way incompatible with a highly spiritual outlook.

The Bible contains no systematic treatment of theological problems. Even the Books of Job and Ecclesiastes, with their majestic probing into the terrible question of why the righteous suffer, have little to say on the more fundamental difficulty of why there should be any suffering or evil at all. That nothing is impossible for God is stated in the Bible (Gen. 18:14; Jer. 32:27), but it is foreign to biblical thought to consider the problem, widely discussed by the medieval thinkers, whether this means that God can do the logically impossible, and whether things involving a contradiction fall under the scope of divine omnipotence. With very few exceptions the biblical books are silent on the whole question of the hereafter. The biblical picture is of the all-pervading presence of God: His footsteps heard in the wind and storm, His being felt in the dealings of man. The Bible, however, contains no command to believe and has no interest in theological speculations as to His true nature. All this is largely due to the severely concrete, "organic" nature of ancient Hebraic thought which hardly bears any resemblances to the philosophical thinking that is the heritage of the Greeks and to which the Western world owes its theology. To a greater or lesser extent the same is true of rabbinic thought.

Rabbinic Theology

The rabbinic period saw the emergence of new theological ideas and the strengthening of older ones. The Torah became the name for the sum total of Jewish religious teaching and its study the supreme religious duty. Rabbinic Judaism, according to some interpretations, is not a "religion of salvation": for the rabbis, this life is good in itself, not merely a school for the eternal life, yet the rabbinic approach to Judaism is distinctly otherworldly. The "eternal life" of the world to come is always contrasted with the transient nature of this life. The biblical doctrines of sin and repentance are deepened, especially by the doctrine of the two inclinations in man: the "good inclination," *yeẓer ha-tov*, which pulls him upward, and the "evil inclination," *yeẓer ha-ra*, which drags him down. In the thought of this period biblical universalism is to some extent obscured by a particularistic emphasis typical of a minority group struggling for its survival. Anthropomorphic descriptions of God abound in rabbinic literature, though they are generally qualified by the suggestion that they cannot really be applied to God. In his dealings with man God operates by the principle of "measure for measure": as man behaves so does God behave toward him. The notion of God as king is found in the Bible. In rabbinic literature, however, the term "the kingdom of God" (*malkhut shamayim*) expresses both an attitude of mind in which man acknowledges God's sovereignty and the ultimate reign of God over all His creatures.

In dealing with the difficult subject of rabbinic theology one must always be aware of the rough and ready spontaneous nature of rabbinic thinking and guard against imposing on the sources a system that is basically alien to them. G.F. Moore's warning (*Judaism*, 1 (1927), 357) is apposite:

> Judaism, in the centuries with which we are concerned, had no body of articulated and systematized doctrine such as we understand by the name theology. Philo, indeed, endeavored to harmonize his hereditary religion with a Hellenistic philosophy, but the resulting theology exerted no discoverable influence on the main current of Jewish thought. As in the case of the Bible itself, any exposition of Jewish teaching on these subjects, by the very necessity of orderly disposition, unavoidably gives an appearance of system and coherence which the teachings themselves do not exhibit, and which were not in the mind of the teachers. This fact the reader must constantly bear in mind. It must further be remarked that the utterances of the rabbis on this subject are not dogmatic, carrying an authority comparable to the juristic definitions and decisions of the Halakah; they are in great part homiletic, often drawing instruction or edification from the words of Scripture by ingenious turns of interpretation, association, and application, which seized upon the attention and fixed themselves in the memory of the hearers by the novelty, not of the lesson, but of the way the homilist got it into the text and out again. Large liberty in such invention has always been accorded to preachers, and every one knows that scholastic precision is not to be looked for in what is said for impression.

The warning has been so strongly reinforced by Max *Kadushin's researches (*Rabbinic Mind*, 1965[2]) into the nature of rabbinic thought and the extreme difficulty of distinguishing between authentic rabbinic dogma and the mere operation of concepts as a dynamic exercise, that a case can be made for denying altogether that there is a rabbinic theology. Summing up, it may be said that the rabbis were certainly much concerned with theological themes, but one would look in vain in rabbinic literature for any kind of systematic treatment of these themes.

Medieval Jewish Theology

Influenced by Aristotelian and Neoplatonic philosophy and by the Arabic *Kalām, the medieval Jewish thinkers produced important systematic treatises on Jewish theology. It was in this period that Jewish theology had its true birth. The term "medieval Jewish philosophy" is, in reality, a misnomer. The medieval thinkers pursued theology rather than philosophy in that, despite being undoubtedly influenced by Greek thinking, they began and ended with faith. Their use of reason was not consciously directed toward the working out of new philosophical positions, but to establish traditional ones, securely grounded in faith. They were religious believers writing for religious believers. What they sought to offer their readers was a reasoned defense of Jewish beliefs even if in the process they arrived at very unconventional attitudes.

The first great systematic Jewish theologian, *Saadiah b. Joseph Gaon, wrote his *Emunot ve-De'ot* ("Beliefs and Opinions") in Arabic in 933. *Baḥya b. Joseph ibn Paquda's *Ḥovot ha-Levavot* ("Duties of the Heart"), though in the main an ethicoreligious tract, is theological in content, especially in its treatment of the unity theme in the first part (*Sha'ar ha-Yiḥud*, "Gate of Unification"). *Judah Halevi's able defense of Judaism in the *Kuzari* deals with many theological topics. The work of the Jewish Aristotelian thinker Abraham *Ibn Daud, *Emunah Ramah* ("Sublime Faith"), is entirely of a theological nature. All of *Maimonides' writings, with the exception of his medical treatises, are of theological import; the three most important works, from the theological point of view, are a commentary to the Mishnah (the most significant of the three) in which he expounds the 13 principles of the Jewish faith as he saw them and accords theology the status of law; *Moreh Nevukhim* ("Guide of the Perplexed"); and a code of Jewish law, *Mishneh Torah* or *Yad ha-Ḥazakah* ("The Strong Hand"). *Levi b. Gershom's *Milḥamot Adonai* ("Wars of the Lord") is a particularly bold series of theological speculations. Ḥasdai *Crescas wrote *Or Adonai* ("Light of the Lord"), a theological statement in which Aristotelianism is vigorously criticized. His pupil, Joseph *Albo, wrote *Sefer ha-Ikkarim* ("Book of the Principles"), a full-scale investigation into the dogmas of Judaism. Isaac b. Moses *Arama's *Akedat Yiẓḥak* ("The Sacrifice of Isaac") is a collection of philosophical sermons on the Pentateuch containing much, though not very original, theological material. Isaac *Abrabanel produced a number of similar works. Joseph b. Ḥayyim *Jabez was a Spanish theologian, hostile to philosophy. R. Moses b. Joseph di *Trani (*Mabbit*) in his *Beit Elohim* ("House of God") deals with three major theological themes: prayer, repentance, and the dogmas of Judaism.

The God of the medieval thinkers is, in the main, impersonal, impassionate, and utterly beyond all human associations. His is a unity "simple to the furthest extent of simplicity" with not the slightest trace of multiplicity. Granted such a conception, the biblical anthropomorphisms presented a serious obstacle. How could one speak of God as "good" and "wise" or even as "one" or say that He "exists," since all these are terms taken from human experience and their attribution to God *in toto* suggests plurality in His being? A dominant theme, consequently, though not followed by all the medieval thinkers, is the negation of God's attributes in any positive form. It is permitted to say what God is not; never should an attempt be made to describe Him as He really is. Typical of this approach are Maimonides' observations: "All men, those of the past and those of the future, affirm clearly that God, may He be exalted, cannot be apprehended by the intellects, and that none but He Himself can apprehend what He is, and that apprehension of Him consists in the inability to attain the ultimate term in apprehending Him. Thus all the philosophers say: We are dazzled by His beauty, and He is hidden from us because of the intensity with which He becomes manifest, just as the sun is hidden to eyes that are too weak to apprehend it" (Guide 1:59). "If I knew Him I would be Him" (Albo, *Ikkarim*, 2:30) is another typical medieval summation of theological limitation. Yet so much thought is given to the doctrine of negation in these works that this, too, has to be treated as an important branch of medieval Jewish theology.

Medieval thought is even more otherworldly than that of the rabbis. The dichotomy of body and soul is especially pronounced. The pleasures of the world are seen as a hindrance to spiritual perfection. The sage has to resort to them but only in great moderation and to keep body and soul together. Eternal bliss is in direct proportion to man's efforts on earth to grasp metaphysical truth and make it his own. The contradiction between these ideas and those of traditional Judaism, as found in the Bible and the Talmud, was acutely sensed and the usual device adopted was to declare that the Bible and the rabbis, when they dealt with theological matters, were not to be understood literally but allegorically. For the first time the mechanics of revelation were discussed in detail. Can one become a prophet even after the close of the Bible? Is prophecy a gift or an attainment? How does God communicate with the prophet? Since God has no vocal organs, what meaning can be given to those biblical passages in which He is said to "speak" to man? What is the difference between the state of prophecy attained by Moses and that of the other prophets? In what way can apparently irrelevant passages in the Pentateuch be considered the word of God? What were God's reasons for ordaining rules such as the dietary laws which on the surface seem to have no rational or ethical justification?

The problems of creation and free will exercised the minds of these thinkers to an extraordinary degree because it was in these areas especially that philosophical thought appeared to contradict traditional Jewish views more strongly. Is matter eternal, as Aristotle suggested, or is it created? Can the believing Jew agree with Plato that from all eternity there exists a hylic substance upon which God imposed form or is the doctrine of *creatio ex nihilo* essential to Jewish faith? Is time a creation or was it always "there"? Is man really free and, if he is, how is this compatible with God's foreknowledge of his actions? Can a man be blamed for entertaining false beliefs since he cannot have any control over what he believes? These questions were not only new in the history of Jewish thought but entirely inconceivable in the earlier, unreflective biblical and rabbinic periods.

The kabbalists produced their own systems, but insofar as these are closed, with little room for rational or critical assent or dissent and with many a warning against the introduction of human reason into the spheres of the divine mysteries conveyed by revelation, they belong to theosophy rather than to theology. For all that, profound theological themes were considered by the kabbalists. The central problem to which the kabbalists addressed themselves was theological. It comprised such queries and answers as: How can the finite world of error and multiplicity have emerged from the Infinite? The reply of the Zohar in terms of emanation and the Lurianic answer in terms of God's withdrawal "from Himself into Himself" to leave room for the emergence of the finite; the Lurianic contemplation of how evil has its source in the divine contraction; the kabbalistic views on man's soul and its relationship to God; the aim of divine worship as conceived by the kabbalists – for God's sake not for man's. All of these questions are theological and demand that a Jewish theology examine them, albeit in a critical light; accepting the insights they contain and rejecting those ideas which cannot defend themselves at the bar of consistency and coherence.

Another theological question raised by kabbalistic teachings is how far Judaism can sustain dualistic ideas. The doctrine of the Ten *Sefirot*, for example, comes close to affirming that there is multiplicity and dynamism in the Godhead and was, in fact, attacked on these grounds by the opponents of the Kabbalah. They went so far as to compare kabbalistic ideas on these matters with Christian speculations on the Trinity. The kabbalists themselves are naturally at pains to deny any suggestion of dualism. **Ein Sof* and the *Sefirot*, they repeatedly declared, are one, expounding their ideas in the famous illustration of water poured into bottles of different hue.

Audacious theological speculations are to be found in ḥasidic thought. R. *Naḥman of Bratslav, for instance, believed that it is inherent in man's finite situation that he encounter difficulties when confronted by the Infinite. For this thinker, doubt, paradoxically, is not faith's foe but its vindication (J.G. Weiss, in *Alei Ayin… li-Shelomo Salman Schocken* (1952), 245–91). R. Mordecai Joseph Leiner of *Izbica was a religious determinist, holding that, in reality, "everything is in the hands of Heaven, even the fear of Heaven" (J.G. Weiss, in: *Sefer Yovel le-Yiẓḥak Baer* (1960), 447–53). In Ḥabad Ḥasidism God alone enjoys ultimate existence, all creatures being included in His blessed unity. The attitude approaches Far Eastern religious ideas on the illusionary nature of worldly existence and it was attacked by the opponents of Ḥasidism as rank heresy. This type of ḥasidic pantheism (more correctly, panentheism) finds its consistent advocacy in the writings of *Shneur Zalman of Lyady and his disciple R. *Aaron b. Moses ha-Levi of Starosielce. The acute ḥasidic explorations into the nature of the love and fear of God and the ḥasidic teachings on contemplative prayer are major contributions to a Jewish mystical theology.

Modern Jewish Theology

From the days of Moses *Mendelssohn onward the scope of Jewish thought in the Western world embraced theology. The closer contacts with Christian thought brought in their wake a fresh consideration of the vexed question of dogma in Judaism; of the true significance of ethical monotheism; of the relationship between Judaism and Christianity and between religion and culture; and of the meaning of revelation. Mendelssohn himself wrote on these topics and on the immortality of the soul. In the 19th century the main theological thinkers were in Germany. They were influenced by the philosophers Kant and Hegel, especially, and by the theologians Friedrich Schleiermacher and Albrecht Ritschl. Thinkers such as Abraham *Geiger, Zacharias *Frankel, Leopold *Zunz, Nachman *Krochmal, Solomon Ludwig *Steinheim, Samuel *Hirsch, Solomon *Formstecher, Samson Raphael *Hirsch, and Hermann *Cohen made their contribution to theology even though many of their interests lay in other directions such as history, philosophy, or apologetics. In particular, the thinkers of the Reform movement were compelled to think through the logic of their new positions and hence were moved to concentrate on theological questions. An incidental result was that the Orthodox leaders were obliged to treat theological problems seriously. An outstanding Orthodox theologian in the 20th century, Rabbi A.I. *Kook, placed the problems of religious Zionism and the challenges presented by modern science and technology at the center of his thought. For example, Kook saw evolutionary theory as being compatible with the optimistic views of the Kabbalah. Isaac *Breuer was another 20th-century Orthodox thinker, with an interest in the religious interpretation of human history and with a view of the Jewish people as "meta-historical." The Lithuanian *Musar movement produced a galaxy of religious thinkers, operating, to be sure, within strictly traditional limits, but striving to uncover the psychological motivations of religious life. The writings of the somewhat nonrepresentative members of this school, Rabbi J.L. *Bloch (*Shi'urei Da'at*, 2 vols., 1949–56) and Rabbi E.E. *Dessler (*Mikhtav me-Eliyahu*, 3 vols., 1955–64), contain detailed and searching examinations of purely theological problems, such as the nature of miracles, free will and God's foreknowledge, and the relationship between human time and God's eternity.

For the majority of contemporary Jewish theologians the central theme is the defense of traditional theism. This is the doctrine of God as both transcendent and immanent in the universe, involved in all its processes, but also beyond the universe. If there were no universe there would still be a God, but without God there could be no universe. Theism involves the rejection of the following doctrines as untrue: deism – God is only wholly immanent; polytheism – there are many gods; dualism – there are two gods, one good, the other evil; atheism – there is no God; and agnosticism – man by his nature cannot know whether or not there is a God. Many Jewish theologians have followed Kant and Protestant theologians in declaring that the truth of God's existence cannot be determined by rational proofs, as in medieval theology, but that it is to be accepted through mystical intuition, tradition, or the existentialist "leap of faith."

Twentieth-century interest in existentialism is reflected in Jewish theological works. Of the three outstanding theologians produced by German Jewry in this century, Leo *Baeck is the exponent of the more classical type of religious thought; Franz *Rosenzweig represents the "new thinking" associated with existentialism; and Martin *Buber can be described as a religious existentialist. Less influenced by continental philosophy, Milton *Steinberg, on the other hand, is emphatic that the views of a Kierkegaard, for example, are incompatible with the Jewish approach to religion and ethics, and some thinkers have scorned Jewish preoccupation with religious existentialism, dubbing it "Kierkegaard with a *yarmulka*."

Two prominent theologians with a worldwide influence are A.J. *Heschel and J.B. *Soloveitchik. Heschel's numerous theological works have as their theme "God in Search of Man," which is the title of his best-known book. Heschel is opposed to that liberal theology which avows that man is capable of raising himself spiritually by his own unaided efforts. Like Reinhold and Helmut Richard Niebuhr, and with an almost Barthian ruthlessness, Heschel roundly declares that an over-optimistic view of man's potentialities is thoroughly unbiblical. The nature of man's heart is evil from his youth. Even the saintliest of men is tainted by sin and God alone gives man the power to survive in the struggle. Heschel also stresses the sense of wonder as an essential ingredient in religious life.

With the exception of his two essays, *Ish ha-Halakhah* ("The Man of Law," 1965) and *Ish ha-Emunah* ("The Man of Faith," 1968), Soloveitchik wrote little, but as the mentor of more than a generation of Orthodox rabbis he was responsible, above any other contemporary thinker, for defending the sober, painstaking, unemotional approach typical of halakhic Judaism. The halakhic man sees his greatest good and highest privilege in obeying God's will as it is revealed in Jewish law. Religious ecstasy is viewed with a degree of suspicion and as supererogatory. Of all Jewish thinkers, Soloveitchik is undoubtedly closest to the idea of Kierkegaard's "knight of faith."

Religious naturalism finds its most powerful advocate in Mordecai M. *Kaplan. The doctrine of a finite God has its Jewish followers, notably in Levi Olan. Among other modern theologians mention should be made of Louis *Jacobs and Will *Herberg. There is also considerable influence on Jewish thought, especially in the United States, of the ideas of A.N. Whitehead and of process philosophy. The more recent "death of God" theology is generally rejected by Jewish theologians with the exception of Richard L. *Rubenstein. Two questions of especial concern, for obvious reasons, to contemporary Jewish theologians are the Holocaust and the State of Israel. How can theology make sense out of the horrors in which a third of the Jewish people was murdered? Can it still be maintained that God works in human history? If the hand of God is to be discerned in the emergence of the State of Israel why was it powerless to intervene during the Hitler regime? Modern scientific theories raise theological problems of their own, particularly in the area of miracles and petitionary prayer, and these have been considered by Jewish theologians. While the logical positivists have been refuted, there has hardly been any reaction in the Jewish theological camp to the problems of religious language rendered acute by modern linguistic analysis.

A number of symposia on Jewish beliefs have been published, notably, *Rediscovering Judaism: Reflections on a New Jewish Theology* (ed. by A.J. Wolf, 1965); *Varieties of Jewish Belief* (ed. by I. Eisenstein, 1966); and *The Condition of Jewish Belief* (1966) originally published in *Commentary* (Aug. 1966). The questions in the *Commentary* symposium, addressed and replied to by rabbis of the Orthodox, Conservative, and Reform groups in the United States, throw light on the particular subjects of contemporary theological interest. They are the following:

(1) In what sense do you believe the Torah to be divine revelation?

(2) In what sense do you believe that the Jews are the chosen people of God?

(3) Is Judaism the one true religion?

(4) Does Judaism as a religion entail any particular political viewpoint?

(5) Does the "God is dead" question have any relevance to Judaism?

There is, and has been, no Jewish journal devoted only to Jewish theology but *Judaism, Conservative Judaism, Central Conference of American Rabbis Journal*, and *Tradition* in the United States, and *Perozedor, Petaḥim*, and *De'ot* in Israel contain many articles of a theological nature.

[Louis Jacobs]

Feminist Theology

First articulated in the 1980s by a number of U.S. Jewish feminists trained in a variety of academic disciplines, this theological discourse turned the feminist critique of American society, religion, and culture inward by focusing on Judaism itself. While specific concerns differ, Jewish feminist theologians share an understanding of religion as rooted in personal experience, leading to a reluctance, if not refusal, to assert universal truths or make universal claims. Their goal is not to persuade others to share any predetermined vision, but to articulate their own understanding of the self, God, and the world, and to view these realities through the lens of Jewish female experience.

This theology is feminist because it is consciously rooted in the conviction that personal experience is shaped by gender as well as by cultural, historical, and economic factors. It presupposes, as well, that traditional Jewish theology, like traditional Christian theology, is androcentric. Using the experiences of Jewish men as a lens through which the world is viewed, such theology minimizes or ignores ways in which Jewish women's piety has gained expression. The Jewish feminist theologian attempts to hear her own voice and feel her own presence within the sources of Jewish tradition. Before she can reform or transmit Judaism's religious teachings, she tries to discover what women's religious experiences have been. She does so by reading between the lines of traditional texts, filling in stories, writing new ones, and making conjectural leaps. Consequently, Jewish feminist theology, as Jewish theology in general, can best be described as responsive. Its commitment to Judaism need not be a commitment either to the past norms of Jewish tradition or to their current articulations as expressed by Judaism's major religious movements. Rather, its allegiance is to the fundamental categories of God, Torah, and Israel, shaped by the experiences of the theologian as woman and as Jew.

Since feminist theology is self-consciously rooted in the theologian's life story, it can also be understood as contextual. Instead of attempting to create theological systems that transcend personal experience, feminist theologians have firmly grounded their theologies in the realities of their lives. The similar concerns of such contemporary Jewish feminist theologians as Judith Plaskow, Marcia *Falk, Rachel Adler, Rebecca Alpert, and Ellen Umansky can thus be attributed to their writing in a similar context, as white, middle-class, religiously liberal, university-educated U.S. women of the late 20th and early 21st centuries. This does not mean that feminist theological claims have relevance only for the theologian herself. On the contrary, she hopes that by drawing on her experiences and sharing her stories, she will encourage others to draw on their experiences as well. In so doing, she offers women and men a means of formulating their own articulated and unarticulated responses to the categories of God, Torah, and Israel. She also offers women and men a means of viewing their own experience as Jewish experience, enabling them to recognize, as Rabbi Laura Geller has written, the "Torah of our lives as well as the Torah that was written down."

One of the greatest contributions of Jewish feminist theology is its insistence that it is possible for diverse groups of people to talk seriously about Jewish theology outside of a legal framework. While religiously liberal rabbis have long discussed the creation of a non-halakhic Jewish self-identity, feminist theologians have been the first to create, however loosely, a network of religiously liberal theologians, both modern and post-modern, who have formally and informally examined traditional and liberal Jewish theological claims together. Further, in attempting to ground this theology in their experiences as women, feminist theologians like Plaskow, Adler, Melissa Raphael, Laura Levitt, and Miriam Peskowitz have called into question not only traditional male, hierarchically dominant, theological language, but also the ways in which theology is created. Through new blessings (Falk), midrashim (Plaskow, Adler, Umansky), poems (Merle Feld), and rituals intended for specific moments in women's lives (Levitt, Penina Adelman, Savina Teubal et. al.), feminist theologians have added a vibrancy to late 20th and early 21st century liberal Jewish theology.

[Ellen M. Umansky (2nd ed.)]

BIBLIOGRAPHY: S. Schechter, *Some Aspects of Rabbinic Theology* (1909); K. Kohler, *Jewish Theology* (1918); G.F. Moore, *Judaism…* 3 vols. (1927–30); W. Herberg, *Judaism and Modern Man* (1951); J.J. Petuchowski, *Theology of Haham David Nieto* (1954); A.J. Heschel, *God in Search of Man* (1955); idem, *Torah min ha-Shamayim be-Aspaklaryah shel ha-Dorot*, 2 vols. (1962–65); M. Steinberg, *Anatomy of Faith* (1960); A.A. Cohen, *Natural and Supernatural Jew* (1962); J. Guttmann, Philosophies; I. Maybaum, *Face of God after Auschwitz* (1965); E.L. Fackenheim, *Quest for Past and Future* (1968); E.B. Borowitz, *New Jewish Theology in the Making* (1968); E.E. Urbach, *Ḥazal – Pirkei Emunot ve-De'ot* (1969); L.H. Silberman, in: AJYB 70 (1969), 37–58. **ADD. BIBLIOGRAPHY:** R. Adler, *Engendering Judaism: An Inclusive Theology and Ethics* (1998); M. Falk, *The Book of Blessings* (1996); L. Levitt, *Jewish Feminism: The Ambivalent Search for Home* (1997); J. Plaskow, *Standing Again a Sinai: Judaism from a Feminist Perspective* (1990); M. Raphael, *The Female Face of God in Auschwitz* (2003); E.M. Umansky and D. Ashton (eds.), *Four Centuries of Jewish Women's Spirituality* (1992).

°THEOPHILUS. Josephus (Apion, 1:216) includes one Theophilus in a list of Greek authors who mentioned the Jews at some length and whose writings testify to the antiquity of the Jewish people. His date and nationality are unknown but he may be identical with the Theophilus whom Alexander Polyhistor cites as a source for the story that King Solomon sent the gold left over from the building of the Temple to the king of Tyre. It is also possible that he is the Theophilus who is known to have been of the school of Zenodotus, the great Alexandrian scholar of the third century B.C.E.

THEOPHILUS (Heb. **Yedidiah**), high priest from 37 to 41 C.E. Theophilus, the son of Hanan son of Seth, was appointed by Vitellius, the Roman governor of Syria, in place of his brother Jonathan (Jos., Ant., 18:123) and served in that office until removed by King *Agrippa I (*ibid.*, 19:297). Mattathias, the son of Theophilus, was high priest when the war against Rome broke out (66 C.E.).

BIBLIOGRAPHY: Schuerer, Gesch, 2 (1907[4]), 271; Klausner, Bayit Sheni, 5 (1951[2]), 22; E. Bammel, in: ZDPV, 70 (1954), 147ff.; E.M. Smallwood, in: JTS, 13 (1962), 14–34.

[Uriel Rappaport]

°THEOPHRASTUS OF ERESOS (372/369–288/285 B.C.E.), a pupil of *Aristotle and his successor. The Jews, he said, are "philosophers by race," a comment reminiscent of remarks ascribed to Aristotle and *Megasthenes. Quotations from him are found in various authors; two of these deal with Jewish sacrificial practices (Jos., Apion, 1:167, and Eusebius, *Praeparatio Evangelica*, 9:21). The main purpose of these descriptions is to demonstrate the incongruous nature of the customs of different peoples, a point made by ethical and legal relativists since Herodotus, if not earlier. Little importance is to be attached to the details he gives with regard to Jewish sacrifices which are in conflict with the injunctions of the Bible, e.g., that the Jews offered sacrifices at night and that honey was used for libations (cf. Lev. 2:11). Such details were subordinate to his main purpose.

BIBLIOGRAPHY: J. Bernays, *Theophrastos' Schrift ueber Froemmigkeit* (1866); Reinach, Textes, 7–9; J. Gutmann, *Ha-Sifrut ha-Yehudit ha-Helenistit*, 1 (1958), 74–88; W. Poetscher, *Theophrastos peri Eusebeias* (Gr. and Ger., 1964), 122f. and passim.

[Daniel E. Gershenson]

THERAPEUTAE, a name given to a group of Jewish ascetics who lived in a community close to Alexandria in the first century C.E. This particular group is described specifically only by the Hellenistic Jewish philosopher Philo in his treatise *De Vita Contemplativa* ("On the Contemplative Life"). The treatise explores one of the perfect philosophical lives as defined by the Stoics, and follows on from a lost treatise on the active life of philosophy in which the Essenes were used as the definitive Jewish example of excellence. The group of *De Vita Contemplativa* may itself have used the name *therapeutai* as a self-reference, though Philo indicates that all those who follow a contemplative life of philosophy may be called *therapeutai* (*Contempl.* 2). In Greek *therapeutai* has a general meaning of "one who serves [God/the gods]," a sense found widely in Philo's work and elsewhere in contemporaneous Greek literature and inscriptions. This relates to the life they lead of total service to God through an ascetic and spiritually focused existence. Philo also plays on the double-entendre of the word in noting that people engaged in a contemplative life in some way "heal" souls.

Philo describes those who follow the contemplative lifestyle as leaving behind their ordinary lives and homes, distributing their belongings to their children, relatives or friends, in order to pursue philosophy elsewhere. They find a place away from their home city in a quiet, rural location in which their contemplative practice can be pursued. While Philo notes that those who follow this lifestyle exist in many parts of the world, he stresses that it is abundantly seen in Egypt, particularly around Alexandria. At this point in the treatise Philo introduces the Jewish group he would focus upon as "the best" of all the contemplative philosophers (*Contempl.* 22). He notes that their particular community is situated in a healthy, breezy spot on a flat, low-lying hill (probably south-west of Alexandria), in between Lake Mareotis and the Mediterranean Sea. Philo writes that their location is surrounded by dwellings and villages and implies that there are cultivated fields and pastures (factors that differentiate them from later Christian ascetics who sought more extreme solitude in desert regions). The architecture of the community settlement is described as consisting of a central building – most likely originally a country villa – incorporating a sacred meeting room (*semneion*) and dining hall (*sumposion*), along with numerous individual hut-like dwellings divided into two rooms: an outer and an inner, the latter called a *monasterion* or *semneion*. In the inner room they keep sacred writings for study and inspiration.

In terms of their spiritual and philosophical exercises, Philo describes the Therapeutae as praying twice every day, at sunrise and sunset. At sunrise they pray to have their minds illuminated by heavenly light, and for the soul to be relieved of the disturbance of the physical senses, in order to follow truth. They interpret "the sacred instructions of the prophet Moses" (*Contempl.* 64) allegorically in order to discover deeper meanings, using works written by predecessors as guides. They compose and write down hymns. Engaged in this practice, they remain within their rough huts for six days, and on seventh days (Sabbaths) they assemble in the meeting room to hear a discourse from the most senior elder. Philo notes that both men and women are equally members of the group, and that this meeting room is divided by a wall 3–4 cubits high, probably with men on one side and women on the other.

They do not eat until after sunset, since the body and its needs are associated with darkness, while their practice of spiritual philosophy is associated with light. They eat only bread seasoned with salt (and sometimes hyssop), and drink only spring water. Philo notes that some Therapeutae can be so preoccupied with contemplation that they do not think of food for three days, and that they can utter precepts of philosophy in their sleep while dreaming. Their clothing is very basic: a short *exomis* or linen wrap in summer, covered with a cloak of woolly sheep or goat skin in winter. It is clear from such comments that Philo wished to emphasize aspects of the group that would impress those who followed Stoic philosophy, in which asceticism, detachment from the world, intellectual clarity, and concentration on the essence of the universe (Nature/God) were prime interests.

A large part of Philo's treatise is taken up with a description of a special event that takes place every 49th evening (the Sabbath of Sabbaths). Like the Pythagoreans, the group apparently venerated not only the number seven but its square. On this occasion, they dress themselves in white clothing (also like Pythagoreans, and also serving Levites or Egyptian cultic priests). At this point in the treatise it becomes clear that the community Philo describes is hierarchical with each member allocated a particular place. There is a lower order of Therapeutae: the "dailies" (*Contempl.* 66). These junior members are chosen to maintain the senior members and wait on them during dinner as *diakonoi* who take the place of slaves. The dining hall is divided, like the meeting room, into two parts, with men on the right and women on the left. They recline on very rough couches: wooden benches strewn with local papyrus, slightly raised for leaning upon.

The procedure at the 49th evening celebration is carefully described by Philo. The president of the community, while reclining, gives a lecture, using allegorical interpretation, on a passage of Scripture or on a philosophical proposition. The community listens in silence, with occasional utterings of approval. The seniors recline and the juniors stand during the address, and afterwards the president is applauded by clapping. He then stands up and sings a hymn, either an ancient one or something recently composed, and then all the others take a turn in singing, with everyone joining in for closing lines and choruses. The meal – bread, salt, hyssop, spring water – is then brought in on a table and served out by the juniors. The table seems to be symbolic of the table of shewbread in the Temple sanctuary. After dinner, the entire company stand and join together in the middle of the dining room in two choirs, one of men and one of women, each with their own choir-leader. The leaders stand in the places of Moses and Miriam respectively who led Israel in songs of praise after the escape from Egypt (Exod. 15). Everyone sings, claps and dances, eventually forming one harmonious choir, singing songs of thanksgiving to God in an ecstatic state. At dawn they greet the arrival of the 50th day by all standing turned toward the rising sun. They pray for a bright day of truth and intellectual illumination, after which they return to their huts.

Questions have been raised about how much Philo is creating an ideal community out of hearsay or accurately representing an actual group. Philo is clearly using elements he believed would appeal to a Stoic audience and others trained in Graeco-Roman philosophy, but it is not improbable that Philo visited such a community close to Alexandria himself and reported what he saw. Philo himself may not have agreed with every aspect of the group's practice. The group seemed to have followed an older or heterodox solar calendar that has the new day beginning at dawn, and its repetition of the 49th evening as the time for festivity is difficult to reconcile with the usual feasts of the Jewish calendar. The group reveres the number 50 as "the most holy and natural of numbers" (*Con-*

templ. 65), like the Pythagoreans, and celebrates the 50th day's regular arrival. The presence of women in the group on an equal or near equal footing with men is striking, but nothing is provided by Philo to explain the group's rationale for such inclusivity, though there may be some implication that both men and women, divested of material connections, aim to be cultic attendants (*therapeutai*) in a true, spiritual Temple. Philo works hard to ensure that the women are presented as a modest ideal, describing them as "mostly elderly virgins" (*Contempl.* 68) and thereby somewhat de-sexualized.

It seems likely that if a real group is in fact described in *De Vita Contemplativa* then it should be seen as part of a larger exegetical and philosophical tradition within Alexandrian Judaism, in which allegorical exegesis, asceticism and an accommodation with Graeco-Roman philosophy is attested. The individual group Philo describes would represent one school of thought within this tradition, but at present much still needs to be learnt about the characteristics of Alexandrian Judaism in the late Hellenistic and early Roman periods before the place of the Therapeutae in this context is properly understood.

BIBLIOGRAPHY: F.C. Conybeare, *Philo About the Contemplative Life* (1895; repr. 1987); F. Daumas and P. Miquel, *De Vita Contemplativa* (Les Oeuvres de Philon d'Alexandrie; Paris, Éditions du Cerf, 1963); T. Engberg-Pedersen, "Philo's *De Vita Contemplativa* as a Philosopher's Dream," in: JSJ, 30 (1999), 40–64; D. Hay, "Things Philo Said and Did Not Say about the Therapeutae," in: *Society of Biblical Literature Seminar Papers*, 31 (1992), 673–83; idem, "The Veiled Thoughts of the Therapeutae," in: R.M. Berchman (ed.), *Mediators of the Divine: Horizons of Prophecy, Divination, Dreams and Theurgy in Mediterranean Antiquity* (1998), 167–84; R.S. Kraemer, "Monastic Jewish Women in Greco-Roman Egypt: Philo Judaeus on the Therapeutrides," in: *Signs*, 14 (1989), 342–70; J. Riaud, "Les Thérapeutes d'Alexandrie dans la Tradition et dans la recherche critique jusqu'aux découvertes de Qumran," in: ANRW, 2: 20: 2 (1987), 1189–1295; G.P. Richardson, "Philo and Eusebius on Monasteries and Monasticism: The Therapeutae and Kellia," in: B.H. McLean (ed.), *Origins and Method: Towards an Understanding of Judaism and Christianity: Essays in Honour of John C. Hurd* (1993), 334–59; H. Szesnat, "'Mostly Aged Virgins': Philo and the Presence of the Therapeutrides at Lake Mareotis," in: *Neotestamentica*, 32 (1998), 191–201; J.E. Taylor, *Jewish Women Philosophers of First-Century Alexandria: Philo's "Therapeutae" Reconsidered* (2003); idem, "Virgin Mothers: Philo on the Women Therapeutae," in: *Journal for the Study of the Pseudepigrapha*, 12 (2001), 37–63; idem, "The Women 'Priests' of Philo's *De Vita Contemplativa*: Reconstructing the Therapeutae," in: J. Schaberg, A. Bach, and E. Fuchs (eds.), *The Cutting Edge* (2004), 102–22; J.E. Taylor and P.R. Davies, "The So-Called Therapeutae of *De Vita Contemplativa*: Identity and Character," in: HTR, 91 (1998), 3–24.

[Joan E. Taylor (2nd ed.)]

THERESIENSTADT (Czech **Terezín**), town in the Czech Republic, which served as a ghetto between 1941 and 1945. About 150,000 Jews, mainly from Central Europe, Holland, and Denmark were deported there by the Nazis. The town, located near the point where the Eger flows into the Elbe, was built as a garrison in 1780 by Emperor Joseph II and half of its inhabitants were soldiers. The first Jew arrived there after 1848. In 1852 there were three Jewish families in the town and in 1930, 98 Jews, mostly soldiers, were recorded there. In 1941, before the town became a ghetto, it had 3,700 inhabitants, including ten Jewish families.

The first indication of the Nazi plan to establish a ghetto in Theresienstadt is to be found in a document dated Oct. 10, 1941. According to acting *Reichsprotektor* Reinhard *Heydrich, Theresienstadt would serve as a temporary transit camp for Jews of the Protectorate of Bohemia and Moravia until their final deportation to the East. At the *Wannsee Conference of January 21, 1942, Heydrich mentioned the second purpose of Theresienstadt: Jews from the Reich and the Ostmark over the age of 65, invalids of World War I, and Jews with war decorations would be concentrated there in a ghetto for the elderly (while all the other deportees were to be sent "for work" near the eastern front). The third purpose, to represent Theresienstadt as a model ghetto and show the world how humanely the Jews were treated, came to the fore after the first official proclamation of the Allies about the destruction of the Jews of Europe was published on December 17, 1942.

The Jews of the Protectorate hoped that the establishment of the ghetto in Theresienstadt would halt the deportations to Poland, which had started in October 1941, and that they would remain in their native country until the war ended. The first deportees reached Theresienstadt from Prague late in November 1941, and by the end of May 1942, one third of the Protectorate Jews (28,887) had been deported there. During the first seven months of the ghetto's existence, living conditions differed little from those in Nazi concentration camps. Families were torn apart; men and women with children were housed in separate barracks and were not allowed to meet. The hopes that the ghetto would serve as a safeguard against future deportations were soon dashed. In January 1942 the first two transports of 1,000 deportees each left Theresienstadt for Riga and from then on the threat of deportation to the East hung over the ghetto inhabitants. Conditions in the ghetto improved after the entire non-Jewish population of Terezin was evacuated and from July 1942 the inmates were at least free to move inside the ghetto walls and to meet their families after work. In June 1942 thousands of Jewish deportees from Germany and Austria began arriving. Most of them were in the special categories mentioned above. They were brought to Theresienstadt under the pretext they would be well taken care of in old age homes. The populations of the ghetto reached its height in September 1942, when 53,000 persons were crowded into its approximately 150,000 sq. yds. (114,000 sq. m., an average density of 2.9 sq. yds – 2.15 sq. m. per person). During that months 18,639 person arrived in Theresienstadt; 3,941 persons, mostly the old, died in the ghetto itself and 13,004 were deported from there to Sobibor, Treblinka, Maly Trostinec, and other extermination camps in the Lublin region. From October 1942 all transports from Theresienstadt were sent to Auschwitz-Birkenau. Deportations from the ghetto were stopped between February and September 1942. After the interlude 17,500 Theresienstadt inmates were sent in September

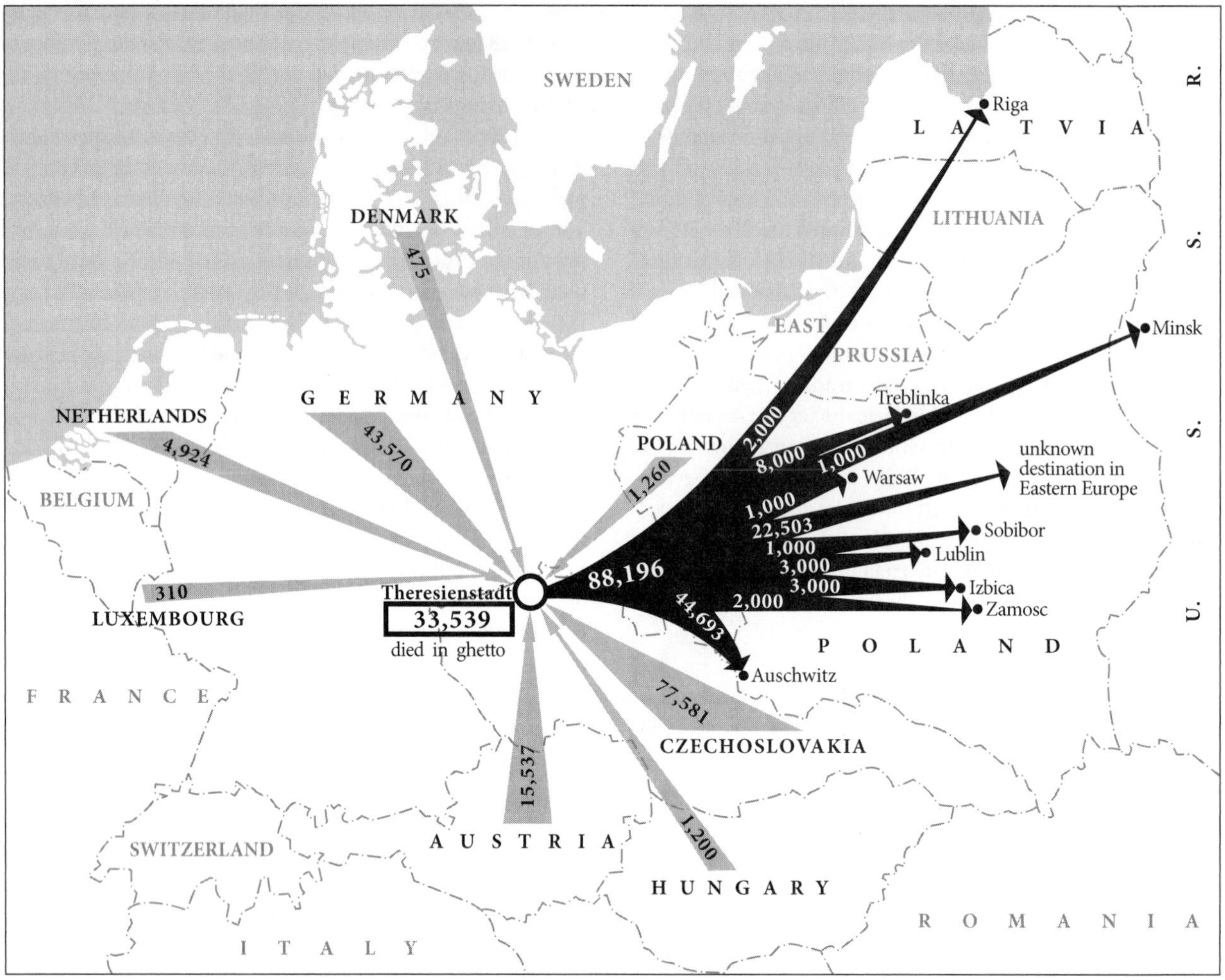

Deportations of Jews to Theresienstadt, and from it to death camps and other ghettos. Territorial boundaries are those of 1937. Main sources: Z. Lederer, Ghetto Theresienstadt, *London, 1953; H.G. Adler,* Theresienstadt 1941–1945, *1960*[2]*.*

and December 1943 and in May 1944 to the so-called "family camp" in Auschwitz-Birkenau and most of them were sent to the gas chambers in March and July 1944. In the last wave of deportations 18,412 ghetto inmates were sent to Auschwitz; only 1,496 of them survived. In Theresienstadt there remained 11,068 inmates, including 456 Danish Jews who were protected from deportation.

Most of the deported to Theresienstadt were assimilated Jews, but there were some strictly Orthodox and many partly observant Jews too. The Zionists constituted a small minority, but influenced ghetto life strongly, because some of them had come to the ghetto voluntarily with Jacob *Edelstein, the first *Judenaeltester* (elder of the Jews), an ardent Zionist, and took special care of the young and the working population as the kernel of future Jewish life.

Organization and Administration

The ghetto was administered by the SS. The first commandant appointed by Reinhard Heydrich was Siegfried Seidl (December 1941–June 1943), who was replaced on Adolf Eichmann's orders by Anton Burger (June 1943–February 1944). The last commandant was Karl Rahm (February 1944–May 1945). Seidle and Rahm were executed after the war. The ghetto was guarded by Czech gendarmes, but internal affairs were run by the *Aeltestenrat* (Council of Elders), composed of Jewish leaders. It was headed by the *Judenaelteste,* appointed by Eichmann and his superiors. Jacob Edelstein, the first elder of Jews (Dec. 4, 1941–Jan. 28, 1943), was executed in Auschwitz in June 1944; the second, Paul *Eppstein (Jan. 28, 1943–Sept. 9, 1944), was shot by the SS in September 1944; the last, Benjamin Murmelstein (Sept. 7, 1944–May 3, 1945), survived. During the third period and after the liberation, the Council was composed of representatives of five groups according to country of origin, i.e., German, Austrian, Czech, Dutch, and Danish Jews, headed by Rabbi Leo *Baeck. On May 10, 1945, Jiri Vogel was appointed head of the community by the Council and was responsible for the liquidation of the ghetto.

The various departments of the Council dealt with the organization of work, food distribution, accommodation, sanitation and public health, care of the aged and the young, and cultural activities. Its greatest achievements were in public health, education of the children, and organization of cultural life. One of the cruel duties imposed on the Council of Elders was the compilation of candidates for deportation after receiving instructions from the SS command as to the number of persons, their age groups, and country of origin to be included in the next transport.

Education and Cultural Life

One of the main concerns of the Jewish administration was the education of the young, which was carried out mainly by young instructors, members of the Zionist youth movements. Children's homes were established, inhabited by a large proportion of children between the ages of 10 and 14 where the instructors tried to shield them from the harsh realities of the ghetto as far as possible. Despite the prohibition of teaching, a school curriculum was secretly followed in the children's homes. The educational system of Theresienstadt was imbued with a spirit of dedication and optimism that the children would survive. The deportees to Theresienstadt included many musicians, painters, actors, writers, and scholars, with whose aid an intensive cultural life was gradually organized in the ghetto. This included several orchestras and theater groups, opera performances (without staging), choirs, and satirical entertainment. Series of lectures and study circles were organized, and a library of 60,000 volumes (confiscated from their deported owners) was established. The study programs, which comprised any Jewish subject, opening for the participants new dimensions in Judaism and strengthening their moral and religious life in the Theresienstadt ghetto, was conducted under difficult conditions, but was not officially restricted. A small Catholic and Protestant community of inmates also existed in the ghetto.

Concealment of Extermination

The intensive effort of the ghetto inhabitants to improve their living conditions was exploited by the Nazis for their own ends. In 1943, when information on the extermination camps began to spread in the free world, the Nazi authorities decided to show off Theresienstadt to representatives of the International Red Cross. For this purpose the external appearance of the ghetto had to be improved: overcrowding was lessened by additional deportations to Auschwitz-Birkenau; a bank, fictitious shops, a café, and a kindergarten were set up and the town underwent the *Verschoenerungsaktion*, a beautification action. The visit of the committee, whose schedule was fixed to the last detail in advance (June 23, 1944), was successful from the Nazi point of views: its three members saw only what the SS wanted them to see and the report of its head, Dr. Maurice Russell, spoke about Theresienstadt as a town like any other. After the visit, a propaganda film on the "new life of the Jews under the protection of the Reich" was filmed. After the filming was finished, most of its participants, almost all the members of the ghetto administration, and most of the ghetto children were sent to the Auschwitz gas chambers.

End of the Ghetto

In the last six months of its existence, 1,454 Jews arrived in the ghetto from Slovakia, 1,200 from Hungary, and 5,932 from the Protectorate, Germany, and Austria who were married to gentiles and had been exempted from deportations until then. The International Red Cross was able to transfer 1,200 Jews from Theresienstadt to Switzerland in February 1945 and 413 Danish deportees to Sweden in April 1945. A last shockwave hit the ghetto when in late April 1945 about 12,700 prisoners of various concentration camps in Germany were dragged by foot or loaded onto freight cars before their liberation by the Allied forces and arrived in Theresienstadt more dead than alive. From them the ghetto inmates heard for the first time the truth about the gas chambers and the extermination of their families and friends. On May 3, 1945, five days before the liberation by the Soviet army, the Nazis transferred command of the ghetto to the Red Cross representative. The last Jew left Theresienstadt on Aug. 17, 1945. After the war a national Czechoslovak cemetery and memorial was established in the Small Fortress outside Theresienstadt which had served as a Gestapo prison. Only after the Communist regime in Czechoslovakia ended in 1989 was a ghetto museum established in the town itself, in the former school which had served as a boys' home in ghetto times. The former main administrative building in the Magdeburg barracks, was renovated and now houses permanent exhibitions on the cultural life of the ghetto.

Between Nov. 24, 1941, and April 20, 1945, around 144,000 Jews were deported to Theresienstadt, of whom approximately 33,000 died in the ghetto and about 88,000 were deported to the death camps; only 4,889 of them survived. There were 18,967 inmates in the ghetto when it was liberated; 12,737 prisoners arrived there from the camps. Of the total deportees to Theresienstadt 76,036 came from Bohemia and Moravia, 43,570 from Germany, 15,537 from Austria, 4,924 from Holland, 475 from Denmark, 1,545 from Slovakia, and 1,200 from Hungary.

BIBLIOGRAPHY: Z. Lederer, *Ghetto Theresienstadt* (Eng. 1953); J. Bor, *Terezín Requiem* (Eng., 1963); Council of Jewish Communities in the Czech Lands, *Terezin* (Eng., 1965); Czechoslovakia, Ministry of Labor and Social Welfare, *Terezin-Ghetto* (Czech and Eng., 1945); Y. Rezniczenko (Ereẓ; ed.), *Theresienstadt* (Heb., 1947); H.G. Adler, *Theresienstadt 1941–1945* (Ger., 1960²), incl. bibl.; idem, *Die verheimlichte Wahrheit: Theresienstaedter Dokumente* (1958).

[Otto Dov Kulka / Ruth Bondi (2nd ed.)]

THEUDAS, a false prophet in Judea during the administration of the Roman procurator Cuspius *Fadus (44–46). Josephus describes how Theudas persuaded the masses (in Acts 5:36 it is stated that they numbered 400) to gather up their possessions and follow him to the Jordan, where at his command the river would part and provide easy passage. Fadus, however, sent a squadron of cavalry after them, and many of the impostor's followers were slain or captured. Theudas himself was caught and decapitated, and his head was sent to Jerusalem. There are certain discrepancies between the accounts of Theudas in Josephus and in Acts. Whereas the former places the incident in 45–46 C.E., the allusion to Theudas in Acts is made by *Gamaliel several years earlier. Furthermore, Acts 5:37 states that Judah the Galilean (d. 6 C.E.) appeared in Galilee after Theudas. Josephus, on the other hand, immediately after recounting the Theudas incident, describes the crucifixion of Judah's sons. It would seem that Josephus is correct (Ant., 20:97–99).

BIBLIOGRAPHY: Schuerer, Hist, 225, 373f.

[Isaiah Gafni]

THIEBERGER, FRIEDRICH (1888–1958), writer and translator. Son of the rabbi of Golčův Jenikov, Bohemia, Thieberger intended to become a rabbi himself, but instead became a teacher of modern languages in German secondary schools in Prague. Influenced by Martin *Buber's visit to Prague in 1910, Thieberger became interested in Jewish religious philosophy, on which he published numerous articles. He was active in *B'nai B'rith and edited its monthly *B'nai B'rith Monatsblaetter fuer den čechoslovakischen Staat*. In 1939, when the Germans entered Prague, Thieberger left for Jerusalem, where he became librarian of the B'nai B'rith library.

Thieberger translated Morris *Rosenfeld's poems into German (1907). His *Juedisches Fest, juedischer Brauch*, published in Germany (1936), was accepted with interest by Jews who had become aware of their Jewish heritage under Hitler's regime. His *King Solomon* was published in English (1947); and *Die Glaubensstufen des Judentums* was published in 1952. He translated Joseph *Klausner's *From Jesus to Paul* into German (1950).

BIBLIOGRAPHY: F. Weltsch, in: *Yad la-Koré*, 5 (1958), 151–2.

[Meir Lamed]

°THIEME, KARL OTTO (1902–1963), historian and theologian. Born in Leipzig, Thieme was a professor at German universities from 1927 to 1933. Believing that the Lutheran Church in Germany was more amenable to National Socialism than the Catholic Church, he converted to Catholicism. His opposition to National Socialism resulted in the loss of his professorship soon after the Nazi ascent to power. In 1935 he immigrated to Switzerland and thereafter devoted the major part of his life's work to bringing about a better understanding between Jews and Christians. He became especially active in pursuit of this ideal on his return to post-World War II Germany where, together with Gertrud Luckner, he founded the *Freiburger Rundbrief*. He also participated in many conventions and inter-denominational dialogues. Although a missionary trait toward the Jews was not entirely absent from his early work, the more he concerned himself with Jewish faith and existence, the more this point of view changed, until he became one of the few Catholics who really prepared the way for Jews and Christians to meet as equals. He played a considerable part in preparing the document of the Vatican Council which revised the attitude of the Catholic Church toward the Jews.

His principal writings on Judaism are *Kirche und Synagoge; Die ersten nachbiblischen Zeugnisse ihres Gegensatzes im Offenbarungsverstaendnis* (1945); *Dreitausend Jahre Judentum; Quellen und Darstellungen zur juedischen Geschichte* (1960). He edited *Judenfeindschaft* (1963), and Franz Rosenzweig's *Die Schrift* (1964).

BIBLIOGRAPHY: *Freiburger Rundbrief*, 53/56 (1962), 7f.; 57/60 (1963/64), 71–73; 73/76 (1968), 5–24; n.s. vol. 9:2 (2002); A. Voegtle, in: *Hochland*, 56 (1963/64), 465–8. **ADD. BIBLIOGRAPHY:** *International Biographical Dictionary of Central Europen Émigrés 1933–1945* (1999), vol. 1, 1161–12.

[Willehad Paul Eckert / Elisabeth Dessauer (2nd ed.)]

THIONVILLE, town in the department of Moselle, N.E. France. There is evidence confirming the presence of Jews in Thionville beginning in the 15th century. In 1546 the physician of the Count of Nassau-Sarrebruck was a Jew who originated from Thionville. A place known as the "cemetery of the Jews" is mentioned about 1560, but by then the Jews had disappeared from the town. After the French conquest, two Jewish families from Metz were authorized to settle in the town in 1656, in spite of the objections of the inhabitants. In 1780 there were about 20 Jewish inhabitants. Four Thionville Jews were compelled to give up their merchant licenses, which they had purchased in 1767, in spite of a famous speech by their counsel Pierre Louis de Lacretelle. There were 14 Jewish families in Thionville in 1795; 40 in 1812; 310 in 1831; 183 in 1880; 332 in 1910; and 281 in 1931. From 1909 to 1940, Thionville was the seat of the regional rabbinate. During the Nazi occupation five Jews were shot and about 30 families were deported. In 1970 the Jewish community consisted of some 450 people. The synagogue, established in 1805, has been rebuilt on several occasions, most recently in 1957, after it had been burned down by the Nazis during World War II.

BIBLIOGRAPHY: A.J. Kohn, *Zur Geschichte der Juden in Diedenhofen…* (1913); Z. Szajkowski, *Franco-Judaica* (1962), index.

[Gilbert Cahen]

THISTLES AND THORNS. Israel, being a Mediterranean and partly a desert country, is rich in prickly plants, which in various locations dominate the landscape. The thorns protect the plant from damage through grazing and in many cases prevent it from drying up, because the prickly leaves or branches limit the surface of the plant and diminish the amount of evaporation. Thorns are found on trees, shrubs, and perennial and annual plants.

Many names are used for prickly plants in Scripture. The identification of the thorns of the Bible is more difficult than that of other plants, because some of the names are general ones and others synonyms. This is especially so with those prickly plants which are mentioned in pairs, such as *koẓ* and *dardar* ("thorns and thistles," Gen. 3:18), *shamir* and *shayit* ("briers and thorns," Isa. 7:24), and *na'aẓuẓim* and *nahalolim* ("thorns and brambles," *ibid.* 19). *Koẓ* ("thorn") is a comprehensive name for plants whose leaves or stalks have prickly projections which pierce anyone touching them (Ezek. 28:24) so that they cannot be taken in the hand (II Sam. 23:6). Thorns of the wilderness (*koẓei ha-midbar*) were used for flagellation (Judg. 8:16). Thorns grow quickly in the fields and supplant the cultivated crop (Jer. 12:13), and only with great labor does the peasant succeed in eradicating them. This is the curse of Genesis 3:18–19, "Thorns also and thistles shall it bring forth to thee… In the sweat of thy face shalt thou eat bread." The industrious peasant tries to uproot the thorns by plowing before sowing his crop (Jer. 4:3), while in desolate lands they spring up in masses (Isa. 32:13; Hos. 10:8). They catch fire easily and spread the flames to the fields of grain (Ex. 22:5). Thorns were used for fuel (Isa. 33:12).

In addition to those prickly trees or shrubs on which there are separate articles (*caper, *jujube, *acacia, *burning bush), the following may be noted. The hawthorn, *Crataegus azarolus*, is a prickly tree which is widespread in Israel. It is not mentioned in the Bible, but in the Mishnah is called *uzrar* or *uzrad* (Ar. *Zaʿrūr*). Growing freely in mountainous areas, it has fruit like a small apple, and fruit trees of its family, the Rosaceae (such as the apple, pear, and quince) can be grafted onto it. The Mishnah states that the *quince belongs to the same species as the hawthorn (Kil. 1:4).

The *atad* ("bramble") is mentioned several times in the Bible. In Jotham's parable of the trees approaching the fruit trees to appoint one of them as king, only the *atad* agrees, on condition that they take refuge in its shadow (Judg. 9:14–15). The reference is to the buckthorn bush – *Lycium eopaeum* – a wild shrub which is common throughout almost the whole of Israel, and is grown by some as a fence around gardens and the threshing floor (cf. Gen. 50:10). Its small berry is eaten by birds. Its thorns are very prickly and it catches fire easily (cf. Judg. *ibid.*; Ps. 58:10). One of the prickly plants exceptionally widespread in Israel is the lowly bush *Poterium spinosum*, the biblical *sirah, sirim* ("thorns"), a name derived from the pot-like shape of the fruit (Lat. *poterium*, "pot"). It flourishes in desolate localities (Isa. 34:13) and densely covers fallow fields, especially in the mountains, in this way preventing soil erosion. It was used for firewood (Nah. 1:10) and for burning lime (cf. II Sam. 3:26). While burning it makes a crackling noise: "As the crackling of thorns under a pot, so is the laughter of the fool" (Eccles. 7:6). The Midrash (Yal. Eccles. 973) comments: "The *sirim* [which are lowly plants] when burning make a noise, as if to say: 'we too are trees.'"

Another lowly prickly bush – the *Alhagi maurorum* – which has long piercing thorns and whose tiny leaves fall off in the summer, grows freely in the vicinity of this plant. It apparently is the *naʿaẓuẓ*, of which Isaiah (55:13) prophesied that the *juniper (*berosh*) would spring up in its stead along the path of the redeemed. The word is derived from נעץ ("to pierce"). In heavy soil this shrub is found together with a lowly shrub called *Prosopis farcata*. This is a weed among summer plants which cannot be uprooted because of its deep roots. According to Saadiah Gaon this is the *nahalolim* mentioned together with the *naʿaẓuẓim* as the dwelling place of the fly and the bee to which the Egyptian and Assyrian armies coming to conquer Israel were compared (Isa. 7:18–19). Possibly the locality Nahalal in the inheritance of Zebulun was called after this shrub (Josh. 19:15, 21: 35). An exceptionally tall prickly bush that beautifies the forests of Israel in the spring with its yellow blossoms is the *Calycotome villosa*. This apparently is the *ḥarul* ("nettle") described as growing in neglected fields and vineyards (Prov. 24:31; Zeph. 2:9; Job 30:7). According to the Targum it is the *higi*, frequently mentioned in rabbinical literature, whose description fits the plant *Calycotome*. These three species as well as the *Ononis leiosperma*, which is apparently *barkanim* ("briers," Judg. 8:7), belong to the family of Leguminosae. The name *barkanim* is connected with *shabraq*, the Arabic name for this plant. It is recognizable by its pinkish blossoms and long thorns and is widespread in all districts of Israel.

All the thorns mentioned above are perennials. There are many annuals in Israel that burgeon in winter and are conspicuous in spring by their prickly leaves and large inflorescence. Most of them belong to the family of Compositae, including the *dardar* ("thistles," *Centaurea*) whose many species are common in the fields throughout Israel (cf. Gen. 3:18; Hos. 10:8). The *ḥoʾaḥ* of the Bible is apparently *Scolymus maculatus*, a tall thorn which grows in heavy soil (cf. Job 40:26). Two species which flourish in fallow fields and are recognizable by their large leaves and whitish veins are the *Silybum marianum*, which is possibly *kommosh* (*kimmosh*, "nettles," Hos. 9:6), and *Notobasis syriaca*, the most common of Israel's thorns, which is possibly the *koẓ* of the Bible when mentioned alone. The plant *Gundelia tournefortii*, the biblical *galgal*, has a unique way of scattering its seed. At the end of the summer it detaches from the ground, and its prickly leaves, resembling sails, fly in the wind and scatter the seeds. This is *galgal lifenei sufah* ("whirling before the wind"; Isa. 17:13; cf. Ps. 83:14).

BIBLIOGRAPHY: Loew, Flora, 1 (1928), 394–415: H.N. and A.L. Moldenke, *Plants of the Bible* (1952), index; J. Feliks, *Olam ha-Ẓomeʾaḥ ha-Mikraʾi* (1968²), 204–30. **ADD. BIBLIOGRAPHY:** Feliks, Ha-Ẓomeʾaḥ, 35, 50, 56.

[Jehuda Feliks]

THOMAS, MICHAEL TILSON (1944–), U.S. conductor and pianist. Thomas was born in Hollywood, his grandparents having been leading players in the New York Yiddish theater. He entered the University of Southern California in 1962, studying both music and scientific subjects. While a student, he accompanied *Heifetz, played at *Piatigorsky's master classes, acted as conducting assistant to Pierre Boulez, and conducted student orchestras. He became chief conductor of the Ojai Festival in 1968 and 1969. After Thomas won the Koussevitzky Prize (1968), his debut came unexpectedly in October 1969, with the Boston Symphony Orchestra, when William *Steinberg was taken ill, and in consequence he was appointed the orchestra's assistant conductor in 1970. Thomas was music director of the Buffalo SO (1971–79), led the New York PO Young People's Concerts on CBS Television (1971–74), and was principal guest conductor at the Los Angeles PO from 1981 to 1985. He was founder and artistic director of the Florida-based New World SO, which gave its first concert in 1988. From 1988 to 1995 Thomas was principal conductor of the LSO. During that time he established an international reputation for innovation and breadth of repertory. In 1990 Thomas and Bernstein co-founded the Pacific Music Festival in Sapporo. Five years later Thomas became music director of San Francisco SO where he performed a great deal of 20th-century music, especially of the American composers. His performance was impressive for its intelligence, emotional energy, and immediate contact with the audiences (whom he often addressed from the podium). Thomas's composition *From the Diary of Anne Frank*, for narrator and orchestra, commissioned by UNICEF, premiered in 1990.

BIBLIOGRAPHY: NG²; M.T. Thomas, *Viva Voce: Conversations with Edward Seckerson*, (1994).

[Max Loppert / Yulia Kreinin (2nd ed.)]

THOMASHEFSKY, BESSIE (1873–1962), renowned Yiddish actress and comedienne. Thomashefsky, who was born Brokhe Baumfeld in Tarashcha, Ukraine, to a Talner ḥasidic family, settled in Baltimore with her family in 1883. She was an enthusiast of English-language theater, enjoying both Shakespeare and African American singers.

Bessie was introduced to Yiddish theater by Boris *Thomashefsky, whose family troupe she joined in 1888. Although she worked briefly with Abraham *Goldfaden in Boston, she rejoined Thomashefsky and married him in Philadelphia at age 16. Bessie Thomashefsky enjoyed her first critical success in Chicago, where she and her husband lived with Jacob P. *Adler. In Chicago, she first performed with legendary comic actor Sigmund *Mogulesco, who influenced her significantly. Settling in New York in 1891, she and her husband established themselves alongside other prominent actors, performing operettas and potboilers by Lateiner [Latayner], Professor Hurwitz, and others, as well as the "literary" dramas of Jacob *Gordin.

In 1900, her husband became a partner in the People's Theater, where Bessie Thomashsky achieved considerable fame. Substituting for the ailing Mogulesco, she proved herself a great comic presence. Though popularly associated with farcical trouser roles, she was acknowledged by critics and colleagues for her dramatic acting. She also played in audacious Yiddish translations of European plays, such as Oscar Wilde's *Salome*. In 1912, she separated from Boris Thomashefsky, an inveterate womanizer. After a brief seclusion, she returned to the stage to reinvent her career, singing and wisecracking in the title role to Rakov's comic operetta *Khantshe in amerike* (Khantshe in America). Its musical score, by Joseph Rumshinsky, has been described as the first to bring American rhythm to the Yiddish stage. Her character, Khantshe, became a template for the many brassy, self-confident working-class women she would play over the next decade, such as Minke the housemaid in *Dem doktors vayber* ("The Doctor's Wives") by Leon *Kobrin. In these roles, she engaged women's suffrage, equal rights, class conflict, gender roles, and even birth control.

From 1915 to 1918, Thomashefsky managed her own theater, in direct competition with her estranged husband, and enjoyed new levels of celebrity. The daily *Warheit*, a New York Yiddish newspaper, serialized her memoirs, which offered candid comments on her marriage and on theater politics. Subsequently published as *Mayn lebns geshikhte: di laydn un freydn fun a yidisher star aktrise* (1916), this autobiography, written with A. Tenenholtz, provides an invaluable history of early Yiddish theater in America. Through the 1920s, Thomashefsky reprised her well-known roles, effectively retiring from the stage by 1930. She moved to Hollywood in retirement, where she made at least one unsuccessful attempt to enter films.

Bessie Thomashefsky was the mother of Yiddish actor Harry Thomashefsky and Hollywood writer Ted Thomas, and grandmother of conductor Michael Tilson *Thomas.

BIBLIOGRAPHY: L. Schlissel. "Thomashefsky, Bessie," in: P.E. Hyman and D.D. Moore (eds.), *Jewish Women in America* (1997), 2:1402–04; L. Kobrin. *Erinerungen fun a yidishn dramaturg* (1925), 2:165–71; "Tomashevski, Besi," in: Zalmen Zylbercweig (ed.) with Jacob Mestel, *Leksikon fun yidishn teater* (1931–1969), 2:840–45.

[Ronald Robboy (2nd ed.)]

THOMASHEFSKY, BORIS (1868–1939), U.S. actor and stage director. Thomashefsky was a pioneer of the Yiddish theater in America and one of its most active figures for nearly 50 years. The son of Pincus Thomashefsky, a Yiddish actor and playwright, he left his native Ukraine for the U.S. in 1881 and a year later sang in a New York synagogue choir. He persuaded a saloon-keeper, Frank Wolf, who was one of the synagogue's trustees, to finance the visit of a Yiddish company from London. This tour is believed to mark the beginning of professional Yiddish theater in the U.S. In 1882 Thomashefsky himself was given a singing part in the first production, Abraham *Goldfaden's *Di Kishefmakhern* ("The Witch"), and as there was a shortage of women on the Yiddish stage, he later often played feminine roles. Thomashefsky's career spanned both highbrow and popular productions. He himself wrote or arranged numerous stage pieces, produced and acted in sentimental melodramas, and revived Goldfaden's operettas. At the same time he brought to the Yiddish-speaking public (often in adaptation) plays like Shakespeare's *Hamlet* (1893), *Richard III* (1895), and Goethe's *Faust* (1902). He also introduced actors of stature, arranged for the Vilna Troupe to perform in the U.S., and staged Israel *Zangwill's *Children of the Ghetto* in Yiddish under Zangwill's supervision (1905).

A flamboyant personality, Thomashefsky liked to appear in romantic, swashbuckling parts. Almost from the start he commanded a large popular following, though critics often deplored the quality of his material, while acknowledging his genuine gifts. His first wife, the actress Bessie (Kaufman) *Thomashefsky (1873–1962), left him in 1912 and opened a rival theater; but in the same year Thomashefsky built the National

Theater in New York, where Yiddish show business flourished for another forty years. With his company he toured other American cities and several European countries. Although some of his productions were ephemeral and even tawdry, Thomashefsky had a reverence for the classics which often launched him on ventures from the world repertoire. In 1923 he made an unsuccessful attempt to establish a Yiddish theater on Broadway. Thomashefsky's autobiography, *Mayn Lebns-Geshikhte*, appeared in 1937.

BIBLIOGRAPHY: Z. Zylbercwaig, *Leksikon fun Yidishn Teater,* 2 (1934), 872–3; B. Gorin, *Geshikhte fun Yidishn Teater,* 2 (1929), 203–4; R.D.S. Lifson, *Yiddish Theater in America* (1965), 149–52, and index.

[David S. Lifson]

°**THOMSEN, PETER** (1875–1954), German Orientalist. From 1894 to 1898 he studied theology at Leipzig University. In 1903 he obtained his doctorate there for a dissertation on the Onomasticon of Eusebius. He remained on the university staff until his death. He visited Palestine in 1909 and 1912 as a member of the German Evangelical Institute.

His works include *Loca Sancta* (1907), an alphabetical list of sources; *Palestina und seine Kultur in fuenf Jahrtausenden* (1909); *Kompendium der palaestinischen Altertumskunde* (1913); a list of Roman milestones in Palestine (1917); and two works on the Greek and Latin inscriptions of Jerusalem (1920, 1941). His main work was the *Systematische Bibliographie der Palaestina-Literatur,* covering the years 1878–1938 (7 vols., 1916–60).

[Michael Avi-Yonah]

THON, ALBERT (1899–1942), Polish lawyer, author, and public worker. Born in Lemberg (Lvov), Thon was a founder of the Zionist youth movement in Austrian-ruled Galicia. After World War I, within the framework of the *American Jewish Joint Distribution Committee, he worked for the rehabilitation of Polish Jews affected by the war. He also participated in the elaboration of aid programs for emigration, such as the establishment of a bank for emigration purposes. In 1922 Thon moved to Lodz, where he became a Zionist leader and was active among the Jewish intelligentsia. With the advent of Hitler, he devoted himself to the organization of the anti-Nazi *boycott, especially in industry. In his capacity as a lawyer, he defended Jews accused of political offenses and published books on law. Arrested by the Gestapo in 1939 because of anti-Nazi activities, he escaped to Lvov in 1941, but was captured a year later and sent to a death camp.

[Moshe Landau]

THON, OSIAS (Jehoshua; 1870–1936), rabbi, early Zionist, and Polish Jewish leader. Born in Lemberg (Lvov), Thon studied philosophy and sociology and was one of George *Simmel's most brilliant students. During his student years, he joined Theodor *Herzl, whom he assisted in preparing the First Zionist Congress. In 1897 he published a philosophical study, the first of its kind, on Zionism, *Zur geschichtsphilosophischen Begruendung des Zionismus*. His Zionist views did not prevent him from being appointed in 1897 to the rabbinate of Cracow, which, like most of the Jewish communities at the time, was under the control of assimilationists. He continued to hold this post until his death. Thon's activities were initially educational and literary. He was a gifted orator, and his influence was not confined to the Jews of Cracow, but spread throughout Galicia and Poland. His literary and scientific activities were conducted in Hebrew, Yiddish, German, Polish, and English and encompassed journalistic essays and articles, as well as academic philosophy. He wrote a book on the philosophical and sociological method of Herbert Spencer (Heb., 1910).

Thon regarded himself as a faithful disciple of *Aḥad Ha-Am, despite the fact that he was not prepared to accept his exclusive concentration on cultural matters. His articles and essays from the 1890s until his death were published in many Jewish newspapers and journals. Thon played a prominent role as the president of the West Galician Zionist Federation and as a member of the Zionist General Council, as well as one of the foremost speakers at the Zionist Congresses. He also dedicated himself to Zionist work in the Diaspora in accordance with the program of the *Helsingfors Conference (1906). In the same year Thon stood as a candidate of the Jewish National Party in the town of Kolomea, East Galicia, in the elections to the Austrian parliament. Although he lost the election to his Polish opponent, Thon continued his political activities and intensified them after World War I. He represented the West Galician Jewish National Council on the Comité des Delegations Juives at the Versailles Peace Conference and shortly afterward (1919) was elected to the first Polish parliament (the Sejm). His parliamentary activities continued until 1931. His speeches in the Sejm received undivided attention and were not interrupted by the many antisemites present. In 1925 Thon, together with Leon *Reich, conducted negotiations with the Polish government and agreed that Jewish members of parliament would guarantee their support of government policy in exchange for certain domestic concessions in favor of Polish Jewry. This agreement (called **ugoda*) aroused a storm of protest in wide sections of the Jewish public, which regarded it as endangering the principle of an independent progressive Jewish policy. In the end the agreement came to nothing due to the coup that established a new regime in Poland and the reactionary and antisemitic direction of Polish policy in the 1930s.

Thon was also one of the leaders of the Hebrew language movement. He helped found the network of *Tarbut schools in Poland and officiated as its president for five years. He was also among the founders of the Institute of Jewish Studies in Warsaw, the foremost academic institution of Polish Jewry. Collections of his articles on Zionism appeared in German in 1930, including the memorable monographs on Zionism and Herzl (the latter first appeared in print in 1914 and was translated into Hebrew, Polish, Yiddish, and Hungarian in 1922). An anthology of his sermons appeared in Polish in 1938. His memoirs appeared in the anthology *Pirkei Galizyah* (edited by I. Cohen and Dov Sadan, 1957, 343–85). Bet Yehoshu'a in Israel is named after him.

BIBLIOGRAPHY: N. Hollander, *Jehoshua Thon* (Eng. 1966); I. Gruenbaum, *Penei ha-Dor*, 1 (1957), 278–94; LNYL 4 (1961) 35–37; J. Tenenbaum, *Galitsie Mayn Alte Heym*, 1 (1952), index; N.M. Gelber, *Toledot ha-Tenu'ah ha-Ẓiyyonit be-Galiẓyah*, 2 (1958), index.

[Aryeh Tartakower]

THON, YA'AKOV YOḤANAN (1880–1950), *yishuv* leader. Born in Lemberg, the younger brother of Osias *Thon, he studied law. In 1904–07 he worked together with Arthur *Ruppin in the Bureau for Jewish Statistics and Demography in Berlin. Thon settled in Ereẓ Israel in 1907 and a year later he was nominated Ruppin's deputy in the management of the Palestine Office of the Zionist Organization. From 1916 to 1920 he filled Ruppin's place during the latter's exile in Turkey. During World War I, Thon adopted a neutral stand toward the conflict and developed contacts with German and Austrian representatives in the country; he thus opposed *Nili's clandestine pro-British activities. In 1917, after the British conquest, he organized the Jewish community council in Jerusalem and became its first chairman. Two years later Thon prepared a long and detailed report on the conditions in Ereẓ Israel during the war entitled *Ereẓ Yisrael bi-Shenot ha-Milḥamah ha-Olamit*. He was a founder and afterward the first chairman of the Provisional Council (Ha-Va'ad ha-Zemanni) of the Jewish community and later of the Va'ad Le'ummi presidium (until 1930). Thon was moderate in his approach to the Mandatory government and tried to come to terms with the Arab National Movement. A founder of *Berit Shalom (from which he later resigned), he was a leader of *Ha-Po'el ha-Ẓa'ir and later joined *Mapai.

Thon's main activities were connected with the Palestine Land Development Corporation, and he was its managing director from 1921 until his death. Under his directorship, the company facilitated the purchasing of land and development and building projects throughout the country. His main works include *Die Juden in Oesterreich* (1908) and *Otto Warburg* (in *Sefer Warburg* (1908), 2–24).

His first wife, SARAH (1881–1920), was a pioneer in the establishment of the handicraft industries employing Oriental women and a leader of the Association of Women for Equal Rights. His second wife, HELENA HANNAH (1886–), was a social worker in Jerusalem and leader in the Women's League for Equal Rights.

THORN, SIR JULES (1899–1980), British industrialist. Born in Vienna, Thorn fought in the Austrian army in World War I and then settled in England about 1920. In 1928, with a modest investment, he opened a retail business in London which sold imported electric light bulbs and radio tubes. Over the next 40 years he built up Thorn Electrical Industries, which became one of Britain's largest concerns.

In 1933, Thorn began to manufacture lamps and lighting products in order to offset the high customs duty on imported varieties. Two years later he started making radio receivers and acquired several famous brands (Ferguson, HMV, Marconi, and Ultra). Concurrently he challenged the light-bulb monopoly of the 1930s and succeeded in breaking it by 1956. After World War II he acquired gigantic holdings through a series of spectacular "takeovers." He built a powerful group of companies producing electric light bulbs, radio valves, domestic appliances, kitchen installations, and catering and fire-fighting equipment. His group of companies led in supplying radio and TV sets in Britain, later controlling 50 percent of the sales of color TV and dominating the TV rental field. His acquisition of Metal Industries led, in 1967, to stricter governmental supervision of stock market deals. He was knighted in 1964. Thorn gave generously to Jewish causes such as the Haifa Technion.

ADD. BIBLIOGRAPHY: ODNB online; DBB, 5, 507–10; S.A. Pandit, *From Making to Music: The History of Thorn EMI* (1996).

[Julian Louis Meltzer]

°THRASYLLUS OF MENDES (d. 36 C.E.), mathematician, astrologer, and philosopher, author of a chronicle quoted by *Clement of Alexandria (Stromateis, 136. 3 = Jacoby, FGr H 2 B. 253), which, according to Jacoby, should perhaps be attributed instead to *Ptolemy of Mende. In it he dates the Exodus as occurring during the reign of the legendary Greek king Inachus, 345 years before the Sothiac cycle (i.e., 1676 or 1666 B.C.E.). The use of the Sothiac cycle suggests an Egyptian origin for the chronology. A similar synchronization of Moses and Inachus was made by Ptolemy of Mende, *Apion, *Justus of Tiberias, *Polybius, *Thallus, and *Varro.

[Louis Harry Feldman]

THREE WEEKS, the period between the 17th of *Tammuz and the Ninth of *Av inclusive. It is a time of mourning called in Hebrew *bein ha-meẓarim* ("between the straits," i.e., the two fasts), and commemorates the destruction of the First and Second Temples in Jerusalem.

The traditional mourning rites during these three weeks are: (1) Not to buy or wear new garments and to abstain from music and entertainment, as well as from bathing for pleasure or sport (except for immersion in a ritual bath, *mikveh*). (2) No new fruits of the season over which the *She-Heḥeyanu* blessing must be pronounced are eaten. (3) Abstention from shaving and from cutting of the hair. (4) No weddings are celebrated. (5) Some very pious Jews abstain also from the consumption of meat and from the drinking of wine, save on the Sabbath.

Generally, these rites are observed only from the first of Av onward (see *Magen Avraham* to Sh. Ar., OḤ 551:18). On the Sabbaths of the Three Weeks ("The Three Sabbaths of Affliction," *Telata de-Furanuta*), special *haftarot* are read from Jeremiah 1:1–2:3; 2:4–3:4 and Isaiah 1:1–27, in which the prophets announce the impending punishment of Israel (see *Sabbaths, Special). Evil spirits were thought to be active during this period, particularly from the first of Av to the ninth. A person is, therefore, advised not to enter into litigation and come before a non-Jewish court in this period, since the result is a matter of luck. Teachers are enjoined not to beat pupils in this period. (Sh. Ar., OḤ 551:18).

BIBLIOGRAPHY: Eisenstein, Dinim, 38–39; H. Schauss, *The Jewish Festivals* (1938), 101–4; ET, 3 (1951), 116–21.

THRONE (Heb. כֵּס, כִּסֵּה, כִּסֵּא; Dan. כָּרְסֵא; cf. Akk. *kussû*), an elevated chair symbolizing the importance and supreme authority of the person seated on it. Thrones were usually elaborate, made from the most expensive materials, and adorned with the personal symbols of the king, of the patron gods of the king, or of the land in which he ruled, or with a description of his deeds and the deeds of his forefathers. In general the throne was set up in a special hall in the palace, the throne hall, which was considered the final and most important place which a common man could reach in his lifetime. Both gods and kings are depicted on various monuments as seated on high thrones. With the widespread use of the word "throne" it became equivalent in meaning to the kingdom itself. In the story of Pharaoh and Joseph, Pharaoh emphasizes to his viceroy: "only with respect to the throne shall I be superior to you" (Gen. 41:40b). The establishment of David as king of Israel is described as the establishment of the throne of David (II Sam. 3:10), and the act of occupying the throne came to indicate the succession to the kingship (I Kings 1:46).

The God of Israel is described metaphorically as sitting upon a royal throne. That He is all-present is expressed by the figure of speech, "Heaven is My throne and earth My footstool" (Isa. 66:1a). From another point of view, however, Jerusalem is called the throne of the Lord (Jer. 3:17).

Only one throne is described in detail in the Bible: the throne of Solomon (I Kings 10:18–20; II Chron. 9:17–19). This throne is described as an elevated seat which had six steps leading up to it. It was made partly of ivory and was overlaid with gold. The throne had a backrest and arms, alongside which were statues of lions. There were also six statues of lions on either side of the steps. According to the Bible no other contemporary king had a similar throne.

Most of the royal thrones which are depicted on monuments from the Ancient Near East are elevated, have high backrests and numerous decorations, and together with their footstools constitute each a single entity.

A very elaborate throne was found in the tomb of Tutankhamen in Egypt. It is made of wood; its feet are in the shape of lions' feet, and its arms are shaped like lion heads. The back and the sides are decorated with the symbol of the king and of the kingdom (see Carter and Mace, in bibl.). The throne of the king of Tyre is depicted on his coffin (see Montet, in bibl.). This throne has a handrest decorated with sphinxes with outstretched wings. The throne of the king Barrakab of Samʿal is square and decorated and has no handrests (see von Luschan, in bibl.). An Assyrian throne is depicted on the relief of the conquest of Lachish by *Sennacherib. In this graphic description, the king sits on a high elevated throne and his feet rest on a wooden footstool. The legs of the throne and its other features are carved and ornamented with various decorations. King Darius is depicted sitting on a throne which has no arms but has an upholstered backrest.

BIBLIOGRAPHY: H. Carter and A.C. Mace, *The Tomb of Tut-Ankh-Amen*, 1 (1923), plates 2, 62, 63; P. Montet, *Byblos et l'Egypte... Atlas* (1929), plates 128–141; F. von Luschan, *Ausgrabungen in Sendschirli*, 4 (1911), plate 60.

[Ze'ev Yeivin]

THRONE OF GOD. The vision of God sitting on a throne (*kisse*) is described by several prophets, among them Micaiah (I Kings 22:19), Isaiah (Isa. 6), Ezekiel (Ezek. 1), and Daniel (Dan. 7:9). Talmudic and midrashic sources developed this theme further, and it entered into religious poetry, liturgy, and mystical *heikhalot* tracts of the early centuries C.E., which speak of the throne as the *merkavah*, or "chariot" (see *Merkabah Mysticism). Among Jewish philosophers, Saadiah and Maimonides, who objected to all anthropomorphic descriptions of God, attempted to explain the visions of the throne allegorically, in contrast to Judah Halevi who accepted a more literal interpretation of the chariot vision (*Kuzari*, 3:65) and who used the image of the throne in his religious poems.

Saadiah did not dismiss the throne vision completely, since he viewed it as part of the true tradition of the prophets, but he gave it a new meaning. In accordance with his principles of biblical interpretation, Saadiah maintained that these visions of the throne of God are not to be taken literally, just as "the sea has spoken" (Isa. 23:4) is a metaphor and should not be understood literally. Saadiah quotes an opponent who asks how it is possible "to put such constructions on an anthropomorphic expression, when the Bible itself mentions a form like that of a human being that was seen by the prophets," and when Ezekiel and Micah describe God being seated on a throne and borne by angels on top of a firmament (*Book of Beliefs and Opinions*, 2:10). In answer to this opponent, who asks Saadiah further whether the prophets did not mean what they said, Saadiah states that a form was created especially for that vision, and it was this form, and not God Himself, that was seen by the prophets. He maintains that "...the throne and the firmament, as well as its bearers, were all produced for the first time by the Creator out of fire for the purpose of assuring His prophet that it was He that had revealed His word to him.... It is a form nobler even than that of the angels, magnificent in character, resplendent with light, which is called the glory of the Lord" (*ibid.*, 2:10: see also Judah b. Barzillai al-Bargeloni, *Perush Sefer Yeẓirah*, ed. by S.Z.H. Halberstamm (1885), 20ff.). It is this form that Daniel describes (Dan. 7:9) and that the talmudic sages characterized as the *Shekhinah*. Thus according to Saadiah, the prophets did not actually see God seated on a throne but they saw either a fire created by God in the form of a throne, or lights that were created by God to give the impression of a throne.

Saadiah described the throne as being of fire rather than of some other material because fire was considered by the Neoplatonists to be the most noble and ethereal of the material substances. He specified that the fire was created, in order to indicate that nothing is coeternal with God. He also wanted to avoid the notion of the logos, i.e., of an intermediary between God and the world which is coeternal with Him. J. Dan suggests that Saadiah's created fires, intermediaries between God and the world, are not hypostases, i.e., they do not have a permanent existence (J. Dan, *Torat ha-Sod shel Ḥasidei Ashkenaz* (1968), 106ff.), and are thus different from Maimonides' ten created separate intelligences that are permanent existents.

Maimonides distinguishes between *Ma'aseh Merkavah* – the account of the chariot – and the specific visions of the throne of God. Dressing his Aristotelian philosophy in traditional terminology, he uses the mishnaic terms (Ḥag. 2:1) *Ma'aseh Bereshit* – the account of creation – and *Ma'aseh Merkavah* to refer to the science of physics and metaphysics respectively (*Guide*, introd., and introd. to pt. 3). The awe that the rabbis associated with *Ma'aseh Merkavah* is related by Maimonides to metaphysics, which he believed was above the understanding of the masses, and should therefore be hidden from them.

Whereas Saadiah considered the throne one of the created forms, Maimonides in his *Mishneh Torah* (Yad, Madda, 2:7) places the throne above them. Dividing the universe into changing substances composed of matter and form, unchanging substances composed of matter and form, and incorporeal intelligences, Maimonides identifies the angels with the incorporeal intelligences. The *ḥayyot* are the highest angelic beings and only God is above them. However, Maimonides also states that the *ḥayyot* are said to be beneath the throne, implying thereby that the throne is identical with God. In his analysis of the term throne in chapter 9 of the first part of the *Guide*, Maimonides gives the term two meanings. According to the first meaning, the throne in biblical usage refers to the sanctuary or the heavens, which are called throne because the grandeur of God manifested itself in these places, and His light and glory descended there. The biblical verse "the heaven is my throne" is interpreted by Maimonides as "the heaven indicates my existence, grandeur, and power": just as a throne indicates the greatness of the individual who is considered worthy of it, so the heavens indicate the existence and grandeur of God. According to the second interpretation, the throne is an allusion to God Himself. For example, when Moses swore "Hand upon the throne of the Lord" (Ex. 17:16), he swore by God Himself. Pointing out that the throne should not be imagined as a thing outside God's essence or as a created being, Maimonides maintains that the throne signifies God's essence. In another passage he identifies the throne with the *aravot* upon which God is said to ride. The *aravot*, according to him, are identical with the all-encompassing celestial sphere, and God's "riding" upon it is interpreted to mean that He exists beyond it and in separation from it (*Guide*, 1:70). Maimonides' interpretation of the throne in his analysis of Ezekiel's vision of the *ḥayyot* (*Guide* 3:7) is different from his interpretation in the other parts of the *Guide* and resembles that of Saadiah. He does not relate the throne to the essence of God, but places the visionary chariot on the level of the separate intelligences. Thus Ezekiel's vision, according to Maimonides, is an apprehension of the glory of God (not of God Himself), of the angels, and the separate intelligences – "the chariot and not the rider." The two meanings of throne in the *Guide* should be compared to the similar meanings of glory in the *Guide* (1:64).

[Rivka G. Horwitz]

THUNDER AND LIGHTNING. Thunder and lightning were looked on as magnificent, awesome, and ominous and hence early man connected these phenomena with the direct activity and manifestation of God. In the Bible the term *barak*, "lightning," is more widespread than the term *ra'am*, "thunder." However, both are mentioned as impressive divine phenomena. In addition, the Bible recognizes the connection between lightning and *rain (e.g., Jer. 10:13; 51:16). The phenomena of thunder, lightning, and rain are also attributed in the Ancient Near East to a single major god: Baal in Canaanite mythology, Hadad in Assyrian and Marduk in Babylonian. Each of these is depicted holding in his hand a lightning trident, as a symbol of his power and of his bestowal of the rain on which the earth depends for fertility and life for survival. The description of the theophany at Mount Sinai is associated with thunder and lightning, cloud and smoke (Ex. 19:16). In biblical poetic literature, lightning is considered to be the arrows of God, which He hurls to the earth in His anger (e.g., II Sam. 22:15; Ps. 144:6; Zech. 9:14). In the same way that lightning is the manifestation of God's power, so also thunder is one of His means of expression (Ps. 81:8).

There are realistic descriptions of lightning in biblical literature: "the lightning, lightening up the world" (Ps. 77:19). The lightning is associated in these descriptions with fire and great bright light (Ezek. 1:13; Dan. 10:6).

[Ze'ev Yeivin]

In the Talmud

Thunder and lightning are classed together in the Mishnah (together with shooting stars, earthquakes, and tempests) as manifestations of the might of God, on seeing or experiencing which one is obliged to recite the blessing "whose strength and might fill the world" (Ber. 9:2). The following varying explanations of the cause of thunder are given: "Clouds in a whirl, clouds pouring water into one another," or "the result of a powerful flash of lightning striking the clouds and breaking off hailstones," or "a blast of wind blowing across the mouth of the clouds." The passage, however, concludes that the third explanation is the most probable one, since "the lightning flashes, the clouds rumble, and then the rain falls." According to Rava, the lightning of which one has to be apprehensive (and therefore utter the prayer to avert danger) is "a single flash, blue lightning, clouds rising in the west and coming from the south, and two clouds facing one another." Thunder was instituted that man should fear God (Bet. 59a).

THURINGIA, state in Germany. Jewish merchants are recorded in Thuringia as early as the 10th century. Jewish communities, however, appeared relatively late. *Erfurt, the oldest Jewish settlement, dates from the 12th century. It became the religious and social center of Thuringian Jewry and constituted one of the largest Jewish communities in Germany in the 13th and 14th centuries. In 1287 *Rudolf I of Habsburg gave jurisdiction over Thuringian Jewry to the archbishop of Mainz. Emperor Louis of Bavaria (1314–47) transferred the jurisdiction to Landgrave Frederick II in 1330. This act, confirmed by *Charles IV (1347–78) in 1350, did not affect the majority of the Jews concentrated in the cities, who did not recognize the landgrave's authority. The southern parts of Thuringia suffered during the *Rindfleisch persecutions (1298). In 1303 Landgrave Frederick I, the Peaceful, personally led the massacre of 126 Jews in Weissensee. Frederick II, the Grave (1323–49), who was deeply in debt to Jewish moneylenders, sent letters to *Dresden, *Meissen, *Nordhausen, and *Muehlhausen during the *Black Death persecutions (1348–49) urging them to massacre the Jews and confiscate their property. The Jewish communities in Thuringia rapidly recuperated, however, and in 1368 Frederick's son extended his protection to the Jewish community. In 1391 a rabbinical assembly took place in Erfurt. That same year the Jews of Eisenach, *Gotha, Langensalza, Jena, Weimar, and Weissensee were freed for six years on the annual payment of 40 gulden from attending the ecclesiastical court of the archbishop of Mainz. In 1416 Rabbi Heller of Erfurt was nominated "Judenmeister" of Thuringian Jewry, with the power of excommunication. In this period, Isaac the Rich of Jena, a moneylender, was agent of Duke Frederick of Saxony, who bought up and annexed estates of nobles who were hopelessly in debt to Isaac.

During the Middle Ages Thuringia produced many scholars who contributed significantly to Jewish learning. Among them were Alefaden b. Isaac ha-Kohen (killed in Erfurt in 1349); Abraham ha-Kohen, rabbi in Erfurt at the end of the 14th century and author of the halakhic work *Kelalot Issur ve-Hetter* (Basle, 1599); and Israel b. Joel Susskin, author of a dirge on the martyrs of the Black Death persecution. In the mid-15th century Thuringia passed to *Saxony. The position of the Jews deteriorated through the expulsions of Jews from Arnstadt (1441), Erfurt (1458), and other cities, and through the preaching of John of *Capistrano (1452). John Frederick the Brave, a fervent supporter of the *Reformation, ordered the total expulsion of Jews in 1536, but this was not enforced finally until 1559. The order was reissued in 1556 and regularly thereafter.

The landgravate of Thuringia subsequently went through a period of disintegration and emerged divided into a large number of minor duchies and principalities, the most important of which were Saxe-Weimar-Eisenach and Saxe-Meiningen-Hildburghausen. Though Jews were prohibited from living in the cities, they were allowed in the latter half of the 17th and in the 18th centuries to settle on the estates of the nobility. In 1737 the duke of Saxe-Weimar was induced by C.F. August, an apostate rabbi and teacher at the University of Jena, to allocate the city of Doenburg for the use of Jews requesting Christian instruction. The former rabbi absconded after a successful tour to raise funds for this project. The *Leibzoll* ("body tax") was abolished in 1808, through the influence of Israel *Jacobson. In 1823 the Jews of the duchy received a charter wherein the office of *Landrabbiner* was established, general education made compulsory, and the use of German in services obligatory. The *Landrabbiner* at the time was Mendel *Hess, publisher of the pro-Reform *Der Israelit des 19 Jahrhunderts* (1840–48). The situation of the Jews of Saxe-Meiningen-Hildburghausen was typical of all the Thuringian principalities (see *Meiningen).

The various principalities granted protection to *court Jews and rich merchants while poor Jews, mostly peddlers, lived on the country estates of the nobility where they constituted between a quarter and a fifth of the population. The cities jealously guarded their privilege of not tolerating Jews. A Jewish charter in 1811 contained modern and medieval elements; the Jews became subjects of the state but citizenship was granted sparingly. In 1833 the Jews numbered 1,524 (of whom only 11 were citizens) and constituted 10 percent of the total population; their decline to 1,487 in 1905 was caused by backward conditions, as well as antisemitism, which encouraged Jewish emigration. The *Burschenschaft* (see *Students Associations) movement was founded at the University of Jena by J.F. *Fries; emancipation became law only with the North German Constitution (1869).

The Thuringian principalities were amalgamated into one state, Thuringia, after World War I. The Jewish population remained stable: 3,335 in 1895 and 3,600 (0.2 percent of the population) in 1932. Thuringia was the first German state where Nazis achieved ministerial office. Dr. Wilhelm Frick (sentenced and executed in 1946) became minister of the interior in 1930. He nominated notorious antisemites and racists to the universities and proposed anti-*Sheḥitah* laws and the dismissal of all Jews from the state bureaucracy. The principal Jewish communities of Thuringia were in *Gotha, Arnstadt, Aschenhausen, Eisenbach, Altenburg, and *Meiningen. These, and many rural Jewish settlements, were annihilated during World War II. After the war a few Jews resided again in Thuringia, East Germany, and there was a synagogue in Erfurt. In 1945 there were 227 Jews living in Thuringia. The membership of the Jewish community declined continuously. It numbered 65 in 1969; 40 in 1982; and 26 in 1990. However, owing to the immigration of Jews from the former Soviet Union, the membership increased to 180 in 1994 and 633 in 2004. Most of the members live in Erfurt.

BIBLIOGRAPHY: *Israelitische Annalen*, 3 (1841), 316–7, 324–5, 333–4, 341–2, 349–5, 357–9; L. Geiger, in: MGWJ, 48 (1904), 641–60; S. Neufeld, *Die Juden im thueringisch-saechsischen Gebiet waehrend des Mittelalters*, 2 vols. (1917–27); idem in: MGWJ, 69 (1925) 283–95; J. Jacobson, in: MGADJ, 6 (1920), 66–97; T. Oelsner, in: JSOS, 4 (1942), 253–64, 358–74; *Germania Judaica*, 1 (1963), index; 3 (1987), 2063 – 73; 2 (1968), 819–21. ANTISEMITIC LITERATURE: A. Human, *Geschichte der Juden im Herzogtum Sachsen-Meiningen-Hildburghausen* (1892); G. Buchmann, *Rudolstaedter Judengeschichte* (1939); idem, *Jenaer Judengeschichte* (1940). **ADD BIBLIOGRAPHY:** T. Bahr (ed.), *Beitraege zur Geschichte juedischen Lebens in Thueringen* (Zeitschrift des Vereins fuer Thueringische Geschichte. Beiheft, vol. 29) (1996); M. Kahl, *Denkmale juedischer Kultur in Thueringen* (Kulturgeschichtliche Reihe, vol. 2) (1997); S. Wolf, *Juden in Thueringen 1933–1945*. Biographische Daten. Vol. 1 + 2 (2000 + 2004); Litt, Stefan: *Juden in Thueringen in der Fruehen Neuzeit (1520–1650)* (Veroeffentlichungen der Historischen Kommission fuer Thueringen. Kleine Reihe, vol. 11) (2003); U. Goedde, *Spurensuche nach juedischem Leben in Thueringen* (Materialien/Thueringer Institut fuer Lehrerfortbildung, Lehrplanentwicklung und Medien, vol. 65) (2004).

[Henry Wasserman / Larissa Daemmig (2nd ed.)]

TIBBON, IBN (Tibbonids), a family of translators, philosophers, and exegetes, based in southern France ("Provence," the Midi, Occitania). JUDAH B. SAUL IBN TIBBON (c. 1120–1190), called the "father of translators," was born in Granada, but fled (most likely due to the Almohad persecutions) and resettled in Lunel, where he worked as physician and merchant. Encouraged (and perhaps supported financially) by *Meshullam b. Jacob, *Abraham b. David of Posquières, and *Asher b. Meshullam, Judah produced Hebrew translations of Bahya Ibn Paquda's *Duties of the Heart* and Solomon Ibn Gabirol's *Improvement of Moral Qualities*. He also translated Saadiah Gaon's *Book of Beliefs and Opinions*, Jonah Ibn Janah's *Book of Roots* and *Sefer ha-Rikmah*, Ibn Gabirol's *Choice of Pearls*, Judah Halevi's *Kuzari*, and possibly a logical work by the Islamic philosopher al-Farabi (his summary of Aristotle's *Posterior Analytics*). Judah's only surviving original composition is his ethical testament, a lively account of his efforts to educate his son according to his cultural and literary ideals. In this testament, he also refers to his book on grammar (no longer extant). A treatise on divine unity, entitled *Sefer Sha'ar ha-Yiḥud*, has been attributed to him.

SAMUEL B. JUDAH IBN TIBBON (c. 1165–1232) was born in Lunel, traveled to Arles, Toledo, Barcelona, and Alexandria, and lived in Marseilles (where he taught his son-in-law and most famous disciple Jacob Anatoli). Like his father, Samuel was a physician, merchant, and translator. His most important translation was the Hebrew rendering of Maimonides' *Guide of the Perplexed*. He issued a first edition in 1204 and revised version, with glossary (*Perush ha-Millot ha-Zarot*), in 1213. But he also translated other writings by Maimonides (Eight Chapters, Commentary on Avot, Letter on Resurrection, Letter to Yemen, Letter on Translation, and possibly the preface to the commentary on Mishnah Sanhedrin, Chapter Ḥelek); and he produced the first Hebrew versions of Aristotle (*Meteorology*) and Averroes ("Three Treatises on Conjunction"). Other translations attributed to him, such as 'Ali b. Ridwan's commentary on Galen's *Ars parva*, are evidently not his work.

Samuel produced original works as well. His *Commentary on Ecclesiastes* (between 1213 and 1221) was the first extensive philosophical commentary written on the book in Hebrew. He explains that Solomon wrote it in order to defend the doctrine of immortality against ancient skeptics who argued that conjunction with the active intellect is impossible. His second major book, *Ma'amar Yikkavu ha-Mayim*, is a similar work of philosophy and exegesis. It begins with a question of cosmology (why is the earth not completely covered by water), then proceeds to answer this question in light of verses from Genesis, Isaiah, Ezekiel, Job, and the Book of Psalms. In addition to these two works, Samuel also wrote a brief "Treatise on the Table and Shewbread," a "Letter on Providence," and "Annotations" to his translation of the *Guide*. He planned two additional projects that were never completed: A commentary on the internal meanings of Proverbs, and an esoteric commentary on Genesis, entitled *Ner ha-Ḥofesh* (see Prov. 20:27).

MOSES B. SAMUEL B. JUDAH IBN TIBBON (fl. 1244–1283) resided in Montpellier, but spent some years in Naples with his brother-in-law Jacob Anatoli. He was the most prolific translator in the family; he produced translations of philosophical as well as technical scientific treatises. The authors he rendered into Hebrew, from Graeco-Arabic, Arabic and Judaeo-Arabic, include the following: Euclid, Geminus, Theodosius, Themistius, Maimonides, Hunayn b. Ishaq, Abu Bakr al-Razi, Ibn al-Haytham, al-Hassar, Ibn al-Jazzar, Al-Farabi, Avicenna, Ibn al-Sid al-Batalyawsi, Averroes, Jabir Ibn Aflah, and al-Bitruji. Like his father, Moses also wrote original works of philosophy and exegesis. Best known is his commentary on Song of Songs, in which he explains the biblical book allegorically as a story about the human intellect's pursuit of conjunction with the active intellect. He wrote several additional works as well, including a commentary on select rabbinic *aggadot* (*Sefer ha-Pe'ah*), a "Letter on Providence" (responding to his father's letter), a responsum on the elements (relating to *Ma'amar Yikkavu ha-Mayim*), various explanations of passages from *Mishneh Torah*, *Book of Knowledge*, *Guide* 2:17, and Psalm 69:32, a philosophical-exegetical work entitled *Sefer ha-Teninim*, a supercommentary on Ibn Ezra, and possibly a treatise about the microcosm (*Olam Katan*) and commentary on the "work of the beginning" (*Ma'aseh be-Reshit*).

JACOB B. MAKHIR (Don Prophet Tibbon, Profatius/Prophacius Judaeus; c. 1236–1306), probably a nephew of Moses, likewise lived in Montpellier, where he had close contacts with Christian physicians in the medical school. In addition to translating Arabic and Graeco-Arabic philosophical and scientific writings (including works by Euclid, Menelaus, Autolycus, Theodosius, Qusta b. Luqa, Ibn al-Haytham, Ibn al-Saffar, Azarquel, Jabir ibn Aflah, and Averroes), he seems to have rendered into Hebrew a Latin medical treatise by his contemporary Arnold of Villanova. Jacob was also engaged in original scientific research. He wrote works of mathematics and astronomy and invented the Quadrant of Israel (*Roba Yisra'el*; *Quadrans novus*), an astronomical instrument that marked an improvement upon the astrolabe. During the communal controversy of 1303–6, he was an outspoken defender of philosophy and the philosophical culture represented by his family.

Three additional members of the Ibn Tibbon family are worthy of mention:

SAMUEL B. MOSES IBN TIBBON was involved in a lawsuit, mentioned in a responsum by Rashba, concerning the marriage of his cousin. JUDAH B. MOSES IBN TIBBON, together with Jacob b. Makhir, was a defender of philosophy during the controversy of 1303–1306. A certain ABRAHAM IBN TIBBON, otherwise unknown, is identified as the translator of Aristotle's *Oekonomika*.

Influence

It is hard to overestimate the influence of the Ibn Tibbon family. With their translations, they created a philosophical library in Hebrew and coined a technical terminology that would be used by translators and original authors throughout the middle ages. Their original works were important as well. This is especially the case with Samuel, Moses, and Jacob Anatoli, who laid the foundations for a Maimonidean tradition of philosophy and exegesis in Europe. Their imprint is found especially in Provence, in the writings of figures such as Levi b. Abraham b. Ḥayyim, Gershom b. Solomon of Arles, Menahem ha-Meiri, and David ha-Kokhavi, but they were important in Italy as well. Moses of Salerno, Zerahiah Hen, Judah Romano, and especially Immanuel of Rome, owe much to the work of their philosophical predecessors. Although some scholars in Spain opposed their work – Jacob b. Sheshet wrote a full-length refutation of *Ma'amar Yikkavu ha-Mayim* – others, such as Isaac Ibn Latif, used them extensively, and in the 14th century they were cited frequently in commentaries on the Bible and supercommentaries on Ibn Ezra. Although their importance, as original philosophers and exegetes, waned in the 15th and 16th centuries, they were still consulted and discussed. Thus Judah Abarbanel (Leone Ebreo) owned a copy of Samuel's *Commentary on Ecclesiastes*, while Judah Moscato cited it several times in *Kol Yehudah*, his commentary on Judah Halevi's *Kuzari*.

See also *Translations and Translators.

BIBLIOGRAPHY: A. Altmann, "The Ladder of Ascension," in: *Studies in Mysticism and Religion Presented to Gershon G. Scholem on his Seventieth Birthday by Pupils, Colleagues and Friends* (1967), 1–32; R. Ben-Meir, "Samuel Ibn Tibbon's Preface to the Commentary on Ecclesiastes," *Maimonidean Studies*, 4 (2000), 13–44 (Heb. section); R. Eisen, *The Book of Job in Medieval Jewish Philosophy* (2004), 79–110; R. Fontaine, "Samuel Ibn Tibbon's Translation of the Arabic Version of Aristotle's *Meteorology*," in: G. Endress and R. Kruk (eds.), *The Ancient Tradition in Christian and Islamic Hellenism* (1997), 85–100; C. Fraenkel, "From Maimonides to Samuel Ibn Tibbon: From the Dalālat al-Ḥā'irīn to the Moreh ha-Nevukhim" (Heb.; Ph.D. diss., Freie University, Berlin, 2000); idem, "The Problem of Anthropomorphism in a Hitherto Unknown Passage from Samuel Ibn Tibbon's 'Ma'amar Yiqqawu ha-Mayim' and in a Newly Discovered Letter by David ben Saul," in: JSQ, 11 (2004), 83–126; O. Fraisse, *Moses Ibn Tibbons Kommentar Zum Hohenlied Und Sein Poetologisch-Philosophisches Programm* (2004); G. Freudenthal, "Les Sciences dans les communautés juives médiévales de Provence: Leur appropriation, leur rôle," in: REJ, 152 (1993), 29–136; idem, "(Al-)Chemical Foundations for Cosmological Ideas: Ibn Sênê on the Geology of an Eternal World," in: S. Unguru (ed.), *Physics, Cosmology, and Astronomy, 1300–1700: Tension and Accommodation* (1991), 47–73; M. Halbertal, *Between Torah and Wisdom: Menahem ha-Me'iri and the Maimonidean Halakhists in Provence* (Heb., 2000); S. Heller-Wilensky, "Towards the Study of Isaac Ibn Latif's Sources," in: *Proceedings of the Fourth World Congress of Jewish Studies*, 2 (1969), 317–26 (Heb.); H. Kreisel, *Ma'aseh Nissim by R. Nissim of Marseilles* (2000); idem, *Levi b. Abraham b. Hayyim, Liwyat Hen 6:3* (2004); J. Kugel, "Some Medieval and Renaissance Ideas about Biblical Poetry," in: I. Twersky (ed.), *Studies in Medieval Jewish History and Literature* (1979), 57–81; T. Lévé, "The Establishment of the Mathematical Bookshelf of the Medieval Hebrew Scholar: Translations and Translators," in: *Science in Context*, 10 (1997), 431–51; I. Loeb, *Un Procés dans la famille des Ibn Tibbon (Marseilles, 1255–6)* (1886); A. Ravitzky, "The Thought of Rabbi Zerahyah b. Isaac b. She'altiel Hen and Maimonidean-Tibbonian Philosophy in the Thirteenth Century" (Heb., Ph.D. diss., Hebrew University, 1978); idem, "On the Sources of Immanuel of Rome's Proverbs Commentary," in: *Kiryat Sefer*, 56 (1981), 726–39 (Heb.); idem, "Samuel Ibn Tibbon and the Esoteric Character of *The Guide of the Perplexed*," in: AJSR, 6 (1981), 87–123; idem, "The Secrets of the *Guide of the Perplexed*: Between the Thirteenth and the Twentieth Centuries," in: I. Twersky (ed.), *Studies in Maimonides* (1990), 159–207; idem, "Aristotle's *Meteorology* and Maimonidean Exegesis of the Account of Creation," in: *Jerusalem Studies in Jewish Thought*, 9 (1990), 225–50 (Heb.); C. Rigo, "Judah Romano's Commentaries on the Bible: His Philosophical System as Contained in Them and His Sources in Jewish Thought and Christian Scholasticism" (Heb., Ph.D. diss., Hebrew University, 1996); J.T. Robinson, "Samuel Ibn Tibbon's *Commentary on Ecclesiastes* and the Philosopher's Prooemium," in: I. Twersky and J. Harris (eds.), *Studies in Medieval Jewish History and Literature*, vol. 3 (2000), 83–146; idem, "Samuel Ibn Tibbon's Commentary on Ecclesiastes" (Ph.D. diss., Harvard University, 2002); idem, "The First References in Hebrew to al-Biṭrūjī's *On the Principles of Astronomy*," in: *Aleph*, 3 (2003), 145–63; idem, "The Ibn Tibbon Family: A Dynasty of Translators in Medieval Provence," in: J. Harris (ed.), *Be'erot Yitzhak: Studies in Memory of Isadore Twersky* (2005), 193–224; idem, "Gershom ben Solomon's *Sha'ar ha-Shamayim*: Its Sources and Use of Sources," in: S. Harvey (ed.), *The Medieval Hebrew Encyclopedias of Science and Philosophy* (2000), 248–74; idem, "From Digression to Compilation: Samuel Ibn Tibbon and Immanuel of Rome on Genesis 1:11, 1:14, 1:20," in: *Zutot*, 4 (2005), 81–97; D. Schwartz, "Kuzari Commentators in Fifteenth-Century Provence," in: I. Twersky and J.M. Harris (eds.), *Studies in Medieval Jewish History and Literature*, vol. 3 (2000) (Heb.); idem, *The Philosophy of a Fourteenth-Century Jewish Neoplatonic Circle* (Heb., 1996); idem, *Studies in Astral Magic in Medieval Jewish Thought* (2005); J. Sermoneta, "Samuel Ibn Tibbon's Critical Remarks on Maimonides' Theory of Intellects," in: *Proceedings of the Sixth World Congress of Jewish Studies* (1977), 3:315–319 (Heb.); J. Shatzmiller, "Contacts et échanges entre savants juifs et chrétiens à Montpellier vers 1300," in: *Juifs et judaïsme de Languedoc, Cahiers de Fanjeaux*, 12 (1977), 337–44; idem, "In Search of the 'Book of Figures': Medicine and Astrology in Montpellier at the Turn of the Fourteenth Century," in: AJSR, 7–8 (1982–3), 383–407; idem, *Jews, Medicine, and Medieval Society* (1994); C. Sirat, "La Pensée philosophique de Moïse Ibn Tibbon," in: REJ, 138 (1979), 505–15; G. Stern, "The Crisis of Philosophic Allegory in Languedocian-Jewish Culture (1304–6)," in: J. Whitman (ed.), *Interpretation and Allegory: Antiquity to the Modern Period* (2000), 187–207; idem, "Philosophy in Southern France: Controversy over Philosophical Study and the Influence of Averroes upon Jewish Thought," in: D. Frank and O. Leaman (eds.), *Cambridge Companion to Medieval Jewish Philosophy* (2003), 281–303; I. Twersky, "Aspects of the Social and Cultural History of Provençal Jewry," in: *Journal of World History*, 11 (1968), 185–207 [reprinted in H.H. Ben-Sasson and S. Ettinger (eds.), *Jewish Society through the Ages* (1971), 185–207; G. Vajda, "An Analysis of the *Ma'amar Yikkavu ha-Mayim* by Samuel b. Judah Ibn Tibbon," in: JJS, 10 (1959), 137–49; idem, *Jacob b. Sheshet, Sefer Meshiv Devarim Nekhohim* (1968); M. Zonta, *La filosofia antica nel Medioevo ebraico: La traduzioni ebraiche medievali dei testi filosofici antichi* (1996). WRITINGS AND TRANS-

LATIONS BY JUDAH IBN TIBBON: *Testament*, ed. and trans. I. Abrahams, in *Hebrew Ethical Wills* (1926); *Sefer Sha'ar ha-Yihud*, in: H. Gad, *Ḥamishah Me'orot Gedolim* (1953), 159–65. Solomon Ibn Gabirol, *Choice of Pearls*, ed. with English trans. by B. Ascher (1859); Ibn Gabirol, *Improvement of the Moral Qualities*, ed. and trans. S. Wise (1902); Ibn Gabirol, *Improvement of Moral Qualities*, ed. A. Zifroni, in *Mekor Ḥayyim* (1925/6); Jonah Ibn Janah, *Sefer ha-Rikmah*, ed. M. Wilensky (1964); Jonah Ibn Janah, *Sefer ha-Shorashim*, ed. W. Bacher (1896); Bahya Ibn Pakudah, *Duties of the Heart*, ed. A. Zifroni (1927/8); Judah Halevi, *Ha-Kuzari*, ed. A. Zifroni (1924); Saadiah Gaon, *Book of Beliefs and Opinions* (1885). WRITINGS AND TRANSLATIONS BY SAMUEL IBN TIBBON: "Letter on Providence," ed. Z. Diesendruck, "Samuel and Moses Ibn Tibbon on Maimonides' Theory of Providence," in: HUCA, 11 (1936), 341–66; *Perush ha-Millot ha-Zarot*, appendix to Maimonides, *Moreh ha-Nevukhim*, ed. Y. Even-Shemuel (1987); "Annotations" on the *Guide*, ed. C. Fraenkel, "From Maimonides to Samuel Ibn Tibbon: From the Dalālat al-Ḥā'irīn to the Moreh ha-Nevukhim" (Ph.D. diss., Freie University, Berlin, 2000); Preface to the Commentary on Ecclesiastes, ed. R. Ben-Meir, "Samuel Ibn Tibbon's Preface to the Commentary on Ecclesiastes," in: *Maimonidean Studies*, 4 (2000), 13–44 (Hebrew section); Commentary on Eccl 1:1, ed. and trans. James T. Robinson, "Samuel Ibn Tibbon's *Commentary on Ecclesiastes* and the Philosopher's Prooemium," in: I. Twersky and J.M. Harris (eds.), *Studies in Medieval Jewish History and Literature*, vol. 3 (2000), 83–146; Complete Commentary on Ecclesiastes, ed. and trans. James Robinson, "Samuel Ibn Tibbon's Commentary on Ecclesiastes" (Ph.D. diss., Harvard University, 2000); Preface to the translation of Maimonides, Commentary on Avot, ed. M. Kellner, "Maimonides and Samuel Ibn Tibbon on Jeremiah 9:22–23 and Human Perfection," in: M. Beer (ed.), *Studies in Halakhah and Jewish Thought Presented to Rabbi Professor Menahem Emanuel Rackman on His Eightieth Birthday* (1994), 49–57; *Ma'amar Yikkavu ha-Mayim*, ed. M. Bisliches (1837); I. Sonne, "Maimonides' Letter to Samuel b. Tibbon according to an Unknown Text in the Archives of the Jewish Community of Veron," in: *Tarbiz*, 10 (1939), 135–54, 309–32 (Heb.); Maimonides, *Treatise on Resurrection (Maqāla fī Tehiyyat ha-Metim): The Original Arabic and Samuel Ibn Tibbon's Hebrew Translation and Glossary*, ed. J. Finkel (1939); Maimonides, *Eight Chapters*, ed. with English trans. by J. Gorfinkle (1912); Maimonides, *Commentary on the Mishnah, Abot*, ed. M. Rabinowitz (1961); Maimonides, *Moreh ha-Nevukhim*, ed. Y. Even-Shemuel (1987); *Moses Maimonides' Epistle to Yemen: The Arabic Original and the Three Hebrew Versions*, ed. A. Halkin, English trans. by B. Cohen (1952); *Otot ha-Shamayim: Samuel Ibn Tibbon's Hebrew Version of Aristotle's Meteorology*, ed. and trans. R. Fontaine (1995); Averroes and 'Abd Allah, "Three Treatises on Conjunction," ed. and trans. J. Hercz, *Drei Abhandlungen ber die Conjunction des seperaten Intellects mit dem Menschen von Averroes (Vater und Sohn), aus dem Arabischen bersetzt von Samuel Ibn Tibbon* (1869); C. Burnett and M. Zonta, "Abu Muhammad 'Abdallah Ibn Rushd (Averroes Junior), On Whether the Active Intellect Unites with the Material Intellect whilst it is Clothed with the Body: A Critical Edition of the Three Extant Medieval Versions together with an English Translation," in: *Archives d'histoire doctrinale et littéraire du moyen âge* 67 (2000), 295–335. WRITINGS AND TRANSLATIONS BY MOSES IBN TIBBON: Moses Ibn Tibbon, *Commentary on Song of Songs*, ed. L. Silbermann (1874); I. Adler, *Hebrew Writings concerning Music in Manuscripts and Printed Books from Geonic Times up to 1800* (1975), 186–90; O. Fraisse, ed. and German trans., in *Moses Moses Ibn Tibbons Kommentar Zum Hohenlied Und Sein Poetologisch-Philosophisches Programm* (2004); *Sefer ha-Teninim, Teshuvah al ha-Yesodot*, ed. and trans. Fraisse, in: *ibid.*; Z. Almog, "Critical Edition of Moses Ibn Tibbon's Olam Katan with an Essay on the History of Microcosm in Medieval Jewish Philosophy" (Ph.D. diss., Dropsie College, 1966). *Maimonides' Treatise on Logic: The Original Arabic and Three Hebrew Translations*, ed. and trans. I. Efros (1938); Maimonides, *Book of Commandments*, ed. Charles Chavel (1981); Maimonides, *Treatise on Poisons and their Antidotes*, ed. S. Muntner (1942); Maimonides, *Commentary on Hippocrates' Aphorisms*, ed. S. Muntner (1961); Maimonides, *Regimen of Health*, ed. S. Muntner (1957); Averroes, Epitome of Aristotle's *Physics* (1559); Averroes, Epitome of Aristotle's *De generatione et corruptione*, ed. S. Kurland (1958); Averroes, Epitome of Aristotle's *Parva naturalia*, ed. H. Blumberg (1954); Averroes, Middle Commentary on Aristotle's *De anima*, ed. Alfred Ivry (2003); *Al-Bitrūjī: On the Principles of Astronomy*, Arabic original with Hebrew trans. by Moses Ibn Tibbon, ed. and trans. by B.R. Goldstein, 2 vols. (1971); *The Problemata physica attributed to Aristotle: The Arabic version of Hunayn b. Ishaq and the Hebrew version of Moses Ibn Tibbon*, ed. and trans. L.S. Filius (1999); Themistius, Commentary on Aristotle's *Metaphysics*, Book Lambda, ed. S. Landauer, *Themistii in Aristotelis Metaphysicorum librum lambda paraphrases hebraice et latine, in Commentaria in Aristotelem Graeca* V/5 (1903); Ibn al-Sid al-Batalyawsī, *Book of Imaginary Circles*, ed. D. Kaufmann, *Die Spuren al-Batlajusis in der jüdischen Religions-Philosophie* (1880); G. Freudenthal, "La philosophie de la géomètrie d'Al-Fārābī. Son commentaire sur le début du 1er livre et le début du Ve livre des *Eléments* d'Euclide," in: *Jerusalem Studies in Arabic and Islam*, 11 (1988), 104–219; al-Fārābī, *Political Regime/Principles of Being* (Hebrew: *Hatḥalot ha-Nimẓa'ot*), ed. J. Filipowski, in *Sefer ha-Assif* (1849), 1–64. TRANSLATIONS BY JACOB B. MAKHIR: J. Millas-Vallicrosa, *Don Profeit Tibbon. Tractat de l'assafea d'Azarquiel* (1933); idem, *Estudios sobre Azarquiel* (1943–50); Averroes, Compendium of Aristotle's *Organon* (1559).

[James T. Robinson and Uri Melammed (2nd ed.)]

TIBERIAS (Heb. טְבֶרְיָה), city on the western shore of Lake Kinneret (the Sea of Galilee), and the largest settlement in the Jordan Valley. The name usually appears in the Jerusalem Talmud as *Tivveryah*, and in the Babylonian Talmud as *Teverya*. The city is built upon a terrace of alluvial soil, lake sediment, and layers of basalt; the last is used as building material. It lies on a broad strip of land along the shore, where the ascent to the top of the mountains is relatively easy. Tiberias is situated approximately 8½ mi. (c. 13½ km.) from the northern tip of Lake Kinneret, and approximately 6 mi. (c. 10 km.) from the southern tip. It is geographically placed to serve as a trade, administrative and cultural center for the surrounding settlements. Because of the steep slopes of the mountains, the built-up part of the city is spread over a relatively large area. The old city lies only a few feet above the level of the lake and 690 ft. (c. 210 m.) below sea level, while the newest part of the city, on the Poriyyah Ridge to the west, reach to approximately 817 ft. (249 m.) above sea level, thus lying 1513 ft. (461 m.) above the level of the lake. This results in noticeable differences in temperature, rainfall, and vegetation within the city limits.

History

Tiberias was founded by Herod *Antipas, son of Herod, king of Judea and tetrarch of Galilee, on the remains of biblical Rakkath (Josh. 19:35, where Rakkath is described as a city of Naphtali between Hammath and Chinnereth; TJ, 1: 1, 70a). The site of Rakkath is probably to be identified with Khirbat

Qunayṭira, N. of the modern city of Tiberias. The city was built between 14 and 18 C.E. It was inaugurated in 18 C.E. and it is from this date that the age of the city was counted; it was named after the then-reigning Roman emperor Tiberius. It was originally unfortified and was planned in the Hellenistic style, with a palace at the highest point overlooking the rest of the city. The new city was declared capital of Galilee, and the government offices and treasury were transferred to it; the richer classes followed. The original population was mixed (Jos., Ant., 18:36ff.), including landless people and freed slaves. Since tombs were found while clearing the area for the building of the city, it was shunned by observant Jews. At the time of the First Jewish War, Jewish fishermen comprised the majority of the population. The territory of Tiberias stretched from the Jordan northward, but its cultivable area was not large and the city relied more on fishing and industry, including glass and pottery making, mat weaving, woodwork, wool weaving, and fish raising in ponds. The city was organized on the Greek model, with a council (*boulé*) headed by an archon, whose members attended a special synagogue. Two royal officials, the hyparchos and agoranomos (market overseer), supervised the city administration; in later centuries there was also a board of strategoi.

From Antipas, Tiberias passed to Agrippa I in 39 C.E.; after his death it came under direct Roman administration. After the death of the Emperor Claudius, it was called Tiberias Claudiopolis ("City of Claudius") in his honor. In 61 C.E. Nero separated Tiberias from Galilee and gave it to Agrippa II, with whom it remained until his death. In 66 the city was split between the Zealots led by Jesus the son of Sapphias, who were opposed to Josephus, the commander in Galilee, and the well-to-do, who favored the Romans and surrendered to them in 67, when Vespasian and his army reached the city. At that time, Tiberias was already the most important city on the lake, which was sometimes called after it (John 6: 1). It had a mint which coined under Antipas (from 19/20 onward) and Claudius (in 53), and from 99 to the reign of Elagabalus, when coinage was municipal. The earlier coins show a wreath of reeds (symbol of the lake), and the later ones have images of Zeus, Tyche, Sarapis, Hygiea, and Poseidon, thus indicating the stronghold of the Romans on the city; Hygiea symbolizes its warm springs, and an anchor or galley its connection with the lake.

The character of the city changed completely in the first half of the second century, when R. Simeon b. Yoḥai purified it; soon afterward it was chosen by the Jewish patriarch and his Sanhedrin as their residence. Tiberias remained the capital of the Jews in the country until the transfer of the religious authorities to Jerusalem after the Arab conquest in the seventh century. The patriarch dominated the city, deciding in tax disputes and raising funds for the building of a wall in the late second century. The so-called Jerusalem Talmud was composed largely at Tiberias. It was the seat of the famous rabbinical academy presided over by R. Johanan and R. Simeon b. Lakish, R. Ammi and R. Assi, and their successors. Thirteen synagogues are mentioned in the sources, including those of the Babylonians and Tarsians residing there. The influence of the rabbis was so strong that the Hadrianeum (temple in honor of Hadrian) was never completed, and the statues in the public baths were destroyed by order of R. Johanan. The attempts of Comes Joseph, a Christian convert, to build a church in Tiberias under Constantine were in vain. The city revolted in 351 against Gallus Caesar; it was occupied by the Roman commander Ursicinus, but suffered no damage.

In the fifth century the Christians established a community with a bishop in Tiberias. At the beginning of that century the Patriarchate was abolished, but in 520, Mar *Zutra, the son of the exilarch of Babylonia, settled in Tiberias and became head of the academy (*Rosh ha-Perek*). *Benjamin of Tiberias was one of the heads of the Jewish uprising against the Byzantines at the time of the Persian invasion in 614. In 636 the city was taken by the Muslim Arabs, and it became the capital of the province of al-Urdunn. In the seventh century it was a center of the Masoretes, who developed a special vocalization there. The great poet Eliezer *Kallir probably lived there at the time. The Jewish community continued to exist under Arab rule, when Tiberias was a center of the tapestry and textile industry, and even under the Crusaders, 50 Jewish families survived. It was the capital of the principality of Galilee from 1100 to 1247. The medieval city, now surrounded by an 18th-century wall, extends north of the Roman town into the cemetery. It was to succor besieged Tiberias that the Crusaders ventured on the expedition which ended in disaster at Hattin in 1187. In the 12th century, Maimonides visited Tiberias and was buried there in 1206. In 1562 the city was given by the Turkish sultan Suleiman I to Don Joseph *Nasi, who tried to reestablish it as a Jewish city, but in the 17th century it fell into complete ruin. It was rebuilt in the 18th century by Sheikh Ẓāhir al-ʿAmr, ruler of Galilee. The Jewish community, which regarded Tiberias as one of the four holy cities of the Land of Israel, revived and was strengthened in 1777 by a group of Ḥasidim. Its walls were built by Ibrāhīm Pasha in 1833.

Tiberias was severely damaged by the violent earthquake of 1837, which destroyed most of the 16th-century city wall and caused the death of many inhabitants (according to one source, 1,000 Jews then lost their lives). Many of the surviving Jews fled to Jerusalem, but returned to Tiberias in the following years; in 1839 the city had 600 Jewish inhabitants. On the site of the old settlement, in addition to the inhabitants belonging to the old *yishuv*, a modern Jewish community was established, given impetus with the founding of Jewish villages in the surrounding areas in eastern Lower Galilee at the beginning of the 20th century. Tiberias served as the center of these settlements. In 1912–14, the first Jewish quarter outside the Old City confines, Shekhunat Aḥvah, was built. After World War I, the town served as a base for *Gedud ha-Avodah ("The Labor Legion"), which was then employed in road building in the vicinity. Throughout Mandate times it was the headquarters of a sub-district. In 1920 the ground was laid for the new Jewish quarter of Kiryat Shemu'el on the slope above the Old City in the northwest; the site was chosen with a view to its relatively cooler climate, and was named after the High Commissioner Sir Herbert Samuel on the occasion of his visit to Tiberias. In the same year, the Tiberias hot springs came into Jewish possession, and the city began to be developed as a modern recreation center. In 1922 the Jewish population of Tiberias was 4,427 out of a total of 6,950.

In the 1936–39 Arab riots, there were repeated Arab assaults on Jews and over 30 persons were killed, although relations between the two communities remained generally tolerable. In 1944 the Jewish population was 6,000 out of a total of 11,310. At the beginning of the War of Independence, an undeclared truce existed between local Jews and Arabs. However, it was broken in April 1948 with an attack by Arabs who anticipated the Syrian invasion of the area. Following the *Haganah's counterattack, all Arab inhabitants left in the same night, making Tiberias the first town of mixed population in the country to become all Jewish in the wake of the war; approximately 4,000 Jewish citizens remained.

In the fall of 1948, many of the Old City's dilapidated buildings were blown up as a first step toward comprehensive city planning. In 1949 a large transit camp for new immigrants (**ma'barah*) was established on the slopes above Kiryat Shemu'el, which absorbed newcomers from southeastern Europe, Yemen, Iraq, Morocco, etc., bringing the number of Tiberias' inhabitants to 16,200 in 1952. In 1960 it increased to 20,843, and in 1968 to 23,600; in the mid-1990s the population reached 35,900, rising further to 39,800 in 2002 and occupying an area of 4 sq. mi (10 sq. km.). After 1952, construction of "Upper Tiberias" (the Poriyyah quarter) centered on a large hospital previously built there, in order to provide permanent housing for the inhabitants of the *ma'barah*, which gradually shrank, to disappear in the early 1960s. Kiryat Shemu'el expanded uphill without, however, linking up with the Poriyyah quarter. Parts of the upper slopes were afforested and an avenue of trees and flower beds was laid out along the shore to the hot springs in the south. Tourism and recreation, based on the hot springs and centering on the winter months, constituted Tiberias' principal economic foundation. New hotels were constructed, mostly in Kiryat Shemu'el, but also on the shore and on the Poriyyah ridge. In the tourist slump that accompanied the al-Aqsa Intifada (see *Israel, State of: Historical Survey), the city experienced severe economic hardship. Fishing continued to be the occupation of some of Tiberias' inhabitants. Local industry was of modest size.

In Tiberias are the traditional and venerated tombs of R. *Johanan b. Zakkai, R. *Meir Ba'al ha-Nes (with two synagogues in its vicinity), R. *Akiva, R. *Ammi, and R. *Assi. *Maimonides and Isaiah *Horowitz are also buried in a Tiberias cemetery.

Excavations were carried out in the southern environs of the city between 1945 and 1956 by Bezalel Rabani and in 1973–74 by G. Foerster. Architectural remains include a colonnaded street (*cardo*), a bathhouse (referred to in talmudic sources), a market place, a large building, possibly a basilica, as well the southern fortified gateway flanked by two round towers (see *Fortifications). Rich finds in pottery, metal and glass, jewelry and coins attest to the city's prosperity until the 11th century C.E. The pottery from Foerster's excavations have been studied by D. Stacey. About 80 meters northeast of the bathhouse A. Druks uncovered in 1964 the remains of a large urban villa complex; it was re-excavated in 1993 by Y. Hirschfeld. A two-chambered mausoleum of the Roman period was uncovered by F. Vitto in 1976 in the Kiryat Shemuel neighborhood. A Roman theater that could have seated 5,000 spectators was probed by Y. Hirschfeld between 1990 and 1994 at the foot of Mount Berenice. Nearby was a rectangular building, dated to between the early third century C.E. and the middle of the Byzantine period, with an adjacent ritual bathing pool (*mikveh*). Hirschfeld has identified it as the *bet midrash* founded by Rabbi Johanan, leader of the Sanhedrin, where the Jerusalem Talmud was redacted. On the summit of Mount Berenice a church and monastery was uncovered by Hirschfeld between 1990 and 1992. The adjacent city wall was constructed during the reign of Justinian in 527–65 C.E., according to Procopius (*Buildings*, 5, 9:21). An excavation led by A. Berman in 1978–79 uncovered a sixth-century building with mosaic floors at the northern edge of the site, which has been identified as one of the 13 synagogues of Tiberias mentioned in the Talmud.

Close to the excavations of 1989 a new excavation was conducted in 1998 by Y. Hirschfeld and O. Gutfeld with the discovery of dwellings from the Abbasid-Fatimid period and a portion of a street with a drainage channel under it. Beneath one of the houses was an incredible find: one of the largest hoards of bronze vessels ever found in the Levant. This hoard included 700 objects consisting of lanterns of different types, table ware, jewelry, and other assorted items.

South of the city are the hot springs of *Hammath Tiberias where two synagogues were uncovered by M. Dothan between 1961 and 1963.

BIBLIOGRAPHY: Schuerer, Gesch, 2 (1906^4), 216ff.; D. Baldi, *Enchiridion*… (1955), nos. 336ff.; S. Klein (ed.), *Sefer ha-Yishuv* (1939), s.v.; G. Le Strange, *Palestine under the Moslems* (1890), 334ff.; M. Avi-Yonah, in: IEJ, 1 (1951), 160ff.; idem, in: *Atlas Yisrael* (1956), Maps 8/9; idem, *Map of Roman Palestine* (1936), 35; A. Kindler, *Coins of Tiberias* (1961); H.Z. Hirshberg (ed.), *Kol Ereẓ Naftali* (1967); Slousch, in: *Koveẓ ha-Ḥevrah*… 1, pt. 1 (1921), 5ff.; 1, pt. 2 (1925), 49–52; W.F. Albright, in: BASOR, 19 (1925), 10. **ADD. BIBLIOGRAPHY:** Y. Tsafrir, L. Di Segni, and J. Green, *Tabula Imperii Romani. Iudaea – Palaestina. Maps and Gazetteer.* (1994), 249–50; D. Pringle, *The Churches of the Crusader Kingdom of Jerusalem. A Corpus.* vol. 21, *L–Z (excluding Tyre)* (1998), 351–66.

[Michael Avi-Yonah, Abraham J. Brawer, and Efraim Orni / Shimon Gibson (2nd ed.)]

TIBERIUS JULIUS ALEXANDER (b. c. 14/16 C.E.), procurator of Judea. Born in Alexandria, Egypt, Tiberius was the son of the *alabarch *Alexander Lysimachus, the brother of *Philo. When a young man he entered Roman military service, thereby becoming in Jewish eyes a man who "did not continue in the religion of his forefathers" (Jos., Ant., 20:100), but there is no knowledge of any formal act of apostasy on his part. In 42 he was appointed *epistrategos* (military commander) of the Thebaid (Upper Egypt). In 46–48 he was appointed procurator of Judea. Josephus (Ant., 10:100 – 03) records only two events about his term of office: the great famine in Judea, relieved with the help of Queen *Helena; and the crucifixion of the sons of *Judah the Galilean at the order of Tiberius, which points to some national ferment at that time, although Josephus states elsewhere (Wars, 2:220) that Tiberius kept the nation at peace "by abstaining from all interference with the customs of the country." In 63 he is mentioned as a high-ranking officer on the staff of the eastern army group of Corbulo. Tiberius reached the peak of his civil service career in 66 when he was appointed by Nero as prefect of Egypt. Shortly after his appointment there was a severe clash between the Jewish and Greek populations of *Alexandria (Jos., Wars, 2:487ff.). Tiberius first tried to mediate, but when his attempt was scornfully rejected by the Jews, he ordered his soldiers to quell the rebels with the utmost rigor. The number of Jewish dead is said to have reached 50,000. In July 69, Tiberius was instrumental in acclaiming *Vespasian, then the commander of the Roman army in Judea, as emperor. Late in 69 or early in 70, Tiberius reached the climax of his military career, when he was promoted by Vespasian to be the highest-ranking officer in *Titus' army in Judea, second only to Titus himself. He is mentioned by Josephus (Wars, 6:236f.) as taking part in the council summoned by Titus to decide about the fate of the Temple, and is said to have voted not to destroy it. There is virtually no information about him after this event.

BIBLIOGRAPHY: Tcherikover, Corpus, 2 (1960), no. 418; Lepape, in: *Bulletin de la Société Archéologique d'Alexandrie*, 8:29 (1934), 331 f.; E.G. Turner, in: *Journal of Roman Studies*, 44 (1954), 54–64; V. Burr, *Tiberius Iulius Alexander* (1955); Schwartz, in: *Annuaire de l' Institut de Philologie et d'Histoire Orientales et Slaves*, 13 (1958), 591ff.; A. Stein, *Die Praefekten von Aegypten in der roemischen Kaiserzeit* (1950), 37ff.

TIBNI (Heb. תִּבְנִי, "man of shredded straw"), *Omri's rival, son of Ginath. He reigned over part of Israel for four years, from the suicide of *Zimri in the 27th year of King Asa of Judah until the accession of Omri in the 31st year of Asa of Judah (c. 873 B.C.E.). Eventually the supporters of Omri prevailed, Tibni died, and Omri's rule was unchallenged (I Kings 16:21–22).

[Mayer Irwin Gruber]

°**TIBULLUS, ALBIUS** (48?–19 B.C.E.), Roman elegiac poet. He mentions Saturn's sacred day in a list of supposed impediments to his leaving Rome (*Elegies* 1:3, 17–18, cf. Ovid). Reinach thought he meant the Sabbath. This is quite possible, for there is no evidence of restriction of movement on Saturday in Roman ritual, and *Augustine (*De consensu Evangelistarum* 1:30) also thought that some pagans confused Saturn and the Jewish God because the Sabbath falls on Saturn's day (cf. Tacitus, *Histories* 5:4).

[Jacob Petroff]

TICHO, ANNA (1894–1980), painter. Born in Brno, Moravia, Ticho began drawing at the age of 12 in Vienna where she was exposed to the 16th-century masterworks in the great museums of the city. At 18 she married her uncle Abraham Albert Ticho, an eye doctor who had immigrated to Ereẓ Israel some months before (see below), and settled with him in Jerusalem. During World War I she moved with her husband to Damascus.

Ticho's artistic style was connected to Jerusalem and its environs. During her initial years in the city Ticho was unable to draw. The harsh sunlight that dimmed the contrast between the color and the outline of the landscape was extremely different from the softly contoured scenery of her childhood years in Europe. The spectacle of indigent people, poverty, and neglected streets paralyzed her desire to paint. Only in Damascus did she return to drawing.

During the 1920s and 1930s she produced mainly pencil drawings of objects in the landscape and portraits of people, some of whom she had met in her husband's clinic. Those drawings are distinguished by their faithfulness to the subject and their accuracy of details (*The Old City of Jerusalem*, 1927, Israel Museum, Jerusalem).

In the 1940s, while most of her Jerusalem scenes were drawn in black and white, she created a series of flower paintings in watercolors. This was her first step toward abstract art, which became more prevalent for her during the 1950s when she stayed at home with her ill husband and painted in a freer style. She used larger sheets of paper than before, and the details in the views she painted spread out almost as if they became pure abstracts.

In her last years, no longer able to go out, she drew landscapes based on her personal interpretation and memory. Towards the end of her life she used new materials such as pastels with very intensive volume. Only in this period did she finally begin to exhibit her works.

Shortly before her death in 1980 Ticho was awarded the Israel Prize.

The Ticho house functioned as a hospital as well as a cultural salon for the German-Jewish immigrants of Jerusalem. Artists, politicians, authors, poets, philosophers, and others, gathered as guests of the Ticho couple. The walls of the home were decorated with her husband's Hanukkah lamps as well as with her pictures. After the Ticho couple passed away the house was dedicated to artistic activities as a part of the Israel Museum.

Her husband, ABRAHAM ALBERT TICHO (1883–1960), founded and headed an ophthalmic hospital in Jerusalem. He was born in Boskovice, Moravia, and immigrated to Palestine in 1912. Until 1918 he was head of the Jerusalem Le-maan Zion society's hospital and eye clinic where he fought an intensive campaign against the scourging disease of trachoma. In 1917 he served as an oculist in the Turkish army. From 1919 to 1921 he was head of the eye department of the Hadassah hospital in Jerusalem, and directed his own hospital and clinic for eye diseases. Part of his Ḥanukkah candelabra collection is now in the Israel Museum.

BIBLIOGRAPHY: I. Salmon, *Ticho House A Jerusalem Landmark* (1994); Anna Ticho, *Jerusalem landscapes: Drawing and Watercolours* (1971).

[Ronit Steinberg (2nd ed.)]

TIDHAR, DAVID (1897–1970), Israeli author and police officer. Born in Jaffa, Tidhar volunteered in 1918 for the Jewish Legion and was also among the defenders of Jaffa Jews during the 1921 Arab riots. He was an early member of the Haganah and joined the Palestine Police in 1922, serving as the commanding officer in the New City of Jerusalem. In 1926 he opened a private investigation bureau. Throughout the years he put his particular knowledge of Arab affairs and of the Mandatory government at the disposal of the *yishuv* institutions and of the Jewish Agency. In 1950 he turned to full-time writing and publishing.

Tidhar was the hero of the first published Hebrew detective stories in a series of 28 stories, *Balash* ("Detective"), written by Shelomo Ben-Israel (Gelfer). Tidhar's major work is *Enẓiklopedyah le-Ḥalutzei ha-Yishuv u-Vonav* (1947ff., of which 19 volumes appeared in his lifetime), a detailed *Who's Who* of Ereẓ Israel. His other writings include *Hot'im veḤata'im be-Ereẓ Yisrael* ("Criminals and Crimes in Ereẓ Israel," 1924); *Bein ha-Pattish ve-ha-Saddan* ("Between Hammer and Anvil," 1932), a collection of articles; *Be-Maddim u-ve-Lo Maddim* ("In and Out of Uniform"), memoirs of public activity from 1912 until 1937, and *Be-Sherut ha-Moledet* ("In the Service of My Country," 1960–61), containing memoirs, documents, and photographs from the period 1912–60.

[Mordechai Shalev]

TIEMPO, CÉSAR (pseudonym of **Israel Zeitlin**; 1906–1980), Argentinean poet and playwright. Born in Yekaterinoslav, Ukraine, he was only nine months old when his family immigrated to Argentina. He became one of the most famous Jewish authors of his generation and was active in literary circles and journalism and known for his struggle against antisemitism both in Argentina and abroad. As a poet, he was aligned with the left-wing literary group Boedo. He published his first volume of poetry as a hoax. Titled *Versos de una…* (1926), it purported to be the poetry of a Jewish prostitute named Clara Beter. The collection was highly praised, and it caused quite a scandal when César Tiempo revealed he was in fact the author. Subsequent volumes of poetry include *Libro para la pausa del sábado* (1930), *Sabatión argentino* (1933), *Sabadomingo* (1938), and *Sábado pleno* (1955), all marked by a deep sense of religiosity. These works constitute a poetic project by the author to critically examine the relationship between immigrant Jewish culture and homegrown Argentine culture, often questioning, criticizing, and praising different aspects of that fusion of identities.

His plays are equally defined by his social conscience. Two of his plays, *Alfarda* (1935) and *Quiero vivir* (1941), feature the return of Clara Beter. His best-known plays are the experimental *El teatro soy yo* (1935) and *Pan criollo* (1938). Tiempo also wrote 14 nonfiction works; one of the most influential was his *La campaña antisemita y el director de la Biblioteca Nacional* (1935), a forceful response to the extreme antisemitism in Argentina at the time. He also wrote a biography of the famous Argentinean actress Berta Singerman, and a number of tangos. Tiempo's major works of poetry, along with a biography and chronology of his life and a CD of the author reciting some of his most famous poems, are collected in *Buenos Aires: esquina Sábado* (1997), edited by Eliahu Toker.

[Darrell B. Lockhart (2nd ed.)]

TIENTSIN, city in Hopeh province, N. China. Before 1917 there were less than ten Jewish families in Tientsin. Refugees from Russia swelled this number until by 1939 there were between 2,000 and 2,500 Jews there, including between 50 and 100 from America and various parts of Europe. The Tientsin Jews generally engaged in commerce, though a few were physicians, teachers, or consular officials. The community had its own synagogue, a Jewish school, and four short-lived journals established between 1930 and 1939. Among them was the weekly supplement *Yevreyskaya Stranitsa* ("The Jewish Page") of the Russian daily *Nash Golos* ("Our Voice"). With the advent of Communism after World War II all Jews left Tientsin.

BIBLIOGRAPHY: H. Dicker, *Wanderers and Settlers in the Far East* (1962), index.

[Rudolf Loewenthal]

TIETZ, German family of department store owners. The development of department stores in Germany was largely the work of two brothers from Birnbaum (Miedzychod), LEONHARDT TIETZ (1849–1914) and OSKAR TIETZ (1858–1923). Each built his own merchandising organization but on the same principle of low but fixed prices, made possible through the direct purchase from manufacturers of a great volume of goods. In 1882, Oskar Tietz, together with an uncle, HERMANN TIETZ (1837–1907), opened a dry goods store in Gera, Thuringia. Hermann soon withdrew from the partnership. The store gradually added other lines and subsequently opened branches in Weimar and Berlin. To defend department stores against discriminatory taxation and attacks, Oskar Tietz became a founder of the Verein Deutscher Waren und Kaufhaeuser, and remained its president until his death. He was succeeded in his business by his sons Georg (1889–1953) and Martin (born c. 1895), and his son-in-law Hugo Zwillenberg, who added the five-store Jahndorf chain and the well-known Kaufhaus des Westens in Berlin to their 13 stores. In 1934 they were forced to relinquish ownership of the group, whose name was changed to Hertie. Leonhardt Tietz started his first small dry goods store in the northwest German town of Stralsund in 1879. Ten years later he opened a branch in Elberfeld, in the economically important Ruhr area. Still carrying mostly textiles, this store developed into one of the largest German department stores with branches in various parts of the country, including Cologne, which became the firm's headquarters. The firm was incorporated in 1905 and in 1909 was the first department store chain to become a public company. At the beginning of the century, operations were extended to Belgium, where the firm of Leonhardt Tietz S.A. remained in the founder's hands until 1918, when it was seized as enemy property. A connection with the De Bijenkorf department store in Amsterdam was retained. Leonhardt was followed as president of the corporation by his son, ALFRED TIETZ. A new era of expansion began in the 1920s, and by 1929 there were 43 stores with 15,000 employees. In 1925 a chain of variety stores called Ehape was started, the first German enterprise of its kind. With the advent of the Nazis in 1933, the members of the family were forced out of control and the organization was renamed West-Deutscher Kaufhof.

BIBLIOGRAPHY: G. Tietz, *Hermann Tietz, Geschichte einer Familie und ihrer Warenhaeuser* (1965); K. Zielenziger, *Juden in der deutschen Wirtschaft* (1930), 208–20; J. Hirsch, *Das Warenhaus in Westdeutschland* (1910); *50 Jahre Leonhardt Tietz* (1929).

[Edith Hirsch]

TIFLIS (Georgian **Tbilisi**), capital city of Georgia. Members of the Georgian Jewish community have lived in Tiflis for many generations. During the 19th century Jews from Russia began to settle there. They were mostly craftsmen and descendants of soldiers who had served in the Caucasus in the Russian army. There was also a small community of Jews of Persian origin. The Georgian Jews maintained their own community which was headed by a *ḥakham*. The attitude of the local Russian authorities to the Jews was favorable because of their usefulness as craftsmen. In 1876 there were 1,276 Jews in Tiflis, increasing to 3,668 (about 2.5% of the population) in 1897. During the early 1920s Tiflis was a transit station for *ḥalutzim* from Russia on their way to Palestine. In the 1959 census 17,311 Jews (2.5%) were registered in Tiflis, of whom 9,328 declared Georgian and 7,600 Russian to be their mother tongue. The Georgian Jews preserved their particular Jewish way of life, many adhering to religious tradition. There were two synagogues, a larger one for the Georgian Jews and a smaller one for the Ashkenazi Jews. The Tiflis Jewish community was regarded as the wealthiest in the Soviet Union. It employed 17 community workers for the synagogue, the *mikveh*, *mazzah* bakery, ritual slaughtering, and cemetery services. About ten students in the Moscow yeshivah (1956–62) came from Tiflis of whom only two or three finished their studies and were appointed as *shoḥatim*. Many Jews in Tiflis applied for exit permits to Israel in the framework of the reunion of families, particularly after 1968. By the early 21st century most of Georgia's remaining 5,000 Jews were living in the city.

Jewish activities in Tiflis are vigorous, and an infrastructure has been established to preserve and develop the heritage of the Georgian Jews. The rabbi and the other heads of the Jewish community participate in all state activities and events, as well as in social events intended to foster a stronger connection between the Georgians and the Jews. There is a synagogue, a Jewish community center, a yeshivah, kindergarten, Sunday school, a women's center, and a youth center.

[Yehuda Slutsky / Ruth Beloff (2nd ed)]

TIGAY, JEFFREY H(OWARD) (1941–), U.S. Bible and ancient Middle East scholar. Born in Detroit, educated at Columbia University (B.A. 1963), the Jewish Theological Seminary of America (M.H.L., rabbinical ordination 1966), and Yale (Ph.D. 1971), Tigay taught from 1971 at the University of Pennsylvania, where he was the Ellis Professor of Hebrew and Semitic Languages and Literatures and graduate chair of the Department of Near Eastern Languages and Literatures. He was the chairman of the Jewish Studies Program (1995–98) and a visiting professor at the Jewish Theological Seminary. He was a scholar in residence of the Jewish Publication Society and a fellow of the Institute for Advanced Studies of the Hebrew University, Jerusalem, and the Center for Judaic Studies at the University of Pennsylvania.

Tigay is widely recognized as a leading Bible scholar and historian. His work on the Gilgamesh epic has been described as "groundbreaking," and his critical, historically informed line-by-line commentary on Deuteronomy, probably his best-known work, is erudite and comprehensive. Tigay believes that the book was written by conservative religious elements to oppose tendencies toward assimilation promoted by the upper classes in the eighth–seventh centuries B.C.E.; his discussion considers linguistic development, literary sources, the evolution of ideas, comparative legal codes, previous commentaries, and much else. Tigay has also been recognized as an outstanding teacher.

Tigay's principal publications are *The Evolution of the Gilgamesh Epic* (1982), *Empirical Models for Biblical Criticism* (principal author and editor, 1985), *You Shall Have No Other Gods: Israelite Religion in the Light of Hebrew Inscriptions* (1986), and *The JPS Torah Commentary: Deuteronomy* (1996). He also co-edited Judah Goldin's *Studies in Midrash and Related Literature* (with Barry L. Eichler, 1988) and *Tehilla le-Moshe: Biblical and Judaic Studies in Honor of Moshe Greenberg* (with M. Cogan and B.L. Eichler, 1997). Tigay is the author of the commentary on Exodus in the Oxford *Jewish Study Bible* (2003) and has published numerous scholarly articles, contributions to symposia and reference works, and reviews. Among his many essays is a 1999 debunking of the recent craze for *Bible Codes as a modern form of bibliomancy.

[Drew Silver (2nd ed.)]

TIGERMAN, STANLEY (1930–), U.S. architect. Born in Chicago, Tigerman studied at MIT, and by his own admission "flunked out." From 1950 to 1954, Tigerman served in the U.S. Navy. After his return to civilian life in 1954, he worked for a number of architectural firms. He returned to study architecture at Yale University and graduated with a master's degree in 1961. His first venture on his own was a small firm in Chicago, Tigerman, Rudolph and Young. In 1962 he established a partnership with Norman Koglin, which lasted two years. After 1964 he was the principal of Stanley Tigerman and Associates Ltd., in Chicago and by 2004 was a principal in the Chicago architectural firm of Tigerman McCurry. He has also taught at several universities in the United States.

Tigerman is best known as founding member of the "Chicago Seven" group of architects who challenged the teachings of Ludwig Mies van der Rohe. Tigerman spoke out about the arrogance and prejudices of the American architectural leaders, especially the American Academy in Rome, which resisted having women members for its first 70 years, as well as no Catholics, Jews or people of color as members.

Tigerman was first recognized for his skill with line and later with organic shapes. From the beginning, he was concerned with the social and political aspects of architecture. The housing project Woodlawn Gardens was sensitive to the issue of density and political empowerment of racial minorities who were the presumed tenants of the complex. Tigerman's firm became known for having a large number of people of color on the permanent professional staff. One of his latest commissions was the Illinois Holocaust Museum and Educational Center in Skokie, the home of many Holocaust survivors in the second half of the 20th century. Tigerman also served on the jury for the Jewish Heritage Community Center to be built near Babi-Yar, a Holocaust killing site in Kiev.

He is the author of several books, including *Architecture of Exile, The Chicago Tribune Tower Competition and Late Entries; Versus: An American Architect's Alternatives; Stanley Tigerman: Buildings and Projects 1966–1989*; and *The California Condition: A Pregnant Architecture.*

Tigerman was chosen to represent the United States at the 1976 and 1980 Venice Biennales and was part of the "New Chicago Architecture" exhibition at the Museo di Castelvecchio in Verona. He received Yale University's first Alumni Arts Award in 1985. In 1976 he was both chairman of the AIA Committee on Design and coordinator of the exhibition and book entitled Chicago Architects. In 1989 he was awarded the Dean of Architecture Award, and in 1992 he received the Illinois Academy of Fine Arts Award. In 1996 he received the American Jewish Committee's Cultural Achievement Award. The International Union of Bricklayers and Allied Craftworkers honored Mr. Tigerman with the Louis Sullivan Award in September 2000. In 1990, his work was exhibited at the Art Institute of Chicago.

In 1994, Tigerman and his wife, Eva Maddox, established Archeworks – the multidisciplinary design school in Chicago. Its aim is to bring a social consciousness to the realm of architecture and design.

BIBLIOGRAPHY: C. Jencks, *The New Paradigm in Architecture* (2002); M. Emmanuel, *Contemporary Architects* (1980); R.A.M. Stern, *Modern Classicism* (1988).

[Stephen C. Feinstein (2nd ed.)]

°**TIGLATH-PILESER II (Tukulti-apil-Esharra** ("My trust is [in] the son of [the Temple] Esharra")) the Third; reigned 745–727 B.C.E.), founder of the Assyrian Empire, which profoundly affected the history of the ancient Near East and in particular the fate of Israel. He is mentioned six times in the Bible (II Kings 15:29; 16:7, 10; I Chronicles 5:6, 26; II Chronicles 28:20), the latter book spelling his name Tillegath-pilneser. He is also mentioned by the name Pul (II Kings 15:19; I Chronicles 5:26), which he assumed upon becoming king of Babylonia in 729 B.C.E.

The Assyrian sources from this period present many difficulties. In 1845, H.A. Layard discovered Tiglath-Pileser's annals in the excavations at Tell Nimrud, ancient Calah (cf. Genesis 10:11), which was the first capital of the Empire. The inscribed stone slabs had already been removed from their original site by *Esarhaddon (680–669 B.C.E.) for reuse in his own palace. Furthermore, since Assyriology was not yet a science, 20 years were to pass before George *Smith was to decipher these inscriptions from Layard's handwritten copies and squeezes and from the few actual inscriptions taken back to the British Museum, the original inscriptions for the most part having been lost. This material has been supplemented by more recently discovered administrative letters and annal fragments found at Calah and at other sites.

In addition to the annals, the Eponym Chronicle for Tiglath-Pileser's reign provides an almost complete framework for reconstructing the king's military activity:

745 – On the 13th of Iyar Tiglath-Pileser sat upon his throne. In Tishri he campaigned against the Land of the Two Rivers

744 – Against Mamri
743 – Defeat of Ararat in the land of Arpad
742 – Against Arpad
741 – Against Arpad. Conquered after three years
740 – Against Arpad
739 – Against the land of Ulluba. The fortress established
738 – Calneh taken
737 – Against the Medes
736 – To the foot of Mount Nal
735 – Against Ararat
734 – Against Philistia (Pilishta)
733 – Against Damascus (Dimashqa)
732 – Against Damascus
731 – Against Sapiya
730 – The king remained at home
729 – The king took the hands of Bel
728 – The king took the hands of Bel
727 – Against the city [....]

Tiglath-Pileser, though probably descended from a collateral royal line, usurped the throne and thereby ended a long period of Assyrian military and economic weakness. During his period, most of *Syria and the Land of Israel had come under the direct influence of *Hazael and his son Ben-Hadad *III of Damascus and later under the northern Israelite kings *Jehoash and *Jeroboam II and finally *Uzziah of Judah. During the latter period, the kingdom of Urartu (*Ararat) challenged Assyrian hegemony by extending its political influence into Syria, forcing Mati'-ilu of Arpad and with him various states of "upper and lower Aram" into vassalage.

Tiglath-Pileser's earlier campaigns were therefore directed against Ararat. After reducing this enemy, he was faced with a new coalition of Syrian states which he subsequently defeated at *Calneh in 738 B.C.E. (cf. Isaiah 10:9). Of importance is the fact that the leader of this league was "Azariyau of Yaudi," who is to be identified with the prominent military and political figure of the day – King Uzziah (Azariah) of Judah. This piece of information sheds light on Uzziah's sphere of influence and military might, documented so far only in the Bible (II Chronicles 26:6 ff).

Furthermore, the mention of Minihummu the Samarian, bringing tribute at this time, provides a synchronism between the biblical account (II Kings 15:19–20) which should be dated to Menahem's ninth year and the Battle of Calneh.

Tiglath-Pileser returned again to the western front between 734 and 732 B.C.E., where he either annexed or reduced to vassalage all the small kingdoms of Syria, Philistia, and *Transjordan. The background of this offensive must be found in a new coalition of these minor kingdoms. The leaders of the resistance were now *Rezin of Damascus and *Pekah the son of Remaliah who had deposed the pro-Assyrian *Pekahiah the son of Menahem (II Kings 15:25). They were joined by Philistine and Edomite allies (see II Kings 16:6; II Chronicles 28:17–18). *Ahaz's refusal to join this alliance precipitated the Syro-Ephramite invasion of Judah and the attempt to place the otherwise unknown Ben *Tabeel on the throne (Isaiah 7:5–6; II Chronicles 28:5 ff.). The latter may have been a Davidic prince of a Transjordanian mother.

While the biblical text suggests that Ahaz initiated Assyrian intervention (II Kings 16:7), the episode must be viewed in the larger context of Tiglath-Pileser's expansionist policy in the west. His strategy was to isolate Rezin by first attacking the Philistine cities. The strategy was the more appropriate since the Phoenician coast, the province of Hamath, and the Judean kingdom already encircled the anti-Assyrian forces. After a two-year campaign *Damascus was taken in 732 B.C.E.

Judging from the contemporary inscription of Barrakab of Sam'al in memory of his father Penamu II, Tiglath-Pileser's vassals were obliged to take part in the siege of Damascus. This might explain Ahaz's presence there as well (II Kings 16:10). Certainly, by this time, Ahaz had accepted Tiglath-Pileser as his suzerain, as suggested already by the treaty terminology found in II Kings 16:7.

The most far-reaching achievements of Tiglath-Pileser were the administrative innovations which became the hallmark of the Assyrian Empire. He reorganized the provincial administration, introduced a more complex tax system, and secured the international lines of trade and communication. The most consequential innovation was the reintroduction of a more efficient method of deportation. This served the dual purpose of removing groups of dissidents from their homeland and also exploiting them for the welfare of the Empire. These exiles were employed in the bureaucracy or army or resettled on farmland in depopulated or border areas.

Tiglath-Pileser was the first who deported large segments of the northern tribes in 732 B.C.E. The Bible specifically mentions that the tribes of *Reuben, *Gad and half of *Manasseh were removed to northwestern Mesopotamia (I Chronicles 5:6,26), which had been depopulated by Ashurnasirpal II (883–859 B.C.E.). Moreover, the Book of Kings gives a more detailed list of his activities in the Galilee. "In the days of Pekah king of Israel, came Tiglath-Pileser king of Assyria, and took Ijon and Abel-beth-maacah, and Janoah, and Kedesh, and Hazor, and Gilead and Galilee, all the land of Naphtali, and he carried them captive to Assyria" (15:29). This list is supplemented by the annals which name among other northern cities Hannattion, Akbara, and Yodefat, probably following the main arteries to the Mediterranean coast.

The recorded number of exiles taken from each site is important, since it provides the first evidence of the population density in this area of Israel.

It was Tiglath-Pileser's success in military and administrative matters that laid the groundwork for the pattern of government that characterized the Assyrian, Neo-Babylonian, and Persian empires over the next 400 years.

BIBLIOGRAPHY: W.F. Albright, in: BASOR, 140 (1955), 34f.; R.D. Barnett and M. Falkner, *The Sculptures of Tiglath Pileser III from the Central and South West Palaces at Nimrud* (1962); S. Loewenstamm, in: *Leshonenu* (1970), 148; B. Oded, in: *Ereẓ Israel*, 10 (1971), 191–7; H. Tadmor, in: PIASH (1967); idem, in; *Scripta Hierosolymitana*, 8 (1961), 252–8; idem, in: *Kol Ereẓ Naphtali* (1967), 62–67 (Heb.).

[Aaron Demsky]

TIGRID, PAVEL (P. Schönfeld; 1917–2003), Czech author, publicist, essayist, politician. Born in Prague, Tigrid started publishing in the *Studentský časopis* ("Students' Review"); his studies at the Faculty of Law were interrupted by the Nazi occupation. His family perished in the Holocaust. He lived in exile in London 1939–45, where he worked for the BBC and for the Czechoslovak government-in-exile. He returned to Prague in 1945. He founded the weekly *Obzory* ("Horizons") with I. Ducháček, editor-in-chief of the journal *Vývoj* ("Progress"). After 1948, Tigrid's second exile was spent in Munich, where he worked for Radio Free Europe; the U.S., where he studied at Columbia University; and Paris from 1960. In 1956 he founded the exile quarterly *Svědectví* ("Testimony"), the main political and cultural review of the Czechoslovak exile. After 1989 he returned to Czechoslovakia and became an adviser to President Václav Havel (1991–92) and minister of culture of the Czech Republic (1994–96). He was also active in Czech-German relations (1998–2000) and was a holder of the T.G. Masaryk Order. For almost five decades, Tigrid provided commentaries on the political and cultural situation in Czechoslovakia as well as analyzing and influencing it from exile or at home.

He published numerous articles and commentaries in the press, on radio and TV, and wrote a considerable number of books, such as *Ozbrojený mír* ("An Armed Peace," 1948); *Marx na Hradčanech* ("Marx at the Castle," 1960, 2001); *Politická emigrace v atomovém věku* ("A Political Emigration in the Era of the Atom," 1968, 1974, 1990); *Le Printemps de Prague* (1968); *La chute irrésistible d' Alexander Dubcek* (1969); *Amère révolution* (1977); *Dnešek je váš, zítřek je náš. Dělnické revolty v komunistických zemích* (1982, 1990; French, *Révoltes ouvrières à l'est 1953–1981*); and *Kapesní průvodce inteligentní ženy po vlastním osudu* ("A Pocket Guide of a Cultured Woman to Her Own Fate," 1988, 1990). A legend of the anti-Communist struggle, Tigrid died in France and was buried there in the presence of Václav Havel, former president of Czechoslovakia and the Czech Republic.

BIBLIOGRAPHY: *Slovník českých spisovatelů* (1982); *Slovník českých spisovatelů* (2000).

[Milos Pojar (2nd ed.)]

TIGRIS (Heb. חִדֶּקֶל; from Old Persian, **Tigra**; Sumerian **Idigna**; Akk. **Idiglat**; Aramaic **Diglat**; Ar. **Dijla**), a major river of S.W. Asia (c. 1,150 mi. (1,850 km.) long). The Tigris is mentioned twice in the Bible, once in Genesis 2:14, as one of the four rivers flowing out of the Garden of Eden: "and the name of the third river is Tigris, which flows east of Ashur"; and a second time in Daniel 10:4, as the scene of Daniel's major vision. In the Targum and the Talmud the Tigris is referred to as Diglat, the earlier form of the name, and Neubauer regards the name Ḥiddekel as compounded of *ḥad* and *Dekel*, i.e., "the swiftly flowing Diklah." Homiletically R. Ashi interprets it in the Talmud as compounded of *ḥad* and *kal*, "sharp and quick." The waters of the Tigris were regarded as healthy both for body and mind (Pes. 59a). Since it is mentioned with regard to creation, it was enjoined that on seeing it one had to recite the blessing "who hath made the work of creation" (Yev. 121a). The Tigris formed the boundary of Babylonia in talmudic times from Baghdad to Apamea (Kid. 71b).

TIKKUN, a Bimonthly Jewish Critique of Politics, Culture, and Society, emerged in the late 20th century as the U.S. leading Jewish leftist magazine. Under the editorial stewardship of Rabbi Michael Lerner, *Tikkun* magazine serves as the literary centerpiece of a larger movement for Jewish social activism and Judaic spiritual renewal. Fashioned as "the voice of Jewish liberals and progressives" and as "the alternative to *Commentary* magazine and the voices of Jewish conservatism," it has published continuously since 1986. After its launching in the San Francisco Bay area, *Tikkun* moved to New York City for a brief stint before returning to its northern California roots.

The magazine adopted the Hebrew word *tikkun* for its masthead, incorporating the Jewish mystical mandate to heal or repair the world. Based upon a kabbalistic notion that viewed the world as a broken vessel, the mandate for *tikkun olam* (repairing the world) obligates every person to fix the world around them. For Lerner, that ethic demanded a magazine steeped in the social protest movements of the 1960s, committed to progressive Jewish political activism, and anchored by the overarching need for greater spirituality in human life.

Tikkun traced its political lineage back to the civil rights movement, the peace movement, feminism, environmentalism, and the labor movement. Yet, the magazine's editorial staff remained concerned about what it perceived as a lack of attention to the spiritual dimension of worldly repair. Positioning itself as an alternative to "society's ethos of selfishness, materialism, and cynicism," *Tikkun* hoped to create a social protest movement "founded on and giving central focus to a spiritual vision." To that end, the magazine features regular contributions in the fields of poetry, literature, and the arts.

In the political world, *Tikkun* has focused much of its attention on the conflict between Israel and the Palestinians. An advocate for a two-state solution, *Tikkun* demanded that the Israeli government end its occupation of the West Bank and Gaza Strip and return to pre-1967 borders. It has also called upon the Palestinians to renounce terror and help build trust with the Israelis. *Tikkun*'s editorials on the Mid-East conflict have positioned the magazine within the awkward and often conflicted left. In an era when some on the left embrace anti-Zionism and sometimes antisemitism, *Tikkun* seeks to define a Jewish and Zionist leftism that will "stand in favor of the rights of Palestinians" just as it will critique "the anti-religious and anti-spiritual biases of the secular Left." The magazine has sought to define a form of left-wing Zionism that envisions co-existence within a two-state solution. For its public condemnations of right-wing Israeli government policies and decisions, *Tikkun* has often been the object of Jewish communal scorn. For its public embrace of Zionism as a legitimate form of Jewish expression, it has often faced rejection from anti-Zionist and non-Zionist American leftist groups.

Much of *Tikkun*'s spiritual activism has been focused on the "Tikkun Community," an interfaith organization (which welcomes, as well, atheists and agnostics) launched by the magazine to foster spiritual consciousness in its larger movement for social change. It recognizes as its central tenet that "the sources of external injustice, suffering, and ecological numbness are to be found not only in economic and political arrangements, but also in our alienation from one another, [and] in our inability to experience and recognize ourselves and each other as holy." With support from intellectuals such as Dartmouth University professor Susanna Heschel and Princeton University professor Cornel West, the *Tikkun* community launched regional conferences and organized college students around the country. *Tikkun* has sought to achieve its political and spiritual reform goals by advancing a post-denominational approach to American Jewish life and politics, and has succeeded in attracting progressive Jewish voices from the Orthodox, Conservative, Reform, Reconstructionist, and Renewal movements in its pages and on its editorial board.

BIBLIOGRAPHY: M. Lerner, *Healing Israel/Palestine: A Path to Peace and Reconciliation* (2003); idem, *Socialism of Fools Anti-Semitism* (1992); idem, *Spirit Matters* (2002); idem, *Tikkun: To Heal, Repair, and Transform the World: An Anthology* (1992).

[Marc Dollinger (2nd ed.)]

TIKKUN ḤAZOT (Heb. תִּקּוּן חֲצוֹת; lit. "institution of midnight [prayer]"), prayers recited at midnight in memory of the destruction of the Temple and for the restoration to the Land of Israel. This custom developed from the rabbinic description of God mourning the destruction. It is recorded that during the night He "sits and roars like a lion, exclaiming: 'Woe to the children, on account of whose sins I destroyed My house and burnt My temple and exiled them among the nations of the world'" (Ber. 3a). The hour of midnight was chosen because David arose at this hour to study and pray, as it is said, "At midnight I will rise to give thanks unto Thee" (Ps. 119:62; Ber. 3b–4a).

This practice became formalized under the influence of the Kabbalah during the period of Isaac *Luria. Two separate forms of the service developed known as *Tikkun Raḥel* and *Tikkun Le'ah. Tikkun Raḥel*, consisting of Psalms 137 and 79 and **Teḥinnot* on the destruction of the Temple, is recited on days when **Taḥanun* is said. On the Sabbath, festivals, and days when *Taḥanun* is omitted, *Tikkun Le'ah*, consisting of more joyful psalms, such as 111 and 126, and selections from the Mishnah (Tamid ch. 1), is recited.

BIBLIOGRAPHY: Eisenstein, Dinim, 142; G. Scholem, *Zur Kabbala und ihrer Symbolik* (1960), 193ff.

TIKKUN SOFERIM, certain changes in the text of the Bible made by the early **soferim* in places which are offensive or show lack of respect to God. Ezra is the first to be referred to as a *sofer* in the Bible. This designation signifies not merely someone expert in the art of writing but also the scholar versed in the Torah. The members of the Great *Synagogue were also *soferim*, and the rabbis attribute to them 18 such *tikkunim*. These are enumerated in *Midrash Tanḥuma* and *Midrash Rabbah*, and Rashi in his commentary on the Bible quotes eight of them on the relevant passages. *Midrash Tanḥuma* begins with the verse: "He that toucheth you toucheth the apple of his eye" (Zech. 2:12); it should have said "My eye," but the Bible puts it in the third person to avoid referring it to God, this being a *tikkun soferim* of the men of the Great Synagogue. On completing the listing of these verses in the Bible, *Midrash Tanḥuma* continues: "but the men of the Great Synagogue altered these verses. And that is why they were called *soferim*, because they counted [Heb. *sofer*] all the letters of the Bible and expounded them." Similarly in Ezekiel 8:17, "Lo, they put the branch to His nose," was adjusted to "their nose." Again with the verse (Gen. 18:22) "but Abraham stood yet before the Lord." R. Simeon said: "This is a *tikkun soferim*, for the *Shekhinah* was actually waiting for Abraham and it should really have read: 'And the Lord stood yet before Abraham.' Similarly the verse (Num. 11:15) 'And if thou deal thus with me, kill me, I pray thee, out of hand, if I have found favor in thy sight; and let me not look upon my wretchedness' should have read 'their wretchedness.'" Rashi *(ad loc.)* language of the Bible. It should have been written 'and they condemned the Omnipresent by their silence,' but the text was amended. Also: 'Thus they exchanged their glory for the likeness of an ox' [Ps. 106:20] should have been written 'His glory' but it was amended."

Words with Diacritical Points above Them

Avot de-Rabbi Nathan, 1 (34,100f.) indicates ten passages in the Bible which have diacritical points over some of the letters. In the view of the rabbis these points were inserted by Ezra the Scribe. "Why? Ezra reasoned thus: 'If Elijah should come and say to me, "Why did you write so?" I shall reply, "Have I not already put dots above them? The dot indicating that the word is as though erased?"' "The dot is an indication that the word is to be omitted." This is the source of the view of Hezekiah b. Manoah in his biblical commentary *Ḥazzekuni*, that dots over words are an indication that Ezra was doubtful about them.

BIBLIOGRAPHY: S. Lieberman, *Hellenism in Jewish Palestine* (1950), 28–37.

[Abraham Arzi]

TIKTIN, rabbinical family originating in Tykocin (Tiktin), near Bialystok, Poland. ABRAHAM BEN GEDALIAH (1764–1820) became a rabbi in his birthplace Schwersenz (Swarzędz), in Łęczyca, and from 1803 in *Glogau (in Silesia). In 1816 he was appointed *Oberlandrabbiner* of Silesia at Breslau. Of 12 rabbinic works, only his *Petaḥ ha-Bayit* was published (Dyhernfurth, 1820; republished 1910, Warsaw). His son SOLOMON (1791–1843) succeeded his father in the Breslau and Silesian rabbinate. He became involved in controversy with the Reform movement when, in 1836, he prohibited the publication in Breslau of M. Brueck's *Reform des Judenthums* (Nagy-Becskerek, 1848), and opposed two years later the appointment of Abraham *Geiger as assistant rabbi, preacher, and *dayyan* in Breslau. He and his son, Gedaliah, conducted a bitter campaign against Geiger, mustering Orthodox circles and having the support of the Prussian conservative bureaucracy and clergy; this struggle became a cause célèbre in both Jewish and gentile circles. Geiger was supported primarily by the patrician, educated Jewish leadership while Tiktin had the support of the majority of the community.

GEDALIAH (c. 1810–1886), Solomon's son, was elected rabbi of Breslau by the Orthodox faction in 1843; this election was confirmed in 1846, and in 1854 his nomination as *Landrabbiner* was confirmed, the government identifying his religious Orthodoxy with political loyalty. When Geiger left Breslau for Frankfurt in 1863, Gedaliah came to terms with his successor Manuel *Joel and a compromise was reached by which separate communal institutions were maintained for both Orthodox and Reform. HEINRICH (1850–1936), Gedaliah's son, was a philologist and Romanian grammarian.

BIBLIOGRAPHY: M. Brann, in: *Jubelschrift ... H. Graetz* (1887), 277f.; E. Schreiber, *Abraham Geiger* (1892), 20ff.; S. Tiktin, in: AZJ, 84 (1920), 452–4 (on Abraham); M. Wiener, *Abraham Geiger and Liberal Judaism* (1962), 17–33.

TIKTINSKI, Lithuanian family associated with the foundation and development of the famous yeshivah of *Mir. In 1815 SAMUEL TIKTINSKI (d. 1835), a merchant of considerable means and a talmudic scholar, gathered together some of the youth of Mir and district and began to lecture regularly to them, defraying from his own pocket the expenses involved in their maintenance. His son ABRAHAM (d. 1835) helped with the teaching and the administration, but with the increase in the number of students, his father in 1823 transferred to him the whole burden of administration. To this task he applied himself with selfless devotion. In addition to teaching, he took particular care to initiate a spirit of concentration in prayer, himself serving as an example. He abolished the prevalent custom of students having meals with a different family each day, in this way raising their status. The fame of the yeshivah spread, and when Abraham could no longer finance it from his own means, he sought outside help. The supporters of the *Volozhin Yeshivah accused Mir Yeshivah of encroaching upon its supporters. The case was put before Abraham *Abele of Vilna who decided in favor of Mir. Both Samuel and Abraham died in 1835 and Joseph David, the rabbi of Mir, was appointed *rosh yeshivah* and was followed in both positions by his son Abraham Moses. In 1850, however, Samuel's second son ḤAYYIM LEIB (1824–1899) was appointed joint principal of the yeshivah with him, and with this appointment a new era began. In addition to his great scholarship, Ḥayyim Leib was distinguished by a gift for teaching and by his method. He eschewed *pilpul*; he insisted that the student must devote himself solely to the texts and the commentaries if he wished to arrive at an understanding of them. Israel *Lipkin said that anyone who wanted to learn a page of Talmud properly should attend Ḥayyim Leib's lectures. On the death of Abraham Moses in 1867, the whole responsibility of Mir Yeshivah devolved upon Ḥayyim Leib. His son SAMUEL (d. 1883) began to help in 1877, but he died six years later, whereupon Ḥayyim's younger son ABRAHAM was appointed lecturer; in the following year his daughter's son, Judah Spira, became *mashgi'ah*. In 1878 and again in 1892 the yeshivah was burnt down in fires which swept the town, and his writings, which were still in manuscript form, were also destroyed. Ḥayyim Leib worked untiringly to replace the buildings. He was able to gain the assistance of Clara de *Hirsch and of the Rothschild family. Among his distinguished disciples was Simeon *Shkop. Ḥayyim Leib died in Warsaw where he had gone for medical treatment.

BIBLIOGRAPHY: M.J. Goldberg, *Toledot ... Ḥayyim Yehudah Leib Tiktinski* (1902); *Yahadut Lita*, 1 (1960), index; 3 (1967), index; Zinovitz, in: *Shanah be-Shanah* 5723 (1962/63), 555–9.

[Mordechai Hacohen]

°TILLICH, PAUL JOHANNES (1886–1965), Protestant philosopher and theologian, born in Starzeddal (Silesia), the son of a Lutheran pastor. He received his education at the universities of Berlin, Tübingen, Halle, and Breslau. Often compared to Martin Buber because they shared a kind of existentialist thought, Tillich made an impact on American Jews comparable to Buber's influence on Christians. Tillich began his teaching career in his native Germany at various universities, but his opposition to Hitler's National Socialism led to him being dismissed from his teaching activities. Vehemently opposed to Nazism, he subsequently went to the United States in 1933 after having, in his own words, "the honor to be the first non-Jewish professor to be dismissed from a German university." Throughout his years of work at the Union Theological Seminary in New York, Harvard University, and the University of Chicago, he maintained his many friendships with Jewish refugees from his native land.

Paul Tillich's numerous writings culminate in his great three-volume *Systematic Theology* (1951–63). In all his work, he employed a "method of correlation" to bring together philosophy and theology. Part idealist, part existentialist, he was a gifted analyst of the human condition in its modern setting. Tillich's concept of "the Protestant principle" self-consciously reproduced elements of Hebrew prophetic tradition, particularly in its stress on criticism of one's own achievements and institutions. Careful to distinguish between Jewish and Christian thought on the messianic question, Tillich was preoccupied with the problem of particularism ("chosenness") and universalism in Judaism. Out of a deep respect for Judaism, he was among the first Christian spokesmen to call for the replacement of attempts at conversion by attempts at dialogue between Christian and Jew.

BIBLIOGRAPHY: Agus, in: *Judaism*, 3 (1954), 80–89; Martin, *ibid.*, 15:2 (1966), 180–8. **ADD. BIBLIOGRAPHY:** C.W. Kegley and R.W. Bretall (eds.), *The Theology of Paul Tillich* (1952); K. Hamilton, *The System and the Gospel: A Critique of Paul Tillich* (1963); D. Ford, *The Modern Theologians* (1997).

[Martin E. Marty / Shimon Gibson (2nd ed.)]

TIM (**Louis Mitelberg**; 1919–2002), French cartoonist and caricaturist. Born in Kaluszyn, Poland, Tim went to Paris to study at the Ecole des Beaux Arts but fled to England at the beginning of World War II. He returned to Paris at the end of the war and became a regular contributor to some of the world's leading newspapers and news magazines, such as the French *L'Express* and *Le Monde* and the American *Time, Newsweek*, and *The New York Times.*

Known for his incisive, courageous, and sometimes poignant style, Tim first achieved world fame in 1967 with his illustration of the words of General de Gaulle describing the Jewish people as "domineering and sure of itself": a skeleton-thin man in the striped garb of the concentration camp inmates throwing out his chest in a swaggering attitude, with his foot on the barbed wire fence. Tim has illustrated the works of Kafka and Zola and published *Pouvoir civil* (1961) and *Autocaricature* (1974) as well as an album on De Gaulle, *Une Certaine Idee de la France* (1969). In 1984 an exhibition of his works was held at the Musee des Arts Décoratifs de Paris, an almost unprecedented honor for a cartoonist.

[Gideon Kouts]

°TIMAGENES OF ALEXANDRIA, historian of Alexandria who also lived in Rome during the Augustan Age. Timagenes was the author of a general history centering on Alexander and his successors. He refers to the Jews and possibly devoted a special section to Jewish history. The three relevant passages preserved from his writings deal with the policy of Antiochus Epiphanes of Judea, *Aristobulus I, and the wars of Alexander Yannai. Timagenes is the only Alexandrian Greek historian who does not evince hostility toward the Jews.

TIME AND ETERNITY. On the subject of time, Jewish medieval philosophers were divided into two broad camps: Those who subscribed basically to the Aristotelian concept of time, and those who favored a concept that goes back ultimately to Plotinus. Included among the former are Isaac Israeli, Saadiah Gaon, Abraham ibn Daud, Maimonides, and Levi b. Gershom, and among the latter are Ḥasdai Crescas and Joseph Albo. Maimonides may be taken as representative of the first group and Crescas of the second.

Maimonides, whose discussion of time appears in his *Guide of the Perplexed* (notably, 1:73), accepts the definition of time laid down by Aristotle as "the number of motion according to 'before' and 'after'" (*Physics* 4:11, 219b). Time, therefore, is neither an independent substance nor identical with motion, although it is totally dependent upon the latter and constitutes an accident of motion, which is itself an accident of body or corporeal substances. Time, consequently, possesses only a quasi-reality. Not only is it an accident of an accident, but it is composed of a past that is gone, a future that does not yet exist, and a present that serves only as a limit between the two. Accordingly, Maimonides rejects the concept of time proposed by the Mutakallimun (see *Kalām) who, basing their thought generally on the atomism of Democritus, maintained that time is composed of time-atoms or instants, which are real entities.

Despite Maimonides' basic agreement with Aristotle on the definition of time, he rejects the latter's attempt to prove the eternity of the universe from the nature of time, and argues instead that time came into existence with the creation of the universe. Prior to creation, God existed alone in timeless eternity, for inasmuch as God is absolutely incorporeal, He has no relation to motion, and consequently none to time.

Crescas' discussion of time appears in his *Or Adonai* as part of his massive critique of the Aristotelian philosophy. The essential distinction between Crescas and Aristotle is that Crescas divorces the existence of time from its essential dependence upon motion. Time, rather than being an accident of motion, is the continuance or duration of the stream of consciousness of a thinking mind. Thus Crescas defines time as "the measure of the continuance [duration] of motion or rest between two instants." Time, therefore, as duration, exists independently of motion. The relation of motion to time is that the former serves to determine or measure some length or part of time. Moreover, as the duration of the activity of mind, time has no extra-mental reality, not even the quasi-reality of Aristotle.

Crescas' definition has two major theological implications. First, it is not the case, as Maimonides, for example, believes, that God cannot be described as existing in time. Since duration is a quality of mind rather than of motion and body, time can be ascribed even to an absolutely incorporeal entity such as God. Second, by similar reasoning, it may be concluded that time did not come into existence with the creation of the universe, but has existed from eternity as the duration of God's infinite consciousness.

Although Albo agrees with Crescas that duration is independent of motion, he maintains that true time is only determinate or measured duration. Hence there was no real time until the creation of the celestial spheres whose corporeality provided the motion necessary to determine a length of duration.

ADD. BIBLIOGRAPHY: H.A. Davidson, *Proofs of Eternity, Creation and the Existence of God in Medieval Islamic and Jewish Philosophy* (1987), chps. 2–3; W.Z. Harvey, *Physics and Metaphysics in Hasdai Crescas* (1998), ch. 1; "Albo's Discussion of Time," in: JQR, 70 (1980), 210–38; S. Feldman, "The Theory of Eternal Creation in Hasdai Crescas and Some of His Predecessors," in: *Viator* (1980), 289–320; T.M. Rudawsky, "The Theory of Time in Maimonides and Crescas," in: *Maimonidean Studies*, 1 (1990), 143–62; W.Z. Harvey, "L'univers infini de Hasday Crescas," in: *Revue de métaphysique et de morale*, 4 (1998), 551–57; T. Lévy, "L'infini selon Rabbi Hasdaï Crescas (1340–1412)," in: *Inquisition et pérennité* (1992), 161–66; S. Stern, "The Rabbinic Concept of Time from Late Antiquity to the Middle Ages," in: G. Jaritz and G. Moreno-Riaño (eds.), *Time and Eternity: The Medieval Discourse* (2003), 129–45; T.M. Rudawsky, "Time and Cosmology in Late Medieval Jewish Philosophy," in: *ibid.*, 147–62; H. Maccoby, "Crescas's Concept of Time," in: *ibid.*, 163–70; J.T. Robinson, "Hasdai Crescas and Anti-Aristotelianism," in: *The Cambridge Companion to Medieval Jewish Philosophy* (2003), 403–4.

TIMERMAN, JACOBO (1923–1999). Argentinean journalist. Born in the small Ukrainian town of Bar, he migrated to Argentina at the age of five with his family. During the years 1948–50 Timerman was a member of the editorial board of *Nueva Sion*, a Socialist-Zionist left-oriented biweekly published in Buenos Aires. He achieved his first great success with the newsmagazine *Primera Plana* (1962–66), followed by *Confirmado* (1965–66), both inspired by *Time* and *Newsweek*. In 1971 Timerman founded the liberal newspaper daily *La Opinión*, on the model of *Le Monde*, and edited the paper until it was shut down by the military regime in 1977. Between 1973 and 1976 *La Opinión* had been closed on a few occasions, because it campaigned against the right-wing populist supporters of the antisemite minister José López Rega as well as the neo-fascist squads known as Triple A (AAA). *La Opinión* was one of the few important newspapers in Argentina to extensively denounce government corruption, state-tolerated antisemitism, and the Junta's flagrant violation of human rights during the repression. Timerman condemned the arbitrary arrests and abductions by military forces, and published the writs of habeas corpus presented to the courts by the families of the *desaparecidos* (the disappeared ones), particularly of journalists. In July 1977 Timerman was arrested, tortured, and held until 1979, first clandestinely, then in a regular military prison, and finally under house arrest, although he was cleared by the judiciary of charges brought against him. Timerman was deported and stripped of his acquired Argentinean citizenship by the military Juntas. During his stay in prison he received moral and spiritual assistance from both Rabbi Marshall *Meyer and diplomats of the Israel Embassy in Buenos Aires. Timerman was released from prison by the Junta thanks to the joint diplomatic efforts of the State of Israel and the United States.

His first place of exile was Israel, and he later moved to New York and Spain. His testimony *Prisoner without a Name, Cell without a Number* (1981) became a worldwide bestseller, describing his personal ordeal and documenting the Argentine institutionalized violence of the military dictatorship in Argentina and its violation of human rights, including the antisemitism among the rank and file of the repressors.

Timerman was outraged by the Israeli invasion of Lebanon, and published a critical book, *Israel, the Longer War* (1982), denouncing the unjust treatment of the Palestinians. This book aroused severe criticism of the author in Israel.

He returned to Argentina in 1984, one year after the restoration of democracy, and testified against the Juntas and violators of human rights. He became editor of the daily *La Razón*. In 1988 Carlos Saul Menem, then governor of the province of La Rioja and presidential candidate, sued him for libel and defamation. He was acquitted in two separate trials, but during the administration of President Menem the case was reopened by the Supreme Court of Argentina, and Timerman decided to flee to Uruguay. The charges against him were finally dropped in 1996.

Timerman wrote books critical of Augusto Pinochet (*Chile, el galope muerto*, 1988) and Fidel Castro (*Cuba, a Journey*, 1990).

BIBLIOGRAPHY: G. Mochkofsky, *Timerman – El periodista que quiso ser parte del poder* (1923–1999), (2003).

[Leonardo Senkman (2nd ed.)]

TIMISOARA (Rom. **Timişoara**; Hung. **Temesvár**), city in the Banat, Transylvania, W. *Romania; between 1552 and 1716 an important center of the Turkish administration; subsequently within *Hungary until 1918. The city comprises several quarters, whose individual development is still evident and affected the history of the local Jews who established separate communal organizations in them. The first Jews arrived in Timisoara before the Turkish conquest by the trade route between *Turkey and Central Europe. At first they came temporarily, on business, but by the first half of the 16th century there were permanent Jewish settlers. The oldest tombstone in the Jewish cemetery dates from 1636 commemorating the "rabbi and surgeon" Azriel Asael. The beginnings of communal organization date from that era. When the Austrians captured the city from the Turks in 1716, the peace treaty included a provision permitting the Jews there to choose either to retreat with the Turks or to remain under the Austrians. Some chose to remain. There were then about 12 Turkish-Sephardi families. In 1736 R. Meir *Amigo of Constantinople and four other Sephardi Jews were authorized to settle in the city. Amigo organized communal life and did much to help the Jews of Timisoara. As the economic situation of Timisoara began to improve, Jews were attracted to the city from other parts of Hungary and as far away as Austria and Moravia. They mainly engaged in commerce.

When under direct Austrian rule, however, the situation of the Jews in Timisoara was more difficult than in any other part of Hungary. The Jewish legislation (Judenordnung) of 1776 for Jews in the Banat region placed many restrictions on the Jews of Timisoara but their situation improved when the region was returned to Hungary in 1779.

Two synagogues, one Sephardi and one Ashkenazi, were built in 1762. The Sephardi congregation continued to exist independently until after World War II. A magnificent synagogue was erected for the main Ashkenazi congregation in 1862. After the Hungarian General Jewish Congress of 1868–69, the community of Timisoara declared itself Neologist. A separate Orthodox congregation was formed in 1871. An Orthodox synagogue was built in 1895. After World War II the congregations were unified by government order.

The Jewish population numbered 155 in 1716; 220 in 1739; 72 families in 1781; 1,200 persons in 1840; 2,202 in 1858; 4,870 (c. 15% of the total population) in 1890; 6,728 (9.2%) in 1910; and 9,368 (10%) in 1930.

In general, the Jews of Timisoara were well-to-do and were able to finance ample communal activities. A ramified educational network was established. Efforts were made to found a Jewish school in 1825. Two schools were opened in different quarters of the city in the 1840s. Between the two world wars, under Romanian administration, two Jewish high schools were established, one general and one commercial. The language of instruction was Romanian, although Hebrew was also taught. The Jews continued to speak Hungarian and German in Timisoara, where German culture was more widespread than in the other towns of Transylvania.

Timisoara was an important Zionist center. A Zionist organization was founded there between the two world wars. Timisoara was the headquarters of the Zionist Organization, *Jewish National Fund (Keren Kayemet le-Israel), and Palestine Foundation Fund (*Keren Hayesod) in Transylvania. The National Jewish Party was active in the city, and won support in the elections. Between 1920 and 1940 the periodical of the Transylvanian Zionist Organization, Uj Kor, was published in Timisoara. These organizations tried to continue after World War II but in 1947–48 they were forced to disband.

Throughout the period between the two world wars the community suffered from antisemitism. In 1936 the *Iron Guard attacked a Jewish theater audience, exploding a bomb in their midst; two Jews were killed and many were wounded.

Holocaust and Contemporary Periods

From 1940 the position of the Jews deteriorated, because of economic restrictions and confiscations. In 1941 many Jewish men were sent to forced labor. The Jewish population, which numbered 10,950 in 1940, increased to 11,788 in 1942 because many Jews from surrounding areas were concentrated in Timisoara, the local Jewish community having to support them. Later all the communal property was confiscated, including land. Until 1945 Timisoara was the center of the German organizations of the Banat region. In 1944 the local German civilian organization also took action against the Jews, but in September of that year the Red Army entered the city.

After the war the National Jewish Organization, formed to assist the Communist Party program, established a branch in Timisoara, and its leaders attempted to liquidate Zionism and impose Communism. Jews were accused of underground Zionist activity, and some were imprisoned, including the author Ezra Fleischer. There were 13,600 Jews in Timisoara in 1947, but their number gradually decreased through emigration to Israel and other countries; 3,000 Jews remained in 1971. The communal organizations still functioned, there was a rabbi, and religious services were held. Although their numbers continued to dwindle, Jews played a part, mostly after 1989, in the renewal of the city's and district's general cultural life.

BIBLIOGRAPHY: MHJ, 3 (1937), docs. nos. 149, 152–3, 227, 354, 360–367, 369, 370–458, 477; 8 (1965), 280; 9 (1966), 429; 10 (1967), 285; 11 (1968), 325, 423, 462; 13 (1970), 45; PK Romanyah, 1 (1969), 308–15 (incl. bibl.); S. Yiẓhaki, *Battei-Sefer Yehudim be-Transylvanyah* (1970), 59–68, 174.

[Yehouda Marton]

TIMNA (Heb. תִּמְנָע), site of intensive ancient copper mining and smelting activities. The Timna Valley (Ar. Wadi Manʿiāyya) is located 12½–18¾ mi. (2030 km.) north of Eilat, and three wadis run through it into the *Arabah: Naḥal Mangan, Naḥal Timna, and Naḥal Neḥushtan. The horseshoe-shaped area, created by tectonic plate movement, spreads out over an area of 23 sq. mi. (60 sq. km.) and is part of the Syrian-African rift. Explorations on the site were carried out by F. Frank and N. Glueck in 1932–34, and by B. Rothenberg from 1959. The ancient mines are situated in the western part of the Timna Valley, and malachite and chalcocite ores can still be found there in white sandstone formations. The mines and mining camps are spread over an area of approximately 4 sq. mi. (c. 10 sq. km.). The ancient smelting camps, where crude copper was produced, are located in the center of the valley, west of Mt. Timna.

During the Chalcolithic period (fourth millennium B.C.E.), tribes of shepherds and hunters with a good knowledge of copper metallurgy settled around Timna, collecting copper ore nodules and smelting them in well-built bowl furnaces. The Chalcolithic copper smelting furnace excavated on the fringes of the Arabah, east of the modern Timna copper mines, is the earliest smelting installation so far found. The next industrial installations for the smelting and casting of copper date to the Late Bronze and Early Iron I periods. These large installations include workshops, storehouses, cisterns, furnaces, and slagheaps. The date of this complex, called "King Solomon's Mines" by N. Glueck, was for some time much disputed. The discovery of numerous hieroglyphic inscriptions in Timna dating to the 14th–12th centuries B.C.E. now indicate that the copper industry of Timna, and probably of most of the other copper-producing sites in the Arabah, was developed by Egyptian mining expeditions during the 19th and 20th Dynasties. The inscriptions were found inside an Egyptian temple dedicated to the Egyptian goddess Hathor and located at the foot of "Solomon's Pillars" in the center of the mining and smelting area; it was probably the central sanctuary of Timna. This temple was built in the reign of Seti I at the end of the 14th century B.C.E. Gifts were also sent to it by Ramses II, Merneptah, and Seti II. It was destroyed in 1216–1210 B.C.E. and was restored only during the reign of Ramses III (1198–1166 B.C.E.). The second temple was short-lived and came to an end with Ramses V (1160–1156 B.C.E.).

Timna, and perhaps also the other copper plants in the eastern Arabah, not yet explored, can now be identified with "Atika, the great copper mines," described in the Papyrus Harris I dating to the time of Ramses III. According to this source, Egyptian copper mining expeditions traveled to Timna from Egypt by way of the sea and by overland caravans. The bay of Jazīrat Farʿun, the only natural anchorage in the Gulf of Eilat, can be identified as the Egyptian mining port before it became the shipyard of King Solomon (see also *Ezion-Geber).

Numerous temple gifts, including a partly gilded copper snake, a *neḥushtan* of Midianite origin, and finds in the smelting camp indicate that the Egyptians operated the copper industry of Timna together with the Midianites, Kenites, and, probably, the Amalekites from the central Negev, i.e., the indigenous inhabitants of the area, possessing metallurgical traditions going back to prehistoric times, as reflected in Genesis 4:22. The Egyptian-Midianite temple and copper industry, built in the Arabah at a time close to the Exodus, and the numerous objects found in the excavations contribute materially to understanding of the cultural and social relations between the tribes of Israel at the time of Moses and the Midianites and Kenites, through the Midianite priest Jethro, father-in-law and adviser to Moses.

The mines of Timna were not operated after the 12th century B.C.E., except during the second to fourth centuries C.E., apparently by soldiers of the third Roman legion (of Cyrenaica). At this time copper ore was transported from Timna to the large copper furnace at Be'er Orah (Ar. Bīr Hindis), south of Timna, the site of which was excavated in 1969.

[Beno Rothenberg]

The modern Timna Copper Works in the hills of Eilat, 15 mi. (25 km.) north of Eilat, were opened in 1959 and produce copper cement (with a content of approximately 80% pure copper) from sedimentary ores mined in open pits and shafts over an area of approximately 8½ sq. mi. (22 sq. km.). The works, employing more than 1,000 persons, increased its production from 5,000 tons (equivalent of pure copper) in 1962 to 14,000 tons in 1968. Nearly all the employees of the

Timna Works were residents of Eilat; the site itself did not have a permanent population. The modern works were first closed in 1976 owing to an economic crisis in the copper industry. They was reopened in 1980 and permanently closed in 1985.

Subsequently the Timna site became a tourist and recreation site, with a park offering visitors numerous attractions: the archaeological antiquities of the Shrine of Hathor and the Chariot Rock Drawings (drawings dating from the Egyptian-Midianite period carved on stones and describing the rituals and lifestyles of people who used to live in the area); the natural phenomenon of The Arches (natural arches formed by erosion); Solomon's Pillars (red sandstone cliffs that have been sculpted into pillar-shaped ridges jutting outward and formed by centuries of water erosion); The Mushroom (a mushroom-shaped rock that was carved by the natural forces of humidity and wind); and a few others, such as the multimedia "Mines of Times" shown in the new visitors' centers and the Timna Lake, an artificial lake designed for recreational activities.

[Efraim Orni / Shaked Gilboa (2nd ed.)]

BIBLIOGRAPHY: J.H. Breasted, *Ancient Records of Egypt*, 4 (1927), 204; F. Frank, in: ZDPV, 57 (1934), 191–280; N. Glueck, *Rivers in the Desert* (1959), 36; B. Rothenberg, in: PEQ, 94 (1962), 5–71; idem, *Ẓefunot Negev* (1967), index; idem, in: *Museum Haaretz. Bulletin*, 8 (1966), 86–93 (Eng. section); B. Rothenberg and A. Lupu, *ibid.*, 9 (1967), 53–70 (Eng. section); B. Rothenberg and E. Cohen, *ibid.*, 10 (1968), 25–35 (Eng. section); B. Rothenberg, *ibid.*, 11 (1969), 22–38 (in Eng. section); *ibid.*, 12 (1970); PEQ, 101 (1969), 57–59; idem, in: *Illustrated London News*, 255 (Nov. 15, 1969), 32–33; 255 (Nov. 29, 1969), 28 **WEBSITE:** timna-park.co.il/heb_timna.html.

TIMNAH (Heb. תִּמְנָה), the name of a number of places mentioned in the Bible.

(1) A Danite city (Josh. 19:43) located on the northern boundary of Judah between Beth Shemesh and Ekron (Josh. 15:10). In the time of the struggle between Dan and the Philistines, Timnah and its vineyards apparently belonged to the latter; Samson went there to marry the daughter of "the Timnite," the lord of Timnah (Judg. 14; 15:6). Later, probably in the days of David, it became an Israelite city, as is evident from its inclusion in the list of cities seized by the Philistines in the time of Ahaz (II Chron. 28:18). Sennacherib conquered it after the battle of Eltekeh in 701 B.C.E. (Annals 2:240). Eusebius places the city between Diospolis (Lydda) and Jerusalem, mistakingly identifying it with (2) below (Onom. 96:24ff.). It is now identified with Tell al-Baṭṭāshī in the Sorek Valley, an almost square mound west of Beth Shemesh with traces of Iron Age pottery and fortifications. Nearby excavations revealed Neolithic to Middle Bronze Age remains.

(2) A Judean city fortified by *Bacchides (I Macc. 9:50). This may be the Timnah to which Judah went for sheepshearing and on the way to which he met Tamar (Gen. 38); some, however, locate this event at (1) above. It is identified with Khirbat al-Tibnā near Beit Nattif.

(3) An unidentified city in the southeastern mountain district of Judah (Josh. 15:57).

BIBLIOGRAPHY: B. Mazar, in: IEJ, 10 (1960), 66; J. Kaplan, in: *Eretz-Israel*, 5 (1959), 9ff.; Y. Aharoni, in: PEFQS, 90 (1958), 27ff. (2) Avi-Yonah, Geog, 36ff.

[Michael Avi-Yonah]

TIMNATH-HERES or **TIMNATH-SERAH** (Heb. תִּמְנַת חֶרֶס, תִּמְנַת סֶרַח), city in the hill-country of the territory of Ephraim, given to Joshua as his inheritance after the division of Canaan among the tribes; he was later buried there. The place is called both Timnath-Heres ("of the sun"; Judg. 2:9) and Timnath-Serah (Josh. 19:50; cf. the name of Asher's daughter, Serah, in Gen. 46:17; I Chron. 7:30). In the Herodian period, it became the headquarters of a toparchy, formerly that of Arimathea (Pliny, *Natural History*, 5:15, 70; Jos., Wars, 3:55). Cassius sold its inhabitants into slavery (Jos., Ant., 14:275). In the Jewish War of 66–70 the city was included within the command of John the Essene (Jos., Wars, 2:567); in the spring of 68 it was occupied by Vespasian (Wars, 4:444). The city continued in existence until Byzantine times (Eusebius, Onom. 100:1ff.). It is identified with Khirbat Tibna, about 7½ mi. (12 km.) north of Beth-Horon; pottery of the early Iron Age and later periods was found there and the traditional tomb of Joshua is shown at the site.

BIBLIOGRAPHY: Abel, in: RB, 34 (1925), 209ff.; Rad, in: PJB, 29 (1933), 32.

[Michael Avi-Yonah]

°**TIMOCHARES** (date unknown), author of a lost history in Greek of Antiochus IV Epiphanes (175–164 B.C.E.) or Antiochus VII Sidetes (138–128). His remarks on Jerusalem's topography are preserved in Eusebius, *Praeparatio Evangelica*, 9:35.

°**TINNEIUS RUFUS**, Roman governor of Judea at the outbreak of the Bar Kokhba War in 132 C.E. In rabbinic sources he is known as "Turnus Rufus." Having failed with the assistance of the Tenth Legion to suppress the revolt, he sought aid from Publicius Marcellus, governor of Syria, and from other provinces. He failed to overcome the rebels, however, and finally the Roman emperor, Hadrian, was obliged to dispatch *Julius Severus, governor of Britain, to Judea.

Talmudic tradition refers to Tinneius Rufus concerning the decree against circumcision (*Bereshit Rabbati* of *Moses ha-Darshan) and as being responsible for plowing up the Temple Mount (Ta'an. 29a). Various Midrashim record his disputations with Akiva, his questions displaying some knowledge of the Torah and of Jewish life, such as: Why does God hate Esau (Tanḥ. Terumah, 3)? Why is man not born circumcised if such be God's will (Tanḥ. Tazri'a, 7)? Why does God not provide sustenance for the poor if He loves them (BB 10a)? Wherein is the Sabbath distinguished from other days (Sanh. 65b; Gen. R. 11:6; Tanh., Tissa, 33; et al.)?

All his questions display an abrasive quality though Akiva is always able to provide an answer. According to the *aggadah* these discussions so disturbed Tinneius Rufus that his wife sought to use her charm in bringing about Akiva's downfall but failed; in the end she became a proselyte, marrying Akiva, to whom she brought a considerable fortune (Av. Zar. 20a; Ned. 50b). Although Tinneius Rufus emerges in Jewish tradition as a wicked man, all the existing sources bear a legendary character, and there are few historical facts about him.

BIBLIOGRAPHY: Eusebius, *Ecclesiasticae Historiae*, 4:6, 1; Pauly-Wissowa, 6 (1937), 1376–79, no. 6.

[Lea Roth]

TIOMKIN, VLADIMIR (Ze'ev; 1861–1927), Zionist leader in Russia. Born to an assimilated family in Yelizavetgrad, Ukraine, Tiomkin qualified as an engineer at the Technological Institute in St. Petersburg in 1886. He was active at first in the Russian revolutionary movement, but the pogroms in southern Russia in 1881 prompted him to join the Jewish national movement, and he was one of the founders of the Ahavat Zion society in St. Petersburg. He was delegate to the Ḥovevei Zion conferences at Druskieniki (1887) and Vilna (1889). In 1891 he was appointed the representative of the *Odessa Committee of Ḥovevei Zion in Ereẓ Israel, and he became head of the executive committee of the Russian Ḥovevei Zion in Jaffa. He initiated land purchases in Ereẓ Israel, but his plans were soon foiled by land speculations and the financial losses incurred by many investors. Tiomkin returned to Russia, where he became **kazyonny ravvin* of Yelizavetgrad in 1893 and did much to develop the institutions of the community. With the appearance of Theodor *Herzl, he joined the Zionist movement and became one of its outstanding supporters and speakers in Russia. He participated in Zionist Congresses, was a member of the Zionist General Council, and was Zionist representative for the Yelizavetgrad region. During the controversy which broke out over the *Uganda Scheme, Tiomkin was a leading member of the oppositionist Ẓiyyonei Zion (1903).

During World War I Tiomkin headed the relief projects in southern Russia on behalf of the Russian Jewish refugees who were expelled from the front region. After the February 1917 Revolution he renewed his activities in the Zionist movement, which had become legalized. During the short period of freedom that followed until the October Revolution, he was one of the foremost speakers at conferences and congresses. He was a member of the presidium of the National Assembly of the Jews of the Ukraine (1918). Due to his great popularity with the Jewish masses, he was not persecuted by the Jewish Communists when in control over the Jews of the Ukraine (1919). In 1920 Tiomkin left Russia and settled in Paris. He became a member of the editorial board of the exiled Russian Zionists' periodical *Razsvet* and joined Vladimir Jabotinsky's *Revisionist Zionist movement. Tiomkin was the first president of the World Union of Zionist-Revisionists. He was an impressive witness in the *Schwarzbard trial. The settlement Ramat Tiomkin near Netanyah is named after him.

BIBLIOGRAPHY: L. Jaffe, *Sefer ha-Congress* (1950^2), 324–6; D. Smilansky, *Im Benei Dori* (1942), 66–70; M.B.H. Hacohen, *Olami*, 2 (1927), 194–8.

[Yehuda Slutsky]

ṬĪRA, AL-, Muslim-Arab village in central Israel, in the southern Sharon Plain N.E. of Kefar Sava. Al-Ṭīra is thought to be the relay station, Mutatio Betthar, mentioned by the fourth-century "Bordeaux Traveler." Under the *Mamluks (14th century) it was a wayfarers' inn (*khān*). The village expanded in the early part of the 20th century, as the spreading of Jewish settlements in its vicinity provided work opportunities and a market for its farm produce. Included within the State of Israel's borders, the village grew from 2,000 inhabitants in 1948 to 7,100 in 1968 and 19,300 in 2002, occupying an area of about 4 sq. mi. (10 sq. km.). Irrigation was introduced, farm branches were variegated, artisan shops and small industries established, and housing conditions greatly improved. Al-Ṭīra's agriculture was based mainly on citrus groves and other fruit orchards, and vegetable and field crops. In 1991 Al-Ṭīra received municipal status.

[Efraim Orni]

TIRADO, JACOB (ca. 1540–1620), one of the founding fathers of the Portuguese community in *Amsterdam. Tirado was born in Portugal into a *Converso family. In 1598 he was living in Amsterdam where he returned to Judaism. In notarial documents he appears as a wealthy merchant under the name of James (Gammez) Lopes da Costa. His trade concentrated on Portugal and Venice. Synagogue services were held in his house, at least in 1610. In about 1608 he must have been among the founders of the Sephardi community, together with Samuel *Palache and the poet Jacob Israel *Belmonte. The community was named Bet Ya'akov. He was among the first *parnassim* of the community and donated a Sefer Torah. After 1612 he left Amsterdam and moved to Venice, where he was active in charity and fund raising for Ereẓ Israel. He might have spent the last years of his life in Jerusalem. According to legendary tradition Tirado left Portugal in 1593 along with a group of Conversos and reached Emden, where R. Moses Uri b. Joseph Ha-Levi helped them to return to Judaism and accompanied them to Amsterdam. Their religious practices led the authorities to suspect that they were holding Catholic services – at that time forbidden – and on the Day of Atonement, 1596, the group was arrested. Tirado was able to communicate with the authorities in Latin and, when he told them the truth, they authorized Jewish worship.

BIBLIOGRAPHY: E.M. Koen, in: *Studia Rosenthaliana*, 3 (1969), 121, 237, 240, 246 (Dutch). **ADD. BIBLIOGRAPHY:** O. Vlessing, in: *Dutch Jewish History*, 3 (1993), 43–75.

TIRASPOL, city in S.E. Moldova. In 1847 the number of Jews amounted to 1,406 and by 1897 it had risen to 8,668 (27% of the total population). In 1910 Tiraspol had two Jewish private schools, one for boys and one for girls. In 1926 there were 6,398 Jews (29.1%) in the town. During the Nazi occupation Tiraspol was under Romanian administration; almost all its Jewish population perished. In the late 1960s the Jewish population of Tiraspol was estimated at about 1,500. The only synagogue was closed by the authorities in 1959, but *kasher* poultry was still available.

TIRAT HA-KARMEL (Heb. טִירַת הַכַּרְמֶל; "Castle of the Carmel"), city in northern Israel. Tirat ha-Karmel is located on the southern slopes of Mt. Carmel, near Haifa. The settlement was established in 1949, received municipal council status in 1951, and municipal status in 1992. Its area is 2.3 sq. mi. (6 sq. km.) and its population in 2002 was 18,700, among them 20% new immigrants. The city has an industrial area housing hi-tech companies.

WEBSITE: www.tirat-carmel.muni.il.

[Shaked Gilboa (2nd ed.)]

TIRAT ẒEVI (Heb. טִירַת צְבִי), kibbutz in central Israel, 6 mi. (10 km.) S.E. of Beth-Shean, affiliated with Ha-Kibbutz ha-Dati. Tirat Ẓevi was founded in 1937 as one of the first, and the southernmost, of the *stockade and watchtower outposts in the Beth-Shean Valley, by Ha-Po'el ha-Mizrachi pioneers from central Europe. In the 1936–39 Arab riots, Tirat Ẓevi had to repulse frequent attacks. In the early stage of the *War of Independence (1948), strong Arab forces commanded by Fawzi al-Kaukji assaulted Tirat Ẓevi but were beaten back after suffering heavy casualties. After the *Six-Day War (1967), the kibbutz became the object of repeated shelling from beyond the nearby Jordan border. Since its founding, Tirat Ẓevi has occupied a central place in the religious settlement movement, and its members are active in religious study and education. In 1968, the kibbutz had 385 inhabitants; in 2002, 666. Kibbutz farming was based on field corps, dates, olives, turkeys, and fishery. The kibbutz also operated a sausage and smoked-meat factory and catering service and developed tourism with a visitor's center and guest rooms. Its name, "Castle of Ẓevi," commemorates Rabbi Ẓevi Hirsh *Kalischer.

WEBSITE: www.tiratzvi.org.il.

[Efraim Orni]

TIRGU-FRUMOS (Rom. **Târgu-Frumos**), town in Jassy district, Moldavia, Romania. In 1763 Jews were granted a special privilege to settle there in order to restore the declining economy of the town. In 1769 Tirgu-Frumos is mentioned in connection with the trade developed by the Jews, who sold cereals, butter, milk, honey, leather, flax, and hemp at the weekly fair. In 1815 the privilege was confirmed and more Jewish settlers arrived; from 280 in 1803 their number increased to 1,258 (31% of the total population) in 1859, and 2,123 (45.6%) in 1899. At the beginning of the 19th century Jews assumed responsible positions in the local council. At the end of the century, however, proceedings were opened against them. For 30 years the Romanian parliament refused to raise Tirgu-Frumos to the status of a town, keeping it a village, because in such a rural environment the Jews had no rights to acquire immovable property. During the Peasants' Revolt in 1907 the synagogue as well as the houses of 59 Jewish families were destroyed. Between the two world wars antisemitism increased, and in consequence many Jews left Tirgu-Frumos. In 1930 there were 1,608 Jews (26.4% of the total) in the town. The members of this community held a central position in trade (cereal, cattle, timber, grocery and other stores, alcoholic beverages), crafts (tailors, cobblers, potters, bakers, furriers, leather cutters, smiths, etc.), small industry and professions (doctors). In 1939 students from the University of Jassy, led by A.C. *Cuza and his son George, attempted to organize anti-Jewish riots but were deterred by an effective *self-defense organization. Among the rabbis of the town were Shalom b. Samuel Shmelke Taubes (1825–1888), who officiated later in Botosani. Three synagogues – the Big Synagogue (of the merchants) founded in 1813, the Cobblers' (1883) and the Poor's – lasted several years more than the community.

In World War II most Jews were expelled to Roman and some also to Botosani. Some 650 victims from the "Death Train" traveling between Jassy and Roman in the days of the Jassy massacre, July 29, 1941, were taken from the train and interred in the Târgu-Frumos cemetery. After the war a community was reconstituted (amounting to 530 persons in 1947) but diminished rapidly through migration to larger cities or emigration. In 1969 about 10 Jewish families remained. The last Jewish inhabitant died in 1998.

BIBLIOGRAPHY: E. Schwartzfeld, *Impopularea, reîmpopulerea și intemeierea târgurilor si târgusoarelor in Moldova* (1914), 17–19, 34; N. Dărângă, *Monografia comunei Târgu Frumos* (1914); V. Tufescu, *Târgușoarele din Moldova, si importanța lor ecomonică* (1942), 92, 104–5, 130, 140; PK Romanyah, 130–2.

[Theodor Lavi / Silviu Sanie (2nd ed.)]

TIRGU NEAMT (Rom. **Târgu-Neamț**), town in Moldavia, Romania. According to local tradition, Jews were authorized to settle by the sovereign Stephen the Great, who ruled from 1457 to 1502. Later, the king (Peter the Lame) issued a decree expelling Jews from the country (1579). Jews returned to Tirgu Neamt in the 17th century. The oldest tombstones date from 1677 and 1689; there were three cemeteries, the last founded in 1838.

In 1859 the Jewish population was 3,006 and in 1899 it reached 3,671 (42% of the total). The oldest synagogue and the *mikveh* were demolished in 1849 by order of the abbot of a nearby monastery. The Jews opposed the order by force and six of them fell during the incidents. The Jewish community then sent a delegation to Constantinople, and obtained an order from the vizir compelling the monastery to pay damages. In 1855–56 the community received from the monastery land, money, and bricks to rebuild the synagogue and the *mikveh*. Among the rabbis who officiated in Tirgu Neamt, most prominent is R. Ḥayyim Mordecai Roller, rabbi between 1895 and 1941. He died in Jerusalem in 1946. Besides the *talmud torah*, a Jewish primary school was founded in 1890 but it was closed down in 1893 because of opposition from the religious circles, supported by the ḥasidic rabbi of *Buhusi. The school was reopened in 1897.

Anti-Jewish feelings in Tirgu Neamt were encouraged by the monks of the local monastery. In 1710 there was a *blood libel, which resulted in the death of five Jews and the pillaging of many Jewish houses. Additional blood libels were instigated in 1765, 1806, 1816, 1836, and 1859. In 1803 the monastery printed pamphlets propagating anti-Jewish agitation. In 1821 Romanian Greeks, in rebellion against Turkish rule, crossed Moldavia, set fire to the town, and assassinated half the Jewish population.

Between the two world wars, after naturalization rights were granted to the Jews, two Jewish representatives served on the local council. In 1931 a Jew acted as vice mayor. On the eve of World War II the community supported eight prayerhouses, an old-age home, a *mikveh*, and premises for a school.

In World War II the Jews were expelled to *Piatra-Neamt. After the war the community gradually came to an end through emigration. The Jewish population numbered 2,900 in 1947, 1,800 in 1950, and about 50 families in 1969. Shalom Dramer was the community's rabbi in 1954. There was one synagogue.

BIBLIOGRAPHY: J. Kaufmann, in: *Fraternitatea*, 7 (1885), 47–48, 54–55, 62–64, 70–71, 78–80, 94–95, 111, 118–9, 158–9; M. Schwarzfeld, *Ochire asupra istoriei evreilor în România* (1887), 14, 42; V. Tufescu, *Târguşoarele din Moldava şi importanţa lor economică* (1942), 92, 118–9; PK Romanyah, 127–9.

[Theodor Lavi]

TIRHAKAH (Heb. תִּרְהָקָה), the "king of *Cush" who, according to the Bible (II Kings 19:9), took part in *Hezekiah's revolt against Sennacherib. These references to Tirhakah (690/89–664 B.C.E.), the fourth pharaoh of the Twenty-Fifth (Ethiopian) Dynasty, appear to be an anachronism. According to a careful interpretation of the problematical biblical passages and Assyrian inscriptions, Hezekiah's uprising started in 703 B.C.E. Sennacherib undertook a successful punitive expedition against Judah's Philistine (II Kings 18:13 ff.) and Egyptian allies in 701, and then besieged all the fortified cities of Judah, ultimately forcing Hezekiah to pay a heavy indemnity. The appearance of "Tirhakah" at the head of another Egyptian contingent only served to cause Jerusalem to be immediately besieged a second time. Although the siege was interrupted because of a plague in the Assyrian camp, Sennacherib, nevertheless, again made Hezekiah and Judah his vassals. In the light of the above-mentioned dates the pharaoh who thus unsuccessfully assisted Hezekiah can only have been Tirhakah's brother and predecessor Shebitku, the Sithos of Herodotus' account of Sennacherib's expedition (2:141). The Bible's references "Tirhakah, king of Cush" however, are not inappropriate, since the citations symbolize the historical role of the entire Ethiopian Dynasty. It was the fate of these kings to make a prolonged but unsuccessful stand against Assyria's advance toward the Mediterranean, and it was Tirhakah who suffered the final defeat 30 years later. Egypt was invaded by Esarhaddon in 671 and by Ashurbanipal in 667; Tirhakah had to withdraw into exile in Nubia, and Thebes was destroyed in 664. Typically, Egyptian historical consciousness refused to recognize the Assyrian invasion; Tirhakah was still considered king of Lower Egypt in 666, and later was listed, like Sesostris, among Strabo's heroes of antiquity (1:3, 21; 2:1, 6). While recognizing the weakness of Egypt vis-à-vis Assyria (cf. the warnings of Isa. 30:1–5; 31:1–3), the Bible also reflects Egypt's gallantry when it telescopes Tirhakah, mythical defender of Egypt, and Shebitku, King Hezekiah's ally.

BIBLIOGRAPHY: G. Goossens, in: *Chronique d'Egypte*, 43–44 (1947), 239–44; M.F.L. Macadam, *The Temples of Kawa*, 1 (1949); H.H. Rowley, in: BJRL, 44 (1962), 395–431.

[Irene Grumach]

TIRZAH (Heb. תִּרְצָה), Canaanite city whose king is mentioned at the end of the list of those defeated by Joshua (Josh. 12:24). Eventually, the city seems to have been joined peacefully to the territory of Manasseh, as is indicated by the story of the daughters of Zelophehad, one of whom is named Tirzah (Num. 26:33; 36:11; Josh. 17:3). In the days of the divided monarchy, it became the residence of Jeroboam I after he left Shechem (I Kings 14:17). Some, however, hold that this is an anachronism and that Tirzah became the capital of Israel only in the days of Baasha. Baasha's son Elah was assassinated when drunk in the house of his steward in Tirzah. Zimri, his assassin and usurper, was besieged by Omri and burnt to death in the palace in 878 B.C.E. (I Kings 15–16). In the sixth year of his reign (c. 872), Omri transferred the capital to Samaria (I Kings 16:24). The rebel Menahem marched from Tirzah against Shallum in 748 B.C.E. (II Kings 15:14, 16). It seems to have been destroyed by the Assyrians at the same time as Samaria (721 B.C.E.). An earlier attack by Shishak in 925 B.C.E. is uncertain, as part of the name is missing in his list of conquered towns, but it is probable in view of the importance of the city at that time.

Tirzah has been identified with Tell al-Fāriʿa (Fārica), about 7 mi. (11 km.) northeast of Shechem, on an important highway near a plentiful spring. Excavations directed by R. de Vaux in 1946–60 revealed remains from the Chalcolithic period and an important Early Bronze Age town with a sanctuary, city wall, and fortified gates. After a gap of several centuries beginning in about 2500 B.C.E., occupation was resumed in the Middle Bronze Age. The town of the Late Bronze Age is poorer. The city was rebuilt in the Israelite period, and in a later phase, a palace was constructed which apparently remained unfinished; this may be due to the removal of the capital to Samaria. The later Israelite level is characterized by large private houses which are in sharp contrast to those of the poor, from which they are separated by a wall. This level was destroyed by the Assyrians in c. 723 B.C.E., after which settlement continued, but on a smaller scale. The site was eventually abandoned in c. 600 B.C.E.

BIBLIOGRAPHY: de Vaux, in: RB, 54 (1947), 394–433, 573 ff.; 69 (1962), 212 ff.; idem, in: PEFQS, 88 (1956), 125 ff.; idem, in: D.W. Thomas (ed.), *Archaeology and Old Testament Study* (1967), 371 ff.; Jochims, in; ZDPV, 76 (1960), 73–96.

[Michael Avi-Yonah]

TISCH, U.S. brothers, entrepreneurs and philanthropists. LAURENCE ALAN TISCH (1923–2003), the older of two brothers, was born in Brooklyn, N.Y. His father, Abraham (Al), was an All-American basketball player at the City College of New

York and owned a garment factory and two summer camps that his wife, Sadye, helped him run. Laurence graduated cum laude from New York University at 18 and a year later earned a master's degree in industrial management from the Wharton School at the University of Pennsylvania. After World War II service in the Office of Strategic Services, he enrolled at Harvard Law School but dropped out after a year. In 1946, the Tisch parents entrusted Larry, as he was known, with $125,000 to invest. He used the money to buy a lackluster resort called Laurel-in-the-Pines in Lakewood, N.J. that he found listed in a Business Opportunities advertisement in the *New York Times*. His brother, PRESTON ROBERT (1926–2005), known as Bob, joined him as a full partner in 1948. The Tisches refurnished the hotel, added amenities like a swimming pool, and dreamed up promotional stunts like importing three reindeer from Finland to pull sleighs in the snow. Over the next dozen years the brothers acquired a dozen hotels in New York, New Jersey, and Florida and in 1956 built the Americana at Bal Harbour, Fla., spending $17 million of their own money. It was in the black the first year, thanks to convention business. In 1961 the brothers gained control of Loews, one of the larger movie-house chains in the country, which was forced to separate its theaters from its filmmaking unit. Larry was attracted to Loews' underlying real-estate assets. In 1961 the brothers knocked down the old Loews Lexington Theater in New York City and used the site to build the 800-room Summit Hotel, the first hotel built in Manhattan in 30 years. In Times Square, they built the Americana, which at 50 stories was the world's tallest hotel upon completion in 1962. In 1968 the Tisches bought Lorillard, then the fifth-largest cigarette company in the United States. Larry shed its non-tobacco interests to increase profit margins. In 1974 Larry acquired a controlling stake in the CNA Financial Corporation, a nearly bankrupt Chicago-based insurance company. Within a few years he transformed it into a company with $16.5 billion in assets and an A-plus credit rating. By 1980 Loews vaulted to more than $3 billion in annual revenue from $100 million a decade earlier, from its 14 hotels, 67 movie theaters, insurance operations, shipping, Bulova watches, and popular cigarette brands like Kent, Newport, and True. Larry did have some setbacks, however. In 1971 Loews invested $40 million in the Franklin National Bank, which was sold to an Italian financier who was later convicted of looting its assets. Loews was sued by the Federal Deposit Insurance Corporation for breach of fiduciary duty and misuse of information. The company paid $1.2 million in an out-of-court settlement. In 1986 Larry was thrust into a new arena when he was invited to discourage a hostile takeover of the Columbia Broadcasting System network. Using Loews as his investment vehicle, Larry acquired almost 25 percent of CBS for $750 million. After a series of disputes with officers of CBS, Larry became acting chairman. Within months he presided over the ouster of 230 of the 1,200 news employees and cut the news division's budget by $30 million. He sold CBS's book publishing units in 1986 to Harcourt Brace Jovanovich for $500 million and its magazines to Diamandis Communications for $650 million the next year. And he also sold CBS Records, the second-largest record company in the world at the time, to the Sony Corporation of Japan for $2 billion. While CBS stock did well, the network faltered, falling to third place among the three major networks. After ten years, CBS was sold to the Westinghouse Electric Corporation for $5.4 billion. In the years after he left CBS Larry took a bearish position in the stock market and posted $2 billion in trading losses for Loews. Larry turned to civic affairs and philanthropy. He was a trustee of the Whitney Museum of Art, the Metropolitan Museum of Art, and the New York Public Library. He was also president of the United Jewish Appeal of New York and was a director of the Legal Aid Society. He became a prolific fundraiser for NYU, helping to provide it with endowment and new buildings. He spent his leisure time with his family, in frequent discussions of Jewish traditions with talmudic scholars. He often invited a rabbi to his Fifth Avenue office to discuss Bible passages and talmudic interpretations.

Bob Tisch worked with his brother to build the multibillion-dollar business empire, but he himself was postmaster general of the United States, half-owner of the New York Giants football team, and leader of many of New York City's top business groups. He was chairman of the host committees for the 1976 and 1980 Democratic National Conventions and led the way in building a new convention center on Manhattan's West Side. His last campaign, Take the Field, to revitalize the ragged athletic fields of the city's public high schools, raised $140 million. Bob Tisch's enthusiasm for convening the city's movers and shakers began during New York City's fiscal crisis in the 1970s with breakfasts at his Park Avenue hotel, the Regency. Major players in that municipal drama such as Lewis *Rudin and Felix G. *Rohatyn were the first regulars and Tisch was credited with coining the term "power breakfast." Among the city organizations Bob Tisch headed were the New York City Convention and Visitors Bureau, the New York City Partnership, and the New York City Chamber of Commerce and Industry. The Tisches were known for their generosity. The medical center and arts school at New York University bear the family name. So does a gallery at the Metropolitan Museum and the children's zoo in Central Park as well as namesake institutions at the University of Michigan, Tufts University, and elsewhere. Bob Tisch attended Bucknell University briefly, joined the army and earned a bachelor's degree from Michigan after his discharge in 1944. When Tisch was postmaster general, from 1986 to 1988, he used his marketing skill to sell stamps by phone and stressed the sale of commemorative stamps, which are financially advantageous for the Postal Service because collectors seldom use them as postage. Bob also founded Meals-on-Wheels in New York, served as its president for 20 years, and many times personally delivered meals to the elderly. His habit of working Sundays prevented him from seeing a professional football game until 1961, but he made up for it. After buying into the Giants in 1991, he loved to attend practices and confer with coaches.

He improved the team's business by sharpening marketing strategies and raising ticket prices.

[Stewart Kampel (2nd ed.)]

TISCHLER, HANS (1915–), musicologist. Born in Vienna, he settled in the United States in 1938 and studied musicology at Yale University with Schrade and Hindemith where he received his Ph.D. in 1942. He held positions in West Virginia at Wesleyan College (1945–47), Roosevelt University in Chicago (1947–65), and Indiana University (from 1965 until his retirement). He was guest lecturer at Tel Aviv University (1972) and Bar-Ilan (1986). Tischler was a leading scholar of late medieval music, editing complete editions and philological studies of the Notre Dame organa as well as of troubadour and trouvère music. His other fields of study were Mozart's piano concertos and the music of Gustav *Mahler. Among his writings are *The Perceptive Music Listener* (1955); *Chanter m'estuet, Songs of the Trouvères* (1981); *The Earliest Motets* (1982); and *Conductus and contrafacta* (2001). His important editions include *A Medieval Motet Book* (1973) and the *Monpelier Codex, PRMMA*, II–VII (1978).

BIBLIOGRAPHY: Grove online.

[Jehoash Hirshberg (2nd ed.)]

TISCHLER, MAX (1906–1989), U.S. industrial research chemist. Tischler was born in Boston. In 1957 he became president of a group of research laboratories. He contributed many papers in the fields of pharmaceuticals and chemical processes. In 1960 he edited the *Organic Syntheses*. He received many medals and awards including the award of the Swedish Royal Academy of Science.

TISHBY, ISAIAH (1908–1992), scholar of *Kabbalah, *Shabbateanism, ethical Hebrew literature, and Ḥasidism. Born as Sándor Schwartz in Sanislo, Hungary, Tishby received a traditional rabbinic education but soon became interested in secular literature and scholarly work. He wrote stories, articles, and poems in Hungarian, publishing a collection of Hungarian poems. He settled in Palestine in 1933 and studied at the Hebrew University, joining its department of Hebrew literature in 1951 (professor from 1955).

His main works include Zohar anthologies (*Mishnat ha-Zohar*, 2 vols., 1949–60); *Pirkei Zohar* (1969); *Torat ha-Ra ve-ha-Kelippah be-Kabbalat ha-Ari* ("The Idea of Evil… in Lurianic Kabbalah," 1942); Azriel of Gerona's exegetical *Perush ha-Aggadot* (1945); and a critical edition – begun by A.Z. Schwarz – of Jacob Sasportas' anti-Shabbatean tract *Ẓiẓat Novel Ẓevi* (1954). A collection of his studies in the fields of Kabbalah and Shabbateanism was published in 1964 as *Netivei Emunah u-Minut* ("Paths of Belief and Heresy"). In 1970 Tishby published *Perakim mi-Sifrei Musar Kabballiyyim*, an anthology of ethical works, with prefaces and commentary, covering from Saadiah to Maimonides. He wrote the article on ḥasidic thought in the *Encyclopaedia Hebraica*, which was also published as a separate book – *Torat ha-Ḥasidut ve-Sifrutah* (1966). Other studies of his deal with the messianic element in Ḥasidism, kabbalistic messianism in 16th-century Italy, and the messianic theology of M.Ḥ. *Luzzatto and his circle. In 1979 he was awarded the Israel Prize for Jewish studies.

[Joseph Dan]

TISHMAN, U.S. family in real estate and construction. Founded by JULIUS TISHMAN (d. 1936) in the United States in 1898, the Tishman family companies constituted a construction behemoth that built 400 million square feet of hotels and skyscrapers that started with tenements. Julius had five sons and six grandsons and, in various guises, the company continued as a major force through the early years of the 21st century. PAUL TISHMAN joined his father's company in 1924 after graduating from Harvard and doing graduate work at the Massachusetts Institute of Technology and Columbia University. He left the company in 1949 to form Paul Tishman Inc., which specialized in urban renewal, buildings for universities and hospitals, and buildings for Federal, state, and local governments. Among his projects was Washington Square Village, where modern apartment buildings replaced several blocks of older housing in Greenwich Village. He retired in 1969 and died in 1996 at the age of 96. He collected African art and the collection was acquired by Walt Disney Productions for Epcot Center in Orlando, Fla.

The Tishman company went public in 1928 and was dissolved in 1978 by a third-generation president, ROBERT TISHMAN, who launched a partnership with his son-in-law, Jerry Speyer. The company was reconstituted in 1980 as a private concern under Robert's cousin, JOHN, who became chief executive officer. John Tishman, a teacher whose father died when he was four, was put in charge of construction, a job the other cousins showed no interest in. In 1965 the Tishmans got a shot at managing the construction of Madison Square Garden in New York. Such high-profile projects begat others, including the first 100-story tower, the John Hancock, in Chicago. The Tishmans were called in as consultants on the World Trade Center. When they suggested ways to cut costs, the Port Authority hired the company as the builder. Tishman continued to develop its own properties but also emphasized research. It invented body-heat detectors that turn lights on and off when people enter or leave rooms. It developed a new roofing installation with Owens Corning Fiberglas, and with U.S. Gypsum it developed an inexpensive fireproof process. During a downturn in the economy John Tishman diversified the company into services. It began managing hotels such as the St. Moritz on Central Park South. It took on financial consulting jobs. John brought in his son, Daniel R., who had been running Tishman's New England projects out of Boston in 1994, and he was put on a direct path to succeed his father. DANIEL TISHMAN (1955–) joined the company in 1990 to lead it into the 21st century. Another Tishman, ALAN V. (1917–2004), was in charge of the leasing arm. The Tishmans were prominent in Jewish philanthropies. Among many campaigns, Alan was a vice president of UJA Federation of New York. Daniel was president of Israel Bonds' Greater New York appeal.

MARGARET (PEGGY) TISHMAN (1919–2004), who was married to Alan V. Tishman, played a prominent role in American Jewish affairs. She was an organizer of the merged UJA-Federation of New York and served as its first president, from 1986 to 1989, becoming one of the first women to gain national recognition as the chief executive of a major charitable federation. She helped found the Jewish Association for the Aged (JASA) in 1968, and she developed an endowment program to support that work. She served on the boards of the American Jewish Joint Distribution Committee and the Jewish Home and Hospital and was president of the Jewish Community Relations Council of New York. As Peggy Westheimer, she graduated from Wellesley College and received a master's degree in education and psychology from Fairfield University. She gained a national reputation in 1954 when she joined the board of the Jewish Home and Hospital amid a growing debate over how society cared for its elderly, and she helped persuade the Jewish Home to build one of the country's first assisted-living residences for older adults. She also served on New York City's Commission on Heroin Addiction and twice was a delegate to the White House Conference on Aging.

[Stewart Kampel (2nd ed.)]

TISHRI (Heb. תִּשְׁרֵי), the post-Exilic name of the seventh month of the Jewish year according to biblical usage which has been retained until the present day even though Tishri is the first month of the chronological year in the current way of dating. Frequently mentioned in Assyrian-Babylonian records and in rabbinic literature (e.g., *Megillat Ta'anit*), it is derived from the Aramaic *shera* or *sherei* ("to begin"). Hence, this name means "beginning of the year." Its zodiacal sign is *Libra*. In the present fixed Jewish calendar it invariably consists of 30 days, 1st of Tishri never falling on Sunday, Wednesday, or Friday in accordance with the system of calendric "postponement" (see *Calendar). In the 20th century, Tishri, in its earliest occurrence, extended from September 6 to October 5 and, in its latest, from October 5 to November 3. Memorable days in Tishri are mainly feasts laid down in the Pentateuch: (1) 1st and 2nd of Tishri, the New Year, Rosh Ha-Shanah (Num. 24:1–6), the second day applying in Ereẓ Israel as well as in the Diaspora (at least since about the tenth century); (2) 10th of Tishri, the *Day of Atonement (Lev. 16:29–34); (3) 1st–10th of Tishri, the *Ten Days of Penitence; (4) 15th of Tishri (in the Diaspora 15th–16th), the first day of Sukkot (the Feast of Tabernacles; Lev. 23:33–43); (5) 16th–21st of Tishri (in the Diaspora 17th–21st), the days of *ḥol ha-mo'ed* ("intermediate days"; Num. 29:17–34), the last of which (6) 21st of Tishri, known as Hoshana Rabba, is of special significance (Suk. 4:4–7); (7) 22nd of Tishri, Shemini Aẓeret ("The Eighth Day of Assembly"; Num. 29:35–38), combined with Simḥat Torah ("Rejoicing with the Torah," which is of post-talmudic origin). In the Diaspora 22nd of Tishri is observed as Shemini Aẓeret, and 23rd of Tishri as Simḥat Torah; (8) 3rd of Tishri, once observed as a minor feast in commemoration of the omission of the Hasmonean title "Priest to the Most High God" (modeled on the title of Melchizedek (Malki Ẓedek) in Gen. 14:18) from the dating of secular documents in the terms of the era of the regnal years of the Hasmonean high-priest kings (Meg. Ta'an. 337, et al.). Later this day reverted to its previous status of a fast in commemoration of the assassination of *Gedaliah (Jer. 41:1–2, et al.), the "fast in the seventh month" in Zechariah 7:5 and 8:19 (RH 18b, et al.) possibly postponed from 1st of Tishri (see Ibn Ezra and Kimḥi, *ibid.*).

[Ephraim Jehudah Wiesenberg]

TIŠMA, ALEKSANDAR (1924–2003), author, novelist. Born in Novi Sad, he had a Jewish mother and a Serbian father. In his novels he depicts, in a realistic style, the multiethnic and multireligious milieu of the mixed population of the Pannonian plain of the Vojvodina Province, including the relative harshness of Jewish existence. In particular he treated the problems of acculturation, identity conflicts, discrimination, and the racial and antisemitic persecutions during the Holocaust. These social phenomena are presented with accuracy and psychological insight. His testimony reveals horrid episodes of murder which occurred during the infamous razzia perpetrated by the Hungarian occupation forces in Novi Sad in January 1942.

Tišma won much praise and many prizes for his work and is counted among the most translated and better-known contemporary Yugoslav writers.

Among his works the following merit mention: *Krivice* ("Guilt," 1961); *Knjiga o Blamu* ("A Book on Blam," 1972); *Upotreba čoveka* ("The Use of a Man," 1976), and *Kapo* (1987).

BIBLIOGRAPHY: D. Katan Ben-Zion, *Presence and Disappearance: Jews and Judaism in Former Yugoslavia in the Mirror of Literature* (2002).

[Zvi Loker (2nd ed.)]

°TISO, JOSEF (1887–1947), prime minister (March–October 1939) and afterward president of Nazi-protected "independent" Slovakia. Trained as a priest, he was an excellent student and earned a doctorate in theology in 1910. A Slovakian nationalist, he began calling for an independent, authoritarian Catholic Slovakia in 1918. Elected to the Czechoslovakian Parliament in 1927, he became minister of health but was dismissed because of his ideology in 1929. Tiso was a Catholic priest at Bánovce and *vôdca* ("leader") of the fascist People's Party of Hlinka. Slovakia became autonomous in 1938 after the Munich Conference and Tiso later became its president. At Hitler's urging, he declared independence in March of 1939 but closely allied Slovakia with Germany. Ironically, he opposed the radicals of the Hlinka Guard and won a power struggle with them. He was one of the people primarily responsible for the deportation of Slovakian Jews to the death camps. His attitude to the "Jewish question" was evident by 1940, when he himself directed the "aryanized" estates in his own parish.

In March 1942 he rejected the appeal of the rabbis of Slovakia imploring him to prevent the mass deportations of Slovakian Jews. The Vatican was embarrassed by his leadership but took no steps to remove him from the priesthood or to excommunicate him. In August 1942, in a speech delivered at Holič, Tiso justified the deportations as "for the good of the Slovak nation, to free it of its pests." He had the power to issue exemptions from deportations and did so for 1,100 people, among them people who had been baptized and also wealthy Jews. After World War II, the National Tribunal of Bratislava found him guilty of several charges, including crimes against humanity, and he was hanged. His record is still a matter of contention in Slovakia and his role still an embarrassment to apologists for the Roman Catholic Church.

BIBLIOGRAPHY: J. Lettrich, *History of Modern Slovakia* (1956), index; L. Rothkirchen, *Ḥurban Yahadut Slovakia* (1961) incl. Eng. summary, index; O.J. Neumann, *Be-Ẓel ha-Mavet* (1958), passim.

[Livia Rothkirchen / Michael Berenbaum (2nd ed.)]

TISZAESZLAR (Hung. **Tiszaeszlár**), town in N.E. Hungary, not far from the provincial capital, Nyiregyhaza. The town became notorious in Jewish history in connection with a *blood libel there which aroused public opinion throughout Europe at the time and became the subject of stormy agitation in Hungary over many years. Its effects were disastrously clear during the White Terror period (1919–21), and even later during the antisemitic activity which culminated in Hungary with the expulsions of World War II. In 1882, when the blood libel occurred, there were about 25 Jewish families living in Tiszaeszlar, which had a total population of approximately 2,700. In 1944, the year of the expulsions, there were 61 Jews in the village.

On April 1, 1882, one of the village inhabitants, Eszter Solymosi, a Christian girl aged 14, disappeared. It was later discovered that she had committed suicide by throwing herself into the River Tisza. A short time after her disappearance, rumors were spread that some of the local Jews had murdered her in the community synagogue for religious requirements in anticipation of the Passover festival. The accusers included the leading local official, the provincial deputy in the parliament in Budapest, and the local Catholic priest, who also published an article which, by implication, accused the Jews of ritual murder. The authorities opened an investigation. The examining magistrate and other representatives of the state, who in principle believed the accusation, carried out their investigation with brutal methods. They succeeded by a ruse in convincing a local 14-year-old Jewish youth, Móric Scharf, to give false evidence: namely that with his own eyes he had witnessed how his father, with local Jews and others who had come from the vicinity, had murdered the girl in the synagogue and gathered her blood in a bowl. The investigation was much publicized, as was the trial which followed. There were also stormy debates on the subject in the Budapest parliament. Antisemitic deputies, such as Győző (Viktor) *Istóczy, fomented a violent agitation. The prime minister Kálmán Tisza did not believe in the libel, but because of political considerations did not dare to impede the judicial proceedings. The minister of justice, Tivadar Pauler, did indeed believe that a few uncivilized Jews employed Christian blood for their religious worship. The state prosecutor-general, Sándor Kozma, a man of liberal opinions, was opposed to the charge. A representative of the prosecution at the trial itself, Ede Szeyffert, also supported this opinion.

The trial was held in Nyiregyhaza during the summer months of 1883. In his summing-up speech the prosecutor proposed that the accused should be acquitted, and the verdict subsequently exonerated the 15 Jews accused. The counsel for the defense was brilliantly led by a non-Jewish advocate, Károly Eötvös, who was also a noted author, politician, and member of the Hungarian parliament. It was as a result of his interventions that the tribunal invalidated the false evidence which had been submitted. After appeals, the verdict was finally upheld by the supreme court of Budapest on May 10, 1884. Instead of subsiding, the wave of antisemitism gathered momentum throughout Hungary after the verdict of the district tribunal. In 1883, there were attacks on Jews in Budapest itself and other localities. These outbreaks reached such proportions that in certain districts the authorities were compelled to proclaim a state of emergency in order to protect the Jews and their property. In the wake of the antisemitic movement concentrated around the trial, and led by Istóczy, a specifically antisemitic party was founded (see *Antisemitism: Antisemitic Political Parties and Organizations), which in the parliamentary elections of 1884 won 17 seats. In the same elections, Eötvös, the defense advocate, was unsuccessful as candidate for the Liberals.

A variety of books and articles on the trial were written by both Jewish and antisemitic authors. In 1904, Eötvös published a history of the trial, a work of literary merit, which was published in a second handsome edition in 1968. The youth who had accused his parents and the members of his community underwent a spiritual and mental crisis. He remained for a while with his parents in Budapest and then left for Amsterdam, where he brought up a family in traditional Judaism and found employment in the diamond industry. His memoirs were published (M. Scharf, in: *Egyenlőség* (Dec. 3, 1927), 13). Numerous articles on the trial appeared in the general and Jewish press in Hungary and the rest of Europe. Its events form the plot of Arnold *Zweig's novel *Ritualmord in Ungarn* (1914). A young Hungarian historian, Sándor Hegedüs, published a monograph on the trial in Budapest in 1966. In the conclusion, he points out that he visited the village in search of material and to his regret still found "negative memories" of the trial among the elderly inhabitants.

BIBLIOGRAPHY: P. Nathan, *Der Prozess von Tisza-Eszlár* (1892); K. Eötvös, *A nagy per…*, 3 vols. (1904); S. Hegedüs, *A tiszaeszlári vérvád* (1966); J. Kubinszky, in: *Századok*, 1–2 (1968), 158–77; N. Katzburg, *Antishemiyyut be-Hungaryah* (1969), 106–55. **ADD. BIBLIOGRAPHY:** A. Handler, *Blood Libel at Tiszaeszlar* (1980); E. Stern, *Glorious Victory of Truth: The Tiszaeszlar Blood Libel Trial, 1882–3: A Historical-Legal-Medical Research* (1998).

[Yehouda Marton]

TITANS, Greek mythological figures, offspring of Uranus and Gaia. They warred against Zeus and were afterward imprisoned in Tartarus. The Septuagint translated Emek Refaim (II Sam. 5:18, 22) as "valley of the Titans" (elsewhere it is translated "valley of the Giants," I Chron. 11:15; 14:9; see also Jos., Ant., 7:71). In the apocryphal book of *Judith the phrase "sons of Titans" is used to represent forces of great power (16:7). *Philo in interpreting Genesis 10:8–9, makes reference to the Titans (*Quaestiones et Solutiones in Genesin* 2:82) and *Josephus alludes to them in *Contra Apionem* 2:240, 247. The Jewish author of the *Sibylline Oracles* describes the war between the Titans and the sons of Cronos, which ends with God's punishing the warring parties (3:106ff.).

BIBLIOGRAPHY: Lanchester, in: Charles, Apocrypha, 2 (1913), 371f.

[Howard Jacobson]

TITHE.

General

The rendering of tithes of property for sacral purposes was common all over the ancient Near East, though well-documented and first-hand evidence concerning tithes comes mainly from Mesopotamia (*ešrû/eširtu*; cf. Dandamaev, in bibl.). Although these Mesopotamian documents come from the neo-Babylonian period (sixth century B.C.E.), there is no doubt that the institution as such is much older. In the Syro-Palestine area the tithe (*mʿa šārtu*; cf. Heb. *maʿser*) is found in Ugarit in the 14th century B.C.E. (*Palais royal d'Ugarit*, 3 (1955), 147:9–11). The tithe was not assigned to temples only. As may be learned from I Samuel 8:15, 17 and from Ugarit (in the aforementioned example), the tithe could also be a royal tax which the king could exact and give to his officials. This ambiguity of the tithe, as a royal due on the one hand and as a sacred donation on the other, is to be explained by the fact that the temples to which the tithe was assigned were royal temples (cf. esp. Amos 7:13) and, as such, the property and treasures in them were put at the king's disposal. This can best be exemplified by the two instances of tithe mentioned in older sources of the Pentateuch (JE). In Genesis 14:20 Abraham gives a tithe (after his battle with the four kings of the north) to Melchizedek the king-priest of Shalem (= Jerusalem) and in Genesis 28:22 (cf. also Amos 4:4) Jacob vows to pay a tithe at Beth-El, the "royal chapel" of the Northern Kingdom (Amos 7:13). The mention of specifically these two "royal temples" in connection with the tithe is not a coincidence. It seems that these two traditions have an etiological slant. The institution of collecting tithes in the northern royal chapel Beth-El is linked to Jacob, the ancestor hero par excellence of the northern tribes, while the institution of the tithe in the royal sanctuary of Jerusalem is traced back to Abraham, whose traditions are mainly attached to the south. As is well known, the kings controlled the treasures of palace and temple alike (I Kings 15:18; II Kings 12:19; 18:15), which is understandable, since they were responsible for the maintenance of the sanctuary and its service not less than for the service of the court (cf. Ezek. 45:17, etc.). It stands to reason that the tithe, which originally was a religious tribute, came to be channeled to the court, and was therefore supervised by royal authorities. This is actually attested in II Chronicles 31:4ff. where Hezekiah is said to organize the collection and the storage of the tribute including the tithe. Though the description of the event comes from a late and tendentious source, its authenticity is supported inasmuch as the Mesopotamian tithe was organized along similar lines (cf. also the organization of Neh. 10:38; 12:44, 47; 13:5, 12). The annual tithe of the Carthaginians, which was sent to the Temple of Melqart in Tyre (Diodorus 20:14), is to be understood in a like manner. The Temple of Melqart was the state treasury of Tyre, and so the tribute paid by the Carthaginians had a political character besides its sacred one.

A further analogy between the sacred tithe and the royal one may be found in the priestly ordination, according to which the tithes of grain and "flow from the vat" are allocated to the levites in return for the services that they perform in the Tabernacle (Num. 18:21). A similar procedure is attested in the Ugaritic grants where the king of Ugarit gives the tithe of a whole city to his official for his loyal service (*Palais royal d'Ugarit*, 3 (1955), 16:153, 244; cf. 16:132, etc.), and, like the tithe given to the levites, it consists of grain and beverage. The same phenomenon is encountered in I Samuel 8:15 where the king is said to give away the tithe (grain and wine) taken from the people to his servants. The levites were actually the faithful officials of David whom he put in charge of the sacred treasures (I Chron. 26:20ff.; cf. B. Mazar, in: VTS, 7 (1960), 197ff.) and the law in Numbers 18 might reflect a Davidic grant (see JAOS, 90 (1970), 202) of a tithe to the levites. Grants to temple personnel are also known from Mesopotamia, and, as in the case of the levites, the property given passes on to their sons.

The property that was subject to tithe in Israel was grain, new wine, and new oil (Deut. 14:23, etc.), as well as cattle and sheep (Lev. 27:32). However, in a general context the tithe appears to embrace all kinds of property. Abraham gives Melchizedek a tenth of everything, which seems to refer to the booty of the war, and Jacob vows that "he will set a tithe from all that God will give him" (Gen. 28:22). In Mesopotamia, there is evidence of tithes from agricultural produce, cattle and sheep, slaves, donkeys, wool, cloth, wood, metal production, silver, gold, et al. It seems, therefore, that the specification in the Priestly and Deuteronomic codes refers only to the most common objects of tithing in Israel.

From the foregoing, it might seem that the tithe was an obligatory tribute, as is actually stated in Deuteronomy 14:22 and as conceived at the time of the Second Temple. However as Y. Kaufmann observed (see bibl.), the impression gained from the earlier sources (JE and P) is that the tithe is a kind of vow or voluntary gift. Thus Jacob's tithe in Genesis 28 is clearly linked to a vow, and by the same token Abraham gives the tithe to Melchizedek of his own free will (Gen. 14:19–20). Amos also mentions the tithe within the framework of voluntary offerings (4:4–5), while the law of tithe in Leviticus 27:32–33 occurs in a chapter dealing with sacred free gifts of various kinds (the firstlings there, verses 26–27, are an exception to the rule: these cannot be dedicated since they are holy by virtue of their birth as firstlings). The evidence of Numbers 18:21ff. is less conclusive. The general impression of the tithe here is one of an obligatory gift because it occurs side by side with first fruit and firstlings due to the priests (18:12ff.). It seems that the tithe, whose main purpose was the maintenance of the Temple and its personnel (see below), was provided by way of an obligatory tax as well as by voluntary donation. It is only Deuteronomy which stripped the tithe of its original purpose and turned it into an obligatory gift to the destitute and the poor (see below).

The Way of Processing and Spending the Tithe

Underlying all the sources in the ancient Near East dealing with the tithe is the notion of a tax indispensable for the maintenance of the temple and its personnel (except Deuteronomy to be discussed below). As may be learned from the Mesopotamian documents, the tithe was stored in the treasuries of the temple, and some of the temple representatives were put in charge of these stores. The cattle were marked with a temple mark, and the tithe of grain and dates could be converted into money when desirable. In the Babylonian documents, evidence is also to be found on the question of how the tithe was spent by the temple. Agricultural produce was mostly destined for consumption by the temple personnel but was also applied to the maintenance of various enterprises and institutions attached to the temple. Cattle and sheep were mainly used for sacrificial purposes. The tithe was collected by representatives of the temple authorities, who were also responsible for the transportation of the products to the temple. Every citizen was obliged to pay tithes and even the temple personnel and the collectors of the tithes themselves were not exempted from the due.

A similar picture is obtained when the biblical sources dealing with the tithe are examined in conjunction with the outside sources. Admittedly, as will be shown, one has to take into account the different attitudes to tithe in the various sources of the Pentateuch, and also the development of this institution at the period of the Second Temple. However, in general, the nature of the tithe and the way of processing and spending it is quite similar to that known from the outside sources, as presented in the previous paragraph. That the tithe was stored in the storehouse of the Temple may be learned from Malachi 3:10; Nehemiah 10:38–39; 12:44; 13:5, 12–13; and II Chronicles 31:4ff. The same sources provide information about the custodians of these stores and about the way in which the tithe was distributed among the Temple personnel (Neh. 13:13). Furthermore, the evidence in Nehemiah 10:38 about levites as tithe collectors in the provincial cities, which some have regarded as a gloss, is now corroborated by Mesopotamian data, according to which tithe collectors were recruited from the temple administration. Although this data is from later sources, this does not mean that the whole procedure was a late invention, especially in view of the fact that the same procedure is attested in outside sources. In fact this is the only realistic way in which the tithe can be conceived. The conversion of tithes of the produce of the land into money found in Mesopotamia is also mentioned in Leviticus 27:31 and Deuteronomy 14:24–25 (though with the difference that in Deuteronomy one is not bound to pay an additional fifth of the tithe for the redemption), and the fact that the tithe collectors themselves are bound to pay tithes is quite instructive for understanding the law about the tithes that the levites have to remove from their income (Num. 18:25ff.).

The Tithe According to the Various Pentateuchal Sources

There is no law about the tithe in the JE source (see *Pentateuch), but its view of the tithe is revealed in Genesis 14:20 and 28:20–22. As already indicated, the tithe in these passages is seen as tribute to the royal chapel.

In the Priestly literature, laws of tithe are found in two places: Leviticus 27:30–33 and Numbers 18:21–32. According to the former law, the tithe is given from "the seed of the ground," from "the fruit of the tree," and from "the cattle and the sheep." The tithe is "holy to the Lord," and if one wishes to redeem the tithe from the seed or from the fruit, he must add one fifth; the tithe from the herd or the flock cannot be redeemed. Here the tithe turns into the property of the Sanctuary, which also accounts for the fact that the tithe of the animals cannot be redeemed since these are considered as potential sacrifices. The tithe of the seed and fruit is mainly assigned to the priests and their household (cf. Lev. 22:11), and this actually explains the fifth one has to add if he wishes to redeem the tithe. According to Leviticus 22:14, if a layman consumes sacred food (unwittingly), he has to pay the value of the food plus one fifth. That gifts "to the Lord" are identical with gifts "to the priest" may be deduced clearly from those instances in which the phrase *le-YHWH* is supplemented with the word *la-Kohen* (Lev. 23:20; Num. 5:8), and from the verses in which it is explicitly said that donations brought to the Lord belong to the priests (Num. 18:12, 13, 14). Indeed the whole chapter of Leviticus 27 deals with dedications to the Temple treasury, which include the holy donations assigned to the priest (cf. verse 26).

According to the law in Numbers 18:21ff., the tithe of the grain and "the flow from the vat" (i.e., wine and oil) has to be given to the levite, who in turn has to set apart one-tenth of the tithe which they received "to the Lord," that is to the priests. It is thus apparent that in the Priestly literature two different views concerning the tithe are to be discerned. According to the stratum embodied in Leviticus 27 (an appendix to the Holiness Code which chronologically antedates the Priestly Code), the tithe is considered the property of the Sanctuary and the priesthood. According to the later stratum (Num. 18:21ff.), the tithe is given to the levites who were the non-officiating class of the Temple personnel. It is not known exactly what caused this change. According to M. Weinfeld, the tithe given to the levites is related to the levitical cities (see bibl.), which were given to the levites (Num. 35:1–8) out of the land apportioned to the Israelites. As is now known, the levitical cities as listed in Joshua 21 (cf. I Chron. 6:39–66) reflect the Davidic period. Some of the listed cities were not occupied before David, and, on the other hand, the geographic scope of the list could not be imagined in the post-Solomonic period (see W.F. Albright, in: *L. Ginzberg Jubilee Volume* (1945), 49–73 (Eng. sect.)). According to B. Mazar (in: VTS, 7 (1960), 193–205), these were the fortified cities where royal granaries and warehouses were kept under the supervision of the levites. Since the tithe in its original form was a tax associated with palace and Temple alike (see above), it stands to reason that these cities, which were counted as temple cities (cf. the high priest in the levitical cities of refuge, Num. 35:9ff. and see Mazar, *ibid.*), served as storages of the tithe. As already indicated, the practice of granting a city together with its tithe to the loyal official of the king is known from Ugarit, which might corroborate evidence concerning David's granting of cities with their tithes to the levites. These were his loyal functionaries and representatives, especially in the newly occupied areas and on the borders (I Chron. 23–26, esp. 26:20ff.; cf. Mazar, *ibid.*), and therefore were entrusted with supervising the collection of the tithe and guarding it. It seems that the tithe given to the levites was not only assigned to them for private consumption but was mainly destined for the upkeep of these royal temple cities. On the other hand, the tenth of the tithe which was given by the levites to the priesthood was needed for the maintenance of the central shrine in Jerusalem. (Before the Temple had been built, the "tent of David" served as the central sanctuary of Israel, II Sam. 6:17; I Kings 3:15; cf. Isa. 16:5; Amos 9:11.)

The Wellhausenian view that the priestly tithe is a reflection of post-Exilic reality (see Wellhausen, Proleg, 152ff.) does not hold for several reasons. (1) The general hypothesis about the post-Exilic background of the Priestly literature has been severely questioned (see *Pentateuch; cf. Kaufmann, Y., Religion). (2) The number of the levites in the Second Temple period was very small, and it is inconceivable that at this time the tithe would be assigned to this small minority, while the priests who exceeded the levites in large proportion received only a tenth of the levite tithe. (3) Even in the period of the Second Temple, the tithe was not given to the levites but to the priests (see below), and there was a general slackness in the fulfilling of the tithe duty in this period because of the justified feeling that the allocation of the tithe to the levites did not fit the new reality, i.e., the period of Restoration. (4) The evidence about the tithe from the ancient Near East, especially from Mesopotamia, completely refuted the arguments of Wellhausen, according to which the tithe was originally eaten by its owner and only during the Second Temple period appropriated by the priests and the Temple personnel. As the evidence cited above indicates, the appropriation of the tithe by the Temple and its personnel was a natural feature of this institution and not vice versa. (5) Wellhausen's contention that the tithe of the cattle and sheep is a late invention which was not in existence even at the time of Nehemiah (10:38–39, etc.) is very strange and actually contradicted by the evidence of the Bible (I Sam. 8:17 – although this refers to royal tithe) and by the Mesopotamian texts in which tithe of animals is referred to very often. (6) As will be shown below, the development of the tithe – like other sacred institutions in ancient Israel – reflects a trend toward secularization and not as Wellhausen argued toward sacralization (see *Pentateuch).

Tithe in the Deuteronomic Code

The law of Deuteronomy (14:22ff.) prescribes the setting aside of a tithe of grain, wine, and oil every year and its consumption at the chosen place (i.e., the central sanctuary). The tithe may be converted into money which is to be spent on the festive meal in the chosen place. Every third year, however, the tithe has to be left in the local settlement, for the benefit of the levite, who has no land of his own, and the stranger, the fatherless, and the widow (14:28–29). After giving away the tithe to these *personae miserabiles*, the owner has to proclaim a confession in which he declares that he has given it to the indigent and not desecrated it by using it for impure purposes (26:12–14).

This novelty of eating the tithe instead of giving it away to the Sanctuary and its ministrants (as was the case before) is to be explained against the background of the cultic reform which stands at the basis of the Deuteronomic law code and especially Deuteronomy 12–19. After the abolition of the provincial sanctuaries (in the levitical cities) and the provincial cultic officials there (levites), there was no more need for the tithe, which was destined for the maintenance of these institutions. However, in order to preserve this old sacred institution, the Israelite is commanded to observe the custom of setting aside a tithe from his yield and guarding its holiness by eating it only in the chosen place and not letting it be defiled. The preservation of another old feature of the tithe is also expressed by the allocating of the tithe every third year to the levite. This year is called "the year of the tithe" (26:12), which seems to preserve the old notion of the connection between the levite and the tithe. It must, however, be admitted that the levite appears here not as a sacred official but as a destitute person, that is, on the same level as the stranger, orphan, and widow.

A similar development in the Deuteronomic code may be recognized in connection with the law of the firstling (15:19–23). The JE law code (Ex. 13:2, 12, 15; 22:29; 34:19) prescribes the allocation of the firstling "to the Lord," that is to the Sanctuary, as a sacrifice (cf. Ex. 13:15), while the Priestly code commands that it be given to the priest who offers the blood and the fat on the altar but keeps the meat for himself (Num. 18:17–18). The Deuteronomic code prescribes the eating of the firstling by its owner at the chosen place (15:19–23), but he is also warned not to violate the holiness of the firstling before bringing it to the chosen place (15:19). A gradual severance of the institution from the sanctum may be discerned here, similar to the development of the tithe.

One must say that the Deuteronomic type of tithe is unique and unprecedented. Whereas the tithe is always a tax or gift for the maintenance of a temple or its personnel, here it is simply a philanthropic gift. The question, of course, is what the sources for the maintenance of the central sanctuary were if tithe did not continue to fulfill its normal function. One wonders whether the law of tithe in Deuteronomy was not formulated in a utopian manner (like a few other Deuteronomic laws, cf., e.g., 15:7–11). In fact, even the tithe according to the Priestly Code seems to contain utopian features. The law (Num. 18) might fit well – as shown above – the period of the United Monarchy, but there is no evidence concerning the levites and their cities after this period, and it is quite possible that the priestly law was not implemented at all after the disruption of the monarchy. One has to keep in mind the fact that the Israelite law codes, like the Mesopotamian ones, were formulated in an idealistic way and therefore cannot be judged against a realistic and pure historical background.

Tithe at the Period of the Second Temple

At the beginning of the Second Temple period the tithe was considered indispensable for the maintenance of the Sanctuary and its personnel. Thus Malachi urges the people to bring "the whole tithe into the storehouse" that there may be food in the house of God (3:10), apparently for the priests. Nehemiah stands on guard so that the people give their tithe to the levites and do not neglect it (Neh. 10:38; 12:44; 13:10–13). As has already been indicated, the method of organizing the tithe in this period was not different from what is known about the organization of the tithe in Mesopotamia. Representatives of the Temple were in charge of collecting the tithes from the fields (Neh. 10:38b), and the tithes were stored in the storehouses of the Temple (Mal. 3:10; Neh. 10:39–40; 12:44; 13:5, 12–13; cf. II Chron. 31:6ff.) under the supervision of priestly officials, who were in charge of their proper distribution (cf. Neh. 13:13). In contrast to the common view, there is no real contradiction between Nehemiah 10:38, which says that "the levites are collecting the tithe in all the cities," and Malachi 3:10; Nehemiah 12:44; 13:12, etc. which speak of the people bringing tithes to the storehouses. The latter statements mean that people made their contribution and not that the people brought the tithes with them in the literal sense of the word. According to the Mesopotamian practice, the temple authorities were responsible for the transportation of the tithe and there is no reason why the same practice should not have prevailed in Judah, especially when this is explicitly stated in Nehemiah 10:38. Moreover, this is supported by the rabbinic tradition, according to which the tithe was given to the levites (or rather to the priests, see below) on the threshing floor (Tosef., Pe'ah 4:3–6; Ket. 26a; TJ, Ket. 2:7, 26d; cf. Jos., Ant., 20:181, etc.). On the other hand, it is possible that the petty farmers brought their tithes with them to Jerusalem.

Though the purpose of the tithe and its method of organization in the discussed period seem quite clear, serious problems from the religious-halakhic standpoint complicated the issue. From Ezra's time the whole pentateuchal literature was considered a total unity (the Law of Moses) and the people had to comply with the Torah as a whole. The various attitudes toward the tithe as reflected in the different sources and especially in the Priestly code, on the one hand, and the Deuteronomic code on the other, had to be combined and the contradictions to be harmonized. Thus for instance the two types of tithes prevalent at this period: "the first tithe" (*ma'aser ri'shon*) and "the second tithe" (*ma'aser sheni*) are the outcome of the contradiction between Numbers 18:21ff. and Deuteronomy 14:22ff. According to the priestly ordination, the tithe is to be given to the levite, whereas according to the Deuteronomic code, it is to be consumed by the owner at the central sanctuary. The rabbis, taking it for granted that both laws are of Mosaic origin and therefore equally binding, interpreted them as two different tributes: one to be given to the levite, "the first tithe"; and the other to be brought to Jerusalem and consumed there, "the second tithe." Theoretically, this was an excellent solution. However, from the practical point of view the implementation of these laws was almost impossible. The excise of 20% of the yield was too high, while a more serious problem was the destination of the tithe. There were very few levites in the Second Temple period – in contrast to the situation at the monarchical period – and so the tithe was automatically shifted to the priests. Because this does not comply with the Law, all kinds of explanations had to be provided in order to do away with this legal anomaly. A common explanation was that Ezra punished the levites because they did not go up from Babylon to Jerusalem and therefore allocated the tithe to the priests (Yev. 86b). There were other harmonistic solutions, for example, that the priests are also levites since they are also descended from the tribe of Levi. But for obvious economic reasons, very few people observed the laws of tithe properly, and the common people were suspected for not putting aside the sacred portion from their yield, so that a conscientious observer of the Law could not partake of it without first tithing it himself. This situation caused a lot of problems whose legal aspects are dealt with extensively in a special tractate called *Demai*.

For post-biblical aspects, see **Terumot* and *Ma'aserot*.

BIBLIOGRAPHY: W. Robertson-Smith, *The Religion of the Semites* (1894[2]); Wellhausen, Proleg, 152ff.; O. Eissfeldt, *Erstlinge und Zehnten…* (1917); F. Horst, *Privilegrecht Jahves* (1930), 51–56 (= *Gottes Recht…* (1961), 73ff.); Pedersen, Israel, 3–4 (1947[2]), 70, 307–13; Kaufmann Y., Toledot, 1 (1960), 147–59, 181–2; de Vaux, Anc Isr, 140–1, 380–2, 403–5; M. Weinfeld, in: *Tarbiz*, 31 (1961), 4–5; idem, in: JAOS, 90 (1970), 202; M.A. Dandamaev, *Vestnik Dreney Istorii* (1965), 14–32; M. Haran, in: EM, 5 (1968), 204–12.

[Moshe Weinfeld]

TITHES, CHURCH, customary institution or article of canon law according to which one tenth of the income from buildings of every category was to be paid to the parish church. The theorists of canon law claim that the ecclesiastic tithe was derived from the tax instituted in the Bible (Lev. 23:30ff.; Deut. 14:22ff.). The real estate owned by Jews in Western Europe during the tenth and eleventh centuries, particularly the agricultural land and vineyards, was substantial. From the second half of the 11th century, there was a migration of Jews from the countryside to the towns and a consequent voluntary and progressive abandonment of agricultural occupations, Jews increasingly restricting themselves in this sphere to occupations of a ritual interest (particularly those connected with vineyards for the production of *kasher* wine). It was precisely at that time that the obligation to surrender the tithe on the produce of their lands to the local church was first imposed on the Jews. The Church Council of Gerona of 1067 (or 1068) restricted this obligation to the lands purchased from Christians. In 1078 another Council of Gerona extended the obligation of the ecclesiastic tithe to all the land in the possession of the Jews. The Fourth Lateran Council held in 1215 (canon 67) declared that this decision was applicable in all the lands of Christendom, with respect to estates formerly owned by Christians that were in the possession of Jews at the time. It appears to have been enforced with considerable severity in southern France. In Spain, however, the Jews were supported by Alfonso VIII, king of Castile, in their refusal to make the payment; in 1205, Pope Innocent III intervened in connection with this.

When the payment of the tithe was first imposed, the Jews adopted a subterfuge in the case of houses: they destroyed the old houses acquired from Christians and erected new ones. In 1219 Honorius III intervened in this matter, at least where the diocese of Toledo was concerned. In 1233 Gregory IX once more enforced the prescription laid down by the Council of Gerona of 1078; even with respect to Jewish land in formerly Muslim regions, where there was no reason to assume that it had been purchased from Christians, the tithe obligation was fully applied. In England, and in the Germanic countries, the tithe appears to have been exacted from the Jews with severity. In England the problem was solved from the second half of the 13th century by the general prohibition on the owning of land by Jews. When the Jews returned to France during the 14th century, they could no longer own any lands, while in the German countries, the prohibition was applied only from the first half of the 14th century. The problem could have arisen again in France from the time the Revolution granted the Jews the rights of citizenship, which included the right of owning land, had not the Revolution already abolished ecclesiastic tithes, by a law of April 4, 1789.

BIBLIOGRAPHY: J.B. Saegmueler, *Lehrbuch des katholischen Kirchenrechts* (1914^{3}), 442–4; J. Parkes, *Jew in the Medieval Community* (1938); G. Lepointe, in: *Dictionnaire de droit canon*, 4 (1949), 1231–44; B. Blumenkranz, *Juifs et chrétiens…* (1960), 349; S. Grayzel, *Church and the Jews…* (1966^{2}), index.

[Bernhard Blumenkranz]

TITIEV, MISCHA (1901–1978), U.S. anthropologist. Born in Kremenchug, Russia, Titiev moved to Boston with his family when he was six years old. He received a B.A. (1923), an M.A. in English literature (1924), and a Ph.D. in anthropology (1935), all from Harvard University. Titiev served as assistant museum curator and junior archaeologist for the National Park Service (1935–36). He joined the faculty of the University of Michigan in 1936, rising to professor in 1951. He conducted field studies among the Hopi Indians in Arizona, the Araucanian Indians in Chile, the Japanese in Peru, and the natives in rural Okayama, Japan.

During World War II he served in the Office of Strategic Services (OSS). In 1954 he was a Fulbright professor at the Australian National University. After retiring from teaching he was named professor emeritus at the University of Michigan.

His principal academic interests were the ethnology of the Hopi Indians, the social organization of the Japanese in Japan and Peru, and the ethnology of the Araucanian Indians of Chile. He conducted research in East Asian anthropology and participated in founding the Japanese Study Center at the University of Michigan. Titiev was so highly respected by the Hopi Indians that he was adopted into the tribes of the Third Mesa and the Sun Clan.

Among his written works are *Old Oraibi* (1944); *Araucanian Culture in Transition* (1951); *The Science of Man* (1954, 1963^{2}); and *Introduction to Cultural Anthropology* (1959).

The Mischa Titiev Library, established in 1976 at the College of Literature, Science, and the Arts (LSA), regents of the University of Michigan, contains a wide collection of material for anthropological research.

[Ephraim Fischoff / Ruth Beloff (2nd ed.)]

TITLES.

In the Talmud

The many titles appearing in talmudic literature may be roughly classed into two (sometimes overlapping) categories: titles of respect and titles of office. Almost all these titles make their first appearance not earlier than in the middle or late part of the first century C.E. Thus all "pre-tannaitic" personalities, with the exception of Simeon the Just, bore no titles, unless the term *ish* (lit. "man [of]") in *Avot* 1:4 designates some high office rather than merely meaning "native of." Other titles of the Temple period refer mainly to the priestly hierarchy, e.g., *Kohen gadol, segan ha-kohanim*, among others.

TITLES OF RESPECT. The most important in this category is a group of three related terms: *rabban*, *rabbi*, and *rav*.

According to the Tosefta (Eduy. end) "he who has disciples, and his disciples have disciples, is called *rabbi*. If his disciples are forgotten (but his statements are handed down) he is called *rabban*. If both are forgotten he is quoted by his name." No such use of *rabban*, however, occurs in rabbinic literature, and Allon suggests that this *baraita* refers to the manner in which a disciple referred to the teachings of his teacher which he had heard or which had been transmitted to him, but not to the titles accorded them by the people as a whole. In point of fact, the only sages upon whom the title *rabban* was conferred were heads of the central academy, or the Sanhedrin after Hillel, including Rabban Johanan b. Zakkai and Hillel's descendants, Gamaliel I, II, III, and Simeon b. Gamaliel III (cf. *Iggeret Sherira Ga'on*, ed. by B.M. Lewin (1921), 125f.). It was then a title of supreme distinction granted to the head of the academy. The term *rabbi* was granted to all Palestinian scholars from the late first century onward who had received **semikhah* ("ordination"). Its use in Matthew 23:7, 8 is generally regarded as anachronistic. (Rabbi, without a proper name, refers to Judah ha-Nasi I.) The Ashkenazim vocalize the name as *rabbi* (רַבִּי), which may mean "my master." The Sephardim, however, vocalize it *ribbi* (רִבִּי) with no suggestion that it is the first person suffix of "master." Some of the talmudic sages, in fact, have the cognomen *be-ribbi* added to their name; cf. Yose b. Ḥalafta (Suk. 26a), Judah b. Ilai (Men. 34b), Eleazar ha-Kappar (Av. Zar. 43a), and Joshua b. Levi (Kid. 80). Rashi explains *be-ribbi* as "a scholar of outstanding acumen" (Suk. 26a) and Samuel b. Meir as "a leading scholar of his generation" (Pes. 100a). Ezekiel Landau (*Noda bi-Yhudah, mahadura tinyana*, OḤ no. 113) differentiates between *be-ribbi* as a title added to a name, which means a leading scholar, and *biribbi* unattached to a name, which refers to an individual. In Babylon, however, where scholars were not ordained, they were only called *rav* ("master"; see Arukh, s.v. אביי, but cf. Tosef., Eduy. ad. fin.).

The term *abba* ("father"), originally an address of esteem and affection, came to mean something less than *rabbi* (*Abba* Saul, Judah, etc.). The term *mar* (or *mari*, "my lord") seems to have had a similar semantic history, though when used in Babylon (*Mar* Samuel, Ukba, Zutra) probably meant more than just *rav*. Other appellations of respect are *he-ḥasid* ("the righteous"; cf. Suk. 52b), and the more technical *ḥakham, talmid ḥakham* ("scholar") and others.

TITLES OF OFFICE. The biblical *nasi* ("prince") was used in tannaitic times to designate the president of the Palestinian community. In Babylon, the exilarch was called *resh galuta* (lit. "head of the Diaspora"). The head of the Sanhedrin was entitled *av bet din*, and members of the court *zekenim* ("elders"). There were also the following Palestinian titles: *rosh keneset* ("head of a synagogue"?); **parnas* ("communal administrator"); and *gabbai ẓedakah* ("public collector and distributor of charity"). A *ḥazzan* was a synagogue sexton (Suk. 51b), a school superintendent (Shab. 1:3) or, in collegiate debates, a chairman (TJ, Ber. 4:1, 7d). In Babylon, the president of the students assembled to study in Adar and Elul was called *resh kallah*, and was second only to the *resh sidra*; an assistant teacher was called *resh dukhan* (BB 21a), a college janitor *maftir keneset*, and the town guard *ḥazzan mata*.

Finally, "a member of the order for the observance of levitical purity in daily intercourse" was known as a **ḥaver*. However, in amoraic times, both in Palestine (TJ, Ta'an. 1:6, 64c: "fellow of the rabbis") and Babylon (Beẓ. 25a), it could simply mean a fellow student. Often honorific epithets were assigned to outstanding personalities, but these are descriptive rather than titles proper.

[Daniel Sperber]

In the Middle Ages

Among Jews in the Middle Ages, titles stemmed from community leadership, from scholarship, or from a pious way of life. Titles would be transferred from one of those spheres to express admiration for an individual. Among titles designating both scholarship and office was the *archipherecites or *resh pirka*, head of the academy, mentioned in the sixth century. From the academies of Babylonia, as well as from participation in the leadership functions of the geonic period, come the titles **gaon, *av bet din* (ABaD), **alluf* or **resh kallah*, as well as the leadership titles *resh golah* ("*exilarch") in Babylonia, *nasi* in other lands, and **nagid* in Egypt, Kairouan, and Spain. The community leaders held a variety of titles in many languages. Some of the Hebrew ones are **parnas, kahal, rosh, ne'eman, manhig, tuv, ikkor, *alluf,* and **gabbai*. The communal functionaries were *shoḥet u-vodek, moreh ẓedek, *dayyan, *shammash, *ḥazzan, *rav, rosh yeshivah*, and **maggid*. Since the 15th century, among Ashkenazi Jewry the titles *ḥaver, morenu*, and *rav* appear in connection with the Ashkenazi **semikhah*. The rabbi of the local community is defined as the *mara de-atra*. In the 15th century the title *manhig* ("leader") for rabbis appeared, only to disappear in the 16th, and for a short period *rosh golah* reappeared as an honorific title. Appellations denoting special attributes were *ha-navi, he-ḥasid, ha-sar ha-gadol, ha-go'el ha-malakh, ha-kadosh* ("martyr"). For Sephardi Jewry **ḥakham* and *marbiẓ torah* are the main functional titles for scholars. Among the ḥasidic appellations are **admor (adonenu morenu ve-rabbenu)*, and *ba'al shem tov*. Among the Sephardi Jews **ḥakham bashi* was in use for the Turkish chief rabbi. In modern times the appellation *rav rashi* ("chief rabbi") appears.

[Isaac Levitats]

BIBLIOGRAPHY: A. Orenstein, *Enẓiklopedyah le-To'orei Kavod be-Yisrael* (1958–); Allon, Meḥk, 1 (1957), 253–5. IN THE MIDDLE AGES: Baron, Community, 3 (1942), index; Eisenstein, Yisrael, s.v. *To'orei Kavod*.

TITLES OF NOBILITY. Titles of nobility in Europe were originally bound up with land tenure, and if only for this reason Jews were automatically excluded from holding them in the Middle Ages. A Jew, Ḥayyim (Cham), is referred to in a fifth-century epitaph found in Venice as *clarissimus*, which implies that he had the rank of knight (*eques*), but in the circumstances this may have been no more than a formal courtesy (Frey, 103, p. 593). A number of Jews in 12th- and 13th-century England were designated *miles*, which in the opinion of Joseph Jacobs implied "soldier," but in fact was the common agnomen of the Hebrew "Meir," e.g., Meles of Marseilles (Samuel b. Judah b. Meshullam). There were also various scholars and others called Sir Leon (i.e., Sir Judah, referring to Judah called a lion by his father: Gen. 49:9). This was probably no more than a conventional title attached to the name Judah in accordance with the biblical designation of Judah's supremacy (Gen. 49:10; Deut. 33:7), e.g., Judah Sir Leon of *Paris, Judah Sir Leon le Blund of London (12th century), and *Judah b. Jehiel ("Messer Leon"). Sir Morel, presumably a slurring – possibly jocular – mispronunciation of the biblical Samuel, was also popular, e.g., *Samuel b. Solomon of Falaise (Sir Morel). Sometimes lands which were held as knights' fees passed into Jewish hands, whether by mortgage or otherwise, but that Jews enjoyed or used the knightly title attached to them is out of the question. In Spain many Jews in the Middle Ages had a status not dissimilar to that of the court nobility, but it is certain that none had a title conferred on him. Noah-Manuel Norsa (of the *Norzi family of Ferrara, Italy) was referred to in an official document in 1409 as *nobilem virum*, implying a patent of nobility.

The earliest Jew to be formally ennobled was apparently Joseph (Ippolito) da *Fano (late 16th century) who according to Immanuel Aboab was created – presumably by the Holy Roman Emperor – marquis of Villimpenta (in Mantua), but the circumstances are obscure. About 1622 the financier Jacob *Bassevi of Prague was ennobled by Emperor Ferdinand II, receiving the title Von Treuenburg, in recognition of his financial assistance at the time of the Thirty Years' War. *Marranos, who at this time escaped from Spain and Portugal and professed Judaism abroad, sometimes already enjoyed nobiliary titles: Mordecai da Modena had been created Knight of the Golden Fleece by Charles V. Others were or fancied themselves to be closely connected with Spanish and Portuguese noble families, so that personal titles of nobility came naturally to them. More than one member of the Spanish and Portuguese community in Holland was raised, somewhat paradoxically, to the nobility for his services, while a Jew, to the Spanish crown, among them Manuel (Isaac Nuñez) *Belmonte, who was created Count Palatine by Leopold III in 1693 and passed on the title to his heirs, pillars of the synagogue; and Antonio (Isaac) Lopes *Suasso, who was made baron of Avernas de Gras by Charles II of Spain. Francisco da Silva Solis, son of the Portuguese Marrano financier Duarte da Silva Solis, was created marquis de Montfort in 1682 in return for his military services; his son, the second marquis, returned to Judaism under the name Isaac (Fernando) da Silva *Solis, naturally preserving the ancestral title. King William III of England, following Dutch precedent, knighted the financier Solomon de *Medina in 1711, but this precedent was not followed in England for over a century. In France titles were attached to some estates: hence when Liefmann *Calmer purchased certain lands from the duc de Chaulnes in 1774, he automatically became viscomte d'Amiens and baron de Picquigny. By a similar process there emerged in the period of Enlightenment the barons *d'Aguilar, von *Arnstein, *Eskeles, etc., and the baron Albert Treves in Italy. Turkey, however, had long before conferred not merely the title but the substance of nobiliary status on professing Jews, when Joseph *Nasi was created duke of Naxos in 1566, to be followed not long after by the Marrano Solomon *Abenaes, who as a Christian had been a knight of Santiago but after reverting to Judaism was created duke of Mytilene by the sultan.

Although the 13th-century kings of Hungary had given titles of nobility along with estates to their Jewish chamberlains (e.g., Woelfel of Komárom), there were comparatively few Jewish nobles in the Austro-Hungarian Empire up to the end of the 18th century; outstanding among them were the barons Dirsztay, Kohner, *Hatvany, and Weiss, and the Austrian barons *Koenigswarter, *Hofmannsthal, and *Morpurgo. In Germany as well (especially Prussia) most Jews were granted titles only after baptism, as were Cohn-Oppenheimer, Von Weinberg, Von *Simson, Fritz Victor von Friedlaender-Fuld, Von Heine-Geldern, and Von Mendelssohn, though notable exceptions were Gerson *Bleichroeder, Maximilian Goldschmidt Rothschild, and Jacob von Hirsch. The ennobling of Jewish families was greeted contemptuously by the German antisemites, who recorded the process in the Semi-Gotha, a handbook of the "nobility" who were Jews or of Jewish blood, closely imitating the annual Gotha Almanac which chronicled Europe's aristocracy.

The 19th century witnessed two tendencies: on the one hand the acquisition of nobiliary titles by some wealthy Jews from impoverished governments, and on the other hand the elevation of Jewish notables to the nobility in recognition of public services.

In England, Sir Moses *Montefiore was knighted by Queen Victoria in 1837, when he was sheriff of London; Isaac Lyon *Goldsmid, the first Anglo-Jewish baronet (1841), was made baron de Palmeira in 1846 by the Portuguese government. An interesting case is that of the Jamaican Jew Issac de Lousada (d. 1857), descended from the 17th-century Spanish New Christian duke de Lousada, chamberlain to Charles III, who succeeded in getting this title revived in 1848. This is the highest title of nobility ever granted to a Jew in the West. The first Russian Jew to be ennobled was Baron Horace *Guenzburg in 1871, while his father, Joseph Yozel *Guenzburg, was likewise created a baron three years later; shortly afterward Alexander III made the title hereditary. The Rothschild family, ennobled in Austria early in the 19th century, bore in most countries the formal but not very meaningful hereditary title of baron. Nathaniel Mayer de Rothschild was created the first Anglo-Jewish peer in 1885 as Lord (Baron) Rothschild. Thereafter the elevation of English Jews to the peerage for social or political services was not uncommon; Rufus Isaacs, after being made baron in 1914 and viscount in 1916, was created marquis of *Reading in 1926. Similarly, Herbert *Samuel's political career was crowned by his being created Viscount Samuel in 1937. Lords Swaythling, *Melchett, Wadsworth (see Sydney James *Stern), *Silkin, M.S. *Bearsted, *Jessel, *Mancroft, and H.L. *Nathan also exemplify this process. On the other hand, it is noteworthy that many of the Jewish peerages in the English creations are now extinct through lack of male issue, while in some cases the present holders of the titles are no longer Jews. After the institution of life peerage began in England, in order to strengthen the House of Lords, a number of Jews had their distinction recognized in this fashion.

[Cecil Roth]

TITUS, ARCH OF.

(1) A triumphal arch commemorating *Titus' victory over the Jews and his conquest of Jerusalem, erected in 80 C.E. during his reign as emperor, apparently at the eastern end of the Circus Maximus in Rome. This arch, no longer extant, is known from its inscription, which was copied in the Middle Ages. Dedicated by the senate and the Roman people in honor of Titus, the inscription enumerates his virtues and refers to the submission of the Jews and the destruction of Jerusalem as a feat unparalleled among the achievements of former kings and commanders.

(2) At a later stage, during the reign of Titus' brother Domitian, another triumphal arch was either erected or completed to commemorate this victory. This arch, which is extant, was set up at the western end of the Via Sacra. While it may have been started before the time of Domitian, it was definitely completed after Titus' death, since the inscription refers to him as divine (*Divo Tito*). Regarded as an architectural masterpiece, it influenced the architecture of the following period. It has a dedicatory inscription and various bas-reliefs, the best known being the one on the inner wall of the arch which shows the Temple vessels carried in a triumphal procession as spoils. These consist of the table of shewbread, the trumpets, the censers, and the seven-branched candlestick, which is especially conspicuous, being carried aloft by the victors. The design of the candlestick has raised many problems and much has been written on it, the authenticity of the base in particular being called in question, as it consists of two hexagons, the one superimposed on the other, on whose sides dragons are depicted. Some regard this design as authentic, others as the fruit of the artist's imagination (see *Menorah). On the inner wall, opposite the bas-relief of the Temple vessels, Titus is portrayed as the victor riding in a chariot drawn by four horses and being garlanded by the goddess of victory. The arch of Titus, symbolizing and glorifying the victory of Rome, has been for the Jews the symbol of their defeat and tragedy consequent on the failure of the war against Rome and the destruction of Jerusalem and the Temple. During the Middle Ages no Jew was allowed to, or would, pass under the Arch, paying instead a fee to be allowed to go through a neighboring house.

BIBLIOGRAPHY: Pauly-Wissowa, Suppl. 4 (1924), 479f. no. 9; S.B. Platner, *Topographical Dictionary of Ancient Rome* (1929), 45–47; CAH, 11 (1936), 787f.; S. Reinach, in: REJ, 20 (1890), lxv–xci.

[Uriel Rappaport]

°**TITUS, FLAVIUS VESPASIANUS,** emperor of Rome, 79–81 C.E., destroyer of the Second *Temple in 70. Titus was the son of *Vespasian and accompanied him to Judea when he was appointed by *Nero to suppress the uprising there (66). Arriving in Judea with legions from Alexandria, Titus took an active part in the conquest of Galilee, under the command of Vespasian. He captured Jotapata (where he spared the life of *Josephus, who had been in command) and other cities, including Tarichea and Gamala, leaving Giscala (גּוּשׁ חָלָב) the only Galilean city still to be subdued. Seeking the surrender of the city without resort to battle, he succumbed to a ruse of its commander *John of Giscala, who asked for surrender negotiations to be delayed until after the Sabbath and used the opportunity to escape to Jerusalem together with those of his followers who survived the pursuit of Titus. When Vespasian became emperor in 69, he entrusted Titus with the suppression of the revolt. Titus was in Egypt at the time, and left by sea for Caesarea, where he organized his forces.

At Jerusalem

Titus had at his disposal four legions, supplemented by auxiliary forces, including the army of *Agrippa II. *Tiberius Alexander acted as the Roman commander's chief adviser and assistant. Moving on Jerusalem, he encamped on Mount Scopus shortly before Passover, 70, and after surveying the scene decided to make his way to the city's walls through the less densely populated new city. He gave orders for embankments to be built from which to attack the (outer) wall, for which purpose most of the trees in the vicinity were uprooted.

The Roman soldiers were constantly harassed by the Jews, who succeeded in undermining and destroying the embankments. The enraged Titus led a cavalry charge against the Jews, in which he personally killed 12 of his opponents (Jos., Wars, 5:287ff.; Suetonius, Titus, 5). Titus then launched his attack on the second wall, from an area known as the "Assyrian Camp," the Romans being obliged to storm the wall for a second time, after it was recaptured from them by the Jews. Titus gave instructions that everything was to be destroyed. Realizing that the city could not be conquered by storm, Titus decided to vanquish its citizens by starvation, calling for the erection of a further wall to seal off all access to and from the Jews concentrated in the Temple area. At the same time the Romans again erected embankments, which necessitated the carrying of logs over great distances. Many Jews who sought to escape the rigors of the famine were caught and severely tortured by the Romans, who even disemboweled their victims in the hope of extricating gold which they believed the Jews to have swallowed (Jos., Wars, 5:548ff.).

The daily sacrifices in the Temple, which had continued without interruption, finally ceased on the 17th day of Tammuz. At various stages during the battle for Jerusalem, Josephus was sent by Titus to appeal to the Jews to surrender. The Jews scornfully rejected his pleas, but in the end some members of the high priestly families were persuaded to surrender (Jos., Wars, 6:96ff.). Titus harangued his own troops, offering prizes to the first of them to scale the wall surrounding the Temple court, which he set about battering as a prelude to his final assault on the rebels.

Destruction of the Temple

Various degrees of responsibility have been assigned to Titus for the events that followed his order (on the Ninth of Av) to set the Temple gates on fire. Josephus (*ibid.*) relates that (on the eve of the Ninth of Av) Titus called a council of war to determine the Temple's fate, and after hearing divided opinions, decided that it should be preserved. Josephus ascribes the actual setting alight of the Temple to the unauthorized act of a Roman soldier who flung a burning torch at the Temple, and states that Titus' subsequent efforts to persuade his soldiers to extinguish the flames were in vain, their desire for revenge allegedly overcoming their sense of discipline. *Sulpicius Severus, however, maintains that the destruction of the Temple was the premeditated act of Titus, based on his conviction that its fall would be accompanied by that of the rebellious people, whose fount of strength it was. His source is thought to be the lost writings of Tacitus, to which he lent a Christian interpretation. This version appears to approximate the truth rather than that of Josephus, which was probably written with the desire to clear Titus of blame.

The Temple's destruction signaled the end of organized Jewish resistance and Titus, after capturing also the upper city, ordered the destruction of the whole city and its walls. Only three towers were left as a reminder of past glory. Titus was hailed as emperor by his soldiers; he distributed awards and held a three-day victory celebration and other festivities, including gladiatorial contests, at which many of the Jews who had been taken prisoner were killed. He held similar festivities in the capital and other cities of Syria, from where he continued his journey through the Euphrates area to Alexandria and Rome. In Antioch he rejected a request to have the Jews banished from the city. Josephus ascribes this to his humanitarian feelings (Wars, 7:100ff.) but more probably, it was to avoid incurring the enmity of the Jews in various parts of the empire toward Rome. He took with him the two leaders of the revolt, John of Giscala and Simeon b. Giora, together with a large number of young and healthy prisoners, who were included in the victory procession given by Rome to conquerors, at which sacred vessels taken from the Temple were also displayed. An arch (depicting scenes from the procession) was erected to commemorate Titus' victory over the Jews, and is still to be seen in Rome (Arch of *Titus).

When he became emperor, Titus severed his relationship with *Berenice, sister of Agrippa II, whose lover he had been while in Judea. Tacitus and Suetonius testify to the general approval he met with during his short reign, remarking on the great generosity he displayed when a number of disasters struck Rome and other parts of the empire. He is described by Suetonius as the "delight of the human race," whose death caused much sorrow to the whole world. Jewish scholars, however, see him as a ruthless enemy of their people, to whom he displayed no feelings of mercy or generosity, and the cruel treatment he meted out to his prisoners is reflected even in the writings of Josephus. In talmudic tradition he is termed "the wicked descendant of the wicked Esau," and is denounced for insulting and blaspheming the God of Israel and for not hesitating to enter and desecrate even the Holy of Holies (cf. Jos., Wars, 6:260). His name is engraved in Jewish memory as the destroyer of the Temple.

[Lea Roth]

In the *Aggadah*

After the fall of the Temple, Titus entered the Holy of Holies, his drawn sword in his hand, slashed the *parokhet*, and spreading out a Scroll of the Law on the top of the altar, had intercourse with two harlots he had brought in. Titus attributed the bloodstains on his sword to his having slain the Almighty (Git. 56b). Some of the sources, however, point out that in reality it was either the blood of the daily sacrifices or of those of the Day of Atonement (Lev. R. 22:3). Titus began to revile and blaspheme God, boasting that he had vanquished "the king in his own palace." He next collected all the vessels of the Temple, placed them in a net, and sailed for Rome. After he embarked a violent gale blew, and Titus claimed that God possessed power only over water since He had smitten the generation of the flood and Pharaoh by water. Thereupon the Almighty caused the sea to cease from its raging. When Titus landed, a tiny gnat entered his nose and fed on his brain for seven years, growing in size until it caused his death. When he died, the physicians opened his skull and found a creature resembling a sparrow weighing two selas, or according to another account, a young dove two pounds in weight. Its beak was of brass and its claws of iron. Before his death, Titus commanded that his remains be burnt and scattered over the seven seas so that the God of the Jews would not find him and bring him to trial.

When *Onkelos, who according to the Talmud was the son of Titus' sister, desired to convert to Judaism, he raised Titus from the dead to seek his guidance. Titus informed him that Israel is the most reputable nation in the other world, but that their observances are burdensome. He advised his nephew to attack them so that he would become a leader in the temporal world, since adversaries of the Jews become masters. Titus informed him that his punishment was, ironically, in accordance with his own wish that his body be burned and his ashes scattered (so as to escape *punishment after death). Every day his ashes are collected, sentence is passed, and he is burnt and his ashes scattered again over the seven seas (Git. 56b–57a; Lev. R. 22:3; ARN2[7], 20f. et al.).

[Aaron Rothkoff]

In the Arts

From medieval times onward Titus has played a double role in literature, art, and music: as the lover of *Berenice and as the conqueror of Jerusalem. Literary exploitation of the first theme, based on *Josephus, Suetonius, and other ancient sources, mainly dates from the 17th century. Probably the earliest serious treatment of the Titus-Berenice romance was *Bérénice* (1648–51), a four-volume French novel by Jean Renault de Segrais which is said to have partly inspired the dramatic interpretations of Pierre Corneille and Jean *Racine. Racine's outstanding five-act tragedy, *Bérénice*, was performed eight days before Corneille's *Tite et Bérénice* in November 1670. The former's drama maintains that Titus finally gave up Berenice in deference to Roman public opinion, while the latter's (staged by Molière's troupe) makes Berenice voluntarily give Titus his freedom. The appearance of these two dramatic works gave rise to considerable interest and debate, not least on account of the topical theme of a monarch's conflict between love and duty. The contemporary literary discussions gave rise to an anonymous three-act prose comedy, *Tite et Titus, ou Critique sur les Bérénice* (Utrecht, 1673), and to Fatouville's parody, *Bérénice* (Paris, 1683). The works that followed include Thomas Otway's *Titus and Berenice*, a tragedy based on that of Racine, which was staged in London in 1677, and *La clemenza di Tito* (1734), an 18th-century text by Pietro Metastasio that was often copied or adapted by other writers. In the late 19th century, Heinrich Vollrat Schumacher wrote the German novel *Berenice* (1892²), an abridged Hebrew version of which (*Be-a'arat ha-Milḥamah*, 1905) was published in Jerusalem. Hans Kyser's German tragedy, *Titus und die Juedin* (1911), was a significant modern treatment of the subject. Other works by 20th-century writers include John Masefield's play, *Berenice* (with *Esther*, 1922), which was based on Racine; *Birinikah* (1945), Eisig *Silberschlag's Hebrew translation of an unpublished German drama by Carl de Hass; and the U.S. novelist Leon Kolb's *Berenice, Princess of Judea* (1959) and *Mission to Claudius* (1963), the latter of which was illustrated by Jakob *Steinhardt.

The second theme, that of the destruction of Jerusalem, attracted many writers not only because of its theological implications for the Christian – who saw in the Jewish disaster the fulfillment of Jesus' prediction – but also by virtue of its sheer drama and pathos. The subject was mainly exploited by English and French poets during the Middle Ages. An early English (15th-century) poem on the theme, attributed to John Lydgate and Adam Davy, was *Titus and Vespasian; or, The Destruction of Jerusalem*. In France, *Le livre Titus et Vespasianus*, an epic *chanson de geste*, possibly dates from the 14th century. During the Puritan era, English writers anxious to circumvent religious objections to the staging of biblical plays often found it convenient to acknowledge their indebtedness to Josephus' *Jewish Wars* in preambles to works on the theme. William Heminge (or Hemings), son of an actor friend of Shakespeare, wrote a drama based on Josephus and *Josippon entitled *The Jewes Tragedy, or their Fatal and Final Overthrow by Vespasián and Titus his Son...* (1662). Two other 17th-century treatments were Joost van den Vondel's drama, *Hierusalem Verwoest* (1620), and an anonymous Mexican (Aztec) *Auto de la destrucción de Jerusalén* (published in 1907).

The Roman assault on Jerusalem inspired many notable works of the 19th and 20th centuries, several of which were written by Jews. Two English treatments were Lord *Byron's poem, "On the Day of the Destruction of Jerusalem by Titus" (in *Hebrew Melodies*, 1815), and *The Fall of Jerusalem* (1820), a dramatic poem by Henry Hart Milman, dean of St. Paul's. A work of the same period was Manoel Caetano Pimenta de Aguiar's Portuguese tragedy *Destruiçãao de Jerusalem* (Lisbon, 1817). Two treatments that followed were *Titus; oder, Die Zerstoerung Jerusalems* (1855), a four-act German verse drama by Julius Kossarski, and *Az utolsó próféta* ("The Last Prophet," 1869), a historical play by the Hungarian convert Lajos *Dóczy. The South African rabbi and author Judah Loeb *Landau's five-act Hebrew drama, *Aḥarit Yerushalayim* (1886), was written when the author was barely 20. Among 20th-century treatments were Sir Henry Rider Haggard's late novel, *Pearl Maiden; A Tale of the Fall of Jerusalem* (1903), and J.A. Herbert's poetic *Titus and Vespasian* (1905), which was based on the 15th-century *Bataile of Jerusalem*. Max Jacob's French poem, *Le siège de Jérusalem, drame céleste*, appeared in 1914. The destruction of Jerusalem also forms the background to Lion *Feuchtwanger's trilogy about Josephus.

In art Titus is chiefly celebrated in the famous Arch of *Titus in Rome. Reliefs adorning the arch depict the victories and glory of Titus, most notably his campaign in Judea. A later, more stylized depiction of the fall of Jerusalem and the capture of the Temple by Titus is contained in a panel of the *Franks Casket* (c. 700 C.E.; British Museum), a remarkable example of early English carving in whalebone. Josephus' description of the triumphal procession after Jerusalem's fall inspired *The Triumph of Caesar*, a painting by Andrea Mantegna (1431–1506; Hampton Court Palace, England).

The subject has provided less significant inspiration in music. Metastasio's libretto, *La clemenza di Tito*, was first set by Antonio Caldara (1734) and subsequently by other 18th-century composers, including Scarlatti, Hasse, and Gluck. Mozart's setting of a libretto by C. Mazzola after Metastasio (*La clemenza di Tito*, 1791; Koechel 621) in the year of his death was already an anachronism in its time. This composition for Leopold II's coronation as king of Bohemia was both Mozart's last opera and the last of its kind in European musical history to follow the baroque *opera seria* style.

See also *Josephus in the Arts.

BIBLIOGRAPHY: Weynand, in: Pauly-Wissowa, 12 (1909), 2695–729, no. 207; *Oxford Classical Dictionary* (1970), s.v. *Titus*; R. Symes, *Tacitus* (1958), index; Reinach, Textes, index; Schuerer, Hist, index; Klausner, Bayit Sheni, 5 (1951²), 20, 180–202, 222–65. IN THE AGGADAH: Ginzberg, Legends, 5 (1925), 60, 287. IN THE ARTS: C. Raphael, *Walls of Jerusalem* (1968), deals with the destruction of Jerusalem in history and legend; M. Roston, *Biblical Drama in England* (1968), 118–9, 173–5, 222.

TIVOLI, SERAFINO DA (1826–1890), Italian painter, founder and leader of the *macchiaioli* school. He was a leader of the young Italians who, inspired by the political revolutions of 1848, wanted to change the character of Italian painting. They hoped to lead it in a new direction, away from outworn neoclassic formulas. Da Tivoli went to Florence at the age of 12 and soon decided that painting was his vocation. He adopted the *macchiaioli* method of painting: that is, he applied his paint in rapid dots or spots (*macchie*). He painted fresh, spontaneous landscapes, full of movement, but the critics and public were hostile to his technique. Da Tivoli fought in the wars of the Italian Risorgimento. From 1860 until his death he lived in Paris. There his art became increasingly realistic, and landscapes such as "The Seine at St. Denis" and

"The Old Fish-House at Bougival" were painted under the influence of Corot.

BIBLIOGRAPHY: A. Franchi, *Arte e artisti toscani dal 1850 ad oggi* (1902), 92–95; idem, *I macchiaioli toscani* (1945); A.M. Comanducci, *I pittori italiani dell'Ottocento* (1934), 199; M. Girardelli, *I macchiaioli e l'epoca loro* (1958).

TIVON (Heb. טִבְעוֹן), a locality in Galilee. Tivon is mentioned several times in talmudic literature in connection with various sages, some of whom lived there, including Abba Yose, R. Hanina son of Gamaliel, R. Judah of Tivim, R. Zadok the physician, and others, like R. Meir, who visited the local synagogue (Makhsh. 1:3; Tosef., Meg. 2:5; Tosef., Nid. 4:3; Meg. 24b). The people of Tivon were said to have suffered from a defect in their pronunciation which rendered them unsuitable for officiating as precentors. The site of Tivon has been identified with the ruins of Ṭab'un 10 mi. (16 km.) east of Haifa. The lands of Tab'un were acquired by the Jewish National Fund after long litigation, and a garden city, originally called Tivon but later *Kiryat Tivon, was established in the vicinity in 1936.

BIBLIOGRAPHY: S. Klein (ed.), *Sefer ha-Yishuv* (1939), s.v.; idem, *Palaestina-Studien*, 1 (1923), passim; Press, Ereẓ, s.v.; Avi-Yonah, Geog, 133.

[Michael Avi-Yonah]

TKATCH, MEIR ZIML (1894–1967), Yiddish poet. Born in Priborsk (Ukraine), Tkatch immigrated to New York in 1913. He began his literary career with Russian lyrics in 1914, later changing to Yiddish, in which language he published poems and fables in dozens of Yiddish periodicals, and nine volumes of poetry between 1927 and 1960. In 1963 he published his selected poetry in the two-volume *Mayn Hob un Gob* ("My Belongings and Bounty," 1962–63); additionally, *Elterfrukht fun Yugntsvit* ("Old Age's Fruit from Youth's Bloom," 1971) and *Eygns un Fremds* ("One's Own and Another's," 1977). Tkatch's fables, among the finest in Yiddish, are cast in the form of dialogues and miniature dramas. Each teaches a lesson by means of a vivid picture of animal life and affords bitter insight into the psychic realms that are the substratum of human behavior. Tkatch's mastery of difficult verse forms is also evident in his sonnet sequences, triolets, and translations of Yessenin and Robert Frost.

BIBLIOGRAPHY: LNYL, 4 (1960), 111–12; J. Glatstein, *In Tokh Genumen* (1947), 266–72; I.Ḥ. Biletzki, *Massot* (1963), 106–12; Y. Yeshurin, *Meyer Ziml Tkatsh Bibliografye* (1963).

[Sol Liptzin / Jerold C. Frakes (2nd ed.)]

TKHINES (Yid., from Hebrew *teḥinnot*, "supplications"), private devotions and paraliturgical prayers in Yiddish, written by women and men, recited primarily by women. As texts in the vernacular, *tkhines* are important sources for the history of popular Judaism in the 17th, 18th, and 19th centuries, and are particularly useful in studying the history of women's religion. Most Jewish men attained basic literacy in Hebrew, and a significant minority went on to full mastery of the classic literary tradition. However, only a small number of women learned more than the rudiments of Hebrew, and those Central and East European Jewish women who could read were usually literate only in the vernacular Yiddish. Jewish liturgy and other devotional and scholarly works were written by men and were almost always in Hebrew or Aramaic, making them inaccessible to most women.

In books of *tkhines*, each individual prayer begins with a heading directing when and sometimes how it should be recited: "A pretty *tkhine* to say on the Sabbath with great devotion"; "A confession to say with devotion, not too quickly; it is good for the soul"; "A *tkhine* that the woman should pray for herself and her husband and children"; "When she comes out of the ritual bath"; "What one says on the Eve of Yom Kippur in the cemetery." Scholars are divided as to whether these prayers were meant as a women's substitute for the Hebrew liturgy, or as voluntary, supplementary prayers, recited when women wished. Although some *tkhines* were intended to be recited in the synagogue ("When the shofar is blown on Rosh ha-Shanah, say this"), and a few were for male worshipers ("A lovely prayer for good livelihood to be said every day by a businessman"), the majority were associated with women's domestic lives: prayers to be recited privately daily and on Sabbaths, festivals, fasts, and New Moons, for the three so-called "women's commandments" (**ḥallah*, **niddah*, *hadlakat ha-nerot* [candle lighting]); for pregnancy and childbirth, for visiting the cemetery; for private griefs such as childlessness and widowhood; for recovery from illness; for sustenance and livelihood; for confession of sins. *Tkhines* framed women's domestic lives and roles as sacred, and also connected them with grander themes from Jewish thought, especially the hope for the messianic redemption and the end of exile.

Background

During the 16th and 17th centuries, new rituals and new genres of religious literature emerged, whose audience was a sort of intellectual "middle class." This parallels the emergence of similar literature in Christian Europe, enabled in part by the rise of printing. Works of *musar*, collections of *hanhagot*, *tikkunim*, and other new liturgies and rituals, often in abridged and simplified form, were published both in Hebrew, for an audience of men with a basic education in classical Jewish texts, and in Yiddish, the vernacular, for women and non-scholarly men. Many of these new publications (including Hebrew **teḥinnot*, supplemental prayers for men) developed out of and popularized a mystical pietism originating among the kabbalists of Safed, Palestine, in the 16th century; others originated among secret Shabbetians. *Tkhines* were an important form of women's participation in this pietistic revival and its popular literature. By contrast, however, *tkhines* published in the 18th and 19th century show little evidence of influence from Ḥasidism.

History of the Genre

Although there are manuscript *tkhines*, this is primarily a print genre. The two main groups of *tkhines* comprise those that were printed in Western Europe in the 17th and 18th centuries, which, although published anonymously, were probably written or compiled by men for women; and those that appeared in Eastern Europe in the 17th, 18th, and early 19th centuries, often with named authors or compilers, some of whom were women. The geographical designation refers primarily to place of *printing,* rather than place of *composition,* which is more difficult to determine; it is also intended to suggest a rough periodization, with certain overlaps. The language of the *tkhines* (known from the 17th century on as "*tkhine-loshn*") is relatively fixed, rather like an increasingly archaic "prayer-book English," and displays few of the distinctive linguistic features of the developing East European varieties of Yiddish; thus, linguistic analysis is of little help in determining place of composition.

Other differences between Eastern and Western *tkhines* include the fact that West European *tkhines* were published in collections addressing many topics, either in small books or as appendices to Hebrew prayer books. The first major collection (containing 36 prayers), entitled simply "*Tkhines,*" was published in Amsterdam in 1648; reprints (usually entitled *Seyder Tkhines*), expansions, and additional collections followed. In the mid-18th century, a comprehensive collection containing 123 prayers emerged, entitled *Seyder Tkhines u-Vakoshes* ("Order of Supplications and Petitions" (Fuerth 1762), although there may be one or two earlier editions) and was repeatedly reprinted, with alterations, over the next 150 years, first in Western and then in Eastern Europe. The West European texts depict the holiness to be found in the domestic and the mundane, in the activities of a wife and mother, but they also invoke the angels, the patriarchs and heroes of Jewish history, and the ancient Temple that stood in Jerusalem. The very earliest East European *tkhines* were published in Prague. *Eyn Gor Sheyne Tkhine* ("A Very Beautiful Tkhine," ca. 1600) is one of the first to claim female authorship: it is attributed to "a group of pious women." Two other Prague imprints, one from the turn of the 18th century, and the other from 1705, are attributed to women: Rachel bat Mordecai Sofer of Pinczow, and Beila bat Ber Horowitz. Like many other East European texts, all three of these Prague *tkhines* were short, and dealt with only a single subject each, such as a *tkhine* "to be recited with devotion every day." However, one notable work, *Seyder Tkhines* (Prague 1718), was written by a man, Matthias ben Meir, formerly rabbi of Sobota, Slovakia, explicitly for a female audience. "My dear women," he writes, "…I have made this *tkhine* for you in Yiddish, in order to honor God and … to honor all the pious women. For there are many women who would gladly awaken their hearts by saying many *tkhines*." This work contains 35 prayers, on a variety of topics. Many later editions, entitled *Preger Tkhine* ("Prague Tkhine"), were published without the name of the author.

Except for the Prague imprints, the East European *tkhines* were usually small pamphlets printed on bad paper with poor type, often with no imprint, making their bibliographic history difficult to trace. Books of *tkhines* originating in 18th-century Eastern Europe, especially in Galicia, Volhynia, and Podolia (now parts of Poland, Belarus, and Ukraine), tended to deal with a smaller number of subjects (such as the High Holidays and the penitential season), often by a single author, and were usually under 20 pages long. Because a significant number of these authors were women, these texts allow us to hear women's voices directly. Important examples include *Tkhine Imohes* ("*Tkhine* of the [Biblical] Matriarchs") for the Sabbath before the New Moon, by Leah *Horowitz (18th century), which argues for the power of women's prayer and quotes from rabbinic and kabbalistic sources; *Tkhine Imohes fun Rosh Khoydesh Elul* ("*Tkhine* of the Matriarchs for the New Moon of Elul" [and the entire penitential season]; Lviv, n.d.), by Serl daughter of Jacob ben Wolf Kranz (the famed Preacher of Dubno, 1741–1804), which calls on the four biblical matriarchs (Sarah, Rebecca, Rachel, and Leah) to come to the aid of the worshiper and plead her case before the heavenly court; and *Shloyshe Sheorim* ("The Three Gates"), attributed to the legendary Sarah *Bas Tovim (she probably lived in Podolia in the 18th century), which contains three sections: one for the three "women's commandments," one for the High Holidays, and one for the Sabbath before the New Moon. Some East European *tkhines* suggest that women should take part – in some fashion – in such traditionally male activities as synagogue prayer and Torah study.

By the mid-19th century, the genre had undergone significant change. Jews in Central and Western Europe had largely abandoned Yiddish; books comparable to *tkhines* were published first in Germanized Yiddish, then in German in Yiddish characters, and finally in German. However, these texts exhibited an entirely new sensibility, influenced by the rising ideal of the bourgeois family, with its stress on sentiment and emotional family ties, and its new definition of gender roles. Similarly, in Eastern Europe, the ideal of the bourgeois family came into play, but in a somewhat different fashion. *Maskilim* wrote *tkhines* to reach the "benighted" traditional women with their reform program. Unlike earlier *tkhine* authors, female or male, they scorned their audience and the genre. Often, because they thought they could sell more books, they attributed their works to female authors, either those who had actually written *tkhines* a century earlier, or to creations of their own imagination. (Because the maskilic practice of using female pseudonyms was well known, earlier scholars were skeptical of any attributions to female authorship. However, many 17th and 18th century women authors can be authenticated.) Alongside these newer maskilic *tkhines*, older texts and collections, both those originally published in Western Europe and those originally published in Eastern Europe, continued to be reprinted in Eastern Europe in numerous editions, often revised or garbled by the printers.

Significance

The *tkhines* reveal a whole world of women's religious lives, concerns, customs, and settings for prayer. The women (and men) who composed these prayers for women addressed the spiritual issues of their day, whether on the level of domestic piety or national redemption. The *tkhines* themselves are at home in the literature produced for the intellectual "middle class" of this period; they belong among the guides to the upright life, books of customs, condensations of guides to pious practices, and digests of mystical teachers that were read by householders and artisans. Indeed, the *tkhines* show just how much women were a part of this intellectual and spiritual world.

Recent Developments

As the use of Yiddish declined among emigrants from Eastern Europe in the late 19th and the 20th centuries, and the Yiddish-speaking heartland was destroyed by the Holocaust, the genre of *tkhines* nearly disappeared, except among Ḥasidim and other isolated traditional Yiddish-speaking populations. Since the 1980s, however, the *tkhines* have aroused new interest both in scholars and in members of the Jewish public in Europe and North America. Jewish women, in particular, have sought to find a "usable past" in which to root themselves. Orthodox women have turned to the historical *tkhines* as a direct expression of "traditional" Jewish women's spirituality. This has occurred despite the fact that, unlike their European ancestors, many young Orthodox women in America today are well educated in the Hebrew prayer book and classical sources in Hebrew, and may not know Yiddish at all. Liberal Jewish feminists have sought role models in the *tkhines* uncovered by scholars, and some have also written and published new *tkhines*, some of which have been incorporated into recent editions of Conservative and Reconstructionist prayer books.

BIBLIOGRAPHY: D. Kay, *Seyder Tkhines: The Forgotten Book of Common Prayer for Jewish Women* (2004); C. Weissler, *Voices of the Matriarchs: Listening to the Prayers of Early Modern Jewish Women* (1998); B. Kratz-Ritter, *Fuer "fromme Zionstoechter" und "gebildete Frauenzimme"* (1995).

[Chava Weissler (2nd ed.)]

TLEMCEN (Lat. **Pomaria**), city in N.W. *Algeria; Judeo-Berber center. The *Berber tribes in the neighboring areas of Tlemcen professed Judaism. Judeo-Muslim saints were worshiped there for a long time. In the 10th and 11th centuries scholars of the community corresponded with the *geonim* of Mesopotamia. The city was destroyed by the *Almohads in 1146. Jews settled there again only in 1248, when it became the capital of the Zeiyanid kingdom. The Jews of Tlemcen lived outside the city in a suburb or village called *Agadir. Abraham Ben-Jalil, ambassador of Aragon, settled there with his family in 1291. In 1415 R. Saadiah ha-Cohen Sullal served as a rabbi in Tlemcen. In the middle of the century his son Nathan took the rabbinate. The community's rabbis in the 14th century were Abraham b. Ḥakun and Moses b. Zakar. When Ephraim b. Israel Al-Nakawa (Enquaua), a Spanish refugee who was the son of the author of *Menorah*, settled in Agadir, he obtained permission for Jews to settle in the city of Tlemcen, where he built a synagogue. Among its outstanding scholars were Judah Najjār, Marzuk b. Tāwa, Saadiah Najjār, the Ankawas, Zerahia Zalmati, and the Alashkars. The Arab traveler 'Abd al-Bāsit remarks that he studied medicine with the famous teacher, Moses *Alashkar (1465). However, in 1467 this coexistence was disrupted by persecutions of the Jews by Muslim religious brotherhoods. At this time many Jews left for Castile. The appointment of R. Isaac bar Sheshet as a *dayyan* of Algerian Jewry was issued in Tlemcen. In the 15th century well-known rabbis lived there. Rabbi Joseph Sasportas (son of Abraham Sasportas) was born in the first decade of the 15th century in Tlemcen. He was the student of the *dayyan* R. Ephraim Enquaua. His son Judah and his grandson Moses studied in Tlemcen. Their teacher was R. Amram Najjari. The Jews had political influence in the court in Tlemcen during the 15th century. R. Joseph Sasportas was appointed *dayyan* by the king. The family of R. Abraham *Gavison settled in Tlemcen 50 years after the death of R. Ephraim Enquaua. In 1493, the Spanish rabbi Judah Khalass (Chalaz, *Khalaz), the author of *Mesi'aḥ Illemim,* settled in the city. In 1492 many Spanish refugees settled in Tlemcen, including the *Gavison, *Levy-Bacrat, and Khallas families. Some of them, including Stora, Ben-Mahiya, and Sasportas, assumed important diplomatic functions. The *nagid* Abraham ben Saadon helped the refugees, aiming to make Tlemcen a center of Torah study. R. Jacob Beirav and his son Joseph settled for a short time in Tlemcen after 1492. R. Jacob served there as a rabbi. Jacob Alegre was sent on a mission to Charles V (1531). In the treaties they negotiated a clause granting religious liberty to the Jews who wished to settle in Spanish territory. In the mid-15th century Rabbi Jacob ha-Kohen Ashkenazi from Ashkenaz settled in the city. He became a famous figure in the community, a kabbalist and teacher. His best-known student was R. *Jeshua ben Joseph ha-Levi, the author of *Halikhot Olam*. In the early 16th century Tlemcen suffered a series of disasters, from which it never completely recovered. In 1517 the Turks pillaged the city, destroyed Jewish property, and obliged the Jews to wear a piece of yellow material on their headgear. By 1520 there were no more than 500 "houses" (families) of Jews. In 1534 the Spanish army captured the town; massacres took place and 1,500 Jews were enslaved. Their coreligionists of *Fez and *Oran paid a ransom to set them free. In the second half of the 16th century the *dayyan* Solomon Khallas II was active in Tlemcen. Other scholars in that period were Solomon Enquaua, Maimon Khallas, and Judah Khallas III. At the beginning of the 17th century the *dayyan* Moses Shuraqi lived in Tlemcen. Although the Jewish community of Tlemcen was sacked by the Turks in 1670, it still produced such scholars as Nathan Djian and Isaac Moatti in the 1700s. When the French entered the city in 1830, they found 1,585 Jews and five synagogues, one of which they turned into a church in 1842. In the 18th century the community was organized and the local rabbis were David Djian, Jacob Benichou, Shalom Elashkar, Judah Djian, Nissim Elhaik, Messas Touati, and Joshua Allkabetz. The leader of the community was called *Sheikh -al-Yahud.* At the beginning of the 19th century, the chief rabbi of the community was Ḥayyim Kasbi, the author of *Ẓeror ha-Ḥayyim* (published in 1807). He immigrated to Oran. In the 19th century R. Abraham Enquaua founded a yeshiva, Eẓ Ḥayyim. In the second half of the century the rabbis Ḥayyim Blia'h, Nathan Assiag, and Masud Benishou lived there. The French authorities (from 1842) set up a consistoire in Tlemcen. In 1846 the Muslims slaughtered Jews in a pogrom. In 1851, 2,688 Jews lived in Tlemcen with eight synagogues and two schools. In the 19th century modernism spread in Jewish society. In 1866, 200 Jewish students studied in the French-Jewish school. The president of the consistoire was Simon Kanoui. There were local parents who sent their children to Christian schools. Jews from Tlemcen served in the French army. During the 1881 uprisings the Jews fought back their Christian adversaries. They were not attacked again until 1940, when legal discrimination was instituted. Their rights were restored later along with those of the rest of Algerian Jewry. In 1911 the Jews in Tlemcen numbered 5,000 and, in 1941/42, 4,907. The community was never larger than 6,000 persons, and its members were mostly workers and salaried employees. The *Alliance Israélite Universelle founded schools in the city, but at the end of the 19th century no yeshivah existed there. In 1902, the local rabbi, Abraham Meir, who came from France to Tlemcen in 1890, published a book there. He criticized the *minhagim* of the community and emphasized the backward character of the native Jews and the cultural difference between them and the European Jews in the city, in spite of the *Crémieux Decree giving Algerian Jews French citizenship. The local Jews in response to the book dismissed R. Meir and he returned to France. At the end of the 19th century the French rabbi Moïse Weil served in Tlemcen. He was the consistoire rabbi and after his departure R. Ḥayyim Blia'h (1832–1919) served as the local rabbi. Other rabbis of the period were Isaac Shuraky, Zemah Amselem, Aaron Alkobi, Saadiah Shuraki, and Judah Sultan. Another important rabbi was David Cohen Sekely. His disciples were the rabbis Ḥayyim Touati, Jacob Sharvit, Saadiah Sharvit, and Samuel Benichou. The traveler Jacob Goldman visited Tlemcen in 1890 and published a description of the community in the Jewish press in Europe. The Jews lived in a crowded quarter in single-story buildings. The wealthy Jews lived in other quarters in large houses. The Jewish cemetery on the outskirts of Tlemcen was the most important place of pilgrimage for Jews and non-Jews. Located there is the tomb of Rabbi Ephraim Enquaua. Sometimes more than 10,000 people from many parts of the world convened there on Lag ba-Omer. In 1903 there is a description of the community as a conservative entity. Rabbi Ḥayyim Serehen published a phonetic *siddur* there in 1931. In 1924–40 the chief rabbi of Tlemcen was Joseph Mashash. The Alliance Israélite Universelle school was closed down in 1934. The last local rabbis of Tlemcen were Jacob Sharvit and Isaac Rouch. After 1962 no Jews lived in Tlemcen. A yeshivah was active in Tlemcen in the 20th century. R. David Ibn Halifa (b. 1906) studied in this yeshivah in his youth.

BIBLIOGRAPHY: L. Marmol de Carvajal, L'Afrique, 2 (1667), 329; Abbé Bargés, *Tlemcen, ancienne capitale du royaume de ce nom* (1859), passim; A. Cohen, *Les juifs dans l'Afrique septentrionale* (1867), passim; Revue Africaine (1870), 376–83; M. Weil, *Le cimetière Israélite de Tlemcen* (1881); E. Doutte, *Les Marabouts* (1900), 64–69; A. Meyer, *Etude sur la communauté de Tlemcen* (1902); SIHM, Espagne, index; R. Brunschvig (ed.), *Deux récits de voyage inédits…* (1936), 44–107; A.M. Hershman, *Rabbi Isaac ben Sheshet Perfet and his Times* (1943), 161ff.; A. Ashtor, Toledot, 2 (1551), pp. 449, 471; *Revue Africaine* (1955), 177f.; G. Shukron, in: *Qorot*, 3 (1963), pp. 86–88; Hirschberg, Afrikah, index; A. Chouraqui, *Between East and West* (1969), passim. **ADD. BIBLIOGRAPHY:** H. Chemouli, *Une Diaspora Méconnue* (1976), 7–64; M. Abitboul, in: *Pe'amim*, 2 (1979), 77ff.; J. Hacker, in: *Zion*, 45 (1980), 118–32; M. Bar-Asher, *La composante hébraïque du Judéo-Arabe algérien* (1992); S. Slymovics, in: *Jewish Folklore and Ethnology Review*, 15:2 (1993), 4–88; N. Aminoah, *Rabbi Yosef Sasportas Ḥakham ve-Dayyan be-Malkhut Tlemcen ve-Sefer Teshuvotav* (1995); E. Bareket, *Shafrir Miẓrayim* (1995), index; Y. Charvit, *Elite rabbinique d'Algérie et modernization 1750–1914* (1995); S. Schwarzfuchs, *Tlemcen mille ans d'histoire d'une communauté Juive* (1995); Y. Charvit, *Elite rabbinique d'Algérie et Erez Israël au XIXème siècle*, 3 vols. (1998); S. Schwarzfuchs, in: *Kountrass*, 78 (May-June 2000), 43–48; A.R. Marciano, *Sefer Malkhei Yeshurun ve-Shivḥei Ḥakhmei Aljeria* (2000); S. Bar Asher, in: *Pe'amim*, 86–87 (2001), 244; Y. Sharvit, *Me-Ereẓ ha-Yam le-Ereẓ Israel – Yehudei Aljeria u-Medinat Yisrael (1948–1998)* (2002); A. Rodrigue, *Ḥinnukh, Ḥevrah ve-Historyah* (1991), 147–48.

[David Corcos / Leah Bornstein-Makovetsky (2nd ed.)]

TLUMACH (Pol. **Tlumacz**; Yid. **Tlomats**), town in Ivano-Frankovsk (formerly Pol. Stanisławów) district, Ukraine; passed to Austria in 1772, and reverted to Poland between the two world wars. An organized community existed there from the 18th century. In 1765, there were 102 houses, of which 59 belonged to Jews; 372 Jews then lived in Tlumach and 148 in the surrounding area. The Jews in Tlumach were mainly occupied in small-scale commerce and crafts, the wealthier ones engaging in trade in timber and the production of alcoholic beverages. Ḥasidism gained adherents there during the 19th century. The Jewish population numbered 1,756 (43% of the total) in 1880; 2,097 (39%) in 1900; and 2,082 (36%) in 1910. The *Baron de Hirsch Fund established a school and a bank in the town. During World War I the Jews in Tlumach suffered from the invasion of the Russian armies, and in 1918 from the Ukrainian nationalists. There were 2,012 Jews living in Tlumach (35% of the total) in 1921. In the interwar period Zionism gained influence within the community.

[Shimon Leib Kirshenboim]

Holocaust and Contemporary Periods

On July 7, 1941, after the outbreak of the German-Soviet war, Tlumach was taken by the Hungarian allies of Germany. At the beginning of August 1941 Jewish refugees from Hungary were brought to the city. During the same period the Ukrainian population expelled the Jews from the city and robbed them of their property. They returned only after the intervention of the Hungarian army. In September 1941 Tlumach was handed over to direct German administration. The leaders of the Jewish intelligentsia were killed, including the chairman of the Judenrat, Eliasz Redner. In the winter of 1941–42 many Jews were seized and sent to work camps in the area. On April 3, 1942, 1,200 Jews were deported to Stanislav, where they were murdered. Subsequently a ghetto was established, in which 3,000 Jews, including those from the surrounding area, were concentrated. On May 18 another *Aktion* took place, in which about 180 Jews were killed on the spot and about 350 were deported to work camps in the area. The murder of individuals in the ghetto continued, and many there suffered from disease and hunger. At the end of November 1942 the ghetto was destroyed. A few escaped to the forests, but fell victims to Ukrainian nationalists.

The community in Tlumach was not reconstituted after the war.

[Aharon Weiss]

BIBLIOGRAPHY: B. Wasiutyński, *Ludność żydowska w Polsce w wiekach XIX i XX* (1930), 124, 148, 155.

TNUVA (Heb. תְּנוּבָה; "produce"), a cooperative association affiliated to the *Histadrut, which markets the agricultural produce of most of the Jewish villages in Israel. It operated at first as the agricultural marketing department of *Hamashbir, and became an independent organization in 1927. Any village, whatever its political color or organizational affiliation, can join Tnuva and market its produce through it. In 1968, 500 settlements marketed their produce through the cooperative. In addition, individual farmers, fishermen, and food-products industries, etc., availed themselves of Tnuva's services. It had departments for milk and milk products, poultry and poultry produce, vegetables, fruits, and other branches of agriculture, each department having a separate administration. Tnuva also operated through subcompanies and by having a share in industrial enterprises, commercial enterprises, and various services.

The governing body of the cooperative is a general assembly of its members that must convene at least once every two years. The general assembly elects a council, whose membership in 1969 was 105. The council chooses a governing board of 35 members and a secretariat of 17 members. The *Ḥevrat ha-Ovedim of the Histadrut is represented in Tnuva by Nir Shittufi, which is a member of the cooperative without responsibility for its debts and without the full rights of membership (profit sharing, etc.). Nir Shittufi participates in the general assembly, however, with the right to reject candidates for membership in Tnuva. It is also responsible for guarding the cooperative principles of Tnuva.

Tnuva markets approximately 70% of local agricultural produce. In 1968 the cooperative's turnover (not including subcompanies) reached $180,000,000). The company maintained a laboratory for the improvement of quality and for industrial processing of agricultural produce. In addition, much agricultural produce was processed through its dairy industry, fruit and vegetable canning industries, etc.

Tnuva's marketing policy attempted to ensure a suitable balance between supply and demand, in order to ensure that the producer receives a reasonable price, that there be a balance between prices in various parts of the country, and that marketing be speedy and complete while scrupulously supervising quality.

In the early 2000s Tnuva was the biggest marketing and trading company in Israel, with sales of $1.5 billion. Though still owned as a cooperative by the kibbutzim and moshavim it operated as a profit-oriented company under modern management, in four major divisions: milk and dairy; meat; fruit and vegetables; and eggs. It also had a number of subsidiaries, such as Sunfrost, Tiv Tirat Zvi, and Harduf Organic Foods.

BIBLIOGRAPHY: Histadrut, Makhon le-Meḥkar Kalkali ve-Ḥevrati, *Meshek ha-Ovedim 1960–65* (1967); I. Avneri (ed.), *Ha-Lu'aḥ ha-Ko'operativi shel Medinat Yisrael* (1968). **WEBSITE:** www.tnuva.co.il.

[Leon Aryeh Szeskin / Shaked Gilboa (2nd ed.)]

ABBREVIATIONS

GENERAL ABBREVIATIONS

This list contains abbreviations used in the Encyclopaedia (apart from the standard ones, such as geographical abbreviations, points of compass, etc.). For names of organizations, institutions, etc., in abbreviation, see Index. For bibliographical abbreviations of books and authors in Rabbinical literature, see following lists.

*	Cross reference; i.e., an article is to be found under the word(s) immediately following the asterisk (*).
°	Before the title of an entry, indicates a non-Jew (post-biblical times).
‡	Indicates reconstructed forms.
>	The word following this sign is derived from the preceding one.
<	The word preceding this sign is derived from the following one.

ad loc.	*ad locum*, "at the place"; used in quotations of commentaries.
A.H.	*Anno Hegirae*, "in the year of Hegira," i.e., according to the Muslim calendar.
Akk.	Addadian.
A.M.	*anno mundi*, "in the year (from the creation) of the world."
anon.	anonymous.
Ar.	Arabic.
Aram.	Aramaic.
Ass.	Assyrian.
b.	born; *ben, bar.*
Bab.	Babylonian.
B.C.E.	Before Common Era (= B.C.).
bibl.	bibliography.
Bul.	Bulgarian.
c., ca.	Circa.
C.E.	Common Era (= A.D.).
cf.	*confer*, "compare."
ch., chs.	chapter, chapters.
comp.	compiler, compiled by.
Cz.	Czech.
D	according to the documentary theory, the Deuteronomy document.
d.	died.
Dan.	Danish.
diss., dissert,	dissertation, thesis.
Du.	Dutch.
E.	according to the documentary theory, the Elohist document (i.e., using Elohim as the name of God) of the first five (or six) books of the Bible.
ed.	editor, edited, edition.
eds.	editors.
e.g.	*exempli gratia*, "for example."
Eng.	English.
et al.	*et alibi*, "and elsewhere"; or *et alii*, "and others"; "others."
f., ff.	and following page(s).
fig.	figure.
fl.	flourished.
fol., fols	folio(s).
Fr.	French.
Ger.	German.
Gr.	Greek.
Heb.	Hebrew.
Hg., Hung	Hungarian.
ibid	*Ibidem*, "in the same place."
incl. bibl.	includes bibliography.
introd.	introduction.
It.	Italian.
J	according to the documentary theory, the Jahwist document (i.e., using YHWH as the name of God) of the first five (or six) books of the Bible.
Lat.	Latin.
lit.	literally.
Lith.	Lithuanian.
loc. cit.	*loco citato*, "in the [already] cited place."
Ms., Mss.	Manuscript(s).
n.	note.
n.d.	no date (of publication).
no., nos	number(s).
Nov.	Novellae (Heb. *Ḥiddushim*).
n.p.	place of publication unknown.
op. cit.	*opere citato*, "in the previously mentioned work."
P.	according to the documentary theory, the Priestly document of the first five (or six) books of the Bible.
p., pp.	page(s).
Pers.	Persian.
pl., pls.	plate(s).
Pol.	Polish.
Port.	Potuguese.
pt., pts.	part(s).
publ.	published.
R.	Rabbi or Rav (before names); in Midrash (after an abbreviation) – *Rabbah.*
r.	recto, the first side of a manuscript page.
Resp.	Responsa (Latin "answers," Hebrew *She'elot u-Teshuvot* or *Teshuvot*), collections of rabbinic decisions.
rev.	revised.

Rom.	Romanian.
Rus(s).	Russian.
Slov.	Slovak.
Sp.	Spanish.
s.v.	*sub verbo, sub voce*, "under the (key) word."
Sum	Sumerian.
summ.	Summary.
suppl.	supplement.
Swed.	Swedish.
tr., trans(l).	translator, translated, translation.
Turk.	Turkish.
Ukr.	Ukrainian.
v., vv.	*verso*. The second side of a manuscript page; also verse(s).
Yid.	Yiddish.

ABBREVIATIONS USED IN RABBINICAL LITERATURE

Adderet Eliyahu, Karaite treatise by Elijah b. Moses *Bashyazi.

Admat Kodesh, Resp. by Nissim Ḥayyim Moses b. Joseph |Mizraḥi.

Aguddah, Sefer ha-, Nov. by *Alexander Suslin ha-Kohen.

Ahavat Ḥesed, compilation by *Israel Meir ha-Kohen.

Aliyyot de-Rabbenu Yonah, Nov. by *Jonah b. Avraham Gerondi.

Arukh ha-Shulḥan, codification by Jehiel Michel *Epstein.

Asayin (= positive precepts), subdivision of: (1) *Maimonides, *Sefer ha-Mitzvot;* (2) *Moses b. Jacob of Coucy, *Semag.*

Asefat Dinim, subdivision of *Sedei Ḥemed* by Ḥayyim Hezekiah *Medini, an encyclopaedia of precepts and responsa.

Asheri = *Asher b. Jehiel.

Aeret Ḥakhamim, by Baruch *Frankel-Teomim; pt, 1: Resp. to Sh. Ar.; pt2: Nov. to Talmud.

Ateret Zahav, subdivision of the *Levush*, a codification by Mordecai b. Abraham (Levush) *Jaffe; *Ateret Zahav* parallels Tur. YD.

Ateret Ẓevi, Comm. To Sh. Ar. by Ẓevi Hirsch b. Azriel.

Avir Ya'akov, Resp. by Jacob Avigdor.

Avkat Rokhel, Resp. by Joseph b. Ephraim *Caro.

Avnei Millu'im, Comm. to Sh. Ar., EH, by *Aryeh Loeb b. Joseph ha-Kohen.

Avnei Nezer, Resp. on Sh. Ar. by Abraham b. Ze'ev Nahum Bornstein of *Sochaczew.

Avodat Massa, Compilation of Tax Law by Yoasha Abraham Judah.

Azei ha-Levanon, Resp. by Judah Leib *Zirelson.

Ba'al ha-Tanya – *Shneur Zalman of Lyady.

Ba'ei Ḥayyei, Resp. by Ḥayyim b. Israel *Benveniste.

Ba'er Heitev, Comm. To Sh. Ar. The parts on OḤ and EH are by Judah b. Simeon *Ashkenazi, the parts on YD AND ḤM by *Zechariah Mendel b. Aryeh Leib. Printed in most editions of Sh. Ar.

Baḥ = Joel *Sirkes.

Baḥ, usual abbreviation for *Bayit Ḥadash*, a commentary on Tur by Joel *Sirkes; printed in most editions of Tur.

Bayit Ḥadash, see *Baḥ*.

Berab = Jacob Berab, also called Ri Berav.

Bedek ha-Bayit, by Joseph b. Ephraim *Caro, additions to his *Beit Yosef* (a comm. to Tur). Printed sometimes inside *Beit Yosef*, in smaller type. Appears in most editions of Tur.

Be'er ha-Golah, Commentary to Sh. Ar. By Moses b. Naphtali Hirsch *Rivkes; printed in most editions of Sh. Ar.

Be'er Mayim, Resp. by Raphael b. Abraham Manasseh Jacob.

Be'er Mayim Ḥayyim, Resp. by Samuel b. Ḥayyim *Vital.

Be'er Yiẓḥak, Resp. by Isaac Elhanan *Spector.

Beit ha-Beḥirah, Comm. to Talmud by Menahem b. Solomon *Meiri.

Beit Me'ir, Nov. on Sh. Ar. by Meir b. Judah Leib Posner.

Beit Shelomo, Resp. by Solomon b. Aaron Ḥason (the younger).

Beit Shemu'el, Comm. to Sh. Ar., EH, by *Samuel b. Uri Shraga Phoebus.

Beit Ya'akov, by Jacob b. Jacob Moses *Lorberbaum; pt.1: Nov. to Ket.; pt.2: Comm. to EH.

Beit Yisrael, collective name for the commentaries *Derishah*, *Perishah*, and *Be'urim* by Joshua b. Alexander ha-Kohen *Falk. See under the names of the commentaries.

Beit Yiẓḥak, Resp. by Isaac *Schmelkes.

Beit Yosef: (1) Comm. on Tur by Joseph b. Ephraim *Caro; printed in most editions of Tur; (2) Resp. by the same.

Ben Yehudah, Resp. by Abraham b. Judah Litsch (ליטש) Rosenbaum.

Bertinoro, Standard commentary to Mishnah by Obadiah *Bertinoro. Printed in most editions of the Mishnah.

[Be'urei] Ha-Gra, Comm. to Bible, Talmud, and Sh. Ar. By *Elijah b. Solomon Zalmon (Gaon of Vilna); printed in major editions of the mentioned works.

Be'urim, Glosses to Isserles *Darkhei Moshe* (a comm. on Tur) by Joshua b. Alexander ha-Kohen *Falk; printed in many editions of Tur.

Binyamin Ze'ev, Resp. by *Benjamin Ze'ev b. Mattathias of Arta.

Birkei Yosef, Nov. by Ḥayyim Joseph David *Azulai.

Ha-Buẓ ve-ha-Argaman, subdivision of the *Levush* (a codification by Mordecai b. Abraham (Levush) *Jaffe); *Ha-Buẓ ve-ha-Argaman* parallels Tur, EH.

Comm. = Commentary

Da'at Kohen, Resp. by Abraham Isaac ha-Kohen. *Kook.

Darkhei Moshe, Comm. on Tur Moses b. Israel *Isserles; printed in most editions of Tur.

Darkhei No'am, Resp. by *Mordecai b. Judah ha-Levi.

Darkhei Teshuvah, Nov. by Ẓevi *Shapiro; printed in the major editions of Sh. Ar.

De'ah ve-Haskel, Resp. by Obadiah Hadaya (see *Yaskil Avdi).*

Derashot Ran, Sermons by *Nissim b. Reuben Gerondi.
Derekh Ḥayyim, Comm. to *Avot* by *Judah Loew (Lob., Liwa) b. Bezalel (Maharal) of Prague.
Derishah, by Joshua b. Alexander ha-Kohen *Falk; additions to his *Perishah* (comm. on Tur); printed in many editions of Tur.
Derushei ha-Ẓelaḥ, Sermons, by Ezekiel b. Judah Halevi *Landau.
Devar Avraham, Resp. by Abraham *Shapira.
Devar Shemu'el, Resp. by Samuel *Aboab.
Devar Yehoshu'a, Resp. by Joshua Menahem b. Isaac Aryeh Ehrenberg.
Dikdukei Soferim, variae lections of the talmudic text by Raphael Nathan*Rabbinowicz.
Divrei Emet, Resp. by Isaac Bekhor David.
Divrei Ge'onim, Digest of responsa by Ḥayyim Aryeh b. Jeḥiel Ẓevi *Kahana.
Divrei Ḥamudot, Comm. on *Piskei ha-Rosh* by Yom Tov Lipmann b. Nathan ha-Levi *Heller; printed in major editions of the Talmud.
Divrei Ḥayyim several works by Ḥayyim *Halberstamm; if quoted alone refers to his Responsa.
Divrei Malkhi'el, Resp. by Malchiel Tenebaum.
Divrei Rivot, Resp. by Isaac b. Samuel *Adarbi.
Divrei Shemu'el, Resp. by Samuel Raphael Arditi.

Edut be-Ya'akov, Resp. by Jacob b. Abraham *Boton.
Edut bi-Yhosef, Resp. by Joseph b. Isaac *Almosnino.
Ein Ya'akov, Digest of talmudic *aggadot* by Jacob (Ibn) *Habib.
Ein Yiẓḥak, Resp. by Isaac Elhanan *Spector.
Ephraim of Lentshitz = Solomon *Luntschitz.
Erekh Leḥem, Nov. and glosses to Sh. Ar. by Jacob b. Abraham *Castro.
Eshkol, Sefer ha-, Digest of *halakhot* by *Abraham b. Isaac of Narbonne.
Et Sofer, Treatise on Law Court documents by Abraham b. Mordecai *Ankawa, in the 2nd vol. of his Resp. *Kerem Ḥamar.*
Etan ha-Ezraḥi, Resp. by Abraham b. Israel Jehiel (Shrenzl) *Rapaport.
Even ha-Ezel, Nov. to Maimonides' *Yad Ḥazakah* by Isser Zalman *Meltzer.
Even ha-Ezer, also called *Raban* of *Ẓafenat Pa'ne'aḥ,* rabbinical work with varied contents by *Eliezer b. Nathan of Mainz; not identical with the subdivision of Tur, Shulḥan Arukh, etc.
Ezrat Yehudah, Resp. by *Isaar Judah b. Nechemiah of Brisk.

Gan Eden, Karaite treatise by *Aaron b. Elijah of Nicomedia.
Gersonides = *Levi b. Gershom, also called Leo Hebraecus, or Ralbag.
Ginnat Veradim, Resp. by *Abraham b. Mordecai ha-Levi.

Haggahot, another name for *Rema.*
Haggahot Asheri, glosses to *Piskei ha-Rosh* by *Israel of Krems; printed in most Talmud editions.
Haggahot Maimuniyyot, Comm,. to Maimonides' Yad Ḥazakah by *Meir ha-Kohen; printed in most eds. of Yad.
Haggahot Mordekhai, glosses to *Mordekhai* by Samuel *Schlettstadt; printed in most editions of the Talmud after *Mordekhai.*
Haggahot ha-Rashash on Tosafot, annotations of Samuel *Strashun on the Tosafot (printed in major editions of the Talmud).
Ha-Gra = *Elijah b. Solomon Zalman (Gaon of Vilna).
Ha-Gra, Commentaries on Bible, Talmud, and Sh. Ar. respectively, by *Elijah b. Solomon Zalman (Gaon of Vilna); printed in major editions of the mentioned works.
Hai Gaon, Comm. = his comm. on Mishnah.
Ḥakham Ẓevi, Resp. by Ẓevi Hirsch b. Jacob *Ashkenazi.
Halakhot = Rif, *Halakhot.* Compilation and abstract of the Talmud by Isaac b. Jacob ha-Kohen *Alfasi; printed in most editions of the Talmud.
Halakhot Gedolot, compilation of *halakhot* from the Geonic period, arranged acc. to the Talmud. Here cited acc. to ed. Warsaw (1874). Author probably *Simeon Kayyara of Basra.
Halakhot Pesukot le-Rav Yehudai Ga'on compilation of *halakhot.*
Halakhot Pesukot min ha-Ge'onim, compilation of *halakhot* from the geonic period by different authors.
Ḥananel, Comm. to Talmud by *Hananel b. Ḥushi'el; printed in some editions of the Talmud.
Harei Besamim, Resp. by Aryeh Leib b. Isaac *Horowitz.
Ḥassidim, Sefer, Ethical maxims by *Judah b. Samuel he-Ḥasid.
Hassagot Rabad on Rif, Glosses on Rif, *Halakhot,* by *Abraham b. David of Posquières.
Hassagot Rabad [on Yad], Glosses on Maimonides, *Yad Ḥazakah,* by *Abraham b. David of Posquières.
Hassagot Ramban, Glosses by Naḥmanides on Maimonides' *Sefer ha-Mitzvot;* usually printed together with *Sefer ha-Mitzvot.*
Ḥatam Sofer = Moses *Sofer.
Ḥavvot Ya'ir, Resp. and varia by Jair Ḥayyim *Bacharach
Ḥayyim Or Zaru'a = *Ḥayyim (Eliezer) b. Isaac.
Ḥazon Ish = Abraham Isaiah *Karelitz.
Ḥazon Ish, Nov. by Abraham Isaiah *Karelitz
Ḥedvat Ya'akov, Resp. by Aryeh Judah Jacob b. David Dov Meisels (article under his father's name).
Heikhal Yiẓḥak, Resp. by Isaac ha-Levi *Herzog.
Ḥelkat Meḥokek, Comm. to Sh. Ar., by Moses b. Isaac Judah *Lima.
Ḥelkat Ya'akov, Resp. by Mordecai Jacob Breisch.
Ḥemdah Genuzah, , Resp. from the geonic period by different authors.
Ḥemdat Shelomo, Resp. by Solomon Zalman *Lipschitz.
Ḥida = Ḥayyim Joseph David *Azulai.
Ḥiddushei Halakhot ve-Aggadot, Nov. by Samuel Eliezer b. Judah ha-Levi *Edels.
Ḥikekei Lev, Resp. by Ḥayyim *Palaggi.
Ḥikrei Lev, Nov. to Sh. Ar. by Joseph Raphael b. Ḥayyim Joseph Ḥazzan (see article *Ḥazzan Family).
Hil. = Hilkhot ... (e.g. *Hilkhot Shabbat).*
Ḥinnukh, Sefer ha-, List and explanation of precepts attributed (probably erroneously) to Aaron ha-Levi of Barcelona (see article *Ha-Ḥinnukh).*
Ḥok Ya'akov, Comm. to Hil. Pesaḥ in Sh. Ar., OḤ, by Jacob b. Joseph *Reicher.
Ḥokhmat Sehlomo (1), Glosses to Talmud, *Rashi* and Tosafot by Solomon b. Jehiel "Maharshal") *Luria; printed in many editions of the Talmud.
Ḥokhmat Sehlomo (2), Glosses and Nov. to Sh. Ar. by Solomon b. Judah Aaron *Kluger printed in many editions of Sh. Ar.
Ḥur, subdivision of the *Levush,* a codification by Mordecai b. Abraham (Levush) *Jaffe; *Hur* (or *Levush ha-Hur)* parallels Tur, OḤ, 242–697.
Ḥut ha-Meshullash, fourth part of the *Tashbeẓ* (Resp.), by Simeon b. Zemaḥ *Duran.

Ibn Ezra, Comm. to the Bible by Abraham *Ibn Ezra; printed in the major editions of the Bible *("Mikra'ot Gedolot").*
Imrei Yosher, Resp. by Meir b. Aaron Judah *Arik.
Ir Shushan, Subdivision of the *Levush,* a codification by Mordecai b. Abraham (Levush) *Jaffe; *Ir Shushan* parallels Tur, ḤM.
Israel of Bruna = Israel b. Ḥayyim *Bruna.
Ittur. Treatise on precepts by *Isaac b. Abba Mari of Marseilles.

Jacob Be Rab = *Be Rab.
Jacob b. Jacob Moses of Lissa = Jacob b. Jacob Moses *Lorberbaum.
Judah B. Simeon = Judah b. Simeon *Ashkenazi.
Judah Minz = Judah b. Eliezer ha-Levi *Minz.

Kappei Aharon, Resp. by Aaron Azriel.
Kehillat Ya'akov, Talmudic methodology, definitions etc. by Israel Jacob b. Yom Tov *Algazi.
Kelei Ḥemdah, Nov. and *pilpulim* by Meir Dan *Plotzki of Ostrova, arranged acc. to the Torah.
Keli Yakar, Annotations to the Torah by Solomon *Luntschitz.
Keneh Ḥokhmah, Sermons by Judah Loeb *Pochwitzer.
Keneset ha-Gedolah, Digest of *halakhot* by Ḥayyim b. Israel *Benveniste; subdivided into annotations to *Beit Yosef* and annotations to Tur.
Keneset Yisrael, Resp. by Ezekiel b. Abraham Katzenellenbogen (see article *Katzenellenbogen Family).
Kerem Ḥamar, Resp. and varia by Abraham b. Mordecai *Ankawa.
Kerem Shelmo. Resp. by Solomon b. Joseph *Amarillo.
Keritut, [Sefer], Methodology of the Talmud by *Samson b. Isaac of Chinon.
Kesef ha-Kedoshim, Comm. to Sh. Ar., ḤM, by Abraham *Wahrmann; printed in major editions of Sh. Ar.
Kesef Mishneh, Comm. to Maimonides, *Yad Ḥazakah,* by Joseph b. Ephraim *Caro; printed in most editions of *Yad Ḥazakah.*
Keẓot ha-Ḥoshen, Comm. to Sh. Ar., ḤM, by *Aryeh Loeb b. Joseph ha-Kohen; printed in major editions of Sh. Ar.
Kol Bo [Sefer], Anonymous collection of ritual rules; also called *Sefer ha-Likkutim.*
Kol Mevasser, Resp. by Meshullam *Rath.
Korban Aharon, Comm. to *Sifra* by Aaron b. Abraham *Ibn Ḥayyim; pt. 1 is called: *Middot Aharon.*
Korban Edah, Comm. to Jer. Talmud by David *Fraenkel; with additions: *Shiyyurei Korban;* printed in most editions of Jer. Talmud.
Kunteres ha-Kelalim, subdivision of *Sedei Ḥemed,* an encyclopaedia of precepts and responsa by Ḥayyim Hezekiah *Medini.
Kunteres ha-Semikhah, a treatise by *Levi b. Ḥabib; printed at the end of his responsa.
Kunteres Tikkun Olam, part of *Mispat Shalom* (Nov. by Shalom Mordecai b. Moses *Schwadron).

Lavin (negative precepts), subdivision of: (1) *Maimonides, *Sefer ha-Mitzvot;* (2) *Moses b. Jacob of Coucy, *Semag.*
Leḥem Mishneh, Comm. to Maimonides, *Yad Ḥazakah,* by Abraham [Ḥiyya] b. Moses *Boton; printed in most editions of *Yad Ḥazakah.*
Leḥem Rav, Resp. by Abraham [Ḥiyya] b. Moses *Boton.
Leket Yosher, Resp and varia by Israel b. Pethahiah *Isserlein, collected by *Joseph (Joselein) b. Moses.
Leo Hebraeus = *Levi b. Gershom, also called Ralbag or Gersonides.
Levush = Mordecai b. Abraham *Jaffe.
Levush [Malkhut], Codification by Mordecai b. Abraham (Levush) *Jaffe, with subdivisions: *[Levush ha-] Tekhelet* (parallels Tur OḤ 1–241); *[Levush ha-] Ḥur* (parallels Tur OḤ 242–697); *[Levush] Ateret Zahav* (parallels Tur YD); *[Levush ha-Buẓ ve-ha-Argaman* (parallels Tur EH); *[Levush] Ir Shushan* (parallels Tur ḤM); under the name *Levush* the author wrote also other works.
Li-Leshonot ha-Rambam, fifth part (nos. 1374–1700) of Resp. by *David b. Solomon ibn Abi Zimra (Radbaz).
Likkutim, Sefer ha-, another name for *[Sefer] Kol Bo.*

Ma'adanei Yom Tov, Comm. on *Piskei ha-Rosh* by Yom Tov Lipmann b. Nathan ha-Levi *Heller; printed in many editions of the Talmud.
Mabit = Moses b. Joseph *Trani.
Magen Avot, Comm. to *Avot* by Simeon b. Ẓemaḥ *Duran.
Magen Avraham, Comm. to Sh. Ar., OḤ, by Abraham Abele b. Ḥayyim ha-Levi *Gombiner; printed in many editions of Sh. Ar., OḤ.
Maggid Mishneh, Comm. to Maimonides, *Yad Ḥazakah,* by *Vidal Yom Tov of Tolosa; printed in most editions of the *Yad Ḥazakah.*
Maḥaneh Efrayim, Resp. and Nov., arranged acc. to Maimonides' *Yad Ḥazakah ,* by Ephraim b. Aaron *Navon.
Maharai = Israel b. Pethahiah *Isserlein.
Maharal of Prague = *Judah Loew (Lob, Liwa), b. Bezalel.
Maharalbaḥ = *Levi b. Ḥabib.
Maharam Alashkar = Moses b. Isaac *Alashkar.
Maharam Alshekh = Moses b. Ḥayyim *Alashekh.
Maharam Mintz = Moses *Mintz.
Maharam of Lublin = *Meir b. Gedaliah of Lublin.
Maharam of Padua = Meir *Katzenellenbogen.
Maharam of Rothenburg = *Meir b. Baruch of Rothenburg.
Maharam Shik = Moses b. Joseph Schick.
Maharash Engel = Samuel b. Ze'ev Wolf Engel.
Maharashdam = Samuel b. Moses *Medina.
Maharḥash = Ḥayyim (ben) Shabbetai.
Mahari Basan = Jehiel b. Ḥayyim Basan.
Mahari b. Lev = Joseph ibn Lev.
Mahari'az = Jekuthiel Asher Zalman Ensil Zusmir.
Maharibal = *Joseph ibn Lev.
Mahariḥ = Jacob (Israel) *Ḥagiz.
Maharik = Joseph b. Solomon *Colon.
Maharikash = Jacob b. Abraham *Castro.
Maharil = Jacob b. Moses *Moellin.
Maharimat = Joseph b. Moses di Trani (not identical with the Maharit).
Maharit = Joseph b. Moses *Trani.
Maharitaẓ = Yom Tov b. Akiva Ẓahalon. (See article *Ẓahalon Family).
Maharsha = Samuel Eliezer b. Judah ha-Levi *Edels.
Maharshag = Simeon b. Judah Gruenfeld.
Maharshak = Samson b. Isaac of Chinon.
Maharshakh = *Solomon b. Abraham.
Maharshal = Solomon b. Jeḥiel *Luria.
Mahasham = Shalom Mordecai b. Moses *Sschwadron.
Maharyu = Jacob b. Judah *Weil.
Maḥazeh Avraham, Resp. by Abraham Nebagen v. Meir ha-Levi Steinberg.
Maḥazik Berakhah, Nov. by Ḥayyim Joseph David *Azulai.

*Maimonides = Moses b. Maimon, or Rambam.
*Malbim = Meir Loeb b. Jehiel Michael.
Malbim = Malbim's comm. to the Bible; printed in the major editions.
Malbushei Yom Tov, Nov. on *Levush*, OḤ, by Yom Tov Lipmann b. Nathan ha-Levi *Heller.
Mappah, another name for *Rema.*
Mareh ha-Panim, Comm. to Jer. Talmud by Moses b. Simeon *Margolies; printed in most editions of Jer. Talmud.
Margaliyyot ha-Yam, Nov. by Reuben *Margoliot.
Masat Binyamin, Resp. by Benjamin Aaron b. Abraham *Slonik Mashbir, Ha- = *Joseph Samuel b. Isaac Rodi.
Massa Ḥayyim, Tax *halakhot* by Ḥayyim *Palaggi, with the subdivisions *Missim ve-Arnomiyyot* and *Torat ha-Minhagot.*
Massa Melekh, Compilation of Tax Law by Joseph b. Isaac *Ibn Ezra with concluding part *Ne'ilat She'arim.*
Matteh Asher, Resp. by Asher b. Emanuel Shalem.
Matteh Shimon, Digest of Resp. and Nov. to Tur and *Beit Yosef,* ḤM, by Mordecai Simeon b. Solomon.
Matteh Yosef, Resp. by Joseph b. Moses ha-Levi Nazir (see article under his father's name).
Mayim Amukkim, Resp. by Elijah b. Abraham *Mizraḥi.
Mayim Ḥayyim, Resp. by Ḥayyim b. Dov Beresh Rapaport.
Mayim Rabbim, , Resp. by Raphael *Meldola.
Me-Emek ha-Bakha, , Resp. by Simeon b. Jekuthiel Ephrati.
Me'irat Einayim, usual abbreviation: *Sma* (from: *Sefer Me'irat Einayim*); comm. to Sh. Ar. By Joshua b. Alexander ha-Kohen *Falk; printed in most editions of the Sh. Ar.
Melammed le-Ho'il, Resp. by David Ẓevi *Hoffmann.
Meisharim, [*Sefer*], Rabbinical treatise by *Jeroham b. Meshullam.
Meshiv Davar, Resp. by Naphtali Ẓevi Judah *Berlin.
Mi-Gei ha-Haregah, Resp. by Simeon b. Jekuthiel Ephrati.
Mi-Ma'amakim, Resp. by Ephraim Oshry.
Middot Aharon, first part of *Korban Aharon,* a comm. to *Sifra* by Aaron b. Abraham *Ibn Ḥayyim.
Migdal Oz, Comm. to Maimonides, *Yad Ḥazakah,* by *Ibn Gaon Shem Tov b. Abraham; printed in most editions of the *Yad Ḥazakah.*
Mikhtam le-David, Resp. by David Samuel b. Jacob *Pardo.
Mikkaḥ ve-ha-Mimkar, Sefer ha-, Rabbinical treatise by *Hai Gaon.
Milḥamot ha-Shem, Glosses to Rif, *Halakhot,* by *Naḥmanides.
Minḥat Ḥinnukh, Comm. to *Sefer ha-Ḥinnukh,* by Joseph b. Moses *Babad.
Minḥat Yiẓḥak, Resp. by Isaac Jacob b. Joseph Judah Weiss.
Misgeret ha-Shulḥan, Comm. to Sh. Ar., ḤM, by Benjamin Ze'ev Wolf b. Shabbetai; printed in most editions of Sh. Ar.
Mishkenot ha-Ro'im, Halakhot in alphabetical order by Uzziel Alshekh.
Mishnah Berurah, Comm. to Sh. Ar., OḤ, by *Israel Meir ha-Kohen.
Mishneh le-Melekh, Comm. to Maimonides, *Yad Ḥazakah,* by Judah *Rosanes; printed in most editions of *Yad Ḥazakah.*
Mishpat ha-Kohanim, Nov. to Sh. Ar., ḤM, by Jacob Moses *Lorberbaum, part of his *Netivot ha-Mishpat;* printed in major editions of Sh. Ar.
Mishpat Kohen, Resp. by Abraham Isaac ha-Kohen *Kook.
Mishpat Shalom, Nov. by Shalom Mordecai b. Moses *Schwadron; contains: *Kunteres Tikkun Olam.*
Mishpat u-Ẓedakah be-Ya'akov, Resp. by Jacob b. Reuben *Ibn Ẓur.
Mishpat ha-Urim, Comm. to Sh. Ar., ḤM by Jacob b. Jacob Moses *Lorberbaum, part of his *Netivot ha-Mishpat;* printed in major editons of Sh. Ar.
Mishpat Ẓedek, Resp. by *Melammed Meir b. Shem Tov.
Mishpatim Yesharim, Resp. by Raphael b. Mordecai *Berdugo.
Mishpetei Shemu'el, Resp. by Samuel b. Moses *Kalai (Kal'i).
Mishpetei ha-Tanna'im, Kunteres, Nov on *Levush,* OḤ by Yom Tov Lipmann b. Nathan ha-Levi *Heller.
Mishpetei Uzzi'el (Uziel), Resp. by Ben-Zion Meir Hai *Ouziel.
Missim ve-Arnoniyyot, Tax *halakhot* by Ḥayyim *Palaggi, a subdivision of his work *Massa Ḥayyim* on the same subject.
Mitzvot, Sefer ha-, Elucidation of precepts by *Maimonides; subdivided into *Lavin* (negative precepts) and *Asayin* (positive precepts).
Mitzvot Gadol, Sefer, Elucidation of precepts by *Moses b. Jacob of Coucy, subdivided into *Lavin* (negative precepts) and *Asayin* (positive precepts); the usual abbreviation is *Semag.*
Mitzvot Katan, Sefer, Elucidation of precepts by *Isaac b. Joseph of Corbeil; the usual, abbreviation is *Semak.*
Mo'adim u-Zemannim, Rabbinical treatises by Moses Sternbuch.
Modigliano, Joseph Samuel = *Joseph Samuel b. Isaac, Rodi (Ha-Mashbir).
Mordekhai (Mordecai), halakhic compilation by *Mordecai b. Hillel; printed in most editions of the Talmud after the texts.
Moses b. Maimon = *Maimonides, also called Rambam.
Moses b. Naḥman = Naḥmanides, also called Ramban.
Muram = Isaiah Menahem b. Isaac (from: Morenu R. Mendel).

Naḥal Yiẓḥak, Comm. on Sh. Ar., ḤM, by Isaac Elhanan *Spector.
Naḥalah li-Yhoshu'a, Resp. by Joshua Ẓunẓin.
Naḥalat Shivah, collection of legal forms by *Samuel b. David Moses ha-Levi.
*Naḥmanides = Moses b. Naḥman, also called Ramban.
Naẓiv = Naphtali Ẓevi Judah *Berlin.
Ne'eman Shemu'el, Resp. by Samuel Isaac *Modigilano.
Ne'ilat She'arim, concluding part of *Massa Melekh* (a work on Tax Law) by Joseph b. Isaac *Ibn Ezra, containing an exposition of customary law and subdivided into *Minhagei Issur* and *Minhagei Mamon.*
Ner Ma'aravi, Resp. by Jacob b. Malka.
Netivot ha-Mishpat, by Jacob b. Jacob Moses *Lorberbaum; subdivided into *Mishpat ha-Kohanim,* Nov. to Sh. Ar., ḤM, and *Mishpat ha-Urim,* a comm. on the same; printed in major editions of Sh. Ar.
Netivot Olam, Saying of the Sages by *Judah Loew (Lob, Liwa) b. Bezalel.
Nimmukei Menaḥem of Merseburg, Tax *halakhot* by the same, printed at the end of Resp. Maharyu.
Nimmukei Yosef, Comm. to Rif. *Halakhot,* by Joseph *Ḥabib (Ḥabiba); printed in many editions of the Talmud.
Noda bi-Yhudah, Resp. by Ezekiel b. Judah ha-Levi *Landau; there is a first collection *(Mahadura Kamma)* and a second collection *(Mahadura Tinyana).*
Nov. = Novellae, Ḥiddushim.

Ohel Moshe (1), Notes to Talmud, *Midrash Rabbah,* Yad, *Sifrei* and to several Resp., by Eleazar *Horowitz.

Ohel Moshe (2), Resp. by Moses Jonah Zweig.
Oholei Tam. Resp. by *Tam ibn Yaḥya Jacob b. David; printed in the rabbinical collection *Tummat Yesharim.*
Oholei Ya'akov, Resp. by Jacob de *Castro.
Or ha-Me'ir Resp by Judah Meir b. Jacob Samson Shapiro.
Or Same'aḥ, Comm. to Maimonides, *Yad Ḥazakah,* by *Meir Simḥah ha-Kohen of Dvinsk; printed in many editions of the *Yad Ḥazakah.*
Or Zaru'a [the father] = *Isaac b. Moses of Vienna.
Or Zaru'a [the son] = *Ḥayyim (Eliezer) b. Isaac.
Or Zaru'a, Nov. by *Isaac b. Moses of Vienna.
Orah, Sefer ha-, Compilation of ritual precepts by *Rashi.
Oraḥ la-Ẓaddik, Resp. by Abraham Ḥayyim Rodrigues.
Oẓar ha-Posekim, Digest of Responsa.

Paḥad Yiẓḥak, Rabbinical encyclopaedia by Isaac *Lampronti.
Panim Me'irot, Resp. by Meir b. Isaac *Eisenstadt.
Parashat Mordekhai, Resp. by Mordecai b. Abraham Naphtali *Banet.
Pe'at ha-Sadeh la-Dinim and Pe'at ha-Sadeh la-Kelalim, subdivisions of the *Sedei Ḥemed,* an encyclopaedia of precepts and responsa, by Ḥayyim Hezekaih *Medini.
Penei Moshe (1), Resp. by Moses *Benveniste.
Penei Moshe (2), Comm. to Jer. Talmud by Moses b. Simeon *Margolies; printed in most editions of the Jer. Talmud.
Penei Moshe (3), Comm. on the aggadic passages of 18 treatises of the Bab. and Jer. Talmud, by Moses b. Isaiah Katz.
Penei Yehoshu'a, Nov. by Jacob Joshua b. Ẓevi Hirsch *Falk.
Peri Ḥadash, Comm. on Sh. Ar. By Hezekiah da *Silva.
Perishah, Comm. on Tur by Joshua b. Alexander ha-Kohen *Falk; printed in major edition of Tur; forms together with *Derishah* and *Be'urim* (by the same author) the *Beit Yisrael.*
Pesakim u-Khetavim, 2nd part of the *Terumat ha-Deshen* by Israel b. Pethahiah *Isserlein' also called *Piskei Maharai.*
Pilpula Ḥarifta, Comm. to *Piskei ha-Rosh, Seder Nezikin,* by Yom Tov Lipmann b. Nathan ha-Levi *Heller; printed in major editions of the Talmud.
Piskei Maharai, see *Terumat ha-Deshen,* 2nd part; also called *Pesakim u-Khetavim.*
Piskei ha-Rosh, a compilation of *halakhot,* arranged on the Talmud, by *Asher b. Jehiel (Rosh); printed in major Talmud editions.
Pitḥei Teshuvah, Comm. to Sh. Ar. by Abraham Hirsch b. Jacob *Eisenstadt; printed in major editions of the Sh. Ar.

Rabad = *Abraham b. David of Posquières (Rabad III.).
Raban = *Eliezer b. Nathan of Mainz.
Raban, also called *Ẓafenat Pa'ne'aḥ* or *Even ha-Ezer,* see under the last name.
Rabi Abad = *Abraham b. Isaac of Narbonne.
Radad = David Dov. b. Aryeh Judah Jacob *Meisels.
Radam = Dov Berush b. Isaac Meisels.
Radbaz = *David b Solomon ibn Abi Ziumra.
Radbaz, Comm. to Maimonides, *Yad Ḥazakah,* by *David b. Solomon ibn Abi Zimra.
Ralbag = *Levi b. Gershom, also called Gersonides, or Leo Hebraeus.
Ralbag, Bible comm. by *Levi b. Gershon.
Rama [da Fano] = Menaḥem Azariah *Fano.
Ramah = Meir b. Todros [ha-Levi] *Abulafia.
Ramam = *Menaham of Merseburg.
Rambam = *Maimonides; real name: Moses b. Maimon.
Ramban = *Naḥmanides; real name Moses b. Naḥman.
Ramban, Comm. to Torah by *Naḥmanides; printed in major editions. ("Mikra'ot Gedolot").
Ran = *Nissim b. Reuben Gerondi.
Ran of Rif, Comm. on Rif, *Halakhot,* by Nissim b. Reuben Gerondi.
Ranaḥ = *Elijah b. Ḥayyim.
Rash = *Samson b. Abraham of Sens.
Rash, Comm. to Mishnah, by *Samson b. Abraham of Sens; printed in major Talmud editions.
Rashash = Samuel *Strashun.
Rashba = Solomon b. Abraham *Adret.
Rashba, Resp., see also; *Sefer Teshuvot ha-Rashba ha-Meyuḥasot le-ha-Ramban,* by Solomon b. Abraham *Adret.
Rashbad = Samuel b. David.
Rashbam = *Samuel b. Meir.
Rashbam = Comm. on Bible and Talmud by *Samuel b. Meir; printed in major editions of Bible and most editions of Talmud.
Rashbash = Solomon b. Simeon *Duran.
*Rashi = Solomon b. Isaac of Troyes.
Rashi, Comm. on Bible and Talmud by *Rashi; printed in almost all Bible and Talmud editions.
Raviah = Eliezer b. Joel ha-Levi.
Redak = David *Kimḥi.
Redak, Comm. to Bible by David *Kimḥi.
Redakh = *David b. Ḥayyim ha-Kohen of Corfu.
Re'em = Elijah b. Abraham *Mizraḥi.
Rema = Moses b. Israel *Isserles.
Rema, Glosses to Sh. Ar. by Moses b. Israel *Isserles; printed in almost all editions of the Sh. Ar. inside the text in Rashi type; also called *Mappah* or *Haggahot.*
Remek = Moses Kimḥi.
Remakh = Moses ha-Kohen mi-Lunel.
Reshakh = *Solomon b. Abraham; also called Maharshakh.
Resp. = Responsa, *She'elot u-Teshuvot.*
Ri Berav = *Berab.
Ri Escapa = Joseph b. Saul *Escapa.
Ri Migash = Joseph b. Meir ha-Levi *Ibn Migash.
Riba = Isaac b. Asher ha-Levi; Riba II (Riba ha-Baḥur) = his grandson with the same name.
Ribam = Isaac b. Mordecai (or: Isaac b. Meir).
Ribash = *Isaac b. Sheshet Perfet (or: Barfat).
Rid= *Isaiah b. Mali di Trani the Elder.
Ridbaz = Jacob David b. Ze'ev *Willowski.
Rif = Isaac b. Jacob ha-Kohen *Alfasi.
Rif, *Halakhot,* Compilation and abstract of the Talmud by Isaac b. Jacob ha-Kohen *Alfasi.
Ritba = Yom Tov b. Abraham *Ishbili.
Riẓbam = Isaac b. Mordecai.
Rosh = *Asher b. Jehiel, also called Asheri.
Rosh Mashbir, Resp. by *Joseph Samuel b. Isaac, Rodi.

Sedei Ḥemed, Encyclopaedia of precepts and responsa by Ḥayyim Ḥezekiah *Medini; subdivisions: *Asefat Dinim, Kunteres ha-Kelalim, Pe'at ha-Sadeh la-Dinim, Pe'at ha-Sadeh la-Kelalim.*
Semag, Usual abbreviation of *Sefer Mitzvot Gadol,* elucidation of precepts by *Moses b. Jacob of Coucy; subdivided into *Lavin* (negative precepts) *Asayin* (positive precepts).
Semak, Usual abbreviation of *Sefer Mitzvot Katan,* elucidation of precepts by *Isaac b. Joseph of Corbeil.

Sh. Ar. = *Shulḥan Arukh,* code by Joseph b. Ephraim *Caro.

Sha'ar Mishpat, Comm. to Sh. Ar., ḤM. By Israel Isser b. Ze'ev Wolf.

Sha'arei Shevu'ot, Treatise on the law of oaths by *David b. Saadiah; usually printed together with Rif, *Halakhot;* also called: *She'arim of R. Alfasi.*

Sha'arei Teshuvah, Collection of resp. from Geonic period, by different authors.

Sha'arei Uzzi'el, Rabbinical treatise by Ben-Zion Meir Ha *Ouziel.

Sha'arei Ẓedek, Collection of resp. from Geonic period, by different authors.

Shadal [or Shedal] = Samuel David *Luzzatto.

Shai la-Moreh, Resp. by Shabbetai Jonah.

Shakh, Usual abbreviation of *Siftei Kohen,* a comm. to Sh. Ar., YD and ḤM by *Shabbetai b. Meir ha-Kohen; printed in most editions of Sh. Ar.

Sha'ot-de-Rabbanan, Resp. by *Solomon b. Judah ha-Kohen.

She'arim of R. Alfasi see *Sha'arei Shevu'ot.*

Shedal, see Shadal.

She'elot u-Teshuvot ha-Ge'onim, Collection of resp. by different authors.

She'erit Yisrael, Resp. by Israel Ze'ev Mintzberg.

She'erit Yosef, Resp. by *Joseph b. Mordecai Gershon ha-Kohen.

She'ilat Yavez, Resp. by Jacob *Emden (Yaveẓ).

She'iltot, Compilation arranged acc. to the Torah by *Aḥa (Aḥai) of Shabḥa.

Shem Aryeh, Resp. by Aryeh Leib *Lipschutz.

Shemesh Ẓedakah, Resp. by Samson *Morpurgo.

Shenei ha-Me'orot ha-Gedolim, Resp. by Elijah *Covo.

Shetarot, Sefer ha-, Collection of legal forms by *Judah b. Barzillai al-Bargeloni.

Shevut Ya'akov, Resp. by Jacob b. Joseph Reicher.

Shibbolei ha-Leket Compilation on ritual by Zedekiah b. Avraham *Anav.

Shiltei Gibborim, Comm. to Rif, *Halakhot,* by *Joshua Boaz b. Simeon; printed in major editions of the Talmud.

Shittah Mekubbeẓet, Compilation of talmudical commentaries by Bezalel *Ashkenazi.

Shivat Ẓiyyon, Resp. by Samuel b. Ezekiel *Landau.

Shiyyurei Korban, by David *Fraenkel; additions to his comm. to Jer. Talmud *Korban Edah;* both printed in most editions of Jer. Talmud.

Sho'el u-Meshiv, Resp. by Joseph Saul ha-Levi *Nathanson.

Sh[*ulḥan*] Ar[*ukh*] [of Ba'al ha-Tanya], Code by *Shneur Zalman of Lyady; not identical with the code by Joseph Caro.

Siftei Kohen, Comm. to Sh. Ar., YD and ḤM by *Shabbetai b. Meir ha-Kohen; printed in most editions of Sh. Ar.; usual abbreviation: *Shakh.*

Simḥat Yom Tov, Resp. by Tom Tov b. Jacob *Algazi.

Simlah Ḥadashah, Treatise on *Sheḥitah* by Alexander Sender b. Ephraim Zalman *Schor; see also *Tevu'ot Shor.*

Simeon b. Ẓemaḥ = Simeon b. Ẓemaḥ *Duran.

Sma, Comm. to Sh. Ar. by Joshua b. Alexander ha-Kohen *Falk; the full title is: *Sefer Me'irat Einayim;* printed in most editions of Sh. Ar.

Solomon b. Isaac ha-Levi = Solomon b. Isaac *Levy.

Solomon b. Isaac of Troyes = *Rashi.

Tal Orot, Rabbinical work with various contents, by Joseph ibn Gioia.

Tam, Rabbenu = *Tam Jacob b. Meir.

Tashbaẓ = Samson b. Zadok.

Tashbeẓ = Simeon b. Zemaḥ *Duran, sometimes also abbreviation for Samson b. Zadok, usually known as Tashbaẓ.

Tashbeẓ [*Sefer ha-*], Resp. by Simeon b. Ẓemaḥ *Duran; the fourth part of this work is called: *Ḥut ha-Meshullash.*

Taz, Usual abbreviation of *Turei Zahav,* comm., to Sh. Ar. by *David b. Samnuel ha-Levi; printed in most editions of Sh. Ar.

(Ha)-Tekhelet, subdivision of the *Levush* (a codification by Mordecai b. Abraham (Levush) *Jaffe); *Ha-Tekhelet* parallels Tur, OḤ 1-241.

Terumat ha-Deshen, by Israel b. Pethahiah *Isserlein; subdivided into a part containing responsa, and a second part called *Pesakim u-Khetavim* or *Piskei Maharai.*

Terumot, Sefer ha-, Compilation of *halakhot* by Samuel b. Isaac *Sardi.

Teshuvot Ba'alei ha-Tosafot, Collection of responsa by the Tosafists.

Teshjvot Ge'onei Mizraḥ u-Ma'aav, Collection of responsa.

Teshuvot ha-Geonim, Collection of responsa from Geonic period.

Teshuvot Ḥakhmei Provinẓyah, Collection of responsa by different Provencal authors.

Teshuvot Ḥakhmei Ẓarefat ve-Loter, Collection of responsa by different French authors.

Teshuvot Maimuniyyot, Resp. pertaining to Maimonides' *Yad Ḥazakah;* printed in major editions of this work after the text; authorship uncertain.

Tevu'ot Shor, by Alexander Sender b. Ephraim Zalman *Schor, a comm. to his *Simlah Ḥadashah,* a work on *Sheḥitah.*

Tiferet Ẓevi, Resp. by Ẓevi Hirsch of the "AHW" Communities (Altona, Hamburg, Wandsbeck).

Tiktin, Judah b. Simeon = Judah b. Simeon *Ashkenazi.

Toledot Adam ve-Ḥavvah, Codification by *Jeroham b. Meshullam.

Torat Emet, Resp. by Aaron b. Joseph *Sasson.

Torat Ḥayyim, , Resp. by Ḥayyim (ben) Shabbetai.

Torat ha-Minhagot, subdivision of the *Massa Ḥayyim* (a work on tax law) by Ḥayyim *Palaggi, containing an exposition of customary law.

Tosafot Rid, Explanations to the Talmud and decisions by *Isaiah b. Mali di Trani the Elder.

Tosefot Yom Tov, comm. to Mishnah by Yom Tov Lipmann b. Nathan ha-Levi *Heller; printed in most editions of the Mishnah.

Tummim, subdivision of the comm. to Sh. Ar., ḤM, *Urim ve-Tummim* by Jonathan *Eybeschuetz; printed in the major editions of Sh. Ar.

Tur, usual abbreviation for the *Arba'ah Turim* of *Jacob b. Asher.

Turei Zahav, Comm. to Sh. Ar. by *David b. Samuel ha-Levi; printed in most editions of Sh. Ar.; usual abbreviation: *Taz.*

Urim, subdivision of the following.

Urim ve-Tummim, Comm. to Sh. Ar., ḤM, by Jonathan *Eybeschuetz; printed in the major editions of Sh. Ar.; subdivided in places into *Urim* and *Tummim.*

Vikku'aḥ Mayim Ḥayyim, Polemics against Isserles and Caro by Ḥayyim b. Bezalel.

Yad Malakhi, Methodological treatise by *Malachi b. Jacob ha-Kohen.

Yad Ramah, Nov. by Meir b. Todros [ha-Levi] *Abulafia.
Yakhin u-Vo'az, Resp. by Ẓemaḥ b. Solomon *Duran.
Yam ha-Gadol, Resp. by Jacob Moses *Toledano.
Yam shel Shelomo, Compilation arranged acc. to Talmud by Solomon b. Jehiel (Maharshal) *Luria.
Yashar, Sefer ha-, by *Tam, Jacob b. Meir (Rabbenu Tam); 1st pt.: Resp.; 2nd pt.: Nov.
Yaskil Avdi, Resp. by Obadiah Hadaya (printed together with his Resp. *De'ah ve-Haskel).*
Yaveẓ = Jacob *Emden.
Yehudah Ya'aleh, Resp. by Judah b. Israel *Aszod.
Yekar Tiferet, Comm. to Maimonides' *Yad Ḥazakah,*by David b. Solomon ibn Zimra, printed in most editions of *Yad Ḥazakah.*
Yere'im [*ha-Shalem*], [*Sefer*], Treatise on precepts by *Eliezer b. Samuel of Metz.
Yeshu'ot Ya'akov, Resp. by Jacob Meshullam b. Mordecai Ze'ev *Ornstein.
Yiẓhak Rei'aḥ, Resp. by Isaac b. Samuel Abendanan (see article *Abendanam Family).
Ẓafenat Pa'ne'aḥ (1), also called *Raban* or *Even ha-Ezer,* see under the last name.
Ẓafenat Pa'ne'aḥ (2), Resp. by Joseph *Rozin.
Zayit Ra'anan, Resp. by Moses Judah Leib b. Benjamin Auerbach.
Ẓeidah la-Derekh, Codification by *Menahem b. Aaron ibn Zerah.
Ẓedakah u-Mishpat, Resp. by Ẓedakah b. Saadiah Huẓin.
Zekan Aharon, Resp. by Elijah b. Benjamin ha-Levi.
Zekher Ẓaddik, Sermons by Eliezer *Katzenellenbogen.
Ẓemaḥ Ẓedek (1) Resp. by Menaham Mendel Shneersohn (see under *Shneersohn Family).
Zera Avraham, Resp. by Abraham b. David *Yiẓḥaki.
Zera Emet Resp. by *Ishmael b. Abaham Isaac ha-Kohen.
Ẓevi la-Ẓaddik, Resp. by Ẓevi Elimelech b. David Shapira.
Zikhron Yehudah, Resp. by *Judah b. Asher
Zikhron Yosef, Resp. by Joseph b. Menahem *Steinhardt.
Zikhronot, Sefer ha-, Sermons on several precepts by Samuel *Aboab.
Zikkaron la-Rishonim . . ., by Albert (Abraham Elijah) *Harkavy; contains in vol. 1 pt. 4 (1887) a collection of Geonic responsa.
Ẓiẓ Eliezer, Resp. by Eliezer Judah b. Jacob Gedaliah Waldenberg.

BIBLIOGRAPHICAL ABBREVIATIONS

Bibliographies in English and other languages have been extensively updated, with English translations cited where available. In order to help the reader, the language of books or articles is given where not obvious from titles of books or names of periodicals. Titles of books and periodicals in languages with alphabets other than Latin, are given in transliteration, even where there is a title page in English. Titles of articles in periodicals are not given. Names of Hebrew and Yiddish periodicals well known in English-speaking countries or in Israel under their masthead in Latin characters are given in this form, even when contrary to transliteration rules. Names of authors writing in languages with non-Latin alphabets are given in their Latin alphabet form wherever known; otherwise the names are transliterated. Initials are generally not given for authors of articles in periodicals, except to avoid confusion. Non-abbreviated book titles and names of periodicals are printed in *italics*. Abbreviations are given in the list below.

AASOR	*Annual of the American School of Oriental Research* (1919ff.).
AB	*Analecta Biblica* (1952ff.).
Abel, Géog	F.-M. Abel, *Géographie de la Palestine,* 2 vols. (1933-38).
ABR	*Australian Biblical Review* (1951ff.).
Abr.	Philo, *De Abrahamo.*
Abrahams, Companion	I. Abrahams, *Companion to the Authorised Daily Prayer Book* (rev. ed. 1922).
Abramson, Merkazim	S. Abramson, *Ba-Merkazim u-va-Tefuẓot bi-Tekufat ha-Ge'onim* (1965).
Acts	Acts of the Apostles (New Testament).
ACUM	*Who is who in ACUM* [*Aguddat Kompozitorim u-Meḥabbrim*].
ADAJ	*Annual of the Department of Antiquities, Jordan* (1951ff.).
Adam	Adam and Eve (Pseudepigrapha).
ADB	*Allgemeine Deutsche Biographie,* 56 vols. (1875–1912).
Add. Esth.	The Addition to Esther (Apocrypha).
Adler, Prat Mus	1. Adler, *La pratique musicale savante dans quelques communautés juives en Europe au XVIIe et XVIIIe siècles,* 2 vols. (1966).
Adler-Davis	H.M. Adler and A. Davis (ed. and tr.), *Service of the Synagogue, a New Edition of the Festival Prayers with an English Translation in Prose and Verse,* 6 vols. (1905–06).
Aet.	Philo, *De Aeternitate Mundi.*
AFO	*Archiv fuer Orientforschung* (first two volumes under the name *Archiv fuer Keilschriftforschung)* (1923ff.).
Ag. Ber	*Aggadat Bereshit* (ed. Buber, 1902*).*
Agr.	Philo, *De Agricultura.*
Ag. Sam.	*Aggadat Samuel.*
Ag. Song	*Aggadat Shir ha-Shirim* (Schechter ed., 1896).
Aharoni, Ereẓ	Y. Aharoni, *Ereẓ Yisrael bi-Tekufat ha-Mikra: Geografyah Historit* (1962).
Aharoni, Land	Y. Aharoni, *Land of the Bible* (1966).

Ahikar	Ahikar (Pseudepigrapha).
AI	*Archives Israélites de France* (1840–1936).
AJA	*American Jewish Archives* (1948ff.).
AJHSP	*American Jewish Historical Society – Publications* (after vol. 50 = AJHSQ).
AJHSQ	*American Jewish Historical (Society) Quarterly* (before vol. 50 =AJHSP).
AJSLL	*American Journal of Semitic Languages and Literature* (1884–95 under the title *Hebraica,* since 1942 JNES).
AJYB	*American Jewish Year Book* (1899ff.).
AKM	Abhandlungen fuer die Kunde des Morgenlandes (series).
Albright, Arch	W.F. Albright, *Archaeology of Palestine* (rev. ed. 1960).
Albright, Arch Bib	W.F. Albright, *Archaeology of Palestine and the Bible* (1935^{3}).
Albright, Arch Rel	W.F. Albright, *Archaeology and the Religion of Israel* (1953^{3}).
Albright, Stone	W.F. Albright, *From the Stone Age to Christianity* (1957^{2}).
Alon, Meḥkarim	G. Alon, *Meḥkarim be-Toledot Yisrael bi-Ymei Bayit Sheni u-vi-Tekufat ha-Mishnah ve-ha Talmud,* 2 vols. (1957–58).
Alon, Toledot	G. Alon, *Toledot ha-Yehudim be-Ereẓ Yisrael bi-Tekufat ha-Mishnah ve-ha-Talmud,* I (1958^{3}), (1961^{2}).
ALOR	Alter Orient (series).
Alt, Kl Schr	A. Alt, *Kleine Schriften zur Geschichte des Volkes Israel,* 3 vols. (1953–59).
Alt, Landnahme	A. Alt, *Landnahme der Israeliten in Palaestina* (1925); also in Alt, Kl Schr, 1 (1953), 89–125.
Ant.	Josephus, *Jewish Antiquities* (Loeb Classics ed.).
AO	*Acta Orientalia* (1922ff.).
AOR	*Analecta Orientalia* (1931ff.).
AOS	American Oriental Series.
Apion	Josephus, *Against Apion* (Loeb Classics ed.).
Aq.	Aquila's Greek translation of the Bible.
Ar.	*Arakhin* (talmudic tractate).
Artist.	Letter of Aristeas (Pseudepigrapha).
ARN^{1}	*Avot de-Rabbi Nathan,* version (1) ed. Schechter, 1887.
ARN^{2}	*Avot de-Rabbi Nathan,* version (2) ed. Schechter, 1945^{2}.
Aronius, Regesten	I. Aronius, *Regesten zur Geschichte der Juden im fraenkischen und deutschen Reiche bis zum Jahre 1273* (1902).
ARW	*Archiv fuer Religionswissenschaft* (1898–1941/42).
AS	*Assyrological Studies* (1931ff.).
Ashtor, Korot	E. Ashtor (Strauss), *Korot ha-Yehudim bi-Sefarad ha-Muslemit,* 1(1966^{2}), 2(1966).
Ashtor, Toledot	E. Ashtor (Strauss), *Toledot ha-Yehudim be-Miẓrayim ve-Suryah Taḥat Shilton ha-Mamlukim,* 3 vols. (1944–70).
Assaf, Ge'onim	S. Assaf, *Tekufat ha-Ge'onim ve-Sifrutah* (1955).
Assaf, Mekorot	S. Assaf, *Mekorot le-Toledot ha-Ḥinnukh be-Yisrael,* 4 vols. (1925–43).
Ass. Mos.	Assumption of Moses (Pseudepigrapha).
ATA	Alttestamentliche Abhandlungen (series).
ATANT	Abhandlungen zur Theologie des Alten und Neuen Testaments (series).
AUJW	*Allgemeine unabhaengige juedische Wochenzeitung* (till 1966 = AWJD).
AV	Authorized Version of the Bible.
Avad.	*Avadim* (post-talmudic tractate).
Avi-Yonah, Geog	M. Avi-Yonah, *Geografyah Historit shel Ereẓ Yisrael* (1962^{3}).
Avi-Yonah, Land	M. Avi-Yonah, *The Holy Land from the Persian to the Arab conquest (536 B.C. to A.D. 640)* (1960).
Avot	*Avot* (talmudic tractate).
Av. Zar.	*Avodah Zarah* (talmudic tractate).
AWJD	*Allgemeine Wochenzeitung der Juden in Deutschland* (since 1967 = AUJW).
AZDJ	*Allgemeine Zeitung des Judentums.*
Azulai	Ḥ.Y.D. Azulai, *Shem ha-Gedolim,* ed. by I.E. Benjacob, 2 pts. (1852) (and other editions).
BA	*Biblical Archaeologist* (1938ff.).
Bacher, Bab Amor	W. Bacher, *Agada der babylonischen Amoraeer* (1913^{2}).
Bacher, Pal Amor	W. Bacher, *Agada der palaestinensischen Amoraeer* (Heb. ed. *Aggadat Amora'ei Ereẓ Yisrael),* 2 vols. (1892–99).
Bacher, Tann	W. Bacher, *Agada der Tannaiten* (Heb. ed. *Aggadot ha-Tanna'im,* vol. 1, pt. 1 and 2 (1903); vol. 2 (1890).
Bacher, Trad	W. Bacher, *Tradition und Tradenten in den Schulen Palaestinas und Babyloniens* (1914).
Baer, Spain	Yitzhak (Fritz) Baer, *History of the Jews in Christian Spain,* 2 vols. (1961–66).
Baer, Studien	Yitzhak (Fritz) Baer, *Studien zur Geschichte der Juden im Koenigreich Aragonien waehrend des 13. und 14. Jahrhunderts* (1913).
Baer, Toledot	Yitzhak (Fritz) Baer, *Toledot ha-Yehudim bi-Sefarad ha-Noẓerit mi-Teḥillatan shel ha-Kehillot ad ha-Gerush,* 2 vols. (1959^{2}).
Baer, Urkunden	Yitzhak (Fritz) Baer, *Die Juden im christlichen Spanien,* 2 vols. (1929–36).
Baer S., Seder	S.I. Baer, *Seder Avodat Yisrael* (1868 and reprints).
BAIU	*Bulletin de l'Alliance Israélite Universelle* (1861–1913).
Baker, Biog Dict	*Baker's Biographical Dictionary of Musicians,* revised by N. Slonimsky (1958^{5}; with Supplement 1965).
I Bar.	I Baruch (Apocrypha).
II Bar.	II Baruch (Pseudepigrapha).
III Bar.	III Baruch (Pseudepigrapha).
BAR	*Biblical Archaeology Review.*
Baron, Community	S.W. Baron, *The Jewish Community, its History and Structure to the American Revolution,* 3 vols. (1942).

Baron, Social	S.W. Baron, *Social and Religious History of the Jews,* 3 vols. (1937); enlarged, 1-2(1952^{2}), 3-14 (1957–69).
Barthélemy-Milik	D. Barthélemy and J.T. Milik, *Dead Sea Scrolls: Discoveries in the Judean Desert,* vol. 1 *Qumram Cave* I (1955).
BASOR	*Bulletin of the American School of Oriental Research.*
Bauer-Leander	H. Bauer and P. Leander, *Grammatik des Biblisch-Aramaeischen* (1927; repr. 1962).
BB	(1) *Bava Batra* (talmudic tractate). (2) *Biblische Beitraege* (1943ff.).
BBB	Bonner biblische Beitraege (series).
BBLA	*Beitraege zur biblischen Landes- und Altertumskunde* (until 1949–ZDPV).
BBSAJ	*Bulletin,* British School of Archaeology, Jerusalem (1922–25; after 1927 included in PEFQS).
BDASI	*Alon* (since 1948) or *Hadashot Arkheologiyyot* (since 1961), bulletin of the Department of Antiquities of the State of Israel.
Begrich, Chronologie	J. Begrich, *Chronologie der Koenige von Israel und Juda* (1929).
Bek.	*Bekhorot* (talmudic tractate).
Bel	Bel and the Dragon (Apocrypha).
Benjacob, Oẓar	I.E. Benjacob, *Oẓar ha-Sefarim* (1880; repr. 1956).
Ben Sira	see Ecclus.
Ben-Yehuda, Millon	E. Ben-Yedhuda, *Millon ha-Lashon ha-Ivrit,* 16 vols (1908–59; repr. in 8 vols., 1959).
Benzinger, Archaeologie	I. Benzinger, *Hebraeische Archaeologie* (1927^{3}).
Ben Zvi, Eretz Israel	I. Ben-Zvi, *Eretz Israel under Ottoman Rule* (1960; offprint from L. Finkelstein (ed.), *The Jews, their History, Culture and Religion* (vol. 1).
Ben Zvi, Ereẓ Israel	I. Ben-Zvi, *Ereẓ Israel bi-Ymei ha-Shilton ha-Ottomani (1955).*
Ber.	*Berakhot* (talmudic tractate).
Beẓah	*Beẓah* (talmudic tractate).
BIES	Bulletin of the Israel Exploration Society, see below BJPES.
Bik.	*Bikkurim* (talmudic tractate).
BJCE	Bibliography of Jewish Communities in Europe, catalog at General Archives for the History of the Jewish People, Jerusalem.
BJPES	Bulletin of the Jewish Palestine Exploration Society – English name of the Hebrew periodical known as: 1. *Yedi'ot ha-Ḥevrah ha-Ivrit la-Ḥakirat Ereẓ Yisrael va-Attikoteha* (1933–1954); 2. *Yedi'ot ha-Ḥevrah la-Ḥakirat Ereẓ Yisrael va-Attikoteha* (1954–1962); 3. *Yedi'ot ba-Ḥakirat Ereẓ Yisrael va-Attikoteha* (1962ff.).
BJRL	*Bulletin of the John Rylands Library* (1914ff.).
BK	*Bava Kamma* (talmudic tractate).
BLBI	*Bulletin of the Leo Baeck Institute* (1957ff.).
BM	(1) *Bava Meẓia* (talmudic tractate). (2) *Beit Mikra* (1955/56ff.). (3) British Museum.
BO	*Bibbia e Oriente* (1959ff.).
Bondy-Dworský	G. Bondy and F. Dworský, *Regesten zur Geschichte der Juden in Boehmen, Maehren und Schlesien von 906 bis 1620,* 2 vols. (1906).
BOR	*Bibliotheca Orientalis* (1943ff.).
Borée, Ortsnamen	W. Borée *Die alten Ortsnamen Palaestinas* (1930).
Bousset, Religion	W. Bousset, *Die Religion des Judentums im neutestamentlichen Zeitalter* (1906^{2}).
Bousset-Gressmann	W. Bousset, *Die Religion des Judentums im spaethellenistischen Zeitalter* (1966^{3}).
BR	*Biblical Review* (1916–25).
BRCI	*Bulletin of the Research Council of Israel* (1951/52–1954/55; then divided).
BRE	*Biblical Research* (1956ff.).
BRF	*Bulletin of the Rabinowitz Fund for the Exploration of Ancient Synagogues* (1949ff.).
Briggs, Psalms	Ch. A. and E.G. Briggs, *Critical and Exegetical Commentary on the Book of Psalms,* 2 vols. (ICC, 1906–07).
Bright, Hist	J. Bright, *A History of Israel* (1959).
Brockelmann, Arab Lit	K. Brockelmann, *Geschichte der arabischen Literatur,* 2 vols. 1898–1902), supplement, 3 vols. (1937–42).
Bruell, Jahrbuecher	*Jahrbuecher fuer juedische Geschichte und Litteratur,* ed. by N. Bruell, Frankfurt (1874–90).
Brugmans-Frank	H. Brugmans and A. Frank (eds.), *Geschiedenis der Joden in Nederland* (1940).
BTS	*Bible et Terre Sainte* (1958ff.).
Bull, Index	S. Bull, *Index to Biographies of Contemporary Composers* (1964).
BW	*Biblical World* (1882–1920).
BWANT	*Beitraege zur Wissenschaft vom Alten und Neuen Testament* (1926ff.).
BZ	*Biblische Zeitschrift* (1903ff.).
BZAW	*Beihefte zur Zeitschrift fuer die alttestamentliche Wissenschaft,* supplement to ZAW (1896ff.).
BŻIH	*Biuletyn Zydowskiego Instytutu Historycznego* (1950ff.).
CAB	*Cahiers d'archéologie biblique* (1953ff.).
CAD	*The* [*Chicago*] *Assyrian Dictionary* (1956ff.).
CAH	*Cambridge Ancient History,* 12 vols. (1923–39)
CAH^{2}	*Cambridge Ancient History,* second edition, 14 vols. (1962–2005).
Calwer, Lexikon	*Calwer, Bibellexikon.*
Cant.	Canticles, usually given as Song (= Song of Songs).

Cantera-Millás, Inscripciones	F. Cantera and J.M. Millás, *Las Inscripciones Hebraicas de España* (1956).
CBQ	*Catholic Biblical Quarterly* (1939ff.).
CCARY	Central Conference of American Rabbis, *Yearbook* (1890/91ff.).
CD	*Damascus Document* from the Cairo *Genizah* (published by S. Schechter, *Fragments of a Zadokite Work*, 1910).
Charles, Apocrypha	R.H. Charles, *Apocrypha and Pseudepigrapha . . .*, 2 vols. (1913; repr. 1963–66).
Cher.	Philo, *De Cherubim*.
I (or II) Chron.	Chronicles, book I and II (Bible).
CIG	*Corpus Inscriptionum Graecarum*.
CIJ	*Corpus Inscriptionum Judaicarum*, 2 vols. (1936–52).
CIL	*Corpus Inscriptionum Latinarum*.
CIS	*Corpus Inscriptionum Semiticarum* (1881ff.).
C.J.	Codex Justinianus.
Clermont-Ganneau, Arch	Ch. Clermont-Ganneau, *Archaeological Researches in Palestine*, 2 vols. (1896–99).
CNFI	*Christian News from Israel* (1949ff.).
Cod. Just.	Codex Justinianus.
Cod. Theod.	Codex Theodosinanus.
Col.	Epistle to the Colosssians (New Testament).
Conder, Survey	Palestine Exploration Fund, *Survey of Eastern Palestine*, vol. 1, pt. I (1889) = C.R. Conder, *Memoirs of the . . . Survey*.
Conder-Kitchener	Palestine Exploration Fund, *Survey of Western Palestine*, vol. 1, pts. 1-3 (1881–83) = C.R. Conder and H.H. Kitchener, *Memoirs*.
Conf.	Philo, *De Confusione Linguarum*.
Conforte, Kore	D. Conforte, *Kore ha-Dorot* (1842^2).
Cong.	Philo, *De Congressu Quaerendae Eruditionis Gratia*.
Cont.	Philo, *De Vita Contemplativa*.
I (or II) Cor.	Epistles to the Corinthians (New Testament).
Cowley, Aramic	A. Cowley, *Aramaic Papyri of the Fifth Century B.C.* (1923).
Colwey, Cat	A.E. Cowley, *A Concise Catalogue of the Hebrew Printed Books in the Bodleian Library* (1929).
CRB	*Cahiers de la Revue Biblique* (1964ff.).
Crowfoot-Kenyon	J.W. Crowfoot, K.M. Kenyon and E.L. Sukenik, *Buildings of Samaria* (1942).
C.T.	Codex Theodosianus.
DAB	*Dictionary of American Biography* (1928–58).
Daiches, Jews	S. Daiches, *Jews in Babylonia* (1910).
Dalman, Arbeit	G. Dalman, *Arbeit und Sitte in Palaestina*, 7 vols.in 8 (1928–42 repr. 1964).
Dan	Daniel (Bible).
Davidson, Oẓar	I. Davidson, *Oẓar ha-Shirah ve-ha-Piyyut*, 4 vols. (1924–33); Supplement in: HUCA, 12–13 (1937/38), 715–823.
DB	J. Hastings, *Dictionary of the Bible*, 4 vols. (1963^2).
DBI	F.G. Vigoureaux et al. (eds.), *Dictionnaire de la Bible*, 5 vols. in 10 (1912); Supplement, 8 vols. (1928–66)
Decal.	Philo, *De Decalogo*.
Dem.	*Demai* (talmudic tractate).
DER	*Derekh Ereẓ Rabbah* (post-talmudic tractate).
Derenbourg, Hist	J. Derenbourg *Essai sur l'histoire et la géographie de la Palestine* (1867).
Det.	Philo, *Quod deterius potiori insidiari solet*.
Deus	Philo, *Quod Deus immutabilis sit*.
Deut.	Deuteronomy (Bible).
Deut. R.	*Deuteronomy Rabbah*.
DEZ	*Derekh Ereẓ Zuta* (post-talmudic tractate).
DHGE	*Dictionnaire d'histoire et de géographie ecclésiastiques*, ed. by A. Baudrillart et al., 17 vols (1912–68).
Dik. Sof	*Dikdukei Soferim*, variae lections of the talmudic text by Raphael Nathan Rabbinovitz (16 vols., 1867–97).
Dinur, Golah	B. Dinur (Dinaburg), *Yisrael ba-Golah*, 2 vols. in 7 (1959–68) = vols. 5 and 6 of his *Toledot Yisrael*, second series.
Dinur, Haganah	B. Dinur (ed.), *Sefer Toledot ha-Haganah* (1954ff.).
Diringer, Iscr	D. Diringer, *Iscrizioni antico-ebraiche palestinesi* (1934).
Discoveries	*Discoveries in the Judean Desert* (1955ff.).
DNB	*Dictionary of National Biography*, 66 vols. (1921–222) with Supplements.
Dubnow, Divrei	S. Dubnow, *Divrei Yemei Am Olam*, 11 vols (1923–38 and further editions).
Dubnow, Ḥasidut	S. Dubnow, *Toledot ha-Ḥasidut* (1960^2).
Dubnow, Hist	S. Dubnow, *History of the Jews* (1967).
Dubnow, Hist Russ	S. Dubnow, *History of the Jews in Russia and Poland*, 3 vols. (1916 20).
Dubnow, Outline	S. Dubnow, *An Outline of Jewish History*, 3 vols. (1925–29).
Dubnow, Weltgesch	S. Dubnow, *Weltgeschichte des juedischen Volkes* 10 vols. (1925–29).
Dukes, Poesie	L. Dukes, *Zur Kenntnis der neuhebraeischen religioesen Poesie* (1842).
Dunlop, Khazars	D. H. Dunlop, *History of the Jewish Khazars* (1954).
EA	El Amarna Letters (edited by J.A. Knudtzon), *Die El-Amarna Tafel*, 2 vols. (1907 14).
EB	*Encyclopaedia Britannica*.
EBI	*Estudios biblicos* (1941ff.).
EBIB	T.K. Cheyne and J.S. Black, *Encyclopaedia Biblica*, 4 vols. (1899–1903).
Ebr.	Philo, *De Ebrietate*.
Eccles.	Ecclesiastes (Bible).
Eccles. R.	*Ecclesiastes Rabbah*.
Ecclus.	Ecclesiasticus or Wisdom of Ben Sira (or Sirach; Apocrypha).
Eduy.	*Eduyyot* (mishanic tractate).

EG	*Enziklopedyah shel Galuyyot* (1953ff.).
EH	*Even ha-Ezer.*
EHA	*Enziklopedyah la-Ḥafirot Arkheologiyyot be-Ereẓ Yisrael,* 2 vols. (1970).
EI	*Enzyklopaedie des Islams,* 4 vols. (1905–14). Supplement vol. (1938).
EIS	*Encyclopaedia of Islam,* 4 vols. (1913–36; repr. 1954–68).
EIS[2]	*Encyclopaedia of Islam, second edition (1960–2000).*
Eisenstein, Dinim	J.D. Eisenstein, *Oẓar Dinim u-Minhagim* (1917; several reprints).
Eisenstein, Yisrael	J.D. Eisenstein, *Oẓar Yisrael* (10 vols, 1907–13; repr. with several additions 1951).
EIV	*Enẓiklopedyah Ivrit* (1949ff.).
EJ	*Encyclopaedia Judaica* (German, A-L only), 10 vols. (1928–34).
EJC	*Enciclopedia Judaica Castellana,* 10 vols. (1948–51).
Elbogen, Century	I Elbogen, *A Century of Jewish Life* (1960[2]).
Elbogen, Gottesdienst	I Elbogen, *Der juedische Gottesdienst ...* (1931[3], repr. 1962).
Elon, Mafte'aḥ	M. Elon (ed.), *Mafte'aḥ ha-She'elot ve-ha-Teshuvot ha-Rosh* (1965).
EM	*Enẓiklopedyah Mikra'it* (1950ff.).
I (or II) En.	I and II Enoch (Pseudepigrapha).
EncRel	*Encyclopedia of Religion,* 15 vols. (1987, 2005[2]).
Eph.	Epistle to the Ephesians (New Testament).
Ephros, Cant	G. Ephros, *Cantorial Anthology,* 5 vols. (1929–57).
Ep. Jer.	Epistle of Jeremy (Apocrypha).
Epstein, Amora'im	J N. Epstein, *Mevo'ot le-Sifrut ha-Amora'im* (1962).
Epstein, Marriage	L M. Epstein, *Marriage Laws in the Bible and the Talmud* (1942).
Epstein, Mishnah	J. N. Epstein, *Mavo le-Nusaḥ ha-Mishnah,* 2 vols. (1964[2]).
Epstein, Tanna'im	J. N. Epstein, *Mavo le-Sifruth ha-Tanna'im.* (1947).
ER	*Ecumenical Review.*
Er.	*Eruvin* (talmudic tractate).
ERE	*Encyclopaedia of Religion and Ethics,* 13 vols. (1908–26); reprinted.
ErIsr	*Eretz-Israel,* Israel Exploration Society.
I Esd.	I Esdras (Apocrypha) (= III Ezra).
II Esd.	II Esdras (Apocrypha) (= IV Ezra).
ESE	*Ephemeris fuer semitische Epigraphik,* ed. by M. Lidzbarski.
ESN	*Encyclopaedia Sefaradica Neerlandica,* 2 pts. (1949).
ESS	*Encyclopaedia of the Social Sciences,* 15 vols. (1930–35); reprinted in 8 vols. (1948–49).
Esth.	Esther (Bible).
Est. R.	*Esther Rabbah.*
ET	*Enẓiklopedyah Talmudit* (1947ff.).
Eusebius, Onom.	E. Klostermann (ed.), *Das Onomastikon* (1904), Greek with Hieronymus' Latin translation.
Ex.	Exodus (Bible).

Ex. R.	*Exodus Rabbah.*
Exs	Philo, *De Exsecrationibus.*
EẒD	*Enẓiklopeday shel ha-Ẓiyyonut ha-Datit* (1951ff.).
Ezek.	Ezekiel (Bible).
Ezra	Ezra (Bible).
III Ezra	III Ezra (Pseudepigrapha).
IV Ezra	IV Ezra (Pseudepigrapha).
Feliks, Ha-Ẓome'aḥ	*J. Feliks, Ha-Ẓome'aḥ ve-ha-Ḥai ba-Mishnah* (1983).
Finkelstein, Middle Ages	L. Finkelstein, *Jewish Self-Government in the Middle Ages* (1924).
Fischel, Islam	W.J. Fischel, *Jews in the Economic and Political Life of Mediaeval Islam* (1937; reprint with introduction "The Court Jew in the Islamic World," 1969).
FJW	*Fuehrer durch die juedische Gemeindeverwaltung und Wohlfahrtspflege in Deutschland* (1927/28).
Frankel, Mevo	Z. Frankel, *Mevo ha-Yerushalmi* (1870; reprint 1967).
Frankel, Mishnah	Z. Frankel, *Darkhei ha-Mishnah* (1959[2]; reprint 1959[2]).
Frazer, Folk-Lore	J.G. Frazer, *Folk-Lore in the Old Testament,* 3 vols. (1918–19).
Frey, Corpus	J.-B. Frey, *Corpus Inscriptionum Iudaicarum,* 2 vols. (1936–52).
Friedmann, Lebensbilder	A. Friedmann, *Lebensbilder beruehmter Kantoren,* 3 vols. (1918–27).
FRLT	*Forschungen zur Religion und Literatur des Alten und Neuen Testaments* (series) (1950ff.).
Frumkin-Rivlin	A.L. Frumkin and E. Rivlin, *Toledot Ḥakhmei Yerushalayim,* 3 vols. (1928–30), Supplement vol. (1930).
Fuenn, Keneset	S.J. Fuenn, *Keneset Yisrael,* 4 vols. (1887–90).
Fuerst, Bibliotheca	J. Fuerst, *Bibliotheca Judaica,* 2 vols. (1863; repr. 1960).
Fuerst, Karaeertum	J. Fuerst, *Geschichte des Karaeertums,* 3 vols. (1862–69).
Fug.	Philo, *De Fuga et Inventione.*
Gal.	Epistle to the Galatians (New Testament).
Galling, Reallexikon	K. Galling, *Biblisches Reallexikon* (1937).
Gardiner, Onomastica	A.H. Gardiner, *Ancient Egyptian Onomastica,* 3 vols. (1947).
Geiger, Mikra	A. Geiger, *Ha-Mikra ve-Targumav,* tr. by J.L. Baruch (1949).
Geiger, Urschrift	A. Geiger, *Urschrift und Uebersetzungen der Bibel* 1928[2]).
Gen.	Genesis (Bible).
Gen. R.	*Genesis Rabbah.*
Ger.	*Gerim* (post-talmudic tractate).
Germ Jud	M. Brann, I. Elbogen, A. Freimann, and H. Tykocinski (eds.), *Germania Judaica,* vol. 1 (1917; repr. 1934 and 1963); vol. 2, in 2 pts. (1917–68), ed. by Z. Avneri.

GHAT	*Goettinger Handkommentar zum Alten Testament* (1917–22).
Ghirondi-Neppi	M.S. Ghirondi and G.H. Neppi, *Toledot Gedolei Yisrael u-Ge'onei Italyah ... u-Ve'urim al Sefer Zekher Ẓaddikim li-Verakhah* . . .(1853), index in ZHB, 17 (1914), 171–83.
Gig.	Philo, *De Gigantibus.*
Ginzberg, Legends	L. Ginzberg, *Legends of the Jews,* 7 vols. (1909–38; and many reprints).
Git.	*Gittin* (talmudic tractate).
Glueck, Explorations	N. Glueck, *Explorations in Eastern Palestine,* 2 vols. (1951).
Goell, Bibliography	Y. Goell, *Bibliography of Modern Hebrew Literature in English Translation* (1968).
Goodenough, Symbols	E.R. Goodenough, *Jewish Symbols in the Greco-Roman Period,* 13 vols. (1953–68).
Gordon, Textbook	C.H. Gordon, *Ugaritic Textbook* (1965; repr. 1967).
Graetz, Gesch	H. Graetz, *Geschichte der Juden* (last edition 1874–1908).
Graetz, Hist	H. Graetz, *History of the Jews,* 6 vols. (1891–1902).
Graetz, Psalmen	H. Graetz, *Kritischer Commentar zu den Psalmen,* 2 vols. in 1 (1882–83).
Graetz, Rabbinowitz	H. Graetz, *Divrei Yemei Yisrael,* tr. by S.P. Rabbinowitz. (1928 1929²).
Gray, Names	G.B. Gray, *Studies in Hebrew Proper Names* (1896).
Gressmann, Bilder	H. Gressmann, *Altorientalische Bilder zum Alten Testament* (1927²).
Gressmann, Texte	H. Gressmann, *Altorientalische Texte zum Alten Testament* (1926²).
Gross, Gal Jud	H. Gross, *Gallia Judaica* (1897; repr. with add. 1969).
Grove, Dict	*Grove's Dictionary of Music and Musicians,* ed. by E. Blum 9 vols. (1954⁵) and suppl. (1961⁵).
Guedemann, Gesch Erz	M. Guedemann, *Geschichte des Erziehungswesens und der Cultur der abendlaendischen Juden,* 3 vols. (1880–88).
Guedemann, Quellenschr	M. Guedemann, *Quellenschriften zur Geschichte des Unterrichts und der Erziehung bei den deutschen Juden* (1873, 1891).
Guide	Maimonides, *Guide of the Perplexed.*
Gulak, Oẓar	A. Gulak, *Oẓar ha-Shetarot ha-Nehugim be-Yisrael* (1926).
Gulak, Yesodei	A. Gulak, *Yesodei ha-Mishpat ha-Ivri, Seder Dinei Mamonot be-Yisrael, al pi Mekorot ha-Talmud ve-ha-Posekim,* 4 vols. (1922; repr. 1967).
Guttmann, Mafte'aḥ	M. Guttmann, *Mafte'aḥ ha-Talmud,* 3 vols. (1906–30).
Guttmann, Philosophies	J. Guttmann, *Philosophies of Judaism* (1964).
Hab.	*Habakkuk* (Bible).
Ḥag.	*Ḥagigah* (talmudic tractate).
Haggai	*Haggai* (Bible).
Ḥal.	*Ḥallah* (talmudic tractate).
Halevy, Dorot	I. Halevy, *Dorot ha-Rishonim,* 6 vols. (1897–1939).
Halpern, Pinkas	I. Halpern (Halperin), *Pinkas Va'ad Arba Araẓot* (1945).
Hananel-Eškenazi	A. Hananel and Eškenazi (eds.), *Fontes Hebraici ad res oeconomicas socialesque terrarum balcanicarum saeculo XVI pertinentes,* 2 vols, (1958–60; in Bulgarian).
HB	*Hebraeische Bibliographie* (1858–82).
Heb.	Epistle to the Hebrews (New Testament).
Heilprin, Dorot	J. Heilprin (Heilperin), *Seder ha-Dorot,* 3 vols. (1882; repr. 1956).
Her.	Philo, *Quis Rerum Divinarum Heres.*
Hertz, Prayer	J.H. Hertz (ed.), *Authorised Daily Prayer Book* (rev. ed. 1948; repr. 1963).
Herzog, Instit	I. Herzog, *The Main Institutions of Jewish Law,* 2 vols. (1936–39; repr. 1967).
Herzog-Hauck	J.J. Herzog and A. Hauch (eds.), *Real-encyklopaedie fuer protestantische Theologie* (1896–1913³).
HḤY	*Ha-Ẓofeh le-Ḥokhmat Yisrael* (first four volumes under the title *Ha-Ẓofeh me-Ereẓ Hagar)* (1910/11–13).
Hirschberg, Afrikah	H.Z. Hirschberg, *Toledot ha-Yehudim be-Afrikah ha-Zofonit,* 2 vols. (1965).
HJ	*Historia Judaica* (1938–61).
HL	*Das Heilige Land* (1857ff.)
ḤM	*Ḥoshen Mishpat.*
Hommel, Ueberliefer.	F. Hommel, *Die altisraelitische Ueberlieferung in inschriftlicher Beleuchtung* (1897).
Hor.	*Horayot* (talmudic tractate).
Horodezky, Ḥasidut	S.A. Horodezky, *Ha-Ḥasidut ve-ha-Ḥasidim,* 4 vols. (1923).
Horowitz, Ereẓ Yis	I.W. Horowitz, *Ereẓ Yisrael u-Shekhenoteha* (1923).
Hos.	Hosea (Bible).
HTR	*Harvard Theological Review* (1908ff.).
HUCA	*Hebrew Union College Annual* (1904; 1924ff.)
Ḥul.	*Ḥullin* (talmudic tractate).
Husik, Philosophy	I. Husik, *History of Medieval Jewish Philosophy* (1932²).
Hyman, Toledot	A. Hyman, *Toledot Tanna'im ve-Amora'im* (1910; repr. 1964).
Ibn Daud, Tradition	Abraham Ibn Daud, *Sefer ha-Qabbalah – The Book of Tradition,* ed. and tr. By G.D. Cohen (1967).
ICC	International Critical Commentary on the Holy Scriptures of the Old and New Testaments (series, 1908ff.).
IDB	*Interpreter's Dictionary of the Bible,* 4 vols. (1962).
Idelsohn, Litugy	A. Z. Idelsohn, *Jewish Liturgy and its Development* (1932; paperback repr. 1967)
Idelsohn, Melodien	A. Z. Idelsohn, *Hebraeisch-orientalischer Melodienschatz,* 10 vols. (1914 32).
Idelsohn, Music	A. Z. Idelsohn, *Jewish Music in its Historical Development* (1929; paperback repr. 1967).

IEJ	*Israel Exploration Journal* (1950ff.).
IESS	*International Encyclopedia of the Social Sciences* (various eds.).
IG	*Inscriptiones Graecae,* ed. by the Prussian Academy.
IGYB	*Israel Government Year Book* (1949/50ff.).
ILR	*Israel Law Review* (1966ff.).
IMIT	*Izraelita Magyar Irodalmi Társulat Évkönyv* (1895 1948).
IMT	International Military Tribunal.
INB	*Israel Numismatic Bulletin* (1962–63).
INJ	*Israel Numismatic Journal* (1963ff.).
Ios	Philo, *De Iosepho.*
Isa.	Isaiah (Bible).
ITHL	Institute for the Translation of Hebrew Literature.
IZBG	*Internationale Zeitschriftenschau fuer Bibelwissenschaft und Grenzgebiete* (1951ff.).
JA	*Journal asiatique* (1822ff.).
James	Epistle of James (New Testament).
JAOS	*Journal of the American Oriental Society* (c. 1850ff.)
Jastrow, Dict	M. Jastrow, *Dictionary of the Targumim, the Talmud Babli and Yerushalmi, and the Midrashic literature,* 2 vols. (1886 1902 and reprints).
JBA	*Jewish Book Annual* (19242ff.).
JBL	*Journal of Biblical Literature* (1881ff.).
JBR	*Journal of Bible and Religion* (1933ff.).
JC	*Jewish Chronicle* (1841ff.).
JCS	*Journal of Cuneiform Studies* (1947ff.).
JE	*Jewish Encyclopedia,* 12 vols. (1901–05 several reprints).
Jer.	Jeremiah (Bible).
Jeremias, Alte Test	A. Jeremias, *Das Alte Testament im Lichte des alten Orients* 1930[4]).
JGGJČ	*Jahrbuch der Gesellschaft fuer Geschichte der Juden in der Čechoslovakischen Republik* (1929–38).
JHSEM	Jewish Historical Society of England, *Miscellanies* (1925ff.).
JHSET	Jewish Historical Society of England, *Transactions* (1893ff.).
JJGL	*Jahrbuch fuer juedische Geschichte und Literatur* (Berlin) (1898–1938).
JJLG	*Jahrbuch der juedische-literarischen Gesellschaft* (Frankfurt) (1903–32).
JJS	*Journal of Jewish Studies* (1948ff.).
JJSO	*Jewish Journal of Sociology* (1959ff.).
JJV	*Jahrbuch fuer juedische Volkskunde* (1898–1924).
JL	*Juedisches Lexikon,* 5 vols. (1927–30).
JMES	*Journal of the Middle East Society* (1947ff.).
JNES	*Journal of Near Eastern Studies* (continuation of AJSLL) (1942ff.).
J.N.U.L.	Jewish National and University Library.
Job	Job (Bible).
Joel	Joel (Bible).
John	Gospel according to John (New Testament).
I, II and III John	Epistles of John (New Testament).
Jos., Ant	Josephus, *Jewish Antiquities* (Loeb Classics ed.).
Jos. Apion	Josephus, *Against Apion* (Loeb Classics ed.).
Jos., index	*Josephus Works,* Loeb Classics ed., index of names.
Jos., Life	Josephus, *Life* (ed. Loeb Classics).
Jos, Wars	Josephus, *The Jewish Wars* (Loeb Classics ed.).
Josh.	Joshua (Bible).
JPESB	Jewish Palestine Exploration Society Bulletin, see BJPES.
JPESJ	Jewish Palestine Exploration Society Journal – Eng. Title of the Hebrew periodical *Kovez ha-Ḥevrah ha-Ivrit la-Ḥakirat Erez Yisrael va-Attikoteha.*
JPOS	*Journal of the Palestine Oriental Society* (1920–48).
JPS	Jewish Publication Society of America, *The Torah* (1962, 1967[2]); *The Holy Scriptures* (1917).
JQR	*Jewish Quarterly Review* (1889ff.).
JR	*Journal of Religion* (1921ff.).
JRAS	*Journal of the Royal Asiatic Society* (1838ff.).
JHR	*Journal of Religious History* (1960/61ff.).
JSOS	*Jewish Social Studies* (1939ff.).
JSS	*Journal of Semitic Studies* (1956ff.).
JTS	*Journal of Theological Studies* (1900ff.).
JTSA	Jewish Theological Seminary of America (also abbreviated as JTS).
Jub.	Jubilees (Pseudepigrapha).
Judg.	Judges (Bible).
Judith	Book of Judith (Apocrypha).
Juster, Juifs	J. Juster, *Les Juifs dans l'Empire Romain,* 2 vols. (1914).
JYB	*Jewish Year Book* (1896ff.).
JZWL	*Juedische Zeitschift fuer Wissenschaft und Leben* (1862–75).
Kal.	*Kallah* (post-talmudic tractate).
Kal. R.	*Kallah Rabbati* (post-talmudic tractate).
Katz, England	*The Jews in the History of England, 1485-1850 (1994).*
Kaufmann, Schriften	D. Kaufmann, *Gesammelte Schriften,* 3 vols. (1908 15).
Kaufmann Y., Religion	Y. Kaufmann, *The Religion of Israel* (1960), abridged tr. of his *Toledot.*
Kaufmann Y., Toledot	Y. Kaufmann, *Toledot ha-Emunah ha-Yisre'elit,* 4 vols. (1937 57).
KAWJ	*Korrespondenzblatt des Vereins zur Gruendung und Erhaltung der Akademie fuer die Wissenschaft des Judentums* (1920 30).
Kayserling, Bibl	M. Kayserling, *Biblioteca Española-Portugueza-Judaica* (1880; repr. 1961).
Kelim	*Kelim* (mishnaic tractate).
Ker.	*Keritot* (talmudic tractate).
Ket.	*Ketubbot* (talmudic tractate).

Kid.	*Kiddushim* (talmudic tractate).
Kil.	*Kilayim* (talmudic tractate).
Kin.	*Kinnim* (mishnaic tractate).
Kisch, Germany	G. Kisch, *Jews in Medieval Germany* (1949).
Kittel, Gesch	R. Kittel, *Geschichte des Volkes Israel,* 3 vols. (1922–28).
Klausner, Bayit Sheni	J. Klausner, *Historyah shel ha-Bayit ha-Sheni,* 5 vols. (1950/512).
Klausner, Sifrut	J. Klausner, *Historyah shel haSifrut ha-Ivrit ha-Ḥadashah,* 6 vols. (1952–582).
Klein, corpus	S. Klein (ed.), *Juedisch-palaestinisches Corpus Inscriptionum* (1920).
Koehler-Baumgartner	L. Koehler and W. Baumgartner, *Lexicon in Veteris Testamenti libros* (1953).
Kohut, Arukh	H.J.A. Kohut (ed.), *Sefer he-Arukh ha-Shalem,* by Nathan b. Jehiel of Rome, 8 vols. (1876–92; Supplement by S. Krauss et al., 1936; repr. 1955).
Krauss, Tal Arch	S. Krauss, *Talmudische Archaeologie,* 3 vols. (1910–12; repr. 1966).
Kressel, Leksikon	G. Kressel, *Leksikon ha-Sifrut ha-Ivrit ba-Dorot ha-Aḥaronim,* 2 vols. (1965–67).
KS	*Kirjath Sepher* (1923/4ff.).
Kut.	*Kuttim* (post-talmudic tractate).
LA	Studium Biblicum Franciscanum, *Liber Annuus* (1951ff.).
L.A.	Philo, *Legum allegoriae.*
Lachower, Sifrut	F. Lachower, *Toledot ha-Sifrut ha-Ivrit ha-Ḥadashah,* 4 vols. (1947–48; several reprints).
Lam.	Lamentations (Bible).
Lam. R.	*Lamentations Rabbah.*
Landshuth, Ammudei	L. Landshuth, *Ammudei ha-Avodah* (1857–62; repr. with index, 1965).
Legat.	Philo, *De Legatione ad Caium.*
Lehmann, Nova Bibl	R.P. Lehmann, *Nova Bibliotheca Anglo-Judaica* (1961).
Lev.	Leviticus (Bible).
Lev. R.	*Leviticus Rabbah.*
Levy, Antologia	I. Levy, *Antologia de liturgia judeo-española* (1965ff.).
Levy J., Chald Targ	J. Levy, *Chaldaeisches Woerterbuch ueber die Targumim,* 2 vols. (1967–68; repr. 1959).
Levy J., Nuehebr Tal	J. Levy, *Neuhebraeisches und chaldaeisches Woerterbuch ueber die Talmudim . . .,* 4 vols. (1875–89; repr. 1963).
Lewin, Oẓar	Lewin, *Oẓar ha-Ge'onim,* 12 vols. (1928–43).
Lewysohn, Zool	L. Lewysohn, *Zoologie des Talmuds* (1858).
Lidzbarski, Handbuch	M. Lidzbarski, *Handbuch der nordsemitischen Epigraphik,* 2 vols (1898).
Life	Josephus, *Life* (Loeb Classis ed.).
LNYL	*Leksikon fun der Nayer Yidisher Literatur* (1956ff.).
Loew, Flora	I. Loew, *Die Flora der Juden,* 4 vols. (1924 34; repr. 1967).
LSI	*Laws of the State of Israel* (1948ff.).
Luckenbill, Records	D.D. Luckenbill, *Ancient Records of Assyria and Babylonia,* 2 vols. (1926).
Luke	Gospel according to Luke (New Testament)
LXX	Septuagint (Greek translation of the Bible).
Ma'as.	*Ma'aserot* (talmudic tractate).
Ma'as. Sh.	*Ma'ase Sheni* (talmudic tractate).
I, II, III, and IVMacc.	Maccabees, I, II, III (Apocrypha), IV (Pseudepigrapha).
Maimonides, Guide	Maimonides, *Guide of the Perplexed.*
Maim., Yad	Maimonides, *Mishneh Torah (Yad Ḥazakah).*
Maisler, Untersuchungen	B. Maisler (Mazar), *Untersuchungen zur alten Geschichte und Ethnographie Syriens und Palaestinas,* 1 (1930).
Mak.	*Makkot* (talmudic tractate).
Makhsh.	*Makhshrin* (mishnaic tractate).
Mal.	Malachi (Bible).
Mann, Egypt	J. Mann, *Jews in Egypt in Palestine under the Fatimid Caliphs,* 2 vols. (1920–22).
Mann, Texts	J. Mann, *Texts and Studies,* 2 vols (1931–35).
Mansi	G.D. Mansi, *Sacrorum Conciliorum nova et amplissima collectio,* 53 vols. in 60 (1901–27; repr. 1960).
Margalioth, Gedolei	M. Margalioth, *Enẓiklopedyah le-Toledot Gedolei Yisrael,* 4 vols. (1946–50).
Margalioth, Ḥakhmei	M. Margalioth, *Enẓiklopedyah le-Ḥakhmei ha-Talmud ve-ha-Ge'onim,* 2 vols. (1945).
Margalioth, Cat	G. Margalioth, *Catalogue of the Hebrew and Samaritan Manuscripts in the British Museum,* 4 vols. (1899–1935).
Mark	Gospel according to Mark (New Testament).
Mart. Isa.	Martyrdom of Isaiah (Pseudepigrapha).
Mas.	Masorah.
Matt.	Gospel according to Matthew (New Testament).
Mayer, Art	L.A. Mayer, *Bibliography of Jewish Art* (1967).
MB	*Wochenzeitung* (formerly *Mitteilungsblatt*) *des Irgun Olej Merkas Europa* (1933ff.).
MEAH	*Miscelánea de estudios drabes y hebraicos* (1952ff.).
Meg.	Megillah (talmudic tractate).
Meg. Ta'an.	*Megillat Ta'anit* (in HUCA, 8 9 (1931–32), 318–51).
Me'il	*Me'ilah* (mishnaic tractate).
MEJ	*Middle East Journal* (1947ff.).
Mehk.	*Mekhilta de-R. Ishmael.*
Mekh. SbY	*Mekhilta de-R. Simeon bar Yoḥai.*
Men.	*Menaḥot* (talmudic tractate).
MER	*Middle East Record* (1960ff.).
Meyer, Gesch	E. Meyer, *Geschichte des Alterums,* 5 vols. in 9 (1925–58).
Meyer, Ursp	E. Meyer, *Urspring und Anfaenge des Christentums* (1921).
Mez.	*Mezuzah* (post-talmudic tractate).
MGADJ	*Mitteilungen des Gesamtarchivs der deutschen Juden* (1909–12).
MGG	*Die Musik in Geschichte und Gegenwart,* 14 vols. (1949–68).

MGG^{2}	*Die Musik in Geschichte und Gegenwart, 2nd edition (1994)*
MGH	*Monumenta Germaniae Historica* (1826ff.).
MGJV	*Mitteilungen der Gesellschaft fuer juedische Volkskunde* (1898–1929); title varies, see also JJV.
MGWJ	*Monatsschrift fuer Geschichte und Wissenschaft des Judentums* (1851–1939).
MHJ	*Monumenta Hungariae Judaica,* 11 vols. (1903–67).
Michael, Or	H.Ḥ. Michael, *Or ha-Ḥayyim: Ḥakhmei Yisrael ve-Sifreihem,* ed. by S.Z. Ḥ. Halberstam and N. Ben-Menahem (1965^{2}).
Mid.	*Middot* (mishnaic tractate).
Mid. Ag.	*Midrash Aggadah.*
Mid. Hag.	*Midrash ha-Gadol.*
Mid. Job.	*Midrash Job.*
Mid. Jonah	*Midrash Jonah.*
Mid. Lek. Tov	*Midrash Lekaḥ Tov.*
Mid. Prov.	*Midrash Proverbs.*
Mid. Ps.	*Midrash Tehillim* (Eng tr. *The Midrash on Psalms* (JPS, 1959).
Mid. Sam.	*Midrash Samuel.*
Mid. Song	*Midrash Shir ha-Shirim.*
Mid. Tan.	*Midrash Tanna'im* on Deuteronomy.
Miége, Maroc	J.L. Miège, *Le Maroc et l'Europe,* 3 vols. (1961 62).
Mig.	Philo, *De Migratione Abrahami.*
Mik.	*Mikva'ot* (mishnaic tractate).
Milano, Bibliotheca	A. Milano, *Bibliotheca Historica Italo-Judaica* (1954); supplement for 1954–63 (1964); supplement for 1964–66 in RMI, 32 (1966).
Milano, Italia	A. Milano, *Storia degli Ebrei in Italia* (1963).
MIO	*Mitteilungen des Instituts fuer Orientforschung* 1953ff.).
Mish.	Mishnah.
MJ	*Le Monde Juif* (1946ff.).
MJC	see Neubauer, Chronicles.
MK	*Mo'ed Katan* (talmudic tractate).
MNDPV	*Mitteilungen und Nachrichten des deutschen Palaestinavereins* (1895–1912).
Mortara, Indice	M. Mortara, *Indice Alfabetico dei Rabbini e Scrittori Israeliti ... in Italia ...* (1886).
Mos	Philo, *De Vita Mosis.*
Moscati, Epig	S, Moscati, *Epigrafia ebraica antica* 1935–1950 (1951).
MT	Masoretic Text of the Bible.
Mueller, Musiker	[E.H. Mueller], *Deutisches Musiker-Lexikon* (1929)
Munk, Mélanges	S. Munk, *Mélanges de philosophie juive et arabe* (1859; repr. 1955).
Mut.	Philo, *De Mutatione Nominum.*
MWJ	*Magazin fuer die Wissenshaft des Judentums* (18745 93).
Nah.	Nahum (Bible).
Naz.	*Nazir* (talmudic tractate).
NDB	*Neue Deutsche Biographie* (1953ff.).
Ned.	*Nedarim* (talmudic tractate).
Neg.	*Nega'im* (mishnaic tractate).
Neh.	Nehemiah (Bible).
NG^{2}	*New Grove Dictionary of Music and Musicians* (2001).
Nuebauer, Cat	A. Neubauer, *Catalogue of the Hebrew Manuscripts in the Bodleian Library ...,* 2 vols. (1886–1906).
Neubauer, Chronicles	A. Neubauer, *Mediaeval Jewish Chronicles,* 2 vols. (Heb., 1887–95; repr. 1965), Eng. title of *Seder ha-Ḥakhamim ve-Korot ha-Yamim.*
Neubauer, Géogr	A. Neubauer, *La géographie du Talmud* (1868).
Neuman, Spain	A.A. Neuman, *The Jews in Spain, their Social, Political, and Cultural Life During the Middle Ages,* 2 vols. (1942).
Neusner, Babylonia	J. Neusner, *History of the Jews in Babylonia,* 5 vols. 1965–70), 2nd revised printing 1969ff.).
Nid.	*Niddah* (talmudic tractate).
Noah	Fragment of Book of Noah (Pseudepigrapha).
Noth, Hist Isr	M. Noth, *History of Israel* (1958).
Noth, Personennamen	M. Noth, *Die israelitischen Personennamen.* ... (1928).
Noth, Ueberlief	M. Noth, *Ueberlieferungsgeschichte des Pentateuchs* (1949).
Noth, Welt	M. Noth, *Die Welt des Alten Testaments* (1957^{3}).
Nowack, Lehrbuch	W. Nowack, *Lehrbuch der hebraeischen Archaeologie,* 2 vols (1894).
NT	New Testament.
Num.	Numbers (Bible).
Num R.	*Numbers Rabbah.*
Obad.	Obadiah (Bible).
ODNB online	*Oxford Dictionary of National Biography.*
OḤ	*Oraḥ Ḥayyim.*
Oho.	*Oholot* (mishnaic tractate).
Olmstead	H.T. Olmstead, *History of Palestine and Syria* (1931; repr. 1965).
OLZ	*Orientalistische Literaturzeitung* (1898ff.)
Onom.	Eusebius, *Onomasticon.*
Op.	Philo, *De Opificio Mundi.*
OPD	*Osef Piskei Din shel ha-Rabbanut ha-Rashit le-Ereẓ Yisrael, Bet ha-Din ha-Gadol le-Irurim* (1950).
Or.	*Orlah* (talmudic tractate).
Or. Sibyll.	Sibylline Oracles (Pseudepigrapha).
OS	*L'Orient Syrien* (1956ff.)
OTS	*Oudtestamentische Studien* (1942ff.).
PAAJR	*Proceedings of the American Academy for Jewish Research* (1930ff.)
Pap 4QS^{e}	A papyrus exemplar of IQS.
Par.	*Parah* (mishnaic tractate).
Pauly-Wissowa	A.F. Pauly, *Realencyklopaedie der klassichen Alertumswissenschaft,* ed. by G. Wissowa et al. (1864ff.)

PD	*Piskei Din shel Bet ha-Mishpat ha-Elyon le-Yisrael* (1948ff.)
PDR	*Piskei Din shel Battei ha-Din ha-Rabbaniyyim be-Yisrael.*
PdRE	*Pirkei de-R. Eliezer* (Eng. tr. 1916. (1965^{2}).
PdRK	*Pesikta de-Rav Kahana.*
Pe'ah	*Pe'ah* (talmudic tractate).
Peake, Commentary	A.J. Peake (ed.), *Commentary on the Bible* (1919; rev. 1962).
Pedersen, Israel	J. Pedersen, *Israel, Its Life and Culture,* 4 vols. in 2 (1926–40).
PEFQS	*Palestine Exploration Fund Quarterly Statement* (1869–1937; since 1938–PEQ).
PEQ	*Palestine Exploration Quarterly* (until 1937 PEFQS; after 1927 includes BBSAJ).
Perles, Beitaege	J. Perles, *Beitraege zur rabbinischen Sprach- und Alterthumskunde* (1893).
Pes.	*Pesaḥim* (talmudic tractate).
Pesh.	Peshitta (Syriac translation of the Bible).
Pesher Hab.	Commentary to Habakkuk from Qumran; see 1Qp Hab.
I and II Pet.	Epistles of Peter (New Testament).
Pfeiffer, Introd	R.H. Pfeiffer, *Introduction to the Old Testament* (1948).
PG	J.P. Migne (ed.), *Patrologia Graeca,* 161 vols. (1866–86).
Phil.	Epistle to the Philippians (New Testament).
Philem.	Epistle to the Philemon (New Testament).
PIASH	*Proceedings of the Israel Academy of Sciences and Humanities* (1963/7ff.).
PJB	*Palaestinajahrbuch des deutschen evangelischen Institutes fuer Altertumswissenschaft,* Jerusalem (1905–1933).
PK	*Pinkas ha-Kehillot,* encyclopedia of Jewish communities, published in over 30 volumes by Yad Vashem from 1970 and arranged by countries, regions and localities. For 3-vol. English edition see Spector, *Jewish Life.*
PL	J.P. Migne (ed.), *Patrologia Latina* 221 vols. (1844–64).
Plant	Philo, *De Plantatione.*
PO	R. Graffin and F. Nau (eds.), *Patrologia Orientalis* (1903ff.)
Pool, Prayer	D. de Sola Pool, *Traditional Prayer Book for Sabbath and Festivals* (1960).
Post	Philo, *De Posteritate Caini.*
PR	*Pesikta Rabbati.*
Praem.	Philo, *De Praemiis et Poenis.*
Prawer, Ẓalbanim	J. Prawer, *Toledot Mamlekhet ha-Ẓalbanim be-Ereẓ Yisrael,* 2 vols. (1963).
Press, Ereẓ	I. Press, *Ereẓ-Yisrael, Enẓiklopedyah Topografit-Historit,* 4 vols. (1951–55).
Pritchard, Pictures	J.B. Pritchard (ed.), *Ancient Near East in Pictures* (1954, 1970).
Pritchard, Texts	J.B. Pritchard (ed.), *Ancient Near East Texts* ... (1970^{3}).
Pr. Man.	Prayer of Manasses (Apocrypha).
Prob.	Philo, *Quod Omnis Probus Liber Sit.*
Prov.	Proverbs (Bible).
PS	*Palestinsky Sbornik* (Russ. (1881 1916, 1954ff).
Ps.	Psalms (Bible).
PSBA	*Proceedings of the Society of Biblical Archaeology* (1878–1918).
Ps. of Sol	Psalms of Solomon (Pseudepigrapha).
IQ Apoc	The *Genesis Apocryphon* from Qumran, cave one, ed. by N. Avigad and Y. Yadin (1956).
6QD	*Damascus Document* or *Sefer Berit Dammesk* from Qumran, cave six, ed. by M. Baillet, in RB, 63 (1956), 513–23 (see also CD).
QDAP	*Quarterly of the Department of Antiquities in Palestine* (1932ff.).
4QDeut. 32	Manuscript of Deuteronomy 32 from Qumran, cave four (ed. by P.W. Skehan, in BASOR, 136 (1954), 12–15).
4QEx^{a}	Exodus manuscript in Jewish script from Qumran, cave four.
4QEx$^{\alpha}$	Exodus manuscript in Paleo-Hebrew script from Qumran, cave four (partially ed. by P.W. Skehan, in JBL, 74 (1955), 182–7).
4QFlor	*Florilegium,* a miscellany from Qumran, cave four (ed. by J.M. Allegro, in JBL, 75 (1956), 176–77 and 77 (1958), 350–54).).
QGJD	*Quellen zur Geschichte der Juden in Deutschland* 1888–98).
IQH	*Thanksgiving Psalms* of *Hodayot* from Qumran, cave one (ed. by E.L. Sukenik and N. Avigad, *Oẓar ha-Megillot ha-Genuzot* (1954).
IQIs^{a}	Scroll of Isaiah from Qumran, cave one (ed. by N. Burrows et al., *Dead Sea Scrolls* ..., 1 (1950).
IQIs^{b}	Scroll of Isaiah from Qumran, cave one (ed. E.L. Sukenik and N. Avigad, *Oẓar ha-Megillot ha-Genuzot* (1954).
IQM	The *War Scroll* or *Serekh ha-Milḥamah* (ed. by E.L. Sukenik and N. Avigad, *Oẓar ha-Megillot ha-Genuzot* (1954).
4QpNah	Commentary on Nahum from Qumran, cave four (partially ed. by J.M. Allegro, in JBL, 75 (1956), 89–95).
IQphyl	Phylacteries *(tefillin)* from Qumran, cave one (ed. by Y. Yadin, in *Eretz Israel,* 9 (1969), 60–85).
4Q Prayer of Nabonidus	A document from Qumran, cave four, belonging to a lost Daniel literature (ed. by J.T. Milik, in RB, 63 (1956), 407–15).
IQS	*Manual of Discipline* or *Serekh ha-Yaḥad* from Qumran, cave one (ed. by M. Burrows et al., *Dead Sea Scrolls* ..., 2, pt. 2 (1951).

IQS^{a}	The *Rule of the Congregation or Serekh ha-Edah* from Qumran, cave one (ed. by Burrows et al., *Dead Sea Scrolls* ..., 1 (1950), under the abbreviation IQ28a).
IQS^{b}	*Blessings* or *Divrei Berakhot* from Qumran, cave one (ed. by Burrows et al., *Dead Sea Scrolls* ..., 1 (1950), under the abbreviation IQ28b).
4QSam^{a}	Manuscript of I and II Samuel from Qumran, cave four (partially ed. by F.M. Cross, in BASOR, 132 (1953), 15–26).
4QSam^{b}	Manuscript of I and II Samuel from Qumran, cave four (partially ed. by F.M. Cross, in JBL, 74 (1955), 147–72).
4QTestimonia	Sheet of Testimony from Qumran, cave four (ed. by J.M. Allegro, in JBL, 75 (1956), 174–87).).
4QT.Levi	*Testament of Levi* from Qumran, cave four (partially ed. by J.T. Milik, in RB, 62 (1955), 398–406).
Rabinovitz, Dik Sof	See Dik Sof.
RB	*Revue biblique* (1892ff.)
RBI	*Recherches bibliques* (1954ff.)
RCB	*Revista de cultura biblica* (São Paulo) (1957ff.)
Régné, Cat	J. Régné, *Catalogue des actes . . . des rois d'Aragon, concernant les Juifs* (1213–1327), in: REJ, vols. 60 70, 73, 75–78 (1910–24).
Reinach, Textes	T. Reinach, *Textes d'auteurs Grecs et Romains relatifs au Judaïsme* (1895; repr. 1963).
REJ	*Revue des études juives* (1880ff.).
Rejzen, Leksikon	Z. Rejzen, *Leksikon fun der Yidisher Literature,* 4 vols. (1927–29).
Renan, Ecrivains	A. Neubauer and E. Renan, *Les écrivains juifs français* ... (1893).
Renan, Rabbins	A. Neubauer and E. Renan, *Les rabbins français* (1877).
RES	*Revue des étude sémitiques et Babyloniaca* (1934–45).
Rev.	Revelation (New Testament).
RGG^{3}	*Die Religion in Geschichte und Gegenwart,* 7 vols. (1957–65^{3}).
RH	*Rosh Ha-Shanah* (talmudic tractate).
RHJE	*Revue de l'histoire juive en Egypte* (1947ff.).
RHMH	*Revue d'histoire de la médecine hébraïque* (1948ff.).
RHPR	*Revue d'histoire et de philosophie religieuses* (1921ff.).
RHR	*Revue d'histoire des religions* (1880ff.).
RI	*Rivista Israelitica* (1904–12).
Riemann-Einstein	*Hugo Riemanns Musiklexikon,* ed. by A. Einstein (1929^{11}).
Riemann-Gurlitt	*Hugo Riemanns Musiklexikon,* ed. by W. Gurlitt (1959–67^{12}), Personenteil.
Rigg-Jenkinson, Exchequer	J.M. Rigg, H. Jenkinson and H.G. Richardson (eds.), *Calendar of the Pleas Rolls of the Exchequer of the Jews,* 4 vols. (1905–1970); cf. in each instance also J.M. Rigg (ed.), *Select Pleas* ... (1902).
RMI	*Rassegna Mensile di Israel* (1925ff.).
Rom.	Epistle to the Romans (New Testament).
Rosanes, Togarmah	S.A. Rosanes, *Divrei Yemei Yisrael be-Togarmah,* 6 vols. (1907–45), and in 3 vols. (1930–38^{2}).
Rosenbloom, Biogr Dict	J.R. Rosenbloom, *Biographical Dictionary of Early American Jews* (1960).
Roth, Art	C. Roth, *Jewish Art* (1961).
Roth, Dark Ages	C. Roth (ed.), *World History of the Jewish People,* second series, vol. 2, *Dark Ages* (1966).
Roth, England	C. Roth, *History of the Jews in England* (1964^{3}).
Roth, Italy	C. Roth, *History of the Jews in Italy* (1946).
Roth, Mag Bibl	C. Roth, *Magna Bibliotheca Anglo-Judaica* (1937).
Roth, Marranos	C. Roth, *History of the Marranos* (2nd rev. ed 1959; reprint 1966).
Rowley, Old Test	H.H. Rowley, *Old Testament and Modern Study* (1951; repr. 1961).
RS	*Revue sémitiques d'épigraphie et d'histoire ancienne* (1893/94ff.).
RSO	*Rivista degli studi orientali* (1907ff.).
RSV	Revised Standard Version of the Bible.
Rubinstein, Australia I	*H.L. Rubinstein, The Jews in Australia, A Thematic History, Vol. I (1991).*
Rubinstein, Australia II	*W.D. Rubinstein, The Jews in Australia, A Thematic History, Vol. II (1991).*
Ruth	Ruth (Bible).
Ruth R.	*Ruth Rabbah.*
RV	Revised Version of the Bible.
Sac.	Philo, *De Sacrificiis Abelis et Caini.*
Salfeld, Martyrol	S. Salfeld, *Martyrologium des Nuernberger Memorbuches* (1898).
I and II Sam.	Samuel, book I and II (Bible).
Sanh.	*Sanhedrin* (talmudic tractate).
SBA	Society of Biblical Archaeology.
SBB	*Studies in Bibliography and Booklore* (1953ff.).
SBE	*Semana Biblica Española.*
SBT	*Studies in Biblical Theology* (1951ff.).
SBU	*Svenkst Bibliskt Uppslogsvesk,* 2 vols. (1962–63^{2}).
Schirmann, Italyah	J.Ḥ. Schirmann, *Ha-Shirah ha-Ivrit be-Italyah* (1934).
Schirmann, Sefarad	J.Ḥ. Schirmann, *Ha-Shirah ha-Ivrit bi-Sefarad u-vi-Provence,* 2 vols. (1954–56).
Scholem, Mysticism	G. Scholem, *Major Trends in Jewish Mysticism* (rev. ed. 1946; paperback ed. with additional bibliography 1961).
Scholem, Shabbetai Ẓevi	G. Scholem, *Shabbetai Ẓevi ve-ha-Tenu'ah ha-Shabbeta'it bi-Ymei Ḥayyav,* 2 vols. (1967).
Schrader, Keilinschr	E. Schrader, *Keilinschriften und das Alte Testament* (1903^{3}).
Schuerer, Gesch	E. Schuerer, *Geschichte des juedischen Volkes im Zeitalter Jesu Christi,* 3 vols. and index-vol. (1901–11^{4}).

Schuerer, Hist	E. Schuerer, *History of the Jewish People in the Time of Jesus,* ed. by N.N. Glatzer, abridged paperback edition (1961).
Set. T.	*Sefer Torah* (post-talmudic tractate).
Sem.	*Semaḥot* (post-talmudic tractate).
Sendrey, Music	A. Sendrey, *Bibliography of Jewish Music* (1951).
SER	*Seder Eliyahu Rabbah.*
SEZ	*Seder Eliyahu Zuta.*
Shab	*Shabbat* (talmudic tractate).
Sh. Ar.	J. Caro Shulḥan Arukh. OḤ – *Oraḥ Ḥayyim* YD – *Yoreh De'ah* EH – *Even ha-Ezer* ḤM – *Ḥoshen Mishpat.*
Shek.	*Shekalim* (talmudic tractate).
Shev.	*Shevi'it* (talmudic tractate).
Shevu.	*Shevu'ot* (talmudic tractate).
Shunami, Bibl	S. Shunami, *Bibliography of Jewish Bibliographies* (1965^{2}).
Sif.	*Sifrei Deuteronomy.*
Sif. Num.	*Sifrei Numbers.*
Sifra	*Sifra* on Leviticus.
Sif. Zut.	*Sifrei Zuta.*
SIHM	Sources inédites de l'histoire du Maroc (series).
Silverman, Prayer	M. Silverman (ed.), *Sabbath and Festival Prayer Book* (1946).
Singer, Prayer	S. Singer *Authorised Daily Prayer Book* (1943^{17}).
Sob.	Philo, *De Sobrietate.*
Sof.	*Soferim* (post-talmudic tractate).
Som.	Philo, *De Somniis.*
Song	Song of Songs (Bible).
Song. Ch.	Song of the Three Children (Apocrypha).
Song R.	*Song of Songs Rabbah.*
SOR	*Seder Olam Rabbah.*
Sot.	*Sotah* (talmudic tractate).
SOZ	*Seder Olam Zuta.*
Spec.	Philo, *De Specialibus Legibus.*
Spector, Jewish Life	*S. Spector (ed.), Encyclopedia of Jewish Life Before and After the Holocaust (2001).*
Steinschneider, Arab lit	M. Steinschneider, *Die arabische Literatur der Juden* (1902).
Steinschneider, Cat Bod	M. Steinschneider, *Catalogus Librorum Hebraeorum in Bibliotheca Bodleiana,* 3 vols. (1852–60; reprints 1931 and 1964).
Steinschneider, Hanbuch	M. Steinschneider, *Bibliographisches Handbuch ueber die . . . Literatur fuer hebraeische Sprachkunde* (1859; repr. with additions 1937).
Steinschneider, Uebersetzungen	M. Steinschneider, *Die hebraeischen Uebersetzungen des Mittelalters* (1893).
Stern, Americans	M.H. Stern, *Americans of Jewish Descent* (1960).
van Straalen, Cat	S. van Straalen, *Catalogue of Hebrew Books in the British Museum Acquired During the Years 1868–1892* (1894).
Suárez Fernández, Docmentos	L. Suárez Fernández, *Documentos acerca de la expulsion de los Judios de España* (1964).
Suk.	*Sukkah* (talmudic tractate).
Sus.	Susanna (Apocrypha).
SY	*Sefer Yeẓirah.*
Sym.	Symmachus' Greek translation of the Bible.
SZNG	*Studien zur neueren Geschichte.*
Ta'an.	*Ta'anit* (talmudic tractate).
Tam.	*Tamid* (mishnaic tractate).
Tanḥ.	*Tanḥuma.*
Tanḥ. B.	*Tanḥuma.* Buber ed (1885).
Targ. Jon	Targum Jonathan (Aramaic version of the Prophets).
Targ. Onk.	Targum Onkelos (Aramaic version of the Pentateuch).
Targ. Yer.	Targum Yerushalmi.
TB	Babylonian Talmud or Talmud Bavli.
Tcherikover, Corpus	V. Tcherikover, A. Fuks, and M. Stern, *Corpus Papyrorum Judaicorum,* 3 vols. (1957–60).
Tef.	*Tefillin* (post-talmudic tractate).
Tem.	*Temurah* (mishnaic tractate).
Ter.	*Terumah* (talmudic tractate).
Test. Patr.	Testament of the Twelve Patriarchs (Pseudepigrapha). Ash. – Asher Ben. – Benjamin Dan – Dan Gad – Gad Iss. – Issachar Joseph – Joseph Judah – Judah Levi – Levi Naph. – Naphtali Reu. – Reuben Sim. – Simeon Zeb. – Zebulun.
I and II	Epistle to the Thessalonians (New Testament).
Thieme-Becker	U. Thieme and F. Becker (eds.), *Allgemeines Lexikon der bildenden Kuenstler von der Antike bis zur Gegenwart,* 37 vols. (1907–50).
Tidhar	D. Tidhar (ed.), *Enẓiklopedyah la-Ḥalutẓei ha-Yishuv u-Vonav* (1947ff.).
I and II Timothy	Epistles to Timothy (New Testament).
Tit.	Epistle to Titus (New Testament).
TJ	Jerusalem Talmud or Talmud Yerushalmi.
Tob.	Tobit (Apocrypha).
Toh.	*Tohorot* (mishnaic tractate).
Torczyner, Bundeslade	H. Torczyner, *Die Bundeslade und die Anfaenge der Religion Israels* (1930^{3}).
Tos.	*Tosafot.*
Tosef.	Tosefta.
Tristram, Nat Hist	H.B. Tristram, *Natural History of the Bible* (1877^{5}).
Tristram, Survey	Palestine Exploration Fund, *Survey of Western Palestine,* vol. 4 (1884) = *Fauna and Flora* by H.B. Tristram.
TS	*Terra Santa* (1943ff.).

TSBA	*Transactions of the Society of Biblical Archaeology* (1872–93).
TY	*Tevul Yom* (mishnaic tractate).
UBSB	United Bible Society, *Bulletin.*
UJE	*Universal Jewish Encyclopedia*, 10 vols. (1939–43).
Uk.	*Ukẓin* (mishnaic tractate).
Urbach, Tosafot	E.E. Urbach, *Ba'alei ha-Tosafot* (1957²).
de Vaux, Anc Isr	R. de Vaux, *Ancient Israel: its Life and Institutions* (1961; paperback 1965).
de Vaux, Instit	R. de Vaux, *Institutions de l'Ancien Testament,* 2 vols. (1958 60).
Virt.	Philo, *De Virtutibus.*
Vogelstein, Chronology	M. Volgelstein, *Biblical Chronology (1944).*
Vogelstein-Rieger	H. Vogelstein and P. Rieger, *Geschichte der Juden in Rom,* 2 vols. (1895–96).
VT	*Vetus Testamentum* (1951ff.).
VTS	*Vetus Testamentum* Supplements (1953ff.).
Vulg.	Vulgate (Latin translation of the Bible).
Wars	Josephus, *The Jewish Wars.*
Watzinger, Denkmaeler	K. Watzinger, *Denkmaeler Palaestinas,* 2 vols. (1933–35).
Waxman, Literature	M. Waxman, *History of Jewish Literature,* 5 vols. (1960²).
Weiss, Dor	I.H. Weiss, *Dor, Dor ve-Doreshav,* 5 vols. (1904⁴).
Wellhausen, Proleg	J. Wellhausen, *Prolegomena zur Geschichte Israels* (1927⁶).
WI	*Die Welt des Islams* (1913ff.).
Winniger, Biog	S. Wininger, *Grosse juedische National-Biographie ...,* 7 vols. (1925–36).
Wisd.	Wisdom of Solomon (Apocrypha)
WLB	*Wiener Library Bulletin* (1958ff.).
Wolf, Bibliotheca	J.C. Wolf, *Bibliotheca Hebraea,* 4 vols. (1715–33).
Wright, Bible	G.E. Wright, *Westminster Historical Atlas to the Bible* (1945).
Wright, Atlas	G.E. Wright, *The Bible and the Ancient Near East* (1961).
WWWJ	*Who's Who in the World Jewry* (New York, 1955, 1965²).
WZJT	*Wissenschaftliche Zeitschrift fuer juedische Theologie* (1835–37).
WZKM	*Wiener Zeitschrift fuer die Kunde des Morgenlandes* (1887ff.).
Yaari, Sheluḥei	A. Yaari, *Sheluḥei Ereẓ Yisrael* (1951).
Yad	Maimonides, *Mishneh Torah (Yad Ḥazakah).*
Yad	*Yadayim* (mishnaic tractate).
Yal.	*Yalkut Shimoni.*
Yal. Mak.	*Yalkut Makhiri.*
Yal. Reub.	*Yalkut Reubeni.*
YD	*Yoreh De'ah.*
YE	*Yevreyskaya Entsiklopediya,* 14 vols. (c. 1910).
Yev.	*Yevamot* (talmudic tractate).
YIVOA	*YIVO Annual of Jewish Social Studies* (1946ff.).
YLBI	*Year Book of the Leo Baeck Institute* (1956ff.).
YMḤEY	See BJPES.
YMḤSI	*Yedi'ot ha-Makhon le-Ḥeker ha-Shirah ha-Ivrit* (1935/36ff.).
YMMY	*Yedi'ot ha-Makhon le-Madda'ei ha-Yahadut* (1924/25ff.).
Yoma	*Yoma* (talmudic tractate).
ZA	*Zeitschrift fuer Assyriologie* (1886/87ff.).
Zav.	*Zavim* (mishnaic tractate).
ZAW	*Zeitschrift fuer die alttestamentliche Wissenschaft und die Kunde des nachbiblishchen Judentums* (1881ff.).
ZAWB	*Beihefte* (supplements) to ZAW.
ZDMG	*Zeitschrift der Deutschen Morgenlaendischen Gesellschaft* (1846ff.).
ZDPV	*Zeitschrift des Deutschen Palaestina-Vereins* (1878–1949; from 1949 = BBLA).
Zech.	Zechariah (Bible).
Zedner, Cat	J. Zedner, *Catalogue of Hebrew Books in the Library of the British Museum* (1867; repr. 1964).
Zeitlin, Bibliotheca	W. Zeitlin, *Bibliotheca Hebraica Post-Mendelssohniana* (1891–95).
Zeph.	Zephaniah (Bible).
Zev.	*Zevaḥim* (talmudic tractate).
ZGGJT	*Zeitschrift der Gesellschaft fuer die Geschichte der Juden in der Tschechoslowakei* (1930–38).
ZGJD	*Zeitschrift fuer die Geschichte der Juden in Deutschland* (1887–92).
ZHB	*Zeitschrift fuer hebraeische Bibliographie* (1896–1920).
Zinberg, Sifrut	I. Zinberg, *Toledot Sifrut Yisrael,* 6 vols. (1955–60).
Ẓiẓ.	*Ẓiẓit* (post-talmudic tractate).
ZNW	*Zeitschrift fuer die neutestamentliche Wissenschaft* (1901ff.).
ZS	*Zeitschrift fuer Semitistik und verwandte Gebiete* (1922ff.).
Zunz, Gesch	L. Zunz, *Zur Geschichte und Literatur* (1845).
Zunz, Gesch	L. Zunz, *Literaturgeschichte der synagogalen Poesie* (1865; Supplement, 1867; repr. 1966).
Zunz, Poesie	L. Zunz, *Synogogale Posie des Mittelalters,* ed. by Freimann (1920²; repr. 1967).
Zunz, Ritus	L. Zunz, *Ritus des synagogalen Gottesdienstes* (1859; repr. 1967).
Zunz, Schr	L. Zunz, *Gesammelte Schriften,* 3 vols. (1875–76).
Zunz, Vortraege	L. Zunz, *Gottesdienstliche vortraege der Juden ...* 1892²; repr. 1966).
Zunz-Albeck, Derashot	L. Zunz, *Ha-Derashot be-Yisrael,* Heb. Tr. of Zunz Vortraege by H. Albeck (1954²).

TRANSLITERATION RULES

HEBREW AND SEMITIC LANGUAGES:

	General	*Scientific*
א	not transliterated[1]	ʾ
בּ	b	b
ב	v	v, b̲
גּ	g	g
ג		ḡ
דּ	d	d
ד		d̲
ה	h	h
ו	v – when not a vowel	w
ז	z	z
ח	ḥ	ḥ
ט	t	ṭ, t
י	y – when vowel and at end of words – i	y
כּ	k	k
כ, ך	kh	kh, k̲
ל	l	l̲
מ, ם	m	m
נ, ן	n	n
ס	s	s
ע	not transliterated[1]	ʿ
פּ	p	p
פ, ף	f	p, f, ph
צ, ץ	ẓ	ṣ, ẓ
ק	k	q, k
ר	r	r
שׁ	sh[2]	š
שׂ	s	ś, s
תּ	t	t
ת		t̲
ג׳	dzh, J	ğ
ז׳	zh, J	ž
צ׳	ch	č
◌ָ		å, o, ȯ (short) â, ā (long)
◌ַ	a	a
◌ֲ		a, ^{a}
◌ֵ		e, ẹ, ē
◌ֶ	e	æ, ä, ę
◌ֱ		œ, ĕ, ^{e}
◌ְ	only *sheva na* is transliterated	ə, ĕ, e; only *sheva na* transliterated
◌ִ, ◌ִי	i	i
◌ֹ, וֹ	o	o, o, o
◌ֻ, וּ	u	u, ŭ û, ū
◌ֵי	ei; biblical e	
‡		reconstructed forms of words

1. The letters א and ע are not transliterated.
An apostrophe (') between vowels indicates that they do not form a diphthong and are to be pronounced separately.
2. *Dagesh ḥazak* (forte) is indicated by doubling of the letter, except for the letter שׁ.
3. Names. Biblical names and biblical place names are rendered according to the Bible translation of the Jewish Publication Society of America. Post-biblical Hebrew names are transliterated; contemporary names are transliterated or rendered as used by the person. Place names are transliterated or rendered by the accepted spelling. Names and some words with an accepted English form are usually not transliterated.

YIDDISH

א	not transliterated
אַ	a
אָ	o
בּ	b
בֿ	v
ג	g
ד	d
ה	h
ו, וּ	u
וו	v
וי	oy
ז	z
זש	zh
ח	kh
ט	t
טש	tsh, ch
י	(consonant) y (vowel) i
יִ	i
יי	ey
ײַ	ay
כּ	k
כ, ך	kh
ל	l
מ, ם	m
נ, ן	n
ס	s
ע	e
פּ	p
פֿ, ף	f
צ, ץ	ts
ק	k
ר	r
ש	sh
שׂ	s
תּ	t
ת	s

1. Yiddish transliteration rendered according to U. Weinreich's Modern *English-Yiddish Yiddish-English* Dictionary.
2. Hebrew words in Yiddish are usually transliterated according to standard Yiddish pronunciation, e.g., חזנות = *khazones.*

LADINO

Ladino and Judeo-Spanish words written in Hebrew characters are transliterated phonetically, following the General Rules of Hebrew transliteration (see above) whenever the accepted spelling in Latin characters could not be ascertained.

ARABIC

ا ء	a[1]	ض	ḍ
ب	b	ط	ṭ
ت	t	ظ	ẓ
ث	th	ع	c
ج	j	غ	gh
ح	ḥ	ف	f
خ	kh	ق	q
د	d	ك	k
ذ	dh	ل	l
ر	r	م	m
ز	z	ن	n
س	s	ه	h
ش	sh	و	w
ص	ṣ	ي	y
ـَ	a	ـَا ى	ā
ـِ	i	ـِي	ī
ـُ	u	ـُو	ū
ـَو	aw	ـِيّ	iyy[2]
ـَي	ay	ـُوّ	uww[2]

1. not indicated when initial
2. see note (f)

a) The EJ follows the *Columbia Lippincott Gazetteer* and the *Times Atlas* in transliteration of Arabic place names. Sites that appear in neither are transliterated according to the table above, and subject to the following notes.

b) The EJ follows the *Columbia Encyclopedia* in transliteration of Arabic names. Personal names that do not therein appear are transliterated according to the table above and subject to the following notes (e.g., Ali rather than ʿAlī, Suleiman rather than Sulayman).

c) The EJ follows the *Webster's Third International Dictionary, Unabridged* in transliteration of Arabic terms that have been integrated into the English language.

d) The term "Abu" will thus appear, usually in disregard of inflection.

e) Nunnation (end vowels, *tanwīn*) are dropped in transliteration.

f) Gemination (*tashdīd*) is indicated by the doubling of the geminated letter, unless an end letter, in which case the gemination is dropped.

g) The definitive article *al-* will always be thus transliterated, unless subject to one of the modifying notes (e.g., El-Arish rather than al-ʿArīsh; modification according to note (a)).

h) The Arabic transliteration disregards the Sun Letters (the antero-palatals (*al-Ḥurūf al-Shamsiyya*).

i) The *tā-marbūṭa* (o) is omitted in transliteration, unless in construct-stage (e.g., *Khirba* but *Khirbat Mishmish*).

These modifying notes may lead to various inconsistencies in the Arabic transliteration, but this policy has deliberately been adopted to gain smoother reading of Arabic terms and names.

GREEK

Ancient Greek	*Modern Greek*	*Greek Letters*
a	a	*Α; α; ᾳ*
b	v	*Β; β*
g	gh; g	*Γ; γ*
d	dh	*Δ; δ*
e	e	*Ε; ε*
z	z	*Ζ; ζ*
e; e	i	*Η; η; ῃ*
th	th	*Θ; θ*
i	i	*Ι; ι*
k	k; ky	*Κ; κ*
l	l	*Λ; λ*
m	m	*Μ; μ*
n	n	*Ν; ν*
x	x	*Ξ; ξ*
o	o	*Ο; ο*
p	p	*Π; π*
r; rh	r	*Ρ; ρ; ῥ*
s	s	*Σ; σ; ς*
t	t	*Τ; τ*
u; y	i	*Υ; υ*
ph	f	*Φ; φ*
ch	kh	*Χ; χ*
ps	ps	*Ψ; ψ*
o; ō	o	*Ω; ω; ῳ*
ai	e	*αι*
ei	i	*ει*
oi	i	*οι*
ui	i	*υι*
ou	ou	*ου*
eu	ev	*ευ*
eu; ēu	iv	*ηυ*
–	j	*τζ*
nt	d; nd	*ντ*
mp	b; mb	*μπ*
ngk	g	*γκ*
ng	ng	*γγ*
h	–	‘
–	–	’
w	–	*Ϝ*

RUSSIAN

А	A
Б	B
В	V
Г	G
Д	D
Е	E, Ye[1]
Ё	Yo, O[2]
Ж	Zh
З	Z
И	I
Й	Y[3]
К	K
Л	L
М	M
Н	N
О	O
П	P
Р	R
С	S
Т	T
У	U
Ф	F
Х	Kh
Ц	Ts
Ч	Ch
Ш	Sh
Щ	Shch
Ъ	omitted; see note [1]
Ы	Y
Ь	omitted; see note [1]
Э	E
Ю	Yu
Я	Ya

1. Ye at the beginning of a word; after all vowels except ***Ы***; and after **Ъ** and ***Ь***.
2. O after ***Ч***, ***Ш*** and ***Щ***.
3. Omitted after ***Ы***, and in names of people after ***И***.

A. Many first names have an accepted English or quasi-English form which has been preferred to transliteration.
B. Place names have been given according to the *Columbia Lippincott Gazeteer*.
C. Pre-revolutionary spelling has been ignored.
D. Other languages using the Cyrillic alphabet (e.g., Bulgarian, Ukrainian), inasmuch as they appear, have been phonetically transliterated in conformity with the principles of this table.

GLOSSARY

Asterisked terms have separate entries in the Encyclopaedia.

Actions Committee, early name of the Zionist General Council, the supreme institution of the World Zionist Organization in the interim between Congresses. The Zionist Executive's name was then the "Small Actions Committee."

***Adar**, twelfth month of the Jewish religious year, sixth of the civil, approximating to February–March.

***Aggadah**, name given to those sections of Talmud and Midrash containing homiletic expositions of the Bible, stories, legends, folklore, anecdotes, or maxims. In contradistinction to **halakhah.*

***Agunah**, woman unable to remarry according to Jewish law, because of desertion by her husband or inability to accept presumption of death.

***Aharonim**, later rabbinic authorities. In contradistinction to **rishonim* ("early ones").

Ahavah, liturgical poem inserted in the second benediction of the morning prayer *(*Ahavah Rabbah)* of the festivals and/or special Sabbaths.

Aktion (Ger.), operation involving the mass assembly, deportation, and murder of Jews by the Nazis during the *Holocaust.

***Aliyah**, (1) being called to Reading of the Law in synagogue; (2) immigration to Ereẓ Israel; (3) one of the waves of immigration to Ereẓ Israel from the early 1880s.

***Amidah**, main prayer recited at all services; also known as *Shemoneh Esreh* and *Tefillah.*

***Amora** (pl. **amoraim**), title given to the Jewish scholars in Ereẓ Israel and Babylonia in the third to sixth centuries who were responsible for the **Gemara.*

Aravah, the *willow; one of the *Four Species used on *Sukkot ("festival of Tabernacles") together with the **etrog, hadas,* and **lulav.*

***Arvit**, evening prayer.

Asarah be-Tevet, fast on the 10th of Tevet commemorating the commencement of the siege of Jerusalem by Nebuchadnezzar.

Asefat ha-Nivḥarim, representative assembly elected by Jews in Palestine during the period of the British Mandate (1920–48).

***Ashkenaz**, name applied generally in medieval rabbinical literature to Germany.

***Ashkenazi** (pl. **Ashkenazim**), German or West-, Central-, or East-European Jew(s), as contrasted with *Sephardi(m).

***Av**, fifth month of the Jewish religious year, eleventh of the civil, approximating to July–August.

***Av bet din**, vice president of the supreme court (*bet din ha-gadol*) in Jerusalem during the Second Temple period; later, title given to communal rabbis as heads of the religious courts (see **bet din*).

***Badḥan**, jester, particularly at traditional Jewish weddings in Eastern Europe.

***Bakkashah** (Heb. "supplication"), type of petitionary prayer, mainly recited in the Sephardi rite on Rosh Ha-Shanah and the Day of Atonement.

Bar, "son of . . . "; frequently appearing in personal names.

***Baraita** (pl. **beraitot**), statement of **tanna* not found in *Mishnah.

***Bar mitzvah**, ceremony marking the initiation of a boy at the age of 13 into the Jewish religious community.

Ben, "son of . . . ", frequently appearing in personal names.

Berakhah (pl. **berakhot**), *benediction, blessing; formula of praise and thanksgiving.

***Bet din** (pl. **battei din**), rabbinic court of law.

***Bet ha-midrash**, school for higher rabbinic learning; often attached to or serving as a synagogue.

***Bilu**, first modern movement for pioneering and agricultural settlement in Ereẓ Israel, founded in 1882 at Kharkov, Russia.

***Bund**, Jewish socialist party founded in Vilna in 1897, supporting Jewish national rights; Yiddishist, and anti-Zionist.

Cohen (pl. **Cohanim**), see Kohen.

***Conservative Judaism**, trend in Judaism developed in the United States in the 20th century which, while opposing extreme changes in traditional observances, permits certain modifications of *halakhah* in response to the changing needs of the Jewish people.

***Consistory** (Fr. *consistoire*), governing body of a Jewish communal district in France and certain other countries.

***Converso(s)**, term applied in Spain and Portugal to converted Jew(s), and sometimes more loosely to their descendants.

***Crypto-Jew**, term applied to a person who although observing outwardly Christianity (or some other religion) was at heart a Jew and maintained Jewish observances as far as possible (see Converso; Marrano; Neofiti; New Christian; Jadīd al-Islām).

***Dayyan**, member of rabbinic court.

Decisor, equivalent to the Hebrew *posek* (pl. **posekim*), the rabbi who gives the decision (*halakhah*) in Jewish law or practice.

***Devekut**, "devotion"; attachment or adhesion to God; communion with God.

***Diaspora**, Jews living in the "dispersion" outside Ereẓ Israel; area of Jewish settlement outside Ereẓ Israel.

Din, a law (both secular and religious), legal decision, or lawsuit.

Divan, diwan, collection of poems, especially in Hebrew, Arabic, or Persian.

Dunam, unit of land area (1,000 sq. m., c. ¼ acre), used in Israel.

Einsatzgruppen, mobile units of Nazi S.S. and S.D.; in U.S.S.R. and Serbia, mobile killing units.

***Ein-Sof**, "without end"; "the infinite"; hidden, impersonal aspect of God; also used as a Divine Name.

***Elul**, sixth month of the Jewish religious calendar, 12th of the civil, precedes the High Holiday season in the fall.

Endloesung, see *Final Solution.

***Ereẓ Israel**, Land of Israel; Palestine.

***Eruv**, technical term for rabbinical provision permitting the alleviation of certain restrictions.

***Etrog**, citron; one of the *Four Species used on *Sukkot together with the **lulav, hadas,* and *aravah.*

Even ha-Ezer, see Shulḥan Arukh.

***Exilarch**, lay head of Jewish community in Babylonia (see also *resh galuta*), and elsewhere.

***Final Solution** (Ger. *Endloesung*), in Nazi terminology, the Nazi-planned mass murder and total annihilation of the Jews.

***Gabbai**, official of a Jewish congregation; originally a charity collector.

***Galut**, "exile"; the condition of the Jewish people in dispersion.

*__Gaon__ (pl. **geonim**), head of academy in post-talmudic period, especially in Babylonia.

Gaonate, office of *gaon.

*__Gemara__, traditions, discussions, and rulings of the **amoraim*, commenting on and supplementing the *Mishnah, and forming part of the Babylonian and Palestinian Talmuds (see Talmud).

*__Gematria__, interpretation of Hebrew word according to the numerical value of its letters.

General Government, territory in Poland administered by a German civilian governor-general with headquarters in Cracow after the German occupation in World War II.

*__Genizah__, depository for sacred books. The best known was discovered in the synagogue of Fostat (old Cairo).

Get, bill of *divorce.

*__Ge'ullah__, hymn inserted after the **Shema* into the benediction of the morning prayer of the festivals and special Sabbaths.

*__Gilgul__, metempsychosis; transmigration of souls.

*__Golem__, automaton, especially in human form, created by magical means and endowed with life.

*__Ḥabad__, initials of *ḥokhmah, binah, da'at*: "wisdom, understanding, knowledge"; ḥasidic movement founded in Belorussia by *Shneur Zalman of Lyady.

Hadas, *myrtle; one of the *Four Species used on Sukkot together with the **etrog*, **lulav*, and *aravah*.

*__Haftarah__ (pl. **haftarot**), designation of the portion from the prophetical books of the Bible recited after the synagogue reading from the Pentateuch on Sabbaths and holidays.

*__Haganah__, clandestine Jewish organization for armed self-defense in Ereẓ Israel under the British Mandate, which eventually evolved into a people's militia and became the basis for the Israel army.

*__Haggadah__, ritual recited in the home on *Passover eve at seder table.

Haham, title of chief rabbi of the Spanish and Portuguese congregations in London, England.

*__Hakham__, title of rabbi of *Sephardi congregation.

*__Hakham bashi__, title in the 15th century and modern times of the chief rabbi in the Ottoman Empire, residing in Constantinople (Istanbul), also applied to principal rabbis in provincial towns.

Hakhsharah ("preparation"), organized training in the Diaspora of pioneers for agricultural settlement in Ereẓ Israel.

*__Halakhah__ (pl. **halakhot**), an accepted decision in rabbinic law. Also refers to those parts of the *Talmud concerned with legal matters. In contradistinction to **aggadah*.

Ḥaliẓah, biblically prescribed ceremony (Deut. 25:9–10) performed when a man refuses to marry his brother's childless widow, enabling her to remarry.

*__Hallel__, term referring to Psalms 113-18 in liturgical use.

*__Ḥalukkah__, system of financing the maintenance of Jewish communities in the holy cities of Ereẓ Israel by collections made abroad, mainly in the pre-Zionist era (see *kolel*).

Ḥalutz (pl. **ḥalutzim**), pioneer, especially in agriculture, in Ereẓ Israel.

Ḥalutziyyut, pioneering.

*__Ḥanukkah__, eight-day celebration commemorating the victory of *Judah Maccabee over the Syrian king *Antiochus Epiphanes and the subsequent rededication of the Temple.

Ḥasid, adherent of *Ḥasidism.

*__Ḥasidei Ashkenaz__, medieval pietist movement among the Jews of Germany.

*__Ḥasidism__, (1) religious revivalist movement of popular mysticism among Jews of Germany in the Middle Ages; (2) religious movement founded by *Israel ben Eliezer Ba'al Shem Tov in the first half of the 18th century.

*__Haskalah__, "enlightenment"; movement for spreading modern European culture among Jews c. 1750–1880. See *maskil*.

*__Havdalah__, ceremony marking the end of Sabbath or festival.

*__Ḥazzan__, precentor who intones the liturgy and leads the prayers in synagogue; in earlier times a synagogue official.

*__Ḥeder__ (lit. "room"), school for teaching children Jewish religious observance.

Heikhalot, "palaces"; tradition in Jewish mysticism centering on mystical journeys through the heavenly spheres and palaces to the Divine Chariot (see Merkabah).

*__Ḥerem__, excommunication, imposed by rabbinical authorities for purposes of religious and/or communal discipline; originally, in biblical times, that which is separated from common use either because it was an abomination or because it was consecrated to God.

Ḥeshvan, see Marḥeshvan.

*__Ḥevra kaddisha__, title applied to charitable confraternity (**ḥevrah*), now generally limited to associations for burial of the dead.

*__Ḥibbat Zion__, see Ḥovevei Zion.

*__Histadrut__ (abbr. For Heb. **Ha-Histadrut ha-Kelalit shel ha-Ovedim ha-Ivriyyim be-Ereẓ Israel**). Ereẓ Israel Jewish Labor Federation, founded in 1920; subsequently renamed Histadrut ha-Ovedim be-Ereẓ Israel.

*__Holocaust__, the organized mass persecution and annihilation of European Jewry by the Nazis (1933–1945).

*__Hoshana Rabba__, the seventh day of *Sukkot on which special observances are held.

Ḥoshen Mishpat, see Shulḥan Arukh.

Ḥovevei Zion, federation of *Ḥibbat Zion, early (pre-*Herzl) Zionist movement in Russia.

Illui, outstanding scholar or genius, especially a young prodigy in talmudic learning.

*__Iyyar__, second month of the Jewish religious year, eighth of the civil, approximating to April-May.

I.Ẓ.L. (initials of Heb. *__Irgun Ẓeva'i Le'ummi__; "National Military Organization"), underground Jewish organization in Ereẓ Israel founded in 1931, which engaged from 1937 in retaliatory acts against Arab attacks and later against the British mandatory authorities.

*__Jadīd al-Islām__ (Ar.), a person practicing the Jewish religion in secret although outwardly observing Islām.

*__Jewish Legion__, Jewish units in British army during World War I.

*__Jihād__ (Ar.), in Muslim religious law, holy war waged against infidels.

*__Judenrat__ (Ger. "Jewish council"), council set up in Jewish communities and ghettos under the Nazis to execute their instructions.

*__Judenrein__ (Ger. "clean of Jews"), in Nazi terminology the condition of a locality from which all Jews had been eliminated.

*__Kabbalah__, the Jewish mystical tradition:

Kabbala iyyunit, speculative Kabbalah;

Kabbala ma'asit, practical Kabbalah;

Kabbala nevu'it, prophetic Kabbalah.

Kabbalist, student of Kabbalah.

*__Kaddish__, liturgical doxology.

Kahal, Jewish congregation; among Ashkenazim, *kehillah*.

*__Kalām__ (Ar.), science of Muslim theology; adherents of the Kalām are called *mutakallimūn*.

*__Karaite__, member of a Jewish sect originating in the eighth century which rejected rabbinic (*Rabbanite) Judaism and claimed to accept only Scripture as authoritative.

*__Kasher__, ritually permissible food.

Kashrut, Jewish *dietary laws.

*__Kavvanah__, "intention"; term denoting the spiritual concentration accompanying prayer and the performance of ritual or of a commandment.

*__Kedushah__, main addition to the third blessing in the reader's repetition of the *Amidah* in which the public responds to the precentor's introduction.

Kefar, village; first part of name of many settlements in Israel.

Kehillah, congregation; see *kahal*.

Kelippah (pl. **kelippot**), "husk(s)"; mystical term denoting force(s) of evil.

*__Keneset Yisrael__, comprehensive communal organization of the Jews in Palestine during the British Mandate.

Keri, variants in the masoretic (*masorah) text of the Bible between the spelling (*ketiv*) and its pronunciation (*keri*).

*__Kerovah__ (collective plural (corrupted) from **kerovez̧**), poem(s) incorporated into the *__Amidah__.

Ketiv, see *keri*.

*__Ketubbah__, marriage contract, stipulating husband's obligations to wife.

Kevuz̧ah, small commune of pioneers constituting an agricultural settlement in Erez̧ Israel (evolved later into *kibbutz).

*__Kibbutz__ (pl. **kibbutzim**), larger-size commune constituting a settlement in Erez̧ Israel based mainly on agriculture but engaging also in industry.

*__Kiddush__, prayer of sanctification, recited over wine or bread on eve of Sabbaths and festivals.

*__Kiddush ha-Shem__, term connoting martyrdom or act of strict integrity in support of Judaic principles.

*__Kinah__ (pl. **kinot**), lamentation dirge(s) for the Ninth of Av and other fast days.

*__Kislev__, ninth month of the Jewish religious year, third of the civil, approximating to November-December.

Klaus, name given in Central and Eastern Europe to an institution, usually with synagogue attached, where *Talmud was studied perpetually by adults; applied by Ḥasidim to their synagogue ("*kloyz*").

*__Knesset__, parliament of the State of Israel.

K(c)ohen (pl. **K(c)ohanim**), Jew(s) of priestly (Aaronide) descent.

*__Kolel__, (1) community in Erez̧ Israel of persons from a particular country or locality, often supported by their fellow countrymen in the Diaspora; (2) institution for higher Torah study.

Kosher, see *kasher*.

*__Kristallnacht__ (Ger. "crystal night," meaning "night of broken glass"), organized destruction of synagogues, Jewish houses, and shops, accompanied by mass arrests of Jews, which took place in Germany and Austria under the Nazis on the night of Nov. 9–10, 1938.

*__Lag ba-Omer__, 33rd (Heb. **lag**) day of the *__Omer__ period falling on the 18th of *Iyyar; a semi-holiday.

Leḥi (abbr. For Heb. *__Loḥamei Ḥerut Israel__, "Fighters for the Freedom of Israel"), radically anti-British armed underground organization in Palestine, founded in 1940 by dissidents from *I.Z.L.

Levir, husband's brother.

*__Levirate marriage__ (Heb. *yibbum*), marriage of childless widow (*yevamah*) by brother (*yavam*) of the deceased husband (in accordance with Deut. 25:5); release from such an obligation is effected through *ḥaliz̧ah*.

LHY, see Leḥi.

*__Lulav__, palm branch; one of the *Four Species used on *Sukkot together with the *__etrog__, *hadas*, and *aravah*.

*__Ma'aravot__, hymns inserted into the evening prayer of the three festivals, Passover, Shavuot, and Sukkot.

Ma'ariv, evening prayer; also called *__arvit__.

*__Ma'barah__, transition camp; temporary settlement for newcomers in Israel during the period of mass immigration following 1948.

*__Maftir__, reader of the concluding portion of the Pentateuchal section on Sabbaths and holidays in synagogue; reader of the portion of the prophetical books of the Bible (*__haftarah__).

*__Maggid__, popular preacher.

*__Maḥzor__ (pl. **maḥzorim**), festival prayer book.

*__Mamzer__, bastard; according to Jewish law, the offspring of an incestuous relationship.

*__Mandate, Palestine__, responsibility for the administration of Palestine conferred on Britain by the League of Nations in 1922; mandatory government: the British administration of Palestine.

*__Maqāma__ (Ar. pl. **maqamāt**), poetic form (rhymed prose) which, in its classical arrangement, has rigid rules of form and content.

*__Marḥeshvan__, popularly called Ḥeshvan; eighth month of the Jewish religious year, second of the civil, approximating to October–November.

*__Marrano(s)__, descendant(s) of Jew(s) in Spain and Portugal whose ancestors had been converted to Christianity under pressure but who secretly observed Jewish rituals.

Maskil (pl. **maskilim**), adherent of *Haskalah ("Enlightenment") movement.

*__Masorah__, body of traditions regarding the correct spelling, writing, and reading of the Hebrew Bible.

Masorete, scholar of the masoretic tradition.

Masoretic, in accordance with the masorah.

Meliz̧ah, in Middle Ages, elegant style; modern usage, florid style using biblical or talmudic phraseology.

Mellah, *Jewish quarter in North African towns.

*__Menorah__, candelabrum; seven-branched oil lamp used in the Tabernacle and Temple; also eight-branched candelabrum used on *Ḥanukkah.

Me'orah, hymn inserted into the first benediction of the morning prayer (*Yoz̧er ha-Me'orot*).

*__Merkabah__, *merkavah*, "chariot"; mystical discipline associated with Ezekiel's vision of the Divine Throne-Chariot (Ezek. 1).

Meshullaḥ, emissary sent to conduct propaganda or raise funds for rabbinical academies or charitable institutions.

*__Mezuzah__ (pl. **mezuzot**), parchment scroll with selected Torah verses placed in container and affixed to gates and doorposts of houses occupied by Jews.

*__Midrash__, method of interpreting Scripture to elucidate legal points (*Midrash Halakhah*) or to bring out lessons by stories or homiletics (*Midrash Aggadah*). Also the name for a collection of such rabbinic interpretations.

*__Mikveh__, ritual bath.

*__Minhag__ (pl. **minhagim**), ritual custom(s); synagogal rite(s); especially of a specific sector of Jewry.

*__Minḥah__, afternoon prayer; originally meal offering in Temple.

*__Minyan__, group of ten male adult Jews, the minimum required for communal prayer.

*__Mishnah__, earliest codification of Jewish Oral Law.

__Mishnah__ (pl. __mishnayot__), subdivision of tractates of the Mishnah.

__Mitnagged__ (pl. *__Mitnaggedim__), originally, opponents of *Ḥasidism in Eastern Europe.

*__Mitzvah__, biblical or rabbinic injunction; applied also to good or charitable deeds.

__Mohel__, official performing circumcisions.

*__Moshav__, smallholders' cooperative agricultural settlement in Israel, see moshav ovedim.

__Moshavah__, earliest type of Jewish village in modern Ereẓ Israel in which farming is conducted on individual farms mostly on privately owned land.

__Moshav ovedim__ ("workers' moshav"), agricultural village in Israel whose inhabitants possess individual homes and holdings but cooperate in the purchase of equipment, sale of produce, mutual aid, etc.

*__Moshav shittufi__ ("collective moshav"), agricultural village in Israel whose members possess individual homesteads but where the agriculture and economy are conducted as a collective unit.

__Mostegab__ (Ar.), poem with biblical verse at beginning of each stanza.

*__Muqaddam__ (Ar., pl. __muqaddamūn__), "leader," "head of the community."

*__Musaf__, additional service on Sabbath and festivals; originally the additional sacrifice offered in the Temple.

__Musar__, traditional ethical literature.

*__Musar movement__, ethical movement developing in the latter part of the 19th century among Orthodox Jewish groups in Lithuania; founded by R. Israel *Lipkin (Salanter).

*__Nagid__ (pl. __negidim__), title applied in Muslim (and some Christian) countries in the Middle Ages to a leader recognized by the state as head of the Jewish community.

__Nakdan__ (pl. __nakdanim__), "punctuator"; scholar of the 9th to 14th centuries who provided biblical manuscripts with masoretic apparatus, vowels, and accents.

*__Nasi__ (pl. __nesi'im__), talmudic term for president of the Sanhedrin, who was also the spiritual head and later, political representative of the Jewish people; from second century a descendant of Hillel recognized by the Roman authorities as patriarch of the Jews. Now applied to the president of the State of Israel.

*__Negev__, the southern, mostly arid, area of Israel.

*__Ne'ilah__, concluding service on the *Day of Atonement.

__Neofiti__, term applied in southern Italy to converts to Christianity from Judaism and their descendants who were suspected of maintaining secret allegiance to Judaism.

*__Neology; Neolog; Neologism__, trend of *Reform Judaism in Hungary forming separate congregations after 1868.

*__Nevelah__ (lit. "carcass"), meat forbidden by the *dietary laws on account of the absence of, or defect in, the act of **sheḥitah* (ritual slaughter).

*__New Christians__, term applied especially in Spain and Portugal to converts from Judaism (and from Islam) and their descendants; "Half New Christian" designated a person one of whose parents was of full Jewish blood.

*__Niddah__ ("menstruous woman"), woman during the period of menstruation.

*__Nisan__, first month of the Jewish religious year, seventh of the civil, approximating to March-April.

__Niẓoẓot__, "sparks"; mystical term for sparks of the holy light imprisoned in all matter.

__Nosaḥ__ (__nusaḥ__) "version"; (1) textual variant; (2) term applied to distinguish the various prayer rites, e.g., *nosaḥ Ashkenaz*; (3) the accepted tradition of synagogue melody.

*__Notarikon__, method of abbreviating Hebrew works or phrases by acronym.

__Novella(e)__ (Heb. **ḥiddush (im)*), commentary on talmudic and later rabbinic subjects that derives new facts or principles from the implications of the text.

*__Nuremberg Laws__, Nazi laws excluding Jews from German citizenship, and imposing other restrictions.

__Ofan__, hymns inserted into a passage of the morning prayer.

*__Omer__, first sheaf cut during the barley harvest, offered in the Temple on the second day of Passover.

__Omer, Counting of__ (Heb. *Sefirat ha-Omer*), 49 days counted from the day on which the *omer* was first offered in the Temple (according to the rabbis the 16th of Nisan, i.e., the second day of Passover) until the festival of Shavuot; now a period of semi-mourning.

__Oraḥ Ḥayyim__, see Shulḥan Arukh.

*__Orthodoxy__ (Orthodox Judaism), modern term for the strictly traditional sector of Jewry.

*__Pale of Settlement__, 25 provinces of czarist Russia where Jews were permitted permanent residence.

*__Palmaḥ__ (abbr. for Heb. *peluggot maḥaz*; "shock companies"), striking arm of the *Haganah.

*__Pardes__, medieval biblical exegesis giving the literal, allegorical, homiletical, and esoteric interpretations.

*__Parnas__, chief synagogue functionary, originally vested with both religious and administrative functions; subsequently an elected lay leader.

__Partition plan(s)__, proposals for dividing Ereẓ Israel into autonomous areas.

__Paytan__, composer of **piyyut* (liturgical poetry).

*__Peel Commission__, British Royal Commission appointed by the British government in 1936 to inquire into the Palestine problem and make recommendations for its solution.

__Pesaḥ__, *Passover.

*__Pilpul__, in talmudic and rabbinic literature, a sharp dialectic used particularly by talmudists in Poland from the 16th century.

*__Pinkas__, community register or minute-book.

*__Piyyut__, (pl. __piyyutim__), Hebrew liturgical poetry.

*__Pizmon__, poem with refrain.

__Posek__ (pl. *__posekim__), decisor; codifier or rabbinic scholar who pronounces decisions in disputes and on questions of Jewish law.

*__Prosbul__, legal method of overcoming the cancelation of debts with the advent of the *sabbatical year.

*__Purim__, festival held on Adar 14 or 15 in commemoration of the delivery of the Jews of Persia in the time of *Esther.

__Rabban__, honorific title higher than that of rabbi, applied to heads of the *Sanhedrin in mishnaic times.

*__Rabbanite__, adherent of rabbinic Judaism. In contradistinction to *Karaite.

__Reb, rebbe__, Yiddish form for rabbi, applied generally to a teacher or ḥasidic rabbi.

*__Reconstructionism__, trend in Jewish thought originating in the United States.

*__Reform Judaism__, trend in Judaism advocating modification of *Orthodoxy in conformity with the exigencies of contemporary life and thought.

Resh galuta, lay head of Babylonian Jewry (see exilarch).

Responsum (pl. ***responsa**), written opinion (*teshuvah*) given to question (*she'elah*) on aspects of Jewish law by qualified authorities; pl. collection of such queries and opinions in book form (*she'elot u-teshuvot*).

***Rishonim**, older rabbinical authorities. Distinguished from later authorities (**aḥaronim*).

***Rishon le-Zion**, title given to Sephardi chief rabbi of Ereẓ Israel.

***Rosh Ha-Shanah**, two-day holiday (one day in biblical and early mishnaic times) at the beginning of the month of *Tishri (September–October), traditionally the New Year.

Rosh Hodesh, *New Moon, marking the beginning of the Hebrew month.

Rosh Yeshivah, see *Yeshivah.

***R.S.H.A.** (initials of Ger. *Reichssicherheitshauptamt*: "Reich Security Main Office"), the central security department of the German Reich, formed in 1939, and combining the security police (Gestapo and Kripo) and the S.D.

***Sanhedrin**, the assembly of ordained scholars which functioned both as a supreme court and as a legislature before 70 C.E. In modern times the name was given to the body of representative Jews convoked by Napoleon in 1807.

***Savora** (pl. **savoraim**), name given to the Babylonian scholars of the period between the **amoraim* and the **geonim*, approximately 500–700 C.E.

S.D. (initials of Ger. *Sicherheitsdienst*: "security service"), security service of the *S.S. formed in 1932 as the sole intelligence organization of the Nazi party.

Seder, ceremony observed in the Jewish home on the first night of Passover (outside Ereẓ Israel first two nights), when the *Haggadah is recited.

***Sefer Torah**, manuscript scroll of the Pentateuch for public reading in synagogue.

***Sefirot, the ten**, the ten "Numbers"; mystical term denoting the ten spheres or emanations through which the Divine manifests itself; elements of the world; dimensions, primordial numbers.

Selektion (Ger.), (1) in ghettos and other Jewish settlements, the drawing up by Nazis of lists of deportees; (2) separation of incoming victims to concentration camps into two categories – those destined for immediate killing and those to be sent for forced labor.

Seliḥah (pl. ***seliḥot**), penitential prayer.

***Semikhah**, ordination conferring the title "rabbi" and permission to give decisions in matters of ritual and law.

Sephardi (pl. ***Sephardim**), Jew(s) of Spain and Portugal and their descendants, wherever resident, as contrasted with *Ashkenazi(m).

Shabbatean, adherent of the pseudo-messiah *Shabbetai Ẓevi (17th century).

Shaddai, name of God found frequently in the Bible and commonly translated "Almighty."

***Shaḥarit**, morning service.

Shali'aḥ (pl. **sheliḥim**), in Jewish law, messenger, agent; in modern times, an emissary from Ereẓ Israel to Jewish communities or organizations abroad for the purpose of fund-raising, organizing pioneer immigrants, education, etc.

Shalmonit, poetic meter introduced by the liturgical poet *Solomon ha-Bavli.

***Shammash**, synagogue beadle.

***Shavuot**, Pentecost; Festival of Weeks; second of the three annual pilgrim festivals, commemorating the receiving of the Torah at Mt. Sinai.

***Sheḥitah**, ritual slaughtering of animals.

***Shekhinah**, Divine Presence.

Shelishit, poem with three-line stanzas.

***Sheluḥei Ereẓ Israel** (or **shadarim**), emissaries from Ereẓ Israel.

***Shema** ([Yisrael]; "hear… [O Israel]," Deut. 6:4), Judaism's confession of faith, proclaiming the absolute unity of God.

Shemini Aẓeret, final festal day (in the Diaspora, final two days) at the conclusion of *Sukkot.

Shemittah, *Sabbatical year.

Sheniyyah, poem with two-line stanzas.

***Shephelah**, southern part of the coastal plain of Ereẓ Israel.

***Shevat**, eleventh month of the Jewish religious year, fifth of the civil, approximating to January–February.

***Shi'ur Komah**, Hebrew mystical work (c. eighth century) containing a physical description of God's dimensions; term denoting enormous spacial measurement used in speculations concerning the body of the **Shekhinah*.

Shivah, the "seven days" of *mourning following burial of a relative.

***Shofar**, horn of the ram (or any other ritually clean animal excepting the cow) sounded for the memorial blowing on *Rosh Ha-Shanah, and other occasions.

Shoḥet, person qualified to perform **sheḥitah*.

Shomer, *Ha-Shomer, organization of Jewish workers in Ereẓ Israel founded in 1909 to defend Jewish settlements.

***Shtadlan**, Jewish representative or negotiator with access to dignitaries of state, active at royal courts, etc.

***Shtetl**, Jewish small-town community in Eastern Europe.

***Shulḥan Arukh**, Joseph *Caro's code of Jewish law in four parts:
Oraḥ Ḥayyim, laws relating to prayers, Sabbath, festivals, and fasts;
Yoreh De'ah, dietary laws, etc;
Even ha-Ezer, laws dealing with women, marriage, etc;
Ḥoshen Mishpat, civil, criminal law, court procedure, etc.

Siddur, among Ashkenazim, the volume containing the daily prayers (in distinction to the **maḥzor* containing those for the festivals).

***Simḥat Torah**, holiday marking the completion in the synagogue of the annual cycle of reading the Pentateuch; in Ereẓ Israel observed on Shemini Aẓeret (outside Ereẓ Israel on the following day).

***Sinai Campaign**, brief campaign in October–November 1956 when Israel army reacted to Egyptian terrorist attacks and blockade by occupying the Sinai peninsula.

Sitra aḥra, "the other side" (of God); left side; the demoniac and satanic powers.

***Sivan**, third month of the Jewish religious year, ninth of the civil, approximating to May–June.

***Six-Day War**, rapid war in June 1967 when Israel reacted to Arab threats and blockade by defeating the Egyptian, Jordanian, and Syrian armies.

***S.S.** (initials of Ger. *Schutzstaffel*: "protection detachment"), Nazi formation established in 1925 which later became the "elite" organization of the Nazi Party and carried out central tasks in the "Final Solution."

***Status quo ante** community, community in Hungary retaining the status it had held before the convention of the General Jewish Congress there in 1868 and the resultant split in Hungarian Jewry.

*__Sukkah__, booth or tabernacle erected for *Sukkot when, for seven days, religious Jews "dwell" or at least eat in the *sukkah* (Lev. 23:42).

*__Sukkot__, festival of Tabernacles; last of the three pilgrim festivals, beginning on the 15th of Tishri.

Sūra (Ar.), chapter of the Koran.

Ta'anit Esther (Fast of *Esther), fast on the 13th of Adar, the day preceding Purim.

Takkanah (pl. ***takkanot**), regulation supplementing the law of the Torah; regulations governing the internal life of communities and congregations.

*__Tallit (gadol)__, four-cornered prayer shawl with fringes (*ẓiẓit*) at each corner.

*__Tallit katan__, garment with fringes (*ẓiẓit*) appended, worn by observant male Jews under their outer garments.

*__Talmud__, "teaching"; compendium of discussion on the Mishnah by generations of scholars and jurists in many academies over a period of several centuries. The Jerusalem (or Palestinian) Talmud mainly contains the discussions of the Palestinian sages. The Babylonian Talmud incorporates the parallel discussion in the Babylonian academies.

Talmud torah, term generally applied to Jewish religious (and ultimately to talmudic) study; also to traditional Jewish religious public schools.

*__Tammuz__, fourth month of the Jewish religious year, tenth of the civil, approximating to June-July.

Tanna (pl. ***tannaim**), rabbinic teacher of mishnaic period.

*__Targum__, Aramaic translation of the Bible.

*__Tefillin__, phylacteries, small leather cases containing passages from Scripture and affixed on the forehead and arm by male Jews during the recital of morning prayers.

Tell (Ar. "mound," "hillock"), ancient mound in the Middle East composed of remains of successive settlements.

*__Terefah__, food that is not **kasher*, owing to a defect on the animal.

*__Territorialism__, 20th century movement supporting the creation of an autonomous territory for Jewish mass-settlement outside Ereẓ Israel.

*__Tevet__, tenth month of the Jewish religious year, fourth of the civil, approximating to December–January.

Tikkun ("restitution," "reintegration"), (1) order of service for certain occasions, mostly recited at night; (2) mystical term denoting restoration of the right order and true unity after the spiritual "catastrophe" which occurred in the cosmos.

Tishah be-Av, Ninth of *Av, fast day commemorating the destruction of the First and Second Temples.

*__Tishri__, seventh month of the Jewish religious year, first of the civil, approximating to September–October.

Tokheḥah, reproof sections of the Pentateuch (Lev. 26 and Deut. 28); poem of reproof.

*__Torah__, Pentateuch or the Pentateuchal scroll for reading in synagogue; entire body of traditional Jewish teaching and literature.

Tosafist, talmudic glossator, mainly French (12–14th centuries), bringing additions to the commentary by *Rashi.

*__Tosafot__, glosses supplied by tosafist.

*__Tosefta__, a collection of teachings and traditions of the *tannaim*, closely related to the Mishnah.

Tradent, person who hands down a talmudic statement on the name of his teacher or other earlier authority.

*__Tu bi-Shevat__, the 15th day of Shevat, the New Year for Trees; date marking a dividing line for fruit tithing; in modern Israel celebrated as arbor day.

*__Uganda Scheme__, plan suggested by the British government in 1903 to establish an autonomous Jewish settlement area in East Africa.

*__Va'ad Le'ummi__, national council of the Jewish community in Ereẓ Israel during the period of the British *Mandate.

*__Wannsee Conference__, Nazi conference held on Jan. 20, 1942, at which the planned annihilation of European Jewry was endorsed.

Waqf (Ar.), (1) a Muslim charitable pious foundation; (2) state lands and other property passed to the Muslim community for public welfare.

*__War of Independence__, war of 1947–49 when the Jews of Israel fought off Arab invading armies and ensured the establishment of the new State.

*__White Paper(s)__, report(s) issued by British government, frequently statements of policy, as issued in connection with Palestine during the *Mandate period.

*__Wissenschaft des Judentums__ (Ger. "Science of Judaism"), movement in Europe beginning in the 19th century for scientific study of Jewish history, religion, and literature.

*__Yad Vashem__, Israel official authority for commemorating the *Holocaust in the Nazi era and Jewish resistance and heroism at that time.

Yeshivah (pl. ***yeshivot**), Jewish traditional academy devoted primarily to study of rabbinic literature; *rosh yeshivah*, head of the yeshivah.

YHWH, the letters of the holy name of God, the Tetragrammaton.

Yibbum, see levirate marriage.

Yiḥud, "union"; mystical term for intention which causes the union of God with the **Shekhinah*.

Yishuv, settlement; more specifically, the Jewish community of Ereẓ Israel in the pre-State period. The pre-Zionist community is generally designated the "old yishuv" and the community evolving from 1880, the "new yishuv."

Yom Kippur, Yom ha-Kippurim, *Day of Atonement, solemn fast day observed on the 10th of Tishri.

Yoreh De'ah, see Shulḥan Arukh.

Yoẓer, hymns inserted in the first benediction (*Yoẓer Or*) of the morning **Shema*.

*__Ẓaddik__, person outstanding for his faith and piety; especially a ḥasidic rabbi or leader.

Ẓimẓum, "contraction"; mystical term denoting the process whereby God withdraws or contracts within Himself so leaving a primordial vacuum in which creation can take place; primordial exile or self-limitation of God.

*__Zionist Commission (1918)__, commission appointed in 1918 by the British government to advise the British military authorities in Palestine on the implementation of the *Balfour Declaration.

Ẓyyonei Zion, the organized opposition to Herzl in connection with the *Uganda Scheme.

*__Ẓiẓit__, fringes attached to the **tallit* and **tallit katan*.

*__Zohar__, mystical commentary on the Pentateuch; main textbook of *Kabbalah.

Zulat, hymn inserted after the **Shema* in the morning service.

ISBN-13: 978-0-02-865947-3
ISBN-10: 0-02-865947-3